CONTEMPORARY
DESIGNERS

CONTEMPORARY ARTS SERIES

Contemporary Artists
Contemporary Architects
Contemporary Photographers
Contemporary Designers
International Contemporary Arts Directory
Contemporary Masterworks (in preparation)

CONTEMPORARY
DESIGNERS

SECOND EDITION

Editor:
Colin Naylor

Advisers:
Andrea Arsenault, Kenji Ekuan
Arnold Friedmann, Norman Gambill
Jack Lenor Larsen, Lennart Lindkvist
Per Mollerup, Jukka Pellinen
Tapio Periäinen, Arthur J. Pulos

St J

ST. JAMES PRESS
CHICAGO AND LONDON

Front cover: Alexander Neumeister—TR06 magnetic levitation train, for Thyssen Menschel, 1982 (model).

© 1990 by St. James Press
All rights reserved. For information, write:

ST. JAMES PRESS
233 East Ontario Street
Chicago 60611, U.S.A.
or
2–6 Boundary Row
London SE1 8HN, England

British Library Cataloguing in Publication Data

Contemporary designers.—2nd ed.—
 1. Designer—Biographies
 I. Naylor, Colin, *1944–*
746'.092'2

 ISBN 0-912289-69-4

First edition published 1984; second edition 1990.

CONTENTS

Editor's Note	*page*	vii
Advisers and Contributors		ix
CONTEMPORARY DESIGNERS		1
Notes on Advisers and Contributors		637

EDITOR'S NOTE

The selection of entrants in this second edition of *Contemporary Designers* is based on the recommendations of the Advisers whose names are listed on page ix. In some instances they have deferred to the judgement of contributors from particular countries or specialists in specific areas of design, but, overall, there has been a remarkable consensus. The choice of more than 600 entrants is intended to reflect the best and most prominent of contemporary designers (those who are currently active, as well as many who have died since 1970, but whose reputations remain essentially contemporary). Virtually every field of design—architectural, interior, display, graphic, textile, fashion, product, industrial, stage and film—is represented in this book. The Advisory Board has tried to suggest the diversity as well as continuity in the world of design.

Entries consist of: personal and professional biography; a list of important and representative design works; a bibliography of books and writings by and about the entrant. As well, living entrants have been invited to make a statement on their work or on contemporary design in general, and to choose an illustration of a representative work. Some 125 design critics and historians have contributed evaluative essays to this edition.

Our research was carried out mainly in the libraries of the Art Institute of Chicago, Victoria and Albert Museum, British Library, Royal Institute of British Architects, Royal Society of Arts, Tate Gallery, St. Bride Printing Library and the London College of Fashion. To find accurate information we frequently had to rely on the entrants themselves. When the entrants were dead, we had to appeal to the essayist, as well as to families and colleagues of the entrants. Thanks are due to these many collaborators; without their generosity, patience and enthusiasm, this book would have been impossible.

ADVISERS/CONTRIBUTORS

Advisers

Andrea Arsenault, Kenji Ekuan, Arnold Friedmann
Norman Gambill, Jack Lenor Larsen, Lennart Lindkvist
Per Mollerup, Jukka Pellinen, Tapio Periäinen
Arthur J. Pulos

Contributors

Marianne Aav, Sandra Michels Adams, James M. Alexander
Arnold Aronson, Adrea Arsenault, Clive Ashwin
Carl Auböck

John Barnicoat, Reed Benhamou, Charlotte Blauensteiner
Sarah Bodine, Szymon Bojko, Monico Boman
Nina Bremer, Jarka M. Burian, Frances Butler
Elizabeth Douthitt Byrne

Ralph Caplan, Ken Carls, Noel Carrington
Stefano Casciani, Barbara Cavaliere, Hazel Clark
Mildred Constantine, Hazel Conway, Anthony J. Coulson
Catherine I. Currier

Helena Dahlback Lutteman, Haig David-West, Toni del Renzio
Diana de Marly, Friedrich Dieckmann, Magdalena Droste

Carla Enbom, Lloyd C. Engelbrecht

Lydia Ferrabee, Jorge Frascara, Arnold Friedmann

Norman Gambill, Madge Garland, Kenneth Gaulin
Grant Greapentrog, Gertrud Gustafsson

Shukuro Habara, John Halas, Ulf Hård af Segerstad
Richard Hayhurst, John E. Hirsch, Augustine Hope
Nancy House

Dennis Ichiyama, Eumie Imm, Alaboigoni Inko-Dokubo

Jan Jennings

Deirdre Kerr, Robin Kinross, Sheila Klos
Harold Koda, Marjorie Kriebel, William Victor Kriebel

Wolfgang Lange, Edith Cortland Lee, Maud Lindgren
Lennart Lindkvist, Ake Livstedt, Gunilla Lundahl

Floyd W. Martin, Leena Maunula, Catherine McDermott
Anne McLean, Philip B. Meggs, Gloria Menard
Russell Merzdorf, Lois Irene Miklas, Tom Mikotowicz
Elena G. Millie, Karen Moon

Eckhard Neumann

Ronald C. Olson

Kristiina Paatero, Philip Pacey, Juhani Pallasmaa
Jukka Pellinen, Tapio Periäinen, Ingeborg Pietzsch
André Pozner, Arthur Pulos

Roger R. Remington, Richard V. Riddell, Virginia Rose
Patricia A. Russac, Douglas A. Russell

Kunio Sano, Jan Sawka, Pamela Scheinman
Helmut Schmid, Paul Shaw, Harlan Sifford
Carin Sjölander, Gillian Skellenger, Michael Robert Soluri
Jukka Sorjo-Smeds, Herbert Spencer, Mafalda Spencer
Raymond Spilman, Gordon Steele, Jerry Steimle
Ivar Stranger, Zenobiusz Strzelecki, Barbara Sudick

Masaaki Tanaka, Benjamin de Brie Taylor, Teal Ann Triggs
Maria Tulokas

Gregory Votolato

George Walsh, Hiroshi Watanabe, David W. Weiss
Kerstin Wickman, Dag Widman, Danuta Wroblewska
Liz Wylie

Barbara Young

CONTEMPORARY
DESIGNERS

Alvar Aalto
Eero Aarnio
Ken Adam
Adolfo
Mehemed Fehmy Agha
Agnès B.
Lis Ahlmann
Tom Ahlström
Otl Aicher
Gil Aimbez
Anni Albers
Franco Albini
Walter Albini
Theoni Aldredge
Alan Aldridge
Walter Allner
Emilio Ambasz
Junichi Arai
Bruce Archer
Giorgio Armani
Boris Aronson
Laura Ashley
Brian Asquith
Associated Space Design
Sergio Asti
Carl Auböck
Gae Aulenti
Kiyoshi Awazu
Åke Axelsson

Cristobal Balenciaga
Boguslaw Balicki
Walter Ballmer
Pierre Balmain
Scott Barrie
Carlo Bartoli
James Basevi
Basile
Saul Bass
John Bates
Hans Theodor Baumann
Edward Bawden
Howard Bay
Herbert Bayer
Geoffrey Beene
Melchiorre Bega
Gretchen Bellinger
Mario Bellini
Félix Beltrán
Maria Benktzon
Ward Bennett
Anne-Marie Beretta
Sigvard Bernadotte
Lucian Bernhard
Harry Bertoia
Betanova
Laura Biagiotti
Max Bill
Joseph Binder
Acton Bjørn
Karin Björquist
Misha Black
Robert Blaich
Karl Oskar Blase
Bill Biass
Cini Boeri
Antonio Boggeri
Marc Bohan
Jonas Bohlin
Rodolfo Bonetto
Gui Bonsiepe
John Box
Robert Boyle
Bruno Bozzetto
Marianne Brandt
Pieter Brattinga
Marcel Breuer
Alexey Brodovich
Erik Bruun
Rut Bryk
Torun Bülow-Hübe
Aaron Burns
Stephen Burrows
Will Burtin

John Bury
Rido Busse
Frances Butler

Jean Cacharel
Henry Thomas Cadbury-Brown
Max Caflisch
Pierre Cardin
Jean Carlu
Eugenio Carmi
Ben Carré
Edward Carrick
Hugh Casson
Anna Castelli-Ferrieri
Achille Castiglioni
Livio Castiglioni
Pier Giacomo Castiglioni
Chamberlin, Powell and Bon
Gabrielle Chanel
Pierre Charbonnier
Chermayeff and Geismar Associates
Ivan Chermayeff
Serge Chermayeff
Paolo Chessa
Seymour Chwast
Roman Cieslewicz
Paul Colin
David Colley
Susan Collier/Sarah Campbell
Joe Colombo
Giulio Confalonieri
Terence Conran
Muriel Cooper
André Courrèges
Lucien Coutaud
Enrico Coveri
Theo Crosby
Wim Crouwel
Gunnar Cyrén

Louis Danziger
Haig David-West
Lucienne Day
Richard Day
Robin Day
Jean d'Eaubonne
Jean-Charles de Castelbajac
Hubert de Givenchy
Rudolph de Harak
Oscar de la Renta
Sonia Delaunay
Jean-Claude de Luca
Michele De Lucchi
W.M. de Majo
Design Research Unit
Donald Deskey
Ingrid Dessau
Niels Diffrient
Jay Doblin
Danilo Donati
Rinaldo Donzelli
Louis Dorfsman
Henry Dreyfuss
Raoul Pene Du Bois
Duffy-Eley-Giffone-Worthington
Joseph Paul D'Urso
Karl Duschek
Roman Duszek

Charles Eames
Ray Eames
Tom Eckersley
Tias Eckhoff
Heinz Edelmann
Hans Ehrich
Hermann Eidenbenz
Kenji Ekuan
Perry Ellis
Environetics International
Hans Erni
Erté
Vuokko Eskolin-Nurmesniemi

Age Faith-Ell

Abdelkader Farrah
Gene Federico
Fendi
Perry Ferguson
Gianfranco Ferré
Edward Fields
Jochen Finke
Elio Fiorucci
Tazeena Firth
Richard Fischer
Jules Fisher
Willy Fleckhaus
Allan Fleming
Alan Fletcher
Jean-Michel Folon
Colin Forbes
Gregory Fossella
Kaj Franck
André François
Gina Fratini
Gianfranco Frattini
Achim Freyer
Friedrich Friedl
Arnold Friedmann
Sven Fristedt
A. G. Fronzoni
Anthony Froshaug
Adrian Frutiger
S. Neil Fujita
Shigeo Fukuda
Buckminster Fuller
James Fulton
Margaret Furse
Roger Furse

James Galanos
Abram Games
James Gardner
Ken Garland
Jean-Paul Gaultier
Thomas Geismar
Steff Geissbuhler
Rudi Gernreich
Robert P. Gersin
Karl Gerstner
Piero Gherardi
Ghia
Dante Giacosa
Bill Gibb
Bob Gill
Alexander Girard
Giorgetto Giugiaro
Milton Glaser
Ernö Goldfinger
Guillermo Gonzalez Ruiz
Mordecai Gorelik
Mieczyslaw Górowski
Gottschalk and Ash International
Kenneth Grange
Grapus
Michael Graves
Eileen Gray
Milner Gray
Malcolm Grear
Vittorio Gregotti
April Greiman
Madame Grès
Franco Grignani
Anton Grot
Maija Grotell
Jerzy Gurawski

Halston
Rolf Harder
Cathy Hardwick
Elisabet Hasselberg-Olsson
Ashley Havinden
Yoshio Hayakawa
Edith Head
Hein Heckroth
Desmond Heeley
Simo Heikkila
Pieter Hein
Dale Hennesy

F.H.K. Henrion
Jocelyn Herbert
Robert Heritage
Erik Herløw
Helena Hernmarck
Karl-Ernst Herrmann
David Hicks
Ernst and Ursula Hiestand
Hans Hillmann
Hubert Hilscher
George Him
Hipgnosis
Catherine Hipp
Hans Peter Hoch
Armin Hofmann
Erik Höglund
James Holland
Hans Hollein
Knud Holscher
Harry Horner
Max Huber
Johan Huldt
Allen Hurlburt
Ulrica Hydman-Vallien

Takenobu Igarashi
Giancarlo Iliprandi
ISD (Interior Space Design)
Fujiwo Ishimoto
Alec Issigonis
Shima Ito

Sally Jacobs
Arne Jacobsen
George Jenkins
Finn Juhl
Sven-Eric Juhlin
Dora Jung

Norma Kamali
Yusaku Kamekura
Tadeusz Kantor
Herbert W. Kapitzki
Albert Kapr
Donna Karan / Louis Dell'Olio
Toshi Katayama
György Kemény
Kenzo
Gyorgy Kepes
Leo Kerz
Emanuelle Khanh
Gunther Kieser
Kazuo Kimura
Jock Kinneir
Mark-Lee Kirk
Poul Kjaerholm
Anne Klein
Calvin Klein
Werner Klemke
Andrzej Klimowski
Vincent Kling
Florence Klotz
Peter Kneebone
Florence Knoll
Iwataro Koike
Ralph Koltai
Henning Koppel
Vincent Korda
Markku Kosonen
Boris Kroll
Yrjo Kukkapuro
Irma Kukkasjarvi
Mervyn Kurlansky

Karl Lagerfeld
Claude and François- Xavier Lalanne
Pino Lancetti
Walter Landor
Ted Lapidus
Ugo La Pietra
Jean Larcher
Anya Larkin
Jack Lenor Larsen
Ralph Lauren

Maija Lavonen
Michael Lax
Bernard Leach
Eugene Lee
Ming Cho Lee
Harold Leeds
Jan Lenica
Krzysztof Lenk
Dennis Lennon
Alain Le Quernec
Olaf Lèu
Herbert Leupin
Boris Leven
Jan Le Witt
Borge Lindau
Stig Lindberg
Bo Lindekrantz
Vicke Lindstrand
Leo Lionni
Raymond Loewy
Ian Logan
George Lois
Santa Loquasto
Peter Lord
Eugène Lourié
Herbert Lubalin
Gerald Luss
Hans-Rudolf Lutz
Emanuele Luzzati

Vico Magistretti
Erik Magnussen
Mainbocher
Tomás Maldonado
Carl Malmsten
Leonard Manasseh
Mariuccia Mandelli
Karl Mang
Angelo Mangiarotti
Michael Manwaring
Giovanni Mardersteig
Enzo Mari
Javier Mariscal
Noel Martin
Enid Marx
John Massey
Massin
Bruno Mathsson
Minoru Matsuba
Takaaki Matsumoto
Herbert Matter
Holger Matthies
Aimir Mavignier
Mary McFadden
David Mellor
Perttu Mentula
Marjatta Metsovaara
Grethe Meyer
Francis Meynell
Jo Mielziner
James Miho
Tomoko Miho
Masa Minagawa
Marcello Minale
Wilfried Minks
Ottavio Missoni
Rosita Missoni
Issey Miyake
Jan Młodozeniec
Børge Mogensen
Tanya Moisewitsch
Carlo Mollino
Bruno Monguzzi
Rune Mono
Claude Montana
Gene Moore
Hanae Mori
Alex Moulton
Olivier Mourgue
Jozef Mroszczak
Marcìn Mroszczak
Thierry Mugler
Jean Muir
Rolf Felix Müller

Josef Müller-Brockmann
Bruno Munari
Tharon Musser
Martti Mykkanen

Kazumasa Nagai
Makoto Nakamura
John Napier
George Nelson
Hans Neuburg
Alexander Nesmeister
Barbro Nilsson
Bob Noorda
Norman Norell
Eliot Noyes
Antti Nurmesniemi

Timothy O'Brien
Siegfried Odermatt
Donald Oenslager
Herbert Ohl
Tomoji Okada

Sven Palmqvist
Verner Panton
Victor Papanek
Ico Parisi
Art Paul
Andrzej Pawlowski
Pentagram Design
Studio PER
Sigurd Persson
Signe Persson-Melin
Gaetano Pesce
Cipe Pineles
Pininfarina
Giovanni Pintori
Markku Piri
Warren Platner
William Lansing Plumb
Walter Plunkett
Gianni Polidori
Edward Pond
Jean-Pierre Ponnelle
Gio Ponti
Ferdinand Porsche
Anthony Powell
Benno Premsela
James Prestini
Emilio Pucci
Arthur J. Pulos
Ritva Puotila
Andrée Putman

Mary Quant

Peter Raacke
Paco Rabanne
Gunter Rambow
Bieter Rams
Paul Rand
Jorgen Rasmussen
John Reid
Zandra Rhodes
Jens Risom
Carrie Robbins
M. Clark Robertson
Terence Harold Robsjohn- Gibbings
Ernst Roch
Alberto Rosselli
Ann Roth
Martyn Rowlands
Emil Ruder
Cinzia Ruggeri
Gordon Russell
Erkki Ruuhinen
Sonia Rykiel

Horst Sagert
Yves Saint Laurent
Kiyoshi Sakashita
John F. Saladino
Juhani Salovaara
Roberto Sambonet

Willem Sandberg
Giorgio Sant'Angelo
Richard Sapper
Timo Sarpaneva
Jan Sawka
Carlo Scarpa
Tobia Scarpa
Mario Scheichenbauer
Hans Schleger
Douglas W. Schmidt
Hans Schmoller
Paul Schuitema
Leokadia Serafinowicz
Raul Shakespear
Ronald Shakespear
Ronaldus Shamask
Irene Sharaff
Adele Simpson
Jack Martin Smith
Oliver Smith
Jerome Synder
Yuri Soloviev
Luciano Soprani
Johnny Sorensen
Ettore Sottsass, Jr.
Space Design Group
Basil Spence
Herbert Spencer
Jurgen Spohn
Klaus Staeck
Anton Stankowski
Philippe Starck
Franciszek Starowieyski
Alberto Steiner
Henry Steiner
Magnus Stephensen
Richard Stevens
Reynolds Stone
Giotto Stoppino
William Stumpf
Kohei Sugiura
Yoichi Sumita
Inez Svensson

Josef Svoboda
Waldemar Swierzy
Richard Sylbert
Jozef Szajna

TAC Interior Architecture and Graphic Communication
Roger Tallon
Ikko Tanaka
Masaaki Tanaka
Tan Guidicelli
Ilmari Tapiovaara
Brian Tattersfield
Dean Tavoularis
Rouben Ter-Arutunian
Eduardo Terrazas
Armando Testa
Chantal Thomass
Bradbury Thompson
Rud Thygesen
Rosmarie Tissi
Oiva Toikka
Henryk Tomaszewski
Carl Toms
Alexandre Trauner
Pauline Trigère
Gero Troike
Niklaus Troxler
George Tscherny
Jan Tschichold
Alan Tye

Emanuel Ungaro
Maciej Urbaniec
Leon Urbanski

Valentino
Bertil Vallien
Koos van den Akker
John Vassos
Gianni Versace
Nelson Vigneault
Lella Vignelli

Massimo Vignelli
Madeleine Vionnet
Karl Von Appen
Pekka Vuori
Ladislav Vychodil

Wilhelm Wagenfeld
Robin Wagner
Don Wallance
Hermann Warm
Tokuji Watanabe
Jon Wealleans
Bjorn Weckstrom
Hans Wegner
Wolfgang Weingart
John Weitz
Robert Welch
Lyle Wheeler
Albert Whitlock
Zofia Wierchowicz
B.K. Wiese
Tapio Wirkkala
Henry Wolf
Ann Wolff
Lewis Woudhuysen
Russel Wright
Lance Wyman

Kansai Yamamato
Sori Yanagi
Jay Yang
Shoei Yoh
Tadanori Yokoo

Marco Zanuso
Hermann Zapf
Franco Zeffirelli
Eva Zeisel
Reinhart Zimmermann
Patricia Zipprodt
Piet Zwart

Alvar Aalto: *Scroll Chair,* **for Artek, 1934**

A

AALTO, Alvar.

Finnish architect, exhibition, furniture and glassware designer. Born Hugo Alvar Henrik Aalto, in Kuortane, near Jyvaskyla, 3 February 1898. Studied architecture, under Armas Lindgren, at the Technical University of Helsinki, 1916–21: Dip. Arch. 1921. Served in the Finnish Army, 1939. Married the architect Aino Marsio in 1924 (died, 1949); children: Johanna and Hamilkar; married the architect Elissa Makiniemi in 1952. Worked as an exhibition designer, in Göteborg, Tampere and Turku, 1921–22; architect from 1923, and furniture designer from 1925, establishing office in Jyvaskyla, 1923–27, in Turku, 1927–33, and in Helsinki, 1933 until his death in 1976; in partnership with Aino Aalto, 1924–49, and with Elissa Aalto, 1952–76; established experimental plywood workshop with Otto Korhonen, Turku, 1929, and Artek furniture design company with Aino Aalto and Mairea Gullichsen, Helsinki, 1935. Professor of Architecture, Massachusetts Institute of Technology, Cambridge, 1946–48. President of the Academy of Finland, 1963–68. **Exhibitions:** Museum of Modern Art, New York, 1938; Kunstgewerbemuseum, Zurich, 1948 (with Aino Aalto); Gewerbemuseum, Basel, 1957 (with Mies van der Rohe); Keski-Suomen Museum, Jyvaskyla, 1962; Akademie der Künste, Berlin, 1963; Kunsthaus, Zurich, 1964; Palazzo Strozzi, Florence, 1965; Ateneum, Helsinki, 1967; Moderna Museet, Stockholm, 1969; Finlandia Hall, Helsinki, 1978 (toured); Museum Folkwang, Essen, 1979; Museum of Modern Art, New York, 1984 (toured). Recipient: First prizes in Finnish and European architectural competitions, 1923, 1927, 1928, 1936, 1938, 1948, 1950, 1951, 1952, 1953, 1955, 1958, 1959, 1967; Royal Gold Medal, Royal Institute of British Architects, 1957; Sonningpriset, Denmark, 1962; Gold Medal, American Institute of Architects, 1963; Gold Cube, Svenska Arkitekters Riksforbund, Sweden, 1963; Gold Sash, Sociedad de Arquitetos, Mexico, 1963; Gold Medal, City of Florence, 1965; Palme d'Or du Mérite de l'Europe, 1966; City of Helsinki Prize, 1966; Thomas Jefferson Medal, University of Virginia, 1967; Litteris et Artibus Award, Sweden, 1969; Gold Medal, Academie d'Architecture, Paris, 1972; Tapiola Medal, 1975; National Arts Foundation Award, Liechtenstein, 1975. Honorary Doctorates: Princeton University, New Jersey, 1947; Technical University, Helsinki, 1949; Norges Tekniske Hojskole, Trondheim, 1960; Eidgenossische Technische Hochschule, Zurich, 1963; Columbia University, New York, 1964; Politecnico, Milan, 1964; Technische Hochschule, Vienna, 1965; University of Jyvaskyla, 1969. Honorary Royal Designer for Industry, Royal Society of Arts, London, 1947; Senior Fellow, Royal College of Art, London, 1950; Honorary Fellow, American Institute of Architects, 1958; Fellow, World Academy of Arts and Sciences, Israel, 1963. Honorary Member: Royal Institute of British Architects, 1937; American Academy of Arts and Sciences, 1957; Södra Sveriges Byggnadstekniska Samfund, Stockholm, 1957; Association of Finnish Architects, 1958; Accademia di Belle Arti, Venice, 1958; Norske Arkitekterns Landsforbund, Oslo, 1959; Västmanlands Dala Nation, Uppsala, 1965; Colegio de Arquitetos, Peru, 1965; Bund Deutscher Architekten, Germany, 1966; Engineering Society of Finland, 1966; American Academy of Arts and Letters, 1968; Akademie de Bildenden Künste, Vienna, 1975; Royal Scottish Academy, 1975. Chevalier of the Légion d'Honneur, France, 1939; Kommendors Korset av Danebrog, Denmark, 1957; Grand Cross of the Lion of Finland, 1965; Grande Ufficiale al Merito, Italy, 1966; Grand Croix de l'Ordre du Faucon, Iceland, 1972. *Died* (in Helsinki) *11 May 1976.*

Works:

Industrial Art exhibition layouts, Tampere, 1922.
7th Centenary Exhibition layouts, Turku, 1929.
Linked Chair 611 stackable chair in birch and plywood, for Jyvaskyla Civil Guards House, 1929–30.
Armchair 15 stackable upholstered chair in birch and plywood, 1929–30.
Convertible upholstered sofa with metal frame, for Wohnbedarf AG, Zurich, 1930.
Armchair 31 scroll chair in laminated birch and plywood with cantilever sides, for Paimio Sanatorium, 1931–32.
Savoy vase in green bottle glass, for Karhula, 1936.
Tea Trolley 900 with laminated sides and wicker or basketwork top, 1936–37.
Armchair 39 with laminated cantilever supports and wicker seat, 1936–37.
Forestry Pavilion, at the *Agricultural Exhibition,* Lapua, 1938.
Finnish Pavilion at the *World's Fair,* New York, 1938–39.
Aalto-kukka vases and dishes in clear glass, for Riihimaki, 1939.
Artek Exhibition pavilion, Hedemora, Sweden, 1945.
Armchair 406 with laminated supports, for Villa Mairea, 1946–47.
Chair 612 with solid wood Y-leg supports, 1946–47.
Armchair 45 with laminated armrest structure and webbing or rattan seat and back, 1946–47.
Stool X66 in ash veneer with three X-legs, 1954.
Stool X601 in ash with four fan-shaped X-legs, 1954.
Finnish Pavilion, at the *Biennale,* Venice, 1956.
X-leg armchair in birch with upholstered seat and back, for the National Pensions Institute, 1956.

(for a complete list of Aalto's buildings and architectural projects, see *Contemporary Architects*)

Publications:

By AALTO: books—*An Experimental Town,* Cambridge, Massachusetts 1940; *Postwar Reconstruction,* New York 1941; *Alvar Aalto Synopsis,* edited by Bernard Hoesli, Basel and Stuttgart 1970; *Alvar Aalto: Sketches,* edited by Göran Schildt, Helsinki 1972, London and Cambridge, Massachusetts 1978.

On AALTO: books—*Alvar Aalto: Architecture and Furniture,* exhibition catalogue, New York 1938; *Alvar Aalto* by Giorgio Labo, Milan 1948; *Alvar Aalto and Finnish Architecture* by E. and C. Neuenschwander, London and New York 1954; *Alvar Aalto* by Frederick Gutheim, London and New York 1960, Milan 1963; *Alvar Aalto* by Göran Schildt and Leonardo Mosso, Jyvaskyla 1962; *Alvar Aalto 1922–62,* edited by Karl Fleig, Zurich, London and New York 1963; *L'Opera di Alvar Aalto,* exhibition catalogue by Leonardo Mossor, Florence 1965; *Alvar Aalto* by Yukio Futagawa and others, Tokyo 1968, London 1970; *Alvar Aalto vol. II: 1963–70,* edited by Karl Fleig, London 1971; *Alvar Aalto* by Karl Fleig (adaptation of previous books), London 1975, Zurich 1979; *Alvar Aalto* by Carlo Cresti, Florence 1975; *Architecture by Alvar Aalto,* Helsinki, no. 1, from 1976; *Alvar Aalto and the International Style* by P. D. Pearson, London and New York 1978; *Architectural Monographs 4: Alvar Aalto* by Steven Groak, Liisa Heihonen and Demetri Porphyrios, London 1978; *Alvar Aalto 1898–1976,* exhibition catalogue by Aarno Ruusuvuori, Helsinki 1978; *Alvar Aalto,* edited by Göran Schildt, London and Cambridge, Massachusetts 1978; *Alvar Aalto—The Inner Process,* lecture paper by Malcolm Quantrill, London 1978; *Alvar Aalto* by David Dunster, New York 1979; *Alvar Aalto: das architektonische Werk,* exhibition catalogue edited by Zdenek Felix, Essen 1979; *Alvar Aalto: tutto il design* by Luciano Rubino, Rome 1980; *Alvar Aalto versus the Modern Movement,* edited by Kirmo Mikkola, Helsinki 1981; *Alvar Aalto als Designer* by Werner Blaser, Stuttgart 1982; *Studies on Alvar Aalto* by Demetri Porphyrios, London 1982; *Det vita bordet* by Göran Schildt, Stockholm 1982, as *Alvar Aalto: The Early Years,* New York 1984; *Alvar Aalto: A Critical Study* by Malcolm Quantrill, London 1983.

Bibliography: *Alvar Aalto: A Bibliography* by William C. Miller, Monticello, Illinois 1976, as *Alvar Aalto: An Annotated Bibliography,* Monticello, Illinois 1984; *Alvar Aalto: Designer and Architect,* Monticello, Illinois 1980.

Although a sense of personal expression permeates Alvar Aalto's work, in fact he developed close creative partnerships with both his first and second wives, who, like him, were trained as architects. After marrying for the first time, in 1924 to Aino Marsio (1894–1949), they worked so closely together that it is impossible to identify their separate roles in their joint projects, or even to be certain which were joint projects and which were not. The historian and theorist Siegfried Giedion, who knew them both well, once wrote that Alvar was "restless, effervescent, incalculable," while "Aino was thorough, persevering, and contained." He added, "Sometimes it is a good thing when a volcano is encircled by a quietly flowing stream."

Aalto progressed from an early classicism, influenced by neo-classic buildings in Northern Europe as well as by the late Renaissance and early Baroque architecture of Italy, to mature work which was not at all revivalist, but which benefited from the possibilities suggested by traditional expression and materials as well as from the new expressive and technical means revealed to him by his association with the architects of the Congrès Internationaux d'architecture Moderne. A similar progression can be seen in his furniture, which became more daring and original after his association with C.I.A.M.

Aalto's earliest furniture designs were based on traditional models derived from the eighteenth century or the early nineteenth century. There was also a resemblance to some of the furniture produced by the English Arts and Crafts movement. Only a tendency to make his designs simpler than comparable pieces gave a hint of Aalto's future mastery of furniture design. It is probable that his first contacts with experimental furniture were the bent-plywood chairs produced in Tallin, Estonia, by Luterma. This firm had once been headed by Christian Luther, whose late-nineteenth-century experiments with casein bonding techniques and hot plate presses had led to a line of mass-produced chairs with bent-plywood, one-piece back-and-seat units. These units, still marketed in the 1920's, had stimulated Aalto's imagination at just about the time he became interested in the C.I.A.M. (He joined the group in 1928 and attended its annual meeting in Frankfurt in 1929.) While there was some direct influence on Aalto from C.I.A.M. designers, such as Marcel Breuer, who developed a cantilever chair, the ability of Breuer and others in the group to create a sense of excitement about experimental furniture was more important.

The first product of Aalto's interest in plywood was a stacking chair, which had traditional, solid, wood legs, placed outside the limits of the seat to permit stacking; the seat was of formed plywood mounted on traditional seat rails. The chair was patented in 1929 and went into production that year in a factory in Turku, Finland, where the Aaltos maintained their office at that time. They worked closely with the factory manager, Otto Korhonen, in producing this chair. Another 1929 design for Korhonen's factory was a chair with a one-piece, bent-plywood seat-and-back unit mounted on a cantilevered, tubular-steel base. Its seat-and-back unit closely resembled one of Luther's units. In variation, portions of the L-shaped, curving plane of the back-and-seat unit were cut and folded forward to form arms, thus also providing greater strength because of the resulting multi-planar curve. At about the same time, the Aaltos initiated experiments which were more in the nature of sculpture than design; these were aimed at exploring some of the possibilities of bending and laminating strips of veneer and thin, wood rods.

Little of Aalto's furniture was conceived for his specific buildings, but his plans for interiors often included pieces of his furniture which had been put into production. However, some of Aalto's furniture, including some of the best known, was designed for individual buildings and later put into production for general sale. Examples are the furniture for the tuberculosis sanitorium at Paimio, Finland and for the mu-

nicipal library at Viipuri (now Vyborg in the Soviet Union).

Aalto was awarded the contract for the design of the sanitorium at Paimio, along with its furnishings and equipment, in 1929, as the result of a competition. As it was constructed and outfitted from 1930 to 1933, he took special care with details. For example, the lighting fixtures were located for the benefit of reclining persons, and the plumbing was designed to minimize noise when it was used. The all-plywood scroll chair, conceived for this sanitorium, avoided metal parts so that it would be less noisy when moved, while its open structure and lack of upholstery aided in maintaining sanitary conditions. It consists of a bent-plywood back-and-seat unit, curving under the front and behind the back. Each end of this scroll-form unit is supported by stretchers, which are attached to supports in the form of laminated-wood loops, which serve as armrests besides and which are also joined by a stretcher in the rear.

For the library commission at Viipuri, also awarded as the result of a competition, Aalto took similar pains. The competition entry was submitted in 1927, the results were announced the following year, and in 1929 Aalto completed his revised plans. Subsequently, the site was changed, and the redesign of the building for the new site was not completed until 1933; construction and furnishing were completed in 1935. The main reading room was enlivened by dramatic changes of floor levels and was illuminated by roof-lights, developed earlier by Aalto, which employed cylindrical openings in the roof. These openings were deep enough to prevent direct sunlight from entering, and reflections off the sides provided diffused natural light. Lighting fixtures were placed above these roof-lights, so that artificial light was diffused as well. The long, narrow lecture-discussion hall on the ground story had an undulating wooden ceiling, formed of slats of wood and designed for acoustic effect. Aalto's experiments with plywood furniture had led to this ceiling; and the integration of wood into buildings designed and constructed according to modern ideas and methods was to become a hallmark of Aalto's practice.

The furniture for the library included lounge chairs which were developed from the Paimio scroll chair. There was also a related series of stackable, wood, three-legged stools and four-legged chairs and tables with circular tops and seats. They rested on hook-shaped supports of birch, which had been formed by precision-sawing them at one end into thin leaves separated by grooves. Thin pieces of wood were then glued into the grooves. Until the glue set, the supports could be easily bent, but when attached to the undersides of the stools, tables, and chairs, they resulted in furniture that was nearly indestructible. Moreover, the cost was low. Although the library was severely damaged in World War II, excellent vintage photographs record its appearance.

International recognition began to come to the Aaltos in 1933, when they showed their furniture in a London exhibition set up by the *Architectural Review* and at the *Triennale* in Milan. Also in that year, they moved their office to Helsinki. Here in the Finnish capital, they were introduced to Harry and Maire Gullichsen, with whom they formed the Artek Company to manufacture and distribute their furniture. (Some production continued simultaneously at Korhonen's factory.) Aino Aalto became supervisor of production, and sales increased greatly in Great Britain and in other European countries as well as in the United States, where their furniture was featured at an exhibition in the Museum of Modern Art in 1938.

The best-known of Aalto's exhibition designs

was the Finnish Pavilion at the New York World's Fair in 1939, a joint commission with Aino. Its most striking feature was the exhibition court, highlighted by a dramatic, undulating, wood screen cantilevered out over a ground-level exhibition of Finnish products. The wood screen had three registers of splayed ribs, on which photographs of Finnish scenes were mounted. Aalto returned to New York in 1940 to revise the exhibition to reflect changes wrought by the first Russo-Finnish War.

The Artek firm was revived after World War II, and Aalto's last two bursts of activity as a furniture designer occurred in 1947 and in 1954–56. During 1947, he developed the "Y" leg, essentially a further development of the supports for his library tables and chairs at Viipuri. The "Y" leg was formed from two joined pieces of solid wood, bent at the knees to diverge at right angles. The bend was accomplished in a manner similar to that used for the library furniture, except that a pattern of thin leaves projected beyond the bend; into these, horizontal members of solid wood, also precision-sawed at the ends into thin leaves, could be dovetailed and glued into position. Thus, a frame was provided for stool or table, and a chair variation allowed supports for the back to be integrated into two of the legs. In the mid-1950's, Aalto developed five-part uprights splayed at the top into a fan shape, thus permitting greater integration of vertical and horizontal members than was possible with the "Y" support.

In 1949, Aalto won a competition for the design of the village center of Säynätsalo, which was to become one of his finest and best-known achievements. It was also during 1949 that Aino Aalto died. During the next two years, construction at Säynätsalo took place, supervised by a young architect, Elissa Mäkiniemi, who became Aalto's second wife in 1952. They, too, developed a close creative partnership, working together on architectural and planning commissions, and she supervised the production of her husband's furniture at Artek.

The architects and designers of the C.I.A.M. were strongly influenced by the Utopian social ideas current in Europe during the 1920's. Nevertheless, their International style work, and that of their followers, has often been criticized as rigid and lifeless. Whether that is a fair assessment or not, it is clear that nowhere were the humanistic intentions of the C.I.A.M. group more readily apparent than in Aalto's work and in the high regard its members had for his work. Aalto's particular achievement is that he maintained his roots in Finland and in the Baltic region while absorbing international influences and working with new technological means.

—Lloyd C. Engelbrecht

AARNIO, Eero.
Finnish industrial and interior designer. Born in Helsinki, 21 July 1932. Studied at the Institute of Industrial Arts, Helsinki, 1954–57: Dip. 1957. Freelance interior and industrial designer, specializing in chair design, Helsinki, since 1962; also photographer and graphic artist. **Exhibitions:** *Rattan Stools,* Asko Company, Helsinki, 1961; *7 x 7 Arkitekter,* Stockholm, 1964; Milan Triennale, 1964; *Fibreglass Furniture,* Asko Company, Helsinki, 1968 (travelled to Stockholm); *Eurodomus,* Milan, 1970; *Mod-*

ern Chairs 1918–1970, Whitechapel Art Gallery, London, 1970; *Plastic as Plastic,* Museum of Modern Art, New York, 1970; *Design in Finland,* Asko Company, Cologne, 1979; *Scandinavian Modern Design 1880–1980,* Cooper-Hewitt Museum, New York, 1982; *Design Since 1945,* Philadelphia Museum of Art, 1983. **Collections:** Suomen Taideteollisuusmuseo, Helsinki; Louisiana Museum, Humlebaek; Stedelijk Museum, Amsterdam; Musee d'Art Moderne, Paris; Victoria and Albert Museum, London; Museum of Decorative Arts, Prague; Israel Museum, Jerusalem. Recipient: First Prize, Trade Mark Competition, Helsinki, 1958; First Prize, Scandinavian Street Furniture Competition, Stockholm, 1965; First Prize, International Furniture Competition, Cantu, 1965; International Design Award, American Institute of Interior Designers, 1968. Address: Riipakoivuntie 24, 02130 Espoo 13, Finland.

Works:

Logotype symbol, for Valmety steel factory, Helsinki, 1958.
Appletree chair, 1959.
Jattujakkare stool in wicker, 1961.
Tomato chair, for Asko, 1964.
Mushroom chair and stool in wicker, 1965.
Thunderball (also called *Bomb* or *Globe*) chair in upholstered fibreglass and metal, for Asko, 1965–66.
Bubble chair, for Asko, 1967.
Pastilli (also called *Gyro* or *Rock n' Roll*) chair in fibreglass, for Asko, 1968.

Publications:

On AARNIO: books—*Modern Furniture* by Ella Moody, London 1966; *The Modern Chair, 1850 to Today* by Gilbert Frey, London and Niederteufen 1970; *Modern Chairs 1918–1970,* exhibition catalogue with text by Carol Hogben, Dennis Young and others, London 1970; *New Design in Wood* by Donald J. Willcox, New York

and London 1970; *The Modern Chair: Classics in Production* by Clement Meadmore, London 1974; *Scandinavian Design: Objects of a Life Style* by Eileene Harrison Beer, New York and Toronto 1975; *Modern Furniture* by John F. Pile, New York and Toronto 1979; *Twentieth-Century Furniture* by Philippe Garner, London 1980; *The Form and Substance of Finnish Furniture* by Riitta Miestamo, Lahti 1981; *Neue Moebel 1950–1982,* edited by Klaus-Jürgen Sembach, Stuttgart 1982, as *Contemporary Furniture,* New York 1982; *Design Since 1945,* edited by Kathryn Hiesinger and George Marcus, Philadelphia and London 1983; *The Conran Directory of Design,* edited by Stephen Bayley, London 1985.

Finnish design since the National Romantic movement of the early 1900's has retained throughout its development close links with the country's native materials and traditions. Aalto's classic furniture of the 1930's, for example, despite its exploitation of wood bending and laminating technology is still firmly rooted in the centuries-old tradition of the Finnish farmhouse.

Eero Aarnio started from this same tradition. One of his first works, the Jattujakkare wickerwork stool, is a simple, straightforward adaption for multiple production of handcraft work, and the Apple tree chair of the 1950's is a direct modern interpretation of the wooden chairs made by local craftsmen for centuries.

But Aarnio goes further. "Design," he says, "means constant renewal, realignment, growth." In support of this principle, he experimented in the 1960's with furniture in plastics and, in tune with the iconoclastic mood of the time, designed a series of chairs whose exotic names—Tomato, Pastille, Bubble, Thunderball—underline their complete departure from traditional forms of seating; in these, he achieved visual excitement, practicality, and comfort with a logical and economic use of his material.

He has now gone yet further: "The materials of the year 2000 are wood, metal, and plastics, upholstered with foam plastic and covered with fabric, leather, and artificial materials." In pur-

suance of this idea, he has evolved a system whereby the components of a chair—legs, seat, arms and back—become modules that may be manipulated by computer; with the use of natural and artificial materials for structure and finish, a vast range of variations can be had.

Aarnio is always ahead of his time. Although perhaps the most international of Finnish designers of furniture, he is nevertheless intensely individual. Not a follower of any school, but conceivably the founder of one, he nevertheless acknowledges his place as a link in a constantly evolving chain. Although Finnish at heart, he sees his country and its products objectively, within a wider, international context. He acknowledges without reservation the importance of the individual, and he sees how modern technology can serve the individual's way of life. "The personal approach of the past and the robot manufacture of the future clasp hands." Everyone can have the chair, say, that he wants. We have come full circle. Industrial production will be so completely mastered that we can forget it," he predicts.

—Gordon Steele

ADAM, Ken.
British film designer. Born Klaus Adam, in Berlin, Germany, 5 February 1921; emigrated to Britain in 1934: naturalized. Educated at Le College Français, Berlin; Craigend Park School, Edinburgh; St. Paul's School, London; studied at Bartlett School of Architecture, University of London, 1937–39: articled in architectural firm C. W. Glover and Partners, London, 1939–40. Served in the Pioneer Corps, 1940, and as fighter pilot in the Royal Air Force, 1941–46: Flight Lieutenant. Married Maria-Letizia Moanro

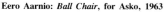
Eero Aarnio: *Ball Chair*, for Asko, 1963

in 1952. Joined film industry as a draughtsman, 1947–48, as art director from 1948, and as production designer from 1959; also freelance architectural and interior designer, London, from 1953. Recipient: Best Art Direction/Costume Design for *The Trials of Oscar Wilde,* Moscow Film Festival, 1960; British Academy Award for *Dr. Strangelove,* 1964, and for *The Ipcress File,* 1965; American Academy Award for *Barry Lyndon,* 1975; Best Production Award for *Pennies from Heaven,* New York Film Critics, 1981. **Collection:** Cinemathèque, Paris. Address: 34 Montpelier Street, London SW7, England.

Works:

Adams and Harvey exhibition stand, at Olympia, London, 1953.
Harlequin espresso bar, Oxford, 1953.
Cul de Sac espresso bar, London, 1956.
The Gondola espresso bar, Richmond, Surrey, 1956.
Mike Todd's "First Night" party, London Festival Gardens, 1957.
K.R.S. offices and boardroom, Dean Street, London, 1958.
House and apartment conversions, London, from 1958.
La Fanciulla del West opera production, Royal Opera House, London, 1977 and 1982.

(films—as draughtsman, art director or production designer): *This Was a Woman,* 1947; *Lucky Mascot (The Brass Monkey),* 1948; *Third Time Lucky,* 1948; *The Queen of Spades,* 1948; *Obsession (The Hidden Room),* 1948; *Dick Barton Strikes Back,* 1949; *Now Barabbas (Now Barabbas Was a Robber . . .),* 1949; *Three Men and a Girl (Golden Arrow),* 1949; *Your Witness (Eye Witness),* 1950; *The Crimson Pirate,* 1952; *The Master of Ballantrae,* 1953; *The Intruder,* 1953; *Star of India,* 1953; *Helen of Troy,* 1955; *Soho Incident (Spin a Dark Web),* 1956; *Child in the House,* 1956; *Around the World in Eighty Days,* 1957; *The Devil's Pass,* 1957; *Night of the Demon (Curse of the Demon),* 1957; *Battle of the V.1 (Missiles from Hell),* 1958; *Gideon of Scotland Yard (Gideon's Day),* 1959; *Beyond This Place (Web of Evidence),* 1959; *The Angry Hills,* 1959; *Ten Seconds to Hell,* 1959; *The Rough and the Smooth (Portrait of a Sinner),* 1959; *In the Nick,* 1959; *John Paul Jones,* 1959; *Ben Hur,* 1959; *Let's Get Married,* 1960; *The Trials of Oscar Wilde (The Green Carnation),* 1960; *The Hellions,* 1962; *Sodoma e Gomorra (Sodom and Gomorrah),* 1962; *Dr. No,* 1962; *In the Cool of the Night,* 1962; *Dr. Strangelove,* 1964; *Woman of Straw,* 1964; *Goldfinger,* 1964; *The Long Ships,* 1964; *The Ipcress File,* 1965; *Thunderball,* 1965; *Funeral in Berlin,* 1966; *You Only Live Twice,* 1967; *Chitty Chitty Bang Bang,* 1968; *Goodbye Mr. Chips,* 1969; *The Owl and the Pussycat,* 1970; *Sleuth,* 1972; *The Last of Sheila,* 1973; *Barry Lyndon,* 1975; *The Seven-Per-Cent Solution,* 1976; *Salon Kitty (Madam Kitty),* 1977; *The Spy Who Loved Me,* 1977; *Moonraker,* 1979; *Pennies from Heaven,* 1981; *King David,* 1985; *Agnes of God,* 1985.

Publications:

By ADAM: articles—"Designing Sets for Action" in *Films and Filming* (London), August 1956; interviews in *Screen International* (London), 12 February 1977; *Positif* (Paris), March 1977; *Cinema* (Paris), January 1978; *Film Comment* (New York), January/February 1982.

On ADAM: books—*Dictionary of Film Makers* by Georges Sadoul, Paris 1965, Los Angeles 1972; *Le Décor der Film* by Leon Barsacq, Paris 1970, as *Caligari's Cabinet and Other Grand Illusions,* Boston 1976; *The Film Encyclopedia* by Ephraim Katz, New York and London 1979; articles—"Three Designers" by R. Hudson in *Sight and Sound* (London), Winter 1964/65; "20 Leading Film Designers" by B. Pattison in the *International Film Guide 1968,* edited by Peter Cowie, London 1967; in *National Film Theatre* (London) booklet, October/November 1979.

Few have contributed more to the success of the British postwar cinema than Ken Adam. His credits as a designer, stage and artistic director on feature films seem hardly credible, since it is difficult to conceive that any single designer could ever create so many major productions with such diverse disciplines and styles—ranging from the large-scale and expensive James Bond pictures like *Moonraker* to intimate and comparatively modest ones like *Queen of Spades.* The number of top name directors with whom Adam has collaborated proves him to be one of the most sought-after production designers in the Western hemisphere. What makes Ken Adam's contribution so vital is his widely based talent and capabilities on so many essential levels. As a trained architect, he understands space and construction. His spirited sketches already contain an understanding of these and other problems that usually become evident only after the set design has finally been constructed. Technically, he is fully competent—knowing the filmic value of different materials from metal to plastic, from hard to soft materials. He has a highly inventive imagination, as shown by the plethora of astounding gadgets in his Bond pictures. His thinking is instinctively large-scale, and one can sense the tradition of the masters of early German expressionist and abstract styles of the 1920s in much of his work. He understands film timing, continuity and movement—which is why he is able to work with the most talented directors. He is also keenly aware of the distinctions between fantasy and reality, using realism as a starting point, a departure to take the audience toward a world of visual fantasy to which film is so eminently suitable. Here, he is able to expand his own inherent skills to enlarge on life. He is also practical—an attitude producers appreciate. He can adapt his work to budgets big or small by understanding the objectives and circumstances of a production. These values have made Ken Adam, for nearly fifty years, one of the most successful production designers on both sides of the Atlantic.

—John Halas

ADOLFO.
American fashion designer. Born Adolfo F. Sardiña in Cardenas, Matanzas, Cuba, 15 February 1933; emigrated to the United States in 1951: naturalized, 1958. Educated at St. Ignacious de Loyola Jesuit School, Havana, B.A. 1950. Served 3 years in the Cuban Army. Apprentice, Cristobal Balenciaga hat salon, Paris, 1950–52; apprentice millinery designer, Bergdorf Goodman, New York, 1953–54; designer Emme millinery shop, New York, 1954–62; also worked as an unpaid apprentice for Chanel, 1956 and 1957. Owner and head designer, Adolfo Inc., New York, since 1962; also designer, Adolfo Menswear Inc., and Adolfo Scarves Inc., New York, since 1978; established fragrance line for Frances Denny, New York, 1979. Member of the Council, Fashion Designers of America, 1962. Recipient: Coty Award for hats, 1955, for costume, 1969; Neiman Marcus Award, 1956. **Exhibition:** *Fashion: An Anthology by Cecil Beaton,* Victoria and Albert Museum, London, 1971. **Collections:** Metropolitan Museum of Art, New York; Smithsonian Institution, Washington, D.C.; Dallas Museum of Fine Arts; Los Angeles County Museum of Art. Address: 36 East 57th Street, New York, New York 10022, U.S.A.

Publications:

On ADOLFO: books—*Fashion: An Anthology by Cecil Beaton,* exhibition catalogue, compiled by Madeleine Ginsburg, London 1971; *With Tongue in Chic* by Ernestine Carter, London 1974; *The World of Fashion: People, Places, Resources,* edited by Eleanor Lambert, New York 1976; *The Changing World of Fashion: 1900 to the Present* by Ernestine Carter, London 1977; *McDowell's Directory of Twentieth Century Fashion* by Colin McDowell, London 1984; *The Encyclopaedia of Fashion from 1840 to the 1980s* by Georgina O'Hara, London 1986.

To make clothes that are long-lasting and with subtle changes from season to season—this is my philosophy.

—Adolfo

Of the two designers who directly shaped his approach, Chanel and Balenciaga, Chanel affected Adolfo more. Her type of classic suit was a regular feature of Adolfo's collections throughout the 1970's, and his 1976 collection was Chanel even down to the two-tone shoes. Among the models were a striped cardigan and blouse with a plain skirt and a navy knit suit with a white silk crepe blouse, combinations that spoke the essence of Chanel. Nancy Reagan bought both outfits. During the subsequent presidential election campaign, Mrs. Reagan gave Adolfo front-page publicity, saying that she took his clothes on the campaign because they travelled well and remained impeccable. Between them, Adolfo and Mrs. Reagan aim at a trim look, somewhat in the tradition of Mainbocher and the Duchess of Windsor, for an important lady who is most satisfied with the designer who can create the image she considers appropriate for her station in life. A little daring is permissible, as in Adolfo's off-one-shoulder evening gown which Mrs. Reagan wore as First Lady Elect, but the exposure was modest and most of the chest was covered. The fact that Adolfo does not strive for originality and sensation is greatly to his advantage when dressing the head of state's consort, whose clothes must have dignity and taste. In addition, Adolfo keeps himself in the background and is not a self-publicist to the extent that his chief American rival Halston is, wherefore Adolfo was the one to win presidential patronage. At any court, the appointed purveyors are expected not to exploit their privilege.

Adolfo is an excellent example of the creator of good-quality clothes achieving a very successful career without gimmickry. He presents variations on established themes, not new ideas which seek to overthrow existing norms. As a conservative designer, he accords fully with the regime for which he works. He gives Mrs. Reagan a conservative look, which expresses her political stance. Any time that a designer becomes associated with a particular government, he or she becomes responsible for part of the image of that regime, as has been seen time and time again, with Rose Bertin and Queen Marie

Adolfo: Crocheted suit, 1983

Antoinette, Leroy and Empress Josephine, Charles Frederick Worth with Empress Eugénie, and Edward Molyneux with the Duchess of Kent. Such a position very few couturiers can hope to attain, and on Adolfo's shoulders rests the responsibility of designing an image that will seem elegant in future history books; he fulfills this charge by following the established principles of his teachers.

—Diana de Marly

AGHA, Mehemed Fehmy.

American photographer, art director, graphic and typography designer. Born of Turkish parents, in Nicolaieff, Ukraine (now in the U.S.S.R.), 11 March 1896; emigrated to the United States in 1929: naturalized, 1936. Studied at the Emperor Alexander Technical School, Nicolaieff, 1909–13; economics, Polytechnic Institute of Emperor Peter the Great, Petrograd, 1914–18; political science, Ecole Nationale des Langues Orientales Vivantes, Paris, 1920–23: Dip. 1923. Studio Chief, Dorland Advertising Agency, Paris, 1924–27; chief assistant and layout artist, *Vogue* magazine, German edition, Berlin, 1927–29; Art Director, Conde Nast Publications, working on *Vogue, Vanity Fair,* and *House and Garden,* in New York, 1929–42; freelance design consultant and art director, establishing M. F. Agha design studio, New York, 1943–70: worked principally for *Better Homes and Gardens, Seventeen, McCall's, Newsweek,* Saks Fifth Avenue, Bloomingdale's, Leo Burnett, Hart Schaffner and Marx, and Franklin Simon. Founder-Member, National Society of Art Directors, New York; Advisory Board Member, Cooper Union, New York. President, Art Directors Club of New York, 1934–35, and American Institute of Graphic Arts, New York, 1943–45, 1954–55. Recipient: American Institute of Graphic Arts Medal, 1957; Art Directors Club of New York Hall of Fame Award, 1972. Honorary Member, Institute of Graphic Arts, New York. *Died* (in Malvern, Pennsylvania) *27 May 1978.*

Publications:

By AGHA: articles—"A Word on European Photography" in *Pictorial Photography in America* (New York), no. 5, 1929; "Surrealism or the Purple Cow" in *Vogue* (New York), November 1936; "Whistler's Hippopotamus: A Japing Dialogue on Photography, New and Old" in *Vogue* (New York), March 1937; "Woman's Place is in the Dark Room" in *Vogue* (New York), October 1938; "George Melies: Movie Pioneer Fantasist" in *Vogue* (New York), March 1939; "Raphaels Without Hands" in *Vogue* (New York), June 1941; "Horseless Photography" in *Harper's Bazaar* (New York), November 1944; "Fashion Photography Today" in *Photography* (New York), Fall 1947; "Creative Rebellion Under Five Dollars" in *Architecture and Engineering* (New York), March 1948; "Remarks on Modern Decorative Design" in *Design* (London), March 1948.

On AGHA: books—*In Vogue: Sixty Years of Celebrities and Fashion* by Georgina Howell, London 1975, 1978; *The Man Who Was Vogue* by Caroline Seebohm, New York 1982; *The Encyclopaedia of Fashion from 1840 to the 1980s* by Georgina O'Hara, London 1986; articles—"Agha's American Decade" in *PM* (New York), no. 8, 1939; "Young Turk" in *Time* (New York), 16 October 1939; "Mehemed Fehmy Agha" by J. Morrow in *Communication Arts* (Palo Alto), no. 4, 1972; "Art Directors Club of New York: 51st Annual Hall of Fame" in *Graphis* (Zurich), no. 163, 1972; "Profile: M. F. Agha" in *Upper and Lower Case* (New York), December 1978; "M. F. Agha" by S. Bodine and M. Dunas in *AIGA Journal* (New York), no. 3, 1985.

An astute and learned man, who spoke five languages fluently and conversed in many more visually, Dr. Mehemed Fehmy Agha pioneered the profession of art direction in the United States. Born of Turkish parents in the Russian Ukraine at the turn of the century, Agha, who received his doctorate in Political Science (thus the term of address), started his career in Paris as a studio chief for the Dorland Advertising Agency. Due to his strong artistic and photographic work, he was sent to Berlin as chief assistant and layout man for the new German *Vogue.* And although this magazine was short-lived, Agha's skills were noticed by Conde Nast, who offered him the job of redesigning American *Vogue.*

Upon his arrival in New York early in 1929, Agha took over not only the design of *Vogue* but also that of *Vanity Fair* and *House & Garden.* He applied his first-hand knowledge of Russian and European avant-garde art and design, as well as innovative magazines such as *Verve, Arts et Metiers Graphiques, Gebrauchsgraphik,* and *Novyi Lef,* to the visual needs of a modern American fashion magazine.

Avant-garde design ideas flooded Agha's treatment of *Vanity Fair.* He employed the asymmetric page layout already exploited by artistic movements such as De Stijl and Dada to add visual dynamism, lower-case letters to rejuvenate headlines and captions, and typecase dingbats to add visual shifts, reminiscent of El Lissitzky's layouts for Mayakovsky's poetry. He treated page layouts afresh as spreads rather than single entities, extending the format and developing a new visual orientation—a design idea that was concurrently employed by Alexey Brodovitch at *Harper's Bazaar.* (The first double-page spread appeared in the May, 1930 *Vanity Fair,* with a photograph taken by Edward Steichen.)

In typography, Agha abolished the affected italic in favor of the more legible roman in titles, stretched out letter spacing and flushed the type lines to the page margins. He substituted heavy black for decorative rules and eliminated clutter in illustrations and ornaments. Paralleling the theories of International Style architecture, the structural bones of typography were geometrically arranged within the taut skin of the page, providing a clean, spacious context for editorial content: the "less is more" mentality applied to layout.

At *Vogue,* Agha installed an in-house photography studio, which incorporated a system of dramatic lighting that could emphasize shadows and stark, planar shafts of light, a translation of chiaroscuro to photography. To encourage his staff to think in terms of snapshots rather than portraits, he introduced extraneous props, such as a stepladder or planks of woods. In the studio shots of the early 30s, subjects became noticeably more animated, gestural and expressionistic. In layout, Agha eliminated border on the photographs and instituted bleeds while often radically cropping the images to show details of a face or silhouetted parts of the body.

Shots taken outside the studio, such as landscapes and cityscapes were also introduced to the pages of *Vanity Fair* by Agha. Aerial photo- graphs of traffic taken from atop the newly constructed Chrysler Building or stark constructivist homages to the George Washington Bridge provided constant reminders of the machine age that he felt modern readers of a stylish magazine should appreciate.

Agha made an important contribution in securing a place for fine artists and art photographers in the popular world of magazine publishing. He invited the now-famous photographers George Hoynignen-Huene and Horst to work for the Conde Nast publications, as well as working with established photographers such as Cecil Beaton, Edward Weston, Berenice Abbott and Steichen. He reproduced drawings by Picasso, Modigliani, George Kolbe and Louis Lozowick, occasionally cajoling them into doing something original for the magazines: Cipe Pineles, who worked under Agha in the early 30s, remembers: "Though the subject may have been fashion, the idea was that great artists could be given the freedom and challenge to work on its presentation."

Dr. Agha laid the groundwork for a new level of design participation in the popular magazine. The art director arose with the need to forge a "cultural commodity" in tune with the changing tastes of a sensitized and consumptive American public during the 1920s. His orchestration of design elements and editorial interpretation created an unprecedented empathy with the audience of his age. After Agha, the art director became an indispensable ingredient in popular magazine publishing.

—Sarah Bodine

AGNÈS B. (Agnès Claret de Fleurieu).

French fashion designer. Born Agnès Troublé, in Versailles, 26 November 1941. Married Christian Bourgeois in 1960; children: Etienne, Nicolas, Ariane and Aurore; married Jean Rene Claret de Fleurieu in 1979; daughter: Iris. Worked as junior editor, *Elle* magazine, Paris, 1958; designer with the Jacobsons, for Dorothee Bis, Paris, 1958–60; freelance designer, working for Limitex, Pierre d'Alby, and V de V, Paris, 1966–75; established own fashion design shop in Les Halles, Paris, 1975: has opened 2 branch shops in Paris, 4 elsewhere in France, and others in New York, Los Angeles, London, Düsseldorf and Tokyo. **Collections:** Musée des Arts de la Mode, Paris; Musée du Louvre, Paris. Address: 194 rue de Rivoli, 75001 Paris, France.

Publications:

On AGNÈS B: books—*25 Ans de Marie-Claire de 1954 a 1979,* compiled by Francoise Mohrt, Paris 1979; *The Encyclopaedia of Fashion from 1840 to the 1980s* by Georgina O'Hara, London 1986; article—"Succès par Excellence" by R. Voight in *Passion* (Paris), March 1983.

Agnès B. is a French sportswear designer who has catapulted herself to fame by challenging the need for fashion in clothing design. She denies the tenet that clothes must be stylized, highly detailed and ephemeral in order to catch the public imagination. Her ascent began in the mid-1970s when, after only a few years in the fashion business, first as a junior editor at *Elle* magazine and then briefly as an assistant to

Dorothee Bis, she opened her own boutique in a converted butcher shop in Les Halles to sell recut and redyed French workers' uniforms, black leather blazers, and T-shirts in striped rugby fabric. Her reputation grew as one of the first young French clothing designers to sell fashion to those who do not want to look too fashionable. In fact, her clothes, while identifiably French in no-nonsense cut, simple, subdued colors (often black), and casual mood, have an undated quality that keeps them current. The wrinkling common to natural materials, the "already worn" look that characterized the hippie ethos was translated by Agnès B. into a timeless chic—common sense with a flair.

In the age of name identification and personal marketing, Agnès B. is as well respected for her business sense as she is for her easy clothing designs. The spontaneous, childlike hand with which she quickly fashioned the logo for her stores belies a sophisticated business savvy. Retaining her own independent boutiques rather than being swallowed up in larger department stores, she astutely perceived that the un-design of her clothes was too "fragile," that they would blend in with the other, trendier lines and be lost. She has opened over 20 shops around the world, including a number in Paris, London, Tokyo, and two in New York City.

Her understated formula to design for real people (men and children as well as women) extends to her shows, which she calls "working sessions," where professional models are rarely used, and to her stores, in which casual and friendly salespeople mix their own antique or mod clothes with her separates. All the stores exude the same comfortable look, with pale wooden floors, white walls and the occasional decorative tile. The flimsy curtain that separates the display area from the communal dressing rooms is an implication of the marginal distinction between Agnès B. clothes and what everyone else is wearing.

Agnès B. strikes a commercial and creative balance—a radical chic. "I have no desire to dress an elite," she states. "It's all a game. I work as if I were still in my grandmother's attic, dressing up. Clothes aren't everything. When they become too important, when they hide the person wearing them, then I don't like them. Clothes should make you feel happy, relaxed and ready to tackle other problems."

—Sarah Bodine

AHLMANN, Lis.
Danish textile designer. Born Mathilde Elisabeth Ahlmann, in Aarhus, 13 April 1894. Studied painting under Harald Giersing. Worked as a ceramics painter in the Herman A. Kahlers workshop, Naestved, 1917–21; apprentice textile weaver, in the Gerda Henning workshop, Copenhagen, 1922–29; freelance textile designer, working with Kaare Klint, Mogens Koch and Borge Mogensen, and establishing her own workshop in Copenhagen, from 1930: design consultant to C. Olesen Textiles and Cotil Textiles, Copenhagen. **Exhibitions:** Milan Triennale, from 1957; *Formes Scandinaves,* Musée des Arts Decoratifs, Paris, 1958; *Ler, trae og vaev,* Danske Kunstindustrimuseet, Copenhagen, 1959 (with B. Mogensen and A. Fischer); *Nordisk Industridesign,* Kunstindustrimuseet, Oslo, 1976; *Design Since 1945,* Philadelphia Museum of Art, 1983. **Collec-**

tions: Danske Kunstindustrimuseet, Copenhagen. Recipient: Tagea Brandt Prize, Copenhagen, 1948; Eckersberg Medal, Copenhagen, 1964; Cotil Prize, Copenhagen, 1974; C. F. Hansen Medal, 1978. *Died* (in Copenhagen) *15 January 1979.*

Publications:

On AHLMANN: books—*Modern Danish Textiles* by Bent Salicath and Arne Karlsen, Copenhagen 1959; *Made in Denmark* by Arne Karlsen and Anker Tiedemann, Copenhagen 1960; *A Treasury of Scandinavian Design,* edited by Erik Zahle, New York 1961; *New Design in Weaving* by Donald J. Willcox, New York and London 1970; *Lis Ahlmann: tekstiler* by Thomas Mogensen, Copenhagen 1974; *Danish Design,* edited by Svend Erik Moller, Copenhagen 1974; *Scandinavian Design: Objects of a Life Style* by Eileene Harrison Beer, New York 1975; *Design Since 1945,* edited by Kathryn Hiesinger and George Marcus, Philadelphia and London 1983.

AHLSTRÖM, Tom (Erik Torbjörn).
Swedish industrial designer. Born of Swedish parents, in Helsinki, Finland, 30 May 1943. Studied metalwork, National College of Art, Craft and Design (Konstfackskolan), Stockholm, 1964–68; apprentice designer, Ogle design office, London, 1967. Married Gun Dahlberg in 1988; daughter: Amanda. Founder-Director, with Hans Ehrich, A & E Design AB, Stockholm, from 1968, and Interdesign AB, Stockholm, from 1982, designing for Gustavsberg, Jordan, Arjo, Anza, Fagerhults, RFSU, ASEA, Colgate, Norwesco, Yamagiwa, etc. **Exhibitions:** *From Idea to Finished Product,* Form Design Center, Malmo, 1977 (travelled to Stockholm); *Contemporary Swedish Design,* Nationalmuseum, Stockholm, 1983 (toured); *Faces of Swedish Design,* Cranbrook Academy of Art, Bloomfield Hills, Michigan, 1988 (toured); *From Revolution to New Expressions 1968–1988,* Nationalmuseum, Stockholm, 1989. **Collections:** Nationalmuseum, Stockholm; Tekniska Museet, Stockholm; Röhsska Konstslöjdmuseet, Göteborg. Recipient: Swedish State Award to Artists, 1971, 1972; Industrial Designer of the Year Award, 1987. Address: A & E Design AB, Tulegatan 19 G VI, 113 53 Stockholm, Sweden.

Works: (with Hans Ehrich)

Paintbrushes, for Anza, 1968.
Shower trolley and roll-in bath system, for Arjo Hospital Equipment, 1969.
Bam-Bam plastic stacking chairs, for Arjo Hospital Equipment, 1970.
Dikken plastic outdoor sofa, for Lammhults, 1970.
Queue ticket dispenser and number indicator, for Turn-O-Matic, 1974.
Pilot lift and transport chair, for Arjo Hospital Equipment, 1975.
1230 dishwashing brush, for Jordan, 1975.
Lucifer desk lamp, for Fagerhults Belysning, 1975/76.
Lift-Ride Chair, for Arjo Hospital Equipment, 1980.

Mobil shower and toilet wheelchair, for RFSU Rehab, 1980.
Stella Polaris floor lamp, for Yamagiwa, 1983.
Paint scrapers and putty knives, for Anza, 1984/85.
Giro desk lamp, for Fagerhults Belysning, 1987.
Rufus shower and bathroom aids for the disabled, for RFSU Rehab, 1987.
Orbit floor lamp, for Ateljé Lyktan, 1988.
F1 table lamp, for Belysia, 1989.

Publications:

On AHLSTRÖM/EHRICH: books—*Design in Sweden* by Lennart Lindkvist, Stockholm 1972; *Design* by Jocelyn de Noblet, Paris 1974; *Contemporary Swedish Design,* exhibition catalogue by Monica Boman, Lennart Lindkvist and others, Stockholm 1983; *Industry is Sweden,* edited by Gullers Pictorial Inc., Stockholm 1985; *Den Svenska Formen* by Monica Boman and others, Stockholm 1985; *The Conran Directory of Design,* edited by Stephen Bayley, London 1985; *Sweden in Fact 1987,* edited by Gustaf Olivecrona, Stockholm 1986; *Design Art,* West Berlin 1988; *International Design Yearbook 1988/89,* edited by Arata Isozaki, London 1988; *Faces of Swedish Design,* exhibition catalogue edited by Monica Boman, Stockholm 1988; articles—in *Form* (Stockholm), no. 3, 1970; *Domus* (Milan), no. 489, 1970; *Domus* (Milan), no. 505, 1971; *Abitare* (Milan), no. 105, 1972; *Form* (Stockholm), no. 1, 1975; *Domus* (Milan), no. 555, 1976; *Japan Interior Design* (Tokyo), no. 261, 1980; *Domus* (Milan), no. 614, 1981.

See EHRICH, Hans

Since 1982 A & E Design has been located on Tulegatan in downtown Stockholm. You enter through an unrevealing archway to find yourself in the midst of a craftsmen's quarter, full of studios, printing shops and small factories. With two storeys and a roof garden at their disposal, Hans and Tom were able to plan their own, customized interior, comprising a drawing office and a large, exceptionally well-equipped model workshop for producing every conceivable kind of model and prototype. This workshop is something of a nerve center for A & E, and the secret of many of Tom's and Hans' successes. Patient modelling is A & E's specialty. Their meticulous working models are constructed fullscale from the very outset, in order to penetrate technical and ergonomic functions.

The first thing one sees on entering the studio is a big showcase containing all the well-known products. Bright red, which has become something of a signature for A & E, dominates everything. Red plastic products with an unmistakable design, for instance. But one is easily deceived. Many of the products on display are hand-made presentation models or prototypes, meticulously fabricated in wood and then perfectly painted with a plastic-like surface. Here are all the products which have made the A & E design team well known far beyond the borders of Sweden: dish-washing brushes, paint brushes and painter's equipment, queuing systems, light fittings, implements for the handicapped and bathing and transport equipment for the disabled.

When the presentation models are tested and ready, exquisite boxes are made for each item. This reminds me of the Japanese stoneware masters who pack their materials in beautiful wooden boxes.

Whenever Tom and Hans present a new model, you are always fully convinced that this is the ultimate solution both to technical problems and to problems of design. And yet, after a few more years, they contrive to improve their product. The dish-washing brush for Jordan, for example, has undergone several successive improvements.

Hans and Tom specialized in using plastic at an early stage. Their very first assignment, for paint brushes, led them to acquire a specialist knowledge of plastics. Few other people have succeeded in treating plastic with such a degree of awareness, devising a formal language which seems appropriate to the material.

Hans and Tom have spent much of their time designing aids and implements for the disabled. Their painstaking working methods and their frequently ingenious technical solutions have resulted in many fine products in this connection—among other things, a folding, locking armrest for toilets used by the disabled, extension handles for persons who cannot grip properly, and a lift-and-ride chair for transporting patients to the shower.

Most of A & E's products are admirably presented in fact sheets describing how they work. "Background," "Aims," "Research," and "The Design Process" are headings which make the whole thing look so simple and self-evident. Behind all this, however, there may be years of designing effort. Tom and Hans often develop product ideas on their own initiative. They devote at least 15–20% of their working hours to developing projects of their own.

What are the distinguishing qualities of A & E as designers? They attempt the following an-swer:

"To a great extent our products are characterized by a strict geometrical formal language. We will have nothing whatsoever to do with imitation materials or décors, or other effects which do nothing to improve the functional properties of the product."

Many Swedish industrial designers would genuinely endorse these aims, but it is abundantly clear that A & E have a formal language of their own, and one which I find highly distinctive. We see little here of what is commonly associated with "Scandinavian Design." Their mentors, especially when they started, were unmistakably Italian. Hans Ehrich himself mentions Joe Colombo, and they have always been on close terms with Milan and the journal Domus. Few Swedish industrial designers have reaped so much attention from the international design magazines, but then few of their contemporaries have worked as hard as Hans and Tom to cultivate international contacts or to keep abreast of design developments in the world at large.

—Lennart Lindkvist

AICHER, Otl.

German graphic designer. Born Otto Aicher, in Ulm, 13 May 1922. Studied at the Akademie der Bildenden Künste, Munich, 1946–47. Married Inge Scholl in 1952; children: Eva, Florian, Julian and Manuel. Freelance graphic designer, establishing studio in Ulm, from 1948: has designed for the Ulm Volkshochschule, Ulm Stadtmuseum, BMW, Clima, Lufthansa, Erco, König Pilsner, Westdeutsche Landesbank, etc. Co-founder and developer, 1949–54, Lecturer, 1954–65, Rektoratskollegium Member, 1956–59, and Vice-Chancellor, 1962–64, Hochschule für Gestaltung, Ulm; visiting lecturer, Yale University, New Haven, Connecticut, 1958. **Exhibitions:** Yale Univer-

sity, New Haven, Connecticut, 1959; Museu de Arte Moderna, Rio de Janeiro, 1959; *Entschlüsselte Landschaften*, Paedagogische Hochschule, Weingarten, 1976; *Design Since 1945*, Philadelphia Museum of Art, 1983. **Collections:** Museum of Modern Art, New York; Museu de Arte Moderna, Rio de Janeiro. Recipient: Prize of Honour, Milan Triennale, 1954; Best German Poster Prize, 1955; First Prize, European Typography Competition, Innsbruck, 1958. Address: Rotis 12, 7970 Leutkirch 1, West Germany.

Works:

Posters, for the Volkhochschule, Ulm, 1946–62.
Typographic layouts, for the *Allgemeine Sonntagszeitung* newspaper, Dusseldorf, 1956.
Total graphic design, for *Stuttgarter Gardinen* magazine, 1959.
Corporate identity graphics, for Firma Clima, Innsbruck and Vienna, 1960.
Colour coordination system, for the elevated railway, Hamburg, 1961.
Corporate identity graphics, for Lufthansa Airlines, 1962–64.
Corporate identity graphics, for the Westdeutsche Landesbank, Düsseldorf, 1964–75.
Signage system, for Frankfurt airport, 1967–70.
Total graphics system, for the 20th Olympic Games, Munich, 1972.
Corporate identity graphics, for Bayrische Ruchversicherung, Munich, 1972–75.
Graphic design of *PR* magazine, for BMW, Munich, from 1975.
Corporate identity graphics, for König Pilsner, Duisburg, 1975–76.
Total graphics system, for Erco, Ludenscheid, 1975–77.
Corporate identity graphics, for Sutex Textil Cooperative Society, Sindelfingen, 1977–78.
Colour coordination, architectural design and orientation, for Krupp Hospital, Essen, 1978–79.

Publications:

By AICHER: book—*Kritik am Auto*, Munich 1984.

On AICHER: books—*Die neue Grafik/The New Graphic Art* by Karl Gerstner and Markus Kutter, Teufen and London 1959; *Who's Who in Graphic Art,* edited by Walter Amstutz, Zurich 1962, Dubendorf 1982; *Design Coordination and Corporate Image* by F. H. K. Henrion and Alan Parkin, London and New York 1967; *Monografie des Plakats: Entwicklung, Stil, Design* by Herbert Schindler, Munich 1972; *The Language of Graphics* by Edward Booth-Clibborn and Daniele Baroni, London 1980; *Design Since 1945,* edited by Kathryn Hiesinger and George Marcus, Philadelphia and London 1983; *The Conran Directory of Design,* edited by Stephen Bayley, London 1985.

German graphic designer Otl Aicher communicates each idea in a disciplined, organized and readable style. A style developed early in his career and subtly refined through experience.

Associated with the Hochschule für Gestaltung at Ulm, Aicher was a lecturer in visual communication. He was influenced by Max Bill who served as director. Bill, a former student of the Bauhaus, brought with him the esthetic of functionalism which included regular geometric forms, simple silhouettes, flat finishes and no extraneous ornament. The Hochschule für Gestaltung was the New Bauhaus. After Bill left in 1957, Aicher became co-director. While at the

Hochschule für Gestaltung, among other projects, Aicher collaborated with Hans Gugelot on the design and display of products for Braun. The design was geometric, simple, without extraneous ornament and represented the successful expression of the esthetic of functionalism. Clarity of form and construction is evident in the work Aicher did for the Volkshochschule in Ulm. In a series of street posters, the designs go through a geometric mutation or evolution based on flat, simple, large forms which inform the public with a minimum of words. The message was designed to be absorbed by the passing public, rather than read in detail.

Aicher developed the graphic program for the XX Olympics held in Munich in 1972. The entire design program was co-ordinated by logo, typography, and specified colors, used on standard paper sizes, following specific rules of type and space distribution grids. Working within these design parameters, posters utilizing new photographic technology, street signs, program covers, informational maps and pictographic symbols for the individual sporting events were created. Not only did the design team headed by Aicher work on the graphic designs, they developed all visual expressions of the games, including uniforms and interior decoration of the buildings. By working within this set of design limitations, the result was a clear coherent, easily understood means of communication usable by the international audience.

Because of his success with the Olympic signage Aicher was hired to develop a system of pictograms for ERCO Leuchten. He created culturally neutral signs, understood by people of differing educational backgrounds that communicate the necessary information. These were not illustrations, but signs. Aicher created designs for the town of Isny in Allgäu, West Germany, to be used on posters and tourist literature. The flat black and white pictographs, move beyond geometric forms based on a grid system to incorporate more pictorial images representing the town, its mountains, industry and seasons. Aicher maintained the elements of clarity and concise communication.

Illustrations for the book *Wilhelm von Occam, the Risk of Thinking Modern,* though less geometric, retain the flat forms seen in Aicher's earlier work. Soft colors are utilized, as the images move across the panels, telling the story. The shapes are simple, flat, and devoid of extraneous ornamentation.

Clarity of form and concise communication based on flat, geometric forms and spaces, are adjectives used to describe Aicher's work. His style evolved slowly, becoming less rigid. Elements of the esthetic of functionalism are evident in all of his work. He does not seek to be exciting, dramatic or unique. He does not seek a new language of communication. He does not seek to be so innovative that the message is lost. Aicher's work does communicate an idea, directly and simply.

—Nancy House

AIMBEZ, Gil.
American fashion designer. Born in Los Angeles, California, 19 May 1940. Studied art and design, Chouinard School of Art, Los Angeles (on scholarship); fashion design, Frank Wiggins Trade School, Los Angeles. Assistant designer, at age 19, for Dominique Jones, Los

Gil Aimbez: Pucker-knit mohair top, for Static Knitwear, 1983

Angeles; moved to New York when the west coast office was closed and became a pattern-maker for Anne Klein, *q.v.*; subsequently partner, with Peter Clements, at Genre sportswear firm, New York, until 1980: established Bon Menage dress line, 1977, Snafu outerwear and rainwear line, 1978, and G.A.I. tops, 1979; founder-director and designer, Fezbez design and consulting firm, New York, since 1980: has designed coats, suits, and sweaters for Braefair and Braesport, and knitwear for Static. Address: c/o Jody Donohue Associates, 32 East 57th Street, New York, New York 10022, U.S.A.

Publications:

On AIMBEZ: book—*Fairchild's Who's Who in Fashion* by Anne Stegemeyer, New York 1980.

With a soft voice and a smile to melt hearts, this gentle man emerges with power and strength. A romantic at heart, Gil Aimbez, is consumed by love of history; in folklore, ethnic dress, architecture, furniture, and objects. Rich textures and colors pass through his fingers like a weaver always balancing proportion with style. A master of combining design and technology he can easily produce any effect he wants. He is an artist surrounded by many kinds of collectables from books to antiques to

broaden the sphere of his imagination. His shelves are filled with hundreds, perhaps thousands, of books on every subject. He shares a mutual love for antiques particularly of primitive American and ethnic origin. His world travels have also played a major part in contributing to his design influence. Yet he designs with strict discipline and a keen sense of order.

From his beginnings at Dominique Jones in L.A. he was passionate about designing unique clothes, at times using ethnic influences, always with a romantic sensibility. Being born in Los Angeles of Japanese, Filipino and Mexican heritage of a very large family he was no doubt surrounded by a lifestyle that demanded striving for individuality. After a move to the east coast and positioning himself with various designers including Anne Klein he solidified his position as an eminently contemporary designer.

Aimbez's style is one of comfort and ease. His clientele is ageless, young at heart and in spirit. They embody his choice of natural fabrics, his comfortable shapes whether they are voluminous or body conscious. His variation of style offers clothes that are adaptable to different moods and lifestyles. He takes clothes as seriously as he takes life, but with a relaxed attitude. Affordable prices for good quality clothing is essential in his philosophy.

Gil Aimbez's fashions are closely related to

what he admires most; the past. But they do not lie dormant in a time capsule. On the contrary they supply a contemporary woman at times with an ethnic direction; at other times a romantic softness; and still at others with a primitive influence, always with respect for comfort, versatility and beauty.

—Andrea K. Arsenault

ALBERS, Anni.
American graphic artist and textile designer. Born Anni Fleischmann, in Berlin, Germany, 1899; emigrated to the United States in 1933: naturalized, 1937. Studied art, under Martin Brandenburg, Berlin, 1916–19; Kunstgewerbe-schule, Hamburg, 1919–20; Bauhaus, in Weimar and Dessau, 1922–29: Dip. 1929. Married the painter Josef Albers in 1925 (died, 1976). Instructor and acting director, Bauhaus weaving workshop, Dessau and Berlin, 1930–33; Assistant Professor, Black Mountain College, North Carolina, 1933–49. Independent artist and de-

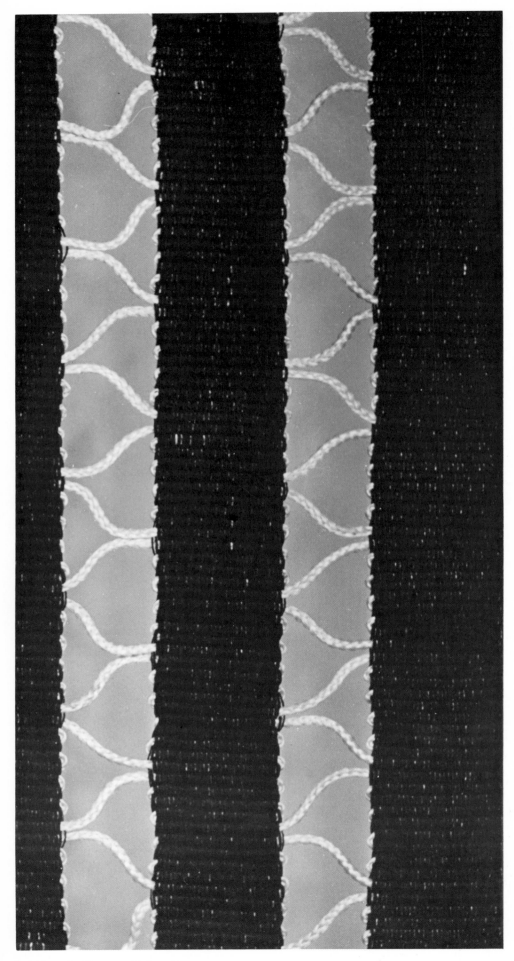

Anni Albers: *Partition* woven fabric, c. 1949

signer, in New Haven, Connecticut, since 1950. **Exhibitions:** Museum of Modern Art, New York, 1949 (toured); Wadsworth Atheneum, Hartford, Connecticut, 1953 (with Joseph Albers); Honolulu Academy of Arts, 1954; Currier Gallery of Art, Manchester, New Hampshire, 1956 (with Mary Callery and Sue Fuller); Massachusetts Institute of Technology, Cambridge, 1959; Carnegie Institute, Pittsburgh, 1959; Baltimore Museum of Art, 1959; Yale University Art Gallery, New Haven, Connecticut, 1959; Colorado Springs Fine Arts Center, Colorado, 1959; Contemporary Arts Museum, Houston, 1960; University of Bridgeport, Connecticut, 1971; Pollock Gallery, Toronto, 1973; Kunstmuseum, Dusseldorf, 1975; Bauhaus-Archiv, West Berlin, 1975; Brooklyn Museum, New York, 1977; Monmouth Museum, New Jersey, 1979; University of Hartford, Connecticut, 1979; Mattatuck Museum, Waterbury, Connecticut, 1979. **Collections:** Museum of Modern Art, New York; Metropolitan Museum of Art, New York; Brooklyn Museum, New York; Busch-Reisinger Museum, Harvard University, Cambridge, Massachusetts; Wadsworth Atheneum, Hartford, Connecticut; Yale University Art Gallery, New Haven, Connecticut; National Gallery, Washington, D.C.; St. Louis Art Museum; Fort Worth Art Museum, Texas; Art Gallery of Ontario, Toronto; Kunstmuseum, Düsseldorf; Israel Museum, Jerusalem. Recipient: Craftsmanship Medal, American Institute of Architects, 1961; Tamarind Lithography Workshop Fellowship, Los Angeles, 1964; Decorative Arts Book Award, 1965; Outstanding Achievement Award, Women's Caucus for Art, New Orleans, 1980; Gold Medal, American Craft Council, 1981. Honorary doctorates: Maryland Institute College of Art, Baltimore, 1972; York University, Toronto, 1973; Philadelphia College of Art, 1976; University of Hartford, Connecticut, 1979. Address: 808 Birchwood Drive, Orange, Connecticut 06477, U.S.A.

Publications:

By ALBERS: books—*On Designing,* New Haven, Connecticut 1959, Middletown, Connecticut 1962; *On Weaving,* Middletown, Connecticut 1965, London 1966 and 1974; articles—"Weaving" in *Junge Menschen,* edited by Walter Hammer, Hamburg 1924, Walluf 1979; "Work with Material" in *Black Mountain Bulletin* (North Carolina), no. 5, 1937; "Weaving at the Bauhaus" in *Bauhaus 1919–28,* edited by Herbert Bayer and others, New York 1938, Boston 1959; "Handweaving Today" in *Weaver* (Concord), January/February 1941; "Designing" in *Craft Horizons* (New York), May 1943; "We Need Crafts" in *Design* (Columbus), December 1944; "Constructing Textiles" in *Design* (Columbus), April 1946; "Design—Anonymous and Timeless" in *Magazine of Art* (New York), February 1947; "Weaving" in *Art and Architecture* (Los Angeles), February 1949; "The Pliable Plane" in *Perspecta* (New Haven), 1957; "On the Designing of Textiles" in *American Fabrics* (New York), Summer 1960; "Conversation with Anni Albers" in *Craft Horizons* (New York), July/August 1965.

On ALBERS: books—*Tapis et Tissus* by Sonia Delaunay, Paris c. 1926; *Josef and Anni Albers: Paintings, Tapestries and Woven Textiles,* exhibition catalogue, Hartford, Connecticut 1953; *Anni Albers: Pictorial Weavings,* exhibition catalogue, Cambridge, Massachusetts 1959; *Artists at Work* by Bernard Chaet, Cambridge, Massachusetts 1960; *Anni Albers,* exhibition catalogue, Düsseldorf 1975; *Anni Albers,* exhibition catalogue by Gene Baro, Brooklyn 1977; *Americans from Germany* by Gerard Wilk, New

York 1977; *The Art Fabric: Mainstream* by Mildred Constantine and Jack Lenor Larsen, New York 1981.

Design is often regarded as the form imposed on the material by the designer. But if we, as designers, cooperate with the material, treat it democratically, you might say, we will reach a less subjective solution of this problem of form and therefore a more inclusive and permanent one. The less we, as designers, exhibit in our work our personal traits, our likes and dislikes, our peculiarities and idiosyncrasies, in short, our individuality, the more balanced the form we arrive at will be. It is better that the material speaks than that we speak ourselves. The design that shouts "I am a product of Mr. X" is a bad design. As consumers, we are not interested in Mr. X but in his product, which we want to be our servant and not his personal ambassador. Now, if we sit at our desk designing, we cannot avoid exhibiting ourselves for we are excluding the material as our co-worker, as the directive force in our planning.

The good designer is the anonymous designer, so I believe, the one who does not stand in the way of the material; who sends his products on their way to a useful life without an ambitious appearance. A useful object should perform its duty without much ado. The table-cloth that calls "Here I am, look at me," is invading the privacy of the consumer. The curtains that cry "We are beautiful, your attention please," but whisper "though not very practical, we will need much of your time to keep us in shape," are badly designed. The unknown designer or designers of our sheets or of our light bulbs performed their task well. Their products are complete in their unpretentious form.

The more we avoid standing in the way of the material and in the way of tools and machines, the better chance there is that our work will not be dated, will not bear the stamp of too limited a period of time and be old-fashioned some day instead of antique. The imprint of a time is unavoidable. It will occur without our purposely fashioning it. And it will outlast fashions only if it embodies lasting, together with transitory, qualities. (*Reprinted from "Design: Anonymous and Timeless"* (1947) in On Designing, *1959.*)

—Anni Albers

Anni Albers' abstract, grid-structured textile designs are based on the belief that high standards and philosophical underpinnings are necessary for modern crafts to become aesthetically satisfying works of art. She advocates the importance to today's designer of maintaining direct experience of the medium, cooperating with and working through the material to attain a holistic design which focuses on the forms' inherent qualities.

In an approach which was new to her craft, Albers emphasized the thread as the beginning and the end in textile-making. Working through the weaving process, she believed, not imposing self on it and not letting oneself become influenced by the judgments of others, the maker who faced the work with an open mind and let the imagination take hold could attain a unified whole which is both ordered and mysterious. In Albers' view, the individual craftsman should carry through the design from beginning to end in order to avoid the fragmentation which results from division of work as practiced in industry. She also helped lead a move to have designs carried out in this fashion enter into American textile production so that more people could be exposed to higher artistic standards of work.

Albers credits weavers of ancient Peru as a major inspiration for her work, but the most direct influence on it was her personal experience of the philosophical ideas and practical applications expounded at the German Bauhaus, where she studied from 1922 to 1929. The spirit of unprejudiced experimentation and the study of universally meaningful, abstract form-building, which pervaded the fertile atmosphere at the Bauhaus, laid the groundwork for her lifelong achievement in bridging the gap between craft and art. Albers' intricately textured, subtly variegated all-over patterns are much more than sheer decorations. They are the embodiment of the ideas and metaphysical ideals promulgated at this meeting place of the early twentieth-century avant-garde.

Albers' textile designs, along with her writings and teachings on the history and practice of weaving and on the theoretical approach to design, have exerted a deep influence on the generation of American weavers who matured during the decades of the 1930's to the 1960's. She also had a prominent effect on the American textile industry of the same period. It should in addition, be noted that she has also been a factor in the abstract painting of our time; a glimmer of her work is evoked in delicate grid pictures of such artists as the American abstractionist Agnes Martin.

—Barbara Cavaliere

ALBINI, Franco.

Italian architect, exhibition and furniture designer. Born in Robbiate, Como, 17 October 1905. Studied architecture at the Politecnico, Milan: Dip. Arch. 1929. Married; son: Marco. In private practice as architect and designer, Milan, from, 1930: subsequently joined by the firm's current partners Franca Helg, 1952, Antonio Piva, 1962, and Marco Albini, 1965; designed numerous exhibitions in Italy, especially the Milan Triennale, from 1936, and furniture for Rinascente, Brionvega, BBB Bonacina, Poggi, Sirrah, Knoll International, etc., from 1940. Lecturer, American-Italian Commission of Cultural Exchange, Rome, 1954–63; Professor of Architectural Composition, Politecnico, Milan, 1963–77. Member, UNESCO Commission for the Renewal of the Museums of the United Arab Republic, 1968–69. Member, CIAM Congres Internationaux d'Architecture Moderne. **Exhibitions:** *Italian Contemporary Art, Design and Architecture,* Stockholm and Helsinki, 1953; *Ten Italian Architects,* Los Angeles, 1967; *28/78 Architettura,* Milan, 1979; *Design and design,* Milan and Venice, 1979; *Franco Albini: Architettura per un Museo,* Galleria Nazionale d'Arte Moderna, Rome, 1980. Recipient: First Prize, Main Hall Competition, Milan Triennale, 1954; Compasso d'Oro Award, Milan, 1955, 1958, 1964; Olivetti National Architecture Medal, Milan, 1957; IN/ARCH Award, Milan, 1963, 1965; Biscione d'Oro Award, Milan, 1971; First Prize, Municipal Theatre Competition, Vicenza, 1971. Honorary Royal Designer for Industry, Royal Society of Arts, London, 1971; Honorary Fellow, American Institute of Architects; Member, Accademia di San Luca. Member: Italian Institute of Town Planning; Scientific Institute of the Italian National Research Centre of Museography. *Died* (in Milan) *1 November 1977.*

Works:

Lacquered wood furniture at the Milan Trade Fair, for the Dassi Company, 1932.
Dwelling Exhibition layouts, at the Milan Triennale, 1936.
Tensile structure suspended bookshelves in glass and brass cable, 1940.
Criteria for the Modern Home exhibition layouts, at the Milan Triennale, 1940.
Home Furnishings exhibition layouts, at the Palazzo dell'Arte al Parco, Milan, 1946.
Desk with metal frame and glass top, for Knoll International, 1950.
Armchair with upholstered movable seat and back, for La Rinascente, 1950.
Easy chair in rattan, for BBB Bonacina, 1951.
Folding wooden dining table, for La Rinascente, 1951.
Italian Contemporary Art, Design and Architecture exhibition layouts, in Stockholm and Helsinki, 1953.
Folding table in wood with woollen cloth cover, for Carlo Poggi, 1954–55.
Luisa upholstered armchair with wood frame, for Carlo Poggi, 1955.
Councilman Chair, for the Council of Genoa, 1955.
Premio La Rinascente/Compasso d'Oro exhibition layouts, at the *World's Fair,* New York, 1956.
Tre Pezzi chair in tubular steel and foam rubber, for Carlo Poggi, 1959.
International Glass and Steel Exhibition layouts, at the Triennale, Milan, 1960.
Why Steel pavilion at the Milan Trade Fair, for Italsider, 1968.
The School of Leonardo exhibition layouts, Palazzo Reale, Milan, 1973.

(for a complete list of Albini's buildings and architectural projects, see *Contemporary Architects*)

Publications:

On ALBINI: books—*Forme Nuove in Italia* by Agnoldomenico Pica, Milan and Rome 1957; *Public Interiors* by Misha Black, London 1960; *Design for Modern Living* by Gerd and Ursula Hatje, Munich and Zurich 1961, London 1962; *Franco Albini* by Giulio Carlo Argan, Milan 1962; *Il Design in Italia 1945–1972* by Paolo Fossati, Turin 1972; *Tubular Steel Furniture,* edited by Barbie Campbell-Cole and Tim Benton, London 1979; *Franco Albini 1930–1970* by Franca Helg, Cesare De Seta and Marcello Fagiolo, Florence 1979, 1981, London 1981; *Atlante del Design Italiano 1940/1980* by Alfonso Grassi and Anty Pansera, Milan 1980; *Franco Albini: Architettura per un Museo,* exhibition catalogue, Rome 1980; *The Conran Directory of Design,* edited by Stephen Bayley, London 1985.

Franco Albini was one of a talented group of architects, designers, and critics who emerged in Milan during the 1930's and who did so much to give Italian design its dominant characteristics and to gain its international reputation. Compared to many of his fellows, of his own and successive generations, he was remarkably sparing with opinions in print, and the few occasions when he made such contributions were largely due to strong persuasion by others. This is not to say, however, that he was not aware of theoretical problems and their bearing upon his practice, which stemmed from a critical appreciation of the aims of Italian Rationalism, corrected by an understanding of the Bauhaus and of Russian avant-garde architecture and design.

His methods were rigorous but sufficiently flexible to lead him ever to invention rather

Walter Albini: Outfits from the Autumn/Winter 1982 collection

than to any conventional resolution of so-called problems. His work thus always acquired a stylishness beyond any notions of forms arising from function, for he recognized that the designer's intervention modified, if not transformed, both function and form, through its structural proposals which constituted a sort of renewal of the object and of the meaning of its function.

Even the 1940 "suspension bookshelves" show this process of "resemantisation" through the structure Albini adopted. Utterly unlike any previous book storage, with which only the level planes have any similarity (and that, minimised by making them of plate glass) the structure also proposed a new function for itself; it acted as a room-divider, of the sort destined to become a cliché of interior decoration through the 1950's and 1960's. The structure, itself, of carefully shaped, complex members of wood and brass and steelcables both for suspending the shelves and as stays to the wooden members, recalls not only suspension bridges but sailing ship architecture. This is true, also, of much of Albini's earlier work and, in the case of spiral staircases, it persisted throughout his career, as can be seen in the Villa Neufer, Ispra (1940); in the Palazzo Rosso, Genoa (1952–61); in one of reinforced concrete, marble, and wood, Parma (1950); and one of steel and white marble, Genoa (1970).

Perhaps another aspect of Albini's methods was his respect for materials and forms; this did not, however, appear to him as a constraint demanding slavish imitation. The cane-and-rush chairs of the 1950's are elegant examples of this sensitivity, while the remarkable room at the Palazzo Bianco for introductory, temporary, and largely documentary exhibitions is a particularly rich exploitation of structural and material promptings. Elsewhere in this museum, the flooring is in white marble, punctuated by little slate squares set diagonally; the lighting, mainly by cold, cathode tube; the walls, pale; the atmosphere, airy. This room reverses the floor pattern, the walls are dark, and the lighting falls in strong spots. The supports for the displays derive their module from the floor pattern.

—Toni del Renzio

ALBINI, Walter.
Italian fashion designer. Born Gualtiero Albini in Busto Arsizio, near Milan, 9 March 1941. Studied fashion and costume design, Istituto Statale di Belle Arti e Moda, Turin. Sketch artist and illustrator, working for Italian publications *Novita* and *Corriere Lombardo* and as apprentice to a fashion house, Paris, 1961–64; freelance fashion designer, Milan, 1964 until his death in 1983: established Walter Albini Fashion House, designing for various firms including Krizia, Billy Ballo, Basile, Callaghan, Escargots, Mister Fox, Diamantis, Trell, Mario Ferari, Lanerossi, Kriziamaglia, Montedoro, and Princess Luciana; launched ready-to-wear collection, 1978; established branches of Walter Albini Fashions in London, Rome, and Venice. *Died* (in Milan) *31 May 1983.*

Publications:

On ALBINI: books—*In Vogue: Sixty Years of Celebrities and Fashion from British Vogue* by Georgina Howell, London 1975, 1978, New York 1976; *Magic Names of Fashion* by Ernestine Carter, Englewood Cliffs, New Jersey and London 1980; *McDowell's Directory of Twentieth Century Fashion* by Colin McDowell, London 1984; *The Encyclopaedia of Fashion from 1840 to the 1980s* by Georgina O'Hara, London 1986; articles—"Walter Albini" in *The Sunday Times* (London), 15 October 1972; "Walter Albini: Italian RTW Designer, Is Dead" in *Women's Wear Daily* (New York), 3 June 1983.

Walter Albini began his formal association with the fashion world by insisting that he be admitted to study at a fashion school in Turin, initially being unaware that it was an all-girls school. For three years, he lived in school rooms with walls covered with copies of drawings by Erté and pages from *La Gazette du Bon Ton,* both of which represent a period that later influenced him strongly.

Respected as a perfectionist, Albini created exciting clothing, which was influenced by his admiration for the style of the glamorous actresses of the 1930's and 1940's, an attachment that dated back to the endless afternoons when he and his mother sat through the films of such stars as Garbo, Dietrich, and Hepburn. He considered this to be the last revolutionary time of change in style, and his great devotion to Coco Chanel stemmed from the fact that she was one of those revolutionaries. He paid homage to her in the Walter Albini High Fashion show in Rome in 1975.

Previous to that, his motto, "dare to die," led him to risks in designing collections, basically sportswear, with specific allusions to yachting and sailor uniforms, to Chanel, the Duchess of Windsor, and the British Air Force. For Krizia, he designed long, pleated, crepe skirts and cardigans with sequins in the early 1960's, and for Billy Ballo in 1968, he concentrated on drawings for fabrics. For Cadette he created black cotton dresses with white cuffs. Later came successes for Basile, Misterfox, Sportfox, Callaghan, and Escargot.

Albini was always truthful to his belief in the need for mystery in women, and he continually observed the ways they express themselves in sitting, moving, and standing. Each of his early dresses and following sportswear lines was known for fantasy and pure femininity, but all were notable, too, for their attention to quality of natural fibers, fine tailoring, and details in construction.

—Gillion Skellenger

ALDREDGE, Theoni.
American stage and film costume designer. Born Theoni Vachliotis, in Athens, Greece, 22 August 1932. Studied at the American School, Athens, until 1948; Goodman Memorial Theatre School, Chicago, 1949–52. Married the actor Thomas E. Aldredge in 1953. Independent costume designer, in Chicago, 1950–57, and in New York since 1958: worked for the Goodman Theatre, Chicago, 1951–53, the Studebaker Theatre, Chicago, 1956–57, and the New York Shakespeare Festival from 1962; has designed costumes for numerous Broadway and off-Broadway plays, ballets, operas, television specials and films. Recipient: Academy Award, Hollywood, 1975; Theatre World Award, 1976; British Motion Picture Academy Award, 1976; Obie Award, *Village Voice,* New York, 1976; Tony (Antoinette Perry) Award, 1977. Address: 240 East 27th Street, Apt. 12G, New York, New York 10016, U.S.A.

Works:

Stage designs include—*The Distaff Side,* Goodman Theatre, Chicago, 1950; *The Immoralist,* Studebaker Theatre, Chicago, 1956; *Much Ado About Nothing,* Studebaker Theatre, Chicago, 1957; *A View from the Bridge,* Studebaker Theatre, Chicago, 1957; *Lysistrata,* Studebaker Theatre, Chicago, 1957; *The Guardsman,* Studebaker Theatre, Chicago, 1957; *Heloise,* Gate Theatre, New York, 1958; *The Golden Six,* York Playhouse, New York, 1958; *Sweet Bird of Youth,* Martin Beck Theatre, New York, 1959; *The Geranium Hat,* Orpheum Theatre, New York, 1959; *The Nervous Set,* Henry Miller's Theatre, New York, 1959; *Silent Night, Lonely Night,* Morosco Theatre, New York, 1959; *A Distant Bell,* Eugene O'Neill Theatre, New York, 1960; *The Best Man,* Morosco Theatre, New York, 1960; *Measure for Measure,* New York Shakespeare Festival, 1960; *Hedda Gabler,* Fourth Street, Theatre, New York, 1960; *Mary, Mary,* Helen Hayes Theatre, New York, 1961; *Under Milk Wood,* Circle in the Square, New York, 1961; *Ghosts,* Fourth Street Theatre, New York, 1961; *I Can Get It For You Wholesale,* Shubert Theatre, New York, 1962; *King Lear,* New York Shakespeare Festival, 1962; *Who's Afraid of Virginia Woolf?,* Billy Rose Theatre, 1962; *Strange Interlude,* Hudson Theatre, New York, 1963; *Antony and Cleopatra,* New York Shakespeare Festival, 1963; *The Trojan Women,* Circle in the Square, New York, 1963; *The Three Sisters,* Morosco Theatre, New York, 1964; *Hamlet,* New York Shakespeare Festival, 1964.

film costumes include—*Girl of the Night,* 1960; *You're a Big Boy Now,* 1967; *No Way to Treat a Lady,* 1968; *Up Tight,* 1968; *Last Summer,* 1969; *I Never Sang for my Father,* 1969; *Promise at Dawn,* 1970; *The Great Gatsby,* 1974; *Network,* 1976; *Semi-Tough,* 1977; *The Cheap Detective,* 1978; *The Fury,* 1978; *Eyes of Laura Mars,* 1978; *The Champ,* 1979; *The Rose,* 1979.

Publications:

On ALDREDGE: books—*The Biographical Encyclopaedia and Who's Who of the American Theatre,* edited by Walter Rigdon, New York, 1966; *Who's Who in the Theatre,* edited by Ian Herbert, London 1982; articles—"Network Designer Theoni Aldredge" by E. L. Gross in *Vogue* (New York), August 1978; "Theater's Top Twofer is Tom and Theoni Aldredge: He Emotes, She Keeps Broadway in Stitches" by K. McMurran in *People Weekly* (Chicago), 29 June 1981; "Architectural Digest Visits: Theoni V. Aldredge" by Peter Carlsen in *Architectural Digest* (Los Angeles), December 1982.

Theoni Aldredge appeared upon the design scene in New York at that moment when both detailed realism and a lush and spectacular romanticism in costume design were being replaced by costumes that were more closely integrated with direction, actor-movement, and the subtext of the drama. Aldredge seemed to have an innate sense of how to design costumes that were not just character clothes but integral visual support for the underlying soul of the play. From Tennessee Williams' *Sweet Bird of Youth* early in her career to the now-famous *Chorus Line,* through many Shakespearean productions and a host of major and minor Broadway scripts, the one thing that characterized Aldredge's costumes was visual projection of the inner life of the play and its action. The many production designs for Shakespeare-in-the-Park undoubtedly solidified this costume sensitivity, since Shakespeare's plays, when performed on an open stage, demand much from the costumes in the way of information and mood, subtext and stage action. Possibly Aldredge's Greek heritage with its mystic, mythic sense of what underlies even the simplest tales and stories also strengthened her sense of the underlying appropriateness of each of her designs.

She has also undoubtedly been influenced by much of what went on in the art world of the 1960's and 1970's but never in a direct way. Her work reflected the prevailing interest in texture, in physicality, in presenting several visual ideas simultaneously, but these were never obvious nor presented so as to step forward from the production. Thus, Aldredge has been less the innovator than a subtle mirror for her times—reflecting in her costumes the visual moods and attitudes of our day within the essentially visual world of the drama.

—Douglas A. Russell

ALDRIDGE, Alan.

British illustrator, poster, book and graphic designer. Born in Aylesbury, Buckinghamshire, in 1943. Studied at Romford Technical College, Essex. Married; children: Miles and Saffron. Worked as an insurance clerk, barrow-boy, repertory actor, etc., in London, 1960-63; freelance designer and illustrator, London, since 1963: designed for The Great American Disaster Restaurant, Jonathan Cape publishers, Penguin Books, Macdonald publishers, *Melody Maker, Mirror Magazine, Daily Telegraph, Esquire,* etc. **Exhibitions:** Galerie Priebut, Amsterdam, 1967; *European Illustrators,* New York, 1968; *12 Illustrators,* Galerie Germain, Paris, 1969; Seibu Gallery, Tokyo, 1970; Galerie Bijenkorf, Amsterdam, 1971; Institute of Contemporary Arts, London, 1973; *The Contemporary Illustrator's Art,* The Minories, Colchester, 1978. Recipient: Children's Book of the Year Award, London, 1974; Silver Medals, Designers and Art Directors Association, London; Scotsman International Awards, London. Address: c/o Jean-Howard-Spink, 5 Rosenau Road, London SW11, 4QN, England.

Works:

The Penguin Book of Comics book design, for Penguin Books, 1967.
Doctor Robert in *The Beatles Illustrated Lyrics* book, Macdonald, 1969.
Being for the Benefit of Mr. Kite in *The Beatles Illustrated Lyrics,* Macdonald 1969.
What Goes On in *The Beatles Illustrated Lyrics,* Macdonald, 1969.
A Great Place for Hamburgers poster, for the Great American Disaster Restaurant, London, 1970.
I'm Happy Just to Dance with You in *The Beatles Illustrated Lyrics 2,* Macdonald, 1971.
Across the Universe in *The Beatles Illustrated Lyrics 2,* Macdonald, 1971.
The Ship's Cat book design, for Jonathan Cape, 1977.

Lion's Cavalcade book design, for Jonathan Cape, 1980.
Phantasia of Dockland, Rockland and Dodos book design, for Jonathan Cape, 1981.

Publications:

By ALDRIDGE: books—*The Penguin Book of Comics,* editor, with George Perry, London 1967, 1971, 1975; *The Beatles Illustrated Lyrics,* London 1969; *Ann in the Moon,* with text by D. Francis, London 1970; *The Beatles Illustrated Lyrics, 2,* London 1971; *The Butterfly Ball and the Grasshopper's Feast,* with poems by William Plomer and notes by Richard Fitter, London 1973; *Bernie Taupin: The One Who Writes the Words for Elton John,* editor, with Mike Dempsey, London, 1976; *The Adventures and Brave Deeds of the Ship's Cat on the Spanish Maine,* with text by Richard Adams, London 1977; *The Peacock Party,* with Harry Willock, poems by George F. Ryder, London 1979; *The Lion's Cavalcade,* with Harry Willock, poems by Ted Walker, London 1980; *Phantasia of Dockland, Rockland and Dodos,* with Harry Willock, London 1981.

On ALDRIDGE: books—*Graphic Design Britain,* edited by Frederick Lambert, London 1967; *The Poster: An Illustrated History from 1860* by Harold F. Hutchison, London and Toronto 1968; *Graphic Design Britain 70,* edited by Frederick Lambert, London and New York 1970; *Alan Aldridge: An Exhibition of Illustrations 1968-1973,* exhibition folder, London 1973; *Graphis Record Covers,* edited by Walter Herdeg, Zürich 1974; *The Contemporary Illustrator's Art: Six Artists and Their Books for Children,* exhibition folder, with introduction by Alasdair Dunlop, Colchester 1978; *Album Cover Album: The Book of Record Covers,* edited by Storm Thorgerson and Roger Dean, Limpsfield, Surrey 1979; *The Language of Graphics* by Edward Booth-Clibborn and Daniele Baroni, London 1980.

Alan Aldridge's success undoubtedly lies in his natural skill in inventing grotesque compositions which have great popular appeal. The combination of a talent that everyone can recognise, together with his ability to produce endless inventions, have ensured him a place in his generation. Not only has he provided many outstanding illustrations for children's books, but it might well be said that all his works are visual fairy tales and that they belong to the fantasies of every age group. In much the same way as the lyrics of the Beatles' songs have a place in everyone's personal experience, so Aldridge's strange designs give tangible forms to universal fantasies. His imagery takes its place in the psychedelic dreams of the 1960's and there is a strong element of hallucination in his visions of insects and grotesque monsters. Many of his paintings have an illusion of roundness and solidity as though to give added weight to an ephemeral vision. Aldridge has also given additional dimensions to the human form, as in his poster for the film *Chelsea Girls* by Andy Warhol or in the actual body-painting in his illustration of "Sexy Sadie" from *The Beatles Illustrated Lyrics,* which he also edited. Although very much a product of his time, he has drawn on the past so frequently that his work, which is full of quotations, takes on a timeless quality. For example, his work sometimes recalls the exaggerations of Tenniel's drawings for Lewis Carroll's poem "Jabberwocky." Even further away in time, Giuseppe Archimboldo's grotesque heads composed of vegetables find a parallel in Aldridge's illustration to Dr. Robert in the *Beatles Lyrics.* Certainly, the bizarre carvings of the Gothic cathedrals' anon-

ymous stonemasons also lie behind the visions of this inventive artist. The exaggerated features of the part-human, part-mythical beasts of the medieval gargoyles find modern descendants in his powerfully grimacing figures.

In spite of the sculptural references in his work—and many of the images are based on three-dimensional models—the finished work is firmly related to the small scale of illustration on a printed page. While its concept can often be monumental, the actual image is often as detailed as that of a miniature. As in the universal images that Hieronymus Bosch contained in a single panel, so within the covers of a book one can travel through an immense world of fantasy in Aldridge's illustrations, as for example to the verses of William Plomer in *The Butterfly Ball and the Grasshopper's Feast* (1973).

—John Barnicoat

ALLNER, Walter.
American painter and graphic designer. Born in Dessau, Germany, 2 January 1909; emigrated to the United States in 1949: naturalized, 1957. Studied under Josef Albers, Vasily Kandinsky, Paul Klee and Joost Schmidt, at the Bauhaus, Dessau, 1927-30. Married Colette Vasselon in 1938 (divorced, 1951); son: Michel; married Jane Booth Pope in 1954; son: Peter. Apprentice designer, Gesellschafts- und Wirtschafts-museum, Vienna, 1929; assistant to the typographer and designer Piet Zwart, in Wassenaar, Netherlands, 1930; assistant to poster artist Jean Carlu, Paris, 1932-33; partner and art director, Omnium Graphique design firm, and art director of Formes Editions d'Art Graphique et Photographique publishers, Paris, 1933-36; independent graphic designer and consultant, New York, since 1949: art director, *Fortune* magazine, 1963-74. Paris editor, *Graphis* magazine, Zurich, 1945-48; co-director, Editions Paralleles, Paris, 1948-51; founder-editor, *International Poster Annual,* for Zollikofer publishers, St. Gallen, 1948-52. Professor, Parsons School of Design, New York, from 1974; visiting critic, Yale University School of Art, New Haven, Connecticut, 1972, 1974, and Ecole Supérieure d'Arts Graphiques, Paris, 1979, 1982, 1985; visiting lecturer, Swinburne Institute of Technology, in Melbourne, Adelaide and Sydney, 1983. United States President, 1972, and International President, 1974, Alliance Graphique Internationale; Member of the Comite de Parrainage, Ecole Supérieure d'Arts Graphiques, Paris, 1985. **Exhibitions:** *Bauhausler in Amerika,* Bauhaus-Archiv, Darmstadt, 1969 (with Josef Albers and Fritz Goro); Musée d'Art Ancien, Brussels, 1974; Gallery Estel, Tokyo, 1974; *Bauhausler in Amerika,* Bauhaus Museum für Gestaltung, West Berlin, 1976; Hemisphere Club Gallery, New York, 1976; Cooper-Hewitt Museum, New York, 1976; Kunstbibliothek der Staatlichen Museen, West Berlin, 1980. **Collections:** Museum of Modern Art, New York; Cooper-Hewitt Museum, New York; Bauhaus Museum für Gestaltung, West Berlin; Deutsches Plakatmuseum, Essen; Israel Museum, Jerusalem. Recipient: Chicago Art Directors Club Award, 1952, 1960; Art Directors Club of New York Award, 1956, 1958, 1960. Addresses: 110 Riverside Drive, New York, New York 10024, U.S.A.; Box 167, Truro, Massachusetts 02666, U.S.A.

Works:

Time and Life Building "500" cover design, for *Fortune,* July 1964.

Computer-generated "500" cover design, for *Fortune,* July 1965.

35th anniversary "Wheel" collage cover design, for *Fortune,* February 1965.

Light-generated cover design, for *Fortune,* June 1968.

"500" consumer products collage cover design, for *Fortune,* May 1972.

(Allner designed 79 covers for *Fortune* between 1951 and 1973).

Publications:

By ALLNER: books—*International Poster Annual,* St. Gallen 1948–52; *A. M. Cassandre: Peintre d'Affiches,* St. Gallen 1948; *Posters: Fifty Artists and Designers,* editor, New York 1952.

On ALLNER: books—*Die Neue Graphik/The New Graphic Design* by Karl Gerstner and Markus Kutter, Teufen and London 1959; *Monografie des Plakats* by Herbert Schindler, Munich 1972; *Who's Who in Graphic Art,* edited by Walter Amstutz, Dubendorf 1982; *Inside Time Inc.* by Julia Lieblich and others, New York 1986; articles—"Computer Graphics at Fortune" by J. Lahr in *Print* (New York), November/December 1966; "Covers of Fortune Magazine" in *Idea* (Tokyo), no. 89, 1968; "Walter Allner in Tokyo" by S. Fukuda in *Idea* (Tokyo), no. 129, 1975; "Walter Allner" by R. Newman in *Design in Australia* (Sydney), February 1984.

Walter Allner's imagination, artistic know-how, and creativity have produced inspired graphics, logos, magazine covers, car cards, and one- to 24-sheet posters. In his own words, "The contribution of the individual—the artist, the designer—in graphic originality, excellence, inventiveness and even audacity alone . . . stimulates interest and establishes the bond between the advertiser and the public. . . . In all my work, whether it concerns a poster, a magazine cover or any other design—I try to be concise."

In this precise and concise way, Allner follows the principles he learned while at the Bauhaus in Dessau. He reveals the essence of each assignment clearly and simply, often using forceful graphic symbols. The message of text is always brief and to the point. His forms tend toward the abstract, with clear line and geometric shape enhanced by solid areas of pure color. In each instance, the design is unmistakable, and at once recognizable, as being a symbol of the product under consideration.

Before coming to the United States in 1949, Allner was already a noted painter, designer, and poster authority. While in Paris, he had assisted the posterist Jean Carlu and had worked with A. M. Cassandre. He had started his own design firm, Omnium Graphique, and was the art director for Formes, Editions d'Art Graphiques et Photographique.

Allner, along with the others, has been credited with continuing the work of the Bauhaus in America. The spirit of functional design, which was so forcefully practiced there, can be seen particularly in the covers he created for *Fortune.* These covers demonstrate the range of possibilities in such an artistic medium. Allner believed every cover should be "something of a surprise." For one, he specified a program for a computer to design the cover. For the Thirty-fifth anniversary issue, he designed a fold-out, using mangled cans to create an assemblage. Shortly after this was published, Allner re-

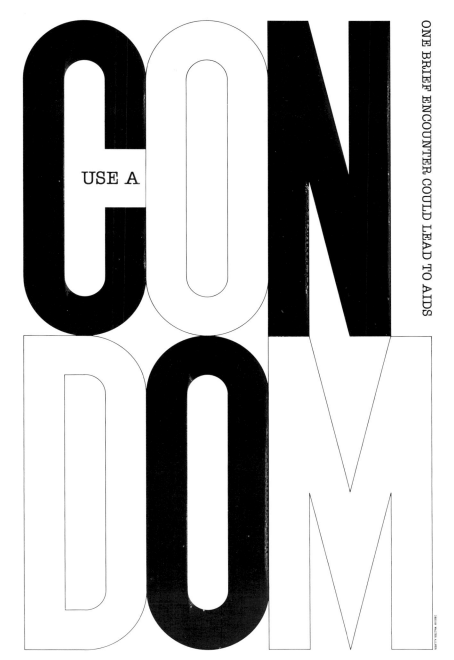

USE A **CON DOM**

ONE BRIEF ENCOUNTER COULD LEAD TO AIDS

Walter Allner: *Use a Condom* poster, 1988

ceived recognition for this work and was honored with an invitation to participate in the United States Information Agency's exhibit at the Berlin Industries Fair.

Recently, Allner was commissioned to design the inauguration poster for the new Bauhaus-Museum in West Berlin. Concurrently, a major exhibition of his editorial graphics and poster designs was held at the Kunstbibliothek of the Staatliche Museum in Berlin. His poster for this exhibition is a large, off-center "A", created out of the negative space of the white paper and defined by three colors: brown, green, and blue. The type in gray ink runs across the bar of the "A". A perfect example of his philosophy, created simply, directly, imaginatively, and concisely, the poster is logically symbolic of the product: Allner.

—Elena Millie

AMBASZ, Emilio.

Argentinean architect, industrial, graphic and exhibition designer. Born in Resistencia, Chaco, 13 June 1943. Studied architecture, Princeton University, New Jersey: MFA 1966. Curator of Design, Museum of Modern Art, New York, 1970–75; freelance designer, establishing architectural practice in New York, and industrial design office in Bologna, Italy, from 1976: founder-president, Emilio Ambasz and Associates, and Emilio Ambasz Design Group, New York, since 1981. Chief Design Consultant, for Cummins Engine Company, Columbus, Indiana, since 1981. Assistant Professor of Architecture, 1966–67, and Philip Freneau Professor, 1967–69, Princeton University, New Jersey; Visiting Professor, Hochschule fur Gestaltung, Ulm 1967. Co-founder, 1967, and Fellow, 1970–72, Institute for Architecture and

Urban Studies, New York; President, Architectural League, New York, 1981–85. **Exhibitions:** Max Protetch Gallery, New York, 1980; Leo Castelli Gallery, New York, 1980, 1983; Centro Domus, Milan, 1983; MAD Centro de Diseno/Galeria Ynguanzo, Madrid, 1984; Halle Sud, Geneva, 1987; Museum of Modern Art, New York, 1989; La Jolla Museum of Art, California, 1989 (toured). **Collections:** Museum of Modern Art, New York. Recipient: Print Casebooks Certificate of Excellence, 1966, 1974; American Institute of Graphic Arts Award, 1973, 1976; Prix Jean de la Fontaine, 1975; *Progressive Architecture* Award, 1976, 1980, 1987; Resources Council Award, New York, 1977; International Business Designers Gold Award, 1977; Smau Prize, 1979; U.S. National Design Award, 1980; Designers Choice Award, 1981; Compasso d'Oro Award, Milan, 1981; Annual Interiors Award, 1981; Industrial Design Excellence Award, 1982, 1983; Merit Award, Art Directors Club of New York, 1983. Address: Emilio Ambasz and Associates, 636 Broadway, New York, New York 10012, U.S.A.

Works:

Arrow graphics poster, for Geigy, 1966.
Italy: The New Domestic Landscape exhibition design, for the Museum of Modern Art, New York, 1972.
The Chairs of Charles R. Mackintosh exhibition design, for the Museum of Modern Art, New York, 1974.
Center for Applied Computer Research and Programming, Las Promesas, Mexico, 1975.
Grand Rapids Art Museum, Michigan, 1975.
The Taxi Project: Realistic Solutions for Today exhibition design, for the Museum of Modern Art, New York, 1976.
Vertebra seating system, for Open Ark, 1977.
Banque Lambert interiors, in Milan, Lausanne and New York, 1979–83.
Museum of American Folk Art, New York, 1980.
Dorsal seating system, for Open Ark, 1981.
Spotlights, for Logotec, 1981.
Mimar architecture magazine design, from 1981.
Lucile Halsell conservatory, for San Antonio Botanical Gardens, Texas, 1982.
Oseris lighting system, for Erco Leuchten, 1983.
Car showroom, for Mercedes Benz, New Jersey, 1985.
Obihiro department store, Hokkaido, Japan, 1988–91.

Publications:

By AMBASZ: books—*Italy: The New Domestic Landscape,* exhibition catalogue, New York 1972; *Walter Pichler: Projects,* exhibition catalogue, New York 1975; *The Architecture of Luis Barragan,* exhibition catalogue, New York 1976; *The Taxi Project: Realistic Solutions for Today,* exhibition catalogue, New York 1976; *Architecture 1,* exhibition catalogue, New York 1977; *Il Disegno Oggi In Italia tra Produzione, Consumo e Qualcos'altro,* Rome 1982; *Emilio Ambasz,* Milan 1984; *The 1986 Design Zoo,* editor, New York 1986.

On AMBASZ: books—*The Print Casebooks: The Best in Posters,* by Martin Fox, Washington, D.C. 1975; *Emilio Ambasz* by Marina Waisman, Buenos Aires 1977; *Furniture by Architects,* exhibition catalogue, Cambridge, Massachusetts 1981; *Emilio Ambasz: 10 Anni di Architettura, Grafica e Design,* exhibition poster with text by Fulvio Irace, Milan 1983; *Concepts of*

Urban Design by David Gosling and Barry Maitland, New York 1984; *Emilio Ambasz 1984: Arquitectura, Diseno Grafico e Industrial,* exhibition catalogue, Madrid 1984; *Twentieth Century Style and Design* by Stephen Bayley, Philippe Garner and Deyan Sudjic, London and New York 1986; *Emilio Ambasz,* exhibition catalogue edited by Giordano Tironi, Geneva 1988; *Emilio Ambasz: The Poetics of the Pragmatic,* with texts by Mario Bellini, Alesandro Mendini, Michael Sorkin and Ettore Sottsass, New York 1989.

*

I am an object maker, whether of graphic designs, products or buildings. As for my attitude toward problem-solving in design, I can distinguish two features. First, I try, not always successfully, to go beyond the problem at hand. Second, since I am so lazy, I always look around to see whether there is not something already existent which I may re-utilize.

Since I feel slightly guilty for having betrayed our forefathers' blind trust in progress and their belief in new products as the healers of mankind's problems, I have felt compelled to develop a little philosophical theory to justify such behaviors. It goes, more or less as follows:

Europe's eternal quest remains Utopia, the myth of the end. America's returning myth is Arcadia, the eternal beginning. While the traditional vision of Arcadia is that of a humanistic garden, America's Arcadia has turned into a man-made nature, a forest of artificial trees and of mental shadows.

Like the first chair-maker who used the wood of surrounding trees, so now are some of America's designers beginning to use objects and processes (and sometimes, the memories) surrounding them. But, since no more trees remain, just chairs, they have to be careful that their creations are either capable of returning to their previous state, or of being re-utilized, lest they find themselves the gardeners of a man-made desert. The designer, that old thaumaturgus of the eternal gesture, must now learn both how to celebrate the ritual of the beginning and how to design for the ceremony of the end.

The principle underlying such notions of order is the concept of open-ended systems, where the possibilities for changing patterns of relationships remain always open, but where

Emilio Ambasz: *Vertebra* office chair, for Open Ark, 1977

each of the component elements maintains its irreducible identity.

The methodological principle guiding my work is the search for basic principles and prototypical or pilot solutions which can first be formulated into a general method and then applied to solve specific problems.

A notion of design in dynamic consonance with a man-made nature in a constant state of becoming involves specialized tasks. First, *empirical,* to construct a cartography of the products and production techniques which populate the man-made garden. Second, *normative,* to develop a program of individual needs and desires in the context of a larger program of social necessities, in order to guide the utilization of the empirical cartography. Third, *synthetic,* to give form to new structures which will allow man to reconcile his fears and desires within the limitations imposed by the empirical realm and the pressure of the normative domain.

I believe that the designer's real task begins once functional and behavioral needs have been satisfied. We create objects not only because we hope to satisfy the pragmatic needs of man, but mainly because we need to satisfy the demands of our passions and imagination. It is not hunger, but love and fear, and sometimes wonder, which make us create. The poetic principle is the fundament of our creating objects. The designer's milieu may have changed, but the task, I believe, remains the same: to give poetic form to the pragmatic.

—Emilio Ambasz

Emilio Ambasz is one of the handful of interdisciplinary practitioners in the last half-century to make contributions to industrial, exhibit, and graphic, as well as architectural design.

Born in Argentina and trained in the United States, Ambasz is nevertheless linked with the current vanguard of Italian design. As Curator of Design at New York's Museum of Modern Art, he organized *Italy: The New Domestic Landscape* (1972), which first exposed the conceptual backbone of Italy's rebirth in consumer markets post World War II. As a polemic, and one that circumscribes Ambasz's own design efforts, the show demonstrated the shifting emphasis from the discrete, autonomous object to objects that function as part of a total environment, claiming for design roots in sociology, politics, and anthropology.

Ambasz established his reputation in industrial design with the Vertebra chair (1976), the first automatic, articulated office chair in the world. Vertebra represented a new important restatement of the role of ergonomics in modern seating. Rather than manipulating controls and levers to adjust the configuration of the chair, the user senses the chair as a dynamic organism as it responds automatically to the body's motions. The shift in Ambasz's approach is one from man's willful dominance over his environment to a more congenial, natural appreciation of his own physical condition in cooperation with the environment.

This same environmental consideration informs Ambasz's architectural projects. Rendered as visionary landscapes of mytho-poetic proportions, many of his projects remain unbuilt, promising a future rather than a present, where technological man finds a reconciliation with his rural past. With Luis Barragan as his closest influence, Ambasz pushes the idea of the machine in the garden to Surrealist conclusions. His sites are often dotted with technological monuments that resemble Neolithic menhirs, cartographic markers that are modern celestial notations of architectural mythology. The program, however, is visually concentrated underground, or in-ground, where the open-ended

configuration of spaces and social patterns derives as much from the natural formation of the site as it does from man's appreciation of it. In an almost primitive reductionism, roofs dissolve into open sky, while containing walls are either transparent when above ground or bounded as excavated ruins; in either case, the artifice of the architect's facade is denied. What is left is the rhythm of utility and psyche that is Ambasz's ritual goal.

Ambasz maintains a belief in the technological necessity of this romantic idealism. His most notable project to date, the San Antonio Botanical Garden Conservatory (1982), is a theater of virtuoso engineering. The truncated glass pyramids that signal its emergence above ground seem homages to the Crystal Palace, that temple of 19th-century technology, ironically constructed to a height to accommodate full-grown trees among the exhibits. Functioning as a presentation of nature, Ambasz's conservatory offers downward views, upward views, as well as normative views, as foliage seems to emerge from underground or descend from the landscape. A sunken court with a natural pool at its center is surrounded by arcades with recessed viewing chambers acting as natural dioramas imbedded in cavernous rock. Access is provided underground through a bunker portal, from above via ramps that slice into the earth like natural fissures, or from a processional staircase that creates the effect of entering a Greek amphitheater.

Ambasz's intentions of giving poetic form to the pragmatic are evident in the dilemma he recognizes: "Europe's eternal quest remains Utopia, the myth of the end. America's returning myth is Arcadia, the eternal beginning. While the traditional vision of Arcadia is that of a humanistic garden, America's Arcadia has turned into a manmade nature, a forest of artificial trees and of mental shadows."

—Sarah Bodine

ARAI, Junichi.

Japanese textile designer. Born in Kiryu City, Gunma Prefecture, 13 March 1932. Trained in weaving at his father's textile factory, Kiryu, 1950–55; also studied at the Theatre Art Institute, Tokyo, 1953. Married Riko Tanagawa in 1958; children: Motomi and Mari. Independent textile designer, Tokyo, from 1955: developed new metallic yarn techniques, 1955–66; worked with fashion designers Comme des Garcons, Issey Miyake, Rei Kawakubo, Shin Hosokawa, Yoshiki Hishinuma, etc., from 1970; created computer-designed woven fabrics, from 1979; founder, Anthology textile design and production studio, Tokyo, 1979, and Arai Creation System textile production company, Tokyo, 1987; opened Nuno fabrics shop, in Roppongi, Tokyo, 1984. Advisor to the Yuki Tsumugi Producers Association, Japanese Ministry of Trade and Industry, and the International Wool Secretariat, from 1987, and to several textile mills in Japan, from 1989. Also formed Tomodachi Za puppet theatre group, Kiryu, 1950. **Exhibitions:** Gen Gallery, Tokyo, 1983; Nichifutsu Gallery, Kyoto, 1984; Sagacho Exhibit Space, Tokyo, 1984; Shimin Gallery, Sapporo, 1985; Takashimaya Store, Osaka, 1985; *Fabrics for the 80s,* Rhode Island School of Design, Providence, 1985; Axis Gallery, Tokyo, 1986; Apita

Studio, Nagoya, 1986; Daimaru Store, Fukuoka, 1986; *Textile Convergence 88,* Chicago, 1988; La-Porte Hall, Kobe, 1989. **Collections:** Fashion Institute of Technology, New York; Cooper-Hewitt Museum, New York; Rhode Island School of Design Museum, Providence; Victoria and Albert Museum, London. Recipient: Recognition Award, Japanese Association for the Welfare of the Blind, 1977; Special Prize, Mainichi Fashion Awards, Tokyo, 1983. Honorary Royal Designer for Industry, Royal Society of Arts, London, 1987. Address: K. K. Arai Creation System, 301 Esyc Hights, 5–16–8 Roppongi, Minato-ku, Tokyo, Japan.

Works:

Bubble Blocks/103 bubble-structure fabric, for Rei Kawakubo, 1981.

Cast Concrete/52 multiple-weave structure fabric, for Rei Kawakubo, 1981.

Diagonal Fukure/106 bubble fabric with diagonal pattern, for Rei Kawakubo, 1982 (with Timney and Fowler).

Split Rope/40 fabric with split warps and wefts, for Issey Miyake, 1982.

Nuno Me Gara computer-designed patterned fabric, for Nuno, 1983.

Big Hole/86 thick wool fabric with big holes, for Reiko Kawakubo, 1983.

Organdie/139 puckered organdie fabric, for Nuno/Shin Hosokawa, 1983.

Fringe/22 random cotton fringe on plain weave, for Issey Miyake, 1983.

Warp Dye Marble/107 warp dye technique fabric, for Nuno/Hanae Mori, 1984 (with Timney and Fowler).

Big Check/36 transparent fabric of 4 thread types, for Yoshiki Hishinuma, 1984.

Basket Weave Big Pockets/54 basket-texture fabric with large soft pucker, for Nuno, 1984.

Spider Web/63 web-knit fabric, for Nuno/Koshino Hiroko, 1984 (with Riko Arai).

Peach Fuzz/59 fluffy-surfaced fabric, for Osamu Maeda, 1985.

Bell/28 thick wool fabric with pucker, for Shin Hosokawa, 1986.

Big Sheep/29 thick wool fabric with big fringe, for Issey Miyake, 1986.

Titanium Poison/32 double-sided thick wool/titanium lame pucker fabric, Issey Miyake, 1986.

Four-Layered Woven Magic double-sided 4-layer patterned weave fabric, for Nuno, 1988.

Publications:

By ARAI: article—"Nuno Choryu" in *Ginka Bunka Shuppan* (Tokyo), no. 63, 1985.

On ARAI: books—*Fabrics for the 80s,* exhibition catalogue with text by Maria Tulokas, Providence 1985; *International Design Yearbook 1987/88,* edited by Philippe Starck, London 1987; *International Design Yearbook 1988/89,* edited by Arata Isozaki, London 1988; *Ideas in Weaving* by Ann Sutton and Diane Saheenan, Loveland, Colorado, and London 1989; articles—"Textiles for the Eighties" by M. Tulokas in *Textilforum* (Hannover), September 1985; "Fabric About Fabric: Junichi Arai's Computer Creates a Textile for the 80s" by D. Cannarella in *Threads* (Newtown, Connecticut), November 1985; "Man of Cloth" by P. Popham in *Blueprint* (London), December 1987/January 1988; "Junichi Arai" by S. Anderson Hay in *Handbook of the Museum of Art, Rhode Island School of Design,* Providence 1989; "Textiles by Junichi Arai, 1979–1988" by M. Tulokas in *Textilforum* (Hannover), June 1989.

Junichi Arai: *Nuno Me Gara* double-weave jacquard fabric, 1983

From ancient times to the present day, mankind has been deeply concerned with fabric, from the cloth we are wrapped in at birth to the cloth we are wrapped in at death. If people were naked they would be like animals. By wearing fabric, we become aware of the changing weather and of sensations on the skin; we also derive feelings of joy and sadness from our clothing. Fabric clothes not only the body but also the spirit. Clothes are the proud emblem that connects us to God, and the weaver is the standard bearer. Weavers were the standard-bearers for both the Renaissance and the Industrial Revolution.

Thus, the present technological world began from the relationship of people to fabric. And if we can properly understand both the advantages and pitfalls of new technology, we can start to make truly contemporary fabric. When things are made which look only backwards, to the supposedly golden past, they are the products of the nostalgia of weak people. Making a contemporary weave is like planting a seed into a new, uncultivated field. When the seed sprouts, the resulting fabric is a fruit which communicates with all our senses and makes us rejoice. Newly conceived fabrics change our consciousness, change our spirit and so can change future

society. This, therefore, is the mission of the weaver today: to pose the challenge of a new human revolution. Weaver—you are carrying the responsibility of beauty. What will you say if you cannot say, "this is a weaver's honour"?

A poet cannot write a poem if he has no words. In the same way, a contemporary weaver cannot create cloth without ideas. We cannot fulfil the needs of people today by mere nostalgia. We must understand the desires of the modern spirit so that we can create a truly appropriate contemporary fabric. Creating an image is the first step in making a work of art. But image alone cannot produce fabric; we need much more basic information in order to start to create: fibre, colour and twist of thread, weave structure, sett and possible effect of finishing. We cannot start to create without our experience being applied to this information. But selecting from the possibilities offered by this information is essentially an ability of the soul. Fine contemporary cloths are the results of the human spirit and new technology working hand in hand.

We are asked about the ability of our soul to make such selections. The most enjoyable part of a weaver's task is transforming an idea into cloth. If a poet has only a limited amount of

inspiration, he flounders: similarly, weavers must do more thinking and develop their ideas. Fortunately, the contemporary weaver has much new technology at his disposal, but this is also his greatest misfortune. He is confused and afraid of the tool that is the computer. This can only lead into a labyrinth with no exit.

How do we create ideas? How do we become inspired and cultivate the wasteland? The answer lies in the ability of the spirit to create and to nurture.

—Junichi Arai

Master of traditional textile methods as well as a pioneer of modern technology, Junichi Arai has expanded the field of fabric design through his exploration of structure and materials. Arai's technical skill, unbridled imagination, and ability to achieve new and surprising effects in the interlacings of yarns—varying from wool and silk to plastic and other synthetic fibres—displays both his virtuosity and authority in textile design. When applied to fashion, the fluid fabrics seem to be made expressly for the body, allowing it to create its own form.

Arai's work was brought to public prominence by the Japanese avant-garde fashion movement, led by Rei Kawakubo and Issey Miyake in the 1970s and early 1980s. He collaborated with fashion designers, producing textiles that emphasized irregular texture and a hand-made look with reference to tribal cultures. Working closely with mill-owners and skilled technicians in his native town of Kiryu, traditionally a centre for the textile industry, Junichi Arai became influential not only in creating this new look in fabric but also in the redesign of highly technical machinery that had originally been developed to produce flawlessly uniform fabric. The computer, which the advanced textile industry had earlier adopted for design and weaving processes, became Arai's indispensable tool. Not only could the computer speed up the adaptation of a design for the loom, it enabled him to conceive structures whose complexity would be almost impossible to draft by hand.

With the computer, according to Arai, drafting the designs of his own multilayered fabrics, where patterns change from one side to another (with equal interest on both sides), takes only a fraction of the time it would take by conventional means. The fabric *Nuno me Gara (Fabric about Fabric)* is a perfect example of his working process. Arai discovers an image he wishes to integrate into a fabric, then records it with a copying machine, and produces a design that interlocks with itself to form a continuous pattern in repetition. The design is scanned by a computer to translate it into a double weave structure where two layers interchange in the black and white configurations of the design. Arai applies this pattern to a variety of special fabrics. In one, he uses overspun cotton yarn that curls back on itself when relaxed after the weaving process—making the fabric denser and richer with stretch. Not only do Arai's fabrics show his remarkable facility for thinking three-dimensionally in terms of woven structures, but they also demonstrate his ability to envision the end results through many phases of a mechanical and indirect process. Arai's early experience with intricate and technically complex kimono fabrics most likely contributed to his prowess.

The relatively small textile mills of Kiryu with their modern technology have offered Junichi Arai ideal working conditions. Small scale production allows flexibility, experimentation at the loom, and finished samples within hours of the idea conception. In response to the needs of designers, manufacturers have developed a new range of yarns from natural and man-made fibres, making it possible for the weaving industry to achieve new effects. Texture, an important part of Arai's work, is accomplished with structure and, more often, with materials.

Arai has continued to design and produce fabrics for fashion designers as well as for his store in Tokyo. In 1987, he concentrated his production with a newly-formed company, K. K. Arai Creation System. He has also expressed interest in designing interior fabrics.

While Arai's work expands the aesthetic and functional potential of fabric, it also carries with it the maker's inherent artistic vision. The distinction of the work lies in the directness of expression, his ability to convey experiences from the strength of his individuality. A variety of ingredients make up this character. Strongly organic surface of fabric, light reflected from synthetic material (at times juxtaposed with an organic texture), tactile quality, and black-and-white patterns with occasional organic colour bring a timeless quality to the work. Despite Arai's pioneering in textile technology, he remains firmly rooted in the human vision of his work.

—Maria Tulokas

ARCHER, (Leonard) Bruce.

British industrial designer. Born in London, 22 November 1922. Educated at Henry Thornton School, Clapham, London, 1932–37; studied at the University of London, 1938–39; mechanical engineering, Northampton Polytechnic (now City University), London, 1945–50. Served in the Scots Guards, British Army, 1941–44. Married Joan Henrietta Allen in 1950; 1 daughter. Worked in various industries as an engineering designer, 1946–50, and as a design and management researcher, 1950–53; freelance design and management consultant, London, 1953–57. Lecturer, then Senior Lecturer in Industrial Design Engineering, Central School of Arts and Crafts, London, 1957–60; Guest Professor, Hochschule fur Gestaltung, Ulm, 1960–61; research fellow, 1961–71, and Professor of Industrial Design from 1972, Royal College of Art, London; also visiting lecturer at several colleges and design institutions throughout the world, since 1956. Member, Science Policy Foundation, London, and Design Council, London, since 1972. Recipient: National Prize, Institute of Engineering Designers, 1951; Kaufmann International Design Research Award, New York, 1964. Member, Institute of Mechanical Engineers; Institute of Engineering Designers; Associates, Chartered Institute of Designers, London. Commander, Order of the British Empire, 1976. Address: 43 Avenue Road, London N6 5DF, England.

Publications:

By ARCHER: books and papers—*Training of the Industrial Designer,* Paris, 1963; *A Systematic Method for Designers,* London 1964; *Design and the Community,* Vienna 1965; *Architects Restructuring their Problems,* Cranbrook, Michigan 1966; *Exploiting Instrument Development,* Eastbourne 1966, 1970; *Design Methods in Architecture,* Portsmouth 1967; *Structure of Design Processes,* Springfield, Virginia 1968, Tokyo 1970, Paris 1971; *Technological Innovation and the Growth of the Economy,* Poconos, New York 1970; *Design for Production,* Glasgow 1970; *The Predicament of Man,* London 1971; *Technological Innovation—A Methodology,* Frimley, Surrey 1971; *Design Awareness and Planned Creativity in Industry,* Ottawa and London 1974.

On ARCHER: books—*Industrial Design and the Community* by Ken Baynes, London 1967; *All Things Bright and Beautiful: Design in Britain 1880 to Today* by Fiona MacCarthy, London 1972; *Industrial Design* by John Heskett, London 1980; *Design by Choice* by Reyner Banham, London 1981; *The Conran Directory of Design,* edited by Stephen Bayley, London 1985; *Electrical Appliances* by Penny Sparke, London 1987.

Professor Bruce Archer's early career as a designer and teacher needs to be seen in the context of the growing enthusiasm for rigorous, systematic design methods, as voiced by J. Christopher Jones (*Design Methods: Seeds of Human Futures,* 1970) and the Design Research Society in Britain through the 1960's. It was hoped that if all the minute decisions involved in creating a design were recorded, it would be possible to build up a complete picture of the design process that would be explicable at all points. More recently, Archer has been advocating a position that goes beyond this extreme to the ethical concerns and intuitive elements of "planned creativity." "Good design is holistic design, in which all the functional, cultural, social and economic interests of all those who are directly or indirectly touched by it are enriched as much, or impoverished as lit-

tle, as human ingenuity can contrive," he has written.

Through his teaching at the Royal College of Art and many international seminars and papers, he has stressed the vital role of design planning and organization in industrial management and company development. Increasingly, this has led him into the more general problems of "design awareness" and the place of design in education as a whole. Following a two-year research programme, Design in General Education, funded by the Ministry of Education, he has argued that designing is a skill comparable to numeracy and literacy. He has proposed that design should be treated as an academic discipline separate from the humanities and the sciences with a focus on Design technology or "the study of the phenomena to be taken into account within the area of design application." He sees these to be the following: "1. Design praxiology—the study of design techniques, skills and judgment applied in a given area. 2. Design language—the study of the vocabulary, syntax and media for recording, devising, assessing and expressing design ideas in a given area. 3. Design taxonomy—the study of the classification of design phenomena. 4. Design metrology—the study of the measurement of design phenomena, with special emphasis on the means for ordering or comparing nonquantifiable phenomena. 5. Design axiology—the study of goodness or value in design phenomena, with special regard to the relations between technical, economic, moral and aesthetic values. 6. Design philosophy—the study of the language of discourse on moral principles in design. 7. Design epistemology—the study of the nature and validity of ways of knowing, believing and feeling in design. 8. Design history—a study of what is the case, and how things came to be the way they are, in the design area. 9. Design pedagogy—the study of principles and practice of education in the design area."

Although the precise structure may be the subject of long dispute, this proposal may prove to be his most important contribution to design education.

—Anthony J. Coulson

ARMANI, Giorgio.

Italian fashion designer. Born in Piacenza, in July 1934. Studied medicine, University of Bologna, 1952–53; also studied photography. Served in the Italian Army, 1953–54. Menswear buyer, for La Rinascente department store chain, Milan, 1954–60; worked for Hitman menswear manufacturer of the Cerrutti group, in Milan, 1960–70; freelance designer, working with Sergio Galeoti to establish company manufacturing for Italian clothing factories, from 1970; created first collection under Giorgio Armani label, 1974; expanded design range to include womenswear, 1975. Also film costume designer, for *American Gigolo, Thief,* and *48 Hours.* **Exhibition:** *Intimate Architecture: Contemporary Clothing Design,* Massachusetts Institute of Technology, Cambridge, 1982. **Collection:** Costume Institute, University of Parma (sketches). Recipient: Neiman Marcus Award, 1979; Cutty Sark Award, 1980, 1981; Manstyle Award, *Gentleman's Quarterly,* 1982. Address: Via Durini 24, 20122 Milan, Italy.

Publications:

On ARMANI: books—*The Changing World of Fashion: 1900 to the Present* by Ernestine Carter, London 1977; *I Mass-Moda: Fatti e Personaggi dell' Italian Look/The Who's Who of Italian Fashion* by Adriana Mulassano, Florence 1979; *Armani* by Richard deCombray, Milan 1982; *The Collector's Book of Twentieth Century Fashion* by Frances Kennett, London and New York 1983; *McDowell's Directory of Twentieth Century Fashion* by Colin McDowell, London 1984; *The Conran Directory of Design*, edited by Stephen Bayley, London 1985; *The Encyclopaedia of Fashion from 1840 to the 1980s* by Georgina O'Hara, London 1986; *Design Source Book* by Penny Sparke and others, London 1986; *International Design Yearbook 1988/89*, edited by Arata Isozaki, London 1988.

I do not design for a tall person or a short person, ugly or beautiful, jet-set or middle class. I aim at a client who dresses from individual choice, not imposed fashion, and not simply because something was designed by Armani. One must make one's own very eclectic and very subjective definition of style. A suit may now be a jacket with a pair of subtly contrasting sports trousers worn with a printed shirt and a zip-front vest. There should be no dictates, no rules.

My ideas come from unimportant things, from a book, a film, from talking to my staff, or from watching how people behave and live. I cannot allow myself the luxury of waiting for the "moment of inspiration." I design clothes that can be produced at a certain cost, that can be sold and worn.

—Giorgio Armani

Since he began to design clothing in 1974, Giorgio Armani has become one of the most influential European fashion designers. In a reverse of the usual progression from women's to men's clothing, Armani began with men's suiting and accessories. He brought into fashion the tiny, rounded shirt collar which was an important move to slim down proportions, and he created a soft, easy-to-wear alternative to the mode prevalent in the 1960's; notable in this new approach were longer proportions and precise cut to show a man's body without restricting free movement. The most distinguishing feature of Armani's designs is the flawless tailoring, done with an attention to detail possible only by hand. He modified the inner structure of the jacket by not gluing the lining to the fabric's underside, a strategy which resulted in a free-flowing fall fundamental to the Armani style. He sloped the shoulders, dropped lapels, employed the lightweight fabrics which he often layers according to texture, color, and pattern. He frequently uses shimmering colors; his hooded sweatshirts, for example, are called "the jelly beans" because of their bright hues, and his linen suit has an iridescent cast. In addition to his famous alternatives to men's suiting, Armani has also offered his unique versions of leisure wear. His loosely draped, leather/bomber jacket and big-brimmed fedora over baggy slacks recalls the *Raiders of the Lost Ark* sensibility, modified into an up-to-date tone. Another relaxed outfit consists of a velour sweatshirt paired with classic, white duck pants.

In a move perhaps even more innovative than his designs for men, Armani has translated men's basic classic clothing into a look for women which highlights the relaxed, revisionist, refined flair for which he is so well known. Big, flat-rimmed hats top loosely draped jackets, in gold silk lame and wickerwork wool for dress and in subtle tones and stripes for busi-

Giorgio Armani: Jacket in rose and taupe with T-pleat grey wool pants and silk blouse, 1983

ness. These may be accompanied by long, freeflowing shirts or puffy, gaucho pants with classic, low-heeled boots. The look is definitely feminine, sensuous, and emancipating in its practicality and comfort. Like his men's clothing, it too encourages diverse combinations to create for the wearer a feeling of self which is not totally dictated by designer regimes.

Armani has taken the basics of "everyman's" wardrobe and given them possibilities for new varieties, open-ended and in tune with the freedom desired by the client who wants style without stricture. His is a fashion revolution as prominent as that of Yves Saint Laurent or Pierre Cardin, less wildly severe or flamboyant than their approaches, more subtle yet emphatic and timeless. In a way very different from the methods of Elio Fiorucci, Armani has changed the bohemian into the fashionable, reshaping clothes from the ordinary world with a touch of the thrift shop but no hint of the cheap or gaudy. It seems totally appropriate that Armani's influence is both pervasive and subtle, felt by a young adult sector which is both professionally tuned in and relaxed in undogmatic independence. That influence extends to many who do not even know his name.

—Barbara Cavaliere

ARONSON, Boris.
American painter, sculptor and stage designer. Born in Kiev, Russia, 15 October 1898; emigrated to the United States in 1923: naturalized, 1930. Studied at the State Art School, Kiev:

Dip. 1916; worked under Alexandra Exter, School of the Theatre, Kiev; trained with Ilya Mashkov, School of Modern Painting, Moscow; studied etching and allied arts under Hermann Struck, Berlin, 1922. Married Lisa Jalowetz in 1945; son: Marc-Henry. Co-founder, Museum of Modern Art, Kiev, 1917; artist with the Culture League, Kiev, 1918; government artist and designer, making decorations and posters for street festivals and pageants, in Kiev and Moscow, 1918; principal technical and research assistant to Alexandra Exter, School of the Theatre, Kiev, 1919; freelance stage designer, in Moscow, 1919–22, and in New York, 1923–77: commissioned to design synagogue interiors and decors, in Washington, D.C., and Sands Point, New York, in 1959. Founder-member, German Artists' Association, Berlin, and Moscow Artists' Association. **Exhibitions:** Anderson Galleries, New York, 1927; Odeon Theatre, Paris, 1928; Museum of Modern Art, New York, 1947; Storm King Art Center, Mountainville, New York, 1963; Wright/Hepburn/Webster Gallery, New York, 1963; Vincent Astor Gallery, New York Public Library, 1981. **Collections:** Museum of Modern Art, New York; Museum of the City of New York; Library of the Performing Arts, Lincoln Center, New York; Theatre Collection, Harvard University, Cambridge, Massachusetts. Recipient: Guggenheim Fellowship, New York, 1950; Antoinette Perry (Tony) Awards, 1951, 1967, 1969, 1971, 1972, 1976; Ford Foundation Grant, 1962; Joseph Maharam Foundation Awards, 1965, 1967, 1970, 1971, 1976; Creative Arts Award, Brandeis University, Waltham, Massachusetts, 1969. *Died* (in Nyack, New York) *16 November 1980.*

Works:

Stage designs include—*Romeo and Juliet,* Ka-

merny Theatre, Moscow, 1919; settings for the Yiddish Kamerny Theatre, Moscow, 1922; *Day and Night,* Unser Theatre, Bronx, New York, 1924; *Final Balance,* Unser Theatre, Bronx, New York, 1925; *Bronx Express,* Schildkraut Theatre, Bronx, New York, 1925; *Tenth Commandment,* Yiddish Art Theatre, Bronx, New York, 1926; *Tragedy of Nothing,* Irving Place Theatre, New York, 1927; *Angels on Earth,* Yiddish Art Theatre, Bronx, New York, 1929; *Jim Cooperkop,* Princess Theatre, New York, 1930; *Walk a Little Faster,* Schubert-Majestic Theatre, New York, 1932; *Small Miracle,* John Golden Theatre, New York, 1934; *Battleship Gertie,* Lyceum Theatre, New York, 1935; *Paradise Lost,* Longacre Theatre, New York, 1935; *Western Waters,* Hudson Theatre, New York, 1937; *The Merchant of Yonkers,* Guild Theatre, New York, 1938; *The Gentle People,* Belasco Theatre, New York, 1939; *Cabin in the Sky,* Martin Beck Theatre, New York, 1940; *The Night Before Christmas,* Morosco Theatre, New York, 1941; *The Snow Maiden,* Metropolitan Opera, New York, 1942; *The Red Poppy,* Music Hall, Cleveland, 1943; *Pictures at an Exhibition,* Metropolitan Opera, New York, 1944; *The Desert Song,* Philharmonic Auditorium, Los Angeles, 1945; *Sweet Bye and Bye,* Shubert Theatre, New Haven, 1946; *The Changeling,* Project Theatre, New York, 1947; *Love Life,* 46th Street Theatre, New York, 1948; *Detective Story,* Hudson Theatre, New York, 1949; *Season in the Sun,* Cort Theatre, New York, 1950; *Country Girl,* Lyceum Theatre, New York, 1950; *The Rose Tattoo,* Martin Beck Theatre, New York, 1951; *Ballade,* New York City Center, 1952; *The Crucible,* Martin Beck Theatre, New York, 1953; *The Master Builder,* Phoenix Theatre, New York, 1955; *Orpheus Descending,* Martin Beck Theatre, New York, 1957; *The Firstborn,* Coronet Theatre, New York, 1958; *Coriolanus,* Shakespeare Memorial Theatre, Stratford-upon-Avon, 1959;

Boris Aronson: Stage set for Stephen Sondheim's *Company*, Alvin Theatre, New York, 1970

Do Re Mi, St. James Theatre, New York, 1960; *Judith,* Her Majesty's Theatre, London, 1962; *Fiddler on the Roof,* Imperial Theatre, New York, 1964; *Cabaret,* Broadhurst Theatre, New York, 1966; *Mourning Becomes Electra,* Metropolitan Opera, New York, 1967; *Zorba,* Imperial Theatre, New York, 1968; *Company,* Alvin Theatre, New York, 1970; *Follies,* Winter Garden, New York, 1971; *A Little Night Music,* Sam S. Shubert Theatre, New York, 1973; *Pacific Overtures,* Winter Garden, New York, 1976; *The Nutcracker,* Kennedy Center, Washington, D.C., 1976 and for CBS Television, 1977.

Publications:

By ARONSON: books—*Marc Chagall,* Berlin 1923; *Contemporary Jewish Graphic Art,* Berlin 1924; book illustrated—*Theatre in Life* by Evreinoff, New York 1929.

On ARONSON: books—*Boris Aronson et l'Art du Theatre* by Waldemar George, Paris 1928; *Boris Aronson: Recent Paintings,* exhibition catalogue by Marcel E. Landgren, New York 1938; *Boris Aronson,* exhibition catalogue by Cecil Allen, Philadelphia 1938; *Boris Aronson: From His Theatre Work,* exhibition catalogue with texts by Harold Clurman and others, New York 1981.

In a tribute, the late director Harold Clurman said, "I know of no designer since (Robert Edmond) Jones who unequivocally deserves the title of master visual artist of the stage than Boris Aronson." Kenneth MacGowan, as early as 1926, referred to Aronson's work in the *New York Times* as "futuristic." Born in Kiev in 1898, Aronson studied art and stage design with Alexandra Exter, Tairov's leading designer and an exponent of radical stage design. From this exposure to the Russian experimental school (circa World War I), he began to formulate his theories of stage design: the set should permit varied movement, each scene should contain the mood of the whole play, and through the fusion of color and form, the setting should be beautiful in its own right. He would add, however, that a set is only complete when the actors move through it.

After brief stays in Berlin and Paris, he came to America to ply his craft with the Yiddish Art Theater and the Unser Theater, where he designed sets and costumes. While creating costumes for *A Chassidic Dance,* he said that it was necessary to examine the rhythm of the dancer, then to turn it into scenic construction. Design, to Aronson, dealt with the relationship of the actor to his environment. This inward approach, through the performer, marked most of his work. His early designs, however, reflected the Russian constructivism in his training. These influences can easily be seen in the sets for *Tenth Commandment,* in which he represented Hell as inside a human skull, or in *Little House in the Woods,* which takes place inside a house with walls and a roof that open up in full view of the audience.

For the Broadway stage, his work was equally inventive. *Walk a Little Faster* featured curtains, one of which was shaped like an iris lens, one that unzipped from top to bottom, and another which covered the performers' bodies except their dancing feet. *Do Re Mi's* curtain of juke boxes evoked a cathedral's stained glass effect.

Aronson stated that his settings stemmed from either a "documentary," researched approach or from his imagination. The productions that he did with Harold Clurman during his Group Theater days, *Awake and Sing* and *Paradise Lost,* for example, showed the naturalistic, poor dwellings of the Depression era,

while many of his other shows, such as Archibald MacLeish's *J. B.,* with its starry circus tent, explored the reaches of his and the audience's imagination.

He often stated that the theater is a collective art, and nowhere was this more evident than in his relationship with Harold Prince toward the latter years of his career. Aronson's Yiddish Art Theater experience came full circle with Prince's production of *Fiddler On the Roof* and his Berlin days, as well, with *Cabaret.* Prince brought out the pure versatility of his designer as evidenced by *Zorba's* monochromatic settings and *Company's* steel, plexiglas, and projections, which contrasted with the pastoral color of *A Little Night Music,* *Follies'* "Loveland," and the Japanese-print style of *Pacific Overtures.*

Aronson was a technical innovator who, by employing projected scenery in *Battleship Gertie* (1935) and in Eugene Loring's ballet *The Great American Goof* (1940), became one of the first exponents of its use. In 1947, the Museum of Modern Art featured his projected scenery for the stage in a show called *Painting With Light.* He used modern materials to solve design problems, such as in deciding to build a giant mirror for *Cabaret* (in which the audience was to see itself) out of lightweight mylar instead of the usual weighty, and thus dangerous, glass. He even took advantage of new technology to aid the design process, as is illustrated by his use of a color copying machine to work out the pattern designs on the model of *Pacific Overtures.*

His work in ballet and opera, especially Mikhail Baryshnikov's *Nutcracker* and the Metropolitan Opera's *Mourning Becomes Electra,* proved that he was a well-rounded designer. Aronson's design of two synagogue interiors, writing of two books, and successful career as a painter and sculptor who had many one-person shows further distinguished him as one of the few leading figures in twentieth-century scene design.

—Tom Mikotowicz

ASHLEY, Laura.
British textile, clothing and product designer. Born Laura Mountney, in Dowlais, Glamorgan, Wales, in 1925. Educated at schools in London and Glamorgan; mainly self-taught in design, from 1953. Married Bernard Albert Ashley in 1949; children: Jane, David, Nick and Emma. Founder and partner, with Bernard Ashley, of Ashley-Mountney Limited printed textile company, 1954–68, and Laura Ashley Limited, from 1968, in Pimlico, London, 1954–56, in Kent, 1956–61, and in Machynlleth, Wales, from 1961: opened retail shops in London, Edinburgh, Bath, Cheltenham, Cambridge, Norwich, Oxford, Aix-en-Provence, Munich, Vienna, Boston, etc., from 1967 (now more than 100 shops and 10 factories); range expanded from scarves, smocks, dresses and aprons to include home furnishing textiles, wallpapers, tiles and perfumes. Recipient: Queen's Award for Export Achievement, London, 1977. *Died* (in Coventry, Warwickshire) *17 September 1985.*

Publications:

By ASHLEY: books—*The Laura Ashley Book of home Decorating,* edited by Elizabeth Dickson and Margaret Colver, London 1982, New York 1984.

On ASHLEY: books—*A History of Fashion* by J. Anderson Black and Madge Garland, London 1975, 1980; *The World of Fashion: People, Places, Resources* by Eleanor Lambert, New York and London 1976; *Magic Names of Fashion* by Ernestine Carter, London 1980; *British Design Since 1880: A Visual History* by Fiona MacCarthy, London 1982; *The Collector's Book of Twentieth Century Fashion* by Frances Kennett, London and New York 1983; *McDowell's Directory of Twentieth Century Fashion* by Colin McDowell, London 1984; *The Encyclopaedia of Fashion from 1840 to the 1980s* by Georgina O'Hara, London 1986.

Admittedly more of an adapter than a designer, the Welsh wonderwoman of country cottage prints has been the inspiration of millions. Laura Ashley's simplicity of pattern and design combined with a romantic nature, has inspired many to walk into a lifestyle where clothing is emotionally appealing, whimsical, and fun, yet practical, where home furnishings are traditional and frilly, yet comfortable and liveable. A love of nature dictates her style, as her designs are floral, soft, and organic, but much of her inspiration actually comes from museum libraries, antique fabric pieces, old books, and the work of the pre-Raphaelite William Morris.

Laura Ashley as a business covers textiles, fashion, and home furnishings. With a goal of becoming one of the best textile printers in the world, the company owns two textile plants with the capacity to bleach, print, and dye more than a million meters per week. To its line of the country collage Victorian prints, the firm recently added a collection of distinct English Drawing Room prints to augment the seemingly endless possible mixtures of beautiful fabric combinations.

While the 1930's revival was dictating a sexy look in fashion, Ashley's clothing emerged fresh as spring air. The lovely garments brought a naiveté to all who wore them, as in her world, innocence and nature were synonymous. Expanding on this perception, wall coverings, furnishing fabrics (which take the company back to its origin in the 1950's in London), linens, bedding, and other numerous items from dishes to personal paraphernalia. There are even Laura Ashley perfumes to extend the essence of nature.

As for Ashley the woman, it is not difficult to imagine her in the countryside in a soft, romantic, country dress billowing in the gentle winds. As she picks flowers and concentrates on color combinations encompassing her, we wonder how these will be used in her next collection. These ideas descending from William Morris must bring all of us to feel a nostalgia for medieval art and pre-industrial values and to desire to get back to nature. In an increasingly computerized world, it's calming to know that Ashley has saved a bit of nature for us all to enjoy. We must admire her sensitivity to style, her love of harmony, her respect for the past, while all the while she produces a totally contemporary environment.

—Andrea Arsenault

ASQUITH, Brian (Anthony).
British industrial designer. Born in Sheffield, Yorkshire, 23 February 1930. Studied at Shef-

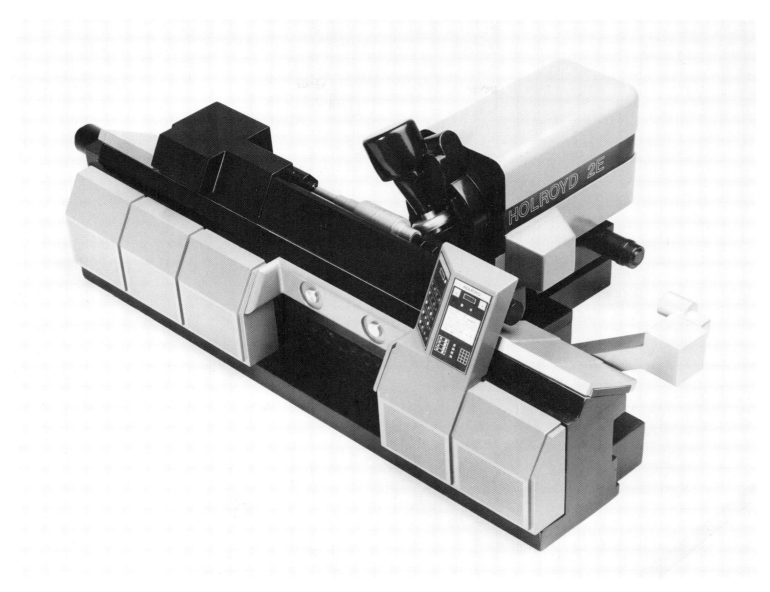

Brian Asquith: *Holroyd 2E* **rotor milling machine casing, for Renold Transmission, 1983**

field College of Art, 1942–47; studied sculpture, under Frank Dobson and John Skeaping, at the Royal College of Art, London, 1947–51: ARCA 1951. Served in the Royal Army Education Corps, Colchester, 1953–55: Sergeant Instructor. Married Barbara T. L. Tonge in 1949; sons: Nicholas, Jeremy and Patrick. Partner, with David Mellor, metalware and product design workshop and office, Sheffield, 1955–60; established own design office, Sheffield, 1960–63, and in Youlgreave, Derbyshire, from 1963: has designed for Redfyre, Spear and Jackson, British Airways, L.B. Plastics, Worshipful Company of Goldsmiths, International Tennis Federation, the Post Office, Baxi Heating, Renold Engineering and the Royal Family. **Exhibitions:** Crafts Centre, London, 1968; Design Centre, London 1978. **Collections:** Victoria and Albert Museum, London; Worshipful Company of Goldsmiths, London; Sheffield City Museum. Fellow: Society of Industrial Artists and Designers, 1965; Royal Society of Arts, London, 1980. Address: Turret House, Youlgreave, Derbyshire, England.

Publications:

On ASQUITH: books—*Modern Silver Throughout the World 1880–1967* by Graham Hughes, London and Toronto 1967; *All Things Bright and Beautiful: Design in Britain 1830 to Today* by Fiona MacCarthy, London 1972; *Modern Design in Metal* by Richard Stewart, London 1979; *The Contemporary Decorative Arts from 1940 to the Present Day* by Philippe Garner, London 1980.

My prime consideration in all designs is to communicate the idea in simple, direct terms. I try to humanize the concept, to give balance and permanence to the object-form, which should be visually colourful and alive, and to communicate quality and precision. The design should be appropriate to the market for which it is intended, be economical to produce, reflect the age, and above all, be a statement about our future hopes. I am interested in forms and shapes that have timeless qualities and in solutions that involve exact geometry. On looking at an object, I try to analyze its meaning to the eventual universal user and its logic, to bring out only areas of importance, and to subdue other nonessential parts. The ultimate is to balance form, colour, and use, so that an uplifting experience is associated with the object or design. New technology brings forth limitless possibilities, but the criteria of planned obsolescence will be neutralized by world resources, both natural and economic. Designs will need to be timeless, simple statements that relate to their use, their material surroundings, and people.

—Brian Asquith

Brian Asquith studied sculpture at Sheffield College of Art and the Royal College of Art. The Keeper of Sculpture at the Victoria and Albert Museum, the sculptor Richard Bedford, told him "I come from Devon so I use marble, you come from Sheffield so sculpt in steel." This Asquith did, notably with his monumental stainless steel and bronze sculpture for national Westminster Bank in Sheffield.

Asquith joined David Mellor in 1955 and opened on his own in 1960. In 1963, he moved out of Sheffield to the village of Youlgreave where he set up in the coach house of Turret House. In 1968, Asquith started making his silverware, applying an industrial approach with some basic components; the smooth, circular sections and the cast ribbed sections can be used in a variety of items. He has been very successful with silver, making a set of water jugs for Salford University, a silver centrepiece as a gift from the British government to Mauritius, a range of silver and gold boxes commissioned for the Prince of Wales' Investiture as personal gifts, a silver centrepiece presented by the Goldsmiths' Company to the City of Sheffield, a pair of silver wine coasters for the Officers' Mess of the Welsh Guards, a set of silver candlesticks presented by Darlington Corporation to Princess Anne, the ciborium, chalice, and alms plate for Derby Cathedral, and the chalice, paten, and ciborium for the nine hundredth anniversary of Winchester Cathedral in

1979. Asquith silver has also been ordered for sporting trophies, the Hamilton Formula Ford trophy, the Welsh squash trophy at Lancaster University, the World Tennis Championship trophies presented to Bjorn Borg and Chris Evert Lloyd in Paris (1981), and four cups for Davies Cup Zonal Competitions. For the Queen Mother's Eightieth birthday he was commissioned by the Victoria Cross and George Cross Associations to create a sundial of marble and bronze.

The bulk of the firm's business is with industrial work, machine tools, and domestic gas heating, but he keeps the craft work price down by using the stock components for the silverware in the industrial way. Asquith likes the contrast of shining plain silver with the textured sections deeply grooved like tree bark. He uses symbolism in some of his official commissions. The mayor's chain for the Ribble Valley Council (1974) has green agates to represent the countryside linked by wedges to represent the River Ribble. As the council is in Yorkshire the mayoress's chain bears the rose of York and Lancaster in gold. He loves stainless steel for its finish and toughness and for the contrast he can achieve with it, as in his stainless steel cross for St. Augustine's, Nottingham; its sharp lines contrast with the Victorian tracery. While he has had to diversify for practical reasons, Asquith is at base a sculptor interested in textures and an innovator in giving the silver craft industrial methods.

—Diana de Marly

ASSOCIATED SPACE DESIGN.

American corporate planning and interior design firm. Founded as the interior design department of Finch, Alexander, Barnes, Rothschild and Pashal architectural firm; Associated Space Design was incorporated as a separate firm, with offices in Atlanta, Georgia and Tampa, Florida, in 1963: Chairman, Cecil Alexander; President, William Pulgram; General Manager and Senior Designer, Leonard Harding. ASD Incorporated has designed office spaces, corporate headquarters, churches, restaurants and clubs, including projects for Coca-Cola, Gulf States Paper Corporation, Neiman-Marcus stores, Island Creek Coal Company, McDonald Corporation, etc. Address: 100 Peachtree Street N.W., Atlanta, Georgia 30303, U.S.A.

Publications:

On ASSOCIATED SPACE DESIGN: book—*Interior Design: An Introduction to Architectural Interiors* by Arnold Friedmann, John Pile and Forrest Wilson, New York and Amsterdam 1970, 1976; articles—in *Interiors* (New York), August 1969, September 1970, January 1971, December 1973, August 1974, January 1976; *Domus* (Milan), October 1973; *Contract Interiors* (New York), March 1978; *Interior Design* (New York), January 1982.

With its main office in Atlanta and a branch in Tampa, Florida, Associated Space Design, one of the largest interior design firms in the country, is most likely the leading firm in the South. Founded in 1963, the firm had previously existed as an interior design department within an architectural firm for five years. Its president and chief executive officer William T. Pulgram

has not only built up a first-rate interior design firm but has contributed enormously as a designer and leader in the field to many national causes. He is one of the most respected designers, and his activities with various governmental bodies, the American Institute of Architects, and a number of other civic and public groups have immeasurably advanced the recognition of the field of interior design.

Associated Space Design offers complete design services, including product and graphic design. The firm's clients include many leading corporations, banks, public institutions, and a number of governmental agencies. Known as a progressive and forward-looking firm since its inception, the firm won national attention for its McDonald Corporation in Oakbrook, Illinois in 1970. The open-office scheme for that project included the spaces for the top executives. The project also contained a highly publicized "think tank" and meditation room for those executives who needed to get away from their everyday work environment. In connection with the McDonald job, Associated Space Design developed a handsome and sophisticated line of systems furniture, which was subsequently marketed by a furniture manufacturer.

The success of the firm is partially due to the fact that it does not approach clients and projects with preconceived ideas. Pulgram stated in a recent interview that the firm does not have a marketing staff and that "we don't even have a decent brochure." He added, "We are involved more on a personal level." Most of the firm's new work is obtained by referral, which is about the highest compliment a firm of this size can receive. There are about forty members in the firm; some were trained as architects, including Pulgram, and some as interior designers, including vice-president Richard Stonis. One cannot ascribe a specific style to Associated Space Design; although the majority of its projects are work environments, it is remarkable to see the creative variety achieved among them.

—Arnold Friedmann

ASTI, Sergio.

Italian architect, exhibition and industrial designer. Born in Milan, 25 May 1926. Educated at high school, Como, 1942–45; studied art and architecture, Politecnico, Milan, 1947–53. Married Mariangela Erba in 1956; children: Marco, Paolo, Andrea and Nicola. Freelance architect and designer, Milan, since 1953: consultant to Ignis-Philips, 1956–67, ITT Europe, 1967, Ariston, 1968, Jabik wallpapers, 1975, Lange Italia sports goods, 1975–77, Lodi Gav, 1976–77, Corning france (Pyrex), 1978–81, and Alfa Romeo, 1981–82. Assistant instructor in interior design, Politecnico, Milan, 1953–58; guest instructor in industrial design and furnishing, at Shizuoka Experimental Institute, Japan, 1962, and at the National Institute for Industrial Research, Lisbon, 1966; visiting instructor in planning and design, State Art Institute, Venice, 1968–69; also visiting lecturer on design at professional institutes, throughout Italy, Belgium, China and Japan, since 1962. Management Committee Member, Associazione Disegno Industriale, Milan, since 1956; Italian correspondent, *Japan Interior Design* magazine, Tokyo, since 1968. **Exhibitions:** Galleria Quattrifolio, Milan, 1967; Design Re-

search, New York, 1970; Georg Jensen Inc., New York, 1972; Centro Cedit, Milan, 1975; Matsuya Design Gallery, Tokyo, 1981; Kyoto International Craft Center, Japan, 1983. **Collections:** Museum of Modern Art, New York; Victoria and Albert Museum, London; Kyoto International Craft Center, Japan. Recipient: Compasso d'Oro Awards, Milan, 1955, 1956, 1959, 1962, 1970; Gold and Silver Medals, Milan Triennale, 1957; MACEF Prize, Milan, 1972; Industrial Design Award, *Bio 5*, Liubliana, 1973; World Crafts Council Prize, Toronto, 1974; Furniture Prize, Hannover, 1980; Honour Award, Institut d'Esthetique Industrielle, Paris, 1982; Board of Trade and Industry Prize, Tokyo, 1983. Address: Via Bernardino Luini 12, 10123 Milan, Italy.

Works:

Marano shoe shop interiors, Milan, 1955.
Kitchen units, for Boffi, 1956.
Tizianella apartment block, Milan, 1958.
Exhibition display, for Pirelli, in Teheran, 1958, 1969.
Charlie Max nightclub interiors, Milan, 1963.
FIAT showroom interiors, Milan, 1964.
Villa Brienno, Lake Como, 1967.
Fitzgerald nightclub interiors, Milan, 1967–68.
La Rinascente store interiors, Milan, 1969.
Crystal glassware, for Arnolfo di Cambio, 1969–83.
Colour television set, for Brionvega, 1973.
Stainless steel tableware, for I.C.M., 1975–83.
Car dashboard, for Alfa Romeo, 1981–82.
Stainless steel tableware, for Hiromori of Tokyo, 1981–82.
Main Street Uno wall lamp, for Eleusi, 1982–83.
Alice glassware collection, for Salviati, 1984.
Alice marble dining-table, for Up and Up, 1986.

Publications:

On ASTI: books—*Forme nuove in Italia* by Agnoldomenico Pica, Milan and Rome 1957; *Architettura ultima* by Agnoldomenico Pica, Milan 1959; *International Modern Glass* by Geoffrey Beard, London 1976; *Atlante del design italiano 1940/1980* by A. Grassi and A. Pansera, Milan 1980; *Il disegno del prodotto industriale* by Vittorio Gregotti, Milan 1982; *The World of Sergio Asti,* exhibition catalogue with texts by Vittorio Gregotti and Ettore Sottsass, Kyoto 1983; *International Design Yearbook 1988/89,* edited by Arata Isozaki, London 1988.

AUBÖCK, Carl.

Austrian architect, clothing and industrial designer. Born in Vienna, 6 January 1925. Educated at the Neustiftgasse High School, Vienna, graduated 1942; studied architecture, Technische Universität, Vienna: Dip. Ing. 1949; postgraduate studies at the Massachusetts Institute of Technology, Cambridge, 1952. Served in the Alpine Division of the German Army, 1942–43: Private. Married Justine Krunes; children: Carl and Maria. Freelance architect and designer, Vienna, since 1955: has designed for Ultra, Tyrolia, Wiesner-Hager, Schuhfabrik Koflach, Rosenthal, Radio Kock, Team 7,

Sergio Asti: *Alice* **dining table in marble, for Up & Up, 1986**

Firma Sowitsch, Ostovics, Philips, Tiroler Glashutte, Grabner, Firma Krotz, etc. Assistant Lecturer, under Professor Merinsky, Institut für Baukunst und Ingenieurwesen, Technische Universität, Vienna, 1950–55; Professor of Architecture and Design, Hochschule für Angewandte Kunst, Vienna, since 1969. President, ICSID International Council of Societies of Industrial Design, 1973–76; President of the College of Delegates, Union Internationale des Architectes, 1982; President, Austrian Institute of Design, 1983. **Exhibitions:** Knoll International, Frankfurt, 1962; Design Centre, Brussels, 1968; Österreichische Werkstätten, Vienna, 1980; *Design Since 1945,* Philadelphia Museum of Art, 1983. **Collections:** Museum für Angewandte Kunste, Vienna; Museum of Modern Art, New York. Recipient: Gold Medal and Diploma of Honour, Brussels World's Fair, 1958; Silver Medal, Milan Triennale, 1961; Federal Design Awards and Awards of Honour, Austrian Ministry of Trade, 1962, 1964, 1966; Gold Medal, Liubliana Design Biennale, 1964; Austrian Coat of Arms Award, Austrian Ministry of Industry, Trade and Commerce, 1975; International Design Award, Tokyo, 1978. Honorary Fellow: American Institute of Architects, 1971; Instituto Tecnico Politico National de Diseno, Universidad de Guadalajara, Mexico, 1981; Kansas City Art Institute, Missouri, 1982; Bulgarian Architects Association, 1983. Address: Bernardgasse 21, 1070 Vienna, Austria.

Works:

Amboss 2060 steel cutlery, for Neuzeughammer Ambosswerk, 1957.
Amboss 2080 steel cutlery, for Neuzeughammer Ambosswerk, 1961.

Burg glassware, for Tiroler Glashütte Claus J. Riedel AG, 1961.
Electric food warmer, for Ultra, 1961.
Tyrolia, Tyrolia Rocket and *Super Rocket* safety bindings, for Tyrolia, 1962–68.
Neopan research microscope, for C. Reichert Optische Werk, 1963.
School furniture and stacking chairs, for Wiesner-Hagner, 1963–65.
Construction/furniture programme, for Firma Grabner, 1964.
MC polyspray machine, for Firma Coudenhove, 1966.
Ski-boots in plastic, for Schuhfabrik Koflach, 1969.
Package design, for Radio Kock, 1975.
Enamel tableware, for Firma Riesswerke, 1975.
Culinar range of tableware and accessories in ceramic, cast iron, glass, wood and textile, for Firma Ostovics, from 1979.
Furnishing fabrics, for Atelier Kindermann, 1981.
Tennis rackets, for Top Hit, 1982.
Floor and table lamps, for Philips, 1983.
Wall and freestanding electric clocks, for Firma Ostovics, 1983.

(Aubock has also designed numerous private houses, apartments, public and industrial buildings throughout Europe and the United States, from 1952.)

Publications:

By AUBÖCK: articles—in *MD Moebel Interior Design* (Stuttgart), no. 7, 1961, no. 11, 1982; *Ski Welt* (Solothurn), November 1971; *Brigitte* (Hamburg), December 1971; *Mosaik* (Zurich),

March 1972; *Austria Today* (Vienna), no. 3, and no. 4, 1975; *Werbung und Marktwirtschaft* (Vienna), June 1979; *Form und Zweck* (West Berlin), no. 5, 1981.

On AUBÖCK: books—*Mobili Tipo* by Robert Aloi, Milan 1956; *Mercati e Negozi* by Robert Aloi, Milan 1959; *International Shop Design* by Karl Kasper, Stuttgart and London 1967; *Design* by Jocelyn de Noblet, Paris 1974; *Contemporary Furniture,* edited by Klaus-Jürgen Sembach, Stuttgart and New York 1982; *Design Since 1945,* edited by Kathryn Hiesinger and George Marcus, Philadelphia and London 1983; *International Design Yearbook 1987/88,* edited by Philippe Starck, London 1987.

In the process of trying to increase and intensify the industrial potential of a country or a region, to achieve a better socio-economic balance, long-range success without a growing element of planning for the future seems hard to imagine. Things simply have to be planned—designed—before they can be produced, and the capability, the know-how and the professional qualities of the designer will to a great extent influence the success or failure of industrial production in the future. Therefore, the future of industrial design, and with it the socio-economic scene in a country—good or bad—will be the direct result of the planning efforts of today, and it will be up to the decision makers and their sense of responsibility to provide the choice and, indeed a future for the community that will add to the quality of life. This will be true not only for highly industrialized countries, but certainly even more so for the developing areas in the world.

My own work as an architect and designer over the last thirty years has shown clearly a

Carl Auböck: *Amboss 2060* cutlery in stainless steel, for Neuzeughammer Ambosswerk, 1957

or the design of furniture, tableware and sports articles, not in their appearance but rather in his approach to the problem, for example in the selection of materials, understood and put in the service of a function.

His direct relationships to materials is understandable against the background of his personal development, in the tradition of his father's workshop, where bronze casting was carried out and where it was quite natural for the son to learn a craft along with his academic education. Craftsmanship is still necessary today in all the objects in metal, wood, leather and horn which are produced to the design of Carl Auböck in the workshop of an old Biedermeier house in Vienna. This natural tradition is particularly important in Austria where tradition is often misunderstood: because it does not rest on formal qualities but sees itself as the promotion of quality in any work. The appointment of Carl Auböck as leader of a master class in metal design at the 'University' for applied arts was a logical consequence, as was the fact that the students attending learn more than metalwork—meanwhile the master class is also called "Product design-metal".

While Carl Auböck's work is deeply rooted in Austrian culture with all its layers of art, literature and history, it is not bound by frontiers. Postgraduate studies in the USA, a good knowledge of languages and his personal curiosity have taken his activities far beyond Austria. It is perhaps indicative that he has built and furnished a cultural institute for the country abroad; his design work for international firms, his function as president of ICSID, his lectures and publications abroad are also typical of him. The consequence is that he is much travelled and has the knowledge resulting from collaboration with and respect for alien mentalities. It is therefore understandable that Carl Auböck has worked out a "design policy" and long term concepts not only for Austria but also for other countries (Brazil, Indonesia) and that he is frequently called into consultation by international organizations like UNIDO.

Carl Auböck cannot be fitted into any group or "direction", yet, or just for that reason, his works are contemporary. They are as new as possible in terms of materials, technology and purpose; in their design and expression they are timeless. They do not deny their geographical and intellectual origins but they leave open every possibility for development in the future.

—Charlotte Blauensteiner

growing interest in the wider aspects and inter-relations of the planning disciplines. The ideas expressed in this statement are intended to exemplify the interlocking aspects of evolution both in architecture and industrial design as an ongoing process rather than a series of accomplishments.

Although conducted as an international practice based in Vienna, my work inevitably reflects its Austrian background in the sense that there is a recognizable continuity with the twentieth-century tradition of architecture and design in Vienna, as established by pioneers and protagonists such as Otto Wagner, Adolf Loos, Josef Hoffmann, Oskar Sternad, Josef Frank, and others in the first half of the century. The intention of this statement is to explain the concern for quality in planning as well as in execution of buildings, products, and general environment as a contribution for an increased quality of life in the complex context of the second half of the twentieth century.

Although I am equipped with specialized qualifications, my attitude as a problem-solver is that of a generalist being able to deal with the

problems on hand by inventing one's own working method and approach—rather than that of a specialist with a narrowed-down range of activities. The intentions and achievements in my work should therefore be considered as examples in a vital process of developing the creative potential of somebody who never was, nor in all probability never will be, very much bound by the limits of professional or academic categories.

—Carl Auböck

Presented here as a designer, Carl Auböck is also an architect, entrepreneur and university teacher. He himself sees no contradiction in these activities—they are all concerned with man's environment, and any separation of these activities seemed to him an impoverishment. The description of designer is perhaps the most appropriate because in its broadest sense it best expresses the unity of interest and action, of plan and execution.

His works in all their variety always bear his personal "handwriting" whether they are buildings for groups of individuals, major planning,

AULENTI, Gae(tana).
Italian architect, interior, stage, exhibition and industrial designer. Born in Palazzolo della Stella, Udine, 4 December 1927. Studied at the Faculty of Architecture, Politecnico, Milan: Dip.Arch. 1954. Freelance designer and architect in private practice, Milan, since 1954: has designed interiors for Fiat, Banca Commerciale Italiana, Pirelli, Olivetti, Knoll International, and products for Poltronova, Candle, Ideal Standard, Louis Vuitton, Artemide, etc. Member of the Movimento Studi per l'Architettura, Milan, 1955–61; editorial staff member, *Casabella-Continuita* magazine, Milan, 1955–65; Directive Board Member, *Lotus International* magazine, Milan, since 1974; Executive Board Member, Milan Triennale, 1977–80. Assistant instructor in architectural composition, Faculty of Architecture, Venice, 1960–62, and Politecnico, Mi-

lan, 1964–67; collaborator in figurative research, with Luca Ronconi, Laboratorio di Progettazione Teatrale, Prato, Florence, 1976–79; also visiting lecturer at congresses and professional institutes, in Europe and North America, since 1967. Vice-President, Associazione per il Disegno Industriale, Milan, 1966. **Exhibitions:** *Aspetti dell'Arte Contemporanea,* l'Aquila, Italy, 1963; *Gae Aulenti,* Gimbels Department Store, New York, 1967; *Italian Design,* Hallmark Gallery, New York, 1968; *Italy: The New Domestic Landscape,* Museum of Modern Art, New York, 1972; *Gae Aulenti,* Padiglione d'Arte Contemporanea, Milan, 1979; *Le Affinite Elettive,* at the Milan Triennale, 1985; *10 Proposte per Milano,* at the Milan Triennale, 1985. Recipient: Grand International Prize, Milan Triennale, 1964; Ubu Prize for Stage Design, Milan, 1980; Architecture Medal, Académie d'Architecture, Paris, 1983; Josef Hoffmann Prize, Hochschule für angewandte Kunst, Vienna, 1984. Honorary Member, American Society of Interior Designers, 1967; Chevalier de la Légion d'Honneur, France, 1987; Commandeur, Ordre des Arts et Lettres, France, 1987; Honorary Dean of Architecture, Merchandise Mart of Chicago, 1988; Accademico Nazionale, Accademia di San Luca, Rome, 1988. Address: Piazza San Marco 4, 20121 Milan, Italy.

Works:

Sgarsul rocking chair, for Poltronova, 1962.
April chair and stool, for Zanotta, 1964.
Italian Pavilion layout, XII Milan Triennale, 1964.
Pipistrello lamp, for Martinelli Luce, 1965.
Olivetti showroom interiors, in Paris, 1966, and Buenos Aires, 1967.
Rimorchiatore lamp, for Candle, 1967.
Knoll International showroom interiors, in Boston and New York, 1969.
Fiat showroom interiors, in Turin and Brussels, 1970.
Sanitary fittings, for Richard Ginori, 1973.
Otto A handles, for Fusital, 1977.
Parola lamps, for Fontana Arte, 1980.
Universal drafting device and drawing-board, for Zucor and Bieffe, 1980.
Tea-service, for Rossi Arcandi, 1980.
Jumbo table, for Knoll International, 1985.
Bench in marble, for Ultima Edizione, 1987.
Sanitary fittings, for Ideal Standard, 1988.
Watch, pen, pencil and fountain-pen, for Louis Vuitton, 1988.

(for a chronological list of Aulenti's buildings and architectural projects, see *Contemporary Architects*)

Publications:

By AULENTI: books—*Un Nuova Scuola di Base,* with others, Milan 1973; *Il Laboratorio di Prato,* with Franco Quadri and Luca Ronconi, Milan 1981; *Il Quartetto della Maledizione,* with others, Milan 1985; *Progetto Bicocca,* with others, Milan 1986.

On AULENTI: books—*Design Italia '70* by Davide Mosconi, Milan 1970; *Design Process Olivetti 1908-1978* by Nathan H. Shapira, Los Angeles 1979; *Gae Aulenti,* exhibition catalogue by Vittorio Gregotti, Emilio Battisti and Franco Quadri, Milan 1979; *Interior Views* by Erica Brown, London 1980; *Knoll Design* by Eric Larrabee and Massimo Vignelli, New York 1981; *Gae Aulenti e il Museo d'Orsay,* Milan 1987; *International Design Yearbook 1988/89,* edited by Arata Isozaki, London 1988.

One of Italy's few women architects, Gae Aulenti is a multi-faceted designer, teacher, and theoretician. She is a member of that second wave of postwar Italian designers who, stimulated and promoted by *Casabella* and *Domus* magazines, rejected the industry-oriented functionalism of the previous generation in favor of a more far-reaching experimental approach to the problems of design. She has produced a large body of work in such diverse fields as urban planning, scenic design, landscape architecture, furniture, and other consumer products, but her international reputation rests primarily on her accomplishments as an interior designer. Her radical style is unremittingly modernist, though she rejects, along with many of her contemporaries, the philosophical pretensions of the modern movement. Basic to this rejection is the rather poignant realization that the International Style is no longer experimental or avantgarde. Aulenti's work reveals a desire to invest the by now traditional modern style with a humanistic dimension, with aspects of humor, mystery, ambiguity, and allusion that it has always lacked.

In her best-known interiors, whether private dwellings such as the Agnelli apartment in Milan (where a flock of sheep by French sculptor-designer François-Xavier Lalanne are "pastured" in a hallway), or showrooms for Olivetti, Fiat, or Knoll from Buenos Aires to Boston, Aulenti has materialized the desire for a metaphysical dimension. Running through these works are features suggesting that the interior be viewed as a microcosmic landscape, a kind of interior "city." She has taken a formal, architectural approach to constructing domestic space as though it were urban space. She shapes and animates this space with purposely intrusive forms and protruberances, angled ceilings, carpeted platforms, etc., which become the symbolic "buildings" of her cityscape, so that the interior becomes a background to "the daily scene" of living. She says, "Any man-made object, whether monument or hovel, cannot but allude to its relationship with the city, the place where [all] human conditions are found."

For Aulenti, the space should stand on its own and not need furniture to be defined. "It doesn't interest me to embellish walls that remain bare and useless and without meaning until the furniture and paintings arrive. What does matter to me is . . . to define a structure that in itself is . . . complete [so] that when you enter such empty surroundings they seem perfectly filled." Aulenti's environments, selfcontained as they are, in fact, sometimes fight the furnishings that are brought in; this can be a serious liability for furniture showrooms in particular. Yet, the uniqueness of conception, the originality of the underlying motive, imbues each space with evidence of a complex sensibility at work behind the scene. The surfaces, frequently lacquered white and reflective, radiate an intellectual glow that reassures the inhabitant of the space and justifies its existence.

—Kenneth Gaulin

AWAZU, Kiyoshi.
Japanese graphic, stage, film and environmental designer. Born in Tokyo, 19 February 1929. Studied at Hosei University, Tokyo, 1946–47. Married Yaeko Shibuya in 1955; children: Miho and Ken. Freelance designer, from 1955: organized *Persona* exhibit, Tokyo, 1965; art director, *Expo 70,* Osaka, 1970, and *Great Japan Exhibition,* Royal Academy, London, 1982; producer, *World Exposition of Science and Technology,* Tsukuba, 1982–83. Assistant Professor of Design, Musashino Art College, Tokyo, 1964–70; Professor of Design, Kyoto Junior College of Art, since 1980. Director, National Anthropology Museum, Osaka, 1980–83. **Exhibitions:** *Japan Advertising Artists' Club Exhibition,* Matsuzakaya Department Store, Tokyo, 1955; *Future City,* Seibu Department Store, Tokyo, 1962; *From Space to Environment,* Matsuya Department Store, Tokyo, 1966; *Trends in Modern Art,* National Museum of Contemporary Arts, Kyoto, 1968; *Graphic Image 74,* Matsuya Department Store, Tokyo, 1974; Watari Gallery, Tokyo and Nagoya, 1974; *Intergrafik Ausstellung,* Berlin, 1976; *Traces and Memories: Prints by Kiyoshi Awazu,* Art Front Gallery, Tokyo, 1981. Recipient: Grand Prize, Japan Advertising Artists' Club, 1956; Film Poster Prize, Paris, 1958; Silver Medal, Milan Triennale, 1962; Mainichi Industrial Design Prize, Tokyo, 1966; Kisaku Ito Film Prize, Tokyo, 1969; Silver Medal and Special Award, Warsaw Poster Biennale, 1970; Book Design Award, Japanese Ministry of Trade and Industry, 1973; Grand Prize, Leipzig Book Fair, 1974; Nihon Academy Film Design Award, Tokyo, 1980. Address: 1–5–24 Minami Ikuta, Tama-ku, Kawasaki City, 214 Kanagawa, Japan.

Works:

Iron gate, for the Izumo shrine, Izumo-shi, 1962.
Persona Exhibit design and layouts, Tokyo, 1965.
Playground, for *Expo 70,* Osaka, 1967–70.
Inugami stage design, for the Tenjo Sajiki theatre group, 1969.
Akyu Gaiden stage design, for the Bungakuza theatre group, 1969.
Tokyo Three-Penny Operetta stage designs, for the Geinoza, 1976.
Great Japan Exhibition design and layouts, Royal Academy of Art, London, 1982.
World Exposition of Science and Technology design and layouts, Tsukuba, 1982–83.
Gaudi exhibition design and layouts, Tokyo and Okinawa, 1978.

film designs include—*Shinjo Ten no Amijima,* 1969; *Himiko,* 1974; *Denen ni Shisu,* 1975; *Hanaregoze Orin,* 1977; *Gaudi,* 1977; *Yashaga-ike,* 1980.

Publications:

By AWAZU: books—*Hiroshima/Nagasaki Document,* editor, with Kohei Sugiura and Shomei Tomatsu, Tokyo 1961; *The Discovery of Design,* Tokyo 1964; *What Can Design Do?,* Tokyo 1969; *Scrapbook of Kiyoshi Awazu's Designs,* Tokyo 1970; *Talks on Design,* Tokyo 1974; *The Thinking Eye,* Tokyo 1975; *The Works of Kiyoshi Awazu,* 3 vols., Tokyo 1978; *Gaudi Sanka,* Tokyo 1981; *Design Junyu,* Tokyo 1982; book illustrated—*Remi is still alive* by I. Hiramo, Tokyo 1958.

On AWAZU: books—*Films and TV Graphics,* edited by Walter Herdeg, Zurich 1967; *Modern Graphics* by Keith Murgatroyd, London 1969; *Monografie des Plakats: Entwicklung, Stil, Design* by Herbert Schindler, Munich 1972; *Archigraphia: Architectural and Environmental Graphics,* edited by Walter Herdeg, Zurich 1978; *Who's Who in Graphic Art,* edited by Walter Amstutz, Zurich 1982; *Japanese Design* by Penny Sparke, London 1987.

Kiyoshi Awazu: *Graphism* oil and silkscreen print, 1977

Graphic design should be dedicated to human existence because it enriches life and makes it more beautiful. I have been mainly concerned with cultural themes—exhibitions, theater, cinema, and architecture—in my works, which are contributed to society rather than to commercialism. I firmly believe that graphic design should not only be used for commercial purposes but also for our daily life. Also, I believe that graphic design represents our ethnic backgrounds, history, and traditions. Needless to say, contemporary design has to make use of international methods. On the other hand, we still have to search for our own national identity in graphic design.

—Kiyoshi Awazu

Kiyoshi Awazu's early poster "Give Back the Sea," which won first prize in the Japanese Advertising Artists Club 1956 exhibition, revealed the passion he thereafter set out to make the basis of his design. Awazu's theme has been to continue to produce works, created by means of his own strong intentions, while questioning the methods of expression in design.

In 1961, along with Kohei Sugiura and Shomei Tomatsu, he edited and produced the book *Hiroshima-Nagasaki Document*, which exemplifies the human conscience that wells up unavoidably in an individual in society where one is powerless to do anything alone, even though there may be a high level of scientific technique. Aware of non-rational and unconscious desires, he believes that even in fields such as science and mathematics, people are guided by their emotions. His work is motivated by the conviction that the expression of the passion of a single individual can shed a sacred light on modern, increasingly barren society.

Awazu's studio, built as an addition to his house ten years ago by the architect Hiroshi Hara, and fast becoming a well-known example of recent Japanese architecture, in itself speaks of Awazu's discernment and profound erudition. What particularly fascinates me among his numerous writings is an article on those who have influenced him, from Ben Shahn to Herbert Bayer and Antonio Gaudi, among others. In each case, Awazu has allowed them to pass through his sensibilities, analyzed them, and articulated their work through his own. It is as if they have all come together in fold upon fold, like the ripples created by many stones being thrown at once onto the surface of a lake, then been carefully considered, expanded, and given expression.

—Shukuro Habara

AXELSSON, Åke.
Swedish furniture and interior designer. Born in Visby in 1932. Studied cabinetmaking, City Industrial Training School, Visby, 1958–59, and interior design, School of Arts, Crafts and Design, Stockholm, 1959–62. Worked in an architectural office, Stockholm, 1960–62; independent interior and furnishing designer, establishing own office in Stockholm, from 1962, and workshop in Vaxholm, from 1970. Instructor in interior and furniture design, School of Arts, Crafts and Design, Stockholm, 1970–79. **Exhibitions:** Hantverket Gallery, Stockholm, 1968;

Ararat, Moderna Museet, Stockholm, 1976; *Contemporary Swedish Design,* Nationalmuseum, Stockholm, 1983 (toured); *Faces of Swedish Design,* IBM Gallery, New York, 1988 (toured). Address: Galleri Stolen, Tyska Brunnsplan 1–3, 111 29 Stockholm, Sweden.

Works:

S 217 stackable beech chair with leather upholstery, for Gärsnäs AB, 1963.
S 233 red beech armchair with leather upholstery, for Gärsnäs AB, 1967.
Vaxholmaren beech and leather armchair, for Gärsnäs AB, 1978.
Scandinavian stackable armchair, for Gemla Möbler AB, 1982.
Kalmarsund 1 knock-down chair in steamed beech, for Gemla Möbler AB, 1983.
SAR stackable lacquered red beech armchair with leather seat, for Garsnas AB, 1984.
Journalism House interiors, Stockholm, 1985.
Classic Greek teak and rope chair with linen cushion, for Skandia Insurance Company, Stockholm, 1986.

Publications:

On AXELSSON: books—*Form och Tradition i Sverige,* edited by Birgitta Walz, Stockholm 1982; *Contemporary Swedish Design,* exhibition catalogue by Monica Boman, Lennart Lindkvist and others, Stockholm 1983; *Den Svenska Formen* by Monica Boman and others, Stockholm 1985; *Made in Sweden: Art, Handicrafts, Design* by Anja Notini, London 1987; *Faces of Swedish Design,* exhibition catalogue edited by Monica Boman, Stockholm 1988.

Chairs hang in bunches from the ceiling of Åke Axelsson's studio in the little town of Vaxholm. It is a peculiar collection, scarcely like any other Swedish furniture designer's. High up fly the ideas and prototypes—the inspiration. On the floor are the completed projects.

Åke Axelsson designs and handcrafts furniture, and is an interior designer. He is also a student of the history of the craft of furniture making. He claims he is driven by curiosity, a compulsion to test new solutions, but also respect for craftsmanship, the need to retain an open-minded relationship with tradition. He speaks of learning from history, seeking the common factor in different cultures in order to begin again from the beginning and peel away the inessential.

Åke believes in the future of utilitarian handicraft. Handcrafted furniture has so far been done mostly by exclusive loners. But Åke feels that it does not need to be like that. He himself has proven that handcrafted furniture is perfectly feasible, and a very attractive alternative to the mass-produced furniture of today. When the units become bigger and bigger, and production more and more rational, the products become impoverished: technology and the forces of distribution take over. "We need small-scale manufacture with limited resources," performed by people directly for other people, says Åke.

For a few years in the 70's, together with an assistant, Åke Axelsson could accomplish one of his dreams—starting small-scale production of simple handcrafted chairs, reasonable in price, and developed in close contact with the user.

In 1970 Åke Axelsson became a teacher at the National College of Art and Design in Stockholm. To teach others, one must teach

oneself. Åke knew about the handicraft of today, but not that of history. He worked his way back to the earliest types of chair in our civilization, those of ancient Egypt and Greece. Hitherto they had been defined in the terms of the art historian, but Åke looked at them with the eyes of a craftsman. He wanted to see how these chairs actually worked beneath the veneer of antiquity, how they were constructed and how they had come to be designed as they were.

He did this by reconstructing the chairs themselves as full-scale models—a kind of basic research in which hand and brain together revived the knowledge of vanished eras.

He found a highly developed, refined technique, the result of a long process of historical evolution. He was impressed by the way in which people derived the utmost possible return from their material, and by the interaction between the structure and the weight of the person sitting on it. He has transferred this experience into his own handmade chairs.

Åke Axelsson has had many commissions over the years. In the 60's he was involved in the renovation of the Operakällaren restaurant in Stockholm, under the direction of Peter Celsing. In this lavishly rich, dramatic 19th century setting, he learned how restoration could be combined with innovation. In the 80's Sweden's Parliament Building in Stockholm was one of his major commissions.

In Australia, the Parliament Building in Canberra will be inaugurated in 1988. It will have 2,400 seats, all designed by Åke Axelsson. The furniture is produced by Gärsnäs but manufactured on licence in Australia.

His interior design projects have generated several chairs which have entered mass production. But Åke's great desire has been to immerse himself in unique furniture—the type that does not have to defer to a predetermined environment. He has made experimental furniture so bold that no manufacturer has yet dared to produce it: lightweight, steel strip constructions with seats and backs of beech slats—simple, clearly outlined designs, with spring and elasticity which shape themselves according to the movement of the body.

But at the same time Åke Axelsson continues to make new industrial chairs—among others, a knock-down chair for Gemla, highly economical to produce. The same leg design can be used for three different models. But the essentials of craftsmanship are still there, and the source of inspiration was the old brewery chair. Tradition, rational production and craftsmanship do not have to be mutually exclusive.

At the same time he is experimenting to endow the purely industrial product with an artistic dimension. On the floor of his studio at the moment stands an extremely rudimentary chair with a seat and back of plywood boards. The parts can be put together like a Meccano construction, and the boards can be freely chosen from a color system devised by the concretist painter and color theorist K. G. Nilsson, who has also designed a décor of colored triangles to be printed on them.

The tension between craft and industrial design, art and mass production, furniture and space, is ever present in Åke Axelsson's work. Hitherto this has been a fruitful tension, resembling a magnetic field in which particles of ideas are constantly in motion, forming new patterns.

The dialogue between space and the chair is necessary, says Åke. It would be wrong to lose contact with the environment in which furniture is used.

—Monica Boman

Biuro Wystaw Artystycznych w Łodzi
Łódzkie Towarzystwo Przyjaciół Książki

Galeria Sztuki BWA, Łódź, ul. Wólczańska 31/33
Czerwiec – sierpień 1983

Małe Formy Grafiki
Polska – Łódź'83

Boguslaw Balicki: Exhibition poster for the BWA Gallery, Lodz, 1982

BALENCIAGA, Cristobal.

Spanish fashion designer. Born in Guetaria, near San Sebastian, 21 January 1895. Studied needlework and dressmaking with his mother in Guetaria, until 1910. Established tailoring business, with sponsorship of the Marquesa de Casa Torres, San Sebastian, 1915–21; founded Eisa fashion house, in Barcelona, 1922–31, and in Madrid, 1932–37; director, Maison Balenciaga fashion house, on Avenue George V, Paris, 1937–40, 1945–68 (lived in Madrid, 1940–45); lived alternately in Madrid and Paris, 1968–72. Also designed film costumes for *The Empty Star,* 1962. **Exhibitions:** *Fashion: An Anthology,* Victoria and Albert Museum, London, 1971; *The World of Balenciaga,* Metropolitan Museum of Art, New York, 1973. Recipient: Chelvaier de la Légion d'Honneur, France; Commander, L'Ordre d'Isabelle-la-Catholique. *Died* (in Javea, Spain) *23 March 1972.*

Publications:

On BALENCIAGA: books—*Always in Vogue* by Edna Woolman Chase and Ilka Chase, London 1954; *Kings of Fashion* by Anny Latour, Stuttgart 1956, London 1958; *The Wheels of Fashion* by Phyllis Lee Levin, New York 1965; *The Fashionable Savages* by John Fairchild, New York 1965; *The Fashion Makers* by Leonard Halliday, London 1966; *Fashion: An Anthology by Cecil Beaton,* exhibition catalogue compiled by Madeleine Ginsburg, London 1971; *Paris Fashion: The Great Designers and Their Creations,* edited by Ruth Lynam, London 1972; *The World of Blaenciaga,* exhibition catalogue with texts by Diana Vreeland and others, New York 1973; *In Vogue: Sixty Years of Celebrities and Fashion,* edited by Georgina Howell, London 1975, 1978, New York 1976; *The History of Haute Couture 1850–1950* by Diana de Marly, London 1980; *Magic Names of Fashion* by Ernestine Carter, London 1980; *McDowell's Directory of Twentieth Century Fashion* by Colin McDowell, London 1984; *The Conran Directory of Design,* edited by Stephen Bayley, London 1985; *The Encyclopaedia of Fashion from 1840 to the 1980s* by Georgina O'Hara, London 1986.

Cristobal Balenciaga was a master couturier whose perfected skills and Spanish heritage resulted in abstract sculpture in silk and wool, wearable monuments to feminine dignity and elegance. His seamstress-mother taught him to cut and sew skillfully. As a young teenager, he so impressed the Marquesa Casa de Torres that she financed his first trip to Paris and also his first tailoring shop. Later, as a buyer for a Spanish store, he traveled often to Paris to purchase couture clothes. In the 1920's, this experience culminated in the opening of the first of two Spanish couture establishments, both named Eisa.

The Spanish Civil War hastened his move to Paris, where in 1937, Spanish friends backed the opening of the couture house bearing his name. The fashion press was hesitant to accept this newcomer to French couture, but Balenciaga found an immediate and lifelong champion in the Americas *Harper's Bazaar* editor, Carmel Snow. During the late 1930's, the pages of *Bazaar* featured Balenciaga designs, such as his Infanta gown of dramatic black and white silk, its padded hips and exaggerated sleeves achieving a popular, romantic silhouette.

Balenciaga's was one of the few Paris couture houses permitted to remain open during the German occupation. During this time he created lavishly embellished matador jackets worn with black evening gowns. He showed, too, closely molded bodices and bouffant skirts which would achieve their most popular expression in Christian Dior's New Look of 1947.

Balenciaga was, more importantly, the first couturier to experiment, as early as 1946, with prophetic, semi-fitted silhouettes. He initiated a gradual evolution towards minimal shaping. His lace chemise dress with dropped waistline was atypical for 1951. It looked ahead to the popularization of unfitted dresses in the late 1950's, notably the famous "sack" dress.

After Dior's death in 1957, Balenciaga was regarded as the world's foremost couturier. Always an innovator of silhouettes, in this period he designed idiosyncratic evening gowns that were aesthetic and technical masterworks. He cut and draped stiff, lightweight silk gazar into abstract volumes which hovered about the wearer and floated majestically as she moved. His released sheaths of flowered taffeta undulated from knee-length hems in front to buoyant, curved trains in back. These pure inventions in silk were likened by fashion writers to banked clouds, giant flowers, and gliding swans.

For day wear, Balenciaga tailored textured woollens into loose and supple suits and coats, featuring flattering, round-mounted collars and shortened sleeves. These garments were prized for their easy fit, which concealed imperfections of the mature figure, and for their understated elegance, which assured their wearers fashion longevity. Moreover, Balenciaga's grandly dignified creations respected the social position of his privileged clientele, which included royalty, aristocracy, socialites, and film actresses.

Indeed, exclusivity was the tone of the entire Balenciaga operation. He and his disciplined staff worked in near-total privacy, shunning publicity and admitting to their showings only a carefully-screened elite. Accordingly, Balenciaga's gowns were among the world's most expensive. Though Balenciaga's silhouettes were widely copied, mass-manufactured versions could offer only generalizations of his subtle construction, for his apparently simple shapes were realized only through painstaking precision. Noteworthy is his design for a coat made with only one seam, including collar and sleeves. Balenciaga himself cut, draped, and re-

fined his toiles until they met his impossibly high standards. He insisted that these skills be mastered by his assistants, who included André Courrèges and Emanuel Ungaro. Hubert de Givenchy was another Balenciaga disciple and a close friend who has maintained devotion to the couture.

While Balenciaga's influence on world fashion was greatest during the late 1950's, his inventions continued into the 1960's, expressing social transitions then occurring. His youthful, patterned tights and knee-boots were couture firsts in 1962, but he also continued to create austerely formal wedding gowns. By this time, sensing the demise of the privileged society which had patronized him, Balenciaga announced his retirement and closed his house in 1968. It was no longer economically feasible to dress the dwindling number of women who could afford his perfection. Socially, such conspicuous consumption had become unacceptable, and high fashion had become unfashionable. Elegant traditions seemed out of place in a world dominated by rebellious youth. Significantly, Balenciaga came out of retirement briefly in 1972 to create a white satin princess-gown for the wedding of Generalisimo Franco's granddaughter.

A year after his death in 1972, a major exhibition of Balenciaga's designs at the Metropolitan Museum of Art provoked new critical appreciation of his work. In the years since, Balenciaga has been lauded as a sculptor in fabric, perhaps the last great couture tradition. As a couturier and as a person, Balenciaga ventured into the realm of pure creativity without denying human grace and dignity.

—Sandra Michels Adams

BALICKI, Boguslaw.

Polish painter, poster and graphic designer. Born in Czortkow, 25 June 1937. Studied painting and design, College of Fine Arts, Lódź, 1957–62. Married Ewa Stanislawska in 1973; son: Jakub. Independent painter and designer, Lódź, 1964–67; partner, with Stanislaw Labecki, in Balicki and Labecki design studio, Lódź, 1967–75; freelance graphic designer, working principally for the Lódź Office of Art Exhibitions and the Muzeum Sztuki, Lódź, since 1975. Assistant Professor, under Stanislaw Fijalkowski, 1963–70, and Associate Professor since 1976, College of Fine Arts, Lódź. **Exhibitions:** *Polish Poster Biennale,* Katowice, 1970, 1972, 1973, 1975, 1977, 1979, 1983; *International Poster Biennale,* Warsaw, 1970,

1972, 1974, 1976, 1980; *Polnische Plakate Heute,* Wilhelm-Lehmbruck Museum, Duisburg, 1971; *Best Poster Exhibition,* Warsaw, 1974, 1975; *l'Art de l'Affiche en Pologne,* Musee d'Art Moderne de la Ville, Paris, 1974; *Balicki and Labecki,* Gallery of Contemporary Art, Lódź, 1975; *The Polish Poster,* Kamakura Museum of Modern Art, 1975 (toured); *Balicki and Labecki,* Gallery of Contemporary Art, Warsaw, 1975; *The Polish Poster,* Kilkenny Castle, Ireland, 1976; *Poster Biennale,* Lahti, Finland, 1977, 1979, 1981; *International Poster Exhibition,* Listowel, Ireland, 1978, 1980. **Collections:** National Museum, Warsaw; National Museum, Poznan; National Museum, Wroclaw; Muzeum Sztuki, Lódź; Kamakura Museum of Modern Art, Japan; Lahti Museum, Finland; Musee de l'Affiche, Paris. Recipient: Painting Award, Lódź, 1966; First Prize, *Eksperyment 66,* Lublin, 1967; Union of Polish Artists Medal, Lódź, 1968, 1969; Poster Medal, Union of Polish Artists, Przemysl, 1972; Silver Medal, Katowice Poster Biennale, 1973; Poster of the Month Award, Warsaw, 1973, 1974; Teaching Achievement Award, Polish Ministry of Culture, 1979. Address: Art Studio nr. 3, Inowroclawska Street 9/163, 91–020 Lódź, Poland.

Works:

Alain Jacquet exhibition poster, for the Muzeum Sztuki, Lódź, 1969.
Henryk Stazewski exhibition poster, for the Muzeum Sztuki, Lódź, 1969.
Aiko Miyawaki exhibition poster, for the Muzeum Sztuki, Lódź, 1970.
Collection of 20th Century Art in the Lódź Fine Arts Museum exhibition poster, for the Muzeum Sztuki, Lódź, 1971.
Japanese Graphics exhibition poster, for the Muzeum Sztuki, Lódź, 1973.
Pieter Brattinga exhibition poster, for the Muzeum Sztuki, Lódź, 1974.

Publications:

On BALICKI: *Balicki and Labecki,* exhibition catalogue with foreword by Janina Filjakowska, Lódź 1975; *Graphis Poster 76,* edited by Walter Herdeg, Zurich 1976; *Plakat Polski/The Polish Poster 1970–1978,* with introduction by Zdzislaw Scubert, Warsaw 1979; *Czy to juz historia? 20 Years of GPD and ZPAP in Lódź,* exhibition catalogue with foreword by Michael Kuna, Lódź 1980.

Boguslaw Balicki's artistic career is connected with Lódź, a center of light industry, named before the war the "Polish Manchester," a term comprehensible to anyone who knows the cultural geography of Poland. This city, which survived the war by luck, preserved not only its buildings but also the character of an industrial center of the end of the nineteenth century. Like American cities, its topography consists of a geometric pattern of streets intersecting at right angles. Accented with factory chimneys, its landscape comprises rows of monotonous, redbrick apartment houses, as well as the roar of spindles and machines. So, it was not incidental that this city was the seat of Polish constructivism, which stressed the new, attractive qualities of the machine epoch, deriving from the logic of construction, organization, function, and economy. Here also was introduced the concept of a functional print, partly influenced by Jan Tschichold and formulated at the beginning of 1930's by Wladyslaw Strzemiński. While still a student in the Lódź School of Design, Balicki was influenced, through the intermediary of Professor S. Fijalkowski, by Strzemiński's theory of

seeing, unism. This theory rejected the "pathos of dramatic outbursts" on behalf of the picture where all parts are organically connected, as in nature. Strzemiński was convinced that form in art should be derived from machinery techniques and that the geometrization of form would secure the objectivism and precision of illustration. The axiom of geometrism corresponding to the mood of that time, has preserved its intellectual and artistic reasons for half a century since it was introduced into the constructivistic model of art. These reasons appealed to the imagination of the young, promising painter and graphic artist, and these principles of geometric order guided Balicki in his formulation of a visual code that could be applied in poster graphics as the transmitter of maximally objectivized, "machine-sembling" information. The co-author of this conception was Stanislaw Labecki, a graduate of the same school and also an admirer of Strzemiński's theory.

In the second half of the 1960's, the two of them formed a team and started to design posters and typography according to abstract conventions. Thus, their approach was totally different from that of the world-known "Polish poster school." However, the Balicki-Labecki team introduced some valuable concepts with regard to the structural layer of the picture. This included the exchangeability of elements of flat geometric forms with sharply contoured edges, as if reduced to a limited number of combinations of shapes. Designing resembled an engineer's work by such functions as adding, deleting, multiplying, setting, contracting, or expanding-on the axis of symmetry, on the diagonal, centrally, or in dispersion, in combinations with patterns of check, mesh, square, etc. Lettering, being a part of that structure, was subjected to the same rigors of setting, with no departures regarding the arrangement of inscriptions, types and sizes of letters, spacing, accentuation, and interlineation. The authors were inspired to develop this "cool" mode of designing when working for the Lódź Arts Museum, which favored the traditions of constructivism and insisted on a homogeneous form for its printed material. As a result, the Balicki-Labecki team developed a system of identification which encompassed catalogues, posters, invitations, ideograms, and logograms. It was one of the first such systems ever used by a museum.

The separation of the team in 1975 did not cause any changes in the Balicki's graphic and typographic work. His posters, made for exhibits and museums in Lódź, are still based on the same repertoire of arrangements.

—Szymon Bojko

BALLMER, Walter.
Swiss graphic, packaging, exhibition and display designer. Born in Liestal, 22 July 1923; emigrated to Italy in 1947. Studied under Hermann Eidenbenz, at the Kunstgewerbeschule, Basel, 1940–44. Worked for C. J. Bücher Verlag printers and publishers, Lucerne, 1945–47; graphic designer, Studio Boggeri, Milan, 1947–48; freelance graphic designer, working for Pirelli, Geigy, Olivetti, Montecatini, La Roche, etc., in Milan, 1948–56; staff designer of graphics, packaging and displays, Olivetti, Milan, 1956–81; founder-director, Unidesign graphics studio, working for Agusta, Hoffman-La Roche, Valentino, Weber, Wertheim, etc., in Milan, since 1981. **Exhibitions:** *Forme et Re-*

cherche, Paris, 1970; *Graphisme Design Suisse,* Paris, 1971; *107 Grafici dell'AGI,* Castello Sforzesco, Milan, 1974; Galleria Sincron, Brescia, 1974; Galleria A, Parma, 1974; Galleria Zen, Milan, 1975; Centro del Portello, Genoa, 1978; Kantonmuseum Baselland, Liestal, 1989. **Collection:** National Museum, Warsaw. Recipient: Compasso d'Oro Award, Milan, 1954; Merit Award, National Swiss Exposition, Lausanne, 1964, 1971; Gold Medal, *Bio 5,* Liubliana, 1973. Member: Arbeitsgemeinschaft Schweizer Graphiker, 1958; Associazione per il Disegno Industriale, 1963; Alliance Graphique Internationale, 1970. Address: Unidesign, via Revere 16, 20123 Milan, Italy.

Works:

Olivetti Spazio showroom interiors, Milan, 1959.
Stile Olivetti touring exhibition layouts, in Switzerland, Germany and Sweden, 1961.
Wert und Haben display at the Swiss National Exposition, Lausanne, 1964.
Olivetti Innovates touring exhibition layouts, in Greece, Africa and the Far East, 1965.
Logo and corporate identity programme, for Olivetti, Milan, 1970.
Logo, for Wertheim stores, Barcelona, 1973.
Graphis Packaging 3 cover design, Zurich, 1977.
Trade mark and corporate identity programme, for Valentino couture, Rome, 1978.
Trade mark and corporate identity programme, for Weber carburettors, Bologna, 1978.
Graphis 204 magazine cover design, Zurich, 1980.
International publicity campaign, for Olivetti ET201 and ET221 typewriters, Milan, 1980.
75th Anniversary book design, for Agusta Helicopters, Milan, 1982.
Logo and corporate identity programme, for Sestrieres holiday centre, Milan and Turin, 1983.
Annual report, for ERG Benzine Company, Genoa, 1987.
Annual report, for Hoffman-La Roche, Basel, 1988.
Annual report, for Zurigo Assicurazioni, Zurich, 1988.
Walter Ballmer: un designer tra arte e grafica exhibition layouts, Liestal, 1989.

Publications:

By BALLMER: articles—statement in *Art and Graphics,* edited by Willy Rotzler, Zurich 1983; "Come s'inventa la 'firma' di un 'Azienda" in *Sole—24 ore* (Milan), 8 January 1984; "Walter Ballmer ratselhafte Bildersprache" in *High Quality* (Heidelberg), no. 5, 1985; text in *Walter Ballmer: un designer tra arte e grafica* brochure, Milan 1989.

On BALLMER: books—*Die neue Grafik/The New Graphic Design* by Markus Kutter and Karl Gerstner, Teufen and London 1959; *Design Coordination and Corporate Image* by F. H. K. Henrion, London 1967; *Signet Signal Symbol* by Waltr Diethelm, Zurich 1970; *107 Grafici dell'AGI,* exhibition catalogue with texts by Renzo Zorzi and Franco Grignani, Venice 1974; *Who's Who in Graphic Art,* edited by Walter Amstutz, Dubendorf 1982; *World Trademarks and Logotypes,* edited by Takenobu Igrashi, Tokyo 1983; *Design Process—Olivetti 1908–1983,* Milan 1984; *Posters by Members of the Alliance Graphique Internationale,* edited by Rudolph de Harak, New York 1986; *Alle radici della communicazione visiva in Italia* by Heinz Waibl, Como 1988.

Printed in Italy, Lucini srl Milano

Walter Ballmer: Retrospective exhibition poster, Liestal, 1989

BALMAIN, Pierre (Alexandre Claudius).
French fashion designer. Born in Saint-Jean-de-Maurienne, Savoie, 18 May 1914. Educated in Saint-Jean-de-Maurienne, 1920–25, and at the Lycée National, Chambéry, 1925–33; studied architecture, Ecole Nationale Supérieure des Beaux-Arts, Paris, 1933–34. Served in the French Air Force, in Bron and Paris, 1936–38, and in the Pioneer Corps of the French Army, in Saint-Jean-de-Maurienne, 1939–40. Freelance fashion sketch artist, working for designer Robert Piguet, Paris, 1934; sketch artist and assistant designer, studio of Edward Molyneaux, Paris, 1934–38; designer, studio of Lucien Lelong, Paris, 1939 and 1941–45; founder-director, Maison Balmain fashion house, on the rue François Premier, Paris, 1945–82, and Balmain Fashions in New York, 1951–55, and in Caracas, 1954; Director General, Pierre Balmain S.A., Paris, 1977–82. Also stage and film costume designer from 1950. **Exhibition:** *Fashion: An Anthology,* Victoria and Albert Museum, London, 1971. Recipient: Knight of the Order of Dannebrog, Copenhagen, 1963; Cavaliere Ufficiale del Merito Italiano, Rome, 1966; Officier de la Légion d'Honneur, Paris, 1978; Vermilion Medal, City of Paris. *Died* (in Paris) *29 June 1982.*

Works:

Film costume designs include—*Night Without Stars,* 1951; *Betrayed,* 1954; *The Deep Blue Sea,* 1955; *Foreign Intrigue,* 1956; *The Happy Road,* 1956; *Fire Down Below,* 1957; *The Reluctant Debutante,* 1958; *Mr. Topaz,* 1961; *Tender is the Night,* 1961; *The Roman Spring of Mrs. Stone,* 1961; *Time Bomb,* 1961; *The Happy Thieves,* 1961; *The Millionairess,* 1961; *Two Weeks in Another Town,* 1962; *I Like Money,* 1962; *Come Fly With Me,* 1963; *In the Cool of the Day,* 1963; *Adorable Julia,* 1964; *Joy House,* 1964; *Arriverderci Baby (Drop Dead Darling),* 1966; *Mozambique,* 1966; *Topaz,* 1969.

Publications:

By BALMAIN: book—*My Years and Seasons,* London 1964, New York 1965.

On BALMAIN: books—*Dressmakers of France* by Mary Brooks Picken and Dora Louise Miller, New York 1956; *Kings of Fashion* by Anny Latour, Stuttgart 1956, London 1958; *The Fashion Makers* by Leonard Halliday, London 1966; *Fashion: An Anthology by Cecil Beaton,* exhibition catalogue compiled by Madeleine Ginsburg, London 1971; *Paris Fashion: The Great Designers and Their Creations,* edited by Ruth Lynam, London 1972; *Costume Design in the Movies* by Elizabeth Leese, Bembridge 1976; *The World of Fashion: People, Places, Resources* by Eleanor Lambert, New York and London 1976; *The History of Haute Couture 1850–1950* by Diana de Marly, London 1980; *McDowell's Directory of Twentieth Century Fashion* by Colin McDowell, London 1984; *The Encyclopaedia of Fashion from 1840 to the 1980s* by Georgina O'Hara, London 1986.

Pierre Balmain was a very successful designer for ladies. Captain Edward Molyneux taught him that no lady should look too fashionable. It was bad form to be avant-garde. A lady dressed with taste, not vulgar ostentation. The fashion press might give the impression that the most sensational designers were the most successful, but a discreet house might outlive the lot of them.

In 1934, when Balmain was accepted by Molyneux, the press was full of Elsa Schiaparelli's shocks, but Balmain as a Frenchman chose to study under a British courtier because royalty and the aristocracy dressed at Maison Molyneux.

The Captain's beautiful but unsensational clothes were regarded as the essence of good taste and were perfect for high society. Balmain learned that sophisticated elegance meant restraint. He applied this lesson in his own house and, consequently inherited the same sort of clientele that Molyneux had had, starting in 1964 with the clothes for the marriage of Viscount Edman to Miss Carcano and leading on to the wardrobe for Thai Queen Sirikit's state visits to Europe and the United States and to the Wedding Dress for Princess Irene of the Netherlands on her Marriage to Prince Charles de Bourbon de Parme.

Balmain did not seek to be the first to raise the hemline or drop it. He would wait, like his teacher, to see whether the new length was lasting or was simply a flash in the pan. Only if it began to be accepted would Balmain adjust his hemlines accordingly. This conservative approach suited a conservative clientele who did not want to be rushed into a new look every year. The gradual approach was the correct one, for it avoided any rash mistakes. When Balmain was involved in designing for the stage and cinema, it was only for characters who were ladies. He dressed Katharine Hepburn in a stage production of Shaw's *The Millionaires* and, in film, Jennifer Jones in *Tender is the Night,* Kay Kendall in *The Reluctant Debutante,* and Vivien Leigh in *The Roman Spring of Mrs. Stone.*

Thus, Balmain was not a leader of fashion. He endorsed new trends but did not start them. Experimentation was for young designers as they floundered about to find their style and make an impact. A senior house kept away from the throng, and today there are still courtiers with this careful approach—Givenchy in Paris and Hardy Amies in London. The school of restrained dress design continues.

—Diana de Marly

BARRIE, Scott.
American fashion designer. Born in Philadelphia, 16 January 1946. Studied applied arts, at Philadelphia Museum College of Art, and fashion design, at Mayer School of Fashion. Designer, at Allen Cole boutique, 1966–69; founder-partner, with Robbie Wolfe, of Barrie Sports, 1969: business expanded to include Barrie menswear, and Barrie Plus, from 1974; also designs loungewear for Barad, and furs for Barlan. Designer of stage and film costumes and accessories, including work for the film *Blood,* 1972, and the Joffrey Ballet production *Deuce Coup,* 1973. Address: 575 Seventh Avenue, New York, New York 10018, U.S.A.

Publications:

On BARRIE: books—*The World of Fashion: People, Places, Resources* by Eleanor Lambert, New York and London 1976; *The Fashion Makers* by Bernardine Morris, New York 1978; *Fairchild's Who's Who in Fashion,* edited by Anne Stegemeyer, New York 1980; *Fashion 2001* by Lucille Khornak, London 1982; *Mc-*

Dowell's Directory of Twentieth Century Fashion by Colin McDowell, London 1984.

The Art Deco style dominates Scott Barrie's imagination and lifestyle, for he lives with an Art Deco décor in his flat and has been using jersey, that fabric associated with the 1920's and 1930's, since 1966 as his preferred textile for clothes. His grandmother's career dressing such singers as Dinah Washington and Sarah Vaughan has conditioned Barrie. He himself dressed the films *Blood* (1972) and the ballet *Deuce Coup* (1973) and was commissioned, most appropriately, to dress Bessie Smith herself.

He admitted in 1974 that his collection was pure 1930's, with its evening pyjamas, Vionnet cowl necklines, little hats, day dresses to below the calf, and, of course, flowing, jersey evening gowns. This preoccupation with 1930's glamour manifested itself in 1975 with a summer collection devoted exclusively to evening wear, with slinky black frocks, the blouson look, and inevitably jersey, for Barrie declared he was a designer of soft, feminine clothes. He has had to admit that his fondness for slender fluidity does not suit all women, but his ideal woman is very much the cinematic one of his favourite period. However, as that lady could be improved by retouching her film negatives or by being photographed through silk screens, her look not really possible, in all its essence, outside the studio. He is a designer of dreams.

Barrie designs loungewear for Barad, furs for Barlan, accessories for his own Barrie Plus, and his menswear range. Barrie is happiest doing glamour, so the lounge or evening dress inspires him most, and he is not known for innovative daywear. If television decided to do a soap opera set in the 1930's, Barrie would be in his element designing the wardrobe. Failing that, Barrie had better take a look at what is the most popular period of revival for the early 1980's—the 1950's—or else he could be left high and dry.

—Diana de Marly

BARTOLI, Carlo.
Italian architect and industrial designer. Born in Milan, 28 June 1931. Studied architecture at the Politecnico, Milan, 1951–57: Dip.Arch. 1957. Married Albertina Amadeo in 1960; children: Anna and Paolo. Established own office for architecture, furniture and industrial design, in Milan, 1959–81, and in Monza, near Milan, since 1981: consultant to Arflex, Con and Con, Arclinea, Confalonieri UCG, Kartell, Oscam, Rossi di Albizzate, and Tisettanta. Instructor, Advanced Industrial Design Course, Florence, 1967–70, and Rome since 1988. **Exhibitions:** Milan Triennale, 1968; *Plastic as Plastic,* Museum of Contemporary Crafts, New York, 1968; Biennale of Industrial Design, Liubliana, 1968; *The Modern Chair 1918–1970,* Whitechapel Art Gallery, London, 1970; *Design and Plastic,* Museum of Decorative Arts, Prague, 1972; *Italian Office Design,* Kyoto, 1979 (traveled to Hong Kong); *Italienisches Möbel Design 1950–1980,* Milan, 1981 (traveled to Cologne); *From Spoon to City: 100 Designers,* at the Milan Triennale, 1983; *Kartell 1949–1983: Products for the Present,* Noviglio, 1983; *Kitchens in the Shop Window,* Milan, 1988. **Collection:** Museum of Modern Art, New York. Address: via Grigna 2, 20052 Monza (Milan), Italy.

Carlo Bartoli: *Carol* chairs in leather, for Matteo Grassi, 1987

Works:

Gaia fibreglass armchair, for Arflex, 1967.
Set 1 office furniture, for Oscam, 1972.
Chair 4875 in polypropylene, for Kartell, 1974.
Blop sofa, for Rossi di Albizzate, 1975.
Knock Down kitchen, for Arclinea, 1980.
Flap chair, for Arclinea, 1980.
Bingo wardrobe, for Confalonieri, 1984.
Slang shelf bracket, for Confalonieri, 1984.
Atlante table legs, for Confalonieri, 1985.
Programma Coba handrail, for Confalonieri, 1985.
Roll armchair and divan, for Rossi di Albizzate, 1986.
Odeon furniture range, for Arclinea, 1987 (with Giulio Ripamonti).
Mix unit bookshelves, for Tisettanta, 1987.
Giunto furniture range, for Confalonieri, 1987.
Carol chair and small armchair, for Matteo Grassi, 1987.
Agora office furniture, for Nobili Arredamenti, 1987.
Junior divan, for Rossi di Albizzate, 1987.
Connly divan, for Matteo Grassi, 1988.
Sophia chair, for Bonaldo, 1988.

Publications:

By BARTOLI: articles—"Quale sara l'avvenire della plastica" in *Corriere della Sera* (Milan), 20 February 1971; "Incontro con Carlo Bartoli" in *Casa* (Milan), September 1980; "Allora questo Italian Style?" in *Modo* (Milan), May 1981; "I designer degli anni 80" in *Brava-Casa* (Milan), May 1982; "Carlo Bartoli, prodotti non emergenti" in *Gap Casa* (Milan), March/April 1983; "I protagonisti dell'arredo/ufficio" in *Ufficio Stile* (Milan), May 1985; "La cucina oggi e domani" in *l'Ambiente Cucina* (Milan), January/February 1986; "Incontro con Carlo Bartoli" in *Casa e Giardino* (Milan), April 1988; "Magnificenza ed efficienza del nuovo centro di Colonia" in *Folia di Acer* (Milan), September/October 1988.

On BARTOLI: books—*The Modern Chair 1918-1970,* exhibition catalogue with texts by Carol Hogben and others, London 1970; *Atlante del Design Italiano* by Alfonso Grassi and Anty Pansera, Milan 1980; *Contemporary Furniture* by Klaus-Jürgen Sembach, Stuttgart and New York 1982; *Dal progetto al prodotto: plastiche e design* by A. Morello and A. Castelli Ferrieri, Milan 1984; *Made in Italy* by L. Massoni, Milan 1986; *Italian Industrial Design* by F. Shimizu and M. Thun, Tokyo 1987; *I Progettisti Italiani: Carlo Bartoli* by Flavio Conti, Milan 1988.

Objects destined for widespread use have to become part of the users' daily view in a non-agressive and non-prevaricating way. While the introduction of new materials and technologies in a field for which they had not been previously employed can justify violent breaks with the expressive tradition, when the use of the same materials and technologies is consolidated and applied to objects destined to enter every house, the project language must necessarily be "non-emerging". This does not mean that one should make the expression banal; rather, one should strive for a proper balance, transferring to the product what is valued in the culture and respecting the human dignity of tradition.

—Carlo Bartoli

BASEVI, James.

American film art director and special effects designer. Born in Plymouth, England, in 1890; emigrated to Canada, then to the United States, c. 1924. Studied architecture. Served in the British Army, in World War I: Colonel. Worked as a draftsman, then as special effects director, Metro-Goldwyn-Mayer film company, Hollywood, California, 1924–36; special effects director, 1937–39, art director, 1939–43, and supervising art director, 1943–44, 20th Century-Fox film company, Hollywood, California; Head of the Art Department, Vanguard Films, Hollywood, 1945. Recipient: Academy Award, for *The Song of Bernadette,* 1943.

Works:

Film designs include—*Soul Mates,* 1925; *Fine Clothes,* 1925; *The Circle,* 1925; *The Big Parade,* 1925; *Confessions of a Queen,* 1925; *The Tower of Lies,* 1925; *Bardelys The Magnificent,* 1926; *Dance Madness,* 1926; *Love's Blindness,* 1926; *The Temptress,* 1926; *The Mysterious Island,* 1929; *History Is Made at Night,* 1937; *Dead End,* 1937; *The Hurricane,* 1937; *The Cowboy and the Lady,* 1938; *The Adventures of Marco Polo,* 1938; *Blockade,* 1938; *Raffles,* 1939; *Wuthering Heights,* 1939; *The Real Glory,* 1939; *The Long Voyage Home,* 1940; *The Westerner,* 1940; *Tobacco Road,* 1941; *A Yank in the R.A.F.,* 1941; *The Black Swan,* 1942; *Moontide,* 1942; *Thunder Birds,* 1942; *China Girl,* 1942; *Son of Fury,* 1942; *Bomber's Moon,* 1943; *Claudia,* 1943; *The Dancing Masters,* 1943; *Guadalcanal Diary,* 1943; *The Gang's All Here,* 1943; *Happy Land,* 1943; *Heaven Can Wait,* 1943; *Hello, Frisco, Hello,* 1943; *Holy Matrimony,* 1943; *Jitterbugs,* 1943;

The Moon Is Down, 1943; *The Ox-Bow Incident*, 1943; *Paris After Dark*, 1943; *The Song of Bernadette*, 1943; *Stormy Weather*, 1943; *Sweet Rosie O'Grady*, 1943; *They Came to Blow Up America*, 1943; *Wintertime*, 1943; *Lifeboat*, 1944; *Bermuda Mystery*, 1944; *Buffalo Bill*, 1944; *The Eve of St. Mark*, 1944; *Four Jills in a Jeep*, 1944; *Greenwich Village*, 1944; *Home in Indiana*, 1944; *Jane Eyre*, 1944; *In the Meantime, Darling*, 1944; *Ladies of Washington*, 1944; *The Keys of the Kingdom*, 1944; *The Lodger*, 1944; *Pin-Up Girl*, 1944; *The Purple Heart*, 1944; *Roger Touhy, Gangster*, 1944; *The Sullivans*, 1944; *Tampico*, 1944; *Wilson*, 1944; *Spellbound*, 1945; *Claudia and David*, 1946; *The Dark Corner*, 1946; *Duel in the Sun*, 1946; *My Darling Clementine*, 1946; *Home, Sweet Homicide*, 1946; *It Shouldn't Happen to a Dog*, 1946; *Johnny Comes Flying Home*, 1946; *Somewhere in the Night*, 1946; *Strange Triangle*, 1946; *Margie*, 1946; *13 Rue Madeleine*, 1946; *If I'm Lucky*, 1946; *The Brasher Doubloon*, 1947; *Captain from Castile*, 1947; *The Homestretch*, 1947; *Carnival in Costa Rica*, 1947; *The Late George Apley*, 1947; *The Shocking Miss Pilgrim*, 1947; *Boomerang*, 1947; *Thunder in the Valley*, 1947; *Fort Apache*, 1948; *Three Godfathers*, 1948; *Mighty Joe Young*, 1949; *She Wore a Yellow Ribbon*, 1949; *To Please a Lady*, 1950; *Wagonmaster*, 1950; *Across the Wide Missouri*, 1950; *Night into Morning*, 1951; *The People Against O'Hara*, 1951; *Just This Once*, 1951; *My Man and I*, 1952; *Battle Circus*, 1953; *Island in the Sky*, 1953; *East of Eden*, 1954; *The Searchers*, 1956.

Publications:

On BASEVI: books—*Ragionamenti sulla Scenografia* by B. Bandini and G. Viazzi, Milan 1945; *Filmlexicon degli Autore e delle Opere*, edited by Michel Lacalamita, and others, Rome 1958–67; *Hollywood in the Thirties* by John Baxter, London and New York 1968; *Le Decor de Film* by Leon Barsacq, Paris 1970, as *Caligari's Cabinet and Other Grand Illusions*, Boston 1976; *The International Film Encyclopedia* by Ephraim Katz, London and New York 1980; *International Dictionary of Films and Filmmakers*, London and Chicago 1985, 1991.

During Hollywood's Golden Age, James Basevi was one of the most successful and innovative set designers and special-effects men in the employ of the major studios. He worked with many of the greatest directors of his time including William Wyler, William Wellman, John Ford, and Elia Kazan. Both in collaboration with other leading designers and on his own, Basevi created some of the most memorable visual images in American film history.

Within a short time after his arrival in Hollywood around 1924, Basevi was an assistant to the highly influential Cedric Gibbons, working on silent classics such as *The Big Parade* (1935). Among numerous consultancies and collaborations, Basevi's work with Richard Day is particularly notable. Their films together include *Bardelys the Magnificent* (1926), *Hurricane* (1937), and *The Captain from Castile* (1947).

During the 1930's, Basevi proved to be one of the greatest masters of special effects. In 1935, as head of MGM's special effects department, he collaborated with Arnold Gillespie on the effects for the lengthy and memorable earthquake sequence in *San Francisco*. This was, at that time, the most ambitious and technically exacting recreation of a natural catastrophe ever attempted; and even with the passage of many years, it remains extremely convincing. For John Ford's *Hurricane*, a 1937 vehicle for Dorothy Lamour, Basevi devised a 600-foot miniature set representing a tropical island village which was to be deluged by a gigantic tidal wave. The wave effect was produced by releasing many thousands of gallons of water onto the model in a controlled manner through tall, specially designed and constructed channels. The result is one of the most believable storms ever filmed using studio miniatures.

As Art Director at Twentieth Century Fox Studios from 1939–1944 later as Head of the Art Department at Vanguard Films and in subsequent freelance work, Basevi demonstrated a special skill in creating highly atmospheric images of the Old West. His sets for John Ford's *My Darling Clementine* (1946) and *She Wore a Yellow Ribbon* (1949) display the visual conventions of the Western genre at their most refined and persuasive.

—Gregory Votolato

BASILE.
Italian fashion design company. Founded as Gianfranco Basile men's tailors, Milan, 1951; taken over by FTM menswear manufacturers, with Aldo Ferranti as manager-director, 1969; autonomous company Basile S.p.A., established in Milan, 1976: opened boutiques on Via della Spiga, Milan, in Bergdorf Goodman's of New York, on the Via Borgogna, Rome, etc. Launched jacket and trouser production, 1969, and the Basile suit for women, 1970; collections Basile, Misterfox, Sportfox, Callaghan and Escargot, designed by Walter Albini, 1971–73; has also produced collections by designers Muriel Grateau and Luciano Soprani. **Exhibition:** *Italian Re-Evolution*, La Jolla Museum of Art, California, 1982. Address: Viale Jenner 51, 20159 Milan, Italy.

Publications:

On BASILE: books—*The World of Fashion: People, Places, Resources* by Eleanor Lambert, New York and London 1976; *Il Tessuto Moderno: Disegno, Moda, Architettura* by Giovanni and Rosalia Fanelli, Florence 1976; *I Mass Moda: Fatti e Personaggi dell'Italian Look/The Who's Who of Italian Fashion* by Adriana Mulassano and Alfa Castaldi, Florence 1979; *Who's Who in Fashion*, edited by Karl Strute and Theodor Doelken, Zurich 1982; *Italian Re-Evolution: Design in Italian Society in the Eighties*, exhibition catalogue edited by Piero Sartogo, La Jolla 1982; *McDowell's Directory of Twentieth Century Fashion* by Colin McDowell, London 1984; *The Encyclopaedia of Fashion from 1840 to the 1980s* by Georgina O'Hara, London 1986.

It was Italian fashion designer Aldo Ferrante who was instrumental in propelling the fashion house called Basile into a position of worldwide acclaim. In 1949, Ferrante had begun by designing an inventive line of men's neckwear. He had previously been a corset salesman, and he subsequently worked with textiles. Next, he worked as sales agent for Krizia and Missoni. It is Krizia's Marriuccia Mandelli who is credited with having given Ferrante his real start in the business of fashion design. In 1969, Ferrante was concentrating on menswear with a characteristically tweedy and wide-shouldered approach that soon became influential in his later designs for women, as in his 1978 low-keyed, tweed jacket, which is pepped up by shiney blue and red silk tweeds woven into the fabric. Ferrante's typical evening wear is by comparison more flamboyant and feminine, done in softly clinging, embroidered silks of bold colors.

By the mid-1970's, Basile had achieved key status in the influential sphere of Milanese fashion under the ownership of FTM, a partnership including Ferrante, Monti, and Tositi. FTM had been created in 1967, operating as production organization for knitwear by well-known designers such as Cerruti, Albini, and Missoni.

In 1980–81, with Gigi Monti at the forefront of the highly successful Basile business, the collection continued to stress its characteristic blend of fine tailoring, classic lines, and high quality, along with fresh and new contemporary details. Slim pants, tunics, waistcoats, and long jackets work together to produce the soft, layered effect preferred by Basile as well as by a number of other designers active in the Milanese fashion front of the period. The collection included a group of softly curved, romantic silhouettes with jackets shorter than earlier, shoulders curved and waists fitted. It also showed fashions with a minimum of details, using plain necklines, natural shoulders, and low waists.

The house of Basile has recently been well represented by the fashions of Luciano Soprani, whose distinctive designs fall into the highly touted recent trends of the Milanese scene. Soprani's work for Basile includes his 1982 light wool black tuxedo jacket with black silk short pants, his 1983 collection of subdued sportswear and tailored clothing including ensembles for men incorporating the Basile square-ended tie and a wonderful (and characteristic) twist on the classic duffel coat with exaggerated shoulders and lots of flowing black wool. In its brief but impressive history, Basile has made a considerable contribution to contemporary Italian fashion created with the Milanese touch for classic quality and earthy, very modern flair.

—Barbara Cavaliere

BASS, Saul.
American graphic designer. Born in New York City, 8 May 1920. Studied under Howard Trafton, at the Art Students League, New York, 1936–39; under Gyorgy Kepes, at Brooklyn College, New York, 1944–45. Married Elaine Makatura in 1961; children: Jennifer and Jeffrey. Freelance designer, New York, 1936–46; founder and president, Saul Bass and Associates, Los Angeles, 1946–78, and Saul Bass/Herb Yager and Associates, Los Angeles, since 1978: has designed for United Airlines, Alcoa, American Telephone and Telegraph, Rockwell International, Warner Communications, Dixie Paper Products, Lawry's Foods, Exxon/Esso, Minolta, etc.; also filmmaker and film title designer, from 1954. Executive Board Member, International Design Conference, Aspen, Colorado; Sundance Film Institute, Utah. **Exhibitions:** film retrospectives—Rotterdam Film Festival, 1981; Cinematheque Francaise, Paris, 1982; Zagreb Film Festival, Yugoslavia, 1984. **Collections:** Museum of Modern Art, New

York; Library of Congress, Washington, D.C.; Stedelijk Museum, Amsterdam; Prague Museum, Czechoslovakia. Recipient: Art Director of the Year Award, National Society of Art Directors, 1957; Artistic Design Award, Museu de Arte Moderno, Rio de Jabneiro, 1959; Philadelphia Museum of Art Award, 1960; Gold Hugo Award, Chicago Film Festival, 1964; Academy Award, 1969; Gold Medal, Moscow Film Festival, 1970; Silver Design Medal, Tokyo, 1971; Hall of Fame Award, Art Directors Club of New York, 1978. Honorary Doctorates: Philadelphia College of Art; Los Angeles Art Center College of Design. Honorary Royal Designer for Industry, Royal Society of Arts, London, 1964; Honorary Fellow, Bezalel Academy, Jerusalem, 1984. Address: 7039 Sunset Boulevard, Los Angeles, California 90028, U.S.A.

Works:

Rose-and-flame motif and advert campaign of film *Carmen Jones,* for Otto Preminger, 1954.
Title sequences and posters of film *Man With the Golden Arm,* for Otto Preminger, 1955.
Title and shower sequences of film *Psycho,* for Alfred Hitchcock, 1960.
Stalking cat title sequences of film *Walk on the Wild Side,* for Edward Dmytryk, 1962.
Car race sequences of film *Grand Prix,* for John Frankenheimer, 1966.
Logotype symbol, for the U.S. Government White House Council for Energy Efficiency, 1981.
Art and Industry commemorative postage stamp, for the U.S. Post Office, 1983.
Architectural design of gasoline station network, for Exxon/Esso, 1983.
Posters and graphics, for the Los Angeles Olympics, 1984.

films (as director)—*The Searching Eye,* 1964; *From Here to There,* 1964; *Why Man Creates,* 1968; *Phase IV,* 1974; *Notes on the Popular Arts,* 1978; *The Solar Film,* 1980; *Quest,* 1984.

Publications:

By BASS: articles—in *Graphis* (Zurich), no. 89, 1960; *Cinema* (Beverly Hills), Fall 1968; *Film Dope* (London), August 1973; *American Cinematographer* (Hollywood), March 1977; *Banc-Titre* (Paris), April 1984.

On BASS: books—*The Silent Salesman* by James Pilditch, London 1961; *Saul Bass* by G. Nelson, New York 1967; *An International Survey of Packaging* by Wim Crouwel and Kurt Weidemann, London 1968; *Design in America* by Ralph Caplan, New York 1969; *The Corporate Search for Visual Identity* by Ben Rosen, New York and London 1970; *Who's Who in Graphic Art,* edited by Walter Amstutz, Dubendorf 1982; *The Conran Directory of Design,* edited by Stephen Bayley, London 1985; *International Dictionary of Films and Filmmakers,* London and Chicago 1985, 1991; *The American Design Adventure 1940-1975* by Arthur J. Pulos, London and Cambridge, Massachusetts 1988.

Saul Bass belongs to the generation of American designers—including Paul Rand, Bradbury Thompson, and Alvin Lustig—who emerged during and after World War II to establish an American approach to modern graphic design. Strong, elemental visual properties characterize Bass's designs, which have been successful in two-dimensional graphics that are static, frozen moments; in kinetic visual communications that exist in time and space (these include animated graphics and a full-length motion picture); and in three-dimensional works including packaging and exhibition design.

Particular to Bass' genius is an ability to arrive at an uncomplicated and immediate expression of the essence of the subject. This simple graphic configuration is then extended into a whole range of communications needs. Bass's motion picture projects also pioneered the visual unity of all graphic materials associated with a film: logo, titling, advertising, theatre poster, etc. His film logotypes frequently feature an elementary, symbolic image that captures the theme of the film, as did the jagged, angular arm of the Otto Preminger film, *The Man with the Golden Arm.* This pictographic arm conveys the drug addiction theme as it jabs downward, contorted and painful, into a rectangle of slablike bars, in the film titles, abstract bars move in staccato rhythm to jazz music, as they form and reform patterns on the screen. These are joined by typography listing the film credits. Finally, the bars metamorphose into the pictographic arm. A milestone in graphic design, these film titles demonstrated that an abstract language of form and rhythm could become a powerful and expressive tool for visual communications, and that two-dimensional graphics could be successfully translated into kinetic form. Equally innovative was the consistency of all publicity and titling material produced for this motion picture.

Bass achieves surprising unity as he integrates image and letterforms in motion-picture graphics and corporated identification work. Just as the heavy, blocky, stencil letters of the film title *Exodus* amplify the form and message of the raised arms, so are Alcoa's virtues emphasized by the geometric perfection of its trademark, tempered by subtle, curved corners, and the smooth, curved transitions in the letterforms of the word "Alcoa".

Bass proved that the insights and visual interests of the graphic designer could be translated into the motion-picture media. This was remarkably demonstrated by his film commissioned by Kaiser Aluminum, *Why Man Creates,* which received an Academy Award. Each segment in the film uses a different cinematic style and technique to express its content. In the particularly notable opening portion, "The Edifice" gives a history of man's major ideas and inventions by a scrolling animation that portrays man's accomplishments as a colossal structure that builds upon itself.

—Philip B. Meggs

BATES, John.
British fashion designer. Born in Ponteland, Northumberland, in 1935. Educated in Newcastle-upon-Tyne. Served in the British Army, 1953–55. Worked as a trainee journalist and office assistant, London, 1951–52; sketch artist, at Herbert Siddon design house, Chelsea, London, 1956–58; freelance fashion sketch artist and designer, selling to wholesale firms, London, 1959–63; partner-designer, in Jean Varon wholesale fashion house, London, 1964–80; founder-director, Capricorn fashion company, for the John Bates label, London, from 1981; designer, for Cojana wholesale fashions, London, from 1983. Also costume designer, for *The Avengers* television series, in the 1960s. **Exhibition:** *Fashion: An Anthology,* Victoria and Albert Museum, London, 1971. **Collection:** Museum of Costume, Bath, Avon. Recipient: Dress of the Year Award, Fashion Critics Association, London, 1965. Address: c/o Cojana Limited, 18 Great Marlborough Street, London W1, England.

Publications:

On BATES: books—*Fashion: An Anthology by Cecil Beaton,* exhibition catalogue compiled by Madeleine Ginsburg, London 1971; *With Tongue in Chic* by Ernestine Carter, London 1974; *Fairchild's Dictionary of Fashion,* edited by Charlotte Calasibetta, New York 1975; *The World of Fashion: People, Places, Resources* by Eleanor Lambert, London and New York 1976; *Fashion in the 60s* by Barbara Bernard, London and New York 1978; *The Guinness Guide to 20th Century Fashion,* edited by David Bond, Enfield 1981; *McDowell's Directory of Twentieth Century Fashion* by Colin McDowell, London 1984; *The Encyclopaedia of Fashion from 1840 to the 1980s* by Georgina O'Hara, London 1986.

John Bates states very firmly that the foundation of good design is balanced proportion and quality of construction. In view of the arrival of the financial depression in the 1970's, he argues that designers must avoid extraordinary fantasies and concentrate on durable clothes that can be worn time and time again. His success is due precisely to this attitude, for his safe clothes in good style at moderate prices bring the customers to the door. This, temperate approach, so typical of British couturiers, can be traced back to the Puritan Revolution which stressed plain chapels, as opposed to gaudy Catholic churches. This stress on simplicity and modesty, which has marked British clothes ever since, does not mean that a dress by Bates is dull. He may stamp a black dress in pleated silk with yellow or red features, but the shape will be simple; the line, uncluttered; and the colour, controlled. In 1982, he showed an evening jacket and skirt in red and white Ascher silk; the jacket had a frilled front and cuffs, but the skirt was kept absolutely plain. This self-discipline, this avoidance of excess even when being romantic, is the basis of Bates's approach.

Appreciating that women come in different shapes and sizes, he designs for all women of all ages and types, not only for the young and slender seen in fashion magazines. He creates for the fat and the thin, and many of his dresses are available with or without belts; full enough for the plump, they can be pulled in for the slim. Thus, his black dress with a while sailor collar could be worn loose like a smock or belted to form a bloused top. Such dresses are a principal feature of Bates's collections, and they guarantee a faithful clientele.

Common sense and an appreciation of the real world have made Bates a greatly appreciated designer, for he respects women and does not try to subject them to grotesque distortions. This, too, is very much in the British tradition, and if some foreign correspondents have complained that British designers lack colourful vibrations, it is precisely because Bates and his compatriots design for real people and not for Parisian circus freaks. The Puritan avoidance of excess has created a school of design in Britain. The line has flowed from Worth to Creed and Redfern to Molyneux to Cavanagh and Hardy Amies, and now Jean Muir and Bates pass the tradition to the rising generation.

—Diana de Marly

BAUMANN, Hans Theodor.
German industrial designer. Born in Basel, Switzerland, 27 October 1924. Studied painting, sculpture and design in Dresden, until 1945; painting, graphics, glasswork and interior design, at the Kunstgewerbeschule, Basel, 1946–50. Married Luise Luz in 1947; daughters: Luise, Christine and Sabine. Worked with Egon Eiermann on stained glass for the Pforzheimer Kirche and the Gedächtniskirche, West Berlin, 1953; freelance designer, establishing Baumann Design Studio, in Schopfheim, from 1955; director, Baumann Product Design, Basel, since 1971; also established design studio in Gaillan en Medoc, France. Professor, Hochschule der Künste, West Berlin, since 1983. Founder-member, 1959, President, 1959–61, business manager, 1964–68, and member of honour from 1979, Verband Deutscher Industrie-Designer; founded chair for teaching of ceramics, National Institute of Design, Ahmedabad, 1970. **Exhibitions:** Milan Triennale, 1954, 1956, 1960; World's Fair, Brussels, 1958; *Glas,* Neue Sammlung, Munich, 1959; *Design in Germany Today,* Smithsonian Institution, Washington, D.C., 1960 (toured); *H. Th. Baumann: Arbeiten,* Institut fur neue technischen Form, Darmstadt, 1961; *Concorso Ceramica,* Faenza, Italy, 1964, 1966, 1967, 1968, 1970, 1971, 1974, 1975, 1976; *Made in Germany,* Deutscher Werkbund, Munich, 1970; *Funf Jahre Gute Form,* Deutsches Museum, Munich, 1970; *Die Gute Industrieform,* at the Hannover Fair, 1974, 1976, 1977; *Deutscher Designertag: Design und Designer,* Karlsruhe, 1977; *New Glass,* Corning Museum, New York, 1979; *H. Th. Baumann: Design,* Kunstgewerbemuseum, Cologne, 1979 (traveled to Vienna); Museum of Applied Art, Belgrade, 1981; Galerie L, Hamburg, 1981; Museum of Applied Art, Zagreb, 1981; *Design Since 1945,* Philadelphia Museum of Art, 1983. **Collections:** Kunstgewerbemuseum, Hamburg; Kunstgewerbemuseum, Cologne; Kunstgewerbemuseum, West Berlin; Kestner-Gesellschaft, Hannover; Neue Sammlung, Munich; Coburg Glasmuseum, Stuttgart; Landesmuseum, Karlsruhe; Museum of Modern Glass, Valencia. Recipient: Sculpture and glass prizes, World's Fair, Brussels, 1958; Honour Award, Liubliana Biennale, 1966; Premio Internazionale, Vicenza, 1966; *Daily Mail* Blue Ribbon Award, London, 1966; Wirtschaftsministeriums Bundespreis, West Germany, 1969, 1973; Porcelain Competition Prize, Tokyo, 1973; International Design Prize, Spanish Government, 1975; Coburg Glaspreis, Germany, 1977; Gold Medal, Zagreb International Fair, 1979. Addresses: Schutzmattstrasse 44, 4051 Basel, Switzerland; Frieseneggerweg 7, 7860 Schopfheim, West Germany.

Works:

Designs include porcelain for Staatliche Porzellanmanufaktur, Berlin; Rosenthal AG, Selb, West Germany; Schönwald; Arzberg; Hutschenreuther, Selb, West Germany; Tirschenreuth; glass for Glashütte Waldsassen; Glashütte Gral, Dürnau; Glashütte Rheinkristall, Leichlingen; Thomas, Selb, West Germany; Rosenthal, Selb, West Germany; Daum, Nancy, France; Glashütte Süssmuth, Immenhausen; ceramics for Staatliche Majolika; Manufaktur Karlsruhe; metal for Rosenthal, Selb, West Germany; Gebr. Deyhle, Schwäbisch-Gmünd, West Germany; Gebr. Hepp, Pforzheim, West Germany; plastics for Benzing, Ehingen, Vitra, Weil/Rhein; wood products for Design Continens; Schwarzwälder Holzwaren, Bernau, East Germany; lamps for Vitra, Weil/Rhein; Trischmann, Stuttgart; Stölzle, Vienna; furniture for Sedus/Stoll, Waldshut; Domus, Schwaikheim; Walter Knoll, Herrenberg; Schwarzwälder Holzwaren, Bernau, East Germany; Holz Henkel, Göttingen, West Germany; Vitra, Weil/Rhein; Wilde und Spieth, Esslingen, West Germany; textiles for Irisette, Zell-Schönau; Contens Design, Schopfheim, West Germany; Erbe, Erlangen, West Germany; stained glass and wall-hangings.

Publications:

On BAUMANN: books—*Gestaltete Industrieform in Deutschland,* Dusseldorf 1954; *Die Gute Industrieform,* exhibition catalogue with texts by Hans Eckstein and Robert Gutmann, Hamburg 1955; *H. Th. Baumann: Arbeiten aus einem Werkstudio,* exhibition catalogue with text by Mia Seeger, Darmstadt 1961; *Praxis der Porzellanmalerei* by Martin Mield and Rudolf Lanschke, Munich 1965; *Made in Germany: Produktform Industrial Design,* exhibition catalogue, Munich 1970; *New Glass: An International Survey,* exhibition catalogue, Corning, New York 1979; *H. Th. Baumann: Design,* exhibition catalogue with introduction by Hans Mayr, Cologne 1979; *Neue Moebel 1950–1982/ Contemporary Furniture,* edited by Klaus-Jurgen Sembach, Stuttgart and London 1982; *Design Since 1945,* edited by Kathryn Hiesinger and George Marcus, Philadelphia and London 1983.

All things that we shape or design are the result of human activity. They find their proper place within the bounds of their environments. The importance of a design does not spring from the formulas of mathematical calculation—it is solely the result of the ability of the human being to add to or take away. It is possible to bring weight, material, purpose, and function into such a relationship with one another that the object which results is beautiful. The path which leads to that beautiful thing doesn't matter—it can be known or unknown. What is important to recognize, however, is where it leads.

—H. Th. Baumann

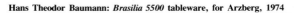

Hans Theodor Baumann: *Brasilia 5500* tableware, for Arzberg, 1974

BAWDEN, Edward.
British painter, printmaker, illustrator, book, mural, textile and advertising designer. Born in Braintree, Essex, 10 March 1903. Educated at Braintree High School, 1910–13, and Friends School, Saffron Walden, Essex, 1913–19; studied at the School of Art, Cambridge, 1919–21; Royal College of Art, London, 1922–25. Served as an official war artist, British Army, in the Middle East, 1940–45. Married the potter Charlotte Epton in 1932 (died, 1970); children: Joanna and Richard. Freelance illustrator and designer, in London, 1925–32, in Great Bardfield, 1932–70, and in Saffron Walden from 1970: designed for Curwen Press, Chatto and Windus, Faber and Faber, Penguin Books, Nonesuch Press, Lion and Unicorn Press, *Architectural Review, Burlington Magazine, Signature, House and Garden, The Listener,* Cole and Sons, Imperial Airways, London Transport, Modern Textiles, Shell-Mex and British Petroleum, Twinings Teas, etc. Instructor in illustration, Goldsmith's College and Royal College of Art, London, from 1930, and Royal Academy Schools, London, 1963–70; visiting instructor, Banff School of Fine Arts, Alberta, 1949–50. Trustee, Tate Gallery, London, 1951–

Edward Bawden: *Aesop's Fables—The Ant and the Grasshopper* linocut print

58. **Exhibitions:** Zwemmer Gallery, London, 1934, 1963; Leicester Galleries, London, 1938, 1949, 1952; Fine Art Society, London, 1968, 1975, 1978, 1979; Minories Gallery, Colchester, 1973 (toured); Fitzwilliam Museum, Cambridge, 1978. **Collections:** Tate Gallery, London; Victoria and Albert Museum, London; National Gallery of South Australia, Adelaide; Art Gallery of Ontario, Toronto. Recipient: Giles Bequest Print Prize, London, 1958; Silver Medal, Society of Industrial Artists and Designers, London, 1964. Honorary Doctorates: Royal College of Art, London, 1970; University of Essex, 1974. Commander, Order of the British Empire, 1946; Associate, 1947, and Academician, 1956, Royal Academy of Art, London; Royal Designer for Industry, Royal Society of Arts, London, 1949. *Died* (in Saffron Walden, Essex) *21 November 1989.*

Works:

Wallpaper designs, for Curwen Modern Textiles, 1926–39.
The Life and Adventures of Peter Wilkins (R. Paltock) book design, for J. M. Dent, 1928.
Adam and Evelyn at Kew or Revolt in the Gardens (R. Herring) book design, for Elkin Mathews and Marrot, 1930.
Posters, promotional leaflets and flight maps, for Imperial Airways, 1930s.
East Coasting (D. Leigh) book design, for London and North Eastern Railway, 1931.

Kynoch Press Note Book 1935 book design, for Kynoch Press, 1934.
Posters, advertisements and booklet covers, for London Transport Passenger Board, 1935–55.
The Weekend Book (F. and V. Meynell) book design, for Nonesuch Press, 1939.
The Voyages of Lemuel Gulliver (J. Swift) book design, for The Folio Society, 1948.
Life in an English Village (E. Bawden and N. Carrington) book design, for Penguin Books, 1949.
The Sundour Diary and Notebook 1953 book design, for Morton Sundour Fabrics, 1952.
How Animals Move (J. Gray) book design, for Cambridge University Press, 1953, and Penguin Books, 1959.
The Histories of Herodotus of Halicarnassus book design, for the Limited Editions Club, 1958.
Postcards and Christmas cards, for Blackwell's Booksellers, 1973–77.

Publications:

By BAWDEN: books—*Life in an English Village*, with introduction by Noel Carrington, London 1949; *Take the Broom*, London 1952; *The Sundour Diary and Notebook 1953*, Carlisle 1952; *Hold Fast By Your Teeth*, London 1963; *A Book of Cuts by Edward Bawden*, with text by Ruari McLean, London 1979.

On BAWDEN: books—*Water Colour Drawings*

by Edward Bawden, exhibition catalogue, London 1933; *The Art of the Book* by Bernard H. Newdigate, London 1938; *British Textile Designers Today* by H. G. Hayes Marshall, Leigh-on-Sea 1939; *Edward Bawden* by J. M. Richards, London 1946; *Edward Bawden* by Robert Harling, London 1950; *Design in British Industry: A Mid-Century Survey* by Michael Farr, Cambridge 1955; *Modern Book Design* by Ruari McLean, London 1958; *London Transport Posters* by Harold Hutchins, London 1963; *Magazine Design* by Ruari McLean, London and New York 1969; *The World of Edward Bawden,* exhibition catalogue with texts by M. Chase and D. P. Bliss, London 1973; *Industrial Design in Britain* by Noel Carrington, London 1976; *Artists at Curwen* by Pat Gilmour, London 1977; *Edward Bawden: A 75th Birthday Exhibition,* catalogue by Carel Weight, London 1978; *Edward Bawden* by Douglas Percy Bliss, London 1980; *British Art and Design 1900–1960,* exhibition catalogue with introduction by Carol Hogben, London 1983; *Eye for Industry: Royal Designers for Industry 1936–1986,* exhibition catalogue by Fiona MacCarthy and Patrick Nuttgens, London 1986.

From an early stage, Edward Bawden created an unmistakably individual style, range of techniques, and broad humour. As his biographer Douglas Percy Bliss has noted "Bawden had his own way of seeing things. It was daft and original. Anyone could tell a Bawden . . ." Even though his work often seems far removed from any contemporary fashion, it nevertheless frequently seems modern and of the moment in its direct simplicity and crisp line. On the one hand, there is in his work the miniaturist's refinement of detail and technique, whilst on the other, there is the impressive ability to reduce complex forms to bold shapes and sprightly lines without needing theatrical effects of light and shade. Throughout, there is a strong interest in texture and pattern that shows itself most forcibly in the larger murals, such as the ingenious screen designed for the Lion and the Unicorn pavilion of the 1951 Festival of Britain.

As many of his illustrations and designs concentrate on well-known and often humorous aspects of British character and tradition, Bawden has been a popular choice to decorate British pavilions at international exhibitions, to brighten public places in colleges and large companies with murals, and, with posters and leaflets, to promote travel to the various parts of England.

He illustrated a very wide range of books, from Thomas More's *Utopia* (1970) to *Buttercups and Daisies* by Compton Mackenzie (1931), but he never concentrated on any particular author's work. It is noticeable that the vitality of his illustrations comes from the graceful interplay of equally stressed shapes, not from exaggeration or caricature. This facility with pattern and balance of detail, which can be traced back to his early work on borders and printing decoration for Harold Curwen, is often used with great effect in his more occasional work designing wallpapers, menus, small advertisements, leaflets, and even pottery decoration.

Although it is difficult to trace direct influences, his virtuosity and range of skills clearly recall the great illustrators of the nineteenth century, and he has done much to revive and revitalise many of their techniques for the present century by his example of patient and industrious craftsmanship.

—Anthony J. Coulson

BAY, Howard.
American stage and film designer. Born in Centralia, Washington, 3 May 1912. Studied at the University of Washington, Seattle, 1928; Chappell School of Art, Denver, Colorado, 1928–29; University of Colorado, Boulder, 1929; Marshall College, Huntington, West Virginia, 1929–30; Carnegie Institute of Technology, Pittsburgh, 1930–31; Westminster College, New Wilmington, Pennsylvania, 1931–32; also studied in Europe, 1939. Married Ruth Jonas in 1932 (died, 1978); children: Ellen and Timothy. Freelance set and lighting designer for Broadway plays, operas, touring companies and film companies, from 1933: designer, working for the WPA project, at the Federal Theatre, New York, 1936–39; designed operas for the National Orchestral Association, 1940; art director, Universal-International Pictures, 1946–48; also freelance producer and director for touring companies and art director for television productions. Instructor, University of Michigan, Ann Arbor, 1941; Guest Lecturer, Purdue University, Lafayette, Indiana, 1962; instructor, Circle-in-the-Square Theatre School, New York, 1962–63; Andrew Mellon Guest Director, Carnegie Institute of Technology, Pittsburgh, 1963; Lecturer, University of Oregon, Eugene, 1963; instructor, director and designer, Ohio University, Athens, 1964; Pro-

fessor of Theatre Arts, 1965–82, Alan King Professor and Chairman of the Theatre Department, 1966–69, Brandeis University, Waltham, Massachusetts; Visiting Professor, Yale University Drama School, New Haven, Connecticut, 1966–67; instructor, Cooper-Hewitt Museum, New York, 1976. President, United Scenic Artists, New York, 1940–46 and 1952–53; National Advisory Board Member, International Theatre Institute, 1980–83. **Exhibitions:** New Gallery, New York, 1955; American Theatre Association, New York, 1968 (toured); Astor Gallery, Lincoln Center, New York, 1970. Recipient: Guggenheim Fellowship, New York, 1939, 1940; New York Drama Critics Poll Award, *Variety* magazine, 1942; Donaldson Award, 1944, 1945; Antoinette Perry (Tony) Award, 1960, 1966; Mahram Award, 1966. *Died* (in New York City) *21 November 1986.*

Works:

Stage designs include—*Chalk Dust,* Experimental Theatre, New York, 1936; *Power,* Ritz Theatre, New York, 1937; *Native Ground,* Venice Theatre, New York, 1937; *One Third of a Nation,* Adelphi Theatre, New York, 1938; *Trojan Incident,* St. James Theatre, New York, 1938; *Sunup to Sundown,* Hudson Theatre, New York, 1938; *Life and Death of an American,* Maxine Elliott's Theatre, New York, 1939; *The Little Foxes,* National Theatre, New York, 1939; *Morning Star,* Longacre Theatre, New York, 1940; *Brooklyn USA,* Forrest Theatre, New York, 1941; *Johnny 2 x 4,* Longacre Theatre, New York, 1942; *The Moon Is Down,* Martin Beck Theatre, New York, 1942; *The Eve of St. Mark,* Cort Theatre, New York, 1942; *Something for the Boys,* Alvin Theatre, New York, 1943; *The Merry Widow,* Majestic Theatre, New York, 1943; *Carmen Jones,* Broadway Theatre, New York, 1943; *Follow the Girls,* Century Theatre, New York, 1944; *Ten Little Indians,* Broadhurst Theatre, New York, 1944; *Catherine Was Great,* Shubert Theatre, New York, 1944; *The Visitor,* Henry Miller's Theatre, New York, 1944; *Up in Central Park,* Century Theatre, New York, 1945; *Show Boat,* Ziegfeld Theatre, New York, 1946; *The Big Knife,* National Theatre, New York, 1949; *Come Back Little Sheba,* Booth Theatre, New York, 1950; *Two on the Aisle,* Mark Hellinger Theatre, New York, 1951; *The Shrike,* Cort Theatre, New York, 1952; *Les Noces,* Brandeis University, 1952; *The Desperate Hours,* Ethel Barrymore Theatre, New York, 1955; *A Very Special Baby,* Playhouse Theatre, New York, 1956; *Jolly Anna,* Philharmonic Auditorium, Los Angeles, 1959; *Toys in the Attic,* Hudson Theatre, New York, 1960; *Milk and Honey,* Martin Beck Theatre, New York, 1961; *Carmen,* San Francisco Opera, 1961; *Isle of Children,* Cort Theatre, New York, 1962; *My Mother, My Father and Me,* Plymouth Theatre, New York, 1963; *Never Live Over a Pretzel Factory,* Eugene O'Neill Theatre, New York, 1964; *Natalya Petrovna,* New York City Opera, 1964; *Man of La Mancha,* ANTA Theatre, New York, 1965; *Knickerbocker Holiday,* Curran Theatre, San Francisco, 1971; *Volpone,* Asolo Theatre, Sarasota, Florida, 1977; *Oedipus,* Florida State University, Tallahassee, 1979; *The Speckled Band,* Missouri Repertory Company, Kansas City, 1983; film designs—*The Exile,* 1947; *Up in Central Park,* 1948; *Go, Man, Go,* 1955; *Mr. Broadway* (television series), 1965; *A Midsummer Night's Dream,* 1966; *The Pueblo Incident,* 1973.

Publications:

By BAY: book—*Stage Design,* New York 1974.

On BAY: books—*The Biographical Encyclopaedia and Who's Who of the American Theatre,* edited by Walter Rigdon, New York 1966; *Contemporary Stage Design,* edited by Elizabeth Burdick, Peggy Hansen and Brenda Zanger, Middletown, Connecticut 1974; *Who's Who in the Theatre,* edited by Ian Herbert, London and Detroit 1977.

Dramatic design is somewhere between a craft and an art. The graphic sketch is not an end in itself but a promise of the finished product—an intention of just how the visual arm will complement the script, the music, the acting, and the direction of a given theatrical event and progress as the drama unfolds. That is why—with the exception of Picasso who adapted to the demands of the stage—the giants of modern art were poor scenic artists. Their self-contained constructions didn't mix with the round actors and dancers. The looser pictorialists fared better behind the footlights: Dufy, Cocteau, Bérard, Tchelichev, Steinberg, Rauschenberg, Hockney, et al.

To serve the variety of dramatic fare, a designer must not polish a single style. The demands of dramaturgy are too assorted to be squeezed into a rigid, painterly manner. Incidentally, watercolor best captures the luminosity of a stage picture under lights. Immersion in research of time and place conditions the designer to think and draw, and then to create a relevant scenic environment.

Naturally, dramatic design is a plastic effort—we deal in three dimensions, and a model may be more appropriate than a rendering. Other hands execute our work, so our directions must be precise—working drawings are a large part of our labors.

Film art direction is a very realistic medium and everything must be measured by the human scale. The problem is to impregnate the naturalistic material with the emotional tenor of the scene.

Dramatic design is automatically a popular art form, partly because actors are not abstractions.

—Howard Bay (1984)

As with many designers, early influences seem to have made a great impression on Howard Bay's subsequent career, and thus the aims of his early work with the Federal Theatre—where beauty and style were secondary to the presentation of ideas, information, characters, and story—seems to have infused all the best work of his mature years. Though he admired the work of Robert Edmond Jones, who was the dean of American designers in the late 1920's and early 1930's, his eminently practical personality did not suit him to follow the older man's moody, symbolist, poetic style. What he did learn from Jones was the directness and simplicity that one could achieve through massive research followed by painstaking refinement.

Even though he became noted for his charming, nostalgic, painterly musicals during the late 1940's and early 1950's, it was eventually his innate pragmatism, realism, and practicality in solving design problems that made him a distinctive American designer with much to offer to students at Brandeis and to audiences of the American theatre. As an example of this practical brilliance, one should examine what he accomplished with his most famous design, that for *The Man of La Mancha.* He needed a prison entrance that was dramatic, that immediately set the feeling of a prison, that gave a long entrance, and that seemed to appear from nowhere. He satisfied this set of requirements with an unusual drawbridge lowered into the center of the action from the darkness at the upper back of the stage—for an effect that made persons from the outside world seem as if they

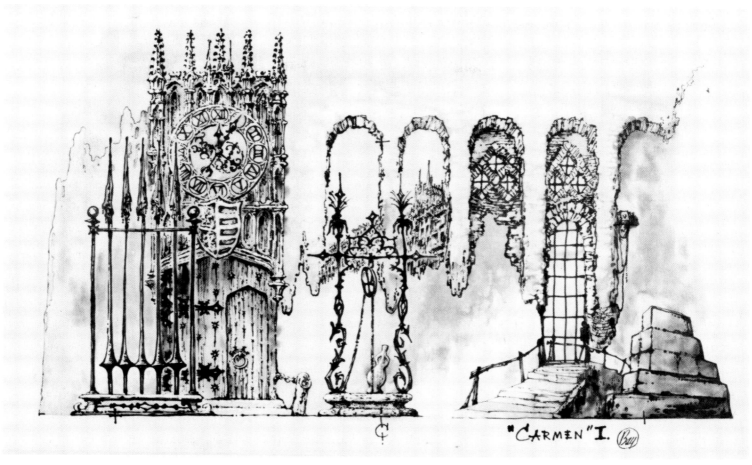

Howard Bay: *Carmen* stage set sketch, for the San Francisco Opera, 1959

came from another planet. It was a brilliant artistic solution that stemmed from the practical and realistic approach that Bay has always taken with his design assignments.

Except for his connection with the Federal Theatre, Bay has not been a political or social commentator in his work, nor has he presented vanguard artistic ideas. On the other hand, he has always been fully contemporary in his work and receptive to new technology and new esthetic concepts when they should be useful in the solution of particular design problems.

—Douglas A. Russell

BAYER, Herbert.
American photographer, architect, interior, graphic and product designer. Born in Haag, Austria, 5 April 1900; emigrated to the United States in 1938: naturalized, 1944. Educated in Linz, Austria, 1911–17; apprentice in architecture and decorative arts, under Georg Schmidthammer, Linz, 1919; graphic design and typography assistant to Emanuel Margold, Darmstadt, 1920; studied mural painting and design, with Vasily Kandinsky, at the Staatliche Bauhaus, in Weimar, 1921–23. Served in the 14th Infantry Regiment, Austrian Army, 1917–18. Married Irene Hecht in 1925 (divorced); daughter: Julia; married Joella Haweis Levy in 1944. Young Master of Typography and Graphic Design, Staatliche Bauhaus, Dessau,

1925–28; Director, Dorland Studio of Design, Berlin, 1928–38; Art Director, *Vogue* magazine, Berlin, 1928–30; freelance photographer, contributing to *Die Linie,* etc., Berlin, 1930–36; painter, photographer, graphic designer and exhibition architect, in New York 1938–45; Director, Dorland International design company, New York, 1945; consultant designer, 1945–56, and Chairman of the Department of Design, 1956–65, Container Corporation of America, Chicago; consultant and architect, Aspen Institute of Humanistic Studies, Colorado, 1964–85; art and design consultant, Atlantic Richfield Company, Los Angeles, 1966–85. **Exhibitions:** Kunstverein, Linz, 1929; Staatliche Bauhaus, Dessau, 1931; Kunstverein, Salzburg, 1936; Black Mountain College, North Carolina, 1939; Yale University, New Haven, Connecticut, 1940; North Texas State Teachers College, Denton, 1943; Brown University, Providence, Rhode Island, 1947 (retrospective; toured); Cleveland Institute of Art, 1952; Aspen Institute for Humanistic Studies, 1955, 1964; Germanisches Nationalmuseum, Nuremberg, 1956 (retrospective; toured); 1970; Fort Worth Art Museum, Texas, 1958 (toured); Städtische Kunsthalle, Düsseldorf, 1960; Museum am Ostwall, Dortmund, 1960; Bauhaus Archiv, Darmstadt, 1961; Städtisches Kunstmuseum, Duisburg, 1962; Neue Galerie, Linz, 1963, 1976, 1980; University of New Hampshire, Durham, 1966; Philadelphia Art Alliance, 1967; University of California at Santa Barbara, 1969; Hudson River Museum, Yonkers, New York, 1969; Centre Culturel Allemand, Paris, 1971; Oesterreichisches Museum fur Angewandte Kunst, Vienna, 1971; Landesbildstelle, Hamburg, 1973 (toured); Saarland Museum, Saarbrucken, 1973; Denver Art Museum, Colorado, 1973, 1980; Deutscher Ring, Hamburg, 1974 (retrospective; toured);

Dartmouth College, Hanover, New Hampshire, 1977 (toured); Centre Georges Pompidou, Paris, 1981; Bauhaus Archiv, West Berlin, 1982 (toured); Museum für Gestaltung, West Berlin, 1986; Kiusthaus, Zug, 1987; Oberösterreichisches Landesmuseum, Linz, 1987. **Collections:** Denver Art Museum, Colorado (archives); Museum of Modern Art, New York; San Francisco Museum of Modern Art; Neue Galerie der Stadt Linz; Museum Folkwang, Essen; Bauhaus Archiv, West Berlin. Recipient: First Prize, *Foreign Advertising Photography* exhibition, New York, 1931; City of Salzburg Medal, 1936; Gold Medal, Art Directors Club of Denver, 1957; Gold Medal, Art Directors Club of Philadelphia, 1961; Trustees Award, Aspen Institute for Humanistic Studies, Colorado, 1965; Ambassador's Award for Excellence, London, 1968; Kulturpreis for Photography, Cologne, 1969; Gold Medal, American Institute of Graphic Arts, 1970; Adalbert Stifter Prize, Linz, 1971; Austrian Cross of Honour, 1978. Honorary Doctorates: Technische Hochschule, Graz, 1973; Philadelphia College of Art, 1974; Art Center College of Design, Pasadena, 1979. Honorary Member, Alliance Graphique Internationale, 1975; Honorary Fellow, Royal Academy of Fine Art, The Hague, 1975; Fellow, American Academy of Arts and Sciences, 1979. *Died* (in Montecito, California) *30 September 1985.*

Works:

Universal typeface, 1925.
Elementare Buchtechnik displays at the *Pressa Ausstellung,* Cologne, 1928.
Deutscher Werkbund displays, at the *Exposition de la Societé des Artistes Décorateurs,* Paris, 1930.

Building Workers Union Exhibition layouts, Berlin, 1931.

Das Wunder des Lebens exhibition catalogue and poster, Berlin, 1935.

Gesunde Kost—Gesunde Menschen advertisement, for Chlorodont Toothpaste, 1937.

Gas und Wasser Ausstellung exhibition layouts in Leipzig, for Junkers Industries, 1937.

Bauhaus 1919-1928 exhibition layouts and catalogue, for the Museum of Modern Art, New York, 1938.

Road to Victory exhibition layouts, for the Museum of Modern Art, New York, 1942.

Series of press advertisements, for Cohama Neckties, 1943-45.

Modern Art in Advertising exhibition layouts at the Art Institute of Chicago, for the Container Corporation of America, 1945.

Office interiors, for the Title Insurance and Trust Company, Chicago, 1948.

Series of press advertisements, for Noreen Hair Color Rinse, 1953.

Seminar Building and Health Center, for Aspen Institute for Humanistic Studies, Colorado, 1953-55.

Paper mills and factory plants in California, Alabama, Washington, Illinois, Texas, Oklahoma and West Germany, for the Container Corporation of America, 1955-57.

Aspen Meadows Hotel complex, for Aspen Institute for Humanistic Studies, Colorado, 1964.

50 Jahre Bauhaus exhibition layouts, catalogue and posters, for the Württembergischer Kunstverein, Stuttgart, 1968.

ARCO Towers and Plaza, for the Atlantic Richfield Company, Los Angeles, 1972-73.

(for information on Bayer's activity as a fine artist and as a photographer, see *Contemporary Artists* and *Contemporary Photographers*)

Publications:

By BAYER: books—*Fotomontagen*, portfolio of 11 photomontages, Berlin 1932; *Fotoplastiken*, portfolio of 10 photographs, Berlin 1937; *Bauhaus 1919-1928*, with Ise and Walter Gropius, New York 1938, 1959, 1975; *Seven Convolutions*, portfolio of lithographs, Colorado Springs 1948; *World Geo-Graphic Atlas*, Aspen, Colorado 1953; *Book of Drawings*, Chicago 1961; *Eight Monochrome Suite*, portfolio of lithographs, Los Angeles 1965; *Herbert Bayer: Paintings*, portfolio of reproductions, Chicago 1965; *Herbert Bayer: Painter/ Designer/Architect*, New York, Ravensburg, West Germany, London and Tokyo 1967; *Herbert Bayer*, portfolio of 6 silkscreens, with introduction by Dieter Honisch, Stuttgart 1968.

On BAYER: books—*The Way Beyond Art: The Work of Herbert Bayer* by Alexander Dorner, New York 1947; *Seven Designers Look at Trademark Design*, edited by Egbert Jacobson, Chicago 1952; *Fotoauge Herbert Bayer*, exhibition catalogue edited by Jan Tschichold, Munich 1967; *Herbert Bayer*, exhibition catalogue with text by Ludwig Grote, London 1968; *Two Visions of Space: Herbert Bayer and Ingeborg ten Haeff*, exhibition catalogue with introduction by Carl Black Jr., New York 1969; *Herbert Bayer: A Total Concept*, exhibition catalogue with introduction by Karl Otto Bach, Denver 1973; *Herbert Bayer: Das Druckgrafische Werk bis 1971*, with text by Hans Wingler and Peter Hahn, West Berlin 1974; *Herbert Bayer: Neue Werk und Projekte*, exhibition catalogue by Ida Rodriguez Prampolini, Zurich, 1974; *Herbert Bayer: un concepto total* by Ida Rodriguez Prampolini, Mexico City 1975; *Herbert Bayer: Beispiele aus dem Gesamtwerk 1919-1974*, exhibition catalogue with introduction by Peter Baum, Linz 1979; *Herbert Bayer: From Type to Landscape*, exhibition catalogue by Jan van der Marck, New York 1977; *Herbert Bayer: Photographic Works*, exhibition catalogue with text by Leland Rice and Beaumont Newhall, Los Angeles 1977; *Herbert Bayer: Das Künstlerisches Werk 1918-1938*, exhibition catalogue, West Berlin 1982; *Herbert Bayer: The Complete Work* by Arthur A. Cohen, Cambridge, Massachusetts 1984; *Herbert Bayer and Modernist Design in America* by Gwen F. Chanzit, Ann Arbor 1987.

*   *   *

We may count Herbert Bayer as one of the few artists whose whole life's work was decisively influenced by the Bauhaus. This is confirmed in the universality of his artistic creation and his basic stylistic attitude through all the decades of this activity. He draws on the whole range of environmental design for his work.

Bayer's first typographical works at the Bauhaus at the beginning of the 1920's still show the influence of "elementary typography", such as Lissitzky's, but he soon advanced beyond this. He developed his own typographical style which became typical of the Dessau Bauhaus graphic image under Gropius. In the introduction of DIN norms, lower case script and the inclusion of photography, Bayer's work set standards and acted as a direction pointer.

As head of the Dessau Bauhaus print shop he was able to put his ideas into practice; among the many innovations he introduced into his teaching was the inclusion of advertising. In 1927 Bayer left the Bauhaus to work independently. He was active as painter and photographer—the photomontage of his self portrait of 1932 is well known. There were also the series of photo-sculptures and photo-montages.

From 1929 on he collaborated on the image of the "New Line", at that time the most modern family journal for which he designed not only the print but also innumerable title pages. During his ten year activity with the Dorland advertising agency he introduced, in the use of photography, retouch and montage, the images of surrealism to advertising and decisively marked the advertising style of the 1930's to whose leading graphic designers he belongs.

His collaboration on exhibition design also acted as a direction pointer. The Paris exhibition of the "German Section" for the German Labour Union in 1930 is one of the summits in exhibition design. The principles were further developed for the first Bauhaus exhibition at the Museum of Modern Art in New York in 1938.

After his emigration to the United States in 1938 Bayer extended his field of work. He fought against the American advertising business which to him was excessively oriented towards the "hard sell".

From 1946 he was successfully active as an architect in Aspen (Colorado). Until well into the 1960's he created a series of buildings for the "Aspen Institute for Humanistic Studies" which combine harmoniously with the mountain landscape. Bayer created large sculptural designs—a marble garden and a grass wall formed from the landscape—both in 1955.

In his painting which he intensified in later years Bayer is occupied in the broadest sense with form and colour relationship. His painting since the 1960's can be seen as his own constant variation within the constructivist painting after 1945. Bayer designed large series of advertisements and information sheets for the Container Corporation of America and for General Electric which demonstrate his talent for the visualization of complex facts.

In 1957-58 Bayer designed a world atlas which is constructed on entirely new principles.

—Magdalena Droste

BEENE, Geoffrey.

American fashion designer. Born in Haynesville, Louisiana, 30 August 1927. Studied medicine, Tulane University, New Orleans, 1943-46; University of Southern California, Los Angeles, 1946; Traphagen School of Fashion, New York, 1947-48; Chambre Syndicale d'Haute Couture, and Académie Julien, Paris, 1948. Display assistant, I. Magnin store, Los Angeles, 1946; apprentice tailor, Paris, 1948-50; assistant to Mildred O'Quinn, Samuel Winston, Harmay and other Seventh Avenue fashion houses, New York, 1951-54; designer, for Teal Traina, New York, 1954-63; founder-director, Geoffrey Beene Inc. fashion house, New York, from 1963: first menswear collection, 1969; beenebag sportswear collection, 1971; men's fragrances Grey Flannel, 1975, and Bowling Green, 1987. **Exhibitions:** *Geoffrey Beene: 25 Years of Discovery,* Los Angeles, 1988; Western Reserve Historical Society, Cleveland, Ohio, 1988; National Academy of Design, New York, 1988; Musashino Museum, Tokyo, 1988. **Collections:** Metropolitan Museum of Art, New York; Los Angeles County Museum of Art; Chicago Historical Society; Western Reserve Historical Society, Cleveland, Ohio; Lyndon Baines Johnson Library, Austin, Texas. Recipient: Coty Award, New York, 1964, 1966, 1968, 1974, 1975, 1977, 1981, 1982; Cotton Council Award, 1964, 1969; Neiman-Marcus Award, 1965; Ethel Traphagen Award, New York, 1966; Designer of the Year Award, 1986, 1987, and Special Award, 1988, Council of Fashion Designers of America. Address: Geoffrey Beene Inc., 550 Seventh Avenue, New York, New York 10018-3295, U.S.A.

Publications:

On BEENE: books—*Fashion: Dress in the Twentieth Century* by Prudence Glynn, London 1978; *The Fashion Makers* by Bernardine Morris, New York 1978; *Fashion: The Inside Story* by Barbaralee Diamondstein, New York 1985; *Couture: The Great Designers* by Caroline Rennolds Milbank, New York 1985; *The Encyclopaedia of Fashion from 1840 to the 1980s* by Georgina O'Hara, London 1986; articles—"It's a Beene" by J. Bowles in *Vogue* (New York), January 1977; "American in Paris: Beene's Private Showing" by B. Morris in the *New York Times*, 9 April 1978; "Architectural Digest Visits Geoffrey Beene" by P. Carlsen in *Architectural Digest* (Los Angeles), September 1979; "Paradise Found: Geoffrey Beene's Long Island Retreat" in *Architectural Digest* (Los Angeles), February 1984; "Designer Profile: 1988 Marks 25th Year in American Fashion for Geoffrey Beene" by K. Monget in *New York Apparel News*, May 1987; "American Beauty: The World of Geoffrey Beene" by P. Morrisroe in *New York*, 30 May 1988.

*   *   *

The most important style to come from Geoffrey Beene was his relaxed look in 1977, when he stressed easy, pull-on clothes, as in his pullover shirt dress. He also expressed this look in several types of trouser-suit for women—the town suit with a short navy jacket, his white silk evening trouser suit, and his most relaxed version of the softly full pyjama suit worn with a long mackintosh. The following year, he made the pyjama his major theme in plain fabrics for day and in silks for evening. The easy look was also shown in short-sleeved shirtdresses with full skirts and in his sweater coat, which was a giant polo-necked jumper to the knee. All this was regarded as his most original contribution to fashion—presenting a casual wearability, an informal ease of attire.

Americans dubbed him the creator of liberated clothes for women, as his billowing frocks

and unstructured suits did not impose any unnatural forms on them; these clothes could be
moved in with ease, which could not be said for
many of the ideas coming from Paris. These
were clothes for working mothers who need
clothes they can forget about once they are on.
That they do not get in the way was a major
attraction for the ordinary woman and a departure from the theatrical and sexist versions of
women too often promoted in contemporary
Paris, invariably by male designers exercising
their own fantasies. However, Beene has matured enough to appreciate what life is really
like for most women, and so he provides them
with clothes that do not imprison or impede.

The American press has termed his clothes
the essence of simplicity, but he cannot avoid
some decorative touches, such as bejewelled
girdles, double belts, and clustered necklaces—
touches which to British eyes spoil the line. Nevertheless, Beene has made an important innovation in conventional clothes, one which, added
to Norma Kamali's adaptation of sports clothes,
creates the most original American statement in
today's fashion—the relaxed and informal look.

—Diana de Marly

BEGA, Melchiorre.
Italian architect, interior and furniture designer.
Born in Crevalcore, Bologna, 20 July 1898.
Studied architecture, Istituto di Belle Arti, Bologna, 1919–22: Dip.Arch. 1922. Served as an
artillery lieutenant, Italian Army, 1914–18.
Married Maddalena Galimberti in 1931 (died
1976); children: Maria, Paola, Anna and Vittorio. Freelance architect and designer, establishing own studio in Bologna, 1920–34, and in
Milan, 1935–69; founded Bega Architetti Associati, Milan, 1969–76 (the studio continues at
via Benedetto Marcello 20, 20124 Milan): concentrated on interior and furniture design, from
1950. Co-director with Carlo Pagani, 1941–42,
and director, 1943–44, of *Domus* magazine,
Milan; President, Accademia di Belle Arti, Bologna, 1950–61. **Exhibitions:** Milan Triennale,
1933, 1940, 1951; *28/78 Architettura,* Palazzo
delle Stelline, Milan, 1979; *Europäische
Keramik seit 1950,* Museum für Kunst und Gewerbe, Hamburg, 1979 (traveled to Düsseldorf); City Hall, Bologna, 1984. Recipient:
Gold Medal for Education, Culture and Art,
Rome, 1968; Gold Medal and Merit Award,
Province of Bologna, 1968; INARCH Design
Prize, Rome, 1970. Honorary Academician,
Clementina Academy, Bologna, 1969; Academician, National Academy of San Luca, Rome,
1963. *Died (in Milan) 26 February 1976.*

Works:

Albergo degli Ambasciatori interiors, Rome,
1926.
Savoia Hotel interiors, Florence, 1931.
Savoia yacht interiors, for the Royal Family of
Italy, 1932.
Conte di Savoia Atlantic liner interiors, 1935.
Uaddan Casino and Theatre interiors, Tripoli,
1936.
Birreria Forst bar interiors, Milan, 1949.
Galtrusco fabric shop interiors, Milan, 1950.
Motta Bar interiors, Milan, 1955.
La Residenza administration centre, for the Mi-
lan Fair, 1958.

Geoffrey Beene: Dinner coat in wool melton with satin quilting, 1983

Galfa skyscraper building, Milan, 1959.
Office suite, for the Ridotto dei Cineconvegni, Milan, 1960.
Shops interiors in New York, for Perugina, 1962.
Office interiors in Hamburg and Berlin, for Axel Springer, 1962–66.
Motta Grill restaurants on the Autostrada del Sole and Autostrada La Serenissima, Italy, 1967.
Palace of Congress interiors, Algiers, 1968.
Anita M oil-tanker cabin interiors, 1969.
Office building in Milan, for *Selezione/ Reader's Digest,* 1970.
IRI Pavilion at the *Italian Produce* exhibition, Beijing, for the IRI/Finsider Group, 1973.

Publications:

On BEGA: books—*Melchiorre Bega architetto* by Giorgio Ramponi, Milan 1931; *Melchiorre Bega: Architettura,* Milan 1937; *Negozi d'Oggi* by Roberto Aloi, Milan 1950; *Mobili Tipo* by Roberto Aloi, Milan 1956; *Forme Nuove in Italia* by Agnoldomenico Pica, Milan and Rome 1957; *Mercati e Negozi* by Roberto Aloi, Milan 1959; *Public Interiors* by Misha Black, London 1960; *Catalogo Bolaffi dell'Architettura Italiana 1963-1966,* edited by Pier Carlo Santini and Giuseppe Luigi Marini, Turin 1966; *Forme Nuove nell'Arredamento Italiano,* edited by Paolo Portoghesi and Marino Marini, Rome 1978; *Melchiorre Bega, Architetto* by Stefano Zironi, Milan 1983.

Coming from a family of Bolognese shop and interior fitters with some famous commissions to their credit, Melchiorre Bega brought this unique experience to bear upon his architectural training. It was natural that he should turn to shop and bar interior design in that period of change and expansion that followed on the Liberation. Even so, those early designs, which sought to use the refined means that Italian craftsmanship afforded, were extremely accomplished. He made use of the whole range of ceramics—as tiles for both floors and walls, with rich glazes and many high-relief panels—and set these off against elegant metal fittings. However, this dazzling surface was supported by a rational structure arising from a serious analysis of the purpose the spaces were to serve.

This latter aspect of his gifts is best seen in the Galfa Skyscraper, which derives its name from the two streets forming the corner on which it stands. A tall, curtain-walled block, its finely wrought details on regular grid elevations are subtly accented by the discreet use of colour. The adroit planning of the floors manages access, lifts, stairs, and services in a way that is both logical and pleasant.

Perhaps the senior administration block for the Milan Fair, La Residenza, shows Bega's talents at full stretch. Again, the elegant geometry of the exteriors encloses very subtle planning of interior spaces, each skillfully attuned to its particular purposes which are also reflected in the carefully considered furnishings and fittings. This is especially noticeable in those areas that serve several functions without showing any sign of compromise. The spaces appear to adapt without undue forcing, and the fittings and furnishings seem to serve only that particular function. Again the colors are discreet, but being quite positive, they underline the disposition of the spaces.

The Ridotto dei Cineconvegni, though in actual forms quite different from La Residenza which preceded it by a couple of years, nevertheless is the result of the same design considerations, the same logical development from the requirements and integration of different functions and purposes within a unitary block.

Melchiorre Bega: Galfa headquarters tower, Milan, 1959

Some of the specialized demands could be met only by purpose-built accommodation, but against these fixtures, the rest of the space is allowed maximum flexibility to meet the different uses. Again, furniture, fittings, and color elegantly announce unity in diversity.

—Toni del Renzio

BELLINGER, Gretchen.
American textile designer. Born in Hartford, Connecticut, 22 April 1946. Educated at the MacDuffie School for Girls, Springfield, Massachusetts, 1962–64; Skidmore College, Saratoga Springs, New York, 1964–68: BS 1968; Sophia University, Tokyo, 1967; Cranbrook Academy of Art, Bloomfield Hills, Michigan,

1968–70: MFA 1970. Director of the Material Resource Center, Skidmore, Owings and Merrill architects, Chicago, 1970–73; Manager of Textile Development, Knoll International, New York, 1973–74; Promotion Director, V'Soske Incorporated, New York, 1974–76; Founder-President, Gretchen Bellinger Inc. textile design firm, New York, since 1976. **Exhibitions:** *Contemporary Weaving,* Oneonta State University, New York, 1969; Lawrence Stevens Gallery, Detroit, 1970; *Beautiful Possessions,* Fine Arts Gallery, Birmingham, Michigan, 1970; *Fur and Feathers,* Sheboygan, Wisconsin, 1971; *Master Weavers and Proteges,* Birmingham, Michigan, 1971. **Collections:** Art Institute of Chicago; Cranbrook Academy of Arts Museum, Bloomfield Hills, Michigan; Metropolitan Museum of Art, New York; Museum of Decorative Arts, Montreal. Recipient: Marguerite Mergentine Award, Skidmore College, 1968; Connecticut Draftsmen Merit Award, Hartford, 1970; Harold Bartlett Award, Rockford, Illinois, 1970; Institute of Business Designers/*Contract Magazine* Silver Award, 1978; American Society of Interior Designers Product Award, 1979; Roscoe Product Design Award, Resources Council, New York, 1981, 1983, 1984, 1985, 1988; Distinguished Alumnae Award, MacDuffie School for Girls, 1986. Address: Gretchen Bellinger Inc., 330 East 59th Street, New York, New York 10022, U.S.A.

Works:

Limousine Cloth wool broadcloth, 1976.
Corde du Roi wool and cotton vertical cut-pile fabric, 1978.
Mazurka silk cloque, 1983.
Diva silk with rhinestone or faux pearl application, 1985.
Can Can swiss dot cotton, 1986.
Prima Donna lurex on silk, 1986.
Wigwam wool textured weave, 1986.
Buzz Buzz wool jacquard, 1988.
Fleur de Lis silk tissue taffeta, 1988.
Imperiale wool and acrylic base epingle, 1988.
Queen Bee silk mousseline, 1989.
Starry Night wool jacquard, 1989.
Stepping Out wool jacquard, 1989.

Publications:

By BELLINGER: article—statement in *Manhattan Catalogue* (New York), October 1981.

On BELLINGER: book—*Material Wealth* by Jack Lenor Larsen, New York 1989; articles—"The Manhattan Showroom of Gretchen Bellinger" in *Interior Design* (New York), November 1976; "Gretchen Bellinger is a Weaver who Doesn't Use her Loom" by M. Carroll in the *Chicago Tribune,* 19 September 1977; "A Gretchen Bellinger Premier: The Ballets Russes Collection" in *Interior Design* (New York), December 1980; "Gretchen Bellinger: Subtleties of Color and Weave" by J. Simpson in *Architectural Digest* (Los Angeles), May 1983; "Ads from Whole Cloth Attract Fabrics Designer" in *Advertising Age* (New York), 30 January 1986; "Elements of Style" in *Metropolitan Home* (New York), April 1988.

Gretchen Bellinger Inc's textile collection was founded in 1976 on the philosophy of quality fabrics in subtle weaves and distinctive palettes. After a decade in business, this initial philosophy continues as the guiding point of view.

Our opening collection included ten fabrics in neutral tones. In part, financial restraints negated extensive palettes. Thus, it was necessary to carefully consider the initial coloration of each fabric. The first colors were grayed tones of pink, blue and green. Bellinger Inc. was instrumental in introducing this new palette (now referred to as "post modern") to architectural and design thinking. Because of this innovative approach to color, I established a reputation as a leading colorist in the furnishings industry. From the grayed tones of 1976, I proceeded to lead the way to bright primaries, clear pastels, and rich jewel tones. These directions are evident in the palettes of *Caravan* venetian worsted, *Skimmer* plain weave, and *Applause* cotton velvet.

In addition to creative colorations, Bellinger Inc. is noted for the adaptation of classic weaves and design motifs for contemporary interiors. *Limousine Cloth* broadcloth, the first fabric in the collection, was woven originally for luxury automobiles of the 1930s and 1940s. The more recent introductions of *Buzz Buzz* jacquard and *Imperiale* epingle take classic motifs—the Napoleonic bee and fleur de lis—and transfer them into contemporary statements. The wool jacquard *Buzz Buzz* combines a predominantly neutral palette with a stylized bee. *Imperiale* epingle uses the fleur de lis in a hardwearing looped pile construction. *Imperiale*'s two-toned coloration is based on the *Pullman Cloth* epingle and *Carriage Cloth* bedford cord palettes.

As with *Buzz Buzz* and *Imperiale,* approximately 90% of the Bellinger collection is custom designed and custom colored. This specialty approach gives the collection a cohesive quality. While fibers, colors and patterns vary, the philosophy behind all of the fabrics is singular. This unique perspective has resulted in many innovations.

The *Window/Wall* collection, originally envisioned as a group of tailored yet luxurious fabrics for contract applications, has expanded to incorporate fanciful, award-winning designs. Particularly creative statements include the permanently pleated silk, *Isadora,* and the rhinestone or faux pearl studded silk, *Diva.* A new fabric in this direction is *Queen Bee* silk mousseline. Inspired by combs of the worker bee, three different weaves represent full, partially full, and empty compartments. The honey-toned silk also features the queen bee overseeing her hive.

Perfection is a key aspect of the Bellinger program: each fabric is designed and refined. If I select a "me too" item, such as cotton pile or mohair plush, the goal is to offer the design community the best possible fabric in the style. *Applause* cotton velvet is an extremely rich velvet, while *La Scala* mohair plush is the epitome of mohairs.

Gretchen Bellinger: *Isadora* pleated silk fabric, 1981

Bellinger Inc's total commitment to design has been widely recognized. Major museums have selected Bellinger fabrics for their collections, and the firm has received seven industry awards for product design excellence. Important design commissions include developing the colors and materials for the restyled British Airways Concorde.

From the beginning, the concept of total design has been vital to my program. I have marketed the product through stylized offices and showrooms. The design concepts are further reinforced through a well thought-out graphic image, complete from stationery through sample tickets to customized gift wrapping . . . and infamous pencils.

—Gretchen Bellinger

Gretchen Bellinger started her business with a courageous conviction. With a vision considerably ahead of its time, she decided to use only natural fibers—cotton, linen, silk and wool—in a collection of luxurious, high-quality fabrics for furniture and interiors, although fabric preference during the 1970's was for synthetic fibers. Bellinger felt that the consumer ultimately would return to natural fibers in furnishings as well as clothing for reasons of comfort, esthetics, and prestige. As she predicted, this eventually occurred.

Determined that her collaborations express a consistent visual attitude, she works methodically, thoughtfully, and logically towards this goal. This simple, straightforward approach gives clarity to her work, which shows integrity of fiber, weave, texture, and color. Exercising great control over the character of her fabrics, she takes the long-range view, one which is consistent with her philosophy of understated high quality and value. She has a special ability to define and interpret classic weaves in her contemporary fabrics, which have themselves become new classics. Among these are a sturdy, wool-faced corduroy; a luxurious, 100 percent linen chenille; and a wool "nun's veiling" woven in Scotland. Her Transportation Collection includes Pullman cloth, with a springy wool pile, and Limousine cloth, a napped wool broadcloth in sophisticated colors. Yachting Cotton, a cotton repp woven in the Netherlands, recalls boating fabrics of an earlier time. A successful exception to her insistence on all-natural fibers is Vicille Garde, a sheer wool casement with lurex yarn forming a discreet grid. Her silk fabrics are usually quiet and restrained, although Isadora, a thin, irregularly pleated curtain fabric, is very lively in character and color range.

Most of her weaves are in solid colors. Patterns, when they occur, are structural, never applied. She generates an individual color palette for each fabric, based on the idea that there is a relationship between the fabric character and the color range offered. She realizes that certain colors in a new fabric may not sell well but feels they are necessary to complete the balance of the line. As a result, her collection has an unusual cohesiveness. At the same time, the stylishness of her fabrics is remarkable.

Bellinger exercises great attention to detail in just about everything. The company offices, furnishings, stationery, and graphics, as well as the warehouse operation, indicate that she has no time for the ordinary or slipshod. She insists on the highest possible quality in everything connected with her name. Instead of the customary greeting card which most businesses send during the holidays, Bellinger sends out a Thanksgiving card. Such individuality in combination with consistent, extraordinary quality characterizes her entire design life.

—Grant Greapentrog

BELLINI, Mario.

Italian industrial designer. Born in Milan, 1 February 1935. Studied architecture at the Politecnico, Milan: Dip.Arch. 1959. Married Giovanna Agrati in 1960; children: Elena, Chiara, Claudio and Marco. Director of Design, La Rinascente department stores, Milan, 1961-63; partner, with Marco Romano, in architectural design studio, Milan, 1963-73; established Studio Bellini architecture and industrial design office, Milan, from 1973: has designed for Artemide, B & B Italia, Brionvega, Olivetti, Cassina, Flos, Lancia, Marcatre, Yamaha, etc.; chief industrial design consultant for office equipment, Olivetti, Milan, from 1963; research and design consultant, Renault cars, from 1978. Director of *Album* monograph yearbook, for Electra Publishers, Milan, since 1979; editor-in-chief, *Domus* magazine, Milan, since 1986. Professor of Design, Istituto Superiore di Disegno Industriale, Venice, 1962-65; visiting lecturer, Unione Costruttori Italiani Macchine Utensili, Cinisello Balsamo, 1971, Università Internazionale dell'Arte, Florence, 1973, 1976, National Hoger Instituut, Antwerp, 1977, Royal College of Art, London, 1978, University of California at Los Angeles, 1979, and Hochschule für Angewandte Kunst, Vienna, 1982-83. Vice-President, ADI Associazione per Disegno Industriale, Milan, 1969-71; Founder-member, Environmedia, Milan, since 1973; Scientific Council Member, Milan Triennale design section, since 1979. **Exhibitions:** *The Modern Chair 1918-1970,* Whitechapel Art Gallery, London, 1970; *Italy: The New Domestic Landscape,* Museum of Modern Art, New York, 1972; *Design Process Olivetti 1908-1978,* University of California at Los Angeles, 1979; *Design and design,* Palazzo delle Stelline, Milan, 1979 (traveled to Venice): *Culture and Technology of Italian Furniture 1950-1980,* Stadtmuseum, Cologne, 1980; *Italian Re-Evolution,* La Jolla Museum of Art, California, 1982; *Design Since 1945,* Philadelphia Museum of Art, 1983; *Mario Bellini: Designer,* Museum of Modern Art, New York, 1987; *Architects Inside: From Mies to Memphis,* International Design Center, New York, 1988. **Collections:** Studi e Archivo della Comunicazione, Parma; Museum of Modern Art, New York; Philadelphia Museum of Art; Musée des Arts Décoratifs, Montreal. **Recipient:** Compasso d'Oro award, Milan, 1962, 1964, 1970, 1979, 1981; Gold Medal, Liubliana Industrial Design Biennale, 1968; Bolaffi Design Prize, Turin, 1973; SMAU Prize, Milan, 1978; ADI-FAD Delta de Oro Award, Barcelona, 1977, 1979; INARCH Prize, Rome, 1979. **Member:** Architects' Association of Milan, 1964; Gestione Case per Lavoratori architectural section, Milan, 1967. **Address:** Corso Venezia 11, 20121 Milan, Italy.

Works:

Programma 101 microcomputer, for Olivetti, 1965.
Amanta, Bambole chairs and *Quattro Gatti* tables, for B & B Italia, 1966-72.
TVC 250 computer terminal, for Olivetti, 1967.
Totem radio and record player in lacquered wood housing, for Brionvega, 1971.
Logos 50/60 series of calculators, for Olivetti, 1973.
Divisumma 18 calculator, for Olivetti, 1973.
The Office World furniture, for Marcatre, 1974.
Area 50 table lamps in porcelain and plastic, for Artemide, 1975.
TC 800 cassette deck in ABS plastic, for Yamaha, 1975-77.
Logos 40 and *Logos 80* series of electronic calculators, for Olivetti, 1976.

Cab chair in steel and leather, for Cassina, 1977.
TES 401 word processor equipment, for Olivetti, 1977.
Monitor television set, for Brionvega, 1977.
ET 101 electronic typewriter, for Olivetti, 1978-79.
Showroom in Tokyo, for Interdecor, 1981.
Praxis portable electric typewriter, for Olivetti, 1981.

Publications:

By BELLINI: articles—in *Gran Bazaar* (Milan), December 1979; *Abitare* (Milan), September 1980; *Corriere della Sera* (Milan), September 1980; *Album* (Milan), November 1981, September 1983; *Le Grandi Automobili* (Milan), Fall 1982.

On BELLINI: books—*Il Disegno Industriale e la sua Estetica* by Gillo Dorfles, Bologna 1963; *Design Italiano: I Mobili* by Enrichetta Ritter, Milan and Rome 1968; *The Modern Chair 1918-1970,* exhibition catalogue with texts by Carol Hogben and others, London 1970; *Design in Italia 1945-1972* by Paolo Fossati, Turin 1972; *The Modern Chair: Classics in Production* by Clement Meadmore, London 1974; *Atlante del Design Italiano 1940-1980* by Alfonso Grassi and Anty Pansera, Milan 1980; *Contemporary Furniture,* edited by Klaus-Jürgen Sembach, Stuttgart and London 1982; *An Industry for Design: The Research, Design and Corporate Image of B & B Italia,* edited by Mario Mastropietro, Milan 1982, 1986; *Design Since 1945,* edited by Kathryn Hiesinger and George Marcus, Philadelphia and London 1983; *Design Process Olivetti 1908-1983,* with text by Renzo Zorzi, Milan 1983; *Mario Bellini: Designer,* exhibition catalogue edited by Susan Weiley, New York 1987; *Design in Italy: 1870 to the Present* by Penny Sparke, London and New York 1988.

The idea of a discipline that deals with the physical environment for the purpose of improving man's habitat, by changing spatial structures, services, facilities and products, is only a relatively recent one. It is almost sixty years since Walter Gropius had the intuition that later led him to state: "The term 'design' encompasses in general the whole orbit of our surroundings and of man's handiwork, from ordinary hold goods to the complex planning of an entire city."

Yet, half a century after the closing of the Bauhaus, the nineteenth-century, academic classification of disciplines still prevails. Architecture has remained a second-class activity useful for decorating its own empty spaces, and civil and transport engineering, a tightly enclosed field of applicational science and technology. All the while, the designing of machines and consumer products is treated as a world unto itself; it stubbornly clings to the mythical connotations of mass production, industrial manufacturing processes, and project methodology, with a now conspicuously outdated propaedeutic and Messianic streak.

Now, if this fragmentation may be justified within a narrow professional scope for reasons to do with operative skills, it is much less acceptable in schools, in their structures and curricula, where it nevertheless remains habitual. Witness the inviolate engineering and architectural schools, some of which may occasionally introduce a supplementary industrial design course in order to be abreast of progress. Witness the schools of industrial design proper, secluded within their reassuring methodological boundaries, which may at times be enriched to the point of providing some rudiments of archi-

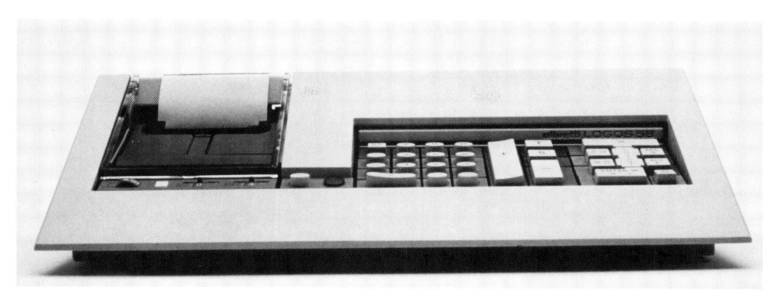

Mario Bellini: *Logos 50-60* desktop calculator, for Olivetti, 1972

tecture. And again, the many—too many—industrial design schools that germinated during modernization in academies or art schools, but which are often suffocated in a context inconsistent with their aims.

To complicate matters further, for us aspiring environment-designers (in Gropius' sense of the term) or heirs—even despite ourselves—to the modern movement, the unifying process is by no means under way. Indeed, the very ideological premises, the functionalistic doctrine and ensuing positivistic faith in a reassuring project methodology, upon which we wishfully thought we could establish a combined design discipline, now appear increasingly disputable and inadequate since the renewed enthusiasm of the early postwar years. It was in this prospect that I found myself, having been trained as an architect, starting out as a machine and consumer goods designer on the one hand, and as a chair and interior products designer on the other, while progressively and deliberately giving up architectural work.

Through research and practice, I had to explore branches of design that were different from my architectural background, as well as from one another—in my opinion, a calculating machine and a chair are further apart than a chair and a church. In an effort not to lose my identity, this led me to the constant quest for a common base which I have come to regard as intersecting these parallel activities, in a wider dimension that also now includes the notion of architecture, which I have taken up again with renewed interest. This dimension, aside from its value to me personally, could constitute a fresh contribution to the still open debate on the cultural unity of all design . . .

An effective improvement in the quality of our environment may be obtained from the reunification of design standards. However, it is my firm belief that such reunification can be accomplished only by superseding the compartmentalization of sectors and moving instead towards a more anthropocentric view of man's environment, at least as far as disciplinary and didactic, or cultural, aspects are concerned. (Excerpted from a speech made at the International Design Conference, Aspen, Colorado, June 1981.)

—Mario Bellini

On a recent (1989) trip, I had the chance to visit the Château Dufresne (Musée des Arts Décoratifs de Montréal). I was surprised and delighted to find an old "friend," *Chiara,* a not-

quite-five-foot high, twenty-five year old, cylindrical light sculpture formed from a sheet of mirror-finished stainless steel, developed by Mario Bellini in 1964. It is part of the museum's permanent collection of modern design. It has always been one of my favorite designs, if for no other reason that, in looking at it, one asks: "It is *so simple,* why didn't I think of that?" Evoking the image of a futuristic nun, the design could only have been made as a result of countless studies in folding paper cutouts. It would not seem possible to create such a form on a drafting board, regardless of the talent of its creator, and thus it truly expresses one aspect of that person.

Although trained as an architect, Mario Bellini is probably best known for his furniture and industrial design products. He apparently prefers working as a "sculptor"—using a series of models, including full-size prototypes—to design, experiment with, and develop his concepts. Tactile surfaces and materials providing direct physical contact between the designer and the product, help to insure a positive and comforting reaction on the part of the eventual user.

Bellini has developed a playful attitude toward the workplace in many of his industrial designs. In 1972 for Olivetti, he and some associates developed the *Divisumma 18* Electronic Printing Calculator, a small, bright-yellow object, barely two inches high, with a continuous flexible, rubberskinned keyboard. The skin is to protect the machine from dust, but it serves the design function of "feel," with the articulated buttons (keys) resembling nipples. It is almost impossible not to want to touch it.

Bellini produced other designs, for Olivetti and Yamaha (stereo equipment), that in triangular form and strong graphic communication also tempted the viewer to want to touch and play with them. He has taken a very similar attitude toward his furniture designs, especially chairs which he finds are both difficult and fascinating objects.

The *Amanta* series (1966) represents his early experiments with fiber glass reinforced polyester. A shell, with turned-up edges to snare fabric-covered cushions, was carefully studied to allow for anatomical demands within the limitations of the material. Elasticity of form, to accommodate the movement of the user, was attained by a deep slit in the back which lends a certain distinction to the resultant design.

One of his best known designs, the *932 series* (1967), destroys all previous notions of furni-

ture as a "structural" object. Here there is no evidence of structure save for blocks of polyurethane foam (stiffness was achieved by inserting a plywood cartilage within the foam) covered in rich leather and cinched around the "waist" with a leather belt. It could be assembled in a variety of sizes. There are no legs, no feet—none are necessary. Like a fashion designer, Bellini has thus "dressed" the foam and offered it as an irresistible haven, harkening back to Le Corbusier's *Grand Comfort,* but without the metal.

Le Bambole [The Dolls] (1972) continued the idea of the apparently structureless, overstuffed chair, using different density foams, now "dressed" in fabric, to generate a form suitable enough to, again, entice you to use it. It was produced in a variety of sizes and shapes. The advertising campaign that introduced it—featuring a bare-topped, female model in various poses—expressed the strength and flexibility of the seemingly nonstructured form, while enticing the viewer with the slogan: "Dolls that go . . . on dolls that stay." The viewer soon realized that, although visually attracted to the model, they were really looking at the furniture—the model was subordinate—unlike similar instances of fashion photography where the model/clothing is, rightfully, paramount.

In 1976, again like a fashion designer, Bellini's *CAB* totally "dressed" a simple, welded-steel frame in leather. Joint stitches were exposed for a demonstration of quality and feel, and the legs were treated with boot-like zippers. Originally a dining chair, it has been developed into an arm chair (1979) and sofa (1982). The almost planer-like quality of the *CAB* design was further developed in *Break,* a dining chair which again conceals its construction and is held together by zippers.

Bellini has recently directed his attention to lighting, interior fittings and tableware items. His furniture designs in the 80's seem to be taking on a more monumental, architectural form. This may be a parallel with the fact that he has had some architectural commissions in recent years. Whether or not this will conflict with his previous notions that when one sits one should not be aware of the structure of the seat, but be supported with a sense of elasticity and comfort, remains to be seen. I have no doubt, in either case, that one will want to sit and will be very comfortable in doing so.

—William Victor Kriebel

BELTRÁN, Félix (Juan Alberto).
Cuban graphic designer. Born in Havana, 23 June 1938. Studied advertising design and layout, under Ivan Chermayeff, Bob Gill and George Tscherny, School of the Visual Arts, New York, 1956–60: Dip. 1960; painting, American Art School, New York, 1961–62: Dip. 1962; life drawing, New School for Social Research, New York, 1962; printmaking, Pratt Graphic Center, New York, 1962; life drawing, Circulo de Bellas Artes, Madrid, 1965–66; politics, Centro Nacional de Investigaciones Cientificas, Havana, 1978–80. Married Lassie Sobera in 1963; daughter: Milena. Professional graphic designer, from 1959: Associate Art Director, American Publishing Company, New York, 1959–62, and Cypress Books Company, New York, 1960–62; designer, Editorial Nacional de Cuba, Havana, 1962–63; Art Director, Ministerio de la Construccion, Havana, 1963–65; chief of promotion, *Exposicuba* exhibition, Havana, 1966–67; chief of design team, Comision de Orientacion Revolucionaria, Havana, 1967–77. President of the Fine Arts section, UNEAC Union de Escritores y Artistas de Cuba, Havana, 1977–81; Cuban President, UNESCO International Association of Art, in Havana, 1979–82. Professor, Escuela de Instructores de Arte, Havana, 1963–65; Escuela National de Diseno Industrial, Havana, 1964–65; Escuela Nacional de Arte, Havana, 1966–69; in the School of Journalism, 1967–73, and the School of Architecture, 1972–76, at the Universidad de la Habana, Havana; Curso Nacional de Cuadros, Havana, 1973–81; in the Faculty of Plastic Arts, at the Instituto Superior de Arte, Havana, 1976–81; Universidad Autonoma Metropolitana and Escuela Nacional de Diseno, Mexico City, 1982–85. **Exhibitions:** UNEAC Gallery, Havana, 1967, 1971; Dum Kultury, Prague, 1969; Museo Nacional, Havana, 1971; Hochschule für Grafik und Buchkunst, Leipzig, 1971; Academia de Bellas Artes, Sabadell, Spain, 1972; Nairobi University, 1973; Fachhochschule, Darmstadt, 1973; Biblioteca Municipal, Havana, 1974, 1975; UAEM Gallery, Mexico City, 1976; Biblioteca Comunale, Milan, 1976; Laval University, Quebec, 1979. Recipient: American Institute of Graphic Arts Awards, New York, 1961; Communication Arts Award, Palo Alto, 1962; Annual Type Directors Award, New York, 1962; Typomundus Awards, Stuttgart, 1969; Leipzig Book Design Award, 1971; Brno Graphics

Biennale Award, 1972; World Symbol and Trademarks Award, Milan, 1974; Cinema Poster Award, Cannes, 1974; International Letterhead Design Awards, Kentucky, 1977; Olympic Poster Award, Moscow, 1980; Listowel Print Biennale Award, Ireland, 1980; Creativity Awards, New York, 1980, 1981, 1982, 1983; Gold Medal, 1980, Golden Centaur Award, 1982, and National Prize, 1983, Accademia Italiana dell'Arte, Parma; Ministerio de Cultura Medal, Havana, 1981; Artistic Merit Medal, Washington, D.C., 1982. Order of the Trabajadores de Cuba, 1975; Order of the Union de Periodistas de Cuba, 1978. Addresses: Apartado de Correos 4109, Zona 4, Havana 4; and Calzada 302, 1/2 Entre H e I, Vedado, Havana 4, Cuba.

Works:

The Sign Shows Where Danger Is traffic safety poster, Cuba, 1969.
Return Used Oil—It's Re-usable public information poster, Cuba, 1970.
OEA logotype of the campaign to dismantle the Organization of American States, for the Comision de Orientacion Revolucionario, 1973.

Publications:

By BELTRÁN: books—*Desde el Diseno,* Havana 1970; *Letragrafia,* Havana 1973; *Acerca del Diseno,* Havana 1974; *Artes Plasticas,* with Ramon Cabrera, Havana 1981; articles—in *Bohemia* (Havana), June 1964, March 1965, July 1965; *La Gaceta* (Havana), February 1970, April 1972, February 1973; *Propaganda* (Havana), February 1973, April 1979; *Revolucion y Cultura* (Havana), April 1974, March 1977; *Union* (Havana), August 1974, June 1979; *Bildende Kunst* (Berlin), April 1979, August 1979; *Punto Grafico* (Valencia), June 1979, May 1980; *Casabella* (Milan), March 1981; *Diseno* (Havana), Spring 1983.

On BELTRÁN: books—*Simbolos, Simbolos y mas Simbolos* by Servando Gonzales, Havana 1970; *Who's Who in Graphic Art,* edited by Walter Amstutz, Dubendorf 1982; *Los Simbolos de Félix Beltrán* by Ramon Cabrera, Havana 1983; articles—in *Idea* (Tokyo), June 1962,

January 1967, May 1970, July 1971; *Gebrauchsgraphik* (Munich), June 1963, September 1971, May 1977; *Neue Werbung* (Berlin), August 1975; *Diseno* (Mexico City), June 1983.

In the history of man-created images, two main types are evident: arbitrary and equivalent images. Arbitrary images do not represent the content directly, but rather substitute an appearance arbitrarily, as in the case of writing, whereas equivalent images more or less correspond to the appearance of the content.

As contents become more complex and diverse in their parts, it is more difficult to find completely equivalent images. That is why symbols, as indirect reflections, play a decisive role in evoking what is most striking in the contents of an entity.

At present, there is a certain tendency to create images which, though simple and attractive, diverge from their essential goal of reflecting an entity. This is partly due to an overestimation of the creative act as an end in itself rather than as a means. This conflict stems essentially from the divergence between emotionalism and functionalism in the field of design. Functionalism is not a style—it does not eliminate imaginative possibilities; on the contrary, it channels them according to needs and conditions. Creation constitutes a decisive step toward the achievement of adequate images should reflect that essence. Besides the images themselves, such qualities as size, position, and color determine effectiveness. Size can reflect content and is relative in relation to context. Position within the context also has communicative implications; this is also true of color, which is an inseparable property of images.

With time, visual images are learned, and they become rooted in the public mind, which responds to the messages, and thus the cycle is completed. Images are grasped by means of the perceptive act, which can be defined as the reflection of the qualities and parts of images directly acting upon the sensory organs. Sensation is a rather frequent partial level of perception. Sensation is also the reflection of isolated and striking qualities of the images, but what is striking does not always agree with what is fundamental. Perception is rendered complete with the public's previous experiences. A single phenomenon may be interpreted in different ways. This is vitally important so that images may be rendered as unambiguous as possible. This aspect is one of the main problems the designer has to face—cultural, social and even biological questions impinge on it. Despite the recent progress of science, enough objective data for the making of decisions in this sense are not always available. The search for images is to a great extent subject to the designer's relative deductive capacity.

—Félix Beltrán

Félix Beltrán came to New York as a student in 1956, as it was becoming the art capital of the world. Not content with a single source of influence, he graduated from the School of Visual Arts in advertising design, earned an additional diploma in easel painting at another school, and attended classes at the Art Students League, the New School for Social Research and the Pratt Graphic Center. His particular mentors were Will Barnet, Ivan Chermayeff, Bob Gill, and George Tscherny. During the same period, he worked as an art director for two publishers. After an additional year of study in Madrid, he returned to Cuba, just prior to the revolution. Whether intentionally or accidentally, he has always been in the place where history was being made.

Beltrán has been the major influence on Cu-

Felix Beltran: *Dismantling the Organization of American States* campaign logo, for the Comision de Orientacion Revolucionario, Havana, 1973

ban design standards in pedagogy and professional practice, and he has organized many unusual exhibitions. The blockade of goods into Cuba has required that visual message for many public programs from films to health and agriculture be produced with readily available materials. Often the paper is made from rice, and there is little variety in inks and virtually no modern typography. Combining these handicaps with his commitment to socialism, Beltrán has helped to create a unique socialist style with color, typography, power, and a total absence of heavy-limbed workers. He has also reconciled the conflict between what he calls "emotionalism and functionalism" in his own work—the difference between art and design.

He considers his greatest contributions to be introducing the first basic design course in Cuba in 1964, his first one-man show of trademarks in Cuba in 1967, the publication in 1970 of his book, the first, on Cuban graphic design, the creation of the first Cyrillic typeface produced in Latin America, and the organization of the first Exhibition of Latin American Trademarks with the participation of seven countries.

—Al Gowan

BENKTZON, Maria.
Swedish industrial designer. Born in Nyköping, 17 June 1946. Studied textile design, National College of Art and Design, Stockholm, 1965–69. Married Erling Ericsson in 1980; children: Emeli and Isak. Freelance design consultant, Stockholm, 1969–72; partner, Ergonomi Design Gruppen, Bromma, since 1973: has collaborated with designer Sven-Eric Juhlin, since 1972. Visiting speaker and lecturer at numerous design congresses and professional institutes, throughout Europe and North America, since 1974. **Exhibitions:** *A Society Open to All,* Kharkov, U.S.S.R., 1977 (toured the Soviet Union, Poland and Czechoslovakia); *Swedish Craft and Design,* Victoria and Albert Museum, London, 1980; *Scandinavian Modern Design 1880–1980,* Cooper-Hewitt Museum, New York, 1982; *Contemporary Swedish Design,* Nationalmuseum, Stockholm, 1983 (toured Scandinavia); *Design Since 1945,* Philadelphia Museum of Art, 1983; *International Design Exhibition,* Osaka, Japan, 1985; *Design in Sweden Now,* toured Canada and Australia, 1985–86; *Scandinavian Design: A Way of Life,* Toyama Museum of Modern Art, Japan, 1987; *Faces of Swedish Design,* IBM Gallery, New York, 1988 (toured the United States); *Designs for Independent Living,* Museum of Modern Art, New York, 1988; *Art and Design,* Internationales Design Zentrum, West Berlin, 1988. **Collections:** Museum of Modern Art, New York; Nationalmuseum, Stockholm; Design Museum, London. Recipient: First International Design Award, 1983 (with Sven-Eric Juhlin), and International Design Competition Prize, 1984 (with Sven-Eric Juhlin and Håkan Bergkvist), Japan Design Foundation; Bruno Mathsson Prize, Sweden, 1984; Swedish Design Excellence Award, 1988. Address: Ergonomi Design Gruppen, Box 14021, 161 14 Bromma, Sweden.

Works:

Training toys and interiors, for Eugeniahemmet-

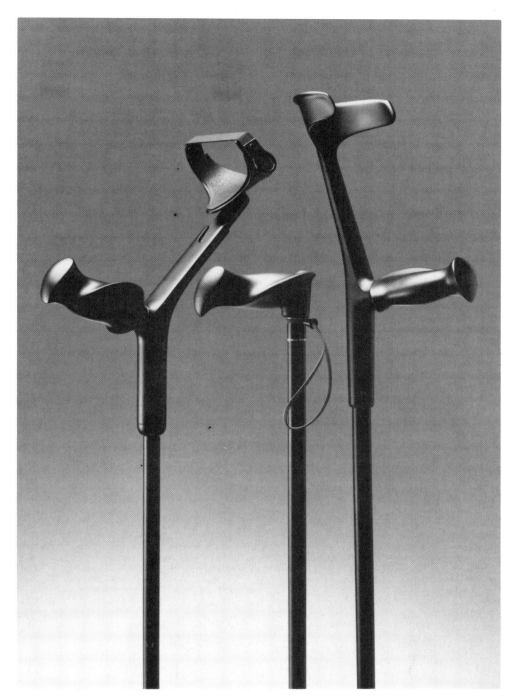

Maria Benktzon and Sven Eric Juhlin: Walking stick and elbow crutches, for RFSU Rehab, 1989

Karolinska sjukhuset handicapped children's ward, 1969.
Handles and Grips project, for Swedish Institute for the Handicapped, 1973.
Kitchen knife and cutting-board, for AB Gustavsberg, 1974.
Pots and pans project, for STU Swedish National Board for Technical Development, 1977.
Eating and drinking implements project, for Folksam Research Foundation/STU Swedish National Board for Technical Development, produced by RFSU Rehab, 1980.
Clothing and Disability book, for STU Swedish National Board for Technical Development, 1980.
Gripping tongs project, for STU Swedish National Board for Technical Development, 1985.
Fix food preparation board, for STU Swedish National Board for Technical Development, produced by RFSU Rehab, 1985.

Cane for arthritics, for STU Swedish National Board for Technical Development, produced by RFSU Rehab, 1987.
Coffee- and teapot, for SAS Scandinavian Airlines System, 1988.
Knife for quadraplegics, for STU Swedish National Board for Technical Development, produced by RFSU Rehab, 1989.
Elbow crutch, for STU Swedish National Board for Technical Development, produced by Etac, 1989.
Eating and drinking implements for multihandicapped children, for Swedish Institute for the Handicapped, produced by RFSU Rehab, 1989.

Publications:

By BENKTZON: books—*Kläder och handikapp/ Clothing and Disability,* Stockholm 1980; articles—"Redskap for hander", with Sven-

Eric Juhlin, in *Form* (Stockholm), no. 10, 1973; "What Can Design Contribute to the Human Society of the Near Future?", with Sven-Eric Juhlin, in *Design Quarterly* (Tokyo), no. 2, 1984; "Ur behoven föds ideerna" in *Form* (Stockholm), no. 8, 1987.

On BENKTZON: books—*Konsthantverk, Konstindustri, Design 1875-1975* by Dag Widman, Stockholm 1975; *Design Since 1945*, edited by Kathryn Hiesinger and George Marcus, Philadelphia and London 1983; *Contemporary Swedish Design*, exhibition catalogue by Monica Boman, Lennart Lindkvist and others, Stockholm 1983; *Design Source Book* by Penny Sparke and others, London 1986, *Faces of Swedish Design*, exhibition catalogue edited by Monica Boman, Stockholm 1988; *Art and Design*, exhibition catalogue, West Berlin 1988; articles—"Världmästare i hjälpmedel for handikappade" in *Svenska Dagbladet* (Stockholm), 7 October 1983; "Designing for the Disabled" in the *Irish Times* (Dublin), 11 April 1989.

*

Essentially, we feel in Ergonomi Design Gruppen that the industrial designer can make a contribution in almost any area that involves industrially manufactured products. We think it is vital to work in areas where there are unsolved problems, or where the solutions that exist do not satisfy the demands that the user is entitled to make. We think it is important to develop everyday products and environments for a "broader average"—including those who are elderly or disabled.

We believe in a collaborative approach to product development as a basis for creativity, aesthetics and intuition. To achieve meaningful results, we feel that it is essential to involve the end user in the design process. The functional requirements of the user determines which design constraints must be met in the final product or environment. To design for a "broader average" means taking the disabled into consideration in the design of products, machines and environments.

—Maria Benktzon/Sven-Eric Juhlin

See JUHLIN, Sven-Eric.

*

When EDG was founded in 1979, the firm moved into a huge 19th-century gingerbread house in Traneberg, just outside Stockholm, which had previously housed a missionary institute. About half of the building's 1,350 sq m of floor space is used for model workshops. The former chapel contains large printing presses and full-scale agricultural machines.

The group develops products and equipment for different work environments in industry, health care, care of the disabled, energy and transportation. They receive commissions from industry, but what distinguishes the group more than anything is that many of its research and development projects are financed by institutions and government authorities. A method has been developed which integrates the know-how and opinions of the users into the product development phase. The existing work situation is systematically surveyed and measured. Then three-dimensional mock-ups are built in full scale for evaluation and simulation of the work process.

The working method of the group is illustrated here by Maria Benktzon and Sven-Eric Juhlin, who have collaborated for over 15 years, all the time specializing in equipment for the handicapped.

To most people, the team of Maria Benktzon and Sven-Eric Juhlin is synonymous with Swedish design for the disabled. They are pioneers in this field and their studies are among the few projects in Sweden which really deserve

the title of design research. Maria and Sven-Eric have created a methodology of design which has been an inspiration to many other designers, outside Sweden as well.

Maria Benktzon and Sven-Eric Juhlin began working together in 1972 on a research project entitled "Handles/Grips," under the aegis of the Swedish Institute for the Handicapped. Their task was to study the need for technical aids for people suffering from impaired muscular strength and mobility, mainly as a result of rheumatoid arthritis. The aim was, if possible, to design products which could be used by everybody instead of constructing special aids in the form of accessories for standard products.

The survey concentrated on grips and handles. Comprehensive studies were undertaken in the homes of disabled persons, and among other things tests were performed on various types of handle in order to discover which type required the least strength. The results were also discussed with medical experts and provided the starting point for the development of two new products. One of these was a kitchen knife with an extra wide blade, good balance, and a new type of handle for maximum utilization of the hand's strength—a classic example of Swedish design for the disabled.

As a direct sequel to the "Handles/Grips" project, Maria and Sven-Eric embarked a few years later on a new project aimed at developing products for eating and drinking. It resulted in a research report and several interesting new products. These included two items of cutlery, a transparent plastic drinking glass which had a high stem and weighed very little, a beaker comprising a glass and a holder, and a plate with a raised rim.

Both projects are based on the same working methods. A survey of physical resources and needs is followed by an analysis of functional requirements. The next stage is to prepare sketches and work out models which are tested in the homes of a number of experimental subjects. Maria and Sven-Eric take pains to stress that just fingering or looking at a product is not enough. Real-life testing is the only possible way of achieving a meaningful evaluation and useful results.

This approach has been made possible by research grants from government authorities, institutions and foundations. Equally indispensable, however, has been the interest taken by the designers in methodically penetrating problems, and compiling and analysing facts on which to base their design of new products.

Their latest project is a support cane for people with arthritis. In collaboration with a doctor, a physiotherapist and a number of patients, they took inventory of what was lacking in ordinary canes. They discovered that canes which took the weight off the weak leg also increased the load on the arms and hands. Many people who start using a cane find they develop pain in their wrists and shoulders because the cane's support surface against the palm of the hand is too small. The next stage was to design test canes to see how the handle could best fit into the hand.

The result was an entirely new cane, in which the handle is a hand-sculpture which organically follows the irregular shape of the palm and thus provides broader support than other canes. The handle is attached to the cane by an articulated joint which can be set at an exact angle suited to the individual. The shaft of the cane is based at the rear of the handle so that it will not be in the way of the fingers.

A large and important portion of Maria's and Sven-Eric's time has been spent in spreading their experience and their knowledge. For several years Sven-Eric was a tutor in design methods and ergonomics at the National College of Art and Design. Together they have lectured on

ergonomics at the Gothenburg School of Arts and Crafts. They have also been much in demand as lecturers in other countries, in conjunction with international conferences dealing with design and the disabled. Their approach to problems of design is constantly reaching new groups and winning new converts.

The former missionary institute is sending out missionaries of a new kind, to spread the word about Swedish design at its best.

—Lennart Lindkvist

BENNETT, Ward.

American sculptor, furniture, interior, fashion, jewelry, textile and advertising designer. Born in New York City, 17 November 1917. Studied at the Porto Romano School of Art, Florence, 1937; Academie de la Grande Chaumiere, and with the sculptor Constantin Brancusi, Paris, 1937–38; painting, under Hans Hofmann, in New York, 1943; apprentice, in the studio of architect Le Corbusier, Paris, 1948–50. Served in the United States Army, 1940–43. Worked in the fashion industry, for Chin Chin Crepe, Saks Fifth Avenue, and Joe Junior, in New York, 1930–33; freelance sketch artist, for American fashion buyers, in Paris, 1937–38; window dresser, for I. Magnin stores, in Los Angeles and San Francisco, 1939–40; clothing designer and window dresser, for Hattie Carnegie, New York, 1943–45; freelance jewelry designer, in Mexico, 1945–46, and interior designer, working in Europe and New York, 1947–50; independent designer, New York, from 1950: has designed for Lehigh Furniture, Chase Manhattan Bank, Gensler Company, Skidmore Owings and Merrill, Tiffany and Company, Brickel Associates, Supreme Cutlery, etc. Visiting Professor, Yale University, New Haven, Connecticut, 1962–63; instructor, 1969–71, and Associate Professor from 1971, Pratt Institute, Brooklyn, New York. **Exhibitions:** *Annual Exhibition of Painting and Sculpture,* Whitney Museum, New York, 1944; Riverside Museum, New York, 1944; Baldwin-Kingrey Gallery, Chicago, 1945; Museum of Modern Art, New York, 1945; *High Style: 20th Century American Design,* Whitney Museum, New York, 1985. **Collection:** Museum of Modern Art, New York. Address: 1 West 72nd Street, New York, New York 10023, U.S.A.

Works:

Penthouse interiors in New York, for Harry Jason, 1947.

1148/58 Mobius range of office furniture, for Brickel Associates, 1970.

University Chair, for the L. B. Johnson Library at the University of Texas, produced by Brickel Associates, 1971.

Sage mohair fabric, for Brickel Associates, 1975.

Sufi wool viscose fabric, for Brickel Associates, 1975.

Metro stainless steel cutlery, for Supreme Cutlery, 1977–78.

Cadet wool broadcloth fabric, for Brickel Associates, 1978.

University 1550 armchair in kiln-dried ash, for Brickel Associates, 1978.

Ankara mohair fabric, for Brickel Associates, 1979.

Ward Bennett: *University Chair 550* **in kiln-dried ash, for Brickel Associates, 1978**

Trylon stainless steel cutlery, for Supreme Cutlery, 1980.
Hollandaise cotton velvet fabric, for Brickel Associates, 1980.
Helex stainless steel cutlery, for Supreme Cutlery, 1981.
Pentimento wool twill fabric, for Brickel Associates, 1981.

Publications:

By BENNETT: articles—in *Interiors* (New York), October 1952, November 1965, January 1977; *Interior Design* (New York), September 1972.

On BENNETT: books—*Design for Modern Living* by Gerd and Ursula Hatje, Munich and Zurich 1961; *Interior Design: An Introduction to Architectural Interiors* by Arnold Friedmann, John F. Pile and Forrest Wilson, New York and Amsterdam 1970, 1976; *Modern Furniture* by John F. Pile, New York and Toronto 1979; *Interior Views* by Erica Brown, London 1980; *The Conran Directory of Design*, edited by Stephen Bayley, London 1985; *High Style: 20th Century American Design*, exhibition catalogue by David Gebhard, Esther McCoy and others, New York 1985.

Ward Bennett's life is a design testimony in itself, to a mode of living not often encountered, especially not today, when more compartmentalized patterns dominate the expectations of most individuals. His life has been one of continued exploration of all the possibilities for finding life interesting, and in the pursuit of that interest, he has produced a wide range of useful, comfortable, and expressive products, from jewelry to buildings, from window decoration to interior design. In all of the varied products of his imagination, his guiding design principle is attention to the structure of space, both to the line that by bounding it makes space visible and to the way in which space extends outward from the person who inhabits it, shaping the range of his actions. Thus, his furniture, designed for comfort, is made up of the minimum skeleton of elements necessary to hold the body with the requisite level of support. These chairs are generally visible as lines in space, rather than as bulky objects filling space. (Those furnishings that are solid, covered objects still present a fine edge, as, for example, the curve at the top of the Alexandra chair; this invigorates their surrounding space with the delicate tension of their own proportions.)
Bennett designs interiors that emphasize both freedom and the shape of the space. His spaces are carefully lit, to allow the orchestration of walls and planes into sequences of expansiveness then constraint, of open spaces then charged by the unexpected detail, such as an edge or corner which projects into visibility and which invites curiosity, or a dark wall cut by a wide door which frames a brilliant garden. He has learned from many sources that the sense of intrigue is the central joy of being human and that this interest is stimulated by the presence of the unusual, accompanied by the sense of personal time and space in which to pursue its contemplation.
All of his projects center on the pleasures of detail and incorporate fine craftsmanship, in woods or textiles with variegated coloration or mottled papers from Japan, in a juxtaposition of rough and smooth, shiny and soft that, by extension, allows him to incorporate into one room the products of heavy industry with the drawings of Paul Klee. While he is known as the originator of the high-tech interior style, those who followed his original esthetic have not managed to retain the quality of collage that

made his most simplified spaces memorable and capable of being the site of creative contemplation. Ultimately, Bennett's knowledge of the components of interest for his own life has been translated into his designs for other people.

—Frances Butler

BERETTA, Anne-Marie.
French fashion designer. Born in Beziers in 1935. Studied dressmaking in Beziers, 1951–53. Married Sandro Beretta in 1966; son: Darius. Designer, for Jacques Esterel and Castillo fashion houses, Paris, 1958–64; stylist and designer, for the firms of Pierre d'Alby, Georges Edelman, Ramosport, MacDouglas, Bercher, and Georges Kay, in Paris, 1965–74; launched brand name Anne-Marie Beretta, designing suits, coats, rainwear, menswear and accessories, Paris, 1974, and Anne-Marie Beretta Mediane label for everyday wear, Paris, 1983: established Left Bank boutique on Boulevard Saint-Sulpice, 1974, and Right Bank boutique on Rue d'Anjou, 1987. Also stylist for Ramosport and Ramowear collections, Paris, from 1974. **Exhibitions:** Musée des Arts Decoratifs, Paris, 1987. **Collection:** Museum of Fashion Arts, Paris. Chevalier des Arts et des Lettres, France, 1987. Address: 1 Boulevard Saint-Martin, 75003 Paris, France.

Publications:

On BERETTA: books—*Who's Who in Fashion* by Karl Strute and Theodor Doelken, Zurich 1982; *Fairchild's Who's Who in Fashion*, edited by Ann Stegemeyer, New York 1983; *McDowell's Directory of Twentieth Century Fashion* by Colin McDowell, London 1984; *The Encyclopaedia of Fashion from 1840 to the 1980s* by Georgina O'Hara, London 1986.

Anne-Marie Beretta began as a very successful designer of sports clothes, with leather garments for McDouglas, rainwear for Ramosport, and ski clothes for Skimmer, but she opened her boutique in 1974 to confront the challenge of city clothes. She believes that fashion in the future must be simple, comfortable, and sympathetic. Her approach is based on restraint, for she does not change her look every season, preferring as she does the continuity and evolution preached by prewar couturiers. She is sensitive to painting and architecture, and both arts are reflected in her dress design. The most daring thing she has done is to abolish traditional lining and interlinings; thus, the fabric must have body of its own, wherefore she uses the very best quality textiles. This gives her clothes a particularly soft look in silhouette, which, together with simplicity, absence of decoration, and her neutral tones—the misty melancholia of autumn shades or the soft harmonies of sunrise—amount to her signature. Nature's colours matter to her, and so do natural fabrics, particularly wool, to the delight of the International Wool Secretariat in London.
Showing a strong British influence are Beretta's simple woollen garments—the duffle coats, the peaked tweed caps, the plain wool overcoats, the cotton mackintoshes, the chunky sweaters, and the tartan trousers, but she has also made gestures to the United States with checked shirts and whipcord skirts. She looks back to ancient Greece for many ideas, but her

Anne-Marie Beretta: Fashion sketch, 1989

recreations of classical drapery are not in the silks used by haut couturiers but in the rustic cloth the Greeks themselves had used. She concedes that taste is difficult to define for it depends on one's education and purse, but "there are a lot of women who want to wear something that resembles them intellectually." Her greatest pleasure comes from a customer saying, "I found myself in your clothes." Thus, she creates for individuals, but they have to be the sort who appreciate her basic approach of simple garments and subtle colours. However, she can be dramatic for evening, as in her 1978 barebacked, black, velvet gown with enormous sleeves reminiscent of the 1830's, and in her 1979 streamlined, lacquered, black-leather sheath with steel jewellery, absolutely simple but stunning. Therein lies her talent; to achieve much by being plain. This makes her the most interesting young designer in Paris today.

—Diana de Marly

BERNADOTTE, Prince Sigvard (Oscar Fredrik).
Swedish industrial designer. Born Count of Wisborg, in Stockholm, 7 June 1907. Studied at the University of Uppsala, 1926–29: BA 1929; Academy of Fine Arts, Stockholm, 1929–31; Staatschule für Angewandte Kunst, Munich, 1931. Served in the Swedish Army, 1929: Lieutenant. Married Marianne Lindberg (second wife) in 1961; son: Michael. Freelance designer of silverware, textiles, bookbindings, glass and porcelain, in Stockholm, from 1929: partner, with Acton Bjørn, in Bernadotte and Bjørn industrial design studio, Copenhagen and Stockholm, 1949–64; independent designer, as Bernadotte Design, Stockholm, since 1964. President, ICSID International Council of Societies of Industrial Design, 1961–63. **Exhibitions:** *Die Gute Industrieform*, Kunstverein,

Hamburg, 1955; *Nordisk Industridesign,* Kunstindustrimuseet, Oslo, 1976; Georg Jensen, Copenhagen, 1980; *Scandinavian Modern Design 1880–1980,* Cooper-Hewitt Museum, New York, 1982. **Collections:** Moderna Museet, Stockholm; Metropolitan Museum of Art, New York. Recipient: Gold Medal, 1952, and Silver Medal, 1955, Milan Triennale. Address: Villagatan 10, 114 32 Stockholm, Sweden.

Publications:

By BERNADOTTE: books—*Industrial Design: Modern Industriell Formgivning,* Goteborg 1953; *Heads or Tails,* Stockholm 1975.

On BERNADOTTE: books—*Konsthantverk och Hemslöjd i Sverige 1930–1940,* edited by Åke H. Huldt, Mattis Horlén and Heribert Seitz, Göteborg 1941; *Fifty Years of Silver in the Georg Jensen Tradition* by Edgar Kauffmann Jr., Erik Lassen and Christian Reventlow, Copenhagen 1956; *Svensk Form,* edited by Åke H. Huldt and Åke Stavenlow, Stockholm 1961; *Design in Sweden,* edited by Lennart Lindkvist, Stockholm 1972; *Scandinavian Design: Objects of a Life Style* by Eileene Harrison Beer, New York and Toronto 1975; *Scandinavian Modern Design 1880–1980,* edited by David Revere McFadden, New York 1982.

One of the pioneers who helped to establish the industrial design profession in Europe, Swedish designer Prince Sigvard Bernadotte has enriched the lives of many individuals with a broad range of products designed for everyday use. For Bernadotte, good design is as necessary as food and drink. To him, the designer is someone who, through talent, education, inspiration, and hard work, creates something that is pleasing to the eye and easy on the hand. His products are not just ornamental objects that stand on a shelf or a table to be admired; instead, they are designed to have a purpose and to be used.

When Bernadotte began working for Georg Jensen in Copenhagen, the prevailing school of design was much the style of "grapes and flowers." His first efforts in silver, as a result, were an absolute revolution. Leaving out all the bulges and decorations, Bernadotte let the inherent beauty of the metal emerge. One of his most important pieces is the silver coffee service owned by the Metropolitan Museum of Art. The beautiful proportion and tasteful spacing of the ornament enhance the verticality, both in form and detail, without interrupting the quiet simplicity of the design.

Bernadotte was also interested in the effects of color on an object, but because color did enter into the design of silver, he turned to textiles. His inspiration for the blended colors and beautiful gradation of tones in his handwoven, wool rugs was the Swedish landscape. For Bernadotte, using colors was like painting. The lyrical quality of his simple designs depended on the blending of rich reds, silver-greys, and moss greens. By designing rugs, Bernadotte not only had the opportunity to demonstrate the effects of colors when placed next to one another but also was able to work in two dimensions instead of three.

The final and all-embracing widening of his career was the beginning of his own industrial design company. His knowledge of materials and production methods was a valuable asset in helping him to understand new ways of manufacturing. Bernadotte was able to make the difficult journey from artisanship to mass production, first designing in silver, then textiles, and finally for industry.

—Patricia A. Russac

BERNHARD, Lucian.
American painter, illustrator, interior, type and graphic designer. Born Emil Kahn, in Stuttgart, Germany, 15 March 1883; emigrated to the United States in 1923: subsequently naturalized. Studied painting, Akademie der Kunst, Munich, but mainly self-taught in design, from 1905. Worked as a freelance graphic designer, adopting pseudonym Lucian Bernhard, in Berlin, from 1905; designer, under E. Growald, at Hollerbaum und Schmidt printers, Berlin; also freelance type designer, for Bauer of Frankfurt, Berthold of Berlin, Flinsch of Frankfurt, and American Type Founders of New Jersey; co-founder, with Hans Sachs, of *Der Plakat* (later titled *Gebrauchsgraphik*) magazine, Berlin, 1909; artistic leader, German Handicrafts Workshops, Berlin; co-founder, with Rockwell Kent, Paul Poiret and Bruno Paul, of Contempora graphic and interior design firm, New York. Professor of Advertising and Poster Design, Akademie der Kunst, Berlin, 1920–23; instructor, New York University, and Art Students League, New York. **Exhibitions:** Deutsches Museum, The Hague, 1913; *Three Rooms Designed in the Contemporary Spirit,* Rochester Memorial Art Gallery, New York, 1950 (with P. Poiret and B. Paul); *The 20th-Century Poster,* Walker Art Center, Minneapolis, 1984; *The Machine Age in America 1918–1941,* Brooklyn Museum, New York, 1986. Member: Deutscher Werkbund; American Institute of Graphic Arts; New York Society of Illustrators. *Died* (in New York City) *29 May 1972.*

Works:

Stiller-Schuh posters, for Stiller shoes, 1908, 1912.
Kaffee Hag poster, for Hag coffee, 1909.
Typewriter poster, for the Adler Factory, 1909.
Bernhard-Antiqua typeface, for Bauer/Flinsch, 1911.
Bernhard-Schmuck typeface, for Bauer, 1911.
Automobile poster, for Audi, 1912.
Bernhard-Fraktur typeface, for Bauer, 1913.
Spark plugs poster, for Bosch, 1915.
Manoli cigarettes poster, 1915.
Flinsch-Privat typeface, for Flinsch, 1920.
Bernhard-Schonschrift typeface, for Bauer, 1924.
Bernhard Roman typeface, for Bauer, 1925.
Kursiv typeface, for Bauer, 1925.
Bernhard-Handschrift typeface, for Bauer, 1928.
Lucian typeface, for Bauer, 1928.
Fashion typeface, for American Typefounders, 1929.
Gothic typeface, for American Typefounders, 1929–31.
Negro typeface, for Bauer, 1931.
Bernhard-Buchschrift typeface, for Bauer, 1933.
Tango typeface, for American Typefounders, 1933.

Publications:

By BERNHARD: article—"What's Wrong with the American Poster?" in *PM* (New York), 1936.

On BERNHARD: books—*Lucian Bernhard,* exhibition catalogue by F. Plietzsch, The Hague 1913; *Art Deco Posters* by Nina Weinstock, Basel 1967; *The Poster: An Illustrated History from 1860* by Harold F. Hutchinson, London and Toronto 1968; *History of the Poster* by Josef and Shizuko Muller Brockman, Zurich 1971; *Second World War Posters,* edited by Joseph Darracott and Belinda Loftus, London 1972; *The Thames and Hudson Manual of Ty-*pography by Ruari McLean, London 1980; *The 20th-Century Poster: Design of the Avant-Garde* by Dawn Ades, New York 1984; *The Machine Age in America 1918–41,* exhibition catalogue by Richard Guy Wilson and Dianne H. Pilgrim, New York 1986.

Lucian Bernhard originally gained fame as a poster designer in Germany at the turn of the century. Influenced by art nouveau posters, especially the work of the Beggarstaff Brothers (James Pryde and William Nicholson), Bernhard's early designs, such as those for Manoli cigarettes and Stiller shoes, were noteworthy for their simple product images dramatically silhouetted against pale, monochrome backgrounds. These designs, beginning with one for Priester matches, employed bold roman letterforms instead of the more traditional Fraktur ones. The motifs were reduced to essentials and often outlined in thick, black strokes to match the bold letterforms. During these years, Bernhard helped launch *Das Plakat* to promote poster design, including his own esthetic of the "poster-object." His success as a poster designer culminated in an appointment as a teacher of poster design at the Royal Art Institute in Berlin.

His subsequent poster work exhibited a strikingly different style, yet was equally influential. During World War I, his posters reintroduced Fraktur letterforms, often used in a large outlined manner, and relied almost exclusively on slogans rather than objects for their content. Their design echoed medieval German woodcuts. The subtle colors of the prewar posters were replaced with bright, bold colors. The final stage in his evolution as a poster designer opened when Roy Latham invited him to work the United States, where he eventually settled. Bernhard's American work, starting with his advertising for Rem cough syrup in 1926, was distinguished by a preference for red, white, and blue as the sole colors.

Bernhard used his success as a poster designer as a jumping off point to design type, packaging, fashions, and furniture. For the Bauer typefoundry in Germany, he designed Bernhard Antiqua (1911), Bernhard Fraktur (1913), Bernhard Roman (1925), Bernhard Cursive (1925), and Bernhard Brush Script (date unknown). The first two were derived from his poster lettering of the period. In the United States, for the American Typefounders, he designed several faces, of which the best known are Bernhard Fashion (1929), Bernhard Gothic (1929–1931), and Bernhard Tango (1933). These latter typefaces constitute his strongest American legacy. By 1930, he had become disenchanted with the increased emphasis on specialization in design and had turned his attention to sculpture and painting.

—Paul Shaw

BERTOIA, Harry.
American sculptor, architectural, furniture, jewelry and graphic designer. Born in San Lorenzo, Udine, Italy, 10 March 1915; emigrated to the United States in 1930. Studied at Cass Technical High School, Detroit, 1932–36; Society of Arts and Crafts, Detroit, 1936; Cranbrook Academy of Art, Bloomfield Hills, Michigan, 1937–39. Married Brigitta Valentiner in 1943; children: Mara, Val and Celia.

Instructor and founder of metal workshop, Cranbrook Academy of Art, Bloomfield Hills, Michigan, 1939–43; worked with Charles Eames in molded plywood division of Evans Products Company, Venice, California, 1943–46; graphics designer, at Point Loma Naval Electronics Laboratory, 1947–49; established own art and design studio, with support from Knoll International, in Bally, Pennsylvania, from 1950. **Exhibitions:** Karl Nierendorf Gallery, New York, 1940, 1943, 1947; Museum of Non-Objective Art, New York, 1943; Smithsonian Institution, Washington, D.C., 1943 (toured); Knoll International, New York, 1951; Fairweather-Hardin Gallery, Chicago, 1956, 1961, 1968, 1975; Staempfli Gallery, New York, 1959, 1961, 1963, 1968, 1970, 1976, 1978, 1981; Knoll International, Paris, 1964; Knoll International, Amsterdam, 1968; Knoll International, Zurich, 1968; K. B. Gallery, Oslo, 1972, 1975; Wadsworth Atheneum, Hartford, Connecticut, 1974; Art Institute of Chicago, 1975; Allentown Art Museum, Pennsylvania, 1975, 1986; Robert Kidd Associates, Birmingham, Alabama, 1982; Lancaster Community College, Pennsylvania, 1982; Benjamin Mangel Gallery, Philadelphia, 1983; Michigan State University, East Lansing, 1987. **Collections:** Museum of Modern Art, New York; Albright-Knox Art Gallery, Buffalo, New York; Massachusetts Institute of Technology, Cambridge; Philadelphia Museum of Art; San Francisco Museum of Modern Art. Recipient: Fine Arts Medal, 1955, Craftsmanship Medal, 1956, Pennsylvania Chapter Fine Arts Medal, 1963, and Gold Medal, 1973, American Institute of Architects; Graham Foundation Grant, New York, 1957. Honorary Doctorate: Muhlenberg College, Allentown, Pennsylvania, 1971. *Died 6 November 1978.*

Works:

420 and *421* (the *Bertoia Chair*) series of chairs in steel rod with wire-formed seats, for Knoll, 1951–52.
423 lounge chair in steel rod with wire-formed seat, for Knoll, 1952.
424 stool in steel rod with wire-formed seat, for Knoll, 1952.
427P chair in metal with plastic seat shell, for Knoll, 1955.

Publications:

On BERTOIA: books—*An Exhibition for Modern Living,* catalogue edited by A. H. Girard and W. D. Laurie Jr., Detroit 1949; *Mobili Tipo* by Robert Aloi, Milan 1956; *Stahlmoebel* by Gustav Hassneplug, Dusseldorf 1960; *Harry Bertoia, Sculptor* by June Kompass Nelson, Detroit 1970; *The Modern Chair 1918–1970,* exhibition catalogue with texts by Carol Hogben and others, London 1970; *Harry Bertoia: An Exhibition of His Sculpture and Graphics,* catalogue by Beverly H. Twitchell, Allentown 1975; *Knoll Design* by Eric Larrabee and Massimo Vignelli, New York 1981; *Neue Moebel 1950–1982/Contemporary Furniture,* edited by Klaus-Jurgen Sembach, Stuttgart and London 1982; *Design Since 1945,* edited by Kathryn Hiesinger and George Marcus, Philadelphia and London 1983; *High Style: 20th Century American Design,* exhibition catalogue by David Gebhard, Esther McCoy and others, New York 1985; *Design Source Book* by Penny Sparke and others, London 1986; *The American Design Adventure 1940–1975* by Arthur J. Pulos, London and Cambridge, Massachusetts 1988.

Harry Bertoia worked alongside Charles Eames at Evans Products in Venice, California during the war years, at first utilizing the newly developed plywood techniques in the manufacture of splints and the like for the military medical services. Later, they moved on to use this technology for furniture, such as the chairs to which Eames gave his name. Bertoia spent another three years at graphic design in the Point Loma Naval Electronics Laboratory before setting up a studio in Pennsylvania with the support of Knoll International, which gave him an exhibition in 1951 and launched the chair that bears his name the following year. After that, he had to his credit a string of commissions, largely for sculpture, exhibitions on an international scale, and a film dealing with his sculpture.

The chairs Bertoia designed for Knoll International linked closely to his sculptural thinking, to lightness and airiness and away from heavy objects bearing hard upon the ground. All following certain basic principles and methods. The chairs are made of a shaped, wire lattice supported by a refined, metal frame which, though consistent in conception, varies somewhat in the bending of the metal and its attachment to the latticework, which can be wholly or partially covered with minimal upholstery, or not. The frame consists of one piece of metal bent to make a front support and side legs linked by runners on the floor, welded to the other supporting elements. The structure is wonderfully clear and articulated, underscored by the transparency of the latticework.

Throughout the 1950's and 1960's, these chairs were part of the iconographic expression of modernity, almost cult objects, though a great many people daily sat on them happily. Though they show clear parallels with the sculpture, they were and still are extremely practical and elegant seats, which is what they were designed to be.

—Toni del Renzio

BETANOVA.
American exhibition, display and graphic designer. Born Elizabeth Lydia Csintalan, in Bratislava, Czechoslovakia, 5 June 1954; emigrated to the United States in 1969: naturalized, 1974. Educated at Ridgefield Park High School, New Jersey, 1969–72; studied art and languages, New York University, 1972–75: BA 1975. Married the designer Haig David-West in 1974; children: Alzo, Hegulka and Gizelka. Designer and director of Haig-Betanova design and publishing firm, Port Harcourt, Nigeria, since 1975: has designed for the Port Harcourt Arts Council, Port Harcourt Contemporary Arts Gallery, Komsky Enterprises, WI-Verlag, Seiyefa Publishers, etc. Instructor in visual education and display, 1976, and gallery manager, 1977–79, Arts Council, Port Harcourt program coordinator, Artgroup, Port Harcourt, 1979–80; lecturer in creative arts, College of Education, Port Harcourt, since 1980. **Exhibitions:** *Eight Contemporary Rivers State Artists,* Contemporary Arts Gallery, Port Harcourt, 1977; Gong Gallery, Lagos, 1979. **Collections:** Gong Gallery, Lagos; Patricia Ellah Collection, Port Harcourt. Recipient: Raymond Miller Fencing Championship Award, New York University, 1973; Junior Olympic Fencing Honor Award, Los Angeles, 1973. Address: Haig-Betanova, P.O. Box 4289, 24A Ellah Place, Trans-Amadi, Port Harcourt, Nigeria.

Works:

Visual Arts Office interiors, for the Port Harcourt Arts Council, 1975.
Contemporary Arts Gallery exterior design, for the Port Harcourt Arts Council, 1976.
Traditional Woven Fabrics exhibition layouts, for the Port Harcourt Arts Council, 1977.
Souvenir Shop interiors, for the Port Harcourt Arts Council, 1977.
Coordinated visual identity system, for Komsky Enterprises, Lagos, 1978.
Akifpo Masks exhibition layouts, for the Port Harcourt Arts Council, 1978.
African Spirits series of greeting cards, for WI-Verlag, Düsseldorf, 1979.
Krieg macht blutige Hande poster, for WI-Verlag, Düsseldorf, 1980.
Francis and Patricia 25 total environment exteriors in Port Harcourt, for Senator Francis Ellah, 1981.
Poetry Trilogy book covers, for Seifeya Publishers, Port Harcourt, 1982.

Publications:

By BETANOVA: book—*Careers in Art,* Port Harcourt 1979; article—"Graphic Design of the City of Port Harcourt" in *Dialogue on Graphic Design Problems in Africa,* edited by Haig David-West, London 1983.

On BETANOVA: book—*Arts Council Information,* booklet, Port Harcourt 1977; articles—"Evolving a New Lyricism" by S. Agioubu-Kemar in the *Daily Times* (Lagos), March 1979; "African Symbolic Design at Play" by F. Balogun in *The Punch* (Lagos), March 1979.

What I have tried to do since my arrival in Africa is to translate the vitality of material vernacular structure into new functional form under controlled circumstances, such as modern interiors, without losing the essential character of the culture. I think that the work I did for the *Afikpo Masks* exhibition (1978) may be considered as a major contribution of my career in exhibit and display design. In a culture where even the most spacious natural environments sometimes tend to be crowded, a new orientation to space needs to be learned, as such a culture progresses from the vernacular level of growth to a technological one within the framework of international currents that no society can deliberately neglect. I think that I am contributing to the introduction of the new orientation in Nigeria. The teaching methodology that I employ at the College of Education (Faculty of Primary Education—Creative Arts Section) seeks to translate craft into design, and is aimed at preparing future creative arts teachers for the task before them—that of contributing towards cultural growth.

An imaginative use of space is vital for meaningful interpersonal relationships in our contemporary world. As modern living standards steadily replace traditional standards, deliberate effort must be made to discourage an erasure of traditional tendencies which ultimately differentiate one culture from the other. This is perhaps most important to the younger countries of the world (such as Nigeria) which tend to be on the consuming end of standards prescribed by the technological explosion of our generation.

What could be done is to introduce change gradually without altering the essential structure of vernacular design content. I believe that the manner in which people arrange their environments reflects on the manner in which they organize their lives, and that in turn reflects on the manner in which they respond to political and social responsibilities. Therefore, in my designs, I try to show examples of how environments can be re-ordered to reflect the basic vernacular philosophies of art and design in unity with the excitement and worries of contemporary civilization.

—Betanova

Arriving in Nigeria in 1974, Betanova brought with her background mixing Slovak lyricism with New World excitement, the romantic aura of her native Bratislava with the electronic tempo of New York City, and the socialist ideological system with the capitalist one. Perhaps this interesting background has enabled her to operate at ease in Nigeria which, like most Third World countries, demonstrates an admixture of all the elements of her background, and to introduce a new dimension to exhibit and display design in this country, thereby placing her among the innovative contemporary designers of our times.

In 1975, she began collecting examples of indigenous Nigerian art and crafts—from wood carvings to thorn carvings, from bead work to masquerade embellishments, and from shell-work to fish traps. Her art-and-crafts collecting was punctuated by discussions with old people in village settlements. Examining her collection in conjunction with these discussions, she noted that the naive, geometric formalism of vernacular art and design was fundamentally perceived first on a functional level, then in terms of visual appeal. She also noted that the formal "fear of space" in vernacular design reflected "togetherness" in social behavior. Further inquiry led her to conclude that in contemporary circumstances, freedom of mobility, which suggested "nonfear of space," was tolerable as a function of a new "fear" introduced by the technological age as evidenced by mechanics and automation.

These findings have greatly influenced Betanova's work in exhibit and display design, for, while retaining the general tempo of vernacular lyricism in indigenous art and design, she introduces the element of space-time as a functional mobility factor. Her environments are therefore a dialectical blend of tradition and contemporaneity; of naive "togetherness" and "togetherness" unmitigated by space-time control. Tangibly, this blend has introduced a new design format and a new functional excitement to the Nigerian contemporary experience. A most vivid example of this was her 1978 design for the *Afikpo Masks* exhibition in Port Harcourt's contemporary arts gallery; there, her innovative exhibition stands blended with the lyrical naive abstraction of vernacular wood carvings.

Besides interesting work in exhibit and display design, she has also produced outstanding work in graphic design and painting. Her paintings—notably the *Mat Motif* and *Mask Form* series which were exhibited in 1979 at the Gong Gallery in Lagos—are a direct offshoot from her research into vernacular lyricism, and, according to Sereba Agiobu-Kemar, art critic of Lagos, they pointed toward a new lyricism in Nigerian art. As a creative arts lecturer at Port Harcourt's College of Education, she lays emphasis on basic understanding of geometry with a blend of vernacular formal arrangements in solving design problems. This teaching strategy may create a new and more effective generation of art and design teachers in Nigeria.

In a society in which the socio-political temperament is still in formative stages, Betanova's work in exhibit and display design—which increasingly influences the way in which people perceive art and design generally and organize their lives and their environments specifically—may become increasingly useful in this process of development.

—Haig David-West

BIAGIOTTI, Laura.

Italian fashion designer. Born in Rome, 4 August 1943. Studied literature, Rome, 1960–62. Married, with one daughter, Lavinia. Worked with her mother Delia Biagiotti, in the family ready-to-wear fashion export firm, Rome, 1962–65; partner and designer, with Gianni Cigna, in clothing firm designing for Schuberth, Barocco, Cappucci, Heinz Riva, Litrico, etc., in Rome 1965–72; founder-designer, Laura Biagiotti Fashions, Rome, since 1972: took over Mac-Pherson knitwear firm, Pisa, 1974; established headquarters at the castle of Marco Simone, Guidonia, 1980; created Portrait collection, 1981, Laurapiu collection, 1984, and Biagiotti Uomo collection, 1987, for Lebole Moda ready-to-wear clothing group; launched perfumes *Laura,* 1982, *Night,* 1986, and *Roma,* 1988. Recipient: Golden Lion Award, Venice, 1985; Commendatore Award, Republic of Italy,

1987. Address: Biagiotti Export S.p.A., Via Palombarese Km. 17. 300, 00012 Guidonia, Rome, Italy.

Works:

Handbags and luggage range, for Copel, 1978.
Sunglasses, for Safilo Group, 1980.
Perfumes and cosmetics, for Eurocos, 1981.
Shoes, for Colette, 1982.
Scarves, for Isa, 1983.
Ceramics and tiles, for Tagina, 1983.
Laurapiu women's clothing collection, for Lebole Moda, 1984.
Household linens collection, for Eliolona, 1984.
MacPherson's Diffusion collection of pullovers, 1985.
Furniture, for Corsini, 1985.

Laura Biagiotti: *Sahara* jacket with classic trousers, 1989

Linea Junior children's sports and leisure wear, for Italiangriffe, 1986.
Jeans collection, for I.T.S.A., 1986.
Costume jewellery, for Enny Bijoux, 1986.
Tights, for Levante, 1986.
Knitwear, for Ghinea, 1987.
Menswear collection, for Lebole Moda, 1987.
Ties, for Guarisco, 1987.
Hair accessories, for Santa Monica, 1988.
Leather wear, for Sicons, 1988.
Beach wear, for Karibe, 1988.
Ladies' lingerie, for Magnolia, 1988.
Bear's Bazaar young ladies' clothing, for Fim, 1988.

Publications:

On BIAGIOTTI: books—*I Mass-Moda: fatti e personaggi dell'Italian Look/The Who's Who of Italian Fashion,* with text by Adriana Mulassano, photos by Alfa Castaldi, Florence 1979; *Who's Who in Fashion,* edited by Karl Strute and Theodor Doelken, Zurich 1982; *McDowell's Directory of Twentieth Century Fashion* by Colin McDowell, London 1984; *The Encyclopaedia of Fashion from 1840 to the 1980s* by Georgina O'Hara, London 1986.

At Guidonia, in the Roman countryside, ready-to-wear designer Laura Biagiotti fell in love with an eleventh-century castle she passed on her daily drive to and from her factory. Once inhabited by a Vatican cardinal and most recently by a family of farmers who had whitewashed the fifteenth-century frescos, when it came up for sale. Biagiotti and her business manager Gianni Cigna agreed that to purchase it would be a wise investment. Today, the sixty-nine room Castello di Marco Simone serves as factory, showroom, and offices as well as residence for Biagiotti, her daughter Lavinia, and a housekeeper.

Biagiotti had planned one day to have been an archaeologist, but as her mother Delia, a Roman couturiere, tired of business demands, Laura interrupted her studies to turn her attention to fashion. Since then, living in her romantic factory/castle, she has successfully joined her love of antiquity with her professed virtues of discipline and hard work in order to succeed as a contemporary businesswoman.

When the time comes to develop a new line, Biagiotti reveals a mania for research. She studies fabrics—in particular, natural fibers—which are often combined with custom patterns and distinctive top-stitching. The work of Laura Biagiotti Exports has never been known to be shocking, but always feminine, luxurious, and finely constructed. The designer has innovated in the form and construction of cashmere dresses, which need minimal attention to sizing, as well as cardigans, sweaters, and recently, jogging outfits. Her particular preference for white was very visible in a recent collection of New England lattice-work linen dresses.

Since her "outsider" showings in Florence in 1972, she presents semiannual, two hundred-piece collections, which are always expected to emphasize high quality, sumptuousness, and femininity. Her 1983 cashmere dresses resemble long, easy sweaters; frequently they display frilled or scarf necklines, cross-over bib detailing, or oversized, knitted cables. To cover all, she takes the softest of cashmere blankets and creates capes or beehive jackets with trellis-top stitching. In 1983, she also introduced rainproof satin and an amusing leopard-skin pattern printed on cotton satin. The voluminous silhoutte of the "*bambola*" or doll dress has become one of her classics, which she varies with detailing and fantasy-patterns.

In 1978 at Castello di Marco Simone, the scent Laura was introduced. This perfume, which combines lilacs, jasmine, tuberoses, and orchids, adds to her romantic image. Recently, fifteen forms were developed into more than one hundred items of clothing to create Portrait by Laura Biagiotti, her line made for large production and distribution. As she developed Portrait, she combined her admiration of Matisse cut-outs and colors with inspiration drawn from flower photographs by Irving Penn to design a collection with classic lines in natural fibers.

—Gillian Skellenger

BILL, Max
Swiss painter, sculptor, architect, stage, exhibition and industrial designer. Born in Winterthur, 22 December 1908. Trained as a silversmith, at the Kunstgewerbeschule, Zurich, 1924–27; studied art, Staatliche Bauhaus, Dessau, 1927–29. Served in the Swiss Army, 1939–45. Married Binia Spoerri in 1931; son: Johann. Independent artist, architect and exhibition designer from 1929, and industrial designer from 1944, in Zurich: member of the Abstraction-Creation group, Paris, 1932–36; Allianz, Zurich, 1937; CIAM Congrès Internationaux d'Architecture Moderne, 1938; UAM Union des Artistes Modernes, Paris, 1949; Deutscher Werkbund, 1956. Lecturer on the Theory of Form, Kunstgewerbeschule, Zurich, 1944–45; co-founder and Rector, Hochschule für Gestaltung, Ulm, 1951–56; Professor of Environmental Design, State Institute of Fine Arts, Hamburg, 1967–74. Central Board Member, Schweizerische Werkbund, 1952–62; Communal Council Member, City of Zurich, 1961; member of the Swiss Federal Art Commission, 1961–69; Board Member, Geschwisten-School Foundation, Ulm, 1964; National Councillor, in the Swiss Parliament, 1967–74; Superior Council Member, Creation Esthètique Industrielle, Paris, 1971–73. **Exhibitions:** Kunstmuseum, Basel, 1949; Museu de Arte Moderno, Sao Paulo, 1950; Ulmer Museum, Ulm, 1956 (toured); Helmhaus, Zurich, 1957; Städtisches Museum, Leverkusen, 1959; Staatsgalerie, Stuttgart, 1960; Kunstmuseum, Winterthur, 1960; Kunsthalle, Bern, 1968; Kunstverein, Düsseldorf, 1968; Kunsthaus, Zurich, 1968; Gemeentemuseum, The Hague, 1968; Kunsthalle, Nuremeberg, 1968; Arts Club, Chicago, 1969; Centre National d'Art Contemporain, Paris, 1969; San Francisco Museum of Art, 1970; Musée Rath, Geneva, 1972; Kunstmuseum, Aarhus, 1972; Albright-Knox Art Gallery, Buffalo, New York, 1974 (toured); San Francisco Art Institute; Museum für Kunst und Gewerbe, Hamburg, 1976 (toured); Akademie der Künste, West Berlin, 1976; University of Parma, Italy, 1977; Museo de Bellas Artes, Caracas, 1979; Mucsarnok Art Gallery, Budapest, 1986; National Gallery, Belgrade, 1987; Kunsthalle, Frankfurt, 1987. **Collections:** Kunstmuseum, Winterthur; Kunsthaus, Zurich; Musée d'Art et d'Histoire, Geneva; Galleria Nazionale d'Arte Moderna, Rome; Centre Georges Pompidou, Paris; Wilhelm Lehmbruck Museum, Duisburg; Art Institute of Chicago; Museum of Modern Art, New York. Recipient: Grand Prize, Milan Triennale, 1936, 1951, 1954; Kandinsky Prize, 1949; Sculpture Prize, Bienal of São Paulo, 1951; Gold Medal, Verucchio, 1966; City of Zurich Art Prize, 1968; Misha Black Medal, Society of Industrial Artists and Designers, London, 1982. Honorary Fellow, American Institute of Architects, 1964; Extraordinary Member, Akademie der Künste, West Berlin, 1972; Honorary Member, Royal Flemish Academy of Science, Literature and Art, 1973. Address: Albulastrasse 39, 8048 Zurich, Switzerland.

Works:

Swiss Pavilion design, at the Milan Triennale, 1936, 1951.
Swiss Pavilion design, at the *World's Fair,* New York, 1938.
City Building and National Planning display, at the *Swiss National Exhibition,* Zurich, 1939.
Three-legged table, for Wohnbedarf AG, Zurich, 1949–50.
Chair with wood frame and moulded plywood seating unit, for Horgen-Glarus, 1950.
The Unknown Present exhibition layouts, at Globus Department Stores, in Basel, St. Gallen, Chur and Aarau, 1957.
Fountain courtyard design, at the *International Hydraulic Engineering Exhibition,* West Berlin, 1961.
Oedipus stage designs, at the Municipal Theatre, Ulm, 1963.
Bilden und Gestalten displays, at the *Swiss National Exhibition,* Lausanne, 1964.
Zurcher Kunstler annual exhibition layouts, Zurich, 1968–70.

(for a complete list of Bill's buildings and architectural projects, see *Contemporary Architects;* for his activity as a painter and sculptor, see *Contemporary Artists*)

Publications:

By BILL: books and portfolios—*Quinze Variations sur même thème,* Paris 1938; *Le Corbusier: Oeuvre Complete,* vol. 3, editor, Zürich 1939, London 1964; *5 Konstruktionen & 5 Kompositionen,* Zurich 1941; *10 Original Lithos,* Zürich 1941; *X & X,* Zürich 1942; *Leo Luppi: 10 Kompositionen,* Zürich 1943; *Konkrete Kunst,* exhibition catalogue, with others, Basel 1944; *Hans Arp: 11 Configurations,* with others, Zürich 1945; *Wiederaufbau,* Zürich 1945; *Wassily Kandinsky: 10 Farbige Reproduktionen,* Basel 1949; *Robert Maillart: Brucken und Konstruktionen,* Zürich 1949, New York 1969; *Moderne Schweizer Architektur 1925–45,* Basel 1950; *Wassily Kandinsky,* editor, Paris 1951; *Form: A Balance Sheet of Mid-20th Century Trends in Design,* Basel 1952; *Über das Geistige in der Kunst,* editor, Bern 1952; *Mies van der Rohe,* Milan 1955; *Essays über Kunst und Künstler,* editor, Stuttgart 1955, Bern 1963; *Die gute Form,* Winterthur 1957; *Punkt und Linie zu Flache,* editor, Bern 1959; *Enzo Mari,* with Bruno Munari, Milan 1959; *Konkrete Kunst: 50 Jahre Entwicklung,* exhibition catalogue, with Rene Wehrli and Margit Staber, Zürich 1960; *7 Scarions,* Genoa 1967; *Zürcher Künstler,* exhibition catalogue, Zürich 1968, 1969; *11 x 4,* Zürich 1970; *Jahresgabe 1972,* Bern 1972; *System mit funf vierfarbigen Zentren,* St. Gallen 1972; *8 = (2 x 4/4) = 8,* Neuchâtel 1974; *16 Constellations,* Paris 1974; *7 Twins,* Neuchâtel 1977; article—"The Bauhaus Idea: From Weimar to Ulm" in *The Architects' Year Book,* vol. 5, London 1953.

On BILL: books—*Max Bill* by Tomas Maldonado, Buenos Aires 1955; *Die Gute Industrieform,* exhibition catalogue by Hans Eckstein and Robert Gutmann, Hamburg 1955; *Max Bill* by Max Bense and others, Teufen 1958; *Moderne Deutsche Industrieform* by Heinz Spielmann, Hamburg 1962; *Who's Who in Graphic Art,* edited by Walter Amstutz, Zurich

1962; *Max Bill* by Margit Staber, St. Gallen 1971; *Max Bill* by Eduard Huttinger, Zurich 1977, 1978; *Design Since 1945,* edited by Kathryn Hiesinger and George Marcus, Philadelphia and London 1983; *The Conran Directory of Design,* edited by Stephen Bayley, London 1985.

For Max Bill, geometry is the foremost foundation for form, geometry made visual as the mutual relationships of rhythmic elements on a surface or in space. Bill's work concentrates on showing the possibilities for endless variation within this philosophical and structural model, to which he adheres rigidly as symbolic of universal order and collective freedom. His choice of anti-illusionistic, mathematical/scientific form is not based on an art-for-art's sake mentality, but rather is viewed by Bill as the systemic basis capable of conveying high ideals which all can share and comprehend through their experience of all the arts. His faith in geometry as communicator of order and unity also allows for the element of the indecipherable, a mysticism inherent in the very nature of the forms.

Bill's multi-media oeuvre demonstrates his position in history as a faithful and productive second-generation practitioner of Bauhaus philosophy and practice. From his earliest to his latest work as painter, sculptor, architect, industrial designer, and writer, Bill has transmitted a direct kinship with his mentors, Josef Albers, László Moholy-Nagy, Piet Mondrian, Paul Klee, and Walter Gropius, among others. Consider his design for Ulm's Hochschule für Gestaltung buildings, which equate so closely with the earlier work of Gropius at the Bauhaus. The no-frills simplicity of his door handle, electric plugs, and medical lamp, no differently than the strict, geometrical structures of his paintings, sculpture, and architecture, are all homages to the ongoing viability of the Bauhaus spirit of pro-technological experimentation. Bill's is not the work of the innovator. His contribution to art and design is as follower of an already established idea and visualization, and he remains tightly within the tradition and its systems while searching out possible variables which are direct extensions of the pre-established ideas and approaches.

The anti-individualist philosophy underlying Bill's work has resulted in an output which stays very close in both look and conception to his artist-teachers at the Bauhaus. He has located some variables which are subtly realized and which never relax in their affirmation of the exclusive principles on which they are based. As painter and sculptor, Bill has made a limited contribution, laudable for its tenacity of belief, yet too often openly dependent on the constructivist, neo-Plasticist tradition he inherited quite literally. There is greater feeling of success in Bill's industrial designs; their impersonal feeling, formal simplicity, use of industrial materials, and crisp sleekness speak of a period mode which has found pertinence for its infusion of high art ideas into popular culture with wide distribution. Bill has stated that at the Bauhaus he found clarity, confirmation of his own views. There can be little doubt of his commitment to a tradition which is among the most fruitful of its time. Yet that tradition, like all others, yearns and needs to be broken, to be used conceptually as a route into future directions for the following generations, not to be adopted or co-opted in a literal fashion. The originators of the Bauhaus proclaimed a post-past view, one in which new discoveries in technology and science are adapted to art and design with an attitude of adventurous experimentation. Such an adventure is considerably watered down by a second-generation vantage point.

—Barbara Cavaliere

BINDER, Joseph.

American painter, typographer and graphic designer. Born in Vienna, Austria, 3 March 1898; emigrated to the United States in 1935: naturalized, 1944. Studied painting, under Berthold Loffler, at the Kunstgewerbeschule, Vienna, 1922–26: Staatspreis 1926. Served in the Austrian Army, 1916–18. Married Carla Neuschil in 1925. Apprenticed to lithographer Robert Scheffler, Vienna, 1912–16; freelance designer, establishing Joseph Binder Graphic Studio, in Vienna, 1924–35, and in New York, 1936–72: designed for Zuntz Kaffee Import, Julius Meinl, Milchgenossenschaft, the American Red Cross, United Airlines, United Nations, *American Graphics, Fortune, Graphis,* etc.; art director and designer, United States Navy Department, Washington, D.C. 1948–58. Visiting lecturer: School of the Art Institute of Chicago; Society of Typographic Arts, Chicago; Minneapolis School of Art; Chouinard School of Art, Los Angeles; Teachers College, Columbia University, New York; Pratt Institute, Brooklyn, New York. National Poster Campaign Committee Member, *Fortune* magazine, New York, 1942. **Exhibitions:** Austrian Werkbund, Vienna, 1935; Architectural League, New York, 1937; Academy of Art, Vienna, 1963; Rose Fried Gallery, New York, 1965, 1967, 1969; Austrian Institute, New York, 1966; Bucknell University, Lewisburg, Pennsylvania, 1967; Austrian Museum of Art and Industry, Vienna, 1972. **Collections:** Cornell University, Ithaca, New York; Metropolitan Museum of Art, New York; Museum of Modern Art, New York; Neuberger Museum, Purchase, New York; Library of Congress, Washington, D.C.; Smithsonian Institution, Washington, D.C.; Austrian Museum of Applied Arts, Vienna. Recipient: Vertex Bulbs Poster Prize, Vienna, 1915; Vienna Music and Theatre Poster Prize, 1924; Baron C. Collier Medal, 1939, Annual Award Medal, 1944, and Certificate of Merit, 1956, Art Directors Club of New York; New York World's Fair Poster Prize, 1939; National Defense Department Poster Prize, Museum of Modern Art, New York, 1941; Direct Mail Certificate of Merit, New York, 1948; American Red Cross Poster Prize, 1952; Outdoor Advertising Award, Art Directors Club of Chicago, 1953; United States Navy Department Poster Prize, 1956; City of Vienna Medal of Honour, 1969. Honorary Professor, Austrian Ministry of Education, 1952; Honorary Member, BOEG Society of Graphic Designers, Vienna, 1952. *Died* (in Vienna) *26 June 1972.*

Works:

Meinl Kaffee poster, for Julius Meinl AG, Vienna, 1923.
Musik und Theaterfest poster, for the Buro des Festes, Vienna, 1924.
Meinl Tee poster, for Julius Meinl AG, Vienna, 1925.
Milch gibt Kraft poster, for the Milchgenossenschaft, Vienna, 1928.
Asko 1931 poster, for the Asko Zweite Arbeiter-Olympiade, Vienna, 1931.
Zunzt Kaffee poster, for Zuntz Kaffee Import, Munich, 1932.
Tank Tracks cover, for *Fortune* magazine, New York, 1938.
A & P Iced Coffee series of advertisements, for Paris and Pearl Advertising Agency, New York, 1939.
Buy American Art poster, for *Fortune* National Poster Campaign Committee, New York, 1942.
Skyscraper cover, for *Graphis* magazine, Zurich, no. 32, 1948.
Pax United Nations poster, for the Museum of Modern Art competition, New York, 1948.

Answer the Call poster, for the American Red Cross, 1952.
The Most Important Wheels in America poster, for the Association of American Railroads, Washington, D.C., 1952.
Join the New Era poster, for the United States Navy Department, Washington, D.C., 1955.

Publications:

By BINDER: book—*Colour in Advertising,* London 1934; book designed—*Internationale Buchkunst Ausstellung,* exhibition catalogue, Leipzig 1927.

On BINDER: books—*Die neue Grafik/The New Graphic Design* by Karl Gerstner and Markus Kutter, Teufen and London 1959; *The Poster: An Illustrated History from 1860* by Harold F. Hutchinson, London and Toronto 1968; *Joseph Binder, New York: Non-Objective Art,* exhibition catalogue with introduction by Wilhelm Mrazek, Vienna, 1972; *Joseph Binder: An Artist and a Lifestyle* by Carla Binder, Vienna 1976; *Advertising: Reflections of a Century* by Bryan Holme, London 1982.

Joseph Binder belongs to the generation of graphic designers, including A. M. Cassandre and E. McKnight Kauffer, that brought the vitality and design qualities of modern art to the European poster. Binder's posters are based on close and careful observation of the world, but these observations are translated into a graphic language of great visual impact and energy. This is achieved through simplification that Binder learned from early modern European design and painting.

During his Vienna period, Binder applied several influences to pictorial poster design. From the Wiener Werkstätte, he learned simplified composition and the use of geometric patterns as design elements. Cubism's planar reduction of figurative subjects, constructivism's diagonal movements, and the asymmetrical balance of de Stijl were other important influences.

Figures and objects in his work are simplified into basic forms, consistent with Cézanne's precept that all objects in nature are based on the elemental geometric forms of cone, cube, and sphere. Binder expressed dimension by placing two flat planes of color side by side to represent light and shadow on the subject. To strengthen the graphic quality of objects in his posters, Binder rejected traditional perspective drawing in preference for orthogonal or parallel perspective construction.

Binder favored the presentation of symbolic persons or objects placed against a simple background of flat or modulated color. His posters are generally organized with strong horizontal, vertical, or diagonal construction lines.

During the 1930's, American design was markedly affected by immigrants from Europe. Due to his early arrival and the more pictorial and accessible nature of his work (as compared to the more formal and geometric work of constructivist and Bauhaus designers who came to America), Binder had an important early impact upon the development of modernist graphic design in America. After coming to the United States, Binder used the airbrush to execute his poster designs. This introduced the refined, modulated form and color that are characteristic of pictorial graphic design from the 1930's and 1940's.

—Philip B. Meggs

Acton Bjørn: *Margarethe Bowl* in melamine, for Rosti, 1955

BJØRN, Acton.

Danish industrial designer. Born in Copenhagen, 23 September 1910. Studied at the Technical High School, Copenhagen, 1926–30; Royal Academy of Fine Arts, Copenhagen, 1931–32. Married Maureen Egeland in 1950; children: Juliane, Thomas and Andreas. Freelance designer, Copenhagen, since 1949: partner, with Prince Sigvard Bernadotte, in Bernadotte and Bjørn industrial design firm, with offices in Stockholm and Copenhagen, from 1950: also independent designer, establishing Acton Bjorns Tegnestue ApS, Copenhagen, from 1966. **Exhibitions:** *Design Since 1945,* Philadelphia Museum of Art, 1983; *Industrial Design in Focus,* Kunstindustrimuseum, Copenhagen, 1989. Recipient: American Society of Industrial Designers Award, 1958; Eurostar Award, 1963, 1968; World Star Award, 1970; Dunhill Prize, London, 1980; ID Classics Prize, Danish Design Council, 1985. Address: Toldbodgade 89, 1253 Copenhagen, Denmark.

Works:

Kitchen utensils, for Rosti, from 1955.
Office machinery, for Facit, from 1958.
Kitchen utensils, for Morsoe, from 1960.
Glassware, for Nordfalk, from 1960.
Radiator thermostats, for Danfoss, from 1963.
Glassware, for Vega, from 1965.
Transformer stations in Denmark, for Siemens, from 1972.
Bathroom equipment and fixtures, for Dansk Pressalit, from 1973.
Carpets, from EGE-Taepper, from 1979.

Publications:

On BJØRN: books—*Dansk Møbelkunst* by Viggo Sten Moller and Sven Erik Møller, Copenhagen 1951; *Packaging: An International Survey of Package Design,* edited by Walter Herdeg, Zurich 1959; *Svensk Form/Forma Sueca,* edited by Ake Stavenlow and Ake H. Huldt, Stockholm 1961; *A Treasury of Scandinavian Design,* edited by Erik Zahle, New York 1961; *Konsten i Sverige: Konsthantverk, Konstindustri, Design 1875–1975* by Dag Widman, Stockholm 1975; *Industrial Design* by John Heskett, London 1980; *Design Since 1945,* edited by Kathryn Hiesinger and George Marcus, Philadelphia and London 1983.

BJÖRQUIST, Karin.

Swedish ceramics designer. Born in Saffle, 2 January 1927. Studied at the National School of Art, Craft and Design, Stockholm, 1945–50. Married Lennart Lindkvist in 1954; children: Jonas and Sara. Designer at Gustavsberg Porcelain Factory, Stockholm, since 1950: assistant designer to Wilhelm Kage, 1950–60, chief designer, 1960–80, and artistic director, 1980–85. **Exhibitions:** Milan Triennale, 1954; *H55,* Helsingborg, 1955; Nordiska Kompaniet, Stockholm, 1956; *Nordisk Keramik 1,* Lunds Konsthall, Sweden, 1961; Malmö Museum, Sweden, 1961; Georg Jensen Inc., New York, 1964; *Hantverkets, 60-tal,* Nationalmuseum, Stockholm, 1968; *Gustavsberg 150 Ar,* Nationalmuseum, Stockholm, 1975; *Svensk Form: Swedish Craft and Design,* Victoria and Albert Museum, London, 1980 (toured); *Contemporary Swedish Design,* Nationalmuseum, Stockholm, 1982 (toured); *Scandinavian Modern Design 1880–1980,* Cooper-Hewitt Museum, New York, 1982 (toured); *Design in Sweden Now,* toured Canada and Australia, 1985–87; *The Lunning Prize,* Nationalmuseum, Stockholm, 1986; *Scandinavian Design: A Way of Life,* Seibu Museum of Art, Tokyo, 1987 (toured); *Faces of Swedish Design,* IBM Gallery, New York, 1988 (toured); *Scandinavian Ceramics and Glass,* Victoria and Albert Museum, London, 1989. **Collections:** Nationalmuseum, Stockholm; Röhsska Konstslöjdmuseet, Goteborg; Malmö Museum; Museum of Applied Art, Copenhagen; Museum of Applied Art, Trondheim; Victoria and Albert Museum, London; Museum of Applied Art, Vienna; Museum of Modern Art, New York; Cooper-Hewitt Museum, New York. Recipient: Gold Medal, Milan Triennale, 1954; Svensk Form/Good Form Prize, Stockholm, 1961; Lunning Prize, 1963; Gregor Paulsson Statuette, Stockholm, 1973; Prince Eugen Medal, 1982; *Vi* Magazine Design Prize, Stockholm, 1986; Design Excellence Award, Swedish Society of Crafts and Design, 1986. Address: Johannesgatan 26, 111 38 Stockholm, Sweden.

Works:

Everyday tableware, for Gustavsberg, 1957.
Ceramic murals, for Nacka Hospital, Sweden, 1962.
Ceramic murals, for the Mariatorget underground station, Stockholm, 1963.

Ceramic murals, for SKS offices, Göteborg, Sweden, 1966.
Ceramic fountains, for the municipality of Valbo, Sweden, 1967.
Octagon tableware, for Gustavsberg, 1968.
Ceramic murals, for Löwenströmska Hospital, Göteborg, Sweden, 1968.
Ceramic mural, for the *Arbetet* newspaper offices, Malmö, Sweden, 1968.
Ceramic mural, for Österåker prison, Sweden, 1970.
Ceramic murals and fountains, for Östrabo School, Udevalla, Sweden, 1970.
Ceramic mural, for the *Aftonbladet* newspaper offices, Göteborg, Sweden, 1970.
Ceramic stove, for the Swedish Embassy, Moscow, 1970.
Ceramic stove, for the Swedish Embassy, Paris, 1973.
BT stoneware, for Gustavsberg, 1973–82.
Octavius stoneware, for Gustavsberg, 1974.
Ceramic mural, for the Sveriges Riksbank, Stockholm, 1975–76.
BV bone chinaware, for Gustavsberg, 1978.
BV stoneware, for Gustavsberg, 1979.
BA Stockholm bone chinaware, for Gustavsberg, 1987.
Ceramic murals, for the Sturebadet public baths, Stockholm, 1988.

Publications:

On BJÖRQUIST: books—*Svensk Form/Forma Sueca* by Åke Stavenlow and Åke H. Huldt, Stockholm 1961; *Karin Björquist of Gustavsberg,* booklet edited by Georg Jensen Inc., New York 1965; *Design in Sweden,* edited by Lennart Lindkvist, Stockholm 1972, 1977; *Scandinavian Design: Objects of a Life Style* by Eileene Harrison Beer, New York 1975; *Konsthantvek, Konstindustri, Design 1875–1975* by Dag Widman, Stockholm 1975; *Keramik* by Ulf Hård af Segerstad, Stockholm 1976; *Scandinavian Modern Design 1880–1980,* edited by David Revere McFadden, New York 1982; *Contemporary Swedish Design,* exhibition catalogue by Monica Boman, Lennart Lindkvist and others, Stockholm 1982; *Serviser fran Gustavsberg* by Inga Arno-Berg, Stockholm 1985; *The Lunning Prize,* exhibition catalogue edited by Helena Dahlbäck Lutteman and Marianne Uggla, Stockholm 1986; *Made in Sweden: Art, Handicrafts, Design* by Anja Notini, London 1987; *Faces of Swedish Design,* exhibition catalogue edited by Monica Boman, Stockholm 1988.

People are different, so designers should not create finished, unchangeable interiors. But creating a beautiful basis for a home gives something which can be built upon. Most people have jobs in which they have no creative opportunities, so they have a need to express themselves when they get home. It is wrong to make decisions for people. They must be able to create their own personal profile.

The two most important pieces of furniture in the home are the bed and the set table. About beds I need say no more. At the table one meets one's friends, who enjoy sitting at a well-decorated, functional table. And since the world today is so full of products, it is important that designers create meaningful articles. Above all, it is important to accept the age one lives in, to be neither nostalgic nor hypnotized by passing fashions.

—Karin Björquist

In principle Karin Björquist works in only one field: ceramics. And she prefers working for mass production. Karin had already opted for industry when she graduated: "I wanted the anonymous."

Some prototypes of her "Everyday" service were presented at the Helsingborg exhibition H55 in 1955. This service had everything one could ask for. "Everyday" is pure and practical, yet nonetheless friendly and human. Since then, Karin Björquist has produced many variants of her excellent base products. Her services usually tend to be white. The decorations she has occasionally added are simple and discrete, especially for services. Superimposing a fish on something sky blue or patterned does not fit in with Karin's philosophy. Her ceramic output is simple and self-evident. In a way it is

eternally youthful. But the fact is that she is acquiring the status of the great classicists, though she wears the mantle lightly. With more than 30 years' good and prominent output behind her, she cannot help becoming something of a historical figure. Don't make any mistake: with her working methods, she is more up-to-date than most others.

Karin Björquist is not afraid of simplicity. But she combines it with a purity and practicality which are poles apart from the dryness and dogmatism that functionalism can sometimes lapse into. Hers is not a clinical purity but a simplicity full of affection and feeling. Moreover, she has passed through a process of development, today emphasizing things which she did not use to. It is partly due to her sterling contribution that baseware has become more of a self-evident phenomenon. Now there are other things to be brought out—our perpetual need of a feast for the eye, for example. She herself says that one becomes less dogmatic with advancing age. But this change is also connected with the attainment of ambitions, added to the realization that beauty is one of the essentials of life.

Who can lay a table with such inspiration as Karin? Who can make such wonderful floral arrangements? Generous bunches of the driest straws or overwhelmingly magnificent lilies and roses help us to understand how fine her jardinières and pots are. When Karin lays the table for a meal, she naturally uses her own service, but she likes to add items by kindred spirits in her arrangements or collages. Gunnar Wennerberg's hepatica decorations from the turn of the century fit well into her world. So do pictures of English gardens, in which the correct flowers thrive together with beautiful stones and shells. And, of course, the ceramics of Wilhelm Kåge.

Karin inherited Kåge's studio at Gustavsberg. He was her great predecessor, active from 1917

until his death in 1960. He introduced "Argenta"—silver ornamentation on a green background. In 1987 Karin took up this special technique in her own way: silver strips on large dishes with folded brims, on the edges of spouts, and as a silver accentuation on the feet of shell-shaped vessels. Karin's color scale is black, white, or pale tints with silver or gold. Kåge can be discerned in the background as a source of inspiration. The strict forms of the Empire style, which so well suit the late 1980's, may also be in the background. Or is it only Karin Björquist?

There is a great deal of responsibility involved in producing new things when so many exist already. But this does not lead her to refrain from new production. Everything has to be properly thought out. And, of course, the production of a new service nowadays is an immense undertaking. It may take years. The task is not only to devise an attractive new form, or to combine saleable parts into a whole: the starting point is the existence of a need.

It is quite an experience listening to Karin's deliberations about new restaurant tableware. Strength and stackability are fairly obvious requirements, but there is also the need for light weight—to save the backs of the waiting staff—refinements of manufacturing technique, and the overall appearance of the finished product. This is how classics are made.

In 1986 Karin Björquist's new bone china service was given the award for Excellent Swedish Design by the Swedish Society of Crafts and Design. The jury said that "the service skilfully utilizes the possibilities of bone china for combining strength with thinness and elegance. The design is pure and universal, and carries the decoration well. The functions are well tested. This service may become a classic."

It is an elegant service for formal use, with sparse decoration in black and gold by Jonas Lindkvist or her own celadon green brim ac-

Karin Björquist: Bowl in glazed porcelain with silver decoration, for Gustavsberg, 1986

centuated by thin gold edges. Even such a representative of simplicity and basic function as Karin Björquist can be seen in the 80's as showy and retrospective. Because what is the celadon decoration "Paris" if not a look at the 30's, the decade of *art déco*? Karin knows she has done right in creating a formal service. The need is there—she feels this herself—so why should we accept anything less than the very best?

—Helena Dahlbäck Lutteman

BLACK, Misha.

British architect, exhibition and industrial designer. Born in Baku, Azerbaydzhan, Russia, 16 October 1910; emigrated to Britain in 1912: subsequently naturalized. Studied at Central School of Arts and Crafts, London, but mainly self-taught in design, from 1929. Married Helen Lilian Evans in 1935 (divorced, 1952); children: Jacob and Julia; married Edna Joan Fairbrother in 1955; son: Oliver. Architect and designer, in London, from 1929; partner, Industrial Design Partnership, 1933–39; Principal Exhibition Architect, Ministry of Information, 1940–45; founder-partner, with Milner Gray, Design Research Unit, 1945–77; partner, in Black, Bayes and Gibson architects, 1963–77: design consultant to the Gas, Light and Coke Company, Kardomah Limited, Tea Bureau, Festival of Britain, British Overseas Airways Corporation, British Railways Board, Beagle Aircraft, London Transport, South Wales Switchgear Limited, Vickers Limited, Hong Kong Rapid Transit Railways, etc. Professor of Industrial Design, 1959–75, and Emeritus, 1975–77, Royal College of Art, London. Chairman, Artists International Association, London, 1934–40; Council Member, 1938–52 and 1956–57, and President, 1954–56, Society of Industrial Artists and Designers, London; Advisory Council Member, Society of Education in Art, London, 1942–59, and Institute of Contemporary Arts, London, 1951–67; National Council Member, 1952–54, and President, 1974–76, Design and Industries Association, London; Member, Council of Industrial Design, London, 1955–64; Executive Board Member, 1957–65, President, 1959–61, and Education Commission Chairman, 1965–69, ICSID International Council of Societies of Industrial Design; Vice-President, Modular Society, London, 1965–77; Advisory Council Member, Science Museum, London, 1966–77; Trustee, 1968–77, and Conservation Committee Chairman, 1974–77, British Museum, London; Member, 1969–77, and Chairman, 1973–77, Culture Advisory Committee, United Kingdom Commission for UNESCO; Council Member, Polytechnic of Newcastle-upon-Tyne, 1969–73; Engineering Design Advisory Committee Member, Design Council, London, 1971–74; Scientific Advisory Committee Member, Experimental Cartography Unit (NERC), London, 1973–75; Master of the Faculty of Royal Designers for Industry, Royal Society of Arts, London, 1973–75; Engineering Section President, British Association for the Advancement of Science, London, 1974; National Theatre Advisory Committee Member, London, 1974–76. Recipient: Fellow, 1945, and Gold Medal, 1965, Society of Industrial Artists, London; Officer, Order of the British Empire, 1945; Royal Designer for Industry, Royal Soci-

ety of Arts, London, 1957; Fellow, Royal College of Art, London, 1960; Companion of the Institute of Mechanical Engineers, London, 1969; Knight Bachelor, 1972; Fellow, Faculty of Architects and Surveyors, London, 1974. Honorary Doctorates: Royal College of Art, London, 1968; University of Bradford, 1974. *Died* (in London) *11 August 1977.*

Works:

Pavilion at the Spanish-American Exhibition in Seville, for Rio-Tinto, 1929.
Kardomah Coffee bars in London and Manchester, for the Liverpool and China Tea Company Limited, 1936–50.
Peace Pavilion interiors, at the International Exposition, Paris, 1937.
Interiors of the United Kingdom Steel, Coal, Shipbuilding and Public Welfare Halls, at the Empire Exhibition, Glasgow, 1938.

British Pavilion Public Welfare and Maritime Halls, at the World's Fair, New York, 1939.
The Birth of an Egg-Cup display, at the *Britain Can Make It* exhibition, Victoria and Albert Museum, London, 1946.
Regatta Restaurant and Dome of Discovery displays, at the Festival of Britain, London, 1948–51.
Darkness into Daylight exhibition layouts, Science Museum, London, 1948.
United Kingdom Pavilion, at the Rhodes Centenary Exhibition, Bulawayo, Southern Rhodesia, 1953.
Public rooms interiors on the liner *Oriana,* for Pacific and Orient Shipping Company, 1957–60.
Ontario Government Pavilion at *Expo 67,* Montreal, 1966–67.
Charles Clore Pavilion mammal house at London Zoo, for the Zoological Society, 1967.
Synagogue interiors on the liner *Queen Elizabeth 2,* for Cunard Shipping, 1969.

Misha Black: *Birth of an Egg Cup* exhibit, at *Britain Can Make It*, Victoria and Albert Museum, London, 1946

Publications:

By BLACK: books—*Physical Planning,* with others, London 1945; *The Practice of Design,* with others, London 1946; *Exhibition Design,* editor, London 1950; *Public Interiors: An International Survey,* editor, London 1960; *The Architect's Anguish,* Leicester 1962; *Group Practice of Design,* with others, London 1967; *Industrial Design—An International Survey,* editor, London and Paris 1967; *The Misha Black Australian Papers,* edited by Trevor Wilson, Sydney 1970; *Papers on Design: Selected Writings,* edited by A. Blake, Oxford 1983.

On BLACK: books—*Modern Furniture* by E. Nelson Exton and Frederic H. Littman, London, 1936; *Design in British Industry: A Mid-Century Survey* by Michael Farr, Cambridge 1955; *Window Display 2,* edited by Walter Herdeg, Zurich 1961; *Modern Graphics* by Keith Murgatroyd, London 1969; *The Aspen Papers: Twenty Years of Design Theory,* edited by Reyner Banham, London 1974; *A Tonic to the Nation: The Festival of Britain 1951* by Mary Banham and Bevis Hillier, London 1976; *Industrial Design* by John Heskett, London 1980; *Misha Black* by Avril Blake, London 1984; *The Conran Directory of Design,* edited by Stephen Bayley, London 1985; *Eye for Industry: Royal Designers for Industry 1936–1986,* exhibition catalogue by Fiona MacCarthy and Patrick Nuttgens, London 1986; *Design Source Book* by Penny Sparke and others, London 1986.

Fluent and highly articulate Misha Black favoured radical but pragmatic solutions to design problems. "The difference between an arrogant conscious aesthetic and a conscientious searching for the most elegant solution is fundamental to my argument," he said. Black was the champion of many causes, from the prewar, left-wing Artists International Association to the most august, postwar International Council of Societies of Industrial Design. He relished the challenge of exhibition design, with its opportunity to express complex ideas in fresh and straightforward ways, its problems of coordinating a team of different skills, its pressures of limited time and resources, and its chance to present temporary, showcase solutions to a number of design problems. In his hands, a deceptively simple exhibition on the making of an eggcup (at the *Britian can make it* exhibition of 1946) became a revealing object-lesson on the problems confronting the designer of a simple, mass-produced object and on the necessary stages of industrial production.

This ability to design with simplicity and ingenuity but not extravagance made him a popular choice with cost-conscious organisations wishing to improve their corporate images and public places. His prewar designs, ranging from radios to the highly regarded Kardomah cafés, had already established a reputation for elegant combination of simple elements. Many of the larger projects that followed owed much to his ability to coordinate and enthuse designers and clients. His long association with Milner Gray before and after the Industrial Design Partnership (the first multi-skill design partnership, founded in the 1930's) and through the privations of wartime exhibition work laid the foundations for the highly innovative and successful postwar Design Research Unit, which they led. As well as building up a large portfolio of architectural work, interior design commissions, and consultancies with large organisations, such as British Rail, he became passionately involved with his later role as a teacher at the Royal College of Art. There, he was very important in developing its contacts with industry and industrial research. This helped to change

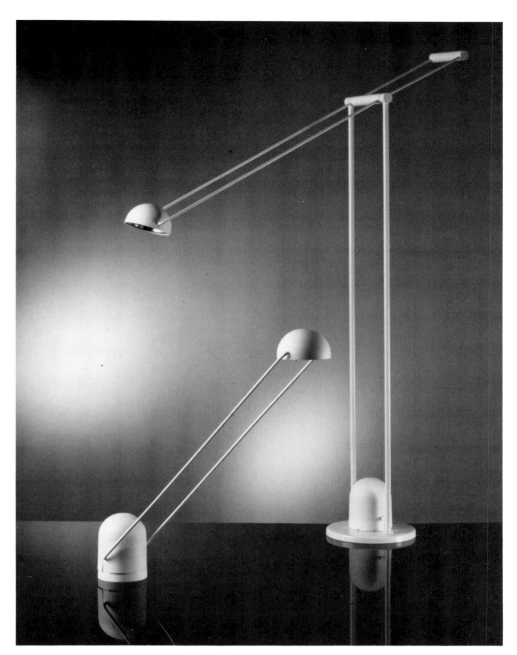

Robert Blaich: *Dimmlite* desk lamps, for Philips, 1987

the basic training of many future industrial designers.

Within his own profession and on public advisory bodies, he was much in demand for his skills as a chairman; he possessed the knack of extracting the essence of ideas, the ability to control unruly meetings with humour and purpose, and a talent for drawing together the threads of an argument and translating discussion into positive action.

—Anthony J. Coulson

BLAICH, Robert I(an).

American industrial, graphic and packaging designer. Born in Syracuse, New York, 25 February 1930. Studied architecture, Syracuse University, New York, 1948–52: BFA 1952.

Married Janet Streithof in 1953; children: Robert, David and James. Designer, 1953–60, Manager of Special Products Division, 1960–68, Vice President in Charge of Design and Development, 1968–79, and Vice President in Charge of Corporate Design and Communications, 1976–79, Herman Miller Inc., Zeeland, Michigan; also Managing Director, Herman Miller AG, Basle, Switzerland, 1969–70; Founder-President, Connectives Inc., communications and design consultants, Grand Rapids, Michigan, 1979–80; Managing Director of Corporate Design, N. V. Philips, Eindhoven, Netherlands, since 1980. Advisory Panel Member, National Endowment for the Arts, Washington, D.C., 1968–78; Trustee, Kendall School of Design, Grand Rapids, Michigan, 1970–75; Trustee and Vice President, Grand Rapids Art Museum, Michigan, 1970–80; Trustee, American Federation of Arts, New York, 1975–80; Environmental Arts Panel Chairman, Michigan Council for the Arts, 1976–78; Art Advisory Committee Member, Cranbrook Academy of Art, Bloomfield Hills, Michigan, 1976–78; Chairman, Design Michigan Program, 1977–78; Board Member and Vice President, 1983, and President, 1987, International Council of Societies of Industrial Design (ICSID); Design Management Advisory Board Member, London Business School, from 1984; Design Advisory Board Member, Formica Corporation, 1984–86; Advisory Board Member, Art Center College of Design, Vevey, Switzerland, from 1984; Advisory Board Member, Design Management Institute, Boston, 1987; Director, International Design Education Foundation, U.S.A., 1989. Visiting Lecturer and Speaker, at numerous universities, congresses and professional institutes, in Europe and the United States, since 1980. **Exhibitions:** *Design in Michigan 1967/1977*, Cranbrook Academy of Art, Bloomfield Hills, Michigan, 1978 (toured); *New Design for Old*, Boilerhouse/ Victoria and Albert Museum, London, 1986; *Natural Design*, Boilerhouse/Victoria and Albert Museum, London, 1986; *Natural Design*, Museum Boymans-van Beuningen, Rotterdam, 1987. Recipient: Governor's Recognition Award, Michigan, 1977; President's Medal, International Council of Graphic Design Associations (ICOGRADA), 1983; *Time* magazine Man of the Year Award, 1984. Fellow, Industrial Designers Society of America, 1981; Fellow, Royal Society of Arts, London, 1982. Member: Industrial Designers Society of America, 1967; American Society of Interior Designers, 1975; American Institute of Graphic Arts, 1978; Kring Industriele Ontwerpers, Netherlands, 1981. Address: N. V. Philips, Corporate Industrial Design, Postbus 218, 5600 MD Eindhoven, Netherlands.

Works (as Director of Design):

All Charles Eames products, for Herman Miller, 1960–78.
All George Nelson products, for Herman Miller, 1960–78.
All Alexander Girard textiles, for Herman Miller, 1960–78.
Action Office System, for Herman Miller, 1964–78.
Chadwick Seating, for Herman Miller, 1971.
Ergon Seating, for Herman Miller, 1972.
Wilkes Seating, for Herman Miller, 1972.
Burdick Office System, for Herman Miller, 1979.
All products, systems, packaging and graphics, for N. V. Philips, 1980–89.

Publications:

By BLAICH: articles—"Design: The Best of '83" in *Time* (New York), January 1984; "Design as a Corporate Strategy" in *Design Talks,* edited by Peter Gorb, London 1988; "Corporate Industrial Design" in *Interieur 88,* conference booklet, Brussels 1988; numerous articles in *ICSID News* (Helsinki), 1988–89; "Design— A Personal Account" in *Design Issues* (Cambridge, Massachusetts), Spring 1989; "Philips is not Guilty of Design Imperialism", in *Designweek* (London), 26 May 1989.

On BLAICH: books—*Design in Michigan 1967/1977* by Katherine McCoy, Detroit 1978; *New Design for Old,* exhibition catalogue with texts by Helen Hamlyn. Eric Midwinter and others, London 1986; *Philips: A Study of Corporate Management Design* by John Heskett, London 1989; *The Design of Herman Miller* by Ralph Caplan, New York 19..?; articles—in *The Wall Street Journal* (New York), 13 January 1988; *Designweek* (London), 21 April 1989.

In his book Nelson on Design, the late architect and designer George Nelson said, "The de-

signer is the latest of the human resources available to business in its eternal struggle to remain successfully competitive. Design is seen as a legitimate and effective tool for business and industry."

The premise that design has an important strategic role to play in business management is one that is still relatively unexplored by most businesses and underutilized by all but a few companies worldwide. Perhaps some of the problem begins with failure to make a connection between design and innovation. Indeed, there seem to be differing opinions about what constitutes innovation.

Christopher Lorenz, management editor of The Financial Times, states: "Good product design includes ease of manufacture, marketability, maintenance, reliable performance and cost effectiveness to both producer and user. Of course it includes a well-designed exterior . . . most often referred to as 'styling' ". Too often design and styling have been seen as synonymous. Actually, styling traditionally has represented a much more limited set of activities in the final phase in a sequential development process, after all the important decisions have already been made.

However, the Japanese gave a new interpretation to the concept of styling in their success with consumer electronics. They did not invent the technologies. These came from the United States and Europe. But the Japanese were innovative in their application of design, which in this case was styling, and in their marketing. The difference had to do with the process. The Japanese integrated the design activity into the whole process of market strategy and product development at the initial stages. In this sense, styling was innovative.

I can best analyze the design management process by telling you something about my own experiences. Although educated as an architect, I gravitated towards industrial design and communications design and have developed experience in design management over a 35 year period. I was associated with Herman Miller for 27 years and with Philips for the past nine. Even though what I was doing during the 35-year period was design management, it has only been recently—about the past ten years—that design management has been defined as an activity. Design management is a relatively new element in design professionalism, growing out of the recognition of increasingly sophisticated interaction with other areas of corporate planning and implementation. Successful innovations are essentially impossible today without an interrelationship between engineering, marketing, manufacturing and design. Design management establishes the possibility that a company has a design program instead of an informal activity.

As the managing director of Corporate Industrial Design (CID), it is my responsibility to ensure that design is an integral part of the company's strategy and policy. CID is responsible for the design, graphics and packaging of all Philips' products for consumer electronics, domestic appliances, personal care, lighting, telecommunications, data systems, medical systems and scientific and industrial equipment. Our goal is to produce the highest quality designs of which we are capable. A goal for Philips is to produce high-quality products.

To accomplish this the design management process involves not only ensuring that CID achieves its goal of producing high-quality designs, but that the design value added to the product is seamlessly and efficiently integrated into the entire design-to-market process so that the corporate goal of producing top-quality products can be achieved. Thus, the design management process is very largely about managing to achieve quality results. The design attributes of

a product constitute a value that is quickly observable to consumers.

I believe that the product is the most important statement a company can make about its image—it is the image.

—Robert I. Blaich

In the best possible sense Robert Ian Blaich represents the transformation of a competent design manager into a corporate design director with a broadened perspective of the global importance of design and a personal conviction of a designer's social and cultural responsibilities.

In 1952, after receiving the BFA degree from Syracuse University in Syracuse, New York, he accepted a position in New York city where he became familiar with show-casing and marketing aspects of furniture. From there he joined Herman Miller Company of Zeeland, Michigan, manufacturers of modern furniture, that was expanding into products and product systems for institutional and office environments. The company appointed him in 1960 to be Manager of its Special Products Division for new product development for educational and institutional fields. He worked directly with consultant designers such as Robert Propst, George Nelson, Charles Eames and Alexander Girard to develop and bring to market new furniture systems for storage and seating for schools, libraries and business offices.

In 1968 Blaich became Vice President of Design and Development for Herman Miller and was given responsibility for long range product planning and development. This search and development of new designers for the company as well as the selection and design of all corporate facilities from administration and manufacturing to offices and showrooms of the corporation in the United States and abroad. After 1976 his responsibility expanded to include Corporate Design and Communications related to the image and presentation of Herman Miller to its various publics. Between 1969 and 1970 he also served as Managing Director of Herman Miller A.G. at Basle, Switzerland, developing new design resources and introducing new products and systems into European markets.

On the public service side of his career, by the mid 1970s Robert Blaich was active in Washington as a member of selection panels reviewing applicants for grants from the National Endowment for the Arts. Over the period of celebration of the nation's Bicentennial in 1976, Federal Design Assemblies were held in Washington to focus the attention of elected officials and career employees of the government on design as an indispensable element in the quality and image of the federal government in the eyes of the public at home and abroad. An outcome of this was that Blaich initiated a similar program, Design Michigan, in his home state to increase an awareness of the designed environment among government and business people as well as the general public.

Robert Blaich elected to leave his position with Herman Miller in 1979 in order to establish Connectives Inc., an independent organization offering consulting services in corporate communications, publishing, graphics, product design, interiors and marketing. This move as well as his public service and the range of his experience, with Herman Miller brought him to the attention of the N. V. Philips Company of the Netherlands that was seeking for a new director to reorganize its design activities on a global basis. The result was an offer from Philips to him that was too challenging to pass up.

In 1980, Robert Blaich became Director of Design for the Philips Company in charge of product and packaging design for all of the company's product divisions. In this capacity he was instrumental in restructuring the design programs into one that designs and develops products on a global scale thus anticipating the entire company's shift to a global strategy. In order to implement this program within the Corporate Design program Blaich organized design workshops and seminars that brought outside consultants into a working and communicating relationship with internal designers and technicians of the design center on such subjects as Youth Markets, User Interface, Product semantics and Communications in product design. Another program of the Center invites internationally recognized speakers to share their special expertise.

Blaich organized the Professional Harmonization Program in 1986 that brought all of the Philips professional products for Telecommunications and Data systems, Test and Measurement and Medical Systems under a Professional House Style that integrated all related products. This program was awarded the 1st prize for Ergonomics at *Ergodesign 86* in Montreaux, Switzerland. In addition to this award, the Philips Company has received over 250 prizes since Blaich joined. He is, indeed, a global force for design.

—Arthur J. Pulos

BLASE, Karl Oskar.
German book, advertising, display, packaging and typographic designer. Born in Cologne, 24 March 1925. Studied design, Staatliche Werkkunstschule, Wuppertal, 1945–49. Served in the German Army, 1944–45. Married Margarete Speckenbach in 1952; sons: Christoph, Boris and Benjamin. Worked as design assistant, Jupp Ernst Studio, Wuppertal, 1949–50; founder-partner, with Felix Müller, of Müller-Blase Studio, Wuppertal, 1950–52; director of Amerika-Haus graphics studio, in Frankfurt, 1952–54, and in Bonn, 1954–58; also freelance designer, in Bonn, 1954–58, and in Kassel, from 1958: has worked for *Form* magazine, 1957–60, Hessische Metallwerke, 1958–74, Atlas Film Distributors, 1959–66, Igus textile company, from 1963, Kassel *Documenta* exhibitions, from 1964, and Kassel Staatstheater, 1966–78; Art Consultant to the German Postal Service, 1988. Founder-Member, Novum Gesellschaft fur neue Graphik, Frankfurt, 1959. Professor of Applied Arts, Kunstakademie, Kassel, since 1958. **Exhibitions:** Museum Schloss Morsbroich, Leverkusen, 1952; Kunstsammlungen, Bonn, 1958, 1969; Landesmuseum, Oldenburg, 1965; Kunstverein, Kassel, 1967, 1984, 1986; Galerie Porta, Wuppertal, 1968, 1970; Galerie Wendelin Niedlich, Stuttgart, 1970, 1972; Studio Kausch, Kassel, 1971, 1972; Musée Palais de l'Athenée, Geneva, 1971; Staatstheater, Kassel, 1972; Kunstverein, Bonn, 1974; Haus am Lutzowplatz, West Berlin, 1981; Kunstverein, Offenbach, 1983; Galerie Circulus, Bonn, 1984; Kunsthaus am Museum, Cologne, 1986; Gesellschaft für Kunst und Gestaltung, Bonn, 1987; Mönchehaus Museum, Goslar, 1987. **Collections:** Städtische Kunstsammlungen, Bonn; Städtisches Museum, Leverkusen; Landesmuseum, Oldenburg; Staatliche Museum, West Berlin; Neue Sammlung, Munich; Deutsches Plakatmuseum, Essen; Stedelijk Museum, Amsterdam; University of California, Berkeley. Recipient: Best

German Poster Prize, 1956, 1957, 1958, 1961, 1965, 1966, 1976, 1980; Gold Medal, Milan Triennale, 1957; First Prize, Fédération Internationale de la Presse Périodique, Rome, 1965. Member: Deutscher Werkbund, Cologne, 1952; Alliance Graphique Internationale, 1964. Address: Kuhbergstrasse 47, 3500 Kassel, West Germany.

Works:

Exhibition posters, for Amerika-Haus, in Frankfurt and Bonn, 1953–58.
55 postal stamp designs, for the Deutsche Bundespost, Bonn, 1955–83.
Form magazine design, for Westdeutscher Verlag, Opladen, 1957–68.
Logotype, packaging and poster design, for Hessische Metallwerke, Schwalmstadt, 1958–74.
Display stand at the Düsseldorf Kunststoffmesse, for Bayer Farbenfabriken, Leverkusen, 1959.
Film posters, for Atlas Filmverleih, Duisburg, 1959–66.
German displays at the Turin International Exposition, for the Bundesarbeitsministerium, Bonn, 1961.
Corporate design, for Igus textile firm, Bergisch-Gladbach, 1963–89.
Graphic Design—Documenta III exhibition layouts, for the Documenta Organization, Kassel, 1964.
Theatre posters, for the Staatstheater, Kassel, 1966–78.
Documenta 4 poster and catalogue, for the Documenta Organization, Kassel, 1968.
Baumpate—Grün ist Leben action/demonstration designs, for the cities of Berlin and Kassel, 1976–81.
Documenta 6 poster and catalogue, for the Documenta Organization, Kassel, 1977.
Documenta 8 visual images, for the Documenta Organization, Kassel, 1987.
Corporate design, for the Kasseler Musiktage, Kassel, 1988–89.
Corporate design, for Kultursommer Nordhessen, Kassel, 1989.

Publications:

By BLASE: books and catalogues—*Bodies and Stripes Variations, Karl Oskar Blase,* Kassel 1966; *Arnold Bode zum 75. Geburstag,* Kassel 1975; *Dokumentation 1 zur 200 jahrfeier der Kasseler Kunsthochschule,* Kassel 1977; *Hommage a Kassel,* Kassel 1978; *Bonner Politiker-Porträts,* Kassel 1979; *Karl Oskar Blase, Briefmarken-Design,* Cuxhagen, 1981; *Karl Oskar Blase, Baumbilder,* Kassel 1981; *Torso als Prinzip,* Kassel 1982.

On BLASE: books—*Who's Who in Graphic Art,* edited by Walter Amstutz, Zurich 1962, Dübendorf 1982; *Karl Oskar Blase Graphik,* exhibition catalogue with text by Alfred Nemeczek, Oldenburg 1965; *German Advertising Art,* edited by Eberhard Holscher, Munich 1967; *Karl Oskar Blase,* exhibition catalogue with text by Alfred Nemeczek, Kassel 1967; *Karl Oskar Blase,* exhibition catalogue with text by Rolf-Gunter Dienst, Wuppertal 1968; *Monographie des Plakats* by Herbert Schindler, Stuttgart 1978; *AGI Posters 1961–1985,* edited by Rudolph de Harak, New York 1986.

"Doing graphic design" and "painting pictures"; I have always looked at these two apparently dissimilar kinds of art as a single activity, as a unity. The informative aim of a poster for example certainly demands more dependence and more restriction in relation to the desire for freedom of design, but it also provokes a clear, possibly distinct expression. But it is also the

"art of the art" to work out what verbal language only imperfectly achieves, and there is the opportunity of working up subjective experiences which one can assume will be perceived by many as new information.

However obvious this formulated unity of graphic design and "free" art may appear, in professional reality it often comes up against a deep-rooted opposition. Keeping them separate is particularly cultivated in the German culture lobby. And for many artists of such a divided art, the decision in favour of a perhaps one-track stylistic form as a necessary prerequisite in the recipe for success sets in at an early stage, frequently even during studies.

My first contact with the works of the Bauhaus artists however, with those of De Stijl for example, but also the preoccupation with Jugendstil has had a lasting influence on me and has possibly marked my artistic practice, both the free and applied equally. In the early postwar years, when we in Germany were looking for new artistic avenues, functional same exhibition: an understanding of art which the German Labour Union to which I have belonged since 1952 has defended and promoted. As both these categories have to some extent had a dual influence on my work, my stylistic intention remains free from overly doctrinaire limitations. Yet in constructive compositions, I use the available artistic possibilities and media. I use illustrative drawing and systematic typography, painting and photography according to the desired effect. Looking back on my work, I find in spite of the multiplicity an always recognisable structural concept and a constructive artistic element.

There remains my theoretical interest in aesthetic questions which expresses itself in a collection of smaller and larger statements. Problems of visual communication, of modern art, of our contemporary aesthetic and of social and political relations are their subjects. In my recent pictures, I also include theoretical matters: "upheaval/radical change pictures" are on the one hand recognisable as text and lay out pictures, but also as trivial images from books and newspapers or simply as pictures.

—Karl Oskar Blase

In the 1950's and 1960's, Karl Oskar Blase was among the important graphic talents in Germany—especially in poster design. In 1956 for his poster "American Primitive," he received the Bund Deutscher Graphiker prize for best poster of the year, followed in subsequent years by many further distinctions.

Formal versatility and great sensitivity apply in all areas of his extensive work: stamp design, packaging and exhibition design. Blase's works can never be arranged in a narrow order, just as he largely evades categories of period style. Clarity of expression is combined with great graphic talent. The penetration effect of his works results mainly from an equilibrium between text and image. They are in harmony, enhance each other mutually and are immediately understandable. The function of the visual image can, however, be taken over by a graphic symbol—as, for example, in the poster for the 1961 Turin Labour Exhibition. His packaging for Peter Raacke's Mono cutlery, designed in 1968, has still lost nothing of its clear, simple beauty. For *Documenta 4* in 1968, Blase developed a logo based on a design which could also serve as a signpost, indicator board or entrance ticket. In this way, this great international art exhibition, taking place every four years, received an optical image sufficient to its exhibitors and distinguished by a great visual significance.

Blase draws on many ideas for his graphic works from his paintings. In his work as teacher at the Kassel Academy, he continues the tradi-

Karl Oskar Blase: *Dokumenta 8* neon exhibition logotype, Kassel, 1987

tion of the "Kassel School" which, in postwar Germany, developed into a centre of gravity for modern poster design.

—Magdalena Droste

BLASS, Bill.

American fashion designer. Born William Ralph Blass, in Fort Wayne, Indiana, 22 June 1922. Educated at Fort Wayne High School, 1936–39; studied fashion design, Parsons School of Design, New York, 1939. Served in the United States Army, 1941–44: Sergeant. Worked as a sketch artist, David Crystal Sportwear, New York, 1940–41; designer, Anna Miller and Company Limited, New York, 1945; designer, 1959–70, and vice-president, 1961–70, of Maurice Rentner Limited, New York; owner-director, Bill Blass Limited(took over Rentner Limited), from 1970: licensed products include menswear, womens sportswear, Vogue Patterns, candies, furs, swimwear, jeans, bedlinens, towels, shoes, loungewear, perfumes and an automobile. **Collections:** Metropolitan Museum of Art, New York; Indianapolis Museum of Art, Indiana; Phoenix Museum of Art, Arizona. Recipient: American Fashion Critics (Winnie) Award, 1961, 1963, 1970, Menswear Award, 1968, Fashion Hall of Fame Award, 1970, and Special Citations, 1971, 1982, 1983, Coty, New York; Gold Coast Fashion Award, Chicago, 1965; Cotton Council Award, New York, 1965; Neiman-Marcus Award, 1969; Print Council Award, 1971; Martha Award, New York, 1974; Ayres Look Award, 1978; Gentleman's Quarterly Manstyle Award, New York, 1979; Cutty Sark Hall of Fame Award, New York, 1979. Honorary Doctorate: Rhode Island School of Design, Providence, 1977. Address: 550 Seventh Avenue, New York, New York 10018, U.S.A.

Publications:

On BLASS: books—*The Fashionable Savages* by John Fairchild, New York 1965; *With Tongue in Chic* by Ernestine Carter, London 1974; *Fashion: The Changing Shape of Fashion Through the Years* by Jane Dorner, London 1974; *20th Century Fashion: A Scrapbook 1900 to Today* by Ernestine Carter, London 1975; *A History of Fashion* by J. Anderson Black and Madge Garland, London 1975, 1980; *The Changing World of Fashion: 1900 to the Present* by Ernestine Carter, London 1977; *The Contemporary Decorative Arts from 1940 to the Present Day* by Philippe Garner, London 1980; *McDowell's Directory of Twentieth Century Fashion* by Colin McDowell, London 1984; *The Encyclopaedia of Fashion from 1840 to the 1980s* by Georgina O'Hara, London 1986.

American fashion designer Bill Blass learned his craft and developed his approach in New York's garment district, where he made his way from sketch artist in 1940 to owner of Bill Blass Limited in 1970. His work concentrates ready-to-wear outfitting for an elegant and worldly social class that he cultivated for the Seventh Avenue scene, which had always made clothing for mass-market consumers. Blass's approach includes the interaction of the designer with his clientele; he furthered the role of the fashion designer as a socially desirable friend and guest, practicing his idea that one must see how

Bill Blass: Trench jacket in check silk crepe jacquard with knee-length skirt, 1984

the rich live in order to make the proper clothing for them. His designs for women's evening wear are, as a result, extremely glamorous and filled with feminine touches such as ruffles and laces. His sportswear division, Blassport, produces a classic, tweedy look for women and men alike, using men's fabrics for both, for a coordinated packaging from top to bottom.

Blass has been the recipient of numerous awards, including one for his overall excellence in many fields. He has made a name in a wide variety of items and was one of the first fashion designers to do sheets and towels. With Hubert de Givenchy and Emilio Pucci, Blass worked on interiors for the Lincoln Continental's Mark IV and Mark V. Blass has noted: "In the seventies, the designer became a brand name. His name on products gave them validity. This helps establish design standards and, on the whole, is a good thing, providing it is not abused." Along with an ever-growing list of designers such as Pierre Cardin, Gucci, Fiorucci,

Sassoon, Calvin Klein, and so on, Blass has become a trademark, a name to be sported almost regardless of what it appears on. As his statement goes, that practice could be good if not abused.

Blass's clothes show many influences, perhaps a few too many to put them in the class of true originals. His inventiveness has been more in the field of the designer's role and, most important, in the role of ready-to-wear's possibilities for upward mobility. He stands out almost more for his celebrity stature than for his particular designs, which basically alter previous and concurrent fashions invented by others. Blass is, after all, not someone who will be revered as an intellect or artist of the highest stature, yet he has developed a place among the gentry who want a classic look with room for glamour while avoiding anything too new or too different.

—Barbara Cavaliere

BOERI, Cini.

Italian architect, furniture and product designer. Born Cini Mariani, in Milan, 19 June 1924. Studied architecture, at the Politecnico, Milan, 1945-51: Dip.Arch. 1951. Married A. Boeri in 1949 (divorced, 1969); children: Sandro, Stefano and Tito. Director of interior design and furnishings, studio of Marco Zanuso, Milan, 1952-63; freelance architect and industrial designer, working for Arflex, Arnolfo di Cambio, Artemide, Fiam, Fusital, ICF, Knoll International, Rosenthal, Venini, etc., in Milan, since 1963. Member, ADI Associazione per il Disegno Industriale, Milan, since 1963. Visiting Professor in Architecture, Industrial and Interior Design, Politecnico, Milan, 1980-83; also guest lecturer at universities in Spain, Brazil and the United States. **Exhibitions:** Milan Triennale, 1965, 1968, 1973, 1986; *Italy: The New Domestic Landscape,* Museum of Modern Art, New York, 1972; *Knoll au Musée,* Musée des Arts Decoratifs, Paris, 1972; *Design in Plastic,* Museum of Decorative Arts, Prague, 1972; *Desenho Industrial Italiano,* Porto Alegre, Brazil, 1975 (toured); *Design and design,* Palazzo delle Stelline, Milan, 1979 (travelled to Venice); *Cini Boeri,* Galerie Hans Schmuller, Bonn, 1980; *Italienische Moebel,* Kölnisches Stadtmuseum, Cologne, 1981; *Italian Re-Evolution,* La Jolla Museum of Art, California, 1982; *Design Since 1945,* Philadelphia Museum of Art, 1983; *Italian Design,* Sogetsu Kaikan Palace, Tokyo, 1984; *16 Italian Women Designers,* Takashimaya Stores, Tokyo, 1985. **Collection:** Museum of Modern Art, New York. Recipient: Compasso d'Oro Award, Milan, 1970; Roscoe Award, New York, 1978, 1985; *Design 85* Award, Stuttgart, 1985. Address: via De Grassi 4, 20123 Milan, Italy.

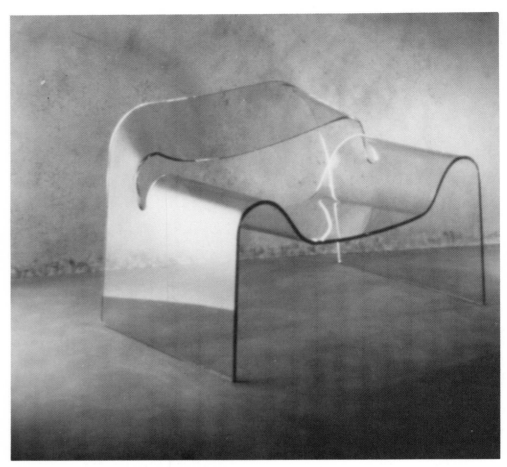

Cini Boeri: *Ghost* easy chair in crystal sheet, for Fiam, 1987

Works:

Cube storage containers in wood and plastic, for Arflex, 1967.
Partner suitcases in ABS plastic and aluminium, for Franzi, 1967.
Lamp 602 and *Lamp 1098* in PVC and metal, for Arteluce, 1968.
Lunar table with steel base and wood/crystal top, for Knoll, 1970.
Gradual sofa system with triangular junction table, for Knoll, 1970.
Serpentone flexible sofa in polyurethane foam, for Arflex, 1971.
Strips armchair, sofa and bed collection, for Arflex, 1972.
Abat-Jour lamp with stone base and perspex opaline shade, for Tronconi, 1978.
Strips 79 relaxer armchair with quilted cover, for Arflex, 1979.
Folio hinged panel dining-chair, for Rosenthal, 1980.
Otto B series of door handles and window pulls, for Fusital, 1980.
Rever symmetric round-edged door with rubber gasket trim, for Tre Piu, 1981.
Prisma collection of office furniture, for Rosenthal, 1981.
Chiara suspension and table lamps in blown glass, for Venini, 1984.
Voyeur free-standing room screen in sandblasted glass, for Fiam, 1987.
Ghost single-piece easy chair in crystal sheet, for Fiam, 1987 (with Tomu Katayanagi).

(Boeri's architectural and interior design work comprises numerous villas, family houses and public buildings in Italy, as well as showrooms for: Franzi in Rome, 1965; Mosel in Bilbao, 1974; Knoll International in Los Angeles, Stuttgart and Paris, 1975, in Milan 1984, in Foligno, 1985, and in New York, 1989; Arflex in Milan, 1977, and in Tokyo, 1981; Abati in

Perugia, 1980; Venini in Frankfurt, 1988, and in Venice, 1989).

Publications:

By BOERI: books—*Le Dimensioni Umane dell' Abitazoine,* Milan 1980; *Cini Boeri: Quaderni di lavoro/Workbook,* Milan 1982.

On BOERI: books—*Design Italiano: I Mobili,* edited by Enrichetta Ritter, Milan and Rome 1968; *Italy: The New Domestic Landscape,* edited by Emilio Ambasz, New York and Florence 1972; *Atlante del Design Italiano 1940-1980* by Alfonso Grassi and Anty Pansera, Milan 1980; *Knoll Design* by Eric Larrabee and Massimo Vignelli, New York and London 1981; *International Design Yearbook 1988/89,* edited by Arata Isozaki, London 1988; articles—"Milanese Woman Architect Specialized in Deco" by J. Rosenthal in *Christian Science Monitor* (Boston), 8 August 1969; "People in Design" by J. R. Guilfoyle in *Industrial Design* (New York), November 1972; "Cini Boeri: Design Activity in Architecture and Furniture" in *Japan Interior Design* (Tokyo), April 1980; "Design Community in Italy: Cini Boeri", special issue of *Idea* (Tokyo), April 1980; "Cini Boeri: Vent'anni di progetti" in *Corriere della Sera* (Milan), 12 June 1984; "Cini Boeri" in *Casa e Giardino* (Milan), November 1987.

I would like to think that the concern of the designer will continue to aim at creating furniture, machines and other accessories necessary to human life. I would also like to be sure that this work will espouse a method whereby production techniques cut the costs to a level acceptable to many rather than to the privileged few. Moreover, I would like to foresee, with in-

telligent and deliberate work, a direction toward an easier and simpler way of life.

I would like all this, even though here and there a type of ironic deformation of these concepts is currently evident, expressing itself in distorted tables, embroidered chairs or in perforated beds. But this is certainly not design. To realize the aims I have mentioned, it is necessary to actively work with industries whose intentions and interests coincide with those of the designers—not the opposite, as often happens. I feel it is important for the designer to be regarded as a technician who works alongside industry to optimise the use and image of its products.

—Cini Boeri

BOGGERI, Antonio.

Italian photographer, art director and graphic designer. Born in Pavia, 8 April 1900. Studied violin at the Conservatorio di Musica, Milan, 1919-22; mainly self-taught in photography and design, from 1924. Served in the Italian Army School for Officers, 1917-18. Married Lidia Giampiccoli in 1937; daughter: Anna. Director, Alfieri e Lacroix printing firm, Milan, 1924-32; founder-director, Studio Boggeri design firm, working with designers Walter Ballmer, Xanti Schawinsky, Max Huber, Aldo Calabresi, Bruno Monguzzi, Ezio Bonini, etc., in Milan, from 1933: has designed for Società Nazionale Gasometri, Olivetti, Kardex, Fran-chi, Marxer, Roche, Glaxo, Richard-Ginori, Dalmine, Glaxo, Pirelli, etc. **Exhibitions:** Milan Triennale, 1951, 1957, 1981; Galleria del Levante, Milan, 1980; *La Sperimentazione Fotografica Italia 1930–1980,* Galleria d'Arte Moderna, Bpologna, 1983. Recipient: Grand Prize, 1951, and Gold Medal, 1957, Milan Triennale; Vita di Pubblicitario, Federazoine Italiana di Pubblicità, Milan, 1967. Member of Honour, Art Directors Club of Milan, 1970. Address: Via Soetti 19, 16038 Santa Margherita Ligure, Genoa, Italy.

Works (from Studio Boggeri):

L'Uovo di Colombo brochure, for Studio Boggeri, 1933 (A. Boggeri).
L'Ete sur Mer poster, for Società Italia di Navigazinone, 1933 (X. Schawinsky).
Cover, for *Campo Grafico* magazine, December 1934 (A. Boggeri and Rossi).
Poster, for *Esposizione Aeronautica Italiana,* Milan, 1934 (X. Schawinsky).
Illy Caffe poster, for Società Hausbrandt, 1934 (X. Schawinsky).
Publicity posters, for Rodina, 1937 (A. Boggeri).
Gas poster, for Società Nazionale Gasometri, 1939 (F. Depero).
Office furniture catalogue, for Kardex, 1940 (R. Muratore).
Vitaplex brochure, for Glaxo, 1946 (C. Vivarelli).
Logotype trademark, for Isis waterproof fabrics, 1948 (A. Boggeri).
Becozym brochure, for Roche, 1950 (E. Bonini).
Bili Complessi brochures and packaging, for Marxer, 1956 (R. Martinelli).
Redoxon Effervescente brochures and packaging, for Roche, 1959 (A. Calabresi).
Eupradyn brochures and packaging, for Roche, 1961 (Calabresi).
Guanti Satinati advertisement, for Pirelli, 1962 (B. Monguzzi).

Publications:

By BOGGERI: books—*Mostra fotografica di Franco Grignani,* exhibition catalogue, Milan 1958; *Mostra di manifesti stranieri,* exhibition catalogue, Milan 1968; articles—in *Natura* (Milan), 1930, 1931; *Campo Grafico* (Milan), no. 12, 1934; *La Pubblicità d'Italia* (Milan), nos. 5–6, 1937, nos. 50–54, 1939; *Graphis* (Zurich), no. 18, 1948, no. 209, 1980; *Linea Grafica* (Milan), 1948, 1949, 1969, 1974; *Typographica* (London), no. 2, 1960; *Incontri* (Milan), nos. 1–3, 1966; *Due Dimensioni* (Milan), no. 8/9, 1973; *Rassegna* (Milan), no. 6, 1981.
On BOGGERI: books—*Die neue Grafik/The*

New Graphic Design by Karl Gerstner and Markus Kutter, Teufen and London 1959; *Lo Studio Boggeri 1933–1973,* edited by Paolo Fossati, Milan 1974; *Storia e Cronaca della Triennale* by Anty Pansera, Milan 1978; *Lo Studio Boggeri 1933–1981,* edited Bruno Monguzzi, Milan 1981; *La Sperimentazione Fotografica in Italia 1930–1980,* exhibition catalogue with text by Carlo Gentili, Bologna 1983.

I worked for eight years with Alfieri and Lacroix, an important graphic arts firm famous for the accurate quality of its production. There, I was able to follow closely the techniques of composing and printing, the processes of photoengraving and reproduction, and I acquired the knowledge that I was later to find so extremely important. That was when I had the idea of the future Studio and of the kind of services it would provide.

I realized that, in the end, the object of the typographical firm consisted primarily of the precise technical carrying-out of the requirements of a demanding clientele in accordance with the precepts of established craft procedures, with no consciousness of any new relationship between object and graphic form. In contrast to the extreme conservatism of the printers, the work of the *maîtres d'affiche* had an extraordinary imaginative liveliness, for they were masters of a complete creative independence clearly pictorial in origin. The area of their free exercises, projects not strictly subject to any particular task, had no place in the Studio's research, which explains why we concerned ourselves with them so seldom.

For me, "graphics" meant the acquisition not merely of a different language, but of a language opposite to the repertoire accumulated on the untouchable remains of classical typography. It was something that had to reckon with the new demands of communication through the picture, whose visuality was far removed from the traditional visuality of reading: to say little, with the introduction of the photograph into the page.

—Antonio Boggeri

BOHAN, Marc (Roger Maurice Louis).
French fashion designer. Born in Paris, 22 August 1926. Educated at the Lycée Lakanal, Sceaux, until 1944. Married Dominique Gaborit in 1950 (died, 1962); married Huguette Rinjonneau (died); daughter: Marie-Anne.

Worked as assistant designer in Robert Piguet fashion house, Paris, 1945–49, and for Edward Molyneux, Paris, 1949–51; also briefly designed in the salon of Madeleine de Rauch, Paris, 1952; opened own fashion salon, producing one collection, Paris, 1953; head designer of haute couture, Jean Patou fashion house, Paris, 1954–58; creator of London collections, under Yves Saint-Laurent, at Christian Dior fashion house, Paris, 1958–59; dress and furs designer, for Révillon fashion house, Paris, 1960; art director and chief designer, Christian Dior S.A., Paris, 1960–89; also freelance stage and film costume designer. Recipient: *Sports Illustrated* Designer of the Year Award, New York, 1963; Schiffli Lace and Embroidery Institute Award, 1963. Chevalier of the Legion d'Honneur, France, and of the Ordre de Saint Charles, Monaco. Address: 71 rue des Saint-Peres, 75006 Paris, France.

Works:

Stewardess uniforms, for Air France, 1962.
Roman Catholic habits, for the Daughters of Charity of Saint Vincent, 1964.

film costume designs include—*Phedre,* 1961; *Topkapi,* 1963; *Arabesque,* 1966; *The Countess from Hong Kong,* 1966; *Secret Ceremony,* 1968; *l'Ours et la Foupee,* 1970; *The Lady in the Car with the Glasses and the Gun,* 1970; *Le Beau Monstre,* 1971; *Rude Journee pour la Reine,* 1974; *Verdict,* 1974; *l'Ironie du Sort,* 1974; *La Race des Seigneurs,* 1974; *l'Aggression,* 1975; *Le Chat et la Souris,* 1975; *Cassandra Crossing,* 1975; *Le Dernier Amant Romantique,* 1977; *Tour feu—Tout Flamme,* 1981; *The Moon in the Gutter,* 1982. stage designs include—*Apres la Chute,* Theatre du Gymnase, 1963; *Le Cheval Evanoui,* Theatre du Gymnase, 1966, 1974; *Madame Princesse,* Theatre du Gymnase, 1966; *Fleur de Cactus,* Theatres des Bouffes Parisiens, 1966; *Le Misanthrope,* Theatre de l'Oeuvre, 1967; *40 Carats,* Theatre de la Madeleine, 1967; *l'Ascension du General Fritz,* Theatre des Ambassadeurs, 1967; *Les Yeux Creves,* Theatre du Gymnase, 1968; *Le Vision Voyageur,* Theatre du Gymnase, 1969; *Le Canard a l'Orange,* Theatre du Gymnase, 1970; *Du Cote de Chez l'Autre,* Theatre de la Madeleine, 1971; *Jean de la Lune,* Theatre du Palais Royal, 1972; *Ne Coupez pas mes Arbres,* Theatre du Gymnase, 1973; *Chat,* Theatre du Gymnase, 1973; *La Polka,* Theatre du Gymnase, 1974; *Cher Menteur,* Theatre du Gymnase, 1974; *Arret ton Cinema,* Theatre du Gymnase, 1977.

Publications:

On BOHAN: book—*The Fashionable Savages*

Antonio Boggeri and Ezio Bonini: New Year address announcement, 1948

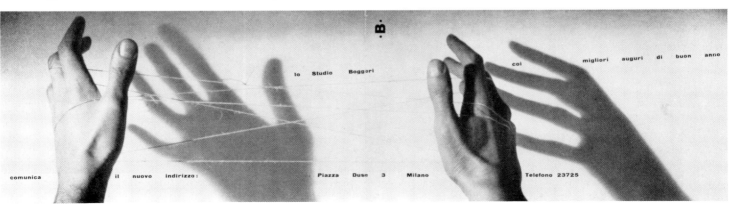

Marc Bohan: Evening dress in black velvet and fake chinchilla, for the House of Dior, 1983

by John Fairchild, New York 1965; *A View of Fashion* by Alison Adburgham, London 1966; *With Tongue in Chic* by Ernestine Carter, London 1974; *In Fashion: Dress in the Twentieth Century* by Prudence Glynn, London 1978; *The Fashionable Mind: Reflection on Fashion 1970–1981* by Kennedy Fraser, New York 1981; *Who's Who in Fashion,* edited by Karl Strute and Theodor Doelken, Zurich 1982; *McDowell's Directory of Fashion* by Colin McDowell, London 1984; *The Encyclopaedia of Fashion from 1840 to the 1980s* by Georgina O'Hara, London 1986.

By taking on the mantle of Dior, Marc Bohan committed himself to perfection of cut, finish, and appearance. For 29 years (1960–89), he continued the tradition, begun by Christian Dior, of producing classic, often luxurious, always finely made clothes for individual customers. His early career at Robert Piguet, as assistant to Captain Molyneux, and at Patou gave him a good grounding. Piguet's advice to him to design clothes which would tempt women provided him with a working motto. By doing so, he has played an important part in helping couture to survive in face of the growing importance of ready-to-wear. He offers his clients what they want, rather than follow every new change of style.

While perpetuating the essence of couture through delicate workmanship, superb cut, and extravagant embroidery, his designs have always been faithful to the times in which they were created. As early as 1961, his slim look acknowledged that finances were more restrained than in the past and that women were leading more active lifestyles. While remaining aware of modern life, Bohan has shown many and varied influences in recent years. The narrow, mid-calf-length coats with epaulettes, worn with boots and slanted berets in 1966, were nicknamed his "Tin Soldier" look. The following year saw the introduction of safari-style suits and dress pants derived from African art and totem motifs. In classic couture tradition, fabrics and colour are both prime factors in Bohan's work. The Gigi suit, for instance, relied for its pretty, romantic effect on softly draping black velvet and wool. Even in the more tailored suits, the attention to detail signifies that they are part of the long-established heritage of haute couture. Gathered Pierrot collars have adorned velvet, taffeta, and satin capes, frilled white chiffon Bertha collars have similarly topped fitted, black velvet dresses.

Bohan has achieved a rare success in these days of faster living and dwindling resources by proving that exclusive dressing can still exist in its own right. Today the House of Dior is a huge business complex covering fashion, perfume, and cosmetics. At its very core was Bohan's domain—haute couture, the fine art of creating clothes.

—Hazel Clark

BOHLIN, Jonas.
Swedish architect, furniture, interior and stage designer. Born in Stockholm, 10 February 1953. Studied construction engineering, Aso Technical College, Sweden, 1970–74; interior architecture, National College of Art and Design (Konstfackskolan), Stockholm, 1976–81. Freelance designer, working mainly with the

Kallemo Furniture Company, in Stockholm, from 1981. Co-founder, Mobile art and design gallery, Stockholm, 1985–87. **Exhibitions:** *Labyrintformeln,* National College of Art and Design, Stockholm, 1981; *Provokationer,* Kulturhuset, Stockholm, 1982; *Utmarkt Svensk Form,* Galleri Heland, Stockholm, 1983; *New Swedish Furniture,* ASF-Gallery, New York, 1985; *Material Pleasure,* Queens Museum, New York, 1985; *Nordisk Möbeldesign,* Form/Design Center, Malmo, 1986; *Scandinavian Design: A Way of Life,* Toyama Museum of Modern Art, Japan, 1987 (toured Japan); *Asplund/Bohlin/Kandell,* Svensk Tenn, Stockholm, 1988; *Georg Jensen Prisen,* Illums Bolighus, Copenhagen, 1988; *Trois Generations: Asplund/Kandell/Bohlin,* Swedish Cultural Centre, Paris 1989. **Collections:** Nationalmuseum, Stockholm; Röhsska Konstslöjdmuseet, Göteborg; Jonkopings Lans Museum, Sweden; Visby Konsthall, Sweden; Malmö Konstmuseer, Sweden; Kunstindustrimuseet, Copenhagen. Recipient: National College of Art and Design Stipend, Stockholm, 1981; Stipend, 1981, and Award of Honour, 1983, Föreningen Svensk Form, Stockholm; Swedish State Cultural Stipend, 1984; Estrid Eriksson Foundation Stipend, Stockholm, 1985; Swedish Artist's Stipend, 1986; Georg Jensen Prize, Copenhagen, 1988. Address: Jonas Bohlin Arkitektkontor AB, Nybrogatan 25, 114 39 Stockholm, Sweden.

Works:

Concrete chair in birch and steel, for Kallemo, 1980.
Concrete chair in concrete and steel, for Kallemo, 1981 (limited edition).
Concrete table in birch and steel, for Kallemo, 1982.
Concave couch in leather, canvas, beech and steel, for Kallemo, 1983.
Concrete table in concrete, glass and steel, for Kallemo, 1984.
Zink wall-shelf in birch, for Kallemo, 1984.

Zink floor-shelf in birch, concrete and steel, for Kallemo, 1984.
Point chair in leather and steel, for Kallemo, 1985.
Contact table in birch and steel, for Kallemo, 1985.
Espresso wall-lamp in pine and porcelain, for Kallemo, 1987.
Double Espresso floor-lamp in aluminum, steel and porcelain, for Kallemo, 1987.
Nonting couch in leather, canvas and steel, for Kallemo, 1987.
Slottsbacken cupboard in oak, glass and steel, for Kallemo, 1987 (limited edition).
Kabin wall-cupboard in parchment and ashwood, for Svenska Arkitekt Forbundet, 1987 (limited edition).
Magasin magazine rack in birch, for Kallemo, 1988.
Triptyk table in birch and steel, for Kallemo, 1988.

Publications:

On BOHLIN: books—*Den Svenska Formen* by Monica Boman and others, Stockholm 1981; *International Design Yearbook 1985/1986,* edited by Robert A. M. Stern, London 1985; *Made in Sweden: Art, Handicrafts, Design* by Anja Notini, London 1987; *International Design Yearbook 1987/1988,* edited by Philippe Starck, London 1987; *High Touch: The New Materialism in Design* by Robert Janjigian, London 1987; *International Design Yearbook 1988/1989,* edited by Arata Isozaki, London 1988; articles—"Jonas Bohlin" by C. Christiansson in *Sweden in Fact* (Stockholm), 1987; "Jonas Bohlin: Between Two Different States" by G. Lundahl in *Scandinavian Review* (Stockholm), no. 2, 1989.

My work, my furniture, is an expression of my need and desire to channel my energy. My friend Sven Lundh, who is also the manufacturer of my furniture, once said: "Jonas Bohlin wants to create a subtle balance between ab-

stract shapes for meditative purposes. The few elements keep precisely to the rules which give harmony and equilibrium, and a revelation of the exact (which we find outside ourselves), and the universal (which we find in ourselves)." This is a formulation which still pleases me greatly. I myself have difficulty in formulating my work through words and opinions. Furniture is a language in itself.

—Jonas Bohlin

Jonas Bohlin has been the centre of many storms. He made his debut with an armchair of concrete and iron tubing. The new impertinent chair was equally uncomfortable. Echoes of Picasso's handlebars and the Readymades of Duchamp. The champions of comfort raged.

A recent challenge to the public is a tall cupboard with double doors. It is made from softly polished rusty steel, bowed and joined like ship's plates and fastened with heavy brass bolts. When the doors are opened, a fragile, elegantly finished interior with glass shelves is revealed. The cupboard was originally named *Mutter.* Maybe it suggested Mother Earth with her ravaged exterior and her vulnerability. One day, however, the name was changed to *Slottsbacken:* a bus stop in Stockholm and a pretentious beer crate. "What is 'nice'? What is beautiful?," it whispers. And the fact that Jonas has signed and numbered the cupboard—just as he did with the concrete chair—is a constant minor provocation. Beauty contained in ugliness, ugliness in beauty excites Jonas. It is in contrasts that discoveries are made, he says.

Another contribution to the 1989 Stockholm Furniture Fair was a table of undisputed beauty, with elegant lines and personality. It is called *Triptyk.* The three parts consist of two iron pedestals cast in one piece with medium-sized tabletops. Each iron top may be surrounded by a somewhat larger ring of massive wood, which covers up the self-consciously moulded decorative letters that spell out "Jonas Bohlin". The assertive capitals are reminiscent of those found on a cannon or a wood stove. The third part

Jonas Bohlin: *Triptyk* table in birch and steel, for Kallemo, 1988

consists of a long massive plank for the two stands. The wood is untreated. "Won't you get wine stains?", someone asks. To Jonas, furniture is serious business. It is about life, about working out your experiences.

Jonas Bohlin was born in Stockholm in 1953. He attended the College of Fine Arts from 1976 to 1981, but before that he had studied to become a construction engineer. Those were active and busy years as part of an intensive group. His concrete chair made its debut at the senior show, as part of an installation highlighting the juxtaposition of different materials. At that time, stage craft was Jonas' main interest. Now it is furniture.

The concrete chair immediately found a manufacturer, Sven Lundh at the Kallemo Furniture Company who, with an unerring instinct for new things, has sought out the most talented and startling designers. Jonas Bohlin and John Kandell are his superstars. The collaboration between Sven Lundh and Jonas Bohlin is very important. Sven's assessments of Jonas' ideas are on-the-mark: he supports or criticizes them, launching them enthusiastically and with personal commitment. "I wait until I have a good idea. Then I turn it over to Kallemo. I make furniture for him, and I have just enough ideas for one company."

In addition, Jonas works with interior design—offices, private dwellings and, quite recently, a restaurant. His resume also lists a couple of exhibitions. His office is in a converted mid-town factory. He is surrounded by designers and architects of different kinds but also by a printing shop and a candy factory. Sometimes the proximity invites collaboration, but usually Jonas is a loner in his work. "I don't fit in an architect's office," he says.

During the period 1985–87 a lot of time was taken up by a gallery, *Mobile.* Jonas started it together with three like-minded friends from various fields. They bought a windowless space next to the entrance of a parking garage. They painted it black and equipped it with dramatic lighting. The idea was to provide exhibition space for radical artists and designers. In between, the space would be available for rent to companies which would receive help in exhibiting their products. This would pay the rent. In addition, "ordinary people" with design ideas were to be offered exhibition space. The idea did not catch on either with the establishment or among radicals. However, there was time for a couple of exciting exhibitions before the adventure was over after two years. *Mobile* became part of history.

Jonas put on his most beautiful and expressive exhibit for the furniture fair in February 1989. Because of the Georg Jensen Prize, he was honoured with two podiums in the large entrance hall. One of the two white circles was taken up by birch and steel predecessors to the concrete chair, painted blue and black. They were arranged haphazardly with a shiny brown string instrument leaning against each one as if an orchestra had just left. Puzzling and beautiful, they left a strong impression on the viewer. The other podium housed a larger selection of Jonas' furniture production, among them the shelf system *Zink* zigzagging upwards on a diagonal. There were also the magazine rack, *Magasin,* a board with slots for newspapers. *Nonting,* a couch, was stood on end. It is reminiscent of a steam roller, and should maybe always be in motion. Upended, its precise geometry became the main message. *Kabin,* a wall cupboard, is a delicate little collector's item for the members of the Architects' Association. A neat little row of shelves of smoothly sanded ash is wrapped in a sheet of cardboard leather which may be tied shut by means of two cotton ribbons. A lamp, *Espresso,* is introduced as an offhanded joke. A small white porcelain

bowl, balanced on a rustic console, throws light at the ceiling. The floor version is a doubled espresso. It feels good to do something tacky, too.

"Too many neat and elegant things are made today. We seem to have settled comfortably on our duffs. Time to venture out and make discoveries: to overthrow the law of gravity."

Success has come to Jonas in unanticipated measure, but then, he has long been in the habit of working seven days a week. He says the Georg Jensen Prize took him by surprise. Jonas Bohlin is an exception in the world of Swedish furniture. The prize was a recognition of his excellence and willingness to break the rules. It is to be hoped that his success will prepare the way for an even younger generation trying to find a profile for its own time.

—Gunilla Lundahl

BONETTO, Rodolfo.

Italian furniture, product and industrial designer. Born in Milan, 18 September 1929. Educated at Liceo, Milan until 1947. Married Evy Musmanno in 1959; son: Marco. Design consultant, working for Pininfarina and other car body firms, Milan, 1951–58; founder-director, Bonetto Design SRL, working for Autovox, Voxson, Elscint, Fiamm, Fiat, IPM, Lancia, Nordica, Novotecnica, Schick, Selenia, Sweda, Veglia Borletti, Zanussi, etc., in Milan, since 1958. Lecturer in Product Design, Hochschule für Gestaltung, Ulm, 1961–65; Instructor in Industrial Design, 1971–87, and Board Member, 1974–89, Istituto Superiore Disegno Industriale, Rome. Executive Board Member, 1963–69, Executive Board President, 1971–73, and President, 1979–82, ADI Associazione Disegno Industriale, Milan; Executive Council Member, Creation Esthètique Industrielle, Paris, 1971; Executive Board Member, 1971–73, Vice-President, 1973–75, President, 1981, and Member of the Senate, 1988, ICSID International Council of Societiés of Industrial Design. **Exhibitions:** *Design and Design,* Palazzo delle Stelline, Milan, 1979 (traveled to Venice); *Design Process: Olivetti 1908–1978,* University of California, Los Angeles, 1979; *Italian Re-Evolution,* La Jolla Museum of Art, California, 1982; *Design Since 1945,* Philadelphia Museum of Art, 1983; *Italia 2000,* Moscow, 1988. **Collections:** Museum of Modern Art, New York; Philadelphia Museum of Art. Recipient: Compasso d'Oro Award, Milan, 1964, 1967, 1970, 1976, 1979, 1981. Address: Bonetto Design SRL, Ripa di Porta Ticinese 55, 20143 Milan, Italy.

Works:

Iveco car instruments, for Veglia Borletti, 1970.
LM and *VP80* elevators, for Stigler-Otis, 1975.
Supermirafiori 131 car interiors, for Fiat, 1975.
Mostro radio, for Voxson, 1978.
Picchio one-piece table telephone, for Sime, 1980.
L20 cash register, for Sweda, 1986.
Inspector 820 measuring machine, for Olivetti-OCN, 1987.
Ala halogen table lamp, for Guzzini, 1987.
Rotor 2 public telephone, for IPM, 1987.

Tipo car interiors, for Fiat, 1988.
Excel 2400 music console, for Elscint, 1988.
TB2 microchip process machine, for Tegal-Motorola New Enterprises, 1988.
Premium Top maintenance-free car battery, for Fiamm, 1989.
Cross 6E geared motor for sliding gates, for Novotecnica, 1989.

Publications:

By BONETTO: articles—"Rodolfo Bonetto" in *Design Quarterly* (Tokyo), no. 2, 1982; "Waking Up: facing the objects of the day", with A. Rossari, in *Italian Re-Evolution,* exhibition catalogue, La Jolla 1982.

On BONETTO: books—*Italy: The New Domestic Landscape,* edited by Emilio Ambasz, New York and Florence 1972; *Design e forme nuove nell'arredamento italiano,* edited by Paolo Portoghesi and Marino Marini, Rome 1978; *Design Process: Olivetti 1908–1978,* exhibition catalogue, Los Angeles 1979; *Atlante del Design Italiano 1940–1980* by Alfonso Grassi and Anty Pansera, Milan 1980; *Design Since 1945,* edited by Kathryn Hiesinger and George Marcus, Philadelphia and London 1983; *The Conran Directory of Design,* edited by Stephen Bayley, London 1985; *International Design Yearbook 1987/88,* edited by Philippe Starck, London 1987.

Rodolfo Bonetto represents in Italy the figure of the designer who works in the modern tradition, resolving functional problems of great complexity by applying a strict design methodology based on a technical and scientific approach to the creation of form.

In fact, he owes his cultural development largely to the Hochschule für Gestaltung at Ulm, to which he was appointed while still very young to teach product design, from 1961 to 1965; the efforts made in that school to unite science and creativity and the powerful influence there of the psychological, ergonomic, social, economic, mathematical, and technological disciplines are all elements found now in Bonetto's own professional practice and in his various productions. This development and his first experiments in the field of automobile design allowed Bonetto always to take on projects of high technological and practical complexity, with the related problems of large-scale mass production; working in the field of machine tools and measuring instruments, for instance, he has been able to find a formal answer to the evolution of the technology, not only that "external" to the object in its production but also that which is "internal." In his designs, in fact, Bonetto has lived through the whole period of the change-over from the electro-mechanical operation of plants to the electronic. He always creates products that are less forms imposed on the machinery than they are complex systems, which tend to be anonymous in form, but in which the design is principally decided by consideration of the point at which machine and operator meet, something on which Bonetto's design work has largely concentrated in the latest years, with important results.

Bonetto seems to be averse to intellectual classification and has always preferred to work in the professional field rather than the critical. This practical activity, however, is always accompanied by an active presence in situations which, at an international level, afford opportunities for publicity and discussion on the subject of industrial design. Besides teaching in the school at Ulm, Bonetto has for many years been a lecturer and member of the Scientific and Educational Committee at Rome's Istituto Superiore Disegno Industriale, the only national

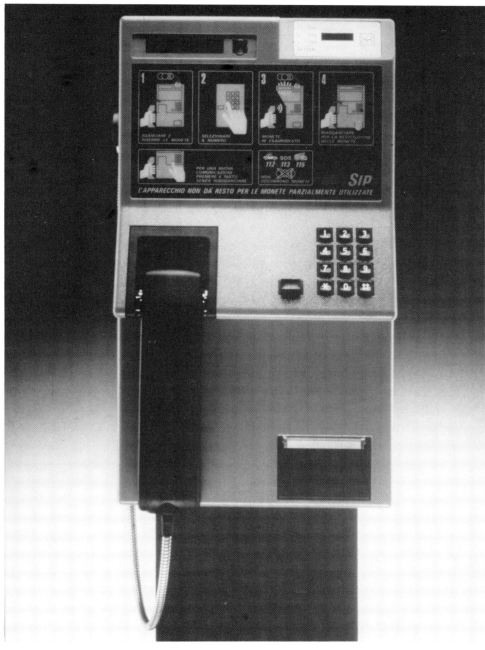

Rodolfo Bonetto: *Rotor 2* **public telephone, for IPM, 1987**

school of design at university level in Italy. There he has conducted on an experimental level research on the defining of new design methodologies. The subject matter of his work and the experience acquired on an international level by his professional activity are publicized by a constant presence at enterprises for the promotion of design, in particular in the Italian Association for Industrial Design, in which he has promoted meetings between the different forces operating in the field of design, and in the International Council of Societies of Industrial Design, for which he has addressed conferences and meetings all over the world and for which he promoted the organization of the Thirteenth World Congress at Milan.

Through this activity Bonetto has become an outstanding figure, designer and propagandist, making an indirect critical contribution to the evolution of design with his professional practice and promoting the discussion and enhancement of the study of design directly by his educational activities.

—Stefano Casciani

BONSIEPE, Gui (Georg).

German product designer. Born in Glucksburg, 23 March 1934. Studied classical languages, Karlsgymnasium, Stuttgart, until 1949; graphics and architecture, Akademie der Schönen Künste and Technische Universität, Munich, 1954–55; design theory, under Tomas Maldonado, Hochschule für Gestaltung, Ulm, 1955–59: Dip. 1959. Married Jovita Alicia Hemmingsen in 1966; children: Jovita, Santiago and Juan. Freelance industrial designer, in Ulm, 1959–68, in Santiago de Chile, 1968–74, in Buenos Aires, 1974–81, and in Brasilia, since 1981: industrial design consultant, International Labor Organization, Santiago, 1968–71; divisional head, INTEC Comite de Investigaciones Technologias, Santiago, 1971–73; divisional chief, Instituto Nacional de Tecnologia Industrial, Buenos Aires, 1974–76; partner and technical director of Studio MM/B Diseno (Mendes Mosquera/Bonsiepe/Kumcher), Buenos Aires, 1975–81; consultant, National Council for Scientific and Technological Development, Brasilia, since 1981. Assistant instructor, 1960–64, and Professor, 1965–68,

Hochschule für Gestaltung, Ulm; Guest Professor of Engineering, Catholic University, Santiago, 1971–72; head of product development workshop, Universidad Federal de Santa Catarina, Florianapolis, Brazil, since 1982. Consultant, UNIDO United Nations Industrial Development Organization, 1973–74, 1979, UNESCO, 1973, 1982, and OECD Organization for Economic Cooperation and Development, 1977, 1978. Editor, *Ulm* magazine, 1964–68, *INTEC* magazine, Santiago, 1971–73, and design section of *Summa* magazine, Buenos Aires, 1979–81. Vice-President, ICSID International Council of Societies of Industrial Design, 1973–75. Recipient: Berlin Senate Award for Design Methodology, 1967; ACELCO Prize, Buenos Aires, 1977; Harvesting Machine Competition Prize, Development Bank of Misiones, 1979. Member: Vereinigung Deutscher Industrie-Designer, 1967. Address: Conselho Nacional de Desenvolvimento Cientifico e Tecnologico, CNPq SDI/CDI, C.P. 11 1142, 70750 Brasilia, D.F., Brazil.

Publications:

By BONSIEPE: books—*Design im Übergang zum Sozialismus*, Hamburg 1974; *Diseno Industrial: Artefacto y Proyecto*, Madrid 1975, as *Diseno Industrial, Tecnologia y Dependencia*, Mexico City 1978; *Teoria e Pratica del Disegno Industriale*, Milan 1975, Barcelona 1978; *A'tecnologia da tecnologia*, Sao Paulo 1983, as *Periferia del Diseno*, Barcelona 1984; articles—in *Ulm* (Ulm), no. 10/1, 1964, no. 12/13, 1965, no. 19/20, 1967; *Contribuciones Tecnicas* (Buenos Aires), no. 3, 1966; *La Gazeta de Cuba* (Havana), no. 78, 969; *Form und Zweck* (Berlin), no. 2, 1976, nos. 1 and 2, 1979.

On BONSIEPE: books—*Die Geschichte des Design in Deutschland* by Gert Selle, Cologne 1978; *Industrial Design* by John Heskett, London 1980; *An Introduction to Design and Culture in the Twentieth Century* by Penny Sparke, London 1986.

I consider the term "design" rather misleading as long as it is not accompanied by a specifier: Design for whom? In which context? In a Eurocentric frame of reference, one might be seduced to suggest a universally valid definition of design, but there is no concept applicable to both of the two profoundly different situations in the Centre and in the Periphery.

The universe of the Centre is one-eyed, often even blind to the realities beyond itself. Of course, the design scene is dominated by the output from the Centre, which defines product types and physiognomies that the industrial system spits out in ever-increasing rhythms. Much of that output touches the fringe of a pathology of consumption and can be interpreted as a symptom of the desire to discover small areas of need not yet occupied by material artifacts. The Centre also produces the theoretical output. After all, experiences with industrial design started in industrialized countries. Compared with that situation, the design scene in the Periphery is almost non-existent, trying desperately to find its own ways because the design solutions it needs are not available elsewhere and so must be invented here. Thus, I sustain the thesis that we have today two kinds of design: the design developed in and for the Centre and the design we hope is developing in and for the Periphery, matching local needs with local resources (materials, know-how, machinery).

The two design worlds have rather little in common. The circle of design maturation in the Centre is complete. The responsibilities of the professional are well-established, educational programmes are consolidated, design events fill

Gui Bonsiepe: Furniture for low-cost housing, developed for INTEC, 1971

design publications, and design centres go on in their daily routine. We may expect more perfection in the vertical direction—digging deeper in a well-marked field. But the designer's "universe of intervention" seems to me to be finite.

Controversies have arisen as to the validity of the modern movement, functionalism, and design rationalism, the death notices of which we find in almost every opportunity given to those who consider themselves beyond modernism. (I would rather think that we face a new type of pre-modernism.) In the end, these discussions seem to be simple attempts to put into brackets the social dimension of design under the cover of arguments about form and style. Passionate discussions of *stilemi* are the counterpart to political conservatism; "retro" in design corresponds to the "retro" in the social quality of the society in which we live.

Style is not a design priority in the Periphery. The question of design in the Periphery is linked to the problem of technological dependence (and, by implication, financial dependence). I came to interpret industrial design as technological variable. Design and technology go beyond product esthetics. They touch the nerve centre of the quality of the material culture—with proper characteristics, not simply of form, but of structure as well. The role of design in the Periphery is emancipatory, helping to get rid of domination. There are temptations to fall into the trap of technological primitivism (after all, rattan is technologically a rather limited material), though some priests of the new simplicity would have us do so. But much of the Centre's criticism of technology is essentially romantic because it is not ready to renounce the advantages modern technology offers. There is also the trap of "good design"—a

cultural export of dubious value in the Periphery. The material culture of the Periphery has to be created; it cannot be found in the past. I doubt, for instance, that the study of pre-Colombian art can orient the Latin American designer in the design of a water tap or a metal-bending machine.

I favor an anti-narcissistic posture similar to Brecht's recommendation to the actor: not to confuse his personality with the role of the character he represents. Products produced by mass-production methods for everyday use are too important to serve as billboards for individuality. In designing a product, there are many more people involved than those labeled "designers." Design is the result of teamwork, and we use the designer's name mainly as a practical shorthand.

At present, I am interested in the zone of transition between (mechanical) engineering and industrial design. Some colleagues consider design as a kind of mini-architecture or sub-discipline of engineering—with esthetics added. I don't share these reductionist views. Architecture differs from design in its variable space and scale, whereas engineering differs in its approach to artifacts. Industrial design is user-centered and concerned with the efficiency of needs in a way that parallels the interest in physical efficiency prevalent in traditional "hard" disciplines. Industrial design is linked to the interface between product and user. Of course, interfaces imply an esthetic dimension (understood as a non-normative concept), and this dimension cannot be added or subtracted at will from a product. Esthetics are intrinsically interwoven with the manner in which we experience products; recognizing that, however, does not mean putting esthetics on a pedestal and

declaring it the dominating factor in design.

We handle esthetic aspects through non-discursive codes which are unfortunately heavily underrepresented in our educational system. It is hardly understood how we acquire these codes and become proficient in their use. That is one of the most conspicuous shortcomings of design methodology as we know it today.

One scenario of the future of our profession presents the designer of tomorrow as a professional heavily relying on computers. But I wonder whether this view isn't overstating the influence of a tool on the quality of design solutions. Like radical phraseology, tools can be quite conservative. Car design continues as conservative as ever in spite of computer-aided design. We may reach destinations faster, but not necessarily new destinations. Tomás Maldonado once described the designer as a troublemaker. I agree with that; it is the essence of design.

—Gui Bonsiepe

BOX, John.
British film designer. Born in London, 27 January 1920. Educated at schools in Ceylon; studied architecture, Bartlett School of Architecture,

University of London. Served in the British Army, 1939–45. Worked as a film draughtsman for London Films, Denham Studios, Buckinghamshire, 1947–49; assistant art director to Alex Vetchinsky and Carmen Dillon, 1950–53; art director, working on the films of Terence Young, Franklin Schaffner, Mark Robson, Carol Reed, Richard Quine, David Lean, John Cromwell, Fred Zinnemann, etc., from 1953. Recipient: Academy Award, 1962, 1965, 1968, 1971. British Academy Award, 1967, 1974, 1975; Moscow Film Festival Award, 1968. Addresses: c/o William Morris Agency, 147 Wardour Street, London W1; 28 Scarsdale Villas, London W8 6PR, England.

Works:

Film designs include—*The Million Pound Note* (Neame), 1953; *The Black Knight* (Garnett), 1954; *A Prize of Gold* (Robson), 1955; *Cockleshell Heroes* (Ferrer), 1956; *The Gamma People* (Gilling), 1956; *Zarak* (Young), 1957; *Fire Down Below* (Parrish), 1957; *How to Murder a Rich Uncle* (Patrick and Varnel), 1958; *High Flight* (Gilling), 1958; *No Time to Die* (Young), 1958; *The Inn of the Sicxth Happiness* (Robson), 1958; *Our Man in Havana* (Reed), 1959; *Two-Way Street* (Day), 1960; *The World of Suzie Wong* (Quine), 1961; *Lawrence of Arabia* (Lean), 1962; *Of Human Bondage* (Hughes), 1964; *The Wild Affair* (Krish), 1965; *A Man for All Seasons* (Zinnemann), 1966; *Oliver* (Reed), 1968; *The Looking Glass War* (Pierson), 1970; *Nicholas and Alexandria* (Schaffner), 1971; *Travels with my Aunt* (Cukor), 1972; *The Great Gatsby* (Clayton), 1974; *Rollerball* (Jewison), 1975; *Sorcerer* (Friedkin), 1977; *The Keep* (Mann), 1983; *A Passage to India* (Lean), 1984.

Publications:

By BOX: articles—interview in *Film Review* (London), January 1975; *Cinematograph* (Paris), February 1982.

On BOX: books—*Le Decor de Film* by Leon Barsacq, Paris 1970, as *Caligari's Cabinet and Other Grand Illusions,* Boston 1976; *The International Film Encyclopedia* by Ephraim Katz, London 1980; *The International Dictionary of Films and Filmmakers,* London and Chicago 1987, 1991.

John Box's designs evidence that selection, care, and craftsmanship can make motion pictures artistic, even when apparent realism is the overall visual style desired by a director. For *Doctor Zhivago* (1965), for example, not only was Russia created in Spain, it was done so in a way that emphasized the color red at key points in the film. That film, too, is the haunting image of the icy villa at the edge of the steppes. This image not only fulfills the need for a setting described in the script, but also is suggestive of a doomed way of life.

Box works in the tradition of the big costume pictures of the 1930's, and, to go further back, in the tradition of nineteenth- and early twentieth-century paintings and illustrations of historical or exotic locations, carefully researched, yet artfully presented. One such nineteenth-century example is the set of illustrations of London districts by Gustave Doré. These were in fact used by Box in designing *Oliver!* (1968) in which he maintained a program of simplified forms and selected colors suitable for the artificial quality of a musical with production numbers. The artificial qualities are more subtly integrated into most of Box's films, as seen in two examples that con-

vincingly show illusions of past times, the sixteenth-century England of *A Man for All Seasons* (1966) and early twentieth-century America of *The Great Gatsby* (1974). Box's sweeping and grand treatment of the past has influenced more recent epic films, such as *Reds* (1981) and *Gandhi* (1982). Perhaps Box's major contribution to motion picture design has been in maintaining artistic qualities associated with earlier periods of art and film without sacrificing the versimilitude of particular historical periods.

—Floyd W. Martin

BOYLE, Robert.

American film designer. Born in Los Angeles, California, in 1910. Studied at the University of Southern California, Los Angeles: B.Arch. 1933. Served in the United States Army Signal Corps, 1942–45. Worked for several architectural firms, then as a film extra, sketch artist, and draughtsman, at Paramount Studios, Hollywood, California; assistant art director, under Wiard Ihnen, at Universal Studios, Hollywood, from 1933–36; art director, at Universal Studios, 1936–42, at RKO Studios, 1946–47, and again at Universal Studios, from 1947: worked with directors Alfred Hitchcock, Bud Boetticher, Norman Jewison, Richard Brooks, Ernest Lehman, Douglas Sirk, etc. Address: 6904 Los Tilos Road, Los Angeles, California 90028, U.S.A.

Works:

Film designs include—*Saboteur* (Hitchcock), 1942; *Flesh and Fantasy* (Duvivier), 1943; *Shadow of a Doubt* (Hitchcock), 1943; *Good Morning, Judge* (Yarbrough), 1943; *South of Tahiti* (Waggoner), 1943; *Nocturne* (Marin), 1946; *They Won't Believe Me* (Pichel), 1947; *Ride the Pink Horse* (Montgomery), 1947; *Another Part of the Forest* (Gordon), 1948; *An Act of Murder* (Gordon), 1948; *For the Love of Mary* (de Cordova), 1948; *The Gal Who Took the West* (de Cordova), 1949; *Abandoned* (Newman), 1949; *Buccaneer's Girl* (de Cordova), 1950; *Louisa* (Hall), 1950; *The Milkman* (Barton), 1950; *Sierra* (Grenen), 1950; *Mystery Submarine* (Sirk), 1950; *Iron Man* (Pevney), 1951; *Mark of the Renegade* (Fregonese), 1951; *The Lady Pays Off* (Sirk), 1951; *Weekend with Father* (Sirk), 1951; *Bronco Buster* (Boetticher), 1952; *Lost in Alaska* (Yarbrough), 1952; *Yankee Buccaneer* (de Cordova), 1952; *Back at the Front* (Sherman), 1952; *Girls in the Night* (Arnold), 1953; *The Beast from 20,000 Fathoms* (Lourie), 1953; *Gunsmoke* (Juran), 1953; *Abbott and Costello Go to Mars* (Lamont), 1953; *Ma and Pa Kettle on Vacation* (Lamont), 1953; *It Came from Outer Space* (Arnold), 1953; *East of Sumatra* (Boetticher), 1953; *Ma and Pa Kettle at Home* (Lamont), 1954; *Johnny Dark* (Sherman), 1954; *Ride Clear of Diablo* (Hibbs), 1954; *Chief Crazy Horse* (Sherman), 1955; *Kiss of Fire* (Newman), 1955; *The Private War of Major Benson* (Hopper), 1955; *Lady Godiva* (Lubin), 1955; *Running Wild* (La Cava), 1955; *Never Say Goodbye* (Hopper), 1956; *A Day of Fury* (Jones), 1956; *Congo Crossing* (Pevney), 1956; *The Night Runner* (Biberman), 1957; *The*

Brothers Rico (Karlson), 1957; *Operation Mad Ball* (Quine), 1957; *Buchanan Rides Alone* (Boetticher), 1958; *Wild Heritage* (Haas), 1958; *The Crimson Kimono* (Fuller), 1959; *North by Northwest* (Hitchcock), 1959; *Cape Fear* (Lee Thompson), 1962; *The Birds* (Hitchcock), 1963; *The Thrill of It All* (Jewison), 1963; *Marnie* (Hitchcock), 1964; *Do Not Disturb* (Levy), 1965; *The Reward* (Bourguignon), 1965; *The Russians Are Coming, the Russians Are Coming* (Jewison), 1966; *Fitzwilly* (Delbert Mann), 1967; *In Cold Blood* (Brooks), 1967; *How to Succeed in Business Without Really Trying* (Swift), 1967; *The Thomas Crown Affair* (Jewison), 1968; *Gaily, Gaily* (Jewison), 1969; *The Landlord* (Ashby), 1970; *Fiddler on the Roof* (Jewison), 1971; *Portnoy's Complaint* (Lehman), 1972; *Mame* (Saks), 1974; *Bite the Bullet* (Brooks), 1975; *Leadbelly* (Parks), 1976; *Winter Kills* (Richert), 1978.

Publications:

By BOYLE: articles—in *America* (New York), 19 November 1960, 2 February 1974; *Film Comment* (New York), May/June 1978; *Cahiers du Cinema* (Paris), June 1982.

On BOYLE: books—*Le Decor de Film* by Leon Barsacq, Paris 1970, as *Caligrai's Cabinet and Other Grand Illusions,* Boston 1976; *The International Film Encyclopedia* by Ephraim Katz, London 1980; *The International Dictionary of Films and Filmmakers,* London and Chicago 1987, 1991.

Art director Robert Boyle collaborated with director Alfred Hitchcock in five films in which the suspense and heightened emotional response to the narrative is caused to a great extent by the design elements. Two examples from Boyle's and Hitchcock's work show how their total control of the imagery established convincing illusions heightened by viewpoints impossible to achieve on location. In *North by Northwest,* much of the Mount Rushmore sequence was filmed on a stage, using rear projections to create the illusion that it was filmed in South Dakota. Boyle first made stills of the actual site, and from these then made detailed portions of the carvings in the studio. In *The Birds,* there is a sequence, seen from a bird's eye view showing the center of the town of Bodega Bay, when a man is attacked by birds as he is using a gas pump. He drops the pump and gasoline spreads to where another man, getting out of a car, lights a cigar and throws down the match, thereby starting a fire. Simultaneously the heroine, in a phone booth, is attacked by birds. In comments published in 1978, Boyle explained that the only real objects in the fire scene were the phone booth, one car, gasoline, and fire. All the rest—including a matte painted by Albert Whitlock, a shot of birds attacking, and miniature smoke—was an illusion. This short sequence is an important one in the film, and its construction underscores the importance Boyle placed on absolute control of the image. This is also seen in his use of mattes simply to change the coloring of a sky to set a particular mood.

The apparent realism of Boyle's images is typical of Hollywood films of the 1950's and 1960's, when actual locations were more frequently used, or designed sets were made to be detailed illusions of real places. However, the care and selection that undergirds this apparent realism is suggestive of the methods of earlier film designers, who were very aware of the effect certain colors, shapes, or viewpoints can have on an audience.

—Floyd W. Martin

BOZZETTO, Bruno.

Italian advertising and animation film designer.
Born in Milan, 3 March 1938. Studied the classics, law and geology, in Milan; also studied animation under John Halas, 1959-60. Freelance animated film designer, Milan, 1958-59; founder-director, Bruno Bozzetto Film advertising and entertainment film company, Milan, since 1959. President, European Association of Animated Film, 1988. Recipient: Gold Plaque, International Film Festival, Chicago, 1976; Bronze Statuette, Tampere Film Festival, Finland, 1977; Jury Prize, 1978, and Diploma of Honour, 1979, MIFED Film Festival, Milan; Prix du Public, Chamrousse, France, 1978; Grand Prix Golden Kuker, First World Animated Film Festival, Varna, Bulgaria, 1979; Blue Ribbon, Los Angeles Film Festival, 1979; Gold Medal, Marburg Film Festival, Germany, 1982; Annual Annie Award, ASIFA, Hollywood, 1982. Address: Bruno Bozzetto Film, via Melchiorre Gioia 55, 20124 Milan, Italy.

Works:

Animated and live-action films include—
Tapum, la storia delle armi, 1958; *La storia delle invenzioni,* 1959; *Un Oscar per il Signor Rossi,* 1960; *Alpha Omega,* 1961; *I due castelli,* 1963; *Il Signor Rossi va a sciare,* (1963); *Il Signor Rossi al mare,* 1964; *West and Soda,* 1965; *Il Signor Rossi compra l'automobile,* 1966; *Una vita in scatola,* 1967; *L'Uomo e il suo mondo,* 1967; *Vip mio fratello superuomo,* 1968; *Ego,* 1969; *Il Signor Rossi al camping,* 1970; *Sottaceti,* 1971; *Oppio per oppio,* 1972; *Il Signor Rossi al safari fotografico,* 1972; *Opera,* 1973; *La Cabina,* 1973; *Self Service,* 1974; *Il Signor Rossi a Venezia,* 1974; *Gli sport del Signor Rossi,* 1975; *La piscina,* 1976; *Il Signor Rossi cerca la felicita,* 1976; *Allegro non troppo,* 1976; *I sogni del Signor Rossi,* 1977; *Le vacanze del Signor Rossi,* 1977; *Striptease,* 1977; *Baby Story,* 1978; *Happy Birthday,* 1979; *Giallo automatico,* 1980; *Sandwich,* 1980; *Ma come fanno a farli cosi belli?,* 1980; *Lilliput-put* (13 films), 1980; *Quark* (series of 45 films), 1981-88; *Tennis Club,* 1982; *Sporting,* 1982; *La Pillola,* 1983; *Sigmund,* 1983; *Nel centro del mirino,* 1983; *Milano Zero,* 1983; *Moa Moa,* 1984; *Sandwich* (12 films), 1984; *Eldorado,* 1985; *Spider,* 1986; *Quark Economia* (13 films), 1986; *Baeus,* 1987; *Sotto il Ristorante Cinese,* 1987; *MiniQuark* (29 films), 1988; *Mister Tao,* 1988.

Publications:

By BOZZETTO: articles—interview in *Cinema International* (London), no. 16, 1967; *Filmblatter* (Berlin), 2 February 1968; *Banc-Titre* (Paris), October 1982.

On BOZZETTO: books—*Film and TV Graphics,* edited by Walter Herdeg, with texts by John Halas and Robert Delpire, Zurich 1967; *Bruno Bozzetto: Animazione primo amore* by G. Bendazzi, Milan 1972; *Full Length Animated Feature Films* by Bruno Edera, London and New York 1977.

Bruno Bozzetto's first period of schooling consisted of classical studies and some years at university devoted to law and geology, but since entering animation and design at the age of seventeen, he has succeeded in a field which was primarily dominated by the Hollywood-based studios, such as those of Walt Disney, Hanna Barbera, and, more recently, Filmation and Ralph Bakshi.

Bozzetto's main attributes are his consistency of output and his inimitable style of grotesque,

Bruno Bozzetto: Still from the film *Mister Tao,* 1988

highly individual caricature. He can define with simple outlines the true essence of a personality which is instantly recognizable and commands interest. As a film cartoonist, he is able to expand a character with the right behaviour patterns and to create a complementary personality in depth. One of his stock characters, Il Signor Rossi, who appeared in numerous short cartoons from 1963 onwards and in three of his feature-length films, became the symbol of the Italian "little man"; resourceful, determined, greedy, and vain, he charmingly puts his family interests above all others.

Bozzetto's rare asset is his ability to coordinate and control story continuity, characterization of personalities, development of story, complementary sound effects and music (which underline the behaviour of his figures), humour (which never steps out of context of the subject), and ideas (which are within the bounds of the technical flexibility of animation) to achieve the final effect. His sharp, European wit differs from the American (which is more physical), inasmuch as he comments satirically on human shortcomings, such as greed and stupidity. Nevertheless, his humour is light, it never swings over into preaching, it remains within the limits of traditional Italian comedy.

His large output, which includes several series for television and six full-length animated feature films, reached a peak with *Allegro non troppo* in 1976. A parody on a grand symphony concert, it plays on the unexpected happenings which could occur during such a concert. The film combines pleasing graphic design, close relationships between choreography of movement and music, and a degree of visual progression which few animated films have achieved so far. His recent productions include his first full-length live-action film *Under the*

Chinese Restaurant (1987). Several of his shorter films, such as *Alpha Omega, Opera, Ego, Baeus,* and *Self Service,* all classic cautionary tales for our time, exemplify his integration of graphic design, story telling, and European humour. In 1988, he produced his longest television series to date, *MiniQuark,* consisting of 29 thirty-minute episodes.

In 1988 Bruno Bozzetto became president of the European Association of Animation Film.

—John Halas

BRANDT, Marianne.

German painter, collagist and industrial designer. Born Marianne Liebe, in Chemnitz (now Karl-Marx-Stadt), 1 October 1893. Studied painting and sculpture, under Fritz Mackensen, Robert Wiese and Richard Engelmann, at the Kunsthochschule, Weimar, 1911-14; metalwork, under Laszlo Moholy-Nagy and Wilhelm Wagenfeld, at the Staatliche Bauhaus, Weimar, 1923-25. Married the Norwegian painter Erik Brandt in 1919 (separated). Independent painter, living in Norway and France, 1919-22; metalware product and industrial designer, working Weimar and Paris, 1924-27, in Dessau and Berlin, 1927-29, and in Gotha, 1929-33; independent painter, tapestry and product designer, in Chemnitz, 1933-49, in Dresden, 1949-51, and in East Berlin, 1951-54: design assistant in office of Walter Gropius, working on the Dammerstock housing development, Berlin, 1929; head of design office, Ruppelwerk AG metalware factory, Gotha, 1929–33. Instructor, 1927–28, and head of metal workshops, Staatliche Bauhaus, Dessau; instructor in wood, metal and ceramics workshops, Hochschule der Bildenden Kunste, Dresden, 1949–51, and at the Institut fur Industrie-formgestaltung, East Berlin, 1951–54: retired to Karl-Marx-Stadt, 1954–76, and to Kirchberg, 1976–83. **Exhibitions:** *Moderne Formgestaltung,* Staatliche Galerie, Dresden, 1967; *50 Jahre Bauhaus,* Württembergischer Kunstverein, Stuttgart, 1968; *Die Zwanziger Jahre,* Kunstgewerbemuseum, Zurich, 1973; *Bauhaus 2,* Galerie am Sachsenplatz, Leipzig, 1977; *Tendenzen der Zwanziger Jahre,* Nationalgalerie, West Berlin, 1977; *Drei Künstler aus dem Bauhaus,* Kupferstichkabinett, Dresden, 1978; *Revolution und Realismus,* Nationalgalerie, East Berlin, 1978. **Collections:** Wissenschftlich-kulturelles Zentrum Bauhaus, Dessau; Kupferstichkabinett, Dresden; Bauhaus-Archiv, West Berlin. *Died* (in Kirchberg, German Democratic Republic) *18 June 1983.*

Works:

Spherical teapot in bronze, silver and ebony, 1923–24.
Ashtray with tilting top, in bronze and silver alloy, 1924.
Hemi-spherical teapot in bronze, silver and ebony, 1924.
Six-piece coffee and tea service in silver, 1924.
Four-piece tea set in brass, silver and ebony, 1924.
Adjustable pendant lamp in aluminium, 1926 (with Hans Przyembel).
Four-piece hotel tea service in nickel silver, 1926.
Kandem night table lamp in lacquered steel, 1928.

(Most of Brandt's Bauhaus period designs were produced by Korting und Matthiesson of Leipzig, 1927–32, and lighting appliances were re-editioned by Tecnolumen of Bremen, 1980).

Publications:

On BRANDT: books—*Bauhausbuch nr. 7: Neue Arbeiten der Bauhauswerkstatten,* Munich 1925; *Bauhaus Weimar 1919–1924: Werkstattarbeiten* by Walther Scheidig, Leipzig 1966, as *Crafts of the Weimar Bauhaus 1919–1924,* London 1967; *The Bauhaus* by Hans Maria Wingler, Cambridge, Massachusetts 1968; *Bauhaus and Bauhaus People,* edited by Eckhard Neumann, New York and London 1970; *Goldsmiths and Silversmiths* by Hugh Honour, London 1971; *Tendenzen der Zwanziger Jahre,* exhibition catalogue by Dieter Honisch, Eberhard Roters and others, West Berlin 1977; *Marianne Brandt, Hajo Rose, Kurt Schmidt: Drei Künstler aus dem Bauhaus,* exhibition catalogue with introduction by Werner Schmidt, Dresden 1978; *Die Geschichte des Design in Deutschland von 1870 bis heute* by Gert Selle, Cologne 1978; *In Good Shape: Style in Industrial Products 1900 to 1960* by Stephen Bayley, London 1979; *Design Source Book* by Penny Sparke and others, London 1986.

Perhaps most widely known for her early silver and bronze service vessels, Marianne Brandt deserves to be remembered also for her contribution to modern lamp and lighting fixture design. Her work directly reflects the evolution of Bauhaus philosophy from the arts-and-crafts bias of the Weimar period (1919–25) to the concern for industrial design and technology of the Dessau period (1925–32). During the Weimar years, Brandt was a successful pupil of Christian Dell, and after 1925 she was influenced by László Moholy-Nagy, who was deeply interested in the phenomenon of light, both aesthetically and practically.

During the early Bauhaus years, the theme "form follows function" had frequently been treated as an intellectual idea rather than as a guiding principle to successful design. Some of Brandt's early craft-oriented work, such as her 1924 tea service reflects this puristic thinking, which resulted in vessels composed of her favorite design forms—sphere, hemisphere, and cylinder—treated as geometric units without integrational considerations. This led at times to awkward results visually, structurally, and functionally, as is exemplified by the teapot of her 1924 service.

From 1925, when Moholy-Nagy took complete charge of the metal workshop, the Bauhaus developed a new relationship with industry; silver and bronze were set aside in favor of industrial metals, such as nickel-plated brass and aluminium. Even though she had designed lamps as early as 1924, Brandt's work underwent a change in direction at this time, as she ceased designing for appearance, or the modern look, and became involved with solving problems related to consumer use. Henceforth, her design effort was put to producing prototypes for mass production.

In 1925, Brandt designed a movable wall fixture with adjustable reflector and a simple wall fixture composed of a frosted-glass cylinder mounted on a metal base. Also concerned with area lighting, she designed for walls or low ceilings a lighting fixture which consisted of a shallow, opaque-glass shield mounted in a simple, metal frame. In the following year, she devised, for shaving or makeup, an ensemble composed of a dull aluminium reflector lit by an electric bulb placed behind a mirror, as well as a lamp with a rise-and-fall cable, pull handle, and aluminium shade. One of her most successful designs, a small, metal-shaded bedside lamp set on a flexible stem for adjustability, was manufactured by Körting and Mathiesson in Leipzig in 1927. By this time, the modern lamp was in wide use in Germany and Switzerland, as is evidenced by the fact that between 1928 and 1932, Körting and Mathiesson made approximately 50,000 lamps based on prototypes of Bauhaus metal workshop students and staff. After 1925, Brandt continued to design serving vessels though none of these were truly innovative nor aimed at solving particular user-problems, such as her lamp and lighting-fixture design were.

—Barbara Young

BRATTINGA, Pieter (Dirk).
Dutch graphic and exhibition designer. Born in Hilversum, 31 January 1931. Educated at the International Quaker School, Castle Eerde, Ommen, 1946–49. Served in the Dutch Corps of Engineers, training with the British Army On the Rhine and the United States Army in Europe, 1950–52: First Lieutenant. Married Wilhelmina Kooy in 1951 (divorced, 1971); Annette Aeneae Venema in 1975; children: Pieter, Anne and Maartje. Director of Design, Steendrukkerij de Jong and Company, Hilversum, 1951–74; Senior Partner, Form Mediation International art and design consultants, Amsterdam, since 1964; Managing Director, Mercis bv., Amsterdam, since 1971. Professor and Chairman, Visual Communications Department, Pratt Institute, Brooklyn, New York,

Marianne Brandt: Hotel tea service in nickel silver, 1926

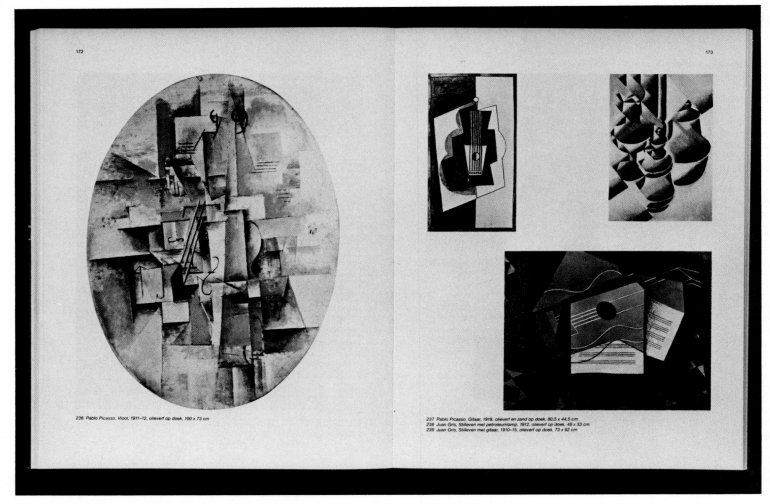

Pieter Brattinga: *Kroller-Muller* book layout, for J. Enschede en Zonen, 1988

1960–64; Visiting Professor, Technical Institute, Eindhoven, 1980–82. Secretary-General, ICOGRADA International Council of Graphic Design Associations, 1966–70; President, Art Directors Club of the Netherlands, 1968–71, and Netherlands Art Foundation, 1969–75. **Exhibitions:** Southern Illinois University, Carbondale, 1961; Lodz Museum of Modern Art, Poland, 1974; Otto Nagel Haus, East Berlin, 1976; Kroller-Muller Museum, Otterlo, 1980. **Collections:** Stedelijk Museum, Amsterdam; Kunstgewerbemuseum, Zurich; Wilanowa Palace, Warsaw; Museum of Modern Art, New York; Library of Congress, Washington, D.C.; Musashimo Art Museum, Tokyo. Recipient: Grand Prix, *International Survey of Exhibition Design,* at the Brno Biennale, 1968. Address: Prinsengracht 628, 1017 KT Amsterdam, Netherlands.

Works:

Series of exhibition announcements and posters, for Steendrukkerij de Jong, 1958–72.
Typographic calendar, for Steendrukkerij de Jong, 1962.
Exhibition announcements and posters, for the Riksmuseum Kroller-Muller, Otterlo, since 1965.
Postage stamps, for the Netherlands Post Office, since 1969.
10 Europa 9 annual book design, for Grafisch Nederland, 1972.
Sandberg: A Documentary book design, for Kosmos, 1975.
De Stijl exhibition design, for the Rijksmuseum Kroller-Muller, Otterlo, 1982.

The Graphic Image of Britain 1900–1970 chart supplement, for Idea Publishers, Tokyo, 1985.
Kroller-Muller book design, for Johannes Enschede en Zonen, 1988.

Publications:

By BRATTINGA: books—*Industrial Design in the Netherlands,* Minneapolis 1964; *Elements of Consideration for the Training of the Visual Communication Designer,* Warsaw 1966; *Artypo: Kunst gemaakt met behulp van grafisch technieken,* Eindhoven 1967; *A History of the Dutch Poster 1890–1960,* with Dick Dooijes, Amsterdam 1968; *De Toekomst van de Grafische Industrie in Nederland,* Amsterdam 1972; *50 Plakate, neun Hollandische Graphiker,* Munich 1972; *A Portrait of Sandberg,* Amsterdam 1972; *The Visual Rhythm of the Newspaper,* Amsterdam 1974; *Sandberg: A Documentary,* with Ad Petersen, Amsterdam 1975; *Influences on Dutch Graphic Design 1900–1945,* Burgenstock 1987.

On BRATTINGA: books—*The First International Poster Biennale,* with introduction by Jozef Mroszczak, Warsaw 1968; *European Designers,* edited by Idea Publishers, Tokyo 1970; *History of the Poster* by Josef and Shizuko Muller-Brockman, Zurich 1971; *Who's Who in Graphic Art,* edited by Walter Amstutz, Dubendorf 1982; *45–80: Typografisch Nederland* by C. Jongejans, Nijmegen 1984; *Posters* by D. Adams, Minneapolis 1984; *The Activities of Pieter Brattinga: Portrait of an Era* by G. Waldmann, Tokyo 1989.

The facet which is most important to the visual communication designer is his thinking. He must have a flexible and well-organized mind to enable him to: 1) distinguish the real truth in a blurred and coloured presentation; 2) abstract its essential points; 3) translate these points, in their order of importance, into a coherent solution—it is quite possible, in fact, that if he is able to make a very clear summarized statement about his commission, he will have solved his problem.

The visual communication designer must have a knowledge of related fields, as well as of the major developments in science, art, and philosophy. Only if he has the ability to select those items of information from which he can draw his own conclusions will he be the right person to give form to communication between people. Unlike the fine artist, most concerned with expressing his own inner feelings, the visual communication designer is primarily an intermediary in the communication of ideas. His education, therefore, must enable him to understand the language of scientists, artists, and officials, so that he can translate their thoughts and ideas into visual terms.

Specialization is one of the aspects of the visual communication field. Whereas the commercial artist of the 1920's was his own illustrator, letterer, and typographer, the designer of today usually occupies himself with only one segment of a project. Or, while functioning as an art director, he must be able to engage and coordinate the services of other specialists for specific tasks. The designer of today very rarely makes an end product. His sketch, script, or layout, unlike the autographic production of the fine artist, is only a plan for technical realization.

He must develop his plan, therefore, within the limitations of a specific technical process.

—Pieter Brattinga

The son of the owner of a printing press, Pieter Brattinga at an early age was made design director of a printing firm, where he became known for the non-commercial Quadrat Prints, first published in 1955 and featuring the work of many different designers. As they were of particularly high quality, the prints thus publicized the skill of the firm. In drawing attention to the quality of the work, Brattinga used the opportunity to further avant-garde ideas that would otherwise not have received such publicity. In addition, Brattinga has designed a number of exhibitions for such museums as the Stedelijk in Amsterdam and the Kröller-Müller in Otterlo. It is significant that his concern in this context is as much for the feelings of the audience as for the professional care of the objects: he is a natural propagandist. He has also had considerable experience as a teacher and writer on education and has produced significant statements on the programme for training designers. These insist on the all-around development of the student, as well as the acquisition of skills.

Brattinga's particular influence, however, derives from his special expertise in typography and graphic design. Examples of his important work include his posters for the work of Mies van der Rohe (1959), for the Netherlands Post Office (1960), and for the Nippon Design Center (1963), their quite different concepts are linked by a high standard of typographical design. His characteristic approach lies in the clear presentation of an idea, usually using typographical elements, which often form a pattern as well as convey a message, as they did when he spread a large, single typeface across an entire wall in the Stedelijk Museum to produce a mural developing from left to right into a series of endless permutations. One was reminded of the tradition established by Hendrik Werkman.

In spite of the skills demonstrated by Brattinga as a designer, he has demonstrated also an ability to handle committees and organizations and to act as a force in spreading good design internationally. His reputation rests on the combination of these factors but first of all, on the respect owed to him as a professional designer.

—John Barnicoat

BREUER, Marcel (Lajos).
American architect, interior and industrial designer. Born in Pecs, Hungary, 22 May 1902; emigrated to the United States in 1937: naturalized, 1944. Educated at the Allami Foreaiskola, Pecs, 1912–20; studied at the Bauhaus, Weimar, 1920–24. Married Martha Erps in 1926; Constance Crocker Leighton in 1940; children: Thomas and Francesca. Freelance architect, planner and designer, in Dessau, 1925–28, in Berlin, 1928–31, and in London, 1935–36; founder and principal, Marcel Breuer and Associates, Cambridge, Massachusetts, 1937–46, and in New York, 1946 until his retirement in 1976. Master of the Bauhaus, in Weimar, 1924, and in Dessau, 1925–28; Associate Professor, Harvard University School of Design, Cambridge, Massachusetts, 1937–46.

Member, National Council of Architectural Registration Boards, 1947. **Exhibitions:** *Exposition Werkbund,* Grand Palais, Paris, 1930; *Bauausstellung,* Berlin, 1931; *Bauhaus 1919-1928,* Museum of Modern Art, New York, 1938; *Marcel Breuer: Architect,* Museum of Modern Art, New York, 1949; *Marcel Breuer,* Metropolitan Museum of Art, New York, 1972; *Marcel Breuer: Architectures,* Musee du Louvre, Paris, 1973; Bauhaus Archives, West Berlin, 1974; Museum of Modern Art, New York, 1981 (retrospective). Recipient: First Prize, International Aluminium Competition, 1930, 1933; Medal of Honor, 1965, Gold Medal, 1968, Award of Excellence, 1970, and Honor Awards, 1970, 1972, 1973, American Institute of Architects; New York State Council on the Arts Award, 1967; Bard Award, City Club of New York, 1968; Thomas Jefferson Medal, University of Virginia, 1968; Metropolitan Washington Board of Trade Award, 1969; Gold Medal, French Academy of Architecture, 1976. Honorary Doctorates: Pratt Institute, Brooklyn, New York, 1950; University of Budapest, 1957; University of Notre Dame, Indiana, 1968; Harvard University, 1970. Honorary Member, Association of Argentine Architects, 1946, and Association of Architects of Colombia, 1947; Fellow, American Institute of Architects; Member, National Institute of Arts and Letters. *Died* (in New York City) *1 July 1981.*

Works:

Wassily collapsible easy chair in tubular steel and leather, 1926, produced by Gavina.
Laccio coffee table in tubular steel with wood or laminate top, 1925–26, produced by Knoll International and Thonet.
B4 club armchair in tubular steel and canvas, for Standard-Mobel, 1926.
B6 side chair in tubular steel and wood, for Standard-Mobel, 1926–27.
B32 (Cesca) cantilever side chair in tubular steel, wood and canework, 1928, produced by Thonet and Gavina.
S286 desk in tubular steel and wood, 1928, produced by Thonet.
Reclining lounge chair in aluminium, for Tubecraft Limited, 1935.
Long upholstered chair in laminated wood, for Isokon, 1935.
Nesting tables in plywood, for Isokon, 1936.
Stacking chair in plywood, for Isokon, 1936.
Stacking chair in plywood and cane with rubber mounts, for the Museum of Modern Art Low-Cost Furniture Competition, 1945–48.
New Canaan desk, 1951, produced by Gavina.

(for a complete list of Breuer's buildings and architectural projects, see *Contemporary Architects*)

Publications:

By BREUER: books—*Sun and Shadow: The Philosophy of an Architect,* edited by Peter Blake, New York and London 1956; *Marcel Breuer: Buildings and Projects 1921–62,* Stuttgart and New York 1962.

On BREUER: books—*The New Interior Decoration* by Dorothy Todd and Raymond Mortimer, London 1929; *Modern Furniture* by E. Nelson Exton and Fredric H. Littman, London 1936; *Marcel Breuer and the American Tradition in Architecture* by Henry Russell Hitchcock, Cambridge, Massachusetts 1938; *Marcel Breuer: Architect and Designer* by Peter Blake, New York 1949; *Marcel Breuer: Disegno Industriale e Architettura* by Giulio Carlo Argan, Milan 1957; *Marcel Breuer 1921-1962* by

Cranston Jones, London 1962; *Marcel Breuer: New Buildings and Projects* by Tician Papachristou, New York 1970; *Marcel Breuer,* exhibition catalogue by Hans Wingler, West Berlin 1975; *GA 5: Marcel Breuer—Koerfer House, Tessin, Switzerland; Stillman House III, Litchfield, Connecticut,* with text by Stanley Abercrombie, Tokyo 1977; *Tubular Steel Furniture* by Barbie Campbell-Cole and Tim Benton, London 1979; *Marcel Breuer: Furniture and Interiors* by Christopher Wilk, New York 1981.

Marcel Breuer's furniture designs so bespeak the philosophy of the Bauhaus that it is difficult to separate the two. His furniture designs were intended to become part of the architectural environment, not to perform as virtuoso, separate entities. Moreover, like other architecture of the modern movement, it intends to solve problems posed within the society it will serve. Breuer proceeded by searching for the fundamental design problem, then solving it in innovative ways. He thereby sometimes substantively changed for society the very concept on which he was working. He did not merely modify another style, nor even intend to create a new style. This approach to design is evident in both his tubular metal chairs for instance, (Wassily and Cesca) and in his modular storage units. His free-standing storage pieces, usually of wood, divide space and indicate changes of use, while his wall-hung units define perimeters.

Breuer's aim was always to reach a broad market whose life would be bettered by his furniture designs, which were all conceived to be industrially produced, easily shipped, and economical. As space in modern low-cost dwellings was limited, the occupant, Breuer felt, must be relieved of clutter, both visual and actual. Tubular metal furniture, light in weight, relatively indestructable, and transparent, was his solution. Breuer chairs moved easily into every room and could be used in a variety of circumstances.

In 1926, a mock film strip with six "frames" by Breuer was published in the *Bauhaus Journal.* The first five frames each contain a date and a Breuer chair, while the sixth shows a sitter floating in a void. The caption explains:
Bauhaus movie lasting five years.
Author: Life demanding its rights.
Operator: Marcel Breuer who recognizes these rights better and better every year: In the end we will sit on air cushions.

Influences upon Breuer, apart from ideological coincidences between Bauhaus philosophy and his own, are easy to see. Earliest is that of de Stijl and Rietveld. At first (1921–24), he borrowed Reitveld materials—boards and plywood. But even in these early designs, Breuer added consideration of the occupant, using upholstery for comfort. Breuer thought of himself as the humanist of modern design.

Never admitted by Breuer is the apparent influence from Le Corbusier (for instance, his furnishing in the Pavillon de l'Esprit Nouveau). Here, Le Corbusier chose Thonet chairs and designed space-dividing cabinets. These may account for Breuer's storage units used to define space and, in part, for his intensified effort to create a chair which, like the Thonets, would not interrupt the flow of space. Nevertheless, his solution, the Wassily, is revolutionary, not imitative.

Influences emanating from Breuer are legion. Imitators and adaptors of his tubular designs appeared immediately. More important, significant designers found tubular metal useful for their own designs once Breuer's work was seen. Among those influenced by Breuer in this way were Mart Stam in Holland, Mies van der Rohe in Germany, Le Corbusier in France, and Aalto in Finland.

During the 1960's a revival of interest in tubular metal designs from the 1920's and 1930's led Breuer to contract licensees to manufacture his furniture. The Cesca Chair became enormously popular, outstripping all other revived designs. Breuer-licensed models are available now only to the wealthiest clients, but cheap imitations appear all over. Although Breuer deplored the poor workmanship in these, he rejoiced that the Cesca could reach the public he always hoped to serve.

—Nina Bremer

BRODOVITCH, Alexey.

American photographer and graphic designer. Born in Ogolitchi, Russia, in 1898; emigrated to the United States in 1930: subsequently naturalized. Educated at Gymnase Tenichev, 1914–15, and the Corps des Pages Military Academy, Saint Petersburg, 1915. Served in the 12th Archtirsky Hussars, in Rumania, Austria and Russia, 1916–18: Captain. Married Nina Brodovitch in 1920 (died, 1959); son: Nikita. Worked as a house-painter, stage scenery artist, furnishing, book and poster designer, etc., in Paris, 1920–26; graphic designer, in Maximilien Vox advertising agency, Paris, 1926–28; art director, Trois Quartiers department store, Paris, 1928; freelance book illustrator, working for Paris and London publishers, in Paris, 1928–30; designer, N. W. Ayer advertising agency, Philadelphia and New York, 1931–38; art director, under editor Carmel Snow, Harper's Bazaar magazine, New York, 1934–58: art director, Saks Fifth Avenue department store, New York, 1939–41; consultant, American Red Cross, United States Treasury Department, Office of Government Reports, and United Services Organization, 1941; art director, I. Miller and Sons, New York, 1941–43; art director and art editor, with Frank Zachery, of Portfolio magazine, New York, 1949–51; consultant, Art in America magazine, New York, 1965. Founder, Le Cercle designers Association, Paris, 1929–30, and Design Engineers designers' association, Philadelphia, 1932–34. Director, Advertising Arts Department, Philadelphia Museum School of Industrial Art (now Philadelphia College of Art), 1930–38; instructor in design, Donnelly Publishers, Chicago, 1939; visiting lecturer in design, at Cooper Union, New York University, and Pratt Institute, New York, 1940; instructor, Brodovitch Design Laboratory, New School for Social Research, New York, 1941–49 (at the Richard Avedon photo studio, 1947–49); instructor, Print Club of Philadelphia, 1946–48; visiting critic, Yale University, New Haven, Connecticut, 1955; instructor, Brodovitch Design Laboratory, American Institute of Graphic Arts (at the Avedon studio, New York), 1964; School of Visual Arts, New York, 1964–65, and Corcoran Gallery, Washington, D.C., 1965; also held design classes at the Avedon studio, New York, 1966. Retired to Oppede-les-Vieux, 1967–69, and to Le Thor, France, 1969–71. **Exhibitions:** Librairie Povolotski, Paris, 1928 (with A. Alexieff); Advertising Designs, Ayer Gallery, Philadelphia, 1931; Crillon Gallery, Philadelphia, 1933; Cosmopolitan Club, Philadelphia, 1933; Altman Department Store, Philadelphia, 1936; New Poster Show, Franklin Institute, Philadelphia, 1937; Design for the Machine, Philadelphia Museum of Art, 1937; Education Pavilion, at the World's Fair, New York, 1939; Alexey Brodovitch and His Influence, Philadelphia College of Art, 1972 (traveled to Montreal); Hommage a Alexey Brodovitch, Grand Palais, Paris, 1982. **Collections:** Philadelphia College of Art; Fashion Institute of Technology, New York. Recipient: First Prize, Bal Banal Poster Competition, Paris, 1924; 5 medals, Exposition Internationale des Arts Decoratifs, Paris, 1925; Book of the Year Award, American Institute of Graphic Arts, 1945; Robert Leavitt Award, American Society of Magazine Photographers, 1954; Hall of Fame Award, Art Directors Club of New York, 1972. DFA: Philadelphia College of Art, 1972. Died (in Le Thor, France) 15 April 1971.

Publications:

By BRODOVITCH: books illustrated and/or designed—Monsieur de Bougrelon by Jean Lorrain, Paris 1928; Contes Fantastiques by Dostoievsky, Paris 1928; A Brief History of Moscovia by John Milton, London 1929; Ballet, with text by Edwin Denby, New York 1945; Paris by Day by André Kertész, New York 1945; Paris by Fritz Henle and Eliott Paul, New York 1947; Sun and Shadow by Marcel Breuer, edited by Peter Blake, New York 1956; Observations by Truman Capote, with photographs by Richard Avedon, New York and Lucerne 1959; Saloon Society by Bill Manville and David Attie, New York 1960; The World of Carmel Snow by Carmel Snow and Marie-Louise Aswell, New York 1962; Calder by P. Guerrero and H. H. Arnason, New York 1966.

On BRODOVITCH: books—Advertising Directions, edited by Edward M. Gottschall and Arthur Hawkins, New York 1959; Buchgestaltung by Albert Kapr, Dresden 1963; Alexey Brodovitch and His Influence, exhibition catalogue by George Bunker, Philadelphia 1972; Alexey Brodovitch, His Work, His Influence, thesis by Karim H. Sednaoui, Derby 1974; The Language of Graphics by Edward Booth-Clibborn and Daniele Baroni, London 1980; Contemporary Photographers, London and Chicago, 1982, 1988; Brodovitch by Andy Grundberg, New York and London 1989.

Alexey Brodovitch's impact upon editorial design, particularly magazine art direction, has been phenomenal. The revolution that he brought to this area of graphic design is based not upon a philosophy or style but upon his perception and sensitivity. Brodovitch's intuitive vision, keen understanding of photography, and unerring sense of balance and visual flow marked his art direction of Harper's Bazaar for a quarter of a century. His unexpected cropping of photographs, use of white space as a design element, and classical purity of typographic layout permeated American graphic design and continues to be a major influence. During the 1930's, Brodovitch exposed Americans to the European avant-garde by commissioning art and photography from leading European artists and photographers, including A. M. Cassandre, Salvador Dali, Henri Cartier-Bresson, and the American expatriate Man Ray.

Brodovitch shaped our understanding and perception of photography as editorial communication. The manner in which he cropped photographs, juxtaposed them, and related a photograph's compositions and tones to the accompanying typography are his hallmarks, which since have been absorbed and assimilated by other designers. Photographer Irving Penn has observed, "All photographers are, whether they know it or not, students of Brodovitch." As a teacher, Brodovitch influenced a generation of designers and photographers at his Design Laboratory, which began with informal classes held in his home, then moved to the New School for Social Research. From the ranks of his students emerged leaders in visual communications, including photographers Penn, Richard Avedon, Art Kane, and Hiro; editorial art directors Otto Storch, Henry Wolf, and Sam Antiput; and advertising designers Bog Gage, Helmut Krone, and Steve Frankfurt.

There is an almost oriental simplicity about many of Brodovitch's layouts. He was able to convey the essence of the subject with an economy rarely found in graphic design. Thus, it seems appropriate that his influence has not taken the form of stylistic mannerisms. Rather, Brodovitch stimulated the perceptual understanding and intuitive problem-solving of an entire generation of graphic designers.

—Philip B. Meggs

BRUUN, (Rolf) Erik.

Finnish graphic, exhibition and corporate designer. Born in Viipuri, 7 April 1926. Studied graphic design, Institute of Industrial Arts, Helsinki, 1944–49. Married the artist Sinikka Kinnunen in 1964; children: Jan-Erik, Peter, Daniel, Vega and Sebastian. Worked in an exhibition and display design studio, Helsinki, 1949–50; freelance graphic designer, working principally for Annonscentral AB, Helsinki, 1950–53; established own poster, graphics and corporate design studio, working for Finncell, Finnish Wood Pulp Industry, Frederika Publishing Company, Kymmene-Stromberg Corporation, Tikkurila Oy, Union Bank of Finland, etc., in Helsinki, since 1953. Instructor in poster design, Commercial Graphic Designers' School, Helsinki, 1956–64. Chairman, Union of Commercial Graphic Designers, Finland, 1958–59; Board Member, Ornamo Association of Finnish Designers, 1961–65. **Exhibitions:** Erik Bruun: Posters, Ministry of Foreign Affairs exhibition, toured Europe and the United States, from 1978; also in shows in Copenhagen, 1955, 1987, Weimar and West Berlin, 1965, Helsinki, 1967, 1981, 1985, Tel Aviv, 1973, Göteborg, 1977, 1987, Peking, 1981, and Tallinn, 1989. **Collections:** Poster Museum, Warsaw; Stedelijk Museum, Amsterdam. Recipient: Best Poster of the Year Award, 1953, 1955, 1957, 1958; Finnish State Industrial Design Award, 1974; Björn Landström Award, Helsinki, 1989. Honorary Professor, Helsinki, 1989. Address: Suomenlinna 24 D, 00190 Helsinki, Finland.

Works:

Destination North Finland poster, 1957.
Helsinki, the Capital of Finland poster, 1962.
Sea Eagle poster, 1962.
Turku Abo poster, 1964.
Statistics reports, for Finncell, from 1964.
Kymi-Kymmene International house magazine, for Kymenne-Stromberg Corporation, 1976–85.
Posters and publications, for Savonlinna Opera Festival, from 1976.
Book designs, for Books from Finland, from 1976.
Kemira Paints graphic design, for Tikkurila Oy, from 1982.
New Finnish banknotes, for Finlands Bank, 1984–86 (with others).
Kalevala poster series, 1985 (with poet Lassi Nummi).

Erik Bruun: *Sea Eagle* **poster, 1962**

Save Our Bears poster, 1986.
Graphics, for Metsa-Serla, from 1986.
Graphics, for Union Bank of Finland, 1987.

Publications:

By BRUUN: books—*What We Have Here: Finnish Impressions,* Helsinki 1973; *100 Years of Finnish Industrial Design,* with Timo Sarpaneva, Helsinki 1975; *Kaija and Heikki Siren,* with Sara Popovits, Helsinki 1976; *Face Finland: Finnish Impressions,* Helsinki 1986.

On BRUUN: books—*Finland Creates,* edited by Jack Fields and David Moore, Jyvaskyla 1977; *Who's Who in Graphic Art,* edited by Walter Amstutz, Zurich 1982; *Erik Bruun: Finland,* with texts by Tapio Periainen and others, Espoo 1987; articles—in *Form Function Finland* (Helsinki), no. 4, 1985; *Welcome to Finland,* Helsinki 1987; *Graphics World* (Maidstone), May/June 1988.

BRYK, Rut.
Finnish ceramics designer. Born in Stockholm, Sweden, 18 October 1916. Studied graphics, Central School of Industrial Art, Helsinki, 1936–39. Married the designer Tapio Wirkkala in 1945 (died, 1985); children: Sami and Maaria. Ceramics designer, Arabia factory, Helsinki, since 1942; also designed woven textiles, for Finlaysson Forssa factory, Tampere, 1960–70, and ceramic ware decorations for Rosenthal AG Design Studio, Selb, West Germany, from 1960. **Exhibitions:** Gallery exhibitions, in Helsinki, 1949, 1953, 1962, 1968, 1970, 1985; Kunstnernes Hus, Oslo, 1952; Smithsonian Institution, Washington D.C., 1956 (with Tapio Wirkkala; toured); Georg Jensen Inc., New York, 1964; Malmo Museum, Sweden, 1965; Stedelijk Museum, Amsterdam, 1970; Amos Anderson Art Museum, Helsinki, 1986; Rovaniemi Art Museum, Finland, 1987. **Collections:** Museum of Applied Arts, Helsinki; City Art Museum, Helsinki; Sara Hilden Art Museum, Tampere; Nationalmuseum, Stockholm; Rohsska Konstslojdmuseet, Goteborg; Nordenfjeldske Kunstindustrimuseum, Trondheim; Stedelijk Museum, Amsterdam; Kunstgewerbemuseum, Zurich; Bayerische Landesgewerbeanstalt, Nuremberg; Landesmuseum für Kultur und Kulturgeschichte, Oldenburg; Museo Internazionale delle Ceramiche, Faenza, Italy; Ceramics Museum, Vallauris, France; Victoria and Albert Museum, London; Everson Museum, Syracuse, New York; University of Calgary, Alberta. Recipient: Grand Prix, 1951, and Diploma of Honour, 1954, Milan Triennale; International Ceramics Prize, Everson Museum, Syracuse, New York, 1958; A.I.D. International Design Award, New York, 1960, 1962; Domus Golden Obelisk Award, Milan, 1963; Premio Ravenna, Faenza, 1967; Grand Prix, Vallauris, 1972; State Award for Craft and Design, Helsinki, 1974; Exempla Prize, Munich, 1977; City of Helsinki Medal, 1978; Cultural Prize of the Year, Finnish Church, Helsinki, 1987. Pro Finlandia Medal, Helsinki, 1968; Commander, Ordre des Arts et des Lettres, France, 1980; Order of the Finnish White Rose, Helsinki, 1982. Address: Itaranta 24, 02100 Espoo, Finland.

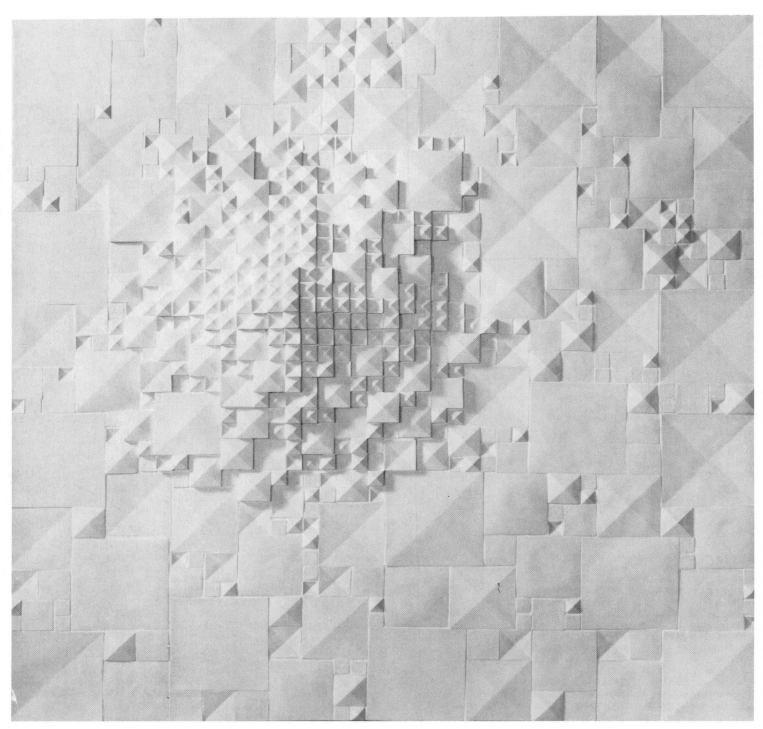

Rut Bryk: *The White Mountain* **ceramic wall relief, 1978**

Works (public commissions):

Banquet Table wall relief, for Rosenthal AG, Selb, 1960.
Fireplace, for the Bank of Finland, Helsinki, 1962.
Thunder Clouds wall relief, for *M/S Finlandia,* 1967.
Gethsemane wall relief, for Sipoo Burial Chapel, Finland, 1971.
Blue Clouds two-piece wall relief, for *M/S Viking,* 1973.
Summer Rain wall relief, for Turku Internal Hospital, Finland, 1973.
Blue Spring wall relief, for the Bahlsen Factory, Hannover, 1974.
City in the Sun wall relief, for the City Hall, Helsinki, 1976.

City by the Water wall relief, for Volvo Head Office, Vantaa, 1982.
The Tree wall relief, for the Bank of Finland, Helsinki, 1982.
Spring Comes to the North wall relief, for the Finnish Embassy, New Delhi, 1985.

Publications:

On BRYK: books—*Rut Bryk,* exhibition catalogue with text by Lisa Licitra Ponti, Amsterdam 1970; *Finnish Design 1875–1975* by Timo Sarpaneva, Erik Bruun and Erik Kruskopf, Helsinki 1975; *Nordenfjeldske Kunstindustrimuseum 1946–1979* by Jan Lauritz Opstad, Trondheim 1980; *Scandinavian Modern Design 1880–1980,* edited by David Revere McFadden,

New York 1982; *Finnish Vision,* with texts by Pekka Suhonen and others, Helsinki 1983; *Rut Bryk,* exhibition catalogue with text by Juhani Pallasmaa, Helsinki 1986; articles—"Rut Bryk" by S. Kallio-Visapaa in *Graphis* (Zurich), no. 35, 1951; "Painter Adopts Ceramic Medium" by A. Toikka-Karvonen in *Craft Horizons* (New York), October 1953; "Fifteen Contemporary Finnish Designers" in *Design Quarterly* (Tokyo), no. 37, 1957; "Pair of Designing Finns" by R. Moss in *Horizon* (New York), July 1963.

Rut Bryk has become so known for her abstract glazed tile reliefs that the other side of her personality and production, the earlier colourful tales in ceramics, has faded into the background. Seldom is an artist's work so clearly divisible into two style periods as Rut Bryk's. Her ceramic reveries and tile compositions form a kind of inverse symmetry.

Whereas her earlier works began with a pictorial theme in which colour was paramount, later works are built around abstract composition, shallow relief and the sensitive interplay of light and shade. If the works in her first period were a kind of ceramic painting, then those in the second come nearer to sculpture. Whereas her pictorial miniatures invited viewers to hear intimate stories whispered close at hand, the newer works reach out into space—the picturesque has been transformed into the architectonic.

In spite of this external dualism, the artist's work tells of an exceptionally single-minded journey towards extreme sensitiveness in expression and mastery of method towards the landscape of tranquillity in which all condenses into nothingness, as in Eastern art and mystic thought, and finally there is always the oneness, one colour, time stood still, silence. Rut Bryk's artistic development is so logical it is like the humble fulfillment of a predestined pattern.

Rut Bryk was trained as a graphic artist, but like so many other designers of her generation, including her husband Tapio Wirkkala, she has worked more outside her vocation than within. In the years before and immediately after World War II, designing was considered more an attitude to life than a profession, and out of this idealism emerged the unique enthusiasm and strength of Finnish applied art during those decades. In recalling the architectonic features of Rut's works, it is not surprising to learn that she originally intended becoming an architect and had even passed the entrance exam before her instinct drew her in the direction of the applied arts.

In addition to ceramic art—into which she came by accident following an invitation from Kurt Ekholm in 1942 to experiment with ceramics at the Arabia Factory—Rut Bryk has made lino-print textiles, church textiles, ryijy rugs and designed woven fabrics for industrial production. Her career in textiles also began by chance when a colleague told her that the Vaasa Cotton Company was looking for a textile designer. Her refined *Seita* series from the 1960's is one of the classics of Finnish textile art, and there is reason to hope that the best from her ten years of fabric designing will again be produced. The very timelessness of their elegant colour combinations can never wilt like fashions.

She designed some exquisitely tasteful patterns for the porcelain objects made by Tapio Wirkkala for the Rosenthal Factory. The decoration of an object is a kind of architectonic art in miniature—it may no more violate the shape of an object than a work of art fixed to the wall may ruin a room. In the Rosenthal series of artists, Rut Bryk appears alongside such illustrious names as Salvador Dali and Victor Vasarely. Philip Rosenthal, who commissioned the first monumental work now located in the studio of the Rosenthal Factory, suggested that the theme should be the company's products. These ordinary household objects the artist metamorphosized into the dishes and drinks, fruits and flowers on a table set for some fantastic banquet.

Colour is an essential motif of Rut Bryk's work. The luxuriance of colour and sense of depth have been achieved through successive layers of different coloured glazes. It is difficult to believe that these powerful and superbly balanced colours were created "blindly" from almost colourless glazing powders. The final colour appears only in the firing process, and so coloration depends on a skillful blend of imagination, memory and experience. The artist can draw on some two hundred numbered,

different coloured glazes developed in Arabia's laboratory. These she refers to by number as easily as a painter talks of "Lemon Yellow" or "Louis XV Green"—just as Vincent Van Gogh did in his letters to his brother. So "72 B" is a pine green, and "M 6" a dangerous and now forbidden uranium colour, an intense reddish-orange that the artist used in many of her earlier works. A carefully kept book from decades past records the colours of her works in a series of numbers and letters, mysterious to an outsider.

All in all, Rut Bryk's output is an impressive example of work demanding unbelievable industry and patience on the odyssey towards supreme simplicity and clarity. Her works are masterpieces of patience. Each square block unit with its recesses, protrusions and patterns is made individually. The surface patterns are scratched or pressed with an incredible variety of makeshift tools, ranging from nails and sticks to pan scrapers. Afterwards, each block receives its colour and glaze. Only then, when each single piece has been precast by hand, can the assembly begin. The whole work, which can measure up to 3 by 5 metres, is composed of thousands and thousands of carefully measured and completed blocks—just like a building. For reasons of transportation and assembly, it is necessary to divide the work into parts, and the work of concealing the seams within the divisions of the mosaic surface demands great accuracy. When, after painstaking alterations and repairs, the work has found its final configuration, the cells of the mosaic may be fixed to the base board and finally jointed.

Only a friend who has experienced Rut's patience and perseverance, be it over a conversation or the detail of a meal, can understand the silent concentration and unyielding strength concealed in her frail figure.

—Juhani Pallasmaa
(from *Journey to Landscapes of Tranquillity*, exhibition catalogue, Helsinki, 1986)

BÜLOW-HÜBE, Torun (Vivianna).
Swedish silversmith, ceramic, glass and jewellery designer. Born in Malmö, 4 December 1927. Studied at the National College of Art, Craft and Design (Konstfackskolan), Stockholm, 1948–51. Married in 1946 (divorced) and in 1951 (divorced); 4 children. Freelance designer, establishing own workshop in Stockholm, 1951–56, in Paris and Biot, France, 1956–68, in Wolfburg and Wendhausen, Germany, 1968–78, and in Jakarta, Indonesia, since 1978: has designed for Christofle, Orrefors, Glashütte Lohnberg, Hutschenreuther, Georg Jensen and Dansk International. **Exhibitions:** Nordiska Kompaniet, Stockholm, 1951, 1961, 1981 (retrospective); Cercle d'Arts, Paris, 1952; Galerie du Siècle, Paris, 1954; Musée Picasso, Antibes, 1958; Georg Jensen Inc., New York, 1963, 1964; La Petite Galerie, Rio de Janeiro, 1963; Hantverket, Stockholm, 1964; Georg Jensen, Copenhagen, 1969; Georg Jensen, Düsseldorf, 1970; Georg Jensen, Stockholm, 1971; La Boutique Danoise/Georg Jensen, Paris, 1973 (retrospective); Malmö Museum, Sweden, 1981 (retrospective); *Torun: 40 Years of Jewelry*, Georg Jensen, Stockholm, 1987 (retrospective; world tour, 1987–90). **Collections:** Nationalmuseum, Stockholm; Malmö Museum, Sweden; Röhsska Konstslöjdmuseet, Göteborg; Kunstindustrimuseet, Oslo; Kunst-

industrimuseum, Copenhagen; Cooper-Hewitt Museum, New York; Museum of Modern Art, New York. Recipient: Silver Medal, 1954, and Gold Medal, 1960, Milan Triennale; Lunning Prize, 1960; Swedish State Grand Prize for Artists, 1965; Honorary Silversmith Award, Foundation for Contemporary Swedish Silver, 1983. Member: Slöjdföreningens Facksektion, Stockholm, 1951; Societé des Artistes Décorateurs, Paris, 1962; Gesellschaft der Goldschmiedekunst, Hamburg, 1970. Address: Wisma Subud 17, Jalan Fatmawati 52, Jakarta 12430, Indonesia.

Works:

Rigid circular necklace in silver with stone pendant, 1948.
Moebius strip bracelet in silver, 1954.
Asymmetrical spiral necklace/sculpture in silver, 1954.
Collar and cuff circlet in silver, 1959.
Coffee service in silver, for Georg Jensen, 1960.
Figure-of-Eight glass spectacles, 1963.
Coffer-boxes in silver, 1963.
Wristwatches in stainless steel, for Georg Jensen, 1969.
Torun Silverplate cutlery in stainless silver, for Dansk International, 1985.
Spiral movement earrings in silver, for Georg Jensen, 1987.
Ovation Music Award in silver and crystal, for Georg Jensen, 1989.

Publications:

On BÜLOW-HÜBE: books—*Contemporary Swedish Design: A Survey in Pictures* by Arthur Hald and Sven Erik Skawonius, Stockholm 1951; *Svensk Form/Forma Sueca* by Ake Stavenlow and Ake H. Huldt, Stockholm 1961; *Modern Jewelry: An International Survey 1890–1964* by Graham Hughes, London 1963, 1964; *Modern Silver Throughout the World 1880–1967* by Graham Hughes, London and Toronto 1967; *Design in Sweden* by Lennart Lindkvist, Stockholm 1972; *Scandinavian Design: Objects of a Life Style* by Eileene Harrison Beer, New York 1975; *Modern Design in Metal* by Richard Stewart, London 1979; *Scandinavian Modern Design 1880–1980*, edited by David Revere McFadden, New York 1982; *Den Svenska Formen* by Monica Boman and others, Stockholm 1985; *Twentieth Century Jewelry* by Barbara Cartlidge, New York, 1985; *The Lunning Prize*, exhibition catalogue edited by Helena Dahlback Lütteman and Marianne Uggla, Stockholm 1986.

Torun Bülow-Hübe is a Scandinavian with an international air but her roots are in Sweden. She trained at the State School of Arts, Crafts and Design and worked in Stockholm from 1948 to 1956, piecing together the uniqueness that made her into an international designer of jewelry and silver.

The simple neck rings with pebbles and fossils suspended on a tongue belong to her first period, as do the superb mounts for pieces of flashed glass by Edward Hald. A broad, smooth bracelet to balance the shimmering glass, or a simple silver loop by which a glass drop dangles from the ear, are examples of her congenial settings for these starry amulets.

On a beach in France Torun Bülow-Hübe found pebbles that fascinated her because they were beautiful without being costly. She used them for ornaments in the true sense of the word: lovely, enticing, pleasurable, without also being an investment. "A simple silver coil that highlights the line of a neck is more beautiful

Torun Bülow-Hübe: *Torun Silverplate* flatware, for Dansk International, 1985

than all the diamonds in the world." Then, without recognizing him, she had a fairytale meeting with Picasso on the beach where she was picking pebbles. He was fascinated and in 1958 she had an exhibition at the Picasso museum in Antibes. She had then spent two years in France and moved to Biot.

In Biot she built up a workshop with five assistants and stayed there until 1968. In an inspiring atmosphere, reverberating with the intensity of jazz, her work became increasingly sculptural. The mobile necklace was conceived here, floating freely about its own axis, wrought in one piece. This was the birthplace of rings that are pieces of sculpture, forms in their own right, made to be worn on a finger. It was here that she started to work with shifted forms—paper models were rotated on a disc so that the play of the form was revealed, corrected and fashioned into a supreme cigarette case (a typical example of shifted design), a coffee service or liquer cups, with a gentle sheen in the smooth metal surface.

This was followed by a period as a designer for Georg Jensen and others. The sculptural wristwatches are outstanding but still no more than a small part of her output as a designer.

Torun Bülow-Hübe is now known as Vivianna and lives in Djarkarta. Just as she once used glass amulets, fossils and pebbles in Europe, so she now works with mother of pearl, horn, mystical stones and shells in her new country. With complete simplicity. "The little smile that radiates from a thing."

—Helena Dahlback Lutteman

Aaron Burns: Type specimen booklet, for The Composing Room, New York, 1953

BURNS, Aaron.
American graphic designer. Born in Passaic, New Jersey, 25 May 1922. Educated at Passaic High School, New Jersey, until 1940; studied at Newark Evening School of Fine and Industrial Arts, New Jersey, 1941–43; United States Armed Forces Institute, Brigham Young University, Provo, Utah, 1945. Served in the United States Army, in Panama and Ecuador, 1943–46: Technical Sergeant. Married Florence Browner in 1952; children: Laurie and Andrew. Apprentice graphic designer, in the Alexander Ross Design Studio, New York, 1946–48; assistant graphic designer to Herb Lublin, at Sudler and Hennessy, New York, 1948; senior art director, Monogram Art Studio, New York, 1948–49; director of design and typography, at Empire State Craftsmen, New York, 1949–52, and at The Composing Room, New York, 1952–60; president and creative director, Graphic Arts Typographers, New York, 1960–62; president, Aaron Burns and Company, a division of Rapid Typographers, New York, 1963–67; senior vice-president and creative director, 1967–69, and computer photosetting consultant, 1971–77, TypoGraphics Communications, New York; founder, with Herb Lubalin, and president, of Lubalin, Burns and Company, New York, since 1970, of International Typeface Corporation, New York, since 1970, and of Design Processing International, New York, since 1976. Editorial director, *Upper and Lower Case* magazine, New York, 1973–78. Instructor in advanced and experimental typographic design, Pratt Institute, Brooklyn, New York, 1955–60. Educational chairman, Type Directors Club of New York, 1956; founder, International Center for the Typographic Arts, New York, 1960; United States delegate, 1960–64, and board member, 1976–83, Association Typographique Internationale, Paris and Geneva; board member, American Institute of Graphic Arts, New York, 1963–66, 1978–81. Recipient: Hall of Fame Award, Art Directors Club of New York, 1983. Address: 2 Hammarskjöld Plaza, New York, New York 10017, U.S.A.

Publications:

By BURNS: book—*Typography,* New York 1961; articles—"William Sandberg: Explorations in Typography" in *Print* (New York), January 1969.

On BURNS: articles—"Typography 1978" in *Print* (New York), May 1968; "The New York of Herb Lubalin and Aaron Burns" by H. Hara in *Graphic Design* (Tokyo), September 1971; "Aaron Burns" in *Art Directors Club Annual,* New York 1983.

BURROWS, Stephen (Gerald).
American fashion designer. Born in Newark, New Jersey, 15 September 1942. Studied at the Philadelphia Museum College of Art, 1961–62; Fashion Institute of Technology, New York, 1964–66. Designer, at Weber Originals, New York, 1966–67; founder-proprietor, with Roz Rubenstein, of "O" fashion boutique, New York, 1968; designer-in-residence, at Henri Bendel, New York, 1969–73; founder-director, with Roz Bernstein, of Burrows Inc., New York, 1973: has also worked with Pat Tennant, at Henri Bendel, New York, from 1977. Recipient: Coty Winnie Award, 1973, 1977, and special award, 1974, American Fashion Critics Association, New York; Crystal Ball Award, Knitted Textile Association, New York, 1975. Address: 550 Seventh Avenue, New York, New York 10013, U.S.A.

Publications:

On BURROWS: books—*Fairchild's Who's Who in Fashion,* edited by Ann Stegemeyer, New

York 1980; *McDowell's Directory of Twentieth Century Fashion* by Colin McDowell, London 1984; *The Encyclopaedia of Fashion from 1840 to the 1980s* by Georgina O'Hara, London 1986; articles—"The Story of Stephen Burrows" by M. R. Carter in *Mademoiselle* (New York), March 1975; "Burrows is Back" by J. Butler in the *New York Times Magazine*, 5 June 1977.

"I make colorful adult toys because I think fashion should have a sense of humor, and I want people to be happy in my clothes," says Stephen Burrows who is something of an innocent in his approach to business. After a time at Bendel's, he spent three-and-one-half years working for a mass-market manufacturer but found it stultifying, as the employer was afraid of new ideas and would use only cheap, artificial fabrics. In 1977, Burrows went back to Bendel's, where he could design as he pleased and could leave the difficulty of converting his ideas for the mass market to others. Thus, Burrows is the sort of designer who has to be shielded from the world if he is to create anything, and not one of those who can work in the midst of a crowd.

Influenced by the 1930's, he made his name with body-clinging dresses in jersey or velour. In 1975, his wrap-over, summer evening gown in jersey was a best-seller. Beachgowns, leisure gowns, and informal evening gowns were full of 1930's fluidity. His 1977 collection showed better feeling for cut, with the bias, zigzag seams, and shirring all prominent. He also showed a reversible look in T-shirts and blousons which were one colour on one side and multi-colour on the other. By 1979, he was making the asymmetrical neckline his signature, as in a T-shirt with the shoulder straps set aslant. He took the traditional, Scottish tweed jacket and gave it asymmetrical lapels, so he had better beware of claymores at dawn.

He maintains that he gets his greatest inspiration from the American craze for sports and athletics, so he wants to give his clothes some of the ease and enjoyment found in sportswear, and he has his own sportswear range, too, offering such garments as his tweed blouson baseball jacket. Nineteen eighty saw him adopting the London Romantics' look in a white, silk, crepe de chine tunic with a deep collar and cuffs of lace to wear with narrow, olive satin trousers. Burrows, an adaptor of existing styles, gives them his own look by a modification or two, a policy that has paid off for designers before him. Comfortable clothes can achieve a comfortable turn-over.

—Diana de Marly

BURTIN, Will.

American typographic, exhibition and graphic designer. Born in Cologne, Germany, 27 January 1903; emigrated to the United States in 1938: naturalized, 1943. Studied at Werkschulen in Cologne, 1927–30. Married Hilda Munk in 1932 (died, 1960); daughter: Carol; married the graphic designer Cipe Pineles in 1961; stepson: Thomas Golden. Worked as a typographic apprentice, Cologne, 1931–38; freelance graphic designer, New York, 1938–43; worked for the United States Army Air Force, 1943–44, and for the Office of Strategic Services, 1944–45; art director, *Fortune* magazine, New York,

1945–49; freelance exhibition and graphic designer, establishing own studio, and working for the Federal Works Administration, Eastman Kodak, Upjohn and Company, Union Carbide, the United States Government, etc., in New York, from 1949: design director and consultant, Upjohn Company, Kalamazoo, Michigan, 1950. Professor of design and chairman of the department of visual communications, Pratt Institute, Brooklyn, New York, from 1959. Program chairman, International Design Conference, Aspen, Colorado, 1955, 1956; chairman, First World Seminar on Typography, Silvermine, Connecticut, 1958. **Exhibitions:** A-D Gallery, New York, 1949; Art Directors Club of Chicago, 1949. Recipient: New York Art Directors Club Medals, 1941, 1955, 1958; Detroit Art Directors Club Medal, 1953; Gold Medal, American Medical Association, 1958; Gold Medal, American Institute of Graphic Arts, 1971; and awards from the Alliance Graphique Internationale, American Society of Industrial Designers, and New York Type Directors Club. Member: American Institute of Graphic Arts; New York Art Directors Club; Society of Typographic Arts, Chicago; Typographic Designers of Canada; Alliance Graphique Internationale. *Died* (in New York City) *18 January 1972.*

Works:

Kristallspiegelglas promotional brochure, for a plate glass company, 1932.
WPA Pavilion at the New York World's Fair, for the Federal Works Agency, 1939.
Scope magazine design, for Upjohn Company, 1952–58.
The Cell exhibition layouts, for Upjohn Company, 1958.
The Brain exhibition layouts, for Upjohn Company, 1960.
DNA exhibition layouts, for Upjohn Company, 1962.
Exhibition displays at the New York World's Fair, for Eastman Kodak, 1964.
The Atom in Action exhibition layouts, for Union Carbide Company, 1964.

Publications:

By BURTIN: book—*Seven Designers Look at Trademark Designs*, edited by Egbert Jacobson, Chicago 1952; articles—in *Graphis* (Zurich), no. 27, 1949, September 1959, November 1962, no. 148, 1970; *Print* (New York), July 1955, January 1960, January 1964; *Design* (London), October 1963.

On BURTIN: books—*Posters: 50 Artists and Designers*, edited by W. H. Allner, New York 1952; *Advertising Directions*, edited by Edward M. Gottschall and Arthur Hawkins, New York 1959; *Die neue Grafik/The New Graphic Design* by Karl Gerstner and Markus Kutter, Teufen and London 1959; *Who's Who in Graphic Design*, edited by Walter Amstutz, Zurich 1962; *Design in America*, edited by Ralph Caplan, New York 1969; *Graphic Design for the Computer Age* by Edward A. Hamilton, New York 1970; *Monografgie des Plakats* by Herbert Schindler, Munich 1972; *A History of Graphic Design* by Philip B. Meggs, New York and London 1983; *The American Design Adventure 1940–1975* by Arthur J. Pulos, London and Cambridge, Massachusetts 1988.

Will Burtin believed that science and the scientific method should be applied to all areas of human social and personal life, including art. Science allows people to "see the workings of nature, makes transparent the solid, and gives substance to the invisible." As a graphic and

exhibition designer, Burtin sought to become the "communicator, link, interpreter, and inspirer" who is able to make scientific knowledge comprehensible. Burtin visualized that which was known but could not be seen, as he interpreted cell structures, molecular construction, and natural processes graphically. The "hand" of the designer was often unseen in Burtin's work, for he often used such techniques as photomontage, models, cutaway views, geometric diagrams, photographic blow-ups of microscopic forms, and overprinting as graphic devices to interpret and convey information.

The linking of science and art was expressed in his 1948 exhibition, *Integration—A New Discipline in Design*. It presented the four major realities upon which visual communications should be based: the reality of man, as measure and measurer; the reality of light, color, and texture; the reality of space, motion, and time; and the reality of science.

Soon after Burtin left *Fortune* in 1949 to concentrate on his growing design consultations and commissions, the Upjohn Company asked him to analyze its communications for development of an unmistakable character which would project a cohesive image for the company. The most ambitious of Burtin's projects for Upjohn was the 1958 cell exhibit. Developed from indistinct microphotographs and consultations with scientists, this twenty-four-foot-diameter model of one-half of a human blood cell (enlarged approximately one million times) was made to be entered by the viewer, for the purpose of observing and understanding the minute structures that make up the fundamental units of life. Moving, pulsating lights glowing within the model interpreted elemental life processes.

—Philip B. Meggs

BURY, John.

British stage designer. Born in Aberystwyth, Wales, 27 January 1925. Educated at the Cathedral School, Hereford, 1935–40; studied chemistry, University College, London, 1941–42. Served in the Fleet Air Arm, Royal Navy, 1942–46. Married Margaret Leila Greenwood in 1947 (divorced, 1962); Elizabeth Rebecca Blackborrow Duffield in 1966; children: Adam, Abigail and Matthew. Actor and resident designer, Joan Littlewood's Theatre Workshop, Stratford, East London, 1946–63; associate designer, 1963–73, and head of design, 1965–68, Royal Shakespeare Company, London; associate director and head of design, National Theatre, London, 1973–85; also freelance designer for the commercial theatre, from 1964: has worked for the Royal Opera House, London; Glyndebourne Festival Opera, England; Metropolitan Opera, New York; Santa Fe Opera, New Mexico; Los Angeles Opera; San Francisco Opera; and the Chicago Opera. Member of the Drama Panel, 1960–68 and 1975–77, and Chairman of the Designers' Working Group, 1962–78, Arts Council, London; Chairman, Society of British Theatre Designers, London, 1975–85. Recipient: 2 Antoinette Perry (Tony) Awards, New York; Gold Medal, Theatre Quadriennale, Prague, 1975. Fellow, Royal Society of Arts, London, 1970; Officer, Order of the British Empire, 1979. Address: 14 Woodlands Road, Barnes, London SW13, England.

Works:

Stage designs include—*A Taste of Honey*, Theatre Workshop, Stratford, 1958; *Fings Ain't What They Used T'Be*, Theatre Workshop, Stratford, 1959; *Oh—What A Lovely War*, Theatre Workshop, Stratford, 1963; *The Wars of the Roses (Henry VI*, parts 1, 2 and 3; *Richard III)*, Royal Shakespeare Company, London, 1963; *The Quatrecentennial History Cycle (Richard II to Richard III)*, Royal Shakespeare Company, London, 1964; *Hamlet*, Royal Shakespeare Company, London, 1965; *Macbeth*, Royal Shakespeare Company, London, 1967; *Hamlet*, Shiki Company, Tokyo, 1969; *Calisto*, Glyndebourne Festival Opera, Sussex, 1970; *Tristan und Isolde*, Royal Opera House, London, 1971; *The Doll's House*, for Claire Bloom, New York, 1971; *Hedda Gabler*, for Claire Bloom, New York, 1971; *Phedre*, Shiki Company, Tokyo, 1973; *The Mozart Cycle (Figaro; Don Giovanni; Cosi fan Tutte)*, Glyndebourne Festival Opera, Sussex, 1973–75; *The Tempest*, National Theatre, London, 1974; *Tamburlane the Great*, National Theatre, London, 1976; *Amadeus*, National Theatre, London, 1979; *Amadeus*, Broadhurst Theatre, New York, 1979; *Boris Gudenov*, Australian Opera Company, 1980; *Macbetto*, Metropolitan Opera, New York, 1982; *The Bartered Bride*, English National Opera, London, 1985; *Romeo and Juliet*, Shiki Company, Tokyo, 1987; *Salome*, Royal Opera House, London, 1988; *Cosi fan Tutte*, Los Angeles Opera, 1988.

Publications:

By BURY: article—"John Bury OBE" in *The Designer* (London), March 1979.

On BURY: book—*Who's Who in the Theatre*, edited by Ian Herbert, London 1977; article—"Contemporary British Scenography" by J. Burian in *Theatre Design and Technology* (Charlottesville), Spring and Fall 1983.

*   *   *

John Bury is perhaps the outstanding British example of a successful scenographer with no formal training in art, theatre design, or even architecture. His early work, for Joan Littlewood's Theatre Workshop, was characterized by improvisational ingenuity in the face of minimal budgets and by functionalism rather than artful design. He became known for assembling authentic raw materials and elements for the construction of sets.

Actually, Bury's chief interest was originally in lighting, which depends on the sets—especially their textured surfaces—for its maximum effect. Unlike almost all British designers, Bury continued to light his own sets until the pressures of his many administrative duties forced him to concentrate on sets and sometimes costumes.

For the *Wars of the Roses* productions, he provided a scenography that radically departed from the prevailing romantic, decorative designs of the 1950's at Stratford-upon-Avon. It was harsher, more realistic, sparer. Its powerful imagery and expressiveness was based on his use of a dominant material, steel, which covered the floor, segments of wall, and even some furniture, but was most evident in two huge periaktoi constructions that could rotate as well as move along curved tracks.

Bury was also involved in the development of a lighter, more abstract "box" approach to staging Shakespeare for the Royal Shakespeare Company. A basic box with a standard rake was used as a stage within the stage for a whole season of plays, providing permanent masking and an esthetically neutral environment within which each play might make its own statement.

Bury refers to his approach as selective, abstract realism. He is not attracted to fantasy, romanticism, or devices such as masks. Because the human actor is for him the basic measure, Bury rarely introduces marked distortion into his sets. Although he disclaims conscious artistry in his work, many of his productions reveal a fine sense of form and style, as was evident in the recurrent form of a Celtic brooch in the scenes of *Tristan and Isolde* (Covent Garden, 1971), the mirrored floor and reflective screen suspended above it for Pinter's *The Silence* (National Theatre, 1969), the stylized decor based on flown and projected scenery for *Amadeus* (London, 1979; New York, 1980), the pastiche of Victorian drop and wing settings for Verdi's *Macbeth* (Metropolitan Opera, 1982).

Bury departed from the National Theatre in 1986, his last production there being Peter Shaffer's *Yonodab*. Since then he has worked closely with Peter Hall on opera productions in North America *(Salome, Figaro, Cosi fan Tutte)*, as well as with other directors in England, Scotland and Israel.

—Jarka M. Burian

BUSSE, Rido.

German industrial designer. Born in Wiesbaden, 14 August 1934. Studied design, Hochschule für Gestaltung, Ulm, 1953–56. Founder-director, Busse Design, Ulm, since 1959: has designed electronics and machinery for the West German Railways, Klocker-Moeller, Osram, Pelikan, Sennheiser, Siemens, Soehnle, Stihl und Vaillant, etc. Central Council Member, VDID Verband Deutscher Industrie-Designer. **Collection:** Museum of Modern Art, New York. Address: Robert-Bosch-Strasse 10, 7915 Elchingen, West Germany.

Publications:

By BUSSE: book—*Der gewerbliche Rechtsschütz als Monopolinstrument der Unternehmensführung*, editor, Ulm 1985; articles—in *Absatzwirtschaft* (Düsseldorf), October 1977; *Frankfurter Allgemeine Zeitung* (Frankfurt), April 1978, August 1982; *Harvardmanager* (Hamburg), March 1979; *Verband Deutscher Industrie-Designer* (Düsseldorf), 1980; *Nurnberger Bund* (Essen), 1981; *Der Erfolgsberater* (Bonn), October 1983; *Form* (Leverkusen), 1983.

On BUSSE: books—*Il Disegno Industriale e la sua Estetica* by Gillo Dorfles, Bologna 1963; *Fewerblicher Rechtsschutz* by A. Danner, Ulm 1984; articles—in *Handelsblatt* (Düsseldorf), August 1977; *Wirtschaftswoche* (Düsseldorf), May 1980; *Technische Rundschau* (Bern), May 1982; *Zeitmagazin* (Hamburg), November 1982; *Maschine und Werrkzeug* (Coburg), July 1983; *Industriemagazin* (Munich), August 1983; *Scala* (Bonn), November 1983.

*   *   *

I am the owner of Busse Design Ulm GmbH, founded in 1959: we now have 52 collaborators, and at our disposal an efficient establishment for mechanical engineering, precision engineering, electro-mechanics and electronics. With our own tooling as well as model and prototype workshops, Busse Design Ulm carries out complete developments up to readiness for fabrication. The enterprise annually awards the "Plagiarius", a negative distinction (booby prize) for imitators. Every three years we give the Busse Longlife Design Award as prize for products which remain on the market for a long time. I am also active as expert consultant, competition juror, publicist, and member of the presidency of the Association of German Industrial Designers (VDID).

—Rido Busse

BUTLER, Frances.

American textile, graphic and garden designer. Born Frances Marie Clark, in St. Louis, Missouri, 28 November 1940. Educated at the American High School, Beirut, Lebanon, and at Berkeley High School, California; studied history and design, University of California, Berkeley, 1957–59, 1964–66: BA 1959, MA 1966; history, Stanford University, California, 1961–64: MA 1964. Married Jonathan Butler in 1964 (died, 1974). Owner and fabric designer, Goodstuffs Handprinted Fabrics, Emeryville, California, 1972–79; owner and publisher, Poltroon Press, Oakland, California, since 1975. Instructor in typography, University of California at Berkeley, 1966–69; Professor of book design, University of California at Davis, since 1970; artist-in-residence: Visual Studies Workshop, Rochester, New York, 1984; San Francisco Center for Interdisciplinary and Experimental Studies, 1985; School of the Art Institute of Chicago, 1986–87; Banff Centre for the Arts, Alberta, 1987. **Exhibitions:** *Pop Fabrics*, Victoria and Albert Museum, London, 1972; *Anatomy in Fabric*, Los Angeles County Museum of Art, 1973; *Art for Wearing*, San Francisco Museum of Modern Art, 1979; *Frances Butler: Retrospective Show*, University of California, Davis, 1982; *American Bookworks in Print*, USIA travelling exhibition, 1984–86; *Typo-Graphisme*, Centre Georges Pompidou, Paris, 1985; *Forwarding the Book in California*, Victoria and Albert Museum, London, 1988. **Collections:** Museum of Modern Art, New York; New York Public Library; Cooper-Hewitt Museum, New York; Los Angeles County Museum of Art; Victoria and Albert Museum, London; British Museum, London; Stedelijk Museum, Amsterdam. Recipient: National Endowment for the Arts Grant, Washington, D.C., 1973, 1975, 1977, 1981. Address: 950 57th Street, Oakland, California 94608, U.S.A.

Works:

Cooked Goose Graphics poster, for the University of California, Davis, 1970.
Acute Angle, Try Using It poster, for the University of California, Davis, 1971.
Beat in the Jungle printed cotton fabric, for Goodstuffs Handprinted Fabrics, 1971.
Japanese Posters silkscreen poster, for the University of California, Davis, 1971.
In the Yellow River printed cotton fabric, for Goodstuffs Handprinted Fabrics, 1972.
Nippon Moon Landing printed cotton fabric, for Goodstuffs Handprinted Fabrics, 1973.
There's No Place to Rest Your Eyes silkscreen poster, for Goodstuffs Handprinted Fabrics, 1973.

Frances Butler: *Shadow Garden*, Berkeley, California, **1980–89**

Worried Man printed cotton fabric, for Goodstuffs Handprinted Fabrics, 1974.
Confracti Mundi Rudera book design, for Poltroon Press, 1975 (with Alastair Johnston).
Logbook (T. Raworth) book design, for Poltroon Press, 1976.
New Dryads (Are Ready for Your Call) book design, for Poltroon Press, 1979.
Shadow Gardens garden layout, for the Butler residence, Berkeley, California, 1980–89.
Career Options book design, for Poltroon Press, 1985.
Various Light garden layout at Seattle University Hospital, for the Washington project for the Arts, 1986–89.
Water Table cement and tile mosaic sculpture, for San Francisco Art Institute, 1989.
Mosaic installation, for Mendelsohn House, San Francisco, 1989.

Publications:

By BUTLER: books—*Confracti Mundi Rudera*, with text by Alastair M. Johnston, Berkeley 1975; *Colored Reading: The Graphic Art of Frances Butler*, Berkeley 1979; *New Dryads*, with text by Alastair M. Johnston, Berkeley 1981; *Occult Psychogenic Misfeance*, Berkeley 1981; *Light and Heavy Light: Contemporary Shadow Use in the Visual Arts*, Berkeley and Davis 1985; *Career Options: A Catalog of Screens*, Rochester, New York 1985; *Territorial Inventions*, Oakland 1988; articles—in *Journal of the Society of Typographic Arts* (Chicago), January 1981, May 1989; *Arts and Architecture* (Los Angeles), Spring 1983; *Design Issues* (Chicago), no. 1, 1984; *Design Book Review* (Berkeley), Spring 1984, Winter 1985, Spring

1986; Fall 1987; *Fine Print* (San Francisco), January 1985; *American Craft* (New York), February/March 1985; *Places* (Cambridge, Massachusetts), Summer 1984, September 1987; *Via* (Philadelphia), September 1989.

On BUTLER: books—*Craftsman Life Style: The Gentle Revolution* by O. Emery and T. Andersen, Pasadena 1978; *Design on Fabric* by Meda Parker Johnston and Glen Kaufman, New York 1981; *Typo-Graphisme: l'Image des Mots*, exhibition catalogue, Paris 1985; *Women in Design: A Contemporary View* by Liz McQuiston, London 1988; articles—in *Fiberarts* (Albuquerque), October 1978; *Idea* (Tokyo), November 1980; *Studio International* (London), no. 195, 1982; *Process Architecture* (Tokyo), Fall 1985.

My interests for many years centered on the observation of human activity of the most quiet and ordinary kinds, and the incorporation of these observations into printed graphics on a wide variety of surfaces, most often fabric and paper. I opened a press so that I could publish books incorporating the kind of illustrations that I felt would expand the available range of expressive human gesture from the stereotyped to the idiosyncratic.

I then moved to the study of visual forms used, not to record experience, but to generate new ideas, visual tools to think with. I concentrated on the study of shadow as an old, multifarious, and continually changing formal image with which to define presence and power in the material and spiritual worlds. Writing articles and a catalog on the subject encouraged my development of a shadow garden in which I exploited some of the folk lore of shadow and its perceptual qualities. Finally, my own use of

shadow as a creative subject extended to the development of shadow plays and giant shadow puppets made to perform them.

In the last five years my interests have shifted from observation of and recreation of expressions of the already known, whether it be experiences, prejudices, or fears, to exploration of human cognitive tactics, and to both the material and the immaterial aids used to encourage and to support learning and thinking. I am especially interested in the ways devised by immigrants to learn how to understand and use their new culture, and the ways in which they both keep and modify their old cultures. My emphasis has been on the ways in which arrangement of both work and leisure spaces are structured by people to express their views of the world and how they fit into it. Immigrant gardens, produced by groups ranging from the Portuguese to the South East Asians, being quite different from the English vernacular garden which dominates the popular media, make the cognitive tactics of gardening startlingly visible. And, as usual, while writing on this subject (articles and a book, *Contemporary Vernacular Gardens*, with photographer Travis Amos) I am producing garden designs influenced by these immigrant gardens. Presently I am working on mosaics in the pictorial and ornamental traditions of the Mediterranean for gardens and some public buildings.

—Frances Butler

A prolific and versatile designer, Frances Butler is also an artist, scholar, educator and writer on design. She has received wide recognition for her work in a number of media: fabric and textile design, managing her own textile design company; graphic design, typography and book design, managing her own small press with partner Alastair Johnston; and more recently, garden design, practicing alone and with others. In addition, her writing on design is well received by a wide audience which ranges from practicing designers to art and social/cultural historians.

Butler's unusual combination of practical and theoretical knowledge and skill in design evolved from her education in both history and design. (Her dissertation toward the Ph.D. in architecture at the University of California, Berkeley, on Portuguese vernacular gardens is in progress at this date.) Her teaching and research, as well as extensive travels and a wide range of intellectual interests, also provide her with an appropriate and supportive base for this duality.

Her flaunting of the usual pattern of success in design—selection of one aspect of design and sticking to it—has also not been a detriment to her career. Rather, unconventionality and experimentation are a vital and integral part of her work which have contributed to her unique style in both design and writing about design.

Readily apparent in her teaching of design, Butler's philosophy is to combine the understanding of creativity and the processes of design with the critical and analytical approaches of design theory to expand the usually narrowly defined field of design.

Recurring themes in her work are sequential movement, time and order in space; light and shadow; complex, overlapping layers of pattern; and an underlying humanistic concern. Human and animal figures almost always play a role in each piece. Despite the often whimsical and highly personal nature of her work, a deeper, intellectual content is communicated through literary, musical, or historical allusions and symbolism from the Orient and the West.

Butler's textile designs, bold and innovative, were sold internationally, most often as wall hangings or art, in single panels or yardage. "Beast in the Jungle" (1971), based on the Henry James novel, uses decorative, repetitive patterns to effectively create a sense of tension in the depiction of two tigers, one barely discernible, stealthily approaching a tea party. In her own words, "In the Yellow River" (1972) is a decorative, repeated image of "an Oxford educated (Chinese) princess (who) still winds up in a maze of packaging near the isle of Deshima and Mao-Tse-tung in the current, moving continuously."

Incorporating many of the same themes and patterns from her textile work into her graphic design, Butler created a structure for the organization of her work in direct contrast to the popular Swiss grid approach. She uses borders, but varies their relationship to the image and the page, breaking images through the borders, overlapping them, inserting text on the images, using text as borders. She also emphasizes size and relationship of images to one another and to the page, frequently as she has stated, ". . . grouping small images into large shapes to lead the viewer through the sequential reading of all the little goodies that make up the whole story. I wanted to create an experience that was 'just like at the movies,' where one sees the entire screen constantly while refocusing on subtle gestures." Color and experimentation with color are other characteristics of her work, and her revival of the nearly obsolete and labor-intensive pochoir technique, brings an unusual richness to the palette of her printed work.

Her early studies in history led her to medieval manuscripts, which spurred an interest in calligraphy, then typography, and later book design and printing. Book design allowed her to experiment further with the themes of sequential movement and continuing patterns and images through the turning of the pages. "Confracti Mundi Rudera," (1975) the first book produced by her Poltroon Press, uses parallel interacting texts, one visual, one verbal. "Career Options, a Catalog of Screens Including the Gesture of Outward" (1985) is a beautifully crafted book full of surprises, like pop-up folded figures and a pocket of postcard-like images related to the images in the book itself. Mostly black and white, the pages are composed of photographic images of cut-out figures, some acrobatic, all casting strong shadows. Brief texts give light-hearted and poetic, but sound advice about the jobs represented by each screen. Many of the images depicted have been used previously in her other work.

Butler has worked on her own private garden since 1980, constantly changing both the plantings and sculptural elements in it. Again emphasizing shadow and light, color, and the interplay of the visual and the verbal, her gardens are filled with many of the images and themes of her other work: order, movement, time, borders, sequence and pattern. Trellises with large letters or words cast moving shadows across whimsically tiled plant beds, and light and color flow through cut-out screens and open-work tables. She incorporates her knowledge of history and literature into the words and quotes tiled into mosaic planters and borders. Influenced by the sophisticated poetry gardens and the naive and eccentric gardens she has researched, her gardens are delightful and ever changing. From her book "Career Options" she sums up what a garden should be: "Once the possibilities are surveyed, make a garden or a stage. Now there is the possibility of entrance and exit and fragments of action can become stories."

Butler has also experimented with photography and photoprint collages, etchings, sculpture, furniture making and mosaics, incorporating many of the themes and images from her graphic work into these forms.

Frances Butler's work is eclectic, idiosyncratic, and impossible to categorize, but intriguing, analytical, humorous, delightful and intelligent.

—Elizabeth Douthitt Byrne

C

CACHAREL, Jean.

French fashion designer. Born Jean Louis Henri Bousquet, in Nîmes, 30 March 1932. Studied at the Ecole Téchnique, Nîmes, 1951–54. Married Dominique Sarrut in 1956; children: Guillaume and Jessica. Worked as a cutter and stylist, for Jean Jourdan, Paris, 1955–57; founder and director, Societé Jean Cacharel ready-to-wear fashions, Paris, since 1964; worked with designer Corinne Sarrut, specializing in separates, dresses, shirts, sweaters, trousers and ties, from 1966. Recipient: Export Trade Oscar, Paris, 1969. Addresses: 49 rue Etienne Marcel, 75001 Paris; 62 rue de Verneuil, 75007 Paris, France.

Publications:

On CACHAREL: books—*The World of Fashion: People, Places, Resources* by Eleanor Lambert, New York and London 1976; *In Fashion: Dress in the Twentieth Century* by Prudence Glynn, London 1978; *Mode im 20. Jahrhundert* by Ingrid Loschek, Munich 1978; *25 Ans de Marie-Claire de 1954 a 1979,* compiled by Francoise Mohrt, Paris 1979; *Fairchild's Who's Who in Fashion,* edited by Ann Stegemeyer, New York 1980; *Who's Who in Fashion,* edited by Karl Strute and Theodor Doelken, Zurich 1982; *McDowell's Directory of Twentieth Century Fashion* by Colin McDowell, London 1984; *The Encyclopaedia of Fashion from 1840 to the 1980s* by Georgina O'Hara, London 1986.

CADBURY-BROWN, Henry Thomas.

British architect, interior and exhibition designer. Born in London, 20 May 1913. Educated at Westminster School, London, until 1930; studied at the Architectural Association School, London, 1931–35; Dip. 1935. Served in the Royal Artillery, British Army, 1939–45: Major. Married Elizabeth Romeyn in 1953. Worked in the office of architect Erno Goldfinger, London, 1936–37; in private architectural and design practice, London, 1937–39, and since 1945: partner, with John F. Metcalfe, in H. T. Cadbury-Brown Partnership, from 1962; also with Eric Lyons Cunningham Partnership, 1977. Instructor, Architectural Association School, London, 1946–49, and Royal College of Art, London, 1952–61; visiting critic, Harvard University School of Architecture, Cambridge, Massachusetts, 1956; Professor of Architecture, Royal Academy, London, 1938; council member, Royal Institute of British Architects, 1951–53; committee member from 1953, and President, 1959–60, Architectural Association, London; British committee member, Union Internationale des Architectes, 1951–54. Recipient: London Architecture Bronze Medal, 1963. Fellow, Royal Institute of British Architects; Honorary Fellow, Royal College of Art, London; Officer, Order of the British Empire, 1967; Associate, 1971, and Academician, 1975, Royal Academy of Art, London. Address: 18 Fentiman Road, London SW8.

Works:

Exhibition displays at the *Design in Industry* exhibition, Olympia, London, 1938.
Origins of the People pavilion at the *Festival of Britain,* London, 1951.
Royal Pavilion at the *Royal Norfolk Agricultural Show,* 1952.
Chance Glass displays at the *Building Exhibition,* London, 1953.
National Farmers Union pavilion at the *Royal Agricultural Society Annual Show,* 1955.
Portland Library and Art Gallery interiors, Nottingham University, 1955.
Conference room interiors, Time-Life Building, London, 1956.
Directors dining-room interiors, Shell Centre, London, 1961.
Kurt Geiger shoe shop interiors in Bond Street and Sloane Street, London, 1965, 1969.
Royal Lancaster Hotel banquet room interiors, London, 1966.
Monk and Dunstone office interiors, Bristol, 1972.

Buildings and architectural works include:— British Railways offices, London, 1937–39; School and housing, Harlow New Town, Essex, 1953–54; Honrsey Lane School, London, 1955; Housing, Hatfield, Hertfordshire, 1959; Shops and housing, Basildon New Town, Essex, 1960; Royal College of Art buildings, London, 1962–63; Birmingham University halls of residence, 1964; Civic Centre, Gravesend, Kent, 1968; Ashburnham School, Chelsea, London, 1973; World's End complex, Chelsea, London, 1977.

Publications:

By CADBURY-BROWN: article—"Ludwig Mies van der Rohe" in the *Architectural Association Journal* (London), July/August 1959.

On CADBURY-BROWN: articles—"The Wrong Decision: Project for the New Royal College of Art Building" in *Architectural Review* (London), July 1973; "Crosland Sets Important Listed Building Precedent" in *Architects' Journal* (London), 26 November 1975; "V & A: History and Future Development" by Johnny Grey in *Architectural Design* (London), no. 7/8, 1977; "It's a Blue Ribbon Scheme" in *Building Design* (London), 5 June 1981.

H. T. Cadbury-Brown, although personally modest to the point of reticence, has developed an authoritative architectural personality that few of his collaborators have been able to resist, though there is an impression that it was somewhat frustrated by Casson and Gooden, and maybe by the Senate of the Royal College of Art as well, in the Kensington Gore buildings where (as for instance in the Senior Common Room) other decorative schemes were imposed. One has only to contrast this with the student refectory area as Cadbury-Brown left it or with the Gulbenkian Hall interior (where he was helped by Elizabeth Cadbury-Brown) to realise what the Royal College of Art undoubtedly lost elsewhere in the building. The two residence halls at Birmingham University, commenced in 1963, also bear witness to his strength, and the commendation they received emphasises how much Cadbury-Brown had contributed to gain the Gold Medal awarded to the Royal College of Art buildings.

In all Cadbury-Brown's work, an eloquent geometry, largely polygonal, invests it with all the decoration it requires. In this respect, his work relates more to Mackintosh and to the Horta of the Palais du Peuple than to the usual masters of the International Style. In some ways, even, the World's End complex of dwellings, offices, school, children's home, and shops—designed in collaboration with the Lyons and Cunningham partnership but owing much in its polygonal effects to Cadbury-Brown—recalls no other building so much as Mackintosh's Glasgow School of Art, which it in no way resembles, however.

Along with many other British architects of the time, following the break-through of the Festival of Britain on London's South Bank, Cadbury-Brown undertook a number of civic commissions for educational buildings. The list is impressive as much for the quality of the individual buildings as for their number—a primary school in West Bromwich, the RCA buildings in Kensington Gore, two residence halls, at Birmingham University, the sixth-form accommodation for Felixstowe College, the lecture theatre block for Essex University, as well as student housing there—all designed within the space of nine or ten years.

Before coming to the design of the World's End development, he had already earlier designed the Taistock Crescent scheme for the same municipality. This had made ingenious use of the site to pack in some 132 dwellings, along with a social services unit. He learned much from the experience, which underlay his obvious contributions to the World's End site. He has also produced distinguished buildings for the Gravesend and Cranbrook Councils.

—Toni del Renzio

CAFLISCH, Max.

Swiss book, typographic and lettering designer. Born in Ilanz, 25 October 1916. Studied typography, as an apprentice compositor, at the Studer-Schlapfer printing works, Horgen, 1932–36, and at the Kunstgewerbeschule, Zurich, until 1938. Married Aline Lüthi in 1943; children: Regula and Ulrich. Worked as a typographer, under Jan Tschichold and Imre Reiner, at the Benno Schwabe and Birkhauser printing works, Basel, 1938–40; typographer, then art director, Benteli AG publishers and printers, Bern-Bumpliz, 1941–62; also freelance designer and typographic consultant, working for Bauer typefoundry of Frankfurt, Holbein of Basel, IBM World Trade of New York, Francke Herbert Lang and the Staatliche Lehrmittelverlag of Bern, from 1943, and for Hell of Kiel, from 1972. Lecturer, Allgemeine Gewerbeschule, Basel, 1940–41; instructor in typography, Kunstgewerbeschule, Zurich, 1962–81. Contributor to *Schweizer Graphische Mitteilungen,* St. Gallen, 1938–40, *Typographische Monatsblätter,* St. Gallen, 1940–89, *Graphische Revue Oesterreichs,* Vienna, 1962, and *Fine Print,* San Francisco, 1983. **Exhibitions:** Stiftung Buchkunst, Frankfurt, 1968; Fachhochschule, Hamburg, 1968; Stadtbücherei Wilhelmspalais, Stuttgart, 1968; Gutenbergmuseum, Bern, 1969; Centro del Libro, Ascona, 1981; Universiteits-Bibliotheek, Amsterdam, 1983; Sankt Kathrinen, St. Gallen, 1989. **Collections:** Stiftung Buchkunst, Frankfurt; Deutsche Bücherei, Leipzig; Klingspor Museum, Offenbach. Recipient: 2 Gold Medals, 1965, and Golden Letter Award, 1970, Leipzig International Book Fair; Preis der Schweizer Buchhandels, 1985; and more than 100 book awards in Switzerland and Germany. Member: Bund Deutscher Buchkünstler, Frankfurt; Association Typographique Internationale. Address: 12 In der Halden, 8603 Schwerzenbach, Switzerland.

Works:

Gedichte vom Mittelalter bis zur Neuzeit book design, for Staatlischer Lehrmittelverlag, Bern, 1953.
Columna typeface, for Bauer, Frankfurt, 1955.
Handbuch der Schweizerischen Volkswirtschaft 2-volume book design, for Benteli-Verlag, Bern, 1955.
Conrad Ferdinand Meyer: Samtliche Werke book design, for Benteli-Verlag, Bern, 1958.
Elegies et Sonnets de Lovize Labe Lionnoize book design, for Alain Berlincourt, Bern, 1961.
The Magic Mountain (Thomas Mann) 2-volume book design, with engravings by Felix Hoffmann, for Limited Editions Club, New York, 1962.
Der abenteuerliche Sinmplicius Simplicissimus (Hans Jakob Christoph von Grimmelshausen) book design, with etchings by Max Hunziker, for Flamberg-Verlag, Zurich, 1964.
Das Höhe Lied book design, with woodcuts by Felix Hoffmann, for Flamberg-Verlag, Zurich, 1964.
The Discourses of Epictetus book design, for Limited Editions Club, New York, 1966.
Der Psalter book design, with illustrations by Max Hunziker, for Württembergische Bibelanstalt, Stuttgart, 1966.
Der Bibel (Hausbibel) book design, for Württembergische Bibelanstalt, Stuttgart, 1967.
Die Bibel (Perlbibel) book design, for Württembergische Bibelanstalt, Stuttgart, 1967.
Die Bibel (altar and chancel bible) design, for Württembergische Bibelanstalt, Stuttgart, 1968.
Atlas de mycologie medicale book design, for Editions Hans Huber, Bern, 1974.
Digiset-Schriften der Firma Meier et Cie AG catalogue design, for Meier et Cie, Schaffhausen, 1982.
Heinrich Bullinger: Werke book design, for Theologischer Verlag, Zurich, 1983.
Mengensatz-Schriftprobe der Firma Typopress book design, for Typopress, Zurich, 1983.
Wilhelm Meisters Lehrjahre (Johann Wolfgang Goethe) 2-volume book design, with illustrations by Felix Hoffmann, for Verlag Mirio Romano, Kilchberg, 1983.
Johannes Gessners Pariser Tagebuch 1727 book design, for Hans Huber Verlag, Bern, 1985.
Romeo und Julia auf dem Dorfe (Gottfried Keller) book design, with illustrations by Karl Walser, for Verlag Mirio Romano, Kilchberg, 1989.

Publications:

By CAFLISCH: books—*The Art of the Book,* with others, London 1951; *Die Antiqua und*

Max Caflisch: *Atlas de Mycologie Medicale* book design, for Editions Hans Huber, Bern, 1974

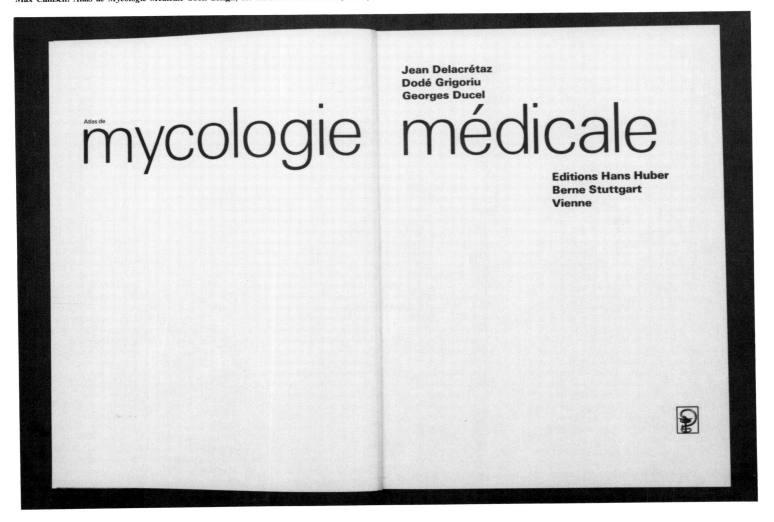

Kursiv des Buchhändlers, Verlegers, Schrift-giessers und Druckers John Bell, Bern 1957; *William Morris, der Erneuer der Buchkunst,* Bern 1959, 1965; *Kleines Spiel mit Ornamenten,* Bern 1965; *Fakten zur Schriftges-chichte,* Bern 1972; *Schrift und Papier,* Grellingen 1973; *Typographie braucht Schrift/Typography Needs Type/Typographie a besoin des caractères,* Lausanne, Switzerland 1977. Kiel, West Germany 1978.

On CAFLISCH: books—*Modern Lettering and Calligraphy,* edited by Rathbone Holme and Kathleen M. Frost, London and New York 1954; *Manuale Typographicum* by Hermann Zapf, Frankfurt 1954, 1968, New York 1968, Cambridge, Massachusetts and London 1970; *A Book of Type and Design* by Oldrich Hlavsa, New York 1960; *Who's Who in Graphic Art,* edited by Walter Amstutz, Zürich 1962, 2nd edition, Dübendorf, Switzerland 1982; *Buch-gestaltung* by Albert Kapr, Dresden 1963; *Calligraphy Today* by Heather Child, London 1963, 1976; *Lettering Today: A Survey and Reference Book,* edited by John Brinkley, London 1964; *Letter Forms: 110 Complete Alphabets,* edited by Frederick Lambert, London 1964, New York 1972; *A Manual of Decorated Type-faces* by R. S. Hutchings, London and New York 1965; *Kürschners Graphiker Handbuch,* edited by Charlotte Fergg-Frowein, West Berlin 1967; *The Art of Written Forms: The Theory and Practice of Calligraphy* by Donald M. Anderson, New York 1969; *Schriftkunst* by Albert Kapr, Dresden 1971; *Architectural Signing and Graphics* by John Follis and Dave Hammer, New York and London 1979; *The Thames and Hudson Manual of Typography* by Ruari McLean, London 1980; *Max Caflisch: Typo-graphica practica,* Hamburg 1988.

Script and form have a decisive influence on the understanding of a text, and therefore on the legibility of a printed work. The activity of the typographer takes place in obscurity. It is true that his hand may be detected in the printed work but it should not intrude upon the reader. It is the typographer's prime task to serve the readers of every age and to produce printed matter which is as comfortable as possible. The more natural typography appears the more the typographer's work can be regarded as successful. In this sense, each typographical task is for me a constantly new challenge.

—Max Caflisch

Max Caflisch's work in book design shows mastery of all aspects of the task: the arrangement and setting of text (with meticulous attention to fine details of spacing and of editorial decision), the choice of paper and other materials, the design of binding and jacket. These skills can be attributed in part to his training as a compositor, as well as to his subsequent design education, and then to his years as an in-house designer with the printer and publisher Benteli A G. Caflisch is a notable product of the Swiss system of typographic training, which marries the instruction of technical printer's skills to a full education in design. But if Caflisch's work is an exemplary product of Swiss typographic culture, it nevertheless has little connection with the school of modernist graphic design and typographic that, during the 1950's and 1960's, made "Swiss" typography famous as a dogmatic style.

Caflisch has designed generally within the assumptions of "classical" or "traditional" typography. He worked under Jan Tschichold in the late 1930's, just at the point when Tschichold was adopting a "traditional" typography, and he has sometimes been seen as having stayed in the shadow of Tschichold's influence.

But though Caflisch's early work (at least as reproduced) does in some respects recall Tschichold's manner, the more important point is that both were working within the same large tradition. Caflisch's published statements make clear his conception of a broad and almost eternal historical sequence, in which his and much other work stands; the contribution of any individual is seen as subservient to this larger phenomenon, and the designer deviates from it at the risk of mere self-expression and disregard for the text and the reader. This doctrine is outlined in Stanley Morison's *First Principles of Typography,* a German-language edition of which Caflisch has translated and designed. The range of Caflisch's typographic skills and interests further recalls Tschichold—especially his lettering and calligraphy but also his published work on the history of the subject—though he has not shown the polemical urge that characterized Tschichold's career, during the heyday of modernist "Swiss typography", he continued his work untroubled by any wish to attack heresies. However, this description of Caflisch's work is not a final one. In more recent work (particularly in display typography), there are signs of a loosening of approach, away from any rigid application of "classical" solutions and towards arrangements that find their own, less symmetrical form.

—Robin Kinross

CARDIN, Pierre.
French fashion designer. Born, of French parents, in San Andrea da Barbara, Italy, 2 July 1922. Educated in Saint-Etienne, France; studied architecture, Saint-Etienne. Worked as an accountant, then as a tailor's cutter, Paris; designer, for Paquin fashion house and for Schiaparelli, Paris, 1945–46; head of workrooms, Christian Dior fashion house, Paris, 1946–50; founder-director, Pierre Cardin fashion house, Paris, from 1950: first ready-to-wear collections, 1959; also film costume designer, from 1946. Founder-director, Theâtres des Ambassadeurs-Cardin (now Espace Cardin complex), Paris, from 1970; chairman, Maxim's Restaurant, Paris, from 1981. **Exhibition:** *Fashion: An Anthology,* Victoria and Albert Museum, London, 1971. Recipient: Gold Thimble Award, Paris, 1977, 1979, 1982; Fashion Oscar, Paris, 1985; Prize of the Foundation for Garment and Apparel Advancement, Tokyo, 1988. Chevalier de la Légion d'Honneur, France, 1983; Grand Officer, Order of Merit, Italy, 1988. Address: 59 Faubourg Saint-Honoré, 75008 Paris, France.

Works:

Film costume designs include—*La Belle et la Bête* (Cocteau), 1946; *A New Kind of Love* (Shavelson), 1963; *The VIPs* (Asquith), 1963; *Eva* (Hakim), 1964; *The Yellow Rolls-Royce* (Asquith), 1965; *Mata Hari Agent H-21* (Lepicier), 1967; *A Dandy in Aspic* (Mann), 1968; *The Immortal Story* (Rozan), 1969; *You Only Love Once* (Sanders), 1969; *Little Fauss and Big Halsy* (Ruddy), 1970.

Publications:

On CARDIN: books—*Dressmakers of France* by Mary Brooks Picken and Dora Loues Miller, New York 1956; *The Beautiful People* by Marilyn Bender, New York 1967; *Fashion: An Anthology by Cecil Beaton,* exhibition catalogue compiled by Madeleine Ginsburg, London 1971; *Paris Fashion: The Great Designers and Their Creations,* edited by Ruth Lynam, London 1972; *The World of Fashion: People, Places, Resources* by Eleanor Lambert, London and New York 1976; *Magic Names of Fashion* by Ernestine Carter, London 1980; *McDowell's Directory of Twentieth Century Fashion* by Colin McDowell, London 1984; *The Conran Directory of Design,* edited by Stephen Bayley, London 1985; *The Encyclopaedia of Fashion from 1840 to the 1980s* by Georgina O'Hara, London 1986.

Intellectual, avant-garde, prolific Parisian fashion designer Pierre Cardin has built a worldwide fashion empire which has achieved continuous success from the late 1950's through the present in both couture and ready-to-wear fashions and a wide variety of accessories and goods. His earliest innovations in women's clothes include the chemise, mini-dress, and cartridge-pleated wools with scalloped edges. He also fashioned coats with draped hemlines and loose back panels. Cardin is credited with launching the Space Age theme in women's fashion; this included such experimental clothing as the short, stark tunic and smock worn over tights and boots, unisex astronaut suits, the batwing jumpsuit, vinyls with hard helmets and goggles, and metal body jewelry. He made wide use of man-made materials in his pursuit of this approach. Soon after he commenced his work for women, Cardin added clothes for men. He is considered the top designer to accomplish influential work for both sexes and was the first designer from Paris to sell ready-to-wear to department stores.

After World War II, Cardin had done costume designs based on the sketches of Christian Bérard for the film *La Belle et la Béte* by Jean Cocteau. He also was well acquainted with the cultural milieu of the period and had studied architecture. It is not, therefore, surprising that he would, in 1970, expand into the fields of art and entertainment. He redesigned a 1930's Paris nightclub called Les Ambassadeurs, turning it into a complex which includes a restaurant, cinema for experimental art, concert hall, art gallery, and meeting rooms, and called it Espace Cardin. Besides designing costumes for movies, Cardin himself has acted in a film with the famous star Jeanne Moreau.

All over the world, Cardin controls boutiques which have arrangements to sell his merchandise exclusively. This includes, of course, his renowned clothes for women, his characteristic men's suits with tight contours of cut and line, always precisely tailored, and the children's clothes he began making during the late 1960's. But the Cardin label can also be seen on jewelry, shoes, leather goods, toiletries such as aerosel deodorant and after-shave lotion, wigs, towels, sheets, luggage, candy, furniture, and even wine. He was one of the first designers to put his name on such a wide assortment of things, at the beginning of a trend which is currently pervasive in the area of ready-to-wear fashions of subsequent designers. Aptly called the *fauve* (wild one) of post-World War II Paris designers, Cardin will be best remembered as a major creator of clothes for the Space Age, apparel to be found in science fiction films but not yet popularized in your local town or city on earth.

—Barbara Cavaliere

CARLU, Jean (Georges Leon).

French illustrator, display and graphic designer. Born in Bonniers-sur-Seine, 3 May 1900. Educated at the College de Saint-Germain-en-Laye; studied architecture, Ecole Nationale Supérieure des Beaux-Arts, Paris. Married Marcelle Dorval in 1943. Freelance and contract designer, mainly in Paris, from 1917: worked for B. Sirven printers, Toulouse, 1919-20, Avenir Publicité agency, Paris, 1921-23, W. S. Crawford agency, London, 1929-31, France Libre organization and American Office of War Information, 1940-45, Agence de Plas advertising, Paris, 1949-52, Larousse publishers, Paris, 1952-72, Publicité Vanypeco agency, Brussels, 1953-72, and Affiche S.A., Brussels, from 1958; also designed graphics and illustrations for the periodicals *La Lumière, La République, What's New, Flair, The Times*, etc. International President, Alliance Graphique Internationale, Paris, 1945-46; President, Syndicat Nationale des Graphistes Publicitaires, Paris. **Exhibitions:** *Exposition des Arts Decoratifs*, Paris, 1925; *Exposition Union des Artistes Modernes*, Musée du Louvre, Paris, 1931; *Exposition Internationale*, Paris, 1937; *France Come Back*, New York, 1946; *France Comes to You*, toured the United States, 1947; *Second World War Posters*, Imperial War Museum, London, 1972; *Jean Carlu*, Musée de l'Affiche, Paris, 1980; *The Twentieth Century Poster*, Walker Art Center, Minneapolis, 1984. **Collections:** Bibliotheque Nationale, Paris; Gewerbemuseum, Basel; Deutsches Plakat-Museum, Essen. Recipient: Gold Medal, Art Directors Club of New York, 1941. Honorary Fellow, Royal College of Art, London; Officier de la Legion d'Honneur, France; Officier des Arts et des Lettrés, France. Address: Villa Les Cypres, Route de Saint-Blaise, Castagniers, 06670 Saint-Martin-du-Var, France.

Works:

Automobiles Talbot poster, for Avenir Publicité, 1923.
Waterman-Jif posters, for Avenir Publicité, 1923.
Monsavon poster, for Monsavon Soap, 1925.
Mobil Oil (Lindberg monoplane) poster, for Mobil Oil Company, 1926-27.
Eclairages-Machineries and *Feu du Ciel* posters, for Theatre Pigalle, Paris, 1929.
4 Routes to the Continent poster, for London and North-Eastern Railways/Crawford Agency, 1930.
Railway signals poster, for Disques Odeon, Paris, 1930.
L'Atlantide (Pabst) film poster, Paris, 1932.
Cuisine Electrique poster, Paris, 1934-35.
L'Optimiste posters, for Cinzano, 1937-38.
America's Answer—Production poster, for the Office of Emergency Management, 1941.
Entre le Marteau et l'Enclume poster, for the Commisariat de l'Information, 1944.
Poster series, for Pan American Airways, 1947-48.
L'Eau qui fait Pschitt . . . Perrier poster, for Agence De Plas, 1949.
Shell X100 Motor Oil posters, for Agence De Plas, 1950.
Poster series, for Air France, 1957-59.
Philips Auto-Radio poster, for Publicité Vanypeco, 1958.

Publications:

By CARLU: articles—in *Arts et Metiers Graphiques* (Paris), no. 7, 1928; *Vendre* (Paris), March 1930; *L'Affiche* (Paris), May 1934; *Le Miroir du Monde* (Paris), 21 March 1936; *World's Press News* (London), 25 June 1936.

On CARLU: books—*Exposition de l'Affiche en Couleur, de Cheret a nos Jours*, exhibition catalogue, Paris 1939; *The Story of Modern Applied Art* by Rudolph Rosenthal and Helena Ratzka, New York 1948; *Die neue Grafik/The New Graphic Design* by Karl Gerstner and Markus Kutter, Teufen and London 1959; *Who's Who in Graphic Art*, edited by Walter Amstutz, Zurich 1962; *History of the Poster* by Josef and Shizuko Müller-Brockmann, Zurich 1971; *Retrospective Jean Carlu*, exhibition catalogue with texts by Alain Weill and Génevieve Gaetan-Picon, Paris 1980; *Advertising: Reflections of a Century* by Bryan Holme, London 1982; *The Twentieth-Century Poster: Design of the Avant-Garde* by Dawn Ades, New York 1984; *Typographic Design: Form and Communication* by Rob Carter, Ben Day and Philip Meggs, New York 1985.

Perhaps Jean Carlu's original study of architecture gave him his lasting interests in making monumental images, in sometimes experimenting with combinations of different media, and in the use of actual material such as aluminum and mosaic in his work. Certainly, many of his images have the power to make effective mural art. His famous design "Cuisine electrique" (1935) was made of patterned aluminum, aluminum sheet, beaten copper sheet, polished copper, mosaic, and luminous neon tubing. The image behind this mixed media was of a simple, formalised figure, as used by many cartoonists, but made possible by the visual languages of the cubists. The multiple textures used were given cohesion by a strong unifying design which was always Carlu's strength. There was also an intellectual rigour in his work, although he often introduced an element of humour into his designs. Without this element, his works might have become simply heroic.

His work is in any case as vital as that of many of his contemporaries working in other countries with political posters and murals. But Carlu worked as many of his French contemporaries did, with a more gently, acceptable form of expression. However, an example of the possibilities of his strength as a political muralist is the poster that he designed in the United States in 1945: "America's Answer—Production." The title of the poster is displayed across the work. Beyond this, a large, gloved hand grasps a wrench which is fastened around the first "o" of the word "production," as though it were a nut. In this way, the typography literally links with the message. This ingenious and sophisticated simplification typifies Carlu's work.

His designs, although suitable for large-scale interpretation, were still effective on the printed page. His skillful use of typography, which was always successfully integrated with his imagery, looks immaculate on the page of a magazine. It is a tribute to this design skills that such an image could operate on any scale while still maintaining its vitality. He supplied illustrations for *Le Bourgeois Marie* by C. Villier as well as for giant billboards in the United States.

—John Barnicoat

CARMI, Eugenio.

Italian painter, sculptor, graphic and industrial designer. Born in Genoa, 17 February 1920. Studied chemistry, at the ETH Eidgenossische Technische Hochschule, Zurich, 1940-44:

Dip.Ing.Chem. 1944; painting, in the studio of artist Felice Casorati, Turin, 1947-48. Married Maria Vittoria Vices Vinci in 1950; children: Francesca, Antonia, Stefano and Valentina. Freelance artist and designer, in Genoa, 1950-65, and in Milan, since 1970; art director, Italsider company, Genoa, 1958-64. Founder-Member, Gruppo Cooperativo di Bocadasse, and Galleria del Deposito, Genoa, 1963-70. Instructor in visual art, Academy of Macerata, 1972-73, and Academy of Ravenna, 1977-79; also visiting lecturer at colleges in the United States, from 1965. **Exhibitions:** Galleria Numero, Florence, 1963; Museum of Modern Art, Zagreb, 1964; Galeria Universitaria, Mexico City, 1967; Musee d'Art Moderne, Paris, 1971; Muzeum Sztuki, Lodz, 1971; Palazzo dei Diamanti, Ferrara, 1975; Centro Comunale di Cultura, Valenza, 1979; Italian Cultural Institute, New York, 1980; Palazzo della Commenda, Genoa, 1982; Andome Wohndesign, Zurich, 1984; Italian Cultural Institute, Zagreb, 1985; Galleria Ponte Pietra, Verona, 1987; Atlantic Hotel Kempinski, Hamburg, 1988. **Collections:** Galleria Nazionale d'Arte Moderna, Rome; Muzeum Sztuki, Lodz; Victoria and Albert Museum, London; Museum of Modern Art, New York. Recipient: First Prize, Milan Poster Triennale, 1957; First Prize, International Drawing Triennale, Wroclaw, 1974. Address: Corso di Porta Vigentina 6, 20122 Milan, Italy.

Works:

Corporate identity programme, for Italsider, 1958-64.
The Bomb and the General book design, for Bompiani, 1966, and Secker and Warburg, 1988 (with Umberto Eco).
The Three Astronauts book design, for Bompiani, 1966, and Secker and Warburg, 1988 (with Umberto Eco).
Experimental colour television programmes, for RAI, 1973-74.
Mirrors, for Acerbis International, 1982-83.
Carpets, for Sisal Collezioni, 1987-88.

Publications:

By CARMI: books—*Stripsody*, with Cathy Berberian and Umberto Eco, Rome and Houston 1966; *La Bomba e il Generale*, with Umberto Eco, Milan 1966, London 1988; *I Tre Cosmonauti*, with Umberto Eco, Milan 1966, London 1988.

On CARMI: books—*Eugenio Carmi*, exhibition catalogue with text by Vera Horvat-Pintaric, Zagreb 1964; *Eugenio Carmi: Chromosynclasma*, with text by Michelangelo Antonioni, Milan 1971; *Apropos d'Eugenio Carmi*, exhibition catalogue by Pierre Restany, Paris 1971; *Eugenio Carmi—una pittura di paesaggio?* by Umberto Eco, Milan 1973; *Carmi*, with texts by Carmine Benincasa, Umberto Eco and others, Milan 1982; *Gli Specchi di Carmi*, trade catalogue with texts by Alessandro Mendini and Daniele Baroni, Bergamo 1983.

1. *Exodus 25:* "And the Lord spake unto Moses saying . . . that they bring me an offering: of every man that giveth it willingly with his heart ye shall take my offering. And this is the offering which ye shall take of them; gold and silver, and brass. And blue, and purple, and scarlet, and fine linen, and goat's hair; and rams' skins dyed red, and badgers' skins, and shittim wood. Oil for the light, spices for anointing oil, and for sweet incense. Onyx stones, and stones to be set in the ephod, and in the breastplate. And let them make a sanctuary; that I may dwell

among them. According to all that I shew thee, after the pattern of the tabernacle and the pattern of all the instruments thereof, and even so shall ye make it. And they shall make an ark of shittim wood: two cubits and a half shall be the length thereof, and a cubit and half the height thereof. And thou shalt overlay it with pure gold, within and without shalt thou overlay it, and shalt make upon it a crown of gold round about. And thou shalt cast four rings of gold for it, and put them in the four corners thereof; and two rings shall in the one side of it, and two rings in the other side of it. And thou shalt make staves of shittim wood, and overlay them with gold. And thou shalt put the staves into the rings of the sides of the ark, that the ark may be borne with them. The staves shall be in the rings of the ark: they shall not be taken from it. And thou shalt put into the ark the testimony which I shall give thee." There follows a detailed description of models for the mercy seat of pure gold, of the table in shittim wood, of the gold candlestick, of the tabernacle of fine twined blue, purple, and scarlet, of cunning work with cherubims upon it.

2. God therefore is an artist and an architect. Probably he knew the earliest aesthetic manifestations of men, when they drew animals on cave rocks, and must have asked himself the old question: why produce aesthetic activity by using up energy needed for the primary business of survival?

3. A careful reading of the project which God the artist proposes to Moses supplies us with an original answer. While, almost bored, he reminds him of the codes of human behaviour, in ten points, he takes a lingering pleasure in giving Moses a graphic description rich with practical details (colours, measurements, materials) of his design for objects that he wants. The Ark must be in shittim wood and covered in pure gold, the linen for the tabernacle shall be of blue, purple and scarlet; the candlestick shall be in beaten gold; the table, too, shall be of shittim wood covered in gold and with a golden crown and a border of a hand's breadth around it.

4. Thou shalt not kill, nor steal, nor covet they neighbour's wife. These are *negative* commands hastily pronounced. Blue, purple, scarlet, pure gold, a crown and shittim wood are the attributes of a reality to be invented; *positive* desires expressed with an enjoyment taken in the abundance of constructive details, gentle and consolatory images (linen cloths, crowns), and emotive stimuli (purple, scarlet). Desires.

5. And therefore: negative and positive.

6. The Negative. "Thou shalt NOT kill, NOT commit adultery. NOT steal. NOT bear false witness against thy neighbour. NOT covet thy neighbour's house. NOT covet thy neighbour's wife, NOR his manservant, NOR his maidservant, NOT his ox, NOR his ass NOR anything that is thy neighbour's" (*Exodus 20*). For the spectacle of the negative, God the artist constructs a dramatic stage set: a mass audiovisual piece with a great author, a consummate producer, and an audience overcome by the emotions of a rising state. "And it came to pass on the third day in the morning, that there were thunders and lightnings, and a thick cloud upon the mount, and the voice of the trumpet exceeding loud; so that all the people that was in the camp trembled" (*Exodus 19*). God knows human nature. And he confronts the people with his own behaviour. It is a people of peasants and servants, who make little use of their minds (as today). For this small part of their minds to work, they require the law of God. Desire belongs to the few. The law works on the negative.

7. The positive. God is intellectual, he is a nonconformist, and aesthete. He desperately seeks that minority which moves the other part

Eugenio Carmi: Carpet for Sisal Collezioni, Piacenza, 1987

of its mind. When Moses comes before him, he speaks to him and gives him a desperate warning: "Go down, charge the people, lest they break through unto the Lord to gaze, and many of them perish" (*Exodus 19*). Desperately, he knows that they would not understand. He knows that Moses alone, by using his mind, can live by art. And, abandoned to the total use of his being, he talks art to him. He imparts his wishes to him, supplies him with images and asks him for forms and colours. His speech grows tender, transformed into a longing for poetry; nature at last releases aesthetic energy. Do theft or adultery still mean anything in the moment of creative inebriation? By now it is the positive, the emission of an energy that will never run out; it is art, the project. "And thou shalt speak unto all that are wise hearted, whom I have filled with the spirit of wisdom, that they may make Aaron's garments to consecrate him, that he may minister unto me in the

priest's office. And these are the garments which they shall make; a breastplate and an ephod, and a robe and a broidered coat, a mitre, and a girdle: and they shall make holy garments for Aaron thy brother, and his sons, that he may minister unto me in the priest's office. And they shall take gold, and blue, and purple, and scarlet, and fine linen. And they shall make the ephod of gold, of blue and of purple, of scarlet, and fine twined linen, with cunning work. It shall have two shoulder pieces thereof joined at the two edges thereof; and so it shall be joined together" (*Exodus 28*). End of metaphor. Moses, like Giotto or Galileo or Bach, is certainly an extraordinary man who lives with the fantastic and dramatic contradiction of being an intelligent man and of feeling his mind "move." He goes up into Mount Sinai and imagines he is God. And invents. And he sees his people waiting for the law. But immediately afterwards he abandons himself to imagination and sees, or rather perceives, invents, raiments of marvellous colours, tables constructed in every minute detail with precious materials. He pursues happiness which only the vision of an imaginary environment can bring him. He becomes a maker of images for a different use of the mind. And in his aesthetic ecstasy he forgets the law of the NO, letting himself be drawn by the invention of happy behaviour. Is this perhaps what the people are waiting for?

9. The people. The people do not know.

10. The mind. The complexity of the cerebral machine is beyond the perceptive possibilities of the mind itself. The keystone of its working is synapsis (multiple interconnection which puts neurons into reciprocal contact). "The number of synapses is estimated to be around sixteen million billions. This staggering network of interneuronal connections gives rise in its turn to an inconceivable figure of possible preferential and contemporary combinations of nerve impulses. These constitute the continuous main operative cerebral state from which emerges the various activities required by environmental situations as they arise. This unpronounceable figure is assumed to be equal to 1.5 followed by three billion zeros" (Luigi Valzelli, L'Uomo e il rettile, Turin, 1978). To print three billion zeros one would need five thousand books of three hundred pages each.

11. Art. Art is a desperate and happy attempt at the identification of man with himself, that is to say, with the great God. It is a continuous reading of this open book containing three billion zeros. Other gods oppose this long and doubtful reading, seducing the people with false desires with few zeros, granted with the certainty of ignorance. But art is ambiguous; it allows the error and the doubts, and with them love.

12. Love. Love is being.

13. Imaginary signals. They are circles. They are hope, Utopia, dreams. They are the project of a thousand colours for the great fine twined cloth.

14. The people. The people are still under the mount. They see the great cloud and hear the trumpets sound, while paranoia prevents them from opening their great book of zeros. Slaves of the great omni-electronic God, they see no colours and do not love. Indeed, not all women can meet Dante and be Beatrice.

15. Reply to God's questions. Man is such only when the production of aesthetic energy becomes a primary activity for survival. In its albeit very brief existence, the history of this world is the history of the image of God the artist, that is to say, of creative man. And the rest is only a chronicle of the negative.

—Eugenio Carmi

The impressive list of exhibitions that Eugenio Carmi has to his credit bears witness to his prowess as an artist, but there has been an intimate connection between his painting and sculpture on the one hand and his designs on the other, as both call upon the same talents and creative resources. Carmi's work tends toward positive, geometric statements, sometimes of an almost abstract simplicity, but they are always much more complex than it at first seems. He is ever concerned to find an apt visual equivalent for quite intricate conceptual notions. These equivalents, however, are rarely reduced to isomorphism; instead, he achieves a subtle resonance out of primarily fairly simple forms in proximity. The richness of signifying is created, therefore, less by straightforward and simplistic denotation than by shapes that suggest a constantly renewed set of relations with the developing context,—that is, the full process of connotation.

It is obvious that Carmi's practice is directed by a theoretical concern for his materials and means, and approach which often sparks off quite interesting byproducts. He became fascinated by the effects of silkscreen printing upon tinplate, a process which he used for many different types of work. During his visits to the shops where this work was carried out, his eye, sharpened by his technical inquisitiveness and appreciation of a technological process, fed to his sensibility something of a shock of recognition upon seeing discarded sheets, out of register, overprinted or otherwise faulty, having served various purposes in setting the machines in motion. In their "Baroque" complexity and intricacy, these sheets were utterly unlike his usual work, yet he employed them as the material of an exhibition.

This ability to turn away from the expected and to prospect the unknown has been an important characteristic, not always leading to what might at first sight appear to be a stylistic volte-face, so much as bringing into his visual repertoire notions and ideas not normally thought to be expressible by those means. Neither in design nor painting, therefore, should his work be considered "abstract," since he is not concerned solely with forms and their relations but rather with the forms as a code, a perceptual code, and their relations which constitute the grammar or syntax appropriate to that code. Thus, his work is to be thought of as a scheme of figuration, geometric for the most part, able to comment upon most complicated matters. The internal posters for Italsider are exciting examples of this approach, and their success is to be measured by the ease with which a bold typographical element can be inserted within the structure and complement it.

—Toni del Renzio

CARRÉ Ben.

American art director and film designer. Born in Paris, France, in 1883; emigrated to the United States in 1912. Studied scenic painting at the Académie Amable studios, Paris. Worked as a scene painter at the Paris Opéra, Comédie Française, and other theatres, Paris, 1901–06; designer and scene painter, Pathé Gaumont film studios, Paris, 1906–12; designer, working mainly with director Maurice Tourneur, at Eclair Studios, Fort Lee, New Jersey, 1912–18; art director, again working with Tourneur, at several film studios, Hollywood, California, 1918–37; background designer and painter for Metro-Goldwyn-Mayer film studios, Hollywood, California, 1937–69; designed murals for General Motors pavilion at New York World's Fair, 1964; retired to concentrate on easel painting, Hollywood, 1969. **Exhibitions:** film retrospectives—Telluride Film Festival, Colorado, 1977; Museum of Modern Art, New York, 1978. *Died* (in Hollywood, California) *28 May 1978.*

Works:

film designs include—*La Course aux Potirons* (Cohl), 1907; *Le Huguenot* (Feuillade), 1909; *La Mort de Mozart* (Feuillade), 1909; *Le Festin de Balthazar* (Feuillade), 1910; *Aux Lions les Chrètiens* (Feuillade), 1911; *The Dollar Mark* (Lund), 1914; *Mother* (Tourneur), 1914; *The Man of the Hour* (Tourneur), 1914; *The Wishing Ring* (Tourneur), 1914; *The Pit* (Tourneur),

1914; *Alias Jimmy Valentine* (Tourneur), 1915; *Hearts in Exile* (Young), 1915; *The Boss* (Chautard), 1915; *The Ivory Snuff Box* (Tourneur), 1915; *A Butterfly on the Wheel* (Tourneur), 1915; *The Pawn of Fate* (Tourneur), 1915; *Camille* (Capellani), 1915; *A Girl's Folly* (Tourneur), 1916; *The Hand of Peril* (Tourneur), 1916; *The Closed Road* (Tourneur), 1916; *La Vie de Boheme* (Capellani), 1916; *The Rail Rider* (Tourneur), 1916; *The Velvet Paw* (Tourneur), 1916; *The Dark Silence* (Capellani), 1916; *The Deep Purple* (Young), 1916; *The Rack* (Chautard), 1916; *Trilby* (Tourneur), 1917; *The Cub* (Tourneur), 1917; *The Undying Flame* (Tourneur), 1917; *The Whip* (Tourneur), 1917; *The Law of the Land* (Tourneur), 1917; *Exile* (Tourneur), 1917; *Barbary Sheep* (Tourneur), 1917; *The Rise of Jenny Cushing* (Tourneur), 1917; *The Pride of the Clan* (Tourneur),1917; *Poor Little Rich Girl* (Tourneur), 1917; *The Blue Bird* (Tourneur), 1918; *Rose of the World* (Tourneur), 1918; *Prunella* (Tourneur), 1918; *A Doll's House* (Tourneur), 1918; *Woman* (Tourneur), 1918; *Sporting Life* (Tourneur), 1918; *The White Heather* (Tourneur), 1919; *The Life Line* (Tourneur), 1919; *Victory* (Tourneur), 1919; *The Broken Butterfly* (Tourneur), 1919; *Stronger Than Death* (Bryant and Blache), 1920; *The River's End* (Neilan), 1920; *In Old Kentucky* (Neilan and Green), 1920; *Go and Get It* (Neilan and Symonds), 1920; *For the Soul of Rafael* (Garson), 1920; *My Lady's Garter* (Tourneur), 1920; *Treasure Island* (Tourneur), 1920; *Don't Ever Marry* (Neilan and Heerman), 1921; *Dinty* (Neilan and McDermott), 1921; *Man, Woman, and Marriage* (Holubar), 1921; *Custer's Last Stand* (Neilan), 1921; *The Wonderful Thing* (Brenon), 1921; *The Light in the Dark* (Brown), 1922; *When the Desert Calls* (Smallwood), 1922; *Queen of the Moulin Rouge* (Smallwood), 1922; *What Fools Men Are* (Terwilliger), 1922; *Wife in Name Only* (Terwilliger), 1923; *Thy Name is Woman* (Niblo), 1924; *The Goldfish* (Storm), 1924; *Cytherea* (Fitzmaurice), 1924; *Tarnish* (Fitzmaurice), 1924; *The Red Lily* (Fitzmaurice), 1924; *So This is Hollywood* (Green), 1924; *Lights of Old Broadway* (Bell), 1925; *The Phantom of the Opera* (Julian), 1925; *The Masked Bride* (Cabanne and von Sternberg), 1925; *Mare Nostrum* (Ingram), 1926; *La Boheme* (K. Vidor), 1926; *The Book* (Wellman), 1926; *Don Juan* (Crosland), 1926; *The Better 'ole* (Reisner), 1926; *My Official Wife* (Stein), 1926; *When a Man Loves* (Crosland), 1926; *The King of Kings* (DeMille), 1927; *Old San Francisco* (Crosland), 1927; *Soft Cushions* (Cline), 1927; *The Jazz Singer* (Crosland), 1927; *The Red Dance* (Walsh), 1928; *The River Pirate* (Howard), 1928; *The Air Circus* (Hawks and Seiler), 1928; *The Iron Mask* (Dwan), 1929; *The Woman from Hell* (Erickson), 1929; *The Valiant* (Howard), 1929; *The Cockeyed World* (Walsh), 1929; *Frozen Justice* (Dwan), 1929; *Hot for Paris* (Walsh), 1929; *City Girl* (Murnau), 1930; *River's End* (Curtiz), 1930; *Women of All Nations* (Walsh), 1931; *The Black Camel* (MacFadden), 1931; *Riders of the Purple Sage* (MacFadden), 1931; *Sailor's Luck* (Walsh), 1933; *Dante's Inferno* (Lachman), 1935; *A Night at the Opera* (Wood), 1935; *Let's Sing Again* (Neumann), 1936; *The Mine with the Iron Door* (Howard), 1936; *Great Guy* (Blystone), 1936; *23 1/2 Hours Leave* (Blystone), 1937; *The Wizard of Oz* (Le Roy), 1939; *Meet Me in St. Louis* (Freed), 1944; *An American in Paris* (Freed), 1951.

Publications:

By CARRÉ: article—interview in *Film Comment* (New York), May/June 1978.

On CARRÉ: books—*Le Décor de Film* by Leon Barsacq, Paris 1970, as *Caligari's Cabinet and Other Grand Illusions,* Boston 1976; *American Silent Film* by William K. Everson, New York 1978; *The Art of Hollywood* by John Hambley, London 1979; *The International Dictionary of Films and Filmmakers,* London and Chicago 1987, 1991.

Ben Carré contributed to film design with his expertise in painting. Trained as a painter, he began his career producing elaborate theater backgrounds. This experience prepared him for the tromple l'oeil effects that early French filmmakers needed for their primitive productions; thus, he came to be employed by Pathé Gaumont Studio in 1901 to paint film scenery. There, Carré instituted the practice of painting the sets in color, even though they were photographed in black and white. Originally his purpose was to enliven the actors' performances; it was later realized that the range of colors actually photographed better.

Carré went to America in 1912 at the invitation of Eclair Studios. In 1914, he struck up a thirty-one film partnership with Maurice Tourneur. Their films are basically of two types. Some, such as the fairy tale *The Bluebird* (1918) demanded a fantastic treatment, which they achieved with stylized sets, silhouetted backdrops, and special effects. On the other hand, some, such as *Trilby* (1917), the story of Bohemian Parisians, has an almost documentary look. For this film, Carré recreated the back streets of Paris in Greenwich Village and duplicated a Parisian art studio with a realism of the sort that influenced the work of director Erich von Stroheim.

Carré moved with Tourneur to Hollywood in 1918, and after 1920, he began working with other directors. One of his greatest creations from this period is the underground scene from *The Phantom of the Opera* (1925). Carré was called upon because of his knowledge of the Paris Opera House. Sketches of the watery caverns of the Phantom, however, came largely from Carré's imagination.

After the sound era began, Carré lost interest in art direction, in large part because the studio art departments became larger and specialized, whereas Carré had been used to working alone. He may also have felt that sound drew emphasis away from the visual image. He worked at various studios designing parts of films for other art directors. For example, he did the glass paintings that gave the appearance of a raging fire in *Dante's Inferno* (1935).

Working as a background painter for MGM from 1937 to 1965, Carré created several memorable images: the shimmering Emerald City in *The Wizard of Oz* (1939) the large Victorian house in *Meet Me in St. Louis* (1944), and the pseudo-Impressionist background for the dream ballet in *An American in Paris* (1951). Carré's retreat to background painting at the end of his career demonstrates that he considered himself primarily a painter.

—Lois Miklas

CARRICK, Edward.

British illustrator, film and stage designer. Born Edward Anthony Craig, in London, 3 January 1905. Studied art, photography and theatre history, in Italy, Germany and France, 1917-26.

Married Mary Timewell in 1960; has 2 children. Photographer and sub-editor, *The Mask* magazine, London, 1926-28; art director, Welsh Pearson Film Company, London, 1928-29; designer of Basil Dean productions, for Associated Talking Pictures, London, 1931-35, and for Douglas Fairbanks Jr. productions, at Criterion Films, London, 1936-39; art director, Crown Film Unit, for the Ministry of Information, London, 1939-46; executive art director, Independent Producers (Rank Organization), London, 1947-49; art director, Ealing Films, London, from 1949; subsequently, freelance film and stage director, working for Hammer Films, Grand National Pictures, Independent Artists, Warwick Films, etc. Founder-President, Grubb Group of modern artists, London, 1928-38; founder, AAT School of English Film, London, 1938; film critic of *International Film Review,* London, and contributor to *Architectural Review, Architectural Record, Theatre Notebook, Penrose Annual, La Tribuna,* etc. **Exhibitions:** St. Georges Gallery, London, 1927, 1928; Redfern Gallery, London, 1929, 1931, 1938. **Collections:** British Museum, London; Victoria and Albert Museum, London; Metropolitan Museum of Art, New York; Yale University, New Haven, Connecticut; University of Texas, Austin. Fellow, Royal Society of Arts, London. Member: Architectural Association, London; Society of Authors, London; Association of Cine Technicians, London; Society for Theatre Research, London. Address: Cutler's Orchard, Bledlow, Aylesbury, Buckinghamshire HP17 9PA, England.

Works:

film designs include—*Laburnum Grove* (Reed), 1936; *Jump for Glory* (Czinner and Garmes), 1937; *Target for Tonight* (Watt), 1941; *Western Approaches* (Jackson), 1944; *Captain Boycott* (Launder), 1947; *The Red Beret* (Young), 1953; *Bachelor of Hearts* (Riller), 1958; *Blind Date* (Losey), 1959; *Macbeth* (Schaefer), 1961; *Maniac* (Carreras), 1963; *Seaside Swingers* (Hill), 1964; *Hysteria* (Francis), 1965; *The Nanny* (Holt), 1965; stage designs include—*In Abraham's Bosom,* London, 1930; *Volpone,* Old Vic, London, 1932; *Queer Cattle,* Old Vic, London, 1932; *Macbeth,* Old Vic, London, 1932; *Cornelius,* London, 1932; *Night Must Fall,* London, 1935; *Autumn,* London, 1937; *Death on the Table,* London, 1938; *Last Train South,* London, 1938; *Henry V,* Old Vic, London, 1938; *Johnson Over Jordan,* London, 1939; *Macbeth,* Shakespeare Memorial Theatre, Stratford on Avon, 1948.

Publications:

By CARRICK: books—*Nothing or the Bookplate,* contributor, edited by Gordon Craig, London 1925; *Theatre Machines in Italy 1400-1800,* London 1931; *The Theatre of Parma,* London 1931; *Designing for Moving Pictures,* London 1941, as *Designing for Films,* London 1950; *Meet . . . the Common People,* compiler, with Gerry Bradley, London 1942; *Art and Design in the British Film,* London 1948; *Oxford Companion to the Theatre,* contributor, London and New York 1951; *Gordon Craig, The Story of His Life,* London 1968; *Fabrizio Carini Motta, Trattato sopra la struttura di teatri,* Milan 1971; *Baroque Theatre Construction,* Aylesbury 1982; books illustrated—*Voyage to the Island of the Articoles* by André Maurois, London 1928; *The Poems and Verse of John Keats,* edited by John Middleton Murry, London 1929; *The Review of Revues,* edited by Charles B. Cochrane, London 1930; *The Georgics of Virgil,* translated by R. D. Blackmore,

London 1931; *In Spring* by Edith Sitwell, London 1931; *In Summer* by Edmund Blunden, London 1931; *In Autumn* by Herbert Palmer, London 1931; *In Winter* by W. H. Davies, London 1931; *Above the River* by John Gawsworth, London 1931; *Fifteen Poems, Three Friends* by John Gawsworth, London 1931; *So Far So Glad* by E. Selsey, London 1934; *The Life of Henry V* by William Shakespeare, London 1939.

On CARRICK: books—*La Scenografia nel Film,* edited by Mario Verdone, Rome 1956; *Who's Who in the Theatre,* 12th edition, edited by John Parker, London 1957; *Filmlexicon degli autore e delle opere,* 7 vols., edited by Michele Lacalamita, Fernaldo Di Giamatteo and others, Rome 1958-67; *Le Décor de Film* by Léon Barsacq, Paris 1970, as *Caligari's Cabinet and Other Grand Illusions,* Boston 1976.

Filmgoers and critics may rhapsodize about the stars, worship the writers, and idealize directors, yet they usually neglect the role of the filmdesigner! Do audiences assume that characters wander into rooms fully formed, without the plan of a human hand determining these celluloid habitations? Edward Carrick crusaded against this image, striving to educate public and artist alike on the art of the motion picture.

Carrick's father, Gordon Craig, no doubt influenced this viewpoint, since he had named the art director as the unifying force behind theatrical productions. Both prolific writer and innovative designer, Craig had revolutionized the English stage.

Carrick began by designing theatrical sets and costumes, as his father did, but motion pictures soon captured his attention. Carrick not only designed for films but published classic statements on the role of the film designer. He replaced his father's poetic tongue with a clear, no-nonsense language appropriate to the modern generation.

Carrick divided screen design into three types. The American or spectacular school derived from Italy. Heir to the tradition of pageantry, it was based on the traditional supposition that displays of wealth bring pleasure. The unreal dominated the German or Imaginist school, currently defined as Expressionistic. Carrick declared this to be the painter's turf, with artists achieving their effects through the power of suggestion. Carrick originated the Realist school with early westerns. Russians later adapted it for propaganda films. It succeeded in France where, Carrick claimed, the people have a natural appreciation for the everyday. World War II documentaries (in the making of which Carrick himself had participated) stimulated its appearance in England. Carrick noted the Realists drew from architects and those interested in sociology, due to their "concrete" concerns.

Carrick believed that "a design for motion pictures should always be the background to an emotion . . . It is the mental state of the character that interests the audience and your background can help his." Carrick emphasized the importance of light sources, the quality of camera movement, and the differences between the film and theatre. He pragmatically analyzed studio structure and the positions of its artists. Carrick's fascination with special effects produced a virtual guidebook to the creation of screen images, illustrated with pictorial examples by much admired colleagues.

Carrick's filmography stands unimpressively next to the richly studded successes of his cohorts. However, as author and educator, Carrick reigns as the "Gordon Craig" of the cinema.

—Edith Cortland Lee

CASSON, Hugh (Maxwell).

British architect, interior, exhibition and stage designer. Born in London, 23 May 1910. Studied at Eastbourne College, Sussex, 1924–27; St. John's College, Cambridge, 1929–31: MA 1931; Bartlett School of Architecture, University College, London, 1931–32; British School, Athens, 1933. Served as a camouflage officer, Air Ministry, London, 1940–44, and as technical officer, Ministry of Town and Country Planning, London, 1944–46. Married the architect Margaret MacDonald Troup in 1938; daughters: Carola, Nicola and Dinah. In private practice as architect and designer, since 1933: with Christopher Nicholson, London, 1937–39; senior partner, Casson Conder Partnership, architects, London, from 1946. Director of Architecture, Festival of Britain, London, 1948–51; Professor of Environmental Design, 1953–75, and Provost, 1980–85, Royal College of Art, London; design consultant and committee member, Bath, Brighton and Windsor Festivals, from the 1960s; member of the Royal Fine Art Commission, London, 1960–83; Royal Mint Advisory Committee, London, from 1972; trustee, British Museum (Natural History), London, from 1976; National Portrait Gallery, London, from 1976; Past President, Royal Academy of Art, London. **Exhibitions:** annual one-person shows of paintings at the Workshop Gallery, London, and elsewhere; regular exhibitor at Royal Academy Summer Exhibitions, London. Recipient: Fellow, Society of Industrial Artists and Designers, London, 1950; Royal Designer for Industry, 1951, and Master of the Faculty, 1969–71, Royal Society of Arts, London; Knight of the Order of the British Empire, 1952; Member of the Royal Danish Academy, 1954; Honorary Associate, American Institute of Architects, 1968; Royal Academician, London, 1970; Knight Commander of the Royal Victorian Order, London, 1978; Italian Order of Merit, 1980; Companion of Honour, London, 1985. Honorary Doctorates: Royal College of Art, London, 1975; University of Birmingham, 1977. Member, Royal Institute of British Architects. Addresses: (office) Casson Conder Partnership, 35 Thurloe Place, London SW7 2HJ; (home) 6 Hereford Mansions, Hereford Road, London W2 5BA, England.

Works (with Casson Conder Partnership):

British pavilion, Van Riebeck Festival Fair, Cape Town, 1952.
Arts faculty site, development plan and 8 buildings, Cambridge University, 1952–82.
Queen Elizabeth II coronation street decorations, Westminster, London, 1953.
Royal apartments on *HMY Britannia,* 1953, 1983.
Royal apartments and guest suites at Windsor Castle, 1954–83.
King George V Memorial Hostel, London, 1960.
Public rooms and first class accommodations on *S.S. Canberra,* for P & O Orient Lines, 1961.
Hall of Residence at Worcester College, Oxford, 1962.
Elephant and Rhinoceros Pavilion at London Zoo, 1965.
Northwest Regional Headquarters Building in Manchester, for National Westminster Bank, 1970.
Science section displays in the British pavilion, *World's Fair,* Osaka, 1970.
Library at Badminton School, Bristol, 1974.
Study Centre at London Zoo, 1976.
Headquarters building, for W. H. Smith Ltd., London, 1976.
Royal apartments on the Royal Train, 1977.

Stage designs—*Alceste,* Glyndebourne Opera, Sussex, 1954; *The Burning Boat,* Royal Court Theatre, London, 1955; *Troilus and Cressida,* Royal Opera House, London, 1956; *The World of Paul Slickey,* Palace Theatre, London, 1959; *The Golden Touch,* Piccadilly Theatre, London, 1960; *Incoronazione di Poppea,* Glyndebourne Opera, Sussex, 1963–64; *La Fedelta Premiata,* Glyndebourne Opera, Sussex, 1979–80.

(for a complete list of buildings and architectural projects, see *Contemporary Architects*)

Publications:

By CASSON: books—*New Sights of London,* London 1937; *Bombed Churches,* London 1946; *Houses by the Millions: An Account of the Housing Achievement in the USA 1940–1945,* London 1947; *Houses: Permanence and Prefabrication,* with Anthony Chitty, London 1947; *An Introduction to Victorian Architecture,* London 1948; *Red Lacquer Days,* London 1956; *The Unseeing Eye,* London 1958; *Museums,* editor, London 1964; *Inscape: The Design of Interiors,* editor, London 1968; *Nanny Says,* with Joyce Grenfell, London 1972; *Sketchbook,* London 1975; *Diary,* London 1981; *Hugh Casson's London,* London 1983; *Hugh Casson's Oxford,* London 1988.

On CASSON: books—*Design in British Industry: A Mid-Century Survey* by Michael Farr, Cambridge 1955; *Public Interiors* by Misha Black, London 1960; *Lettering Today,* edited by John Brinkley, London 1964; *All Things Bright and Beautiful: Design in Britain 1830 to Today* by Fiona MacCarthy, London 1972; *A Tonic to the Nation: The Festival of Britain 1951,* edited by Mary Banham and Bevis Hillier, London 1976; *Design By Choice* by Reyner Banham, London 1981.

Hugh Casson, Neville Conder and Montague Turland: Elephant and Rhinoceros Pavilion, London Zoo, 1965

In private practice since 1933, first with the late Christopher Nicholson and later with several partners under the name of Casson Conder Partnership.

The work of the practice largely concentrated after the war in planning and building universities—Belfast, Birmingham, Cambridge, and Oxford—but has tended to specialise in "non-specialisation," winning principal, large commissions in open and limited competitions. We have consequently covered a wide range of architectural design, including commercial, industrial, and domestic buildings, landscapes, conservation, interior design, exhibitions, and product design.

I have personally been concerned as consultant on the conservation of Bath, Chichester, Winchester, and Salisbury, and the practice has won several awards for work in historically sensitive areas.

—Hugh Casson

It is not easy to give a balanced account about Sir Hugh Casson. There are so many of them. There is Hugh Casson the architect, there is the interior designer, the stage designer, the painter, the illustrator, and writer, the lecturer, the teacher and not last the watercolour painter in which he excelled so brilliantly. And the list is far from complete. His contribution as a planner of universities and colleges has revealed his progressive, original mind, being able to look forward with a clear vision towards the future. But it wasn't until his appointment as the president of the Royal Academy of Arts in 1976 when he became aware that there's yet a further dimension there; the supreme organiser and his capability of skillful handling of such an important assignment. It appears that each Casson was able to enrich the other as his activities expanded.

As the Director of Architecture for the Festival of Britain he brought originality and freshness into that profession; as a Committee member for the Bath, Windsor and Brighton Festivals he opened up these communities to high quality arts; his development plans at Cambridge University's Arts Faculty site and those at Worcester College Hall in Oxford gave a lift to those sites, as well as in many other situations where he combined good architecture with excellent interior design updating these establishments to modern times. The Windsor Castle Royal Apartments and Prince Philip's Library in Buckingham Palace come into this category. These qualities have been utilised in a number of occasions not as permanent as the former, like the street decoration of the Queen's Coronation in 1953, British Pavilion design in the World Expo 70 at Osaka. His stage performances include a number of productions both in Glyndebourne, in the Royal Opera House, Covent Garden, London. One of his last stage designs was *La Fedelta Premiata* for Glyndebourne in 1979/80.

His numerous books, mainly on architecture and visual appreciation include some classics like *Bombed Churches, The Unseeing Eye* and *Hugh Casson's London.* His latest book on Oxford has been published by Phaidon in 1988, a follow up of an illustrated book on Cambridge.

Sir Hugh Casson's contribution on so many levels of arts, and to the cultural level of the nation is without parallel. He has enriched the standard of each of these categories and especially during his presidency of the Royal Academy of Arts opened the doors of the establishment to the general public and democratised fine art making it accessible to the people. It is fortunate that his prolific contribution is still continuing and he is still as active as ever.

—John Halas

CASTELLI-FERRIERI, Anna.

Italian architect and industrial designer. Born Anna Ferrieri, in Milan, 6 August 1920. Studied at the University of Milan, 1938–43: Dip. Arch. 1943. Married Giulio Castelli in 1943; children: Valerio and Maria. Freelance architect, establishing office in Milan, since 1946, and industrial designer, since 1965: has designed for Kartell, Nirvana, Apelli e Varesio, Oltolini, Lanerossi, etc; associated with architect Ignazio Gardella, 1959–73. Assistant Editor, *Casabella-Continuita,* Milan, 1946–47; Italian correspondent, *Architectural Design* (London), in Milan, 1955–60. Founder-member, Movimento Studi per l'Architettura, Milan, 1945; member, Istituto Nazionale di Urbanistica, since 1952; founder-member from 1956, and President, 1969–71, Associazione Disegno Industriale, Milan; International President, United Nations Committee of Soroptimist International, 1973–75. Guest Professor, University of Milan, Faculty of Architecture, 1984–86; Professor, Domus Academy School of Postgraduate Design, Milan, since 1987. **Exhibitions:** *Design Italian Style,* Hallmark Gallery, New York, 1968; *Italy: The New Domestic Landscape,* Museum of Modern Art, New York, 1972; *Design and design,* Palazzo delle Stelline, Milan, 1979 (travelled to Venice); *Italienisches Moebel Design,* Stadtmuseum, Cologne, 1980; *Dal Cucchiaio alla Città,* at the Milan Triennale, 1983; *Italian Women Designers,* Takashimaya Stores, Tokyo, 1985; *Anna Castelli-Ferrieri per Kartell,* Galliano, Turin, 1985; *Sedersi Kartell,* La Rinascente, Milan, 1988. **Collections:** Museum of Modern Art, New York; Stadtmuseum, Munich; Kunstindustrimuseet, Copenhagen; Israel Museum, Jerusalem; Design Museum, London. Recipient: Gold Medals, Milan Triennale, 1947, 1950; Oscar Plast Award, Milan, 1968; Silver Medal, Oesterreichisches Bauzentrum, Vienna, 1969; Gold Medal, Monza, 1972; MACEF Award, Milan, 1972; Gute Form Prize, Bonn, 1973; SMAU Award, Milan, 1977; Product Design Award, Resources Council, New York, 1979, 1984; Compasso d'Oro Awards, Milan, 1979, 1987; American Societies of Industrial Design Award, San Diego, 1981; Furniture Fair Design Award, Cologne, 1982, 1987; *Industrial Design* Magazine Annual Award, New York, 1983; Fine Furniture of the Year Award, Hamburg, 1984. Address: Corso di Porta Romana 87B, 20122 Milan, Italy.

Works:

Modular system kitchen furniture, for Oltolini, 1950.

Four-storey house at QT8 pilot neighborhood, for the Municipality of Milan, 1954.

Four-storey office block in Milan, for Castelli Acciai, 1958.

La Rotonda apartments at Arenzano, for Cemadis, 1963.

Square stacking units in ABS plastic, for Kartell, 1967.

Canteen building at Podenzano, for Tecnitub, 1968.

Oval table in fibreglass, for Kartell, 1969.

Workshop and warehouse at Limbiate, Milan, for Castelli Acciai, 1970.

Five-storey engineering offices at Arese, Milan, for Alfa Romeo, 1970–72.

Corporate headquarters buildings at Noviglio, Milan, for Kartell, 1973.

Outline wallpeg strip system in high-impact polystyrene, for Kartell, 1977.

Multi-use stools in polypropylene and metal, for Kartell, 1979.

Four-leg square table in polypropylene and ABS plastic, for Kartell, 1982.

Central-leg square table in injection-moulded plastic, for Kartell, 1983.

Corporate offices in Milan, for Castek, 1983–85.

Occasional tables in ABS plastic, for Kartell, 1985.

Stacking chair in injection-moulded polypropylene, for Kartell, 1985.

Silent Servant valet/wardrobe in ABS plastic and steel, for Kartell, 1985.

Stooble stacking stool/table in injection-moulded polypropylene, for Kartell, 1987.

Armchair in injection-moulded plastics, for Kartell, 1988.

Publications:

By CASTELLI-FERRIERI: book—*From Project to Product: Plastic and Design,* with Augusto Morello, Milan 1984, 1988; articles—"Case prefabbricate inglesi" in *Casabella* (Milan), no. 193, 1946; "L'avvio della ricostruzione" in *Casabella* (Milan), nos. 440 and 441, 1978; "Industrial Design: una mostra per capire" in *Habitat* (Milan), no. 1, 1985; "Dallo hard al soft—il design italiano come sistema culturale" in *Nuovo* (Milan), no. 14, 1988.

On CASTELLI-FERRIERI: books—*Italy: The New Domestic Landscape,* edited by Emilio Ambasz, New York and Florence 1972; *Design e Forme Nuove nell'Arredamento Italiano,* edited by Paolo Portoghesi and Marino Marini, Rome 1978; *Design and design,* exhibition catalogue with texts by Angelo Cortsei, Arthur Pulos and others, Florence 1979; *Italienisches Moebel Design,* exhibition catalogue with texts by Ignazio Gardella, Gillo Dorfles and others, Cologne 1980; *L'Alfa Romeo: Disegni e Progetti degli Uffici Alfa Romeo di Arese,* Milan 1982; *Paesaggio del Design Italiano 1972–1988* by Giampiero Bosoni, Milan 1988.

I don't understand why believing in design today is out fashion. It seems to me that in a world where total information "in real time" makes a void of any communication, one of the few real ways to communicate is by thinking of and achieving projects that are lived in and used and transformed and reinvented by someone else in a sort of design continuum. I feel it is a serious matter. There is so much talk about energy waste without considering that waste begins in our brains.

I find it useful to study, to research, and to think about new functions which may help us to live in a different way; to take into consideration economic problems which are fundamental to making a project usable, to recognize the opportunities which are offered to us by technological and scientific research; and to carry out something which might suggest to somebody else a solution to his actual concrete problems. This seems to me to be the function I chose for myself when I decided to become a designer.

—Anna Castelli Ferrieri

CASTIGLIONI, Achille.

Italian architect, exhibition and industrial designer. Born in Milan, 16 February 1918. Studied architecture at the Politecnico, Milan: Dip. Arch. 1944. Married Anna Maria Peraldo; Irma Barni; children: Carlo, Monica and Gio-

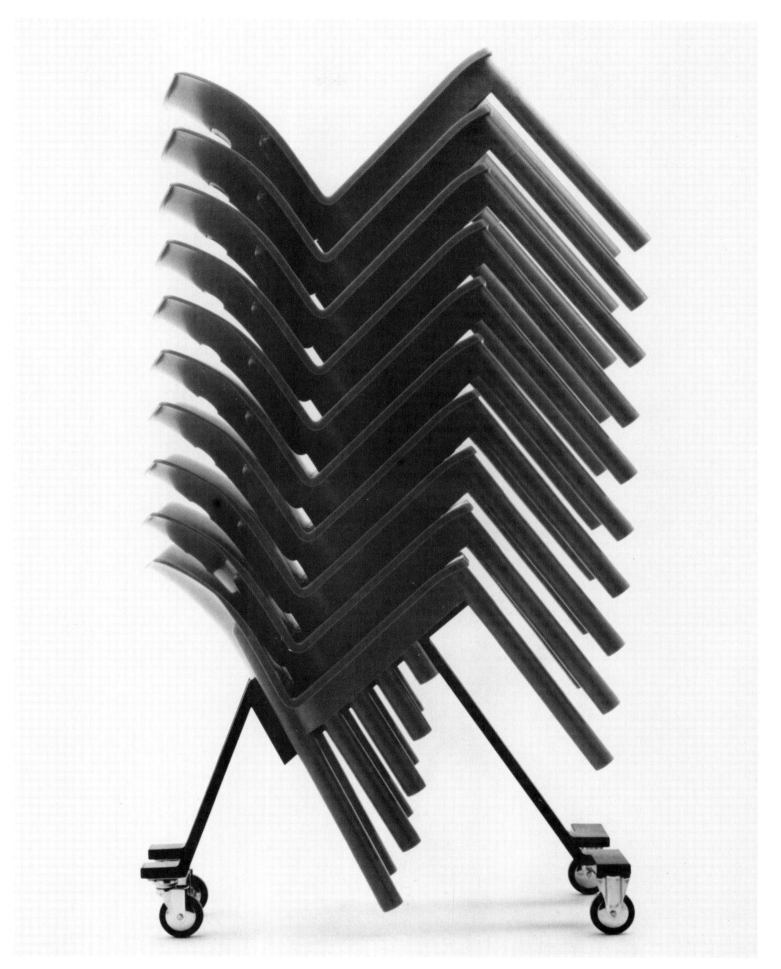

Anna Castelli-Ferrieri: *4870* **stacking chairs in polypropylene, for Kartell, 1985**

Achille and Piergiacomo Castiglioni: *KD51/Teli* lamp in polypropylene fabric, for Kartell, 1959

Works:

Hotel guestroom furniture range, for Zari, 1946.
Tubino lamp, 1951, produced by Flos, 1974.
Luminator lamp, 1955, produced by Gilardi and Arform, 1957.
Cubo armchair with polyfoam block upholstery, for Arflex, 1957.
Mezzadro stool in steel, 1957, produced by Zanotta, 1971.
Sella stool with bicycle seat, 1957, produced by Zanotta, 1983.
Mariano bookcase, produced by Brenna, 1958, and Gavina, 1961.
KD51/Teli lamp, produced by Kartell, 1959, and Flos, 1973.
Lierna chair, produced by Gavina, 1960, and Knoll International, 1969.
Pitagora espresso coffee machine, for Cimbali, 1961.
Arco lamp, produced by Flos, 1962.
Giro swivel armchair, for Gavina, 1962.
Cyrius television set, for Brionvega, 1964.
RR126 stereo equipment unit, for Brionvega,
Leonardo work desk with glass or plastic laminate top, for Zanotta, 1968.
Parentesi floor-to-ceiling suspension lamp, for Flos, 1971.
Ipotenusa halogen desk lamp, for Flos, 1975.
Bipbip standard lamp, for Flos, 1977.
Rosacamuna folding chair, for Zanotta, 1983.

Publications:

By CASTIGLIONI: books—*Design e la sua Prospettive Disciplinari*, Milan 1977; *Progetto e Produzione*, with E. Battinelli and P. Ferrari, Linz 1980.

On CASTIGLIONI: books—*Forme nuove in Italia* by Agnoldomenico Pica, Milan and Rome 1957; *Disegno Industriale* by P. Tedeschi, Bologna 1965; *Design Italiano: i mobili* by Enrichetta Ritter, Milan and Rome 1968; *Il Design in Italia 1945-1972* by Paolo Fossati, Turin 1972; *In Good Shape: Style in Industrial Products 1900 to 1960* by Stephen Bayley, London 1979; *Atlante del Design Italiano 1940-1980* by Alfonso Grassi and Anty Pansera, Milan 1980; *Il Disegno del Prodotto Industriale* by Vittorio Gregotti, Milan 1982; *An Industry for Design: The Research, Design and Corporate Image of B & B Italia* by Mario Mastropietro, Milan 1982, 1986; *Achille Castiglioni*, with texts by Vittorio Gregotti and Paolo Ferrari, Paris and Milan 1985; *Design in Italy: 1870 to the Present* by Penny Sparke, London and New York 1988; *The Adventure of Design: Gavina* by Virgilio Vercelloni, New York 1989.

The need for a new and original approach in contemporary design is emerging more and more urgently. Such a new approach can be effected through design activity on two different levels. On the one hand, there is design for mass production; on the other, design for the production of a limited quantity.

In the first case, research faces the task of large-scale production and is broken off whenever the problems of constructional and commercial production do not arise. It goes without saying that the quality of the product will be closely connected with questions of use and of sales.

In the second case, however, research is carried out on all the problems and complexities. The product that results from it reflects the quality of the research, the standard of production, for the actual product may be regarded as a materialization of the standards of design.

—Achille Castiglioni

vanna. Freelance designer, in Milan, from 1944, working with his brothers Livio Castiglioni, 1944-54, and Pier Giacomo Castiglioni, 1944-68: designed for Aerotecnica Italiana, Alessi, Arnolfo di Cambio, Arteluce, BBB Bonacina, Bernini, Brionvega, Cassina, Cedit, Danese, Ferrania, Flos, Gavina, Gilardi, Ideal Standard, Kartell, Knoll, Lancia, Marcatre, Nova Radio, Palini, Petruzzi e Branca, Poretti, Siemens, Zanotta, Zari, etc.; artistic consultant, Associazione Nazionale Industrie Elettroniche, 1949-80; RAI Radio Televisione Italiana, 1950-69; Internazionale Elettronica, 1977-80; Lanerossi furniture, 1978-80; and to the Comitato Elettronica Italiano and the Istituto Italiana del Marchio di Qualita; project chief, Illuminazione della Citta programme, Turin, 1982-83. Professor of Industrial Design and Head of the Faculty of Architecture, 1969-77, Head of Interior Design, 1977-78, Professor Extraordinary of Industrial Design, 1978-80, and Ordinary Professor of Industrial Design, 1980, Politecnico of Turin; External Professor of Design, Universita Internazionale dell'Arte, Florence, 1973; Ordinary Professor of Design, Politecnico of Milan, since 1981. Coordination Committee Member, 1947-64, Scientific Committee Member, 1979-80, Milan Triennale; Founder-member, 1956, Directive Committee Member, 1963-64, Exhibitions Committee President and Documentation Committee Member, 1965, and Compasso d'Oro Jury Member, 1970, ADI Associazione Disegno Industriale, Milan; Directive Committee Member, Collegio degli Architetti, Milan, 1960-61; Committee Member, Centro Studi e Archivio dell Comunicazione, University of Parma, 1979-80. **Exhibitions:** *La Casa Abitata,* Palazzo Strozzi, Florence, 1965; *Oggetti per la Casa,* Centro Fly, Milan, 1966; *Fem Italienska Designer,* Stockholm, 1974; *Il Design dei Castiglioni,* Centro Masters, Lissone, 1978; *Art and Industry,* Victoria and Albert Museum, London, 1982; *Design Since 1945,* Philadelphia Museum of Art, 1983; *Achille Castiglioni: Form and Expression,* Paris, Milan and London, 1985. **Collections:** Museum of Modern Art, New York; Victoria and Albert Museum, London; Staatliches Museum für Angewandte Kunst, Munich; Kunstgewerbemuseum, Zurich; Israel Museum, Jerusalem. Recipient: Grand Prize, 1951, 1957, Gold and Silver Medals, 1957, 1960, 1963, Milan Triennale; Compasso d'Oro Awards, Milan, 1955, 1957, 1960, 1962, 1964, 1967, 1979, 1981; Architecture Prize, Bienal of Sao Paulo, 1957; Vis Securit Prize, Milan, 1957; First Prize, Reed and Barton Competition, 1960; European Design Prize, Seattle, 1961; Good Design Prize, New York, 1966, 1972; Graphic Prize, Brno, 1968; Gold Medal, Rimini, 1968; Siemens Telephone Competition Prize, Milan, 1977; Ikea Interiors Prize, Zurich, 1981. Address: Piazza Castello 27, 20121 Milan, Italy.

Although trained as an architect, Achille Castiglioni, is probably best known for his furniture and lighting designs (most in conjunction with his older brother, Pier Giacomo, with whom he collaborated from 1944 until the latter's death in 1968) and his exhibition work [see Castiglioni, Pier Giacomo].

Since his brother's untimely death, Achille has continued to produce the fine-styled, highly imaginative designs for which they had become famous. Not limited to furniture or lighting, and continuing in their tradition of producing simple, obvious, and elegant design solutions, his bathroom fixtures for Ideal Standard (1971) demonstrated that such items could be both functional and well designed. In a similar fashion, his handsome flatware for Alessi (1982) brough his aesthetic integrity to the dining table in a comfortable, sculptural form, and was available in both silver and stainless steel. His oil and vinegar set (1984), for the same item, again combined his technical expertise (the stainless steel lids opened as the glass containers were turned over) with his selective eye.

He has also designed a free-standing wine/drink cooler—a bent metal shaft which supports an ice bucket—which has been described as looking "faintly like an attentive but anorexic waiter." It bears a resemblance in thought to a suspended, adjustable light, Parentesi, which he developed (with Pio Manzu) in 1970. Similarly, many of his recent lights take on other identities: Gibigiana (1981) looks more like a bird sculpture than a desk lamp, utilizing an angled mirror to reflect the light (housed in flared, metal "skirt") downwards. He has combined metal and ceramics in an innovative floor lamp, Bibip (1976), and in its recent companion piece, an uplight/wallwasher called Bisbi. One of his recent furniture favorites is Basello (1987), a tiered table which can be pivoted about a connecting point and set at different angles, like a spiral "stairway," for which its name is Milanese slang.

Castiglioni, who has been honored seven times with the Compasso d'Oro, remains through his teaching and unerring design output a highly influential participant in the design world.

—William Victor Kriebel

CASTIGLIONI, Livio.
Italian architect and industrial designer. Born in Milan, 16 January 1911. Studied architecture at the Politecnico, Milan: Dip.Arch. 1936. Served in the Italian Army, 1940-44. Married Xenia Bignami; Giuseppina Ramponi; sons: Giannino and Piero. Freelance designer, Milan, 1936-79, working the architect Luigi Caccia Dominioni, 1938-40, and with his brothers Pier Giacomo Castiglioni, 1937-54, and Achille Castiglioni, 1944-54: designed for Artemide, ENI, Italsider, Montedison, Philips, RAI Radio Televisione Italiana, etc.; design consultant to Phonola Radio, 1939-60, Brionvega, 1960-64; Osram Lamps, 1974-79, and Gulf International/Meridien Hotels, 1975-79. Founder-member, 1956, and President, 1959-60, ADI Associazione Disegno Industriale, Milan. **Exhibitions:** *Il Design dei Castiglioni,* Centro Masters, Lissone, 1978; *Culture and Technology of Italian Furniture,* Stadtmuseum, Cologne, 1980; *Design Since 1945,* Philadel-

phia Museum of Art, 1983. **Collections:** Museo della Scienza e della Tecnica, Milan; Museum of Modern Art, New York. Recipient: Silver Medal, 1936, Golf Medal and Grand Prize, 1940, and Diploma, 1973, Milan Triennale; Gold Medal, Arts Convention, Rimini, 1968; Bolaffi Art Prize, Turin, 1974. *Died* (in Milan) *in 1979.*

Publications:

By CASTIGLIONI: articles—in *Domus* (Milan), no. 151, 1940, no. 196, 1944, no. 197, 1944 and no. 198, 1944; *Architecture d'Aujourd'hui* (Paris), no. 48, 1953; *Stile Industria* (Milan) no. 1, 1957.

On CASTIGLIONI: books—*Design e Forme Nuove nell'Arredamento Italiano,* edited by Paolo Portoghesi and Marino Marini, Rome 1978; *Plastics: Design and Materials* by Sylvia Katz, London 1978; *Il Design Italiano degli Anni 50,* edited by Centro Kappa, Milan 1980; *Atlante del Design Italiano 1940–80* by Alfonso Grassi and Anty Pansera, Milan 1980; *Il Disegno del Prodotto Industriale* by Vittorio Gregotti, Milan 1982; *Il Disegno Industriale Italiano 1928–1981* by E. Fratelli, Milan 1983; *Design Since 1945,* edited by Kathryn Hiesinger and George Marcus, Philadelphia and London 1983.

Livio Castiglioni was a somewhat retiring person whose collaboration has not always been acknowledged; yet over forty years or so his influence has been pervasive. The flowing lines and harmonious detail, years ahead of time, devised for the radio sets of Phonola in 1939 and 1940, have found echoes in the pressure beer dispenser designed for Splügen Brau in 1964 by his brothers, in some of the designs for radio

and television sets by Marco Zanuso and Richard Sapper, in these same designers' Grillo telephone (1967), and in Mario Bellini's Logos 270 data processing machine for Olivetti (1970). None of these were cases of plagiarism; rather, they represent a cultural debt these designers owe to Livio Castiglioni.

Once the novelty of the Boalum lamp ceases to be in the forefront of one's appreciation, it, too, demonstrates the underlying preoccupation of Castiglioni's practice of design—that is, to achieve an object (however pleasing and, for that matter, attention-demanding the final form may be) which is essentially reduced to a unity in which no detail is obtrusive. In each case, the form created is certainly determined by its components, but these are harmonised into the whole, so that the final form is not the sum of these, nor could any of them be happily removed or separated. Such is the case with Phonola radio, for example, in which the components (the raised and angled perforated disk of the loudspeaker, the tuning dial, the ordered distribution of the button controls) achieve clear expression within a unified final design.

Moreover, the intention that the radio might either sit on the table or hang on the wall has been allowed to play a predominant role in the manner in which the angles of the speaker and dial are set, in relation to each other and to the base.

The Boalum lamp is a ninety-centimeter, flexible, metal-and-plastic tube. That is all there is to it. Any number may be fitted together and slung about however one wishes, in tangled coils, in festoons, draped over furniture, heaped in a corner, hung on the wall. Yet, one distinguishes, if not components, then the elements of which it is made—the metals stiffening and the translucent plastic skin.

—Toni del Renzio

Livio Castiglioni: *Model 547* **five-channel radio receiver, for Phonola, 1939–40**

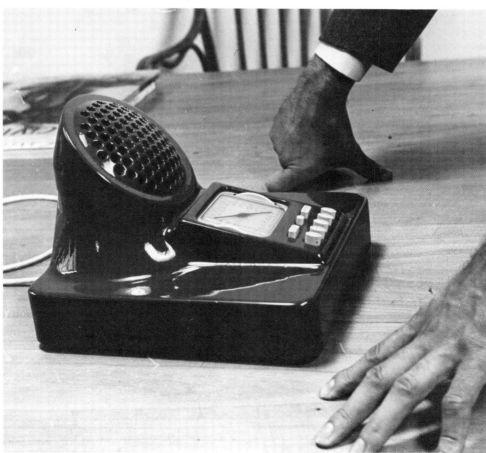

CASTIGLIONI, Pier Giacomo.

Italian architect, exhibition, interior and industrial designer. Born in Milan, 22 April 1913. Studied architecture at the Politecnico, Milan: Dip.Arch. 1937. Married Maria Coduri de Cartosio; daughter: Giorgina. Independent architect and designer, Milan, 1937–68, working with the architect Luigi Caccia Dominioni, 1937–45, and with his brothers Livio Castiglioni, 1937–53, and Achille Castiglioni, 1944–68; also collaborated with the architect Carlo Pagani: designed for Arteluce, Brionvega, Cassina, Ferrania, Gavina, Gilardi, Ginori, Kartell, Krupp, Leuci, Palini, Phonola, Rem, Zanotta, etc.; design consultant to Associazione Nazionale Industrie Elettroniche, 1949–68, and RAI Radio Televisione Italiana, 1950–68. Professor of Design, Politecnico of Milan, 1946–68. Member, Gruppo Domus, Milan, 1944–45; founder-member, Movimento Studi Architettura, Milan, 1945; board member, Architetti della Lombardia, 1949–51; founder-member, ADI Associazione Disegno Industriale, Milan, 1956; vice-president, Consiglio Regionale Lombardo degli Architetti, 1957–58. **Exhibitions:** *Colori e Forme nella Casa d'Oggi*, Villa Olmo, Como, 1952, 1954; *Italian Industrial Design*, Paris, 1957; *Contemporary Italian Design*, Tokyo, 1965; *P. G. Castiglioni: La Casa Abitata*, Palazzo Strozzi, Florence 1965; *Oggetti per la Casa*, Centro Fly, Milan, 1966; *Originale und Plagiate*, Vienna, 1974; *Il Design dei Castiglioni*, Centro Masters, Lissone, 1978; *Culture and Technology of Italian Furniture*, Stadtmuseum, Cologne, 1980; *Design Since 1945*, Philadelphia Museum of Art, 1983. **Collections:** Museo della Scienza e della Tecnica, Milan; Kunstgewerbemuseum, Munich; Kunstgewerbemuseum, Zurich; Victoria and Albert Museum, London; Israel Museum, Jerusalem; Museum of Modern Art, New York. Recipient: Grand Prize, 1951, 1954, Gold and Silver Medals, 1957, 1960, 1963, Milan Triennale; Compasso d'Oro Award, Milan, 1955, 1957, 1960, 1962, 1964, 1967; First Prize, Reed and Barton Competition, 1960; Graphics Prize, Brno, 1968; Gold Medal, Arts Convention, Rimini, 1968. *Died* (in Milan) *27 November 1968*.

Works:

Cavalletto table, produced by Gavina, 1955.
KD51/Teli lamp, produced by Kartell, 1959, and Flos, 1973.
Sanluca chair, produced by Gavina, 1960.
Viscontea lamp, produced by Gavina, 1960.
Gatto lamp, produced by Gavina, 1960.
Taraxacum lamp, produced by Gavina, 1960.
Splugen Brau table lamp, produced by Gavina, 1961.
Toio standard lamp, produced by Gavina, 1962.
Arco lamp, produced by Flos, 1962.
Relemme pendant lamp, produced by Flos, 1962.
Taccia lamp, produced by Flos, 1962.
Black and White glass pendant lamp, produced by Flos, 1965.
Snoopy table lamp, produced by Flos, 1967.

Publications:

By CASTIGLIONI: book—*Colori e Forme nella Casa di Oggi,* exhibition catalogue, Como 1952.

On CASTIGLIONI: books—*Introduction to Design* by Arthur Drexler and Greta Daniel, New York 1959; *Graphic Design in Advertising* by Pier Carlo Santini, Milan 1962; *Disegno e Progettazione* by M. Petrignani, Bari 1967; *Idee per la Casa/Modern Interiors,* edited by

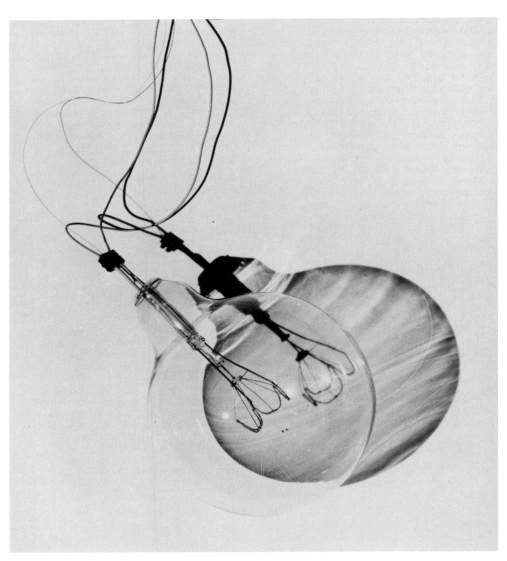

Piergiacomo Castiglioni: *Bulb Lamp*, for the XI Milan Triennale, 1957

Franco Magnani, Milan and London 1969; *History of Modern Furniture* by Karl Mang, Stuttgart 1978, London 1979; *Atlante del Disegno Italiano 1940–1980* by Alfonso Grassi and Anty Pansera, Milan 1980; *An Industry for Design: The Research, Design and Corporate Image of B & B Italia*, edited by Mario Mastropietro, Milan 1982, 1986; *Design Since 1945,* edited by Kathryn Hiesinger and George Marcus, Philadelphia and London 1983; *Design in Italy: 1870 to the Present* by Penny Sparke, London and New York 1988; *The Adventure of Design: Gavina* by Virgilio Vercelloni, New York 1989.

Twenty years ago I ordered an interior light for a bank project that I was working on. It arrived early at my office (the bank was not yet completed) and the rear truck doors were opened to reveal two cardboard boxes. Both about a foot square in area, one about six feet high, the other only about eighteen inches high. The trucker braced himself to pick up the larger box. Low and behold, it almost floated into the air. He returned for the little box, attempting to grip it under one arm. Alas, it would not move. This was my first physical introduction to the work of Pier Giacomo Castiglioni (and his younger brother, Achille). The boxes contained the parts of Arco: the taller, the stainless steel shaft/arm and spun aluminum shade; the smaller, a chamfer-cornered block of white Carrara marble, the base and "anchor" for the adjustable, cantilevered arm. (The lamp has

been poorly copied ever since.) I assembled the lamp to check it, and fell in love with it. The design, materials and detailing were exquisite. It has been here ever since; another was ordered for the project.

Ten years earlier, the names of the Castiglioni brothers were only related to designs shown in handsome photos in *DOMUS* magazine. The Dino Gavina company, which had been producing jeep hoods and the railroad car upholstery, added a few pieces of furniture, including, in 1955, Pier Giacomo Castiglioni's Cavalletto (sawhorse). This was literally a table formed of a flat plane supported on two finely-made, wooden sawhorses. It was the start of a successful collaboration between designer and fabricator. In 1960, Gavina SpA was born with Carlo Scarpa as its president. Pier Giacomo, his brother Achille, Scarpa's son, Tobia, and a few others formed the nucleus of what would become one of the best known furniture producers in the country. The designs were aimed at mass production with careful attention to detail. The Castiglioni's segmented chair, Sanluca, one of the company's first products, was praised by Carlo Scarpa: ". . . this is an armchair for which a formalist like myself would gladly take credit."

It soon became apparent to Gavina that there were few lighting products, then on the market, which were compatible, either in quality or design, with the furniture he was now producing. In 1962, in consort with another furniture manufacturer, Cesare Cassina, a new company,

Flos, was born. However, Pier Giacomo had already started innovative experiments with both old and new materials. Rethinking a material developed for protecting vehicles transported on sea-going vessels—a plastic foam film that turned solid upon being sprayed with air—Viscontea, Gatto and Taraxacum appeared (1960). The Castiglioni's fabric lamp, Teli (1959), a classic design recently returned to the marketplace, was purportedly in answer to Gavina's desire to rid the warehouse of some leftover fabric! More designs, more innovations, more ingenuity, more experiments, more products: Splugen Bräu (1961) effectively directed the light, projector-like, only on the table below and provided an architectural character for a Milan restaurant of the same name; Toio (1962) turned a low voltage lamp, pointed straight up, mounted in a chrome harness, into an art sculpture; Arco (1962), a floor lamp intended to light a table by hanging over it from the corner of a room; Relemme (1962), a counterbalanced, adjustable pendant lamp; Taccia (1962), a shimmering glass/metal table lamp; Black & White (1965), an opal glass pendant lamp; and Snoopy (1967), a jaunty little table lamp with a canted base and "hat," a stylized three-dimensional cartoon character.

About 1967, these designs started to be marketed in the U.S. Now the ingenuity, the quality, the materials, and the details could be appreciated at first hand. Regrettably, Pier Giacomo died the following year at the age of 55, a great loss to the design world. Fortunately, he has left us with a great legacy—his work—which we can continue to appreciate.

—William Victor Kriebel

CHAMBERLIN POWELL AND BON.

British architectural, interior and graphic design partnership. Established in London, 1952, by Peter Chamberlin (born 1919; died 1978), Geoffrey Powell (born 1920), and Christoph Bon (born 1921); additional partner, Frank Woods. Associate company: Chamberlin, Powell and Bon (Barbican), London, established 1960; additional partner, Charles Greenburg. Recipient: Bronze Medal, 1956, 1957, and Architecture Award, 1973, 1974, Royal Institute of British Architects; Ministry of Housing and Local Government Medal, 1965; Civic Trust Commendation, 1973; Concrete Society Award, London, 1983. Address: 1 Lamont Road Passage, Kings Road, London SW10 0HW, England.

Works:

Bousefield Primary School, South Kensington, London, 1957.
Shipley Salt Grammar School, Yorkshire, 1963.
Buildings and furnishings, for the University of Leeds, Yorkshire, 1963–75.
New Residential College, Cambridge University, 1966–67.
The Barbican Arts Centre and commercial development, London, 1966–82.
J. Sainsbury Shop, Folkestone, Kent, 1970.
General Electric Technical Marketing Centre, Warrington, Lancashire, 1974.
Napp Pharmaceutical Laboratories, Cambridge, 1981.

(for a full list of Chamberlin, Powell and Bon's buildings, see *Contemporary Architects*)

Publications:

By CHAMBERLIN POWELL AND BON: reports—*Residential Development within the Barbican Area* by Peter Chamberlin and others, London 1956; *Barbican Redevelopment 1959* by Peter Chamberlin and others, London 1959; *University of Leeds Development Plan,* Leeds 1960; *Proposals for the redevelopment of central Weston-super-Mare* by Peter Chamberlin and others, London 1961; *University of Leeds Development Plan Review 1963* by Peter Chamberlin and others, Leeds 1963; *Barbican Arts Centre 1968,* London 1968.

On CHAMBERLIN POWELL AND BON: book—*Public Interiors* by Misha Black, London 1980; articles—in *Bauen und Wohnen* (Zurich), April 1974; *New Civil Engineer* (London), August 1975; *Progressive Architecture* (New York), July 1977; *Building Design* (London), November 1977, June 1981, September 1981; *Building* (London), 16 June 1978, 29 February 1980, 5 March 1982; *Architecture + Urbanism* (Tokyo), September 1979; *Design* (London), September 1981; *London Architect* (London), March 1982.

Chamberlin Powell and Bon were engaged upon the finishing stages of their work on the Barbican when death lost them Chamberlin. Inevitably, such a vast and complicated but unitary development, first projected in the 1950's, has aroused contradictory reactions. The largest redevelopment undertaken all of a piece in London, the complex as finished remained true to the spirit of the original concept, even though it had changed somewhat in detail in response to the client's evolving understanding of their requirements; the finished building, particularly the Arts Centre, in a very few instances needed hurried adaptation at the eleventh hour. Much has been made of this by the scheme's detractors, often unfairly at the expense of the architects.

The scale of Barbican required a certain variety in the treatment of its space and in the relations of those spaces to the different functions they were to serve. This meant that the design activity at the level of detail, fittings, and furniture, in the public areas of the Arts Centre particularly, had to perform in two ways; it had to link architecturally distinct spaces with a visual coherence, and it had to be sufficiently varied to avoid confusion. The relations of the complex to its site and to its neighbours are such that even terms such as "ground floor" would have little meaning, so reference has had to be made to numbered levels. This has led to problems of orientation and direction which have been brilliantly solved at the design level, but there has remained a psychological inhibition among sections of the public; only continued practice in the use of the building may overcome this problem.

The scale, too, has meant that the office could not, on its own, have undertaken all the subsidiary design work, but it has clearly coordinated this work within its own overall vision. Again, this is especially true of the Arts Centre, where the successive stages of the client's maturing specifications of the Centre's roles led to modifications of original solutions. The various spaces are brought into order by a variety of means. Colour is used to define the concert hall conference area, and the theatre, the foyers, library, cinema, and exhibition space relate to this and are linked by a spatial core articulated by flying staircases. These have been likened by many, to the Centre's detriment, to Piranesi's

Carceri, though critics might with more justice and less malice have referred to some of this artist's architectural fantasies. This would have been even a reasonable aim, in view of the undoubted debt the Bank of England owed to Piranesi's architectural theories and suggestions.

—Toni del Renzio

CHANEL, Gabrielle (Bonheur).

French fashion designer. Nicknamed Coco Chanel. Born in Saumur, Auvergne, 19 August 1883. Educated at Convent Orphanage, Aubazine, 1895–1900; Convent School, Moulins, 1900–02. Worked as a clerk, Au Sans Pareil hosiery shop, Moulins, 1902–04; café-concert singer, with nickname "Coco", in Moulins and Vichy, 1905–08; lived with Etienne Balsan, in Château de Royallieu and in Paris, 1908–09; established millinery business and fashion house, with sponsorship of Arthur "Boy" Capel (died 1919), in Boulevard Malesherbes, Paris, 1909–10, Avenue Gabriel, then rue Cambon, Paris, 1910–40, 1954–71: established fashion shops in Deauville, 1913–15, and Biarritz, 1915–20; marked *No. 5* perfume (by chemist Ernest Beaux), from 1920. Also stage costume designer, 1912–37, and film costume designer, 1931–62. Lived as exile in Lausanne and Paris, 1945–53. **Exhibitions:** *Les Grands Couturiers Parisiens 1910–1939,* Musée du Costume, Paris, 1965; *Fashion: An Anthology,* Victoria and Albert Museum, London, 1971; *The Tens, Twenties, Thirties,* Metropolitan Museum of Art, New York, 1977. Recipient: Neiman-Marcus Award, New York, 1957; *Sunday Times* International Fashion Award, London, 1963. *Died* (in Paris) *10 January 1971.*

Works:

stage costumes include—*Bel Ami* (Nozière), Paris, 1912; *Antigone* (Cocteau), Paris, 1923; *Le Train Bleu* (Diaghilev), Paris, 1924; *Orpheus* (Cocteau), Paris, 1926; *Apollo Musagette* (Stravinsky/Balanchine), New York, 1929; *Oedipus Rex* (Cocteau), Paris, 1937; film costumes—*Tonight or Never* (Le Roy), 1931; *La Regle du Jeu* (Renoir), 1939; *Last Year at Marienbad* (Resnais), 1962.

Publications:

On CHANEL: books—*The Ways of Fashion* by M. D. C. Crawford, New York 1948; *Dressmakers of France* by Mary Brooks Picken and Dora Loues Miller, New York 1956; *Grands Couturiers Parisiens 1910-1939,* exhibition catalogue edited by Madeleine Delpierre and Henriette Vanier, Paris 1965; *The Fashion Makers* by Leonard Halliday, London 1966; *Coco,* stage musical by Alan Lerner, New York 1969; *Fashion: An Anthology* by Cecil Beaton, exhibition catalogue compiled by Madeleine Ginsburg, London 1971; *Chanel Solitaire* by Claude Baillen, Paris 1971, London 1973; *Coco Chanel: Her Life, Her Secrets* by Michael Haedrich, Boston and London 1972; *L'Irregulière* by Edmond Charles-Roux, Paris 1974, as *Chanel: Her Life, Her World,* New York, 1975, London 1976; *L'Allure de Chanel* by Paul Morand, Paris 1976; *Inventive Paris Clothes 1909-1939* by Diana Vreeland, with photos by

Irving Penn, London and New York 1977; *Chanel and Her World* by Edmond Charles-Roux, Paris 1979, London 1981; *Magic Names of Fashion* by Ernestine Carter, London 1980; *McDowell's Directory of Twentieth Century Fashion* by Colin McDowell, London 1984; *The Conran Directory of Design,* edited by Stephen Bayley, London 1985; *The Encyclopaedia of Fashion from 1840 to the 1980s* by Georgina O'Hara, London 1986.

Even in her youth, Gabrielle Chanel was an original. She grew up during the ornate Belle Époque but despised its fussy creations. She was a bit of a tomboy and the mistress of young men in the horsey set, where the way of life necessitated practical clothing. She did not hesitate to adopt masculine garments and, having started as a shop-girl, was not bothered about being a lady. Riding breeches, hacking jackets, men's sweaters, matelot tunics all gave the freedom of movement that fashionable clothes for women did not. Chanel's great impact came from conveying this masculine freedom into feminine attire. Her fundamental rule was that clothes must be easy to wear, and she made sure they were by starting them on the body, not in an abstract drawing, as did male designers. She was wrong in thinking that no male had ever modelled fabrics on a woman because the founding father of French haute couture, Charles Frederick Worth, had done so, but he was long since in his grave. He had created the woman's suit with a mannish shirt back in 1869; in the 1920's Chanel translated this into the cardigan, shirt, and skirt ensemble which has been a classic combination ever since. Subsequently, she made the cardigan of tweed, and the Chanel suit was born; this outfit is probably still the most easily recognised couture creation in the world.

Having discovered these practical combinations, Chanel kept to them, and this consistency became an important feature of her house. She did not change her designs every year, and if one wished today to wear a Chanel jersey suit of 1929, the only alteration one would need to make would be to raise the jumper level from hip to waist. The Chanel suit has been copied by other designers in France and the United States for so long that it has become a standard. Moreover, with such simple clothes, Chanel showed older women how to remain young. The 1920's saw an enormous change from the rule that older women had to wear lace caps and black dresses. Like a schoolgirl, with a white blouse, navy suit, and a bow in her hair, when she was in her fifties, she rejuvenated a whole generation and pointed the way for its daughters.

—Diana de Marly

CHARBONNIER, Pierre.

French filmmaker, painter, stage and film designer. Born in Vienne, Isère, 24 August 1897. Studied at the Collège de Vienne; painting, at the Ecole des Beaux-Arts, Lyons, Ecole des Beaux-Arts, Paris, and Académie Ranson, Paris. Married Annette Natanson in 1920 (divorced); son: the photographer Jean-Philippe Charbonnier; married Regina Centellas in 1950. Independent painter and designer, working with architect Auguste Perret and others, Paris, 1921–28; publicity consultant, Centrales Electriques des Flandres, Ghent, from 1928; stage designer, working with Serge Diaghilev and others, Paris, from 1928, and film designer from 1950. Also filmmaker, collaborating with screenwriter Jean Aurenche, Paris, 1928–55. **Exhibitions:** Théâtre de l'Oeuvre, Paris, 1922; Galérie Percier, Paris, 1924; Galerie Zborovsky, Paris, 1926; Cercle Artistique, Ghenet, 1928; Palais des Beaux-Arts, Brussels, 1933; Musée de Valence, France, 1939; Galérie Folklore, Lyons, 1939–57; Galérie Katia Granoff, Paris, 1951; Galérie Cahiers d'Art, Paris, 1956; Galérie Benador, Geneva, 1965; Galérie Albert Loeb, Paris, 1975. Recipient: Chevalier de la Légion d'Honneur, France; Chevalier des Arts et des Lettres, France. *Died* (in Paris) *2 July 1978.*

Works:

Film designs include—*Diary of a Country Priest* (Bresson), 1950; *A Condemned Man Escapes* (Bresson), 1956; *Pickpocket* (Bresson), 1959; *Les Mauvais Coups* (Leterrier), 1961; *The Trial of Joan of Arc* (Bresson), 1962; *Balthazar* (Bresson), 1966; *Une Femme Douce* (Bresson), 1969; *Four Nights of a Dreamer* (Bresson), 1971; *Lancelot of the Lake* (Bresson), 1974.

Publications:

By CHARBONNIER: books illustrated—*Almanach de Cocagne,* Paris 1922; *Atala* by Chateaubriand, Paris 1925; *Les Noces exemplaires de mie saucée* by A. Salmon, Paris 1926; *Quatre Fascinantes* by Rene Char, Paris 1951; *Le Fenêtre* by Francis Ponge, Paris 1955; films—*Ode,* 1928; *Contact,* 1930; *Ce Soir a Huit Heures,* 1931; *Pirates du Rhône,* 1955; *Bracos de Sologne,* 1955; *La Fortune Enchantée* (animated film), 1955.

On CHARBONNIER: books—*Filmlexicon degii autore e delle opere,* edited by Michel Lacalamita, Fernaldo Giametteo and others, Rome 1958; *Pierre Charbonnier: peintures de 1955 à 1965,* exhibition catalogue, with texts by René Char, Francis Ponge and Jacques Prévert, Geneva 1965; *Le Décor de Film* by Léon Barsacq, Paris 1970, as *Caligari's Cabinet and Other Grand Illusions: A History of Film Design,* revised and edited by Elliott Stein, Boston 1976.

CHERMAYEFF & GEISMAR ASSOCIATES.

American architectural, exhibition, graphic and corporate design firm. Founded in New York, as Brownjohn, Chermayeff & Geismar Associates, 1956–59, and Chermayeff & Geismar Associates, since 1962: current partners—Ivan Chermayeff, Thomas H. Geismar, John Grady and Steff Geissbuhler. The firm has designed for Burlington Industries, Pan American World Airways, Best Products, Perkins-Elmer, New York University, Museum of Modern Art, United States Environmental Protection Agency, Smithsonian Institution, Mobil, Philip Morris, IBM, etc. Recipient: First International Design Award, Japan Design Foundation, 1983. Address: 15 East 26th Street, New York, New York 10010, U.S.A.

Works:

Corporate identity program, for the Chase Manhattan Bank, 1959.
Corporate identity program, for the Mobil Corporation, 1962.
Corporate identity program, for the Xerox Corporation, 1965.
United States pavilion displays at *Expo 70,* Osaka, 1970.
Corporate identity program, for the Museum of Modern Art, New York, 1970.
Sculpture, for the Philip Morris Tower, 1972.
Mobil Masterpiece Theatre posters, for the Mobil Oil Corporation, from 1972.
Red 9 sculpture at 9 West 57th Street, New York, for the Solow Building Corporation, 1974.
Exhibition displays at the JFK Library in Boston, for the Kennedy Family, 1980.
Corporate identity program, for Morgan Stanley and Company, 1982.
Corporate identity program, for Paine Weber, 1985.
PBS corporate identity program, for Public Broadcasting Systems, 1985.
Exhibition displays, for the Statue of Liberty Museum, 1985.
NBC symbol, for National Broadcasting Corporation, 1987.
Corporate identity program, for the Lincoln Center, New York, 1988.

Publications:

On CHERMAYEFF & GEISMAR: books—*Packaging: An International Survey of Package Design,* edited by Walter Herdeg, Zurich 1959; *Typography* by Aaron Burns, New York 1961; *Design Through Discovery* by Marjorie Elliott Bevlin, New York 1963, 1977; *Design in America,* edited by Ralph Caplan, New York 1969; *Graphic Designers in the USA: 2,* edited by Henri Hillebrand, London 1971; *Packaging and Corporate Identity,* edited by Idea Publishers, Tokyo 1971; *107 Grafici dell'AGI,* exhibition catalogue, with texts by Renzo Zorzi and Franco Grignani, Venice 1974; *Chermayeff & Geismar Associates: Trade Marks* by Ivan Chermayeff, New York 1979; *Who's Who in Graphic Art,* edited by Walter Amstutz, Dubendorf 1982; *The Conran Directory of Design,* edited by Stephen Bayley, London 1985; *The American Design Adventure 1940–1975* by Arthur J. Pulos, Cambridge, Massachusetts 1988.

(The following is the introductory statement to Chermayeff & Geismar's Trademarks.) The trademarks presented in this monograph have been developed by Chermayeff & Geismar Associates over a period of many years for a diverse range of clients. Large and small corporations, cultural institutions, government agencies, banks, stores, hotels, real estate developments, and even national celebrations are included. Each has presented a special identification problem to be solved. Thus the designs take many forms—symbols, logotypes, acronyms, monograms—and encompass a variety of styles.

Many of the marks are part of large identification programs. This is only hinted at with the occasional illustration. But common to all is the underlying philosophy that design is partly a problem-solving procedure, and that appropriate trademarks cannot be developed until the client's identification problem has been clearly defined.

Therefore each design, while simple in form, is the culmination of a complex process we believe in. That process can be outlined as:

—listening objectively to the problem as described by the client;

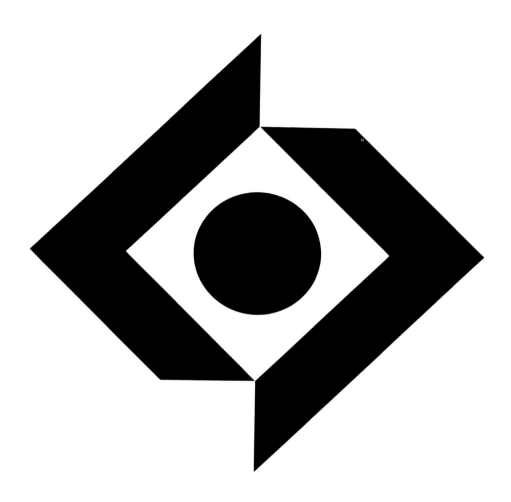

Lincoln Center

Chermayeff and Geismar: Logo for the Lincoln Center, New York, 1988

eff and Geismar, both born in 1932, both products of Ivy League educations, both graduates of Yale, where they met, brought with them broad esthetic backgrounds and vitality of interests; these supply a reservoir of new and old approaches to their commissions. Intellectual and esthetic influences came not only from formal training, but also through personal connections, as Chermayeff's father, noted architect Serge Chermayeff, and his friends, Marcel Breuer and Eliot Noyes among others, were able to introduce an ever-widening circle of influence to the younger designers.

The basic philosophy upon which the firm operates is one which they have inherited from Bauhaus tradition: problem-solving. Thus, designs differ to suit clients. Although they declare that they have no office style, in fact their work has set standards for the period. Moreover, it evinces strong kinships with the visual arts, as is evident, for example, in some designs related to the architecture of Mies van der Rohe, the geometric abstractionist, and to minimal art, on the one hand, and in others that reflect dada and Pop art on the other.

The Chermayeff and Geismar messages are not only clear but often multilayered, surprising, and evocative. Abstract logos by the firm are a case in point. A difficult problem was the Chase Manhattan Bank logo, which had to act as signature, convey a sense of reliability and security, express the essence of a bank, and suit all sorts of presentations from stationery to displays, matchbooks, and so forth. Their solution to the problem was a symbol that is made up of four wedges which enclose a square like guardian walls and that make reference to an ancient coin in the octagonal shape they form, thereby suggesting money, the real business of the bank. The abstract American Bicentennial logo used elements of the flag, with central star surrounded by entwined stripes in red and white. Clear to any American that it connotes patriotism, yet it is pictorially akin to Jasper John's celebrated flag paintings and to the stripe paintings of other American artists.

The "supermarket principle" of collections of objects is used with a nod to Warhol and Johns, as well as other artists. The 1979 International Design Conference poster displaying a collection of baggage tags is one well-known example, but others vary greatly. For example, the 1974 poster for the National Park Service Museum of Immigration utilizes souvenir Statues of Liberty printed in many colors to suggest the diverse groups of immigrants the venerable Miss Liberty has greeted.

Recent designs from Chermayeff and Geismar show their continuing sensitivity to cultural changes. More loosely constructed, these tend to reveal the designer's process informally. A 1979 poster for the New York Art Expo purports to be the designer's working surface, yet conveys all sorts of information. As if mounted on a yellow background, the message appears to be on drawing paper attached by bits of tape. A felt-tipped pen forms the words "Art Expo, New York, 1979." Interspersed are notes in Chermayeff's handwriting, giving not only instructions but also references to various art styles, thus implying both associations of typeface in the finished product and the art styles which may be seen at the Expo. And to emphasize the message, place and dates of the event are printed in bold type on the "background" below.

Chermayeff and Geismar show no signs of falling out of tune with changing times. Since their philosophy is to accept the challenge of each new problem, rather than to be trendy or stylish, they remain among the leaders in design.

—Nina Bremer

—reviewing and evaluating that description against past performances and future intentions;

—defining an attitude or direction from which design development can begin;

—creating a series of design possibilities, continually sifting out the merely fashionable;

—presenting a proposed design by demonstrating its effectiveness within the context in which it will eventually appear;

—developing guidelines and specifications for implementation;

—helping to establish police protection against pressures, both external and internal, that tend to diminish effectiveness.

It should go without saying that the greatest effort is made to assure that each trademark design will be appropriate to the purpose of the business or institution it represents, and meaningful to the audiences it will be seen by.

Within these constraints, the final image should be succinct, memorable, and elegant in either conception or visualization, or if feasible, both.

—Ivan Chermayeff
—Tom Geismar

Probably the most influential graphic designers in the United States, if not the world, the legendary principals Ivan Chermayeff and Thomas H. Geismar prefer to call their firm a "design office," since their work is so varied. Chermay-

Ivan Chermayeff: Masterpiece Theatre television program poster, for Mobil Oil, 1982

CHERMAYEFF, Ivan.

American architectural, graphic and exhibition designer. Born in London, England, 6 June 1932; emigrated to the United States, 1939: naturalized, 1947. Studied at Harvard University, Cambridge, Massachusetts, 1950–52; Institute of Design, Illinois Institute of Technology, Chicago, 1952–54 (Moholy-Nagy Scholarship); Yale University, New Haven, Connecticut, 1954–55: BFA 1955 (Mohawk Paper Company Fellowship). Married Sara Ann Duffy in 1956; children: Catherine, Alexandra and Maro; married Jane Clark in 1978; son: Sam. Assistant to designer Alvin Lustig, New York, 1955; assistant art director, Columbia Records, New York, 1956; founder and partner, in Brownjohn, Chermayeff & Geismar Associates, New York, since 1960, and in Cambridge Seven Associates, Cambridge, Massachusetts, since 1962. Director, American Republic Insurance Company, New York, 1971–80. Instructor in Design, Brooklyn College, New York, 1956–57; School of Visual Arts, New York, 1959–65. Board Member, 1960–63, and President, 1963–64, American Institute of Graphic Arts; Trustee, Museum of Modern Art, New York, from 1965; Board Member, 1967–78, and Co-Chairman, 1968, Aspen Design Conference, Colorado; Vice-President, Yale Arts Association, 1970–74; Committee Member, Yale University Council on Art and Architecture, 1971; Board of Overseers Member, Harvard University Committee for Visual and Environmental Studies, 1972. **Exhibitions:** *107 Grafici dell' AGI,* Casteloo Sforzesco, Milan, 1974; Addison Gallery of American Art, Andover, Massachusetts, 1984; Ingber Gallery, New York, 1987; Jamileh Weber Gallery, Zurich, 1988; Cooper Union, New York, 1989. Recipient: Industrial Arts Medal, American Institute of Architects, 1967; Gold Medal, Philadelphia College of Art, 1971; Visual Environment Award, Fifth Avenue Association, New York, 1974; Fuess Award, Phillips Academy, Andover, Massachusetts, 1979; Gold Medal, American Institute of Graphic Arts, 1979; President's Fellowship, Rhode Island School of Design, Providence, 1981; Benjamin Franklin Fellowship, Royal Society of Arts, London. Address: Chermayeff & Geismar Associates, 15 East 26th Street, New York, NY 10010, U.S.A.

Publications:

By CHERMAYEFF: books—*Observations on American Architecture,* with photographs by Elliott Erwitt, New York 1972; *The Design Necessity,* with Richard Wurman, Ralph Caplan, Peter Bradford and Jane Clark, London and Cambridge, Massachusetts 1973; children's books illustrated—*The Thinking Book* by Sandol Stoddard Warburg, New York 1960; *Keep It Like A Secret* by Sandol Stoddard Warburg, New York 1961; *Blind Mice and Other Numbers,* New York 1961; *The New Nutcracker Suite and Other Innocent Verses* by Ogden Nash, Boston 1962; *Peter Pumpkin* by John Ott and Peter Coley, New York 1963; *Ho for a Hat!* by William J. Smith, New York 1964; *Chermayeff and Geismar Associates: Trademarks,* New York 1979; article—"How Designers See Themselves" in *Print* (New York), January 1967.

See CHERMAYEFF & GEISMAR ASSOCIATES

CHERMAYEFF, Serge.

American architect, interior, exhibition and furniture designer. Born in Grosby Dagestan, Caucasus, Russia, 8 October 1900; sent to school in Britain in 1910: naturalized, 1928; emigrated to the United States in 1939: naturalized, 1946. Educated privately in Moscow, until 1910; at Peterborough Lodge preparatory school, Hampstead, London, 1910–13; Harrow School, Middlesex, 1914–17; studied art and architecture in Europe, 1922–25. Married Barbara May in 1928; sons: the graphic designer Ivan Chermayeff, and the architect Peter Chermayeff. Worked as a journalist for the Amalgamated Press, London, 1918–23; chief designer, for decorators E. Williams Ltd., London, 1924–27; director of the Modern Art Department, Waring and Gillow furnishers, London, 1928–29; in private architectural and design practice, London, 1930–39 (in partnership with Eric Mendelsohn, 1933–36), in San Francisco, 1940–41, and in New York, 1942–46. Professor of Design, Brooklyn College, New York, 1942–46; President and Director of the Institute of Design, Chicago, 1946–51; Lecturer, Massachusetts Institute of Technology, Cambridge, 1952–62; Professor of Architecture, 1962–71, and Emeritus since 1971, Yale University, New Haven, Connecticut; Gropius Lecturer, Harvard University, Cambridge, Massachusetts, 1974; Distinguished Visiting Professor, Ohio State University, Columbus, 1979. Consultant on Planning, Architecture and Industrial Design, Museum of Modern Art, New York, 1942–47; Editorial Board Member, American Federation of Art, New York, 1942–47; Consultant, Chicago Plan Commission, 1946–48; Founder, 1942, and Executive Council Member, 1942–47, American Society of Planners and Architects. **Exhibitions:** *First London Exhibition of Art,* 1929; *White City Exhibition,* London 1936; *Tomorrow's Small House,* Museum of Modern Art, New York, 1945; *The Chicago Plan,* City Hall, Chicago, 1949; *Thirties,* Hayward Gallery, London, 1979; *British Art and Design 1900–1960,* Victoria and Albert Museum, London 1983. Recipient: Gold Medal, Royal Canadian Institute of Architects, 1974; Architectural Education Award, Association of Schools of Architecture and American Institute of Architects, 1980; Misha Black Award, Society of Industrial Artists and Designers, London, 1980. Honorary Doctorates: Washington University, St. Louis, 1974; Ohio State University, Columbus, 1980. Address: Box 1472, Wellfleet, Massachusetts, 02667, U.S.A.

Works:

Modern Furnishings exhibition layouts, Waring and Gillow, London, 1928.
Cambridge Theatre interiors, Seven Dials, London, 1930.
S.S. Atlantique ship interiors, 1931.
R.P.7. steel frame armchair, for Pel Limited, 1932.
Bestlite lamps, for Best and Lloyd, 1933.
Ekco bakelite radio cabinets, for E.K. Cole Limited, 1933–35.
M-7 and *M-11* tubular steel frame armchairs, for Plan Limited, 1934.
De La Warr Pavilion, Bexhill-on-Sea, Sussex, 1935 (with Eric Mendelsohn).
W. and A. Gilbey office building, Camden Town, London, 1937.
Imperial Chemical Industries research laboratories, Blakely, Manchester, 1938.
Design for Use exhibition layouts, Museum of Modern Art, New York, 1944.
The Chicago Plan exhibition layouts, City Hall, Chicago, 1949.
British Railways office interiors, Rockefeller Center, New York, 1950.

Chermayeff House, New Haven, Connecticut, 1962.

(for a complete list of buildings and architectural projects, see *Contemporary Architects*)

Publications:

By CHERMAYEFF: books and pamphlets—*Color and its Application to Modern Building,* London 1936; *Plan for A.R.P.—A Practical Policy,* London 1939; *Report on the Future Development of Diamond K. Ranch,* Cambridge, Massachusetts 1955; *The Shape of Privacy,* Cambridge, Massachusetts 1961; *Community and Privacy,* with Christopher Alexander, New York 1963; *Advanced Studies in Urban Environments,* with Alexander Tzonis, New Haven, Connecticut 1967; *Synopsis of Conclusions and Record of Progress: The Chermayeff Studio,* edited by W. Mitchell, New Haven, Connecticut 1969; *The Shape of Community,* with Alexander Tzonis, New York 1970; *Verse of Anger and Affection 1957–73,* Orleans, Massachusetts 1973; *Design and the Public Good: Selected Writings 1930–1970,* Cambridge, Massachusetts 1982.

On CHERMAYEFF: books—*Design in the Home,* edited by Noel Carrington, London 1933; *20th Century Houses* by Raymond McGrath, London 1934; *The House: A Machine for Living In* by Anthony Bertram, London 1935; *The Practical Idealists: 25 Years of Designing for Industry* by John and Avril Blake, London 1969; *Projects and Theories of Serge Chermayeff* by Richard Plunz, Cambridge, Massachusetts 1972; *Pel and Tubular Steel Furniture of the Thirties* by Tim Benton and others, London 1977; *British Design Since 1880: A Visual History* by Fiona MacCarthy, London 1982; *The American Design Adventure 1940–1975* by Arthur J. Pulos, Cambridge, Massachusetts 1988.

In addition to his work as a designer, Serge Chermayeff was active as fine artist, architect, planner, educator, and writer of prose and poetry. His design work includes interiors, theatre settings, displays and exhibitions, as well as designs for mass production of textiles, furniture, lighting fixtures and radio cabinets.

It is in the breadth of his interests, and in his deep involvement with the human concerns underlying design, as well as in his innovative, open-ended approach to the creative process, that Serge Chermayeff best displays the strong influence on him of leading figures from the first generation of European modernists. Born in 1900, and hence a bit younger than the pioneers, Chermayeff extended their vision, through his own career, well into the latter part of the twentieth century. He was strongly influenced by such leading pioneer modernists as Eric Gill, during the early years of his work in England; by Eric Mendelsohn, with whom Chermayeff practiced in England from 1933 to 1936; and by Walter Gropius, founder of the German Bauhaus and a close friend during the years both lived in the United States.

A native of Grozny in the Caucasus (now part of the Soviet Union), Chermayeff had little formal education in art, and none in design or architecture. After private studies in Moscow, he was sent to England at age ten and enrolled at the Peterborough Lodge Preparatory School, and at the Royal Drawing Society. He completed his formal studies at the Harrow School. As a young man, much of his attention was devoted to painting and to ballroom dancing. The latter interest brought him to Buenos Aires in 1922, where he was a partner in a dance-hall enterprise. Shortly after his return to London in

1924 Chermayeff was hired by Ernest Williams, Ltd., an interior decorating firm. In 1926 he designed stage sets for actor-director Gerald du Murier.

The London furnishing studio of Waring & Gillow hired Chermayeff to direct a Modern Art Studio, and to create a suite of ten rooms for the 1928 Exhibition of Modern Art in Decorating and Furnishing. Chermayeff moved the firm away from its reliance on an eclectic historicism, working closely, he later recalled, with the firm's "group of elderly cabinet makers of great knowledge and skill . . ." who, ". . . to my surprise, welcomed the change from a tradition reaching back to the eighteenth century." He added, "they became enthusiastic collaborators. I never learned so much so fast. . ." Other work for Waring & Gillow included a number of commercial and domestic interiors, as well as carpet designs manufactured by Wilton, and, in 1931, interiors on the French liner *l'Atlantique*, in collaboration with Paul Follot.

Much of Chermayeff's early work could be described as "déco moderne," derived from the famed decorative arts exhibition held in Paris in 1925. In 1929 he came under the influence of Gill, who was his mentor for several years, and Chermayeff also developed close ties with a number of English artists, including Henry Moore, Ben Nicholson, and Barbara Hepworth. On his travels on the Continent for Waring & Gillow he met leading figures of the Modern Movement, including Eric Mendelsohn, then still living in Berlin. The result was an informal education in the creative process and in the social basis of art and design, through which Chermayeff matured as a designer.

In 1930 Chermayeff renovated a house for himself and his wife, Barbara, as a study of what could be accomplished in new materials and furnishings. During the same year he designed the interior, the lighting, some of the sets, and the opening-night program for the Cambridge Theatre in London. In 1931 he began collaboration on designs for a number of prototypes for mass-produced furniture for the London firms of Plan, Ltd., and PEL, Ltd., and the following year began designs for a number of studio interiors for the BBC, utilizing some of the PEL furniture. In 1933 he began designing molded thermoplastic, metal-trimmed Ecko radio cabinets for E. K. Cole; more than 140,000 of the most successful of these, "Model 74," were sold.

From 1933 to 1936 Chermayeff was in partnership with Mendelsohn. This was Chermayeff's real initiation into the practice of architecture. The most significant contribution of Chermayeff to the work of the partnership was the interior of the Entertainment Hall at Bexhill, in 1935. Chermayeff's design origins were evident here; well-planned interior space proved to be a hallmark of his architectural work throughout his career.

Chermayeff immigrated with his family to the United States in 1940, and was appointed to Brooklyn College in 1942 as chair of the Art Department, which he soon renamed the Department of Design. His innovations at Brooklyn College included the first comprehensive attempt to implement a liberal-arts design curriculum. He designed two exhibitions for the Museum of Modern Art in New York: "Design for Use" in 1944, and "Tomorrow's Small House" in 1945.

In 1947 Chermayeff left Brooklyn College and moved to Chicago as successor to Laszlo Moholy-Nagy as head of the Institute of Design, which had recently expanded in size due to the influx of returning war veterans. He retained many of Moholy's innovations, including a stress on the foundation course and on photography, but placed greater emphasis on archi-

tecture and environmental design, and developed a successful graduate program. In 1949 he helped to bring the I. D. into the Illinois Institute of Technology, where it still operates. Most importantly, he managed to sustain the creative ferment which characterized the I. D. under Moholy. Gropius credited Chermayeff with achieving in Chicago, to a greater extent than elsewhere, the kind of education offered by the German Bauhaus.

In Chicago, Chermayeff began an intense period of activity as a painter, exhibiting widely in Chicago and elsewhere. From 1948 to 1955 he designed fabric patterns for L. Anton Maix of New York. In 1949 Robert Brownjohn of the I. D. faculty assisted Chermayeff in organizing an exhibition for the Chicago Planning Commission on planning in Chicago.

After leaving the Institute of Design in 1951, Chermayeff concentrated on his architectural practice and his writing, and taught architecture at Massachusetts Institute of Technology, and Harvard and Yale universities. His architectural work continued to be inseparable from his concern with interiors, as is evident in his innovative schemes for alternatives to the detached suburban house and the urban highrise apartment.

—Lloyd C. Engelbrecht

CHESSA, Paolo (Antonio).
Italian architect, interior and exhibition designer. Born in Milan, 24 February 1922. Studied architecture in Milan 1940–45: Dip.Arch. 1945. Freelance architect and designer, Milan, since 1945: adviser on architecture to the Royal Afghan Government, Kabul, 1957–59. Editor, *Domus* magazine, Milan, 1945–47; also contributor to *Architectural Design, Bauen und Wohnen, Comunita, Interiors, Architecture d'Aujourd'hui, The Architect, Architettura,* and *Nuestra Arquitectura,* from 1945. Instructor architectural, interior and furniture design, at the Politecnico of Milan. **Exhibitions:** *28/78 Architettura,* Palazzo delle Stelline, Milan, 1979. Recipient: Grand Prize, Milan Triennale, 1947; First Prize, Teatro Carlo Felice competition, Genoa, 1949; First Prize, University of Bologna competition, 1950. Address: Via di Villa Basile 2/D, 65100 Pescara, Italy.

Works:

Armchair with metal frame and slung canvas
    seat, for J. G. Furniture, 1950.
Teatro Carlo Felice, Genoa, 1950–53.
Youth Hostel in the Park, Milan.
General Roca Hydro-Electric Centre, Rio Negro, Argentina.
Chiavari Housing Block, Genoa.
Carimate Residential Centre, Como.
Ethioplast Building, Addis Abbaba.
Westfalia Separator Company Headquarters, Milan.
Hitman Factory, Milan-Corsico.

Publications:

On CHESSA: books—*Stahlmöbel* by Gustav

Hassenpflug, Düsseldorf 1960; *Architettura moderna in Milano* by Agnoldomenico Pica, Milan 1964; *Catalogo Bolaffi dell'architettura italiana 1963–1966,* edited by Pier Carlo Santini and Guiseppe Luigi Marini, Turin 1966; *Design e forme nuove nell'arredamento italiano,* edited by Paolo Portoghesi and Marino Marini, Rome 1978; *Storia e cronaca della Triennale* by Anty Pansera, Milan 1978; *Modern Furniture* by John F. Pile, New York and Toronto 1979; *28/78 Architettura,* exhibition catalogue, edited by Maria Grazia Mazzocchi Bonadonna, Milan 1979; *Neue Möbel 1950–1982,* edited by Klaus-Jürgen Sembach, Stuttgart 1982, as *Contemporary Furniture: An International Review of Modern Furniture, 1950 to the Present,* New York and London 1982; articles—"Il Carlo Felice de Genova" in *Domus* (Milan), no. 252, 1950; "Centro Idroelettrica in Patagonia" in *Domus* (Milan), no. 256, 1951.

Paolo Chessa brought intelligence, sensitivity, and literacy to everything he tackled, and though he spent only two years as an editor at *Domus,* he carried on writing for architectural publications. In that magazine in 1956, he was able to present some of his observations on and experiences in the Sila, in southern Italy; This combined a critical account with acute perception of the historical, cultural, and practical dimensions of "the problem of the mezzogiorno." In 1961, in another magazine, he posed a social problem that an architect ought to be able to ameliorate in terms of its relation to the lifestyle of most Italians. At that time, thirty-five percent of dwellings in Milan were without individual sanitation, yet the average Italian, he argued, would rather have a Fiat to park under the noses of his neighbours, go to the tailor for a made-to-measure, hand-sewn suit, have a television set with umpteen controls, and so on.

Though most of his work was tempered by such humane considerations, they were not allowed to have detrimental effect upon his design, which concentrated upon the best possible results from the most readily available materials. This was to be achieved by a system of planned interrelating units with exchangeable elements. The designs of the early 1950's were a step on the way to the high point of his 1955 kitchen furniture, which anticipated many ideas later taken up elsewhere.

His furniture designs, however, must be seen as only part of his activity, which remained very much concerned with architecture as far as it was possible to practise. He was in no sense utopian. He played a vital part in the development of Ligano, at the head of the Gulf of Venice and almost opposite Trieste. With the architect d'Olivo, he produced the overall control plan, carefully siting the zones for development into the amenities for a resort and aiming to avoid haphazard building and other development damaging to the environment and the interests of the local population, who, on the contrary, were to benefit from the transformation.

He, himself, designed two interesting groups of holiday homes, both of which demonstrated the fine qualities of his architectural imagination and his concern for the quality of life. Planned as small communities, this fact was expressed in the aesthetic as well as social considerations of the schemes. An interesting interplay of curved brick walls, for instance, ensured privacy as well as collective services. The other group achieved similar ends by a circular arrangement of six rectangular dwellings somehow staggered and athwart the circle.

—Toni del Renzio

CHWAST, Seymour.
American graphic designer. Born in New York, 18 August 1931. Educated at Abraham Lincoln High School, Brooklyn, New York, until 1948; studied illustration and design, under Will Barnet and Antonio Frascosi, at Cooper Union, New York, 1948–51: Dip. 1951. Married Jacqueline Weiner in 1953; daughters: Eve and Pamela. Founder-partner, with Milton Glaser and Edward Sorel, 1954–82, and President, 1974–82, Push Pin Studios, New York; founder, with Milton Glaser and Reynold Ruffins, 1954, art director, 1955–81, and publisher-editor, 1974–81, *Push Pin Graphics* magazine, New York; founder and publisher, Push Pin Press, New York, 1976–81; director and president, The Pushpin Group Inc., New York, since 1982. Visiting Lecturer, School of the Visual Arts, New York, 1972–74; Visiting Professor, Cooper Union, New York, since 1975. Vice-President, American Institute of Graphic Arts, New York, 1974–78. **Exhibitions:** *The Push Pin Style,* Musee des Arts Decoratifs, Paris, 1970; *A Century of American Illustration,* Brooklyn Museum, New York, 1973; *107 Grafici dell'AGI,* Castello Sforzesco, Milan, 1974; Galerie Delpire, Paris, 1975, 1981; Kunstgewerbemuseum, Zurich, 1981; Royal Palm Gallery, Palm Beach, Florida, 1983; Gutenberg Museum, Mainz, 1983; Jack Gallery, New York, 1987. **Collections:** Museum of Modern Art, New York; Cooper-Hewitt Museum, New York; Library of Congress, Washington, D.C.; Gutenberg Museum, Mainz, Israel Museum, Jerusalem. Recipient: Saint-Gaudens Medal, Cooper Union, New York, 1971; Hall of Fame Award, Art Directors Club of New York, 1983; Gold Medal, American Institute of Graphic Arts, 1986. Address: The Pushpin Group Inc., 215 Park Avenue South, New York, New York 10003, U.S.A.

Works:

Nicholas Nickelby poster, for Mobil Oil Corporation, 1983.
I, Claudius poster, for Mobil Oil Corporation, 1984.
Rumpole of the Bailey posters, for Mobil Oil Corporation, 1984–89.
Forbes Fuels Your Drive poster, for *Forbes Magazine,* New York, 1986.
War Is Madness poster, New York, 1986.
Design and Style mixed media brochures, issues 1–5, for Mohawk Paper Mills Inc., 1986–89.
Sam's Bar woodcut book illustrations, for Doubleday Inc., 1987.
Star Quality—Noel Coward poster, for Mobil Oil Corporation, 1987.
The Baseball Poster poster, for Museum of the Borough of Brooklyn, 1987.
The Charmer poster, for Mobil Oil Corporation, 1989.

Publications:

By CHWAST: books designed or illustrated— *Sara's Granny and the Groodle,* New York 1967; *Pancake King,* New York 1970; *Still Another Alphabet Book,* New York 1970; *Still Another Number Book,* New York 1971; *Mother Goooose,* Boston 1971; *Still Another Children's Book,* New York 1972; *Limerickricks,* New York 1973; *The House That Jack Built,* New York 1974; *Which One Is Different?,* New York 1975; *Sweetheart Book and Others,* New York 1975; *The Illustrated Cat,* New York 1976; *Sleepy Ida,* New York 1977; *The Literary Dog,* New York 1978; *Zabar's Deli Book,* New York 1979; *Art of New York,* co-editor, New York 1983; *Happy Birthday Bach,* New York 1985; *Graphic Style,* New York 1988; *Just Enough Is Plenty,* New York 1988; *Trylon and Perisphere,* New York 1989.

On CHWAST: books—*Packaging: An International Survey of Package Design,* edited by Walter Herdeg, Zurich 1959; *The Push Pin Style* by Communication Arts editors, with introduction by Jerome Snyder, Palo Alto 1970; *Seymour Chwast* by T. Nishio, Tokyo 1974; *107 Grafici dell'AGI,* exhibition catalogue with texts by Renzo Zorzi and Franco Grignani, Venice 1974; *Seymour Chwast: The Left-Handed Designer,* edited by Steven Heller, New York 1985; *New American Design* by Hugh Aldersley-Williams, New York 1988.

What motivates me is the challenge of converting information that has to be conveyed from one form to creative visual form. It is very important that my own graphic personality be imparted in whatever I do. While I am not particularly disposed to any style or type of image, I still follow the basic elements of design in my work. Good drawing is essential. Stylistic direction is dependent upon the concept. The concept is the content, while the style is the packaging. They are inseparable.

—Seymour Chwast

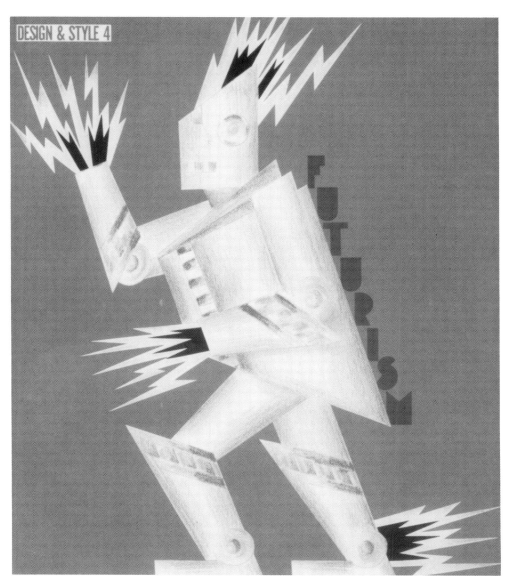

Seymour Chwast: Futurism cover of *Design & Style* magazine, for Mohawk Paper Mills, 1989

In a 1970 exhibition of the work of Push Pin Studios at the Musée des Arts Décoratifs in Paris, it was at once obvious that the group as a whole consisted of creative artists—painters and sculptors—working in the field of design. Notable among the group was the work of co-founder, Seymour Chwast whose own contribution consisted in the particular humour with which he made skillful use of the techniques of both painter and sculptor. The aim of Push Pin was to find an alternative to the established canon of design forms derived from Bauhaus and Swiss sources. By substituting for this free-ranging licence to choose any imagery from any period and to mix sophisticated designs and bad taste with quotations from the imagery of the great painters of the past, Push Pin provided a thoroughly eclectic programme. It is to Chwast's credit that this magpie behaviour with the acquisition of raw material was constructive and not merely tiresome. Basing their methods on the example of Picasso, who had established the worth of finding a solution from whatever comes to hand, instead of continuously searching for the absolute, Chwast and his associates brought this innovative technique into publicity. They also never forgot the debt which all public advertising owes to its popular origins, the broadsheet and the circus poster.

In the work of Chwast, humour plays a more significant part than in the sometimes whimsical or purely poetic notions of others in his group. Even his political posters carry a satirical message, as in the case of "End Bad Breath" or "War Is Good Business—Invest Your Son." Chwast's great contribution has been to bring back into publicity the vitality of the popular voice without degrading the sophisticated high standards of professional design. In the brief history of the poster, there have been those masters, such as Cheret, Toulouse-Lautrec, or Cassandre, who have set standards and lifted the role of the publicist to that of artist; but there have also always been those anonymous but spirited minor artists who have given the street its perennial vitality in the local commercial advertisement, as well as those amateurs who have energized public surfaces with graffiti. To bridge the gap between these extremes of high design and the vernacular requires the unusual technical skill and talent that Chwast has demonstrated. His great natural ability as an artist precedes his comments on and parodies of the language of publicity.

—John Barnicoat

CIESLEWICZ, Roman.

French cartoonist, illustrator, packaging and graphic designer. Born in Lvov, Poland (now in the U.S.S.R.), 13 January 1930; emigrated to France in 1963: naturalized, 1971. Worked at the Groszowice Cement Works, Opole, 1946–47; freelance graphic designer, working for WAG, WAF, RSW, Czytelnik and Iskry publishers, CWF Central Film Distributors, the Chamber of Foreign Commerce and other government institutions, in Warsaw, 1955–63, and designer of *Ty i Ja* magazine, Warsaw, 1959–63; freelance graphic designer in Paris, since 1963: chief layout artist, 1964–66, and art director, 1967–69, *Elle* magazine; graphic designer, *Vogue* magazine, 1966–67; art director, MAFIA (Maime, Arnodin, Fayolle, International Associes) publicity agency, 1969–72; designer of the magazines *Opus International,* 1967–69, *Kitsch,* 1970–71, *Musique · en Jeu,* 1970–73, *CNAC-Archives,* 1971–74, *Kamikaze,* 1976, and *XX Siecle,* 1976; has also designed for the Centre National d'Art Contemporain, Féstival d'Automne, Centre Georges Pompidou, and the publishers Christian Bourgeois, G. Tschou, Julliard, J. J. Pauvert, Adam, Plon, Tolmer, etc. Professor, Ecole Nationale Supérieure des Arts Décoratifs, Paris, 1973–75; Ecole Supérieure des Arts Graphiques, Paris, from 1975. **Exhibitions:** Goethe-Institut, Frankfurt, 1963; Club Synergie, Paris, 1964; Théâtre de la Cité, Villeurbanne, 1965; Muzeum Sztuki, Lodz, 1971; Musée des Arts Décoratifs, Paris, 1972; Stedelijk Museum, Amsterdam, 1973, 1978; Musée de l'Affiche, Vilanov, 1974; Centre Jean Prevost, Saint-Etienne-du-Rouvray, 1976; French Institute, Stockholm, 1977; Konsthall, Lund, 1978; Maison de la Culture, Grenoble, 1979, 1980; Teatr Narodowy, Legnica, 1980; Chelsea School of Art, London, 1981. **Collections:** Stedelijk Museum, Amsterdam; Moderna Museet, Stockholm; Musée des Arts Decoratifs, Paris; Museum Narodowe, Warsaw; Muzeum Sztuki, Lodz; Museum of Modern Art, New York. Recipient: Trepkowski Prize, Poland, 1955; Grand Prix, Czech Cinema Posters Award, 1964; Grand Prize, Warsaw Poster Biennale, 1972; Special Cinema Poster Prize, Cannes, 1973; Grand Prix, Photomontage Biennale, Poland, 1979; Grand Prix, French Poster Awards, 1980. Address: c/o *Elle,* 100 rue Reaumur, 75002 Paris, France.

Works:

Don Juan (Mozart) poster, for the Warsaw Opera, 1961.
Kanal (Wajda) film poster, for Polski Film, Warsaw, 1967.

Publications:

On CIESLEWICZ: books—*L'Affiche Polonaise du Cinema* by Tadeusz Kowalski, Warsaw 1957; *Polnische Plakatkunst* by Josef Mroszczak, Dusseldorf 1962; *Roman Cieslewicz* by Alexander Wojciechowski, Warsaw 1966; *History of the Poster* by Josef and Shizuko Muller-Brockman, Zurich 1971; *Roman Cieslewicz: Wystawa foto-grafiki,* exhibition catalogue by Ursula Czartoryska, Lodz 1971; *Roman Cieslewicz: Graphismes,* exhibition catalogue by Alain Jouffroy, Paris 1972; *The Polish Poster 1970-1978,* with introduction by Zdzislaw Schubert, Warsaw 1979; *Roman Cieslewicz: plakaty, fotomontaze,* edited by Zdzislaw Schubert and Wanda Nelke, Poznan 1981.

*

In the profession which I practice, the pleasure of creating has always been the principal argument in its favour. For that reason, I cannot remember a single occasion on which my work has been conditioned by a client's demands at the expense of my own "research." I do not make a distinction between my so called "studio" work and graphic work said to be "commercial." I try, through my profession, to defer to the essential.

My work does not in any case, need today's abundant and sophisticated techniques. For twenty years, all my work has been carried out on the basis of photographic montage and leaves my studio without any prior commercial agreement. Furthermore, my intervention as "visualist" has never occurred in relation to any object or action that I did not believe in. It is true that the number of my clients is limited and that I concentrate mainly on cultural themes. So, according to the stated principals—whether of Hieronymus Bosch, Capiello, Marcel Duchamp, or Rodchenko (and many others!)—which says that any image that doesn't shock is worth nothing, I try to carry on working.

—Roman Cieslewicz

*

The posters and graphic designs of Roman Cieslewicz have undergone dramatic changes over a two-decade period. During the initial phase of his career in his native Poland, Cieslewicz worked in the prevalent style of Polish poster design that was recognized as an important art form in Poland and acclaimed throughout Europe as an original, national contribution to graphic design. An important influence on Cieslewicz and other younger Polish graphic designers during this period was Henryk Tomaszewski, whose informally composed posters using colorful collage elements set the tone for the era.

After Cieslewicz settled in Paris, his posters began to move toward Surreal juxtapositions of imagery. Nineteenth-century engravings, Old Master art, and high-contrast photographs are graphic materials used by Cieslewicz in assembling images for posters and illustrations. Greatly enlarged halftones became a signature element in works, which produce a dual response. In addition to recognizing the image formed by the tonal values of the halftone, the viewer is also cognizant of the vibrant optical pattern of the enlarged halftone dots, which became concrete forms interacting with the surface of the paper upon which the image is printed.

During the 1970's, the imagery in Cieslewicz's posters became increasingly demonic, conveying a world without joy or hope. Unsettling distortions of the human form, including decapitated and cloned figures, give morbid overtones to many of Cieslewicz's works. A simple graphic device—joining two mirror-image photographs—takes on haunting overtones when the resulting configuration emerges as a cyclopean monster or as a massive authoritarian figure with a dwarfed pinhead. These poignant images evoke the despair of the Existentialist philosophers of the Polish nation, which through much of its history, has been subjugated by its larger and more powerful neighbors or subjected to dictatorial regimes.

—Philip B. Meggs

COLIN, Paul (Hubert).

French painter, illustrator, stage and graphic designer. Born in Nancy, 27 June 1892. Educated at the Ecole Primaire Supérieure, Nancy, studied at the Ecole des Beaux-Arts, Nancy, and the Ecole de Beaux-Arts, Paris. Served in the French Army, 1914–18: Croix de Guerre. Married Marcelle Minot (divorced); daughter: Paule. Independent painter, Paris, 1920–25; freelance illustrator, poster and stage decor designer, in Paris, from 1925: worked for the Theâtre des Champs-Elysées, and others. Founder-director, Paul Colin School of Design, Paris; Executive Council Member, Radiodiffusion-Television Francaise, Paris, 1959–64. **Exhibitions:** Musée de Arts Decoratifs, Paris, 1949; Maison de la Pensée Française, Paris, 1950; Galerie David-Drouant, Paris, 1953; Galerie Blanche, Stockholm, 1954; Galerie Creuze, Paris, 1955; Galerie de la Concorde, Paris, 1960; La Sorbonne, Paris, 1982. Commandeur de la Legion d'Honneur, France. *Died* (in Nogent-sur-Marne, near Paris) *18 June 1985.*

Publications:

By COLIN: books—*La Croute,* Paris 1957; *En Joue, Feu,* Paris 1965; books illustrated—*La Maitresse Noire* by J. C. Roger, *Knock* by J. Romains, *Amies et Filles* by Paul Verlaine, *Nouvelles Théories du Docteur Knock, Scaron,* and *Les Gloriales de Fauchon.*

On COLIN: books—*Paul Colin: Affischer—maquettes originales* exhibition catalogue, Stockholm 1954; *Who's Who in Graphic Art,* edited by Walter Amstutz, Zürich 1962; *Les Années 25,* exhibition catalogue, by François Mathey, Paris 1966; *Der Stil der Zwanziger* by Tina Volmerstein, Milan 1966, Munich 1975; *The Poster: An Illustrated History from 1860* by Harold F. Hutchison, London and Toronto 1968; *Paul Colin: maquettes d'affiches, peintures, dessins,* sales catalogue, Paris 1969; *Geschichte des Plakates/Histoire de l'affiche/History of the Poster* by Josef and Shizuko Müller-Brockmann, Zurich 1971; *A Concise History of Posters* by John Barnicoat, London 1972; *Monografie des Plakats: Entwicklung, Stil, Design* by Herbert Schindler, Munich

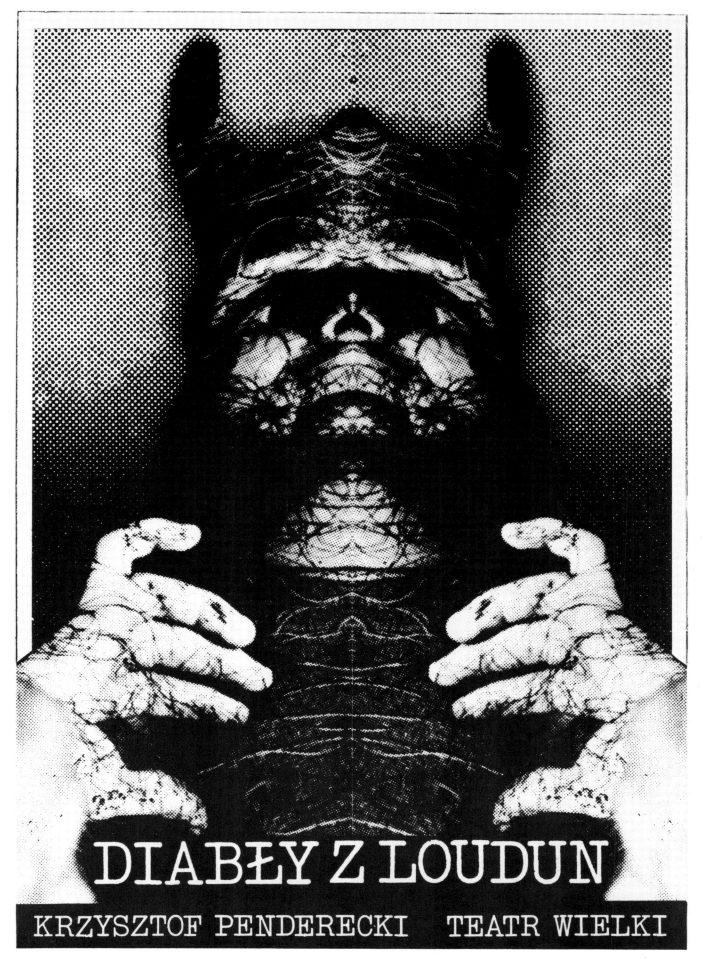

Roman Cieslewicz: *Devils of Loudun* **opera poster, for the Teatr Wielki, Warsaw, 1974**

1972; *The Language of Graphics* by Edward Booth-Clibborn and Daniel Baroni, London 1980; *A History of Graphic Design* by Philip B. Meggs, New York and London 1983.

During his distinguished career in France, Paul Colin exhibited in the Salon d'Automne. However, his reputation was international, as he showed also in London, New York, Liège, Venice, Madrid, and Barcelona, where he gained the Premier Grand Prix. Colin has signed more than five hundred posters and has executed designs for the Opéra, for the Comédie-Française, and for the Théâtre du Champs Elysées, among others. In addition, he has directed a world-famous school in Paris bearing his name.

Following his forceful poster designs for cabarets associated with Josephine Baker in the mid-1920's, Colin is remembered for posters such as "La Cavalier Elsa" (1925), "Jean Borlin" (1925), "Maya" (1927), "Lifar" (1934), "Line Viala" (1937), and "Musée d'Ethnographie Trocadére" (1938). His majestic tribute to the recovery of France from the Occupation in 1944 was his painting for the poster "Liberation" (1944). His major contribution to the poster generally has been achieved through his ability to make a single forceful image which a distillation of many aspects brought together in a single statement—the essence of effective poster design.

—John Barnicoat

COLLEY, (John) David.

American photographer, typographic and graphic designer. Born in Mayfield, Kentucky, 13 August 1940. Studied at Columbia University, New York, 1962–64; University of Illinois, Champaign-Urbana, 1966–69; University of California, Santa Cruz, 1967; Harvard University, Cambridge, Massachusetts, 1972; also studied with the artist-musician John Cage, 1968–69, and with the photographer Ansel Adams, 1977. Designer, Container Corporation of America, Chicago, 1972–73, Massachusetts Institute of Technology, Cambridge, 1975–76, and J. C. Penney Corporate Design Office, New York, 1978–79; also graphic design and poster work, for Chicago Symphony, Museum of Contemporary Art, Chicago, etc., from 1969. Assistant Professor, 1969–75, and Associate Professor since 1979, University of Illinois, Champaign-Urbana; Visiting Lecturer, Massachusetts Institute of Technology, Cambridge, 1975–76, Ohio State University, Columbus, 1976–77, and Institute of Design, Illinois Institute of Technology, Chicago, 1977–78. **Exhibitions:** Society for Typographic Arts, Chicago, 1968, 1970, 1974, 1980; *Vision and Expression,* International Museum of Photography, Rochester, New York, 1969; Murray State University, Kentucky, 1972; University of Illinois, Champaign-Urbana, 1973; Tyler School of Art, Temple University, Philadelphia, 1974; *Sailing at MIT,* Mead Paper Company, New York, 1977; *The New Typography,* Ryder Gallery, Chicago, 1978; *Four American Designers,* Amerika Haus, Munich, 1981 (toured West Germany); *Posters,* Institute of Design, Illinois Institute of Technology, Chicago, 1983. **Collections:** Polaroid Collection, Cambridge, Massachusetts; Mead Paper Library of Ideas, New York; International Museum of Photography at

George Eastman House, Rochester, New York; Museum of Modern Art, New York; Smithsonian Institution, Washington, D.C.; Kennedy Center for Performing Arts, Washington, D.C.; Staatliches Museum fur Angewandte Kunst, Munich; Musée National d'Art Moderne, Paris. Recipient: Artist Grant, Polaroid Corporation, Cambridge, Massachusetts, 1970, 1972, 1980; Award of Excellence, United National International Children's Education Fund (UNICEF), New York, 1982. Member: American Institute of Graphic Arts, New York; Society for Typographic Arts, Chicago. Address: 705 West Nevada Street, Urbana, Illinois 61801, U.S.A.

Works:

Blessed Light: Shaker Architecture book design, for University of Kentucky Press, 1970.
Wednesday Night at the Lab book design, for Harper and Row, 1971.
Poster, for the Joffrey Ballet, 1971.
Technology Review magazine design, for Massachusetts Institute of Technology, 1975.
The New Earth Sciences book design, for Massachusetts Institute of Technology, 1976.
Poster, for the American Library Association, 1976.
Visual identity program, for Edward Durell Stone Associates, 1978.
Visual identity program, for Boston Acoustics, 1979.
Billy Budd poster, for the Metropolitan Opera, New York, 1979.
The Bartered Bride poster, for the Metropolitan Opera, New York, 1979.
Visual identity program, for the Apt Corporation, 1980.
The Educational Wastelands book design, for University of Illinois Press, 1987.
Marxism and the Interpretation of Culture book design, for University of Illinois Press, 1989.
Hall of the South American People poster, for the American Museum of Natural History, 1989.

Publications:

By COLLEY: books—*A Was an Apple Pie,* Urbana 1967; *Twelve Photographs,* Urbana 1968; *Faulkner: A Photographic Representation,* Urbana 1968; *Jardin des Tuileries: 12 Photographs 1984–1988,* Urbana 1988; articles— "The Graphic Film" in *Novum Gebrauchsgraphik* (Munich), no. 45, 1974; "Twenty Years of Design in Chicago" in *Chicago Magazine,* November 1977; "Bill Bonnell: Designer, New York" in *Graphis* (Zurich), no. 224, 1983; "Graphic Design Education USA" in *Novum Gebrauchsgraphik* (Munich), no. 54, 1982; "Graphic Design: Undergraduate Education/Graduate Education" in *Journal of the Graphic Design Education Association,* no. 2, 1989.

On COLLEY: books—*Form and Expression,* edited by Nathan Lyons, New York 1969; *Typographic Design: Form and Communication* by Phillip Meggs, Ben Day and Robert Carter, New York 1985; *American Typographers* by Robert Carter, New York 1988; *Type and Image* by Phillip Meggs, New York 1988; articles—in *WFMT Guide* (Chicago), December 1968; *Art in America* (New York), July/August 1969; *Parnassus* (New Haven), no. 2, 1980; *Novum Gebrauchsgraphik* (Munich), no. 52, 1981; *Art Direction* (New York), January 1981; *American Institute of Graphic Arts Journal of Graphic Design* (New York), January 1988.

The primary problems that my work addresses

are those related to educational and other cultural institutions. To this end, the design has directed itself most often toward the problem of complicated information which finds for itself a rather abstract or structural manifestation.

Most visual information can best be universally expressed as a distilled and refined sign of the content it represents, and it is in this manner of representation that I have most often turned in solving problems. I view graphic design as visual communication—the articulation of specific visual languages. And while my work may well articulate within a specific visual language, that articulation must—by the definition language—become an intelligible transformation of known sensations, structures and forms. It is precisely the process of transformation which continues to hold my interest in visual communication. The changing and reforming of existing sensations and structures to create new forms seems not only a difficult task, but also one of magic and therefore one which cannot ever be completed or understood.

I see contemporary graphic design's task as addressing more and more what may well become known as information design—leaving the lesser tasks of visual communication to an automatic following or restating of the visual languages that have become part of the vernacular.

—David Colley

The work of David Colley presents a unique blend of structure and objectivity, while deriving a sense of playfulness and beauty from within its structure. Deceptively simple, his designs extend the realm of visual language and typographic message by allowing the evolution of structure to come from its content.

Colley is proud to claim the formative experiments in the Bauhaus and the methodology of the Swiss school as major influences on his development as a designer. The work of Joseph Mueller-Brockman, in particular, enhanced his appreciation of clarity and beauty which are attainable in rational design. American designer Massino Vignelli inspired a sense of joy and elegance that can be found within the objectivity of design.

Colley considers the opportunities from institutions such as Container Corporation of America, Massachusetts Institute of Technology, and the J. C. Penney Company pivotal in his career, as these institutions were whole-heartedly dedicated to creating fine design. Each of these experiences helped him to develop his distinctive use of visual language. German-educated designer Dietmar Winkler particularly influenced Colley while at MIT, introducing him to a new level of typographic achievement.

In his philosophy toward his work, Colley states that a thorough understanding of any problem provides the means for the solution. He looks for visual metaphors that communicate a highly complex message through seemingly simple components and relationships. These metaphors are based on understood structures and structural laws which cross the line between verbal and visual communication. A poster design for an American music concert, for example, presents a slightly undulating title, indicative of flowing music or a fluttering flag. The interpretive colors of red, white, and blue enhance the meaning. Another example illustrating the highly expressive quality of Colley's approach is a poster created for Joffrey Ballet. Three parallel lines of typography create a zig-zag shape similar to the contrapposto of classical Greek sculpture. Gradation of type weight and size create a sense of choreographed motion and depth.

David Colley sets out to communicate new ideas by challenging the viewer to participate in his work. Going beyond the boundaries of

David Colley: *Alban Berg* **poster, for the University of Illinois, 1985**

everyday language, the viewer must interact with what he knows in order to understand what he does not.

—R. Merzdorf

COLLIER, Susan/CAMPBELL, Sarah.

British textile and furnishing designers. Susan Collier: born in London in 1938. Studied catering and hotel management in London. Worked as a wardrobe assistant, then as assistant costume designer to Peter Rice and Pat Albeck, London; staff textile designer, Liberty's store, London; freelance designer, working with Soieries Nouveautées, Jaeger, Habitat, Martes, Fischbacher, Richard Allans, Rodier, Liberty Fabrics, etc; founder-partner, with her sister Sarah Campbell, of Collier Campbell Limited design firm, London. Sarah Campbell: born in London in 1946. Studied painting and graphics, Chelsea School of Art, London. Freelance designer, concentrating on wallpapers and furnishing fabrics for Liberty's, Osborne and Little, etc; founder-partner, with her sister Susan Collier, of Collier Campbell Limited design firm, London. **Exhibitions:** *Liberty's 1875-1975*, Victoria and Albert Museum, London, 1975. Address: Collier Campbell Limited, 63 Old Town, London SW4, England.

Publications:

By COLLIER: articles—in *Design* (London), July 1975; *The Designer* (London), July/August 1978.

On COLLIER/CAMPBELL: books—*Liberty's 1875-1975*, exhibition catalogue with texts by R. Strong, B. Morris, V. Mendes and others, London 1975; *Liberty's: A Biography of a Shop* by Alison Adburgham, London 1975; *The 1978 Fashion Guide* by Kaori O'Connor and Farrol Kahn, London 1978; *The Conran Directory of Design*, edited by Stephen Bayley, London 1985; *International Design Yearbook 1987/88*, edited by Philippe Starck, London 1987; articles—in *Sunday Times Magazine* (London), 14 July 1974; *Design* (London), May 1976; *The Designer* (London), July/August 1983.

Susan Collier thinks that textiles should be an inspiration in one's daily life and has successfully proved, in the work of Collier/Campbell, that this can be true. Observing the ugliness of fabrics sold in London stores encouraged Collier in her fresh, personal approach. When she joined Liberty's they were selling furnishing fabrics printed with staid designs from the 1950's. By setting herself the task of updating the patterns, she brought Liberty's furnishings into focus and gave them a reputation equal to that of their dress prints. The new floral look which she and her sister Sarah Campbell invented was inspired by a love of the English countryside, as is illustrated in their Cottage Garden range. At Liberty's, Collier's talents were nurtured and developed by the head of design production, Blair Pride, who died an untimely death in 1973. It was he who made her realise that she and her sister would have greater opportunity to experiment with colour and design if they were working for themselves. When they established their own firm, they had already a reputation backed by a confidence in

their own ability as designers and business-women.

While their skill as innovators with colour and design, as shown in their new collection Six Views, has put them in the forefront of British textile design, they have also proved that creative people can successfully run a business. It is rare that Collier/Campbell take their inspiration from an acknowledged source. With the exception of those evident in Bauhaus and the recent, Matisse-like print Cote d'Azure, few direct influences can be detected. Collier Campbell are not confined by fashionable colours, but produce their collections in different, coordinating ranges. This said, they are best seen as painters who are intuitively in touch with the feeling of their times and practically aware of the means of production (chiefly rotary silk-screen). Collier/Campbell respect the discipline of having to use the limited colour range of a manufacturer such as Jaeger, who introduce only three new colours a season, but have confidence in their own instincts and experiments. Their ability in the fields of design, marketing, and manufacture is illustrated in the variety and vitality of their work, which has attracted clients such as the Swiss cloth manufacturer Fischbacher and the American Martex (bed linens), to which they sell designs under licence. Collier/Campbell's love and understanding of colour and pattern has already put Six Views into consideration for the 1984 Design Council Awards.

—Hazel Clark

COLOMBO, Joe.

Italian architect, interior, exhibition and industrial designer. Born Cesare Colombo, in Milan, 1930. Studied at the Accademia de Brera, and at the Politecnico, Milan, 1950-54. Active as independent painter and sculptor, Milan, 1951-55; established his own industrial and commercial firm, Milan, 1955-62; freelance designer, establishing own studio in Milan, 1962-71: designed for Arflex, Elco, Kartell, La Linea, O-Luce, La Rinascente, Alitalia, Bayer, etc. Founder-member, Arte Concreta group of painters and sculptors, Milan, 1955. **Exhibitions:** Stedelijk Museum, Amsterdam, 1966; Design Research, New York, 1966; Musee des Arts Decoratifs, Paris, 1968; *Modern Chairs*, Whitechapel Art Gallery, London, 1970; *Italy: The New Domestic Landscape*, Museum of Modern Art, New York, 1972; *Design and design*, Palazzo delle Stelline, Milan, 1979; *Design Since 1945*, Philadelphia Museum of Art, 1983. Recipient: IN/ARCH Award, National Institute of Architecture, Rome, 1963; Silver Medal, Milan Triennale, 1964, 1967; Compasso d'Oro Award, Milan, 1967; Association of Industrial Designers Award, New York 1968. *Died (in Milan) in 1971.*

Works:

Colombo table lamp in brass and perspex, for O-Luce, 1962.
Portable mini-kitchen in wood and stainless steel, for Boffi, 1963.
4801 easy chair in moulded plywood, for Kartell, 1963.
Hotel Pontinental interiors, Sardinia, 1963.
Elda 1005 swivel easy chair in plastic with leather upholstery, for Comfort, 1964.

Foldable container furniture, for Arflex, 1964-65.
4868 stacking and linking chair in plastic, for Kartell, 1965.
Supercomfort 1000 easy chair in bent plywood with leather cushions, for Comfort, 1966.
Flexible magnetic furniture system with plastic laminate finish, for La Rinascente, 1966-67.
Triangular System shelf/container units, for Elco, 1967.
Poker twin-top gaming and dining table in steel and plastic laminate, for Zanotta, 1967.
Box 1 combined bedroom/study/livingroom furniture unit, for La Linea, 1967-68.
Display stand at the Turin *Eurodomus* exhibition, for the ADI Italian Association for Industrial Design, 1968.
Square Plastic System unit container furniture, for Elco, 1968-69.
Additional System seating in upholstered polyfoam segments, for Sormani, 1969.
Living Center furniture range in tubular steel with angular cushions, for Rosenthal, 1971.

Publications:

By COLOMBO: books—*New Form Furniture: Japan*, with Sori Yanagi and others, Tokyo 1970; article—interview with A. Bellini in *MD Moebel Interior Design* (Leinfelden), January 1966.

On COLOMBO: books—*Il Disegno Industriale e la sua Estetica* by Gillo Dorfles, Bologna 1963; *The Modern Chair: 1850 to Today* by Gilbert Frey, London and Niederteufen 1970; *Modern Chairs 1918-1950*, exhibition catalogue by Carol Hofgben and others, London 1970; *Italy: The New Domestic Landscape*, edited by Emilio Ambasz, New York and Florence 1972; *History of Modern Furniture* by Karl Mang, Stuttgart 1978, London 1979; *In Good Shape: Style in Industrial Products 1900-1960* by Stephen Bayley, London 1979; *Atlante del Design Italiano 1940/1980* by Alfonso Grassi and Anty Pansera, Milan 1980; *Design Since 1945*, edited by Kathryn Hiesinger and George Marcus, Philadelphia and London 1983; *The Conran Directory of Design*, edited by Stephen Bayley, London 1985; *Design Source Book* by Penny Sparke and others, London 1986.

One of the first industrial designers to achieve an international reputation, Colombo was trained as a painter and architect. A precocious student, he had his first building completed while he was still in architecture school. Although active and successful as an avant-garde painter (he was a member of the "Movimento Nucleare," a group of painters founded in 1951 by Enrico Baj and Sergio Dangelo), sculptor and architect, he concentrated on product and furniture design from 1962 until his death in 1971. In this short period he produced many influential and internationally recognized works. His early focus on interior architecture led to his interest in furnishings and household objects, and later to research on efficient, modular and mass-produced living units.

Bold and innovative, his designs were simple, flexible, brightly colored, functional and appropriately futuristic for the times. Although Colombo claimed that his development process emphasized technical design and choice of materials so that his products could be inexpensively mass produced, his artistic eye was evident in the sculptural and well-proportioned qualities of his designs. Other characteristics of his work were variety and fine craftsmanship, the experimentation and use of new materials (injection-molded plastics, plastic laminates, etc.), clearly articulated structure, and a systems approach that extended to the perception of living space as a whole.

Attempting to make good design accessible and acceptable to the masses, Colombo collaborated with industry and large department stores, in Italy and other countries, to produce furniture and household objects which would appeal to all tastes and budgets. In 1967 Gimbel's, then one of the largest department stores in the United States, held a Joe Colombo week, promoting some of his most popular works, including injection-molded plastic chairs with adjustable legs and a variety of other seating, numerous kinds of lamps, clocks, stemware, and flexible storage cubes. Exhibitions at Design/Research International in New York, the Stedelijk Museum in Amsterdam, and the Musee des Art Decoratifs in Paris also contributed to his widespread success. The New York Museum of Modern Art selected one of his arm chairs and his cubic, rolling mini kitchen for its permanent design collection. His work was influential and widely copied. He was the recipient of numerous awards, including 2 Compassi d'Oros and 2 International Design Awards from the U.S.A.

His application (with designer Ignazia Favata, one of the few designers with whom Colombo collaborated) of ecologically and ergonomically sound design principles to the problems of dwelling space resulted in a system of coordinated, flexible structures which created a dynamic, "total" living environment composed of four dwelling units: kitchen, cupboard, bed and privacy, and bathroom. Each was designed for maximum economy and flexibility in interior arrangement. Evolving through several variations, including a well-publicized one called "Visiona 69," a form of this futuristic, yet practical system was installed in his own home in Milan. In his attempt to create the perfect living space, Colombo increasingly concentrated on the utopian, humanistic needs of environmental design, emphasizing not only the relationship between city and dwelling, and between green spaces and dwelling units, but also the relationship between man and the dwelling unit.

Among his best known works many were highly experimental, such as the Spider Lamp (1965) which was the first lamp to use the halogen bulb for interior lighting; the Elda Chair (1964) which was the first large armchair shell made entirely of fiberglass; and the Universale chair (1965) which was the first chair manufactured entirely of molded plastic.

Colombo was brilliant, dashing, iconoclastic and charismatic. He developed almost a cult following from the 1960s until his death. Even though some of his pieces may appear dated to 1980s sensibilities, his clear and logical solutions with tasteful appearance and reasonable prices have rarely been matched in the history of contemporary design.

—Elizabeth Douthitt Byrne

CONFALONIERI, Giulio.
Italian graphic and industrial designer. Born in Milan, 20 August 1936. Studied political economy, Università Bocconi, Milan; mainly self-taught in typography and design. Independent painter, Milan, 1957–64; freelance designer, establishing own graphics studio in Milan, 1964–83: has designed publicity for Olivetti,

Pirelli, Bassetti, Roche, Westinghouse, Total, Esso, Fulget, Mondadori, *PM* and *Domus* magazines, and products for Tecno, Boffi, Marcatre, Italsider, AGIP Petrols, and Ratti Silks. Member, with Franco Grignani, Bruno Munari, Pino Tovaglia and Silvio Coppola, of the Gruppo di Ricerca Exhibition Design, Milan, 1969–78. **Exhibitions:** *Plastic Design Research,* Palazzo Reale, Milan, 1969; *Design 1970,* Musée d'Art Moderne, Paris, 1970; *Design 20. Jahrhundert,* Museum des 20. Jahrhunderts, Vienna, 1972; *107 Grafici dell'-AGI,* Castello Sforzesco, Milan, 1974. Recipient: Graphic Award, 1957, and Gold Medal, 1969, Milan Triennale; Gold Medal for Book Design, Viareggio, 1959. Member: Alliance Graphique Internationale; Associazione Disegno Industriale, Milan; American Institute of Graphic Arts, New York; Art Directors Club of New York. Address: Via Lanzone 13, 20123 Milan, Italy.

Publications:

By CONFALONIERI: books—*Baldassare, Melchiorre, Gaspare,* with Ilio Negri, Milan 1956; *Racconti italiani,* with Ilio Negri, Milan 1958; *Primo catalogo dei caratteri de assa,* with Ilio Negri, Milan 1960; *Immagine di un libro,* Milan 1965; *12 Finestre,* Milan 1965; *Towns,* Milan 1978; *Graphic Adventure,* Milan 1978.

On CONFALONIERI: books—*Who's Who in Graphic Art,* edited by Walter Amstutz, Zurich 1962, Dübendorf 1982; *Monografie des Plakats* by Herbert Schindler, Munich 1972; *Due Dimensioni* by Felice Nava, Milan 1973; *107 Grafici dell'AGI,* exhibition catalogue with texts by Franco Grignani and Renzo Zorzi, Venice 1974; *Design e Forme Nuove nell'Arredamento Italiano,* edited by Paolo Portoghesi and Mario Marini, Rome 1978; *The Language of Graphics* by Edward Booth-Clibborn and Daniele Baroni, London 1980.

Giulio Confalonieri has tended to exploit somewhat stark contrasts: abrupt passages from black to white, juxtapositions of sharply differentiated colours or textures, powerful images and bold typography held in precarious equilibrium by generous white space. This way of working adds up to an individual use of the characteristics of Italian graphic design to which Confalonieri has, of course, very strongly contributed, along with Erberto Carboni, Max Huber and Giovanni Pintori. However, his work for Cassina, especially, perhaps more nervy and gentler in its contrasts, has contributed as much to the style of that house as any of the designers of its furniture. Or, perhaps more precisely, he has helped to define and project that style, a subtle excitement urbanely contained.

A sophisticated taste informs all Confalonieri's work and thus controls his bold pattern-making, which never gets out of hand and is never made simply for effect. Finely tuned statements in visual terms, however bold and contrasty, his patterns never seek to bludgeon the sensibility.

Not blunt instruments, then, but precision tools, each design—calculated in terms of client, purpose, context—is elegantly appropriate. What will do for Cassina, what will do for Pirelli, and what, for Eurodomus, are highly differentiated, though, to be sure, his sophisticated and fastidious mark is always there. Whereas the work for Cassina creates patterns of an urbane lifestyle, that for Pirelli, something of the ruggedness of the tyre as well as its suggestion of elegant motoring, the designs for Eurodomus somehow manage to express a qual-

ity of European furniture in creative rivalry and diversity.

It is obvious that intelligence guides hand and eye in this process of creative pattern-making, but that intelligence is, in its turn, advised by a sophisticated sensibility. Though the patterns may almost be enjoyed purely aesthetically, that is not their purpose, and there is always something in their nature and in the nature of their components that halts any slide away from function. The patterns are not just vehicles but are themselves vital components of the message and are derived from it. That is to say, they are not arbitrary and imposed but result from an analysis of the complex interaction of the nature of client, brief, and cultural context, and none of these messages could be as well expressed without the particular pattern that has been created.

—Toni del Renzio

CONRAN, Terence (Orby).
British architectural, interior, graphic and industrial designer. Born in London, 4 October 1931. Educated at Bryanston School, Dorset, 1944–49; studied textile design, Central School of Arts and Crafts, London, 1949–50. Married Shirley Ida Pearce in 1955 (divorced, 1962); sons: Sebastian and Jasper; married Caroline Herbert in 1963; children: Tom, Sophie and Edmund. Worked as a textile designer for the Rayon Centre, London, 1950–51; interior designer, Dennis Lennon studio, London, 1951–52; freelance furniture designer, as Conran and Company, working for John Lewis Partnership, Edinburgh Weavers, Simpsons of Piccadilly, etc., in London and Thetford, 1952–56; founder-proprietor, with Ian Storey, of Soup Kitchen restaurants, London, 1953–56; founder-director, with John Stephenson, 1956–71, and Chairman from 1971, Conran Design Group, London; founder-director, 1964–71, and Chairman from 1971, Habitat furnishing stores, in London, and subsequently throughout the world; Joint-Chairman, Ryman Conran Limited, London, 1968–71; managing director, Neal Street Restaurant, London, from 1972; Chairman, Conran Stores, Inc., since 1977; Chairman, Jasper Conran fashion company, London, from 1977; Director from 1979, and Chairman, 1981–83, J. Hepworth and Son, London; Chairman, Habitat Mothercare Limited, London, from 1982; Director, Conran Roche architectural and city planning firm, London, from 1982; Chairman, Conran Octopus publishing company, London, from 1983; Chairman, Butlers Wharf Development, London, from 1984; Director of Michelin House Development, London, from 1985, and Chairman of Bibendum Restaurant, from 1986; Director of British Home Stores PLC, and Savacentre Limited, London, from 1986. Founder-trustee, Conran Foundation for design and industry, from 1982, and the Design Museum, London, from 1989. Member, Royal Commission on Environmental Pollution, 1973–75; Council Member, Royal College of Art, London, 1978–81, and since 1986; Advisory Council Member, 1979–83, and Trustee since 1984, Victoria and Albert Museum, London. Recipient: Presidential Medal, 1968, 1975, and Bicentenary Medal, 1983, Royal Society of Arts, London; Society of Industrial Artists and Designers Medal, London, 1980;

Terence Conran: Logo for the Habitat shops

Daily Telegraph/Association for Business Sponsorship award, London, 1982. Knighthood, 1983; Honorary Fellow, Royal Institute of British Architects, 1984. Address: 196 Tottenham Court Road, London W1P 9LD, England.

Publications:

By CONRAN: books—*The House Book,* London 1974; *The Vegetable Book,* with Maria Kroll, London 1976; *The Kitchen Book,* London 1977; *The Bed and Bath Book,* London 1978; *The Cook Book,* with Carolin Conran, London 1980; *The New House Book,* London 1985; *The Conran Directory of Design,* edited by Stephen Bayley, London 1985; *Plants at Home,* London 1986; *The Soft Furnishings Book,* London 1986; *Terence Conran's France,* London 1987.

On CONRAN: books—*Gute Moebel—Schoene Raume,* edited by Mia Seeger, Stuttgart 1953; *Public Interiors* by Misha Black, London 1960; *Looking at Furniture* by Gordon Russell, London 1964; *Design 1900–1960,* edited by Thomas Faulkner, Newcastle 1976; *Twentieth Century Furniture* by Philippe Garner, London 1980; *The Entrepreneurs* by E. Hennessy, Newbury 1980; *Neue Moebel 1950–1982/ Contemporary Furniture,* edited by Klaus-Jurgen Sembach, Stuttgart and London 1982;

Conran and the Habitat Story by Barty Phillips, London 1984.

As creative retailers, our policy simply amounts to a belief that if reasonable and intelligent people are offered products for their home that are well made, well designed, work well, are of decent quality and at a price they can afford, then they will like and buy them.

—Terence Conran

Terence Conran's belief in offering well-designed products at reasonable prices has been proved correct many times over by a commercial empire now reaching from England to the United States and Japan. The Habitat range offers furniture to be used from bedrooms to kitchens, household linen and curtains, carpets, china and cutlery, casseroles and pots, glassware, lamps, spaghetti-makers, and plastic buckets. All the goods are simple in shape, and Conran sees the main influences on his style as the 1930's streamlined look and the plan, functional furniture found in servants' quarters before the war. One can also detect a strong influence from the United Kingdom's government-sponsored 1942 Utility scheme, which set out to offer plain but good-quality household and clothing products despite wartime shortages.

With his acquisition of Mothercare in 1982,

Conran entered the clothing area as well, and he plans to give mothers and children fashionable garments in addition to functional ones. The design of all these articles is handled by Conran Associates, the largest design organisation in Europe; it covers Habitat and Mothercare products, office products, and graphic design projects, Conran still likes to approve designs.

In the 1950's before Habitat existed, modern design consisted of very expensive items from Sweden or Italy, while most shops stocked highly conservative furniture. Conran was able to break this pattern by producing and inexpensive range of modern furniture so that the young couple starting up could acquire a stylish home. With the expansion overseas, Conran has become an authority on national nuances. The English like bedroom furniture, the French use little. English saucepans have lids, the French ones do not. Mothercare found the same variations in national attitudes toward baby clothes. The bulk of Conran's creations do appeal over frontiers, but an awareness of what will not is essential also, so that particular items can be designed for particular markets. A universal provider, Conran now has a design empire.

—Diana de Marly

COOPER, Muriel.
American graphic and book designer. Born in Brookline, Massachusetts. Studied at Ohio State University, Columbus; Massachusetts College of Art, Boston, BS 1949; Southampton College summer sessions in experimental film, Hampshire, England; Massachusetts Institute of Technology summer sessions in computer graphics, Cambridge; Fulbright scholar in exhibition design, Milan, 1957–58. Art director and designer, Massachusetts Institute of Technology Office of Publications (now Design Services), Cambridge, 1950–57; founder-director, Muriel Cooper/Media Design, Cambridge, Massachusetts, since 1958; Design Director/ Media Director, from 1967, and subsequently Special Projects Director, MIT Press, Cambridge, Massachusetts. Instructor, University of Maryland, College Park; Boston University; Simmons College, Boston; Museum School of Fine Arts, Boston; Massachusetts College of Art, Boston; Massachusetts Institute of Technology Department of Architecture, Cambridge; Lecturer, Director and Professor of Graphics, Visible Language Workshop, Massachusetts Institute of Technology, Cambridge. Member of the Board of Trustees, Massachusetts College of Art, Boston, 1981–87; member of the Undergraduate Advisory Board, Department of Communications, Simmons College, Boston, since 1983. Recipient: Silver Medal, Israel Book Biennale; Grand Prix d'Arles for book design; Distinguished Alumni Award, Massachusetts College of Art, 1983. Member: American Institute of Graphic Arts, New York (board member, 1974–77); Alliance Graphique Internationale, Paris. Address: Visible Language Workshop, Media Laboratory, E15-443, 20 Ames Street, Cambridge, Massachusetts 02139, U.S.A.

Works:

Is Anyone Taking Notice? (McCullin) book design, for MIT Press, 1973.

Travelogue (Harbutt) book design, for MIT Press, 1973.

Muriel Cooper was inspired by the richness of the twenties—Gertrude Stein, Alfred Stieglitz, dadaism—and Gyorgy Kepes was an influence during his early years at the Massachusetts Institute of Technology. She is convinced that an internal structure is necessary to produce anything of lasting value. Although her designs are sometimes described as "Swiss," she has been called a "method actress of design." Her attraction to books satisfies her need to design with time, as represented by the kinetic act of turning pages, yet enables her to create a lasting product.

Her practice, including print, photography, video, and three-dimensional work, has always been synthesized with media and technology. She has interwoven her professional activities with teaching and is at present at the Massachusetts Institute of Technology, where she is a professor of graphics and director of the Visible Language Workshop.

If creativity is the ability to combine unlikely elements, then her unlikely combinations are evidenced in the people, equipment, and products of the Visible Language Workshop, where a concrete poem might be wrapped around a human figure or a gigantic image produced from a slide, altered, and recreated with jets of ink in Ron MacNeil's Architecture Machine. Her special summer sessions at the MIT/VLW, held since 1979, were the first computer-design workshops in the United States. The Visible Language Workshop produces ideas and images that would be impossible in a more conventional setting.

—Al Gowan

COURRÈGES, André.

French fashion designer. Born in Pau, Pyrenées Atlantiques, 9 March 1923. Studied engineering at the Ecole des Ponts-et-Chaussées; apprenticed with Cristobal Balenciaga, Paris, 1948–59. Married Jacqueline Barrière in 1966; daughter: Marie. Independent fashion designer from 1959, founding Courrèges fashion house, Paris, from 1961: designed Couture Future line, 1963; factory with futuristic architecture, Pau, 1968; perfume range, 1971; menswear line, 1973; bathrooms, cars and windsurfing equipment, from 1980; Hyperbole line, 1980. **Exhibition:** *Fashion: An Anthology,* Victoria and Albert Museum, London, 1971. **Collections:** Musee Carnavalet, Paris; Musée du Costume, Paris. Recipient: Couture Award, London, 1964. Address: 40 rue François Premier, 75008 Paris, France.

Publications:

On COURRÈGES: books—*The Fashion Makers* by Leonard Halliday, London 1966; *Fashion: An Anthology by Cecil Beaton,* exhibition catalogue compiled by Madeleine Ginsburg, London 1971; *Paris Fashion: The Great Designers and Their Creations,* edited by Ruth Lynam, London 1972; *In Vogue: Sixty Years of Celebrities and Fashion* by Georgina Howell, London 1975, 1978, New York 1976; *A History of Fashion* by J. Anderson Black and Madge Garland, London 1975, 1980; *Magic Names of Fashion* by Ernestine Carter, London 1980; *The*

History of Haute Couture 1850–1950 by Diana de Marly, London 1980; *The Collector's Book of Twentieth Century Fashion* by Frances Kennet, London and New York 1983; *McDowell's Directory of Twentieth Century Fashion* by Colin McDowell, London 1984; *The Encyclopaedia of Fashion from 1840 to the 1980s* by Georgina O'Hara, London 1986; *Design Source Book* by Penny Sparke and others, London 1986.

What will the future fashion trend be? Garments must be made in bright colors, youthful styles, and they must be easy to take care of, full of spirit, and dynamic. Clothes must be liberating—they must escape conventions.

The evolution of clothes toward the year 2000 will be distinguished by the use of new materials. Fabrics will be softer, and knits will be common because of their softness and their comfort—like second skins.

—André Courrèges

It took Courrèges only a short time to shake off the influence of his master, Balenciaga. In 1962, he began creating his own style, and during the next three years, he presented Paris with the shortest skirts around. His visionary image, rather than momentary fashion, showed an awareness of the need for greater freedom of movement. His approach was essentially that of a couturier, interested in cut and in making the most of the inherent qualities of his fabrics. Whether in the welted seams of his coats or the fit of his trousers, the cut was impeccable, the work of an architect.

Courrèges' predominant use of white enhanced the purity of his line. The palest blue, pink, strong green, red, or black were used sparingly, for emphasis. Like Mary Quant in England, he created a "little girl" look, consisting of short skirts, flat shoes, and little caps which epitomised the youthful exhuberance of the 1960's. The popularity of the look meant that his work was widely copied. Crisp, geometric dresses were reproduced in soft double jersey; tiny, well-fitting baby caps became lumpy, hand-knitted and crocheted bonnets. The mass-market succeeded in adapting Courrèges' ideas at such an alarming rate that he has turned from being a strictly couture designer to making a three-pronged attack on the world of fashion by dividing up his work into couture and two lines of ready-to-wear.

By 1967, the white moon-girls and the silver sequined, space-age outfits had fallen from grace and Courrèges had begun to pay more attention to the body itself. Subsequently, he has experimented with knitted body coverings which create the effect of a second skin and give total freedom of movement. Once again, he is looking to the future, where he sees us wearing more warm, ventilated, knitted fabrics. The present popularity of sweatshirts, tracksuits, bodywarmers and the like show that Courrèges is no visionary but, as in the 1960's, a man of his time.

—Hazel Clark

COUTAUD, Lucien.

French painter, mural, tapestry and stage designer. Born in Meynes, Gard, 12 December 1904. Studied at the Collège Saint-Stanislas,

Nîmes, Ecole des Beaux-Arts, Nîmes, and the Ecole des Beaux-Arts, Paris. Married Denise Bernollen in 1936. Independent painter and stage designer, Paris, from 1928: worked with Charles Dullin's Atelier Théâtre, Paris, the Boboli Gardens, Florence, Comèdie Francaise, Paris, and for the Maggio Fiorentino, Florence; created three tapestries for the liner *France,* and murals for the National Institute of Deaf-Mutes and for the Palace of Discovery, Paris. Founder-member of the Salon de Mai, Paris. Professor of etching, Ecole Nationale Supérieure des Beaux-Arts, Paris, from 1964. **Exhibitions:** *Coutaud, Labisse, Couturier,* Musée Galliera, Paris, 1962; Musée d'Ingres, Montauban, France, 1969; also exhibited at Galerie Roux, Galerie Hentschel, Galerie Bonaparte, Galerie Maeght, David et Garnier, Sagotle Garrec, and Galerie Lucie Weill, all in Paris. **Collections:** Centre Georges Pompidou, Paris; Musee d'Art Moderne de la Ville, Paris. Recipient: Grand Prix des Beaux-Arts de la Ville de Paris; Prix Daniel Wildenstein, Paris, 1971. Chevalier de la Légion d'Honneur, France; Officer des Arts et des Lettres, France. *Died* (in Paris) *June 1977.*

Publications:

By COUTAUD: book—*J'aime le théâtre,* Lausanne 1962.

On COUTAUD: books—*Décors de théâtre* by Raymond Cogniat, Paris 1930; *La Tapisserie française,* edited by P. Tisne, Paris 1946; *Réflexions sur le théâtre* by Jean-Louis Barrault, Paris 1949; *Les Cahiers d'Art-Documents, No. 32: Lucien Coutaud 1904,* edited by Pierre Caillier, Geneva 1956; *Cinq peintres et le théâtre* by Hélène Parmelin, Paris 1956; *La Tapisserie* by Roger-Armand Weigert, Paris 1956; *Catalogue raisonné de l'oeuvre gravé et lithographie de Lucien Coutaud* by Jean Adhémar, Geneva 1960; *Coutaud, Labisse, Couturier,* exhibition catalogue, by Georges Charbonnier and others, Paris 1962; *Lucien Coutaud* by Pierre Mazans, Geneva 1964; *Coutaud: peintures, dessins et gravures,* exhibition catalogue, by Pierre Barbousse, Montauban 1969; *The Decorative Thirties* by Martin Battersby, London 1969, 1974, 1976.

COVERI, Enrico.

Italian fashion designer. Born in Prato, 26 February 1952. Studied stage design, Accademia di Belle Arti, Florence, 1971–74. Freelance fashion designer, working for Tikos, Touche, Acquarius, Lux Sports, Gentry, and Ilaria Knitwear, in Milan, 1972–79; established Enrico Coveri S.p.A. fashion firm, Milan, 1978, and Enrico Coveri France S.A.R.L., Paris, 1983: opened boutique the via San Pietro all'Orto, Milan, in 1981, and subsequent shops in Genoa, Viareggio, Piacenza, Paris, Saint Tropez, Beirut and New York; launched perfumes *Paillettes,* 1982, and *Dollars,* 1983. **Exhibitions:** *Consequenze Impreviste,* Prato, 1982; *Italian Re-Evolution,* La Jolla Museum of Art, California, 1982; San Francisco Museum of Modern Art, 1982; Museum of Contemporary Art, Hartford, Connecticut, 1983; Musée d'Art Contemporain, Montréal, 1983. Recipient: World's Most Elegant Man Award, Paris, 1980; Uomo Europeo Award, Rome 1982; Fil d'Or,

Enrico Coveri: Coat in herringbone wool with black panels, 1983

Munich, 1982. Addresses: Via Visconti di Mo-
drone 26, 20122 Milan; Via Tevere 60, 50019
Osmannoro Sesto Fino, Florence, Italy.

Publications:

On COVERI: books—*I Mass-Moda: Fatti e
Personaggi dell'Italian Look/The Who's Who of
Italian Fashion,* with text by Adriana Mulassano, Florence 1979; *Italian Re-Evolution: Design in Italian Society in the Eighties,*
exhibition catalogue edited by Piero Sartogo,
La Jolla 1982; *McDowell's Directory of Twentieth Century Fashion* by Colin McDowell, London 1984; articles—in *Hommes Vogue* (Paris),
March/April 1978; *Arbiter* (Milan), March/
April 1982; *Il Tempo* (Milan), 17 September
1982; *Il Messagero* (Rome), 21 March 1983;
La Nazione (Florence), 14 June 1983.

CROSBY, Theo.

British architect, interior, exhibition and industrial designer. Born in Mafeking, South Africa,
3 April 1925; settled in England, 1947. Studied
at the University of Witwatersrand, Johannesburg, 1940–47: B.Arch. 1947; Sir John Cass
School, Central School of Art, and St. Martin's
School of Art, all London, 1947–56. Served in
the British Army in the 6th South Africa Armored Division, 1944–46: Signaller. Married
Anne Buchanan in 1960 (separated, 1977);
children: Dido and Matthew. Assistant architect, Fry, Drew and Partners, then Fry, Drew,
Drake and Lasdun, London, 1947–52; Technical Editor, *Architectural Design* magazine,
London, 1953–62; Chief architect, Taylor
Woodrow Euston Station project, London
1962–64; Founder-Partner, with Alan Fletcher
and Colin Forbes, of Crosby/Fletcher/Forbes,
London, 1965–72, and with Fletcher, Forbes,
Kenneth Grange and Mervyn Kurlansky, of
Pentagram Design, London and New York,
since 1972. **Exhibition:** Institute of Contemporary Arts, London, 1960. Recipient: Grand
Prize, Milan Triennale, 1963; two Architectural Heritage Year Awards, 1973. Associate,
Royal Institute of British Architects, 1944; Fellow, Society of Industrial Design, 1963; Member, Akademie der Kunste, Berlin, 1978;
Associate, Royal Academy of Art, London,
1983. Address: Pentagram Design Limited, 11
Needham Road, London W11 2RP, England.

Works:

This Is Tomorrow exhibition layouts, White-
  chapel Art Gallery, London, 1956.
The Architecture of Technology exhibition lay-
  outs, for the International Union of Archi-
  tects, London, 1961.
British section displays, at the Milan Triennale,
  1964.
Industry displays at the British pavilion, *Expo
  67,* Montreal, 1967.
The Lookout observation lounge interiors at the
  Queen Elizabeth II, 1968.
Cape Universal Building Products display at the
  International Building Exhibition, Olympia,
  London, 1969.
Office interiors, for Rowe Rudd, Moorgate,
  London, 1969.
Office conversion and interiors, for Boase Mas-
  simi Pollitt advertising agency, Paddington,
  London, 1972, 1979.

Theo Crosby: Unilever House interiors, Blackfriars, London, 1978–82

The Environment Game exhibition layouts, Hayward Gallery, London, 1973.
Office interiors, for Geers Gross advertising agency, London, 1975, 1982.
British Genius exhibition layouts, Battersea Park, London, 1976.
Unilever House refurbishment and interiors, London, 1978–83.
Globe Theatre reconstruction and museum complex, South Bank, London, from 1982.
Headquarters building interiors, for Nederlandse Middelstande Bank, Amsterdam, 1984.
Battle of Britain monument, London, 1987 (project).

(for a complete list of buildings and architectural projects, see *Contemporary Architects*)

Publications:

By CROSBY: books—*This Is Tomorrow,* exhibition catalogue, London 1956; *Le Corbusier,* exhibition catalogue, London 1959; *An Anthology of Houses,* with Monica Pidgeon, London 1960; *The Architecture of Technology,* designer, London 1961; *Architecture: City Sense,* London and New York 1964; *The Necessary Monument,* London 1969; *A Sign Systems Manual,* with Alan Fletcher and Colin Forbes, London 1970; *Pentagram: The Work of Five Designers,* with Pentagram partners, London 1972; *How to Play the Environment Game,* London 1973; *Living with Design,* with Pentagram partners, London 1978; *Ideas on Design,* with Pentagram partners, London 1986; *Let's Build a Monument,* London 1987; *The Battle of Britain Monument,* London 1987.

On CROSBY: books—*Signs in Action* by James Sutton, London and New York 1965; *European Designers: England, France, Italy,* edited by Idea publishers, Tokyo 1970; *History of the Poster* by Josef and Shizuko Muller-Brockmann, Zurich 1971; *Design by Choice* by Reyner Banham, London 1981.

My work as a designer originates in a nine-year period as an editor of *Architectural Design* with Monica Pidgeon. I did the layouts, covers, and some writing—and learned a great deal about graphics, particularly from my friend Edward Wright.

The general basis of my work is collaborative in the sense that I see the designer's work as creating complex ensembles which many other talents can be deployed. Diaghilev would be an exemplar.

I thus try to see all my tasks as an opportunity to extend the nature of a problem by involving the best people I know and by setting up the work in such a way as to make it easier for them to do good work. In most cases, this approach is rewarding and successful, and the client is often conspicuously well served.

In the general run of my practice, which consists of generally small-scale and complex interiors, I indulge in the design work myself. The task is often too small to involve someone else with dignity. These little tasks have developed into modest examples of furniture, stained glass, and other decorative works.

My main ambition is to re-engage the arts and crafts into the fabric of architecture, to make it as ordinary and integral a process as it used to be. This means relearning a great deal of architectural history, of the grammar of an ornament which has been discarded by the modern movement, and trying to make each task a practical demonstration.

—Theo Crosby

The nine years Theo Crosby worked for the magazine *Architectural Design* introduced him to the British design establishment, and in 1956, he was appointed secretary and organiser of the influential exhibition *This is Tomorrow,* held at the Whitechapel Art Gallery. Working with more than thirty of Britain's most avant-garde architects, designers, and fine artists placed him firmly at the centre of new directions. This experience also initiated a successful exhibition-design career, which has included The British Section (with others) of the 1964 Milan *Triennale,* which was award a Gran Premio; the section of the British Industry Pavilion at *Expo '67,* for which he collaborated on films as well as the exhibition design; and the *British Genius* exhibition at Battersea Park for the Jubilee Year in 1978. In the mid-1960's, Crosby decided not to enter an architectural practice but to team up with graphic designers Alan Fletcher and Colin Forbes to form the nucleus of the group that became Pentagram in 1972. As a team, this firm of distinguished individualists have had an enormous impact on British design. Crosby took responsibility for such areas as exhibition, interior, and environmental design, which he carried out, like the other partners, with his own team of designers. Throughout his career, he has stressed the importance of teamwork, seeing design as "the product of many inputs." Typical work includes a shopping centre at Lewisham and the Arts Council bookshop in London.

Recently, however, Crosby has become the outspoken champion for decoration. Speaking at a seminar on art and architecture at the Institute of Contemporary Art in London, he talked about the important role the arts and crafts play in contemporary architecture and about his faith in the role of architectural history and its models, such as 19th-century books on the grammar of ornament. This rejection of the modernist ideology has also been present in his work; the 1970's renovation of Nash House included decorative corbels, and he has written on the need for a return to embellishment. However, the project that has brought these ideas to fruition is his work for Unilever in London. In the late 1970's, Unilever decided to refurbish their 1939 head office, rather than move out of the city, and they picked Crosby to design the scheme. Choosing to highlight and expand the Art Deco element with the large budget he had, Crosby designed carpets, Art Deco railings, diamond-shaped acrylic light fittings, and stylishly mirrored lifts. The tour-de-force main entrance with its blue-plaster ceilings topped with gold leaf and its white exotic columns opened in 1982 to acclaim in the design and architectural press, partly because the scale of the work was unusual in Britain but mainly because the ensemble was not a pastiche of the 1930's elements but an assembly of design motifs synthesized in a radically new way.

—Catherine McDermott

CROUWEL, Wim (Willem Henrick).

Dutch exhibition, industrial and graphic designer. Born in Groningen, 21 November 1928. Educated in Groningen, until 1946; studied at Akademie Minerva, Groningen, 1947–49; Institut voor Kunstnijverheidsonderwijs, Amsterdam, 1951–52. Served in the Dutch Army, 1949–51. Freelance designer, specializing in exhibition design, Amsterdam, 1952–57; established design studio with architect Kho Liang le, Amsterdam, 1957–61; founded Wim Crouwel design studio, Amsterdam, 1961–63; founder and co-director, Total Design studio, Amsterdam, since 1963. Exhibitions and publications designer, for the Van Abbemuseum, Eindhoven, 1955–63, and Stedelijk Museum, Amsterdam, from 1963. Instructor, Koninklijke Akademie voor Kunst en Vormgeving, Den Bosch, 1954–57, and Institut voor Kunstnijverheidsonderwijs, Amsterdam, 1955–63; instructor in industrial design, Technical High School, Delft, since 1965. Graphics and design series editor, for Uitgeverij Lecturis, Eindhoven, 1974–79. Secretary General, ICO-GRADA International Council of Graphic Design Associations, 1963–66; board member, Stichting Bond voor Kunst en Industrie Prijs, from 1974; Coordinating Commission member from 1976, and Advisory Committee Chairman from 1980, Buitenlandse Tentoonstellingen CRM; President, Stichting Openbaar Kunstbezit, since 1977; Commission member, Museum Boymans-van Beuningen, Rotterdam, from 1980; President, Stichting Rietveld Schroderhuis, Utrecht, and the Stichting Van Doesburghuis, Paris, since 1980. **Exhibitions:** *20 Jaar Kalenders Drukkerij Van de Geer,* Printgallery Pieter Brattinga, Amsterdam, 1976; *Bladen en Spaties,* Printgallery Pieter Brattinga, Amsterdam, 1976; *Overzichts-tentoonstelling,* Stedelijk Museum, Amsterdam, 1979; *Overzichts tentoonstelling,* TNO, Apeldoorn, 1979. Address: Herengracht 567, 1017 CD Amsterdam, Netherlands.

Publications:

By CROUWEL: books—*Nieuw Alfabet: een mogelijkheid voor de nieuwe ontwikkeling,* Hilversum 1967; *An International Survey of Packaging,* with Kurt Weidemann, London and Teufen 1968; *3 x Trademarks,* with others, Stuttgart 1968; *Ontwerpen en drukken,* Amsterdam 1974; articles—in *Drukkersweekblad* (Amsterdam), January 1958; *Forum* (Amsterdam), July 1961; *Print* (New York), no. 1, 1964; *Artscanada* (Toronto), June 1968; *Delta* (Amsterdam), no. 1, 1969; *Visible Language* (Cleveland), Summer 1974; *Holland Herald* (Amsterdam), December 1975; *TD-Publikatie* (Amsterdam), January 1977; *De Tijds* (Amsterdam), 13 July 1979.

On CROUWEL: books—*Advertising Directions* by Edward M. Gottschall and Arthur Hawkins, New York 1959; *Buchgestaltung* by Albert Kapr, Dresden 1963; *An International Survey of Press Advertising* by Kurt Weidemann, Stuttgart and London 1966; *Monografie des Plakats* by Herbert Schindler, Munich 1972; *Wim Crouwel: Ontwerpen en Drukken,* edited by Gerrit Jan Theimefonds, Amsterdam 1974; *Archigraphia: Architectural and Environmental Graphics,* edited by Walter Herdeg, Zurich 1978; *The Language of Graphics* by Edward Booth-Clibborn and Daniele Baroni, London 1980.

Wim Crouwel designs with the general public in mind. For more than three decades, he has imaginatively designed esthetic solutions to design and communication problems encountered in museum exhibitions and signage systems, in publications such as catalogues and books, in letterforms and symbols, as well as in environmental displays. Crouwel believes that messages are relayed most effectively through plain and clear, yet creative, solutions. The unifying element running through all of Crouwel's work, and in particular his widely circulated promotional posters, is his reliance on the geometry of a grid system.

In 1963, Crouwel was a founding partner in Total Design, the first Dutch design firms sufficiently large and diversified to take on comprehensive design projects in both public and private sectors. Almost simultaneously, he launched his influential design activities at the Stedelijk Museum in Amsterdam, thereby initiating a second long-term association with which his work has been particularly identified.

Before Total Design was formed, Crouwel worked in partnership with Kho Liang le, with whom he figured prominently in Pieter Brattinga's progressive gallery at de Jong lithographers in Hilversum. They re-designed the gallery space in 1958, and for the succession of exhibits that followed, they frequently contributed to the design of the exhibitions themselves.

In his 1967 publication *Nieuw Alfabet* [New Alphabet], Crouwel advocates a new type design aimed at the requirements of modern communication. He points out the efficiency and importance of updating type design to meet the demands of the computer age. The alphabet that he proposed "merely as an initial step" consists entirely of horizontal and vertical lines so that the letters may be clearly displayed on cathode ray tubes for the benefit of computer users and television viewers. Crouwel's ultimate goal is a simple and basic alphabet of universal application. He feels that mechanical reproduction will never match the perfection of which the human eye is capable in producing legibility and esthetic feeling. He further suggests that our type design should reflect the current culture, which, of course, cannot be seen in its entirety today but may be sensed. It is unlikely, therefore, that one alphabet will satisfy our needs for any length of time. Crouwel goes so far as to suggest that a counter-language of pictograms might one day fulfill our needs, for in principle his concern is with "communication symbols."

Crouwel has also focused his attention on package design—in effect, a three-dimensional means of communication. A year's work of critical analysis in collaboration with Kurt Weidemann produced the 1968 book *An International Survey of Packaging.* Here, the authors put forth their conception of the ideal package as one that comprises "a sound product, a new idea, a pleasing, functional and easily-handled shape, and good graphics."

Crouwel consistently puts his many talents as designer, writer, thinker, and educator into his work as a communicator. He always demonstrates a knack for projecting information in the most rational and analytical of formats. The messages he sends are understandable and meaningful, and they reach the audiences for which they are intended.

Crouwel has demonstrated that a market exists for clear, concise, and consistent design work, as may be demonstrated by his work for the Dutch government. Having worked with public agencies for several years, in 1967 he was appointed designer for the Dutch pavilion at the 1970 World's Fair in Osaka. Working with Eli Gros, he engineered an audio-visual display depicting Rotterdam's urban planning scheme through the year 2000. The pavilion might be seen as the "package" with which the Netherlands was presented for all to see and understand.

—Catherine L. Currier

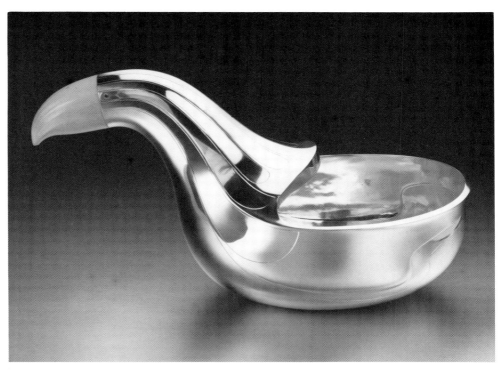

Gunnar Cyrén: *Bird* bowl in silver with whaletooth and sapphire decoration, 1988

CYRÉN, Gunnar (Carl).

Swedish silversmith and glass designer. Born in Gävle, 23 July 1931. Studied at the National College of Art, Craft and Design (Konstfackskolan), Stockholm, 1951–56: goldsmith diploma, 1951, silversmith diploma, 1956; apprenticed to silversmith Sven-Arne Gillgren, Stockholm, 1953–56; studied at Kölner Werkschule, Cologne, 1954. Married Birgitta Bäckström in 1957; children: Marten, Henrik and Gustav. Freelance designer, in Stockholm, 1956–59; designer, Orrefors Glassworks, Sweden, 1959–70, and since 1976; also freelance designer, for Dansk Design Ltd., New York, from 1970; established own silversmith's studio, Gavle, from 1975. Co-owner and director, Gallery Argentum, Stockholm, 1976–80, and Gallery Gamla Stan, Stockholm, 1981–86; owner-director, Gallery Gunnar Cyrén, Gävle, from 1986. **Exhibitions:** *Hantverkets, 60-tal,* Nationalmuseum, Stockholm, 1968; *Scandinavian Modern Design 1880–1980,* Cooper-Hewitt Museum, New York, 1982; *Aktuell Svensk Form,* Ibsenhuset, Skien, 1982; *Design Since 1945,* Philadelphia Museum of Art, 1983; *Contemporary Swedish Design,* Nationalmuseum, Stockholm, 1983 (toured Sweden); *The Lunning Prize,* Nationalmuseum, Stockholm, 1986; *Faces of Swedish Design,* IBM Gallery, New York, 1988 (toured the United States). **Collection:** Nationalmuseum, Stockholm. Recipient: Medal for Proficiency and Industry, Swedish Society of Industrial Design, 1956; Lunning Prize, 1966; Prince Eugen Medal, 1988. Addresses: (workshop) Nedre Bergsgatan 11, 802 22 Gävle, Sweden; (studio) Box 8056, 800 08 Gävle, Sweden.

Works:

Pop Glass wine glasses with coloured stems, for Orrefors, 1965.
Painted glass bowls, for Orrefors, 1967.
Frescati wine glasses, for Orrefors, 1968.
Serpent silver goblet, 1976.
Helena wine glasses, for Orrefors, 1977.
Collection of 24 silver boxes with crystal lids, 1982–83.
Harmony half crystal service, for Orrefors, 1983.
Collection of graal vases with figuring in crystal over- and underlay, for Orrefors, 1987.
Boat-shaped bowl in crystal, for Orrefors, 1987.
Symphony half crystal service, for Orrefors, 1987.
Temples in crystal and silver, 1989.
Animals in bronze and silver, 1989.

Publications:

On CYRÉN: books—*Svensk Form/Forma Sueca* by Ake Stavenlow and Ake H. Huldt, Stockholm 1961; *Scandinavian Design: Objects of a Life Style* by Eileene Harrison Beer, New York 1975; *Form och Tradition i Sverige,* edited by Birgitta Walz, Stockholm 1982; *Scandinavian Modern Design 1880–1980,* edited by David Revere McFadden, New York 1982; *Design Since 1945,* edited by Kathryn Hiesinger and George Marcus, Philadelphia and London 1983; *Contemporary Swedish Design,* exhibition catalogue by Monica Boman, Lennart Lindkvist and others, Stockholm 1983; *Den Svenska Formen* by Monica Boman and others, Stockholm 1985; *The Lunning Prize,* exhibition catalogue edited by Helena Dahlback Lütteman and Marianne Uggla, Stockholm 1986; *Faces of Swedish Design,* exhibition catalogue edited by Monica Boman, Stockholm 1988.

When Gunnar Cyrén emerged from the National College of Art and Design in the mid-1950's, the age of perfect craftsmanship was still in full swing. Soon, however, new winds began to blow. The only form accepted during the 1960's was the "rustic's rustic"—or at least that is how it seemed to Gunnar Cyrén. If you are something of a perfectionist, and enjoy working on a design until you've got everything right, it is not much fun living in a period when skill and precision are looked down on.

During the 60's Gunnar Cyrén made a very firm imprint on the glassware produced at Orrefors. And in his own way he broke with traditions and prejudice. He produced cheerful enamelled decorations and created "Pop Glasses" with their opalescent bowls and colored stems. They are deliberately and confidently designed, with nothing left to chance. Everything he did was elegant in the positive sense of the term.

Gunnar Cyrén has never been interested in industry as a vehicle of personal expression and manifestation. He was unwilling to give excessively wide distribution to things which were highly personal. "You add something which nobody wants." He simply wishes "to be a designer for an industry." For him, this evidently means producing a good basic commodity which respects its purpose and perhaps endows the pieces with "correct" patterns. This may sound functionalistic and tediously impersonal, but look at the "Frescati" wine glasses, based on some jubilee glasses he made in 1968. A couple of rounds on the bowl and he has produced a good basic commodity which respects its function. And yet they are highly personal, though in Cyrén's own way, without flamboyance.

Gunnar Cyrén has never compromised on workmanship. "True content is not improved by leaving anything unfinished," he says. So much for the ignorant and the slapdash. Chance and coincidence can sometimes produce very attractive results, but Gunnar Cyrén does not work that way. His approach is strictly intellectual, though his forms are never overloaded. It is simply that his personal mode of expression operates this way.

Gunnar Cyrén went in for silver in the mid-1970's. He studied metalworking at the National College of Art and Design, and was an apprentice silversmith. He started working with silver so as to experience complete independence. He was tired of merely adapting himself to other people's projects and making decisions together with others. An industrial designer has to defer to the market and the company's finances. Gunnar Cyrén's first silver was inspired by nature, though defiantly not natural-romantic. Its relationship to nature is highly disciplined and stylized; nature is hardly discernible and yet these pieces are manifestly inspired by pine cones, leaves, or writhing snakes. Birds and the occasional fish came next. The birds do not admit of zoological classification, though they possibly belong to the "ale goose" family. Gunnar Cyrén discovered that he and the people carving the old birdlike wooden vessels for beer drinking had had the same problems with the transition from body to head and beak.

His production in the 80's includes a series of austere, almost rectangular, boxes of silver with glass lids cut to an exact fit. When the lid takes the form of an open book, the spiritual subtlety of the box is accentuated. Cyrén's perfection makes the closed, architecturally constructed boxes into worthy bearers of expression. Function is a stage which was passed long ago. The final form seems self-evident, as if it could not have been made in any other way.

Gunnar Cyrén has a sense of the grandiose and magnificent. He is not reluctant to work with gold, but he always uses his own disciplined language. In the summer of 1987 an old Swedish castle, Gripsholm, celebrated its 450th anniversary. Cyrén was one of the silversmiths who were commissioned to produce an object from our time yet linked to the court and state silver tradition of old. His ceremonial staff is over a meter long, heavy and imposing, crowned by a naturalistically designed castle having a large green lawn of plexiglass. The language is the same that he uses for his enamelled glass. And it is an example of Gunnar Cyrén's extravagant style.

—Helena Dahlback Lutteman

D

DANZIGER, Louis.
American print and graphic designer. Born in New York City, 17 November 1923. Educated at high school and Federal Art Project classes, New York, 1938–41; apprentice at a printing firm and a silk-screen printers, New York, 1938–39; studied graphics, under Alvin Lustig, Art Center College of Design, Los Angeles, 1947–48; studied magazine design, under Alexey Brodovitch, New School for Social Research, New York, 1948. Served in the United States Army, 1942–45. Married Dorothy Patricia Smith in 1954. Worked as a stage designer for summer stock companies, New York, 1940–41; assistant to the art director, Delehanty Institute, New York, 1942; assistant art director, War Assets Administration, Los Angeles, 1946; designer, *Esquire* magazine, New York, 1948; freelance designer, establishing own office in Los Angeles, since 1949: corporate design consultant, Atlantic Richfield Company, since 1978; design consultant on the Olympic Games in Los Angeles, 1984; has also designed for the Container Corporation of America, Vivitar, Gelvatex, Los Angeles County Museum of Art, System Development Corporation, Clinton Laboratories, Champion Paper Company, etc. Instructor in advertising design, Art Center College of Design, Los Angeles, 1956–60, and since 1988; director of graphic design program, 1972–79, and senior faculty member, 1979–88, California Institute of the Arts, Valencia; visiting professor of visual and environmental studies, Harvard University, Cambridge, Massachusetts, 1978–88. Member of the graphics panel, Federal Design Improvement Program, since 1975, and of the Design Arts Award panel, since 1980, National Endowment for the Arts, Washington, D.C. **Exhibition:** Society of Typographic Arts, Chicago, 1955. **Collections:** Museum of Modern Art, New York; Library of Congress, Washington, D.C.; Los Angeles County Museum of Art. Recipient: Distinguished Achievement Award, Contemporary Art Council, Los Angeles, 1982; Distinguished Designer Award, National Endowment for the Arts, 1985; and numerous New York Art Directors Club awards; Los Angeles Art Directors Club awards; Type Directors Club awards; American Institute of Graphic Arts awards. Member: Alliance Graphique Internationale; American Institute of Graphic Arts; Art Directors Club of Los Angeles. Address: 7001 Melrose Avenue, Los Angeles, California 90038, U.S.A.

Works:

Poster and announcements, for the International Design Conference, Aspen, Colorado, 1955.
The Light Touch—Hard Sell advertising campaign, for the Dreyfus Agency, 1956.
Logo, advertising, packaging and design program, for Gelvatex Paint Company, 1956.

Great Ideas of Western Man advertisement, for the Container Corporation of America, 1958.
Logo, advertising, packaging and design program, for Clinton Laboratories, 1958–63.
Advertising campaigns, for SDC Systems Development Company, 1960–63.
Packages advertisement, for the Container Corporation of America, 1961.
Vivitar packaging, brochures and advertisements, for Ponder and Best, 1962–68.
The New York School exhibition catalogue and poster, for the Los Angeles County Museum of Art, 1965.
Kobena advertisements, for Ponder and Best, 1965.
American Paintings from the Metropolitan Museum exhibition catalogue and poster, for the Los Angeles County Museum of Art, 1966.
Sculpture of the 60s exhibition catalogue and poster, for the Los Angeles County Museum of Art, 1967.
Mamiya-Sekor packaging and advertisements, for Ponder and Best, 1967–69.
Gerhard Marcks exhibition catalogue, for the University of California at Los Angeles Art Gallery, 1969.
Transparency, Reflection, Light, Space: 4 Artists exhibition catalogue, for the University of California at Los Angeles Art Gallery, 1970.
Art and Technology exhibition catalogue, for the Los Angeles County Museum of Art, 1971.
The Navajo Blanket exhibition catalogue, for the Los Angeles County Museum of Art, 1972.
The Russian Avant Garde exhibition catalogue, for the Los Angeles County Museum of Art, 1980.
Los Angeles in the 60s exhibition catalogue, for the Los Angeles County Museum of Art, 1981.

Publications:

On DANZIGER: books—*Packaging: An International Survey of Package Design,* edited by Walter Herdeg, Zurich 1959; *Exhibitions: An International Survey,* edited by Klaus Frank, New York, 1961; *Who's Who in Graphic Art,* edited by Walter Amstutz, Zurich 1962, Dubendorf 1982; *An International Survey of Press Advertising,* edited by Kurt Weidemann, Stuttgart and London 1966; *Graphic Designers in the USA: 1,* edited by Henri Hillebrand, London 1971, New York 1972; articles—in *Graphis* (Zurich), no. 70, 1957; *Stile Industria* (Milan), no. 11, 1957; *Graphis* (Zurich), no. 191, 1978; *Graphics Today* (New York), vol. 3, no. 1, 1978.

The problem of the graphic designer is quite different from that of the artist who deals essentially in private images. Because of the public nature of our work and because our commissions are generally problems of a specific nature, we find that we are continually trying to satisfy three distinctly different but not necessarily antagonistic judges. The three are the client, the audience, and one's self.

We must, if we accept a commission, use our skill and judgment to achieve our clients' objectives. As socially responsible people, we try to accomplish these aims in a positive way. We do this by performing some service for our audience. We provide information, entertainment, and esthetic pleasure.

Most designers will, I believe, agree with the above. It is in the area of self-satisfaction that the methods and goals of designers vary. The concerns and approaches which provide satisfactions for me and direct the nature of my work are as follows:

I am concerned with finding an image which is visually strong and esthetically gratifying, yet so pertinent to the idea that it becomes difficult to separate form from content.

There is a sense of achievement when one can solve a design problem in an elegant way (The word "elegant" is used here in the scientific sense, as the accomplishment of a great deal with a minimum of means.)

I am concerned with the production of work that demonstrates intelligence. There is continually a search for clarity and depth rather than cleverness.

Although I recognize that the work we do is essentially ephemeral, it is a source of satisfaction to produce work which avoids faddishness and looks fresh over a period of twenty years or longer.

The pressures imposed by the volume of work and the sheer magnitude of the clients move most successful designers more and more into the areas of direction and administration rather than the actual execution of work. For myself, I prefer to do less work and continue to remain more directly involved in its production. This involvement extends into photography. With but few exceptions, I produce all of the photographs seen in my work.

Designing is a source of much satisfaction and many frustrations, but I have always felt that it makes one useful and very special, and that, of course, provides the greatest satisfaction.

—Louis Danziger

In a 1978 article about Louis Danziger, the Swiss *Graphis* cited his answers to a series of questions. From this, we learn that Danziger's typographical instinct was formed from the annual *Gebrauchsgraphik,* which he used to look at in his youth, whereas to the question of who influenced him, he named Alvin Lustig and Alexey Brodovitch. Both pieces of information serve as keys to the understanding of this eminent American graphic designer's genealogy and way of thinking. In truth, several genera-

American Sculpture of the Sixties

Lou Danziger: *American Sculpture of the Sixties* exhibition catalogue, for the Los Angeles County Museum of Art, 1981

understand the essence of Danziger's style. This is exemplified in magazine advertisements for the Container Corporation of America, Clinton Laboratories, the Dreyfus Company, and in booklets for Champion Paper Company, as well as catalogues and posters for the Los Angeles County Museum of Art.

—Szymon Bojko

DAVID-WEST, (Pryde) Haig.
Nigerian graphic designer. Born in Port Harcourt, 18 June 1946. Studied at Bali College, Republic of Cameroun, 1960–64; Ahmadu Bello University, Zaria, Nigeria, 1965–70: BA 1970; art and design, University of Wisconsin, Madison, 1970–71: MA 1971; graphic design, under Henryk Tomaszewski and Jozef Mroszczak; Academy of Fine Arts, Warsaw, 1971–72; art education, under Jerome Hausman and David Exker, New York University, 1973–75: PhD 1975. Married Elizabeth Lydia Csintalan in 1974; children: Alzo, Hegulka and Gizelka. Graphic designer, Nigerian Television, Lagos, 1966–69; art editor, Normedia Group, Lagos, 1967–69; freelance graphic designer, Port Harcourt, from 1970: consultant to Concert Managers of Wisconsin, 1970–71, Mountain Health Services of Georgia, 1973, Prince Street Center of New York, 1973–75, and JDR III Fund of New York, 1974. Chief Executive, Arts Council of Port Harcourt, 1977–79. Instructor in graphic design, University of Georgia, Athens, 1972–73; lecturer in graphic design, University of Nigeria, Nsukka, 1975–76; head of fine and applied arts, College of Education, Port Harcourt, from 1981. Executive Board Member from 1980, vice-president and Africa Regional coordinator from 1981, and convener/moderator of the conference on Design Problems in Africa, 1982, ICOGRADA International Council of Graphic Design Associations. **Exhibitions:** Arts Building, Zaria, 1969; United States Information Center, Kano, 1970; Government Hall, Port Harcourt, 1970; Black History Gallery, Madison, Wisconsin, 1971; Three Continents Gallery, Warsaw, 1972; Klub Kropka, Gliwice, 1972; Goethe Institut, Lagos, 1980. **Collections:** National Gallery and Museum of Modern Art, Lagos; National Gallery, Baghdad; Poster Museum, Warsaw; Lahti Art Museum, Finland. Recipient: Bali College Graduation Award, Cameroun, 1964; International Labour Organization Stamp Design Prize, Lagos, 1969; Rivers State Award for International Studies, Nigeria, 1970; ICOGRADA/Polish Government Scholarship, 1970. Address: PMB 5047, Port Harcourt, Nigeria.

Publications:

By DAVID-WEST: books—*Russian Constructivist Art and Its Impact on Contemporary Poster Design*, PhD dissertation, New York University, 1976; *Haig David-West: Posters*, with foreword by Ronald Ruprecht, Port Harcourt 1980; *New Visual Arts Programme*, Port Harcourt 1981; *Dialogue on Graphic Design Problems in Africa*, editor, London 1983; articles—in *Corpscope* (Port Harcourt), no. 1, 1977; *Creative Communicator* (Chicago), no. 62, 1979; *Design Integration* (Helsinki), no. 1, 1982; *Symposium 82*, Brno 1982.

On DAVID-WEST: books—*Modern Publicity*,

tions of graphic artists, typographers, poster designers, and, in general, lovers of print were raised on this German journal, which represented the highest graphic standard of the 1920's and 1930's. It was not only a source of information but a school of good taste. Something like a continuation of this informal education can be seen in his cooperation with Brodovitch in New York on the layout of the elite monthly *Esquire*.

Along with George Tscherny, Louis Dorfsman, Paul Rand, and perhaps a few other representatives of his generation, he has sound historical erudition in the field of his discipline. This outlook on the evolution of graphic language in our century, deepened by his own experience, Danziger has for many years transmitted to students, and on this foundation, he has been able to develop in them a consciousness of the social, cultural, and artistic bases of visual mass-media. Not by accident does Danziger have in professional circles the reputation of a charismatic pedagogue.

Erudition, scientific interests, and synthesis of disparate elements into one visual, orderly whole: these characterize his works. To this, we must add a subtle feeling for the climate of a

given design problem, for its stylistic framework, or just for its emotional context. An example is the catalogue for the exhibit *The Avant-Garde in Russia, 1910–1930: New Perspectives,* organized by the Los Angeles County Museum. The graphic and typographic concept of this nearly 300-page publication had to take into consideration the particular character of the exhibit, which reconstructed a closed epoch of art. The catalogue was to fulfill this same task, as well as a second, derivative goal: to express the general artistic tendency—in this case constructivist—of the documented exhibit by means of the language of typography. The designer, having at his disposal textual and iconographic material of varying derivation—without cohesion, from the point of view of graphic matter—manifested an important sensitivity for *Zeitgeist*. This is not something that can be learned; it does not belong to the technology of craft. We are dealing here with a work of great restraint and rational discipline, a work puristically economical and in its own way elegant. The concept of elegance appears anyway, in Danziger's terminology, as "accomplishment with minimum means." If by elegance, we mean "esthetic order," we will ·

edited by Felix Gluck, London 1978; *The Nucleus*, edited by the Department of Culture, Lagos, 1982; articles—in *Projekt* (Warsaw), no. 131, 1978; *Graphis* (Zurich), no. 203, 1980; *UR* (London), no. 1, 1980; *The Nation* (Aba, Nigeria), no. 17, 1982.

All art forms are intended to communicate. They are created to "say" something to the viewer or audience. In this process, the creator manipulates form to the point where satisfaction is reached. When the manipulation is individualistic, where the creator responds only to his or her "free" sensations regardless of social issues, the something which the work communicates or "says" tends to be limited to levels of consciousness that may not be tangibly functional to the cause of social progress. With the poster and other forms of committed graphic design, the manipulation process is guided by the creator's sense of social responsibility. The work must be tangibly functional; it must appeal to the conscience of society.

Typically, the poster demonstrates the use of two types of communication—namely, the word-symbol and the picture-symbol, which must be organised in such a manner that a "quantum wholeness" and empathy are maintained. This suggests a dialectical situation in which a whole cannot be equated with the sum of X and Y sensations and reflexes—and in which the aesthetic experience where form fuses with moods, feelings, and emotions aroused by form remains at an equilibrium. Indeed, there are posters which do not demonstrate the word-picture or semantic-iconographic dialogue, but rather, rely completely on the picture or iconographic level of communication. This occurs when the word or semantic addition would appear to blur the message being communicated. Here again, quantum wholeness is a significant factor.

Two groups of contemporary designers are immediately visible in the Nigerian experience. One group reduces itself to the level of disgusting subservience to the whims of its client, totally oblivious of its training and experience, thus edging toward creative prostitution. The other group elevates itself to the level of progressive and systematic educator or pedagogue, regarding designs as a process during which an equation would be established between the old and the new—between vernacular culture and the main currents of world culture—while constantly guarding the elasticity of the equation, ensuring that a certain equilibrium is maintained. Critical to the world view of the latter is the concern to improve, by control processes, the general disposition of the non-literate stratum of society, while constantly ensuring that the literate stratum is not fed with banal material. It is this latter group that may be said to be addressing itself to the tangible problems of contemporary Nigeria.

In Europe's search for new artistic departures at the opening of the twentieth century, the primal geometry of masks from Africa had provided ready answers. In this search, which was essentially a feverish one, lay a restlessness that tended to becloud sound and systematic study. Hence, salient qualities of the art of the traditional African were slighted in favor of qualities that met with the European immediate expectation. Essentially, the mask was at no time regarded as a decorative device and was therefore not "art" to the traditional African. It was more of a ritualistic experience, which, in most instances, was variegated with "calligraphic" forms reflective of the general social dispositions and world outlook of traditional man. In the vernacular culture of the African experience, therefore, it was this calligraphy that was intended as a language of visual communication. Herein lay the most positive evidence of a

Haig David-West: Examples of vernacular calligraphy, 1983

developed form of vernacular visual communication design in Africa, thriving before the advent of modern forms of civilisation. In that culture, which now appears to co-exist with technological changes, the visual representation of the beautiful maintained a plastic equilibrium with inter-personal and inter-group communication.

Colonialist administrative policies succeeded in creating generations of cultural invalids in Nigerian society. To a large extent, the performing arts—drama, dance, gymnastics, etc.—were perceived by the colonialists as nothing more than dispositions developed for their entertainment. The intrinsic didactic content of these performances and their socialising tendency were disregarded. Our ancestors were encouraged to dance, sing, and perform for the enjoyment of the colonialist "spectator." Apparently, this tendency grew with our society—a lot of people still regard the performing arts as having only entertainment functions. There had been a systematic process of indoctrination through the generations.

Identifying the visual arts as a powerful medium for mobilising the masses of people, if encouraged along progressivist (and pluralist) growth lines, colonialist administrators infused an attitude of apathy toward this creative disposition among our people. Again, this apathy was transmitted to our time.

Perhaps the core of the controversy is found in the problem that grows out of the fact that subsequent formulators of our educational policies approached the matter of aesthetic inquiry with a cobweb attitude in which their view of global culture was astigmatic, thereby suggesting their inability to inculcate the idea that creative art and design are indeed fundamental to human growth and co-existence.

—Haig David-West

Haig David-West's work first came to national prominence fourteen years ago when, still an under-graduate at Ahmadu Bello University in the Northern Nigerian city of Zaria, he won all the prizes at the International Labour Organization postage stamp design contest organized by the Nigerian government. One year later, he made history again at the University by becoming the first student ever to graduate with first Class Honours in graphic design. He proceeded abroad for graduate study in the United States and Poland, where he was exposed to the social and political influences which were later to enable him to re-shape the direction of graphic design in Nigeria.

David-West's Polish experience seems to have been most significant for the development of his work. There, he learned that graphic design, if seen in the context of the social sciences, could play a crucial role in mobilising people for action. While in Poland, he also came into contact with Marxism-Leninism as an aesthetic philosophy and felt the significant impact of the work of his Warsaw Academy teachers. These influences crystalised in his doctoral work at New York University, where he formulated his principle of "quantum wholeness"—the equilibrium of the conjunction of social responsibility and artistic form—while studying aesthetics under David Ecker.

In its practical application, quantum wholeness has taken the form in his work of an explosive, didactic iconography bathed in the indigenous Nigerian symbolism. This is most evident in the work that resulted from his investigation of vernacular calligraphy, as exemplified by such outstanding posters as Regatta, Rex Lawson, Iria, Tam, and Tonjo Daye. Regatta, which is a promotional poster for the regatta theatrical event, takes account of the fact that this occurrence, which epitomises creative activity in the Niger Delta, articulates the visual, kinetic, corporal, and linguistic expressions of the people simultaneously. The poster emphasises the rhythm of a choreography of silhouetted paddles in juxtaposition with vernacular calligraphic forms. Another indigenous symbol prominent in some of David-West's posters is derived from naive hieroglyphics predominantly found on which makes a concise political statement, decrying the continued cultural and ideological enslavement of African peoples and warning against the humiliation of neo-colonialist adventurism in Africa.

From designs that are now being produced by David-West's students at the Port Harcourt College of Education, it is obvious that a new generation of designers will reflect the innovative character of the David-West posters. The increasingly influential design curriculum that he has formulated allows for graphic design to be studied in conjunction with political science.

An evaluation of Haig David-West's work and philosophy cannot be complete without mentioning the role he has played in international design diplomacy. He has addressed a UNESCO conference and has convened an international conference in Africa in his capacity as ICO-GRADA Vice President and Regional Coordinator for Africa. His work in this area culminates in his call for committed and socially relevant graphic design, which will assist in consolidating national socio-cultural liberation struggles and ultimately serve as an anchor in international relations. In all he does, his central belief is that a designer operating in a third-world society cannot afford to be apolitical.

—Alaboigoni Inko-Dokubo

DAY, Lucienne.

British textile designer. Born Lucienne Conradi, in Coulsdon, Surrey, 1 January 1917. Educated at the Convent of Notre Dame de Sion, Worthing, 1929–34; studied at Croydon School of Art, London, 1934–37; Royal College of Art, London, 1937–40; ARCA 1940. Married the designer Robin Day in 1942; daughter: Paula. Worked as a teacher, Beckenham School of Art, Kent, 1942–47; freelance designer, establishing studio in London, since 1948: has designed for Edinburgh Weavers, Heal's Fabrics, Wilton Royal Carpet Company, Cavendish Textiles, Tomkinson's Carpets, Thomas Somerset, John Lewis, Rosenthal Porcelain, etc. Selection panel member, Duke of Edinburgh's Elegant Design Awards, 1960–63; jury member, Rosenthal Porcelain Studio-Line, 1960–68; council member, Royal College of Art, London, 1963–68; textile consultants committee member, at Central School of Art, Croydon College of Art, and Kingston School of Art. **Exhibitions:** Prescote Gallery, Banbury, 1979; Lyttelton Gallery, National Theatre, London, 1981; Rohsska Konstslöjdmuseet, Goteborg, 1983; Chelsea Crafts Fair, London, 1983; Oscar Woollens International, London, 1984; St. John's Smith Square, London, 1986. **Collections:** Victoria and Albert Museum, London; Art Institute of Chicago; Cranbrook Museum, Bloomfield Hills, Michigan; Musee des Arts Decoratifs, Montreal; Kunstindustrimuseet, Trondheim; Röhsska Konstslöjdmuseet, Goteborg. Recipient: Gold Medal, 1951, and Grand Prize, 1954, Milan Triennale; First Award, American Institute of Decorators, 1952; Design Council Awards, London, 1957, 1960, 1968; Gold Medal, California State Fair, 1959, 1960. Fellow, Society of Industrial Artists and Designers, London, 1955; Royal Designer for Industry, Royal Society of Arts, London, 1962. Address: 49 Cheyne Walk, Chelsea, London, SW3 5LP, England.

Works:

Calyx printed furnishing fabric, for Heal Fabrics Ltd., 1950.
Elysian printed furnishing fabric, for Edinburgh Weavers, 1950.
Flotilla printed furnishing fabric, for Heal Fabrics Ltd., 1951.
Graphica printed furnishing fabric, for Heal Fabrics Ltd., 1952.
Ticker Tape printed furnishing fabric, for Heal Fabrics Ltd., 1952.
Florimel printed furnishing fabric, for Edinburgh Weavers, 1952.
Palisade printed furnishing fabric, for British Celanese, 1952.
Spectators printed furnishing fabric, for Heal Fabrics Ltd., 1953.
Linear printed furnishing fabric, for Heal Fabrics Ltd., 1953.
Travelogue printed furnishing fabric, for British Celanese, 1953.
Miscellany printed furnishing fabric, for British Celanese, 1953.
Acres printed furnishing fabric, for Edinburgh Weavers, 1954.
Fall printed furnishing fabric, for Edinburgh Weavers, 1955.
Tesserae carpet, for Tomkinsons Carpets, 1957.
Four Seasons ceramic tableware, for Rosenthal China Ltd., 1958.
Odyssey ceramic tableware, for Rosenthal China Ltd., 1960.
Table linen range, for Thomas Somerset, 1967.
Grey Line ceramic tableware, for Rosenthal China Ltd., 1969.
Tangrams three silk mosaic tapestries in the Commercial Union Building, London, for Shearman and Stirling, 1985.
The Window silk mosaic tapestry at the Queen Elizabeth Conference Centre, London, for Powell Moya and Partners, 1986.
Aspects of the Sun group of silk mosaic tapestries in the John Lewis Building, Kingston, Surrey, for Ahrends Burton Koralek, 1989–90.

Publications:

By DAY: article—"Plain or Fancy" in *Daily Mail Ideal Home Book,* London, 1957.

On DAY: books—*British Textiles* by Frank Lewis, Leigh-on-Sea 1951; *Design in British Industry: A Mid-Century Survey* by Michael Farr, Cambridge 1955; *Printed Textiles* by Pat Albeck, London 1969; *The Contemporary Decorative Arts from 1940 to the Present Day* by Philippe Garner, London 1980; *Design Since 1945,* edited by Kathryn Hiesinger and George Marcus, Philadelphia and London 1983; *A Woman's Touch* by Isabelle Anscombe, London 1984.

In 1951, the Festival of Britain gave many young designers the opportunity to launch successful careers. Stimulated by a feeling of deep frustration with postwar austerity, change was in the air. Lucienne Day had married Robin Day soon after leaving the Royal College of Art, and for their work together on the Festival, she designed her first major commission, the famous Calyx fabric. With its bold, spiky graphics and fresh, bright colour, it was an immediate success and did much to launch postwar, modern textile design in Britain. It was also the beginning of a successful twenty-one-year partnership with Heal's, a London furniture store with a policy of promoting modern design. Through this relationship, Day developed as a skilled and sensitive pattern-maker, with a respect for craft traditions and quality production inspired largely by the Scandinavian tradition. Throughout her career, the textiles she designed for them picked up many international awards, including the gold medal at the ninth *Triennale di Milano* in 1951 and, three years later, the grand prize for another group of textiles: Graphics, Spectator, and Linear. She has also worked as a carpet designer; in 1957, Tesserae, for Tomkinsons, won the Design of the Year award, and more recently, she has produced the Nova range for Wilton Carpets. Neither is Day restricted to work in two dimensions. Between 1957 and 1969, she designed china and dinner services for Rosenthal Porcelain, and she has successfully collaborated with her husband on the interior of the BOAC passenger aircraft and has consulted for John Lewis; currently, she is working on projects for department stores and supermarkets.

Over the last few years, her work has changed direction, towards more craft-based production. Drawing on her experience as a colour consultant to industry, Day began to experiment with one-off wall hangings made up of small pieces of oriental plain or shot silk, sewn together by hand. She first showed this work in 1979; its success encouraged further exhibitions in Tokyo and a solo exhibition at the Röhsska Konstslöjd Museum in Göteborg, Sweden. Most of the pieces use a semi-abstract style, and many have been bought to complement formal architectural interiors.

—Catherine McDermott

DAY, Richard.

American art director and film designer. Born in Victoria, British Columbia, 9 May 1896; emigrated to the United States in 1918. Served as model designer in the United States Marine Corps, 1942–45. Married; 6 children. Set decorator for film director Erich von Stroheim, at MGM, Universal, Paramount and United Artists studios, Hollywood, 1918–28; worked independently for Goldwyn and United Artists, in Hollywood, 1928–38; art director, 1939–40, then supervising art director, 1940–42 and 1945–47, at 20th Century-Fox, Hollywood; freelance designer, working for Goldwyn, RKO, United Artists and Warner Brothers, from 1948. Recipient: Academy Awards, 1935, 1936, 1941, 1942, 1951, 1954. *Died* (in Hollywood, California) *23 May 1972.*

Works:

Film designs include—*Blind Husbands* (von Stroheim), 1918; *The Devil's Passkey* (von Stroheim), 1919; *Foolish Wives* (von Stroheim), 1922; *Merry Go Round* (Julian and von Stroheim), 1923; *Greed* (von Stroheim), 1925; *The Merry Widow* (von Stroheim), 1925; *Bright Lights* (Leonard), 1925; *The Only Thing* (Conway), 1925; *His Secretary* (Henley), 1925; *Beverley of Graustark* (Franklin), 1926; *Bardelys the Magnificent* (K. Vidor), 1926; *The Show*

Lucienne Day: *Their Exits and Their Entrances* **silk mosaic, for the National theatre, London, 1981**

(Browning), 1927; *Mr. Wu* (Nigh), 1927; *Tillie the Toiler* (Henley), 1927; *The Unknown* (Browning), 1927; *Adam and Evil* (Leonard), 1927; *After Midnight* (Bell), 1927; *The Road to Romance* (Robertson), 1927; *Tea for Three* (Leonard), 1927; *The Student Prince in Old Heidelberg* (Franklin), 1927; *The Enemy* (Niblo), 1927; *The Divine Woman* (Sjostrom), 1928; *Wickedness Preferred* (Henley), 1928; *Rose Marie* (Hubbard), 1928; *The Big City* (Browning), 1928; *Circus Rookies* (Sedgwick), 1928; *Laugh, Clown, Laugh* (Brenon), 1928; *The Actress* (Franklin), 1928; *Forbidden Hours* (Beaumont), 1928; *Our Dancing Daughters* (Beaumont), 1928; *Excess Baggage* (Cruze), 1928; *While the City Sleeps* (Conway), 1928; *The Wedding March* (von Stroheim), 1928; *West of Zanzibar* (Browning), 1928; *The Bridge of San Luis Rey* (Brabin), 1929; *The Idle Rich* (W. deMille), 1929; *A Man's Man* (Cruze), 1929; *Wonder of Women* (Brown), 1929; *The Girl in the Show* (Selwyn), 1929; *The Unholy Night* (L. Barrymore), 1929; *The Hollywood Revue of 1929* (Reisner), 1929; *Wise Girls* (Hopper), 1929; *The Thirteenth Chair* (Browning), 1929; *The Kiss* (Feyder), 1929; *Their Own Desire* (Hopper), 1929; *Devil May Care* (Franklin), 1929; *Untamed* (Conway), 1929; *Gus Edwards' Song Revue* (Edwards), 1929; *Song Shop* (Lee), 1929; *Anna Christie* (Brown), 1930; *In Gay Madrid* (Leonard), 1930; *Whoopee* (Freeland), 1930; *Sins of the Children* (Wood), 1930; *Madame Satan* (C. deMille), 1930; *Le Spectre Vert* (Feyder), 1930; *The Devil to Pay* (Fitzmaurice), 1930; *The Front Page* (Milestone), 1931; *Indiscreet* (McCarey), 1931; *Street Scene* (K. Vidor), 1931; *The Unholy Garden* (Fitzmaurice), 1931; *Palmy Days* (Sutherland), 1931; *Arrowsmith* (Ford), 1931; *The Greeks Had a Word for It* (L. Sherman), 1932; *Rain* (Milestone), 1932; *Cynara* (K. Vidor), 1932; *The Kid from Spain* (McCarey), 1932; *Hallelujah I'm a Bum* (Milestone), 1933; *Secrets* (Borzage), 1933; *The Bowery* (Walsh), 1933; *The Masquerader* (Wallace), 1933; *Roman Scandals* (Tuttle), 1933; *Gallant Lady* (La Cava), 1933; *Moulin Rouge* (Lanfield), 1934; *Nana* (Arzner), 1934; *The Affairs of Cellini* (La Cava), 1934; *Born to Be Bad* (L. Sherman), 1934; *The House of Rothschild* (Werker), 1934; *The Last Gentleman* (Lanfield), 1934; *Bulldog Drummond Strikes Back* (Del Ruth), 1934; *Kid Millions* (Del Ruth), 1934; *Looking for Trouble* (Wellman), 1934; *We Live Again* (Mamoulian), 1934; *The Mighty Barnum* (W. Lang), 1934; *Folies Bergere* (Del Ruth), 1935; *Clive of India* (Boleslawski), 1935; *Cardinal Richelieu* (Lee), 1935; *The Call of the Wild* (Wellman), 1935; *The Dark Angel* (Franklin), 1935; *Barbary Coast* (Hawks), 1935; *Metropolitan* (Boleslawski), 1935; *Splendor* (Nugent), 1935; *Strike Me Pink* (Taurog), 1936; *These Three* (Wyler), 1936; *One Rainy Afternoon* (Lee), 1936; *Dodsworth* (Wyler), 1936; *The Gay Desperado* (Mamoulian), 1936; *Come and Get It* (Hawks and Wyler), 1936; *Beloved Enemy* (Potter), 1936; *Woman Chases Man* (Blystone), 1937; *Stella Dallas* (K. Vidor), 1937; *Dead End* (Wyler), 1937; *The Hurricane* (Ford), 1937; *The Goldwyn Follies* (Marshall), 1938; *The Cowboy and the Lady* (Potter), 1938; *The Adventures of Marco Polo* (Mayo), 1938; *Charlie Chan in Honolulu* (Humberstone), 1938; *The Little Princess* (W. Lang), 1939; *The Gorilla* (Dwan), 1939; *The Hound of the Baskervilles* (Lanfield), 1939; *The Return of the Cisco Kid* (Leeds), 1939; *Rose of Washington Square* (Ratoff), 1939; *Young Mr. Lincoln* (Ford), 1939; *Frontier Marshal* (Dwan), 1939; *Quick Millions* (St. Clair), 1939; *The Adventures of Sherlock Holmes* (Werker), 1939; *Charlie Chan at Treasure Island* (Foster), 1939; *The Escape* (Cortez), 1939; *Hollywood Cavalcade* (Cummings), 1939; *Pack Up Your Troubles* (Humberstone),

1939; *Drums Along the Mohawk* (Ford), 1939; *Day-Time Wife* (Ratoff), 1939; *City of Darkness* (Leeds), 1939; *Swanee River* (Lanfield), 1939; *The Honeymoon's Over* (Forde), 1939; *Everything Happens at Night* (Cummings), 1939; *City of Chance* (Cortez), 1939; *Little Old New York* (H. King), 1940; *The Blue Bird* (W. Lang), 1940; *He Married His Wife* (Del Ruth), 1940; *The Grapes of Wrath* (Ford), 1940; *The Man Who Wouldn't Talk* (Burton), 1940; *Charlie Chan in Panama* (Foster), 1940; *Star Dust* (W. Lang), 1940; *Johnny Apollo* (Hathaway), 1940; *Shooting High* (Green), 1940; *I Was an Adventuress* (Ratoff), 1940; *Lillian Russell* (Cummings), 1940; *Girl in 313* (Cortez), 1940; *Earthbound* (Pichel), 1940; *Four Sons* (Mayo), 1940; *Manhattan Heartbeat* (Burton), 1940; *Maryland* (H. King), 1940; *The Man I Married* (Pichel), 1940; *Girl from Avenue A* (Brower), 1940; *The Return of Frank James* (F. Lang), 1940; *Pier 13* (Forde), 1940; *Young People* (Dwan), 1940; *Charlie Chan at the Wax Museum* (Shores), 1940; *Yesterday's Heroes* (Leeds), 1940; *The Gay Caballero* (Brower), 1940; *Down Argentine Way* (Cummings), 1940; *The Great Profile* (W. Lang), 1940; *The Mark of Zorro* (Mamoulian), 1940; *Street of Memories* (Traube), 1940; *Tin Pan Alley* (W. Lang), 1940; *Youth Will Be Served* (Brower), 1940; *Murder Over New York* (Lachman), 1940; *Jennie* (Burton), 1940; *Chad Hanna* (H. King), 1940; *Hudson's Bay* (Pichel), 1940; *Michael Shayne, Private Detective* (Forde), 1940; *For Beauty's Sake* (Traube), 1941; *Remember the Day* (H. King), 1941; *Romance of the Rio Grande* (Leeds), 1941; *Western Union* (F. Lang), 1941; *Tobacco Road* (Ford), 1941; *That Night in Rio* (Cummings), 1941; *The Great American Broadcast* (Mayo), 1941; *Blood and Sand* (Mamoulian), 1941; *The Cowboy and the Blonde* (McCarey), 1941; *Man Hunt* (F. Lang), 1941; *A Very Young Lady* (Schuster), 1941; *Moon Over Miami* (W. Lang), 1941; *The Bride Wore Crutches* (Traube), 1941; *Accent on Love* (McCarey), 1941; *Dance Hall* (Pichel), 1941; *Dressed to Kill* (Forde), 1941; *Charley's Aunt* (Mayo), 1941; *Wild Geese Calling* (Brahm), 1941; *Private Nurse* (Burton), 1941; *Sun Valley Serenade* (Humberstone), 1941; *Belle Starr* (Cummings), 1941; *Charlie Chan in Rio* (Lachman), 1941; *We Go Fast* (McGann), 1941; *The Last of the Duanes* (Tinling), 1941; *Man at Large* (Forde), 1941; *A Yank in the RAF* (H. King), 1941; *Geat Guns* (Banks), 1941; *Riders of the Purple Sage* (Tinling), 1941; *Weekend in Havana* (W. Lang), 1941; *Rise and Shine* (Dwan), 1941; *How Green Was My Valley* (Ford), 1941; *Swamp Water* (Renoir), 1941; *The Lone Star Ranger* (Tinling), 1942; *Son of Fury* (Cromwell), 1942; *Roxie Hart* (Wellman), 1942; *Song of the Islands* (W. Lang), 1942; *Rings on Her Fingers* (Mamoulian), 1942; *My Gal Sal* (Cummings), 1942; *The Man Who Wouldn't Die* (Leeds), 1942; *It Happened in Flatbush* (McCarey), 1942; *Whispering Ghosts* (Werker), 1942; *Moontide* (Mayo), 1942; *The Magnificent Dope* (W. Lang), 1942; *Through Different Eyes* (Loring), 1942; *The Postman Didn't Ring* (Schuster), 1942; *Ten Gentlemen From West Point* (Hathaway), 1942; *This Above All* (Litvak), 1942; *Footlight Serenade* (Ratoff), 1942; *A-Haunting We Will Go* (Werker), 1942; *Little Tokyo USA* (Brower), 1942; *Orchestra Wives* (Mayo), 1942; *The Loves of Edgar Allen Poe* (Lachman), 1942; *Berlin Correspondent* (Forde), 1942; *Careful, Soft Shoulders* (Garrett), 1942; *Just Off Broadway* (Leeds), 1942; *Iceland* (Humberstone), 1942; *Girl Trouble* (Schuster), 1942; *Manila Calling* (Leeds), 1942; *The Man in the Trunk* (St. Clair), 1942; *Tales of Manhattan* (Duvivier), 1942; *Springtime in the Rockies* (Cummings), 1942; *That Other Woman* (McCarey), 1942; *The Ox-Bow Incident* (Wellman), 1942; *Thunder Birds*

(Wellman), 1942; *China Girl* (Hathaway), 1942; *The Undying Monster* (Brahm), 1942; *Time to Kill* (Leeds), 1942; *The Black Swan* (H. King), 1942; *Dr. Renault's Secret* (Lachman), 1942; *Quiet Please, Murder* (Larkin), 1942; *Life Begins at 8.30* (Pichel), 1942; *The Meanest Man in the World* (Lanfield), 1943; *Dixie Dugan* (Brower), 1943; *Immortal Sergeant* (Stahl), 1943; *He Hired the Boss* (Loring), 1943; *Chetniks* (L. King), 1943; *Margin for Error* (Preminger), 1943; *My Friend Flicka* (Schuster), 1943; *Tonight We Raid Calais* (Brahm), 1943; *Crash Dive* (Mayo), 1943; *Coney Island* (W. Lang), 1943; *Up in Arms* (Nugent), 1944; *The Razor's Edge* (Goulding), 1946; *Anna and the King of Siam* (Cromwell), 1946; *Boomerang* (Kazan), 1947; *Moss Rose* (Ratoff), 1947; *Miracle on 34th Street* (Seaton), 1947; *The Ghost and Mrs. Muir* (Mankiewicz), 1947; *Mother Wore Tights* (W. Lang), 1947; *I Wonder Who's Kissing Her Now* (Bacon), 1947; *Captain from Castile* (H. King), 1947; *Joan of Arc* (Fleming), 1948; *Force of Evil* (Polonsky), 1948; *My Foolish Heart* (Robson), 1949; *Our Very Own* (Miller), 1950; *Edge of Doom* (Robson), 1950; *Cry Danger* (Parrish), 1951; *I Want You* (Robson), 1951; *A Streetcar Named Desire* (Kazan), 1951; *Hans Christian Andersen* (C. Vidor), 1952; *On the Waterfront* (Kazan), 1954; *Solomon and Sheba* (K. Vidor), 1959; *Exodus* (Preminger), 1960; *Something Wild* (Garfein), 1961; *Goodbye Charlie* (Minnelli), 1964; *Cheyenne Autumn* (Ford), 1964; *The Greatest Story Ever Told* (Stevens), 1965; *The Chase* (Penn), 1965; *The Happening* (Silverstein), 1966; *The Valley of the Dolls* (Robson), 1967; *The Sweet Ride* (Hart), 1967; *The Boston Strangler* (Fleischer), 1968; *Tora-Tora-Tora* (Fleischer), 1970; *Tribes* (Sargent) 1970.

Publications:

On DAY: books—*The Mighty Barnum: A Screen Play,* with foreword by Gene Fowler, New York, 1934; *Filmlexicon degli Autore e delle Opere,* 7 vols., edited by Michele Lacalamita and others, Rome 1958–67; *Hollywood in the Thirties* by John Baxter, London and New York 1968; *Le Décor de Film* by Leon Barsacq, Paris 1970, as *Caligari's Cabinet and Other Grand Illusions,* Boston 1976; *The Art of Hollywood,* edited by John Hambley, London 1979.

Richard Day put to screen some of the seediest sets in Hollywood history. The constructions for *Dead End* (1937) so appalled producer Samuel Goldwyn that the mogul wondered why his money couldn't have been used to build a better slum! Despite his proclivity for suggesting human blight, Day equally eased into drawing-room dramas and musical extravaganzas. What unities can be found in such versatility?

Day's film career began with his apprenticeship to director Erich von Stroheim, who was possessed by a violent forcefulness akin to the German expressionists. Attracted to fantasy and symbolism, in spirit, he belonged with the German social realists such as George Grosz. Yet von Stroheim's meticulous attention to detail recalled the American realists (such as Thomas Eakins), with their fascination for everyday minutiae. Although Day absorbed these traditions, he equally shared the sensibilities of the American Regionalist school. His classically balanced urban scenes recalled Edward Hopper's works, serene even in their turmoil. His humble, rural environments interpreted the countryside with the same poignancy found in paintings by Thomas Hart Benton.

Day's films were lush with details. His expressions of poverty included every crack in the wall, thick coats of dust, peeling paint, and the fading floral wallpaper of an out-of-date print.

Stairways creaked, and laundry blocked the sky like a Piranesi prison. On the other hand, for the old-world wealthy, Day gilded grand staircases with elaborate ornamentation. His swags of velvet drapery regally dressed the richly veined marble colonnades. The "moderne chic" danced on floors of patent leather-black gleam. White multi-platform steps, kaleidoscopic mirrors, and Deco glass sculpture well served the slick set's "swells." Despite their apparent disparities, each style shared Day's love of the particular.

In the 1950's the "new breed" of actors and directors found Day's work well suited to their needs. Day could capture the brutal snap and underlying sensitivity dominating the works of such directors as Elia Kazan. As always, Day invested the commonplace with potent symbolism. His intensely ambient spaces suggested inner psychologies—a critical factor in artistic works of the time. However, despite Day's topicality, his modus operandi had barely changed since his collaborations with von Stroheim.

Day achieved richness through magnification of the specific. Amassing details, he combined visual intricacy with depth of content. As a result, his tragic visions spoke with the boldest tones. Day filled even his saddest images with a poetry that von Stroheim denied, thus giving his viewer a bittersweet sense of hope.

—Edith Cortland Lee

DAY, Robin.

British industrial, interior and furniture designer. Born in High Wycombe, Buckinghamshire, 25 May 1915. Studied at High Wycombe Art School, 1930–33; Royal College of Art, London, 1934–38: ARCA 1939. Married the designer Lucienne Conradi in 1942; daughter: Paula. Freelance designer, London, since 1945; design consultant, Hille International furniture, from 1950, John Lewis Partnership, from 1962, and Barbican Arts Centre, London, from 1968. Part-time instructor in design, Beckenham College of Art, Kent, 1940–47, and the Regent Polytechnic School of Architecture, London, 1948–50; Governor, London College of Furniture, 1974–80. **Exhibitions:** *Hille: 75 Years of British Furniture,* Victoria and Albert Museum, London, 1981; *Design Since 1945,* Philadelphia Museum of Art, 1983; *New Design for Old,* Victoria and Albert Museum, London, 1986. **Collections:** Museum of Modern Art, New York; Victoria and Albert Museum, London; Konstindustrimuseet, Trondheim; Nationalmuseum, Stockholm. Recipient: Fellow, 1948, Design Medal, 1957, Society of Industrial Artists and Designers, London; First Prize (with Clive Latimer), International Furniture Design Competition, Museum of Modern Art, New York, 1949; Gold Medal, 1951, Silver Medal, 1954, Milan Triennale; two Design of the Year Awards, 1957, and Design Centre Awards, 1961, 1962, 1965, 1966, Council of Industrial Design, London, Royal Designer for Industry, Royal Society of Arts, London, 1959; Officer, Order of the British Empire, 1983. Address: 49 Cheyne Walk, Chelsea, London SW3 5LP, England.

Works:

Hillestak Chair, low-cost stacking chair in beech or ply, for Hille, 1949.

Tip-up auditorium seating in steel, latex foam and uncut moquet, for the Royal Festival Hall, London, 1951.
British art and design displays, at the Milan Triennale, 1951.
Television and radio cabinets, for Pye Ltd., 1958.
Furniture, for Gatwick Airport, Sussex, 1960.
Chair range in injection-moulded polypropylene, for Hille, 1963.
Interiors of the Super VC10 and other passenger aircraft, for the British Overseas Airways Corporation, 1963–74.
Seating, for the Barbican Arts Centre, Concert Hall and Theatre, 1980.
Spectrum seating in steel and polypropylene, for Hille, 1985.
Stadium seating in steel and polypropylene, for Hille, 1985.
Upholstered stacking chair in steel and formed ply, for Mines and West, 1989.

Publications:

On DAY: books—*British Furniture Today* by Erno Goldfinger, London 1951; *The Adventure of British Furniture* by David Joel, London 1953, as *Furniture Design Set Free,* London, 1969; *Packaging: An International Survey of Package Design,* edited by Walter Herdeg, Zurich 1959; *Public Interiors* by Misha Black, London 1960; *Furniture in Britain Today* by Dennis and Barbara Young, London 1964; *Looking at Furniture* by Gordon Russell, London 1964; *Industrial Design in Britain* by Noel Carrington, London 1976; *Hille: 75 Years of British Furniture,* exhibition catalogue by Sutherland Lyall, London 1981; *Design Since 1945,* edited by Kathryn Hiesinger and George Marcus, Philadelphia and London 1983; *The Conran Directory of Design,* edited by Stephen Bayley, London 1985; *New Design for Old,* exhibition catalogue with texts by Helen Hamlyn, Eric Midwinter and others, London 1986.

All man-made things and environments are designed in one way or another. I believe that the quality of this design is important to the well-being of humanity. Designers have responsibilities other than the profit motive, and must be increasingly concerned with conservation and the sensible use of the planet's resources.

I feel that all fields of design are inter-related and I personally prefer to avoid over-specialisation by working in a number of design areas. I am less interested in fashion than in a synthesis of good construction, good function and aesthetics.

—Robin Day

Robin Day: Upholstered stacking chairs in steel and plywood, for the Mines and West Group, 1989

Though the early years of Robin Day's career were spent in display and graphic design, his training and real interest lay in furniture. It is in this field, especially in the development of injection-moulded plastic furniture, that Day made important innovative contributions. Of special interest throughout his career has been mass production of low-cost units that put good design within reach of the everyday householder.

Day was first brought to the attention of British furniture manufacturers in 1949 when he won first prize in a competition sponsored by the Museum of Modern Art in New York for a low-cost storage unit. He shortly became a design consultant to the Hille Company of London and in so doing, established one of the most fruitful collaborative relationships of recent times in the British design field. Sharing with Hille common interests in production of low-cost furniture and in exploring new materials and technical means, Day was placed in the ideal position of being able to carry out research subsidized and encouraged by his employer.

In the early 1950's Day explored the potential of moulded plywood using newly available plastic glues. This research resulted in the highly successful Hillestak chair which was, as its name suggests, stackable, a feature then attracting much interest. However, despite the fact that the design looked simple, the chair required assembly of twenty-two parts. Day further simplified the design of this inexpensive, stackable chair, shortly to produce the Q Stak chair, which had a back and seat made of a single piece of moulded plywood which bolted onto a metal leg-frame.

The liberating principle, which allowed for the seating shell and the base to be separately considered and made of different materials, had been originally established in the mid-1950's by the American designer Charles Eames, who applied the idea first to his moulded plywood chairs and shortly thereafter to his moulded fiberglass chairs. Soon, Hille acquired rights to produce the Eames chair made of moulded, glass-reinforced plastic. Inspired by this chair, Day, wanting to produce a still lower-cost plastic chair, began his research into the properties of polypropylene, a cheap, durable, lightweight plastic invented in 1954 by the Italian Guilio Natta. By the early 1960's Day had successfully developed a shell that could be made of polypropylene and produced by means of injection moulding. This material and method reduced costs considerably over fiberglass.

This versatile shell has been treated to a wide variety of uses (left bare, padded with foam and variously upholstered) and joined to different kinds of bases (four legs and pedestal and swivel bases). The shell has been used in mass seating arrangements both indoors and outdoors, and it has been reduced in scale for child and youth seating.

—Barbara Young

D'EAUBONNE, Jean (Adrien).

French painter and film designer. Born in Talence, Gironde, 8 March 1903. Studied painting and sculpture under Antoine Bourdelle, Paris. Worked as a painter and poster designer, Paris, until 1927; assistant film designer to Lazare Meerson and Jean Perrier, Paris, 1928–30; art director, working on the films of Marcel Carné, Jean Gremillon, Jean Cocteau, Max Ophuls, Maurice Gleizes, Jacques Feyder, Julien Duvivier, Vicente Minnelli and others, in Paris, 1930–39, 1946–71, and in Hollywood, 1957–68; lived in Switzerland, 1940–45. Recipient: Venice Film Festival Prize, 1950; Punta del Este Film Festival Prize, 1950. *Died in July 1970.*

Works:

Film designs include—*Le Perroquet Vert* (Milva), 1928; *Tarakanova* (Bernard), 1930; *Le Sang d'un Poète* (Cocteau), 1930; *Le Defenseur* (Ryder), 1930; *La Ronde des Heures* (Ryder), 1930; *Azais* (Hervil), 1930; *Coup de Roulis* (de la Cour), 1931; *Le Juif Polonais* (Kemm), 1931; *Coquecigrole* (Berthomieu), 1931; *Pour un Sou d'Amour* (Gremillon), 1931; *Amour et Discipline* (Kemm), 1931; *Le Truc du Brésilien* (Cavalcanti), 1932; *Les Vignes du Seigneur* (Hervil), 1932; *L'Amour et al Veine* (Banks), 1932; *Mademoiselle Josette ma Femme* (Berthomieu), 1933; *Mannequins* (Hervil), 1933; *Ame de Clown* (Noe and Didier), 1933; *L'Ami Fritz* (de Baroncelli), 1933; *Coralie et Cie* (Cavalcanti), 1933; *La Femme Idéale* (Berthomieu), 1933; *Maitre Bolbec et son Mari* (Natanson), 1934; *Le Petit Jacques* (Roudes), 1934; *La Reine de Biarritz* (Toulout), 1934; *L'Aristo* (Berthomieu), 1934; *Le Clown Bux* (Natanson), 1935; *Les Beaux Jours* (M. Allegret), 1935; *Le Chant d'Amour* (Roudes), 1935; *Marie des Angoisses* (Bernheim), 1935; *Le Roman d'un Spahi* (Bernheim), 1936; *La Flamme* (Berthomieu), 1936; *Jenny* (Carne), 1936; *L'Amant de Madame Vidal* (Berthomieu), 1936; *Anne-Marie* (Bernard), 1936; *La Chaste Suzanne* (Berthomieu), 1937; *Police Mondaine* (Bernheim and Chamborant), 1937; *L'Habit Vert* (Richebe), 1937; *Un Dejeuner de Soleil* (Cravenne), 1937; *Légions d'Honneur* (Gleize), 1937; *L'Homme sans Nom* (Vallee), 1937; *Les Gens du Voyage* (Feyder), 1938; *Le Train pour Venise* (Berthomieu), 1938; *Carrefour* (Bernhardt), 1938; *Trois Valses* (Berger), 1938; *Un de la Canebière* (Pujol), 1938; *Les Gangsters du Château d'If* (Pujol), 1938; *Nuit de Decembre* (Bernhardt), 1939; *L'Enfer des Anges* (Christian-Jaque), 1939; *De Mayerling a Sarajevo* (Ophuls), 1939; *La Loi du Nord* (Feyder), 1942; *Une Femme Disparait* (Feyder), 1942; *Etoile sans Lumiere* (Blistene), 1945; *Macadam* (Blistene and Feyder), 1946; *La Foix aux Chimères* (Chenal), 1946; *La Chartreuse de Parme* (Christian-Jaque), 1947; *Black Magic* (Ratoff), 1947; *L'Impasse des Deux Anges* (Tourneur), 1948; *Hans le Marin* (Villiers), 1948; *Le Paradis des Pilotes Perdus* (Lapmin), 1949; *Je n'Aime que Toi* (Montazel), 1949; *Pas de Week-end pour notre Amour* (Montazel), 1949; *Lady Paname* (Jeanson), 1949; *Orphée* (Cocteau), 1950; *La Ronde* (Ophuls), 1950; *La Dame Chez Maxim's* (Aboulker), 1950; *Ma Pomme* (Sauvajon), 1950; *Olivia* (Audry), 1950; *Nuits de Paris* (Baum), 1951; *Le Plaisir* (Ophuls), 1952; *Casque d'Or* (Becker), 1952; *Plaisirs de Paris* (Baum), 1952; *La Fête a Henriette* (Duvivier), 1952; *"Lysistrata"* episode of *Destinée* (Christian-Jaque), 1952; *Rue d'Estrapade* (Becker), 1953; *Jeunes Maries* (Grangier), 1953; *Le Mystère du Palace Hôtel* (Steckel and Berna), 1953; *Madame de . . .* (Ophuls), 1953; *Cet Homme est Dangereux* (Sacha), 1953; *Julietta* (M. Allegret), 1953; *Touchez pas au Grisbi* (Grisbi), 1954; *Mam'zelle Nitouche* (Y. Allegret), 1954; *Scenes de Ménage* (Berthomieu), 1954; *Bonnes a Tuer* (Decoin), 1954; *Les Amants du Tage* (Verneuil), 1954; *Marianne de ma Jeunesse* (Duvivier), 1955; *Lola Montes* (Ophuls), 1955; *L'Affaire des Poisons* (Decoin), 1955; *Le Secret de Soeur Angèle* (Joannon), 1955; *Le Long des Trottoirs* (Moguy), 1956; *Paris-Palace-Hôtel* (Verneuil), 1956; *L'Homme aux Cles d'Or* (Joannon), 1956; *Le Mariée est Trop Belle* (Gaspard-Huit), 1956; *Bonsoir Paris, Bonjour l'Amour* (Baum), 1956; *OSS 117 n'est pas Mort* (Sacha), 1956; *Jusqu'au Dernier* (Billon), 1956; *Amère Victoire* (Ray), 1957; *Une Manche et la Belle* (Verneuil), 1957; *Quand la Femme s'en Mêle* (Y. Allegret), 1957; *Montparnasee 19* (Becker), 1957; *The Reluctant Debutant* (Minnelli), 1958; *Christine* (Gaspard-Huit), 1958; *Nina* (Boyer), 1958; *Ein Engel auf Erden* (Radvanyi), 1959; *Suspense au 2e Bureau* (de St.-Maurice), 1959; *Katja* (Siodmak), 1960; *Les Magiciennes* (Friedman), 1960; *Crack in the Mirror* (Fleischer), 1960; *The Big Gamble* (Fleischer), 1960; *Madame Sans-Gène* (Christian-Jaque), 1961; *L'Affaire Nina B* (Siodmak), 1962; *Love is a Ball* (Swift), 1962; *Charade* (Donen), 1963; *Paris When it Sizzles* (Quine), 1964; *Le Repas des Fauves* (Christian-Jaque), 1964; *Lady L* (Ustinov), 1965; *Cartes sur Table* (Franco), 1965; *Galia* (Lautner), 1966; *Avec le Peau des Autres* (Deray), 1966; *Fleur d'Oseille* (Lautner), 1967; *La Pacha* (Lautner), 1967; *Custer of the West* (Siodmak), 1968; *The Girl on a Motorcycle* (Cardiff), 1968; *Johnny Banco* (Y. Allegret), 1968; *Faut pas Prendre les Enfants du Bon Dieu pour des Canards Sauvages* (Audiard), 1968; *Une Veuve en Or* (Audiard), 1969; *Sur la Route de Salina* (Lautner), 1969; *Elle Boit pas, Elle Fume pas, Elle Drague pas, mais . . . Elle Cause* (Audiard), 1970; *Sappho* (Farrel), 1970; *Laisse Aller, c'est une Valse* (Lautner), 1970; *Le Cri du Cormorant le Soir, au-dessus des Jonques* (Audiard), 1970; *Le Drapeau Noir Flotte sur la Marmite* (Audiard), 1971.

Publications:

On D'EAUBONNE: books—*Dictionnaire des Cineastes,* edited by Georges Sadoul, Paris, 1965, 1974; *Le Décor de Film* by Leon Barsacq, Paris 1970, as *Caligari's Cabinet and Other Grand Illusions,* Boston 1976; *Screen Series: France* by Marcel Martin, London and New York, 1971; *The World Encyclopedia of Film,* edited by Tim Cawkwell and John M. Smith, London 1972; *The International Film Encyclopedia* by Ephraim Katz, London 1980.

Jean D'Eaubonne established his credentials as one of France's most talented art directors during his collaboration with Jean Cocteau on *Le Sang d'un poète.* His training as a sculptor and assistantship with Lazare Meerson perfectly suited Cocteau's concept of the film's Surrealism. Reworking this style 20 years later in Cocteau's *Orphée* seemed to provide convenient bookends for the first half of D'Eaubonne's career. Yet neither film truly indicates his strengths of versatility. Designing for many of France's important directors, such as Carné, Ophüls, Feyder, Becker, and Duvivier, D'Eaubonne excelled in extending Meerson's "poetic realism." In many ways similar to the visual strategies and thematic concerns of the German *Kammerspiel,* poetic realism employed sets to complement or advance a film's narrative and humanistic viewpoint. This allowed D'Eaubonne to design in many different fashions, depending on the need of each specific film. His elegant work in *Casque d'or* borders on Impressionism while his few films in the United States, notably *Charade* and *Paris When it Sizzles,* suggest a development of poetic realism towards a rigid naturalism. His collaboration with Georges Annenkov and Christian Matras on Max Ophüls last four films, *La Ronde, Le Plaisir, Madame de . . . ,* and *Lola Montès,* yielded magnificent results. The sets, costumes, and cinematography combined perfectly to reveal a sensitivity to baroque detail in a variation of poetic realism best described as diffused Expressionism. The four began work on a film based on *The Marriage of Figaro*, but abandoned it after Ophüls's death.

Jean D'Eaubonne cannot be easily classified; his designs borrow from many schools and are applied upon narrative and thematic demand. His 40 year career bears testament to his range and skill.

—George Walsh

de CASTELBAJAC, Jean-Charles.

French fashion, interior and furniture designer. Born, of French parents, in Casablanca, Morocco, 28 November 1949. Educated at Catholic boarding schools in France, 1955–66; studied law, Faculté de Droit, Limoges, 1966–77. Married Katherine Lee Chambers in 1979; sons: Guillaume and Louis. Founder and designer, with his mother Jeanne-Blanche de Castelbajac, of Ko and Co ready-to-wear fashion company, Limoges, from 1968; also freelanced for Pierre d'Alby, Max Mara, Jesus Jeans, Etam, Gadgling, Julie Latour, Fusano, Amaraggi, Carel Shoes, Ellesse, Hilton, Levi-Strauss, Reynaud, etc., from 1968; director, Jean-Charles de Castelbajac fashion label, Paris, 1970, and Societé Jean Charles de Castelbajac S.A.R.L., Paris, 1978: established boutiques in Paris, New York and Tokyo, 1975–76. Also film and stage costume designer, notably for musicians Elton John, Talking Heads and Rod Stewart, from 1976; interior and furniture designs, from 1979. Member of Didier Grumbach's Les Créateurs group of designers, Paris, 1974–77. **Exhibitions:** Centre Georges Pompidou, Paris, 1978; *Forum Design,* Linz, Austria, 1980; Laforet Museum, Belgium, 1984. **Collections:** Musee du Costume, Paris; Fashion Institute of Technology, New York. Addresses: 188 rue de Rivoli, 75001 Paris, France; 55 rue de Lisbonne, 75008 Paris, France.

Works:

film costumes include—*Violette et Francois,* 1976; *Annie Hall,* 1977; *Who Killed My Husband?,* 1979; *Charlie's Angels,* television series, 1978–80.

Publications:

On de CASTELBAJAC: books—*The Changing World of Fashion* by Ernestine Carter, London 1977; *Design ist unsichtbar,* edited by Hellmuth Gsollpointer, Angela Hareiter and others, Vienna 1981; *Who's Who in Fashion,* edited by Karl Strute and Theodor Doelken, Zurich 1982; *Le Chic et la Mode* by Delbourg Delpais, Paris 1982; *Flammarion Fashion Dictionary* by Jerome Deslanbre, Paris 1983; *McDowell's Directory of Twentieth Century Fashion* by Colin McDowell, London 1984; *The Encyclopaedia of Fashion from 1840 to the 1980s* by Georgina O'Hara, London 1986.

In 1974 I introduced into fashion the use of numerous materials originally destined for industry—materials like bandages, blankets, car upholstery, cheese cloth, linen sheeting, spinnaker nylon, cleaning fabrics, etc. For daytime sport

Jean-Charles de Castelbajac: Housecoat dress with painted design by Jean Charles Blais, 1982

silhouette looks in 1975, I introduced a line of jogging wear, with quilted jackets, and created the quilted down coat now so famous in the U.S.A. I also made numerous coats and jackets from plaid and blanket materials. Subsequently, I have worked with major artists on painted dresses (like a walking canvas), and have begun designing furniture.

My philosophy is based on timelessness, and my creative work—both in fashion and other fields of design—is informed by the same idea. I am never influenced by folk or ethnic styles, but by lifestyles and elegance. I consider my work akin to that of the painter, and my ideas come from observing nature and people going about their lives. I like working for different industries—in ceramics, automobiles and furniture—because they are part of the puzzle which constitutes my style—a style of freedom.

—Jean-Charles de Castelbajac

A man of passions—for form and function, for color, for comfort and protection,—there lies the basis of this humanistic designer. Jean-Charles de Castelbajac began his obsession by cutting his first garment out of a blanket from boarding school. Because the material already existed, he was left to play with the form. Many times each year, he returns to this first gesture, cutting the cloth, so he remains close to its essence and function. This he must accomplish before thinking of embellishment, so permanence in his garments results. They are never linked to fleeting moments or frivolity. De Castelbajac feels that above all a sentiment must be produced through color. Because of this, he has an affinity with painters, with whom he spends much time to strengthen his creative impulses.

A man of the future, he nevertheless does not make "futuristic" clothing. His designs fulfil the need for practical and unassuming fashion of maximum quality. Favoring soft natural colors, he also uses natural textures and fibers. Innovative but respectful of classics, de Castelbajac has been called a modern traditionalist.

His fondness for architecture is apparent in the harmonious, architectonic shapes that flow through every collection. Since his imagination does not stop with garments, de Castelbajac has decided also to create other objects for the environment. Having a strong revulsion to prints on garments, he humorously solved the predicament by using large-scale motifs of Tom and Jerry or phrases from Nerval or Barbey d'Aurevilly inscribed on silk for very simple dresses. His clothing is identifiable by his manner of being true to himself—that is, being profoundly human and knowing something which is not only style.

—Andrea Arsenault

de GIVENCHY, Hubert (James Marcel Taffin).
French fashion designer. Born in Beauvais, 21 February 1927. Studied at the Collège Felix-Faure, in Beauvais and Montalembert; Ecole National Supérieure des Beaux-Arts, Paris; Faculty of Law, University of Paris. Worked in the fashion houses of Lucien Lelong, 1945-46, Robert Piquet, 1946-48, Jacques Fath, 1948-49, and Elsa Schiaparelli, 1949-51, all in Paris; established Givenchy fashion house in Parc Monceau, Paris, 1952-56, and in Avenue George V, Paris, since 1956: President and director-general of Societe Givenchy-Couture and Société des Parfums Givenchy, Paris, from 1954. Also film costume designer, from 1961. **Exhibition:** *Fashion: An Anthology,* Victoria and Albert Museum, London, 1971. Addresses: 3 Avenue George V, 75008 Paris, France; 4 rue Fabert, 75007 Paris, France.

Works:

Film costume designs include—*Breakfast at Tiffany's* (Edwards), 1961; *Charade* (Donen), 1963; *The VIPs* (Asquith), 1963; *Paris When It Sizzles* (Quine), 1964; *How to Steal a Million* (Wyler), 1966.

Publications:

On GIVENCHY: books—*Paris à la Mode* by Celia Bertin, Paris and London 1956; *Dressmakers of France* by Mary Brooks Picken and Dora Loues Miller, New York 1956; *Kings of Fashion* by Anny Latour, Stuttgart 1956, London 1958; *The Fashionable Savages* by John Fairchild, New York 1965; *The Fashion Makers* by Leonard Halliday, London 1966; *Fashion: An Anthology by Cecil Beaton,* exhibition catalogue compiled by Madeleine Ginsburg, London 1971; *In Vogue: Sixty Years of Celebrities and Fashion* by Georgina Howell, London 1975, 1978, New York 1976; *In Fashion: Dress in the Twentieth Century* by Prudence Glynn, London 1978; *25 Ans de Marie-Claire de 1954 a 1979,* compiled by Francoise Mohrt, Paris 1979; *The Guinness Guide to 20th Century Fashion* by David Bond, Enfield 1981; *The Collector's Book of Twentieth Century Fashion* by Frances Kennet, London and New York 1983; *McDowell's Directory of Twentieth Century Fashion* by Colin McDowell, London 1984; *The Encyclopaedia of Fashion from 1840 to the 1980s* by Georgina O'Hara, London 1986.

Simple mix-and-match separates, which emphasize feminine curves; wide use of accessories such as scarves; blouses and jackets with widened shoulders and puffed sleeves; two-part evening gowns, with choice of either décolleté or plain jersey top; an almost exclusive limitation to black and white; the penchant for basic fabrics, especially cotton: these are some of the early characteristics which helped propel Parisian fashion designer Hubert de Givenchy into instant fame in the early 1950's. Givenchy's debut, accomplished on what was by Parisian couturier standards a shoestring budget, was quite a spectacular, an imaginative display of women's fashions; geared toward originality and affordability for the wearer, the designs accomplished these goals with simple fabrics and outfitting that encouraged interchangeability of parts. A comparison of two of Givenchy's 1952 outfits exemplifies the multiple possibilities he found in black and white. Consider first his wrap bathrobe coat of black net worn over a softly figure-hugging, strapless, floor length, white satin evening gown, and second, his black alpaca skirt with high, stitched Flamenco waist teamed with a white cotton blouse that incorporates black and white Flamenco ruffles at the elbows of the wide sleeves. Accessories introduced at this time included a paper-lantern-pleated babushka, a Garbo-like slouch hat, straw slippers with bandana-knot toes, and a huge, multi-layered, white chiffon scarf bordered with navy-blue satin and worn knotted at the neck of his sleekly fitted, navy-blue gabardine suit.

Givenchy was only twenty-five in 1952 when he opened his own house in Paris, but he was already an accomplished dressmaker, having learned both the practical and theoretical ends of his profession during eight years spent working with Jacques Fath, Robert Piguet, Lucien Lelong (where he took Dior's place), and Elsa Schiaparelli. Four years after the commencement of his own salon, Givenchy met the established "institution" of Parisian couture, Cristobal Balenciaga, and began a lifelong friendship which was an important influence on his ideas and approach to style. Critical opinion during the next years was mixed as to whether Givenchy's resulting move away from the novel and toward a more cautious evolution led him into a kind of premature classicism or into a more timeless and conceptual approach, a steadily pursued course which in the long run would be to his lasting benefit. Following a basic cue from his prime mentor, Givenchy has expressed his beliefs in the nature of fashion design, seeing it as a discipline which should be a slow and steady evolution, dedicated to enhancing the meaning and movement of the human body, attentive to the needs of the changing times and concentrating also on the volume and proportions one puts on the body. He feels that fashion should allow adaption to personal style, resulting in an overall discreet mixture according to the individual's choices. During the 1960's, Givenchy was the choice of many notables such as Jacqueline Kennedy Onassis and Audrey Hepburn, both of whom have since gone on to different couturiers.

However, it is perhaps unfair to judge Givenchy on the basis of fame's currencies. His inventiveness and continuous striving to combine luxury with experiment, while not forgetting tradition, have earned him a prominent place among fashion designers of his time. It should not go unnoted that Givenchy the man—handsome, astute, patrician—is himself symbolic of the grand tradition of twentieth-century Parisian haute couture, which has generally waned with the current generation. Whether it is for his draped satin evening sheaths, his dresses embroidered with fruits, fish or bamboo, his tiny tambourine hats over chiffon scarves, or the touches of fur on many costumes, Givenchy has left an indelible signature in the book of high fashion design.

—Barbara Cavaliere

DE HARAK, Rudolph.
American graphic designer. Born in Culver City, California, 10 April 1924. Self-taught in design. President, Rudolph de Harak and Associates, New York, since 1959. Instructor in design, Parsons School of Design, New York, and Pratt Institute, Brooklyn, New York, 1973-78; Frank Stanton Professor of Design, Cooper Union, New York, from 1979; also visiting professor, School of the Visual Arts, New York, 1962-63, Carnegie-Mellon University, Pittsburgh, 1966, Kent State University, Ohio, 1976, University of Missouri, Virginia Commonwealth University, and Minneapolis College of Art, 1977, Kutztown State College, 1978, and Yale University, 1979, 1980. **Exhibitions:** American Institute of Graphic Arts, New York, 1964; Carnegie Mellon University, Pittsburgh, 1964. **Collections:** Museum of Modern Art, New York; Musée d'Art Moderne de la Ville, Paris; Museum für Angewandte Kunst, Vienna; Museum fur Kunst und Gewerbe, Hamburg; Stedelijk Museum, Amsterdam; National Museum, Warsaw; Israel Museum, Jeru-

Rudolph de Harak: Trademark logotype in mercury and incandescent lighting, for Kurt Versen Company, 1982

salem. Recipient: American Institute of Graphic Arts awards, 1960, 1963, 1964, 1965, 1968, 1970, 1977, 1978, 1979, 1980; Communication Arts awards, Palo Alto, 1969, 1971, 1973; American Institute of Architects award, 1971; Type Directors Club awards, New York, 1976, 1977, 1980; Art Directors Club of New York awards, 1977, 1978, 1980; Brno Graphics Biennale prize, 1979. Member: American Institute of Graphic Arts, 1957; Alliance Graphique Internationale, 1963. Address: 150 Fifth Avenue, New York, New York, 19911, U.S.A.

Publications:

By DE HARAK: book—*Posters by Members of the Alliance Graphique Internationale,* editor, New York, 1986.

On DE HARAK: books—*Graphic Designers in the U.S.A.,* edited by Henri Hillebrand, London, 1971; *Archigraphia* by Walter Herdeg, Zurich, 1978; *Architectural Signing and Graphics* by John Follis and Dave Hammer, New York 1979; *The Language of Graphics* by Edward Booth-Clibborn and Daniele Baroni, New York and London 1980; *Who's Who in Graphic Art,* edited by Walter Amstutz, Dubendorf 1982; *Top Graphic Design* by F. H. K. Henrion, Zurich 1983; *A History of Graphic Design* by Philip Meggs, New York 1983.

To design is to create, organize, and use form in many situations and relationships. Its purpose is to visually communicate diverse categories of information in an increasingly complex environment.

Design is a problem-solving process. But for many of us, it is more than that. It is also a very personal process of searching for and developing new concepts that serve to clarify and extend ideas. Herein lies the creativity of design.

The climate within which the designer works is very complex, and, as in all creative fields, at times, painful and frustrating.

The designer's work must satisfy the tastes and opinions of the client and successfully reach the audience for which it is intended. Even though it should be self-rewarding, frequently, personal preferences have little meaning in the solving of design problems.

To accomplish his or her tasks, the designer must be thoroughly experienced—at once blessed with imagination, and, additionally, familiar with tools, techniques, and production methodologies.

Finally, it is critical that the designer work with a strong commitment, be articulate, have the ability to listen, have human concerns, and be alert to social needs.

—Rudolph de Harak

DE LA RENTA, Oscar.

Dominican fashion designer. Born in Santo Domingo, 22 July 1932. Educated at Santo Domingo University; studied art, Academia de San Fernando, Madrid. Married Françoise de Langlade in 1967 (died, 1983). Staff designer, under Cristobal Balenciaga, Eisa fashion house, Madrid; assistant designer to Antonio Castillo, at Lanvin-Castillo fashion house, Paris, 1961–63; designer, Elizabeth Arden couture and ready-to-wear range, New York, 1963–65; partner-designer, in Jane Derby Incorporated, New York, 1965–69; chief executive and Richton International board member, in Richton's Oscar de la Renta Couture, Oscar de la Renta II, Oscar de la Renta Furs, and Oscar de la Renta Jewelry, New York, 1969–73; director, Oscar de la Renta Limited, New York, from 1973; also owner of Oscar de la Renta specialty shop, Santo Domingo, since 1968. Recipient: Coty American Fashion Critics' Winnie Award, New York, 1967, 1968; Neiman-Marcus Award, New York, 1968; Golden Tiberius Award, 1969; American Printed Fabrics Council Award, New York, 1971; Coty Hall of Fame Award, 1973; Fragrance Foundation Award, New York, 1978. Caballero of the Order of San Pablo Duarte, and Gran Commandante of the Order of Cristobal Colon, Dominican Republic, 1972. Address: 555 Seventh Avenue, New York, New York 10018, U.S.A.

Publications:

On DE LA RENTA: books—*Fairchild's Dictionary of Fashion,* edited by Charlotte Calasibetta, New York 1975; *The World of Fashion: People, Places, Resources* by Eleanor Lambert, London and New York 1976; *The Fashion Makers* by Barbara Walz and Bernardine Morris, New York 1978; *Fairchild's Who's Who in Fashion,* edited by Ane Stegemeyer, New York 1980; *The Collector's Book of Twentieth Century Fashion* by Frances Kennett, London and New York 1983; *McDowell's Directory of Twentieth Century Fashion* by Colin McDowell, London 1984; *The Encyclopaedia of Fashion from 1840 to the 1980s* by Georgina O'Hara, London 1986.

Today one of New York's most influential fashion designers, Oscar de la Renta was born in Santo Domingo of Spanish parents. His father, a successful insurance businessman, was disappointed when his only son failed to follow in his footsteps and instead went to Madrid to study painting. After his mother died, and his father refused to continue to pay for his artistic studies, de la Renta used his drawing skills to earn money, by selling fashion sketches to magazines. Some of his sketches for original dress designs were seen by the American ambassador's wife, Mrs. John Lodge, who hired him to design a debutante gown for her daughter Beatrice. The young woman's appearance in the de la Renta dress on the cover of *Life* magazine in 1956 prompted him to abandon painting and obtain a position on the staff of Balenciaga's world-famous couture house in Madrid. Working with Balenciaga convinced de la Renta to become a fashion designer. In 1961, he went to Paris, and on the strength of his sketches and the boasts about his dressmaking skills, he was hired by Antonio Canovas del Castillo. Before he began this new position, de la Renta returned to Madrid to take an accelerated two-week dressmaking and designing course so he would be prepared to handle the new job at Lanvin-Castillo, where he specialized in tailoring.

In 1963, de la Renta came to New York as a designer of the Elizabeth Arden couture and ready-to-wear collection, which specialized in clothing for elegant, conservative, and wealthy women. Two years later, de la Renta bought into the Seventh Avenue design firm of Jane Derby, where he became designer and partner. After Derby's retirement and subsequent death, that firm evolved into Oscar de la Renta, Incorporated. No longer producing custom designs, the new firm maintained essentially the same clientele: women who purchased simple, elegant, and expensive designs with a custom-made look. He added to this look an unmistakably feminine and romantic quality, which has retained its appeal throughout his work. In 1969, his successful business was brought out by the fashion conglomerate Richton International, under which he served as chief executive of four divisions and also as a member of Richton's board of directors. However, in 1973, de la Renta bought back full control of his organization, which continues to be one of the most profitable and well-known fashion design firms in the world.

De la Renta's flair for lush color and sensuous fabrics is undoubtably the result of his love for art, especially abstract art, and his youthful ambition to be a painter. His training in the European couture houses of Balenciaga and Lanvin-Castillo taught him high standards of taste and quality and a sense of the dramatic. His work for Elizabeth Arden instilled in him an appreciation for casual elegance. The European elitism of haute couture led to his emphasis on designs for "beautiful people." Another influence on his work has been his love of things Far- and Near-Eastern, as evidenced in his gypsy look of the 1960's, and in the decorating of his own home. His late wife Françoise de Langlade, the former editor of French *Vogue,* helped him attract many of the rich, famous, and glamorous women who share the same luxurious lifestyle for which de la Renta designs.

De la Renta has had tremendous influence on the fashion world. In the 1960's, his Russian and gypsy lines initiated the widely popular ethnic look. The very next season, his introduction of the *belle époque* look was also extremely popular and influential worldwide. His use of boldly printed fabrics, lush colors, and see-through fabrics have also been pace-setting.

The innovations with which de la Renta is credited have been successful because of their novelty and beauty but also because of his expert sense of timing. His ability to introduce new lines at just the right time has contributed to the acceptance of his work. Among his major innovations was the introduction in 1966 of a moderately-priced, designer, ready-to-wear line, the Oscar de la Renta Boutique. Other designers followed when they saw its success. De la Renta was also the first American designer to become popular in both the United States and Europe and to cater his designs to the sophisticated woman over thirty. In 1968, he was among the first high-fashion designers of women's clothing to design menswear. In 1969, he was the first high-fashion designer in the United States in whose business enterprise, Richton International, the public could invest on the stock market. He is also among the first to establish a foothold in Japan, where de la Renta is now a big name in fashion.

De la Renta's astute sense of business and design allows him to continue to design clothing that appeals to both the socialite and the working woman. His fashions have evolved from mostly lavish and expensive upper-class fashions to feminine yet practical clothing and accessories for today's active, professional woman. He is also aware that the socially elite are no longer the sole inspiration for fashions of the day. Women seek their own identities and styles. The working woman needs appropriate fashions for her career and her social life, and de la Renta's creations are attuned to these needs.

De la Renta's social conscience is indicated by his commitment to a Boy's Town type of home in Santo Domingo; for his charity there, he was presented the Dominican Republic's Grado Caballero, Order of San Pablo Duarte,

and the Grado Caballero de Commandante, Order of Cristobal Colon, in 1972.

—Elizabeth Douthitt Byrne

DELAUNAY, Sonia.
Russian painter, stage, textile and poster designer. Born Sophie Stern, in Gradizhsk, Ukraine, 14 November 1885; adopted uncle's family name, 'Terk' in 1890. Educated in St. Petersburg, until 1902; studied drawing and anatomy, Kunstakademie, Karlsruhe, 1903–04; painting, at the Académie de la Palette, Paris, 1905. Married the art critic Wilhelm Uhde in 1909 (divorced, 1910); the painter Robert Delaunay in 1910 (died, 1941); son: Charles. Independent painter and graphic artist from 1905, stage designer from 1918, and textile designer from 1921: worked in Paris, 1905–10, 1921–39, 1944–79, in Nantes, 1910–12, in Spain and Portugal, 1914–20, in the Auvergne, 1940–41, and in Grasse, 1942–44. Founder-member, with Robert Delaunay, Fredo Sides, Nelly Van Doesburg and others, of the Salon des Realites Nouvelles, Paris, 1939, and from 1946. **Exhibitions:** Nya Konstgalleriet, Stockholm, 1916; Galerie der Sturm, Berlin, 1920; Stedelijk Museum, Amsterdam, 1938; Städtisches Museum, Bielefeld, 1958; Musée des Beaux-Arts, Lyons, 1959; Galleria Civica d'Arte Moderna, Turin, 1960; Musée Rath, Geneva, 1964; Musée du Louvre, Paris, 1964; National Gallery of Canada, Ottawa, 1965; Musée des Arts Décoratifs, Paris, 1965; Musée National d'Art Moderne, Paris, 1967, 1975, 1985; Maison de la Culture, Amiens, 1968; Museum Arkiv för Dekorativ Konst, Lund, 1968; Maison de la Culture, Rennes, 1969; Carnegie Institute, Pittsburgh, 1969; Musée des Beaux-Arts, Le Havre, 1969; National Gallery of Victoria, Melbourne, 1969 (toured); University of Texas, Houston, 1970; Musée de l'Impression sur Etoffes, Mulhouse, 1971; Fundacao Gulbenkian, Lisbon, 1972; Musée des Beaux-Arts, Nancy, 1972; Musée d'Art Moderne de la Ville, Paris, 1972 (travelled to Washington, D.C.), 1977; Musée des Beaux-Arts, La Rochelle, 1973; New York Cultural Center, 1973; Kunsthalle, Bielefeld, 1974; Musée de Grenoble, 1974; Internationaal Cultureel Centrum, Antwerp, 1975; National Museum of Modern Art, Tokyo, 1979; Albright-Knox Art Gallery, Buffalo, New York, 1980; Art Institute of Chicago, 1981; House of Artists, Leningrad, 1986. **Collections:** Musée National d'Art Moderne, Paris; Musée des Arts Décoratifs, Paris; Centre de Documentation de Costume, Paris; Musée de l'Impression sur Etoffes, Mulhouse; Deutsches Spielkarten Museum, Bielefeld; Stedelijk Museum, Amsterdam; Museum of Modern Art, New York; National Gallery of Canada, Ottawa. Recipient: Gold Medal, Paris International Exposition, 1937; Grand Prix, International Women's Salon, Cannes, 1969; Grand Prix de la Ville de Paris, 1973; Stephan Lochner Medal, Cologne, 1974. Officier de la Légion d'Honneur, France, 1975. *Died* (in Paris) *5 December 1979.*

Works:

Simultaneous Dress body-painting garments, 1912–13.

La Prose du Trans-Siberien et de la Petite Jehanne de France book design, for Editions des Hommes Nouveaux, Paris, 1913 (with Blaise Cendrars).
Chocolat posters, for Chocolat Bensdorp, 1916–22.
Cleopatra ballet costumes, for Diaghilev's Ballets Russes, Paris, 1918.
Le Coeur à Gaz (T. Tzara) costumes, Theatre Michel, Paris, 1923.
B12 car styling and decoration, for Citroen, 1925.
Zig Zag advertisement sculpture in neon, for Société d'Electricité de France, 1936.
Mural panels in the Palais des Chemins de Fer and Palais de l'Air, at the Paris International Exposition, 1937 (with Robert Delaunay).
Exhibition stand at the Salon de l'Automobile, Paris, for Maison Berliet, 1957.
Simultané playing cards, 1959, produced by the Deutsches Spielkarten Museum, Bielefeld, 1964.
Matra B530 sports car styling and decoration, 1967.
International Women's Year poster, for UNESCO, 1975.

Publications:

By DELAUNAY: books—*L'Influence de la Peinture sur l'Art Vestimentaire,* lecture pamphlet, Paris 1927; *Tapis et Tissus,* Paris 1929; *Compositions, Couleurs, Idées,* Paris 1930; *Robes-Poèmes,* Milan 1969; *Alfabeto,* edited by R. Marconi and G. Niccolai, Venice 1970; *Nous Irons Jusqu'au Soleil,* Paris 1978; *The New Art in Colour: The Writings of Robert and Sonia Delaunay,* edited by Arthur Cohen, New York 1978.

On DELAUNAY: books—*New Interior Decoration* by Dorothy Todd and Raymond Mortimer, London 1929; *Sonia Delaunay,* exhibition catalogue by Bernard Dorival, Paris 1965; *Sonia Delaunay: tapis et oeuvres graphiques,* exhibition catalogue with text by Jacques Damase, Paris 1970; *Sonia Delaunay: Rhythms and Colours* by Jacques Damase, Paris 1971, London 1972; *Robert et Sonia Delaunay à Portugal* by Fernando Pernes, Lisbon 1972; *Sonia Delaunay: tapisseries,* exhibition catalogue with texts by Jacques Lassaigne and others, Paris 1972; *Sonia Delaunay* by Arthur Cohen, New York 1975; *La Rencontre: Sonia Delaunay—Tristan Tzara,* exhibition catalogue with texts by Jean Cassou and Jacques Damase, Paris 1977; *Sonia Delaunay: noirs et blancs* by Germain Viatte, Paris 1978; *Sonia Delaunay* by Bernard Dorival, Paris 1980; *Sonia Delaunay: Art in Fashion* by Diana Vreeland and Elizabeth Morano, New York 1986; *Sonia Delaunay: Magique Magicienne* by Dominique Desanti, Paris 1988.

Because she felt that abstract art allows for a wider vision of man and nature and opens new areas of sensitivity and perception, Sonia Delaunay produced from her earliest beginnings the now famous color rhythm series. Because she believed the essential premise that color is the basic element of the world, she used color to express emotion in all her work. The dynamism in her soft-edge geometric work allows both of these—form and color, added to her response to movement and motion—to give essence and character to her concerns.

Hers was no naive understanding of geometry and its relation to color and motion; it was never mechanical, always more organic and thus presented a rhythmic action that served her purposes. She was equally concerned with the spectator's relationship to her work. She felt that it had to be a transformation process, so that the spectator became more than a mere recipient, a responsive viewer who could react to the motion, form, and color. Thus, she did not limit herself to painting, but the painting influenced her other work: posters, illustrations, textiles, and even fashion design. This concern for all of the visual media she espoused as early as 1927 in a lecture she gave at the Sorbonne on fashion design and the importance and contribution of painting to this universal area.

Delaunay was a truly self-contained woman. Working with men at a time when the work of women artists was little known and respected, it never occurred to her that her collaborative and individual work was on anything less than an equal footing with the men and women—people such as Robert Delaunay, Blaise Cendrars, Sophie Tauber-Arp, Jean Arp—with whom she related both in her work and in her personal life.

She was a tireless worker, employing not only her work but also her writings and lectures to project her point of view. It is only within the last few decades that the true importance and meaning of her life's work has gained the belated recognition of scholars and critics. And for other artists of our time, women and men, she remains a source of inspiration.

—Mildred Constantine

DE LUCA, Jean-Claude.

French fashion designer. Born, of French parents, in Barcelona, Spain, 13 October 1948. Educated at Montcel private school, and Lycée Jaccard, Lausanne; studied law, at the University of Milan. Design assistant in Givenchy and Guy Laroche fashion houses, Paris, 1971–74; freelance designer, working with Dorothée Bis, Emanuel Ungaro and others, Paris, 1974–76; founder-director, Jean-Claude de Luca fashion company, Paris, from 1976: first menswear collection, 1983. **Exhibition:** *Design in Lace,* Musée Galliera, Paris, 1983. **Collections:** Musée de la Couture, Paris; Museum of Modern Art, New York. Address: 10 Avenue de l'Opéra, 7501 Paris, France.

Publications:

On DE LUCA: books—*The 1978 Fashion Guide* by Kaori O'Connor and Farrol Kahn, London 1978; *25 Ans de Marie-Claire de 1954 a 1979,* compiled by Francoise Mohrt, Paris 1979; *Fairchild's Who's Who in Fashion,* edited by Ann Stegemeyer, New York 1980; *Fashion 2001* by Lucille Khornak, London 1982; *McDowell's Directory of Twentieth Century Fashion* by Colin McDowell, London 1984; *The Encyclopaedia of Fashion from 1840 to the 1980s* by Georgina O'Hara, London 1986.

I design clothes for everyday wear, but luxurious clothes for the career woman who can afford to buy her own clothes. Clothes have to be like a visitor's card, a way of communicating with people—the clothes one wears being *you* and therefore translating one's character visually.

I try to keep in mind when designing a collection that clothes have to have a note of humour and poetry. The important thing is to remain curious about things at all levels. The

mind has to be inquisitive and alert to new ideas, but foremost I believe in luxurious, natural fabrics used in new ways. My favorite colours are white and black, because they allow numerous possibilities to produce striking, classic, and stylish outfits. I believe in subtle changes of mood and ideas.

I am now very interested in painters as a motivation in my way of working—especially Goya: the colours, the forms, the construction—which goes hand in hand with my passion for the opera. My training in law studies has permitted me to use a certain meticulous and strict way of working—but it has not hindered progress by any means, only helped. I like active women who are sexy but not frivolous, who use their charm but not falsely: I like beautiful city girls, not feminine girls—and I design for these women. I design clothes for the really fulfilled woman, socially and career-wise, who knows how to get ahead. She has her head well sorted out and needs clothes that are stylish, luxurious, but comfortable and sporty, with a hint of humour and harmony of colours. I am a city person who loves the city life, the city's stimulus.

—Jean-Claude de Luca

After spending a year and a half with Givenchy, Jean-Claude de Luca thought that the ready-to-wear world would be the best in which to work, as the majority of women could not afford couture prices. He sold some designs to Dorothée Bis, and Ungaro commissioned a prêt-à-porter collection from him for 1974. After that, in 1976, de Luca opened on his own. He considers Paris a second-rate city, good only at fashion, with no theatre or ballet of note, but knows that fashion is important. "Clothes are your image," he insists, for clothes speak of group identity and social status, as well as fulfilling a fundamental physical necessity. De Luca likes best the basic garments—the waistcoat, jacket, and trousers,—but he updates them by using contrasting fabrics, such as cotton and wool. He believes textiles will be increasingly important, in view of all the research going on to produce new types.

A graduate in law, de Luca can appreciate the needs of the professional woman, but one must query why he expects her to look like Superman. This was the theme of his 1978–79 collections, with shoulders built out like American football players', martial suits, officers' capes, metal buttons, and marching boots. Although this design approach contrasts strongly with his statement that he wants clothes to be practical and to fit daily activity, he repeated the mistake in 1980 with his Space Age look, which included brief tunics, tights, and again, boots. Does he really expect professional women to go to the office attired like Gestapo chiefs or Martians? Practical clothes are those which do not impede the wearer and do not leave her ill-covered in climatic extremes.

The root problem with male designers for women is that they do not wear the garments themselves. Wearing a brief tunic at a bus stop in rain or frost would be a good starting lesson, as would trying to type when loaded with enormous shoulders. Molyneux told Balmain and Dior that the first question to ask is whether the creation if wearable. There is still plenty of time for de Luca to study this approach, as he is still in his early stage, exercising his imagination. One hopes that he will sit down and work out what exactly women have to do and design clothes for that activity, which is mainly humdrum, not filled with romantic adventures at Waterloo or on other planets. It is the same lesson most young designers must learn, as they almost invariably start with fantasy.

—Diana de Marly

DE LUCCHI, Michele.

Italian industrial, interior, exhibition and graphic designer. Born in Ferrara, 8 November 1951. Educated at the Liceo Scientifico Enrico Fermi, Padua, 1964–69; studied architecture, University of Florence, 1969–75: Dip.Arch. 1975. Freelance designer, collaborating with designers Andrea Branzi, Gaetano Pesce, Ettore Sottsass Jr., the Superstudio group and others, in Milan, since 1973: consultant to Centrokappa, Milan, 1978, and Olivetti Synthesis, from 1979. Founder-member, with Piero Brombin, Boris Premru and Valerio Tridenti, of Gruppo Cavart, Padua, 1973–76; founder, with Ettore Sottsass Jr., Barbara Radice and others, of Memphis furniture design group, Milan, 1980. Professor of industrial design, Università Internazionale dell'Arte, Florence, 1976–77. **Exhibitions:** *Un'Idea per i Monti Ricchi,* Galleria Images 70, Abano Terme, 1973; *Esplorazione sul Territorio Corpo,* Galleria Stevens, Padua, 1975; *Laboratorio Indoor,* Studio Eremitani, Padua, 1976; *Il Design negli Anni '50,* Centrokappa, Milan, 1977; *Design Phenomène,* Forum Design, Linz, 1980; *Una Generazione Post-Moderna,* Palazzo Bianco, Genoa, 1982; *Memphis,* Arc 74, Milan, 1982 (toured); *Ricerca per un Ambiente d'Ufficio Olivetti,* at the Milan Triennale, 1983; *Michele De Lucchi: A Friendly Image for the Electronic Age,* Amsterdam, 1985. Addresses: Via Cenisio 40, 20154 Milan; Via Vittoria Colonna 8, 20149 Milan, Italy.

Works:

Il Design Italiano negli Anni '50 exhibition layouts, for Centrokappa, Milan, 1977.
Sinerpica and *La Spaziale* lamps, for Alchymia, 1978.
Tarkin chair, for Thema, 1978 (with M. Matzukase).
Series 45 CR office furniture, for Olivetti Synthesis, 1980 (with Ettore Sottsass Jr.).
Via Giulini office and showroom interiors in Milan, for Olivetti Synthesis, 1980.
Icarus office furniture, for Olivetti Synthesis, 1981 (with Ettore Sottsass Jr.).
Terrific and *Fantastic* ceramic plates, for Abet Print, 1981.
Kristall table, for Memphis, 1981.
Peter Pan armchair, for Thalia, 1981.
Shop interiors in Milan, for Fiorucci, 1981 (with Ettore Sottsass Jr.).
Gabbia furniture system, for Alchymia, 1981.
Fortune trestle table, for Memphis, 1982.
Vega glass lamp, for Vitosi, 1982.
Calcutta marble coffee table, for Up & Up, 1982.
Pool armchair system, for Matau, 1982.
Lido divan, for Memphis, 1982.
President coffee table, for Memphis, 1983.
Rotor, Roll and *Round* lamps, for Bieffeplast, 1983.
Cyclos wall lamp, for Artemide, 1983.

Publications:

By DE LUCCHI: books—*Architetture Verticali,* Florence 1968; *Solid: Un Nuova Collezione di Oggetti per la Casa,* editor, Milan 1987; articles—in *Parametro* (Faenza), June 1976; *Japan Interior Design* (Tokyo), December 1976; *Modo* (Milan), May 1979, January/February 1980; *Space Design* (Tokyo), December 1979; *Donna* (Milan), April 1980, September 1980; *Casa Vogue* (Milan), September 1980; *Abitare* (Milan), November 1981; *Ufficio Stile* (Milan), June 1982; *Domus* (Milan), September 1982; *Nikkei Architecture* (Tokyo), February 1983; *Sumo* (Milan), March 1983; *Interni* (Milan), May 1983.

Michele de Lucchi: *Cyclos* **wall lamp, for Artemide, 1983**

On DE LUCCHI: books—*Homo Trahens* by Gruppo Cavart, Florence 1976; *Dalla Citta la Cucchiaio* by Bruno Orlandoni, Turin 1977; *Memphis: The New International Style* by Barbara Radice, Milan 1981; *Design Process: Olivetti 1908–83,* with text by Renzo Zorzi, Milan 1983; *The Hot House: Italian New Wave Design* by Andrea Branzi, London 1984; *Michele De Lucchi: A Friendly Image for the Electronic Age,* exhibition catalogue Amsterdam 1985; *Memphis: Objects, Furniture and Patterns* by Richard Horn, New York 1986; *Italian Design: 1870 to the Present* by Penny Sparke, London and New York 1988.

The image of technology is different from actual technology, and there exist a lot of possibilities within the image of technology. We are living in an epoch of consumerism. Our way of communicating with each other is mass-produced. We see it as sophisticated technology, for example, when the Japanese produce a stereo that is matte black and silver. We recognize it immediately as such because the "image" of sophisticated technology is matte black. Today we use more images, and the images we use are very sophisticated. People who work with images deal in a kind of iconology, a very sophisticated iconography. The ideal is to have a catalogue of iconography that exists today and to use this iconography to open up possibilities.

I chose household objects that we have in our homes—objects that everybody uses, but no one would think to design—to explore the possibilities. We see a vacuum cleaner, but we don't think about the image of the vacuum cleaner. My feeling is that the vacuum cleaner is a mass-produced object that is also a means of communicating. It is possible to communicate an image with a vacuum cleaner. When I design a vacuum cleaner—even if it is only decorative—it will change the technology. As the design of the shell changes, there will be changes on the inside. The designer creates the job. Technology fills the design. Decoration will change the way the object is perceived, the very nature of design. Not to just make a lamp, but that this lamp will change the very idea of lamps. It's not that this lamp or this vacuum cleaner is the best lamp or best vacuum cleaner, or that this is the final lamp or vacuum cleaner, but that each will change the whole idea—a very little—of the way we conceive design.

I'm working on designing the idea of design. The traditional designer works with the manufacturer whose idea is to produce something that will become a best-seller. Then there are designers with a longer view. Ettore Sottsass was the first to say that when you design an object, you don't just design the object but also the environment in which the object will be put. And you also design the behavior of the people who will use the object. The idea was to open the possibilities of design so that people could exercise their creativity, but we realize that most people need to have models. By seeing a model of change, the consumer is able to see the possibilities of change.

—Michele De Lucchi

At thirty-seven, architect Michele De Lucchi is fairly famous, mostly for his striking, architectural-like furniture and industrial designs. He is probably best known for his work done for Memphis (founded in 1980) and that done in collaboration with his friend and mentor, Ettore Sottsass.

De Lucchi uses bright colors and bold forms in his designs, in an attempt to foster different sensations/responses from the viewer/user, which often appear more like child's toys (his prototypes for a vacuum cleaner and a hair dryer (1979) look like multi-colored pull-toys; *Kristall* (1981) has a bright yellow round table sprouting from a black and white diagonally-striped "box" supported on thin metal feet; *Lido* (1982) a multi-colored sofa which appears to have been resurrected from a psychedelic bus or, perhaps, an amusement park; and *Peter Pan* (1981), a proposed tubular steel frame chair which could be dressed/undressed in upholstery of many patterns and colors) than "serious" furniture. This is perhaps his greatest strength and, potentially, his greatest weakness—whether the eventual user will consider his work more than "fun" or an "object d'art" and really appreciate their value as usable items without all the stereotyped restrictions of the "real" world. His work has often been called "ludicrous," to which De Lucchi replies: ". . . the word 'ludicrous' can certainly be used provided it refers to the demystification of a particular image of technology: the sort of technology that's remote, difficult and inaccessible. After all, technology is really quite simple and banal, and is intended to help you." He elaborates that ". . . Design can push technology, because design can help technology to be understood . . . technology is only a factor which affects design . . . if a lower keyboard is required during the design of a computer, then a technological solution must be found."

De Lucchi sees that products, which may now be in fashion for five years, will soon be "in" for only one year. Replacement will be at a faster pace. He is "a strong believer" in consumerism, "the only factor which we can't eliminate and which assures the success of technology and industry." He does not treat it in the "political or social sense," but "in the context of fashion and consumption." He feels that "this is not decadence," but "a high level of sophistication concerning our relationship with the things around us."

Michele De Lucchi is currently working on a variety of projects for Olivetti and various producers of interior furniture and lighting.

—William Victor Kriebel

DE MAJO, W(illem) M(aks).
British graphic and industrial designer. Born of Yugoslav nationality, in Vienna, Austria, 25 July 1917; emigrated to Britain in 1939: naturalized, 1947. Studied at the Commercial Academy, Vienna; also attended classes on commercial art, under Professor Puchinger, Vienna Urania Polytechnic. Served in Royal Yugoslav Air Force, attached to British Royal Air Force, 1941–43, in War Ministry, London, 1944, and Royal Air Force at SHAEF, in Africa, Middle East and Europe, 1945–46: Flight Lieutenant; MBE. Married Veronica Mary Brooker in 1941 (separated); daughters: Monica, Francesca and Sarina. Freelance designer, in Belgrade 1936–39, and in London since 1946: art director, Moda of Belgrade, 1938–39; former design consultant to Miles-Martin (Biro) Pen Company, Sir Henry Lunn Limited, Miles Aircraft, British Overseas Airways, W. & A. Gilbey, Clayton Brothers, B.N.T. Limited U.K., Philips NV, Charles Letts and Company; currently, to John Millar and Sons (1884) Limited, Ti-Wells Limited, and Micron CA of Caracas. Founder and President, ICOGRADA International Council of Graphic Design Associations, 1963; guest speaker at numerous professional institutes and congresses. **Collections:** Victoria and Albert Museum, London; ICOGRADA Visual Archive, London and Reading, Berkshire. Recipient: Design Medal, Society of Industrial Artists and Designers (now Chartered Society of Designers), London, 1969; Commemorative Medal, ZPAP Association of Polish Artists and Designers, 1983. Honorary Member: GVN Graphic Designers Association, Netherlands, 1959; SAFT/SRF Swedish Advertising Association, 1965; CBG Belgian Chamber of Graphic Designers, 1966; GDA Graphic Design Austria, 1988. Address: 99 Archel Road, London W14 9QL, England.

Works:

Corporate identity programme, for Moda fashion store, Belgrade, 1938–39.
Interiors and gift products, for RAF Air Division Giftshop, Detmold, Germany, 1945–46.
Biro showroom interiors, displays and packaging, for Miles-Martin Pen Company, London, 1946–52.
Cigarette lighter packaging, displays and showroom interiors, for Ronson Products, 1948–63.
Ulster Farm and Factory exhibition layouts at the Festival of Britain, London, for the Government of Northern Ireland, 1950–51.
Fruit drinks and mineral water corporate identity programme and packaging, for Clayton Brothers, 1950–68.
Smirnoff Vodka and Perrier water promotional products and displays, for W. and A. Gilbey, 1950–66.
Exhibition displays at the Bulawayo Rhodes Centenary Exhibition, for the Schlesinger Organization of Johannesburg, 1953.
Corporate identity programme, interiors and displays, for John Millar and Sons (1844) Limited, from 1953.
Hand tools corporate identity programme and packaging, for Brades-Nash and Tyzack Industries, 1954–58.
Animated symbol, for ABC TV television corporation, London, 1956–57.
Corporate identity programme, packaging and displays, for Transparent Paper Limited, 1957–63.
Tricot jersey corporate identity programme, packaging and displays, for Ets. St. Joseph, Paris and Bordeaux, 1960–67.
The BP Story exhibition layout, for the Baden-Powell Memorial Fund, 1961–62.
Design programme and displays at the National Advertising Exhibition in Olympia, London, for Adex Limited, 1962.
Carson's Chocolates gift packaging, for Carson Limited, 1965–66.
Corporate identity programme, packaging, display and product design, for Charles Letts and Company, 1966–68.
Gift matches and presentation packs, for Neiman-Marcus, 1972.
Corporate identity programme, for Brentford Football Club, Middlesex, 1975–76.
Corporate identity programme, packaging and product designs, for Ti-Well paper products, Leather goods, for W. and A. Goold, 1984–86.

Publications:

By DE MAJO: articles—"Light and Structure" in *Print* (New York), July 1955; "Design for Prosperity versus Design for Posterity," *Design Quarterly* (Minneapolis), vol. 36, 1956; "Design of Gift Packs" in *Packaging,* Zürich 1959; "Single Biggest Problem in the Design Field Today" in *Print* (New York), January 1961; "Conquering Export Markets Through Better Package Design" in *International Trade Forum* (Geneva), vol. 2, 1966; "One Man's Paper is Another Man's Problem" in *British Printer* (London), 28 March 1969; "Bibliography: Signs and Sign Systems" in *Print* (Washington, D.C.), November 1969; "Design '81 in Helsinki" in *Graphic Design* (Tokyo), December 1981; "Balloon Graphics" in *Graphic Design* (Tokyo), March 1982.

On DE MAJO: books—*Who's Who in Graphic Art,* edited by Walter Amstutz, Zurich 1962, Dubendorf 1982; *All Things Bright and Beautiful* by Fiona MacCarthy, London 1972; *A Tonic to the Nation* by Mary Banham, London 1976; *Minerva at Fifty* by James Holland, London 1980.

I was not exactly a great scholastic success at school, not being too keen on regimentation and discipline; my fertile mind seemed to get bored rather easily, resulting in my being a somewhat lazy student. However, once I was allowed to do my own thing, I quickly developed single-mindedness of purpose and perseverance which I have retained ever since. From an early age, I showed an interest in forms and colours, and I spent many hours sketching and developing ideas. My father could not see much future in my becoming an "artist" and as he had hoped that I would follow in his footsteps and eventually take over the successful export and import business which he had built up, I was sent to the Commercial Academy in Vienna, where we lived at the time. Alas, I did not enjoy my business training. When around 1935 my father decided that the family should return to Belgrade, his native town, we agreed that I would work half the day for him as personal assistant and sales representative and the other half for myself as a commercial artist. It was a strenuous period, with many late evenings trying to do two jobs and not many design commissions. Even when one did get a job, it was badly paid. But I pressed on. I sold my first poster to one of the local dress-material shops and my first commissions for advertisements followed from a small advertising agency. At the same time, every morning when I had to go out trying to sell my father's range of goods, mainly Czechoslovakian textiles, linoleum from Kirkcaldy, ties from Manchester and Italy, and various other goods, my heart sank. Although the products were all of good quality, their decorative designs were hideous. So I figured that the only way in which I could overcome my dilemma was to try to jump across the fence and become the person who creates the product. I reasoned that if a product were to be well designed, whoever manufactured it would enjoy doing his job. At the same time, the sales representative would be proud to sell it, and the end user happy to buy it. Little by little, I developed and implemented this theory and was lucky to find clients who believed in me and gave me opportunity and encouragement. Thus, quite soon, aided by an inbred flair, and a considerable amount of cheek and courage, believing that almost nothing was impossible if one set one's mind to it, I succeeded in expanding my activities and experience. In early 1939, I had decided to emigrate, and the early war years found me in England where I did a number of unusual jobs. They varied from being a lumberjack in Shropshire to joining the BBC Overseas Service as a news typist and broadcaster. From the end of 1941 until 1946, I served as an Officer and Pilot in the Royal Yugoslav Air Force, seeing war service in Africa, the Middle East and Europe, and was later transferred to the Royal Air Force. On my demobilization and after a brief, not very successful spell as an exporter, I got the chance of a lifetime, which I grabbed with both hands. I was offered the job of display designer for the Miles Martin Pen Company's new Biro showrooms. This was soon followed by my appointment as consultant designer to the company, as well as to Sir Henry Lunn and Miles Aircraft, and things have progressed ever since. By the 1960's, I had been commissioned to design a great variety of items from a visiting card through stationery, publicity materials, products in paper, cardboard, leather, wood, glass, metal, plastics and textiles to point-of-sales material, carpets, ties and leather goods, liveries for transportation fleets, including vehicle bodies and the interior decoration scheme for a four-engined airliner. New challenges were designing the Baden-Powell museum exhibit and a number of extensive corporate identity programmes.

Willem de Majo: Corporate identity, packaging, product and exhibit designs

I have always been a great believer that integrated design plays an important part in any successful business, and by working over such a wide field, I feel that I can be more creative, bringing to the problem on hand a varied experience from different disciplines. The requirements for a successful designer are varied. They will consist, though not necessarily in this order, of some of the following:

An imaginative and quick mind.

The capability of absorbing information and details and a good memory.

A willingness to put in long hours, if necessary, and to try an unusual yet analytical approach.

A methodical mind, keen on attention to detail.

An ability to establish a clear and detailed design brief and to allow sufficient time for the job yet be able to work under pressure when required.

The ability to stay within budgets.

Above all, belief in what he is doing.

He must never lose his integrity even though he may have to make compromises on occasions. He needs to be a good salesman in order to put over his products and proposed solutions. He must be loyal to his client, yet remember the great moral responsibility he has as a designer; in many instances, he is the link between customer and manufacturer, and very often, the difference between success and failure of a job may rest in his hands. Sometimes, it is important that a designer should produce a solution which the client may have never dreamed he wanted or realised that he needed, in preference to just doing what the client may have asked for or thought that he required. Like a Queen's Counsellor, while he is not expected to know all the answers, he must know where to find them.

To me, good design, whether two-dimensional, like visual communication, publicity, or information design, or three-dimensional, like product design, is organic, something which grows and changes, develops and expands. No one part of it can be solved in a vacuum without a thorough understanding of the whole.

—W. M. de Majo

Among W. M. de Majo's many assets, four assure his reputation. First is his organizational ability. Few would deny that the formation of ICOGRADA (the International Council of Graphic Design Associations) in 1963 was Willy de Majo's personal achievement. Without his patience, perseverance, and endless persuasion, the Council would not have come into being. Today, this Council has an important international voice in the world of design, representing as it does more than 40,000 graphic designers from some 30 countries. From 1963 to 1965, de Majo was the first president of ICOGRADA, and he has held many other important posts, among them chairmanship of the first study group of the International Council of Societies of Industrial Design.

Second, one notes his enterprising and progressive outlook. Willy de Majo has the ability to absorb quickly a complex situation and come up with a practical solution to its problems. He is also able to project ahead and, based on his considerable experience, come up with answers to problems which, on the surface, may seem insoluble. These factors make him one of the significant catalysts and pioneers of the design profession. His work covers a spectrum of activity so wide that it would handicap most designers. However, de Majo makes use of this breadth by cross-germinating one medium with another. At the same time, he gives attention to the full range of a client's concerns, from manufacturing to sales to consumer problems. These aspects are always seen in their relations and brought into focus.

Third is his professional competence, manifested by close attention to the minutest detail from the various stages of manufacture to the actual marketing. There is often visual and physical pleasure in the experience of holding an object, such as a book of matches or a diary, which has come through the stages of production supervised by him. In all his work, there is clarity and directness which are, of course, the prime elements of the end product.

Fourth, one remarks his abundant energy. His overall achievement, both in practising design and in international organization, is rare in the business of communication. One assumes that his energy derives from his colourful past in Vienna, Belgrade, and Paris. After forty years of input, the design profession has recognized his rich contribution with numerous awards from many countries.

In the world of design W. M. de Majo has become one of the most sought-after lecturers. In May 1988, for example, as former president, he opened the Oslo ICOGRADA Congress celebrating its 25th anniversary. In June that year he was Guest Speaker at the 13th Biennale of Graphic Design in Brno, Czechoslovakia; in July, a jury member of the Crystal Design Award and Speaker at the design symposium Visual Communication Design; and in October, Guest Speaker at Graphic Design/Austria's Annual General Meeting, *Design is a Profession,* when he was awarded honorary membership of the GDA for outstanding contribution in the field of graphic design and for the advance of the profession.

—John Halas

DESIGN RESEARCH UNIT.

British architectural, interior, graphic and industrial design group. Founded by Marcus Brumwell and Herbert Read, with Misha Black and Milner Gray as founder-partners and senior consultants, in London, 1943. Current directors: William Furbisher (born 1930), James Williams (born 1927), Robert Yull (born 1928), Ian Liddell (born 1933), George Freeman (born 1930), Maurice Green (born 1944), Richard Dragun (born 1945), and Steve Simmons (born 1949). Associates: Peter Anspach and Ray Finch. Consultants: Milner Gray, John Allwood and Basil Fahmi. The group has designed products and programmes for W. and A. Gilbey, Chase Manhattan Bank, British Petroleum, James Catto, Ekco Plastics, Vickers, Morphy Richards, Watney Mann, Carreras, British Railways Board, Unilever, Hong Kong Mass Transit Railway, Mobil Oil, etc. Recipient: Design Centre Awards, London, 1957, 1960, 1967; Silver Medal, Milan Triennale, 1958; Starpacks Merit Awards, 1960, 1962, 1963, 1966; Civic Trust Awards, London, 1962, 1965, 1966, 1967; Shell Award, London, 1966; British Stationery Council Award, 1966; Design and Art Directors Association Award, London 1967. Address: 94 Lower Marsh Street, London SE1 7AB, England.

Works:

Regatta Restaurant and Dome of Discovery displays, at the Festival of Britain, London, 1948–51.
Corporate design programme, for Courage Limited, 1950.

British Rail corporate design programme, for the British Railways Board, 1956–66.
Pyrex ovenware, for James Jobling, 1957.
Public rooms on the liner *Oriana,* for Pacific and Orient Shipping Company, 1957–60.
Guards cigarette packaging, for Carreras, 1960.
Whisky bottles, labels and packaging, for James Catto, 1960–62.
Wine and spirits bottles, packaging and decanters, for W. and A. Gilbey, 1960–66.
Stocking packs, for Berkshire, 1962.
Signposting at West London Air Terminal, Heathrow, for British European Airways, 1965.
Gilbey House distillery and offices at Harlow, for W. and A. Gilbey, 1965.
Logotype symbol and letterhead, for Tarmac Limited, 1966.
Charles Clore Pavilion for Mammals at London Zoo, for the Zoological Society, 1967.
Ilfoprint film processor, for Ilford Photographic Equipment, 1967.

Publications:

On DESIGN RESEARCH UNIT: books— *British Furniture Today* by Erno Goldfinger, London 1951; *Design in British Industry: A Mid-Century Survey* by Michael Farr, Cambridge 1955; *Furniture in Britain Today* by Dennis and Barbara Young, London 1964; *Signs in Action* by James Sutton, London and New York 1965; *Modern Graphics* by Keith Murgatroyd, London 1969; *The Practical Idealists: 25 Years of Designing for Industry* by John and Avril Blake, London 1969; *Communication by Design: A Study in Corporate Identity* by James Pilditch, Maidenhead 1970; *Design Matters* by Bernat Klein, London 1976; *British Design Since 1880* by Fiona MacCarthy, London 1982.

In retrospect, the Design Research Unit can be seen as the logical expansion of the prewar, multi-skill Industrial Design Partnership operated by Misha Black, Milner Gray, and Kenneth Bayes. But it soon became a more idealistic pioneer of flexible and detailed service to meet the more inclusive needs of postwar design. Throughout its existence, the Design Research Unit has led the way in developing the technique and practice of detailed investigation and high-level consultation in creating a design brief. This procedure often involves extensive research, as was the case with the re-design of Bata International's European shoeshops in the 1960's; for this project, two graphic designers and two architects went to 114 shops in eight countries.

Through its wide range of associate designers (often with their own practices) and through internal discussion, the Unit has championed the idea of design as a cooperative activity "since it believes that only by pooling the talent of a team of designers is it possible to offer a service capable of meeting every demand from the wide and varied field of present-day industry." In its long life, the Unit has experienced a number of complete management reorganisations and many changes of staff, but it has always tried to operate on these democratic principles once humourously referred to by Black as "sympathetic disharmony." The idealism has always been matched by a close attention to budgeting and scheduling, largely under the direction of Mary Goslett, whose *Professional Practice for Designers* (1961) has profoundly influenced the practical internal organisations of design practices generally.

Although its early reputation relied heavily on the successful careers and contacts of its senior partners and its part in a number of important postwar exhibitions—including *Britain*

Design Research Unit: Argyle Station, on the Hong Kong Mass Transit Railway, 1979–80

Can Make It (1946), *Design at Work* (1948), and the culminating *Festival of Britain* (1951)—the Design Research Unit's most influential period came later, with the opportunities created by greater economic prosperity. It never fully achieved its ideal of providing a completely comprehensive design service, but competence in handling large interior design contracts made it one of the most respected practices and one of the biggest. The range of these contracts was surprisingly wide—from layouts and decoration of the public areas of the steamship *Oriana* (1959) to the small mammal house for London Zoo (1967). The Unit has also been involved in some environmental planning to refurbish parts of Norwich and Burslem and in a host of small product-design projects, such as the design of a gas meter. Nevertheless, the most influential achievements have been the corporate design programmes worked out for such household names as the brewers Courage (1950) and Watney Mann (1960), the photographic company Ilford (1946–66), Dunlop (1962), tailors Austin Reed (1954), and British Rail (1956–66).

—Anthony J. Coulson

DESKEY, Donald.
American interior, packaging and industrial designer. Born in Blue Earth, Minnesota, 23 No-

vember 1894. Studied at the University of California, Berkeley, 1915–17; Art Institute of Chicago, 1918–19; California School of Fine Arts, San Francisco, 1919–20; Ecole de la Grande Chaumière, Academie Colarossi, and Atelier Leger, all in Paris, 1920–22. Served in the United States Army, 1917–18. Married Mary Douthett in 1921 (divorced, 1946); sons: Michael and Stephen; married Katharine Godfrey Brennan in 1952. Freelance designer, since 1926: established Donald Deskey Associates, New York, 1935–75, opening branch offices in London, Frankfurt, Milan, Copenhagen and Stockholm, in the 1950s and 1960s. Professor of Art, Juniata College, Huntingdon, Pennsylvania, 1922–24; Professor of Industrial Design, New York University, 1930–36; also lecturer at Massachusetts Institute of Technology, Harvard Business School, and other universities. **Exhibitions:** Metropolitan Museum of Art, New York, 1934; *The Machine Age in America 1918–1941,* Brooklyn Museum, New York, 1986. **Collections:** Metropolitan Museum of Art, New York; Art Institute of Chicago; Philadelphia Museum of Art; Yale University Gallery, New Haven, Connecticut; Virginia Museum of Fine Arts, Richmond; Cooper-Hewitt Museum, New York. Address: 270 Island Creek Drive, St. John's Island, Vero Beach, Florida 32963, U.S.A.

Works:

Display windows, for Saks and Company, Fifth Avenue, New York, 1926–27.
Apartment interiors on Park Avenue, New York, for Adam Gimbel, 1927.

Soda fountain and beauty salon in Brooklyn, for Abraham and Straus, 1928–30.
Apartment renovations on West 54th Street, New York, for Abby Aldrich Rockefeller, 1929–31.
Radio City Music Hall interiors, Rockefeller Center, New York, 1932.
Apartment interiors at Radio City Music Hall, New York, for Samuel L. (Roxy) Rothafel, 1932.
House interiors in Mount Kisco, New York, for Richard H. Mandel, 1933–35.
International Casino interiors at 1526 Broadway, New York, 1937.
Development of Weldtex board, for United States Plywood Corporation, 1940.
Design of all U.S. showrooms, for Bigelow-Sanford Carpet Company, 1945–52.
Begins prefabricated housing, for Shelter Industries Incorporated, 1946.
Techniplan office furniture, for Globe-Wernicke Company, 1948–54.
Packaging designs, for Procter and Gamble, 1949–76.
Corporate identity program, for Sinclair Refining Company, 1954–56.
Marco Polo Club interiors at the Waldorf-Astoria Hotel, New York, 1959.
Packaging and interiors, for Johnson and Johnson, 1959.
Wall Street Club interiors on Chase Manhattan Plaza, New York, 1960–62.

Publications:

On DESKEY: books—*The Story of Modern Applied Art* by Rudolph Rosenthal and Helena L.

Ratzka, New York 1948; *Packaging: An International Survey of Package Design,* edited by Walter Herdeg, Zurich 1959; *Design in America* by Ralph Caplan, New York 1969; *The Decorative Thirties* by Martin Battersby, London 1969, 1974, 1976; *The Streamlined Decade* by Donald J. Bush, New York 1975; *80 Years of Ideas and Pleasure from House and Garden,* edited by Mary Jane Pool and Caroline Seebohm, London 1980; *Industrial Design* by John Heskett, London 1980; *American Design Ethic* by Arthur J. Pulos, London and Cambridge, Massachusetts 1983; *The Conran Directory of Design,* edited by Stephen Bayley, London 1985; *Design Source Book* by Penny Sparke and others, London 1986; *The Machine Age in America 1918-1941* by Richard Guy Wilson and Dianne H. Pilgrim, New York 1986; *Donald Deskey: Decorative Designs and Interiors* by David A. Hanks and Jennifer Toher, New York 1987; *American Art Deco* by Alastair Duncan, New York 1987; *The American Design Adventure 1940-1975* by Arthur J. Pulos, Cambridge, Massachusetts 1988.

Despite forty years of an active professional life which has encompassed nearly every phase of design, Donald Deskey is best known—indeed, one might say singularly known—for the furnishings and interiors he developed for Radio City Music Hall in 1931. Readers of design history might even be excused for assuming that his contribution to the field consists solely of the private suite he created for the guiding spirit of that entertainment enterprise, "Roxy" Rothafel, since this environment, which used some of the most advanced materials of the day, is a staple in illustrated texts on the Art Deco period.

Deskey thus appears to have little accomplishment behind him, save for the one interior—although, admittedly, that interior is both a tour de force and a monument to the unabashedly exuberant 1930's. It is only with difficulty that we unearth references to his extensive work in graphics, advertising, display, exhibition, interior architecture, and product design. In his relative anonymity, however—which contrasts with the well-publicized careers of some of his early contemporaries such as Norman Bel Geddes and Raymond Loewy—he is the archetype of today's designers who are generally unknown even though their designs and concepts may have national impact.

He may also be said to be prototypical in that his career mirrors the development of design from applied art to profession. Prior to World War II, Deskey and other American artists blended the *arts décoratifs* of the Paris exposition of 1925 with the typographic inventions of the Bauhaus, and turned to illustration, graphic design, and advertising. The application of art to commerce that was advertising was soon extended to product design, and graphic artists were in great demand when merchants realized that esthetics would be profitable. Suddenly, Deskey and others like him were asked to turn their hand to windows, displays, exhibitions, costumes, products, and interior spaces. The best of them helped to transform merchandising practises and to create the Deco style characteristic of the 1930's.

World War II ended the society to which Deskey responded, and the post-war years were characterized by the faceless monoliths of the International Style. However, the pre-war decorative chutzpah, only partially civilized by a theatrical neo-classicism, has recently resurfaced as post-modernism. Deskey himself is not contributing to this revival, but his work lies as its roots, just as it lies at the roots of the design industry he helped create and to which he was until recently a versatile contributor.

—Reed Benhamou

DESSAU, Ingrid (Peterson).

Swedish textile designer. Born in Svalov, Malmö, 3 March 1923. Studied at the National College of Art, Craft and Design, Stockholm, 1939-45. Worked as a designer, for the Handcraft Society of Kristianstad County, Sweden, 1945-49; designer, Kasthallcarpet factory, Kinna, 1954-75, and for Kinnasand textile company, Kinna, 1970-84; freelance textile designer, working for Hitex, Kinnasand, and as a textile consultant, in Malmo, since 1984. **Exhibitions:** *Hantverkets, 60-tal,* Nationalmuseum, Stockholm, 1968; *The Lunning Prize,* Nationalmuseum, Stockholm, 1986; *Faces of Swedish Design,* IBM Gallery, New York, 1988 (toured). **Collections:** Nationalmuseum, Stockholm. Recipient: Lunning Prize, 1955. Address: Sanekullavägen 40 F, 217 74 Malmö, Sweden.

Works:

Zig Zag double-weave cotton fabric, for Kinnasand, 1981.
Carpets and fabrics, for the Parliament Building, Stockholm, 1983.

Ingrid Dessau: *Herringbones* tapestry, 1981

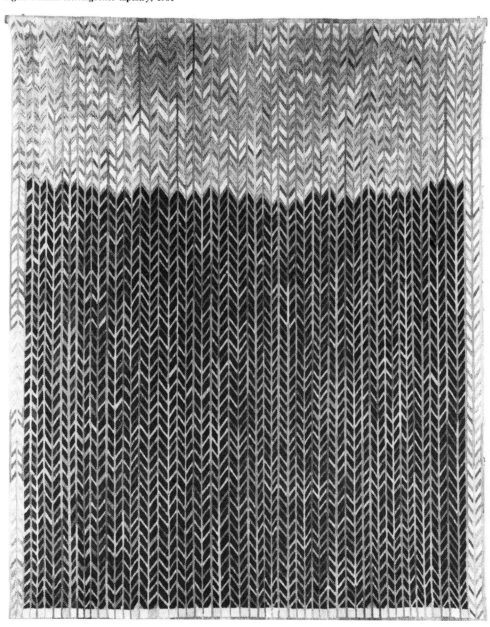

Joplin linen-weave furniture fabric, for Kinnasand, 1985.
Dixie hand-knotted wool carpet, for Kinnasand, 1986.
Basin Street hand-woven high and low pile carpet, 1986.
Blue Swell hand-tufted carpet, for Hitex, 1987.

Publications:

On DESSAU: books—*Svensk Form/Forma Sueca* by Ake Stavenlow and Ake H. Huldt, Stockholm 1961; *Scandinavian Design: Objects of a Life Style* by Eileene Harrison Beer, New York 1975; *Den Svenska Formen* by Monica Boman and others, Stockholm 1985; *The Lunning Prize,* exhibition catalogue edited by Helena Dahlback Lutteman and Marianne Uggla, Stockholm 1986; *Faces of Swedish Design,* exhibition catalogue edited by Monica Boman, Stockholm 1988.

I prefer to work with carpets. They give a room an important base, and they can also serve as a decorative element. Carpets have a scale and architectural dimension which interests me. I have worked to a large extent with architects. My ultimate aim is trying to give vibrancy to what is simple.

—Ingrid Dessau

Suddenly a pattern swarms densely with . . . what? Fish. Fishbones swaying at an angle, fishbones of various sizes, pulsating and lively. Behind them you can imagine Ingrid Dessau's vigorous laughter. Normally, fishbones represent a strict weaving pattern, well under control, a given code. Here they have liberated themselves from the abstraction and swarm freely across the handwoven surface. Thus can a mature artist allow herself to play freely when she has her base in a superb sense of form. And thus can Ingrid Dessau bloom. She has devoted her life to examining the possibilities of weaving techniques, and transforming them into an infinite number of variations in simple, geometrical patterns. Abstract patterns which also resound to the joy and the confirmation of life, patterns which have made her both respected and loved.

The fishbone pattern is part of a collection of handwoven heavy pile carpets which the Swedish textile company Kinnasand has had woven in India.

"Now it's all coming out," says Ingrid Dessau, pleased with her new collection. Several years of intensive development work are now producing the best possible results. India has an unbelievable amount of know-how and fantastic traditions. But the will to do a perfect job lay fallow as long as purchasers asked only for the very cheapest carpets. In this case, the high standard of quality required has given a technical and artistic lift to both Kinnasand and the Indian weavers. In addition the carpets are woven under humane conditions. This was a condition set by Ingrid if she was to take on this task at all.

The first carpets had clean patterns with mirror images, friezes and corners. They were soft as velvet and smooth. Their spare design and simplicity of color brought something new and refreshing to the traditional heavy pile carpets. And they have been highly successful.

They were as simple as possible and that was what was lacking at the time. They could fit in with a variety of settings. They were produced in strong, happy, normal colors.

The latest collection consists of carpets of twisted, double-threaded yarn, which gives a coarser and more grainy surface. These are dense, more individual, and with more detailed patterns. One is characterized by reliefs, another is more "avant garde," and yet another features the fishbones. There is a variety of coloring: dark plum, celadon, blue-gray, charcoal, gray-green, clear, dark purple and dark red.

Ingrid Dessau prefers to work with carpets. They give a room its all-important base, and can also serve as a decoration. They have a scale and architectural dimension which suits Ingrid's temperament. For this reason she has worked to a large extent with architects—a much appreciated colleague who has made the fabrics for many interiors. Her major projects have included the textile program for the Swedish parliament building and Government House, which were renovated in the early 80's. Both were unusually advanced projects, both artistically and from the point of view of organization.

"I have more to do than I have time for," Ingrid says. She retired from Kinnasand in 1984 and has worked as a freelance since then. Her larger works have included the Indian carpets and handtufted carpets for Hitex. Collaboration with Hitex is important for her interior decoration assignments, and usually involves specially composed carpets. Usually such jobs

have to be done quickly: the carpets come into the construction picture at a late stage, and then it's good to be able to do them in Sweden. The handtufted carpets also include much of the life and quality of a handwoven carpet.

Ingrid Dessau's interior fabrics for Kinnasand have so far offered the pleasure of an exquisite use of bindings in understandable geometrical patterns, series of variations in white on white, colorful double weaves and rhythmical humorous striping.

"I often begin with complicated patterns, but I peel them away bit by bit. What I make must fit in with a lot of other things."

Ingrid Dessau began her professional career at a famous hand-weaving factory and with the Swedish Handcraft Association, heavy with tradition. Her strong interest in the technical side gave her new forms of expression. She has since transferred her skill in hand weaving to industry, by testing the technical possibilities to their utmost.

"I am very particular," she admits.

But in the end it's a matter of diligence, discipline, a feeling for quality, and self-criticism based on a solid knowledge of the market. This is balanced by an imaginative flow of patterns which appear in a steady stream of sketches. The ultimate aim is to give vibrancy to what is simple.

—Gunilla Lundahl

DIFFRIENT, Niels.

American industrial designer. Born in Star, Mississippi, 6 September 1928. Educated in Detroit public schools, until 1943; Cass Technical High School, Detroit, 1943–46; Cranbrook Academy of Art, Bloomfield Hills, Michigan, 1948–51 and 1952–53: BFA 1953; Wayne State University, Detroit, 1951–52; Fulbright Fellowship in Design and Architecture, working with designer Marco Zanuso, Milan, 1954–55. Married Lois Newell in 1952 (divorced, 1969); children: Scott, Julie and Emily; married designer Helena Hernmarck in 1976. Designer and modeler, at Eero Saarinen Associates, Bloomfield Hills, Michigan, 1948–53; staff designer, Walter B. Ford Associates, Detroit, 1953–54; designer and partner, Henry Dreyfuss Associates, New York, 1955–81; founder-principal, Niels Diffrient Product Design, Ridgefield, Connecticut, since 1981: consultant to Ford Motor Company, Philips Corporation, Texas Instruments Inc., and Howe Furniture Company. Assistant Professor-in-Residence, University of California at Los Angeles, 1960–69. Board Member, 1970, and Vice-President, 1975, Industrial Design Society of America; Advisory Board Member, Art Center College of Design, Pasadena, California, since 1972; Board Member since 1974, Chairman, 1975, and Treasurer, 1976, International Design Conference, Aspen, Colorado; Advisory Consultant, 1972, and Policy Panel Member, 1980, National Endowment for the Arts, Washington, D.C.; President, International Design Education Foundation, 1976; Editorial Board Member, *Industrial Design* magazine, New York, 1977–89. **Exhibitions:** *Niels Diffrient: Knoll Seating,* Cranbrook Academy of Art Museum, Bloomfield Hills, Michigan, 1980; *New Design for Old,* Boilerhouse/Victoria and Albert Museum, London, 1986; *Ceremonial Lights,* Israel Museum, Jerusalem, 1987; *Furniture as Object,* Aetna Institute/

Gallery Jazz, New York, 1987; *397 Chairs,* Architectural League, New York, 1988. **Collection:** Cranbrook Academy of Art Museum, Bloomfield Hills, Michigan. Recipient: First Medal in Design, Cranbrook Academy of Art, 1949, 1950, 1951; First Prize, Packard Automobile Design Competition, 1951; First Prize, Michigan Recreational Center, 1952; Compasso d'Oro Award, Milan, 1957; United States Government Award for Design for the Handicapped, 1970, 1974; American Institute of Graphic Arts Award, 1972; Design and Environment Award, 1976; Resource Council Award, New York, 1979, 1981; Institute of Business Designers Award, 1979, 1980, 1984; Designers Choice Award, *Industrial Design* magazine, New York, 1980, 1982, 1985; Design Excellence Award, Industrial Design Society of America, 1980, 1985; United States National Award for Transportation Design, 1981; *Time* magazine Best of 1982 Award, 1982; Gold Medal, American Institute of Architects, 1989. DHL: Art Center College of Design, Pasadena, 1975. Fellow, Industrial Design Society of America, 1971; Honorary Royal Designer for Industry, Royal Society of Arts, London, 1987. Address: 879 North Salem Road, Ridgefield, Connecticut 06877, U.S.A.

Works:

Automated portable sewing machine in die-cast metal, for Borletti Company, 1956 (with Marco Zanuso).

High-voltage electricity pylons in steel, aluminium and wood, for the Edison Electric Institute, 1964.

High-voltage sub-station in Covina, California, for the Southern California Edison Company, 1967.

Airplane interiors of the Boeing 747, 767, 727, 707 and Douglas DC-10, for American Airlines, 1968–80.

High capacity lift truck in steel plate and iron castings, for Hyster Company, 1972.

Pneumatic Hyway Vibrating Compactor heavy-duty roller, for Hyster Company, 1974.

Human Factors information product in 3 volumes with graphic selector, for MIT Press, 1974, 1978.

Upholstered executive office chair in steel and aluminium casting, for Knoll International, 1978.

Task Seating series of upholstered office chairs with die-formed steel shell, for Knoll International, 1978.

8-passenger business jet interiors, for Gates Learjet Series 50, 1979.

Reclining upholstered office seating series in steel and aluminium, for Sunar Hauserman Company, 1982.

Reclining task chair and accessories in aluminium, steel and thermoformed plastic, for Sunar Hauserman Company, 1984.

Publications:

By DIFFRIENT: books—*Electrical Transmission Structures,* editor, New York 1965; *Humanscale 1/2/3,* with Alvin R. Tilley and Jean C. Bardgajy, Cambridge, Massachusetts 1974; *Design of Experience,* Minneapolis 1975; *Humanscale 4/5/6,* with Alvin R. Tilley and David Harman, Cambridge, Massachusetts 1981; *Humanscale 7/8/9,* with others, Cambridge, Massachusetts 1981.

On DIFFRIENT: books—*Design and Environment* by Ann Ferebee, New York 1976; *Chair* by Peter Bradford and Barbara Prete, New York 1978; *Niels Diffrient: Knoll Seating,* exhibition catalogue edited by Katherine McCoy, Birming-

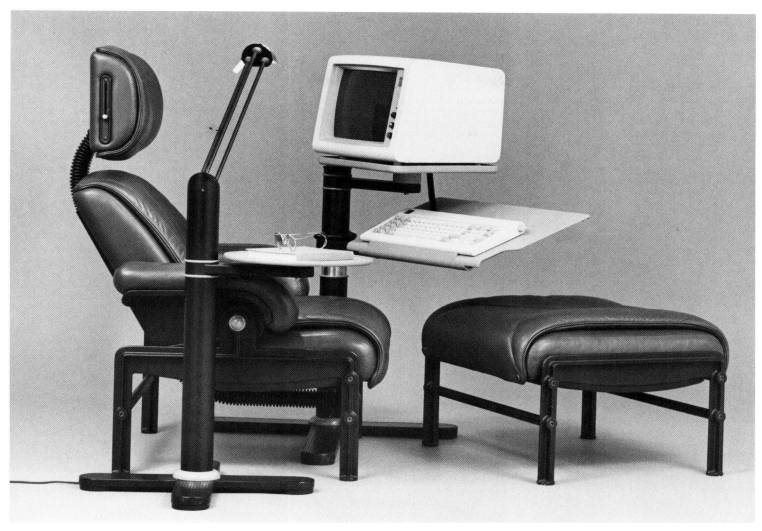

Niels Diffrient: *Jefferson* **reclining task chair system, for Sunar Hauserman, 1984**

ham, Michigan 1980; *Knoll Design* by Eric Larrabee and Massimo Vignelli, New York 1980; *The Conran Directory of Design,* edited by Stephen Bayley, London 1985; *The American Design Adventure 1940–1975* by Arthur J. Pulos, Cambridge, Massachusetts and London 1988.

My principal interest is in design for mass production—the products of daily use manufactured in quantity for large numbers of people. My goal is to achieve a combination of elegance and performance in mass-produced products to equal the fine products of the handcrafts. The constraints inherent in this pursuit are imposed by the separate demands of marketing, manufacturing, and engineering. In contrast to handmade products for which the designer is also the fabricator who transacts directly with the user and, most certainly, gets direct feedback on the product's performance, especially if it fails, those mass-produced products that are my goal must be achieved in the face of certain difficulties: someone else makes the products, they are sold to people you don't know, and you never gain sufficient information about how they work.

Designing is a practical art. In other words, it combines art and practicality. Art, as such, serves no practical purpose. To be successful at designing for practical use, the art as esthetics and amenity must be so inherent and natural in the performance of the product that it is not conceivable to have one without the other except at considerable sacrifice.

Objects that achieve this highly desirable state have been normally approached by one of two paths. The first has been going on for some time and springs from technical goals. Objects which are true to a clear function, such as boats and airplanes, are nearly always handsome. The other avenue is more recent and approaches the task from an esthetic basis on the tacit assumption that the object that looks right will work right. Neither of these paths achieves consistent success and rarely fulfills its potential. Most often the traditional goals of either extreme form the ultimate measure of accomplishment and override concerns of the other.

The missing ingredient is a comprehensive measure of accomplishment. The technician is satisfied if the electro/mechanical performance is successful at a good price, and the esthetic designer is satisfied if the product wins a design award. Neither result is complete, and the simple combination of the two would still leave something out. By better understanding the experience provided by the product, I believe it might be possible to surpass parochial professionalism and achieve designs that are less self-conscious and more elegantly natural. All practical design includes performance, that is, how it functions in relation to the user—not just how the gears mesh or the electrons react, but whether it provides a positive experience, does its job, and possibly satisfies a deeper emotion. When the level of performance between product and person reaches an exquisite level of interaction, conceivably esthetic in nature, then its appearance will be as natural as its technical

elements; it will exceed the need for applied fashion but will at the same time create it.

—Niels Diffrient

Niels Diffrient is an industrial designer whose professional accomplishments include aircraft interiors, construction equipment, high-voltage transmission towers, and sewing machines, but his reputation may rest ultimately on his designs for office seating. Previously well-known within his profession, he has achieved wider notoriety since the introduction of Knoll's Diffrient Seating (1979) and Sunar's Helena chair series (1982). These are technologically sophisticated office chairs engineered for high-volume production and featuring clearly articulated adjustment and control mechanisms. Conceptually, they exemplify Diffrient's thorough knowledge of mechanics and industrial processes: "Once you understand the tools, then you can design the parts."

Diffrient graduated from Cranbrook Academy in the generation following Charles Eames, Florence Knoll, and Eero Saarinen. He went to work for Saarinen in the late 1940's as model maker. It was here, while preparing Saarinen's first Knoll designs for production, that he became aware of the shortcomings of an industry that, paradoxically, utilized traditional handicraft technologies to produce modern furniture. From that experience, Diffrient became convinced that for good design to reach the widest possible audience it must be mass-produced. "To do something . . . that will be produced by the most advanced techniques, and produced in the millions, . . . that is where the fascination (lies) for me," he has stated. His enthusiasm is tempered, however, by a concern for human factors.

Early in his career, he was exposed to the science of human engineering as a protégé of Henry Dreyfuss, a pioneer in that field. Through collaboration with Dr. Janet Travell, who had treated President John F. Kennedy for back problems in the early 1960's, Diffrient has developed a keen, almost evangelical design philosophy which places human comfort above other design criteria. An unabashed functionalist even as the fashion grows to repudiate that thinking, he is nonetheless wary of some easy answers to be found in that approach. Of the Bauhaus pioneers, he says, "I don't think those folks cared whether the chair was comfortable. . . . They were mainly interested in . . . counter-(ing) . . . the Beaux-Arts tradition." Diffrient's own, frequently unusual, design solutions are the result of a mature understanding of an object's intended function. His approach to problem-solving involves the constant reworking of existing solutions until, by one final refinement or inspirational leap, the design becomes uniquely his own—and perhaps uniquely useful.

—Kenneth Gaulin

DOBLIN, Jay.

American design planner and industrial designer. Born in New York City, 10 December 1920. Studied industrial design, under Alexander Kostellow, Rowenna Reed, Donald Dohner and Gordon Lippincott, at the Pratt Institute, Brooklyn, New York, 1939–42: Honor Student Award, 1942. Married Annette Woodward in 1949. Designer of camouflage and other government projects, 1942–49, and of projects for Frigidaire, Shell Oil, Nabisco, Coca-Cola, Singer, British Petroleum, etc., at Raymond Loewy Associates, in New York and Chicago, 1950–55; co-founder, with Ralph Eckerstrom and others, and senior vice-president, of Unimark International design company, Chicago, 1964–72; freelance planning consultant, establishing Jay Doblin and Associates, Chicago, 1972–89; consultant to J. C. Penney, Standard Oil of Indiana, Borg-Warner, General Electric, Xerox Corporation, American Hospital Association, Beatrice Foods, etc. Director of the Industrial Design Evening School, Pratt Institute, Brooklyn, New York, 1948–52; Professor and co-director, 1955–69, and Adjunct Professor of Design Theory from 1978, Institute of Design, Illinois Institute of Technology, Chicago; Professor, School of the Art Institute of Chicago, 1975–78; Visiting Professor, Graduate School for Business Studies, London, 1980. Vice-President, 1956–57, President, 1957–58, Board Member, 1956–64 and 1977–80, and Board Chairman, 1958–59, Industrial Designers Society of America; Design and Education Adviser, Japanese Ministry of International Trade and Industry, 1959; Vice-President, ICSID International Council of Societies of Industrial Design, 1960–80; President, Industrial Design Educa-

tors Association, Chicago, 1963–64; Board Member, International Design Conference, Aspen, Colorado, 1963–67; Advisory Board Member, *Industrial Design* magazine, New York, 1974, and Design Management Institute, New York, 1980. Recipient: Fellow, 1959, Distinguished Design Program Award, 1974, and Personal Achievement Award, 1982, Industrial Designers Society of America; Kaufmann International Design Award, New York, 1964; Distinguished Alumnus Award, Pratt Institute, New York, 1973, Honorary Fellow: Society of Typographic Arts, Chicago, 1979; Royal Society of Arts, London, 1980. *Died* (in Chicago), *11 May 1989.*

Publications:

By DOBLIN: books—*Perspective: A New System for Designers,* New York 1955; *100 Great Product Designs,* New York 1969.

On DOBLIN: books—*Il Disegno Industriale e la sua Estetica* by Gillo Dorfles, Bologna 1963; *Design in America* by Ralph Caplan, New York 1969; *A History of Design from the Victorian Era to the Present* by Ann Ferebee, New York 1970; *The Conran Directory of Design,* edited by Stephen Bayley, London 1985; *An Introduction to Design and Culture in the Twentieth Century* by Penny Sparke, London 1986; *The American Design Adventure 1940–1975* by Arthur J. Pulos, London and Cambridge, Massachusetts 1988.

I began as a hardgoods designer with Raymond Loewy in New York. It was during Loewy's most prolific years; he had a staff of more than 100 and many major accounts, including Pennsylvania Railroad, Studebaker, Coca-Cola, Frigidaire, Greyhound, Singer, etc. He gave me the opportunity to design dozens of major products. After ten years, Loewy made me head of their newly formed marketing group. We did full-scale redesigns of Shell, BP, Nabisco, etc. The experience changed me; I now thought of design as systems composed of integrated disciplines rather than products.

By 1955, after fifteen years, I had lost interest in commercial design for giant companies. I accepted the directorship of the Institute of Design at Illinois Institute of Technology. This school, founded by Moholy-Nagy, was being joined to Mies van der Rohe's School of Architecture in Mies's newly finished Crown Hall. This was a fresh challenge.

During the fourteen-year period at the Institute of Design, I went through two phases. In the beginning, I oriented the school and myself to do simple, clear, uncommercial design. I felt that this was where design would go. It succeeded: the work was fresh and useful. But in the mid-1960's, it became clear that the computer would change design, so we changed the school's central emphasis to systems design methodology. It wasn't the machine itself but the disciplined algorithmic thinking that computer-assisted design required. This was an explosive revelation to me. I worked enthusiastically at this time for ten years at the school and at Unimark (a new design firm I co-founded with Ralph Eckerstrom and others in 1965).

By the mid-1970's, I changed again; I began doing large-scale corporate design planning. One, for J. C. Penney, co-ordinated 300 designers in eight design activities (products, packaging, interiors, exteriors, catalogues, advertising, internal communications, and displays). Later, I did similar assignments for Standard Oil, Xerox, American Hospital Association, Beatrice Foods, Borg-Warner, etc. This history may sound like a straight development from product design to systems of products to corporate de-

sign planning, with an increase of complexity at each stage. But paralleling this has been a deep interest in design theory. Now, no client has ever paid me for theory. They don't want it. In fact, they freeze when they're exposed to it. And yet, this is my central interest. My problem is that I'm not smart enough to solve the essential design-theory problems. And large-scale corporate design planning involves business strategy and organization (which includes politics). Both of these are frustratingly difficult for me; my early background as a hardgoods designer does not support these. So, as someone once said, I've reached my level of incompetence at both theory and design planning. The decision for those who reach this point is to either go back to where they can operate competently or to keep at it and hope one's competence rises to meet the problems. I am confronted by this.

During my early and middle years, I wanted to be where I now am. But now that I'm here, I wonder why I did it when I was so happy and productive in the earlier stages. My present goal is to develop theories of design that will support the emergence of a profession from what is now a practice or trade. Compared to law, management, consulting, architecture, accounting, advertising, and even interior design, product and message design is a small, low-grade activity. The reason I'm so interested in doing this is that product design, the prime control of how industrial output should impact culture, ought to be respected and well supported.

—Jay Doblin (1984)

Designer, planner, professor, theorist, Jay Doblin was in the forefront of the industrial design profession after his graduation from the Pratt Institute in 1942. He was a practical designer, a planner, a visionary. He taught design, wrote about design, and proselytized about the mission of the designer.

Doblin began his career in the 1940's as a product designer for Raymond Loewy, one of the great practitioners, in his heyday. As executive designer, he worked on many product programs and took particular pride in having contributed to such hit products of the 1950's as the Edison Voicewriter. Although a good draftsman and a practical designer, he seems to have found new challenges in establishing and directing Loewy's marketing design group. Later, as Vice-President of Unimark and as a consultant, he worked on design and product planning for large corporations, devising new and original techniques of analysis and problem-solving. His work for J. C. Penney earned the Industrial Design Society of America's 1974 Award for Distinguished Design Programs. He has come to be considered a multi-talented designer, able to analyze highly complex, interactive, business and design problems and to propose innovative and holistic solutions.

Always interested in education and possessing a natural flair for teaching, Doblin maintained a close connection with educational institutions throughout his professional career. At the Institute of Design, where, as Director, he was successor to László Moholy-Nagy and inheritor of the Bauhaus tradition, he brought a new focus to the industrial design program, emphasizing professional orientation and practice. His classroom experience and his love of theory undoubtedly contributed to the fresh and critical evaluations which Doblin brought to a variety of design problems. He lectured widely and wrote about design process, planning and evaluation. Doblin believed in speaking out on issues he considered to be important. Invariably, others listened.

—Benjamin deBrie Taylor

DONATI, Danilo.

Italian stage and film costume designer. Born in Luzzara, in 1926. Studied art in Florence. First stage designs, for opera productions of Luchino Visconti, Rome 1955; film designer, working notably with directors Pier Pasolini and Federico Fellini, in Rome, from 1962; supervising art director, RAO television network, Rome. Recipient: Academy Award and British Academy Award, 1968, 1976. Address: via Due Macelli 31, 00100 Rome, Italy.

Works:

Film costume designs include—*La Steppa* (Lattuada), 1962; *Rogopag* (Pasolini and others), 1962; *Il Vangelo Secondo Matteo* (Pasolini), 1964; *La Mandragola* (Lattuada), 1965; *El Greco* (Salce), 1966; *Uccellacci e Uccellini* (Pasolini), 1966; *The Taming of the Shrew* (Zeffirelli), 1966; *Oedipo Re* (Pasolini), 1967; *Romeo and Juliet* (Zeffirelli), 1968; *La Cintura di Castita* (Festa Campanile), 1968; *Porcile* (Pasolini), 1969; *Medea* (Pasolini), 1969; *Satyricon* (Fellini), 1969; *La Monaca di Monza* (E. Visconti), 1969; *I Clowns* (Fellini), 1970; *Il Decameron* (Pasolini), 1971; *Roma* (Fellini), 1972; *I Racconti di Canterbury* (Pasolini), 1972; *Fratello Sole, Sorella Luna* (Zeffirelli), 1972; *Il Fiore delle Mille e Una Notte* (Pasolini), 1974; *Amarcord* (Fellini), 1974; *Salo, o le 120 Giornate di Sodoma* (Pasolini), 1975; *Caligula* (Brass), 1976; *Casanova* (Fellini), 1976; *Hurricane* (Troell), 1979; *Flash Gordon* (Hodges), 1980; *Ginger e Fred* (Fellini), 1985.

Publications:

On DONATI: books—*Le Decor de Film* by Leon Barsacq, Paris 1970, as *Caligari's Cabinet and Other Grand Illusions*, Boston 1976; *On the Set of ''Fellini-Satyricon''* by Eileene Lanouette Hughes, New York 1971; *The Classic Cinema* by Stanley J. Solomon, New York 1973; *Pier Paolo Pasolini: Trilogia della Vita*, edited by Giorgio Gattei, Bologna 1975; *Luchino Visconti: Il Mio Teatro*, 2 vols., edited by C. D'Amico and R. Renzi, Bologna 1979; *The International Dictionary of Films and Filmmakers*, London and Chicago 1987, 1991.

Danilo Donati has to his credit costume and set designs for an impressive list of memorable cinematic and theatrical productions, many of which depict great classics of opera, the Bible, Greek tragedy, Shakespeare, and others, as interpreted according to some of the most important contemporary film and stage directors of Italy. After his training in Florence as a muralist and fresco painter, Donati spent several years as supervising art director at RAI, Italy's national television network. During the 1960's, he realized some of his finest achievements in the designs he created for the movies of Pasolini, Fellini, and Zeffirelli. During the same period, he also did costumes for the stage, one of the most flamboyant examples being the work he did for *Festa italiana*, a spectacle and ball staged by Gino Landi, Italian choreographer of television spectaculars, and held at New York's Madison Square Garden in 1966. For the occasion, Donati dressed Roman charioteers, flag throwers, gladiators, medieval knights, and more; made wild, orange tarantella costumes; and came up with a resplendently somber, medieval scene in black-and-white for dancers who re-enacted the live chess game which is held every year in Marostica.

One of Donati's more recent projects consists of costumes and sets he created for Dino De Laurentis' adventure-fantasy movie, *Flash Gordon*. It took more than seven months to make the 600-plus original, futuristic costumes for the extravaganza, for which Donati also did massive sets that filled 250,000 square feet at three London studios. From the ancient to the futuristic, Donati's designs have covered the centuries, including contemporary costumes for movies such as Fellini's *Roma* (1972) and early Fascist-era outfittings for Fellini's highly acclaimed portrait of adolescence in the Italy of that time, *Amarcord* (1974).

It is Donati's flair for the lavish and historic which has earned him a serious and lasting position as designer. His five Oscar nominations (including two wins) alone serve as ample exemplar of the central character of his contribution to the history of movie costume and set design. *La Mandragola* (1966), *The Gospel According to Saint Matthew* (1964), *The Taming of the Shrew* (1967), *Romeo and Juliet* (1968), *Casanova* (1976): the list reads like a who's who of outstanding contemporary Italian cinema. The work he has accomplished with Fellini alone is evidence enough of the high-caliber movies with which Donati has been associated. *Satyricon* (1969), *Roma* (1972), *Amarcord* (1974), *Casanova* (1976): this list of some of Fellini's finest achievements demonstrates Fellini's continued confidence in Donati's particular abilities, even as it suggests the breadth of the challenge Donati has faced in his field. It also brings to mind the general situation of the costume and set designer whose work can easily be overlooked in light of the fame of the filmmaker, while the contribution of the costume designer is too often taken for granted. Over his career, Donati's work has been well-researched historically, fittingly elaborate or simple, always attuned to the overall effect of the movie as a whole. And these are the signs which point to a knowledgeable and inventive designer for the entertainment media.

—Barbara Cavaliere

DONZELLI, Rinaldo.

Italian graphic, industrial and corporate designer. Born in Mariano Comense, near Como, 12 September 1921. Educated at the Scuola Secondaria di Avviamento Professionale, Como, 1932–35; mainly self-taught in design. Served in the Italian Army, 1941–45. Married Giuseppina Rosa Molteni in 1948; children: Mariapia, Anna, Silvia, Palo, Elena, Elisabetta, Giovanni and Alberto. Worked in a sawmill and a carpenter's shop, Como, 1936–38; independent portrait painter, Como, 1938–41; freelance designer, from 1945: design consultant, Motogilera motorcycle company, Arcore, Milan, 1950–64, and Motoguzzi motorcycle company, Mandello del Lario, Como, 1965–72. Address: Via Isonzo 87A, 22066 Mariano Comense (Como), Italy.

Publications:

By DONZELLI: books (also illustrator)—*Lavori in legno,* co-author, Milan 1978; *Disegnare una persona,* Bologna 1979.

On DONZELLI: books—*Design e forme nuove dell'arredamento italiano,* edited by Paolo Portoghesi and Marino Marini, Rome 1978; *Atlante del design italiano* by Alfonso Grassi and Anty Pansera, Milan 1980; *Da cosa nascecosa* by Bruno Munari, Bari, Italy 1981.

Find the interesting—the useful—the true—immediately.

To be Donzello
requires Rinaldo
to stay a young fellow.

—Rinaldo Donzelli

Rinaldo Donzelli: Trade mark for Motoguzzi motorcycle company

DORFSMAN, Louis.

American graphic designer. Born in the Bronx, New York, 25 April 1918. Studied at Cooper Union, New York, 1936–39: BFA 1939. Served in the United States Army, 1943–46. Married Ann Hysa in 1940; children: Elissa, Mitchell and Neil. Worked as exhibit and display designer, for the New York World's Fair, 1939, and as director of training films for the United States Navy, 1940–43; joined Columbia Broadcasting System as a designer, New York, 1946: vice-president of advertising and sales promotion, CBS Radio, 1959–69; director of advertising and sales promotion, CBS Television Network, 1960–64; director of design, 1964–68, and vice president of advertising and promotion from 1968, CBS Inc., New York. Instructor, at New York Workshop School of Design, and Cooper Union, New York. Board Member, International Design Conference, Aspen, Colorado; trustee, Cooper Union, New York. **Exhibitions:** American Institute of Graphic Arts, New York; Cooper Union, New York; Washington University, St. Louis. **Collections:** Museum of Modern Art, New York; Metropolitan Museum of Art, New York. Recipient: Special Citation, 1956, and Augustus St. Gaudens Medal, 1963, Cooper Union, New York; Gold Medal, Philadelphia Print Club, 1962; Gold Medal, American Institute of Graphic Arts, 1978; Hall of Fame Award, 1978, and 13 Gold Medals, Art Directors Club of New York. Address: CBS Inc., 51 West 52nd Street, New York, New York 10019, U.S.A.

Works:

Living Off the Main Line newspaper advertisement, for CBS Radio, 1951.
The Importance of Good Connections magazine advertisement, for CBS Radio, 1954.
Summertime Promotion Kit brochure, for CBS Radio, 1955.
Impact magazine advertisement, for CBS Radio, 1957.
CBS Preview 62 promotional packaging, for CBS Television, 1962.
The Rocket's Red Glare . . . magazine advertisement, for CBS Television, 1962.
CBS Mid-Season Promotion promotional packaging, for CBS Television, 1964.
Daytime Program Promotion promotional packaging, for CBS Television, 1963.
Typographic assemblage mural, for the CBS cafeteria, New York, 1963.
What in the World's Going On Here? newspaper advertisement, for CBS Television, 1966.
Of Black America newspaper advertisement, for CBS Television, 1968.

(From 1962, Dorfsman also planned the office and working space interiors of the new CBS building on 52nd Street, as well as re-designing the signage, and all stationery and printed materials for the company).

Publications:

By DORFSMAN: book—*Push Pin Studios,* with Tadanori Yokoo and Masataka Ogawa, Tokyo 1972; articles—in *Graphis* (Zurich), no. 141, 1969, no. 185, 1976; *Communication Arts* (Palo Alto), no. 4, 1972.

On DORFSMAN: books—*Die neue Grafik/The New Graphic Design* by Karl Gerstner and Markus Kutter, Teufen and London 1959; *Advertising Directions,* edited by Edward M. Gottschall and Arthur Hawkins, New York 1959; *Typography* by Aaron Burns, New York 1961; *Who's Who in Graphic Art,* edited by Walter Amstutz, Zurich 1962, Dubendorf

1982; *An International Survey of Packaging* by Wim Crouwel and Kurt Weidemann, London 1968; *The Corporate Search for Visual Identity* by Ben Rosen, New York and London 1970; *Monografie des Plakats: Entwicklung, Stil, Design* by Herbert Schindler, Munich 1972; *The Design Concept* by Allen Hurlburt, New York 1981; *A History of Graphic Design* by Philip B. Meggs, London and New York 1983; *The Conran Directory of Design,* edited by Stephen Bayley, London 1985.

The son of a sign painter, Louis Dorfsman was born and raised in the Bronx and graduated from Cooper Union in New York City. He began working at CBS in 1946, when he was hired directly by William Golden, creative director for the company. Dorfsman's early work centered around identifying and defining opportunities in selling advertising time on the CBS radio network, very much competing for the advertising dollar with CBS-TV. His early ads, such as "Busy Markets," evidenced an approach to problem-solving and visual fact not before seen in radio advertising.

Upon Golden's sudden death in 1959, Dorfsman was named to his position, from which, for the next decade, he produced high-quality tune-in ads, corporate brochures, entertainment packages for the new TV season, books, film, and animation, in all of which taste, craft, and humor more than suggested that a designer could have an esthetic. With the support of William S. Paley, chairman and founder of CBS, and Dr. Frank Stanton, president of CBS through 1973, the art department under Dorfsman's direction flourished as an in-house operation.

His *Gastrotypographicalassemblage* was a major project designed and constructed in the mid-1960's in the new corporate office building for the employee cafeteria. Often collaborating with his lifelong friend, Herb Lubalin, Dorfsman created a mural that was as much an environmental installation as it was a typographic self-portrait of a man whose ease at arranging and designing type is joy and self-expression.

Dorfsman's animation concepts and narrative film interpretations advertising the network are visually stimulating and usually amusing. In one, announcing the beginning of a National Football League game, a television fan is watching a game from his easy chair when suddenly, a football shoots out of the television and is followed by the entire team rushing on the viewer. In another, he used two members of the Broadway mime group Mummenshantz to characterize "happy" and "sad" as a means of announcing the CBS afternoon playhouse.

A sense of classicism, often mixed with the spirit of child-like exploration, taste, and old-world craftsmanship characterize to this day the wide range and qualities of Dorfsman's work for CBS, as well as for the Dansk Company and the design conferences at Aspen. His exploration of alternative mediums to meet the evolving marketing needs and to shape the public perception of CBS has been virtually unique in twentieth-century design, for Dorfsman has worked for the same company for more than thirty years and consistently maintained quality by relying on personal wit, streetside sensitivity, and acute business skills, in addition to his artistic talents.

—Michael Robert Soluri

DREYFUSS, Henry.

American industrial and stage designer. Born in New York City, 2 March 1904. Studied at the Ethical Culture School, New York. Married Doris Marks in 1930; children: John, Gail and Ann. Apprenticed to designer Norman Bel Geddes, New York, 1924; worked as stage presentation designer for the Strand Motion Picture Theatre, New York, and as a guide for American Express in Europe, 1925–27; freelance stage designer for theatres in New York, 1927–30; established own industrial design office, New York, from 1929: designed for Bell Telephone Laboratories, General Electric, the 1939 New York World's Fair, New York Central Railroad, John Deere Company, Mergenthaler Linotype, Hoover, Eversharp, Royal Typewriters, Lockheed Aircraft, American Export Lines, Western Electric, *McCall's* magazine, etc. Professor of Engineering, California Institute of Technology, Pasadena, from 1952; also visiting lecturer at Harvard University, Yale University, and Massachusetts Institute of Technology. Board Member, Ford Foundation Educational Facilities Laboratories, and the Performing Arts Council of Los Angeles Music Center; Executive Committee Member, National Reading Council; Trustee, California Institute of Technology, People to People, and Los Angeles County Art Museum. Recipient: American Designers Institute Award, 1943; Gold Medal, Architectural League of New York, 1951, 1954; American Institute of Graphic Arts Award of Excellence, 1953; Philadelphia Museum College of Art Design Award, 1958, 1962; American Society of Industrial Designers Award, 1960; American Iron and Steel Institute Design Award, 1963, 1965; Ambassador Award for Achievement, London, 1965; National Association of Schools of Art Award, 1969; Jack A. Kraft Award, Human Factors Society, 1971. Benjamin Franklin Fellow, Royal Society of Arts, London; Fellow, Industrial Designers Society of America; Honorary Member, Telephone Pioneers of America. Honorary doctorates: Occidental College, Los Angeles, 1953; Pratt Institute, Brooklyn, New York, 1963; Otis Art Institute, Los Angeles, 1968. Order of the Orange Nassau, Netherlands, 1952. *Died* (in Pasadena, California) *5 October 1972.*

Works:

Upright vacuum cleaner, for Hoover, 1935.
Mercury diesel locomotive, for New York Central Railroad, 1936.
300 combined handset desk telephone, for Bell Telephone Laboratories, 1937.
Engine 5450 diesel locomotive, for New York Central Railroad, 1938.
Twentieth Century Limited train design, for New York Central Railroad, 1938.
Democracity: The City of Tomorrow exhibit, at the New York World's Fair, 1939.
McCall's magazine re-design, New York, 1940.
Embankment compacter and lift truck, for Hyster Company, 1950s.
Constellation and *Electra* passenger airplane interiors, for Lockheed, 1953.
Touch-Tone Trimline telephone, for Bell Telephone Laboratories, 1955.
Injector one-piece safety razor, for ASR Products Company, 1959.

Publications:

By DREYFUSS: books—*Industrial Design: A Pictorial Accounting,* New York 1929, 1958; *Designing for People,* New York 1955, 1967; *The Measure of Man: Human Factors in Design,* New York 1960, 1967; *Henry Dreyfuss*

Symbol Source Book, with Doris Marks Drey-fuss, New York 1972; articles—in The Enamel-ist (Cleveland), November 1933; House Beautiful (London), November 1933; Electrical Manufacturing (New York), May 1934, Febru-ary 1936, October 1937; Architect and Engi-neer (San Francisco), July 1936; Art and Industry (New York), September 1944; Arts and Architecture (San Francisco), September 1947; American Fabrics (New York), no. 38, 1956.

On DREYFUSS: books—Art and the Machine by Sheldon and Martha Cheney, New York 1936; Industrial Design: A Practical Guide by Harold Van Doren, New York and London 1940; Design in British Industry: A Mid-Century Survey by Michael Farr, Cambridge 1955; The Business of Product Design by James Pilditch and Douglas Scott, London 1965; De-sign in America by Ralph Caplan, New York 1969; The Streamlined Decade by Donald J. Bush, New York 1975; Industrial Design by John Heskett, London 1980; Design Since 1945, edited by Kathryn Hiesinger and George Marcus, London and Philadelphia 1983; The Machine Age in America 1918–1941, edited by Richard Guy Wilson and Dianne H. Pilgrim, New York 1986; The American Design Adven-ture 1940-1975 by Arthur J. Pulos, London and Cambridge, Massachusetts 1988.

Henry Dreyfuss, among the first of the great American industrial designers, was always con-cerned with his guiding vision—to make ma-chines to fit people, thus making life more efficient and less irritating. His credo was, sharply stated, "that what we are working on is going to be ridden in, sat upon, looked at, talked into, activated, operated, or in some way used by people individually or en masse." He never shied away from the concept of beauty in the functional and was neither slave to the swings of art and taste nor to the modernistic styles of the times.

His early education at the Ethical Culture school produced in him concern for people and their environment. Later, he studied stage de-sign with Norman Bel Geddes, and it is obvi-ous that, although industrial design was not the theme of his studies, exposure to this seminal designer was a great influence in his life and in his future work.

It was through his mediation as an industrial designer and his insistence on working with en-gineers, that he made the aims of business coin-cide with the needs of people who used the products he designed. Not only did he serve clients as an industrial designer, but he became corporate advisor as well to Hallmark Cards, Polaroid, American Airlines, and American Telephone and Telegraph.

He was on the faculty of the Engineering Di-vision of the California Institute of Technology for many years and lectured annually on indus-trial design to the students in Business Econom-ics. On the Board, he persuaded his fellow Trustees to employ the best architects to design new buildings on the campus. As well, he was a leader in such civic organizations as the Center for the Performing Arts, the Music Center, the Los Angeles County Museum, Los Angeles Beautiful, and Pasadena Beautiful.

No evaluation would be complete without the mention of Doris Marks Dreyfuss, his wife, as many of his accomplishments belong to both of them. Their last and greatest collaborative work, the Henry Dreyfuss Symbol Sourcebook, an international dictionary of symbols, projects his belief that the eye can catch symbols faster and more easily than the mind can catch words. Mrs. Dreyfuss' contribution was her insistence upon absolute clarity of meaning with simplic-ity of expression. Thus, their book was aimed at the literate, the illiterate, at people of many different cultures, and, at the high speed re-quired in our technological world.

—Mildred Constantine

DU BOIS, Raoul Pène (-Henri Charles).

American stage and film designer. Born in Staten Island, New York, 29 November 1914. Studied at the Grand Central Art School, New York, but mainly self-taught in design. Worked as assistant to designer Cleon Throckmorton, at the Christopher Morley Theatre, Hoboken, New Jersey, 1932–33; freelance muralist, fash-ion sketch artist and window display designer, New York, 1933–34; stage set and costume de-signer, from 1934: first designed for the Ziegfeld Follies production at the Shubert The-atre, New York, 1934, then for other musicals, revues, ballets and films; created costumes for performers Ethel Merman, Ginger Rogers, Dorothy Lamour, Paulette Goddard, Sonja Henie, Ed Wynn, etc.; contract film designer, Para-mount Studios, Hollywood, California, 1941–45. Independent painter, in Paris, 1959–65. **Exhibition:** Wright/Hepburn/Webster Gallery, New York, 1968. Recipient: Antoinette Perry Awards, New York, 1953, 1971; Joseph Ma-haram Foundation Award, New York, 1971. Member, United Scenic Artists, New York. Died (in New York City) in 1985.

Works:

Stage designs (Broadway, except as noted) include—Life Begins at 8.40, 1934; Jumbo, 1935; Home and Beauty (London), 1937; The Two Bouquets, 1938; Leave It to Me, 1938; Du Barry Was a Lady, 1939; Too Many Girls, 1939; One for the Money, 1939; Two for the Show, 1940; Panama Hattie, 1940; Hold on to Your Hats, 1940; Liberty Jones, 1941; Carmen Jones, 1943; The Firebrand of Florence, 1945; Are You With It?, 1945; Heaven on Earth, 1948; Lend an Ear, 1948; Alive and Kicking 1950; Call Me Madame, 1950; Make a Wish, 1951; New Faces of 1952, 1952; In Any Lan-guage, 1952; Wonderful Town, 1953; Maggie, 1953; Charley's Aunt, 1953; Mrs. Patterson, 1954; Carmen Jones, 1956; Bells Are Ringing, 1956; The Music Man, 1957; Gypsy, 1959; The Student Gypsy, 1963; PS I Love You, 1964; Royal Flush, 1964; Darling of the Day, 1968; Peter and the Wolf, 1969; Here and Now, 1969; Rondelay, 1969; No, No, Nanette, 1971; Rain, 1972; Irene, 1973; No, No, Nanette (London), 1973; Gypsy (London), 1973; Gypsy (London), 1974; and Doctor Jazz, 1975; for films—Louisiana Purchase, Lady in the Dark, Dixie, Frenchman's Creek, and Kitty; for the ballet—Ghost Town, for the Monte Carlo Ballet, and Jeux, for the New York City Ballet; for revues and spectacles—several editions of the Ziegfeld Follies; John Murray Anderson's Almanac, 1953; Sonja Henie's ice show; Maurice Cheva-lier's New York show, 1963; and numerous Billy Rose entertainments, in New York, Texas, and Cleveland, including several versions of the Aquacade, the Diamond Horseshoe review, and Let's Play Fair (a cabaret-theatre revue) at Casa Manana, New York, 1938.

Publications:

On DU BOIS: books—The Biographical Ency-clopaedia and Who's Who of the American The-atre, edited by Walter Rigdon, New York 1966; Hollywood Costume Design by David Chieri-chetti, New York and London 1976; Who's Who in the Theatre, edited by Ian Herbert, London and Detroit 1977; The Oxford Compan-ion to the American Theatre, edited by Gerald Bordman, New York 1984.

Raoul Pène du Bois was only a youth when he skyrocketed to fame as a costume and set de-signer for theatrical productions. He has gained his widest acclaim for the long list of Broadway musicals on which he has worked over the years, beginning with the world-renowned hit Jumbo (1935) and spanning the next four de-cades with works such as Rodgers and Hart's Too Many Girls (1939), Oscar Hammerstein's Carmen Jones (1943), Leonard Bernstein's Wonderful Town (1953) and The Bells Are Ring-ing (1956), and Jules Styne's Gypsy (1959).

During the 1930's, du Bois had a number of fertile collaborations with director-producer Billy Rose, whose showmanship du Bois matched with his flamboyant displays, such as his sparkling setting for Rose's Aquacade at the New York World's Fair. Here, for the curved stage, he created a backdrop composed of a row of pillars; at the finale of the show, ten foun-tains shot up between the pillars and a curtain of water stained with colored lights arose for a breathtaking effect. Fire blazed from each of the twelve urns above the colonnade and 200 performers paraded in costumes of saffron satin and gold kid. During the same period, du Bois also distinguished himself for his more classic and studied designs such as those for the ballet Ghost Town (1939) which he was commissioned to do by the Monte Carlo Ballet. Du Bois' lav-ish outfittings included women dressed with bustles, deep gathers, and feathered hats; gents garbed in elegant suitings and high hats; and a muscleman in stars-and-stripes tights—all his-torically authentic in the manner of apparel worn in a Nevada mining town of the 1870's and all slightly exaggerated to enhance the ap-propriate entertainment quality.

During the years 1941 to 1945, du Bois was under contract to Paramount studios in Holly-wood, and, while he continued his work for the theatre, he also worked on movies such as Dixie, Frenchman's Creek, Lady In the Dark and Louisiana Purchase. For the latter, du Bois captured the spirit of the story, using as few colors as he could for most scenes and going wild with colorful effects in the Mardi Gras and ballroom sequences.

Except for the period between 1959 and 1965, when du Bois lived in Paris and spent almost all of his time at easel painting, most of his energy in later years has continued to be dedicated to theater design. Outstanding among his numerous achievements is his 1971 produc-tion of No, No, Nanette. Du Bois spent the bet-ter part of two years designing costumes and sets which capture the look and feeling of the mid-1920's with meticulous attention to every detail. Working out of old issues of Harper's Bazaar and Vogue, he came up with 270 cos-tumes, each unique, including those for every member of the chorus. For her Charleston number, star Helen Gallagher wore a fitted, gray wool suit jacket bound in navy braid and a pleated skirt; the ensemble was completed with vest and matching, gray felt fedora. Her partner in the scene, Bobby Van, was outfitted with gaily striped jacket and jaunty white pants and sport shoes. The look of the roaring twenties was also appropriately recreated in the stage sets, with arches as frames and side flats of scenery, for example, used in the authentic manner of the period being depicted.

Du Bois has often discussed the principles which underlie all of his work. He sees costumes for the theater as part of the set, working together with it to communicate a sense of exaggeration and suggestion, not retiring into the background but asserting themselves as a contribution equal to all other elements which compose the overall show. The main thing, he has said, is to "contribute entertainment," "produce a sort of unreal brilliance," because the theater is not suited for realism, morals, or message-making but geared to a more fanciful tone. Theatrical design is different, he has noted, from fashion design to be worn in real life; theater costumes are like "moving scenery" and the costume designer should be a "historian of taste." He also differentiates sharply between theater and movie designing, suggesting, for example, that theater sets are like framed pictures while in movies, they are a part of the action, most often using a real environment and not one that is contrived and constructed. Du Bois has certainly put his theories into practice with long-time commitment and also with a unique ability which has earned him a prominent place in the annals of recent theater design.

—Barbara Cavaliere

DUFFY-ELEY-GIFFONE-WORTHINGTON.
British architectural, interior and furniture design partnership. Founded by the New York design firm JFN Associates, in London, 1974. Founder Partners: Francis Duffy, Peter Eley, Luigi Giffone, and John Worthington; subsequently joined by current partners: Colin Cave in 1977, John Francis in 1982, and Chris Byng-Maddock in 1982; DEGW Overseas, under managing director Luigi V. Mangano, founded in 1981. Clients include American Express, Banco Nacional de Mexico, Barclays Bank, British Nuclear Fuels, British Telecom, Eagle Star Insurance Group, Factory Mutual International, Hewlett Packard, IBM International, London Electricity Board, Port of London Authority, Royal Institute of British Architects, and the United Kingdom Atomic Energy Authority. Address: 8 Bulstrode Place, London W1, England.

Works:

Office interiors, for American Express, London, 1973–74.
Graphics and sign systems, for IBM Netherlands, Amsterdam, 1975–76.
Office interiors, for BBDO Advertising Agency, London, 1978–79.
Office building, for the United Kingdom Atomic Energy Authority, Warrington, Lancashire, 1979.
Birch Wood Science Park, Warrington, Lancashire, 1979.
Warehouse interiors, for British Leyland/Unipart, Coventry, 1979–80.
Headquarters offices, for Factory Mutual International, London, 1979–81.
Offices, for the Digital Equipment Corporation, Evry, France, 1980–81.
Sales and accounts office interiors, for the Ryan Hotel, London, 1980–81.
Salesroom interiors, for Christie's, Amsterdam, 1980–81.

Office interiors and furniture, for the Leagas Delaney Partnership, London, 1981–82.
Fleetway House interiors, for Barclays Bank, London, 1982–83.

Publications:

By DEGW: books—*Planning Office Space*, London 1979; *Industrial Rehabilitation*, London 1980; *Information Technology and Office Design*, London 1983.

On DEGW: articles—in *Building Refurbishment and Maintenance* (London), January/February 1980; *Domus* (Milan), September 1980; *Building Design* (London), 19 December 1980, 15 May 1981; *Design* (London), January 1981; *Building* (London), 19 June 1981; *Interior Design* (Morden), August 1981, December 1981, September 1982; *Techniques et Architecture* (Paris), June 1982.

Duffy says that many existing office buildings are becoming prematurely obsolete, as they were not designed to cope with computer technology. Offices are now being crowded with computer terminals, word processors, printers, graphic generators, and information distributors, with their miles of cable for which office blocks do not have the space. The problems of where to put the wiring and whether the office is to become a factory with workers glued to machines are ones that concern DEGW very closely. In 1982, the group was appointed to the Orbit Study established by the Department of Industry and British Telecom to tackle office research on buildings and information technology. The partner John Worthington sees that buildings will have to be designed to function more flexibly, instead of being erected for a specific process. He points out that buildings must now accommodate mixed functions because technology is changing all the time. More flexible leasing of property must also be organised, as firms expand or condense depending on their new equipment. The electrical engineer must work with the architect to resolve questions of placing power points and masses of cable.

The partnership puts great importance on labour relations in design. The problem with the British Leyland Unipart warehouse was that it had been designed as a vast shell, with little room for workers to make their own nooks, so DEGW broke the central buffet into three, making it possible for workers to have their own without walking all the way to the middle.

DEGW have produced three books, *Information Technology and Office Design*, *Planning Office Space*, and *Industrial Rehabilitation*, and in May 1983 they launched *Facilities*, a monthly digest for building administration managers with Duffy as editor-in-chief. The partners also are regular contributors to *The Architects' Journal*. Thus, they are in the forefront in explaining the new problems offices face and in creating solutions to accommodate technological developments.

—Diana de Marly

D'URSO, Joseph (Paul).
American architectural, interior and industrial designer. Born in Newark, New Jersey, 8 April 1943. Educated at West Side High School, Newark, 1958–61; studied interior design and architecture, at the Pratt Institute, Brooklyn, New York, 1961–66: BFA 1965; Royal College of Art, London, 1966–67; Manchester College of Art and Design, England, 1967–68: MA 1968. Freelance designer, establishing D'Urso Design Inc., in New York, from 1968: has designed private residences, restaurants, art galleries, discotheques, showrooms, offices, and a range of furniture for Knoll International. **Exhibitions:** Museum of Modern Art, New York, 1968; Pratt Institute, Brooklyn, New York, 1968. Recipient: American Institute of Interior Designers Award, 1965; Burlington Industries Designer of the Year Award, 1973; Stuttgart Fair Best in Show Award, 1982; Good Design Prize, Bonn, 1983. Address: D'Urso Design Inc., 80 West 40th Street, New York, New York 10018, U.S.A.

Publications:

By D'URSO: articles—in *Manhattan Catalog* (New York), Summer 1979, November 1979, Fall 1980; *Skyline* (New York), April 1980.

On D'URSO: books—*Interior Design: The New Freedom*, edited by Barbaralee Diamonstein, New York 1982; *Joe d'Urso: Designer*, Minneapolis 1983; *International Design Yearbook 1987/88*, edited by Philippe Starck, London 1987; articles—in *Interior Design* (New York), February 1976, February 1977, January 1979, August 1980, January 1981, March 1981, May 1983; *Progressive Architecture* (Stamford), September 1977; *Avenue* (New York), October 1977; *Skyline* (New York), October 1979; *Interiors* (Radnor), August 1980; *Architectural Record* (New York), December 1980; *Casa Vogue* (Milan), January 1981, February 1982; *Artnews* (New York), February 1981; *Metropolitan Home* (New York), June 1981; *Architectural Digest* (New York), August 1983.

As a designer, I am obviously interested in all aspects of the visual world from the largest scale to the smallest. There is, however, a special excitement for me in three-dimensional spaces on the human scale. By this I mean being in a space or walking in a series of spaces, as opposed to picking up an object, however beautiful.

I have often thought that perhaps it would be simpler to be an artist in the traditional sense—thereby eliminating the client—but no matter how much I am stimulated by great painting and sculpture, I am most stimulated and rewarded by manipulating three-dimensional space within a structural and functional framework.

My experiences in travelling widely, teaching, and researching great architectural works of the past have formed my sensibility and given me a full reserve to draw on in my work. This exposure is essential, but ultimately, I believe most in concentration and hard work. In today's working world full of distractions, I think concentration is the most elusive of all states of mind, and one must work extremely hard at preserving it.

My personal involvement with all of my projects and clients is intense and exhaustive, and I take full responsibility for the work. My feeling is that the best work is produced by a triangle consisting of the space or program involved at the apex, and the client and the designer focusing from the base corners toward the apex.

—Joseph D'Urso

A major talent, Joseph Paul D'Urso is one of the most important and influential designers in

Joseph Paul D'Urso: Living and bathing areas of apartment in Dakota, New York, 1981

America. His international fame is based primarily upon his work in interior design, although he also has been highly acclaimed as a product designer through his development of a line of furniture for Knoll International. D'Urso's meteoric ascent to stardom in design started with a 1968 exhibition at the Museum of Modern Art of the work he had done as a teaching fellow graduate student in Manchester, England. He was twenty-four at that time, and it is doubtful whether there are other interior designers of any age who have had one-person shows of their own at the Museum of Modern Art.

D'Urso has executed projects ranging from houses to apartments to lofts and other residences—all with a strongly personal style. He has also designed a number of commercial projects, including a highly acclaimed showroom for Calvin Klein's menswear and, most recently, the 60,000 square-foot "I" club in Hong Kong. Publications that have featured his work include the *New York Times* (many times) and just about every major design magazine, as well as many other books and magazines, and he has been honored with several awards.

D'Urso is a minimalist, yet his work is strongly architectural and always elegant in an understated way. He creates a three-dimensional work of art in a simple space with just a few elements. Although there is a definite look to his work, he is responsive to the needs of his clients, and he approaches design as a problem-solving activity.

—Arnold Friedmann

DUSCHEK, Karl (Erich).
German graphic and corporate identity designer. Born in Braunschweig, 14 March 1947. Studied graphic design, Staatliche Hochschule für Bildende Künste, Braunschweig, 1963–66: Dip. 1970. Assistant lithography teacher, Staatliche Hochschule für Bildende Künste, Braunschweig, 1968–70; graphic designer, Atelier für Künstlerischen Steindruck, for Edition Pro Litho, Lausanne, 1970–72; freelance designer and partner, with Anton Stankowski, in Atelier Stankowski + Duschek graphic design firm, Stuttgart, since 1972: has designed corporate image for the Deutsche Bank AG, Frankfurt, since 1974, and for Bayern Versicherung insurance company, Munich, 1975–80; city design, for the 11th Olympic Congress, Baden-Baden, 1976–81; sign system image for the Messe-Fair, Frankfurt, since 1982. **Exhibitions:** Galerie Beatrix Wilhelm, Leonberg/Stuttgart, 1978, 1983; Galerie Seestrasse, Rapperswil, 1980 (with A. Stankowski); Kunstverein, Ludwigsburg, 1980 (with H. Treiber); Ausstellungsraume Leitner, Stuttgart, 1982; Galerie Circulus, Bonn, 1985; Städtische Galerie, Stadt Ostfildern, 1986 (with A. Stankowski); Städtische Galerie, Leonberg/Stuttgart, 1987 (with A. Stankowski); Galerie im Burgenlandzentrum, Stuttgart, 1989 (with K. H. Franke and H. Kapitzki). **Collections:** Staatsgalerie, Stuttgart; Deutsches Plakatmuseum, Essen. Address: Bebelstrasse 121, 7000 Stuttgart 1, West Germany.

Works:

Trademark logo, for Zehnder radiators, 1979.
Trademark logo, for Landesausstellung Niedersachsen, 1985.
Logo, for the Berchtesgaden bid for the 1992 Winter Olympics, 1985.
Trademark logo, for Bisterfeld und Weiss, 1985.
Signage system, for Design Tech Jürgen R. Schmid, 1986.

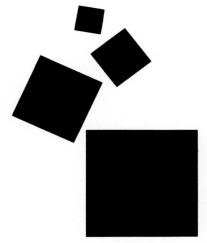

Karl Duschek: Logotype symbol, for the Frankfurt Fair, 1982

Adaptable logo system, for the Volkhochschules of Baden-Württemberg, 1986.
Logo, for the University of Stuttgart, 1987.

Publications:

By DUSCHEK: book—*Die Anzeige,* Stuttgart 1976; articles—"Farbe im visuellen Erscheinungsbild" in *MD: Moebel Interior Design* (Stuttgart), November 1982; "Frankfurter zum Zauberkasten" in *Form* (Seeheim), January 1983.

On DUSCHEK: books—*Karl Duschek: System und Serie,* exhibition catalogue by Matthias Gotz and Friedrich Heckmanns, Leonberg and Aachen 1982; *Kunst im Deutschen Südwesten von 1945 bis zur Gegenwart* by Günther Wirth, Stuttgart 1982; *Braunschweiger Konstruktivisten,* exhibition catalogue by Peter Luft, Braunschweig 1984; articles—in *Novum Gebrauchsgraphik* (Munich), no. 7, 1978; *Idea* (Tokyo), July 1982; *Kunstforum* (Mainz), January 1983; *Revue K* (Alfortville), no. 29, 1987; *Delfin* (Siegen), no. 11, 1988.

1. The importance of thought and perception in design is oriented towards problems of time. Timeless design is quality.
2. Whether thought (logic) or perception (emotion) has more importance may be tested in the contemplation and evaluation of visual objects.
3. Important works contain inventions. These inventions appear frequently as effects. In this case, one has to decide whether these effects are mainly part of the project or whether they come to life by being seen.
4. Every work should reveal a particular aesthetic basis. In a qualified sense, an anti-aesthetic can also make its contribution.
5. Political or social problems are merely suggested by design means.
6. Innovative values need a meaningful or functional quality. Formal elements can act as a support.
7. Logic, geometry, and order are an important part of our thought and action.
8. Producing order has become a natural occurence. Disorder in order can gain acceptance, but on the other hand, order in disorder, rarely.
9. Certain formal results are without tension in the visual statement; monochrome and total symmetry, for example.
10. The quality of a work is often not clear if the overall concept is not perceived.

11. Colours influence the emotions (sympathy value).
12. Colour harmonies work for the moment. Forms or groups of forms support the long-term effect.
13. Forms, especially groups of forms with connections to each other, act as an impetus to visual ideas.
14. Artistic thought should simply be to achieve. Formal quality in signs, symbols is necessary to concise art.
15. In the artistic sense, an ornament cannot be functional. Without the principle of order, the ornament is a way of expressing perception.
16. Purity can be accepted as a criterion of quality; for example, the preference for primary colours over mixed colours. In the academic teaching of design, a work is regarded as impure if, through pure technique, it is overworked (drawn to death, for example).
17. Computer graphics in the sphere of design, despite their roots in geometry and order, are far from convincing.
18. Serial design is largely involved with formal modules. Principles such as rows, groups, development variation, etc. are the basis of industrial production. The time factor, or the process for accomplishing a time phase, is more important compared to stylistic innovations. Serial solutions broaden the working of static individual objects.
19. The reduction of stylistic elements, even in schemes of thought, should lead to solutions which nevertheless fulfil their purpose.
20. Spatial effects in a sign/symbol form do not correspond to the basic principle of concise reduction.
21. Contours of a flat form contradict the unequivocal form.
22. Scientific experiences can only narrowly be turned to account in design work.
23. A qualitative judgment of design must be followed subjectively.
24. Quantitive examinations of design qualities, market research for example, a base design quality and inhibit innovations.
25. The earliest discussion of a problem or theme often leads to the opening up of a preconceived opinion.
26. It is, perhaps, not the maintenance of a consistent understanding but the meaningful analysis of experience that is important to development.
27. Spontaneous commitments can be just as important as spontaneous criticisms.

—Karl Duschek

DUSZEK, Roman.
Polish graphic designer. Born in Warsaw, 8 November 1935. Studied graphic design, Academy of Fine Arts, Warsaw, 1955–59: MA 1959. Married Maria Duszek in 1959; daughters: Eva and Marta. Graphic designer, at Reklama advertising agency, Warsaw, 1960–62; freelance designer, Warsaw, 1962–66; staff designer, with Lonsdale Agency graphic design firm, Paris, 1966–68; art director, Polish Technical School Publishers, Warsaw, 1967–73, Polish School and Educational Publishers, Warsaw, 1973–74, and KAW Polish Publishing Agency, Warsaw, 1976–78; freelance designer, Warsaw, since 1978: visual communications consultant, Lot Polish Airlines, from 1980. Associate Professor of Graphic Design, Academy of Fine Arts, Warsaw, from 1978. Executive Board Member, 1977–79, and Vice-President, 1979–83, ICOGRADA International Council of Graphic Design Associations; expert on graphics, Polish Ministry of Culture and Art. **Collection:** National Museum, Warsaw. Recipient: Award of Distinction, Ministry of Culture and Art, Warsaw, 1962, 1963, 1980; Gold Chestnut Award, Warsaw, 1964; Package Design Prize, Poznan, 1972. Member, ZAIKS Association of Authors, Warsaw. Address: Kleczewska 29, 01–826 Warsaw, Poland.

Works:

La Vache Qui Rit trademark symbol and packaging, for the Lonsdale Agency, Paris, 1967.
Corporate identity program and signage system, for the Intercontinental Hotel Victoria, Warsaw, 1976.
Corporate identity programme, for Lot Polish Airlines, 1977 (with A. Zbrozek).
Identification logotype symbol, for Polish Television, 1978.
Identity programme, for Polish Television News, 1979.
Visual information system and signage, for the Warsaw Subway, 1983 (with others).

Publications:

On DUSZEK: articles—in *Zycie Warszawy* (Warsaw), 17 March 1976, 22 July 1977; *Reklama* (Warsaw), June 1976, January/March 1982; *Magazyn Rodzinny* (Warsaw), December 1972; *Literatura* (Warsaw), no. 1, 1981; *Kaleidoscope* (Warsaw), 15 April 1982; *Kurier Polski* (Warsaw), 16 August 1983.

Roman Duszek's way to designing started, as with most Polish designers, in fine arts. He might have become an artist and enjoyed the charms of aquatint, etching, lithography, woodcutting, or of the noble art of drawing. Instead, he was attracted by the idea of harmonizing art with the material of the human environment. His education developed in him a basic sensitivity of visual perception and an artistic consciousness. Such a humanistic background, without which there is no good, conscious creativity, turned out to be a priceless investment for Duszek and affected the whole body of his creative work. Incidentally, this is what the graduates of even the world-renowned schools of graphic design miss. To be a modern designer, it is not enough to display technical skills; most important is the ability to perceive the world through the prism of human nature, to understand the profound layers of the human psyche, which is the source of our common mythology, of reflexes, preferences, and fascinations.

Duszek acquired the knowledge of his new field first through practice on a modest scale, while designing small forms of commercial

Roman Duszek: Logotype symbol for the Polish National Fund for Health Protection, 1977

the rules and turmoils of free competition. He mastered the techniques of testing preferences. The problem of "how to do it" was not so difficult for him any longer as were the more complex questions regarding the selection of his concepts and of their esthetic values.

At that time, Paris was a good ground for intellectual growth. The world was shaken by conflicts in the midst of prosperity. In art, conceptualism and minimal art—trends appealing to the intellect and not to the emotions—were given preference. Some keen observer would write later about this paradox: "Art was cold and life—hot." A similar situation pertained in the field of mass media. On the one hand, there was a wave of underground prints, graphically lax magazines for young people, "hot" cover designs for pop music records, neo-secession in lettering. On the other, the unquestionable authority Swiss typography; Helvetica was almost a symbol of functional type, cool and ascetic. It seems that Duszek's esthetic disposition oscillated between representation and abstraction, between emotional and rational attitudes. Such preferences would dictate his style in the following years.

In the mid-1970's, some essential changes took place in his work. He won a competition (together with A. Zbrozek) for the system of identification for the Polish Airlines, LOT, and carried it out. In its scale and complexity, this work subdued everything he had done before. Moreover, it was one of the first examples of "corporate identity" applied in Poland. In the opinion of experts, the value of this project lay in a successful solution of the difficult problem of identification in the air and from the ground of the airline sign located on the fuselage. His second great success was his work on the interior decoration of the Warsaw hotel Victoria. Thanks to this work, the image of the hotel was brought up to the international level. His latest complex task is to prepare (together with A. Bojar) an informative system for the future metro in Warsaw.

Trademarks and logotypes have become important forms of expression for Duszek. They form his language of communication with the external world. Many of them are in wide circulation, as are the stamp for the National Fund of Health Protection and the main logotype of Polish Television.

—Szymon Bojko

graphics, such as flyers, labels, insets, trademarks. Then he went on to three-dimensional graphics in the form of package design. In the postwar Polish reality, with socialized, monopolized production, no competition, demand dominating supply, product scarcity, a sophisticated form of package design was a luxury. Duszek was one of those who broke the inertia of the market and who, driven by professional ambitions, introduced their designs into mass production. For his total work on package design, he was granted the first award in the Polish Exhibit of Package Design in Poznań.

The next step in his self-education was a longer, independent practice in Lonsdale, a Paris design agency. This work initiated him into all stages of this profession, including the industry-market-consumer system, as well as

EAMES, Charles.

American architect, filmmaker, interior, exhibition and furniture designer. Born in St. Louis, Missouri, 17 June 1907. Studied at the Washington University School of Architecture, St. Louis, 1924-26. Married Ray Kaiser in 1941; daughter, by previous marriage: Lucia. Worked for Trueblood and Graf architectural firm, St. Louis, 1925-27; in private practice as architect and designer, St. Louis, 1930-36; Fellow, 1936, and Head of Experimental Design Department, 1937-40, Cranbrook Academy of Art, Bloomfield Hills, Michigan; worked in the art department of Metro-Goldwyn-Mayer film company, Los Angeles, 1941; began experimental plywood molding laboratory, with John Entenza, Gregory Ain, Margaret Harris and Griswald Raetz, in Los Angeles, 1942-45; in design partnership with Ray Eames, in Los Angeles and Venice, California, 1944-78: formed Molded Plywood Division of Evans Products Company, Los Angeles, 1944; Consultant Designer, Herman Miller Inc., Los Angeles, from 1946. Lecturer, California Institute of Technology, Pasadena, 1953-56; Charles Eliot Norton Professor of Poetry, Harvard University, Cambridge, Massachusetts, 1970. Member, National Council on the Arts, 1970-78. **Exhibitions:** *Organic Design in Home Furnishings,* Museum of Modern Art, New York, 1941 (toured); *New Furniture Designed by Charles Eames,* Museum of Modern Art, New York, 1946; *An Exhibition for Modern Living,* Detroit Institute of Arts, 1949; *The Modern Chair 1918-1970,* Whitechapel Art Gallery, London, 1970; *Charles Eames,* Museum of Modern Art, New York, 1973; *One Hundred Modern Chairs,* National Gallery of Victoria, Melbourne, 1974; *Connections: The Work of Charles and Ray Eames,* University of California at Los Angeles, 1976; *Design in Michigan 1967/1977,* Cranbrook Academy of Art, Bloomfield Hills, Michigan, 1978 (toured); *Design Since 1945,* Philadelphia Museum of Art, 1983; *High Style: 20th Century American Design,* Whitney Museum, New York, 1985; *The Machine Age in America 1918-1941,* Brooklyn Museum, New York, 1986. **Collections:** Library of Congress, Washington, D.C.; Museum of Modern Art, New York; Philadelphia Museum of Art. Recipient: Furniture Prize, Museum of Modern Art, New York, 1940; Industrial Designers Institute Award, 1951; Gold Medal, 1954, Grand Prize, 1957, Milan Triennale; Kaufmann International Design Award, 1960; National Honor Award, 1964, Los Angeles Chapter Honor Award, 1967, Industrial Arts Medal, 1972, and Distinguished Service Award, 1974, American Institute of Architects; Design Medal, Society of Industrial Artists and Designers of Great Britain, 1967; Elsie de Wolfe Award, American Society of Interior Designers, 1975; Royal Gold Medal, Royal Institute of British Architects, 1979. Honorary doctorates: Kansas City Art Institute, 1955; California College of Arts and Crafts, 1962; Pratt Institute, Brooklyn, 1964;

Washington University, St. Louis, 1970; University of Cincinnati, 1978. Honorary Royal Designer for Industry, Royal Society of Arts, London, 1960; Fellow, Royal College of Art, London, 1960; Member, American Academy of Arts and Sciences. *Died* (in St. Louis) *21 August 1978.*

Works:

Molded plywood chair, for the Museum of Modern Art *Organic Furniture* competition, 1940 (with Eero Saarinen).
Child's chair, for Evans Products Company, 1944.
Dining and side chairs in steel rod and molded walnut plywood with rubber mounts, for Herman Miller, 1946.
Chairs in steel rod and aluminium with molded plastic seats, for Herman Miller, 1949-53.
ESU 275 chest of drawers in steel and birch with walnut or birch top, for Herman Miller, 1950.
Good Design Show exhibition layouts, for the Museum of Modern Art, New York, 1950.
Storage units in steel and plastic-coated plywood, for Herman Miller, 1950.
Chair in wire rod with wire seat and removable cushion, for Herman Miller, 1951.
Eames Storage Unit/ESU desk in steel with walnut or birch, for Herman Miller, 1952.
670 and *671* swivel-base upholstered lounge chair and ottoman in aluminium and molded plywood, for Herman Miller, 1957.
Solar toy, for Alcoa Aluminium, 1957.
675 lobby chair in cast aluminium with leather upholstery, for Herman Miller, 1960.
La Fonda chair in cast aluminium and fibreglass with polyfoam upholstery, for Herman Miller, 1960.
Eames Contract Storage cupboard/bed/study units in birch plywood, for Herman Miller, 1961.
RE-204 sofa in aluminium with polyfoam and plastic upholstery, for Herman Miller, 1962.
Tandem 2600 single/double row seating in aluminium and steel with plastic upholstery, for Herman Miller, 1962.
IBM exhibit design at the *World's Fair,* New York, for International Business Machines, 1964.
Photography and the City exhibition layouts, for the Smithsonian Institution, Washington, D.C., 1968.
Chaise ES106 (Soft Pad group) couch in aluminium with polyfoam and leather cushions, for Herman Miller, 1969.
The World of Franklin and Jefferson touring exhibition layouts, for the American Bicentennial Administration, 1975-76.

(for a list of Eames' buildings and architectural projects, see *Contemporary Architects*)

Films: with Ray Eames—*Traveling Boy,* 1950;

Parade; or, Here they Come Down the Street, 1952; *Blacktop,* 1952; *Bread,* 1953; *Calligraphy,* 1953; *Communications Primer,* 1953; *Sofa Compact,* 1954; *Two Baroque Churches in Germany,* 1955; *House,* 1955; *Textiles and Ornamental Arts of India,* 1955; *Eames Lounge Chair,* 1956; *The Spirit of St. Louis* (aerial sequences only), 1956; *Day of the Dead,* 1957; *Tocatta for Toy Trains,* 1957; *Information Machine,* 1957; *Expanding Airport,* 1958; *Herman Miller at the Brussels Fair,* 1958; *DeGaulle Sketch,* 1959; *Glimpses of the U.S.A.,* 1959; *Jazz Chair,* 1960; *Introduction to Feedback,* 1960; *Fabulous Fifties* (sequences in CBS-TV Special), 1960; *IBM Mathematics Peep Show,* 1961; *Kaleidoscope,* 1961; *Kaleidoscope Shop,* 1961; *ECS,* 1962; *House of Science,* 1962; *Before the Fair,* 1962; *The Good Years* (sequences in CBS-TV Special), 1962; *Think,* 1964; *Think* (revised version), 1965; *IBM at the Fair,* 1965; *Westinghouse ABC,* 1965; *The Smithsonian Institution,* 1965; *The Smithsonian Newsreel,* 1965; *Horizontes,* 1966; *Boeing: The Leading Edge,* 1966; *IBM Museum,* 1967; *A Computer Glossary,* 1967; *National Aquarium Presentation,* 1967; *Schuetz Machine,* 1967; *Lick Observatory,* 1968; *Babbage,* 1968; *Powers of Ten,* 1968; *Photography and the City,* 1969; *Tops,* 1969; *The U.N. Information Center,* 1970; *Man's View of Himself,* 1970; *Memory,* 1970; *The Perry Expedition,* 1970.

Publications:

By EAMES: books—*The Eames Report,* leaflet, with Ray Eames, Los Angeles 1958; *A Computer Perspective,* Cambridge, Massachusetts 1973; *The World of Franklin and Jefferson,* exhibition catalogue, Los Angeles 1976; articles—in *Arts and Architecture* (Los Angeles), September 1941, December 1941; *Interiors* (New York), November 1965; *Domus* (Milan), January 1970; *Film Quarterly* (Berkeley), Spring 1970; *Architectural Forum* (New York), June 1971; *American Scholar* (Washington, D.C.), Summer 1971.

On EAMES: books—*Organic Design in Home Furnishing,* exhibition catalogue with text by Eliot Noyes, New York 1941; *Prize Designs for Modern Furniture* by Edgar J. Kaufmann Jr., New York 1950; *Shaping America's Products* by Don Wallance, New York 1956; *The Modern Chair 1918-1970,* exhibition catalogue with texts by Carol Hogben and others, London 1970; *Charles Eames,* exhibition catalogue by Arthur Drexler, New York 1973; *Connections: The Work of Charles and Ray Eames,* exhibition catalogue by Ralph Caplan and Philip Morrison, Los Angeles 1976; *Furniture Designed by Architects* by Marian Page, New York and London 1980; *Ray and Charles Eames: il collettivo della fantasia* by Luciano Rubino, Rome 1981; *The American Design Adventure 1940-1975* by Arthur J. Pulos, London and Cambridge, Massachusetts 1988; *Eames Design: The Office of Charles and Ray Eames 1941-1978* by Ray Eames, with John and Marilyn Neuhart, London 1989.

Charles Eames and Ray Kaiser first collaborated as designers in 1940, and after their marriage the following year, they worked so closely together that most of their work from 1941, until the death of Charles in 1978, is best considered a joint effort.

Charles Eames studied architecture at Washington University, then stayed in St. Louis to work as an architect before Eliel Saarinen appointed him head of the Experimental Design Workshop at the Cranbrook Academy in Bloomfield Hills, Michigan in 1937. At about the same time, Eames joined the architectural office of Saarinen and his son, Eero. Ray Kaiser studied with the German-American artist Hans Hofmann in New York and Provincetown before enrolling at Cranbrook in 1940.

Charles Eames and Eero Saarinen entered the 1940 exhibition and competition *Organic Design in Home Furnishings* at the Museum of Modern Art in New York. They were assisted by Ray Kaiser in preparing their entries, which won first prizes in two categories. The winning designs included three plywood chairs molded into compound curves, made possible by using thin veneers laminated to layers of glue. It was expected that the winning designs would be put into production, but the entry of the United States into World War II prevented any immediate attempt to overcome production obstacles. Nevertheless, a few prototypes, produced at great expense, were part of an exhibition seen in New York, Cincinnati, and other cities in 1941 and 1942.

Shortly after their marriage, Charles and Ray Eames moved to southern California, where Charles designed sets for the MGM film studios, and they continued during the war years to experiment with plywood. Initially, they used their small apartment as a workshop, but later, with the help of some friends, they moved their workshop to a vacated bakery. In 1942, they began supplying leg splints to the United States Navy. These were made of molded plywood to provide maximum support and comfort to wounded persons. In 1943, their workshop became the southern California branch of the Detroit-based Evans Products Company and expanded into production of laminated glider parts and other items. Meanwhile, the experiments with molded-plywood chairs progressed, and when the war ended, the Evans Products Company was ready to put the first Eames chairs into production.

In 1946, the Museum of Modern Art presented *New Furniture Designed by Charles Eames*, an exhibition that included pieces manufactured by the Evans Products Company, as well as some experimental pieces that were never mass-produced. (As would be the case many times with their joint endeavors, the role of Ray Eames was not credited.) The chairs, designed for a variety of outdoor and indoor uses, attracted the most attention. Some of these were of all-plywood construction, while others were of plywood and metal. The seat and back units of the chairs were made of resin-impregnated plywood, bonded together at the time of molding into compound curves, and stained with brilliant dyes in shades of red, yellow, and blue, which penetrated the wood piles without blurring the natural grain. The parts of the chairs were attached to each other by means of rubber shock-mounts originally developed for engine mountings.

Because the 1946 Museum of Modern Art exhibition was very successful, the Evans Company decided to sell distribution rights for its Eames-designed products to the Herman Miller Furniture Company of Zeeland, Michigan, which had recently appointed George Nelson director of design. Two years later, when the Miller Company purchased production rights, a long association between the Eameses and Herman Miller began. The Eames studio was moved to a converted automobile repair-shop in Venice, California, where Charles and Ray Eames worked with a staff of assistants, usually numbering about twenty.

Two of the chairs designed by Charles and Ray Eames for Herman Miller have become so well known they are often simply called "Eames chairs." One of these is the 1946 dining chair of plywood shock-mounted onto slender steel rods, a variation on some of the chairs exhibited earlier that year. The other, put into production ten years later, is a leather-covered, plywood, lounge chair with a metal swivel base; it is accompanied by a related ottoman. The first Eames-designed chairs with one-piece, molded-plastic, seat-and-back units were put into production by Herman Miller in 1950. Because of their light weight, simple lines, and low cost, a number of Eames-designed chairs were almost equally successful in home and office environments, and consequently millions of them have been sold. (In addition, millions of unauthorized copies made by other manufacturers have been sold.) The Eameses also designed a number of advertisements and showroom displays for Herman Miller, beginning in 1948.

In 1947, Charles and Ray Eames designed a house for themselves in Santa Monica, California. One of a group of "case study" houses with which Charles was involved under the sponsorship of the magazine *Arts and Architecture,* the house was first planned as a box-like structure, utilizing prefabricated parts intended for constructing factories, and was to be suspended between two steel trusses. Later, it was redesigned to utilize the already-delivered parts but to maximize the amount of enclosed volume. The result, with its mass-produced, steel column, window, and door elements, and its modular units of stucco and metal siding, is an open and light-flooded space. The straight lines and right angles of the interior are softened by displays of antique toys, plants, furniture, and fossils, so that the effect is more domestic than industrial. (Some of the Eames collection of antique toys, along with peep-shows, posters, and other items, is displayed in the converted automobile repair-shop studio.)

Among the earliest exhibition designs of the Eameses was a multi-screen slide presentation for the 1959 American National Exhibition in Moscow. Their grid-work of slides, which vividly depicted a cross section of the everyday lives of Americans, was well received by Soviet viewers. A series of exhibitions commissioned by the International Business Machines Corporation ranged from *Mathematica* at the California Museum of Science and Industry in Los Angeles in 1961 to *A Computer Perspective* for the IBM Exhibit Center in New York in 1971. For the latter, there was a related film and a book, *A Computer Perspective,* published in 1973. Another exhibition, *Franklin and Jefferson,* for the American Bicentennial was seen in Paris, Warsaw, and London and in several American cities in 1975-76.

The short films made by the Eameses range from the previously mentioned *A Computer Perspective* and other films, such as *Powers of Ten* (1968, new version 1977-78), that clearly and imaginatively explained complex mathematical and technical concepts, to whimsical films based on the Eames collection of toys; these included *Toccata for Toy Trains* (1957), with original music by Elmer Bernstein, and *Tops* (1969).

Charles and Ray Eames developed a close relationship with India from 1953, when they were invited to investigate its problems and opportunities related to design. *The Eames Report* of 1958 led to the establishment of the National Institute of Design at Amedabad in 1961. In 1964 the Eameses used the N.I.D. as a working base to set up a Jawarharlal Nehru memorial exhibition that opened in New York the following year and was later seen on four continents. Ray Eames last visited India in 1987 to confer the N.I.D.'s first Charles Eames Award.

As significant as the individual achievements of the Eameses are, it is nevertheless the cumulative power of their lives and their work which ultimately will be judged most important. They were not blinded by their success at meeting industrial demands or by the "classical" status some of their designs achieved. Rather, Charles and Ray Eames retained a clear sense of human needs and values. One indication of this is their deep and long-standing attraction to objects embodying the incidental, the humorous, and the whimsical. An extensive Eames archive was established in 1985 at the Library of Congress in Washington, aided by a grant of $500,000 from International Business Machines. Included in the archive are letters, drawings, photographs and films.

—Lloyd C. Engelbrecht

EAMES, Ray.
American artist, filmmaker, exhibition, interior and furniture designer. Born Ray Kaiser, in Sacramento, California, in 1916. Educated at May Friend Bennet School, Mill Brook, New York, 1931–33; studied painting, under Hans Hofmann, in New York and Provincetown, Massachusetts, 1933–39; Cranbrook Academy of Art, Bloomfield Hills, Michigan, 1940–41. Married the architect and designer Charles Eames in 1941. Freelance designer, in partnership with Charles Eames, 1940–78. Founder-Member, American Abstract Artists, New York, 1940. **Exhibitions:** *An Exhibition for Modern Living,* Detroit Institute of Arts, 1949; *The Modern Chair 1918-1970,* Whitechapel Art Gallery, London, 1970; *Connections: The Work of Charles and Ray Eames,* University of California at Los Angeles, 1976; *Design Since 1945,* Philadelphia Museum of Art, 1983. Recipient: Kaufmann International Design Award, 1960; Elsie de Wolfe Award, American Society of Interior Designers, 1975. *Died* (in Venice, California), *21 August 1988.*

See EAMES, Charles.

ECKERSLEY, Tom.
British graphic designer. Born in Newton-le-Willows, Lancashire, 30 September 1914. Studied at Salford School of Art, Lancashire, 1930–34. Served as a cartographer in the Royal Air Force, 1940–45. Married Daisy Mudge in 1937 (divorced, 1965); Mary Kessell in 1966 (died, 1977); sons: Anthony, Richard and Paul. Graphic designer, in partnership with Eric Lombers, London, 1934–40; also designed

Tom Eckersley: Poster for the International Wildlife Film and Television Festival, 1988

posters for the General Post Office, the Ministry of Information and National Service, and for the Royal Society for the Prevention of Accidents, London, 1940–45; freelance graphic designer, London, since 1945: has designed for London Transport, Shell Mex, British Broadcasting Corporation, Austin Reed, etc. Visiting lecturer in graphic design, Westminster School of Art, London, 1938–39; Head of Graphic Design Department, London College of Printing, 1959–75. **Exhibitions:** *Shell Posters,* Shell Mex House, London, 1938; *Eight British Designers,* Nationalmuseum, Stockholm, 1952; *Graphic Art from Britain,* American Institute of Graphic Arts, New York, 1956; *European Design,* University of California at Los Angeles, 1962; *107 Grafici dell'AGI,* Castello Sforzesco, Milan, 1974; *Homage to Tom Eckersley,* London College of Printing, Paperpoint Gallery, 1975; *Tom Eckersley: Posters and Other Graphic Works,* Camden Arts Centre, London, 1980 (toured); Newscastle Gallery of Art, 1983; *Tom Eckersley Past and Present,* Dundee College of Art, Scotland, 1985; *Tom Eckersley: retrospective,* Maidstone College of Art and Design, Kent, 1985; Oxford Polytechnic, 1986; *Eye for Industry: Royal Designers for Industry 1936–1986,* Victoria and Albert Museum, London, 1986. **Collections:** Imperial War Museum, London; Victoria and Albert Museum, London; Museum of Modern Art, New York; Australian National Gallery, Canberra. Recipient: Heywood Medal, Salford School of Art, 1934; Design Award, Slovak Union of Nature Protectors, 1988. Fellow, Society of Artists and Designers, London, 1961; Society of Typographic Designers, New York, 1961; Honorary Fellow, Manchester College of Art and Design, 1961; Humberside College of Higher Education, 1985; Royal Designer for Industry, Royal Society of Arts, London, 1963; Order of the British Empire, 1948. Address: 53 Belsize Park, London NW3 4JL, England.

Works:

His Action Station poster, for the Post Office Savings Bank, 1942.
Good Mornings Begin with Gillette poster series, for Gillette Razor Company, 1948.
Please Pack Parcels Carefully poster series, for the General Post Office, 1954.
Extension of the Piccadilly Line poster, for London Transport, 1970.
Keep an Eye on Valuables poster, for the London College of Printing, 1974.
Open Week poster, for the London College of Printing, 1974.
Long Hair is Dangerous poster, for the London College of Printing, 1975.
Help Lepra Fight Leprosy poster, for LEPRA Medical Charity, 1975.
Ceremonial London poster, for London Transport, 1975.
Murals at Heathrow Airport underground station, for London Transport, 1977.
Artists from London Art Schools 1953–83 Royal Academy exhibition poster, for the Inner London Education Authority, 1983.

Publications:

By ECKERSLEY: book—*Poster Design,* London 1954; books illustrated—*Animals on Parade* by E. A. Cabrelly, London, 1947; *Cat O'Nine Lives* by D. Eckersley, London, 1947.

On ECKERSLEY: books—*Die Neue Grafik/ The New Graphic Design* by Karl Gerstner and Markus Kutter, Teufen and London 1959; *Graphic Design Britain,* edited by Frederick Lambert, London 1967; *107 Grafici dell'AGI,*

exhibition catalogue with texts by Renzo Zorzi and Franco Grignani, Venice 1974; *Tom Eckersley: Posters and Other Graphic Works,* exhibition catalogue with texts by Zuleika Dobson and George Him, London 1980; *Top Graphic Design* by F. H.K. Henrion, Zurich 1983; *Posters by Members of the Alliance Graphique Internationale,* edited by Rudolph de Harak, New York, 1986; *World Graphic Design,* edited by Kodansha Publishers, Tokyo 1988; *The Poster* by Alan Weill, London 1988.

From 1934 until World War II, I worked in partnership with Eric Lombers under the signature Eckersley-Lombers. Since the end of the hostilities, I have worked on my own. My career has been divided equally between my work as a graphic designer and as a teacher. I have always found the two compatible and stimulating. I consider it vital that if you teach, you should also practice. In Europe and the United States, many leading designers and painters have given time to teaching, the Bauhaus being an outstanding example. My aim in my own work has always been to combine aesthetics and purpose in solving a graphic problem. I believe that in any civilized society this should be the aim in all areas of design.

The poster has always had immense appeal for me. The fact that it is mainly the work of one individual suits my temperament and approach to graphic work. I believe strongly in the individuality that most of the great designers have always brought to their work; while solving problems, they have always brought a personal identity to whatever they do.

—Tom Eckersley

Tom Eckersley is arguably the foremost living British poster artist and, through his massive output and his long service in teaching, the most important single influence on the British poster in this century. The style of pictorial poster prevalent in Britain during his youth and training tended to be highly figurative, often featuring human incident and volumetrically rendered landscape. As a student, Eckersley was deeply impressed by a Manchester exhibition of poster design, which included examples by Cassandre, in turn heavily influenced by post-cubist painting in France. He was also much influenced by the exhibition of surrealist art held in London in 1936, and both these traditions, cubism and surrealism, are evident in his mature work.

His early poster designs, some of them undertaken in conjunction with Eric Lombers (with whom he had been a student), show a high degree of simplification and progressive abstraction of form, although they retain stippled half-tones loosely related to the depiction of volume. His mature designs reveal a highly intelligent process of simplification towards the concept of the "visual telegram", as Cassandre put it, in which everything superfluous is eliminated. They often include brilliant exploitation of visual pun and humour, a tendency which has a peculiar strength in the British graphic tradition. His approach to poster design was influential in overthrowing the reigning orthodoxy of strict segregation or stratification of the conventional ingredients of the poster: headline, image, copy. In Eckersley's work, they frequently become inextricably interwoven and interact upon one another in a subtle and complex manner.

His 1975 poster of Lepra, the British Leprosy Relief Appeal, may be taken as a paradigm of this approach. A world map showing the distribution of leprosy is laid over a simple profile of a negro child's head in such a way that the map may be read on one level as information and on another, possibly subliminally, as a metaphor

for the destructive consequences of the disease.

In his early posters, he made extensive use of stencils combined with the brush stipple, a medium which reproduced well in lithography. Following the perfection of silkscreen techniques in the late 1960's he moved to that medium, attracted by its potential for powerful, hard-edge forms in brilliant colour. The recent expansion in the range and quality of coloured papers has permitted him to design by means of a papier collé technique, which has further reinforced the flat, schematic character of his imagery.

Eckersley has never adopted the fulsome and often over-loaded effects of full-colour photography, nor the ruthless exploitation of sex and violence so widespread in contemporary advertising. His persistence with a highly personal and idiosyncratic style of design, the origins of which can be so easily identified and dated, paradoxically still permits him to produce work which is fresh, vigorous, and novel, a welcome counterbalance to the strident hyperbole and the cult of the new which is so prevalent in contemporary publicity graphics.

—Clive Ashwin

ECKHOFF, Tias.
Norwegian ceramics, metalware and furniture designer. Born in Vestre Slidre, 25 June 1926. Studied ceramics, National College of Crafts and Industrial Design, Oslo, 1945–49: Dip. 1949; also trained in the studio of Nathalie Krebs, Saxbo, Denmark, 1947–48. Married Janicke Didrichsen in 1952; children: Eivind, Sigrid and Sven. Designer from 1949, art director, 1953–60, consultant from 1960, and board member since 1974, Porsgrund porcelain factory, Porsgrunn; also freelance designer, for Norsk Stalpress, Georg Jensen, Dansk Knivfabrik, Trio-Ving, Lundtofte Design, etc., in Oslo, from 1957. **Exhibitions:** *Lunning Prizewinners,* Georg Jensen Inc., New York, 1956; *Scandinavian Modern Design 1880–1980,* Cooper-Hewitt Museum, New York, 1982 (toured); *Design Since 1945,* Philadelphia Museum of Art, 1983; *The Lunning Prize,* Nationalmuseum, Stockholm, 1986. **Collections:** Museum of Modern Art, New York; Victoria and Albert Museum, London; Kunstmuseum, Cologne; Landesgewerbemuseum, Stuttgart; Röhsska Konstslöjdmuseet, Göteborg; Danske Kunstindustrimuseum, Copenhagen; Nordenfjeldske Kunstindustrimuseum, Trodheim; Vestlandske Kunstindustrimuseum, Bergen; Kunstindustrimuseet, Oslo. Recipient: Glassware Prize, Hadelands Competition, Oslo, 1951; Cutlery Prize, Georg Jensen Inter-Scandinavian Competition, Copenhagen, 1953; Statens Brugskunststipend, Oslo, 1953; Lunning Prize, 1953; Gold Medals, Milan Triennale, 1954, 1957, 1960; Gold Medal, Deutsche Handwerkmesse, Munich, 1961; Design Prize, Norwegian Export Council, 1961; *Norwegian 10* Prizes, Oslo, 1961, 1965, 1966, 1974, 1976. Addresses: (home) Lyder Sagensgate 6, 0358 Oslo 3, Norway; (office) Fastingsgate 6, 0358 Oslo 3, Norway.

Works:

Det Riflete/The Fluted One porcelain tableware, for Porsgrund, 1952.

Cypress flatware cutlery in sterling silver, for Georg Jensen, 1952.

Glohane/Glowing Cock overproof ware, for Porsgrund, 1955.

Opus flatware cutlery in stainless steel and plastic, for Dansk Knivfabrik, 1959.

Maya flatware cutlery in stainless steel, for Norsk Stalpress, 1961.

Regent porcelain tableware, for Porsgrund, 1961.

Fuga flatware cutlery in stainless steel, for Dansk Knivfabrik, 1962.

Una flatware cutlery in stainless steel, for Norsk Stalpress, 1973.

Tiki flatware cutlery in stainless steel, for Norsk Stalpress, 1974.

Ana chair in plastic and steel with wool upholstery, for Ana-Tomi, 1980.

Tomi chair in plastic and steel with wool upholstery, for Ana-Tomi, 1983.

Chaco flatware cutlery in stainless steel, for Norsk Stalpress, 1989.

Publications:

By ECKHOFF: articles—"Keramiske Materialer i husholdningen" in *Bonytt* (Oslo), no. 15, 1955; "Om smak og behag" in *Glassposten* (Oslo), no. 6, 1962.

On ECKHOFF: books—*Industridesigneren Tias Eckhoff* by Alf Boe, Olso 1965; *Porsgrunds Porcelaenfabrik 1885–1965* by Alf Boe, Oslo 1965; *34 Skandinavske Designere* by Sven Erik Moller, Copenhagen 1967; *Nordisk Kunsthandverk og Design* by Fredrik Wildhagen and others, Oslo 1981; *Scandinavian Modern Design 1880–1980*, edited by David Revere McFadden, New York 1982; *Design Since 1945*, edited by Kathryn Hiesinger and George Marcus, Philadelphia and London 1983; *The Lunning Prize,* exhibition catalogue edited by Helena Dahlbäck Lütteman and Marianne Uggla, Stockholm 1986; *Norge i Form* by Fredrik Wildhagen, Oslo 1988.

My background as a designer is in the postwar Scandinavian design movement. This movement dictated that good design should combine function, aesthetics, economy and social awareness—an engaging and stimulating milieu in which to develop.

However, the most important factor for my subsequent work must have been the fact that I grew up on a farm where the sovereign craftsman of the district had a small cottage. He was able to make anything—from building a violin to repairing and reconstructing agricultural machinery. I spent a considerable part of my childhood in that cottage, where big new problems were solved with small and simple remedies.

And so I have strived in my work to approach tasks in a simple and practical way, and to preserve the tenets of good ergonomic and economical solutions applied to "beautiful articles for everyday use" (the 1950s slogan in Scandinavia), articles that will last for many years. Fortunately, most of my design products from the 1950s and 1960s are still in production and on sale.

—Tias Eckhoff

Born in 1926, Tias Eckhoff is a prominent Norwegian designer whose career has developed from the postwar period to the present day. He was educated as a craftsman in the ceramics department of Oslo's National College of Arts and Crafts. Here, his refined linear draughtmanship soon became noticed.

In 1949, whilst still attending the National College of Arts and Crafts, he was named as designer by Porsgrund porcelain factory. His first table service in feldspar porcelain, *Det Riflede/The Fluted One* (1952), won a gold medal at the Milan Triennale of 1954. Stressing the material quality and purity of design, *The Fluted One* heralded the very essence of "Scandinavian Design". A complementary and contemporary work is *Glohane/Glowing Cock* (1955), a more rustic series of heatproof jugs and servers in bright monochrome colours produced by the sanitary division of the same factory when capacity was available. His undecorated coffee service, *Regent* (1961), has a supple linear grace that makes it an outstanding representative of Eckhoff's ceramic design.

After leaving his position as chief designer at the Porsgrund factory in 1960, Eckhoff established his own design studio in Oslo. As a freelance and consultant designer, he developed designs for different purposes: furniture, kitchen equipment, locking devices, armoured steel doors, etc. For the contract market, Eckhoff not only designed *Tomi* (1983), an easy and elegant chair in steel and plastic with upholstery in woven wool, but also its production machinery and equipment as well.

Cutlery is another field to which Eckhoff has dedicated himself. His first set, *Cypress* (1952), was produced in silver by Georg Jensen of Copenhagen. Later, he created a long series of designs for cutlery ranges in stainless steel. The set *Maya* (1961), produced by Norsk Stalpress of Bergen, is still in production. It represents a balanced conception between elongated and rounded forms. *Fuga* (1962), produced by Dansk Knivfabrik of Copenhagen, is another set characterized by a sophisticated sobriety which bears witness to a simplified process of manufacture. A recent addition to this field is *Chaco* (1989), also produced by Norsk Stalpress.

As a consultant designer, Eckhoff is associated with a long list of widely-differing firms. He has played a major role in the activites of Norwegian design organizations, was elected member of the American Institute of Interior Designers, and has won numerous gold medals and other awards at home and abroad. The greater part of Eckhoff's commissioned work is for the consumer market. The excellence of his design rests on a sound basis of technical and ergonomic analysis. Still, his most compelling virtue as a designer is his exquisite line of draughtmanship.

—Ivar Stranger

Tias Eckhoff: *Chaco* cutlery in stainless steel, for Norsk Stalpress, 1989

EDELMANN, Heinz.

German animated film and graphic designer. Born, of German parents, in Usti nad Labem, Czechoslovakia, 20 June 1934. Studied art, at the Kunstakademie, Düsseldorf, 1953–58; mainly self-taught in design. Married Anna Edelmann; daughter: Valentine. Worked as an advertising agency copywriter, Düsseldorf, 1958–59; freelance graphic designer, working with Anna Edelmann, in Düsseldorf, 1959–70, and in the Hague, since 1970: has designed for Atlas-Film-Verleih, Animations-Filme, Carl Hanser Verlag, Ernst Klett Verlag, Gertraud Middlehauve Verlag, Hoechst, Sandoz, Der Deutsche Ring insurance company, Düsseldorfer Kammerspiele, Westdeutscher Rundfunk, etc. Staff designer, with Willy Fleckhaus, of *Twen* magazine, Cologne and Munich. Instructor, Werklehrseminar, Düsseldorf, 1959–61, Werkkunstschule, Düsseldorf, 1961–63, the Free Academy and Royal Academy, The Hague, from 1971. **Exhibition:** *107 Grafici dell'AGI,* Castello Sforzesco, Milan, 1974. Address: Leuvensestraat 83, s-Gravenhage, Netherlands.

Works:

books designed include—*The Once and Future King* by T. H. White; *The Last Unicorn* by Peter S. Beagle; *The Dream-Quest of Unknown Kadath* by H. P. Lovecraft; *Amadis von Gallien,* 2 vols.; *Die Goldene Kuppel des Comes Arbogast oder Lichtenberg in Hamburg* by Helmut Heissenbuttel; *Die Heiliger Drei Konige auf der Reise* by J. Rausch; *Die Prinzessin aus Elfenland* by Lord Dunsany; *Manuel Gassers Kochleverzeichnis: Die Kuche meine Tante Marie* by Manuel Gasser; *Unter dem Regemond* by Oscar Beni; *Uber die Engel* by Rafael Alberti; *Ökonomie des Arbeit,* 2 vols., by Gerhard Brinkmann; *Der Deutsche Werkbund 1907–1934* by Joan Campbell; *Bemerkungen* by Erwin Chargaff; *Waldstein* by Sven Delblanc; *Der Antike Staat* by Numa Denis and Fustel de Coulanges; *Die Versager* by Henning Grunwald; *Goethe and Cotta; Briefwechsel 1797–1832,* edited by Dorothea Kuhn; *Textbucher 1–6* by Helmut Heissenbuttel; *Sturm* by Ernst Junger; *Rattus Rex* by Colin McLaren; *Verteidigung des Briefes* by Pedro Salinas; *Schulbuch-Schelte* by Gerd Stein; *Sprechmaschine Pechmarie* by Ralf Thenior; *Phonetik* by H. G. Tillmann and P. Mansell; *Handbuch der Kulturanthropologie* by Frank Robert Vivelo.

Publications:

By EDELMANN: book—*Die 51 schönsten Buchumschlage von Heinz Edelmann,* with introduction by Kurt Weidemann, Stuttgart 1982.

On EDELMANN: books—*Das Plakat* by Anton Sailer, Munich 1965; *German Advertising Art,* edited by Eberhard Holscher, Munich 1967; *Book Jackets and Record Sleeves,* edited by Kurt Weidemann, Stuttgart and London 1969; *Monografie des Plakats: Entwicklung, Stil, Design* by Herbert Schindler, Munich 1972; *107 Grafici dell'AGI,* exhibition catalogue with texts by Zenzo Zorzi and Franco Grignani, Venice 1974; *Full Length Animated Feature Films* by Bruno Edera, London and New York 1977; *Who's Who in Graphic Art,* edited by Walter Amstutz, Dubendorf 1982.

Heniz Edelmann combines in his work the spirit and fashion of his time, the traditions of the darker fantasies of Central Europe, and a formidable technical professionalism. At one period, he was a member of the editorial staff of the magazine *Twen,* a pace-setting phenomenon of its time. In addition, he absorbed much of the then-current imagery of Pop art. Later, his work reflected the colourful fantasies of the psychedelic decorations of the 1960's. Edelmann has continuously developed his style but retained the intensity of his vision so that in spite of a wide range of expression his creative output is imprinted with his fundamentally powerful integrity.

Despite his inventiveness, important traditional elements appear in his work. For example, one can sometimes relate his work to the images of the macabre found in the woodcuts and drawings of medieval Germany. Again, he has used the imagery of popular prints of the nineteenth century. His work has frequently been used in children's books, and even among the well-known designs made for WDR it is the posters for children's television programmes that one remembers most forcefully. The traditional themes of violence and cruelty presented in decorative terms so characteristic of the great literary classics for children are given a new currency through Edelmann's designs. His constant stylistic changes, which contain an erratic, often terrifying element, stay abreast of events in design and keep him ahead of his imitators. Never melodramatic, he frequently parodies himself, and his work is, at basis, humorous.

Among his most recent designs are the eighteen posters made for the World Theatre Festival in Cologne in 1981. The designs, which consists of incongruous images, can be used in any context by over-printing text. It is to Edelmann's credit that he has the rare gift of producing images still capable of distrubing the sophisticated tastes of the 1980's. Publicity has relied on such methods now for decades, yet Edelmann's designs are fresh and original. A recent poster for Crazy Programmes on WDR children's television reveals his facility as a linear draughtsman and links the contemporary idioms of montage with the circus drawings of Toulouse-Lautrec.

—John Barnicoat

EHRICH, Hans.
Swedish industrial designer. Born of Swedish and German parents, in Helsinki, Finland, 25 September 1942. Studied metalwork and design, National College of Art, Craft and Design (Konstfackskolan), Stockholm, 1962–68; apprentice designer, in Turin and Milan, 1965. Founder-Director, with Tom Ahlström, A & E Design AB, Stockholm, from 1968, and Interdesign AB, Stockholm, from 1982, designing for Anza, Arjo, Colgate, Fagerhults, Gustavsberg, RFSU, ASEA, Jordan, Norwesco, Yamagiwa, etc. **Exhibitions:** *From Idea to Finished Product,* Form Design Center, Malmo, 1977 (travelled to Stockholm); *Contemporary Swedish Design,* Nationalmuseum, Stockholm, 1983 (toured); *Faces of Swedish Design,* Cranbrook Academy of Art, Bloomfield Hills, Michigan, 1988 (toured); *From Revolution to New Expressions 1968–1988,* Nationalmuseum, Stockholm, 1989. **Collections:** Nationalmuseum, Stockholm; Tekniska Museet, Stockholm; Röhsska Konstslöjdmuseet, Goteborg. Recipient: Swedish State Award to Artists, 1971, 1972; Industrial Designer of the Year Award, 1987. Address: A & E Design AB, Tulegatan 19 G VI, 113 53 Stockholm, Sweden.

See AHLSTRÖM, Tom

Hermann Eidenbenz: Poster for the Mustermesse, Basel

EIDENBENZ, Hermann.
Swiss graphic, lettering and typographic designer. Born, of Swiss parents, in Cannanore, India, 4 September 1902. Apprentice, Orell Füssli printers, Zurich, 1921–22; studied graphics, under Ernst Keller, Kunstgewerbeschule, Zurich, 1919–23. Served in the Swiss Army, 1940–45. Married Lotte Christoffel in 1945; children: Florian, Thomas, Mathias and Franziska. Design assistant, in Wilhelm Deffke's studio, Berlin, 1923–25, and in O. H. W. Hadank's studio, Berlin, 1925–26; founder-partner, with his brothers Reinhold and Willy, studio for graphic design, photography and advertising, Basel, 1923–53; designer and advertising consultant, Reemtsma cigarette manufacturers, Hamburg, 1955–67; freelance designer, Basel, since 1970. Instructor in lettering and graphic design, Kunstgewerbe- und Handwerkschule, Magdeburg, 1926–32; instructor in graphic design, Werkkunstschule, Braunschweig, 1953–55. **Exhibitions:** Helmhaus, Zurich, 1940; Kunstgewerbemuseum, Zurich, 1959; Gewerbemuseum, Basel, 1979; Reinhold Brown Gallery, New York, 1980. **Collections:** Gewerbemuseum, Basel; Kunstgewerbemuseum, Zurich. Address: Mittlere Strasse 7, 4056 Basel, Switzerland.

Works:

Coat of arms, for the City of Basel, 1947.
Coat of arms, for the City of Braunschweig, 1954, 1981.
Ten and twenty franc bank notes, for the Central Swiss Bank, 1956–80.
All West German bank notes, for the Deutsches Bundesbank, from 1964.
Coat of arms, for the City of Trier, 1982.

Publications:

On EIDENBENZ: books—*Packaging: An International Survey of Package Design,* edited by Walter Herdeg, Zurich 1959; *Die Neue Grafik/ The New Graphic Design* by Karl Gerstner and Markus Kutter, Teufen and London 1959; *Moderne Werbe- und Gebrauchs-Graphik* by Hans Neuburg, Ravensburg 1960; *Who's Who in Graphic Art,* edited by Walter Amstutz, Zurich 1962, Dubendorf 1982; *The Western Heritage of Type Design* by R. S. Hutchings, London and New York 1965; *Schriftkunst* by Albert Kapr, Dresden 1971; *History of the Poster* by Josef and Shizuko Müller-Brockmann, Zurich 1971.

EKUAN, Kenji.
Japanese industrial designer. Born in Tokyo, 11 September 1929. Educated at the College of Buddhism, Kyoto, and trained for the priesthood at Chioin Temple, 1947–49; studied design, National University of Fine Arts and Music, Tokyo, 1950–55: BA 1955; studied industrial design, Art Center College of Design, Pasadena, 1956 (Japan External Trade Organization scholarship). Served in the Japanese Navy: cadet. Founder-President, GK (Group Koike) Industrial Design Associates, Tokyo, and subsidiaries GK Sekkei, GK Inc., GK Shop, GK Institute, Kyoto Design Center, and GK Design International (Los Angeles), since 1957. Board Member, from 1962, and Presi-

dent, 1970–72, Japan Industrial Designers Association; Vice-President of the Executive Board, 1973–75, President, 1976–79, and Senate Member from 1979, ICSID International Council of Societies of Industrial Design; Design Advisory Committee Member, Japanese Ministry of International Trade and Industry, since 1975; Board Member of the Japan Design Foundation, Japan Exhibition Association, Japan Livelihood Association, and Japan Society for Future Research; Advisory Committee Member, Art Center College of Design, Pasadena, Japan Ergonomics Association, Hiroshima Metropolitan Museum of Modern Art, and Japan Computer Graphics Association; Organizing Committee Member, Tokyo National Museum of Modern Art; President, Kuwasawa Design School. **Exhibitions:** *Kenji Ekuan and His World,* Axis Gallery, Tokyo, 1982. Recipient: First Prize, Nippon Telegraph and Telephone Competition, 1953; First Prize, 1955, 1958, and Grand Prix, 1974, 1977, Mainichi Industrial Design Competition; Kaufmann International Design Study Grant, New York, 1964; First Prize, Misawa Prefabricated Housing Competition, 1969; Japanese Ministry of International Trade and Industry Awards, 1972, 1975, 1977; ICSID Colin King Grand Prix, 1979; International Design Award, Japan Design Foundation, 1987. Honorary Royal Designer for Industry, Royal Society of Arts, London, 1974; Honorary Fellow, Industrial Design Institute of Australia, 1981; Honorary Member, ORNAMO Finnish Association of Designers, 1981; Member, Mexican Academy of Design, 1984. DSc: Art Center College of Design, Pasadena, 1981. International Member, Industrial Designers Society of America. Address: 2-19-16 Shimo-ochiai, Shinjuku-ku, Tokyo 161, Japan.

Works:

Motorcycles, snowmobiles, powerboat engines and golf carts, for Yamaha Motorcycle Company, from 1953.

Public telephone booth, for Nippon Telegram and Telephone Corporation, 1953.

Bicycles, for Maruishi Cycle Industrial Company, from 1955.

Soy sauce bottle and package design, for Kikkoman Shoyu Company, from 1958.

Office furniture, for Okamura, from 1961.

Opera glasses, binoculars and lens accessories, for Hoya Corporation, from 1963.

Systems kitchens and bathroom fittings, for Nas Stainless Company, from 1963.

Offset printing press and catalogues, for Komori Printing Machinery, from 1965.

World clock, program timers, exhibition displays and *Expo 70* official timer system, for Hattori Company (Seiko), from 1970.

Interiors, signage system and cash dispensers, for Fuji Bank, from 1973.

Kashima Jingu station plaza and environmental plan, for Kashima Cho Office, Tochigi Prefecture, 1975–83.

Sunliner and *Sunpoint* glass display systems, for Asahi Glass Company, 1979.

SLR ZE-X camera, for Mamiya Camera Company, 1981.

Rumina 1460 sewing machine, for Singer Nikko, 1982.

Security alarm systems, for Secom Company, from 1982.

SV-250 community vehicle, for the Japan Small Vehicle Association, 1982.

Publications:

By EKUAN: books—*Dogu Ko,* Tokyo 1967; *Industrial Design: The World of Dogu, its Ori-*

Kenji Ekuan: *SV-250* community vehicle, for the Japan Small Vehicle Association, 1982

gins, its Future, Tokyo 1971; *Design: The Relationship of Man and Technology,* Tokyo 1972; *Ekuan: Dunhill Industrial Design Lecture Series 1973,* Sydney 1975; *The History of Kitchen Utensils,* Tokyo 1976; *Makunouchi Bento No Bigaku/The Aesthetics of the Makunouchi Box Lunch,* Tokyo 1980; *The Philosophy of Tools,* Tokyo 1980; *The World of GK: The Concept and Development of Industrial Design,* Tokyo 1983; *Butsudan to Jidosha/The Buddhist Altar and the Automobile,* Tokyo 1986.

On EKUAN: books—*The Conran Directory of Design,* edited by Stephen Bayley, London 1985; *Japanese Design* by Penny Sparke, London 1987; articles—"Tokyo's Mister Less-Is-More" by S. Braidwood in *Design* (London), January 1981; "Design and Democracy" by J. Fair in *PHP* (Tokyo), September 1982; "Kenji Ekuan Muovailee Esineelle Sielun" in *Helsingin Sanomat* (Helsinki), 10 February 1987; "Kenji Ekuan: Industrial Designer" in *PHP* (Tokyo), November 1988.

*

My primary concern as an industrial designer is to simplify complex elements through design to create things which are easily appreciated and understood by the masses. The widespread diffusion of small cars, sophisticated cameras, and mini-calculators is essentially a democratization of high culture. Technology, by simplifying the operation of complex mechanisms and machineries, has made such products readily available to the masses. It is the designer's task to bring the fruits of civilization to people. He must strive to humanize technology and familiarize it to laymen. By creating a congenial man-machine interface, he can offer cultivated or cultural beauty. Through the power of design the two worlds of man and material things can be made to function together in harmony.

When the historical and cultural references of the design of a nation are, by means of mature techniques and technology, enlivened by products introduced to the world, material things can enrich man's life. When those products are globally appreciated, internationalization of a local culture is achieved. The "cultural connection" through design has been my lifelong pursuit.

I have a great fascination for the communicative quality of design as a tangible medium. Because design is blessed with the power to create a culture of living, serious thought must be given to designing products which can bring living comfort to people. While I am proud to be a designer, I am constantly reminded of the tremendous responsibility demanded by my profession as a creative mediator of man and the material world.

—Kenji Ekuan

*

"To seek the soul in material things" is one of the declared goals of GK (Groupe Koike)—the largest design office in the world. In 1953, under the guidance of Professor Iwatoro Koike, Kenji Ekuan and some other designers and architects formed a team, which developed into GK. Ekuan, who has been President since its founding, can in many ways be considered representative of the postwar generation of Japanese designers.

The wisdom of Ekuan—being not only a designer but also a Buddhist monk—and the determination "to keep the spiritual purity of a novice" has fundamentally influenced the development and growth of GK over thirty years. It would probably lead too far to note all the details of GK's success story—winning many competitions as well as many prizes sponsored by the municipal governments of Tokyo and other major Japanese cities. The group, and Ekuan with it, gained recognition as a leading design practice by working with large industries like Yamaha and others, in Japan and internationally. Cooperation with famous Japanese architects, including Kenzo Tange, Kisho Kurokawa, and others, stimulated Ekuan's already existing interest in urban and environmental matters. Active participation in important design events, such as the 1962 World Design Conference in Tokyo, the EXPO '70 in Osaka, the 1973 International Council of Societies of Industrial Design congress in Kyoto, and the 1983 first International Design Festival in Osaka, has contributed to make Ekuan the internationally well-known design personality that he has become. This development crested with his election as President of the International Council of Societies of Industrial Design at its 1976 assembly in Brussels.

However, nothing could be wronger than to confuse Ekuan with the successful organization man that he sometimes might appear to be. It is his basically reflective and philosophical quality, incorporating the finest elements of Japanese culture and tradition, that leads him into a continuous, ongoing search for a Nirvana of beauty, satisfying infinite desires by seeking the soul beyond the material aspects of things that form the human environment.

An inborn sense of dignified respect for symbolic meaning as well as for methodology and a pronounced lack of satisfaction with achievements and success have—not surprisingly—contributed to make (and keep) Ekuan one of the most interesting figures in the world of design. He gives living proof that spirituality, talent, and future-oriented activity in this particular field can very well rely on the cherished background of one's culture, tradition, and symbolic values in a post-industrial future that—on the face of it—seems far from safe or certain.

—Carl Auböck

ELLIS, Perry (Edwin).

American fashion designer. Born in Portsmouth, Virginia, 30 March 1940. Studied business, College of William and Mary, Williamsburg, Virginia, 1958–61: BA 1961; retailing studies, New York University, 1961–63: MA 1963. Worked as a buyer, Miller and Rhoads department store, Richmond, Virginia, 1963–67; design director, John Meyer, New York, 1968–74; sportswear designer, Vera Companies, New York, 1974–75; sportswear designer, with own "Portfolio" label, Manhattan Industries, New York, 1975–78; independent designer, New York, 1978–86: established Perry Ellis Sportwear, 1978, and Perry Ellis Menswear, 1980; also designed furs, household textiles, toiletries, clothing and patterns for Levi Strauss, Greif, Martex, Visions Stern, *Vogue*, etc., from 1978. Established Perry Ellis fashion studies scholarship, with Marshall Field and Company, at the Art Institute of Chicago. Recipient: Neiman Marcus Fashion Award, 1979; eight Coty American Fashion Critics Awards, and Coty Hall of Fame Award, 1981; Council of Fashion Designers American Sportswear Award, 1981. *Died (in New York City) 30 May 1986.*

Publications:

On ELLIS: books—*Fairchild's Who's Who in Fashion,* edited by Ann Stegemeyer, New York 1980; *McDowell's Directory of Twentieth Century Fashion* by Colin McDowell, London 1984; *The Encyclopedia of Fashion from 1840 to the 1980s* by Georgina O'Hara, London 1986.

Without a doubt, Perry Ellis was the most "charming" of his generation of American designers. A whiff of Victoriana, of crisp linen and gingham is always detectable, even in his most "serious" clothes. He was pre-eminently a designer for the young, but there is nothing

pejorative about this observation. On the contrary, Ellis's sensibilities, while on the surface, "naive," were actually shrewd and sophisticated. It would be wrong to dismiss his work as revivalistic, for it has far more to do with a re-exploration of what simple, traditional clothes were—and can be—about.

Starting with a simple linen dress, Ellis could, by carefully re-aligning the proportions, even exaggerating them, suggest infinite resources and artfulness. Which is why, although on the surface, conservative, his clothes never suggest revivalism. It is the past looked at through the prism of the late twentieth century, with all that the latter quarter has taught us about masculinity, femininity, and the meaning of clothes as ritual, as seduction, as fantasy. The designer's predilection for the slightly "off" in the proportioning of his clothes is the closest he comes to a trademark. He would, for example, give a tweed coat impossibly deep and full cuffs on the sleeve, or place the waist of a dress a couple of inches higher that it "should" be. It is thus, as a highly subtle modifier of our perceptions that Ellis stands out, but his base line was always the status quo.

It is this curious conservatism, which Ellis shared with the other leading American designers of his day, that makes America famous for clothes that are easy, functional, even elegant, but never wildly original or avant-garde. The reason that late twentieth-century American clothes never matched her art or her dance in orginality poses a fascinating question for historians: in the meantime, what is pleasurable, particularly with regard to Ellis, is how masterful is the re-statement and distillation of the main theme of American clothing.

—Peter Carlsen

ENVIRONETICS INTERNATIONAL.

American architectural and interior design firm. Founded, as Michael Saphier Associates, in New York, 1937; incorporated as Saphier, Lerner, Schindler, in 1958; became SLS Environetics, 1962, and Environetics International, in 1981. Chairman, President and Chief Executive: Lawrence Lerner (born 1923); Vice-Chairmen: Richard Korchen (born 1930) and Sidney Resnick (born 1931); Chief Operating Officer: Donald Sachar; Executive Vice-President: Alan Briskman; Senior Vice-President: Edward Bajbek. Addresses: Environetics International Inc., 600 Madison Avenue, New York, New York 10022, U.S.A.; 11110 Ohio Avenue, Los Angeles, California 90925; 1025 Connecticut Avenue N.W., Washington, D.C. 20036; 49 Wigmore Street, London W1H 9LE, England; Environetica S.A., Paseo de la Reforma 76, Piso 16, Mexico 6, D.F., Mexico.

Works:

Sears Roebuck and Company interiors, Chicago, 1973.
United Technologies Corporation interiors, Hartford, Connecticut, 1978.
Swiss Bank Corporation interiors, at the World Trade Center, New York, 1979.
Federated Department Stores, interiors, Cincinnati, Ohio, 1979.
William Collins Publishers interiors, Glasgow, 1979.

W. H. Smith bookshops interiors, London, 1980.
Hanes Corporation interiors, Winston-Salem, North Carolina, 1980.
American Can Company interiors, Stamford, Connecticut, 1981.
Federal Land Bank interiors, St. Paul, Minnesota, 1982.
Planning Research Corporation interiors, Washington, D.C., 1982.
Philips Petroleum interiors, London, 1983.
Bendix Corporation interiors, Rosslyn, Virginia, 1983.
John Paul Getty Museum interiors, Malibu, California, 1983.
DG Bank interiors, New York and London, 1983.

Publications:

By ENVIRONETICS INTERNATIONAL (Lawrence Lerner): articles—in *Office Management* (Beckenham, Kent), July 1958; *The Office* (Stamford, Connecticut), July 1959, August 1960, July 1964; *The Executive* (London), November 1959; *Contract* (New York), July 1962, September 1964, April 1965, March 1966, May 1966, March 1979; *Interior Decorators News* (New York), August 1962, March 1963; *Journal of Property Management* (Chicago), May/June 1964; *The Steelcase Circle* (New York), December 1964; *Business Products* (Arlington, Virginia), January 1966; *Progressive Architecture* (New York), November 1969; *Designers West* (Los Angeles), August 1973; *Management World* (Willow Grove, Pennsylvania), June 1975; *Realty* (New York), June 1979, July 1980; *Administrative Management* (Beckenham, Kent), January 1981; *Index Report* (New York), May 1982; *Words* (Willow Grove, Pennsylvania), September 1982.

Environetics International, Inc. was the first interior architectural firm to organize its administrative management structure into a classic commercial enterprise. It was the first interior architectural professional service to merge with a major American industrial corporation (Litton Industries), all of whose stock was in the hands of the public. Environetics was also the first interior architectural firm to create a network of offices in major cities across the United States and ultimately around the world. The sequence was as follows: Cleveland, 1956; Los Angeles, 1958; Chicago, 1960; San Francisco, 1961; New Orleans, 1962; Boston, 1968; Houston, 1970; London, 1972; Washington, D.C., 1973; Tokyo, 1980; Minneapolis, 1980; Mexico City, 1981. The New Orleans, Minneapolis, Boston, and Houston offices were project-oriented and have been closed.

The company was a forerunner by many years of involvement in computer graphics as applied to architectural working drawings. As far as we know, it was the only company in the profession to have its own in-house software and hardware for the production of architectural working drawings from 1969 on. It was only in the late 1970's and early 1980's that other firms became involved in the state-of-the-art.

In 1955, the Gulf Oil Corporation retained Environetics to plan the use of a projected building, from the inside out. The architect was retained after our study was completed, and the size and shape of this building and its individual floors was determined by our study. Environetics has been known for this basic technique and philosophy. It was applied in 1969 to the creation of the world's largest commercial office building, the Sears Tower, which is 4.4 million square feet. All of the working drawings for the entire interior of the Sears Tower were produced on the Environetics

ENVIRONETICS INTERNATIONAL 157

Environetics International: Swiss Bank Corporation interior, at the World Trade Center, New York, 1979

MAN/MAC computer graphic system. In the years since 1973 when Sears occupied the Tower, the MAN/MAC system has been in continuous use in maintaining major changes in the occupancy of the building.

All of our clients are constrained by budgetary limitations. These limitations, however, do not restrict their need and desire to fulfill all of their functional and aesthetic requirements. We therefore consider it our task to produce an environment for them that permits their employees to work in stimulating, exciting, and beautiful surroundings while satisfying all the constraints of budget and time. In short, we feel that it is a designer's responsibility always to create an aesthetically pleasing environment regardless of functional and budgetary requirements.

—Lawrence Lerner
Environetics International

Environetics International is so closely identified with its chairman and president, Lawrence Lerner, that it is hard to separate the firm from Lerner the designer. Whatever the firm's particular strength and orientation, it is in some way the talent and leadership of this chief executive officer. The firm was started by Michael Saphier, and it was Michael Saphier Associates that Lerner joined in 1948. In 1958, he was made president of the company, and the name

of the practice was changed to Saphier Lerner Schindler.

Environetics International is one of the world's leading firms in interior design and planning. It is also one of the largest, but throughout the past thirty years, the firm could have made its mark simply as an excellent and totally professional firm offering design services to corporate clients in a manner appropriate to any respected by commerce and industry. Until the early 1950's, interior design was not the serious profession that it is now. Lerner was one of the pioneers who made space planning and the design of business environments a highly respected specialty. The firm specialized in the design of office environments at a time when the concept was new, and others were still practicing interior design as decoration.

Under Lerner's leadership, the firm went beyond space planning and interior design to become the recognized expert in the office of the future and the techniques appropriate to that concept. While working on a design project for NASA in 1961, Lerner saw the computer technology used to interpret data supplied from satellites. This sparked the idea which started Environetics International on the road to establishing one of the first and most extensive computer-aided design facilities in architecture and interior design.

Lerner's mind is attuned to technology, and

he is probably the most knowledgeable designer interfacing with computer technology for "high tech" offices. In 1971, he led a design team conducting a feasibility study for an off-shore airport for New York City. This widely acclaimed, imaginative project typifies the accomplishments of the firm and of Lerner the designer.

—Arnold Friedmann

ERNI, Hans.
Swiss painter, sculptor, illustrator, stage, mural, ceramic and graphic designer. Born in Lucerne, 21 February 1909. Educated at the Volksschule, Lucerne, 1915–23; apprentice surveyor and architectural draughtsman, in Lucerne, 1924–27; studied at the Kunstgewerbeschule, Lucerne, 1927–28, Académie Julian, Paris, 1928–30, and under Heinrich Wölfflin, at the Vereinigte Staatschule für Freie und Angewandte Kunst, Berlin, 1929–30. Served in the

transport and camouflage units of the Swiss Army, 1940–45. Married Doris Kessler in 1949. Independent painter and designer, in Lucerne, London and Berlin, 1930–39, and with studio in Lucerne, from 1945: first stage designs, 1946, postage stamp designs, 1949, and ceramic designs, 1950. Founder-member, Allianz group of artists, Zurich, 1938. **Exhibitions:** Galerie Schulthess, Basel, 1935; Kunst- und Gewerbemuseum, Winterthur, 1945; Kunstkring, Rotterdam, 1946; Musée de l'Athenée, Geneva, 1948, 1957, 1961, 1969, 1974; Gutenberg Book Guild, Zurich, 1950; Main Street Gallery, Chicago, 1951, 1953, 1955, 1956, 1959, 1960, 1963, 1967, 1970; Librairie Paul Morihier, Paris, 1950, 1953; Zwemmer Gallery, London, 1956; Musee Royale, Brussels, 1958; Hammer Galleries, New York, 1959, 1964; Kunstverein, Mannheim, 1962; National Gallery of Victoria, Melbourne, 1964; Museum zur Allerheiligen, Schaffhausen, 1966; Musee Rath, Geneva, 1969; Kunstmuseum, Lucerne, 1971; Kulturzentrum Seedamm, Pfaffikon, 1976; German Nationalmuseum, Nuremberg, 1977; Hans-Erni-Museum, Lucerne, 1979. **Collection:** Hans-Erni-Museum, in the Swiss Transport Museum, Lucerne (opened 1979). Recipient: Lucerne Mural Competition Prize, 1935; Rimini Biennale Prize, 1952; Gold Medal, Cannes Ceramics Exhibition, 1955; Warsaw Poster Biennale Prize, 1966. Address: Kreuzbuchstrasse, Meggen, Lucerne, Switzerland.

Works:

Coffee sgraffito mural, for Nestle Building, Vevey, 1959.
Mosaic, for the College Abbaye de Saint-Maurice, Valais, 1961.
Day and Night and *Towards Humanity* murals, for the Bankverein, Geneva, 1963.
Mosaic, for the SRG Swiss Radio and Television Building, Bern, 1964.
Business Organization mural, for the Lausanne Exposition, 1964.
La Noce mural, for the Hotel Intercontinental, Lausanne, 1965.
The Valais mural, for the Union des Banques Suisses, Sion, 1966.
Sgraffito mural, for the Swissair airlines headquarters, Zurich, 1967.
Poseidon mural, for the Municipal Swimming Pool, Lucerne, 1969.
Four Elements mural, for the Winterthur Insurance Company, Winterthur, 1970.
Prometheus metal mural, for the Municipal Electricity Board, Lucerne, 1972.
Man and Progress tapestry, for the Savings Bank of Geneva, 1974.
Man in Flight mural, for the International Civil Aviation Organization, Montreal, 1975.
Penta Rhei mural, for the Hans Erni Museum, Lucerne, 1984–86.

Publications:

By ERNI: books—*Promesse del l'Homme*, with André Bonnard, Paris 1953; *Liebesgedicht*, Lausanne 1962; *Sketchbook I*, Zürich 1963; *The Aldus Encyclopaedia*, 10 vols, editor, London 1958–65; *Hans Erni* portfolio, Zürich 1969; *Sketchbook: Israel*, Zürich 1971; *Sketchbook: India*, Zürich 1973; *Erotidien*, Zürich 1973; *Minuskeln*, Lucerne 1975; *Hans Erni: Gedanken und Gedichte*, Frauenfeld, Switzerland 1978; books illustrated—*Le Banquet* by Plato, Zürich 1941; *Das Lied des Friedens* by Albius Tibullus, Basel 1942; *Work Through the Centuries* by G. Canevascini, Zürich 1943; *Olympiques* by Pindar, Lausanne 1944; *Troy, Tales from Ancient Greece* by Hans Bracher,

Bern 1948; *King Oedipus* by Sophocles, Lausanne 1949; *Antigone* by Sophocles, Lausanne 1950; *Daphnis and Chloe* by Longus, Lausanne 1950; *Anthologie de la nouvelle francaise* by Marcel Raymond, Lausanne 1950; *Histoires naturelles* by Jules Renard, Lausanne 1953; *Fables* by La Fontaine, Lausanne 1955; *Portrait of an Age*, London 1957; *Verheissung des Menschen* by André Bonnard, Berlin 1957; *Metamorphoses* by Ovid, New York and Verona, Italy 1958; *The Golden Ass* by Apuleius, Zürich 1960; *Homer's Odyssey*, New York 1961; *The Trial and Death of Socrates* by Plato, New York and Verona, Italy 1962; *Siddartha* by Hermann Hesse, Paris 1963; *Candide* by Voltaire, Geneva, 1966; *Die Physiker* by Friedrich Durrenmatt, Lausanne 1969; *The Queen of Sheba's Nightmare* by Bertrand Russell, Zürich 1970; *Der Fall Sokrates* by W. W. Schutz, Zürich 1970; *Song of Songs* by Robert Graves, London 1973; *Iliad* by Homer, New York 1974; *Shakespeare l'ancien* by Victor Hugo, Lausanne 1975; and others.

On ERNI: books—*Hans Erni: ein Maler unserer Zeit* by Konrad Farner, Zurich 1945; *Les Fresques de Hans Erni* by Jean Gabus, Neuchatel 1955; *Hans Erni* by Claude Roy, Geneva, 1955; *Hans Erni* by P. F. Schneeberger, Geneva 1961; *Peintures en Relief de Hans Erni* by Walter Ruegg, Geneva 1963; *Hans Erni: Perspectives and Ideas on the Arts* by P. Carroll, Chicago 1963; *Hans Erni* by Claude Roy, Lausanne 1964; *Erni* by Manuel Gasser and Mondo Annoni, Geneva 1969; *Catalogue Raisonné de l'Oeuvre Lthographie et Gravé de Hans Erni*, 2 vols., edited by Peirre Cailler, Geneva 1969, 1971; *Hans Erni* by Carl Burckhardt and Walter Ruegg, Lausanne 1970; *Hans Erni: ein Weg zum Nächsten*, 5 vols., edited by Jean-Christophe Ammann, Lucerne 1976; *Hans Erni: Das Malerische Werk* by Walter Ruegg, Frauenfeld 1979; *Hans Erni: Das Zeichnerische Werk und Offentliche Arbeiten* by John Matheson, Frauenfeld 1981.

Hans Erni is an artist, a designer who has blurred the lines between design art, commercial art, and fine art. His early training as an architectural draftsman gave him a respect for the neat line and the well-defined shape, as well as the clear eye of a naturalist. His contract with artists working in Paris in the late 1920's broadened his vision to abstraction, especially after he joined the Abstraction-Creation group. From these early experiences, he melded a style of graphic expression that included the direct appeal of realistic representation along with the broader scope of abstraction. To this, he added the psychological punch of surrealism. His graphic work was very popular during the 1950's in advertising, book design, and illustration. Characteristically, in this work, the human figure, often painted before a dark background, is suspended in a fine-lined framework of symbolic importance. This same subject and style, easily acceptable, made his lithographs collectable both in the original and in reproduction.

Although his murals are of a more visible and enduring nature, his graphic works are better known and have been more influential. A twentieth-century artist, he nevertheless carries on the nineteenth-century tradition of accommodation between graphic art and design, for he has found no conflict between the two. Because critics from both worlds have had difficulty assigning his work its artistic value, it has as yet to receive a just critical reception. Erni's work has been consistently popular with both the commercial world and the general public, as he moves in and out and sometimes back in the mention of fine art critics, in the world of commercial awards, and in best-of-the-year publications. His multi-faceted style and inter-

est in a gentle sensuality has influenced many illustrators, while concern for subject content may have more influence on the non-commercial artist than is yet evident.

—Harlan Sifford

ERTÉ.
French graphic artist, sculptor, illustrator, fashion, stage and film designer. Born Romain de Tirtoff, in St. Petersburg, Russia, 10 November 1892; emigrated to France in 1911, and subsequently naturalized. Adopted pseudonym Erté from his initials R.T. Studied painting and drawing, under Repine and Lossewsky, at the Academy of Fine Arts, St. Petersburg, from 1906; Academie Julian, Paris, 1912. Worked as a fashion artist for couturier Paul Poiret, Paris, 1912–13; stage costume designer, from 1913, working for Théâtre de la Renaissance, Le Bataclan, Théâtre Femina, Folies Bergeres, Théâtre Sarah Bernhardt, Bal Tabarin, Opéra Comique, Théâtre Palais du Chaillot, Bouffe Parisiens, Théâtre du Châtelet, Théâtre de la Madeleine, and Théâtre du Vieux Colombier, in Paris, for George White's Scandals and the Ziegfeld Follies, in New York, for the San Carlo Opera, in Naples, for the Teatro de Quattro Fontane, in Rome, and for the Saville Theatre, London; freelance illustrator, from 1915, working for *Harper's Bazaar, Vogue, Cosmopolitan, Delineator, Femina, L'Illustration, Art et Industrie, Le Gaulois Artistique, La Gazette du Bon Ton, Plaisir de France, The London Sketch* and *Illustrated London News;* freelance film costume designer, working for William Randolph Hearst's Cosmopolitan Films, 1919, and contract costume designer, Metro-Goldwyn-Mayer film company, Hollywood, California, 1925. **Exhibitions:** Madison Hotel, New York, 1925; Galerie Charpentier, Paris, 1926, 1929; Galerie du Studio, Brussels, 1927; Warren and Cox, New York, 1929; Waldorf Astoria Hotel, New York, 1935; Galerie Ror Volmar, Paris, 1964; Galerie la Motte, Paris, 1965; Galerie Jacques Perrin, Paris, 1966; Galleria Milano, Milan, 1966; Grosvenor Gallery, London, 1967; Galerie Lambert-Monet, Geneva, 1972; Electrum Gallery, London, 1975; Smithsonian Institution, Washington, D.C., 1979; Musee Boulogne-Billancourt, Paris, 1986. **Collections:** Metropolitan Museum of Art, New York; Museum of Modern Art, New York; Victoria and Albert Museum, London. Honorary Member, Motion Picture and Television Costume Designers Guild, New York; Ordre de Mérite Cultural, France, 1972; Officier de l'Ordre des Arts et des Lettres, France, 1976; Chevalier de la Légion d'Honneur, France, 1985. *Died* (in Paris) *21 April 1990*.

Works:

Costumes for the musical comedy star Gaby Deslys, Paris, 1915.
Costumes for *Legendary Kings*, Theatre Femina, Paris, 1919.
Costumes for *Faust*, Chicago Opera Company, 1920.
Sets and costumes for *Awakening the Past*, Alcazar Music Hall, Marseilles, 1923.
Costumes for *Pélleas et Mélisande*, Metropolitan Opera, New York, 1927.
Costumes for *Casanova*, Scala Theater, Berlin, 1930.

Costumes for *Louis XIV,* Alhambra, Paris, 1933.

Costumes for *Joys of the Capitol,* Theatre de la Madeleine, Paris, 1936.

Costumes for *The Bottom of the Sea,* French Casino, New York, 1946.

Costumes for *Capriccio,* Opéra-Comique, Paris, 1957.

Costumes for *Castor et Pollux,* Theatre Antique de Fourvieres, Lyons, 1961.

Illustrated alphabet, completed 1967, published as lithographs, 1977.

La Traviata playing-cards, for Alfred Dunhill Limited, 1969.

Zizi Jeanmaire costumes for *Zizi je t'aime,* Casino de Paris, 1972.

Sets and costumes for Gershwin's *Rhapsody in Blue,* Radio City Music Hall, New York 1988.

Six designs of "De Luxe" cognac bottles, for Courvoisier, 1988.

film designs for MGM—*The Mystic,* 1925; *Bright Lights,* 1925; *Time, the Comedian,* 1925; *Dance Madness,* 1925; *La Bohème,* 1925; *Paris,* 1925.

Publications:

By ERTÉ: books—*Things I Remember: An Autobiography,* New York and London 1975; *Designs by Erté: Fashion Drawings and Illustrations from Harper's Bazaar,* New York and London 1976; *Erté Graphics: Five Complete Suites,* New York 1978; *Erté,* London 1978; *Erté's Theatrical Costumes in Full Color,* edited by Salome Estorick, New York 1979; *Erté's Costumes and Sets for Der Rosenkavalier,* New York 1980; *Erté's Fashion Designs: 218 Illustrations from Harper's Bazaar 1918–1932,* New York and London 1981; *Erté's at Ninety: The Complete Graphics,* London 1982; *Erté Sculpture,* London 1986; *Erté at Ninety-Five: Graphics,* London 1987; book illustrated—*Ermyntrude and Esmeralda* by Lytton Strachey, London 1970.

On ERTÉ: books—*Romain de Tirtoff—Erté,* exhibition catalogue by Giuliana Veronesi, Milan 1966; *Erté* by Charles Spencer, London 1970; *Erté* by Roland Barthes, Parma 1972, New York 1975; *Illustrateurs des Modes et Manières en 1925,* exhibition catalogue with text by Marcel Astruc, Paris 1972; *Romantic and Glamorous Hollywood Design,* exhibition catalogue by Diana Vreeland, New York 1974; *Stage Design* by Donald Oenslager, New York 1975; *Hollywood Costume Design* by David Chierichetti, London 1976; *Designs by Erté,* edited by Stella Blum, New York 1977.

Rather than using his own name, Romain de Tirtoff, when he came to Paris, he called himself Erté (after the French pronunciation of his initials) to avoid offending his aristocratic Russian family who thought an artistic career undignified. Already inspired by the graphic style of Greek vase painting seen in the Hermitage in Leningrad and by the colours and detail of Indian and Persian miniatures, he arrived in a Paris attuned to Orientalism. The influence of Poiret and the Ballets Russes had created an atmosphere into which Erté was quickly absorbed.

His exotic fantasy-figures captured the mood of the moment. Using pen and Indian ink and later gouache, he visualised a stylised ideal of beauty which he based on Marie du Plessis, and eighteenth-century French courtesan. Elegant women were captured in motion, frozen in poses which best display their garments, their jewellery, their accessories, their furs. They are latter-day fashion models springing from the imagination. With his contemporaries such as Iribe, Lepape, and Barbier, Erté created bold fashion illustrations which epitomised the mood of the 1920's. As always, beyond the whims of fashion, Erté's recent work, such as his designs for *Der Rosenkavalier,* still reveals the same exquisite use of line and impact of stark contrast that it did seventy years ago.

His desire to create individual garmets which relied for their detailed perfection on hand craftsmanship made them unsuitable for the mass market. By turning more to the theatre, he was able to continue as he wished. One stage set, titled "Gold," which he produced for the Ziegfeld Follies, required the use of six and a half miles of gold lamé to create the desired impact.

A master of exotic fantasy, Erté is also an innovator who has worked in many areas of design. He was one of the earliest designers in this century to create for total environments. His use of metal detailing on clothes, his fashion version of the caftan, and his one-shoulder and cutout dresses of the 1920's all predated recent trends. Acknowledged as a highly skilled draughtsman, he is also a witty observer. His meeting of the fat and thin lady wearing the same dress show him making a comment on fashion, not just a document of it. The revival of Art Deco in the late 1960's drew new attention and acclaim to his work. This success has inspired him to move into sculptural *formes picturales,* one of which inspired the candelabra appearing in *Der Rosenkavalier.*

—Hazel Clark

ESKOLIN-NURMESNIEMI, Vuokko.
Finnish product, exhibition, fashion and textile designer. Born Vuokko Hillevi Lilian Eskolin, in Helsinki, 12 February 1930. Studied ceramics, Institute of Industrial Arts, Helsinki, 1948–52. Married the designer Antti Nurmesniemi in 1953. Ceramics designer, Wartsila-Arabia, Helsinki, 1952–53; chief fashion and printed textile designer, Printex-Marimekko, Helsinki, 1953–60; own production of printed and woven textiles and rugs, Helsinki, 1960–62; founder-director, Vuokko Oy fashion and textile design company, Helsinki, 1964–88, and head designer of Oy Vuokko AB, Helsinki, since 1988; also glass designs, for Wärtsilä Nuutajärvi Glass, Helsinki, ryijy wall rug designs, for Friends of Finnish Handicrafts, Helsinki, woven and printed fabrics, for Villayhtyma, Helsinki, for Pausa of Germany, and for Borås Väveri of Sweden, 1956–57; exhibition designs, for Nordiska Galleriet, Stockholm, and Design Research, Boston, 1958, and for the Milan Triennale, 1964; clothing designs, for Villayhtyma, Helsinki, 1963–64. **Exhibitions:** Artek Gallery, Helsinki, 1957, 1964; Artek Gallery, Stockholm, 1958; Bonniers, New York, 1966; Nordic House, Reykjavik, 1976; University of Texas, Arlington, 1976; Design Center, Tokyo, 1978; Form i Göteborg, 1979; *30 Years of Design,* Milan, 1980; Konstmuseet, Göteborg, 1980; Glyptotek Museum, Copenhagen, 1981; Malmö Museum, Sweden, 1982; Design Center, Helsinki, 1985; Museu de Arte, Sao Paulo, 1988. **Collections:** Museum of Applied Arts, Helsinki; Museum of Industrial Design, Copenhagen; Malmö Museum, Sweden; Röhsska Konstslöjdmuseet, Göteborg; Royal Scottish Museum, Edinburgh; Victoria and Albert Museum, London; Metropolitan Museum of Art, New York; Musée de l'Impression sur Etoffes, Mulhouse, France. Recipient: Gold Medal, 1957, and Grand Prix, 1964, Milan Triennale; City of Helsinki Bursary, 1958; Danish-American Lunning Prize, 1964; Pro Finlandia Medal, Helsinki, 1968; Finnish State Prize for Design, 1968; Ingrid Jespersen Foundation Prize, 1973; Prince Eugen Medal, 1986. Honorary Member, Academia Mexicana de Diseno, Mexico City, 1981; Honorary Royal Designer for Industry, Royal Society of Arts, London, 1988. Member: Texo Association of Finnish Textile Designers; MTO Association of Finnish Fashion Designers. Address: Hopeasalmentie 27, 00570 Helsinki, Finland.

Works:

Ceramic tableware, for Arabia, 1952.

Clothing and printed cotton fabrics, for Marimekko, 1953–60.

Glass bowls, vases and plates, for Wärtsilä Nuutajärvi, 1957.

Woven woollen household fabrics, for Villayhtyma, 1957.

Exhibition layouts, for Design Research of Boston, 1958.

Clothing, printed and woven fabrics, for Vuokko Oy, 1964–88.

Ecclesiastical textiles, for Kaleva Church, Tampere, 1966.

Ecclesiastical textiles, for Kannelmaki Church, Helsinki, 1968.

Ecclesiastical textiles, for Lieto Church, Finland, 1972.

Publications:

On ESKOLIN-NURMESNIEMI: books—*Finnish Design 1875–1975,* by Erik Bruun, Timo Sarpaneva and Erik Kruskopf, Helsinki 1975; *Finland Creates,* edited by Jack Fields and David Moore, Jyvaskyla, 1977; *One Hundred Great Finnish Designs,* edited by Per Mollerup, Snekkersten 1979; *Finnland Gestaltet,* exhibition catalogue by Tapio Periainen, Simo Heikkila and others, Espoo 1981; *Contemporary Textile Art: Scandinavia* by Charles S. Talley, Stockholm 1982; *Scandinavian Modern Design 1880–1980,* edited by David Revere McFadden, New York 1982; *Design Since 1945,* edited by Kathryn Hiesinger and George Marcus, Philadelphia and London 1983; *Finnish Vision,* with texts by P. Suhonen, J. Lintinen and others, Helsinki 1983; *The Encyclopaedia of Fashion from 1840 to the 1980s* by Georgina O'Hara, London 1986; *The Lunning Prize,* exhibition catalogue edited by Helena Dahlback Lutteman and Marianne Uggla, Stockholm 1986; *Finnish Industrial Design,* edited by Tua Pontasuo, Helsinki 1987; articles—"Thirty-Four Lunning Prizewinners" in *Mobilia* (Snekkersten), September 1967; "Some Call Them Purists" by M. Kaipanen in *Form Function Finland* (Helsinki), no. 2, 1981; "Prince Eugen Medal to Vuokko Nurmesniemi" in *Form Function Finland* (Helsinki), no. 1, 1987.

By training, I am a ceramic artist, a craftsman. In practice, however, I have worked in the textile and garment field, using the many possibilities offered by modern technology. During my professional training to become a ceramic artist, I discovered my interest in clothing design. In the evenings, I began practising cutting clothes.

I have always wanted to experiment, to find and develop new things, to play. I try to look at design as an all-encompassing phenomenon: I cannot think of garments as simply pieces of clothing; I think of them as pieces of material,

Vuokko Eskolin-Nurmesniemi: *Unikko+Kolmio* dress in viscose velvet, 1983

as expressions of colour, as complete entities that I have designed and combined myself.

I love my work which, during the last few years, has mainly been in the textile and garment field. But I have not forgotten the planning of exhibitions and the making of graphics wherever these have had a tangent on the presentation of my own production. I have tried to simplify my creations without forgetting the richness of life itself and its direct influence on my creations.

—Vuokko Eskolin-Nurmesniemi

Vuokko Eskolin-Nurmesniemi represents the ideological principles of design at their purest. She has an unusually sound and harmonious view of the world, which reflects directly on her designs.

Vuokko has a scholarly and theoretically well-founded approach to her work which she has directed to a closely restricted social group. By ecological and humanistic means she has reached the mystic timeless forms. Still in 1989 people keeping up with the times are wearing dresses designed by her in the 50s. Her great strength is the happy synenergy of theory and fantasy, reason and emotion. As a clothes designer Vuokko is a Constructivist, for whom the primary aim of design is simple structure, by which she is able to create uncomplicated everyday garments as well as dramatic effects of fest dresses.

She has had innovative insight, such as: Printing one colour partly on top of another, thus producing a third colour, which in the 50s was to become Marimekko's trademark. Deep research into the characteristic features of fabrics made of natural fibres and the use of this knowledge on the cut. As a result the garment lives and moves with ease and beauty. Designing fabrics, models and garments as a harmonious whole, thus making possible their free variation and combination. Experiments on seams: dresses, skirts, trousers, coats etc. with one seam, two seams, three seams etc. form an interesting part of Vuokko's experimenting with product development. Unprejudiced renovation and simplification of small structural and functional details: off with folds, adhesive bands to replace buttons, zips to speed up dressing, etc.

Vuokko Eskolin-Nurmesniemi was trained at the Institute of Industrial Arts, Section of Ceramic Art, and attended at the same time the Institute for Pattern Design and Cutting. She was one of the youngest students of the Institute of Industrial Arts, taking her exam in 1952. She has designed ceramics for Arabia, Finland (1952), glass for Nuutajärvi Glassworks (1956–57), Ryijy wall rugs for the Friends of Finnish Handicraft, woven fabrics for Villayhtymä, printed fabrics for Marimekko and Printex (1953–60), Borås Väveri in Sweden (1956) and Pansa in FRG, church textiles for Kaleva church (by architect Reima Pietilä) in Tampere, for Kannelmäki church in Helsinki and Lieto church in Lieto. Her longest employment as a designer was in Marimekko, where she was head designer in 1953–60. In 1964 she founded her own company Vuokko Oy, the soul and executive for which she was until 1988. She is presently head designer of Oy Vuokko Finland Ab.

She has held own exhibitions, for instance in the Scandinavian countries, USA, Japan, Brazil and Italy, mostly together with her husband Antti Nurmesniemi, professor and interior designer. She has participated in several design exhibitions and presented her designs on many fashion shows all over the world.

Vuokko believes there is no fashion, just time. We follow our time, and time follows us. "In many ways I don't mind when others call me a purist. I think things must be functional, easy to wear and of high quality." "I've always said there are two sides to me: the very clean Vuokko and the fantasy Vuokko. I must say that I prefer the clean me. If you are too complicated no-one understands you."

Universally thinking Vuokko has been in many respects a predecessor of her field on its many essential levels: technically, socially, functionally, aesthetically, ecologically. All of these are central dimensions of design and designer, and Vuokko takes continually responsibility for them, officially as well as in her own design. She is significant for far more than clothes design only, as her philosophy is basic ideology of design.

—Tapio Periainen

F

FAITH-ELL, Age.
Swedish textile designer. Born Anna Margareta Faith-Ell, in Växjö, 9 July 1912. Educated at Växjö Girls' School, 1919–30: Dip. 1930; studied art-embroidery and dressmaking, Saint Birgitta's School, Stockholm, 1930–31; weaving, at Johanna Brunsson's Weaving School, Stockholm, 1931–34: Dip. 1934; studied under E. J. Wimmer-Wisgrill, Hochschule für angewandte Kunst, Vienna, 1935; studied machine-woven textiles, Staatslehr- und Versuchsanstalt fur Textilindustrie, Vienna, 1943. Textile designer, with the Swedish Handicraft Society, in Malmo, Uppsala, Linköping, Stockholm and Kalmar, 1936–42; textile designer and instructor, R. Atkinson/Irish Poplin House, Belfast, 1946–49; textile designer, AB Kinnasand, Kinna, 1955–56 and 1964–65, Eriksbergs Väveri AB, Kinna (for Nordiska Komapniet department store), 1960–61, AB Marks Jacquardväveri, Björketorp, 1961–63; also freelance designer, Växjö, since 1955: has designed for AB Stobo, 1956–58, Mab and Mya, 1957–60, AB Hagaplast, 1958–64, AB Tidstrands Yllefabriker, 1958–67, AB Kinnasand, 1960, 1970–71 and 1978, Arova of Switzerland, 1967–68. Instructor, Hochschule für angewandte Kunst, Vienna, 1942–45; Higher Secondary School, Växjö, 1962–78. Specialist Committee Member, Swedish Society for Industrial Design, 1957–66. **Exhibitions:** *Our Home*, Röhsska Konstslöjdmuseet, Göteborg, 1938; *Scandinavian Decorative Arts*, Liljevalchs Konsthall, Stockholm, 1946; *Woven/Printed*, Neue Sammlung, Munich, 1959; *Drei Schweden*, Institut fur neue technische Form, Darmstadt, 1959 (with K. E. Ekselius and E. Hoglund; toured); *Woven This Spring*, Nordiska Kompaniet, Stockholm, 1960; *Blankets*, Nordiska Kompaniet, Stockholm, 1962; *Yard-Goods for Public Places*, Swedish Design Centre, Stockholm, 1966; *SID Design Prize*, Sverigehuset, Stockholm, 1974; *The Swedish Handicraft Association*, Liljevalchs Konsthall, Stockholm, 1982; *58 Swedish Industrial Designers*, Design Center, Stockholm and Malmö 1986; *Excellent Swedish Design*, Design Center, Stockholm and Malmö, 1987; *Design/Form/Colour*, Kalmar Art Museum, Sweden, 1988. **Collections:** Nationalmuseum, Stockholm; Röhsska Konstslöjdmuseet, Göteborg; Kalmar Art Museum, Sweden; Neue Sammlung, Munich. Recipient: Silver Medal, Stockholm Crafts Association, 1934; Andersson Fellowship, 1935, 6 textile competition prizes, 1937, and Peter Beijer Fellowship, 1942, Swedish Society for Industrial Design; Swedish Board of Commerce Fellowship, 1942; Swedish Handicraft Association Fellowship, 1942; Gold Medal, Milan Triennale, 1960; Association of Industrial Designers Award, New York, 1963; Växjö Lions Club Fellowship, 1965; Fellowships, 1967, 1968, and Artist's Stipend, 1977, Swedish Artists' Fellowship Committee; Pattern Competition Prize, Sellgrens Vaveri/Norwegian Association for Applied Art, 1976; City of Växjö Cultural Prize, 1984; Excellent Swedish Design Award, 1987. Member: Swedish Society of Industrial Design, 1935; Swedish Society of Artist-Craftsmen and Industrial Designers, 1963; American Institute of Interior Designers, 1963. Address: Kungsvägen 54, 352 33 Växjö, Sweden.

Works:

Ribbon curtain fabric in linen and cotton, for Eriksbergs Väveri, 1960.
Jungfrulin curtain fabric in linen and cotton, for Marks Jacquardväveri, 1961.
Bjornfloka curtain fabric in cotton, for Marks Jacquardväveri, 1961.
Baldersbra curtain fabric in cotton, for Marks Jacquardväveri, 1961.
Knippfryle curtain fabric in cotton, for Marks Jacquardväveri, 1961.
Sjösala curtain fabric in cotton, for AB Kinnasand, 1963.
Malin curtain fabric in linen and cotton, for AB Kinnasand, 1963.
Vävruta curtain fabric in cotton, for AB Kinnasand, 1963.
Lotta curtain fabric in cotton, for AB Kinnasand, 1976.
Onyx curtain fabric in cotton, for AB Kinnasand, 1987.
Opal curtain fabric in cotton, for AB Kinnasand, 1987.
Grafit curtain fabric in cotton, for AB Kinnasand, 1987.
Klitter curtain fabric in cotton, linen and polyester, for AB Kinnasand, 1987.
Safir curtain fabric in polyester, for AB Kinnasand, 1987.
Noja curtain fabric in cotton, for AB Kinnasand, 1988.
Rigg curtain fabric in polyester, for AB Kinnasand, 1988.

Publications:

By FAITH-ELL: article—"Interview mit Age Faith-Ell" in *Moebel Interior Design* (Stuttgart), July 1966.

On FAITH-ELL: books—*Konsthantverk och Hemslöjd i Sverige 1930–1940*, edited by Ake H. Huldt, Mattis Horlen and Heribert Seitz, Göteborg 1941; *Svensk Heminredning* by Lilly Arrhenius, Stockholm 1957; *Scandinavian Design* by Ulf Hård af Segerstad, Stockholm and London 1961; *A Treasury of Scandinavian Design*, edited by Erik Zahle, New York 1961; *Modern Svensk Textilkonst* by Ulf Hård af Segerstad, Stockholm 1963; *Tio Textilkonstnarer* by Gerd Reimers, Falun 1965; *Decorative Art in Modern Interiors* by Ella Moody, London 1969; *New Design in Weaving* by D. J. Willcox, New York and London 1971; *Design in Sweden*, edited by Lennart Lindkvist, Stockholm 1972; *Konsten i Sverige: Konsthantverk, Konst-industri, Design 1875–1975* by Dag Widman, Stockholm 1975.

It has been my good fortune to have been born and raised in an optimal environment. My father was not only a furniture and house architect, but also a revolutionary force in the pedagogics of drawing and school handicraft. Renowned both in Sweden and internationally for his pioneering ideas within this important field, he had strong convictions and was often described as a fiery spirit. Like all pioneers, he had his opponents. Naturally, my father's activity has had great impact on the development of the creative force in my own life. He was absolutely my best teacher. Even in my youth, however, he made me realize that an existence as an artist is no bed of roses. Despite this, I trained to become a designer.

After completing my training, I was employed as a designer by the Swedish Handicraft Society, which is represented in every municipality, and worked in several cities. It was my task to renew collections, but often I was met by resistance. I enjoyed my work, as I felt that I had been given an important assignment, but at that time, the Society did not pay its designers well, and our names were seldom advertised. As to the period I spent within this institution, I would like to quote from the chapter about me, in Gerd Reimer's book, *Tio Textilkonstnärer*:

At first, however, it was the Swedish Handicraft Society that benefited from her work. This was in the 1930s, when the range of colours was boring and drab, and she had to go through a difficult struggle to force through light and airy colours.

Quite a number of the carpets and curtains that the Swedish Handicraft Society delivered to private and public collections during these ten years would have born Age Faith-Ell's name if, at that time, it had been the custom to sign such utility goods. This wasn't the case, and much of the handicraft of the 1930s has therefore faded into anonymity. Among the things that Faith-Ell designed at this time were carpets, curtains, and draperies. This collection has been important for her development as an industrial designer, and as such, she has never lost contact with the tradition that the years within handicraft conveyed.

Tired of moving from one small Swedish town to another, I gladly accepted an offer to work as a teacher at the Hochschule für angewandte Kunst in Vienna, where I previously had been a student. Austria was occupied, there was a war going on, and we worked under difficult conditions, with daily bombing attacks and lack of material and food. Despite this, my period as a teacher at this school was the happiest in my life. Unfortunately, the war situation

Age Faith-Ell: *Opal* cotton curtain fabric, for AB Kinnasand, 1987

forced me to leave the school and Austria after three years.

Following a few years as a designer and instructor at R. Atkinson/Irish Poplin House in Belfast, I returned to Sweden in the early 1950s to take care of my mother, since my father had suddenly passed away. I arrived at the right time. Sweden's rapid recovery from the war brought with it a need for high-quality interior decoration because new theatres, schools, and hotels were being built. Designers were hired—not the least, textile designers—who were now tied to industry, and numerous talented individuals were finally recognized. For many of us, it was the golden era, the period when "Swedish modern" became a concept outside the borders of Sweden. There is a reason that the 1950s are referred to as "the decade of textiles" here in Sweden: I dare say that Swedish textile design more or less set the fashion throughout the world at that time.

However, my debut as an industrial designer occurred in Germany. The Institut für neue technische Form in Darmstadt asked me to have an exhibition there, after having seen my design collection. The success of this exhibition resulted in the Nordiska Kompaniet immediately asking me to have an individual exhibition in Stockholm. The management made arrangements with a factory to manufacture my collection of textiles, and naturally, Nordiska retained sole rights to this production. All of a sudden all doors had opened for me. I had achieved the peak of my career, perhaps also of my life. I was forty-eight years old.

At the end of the 1960s, our luck turned. There was a crisis in the textile industry. Many factories were closed, and many designers lost their jobs. I went back to my work as a teacher,

this time unfortunately not at an art school, but at a secondary school, where I worked until I retired.

I would like to end my narrative with a few more words from *Tio Textilkonstnärer*:

Age Faith-Ell is one of our most versatile textile designers—an uneasy spirit who can never settle down anywhere, it is said by someone who wants to be cruel.

An untiring experimenter who constantly wants to try new roads, says another, more respectful voice.

What is the truth? Perhaps it lies somewhere in between because it is clear that Age Faith-Ell, who undoubtedly can include a long list of company names in her curriculum vitae, is a restless, searching spirit. At the same time, however, her work is more whole than that of many others because in it, one can trace a development, a logical growth, which becomes more and more convincing for each new exhibition, each new collection. Furthermore, she is one of the Swedish industrial designers who is most renowned abroad. She has attained many international awards and participated in numerous exhibitions, both individual and collective.

It may be a fact that the picture of Age Faith-Ell is many-coloured, with respect to the kind and number of assignments she has had, but if one looks at the picture as a whole, her activity becomes more homogeneous. She knows her style and does not diverge from it—her work is not least about devotion to a set purpose.

—Age Faith-Ell

FARRAH, Abdelkader.

Algerian stage designer. Born in Ksar-El-Boukhari, 28 March 1926. Self-taught in painting and design. Freelance designer, since 1953: head of design, Comédie de l'Est, Strasbourg, 1955–61; associate designer, Royal Shakespeare Company, Stratford-upon-Avon, 1962–65; head of design, Royal Lyceum Company, Edinburgh, 1965–66; returned to Royal Shakespeare Company, working in Stratford-upon-Avon and London, since 1969. Head of Design Course, Ecole d'Art Dramatique, Strasbourg, 1955–61; National Theatre School of Canada, Montreal, 1968–69. **Exhibitions:** Prague Quadriennale, 1979; Maison Internationale du Theatre, Paris, 1982; *Contemporary British Theatre Design*, London 1983. **Collection:** Victoria and Albert Museum, London. Recipient: Meilleur Spectacle de l'Annee award, Paris, 1959, 1972; *Plays and Players* magazine award, London, 1971; Society of West End Theatres Award, London, 1976, 1977. Address: Royal Shakespeare Company, Barbican Theatre, Barbican, London EC2Y 8BQ, England.

Works:

Stage designs include—*Samson and Dalila*, Nederlandsche Opera, Amsterdam, 1953; *Caucasian Chalk Circle* and *Mann ist Mann*, Comedie Saint-Etienne, 1955–59; *Mayor of Zalemea*, Comédie de l'Est, Strasbourg; *Prometheus Bound*, Comédie de l'Est, Strasbourg, 1958; *Andromaque*, Comédie de l'Est, Strasbourg, 1959; *Don Giovanni*, Opéra de Strasbourg, 1959; *Oedipus Rex*, Sadler's Wells Opera, London, 1960; *The Cherry Orchard*, Royal Shakespeare Company, 1961; *King Lear*, De Haagsche Comedie, The Hague, 1964; *Three Sisters*, English Stage Company, London, 1965; *Carmen*, Welsh National Opera, Cardiff, 1965; *The Birds*, Royal Lyceum Company, Edinburgh, 1966; *The Dragon*, English Stage Company, London, 1966; *Galileo Galilei*, Royal Lyceum Company, Edinburgh, 1967; *Doctor Faustus*, Royal Shakespeare Company, 1968; *Oh, Calcutta*, Somerford Productions, London, 1970; *The Balcony*, Royal Shakespeare Company, 1971; *Richard III*, Comédie Francaise, Paris, 1972; *Enrico IV*, Sol Hurok Concert Inc., New York, 1973; *Henry IV*, parts 1 and 2, Royal Shakespeare Company, 1975; *Henry V*, Royal Shakespeare Company, 1975; *Othello*, Paris Opera, 1976; *Troilus and Cressida*, Burgtheater, Vienna, 1977; *Coriolanus*, Royal Shakespeare Company, 1977; *As You Like It*, Burgtheater, Vienna, 1979; *Parsifal*, Royal Opera House, London. 1979; *Women Beware Women*, Teatro Stabile, Genoa, 1981; *Julius Caesar*, Royal Shakespeare Company, 1983; *Red Noses*, Royal Shakespeare Company, 1985; *The Danton Affair*, Royal Shakespeare Company, 1986; *Romeo and Juliet*, Royal Shakespeare Company, 1989.

Publications:

By FARRAH: book—*The Rebec Player*, London 1955; article—interview in *Plays and Players* (London), November 1982.

On FARRAH: books—*Stage Design Throughout the World Since 1950*, edited by René Hainaux, Brussels 1964; *Stage Design Throughout the World Since 1960*, edited by René Hainaux, Brussels 1973; *Lights of Western Theatre* by Alfred Farag, Cairo 1989.

I was brought up in a non-European environment; East and West are two complementary realities in my own experience.

For more than 30 years, I have worked on

plays, occasionally on operas, ballets, musicals, reviews, and some popular celebrations.

A designer helps to state that special way of addressing an audience—his work should not be isolated from the general context. The challenge is to reconcile opposites and find out how far one can go without tilting the balance. Objectivity to one person may become subjectivity to the next.

I have been involved with assignments concerned with the following ideas: respect of the classics or their rejection; escapist entertainment or didactic reassessment of political struggle; naturalistic narrative; cult of aesthetics or their demystification; slow exploration process when and if allowed by time, finances, and belief; rigour and ritual on a "bare stage"; disintegration of traditional space by mixing audience and action.

One wave follows the other, and today's avant-garde becomes the corroded cliché of tomorrow. Each design movement reaches a point of crisis and temporary death and is reincarnated later under a new guise. To some, it becomes a revelation, to others it is a rediscovery—I respect a designer who can achieve the right metaphor about a piece.

The needs create the means, and the design alphabet is impressive, bearing in mind stylistic suitability and economics: scenic painting; hard, soft, or pneumatic architecture; timber; textiles; metals; plastics; reflective surfaces; engineering allowing dynamics of all kinds: lights, projections, laser and audio-visual technology—without forgetting the body and voice of the performer.

To conclude, my views about contemporary design are without a clear-cut conclusion, for the theatre, and designers, will still go on, subjected to that never-ending pendulum swing.

—Abdelkader Farrah

Despite Abdelkader Farrah's background in painting, his scenography is distinguished as much by an architectonic and theatrical shaping of space on stage as by a painter's talent for bold design and color in costumes and properties. A Farrah set may occasionally be lean and unobtrusive, almost Brechtian, but it is never anonymous or expressionless. As he has stated, he imitates nature in its inner dynamic rather than its epidermic look.

Explicitly theatrical scenography was evident in Genet's *The Balcony* (Royal Shakespeare Company, 1971), in which a complex series of kinetic panels and boxes, all mirrored, created chambers of illusion in a brothel. A legacy of his association with Michel Saint Denis, masks, too, have fascinated Farrah. The 1963 *Tempest* included half-masks of the conspirators' own features, and the 1968 Royal Shakespeare Company *Doctor Faustus* masked the Seven Deadly Sins. For *Richard III* (Royal Shakespeare Company, 1970), Farrah elaborated the helmets of warriors into enlarged, bust-like masks of heraldic beasts to signify allegiance to opposing armies.

A primarily architectonic approach was evident in *Coriolanus* (Royal Shakespeare Company, 1977), the set consisting almost entirely of large, metallic, mobile blocks with steeply slanted tops; these functioned as walls, gates, and battlements. *Henry V* (Royal Shakespeare Company, 1975) was equally stark and architectonic but included a few striking elements of colorful spectacle. The stage was stripped to its brick walls, which were then painted white. The bare floor contained a platform with a mild rake, encompassed by galleries, bridges, and lighting instruments that were completely exposed. Suspended above the stage was a huge, dull-colored canvas sack, the inner surface of which was richly emblazoned with appliquéd heraldic motifs and emblems. Depending on whether the canvas material was suspended or released, it could represent the nobility of France or, when lowered to the floor, the muddy battleground of France. (Farrah had been inspired by circus tents.) Moreover, part of the floor was laterally hinged, and thus, one whole section of it could lift up to form a steep, dangerous surface to be scaled during the battle scenes.

Similar techniques of variously inclining planes were evident in Royal Shakespeare Company productions of *Richard II* and *As You Like It*. In each, the opening scene occurred on a relatively shallow forestage backed by a wall. For the subsequent scenes, the wall was lowered backward to form the rear part of the stage floor. An added, gracefully expressive element in *As You Like It* were trunks of trees that curved up from the floor to a vertical position to suggest stylized waves or some exotic stringed instrument. Together with other natural and folk motifs, they created an effect that was warmer, softer, more humane than that of many Farrah sets that convey a certain hard-edged, aggressive boldness.

—Jarka M. Burian

Abdelkader Farrah: *Julius Caesar*, for the Royal Shakespeare Company, London, 1983

FEDERICO, Gene.

American graphic designer. Born in New York City, 6 February 1918. Studied under Leon Friend, at Abraham Lincoln High School, New York, until 1936; under Tom Benrimo, at Pratt Institute, New York, 1937–38; under Howard Trafton and Herbert Bayer, at the Art Students League, New York, 1939–41. Served in the United States Army, 1941–45. Married Helen Federico in 1942; daughters: Lisa and Gina. Advertising art director in New York since 1938: art director, Abbott Kimball Company, 1938–40 and 1945–46; associate art director, *Fortune* magazine, 1946–47; art director, Grey Advertising, 1949–51, and Doyle Dane Bernbach, 1951–54; vice president and art director, Douglas D. Simon advertising agency, 1954–59; vice-president and group head, Benton and Bowles agency, 1959–65; vice-president and creative director, Warwick and Legler, 1965–66; executive vice-president and creative director of Lord, Geller, Federico, Einstein agency, since 1966. Recipient: Gold Medal, 1959, 1981, and Hall of Fame Award, 1980, Art Directors Club of New York; Silver Medal, Art Directors Club of Philadelphia. Address: 655 Madison Avenue, New York, New York 10021, U.S.A.

Publications:

On FEDERICO: books—*Posters: 50 Artists and Designers*, edited by W. H. Allner, New York 1952; *Who's Who in Graphic Art*, edited by Walter Amstutz, Dubendorf 1982; articles—in *Communication Arts* (Palo Alto), no. 3, 1972; *Idea* (Tokyo), May 1973.

If an ad isn't seen, it can't be read. And if it isn't seen and read, it won't be believed, and it won't be acted upon. So I begin with the problem of visibility, of working to strip away the nonessentials so that the effect is concentrated and the message stands out in the environment of the medium. Print's more challenging. For a simple reason. It's easier to flip a page than a channel.

—Gene Federico

Graphic designer Gene Federico has worked for more than forty years in advertising. Quick to state that he is a craftsman, not an artist, he seeks to give the client a voice, rather than to project his own "personality" on his designs. However, Federico has consistently aimed to make "elegant" solutions to marketing problems; by this he means "beautiful simplicity, directness and efficacy," qualities that relate his work to precedents by A. M. Cassandre and Paul Rand. Avoiding the "trendy" or merely stylish, he hopes that over years his basic solutions to clients' requests will be effective. Each ad he designs must stand out from the welter of others, must be easily understood and read. At the same time, Federico has attempted to avoid becoming set in a mode; he tries to keep up with what he sees in the social climate and then to apply this within his own philosophy.

Clients who have used his designs over many years include IBM, Hennesy cognac, and Napier, a manufacturer of costume jewelry. The ads designed by this major design partner of the firm Lord, Geller, Federico and Einstein exhibit a tough-minded similarity which marks them as Federico's. For example, an ad done for IBM's electric typewriter in the early 1960s breaks rules of advertising practice yet is one of his most successful. Federico entirely omitted the headline, allowing a centrally located photograph of the typewriter with its prominent IBM logos to state the subject immediately and succinctly. Above the typewriter appears the symbol of Aldus Manutius, the early sixteenth-century Venetian printer, while below the typewriter, rather more copy than is usual is presented in easily readable and classic form to establish a base for the two photographed images and explain the advantages of the new IBM typewriter in light of the history of writing. The background shades from dark blue across the top behind the pale, plaster-cast symbol to medium blue behind the silver typewriter and palest blue behind the copy below. The ad works most effectively to establish the cerebral worth of the typewriter in historical terms.

Federico's clients are for the most part advertising agencies, which must then appeal to seller of product or service, but occasionally the client comes directly to him, as was the case with the Killington ski resort just after it had installed its snow-making system. Federico's assignment was to convince his audience to send for booklets about the resort in order to plan vacations well in advance of the season. For this advertisement, Federico headlined "Killington" in light blue upon a dark blue background of the two-tone page. The background gradually lightens as it descends, until it is virtually white on the bottom third of the page. The whole page is sprinkled with white circles, suggesting artificial snowflakes; these are densest on the darkest blue, become sparser in the middle, and vanish in the field of white "snow" at the bottom. Copy and coupon are set against the white. Headline, text, and coupon are easily readable, and the pictorial image confirms the text. This advertisement succeeded in drawing a high rate of response in coupon return.

—Nina Bremer

FENDI.

Italian fashion design firm. Established as a small leather and fur workshop by Adèle Casagrande (died, 1978), in Rome, 1918; name changed to Fendi on Adèle's marriage to Edoardo Fendi in 1925; offices, workshops and fur studio established in the Via Borgognona, Rome, 1964. Current principals include the 5 daughters of Adele and Edoardo Fendi: Paola (born 1931) and her husband Ciro Saracino; Anna (born 1933); Franca (born 1935) and her husband Luigi Formilli; Carla (born 1937) and her husband Candido Speroni; and Alda (born 1940). The firm now designs and makes leather and fur clothing and accessories, a ready-to-wear line, as well as knitwear and beachwear; the designer Karl Lagerfeld has been chief fur design consultant since 1967. **Exhibitions:** *Art-Fashion-Design*, Prato Museum, Italy, 1982. **Collections:** Metropolitan Museum of Art, New York; Art Institute of Chicago. Address: Via Borgognona 7, 00187 Rome, Italy.

Publications:

On FENDI: books—*I Grandi Personaggi della Moda* by Maria Vittoria Alfonsi, Verona 1974; *The Fashion Makers* by Bernadine Morris, New York 1978; *I Mass-Moda: Fatti e Peronaggi dell'Italian Look* by Adriana Mulassano, Florence 1979; *Moda e Modi* by Adriana Mulassano, Milan 1980; *Pelle a Pelle* by Prudence Glynn Rome 1982; *McDowell's Directory of Twentieth Century Fashion* by Colin McDowell, London 1984; *The Encyclopaedia of Fashion from 1840 to the 1980s* by Georgina O'Hara, London 1986.

Speaking about Fendi furs means speaking about new techniques, about sophisticated research in workmanship, about traditional skins used in an unusual way, and about pelts considered "poor" until yesterday and now revalued through creativity and man's skill.

Therefore, the name "Fendi" is a synonym for leader in fur research. But Fendi also means anticipation of shapes, perception of new colours, lightness, softness, and inventiveness which unpredictably transforms leather, renewing a fashion concept which seemed unchangeable some years ago.

The evolution of Fendi furs is an escalation towards perfection, new colours, and a uniqueness which has always respected the basic principle of discretion. Fendi furs are styled by Karl Lagerfeld.

—Fendi

Walking along various streets around via Borgognona in Rome, you would no doubt notice the prestigious name of Fendi at several boutique entrances. These are accessory and ready-to-wear stores and the glamorous fur salon at no. 39. The salon is office and showroom to the Fendi sisters and their families involved in management, sales, and design. Paola is the technical expert, as she develops new tanning methods, discovers new materials, and invents new stitching techniques. Unique to Fendi furs are unusual combinations, often brightly dyed, with unconventional detailing including dramatic openings, slashes, pleating, ruffling, and appliqué. Anna works as a designer, while Franca works with customer relations. Carla acts as coordinator of the firm, and Alda is sales director. Each one is respectful of the others, and all are particularly reverent in their appraisal of the work. Joined by their husbands and children and close relatives, the clan works very smoothly to introduce each year several collections combining high-fashion furs, ready-to-wear, mass-produced items, and leather accessories. The firm serves eighty sales outlets in the Italian market and others also in America, Canada, Germany, and Switzerland. On Fifth Avenue in New York, Bergdorf Goodman opened a leather-goods boutique repeating the facade of the main store in Rome. Here, one sees the Fendi handbags, immediately recognizable by their trademark of a stamped or printed, repeated double-F motif.

During the fall/winter season of 1982, the firm introduced evocations of a romantic Russian past with voluminous, layered coats, accessorized with flower-shaped brooches and necklaces in fur and leather. That particular year, skins were also joined together to form flower patterns, and fur ruffles were used as detailing. Modeled were Tibetan lamb coats, weasel, marmoridea, fitch, Russian squirrel, beaver, fisher, mink, and lynx. Pants and sweaters were suggested for day, and pants, skirts, and blouses, for evening, with a fur greatcoat in loden green to cover all. Among other fabrics used were velveteen, flannel, embroidered taffetta, cashmere, alpaca, and shetland in loden, black, and coffee.

A year later, in 1983, the shape created was a wide look, which now included constructed shoulders. The furs were shown with soft blousing and dolman or set-in sleeves. The poncho-coat, with long, puffed fur, was matched with sheared pelts flattening in the front and back. Very long fur scarves with tasseled fringe were added. Fur inserts were seen, as were tissue-thin suede and irregular, zigzag stitching for accents. High-waisted sweaters in striped and geometric jaquards were shown, as

NAPIER IS SNOOTIER.

©1983 *Napier*® Fine Fashion Jewelry.

Gene Federico: Advertisement for Napier Jewellery, 1983

Fendi: Fur coat and cap, 1983

well as skirts worn like a second skin and flannel doubled with cashmere. Colors were dusty pastels, copper, lead, and pewter. New additions to exotic fur combinations were marbeled suede, stained suede, and shearling printed in flowered tapestry or ritual and mask designs. Always to be noted are the beautiful fabrics, as well as accessories manufactured to their own design from such companies as Garolini for shoes, Colony for belts, and Portolano for gloves. The Fendi firm is a clan that continues to be a credit to the founder, spiritual leader, and until recently, head of the family, Adele Casagrande Fendi.

—Gillion Skellenger

FERGUSON, Perry (Field).

American film designer. Born in Fort Worth, Texas, 12 November 1901. Married; son: Perry. Art director, 1935–41, and supervising art director, 1941–53, at RKO Studios, Hollywood, California; also worked on films for United Artists, Columbia, Universal and Metro-Goldwyn-Mayer, from 1949; collaborated with designers Van Nest Polglase and George Jenkins.

Works:

Film designs include—*Hooray for Love* (W. Lang), 1935; *Winterset* (Santell), 1936; *Bringing Up Baby* (Hawks), 1938; *Gunga Din* (Stevens), 1939; *The Story of Vernon and Irene Castle* (Potter), 1939; *The Swiss Family Robinson* (Ludwig), 1940; *Citizen Kane* (Welles), 1941; *Ball of Fire* (Hawks), 1942; *They Got Me Covered* (D. Butler), 1943; *North Star* (Milestone), 1943; *Up in Arms* (E. Nugent), 1944; *Casanova Brown* (S. Wood), 1944; *Belle of the Yukon* (Seiter), 1945; *The Kid from Brooklyn* (McLeod), 1946; *The Stranger* (Welles), 1946; *Song of the South* (H. Foster), 1946; *The Best Years of Our Lives* (Wyler), 1946; *The Secret Life of Walter Mitty* (McLeod), 1947; *Desert Fury* (L. Allen), 1947; *The Bishop's Wife* (Koster), 1947; *A Song Is Born* (Hawks), 1948; *Rope* (Hitchcock), 1948; *Without Honor* (Pichel), 1950; *711 Ocean Drive* (J. Newman), 1950; *Sound of Fury* (Endfield), 1950; *The Groom Wore Spurs* (Whorf), 1951; *Queen for a Day* (Lubin), 1951; *The Lady Says No* (Howe), 1951; *The Big Sky* (Hawks), 1952; *Main Street to Broadway* (Garnett), 1953; *The Shaggy D.A.* (Stevenson), 1976; *Herbie Goes to Monte Carlo* (McEveety), 1977.

Publications:

On FERGUSON: books—*Filmlexicon degli Autori e delle Opere*, supplement, edited by Michele Lacalamita and others, Rome 1973; *Le Décor de Film* by Leon Barsacq, Paris 1970, as

Caligari's Cabinet and Other Grand Illusions, Boston 1976.

Perry Ferguson's art direction told stories through style and space. *Ball of Fire* (1942) for example, contrasted a professor's nineteenth-century lodgings (an antiquity enclosed by dusty walls of books and surrounded by a garden like that of a medieval cloister) with New York nightlife (studded with spacious, slick, and fashionable supper clubs). At the same time, Ferguson used circular spaces to complement the ensemble acting and to emphasize Sugarpuss O'Shay as the storyline's pivot.

The artistic credit for Ferguson's greatest achievement, *Citizen Kane* (1941), has not always been properly assigned. On the film, Van Nest Polglase received the art direction credit, with Ferguson named as associate. Moreover, director Orson Welles put his own strong visual stamp on this film as on all of his productions. However, both Welles and photographer Greg Toland have emphasized Ferguson's role as art director, thus validating his right acclaim.

Kane's visual complexity spans volumes of analysis. Perhaps most memorable was Xanadu: a creation of extensive research (including a study of the Hearst mansion) culminating in a tasteless hodge-podge of styles. This frantically electric building symbolized Kane's obsession to possess. Xanadu also captured multiple psychological spaces. For instance, the vacuous, over-sized palace with dwarfing fireplace, high ceilings, and cold, polished floor provided a striking image of loneliness for the bored, idle Susan it engulfed. Her bedroom, suggesting the *horror-vacuui* of a child's mind, interpreted her as a toy trapped in Kane's demonic doll house. She eventually left the claustrophobic atmosphere, but Kane, framed ad infinitum by his own mirrored reflection, would be trapped forever in this ego-prison of his own making.

Styles changed like points of view in this film. Kane grew up with a Currier and Ives childhood, a Beaux-Arts adolescence, an expressionistic adulthood, and a surrealist senility—or were these merely perceptions of his narrators? The film is notable for spatial changes (enhanced by Toland's creative photography): closed, open, horizontally narrow, vertically narrow, dominating characters, overwhelmed by characters, disorienting. Such diverse spaces are the basis of the film's formal design, as well as agents of expression.

Ferguson's enhancement of the narrative in *The Best Years of Our Lives* (1946; in collaboration with George Jenkins) opens with a crowded room of faceless GI's. Eventually, the camera targets on our protagonists, cramped together on the plane ride home. The banker returns to his comfortable, but efficient, high-priced apartment (acknowledging an affluence devoid of ostentation). The local boy enters a homecoming straight out of a Norman Rockwell illustration, with sentimental front porches and shady trees iconographic of small-town folksiness. The ex-soda jerk cum war hero, confused in his father's crowded trailer, out of place in his floozy wife's bachelorette apartment, has no real home. He returns to a womb-like airplane cockpit to relive the pains of the war. Through these sets, Ferguson illustrated the differences and universalities of former GI's returning to once familiar worlds as strangers and each searching for a space to call his own.

—Edith Cortland Lee

FERRE, Gianfranco.
Italian fashion designer. Born in Legnano, in 1944. Studied architecture, Politecnico, Milan. Worked as a freelance jewellery and fashion accessory designer, Milan, 1969–73; fashion designer, Baila Company, Milan, 1974–78; launched Gianfanco Ferre fashion label, Milan, from 1978: first women's collection, 1978; first menswear collection, 1982; launched perfumes and accessories lines, from 1984; first haute couture collection, 1986, and furs collection, 1987; artistic director, Christian Dior fashion house, Paris, since 1989. **Exhibitions:** *Italian Re-Evolution*, La Jolla Museum of Contemporary Art, California 1982 (travelled to Hartford, Connecticut); *Intimate Architecture: Contemporary Clothing Design*, Massachusetts Institute of Technology, Cambridge, 1982; *Creators of Italian Fashion 1920/1980*, Daimaru Museum, Osaka, 1983 (travelled to Tokyo); *The Unpleasant Genius: Creativity and Technology of Italian Fashion 1951/1983*, Sala Congressi del Galoppatoio di Villa Borghese, Rome, 1984; *Moda Italia*, Pier 88, New York, 1988; *Tartan*, Fashion Institute of Technology, New York, 1988. Address: Via Spiga 19/A, 20121 Milan, Italy.

Publications:

On FERRE: books—*I Mass-Moda Fatti e personaggi dell'Italian Look/The Who's Who of the Italian Fashion*, with text by Adriana Mulassano and photos by Alfa Castaldi, Florence 1979; *Italian Re-Evolution*, exhibition catalogue edited by Piero Sartogo, La Jolla 1982; *The Italian Look Reflected*, with text by Silvia Giacomoni and photos by Alfa Castaldi, Milan 1984; *The Unpleasant Genius*, exhibition catalogue edited by Pia Soli, Milan 1984: *McDowell's Directory of Twentieth Century Fashion* by Colin McDowell, London 1984; *The Encyclopaedia of Fashion from 1840 to the 1980s* by Georgina O'Hara, London 1986; *Moda Italia*, exhibition catalogue edited by Bonizza Giordani Argani, Milan 1988.

Gianfranco Ferré has always been faintly uncomfortable with the idea of fashion as a relentlessly changeable phenomenon. He has always claimed that his clothes—even when he was

Gianfranco Ferre: Floral lace jacket, 1989

most involved with abstraction, as in his early women's collections—were meant for "real people," by implication, people who were concerned with style, rather than fashion. While this has become a common-enough claim in an era in which it has become fashionable in itself to decry the idea of being in fashion, Ferré is obviously sincere in his determination to create a serene, even classical point of view, which varies only subtly from season to season.

At the core of the designer's sensibility, one suspects, there is a finely-tuned concern for simplicity. His architectural training is often cited as the root of his exceptionally sober and economical sense of cut, and it is a training which shows in his own environment, in his own style of dressing, and which is indeed the epitome of his fashion esthetic. On this foundation, Ferré has evolved a style which uses traditional fabrics and deceptively conventional tailoring to suggest the mobility and necessary condensed qualities inherent in modern life. To look at a Ferré dress fleetingly is almost like looking at a sketch, a quick impression of line and color. In this sense, he rather resembles his contemporary, Karl Lagerfeld, who has a similar ability to suggest the timeless and whose work on closer inspection reveals vast subtleties. Unlike Lagerfeld, however, Ferré is far less concerned with the sympathetic reinterpretation of the past and more with the intimate relationship between the wearer and the garment.

Another of the designer's hallmarks is his bold use of primary colors, juxtaposed with gray, black, or green. These bright, almost industrial hues—tractor yellow, fire truck red—add an additional energy to Ferré's work, suggesting the bright world of the laboratory or the flash of skyscrapers glimpsed from a highway. And it is this suave modernity, this fast-moving element that most distinguishes Ferré's clothes and makes it possible today, probably even more so in the future, to identify that fugitive gesture, the artist's signature.

—Peter Carlsen

FIELDS, Edward.

American textile designer. Born in New York City, in 1913. Served in the United States Merchant Marine, until 1941. Married Eleanor Fields in 1935. Performer, in Fields Brothers' song-and-dance team at the Ziegfeld Follies, New York, 1922; worked at various jobs in New York, until 1935; opened own rug showroom, New York, 1935; acquired "magic needle" prototype, and began manufacturing own large-scale, high fashion rugs and carpets, from 1941; with his brother Eliot Fields, established Edward Fields Inc. carpet manufacturing firm, Flushing, New York, from 1950 (the firm continues at 232 East 59th Street, New York): designed for the White House, American Airlines, etc. Board Member, Fashion Institute of Technology, New York. Honorary Fellow, American Society of Interior Designers, 1978. *Died* (in Clearwater, Florida) *17 April 1979.*

Publications:

By FIELDS: article—interview in *Interiors* (New York), November 1978.

On FIELDS: articles—in *Interiors* (New York, July 1956, January 1972, June 1979; *Interior Design* (New York), September 1967, February 1971, May 1979; *Residential Interiors* (Radnor), January 1977; *Architectural Digest* (Los Angeles), August 1982.

The day after his marriage in 1935, Edward Fields opened his business as a carpet representative in the New York showroom of Hampton Shops, a fashionable decorating firm. His wholesale carpet and rug business flourished, but he became dissatisfied with the lines he was able to offer. In 1941, he acquired the model

for a rug-making machine with a special needle from Joseph Blumfeld, a Viennese rug-maker. This device evolved into Fields' "magic needle" machine, resembling a miniature handgun, which enabled him to start making his own rugs in 1942–43.

During the 1930s and 1940s, the carpet industry was aggressively and successfully promoting wall-to-wall broadloom as a universal solution to floor covering requirements, but after World War II, furniture began to be arranged in a more organized fashion, so that with increasing frequency, the rug became the central design element. Moreover, the new vogue for radiant heating in floors mandated the need for rugs which did not cover the entire floor surface. Thus, when Fields established his own business in 1950, with more distinctive rug design in mind, he decided that the firm's output would be custom work, produced entirely in the United States under his supervision and handcrafted with the highest standards from 100% wool yarn. Fields felt that a rug should not be the entire center of attention in a room but that it could be treated as a distinctive design element. He often referred to the floor as the room's "fifth wall."

During the 1950s and 1960s, he worked with a number of outstanding designers to produce significant rug designs, which were frequently viewed as a form of art. Marion V. Dorn, who had worked with Elsie de Wolfe and Syrie Maugham, designed rugs that were based on abstract South American motifs. These rugs differed from other contemporary designs in that they were derived from ethnic, rather than *moderne*, sources. Raymond Loewy, a close friend of Fields, encouraged him to produce rugs which would be in keeping with the avant-garde movement of the time. This resulted in a collaboration with William Raiser, an interior designer who had been associated with Loewy. A collection of contemporary rugs was generated, and Fields dubbed them "area rugs." The area rug concept was soon picked up by well-known interior designers and architects, who brought their own designs to Fields for translation into rugs in custom sizes and colors for modern interiors.

In the 1960s, Fields employed Annie Sanders Bohlin, a Cranbrook graduate and Fulbright scholar, to design contemporary rugs for him in the free-form style so popular at the time. Darren Pierce, Percival Goodman, Joan Gerson, Chaim Gross, Van Day Truex, Robert Motherwell, and Helen Frankenthaler also designed for Field's carpets.

Field's rugs for the White House included a blue and gold oval rug, with motifs from each state, for the Diplomatic Reception Room and a floral-bordered carpet in the President's Oval Office. Fields designed the tapestry rugs which were used on the bulkheads of American Airlines' passenger fleet, and his firm wove the large, scenic tapestry for American's passenger terminal at the Dallas-Fort Worth airport.

He established two yearly awards for the Fashion Institute of Technology, where he served as a member of the board—the William G. Raiser Award for interior design and the Edward C. Fields Award for product design. His son, Jack Fields, President of Edward Fields, Inc., and his widow, Eleanor Fields, Chairman of the Board, today continue the strong tradition of excellence for which the company is known. The thousands of designs in the firm's collection now include rugs based on geometry, organic references, interpretations of historic designs, natural motifs, and *trompe l'oeil*, with a palette range from subtly textured monochromatic rugs to examples of highly exuberant designs in brilliant colors with dramatic sculpturing.

—Grant Greapentrog

FINKE, Jochen.

German stage designer. Born in Glogau, Germany (now Glogow, Poland), 3 August 1941. Educated in Grimma, until 1959; studied stage design, under Heinrich Kilger, Kunsthochschule, East Berlin, 1964–69: Dip. 1969; graduate studies, under Karl von Appen, Akademie der Künste, East Berlin, 1969–71. Married Renée Hendrix in 1973; son: Jakob. Worked as a gardener in Dresden, as stage decorator in Stralsund, as technical draughtsman in East Berlin, and several other jobs, 1960–64; first stage designs, Frankfurt on Oder, 1965; resident stage designer, Deutsches Theater, East Berlin, 1971–79; chief designer, Volksbühne, East Berlin, since 1980. Leading member of the stage design group, Verband Bildender Künstler, East Berlin, since 1975; vice-president of the DDR section, and member of International Scenography Commission, OISTAT Organization Internationale des Techniciens et Architects de Theatre, since 1982. Guest instructor, at the Fachschule für Gestaltung, East Berlin, since 1974, Kunsthochschule, East Berlin, 1977–79, Hochschule für Schauspielkunst, East Berlin, since 1980, and Theaterhochschule, Helsinki, 1985. **Exhibitions:** Galerie im Turm, East Berlin, 1979; Kleine Galerie Pankow, East Berlin, 1986; Kleine Galerie, Eberswalde, 1989. **Collections:** Kleist-Museum, Frankfurt on Oder; Goethe Nationalmuseum, Weimar; Gerhart Hauptmann Museum, Erkner. Recipient: Goethe-Prize, 1986. Address: Parkstrasse 64, 1100 Berlin, German Democratic Republic.

Works:

Stage designs include—*Kabale und Liebe*, Deutsches Theater, East Berlin, 1971; *Juno und der Pfau*, Deutsches Theater, East Berlin, 1972; *Torquato Tasso*, Deutsches Theater, East Berlin, 1975; *Ein Sommernachtstraum*, Hans Otto Theater, Potsdam, 1976; *Schwanensee*, Komische Oper, East Berlin, 1977; *Faust*, Mecklenburgisches Staatstheater, Schwerin, 1979; *Berlin Alexanderplatz*, Volksbuhne, East Berlin, 1981; *Tinka*, Berliner Ensemble, East Berlin, 1982; *Die Niebelungen*, Staatsschauspiel, Dresden, 1984; *Mahagonny*, Teatro Sao Carlos, Lisbon, 1985; *Optimistische Tragödie*, Volksbühne, East Berlin, 1985; *Penthesilea*, Staatsschauspiel, Dresden, 1986; *Der Meister und Margarita*, Volksbühne, East Berlin, 1987; *Warten auf Godot*, Volksbühne, East Berlin, 1988; *Romeo und Julia*, Teatro Aberto, Lisbon, 1988; *Hamlet*, Volksbühne, East Berlin, 1989.

Publications:

By FINKE: articles—"Der Spiel-Raum" in *Theater der Zeit* (East Berlin), October 1976; "Verwandlungen" in *Theater der Zeit* (East Berlin), April 1979; "Heinrich Kilger" in *Der Sonntag* (East Berlin), March 1982; "Bestandsaufnahmen" in *Theater der Zeit* (East Berlin), September 1983; "Mahagonny in Portugal" in *Podium* (East Berlin), January 1986; "Szenographie" in *Szenographie der Volksbuhen*, East Berlin 1989.

On FINKE: books—*Stage Design Throughout the World 1970–1975* by René Hainaux and Nicole Leclercq, Brussels and London 1976; *Buhnenbilder* by Friedrich Dieckmann, East Berlin 1978; *Tasso 75* by Christoph Funke, East Berlin 1978; *100 Jahre Deutsches Theater Berlin* by Michael Kuschnia, East Berlin 1983; *Bild und Szene* by I. Pietzsch and others, East Berlin 1988; *Wolfgang Engel inszeniert Penthesilea* by Michael Funke and Dieter Goerne, East Berlin 1989.

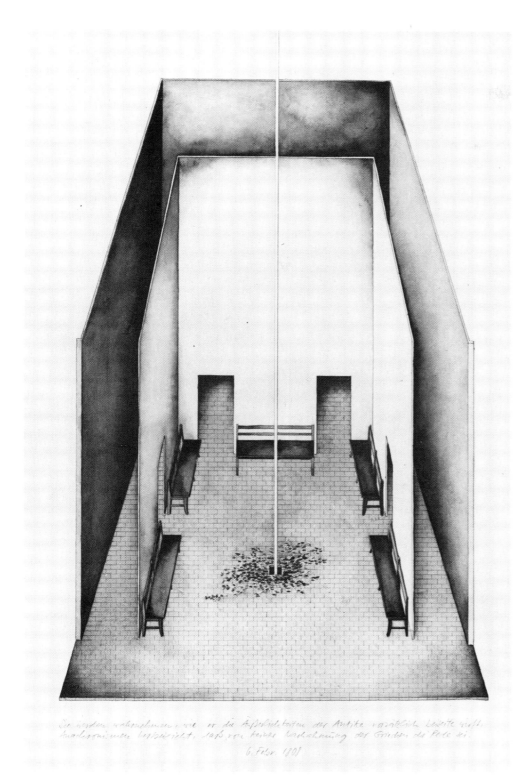

Jochen Finke: Set design for *Penthesilea*, at the Dresden Staatschauspiel, 1986

One cannot exhibit stage design. So one acquires a theatre ticket and attends the only possible stage design exhibition—the theatrical performance. The stage design does not exist without the actor, the singer, the dancer, and the spectator. These are the true producers of the stage design, that is, of that which can be experienced on the stage as a pictorial interpretation of reality.

Stage design is not static. During its short lifetime between the beginning and the end of a theatrical performance, it is subject to continual transformation. Existence on the stage is defined by the event. (*From a text accompanying a theatre design exhibition.*)

Each stage design comes to life in the process of adapting a dramatic work to the present time. If one is successful in shaping the stage as a visible expression of social or historic structures, the actor is given the opportunity in his concrete relation to his surroundings to represent the dramatic figure in its social determination. The space, in making possible and limiting the scene, becomes a lively theatrical means of expression. As a restraint on the presented events, it becomes an aesthetic system of the definition of our relationship to historical material. (*From "Der Spiel-Raum" in* Theater der Zeit.)

The classical definitions of stage design no longer apply. Concepts such as decor, illusion, and history hardly matter. In their place, we talk of space, movement, performance. Stage design statements are better understood as spatial statements. Without space, there is no movement; without movement, no scene. Stage design is now regarded as nothing other than the visual relation between figure and space. In consequence, the stage designer has become not only partner of the director but, even more, partner of the actors. By unequivocally concentrating on the scene in his work, the designer is forced deeper into the production process. The boundaries between stage design and production have become permeable. The actor stands once again at the heart of the theatre.

Like literature and the plastic arts, theatre has title to its existence only if it communicates something, if it says something about reality in a concrete social situation, if it formulates an attitude toward the world. Hence, the necessity for a continual expansion of rules and proven methods. Contemporary theatre is always experimental. And the search for new possibilities is the only form of artistic survival. (*From "Bestandsaufnahme" in* Theater der Zeit.)

—Jochen Finke

In his work, the designer Jochen Finke, a pupil of Karl von Appen and Heinrich Kilger, is primarily interested in giving visual expression to spiritual problems. He feels particularly inspired by the romantic painter Caspar David Friedrich, and by the Surrealists de Chirico and Magritte. Finke renounces imitative and illustrative methods: he likes to bring new meaning to real objects by placing them in unfamiliar juxtapositions, producing a kind of irritation or alienation. The concrete objects on the stage (trees, water, fire, lamps, etc.), through their relationships to each other and to the actions of the players, express new connections which are revealed in prominent and significant ways. Materials are not just imitated—the objects on stage are genuine, concrete material. Finke works analytically: before he paints, he writes. The piece, its dramaturgy, its conceptual information, take prime place in the work process. He learned this methodical approach from his teacher Heinrich Kilger.

For this designer, space is a lively means of expression in the theatre. Spatial changes, disruption of perspectives, light—always in relation to the play of the actors—are consciously-used methods to make clear space/time relationships. Finke's stage designs are imbued with an acute rationalism and clarity. His first work for the Deutsches Theatre in Berlin, the design for Schiller's *Intrigue and Love*, showed stage space and furniture in an even white. Areas of social difference (petit bourgeois and the court) were made meaningful through differing ceiling heights. A sort of passe-partout frame—decorated on its movable upper part with Schiller's writing—gave to the whole a strong, contoured form. The social problems were rendered by optical rhythm. In the design of Goethe's *Torquato Tasso*, Finke returned to the movable scenery of Goethe's time. The relationship of the interiors to nature outside gave particular significance to this production at the Deutsches Theatre. The more Tasso found himself prisoner at the court of Ferrara, the more the naturalistic elements were pushed back, until at the end of the play, with all the scenic devices removed, Tasso took the road to freedom in a clear light on an almost empty stage. The costumes, too, were derived from the original period of the piece. Finke considers the historic circumstances of the plot very precisely, consciously rejecting any contemporary interpretation.

In *Berlin Alexanderplatz* (based on Doblin's novel), which was premiered at the Berlin Volksbühne, the irritations of the large city to which the hero sees himself exposed were expressed in grey-blue steel constructions and scaffolding. These devices were movable, and so from time to time gave out on new vistas and spaces. A few birches hinted at landscape, almost crowded out by the image of the city. *Tinka*, a contemporary piece by the East German author Volker Braun, and performed in 1983 at the Berliner Ensemble, takes place in a large enterprise. Finke designed a space carousel with a deliberately sterile effect, which—when moved by the revolving stage—allowed the scenes to glide easily into one another. The cool high walls between each scenic space isolated people from one another. Finke's offerings are always to the point, concrete and precise. In this, above all, lies their aesthetic effect.

—Ingeborg Pietzsch

FIORUCCI, Elio.

Italian fashion designer. Born in Milan, 10 June 1935. Founder and proprietor, Fiorucci shoe store, Milan, 1962–67; director, Fiorucci fashion shop, Galleria Passerella, Milan, selling clothes by Ossie Clark, Zandra Rhodes and others, from 1967; began first wholesale and retail production of jeans, fashion accessories and household items in 1970: founded Fiorucci S.p.A., Milan, 1974, and Fiorucci Inc., New York, 1976; opened major boutique-cultural centres in New York, 1976, in Boston and Los Angeles, 1978, and shops throughout Europe, the United States, Japan, and Southeast Asia, from 1978. Founder, Technical Design School, Milan, 1977. Contributor to *Donna* magazine, Milan. **Exhibition:** *Italian Re-Evolution*, La Jolla Museum of Art, California, 1982. Address: Fiorucci S.p.A., Galleria Passerella 2, 20122 Milan, Italy.

Publications:

On FIORUCCI: books—*I Mass-Moda: Fatti e Personaggi dell'Italian Look* by Adriana Mulassano, Florence 1979; *Italian Re-Evolution: Design in Italian Society in the Eighties*, exhibition catalogue edited by Piero Sartogo, La Jolla 1982; *McDowell's Directory of Twentieth Century Fashion* by Colin McDowell, London 1984; *The Conran Directory of Design*, edited by Stephen Bayley, London 1985; *The Encyclopaedia of Fashion from 1840 to the 1980s* by Georgina O'Hara, London 1986; *Italian Design: 1870 to the Present* by Penny Sparke, London 1988.

Elio Fiorucci is the guiding light for a fashionable naughty kitsch which has recently become trendy among the chic youth and well-known personalities alike in both the United States and Europe and, in fact, the world around. He is vehemently opposed to haute couture, which he terms "pathetic," yet his outrageously flamboyant clothes and accessories have an inimitable style and attitude which has caught on and been copied both by the fashionable stores and by the types of cheap wholesalers who supply streetvendors with their "plastic" wares. Fiorucci's major innovation is turning ordinary apparel and accessories into flashy transformations for colorful fun and up-to-the-minute, high-tech look achieved by a mix-and-match choice left to the discretion of the individual customer. He is more of a wholesaler, promoter, and distributor than a fashion designer as such; he uses various designers for each class of item which appears in his boutiques and in other stores around the world as well.

His origins lie in the pop culture scene of the mid-1960s, his first clothes being the Carnaby Street look of that period. He helped open the European and Japanese market: to acceptance of the new, and at present, his influence can be seen in the United States as well in nouveau chic areas such as the East Village in New York and in Los Angeles' New Wave scene. He is also preferred by many celebrities, drawing admiration from clients such as Brooke Shields, John Travolta, Jackie Onassis, and even Princess Diana, to whom for the royal wedding, he sent a sweatshirt adorned with a jeweled crown.

Fiorucci's famous stores in New York and Milan are a "total atmosphere," with flashing strobe lights and new wavey/disco music blasting amidst the arrays of loudly colorful and patterned items, all bearing the Fiorucci label. His shoes and boots are his most longstanding trademark items, with patent-leather reds, yellows, blues, greens, and purples predominant, along with animal-skin or bright colored insets on black. The ordinary sweatshirt has never before been so varied and so "smart," going longer, becoming a dress, turning inside out, decorated with abstract patterns or worn with diversely shaped belts and scarves. There are variously emblazoned or solid-colored headbands, socks, gloves, sweatpants, jackets, book bags, looseleaf binders, note pads, magic markers, pencils, license plates, postcards, hats purses, calendars, boxes, and so on, with fringes, zippers, holes, leopard skin designs, fake fur, or fishnet all in plastic, metal, acrylic, netting, or some other new material. It's all Fiorucci's droll expression of the idea that the cheap, gaudy, and slightly kinky be worn as an emblem of "rebellion," a comment on the plastic society of the present.

For Fiorucci, who has been called the "Titan of Trash Flash," thrift-shop clothing and junk-shop accessories can be re-arranged and made over into jazzy outfittings that are both affordable and stylish, and, perhaps most important, appealing to the trendy sets who are "in the know" and want to express themselves with an eyebrow-raising, fun-loving twist. His success over the past decade has been rather phenomenal, and it will be interesting to see if he can continue to capture the world's fashion eye in the future.

—Barbara Cavaliere

FIRTH, Tazeena (Mary).

British stage and exhibition designer. Born in Southampton, Hampshire, 1 November 1935. Educated at St. Mary's School, Wantage, Berkshire, 1943–50; Chatelard School, Les Avents, Switzerland, 1950–52. Designer, Theatre Royal, Windsor, Berkshire, 1954–57, for the English Stage Company, Royal Court Theatre, London, 1957–60, Royal Shakespeare Company, Stratford-upon-Avon, Warwickshire, 1966–74, and for the National Theatre, London, 1974–77; has worked in collaboration with designer Timothy O'Brien, since 1961. **Exhibition:** *British Theatre Design '83–87*, Riverside Studios, London, 1988. **Collections:** Victoria and Albert Museum, London; Theatre Museum, Goteborg. Recipient: Gold Medal, Prague Quadriennale, 1975. Address: 33 Lansdowne Gardens, London SW8 2EQ, England.

Works:

Stage productions (with Timothy O'Brien) include—*The Bartered Bride*, Sadler's Wells Theatre, London, 1962; *Girl of the Golden West*, Sadler's Wells Theatre, London, 1962; *Next Time I'll Sing to You*, Arts Theatre, London, 1963; *Licence to Murder*, Vaudeville Theatre, London, 1963; *Luv*, Arts Theatre, London, 1963; *Poor Bitos*, Arts Theatre, London, 1964; *Hedda Gabler*, Arts Theatre, London, 1964; *Entertaining Mr. Sloane*, Arts Theatre, London, 1964; *A Scent of Flowers*, Duke of York's Theatre, London, 1964; *Poor Bitos*, Arts Theatre, New York, 1964; *Waiting for Godot*, Royal Court Theatre, London, 1964; *Tango*, Aldwych Theatre, London, 1966; *Days in the Trees*, Aldwych Theatre, London, 1966; *Staircase*, Aldwych Theatre, London, 1966; *All's Well That Ends Well*, Royal Shakespeare Company, Stratford-upon-Avon, 1967; *As You Like It*, Royal Shakespeare Company, Stratford-upon-Avon, 1967; *Romeo and Juliet*, Royal Shakespeare Company, Stratford-upon-Avon, 1967; *The Merry Wives of Windsor*, Royal Shakespeare Company, Stratford-upon-Avon, 1968; *Troilus and Cressida*, Royal Shakespeare Company, Stratford-upon-Avon, 1968; *The Latent Heterosexual*, Aldwych Theatre, London, 1968; *Pericles*, Royal Shakespeare Company, Stratford-upon-Avon, 1969; *Women Beware Women*, Royal Shakespeare Company, Stratford-upon-Avon, 1969; *Bartholomew Fair*, Aldwych Theatre, London, 1969; *Measure for Measure*, Royal Shakespeare Company, Stratford-upon-Avon, 1970; *The Knot Garden*, Royal Opera House/Covent Garden, London, 1970; *The Merchant of Venice*, Royal Shakespeare Company, Stratford-upon-Avon, 1971; *Enemies*, Aldwych Theatre, London, 1971; *Man of Mode*, Aldwych Theatre, London, 1971; *La Cenerentola*, Municipal Theatre, Oslo, 1972; *Lower Depths*, Aldwych Theatre, London, 1972; *The Island of the Mighty*, Aldwych Theatre, London, 1972; *As You Like It*, Arts Theatre, Cambridge, 1972; *Richard II*, Royal Shakespeare Company, Stratford-upon-Avon, 1973; *Love's Labours Lost*, Royal Shakespeare Company, Stratford-upon-Avon, 1973; *Summer Folk*, Aldwych Theatre, London, 1974; *Pericles*, Comedie Francaise, Paris, 1974; *The Bassarids*, English National Opera, London, 1974; *Next of Kin*, National Theatre, London, 1974; *The Marrying of Ann Leete*, Aldwych Theatre, London, 1975; *The Bassarids*, Stadt Oper, Frankfurt, 1975; *John Gabriel Borkman*, National Theatre, London, 1975; *Peter Grimes*, Royal Opera House/Covent Garden, London, 1975; *Wozzeck*, Adelaide Festival, South Australia, 1976; *The Zykovs*, Aldwych Theatre, London, 1976; *The Force of Habit*, National Theatre, London, 1976; *Tales from the Vienna Woods*, National Theatre, London, 1977; *Bedroom Farce*, National Theatre, London, 1977; *Falstaff*, Berlin Opera, 1977; *The Cunning Little Vixen*, Stora Theatre, Göteborg, Sweden, 1978; *Evita*, Palace Theatre, London, 1978 (and productions worldwide); *A Midsummer Night's Dream*, Sydney Opera House, Australia, 1978; *The Rake's Progress*, Royal Opera House/Covent Garden, London, 1978; *Lulu*, Royal Opera House/Covent Garden, London, 1981; *A Doll's Life*, Mark Hellinger Theatre, New York, 1982; *Turandot*, Vienna State Opera, 1983; *Katerina Ismailova*, Goteborg, 1984; *La Traviata*, Umeà, 1985; *The Trojan Women*, Göteborg, 1985; *Bluebeard's Castle*, Copenhagen, 1985; *Il Seraglio*, Göteborg, 1986; *The Magic Flute*, Umeà, 1987; *Rigoletto*, Umeà, 1987.

Publications:

On FIRTH: book—*British Theatre Design '83–87*, with texts by Timothy O'Brien and David Fingleton, London, 1988.

A theatre designer's job is to persuade people to think and feel certain things—it could be said, "to prevent them from thinking the wrong thing." It is important to remember that the audience does not have the advantage of having heard the discussions that lead up to a production; they are informed only by what they see and hear in front of them.

Beautiful sets and luxurious costumes, in themselves works of art, are no help unless they reinforce the dramatic intentions. The stage is a deceptive place where the genuine can seem false. The theatre has it own reality where tall poles covered with green carpet can communicate more to an audience than trees cut fresh from the forest. Beware the overly complex unless it looks simple, for the singer or actor is made in the human scale. These all-important humans should complete the design, not compete.

—Tazeena Firth

See O'BRIEN, Timothy.

Precision and a search for an ideal visual image that lies between prosaic reality and conscious art or metaphor underlies all of the work of Timothy O'Brien and Tazeena Firth. A prime example was the scenography for Gorki's *Summerfolk* (Royal Shakespeare Company, 1974). Three walls and the floor were covered with a green wool carpet, which had a variety of subtle shades but no distinct pattern. Trees were represented by absolutely straight columns covered with the same carpet. A genuine feeling of external nature was evoked without a hint of naturalistic detail. A more metaphoric and abstract approach was found in Etheredge's *Man of Mode* (Royal Shakespeare Company, 1971), the chief element of which consisted of a series of polished, silvery spheres in different, neatly organized configurations; these marvellously conveyed both precision and playfulness, even as they helped re-describe the space for various scenes.

O'Brien sees his and Firth's work as having evolved toward greater expressiveness over the years. It has also become technically more complex. For the Michael Tippett opera *The Knot Garden* (Covent Garden, 1970), the set consisted of eleven miles of thick string forming a series of wings and a backdrop in several layers. High-powered projectors cast pointillistic photos of gardens onto the strings, filling the stage with an abstract impression of nature in which the characters stood out in the beams of tightly focussed spotlights. Kinetics contributed to scenes of psychological stress as two concentric arcs of steel rods on substage rails rode around in grooves in the field of projected images, thereby creating a visually disorienting effect.

The set for the musical *Evita* (London, 1978) was a culmination of increased expressiveness for which O'Brien and Firth drew upon both traditional scene painting and sophisticated technology. The scenographically crucial element was a very large projection screen that glided up and down stage at an oblique angle to receive projected images of photographs and documentary newsreels. Also present was a metal bridge construction that served as a ceremonial platform; as wide as the stage, it moved toward the audience from the rear of the stage for several crowd scenes. Framing the total stage picture were huge murals on the proscenium facade, and intensifying the visual effect of the action on stage were not only spot-lights shining up through the stage floor but mirrors that lined the inner surfaces of the proscenium arch as well as the side walls of the stage. Other recent O'Brien/Firth productions that display a heightened expressiveness beyond that of their earlier work include Stravinsky's *The Rake's Progress* (Covent Garden, 1979), Berg's *Lulu* (Covent Garden, 1981), and the musical adaptation of Ibsen's *Doll's House, A Doll's Life* (New York, 1982).

—Jarka M. Burian

FISCHER, Richard.
German industrial and product designer. Born in Neumarkt, Oberpfalz, 30 October 1935. Educated at Grundschule, 1940–45, and Gymnasium, 1946–51, in Neumarkt; studied mechanical engineering, Berufsschule, Neumarkt, 1952–55; product design, Hochschule für Gestaltung, Ulm, 1955–59: Dip. 1959. Married Caecilia Ochsenkuhn in 1960; daughters: Katja and Angela. Designer, for BASF chemical firm, Ludwigshafgen, 1959–60, and for Braun AG, Frankfurt, 1960–68; freelance designer, in Offenbach, since 1968: has designed for Minox, Canton, Keiper, Demolux, Medium and Company, Coronet-Werke, etc. Instructor and Head of Product Design, Werkkunstschule, Offenbach, 1968–72; Professor of Product Design, Hochschule für Gestaltung, Offenbach, since 1972. Recipient: Berliner Kunstpreis Junge Generation, 1965; Design Prize, Zentrum für Produktform, Vienna, 1976; Product Design Awards, Design Center, Stuttgart, 1980. Member, Verband Deutscher Industrie-Designer. Address: Lausitzerstrasse 11, 6050 Offenbach-Burgel, West Germany.

Richard Fischer: Epidiascope projector, for Medium and Company, 1988

Works:

Sixtant S mains/battery electric razors, for Braun AG, 1966.
KM2 range of coffee-grinders, blenders, peelers, and juice-extractors, for Braun AG, 1966.
35 EL 24 x 36mm format camera with flashgun attachments, for Minox, 1975.
Gamma 800 high-performance receiver, for Canton Elektronik, 1976.
Dynavit computer-training equipment, for Keiper, 1976, 1989.
EC 9 x 11mm format camera, for Minox, 1977.
HC 100 home and car compact loudspeaker, for Canton Elektronik, 1977.
City flooring and kitchen cleaner, for Coronet-Werke, 1983.
EC-P pre-amplifier, for Canton Elektronik, 1985.
Computerized calibration equipment for eyeglasses and spectacles, for Eyemetrics-Computer Optik, 1987.
Epidiascope projector with integrated carrying-case, for Medium and Company, 1988.

Publications:

By FISCHER: articles—"Zur Anzeichenfunktion" in *HfG: Bericht 5* (Offenbach), November 1975; "Anzeichenfunktionen" in *HfG: Fachbereich Produktgestaltung* (Offenbach), November 1978; "Formgebung—das Erzeugen einer Produktsprache" in *Konstruktion, Elemente, Methoden* (Leinfelden), October 1981.

On FISCHER: books—*1. Deutscher Designertag 1977, Karlsruhe: Design und Designer,* exhibition catalogue, Dusseldorf 1977; *The Conran Directory of Design,* edited by Stephen Bayley, London 1985.

The work of the designer, based on my twenty-five years of practical experience, presents itself as follows: the designer comes into his own only if he is also a significant member of a team of specialists. In this team, he will be seen as the expert on the appearance of the object—that is, his task will be seen as attending to the object's physical perceptibility. The layman would say that the designer is responsible for the "appeal" of a product, the product's symbolic dimension.

His role, as described here, is in startling contradiction to the usual concept of the designer as coordinator. In my opinion, the designer has to understand and take into consideration a great many of the problems of other disciplines (technology, psychology, sociology, economics), for product appeal rests upon symbolic conversion of the substance of the above-named disciplines. Frequently, the designer will even be entrusted with the complete technical development of simple objects up to the construction of a model. The more areas he can take over from the whole spectrum of development, the more effective and smooth, as well as cost-effective, will be the overall development of a product. But, as these tasks vary from case to case, design becomes an "interdiscipline."

Because the chief task of a designer is to master product appeal, it follows that he must be able not only to interpret meanings which will be transmitted through the object but to realise the essence in his design of the product. By means of product appeal, the consumer can be informed how an object is constructed, how it functions, how to handle it, and whether it is built to last. The consumer can also be reached by appeal to his psychosocial self-image.

Products not only fulfill practical functions but can be the bearers of social symbolism (for example, status symbols) and also of expectations, such as warmth, comfort, etc. All this should be conscious, rather than intuitive, on the part of the professional designer: he should be able to articulate his intentions verbally in order to make these perceptions known to his other team colleagues in marketing, sales, development, and production.

—Richard Fischer

FISHER, Jules (Edward).

American stage lighting designer. Born in Norristown, Pennsylvania, 12 November 1937. Studied at Pennsylvania State University, University Park, 1956; Carnegie Institute of Technology, Pittsburgh, 1957–60: BFA 1960. Assistant stage manager and carpenter, Valley Forge Music Fair, Devon, Pennsylvania, 1955; assistant electrician, at the Shubert Theater, and Circle in the City, Philadelphia, 1956; worked in stock, then at the 74th Street, Theatre, New York, 1958–59; independent lighting designer, in New York, since 1959: President, Jules Fisher Associates theater consultants, working for Circle in the Square, New York, Deauville Star in Miami, Studio Theatre of Brooklyn Academy of Music, California Institute of Arts in Valencia, WJCTV Channel 78, Jacksonville Public Television Studio, and C. W. Post College Concert Theatre at University of Greenville, New York, from 1963; President, Jules Fisher and Paul Marantz architectural and lighting design firm, designing for St. Louis Art Museum, Hubert Humphrey Metrodome in Minneapolis, Lake Placid Winter Olympic Stadium, Boston Museum of Fine Arts, New York Grand Hyatt Hotel, etc., from 1971; President, Jules Fisher Enterprises, New York, from 1973. Recipient: Antoinette Perry (Tony) Award, 1973, 1974, 1978; Drama Desk Award, New York, 1981. Address: 126 Fifth Avenue, New York, New York, 10011, U.S.A.

Works:

Production lighting designs (New York) include—*All of the King's Men,* 1959; *West Side Story* (tour), 1960; *Riding Hood Revisited,* 1961; *Red Roses for Me,* 1961; *O Say Can You See,* 1962; *Porgy and Bess,* 1962; *Six Characters in Search of an Author,* 1963; *Spoon River Anthology,* 1963; *The Trojan Women,* 1963; *Enter Laughing,* 1963; *Don Giovanni,* 1963; *The Subject Was Roses,* 1964; *PS I Love You,* 1964; *Half a Sixpence,* 1965; *The Devils,* 1965; *Searjeant Musgrave's Dance,* 1966; *The Threepenny Opera,* 1966; *Little Murders,* 1967; *South Pacific,* 1967; *Iphigenia in Aulis,* 1967; *The Canterbury Tales,* 1968; *Hair,* 1968; *Butterflies are Free,* 1969; *Steambath,* 1970; *Soon,* 1971; *Hamlet,* 1971; *Lenny,* 1971; *Jesus Christ Superstar,* 1971; *Pippin,* 1972; *Mourning Becomes Electra,* 1972; *The Iceman Cometh,* 1973; *Uncle Vanya,* 1973; *Ulysses in Nighttown,* 1974; *Sergeant Pepper's Lonely Hearts Club Band on the Road,* 1974; *Dancin',* 1978; *Beatlemania,* 1978; *Frankenstein,* 1980; *Rock and Roll: The First 5,000 Years,* 1982; *La Cage aux Folles,* 1983; *The Rink,* 1983; *Big Deal,* 1985; *Song and Dance,* 1986; *Rags,* 1987; *Elvis,* 1988; *Legs Diamond,* 1988.

Publications:

On FISHER: book—*The Art of Stage Lighting* by Frederick Bentham, London 1968, 1980.

Lighting design has been my craft and profession for twenty-five years. It continues to give me rewards as I strive to improve my work. The primary sense of satisfaction comes from witnessing my contribution to the elucidation of the drama by using light to make each moment within the drama better express the intentions of the playwright and the directors; aiding the actor in his performance by providing an environment, a motivation, and an atmosphere in the space he or she inhabits; and assisting the audience to see, through a command of the variables of the light that affect the eye and the brain. The joy in my work has been the process of attempting to fulfill these goals.

As to a future goal, I would hope that improvements in the technical propagation and control of light, paralleled by my own continuing growth and maturity as a craftsperson, will bring about the ability to infinitely mold and sculpt the lightspace to the greatest artistic end.

—Jules Fisher

Jules Fisher developed an attraction to lighting design as a youth. After some initial exposure to theatre in high school, Fisher became involved as a stage manager, carpenter, and assistant electrician in summer stock and local Philadelphia area theatres. His work on three New York musical touring productions that played in the Shubert in Philadelphia led to his becoming lighting designer for three productions at the Circle in the City Theatre there. By the time Fisher received his B.F.A. from the Carnegie Institute for Technology in 1960, he was already designing shows in New York at several Off-Broadway theatres. Unlike other young designers who go to New York City to build a career, Fisher never interned with a major lighting designer. Instead, he forged his training out of practical experience, working on production after production.

His first New York show was *All of the King's Men* (1959). It was during this early stage of his career that he developed the basic tenets of his approach to lighting design. Primarily, Fisher believes that a show "must move an audience emotionally," and he sees the role of the lighting designer as serving that purpose. According to Fisher, the lighting designer must work with a director from the beginning of the production process. The designer must create a plan that supports the whole production by enhancing the director's and playwright's intention. Fisher enjoys working with directors who can easily transmit their ideas to him. Among his favorite directors are the late Bob Fosse, Mike Nichols, and Tom O'Horgan.

Fisher's lighting designs for plays indicate his eclectic tastes. One of Fisher's earliest achievements, and one of his favorites, *Spoon River Anthology* (1963), not only insured his continuing career, but also manifested his simple, economic approach to the craft of lighting. Working with Charles Aidman, who adapted the material and staged it, Fisher created lighting that illuminated the performers without calling attention to itself. The small cast performed a series of monologues on a stage that was sparsely decorated with four rough-hewn benches, a lectern, and two chairs, all of which was illuminated against a blue background. By using different combinations of light from the top, sides, back, and front, each monologue was uniquely lit to suit the material. Fisher's subsequent lighting designs for such successful plays as *Enter Laughing* (1963), *Butterflies Are Free* (1969), *Mourning Becomes Electra,*

Jules Fisher: Production lighting of *La Cage aux Folles*, New York, 1983

(1972) and *Uncle Vanya* (1973) revealed this same straightforward approach to his craft. In *Uncle Vanya*, directed by Mike Nichols at the Circle in the Square Theatre, Fisher's design "illuminated," not only the stage, but the story through subtle shifts in color and intensity. As the show progressed, these slight changes in lighting helped to create the moods and focus necessary to motivate the characters' ultimate realization of the inevitability of life passing. Fisher is very aware that "lighting is constantly in motion in a show," and he uses this kinetic capability to support the transformations that occur through the course of a production.

In contrast to his designs for the lighting of many successful plays, he was involved with the rock musicals, *Hair* (1968), and *Jesus Christ Superstar* (1971). All of these productions displayed a more sophisticated and provocative application of theatrical lighting. *Hair* incorporated one of the earliest uses on Broadway of lighting, with bold deep saturated colors, that shifted and pulsated in time to the music. This is the same presentational technique that is used in rock and roll concerts, and unlike traditional lighting practice in which shifts are logically placed to coincide with the values in a scene. The lighting for *Jesus Christ Superstar* was equally daring. Heralded as a "masterpiece of engineering and design" by Kevin Sanders of WABC-TV in New York, Fisher's design employed highly placed back-lights which shone brilliantly on the heads and shoulders of the performers who walked on set

designer Robin Wagner's steeply raked stage floor. In the London version, Fisher installed multi-colored fluorescent tube lights behind plexiglass panels in the raked floor which would flash and change, similar to those in discotheques. Subsequently, his interest in rock and roll show lighting led to his becoming production supervisor for the *Rolling Stones* tour of the United States in 1975.

Fisher believes in closely coordinating his work with the set designer. Working with Tony Walton who designed the scenography for *Pippin* (1972), he created much more than a workable lighting design. From the opening musical number in *Pippin*, in which only the performer's white-gloved hands were visible against a black void; through the big, splashy production numbers, to the end of the show, where only a work light on a bare stage was seen, Fisher's lighting insinuated itself in an organic manner and became more than mere illumination. In itself it was metaphorical, and integral to the scenic values of the production.

In *Pippin* and his other work for director Bob Fosse, Fisher showed his amazing ability to theatrically light dancers' moving bodies. In *Chicago* (1975), and *Dancin'* (1978), Fisher's talent for lighting the dancing form was duly noted by the critics. In the *New York Times* review for *Dancin'*, Richard Eder stated that Fisher's lighting "is integrated into Mr. Fosses's precise and stylish rhythms." Ted Kalem, of *Time Magazine*, commented about the same show that "Fisher's lighting, like the hand

of a master painter, seems to turn those same bodies into efflorescent still lifes even when they are in dynamic motion." Fisher has employed this same talent in musical shows that Fosse did not direct such as *Ulysses in Nighttown* (1974), for which he won a Tony Award, and *La Cage Aux Folles* (1983). About the latter, Clive Barnes wrote in the *New York Post* that Fisher's lighting, "a flashy flash-load of light, provides the show with its special fashion."

Fisher keeps busy not only with lighting design, but with several other activities related to theatre. He has co-produced such shows as *Lenny* (1971), *Dancin'*, (1978), *Rock and Roll, The First 5,000 Years* (1982), *The Rink* (1983), and *Big Deal* (1985), and most recently *Elvis,* (1988), for which he also co-designed the lights, as well as acted as production supervisor/director. As a theatre building consultant, Fisher has worked on such major performance and entertainment spaces as the Brooklyn Academy of Music, Circle in the Square Theatre, and New York's Palladium Night Club. He is very aware of the dangers inherent in theatre design. He considers it a problem when architects do not consider that the function of a theatre is to provide people with an emotional experience. They may approach theatre design as merely an opportunity to make a "visual statement." Fisher counters this limited approach by affirming that "sometimes a good building for theatre is less dramatic architecturally."

Fisher strives to improve his craft as a designer. He does not want to develop a recognizable style, but wants each of his lighting designs to serve the needs of the various productions. Throughout his career, he has been attracted to the use of film in theatre, influenced by the Czech designer Josef Svoboda. *Beatlemania*, *Rock and Roll*, *The First 5,000 Years*, and *Elvis* have featured live actors and film projections to create what Fisher refers to as a "three-dimensional experience on a two-dimensional plane." Very much concerned with the future of lighting technology, he believes that through developments in stage lighting the lighting designer will more effectively serve the artistic intentions of the playwright, director, performer, and ultimately, the audience.

—Tom Mikotowicz

FLECKHAUS, Willy.

German book, magazine, poster and graphic designer. Born in Velbert, 21 December 1925. Married Ursula Thonnisen in 1951; 4 children. Freelance graphic designer, working for Westdeutscher Rundfunk radio, Cologne mubnicipal theatres, Munich Olympics, etc.; art director, *Twen* magazine, Cologne and Munich, 1959–70; art editor, Suhrkamp Verlag book publishers, Frankfurt; art director, *Frankfurter Allgemeine Zeitung* newspaper, Frankfurt. Professor, at University of Wuppertal, Gesamthochschule of the University of Essen, and the Folkwangschule, Essen; founder-director of the Tuscany Summer School. President, Art Directors Club of Germany, 1972–73. Recipient: Culture Prize, Deutsche Gesellschaft fur Photographie, Cologne; Gold Medal, Art Directors Club of Germany; Hall of Fame Award, Art Directors Club of New York, 1987. Address: 5068 Odenthal, Erberich, West Germany.

Works:

Books designed (for Suhrkamp Verlag) include—*Der Schatten des Korpers des Kutches* (P. Weiss), 1960; *Stucke I/II* (M. Frische), 1962; *Materialen zu Weiss' Marat/Sade*, 1967; *Holderlin: Ein Chronik in Text und Bild*, 1970; *Mein Gamili* (R. Wolf), 1971; *Der Kurze Brief zum Langen Abscheid* (P. Handke), 1972; *Grunverschlossene Botschaft* (H. Atmann), 1972; *Polaris*, 1973; *Philosophische Terminologie* (T. Adorno), 1973; *Herman Hesse: Leben und Werk im Bild*, 1973; *Kinder und Hausmachen* (Grimm), 1974; *Tartarin von Tarasca* (A. Daudet), 1974; *Die Grossen Detektive*, 1975; *Reineke Fuchs* (J. Goethe), 1975.

Publications:

On FLECKHAUS: books—*Magazine Design* by Ruari McLean, London and New York 1969; *Graphis Record Covers*, edited by Walter Herdeg, Zurich 1974; *Der Marianbader Korb: Über di Buchgestaltung im Suhrkamp Verlag* by Siegfried Unseld, Hamburg 1976; articles—in *Graphis* (Zurich), May/June 1987; *Idea* (Tokyo), March 1988.

FLEMING, Allan Robb.

Canadian typographic, book and graphic designer. Born in Toronto, 7 May 1929. Studied advertising art, Western Technical School, Toronto, 1943–46. Married Nancy Chisholm in 1951; children: Martha, Peter and Susannah. Design assistant in Toronto, working for T. Eaton Company, 1946–49, Aiken McCracken advertising agency, 1949–51, and the Art and Design Service, 1951–53; freelance designer, London, 1953–54; designer, John Tait and Partners, London, 1954–55; worked as a freelance designer, Toronto, 1955–57; vice-president and creative director, Cooper and Beatty typographers, Toronto, 1957–62; art director, *Maclean's* Magazine, Toronto, 1962–63; vice-president and creative chief, MacLaren Advertising Company, Toronto, 1963–68; chief designer, University of Toronto Press, 1968–77; associate, Burton Kramer Associates, Toronto, 1973–76, and Burns, Cooper, Donoahue, Fleming and Company, Toronto, 1976–77. Instructor in typographic design, Ontario College of Art, Toronto, 1956–60 and 1977. **Exhibitions:** Gallery of Contemporary Art, Toronto, 1958; *Printing for Commerce*, American Institute of Graphic Arts, New York, 1959; Vancouver Art Gallery, 1976 (toured). *Died* (in Toronto) *31 December 1977.*

Publications:

On FLEMING: books—*Packaging: An International Survey of Package Design*, edited by Walter Herdeg, Zurich 1959; *Who's Who in Graphic Art*, edited by Walter Amstutz, Zurich 1962; articles—in *Canadian Art* (Ottawa), November 1959; *Industrial Design* (New York), July 1961; *Domus* (Milan), June 1962; *Vanguard* (Vancouver), September 1976; *Saturday Night* (Toronto), 11 November 1976; *The Canadian* (Toronto), 6 August 1977; *Graphis* (Zurich), no. 34, 1978.

As an advertising designer, Allan Fleming left scraps of his philosophy behind in writings. Most of his ads, though, were ephemeral, and of his renowned presentations to clients, we also have no record. As a trademark and logo designer, however, he left a legacy that is still very much alive. His CN logo, for instance, has not become dated even after almost twenty-five years of use. Its smooth, controlled shape, its feeling of unity, and its metaphorical suggestion of linked railway cars seen from the air still work well. His 1965 logo for Ontario Hydro uses the "O" and "H" from the company name only as starting points. The letters are shaped

Allan Fleming: Photo spread from *Rural Ontario*, for the University of Toronto Press, 1970

and combined to read as an electrical plug (with the stems of the "H" as its prongs). The letterforms tend to disappear so that the logo becomes a symbol in its own right, as was generally Fleming's method; he usually manipulated essential typographical elements to form a symbol, often with the involvement of metaphor.

Fleming was particularly a book designer during the last ten years of his life. He produced many high-quality works which earned him a reputation in the more erudite or esoteric strata of Canadian society, but his work seems always to have been effective. His 1962 redesign of *Macleans* (a national new magazine), for example, caused its newsstand circulation to more than double.

Fleming's influence has not been so much a stylistic one as it has been an example to younger designers of professionalism and inventive originality. Often regarded as having helped graphic design in Canada to come of age, he helped to establish the field as a respected one in Canada during a time when illustration was popularly considered to be the only commerical "art." Perhaps his most notable public recognition came in the 1976 twenty-year retrospective exhibition of his work organized by the Vancouver Art Gallery and circulated to other provinces.

He was a unique sort of designer, not adhering to any one approach or school. Some have attempted to credit him with creating a distinctively Canadian style in his work. This may be a specious tack, but certainly Fleming's fresh, resolved look in trademark and logo design did a great deal to inspire young designers and to elevate the quality of work being done in what now can be seen to have been Canada's formative years in design.

—Liz Wylie

FLETCHER, Alan (Gerard).

British graphic, packaging, book and typographic designer. Born of British parents, in Nairobi, Kenya, 27 September 1931. Educated at Christ's Hospital School, Horsham, Sussex, 1941–48; studied at the Central School of Arts and Crafts, London, 1950–51; Royal College of Art, London, 1953–56; ARCA 1956; Yale University, New Haven, Connecticut, 1956–57: MFA 1957. Married Paola Biagi in 1956; daughter: Raffaella. Worked at Berlitz language school, Spain, 1952–53; assistant to typographer Herbert Spencer, London, 1956; designer, at Container Corporation of America, Chicago, 1957, at *Fortune* magazine and Time-Life Inc., New York, 1957–59; freelance designer, London, 1959–62; founder-partner, with Colin Forbes and Bob Gill, of Fletcher/Forbes/Gill design firm, London, 1962–65; with Theo Crosby and Colin Forbes, of Crosby/Fletcher/Forbes design firm, London, 1965–72; with Theo Crosby, Colin Forbes, Kenneth Grange and Mervyn Kurlansky, of Pentagram Design partnership, London and New York, since 1972: consultant art director, Time-Life International, London, 1959–64. President, Designers and Art Directors Association, London, 1973, and Alliance Graphique Internationale, Paris, 1982–84. Visiting Lecturer, Yale University, New Haven, Connecticut, 1979. **Exhibitions:** *Graphic Design: London Group,* London, 1960; *International Poster Biennale,* Warsaw, 1966; *107 Grafici dell'AGI,* Castello Sforzesco, Milan, 1974; *Eye for Industry,* Victoria and Albert Museum, London, 1986; *Pentagram's Portfolio,* ITC Center, New York, 1986. **Collections:** Stedelijk Museum, Amsterdam; Museum of Modern Art, New York. Recipient: Federation of British Industries Fellowship, 1956; One Show Gold Award, New York, 1974; Gold Award, 1974, and President's Award, 1977, Designers and Art Directors Association, London; Medal, Society of Industrial Artists and Designers, London, 1982. Fellow, Society of Industrial Artists and Designers (now Chartered Society of Designers), 1964; Royal Designer for Industry, Royal Society of Arts, London, 1972; Senior Fellow, Royal College of Art, London, 1989. Address: Pentagram Design, 11 Needham Road, London W11 2RP, England.

Works:

Packaging, for the Container Corporation of America, Chicago, 1959.
Promotional graphics, for *Fortune* magazine, New York, 1959.
Promotional graphics (articulated symbol), for Pirelli, Milan, 1972.
Poster and calendars, for Olivetti, Milan, 1973.
Logotype and corporate identity, for Reuters international news agency, 1973.
Mural, for Kodak, Harrow, Middlesex, 1975.
Logotype and corporate identity, for the Commercial Bank of Kuwait, 1980.
Signage programme, for IBM Europe headquarters building, Paris, 1983.
Signage programme, for Lloyd's of London building, 1984.
Corporate identity, for Mandarin Oriental Hotel Group, Hong Kong, 1985.
Logotype and corporate identity, for Lloyd's of London, 1986.
Design consultancy programme, for OUN Corporation, Tokyo, 1987.
Symbol and signage programme, for the Victoria and Albert Museum, London, 1988.

Publications:

By FLETCHER: books—*Graphic Design: Visual Comparisons,* with Colin Forbes and Bob Gill, London 1963; *Was ich Sah,* Hamburg 1967; *A Sign Systems Manual,* with Theo Crosby and Colin Forbes, London 1970; *Identity Kits: A Pictorial Survey of Visual Arts,* with Germano Facetti, London 1971; *Pentagram: The Work of Five Designers,* with Pentagram partners, London 1972; *Design and Art Direction 74,* editor with Edward Booth Clibborn, London 1974; *Living By Design,* with Pentagram partners, London 1978; *Ideas on Design,* with Pentagram partners, London 1986.

On FLETCHER: books—*Who's Who in Graphic Art,* edited by Walter Amstutz, Zurich, 1962, Dubendorf 1982; *Signs in Action* by James Sutton, London and New York 1965; *Graphic Design Britain,* edited by Fredrick Lambert, London 1967; *History of the Poster* by Josef and Shizuko Muller-Brockmann, Zurich 1971; *107 Grafici dell'AGI,* exhibition catalogue with texts by Renzo Zorzi and Franco Grignani, Venice 1974; *Top Graphic Design,* edited by F. H. K. Henrion, Zurich 1983; *The Conran Directory of Design,* edited by Stephen Bayley, London 1985; *Eye for Industry: Royal Designers for Industry 1936–1986,* exhibition catalogue by Fiona MacCarthy and Patrick Nuttgens, London 1986.

In his work with Pentagram, Alan Fletcher has demonstrated the value of the designer who is integrated into a total design practice. His enterprise in typography and in packaging, for example, brings together two aspects of design which in practice have to be closely related. The range of work handled by Pentagram spreads from letterheads to interior design, from product design to posters. The solutions arrived at by analysing the problems set by one commission are shared by the group and give an extra dimension to work of the organization as a whole.

Fletcher has brought to the group his own talent as a graphic designer but also his sense of the place for good design in society itself. For example, he is associated with a number of designs that are dependent on their location in the street to bring them to life. These include the long poster for Pirelli that stretched along the side of double-decker buses in London. Appearing just below the upper windows, it supplied the legs and feet of the actual passengers whose profiles appeared in the windows above, thereby creating a graphic joke that incorporated the daily lives of the people who became a living part of Fletcher's design.

In other ways, his designs have become a familiar part of the lives of Londoners and have brought to areas previously dominated by the decorations of the untutored popular design—the cafe or shop—the sophistication and humour of a professional designer. The impeccable standards required of first-rate designers prompted many of their number in the 1950s and 1960s to treat their discipline lightly and turn away from purer aspects of refined design to bring their talents into the marketplace. Fletcher, unlike many of his contemporaries, has achieved this feat not by changing his style or employing the shock tactics of the surrealists but by maintaining clear design standards and giving his work enough social relevance that his design fits naturally into the surroundings of everyday life.

—John Barnicoat

FOLON, Jean-Michel.

Belgian cartoonist, painter, illustrator, stage and graphic designer. Born in Uccle-Brussels, 1 March 1934. Studied at the Ecole Supérieure d'Architecture de la Cambre, Brussels; mainly self-taught in painting and design. Freelance painter and designer in Paris, from 1956; has designed graphics for the magazines *Holiday, Fortune, Time, Graphis, New Yorker, L'Express, Le Nouvel Observateur,* murals for the Brussels Metro and Waterloo Rail Station, London, as well as numerous graphics for books, stage and film. **Exhibitions:** Librairie Le Palimugre, Paris, 1966; Galerie de France, Paris, 1968; Lefebre Gallery, New York, 1969, 1972, 1978, 1980, 1982; Musée des Art Décoratifs, Paris, 1971; Palais de Beaux-Arts, Charleroi, Belgium, 1971; Arts Club of Chicago, 1972; Palais des Beaux Arts, Brussels, 1975; Deutsches Plakat-Museum, Essen, 1976; Museum Boymans van Beuningen, Rotterdam, 1976; Institute of Contemporary Arts, London, 1977; Musée d'Art Moderne, Liège, 1978; Centre d'Action Culturelle, Saint Brieuc, 1980; Musée de la Poste, Paris, 1982. Recipient: Grand Prix, Triennale of Honour in Art, Italy, 1965; Art Directors Club of New York Award, 1966; Grand Prix, Bienal of Sao Paulo, 1973. Address: Burcy, 77890 Beaumont-du-Gatinais, France.

178 FOLON

Publications:

By FOLON: books—*Le Message: dessins de Folon,* Paris 1967, 1974; *La Mort d'un arbre,* Paris 1974; *Les Ruins circulaires,* portfolio, with text by Jorge Luis Borges, Monte Carlo 1974; *Lettres à Giorgio 1967–1975,* Geneva 1976; *Affiches de Folon,* with text by Milton Glaser, Paris, New York and Milan 1978; *Le Regard du temoin,* Paris 1979; *The Conversation,* with Milton Glaser, New York 1983.

On FOLON: books—*Film and TV Graphics,* edited by Walter Herdeg, Zurich 1967; *Folon,* exhibition catalogue with text by Francois Mathey, New York 1969; *Modern Graphics* by Keith Murgatroyd, London 1969; *Graphic Designers in Europe-1,* edited by Henri Hillebrand, London 1971; *Jean-Michel Folon,* exhibition catalogue with text by Francois Mathey, Paris 1971; *Monografie des Plakats: Entwicklung, Stil, Design* by Herbert Schindler, Munich 1972; *Vue Imprenable* by Giorgio Soavi, Paris 1974; *Folon,* exhibition catalogue with text by Andre Fermigier, Geneva 1975; *Who's Who in Graphic Art,* edited by Walter Amstutz, Dubendorf 1982.

Jean-Michel Folon's great popularity has its source in the topicality of his vision. He is able—as few can—to express the taste and bitterness of our times in a concise and almost childishly simple manner. As a result of his ability to perceive the half-conceived ideas, worries, and goals by which people live, the speed with which these are transferred into the iconosphere, Folon's drawings rank as symbols of our *Zeitgeist.* The famous Japanese critic, Masaru Katsumie, called Folon a "*peintre moraliste,*" while his philosophical stance suggests to him analogies of the French thinker "What do I know?."

His first trip to New York in 1967 left a strong imprint on the artist. Here he met the absurd heights of a city—Moloch, cut by cement canyons, a city in which instead of trees grow thickets of signposts, like walls of green in impassible tropical forests. A lonely, tortured, little man gives in to their hypnotic operations. Like the Biblical wife of Lot, he, too, transforms himself into a directional arrow, which grows out in every direction and forms a finely wrought arabesque, a jumble of lines obligatorily ending in the point of an arrow. Another critic, Dino Buzzati, says that the metropolises pictured in Folon's drawings are kingdoms of alienation where man is reduced to the status of a robot:

> A nightmare? yes, definitely. But thanks to the heavens, an artist who does not translate the horrible alienation into dispairing masks or moans of agony. . . . With an inexhaustible eruption of stylistic discoveries, qualitatively not inferior to Steinberg, Folon laughs at it or at least smiles at it, while transforming the nightmare into a stupefying, vertiginous, hallucinating, megalopolitan ballet.

Buzzati also emphasizes the poetry of Folon's imagination. Michel Ragon does the same thing in his book about urbanism of the future, *La Cité de l'an 2000,* which includes a series of the artist's drawings. One of them represents a monotonous panorama of uniform buildings, but at a certain spot there is an open window and in it, a flowerpot, from which a lonely little branch climbs into the distant space.

Folon studied architecture in Brussels; he dropped it for the craft of drawing, which he pursues with mastery. From the beginning of his career, he worked out a style of his own (some critics see in his work Paul Klee's influ-

ence), characterized by a simple designer's line. Ignoring the evolution of contemporary drawing, he does not change it. He began with little pictures, but with time, passed on to large formats, which he continues to execute precisely with pen or brush. Thanks to a transparent facture, the colorful, well-saturated surfaces create the impression of a light, ethereal material. Their open quality reduces the drawings' graphic hardness and it softens their dramatic expression. In these luminous, colorful drawings/reflections, Folon dispels the contemporary electronic and computerized world.

—Szymon Bojko

FORBES, Colin.
British graphic and typographic designer. Born in London, 6 March 1928. Educated at Sir Anthony Browne's School, Brentwood, Essex; studied graphic design, Central School of Arts and Crafts, London. Married Wendy Schneider in 1967: 3 children. Worked as an assistant to the typographer Herbert Spencer, London, 1952; freelance designer, London, 1953–57; art director, Stuart Advertising agency, London, 1957–58; freelance designer, London, 1961–62, founder-partner, with Alan Fletcher and Bob Gill, of Fletcher/Forbes/Gill design firm, London, 1962–65; with Theo Crosby and Alan Fletcher, of Crosby/Fletcher/Forbes design firm, London, 1965–72; with Theo Crosby, Alan Fletcher, Kenneth Grange and Mervyn Kurlansky, Pentagram Design partnership, London and New York, since 1972. Lecturer, 1953–57, and Head of Graphic Design, 1958–61, Central School of Arts and Crafts, London. International President, Alliance Graphique Internationale, 1976–79; Vice-President, American Institute of Graphic Arts, since 1981; Chairman, Stanford Design Forum, California, 1988. **Exhibitions:** *International Poster Biennale,* Warsaw, 1966; *Kinetics,* Hayward Gallery, London, 1970; *107 Grafici dell'AGI,* Castello Sforzesco, Milan, 1974. Member, De-

Colin Forbes: Cover design for *Interiors* magazine, New York

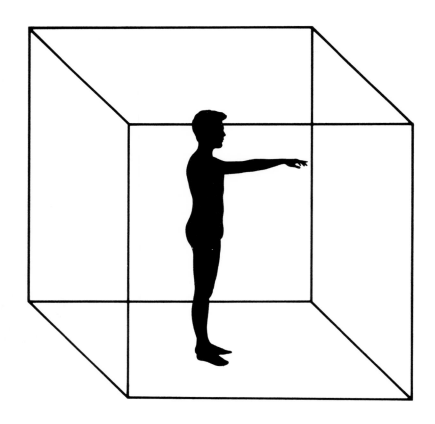

signers and Art Directors Association, London. Address: Pentagram Design, 212 Fifth Avenue, New York, New York 10010, U.S.A.

Works:

Conference signage, for the Zinc Development Association, 1966.
Posters, for Pirelli Tyres, 1966–69.
Campaign poster against museum admission charges, 1970.
Corporate identity programme, for Lucas Industries, 1972–76.
Re-design and consultancy, for *Interiors* magazine, New York, 1982–83.
Logotype, for Nissan, 1984.
Publications designs, for Drexel Burham Lambert, 1986.
Charitable contributions campaign, for IBM, 1987.
NFL catalogue, for USA National Football League, 1989.

Publications:

By FORBES: books—*Graphic Design: Visual Comparisons,* with Alan Fletcher and Bob Gill, London 1963; *A Sign Systems Manual,* with Alan Fletcher and Theo Crosby, London 1970; *Creativity and Communication,* co-author, London 1971; *Pentagram: The Work of Five Designers,* with Pentagram partners, London 1972; *New Alphabets: A to Z,* co-author, London 1973; *Living By Design,* with Pentagram partners, London 1978; *Ideas on Design,* with Pentagram partners, London 1986.

On FORBES: books—*Lettering Today: A Survey and Reference Book,* edited by John Brinkley, London 1964; *Signs in Action* by James Sutton, London and New York 1965; *Graphic Design Britain,* edited by Frederick Lambert, London 1967; *History of the Poster* by Josef and Shizuko Muller-Brockmann, Zurich 1971; *107 Grafici dell'AGI,* exhibition catalogue with texts by Renzo Zorzi and Franco Grignani, Venice 1974; *Who's Who in Graphic Art,* edited by Walter Amstutz, Dubendorf 1982.

*   *   *

The one constant in the work of British graphic designer Colin Forbes is the high quality of design. He believes a visual problem has an infinite variety of solutions, and that many are valid. Just as there are an infinite variety of design solutions, Forbes has used an infinite variety of styles in his work.

Working as a freelance designer in London, Forbes joined Alan Fletcher and Robert Gill in the firm Fletcher, Forbes, Gill in 1962. The firm became Crosby, Fletcher, Forbes in 1965 when architect Theo Crosby replaced Gill in the firm. This group helped define British design of the 60s. It was not the clean, cool design of the Swiss, nor the expressionist work known in America, but was based on irony, wit and humor. In 1972, the firm became known as Pentagram because additional designers joined the group, and they chose not to just add names to the list. The business of Pentagram is design. Colin Forbes currently serves as the chairman of the board in New York City.

Forbes' specialty in the Pentagram design group is graphic and typography design, working on corporate identity programs, packaging, book design, and advertising art. Because the persuasive element of communication art responds to fashion and obsolescence, there is not one unified style or philosophy of design evident in Forbes' work. The design solution emerges from the requirements of the individual problem as determined by the client, the purpose, the longevity of the project, the audience, and cost. Self-expression does not enter into Forbes' design solution. He practices the craft of design.

A change of wording and signatures on a petition being circulated among the populace, became a memorable poster designed by Forbes, against museum charges in Britain. Forbes used the male-female version of the number 6 as the logotype for the Pressure Die Casting Conference held in 1966. In 1983, Forbes chose a post-modern design as the graphic solution for Designer's Saturday, a showcase of ideas for members of the professional design community. He utilized a serif typeface with classic geometric elements employed in a three dimensional manner, combining historical elements with contemporary design vocabulary. Pastel coloring was introduced in the printed materials.

Because of his current position as leader of the major design group, Pentagram, and his affiliation with professional design organizations, Forbes is instrumental in influencing current design trends. Throughout his career Forbes has incorporated new technologies and new design fashions into his work without developing a defined style. Forbes the designer is anonymous, while his work is known. He knows that there are a multiplicity of valid solutions to any design problem. Design is not just a business for Forbes, but a way of life.

—Nancy House

FOSSELLA, Gregory.
American industrial, interior, exhibition and corporate designer. Born in Brockton, Massachusetts, 26 August 1933. Studied at the Rhode Island School of Design, Providence, 1954–58: BFA 1957. Served in the United States Army, 1953: Corporal. Married Janet Ostberg in 1963 (divorced); children: Craig, Dean and Nicole. Founder-President, Gregory Fossella Associates industrial design consultancy, Boston, since 1960: has designed for Acoustic Research, American Optical, Anchor Hocking, Armstrong, Black and Decker, Bristol-Meyers, Colgate-Palmolive, Corning, Data General, Exxon, Ford Motor Company, General Electric, General Motors, Hughes Aircraft, Proctor-Silex, Sears Roebuck, Western Electric, Xerox, etc. Board Member, 1957, Trustee and College Council Member since 1980, Rhode Island School of Design, Providence. Recipient: Merit Award, 1965, and Award of Excellence, 1987, Industrial Designers Society of America; Industrial Design Annual Review Award, New York, 1965, 1968, 1969, 1970, 1972, 1973, 1975; Award of Excellence, 1968, 1970, Silver and Merit Awards, 1975, Art Directors Club of Boston; Merit Award, Art Directors Club of New York, 1968, 1973; United States Government Best in US Design Award, 1969; Communication Arts Award of Excellence, 1973; Packaging Design Award of Excellence, 1973, 1974; Fortune Magazine Best 25 Products Award, 1975; Governor's Award, Design Michigan, 1975; Francis Hatch Award, 1975, 1980; Print Casebook Design Excellence Award, 1979; Hardware Industry Merit Award, 1979; IDEA Prize, 1987. Member, Industrial Designers Society of America. Address: 97 Main Street, Box 838, Osterville, Massachusetts 02655, U.S.A.

Works:

MPD gas pump, for Gilbarco, 1980.
Textile equipment, for Leesona, 1980.
Fishing reel, for Ryobi, 1980.
S-Serve incubators, for GCA, 1980.
CNC Control, for Cincinnati Milocron, 1981.
X–15 pitchers, for Aladdin, 1981.
400 Series matrix printer and robotic systems, for General Electric, 1981.
500D helicopter, for Hughes Aircraft, 1981.
Detergent container, for Colgate, 1981.
Magic Score module and bowling center, for AMF, 1982.
Emergency response center, for Life Time Products, 1982.
Modular printer, for Dennison, 1982.
Sprint CPU, for Four Phase, 1982.

Gregory Fossella: *Fastrak Series 5000* computer keyboard/display unit, for Four-Phase Systems, 1981

Executive terminal, for Exxon, 1983.
Pen set, for Sheaffer, 1983.
Fireplace insert, for AOC, 1983.
Oil container, for Penzoil, 1984.
Airline ticket printer, for Data Products, 1987.
Audio loudspeakers and component range, for Teledyne AR, 1987.

Publications:

On FOSSELLA: books—*The Book of American Trade Marks: 1,* edited by David E. Carter, Ashland 1972; articles—"Designers in Boston" in *Industrial Design* (New York), November 1971; "Business Helicopters: Fossella Styles for Corporate Identity" in *Rotor and Wing International* (Peoria), February 1981; "Gregory Fossella: Industrial Designer Par Excellence" in *Inflight Magazine* (Minneapolis), September/ October 1981; "At Home with Top Designer Gregory Fossella" in *Boston Herald Celebrity Magazine,* 13 June 1983; "Logan Airport Signage System" in the *Boston Globe,* 17 April 1984.

Described as a person with energy to spare, Gregory Fossella has earned the respect of his colleagues for his success in running an industrial design firm with frankness and honesty. As an active participant in the system of his company's designs, Fossella oversees the product division. His most efficient way of working is with his staff in this area. As a result, his firm is effective in the marketplace. Fossella lets his clients know he is not going to make their job difficult. They are informed through formal presentations, at which Fossella encourages feedback. According to him, a company buys a design firm because it is buying a group of minds; therefore, he considers it vital to know how to work with people.

Whether Fossella is designing graphics, packaging, or products for companies such as Brilliant Seafood or International Data Sciences, his designs do not assault the consumer's sensibilities. Conservative in taste, Fossella designs his products to sell by determining the best mix of function, appearance, material, quantity, and consumer preference. For example, his package for Clean Laundry Detergent was designed to convey a certain image. By combining the triangular configuration of the box, integrated handle, and package graphics with clouds, stylized flowers, or abstract soap suds, Fossella was able to communicate a clear and simple, or perhaps a "clean," message. To Fossella, when industrial designers put out a shingle, they had better be ready to solve the client's problem. Judging from the number of design awards he has received, and the broad range of areas in which he works, Fossella has indeed, been successful.

—Patricia A. Russac

FRANCK, Kaj.

Finnish glass, ceramic, furniture, textile and interior designer. Born in Viipuri, 9 November 1911. Studied interior design, Institute of Industrial Arts, Helsinki, 1929–32. Served in the Finnish Army, 1932–33, 1939–40 and 1941–44: Lieutenant. Designer in Helsinki, working for Taito Oy, 1933, Riihimaki Glass, 1934, Oy Tema, 1934–37, Wollfabriken, 1937–

Kaj Franck: Variations on the *Kilta* cup, for Nuutajarvi, c. 1955

39, Wärtsilä-Arabia, 1945–60 and Wärtsilä-Nuutajärvi glassworks, 1950–76: artistic director, Institute of Industrial Arts, Helsinki, 1960–67; art director, Silicab Group of the Oy Wärtsilä Corporation, Helsinki, 1967–73; occasional freelance designer after his retirement in 1976. Art Professor of the Finnish State, Helsinki, 1973–78; also visiting design lecturer in Tokyo, Munich, Jokkmokk, Tbilisi, Amsterdam, Dublin, Krakow and London, 1960–81. **Exhibitions:** Milan Triennale, 1951, 1954, 1957, 1960, 1968; *Design in Scandinavia,* toured the United States and Canada, 1954–57; *Glass 1959,* Corning Glass Museum, New York, 1959; *Fins Glas,* Stedelijk Museum, Amsterdam, 1972 (travelled to Düsseldorf); *100 Years of Finnish Crafts and Design,* Ateneum, Helsinki, 1975; *Metamorphoses Finlandaises,* Centre Georges Pompidou, Paris, 1978; *Finland: Nature, Design, Architecture,* toured the United States, 1981–83; *Scandinavian Modern Design 1880–1980,* Cooper-Hewitt Museum, New York, 1982; *Design Since 1945,* Philadelphia Museum of Art, 1983; *The Lunning Prize,* Nationalmuseum, Stockholm, 1986; *Scandinavia: Ceramics and Glass in the Twentieth Century,* Victoria and Albert Museum, London, 1989. **Collections:** Finlands Glassmuseum, Helsinki; Museum of Applied Arts, Helsinki; Nationalmuseum, Stockholm; Nordenfjeldske Kunstindustrimuseum, Trondheim; Kunstindustrimuseet, Copenhagen; Stedelijk Museum, Amsterdam; Kunstmuseum, Düsseldorf; Victoria and Albert Museum, London; Corning Glass Museum, Corning, New York. Recipient: Gold Medal, 1951, Honour Award, 1954, and Grand Prix, 1957, Milan Triennale; Lunning Prize, Copenhagen, 1955; Compasso d'Oro Award, Milan, 1957; Pro Finlandia Medal, Helsinki, 1957; Prince Eugen Medal, Stockholm, 1964; State Arts and Crafts Prize, Helsinki, 1977; Svenska Kulturfonden Honour Award, Stockholm, 1981. Honorary Doctorate: Royal College of Art, London, 1983. Address: Raunigrand 6, 00610 Helsinki 61, Finland.

Works:

Kilta earthenware kitchen and table service ranges, for Arabia, 1948–53.

Polaris earthenware table service, for Arabia, 1951.
Wärtsilä shop interiors, Helsinki, 1952.
Wärtsilä showroom interiors, Helsinki, 1961.
Walter Runeberg Museum interiors, Porvoo, 1961.
Facet glassware, for Nuutajärvi, 1962.
Amos Andersson Museum interiors, Helsinki, 1965.
Prisma glassware, for Nuutajärvi, 1967.
Luna glassware, for Nuutajärvi, 1972.
Railway car earthenware table service, for Arabia, 1975.
Nuutajärvi Glass Museum interiors, Nuutajärvi, 1978.
Delfoi glassware, for Nuutajärvi, 1978.
Easy Day plastic tableware and cutlery, for Sarvis, 1979.
Teema earthenware kitchen and table service ranges, for Arabia, 1979–81.

Publications:

By FRANCK: book—*Ornamo 1950–1954: Finnish Decorative Art,* editor with others, Helsinki 1955.

On FRANCK: books—*Finnish Designers of Today* by Oili Maki, Helsinki 1954; *The Beauty of Modern Glass* by R. Stenett-Willson, London and New York 1958; *A Treasury of Scandinavian Design,* edited by Erik Zahle, New York 1961; *Finnisches Glas* by K. Niilonen, Helsinki 1966; *34 Scandinavian Designers* by Svend Erik Möller, Copenhagen 1967; *Fins Glas,* exhibition catalogue with text by H. Wakefield, Amsterdam 1972; *Scandinavian Design: Objects of a Life Style* by Eileene Harrison Beer, New York 1975; *One Hundred Great Finnish Designs,* edited by Per Mollerup, Snekkersten 1979; *Scandinavian Modern Design 1880–1980,* edited by David McFadden, New York 1982; *Design Since 1945,* edited by Kathryn Hiesinger and George Marcus, Philadelphia and London 1983; *The Conran Directory of Design,* edited by Stephen Bayley, London 1985; *Twentieth Century Design: Glass* by Frederick Cooke, London 1986; *Scandinavia: Ceramics and Glass in the Twentieth Century* by Jennifer Hawkins Opie, London 1989.

Kaj Franck, one of Finland's most distinguished designers, was educated in Helsinki during the interwar period in which the country made a tremendous contribution to architecture and design, most notably through the work of Alvar Aalto. Franck learned the lessons of functional modernism well.

Unlike the other Scandinavian countries, Finland was not quite so obsessed with the social role of design. In the postwar period, the country developed a powerful and individual design image with a rather purist approach that can be best seen in the work of Franck and firms such as Marrimekko and Vuokko. Part of this success can be attributed to the importance given to design in the structure of the Finnish economy. Because production tended to concentrate around large firms, rather than small workshops, design in Finland has been given a great deal of support. In the mid-1930s, for example, Arabia was employing more than 1,000 workers, and in the period after the war, when it became one of Europe's largest ceramic manufacturers, it employed more than thirty designers. Of these, Franck was the most distinguished, and his work revolutionized modern standards of production for domestic ceramics.

Opposed to the idea of complete, uniform services, he offered the alternative of large numbers of practical and attractive pieces to complement each other. The Kilta range, familiar to a whole generation of Finns in their homes, cafes, and restaurants, is the best example of this approach. Another is a 1953 set of stacking preserve jars in pure cylindrical forms and bright, concordant colours. In 1957, Franck's set of vitreous enamel bowls for Wärtsilä won the Grand Prize at the Milan *Triennale*. Sophisticated, durable, light, stackable, like the other designs, they were intended to be mixed and matched. With their surfaces of pale and dark blue, red, yellow, green, and white, designs such as these show Franck's disciplined functionalism at its best.

Another aspect of Franck's design personality, one interested in playful humour and experimentation, is best expressed in his glass designs, which because of the nature of the material can ignore rational considerations. Franck has also followed a traditional Scandinavian pattern in that he has also produced, besides his industrial designs, a substantial body of craft objects, as for example, his glass Nuuta plate of 1965. In this area, however, his understanding of the potential of the material and his sense of pattern remain consistent with the design principles of his other work.

—Catherine McDermott

FRANÇOIS, André.
French illustrator and graphic designer. Born André Farkas, in Timisoara, Rumania, 9 November 1915; emigrated to France in 1935: naturalized, 1938; adopted name François, 1939. Studied at the School of Fine Arts, Budapest, 1932–34; studied privately with A. M. Cassandre, Paris, from 1935. Married Margaret Edmunds in 1939; children: Pierre and Catherine. Freelance graphic designer, Paris, since 1935: commercial artist, working for Standard Oil, Olivetti, Perrier, Dutch Masters Cigars, etc., 1935–44; caricaturist and cartoonist, for *Vogue*, *Femina*, *Holiday*, *Punch*, *Tribune des Nations*,

1953–60, and for the *New Yorker* (designed more than 50 covers), from 1963; book illustrator from 1946, and author, mainly of children's books, from 1952; stage set and costume designer, working for Roland Petit, 1956, Peter Hall, 1958, Jean Babilee, 1959, Gene Kelly, 1960, etc.; also independent painter and sculptor. **Exhibitions:** Galerie La Hune, Paris, 1955; Bianchini Gallery, New York, 1962; Galerie Delpire, Paris, 1965, 1973, 1981; Stedelijk Museum, Amsterdam, 1967; Wilhelm Busch Museum, Hannover, 1967; Musée des Arts Décoratifs, Paris, 1970; Galerie Melisa, Lausanne, 1971; Galerie Gurlitt, Munich, 1971; Arts Club of Chicago, 1975; Château des Papes, Avignon, 1977, Musée Saint Georges, Liege, 1977; Palais des Beaux-Arts, Brussels, 1977; Musée de Pontoise, 1979; Galerie Mecanorma, Paris, 1979; Galerie Bartsch-Chariau, Munich, 1981; Palais de Tokio, Paris, 1986 (retrospective); Musée-Château de Dieppe, 1989. **Collections:** Musée des Arts Decoratifs, Paris; Wilhelm Busch Museum, Hannover; Musée des Beaux-Arts, Brussels; Stedelijk Museum, Amsterdam; Museum of Modern Art, New York. Recipient: *New York Times* Children's Illustrated Book Award, 1952, 1956, 1958, 1970; Gold Medal, Warsaw Poster Biennale, 1972; Prix Honoré Daumier, Paris, 1979; Grand Prix National des Arts Graphiques, Paris, 1980. Chevalier des Arts et des Lettres, France, 1957; Honorary Royal Designer for Industry, Royal Society of Arts, London, 1975; Honorary Doctorate, Royal College of Art, London, 1977. Member, Alliance Graphique Internationale. Address: 16 Rue Robert Machy, 95810 Grisy-les-Platres, France.

André Francois: *L'Ascendant* painting with collage, 1974

Publications:

By FRANCOIS: books—*Double Bedside Book*, London 1952, as *The Tattooed Sailor and Other Cartoons from France*, New York 1952; *Crocodile Tears*, London 1955, Paris 1956; *The Half Naked Knight*, New York and London 1958; *Heikle Themen*, Zurich 1959; *The Biting Eye of Andre François*, with preface by Ronald Searle, London 1960; *Dapple Gray*, with John Symonds, London 1962; *The Penguin Andre François*, London 1964; *You Are Ri-di-cu-lous*, New York 1970; *Les Rhumes*, Paris 1971; *Qui est le plus marrant?*, Paris 1971; *Santoun*, Paris 1972; *Toi et moi*, Paris 1973; *Mr. Noselighter*, with Roger McGough, London 1977; *Andre François: Graphics, Paintings, Sculpture and Stage Designs*, Paris 1986, London and New York 1987; books illustrated—*Jacques le fataliste* by Diderot, Paris 1946; *William Waste* by J. Symonds, London 1946; *L'Odyssée d'Ulysse* by J. Le Marchand, Paris 1947, London 1960; *Little Boy Brown* by I. Harris, Philadelphia 1949; *The Magic Currant Bun* by J. Symonds, Philadelphia 1952; *Lettres des Iles Baladar*, Paris 1952; *Travellers Three* by J. Symonds, Philadelphia 1953; *Beau Masque* by R. Vailland, Paris 1954; *On vous l'a dit* by J. Anselme, Paris 1955; *Contes drolatiques* by Balzac, Paris 1957; *Roland* by N. Stephane, New York 1958; *Ubu Roi* by A. Jarry, Paris 1958; *Tom and Tabby* by J. Symonds, Paris 1964; *Grodge-Cast and the Window Cleaner* by J. Symonds, New York 1965; *Le meilleur des mondes* by A. Huxley, Paris 1961; *Si tu t'imagines* by R. Queneau, Paris 1979; *L'Arrache coeur* by B. Vian, Paris 1981.

On FRANCOIS: books—*Posters: 50 Artists and Designers*, edited by W. H. Allner, New York 1952; *Window Display 2*, edited by Walter Herdeg, Zurich 1961; *Who's Who in Graphic Art*, edited by Walter Amstutz, Zurich 1962, Dubendorf 1982; *The Poster: An Illustrated History from 1860* by Harold F. Hutchinson, London and Toronto 1968; *107 Grafici dell'AGI*, exhibition catalogue with texts by Renzo Zorzi and Franco Grignani, Venice 1974; *Illustrators of Children's Books 1967–1976* by L. Kingman, G. Allen Horgarth and H. Quimby, Boston 1978.

A millionaire was once asked: "Is it very expensive to run a yacht?" He replied: "If you have to ask, it means you can't."

So when I am asked whether it is possible to practise free art and commercial art side by side, my answer is: no. If the inner drive is strong enough, the question simply does not arise. The attempt to demonstrate the influence of free art on commercial art—and vice versa—seems to me completely superfluous. Both are facts of life, and I can only express myself quite subjectively about their possible division.

In the life of every artist there comes a moment when he no longer feels the urge to jump through hoops or to occupy himself with the problems of others, with all the limitations and obligations that they involve. The artist develops his own rules, and he wants to jump through his own hoops and experience his personal problems on his own. The "commercial" artist's habit of reacting to every impulse from without—be it a telephone call or a written contract—is hard to eradicate. To express oneself and to obey only the impulse from within requires a long process of re-education. It is impossible to work for an advertiser in the morning and be a painter in the afternoon; a long period of continuity is necessary in both cases. Neither training nor technical knowledge divide the free artist from the commercial artist: only the nature of the work and the demands made on the imagination are decisive.

The artist who devotes 80% of his time to painting is a painter, the artist who devotes 80% of his time to posters is a poster artist.

In commercial art an attempt is made to give form to an idea; free art, on the other hand, obtains its meaning in the course of the work and the form does not find its meaning until the work is completed. One activity starts with the idea and is brought into a form, while the other starts with the form and ultimately obtains its meaning.

Depending on my state of mind at the time, I could argue the opposite of the above with equal conviction. It can happen that I take on the adventure of a difficult task of applied graphics with great pleasure and am delighted by a satisfactory solution. It can also happen that I try to turn a serious commitment into a game and work out an illustration or a poster with playful enjoyment. My view is: Whatever I do, I am.

This does not alter the fact that navigation from one harbour to the other can be difficult and dangerous, that the facets of truth are many and contradictory—and liable to many changes between one shore and the other. (*Previously published* in Arts and Graphics, *Zürich 1983*.)

—André François

To assess the accomplishments of André François, one must look back over the years and into almost all categories of design, illustration, painting, and sculpture. In this search a common denominator appears, the François humor—shy and subtle.

Design of sets for a modern ballet, while posing stringent requirements, still offers opportunity for François to be François. This is true also when he addresses the demands of product advertising. Even in these situations, François always is able to create a warm and gentle spirit, which undoubtedly is beneficial as well as distinctive.

François has a penchant for perceptively exploring symbols and endowing inanimate objects with human features and characteristics. In his illustrations for magazine covers, and more recently in his paintings, François evokes a magical gift—possession of a bottomless trove of ideas for transforming parts of the human body—an eye, an ear, a foot—into new roles, in which they are sometimes disconnected and able to prance about independently. Although it appears that he has only to reach into the box, not so, says François. He works and re-works persistently, sometimes not sure where his explorations will lead, not sure when he has arrived. How is it that the final piece can be so fresh, after constant struggle? It is, perhaps, that his work is so individual, such a personal expression, that it is, indeed visually surprising and fresh to anyone else.

He has said, himself, that materials and technique must be subordinate to the thought expressed. Some of his paintings employ pebbles affixed to his canvas. This suggests the plastic, sculptural element in François' work, but in his view, the pebbles are there not to provide three-dimensionality but, to act as visual elements of the thought he is conveying.

No doubt the painter in François was there from the beginning, even though his early work was in applied fields. Still, his illustrations for covers of such magazines as *Punch* and the *New Yorker* can be seen as precursors of his present-day paintings. At least one of his old-broken-clockface paintings, a device which has grown to be a François cachet, also has appeared on the cover of the *New Yorker*.

In all, his has been a phenomenally productive career, one that has been as long as it has been successful. It has given him the opportunity to apply himself in many fields and bring to each his own, special sense of the humor in this life.

—Jerry Steimle

FRATINI, Gina.

British fashion designer. Born Georgia Caroline Butler, of British parents, in Kobe, Japan, 22 September 1931. Educated in Simla, India, until 1943; Hathrop Girls' School, Gloucestershire, 1944–46; studied fashion design, under Madge Garland, at the Royal College of Art, London, 1947–50. Married Renato Fratini in 1960. Assistant set and costume designer, Kathleen Dunham dance group, in London, Italy and the United States, 1951–54; freelance costume and fashion designer, London, since 1954: established Gina Fratini Limited, London, from 1964; also designed costumes for film *Stop The World: I Want to Get Off*, 1966, and for stage productions *Side By Side By Sondheim*, and *Nymphs and Satire*, 1963. **Exhibition:** *Fashion: An Anthology*, Victoria and Albert Museum, London, 1971. **Collections:** Victoria and Albert Museum, London; Bethnal Green Museum, London; Birmingham Museum of Art, Warwickshire; Bath Museum of Costume, Avon. Address: Gina Fratini Limited, 17 Wandle Road, London SW17 7DL, England.

Publications:

On FRATINI: books—*Fashion: An Anthology by Cecil Beaton*, exhibition catalogue compiled by Madeleine Ginsburg, London 1971; *A History of Fashion* by J. Anderson Black and Madge Garland, London 1975, 1980; *The World of Fashion: People, Places, Resources* by Eleanor Lambert, New York and London 1976; *The Magic Names of Fashion* by Ernestine Carter, London 1980; *The Collector's Book of Twentieth Century Fashion* by Frances Kennet, London and New York 1983; *McDowell's Directory of Twentieth Century Fashion* by Colin McDowell, London 1984; *The Encyclopaedia of Fashion from 1840 to the 1980s* by Georgina O'Hara, London 1986; *The Fashion Conspiracy* by Nicholas Coleridge, London 1988; *The History of Twentieth Century Fashion* by J. Mulvagh, London 1988.

Gina Fratini, all British in spite of her name, was born in Japan, where her father was a government official. She spent her childhood in the Far East and received her first schooling in India. Later, she went to one of England's most famous girls' schools, Hathrop Castle in Gloucestershire. Then, she began at the recently founded School of Fashion Design at London's Royal College of Art, from which she graduated with honours. After college, she joined the Kathleen Dunham dance troupe and studied body movements, which later were to be of great assistance to her in designing clothes; her creations always move beautifully, and the natural graces of the body are never hampered by ill-considered cut.

Fratini started dressmaking almost by chance. She had always made her own clothes, and one day an impecunious friend asked her for help in obtaining a ballgown for a very special occasion. She obliged, and her friend's dress was so much admired that several other friends wanted to know its origin. Fratini was besieged by re-

Gina Fratini: Short ballgown in silk taffeta, 1980

quests and for several years continued to work alone, turning out fabulously pretty dresses all made by herself. One day, a friend in the fashion business implored her to make a small collection of a dozen models which he guaranteed he would show to an influential fashion editor. Fratini made the dresses, modelled them herself, and so excited the fashion editor that she arranged for them to be seen by the owner of one of London's most exclusive retail shops. "Madame" bought the lot, sold them immediately, and demanded repeats. Gina had no workroom, no assistants, no knowledge of the international wholesale fabric market, but somehow managed, and success followed success.

Now she sells only to the most exclusive "Madame" shops throughout England and to special departments in such stores as Harrods. Privately, she makes for all the "Royals," including the young duchesses of the Royal family. She has never deviated from her personal choice of a romantic and very feminine style, and it is not surprising that her favourable client is the romantically beautiful Princess of Wales.

—Madge Garland

FRATTINI, Gianfranco.
Italian architect, interior, exhibition, industrial designer. Born in Padua, 15 May 1926. Educated at the Liceo Classico, Milan, 1943–45; studied architecture, at the Politecnico, Milan, 1946–53: Dip. 1953. Married Ingeborg Weber in 1957; children: Emanuela and Marco. Worked as assistant designer, studio of Gio Ponti, Milan, 1951–53; freelance designer, establishing own studio in Milan, since 1953: has designed for Cassina, B. Bernini, Arteluce, Artemide, Molteni, Ricci, Fratelli Faver, Gio Caroli, Fantoni, Insa, Former, Ballato, etc. Exhibition Committee Member, 1958–59, Ethical Council Member, 1972–75, and Directive Committee Member, 1979–82, ADI Associazione Disegno Industriale, Milan; Building Commission Member, Portofino City Council, Genoa, since 1975; Administrative Councillor, Milan Triennale, from 1983. State Examinations Commission Member, Faculty of Architecture, Politecnico of Milan, 1974–75. **Exhibitions:** *Contemporary Italian Architecture,* Malmo Museum, Sweden, 1968; *Domus Design,* Teheran, 1975; *Il Design Italiano negli Anni '50,* Centro Kappa, Milan, 1977; *Design and design,* Palazzo delle Stelline, Milan, 1979 (traveled to Venice); *Dal design all'habitat,* Bari, Italy, 1982; *Il Lavoro del Designer,* Trieste, 1983; *Dal cucchiaio alla città,* Palazzo Triennale, Milan, 1983; *Design Since 1945,* Philadelphia Museum of Art, 1983; *Disegnare il marmo,* Carrara, 1986; *Nouveaux Projets pour l'Habitat,* Paris 1988. **Collections:** Museum of Modern Art, New York; Museum of Contemporary Art, Chicago; Museum of Applied Arts, Helsinki. Recipient: Compasso d'Oro Awards, Milan, 1955, 1956, 1957, 1979, 1981, 1987; Gold Medal, 1957, Grand Prize, 1960, Silver Medal, 1973, Milan Triennale; Gold Medal, Mostra del Vimini, 1959; Plast Oscar Award, Milan, 1968; Award of Honour, Liubliana, 1973, 1981; MACEF Award, Milan, 1974; International Diamond Award, New York, 1976; Casa Amica Award, Milan, 1976; Furniture Award, Valencia, 1987. Address: Via Santa Agnese 14, 20123 Milan, Italy.

Gianfranco Frattini: *Proust* bookcase in black ash and pearwood, for Acerbis International, 1987

Works:

Model 849 armchair, for Cassina, 1957.
Model 530 writing-desk, for G. B. Bernini, 1957.
Model 804 secretaire-desk, for G. B. Bernini, 1964.
Sesann divan and armchair, for Cassina, 1970.
Boalum lamp, for Artemide, 1970.
Larco range of furniture, for Molteni, 1970.
560 Series range of furniture, for G. B. Bernini, 1971.
Kioto table, for Pier Luigi Ghianda, 1974.
Nuela Series range of furniture, for Lema, 1976.
Megaron lamp, for Artemide, 1979.
Simbio range of furniture, for Former, 1979.
Model 45 beaker in handblown glass, for Progetti, 1980.
Sesamo roll-top writing-desk, for G. B. Bernini, 1983.
Capri square table in beech and leather, for Cassina, 1985.
Caprile upholstered seating in beech, for Cassina, 1985.
Proust adaptable worktable in ash, for Acerbis International, 1986.
Proust bookcase in lacquered ash, for Acerbis International, 1987.
Acheo standard lamp in steel and pyrex, for Artemide, 1988.

Publications:

On FRATTINI: books—*Mobili tipo* by Robert Aloi, Milan 1956; *Design for Modern Living* by Gerd and Ursula Hatje, Munich and Zurich 1961, London 1962; *Forme e colore nell'arredamento moderno* by Giulio Peluzzi, Milan 1967, as *The Modern Room,* London 1967; *Design Italiano: i mobili* by Enrichetta Ritter, Milan and Rome 1968; *Italian Look* by G. Bocca and others, Milan 1972; *Design e Forme Nuove nell'Arredamento Italiano,* edited by Paolo Portoghesei and Marino Marini, Rome 1978; *Twentieth Century Furniture* by Philippe Garner, London 1980; *Neue Moebel 1950–1982* edited by Klaus-Jürgen Sembach, Stuttgart 1982, as *Contemporary Furniture,* New York 1982; *Design Since 1945,* edited by Kathryn Hiesinger and George Marcus, Philadelphia and London 1983; *International Design Yearbook 1988/89,* edited by Arata Isozaki, London 1988.

There is an immediate contrast between the present day and the period when I began my career; in the 1950s, there was everything to do and much opportunity to carry out new ideas. New pieces of design often sprang from problems of interior architecture, since the choice of pieces available on the market at that time was limited, and pieces initially produced for a given setting were later appropriately modified and put into industrial production.

Today, however, the production of "so-called design" is exceptional. Very often, perfectly good pieces are scrapped because the continual launching of "novelties" on the market to make a quick profit makes the public so confused that they can no longer identify and distinguish the really good pieces. Today more than ever, it is essential to have a thorough knowledge of the material you are working with and to offer a consistent and fair product.

There is a lot of talk today about the postmodern movement, both in architecture and design. My own view is that it is a phenomenon that is bound to make its mark on the products of design, though on the whole, it seems to me that a symbiosis between industrial design and postmodernism can hardly be put forward. The problem of technological research seems to be deliberately ignored, and the prospects for series production, a basic element in order to talk of design, seem very remote; for these reasons, in my view—and also because of their prices—the products of postmodernism have more the qualities of objects of applied art.

I personally think of myself as a rationalist, and I believe in the validity of the double slogan of "form-function," even if during phases in the planning, the conformation of an object has to pass through a number of filters of an individual nature—the designer's cultural background, his sensibility, aesthetic sense, and mentality. If it were not so, even design problems could be solved by a mathematical formula, whereas, fortunately, even when we start from objective premises, our work leaves room for individual expression.

—Gianfranco Frattini

G. F. Frattini's achievement was summed up by Gio Ponti as *"una bella funzionalità,"* meaning that his close attention to the practicalities of his brief was combined with an equally close attention to elegant design. No detail was overlooked. For instance, his elegant Stork Club in the centre of Milan served a house Scotch for which he designed the label on the bottle. This combination of elegance and functionalism has characterised all his work but has not excluded a certain toughness when, as in the case of the 1976 plastic crash helmet, this was a necessity. Similarly, for all its smart atmosphere designed into it by Frattini, the Ritrovo Saint Andrew's was an eminently workable interior from the point of view of its rapid and easy dispensation of drinks and snacks; everything seemed to happen in a relaxed and relaxing manner, due as much to the nature of the design as to the service personnel.

This is a clue to this designer's achievement—a delight in fine materials finely wrought for specific purposes and embracing an attention to the most mundane aspects of practicalities. In his social interiors as in individual products, they are as they are because that is how they best work but also how they best look and communicate their purposes. That first demountable armchair for Cassina in 1955 clearly announced its evident comfort as an easychair in which to lounge, but it made equally obvious the fact that it could easily be taken apart; both of these attributes were expressed in the elegance of the design which bespoke a characteristic, aesthetic economy of means.

Much this same point of view could be seen in the marvellous, flexible, segmented tube of light that he designed with Livio Castiglioni for Artemide. This Boalum lamp could be coiled, knotted, tangled, stretched out, draped over other pieces of furniture. Its form resided in its minimal character. What are often separable structural members in a lighting fitting are here brought together in one unique unprecedented object that achieves style in its very shapelessness and, at the same time, overcomes the limitations that conventional structures place upon flexibility of use and purpose. All these contradictory demands have been resolved in a truly surprising simplicity whose title to pure functionalism cannot be again said while its elegance arises equally from the boldness of the proposal.

—Toni del Renzio

FREYER, Achim.
German painter, environmental artist, graphic, stage and animated film designer. Born in Berlin, in 1934. Studied at the Meisterschule fur Graphik, East Berlin, 1951–55; stage design, in the studio of Bertolt Brecht, Akademie der Kunste, East Berlin, 1955–57. Freelance designer, working in East Berlin, 1957–72, and in West Berlin from 1972: resident designer, Deutsches Theater, East Berlin, 1964–72; also created room performances and environments, East Berlin, 1965–68; stage designer of plays and operas in West Berlin, from 1972. **Exhibition:** *Documenta 6,* Museum Fridericianum, Kassel, 1977. Address: Kadettenweg 53, 1000 Berlin 45 (West), Germany.

Works:

Stage and environmental designs include—*Zwangsraume, Bilder, Objekte,* West Berlin, 1973; *Monument des Heinrich von Kleist,* Stadttheater, Stuttgart, 1975; *Beethoven Innenraum-Landschaft,* Stadtisches Theater, Frankfurt, 1976; *Mauricio Kagel: Musiktheater,* Städtische Oper, Cologne, 1977; *Faust,* Staatstheater, Stuttgart, 1977.

Publications:

On FREYER: books—*Stage Design Throughout the World 1970–1975* by René Hainaux and Nicole Leclercq, Brussels and London 1976; *Documenta 6: Band 1,* exhibition catalogue with texts by Klaus Honnef and others, Kassel 1977; *Das Theater der Siebziger Jahre: Kommentar, Kritik, Polemik,* edited by Georg Hensel, Stuttgart 1980.

Achim Freyer once described himself as an artist who works in a number of media, the theater being just one of them. He first became involved in the theater in 1954 when Bertolt Brecht showed interest in puppets Freyer had made. After serving as assistant to Brecht and Karl von Appen, the resident designer at the Berliner Ensemble, Freyer left the theater for an extended period of time to work solely on painting and the graphic arts. By the mid-1960s, feeling pressured by the government in East Berlin to comply with the officially accepted style of art, he sought refuge in the company of others by working again in the theater. After several successes with directors Benno Besson and Ruth Berghaus, Freyer again ran afoul of the regime when he designed Goethe's *Clavigo* in an East German-Pop art manner. The production was banned, and shortly thereafter Freyer seized an opportunity to emigrate to West Germany where he once resided.

After a few years of successful freelancing, Freyer settled in Stuttgart and did some of his best work designing for director Claus Peymann at the Staatstheater Stuttgart. For productions such as *Kaethchen von Heilbronn* he created what he called "monuments," visual compositions that reflected his personal reaction to the author. These pieces grew out of Freyer's long-standing interest in contemporary art and music, particularly in the work of Joseph Beuys, Robert Rauschenberg, Mauricio Kagel, Dieter Schnebel, and Philip Glass. He exhibited his monuments in the lobbies of theaters, offering audiences an opportunity to confront purely visual imagery inspired by the designer's encounter with the play. Gradually, the monuments moved out of the theater and into the art gallery, and in 1977 Freyer exhibited a monument, now called a *Raum,* at the Documenta 6 international art exhibition. This work, *Deutschland, ein Lebensraum,* was a conglomeration of associative images representing Freyer's reaction to contemporary German life.

In all its various guises, on stage, in the lobby, or in the gallery, Freyer's art is intensely personal. He considers his work a process of continuous self-exploration. Looking back at an earlier design, he once said, "That was important to me. That brought me further." On another occasion, asked to explain an earlier design for *Pelléas and Melisande,* he answered, "How can I possibly conceive today how I dreamed and worked at that time? The conception has become something else." Although fascinated by many plays and operas, Freyer has said he can design only for those works in which he finds his own themes, those being the conflict between isolation and communion and the conflict between the establishment of order by a state and the disruption of that order by the individual.

—Richard V. Riddell

FRIEDL, Friedrich.
German graphic and exhibition designer. Born of German parents, in Fulnek, Czechoslovakia, 7 September 1944. Educated in Besigheim/Neckar, 1950–54; high school, Stuttgart, 1954–61; studied graphic design, Werkkunstschule, Darmstadt, 1968–72: Dip. 1972. Married Regina Bardt in 1976; sons: Andreas and Christian. Worked as an apprentice, then as typesetter, Stuttgart, 1961–66; freelance graphic designer, Darmstadt, since 1972: has designed for the West Berlin Internationale Design Zentrum, Darmstadt Rat fur Formgebung, Deutscher Werkbund, Letratset Deutschland, Galerie Hoss in Munich, Edition Hoffmann of Friedberg, Edition E of Munich and the Darmstadt Fachbereich Gestaltung. Instructor in typography, basic design and visual communications, at the Fachbereich Gestaltung of the Fachhochschule, Darmstadt, 1972–82; instructor in experimental design, Hochschule für Gestaltung, Offenbach, from 1980; Professor of typography, Fachhochschule, Hildesheim, since 1982. Co-editor, *Schriftwechsel* magazine of typography, Frankfurt, since 1982. **Exhibitions:** Print Gallery Pieter Brattinga, Amsterdam, 1976; Atelier Dawo, Dusseldorf, 1977. **Collections:** Klingspor Museum, Offenbach; Deutsches Plakatmuseum, Essen; Poster Museum, Warsaw. Recipient: Graphic-Design in Deutschland Prize, 1969, 1970, 1971, 1974, 1975, 1977; Warsaw Poster Biennale Prize, 1972, 1974, 1978; Essen Poster Triennale Prize, 1976, 1980. Address: Lucasweg 6, 6100 Darmstadt, West Germany.

Publications:

By FRIEDL: books—*Das Gewöhnliche Design,* Cologne 1979; *Exakte Zeichnungen,* Munich 1981; articles—in *Letratime* (Frankfurt), nos. 1, 2, 1978; *Schriftwechsel* (Frankfurt), nos. 1–6, 1982–83.

On FRIEDL: book—*Modern Publicity 1981,* edited by Felix Gluck, London 1980.

In my design work, I do not try to appear intelligible to the largest possible number of people. Rather, I try to find a form that will do justice to the complicated content and complex connections.

I try to further boundaries in visual communication and not to repeat existing positions. For me, design is an ever new visual and intellectual experiment that has nothing to do with commercial graphics.

—Friedrich Friedl

As a young composer, Friedrich Friedl was influenced by the aesthetic philosophy of Max Bense. From beginnings in informal painting, which he developed along with his daily work in the compositor's workshop of a large printing firm in Stuttgart, there appeared in the 1960s his first structural picture compositions. Consisting of connecting lines, these did not end in systematic networks but were distinguished by a dynamic of form in detail and a repose of form overall.

The use of letters, numbers, and parts of sentences in his recent works gives his attractive collages a highly designed character. In alienating letters from their original function as bearers of information and changing them into variable elements of a concrete design concept, Friedl has created an individual pictography which has extended the accepted ideas of concrete art. His fine-art works are characterised by painterly values to which he has recently added lively colour.

Friedl designs posters and other means of communication for cultural clients with similar results. His chief medium in graphic design is typography. He uses text information also as a structural design element, and with this approach, he has achieved a new and innovative expression.

—Eckhard Neumann

FRIEDMANN, Arnold.
American interior designer. Born in Nuremberg, Germany, 12 May 1925; emigrated to the United States in 1947: naturalized, 1955. Educated at high schools in Europe and Palestine; studied art, Brooklyn Museum of Art School, New York, 1947; interior design, Pratt Institute, Brooklyn, New York, 1949-53: BFA 1953; art education and design, at Pratt Institute and New York University, 1954-60: MS 1960; environmental behavior and design, Union Graduate School, Cincinnati, Ohio: PhD. 1976. Served in the British Army, 1943-46: Sergeant. Married Susanne Kirsch in 1949; sons: Daniel and Ronald. Worked as a cabinet-maker and furniture designer, New York, 1947-49; freelance interior and furniture designer, establishing own office in New York, 1954-72; vice-president, Danco Design Associates, Northampton, Massachusetts, 1975-77; partner, Amherst Design Associates Massachusetts, since 1980. Instructor, then Professor of Design, 1954-72, and Chairman of Interior and Environmental Design Department, 1969-72, Pratt Institute, Brooklyn, New York; Head of Textiles, Clothing and Environmental Arts, 1972-73, then Professor of Design, Director of the Design Program, Graduate Design Program Director, and Adjunct Professor of Landscape Architecture and Regional Planning, from 1973, and Associate Dean of Humanities and Arts since 1984, University of Massachusetts, Amherst; Visiting Professor/Fellow, Southern Illinois University, 1964, Institute for Man and Environment at the University of Massachusetts, 1976-77, Glasgow School of Art, Scotland, 1983, and Royal Melbourne Institute of Technology, Australia, 1984. Editor, International Federation of Interior Architects *Education Newsletter,* since 1981; member since 1972, and Chairman, 1972-74, Standards Committee of the Foundation for Interior Design Education and Research; Editorial Committee Member, *Journal of Interior Design Education and Research,* since 1976. Recipient: Design Project Fellowship, National Endowment for the Arts, 1979; Distinguished Teacher Award, University of Massachusetts, 1980. Honorary Member, American Society of Interior Designers, 1979; Honorary Fellow, Design Institute of Australia, 1985. Address: 42 North Maple Street, Hadley, Massachusetts 021035, U.S.A.

Works:

Corporate offices and showroom in New York, for Henri Polak Diamond Corporation, 1974.
Cooperative residential apartment in New York, for Mr. Milton Gelfand, 1974.
House interiors in Mamaroneck, New York, for Mr. and Mrs. S. Singer, 1975.
Psychiatric practice offices in New York, for Dr. Harold Kaplan, 1976.
Factory workspaces and cafeterias in Greenfield, Massachusetts, for TRW-Greenfield Tap and Die Corporation, 1980.
YMCA Health Club in Greenfield, Massachusetts, for the Young Men's Christian Association, 1981.
Engineering firm office in Greenfield, Massachusetts, for Douglas G. Peterson and Associates, 1983.
National corporate headquarters in Holyoake, Massachusetts, for the American Pad and Paper Company, 1984.
Executive offices and library in Springfield, Massachusetts, for the Basketball Hall of Fame, 1984.
Admissions and waiting-room additions in Northampton, Massachusetts, for the Cooley Dickinson Hospital, 1985.
Medical offices in Springfield, Massachusetts, for Dr. Kenneth Frankel, 1987.
YMCA hotel guestrooms, lobby and public facilities in Springfield, Massachusetts, for the Young Men's Christian Association, 1985-89.

Publications:

By FRIEDMANN: books—*A Critical Study of Interior Design Education,* New York 1968; *Interior Design: An Introduction to Architectural Interiors,* with John Pile and Forrest Wilson, New York 1970, 1982; *Course Outline: A Study Course for NSID Qualifications Examination,* New York 1973; *Commonsense Design,* New York 1976; *Environmental Design Evaluation,* with Craig Zimring and Ervin Zube, New York 1978; *Construction Materials for Interior Design,* with William Rupp, New York 1989.

My primary professional interest and activity has been in education, although I am a designer before anything else. Design is a state of mind and a lifestyle as well as a profession. I have always tried to imbue students with that sense of mission which is very real to me. Perhaps more than the transmission of knowledge and the kindling of creativity, it has always mattered most to me to give students a strong sense of commitment to design and to design excellence.

I have devoted my professional life to design education at two institutions. I have tried to help with the shaping of first-rate programs or have initiated such programs to go beyond the confines of the schools with which I have been associated. I did so, recognizing the need to improve interior design education nationally and internationally. Through the publication of my *Critical Study* in 1968, I had the opportunity to become a moving force in the field of design education and in the professionalization of interior design. In that study, I proposed the accreditation of schools, as well as the accreditation of individual designers. Now that both concepts have been realized, they have measurably strengthened and enhanced the profession of interior design.

In my personal work, I have been more interested in the humanization of the work environment and the personalization of living spaces than in trying to develop a design style recognizable as mine. Through my work as a writer and academician, I have been concerned with the development of theoretical approaches to design—including interior design criticism and environmental/behavior research—and have written extensively on some of these subjects.

—Arnold Friedmann

Arnold Friedmann's commitment to the "improved quality of life that good design can bring to an environment" is evident in his design commissions but finds its fullest expression in his dedication to design education. His seventeen years at Pratt Institute and more than ten at the University of Massachusetts, Amherst have produced a legacy of designers who share his commitment and goal of excellence. Through personal example and close, one-to-one working relationships with his students, Friedmann has promoted the development of many mature designers.

His involvement with teaching has not been limited to the classroom; it encompasses the broadest implications of professionalism. In 1962, Friedmann helped to found the Interior Design Educators Council, which was organized to provide a forum for the improvement of interior design teaching. His report, *A Critical Study of Interior Design Education,* produced for the curriculum research-committee of this organization in 1968, was the first comprehensive research on the topic. This study proposed two instruments essential to the profession: a formal program of accreditation of schools and a national examination for professionals. These proposals and Friedmann's unstinting help initiated today's accrediting agency, the Foundation of Interior Design Education and Research, and examining board, the National Council for Interior Design Qualifications. Friedmann has held major offices or chairmanships in each of these organizations, having been Standards Committee chairman of FIDER and board member and secretary of NCIDQ as well as secretary and president of the Interior Design Educators Council.

Friedmann's encouragement was also a factor in the merger of the American Institute of Interior Designers and the National Society of Interior Designers into the American Society of Interior Designers; this action was another step in uniting and strengthening the profession. As co-chairman of the Education Committee of the International Federation of Interior Architects and editor of the IFI Education Newsletter, he promotes high-quality education internationally as well as nationally. *Interior Design: An Introduction to Architectural Interiors,* which he co-authored, is one of the most concise and complete texts in the field.

Friedmann's concern with the quality of an environment, not just its design style, is reflected in his doctoral work in environmental psychology at Union Graduate School, his investigations of the effect of the environment on

Arnold Friedman: Interior of remodelled 1930 farm woodshed, Massachusetts, 1979

behavior patterns of the institutionalized mentally retarded, and his recent studies of fast food establishments, airports, and other public spaces. Consciousness about design in public and private spaces is fundamental to his research and teaching: "Our ordinary spaces are much more important than the kind pictured in an architectural or design magazine," he says.

—Marjorie Kriebel

FRISTEDT, Sven.
Swedish textile designer. Born in Stockholm, 29 November 1940. Studied textiles at Anders Beckman School, Stockholm, 1957–59. Fabric designer, Mab and Mya, Stockholm, 1959–61; designed clothing fabric patterns, for Katja of Sweden, Stockholm, 1961–1965; woven and printed textile designer, Borås Wäfveri, Sweden, since 1965; also freelance designer, for Ikea, in Simrishamn, from 1970. **Exhibitions:** *Scandinavian Modern Design 1880–1980,* Cooper-Hewitt Museum, New York, 1982; *Faces of Swedish Design,* IBM Gallery, New York, 1988 (toured the United States). **Collections:** Nationalmuseum, Stockholm; Museum of Modern Art, New York. Address: Östergatan 4, 279 00 Simrishamn, Sweden.

Works:

Orinen/Serpent printed cotton fabric, 1972.
Satin Cross collection of printed fabrics, for Borås Wäfveri, 1983.
Puzzle cotton fabric, for Borås Wäfveri, 1986.
Loppcirkus/Flea Circus cotton fabric, for Borås Wäfveri, 1986.
Pram cotton fabric, for Borås Wäfveri, 1986.
Glass and Concrete collection of fabrics, 1986–87.
Living It Up collection of clothing and furnishing fabrics, 1987.

Publications:

On FRISTEDT: books—*Svensk Textilkonst/Swedish Textile Art* by Edna Martin and Beate Sydhoff, Stockholm 1980; *Scandinavian Modern Design 1880–1980,* edited by David Revere McFadden, New York 1982; *Trycka Tyger* by Inez Svensson, Stockholm 1984; *Den Svenska Formen* by Monica Boman and others, Stockholm 1985; *Faces of Swedish Design,* exhibition catalogue edited by Monica Boman, Stockholm 1988.

He's on his way to India when we meet in Stockholm. His eyes shine with curiosity and expectation. He is dressed in an elegant black-and-gray patterned shirt and trousers of cotton, sewn in his own patterns. Spiritually he is already on his journey: he has arrived in Stockholm from his house in southern Sweden in order to get ready for the trip.

He squirms a little, as though facing a chal-

lenge. It is exciting. Memories of his travels usually make a definite impression on his new collections.

Sven always talks luxuriantly and generously. For over 20 years his decorative desires to fill surfaces with symbols, flourishes and colors have raised Swedish interior fabrics to bubbling heights. His patterns are grandly luxuriant or just the opposite: a surface of dense, arcane symbols in the form of prints or screens with the addition of the occasional dot of color.

Sven's first trip after completing his education was to Italy. His teacher, Göta Trägårdh, had encouraged him and arranged financial support. That was in the early 60's, and for Sven it provided an unbelievable kick, and inspiration from which he has luckily never recovered. All the fruits, vegetables and flowers. . . And his meeting with the American designer Ken Scott who created rich patterns in fantastic color combinations.

Flying leaves, flowers, strawberries, melons, gooseberries, suns, sky, clouds, and gay stripes have flooded Sven's patterns in a never-ending stream.

In the intervals he has "washed" his excesses of rich patterns clean with more strict geometrical exercises: large squares, broad stripes, narrow stripes.

His strict discipline is counterbalanced by a joy of color. One example is his *Glass and Concrete* collection which he created together with Vivianne Sjölin. Narrow and wide stripes in a flood of colors is also a recurring theme in many of his collections. *Puzzle* has become a bridge between the different languages of design.

In the 60's it was not easy for young designers to sell patterns to the textile industry. Katja of Sweden opened the door for Sven by asking him to design patterns for her clothes. A few years later he came into contact with Borås Wäfveri after having an argument with one of the directors.

"Why are your patterns so boring and cautious, when the time is now ripe for bolder designs?" he asked—young and green, yet very sure of himself.

"Go home and make some of those designs yourself," replied the manufacturer. "You won't find it so easy!"

He did, and his patterns turned out to be a commercial success. Since then he has had innumerable trips to the city of Borås in southwestern Sweden. Their collaboration has continued without interruption. For both the Swedish and international public, it has become a custom that new collections appear at regular intervals. Today his patterns comprise 25% of Borås' manufacture. He makes patterns for both domestic and public environments. IKEA usually orders a special collection, and it is not unusual to find his fabrics on Italian sofas at the furniture fair in Milan.

At the beginning of the 80's he was in Japan. This made an impression on his *Living it Up* collection, which is one of his favorites—patterns which he both dresses in and surrounds himself with. At home in Simrishamn he entertains himself, his friends, and his neighbors with his fabric collages and arrangements. The washing line in the back garden allows the townspeople to keep up to date on the sheets, tablecloths and other fabrics which Sven is currently working on. Everybody knows that his washing hanging on the line is esthetically entertaining. You can look through the window of his studio, a former painting shop, and see him designing patterns and, when the mood is on him, painting pictures. The frames are always decorated: they present no obstacle to the flow of his imagination.

—Hedvig Hedqvist

FRONZONI, A(ngiolo) G(iuseppe).
Italian architect, interior, graphic, and product designer. Born in Pistoia, 5 March 1923. Self-taught in design. Married Marina Fra in 1947; daughters: Elena, Paola and Camilla. Freelance designer, working in Brescia, 1945–55, and in Milan from 1956. Founder-director, *Punta* magazine, Brescia, 1947–65; editor and designer, *Casabella* magazine, Milan, 1965–67. Coordinator of global design research project, Collegio Regionale Lombardo degli Architetti, Milan, 1964–65; instructor in visual communications, Umanitaria di Milano, 1967–69, Istituto Statale d'Arte, Monza, from 1968, and Istituto Universitario Isia, Urbino, 1975–77; founder and coordinator, Istituto di Comunicazione Visiva, Milan, 1978–79. **Exhibitions:** Libreria Salto, Milan, 1963; London College of Printing, 1965; Instituto de Arte y Comunicacion Visual, Buenos Aires, 1966; Politecnico, Turin, 1969; Moravska Galerie, Brno, 1975. **Collections:** Bibliothèque Nationale, Paris; Musée des Arts Décoratifs, Paris; Kunstgewerbemuseum, Zurich; Stedelijk Museum, Amsterdam; Deutsches Plakatmuseum, Essen; Deutsches Bucherei, Leipzig; Royal Ontario Museum, Toronto; Museum of Modern Art, New York. Recipient: Zanotti Bianco Prize,

Rome, 1978. Address: Corso Magenta 52, 20123 Milan, Italy.

Publications:

By FRONZONI: books designed—*Bonalumi,* Milan 1973; *Arte e Materie Plastiche,* Milan 1975; *Acque di Sicilia,* Milan 1977.

On FRONZONI: books—*A. G. Fronzoni,* exhibition catalogue by Umbro Apollonio, Turin 1969; *A History of Visual Communication* by Josef Muller-Brockmann, Teufen 1971; *Design e Forme Nuove nell'Arredamento Italiano,* edited by Paolo Portoghesi and Marino Marini, Rome 1978; *Atlante del Design Italiano 1940/ 1980* by Alfonso Grassi and Anty Pansera, Milan 1980; *Grid Systems in Graphic Design* by Josef Muller-Brockmann, Teufen 1981.

I began working as a designer in 1945, with the war just over and the reconstruction of Europe under way. It was a particularly stimulating period. I was determined to learn by doing. I believed that I could contribute through my work to the transformation of society, that I could help reduce objects and facts of social meanings. I had faith in the progressive function of applied rationality.

I persevered with my work, acting in a design context of total spatiality conceived as an information system, in a search for the image of contemporary society, for a model for the use of that *Gesamtkunstwerk,* the city. An attitude derived from a personal, critical background led me to regard design as a protest and a transgression; to seek a design that could subject technical tools to cultural choices; not to satisfy the client's needs, but to eradicate them; to relentlessly avoid waste and redundance; to cater to the necessities of the social community as the true client.

I have never given in, although one question remains open: whether the innovative autonomy of this work may not eventually turn out to be really an illusion.

In this situation, the designer's task is an arduous one. But this does not discourage me. Anyone who tries to play a civilised and progressive role is put to a hard test in any environment, especially if his job, as in the case of the designer, is always to put every environment to a hard test and especially if his work consists in continuous designing, which is certainly for him intentionally to exist in the future.

Since 1967, when I added teaching to my activities, I have been increasingly conscious that the true task of the designer is that of an educator more than of a technician. His real purpose is not to create a city but to educate people to build the city, conceived as a sensitive form of civilisation.

—A. G. Fronzoni

A. G. Fronzoni has always tended to refine his designs to a deceptive simplicity, eschewing more and more all unnecessary elements and emphasising the rectangular geometry that is generally apposite. Where it was appropriate, as in the 1964 furniture produced in series by Galli, this natural rectangularity was further accented by the choice of square-section, metal tubing, particularly successful for a chair and a bed frame, which were sparse but not Spartan. In many of these pieces, the airy framework of the supporting structure contrasted with the slab forms of seat or cupboard or drawer unit.

This same aesthetic informed the elegant pages he produced for *Casabella* when he was the editor and art director (1965 to 1967). The simple, logical, sensitively composed pages exploited the somewhat unusual format and held

the bold, sans serif type to reasonable sizes, while page succeeded page in a carefully planned sequence, feature separated from feature by a subtle articulation of internal elements. Much the same could be said of the catalogues and invitation cards designed for the Galleria La Polena in Genoa during the latter years of the 1960's; they managed to achieve, within what in clumsier hands would have been a severely restrictive style, a quite distinct character. The same sort of character had been achieved in the gallery itself which he had designed in 1965 within an old building. Again, careful, minimal detail created an admirable background for the display of works of art. Perhaps the experience gained with this gallery stood him in good stead when he came to some of his later conversions of historical buildings to newer purposes, chiefly as galleries or museums.

In spite of or even because of his quietly uncompromising modernism, he showed a respect and understanding towards these ancient buildings, and his installations drew upon them in a formal dialogue of proportion. Influential here was Ernesto Rogers, who had been the editor of *Casabella,* had researched and set up a small but significant exhibit at the 1951 *Triennale, Architettura, misura d'uomo* [Architecture, the measure of man], which spanned the centuries and saw proportion and rationalism (this word, too, has a link with notions of *ratio,* measure) as civilising elements and as the means by which otherwise contrasting styles could be brought into fruitful formal dialogue. Whether from Rogers himself (who had edited *Casabella* for a number of years) or from the *Triennale* exhibit, Fronzoni certainly learned the lesson and profited from it in the run of restoration work he undertook from the late 1960's into the 1980's.

—Toni de Renzio

FROSHAUG, Anthony.
British typographer and graphic designer. Born in London, in 1920. Studied drawing, book production and engraving, Central School of Arts and Crafts, London, 1937–39; medicine, St. Mary's Hospital School, London, 1940–43; architecture, Architectural Association School, London, 1967–69. Freelance designer, 1941–84: typographer and exhibition designer, London, 1941–47; established own printing press and workshop, Cornwall, 1949–52 and 1953–57; designer in London, 1962–84, establishing own printing workshop, from 1971. Lecturer, 1948–49, senior lecturer in typography, 1952–53, and lecturer in graphic design, 1970–84, Central School of Art and Design, London; docent, Department of Visual Communications, Hochschule für Gestaltung, Ulm, 1957–60; tutor in graphic design, Royal College of Art, London, 1961–64; senior lecturer in graphic design, Watford College of Technology, Hertfordshire, 1964–67; tutor in graphic design, Coventry College of Art and Design, Warwickshire, 1969–70; also guest professor, Technical University of Norway, Trondheim, 1960. Member, Society of Industrial Artists and Designers, London, 1947. **Exhibition:** Watford College of Technology, Hertfordshire, 1965. **Collection:** St. Bride Printing Library, London. *Died* (in London) *15 June 1984.*

A. G. Fronzoni: Contemporary Art Gallery interiors in the Teatro del Falcone, Genoa, 1979–81

Publications:

By FROSHAUG: books—*Typographic Norms*, Birmingham and London 1964; *Typography 1945–65*, Watford 1965; articles—in *Ulm* (Ulm), April 1959; *Design* (London), October 1963; *Ark* (London), June 1964; *The Designer* (London), January 1967; *Typographic* (London), no. 7, 1975.

On FROSHAUG: books—*Design in Britain*, annuals edited by Peter Ray, London 1947, 1951; *Art Without Boundaries 1950–1970*, edited by Gerald Woods, Philip Thompson and John Williams, London 1972; *Typography: Design and Practice* by John Lewis, London 1978.

Anthony Froshaug's typography took its first inspiration from the work of Jan Tschichold. After an initial phase of absorption (with more understanding than other contemporaries in Britain showed), Froshaug began to pursue an approach that was no more than latent in Tschichold's "new typography." Thus, the constraints in a task—the meanings and possible semantic structures of a text and the given elements of standard and optimal sizes of materials employed—come to dominate and determine final form, which is therefore correspondingly less subject to the designer's arbitrary will. This approach comes into its own with material more complex than simple prose: listed items, tabular matter, text integrated with pictorial or diagrammatic illustration. Yet, if Froshaug's work takes its bearings from constraints, it also has qualities of visual and physical distinction that can only be finally explained by positing some "feeling for form."

Although Froshaug has shown a new approach, his work also has quite un-modern traits. The workshop experiment may have been forced by the difficulties of getting trade printers to follow unconventional instructions, but it was also a statement of allegiance with the earliest printers. His early practice of setting text unjustified has modern associations but also ancient ones—the work of the scribes. A further point of reference here is the work René Hague and Eric Gill did between 1931 and 1940; this was another un-private press that tried to do good, everyday work. The larger rationale for Froshaug's workshop was made explicit in Lewis Mumford's *Technics and Civilization:* an acceptance of new technologies, kept small-scale and knowable, directed towards human needs.

The workshop situation allows experiments not otherwise open to a designer, and Froshaug's work of that time has qualities of invention and play that are less evident later. His years at the Hochschule für Gestaltung in Ulm might be considered a factor in this development towards a sterner approach. It was natural that Froshaug should be attracted by the invitation to teach at this reformulation of the Bauhaus, small and limited in scale, politically radical, approaching its work with a seriousness not to be found in Britain. Here, Froshaug began to apply his interest in mathematics to problems of design.

In recent years, Froshaug's mathematical interests have focussed on the uses of small computers (again, as in his printing, there is a concern with the maximal use of very limited machines). Published results of this work have still to surface.

—Robin Kinross

FRUTIGER, Adrian.

Swiss graphic, calligraphic and typographic designer. Born in Interlaken, 24 May 1928. Apprentice type-compositor, under Ernst Jordi and Walter Zerbe, at Otto Schaefli AG, Interlaken, 1944–48; studied illustration, engraving and sculpture, under Walter Kaech and Alfred Willimann, at the Kunstgewerbeschule, Zurich, 1948–50. Typeface designer, Deberny et Peignot printers and typefounders, Paris, from 1951; also freelance type and symbol designer, working for Sofratype, Lumitype, Monophoto, Bauer, D. Stempel, IBM, Mergenthaler-Linotype, Facom Tool Company, Brancher Printing Ink Company, Gaz de France/Electricité de France, Métro de Paris, Air France, British Petroleum, Ahmedabad Institute of Design, etc., from 1959; established own typography and advertising design studio, with Andre Gurtler and Bruno Pfaffli, in Paris, 1962, and in Arceuil, 1965; art director, Editions Hermann publishers, Paris, 1957–67; design consultant, IBM typewriter faces, from 1963; also architectural sculptor, from 1962. Instructor, Ecole Estienne, Paris, 1952–60, and Ecole Nationale Supérieure des Arts Décoratifs, Paris, 1954–68. **Exhibitions:** Monotype House, London, 1964; Galerie Pierre Beres, Paris, 1968; Gewerbemuseum, Bern, 1973; Gutenberg Museum, Mainz, 1977. Address: Atelier Frutiger-Pfaffli, 23 Villa Moderne, 94110 Arceuil, France.

Works:

President typeface, for Deberny et Peignot, 1952.
Phoebus typeface, for Deberny et Peignot, 1953.
Ondine typeface, for Deberny et Peignot, 1953.
Meridien text typeface, for Deberny et Peignot, 1954.
Univers typeface family, for Deberny et Peignot, 1954–55.
Opera text typeface, for Sofratype, 1959.
Concorde text typeface, for Sofratype, 1959.
Alphabet, for Orly Airport, Paris, 1959.
Egyptienne text typeface, for Sofratype, 1960.
Apollo text typeface, for Monophoto, 1962.
Serifa typeface family, for Bauer, 1967.
OCR-B Optical Character Recognition standard typeface, for the European Computer Manufacturers Association, 1968–73.
Alpha-BP typeface, for the British Petroleum Company, 1969.
Dokumenta typeface, for the *National-Zeitung,* Basel, 1969.
Alphabet and lettering plan, for Charles de Gaulle Airport, Paris, 1970.
House typeface, for the Facom Tool Company, Paris, 1971.
Iridium typeface, for D. Stempel AG, 1972.
House typeface, for the Brancher printing ink company, Paris, 1972.
Glypha condensed typeface series, for D. Stempel AG, 1978–79.
Icone typeface series, for D. Stempel AG, 1980.

Publications:

By FRUTIGER: books—*Die Kirchen am Thunersee*, booklet, Interlaken 1948; *The Development of the Roman Alphabet*, Zurich 1951; *Au Commencement*, graphic portfolio, Paris 1960; *Partages*, graphic portfolio, Paris 1962; *The Song of Solomon*, illustrator, Winterthur 1966; *Genesis*, illustrator, Winterthur 1967; *Typographical Training for Technicians and Technical Training for Typographers*, booklet, Copenhagen 1973; *La Cité de Dieu*, illustrator, Paris 1977; *Der Mensch und seine Zeichen*, 3 vols., Echzel and Frankfurt 1978–80, Lausanne 1983; *Type, Sign, and Symbol*, with texts by M. Besset, E. Ruder and H. R. Schneebeli, Zurich 1980.

On FRUTIGER: books—*Who's Who in Graphic Art*, edited by Walter Amstutz, Zurich 1962, Dubendorf 1982; *Graphismes by Frutiger* by John Dreyfus, London 1964; *Letter Forms: 110 Complete Alphabets*, edited by Frederick Lambert, London 1964, New York 1972; *Serifa: Die neue Schrift von Adrian Frutiger* by Emil Ruder, Frankfurt 1967; *Serifa, Vorprobe* by Hermann Zapf, Frankfurt 1967; *Adrian Frutiger: Ein Sternseminar*, edited by the Graphisk Institut, Stockholm 1968; *Schrift, Signet, Symbol: Formgebung in Schwarz und Weiss—Adrian Frutiger*, exhibition catalogue by Walter Zerbe, Bern 1973; *Adrian Frutiger: Zeichen, Schriften, Symbole*, exhibition folder with text by Kurt Weidemann, Mainz 1977; *The Thames and Hudson Manual of Typography* by Ruari McLean, London 1980; *The Conran Directory of Design*, edited by Stephen Bayley, London 1985; *Typographic Design: Form and Communication* by Rob Carter, Ben Day and Philip Meggs, New York 1985.

The typographer can get involved in scientific and technical aspects, particularly with the new composing methods. He can also devote himself to artistic aspects, where he has to solve space problems—problems of a white page that he has to divide and make come alive. The typographer is the one who renders thoughts accessible to everybody; he is the intermediary between the one who thinks, the one who creates, and the one who receives. This is one of the most beautiful professions—and also one of the most difficult.

I became enraptured by the simplicity of the abstract sign, by the magic of these twenty-six letters which, by themselves, can encompass the entire world's thought. I feel, for instance, that the inside white spaces are more important than the outside contours of a letter. The letters of an alphabet are like the various elements of a house: the material of typography is the black, and it is the typographer's task, with the help of this black, to capture space, to create harmonious whites inside the letters as well as between them. A letter only exists in its relation to the others. In addition, the look of a page printed in a given typeface must be the same in all languages. This is where the problem of the frequence of letters arises.

In typography, as in other art forms, the "hand," the "stamp" of the one who creates the character is recognizable. Once the typographer has acquired the full knowledge of his profession and the skill of his hands corresponds to his sensitivity and logic, he can no longer escape from an aesthetic shaped by his temperament, his education, his cultural heritage, and the experiences of many years' work. It is only in retrospect that one realizes that one is the child of one's own epoch, that one submits to one's time. For instance, the style of Univers was in the air after the War. Although this is a bit of an exaggeration, I could almost say that it was anticipated, that there was a need for it to be created.

My way of thinking can be described as organized; everything has to pass through my head. To a degree, I lack spontaneity; my creative mechanism is always based on logic, on a text, on a development; it could well be that this renders my work more understandable than that of others, more communicable.

I believe that in a person's life, his area of specialization becomes more and more demanding and may result, in a certain way, in a loss of his freedom. For me, the retreat from this specialization is in the applied use of ty-

Adrian Frutiger: *Univers* typeface family, 1954–55

Schematischer Aufbau
der Univers-Schriftfamilie.

FUJITA, S(adamitsu) Neil.
American graphic designer. Born in Waimea, Kauai, Hawaii, 16 May 1921. Studied at Chouinard Art Institute, Los Angeles, 1940–42 and 1947–49; Columbia University, New York 1957–59. Served in the United States Army, 442 Infantry Regiment, in Italy and France, 1944–46, and with G-2 Intelligence, in Okinawa, 1946–47: Staff Sergeant. Married Aiko Tamaki in 1949; sons: Kenji, David and Martin. Art Director, at N. W. Ayer and Son, Philadelphia, 1953–54; director of design and packaging, Columbia Records, New York, 1954–60; freelance designer, New York, 1960–63; founder and president of Ruder, Finn and Fujita, New York, 1963–77, and of S. Neil Fujita Design Incorporated and Wisteria Field Incorporated, New York, since 1977. Instructor, Philadelphia College of Art, 1953–54, Pratt Institute, Brooklyn, New York, 1960–62, The New School for Social Research, New York, 1969, and the Parsons School of Design, New York, from 1979. **Exhibitions:** Philadelphia Art Alliance, 1954; Atwater Kent Museum, Philadelphia, 1954; Los Angeles County Museum of Art, 1955; Virginia Museum of Fine Arts, Richmond, 1955; American Institute of Graphic Arts, New York, 1956; Santa Barbara Museum of Art, California, 1956. **Collection:** Atwater Kent Museum, Philadelphia. Recipient: Gold Medal, Art Directors Club of New York, 1952, 1957, Art Directors Club of Chicago, 1953, and Art Directors Club of Philadelphia, 1953, 1954; Merit Award, Art Directors Club of New York, 1953, 1954, and Art Directors Club of Chicago, 1953; Excellence Award, American Institute of Graphic Arts, 1954, 1955, 1977, and Type Directors Club, New York, 1954, 1955, 1957; Service of Freedom Award, International Rescue Committee, 1970. Address: 415 Central Park West, New York, New York 10025, U.S.A.

Publications:

By FUJITA: book—*Aim for a Job in Graphic Art and Design,* New York 1968, 1977; articles—in *Print* (New York), 1964, 1967, 1969; *Financial World* (New York), 26 June 1968; *Idea* (Tokyo), May 1970; *Public Relations Journal* (New York), October 1970; *Publishers Weekly* (New York), 10 April 1972; *Graphics USA* (New York), October 1974, January 1977.

On FUJITA: book—*Printing History* by Gordon Nearill, New York 1979; *Album Covers* by Martina Schmitz, Munich 1987.

The understanding of our purpose in life and work doesn't necessarily apply only to a designer or art director; it applies to everyone. Somehow I feel that the designer, like anyone working in the creative arts, should understand this purpose better. Perhaps I am inclined to think so because people in the creative field are constantly arranging and composing, or drawing things together to make their creativity work.

The designer, for example, graphically starts with a clear white surface. To this surface he brings originality and a purpose. I suggest this is totally irrelevant to what it takes to recognize clearly the complexities of human behavior and make what we have learned about human nature work for us.

Is the designer, who works with an uninterrupted clear white surface, unaware of the role he must also play as a performer on the surface of humanity? I hardly think so; I think the designer is well aware that he is first an individual, an integral part of the human race, who understands his role and function and is capable of meeting his responsibility as a human being.

pography and letters. The studio is very important to me; without it I'd be in an ivory tower. I need contact with the concrete and the daily application of the materials I create, even if, as is obvious, I don't necessarily use my own typefaces or the machines for which I am designing. It's different with the illustration of books. I relinquish the "alphanumeric skeleton" when expressing my personal philosophical or religious thought. It is true that I love this work also, but I would not be unhappy if I had nothing but the "alphanumeric skeleton": it is really so rich. And besides even in the realm of personal aesthetic expression, I'd never be an Artist with a capital "A."

I am of Germanic origin, since I was born in the German section of Switzerland, and have received a German-type scholastic and professional education; for this I am grateful. With the methods and knowledge acquired there, I have been able to do more constructive, rational, better-organized work. And, since I have also led a very active life in a Latin country, the two influences complement each other. The result is a combination of qualities which have undoubtedly contributed to the success of Univers—which is accepted just as favourably in the Latin countries as it is in the Germanic ones.

—Adrian Frutiger

When the historical importance of contemporary typographers is analysed, Frutiger stands out as the designer who led the way in several essential directions. Beyond the usual four options, his Univers offers a set of new possibilities with its twenty-one variations based on slant, proportion, and weight. Unlike most sans-serif alphabets designed before 1954, Univers is based on a geometrical construction thoroughly corrected to meet visual and technological needs. For example, a high x-height reduces the excessive conspicuousness of capitals and increases readability in small sizes; slightly

wider strokes in the capitals than in the lower cases help maintain a similar stroke weight-to-letter size relation; progressive thinning of the strokes as they meet helps maintain constant apparent width. These and many other details show Frutiger's fine sensitivity to typeface design.

His adaptation of Univers for the IBM composer placed in the market a new class of product between typesetting and typewriting, one that revolutionized the visual standards of low technology in typography. To compensate for the distortions occurring in phototypesetting, he introduced new details in type design for this medium. Re-evaluating the actual form of the strokes, their ends, and their encounters, he aimed at maintaining the desirable consistency already pursued through optical corrections in the design of the Univers.

Working with a grid three times finer than the one in use at the time and pushing available technology to its limits, he designed the Optical Character Recognition typeface Class B for the European Computer Manufacturers Association, thereby bringing computer typography back to meet the needs of the reader after a period of hardware-imposed design. His Frutiger series, excellent for signage, shows generous counters and more open ends (particularly in the lower cases a, c, e and s, the upper cases C, G and S, and the numerals 2, 3, 5, 6 and 9); these contribute to a greater distinctiveness for each character and move away from the Bauhaus concept of beauty based on consistency toward the concept of performance based on differentiation within a system.

Much as Claude Garamond opened new avenues to typeface design in 1544 by providing an appropriate response to the technology and the needs of the time, so Frutiger has responded to the needs of our century, with an equally deep understanding of technology and a comparable grace.

—Jorge Frascara

S. Neil Fujita: Title logo for Mario Puzo's *The Godfather*, used for the bookjacket, 1969, and for the film, 1972

The designer is certainly capable of reaching out for goals far greater and richer in human values than to be satisfied with the attainment of a mere visual creation. I think he is capable of grouping and unifying personalities and emotions in a composition of people and relationships. For this reason, improbable as it may seem, a designer who works with ideas, materials, personalities and a surface could very well sit in the General Assembly at the United Nations and function effectively as a designer for a creative unit international in magnitude and diversity. I feel that merely replacing a flat surface with an arena of human dimensions is all it takes to put the designer on not too unfamiliar ground. On both surfaces there are varied shades of colors to work with as well as other related elements required to create harmonious composition.

But the truth is, many of us are still looking for answers and directions on the clear white, unobtrusive surface. We haven't bothered to look beyond the edge of our drawing pads. We haven't learned to bridge the gap between our purpose and function in life. Call this link a rapport—or better still, call this connecting span a translation between people. No matter how we look at it, this transmission between man and the world around him should be bridged, and the job requires, for lack of a better term, a super-engineer.

Human engineering covers a tremendously broad area—an area so big that many of us have failed miserably to understand it. This not only means understanding our purpose in life and work, but also covers the area of understanding others. It is here, I think, where we divide the men from the boys. It is here where we divide the executives from the executors. It is here we learn to give and take. It is also here, in one of the categories of the humanities, where we truly find the purpose of our craft and concepts.

To understand the immediate area of where we stand as designers or art directors, it is a good starting point to learn the meaning of our purpose in life and work. Like everyone, we must start from where we are.

The artist, for example, who paints, functions best when he excludes himself from his society in order to create, but ironically it is the same society that later recognizes his accomplishments. The designer, on the other hand, functions in reverse. He creates for the society he lives in and never excludes himself from it. He is like an actor who needs an audience to speak to with his graphic gesture and iconology.

The painter who expresses and the designer who interprets do have one thing in common: they are both communicators. But they work from different approaches.

It is clear that the painter finds his audience after his work is completed, while the designer knows his audience before he starts. This is, I believe, the general consensus. However, this theory doesn't always hold true because there are painters who paint for a specific audience and there are designers who like to take the role of a painter, neglecting their purpose as graphic communicators of a client's message. I think it is sad when a painter thinks commercially or when a designer thinks purely idealistically.

The respect I hold for both is too great to allow indifference of opinion to nullify their respective positions and functions as craftsmen. My respect for the painter is high because it takes guts and perseverance to paint. My respect for the designer is equally high because it takes guts and diplomacy to survive.

What separates one from the other professionally does not, however, remove them from a common denominator. They are both considered to be craftsmen. Of course, there are others, perhaps not in the creative arts, but nevertheless men who are equally devoted to their craft. There is the carpenter, the blacksmith, the plumber, the typographer, the engraver, the printer, and countless others who perform functions that exemplify an honest and practical definition of the performing craft. I place the role of the designer and painter, in part, in a similar category.

But when the designer removes himself from the category of the craftsman, it is like a plumber talking with verbosity about the esthetic qualities of his wrench, rather than tending to the leak in the pipe. Or, with equal absurdity, it is like the typographer talking about the beauty of a metallic alphabet giving

metal to a word or sentence. This all means that designers shouldn't continue merely to talk about design; they should use it effectively, giving substance to their function and purpose.

It is the substance we put into our purpose in life and work that truly measures the depth of our function. As designers, we approach our duties and responsibilities not only with the understanding of ourselves, but also with the respect of others. And we go on performing our function as craftsmen, devoted to the values of accomplishment, not the volume of accolades. The reward we win will be the satisfaction of knowing that we have done our job as professionals, not tyros; as responsible artists responsible to man. (*Reprinted from "Human Engineering: A Neglected Design Tool" in* Print [*New York*], *1969.*)

—S. Neil Fujita

FUKUDA, Shigeo.

Japanese graphic designer. Born in Tokyo, 4 February 1932. Studied at the National University of Arts and Music, Tokyo, 1952–56. Married Shizuko Fukuda in 1961; daughter: Miran. Freelance graphic designer, Tokyo, from 1960. Instructor, National University of Arts and Music, Tokyo, from 1980, and at Yale University, New Haven, Connecticut, 1983. **Exhibitions:** Cosy Space, Tokyo, 1978; Seibu Department Store, Tokyo, 1978, 1979; Gallery Marronnier, Kyoto, 1978; Gallery Lukoan, Osaka, 1978; Matsuya Design Gallery, Tokyo, 1979; Nick Design Gallery, Fukuoka, 1979; Kokugeki Gallery, Asahikawa City, Hokkaido, 1979; Ikebukuro Parco Gallery, Tokyo, 1980; Space 21, Tokyo, 1980; Green Collections, Tokyo, 1980; Matsuda Rotary Club, Tokyo, 1980; Galery Tosenbo, Kyoto, 1981. **Collections:** Museum of Modern Art, New York; Walker Art Center, Minneapolis; Yale University, New Haven, Connecticut; University of Colorado, Boulder; Musee de l'Affiche, Paris; Modern Art Museum, Warsaw; Modern Art Museum, Brno. Recipient: Brno Graphics Biennale Awards, 1966, 1970, 1974; Gold Medal, Warsaw Poster Biennale, 1972, 1976; 30th Anniversary Poster Competition Prize, Warsaw, 1975; Montreal Olympics Poster Prize, 1975. Honorary Royal Designer for Industry, Royal Society of Arts, London, 1986. Member: Japan Graphic Designers Association; Japan Design Committee; Alliance Graphique Internationale. Address: 3-34-25 Kamikitazawa, Setagaya-ku, Tokyo, Japan.

Publications:

By FUKUDA: books—*Toyo,* Tokyo 1970; *Element of Idea,* Tokyo 1977; *Forms of Shigeo Fukuda,* Tokyo 1977; *Hyohonbako,* Tokyo 1978; *Shigeo Fukuda,* Tokyo 1979; *Visual Illusion,* Tokyo 1982; *Posters of Shigeo Fukuda,* Tokyo 1982; articles—in *Idea* (Tokyo), July 1971; *Graphic Design* (Tokyo), December 1971.

On FUKUDA: books—*Modern Graphics* by Keith Murgatroyd, London 1969; *107 Grafici dell'AGI,* exhibition catalogue with texts by Renzo Zorzi and Franco Grignani, Venice 1974; *Archigraphia: Architectural and Environmental Graphics,* edited by Walter Herdeg, Zurich 1978; *The 20th-Century Poster: Design of the Avant-Garde* by Dawn Ades, New York 1984;

Eye for Industry: Royal Designers for Industry 1936-1986, exhibition catalogue by Fiona MacCarthy and Patrick Nuttgens, London 1986; *Japanese Design* by Penny Sparke, London 1987.

Asked about Shigeo Fukuda, the graphic designer comments, "One of the greatest designers of our time," while a leading New York art dealer states, "Fukuda? Well, an outstanding sculptor," and an art scholar from Yale says, "What a thinker!" Yes, amazingly, they all talk about the same person. When asked about his own opinion as to which part of his work is most important, Fukuda only smiles enigmatically.

The son of a family long known as toy manufacturers, Fukuda was almost destined to follow the tradition. And, so to say, in many respects he does. Especially, one sees in the enormous production of the last twenty years strong currents directly linked to two kinds of toys—a wood puzzle you can play with in many ways and the traditional Japanese *origami* folded-paper craft.

Fukuda's posters first achieved recognition on the international scene at the *Expo '70* in Osaka. Later, when the possibilities were bigger and the invitations from abroad followed, Fukuda grew in a more personal direction. Hundreds of his own *origami* paper constructions were followed by the posters for his own exhibitions of those paper marvels. They were more intimate, disciplined in a strange way, suggesting that indeed, less is better. In the early 1970's, the two-dimensional forms reached a peak of quality.

The "Environmental Pollution" series of black-and-white silkscreen prints was based on real objects Fukuda fashioned from wood, painted, and regularly exhibited. Combined with humorous, paper, cut-out models, to make three variants, they transformed the character of Fukuda's activity from smart designer to avant-garde art. The careful craftsmanship and logical design only reinforced the power of pure artistic imagination.

Another gigantic project followed. Fukuda was co-author of a very risky, almost kamikaze-like attempt to try the tired *Mona Lisa* portrait once more. His installation of 100 transformations of the famous subject was a masterpiece of a gamble of eastern mastery playing with a cult object of western civilization. The effect was striking in its universality.

Recently, Fukuda has concentrated more and more on three-dimensional forms. Using many media, he develops huge public spaces marked by his brisk wit and endless reserves of sophisticated humor. But the most important realization of freestanding objects are wood sculptures, quite large in scale, painted in plain but contrasting colors. They are the puzzles again—two-sided constructions bearing serious messages. From one angle, we see a pianist, from another, the violinist. But in others, the symbols are written on one side, portrayed visually on the other. Often these clash violently—as in real life, theory versus practice.

Viewed in larger numbers, they state Fukuda's philosophy: Nothing is real, every truth has many faces, the symbols don't work, bad is good—pure life indeed.

The artistic breaks all barriers—as between design and fine art—while he happily mixes his Japanese tradition with western meanings. With his witty humor and enormous energy, he hates to pose as the teacher of what is right in art; rather, he tries to puzzle us and gently force us to think. He plays with his toys, with their intellectual means, but he's deeply concerned about the state of our world. A smile with a little tear.

—Jan Sawka

FULLER, Richard Buckminster.

American architectural designer. Born in Milton, Massachusetts, 12 July 1895. Educated at Milton Academy, 1904-13; Harvard University, Cambridge, Massachusetts, 1913-15, and the United States Naval Academy, Annapolis, Maryland, 1917. Served in the United States Navy, 1917-19; Lieutenant. Married Anne Hewlett in 1917; daughters: Alexandra (died) and Allegra. Assistant Export Manager, Armour and Company, New York, 1919-21; National Accounts Sales Manager, Kelly-Springfield Truck Company, 1922; President, Stockade Building System, Chicago, 1922-27; Founder and President, 4D Company, Chicago, 1927-32; Editor and Publisher, *Shelter* magazine, Philadelphia, 1930-32; Founder, Director, and chief engineer, Dymaxion Corporation, Bridgeport, Connecticut, 1932-36; Assistant to the Director of Research and Development, Phelps Dodge Corporation, New York, 1936-38; Technical Consultant on the staff of *Fortune* magazine, New York, 1938-40; Vice-President and Chief Engineer, Dymaxion Company, Delaware, 1940-50; Chief Mechanical Engineer, United States Board of Economic Warfare, Washington, D.C. 1942-44, and Special Assistant to the Deputy Director of the United States Foreign Economic Administration, Washington, 1944; Chairman and Chief Engineer, Dymaxion Dwelling Machine Corporation, Wichita, Kansas, 1944-46; Chairman, Fuller Research Foundation, Wichita, 1946-54; President, Geodesics, Forest Hills, New York, 1949-83, Synergetics, Raleigh, North Carolina, 1954-59, and Plydomes, Des Moines, Iowa, 1957-83; Chairman, Tetrahelix Corporation, Hamilton, Ohio, 1959-83; Senior Partner, Fuller and Sadao, Long Island City, New York, 1979-83; Chairman of the Board, R. Buckminster Fuller, Sadao and Zung Architects, Cleveland, Ohio, 1979-83; Senior Partner, Buckminster Fuller Associates, London, 1979-83. Research Professor, 1959-68, University Professor, 1968-75, Distinguished Service Professor, 1972-75, and University Professor Emeritus, 1975 until his death in 1983, Southern Illinois University, Carbondale; World Fellow in Residence, Consortium of the University of Pennsylvania, Swarthmore College, Bryn Mawr College, and the University City Science Center, Philadelphia, and Consultant to the Design Science Institute, Philadelphia, 1972 until his death in 1983. University Professor Emeritus, University of Pennsylvania, Philadelphia, 1974 until his death in 1983; Tutor in Design Science, International Community College, Los Angeles, 1975. Editor-at-large, *World Magazine,* New York, 1972-75. President, Triton Foundation, Cambridge, Massachusetts, 1967; International President, MENSA, Paris, 1975, and World Society for Ekistics, Athens, 1975; Consultant to Architects Team 3, Penang, Malaysia, 1974 until his death in 1983. Charles Eliot Norton Professor of Poetry, Harvard University, 1962-63; Harvey Cushing Orator, American Association of Neuro-Surgeons, 1967; Nehru Lecturer, New Delhi, 1969; Hoyt Fellow, Yale University, New Haven, Connecticut, 1969; Fellow, St. Peter's College, Oxford, 1970; Distinguished Lecturer, College of Engineering, Villanova University, Pennsylvania, 1976; Distinguished Half Century Lecturer, University of Houston, 1977; Ezra Pound Lecturer, University of Idaho, Moscow, 1977; Grauer Lecturer, University of British Columbia, Vancouver, 1977; Distinguished Lecturer, University of Calgary, Alberta 1979; Adjunct Professor of Humanities, Texas Wesleyan University, Fort Worth, 1980; Regents Lecturer, University of California at Los Angeles, 1982.

Exhibitions: Harvard University, Cambridge, Massachusetts, 1929; American Institute of Architects, Washington, D.C., 1930; World's Fair, Chicago, 1933; Museum of Modern Art, New York, 1937, 1940, 1943, 1959, 1968, 1977; United States Embassy, London, 1962; United States Geodesic Pavilion, at *Expo '67,* Montreal, 1967; Spoleto Festival, Italy, 1967; Museum of Science and Industry, Chicago, 1973 (toured the United States and Canada); Cooper-Hewitt Museum, New York, 1976; Ronald Feldmann Fine Arts Gallery, New York, 1977 (2 shows); Philadelphia Museum of Art, 1977; Carl Solway Gallery, Cincinnati, 1977 (travelled to Carl Solway Gallery, New York); Protetch McIntosh Gallery, Washington, D.C., 1977; Dumont and Kenyon Associates, Van Wezel Performing Arts Center, Sarasota, Florida, 1978; Drawing Center, New York, 1979 (travelled to the Smithsonian Institution, Washington, D.C.); Getler-Pall Gallery, New York, 1981; Carl Solway Gallery, Cincinnati, 1981; DeCordova and Dana Museum, Lincoln, Massachusetts, 1982; Fendrick Gallery, Washington, D.C., 1982; Galerie Watari, Tokyo, 1982.

Collections: Metropolitan Museum of Art, New York; Museum of Modern Art, New York; Museum of Fine Arts, Boston; Fogg Museum, Harvard University, Cambridge, Massachusetts; Philadelphia Museum of Art; Baltimore Museum of Art; Art Institute of Chicago; Museum of Science and Industry, Chicago; Seattle Art Museum; Los Angeles County Museum of Art; Staatliche Museum, West Berlin; Victoria and Albert Museum, London. Recipient: Award of Merit, American Institute of Architects, New York Chapter, 1952; Grand Prize, *Triennale,* Milan, 1954, 1957; Award of Merit, United States Marine Corps, 1955; Gold Medal, National Architectural Society, 1958; Gold Medal American Institute of Architects, Philadelphia Chapter, 1960; Franklin P. Brown Medal, Franklin Institute, Philadelphia, 1962; Allied Professions Gold Medal, 1963, Architectural Design Award, 1968, and Gold Medal, 1970, American Institute of Architects; Plomado de Oro Award, Society of Mexican Architects, 1963; Delta Phi Delta Gold Key, 1964; Creative Achievement Award, Brandeis University, Waltham, Massachusetts, 1965; First Award of Excellence, Industrial Designers Society of America, 1966; Order of Lincoln Medal, Lincoln Academy, Illinois, 1967; Gold Medal for Architecture, National Institute of Arts and Letters, 1968; Royal Gold Medal for Architecture, Royal Institute of British Architects, London, 1968; Citation of Merit, United States Department of Housing and Urban Development, 1969; Citation of Excellence, National Institute of Steel Construction, 1969; Humanist of the Year Award, American Association of Humanists, 1969; McGraw-Hill Master Designer in Product Engineering Award, 1969; Alpha Rho Chi Master Architect Life Award, 1970; President's Award, University of Detroit, 1971; Salmagundi Medal, Salmagundi Club, New York, 1971; Annual Award of Merit, Philadelphia Art Alliance, 1973; Honorary Citizenship Award, City of Philadelphia, 1973; Planetary Citizens Award, United Nations, 1975. Honorary Doctorates; North Carolina State University, Raleigh, 1954; University of Michigan, Ann Arbor, 1955; Washington University, St. Louis, 1957; Southern Illinois University, Carbondale, 1959; Rollins College, Winter Park, Florida, 1960; University of Colorado, Boulder, 1964; Clemson University, South Carolina, 1964; University of New Mexico, Albuquerque, 1964; Monmouth College, West Long Branch, New Jersey, 1965; California State Colleges, 1966; Long Island University, Greenvale, New York, 1966; California College of Arts and Crafts, Oakland, 1966; Clarkson College of Technology, Potsdam, New York, 1967; Dartmouth College, Hanover, New Hampshire, 1968; University of Rhode Island, Kingston, 1968; New England College, Henniker, New

Hampshire, 1968; Ripon College, Wisconsin, 1968; Bates College, Lewiston, Maine, 1969; Boston College, 1969; University of Wisconsin, Madison, 1969; Brandeis University, Waltham, Massachusetts, 1970; Columbia College, Chicago, 1970; Park College, Parkville, Missouri, 1970; Minneapolis School of Art, 1970; Wilberforce University, Ohio, 1970; Southeastern Massachusetts University, North Dartmouth, 1971; University of Maine, Orono, 1972; Grinnell College, Iowa, 1972; Emerson College, Boston, 1972; Nasson College, Springvale, Maine, 1973; Rensselaer Polytechnic Institute, Troy, New York, 1973, Beaver College, Glenside, Pennsylvania, 1973; Pratt Institute, Brooklyn, New York, 1974; McGill University, Montreal, 1974; St. Joseph's College, Philadelphia, 1974; University of Pennsylvania, Philadelphia, 1974; University of Notre Dame, Indiana, 1974; Hobart and William Smith Colleges, Geneva, New York, 1975; Hahnemann Medical College and Hospital, 1978; International College, 1979; Southern Illinois University, Carbondale, 1979; Alaska Pacific University, Anchorage, 1979; Roosevelt University, Chicago, 1980; Georgian Court College, 1980; Newport University, 1980; Texas Wesleyan University, Fort Worth, 1981. Member, National Academy of Design; Fellow, American Institute of Architects, and of the Building Research Institute of the National Academy of Sciences; Life Fellow, American Association for the Advancement of Science. Member, National Institute of Arts and Letters; Fellow, American Academy of Arts and Sciences. R. Buckminster Fuller Chair of Architecture established at the University of Detroit, 1970. Member, Mexican Institute of Architects; Honorary member, Society of Venezuelan Architects, Israel Institute of Engineers and Architects, Zentralvereininung der Architekten Österreichs, and Royal Society of Siamese Architects; Benjamin Franklin Fellow, Royal Society of Arts; Honorary Fellow, Royal Institute of British Architects. *Died* (in Los Angeles) *1 July 1983.*

Works:

United States Air Force Early Warning System Domes, in the Arctic, 1954.
United States Exhibition Pavilion, Sokolniki Park, Moscow, 1959.
Climatron botanical garden, St. Louis, 1960.
Cinerama Theatre, Hollywood, California, 1963.
United States Pavilion, at *Expo 67,* Montreal, 1967.
Airplane Museum, Schipol Airport, Amsterdam, 1969.
Weather Radome, Mount Fuji, Japan, 1973.
Archaeological Site Dome, Ban Chiang, Thailand, 1979.
Fly's Eye Information Center, Los Angeles, 1981.
Spruce Goose Airplane Hanger, Long Beach, California, 1982.
Spaceship Earth Dome, Walt Disney World, Orlando, Florida, 1982.

Patents: Stockade (building structure), 1927; Stockade (pneumatic forming process), 1927; 4D House, 1928; Dymaxion Car, 1937; Dymaxion Bath, 1940; Dymaxion Deployment Unit, 1944; Dymaxion Airocean World, 1946; Fuller House, 1946; Geodesic Dome, 1954; Paperboard Frame, 1959; Plydome, 1959; Catenary, 1959; Octertruss, 1961; Tensegrity, 1962; Submarisle, 1963; Aspension, 1964; Monohex, 1965; Laminar Dome, 1965; Octa Spinner, 1965; Star Tensegrity, 1967; Rowing Device, 1970; Tensegrity Dome with Spaced Lesser Circles, 1973; Geodesic Hexa Pent, with Shoji

Sadao, 1974; Floating Breakwater, 1975; Non-symmetrical Tension-integrity Structures, 1975; Floating Breakwater, 1979.

Publications:

By FULLER: books—*The Time Lock,* privately printed 1928, as *4D Time Lock,* Corrales, New Mexico 1970; *Nine Chains to the Moon,* Philadelphia 1938, London 1973; *Designing a New Industry: A Composite of a Series of Talks,* Wichita, Kansas, 1945-46; *Earth, Inc.,* lecture, New York 1947; *Design for Survival—Plus,* Ann Arbor, Michigan 1949; *Untitled Epic Poem on the History of Industrialization,* Millerton, New York 1962; *Education Automation: Freeing the Scholars to Return to Their Studies,* Carbondale, Illinois 1962; *Ideas and Integrities: A Spontaneous Autobiographical Discourse,* edited by Robert W. Marks, Englewood Cliffs, New Jersey 1963; *No More Secondhand God, and Other Writings,* Carbondale, Illinois 1963; *World Design Science Decade Documents,* 6 vols., Carbondale, Illinois 1963-67; *Comprehensive Thinking,* selected and edited by John McHale, Carbondale, Illinois 1965; *What Am I Trying to Do?,* London 1968; *Reprints and Selected Articles,* Belfast, Maine 1969; *Operating Manual for Spaceship Earth,* Carbondale, Illinois 1969; *Utopia or Oblivion: The Prospects for Humanity,* New York 1969, London 1970; *Fifty Years of Design, Science, Revolution and the World Game,* Carbondale, Illinois 1969; *Planetary Planning,* New Delhi, India 1969; *Approaching the Benign Environment,* with others, University, Alabama 1970; *The Buckminster Fuller Reader,* edited by James Meller, London 1970; *I Seem to Be a Verb,* with Jerome Agel and Quentin Fiore, New York 1970; *The World Game: Integrative Resource Civilization Planning Tool,* Carbondale, Illinois 1971; *Old Man River: An Environmental Domed City,* St. Louis, Missouri 1972; *Intuition,* New York 1972; *Buckminster Fuller to Children of Earth,* New York 1972; *Synergetics: Explorations in the Geometry of Thinking,* with E. J. Applewhite, New York 1975; *And It Came to Pass—Not to Stay,* New York 1976; *Pound, Synergy, and the Great Design,* Moscow, Idaho 1977; *Buckminster Fuller: An Autobiographical Monologue/Scenario,* edited by Robert Snyder, New York 1977, 1980; *R. Buckminster Fuller on Education,* edited by Peter H. Wagschal and Robert D. Kah, Amherst, Massachusetts 1979; *Synergetics 2: Further Explorations in the Geometry of Thinking,* with E. J. Applewhite, New York 1979; *Critical Path,* New York 1982; *Tetrascroll: Goldilocks and the Three Bears: A Cosmic Fairy Tale,* New York 1982; *Grunch of Giants,* New York, 1982; *Inventions,* New York 1983.

On FULLER: books—*The Dymaxion World of Buckminster Fuller* by Robert W. Marks, New York 1959; *R. Buckminster Fuller* by John McHale, New York 1962; *Wizard of the Dome: R. Buckminster Fuller, Designer for the Future* by Sidney Rosen, Boston 1969; *Bucky: A Guided Tour of Buckminster Fuller* by Hugh Kenner, New York 1973; *Mind's Eye of Buckminster Fuller* by Donald W. Robertson, New York 1974; *Buckminster Fuller at Home in the Universe* by Alden Hatch, New York 1974; *Cosmic Fishing: An Account of Writing Synergetics with Buckminster Fuller* by E. J. Applewhite, New York and London 1977; *Pilot for Spaceship Earth* by Athena V. Lord, New York 1978; *Robert Buckminster Fuller: uno spazio per la technologia* by Pier Angelo Cetica, Padua, Italy 1979; *Buckminster Fuller: An Autobiographical Monologue/Scenario* by Robert Snyder, New York 1980; *Synergetic Stew: Ex-*

plorations in Dymaxion Dining, Philadelphia 1982.

Bibliography—*Richard Buckminster Fuller: A Bibliography* by Mary Vance, Monticello, Illinois 1980.

*

It was R. Buckminster Fuller's lifelong belief that humanity is capable of using the high technology it has invented to the positive end of gaining a physical and spiritual world view which would raise life above the barriers of entropy. His premise was based on what he called "dymaxion," an approach to design and ideals. Aimed at using fewer resources to achieve maximum output, this principle, he believed, could regenerate the forces of energy for the planet as a whole. In order to accomplish this goal, Fuller taught, outmoded conventions must be eliminated and the advances of the scientific and technological revolution of the twentieth century must be employed to raise humanity's standard of living.

Many of Fuller's designs were geared to create possibilities of greater mobility geographically, an aim he felt to be highly necessary in attaining his ideals. In 1927, he designed the easily movable and totally self-contained Dymaxion House, a structure hung from a central core. Continuing his search for more inexpensive, resource-saving, and mobile structures, Fuller invented the Dymaxion Car in 1933. His most famous construct, the Geodesic Dome, created in 1947, further advanced the move toward less cost, weight, and material. Used widely by industry and the military during the 1950s, the Geodesic dome remains among the most outstanding design inventions of recent years.

Fuller was as famed as a writer and speaker as he is as a maker and thinker. The inspiring and gregarious lectures he gave around the world until his death left his audiences breathless and inspired with new hope for the positive uses of technology, based on humanistic commitment without nostalgia or dependence on old traditions. Throughout his many books and articles, published over a period of fifty years, Fuller could always be counted on to raise controversy and to purvey insatiable inventiveness and optimism. In *Earth, Inc.* (1973), for example, he wrote passionately and convincingly of the need for a design-science revolution which, he noted, we now have all the resources to accomplish. His is a revolution of education, of the commitment of world youth, and of the creative intelligence of all, working together for the common good. His many designs made practical his idealism, bringing the philosophy into reality.

The main influence on Fuller was his broad study of the history of science and mathematics, which he seems to have combined with the science-fiction genius of H. G. Wells. He can be likened to the Renaissance man who combines broad-based studies to achieve vital artistic invention. Fuller's is also an extension of the beliefs and practices of the great Bauhaus architects and artists whose uses of modern technology for design constitute one of the greatest achievements of the early twentieth century. Fuller's impact has been especially felt by contemporary sculptors who base their monumental abstractions on architectural principles and use new materials to achieve an aura of great mass and weightlessness.

—Barbara Cavaliere

James Fulton: *Bantam 366* excavator, for Koehring. 1980

FULTON, James (Franklin).

American industrial designer. Born in Cincinnati, Ohio, 13 April 1930. Studied industrial design under Alexander Kostellow, Rowena Reed and Eva Zeisel, at the Pratt Institute, Brooklyn, New York, 1948–51: Dean's Medal and Honors, 1951; B. Industrial Design, 1976. Married Mary Sherman Walbridge in 1953 (divorced, 1975); children: Martha, James and Laurel. Designer, at Towle Sterling company, Newburyport, Massachusetts, 1951, and at Owens-Corning Fiberglas Corporation, Toledo, Ohio, 1952–53; senior designer, Harley Earl Associates, Warren, Michigan, 1953–58; design director, then managing director, Compagnie de l'Esthétique Industrielle (C. E. I. Raymond Loewy), Paris, 1958–60; director of product design, transportation and housing components, 1960–62, vice-president, 1962–64, and senior vice president, 1964–66, Loewy/Snaith design firm, New York; founder and president of Fulton + Partners planning and design consultants, New York, from 1966; director, Endt + Fulton Partners, Paris, from 1975. Founder and chairman, Design Publications Incorporated (including *Design Review, Industrial Design,* etc.), New York, since 1977. Trustee from 1968, executive committee member from 1973, and chairman of the planning and development committee from 1977, Pratt Institute, New York; art collection committee member, Owens-Corning Fiberglas Corpora-

tion, Toledo, Ohio, from 1968; founder and chairman, International E22 Class of racing yachts section, New York Yacht Club, from 1968; president, 1975–76, and chairman, 1977–78, Industrial Designers Society of America; trustee, Dime Savings Bank, New York, from 1982. Recipient: Contemporary Achievement Award, Pratt Institute, New York, 1967; Fellow, Industrial Designers Society of America, 1976. Address: Fulton + Partners, 330 West 42nd Street, New York, New York 10036, U.S.A.

Works:

Folding playpen in net and aluminium, for Trimble, 1957.
Corporate visual image, for British Petroleum, 1958–60.
Corporate visual imagery, for Trans World Airlines, 1960–63.
Pattern programme and corporate imagery, for Formica, 1960–65.
Modular FRP bathroom, for Owens-Corning Fiberglas, 1962–64.
Corporate symbol, for Shell Oil Company, 1964.
Agricultural tractor, for Allis Chalmers, 1972–74.
Open-office screening system, for Owens-Corning Fiberglas, 1976.

Construction equipment, for Koehring, 1976–80.
Bantam 366 excavator cab, for Koehring, 1980.

Publications:

By FULTON: articles—in *Reinforced Plastics* (Connecticut), May 1964; *IDSA Journal* (New York), 1968, 1970; *Idea* (Tokyo), June 1974; *Yachting* (New York), October 1978.

Designers are in a unique position to assist industry in the constructive use of technology. The ability to recognize needs and their full implications is basic. An additional strength lies in the ability to maintain an objective point of view and to coordinate various talents in an effective and innovative way. We as designers can and should be the link between maker and user.

As designers, we must accept the responsibility for the practical utilization of resources and the humane use of technology in our projects. This demands a high degree of sensitivity, intelligence, and a broad understanding of the many disciplines which contribute to successful problem solving. We choose to practice design in the context of its impact on the total system and proceed with the conviction that excellence is one quality which does not become obsolete. Our design responsibility begins with planning, the process of developing a detailed program of action. This essential first phase consists of analyzing the overall problem, identifying its design components, and defining objectives which are in harmony with user needs and the producer's technical capabilities. It is only when this effort is thorough that meaningful goals can be set, priorities established, and creative energy usefully directed. With this kind of background, we can proceed to explore and probe for concepts which hold the promise of a solution.

Comprehensive plans and the finest design ideas can be distorted when follow-through is inadequate. The complex matrix of design decisions which produces a solution requires the balancing of many considerations. When changes are needed as a project is carried into production, the designer is best qualified to choose among the available alternatives which will achieve the original intent.

The commitment to excellence in design is an attitude which motivates us in all of our professional activities. Our ideal is to be both responsive and responsible.

—James Fulton

FURSE, Margaret.

British stage and film costume designer. Born Alice Margaret Watts, in London, 18 February 1911. Educated at Miss Campbell's School, Hampstead, London, and in Versailles, France, 1921–27; studied costume design, under Jeanetta Cochrane, at Central School of Arts and Crafts, London, 1928–30. Married the stage and film designer Roger Furse in 1936 (divorced, 1951); the film critic Stephen Watts in 1952. Stage designer, working with the Motley Group of designers, London, 1930–39; assistant stage designer under Roger Furse, at the Old Vic Theatre, London, 1940; film designer, working for British-Gaumont, the Rank Organization, Cineguild, Warner Brothers, Twentieth Century-Fox, Walt Disney, Joseph Levine, Hal Wallis, Universal, and several independents, 1941–73. **Collection:** British Film Institute, London. Recipient: British Film Academy Award, 1965; American Film Academy Award, 1969; American Television Academy Award, 1974. *Died* (in London) *9 July 1974.*

Works:

Film costume designs include—*Henry V* (Olivier), 1944; *Great Expectations* (Lean), 1946; *Blanche Fury* (Allegret), 1948; *The Prince and the Pauper* (Keighley), 1947; *Oliver Twist* (Lean), 1948; *The Passionate Friends* (Lean),1948; *Madeleine* (Lean), 1949; *Night and the City* (Dassin), 1950; *The Mudlark* (Negulesco), 1950; *No Highway* (Koster), 1951; *The House in the Square* (Baker), 1951; *Meet Me Tonight* (Pelissier), 1952; *The Crimson Pirate* (Siodmak), 1952; *The Master of Ballantrae* (Keighley), 1953; *The Million Pound Note* (Neame), 1954; *The Spanish Gardener* (Leacock), 1956; *The Inn of the Sixth Happiness* (Robson), 1958; *Kidnapped* (Stevenson), 1959; *Sons and Lovers* (Cardiff), 1960; *Greyfriars Bobby* (Chaffey), 1960; *The Horsemasters* (Fairchild), 1961; *In Search of the Castaways* (Stevenson), 1961; *The Prince and the Pauper*, 1962; *Becket* (Glenville), 1964; *A Shot in the Dark* (Edwards), 1964; *Young Cassidy* (Cardiff), 1964; *Return from the Ashes* (Lee-Thompson), 1965; *The Trap* (Hayers), 1966; *Cast a Giant Shadow* (Shavelson), 1966; *Great Catherine* (Flemyng), 1968; *The Lion in Winter* (Harvey), 1968; *Sinful Davey* (Huston), 1968; *Anne of the Thousand Days* (Jarrott), 1969; *Scrooge* (Neame), 1970; *Mary Queen of Scots* (Jarrott), 1971; *Bequest to the Nation* (Jones), 1973; *A Delicate Balance* (Richardson), 1975.

Publications:

On FURSE: books—*Filmguide to Henry V*, Bloomington, Indiana 1973; *Costume Design in the Movies* by Elizabeth Leese, Bembridge 1976; *Hollywood Costume Design* by David Chierichetti, London 1976.

Margaret Furse: Still from David Lean's *Great Expectations*, 1946 Courtesy The Rank Organisation PLC

Laurence Olivier's *Henry V* (1944) auspiciously introduced Margaret Furse's film career, since the entire concept of the movie presented great challenges. The story jumped several centuries. It exploited a wide variety of regional, physical, and social types, so actors needed theatrical costumes, military uniforms, liturgical vestments, royal finery, peasant rags, and middle-class, everyday wear. The frequent crowd scenes demanded colorful diversity. Good and evil were to be differentiated through imagery. All this had to be done in the face of wartime restrictions. As easily as applying silver paint to crochetwork to serve as soldiers' chainmail, Furse, along with husband Roger, solved these problems.

For *Henry V,* costumes were based on miniature Elizabethan portraits and International Gothic illuminated manuscripts, but even for simple comedies, such as *The Million Pound Note* (1953), Furse took no less care in research. In that film, characters seem to step from the pages of *Godey's Ladies Book.* Among these well-dressed matrons and self-consciously finely tailored gentlemen, the innocent heroine stands apart. Moderately frilled in virginal white, full of spunk and vigor, she is seen by the audience, as by the hero, visually apart from the crowd.

Crowning her excellence in British period costume, one of Furse's final films, *Mary Queen of Scots* (1971), transcends simple historical design. The film opens with Mary, youthful and naive, cavorting in an unencumbering white nightgown, which flows *à la* Isadora Duncan. Furse developed Mary's character primarily in soft pastels and pale golds, emphasizing Mary's pre-Raphelite-like romanticism. In contrast, clear-headed Elizabeth wore the sharper hues. The foil of Elizabeth's increasing sartorial splendor through time culminates in her final confrontation with Mary. Furse fitted the English queen in a massive, explosively patterned gown, accessorized by an awesome hat, so that Elizabeth recalled the adamant image of her father, Henry VIII. In contrast, Mary dresses like a nun, drained of all color and earthly adornments. Styled with affectation in France, Mary had grown severe in Scotland. As she approaches her death, Furse shrouded her in black. With a final speech at the executioner's block, Mary boasts of her rebirth to a greater life in heaven and triumphantly reveals beneath her cloak a startling, bright red dress, more powerful in color than anything previously seen in the film. At the conclusion, Elizabeth, despite her temporal power and decorations, can conquer neither Mary's spirit nor visual impact.

Furse, the expert at historical costume, never served as its slave. She manipulated her references as metaphors, uniting the academic with the imaginative.

—Edith Cortland Lee

Roger Furse: Still from Laurence Oliver's *Henry V*, 1948   Courtesy The Rank Organisation PLC

FURSE, Roger (Kemble).

British painter, illustrator, stage and film designer. Born in Ightham, Kent, 11 September 1903. Educated at St. George's Choir School, Windsor, Berkshire, 1910–14; Eton School, Buckinghamshire, 1914–20; studied painting, Slade School of Fine Art, London, 1921–24, and in Paris, 1924–27. Served in the Royal Navy, 1940–43. Married Alice Margaret Watts (the designer Margaret Furse) in 1936 (divorced, 1951); Ines Sylvia Perg in 1952. Worked as a portrait painter and commercial artist in Paris, 1925–27, and in New York, 1927–31; stage designer, working for the Gate Theatre, Old Vic, Ambassadors Theatre, Vaudeville Theatre, Queen's Theatre, Strand Theatre, Westminster Theatre, Haymarket Theatre, Piccadilly Theatre, St. James's Theatre, Covent Garden Opera House, Sadler's Wells Opera, and Duke of York's Theatre, in London, and for the Stratford Shakespeare Memorial Theatre, Chichester Festival Theatre, and the Cambridge Festival Theatre, from 1931; art director, Perranporth Summer Theatre, Cornwall, 1936–38; film costume and set designer, in London and Hollywood, California, from 1943. **Exhibition:** Leicester Galleries, London, 1948. Recipient: Academy Award, 1948; Royal Designer for Industry, Royal Society of Arts, London, 1949. *Died* (in Corfu, Greece) *19 August 1972.*

Works:

Film designs include—*Henry V* (Olivier), 1944; *The True Glory* (Reed/Kanin), 1945; *Odd Man Out* (Reed), 1946; *Hamlet* (Olivier), 1948; *Under Capricorn* (Hitchcock), 1949; *The Angel with the Trumpet* (Bushell), 1949; *Ivanhoe* (Thorpe), 1952; *Knights of the Round Table* (Thorpe), 1953; *Helen of Troy* (Wise), 1955; *Richard III* (Olivier), 1955; *The Prince and the Showgirl* (Olivier), 1956; *Saint Joan* (Preminger), 1957; *Bonjour Tristesse* (Preminger), 1957; *Spartacus* (Kubrick), 1960; *The Roman Spring of Mrs. Stone* (Quintero), 1961; *The Road to Hong Kong* (Panama), 1961.

Publications:

By FURSE: articles—in *Films and Filming* (London), April 1955, May 1955.

On FURSE: books—*Roger Furse: Exhibition of Designs for the Film Hamlet,* catalogue, London 1948; *Film Today Books: Screen and Audience,* edited by John E. Cross and Arnold Ketterbury, London 1949; *Le Decor de Film* by Leon Barsacq, Paris 1970, as *Caligari's Cabinet and Other Grand Illusions,* Boston 1976; *Filmguide to Henry V,* Bloomington, Indiana

1973; *Costume Design in the Movies* by Elizabeth Leese, Bembridge 1976; *The International Film Encyclopedia* by Ephraim Katz, New York and London 1980.

Roger Furse produced many fine designs but none more glorious than those achieved in film with Laurence Olivier. Dismiss their final film collaboration, *The Prince and the Showgirl* (1956); these sets sparkle with studied grandeur, but they lack genius. For that, look to their settings of Shakespeare for the screen.

The communal effort of Olivier's production company (unofficial and, later, official as a short-lived theatrical venture called Laurence Olivier Productions, Ltd.) brought forth the Shakespearean series. *Henry V* (1944) credited Paul Sheriff (assisted by Carmen Dillon) as art director while Furse and his wife Margaret served as costume designers. Visually, they transported the spectator from the Elizabethan theatre to the pages of fifteenth-century illuminated manuscripts and back again. For Renaissance England, the Furses recreated elegant gentlemen and ragged braggerts with equal authenticity. For the era of King Henry, they drew an elegant France and noble England, a world both tragic and comic, evil and divine. The Furses painted red and gold against blue and silver, dividing allegiances with a colorful palette.

Assisted by Carmen Dillon, Roger Furse designed sets and costumes for *Hamlet* (1948). Though described by critics as mannered, theatrical, or expressionistic, the film was intended to contrast dramatically with the *Henry V* production. Olivier and Furse conceived *Hamlet* as a black-and-white etching to differentiate it from *Henry V*'s colorfully painted pageantry. A range of tonal values punctuated by recurring shadows and mists accentuated the concept. Furse further echoed Prince Hamlet's moody loneliness with the castle's vast, empty spaces to achieve what he later described as Olivier's desire for "a dream-like cavernous place as the setting for a drama which is centered in the shadowy regions of the hero's mind." He indicated that he had used Norman arches, Byzantine-like wall paintings, and tapestries of an even later period as a setting for the action rather than as period documentation.

Richard III (1956) returned Olivier to technicolor, with Furse serving as costumer and art director. Stark, airy spaces served to highlight those few details that were retained. Emphasizing the crown motif and underlining the story with recurring Christian imagery, Furse contributed an unspoken reinterpretation of Shakespeare's play, even as he created visual unity.

Olivier planned on a fourth film project which, of course, included Furse on its staff. However, he could find no funding for *Macbeth* because potential backers doubted such a title's commercial success. As for the film's possible artistic strides, unfortunately, we shall never know.

—Edith Cortland Lee

GALANOS, James.
American fashion designer. Born in Philadelphia, Pennsylvania, 20 September 1924. Studied art and drapery at Traphagen School of Fashion, New York, 1943. Freelance fashion sketch artist for clothing manufacture, New York, 1942–43; worked for designer Hattie Carnegie, New York, 1944; assistant to designer Jean Louis, Columbia Studios, Hollywood, California, 1946–47; apprentice designer, studio of Robert Piguet, Paris, 1947–48; designer, at Davidow, New York, 1949–50; established Galanos Originals fashion company, in Beverly Hills, 1951–83, and in Los Angeles, from 1983: collaborated with Neustadter Furs on couture collection, 1968; also occasional film and stage costume designer, from 1967. **Exhibitions:** *Fashion: An Anthology,* Victoria and Albert Museum, London, 1971; Los Angeles County Museum of Art, 1974; Fashion Institute of Technology, New York, 1976. **Collections:** Metropolitan Museum of Art, New York; Philadelphia Museum of Art; Art Institute of Chicago; Denver Art Museum, Colorado; Dallas Museum of Fine Arts, Texas; Los Angeles County Museum of Art; Smithsonian Institution, Washington, D.C. Recipient: Neiman Marcus Distinguished Service Award, 1954; Coty American Fashion Critics Winnie Award, 1954, Return Award, 1956, and Hall of Fame Award, 1959; Costume Institute Award, Metropolitan Museum of Art, New York, 1954; International Achievement Fair Creativity Award, 1956; Filene Young Talent Award, Boston, 1958; Cotton Fashion Award, New York, 1958. Address: 2254 South Sepulveda Drive, Los Angeles, California 90064, U.S.A.

Publications:

On GALANOS: books—*The Wheels of Fashion* by Phyllis Lee Levin, New York 1965; *Fashion: An Anthology by Cecil Beaton,* exhibition catalogue compiled by Madeleine Ginsburg, London 1971; *In Fashion: Dress in the Twentieth Century* by Prudence Glynn, London 1975; *Fairchild's Who's Who in Fashion,* edited by Ann Stegemeyer, New York 1980; *McDowell's Directory of Twentieth Century Fashion* by Colin McDowell, London 1984; *The Encyclopaedia of Fashion from 1840 to the 1980's* by Georgina O'Hara, London 1986.

Fashion is a living art form. It is the function of the designer to arrange harmoniously and artistically all the components of design, such as color, line, details, so that the garment becomes one with the human form.

—James Galanos

James Galanos is one of a handful of designers in the world today designing couture-quality clothes for a luxury clientele. Recipient of many fashion awards and owner of his Los An-

geles design establishment for more than thirty years, he achieved success only after years of discouraging attempts to interest buyers in his highly-individualized and necessarily expensive creations.

His designs are distinguished less by any consistency of style than by his adherence to couture standards learned while an apprentice to Robert Piguet in Paris in the late 1940s. He is known for his imaginative handling of distinctive, often boldly-patterned, European fabrics, which sometimes cost $50 a yard. After being cut individually, hand-basted, and sandwiched with layers of interlining, each garment is molded on a form and manipulated into shape with steam and pressing. Since darts are not used, the customer can have simple alterations done without time-consuming fittings. Hand-finishing and silk linings are so meticulous that Galanos garments have actually been modeled inside-out. Evening gowns are hand-embroidered and beaded. Each piece, handled by numerous skilled workers, takes as long as two weeks to make. This is why Galanos prices range in the thousands of dollars.

Before shipment to specialty stores, each garment is inspected by the designer, who sometimes attaches to it a note with suggestions for accessories. Personal attention is an important part of maintaining his diminishing clientele of the few women who appreciate Galanos quality and are able to pay for it. He travels with his collections to New York semi-annually and meets with his customers at showings across the country, consulting individually with regular clients who include film stars and international socialites.

Fashion writers in the 1950s considered Galanos avant-garde. In the 1960s, his subtly molded suits were paragons of constructed chic. By the 1970s, his clientele had matured and his designs became correspondingly conservative, But in the early 1980s, he is once again offering fresh and youthful designs, such as multi-level suits with cropped trousers. Galanos attracted widespread publicity when Nancy Reagan, one of his long-time customers, became First Lady and had Galanos design her inaugural ballgown. Apart from his limited-distribution signature fragrance, the Galanos name is associated exclusively with his own designs.

—Sandra Michels Adams

GAMES, Abram.
British graphic designer. Born in London, 29 July 1914. Educated at the Grocers Company

School, London, 1925–30. Served as infantryman, in the British Army, 1940–41; official War Office poster designer, 1941–46: Captain. Married Marianne Salfield in 1945; children: Daniel, Sophie and Naomi. Freelance designer, working on posters, magazines, logos, advertisements, postage stamps, and corporate identity programmes, London, 1937–40 and since 1946: has designed for BBC Television, the 1951 Festival of Britain, London Transport, British Airways, Guinness, British Aluminium, etc.; inventor of "Imagic" and "RLF" copying processes. Visiting Tutor, Royal College of Art, London, 1946–53. **Exhibitions:** Reklamförening, Stockholm, 1943; Palais des Beaux-Arts, Brussels, 1946; Bezalel Museum, Jerusalem, 1950, 1963; Tel Aviv Museum, 1950; Ben Uri Gallery, London, 1952; *8 British Designers,* Nationalmuseum, Stockholm, 1952; Museu de Arte, Sao Paulo, 1954 (toured Brazil); *Design From Britain,* Florida State University, Tallahassee, 1956; Waldorf-Astoria, New York, 1960; Visual Arts Center, Chicago, 1961; *Second World War Posters,* Imperial War Museum, London, 1972; *Eye for Industry,* Victoria and Albert Museum, London, 1986. **Collections:** Victoria and Albert Museum, London; Imperial War Museum, London; Stedelijk Museum, Amsterdam; Kunstgewerbemuseum, Zurich; Israel Museum, Jerusalem; Australian National Gallery, Canberra; Australian War Memorial Museum, Canberra; Museum of Modern Art, New York; Library of Congress, Washington, D.C. Recipient: Prizes in international poster competitions, 1957–64; First Prize, International Philatelic Competition, Asiago, Italy, 1976; Design Medal, Society of Industrial Artists and Designers, London, 1960; Silver Medal, Royal Society of Arts, London, 1962. Officer, Order of the British Empire, 1957; Royal Designer for Industry, Royal Society of Arts, London, 1959. Address: 41 The Vale, London NW11 8SE, England.

Works:

19 posters for London Transport, 1937–75.
ATS Auxiliary Territorial Service poster, for the War Office, 1941.
Displaced Persons poster, for the Central British Fund, 1946.
13 posters, for British Airways, 1947–59.
Emblem, for the 1951 Festival of Britain, 1948.
Magazine advertisements, for British Aluminium, 1948–53.
8 posters, for the *Financial Times,* London, 1951–59.
Poster, for Osram Lamps, 1952.
Poster, for Guinness, 1956.
Freedom from Hunger poster, for FAO/United Nations, 1960.
3 posters, for *The Times,* London, 1960–62.
Emblem, for the Queen's Award to Industry, 1966.
Emblem, for the GKN Group, 1968.

Cover, for the *Encyclopaedia Judaica*, 1969.
Set of 4 postage stamps, for Jersey, Channel Islands, 1974.
Emblem, for the 1985 Festival of British Jewry, 1984.

Publications:

By GAMES: book—*Over My Shoulder,* London 1960.

On GAMES: books—*Posters: 50 Artists and Designers* by Walter Allner, New York 1952; *Design in British Industry: A Mid-Century Survey* by Michael Farr, Cambridge 1955; *Die Neue Grafik/The New Graphic Design* by Karl Gerstner and Markus Kutter, Teufen and London 1959; *Graphic Design Britain,* edited by Frederick Lambert, London 1967; *History of the Poster* by Josef and Shizuko Muller-Brockman, Zurich 1971; *Who's Who in Graphic Art,* edited by Walter Amstutz, Dubendorf 1982; *Advertising: Reflections of a Century* by Bryan Holme, London 1982; *The Conran Directory of Design,* edited by Stephen Bayley, London 1984; *Design Source Book* by Penny Sparke and others, London 1986; *Eye for Industry: Royal Designers for Industry 1936–1986,* exhibition catalogue by Fiona MacCarthy and Patrick Nuttgens, London 1986; *Did Britain Make It? British Design in Context 1946–86,* edited by Penny Sparke, London 1986.

My personal philosophy on design can be summarised as: "maximum meaning—minimum means."

—Abram Games

Abram Games was designing posters during the 1930s, but he achieved his reputation during World War II and the decades following. In many ways, he followed the inspired example of designers such as Edward McKnight Kauffer, Tom Purvis, and Fred Taylor in Britain, as he extended into the postwar years the new graphic arts language inspired by the avant-garde movements of the earlier part of the century.

However, far from being merely an interpreter of the modern movement for the masses, Games proved to be a powerful propagandist and a forceful salesman. Using many of the devices of the surrealist, for example, he made sophisticated use of symbolism to express his message clearly and without compromise. His war posters advising against careless talk were designed to shock; and in this way, his imagery compares with that of his contemporaries in other countries where imagery had traditionally been more dramatic than in the lyrical designs used in Britain for public transport.

Abram Games: Emblem for Barclay Samson Limited, 1988

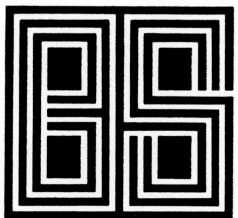

Games is very much the professional designer whose immaculate working methods are always evident in the absolute precision of his final image. He often starts with a sketch that contains the essence of his idea but which is also a creative mark. This eventually becomes a thoroughly rationalised design, from which all traces of the artist's rough indication have been polished away to reveal a clear-cut symbol easily grasped at first sight. Thus, Games the artist sublimates his own reactions and feelings about the subject and channels his skill into the final message required by his client.

For several decades, he produced hundreds of first-class posters at a time when competition was high. His designs for the emblem for the Festival of Britain in 1951 and for British Broadcasting Television both won him first prizes. In his own words, the designer "has the great gift of the artist, the power of the propagandist, the technique and machinery of modern civilisation, printing presses, the cinema, radio, and television."

—John Barnicoat

GARDNER, (Leslie) James.
British exhibition designer. Born in London, 29 December 1907. Educated in London schools until 1922; mainly self-taught in design. Served in the British Army, 1939–45: Chief Camouflage Officer. Married Mary Williams in 1936 (died, 1965); sons: Brian and Neil. Worked as a jewellery designer, for Cartier, London, 1924–31; independent designer, London, since 1947: has designed exhibitions for the Council of Industrial Design, Central Office of Information, Board of Trade, Federation of British Industries, Pilkington Brothers, NV Philips, United Kingdom Atomic Energy Authority, Institute of Geological Sciences, Maryland Academy of Sciences, New York City Council, Cunard Steamship Company, Delta Queen Steamboat Company, etc. **Exhibitions:** *Eye for Industry,* Victoria and Albert Museum, London, 1986. **Collections:** Victoria and Albert Museum, London. Royal Designer for Industry, Royal Society of Arts, London, 1947; Commander, Order of the British Empire, 1959; Senior Fellow, Royal College of Art, London, 1987. Address: The Studio, 144 Haverstock Hill, London NW3 2AY, England.

Works:

Britain Can Make It exhibition at the Victoria and Albert Museum, London, for the Council of Industrial Design, 1946.
United Kingdom pavilion and exhibits at the Brussels World Fair, for the Central Office of Information, 1958.
British Trade Fair in New York, for the Board of Trade/Federation of British Industries, 1960.
Glass Museum at St. Helen's, Lancashire, for Pilkington Brothers, 1965.
Evoluon Technological Museum in Eindhoven, for NV Philips, 1966.
Above-water lines of the *Queen Elizabeth II,* for the Cunard Steamship Company, 1966.
Britain Today exhibit at *Expo 67,* Montreal, for the Central Office of Information, 1967.
The Peaceful Uses of Atomic Energy exhibition in Geneva, for the United Kingdom Atomic Energy Authority, 1971.

The Story of the Earth exhibition at the Geological Museum, London, for the Institute of Geological Sciences, 1972.
Maryland Science Centre in Baltimore, for the Maryland Academy of Sciences, 1974.
Museum of the Jewish Diaspora in Tel Aviv, for the Jewish Congress, 1978.
Shipping Museum in Copenhagen, for A. P. Moller, 1979.
Pavilion at *Expo 85,* Tsukuba, Japan, for the Asian Development Bank of Manila, 1985.
Design concept of butterfly farm at Fort Lauderdale, Florida, 1988.
National Museum of Natural Science in Taiwan, for the Taiwan Government, 1988.
History of Jerusalem exhibition in the Citadel, for the Jerusalem Foundation, 1989.

Publications:

By GARDNER: books—*Exhibition and Display,* with Caroline Heller, London and New York 1960; *Elephants in the Attic,* London 1983.

On GARDNER: books—*Industrial Design in Britain* by Noel Carrington, London 1976; *A Tonic to the Nation: The Festival of Britain 1951,* edited by Mary Banham and Bevis Hillier, London 1976; *Industrial Design* by John Heskett, London 1980; *Design Source Book* by Penny Sparke and others, London 1986; *Eye for Industry: Royal Designers for Industry 1936–1986,* exhibition catalogue by Fiona MacCarthy and Patrick Nuttgens, London 1986; *Did Britain Make It? British Design in Context 1946–86,* edited by Penny Sparke, London 1986.

Designing is the facility to unravel the logic of a situation or problem, coupled with the ability to make mental models of possible answers and motivated by the desire to initiate—not follow the orthodox pattern. Producing what one has designed is hard work; so why work on something that has already been done? I did not aim for any specialist branch of the profession. Things just happened to me, and whatever came, I had a go. A success, and other jobs followed. One is then competing with oneself, with what one did before. As a result, I have shown that within the correct designing facility, one need not specialise—I have designed match-box covers (smallest) and the *Queen Elizabeth II* oceanliner (largest).

In time, one gains experience right across the board, and know-how gathered for one task contributes (maybe with a new look) to another. When in doubt on a technical point, one can always ask the expert; the lesson here is to ask the top expert, someone who actually does it, not a technocrat with a university degree.

The real way to learn is to study a subject for a definite purpose; this programmes the mind on active, meaningful lines and stimulates one's adrenalin, as one must not fail is one is to survive. To learn a subject for, say, an examination, and not for "doing," is a waste of time and leads to mental imbalance, a mind full of facts and theories—aimed at nothing and so, redundant.

Most children are born with a designer's imagination and dexterity, but they lose it when they go to school, where the rewards and punishments are for "taped," ready-made mental programmes. Second hand. A designer who hopes to be creative comes up against the problem that the majority of the people are conformists and fear the unorthodox, so most designers, from practice, end up doing the orthodox.

—James Gardner

James Gardner: Quiz booth at Evoluon Technological Museum, Eindhoven, 1966

James Gardner, who has been one of Britain's top designers for over half a century, can be described as a total designer in the sense that his mental horizon is enormous, his vision is inspired, his technical intelligence and use of material is always up to date, and his design philosophy always original. He certainly has a valid point when he maintains that people can be classed into two types: the "talkers" and the "doers". The division occurs at an early age in ones schooling and formal development. The system turns out scholars who more often than not become visual "delinquents". He maintains that the other side specialises in special dexterity and constructs concepts with visual images. James Gardner certainly fits into the latter category but he may not realise how good he is in the first one. He has to. To battle through half a century of practice in such a difficult discipline as exhibition design one has to be able to absorb a vast amount of information, different scripts of a range of specialised subjects, fight, argue, battle through committees in order to convey your ideas, your concepts and to survive by maintaining a contemporary image in a constantly changing society. There were only two individuals capable of achieving this in our period; Frank Lloyd Wright and Buckminster Fuller, both from the United States. Gardner's work, while containing similar sense in spatial dimension, as well as attention to detail, also contains an element of Britishness which could be detected in Henry Moore's work but it still belongs to Gardner. Gardner's multi-dimensional talent does not prevent him from being totally practical when budgets and costs are being considered. In this sense he is more restricted than an artist who can express himself freely, and is nearer to the restrictions of an architect or an industrial designer. His work in designing exhibitions in three dimensions incorporates all these elements: art, architecture, industrial designs, as well as a great deal of moving media like computer graphics, animation, lasers, robotics, which involve many specialists whose work must be co-ordinated and controlled. One would assume that he would engage a sizeable studio for this. Actually he prefers to work with the smallest possible team of not more than 8 people as he maintains that be delegating too much one may lose control of an assignment.

Although active before, Gardner's contribution to exhibition design started soon after the war with the Dance Pavilion in the Pleasure Gardens of the Festival of Britain in 1951. The period was an important one for British design both internally and outside England. British design was put on the map and followed by other exposures in many parts of the world like the World Fair in Brussels, the Montreal Expo and the British Trade Fair in New York. The Evolution Technological Museum for N. V. Philips in Eindhoven was a feather in Gardner's cap, so was the Conservation Museum and the Maryland Science Centre in Baltimore, as well as the Shipping Museum in Copenhagen.

But the most remarkable project and the latest one which opened in 1988 was the National Museum of Natural Science in Taiwan, ROC. It is possibly the most ambitious assignment for both Taiwan and Gardner. The museum covers the subject of natural science from the origins of life to modern man including sub-sections on colour, sound and numbers of forms in Nature. This project somewhat brings together for most of Gardner's basic interests and according to the reactions stands as a monument to Gardner's artistry and skill.

—John Halas

GARLAND, Kenneth (John).

British graphic designer. Born in Southampton, Hampshire, 12 February 1929. Studied at the West of England Academy of Art, Bristol, 1947–48; under Paul Hogarth, Anthony Froshaug, Herbert Spencer and Jesse Collins, at Central School of Arts and Crafts, London, 1952–54; National Diploma in Design 1954. Art editor, National Trade Press, London, 1954–56, and *Design* magazine, London 1956–62; founder-director, Ken Garland and Associates design consultants, London, since 1962. Visiting lecturer in graphics, Central School of Arts and Crafts, London, 1957–60; visiting tutor in graphics, Reading University, Berkshire, from 1971, and Royal College of Art, London, from 1977. **Collection:** Victoria and Albert Museum, London. Recipient: Gute Form Prize, West Germany, 1971. Address: Ken Garland and Associates, 71 Albert Street, London NW1 7LX, England.

Works:

Publicity programmes, for the Campaign for Nuclear Disarmament, 1962–66.
Book designs, for the Ministry of Technology, London, 1962–67.
Corporate house style, for Barbour Index, 1962–73.
Corporate house style, for James Galt and Company, 1962–82.
Corporate House Style, for Race Furniture, 1963–66.
Book designs, for the Cambridge University Press, 1973–75.
Book and catalogue designs, for the Arts Council of Great Britain, 1978–82.

Ken Garland: Exhibition poster for the London College of Printing, 1975

Publications:

By GARLAND: books—*Lettering Today,* with others, London 1964; *Graphics Handbook,* London and New York 1966; *Graphics Glossary,* London 1980; *Ken Garland and Associates: 20 Years of Work and Play 1962-1982,* London 1982.

On GARLAND: books—*Designers in Britain 5,* edited by Herbert Spencer, London 1957; *Left, Left, Left* by Peggy Duff, London 1971; articles—in *Gebrauchsgraphik* (Munich), July 1960, April 1976; *Der Polygraph* (Frankfurt), no. 14, 1963; *Design* (London), July 1963; *The Designer* (London), April 1967, April 1983.

Every single day since I started work as a graphic designer in 1955, I have gone to my studio in the morning with the keenest sense of pleasure and anticipation. It has always delighted and intrigued me that my clients have been prepared to pay me for doing that which I enjoyed most: what splendid indulgence! What luck!

At the same time, paradoxically, I have to record an almost continuous sense of disappointment in the results of my work. Why could I not have done better? It was not, I believe, for want of trying, nor for the lack of sympathy and support from clients, and certainly not for lack of money since I think that is rarely the determining factor in matters of design quality.

It may be that the paradox is insoluble—an occupational syndrome perhaps—but I would dearly love, some time in my working life, to produce one substantial piece of work which has been well conceived, well handled, well finished and well received; something of which I could feel unreservedly proud.

In the meantime, I look forward to getting to the studio tomorrow, regardless of the results.

—Ken Garland

Ken Garland was of the generation of graphic designers emerging in post-1945 Britain; They were the first to be fully aware of the work of the prewar Continental modernists and also to look towards the work of contemporaries in Europe and the United States. His article, "Structure and Substance" (*Penrose Annual,* 1960) provides a good summary of that moment in British graphic design.

As art editor of *Design* and since then as head of Ken Garland and Associates, his work has been notable for its fresh approaches. For example, he has integrated photography and drawn images as much as possible with text. (The British tradition of illustration had discouraged this.) There is also much care evident in the treatment of details, as also of textual niceties; diagrams are thought out from scratch and have considerable elegance as well as clarity. But the work is not smoothly elegant; the photography employed shows a realist, documentary tendency, rather than a pattern-making one. The "associates" in the practice (which has always stayed small) have made their own initiatives, and this has reduced the possibility of an overbearing style.

Social and political commitments are evident in Garland's work. Active in the Committee of 100 and the Campaign for Nuclear Disarmament, he designed posters, banners, and leaflets for CND in the 1960s. This work, done for love, to tight deadlines, on low budgets has a consequent simplicity and directness. The manifesto "First Things First" that Garland wrote and himself published in January 1964 (cosigned by twenty-one other designers and photographers) was a forthright statement of belief; it stood against the misapplications of graphic design (to high-pressure consumer advertising, in particular) and for socially useful work across the broadest range of tasks. The wish expressed by this statement was not "to take any of the fun out of life" but rather to reverse "priorities in favour of the more lasting forms of communication." Garland's best work has built pleasure into serviceable and useful graphic design.

Garland's written contributions have been of a piece with his practice. The *Graphics Handbook* and *Illustrated Graphics Glossary* are compilations of useful knowledge, but they widen the traditionally limited scope of such books. Among his articles, that on the design of the London Underground diagram (*Penrose Annual,* 1969) is still the best source of information and criticism on this subject.

—Robin Kinross

GAULTIER, Jean-Paul.

French fashion designer. Born in Arceuil, Val-de-Marne, 24 April 1952. Educated at the Ecole Communale, the College d'Enseignement, and at the Lycee d'Arceuil, until 1969; mainly self-taught in design. Worked as a design assistant in the fashion houses of Pierre Cardin, Jacques Esterel and Jean Patou, Paris, 1970-73; designer of United States collections for Pierre Cardin, in Manila, Philippines, 1974-75; independent designer, for Majago and others, Paris, 1976-78; founder, Jean-Paul Gaultier S.A., Paris, from 1978: has designed costumes and videos for R. Chopinot, Rita Mitsuko, Yvette Horner, etc., from 1985. Recipient: Best Designer Oscar Award, Paris, 1987. Address: 70 Galerie Vivienne, 75002 Paris, France.

Jean-Paul Gaultier: Man's suit with coordinated shirt and necktie, 1989

Publications:

On GAULTIER: books—*McDowell's Directory of Twentieth Century Fashion* by Colin McDowell, London 1984; *The Encyclopaedia of Fashion from 1840 to the 1980s* by Georgina O'Hara, London 1986; articles—in *Sunday Times Magazine* (London), 14 October 1984; *Drapers Record* (London), 6 December 1986; *Elle* (London), November 1987; *Harrods Magazine* (London), Spring 1988.

GEISMAR, Thomas H.

American architectural, graphic and exhibition designer. Born in Glen Ridge, New Jersey, 16 July 1932. Studied at Brown University and Rhode Island School of Design, Providence, 1950–53: BFA 1953; Yale University, New Haven, Connecticut, 1954–58: MFA 1958. Served in the United States Army, 1955–57. Married Joan Hyams in 1958; children: Peter, Kathryn and Pamela. Founder-Partner, in Brownjohn, Chermayeff & Geismar Associates, New York, 1956–59, Chermayeff & Geismar Associates, New York, since 1960, Cambridge Seven Associates, Cambridge, Massachusetts, since 1962, and Mea Form, New York, since 1980. Chairman, Advisory Committee on Transport Signs and Symbols, United States Department of Transportation; Committee Member, Yale University Council for the School of Art; Carnegie Professor, Cooper Union, New York; Albert Dorne Visiting Professor, University of Bridgeport, Connecticut; former Vice-President and Director, American Institute of Graphic Arts. **Exhibition:** *107 Grafici dell'AGI,* Castello Sforzesco, Milan, 1974. Recipient: Gold Medal, American Institute of Graphic Arts, 1979. Address: Chermayeff & Geismar Associates, 15 East 26th Street, New York, New York 10010, U.S.A.

See CHERMAYEFF & GEISMAR ASSOCIATES

GEISSBUHLER, Steff.

Swiss graphic designer. Born Stephan Geissbuhler, in Zofingen, 21 October 1942. Studied graphic design, under Armin Hofmann, Emil Ruder, Walter Bodmer and Donald Brun, at the Allgemeine Gewerbeschule, Basel, 1958–64: Dip. 1964. Married Sigrid Bovensiepen in 1966 (divorced, 1974); sons: Marc and Christopher; married Elissa Beth Feuerman in 1983; sons: Alexander and Benjamin. Promotions designer, J. R. Geigy AG pharmaceutical and chemical corporation, Basel, 1964–67; associate and designer, Murphy/Levy/Wurman architectural and urban planning firm, Philadelphia, 1968–71; freelance designer, New York, 1971–73; associate and designer, Anspach/Grossman/Portugal, New York, 1973–75; designer, 1975, associate, 1976, and partner since 1979, Chermayeff & Geismer Associates, New York; also designer and member, GEE Group for Environmental Education, Philadelphia, 1968–73; consultant designer, George Nelson Inc., New York, 1969. Assistant Professor of Graphic Design, 1967–70, Associate Professor, 1970–73,

Design Coordinator, 1971–73, and Chairman of the Graphic Design Department, 1973, Philadelphia College of Art. Vice-President, 1976–78, and President, 1985–86, American Institute of Graphic Arts, New York chapter. **Exhibitions:** *Annual Exhibition of Applied Arts,* Bern, 1966, 1967; *Graphic Design Alumni Allgemeine Gewerbeschule,* Kunstgewerbemuseum, Basel, 1967 (toured); *Color Show,* Whitney Museum, New York, 1974 (toured). **Collection:** Kunstgewerbemuseum, Basel. Recipient: Swiss National Prize for Applied Arts, Bern, 1966, 1967; United States Government Federal Design Achievement Award, 1988; and numerous awards from the American Institute of Graphic Arts, Type Directors Club, Art Directors Clubs of New York and Los Angeles. Member: Alliance Graphique Internationale, Paris; Society of Typographic Designers, Chicago; Poster Society, New York. Address: c/o Chermayeff & Geismar Associates, 15 East 26th Street, New York, New York 10010, U.S.A.

Works:

Product identification, posters and promotional graphics, for J. R. Geigy corporation, Basel, 1964–67.

Corporate logotype, packaging and promotional graphics, for May Department Stores Company, from 1970.

Book 7 and *Process of Choice* book series design, for the GEE Group for Environmental Education, published by MIT Press, 1973.

A Nation of Nations exhibition poster, publications, signage and graphics, for the Museum of Natural History and Technology, Smithsonian Institution, Washington, D.C., 1976.

Taking Things Apart and Putting Things Together exhibition poster and graphics, for the American Chemical Society, 1976.

Corporate identity program, for Morgan Stanley investment bankers, 1977.

Graphic identification system, for the U.S. Environmental Protection Agency, 1977.

Corporate identity program, for the Union Pacific Corporation, from 1978.

Corporate identity program graphics, for the Banco d'Italia, Argentina, 1979.

Convention center logotype, symbol and graphics program, for the Centro de Convenciones de Cartogena, Colombia, 1980.

Corporate identity program graphics, for Barneys, New York, 1981.

25th Anniversary logotype, posters and graphics, for Alvin Ailey American Dance Theater, 1983.

Graphic identification program, for Charles Square multi-use real estate development, Cambridge, Massachusetts, 1983.

Corporate identity program, for PaineWebber investment bankers, 1984.

Louisiana Journey exhibit logotype and graphics at the New Orleans World's Fair, for the State of Louisiana, 1984.

Corporate identity program, for NBC National Broadcasting Company, 1985.

Real estate identity program in Princeton, New Jersey, for Russell Estates, 1985.

Corporate identity program, for Nashua office systems and supplies, 1986.

Peace poster, for the Shoshin Society, 1987.

New York and the Arts: A Cultural Affair series of 9 posters, for the New York Department of Cultural Affairs, 1989.

Publications:

By GEISSBUHLER: books illustrated—*The Process of Choice* by Alan Levy, Cambridge, Massachusetts 1973; *Our Man-Made Environment: Book 7,* Cambridge, Massachusetts 1973.

On GEISSBUHLER: books—*Graphic Design Manual* by Armin Hofmann, Niederteufen 1965; *Publicity and Graphic Design in the Chemical Industry* by Hans Neuburg, Zurich 1967; *15 Graphiker* by Armin Hofmann, Basel 1967; *Signs, Symbols and Signals* by Walter Diethelm, Zurich 1976; *30 Years of Poster Art* by Armin Hofmann, Basel 1982; *Who's Who in Graphic Art,* edited by Walter Amstutz, Dubendorf 1982; *A History of Graphic Design* by Philip B. Meggs, New York 1983.

Post Modern, New Wave, Swiss Punk, Pluralist, West Coast, Avant Garde, Deco. The recent development in graphic design has many labels, depending on your location, point of view, and/or attitude.

Rarely has a direction in design caused such emotional response. Designers whose philosophy of "form follows function" overrides everything are irritated and angry at this overemphasis on decor and sometimes purely visual esthetic treatment of information. Others brush it off as a fading fad and are disturbed at the fact that it doesn't go away and seems even to creep into their own work. To me, the rediscovered freedom in design is a very positive and exciting evolution.

Perhaps some of the clearest changes are to be found in typography. Jan Tschichold, Emil Ruder, Josef Müller-Brockmann, Max Bill and others taught us to deal with verbal information in a disciplined, structured, organized, and readable fashion. We reduced the elements to the minimum necessary to achieve clarity and simplicity, which lead to strong and architectural solutions. We practiced the philosophy of "less is more." We straightened out the crooked pictures on the walls of commercial art. The Swiss did it especially well; to be orderly is our nature.

Wolfgang Weingart, after taking over Emil Ruder's teaching position for typography in Basel, brought with him a fresh, inquisitive approach. Having, as a student, observed Ruder, he could not possibly tighten the system any further, but he started to build on this strong foundation, exploring, challenging, and expanding the design of verbal information. If Gutenberg could invent movable type, Weingart could teach it to dance. Typography became again a means of expression.

During a lecture tour through the United States, Weingart introduced and explained his philosophy at various schools, questioning the current state of the arts in typography. The audience's reaction was very mixed and caused turmoil, confusion, and outright rejection, but the seed had been sown and was welcomed by some as a necessary change.

None of this is really new. We need only to go back to the work of Stéphan Mallarmé, the Italian futurists, Dada, the Russian constructivists, El Lissitzky, and of course, the Bauhaus with Herbert Bayer, Moholy-Nagy, Piet Zwart, et al. What is different is the rediscovered freedom, the playfulness, and the inquisitive daring to try beyond the tested principles, to accept the beauty of an accident and the seemingly uncontrolled. In order to be truly free in the search for expression, readability is often ignored, sacrificing the information, but leading to unusually beautiful and intriguing solutions.

Although it is easier to find acceptance of this work with smaller clients or for more decorative applications, it seems to find its way into the more hardcore corporate world of annual reports, identity programs, and even (up until now untouchable) financial forms and documents.

Of course, as in other design directions,

Steff Geissbuhler: Poster for the Simpson Paper Company, 1989

there are imitators using this kind of visual vocabulary as a surface style. I call this group the "New Wave Surfer Club," trying to ride the waves other people have created to the shores of a new era. The strong talents keep challenging the tested and successful recipes and keep searching for new expressions in solving old problems.

It is impossible to mention all the influences which led to this point. It is a cycle in the evolution of design to which art, architecture, photography, music, and fashion, all contribute and are, in turn, affected. (*By permission of Graphis Press, Zürich, Switzerland.*)

—Steff Geissbuhler

Much of the design and many designers we see today get locked into a particular style of school, but the work of Steff Geissbuhler defies simple classifications. Instead, his work can best be defined by the nature of the design problems he has had to solve for a diversified list of clients.

For Geissbuhler, problem-solving means doing what is appropriate. Each new project brings a new set of parameters and, as the problems constantly change, so too must the solutions. Though his own feelings and ideas will indeed be a part of the finished work, design for him is not merely a means of self-expression. Rather, graphic communication of the ideas and image of the client, with careful consideration of the audience, are of prime importance. Thus, the large variety of clients with

whom Geissbuhler has had an opportunity to work explains the variety and diversity of his design. From his early work at Ciba to the work for the United States Government and large corporations as a partner at Chermayeff and Geismar, his diverse styles have still maintained a consistent quality. Bold, yet clean graphics and innovative integration of type and illustrative material are characteristic of his work.

Drawing has always been important to Geissbuhler, both as a means of self-expression and as a working tool for his design. This fundamental discipline, too often dismissed by designers today, was taught strictly and thoroughly in his native Switzerland. Though the training was rigorous, drawing has never restrained or confined his design because for him, drawing has never been a rigid practice. Even his early student work, seen by designers around the world in Armin Hofmann's *Graphic Design Manual,* was recognizably expressive. Though his drawing is controlled, its spontaneity has actually opened all the applications of graphics to him. Whether the final product is typographic, photographic, or illustrative, drawing is his conceptual and visual starting point and therefore remains integral to his work.

His desire and ability to adapt has made it possible for him to integrate his strict and disciplined European training with the American willingness to experiment, thereby forming a unique foundation from which to solve design problems. This blending, both of cultures and

design ideology, is at the heart of his work and better represents his talent than any simple label.

—Barbara Sudick

GERNREICH, Rudi.
American fashion designer. Born in Vienna, Austria, 8 August 1922; emigrated to the United States in 1938; naturalized, 1943. Studied at Los Angeles City College, 1938–41; Los Angeles Art Center School, 1941–42. Dancer, with the Lester Horton Dance Theatre troupe, 1942–48; fabrics salesman for Hoffman company, and freelance clothing designer, in Los Angeles and New York, 1948–51; designer, at Walter Bass Incorporated, Beverly Hills, California, 1951–59, swimwear designer, for Westwood Knitting Mills, Los Angeles, 1953–59, and shoe designer, for Genesco Corporation, 1958–60; founder-president, GR Designs, 1960–64, and Rudi Gernreich Incorporated, Los Angeles, from 1964: also designed swimwear for Harmon Knitwear of Marinette, Wisconsin, and home furnishings for Knoll International, New York. Member of the Mont-

gomery Ward International Design Advisory Council, from 1967. Recipient: *Sports Illustrated* Designer of the Year Award, 1956; Wool Knit Association Creative Achievement Award, 1960; Coty American Fashion Critics' Special Award, 1960, Winnie Award, 1963, Return Award, 1966, and Hall of Fame Award, 1967; Neiman-Marcus American Fortnight Trophy, 1961; Sporting Look Award, 1963; *Sunday Times* International Special Award, London, 1965; Filene Design Award, Boston, 1966; Knitted Textile Association Crystal Ball Award, 1975. *Died* (in New York) *21 April 1985.*

Publications:

By GERNREICH: articles—interviews in *Forbes Magazine* (New York), 15 September 1970; *Holiday* (New York), June 1975.

On GERNREICH: books—*The Fashionable Savages* by John Fairchild, New York 1965; *A View of Fashion* by Alison Adburgham, London 1966; *In Vogue: Sixty Years of Celebrities and Fashion* by Georgina Howell, London 1975, 1978, New York 1976; *In Fashion: Dress in the Twentieth Century* by Prudence Glynn, London 1978; *The Collector's Book of Twentieth Century Fashion* by Frances Kennett, London and New York 1983; *McDowell's Directory of Twentieth Century Fashion* by Colin McDowell, London 1984; *The Encyclopaedia of Fashion from 1840 to the 1980s* by Georgina O'Hara, London 1986; *Design Source Book* by Penny Sparke and others, London 1986.

Rudi Gernreich was a most important designer in the 1960s of women's clothing. The strong impact of his fashion statements was felt not only in the world of high fashion, where he first received attention, but in the clothing worn by all women, and indirectly, menswear as well.

He produced several startling innovations that received international acclaim. His work as a dancer and his delight as a swimmer led him to explore the advantages of knitted fabrics. He not only freed the bathing suit from its armored understructure but, eventually, from one-half its coverage to make fashion headlines with the topless swimsuit. This momentous design has not to date become a household necessity, but his other uses of knits have. These include the tanksuit, other unstructured swimwear, and the tank top, which has appeared in all guises from sportswear to the most formal wear. The mini-dress in many fabrics, knitted or otherwise, has been a constant of women's wardrobes, whether worn, as Gernreich originally introduced it, alone with boots, those long white boots, or as an overblouse with skirts or slack.

The casualness of the designs that Gernreich introduced in the 1960s, the easy care of most of the fabrics used, and a price range that would fit most budgets have had lasting effects on women's clothing. Daring color, bold and startling, and always lots of white; simple cut: straightforward one-statement styles—with these qualities, his designs did away with richness of detail. But at times, it was replaced by the absurdity of his innovation, particularly in the cutouts. Youthful always, his clothing is designed for movement. At his best startling—the see-through blouse, the Swiss cheese swimsuit—and touched with humor, his ideas, with time, have come to belong to a society that finds the human body as acceptable as the clothes it wears. Although his designs may not be seen on every street corner, there are few corners which are not affected by what was once thought to be his brashness.

Gernreich's youthful clothes that revel in the beauty of the youthful body, its activity and movement, are a strong and lasting statement.

The lack of acceptance of some of his fashion prophecies, such as the soft, flowing, unisex caftan for older persons, has little to do with either its esthetics or practicality.

—Harlan Sifford

GERSIN, Robert P(eter)

American industrial and graphic designer. Born in Boston, Massachusetts, 12 April 1929. Educated at Boston English High School, 1944–47; studied at Massachusetts College of Art, Boston, 1947–51; BA 1951; Cranbrook Academy of Art, Bloomfield Hills, Michigan, 1951–52: MA 1952. Served in the United States Navy Office of Naval Research, Washington, D.C., 1952–56; Lieutenant j.g. Founder-President, Robert P. Gersin Associates design consultancy, New York, 1959–89. Advisory Board Member, Alfred University, Alfred, New York, 1979–89; Editorial Board Member, *Industrial Design* magazine, New York, 1975–88, and *Metropolis* magazine, New York, 1981–88. Recipient: numerous awards from the American Institute of Graphic Arts, American Institute of Interior Designers, *Industrial Design* magazine, Industrial Designers Society of America, New York Museum of American Crafts, New York Art Directors Club, Type Directors Club, etc. Honorary doctorate: Massachusetts College of Art, 1982. *Died* (in New York City) *18 October 1989.*

Works:

Exhibit and corporate identity program, for Avon Books, 1964–66.
Packaging, graphics, exhibits and corporate identity program, for the Xerox Corporation, 1968–80.
Graphics and interiors, for American Telephone and Telegraph, 1971.
Exhibition displays, for Houston Lighting and Power Company, 1972.
United States Pavilion exhibit at *Expo '75*, Okinawa, for the United States Information Agency, 1975.
Exhibit, for the Smithsonian Institution, Washington, D.C., 1975.
Exhibit, for NASA National Aeronautical and Space Administration, 1976.
Product design, for the Timex Corporation, 1976, 1978.
Graphics and packaging, for Myojo Foods, 1979.
Packaging, for Underberg GmbH, 1979.
Signage and graphics, for the City of Niagara Falls, New York, 1980.
Food packaging, for Bloomingdales, 1980–81.
Exhibits and packaging for Miles Pharmaceuticals, 1981.
Exhibition displays, for COMSAT Communications Satellite Corporation, 1982.
Quick Fix packaging and Answer Center interiors, for General Electric, 1982.
Packaging, for the Government of Jamaica, 1983–85.
Graphics and interiors, for the U.S. Shoe Corporation, 1983–89.
Graphics and interiors, for the Great Atlantic and Pacific Tea Company, 1984.
Corporate identity program, interiors, packaging and graphics, for Sears Roebuck and Company, 1984–87.

Corporate identity program, for the United States General Accounting Office, 1985–87.

Publications:

By GERSIN: articles—"Designer's Case Study" in *Industrial Design* (New York), September 1962; "Design and Printing for Commerce" in *AIGA Journal* (New York), Summer 1968; "Packaging: What Lies Ahead" in *Industrial Design* (New York), April 1970; "On Design Values and Self-Analysis" in *Industrial Design* (New York), September/October 1975; "Robert P. Gersin Associates," with L. Ferrabee, in *Idea* (Tokyo), no. 182, 1983; "Corporate Identity and the Latent Visual Memory" in *Directory of International Package Design,* Tokyo 1985; "Shopping Bags Are Walking Billboards" in *Shopping Bag Design,* New York 1987; "The Arrogance of the Right Angle" in *High Quality Magazine* (Heidelberg), January 1988.

On GERSIN: books—*Modern Publicity* annuals, New York 1966, 1967, 1968, 1974, 1977, 1978, 1981; *50 Ads and 50 TV Commercials* by Helmut Krone, New York 1971; *Developing a Corporate Identity* by Elinor Selame, New York 1975; *Casebooks Packaging* annuals, Washington, D.C., 1975, 1977, 1978, 1980, 1982; *International Trademark Design* by Peter Wildbur, London 1979; *Packaging Design* by Stanley Sacharaw, New York 1983; *American Design Classics* by Joan Wessel and Nada Westerman, New York 1985; *World Graphic Design Now* by Katsuo Kimura and Shin Matsunaga, Tokyo 1988; *Information Graphics* by Peter Wildbur, London and New York 1989.

For thirty years, Robert Gersin maintained a successful office in the heart of Manhattan, where the struggle for conspicuous design excellence is probably at its most intense. While the first generation of professional industrial designers was characterized by flamboyant individuals carving out an identity for a struggling new profession, the second generation, to which Gersin belongs, has worked in quite a different context. He worked within an atmosphere in which the value of industrial design programs has become more generally recognized and the demand more widespread. New products are abundant, consumers are better educated and more selective, and a client's products and visual identity must be quickly established in highly competitive markets.

Three areas of Gersin's experience can be identified as having had the greatest influence on his work. His education, derived from the philosophy of the Bauhaus, gave him a respect for innovation, experimentation, the scientific approach, and the honest expression of materials, function, and purpose; his travels, throughout the United States and abroad, enabled him to observe and document many different cultural and regional approaches to design problems; and the social and commercial environment of the last twenty years led him to emphasize understanding the perceptions and needs of the user and meeting these needs first, rather than those of the designer or even the client. This pragmatic approach has been largely responsible for the success of Gersin's projects, whether they be products, packaging, corporate identity programs, graphics, exhibits, or interiors.

Most of his projects combine several disciplines, as did the design of the United States Pavilion at *Expo '75* in Japan; the computer equipment, interiors, graphics, and signage for the Houston Lighting and Power Energy Control Center; and American Telephone and Telegraph's prototype retail program. User-research

Robert P. Gersin: A & P Futurestore in Allendale, New Jersey, 1984

is integral to all of Gersin's projects. In the Quick Fix packaging program for General Electric, his company tested users' desires to repair their appliances and their misgivings about doing so, and then designed a packaging system using symbols, drawings, a simple text, and color-coding to enable users to find and replace parts easily.

Gersin's innovations have included a dramatic 150-ton capacity, circular, acrylic aquarium for the United States Pavilion at *Expo '75*; a durable microscope, produced for less than $1.50, for Xerox Learning Systems; a portable school planetarium, with a dome using fiberglass technology from the sailcraft industry, which could be assembled by children with only a dime as a tool; and a new container for yogurt that doubled the shelf life of the product.

—Lydia Ferrabee

GERSTNER, Karl.
Swiss painter, lettering, typographic and graphic designer. Born in Basel, 2 July 1930. Educated in Basel, 1937–44; studied graphic design and typography, at the Allgemeine Gewerbeschule, Basel, 1945–46; apprentice designer in the Fritz Buhler advertising studio, Basel, 1946–49: influenced by Armin Hofmann, Emil Ruder and Hans Finsler. Served in the Swiss Army, 1946–47. Married Inge Hoechberg in 1958; daughter: Muriel. Freelance designer, working with Max Schmidt, for Geigy pharmaceutical company, Basel, 1949–53; freelance photographer and graphic designer, establishing Bureau Basel design studio,

in Basel, 1953–59; founder-director, with copywriter Markus Kutter, of Gerstner + Kutter advertising agency, Basel, 1959–62, and with industrial designer Paul Gredinger, of GGK (Gerstner-Gredinger-Kutter) agency, Basel, 1962–70: the agency now has 13 branches throughout the world. Retired from GGK to concentrate on painting, from 1970. Visiting lecturer, at San Francisco State College, Massachusetts Institute of Technology, University of Hawaii, University of California, Berkeley, and the Royal College of Art, London, from 1958.
Exhibitions: Club Bel Etage, Zurich, 1957; Galerie Suzanne Bollag, Zurich, 1961; Galerie Denise René, Paris, 1962, 1967, 1969, 1974, 1982, 1986; Haus am Lutzowplatz, West Berlin, 1963, 1970; Staempfli Gallery, New York, 1965, 1967, 1985; Galerie Denise Rene/Hans Mayer, Düsseldorf, 1969, 1971, 1972, 1978, 1981, 1990; Museum of Modern Art, New York, 1973; Kunstmuseum, Dusseldorf, 1974; Kunstmuseum, Solothurn, 1978; Studio Bombelli, Cadaques, 1981; Galerie der Spiegel, Cologne, 1984; Galerie Appel und Fertsch, Frankfurt, 1986. **Collections:** Museum of Modern Art, New York; Tate Gallery, London; Kunstmuseum, Dusseldorf; Staatsgalerie, Stuttgart; Kunstmuseum, Solothurn. Recipient: Gold Medal, Milan Triennale, 1957. Member, Verband Schweizer Graphiker; Schweizerischer Werkbund. Address: Leonhardsgraben 52, 4051 Basel, Switzerland.

Works:

Coporate identity programmes for British Overseas Airways Corporation, Burda, Ringier, Swissair and the Basel *National-Zeitung;* advertising and graphics for Citroen, Holzapfel, Schwitter, Bech Electronic Center, Geigy, Philips, Volkswagen, IBM, Jaegermeister, Dow Chemicals, Boîte à Musique, Sinar Fachkamerabau, Keramikfabrik Felix Handschin, Intermobel, etc.

Publications:

By GERSTNER: books—*Kalte Kunst?*, Teufen 1957; *The New Graphic Design*, with Markus Kutter, Teufen and London 1959; *Gerstner + Kutter: Werbung-Gaphik-Publizitat*, with Markus Kutter, Basel 1959; *Gerstner + Kutter 1960*, with Markus Kutter, Basel 1961; *Designing Programmes*, Teufen and New York 1963; *Mit dem Computer Kunst produzieren*, Zagreb 1968; *Do-it-Yourself Kunst*, Cologne 1970; *Compendium for Literates*, Teufen 1970, Cambridge, Massachusetts 1972; *Typographisches Memorandum*, St. Gallen 1972; *Think Program*, New York 1973; *Andre Thomkins: Inspiration und Methode*, Hannover 1974; *15 Variationen uber einen Satz von Max Bill*, Ulm 1978; *Gute Kunst, schlechte Kunst*, Hamburg 1981; *Kunst in der Demokratie—ein Utopie*, Frankfurt 1981; *Der Wert der Kunst*, Basel 1982; *Der Kunstler und die Mehrheit*, Frankfurt 1986; *The Forms of Color*, Cambridge, Massachusetts 1986.

On GERSTNER: books—*Advertising Directions*, edited by Edward M. Gottschall and Arthur Hawkins, New York 1959; *Typography* by Aaron Burns, New York 1961; *Design Coordination and Corporate Image* by F. H. K. Henrion and Alan Parkin, London and New York 1967; *An International Survey of Packaging* by Wim Crouwel and Kurt Weidemann, London 1968; *History of the Poster* by Josef and Shizuko Müller-Brockmann, Zurich 1971; *Karl Gerstner: Color Sounds*, exhibition catalogue with interview by Wibke von Bonin, New York 1975; *Karl Gerstner: Color Forms*, exhibition catalogue with text by Grace Glueck, Dusseldorf 1981; *The Spirit of Color: The Art of Karl Gerstner*, edited by Henri Stierlin, Stuttgart, Paris, and Cambridge, Massachusetts 1981; *Karl Gerstner's Private Pinakothek*, Solothurn 1983; *Gerstner's Muhle*, Hamburg 1985.

When I was twenty, I set up on my own—with the aim of putting into practice, to the best of my ability, the Bauhaus philosophy of the unity of culture. As a graphic designer, I thought to design things of everyday life like works of art; and as a picture-maker, I thought to design works of art like things of everyday life. Soon after, I established my own office. My objective was to realize my dream, i.e., to found a kind of Bauhaus—not as a school, but as a commercial agency for all kinds of creative tasks, from the visiting card to city planning. This agency, "Bureau Basel," was intended to bring together a team of designers, architects, photographers, sociologists, psychologists, writers, musicians, and so on. All of them were full of ideas and ready to resolve problems in interdisciplinary cooperation. But the dream remained a dream; the Bureau Basel never worked as it should have.

After tha common experience, Markus Kutter and I decided to found a conventional advertising agency—with unconventional work, because neither of us understood anything about advertising. Thus, in 1959, Gerstner + Kutter was founded in Basel, and I concentrated my energy on building up this enterprise. As a consequence of our ignorance, we were obliged to develop our own ideas and principles, which turned out to be the basis of the future success of the agency.

About ten years later, when I was forty, I retired from the agency, for I had realized that the Bauhaus philosophy led to many contradictions. I also wanted to concentrate on what has always been close to my heart: doing nothing, having time, making pictures. What I didn't know at that time was that I was starting on another—rather unexpected—career; as a typographic designer for printed media. I conceived concepts for several monthly, weekly, and daily papers, and these tasks in the communication business gave me much satisfaction.

As both a designer and a picture-maker, I have always accompanied my work with theoretical reflections research, and I have written several articles and books exploring the efficiency of creative processes. This inquiry led to my summarizing formula "Instead of solutions of problems, programs for solutions."

—Karl Gerstner

Today, the process of writing has become increasingly complex, as it combines both science and art, which have spawned a variety of scientific branches as well as art forms. Typography is one of the remarkable results of this combination, and its scientific and artistic connections are still being debated.

In 1959, Karl Gerstner formed an advertising agency in Switzerland and began his investigations into typography, language, and writing. The results have included a series of publications—*Kalte Kunste?* (1957), *Designing Programmes* (1963), *Typographical Memorandum* (1972) and *Compendium for Literates* (1970)—and a 1973 exhibition at the Museum of Modern Art in New York; the latter, titled *Think Program,* included material based on these publications and reinforced his theories on systematizing (programming) the problem-solving process.

In all of these endeavors, typography was viewed as a scientific as well as artistic phenomenon. Gerstner classified typography by separating it into categories—for instance, typography as language, as image, as field, or as sequence. This enabled the reader to see how language and writing changed once they were transformed into type. For example, typography can transform language or writing into a visual idea. Words and sentences can be visually manipulated so that verbal meaning is enhanced.

By a simple distortion of a letter or word, the viewer can be presented with a visual pun.

Gerstner further acknowledges that type alone is an inadequate form of communication. Visual materials such as photographs, drawings, and diagrams support the copy and can make possible its reduction. However, to the proverbial picture that's worth a thousand words, Gerstner retorts that "the text could not be replaced by a thousand pictures."

The subject of space and time is an important one in typography. How long it takes to speak a line or a paragraph is identical to the amount of space required to print it. Thus, a designer must consider spatial organization and type selection, just as a speaker is concerned with speech patterns and briefings. For the designer, the use of a highly developed grid can provide all the flexibility and freedom to arrange and organize typography and other visual material.

Finally, the limitation of space in typography can be solved and expanded by the use of a series of spaces or pages. This process involves the development of a sequence which can be a creative force in design, particularly book design. Though each page is new and different, a sense of similarity and uniformity is sought and maintained.

These summary observations culminated in the publication of Gerstner's *Compendium* in 1972. Though he no longer practices advertising, his outlook is sufficiently wide-ranging to afford him the luxury of pursuing varied forms of creativity. Since 1970, he has been applying these concepts to other art forms, particularly painting and constructions.

—D. Ichiyama

Karl Gerstner: Poster for Felix Handschin Keramik

GHERARDI, Piero.

Italian stage and film designer. Born in Poppi, Arezzo, 20 November 1909. Mainly self-taught in art and design. Worked as an architect, in Rome, 1930s; film set dresser and furnisher, Rome 1945–49; art director, working on the films of Federico Fellini, Duilio Coletti, Mario Soldati, Mario Monicelli, Gianni Francioni, Alberto Lattuada, King Vidor, Luigi Zampa, etc., in Rome, 1950–71; also stage designer, working on productions in Italy, and for the National Theatre, London, from 1953. Recipient: Academy Award, 1961, 1963; Gold Sash Award for Film Design, Italy, 1961, 1965, 1967. *Died* (in Rome) *8 June 1971.*

Works:

Film designs include—*Notte di Tempesta* (Franciolini), 1945; *Eugenia Grandet* (Soldati), 1946; *Daniele Cortis* (Soldati), 1946; *Amanti senza Amore* (Franciolini), 1947; *Senza Pieta* (Lattuada), 1948; *Proibito Rubare* (Comencini), 1948; *Fuga in Francia* (Soldati), 1948; *Campane a Martello* (Zampa), 1949; *Napoli Milionaria* (de Filippo), 1949; *Cinema d'Altri Tempi* (Steno), 1950; *Her Favourite Husband* (Soldati), 1950; *Romanzo d'Amore* (Coletti), *Camicie Rossi* (Alessandrini), 1950; *Sensualita* (Francassi), 1951; *Iolanda la Figlia del Corsaro Nero* (Soldati), 1951; *Anni Facili* (Zampa), 1953; *Proibito* (Monicelli), 1954; *Le Notti di Cabiria* (Fellini), 1956; *War and Peace* (K. Vidor), *Padri e Figli* (Monicelli), 1957; *La Grande Strada Azzurra* (Pontecorvo), 1957; *Il Medico e lo Stregone* (Monicelli), 1957; *I Soliti Ignoti* (Monicelli), 1958; *La Dolce Vita* (Fellini), 1960; *Kapo* (Pontecorvo), 1960; *Risate di Gioia* (Monicelli), 1960; *Sotto Dieci Bandiere* (Coletti), 1960; *Crimen* (Camerini), 1960; *Il Gobbo* (Lizzani), 1960; *Il Carabiniere a Cavallo* (Lizzani), 1961; *Il Re di Poggioreala* (Coletti), 1961; "Renzo e Luciana" episode of *Boccaccio 70* (Monicelli), 1962; *Violenza Segreta* (Moser), 1962; *Otto e Mezzo/8¹/₂* (Fellini), 1963; *La Ragazza di Bube* (Comencini), 1963; "Peccato nel Pomeriggio" episode of *Alta Infedelta* (Petri), 1964; "Fatebene Fratelli" episode of *Tre Notti d'Amore* (Comencini), 1964; "La Telefonata" and "Il Trattato di Eugenetica" episodes of *Le Bambole* (Risi and Comencini), 1964; *Giulietta degli Spiriti* (Fellini), 1965; *Madamigella de Maupin* (Bolognini), 1965; *L'Armata Brancaleone* (Monicelli), 1965; "Fata Armenia" episode of *Le Fate* (Monicelli), 1966; *Se Tutte le Donne del Mondo* (Levin and Maiuri), 1966; *Diabolik* (Bava), 1967; *The Appointment* (Lumet), 1969; *Queimada* (Pontecorvo), 1969; *Infanzia, Vocazione, e Prime Esperienze di Giacomo Casanova, Veneziano* (Comencini), 1969; *Brancaleone alle Corciate* (Monicelli), 1970; *Le Avventure di Pinocchio* (Comencini), 1971.

Publications:

By GHERARDI: article—interview in *Sight and Sound* (London), Winter 1969–70.

On GHERARDI: books—*Federico Fellini's Juliet of the Spirits*, edited by Tullio Kezich, New York 1965; *Dizionario del Cinema Italiano 1945–1969* by Gianni Rondolino, Turin 1969; *Le Décor de Film* by Leon Barsacq, Paris 1970, as *Caligari's Cabiet and Other Grand Illusions*, Boston 1976; *The International Film Encyclopedia* by Ephraim Katz, New York and London 1980; *The International Dictionary of Films and Filmmakers*, London and Chicago 1987, 1991.

Piero Gherardi collaborated with Federico Fel-

Piero Gherardi: Still from Federico Fellini's *Otto e Mezzo/8¹/₂*, 1963

lini on his major films of the late 1950s and early 1960s. The styles of these films show an infusion of new artistic qualities into the established practices of Neorealist films of the late 1940s. In *La Dolce Vita, 8¹/₂,* and *Juliet of the Spirits,* there still was the use of some actual locations and some non-professional actors, characteristics of the Neorealist movement. But Gherardi and Fellini brought certain surrealistic images into their films, such as the opening of *La Dolce Vita,* in which a statue of Christ with outstretched arms is suspended from a helicopter. Though such a situation is plausible the image is striking and memorable because it juxtaposes familiar objects with an unusual context.

The sets and costumes of *8¹/₂* and *Juliet of the Spirits* established the dreamlike quality of the films. The spa in *8¹/₂* is not a real location but a set, modeled not on an existing place but on the memories of one Gherardi had visited as a child. Similarly, the train station is the memory of one—all the viewer sees is a locomotive, a platform, and some steam. In *Juliet of the Spirits,* the conservative heroine's surroundings are mostly white, while the interiors of the house of her liberated friend Suzy are red, yellow, and violet. Juliet's house, an environment of purity, is contrasted to Suzy's, which has the

atmosphere of circus and brothel. Gherardi considered a costume as more than a mere covering for a character; it reveals that character and defines the personality. Likewise, his sets did more than give documentary information about a place. Gherardi often mixed the ordinary with the simplified or the surrealistic. In so doing, he emphasized the artificial quality of films and helped to focus attention on characters and situations whose components were as complex as the visual elements.

—Floyd W. Martin

GHIA.

Italian engineering and car styling firm. Founded as Carrozzeria Ghia, by Giacinto Ghia (1887–1944), in Turin, 1915. Incorporated as Ghia S.p.A., 1945, under directors Mario Felice Boano, 1946–53, Luigi Segre, 1953–63, Gino Rovere, 1963–64, Luigi Gaspardo Moro,

1964–67, Alessandro De Tomaso and the Rowan Controller Company, 1967–72, and under the Ford Motor Company, from 1972; complete manufacturing works founded as Carrosserie Ghia Societe Anonyme Suisse Aigle, in Switzerland; Ghia S.p.A. took over Stabilimento Monviso car styling firm of Turin to create the subsidiary Karmann-Ghia, 1955. Designers: Giacinto Ghia, 1915–44, Mario Revelli de Beaumont, 1946–50, Mario Felice Boano, 1946–53, Filippo Sapino, 1960–67 and 1970s, Giorgio Giugiaro, 1965–68, and Tom Tjaarda, 1968–77. **Exhibitions:** *Carrozeria Italiana,* Palazzina della Promotrice delle Belle Arti, Turin, 1978 (toured); *Die Nützlichen Kunste,* Messegelände am Funkturm, West Berlin, 1981. **Collection:** Museo dell'Automobile, Turin. Address: Ghia S.p.A., Via A. Da Montefeltro 5, Turin, Italy.

Works:

Cars designed include—Itala guida interna, 1928; Fiat Berlina Sport, 1929; Fiat 518A cabriolet, 1933; Fiat 518A Berlina, 1933; Fiat 518A Tre Luci, 1933; Fiat 6C 1500, 1947; Alfa Romeo 6C 2500 cabriolet, 1948; Alfa Romeo 6C 2500S cabriolet, 1949; Fiat 1100 Gioiella coupe, 1949; Lancia Aurelia Berlina President, 1950; Fiat 1400 cabriolet, 1952; Fiat 8V coupe, 1952; Alfa Romeo 1900C coupe, 1952; Dodge Fire Arrow, 1953; Dodge Fire Bomb cabriolet, 1953; Chrysler Dart DS, 1955; Ferrari 410 Superamerica, 1955; Chrysler Gilda prototype, 1955; Chrysler Selene I prototype, 1959; Renault prototype, 1959; Chrysler Selene II prototype, 1960; Chrysler Valiant Asimmetrica, 1961; Chrysler Turbina Turboflite, 1961; De Tomaso Vallelunga, 1964; Plymouth 450SS cabriolet, 1965; Maserati Ghibli, 1965; De Tomaso Pampero Roadster, 1967; De Tomaso Mangusta, 1967.

Publications:

On GHIA: books—*Carrozzieri di Ieri, Carrozzieri di Oggi* by Carlo Biscaretti di Ruffia, Turin 1952; *Il Disegno Industriale e la sua Estetica* by Gillo Dorfles, Bologna 1963; *Fiat* by Michael Sedgwick, London 1974; *Bodies Beautiful: A History of Car Styling and Craftsmanship* by John McLellan, Newton Abbot 1975; *A Source Book of Classic Cars* by G. N. Georgano, London 1977; *Carrozzeria Italiana: Cultura e Progetto,* edited by Angelo Tito Anselmi, Milan 1978; *Cars of the Thirties and Forties* by Michael Sedgwick, London and Göteborg 1979; *Industrial Design* by John Heskett, London 1980; *Die Nützlichen Künste,* edited by Tilmann Buddensieg and Henning Rogge, West Berlin 1981; *The Conran Directory of Design,* edited by Stephen Bayley, London 1985.

GIACOSA, Dante.
Italian car designer. Born in Rome, 3 January 1905. Educated at the Ginnasio and Liceo Classico, Alba, Piedmont, 1914–22; studied mechanical engineering, at the Politecnico, Turin, 1922–27: D.Ing. 1927. Served in the Italian Army Apprentice Cadet School, 1927–28, and as an air force engineer, 1937. Married Laura

Gherzi Paruzza in 1936; daughter: Mariella. Draughtsman, S.P.A. Motor Vehicle Company, Turin, 1928–30; worked for the Fiat Automobile Company, Turin 1930–70: diesel engines engineering, 1930–32; foreman, aero engines engineering, 1932–33; passenger car engineering design chief, 1933–46; director of engineering for Fiat Motor Vehicle and Fiat Styling, 1946–55; principal director of Fiat Styling, 1955–65; member of Fiat Directive Committee, 1960–70; divisional manager of engineering and styling, 1965–70; consultant engineer to Fiat from his retirement in 1970. President, Societa Industriale Ricerche Automotoristiche research and development company, Turin, from 1974. Professor of engineering design, Turin University, 1947–67. President of the Commissione Unificazione Nazionale Autoviecoli, 1955–75, Associazione Tecnica Automobile from 1965, and Federation Internationale des Sociétés d'Ingénieurs des Techniques de l'Automobile, 1968–69. **Exhibitions:** *Carrozzeria Italiana,* Palazzina della Promotrice delle Belle Arti, Turin, 1978 (toured); *Design and design,* Palazzo delle Stelline, Milan, 1979 (travelled to Venice); *Gli Annitrenta,* Palazzo Reale, Milan, 1982. **Collection:** Museo dell'Automobile, Turin. Recipient: Order of Merit, Italian Republic, 1956; Order of Merit, Societe Française pour la Recherche et l'Invention, 1957; Compasso d'Oro Award, Milan, 1959; Gold Medal, Rimini Biennale, 1968; Colombiana Medal, Genoa, 1970; Gold Medal, Societé des Ingénieurs de l'Automobile, Paris, 1981. Honorary Doctorate: Pasadena Art School, California, 1981. Fellow, Society of Automobile Engineers, Pennsylvania, 1948; Institute of Mechanical Engineers, London, 1964. Address: Viale Settimo Severo 30, 10133 Turin, Italy.

Works:

Car designs include—Fiat 1100S, 1933; Fiat 500 Topolino, 1936; Fiat 1400, 1950; Fiat 1100–103 Turbine, 1953; Fiat 600, 1955; Fiat Nuova 500, 1957; Fiat 1800, 1959; Fiat A109-Primula/Autobianchi, 1964; Fiat 124 coupe, 1966; Fiat 128, 1969; Fiat A112/Autobianchi, 1969; Fiat 127, 1971.

Dante Giacosa: *Fiat Nuova 500* two-door saloon, 1957–60

Publications:

By GIACOSA: books—*Motori Endotermici,* Milan 1938, 1984; *Forty Years of Design with Fiat,* Milan 1981; articles—in *Royal Auto* (Brussels), January 1952; *Automobile* (Rome), Summer 1961; *Stile Industria* (Milan), no. 35, 1961; *Form und Technik* (Zurich), August 1961; *Pirelli* (Turin), no. 4, 1962, no. 6, 1965; *First Edition* (Milan), May 1963; *Style Auto* (Milan), December 1963; *Atti del Convegno* (Rome), Winter 1981; *Le Grandi Automobili* (Milan), no. 3, 1982; *Modo* (Milan), no. 55, 1982.

On GIACOSA: books—*Fiat* by Michael Sedgwick, London 1974; *The Library of Motoring: The Designers* by L. J. K. Setright, London 1976; *A Source Book of Classic Cars* by G. N. Georgano, London 1977; *Carrozeria Italiana: Cultura e Progetto,* exhibition catalogue edited by Anfelo Tito Anselmi, Milan 1978; *Cars of the Thirties and Forties* by Michael Sedgwick, London and Goteborg 1979; *Architeture delle Macchine,* Milan 1982; *Italian Design: 1870 to the Present* by Penny Sparke, London 1988.

A design is good when it produces a feeling of true balance between art and engineering. The technician can become good designer only in an environment which inspires him with the idea that a high standard of functional value can be reached only if united with beauty of shape; one who can attain this vital balance between engineering and art will reach the summit in design.

To achieve his purpose, the industrial designer must work in close cooperation with a number of specialists and must, on occasion, coordinate the work of a number of different industries. Ultimately responsible for the work, he is both the leader and a part of a great organisation. He must have the mind of an architect, concerned with both technique and art, and his mode of expression must link technical and artistic language.

An elaborate graph made at any stage in the planning of a modern vehicle, will express clarity, accuracy, geometrical exactitude, and constructural possibility, exactly as though it were an architectural plan. And it is with such a series of drawings that the designer produces ideas in graphic form first for himself and then for the other technical departments, the sales manager, the production manager, and the executive of every other branch concerned. The work of the designer will be more expressive or more technical in character, according to whether the artist or the technician predominates. But if he combines the technician and the artist equally within himself, his most expressive design will always have that technical touch to differentiate it from a similar design produced by the pure artist. It is for the technical design and not for the artist to number in detail the external and internal components required to create a whole; he cannot stop at the purely superficial aspect but is driven on towards the technical considerations and the functional purpose behind the design.

The designer-artist will succeed in harmonising functional value and visual appearance; smoothness of line in a vehicle will be accompanied by a comparable smoothness in running and the style of the body-work will be reflected in the behavior of the machine on the road. That is why I maintain that the automobile industry will achieve its best results when its working conditions allow for the training of designers who can combine technical knowledge with means of artistic expression.

Le Corbusier, in his much-discussed treatise on modern architecture, states, "Basing their work upon calculations, engineers employ geometric shapes which satisfy our eyes by their geometrical construction and our spirit by their mathematical expression; such achievement belongs to great art."

Le Corbusier, in my opinion was right; technique, which has introduced us to "rational" shapes and taught us the use for materials, makes it possible for us, in our closest approach to the field of art, to maintain that sincerity of expression which imbues a piece of work with the spirit of its time.

Today, scientific knowledge has reached the point where the man is capable of creating monuments that have no direct connection with nature but that nevertheless can express new ways of feeling, which can be one day objects of a new history of art. Such a history will deal with the story of engineering as though it were that of architecture, and it will describe the styles adopted, for instance, in the field of automobile design as though they were architectural, for the development of automobile design towards maturity has points of resemblance with the development of design in architecture. (*Excerpted from a paper presented in 1951 before a London conference organized by the Council of Industrial Design.*)

—Dante Giacosa

GIBB, Bill.

British fashion designer. Born William Elphinstone Gibb, in Fraserburgh, Scotland, 23 January 1943. Educated in Fraserburgh until 1960; studied at St. Martin's School of Art, London, 1962–66: Dip.AD. 1966; under Janey Ironside, Royal College of Art, London, 1966–68: Des.RCA. 1968. Founder and partner, with others, of Alice Paul clothing boutique, London, 1967–69; freelance designer, working for

Bill Gibb: Evening dress in crepe de chine and net with embroidered motifs, 1979

Baccarat fashion house, London, 1969-72; founder-chairman, Bill Gibb Fashion Group, London, 1972-88: opened first shop in Bond Street, London, 1975. **Exhibitions:** *British Design,* Musee du Louvre, Paris, 1971; *Fashion: An Anthology,* Victoria and Albert Museum, London, 1971; *Bill Gibb: 10 Years,* Albert Hall, London, 1977. **Collections:** Bath Museum, Avon; Leeds Museum, Yorkshire; Victoria and Albert Museum, London; Royal Ontario Museum, Toronto. Recipient: *Vogue* Designer of the Year, 1970; ITV Best Fashion Show Award, London, 1979. Fellow, Society of Industrial Artists and Designers, London, 1975. *Died* (in London) *3 January 1988.*

Publications:

By GIBB: article—in *The Designer* (London), May 1981.

On GIBB: books—*Fashion: An Anthology by Cecil Beaton,* exhibition catalogue compiled by Madeleine Ginsburg, London, 1971; *In Vogue: Sixty Years of Celebrities and Fashion,* edited by Georgina Howell, London 1975, 1978, New York 1976; *The Changing World of Fashion: 1900 to the Present* by Ernestine Carter, London 1977; *The Guinness Guide to 20th Century Fashion* by David Bond, Enfield 1981; *The Collector's Book of Twentieth Century Fashion* by Frances Kennett, London and New York 1983; *Sixty Years of Faces and Fashion* by Prudence Glynn, London 1983; *McDowell's Directory of Twentieth Century Fashion* by Colin McDowell, London 1984; *The Encyclopaedia of Fashion from 1840 to the 1980s* by Georgina O'Hara, London 1986; *Design Source Book* by Penny Sparke and others, London 1986.

From the age of 12 there was no doubt in my mind that I wanted to pursue a career in fashion. It was an obsession. Arriving in London at the age of 19 from northeast Scotland, I strove for the top and achieved it within ten years. The motivation is inexplicable in the sense that I feel that I have been given a rare gift of talent to design beautiful clothes.

There is nothing comparable to the sheer joy and challenge of confronting a blank sheet of paper in order to create a collection. I discipline myself by deciding on a theme, e.g., a collection based on a porcelain look, a Scottish theme, or, a Byzantine influence (which I used for one of my most successful collections, Autumn/Winter 1975). From many rough sketches, I edit down to what I consider to be a complete, comprehensive, exciting, and desirable amount, i.e., around sixty to seventy outfits. I believe in coordinates that give women a choice and the enjoyment of putting together their own look in the Gibb style. The sensuality of women is important, and I believe my clothes achieve this for them.

I enjoy all aspects of design, and although I am better known for fantasy gowns, my feeling for knitwear is perhaps stronger because to me it is of the earth, more honest—probably being a Celt, the roots cannot be denied.

To travel is to glean knowledge, and I know this is essential in my quest for constant inspiration. I probably belong to the Romantic genre of designers, but I can appreciate and understand street fashion, probably again, because of its honesty.

Fashion designs today, I feel, no longer dictate "The Look." Since 1947 and "The New Look" created by Dior, women have become quite educated in their style of dress and what suits them in particular. I feel, rather than dictate. I create a mood which is taken up by those who like to wear my particular look.

Fashion, being so transient, has a message

for everyone. Now, in the 1980s, fashion still seems to revolve around more awareness of the body which began in the 1970s when health foods and diets were high on the list of priorities—hence the current popularity of sportswear to coincide with the increasing number of people who exercise more and more to attain this eternal "spirit of youth" now dominating our society.

People will always be fascinated by clothes and fashion. They can be varied—frowned upon, unbearable, risqué, dowdy, but always exciting and moving—searching, and a force to be reckoned with.

—Bill Gibb (1984)

Bill Gibb derived his penchant for juxtaposing fabrics and patterns with an out-of-the-ordinary flair from the three years he spent doing freelance designs for Basccarat, an expensive London ready-to-wear fashion house. In the early 1970s, he came up with an adventurous approach to womenswear which gained him a lasting recognition.

Gibb's is not a revolutionary approach but rather stresses the mix-and-match, loose-fitting look which found a general vogue during the 1970s and 1980s. Among the touches for which he is recognized is his use of the monogram, ears of wheat and a bee insignia being among his favorites. He customarily exhibited a flamboyance, well exemplified in outfittings such as his 1976 hooded cape and Byzantine-patterned pullover worn with below-the-knee pants of checked suede and print socks. His smocks, kimonos, capes are usually full and loose, embellished by a variety of eye-catching patterns and fabrics such as tartan plaids, silks, brocades, colored braid trims, chiffon panels, and heavily embroidered nets and laces. Gibb had moments of relative simplicity, such as in his fall 1975 collection which was dominated by more classic silhouettes and muted colors in his daytime wear. Yet, preference for the elaborate and for experimentation in the adorning detail held sway in most cases.

Gibb's ideas for menswear completely differ from those he held for women's fashion. Here, there prevails a minimal tone characterized by earthy colors and comfortable shapes in his casual coats, trousers, and sweaters of wool, chintz and corduroy. In his 1979 first collection for men, there were coordinates, but no suits, and a mix of patterns. These, along with other punctuations in details such as loops and buttons on sleeve tips or floral silk ties, provide subtle hints of Gibb's established strategies for women.

In a 1978 article, Gibb noted, "There's nothing really particularly new, is there?" Notwithstanding what one might think of the general application of this statement, it is revealing of Gibb's position in fashion design. He produced his little trademarks and added his own brand of finesse for detail and fabric/pattern blending, but in no way was Gibb a major style creator. Along with so many others of recent ilk, he left an interesting but rather small contribution to the fashion trends of two decades.

—Barbara Cavaliere

GILL, Bob.
American graphic designer. Born in New York City, 17 January 1931. Studied design, at Phila-

delphia Museum School of Art, 1948-51; painting, at Pennsylvania Academy of Fine Arts, Philadelphia, 1951; City College of New York, 1952, 1955. Served in the United States Army, 1952-54. Married Elizabeth Mills in 1967 (divorced, 1974). Freelance designer and illustrator, New York, 1954-60; art director, at Charles Hobson advertising agency, London, 1960-62; partner, with Alan Fletcher and Colin Forbes, in Fletcher/Forbes/Gill design studio, London, 1962-67; freelance designer, illustrator and filmmaker, in London, 1967-75, and in New York, since 1976. Instructor, School of Visual Arts, New York, 1955-60, Pratt Institute, Brooklyn, New York, 1959, Central School of Art, London, 1967-69, Chelsea School of Art, London, 1969, Royal College of Art, London, 1970-75, Hornsey School of Art, London, 1972-74, and Parsons School of Design, New York, 1981. **Exhibitions:** School of Visual Arts, New York, 1959; American Institute of Graphic Arts, New York, 1966; Stedelijk Museum, Amsterdam, 1970. **Collections:** Museum of Modern Art, New York; Victoria and Albert Museum, London. Recipient: Gold Medal, Art Directors Club of New York, 1954; Silver Medal, Design and Art Directors Association, London, 1968, 1970; numerous American Institute of Graphic Arts and Type Directors Club awards, New York. Address: 1200 Broadway, New York, New York 10001, U.S.A.

Works:

books illustrated and designed include—*New York: Places and Pleasures* (Simon), 1957; *The Millionaires* (Gill/Reid), 1959; *A Balloon for a Blunderbus* (Gill/Reid), 1960; *A to Z* (Gill), 1961; *What Colour Is Your World?* (Gill), 1963; *The Present* (Gill/Fletcher/Forbes), 1963; *The Green-Eyed Mouse and the Blue-Eyed Mouse* (Gill), 1965; *Parade* (Gill/Botsford), 1967; *Bob Gill's Portfolio* (Gill), 1968; *I Keep Changing* (Gill), 1971; *Ups and Downs* (Gill), 1974; *Forget All the Rules You Ever Learned About Graphic Design* (Gill), 1981. Gill has made more than 30 documentaries and industrial films for clients including Olivetti, Pirelli, Singapore Airlines, Holiday Inn, and the Lincoln Center.

Publications:

By GILL: books—*Graphic Design: Visual Comparisons,* with Alan Fletcher and Colin Forbes, London 1963; *Illustration: Aspects and Directions,* with John Lewis, London and New York 1964.

On GILL: books—*The New Graphic Design* by Karl Gerstner and Markus Kutter, Teufen and London 1959; *Graphic Design Britain,* edited by Frederick Lambert, London 1967; *Graphis Record Covers,* edited by Walter Herdeg, Zurich 1974; *The Language of Graphics* by Edward Booth-Clibborn and Daniele Baroni, London 1980.

Bob Gill is more an artist than anything, but he understands how to utilise his creativity, harness it to graphic purposes, and to feed purely "mechanical" typography with inspiration. This is shown very clearly in the many logotypes he has designed, as in the reversed capital "R" for Real Typographers (1953) and the lowercase "e" balanced on the top right of a capital "B" for Blond Educational Books (1963). His value as a graphic designer may depend on his understanding of when not to draw and how far to go with a drawing. The two covers, *Graphis No. 119* and *Design No. 166,* demon-

Forget all the rules you ever learned about graphic design.

Including the ones in this book.

Forget how good design is *supposed* to look. What you think is good design, is what other desi[

Bob Gill: *Forget All the Rules* ... book jacket, 1981

GIRARD, Alexander (Hayden).

American architect, interior and industrial designer. Born in New York City, 24 May 1907. Studied at the Architectural Association School, London, 1925–29; Royal School of Architecture, Rome, 1930–31; New York University, 1932–35. Worked in several architectural offices, in Florence, Rome, London, Paris and New York, 1929–32; independent architect and designer, establishing own architectural office in Florence, 1930, in New York, 1935–37, in Detroit, 1937–52, and in Santa Fe, New Mexico, from 1953: design director, textile division of Herman Miller Inc., Zeeland, Michigan, from 1952. Established Girard Foundation for collections of toys and folkcraft objects, Santa Fe, 1961: donated to State of New Mexico, 1978; Girard Wing of Museum of International Folk Art, Santa Fe, opened 1982. **Exhibitions:** *International Exposition,* Barcelona, 1929; *Printed Textiles for the Home,* Museum of Modern Art, New York, 1947 (toured); *Textiles USA,* Museum of Modern Art, New York, 1956; *The Design Process at Herman Miller: Nelson, Eames, Girard, Probst,* Walker Art Center, Minneapolis, 1975 (toured). Recipient: Gold Medal, Barcelona International Exposition, 1929; Museum of Modern Art Fabrics Prize, New York, 1946; League of New York Trailblazer Award, 1952; Medal of Honor, Architectural League, New York, 1962, 1965; Elsie de Wolfe Award, American Institute of Interior Designers, 1966; Allied Professions Medal, American Institute of Architects, 1966; *Institutions Magazine* Award, Chicago, 1967; Burlington House Award, Los Angeles, 1974; Gold Medal, Honor Fraternity of Tau Sigma Delta, San Antonio, 1980; Governor's Award, New Mexico, 1981. Honorary Royal Designer for Industry, Royal Society of Arts, London, 1965. Address: P.O. Box 2168, Santa Fe, New Mexico 87501, U.S.A.

Works:

Italian exhibit layouts, at the *International Exposition,* Barcelona, 1929.
Junior League shop interiors, Grosse Pointe, Michigan, 1936.
Office and plant interiors, for the Detrola Corporation, Detroit, 1943.
Office interiors, for the Ford Motor Company, Dearborn, Michigan, 1946.
Design for Modern Use: Made in USA travelling exhibition layouts, for the Museum of Modern Art, New York, 1950.
Fabrics and wallpaper ranges, for Herman Miller Inc., 1952.
Michigan Bulletin magazine redesign, for the American Institute of Architects, Detroit, 1953.
Furniture showroom interiors in Grand Rapids, Michigan, for Herman Miller Inc., 1953.
Glassware, ceramics and leather goods design programme, for Georg Jensen Inc., New York, 1955.
Showroom interiors in San Francisco, for Herman Miller Inc., 1958.
Plant and office interiors, for the Cummins Engine Company, Columbus, Indiana, 1960–64.
Textiles shop interiors in New York, for Herman Miller Inc., 1961.
Administration Centre three-dimensional mural, for John Deere and Company, Moline, Illinois, 1964.
Corporate visual programme, for Braniff International Airline, Dallas, 1964.
El Encanto de un Pueblo exhibition pavilion and layouts, for *Hemisfair 68,* San Antonio, Texas, 1967.
Girard Group furniture range, for Herman Miller Inc., 1967.

strate this in exemplary fashion. The *Graphis* cover reproduces the postal wrapper of a packet sent to the editor; it includes stamps and labels and postmarks and all the rest. The *Design* cover is a simple drawing of a black-and-white post for a traffic sign with, instead of such a sign, a rough square with the word "sign" written on it.

As the occasion has demanded, he can go much farther with the drawing. The record cover for George Harrison's *Wonderwall Music* (Apple Records, 1968) is really a charming painting in its own right. It does, of course, also summon a vivid impression of the music.

He also put his talent to good purpose in some of the packaging commissions he undertook. On the boxes for typing paper for Spicers in 1961, stark-white, reverse lettering on red and blue ground gives an effect of torn paper. In 1967 for Pickerings, he devised packages for combinations of a can of filling and a packet of pastry mix sold together in one box; these reproduced the two on its faces as though the box were transparent.

Perhaps the distinctive quality that runs through Gill's work, in addition to the irrepressible wit and irony, is an ability to seize the essential in a memorably condensed image, as in the montage of torn photographs for the film *A Severed Head* (1968), for example, or the record cover for Troubadour Records of the Colin Bates Trio, a seeming photograph of a record with hole and label well off center. However, these imaginatively compressed images are not always all that simple. For instance, Spicers Kingsbury paper was advertised by a rough little drawing in thick outline of one of those Swiss army knives opened up to show all the little gadgets and attachments for the many uses it could serve.

—Toni del Renzio

African Fabrics exhibition layouts, for the Colorado Springs Fine Arts Center, Colorado, 1976.

Multiple Visions inaugural exhibition layouts, for the Girard Wing of the Museum of International Folk Art, Santa Fe, New Mexico, 1982.

Publications:

By GIRARD: book—*The Magic of a People/El Encanto de un Pueblo*, New York 1968; film—*Day of the Dead*, with Charles Eames, 1956.

On GIRARD: books—*House and Garden: The Modern Interior*, edited by Robert Harling, London 1964; *80 Years of Ideas and Pleasure from House and Garden*, edited by Mary Jane Pool and Caroline Seebohm, London 1980; *Knoll Design* by Eric Larrabee and Massimo Vignelli, New York 1981; *The Conran Directory of Design*, edited by Stephen Bayley, London 1985; *The American Design Adventure 1940–1975* by Arthur J. Pulos, London and Cambridge, Massachusetts 1988.

Every new project presents some version of basic order.

In it, the ingredients for the exercise of fantasy and magic may usually be found.

These ingredients, if discovered and used significantly, can give special individuality and identity to the project or the client, or better, both.

When the client joins in the search, the ideal conditions exist for the realization of the best solution to the project.

My greatest enjoyment and satisfaction in the solution of any project is uncovering the latent fantasy and magic in it and convincing my client to join me in this project.

—Alexander Girard

It is impossible to think of Alexander Girard without considering his lifelong collecting of children's toys and folk art, 106,000 items of which now form the Girard Foundation Collection at the Museum of International Folk Art in Santa Fe, New Mexico.

As a designer and as a person, Girard is most often regarded as a humanist. During the period from 1940 to 1960, when American design was mostly enslaved by machine technology and the rigors of the International Style, Girard gave due respect to much that was of worth from both of these sources but distinguished himself by valuing equally childlike joy and the richness of folk art and culture. With his respect for the overall view, his complete and completed designs resulted from a multi-faceted order of details, rich and rewarding. He was as concerned with the buttons on the waiters' coats as he was with the floor plans of the restaurants he designed.

Girard's eye has always seen beyond period style to that which is timeless, not because of its quaintness nor historic value only, but because of its intrinsic human quality that could be continuously used. His turn-of-the-century music hall transformed into the Herman Miller showroom in San Francisco shows well his design thinking. Here was no reconstruction of a music hall atmosphere as a background for displaying, in sharp contrast, the Miller collection but instead the bold openness of the architectural structure, strengthened with clear color, and the sparkle of the brilliant, medallion-cut glass windows. He removed the original murky clutter to reveal not bare bones but a lively and enriched structure, a space, open, bright and right, one that could be an integral part of a display of objects designed fifty years later.

His respect for contemporary technology is obvious in his textile design. He has always esteemed what the machine can produce in quantity and with ease. He has respected the quality of folds and flow that fabric can have and has enriched this surface with geometric and simple, abstracted design. These qualities also are evident in native fabrics, and he has produced outstanding exhibitions of fabrics both native and contemporary.

As a humanist, Girard sees the interrelatedness of human activity through both history and daily living. He gives rightful due to architectural soundness of structure and furnishes that structure with the wit and charm of a child's toy. His interiors are to be lived in, and they also display the lives lived within. The restaurants he designed and other public spaces he has created, while fulfilling the demands of their functions, have also enriched the eye with his carefully chosen and ordered world of visual pleasure. In a time when contemporary design has been most often formalized into an international sameness, Girard has maintained his richness of spirit, his wit, and his childlike wonder at all that the visual world has to offer. As a designer, he brings order to the chaos of wonder.

—Harlan Sifford

GIUGIARO, Giorgetto.

Italian industrial designer. Born in Garessio, Cuneo, 7 August 1938. Studied fine art and technical drawing, Accademia di Belle Arti, Turin, 1953–55. Married Maria Teresa Serra; children: Fabrizio and Laura. Designer, under Dante Giacosa and Bruno Barbero, at Fiat Car Styling Center, Turin, 1955–59; designer, under Nuccio Bertone, Carrozzeria Bertone Car Styling Center, Grugliasco, Turin, 1959–65; head of Styling and Project Center, Carrozzeria Ghia, Turin, 1965–68; founder and director, with Aldo Mantovani, of Ital Design car styling company, Moncalieri, Turin, from 1968; established Ital Design industrial product division, 1970: designed cars for Alfa Romeo, Fiat, Mazda, Isuzu, Iso, Maserati, Lotus, Hyundai, Volkswagen, Lancia, BMW, and Renault, and products for Philips, Sony, Nikon, Necchi, Shoei, Suzuki and Seiko. **Exhibitions:** *The Taxi Project*, Museum of Modern Art, New York, 1976; *Giugiaro: Car Designer*, Lijnbann Centrum, Rotterdam, 1981; *Carrozzeria Italiana*, Pasadena Art Center, California, 1981; *The Italian Idea*, Aspen Design Center, Colorado, 1981; *Die Nutzlichen Kunste*, Messegelande am Funkturm, West Berlin, 1981; *Italian Re-Evolution*, La Jolla Museum of Contemporary Art, California, 1982; *Design Since 1945*, Philadelphia Museum of Art, 1983. Recipient: Gold Medal, Society of Industrial Artists and Designers, London, 1980; Compasso d'Oro Award, Milan, 1981. Address: Ital Design, Via Grandi 11, 10024 Moncalieri, Turin, Italy.

Works:

Cars designed include—Gordon Keeble GT, 1960; Alfa Romeo 2000/2600 Sprint, 1960; BMW 3200 CS, 1961; ASA 1000 coupe, 1961; Simca 1000/1200 coupe, 1962; Iso Rivolta 330/340 GT, 1962; Alfa Romeo Giulia GT, 1963; Iso Grifo, 1963; Bizzarrini GT Strada, 1964; Fiat 850 Spider, 1965; Mazda Luce 1500/1800, 1965; Isuzu 117 coupe, 1966; De Tomaso Mangusta, 1966; Maserati Ghibli, 1966; Fiat Dino coupe, 1967; Iso Rivolta Fidia, 1967; Maserati Ghibli Spider, 1968; Maserati Bora, 1971; Alfa Romeo Alfasud, 1971; Maserati Merak, 1972; Lotus Esprit, 1972; Volkswagen Passat, 1973; Volkswagen Scirocco, 1974; Volkswagen Golf, 1974; Alfa Romeo Alfetta GT/GTV, 1974; Hyundai Pony, 1974; Alfa Romeo Alfasud Sprint, 1976; Maserati Quattroporte, 1976; Audi 80, 1978; BMW M1, 1978; Lancia Delta, 1979; Fiat Panda, 1980; De Lorean DMC 12, 1981; Isuzu Piazza, 1981; Lancia Prisma, 1982; Fiat Uno, 1983; Hyundai Stellar, 1983; Saab 9000, 1984; Seat Ibiza, 1984; Isuzu Gemini coupe, 1984; Isuzu Gemini/Chevrolet Spectrum, 1984; Lancia Thema, 1984; Hyundai Excel, 1985; Hyundai Presto, 1985; Fiat Premio/Duna, 1985; Seat Malaga, 1985; Fiat Croma, 1985; Renault 21, 1986; Fiat Duna Weekend, 1986; Eagle Premier, 1987; ZCZ Florida, 1987.

Publications:

On GIUGIARO: books—*The Library of Motoring: The Designers* by L. J. K. Setright, London 1976; *Art and the Automobile* by D. B. Tubs, Guildford and London 1978; *Atlante del Design Italiano 1940–1980* by Alfonso Grassi and Anty Pansera, Milan 1980; *Giugiaro Design* by Bruno Alfieri, Milan 1980; *Giugiaro and Ital Design* by Akira Fujimoro, Tokyo 1981; *Giugiaro, Car Designer: 20 Years of Research of Form and Function in Car Design*, exhibition catalogue with text by Giuliano Molineri, Rotterdam 1981; *Carrozzeria Italiana*, exhibition catalogue with text by Giuliano Molineri, Pasadena 1981; *Design Since 1945*, edited by Kathryn Hiersinger and George Marcus, Philadelphia and London 1983; *The Conran Directory of Design*, edited by Stephen Bayley, London 1985; *Italian Design: 1870 to the Present* by Penny Sparke, London 1988.

It was the work of Giorgetto Giugiaro as director of Bertone that first drew comments about the Italian combination of eye, hand, and brain. And to be sure, his work from the 1960s right up to the present time has always carried, almost as a hallmark, the stamp of intelligence, sensibility, and fine craftsmanship. Elegance has not been reserved for the outer bodywork alone but has shaped the interior, the seating, the instrument panel, the steering wheel, and other controls; all have been conceived as part of a whole design, meticulous and finely detailed, though on occasion the priorities shock Anglo-Saxon pragmatics. Giugiaro believes that an automobile should *fare una bella figura*, cut a fine figure, but that only a well-engineered vehicle can do it. The finer the car the finer the figure! Put in another way, the dominant concept of design at Bertone and, subsequently, at Ital Design has been the general notion of an elegant box encompassing intelligently disposed components. Of course, the elegance of the box depends upon the particular use that is to be made of it, so none of the automobile bodies have appealed to fanciful streamlining and space-travel effects. Moreover, when aerodynamic considerations have influenced the shape of an automobile, there has never been any question of transferring that shape to some other product. Giugiaro's sewing machines for Necchi are not about to take off for outer space or even to dash along the highway at 100 miles an hour. The elegance of their lines stem from quite other and far more civilized considerations.

Italian design, as in this case exemplified by Giugiaro, has, in the main, been a search after the appropriate without settling for the banal

Giorgetto Giugiaro: *Medusa* prototype car, for Lancia, 1980

and the unadventurous. While function is not to be ignored, it alone cannot ensure the success of a design, which must question that aesthetic assumptions built into definitions of function. Design has to be a cultural product, a part of the civilizing process; it arises not only to meet new functions but to meet new ways of functioning. In this, it fulfills in our time something analogous to the development of good manners in the past. It is in this way and from these cultural considerations that Giugiaro's elegant designs are to be seen as positive and innovating good taste, a conscious stand against "kitsch," "camp," and those substitutes for the positive exercise of eye, hand, and brain which are "metaphorical," such as "high-tech" (now some thirty years or more after its original appropriation), Art Déco, and other revivals.

—Toni del Renzio

GLASER, Milton.

American graphic designer. Born in New York City, 26 June 1929. Educated at the High School of Music and Art, New York, 1943–46; studied at Cooper Union, New York, 1948–51:

Dip. 1951; Accademia di Belle Arti, Bologna, 1952–53 (Fulbright scholarship). Married Shirley Girton in 1957. Founder, with Seymour Chwast and Edward Sorel, 1954, and President, 1954–74, Push Pin Studios, New York; President, Milton Glaser, Inc., New York, since 1974: has redesigned the magazines *Paris Match, Cue, New West, L'Express, L'Europe, Jardin des Modes, Village Voice* and *Esquire*. Also founder, with Reynold Ruffins and Seymour Chwast, 1955, and co-art director, 1955–74, *Push Pin Graphic* magazine, New York; founder, with Clayton Felker, 1968, and design director, 1968–76, *New York Magazine*, New York; vice-president and design director, *Village Voice* magazine, New York, 1975–77. Lecturer, Pratt Institute, Brooklyn, New York, and School of Visual Arts, New York, from 1961. Board Member, Cooper Union, School of Visual Arts, and Aspen Design Conference; former vice-president, American Institute of Graphic Arts, New York. **Exhibitions:** *The Push Pin Style,* Musee des Arts Decoratifs, Paris, 1970; Museum of Modern Art, New York, 1975; Portland Visual Arts Center, Oregon, 1975; Centre Georges Pompidou, Paris, 1977 (toured); Carl Solway Gallery, Cincinnati, 1980; Peabody Gallery, Harvard University, Cambridge, Massachusetts, 1981. **Collections:** Museum of Modern Art, New York; Israel Museum, Jerusalem. Recipient: Society of Illustrators Gold Medal, 1979; St. Gaudens Medal, Cooper Union, New York, 1979; Hall of Fame Award, Art Directors Club of New York, 1979. Honorary Doctorate: Minneapolis Institute of Arts, 1971; Moore College, Philadelphia,

1975; Philadelphia Museum School, 1979; School of the Visual Arts, New York, 1979. Honorary Fellow, Royal Society of Arts, London, 1979. Address: Milton Glaser Inc., 207 East 32nd Street, New York, New York 10016, U.S.A.

Works:

Bob Dylan album insert poster, for Columbia Records, 1966.
Product promotion poster series, for Olivetti S.p.A., from 1968.
Signet Shakespeare book series cover designs, for Signet Classics, 1968–72.
New York Magazine design, layout and art direction, 1968–76.
Childcraft Store interior, exterior and merchandising design, in New York, for Childcraft Stores, 1970.
I ♥ NY tourism campaign symbol, for the New York State Department of Commerce, 1973.
World Trade Center observation deck and restaurants signage, exhibit, theme and graphics system, for INHILCO/Port Authority of New York and New Jersey, 1975.
Supermarket interiors, packaging, merchandising and advertising programs, for The Grand Union Company, from 1978.
Sesame Place educational play park signage, theme and graphics system, in Bucks County, Pennsylvania, for Children's Television Workshop, 1980.
The Rainbow Room identity and graphics program in the Rockefeller Center, New York,

Milton Glaser: *Juilliard III* **poster, for the Juilliard School, New York, 1989**

for the Rockefeller Management Corporation, 1987.

Queens College identity, graphics and advertising program, New York, from 1987.

International AIDS logo and poster, for the World Health Organization, 1988.

Publications:

By GLASER: books—*If Apples Had Teeth,* with Shirley Glaser, New York 1960; *The Underground Gourmet,* with Jerome Snyder, New York 1968, 1970; *Milton Glaser: Graphic Design,* edited by Peter Mayer, New York and London 1973; *The Milton Glaser Poster Book,* with introduction by Giorgio Soavi, New York 1977; books illustrated—*The Smallest Elephant in the World* by Alvin Tresselt, New York 1960; *Cats and Bats and Things with Wings* by Conrad Aitken, New York 1965; *Help, Help, The Gobolinks* by Gian Carlo Menotti, New York 1970; *Fish in the Sky* by George Mendoza, New York 1971; *Rimes de la Mere Ole,* with Seymour Chwast and Barry Zaid, Boston 1971; *The Illustrated Don Juan* by Isaac Asimov, New York 1972.

On GLASER: books—*The Push Pin Style Book,* exhibition catalogue, Palo Alto 1970; *History of the Poster* by Josef and Shizuko Muller-Brockmann, Zurich 1971; *Graphic Designers in the USA: 3,* edited by Henri Hillebrand, London 1972; *Who's Who in Graphic Art,* edited by Walter Amstutz, Dubendorf, 1982; *The Conran Directory of Design,* edited by Stephen Bayley, London 1985; *New American Design* by Hugh Aldersley-Williams, New York 1988.

The distinctions between fine and applied art are frequently blurred, particularly in the historical sense. I don't know how to characterize a Persian rug or an Islamic book illustration or an African ritual sculpture in terms of whether they are fine or applied art, although I know that a study of their form has influenced me. I would say that in my work, both fine and applied arts have been significant influences. In fact, all sorts of random visual material, artifacts, objects, printed ephemera, as well as the history of art itself, have been influential in my graphic work. Drawing has been essential to my work for many years as a tool for understanding visual occurrences and as a basic resource for experiencing form.

The vocabulary of form between professional graphic art on the one hand and fine art on the other share many conventions of structure, texture, scale, and color; what seems to be most significantly different is the fundamental intention that illuminates each form of activity. Fine art metaphysically transforms man. The commercial graphic arts convey information of specific kind that motivates the viewer towards action.

—Milton Glaser

Among international designers whose work came to fruition in the middle 1950s, Milton Glaser remains an outstanding figure. Like many of the best of his contemporaries, he sought to replace the ascendancy of the formal qualities associated with the best design from Switzerland with a new, eclectic approach. Ideas could be borrowed from material past or present using in particular the devices of juxtaposition—already a method used by the surrealists to jolt the imagination. His work is often witty but, unlike that of his associates, seldom comic. Always decorative, Glaser's work frequently contains a message and is not strictly commercial.

His great contribution at Push Pin Studios was to give currency in design to a process already established in painting and sculpture, particularly by Picasso: first a mastery of technical skill and then an imaginative use of quotation and parody. This eclectic use of images can be seen to parallel the proliferation in the middle-twentieth century of fast reproductive graphic processes available to everyone. As well as quotations from as far afield as the work of Piero di Cosimo, one finds in Glaser's work a complete assimilation of more recent art history, including such developments as art nouveau, Art Deco, dada and surrealism. The passage of Pop and Op art have also been absorbed into his work. Glaser is the design counterpart to such artists as Johns, Rauschenberg, Oldenburg, and Lichtenstein, whose search through the archives of museum and daily life alike have produced a new language of expression. Glaser, for all his intelligence and sophistication, has not forgotten the grass roots of mass advertising, and among his impeccably professional designs appears suddenly the unpretentious popular quotation, perhaps from some anonymous sign-writer. In his own words: "My work has achieved its balance through the mixture of chance and professionalism."

—John Barnicoat

GOLDFINGER, Ernö.

British architect, interior, exhibition and furniture designer. Born in Budapest, Hungary, 11 September 1902; emigrated to Britain in 1934: naturalized, 1945. Educated at a gymnasium, Budapest, 1912–19, and at Le Rosay School, Gstaad, Switzerland, 1919–20; studied architecture, at the Atelier Jaussely, Paris, 1922–23, Ecole des Beaux-Arts, Paris, 1923, the Atelier Auguste Perret, 1924, and at the Ecole d'Urbanisme, Sorbonne, Paris, 1927–28. Married Ursula Ruth Blackwell in 1933; children: Peter, Elisabeth and Michael. Freelance architect and designer, in partnership with Andre Sive, Paris, 1924–29, in private practice, Paris, 1930–34, and in London, 1934–79: partnership with Gerald Flower, from 1934. Founder-member, CIAM Congres Internationaux d'Architecture Moderne, 1928–59, and of MARS Modern Architecture Research Society (British section of CIAM), 1935–60: editor, *MARS News,* London, 1944–45. Foreign Relations Committee Member, Royal Institute of British Architects, 1937–45; council member, Architects Registration Council, London, 1941–50, Architectural Association, London, 1960–63, 1965–68, Council of Industrial Design, London, 1961–65, and the Royal Academy of Art, London, 1974. London correspondent, *l'Architecture d'Aujourd'hui* magazine, Paris, 1934–74. **Exhibitions:** *CIAM Exhibition,* Athens, 1934; *Housing Exhibition,* Grand Palais, Paris, 1934 (travelled to London); *MARS Group Exhibition,* Burlington Gallery, London, 1938; *CIAM Exhibition,* Aix-en-Provence, 1952; *This Is Tomorrow,* Whitechapel Art Gallery, London, 1955; *UIA Sport Buildings Commission,* Moscow, 1968; *Thirties,* Hayward Gallery, London, 1979; *Works I: Ernö Goldfinger,* Architectural Association, London 1983. **Collection:** Royal Institute of British Architects, London. Recipient: Fellow, Royal Institute of British Architect, 1966, and Royal Society of Arts, London, 1968; Associate, 1968, and Academician,

1975, Royal Academy of Art, London; Honorary Member: Association of Hungarian Architects, 1963. *Died* (in London) *15 November 1987.*

Works:

Beauty salon interiors in Grafton Street, London, for Helena Rubinstein Beauty Salons, 1926.

Office interiors in rue Godot de Mauroy, Paris, for Central European Express, 1927.

Exhibition stand at the *British Industries Fair,* Olympia, London, for Alpina Limited, 1928.

Offices and apartment interiors in the rue de Varenne, Paris, for Suzanne Blum, 1930.

Stacking chairs in steel, for Entas, Paris, 1931.

Toy showroom in Endsleigh Street, London, for P. and M. Abbatt Company, 1933.

Kitchen fittings and furniture, for Easiwork, 1935.

Children's section of the British Pavilion, at the World's Fair, Paris, 1937.

Exhibition stand at the *British Industries Fair,* Olympia, London, for ICI Imperial Chemical Industries, 1938.

Shop interiors in Shaftesbury Avenue, London, for S. Weiss, 1951.

Showroom interiors in Albemarle Street, London, for Taylor Woods, 1956.

This Is Tomorrow exhibition layouts, for the Whitechapel Art Gallery, London, 1956.

Office interiors in the Haymarket, London, for the French Government Tourist Office, 1958.

Hille House Offices and showrooms in Watford, Hertfordshire, for Hille and Company, 1960.

Office interiors in Piccadilly, London, for the French Government Tourist Office, 1963.

SNCF Travel Offices in the Champs Elysees, Paris, for the French Government Tourist Office, 1967.

(For a complete list of Goldfinger's buildings and architectural projects, see *Contemporary Architects*)

Publications:

By GOLDFINGER: books—*County of London Plan Explained,* with E. J. Carter, London 1945; *British Furniture Today,* London 1951; articles—in *Pester Lloyd* (Budapest), 8 August 1925, 30 December 1925; *l'Architecture d'Aujourd'hui* (Paris), March 1934, July 1938, September 1950, February 1952, February/March 1960; *Architectural Review* (London), November 1941, December 1941, January 1942, May 1954; *The Architects' Journal* (London), April 1942, March 1943, October 1980; *Architect and Building News* (London), January 1943; *Das Werk* (Zurich), April 1947; *Architectural Design* (London), July 1954; *RIBA Journal* (London), September 1969; *Building Design* (London), 7 March 1975.

On GOLDFINGER: books—*Shops* by Brian and Norman Westwood, London 1937; *Modern Houses in England* by F. R. S. Yorke, London 1944; *British Achievement in Design* by Noel Carrington and Muriel Harris, London 1946; *Gute Moebel/Schoene Raume,* edited by Mia Seeger, Stuttgart 1953; *Public Interiors* by Misha Black, London 1960; *Ernö Goldfinger* by Mate Major, Budapest 1970; *Industrial Design in Britain* by Noel Carrington, London 1976; *Hille: 75 Years of British Furniture* by Sutherland Lyall, London 1981; *Architects' Designs for Furniture* by Jill Lever, London 1982; *Ernö Goldfinger: Works I,* compiled by James Dunnett and Gavin Stamp, London 1983.

Ernö Goldfinger had a remarkably long and successful career. Committed to the ideas of the modern movement, he lived for 50 years with his wife and mother in a house he designed in Willow Road, Hampstead in 1937; it was filled with furniture designed by the architect and with paintings by Max Ernst and Amédée Ozenfant. The Paris he knew in the 1920s left a deep impression on his attitudes and taste. He met and socialised with Ernst and Fernand Léger at the Café du Dôme and visited the 1925 Paris International Exposition with Adolf Loos, who encouraged Goldfinger to visit London. There, in 1926, he designed the now-destroyed beauty salon for Helena Rubenstein in Grafton Street. Shopfronts in England were rather conventional at this time, largely as Goldfinger recalls, done up in sage green paint or fake Queen Anne like Fortnum and Mason's; in that context, his sparse, steel-and-glass design was a shock. Sage's, then the biggest shopfitters in London, commissioned to do the work, felt so sorry for Goldfinger, assuming that his lack of decoration indicated an inability to draw, that they added some details. Nevertheless, the final design was admired, particularly by C. H. Reilly who printed a photograph in the *Architectural Review*.

Returning to Paris, Goldfinger worked on shop and apartment interiors, very modern in taste, usually with furniture to his own designs. But in the early 1930s he came to England to build a practice. Some of the early commissions obtained there included a toy shop and toy designs for P. A. Abbatt in Wimpole Street and unit furniture for the Canadian kitchen-furniture manufacturer Easiwork. After the war, he designed exhibition kiosks for the 1951 Festival of Britain, then developed work as an exhibition designer, most notably for the famous 1956 *This is Tomorrow* exhibition, which showed the work of more than thirty of Britain's avant-garde artists, architects, and designers. He also continued to design furniture, most of which actually extended his architectural work. In 1951, he published a small book, *British Furniture Today*, which offers a good idea of his design philosophy and a number of rare photographs of his own work. The book particularly indicates that his design interests were in tune with those of the period, including interchangeable parts, unit furniture, small-scale pieces, new technology, and a concern for the growing awareness of ergonomics. Goldfinger quotes widely from the pioneer ergonomic study by Bengt Akerblom, *Standing and Sitting Posture* (1948), and many of his chairs explore ergonomic devices such as self-adjusting backs.

—Catherine McDermott

GONZALEZ RUIZ, Guillermo.
Argentinian architectural, exhibition and graphic designer. Born in Cascomus, Buenos Aires Province, 18 March 1937. Educated at the Colegio Nacional, Buenos Aires, until 1955; studied architecture and city planning, under Gaston Breyer and Wladimiro Acosta, at the University of Buenos Aires, 1957–65: Dip. Arch. 1965. Married Maria Solanas in 1966 (divorced, 1980); children: Diego, Caroline and Pablo. Freelance designer, establishing first graphics studio with architect Mario Wainstein, in Buenos Aires, 1959–62; staff designer, 1962–64, art director, 1967–68, at Agens Stu-

dio, Buenos Aires; designer, with Cicero Studio, Buenos Aires, 1968–69; partner, with Ronald Shakespear, of Ruiz and Shakespear design studio, Buenos Aires, 1969–73; freelance designer, with own graphic and architectural design studio, Buenos Aires, from 1973: director of design, Municipality of Buenos Aires, 1971–73. **Exhibitions:** Kunstmuseum, Cologne, 1968; Stedelijk Museum, Amsterdam, 1968; Applied Arts Biennale, Montevideo, 1969; Cali Graphics Biennale, Colombia, 1972; Brno Graphics Biennale, Czechoslovakia, 1973, 1975, 1977, 1979; Lapiz de Plata Awards Exhibition, Buenos Aires, 1982. **Collections:** Stedelijk Museum, Amsterdam; Museo de la Ciudad de Mar del Plata, Argentina. Recipient: National Poster Competition Prize, Buenos Aires, 1957, 1960, 1962, 1963; National Symbol and Logotype Competition Awards, Buenos Aires, 1966, 1967, 1971, 1973; Lapiz de Plata Prize, Buenos Aires, 1982. Address: Ricardo Rojas 401, piso 13°, 1001 Buenos Aires, Argentina.

Works:

Graphic identity programme, for the Banco de la Ciudad de Buenos Aires, 1970.
Sign system, for the city of San Juan, 1971.
Sign system, for the city of Buenos Aires, 1971–73.
Argentine regional offices sign system, for the Banco de Italie y Rio de la Plata, 1975–77.
Urban sign system, for Planta Aluar, Puerto Rico, 1976.
Airport buildings sign system and graphic identity, for Austral S.A., Buenos Aires, 1977–78.
Corporate identity programme, for Credibanco, Buenos Aires, 1978.
Corporate identity programme, for Carta Credencial, Buenos Aires, 1978.
Point-of-sales visual identity programme, for Vinilia Wallpapers, 1979.
Graphic sign system, for the Naval Hospital, Buenos Aires, 1980–81.
Plant and workshops sign systems, for Serenisima, Buenos Aires, 1983.

Publications:

By GONZALEZ RUIZ: books—*Sistema de Senales Urbanas de la Ciudad de Buenos Aires*, Buenos Aires 1972; *Sistema de Identificacion Visual de la Municipalidad de la Ciudad de Buenos Aires*, Buenos Aires 1972; *Sistema Tipo de Senalamiento Urbano y Edilicio*, Buenos Aires 1975; articles—in *Summa* (Buenos Aires), no. 1, 1963, no. 16, 1964, no. 28, 1965, no. 50, 1970; *Nuestra Arquitectura* (Buenos Aires), no. 42, 1973; *Graphic Design* (Tokyo), March 1980.

On GONZALEZ RUIZ: books—*Modern Publicity*, London 1976, 1978; *Top Symbols and Trademarks of the World*, Milan 1977, 1978; *Archigraphia: Architectural and Environmental Graphics*, edited by Walter Herdeg, Zurich 1978.

The beginning of my expressive and intellectual development acknowledges various influences:
1) My teachers of the School of Architecture (1957–65). My visual formation is essentially architectural. In school, I learned systematic thought. The rational structure of my thinking is the result of experience at the university, where I learned to think in terms of form and acquired my basic visual cultivation. My first, brilliant teacher was titular professor of vision Gastón Breyer, who introduced me to the psychology of form, to Köler, to Kofka, to the *Gestalt* conception, and to the theory of color. In

the architectural composition class of another beloved teacher, Wladimiro Acosta, now deceased, I learned to use my projectual mechanism, which I later transferred to graphic design. There, I essentially redeemed the humanist sense of design.
2) Publicity agencies (1962–67). There, I learned graphic work and the processes of composition, photoengraving, and printing. I began my apprenticeship at Agens (1962–64) and was at Agens again in 1967 as art director. Though this work was a valuable aid to my learning, I believe I was at this stage experiencing autodidactic growth. Because of the influences and experiences I have mentioned, I consider myself a graphic architect, and not a graphic designer and architect. This process of synthesis demanded a lot of effort for ten years (1960–70), and I got through it with the help of analytic therapy, not without first going through periods of anguish, confusion, frustration, and doubt. The second decade (1970–80) and the beginning of the third found me solid and sure of my convictions (not vocational, because I've had a visual vocation since childhood. When I was nine years old I won a first place prize in drawing. I refer to those that channeled my career toward a particular area of graphic design: systematic design, that is to say, the systems of visual identification and of municipal and urban signage).
3) The Argentine architects (1963–70). The first of these, Carlos Mendez Mosquera, was my initial life-model. He belonged to the generation before mine and was skilled in the graphic-architectural areas that attracted me. Although he wasn't practicing design, he possessed a visual culture that was for me, at that time, undeveloped. I was acquainted with him at Agens in 1964, he gave me work at Cicero, and he financed Shakespear and me during the first months of our independent study (1968). He gave me an assistantship and exposed me to the journal he had just established—*Summa*—so that I could make my first notes about design. All these things he did in order to connect me with the outstanding architects both of the previous generation and of my own. I'm very grateful to Mendez Mosquera for the things he did for me between 1964 and 1968, and I'm grateful to all the architects who in the subsequent years made it possible for me to exercise my expression and enrich my learning.
4) Graphic designers (1960–70). The graphic designers that influenced my work in the first formative stage were Juan Carlos Distefano, Franco Grignani, Silvio Coppola, Joseph Müller-Brockmann, Armin Hofmann, Alan Fletcher, Bob Gill, Heinz Edelman, and Saul Bass. They all possessed that balance of freedom and order, of intuition and rationalism that is so important in graphic expression.
5) My colleagues and collaborators (1969–73). Among the first, I want to mention Ronald Shakespear, with whom I spent two years at Agens and six as an associate in our common study. Gifted with a solid graphic vision, he is a strong defender of the idea-object as generator of all work. By working closely with him on many projects, I embraced the concept of synthesis and strength in graphism. Gabriel Ezcurra Náon, with whom I collaborated for ten years (1970–80) influenced me with his extreme perfectionism in graphic drawing, his silent and invaluable contribution to the final execution of the design and to the constant force in graphic work.
My work as a graphic architect displays particular traits and tendencies: (1) a structuralist conception of graphics, whether two- or three-dimensional. (2) the predominance of formal conceptions based on pure geometric forms. (3) the frequent use of point and line as generator of graphism. (4) the constant seeking for visual

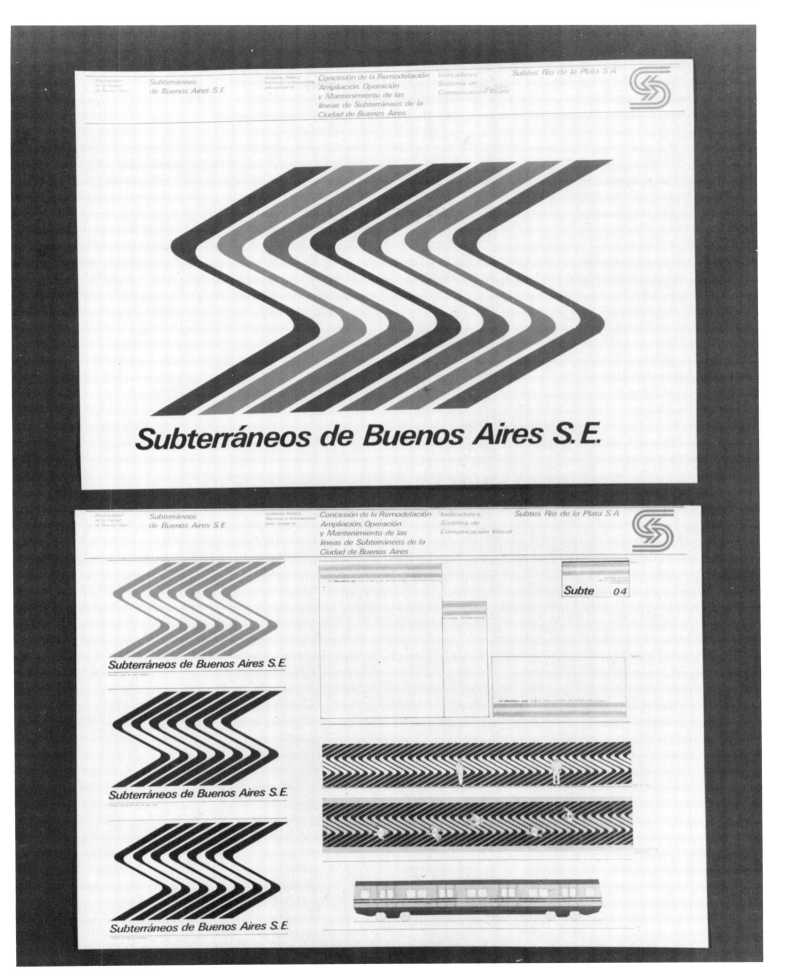

Guillermo Gonzalez Ruiz: Logotype for the Buenos Aires Metro, 1980

potential and synthesis (the tendency the Kepes calls optic scandal). (5) the frequent intention of the balance of form and function, product of a rationalist ideology that I maintain in spite of the new post-modernist esthetic tendencies. Though these are the predominant characteristics of my work, they themselves don't imply a contribution. The distinctive characteristics perhaps should be looked for within the specific sign design project because it is through spatial and material graphics that I have been able to integrate the graphic and architectural components. Signage is for me the visual transcription of the circulatory structures of cities or buildings. Because of this, my ideas for signage systems are based on previous knowledge of the flow of vehicles, persons, and things and on the spatial and constructive nature of the environment where the signage is to be.

I conceive of signage as part of municipal or urban equipment, and this approach induces me to look always for ideas linked to the spatial aspect of the signs. That is why there are these: structures of circular pipe sections in the project for Buenos Aires (to go along with the semaphore and luminaries of the city). For the same reason, the signs of Aluar are of premolded concrete, and those of a commercial gallery are of crystal, due to the fact that its roof is transparent. And the signs of the central market are trapezoidal, like the many doors of its pavilion. And the signals of the San Isidro Hippodrome are rectangular with curved corners, because that is the predominant shape there, from the racetrack to the roof and columns. And the constructive system of the Pediatric Hospital is interchangeable letter for letter because the entire place has a kind of freedom and total interchangeability.

I sincerely believe that herein lies my most significant contribution—graphic-industrial design plans that revolve around the environment in which the objects are to be placed. To project any system of signage, before looking at the paper, I look at the space. Because of this, in my trajectory I can't differentiate the projects by their magnitude, scale, transcendence, or popularity. The approximately fifty systems developed are, independently of their degree of complexity, true expressions of the optic by which my plans are governed. Logically, those that stand out the most are "the big ones," but at times, those aren't exactly the ones that reflect that integrative conception to which I have referred. On the other hand, one project practically unknown, the signage for the Club Hípico in Uruguay, is a symbol for me of my governing ideas: it integrates a series of wood signs composed of horizontal slabs that connote jumping hurdles.

Another possible contribution of my work could be in the spatial, rather than planar, conception of the signs. That is what permitted me to come up with a proposal for Buenos Aires' street signs. It answers with only four joined plaques the most diverse questions about traffic, nomenclature, and numbering. I confess that even now, after twelve years, I continue seeing it as a good proposal. I believe that its massive and indiscriminate diffusion in all the cities of the country, and in Uruguay, Paraguay, and Chile is not accidental. Its surprisingly widespread use should surely not be attributed only to the commercial interest of the sign factories, but to the fact that it resolves the urban street-sign problem. And the third possible contribution could be in my firm belief in using a technological language that grows as a result of the use of national productive processes and materials, and not as a transference of external experiences to local industrial reality.

—Guillermo Gonzalez Ruiz

More than a designer of signage or of visual identities, Guillermo Ruiz is a designer of systems. He devises the macro-structures that establish order, categorize information, and integrate the systems' elements on the basis of sub-ordinations. In his signage system for the Argentinian Social Welfare housing programs, signs link highway access to apartments through five categories of information coded in clear steps. Sub-codes are used within some of those categories to meet different needs.

He designs as a city planner, understanding sign systems as the visual transcription of circulation patterns, where the elements appear as extensions of the architectural environment. Examples of this are the signage for Buenos Aires, for the Aluar aluminum plant, and for the San Isidro Racing Track, where the signage furniture in each case relates to the specific architectural characteristics of the environment.

The individual components of his systems are frequently adopted by other users, as was the signage for the city of Buenos Aires. (That was massively, and often not too wisely, taken over by other cities.) In this system, four metal plates attached to a tubular column display the name of the street, the range of address numbers of the corresponding blocks, and the direction of circulation for vehicles. Appropriate sizing and placing satisfy the needs of the drivers without obstructing pedestrian circulation or overloading the visual environment.

In the 1960s Gonzalez Ruiz worked on graphic products in a variety of areas, including promotion for consumer products and for cultural activities, corporate identities, and film graphics (in Agens, possibly the most inventive advertising agency that ever existed in South America, in Cicero, and in his own studio with Shakespear). In this work, he showed a visual power reminiscent of Müller-Brockmann, Hofmann, Distefano, Coppola, or Bass, particularly in the poster, in the use of strong scale-contrast in typography, and in an expressive but structural use of form and figure-ground relationships. In the 1970s, he concentrated on visual identity programs and signage systems.

Simplicity of form, clarity of language, adjustment in the detail, and integration with the environment are characteristics of Gonzalez Ruiz's present design production, an excellent example of design that works, without imposing itself distractingly between the message and the user.

—Jorge Frascara

GORELIK, Mordecai.

American playwright, stage and film designer. Born in Shchedrin, Minsk Province, Russia, 25 August 1899; emigrated to the United States in 1905: naturalized, 1909. Educated at Boys' High School, Brooklyn, New York, until 1917; studied at the Pratt Institute, Brooklyn, New York, 1918–20; apprenticed at Neighborhood Playhouse and Provincetown Players, New York, 1920–22; studied stage design, under Robert Edmond Jones, Norman Bel Geddes and Serge Soudeikin, in New York, 1920–30. Served in the United States Student Army Corps, 1917, the Office of War Information, 1944, and as theatre consultant to the United States Military Government in Germany, 1949. Married Frances Strauss in 1935 (died, 1966); children: Eugene and Linda; married Lorraine

Kable in 1972. Scene painter and technician, with Provincetown Players, New York, 1920–21; freelance designer, New York, from 1924; also sketch artist and film production designer, working for Metro-Goldwyn-Mayer, 20th Century-Fox, Republic and RKO Pictures, in Hollywood, California, from 1944. Instructor and designer, School of the Theatre, New York, 1921–22; American Academy of Dramatic Arts, New York, 1926–32; research professor in theatre, 1960–72, and professor emeritus from 1972, Southern Illinois University, Carbondale. Visiting lecturer: New School for Social Research, New York, 1940–41; Biarritz American University, France, 1945–46; New York University, and University of Toledo, Ohio, 1956; University of Hawaii and University of Miami, 1958; Bard College, Annandale-on-Hudson, New York, 1959; Brigham Young University, Provo, Utah, 1961; California State University, Los Angeles, 1964; San Jose State University, California, 1965; Buffalo State College, New York, 1967; University of Massachusetts, Boston, 1972; University of Southern California, Los Angeles, 1975. Sponsor, ACTF Mordecai Gorelik Award, 1981; American Theatre Association Fellowship, from 1982; Southern Illinois University Mordecai Gorelik Award, from 1983. **Exhibitions:** *International Theatre Scenic Exhibition,* London, 1925 (toured); Bourgeois Galleries, New York, 1926; *International Scenic Exhibition,* New York, 1927; Harvard Society, Cambridge, Massachusetts, 1932; Montclair Art Museum, New Jersey, 1932; Architectural League, New York, 1932; *International Theatre Arts Exhibition,* New York, 1934; Pratt Institute, Brooklyn, New York, 1936; McCord Theatre Museum, Dallas, Texas, 1936; *International Exhibition of Theatrical Art,* Vienna, 1936. **Collection:** Morris Library Special Collections, Southern Illinois University, Carbondale. Recipient: Guggenheim Fellowship, New York, 1936, 1937; Rockefeller Foundation Grant, New York, 1946, 1950; Fulbright Fellowship, Washington, D.C., 1962; Theta Alpha Phi Award, 1971; United States Institute for Theatre Technology Award, 1981. Member: American Theatre Association; Speech Communication Association. *Died* (in Sarasota, Florida) *7 March 1990.*

Works:

Stage designs include (in New York unless otherwise indicated)—*King Hunger,* Players Club, Philadelphia, 1924; *Processional,* for the Theatre Guild, Garrick Theatre, 1925; *Last Love,* Schildkraut Theatre, Bronx, New York, 1926; *Nirvana,* Greenwich Village Theatre, 1926; *The Moon is a Gong,* Cherry Lane Theatre, 1926; *Loudspeaker,* 52nd Street Theatre, 1927; *The Final Balance,* Provincetown Playhouse, 1928; *God, Man and the Devil,* Yiddish Art Theatre, 1928; *Uncle Moses,* Yiddish Art Theatre, 1930; *1931,* Mansfield Theatre, 1931; *Success Story,* Maxine Elliott's Theatre, 1932; *Big Night,* Maxine Elliott's Theatre, 1933; *Little Ol' Boy,* Playhouse, 1933; *Men in White,* Broadhurst Theatre, 1933; *All Good Americans,* Henry Miller's Theatre, 1933; *Gentlewoman,* Cort Theatre, 1934; *Sailors of Cattaro,* Civic Repertory Theatre, 1934; *Mother,* Civic Repertory Theatre, 1935; *The Young Go First,* Park Theatre, 1935; *Golden Boy,* Belasco Theatre, 1937; *Tortilla Flat,* Henry Miller's Theatre, 1938; *Casey Jones,* Fulton Theatre, 1938; *Thunder Rock,* Mansfield Theatre, 1938; *Rocket to the Moon,* Belasco Theatre, 1939; *The Quiet City,* Belasco Theatre, 1939; *Night Music,* Broadhurst Theatre, 1940; *Walk Into My Parlor,* Sayville, New York 1941; *Volpone,* Actors Laboratory Theatre, Los Angeles, 1944

Mordecai Gorelik: Set design for John Howard Lawson's *Processional*, Garrick Theatre, New York, 1925

(also costume designer; and at Biarritz American University, France, 1946; Rooftop Theatre, New York 1957; Southern Illinois University, Carbondale, 1980, also director); *Doctor Knock*, Biarritz American University, France, 1945 (also director); *All My Sons*, Coronet Theatre, 1947; *Paul Thompson Forever*, Actors Laboratory Theatre, Los Angeles, 1947 (also author and director); *Desire under the Elms*, American National Theatre and Academy, 1952; *Danger, Men Working!*, Circle Workshop, Los Angeles, 1952 (also director); *Saint Joan*, Playhouse, Wilmington, Delaware, 1954 (toured the United States); *The Flowering Peach*, Belasco Theatre, 1954; *A Hatful of Rain*, Lyceum Theatre, 1955; *Born Yesterday*, University of Toledo, Ohio 1956 (also director); *The Sin of Pat Muldoon*, Cort Theatre, 1954; *Plough and the Stars*, Barbizon Plaza Theatre, 1956 (also director); *Guests of the Nation*, Theatre Marquee, 1958; *A Distant Bell*, Eugene O'Neill Theatre, 1960; *The Dybbuk*, Brigham Young University, Provo, Utah, 1961 (also director; and at San Jose State College, California, 1965; Southern Illinois University, Carbondale, 1971); *The Annotated Hamlet*, Southern Illinois University, Carbondale, 1961 (also director); *The House of Bernarda Alba*, Southern Illinois University, Carbondale, 1962 (also director); *Marseilles*, Southern Illinois University, Carbondale, 1963 (also director); *The Good Woman of Setzuan*, Southern Illinois University, Carbondale, 1964 (also director); *The Firebugs*, California State University, Los Angeles, 1964 (also translator and director, and at Southern Illinois University, Cardondale, 1965); *Rainbow Terrace*, Southern Illinois University, Carbondale, 1966 (also author and director; and at Ghost Ranch, New Mexico, 1983); *Andrus and the Image*, Kansas State University, Manhattan, 1977 (also author; and at East Central University, Ada, Oklahoma, 1979); films, as production designer include *Days of Glory*, 1944; *Our Street*, 1944 (not produced); *Salt to the Devil*, Plantagenet Films, London, 1949; *L'Ennemi Publique no. 1/The Most Wanted Man*, Cité Films, France, 1954; *None But the Lonely Heart*, 1955.

Publications:

By GORELIK: books—*New Theatres for Old*, New York 1940, 1962, 1975, London 1947; *Paul Thompson Forever* (one-act play), Boston 1950; *Biedermann and the Firebugs* by Max Frisch, translator, in *Masters of Modern Drama*, edited by M. Block and Robert G. Shedd, New York 1962, as *The Firebugs*, New York 1963, 1980, reprinted in *Best Short Plays of the World Theatre*, edited by Stanley Richards, New York 1968, and in *Classics of Modern Thought: Vol. III; The Modern World*, New York 1980; *The Big Day* (one-act play) in *Best Short Plays 1977*, edited by Stanley Richards, New York 1978; *Rainbow Terrace* (one-act play) in *Wrestling with God*, New Orleans 1984; *Toward a Larger Theatre* (7 plays), privately printed, Smithtown, New York 1984.

On GORELIK: articles—"The Work of Mordecai Gorelik" by Djuna Barnes in *Theatre Guild* (New York), February 1931; "Plough and the Stars" in *Variety* (Hollywood, California), 11 April 1956; "Dramatist Raps 'Absurd Trend' " by Barbara Huddard in the *Denver Post* (Colorado), 21 April 1965; "Theatre: The Search" by Leonard Radic in *The Age* (Melbourne, Australia), 3 October 1967.

Unlike many of the other famous designers of his generation in the United States, Mordecai Gorelik was far more influenced by the ideas behind the development of new theatrical forms than by painting, decorating, or purely visual sources. From the beginning, he wanted his settings to speak to the audience's mind as well as its eye, and he was strongly attracted to plays of ideas that demanded a presentational style. Though he studied and apprenticed with Robert Edmond Jones, Norman Bel Geddes, and Serge Soudeikin, his personal style is closer to that of the Living Newspaper and Epic Theatre, and he has had a lifelong allegiance to Bertolt Brecht's production methods. This devotion to the presentational ideas behind a stage setting led him to shun beautiful, moody pictures in favor of sets that underlined and projected the message

behind the action of a play. His sketches have never been beautiful works of art; they are idea-sketches that state the visual facts of a production very directly.

Though he made his early reputation in the 1930s when Jo Mielziner and Donald Oenslager were also becoming major design figures on Broadway, Gorelik did not participate in their impressionistic symbolism or realism but reached ahead to the new presentational styles inherent in the theatre of ideas. Thus, even in his sixties, he could be an innovator, as he was when he brought to the United States his own adapted translation of a famous absurdist drama, *The Firebugs*, which he co-directed off-Broadway. His keen intellect made him an ideal teacher and writer, and he made many contributions to the development of younger designers through his book, articles, and his many faculty positions held throughout the United States. Thus, his contribution, like that of the fine artists from the years just before World War I until the beginning of the 1960s, has been in the area of intellectual abstraction, presenting the relativity of realities on stage. Probably the key source of his visual thinking, as with so many other artists of his persuasion, has been the college, and we are indebted to him for bringing us the ideas of Brecht and Piscator when they were still little-known theatrical names.

—Douglas A. Russell

GÓROWSKI, Mieczyslaw.
Polish graphic and industrial designer. Born in Milkowa, Novy Sacz, 4 February 1941. Educated at Milkowa Primary School, and Tarnow Secondary School of Fine Arts, 1948–59; studied interior design, painting under Waclaw Taranczewski, and industrial design under An-

drzej Pawlowski, at the Academy of Fine Arts, Krakow, 1959–66: MA 1966. Married Ewa Giza in 1960. Freelance designer, Krakow, from 1969: worked with the Research Center of the Metal Products Industry, Krakow, 1969–78; has concentrated on theatre posters since 1975. Assistant to Andrzej Pawlowski, 1966–69, lecturer in industrial design, 1971–81, and independent lecturer from 1981, Academy of Fine Arts, Krakow. **Exhibitions:** *Polish Poster Biennale,* Katowice, 1969, 1973, 1975, 1977, 1979, 1981; *International Poster Biennale,* Warsaw, 1970, 1972, 1976, 1978, 1980; *Graphics and Posters from Krakow,* Cultureel Centrum, Venlo, 1975; Polish Academy of Science Centre, Paris, 1977; University Library, Caen, 1978; Poets' Club, Paris, 1978; *Designing for Children,* Warsaw, 1979; *Polish Graphics and Posters,* Kamakura Municipal Museum, Japan, 1980; Poster Gallery, Warsaw, 1980; *Kunstler aus Krakau '80,* Staatstheater, Darmstadt, 1980; Galerie Chabin, Paris, 1981; Galerija Schody, Krakow, 1981; University of Illinois, Urbana-Champaign, 1981; Castle of Breton Princes, Nantes, 1982. **Collections:** Academy of Fine Arts, Krakow; Poster Museum, Warsaw; Lahti Poster Museum, Finland; Kungliga Dramatiska Theatern, Stockholm; Musée de l'Affiche, Paris; Centre Georges Pompidou, Paris; Bibliothèque Forney, Paris; Museum of Modern Art, New York. Recipient: Krakow Poster Biennale Grand Prize, 1969; Krakow Folklore Poster Competition Prize, 1974, 1975; Publicity Award, Krakow, 1976; Poster of the Year Award, Krakow, 1976, 1977, 1979; Polish Ministry of Culture and Art Award, 1979; Katowice Poster Biennale Award, 1981; Poster Collectors Club Award, Poznan, 1983. Member, Polish Artists' Union, 1966; Polish Ecological Club, 1980. Address: ul. Slomiana 4/23, 30–316 Krakow, Poland.

Publications:

By GÓROWSKI: articles—in *Wiadomosci IWP* (Warsaw), February/March 1977; *Gazeta Poludniowa* (Krakow), no. 257, 1980; *Form und Zweck* (Berlin), August 1980, February 1981.

On GÓROWSKI: books—*Interdesign '71 ICSID,* Minsk 1971; *Grafiek en Poster uit Krakau,* exhibition catalogue, Venlo 1975; *Polish Graphics and Posters,* exhibition catalogue, Kamakura 1980; *Künstler aus Krakau '80,* exhibition catalogue, Darmstadt 1980; *M. Górowski's Posters* by Anna Szpor-Weglarska, Warsaw 1980.

I agree with the opinions of some critics who suggest that in contemporary times the poster has taken on the role of "commissioned art." Such a role was held years ago by painting, sculpture, or graphics, when they were created mainly by order of great and powerful people or by order of the Church. Subjects (e.g., portraits) were very often settled from the beginning. The artist had the possibility of realizing his own creative attitude only within the framework of a given subject, which had to be treated very respectfully.

The case of today's poster is similar, especially if it is designed for an artistic purpose. By that, I mean posters for certain theatrical productions, films, exhibitions, concerts, etc. In such situations, the poster is realized through the designer's personal experience and understanding, and so, poster art appears to be on the border between pure and applied art. Poster artists should have personal, potential possibilities for creative performance and should be fluent in the rules of designing for utilitarian conditions. They should know visual communication, the technology of the graphic processes, etc.

My choice of direction within artistic activity was probably caused by the character of the studies and their variety at the Academy of Fine Arts in Kraków. Humanism is the leading idea I try to realize in poster design.

The Humanistic idea lights my teaching in the Department of Industrial Design at the Academy of Fine Arts in Kraków. Choosing the subjects and leading the didactic process, I try to support the evolution of creative attitudes in young designers by means of humanistic values and to block technocratic attitudes. The subjects which serve this aim are, for example, designing for crippled people who need medical care or rehabilitation—didactic toys, rehabilitative toys, etc. This aim is also served by a deep penetration into folk art—native and foreign material culture—with its truthful wisdom and symbiotic connection with nature. I am deeply convinced that there is a great need to replace the priority of the technological trend—which

governs the contemporary world—with the humanistic trend.

—MieczysŁaw Górowski

MieczysŁaw Górowski made his debut with graphic works that he composed for local cultural events and festivals, works being more of a decorative than of informative value on a mass scale. However, he proved that his eye was not trained in vain in the visual communication workshop, where he had acquired skill in defining signs or ideograms. And certainly, he must have been also well acquainted with the psychology of perception, ergonomics, and anthropotechnics. He was aware that the task of a designer is different from that of an illustrator. Trained in methods of designing, in solving each problem through reasoning, analysing the usefulness and the function of each single product—a machine or a print, a working envi-

Mieczyslaw Gorowski: *Euripides* poster, for the Slovak Theatre, Krakow, 1976

ronment or a living space—Górowski used methods of abstraction. He treated the poster, and righly so, as an industrial product. Accordingly, he concentrated his attention on the language of message-semantics, syntactics, and pragmatics, exploring the relations between shape and meaning as well as between the graphic representation and the anticipated reaction of the recipient.

In order to avoid a narrative approach, he operated with a highly objective, abstract form, with an archetype of the concept, abstract though not totally free of its informative aspect. However, a sign, even when having the form of a segment of the rainbow, of a circle, or of an isolated letter, must convey some meaning, so that it is not reduced to a mere ornament. This is what Górowski always kept in mind, along with another design doctrine—reliance on the module system and, resulting from it, combinatory sets. Górowski's first posters to appear on the walls of Kraków were so designed that, without additional cost, they could be turned into a series of repeating pictures to intensify the perception. For instance, the poster "Peoples' Holiday" (1972) constituted a graphic rhythm formed with multiple, crisscrossing vertical lines, resembling furrows in the soil, and horizontal lines. He also sought humor, as in his poster "Days of Cracow" (1973) which presents the image of a legendary dragon in the form of a pull-apart toy. The trunk of the dragon, divided into segments and printed on separate sheets of paper, could be freely extended.

The convention of the poster as an impersonal symbol, with emotional tones reduced to minimum, satisfied Górowski only in the initial stage of his creative work. Since the mid 1970s the influence of constructivism, of geometric abstraction, and of Optical art has diminished in his work. Also, his designing has been less associated with posters. One critic described this new period as "a change from design to painting methods, from rationalism to romanticism." Suddenly, this artist became aware of the limitations of the symbol system and of the monotony of its repertoire. He was not able to express himself in it well enough. He found himself as if enclosed in a corset of doctrine, and, in order to get out of it, he had to replace the abstraction with a representation, with pictorial form. This probably suited his visual temperament and his narrative imagination, which had been subdued and restrained so far. When he was offered the opportunity to collaborate with Kraków's J. Słowacki Theater, one of the oldest dramatic theaters in Poland, he decided to express himself in a different visual language, semantically and formally richer, while designing its posters and, later, those for other theaters.

In this city, where since the period of "Young Poland" (art noveau), posters had traditionally been painted by great artists, such as Wyspiański, Frycz, Axentowicz, Mehoffer, suddenly something fresh appeared. The originality of Górowski's visual language was contained in his meaningful, intriguing, artfully designed metaphors that often could be immediately and directly unravelled. The metaphor, though discreet in its expression, set forth commentary on the given drama or the opinion of the poster's author. At the same time, it emphasized the play and its moral message.

A task of this type required changes in formal means, in technology of designing. Thus, his posters were given a new quality; the mood of the picture was created by the texture, with subtle variations of the structure: a wall, a piece of board or stone, a fabric, an eroded rock, flesh, rust, or feathers. Monochromatic textures in hushed tones of grey or brown instill a kind of atmosphere, a blanket from under which shapes

and fragments of human body, objects, and accessories emerge. To achieve this, Górowski has used photography as an initial substance, which he transforms until he has obtained a uniform picture surface.

—Szymon Bojko

GOTTSCHALK AND ASH INTERNATIONAL.

International environmental, graphic, packaging and corporate design group; Founded by Fritz Gottschalk (born 1937) and Stuart B. Ash (born 1942) in Montreal, 1966; established offices in Toronto, 1970, in New York, 1978, and in Zurich 1979. Other current principals: Kenneth Carbone (born 1951), partner from 1978; Leslie Smolan (born 1952), partner from 1980; Peter Steiner (born 1944), partner from 1971; Michael Friedland (born 1952), associate from 1980; Tiit Telmet (born 1942), partner from 1978; Peter Adam (born 1947), partner from 1978; Les Holloway (born 1949), associate from 1981. The firm has provided corporate, environmental, graphic, packaging and design management programmes for Alusuisse, American Stock Exchange, Anca Inc., Bank of Nova Scotia, Ciba-Geigy, Canadian Pacific Enterprises, Contraves AG, Government of Canada, GTE Corporation, Hudson's Bay Company, Maclean Hunter Limited, Northern Telecom, Royal Bank of Canada, Syntex, etc. **Exhibitions:** Mead Library of Ideas, New York, 1967; National Gallery of Canada, Ottawa, 1969; Museum of Fine Arts, Montreal, 1970; Container Corporation of America, Chicago, 1975. Addresses: 2050 rue Mansfield, Montreal, Quebec H3A 1Z3, Canada; 322 King Street West, Toronto, Ontario M5V 1JA, Canada; 170 Fifth Avenue, New York, New York 10010, U.S.A.; Sonnhaldenstrasse 3, 8032 Zurich, Switzerland.

Publications:

On GOTTSCHALK AND ASH: books—*107 Grafici dell'AGI,* with texts by Renzo Zorzi and Franco Grignani, Venice 1974; *Who's Who in Graphic Art,* edited by Walter Amstutz, Dubendorf 1982; articles—in *Graphis* (Zurich), no. 148, 1970; *Communication Arts* (Palo Alto), no. 1, 1973; *Typographische Monatsblatter* (St. Gallen), August/September 1974; *Idea* (Tokyo), January 1975, September 1978, January 1979.

Design is communication. Good design has the power to involve, inform, motivate and sell. It translates emotion into images and creates lasting impressions. How an organization is perceived by all of its audiences depends greatly on the effectiveness of comprehensive design program.

At Gottschalk and Ash International, we believe design must reflect the best basic qualities of each organization, product, or personality. It must speak to the public directly and clearly, yet with great imagination to attract and hold attention.

Because communication requirements are unique and specific audiences, unlike any other, we have assembled a uniquely broad range of design talents and management skills. Each of our offices provides complete design and project coordination services that include a thor-

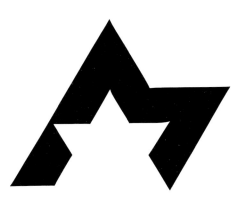

Gottschalk and Ash International: Canadian National Metric Conversion symbol, 1973

ough understanding of local markets as well as access to our international design network. Within each office are the resources to solve corporate identity programs, consumer packaging, environmental design programs, annual reports and print communication.

At Gottschalk and Ash International, we consciously plan not to become unifaceted in any given area of design or with a specific client mix. We pride ourselves on our multidisciplinary approach to all areas of design, working with a diverse range of clients, both large and small, and covering a spectrum of cultural, institutional, and corporate organizations. The firm has a commitment to the design community, and many associates are involved in teaching, lecturing, and judging or working with design organizations, fostering the future of good design.

—Gottschalk and Ash International

Gottschalk and Ash International was formed in Montreal in 1966 by Fritz Gottschalk, a Swiss-born designer, and Stuart Ash, a Canadian specializing in typography. The firm's constant, strong affiliation with Swiss design is evident not only stylistically in their flat, graphic, and precise forms, but also in their rigorous research methods, high level of integration within their programs, and carefully considered applications of their designs. Usually clear and readable, their work has a strong, immediate impact, yet is often lighthearted in tone. Their packaging for various pharmaceutical products made by Anca and Syntex, for example, uses flat shapes in highly saturated, bright colours and simple, clear letter-forms to help remove the medicinal connotations of the products. Their logo designs are versatile, and accompanying manuals outline the various applications possible to the client. A symbol produced in 1981 for Maclean-Hunter, a large Canadian magazine publishing firm, can work alone in some applications or in conjunction with the company name in others. Two zigzag, opposing forces seem to merge as they meet within a two-colour rhomboid, producing a dynamic effect.

The work of Gottschalk and Ash is once rich, yet reductivist, and always contemporary in feeling. At times, though, their programs can be very anonymous in nature, with no human or personal feeling. For example, as designers of the insignia and logo for the Royal Bank of Canada, Gottschalk and Ash also did the interior signage for the Royal Bank Plaza, a downtown office complex built in Toronto in the late 1970s. Their use of Helvetica type throughout this project makes the information very clear but does not alleviate the impersonal, corporate feeling of the environment.

Some would see keeping strictly to a Swiss

approach and style as limiting and monotonous, as a Swiss look is not appropriate for every client or situation. But since Gottschalk and Ash work so frequently for large companies and since their work embodies the best aspects of Swiss design—its clarity, unity and integration of disparate factors, for example—their use of this kind of design seems legitimate. At its best, their work is masterful within the limits of the Swiss method.

—Liz Wylie

GRANGE, Kenneth (Henry).
British industrial and product designer. Born in London, 17 July 1929. Educated at Sir John Cass School, and Wembley Hill Elementary School, London, 1936–44; studied at Willesden School of Arts and Crafts, London, 1944–47. Served as a technical illustrator in the British Army Royal Engineers, 1947–48. Worked as a design assistant, Arcon Chartered Architects, London, 1947; architectural assistant, Bronek Katz and Vaughan, London, 1949–50; designer, with Gordon Bowyer design firm, London, 1950–52, and with Jack Howe and Partners design firm, London, 1952–58; freelance industrial designer, establishing Kenneth Grange Design, London, 1958–71; founder-partner, with Theo Crosby, Alan Fletcher, Colin Forbes and Mervyn Kurlansky, of Pentagram Design partnership, London, from 1972: consultant design director to Wilkinson Sword Company, and to Thorn-EMI major domestic appliances division, since 1982; has designed for Reuters, Plessey, British Rail, Kodak, Kenwood Appliances, Ronson, Morphy Richards, Maruzen, Parker Pens, GEC, Platignum, etc. Industrial design advisor to the Design Council, London, 1979. Master of the Faculty of Royal Designers for Industry, London, 1985–87; President, Chartered Society of Designers, London, 1987–88. **Exhibitions:** Boilerhouse/Victoria and Albert Museum, London, 1983; *Design Since 1945*, Philadelphia Museum of Art, 1983; *Eye for Industry*, Victoria and Albert Museum, London 1986; *New Design for Old*, Boilerhouse/Victoria and Albert Museum, London, 1986. Recipient: ten Design Council Awards, London, 1959–81; Duke of Edinburgh's Elegant Design Award, Council of Industrial Design, London, 1963. Fellow, Society of Industrial Artists and Designers (now Chartered Society of Designers), London, 1959; Royal Designer for Industry, Royal Society of Arts, London, 1969; Honorary Professor, Heriot-Watt University, Edinburgh, 1987. Honorary Doctorates: Royal College of Art, London, 1985; Heriot-Watt University, Edinburgh, 1986. Address: Pentagram Design, 11 Needham Road, London W11 2RP, England.

Works:

44A Camera, for Kodak, 1959.
Parking meter, for Venner, 1960.
Chef food mixer, for Kenwood, 1960.
Milward Courier electric shaver, for Needle Industries, 1963.
Brownie Vecta Camera, for Kodak, 1964.
Window fittings, for Henry Hope and Sons, 1965–67.
Variset hat and coat systems, for A. J. Binns, 1965–70.

Kenneth Grange: *Milward Courier* battery shaver, for Needle Industries, 1963

Chefette handmixer, for Kenwood, 1966.
Mariner instruments, for Taylor Instruments, 1968.
Corporate symbol, typewriters, calculators and sewing machines, for Maruzen, 1968–72.
Instamatic Camera, for Kodak, 1970.
High-speed train exteriors, for British Rail, 1971–73.
Information terminals, for Reuters, 1975.
Pocket Instamatic Camera, for Kodak, 1975.
Royal razor, for Wilkinson Sword, 1977.
Alphatex sign system, for Wood and Wood, 1978.
Parker 25 fountain pen, for Parker Pens, 1979.
Hi-fi speakers, for B & W, 1980.
Electronic parking meter, for GEC, 1982.
Accountant pen, for Platignum, 1983.

Publications:

By GRANGE: books—*Pentagram: The Work of Five Designers,* with Pentagram partners, London 1972; *Living By Design,* with Pentagram partners, London and New York 1978; *Kenneth Grange at the Boilerhouse: An Exhibition of British Product Design,* catalogue edited by Stephen Bayley and Jon Ward, London 1983.

On GRANGE: books—*The Business of Product Design* by James Pilditch and Douglas Scott, London 1965; *Modern Design in Metal* by Richard Steward, London 1979; *Design Since 1945,* edited by Kathryn Hiesinger and George Marcus, Philadelphia and London 1983; *The Conran Directory of Design,* edited by Stephen Bayley, London 1985; *Eye for Industry: Royal Designers for Industry 1936–1986,* exhibition catalogue by Fiona MacCarthy and Patrick Nuttgens, London 1986; *New Design for Old,* exhibition catalogue with texts by Helen Hamlyn, Eric Midwinter and others, London 1986.

Kenneth Grange's concept of the designer's role is one of the most significant aspects of his work and influence. His convictions that product design should be an integral part of the manufacturing process, that the designer is primarily an innovator, and that his authority transcends any narrow specialism have in many cases led to his participation in redevelopment of existing products or creation of the image for a new artifact or technology. For instance, major redevelopment was carried out for the Frister and Rossman 804 sewing machine, for which setting back the main shaft to allow more space in front of the needle exemplifies Grange's fresh approach to component layout. Further, he realigned the ends, so that the machine can be upended and balanced on the handwheel, thus neatly resolving a longstanding servicing problem. For the Post Office's new Confravision studios, Grange created a continuous, L shaped conference table with wings; it unifies the studio, and at the same time, provides camera-viewing space for document display and restricts movement of the participants out of camera range.

Believing that design has social as well as economic function, Grange argues that his emphasis on the consumer's pleasure and satisfaction is an essential element of the designer's responsibility to the manufacturer. These views place Grange squarely within mainstream design thought of the 1960s and 1970s, but the outstanding success of his industrial design practice has lent considerable weight to his arguments and has reinforced the influence of the designer, and particularly the design consultant, in Britain and as far afield as Japan.

While Grange would be the first to deny that industrial design is simply styling, his work has a clearly recognizable visual identity established in the 1960s when the influence of the Italians and of West German companies such as Braun was strong. Close formal links with Italian design can be seen by comparing, for example, Grange's Variset cloakroom hanger system for A. J. Binns (1978) with the Sedia Poeta chair by Gigi Sabadin for Stilwood (both using flat, angular shapes with rounded corners) or again, the nose end of the High Speed Train with Cini Boeri's lamp model 2401 for Stilnovo of Milan. The High Speed Train, the Frister and Rossman 804, and Grange's prize-winning Courier shaver for Milward (1963) all demonstrate his preference for strong, sculptural forms which unify the design. Keeping control areas to a minimum, he uses moulded materials and flush surfaces to promote this effect.

—Karen Moon

GRAPUS.

French graphic design group. Founded by Pierre Bernard (born 1942), Gérard Paris-Clavel (born 1943), and François Miehe (born 1942), in Paris, 1970. Current principals: Pierre Bernard, Gérard Paris-Clavel, Alexander Jordan (born 1947), and Jean-Paul Bacholle (born 1930). Grapus has designed graphics and posters for Secours Populaire Français, Amis de la Terre, Amitiés Franco-Vietnamiennes, Confédération General du Travail, French Communist Party, Renault-Cuincy, Front Démocratique pour le Libération de la Palestine, Festivals of La Rochelle and Avignon, Centre Georges Pompidou, Musée des Arts Decoratifs, Théâtre de la Salamandre, Comédie Française, Radio Lorraine Coeur d'Acier, *La Vie Ouvrière, l'Humanité, La Nouvelle Critique, France Nouvelle, Avant-Garde,* etc.,

since 1970. **Exhibitions:** Comité d'Entreprise de l'Aerospatiale, Chatillon-sous-Bagneux, 1978; Galerie Saluden, Quimper, 1979; *Grapus: l'Image Flottante,* Athens, 1981; Stedelijk Museum, Amsterdam, 1981; *A la Tienne, Estienne,* Ecole Estienne, Paris, 1981; Pecsi Galeria, Pecs, 1982; Dorttya Galeria, Budapest, 1982; Kunstgewerbemuseum, Zurich, 1982; Musée de l'Affiche, Paris, 1982; Forradalmi Museum, Szombathely, 1982; *100 Affiches de Grapus,* Salle de l'Aigalier, Martigues, 1983; Musée des Arts Decoratifs, Lausanne, 1983; Aspen Center of Visual Art, Colorado, 1983. **Collections:** Poster Museum, Vilanov; Museum of Decorative Arts, Prague; Galeria Moravia, Brno; Deutsches Plakatmuseum, Essen; Stedelijk Museum, Amsterdam; Museum of Modern Art, New York; Bibliothèque Nationale, Paris; Musée de l'Affiche, Paris; Bibliothèque Forney, Paris. Recipient: Warsaw Poster Biennale Medals, 1978, 1980; Brno Graphics Biennale Medals and Prizes, 1978, 1980, 1982; Lahti Poster Biennale Awards, 1981, 1983; Colorado Poster Exhibition Prize, 1983. Address: 4 Allée Georges Braque, 93300 Aubervilliers, France.

Publications:

On GRAPUS: books—*Grapus,* exhibition catalogue with text by Alain Weill, Paris 1982; *Images de la Révolte 1965–1975,* with text by Steef Davidson, Paris 1982; *Top Graphic Design* by F. H. K. Henrion, Zurich 1983; articles—in *l'Humanité* (Paris), 11 April 1977; *ATAC Informations* (Paris), no. 96, 1978; *Novum Gebrauchsgraphik* (Munich), August 1979; *Projekt* (Warsaw), August 1979; *The Designer* (London), May 1980; *Idea* (Tokyo), May 1981; *Graphis* (Zurich), no. 213, 1981; *Révolution* (Paris), 30 April 1982; *International Herald Tribune* (Paris), 14 January 1983; *Werbung/Publicité* (Zurich), May 1983; *Direction* (London), March 1987; *Graphics World* (Maidstone), November 1987.

We know once and for all that images are not innocent. We want to show this each time we make one. We give people the opportunity to see the obvious manipulation, the mechanism which produced the emotion. We appeal to their capacity for recognition and to their past expe-

Grapus: Retrospective exhibition poster, for the Musée d'Affiche, Paris, 1982

rience in order to better awaken their critical judgment. We refuse in the mass communication process to consider the public as a mass of consumers or as a public opinion to be manipulated. We want to address everyone, each in *his* or *her* difference, as a "citizen to be moved." But, for this, producers of mass messages—our clients—have to be our accomplices. They must enter into this new and more difficult relationship. It is, thus, by a mutual effort that we can really see that graphic design, rather than simply reflecting power, can truly become an instrument that powers reflection.

—Grapus

Grapus began as an association of three French graphic designers, communists. They were not admen. They have always worked collectively and signed their works as a group. Of the founder-members of the group, two had studied under the renowned Henryk Tomaszewski at Warsaw's Academy of Arts—and the group was fired with the endeavour to cultivate beautiful pictures to change the world, such as they had discovered in Poland. It is a rare thing in the design profession to exchange the well-marked-out future of an illusion-maker for the insecure one of a history-maker. After all, they could have had a good material life working on publicity for tunny fish in mayonnaise or for cars. But they opted for the risky business of fighting against unemployment and for freedom of expression.

As they saw it, the prevailing factor in the production of pictures in France was the promotion of merchandise, the signal-sender not responding to need, but creating it himself in order to conquer a new area of the market. The functional advertisement for a better commodity (one that corresponds better to its utilitarian purpose) had long ceased to exist. One of their difficulties lay in the situation whereby the socio-cultural poster has the marginal status of a squatter. Very few of the unemployed have the means to pay for advertising space. And so, Grapus went for the most sympathetic of established client/sponsors they could find and produced all manner of materials for organizations such as Confédération Générale du Travail, the French Communist Party, the journal *Avant-Garde* and the Théâtre de la Salamandre; they aimed at a constancy of relationship, a continuum instead of just a brief fascination with no future. Their work, too, appeared in various formats: small posters, stickers, stationery, flags, journals, and other economical programmes.

Today, Grapus is not just a group of politically-committed artists or communist semiologists, but artist-communists who want to convey their message at once clearly and subjectively. Having produced more than 1,000 pictures committed to the social and cultural struggle, however, they are aware of a partial irresponsibility on the part of the genuine artist. They believe in Godard's axiom: "This is not a just picture, this is just a picture." Their works, they realize, are freely floating objects, like bottles cast into the sea—but they leave no one indifferent when they reach the opposite shore.

—George Walsh

GRAVES, Michael.
American architect, interior and furniture designer. Born in Indianapolis, Indiana, 9 July

1934. Studied at the University of Cincinnati, Ohio, 1954–58: B.Arch. 1958; Harvard University, Cambridge, Massachusetts, 1958–59: M.Arch. 1959; American Academy, Rome, 1960–62: Prix de Rome; Brunner Fellowship. Worked in the design office of George Nelson, New York, 1962–64; founder-principal, Michael Graves Architect architectural and design firm, Princeton, New Jersey, from 1964. Lecturer, 1962–63, assistant professor, 1963–67, associate professor, 1967–72, and professor of architecture from 1972, Princeton University, New Jersey; visiting fellow, Institute for Architecture and Urban Studies, New York, 1971–72; visiting professor, University of Texas, Austin, 1973, 1974; University of Houston, Texas, 1974, 1978; New School for Social Research, New York, 1975; University of California at Los Angeles, 1977; architect-in-residence, American Academy, Rome, 1979. **Exhibitions:** *40 Under 40*, Architectural League, New York, 1966; *Architecture of Museums*, Museum of Modern Art, New York, 1968; *Five Architects*, Princeton University, New Jersey, 1974 (travelled to Austin, Texas); *The New York Five*, Art Net, London, 1975; *Michael Graves: Projects 1967–76*, Columbia University, New York, 1976; *Beyond the Modern Movement*, Harvard University, Cambridge, Massachusetts, 1977; *Ornament in the Twentieth Century*, Cooper-Hewitt Museum, New York, 1978; *Michael Graves: Progetti 1977–81*, Rome, 1981; *Design Since 1945*, Philadelphia Museum of Art, 1983; *Intuition and the Block Print*, John Nichols Printmakers and Publishers, New York, 1984. Recipient: *Progressive Architecture* Design Award, New York, 1970, 1976, 1977, 1978, 1979; American Institute of Architects National Honor Award, 1975, and Design Award, 1985; Fellow, Society for the Arts, Religion and Culture. Address: 34 Witherspoon Street, Princeton, New Jersey 08540, U.S.A.

Works:

Urban County Nature and Science Museum, Mountainside, New Jersey, 1967.
N.E.S.T. rehabilitation housing, Trenton, New Jersey, 1967–71.
Three murals in Transammonia Inc. offices, New York, 1974.
Mural in the school of architecture, University of Texas, Austin, 1974.
Abrahams Dance Studio, Princeton, New Jersey, 1977.
Mural in the John Witherspoon School, Princeton, New Jersey, 1978.
Newark Museum Children's Museum, New Jersey, 1978.
Furniture showrooms and office in New York and Cleveland, for E. F. Hauserman Corporation, 1978.
San Juan Capistrano Regional Library, California, 1983.
Headquarters building in Louisville, Kentucky, for the Humana Corporation, 1983.
Diane Von Fürstenberg boutique, Fifth Avenue, New York, 1984.

(for a complete list of Graves' buildings and architectural projects, see *Contemporary Architects*)

Publications:

By GRAVES: book—*Michael Graves: Buildings and Projects 1966–81*, New York 1982; articles—in *Journal of Architectural Education* (Washington, D.C.), September 1975, September 1978; *Architectural Design* (London), June 1977, March 1979; *AIA Journal* (Washington,

D.C.), October 1978; *Artsmagazine* (New York), April 1980; *Architectural Record* (New York), June 1980; *Via* (Cambridge, Massachusetts), no. 4, 1980; *Architecture + Urbanism* (Tokyo), December 1982, December 1983; *Connaissance des Arts* (Paris), March 1984.

On GRAVES: books—*40 Under 40*, exhibition catalogue by Robert A. M. Stern, New York 1966; *Five Architects: Eisenman, Graves, Gwathmey, Hejduk, Meier* by Kenneth Frampton and Colin Rowe, New York 1972; *New Directions in American Architecture* by Robert A. M. Stern, New York 1977; *Architectural Monographs 5: Michael Graves* by Alan Colquhoun and others, London 1979; *Collaboration: Artists and Architects* by Barbaralee Diamonstein, New York 1981; *The Conran Directory of Design*, edited by Stephen Bayley, London 1985; *Twentieth Century Design: Furniture* by Penny Sparke, London 1986; *Modern Furniture Classics* by Miriam Stimpson, London 1987; *New American Design* by Hugh Aldersley-Williams, New York 1988.

It is too soon to say whether the environments Michael Graves is now creating will permanently alter our stylistic direction or whether they will testify only to the eclecticism of the 1980s. What can be said is that Graves, first as an architect and then as a designer of interior spaces and furnishing, is currently a force to be reckoned with.

The visual references in his work—"analogies," as Graves calls them—are plain. The forms of Rome and the Renaissance appear often in witty translation whenever structure is, or appears to be, at issue. Furnishings borrow more directly from the stylized forms of the 1930s. However, one may wonder whether even Graves, daring as he seems to be, would have advanced so quickly to such bold combinations had not Robert Venturi plowed the intellectual ground in which Graves' postmodern seed now flourishes. But he probably would have arrived at the scenographic esthetic which is evident in his showroom designs.

In the showroom environments, boundaries are finessed with trompe l'oeil painting and controlled vistas. The techniques can be traced to Rome or to the illusion of the stage. The result should exalt the product, but Graves does his architectural job too well. Rather than gaining importance from their luminous surround, the mass-productions of sponsoring Sunar often seem anticlimactic afterthoughts. This schism between environment and furniture is said to have led Graves to design his own furnishings; and certainly the well-staged outlines of his neo-moderne pieces hold their own against the postmodern backdrop, even in a residential setting (as *Metropolitan Home* proved when it commissioned Graves to transform a boxy apartment). But creating furniture to enhance atmosphere, the architect's traditional means of self-protection, often leads to visually exciting, physically uncomfortable pieces (as Graves, like Frank Lloyd Wright before him, admits). It might be remembered that, historically, styles which have responded only to their own esthetic have not survived outside the museum vignette.

—Reed Benhamou

GRAY, Eileen.
Irish architect, interior, furniture and textile de-

signer. Born at Brownswood, Enniscorthy, County Wexford, 9 August 1879. Studied drawing and painting, at Slade School of Fine Art, London, 1898–1902; lacquerwork, in D. Charles furniture workshops, Soho, London, 1900–02; drawing, at Académie Julian and Académie Colarossi, Paris, 1902–05; lacquerwork and cabinetmaking, with Sugawara, Paris, 1907–14. Served as an ambulance driver, in the French Army, 1914–15. Independent furniture and interior designer from 1908, textile designer from 1910, and architect from 1926, in Paris and southern France: proprietor, with Sugawara, of lacquerwork and furniture studio, in London, 1915–17, and in Paris, 1917–22; director, Jean Desert shop and showrooms, Paris, 1922–30; freelance designer, working mainly on architectural projects with Jean Badovici, in Roquebrune, 1926, in Castellar, 1939–45, and in Paris, 1945–76. **Exhibitions:** *Salon des Artistes Décorateurs,* Paris, 1913, 1922; *Exposition Internationale,* Paris, 1937; Royal Institute of British Architects, London, 1973; *l'Année 1925,* Musee des Arts Décoratifs, Paris, 1976; Victoria and Albert Museum, London, 1979 (travelled to New York). Recipient: Honorary Royal Designer for Industry, Royal Society of Arts, London, 1972; Fellow, Royal Institute of Irish Architects, Dublin, 1973. *Died* (in Paris) *28 November 1976.*

Works:

Suzanne Talbot apartment interiors and furnishings, Rue de Lota, Paris, 1919–22.
Monte Carlo Boudoir, 1923 (project).
Eileen Gray apartment interiors and furnishings, 21 Rue Bonaparte, Paris, 1925–28.
House for an engineer, 1926 (project).
E-1027 (Eileen Gray house) villa and furnishings, Roquebrune, Cap Martin, France, 1927–29 (with Jean Badovici).
Jean Badovici studio and apartment interiors, rue Chateaubriand, Paris, 1930.
Tempe à Pailla (Eileen Gray house) villa and furnishings, Castellar, near Menton, France, 1932–34.
House for two sculptors, 1933 (project).
Tube house, 1937 (project).
Centre des Vacances, 1937 (exhibition project).
Eileen Gray apartment interiors and furnishings, St. Tropez, France, 1939 (destroyed, 1944).
Cultural and Social Centre, 1946–49 (project).

Publications:

By GRAY: article—in *l'Architecture d'Aujourd'hui* (Paris), no. 1, 1930.

On GRAY: books—*Gli Elementi dell'Architettura Funzionale* by Alberto Sartoris, Milan 1932; *Des Canons, des Munitions? Merci: Des Logis . . .* by Le Corbusier, Paris 1938; *Eileen Gray: Designer 1879–1976,* exhibition catalogue by Stewart Johnson, London 1979; *The Conran Directory of Design,* edited by Stephen Bayley, London 1985; *Twentieth Century Design: Furniture* by Penny Sparke, London 1986; *Design Source Book* by Penny Sparke and others, London 1986; *Modern Furniture Classics* by Miriam Stimpson, London 1987.

It is for her originality and her fund of ideas that Eileen Gray is remembered, together with the fact that she was one of the few women working independently in the field of architecture and design in the interwar period. Her interest in lacquer-work led her to settle in Paris (where she had been studying for five years) in 1907, and her furniture designs using this new technique were imaginative and exotic. For example, a dark green lacquer table (1914) had green silk cords with amber beads and tassles looped through the ends; it was supported on legs with stylised white lotus lilies at the top.

Her first interior design commission (1919), for Suzanne Talbot, included the remarkable lacquer pirogue and a screen consisting of 450 thin, lacquer plaques textured with powdered stone. This was used to shorted a long, narrow space in a simple, unexpected way. Four years later, she designed a bedroom-boudoir for the 1923 Salon des Artistes Décorateurs. This featured pierced screens of lacquered plaques and clean-lined furniture. The effect of clarity of line and space was quite different from current French taste in interior design, and it was greeted with derision by the French press but attracted the attention of the de Stijl group. Some of her work had been exhibited in Amsterdam the previous year, and her 1922 table showed that they shared similar concerns. In June 1924, the Dutch art journal *Wendingen* devoted a complete issue to her work.

By this time, her work had come to the attention of members of the modern movement, such as Gropius, Kiesler, and Le Corbusier, and she was encouraged by them to turn to architecture. Her house at Roquebrune, E-1027 (1924–26), designed with Jan Badovici, an architect and editor of *L'Architecture Vivante,* showed close links with the International Style in its flat roof, ribbon windows, and pilotis. In its furniture, which used space economically, she explored cantilevering and the use of such materials as tubular metal, glass, and aluminum. This concern with the potential of new materials could also be seen in her fluid, painted, steel-rod chair with laced canvas seat (1930) and her free-form table of oak on a slender, steel-rod frame (1938). Both of these showed features that came to be emphasized in contemporary design in the 1950's, namely concern with organic form and with the inter-relationship between forms.

—Hazel Conway

GRAY, Milner (Connorton).
British industrial, exhibition and graphic designer. Born in Blackheath, London, 8 October 1899. Studied painting and design, Goldsmith's College of Art, London, 1916–17 and 1919–21. Served in the British Army camouflage unit, 1917–19: Private. Married Gnade Osborne-Pratt in 1934. Founder and Senior Partner, Bassett-Gray Group of Artists and Writers multi-discipline design practice, London, 1922–35, re-named Industrial Design Partnership, 1935–40; Principal Exhibition Designer and Head of Exhibitions Branch, Ministry of Information, London, 1940–44; founder-partner, with Misha Black, from 1945, and senior consultant since 1980, Design Research Unit, London: consultant to Foley China, E. Brain and Company, Royal Staffordshire Pottery, A. J. Wilkinson and Company, etc. Principal, Sir John Cass College of Art, London, 1937–40. Visiting lecturer, Goldsmith's College of Art, London, 1932–40, Chelsea School of Art, London, 1934–37, Reimann School of Art and Design, London, 1937–39, and Royal College of Art, London, 1939–40. Council Member, Design and Industries Association, London, 1935–38; Governor, Central School of Art and Design, London, 1944–46, and Hornsey College of Art and Design, London, 1949–56; Vice-President, 1955–57, and Council Member, 1959–65, Royal Society of Arts, London; Advisor, BBC Schools Broadcasts, London, 1949–55; National Art Examination Committee Member, Ministry of Education, London, 1949–52; Formation Committee Member, ICSID International Council of Societies of Industrial Design, 1956; National Art Education Advisory Council Member, 1959–69; Master of the Art Worker's Guild, London, 1963; Post Office Stamp Committee Member, Council of Industrial Design (now Design Council), London, 1963–67. Founder-Member, 1930, Honorary Secretary, 1932–40, Vice-President, 1940–43, President, 1943–49 and 1966–67, Fellow, 1945, and Chairman of the Board of Trustees, 1963–88, Society of Industrial Artists (now Chartered Society of Designers), London; Advisory Committee Member, Royal Mint, London, 1952–88; Master of the Faculty of Royal Designers for Industry, Royal Society of Arts, London, 1955–57; Council Member from 1959, and Vice-President, 1981, Artists General Benevolent Institution, London; British President, Alliance Graphique Internationale, 1963–71. **Exhibitions:** *British Industrial Art,* Dorland Hall, London, 1933; *107 Grafici dell'AGI,* Castello Sforzesco, Milan, 1974; *Thirties,* Hayward Gallery, London, 1979; *Eye for Industry,* Victoria and Albert Museum, London, 1986. **Collection:** Victoria and Albert Museum, London. Recipient: Design Medal, Society of Industrial Artists and Designers, London, 1955; Diploma, Milan Triennale, 1957; Design Centre Award, London, 1957; Queen's Silver Jubilee Medal, London, 1977. Royal Designer for Industry, Royal Society of Arts, London, 1938; Honorary Fellow, 1963, Senior Fellow, 1971, and Honorary Doctorate, 1979, Royal College of Art, London; Honorary Design Associate, Manchester College of Art and Design, 1965; Fellow, Institute of Packaging, 1987. Commander, Order of the British Empire, 1963. Address: 8 Holly Mount, Hampstead, London NW3 6SG, England.

Works:

London Building Centre symbol, poster and advertising programme, 1932.
Kardomah Cafes murals and decorations, in London, Birmingham and Manchester, 1936–40.
Coal and Steel Halls murals of the United Kingdom pavilion, *Empire Exhibition,* Glasgow, 1938.
Section displays, at *MARS Exhibition of Modern Architecture,* London, 1938.
Design at Home exhibition layouts, National Gallery, London, 1945.
Taxicab and cooking-stove designs, at *Britain Can Make It* exhibition, Victoria and Albert Museum, London, for the Council of Industrial Design, 1946.
Rolex symbol, house style and package designs, for Rolex Watch Company, Geneva, 1946.
Design at Work exhibition layouts at the Royal Academy, London, for the Royal Society of Arts, 1948.
Corporate identity programme, for Austin Reed Limited, London, 1949–50.
Festival of Britain signage system, South Bank, London, 1949–51.
Milk bottle filling and capping machine, for UD Engineering Company, 1950.
Royal Coat-of-Arms engraved glass screen, at the Royal Festival Hall, London, 1951.
Pyrex oven-to-table glassware, for James Joblings Limited, 1955–65.

Milner Gray: Royal Coat of Arms, for the Council of Industrial Design, London, 1951

Corporate identity programme, for Watney-Mann Group of breweries, 1956–70.
Armorial bearings, for the Central Electricity Generating Board, 1963.
Corporate design programme, for the British Railways Board, 1963–68.
Corporate identity programme, for the British Aluminium Company, 1967–72.
Armorial bearings and common seal, for the General Post Office, London, 1970.
Official emblem, for the Queen's Silver Jubilee, 1976–77.

Publications:

By GRAY: books—*The Practice of Design,* with others, London 1946; *Package Design,* London and New York 1955; *Lettering for Architects and Designers,* with Ronald Armstrong, London 1962, Tokyo 1965.

On GRAY: books—*British Achievement in Design,* edited by Noel Carrington and Muriel Harris, London 1946; *Design in British Industry: A Mid-Century Survey* by Michael Farr, Cambridge 1955; *Who's Who in Graphic Art,* edited by Walter Amstutz, Zurich 1962, Dubendorf 1982; *An International Survey of Packaging* by Wim Crouwel and Kurt Weidemann, London 1968; *107 Grafici dell'AGI,* exhibition catalogue with texts by Renzo Zorzi and Franco Grignani, Venice 1974; *Industrial Design in Britain* by Noel Carrington, London 1976; *Milner Gray* by Avril Blake, London 1986.

To designers, I would just like to say that the work we most admire is often the simplest and the most obvious—of the kind that we all know we could have done, had we only thought of it. It is simple and inevitable because, the right question having been asked, there was no longer any difficulty in finding the right answer. As soon as we tackle a design problem, we ourselves become a part of the problem we aim to solve, bringing to its solution our own predilections, which may not coincide with those of the others associated with us in its solution. The solution will seldom be achieved by bulldozing our ideas over the other fellow's, who, too, is as identified with the problem as we are.

I believe that the designer's originative capacity derives from an inward urge to bring new forms into being. His creative contribution differs not in *quality* but in *kind* from that of other industrial workers—the factory manager who evolves a new production-line technique or the business executive who conceives a new sales system. The designer's originative capacity is not necessarily superior or fundamentally different: the difference lies in his application of it. This, which turns the tolerable into the beautiful, the merely functional into the highly desirable, makes him as valuable to industry as his scientific and executive colleagues.

Every design is, in a sense, an act of communication: a statement of a conviction about the nature and the functions of an article, a statement for which the designer accepts responsibility. The greater the intensity with which he

appreciates and the integrity with which he expresses the whole truth about the product as he perceives it, the better his design. Integrity of expression comes from the integration of thought and action, integration of mind, eye, and hand, of honest, disciplined work. The designer's social contribution and responsibility is to realize the true and total value *to the ultimate users* of the products he designs. *(Excerpted from a speech at the summary session of the International Design Conference in Aspen, Colorado, 18–24 June 1961)*

—Milner Gray

In a very productive and successful career, Milner Gray has established a worldwide reputation for his immaculate draughtsmanship and his interest in lettering. Before World War II, he combined a busy career in practice with several important teaching posts. Later, he helped create many of the best-known symbols, packaging materials, and corporated liveries in Britain for large companies from brewers to pottery manufacturers. He is well known for his designs of badges, particularly for royalty. The official emblem for Queen Elizabeth II's Silver Jubilee is a recent example. These types of design show his respect for tradition and attention to detail, as well as a knack for identifying distinctive features that help to make the design feel contemporary and clear-cut.

Perhaps his greatest contribution to twentieth-century design has been what he has accomplished as a planner and organiser of people; drawing colleagues into the first viable professional society of designers in Britain, pulling together very different characters and talents to make effective wartime exhibitions, creating and sustaining design practices—first the Bassett-Gray partnership, then the Industrial Design Partnership, and finally the first large, multi-skill group in Britain, the Design Research Unit. His ability to coordinate many different people, ideas, and interests laid the foundations for the detailed and memorable design schemes and programmes that the Design Research Unit has helped to devise for organisations with such different activities as British Rail, Wedgwood, Imperial Chemical Industries, and the brewers John Courage Ltd.

He is clear about his most positive achievement: "The only thing I have done that I think will stand up is the setting up of the S.I.A.D. (Society of Industrial Artists and Designers) in 1929–30." But he will probably be best remembered for his skillful and persistent advocacy of democratic principles in creating professional organisations, maintaining design practices, and working out design schemes with clients. "The committee should initiate the field of study, establish areas of research, and organise and programme the work of the design development team," he has said. In championing the committee system, he has laid great emphasis on the need for the designer to be a skilled communicator, in both the boardroom and the factory. The designer must be able to argue the case but not assume that he is the only person with the correct solution.

—Anthony J. Coulson

GREAR, J(ames) Malcolm.
American graphic designer. Born in Mill

Springs, Kentucky, 12 June 1931. Studied at the Art Academy of Cincinnati, Ohio, 1955–58. Served as an aviation metalsmith in the United States Navy, 1950–54. Married Clarice Simpson in 1955; children: Jason, Joel, Amie and Leah. Founder and Chief Executive Officer, Malcolm Grear Designers Inc., Providence, Rhode Island, since 1960: has designed corporate image programs, environmental graphics and packaging for medical facilities, museums, corporations, universities, government agencies and communities. Lecturer in basic and graphic design, Art Center Association, Louisville, Kentucky, 1958–60, and Allen R. Hite Institute, University of Louisville, Kentucky, 1959–60; Associate Professor of Graphic Design, 1960–79, Head of Graphic Design Department, 1965–69, Professor of Graphic Design, 1980–88, and Helen M. Danforth Professor since 1988, Rhode Island School of Design, Providence. Member of the Graphic Design Review Panel for Federal Agencies, National Endowment for the Arts, 1973–78; Executive Committee Member, Rhode Island Committee for the Humanities, American Institute of Graphic Arts, 1978–86. **Exhibitions:** *Communication by Design,* Institute of Contemporary Art, Boston, 1964 (toured); *Communication Graphics,* American Institute of Graphic Arts, New York, 1971, 1972, 1981; *International Annual of Poster Art,* Zurich, 1973; *Environmental Design: Signing and Graphics,* American Institute of Graphic Arts, New York, 1977; *Malcolm Grear Designers,* travelling studio exhibit, 1984–86. **Collections:** Cooper-Hewitt Museum, New York; Whitney Museum, New York. Recipient: Annual Book of the Year Award, American Institute of Graphic Arts, 1968, 1970, 1971, 1974, 1977, 1979, 1981, 1985; Governor's Award, Rhode Island State Council on the Arts, 1969; *Print* magazine Poster of the Decade Award, 1971; Art Libraries Society Museum Publication Award, New York, 1976; New England Book Show Design Excellence Awards, 1976; Annual Design Award, Art Society of North America, 1977; Design Excellence Awards, 1979, Design Award, 1981, and Gold Medals, 1983, Art Directors Club of Boston; Typographic Excellence Awards, Type Directors Club, New York, 1980; Design Excellence Awards, Society of Typographic Arts, Chicago, 1980, 1982; Silver Medal, Leipzig Book Design Exhibition, 1982; John R. Frazier Award for Excellence in Teaching, 1986; American Federation of Arts Design Excellence Awards, 1987; Honorary Alumnus Award, Rhode Island School of Design, 1989. Address: 391–393 Eddy Street, Providence, Rhode Island 02903, U.S.A.

Works:

Exhibition design, for Merrimack Valley Textile Museum, Andover, Massachusetts, 1962.
Biology (H. Curtis) book design, for Worth Publishers, New York, 1969.
Biochemistry (A. Lehninger) book design, for Worth Publishers, New York, 1970.
Environmental graphics, for the Comprehensive Training Center, Somerset, Kentucky, 1971.
Outpatient hospital signage and wall murals, for Boston City Hospital, 1971.
Jean Miro: Magnetic Fields exhibition catalogue design, for the Guggenheim Museum, New York, 1972.
Places: Aaron Siskind Photographs exhibition book design, for the Light Gallery, New York, 1976.
Robert Motherwell and Black exhibition catalogue design, for the William Benton Museum of Art, University of Connecticut, 1976.

Tall Ships '76 identity program and image application, 1976.
Henri Matisse: Paper Cut-Outs exhibition catalogue design, for the St. Louis Art Museum and Detroit Institute of Arts, 1977.
Total sign system, dedication book and exhibit, for King Khalid City, Saudi Arabia, 1977–80.
Planar Dimensions exhibition catalogue design, for the Guggenheim Museum, New York, 1979.
Identity program, for the U.S. Department of Health and Human Services, 1980.
Sign system, for the Boston Museum of Fine Arts, 1980.
Dale Chihuly: Glass book design, for Dale Chihuly, 1982.
Series of library book designs, for the Scientific American Library, 1982–86.
Identity program, for the Presbyterian Church of the U.S.A., 1984.
Earth Zero poster commemorating the Hiroshima bombing, for The Shoshin Society Inc., 1986.

Publications:

On GREAR: books—*Trademarks USA,* edited by the Society of Typographic Arts, Chicago 1968; *Signet, Signal, Symbol* by Walter Diethelm, Zurich 1970; *Book of American Trademarks* by David E. Carter, New York 1972, 1973; *Trademark and Symbol* by Yasaburo Kuwayama, Tokyo 1973; *Architectural Signing and Graphics* by John Foulis and David Hammer, New York 1979; *Graphic Art for our Environment* by Takenobu Igarashi, Tokyo 1980; *Visual Puns in Design* by Eli Kence, New York 1982; *American Corporate Identity* by David E. Carter, New York 1988; *Type and Image* by Philip B. Meggs, New York 1988.

Malcolm Grear works closely with his staff of designers to solve a variety of design problems by sharing creativity in a relaxed, familial atmosphere. Although the firm began as a two-dimensional design studio, his expertise has grown to include space planning for hospitals and schools and designs for exhibitions and trade shows. In applying his talents to the more complex problems of environmental planning and architectural graphics programs, Grear goes beyond the traditional role of a graphic designer as one who arranges type and visual elements on a two-dimensional surface.

Grear's ability to bring graphic insight to what have been traditionally non-graphic problems is evident in his large-scale environmental projects, which are problems in use and communication. For Grear, it is a matter of figuring out how people relate to one another and then, designing according to their needs. For the Oakwood Comprehensive Training Center, a state-run facility for emotionally disturbed children in Kentucky, Grear brought together the buildings and grounds by designing an environment with architectural graphics, sculptures, and movable animal cutouts. One of his most ambitious projects, however, was the space planning of the Westminster Center public mall in Providence, Rhode Island. In order to respect the vitality of the area and its architecture, Grear had the project enlarged by one block. In doing this, he avoided making an exhibit of a mall by effecting a response to the cross streets.

As others have noted, Grear brings to his work a strong commitment to moral principle. Just as an art poster or museum catalogue must respect the work of the artist involved, so must the architectural graphics and space planning respect the architecture with which it works. Whether the designs are his crisp, clean

graphic symbols or his large-scale environmental projects, Grear brings to them the same enthusiasm for combining graphic qualities with the personal identities of his clients.

—Patricia A. Russac

GREGOTTI, Vittorio.
Italian architect, interior, exhibition and industrial designer. Born in Novara, 10 August 1927. Studied architecture, at the Politecnico, Milan, 1948–52: Dip.Arch. 1952. Married Marina Mazza in 1975. Partner, with Lodovico Meneghetti and Giotto Stoppino, in Architetti Associati, Novara, 1952–63, and Milan, 1964–67; in private architectural and design practice, Milan, 1968–74; partner, with Pierluigi Carri and Hiromichi Matsui, in Gregotti Associati architects and designers, Milan, since 1974: consultant, Rinascente stores group, Milan, 1968–71; director of the visual arts section, Venice Biennale, 1974–76. Associate editor, with Ernesto N. Rogers, of *Casabella* magazine, Milan, 1952–60; editor, *Edilizia Moderna* monographs, Milan, 1962–64; architectural editor, *Il Verri* magazine, Milan, 1963–65; co-editor, *Lotus* magazine, Venice, from 1974. Professor of architectural composition, Politecnico, Milan, from 1964, and Istituto di Architettura, Venice, from 1978. **Exhibitions:** Milan Triennale, from 1951; *28/78 Architettura,* Palazzo delle Stelline, Milan, 1979 (travelled to Venice); *Vittorio Gregotti: Progetti,* Palermo, 1981; *La Modernite,* Paris, 1982; *Il Mestiere di Architetto: Botta, Piano, Gregotti,* Ferrara, 1984; *Vittorio Gregotti,* Harvard University, Cambridge, Massachusetts, 1984; *The European Iceberg,* Art Gallery of Ontario, Toronto, 1985. Recipient: Grand Prize, Milan Triennale, 1963; Compasso d'Oro Award, Milan, 1968; IACP Housing Development Prize, Palermo, 1970; University of Florence Design Prize, 1971; University of Calabria Design Prize, 1973. Address: Gregotti Associati, Via Bandello 20, 20123 Milan, Italy.

Works:

Exhibition pavilion at the Marketing Fair, Novara, 1953.
Headquarters Building, for the Istituto di Credito, Novara, 1958–59.
Master plan for the City of Novara, 1962–67.
Entrance pavilion, for the Milan Triennale, 1964 (with Peppo Brivio).
Cotton mill building, for Bossi, Novara, 1968.
Headquarters building, for the Instituto di Credito, Bra, 1968.
Two supermarkets, for La Rinascente, Milan, 1969.
Science department buildings, for the University of Palermo, 1972–84.
Offices and warehousing, for Gabel, Como, 1973–74.
New university of Calabria, Cosenza, 1973–75.
Music store, for Ricordi, Milan, 1974–75.
Office building, for Bossi, Novara, 1981–83.

(for a complete list of Gregotti's buildings and architectural projects, see *Contemporary Architects*)

Publications:

By GREGOTTI: books—*Territorio dell'Archi-*

tettura, Milan 1966; *New Directions in Italian Architecture,* London 1968, New York 1969; *Il Disegno del Prodotto Industriale,* Milan 1982; articles—in *Casabella* (Milan), no. 216, 1957, no. 228, 1959, no. 229, 1959, no. 240, 1960, no. 254, 1961 September 1977, July 1978, January 1981, October 1982; *Edilizia Moderna* (Milan), no. 86, 1965; *l'Arte Moderna* (Milan), no. 91, 1967, no. 94, 1967; *l'Architecture d'Aujourd'hui* (Paris), September 1968; *Domus* (Milan), October 1973, May 1974, May 1981; *Parametro* (Bologna), June 1977; *Alfabeta* (Milan), June 1979; *Rassegna* (Milan), July 1981, September 1982; *Daidalos* (Berlin), June 1984.

On GREGOTTI: books—*Design Italiano: i mobili* by Enrichetta Ritter, Milan and Rome 1968; *Design e Forme Nuove nell'Arredamento Italiano,* edited by Paolo Portoghesi and Marino Marini, Rome 1978; *Il Progetto per l'Universita delle Calabrie e Altre Architetture di Vittorio Gregotti,* Milan 1979; *Moderno Postmoderno Millenario,* edited by Andrea Branzi, Milan 1980; *A History of Industrial Design* by Edward Lucie-Smith, Oxford 1983; *The European Iceberg,* exhibition catalogue edited by Germano Celant, Milan 1985; *The Conran Directory of Design,* edited by Stephen Bayley, London 1985; *Italian Design: 1870 to the Present* by Penny Sparke, London 1988.

Perhaps more than most Milanese architects and designers, Vittorio Gregotti has maintained an intellectually valid common denominator to all his many and varied activities, as he has run through all the roles of architect, publicist, editor, critic, historian, designer, impresario, and, above all, apologist. His commitment to the so-called "Neo-Liberty," a "revival" of art nouveau, was particularly courageous, while the theoretical underpinning he sought demonstrated equally his forthright honesty and subtle articulation of the concept of historicism. His intellectual approach was characterized then, as it is now, by a sophisticated understanding that the two intellectual notions alike designated by the term "historicism," are somehow intertwined. Revivalism, the genuine attempt to recreate the style of previous practices, is doomed to failure, but at the same time, history is a key. The point for him was to pick up the possibilities from the presumed moment of deviation without losing the benefit of hindsight. Gregotti's return to art nouveau was a return to principles, and he attempted to proceed with those principles in the light of all that had happened meanwhile. His approach was not at all a rejection of the Italian twentieth-century experience but rather a critical reevaluation of it, an attempt to reinvigorate it with a more precise historical perspective.

By 1964, his section of the Milan *Triennale* the entrance pavilion (with Peppo Brivio), showed the full cultural significance of his departure from any principles and his transcendence of the limitations revivalism might be thought to have imposed. In the light of his recent undertakings, it is clear that at no time did Gregotti think to limit himself to historically prescribed models. There was nothing of the Gothic Revival spirit in his conception of Neo-Liberty, and none of his work shows any sign of slavish imitation, of pastiche. The creative vigour in all his work would have pushed him beyond such limitations even if pure revivalism had ever been his aim.

No discussion of Gregotti can ignore his undoubted achievement of a unity of theory and practice, however precarious, which informs all is work alike, including his most committed book to date, *Territorio dell'Architettura;* the Zen Housing Development, Cardillo, Palermo; the Community Centre at Gibellina in Sicily, which occupied him through the 1970s; the new

university at Cosenza and new buildings for the University at Florence; and, of course, his many activities as an editor.

—Toni del Renzio

GREIMAN, April.

American graphic designer. Born in Rockville Center, New York, 22 March 1948. Studied at Kansas City Art Institute, Missouri, 1966–70: BA 1970; under Armin Hofmann and Wolfgang Weingart, at the Allgemeine Kunstgewerbeschule, Basel, 1970–71. Freelance graphic designer, working for The Architects Collaborative, Boston, Museum of Modern Art, New York, and Anspach/Grossman/Portugal, New York, 1971–75; established own studio in Los Angeles, from 1976. Assistant professor of design, Philadelphia College of Art, 1971–75; design instructor, Otis/Parsons Art Institute, Los Angeles, from 1982. **Exhibitions:** Philadelphia College of Art, 1974; Meghan Williams Gallery, Los Angeles, 1978; University of California at Los Angeles, 1979; Tokyo Gallery, Japan, 1979; Rhode Island School of Design, Providence, 1979; *April Greiman/Michael Graves,* Northern Illinois University, DeKalb, 1982; *April Greiman/Jayme Odgers/Chris Garland,* Kent State University, Ohio, 1983; Kansas City Art Institute, Missouri, 1983. **Collections:** Cooper-Hewitt Museum, New York; Walker Art Center, Minneapolis. Member: American Institute of Graphic Arts, New York, 1978; Society of Typographic Arts, Chicago, 1983. Address: 620 Moulten Avenue, Los Angeles, California 90031, U.S.A.

Works:

Clients include—The Architects Collaborative, Boston; Elizabeth Arden; Fat City Cafe, San Diego; The Fashion Group, New York; Gray Advertising; Denzu Advertising; Pacific Design Center 2; Le Triangle complex of 20 stores, Beverly Hills; Vertigo retail shops, Los Angeles; Optica retail shops, Beverly Hills, Houston, Dallas, Chicago, and Costa Mesa; Society of Typographic Arts, Chicago; China Club restaurant, Los Angeles; 1984 Olympic Culture Committee, Los Angeles; Academy of Television Arts and Sciences; American Film Industries; Sunlight Productions; Robert Abel Productions; Preston Cinema System; Warner Records; A & M Records; Album Graphics Inc.; RSO Records; magazines—*Artforum,* New York; *Time,* New York; *Expedition,* Philadelphia; *Luxe,* Miami, Florida; *McCalls,* New York; *Progresive Architecture,* Stamford, Connecticut; *Wet,* Los Angeles; *Zoetrope,* Chicago; museums and galleries—Museum of Modern Art, New York; Los Angeles County Museum of Art; Philadelphia Museum of Art; La Jolla Museum of Contemporary Art, California; Newport Harbor Museum, Newport Beach, California; Meghan Williams Gallery, Los Angeles; Janus Gallery, Los Angeles; schools—Annenberg School of Communication, Philadelphia; California Institute of the Arts, Los Angeles; State University of New York at Purchase; Yale University, New Haven, Connecticut; Design Institute of San Diego; Philadelphia Academy of Music.

Publications:

By GREIMAN: articles—in *Artifacts at the End of a Decade,* exhibition catalogue by Steve Watson and Carol Huebner, New York 1980; *Kansas City Institute Magazine* (Missouri), Fall 1982.

On GREIMAN: books—*The 20th-Century Poster: Design of the Avant-Garde* by Dawn Ades, New York 1984; *New American Design* by Hugh Aldersley-Williams, New York 1988; articles—in *Typographische Monatsblatter* (St. Gallen), January 1975; *Anan* (Tokyo), no. 267, 1980; *Print* (New York), January 1981; *Idea* (Tokyo), no. 167, 1981, Winter 1983; *Modo* (Milan), Spring 1982; *Studio International* (London), no. 995, 1982; *Graphis* (Zurich), March/April 1983.

As a designer—a channel of/for information—one accepts the challenge of mediating the ever-increasing speed at which time and technology are expanding. To inspire with the language of this vocabulary is to participate/perpetuate the infant/giant of visual consciousness. As a designer/artist one must immerse oneself in technology, alert oneself to the abundance of new definitions, free oneself to move clearly, fluidly, and playfully in the arena of ideas and information. *(Excerpted from an interview with Claire E. Dishman)*

—April Greiman

April Greiman is one of the truly original graphic designers of the late twentieth century. As a young designer, she responded to the inventive dynamic found in the work of her teacher, Wolfgang Weingart. Later, in a series of stunning innovations, Greiman's work rapidly emerged as an original moment in the history of design. Her inventiveness consists mainly in her attitude toward space in graphic design. In her work, the rigid two-dimensionality of modern typography yielded to a dynamic, illusionistic space achieved by overlapping forms, movements in and out of space, lines and planes that seem to recede in perspective or tilt forward from the picture plane, and shadows that are cast onto the page by forms hovering above it. Greiman approaches the page as a complex arena filled with fragments of information placed in intricate balance. Contemporary music and choreography might be considered as formal parallels to Greiman's creation of order out of dissonance in an effort to energize the total space.

The Proun paintings of the Russian Constructivist El Lissitzky are an important inspiration for Greiman. However, whereas Lissitzky used illusionistic space in these paintings, he maintained an absolute flatness in his typographic designs, as Greiman has not.

Greiman has given much consideration to the visual linking of photographic and graphic material. Colored bars overlap or run behind photographs. Graphic elements, such as pictures and colored shapes or forms, appear in photographs as visual counterpoint to the graphic elements surrounding the photographic images. Jayme Odgers' extremely wide-angle photographs, with objects and people thrusting deep into the space or projecting forward, provide a perfect companion for Greiman's innovative vocabulary of form.

—Philip B. Meggs

GRÈS, Madame.

French fashion designer. Born in Paris, in 1899. Studied painting and sculpture, Paris; apprenticed in Premet fashion house, Paris, 1931–33. Married the painter Serge Czerefkov (divorced); daughter: Anne. Established own dress pattern design and cutting business, under the name Alix Barton, in Rue Miromesnil, Paris; designer, then director, Maison Alix fashion house, in the Faubourg Saint-Honore, Paris, 1934–42; director, Grès Couture (after husband's pseudonym "Grès"), in the Rue de la Paix, Paris, 1942, and from 1945: launched perfume *Cabochard*, 1966. Also film costume designer in the 1930s. President, Chambre Syndicale de la Couture Parisienne, Paris, 1972. **Exhibitions:** *Fashion: An Anthology,* Victoria and Albert Museum, London, 1971; *The 10s, 20s and 30s,* Metropolitan Museum of Art, New York, 1974; *Franzosisches Kunsthandwerk Heute,* Overstolzenhaus, Cologne, 1981. Recipient: Chevalier de la Légion d'Honneur, France. Address: 1 Rue de la Paix, 75002 Paris, France.

Publications:

On GRÈS: books—*Always in Vogue* by Edna Woolman Chase and Ilka Chase, London 1954; *Dressmakers of France* by Mary Brooks Picken and Dora Loues Miller, New York 1956; *Kings of Fashion* by Anny Latour, Stuttgart 1956, London 1958; *In My Fashion* by Bettina Ballard, London 1960; *Fashion: An Anthology by Cecil Beaton,* exhibition catalogue compiled by Madeleine Ginsburg, London 1971; *In Vogue: Sixty Years of Celebrities and Fashion,* edited by Georgina Howell, London 1975, 1978, New York 1976; *The World of Fashion: People, Places, Resources* by Eleanor Lambert, New York and London 1976; *Inventive Paris Clothes 1909–1939* by Diana Vreeland, New York and London 1977; *The History of Haute Couture 1850–1950* by Diana de Marly, London 1980; *McDowell's Directory of Twentieth Century Fashion* by Colin McDowell, London 1984; *The Encyclopaedia of Fashion from 1840 to the 1980s* by Georgina O'Hara, London 1986.

The white salon with drawn shades seems to defy time and change. There is no blaring music, there are no gimmicks, nothing to detract from the clothes themselves. Madame Grès lives for her clothes and has no interest in herself. She conducts a love affair with fabric, knowing how each one falls and what each will or will not do. All designs start on the body with the reality of the fabric on a moving form, not in abstract drawings. While she maintains a careful approach to mainstream fashion following a dominant line and despising extreme subfashions, her most famous range is composed of her changeless, Grecian evening dresses. Here, Grès is supreme, the most famous exponent of drapery today. No matter what ornate fantasies other designers create, these classical gowns stand on Olympus, for as the Duchesse d'Orléans remarked, Grès seems to design for Greek goddesses. The simplicity of these dresses comes as close to timelessness as any human being can achieve. Although they are a standard form, such is Grès's invention that each year produces new variations on the theme. They can be white or in two tones of blue or in contrasting black and cerise. After all, the ancient Greeks did colour their statues; the neo-Classical movement was wrong in thinking every thing Greek had to be marble-white.

Grès grew up under Art Deco influence, and this streamlined simplicity has conditioned her own approach. Her clothes are sculptural because she wanted to be a sculptor but was pre-vented. Her shapes are pure because she is a technician. As precise as an engineer, she still does some sewing herself, as well as manipulating the folds to produce that faultless fall of fabric. The purity of perfection is the only standard allowed. The creation is the idol, its creator is but the servant. Every museum with a costume collection would like to be given a Grès gown, for she is regarded as the greatest exponent of her art.

—Diana de Marly

GRIGNANI, Franco.

Italian painter, photographer, graphic and industrial designer. Born in Pieve Porto Morone, Pavia, 4 February 1908. Educated at the Istituto Tecnico and Liceo Scientifico, Pavia, until 1926; studied architecture, at the Politecnico, Turin, 1929–33. Served in the Italian Army Artillery, 1939–43: Lieutenant. Married Jeanne Michot in 1942; daughters: Daniela and Manuela. Independent painter, photographer and designer, Milan, from 1932: art director, *Belleza d'Italia* magazine, Milan, 1948–60; Alfieri e Lacroix printers, Milan, from 1952; and *Pubblicità in Italia* yearbook, Milan, 1956–82. Participated in the second Futurist movement, Milan, in the 1930s; founder-member, Gruppo Exhibition Design, Milan, 1969. Instructor in visual design, Nuova Accademia di Belle Arti, Milan, from 1979. Italian section president, AGI Alliance Graphique Internationale, 1969–81. **Exhibitions:** Libreria Salto, Milan, 1958, 1960; Libreria Comunale, Milan, 1958; Normandy House STA Gallery, Chicago, 1960; Centro Culturale Pirelli, Milan, 1967; 500D Gallery, Chicago, 1970; Museo Rotonda Besana, Milan, 1975; Museo de Bellas Artes, Caracas, 1977; Salone Comunale, Reggio Emilia, 1979; Galleria Flaviana, Locarno, 1981; Lorenzelli Arte, Milan, 1981; Palestra Civica, Pieve Porto Morone, 1983; Galleria Quanta, Milan, 1984; Galleria Municipale di La Salle, Aosta, 1985: Galleria Il Salotto, Como, 1985. **Collections:** Poster Museum, Warsaw; Stedelijk Museum, Amsterdam; Museum of Modern Art, New York; Victoria and Albert Museum, London. Recipient: Grand Prize, 1951, Gold Medal, 1957, Milan Triennale; Gold Medal for Publicity and Advertising, Milan, 1954; Il Ponte Group Silver Lion Award, Venice, 1962; G. Puecher Gold Medal, Milan, 1974. Member, Alliance Graphique Internationale, 1951; Honorary Member, Society of Typographic Arts, Chicago, 1967. Address: Via Bianca di Savoia 7, 20122 Milan, Italy.

Publications:

By GRIGNANI: books—*107 Grafici dell'AGI,* exhibition catalogue with Renzo Zorzi, Venice 1974; *Franco Grignani: Art and Grapics,* edited by Willy Rotzler, Zurich 1983; articles—in *Linea Grafica* (Milan), 1963, no. 3, 1970, no. 5, 1972, no. 1, 1973; *Graphis* (Zurich), no. 108, 1963; *Print* (New York), January/ February 1964; *Soli* (Turin), no. 4, 1967; *Design* (Bergamo), no. 3, 1974; *IBM Review/Italy* (Milan), no. 4, 1976.

On GRIGNANI: books—*Layout* by Raymond A. Ballinger, New York 1956; *Die neue Grafik/ The New Graphic Design* by Karl Gerstner and Markus Kutter, Teufen and London 1959; *Who's Who in Graphic Art,* edited by Walter Amstutz, Zurich 1962, Dubendorf 1982; *Franco Grignani* by Giulio Carlo Argan, Milan 1967; *Franco Grignani: Graphic designer in Europe,* Tokyo 1971; *Franco Grignani: El Sentido de una Larga Busqueda* by Giulio Carlo Argan, Caracas 1977; *Franco Grignani: Il Segno come Matrice* by Giuseppe Turroni, Milan 1978; *Mostra Antologica di Franco Grignani,* exhibition catalogue by Bruno D'Amore and Giuseppe Berti, Reggio Emilia 1979; *Contemporary Photographers,* Chicago and London 1988.

Given that all my activities, covering some decades, have been directed towards experiment and research in graphic communication, using technical knowledge and scientific methods for a broad investigation of visual phenomena, it is clear that what interested me was the existential problems of our technological civilization taken "to the physical limits of the human eye." From this basic starting point, I proceeded to a long and complex accumulation of optical-visual experiments, which revealed to me the importance of reality changed by tensions and distortions, a "skidding" of the pictures, overcoming the mental and visual inertia so as to break down concrete optics.

For these reasons, my graphic designs always have an aesthetic content, in order to give the viewer room for mental manoeuvre. And the graphic symbol, never inert and passive, in old prints, acquires a decisiveness breaking down the bastions of custom so as to constitute an aesthetic training for a social culture and an individual intellective liberation.

Where there exists beauty there can be no wastage of the values; basing myself on this assertion, I seek in symbolical forms a vitality and an influence that makes the eye of the viewer a participant through a challenge to the surrounding world, in a time that creates certainties and can no longer be overtaken and overcome in imagination.

—Franco Grignani

GROT, Anton.

Polish-American film designer. Born Antocz Frantiszek Groszewski, in Kelbasin, Poland, 18 January 1884; emigrated to the United States in 1909. Studied illustration and design, at the School of Art, Krakow, and at the Technisce Hochschule, Königsberg, Germany. Set designer, for Sigmund Lubin Manufacturing Company, Philadelphia, 1913–17, for Blache, 1917–18, and for Pathe, in New Jersey, 1918–21: designed for directors Louis Gasnier, 1918–19, George B. Seitz, 1919–21, and George Fitzmaurice, 1920–22; designer of Fairbanks/ Pickford films, for United Artists, Hollywood, 1922, and for Cecil B. DeMille films, Hollywood, 1922–27; art director, Warner Brothers Films, 1927–48; retired, to concentrate on painting, Los Angeles, 1948–74. **Collection:** University of California at Los Angeles. Recipient: Special Academy Award, 1940. *Died* (in Los Angeles, California) *21 March 1974.*

Works:

Film designs include—*The Mouse and the Lion* (Brooks), 1913; *Arms and the Woman* (Fitz-

franco grignani

La grafica moderna ha sempre tentato di pro-
porre la dimensione plastica in ogni organizzazione visiva. Sul foglio, l'illusorio della terza dimensione esalta la toccabilità fisica delle Corse, le
immagini proiettate entro l'occhio assumono
qualità materiche e, con il movimento virtuale, le
influenze figurali si sottolineano nell'inconscio
dell'uomo. Così fa anche l'esatta e costante stampa dei segni, dei colori stessi nelle loro struttu-
razioni tissurali, vellutate o lucide, il dosaggio
dei rapporti nell'iterativo segno tipografico. Que-
sta è la stampa nella qualità Alfieri & Lacroix.

Franco Grignani: *La Grafica Moderna* advertisement, for Alfieri e Lacroix, Milan

maurice), 1916; *The Recoil* (Fitzmaurice), 1917; *The Iron Heart* (Fitzmaurice), 1917; *The Seven Pearls* (Mackenzie), 1917; *The Naulahka* (Fitzmaurice), 1918; *Sylvia of the Secret Service* (Fitzmaurice), 1918; *Bound and Gagged* (Seitz), 1919; *Pirate Gold* (Seitz), 1920; *Velvet Fingers* (Seitz), 1920; *Robin Hood* (Dwan), 1922; *Tess of the Storm Country* (Robertson), 1922; *Dorothy Vernon of Haddon Hall* (Neilan), 1924; *The Thief of Baghdad* (Walsh), 1924; *A Thief in Paradise* (Fitzmaurice), 1924; *Don Q, Son of Zorro* (Crisp), 1925; *The Road to Yesterday* (DeMille), 1925; *The Volga Boatman* (DeMille), 1926; *Silence* (Julian), 1926; *Young April* (Crisp), 1926; *White Gold* (Howard), 1927; *Vanity* (Crisp), 1927; *The Little Adventuress* (W. DeMille), 1927; *The Country Doctor* (Julian), 1927; *The King of Kings* (DeMille), 1927; *Stand and Deliver* (Crisp), 1928; *Hold 'em Yale* (E. Griffith), 1928; *The Blue Danube* (Sloane), 1928; *Walking Back* (Julian), 1928; *A Ship Comes In* (Howard), 1928; *The Godless Girl* (DeMille), 1928; *The Barker* (Fitzmaurice), 1928; *Show Girl* (Santell), 1928; *Noah's Ark* (Curtiz), 1928; *Why Be Good?* (Seiter), 1929; *Smiling Irish Eyes* (Seiter), 1929; *The Man and the Moment* (Fitzmaurice), 1929; *Her Private Life* (A. Korda), 1929; *Footlights and Fools* (Seiter), 1929; *Lilies of the Field* (A. Korda), 1930; *Playing Around* (LeRoy), 1930; *No, No, Nanette* (Badger), 1930; *A Notorious Affair* (Bacon), 1930; *Song of the Flame* (Crosland), 1930; *Bright Lights* (Curtiz), 1930; *Top Speed* (LeRoy), 1930; *Outward Bound* (Milton), 1930; *Little Caesar* (LeRoy), 1930; *Body and Soul* (Santell), 1931; *Svengali* (Mayo), 1931; *Heartbreak* (Werker), 1931; *Honour of the Family* (Bacon), 1931; *The Mad Genius* (Curtiz), 1931; *Surrender* (Howard), 1931; *One Way Passage* (Garnett), 1931; *Big City Blues* (LeRoy), 1931; *The Hatchet Man* (Wellman), 1932; *Alias the Doctor* (Curtiz), 1932; *Two Seconds* (LeRoy), 1932; *Doctor X* (Curtiz), 1932; *The Match King* (Bretherton/Keighley), 1932; *Scarlet Dawn* (Dieterle), 1932; *Lawyer Man* (Dieterle), 1932; *20,000 Years in Sing Sing* (Curtiz), 1932; *Mystery of the Wax Museum* (Curtiz), 1933; *Grand Slam* (Dieterle), 1933; *The King's Vacation* (Adolfi), 1933; *Gold Diggers of 1933* (LeRoy), 1933; *Baby Face* (Green), 1933; *Ever in My Heart* (Mayo), 1933; *From Headquarters* (Dieterle), 1933; *Footlight Parade* (Bacon), 1933; *Son of a Sailor* (Bacon), 1933; *Easy to Love* (Keighley), 1933; *Mandalay* (Curtiz), 1934; *Gambling Lady* (Mayo), 1934; *Upperworld* (Del Ruth), 1934; *He Was Her Man* (Bacon), 1934; *Dr. Monica* (Keighley), 1934; *The Firebird* (Dieterle), 1934; *Side Streets* (Green), 1934; *British Agent* (Curtiz), 1934; *Six Day Bike Rider* (Bacon), 1934; *The Secret Bride* (Dieterle), 1934; *Gold Diggers of 1935* (Berkeley), 1934; *Red Hot Tires* (Lederman), 1935; *The Florentine Dagger* (Florey), 1935; *Travelling Saleslady* (Enright), 1935; *The Case of the Curious Bride* (Curtiz), 1935; *Stranded* (Borzage), 1935; *Broadway Gondolier* (Bacon), 1935; *Bright Lights* (Berkeley), 1935; *Dr. Socrates* (Dieterle), 1935; *A Midsummer Night's Dream* (Reinhardt/Dieterle), 1935; *Captain Blood* (Curtiz), 1935; *The Golden Arrow* (Green), 1936; *The White Angel* (Dieterle), 1936; *Anthony Adverse* (LeRoy), 1936; *Stolen Holiday* (Curtiz), 1936; *Sing Me a Love Song* (Enright), 1936; *The Life of Emile Zola* (Dieterle), 1937; *Tovarich* (Litvak), 1937; *Confession* (May), 1937; *The Great Garrick* (Whale), 1937; *Fools for Scandal* (LeRoy), 1938; *Hard to Get* (Enright), 1938; *They Made Me A Criminal* (Berkeley), 1939; *Juarez* (Dieterle), 1939; *The Private Lives of Elizabeth and Essex* (Curtiz), 1939; *The Sea Hawk* (Curtiz), 1940; *A Dispatch from Reuters* (Dieterle), 1940; *The Sea Wolf* (Curtiz), 1941; *Affectionately Yours* (Bacon), 1941; *Thank Your Lucky Stars* (Butler), 1943; *The Conspirators* (Negulesco), 1944; *Rhapsody in Blue* (Rapper), 1945; *Mildred Pierce* (Curtiz), 1945; *My Reputation* (Bernhardt), 1946; *One More Tomorrow* (Godfrey), 1946; *Never Say Goodbye* (Kern), 1946; *Deception* (Rapper), 1946; *Nora Prentiss* (V. Sherman), 1947; *The Two Mrs. Carrolls* (Godfrey), 1947; *Possessed* (Bernhardt), 1947; *The Unsuspected* (Curtiz), 1947; *Romance on the High Seas* (Curtiz), 1948; *June Bride* (Windust), 1948; *One Sunday Afternoon* (Walsh), 1948; *Backfire* (V. Sherman), 1948.

Publications:

On GROT: books—*Filmlexicon degli Autore delle Opere,* 7 vols., edited by Michele de Lacalamita and others, Rome 1958; *One Reel a Week* by Fred J. Balshofer and Arthur C. Miller, Berkeley 1967; *Le Decor de Film* by Leon Barsacq, Paris 1970, as *Caligari's Cabinet and Other Grand Illusions,* Boston 1976; *The Hollywood Exiles* by John Baxter, London 1976; *The Warner Brothers Story* by Clive Hirschhorn, New York 1979; *The International Dictionary of Films and Filmmakers,* Chicago and London 1987, 1991.

Anton Grot's special Academy Award in 1940 for his invention of a "ripple machine", which created weather and light effects on water, perhaps symbolizes his particular interest in the expressive qualities of light in motion pictures. Of all the major designers working in Hollywood in the 1930s, Grot was among those whose work was most strongly affected by European modernism in films and painting. The angular shadows and strong, light-and-dark contrast found in *Little Caesar,* for example, help to establish the underworld context of the film. In the pressbook for *Doctor X* (a Technicolor film), Grot explained how he used heavy construction, low arches, dark colors, and shadows to create a mood of mystery and melodrama: "We design a set that imitates as closely as possible a bird of prey about to swoop down upon its victim, trying to incorporate in the whole thing a sense of impending calamity, of overwhelming danger." Similar expressive qualities are found, particularly in scenes of danger or terror, in the melodramatic swashbucklers Grot designed, such as *Captain Blood* (1935), *The Private Lives of Elizabeth and Essex* (1939), and *The Sea Hawk* (1940). In his designs for "The Forgotten Man" production number in *The Gold Diggers of 1933,* Grot cast jagged shadows on the women who sing of their forgotten men, and in the finale of the song, he silhouetted unemployed veterans marching ceaselessly over a machine-like series of curved bridges. Using traditional and natural forms freely in *A Midsummer Night's Dream* (1935), Grot created such memorable images as the entrance of Oberon, king of the fairies, crowned with a spiky headdress, and wearing a sparkling black cloak that sweeps for many yards behind the horse on which he is riding.

Grot's use of stylistic qualities of twentieth-century European art no doubt derived in part from his Polish background, yet this interest parallels that of contemporary American painters such as John Marin, Charles Burchfield, and Georgia O'Keeffe. Just as the abstract qualities found in the paintings of these artists is crucial to the success of their works, so, too, Grot's film designs can be seen as combinations of realistic details built upon abstract formal qualities, particularly those of light and shadow.

—Floyd W. Martin

GROTELL, Maija.

American ceramics, glass and product designer. Born in Helsinki, Finland, in 1899; emigrated to the United States in 1927. Studied painting, sculpture and design, at the Central School of Industrial Art, Helsinki: graduate studies in ceramics. Worked as a draughtsman and textile designer for the National Museum of Finland, Helsinki, until 1926; freelance ceramics and industrial designer, in New York and Michigan, 1927-73. Instructor in ceramics, Henry Street Crafts School, New York, 1929-38, and at the School of Ceramic Engineering, Rutgers University, New Brunswick, New Jersey, 1936-38; director of the department of ceramics, Cranbrook Academy of Art, Bloomfield Hills, Michigan, 1938-67. **Exhibitions:** Museum of Contemporary Crafts, New York, 1963, 1968; Cranbrook Academy of Art, Bloomfield Hills, Michigan, 1967. **Collections:** Museum of Contemporary Crafts, New York; Metropolitan Museum of Art, New York; Detroit Institute of Arts, Michigan; Art Institute of Chicago; Cleveland Museum of Art, Ohio; Cranbrook Academy of Art, Bloomfield Hills, Michigan. Recipient: International Exposition Award, Barcelona, 1929; Paris Salon Medal, 1937; Syracuse Museum Award, New York, 1936, 1946, 1949; Detroit Institute of Art Award, 1955; Charles F. Binns Medal, Alfred University, New York, 1961; Founders Medal, Cranbrook Academy of Art, 1964. *Died in 1973.*

Publications:

On GROTELL: books—*The Art of Interior Design* by Victoria Kloss Ball, New York 1960; *Objects: USA* by Lee Nordness, London and New York 1970; *Twentieth Century Design: Glass* by Frederick Cooke, London 1986; articles—in *Craft Horizons* (New York), September 1968, November 1969, February 1974, February 1977.

Maija Grotell's experimentation in ceramic surface decoration contributed to the creation of the modern American ceramic esthetic, which views clay as an expressive medium. In her constant experimentation with glaze effects, she rediscovered the beauty and subtlety of ancient Oriental glazes, such as copper red, gun metal, and ash, and found substitutions for toxic glaze ingredients, such as chrome and iron for uranium in producing bright oranges. During the 1940s and 1950s, when little information on glazes had been published (except for industrial use), Grotell and some of her peers, including Glen Lukens, Marguerite Wildenhain, and Gertrude and Otto Natzler, revolutionized the ceramic surface by experimenting with rough, textured effects, including bubble and crater glazes and deep, rich colors. Grotell further transformed the surface by making pronounced finger ridges during throwing and by applying sparse, glaze-resist patterns, which emphasized raw clay as a painterly field. For most of her career she concentrated on spherical and cylindrical vessel shapes—heavy, fluid volumes which formed the basis for decoration. Her work of this period was covered with geometric and organic motifs, which she used in abstract patterning of planes, lines, and angles compatible with the scale and proportions of the host vessel. This work achieved international recognition for its simplicity and presence, its statement of the dynamic personality of its maker.

Grotell's teaching methods strongly influenced ceramic instruction in the United States. She rejected the prevailing, structured approach of Arthur Baggs, Myrtle French, and others, championing instead the teaching of productive thought. Her own independent investigations into ceramic surfaces, textures, and patterns challenged the next generation of potters to push further the plastic value of the medium. The ceramics department which she created at Cranbrook Academy is considered one of the nation's finest, and many of her students went on to become noted ceramists; among them are Toshiko Takaezu, John Glick, and Richard DeVore.

Grotell's work brought international recognition to the American artist potter; she is considered responsible for an important philosophic shift in the emphasis from pottery as functional household necessity to pottery as sculpture with esthetic merit.

—Sarah Bodine

GURAWSKI, Jerzy.

Polish architect and stage designer. Born in Lwow (now in the U.S.S.R.), 4 September 1935. Educated at schools in Lwow, Katowice and Bielsko, 1942–54; studied architecture, Technical University, Kraków, 1955–61: M.Arch. 1961. Married Teresa Pankow in 1963; sons: Wojtek and Bartek. Architect of the Laboratory Theatre, in Opole and Wroclaw, 1961–70; designer in the State Architecture Offices, in Opole and Poznań, since 1962. Instructor in architecture, Technical University, Poznań, since 1974. Chairman of the Poznań Jury Council since 1976, and Coordination Council Member since 1980, SARP Association of Polish Architects. **Exhibitions:** *15th Anniversary of Polish Scenography,* Palace of Culture, Warsaw, 1962; *Quadriennale Scenografii,* Prague, 1971; *Moderne polsk scenografi,* Kunstindustrimuseet, Oslo, 1971; *Modern Polish Scenography,* Vienna, 1972; *Theatre of Nations,* Nancy, France, 1984. Recipient: First Prize, Touring Theatre Competition, Association of Polish Architects, 1959; Gold Medal, *Quadriennale of Scenography,* Prague, 1971. Address: ul. Bonin 26/9, 60–658 Poznań, Poland.

Works:

Skansen Museum, Silesia, 1964–70.
City Library, Opole, 1970.
Mountain Resort Guest House, Glucholazy, 1970–75.
Nursery Building, Opole, 1972–77.
Roman Catholic Church and School, Glogow, 1980–89.
Hospital and Clinic, Poznań, 1981–85.
Roman Catholic Church, Leszno, 1981–89.
New University complex, Poznań, 1981–89.
Students' Hostel, Poznań, 1982–85.
Twin Tower Church, Zielona Gora, from 1985.
Excavated Basilica Cathedral Church, Gorzow, from 1987.
Hospice, Monastery and Workshop reconstruction, Glogow, from 1987.
Museum and Educational Pavilion in the Botanical Gardens, Poznań, from 1988.

Stage designs include—*Siakantula,* Theatre Laboratory, Opole/Krakow/Wroclaw, 1960; *Dziady,* Theatre Laboratory, Opole/Wroclaw, 1961; *Kordian,* Theatre Laboratory, Opole/Krakow, 1962; *Akropolis,* Theatre Laboratory, Opole, 1962; *Tragical History of*

Dr. Faustus, Theatre Laboratory, Opole, 1963; *Principe Constante,* Theatre Laboratory, Opole, 1964; *Duke the Unbroken,* Theatre Art Research Institute, Wroclaw, 1965; *Bertha the Fat,* Juliusz Slowacki Theatre, Krakow, 1980; *Phaedra,* Second Wroclaw Studio, 1986.

Publications:

By GURAWSKI: book—*Design of the New University,* with others, Poznań 1978; articles— "On Ethnographic Parks Planning" in *Ethnographic Review* (Opole, Poland), no. 22–24, 1970; "About the Corridor," with others, in *Architektura* (Warsaw) no. 393, 1979; "Designing of Medium-Sized City Centres," with others, in *Miasto* (Warsaw), no. 4, 1979; "Marian Fikus and Jerzy Gurawski," interview, in *Architektura* (Warsaw), no. 407, 1982; "Gurawski on Grotowski", interview with Monika Kuc, in *Kultura* (Warsaw), March 1988.

On GURAWSKI: books—*Polska plastyka teatralna* by Z. Strzelecki, Warsaw and New York 1963; *Toward a Poor Theatre* by Jerzy Grotowski, Holstebro, Denmark 1968; *Kierunki scenografii wspolczesnej* by Z. Strzelecki, Kraków 1970; *Scenic Revolutions of the 20th Century* by Denis Bablet, Paris 1975, Warsaw 1980; *Grotowski e jego Laboratorium* by Z. Osinski, Warsaw 1980; *Wspolczesna scenografia polska* by Z. Strzelecki, Warsaw 1983; articles—"Scenographie nouvelle" by Jacques Polieri in *Aujourd'hui art et architecture* (Paris), no. 42–43, 1963; "Architect in the Theatre Laboratory" in *Dialog* (Warsaw), May 1984.

Theatre—Kraków, 1956–60—a breath of fresh air after Stalinism. Lively movement of the theatrical avant-garde inspired my interests in the variability of the scenic space. First, two theatre designs came into being—the "circular" theatre and "variable audience" theatre competition, the former of which was my diploma design. Then, in 1960, I met Jerzy Grotowski; confrontation of our views resulted in cooperation. The ten scenic spaces that I worked out for his stagings between 1960 and 1974 I regard as my most important professional achievements. The influence of Grotowski's unique personality on intensifying my search for the roots of form has proved essential—in the fields of both theatre and architectural design.

I have been looking for archetypes of form and its place in the time and culture of both region and nation. The direction of my research was the transposition into our time of those historical forms of which the meaning and function has been preserved, both in the "micro" and "macro" scale, from theatrical space, through the forming of architecture, to large-scale urban layouts.

Putting to effect the projects for two large Roman Catholic churches in cooperation with my partner Marian Fikus, I drew largely on the rich store of forms historically connected with sacral buildings, and I attempted to transpose them into modern times, so that the spatial object reveals a logical and hierarchical wholeness—symbolizing the continuity and, simultaneously, the changeability of Time.

—Jerzy Gurawski

The name of Jerzy Gurawski is linked to the theatrical conception of Jerzy Grotowski's Theatre 13 Rzedow in Opole and, later, the Laboratory in Wroclaw. An architect, in contrast to all other Polish scenographers, whose foundation is in painting, that is, color, Gurawski is a builder—a builder of theatrical space; he orga-

nizes both the activity of the actor and the perception of the spectator.

Instead of decorations on a box-like stage, he creates functional constructions in the space of the whole theatre auditorium: territories of actors and territories of spectators in a mutual relationship, different each time, depending on the point of view of a particular staging. He rejects all illusionism (painted views, imitative decorations), employing only authentic material, primarily wood not camouflaged by any painting, and authentic accessories and props (costumes are always designed by Waldemar Krygier). One can perhaps see here a convergence with the interest in the plastic arts in *objets trouvés,* found objects which manifest a similar interest in the authentic. However, one can also find in Gurawski's work a certain element of metaphor in the preference of one territory of acting over another, one world over another. Above all, he continues and realizes twentieth-century dreams, as he turns back from the Italian stage and its illusionism of acting and decorations, its domination of drama, and replaces them with an integral theatrical creation.

The Theatre 13 Rzedow began its activity as an axial and box-like stage. Each spectacle is a step forward in the direction of conquering the total space of the theatre. In *Siakuntala,* the action extends into the audience's space. In *Dziady* [Forefather's Eve], there is no stage; rather the drama plays itself out in the center, among the spectators. In *Kordian,* the auditorium is filled with beds, as in some nightmarish hospital, and the beds are placed in tiers; the national hero's drama is situated in an insane asylum! The audience takes its seats on the beds next to the actors. *Doctor Faustus* takes place as if in a cloister refectory: the audience sits at two rows of table-podiums, thereby to participate in this gathering and confession. At the head on a high chair presides Faust in monk's robes. *Prince Constant* takes place as if in a dissecting room: in the center a table-podium, around which, behind a barrier, are seats for the spectators.

In none of these cases does the "architecture" imitate a hospital, a refectory, or a dissecting-room. Rather, the set is based on the fundamental schema of these places, while utilizing the location of the two theatrical groups: the acting and the perceiving (actors and spectators). But it does not shy away from theatricality and thus from the authenticity of the very place in which we find ourselves.

Gurawski cooperated with Grotowski in his "classic" period. He did not participate either in the early presentations, when Grotowski employed the Italian arrangement, nor in the late, when the spectacle form was discarded. The Theatre 13 Rzedow can be considered, from the spatial point of view, as a continuation of Warsaw's 1933 interwar Zoliborz Theatre, in which Szymon Syrkus, also an architect, created a uniform space—the action took place amidst the audience, while seats for the spectators were placed on podiums. In contrast to many monumental attempts, which were projected in the east and in the west but which were never realized, both of these theatres, though small-audience institutions, were achieved. To a certain degree, they can be traced back to the theatrical conception preached by Adam Mickiewicz in the course of his lesson XVI at the Collège de France in Paris, that is, to a conception of a Polish theatre.

—Zenobiusz Strzelecki

Jerzy Gurawski: Stage setting for *Phaedra*, **1985**

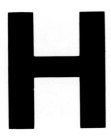

H

HALSTON.

American fashion designer. Born Roy Halston Frowick, in Des Moines, Iowa, 23 April 1932. Studied at Indiana University, Bloomington, and the School of the Art Institute of Chicago, until 1953. Independent hat designer, Chicago, 1952–53; window dresser, for Carson-Pirie-Scott department store, Chicago, 1954–57; designer and manager of the hats division of Lily Dache company, New York, 1958–59; designer for the millinery salon and for the clothing collections, at Bergdorf Goodman, New York, 1959–68; founder and designer, of Halston Limited fashion business, New York, 1962–73; with Henry Pollack Incorporated, established Halston International company for mass-marketing, New York, 1970; with Ben Shaw, founded Halston Originals ready-to-wear business, New York, 1972; Halston Limited re-named Halston Enterprises, a division of Norton Simon Incorporated, New York, 1973: Halston III fashion range initiated for J. C. Penney, 1983. Recipient: Coty American Fashion Critics' Special Award, 1962, 1969, Winnie Award, 1971, Return Award, 1972, and Hall of Fame Award, 1974. *Died* (in San Francisco) *27 March 1990.*

Publications:

By HALSTON: article—in *Harper's Bazaar* (New York), October 1977.

On HALSTON: books—*Fashion Merchandizing* by Mary D. Troxell, New York 1971, 1976; *A History of Fashion* by J. Anderson Black and Madge Garland, London 1975, 1980; *Quest for the Best* by Stanley Marcus, New York 1979; *Fairchild's Who's Who in Fashion,* edited by Ann Stegemeyer, New York 1980; *The Collector's Book of Twentieth Century Fashion* by Frances Kennett, London and New York 1983; *McDowell's Directory of Twentieth Century Fashion* by Colin McDowell, London 1984; *The Encyclopaedia of Fashion from 1840 to the 1980s* by Georgina O'Hara, London 1986.

In an interview in 1972, Halston listed his most admired predecessors as Balenciaga, Chanel, Givenchy, and Saint Laurent, and he condemned Britain for never having produced a major look. He followed this in 1974 by trying to revive the British miniskirt, the most famous look of the 1960s, and went on to claim that he was the creator of the uncluttered elegance he promoted, but that is something for which the British have been celebrated for generations. Maybe there has been more British influence on Halston than he would care to admit. He has had to cope with a degree of unpopularity in the American press for which he left himself wide open by declaring himself the king of American fashion. Not surprisingly, the press then demanded what exactly he had done that was so outstanding. He could claim caftans for evening and hot pants, but what else was new? However, as can be seen with many other couturiers, outstanding originality is not important. There is a market for good quality and for conservative clothes, which Halston is well able to satisfy.

His policy is sensibly based on designing clothes for his customers' lifestyle, in which he participates by going to parties with his patrons, such as Liza Minelli, Marisa Berenson, and Elizabeth Taylor. In 1973, he stated "Women want clothes that have a long life. They want fewer clothes and things to wear for several different seasons. And that goes right across the board. The richest women in the world are now very practical." This sensible approach is good business and because couture houses remain durable by diversifying their interests, Halston now embraces ready-to-wear Halston Originals, Halston furs, Halston luggage, Halston menswear, and the Halston fragrance line.

Halston can lack discipline. His 1980 "ruffle look" saw them used as collars, shoulder wings, skirts, and bustles and even decorating bathing suits; this was an approach hardly in the tradition of Chanel and Balenciaga. One cannot envisage Halston emulating Molyneux in selling one standard, three-quarter length coat for more than thirty years. Such absolute continuity is probably beyond him, as it is so British to retain a popular model in dresses (as in motor cars, such as the Mini) for decades, whereas the United States puts so much stress on novelty. However, American designers can survive this frenzy by following a conservative path, and Halston is of this band.

—Diana de Marly

HARDER, Rolf (Peter).

Canadian graphic designer. Born in Hamburg, 10 July 1929; emigrated to Canada in 1955: naturalized, 1973. Educated at Christianeum high school, Hamburg, until 1948; studied at the Academy of Fine Arts (Landeskunstschule), Hamburg, 1948–52. Married Maria-Inger Rumberg in 1958; children: Christoph and Vivian. Designer, with Rolf Ruehle Werbung, Hamburg, 1952–55, and with Schneider Cardon Ltd., Montreal, 1955–56; Art Director, George Ferguson Associates, Montreal, 1956–57; visualizer, with Lintas GmbH, Hamburg, 1957–59; established Rolf Harder Design, Montreal, 1959–65; co-founder and principal, with Ernst Roch, Design Collaborative Associates graphic design firm, Montreal, 1965–77; founder-director, Rolf Harder and Associates graphic design consultants, working for Hoffmann-La Roche Limited, Alcan Aluminium Ltd., Consolidated Bathurst Inc., Canadian Pulp and Paper Association, Canada Post Corporation, Government of Canada, Bell Canada, Teleglobe Canada, IBM Canada, Grand Prix du Canada, etc., in Montreal, since 1977. Canadian Group President, Alliance Graphique Internationale, since 1975; International Advisory Board Member, *Typos* magazine, London, since 1979. Guest lecturer at colleges and professional institutions, throughout Canada, since 1970. **Exhibitions:** *AIGA Packaging,* American Institute of Graphic Arts, New York, 1960, 1961, 1964, 1965; *Annual Exhibition of Advertising and Editorial Arts,* Los Angeles, 1960, 1961, 1964, 1968, 1982; *Typomundus,* New York, 1965, Munich, 1970; *Annual Exhibition,* Type Directors Club, New York, 1967, 1974, 1981; *Graphic Design by Rolf Harder and Ernst Roch,* Musee des Beaux-Arts, Montreal, 1970 (toured Canada, Germany, Yugoslavia and the United States 1970–74); Royal Canadian Academy of Arts, Toronto, 1970, 1971, 1980, 1987; *107 Graphic Designers of the AGI,* Castello Sforzesco, Milan, 1974 (travelled to Brussels, Toronto, Montreal and Caracas); *Canadian Graphic Design,* Design Gallery, Tokyo, 1975; *100 Years of the Poster in Canada,* Art Gallery of Ontario, Toronto, 1979 (toured Canada); *Rolf Harder: Graphic Design,* Pointe-Claire Cultural Centre, Montreal, 1980. **Collection:** Library of Congress, Washington, D.C. Recipient: First Prize, Canadian Association for Retarded Children Symbol Competition, 1964; Special Prize, Biennale of Graphic Design, Brno, 1970; Special Prize, International Poster Competition, Moscow, 1987. Fellow, Society of Graphic Designers of Canada, 1985. Member: Royal Canadian Academy of Arts; Alliance Graphique Internationale; American Institute of Graphic Arts; International Centre for Typographic Arts. Address: 1638 Sherbrooke Street West, Montreal, Quebec H3H 1C9, Canada.

Works:

Visual identity program, for Hoffmann-La Roche Limited, 1959–77.
Visual identity program, for Canadian pavilion, XIV Milan Triennale, 1968.
Logo, for RoyFund Limited, 1969.
Logo, for Imasco Limited, 1970.
Logo, for Queenswear Limited, 1972.
Numerous postage stamps, for Canada Post Corporation, from 1975.
New alphabet, for Northern Telecom, 1976–77.
Visual identity program, for Grand Prix du Canada, 1977.
Logo, for IBM Eastern Region Productivity Centre, 1978.
Logo, for International Design and Woodcraft, 1978.
Centennial logo, for Bell Canada, 1979.
Logo, for CompuDesign Inc., 1982.
Logo, for McMillan Bathurst Inc., 1983.

Rolf Harder: Souvenir postage stamps, for the Canada Post Corporation, 1985

Visual identity program, for Maison Alcan, 1984.

Symbol and signage, for Protestant School Board of Greater Montreal, 1987–89.

Publications concept, for Transport Canada, 1988.

Publications:

By HARDER: books—*Pitseolak, Pictures Out Of My Life,* co-publisher, Montreal 1971; *Arts of the Eskimo: Prints,* co-publisher, Montreal 1975.

On HARDER: books—*Optical Illusions and the Visual Arts* by Carraher Thurston, New York 1966; *Graphic Design by Rolf Harder and Ernst Roch,* exhibition catalogue with texts by Hans Neuburg and Allan Harrison, Montreal 1977; *International Trade Mark Design* by Peter Wildbur, London 1979; *Letterheads* by Takenobu Igarashi, Tokyo 1986; *World Trade Marks and Logotypes II,* edited by Takenobu Igarashi, Tokyo 1987; *World Graphic Design: Packages,* Tokyo 1988; *World Graphic Design: Corporate Identity,* Tokyo 1989; *Typographic Communications Today* by Edward M. Gottschall, Cambridge, Massachusetts and London 1989.

Let me begin by stating what, in my view, the graphic designer is *not.*

We are not artists who, in solitary struggle, produce a piece of art. Although "art" may be the result, our primary aim is to solve communication problems. Our attitude in approaching an assignment can be compared to that of the architect who, apart from very important aesthetic considerations, always has to keep the building's function in mind as he designs it. In other words, we are first of all pragmatists whose desire for self-expression must not interfere with a clear and unequivocal formulation of a given message.

Aesthetics, craftsmanship, a feeling for an understanding of form, colour and composition, are necessary prerequisites for the designer's work. Beyond this, there is still plenty of room for wit, imagination, intuition and talent. But all this has to be tempered by a healthy amount of intellectual self-control which keeps questioning and reappraising the developing ideas. Contrary to the fine artist, who poses his own problems of concept and content, we graphic designers are given a problem which we have to analyse thoroughly. We have to formulate intellectually and visually the requirements in order to reach the desired objective, which is to communicate a specific message.

Another aspect of the designer's work: he contributes in many ways, some small, others more significant, towards the shaping of our environment; he exerts a certain influence on the thinking and behaviour of his fellow men. Therefore, a sense of responsibility is necessary, if his endeavours are to go beyond the mere purpose of earning a living.

Alan Gussow, an American artist-environmentalist, said: "When our environment is degraded, we are degraded, since we are not distinct from our place—we are that place. The value of the individual tends to decrease along with that of the place."

If a designer's work is aesthetically satisfying, intellectually stimulating, imaginative and at the same time concise and informative—in short, generally in harmony with our needs—he has made a positive contribution towards a more human environment.

—Rolf Harder

Rolf Harder has been a major force in Canadian graphic design since he opened his first studio in Montreal in 1959. German-born, Harder studied at the Hamburg Academy of Fine Arts before emigrating to Canada in the mid-fifties. At that time, design in Canada was strongly influenced by the American approach to advertising and marketing illustration, known as "commercial art". With few exceptions, most efforts were, at best, mediocre. The international style which Harder helped pioneer and the standards of quality he espoused created a new awareness of aesthetics and form that changed the face of graphic design in his adopted country.

For Harder, the purpose of design is not to decorate, but to communicate. His strength as a designer nevertheless owes much to his talent as artist and illustrator. His inspired melding of colour, line and typography is evident in his striking logos, book designs and posters. The postage stamps he has designed for Canada Post are particularly fine examples of his functional, and sensitive, work.

Harder's contention that graphic design has a crucial social role to play was not familiar to the area in which he decided to specialize, industrial and institutional graphics. Acquiring government agencies and some of Canada's major corporations as clients, however, enabled him to spread the message. Granted, those clients may not have been altruistically moved in their choice of Harder as designer of their logos, visual identity programmes and prestigious publications, but their visual environment has nonetheless been enhanced by the chief selling feature of his work—finely-crafted, superbly functional design.

The visual clarity and pristine form that is Harder's trademark belies the depth and complexity of his approach to design development. A painstaking analysis of all aspects of the project is made before any design is begun. It is at this investigative stage that potential solutions to the design problem evolve and their possibilities are weighed. When the optimum resolution finally emerges, then the designer's imagination can take over and develop the graphics "package" that best suits the purpose. One admiring critic has described Harder's technique as "working from the inside out".

It is a technique based on logic. One that calls for systematic thinking and intellectual discipline. To be successful, it also requires a sense of adventure and a commitment to beauty. Harder's postage stamps are fine examples of discipline, artistic achievement. So are the creative packaging designs developed for his pharmaceutical clients.

Harder is a disciple of constructivism, although not in a dogmatic sense. In his work, form never takes precedence over function but he does enjoy experimenting with his designs, often in quite a playful way. Eventually it is how he balances organization of form with the aesthetic elements of the piece that sets his work apart. So is the vitality of his design that captures the viewer's attention and does exactly what Harder has set out to do: communicate. Says one colleague, "Harder consistently produces design solutions that are intellectually satisfying and emotionally pleasing".

Highly respected by colleagues and clients, Harder has been called a "designer's designer". The influence he has had both on the profession and on other designers' work is profound. National and international recognition has come with over 100 awards, exhibitions of his work around the world, review of his designs in the leading professional publications. And after thirty years of imaginative and innovative design, Harder's work is as fresh and as stimulating as ever.

—Gloria Menard

HARDWICK, Cathy.

American fashion and interior designer. Born Cathaline Kaesug Sun, in Seoul, Korea, in 1933; emigrated to the United States in 1952: naturalized, 1959. Mainly self-taught in design. Married Anthony Hardwick in 1966. Clothing designer, for Alvin Duskin, San Francisco, in the 1960s; freelance designer, establishing own boutique in San Francisco, 1968-74; president, Cathy Hardwick Limited, New York, 1975-81, and Cathy Hardwick Design Studio, New York, from 1977. Recipient: Coty Special Award, New York, 1975. Address: Cathy Hardwick Design Studio, 1466 Broadway, Suite 901, New York, New York 10018, U.S.A.

Publications:

On HARDWICK: books—*The Changing World of Fashion: 1900 to the Present* by Ernestine Carter, London 1977; *Fairchild's Who's Who in Fashion,* edited by Ann Stegemeyer, New York 1980; *McDowell's Directory of Twentieth Century Fashion* by Colin McDowell, London 1984; *The Encyclopaedia of Fashion from 1840 to the 1980s* by Georgina O'Hara, London 1986.

I make clothes to celebrate and enhance the woman's body—these are clothes for a very secure, happy person, who is successful in her life, and whose body and mind are in good shape, whatever her age. Of course, anyone can wear my clothes, since I think they are as ageless as my ideal woman.

—Cathy Hardwick

Cathy Hardwick: Evening dress in red matte jersey, 1983

Cathy Hardwick came into her own as one of a group of young, recognized American designers of relatively moderately priced ready-to-wear women's clothing soon after she arrived in New York from San Francisco and opened her own design studio in the early 1970s. The very next year, she launched her line of simple, fluid dresses, pants, jackets, and blouses, by opening her own manufacturing firm on Broadway.

A consistency runs throughout Hardwick's work. She likes simplicity and understatement and most often uses fine, natural fabrics, preferring cotton for summer and wool for winter. She is not what one might call a major innovator, but is rather a subtle stylist who adds her personal, innovative touches to the basic items of wardrobe, incorporating a certain panache into her very wearable and versatile creations. Exemplary of her uses of individualistic variations are her jumpsuits. In her spring 1975 version, loose, midcalf pants were slit to the thighs, topped with a narrow tank tied at the side, and the whole was enlivened by the multicolored stripes on the black, lightweight cotton fabric. Hardwick's fall 1975 modification of the popular jumpsuit was a dropshoulder variety, with frilly ruffled shoulderline; its sensuous lines were enhanced by the choice of pale lavender rayon crepe de chine. Hardwick's penchant for the subtle touch of the exotic was also prominent in her 1976 jumpsuit of raspberry-colored crinkled cotton, strapless and harem-hemmed, light, fluid, and bare for easy yet sophisticated wear. She also often demonstrates her liking for chinoiserie, as in her 1975 wool and silk tunics and frog-closed jackets of quilted florals or embroidered silks.

Another basic in Hardwick's output is the look of total coordination achieved through multiple mix-and-match possibilities. Take, for example, her 1975 knits, which included pullovers cut like T-shirts, soft mohair cardigans, and softly gathered or slim skirts, all dyed to match along with a group of scarf-hats. Also outstanding were her 1978 pale blue silk "waterfall" neckline blouses with rounded collars and narrow wrists to go with navy silk pleated pants for Dessina.

Whether they are playclothes of terrycloth or crinkled cotton or holiday wear of wool challis or red velvet, Hardwick's creations always stress a basic simplicity with elegant feminine touches. They are geared for women of all ages who are looking for clean, solid feminity with a not-too-far-out flash of spirited arrogance.

—Barbara Cavaliere

HASSELBERG-OLSSON, Elisabet.

Swedish textile designer. Born Elisabet Hasselberg, in Göteborg, 15 October 1932. Self-taught in weaving and textile design, from 1960. Married the architect John Olsson in 1956; daughter: Anna. Concentrated on tapestry weaving, initially in Elsa Gullberg's workshop in Vaxholm, from 1964: established own workshop in Täby, 1966. **Exhibitions:** *Why a Brush?,* Hantverket Gallery, Stockholm, 1966; Finnish Design Center, Helsinki, 1969; Form Design Center, Malmo, 1969; Galleri Glaucus, Stockholm, 1971; *Expressions Textiles Nordiques,* Angers, France, 1973; *First World Crafts Exhibition,* Toronto, 1974; Sundsvalls Museum, Sweden, 1975; Södertälje Konsthall, Sweden, 1975; *Swedish Textile Art—Five Temperaments,* toured Cuba, Canada and Mexico, 1976; *Tre Temperament i Väv,* Nationalmuseum, Stockholm, 1976; *Expressions Suédoise,* Brussels, 1977; Centre Culturel Suedois, Paris, 1978; *Scandinavian Crafts Exhibition,* Tokyo, 1978; *Scandinavia Today,* toured the United States, 1982; *Contemporary Swedish Design* Nationalmuseum, Stockholm, 1983; *Scandinavia Today,* toured Japan and the United States, 1987–88; Västerbottens Museum, Umeå, 1988 (travelled to Södertälje and Borås). **Collections:** Nationalmuseum, Stockholm; Malmö Museum, Sweden; Röhsska Könstslöjdmuseet, Göteborg. Address: Arrendevagen 23, 18338 Täby, Sweden.

Works:

Stammar/Trunks linen on cotton warp tapestry, 1964.
Vision I linen and art silk on linen warp tapestry, 1965.
Inscription Vietnam linen on linen warp tapestry, 1968.
Till Havet II/To The Sea II linen and art silk on linen warp tapestry, 1968.
Hemmet/The Home linen on linen warp tapestry, 1970.
Vägen Hem/The Homeward Road linen, art silk and wool on linen warp tapestry, 1970.
Förväntan/Expectation linen on cotton warp tapestry, 1971.
Molnet/The Cloud linen on cotton warp tapestry, 1973.
Kappan/The Coat linen and art silk on cotton warp tapestry, 1973.
Gryning/Dawn linen and art silk on cotton warp tapestry, for Tibble Church, Taby, 1973.
Aker/Farmland linen on cotton warp tapestry, 1974.
Elden/The Fire linen and art silk on cotton warp tapestry, for the Kooperativa Forbundet, 1974.
Trasmattan/The Rag-Carpet linen on cotton warp tapestry, 1975.
Stranden/The Beach linen and art silk on cotton warp tapestry, 1976.
Oppen dorr/Open Door linen on cotton warp tapestry, 1978.

Elisabet Hasselberg-Olsson: *Memory of a Landscape* tapestry, for the Swedish Parliament Assembly Hall, Stockholm, 1982–83

Fabrik/Factory linen on cotton warp tapestry, 1980.

Memory of a Landscape linen, boucle and wool on cotton warp tapestry, for the Swedish House of Parliament, Stockholm, 1982–83.

Horn/Corner linen on cotton warp tapestry, 1986.

Spar/Tracks linen on cotton warp tapestry, 1987.

Stenar/Stones linen on cotton warp tapestry, 1988.

Publications:

On HASSELBERG-OLSSON: books—*Tre Temperament i Väv,* exhibition catalogue by Dag Widman, Helena Lutteman and Katja Walden, Stockholm 1976; *Svensk Textilkonst/ Swedish Textile Art* by Edna Martin and Beate Sydhoff, Stockholm 1980; *Form och Tradition i Sverige,* edited by Birgitta Walz, Stockholm 1982; *Contemporary Swedish Design,* exhibition catalogue by Monica Boman, Lennart Lindkvist and others, Stockholm 1983; *Elisabet Hasselberg-Olsson: Memory of a Landscape,* with text by Gunilla Lundahl, Stockholm 1984; *Den Svenska Formen* by Monica Boman and others, Stockholm 1985; *Elisabet Hasselberg-Olsson: Bildvävar 1965–1988,* exhibition catalogue with texts by Elisabeth Rasch, Beate Sydhoff and Per Drougge, Umeå 1988.

HAVINDEN, Ashley (Eldrid).

British painter, typographer, textile and graphic designer: also known as "Ashley". Born in Rochester, Kent, 13 April 1903. Educated at Christ's Hospital School, Horsham, Sussex, 1912–20; studied drawing and design, Central School of Arts and Crafts, London, 1922–23; also private studies with the sculptor Henry Moore, Hampstead, London, 1933. Served in the British Army camouflage unit, 1941–45: Captain. Married Margaret Kirk Sangster in 1928; children: Michael and Venice. Trainee and designer, 1922–29, art director and board member, 1929–60, and vice-chairman, 1960–67, W. S. Crawford advertising agency, London; director, 1946–48, and chairman, 1948–67, Design International (Sir William Crawford and Partners) industrial design firm, London; freelance designer, with own studio in Hertingfordbury, Hertfordshire, 1967–73: designed for the Milk Marketing Board, General Post Office, London County Council, Central Office of Information, Simpson's of Piccadilly, KLM Royal Dutch Airlines, Morton Sundour Fabrics, Wilton Royal Carpet Factory, Edinburgh Weavers, Duncan Miller Interior Design, Chrysler Motors, Osram Lamps, Pretty Polly Stockings, etc. Council member, 1946–47, and president, 1953, Society of Industrial Artists and Designers, London; governor, 1950–57, and chairman, 1955–56 and 1958–59, London College of Printing; president, Advertising Creative Circle, London, 1955, Double Crown Club, London, 1956, and Alliance Graphique Internationale, Paris, 1957–59; advisory committee member, 1958–65, and governor, 1965–67, Chelsea School of Art, London; governor, Central School of Arts and Crafts, London, 1959–67; master of the faculty of Royal Designers for Industry, Royal Society of Arts, London, 1967–69. **Exhibitions:** *Union des Artistes Modernes,* Paris, 1933; Lund Humphries Gallery, London, 1937; London Gallery, London, 1937; *Exposition Internationale,* Paris, 1937; Leicester Galleries, London, 1938; Alex Reid and Lefevre Galleries, London, 1939; *Golden Gate Exposition,* San Francisco, 1939; *Design at Work,* Royal Academy of Art, London, 1946; *Britain Can Make It,* Victoria and Albert Museum, London, 1946; Marlborough Fine Art, London, 1965; *Second World War Posters,* Imperial War Museum, London, 1972; *Thirties,* Hayward Gallery, London, 1979; *Eye for Industry,* Victoria and Albert Museum, London, 1986. Recipient: Fellow, 1945, and Royal Designer for Industry, 1947, Royal Society of Arts, London; Fellow, Society of Industrial Artists and Designers, London, 1946; Honoured Member, Advertising Creative Circle, London, 1966; Fellow, Institute of Practitioners in Advertising, London, and Central Institute of Art and Design, London. Honorary Doctorate: Manchester University, 1961. Officer, Order of the British Empire, 1951. *Died* (in Hertingfordbury, Hertfordshire) *31 May 1973.*

Ashley Havinden: Poster for the Milk Marketing Board, London, 1936

Publications

By HAVINDEN: books—*Line Drawing for Reproduction,* London 1933, 1941; *MARS Group of Modern Architects,* exhibition catalogue with text by John Summerson, London 1938; *Advertising and the Artist,* with introduction by Stephen Tallens, London 1956; *Advertising and the Motor-Car,* edited by Michael Frostick, London 1970.

On HAVINDEN: books—*British Textile Designers Today* by H. G. Hayes Marshall, Leigh-on-Sea 1939; *Packaging: An International Survey of Package Design,* edited by Walter Herdeg, Zurich 1959; *Who's Who in Graphic Art,* edited by Walter Amstutz, Zurich 1962; *The Poster: An Illustrated History from 1860* by Harold F. Hutchinson, London and Toronto 1968; *Second World War Posters,* exhibition catalogue edited by Joseph Darracott and Belinda Loftus, London 1972; *Industrial Design in Britain* by Noel Carrington, London 1976; *Advertising: Reflections of a Century* by Bryan Holme, London 1982; *Eye for Industry: Royal Designers for Industry 1936–1986,* exhibition catalogue by Fiona MacCarthy and Patrick Nuttgens, London 1986.

At the opening of Ashley Havinden's career, British graphic design was dominated by late Victorian and Edwardian conventions, such as the prominent, obligatory use of tasteless company "nameblocks" in thick script, company slogans, and redundant figurative imagery. As a young designer, he met and fell under the charismatic influence of Stanley Morison, the great typographic designer then engaged upon the systematic revival of classic typefaces for the Monotype Corporation. Partly in response to Morison's influence, Havinden produced a number of designs which were tastefully balanced, symmetrical, and typographically refined.

Although these early designs made progress toward simplification of pictorial imagery and a tauter relationship between text and image, Havinden later recognised the Morison influence as a blind alley. By the mid-1920s, he had become aware of the design innovations of the Bauhaus, the constructivists, and such figures as László Moholy-Nagy and Jan Tschichold. He visited Germany and eventually was to spend a year there absorbing the Continental influence on graphic design. The campaign for Chrysler cars dispensed with many of the conventions of the day and used instead dramatic, highly simplified imagery; a bold, sans-serif typeface; and a strong, constructive alignment in layout. The use of the Chrysler designs internationally necessitated cutting the letterform he designed for it as a typeface.

An important feature of Havinden's career is his intelligent openness to the influence of fine art and architecture. As a young man, he took lessons from the sculptor Henry Moore, and he continued to work and exhibit as a painter. He read and absorbed the foremost theorists of his day, including Tschichold, Gropius, and Le Corbusier, at the same time converting what they had to say to something which was uniquely his own. This, combined with a refined and discriminating taste, made him one of the leading figures in British graphic design for more than four decades.

Prominent in Havinden's early mature work is the machine aesthetic, with its bold, rectilinear letterforms and simple, hard-edge pictorial imagery. By the late 1930s, a more relaxed mood emerged, perhaps in reaction to the extremism of Continental design of the day. In his "Drink Milk Daily" poster of 1936, the text is still set on a diagonal, but the letterform has a pleasantly improvised chalk-and-blackboard look.

Yoshio Hayakawa: *The Face* exhibition poster, for the Imabashi Gallery, Tokyo, 1968

Havinden's postwar designs exhibit a wide variety of approaches and possibilities, ranging from the firmly constructed look of his work for the National Book League, to free, improvisatory motifs reminiscent of graffiti, as in his corporate image for Richard Shops. His designs for Pretty Polly stockings, which utilize a pastiche of rustic *lettres ornées,* are still currently in use and look as vivid and fresh as the day they were produced.

—Clive Ashwin

HAYAKAWA, Yoshio.

Japanese illustrator, display, stage and graphic designer. Born in Osaka, 13 February 1917. Studied at the School of Industrial Design, Osaka, 1931–36. Married Ume Chibata in 1949; son Maku. Window display artist, Mitsukoshi Department Store, Osaka, 1937–38; display designer, Osaka City Administration, 1944–48; advertising designer, Kintetsu Department Store, Tokyo, 1948–52; freelance graphic and stage designer from 1952, establishing Yoshio Hayakawa Design Office, Tokyo, from 1954: consultant, Art Directors Club of Tokyo, from 1980; planning specialist, Osaka in the 21st Century, from 1981. Founder-member, DAS Society of Designers, Tokyo, 1956; co-founder, NIC Japan Illustrators Congress, 1969; planning committee member, *Expo 70* exhibition, Osaka, 1970. Lecturer, University of Fine Arts, Kyoto, 1953–70; part-time lecturer, University of Fine Arts, Osaka, from 1964. **Exhibitions:** *Yoshio Hayakawa: Commercial Design,* Osaka, 1952; *Graphics 55,* Tokyo, 1955; *Japanese Posters,* toured Europe, 1977; *Japan Style,* toured Europe, 1979; *Modern Japa-*

nese Posters, Toyama Museum of Art, Japan, 1982. **Collections:** Museum of Modern Art, New York; Toyama Prefectural Museum of Art, Japan; Musashino University of Fine Art, Japan. Recipient: Mainichi Industrial Design Prize, Tokyo, 1954; Tokyo Art Directors Club Medal, 1957, 1959; Ministry of Industry and Culture Book Design Award, Tokyo, 1978; Kodansha Culture Award, Tokyo, 1981; Shijuho Award, Tokyo, 1982. Member, Alliance Graphique Internationale. Address: Yoshio Hayakawa Design Office, 6-27-113, Akasaka 8 chome, Minato-ku, Tokyo 107, Japan.

Publications:

By HAYAKAWA: book—*Illustrations*, Tokyo 1955; article—in *Print* (New York), January 1967.

On HAYAKAWA: book—*Posters* by W. H. Allner, New York 1952; articles—in *Graphis* (Zurich), no. 46, 1953, no. 55, 1954, March 1956.

It is clear that one function of graphic design is to communicate messages. I believe, however, that it should not end up being just a technique and that it is important that we invite the world of graphic design, with its formative appeal consisting of color and shape, to inject elements of beauty into people's lives. Although my expression takes various forms depending on the purpose of the message, I strive for human warmth in all cases.

— Yoshio Hayakawa

After completing his education at the School of Industrial Design in Osaka, Yoshio Hayakawa entered commercial design. His graphic design compositions are solid and unique works, the result of his individual style and the emotion one can sense in his illustration. He has had a great influence on Japanese graphic design, and there are many who follow his style.

His superlative temperament as an artist is based on solid ideas. At first glance, his work seems all to be in the same style, but each piece has something different about it and possesses an agreeability which serves to calm those who view his works. He on occasion presents exhibits of his drawings and paintings; these always manifest his desire to progress in the creation of new work.

— Masaaki Tanaka

HEAD, Edith.
American film costume designer. Born Edith Claire Posener, in San Bernardino, California, 28 October 1897. Educated in Redding and Los Angeles, California; studied at the University of California at Los Angeles: BA; Stanford University, California: MA; also attended classes at the Otis Art Institute and Chouinard Art School, Los Angeles. Married Charles Head in 1923 (divorced, 1923); the designer Wiard Ihnen in 1940 (died, 1979). Instructor in French, Spanish, and art, at Bishops School for Girls, La Jolla, and at Hollywood School for Girls, Los Angeles, 1923; sketch artist, 1924-27, assistant to Travis Banton, 1927-38, and head of design, 1938-66, Paramount Film Studios, Hollywood; chief costume designer, Uni-

versal Studios, Hollywood, 1967-81. Also designed uniforms for Pan American Airlines, the United States Coastguard and United Nations tour guides. Lecturer, University of Southern California, 1949-51, 1973. Fashion editor, *Holiday* magazine, 1973. **Exhibitions:** *Romantic and Glamorous Hollywood Design*, Metropolitan Museum of Art, New York, 1974; *Hollywood Film Costume*, Whitworth Art Gallery, Manchester, 1977. Recipient: Academy Awards, 1949, 1950, 1951, 1953, 1954, 1960, 1973; Film Designer of the Year Award, Mannequins Association, Los Angeles, 1962; Costume Designers Guild Award, 1967. *Died* (in Los Angeles, California) *26 October 1981*.

Works:

Film designs include—*Peter Pan*, 1924; *The Golden Bed*, 1925; *The Wanderer*, 1925; *Mantrap*, 1926; *Wings*, 1927; *The Saturday Night Kid*, 1929; *The Virginian*, 1929; *The Wolf Song*, 1929; *Along Came Youth*, 1930; *Only the Brave*, 1930; *The Santa Fe Trail*, 1930; *The Big Broadcast of 1932*, 1932; *Love Me Tonight*, 1932; *Undercover Man*, 1932; *She Done Him Wrong*, 1933; *Cradle Song*, 1933; *Hello Everybody*, 1933; *Sitting Pretty*, 1933; *Strictly Personal*, 1933; *Little Miss Marker*, 1934; *The Big Broadcast of 1936*, 1935; *Lives of a Bengal Lancer*, 1935; *Mississippi*, 1935; *Ruggles of Red Gap*, 1935; *Peter Ibbetson*, 1935; *Wings in the Dark*, 1935; *The Big Broadcast of 1937*, 1936; *The Jungle Princess*, 1936; *The Milky Way*, 1936; *Poppy*, 1936; *Woman*, 1936; *Trap*, 1936; *College Holiday*, 1936; *The Barrier*, 1937; *Blond Trouble*, 1937; *Blossoms on Broadway*, 1937; *Borderland*, 1937; *Bulldog Drummond Comes Back*, 1937; *Bulldog Drummond Escapes*, 1937; *Bulldog Drummond's Revenge*, 1937; *Clarence*, 1937; *The Crime Nobody Saw*, 1937; *A Doctor's Diary*, 1937; *Double or Nothing*, 1937; *Ebb Tide*, 1937; *Exclusive*, 1937; *Forlorn River*, 1937; *Girl from Scotland Yard*, 1937; *Murder Goes to College*, 1937; *The Great Gambini*, 1937; *Hideaway Girl*, 1937; *Hills of Old Wyoming*, 1937; *Hold 'Em Navy*, 1937; *Hotel Haywire*, 1937; *Her Husband Lies*, 1937; *Interns Can't Take Money*, 1937; *John Meade's Woman* (with Bridgehouse), 1937; *Last Train from Madrid*, 1937; *Let's Make a Million*, 1937; *Make Way for Tomorrow*, 1937; *Midnight Madonna*, 1937; *Mind Your Own Business*, 1937; *Mountain Music*, 1937; *Souls at Sea*, 1937; *Night Club Scandal*, 1937; *A Night of Mystery*, 1937; *North of the Rio Grande*, 1937; *On Such a Night*, 1937; *Outcast*, 1937; *Partners in Crime*, 1937; *Partners of the Plains*, 1937; *She Asked for It*, 1937; *She's No Lady*, 1937; *Sophie Lang Goes West*, 1937; *Texas Trail*, 1937; *This Way Please*, 1937; *Thrill of a Lifetime*, 1937; *True Confession*, 1937; *Wild Money*, 1937; *Turn Off the Moon*, 1937; *Waikiki Wedding*, 1937; *Wells Fargo*, 1937; *Artists and Models Abroad*, 1938; *The Arkansas Traveler*, 1938; *Bar 20 Justice*, 1938; *Booloo*, 1938; *Born to the West*, 1938; *Bulldog Drummond in Africa*, 1938; *Bulldog Drummond's Peril*, 1938; *Campus Confessions*, 1938; *Coconut Grove*, 1938; *Professor Beware*, 1938; *Prison Farm*, 1938; *Pride of the West*, 1938; *Men with Wings*, 1938; *Love on Toast*, 1938; *Little Orphan Annie*, 1938; *King of Alcatraz*, 1938; *In Old Mexico*, 1938; *Illegal Traffic*, 1938; *Hunted Men*, 1938; *Her Jungle Love*, 1938; *Heart of Arizona*, 1938; *Give Me a Sailor*, 1938; *The Frontiersman*, 1938; *College Swing*, 1938; *Ride a Crooked Mile*, 1938; *Say It in French*, 1938; *Scandal Sheet*, 1938; *Sing You Sinners*, 1938; *Tropic Holiday*, 1938; *Touchdown, Army*, 1938; *Tom Sawyer Detective*, 1938; *Tip-off Girls*, 1938; *Thanks for the Memory*, 1938; *The Texans*, 1938; *Sons of the

Legion*, 1938; *Spawn of the North*, 1938; *Stolen Heaven*, 1938; *Arrest Bulldog Drummond*, 1939; *All Women Have Secrets*, 1939; *Honeymoon in Bali*, 1939; *Heritage of the Desert*, 1939; *Back Door to Heaven*, 1939; *Beau Geste*, 1939; *Boy Trouble*, 1939; *The Great Victor Herbert*, 1939; *Grand Jury Secrets*, 1939; *The Gracie Allen Murder Case*, 1939; *Disputed Passage*, 1939; *Disbarred*, 1939; *Death of a Champion*, 1939; *The Cat and the Canary*, 1939; *Cafe Society*, 1939; *Bulldog Drummond's Secret Police*, 1939; *Bulldog Drummond's Bride*, 1939; *Night Work*, 1939; *The Night of Nights*, 1939; *Hotel Imperial*, 1939; *I'm Missouri*, 1939; *Invitation to Happiness*, 1939; *Island of Lost Men*, 1939; *The Lady's from Kentucky*, 1939; *Law of the Pampas*, 1939; *The Light That Failed*, 1939; *The Llano Kid*, 1939; *The Magnificent Fraud*, 1939; *Man About Town*, 1939; *Million Dollar Legs*, 1939; *Never Say Die*, 1939; *$1,000 a Touchdown*, 1939; *Undercover Doctor*, 1939; *This Man Is News*, 1939; *Television Spy*, 1939; *Sudden Money*, 1939; *St. Louis Blues*, 1939; *Some Like It Hot*, 1939; *The Star Maker*, 1939; *Rulers of the Sea*, 1939; *Our Leading Citizen*, 1939; *Our Neighbors, the Carters*, 1939; *Paris Honeymoon*, 1939; *Persons in Hiding*, 1939; *What a Life*, 1939; *Unmarried*, 1939; *Zaza*, 1939; *Adventure in Diamonds*, 1940; *Buck Benny Rides Again*, 1940; *Cherokee Strip*, 1940; *Christmas in July*, 1940; *Comin' Round the Mountain*, 1940; *Dancing on a Dime*, 1940; *French Without Tears*, 1940; *Doctor Cyclops*, 1940; *Emergency Squad*, 1940; *The Farmer's Daughter*, 1940; *Geronimo*, 1940; *The Ghost Breakers*, 1940; *Rhythm on the River*, 1940; *Remember the Night*, 1940; *Rangers of Fortune*, 1940; *Queen of the Mod*, 1940; *Quarterback*, 1940; *A Parole Fixer*, 1940; *Opened by Mistake*, 1940; *A Night at Earl Carrols*, 1940; *Golden Gloves*, 1940; *The Great McGinty*, 1940; *I Want a Divorce*, 1940; *Love Thy Neighbor*, 1940; *Moon Over Burma*, 1940; *Mystery Sea Raider*, 1940; *Road to Singapore*, 1940; *Safari*, 1940; *Seventeen*, 1940; *The Show Down*, 1940; *Stagecoach War*, 1940; *Those Were the Days*, 1940; *Women Without Names*, 1940; *The Way of All Flesh*, 1940; *Untamed*, 1940; *Typhoon*, 1940; *Three Men from Texas*, 1940; *Aloma of the South Seas*, 1941; *Among the Living*, 1941; *Life with Henry*, 1941; *Las Vegas Nights*, 1941; *The Lady Eve*, 1941; *Kiss the Boys Goodbye*, 1941; *I Wanted Wings*, 1941; *Hold Back the Dawn*, 1941; *Bahama Passage*, 1941; *Birth of the Blues*, 1941; *Buy Me That Town*, 1941; *Caught in the Draft*, 1941; *Doomed Caravan*, 1941; *Flying Blind*, 1941; *Forced Landing*, 1941; *Glamour Boy*, 1941; *Henry Aldrich for President*, 1941; *West Point Widow*, 1941; *World Premiere*, 1941; *You're the One*, 1941; *You Belong to Me*, 1941; *Ball of Fire*, 1941; *Skylark* (with Irene), 1941; *Kiss the Boys Goodbye*, 1941; *Sullivan's Travels*, 1941; *The Road to Zanzibar*, 1941; *Here Comes Mr. Jordan*, 1941; *There's Magic in Music*, 1941; *Virginia*, 1941; *Shepherd of the Hills*, 1941; *Reaching for the Sun*, 1941; *New York Town*, 1941; *One Night in Lisbon*, 1941; *The Gay Sisters* (with Milo Anderson), 1942; *I Married a Witch*, 1942; *The Major and the Minor*, 1942; *The Road to Morocco*, 1942; *This Gun for Hire*, 1942; *Beyond the Blue Horizon*, 1942; *The Remarkable Andrew*, 1942; *The Fleet's In*, 1942; *Young and Willing*, 1942; *My Favourite Blond*, 1942; *Are Husbands Necessary?*, 1942; *Holiday Inn*, 1942; *The Glass Key*, 1942; *Star Spangled Rhythm*, 1942; *Lucky Jordan*, 1942; *Flesh and Fantasy* (with V. West), 1943; *True to Life*, 1943; *Lady of Burlesque* (with Natalie Visart), 1943; *Not Time for Love* (with Irene), 1943; *The Crystal Ball*, 1943; *China*, 1943; *Salute for Three*, 1943; *Five Graves to Cairo*, 1943; *Riding High*,

1943; *Let's Face It*, 1943; *Hostages*, 1943; *Tender Comrade* (with Renie), 1943; *And Now Tomorrow*, 1944; *Going My Way*, 1944; *Here Come the Waves*, 1944; *I Love a Soldier*, 1944; *I'll be Seeing You*, 1944; *Our Hearts Were Young and Gay*, 1944; *The Uninvited*, 1944; *Standing Room Only*, 1944; *Lady in the Dark* (with Du Bois and Leisen), 1944; *Rainbow Island*, 1944; *Double Indemnity*, 1944; *Ministry of Fear*, 1944; *And the Angels Sing*, 1944; *Hour Before Dawn*, 1944; *The Affairs of Susan*, 1945; *The Bells of St. Mary's*, 1945; *Christmas in Connecticut* (with Milo Anderson), 1945; *Duffy's Tavern* (with Dodson), 1945; *Incendiary Blonde*, 1945; *The Lost Weekend*, 1945; *Love Letters*, 1945; *Masquerade, in Mexico*, 1945; *A Medal for Benny*, 1945; *Miss Susie Slagle's* (with Dodson), 1945; *Out of This World*, 1945; *The Road to Utopia*, 1945; *The Stork Club*, 1945; *The Blue Dahlia*, 1946; *My Reputation* (with Rhodes), 1946; *Notorious*, 1946; *The Strange Love of Martha Ivers*, 1946; *To Each His Own*, 1946; *The Virginian*, 1946; *The Well-Groomed Bride*, 1946; *Blue Skies* (with Waldo Angelo), 1946; *The Perfect Marriage*, 1946; *Cross My Heart*, 1946; *The Bride Wore Boots*, 1946; *California*, 1946; *The Road to Rio*, 1947; *The Two Mrs. Carrolls* (with Milo Anderson), 1947; *Welcome Stranger*, 1947; *My Favorite Brunette*, 1947; *Desert Fury*, 1947; *I Walk Alone*, 1947; *Where There's Life*, 1947; *Wild Harvest*, 1947; *Perils of Pauline*, 1947; *Variety Girl*, 1947; *Blaze of Noon*, 1947; *Ramrod*, 1947; *The Big Clock*, 1948; *The Emperor Waltz* (with Gile Steele), 1948; *A Foreign Affair*, 1948; *Miss Tatlock's Millions*, 1948; *The Night Has a Thousand Eyes*, 1948; *Rachel and the Stranger*, 1948; *Sorry Wrong Number*, 1948; *Arch of Triumph*, 1948; *Dream Girl*, 1948; *My Own True Love*, 1948; *Beyond Glory*, 1948; *Sainted Sisters*, 1948; *So Evil My Love*, 1948; *Isn't It Romantic*, 1948; *June Bride* (with Rhodes), 1948; *The Heiress* (with Gile Steele), 1949; *Red, Hot and Blue*, 1949; *Rope of Sand*, 1949; *My Friend Irma*, 1949; *The Great Lover*, 1949; *The Great Gatsby*, 1949; *Beyond the Forest*, 1949; *Copper Canyon* (with Gile Steele), 1950; *Mr. Music*, 1950; *My Foolish Heart* (with Wills), 1950; *My Friend Irma Goes West*, 1950; *Riding High*, 1950; *Samson and Delilah* (with Gile Steele, Jeakins Wakeling, and Elois Jenssen), 1950; *Sunset Boulevard*, 1950; *Paid in Full*, 1950; *September Affair*, 1950; *All about Eve* (with Charles LeMaire), 1950; *The Big Carnival*, 1951; *Branded*, 1951; *Detective Story*, 1951; *Here Comes the Groom*, 1951; *The Lemon Drop Kid*, 1951; *Payment on Demand*, 1951; *A Place in the Sun*, 1951; *That's My Boy*, 1951; *Carrie*, 1952; *The Greatest Show on Earth* (with Jeakins and White), 1952; *Jumping Jacks*, 1952; *Just for You* (with Wood), 1952; *My Favorite Spy*, 1952; *Sailor Beware*, 1952; *Son of Paleface*, 1952; *Something to Live For*, 1952; *The Caddy*, 1953; *Come Back Little Sheba*, 1953; *Off Limits*, 1953; *Road to Bali*, 1953; *Roman Holiday*, 1953; *Sangaree*, 1953; *Scared Stiff*, 1953; *Shane*, 1953; *The Stooge*, 1953; *Red Garters* (with Wood), 1953; *The Stars Are Singing*, 1953; *Elephant Walk*, 1954; *Here Come the Girls*, 1954; *Knock on Wood*, 1954; *Living It Up*, 1954; *Money from Home*, 1954; *The Naked Jungle*, 1954; *Rear Window*, 1954; *Sabrina*, 1954; *White Christmas*, 1954; *The Country Girl*, 1954; *About Mrs. Leslie*, 1954; *Artists and Models*, 1955; *The Bridges at Toko-Ri*, 1955; *The Desperate Hours*, 1955; *The Far Horizon*, 1955; *The Girl Rush*, 1955; *Hell's Island*, 1955; *Lucy Gallant*, 1955; *The Rose Tattoo*, 1955; *Run for Cover*, 1955; *The Seven Little Foys*, 1955; *Strategic Air Command*, 1955; *Three Ring Circus*, 1955; *To Catch A Thief*, 1955; *The Trouble with Harry*, 1955; *You're Never Too Young*, 1955; *Anything Goes*, 1956; *The Birds and the Bees*, 1956; *The*

Court Jester (with Wood), 1956; *Hollywood or Bust*, 1956; *The Leather Saint*, 1956; *The Man Who Knew Too Much*, 1956; *The Mountain*, 1956; *The Proud and the Profane*, 1956; *Pardners*, 1956; *The Rainmaker*, 1956; *The Scarlet Hour*, 1956; *The Search for Bridey Murphey*, 1956; *That Certain Feeling*, 1956; *The Lonely Man*, 1956; *The Rose Tattoo*, 1956; *The Ten Commandments*, 1956; *The Buster Keaton Story*, 1957; *Beau James*, 1957; *The Delicate Delinquent*, 1957; *The Devil's Hairpin*, 1957; *Fear Strikes Out*, 1957; *Funny Face* (with Hubert de Givenchy), 1957; *Gunfight at the O.K. Corral*, 1957; *Hear Me Good*, 1957; *The Joker Is Wild*, 1957; *Loving You*, 1957; *The Sad Sack*, 1957; *Short Cut to Hell*, 1957; *The Ten Commandments* (with Jeakins, Jester, John Jensen, and Arnold Friberg), 1957; *The Tin Star*, 1957; *Three Violent People*, 1957; *Wild Is the Wind*, 1957; *As Young as We Are*, 1958; *The Buccaneer* (with Jester), 1958; *The Geisha Boy*, 1958; *Hot Spell*, 1958; *Houseboat*, 1958; *Splendour in the Grass*, 1958; *The Facts of Life*, 1960; *Pepe*, 1960; *A Pocketful of Miracles*, 1961; *David and Lisa*, 1962; *America, America*, 1963; *Ladybug, Ladybug*, 1963; *Fail Safe*, 1964; *Harvey Middleman*, 1965; *Fireman*, 1965; *The Pawnbroker*, 1965; *The Group*, 1966; *The Oscar* (also personal appearance), 1966; *Bye Bye Braverman*, 1968; *The Night They Raided Minsky's*, 1968; *The Subject Was Roses*, 1968; *The Swimmer*, 1968; *Alice's Restaurant*, 1969; *Sweet Charity*, 1969; *Butch Cassidy and the Sundance Kid*, 1969; *Topaz*, 1969; *Cotton Comes to Harlem*, 1970; *There Was A Crooked Man*, 1970; *Airport*, 1970; *Myra Breckinridge*, 1970; *Sometimes a Great Notion*, 1971; *Hammersmith Is Out*, 1972; *Pete n' Tillie*, 1972; *A Doll's House*, 1973; *The Sting*, 1973; *The Taking of Pelham 123*, 1974; *Airport 1975*, 1974; *Serpico*, 1974; *Rooster Cogburn*, 1975; *The Man Who Would Be King*, 1975; *Gable and Lombard*, 1976; *W. C. Fields and Me*, 1976; *Family Plot*, 1976; *Airport 77*, 1977; *The Big Fix*, 1978; *Olly Olly Oxen Free*, 1978; *Sextette*, 1978; *The Last Married Couple in America*, 1979; *Dead Men Don't Wear Plaid*, 1982.

Publications:

By HEAD: books—*The Dress Doctor*, with Jane Kesner Ardmore, Boston 1959; *How to Dress for Success*, with Joe Hyams, New York 1967; *Edith Head's Hollywood*, with Paddy Calistro, New York 1983; articles—in *Silver Screen* (New York), September 1946, January 1948; *Hollywood Quarterly* (Los Angeles), October 1946; *Photoplay* (New York), October 1948; *Good Housekeeping* (New York), March 1959; *Holiday* (New York), January 1973; July 1973; September 1974; November 1974; January 1975; March 1975; September 1975; March 1976; *Inter/View* (New York), January 1974; *Take One* (Montreal), October 1976; *American Film* (Washington, D.C.), May 1978; *Cine Revue* (Paris), 19 April 1979.

On HEAD: books—*Fashion Is Our Business* by Beryl Williams, New York 1945, London 1947; *Hollywood Speaks: An Oral History* by Mike Steen, New York 1974; *Romantic and Glamorous Hollywood Design*, exhibition catalogue by Diana Vreeland, New York 1974; *Hollywood Costume* by Dale McConathy, New York 1976; *Hollywood Costume Design* by David Chierichetti, London 1976; *Hollywood Film Costume*, exhibition catalogue by Michael Regan, Manchester 1977; *In a Glamorous Fashion: The Fabulous Years of Hollywood Costume Design* by W. Robert La Vine, Boston and London 1981.

Fashion designer Edith Head is probably the

most noted purveyor of Hollywood glamor during its heydey as the epitome of resplendent fashion extravaganza. Her approach to designing fashions and makeup for the stars of the movies was to create the total aura of the special characterization called for by each role. She achieved her aim by adapting her subject so that the viewers would be persuaded to believe the primary reality of the part over the real-life persona of the star. When she worked with Grace Kelly in three very different parts, with Bette Davis in *All About Eve* or with Audrey Hepburn in *Roman Holiday*, she always considered unique, on-camera personality as primary, using what she has called a "cross between camouflage and magic" to dream up the hairstyle, complete outfitting, and type of makeup that would best bring the character in that role to life most vividly.

During the period of Head's reign in Hollywood, the clothes a star wore were the real thing—expensive furs, jewels, hand-beaded gowns—lavishly gorgeous and stressing imaginative appeal over accuracy to ordinary daily lifestyles. While always allowing for the settings and times of the roles, Head also enveloped the actor or actress in a complete image, so as to build a mystique which contributed quite prominently to the total spell of the glamorous Hollywood myth of her time. She was successful in enchanting moviegoers to anticipate the work of her fashion designs almost as much as they would the acting or the script. More than any other single designer for films, Head will always be remembered for the influence of clothes which started fashion rages that swept the country when one of her movies was released. She also gained further influence as a character and journalist in her own right, appearing often in her customary garb of heavily-framed glasses, basic suit, and severe, bun hairdo on television and radio shows over the years and putting out a popular column of fashion commentary which was printed regularly in more than forty newspapers.

Head's basic tenets of design were geared to making people look both younger and thinner. She advocated using darker colors in what she called "the danger areas," the places where the figure is thicker, and she believed that heavier people should never wear tight clothing or choose shiny fabrics or bold patterns for the larger parts of their physiques. During most of her career, Head dressed women, but she also did some outstanding work for male stars, such as Paul Newman and Robert Redford in the 1973 movie, *The Sting*.

In her last year, as the high glamor of Hollywood declined in favor of a "real life" preference for jeans over jewels, Head designed uniforms for Pan American airline stewardesses and women in the Coast Guard. She also designed clothing to appear as Vogue Patterns for women to sew for themselves. But Head will always be synonymous with the era of Hollywood glamor as personified by Joan Crawford and Barbara Stanwyck. During the past few years, as shows such as *Dynasty* gain acclaim, it appears that glamor is making a return which pertinently recalls the original purveyor of Hollywood dreams, Edith Head.

—Barbara Cavaliere

HECKROTH, Hein.
German painter, stage and film designer. Born

Hein Heckroth: Still from Powell and Pressburger's *The Red Shoes*, 1948   Courtesy The Rank Organiasation PLC

in Giessen, 14 April 1901. Educated at the Volksschule, Giessen, until 1914; studied book printing and typography, in Giessen, 1915-19; painting, under Ludwig Gies, at the Städelsche Kunstinstitut, Frankfurt, 1920, and under Reinhold Ewal, at the Zeichen-Akademie, Hanau, 1921. Married the painter Ada Maier in 1924; daughter: Renate. Independent painter and stage designer from 1921, film designer from 1939, and television designer from 1953: worked in Wiesbaden, 1921-23, Munich, 1924-26, Essen, 1927-33, Amsterdam, 1933, Paris, 1934, London, 1935-39 and 1941-54 (interned in Australia, 1940-41), and in Frankfurt, 1955-70. Stage designer, for the Künstlertheater für Rhein und Main, Wiesbaden, 1921, and for choreographer Kurt Joos, in Munich and throughout Europe, 1924-35; art director, Municipal Theatres, in Essen, 1927-33, and in Frankfurt, 1956-70; also guest designer at theatres in Chemnitz, Cologne, Hagen, Düsseldorf, Munich and Paris, 1927-33; and in London, Baltimore, Berlin, Frankfurt and Milan, 1935-70. Art director, for Michael Powell and Emerica Pressburger's Archer Films, then for Rank, London and Lion Films, working in London, Munich and Hollywood, 1945-66. Head of stage design, Folkwangschule, Essen, 1929-33; professor of stage design, Akademie der Bildenden Künste, Dresden, 1932; instructor, Dartington Hall, South Devon, 1935-39. **Exhibitions:** Modern Art Gallery, London, 1943; Kunstverein,

Frankfurt, 1970; Kunsthalle, Kassel, 1977. Recipient: Kunstpreis der Rheinische Sezession, 1932; International Choreography Competition Prize, Paris, 1932; Academy Award, 1948. *Died* (in Alkmaar, Netherlands) *6 July 1970.*

Works:

Film designs include—*Caesar and Cleopatra* (Pascal), 1945; *A Matter of Life and Death* (Powell and Pressburger), 1946; *Black Narcissus* (Powell and Pressburger), 1947; *The Red Shoes* (Powell and Pressburger), 1948; *The Small Back Room* (Powell and Pressburger), 1948; *Gone to Earth* (Powell and Pressburger), 1950; *The Elusive Pimpernel* (Powell and Pressburger), 1950; *The Tales of Hoffmann* (Powell and Pressburger), 1951; *The Story of Gilbert and Sullivan* (Gilliat), 1953; *Ludwig II* (Kautner), 1954; *Oh . . . Rosalinda* (Powell and Pressburger), 1955; *The Sorcerer's Apprentice* (Powell), 1955; *The Battle of the River Plate* (Powell and Pressburger), 1956; *Robinson soll nicht sterben* (von Baky), 1957; *Die Dreigroschenoper* (Staudte), 1962; *Bluebeard's Castle* (Powell), 1964; *Torn Curtain* (Hitchcock), 1966.

Publications:

By HECKROTH: booklet—*Meine Arbeit als*

Bühnebilder, Filmarchitekt und Fernsedesigner, Rotary Club address, Frankfurt 1962; articles— in *Programmheft des Theaters der Stadt Münster* (Münster), no. 3, 1924, no. 5, 1924, no. 10, 1924; *Die Theater-Welt* (Frankfurt), no. 10, 1930; *Programm der Deutschen Oper am Rhein* (Dusseldorf), no. 2, 1957.

On HECKROTH: books—*Surrealist Paintings by Hein Heckroth,* exhibition folder with text by Herbert Read, London 1943; *Art in Modern Ballet* by G. Arbert, New York 1946; *Art and Design in the British Film* by Edward Carrick, London 1948; *The Red Shoes Ballet: A Critical Study* by Monk Gibbon, London 1948; *Hein Heckroth 1901-1970,* exhibition catalogue by Helmut Grosse and Ewald Rathke, Frankfurt 1970; *Le Decor de Film* by Leon Barsacq, Paris 1970, as *Caligari's Cabinet and Other Grand Illusions,* Boston 1976; *Hein Heckroth 1901-1970,* exhibition catalogue by Erich Herzog and Karlheinz Gabler, Kassel 1977; *The International Film Encyclopedia* by Ephraim Katz, New York and London 1980.

Hein Heckroth preserved his German cosmopolitanism in his years of exile, and it formed the cultural base from which his irony could inform his work. There was, thus, a considerable continuity to his work, though his consistency at no time inhibited his development or zest for experiment, which probably underlay the quite considerable success the *Seven Deadly*

Sins enjoyed in its 1960 Frankfurt revival. It was said that his contribution had played an important part in that success, which came on the heels of his two films that also had successful showings in Germany.

Heckroth's freely brushed style of design might lead one to underestimate his meticulous attention to the details of production. However, at no time during his career did he have to revise his designs in the light of practical theatrical requirements. For his films, his foresight was even more striking, as they needed great, labyrinthine sets that could easily have been disastrous failures had he not had a grasp of the spaces they would use. In his designs, he also overcame brilliantly the shortcomings of the colour film process of that time by avoiding the difficult colours and awkward combinations.

In the light of his style of drawing and painting and in view of the somewhat loose terminology used about German art of the early years of the twentieth century, the label "expressionist" has sometimes been attached to his work. As far as this term is taken to mean merely avant-garde art of an alternative tendency to that associated with developments in Paris up to the war, then it probably is not misleading. However, as his association with Kurt Joos demonstrates, his work retained a strong intellectual content, while his sense of irony precluded indulgence in self-expression. Furthermore, his very method of working, although often initiated by sketches of a rudimentary nature, was one of elaboration from initial idea through to finished project, every detail and effect carefully calculated, and nothing left to chance.

Nowhere was this latter aspect of his work more evident than in the film *Red Shoes*, for which he not only had to design the sets and costumes but the angles from which the action would be shot. This, none of your splash-and-dash expressionism could have permitted. It is worth remembering he told a wartime London audience that the calculation that went into *The Cabinet of Dr. Caligari*, along with what he held to be its anti-nationalist message, removed that film from the taint of expressionism. How much more so must we understand that this was to apply as well to his own work for the cinema.

—Toni del Renzio

HEELEY, Desmond.

British stage designer. Born in West Bromwich, Staffordshire, 1 June 1931. Educated at All Saints primary and secondary schools, West Bromwich, 1936–44; studied at Ryland School of Art, West Bromwich, 1945. Worked for the Birmingham Repertory Theatre Company, Warwickshire, 1945–47; wardrobe and property assistant, 1947–52, and designer from 1955, Shakespeare Memorial (now Royal Shakespeare) Theatre Company, Stratford on Avon, Warwickshire; designer, for the Stratford Festival, Ontario, 1957–73, the Old Vic Theatre, London, from 1958, and for the Tyrone Guthrie Theatre, Minneapolis. Also television drama designer. Instructor, Central School of Arts and Crafts, London. Recipient: 2 Tony Awards, New York, 1967. Address: Alexandra Road, London NW8, England.

Works:

Stage productions include—*Toad of Toad Hall,*

Shakespeare Memorial Theatre, Stratford-on-Avon, 1948; *The Lark,* London 1955; *Titus Andronicus,* Shakespeare Memorial Theatre, Stratford-on-Avon, 1955; *Hamlet,* Shakespeare Memorial Theatre, Stratford-on-Avon, 1956; *Titus Andronicus,* London, 1957; *Twelfth Night,* Old Vic, London, 1958; *Macbeth,* Old Vic, London, 1958; *Farewell, Farewell, Eugene,* London, 1959; *The Double Dealer,* Old Vic, London, 1959; *The Merchant of Venice,* Shakespeare Memorial Theatre, Stratford-on-Avon, 1960; *Toad of Toad Hall,* London, 1960; *Much Ado About Nothing,* Shakespeare Memorial Theatre, Stratford-on-Avon, 1961; *The Devils,* London, 1961; *Romeo and Juliet,* Shakespeare Memorial Theatre, Stratford-on-Avon, 1961; *Oh, Dad, Poor Dad,* London, 1961; *Misalliance,* London, 1963; *Divorce a la Carte,* London, 1963; *Gentle Jack,* London, 1963; *Hamlet,* Old Vic, London, 1963; *Carving a Statue,* London, 1964; *La Contessa,* London (and U.K. tour), 1965; *Rosencrantz and Guildenstern Are Dead,* Old Vic, London, 1969; *In Praise of Love,* London, 1973; *Cyrano,* New York, 1973; *The Matchmaker,* Tyrone Guthrie Theatre, Minneapolis, 1976.

Publications:

By HEELEY: book—*The Life of Timon of Athens: Designs by Desmond Heeley,* with introduction by Paul Scofield, London 1976.

On HEELEY: books—*Who's Who in the Theatre,* London 1972, 1977; *Creative Canada,* vol. 1, Toronto and Buffalo 1974; *British Theatre Design,* edited by John Goodwin, London 1989.

Though he began his career in theatre at the Birmingham Repertory Theatre, it was in the shops of the Memorial Theatre, Stratford-on-Avon, working on the spectacular and richly romantic productions of Shakespeare presented there in the late 1940s and early 1950s that Desmond Heeley developed his love of surface textures under light. Since his first work was with stage properties, it is not surprising that his first costume designs—for *Toad of Toad Hall,* first at Stratford and later in London—stressed the idea of costumes as expanded properties, particularly in the wonderful masks, headdresses, hands and feet designed for this production.

From then on, in his many famous productions at Stratford and the Old Vic, his costume designs were always praised for their wonderful sense of movement, layered texture, subtle coloration, and great depth of surface. No matter what the production, the costumes always conjured up a world of lushness and complex richness that spoke with great force to the senses. All kinds of surface techniques were presented—from shredding, painting, and spattering to layering one transparent or open-work surface over other glinting or opalescent textures. The historical sense of these costumes was always very fully developed, but the audience's sense of whatever historical period was being presented was always deepened and strengthened by the extra dimension of textures and tactile richness. His style could be said to be that of impressionistic symbolism, with the added sense of texture that has come to modern art through junk art, collage, action painting, and abstract expressionism. Thus, the overall effect was moodily and impressionistically romantic, but the direct perception of forms and surfaces was deeply physical.

Heeley's work has been seen at its best in Shakespeare and opera where the imagery and poetry of story and character are larger than life and operate upon an audience by making it ex-

pect an enhanced richness and depth of costume effect. Thus, Heeley's work never presents an audience with visual ideas, never relates to the real world of politics, values, or environment, but always operates subliminally to give the spectator a coloristic fantasy-world. His particular influence upon younger Shakespearean designers has been in the area of surface techniques, including costume painting, the use of melted plastics, the outlining of braids and buttons, the highlighting and shadowing of costumes, and the development of laces and nets over other textures to give richness and surface complexity to a production.

—Douglas A. Russell

HEIKKILA, Simo.

Finnish interior, exhibition and furniture designer. Born in Helsinki, 2 May 1943. Studied at the Academy of Applied Arts, Helsinki, 1963–67: Dip. 1967. Assistant designer, Marimekko textile company, Helsinki, 1967–70; freelance designer, establishing own studio in Helsinki, since 1971: has designed furniture for Asko, Avarte, Haimi, Nupponen, Tarzan, Uveka, Vivero/Economic, etc.; collaborated with designer Yro Wiherheimo, 1972–80; has worked with experimental furniture designs, since 1981. Instructor, Institute of Technology, Helsinki, 1971–75, and University of Industrial Arts, Helsinki, since 1975. **Exhibitions:** *Finland Designs 2,* Museum of Applied Arts, Helsinki, 1981; *Finnland Gestaltet,* Museum für Kunst und Gewerbe, Hamburg, 1981 (toured); *Scandinavian Modern Design 1880–1980,* Cooper-Hewitt Museum, New York, 1982 (toured); *Finland: Nature, Design, Architecture,* Cranbrook Academy of Art, Bloomfield Hills, Michigan, 1982 (toured); *Simo Heikkila: Pieces of Wood,* Galleri Bronda, Helsinki, 1984; *Finse Vormgeving,* Van Reekummuseum, Apeldoorn, 1984; *Full-Scale Furniture,* Kluuvi Gallery, Helsinki, 1984; *New Chairs from Scandinavia,* Artek Gallery, Helsinki, 1984; *Simo Heikkila: Pezzi di Legno,* Galleria Carelia, Milan, 1985. **Collections:** Museum of Applied Arts, Helsinki; Kunstindustrimuseet, Oslo; Museum für Kunst und Gewerbe, Hamburg; Cooper-Hewitt Museum, New York; Victoria and Albert Museum, London. Recipient: Asko Furniture Competition Prize, Helsinki, 1968; *Kaunis Koti* magazine award, 1969; Finnish Association of Designers Scholarship, 1976; ESPE Competition Prize, Helsinki, 1980; Abitare Prize, Milan, 1981; Three-Year Finnish State Scholarship, 1981; SIO Interior Architects Award, Helsinki, 1983, 1984; First Prize, Lahti Design Competition, 1985; Finnish State Award for Industrial Design, 1985. Address: Vilhovuorenkatu 11 B, 00500 Helsinki, Finland.

Publications:

By HEIKKILA: books—*Finnland Gestaltet,* exhibition catalogue, with Tapio Periainen and others, Espoo 1981.

On HEIKKILA: books—*Scandinavian Modern Design 1880–1980,* edited by David Revere McFadden, New York 1982; *Finnish Vision,* with texts by P. Suhonen, J. Lintinen and others, Helsinki 1983; *Finnish Industrial Design* by Tuula Pontasuo, Helsinki 1987.

HEIN, Pieter.

German stage and television designer. Born in Berlin, 14 October 1938. Studied stage design, under Willi Schmidt, at the Hochschule für Bildende Kunste, Berlin-Charlottenburg, 1956–61; postgraduate studies, under Karl von Appen, at the Deutsche Akademie der Kunste, East Berlin, 1962–64. Married and divorced; children: Hieronymus, Yvonne and Claudia. Freelance stage designer, working for the Städtische Bühnen, Quedlinburg, and Volksbühne am Luxemburgplatz, East Berlin, 1961–63; assistant to Karl von Appen, 1965–67, and designer, 1968–69, Berliner Ensemble, East Berlin; designer, Volksbühne am Luxemburgplatz, East Berlin, 1970–80; freelance set and costume designer, East Berlin, since 1980: worked with directors Manfred Karge and Matthias Langhoff, 1968–74, and with Fritz Marquardt from 1974. **Exhibitions:** Prague Quadriennale of Scenography, 1967, 1971, 1976; *Die Bühne als szenischer Raum,* Zurich, 1980; *Bild und Szene,* East Berlin, 1981; *IX Kunstausstellung der DDR,* Dresden, 1982. Recipient: *Berliner Zeitung* Critics' Prize, East Berlin, 1969, 1977. Address: Elsa-Brandström-Strasse 38, 1100 Berlin, German Democratic Republic.

Works:

Productions include—*Emilia Galotti,* Volksbühne, East Berlin, 1962; *Die Rundkopfe und die Spitzkopfe,* Landestheater, Halle, 1964; *In der Suche J. R. Oppenheimer,* Berliner Ensemble, East Berlin, 1965; *Der Schuhu und die fliegende Prinzessin,* Student-Ensemble, Staatliche Schauspielhaus, East Berlin, 1967; *Die Gesichte der Simon Machard,* DDR Television, 1968; *Wald,* Volksbuhne, East Berlin, 1971; *Die Rauber,* Volksbuhne, East Berlin, 1971; *Der Brotladen,* Théâtre de la Commune, Aubervilliers, 1972;

Othello, Volksbühne, East Berlin, 1972; *Die Wildente,* Volksbühne, East Berlin, 1973; *Spektakel,* Volksbühne, East Berlin, 1974; *Der Menschenhasser,* Volksbühne, East Berlin, 1975; *Die Bauern,* Volksbühne, East Berlin, 1976; *Danton's Tod,* Institut für Schauspielregie BAT, East Berlin, 1977; *Emilia Galotti,* Burgtheater, Vienna, 1978; *Ein Puppenheim,* Burgtheater, Vienna, and Akademietheater, East Berlin, 1979; *Die Fledermaus,* Schauspielhaus, Bochum, 1980; *Der Bau,* Volksbuhne, East Berlin, 1980; *Gräfin Mariza,* Theater Greifswald, 1981; *Lulu,* Staatstheater, Dresden, 1983; *Gespenster,* Kammerspiele des Deutschen Theaters, East Berlin, 1983.

Publications:

On HEIN: books—*Stage Design Throughout the World 1970–1975* by René Hainaux and Nicole Leclercq, Brussels and London 1976; *Die Schauspieltheater der DDR und das Erbe 1970–1974,* edited by Manfred Nossig, East Berlin 1976; *Streifzuge: Aufsätze und Kritiken* by Friedrich Dieckmann, East Berlin and Weimar 1977; *Bühnebilder der DDR: Arbeiten aus den Jahren 1971–1977,* edited by Friedrich Dieckmann, East Berlin 1978; *Theaterbilder* by Friedrich Dieckmann, East Berlin 1979.

*

The stage designer Pieter Hein, one of the most original talents in the East German theatre, was a master pupil of Professor Karl von Appen. His stage designs are clearly influenced in their intellectual and dramatic content (but not in their practical artistic execution) by his teacher and model. Their rationalism and clear structure allow for telling arrangements, the actor becoming a decisive interpreter between image and scenic process. With extreme economy of decorative elements, Hein achieves a practical

functionalism of the scene and, at the same time, great aesthetic effect. Brecht's epic theatre, the early German painters (particularly Albrecht Altdorfer), and the nineteenth-century Romantic Caspar David Friedrich have all inspired this artist.

Hein sees the stage as space, as a dynamic element that can be quickly and easily transformed. Theatre is presented in its dramatic functionalism. Nothing figurative or imitative is allowed; rather, he finds spatial solutions of expressive simplicity. Colors frequently play a decisive role—a brilliant red for Shakespeare's *Othello;* a stark white for Schiller's *The Robbers;* white, too, for Heiner Müller's *Peasants,* and gray for Müller's production piece *The Building.*

The Robbers produced at the Berlin Volksbühne in 1971 was a sensational success, due not least to Hein's stage design. For the castle scenes, he built an easily adaptable, multilayered, synchronised decor from fabrics and scaffolding. The forest dwelling of the young, rebellious robbers was presented totally bare before a few white hangings on an almost empty stage—until the rich plunder covered it. The theme of the play—young people protesting anarchically against old, inherited hierarchies—came over clearly in the designer's presentation, which deliberately gave free play to the associative fantasies of the audience. At the end, the robbers crouched like enormous, dark birds in the white, burnt frame of the castle from which the fabrics had been torn down: tabula rasa of the proceedings and the play.

Ibsen's *Wild Duck* presented in the first scene a gorgeous winter garden, richly furnished in the style of the period, and in due course, a stage crammed and overstuffed with lumber and torsos. In the background was to be seen a tableau vivante from which the characters stepped out, with a well calculated alternation

Pieter Hein: Production of Ibsen's *The Wild Duck*, at the Volksbuhne am Luxemburgplatz, Berlin, 1973

of private and ceremonial behaviour. For Müller's *Peasants,* in a sequence from the early history of the German Democratic Republic, Hein designed an enormous, white stairway (which clearly called on expressionist precedents) on which figures and properties, historically exact and realistic, presented dramatic effects.

The frequent collaboration with the producers Manfred Karge and Matthias Langhoff, who were also previously active at the Berliner Ensemble and influenced by Brecht's epic theatre, substantially influenced Hein's work; from the effort of these producers to achieve a demonstrative method of acting aimed at alienation, Hein discovered those spatial solutions in which consciously exhibited theatricality and rationally developed action also find their place in stage design.

—Ingeborg Pietzsch

HENNESY, Dale.

American painter and film designer. Born in Washington, D.C., in 1926. Studied painting and motion picture illustration, at the School of Applied Arts, Glendale, California, 1948–50. Sketch artist and illustrator, 20th Century-Fox film studios, Hollywood, from 1952: chief sketch artist for art director John DeCuir, 1956–62; art director, 20th Century-Fox film studios, Hollywood, 1963–81. Also taught private classes in painting. Recipient: Academy Award, 1966. *Died (in Los Angeles, California) in 1981.*

Works:

Films include—*Under the Yum Yum Tree* (Swift), 1963; *Good Neighbor Sam* (Swift), 1964; *John Goldfarb Please Come Home* (Lee-Thompson), 1965; *Fantastic Voyage* (Fleischer), 1966; *In Like Flint* (Douglas), 1967; *Adam at 6AM* (Scheerer), 1970; *Cover Me, Babe* (Black), 1970; *The Christian Licorice Store* (Frawley), 1971; *Simon, King of the Witches,* 1971; *Dirty Harry* (Siegel), 1971; *Everything You Always Wanted to Know About Sex* (Allen), 1972; *A Time to Run* (Adamson), 1972; *Slither* (Zieff), 1973; *Battle for the Planet of the Apes* (Lee-Thompson), 1973; *Sleeper* (Allen), 1973; *Young Frankenstein* (Brooks), 1974; *Logan's Run* (Anderson), 1976; *King Kong* (Guillermin), 1976; *Dog Soldiers* (Reisz), 1978; *The Island* (Ritchie), 1980; *The Competition* (Oliansky), 1980; *Wholly Moses* (Weis), 1980; *Annie* (Huston), 1982.

Publications:

On HENNESY: books—*Le Decor de Film* by Leon Barsacq, Paris 1970, as *Caligari's Cabinet and Other Grand Illusions,* Boston 1976; *Special Effects* by Christopher Finch, New York 1984; articles—in *American Cinematographe* (Paris), 1 January 1977; *Film Comment* (New York), May/June 1978.

HENRION, F(rederick) H(enri) K(ay).

British graphic and industrial designer. Born in Nuremberg, Germany, 18 April 1914; emigrated to Britain in 1936: naturalized, 1946. Educated at the Melanchton Gymnasium, Nuremberg, 1924–33; trained as a textile designer, Paris, 1933–34; studied graphic design, Ecole Paul Colin, Paris, 1934–36. Served as exhibitions consultant, British Ministry of Information, and United States Office of War Information, 1940–45. Married Daphne Hardy in 1947 (separated, 1970); children: Max, Paul and Emma. Independent designer from 1936: chief consultant designer, Sir William Crawford and Partners, London, 1946–47; art editor, *Contact* publication, London, 1947–48; art director, British Overseas Airways Corporation publications, 1949–51, and *Future* magazine, London, 1951; art editor, Bowater Papers, London, 1951–53; principal, Henrion Design Associates, 1951–73, HDA International, 1973–82, and Henrion, Ludlow and Schmidt, London, from 1982; also design consultant to Blue Circle Cement, Braun AG, British Broadcasting Corporation, British Leyland, Coopers and Lybrand, KLM Royal Dutch Airlines, Volkswagen AG, Vorwerk AG, General Post Office, etc. Tutor in graphic design, 1948–50, and Governor, 1957–61, Central School of Arts and Crafts, London; visiting lecturer, Royal College of Art, London, 1951–56; head of visual communications, 1976–79, and visiting lecturer in typography, 1979–83, London College of Printing; guest professor, Universidad Autonoma Metropolitana, Mexico City, 1982, Cooper Union, New York, 1984, and University of Essen, 1984–85. President, Society of Industrial Artists and Designers, London, 1960–62, Alliance Graphique Internationale, Paris, 1963–66, and ICOGRADA International Council of Graphic Design Associations, 1968–70; member of the Council for Industrial Design, London, 1964–67; master of the faculty of Royal Designers for Industry, Royal Society of Arts, London, 1971–73. **Exhibitions:** *Henrion Design,* Institute of Contemporary Arts, London, 1960; *International Design Systems,* Intergraphic Gallery, Munich, 1971 (travelled to Darmstadt); *Corporate Design,* Design Centre, London, 1973, 1976; *Eye for Industry,* Victoria and Albert Museum, London, 1986. **Collections:** Imperial War Museum, London; Victoria and Albert Museum, London; Stedelijk Museum, Amsterdam; Museum fur Kunst und Gewerbe, Hamburg; Museum of Modern Art, New York; Library of Congress, Washington, D.C. Recipient: Japanese Institute of Packaging Award, 1969; Royal Society of Arts Duke of Edinburgh Award, London, 1971, 1973; Design and Art Direction Award, London, 1973; Brno Graphics Biennale Award, 1974; *Packaging* magazine package of the year award, New York, 1975; SIAD Design Medal, London, 1976. Order of the British Empire, 1951; Royal Designer for Industry, Royal Society of Arts, London, 1959; Senior Fellow, Royal College of Art, London, 1988. Address: 35 Pond Street, London NW3 2PN, England.

Works:

Smoke Abatement exhibition layouts, at Charing Cross Station, London, 1939.
Dig for Victory exhibition layouts, London Zoo, 1942.
Magazine covers, for *Harper's Bazaar,* New York, 1942–45.
Advertising campaign, for Harella Fashions, 1942–46.
Design for Living exhibition layouts, London, for the Army Bureau of Current Affairs, 1944 (with Herbert Read).
Electric sewing machine, for *Britain Can Make It* exhibition, Victoria and Albert Museum, London, 1946.
Speedbird magazine layouts and graphics, for British Overseas Airways Corporation, London, 1949–51.
Agriculture and Country Pavilions, at the Festival of Britain, South Bank, London, 1950–51.
US and UK Laugh exhibition layouts, at the London Tea Centre, 1953 (travelled to New York).
Keep Britain Tidy exhibition layouts, at the London Tea Centre, 1962.
British Pavilion exhibits, signs and graphics, at *Expo 67,* Montreal, 1967.
ICOGRADA posters, for the International Council of Graphic Design Associations, 1980–89.
Logotype symbol, for the National Theatre, London, 1983 (with Jan Dennis).

Publications:

By HENRION: books—*Design Coordination and Corporate Image,* with Alan Parkin, London and New York 1969; *Top Graphic Design,* Zurich 1983; *AGI Annals 1989,* Tokyo 1989; articles—in *Print* (New York), August 1956; *Art and Industry* (London), February 1957; *Design* (London), August 1959; *Design for Industry* (London), November 1959; *Industrial Design* (New York), August 1961; *Graphis* (Zurich), no. 129, 1967; *Print* (Washington, D.C.), November 1969.

On HENRION: books—*Who's Who in Graphic Art,* edited by Walter Amstutz, Dubendorf 1982; *The Conran Directory of Design,* edited by Stephen Bayley, London 1985; *An Introduction to Design and Culture in the Twentieth Century* by Penny Sparke, London 1986; *Eye for Industry: Royal Designers for Industry 1936–1986,* exhibition catalogue by Fiona MacCarthy and Patrick Nuttgens, London 1986; *Design Source Book* by Penny Sparke and others, London 1986.

In my fifty years of design practice, I have always believed that a designer's job is to adjust to new conditions and be ready to cope with them, ideally when they happen. Thus, although trained as a poster designer, I went into packaging, exhibition, and product design, into advertising and TV design in the late 1950s, 1960s, and 1970s. I was one of the first to design corporate identity programmes in Europe and am now very interested and involved in computer-generated design. To some degree, my career has been the history and evolution of graphic design over the last fifty years and I hope it will continue to be so.

—F. H. K. Henrion

F. H. K. Henrion can measure up a situation from the periphery and trace it back to the central point of the argument with great speed. He is a lateral thinker, who can summarise clearly. Able also to detach himself from his own personal interest and viewpoint in order to see the interests of others, he can evaluate the consequences of an act in their entirety. These qualities, combined intelligence and patience, account for Henrion's career as a successful designer for nearly half a century. His clients include top advertising agencies, governments, and well-known corporations throughout Europe.

Henrion's work includes exhibition design, typographical and sign systems, and industrial design. Although he was trained initially as a poster designer, he soon widened his interests to include packaging, exhibition and product

META PHOR AND AMBI GUITY

15th Icograda Student Seminar
13/14 February 1989
Odeon Leicester Square London
Speakers: Saul Bass/USA
H. R. Lutz/Switzerland
Richard Hess/USA
Alan Fletcher/UK
Chairman: FHK Henrion
Information from:
Banks Sadler Ltd
9 Delancey Street
London NW1 7NL
tel: 01 388 9101

F.H.K. Henrion: *Metaphor and Ambiguity* **poster, for the International Council of Graphic Design Associations, 1989**

design, and, from the mid-sixties, advertising and television design using computer and video techniques. One of the first to design corporate identity programmes in Europe, he integrated applied graphics over a wide field of uses: in transport, in architecture, and in signs and symbols.

Henrion's style of design incorporates clear, crisp organisation which may be compared to the best of Swiss typography. His method functions on multiple levels, beyond the surface, there is always additional enriching meaning which is identifiable with the client's activities. Henrion's attention to detail is meticulous, and no matter what may be the end product—a brochure or a complex pavilion—it is always well executed to the last detail, technically perfect. This designer's presentations to clients are exemplary, containing as they do not only understanding of the client's problems, but solutions which go beyond the client's expectation in practical terms and spirit.

Henrion's contribution to the new generation of designers has been considerable. Besides teaching at the Royal College of Art, the Central School of Art and Design, and the London School of Printing, he has been a member of the National Council for Diplomas in Art and Design and of the National Advisory Council on Art Education. These and other similar posts gave him a chance to help revolutionise design education in Great Britain to such an extent that by the middle 1970s, Britain had become a leading nation in communication graphics and the quality of teaching, an example for other nations.

Henrion is both the chairman and programme organiser of the International Council of Graphic Design Associations Annual Student Seminar in London and the Alliance Graphique Internationale Student Seminar in Paris and New York, each attended by more than 1,000 students. He is visiting professor at various universities in Europe and the United States.

—John Halas

HERBERT, Jocelyn.

Brtish stage and film designer. Born in London, 22 February 1917. Educated at Saint Paul's Girls School, London, until 1932; studied painting, Académie André L'Hôte, Paris, 1932–33; under Leon Underwood, Slade School of Fine Art, London, 1934–36; stage design, with Michael Saint Denis and George Devine, at the London Theatre Studio, 1936–37. Married Anthony B. Lousada in 1937 (divorced, 1960). Resident stage designer, English Stage Company, Royal Court Theatre, London, 1956–58; freelance designer, London, from 1958. **Exhibitions:** *Eye for Industry,* Victoria and Albert Museum, London, 1986; *British Theatre Design '83-'87,* Riverside Studios, London, 1988. Recipient: Associate, Royal College of Art, London, 1964; Royal Designer for Industry, Royal Society of Arts, London, 1971. Address: 45 Pottery Lane, London W11, England.

Works:

Stage productions (for the Royal Court Theatre, London, unless specified) include—*The Chairs,* 1957; *The Sport of My Mad Mother,* 1957; *The Lesson,* 1958; *Endgame,* 1958; *Roots,* 1959;

Sergeant Musgrave's Dance, 1959; *Chicken Soup with Barley,* 1960; *I'm Talking About Jerusalem,* 1960; *Trials by Logue,* 1960; *The Changeling,* 1961; *The Kitchen,* 1961; *Luther,* 1961; *A Midsummer Night's Dream,* 1962; *Chips With Everything,* 1962; *Happy Days,* 1962; *Baal,* 1963; *Skyvers,* 1963; *Exit the King,* 1963; *The Seagull,* 1964; *Saint Joan of the Stockyards,* 1964; *Inadmissible Evidence,* 1964; *Julius Caesar,* 1964; *A Patriot for Me,* 1965; *The Lion and the Jewel,* 1966; *Heartbreak House,* His Majesty's Theatre, London, 1967; *Life Price,* 1969; *Becket 3,* 1970; *Three Months Gone,* 1970; *Home* (also in New York), 1970; *The Changing Room,* 1971; *Not I,* 1973; *Krapp's Last Tape,* 1973; *Savages,* 1973; *Cromwell,* 1973; *Life Class,* 1974; *What the Butler Saw,* 1975; *Teeth 'n' Smiles,* 1975; *Richard III,* Shakespeare Memorial Theatre, Stratford-on-Avon, 1961; *Othello,* Old Vic, London, 1964; *Mother Courage,* Old Vic, London, 1965; *Inadmissible Evidence,* New York, 1965; *Ghosts,* Aldwych Theatre, London, 1966; *Orpheus and Eurydice,* Sadler's Wells Theatre, London, 1967; *Hamlet,* Round House, London (also in New York), 1969; *A Woman Killed with Kindness,* Old Vic, London, 1971; *Tyger,* Old Vic, London, 1971; *Becket 3,* 1973; *Endgame,* 1973; *Not I,* 1973; *Pygmalion,* Albery Theatre, London, 1974; *The Force of Destiny,* Paris Opera, 1975; *Play and Other Plays,* 1976; *Lulu,* Metropolitan Opera, New York, 1977; *The Abduction from the Seraglio,* Metropolitan Opera, New York, 1979; *Rise and Fall of the City of Mahagonny,* Metropolitan Opera, New York, 1979; *Galileo,* National Theatre, London, 1980; *Early Days,* National Theatre, London, 1980; *The Oresteia,* National Theatre, London, 1981; *Portage to San Cristobal,* Mermaid Theatre, London, 1982; *The Devil and the Good Lord* Lyric Hammersmith, London, 1984; *Gigi,* Lyric Theatre, London, 1985;`*The Mask of Orpheus,* Coliseum, London, 1986; *J. J. Farr,* Phoenix Theatre, London, 1987; *Tracks,* Adelphi Theatre, London, 1988; *Julius Caesar,* Haymarket Theatre, Leicester, 1988; films include—*Tom Jones* (Richardson), *Othello* (Burge), 1965; *Isadora* (Reisz), 1968; *If . .* (Anderson), 1969; *Ned Kelly* (Richardson), 1970; *O Lucky Man* (Anderson), 1973; *Hotel New Hampshire* (Richardson), 1984; *The Whales of August* (Anderson), 1987.

Publications:

On HERBERT: books—*Who's Who in the Theatre,* London 1972, 1977; *Encyclopedia of World Theatre,* New York 1973; *Eye for Industry: Royal Designers for Industry 1936–1986,* exhibition catalogue by Fiona MacCarthy and Patrick Nuttgens, London 1986; *British Theatre Design '83-'87,* with texts by Timothy O'Brien and David Fingleton, London 1988.

Credited by Peter Brook with restoring a new simplicity and purity to the English theatre, Jocelyn Herbert exercises a scrupulous restraint regarding traditional stage decor and seeks a few key elements—usually realistically based, preferably of authentic materials—to capture the essence of a play or its specific scenes. She is attracted to minimal settings because she finds beauty in an empty stage with perhaps a single telling object on it. Both Herbert and the Royal Court Theatre as a whole openly acknowledged their debt to Bertolt Brecht in their work—not only in a concern with social, humanistic issues in the choice of plays, but also in their essentially austere, functional, quietly expressive mode of staging. Theatricality was present but never aggressively so, most often being subordinated to function and cleanness of

form. In this, they augmented their initial commitment to the Copeau-Saint Denis model of discipline, economy, and grace, rather than departing from it.

Herbert's spare, realistically slanted work was especially evident in Royal Court productions such as John Arden's *Sergeant Musgrave's Dance* (1959), Arnold Wesker's *Chips with Everything* (1962), and Brecht's *Baal* (1963), all of which employed a bare stage with cyclorama (sometimes with projections of painted murals) backing up relatively few, carefully selected and composed objects, usually lit by exposed instruments.

Her later work observed the same pattern but became larger in scale and more complex in operation. For Brecht's *Galileo* (1980), she stripped the stage to the bare walls but added a large, flown projection screen and mobile platform to facilitate the flow of action and Epic establishment of the story's context. For *The Oresteia* (1981), she was able to draw upon her extensive work with masks in the Saint Denis school and strove for a balance of abstraction and character flavor. She also created a balance of ancient Greek and universal modern in the setting. In the middle of the stage rose a stark, metallic facade that echoed the huge, stage-shop doors of the Olivier Theatre, thus establishing a striking unity between this contemporary theatre and the Greek setting. Offsetting the rectangular facade was a white circle for the chorus; such interplay of forms is a recurrent motif in her work. In all of Herbert's productions one is aware of a fine sense of spatial proportion and composition; her selectivity is never empty or bland.

—Jarka M. Burian

HERITAGE, Robert.

British furniture and product designer. Born in Birmingham, Warwickshire, 2 November 1927. Studied at Birmingham College of Art, 1942–46; furniture design, at the Royal College of Art, London, 1948–51. Married Dorothy Shaw in 1953; children: Paul, Rachel and Michael. Staff designer, at G. W. Evans furniture manufacturers, London, 1951–53; freelance designer, working with Dorothy Heritage, London, from 1953; founder-partner, with Harold Bartram, Ron Carter, George Cayford and George Freeman, of Design Partners design studio, London, 1960–61: consultant to Archie Shine, Concord/Rotaflex, Elliott's, Race Furniture, Beaver and Tapley, Meurop, Green and Vardy, Slumberland, Cintique, Program Furniture, etc. Instructor in design, Twickenham School of Art, London, 1953–55; professor of furniture design, Royal College of Art, London, 1974–85. **Exhibitions:** *Modern Chairs 1918–1970,* Whitechapel Art Gallery, London, 1970; *Design Since 1945,* Philadelphia Museum of Art, 1983; *Eye for Industry,* Victoria and Albert Museum, London, 1986. **Collections:** Museum of Modern Art, New York; Philadelphia Museum of Art; Victoria and Albert Museum, London; Museu de Arte Moderno, Rio de Janeiro. Recipient: 12 Design Council Awards, London, since 1958; British Aluminium Award, London, 1966; Gute Form Prize, Bonn, 1972. Honorary Designer, Royal College of Art, London, 1951; Fellow, Chartered Society of Designers, London, 1960; Royal Designer for Industry, Royal Society of Arts, London, 1963; Commander, Order of the British Em-

Robert Heritage: *Tipster* stacking and linking chair, for Race Furniture, 1979

pire, 1980. Address: 12 Jay Mews, Kensington Gore, London SW7 2EP, England.

Works:

Heritage wall storage units, for Archie Shine Limited, 1963.
Stainless steel cutlery, for Yote Manufacturing Company, 1963.
Quartet spotlight range, for Concord Lighting International, 1966.
QE2 dining chair, for Race Furniture, 1969.
Powerflood halogen light fitting, for Concorde Lighting International, 1971.
Master clock, for English Clock Systems, 1973.
Superjet bed lamp, for Concorde Lighting International, 1979.
Tipster stacking and linking chair, for Race Furniture, 1980.
Aspect cellular ceiling system, for Interlight International, 1981.
Articula office chair range, for Antocks Lairn, 1981.
Ambit modular lighting system, for Tecnolyte, 1984.

Publications:

By HERITAGE: article—in *The Designer* (London), March 1972.

On HERITAGE: books—*The Adventure of British Furniture* by David Joel, London 1953, as *Furniture Design Set Free,* London 1969; *Furniture in Britain Today* by Dennis and Barbara Young, London 1964; *Modern Chairs 1918-1970,* exhibition catalogue by Carol Hogben and others, London 1970; *Modern Design in Metal* by Richard Stewart, London 1979; *Twen-*

tieth Century Furniture Design by Philippe Garner, London 1980; *Design Since 1945,* edited by Kathryn Hiesinger and George Marcus, Philadelphia and London 1983; *The Conran Directory of Design,* edited by Stephen Bayley, London 1985; *Eye for Industry: Royal Designers for Industry 1936-1986,* exhibition catalogue by Fiona MacCarthy and Patrick Nuttgens, London 1986; *Twentieth Century Design: Furniture* by Penny Sparke, London 1986.

HERLOW, Erik.
Danish architect, exhibition and industrial designer. Born in Helsingør, 5 January 1913. Educated in Helsingør until 1933; studied at the Royal School of Building, Copenhagen, 1933-36; Royal Academy of Fine Arts, Copenhagen, 1937-44. Married Birgit Utzon Frank in 1946; children: Eva, Christian and Camilla. Architect and designer, Cophenhagen, from 1942: consultant to A. Michelsen Metalworks, Copenhagen, 1942-49, Royal Danish Porcelain Factory, Copenhagen, from 1955, and Dart Industries, Europe and the United States, from 1968. Director of design instruction, Guldmedehøjskolen, Copenhagen, 1952-54; lecturer in industrial design, 1957-59, professor and director of industrial design courses, 1959-79, Royal Academy of Fine Arts, Copenhagen; also visiting lecturer throughout Europe, the United States and Japan. Scandinavian team consultant to the Association of Irish Industry and Applied Arts, Dublin, 1956; Committee Member, Danish National Bank Jubilee Fund, Copenhagen, 1968-

75. **Exhibitions:** *An Exhibition for Modern Living,* Detroit Institute of Arts, 1949; Milan Triennale, from 1951; *Scandinavian Design,* toured the United States, 1954; *Formes Scandinaves,* Musée des Arts Décoratifs, Paris, 1958; *Design Since 1945,* Philadelphia Museum of Art, 1983. **Collections:** Kunstindustrimuseet, Copenhagen; Röhsska Konstslöjdmuseet, Göteborg; Nationalmuseum, Stockholm; Kunstindustrimuseum, Bergen; Museum of Modern Art, New York; Victoria and Albert Museum, London. Recipient: C. F. Hansen Prize, Copenhagen, 1948; Knud V. Engelhardt Memorial Grant, Copenhagen, 1949; Grand Prize, 1951, Gold Medal, 1954, 1957, and Silver Medal, 1954, 1960, Milan Triennale; Eckersberg Medal, Copenhagen, 1958; LIfe Stipend, Danish State Fund for the Endowment of the Arts, from 1980. Member, Dansk Designerrad. Address: Erik Herlows Tegnestue, Gothersgade 143, 1123 Copenhagen K, Denmark.

Works:

Danish pavilion displays, at the Milan Triennale, 1951.
United States Embassy building, Copenhagen, 1952.
Coffee pot, for Dansk Aluminium Industri, 1952.
Formes Scandinaves exhibition layouts, for the Musée des Arts Decoratifs, Paris, 1958.
Museum of Forestry, Gavle, Sweden, 1961.
Dansk-Norsk Kvaelstoffabrik building, Grenaa, Denmark, 1961-63.
Shell Oil Refinery, Fredericia, Denmark, 1963-64.
Town Centre redevelopment, Albertslund, Denmark, 1963-67.
Research Centre, Vedbaek, Denmark, 1963-69.

Erik Herlow: Aluminium coffee-pot before and after re-design, for Dansk Aluminium Industri, 1952–53

Superflos factory and ancillary buildings, Vedbaek, Denmark, 1973–82.

Haldor Topsoe buildings, Ravnholm, Denmark, 1975–77.

SAS Airbus 300 interiors, for Scandinavian Airlines System, 1978–79.

Publications:

By HERLOW: books—*Good Things for Everyday Use,* Copenhagen 1949; *Study Designs for Goldsmiths,* with Ibi Trier-Morch, Copenhagen 1952.

On HERLOW: books—*An Exhibition for Modern Living,* catalogue by A. H. Girard and W. D. Laurie, Detroit 1949; *Modern Danish Silver* by Esbjorn Hiort, New York, London and Copenhagen 1954; *Made in Denmark* by Arne Karlsen and Anker Tiedemann, Copenhagen 1960; *A Treasury of Scandinavian Design* by Erik Zahle, New York 1961; *Scandinavian Design* by Ulf Hard af Segerstad, London and Stockholm 1961; *Contemporary Danish Design* by Arne Karlsen, Bent Salicath and Mogens Utzon-Frank, Copenhagen 1966; *Dansk Kunstindustri 1900–1950* by Viggo Sten Moller, Copenhagen 1970; *Danish Design,* edited by Svend Erik Moller, Copenhagen 1974; *Scandinavian Design: Objects of a Life Style* by Eileen Harrison Beer, New York and Toronto 1975; *Design Since 1945,* edited by Kathryn Hiesinger and George Marcus, London and Philadelphia 1983; *The Conran Directory of Design,* edited by Stephen Bayley, London 1985.

My work as an industrial designer has at all times taken the form of teamwork, which contributes by the joint work of a group in the development of products for and together with industry. The main task of the designer is to influence the group work on the basis of a comprehensive view, so that at the earliest possible stage it is possible to assess what will be the consequences of the development work for the enterprise, the consumer, and the society. This implies that work should be performed methodically on the basis of a general knowledge and understanding, with the support of professional ability and artistic faculties. The general knowledge implies that the industrial designer is more freely placed as regards innovation in relation to the more unilateral and highly specialized members of the development group. The industrial designer will in that situation never be able to say, "This is my creation," but he can state, "This development work has been a success for us, for the benefit and pleasure of producer, consumer/user, and society."

The decisive factor is therefore that the designer participates in the collaboration from the very beginning, so that in all phases of development, the group can jointly evaluate the consequences of the work performed. By "consequences" I understand the financial and development results that the product development may have for the enterprise both from a long-term and a short-term point of view. For the consumer, the consequence of the development work will be the satisfaction of a need in the best and finest way and not the establishment of an unnatural need. For society, the consequence must be assessed on the basis of the point of view that the satisfaction of a need will not have decisive, damaging effects on other justified needs and sectors. The physical design of a product will reach the optimum of its usefulness where there is an interrelation between economy, construction, material, function, esthetics, ethics, and use.

—Erik Herlow

HERNMARCK, Helena (Maria).

American weaver and tapestry designer. Born in Stockholm, Sweden, 22 April 1941; emigrated to the United States in 1975: naturalized, 1976. Studied at Handarbets Vänner Weaving School, Stockholm, 1958; School of Art, Craft and Design (Konstfackskolan), Stockholm, 1959–63. Married Jan Barynin in 1963 (divorced, 1967); Michael Maconochie in 1971 (divorced, 1976); Niels Diffrient in 1976. Freelance professional tapestry designer working in Montreal, 1965–72, in London, 1972–73, in Blandford, Dorset, 1973–75, in New York City, 1975–80, and in Ridgefield, Connecticut, since 1980. **Exhibitions:** Quebec Architects Association, Montreal, 1965; Museum of Modern Art, 1973; Los Angeles County Museum of Art, 1974; Museum of Applied Art, Copenhagen, 1977; Hiram Halle Memorial Library, Pound Ridge, New York, 1981; Birmingham Public Library, Alabama, 1986; Galleri Österdahl, Stockholm, 1988; Greenwich Library, Connecticut, 1989. **Collections:** Nationalmuseum, Stockholm; Swedish State Council for the Arts, Stockholm; Röhsska Konstslöjdmuseet, Göteborg; National Gallery of Victoria, Melbourne; Museum of Modern Art, New York; Los Angeles County Museum of Art; Metropolitan Museum of Art, New York. Recipient: Craftsmanship Medal, American Institute of Architects. Address: 879 North Salem Road, Ridgefield, Connecticut 06877, U.S.A.

Works:

The Launching of the QE2 three tapestries, for Cunard Steamship Company, London, 1968.

Newspapers tapestry, for Swedenhouse, Stockholm, 1969.

Rainforest/Vine Covered Maple two tapestries, for Weyerhauser Company, Tacoma, Washington, 1970/71.

Steel 1, 2 and 3 three tapestries, for Bethlehem Steel, Pennsylvania, 1973.

Boston Harbour/Hancock Coat of Arms/Sylt three tapestries, for John Hancock Mutual Life Insurance Company, Boston, 1973/75.

Fields tapestry, for United Services Automobile Association, San Antonio, Texas, 1975.

Sailing tapestry, for Federal Reserve Bank, Boston, 1976.

Journey tapestry, for Lutheran Aid Association, Appleton, Wisconsin, 1977.

Poppies/Bluebonnets two tapestries, for Dallas Centre, Texas, 1978/79.

Wordscape tapestry, for Stanford University Library, California, 1979.

Family Feeling 1/2 two tapestries, for Johnson and Johnson, Skillman, New Jersey, 1981/89.

Six Flags of Texas tapestry, for Texas Commerce Bank, Houston, 1981.

Front Pages tapestry, for Newsday, Melville, New York, 1982.

Oklahoma Suite three tapestries, for Oklahoma First Tower, Oklahoma City, 1982.

Blue Wash 1/2 two tapestries, for Pitney-Bowes, Stamford, Connecticut, 1984.

Divided Landscape tapestry and carpet, for Kellogg's Company, Battle Creek, Michigan, 1986.

Homage to Louis Sullivan tapestry, for Fifield Development Corporation, Chicago, 1986.

1909 Plan of Chicago tapestry, for John Buck Company, Chicago, 1988.

Up and Down four tapestries, for Pepsicola, Somers, New York, 1989.

Publications:

By HERNMARCK: article—"Helena Hernmarck: an interview" in *Fiberarte* (Taos), March/April 1978.

On HERNMARCK: books—*Tre Temperament i Väv,* exhibition catalogue by Dag Widman, Helena Lutteman and Katja Walden, Stockholm 1976; *Swedish Textile Art* by Edna Martin and Beate Sydhoff, Stockholm 1980; *Scandinavian Modern Design 1880–1980,* edited by David Revere McFadden, New York 1982; *Helena Hernmarck,* exhibition catalogue with texts by Jack Lenor Larsen and Joan Barnum, Greenwich, Connecticut 1989; articles—"Helena Barynina Hernmarck" in *Craft Horizons* (New York), March/April 1970; "Helena Hernmarck and the New Pointillism" by P. Blake in *Architecture Plus* (New York), April 1973; "Helena Hernmarck: Tapestry Designer" in *Interior Design* (New York), April 1977; "Photo Realism in a Mediaeval Medium" by A. Knight in *Horizon* (New York), December 1977; "The Artist and the Corporation: A Success Story" by M. Slavin in *Working Woman* (New York), December 1981; "Painting Pictures with Fabric" by W. Von Eckhardt in *Time* (New York), 28 January 1985; "Dialogue with Architecture: Helena Hernmarck" by P. Scheinman in *American Craft* (New York), June/July 1988; "Weaver Scales Down her Art for Show" by B. Liebenson in *New York Times,* 17 May 1989.

My design compositions fall loosely into three categories: photorealism; trompe l'oeil; watercolour designs, calligraphy and collage. Smaller pieces in residential scale tend to be more subtle and contemplative, whereas the corporate commissions, which are viewed in a hurried circumstance, are often large and startling. Landscapes and scenes from nature are used for their timelessness. Most of all, the image must be sympathetic to the architecture. I research for existing images, take photographs and use the colour xerox machine. Lately, I'm experimenting with illusions of folded paper.

The goal is textile art, not production weaving. However, beyond tapestries, I also weave utilitarian textiles such as bedspreads, drapes or upholstery fabrics. I enjoy threads and yarns; I like the way they carry colour. So I choose this medium both for the material and the technique. I am a painter with yarn. Picture and fabric are created at once; the character of the cloth is part of the image. Photorealism is achieved by weaving the way that light and shadows fall on each form.

From the structure of the weaving one gets a different impression, depending on whether it is seen from near or far. Observed from close up, each area is separated into layers, woven as tabby and pattern of blended yarns and colours. The image is defined by passing the bundle of pattern weft through the tabby—creating dots, dark areas against light, one surface under another to achieve translucent effects. Like Pointillism, this technique makes our eyes blend the colours and fill in the missing information. Colour mixes are adjusted constantly, and judged by looking through a reducing glass. Quality is achieved when workmanship, skill of execution and finish look complete, with nothing superfluous. Then the image stands on its own as a woven textile. Additionally, weaving is time-consuming and, in translating the image, nothing of the fleeting moment must be lost. I work at the horizontal warp loom because it handles large work and gives me access to several harnesses and pedals. Choice of warp has bearing on the final look, even if the tapestries are weft faced. For weft, we assemble 500–600 colours of yarn for an average size tapestry of 10 feet by 15 feet, weighing a hundred pounds. It is important that it hangs straight and stays flat, and carries its own weight. The largest

Helena Hernmarck: *Folded Paper No. 1* tapestry, 1988

tapestries are over 400 square feet, and take over nine months to complete.

It is when I undertake these large-scale tapestries that assistants are a help, and almost sixty large pieces have been completed in the past twenty years.

—Helena Hernmarck

Helena Hernmarck has achieved a distinctive contemporary style through her inventive fusion of photorealism and Swedish handweaving techniques. Her unique role has been in adapting the European workshop model to a modern corporate clientele, concentrating on large-scale photographic subjects, meticulously researched and rendered in luminous detail. Accessible and dramatic, her tapestries of striped flags billowing, newspaper pages and wild flowers, among others, serve as vivid icons that enliven the corporate lobby or boardroom with a specific sense of place or history.

Hernmarck's reputation was enhanced by an early and continuous association with prominent U.S. architectural firms, such as I. M. Pei & Partners, and Skidmore, Owings & Merrill—

the fruit of scheduled cross-country trips in 1967 and 1972 to present her portfolio while she resided and worked briefly in Canada and England. Through such influential architects, her work received immediate critical attention, beginning with the widespread publication of her two *Rainforest* commissions (1970–71) for the Weyerhauser Company of Tacoma, Washington, a decisive factor in the establishment of Hernmarck's studio in the Soho area of New York City in 1975.

In a climate sympathetic to Swedish design, and with the added prestige of a one-person exhibition at the Museum of Modern Art in New York in 1973, Hernmarck set out to build a career in an arena closed to most American craftsmen. With a single-minded enthusiasm and professional skill, she created tapestries for top corporations in the United States as well as in Europe and Australia. Her success can be measured not only by the durability of her works in situ—as compared with much fiber art that suffered disintegration or vandalism—but also by its acquisition for major permanent collections of twentieth-century design, including the double-sided *Mao/Yin Yang* (1971) by the

Museum of Modern Art and *Glastonbury Tor* (1973) by the Metropolitan Museum of Art in 1987.

While the preference for custom spun and dyed Swedish wools and an uncompromising care in the weaving process are legacies of Hernmarck's training in Stockholm, her choice and interpretation of images account for her standing as an innovator. After moving to Ridgefield, Connecticut, in 1980, Hernmarck employed a greater variety of media for designing—striving always to respond freshly to each problem. *Blue Wash I* and *II* (1984), a pair of narrow vertical pieces for Pitney Bowes, of Stamford, Connecticut provided a rare opportunity to experiment with abstraction, taken from a liquid watercolour design resembling a cascade. Hernmarck used a symmetrical geometric composition for the first time in a 1986 commission for the Fifield Corporation of Chicago, enlarging a ceiling pattern from the historic Stock Exchange Trading Room in her *Homage to Louis Sullivan*. By 1987, she felt ready to translate more personal images into a series of intimate exhibition pieces.

A resurgent interest in loom weaving, as fiber

art returned to the wall in the 1980s, and notably in the coalescing of an international tapestry movement at a symposium organized in Melbourne, Australia in May 1988, at which Hernmarck was a keynote speaker, highlighted her importance in the evolution of contemporary tapestry. At the same time, a renewed emphasis on the role of the decorative arts in architectural design brings acclaim to Helena Hernmarck's pioneer work in corporate art.

—Pamela Scheinman

HERRMANN, Karl-Ernst.

German stage designer. Born in Berlin, in 1936. Studied at the Meisterschule für Kunsthandwerk, West Berlin, 1953–57; stage design, under Willi Schmidt, at the Hochschule für Bildende Künste, West Berlin, 1957–62. Freelance stage designer, Ulm, 1962; designer, with Wilfried Minks, for the Stadttheater, Bremen, 1963–69; freelance designer, in Braunschweig, 1969–70; head of design, Schaubühne am Hallseschen Ufer, West Berlin, from 1970; also guest designer, at the Hamburg Schauspielhaus, Hamburg Burgtheater, Munich Kammerspiele, and the Salzburg Festivals. Address: c/o Schaubühne am Lehniner Platz, Kurfurstendamm 153, 1000 Berlin 31 (West), Germany.

Works:

Stage productions (at the Schaubühne, West Berlin, unless noted) include—*Jungle in the Cities*, Munich, 1968; *Die Mutter*, 1970; *Der Ritt uber den Bodensee*, 1971; *Peer Gynt*, 1971; *Das gerettete Venedig*, 1971; *Geschicheten aus dem Wiener Wald*, 1972; *Prinz Friedrich von Homburg*, 1972; *Optimistic Tragedy*, 1972; *Fegefeuer in Ingolstadt*, 1973; *Himmel und Erde*, Stuttgart, 1974; *Antiken Projekt: Ubungen für Schauspieler*, 1974; *Sommergäste*, Berlin, 1975; *Shakespeare's Memory*, 1976; *As You Like It*, 1977; *Gross und Klein*, 1978; *The Orestia*, 1980; and *Kalldewey Farce*, 1981.

Publications:

By HERRMANN: books—*Peer Gynt: ein Schauspiel aus den neunzehnt Jahrunderts*, editor, with Ellen Hammer and Botho Strauss, West Berlin 1977.

On HERRMANN: books—*Stage Design Throughout the World 1970–1975*, edited by René Hainaux and Nicole Leclercq, Brussels and London 1976; *William Shakespeare: Wie es euch gefallt/As You Like It* by Northrop Frye, West Berlin 1977; *Theater Lexikon*, edited by Christoph Trilse, Klaus Hammer and Rolf Kabel, West Berlin 1978; *Das Theater der siebziger Jahre: Kommentar, Kritik, Polemik*, edited by Georg Hensel, Stuttgart 1980.

Karl-Ernst Herrmann's name is inextricably linked with director Peter Stein's, since Herrmann has been Stein's principal designer at the Schaubühne in West Berlin since 1971. Herrmann first worked with Stein in 1968 on a production of Brecht's *Jungle in the Cities* in Munich. This came at the end of Herrmann's tenure as the junior designer at the Bremen Stadttheater during the 1960s, a time of great

excitement in Bremen when designer Wilfried Minks was creating daring and innovative theater. Emerging from Minks' shadow when he moved to the Schaubühne in 1971, Herrmann began filling neutral spaces with complete audience-stage environments.

His most famous works, in collaboration with directors Stein, Luc Bondy, and others, were created for the Schaubühne, first in the confines of an old lecture hall (e.g., *Peer Gynt*, 1971; *Optimistic Tragedy*, 1972; and *Summerfolk*, 1974). When the Schaubühne ensemble outgrew this hall, Herrmann designed more extravagant spaces in an old film studio in Spandau (e.g., *Shakespeare's Memory*, 1976; *As You Like It*, 1977; and *Gross und Klein*, 1978). Finally, in the late 1970s, the city of Berlin gave the by then world-renowned ensemble a permanent home in a renovated Erich Mendelsohn movie theater on Lehniner Platz. In this flexible space, outfitted with sophisticated technical machinery that can transform the interior into one, two, or three separate theaters with variable floors, Herrmann designed imaginative spaces for *The Oresteia* (1980) and *Kalldewey Farce* (1981), among others.

Throughout his work at the Schaubuhne, Herrmann has demonstrated a strong regard for the importance of the actor and the text. Unlike other prominent German designers of the 1970s and 1980s who gave their designs independent expression apart from the text and actors, Herrmann's work always played a supportive role within the dramatic hierarchy. Thus, although he has stimulated others to use unconventional rooms for theater productions, Herrmann has always adhered to the traditional, conservative view of the function of stage design, seeing it as subordinate to and supportive of the dramatic action.

—Richard V. Riddell

HICKS, David (Nightingale).

British interior and furnishings designer. Born in London, 25 March 1929. Educated at Charterhouse School, London, until 1937; studied at the Central School of Arts and Crafts, London, 1938–42. Served in the Royal Army Educational Corps. 1949–51: Sergeant. Married Lady Pamela Mountbatten in 1960; children: Edwina, Ashley and India. Independent designer, London, since 1953: founder-principal, Hicks and Parr decorating firm, 1956–59, David Hicks Limited from 1960, and David Hicks International Marketing Limited, with branch offices in Switzerland, France, Belgium, Germany, Pakistan and Australia, from 1970. Designed interiors for Helena Rubinstein, the Prince of Wales, the QE2 liner, British Steel, Aeroflot airlines, the British Embassy in Washington, etc; also designer of clothing and fashion accessories for the Association of Japanese Manufacturers, from 1977, and womenswear collections from 1982. Master, Worshipful Company of Salters, London, 1977–78. Recipient: Design Council Award, London, 1970. Fellow, Royal Society of Arts, London. Address: 13 Albany, Piccadilly, London W1V 9RP, England.

Publications:

By HICKS: books—*David Hicks on Decora-*

tion, London 1966; *David Hicks on Living . . . With Taste*, London 1968; *David Hicks on Bathrooms*, London 1970; *David Hicks on Decoration with Fabrics*, London 1971; *David Hicks on Decoration: 5*, London 1975; *David Hicks Book of Flower Arranging*, London 1976; *David Hicks: Living with Design*, London 1979; *David Hicks Garden Design*, London 1982; *David Hicks Style and Design*, London 1988.

On HICKS: books—*Interior Architecture and Decoration* by Alain Demachy, London 1974; *Design Matters* by Bernat Klein, London 1976; *The Contemporary Decorative Arts from 1940 to the Present Day* by Philippe Garner, London 1980; *Environmental Interiors* by Mary Jo Weale and W. Bruce Weale, New York and London 1982; *The Conran Directory of Design*, edited by Stephen Bayley, London 1985.

HIESTAND, Ernst and Ursula.

Swiss graphic, exhibition and interior designers. Ernst Hiestand—born in Zurich, 16 September 1935. Ursula Hiestand—born in Zurich, 4 April 1936. Both studied graphic design in Zurich and Paris, worked in a Zurich advertising agency, then traveled in the United States, Japan and Africa. Established joint graphic design studio, in Zollikon, Zurich, from 1960. Ernst Hiestand is instructor in graphic design, at the Kunstgewerbeschule, Zurich, and guest lecturer at numerous schools in Basel, Lucerne, Offenbach, etc. **Exhibition:** *107 Grafici dell'AGI*, Castello Sforzesco, Milan, 1974. Address: Chupliweg 6, 8702 Zollikon-Zurich, Switzerland.

Publications:

On the HIESTANDS: books—*An International Survey of Packaging* by Wim Crouwel and Kurt Weidemann, London 1968; *Modern Graphics* by Keith Murgatroyd, London 1969; *107 Grafici dell'AGI*, with texts by Renzo Zorzi and Franco Grignani, Venice 1974; *Archigraphia: Architectural and Environmental Graphics*, edited by Walter Herdeg, Zurich 1978; *Who's Who in Graphic Art*, edited by Walter Amstutz, Dubendorf 1982.

HILLMANN, Hans (Georg).

German illustrator, book and graphic designer. Born in Nieder-Mois, Silesia (now in Poland), 25 October 1925. Studied at the Staatliche Schule für Handwerk und Kunst, Kassel, 1948–49, studied graphics under Hans Leistikow, at the Staatliche Werkakademie, Kassel, 1949–53. Served in the German Army, 1943–45. Freelance graphic designer, working in Kassel, 1953–56, and in Frankfurt from 1956. Founder-member, Novum Gesellschaft für neue Graphik group, Frankfurt, 1959. Professor of graphic art, Staatliche Hochschule für Bildende Künste, Kassel, from 1961. **Exhibitions:** *German Posters of Today,* Baghdad and New Delhi,

Hans Hillmann: Illustration to the book *Flypaper*, 1982

1959-60; *80 Masters: 160 Posters,* Den Bosch, Netherlands, 1960; *Novumgraphik,* Hessisches Landesmuseum, Darmstadt, 1960; *Hans Hillmann,* Kunstverein, Kassel, 1962; *Filmplakate,* Die Neue Sammlung, Munich, 1965; Warsaw Poster Biennale, 1966, 1968, 1970, 1972, 1974; *Hans Hillmann,* National Museum, Poznan, 1973; *Hans Hillmann: Filmplakate,* Neuer Berliner Kunstverein, 1974; *Fliegenpapier,* Institut für Neue Technische Form, Darmstadt, 1982. **Collections:** Landesmuseum, Kassel; Stedelijk Museum, Amsterdam; Royal Ontario Museum, Toronto. Recipient: Best German Poster of the Year Awards, 1958, 1959, 1960; Toulouse-Lautrec Prize, Paris, 1962; Warsaw Poster Biennale Medal, 1966; Cinema 16 Prize, Colombo, 1966. Member: Deutscher Werkbund, 1960; Alliance Graphique Internationale, 1960; Kunstbeirat der Deutschen Bundespost, 1968. Address: Neuhofstrasse 37B, 6000 Frankfurt-am-Main, West Germany.

Works:

Posters, for Neue Filmkunst distributors, 1953-74.
Illustrations, for *Twen* magazine, Frankfurt, 1961-63.
Film magazine design, Frankfurt, 1963-64.
Book designs, for Fischer Verlag, Frankfurt, 1967-68.

Publications:

By HILLMANN: books—*Ich hab Geträumt ich war ein Hund der Träumt,* Frankfurt 1970; *ABC—Geschichten,* Frankfurt 1975; *Ich hab mir in der Besprechung ein Bild gemacht,* Obertshausen 1976.

On HILLMANN: books—*Deutsche Illustratören der Gegenwart* by E. Holscher, Munich 1959; *Who's Who in Graphic Art,* edited by Walter Amstutz, Zurich 1962, Dubendorf 1982; *Graphic Designers in Europe: 2,* edited by Henri Hillebrand, London 1972; *107 Grafici dell'AGI,* with texts by Renzo Zorzi and Franco Grignani, Venice 1974; *The Language of Graphics* by Edward Booth-Clibborn and Daniele Baroni, London 1980; *A History of Graphic Design* by Phililp B. Meggs, New York 1983.

HILSCHER, Hubert.
Polish book, magazine, trademark and graphic designer. Born in Warsaw, 14 October 1924. Studied under T. Kulisiewicz, at the Academy of Fine Arts, Warsaw, 1949-55. Freelance designer, working in Warsaw, since 1956: art director, *Projekt* magazine, Warsaw, from 1962. Chairman of the Warsaw Graphic Arts section, Polish Union of Artists, 1960-63; deputy chairman, Warsaw Poster Biennale Committee, 1965-76. **Exhibitions:** Vienna, 1964; Düsseldorf, 1968; Berlin, 1969; Bratislava, 1969; Prague, 1969; Budapest, 1969; Sofia, 1969; Szczecin, 1971; Royan, 1972. Recipient: Commercial Art Award, Polish Ministry of Culture, 1962; Ljubliana Applied Art Biennale Award, 1964; Manifesto Turistico Award, Milan, 1967, 1970; Warsaw Poster of the Year Award, 1973, 1975, 1980; Mayor's Award, Brno Poster Biennale, 1974; Polish Book Publishers Society Award, 1980; Lahti Poster Biennale Medal,

1981. Polish Gold Cross of Merit, 1955; Polish Anniversary Medal, 1974; Order of Polonia Restituta, Warsaw, 1976. Address: ul. Flitrowa 23, m. 3, 02-057 Warsaw, Poland.

Publications:

By HILSCHER: article—in *Projekt*(Warsaw), no. 3, 1978.

On HILSCHER: book—*Polish Poster Art Today,* by Szymon Bojko, Warsaw 1972; *Contemporary Polish Posters,* edited by Joseph S. Czestochowski, New York 1979; *The Polish Poster 1970-1978,* with introduction by Zdzislaw Schubert, Warsaw 1979.

"I do not consider myself an artist. I practice an artistic craft, and I do so as the result of a combination of circumstances . . . I do my own job as a printer, a carpenter, or a clerk does his. This is how I earn my living." Yes, Hubert Hilscher told this to an interviewer a few years ago.

Though this statement by one of the most renowned Polish designers is spiced with irony, it sounds like a calamity in a country that loves her poster designers and locates them at the very top of an artistic ladder, above the painters, sculptors, and printers. This artist's attitude toward his own profession is very unusual, divergent from that of the majority of his colleagues, who espouse freewheeling creativity and sometimes even personalize commissioned work too much. For them, the rule is "form over function." Hilscher, on the other hand, knows and applies the strict rules of design to each case—the work on the book must serve the subject, not dominate it. The care about clean composition, as well as great control over the placement and function of each letter, are strong points of Hilscher's work.

Besides being a careful and intelligent lay-out person for thousands of issues of various publications, including the leading Polish art magazine, *Projekt,* Hilscher is a brilliant poster designer. The majority of his posters are composed with abstract, linear or geometrical forms. Often, if done for an architectural subject, they look almost three-dimensional. This reminds us that Hilscher studied building construction early in his career. Something lasts.

A leading series of posters—mostly abstract compositions, laboriously crafted, vibrating, and flying at the walls of the concert halls—are dedicated to various musical events. He is also known for posters commemorating exhibitions of architecture, industrial design, and sculpture. However, Hilscher's most popular designs, which sell worldwide, are the zoo posters. Aggressively colorful wild animals—tigers, lions, parrots, elephants—attack everybody's eye. They're funny and mad. One wonders why such a disciplined person as Hilscher bursts with such an avalanche of colors and shapes. Yet, if one makes a little study of them, one sees that all those Op art effects and strange collisions of red and green, yellow and blue, are not accidental. His lions are pure, striking objects achieved through the logical exercise of visual composition. This vibrating shape against the flat field of the basic, sharp color is determined by masterful but simple planning.

Hilscher tries to focus on the real and important role of visual art in society. He is sure that public tastes, good and bad, are shaped by the visual information attacking the eye of everybody everywhere. HIs small, private battle we can compare with the famous ideas of the pre-war Bauhaus. For both, the most important task of any designer is to create correct visual behavior against the existing jungle.

Hilscher is less provocative and egomaniacal

than most of his Polish colleagues, but his calm organized, and sometimes underestimated work on many publications and albums dedicated to Polish graphic art has helped to present this art in the best, cleanest, and most elegant way to the whole world. All of us poster artists of Poland owe something to this friendly and modest gentleman.

—Jan Sawka

HIM, George.
British illustrator, graphic and exhibition designer. Born in Lodz, Poland, 4 August 1900; emigrated to Britain in 1937: naturalized. Studied religious history, at the Universities of Lodz, Warsaw, Berlin, and Bonn, 1918-24: PhD. 1924; graphic design, at the Staatliche Akademie für Graphische Kunst und Buchgewerbe, Leipzig, 1924-28. Married Shirley Elizabeth Rhodes. Freelance designer, working in Germany, 1928-33; partner with Jan LeWitt, in LeWitt-Him design practice, in Warsaw, 1933-37, and in London, 1937-54; freelance designer, in private practice, London, 1955-82: designed posters and graphics for the Ministry of Information, Home Office, General Post Office, Festival of Britain, Schweppes, Haus Neuerburg, De Bijenkorf stores, *The Observer,* etc; design consultant, El Al Israel Airlines, 1952-78. Senior Lecturer, Leicester Polytechnic, 1969-76. **Exhibitions:** London, 1937; Jerusalem and Tel Aviv, 1948; New York and Philadelphia, 1957; *Second World War Posters,* Imperial War Museum, London, 1972; London College of Printing, 1976; Ben Uri Gallery, London, 1978, 1981; *Eye for Industry,* Victoria and Albert Museum, London, 1986. Fellow, Society of Industrial Artists and Designers, London; Society of Typographical Designers, London; Royal Designer for Industry, Royal Society of Arts, London; Member, Alliance Graphique Internationale, Paris. *Died* (in London) *4 April 1982.*

Publications:

By HIM: books—*Locomotive,* with Jan LeWitt, London 1937; *The Little Red Engine,* with Jan LeWitt, London 1942; *Israel, The Story of a Nation,* London 1958; *25 Years of Youth Aliyah,* London 1959; *Squawky,* with S. Potter, London 1964; *Folk Tales,* with Leila Berg, London 1966; *Giant Alexander* books, with F. Herrmann, London 1964-75; *Little Nippers,* edited by Leila Berg, London 1973, 1974; *The Day with the Duke,* with Ann Thwaite, London 1972; *Ann and Ben,* London 1974; *King Wilbur* books, with Jim Rogerson, London 1976; *Don Quixote,* London 1980; book illustrated—*Zuleika Dobson* by Max Beerbohm, London 1960.

On HIM: books—*Window Display 2,* edited by Walter Herdeg, Zurich 1961; *Who's Who in Graphic Art,* edited by Walter Amstutz, Zurich 1962, Dubendorf 1982; *Graphic Design Britain,* edited by Federick Lambert, London 1967; *Film and TV Graphics,* edited by Walter Herdeg, Zurich 1967; *An International Survey of Packaging* by Wim Crouwel and Kurt Weidemann, London 1968; *Advertising: Reflections of a Century* by Bryan Holme, London 1982; *Eye for Industry: Royal Designers for Industry 1936–1986,* exhibition catalogue by Fiona Mac-Carthy and Patrick Nuttgens, London 1986.

To evaluate the design work of Jan LeWitt and George Him, one must consider three aspects of their careers: their joint achievements during their partnership from 1933 to 1954, Him's own work until his death in 1982, and Him's character as a man, a personality, and a philosopher.

Upon his departure from the partnership, Le-Witt kept himself in the background and concentrated on abstract visual art. He had an urge to make up for lost time from his neglected love of painting freely, without the restraint imposed by a brief from a commercial client. Him adopted exactly the opposite policy; he recognized the challenge of a given problem, enjoyed analyzing it as a surgeon does over the operating table, and solving it logically, step by step. Their partnership had come into being through their eccentric plan to walk around the world together, earning their keep by sketching. Instead, they established themselves in London where they collaborated on book covers and children's illustrations. How two characters with such opposing personalities stayed together for seventeen years is still puzzling. One can only assume that through contradiction, argument, and continual friction they found their mutual strength and achieved better and richer solutions than they would have done individually. They made a joint impact with their wartime posters in Britain, especially the one persuading the public to walk; this consisted of the shoe-shaped "Shanks' Pony," head and tail emerging from each end of the shoe, and be-shod lettering. Also a classic was their "Vegeta-bull" character (a bull made up entirely of vegetables), intended to encourage the public to substitute vegetable dishes for meat.

One of the most imaginative advertising campaigns ever to appear in Britain was originated by Him and the humourist Stephen Potter for the soft drinks company Schweppes in the early 1960s. It was based on "Schweppshire," an imaginary county somewhere in England. Potter, the inventor of "gamesmanship" and "lifesmanship," and Him created an English scene out of such nonsense and eccentricity. Later, they followed this with "Europe in Per-Schwepptive," making fun of the Englishman's prejudice against Europe. As with Him's other works, wit and inventiveness dominated both the story and the images for these series. Besides the playful pleasures of content and form, everything the most demanding client needed to convey was there. Him's work, to the end, showed him to be mentally alert, fertile in ideas, and original in concept.

Him was a true amalgam of Eastern and Western Europe. His studies of art and philosophy in German universities, his choice of British soil as a location in which to function mixed to create a uniquely interesting and fascinating personality. Having had the privilege of working with him for some twelve years on animated films, I benefited from his logic and penetrating analytical approach to story-development in arriving at a final conclusion. His brain was continually brimming over with ideas, but he was always able to control them with self-discipline and consideration for the point of view of others. His craftsmanship and sense of colour were superb and his speed of execution, unusually fast, contributing substantially to the fact that everything he created came to life.

Apart from his work in Europe, Him did a great deal in Israel, including the designs for the exhibition at Masada. He also taught at the Academy of Art and Design in Tel Aviv.

—John Halas

HIPGNOSIS.
British graphic design partnership. Founded by Storm Thorgerson (born 1944) and Aubrey Powell (born 1946), in London, 1969; joined by additional partner Peter Christopherson (born 1955) in 1974. Hipgnosis designed record sleeves and publicity material for rock music artists, including Pink Floyd, The Police, 10CC, Sad Café, Led Zeppelin, Genesis, The Alan Parsons Project, Wishbone Ash, Peter Gabriel, Paul McCartney, XTC, Bad company, UFO, etc.; also designed advertising and graphic materials for Polygram, GGK Agencies, Volvo cars, Talbot cars, Colman's mustard, Stella Artois lager, Kronenbourg lager, Rank Xerox, etc. Address: c/o Aubrey Powell Productions, Ilford House, 133 Oxford Street, London W1, England.

Publications:

By HIPGNOSIS: books—*Album Cover Album,* edited by Storm Thorgerson and Roger Dean, Limpsfield 1977; *Wings Tour USA: Hands Across the Water,* edited by Aubrey Powell, Storm Thorgerson and Peter Christopherson, Limpsfield 1978; *The Photodesigns of Hipgnosis: The Goodbye Look,* with text by Storm Thorgerson, London 1982.

On HIPGNOSIS: books—*The Contemporary Decorative Arts from 1940 to the Present Day* by Philippe Garner, London 1980; *The Dictionary of Visual Language* by Philip Thompson and Peter Davenport, London 1980, 1982; *Album Cover Album 2,* edited by Roger Dean and David Howells, New York 1982.

When the children of the 1960s rejected their parents' lifestyles, music communicated that rebellion. The relative affluence of the decade afforded personal stereos for many, as well as the ability to purchase numerous phonograph records. An industry responded, providing music that gave pleasure, escape, and status. In addition, record-jacket art and posters accompanied each hot disc with images as eloquent as the sounds they packaged.

Music stores became galleries of pop culture. Comic book drawings, superficial Indian mysticism, art nouveau nostalgia, scenes of pastoral innocence, and bits of benign decadence were strewn through the record bins. Many covers were designed to shock the middle class right out of its pedal pushers. Psychedelia filled eyes and ears and minds, as brightly colored letterings seemed to melt off the cardboard. By the time Hipgnosis entered the picture, a style had been established.

Even the charming Hipgnosis alluded to contemporary pretenses (hypnosis—influence of the unconscious; hip—modern, with-it; gnosis—ancient wisdom, mystical). Its earliest commission, Pink Floyd's *Saucerful of Secrets,* was typical for 1968. Multiple cosmic images meshed in formless color, while the musicians drifted in an unperturbed bubble. But by the time Pink Floyd released *Ummagumma* the next year, Hipgnosis had dropped the cliché for the daring. Repetitions of the musicians in frames, with slight alterations, played mind games with the viewer. Subtle suggestions of psychological states, such as infinite regression and déjà vu, better suggested mind-expanding experiences than lightshow theatrics.

In the 1970s, Hipgnosis developed those themes established by earlier artists. As surrealism had stimulated the visionaries of the 1960s, so it continued to capture the imaginations of youth. Part of this heritage included the use of pun and collage—both frequent on covers by Hipgnosis. Another surrealist convention—overtly offending the bourgoisie—was not ig-

nored. In fact, what could be called the sexual innocence of the "love children" degenerated into jaded obscenities, continual crotch shots, grapplings, and graspings. This was always, of course, within the cannons of good design. Like fine times on a summer day, absurdity ran rampant.

Hipgnosis created works to which the viewer was forced to react as images played on the mind. Brand X's *Unorthodox Behavior* (1976), with its eye peeking through a venetian blind, affirms the drug-crazed suburbanite's ambiguous paranoia (does he stare at us or do we invade his privacy?). Hipgnosis intruded on our fantasies with narratives like paperback novels or one-second movie scenarios. Viewers who paid the price could dream for free of film noir mysteries, science-fiction illusions, or travels to exotic locales—all illustrated by Hipgnosis—with each purchase of the latest electronic boogie.

In the 1980s, a drop in disposable income has curtailed record sales. Budget cuts and fewer manufactured LP's may spell the end of sophisticated album art. All is transitory. Mind expansion and sensory awareness fade as fads, and the creativity of Hipgnosis falls out of fashion. But during the record industry's peak of influence, Hipgnosis tapped the consciousness of a decade.

—Edith Cortland Lee

HIPP, Catherine.
American fashion designer. Born in Dallas, Texas. Educated in Little Rock, Arkansas; studied liberal arts at the University of North Carolina, Chapel Hill, B.A. in English. Worked as piece goods buyer for Gunne Sax, San Francisco, before becoming an independent fashion designer in San Francisco, and in New York, since 1975; founder-director Catherine Hipp Ltd. knitwear house, from 1975; co-founded, with Jackie Hayman, and designer, Catherine Hipp fashion house, since 1981. Address: 110 West 40th Street, New York New York 10018, U.S.A.

Publication:

On HIPP: article—"Catherine Hipp" in *Women's Wear Daily* (New York), 14 November 1983.

When I was in second grade in Little Rock, Arkansas, we all had to write what we thought everyone else would grow up to be. Everyone agreed I would move to New York and be editor of a fashion magazine.

I never had to make a decision about what I was going to do. I always knew I would design clothes. I started sewing on my mother's little black Singer when I was seven. When I was thirteen, I taught myself to make patterns. I'd sit on the floor and cut newspapers into geometric shapes—cones, triangles, parallelograms, rhombuses—and stick them together into patterns.

At the University of North Carolina at Chapel Hill, I was very hot in trig and math, although I majored in English and took enough art history and religion for each to be a major. It never occurred to me to go to fashion school. I went to college to learn. I really was a student. I still am.

After graduation, I chose to go to San Francisco, *not* New York, and got a nothing job with a big dress company. In two weeks, they made me piece goods buyer. I stayed two and a half years, but I was also designing my own clothes on the side and the boss didn't like that. So, I left and started my own business doing "techy" clothes in slick nylon cire. Bright red, yellow, blue. They sold.

On my first trip to Europe, I was driving through the Rhone Valley and suddenly knew I had to move to New York. One day I went—and cried for two years. It was such a shock. New York has all the support systems for a designer. Top models. Great photographers. Vast libraries. Famous stores. But San Francisco is airy, and New York seemed so dark. That was in 1975. The city is light and open to me now, but it took time.

I've experimented a great deal. Sometimes I've been ahead of the times. My first collection in New York, for instance, included skinny knits that looked like the ballet warm-up clothes that are popular today and also sportswear evocative of clown suits with suspenders. Well, skinny knits weren't in yet. And women weren't ready for humorous sportswear. It was something of a disaster, but I learned more from it than I could have at any fashion school. I've also done collections all in one color and in one fabric. I learned from them how to achieve variety of shapes and treatments working with one material.

In 1981, Jackie Hayman and I started a new business. Jackie had been vice-president of Ann Taylor and has an almost uncanny knowledge of the kind of clothes women need and want. Real women in this real world of ours. We've been making clothes for them ever since, and we've grown into an international company.

I don't like to say that we make tailored clothes because that sounds like gray flannel business suits. But the clothes *are* meticulously tailored. We insist on high-quality workmanship and fabrics. In fact, we have all our fabrics and colors made to order. For me, shape comes first. I never start with color or fabric. I used to design at the barre—I have a passion for ballet—to see how the body looks in motion. I don't have to do that any more. And I no longer cut out geometric forms. With experience has come an interesting dynamic, so that now I'm subconsciously aware of the abstract interaction of shapes and how to relate them to the reality of a woman's body. I see certain planes of the body as more beautiful than others, and I try to show them off in the clothes. The chest, shoulders, hips. In the end, it comes down to making women look good and feel good, to designing clothes that enhance the female form and the female persona.

—Catherine Hipp

There is a laconic elegance to the clothes that suggest something very American, very poised, in the sense of a Katharine Hepburn or a Carole Lombard. One senses that Catherine Hipp is dressing a woman who can fend for herself in the often far-fetched scenarios of American life. But there is more to her clothes than wit or a talent for pastiche. Although Hipp agrees that it is the 1930s and the 1940s which appeal to her most in fashion terms, and specifically the easy, functional, professional working women's clothes of those times, it is not simply comfortable nostalgia that makes her clothes work. There is also a clear-eyed understanding of what fashion means and of the alchemy by which a dress, say, based on a period prototype comes into its own contemporary context, by the addition of a small detail or a subtlety of cut.

Hipp herself believes that the most important source of inspiration for designers today should

Catherine Hipp: Zip-front trouser suit, 1984

be the space program. While realizing that she, along with every other designer, has yet to find a way to resolve the "costume party" overtones inherent in the translation of a space suit into a wearable resolution of that contemporary paradigm, the jump-suit, she believes that there is a causal link between the modest, almost naive dresses she so lovingly collected in local thrift shops as a child and the bone-pure blueprints of functional human covering represented by what men and women wear on space shuttles. She realizes that in terms of what women want and need today, functionalism is a critical element but not the only one. Hipp's work then, is a piquant mix of the outright nostalgic, the shrewdly modern, and the sophisticatedly *soignée*.

Like many other highly gifted designers, Hipp is self-taught. She started with the simplest of cuts and developed as she went along. Yet, unlike a Shamask, there is not a sense of reductionism in her work, which is meant to evoke a rather complicated set of responses—to

America, to fashion, to the role of women in clothes. The clothes, in spite of their surface simplicity, are intellectual in intent, as well as what all clothes should be, esthetically pleasing objects in themselves.

—Peter Carlsen

HOCH, Hans Peter.
Swiss book, exhibition and graphic designer. Born in Aarau, 26 June 1924. Studied at the Höhere Fachschule für das Grafische Gewerbe, Stuttgart, 1946, Arbeitsgemeinschaft Bildender Künstler, Bernstein, 1946–49, and the Akademie der Bildenden Künste, Stuttgart, 1949–51.

Married Margarethe Jerg in 1950; sons: Christoph, Thomas and Andreas. Freelance designer, with own studio for communications, corporate, exhibition, signage and graphic design, Stuttgart, since 1954. Recipient: Best German Poster Prize, Stuttgart, 1963, 1965; Graphic Design in Deutschland Prize, 1971, 1974, 1978, 1981; Kieler Woche Prize, Kiel, 1973; Pro Plakat Poster Prize, 1976; Warsaw Poster Biennale Prizes, 1976; Für den Sport Postage Stamp Prize, 1979, 1980, 1986, 1987, 1989; Beautiful Book Prize, Germany, 1982; Leichtathletik Europameisterschaften Prize, Stuttgart, 1982; Berlin Kunstbibliothek Poster Prize, 1983; World Book Prize, Leipzig, 1983; Gedenkstätte Deutscher Widerstand Prize, Berlin, 1983. Member: Bund Deutscher Grafik Designer; Allianz Deutscher Grafik Designer; Alliance Graphique Internationale; Verband Bildender Künstler; Deutscher Werkbund. Address: Rechbergweg 8, 7066 Höhengehren, West Germany.

Works:

Die Bibel: Gottes Wort im Wandel der Welt exhibition layouts and catalogue, for the Rottenburg Diocese, Stuttgart, 1963.
Bauhaus exhibition layouts, poster and graphics, for the Institut fur Auslandsbeziehungen, Stuttgart, 1974.
Graphics and signage system, for the University of Tubingen, 1975.
John Cranko: Ballett in Stuttgart exhibition layouts, graphics and poster, for the Institut fur Auslandsbeziungen, Stuttgart, 1975.
Kamerun: Konige Masken Feste exhibition layouts, catalogue and poster, for the Institut für Auslandsbeziehungen, Stuttgart, 1977.
Fotografie im Wissenschaft und Technik exhibition layouts and poster, for the Institut für Auslandsbeziehungen, Stuttgart, 1977.
Für den Sport postage stamps, for the German Ministry of Posts and Telecommunications, 1979–80.
Entwicklung der Fotografie catalogue series, for the Institut fur Auslandsbeziehungen, Stuttgart, 1980–83.
Leichtathletik Europameisterschaften Stuttgart 1986 logo, poster and publicity graphics, for the Deutscher Leichtathletik Verband, 1982.
Germans to America series of 14 posters, for the Institut für Auslandsbeziehungen, Stuttgart, 1983.
Kunst Landschaft Architektur exhibition layouts, catalogue and poster, for the Institut für Auslandsbeziehungen, Stuttgart, 1983.

Publications:

On HOCH: books-*European Designers: Germany, Holland, Switzerland,* edited by Idea Publishers, Tokyo 1970; *Who's Who in Graphic Art,* edited by Walter Amstutz, Dubendorf 1982; *Kunst und Design: Hans Peter Hoch,* Stuttgart 1988.

Graphic design today can no longer be understood and judged in its previous meaning, for it is no longer simply an artistic, aesthetic activity, concerned just with form. Today, graphic design must incorporate the new demands of the fields of visual communication and extended information media.

We can separate graphic design into an artistic-emotional field and a functional-methodical one. Graphic design of the former sort strives for pleasant effects, and the work is valued according to its artistry. Graphic design of the latter type is concerned with transmission of information visually, and its value depends on its success in doing so. Over all, we may say

**Leichtathletik-
Europa-
Meisterschaften
Stuttgart 1986**

**26. - 31.
August**

Hans Peter Hoch: Promotional sticker, for the 1986 European Athletics Championships, Stuttgart, 1982

that the extensive range of graphic design today demands that the designer attempt to meet new requirements and conditions. This objective will require new methods of training.

—Hans Peter Hoch

HOFMANN, Armin.
Swiss Sculptor, stage and graphic designer. Born in Winterthur, 29 June 1920. Studied at the School of Arts and Crafts, Zurich. Married Dorothea Hofmann. Freelance designer, working in Basel and Bern, from 1946. Instructor in graphic design, School of Arts and Crafts, Basel, 1947–55 and from 1957; visiting lecturer, Philadelphia Museum School of Art, 1955, Yale University, New Haven, Connecticut, 1955, Aspen International Design Conference, Colorado, 1956, and the National Design Institute, Ahmedabad, 1965. **Exhibitions:** *8 Swiss Graphic Artists,* toured the United States, 1957–58; American Institute of Graphic Arts, New York, 1966; *107 Grafici dell'AGI,* Castello Sforzesco, Milan, 1974; *30 Jahre Plakat Kunst,* Gewerbemuseum, Basel, 1983; *The 20th-Century Poster,* Walker Art Center, Minneapolis, 1984; Swiss Institute, New York, 1986; *The Basel School of Design and Its Philosophy,* Moore College of Art, Philadelphia, 1986. **Collection:** Museum of Modern Art, New York. Recipient: First Prize, Swiss National Exhibition, Lausanne, 1964. Member: Schweizerische Werkbund; Verband Schweizerischer Graphiker; Alliance Graphique Internationale. Address: Nadelberg 19, Bern, Switzerland.

Publications:

By HOFMANN: book—*Graphic Design Manual: Principles and Practice,* Teufen and London 1965; articles—in *Graphis*(Zurich), no. 146, 1969; *Design Quarterly*(Minneapolis), no. 130, 1985.

On HOFMANN: books—*The New Graphic Design* by Karl Gerstner and Markus Kutter, Teufen and London 1959; *Who's Who in Graphic Art,* edited by Walter Amstutz, Zurich 1962, Dubendorf 1982; *Film and TV Graphics,* edited by Walter Herdeg, Zurich 1967; *History of the Poster* by Josef and Shizuko Muller-Brockmann, Zurich 1971; *107 Grafici dell'AGI,* exhibition catalogue with texts by Renzo Zorzi and Franco Grignani, Venice 1974; *Archigraphia: Architectural and Environmental Graphics,* edited by Walter Herdeg, Zurich 1978; *A History of Graphic Design* by Philip B. Meggs, New York and London 1983; *The 20th-Century Poster: Design of the Avant-Garde* by Dawn Ades, New York 1984; *The Basel School of Design and Its Philosophy: The Armin Hofmann Years 1946-1986,* exhibition catalogue, Philadelphia 1986.

Throughout this century, the poster has been a contemporary and viable communication medium, and for the Swiss, it has become an enriching part of their culture and a source of international pride. For the past thirty years, one of its major proponents has been Armin Hofmann whose creative use of word and image has produced scores of outstanding posters.

Because most of Hofmann's posters were commissioned by social and cultural organizations, experimentation and innovation seemed appropriate and was encouraged. His posters for the Kunsthalle in Basel display ingenious and sensitive use of letterforms. He decided at the outset to identify this series by utilizing letters as a common denominator instead of art works. This approach has produced posters which not only display his sensitivity and ability to manipulate letters but also demonstrate the remarkable flexibility and elegance of the alphabet.

Another important aspect of Hofmann's posters is the dramatic and effective use of photography. With Swiss photographer Max Mathys, he has produced an exquisite series for the city theatre in Basel. The distinguishing quality of these posters is the surreal nature of the compositions. Hands, ears, eyes, and faces are enlarged and juxtaposed to create startling and memorable images. For example, one of the posters shows a series of hand gestures emerging from a solid black background. They dramatically express and symbolize all the variety and energy of the theatre. Another promotes the performance of the play *Wilhelm Tell.* Here in a truly elegant composition, a greatly enlarged apple is typographically penetrated by a clever arrangement of the name *Tell.* These examples demonstrate Hofmann's keen understanding of the formal and dynamic aspects of visual communications.

—D. Ichiyama

HÖGLUND, Erik (Sylvester).
Swedish sculptor and glass designer. Born in Karlskrona, 31 January 1932. Studied at the National College of Art, Craft and Design (Konstfackskolan), Stockholm, 1948–53. Married Ingrid Callenberg in 1973; children: Anna, Erika, Albin, Eva-Maria, Ola and Sara. Designer, Kosta Boda Bruks AB glassworks, Boda, 1953–73; independent designer and sculptor, working in glass, bronze, wood, stone and brick, Stockholm, since 1973. **Exhibi-**

Erik Höglund: *Bull's Head* glass, 1988

tions: Smålands Museum, Växjö, 1954; Blekinge Museum, Karlskrona, 1955; Kalmar Museum, Sweden, 1955; Lilla Galleriet, Stockholm, 1957; Illums Bolighus, Copenhagen, 1963; Georg Jensen Inc., New York, 1965; David Jones Gallery, Melbourne, 1965 (toured); Rosenthal, Zurich, 1966; *20 Years of Boda Glass,* Sverigehuset, Stockholm, 1973 (traveled to Gävle); Svensk Form, Malmo, 1974; Galleri Svenska Bilder, Stockholm, 1979; Heller Gallery, New York, 1982; Stadtmuseum, Düsseldorf, 1983; *30 Ar med Glas, Konst och Smide,* Smålands Museum, Växjö, 1984 (toured); Galerie Aix, Stockholm, 1988; Ronneby Kulturcentrum, Sweden, 1989; Finnish Glass Museum, Riihimaki, 1989. **Collections:** Nationalmuseum, Stockholm; Röhsska Konstslöjdmuseet, Göteborg; Konstmuseet Arkiv for Dekorativ Konst, Lund; Smålands Museum, Växjö; Blekinge Landsmuseum, Karlskrona; Landeschaftsmuseum, Darmstadt; Museum Bellerive, Zurich; Cooper-Hewitt Museum, New York; Corning Glass Museum, New York. Recipient: Swedish Crafts Stipend, 1954; Swedish Royal Art Foundation Stipend, 1955; Lunning Prize, 1957. Address: Sigurd Rings Gata 7V, 12651 Hagersten, Stockholm, Sweden.

Works:

Vase in engraved crystal, for Boda, 1953.
Vases in bubbled glass, for Boda, 1954.
Kanotister bowl in engraved crystal, for Boda, 1954.
Drinking vessels in bubbled glass, for Boda, 1954.
Red glass jar with folded rim, for Boda, 1959.
Entrance gates in glass, copper and brass, for Lorensberg Restaurant and Park Hotel, Göteborg, 1962.
Umbrella stand in forged iron and glass, 1963.
Decorative wall in crystal glass, for Ellagård School, Täby, 1964.
Jugs in bubbled glass, for Boda, 1965.
Stone and Water fountain and sculpture installation, for Sollentuna Centre, Stockholm, 1974–75.
Snaps-Glass wineglasses, 1978–79.
Wall reliefs in brick, for the Sparbanken, Linköping, 1979–80.
Circus hanging sculptures in forged iron and glass, for the Government Building, Kristianstadt, 1980–81.

Publications:

On HÖGLUND: books—*Svensk Form/Forma Sueca* by Ake Stavenlow and Ake H. Huldt, Stockholm 1961; *The Story of Boda and Erik Höglund,* booklet edited by Boda Glassworks, Boda 1965; *Scandinavian Design: Objects of a Life Style* by Eileene Harrison Beer, New York 1975; *Form och Tradition i Sverige,* edited by Birgitta Walz, Stockholm 1982; *Scandinavian Modern Design 1880–1980,* edited by David Revere McFadden, New York 1982; *Den Svenska Formen* by Monica Boman, Stockholm 1985; *The Lunning Prize,* exhibition catalogue edited by Helena Dahlback Lutteman and Marianne Uggla, Stockholm 1986; *Från Boda till New York: Konstnären Erik Höglund* by Gunnel Holmer, Stockholm 1986; *Svenskt Glas 1915–1960,* exhibition catalogue with text by Helmut Ricke, Stockholm 1987; *Mellan mörker och Ljus: Erik Höglunds 80-tal* by Björn Ranelid, Stockholm 1988; *Erik Höglund under 40 Ar: Retrospektiv Utställning 1949–1989,* exhibition catalogue by Jan Torsten Ahlstrand, Ronneby 1989.

Erik Höglund is something of an *enfant terrible.* In the 1950s he was one of those who punctured the myth that Scandinavian design is always clean-cut and refined. On leaving art school in 1953 at the age of twenty-one he joined the Boda glass factory. With no previous experience and undaunted by the weight of tradition, he set to with a will. Slender, fragile designs and refined aesthetics were not for him. Solid, earthy forms were the thing right from the start.

His bottles and jugs in thick, clear glass were free and asymmetric, almost always with attached ornaments. Arms were made to project from the shoulders of a glass, the figure of a girl was pressed on or he added a seal ornament as a sort of signature. A preference for coloured glass, somber grey or bright orange appeared early on. To impart more life he soon used bubbly glass, which strictly speaking was a technical imperfection. His glass caused a sensation—tobacco brown, green, grey or red, completed in the glasshouse with an essentially free design. Other pieces were engraved. Erik Höglund often did the work, which meant that he could express himself directly.

Many materials have caught his fancy besides glass—wood, clay, iron and bronze. A turned wooden bed in the baroque spirit and wrought iron candelabra are notable items from the 1960s. He has devoted more and more time to monumental decorations, using glass, metal and brick, and he has also sculpted in bronze.

Many designers and craftsmen see the material as their starting point. Not so Erik Höglund, whose primary concern is the free expression. He likes to try out his sculptural forms in different materials. One example is the head of a girl moulded in glass or set in a brick wall. A lot of his work in the 1980s has been in brick, a hard, yellow type that he sculpts before firing and then combines with standard bricks. Fragments set in high relief are composed into human figures in the manner of ancient

Persian walls. The free fable-making and the search for new effects are reminiscent of his glass from the early 1950s.

—Helena Dahlback Lutteman

HOLLAND, James.

British graphic and industrial designer. Born in Gillingham, Kent, 19 September 1905. Studied painting, Rochester School of Art, Kent, 1922–24; Royal College of Art, London, 1924–28. Married Diana John in 1936(divorced); Jacqueline Arnall in 1953; children: Susan, Vivian, James and Jane. Art director, Lord and Thomas advertising agency, London, 1928–29; freelance painter and designer, London, 1929–40; art master, Beckenham Grammar School, Kent, 1940–42; exhibition designer, Ministry of Information, London, 1942–45; chief designer, Central Office of Information, London, 1945–48; joint chief designer, Festival of Britain, London, 1948–51; art director, Foote, Cone and Belding advertising agency, London, 1951–53; associate design director, Erwin Wasey advertising agency, London, 1956–61. Co-founder, Artists International Association, London, 1933; education officer, Society of Industrial Artists and Designers, London, 1971–79. Head of visual communication, Birmingham Polytechnic, Warwickshire, 1963–71; visiting lecturer, Leicester Polytechnic, 1971–78. **Exhibitions:** *The Thirties,* Hayward Gallery, London, 1979.

Collections: British Museum, London; Victoria and Albert Museum, London; Tate Gallery, London. Associate, Royal College of Art, London; Fellow, Society of Industrial Artists and Designers; Fellow, Royal Society of Arts, London. Order of the British Empire, 1951. Address: Romford Cottage, Romford Road, Pembury, Kent TN2 4BB, England.

Publications:

By HOLLAND: book—*Minerva at Fifty: The Jubilee History of the Society of Industrial Artists and Designers 1930–1980,* London 1980.

On HOLLAND: books—*All Things Bright and Beautiful: Design in Britain 1830 to Today* by Fiona MacCarthy, London 1972; *A Tonic to the Nation: Festival of Britain 1951* by Mary Banham and Bevis Hillier, London 1975; *The Thirties: British Art and Design Before the War,* exhibition catalogue with texts by A. J. P. Taylor, Ian Jeffrey and others, London 1979; *AIA: The Story of the Artists International Association 1933–1953* by Lynda Morris and Robert Radford, Oxford 1983.

Like many of my contemporaries (including Barnet Freedman and James Boswell), I trained at the Royal College of Art as a painter. I turned to design and illustration on leaving, initially to make a living, but later because I came to feel that graphic communication was a more significant social activity in the very disturbed world of the 1930s. With others, I helped to set up the Artists International Association. During the war years, our experience on the social front was useful in the Ministry of Information, where I worked with Misha Black, Milner Gray, and others. From exhibitions to printed ephemera, my interest has been in graphic design as communication, and I am particularly concerned with the relation of word to image. In recent years, I have urged that this relation be considered important in the education of the young designer.

I have become greatly involved in design education as moderator for the art colleges in the South West, from Bournemouth and Gloucester to Cornwall. Design education has never faced such difficult choices as are offered today, largely as a result of the technological explosion. I believe, however, and certainly hope, that the "eternal verities" are still valid and may still point the way for the young designer bewildered by a variety of possible options. In the last resort, the graphic designer, bereft of all traditional tools and media no less that the products of modern technology, should still be able to convey his message by scratching the cave wall or drawing in the sand.

—James Holland

Throughout his career, James Holland has been involved in the institutional promotion of art and design. In the 1930s, he was a founder-member of the influential Artists' International Association, as well as an art director for a major advertising agency. During the 1960s, his energies were increasingly chanelled into advanced design education, as a teacher, head of a major design faculty, examiner, and, subsequently, as Education Officer of the Society of Industrial Artists and Designers, a position from which he retired in 1979.

Holland's work as a graphic designer responds sensitively to the nature of the task in hand and clearly exhibits his training and experience as a painter. His posters, often drawn broadly in four colors, are bold and dramatic in

James Holland: *Campania* aircraft carrier converted to touring exhibition craft, for the Festival of Britain, 1951

conception, with powerful chiaroscuro and contrasts of scale. Many of the subjects offered by his work for government ministries gave scope for strong, dramatic imagery, as was the case, for example, in his posters for exhibitions about the navy and life-saving at sea.

His book jackets similarly make ingenious use of three- or four-color line illustrations, drawn freely and vigorously in a lithographic manner, but these are adjusted to the more intimate scale of the product. Some of his designs are straightforwardly figurative in conception, but the majority use degrees of abstraction, simplification, and overlay of juxtaposition of forms. Emphasising movement, his line illustrations depend on an energetic, wiry line.

One of Holland's foremost preoccupations is the harmonious relation of text and image. This he achieves by means of both discreetly selected type faces and—a forte of British graphic designers of his generation—a good command of hand lettering.

Holland's breadth of experience as a designer and art director, combined with his perceptive but relaxed demeanour as a person, made him a teacher and educational adviser of considerable influence. His activities as Education Officer of the Society of Industrial Artists and Designers were of immense benefit not only to the growing national reputation of that body but to the numerous colleges, schools, and faculties of art and design with which it had connections.

—Clive Ashwin

HOLLEIN, Hans.

Austrian architect, interior and exhibition designer. Born in Vienna, 30 March 1934. Studied civil engineering, Bundesgewerbeschule, Vienna, 1949–53; architecture, Academy of Fine Arts, Vienna, 1953–56; planning and architecture, Illinois Institute of Technology, Chicago, 1958–59; environmental design, University of California, Berkeley, 1959–60: M.Arch. 1960. Worked in several architectural offices, in the United States, Australia, South America, Sweden and Germany, 1960–64; in private architectural and design practice, Vienna, from 1964: design consultant to Herman Miller, American Optical Corporation, Franz Wittmann KG, Alessi, Memphis, Poltronova, Knoll International, Cleto Munari, etc., from 1966. Editor, Bau magazine, Vienna, 1965–70. Professor of architecture, Academy of Fine Arts, Dusseldorf, from 1967; head of the Institute of Design from 1976, and of the master class in architecture from 1979, Academy of Applied Arts, Vienna; also visiting professor, Washington University, St. Louis, 1963–64 and 1966, and Yale University, New Haven, Connecticut, from 1979. Vice-president, Austrian Architects Association, 1965; Austrian State Commission Member for the Venice Biennale, from 1978. **Exhibitions:** Hans Hollein/Walter Pichler, Galerie Nächst St. Stephan, Vienna, 1963; Museum of Modern Art, New York, 1967; Musée d'Art Moderne, Paris, 1968; Lunds Konsthall, Sweden, 1968; Städtisches Museum, Mönchengladbach, 1970, 1975, 1984; Hans Hollein, at the Venice Biennale, 1972; Museum Folkwang, Essen, 1972; Centre Georges Pompidou, Paris, 1986; Museum des 20. Jahrhunderts, Vienna, 1987; Accademia delle Arti del Disegno, Florence, 1988. Recipient: Reynolds Memorial Award, U.S.A., 1966,

1984; Brno Biennale Committee Prize, 1968; Austrian State Award for Design, 1968, 1983; Bard Award, New York, 1970; Rosenthal Studio Prize, Frankfurt, 1973; City of Vienna Prize, 1974; Industrial Design Award of Excellence, New York, 1977; German Architecture Award, 1983; Sunday Times Award, London, 1984; Pritzker Prize, 1985. Honorary Fellow, American Institute of Architects, 1981. Member: Austrian Chamber of Architects; AKNW German Chamber of Architects; BDA League of German Architects. Address: Argentinerstrasse 36, 1040 Vienna 4, Austria.

Works:

Retti Candle Shop, Vienna, 1964–65.
CM Boutique, for Christa Metek, Vienna, 1966–67.
Richard Feigen art gallery, New York, 1967–69.
Austriennale exhibition layouts, at the 14th Milan Triennale, 1968.
Death exhibition layouts, for the Städtisches Museum, Mönchengladbach, 1970.
Section N interior furnishings shop, Vienna, 1971–72.
Paper exhibition layouts, for the Austrian Design Centre, Vienna, 1972.
Schullin jewellery shop 1, Vienna, 1972–74.
Städtisches Museum Abteiberg, Mönchengladbach, 1972–82.
Man Transforms exhibition layouts, for the Cooper-Hewitt Museum, New York, 1974–76.
Central office and three branch offices, for the Austrian Tourist Bureau, Vienna, 1976–79.
Museum of Glass and Ceramics, Tehran, 1977–78.
Alessi exhibit displays, at the Milan Triennale, 1979.
Beck department store, Munich, 1981.
Museum of Energy, Essen, 1981.
Schullin jewellery shop 2, Vienna, 1981–82.
Beck shop at Trump Tower, New York, 1981–83.
National Museum of Egyptian Civilization, Cairo, 1983.
Dream and Reality exhibition layouts, for the Kunstlerhaus, Vienna, 1984.

(for a complete list of Hollein's buildings and architectural projects, see Contemporary Architects)

Publications:

By HOLLEIN: books—GA 47: Otto Wagner, edited by Y. Futagawa, Tokyo 1978; l'Ora di Ginnastica, exhibition catalogue, Mönchengladbach 1984; Friedrich Achleitner: Schriften und Werk, exhibition catalogue, Vienna 1985.

On HOLLEIN: books—Hans Hollein/Walter Pichler: Architektur, exhibition catalogue by Joseph Esherick, Vienna 1963; Hans Hollein: Work and Behavior, Life and Death, Everyday Situations, exhibition catalogue, Vienna 1972; Hans Hollein, booklet by Christoph Makler, Aachen 1978; Architektur aus Österreich seit 1960 by Peter M. Bode and Gustav Peichl, Salzburg 1980; GA 8: Schullin Jewellery Shop, Vienna, edited by Yukio Futagawa, Tokyo 1984; Die Revision der Moderne: Postmoderne Architektur 1960–1980 by Heinrich Klotz, Munich 1984, as Post Modern Visions, New York 1984; Hans Hollein: Works 1960–1988, exhibition catalogue by Gianni Pettena, Milan 1988.

Bibliography—Hans Hollein: A Bibliography of Books and Articles by Carol Cable, Monticello 1983.

Twenty-five years ago some unusual "architectural" projects were publicized. Called "Trans-

formations" by their designer, they used photomontages to change the scale and surroundings of common or known objects: an aircraft carrier in the middle of a rolling landscape, a "high-rise building" which on closer view is clearly an oversized spark-plug, and a sleek, shiny skyscraper on Wall Street—a radiator grille from a Rolls-Royce! Although these fantasies caused some stir in the art world, it was a tiny little shop in Vienna (1965) which brought instant fame to Hans Hollein. Hailed in the architectural press for garnering the coveted Reynolds Metal Award for outstanding use of aluminum, the prize of $25,000, a considerable sum at the time, was said to be worth more than the shop's construction budget!

The Retti candleshop was to be the first of many successful designs that soon followed. Another tiny Vienna boutique, "CM" for Christa Metek (1966–67), utilized a storefront of aluminum, painted metal, and glass to provide a bull's-eye like sign/shop window/front door/air conditioner outlet all in a striking facade. The Richard Feigen Gallery (1967–69) turned the interior and facade of a New York brownstone into a sleek environment of shiny surfaces, bold curves and visually connected multiple levels of exhibition space. Exhibition space. That is the key!

The "Austriennale" at the 14th Triennial in Milan (1968) featured a series of parallel corridors of varying lengths, enclosed at the ends by a row of identical doors. These individual environments offered a variety of physical and psychical experiences through artificial means, not the least of which was a pair of "Austrian (eye) Glasses," produced on the spot, which highlighted the exhibit and became a souvenir for the visitor.

A zeppelin-like tube floating over a rural landscape (1968) turns out, upon inspection to be nothing more than a filter-tipped cigarette juxtaposed in yet another "Transformation." By now, such "architectural" compositions of common objects have started to flow from the fertile mind of friend and artist/sculptor Claes Oldenburg (b.1929), some of which will eventually be realized.

Hollein moves into the 70s with more projects, exhibition designs, shops and competition entries. The "Section N" Showroom (1971) for furniture and objects in Vienna allowed a return to interconnecting volumes on several levels. His design for the Schullin Jewelry Store (1972) on the Graben in Vienna, as a "CM," again provided unusual expression for the air conditioner ventilation—a series of stainless steel/brass tubes piercing a fissure crack in the polished granite facade. Here again a tiny store is turned into an object almost as precious as the wares within.

Hollein's designs for the Munich Olympic Village Subway Entrance Area (1971–72), a first place competition entry, became the guidelines for the entire village. The "Media Linien," an electrified tubular system on steel supports, allowed for the connection of various parts which adapted it to an almost endless variety of urban and climate conditions and displayed his interest in technology to the general public. Meanwhile, his nearby work for the Carl Friedrich von Siemens Foundation facilities brought his high style and attention to details to the semi-private business world.

Another competition produced what may be his largest commission to date—the Municipal Museum Abteiberg Mönchengladbach, Germany (1972–82). Here the design, on a hillside overlooking the town, provides multiple level access to the building dug-in to the hill side to conceal its scale from the structures around it. The complex interior volumes are concealed from downhill by a series of undulating walls—

stepped planters—climbing up to the "walk-on" roof which serves as a major access to the structure, which will be home to Hollein's own exhibition "The Gymnasium Lesson" in 1984.

The Museum of Glass and Ceramics in Tehran (1977–78) gave rise to still more innovations in design and technology in the treatment and lighting of the custom designed display cases. Again, the polished materials of metal and glass strengthen the sense of value of the objects within, while indirect lighting plays off the ornate interior of the building which houses it.

Hollein's work for the Austrian Travel Service of the late 70s, where simulated palm trees provide spatial articulation, as well as suggestions of exotic lands, and pseudo-Rolls-Royce radiator grilles become teller windows, starts his excursion into the Post-Modernism of the period.

The second Schullin Jewelry Store (1981–82) and the shop for Ludwig Beck at Trump Tower, New York City (1981–83) carry these excursions further, while his object/utensil/furniture designs for firms like Alessi, Munari, and Memphis transmute these ideas into a smaller, perhaps more palatable, scale.

Stage sets and exhibit designs flourished. Perhaps the most notable, "Dream and Reality: Vienna, 1870–1930" (1984–85), gave him the opportunity to transform the entire Kunstlerhaus into an informational and atmospheric consciousness of the period. Externally, one wing wall was painted in gold—the dream, while another was in gray—the reality. Internally, the grand staircase greeted the visitor with a parade of mannequins garbed as town burghers while it led one to a succession of rooms, which conveyed the spirit of the Secession, Klimt, Loos, Otto Wagner, Mahler, Schonberg, Freud and the political realities of Red Vienna and World War I. Again the technological features of display and lighting design combined with Hollein's inherent and ingenious design sense.

It is my understanding that his First Place Competition Design for the Frankfurt Museum of Modern Art (1982–83) is currently under construction. It will therefore be arriving at a time when the Post-Modernism surrounding its development is on the wane. It will be interesting to see how, or even if, Hollein will maintain its currency in the 90s. In any event, I look forward to the next work by this man to whom "Alles ist Architektur."

—William Victor Kriebel

HOLSCHER, Knud.
Danish architect, industrial and graphic designer. Born in Rødby, 6 May 1930. Educated in Maribo, until 1949; studied architecture, Royal Academy of Fine Arts, Copenhagen, 1949–55, 1956–57. Married Henny Meyland Rasmussen in 1958; children: Tine, Nils and Rasmus. Draughtsman, then associate, in the office of Arne Jacobsen, in Copenhagen, 1959–60, and in Oxford, 1960–64; partner with Alan Tye, in Holscher-Tye architects, Copenhagen, 1964–66; partner, in Krohn and Hartvig Rasmussen architects, Copenhagen, from 1966; collaborated with the architect Svend Axelsson, from 1978: industrial and graphic designer from 1963; consultant to George Jensen, Højgaard and Schult, Perstorp, IFO Sanitar, Folsgaard Lamps, Thor Radiator, Pevo, Toni Fittings, Dampa, Royal Copenhagen, Nordisk Solar, Dansk Pressalit, Col-

oplast, Bodilsen Furniture, etc. Assistant instructor with E. Christian Sorensen, 1958–60 and 1964–68, and professor of architecture from 1968, Royal Academy of Fine Arts, Copenhagen. **Exhibitions:** *IDD Design Exhibit,* Nikolaj Plads, Copenhagen, 1972; *Danish Handicrat Products,* Sonderborg, 1973; *Nordisk Industriedesign,* Kunstindustrimuseet, Oslo, 1976; *Design Since 1945,* Philadelphia Museum of Art, 1983; Design Center, Stuttgart, 1986. Recipient: British Design Award, London, 1964, 1966, 1970; British Aluminium Industry Prize, 1966; Guild of Architectural Ironmongers Prize, London, 1966, 1969; Theophilus Hansen Scholarship, Copenhagen, 1966; Eckersberg Medal, Copenhagen, 1970; IDD Danis Industrial Design Prize, 1977; Traeprisen Award, Copenhagen, 1979; Scandinavian Lighting Fair Prize, Copenhagen, 1983; Hanover Fair Lighting Design Prize, 1983; Die Gute Industrieform Prize, Bonn, 1984; Goed Industrieel Vorm Prize, Antwerp, 1987; Design Innovation Award, Essen, 1987; IG Design Prize, Copenhagen, 1987; Betonelementprisen Award, Copenhagen, 1989; plus numerous prizes in architectural competitions, from 1965. Address: Teknikerbyen 7, 2830 Virum, Denmark.

Works

Meridian One sanitary fittings, for Adamsez, 1965.
Modric series of fittings, for Allgood, 1966.
Office sign system, for Headway Syncronol, 1971.
D-Line series of fittings, for Carl F. Petersen, 1975.
UFO series of ventilators, for Riscanco, 1977.
Toni series of tap fittings, for Toni sanitary wares, 1979.
Stringline lighting range, for Nordisk Solar, 1983.
Theatre Chair, for Fritz Hansen, 1983.
Ifo Aqua ceramic sanitary wares, for Ifo Sanitar, 1984.

Major architectural works include—Odense University, Denmark, 1966–80; Jos University, Nigeria, 1977; Royal Danish Theatre, Copenhagen, 1978; Bahrain National Museum, 1981; Naestved Town Hall, Denmark, 1981; Copenhagen Airport, Kastrup, 1983; Unicon Beton Headquarters, Roskilde, 1989.

Publications

By HOLSCHER: book—*Culture in a Crisis Time,* with others, Copenhagen 1980.

On HOLSCHER: books—*Nordisk Industridesign,* exhibition catalogue by Lauritz Opstad and Alf Boe, Oslo 1976; *Modern Design in Metal* by Richard Stewart, London 1979; *Design Since 1945,* edited by Kathryn Hiesinger and George Marcus, Philadelphia and London 1983; *The Conran Directory of Design,* edited by Stephen Bayley, London 1985.

People talk about the rational, the causal principle as opposed to the irrational. LeCorbusier looked at this duality in the premises of architecture; he compared it to a river, of which one bank is the rational, the technical side, while the other is the humanist. You have to choose your bank of the river.

Architects express their ideas, their interpretation of a programme, in pictures—some make picturesque drawings, some prefer to create ideas that tower over the landscape of architectonic manifestations like young trees. These ideas are inspirational and may create standards

for the general run of more ordinary architectural work.

Architects also work the opposite way; often they collect pictures to illustrate situations and environments, usually with the aid of the camera, all to help them in their efforts. These pictures sometimes illustrate very clearly all the problems involved, and they act as references.

One of the prettiest pictures I have is one of the south coast of Lolland. Showing a beach after snow, it is a composition showing how clumps of seaweed washed up on the sand have caught the snow, so that each clump of weed has pulled a little snowdrift after it.

At first it looks fine, very pretty, but after you look at it for a while, a marked, rational coherence becomes clear. Near the water the salt has melted the snow, so seaweed and wet sand are dominant; further up the beach the snow is firmer. The whole thing is clear, full of contrasts, very pretty, all rational and calculated. How hard it is to create such an attractive impression! We have to be continually revising, keeping an open mind. And where the snowscape so clearly balances the many sets of parameters against each other in its perfectly rational composition is in the functional requirements that are so hard to harmonize in working out a project—technique, economy, and finally also the administrative burdens that make the creative process so much more difficult.

There are very few master builders who will listen to the aesthetic arguments; they prefer to stick strictly to the rational side in working out their programmes. Relatively few of us are thus alone in striving for a humanist interpretation of the rational and the presumptive.

The seashore is conceived in a single design, a single idea; the eye can pass on to the conception of a wider landscape, in which the shore becomes a detail. This more comprehensive aesthetic experience is generally missing in architecture. Our world is badly off for creators of satisfactory environments, and yet we have classic examples of such complexes, which time has made easier to understand and to accept.

Our world is accelerating technocratically, everything is hurried, and, unfortunately, it is all commonplace. The creative process that used to take months is now all over in days. There is competition for swift solutions. The refinement that developed over a long period, found expression in traditional architecture is missing today. Hence, the few solutions that are outstanding. Hence also, perhaps, the poverty I mentioned earlier in the creation of complete environments; until one set of solutions has been tried out, there is no call for ordinary development to be revised.

The seashore strikes us as aesthetic, but it is not an artistic expression, and it was perhaps its rational coherence that made it comprehensible. A psychologist who has analysed the process tells us that appreciation has certain associations; what happens, according to his analysis, is that we discover in the work an intention, an order, which has lain more or less hidden, and when we recognize it, it offsets the complexity of the work.

Architecture must contain a certain amount of fresh creation, of originality. Otherwise, its information content is reduced, and appreciation with it. Understanding depends on order and on certain known and accepted elements. However, too many familiar elements will transform the conception and it will be regarded as stylistic.

If the idea is too foreseeable, too familiar—if, that is, we say that a conception is stylistic—the idea withers away; thus, there is an implicit need in architecture for continual renewal. I will go so far as to say that the greatest renewal—by which I mean the lowest level of foreseeableness—calls for a maximum of sim-

Knud Holscher: *Ifo Aqua* **ceramic sanitary wares, for Ifo Sanitar, 1984**

plicity, that is to say, a low level of complexity. It is just this conception we should be aiming for; it is what makes the strongest artistic impression.

The picture of the seashore was not a new creation; it was complex, very clearly in line with the psychologist's formula. The postulates of architecture are continually changing, so we must continually revise our own assumptions and causal relationships. Changing associations within society must be appropriately reflected in architecture.

Architecture must thus by nature be creative; if it is to be generally appropriate to its period, it must stand at a distance from what we know and recognize—that is true of questions of form, but as I have mentioned, purely functional elements will also affect development.

Lack of political ability to solve our ecological problems in time has meant that within a decade we have moved from being a growth society to a society with inherited problems and different parameters for their solution. We are, thus, at the beginning of a new period, in which, among other things, the question of energy will have a great influence on planning and building and on our lifestyle.

As in the picture of the seashore, we have parameters for the solution of what is measurable, but up to now, we have had to give way to political-social relationships, which make a synthesis very much harder. The solution lies neither in the familiar round of nostalgic environment nor in pure, suntrap technocracy. The epitome, the synthesis alone will be acceptable. We must sail in the middle of the river, between the rational and the irrational banks. That is where we shall find a synthesis which will provide an answer to problems that are so complex that their formulation is found only in, and with, their solution.

—Knud Holscher

HORNER, Harry.
American stage and film designer. Born in Holicz, Austria-Hungary (now Czechoslovakia), 24 July 1910; emigrated to the United States in 1935: naturalized, 1938. Studied architecture, University of Vienna, 1929–34; stage design, at Max Reinhardt's Seminary for Drama and Stage Direction, State Academy of the Theatre, Vienna, 1932–34; also studied costume design under Professor Roller, Vienna, 1934. Served in the United States Army Air Force, 1942–44: Technical Sergeant. Married Betty Pfaelzer in 1938 (died, 1950); Joan Frankel in 1952; sons: James, Christopher and Antony. Actor and designer, with Max Reinhardt's Repertory Company, Theater in der Josefstadt, Vienna, and at Salzburg Summer Festivals, 1934–35, and with Reinhardt in the United States, 1935–36; freelance stage designer and director from 1935, film designer from 1940, and film director, mainly with 20th Century-Fox and United Artists, from 1951: founder, Enterprise Films of Canada, and Anglo Enterprise Films Limited, London, 1964. **Exhibition:** International Museum of Photography at George Eastman House, Rochester, New York, 1979. **Collections:** Lincoln Center, New York; George Eastman House, Rochester, New York; University of Illinois, Champaign. Recipient: League of Nations Award, 1932; Academy Award, 1949, 1961;

Los Angeles Critics Stage Design Award, 1970. Member, Society of Motion Picture Directors; Canadian Directors Guild. Address: 729 Brooktree Road, Pacific Palisades, California 90272, U.S.A.

Works:

Stage productions (New York, unless noted) include—*Victoria Regina,* for the Italian tour, 1935; *Eternal Road,* 1936; *The Magic Flute,* at the Salzburg Festival, 1937; *Ice Follies* (also director), Cleveland, 1937; *Night People,* 1938; *All the Living,* 1938; *Jeremiah,* 1939; *Family Portrait,* 1939; *Herod,* with Katharine Cornell, 1939; *Railroads on Parade,* at New York's World's Fair, 1939; *Orfeo,* Metropolitan Opera, 1939; *World We Make,* Theatre Guild, 1939; *Il Trovatore,* Metropolitan Opera, 1940; *Little Foxes,* 1941; *Lady in the Dark,* 1941; *Let's Face It* (musical), 1941; *Banjo Eyes* (musical), 1941; *Elektra,* San Francisco Opera, 1941; *Lily of the Valley,* 1942; *Heart of the City, Star and Garter,* 1942; *Kiss for Cinderella,* 1942; *Fidelio,* San Francisco Opera, 1942; *World of Christopher Blake,* 1942; *Winged Victory* (musical; also designed film version) and *You Bet Your Life* (special service production for training camouflage units; also writer), for United States Army Air Force, 1943–45; *Me and Molly,* 1948; *Joy to the World,* 1948; *Turandot* (also director), San Francisco Opera, 1953; *Hazel Flagg* (musical), 1953; *The Portuguese Inn,* San Francisco Opera, 1954; *The Flying Dutchman,* San Francisco Opera, 1955; *The Magic Flute* (also director), Metropolitan Opera, 1956; *Joan at the Stake,* San Francisco Opera, 1956; *Dialogue of the Carmelites* (also director), San Francisco Opera, 1957; *King David* (also director), world premiere at the Hollywood Bowl, 1958; *A Midsummer Night's Dream* (also director), at the Vancouver Music Festival, 1961; *The Magic Flute* (also director), at the Vancouver Music Festival, 1962; *Aida* (also director), for the opening of the Seattle Festival Opera House, 1963; *Idiot's Delight,* 1970; films—*Our Town* (Wood), 1940; *The Little Foxes* (Wyler), 1941; *Tarzan Triumphs* (Thiele), 1943; *Stage Door Canteen* (Borzage), 1943; *Winged Victory* (Cukor), 1944; *A Double Life* (Cukor), 1944; *The Heiress* (Wyler), 1949; *Tarzan and the Slave Girl* (Sholem), 1950; *Outrage* (Lupino), 1950; *Born Yesterday* (Cukor), 1950; *He Ran All the Way* (Berry), 1951; *Androcles and the Lion* (Erskine), 1952; *The Marrying Kind* (Cukor), 1952; *Separate Tables* (Delbert Mann), 1958; *The Wonderful Country* (Parrish), 1959; *The Hustler* (Rossen), 1961; *The Luck of Ginger Coffey* (Kershner), 1964; *They Shoot Horses, Don't They?* (Pollack), 1969; *Who Is Harry Kellerman and Why Is He Saying Those Terrible Things About Me?* (Grobard) 1971; *Up the Sandbox* (Kershner), 1972; *The Blackbird* (Giler), 1975; *Harry and Walter Go To New York* (Rydell), 1976; *Audrey Rose* (Wise), 1977; *The Driver* (Hill), 1978; *Moment by Moment* (Wagner), 1978; *Strangers: The Story of a Mother and Daughter* (Katselas — for TV), 1979; *The Jazz Singer* (Fleischer and Furie), 1980. Films directed—*Red Planet Mars,* 1952; *Beware My Lovely,* 1952; *Vicki,* 1953; *New Faces,* 1953; *A Life in the Balance,* 1954; *Man from Del Rio,* 1956; *The Wild Party,* 1956.

Publications:

By HORNER: articles—in *Theatre Arts* (New York), November 1941, December 1947; *Hollywood Quarterly* (Los Angeles), Fall 1950; *American Film* (Washington, D.C.), February 1977; *Cinematographe* (Paris), February 1982.

On HORNER: books—*La Scenografia nel Film,* edited by Mario Verdone, Rome 1956; *Scene Design for Stage and Screen,* edited by Orvill Kurth Larson, East Lansing 1961; *Le Decor de Film* by Leon Barsacq, Paris 1970, as *Caligari's Cabinet and Other Grand Illusions,* Boston 1976; *Filmmakers on Filmmaking,* edited by Joseph McBride, Los Angeles 1983; *The International Dictionary of Films and Filmmakers,* Chicago and London 1987, 1991.

Just what is the art director's contribution to a play or film? The visual aspect of any dramatic work is an important part of the total effect. In a film, the dramatic effect lies in the camera movement, wheras the effect on the stage often lies in the movement of scenery to give the motion of the locale as part of the illusion. There is no question that the mood of a scene is strongly influenced by the scenic effect.

In a motion picture, camera movement can create the effect of a chase, a train ride, or even the movement of an army—in short, any effect and mood that is brought about by the movement of the camera itself. The stage, however, requires inventions in design in order to simulate motion. The stage might require the creation of devices such as turnable projections in order to move from one scene to another. In short, the designer of stage productions becomes a direct contributor to the creation and mood of a scene, and the audience is required to participate by substituting imagination for reality. In film, realism is expected. Event the trend toward space pictures requires fantasy to be realistic. One of the first modern designer-directors to do this was William Cameron Menzies.

Every imaginative production designer in film has his own favorite design subject. This means that we like to work on stories that particularly appeal to us, that particularly move us more than other stories. Almost every motion picture I've designed falls into this category, and I found I was moved more by character development than by the plot itself. In other words, I look at a script and consider the character description seen by the writer and director to be the most important pre-condition of the design. For example, in the film version of *The Little Foxes,* Regina and the other characters moving around her became the focal elements of my design. The sets were designed to indicate Regina's greed and materialism. In *The Heiress,* the characters of Catherine and her father became the guides for architectural and artistic demands in the designs. The father's domineering personality, his daughter's shyness which later turned into hatred, and her relationship with her lover became the focal points in my concept. The hotel in *Separate Tables* determined again my design by the characterizations of the people who frequented it. Even in a film which concentrated on action, such as *They Shoot Horses, Don't They,* I tried to emphasize the conditions of the various people involved in the dance marathon.

In my interpretation, it is the character of the persons involved that determines the plot of the dramatic action, both on stage and in film, and that guides me in the execution of my designs.

—Harry Horner

In his first film assignment, *Our Town* (1940), Harry Horner was personally introduced to the methods of production design by William Cameron Menzies himself. The young Horner has been assigned the film, but the producer wanted Menzies' experience and thus hired him as the production designer. Instead of re-designing the town, Menzies realized the value of Horner's meticulously researched program: Horner took small-scale views into the lives of the story's townspeople; this was stressed by using mostly

Harry Horner: Set design for *Aida*, at the Seattle Opera, 1963

closeups, and this microcosmic plan was supported by numerous props that became signs of characterization.

But director Sam Wood did not like Horner's unique plan, and so large sets—designed by Horner—were built. Though the original program was thwarted, Menzies maintained much of Horner's design. Nevertheless, visual unity was lost to the expanded scale; Horner's small details were made trite or overpowered.

Ever since the film, it is significant that Horner has remained most interested in visual characterization. He has explained that he emotionally reacts to a script's characters. These very personal, intuitive, expressionistic responses are housed visually within stylistic and iconographic structures. Not only the major contributor to the visual style and iconography of most of his films, Horner also knew how to contrapuntally tie these structures to others, such as the literary/dramatic ones of plot, characterization, and performance.

To isolate Horner's contributions, the stylistic and iconographic elements of his films can be separated and appreciated. Stylistically, it is clear that Horner, like most major film designers, is not a strict realist but an eclectic realist. Horner's best production designs—*The Little Foxes, The Heiress, Born Yesterday, The Hustler, They Shoot Horses, Don't They?* and *The Driver*—are eclectic; except for *Born Yesterday,* all use a mixture of realism and expressionism. Horner also used these two styles and surrealism in his designs for *A Double Life, Up the Sandbox,* and *Who Is Harry Kellerman and Why Is He Saying All Those Terrible Things About Me?* This film eclecticism proves what postmodernist theory has lately rediscovered: that style's humanistic dimensions offers significant meanings in the contemporary world.

To prove Horner is not a realist but an electic realist, his floor plans for many film sets: they are *not* imitations of functional architectural space, even though to most people the room of building may appear to be real. For the illusion of reality, Horner uses highly crafted surface textures, appropriate patterns, and color, and these are also subject to his emotive responses so that they too fit within the design program. In scenes of tension or violence, for example, the floor plans tend toward polygonal forms that create angled walls. But with the "realistic" surfaces, such multi-planed walls, when photographed, will become a tense expressionist-realist environment for the performance.

Iconographically selected or designed objects, spaces, decor, and presentation on the screen also are hidden under these electic realist appearances. For example, in one of Horner's masterworks, *The Heiress* (1949), the meticulously researched, mid-nineteenth century house of Dr. Sloper appears authentic, leading one to accuse Horner of a narrow historicism. But it was only an illusion. As Horner described it, the house was emotionally conceived as an elegant cage in which Catherine Sloper was psychologically interred. The floor plan was given many planes that compress the characters. Linear grids subtly appear in lattices, wallpaper, and in other details; they increase the sense of enclosure. To insure the emotional environment was correctly lit and photographed, Horner made continuity sketches with expressionistic, high-contrast lighting and extreme angles.

The sketches were discussed with Wyler and Leo Tover, the cameraman. Conversations made over these drawings tightly integrated Horner's design program into the photography and performances. This film production from beginning to end met many of Horner's standards for a film's creative social aspect—the artistic family, headed by an esthetically sensitive director.

A spirit of collaboration between the specialized artists has existed in each film Horner has enjoyed working on—one should add, whether or not the film became a box-office success. Horner says that the films with incompatible production members usually become jobs unworthy of being called a production design.

—Norman Gambill

HUBER, Max.
Swiss typographic, industrial, display and graphic designer. Born in Baar, Zurich, 5 June 1919. Studied at the Kunstgewerbeschule, Zurich, 1935–38. Assistant graphic designer in an advertising agency, Zurich, 1937–38; layout artist, for Conzett and Huber magazines, Zurich, 1938–40; designer and art director, Studio Boggeri, Milan, 1940; freelance designer, working mainly on exhibition designs with Max Bill and Werner Bischof, in Zurich, 1942–46; also art director, Artemis Verlag publishers, Zurich, 1943–46; freelance designer, working in Milan, from 1946: designed for La Rinascente stores, Edizioni Einaudi, Legler cotton mills, Automobile Club of Italy, RAI Radiotelevisione Italiana, Supermercatori Italiani, Birra Poretti, Olivetti, etc. **Exhibitions:** *Allianz,* Zurich, 1943; *Salon des Realités Nouvelles,* Paris, 1946; *Arte Astratta e Concreta,* Milan, 1947;

Galleria Il Camino, Milan, 1948; Libreria Salto, Milan, 1950; *Purpose and Pleasure,* London, 1952; *Design and design,* Palazzo delle Stelline, Milan, 1979 (traveled to Venice); *Gli Annitrenta: Arte e Cultura in Italia,* Palazzo Reale, Milan, 1982. Recipient: Gold Medal, Milan Triennale, 1954; Compasso d'Oro Award, Milan, 1954, 1960, 1964. Address: 6831 Sagno (Ticino), Switzerland.

Publications:

On HUBER: books—*Olivetti 1908-1958,* with texts by Adriano Olivetti, Libero Bigiaretti and Franco Forlini, Turin 1958; *The New Graphic Design* by Karl Gerstner and Markus Kutter, Teufen and London 1959; *Moderne Werbe- und Gebrauchs-Grafik* by Hans Neuburg, Ravensburg 1960; *Who's Who in Graphic Art,* edited by Walter Amstutz, Zurich 1962, Dubendorf 1982; *History of the Poster* by Josef and Shizuko Muller-Brockmann, Zurich 1971; *Design and Design,* exhibition catalogue with texts by Angelo Cortesi, Arthur Pulos and others, Florence 1979; *A History of Graphic Design* by Philip B. Meggs, New York and London 1983; *Italian Design: 1870 to the Present* by Penny Sparke, London 1988.

Max Huber established himself in Milan soon after the end of the war and quickly became an influence, leading the way towards a creative use of typographical devices and means. Perhaps the most famous of his works in this respect was the logo and name style for the Milan store, La Rinascente. Utterly stark and simple, it was an elegant combination of a modern face, italic, lower case "la" with a bold, sans serif "Rinascente," the two reduced to "l" and "R" for the logo, which appeared in a repeat pattern for paper bags and wrapping paper.

Another aspect of this strongly typographical approach to design was the label he designed for Frisia, a soft drink; simplified, sans serif capitals in different colours overlapped to make a distinctive but legible namestyle. That was in 1958, the same year he designed the poster for the Bergamo Gran Premio for art films and films on art, and this, too, relied upon large sans serif capitals unusually placed together to form a striking pattern.

Again, this attachment to pattern-making with type added much to those exhibitions for which he was employed to take care of the graphics. Panels of sans serif type for the most part made positive contributions to the display and were not to be relegated to a discrete role of captioning the exhibits. This was particularly so at the *Triennale* in 1951; his collaboration in the section *La forma dell'utile* gave it a distinction it might well not otherwise have attained, while his work on the ENI stand at the 1955 Naples Petrol Exposition strikingly matched its structure.

In many ways, Huber might be thought to have abandoned his Swiss origins, though occasionally there is a fleeting echo of Max Bill's graphic and exhibition design. Rather he sought to build upon an Italian tendency that was initiated in the 1930s and that linked to the work of Giovanni Pintori, for example, and had been much the dominant style in the magazine *Campo grafico,* where the phrase *architettura del'libro,* the architecture of the book, had been coined to encapsulate the aesthetic of using type the way an architect of the modern and rationalist school uses the elements of building. Inevitably, this tendency was modified, both in Huber's own development and in the changing cultural climate since the end of Fascism, but it did provide a link and made possible Huber's career as well as his widespread and deep influence in Italy. His presence served to alert Italian graphic designers to possibilities still to be developed from

their own immediate past and not to be dismissed as having been done under Fascism and therefore to be despised.

—Toni del Renzio

HULDT, Johan (Gunnar Hampus).

Swedish furniture and industrial designer. Born in Stockholm, 1 January 1942. Studied at Lidingö H. A. Läroverket, 1962; Military Naval College, Göteborg, 1963; Kalmar Naval College, 1963; industrial woodwork, Enskede Trade School, 1964; State School of Arts and Design, Stockholm, 1964-68; sociology, University of Stockholm, 1969. Married Elisabeth Hintze in 1972; children: Mikael and Maria. Founder, with Jan Dranger, of Innovator Design Studios, 1968, and Executive Manager of Innovator Design AB, Stockholm, since 1969; Founder of Basic Design shop system, 1978, and Managing Director of Basic Design AB, Stockholm, 1983-89. Lecturer, Royal Swedish School of Design, Stockholm, 1975-78. Director, Swedish Furniture Research Institute, Stockholm, 1974-76; Chairman, National Association of Swedish Interior Architects (S.I.R.), Stockholm, 1983-88. **Exhibitions:** Museu de Arte Moderna, Rio de Janeiro, 1972; Museu de Arte, Sao Paulo, 1973, 1980; Nationalmuseum, Stockholm, 1985, 1989. **Collections:** Nationalmuseum, Stockholm; Museum of Modern Art, New York; Museu de Arte, Sao Paulo; Museu de Arte Moderna, Rio de Janeiro. Recipient: Scandinavian Chair of the Year Award, 1972-74; Gute Form Award, 1974. Honorary Collaborator, International Designers' School, Barcelona. Address: Innovator Design AB/ Johan Huldt Design AB, Stora Skuggans Väg 9, 115 42 Stockholm, Sweden.

Works:

Multoman sofa, for Dux International, 1969.
Tech Trolley enamelled steel multipurpose trolley, for Möbelmontage, 1972.
Stuns upholstered lacquered steel armchair, for Möbelmontage, 1972.
Woodstock upholstered wooden armchair and sofa, for Möbelmontage, 1973.
Balluff sofa, for Möbelmontage, 1974.
Vivaldi folding chair, for Möbelmontage, 1975.
Mari upholstered wooden armchair and sofa, for Innovator Design, 1977.
Columbi table, for Akuma, 1978.
Terminal table, for Akuma, 1979.
Butterfly steel armchair, for Innovator Design, 1981.
Slim steel armchair, for Innovator Design, 1982.
Flight upholstered steel armchair, for Innovator Design, 1985.
Galac Tech steel chair, for Innovator Design, 1986.

Publications:

On HULDT: books—*Design in Sweden* by Katja Walden and others. Stockholm 1972; *Konsthantverk, Konstindustri, Design 1875-1975* by Dag Widman, Stockholm 1975; *Morgondagens Antikviteker* by Anders Neumüller, Stockholm 1982; *The Conran Directory of Design* by Stephen Bayley and others, London 1985; *The International Design Yearbook 1985/1986,* edited by Robert A. M. Stern, London 1985; *Den Svenska Formen* by Monica Boman and others, Stockholm 1985.

Johan Huldt began his professional design career in partnership with a classmate from the Stockholm High School of Design in 1968. For several years, he worked as a freelance designer for some of Sweden's most prominent furniture manufacturers. His reputation grew as his designs became more widely appreciated. Despite this, he still found it difficult to achieve his goals or to fulfil his design ideas as a freelancer; the selling of his own ideas and abilities required too much "design for the sake of design."

Brought up in a home where many famous Scandinavian designers were frequent guests and their works everyday objects, Huldt acquired a profound appreciation of quality in design. He found himself constantly objecting, however, to the fact that good design was so expensive; students and young people like himself were not consumers of good design. In his own work, he therefore dedicated himself to inexpensive design that stressed practical and functional properties.

During the 1970s, Huldt explored many different areas of design, such as the interiors of churches, sex-education shops, civil defence shelters and, of course, more customary disciplines as graphic, textile, furniture and packaging design. His main activity, however, is furniture design—home furnishing for the young and young-in-spirit, people with "more taste than money." Early on, he formulated a comprehensive design concept to which he still remains true: he has to struggle to make the world "a little less ugly" for the many, rather than to design objects for people boasting a professional design taste. To accomplish these ideas, Huldt very soon left freelancing, joined a new partner, and went into the manufacture and retailing of furniture, thus controlling the entire chain from idea to ultimate consumer.

When asked to give his views on design, Huldt says: "Design work must be performed as a subtle balance between very precise human and functional demands, and an austere use of scarce raw materials—all in combination with harmony and beauty. Contemporary furniture design must therefore be based on the modern family in a new society, with its responsibility to nature and energy and an increased need for pleasure and beauty in a materialistic world. Real design work today includes many new fields that must be addressed by every conscientious designer. He has a great responsibility to research and formulate genuine human and social demands. He must also acquire a thorough knowledge of production and distribution techniques, as well as of economic systems and their effects. In my daily work, I find it equally important to consider the designer's view at all stages of a product's life, as well as other aspects of society not usually included in a designer's brief—thus involving problems other than those of shape or mere aesthetics. The task, then, is not only to create new possibilities, constructions and forms, but also to oppose those environmental objects that are produced without honest planning of shape and function. I believe it vital that today's designer should channel his ability to create good designs in terms of elegance and beauty, at the same time attending to the rigid technical and economic conditions which are the base for his work. He must therefore have confidence in himself, since the significance of this work will not be apparent in experimental dynamic shapes, as seen in the 1960s, nor in the scientific modular systems of the 1970s. The effect of his work may not even show in the final product, being instead an essential but unseen part of the process. Good design only differs in form from bad design through small but important details. This does not mean, however, that the end result will be less exciting than before, but we will have to educate ourselves to enjoy less dramatic expressions and to take pleasure in the importance of minor details."

Today, Johan Huldt performs his design work within his own company, Innovator, with manufacturing facilities in Sweden, Japan, Brazil and Spain. His furniture is made in large editions and is to be found in more than 25 countries all over the world. He travels frequently to exchange ideas and keep in touch with the current international scene. It gives him satisfaction to see his furniture displayed in New York, Rio de Janeiro, Zurich, Paris or London—and often more easily accessible there than in his native Sweden. With his very Scandinavian background, Huldt is deeply interested in a new "world culture"—as long as it is interpreted in a bluejeans idea rather than in hamburgers.

—Maud Lindgren

HURLBURT, Allen (Freeman).

American graphic designer. Born in Bridgeport, Connecticut, 24 October 1910. Studied economics, at the University of Pennsylvania, Philadelphia, 1929–32: BS 1932. Married Regina Victoria Rowe in 1953; daughter: Susan. Art Director, Bureau of Advertising, New York, 1937–43, and NBC National Broadcasting Company, New York, 1946–51; art director, 1952–67, editorial board member, 1953–72, director of design, 1968–72, and editorial adviser, 1970–72, *Look* magazine, New York; vice-president, 1962–72, and editorial adviser, 1970–72, Cowles Communications, New York. President, American Institute of Graphic Arts, New York, 1968–69. **Exhibition:** Museum of Modern Art, New York, 1965. Recipient: Gold Medal, Art Directors Club of New York, 1948, 1949, 1955, and 1961–70; Art Director of the Year Award, National Society of Art Directors, 1965; Gold Medal, American Institute of Graphic Arts, 1973. Fellow, Royal Society of Arts, London. Member: Alliance Graphique Internationale; American Institute of Graphic Arts; Art Directors Club of New York. *Died* (in Sarasota, Florida) *30 June 1983.*

Publications:

By HURLBURT: books—*Publication Design,* New York 1971; *Layout: The Design of the Printed Page,* New York 1977; *The Grid,* New York 1978; *The Design Concept,* New York 1981; *Photo/Graphic Design,* New York 1983.

On HURLBURT: books—*The Stars* by Richard Schickel, New York 1962; *The Language of Graphics* by Edward Booth-Clibborn and Daniele Baroni, London 1980.

Allen Hurlburt was open to all contemporary activity in the arts, architecture, literature, and the sciences. A bridge between the visual world and the public, his work in design raised the perception and altered the spectators' vision of verbal and visual material.

Through his own process of discovery and selectivity, he expanded the role and function of the magazine art director, bringing this discipline strongly and equally into the editorial process. He launched this challenge in the pages of *Look* magazine where, during his tenure as art director, he brightened the pages within illustrative material that reflected his broad knowledge and his spirit of investigation of the visual world. He had the rare ability to relate graphic originality to the requirements of journalism.

Concerned with typography and layout, he recognized the heritage of the past but was also responsive to the new technologies as he created his own standards and unified the appearance of the magazine, transforming it dramatically. Thus, he was a pioneer in art direction and possibly the most influential magazine art director of his day. Setting new standards, he gave the magazine not only a distinctive look but a visual identity which appealed to its audience.

Hurlburt never stopped studying and learning. His supportive interest in young designers and his ability to give of himself and his knowledge made him an excellent educator. With clarity of mind, he became the sounding board for precise shades of meaning in graphic design.

—Mildred Constantine

HYDMAN-VALLIEN, Ulrica.

Swedish painter, sculptor, glass, ceramics and textile designer. Born Ulrica Hydman, in Stockholm, 14 March 1938. Studied at the National College of Art, Craft and Design, Stockholm, 1958–63. Married designer and sculptor Bertil Vallien in 1963; children: Hampus and Markus. Ceramics artist, establishing own studio in Eriksmala, from 1963; glass designer, Kosta Boda AB, Sweden, since 1972; ceramics designer, for Rörstrand AB, Lidköping, 1984–86; also freelance designer, working with Weil's, etc. Instructor, Pilchuk Glass School, Seattle, Washington, 1980–88, and at Bildwerk Frauenau, Germany, 1989. **Exhibitions:** *Adventure in Swedish Glass,* toured Australia, 1975; *Scandinavian Modern Design 1880–1980,* Cooper-Hewitt Museum, New York, 1982 (toured); Heller Gallery, New York, 1983; Museu de Arte Moderno, Sao Paulo, 1984; Essener Glasgalerie, West Germany, 1985; New Glass Gallery, New York, 1985; Sweden Center, Tokyo, 1986; Galleri Ikaros, Göteborg, 1987; Liljevalchs Konsthall, Stockholm, 1988; *Faces of Swedish Design,* IBM Gallery, New York, 1988 (toured). **Collections:** Nationalmuseum, Stockholm; Röhsska Konstslöjdmuseet, Goteborg; Kunstmuseum, Düsseldorf; Corning Glass Museum, New York; Victoria and Albert Museum, London; National Museum of Modern Art, Tokyo. Recipient: Young Artist Award, Nationalmuseum, Stockholm, 1972; Major State Scholarship, Stockholm, 1973, 1974; Swedish National Artists Award, 1980; Women in Design Prize, New York, 1983; Swedish Artists Scholarship, 1983–87; Coburg Glaspreis Awards, West Germany, 1985. Address: Afors Glasbruk, Bromsväg 8, 361 04 Eriksmåla, Sweden.

Works:

Tinto Mara hand-blown coloured glassware, for Kosta Boda, 1972.
Romantica hand-blown painted glass tableware, for Kosta Boda, 1973.
Butterfly hand-blown painted glassware, for Kosta Boda, 1976.
Pastell hand-blown coloured glassware, for Kosta Boda, 1978.
Poem hand-blown painted glass tableware, for Kosta Boda, 1978.
Paradise hand-blown painted glassware, for Kosta Boda, 1985.
Poem hand-painted ceramic tableware, for Rörstrand, 1985.
Cleopatra clear glassware with snake decoration, for Kosta Boda, 1986.
Open Minds hand-painted blown vases and cups, for Kosta Boda, 1986.
Caramba hand-painted cotton fabric, for Weil's, 1986.
Caramba hand-painted blown glass vases and bowls, for Kosta Boda, 1987.
Love hand-painted blown glass vases and bowls, for Kosta Boda, 1988.
Jade blown glass vases and bowls, for Kosta Boda, 1988.
Birdy hand-painted glass vases and bowls, for Kosta Boda, 1989.

Publications:

On HYDMAN-VALLIEN: books—*Modern Ceramics* by Geoffrey Beard, London 1969; *Keramik* by Ulf Hård af Segerstad, Stockholm 1976; *I Glasrike* by Bertil Palmqvist, Stockholm 1979; *Glasboken: Historia, Teknik och Form* by Carl F. Hermelin and Elsebeth Welander, Boras 1980; *Scandinavian Modern Design 1880–1980,* edited by David Revere McFadden, New York 1982; *Crystal Clear: New Glass from Sweden* by Helena Dahlbäck Lutteman, Uppsala 1982; *Den Svenska Formen* by Monica Boman and others, Stockholm 1985; *Made in Sweden: Art, Handicraft, Design* by Anja Notini, London 1987; *Contemporary Glass* by Suzanne Franz, New York 1989; articles—"Bertil Vallien and Ulrica Hydman-Vallien: Designs for Art and Living" by K. Chambers in *New Work* (New York) no. 21/22, 1985; "Ulrica Hydman-Vallien" in *Swedish Design Annual,* Stockholm 1987.

As a designer for Kosta Boda, I work closely with the craftsmen in the hot shop. I refuse to work with machines. My intention is to keep alive the old techniques and to add some new ones, and to find ways of extending the potential of the material.

As a designer and in production work, I like to put something of myself into everything—even in mass-production. In the "Artist's Collection" series, I can remain close to my own expression, as in painting. In the glass pieces *Open Minds* (1987) and *Birdy* (1989), I am able to make my personal mark, which is not always the most immediately acceptable to the public; I like to tease and challenge. The series *Cleopatra,* with a snake wound around the stems of hand-blown drinking glasses, are made for especially daring consumers. Although I have complete freedom in my artwork as a painter and sculptor, I want as much as possible to be true to myself in my design work, as well. By holding firmly to this principle, I have today gained acceptance for the idea in industrial design.

—Ulrica Hydman-Vallien

Ulrica Hydman-Vallien: *Cleopatra* glassware, for Kosta Boda, 1986

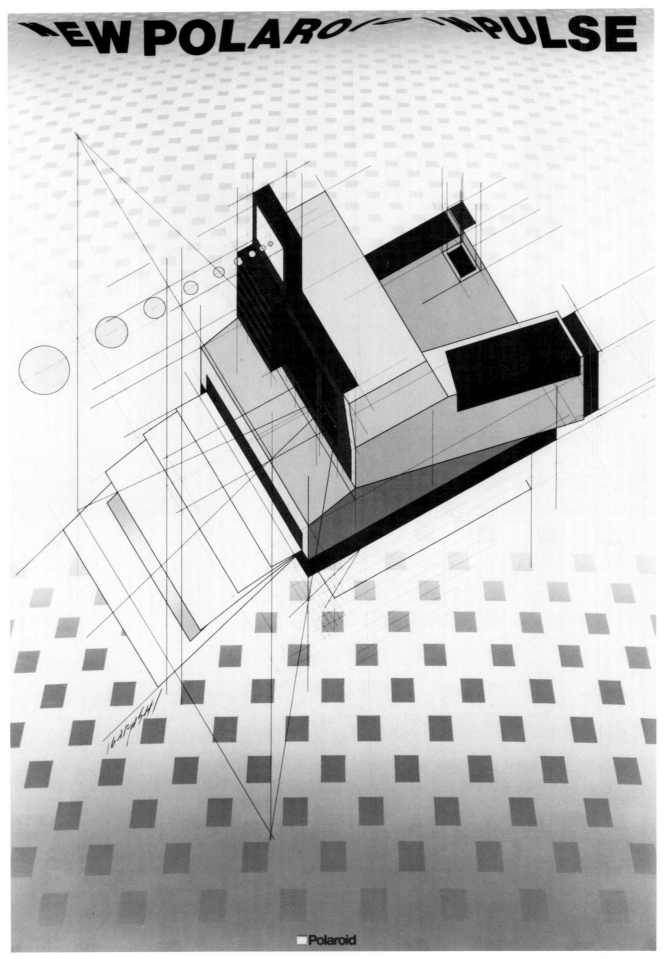

Takenobu Igarashi: *New Impulse Camera* **poster, for the Polaroid Corporation, 1989**

IGARASHI, Takenobu.

Japanese environmental, product, corporate and graphic designer. Born in Hokkaido, 4 March 1944. Studied graphic design, at Tama Art University, Tokyo, 1964–68: BA 1968; University of California at Los Angeles, 1968–69; MA 1969. Married Fumiko Hashimoto in 1980; children: Tomoko and Shoko. Independent designer, establishing own office in Tokyo, since 1970. Lecturer, 1975–76, and visiting professor, 1989, College of Fine Arts, University of California at Los Angeles; instructor, Department of Technology, Chiba University, 1979–83; professor and head of design, Tama University, Tokyo, from 1989. Board member, Japan Graphic Designers Association, Tokyo, 1985–89; vice-president, Alliance Graphique Internationale, Paris, 1985–91. **Exhibitions:** Fujie Gallery, Tokyo, 1972, 1975; *One Day, One Show,* Tokyo Designers Space, 1976; Print Gallery, Amsterdam, 1978; *One Week, One Show,* Tokyo Designers Space, 1979; Tokyo Designers Space Open Gallery, 1980; Parco Street Gallery, Tokyo, 1981; Matsuya Design Gallery, Tokyo, 1981; Reinhold Brown Gallery, New York, 1983; Mikimoto Hall, Ginza, Tokyo, 1983; Portfolio Center, Atlanta, 1984; Ginza Graphic Gallery, Tokyo, 1987; Macquarie Galleries, Sydney, 1987; Asahi Gallery, Tokyo, 1987; Gallery of Arts and Sciences, Keihan Department Store, Osaka, 1988; Von Oertzen Gallery, Frankfurt, 1988. **Collections:** Museum des 20. Jahrhunderts, Vienna; Kunstgewerbemuseum, Zurich; Museum of Modern Art, New York; Cooper-Hewitt Museum, New York; Art center College of Design, Los Angeles; Library of Congress, Washington, D.C.; Toyama Museum of Modern Art, Japan. Recipient: Merit Award, 1976, 1978, and Bronze Prize, 1986, Warsaw Poster Biennale; Bronze Prize, Third Lahti Poster Biennale, Finland, 1979; Bronze Prize, Brno Graphics Biennale, 1980; Outstanding Public Signage Award, Japan Sign Design Association, 1980; Silver Prize, Warsaw Jazz Poster Salon, 1986; Gold and Bronze Prize, 1986, and Silver Prize, 1988, CS Design Award, Japan. Address: Igarashi Studio, 6-6-22 Minami Aoyama, Minato-ku, Tokyo 107, Japan.

Works:

Expo '85 official poster, for the International Science and Technology Exposition Association, 1982.
Signage programme, for the Mita and Hiyoshi campuses of Keio University, Tokyo, 1982, 1985.

Visual identity symbol, for the Kanazawa Institute of Technology, 1983.
Corporate identity programme, for the Mitsui Bank Limited, 1984.
Poster calendar, for the Museum of Modern Art, New York, 1984–88.
3 sculpture in stainless steel, for the Michael Peters Group, 1985.
Signage programme, for the headquarters of the Honda Motor Company, Tokyo, 1985.
Neocon 19 architecture and design convention poster, for the Merchandise Mart, Chicago, 1986.
Visual identity symbol, for the Suntory Classical Music Hall, Tokyo, 1986.
Corporate identity programme, for Meiji Milk Products Company, 1986.
Africa Award for Leadership sculptural trophy in gold-plated aluminum, for the Hunger Project, 1987.
Oun Collection products and accessories range, for the Oun Corporation, from 1987.
Fisso desk accessories range, for the Fujii Company, 1988.
Hyvalysti gardening kit, for the Kai Corporation, 1988.
Zanders calendar, for Zanders Feinpapiere AG, 1988.
Polaroid Impulse poster, for the Polaroid Corporation, 1988.

Publications:

By IGARASHI: books—*Letterheads of the World,* editor, Tokyo 1977; *Graphic Design for Our Environment,* Tokyo 1980; *World Trademarks and Logotypes,* editor, Tokyo 1983; *Letterheads: A Collection from Around the World,* editor, Tokyo 1986; *World Trademarks and Logotypes 2,* editor, Tokyo 1988.

On IGARASHI: books—*Igarashi Space Graphics* by Yoshiro Nakamura, Tokyo 1983; *Seven,* Tokyo 1985; *Igarashi Alphabets,* Zurich 1987.

As can be seen from his personal history, Takenobu Igarashi is one of the young generation who have grown up in the new Japanese world of design and studied in American universities. Igarashi's most distinctive contribution to design lies in his unique lettering and typography. In particular, he has successfully given three-dimensional expression to letters of the alphabet. At first glance, this work, which is decorative rather than functional, suggests the revival of Art Deco, but it is filled with a new sensibility. The manner in which he fashions the shape of each letter just as if he were constructing an edifice

is of great appeal. Moreover, the delightfulness of shape and harmony of color are distinctive.

Igarashi also has a strong interest in graphic design in the environment, from supermarkets to public libraries, and has demonstrated substantial abilities in various types of visual communication design. He has done striking work in poster design, packaging, and editorial design.

—Masaaki Tanaka

ILIPRANDI, Giancarlo.

Italian illustrator, industrial, type and graphic designer. Born in Milan, 15 March 1925. Educated at the Liceo Scientifico, Milan, until 1943; studied medicine, at the University of Milan, 1944–46; painting and stage design, at the Accademia di Brera, Milan, 1946–53; painting, at the Hochschule für Bildende Künste, West Berlin, 1958; also attended seminars in American Studies, Salzburg, 1950. Served in the Freedom Volunteer Corps, Italian Army, 1945; Adjutant-Major. Married Lalla Aldrovandi in 1953 (separated, 1973); daughter: Viviana. Worked as an independent painter and stage designer, Milan, 1945–55; freelance designer, Milan, from 1955: designed for RAI Radiotelevisione Italiana, La Rinascente department stores, Standa department stores, Stanley Works, Arflex, Roche, Bassetti, Grancasa, Electa, Hunter Douglas, Montecatini, Edisport, Rossi di Albizzate, Stilnovo, Olivetti, Pirelli, Honeywell, RB Rossana, etc; art director of magazines *Scinautico,* 1960–64, *Sci,* 1965–70, *Popular Photography Italiana,* 196–72, *Rivista RAI,* 1968–69, *Esquire and Derby,* 1977, *Interni,* 1979–82, *Arbiter,* 1980, *Il Diaframma,* 1980–82, and *Phototeca,* from 1980. Founder and president, Art Directors Club of Milan, 1967–68, 1970–71; board member, 1971–73 and 1985–88, and vice-president, 1985–88, ADI Associazione Disegno Industriale, Milan; scientific didactic committee member, Istituto Superiore Industrie Artistiche, Urbino, 1974–84; scientific committee member, Centro Studi e Archivio Comunicazione, Parma, from 1979; vice-president, 1987–89, and president elect, 1989, ICOGRADA International Council of Graphic Design Associations; chairman, Bureau of European Designers Associations, 1988–89. Instructor, Societa Umanitaria, Milan, 1961–68, Scuola Superiore Pubblicita, Milan, 1965–73, and Istituto Europeo Design, Milan, 1982–83. **Exhibitions:** Saletta del Disegno, Milan, 1951; Galleria dell'Ariete, Milan, 1958; Libreria San Babila, Milan, 1959, 1961; Centro Internazionale della Grafica, Venice, 1975; Galleria Il Diaframma, Milan, 1975; Galleria Il Libraio, Milan, 1978; Galleria Alzaia, Rome, 1987; Museo Civico, Caltagirone, 1987. **Collections:** Vilanov Poster Museum, Poland; Museum of Modern Art, New York; Galleria d'Arte Moderna, Milan; Centro Studi e Archivio Comunicazione, Parma. Recipient: International Award, Milan Triennale, 1964; Milan Art Directors Club Award, 1967; Typomundus 69 Merit Award, 1969; Design Award, Warsaw Poster Biennale, 1976; Compasso d'Oro Awards, Milan, 1979. Address: Via Vallazze 63, 20131 Milan, Italy.

Works:

Exhibition displays and pavilions, for RAI Radiotelevisione Italiana, 1955–65 (with A. and P. G. Castiglioni).

Displays, posters and publicity graphics, for La Rinascente department stores, Milan, 1955–68.

Corporate image programme, displays and graphics, for RB Rossana, Bergamo, 1960–86.

Corporate image programme and graphics, for Ankerfarm, Milan, 1964–74.

Corporate image programme and graphics, for Arflex, Milan, 1966–76.

Forma, Dattilo and *Modulo* typefaces, for Nebiolo Typefoundry, Turin, 1967–78 (with others).

Displays and posters, for Standa department stores, Milan, 1968–72.

Isola, Penisola, Arcipelago, Rossana Night, and *Rossana Sole* kitchen units and furniture, for RB Rossana Cucine, Bergamo, 1969–72.

Corporate image programme, displays and graphics, for Stanley Italia, Como, 1974–79.

131 Mirafiori and *Ritmo Super* car instruments, for Fiat, 1978–81 (with Rodolfo Bonetto).

Square, Round and *Superegg* dot-matrix typefaces, for Honeywell Information Systems, 1981–86 (with Pesenti, Gandolfi and Pizzigoni).

Graphic identity, posters and catalogues, for the Gallerie Civiche Comune di Modena, from 1982.

Graphic identity and exhibition displays, for ADI Associazione Disegno Industriale, Milan, 1985–89.

Exterior and interior decor and displays, for Grancasa department stores, Milan, 1986–89.

Publications:

By ILIPRANDI: books—*Linguaggio Grafico,* vols. 1–4, Milan 1965–83; *Addio Liberty,* Varese 1967; *Creativity Oggi,* Milan 1971; *Storia della Comunicazione Visiva,* vols. 1–6, Urbino 1977–83; *NY Inclusive Tour,* Naples 1978; *Il Progetto Grafico,* with others, Milan 1981; *Visual Design,* with others, Milan 1984; *Omnibook 2,* editor with others, Milan 1985; *Omnibook 4,* editor with others, Milan 1988; *Un Progetto per Milano,* Milan 1988; *Design Italiano,* Milan 1988; *BEDA Dossier,* Milan 1988.

On ILIPRANDI: books—*An International Survey of Packaging* by Wim Crouwel and Kurt Weidemann, London 1968; *Book Jackets and Record Sleeves,* edited by Kurt Weidemann, Stuttgart and London 1969; *Graphis Record Covers,* edited by Walter Herdeg, Zurich 1974; *Archigraphia: Architectural and Environmental Graphics,* edited by Walter Herdeg, Zurich 1978; *Atlante del Design Italiano 1940–1980* by Alfonso Grassi and Anty Pansera, Milan 1980; *Who's Who in Graphic Art,* edited by

Giancarlo Iliprandi: Monobloc kitchen work unit, for Rossana, 1969

Walter Amstutz, Dubendorf 1982; *L'Italia del Design* by Alfonso Grassi and Anty Pansera, Casale 1986; *Alle Radici della Comunicazione Visiva Italiana* by Heinz Waibl, Como 1988.

I regard design as a creative activity aiming at the improvement of the quality of man's life. The design of visual communication is moreover responsible not only for the matter it transmits through its own messages but also for the formal values that in any case represent a "consumerist" cultural heritage.

I believe that every designer ought to play his part, by active presence in associations, by participation in education, by contributing to professional reviews or writing or editing books, as well as by the results of his own work, in the affirmation of these principles: "better social

quality of human life" and "moral responsibility of the productions of culture."

Experimental research and planning methodology seem only abstract theories of work, yet without a continual return to these basic principles, it is useless to hope for a practical, pragmatic meeting between form and function, between technical concepts and free creativity. Between cultures of being rather than of becoming.

The culture of the designer, both what he absorbs and what he transmits, is a culture of doing, a continuous presence of gestures, words, shapes, signs, of writings, activities, commitment, discussion, of openings and closings. An active presence, then, in our case typically Italian, or rather, typically mid-European. (To be or to become?) Our bad habit of debating every problem started long before 1968 (as anyone knows who has read Cato the censor) and will last longer, surviving "Le pouvoir à l'imagination" of the Maggio Francese at the main exhibition *Italy, The New Domestic Landscape* at the Museum of Modern Art in 1972 and even the great retrospective show organized by the municipality of Milan on the occasion of the 13th Congress of the International Council of Societies of Industrial Design under the name of *Visual Design 33–83, Fifty years of Italian Production: A Jubilee.*

Italian design, whether associated with historic rationalism or functionalism or formalism or postmodernism or Memphis, or the fruit of an attachment to a tradition (but which tradition?), or generated by a reaction to the revolution (but which revolution?), will continue to live until the protagonists of it have learned to submit every problem to discussion. More central to the question, it is evident that Italian design will survive as long as it produces culture—as long, that is, as it succeeds in being occupied, even preoccupied, with improving the quality of life and in leaving no empty spaces from which consumerism can enter and begin the systematic destruction of our cultural heritage. The worst opportunism of all ages is ignorance.

—Giancarlo Iliprandi

ISD (INTERIOR SPACE DESIGN).
American interior design firm. Founded as a subsidiary of Perkins and Will architectural firm, in Chicago and New York, 1960; independent corporation since 1973. Chief executives: Michael Pinto, President; J. Harrison Lassiter, Senior Vice President; Mel Hamilton, Senior Vice President; H. Davis Mayfield III, Senior Vice President; Jan Belson, Vice President, Los Angeles; Gary Lee, Vice President, Chicago; John Lijewski, Vice President, New York; Nancy Lindsay, Vice President, Houston. **Collection:** Cooper-Hewitt Museum, New York. Recipient: New York Art Directors Club Award of Merit, 1980; *Industrial Design* Designers Choice Award, New York, 1980; Illuminating Engineering Society Lumen Award, New York, 1980; *Interiors* Design Award, New York, 1982, 1983. Addresses: 305 East 46th Street, New York, New York 10017; 400 North State Street, Chicago, Illinois 60610; Two Shell Plaza, Houston, Texas 77002; 818 West 7th Street, Los Angeles, California 90017, U.S.A.

Works:

First National Bank interiors, Memphis, Tennessee, 1964.
City Hall interiors, Boston, Massachusetts, 1969.
Westinghouse Electric Corporation interiors, Monroeville, Pennsylvania, 1971.
Mercantile Exchange Building interiors, Chicago, 1972–74.
CBS Incorporated office interiors, Washington, D.C., 1976.
American Telephone and Telegraph office interiors, Basking Ridge, New Jersey, 1976–77.
R. J. Reynolds World Headquarters interiors, Winston-Salem, North Carolina, 1978.
General Mills office interiors, Minneapolis, Minnesota, 1979.
Xerox Corporation Headquarters interiors, Stamford, Connecticut, 1979.

American Academy of Arts and Sciences interiors, Cambridge, Massachusetts, 1980.
British Petroleum office interiors, London, 1981.
R. J. Reynold Plaza Tower interiors, Winston-Salem, North Carolina, 1981.
American Telephone and Telegraph Corporate Headquarters interiors, New York, 1983.
PPG Industries Corporate Headquarters interiors, Pittsburgh, 1984.
Chemical Bank interiors, New York, 1988.
ARCO Oil and Gas interiors, Midland, Texas, 1988.
Walt Disney Corporation interiors, Burbank, California, 1989.

Publications:

On ISD: articles—in *Architectural Record* (New York), May 1974; *American Bar Association Journal* (Chicago), April 1976; *Contract Magazine* (New York), December 1976; *Buildings* (Cedar Rapids), October 1979; *Interior Design* (New York), November 1979, December 1981; *The Designer* (New York), November 1980; *Interiors* (New York), January 1983; *New York Post,* 17 February 1983; *Houston Chronicle,* 22 February 1983; *Dallas/Fort Worth Business,* 4 April 1983.

A list of ISD's clients reads like an excerpt of the top corporations from the Fortune 500. The most talked-about building for which ISD has designed the interiors is Philip Johnson's AT & T tower in New York. ISD's rather spectacular creative accomplishments here include the planning and design of millions of square feet of space. In this, the firm carried on the philosophy of design and traditions that had already made its work renowned, so that in its third decade of operation it had become one of the U.S.A.'s largest organizations of design professionals specializing in design of interior spaces.

Some of ISD's most famous interiors include the First National Bank of Memphis, the Boston City Hall, the Academy of Arts and Sciences in Cambridge, Massachusetts, and the Xerox Corporation headquarters in Stamford, Connecticut—to name just a few. Although ISD offers technical services to meet the complex needs of planning and design, one of the firm's major interests in its work is art. ISD has long stressed the need for art in public places and has helped clients assemble major art collections. The firm has the ability to educate corporate clients to use works of art in their buildings and thus to enhance and enrich the quality of corporate environments. ISD is equally concerned with the research and development of

Interior Space Design: Staircase at the American Telephone and Telegraph offices, Basking Ridge, New Jersey, 1977

office furniture and systems, and has a team that continuously monitors the development of new products.

The consistently high quality of ISD's work is due to the symbiotic combination of the firm's design principles and the inspired leadership of its executives. The many successful projects credited to the firm represent team effort of a large design firm at its best.

—Arnold Friedmann

ISHIMOTO, Fujiwo.

Japanese textile designer. Born in Ehime, 10 March 1941. Studied graphic design, National University of Art, Tokyo, 1960-64. Commercial artist, Ichida Company, Tokyo, 1964-70; designer, Decembre Oy, Helsinki, 1970-74; printed textile designer, Marimekko Oy, Helsinki, since 1974. **Exhibitions:** *Designs for Madame Butterfly,* Helsinki, 1980; *Fujiwo Ishimoto + Marimekko,* Tokyo, 1982; *Textile Artist Fujiwo Ishimoto: Sources of Inspiration,* Helsinki and Jyvaskyla, Finland, 1982; *The Great Bear Textiles,* Helsinki, 1984; *Fujiwo Ishimoto: Textile Designs,* Tokyo, 1988; *Designs for Madame Butterfly,* Seinajoki, Finland, 1989; *Fujiwo Ishimoto: Retrospective Fabric Exhibition,* Seinajoki, Finland, 1989. **Collections:** Museum of Applied Arts, Helsinki; Cooper-Hewitt Museum, New York. Recipient: Roscoe Prize, U.S.A., 1983. Member, Ornamo Finnish Society of Applied Arts, 1978. Address: Kauppiaankatu 13 E 25, 00160 Helsinki, Finland.

Works: (all for Marimekko Oy)

Sumo brushstroke pattern fabric, 1977.
Jama brushstroke pattern fabric, 1977.
Taiga brushstroke pattern fabric, 1978.
Seitseman/Seven Flowers patterned fabric, 1978.
Mattailla/Tussock collection of earth-colour pattern fabrics, 1979.
Tuulentupa/Castle of the Winds collection of linear pattern fabrics, 1981.
Ukkospilvi/Thunder Cloud brushstroke pattern fabric, 1982.
Nauru/Laughter brushstroke pattern fabric, 1982.
Kuiskaus/Whispering brushstroke pattern fabric, 1982.
Maisema/Landscape collection of abstract pattern fabrics, 1983.
Iso Karhu/Great Bear collection of ikat-effect fabrics, 1984.
Sinitaivas/Sky collection of graduated pattern fabrics, 1986.
Sydantalvi/Midwinter collection of marble-effect fabrics, 1987.
Aatto/Eve watercolour technique fabric, 1989.

Publications:

On ISIMOTO: books—*Design Since 1945,* edited by Kathryn Hiesinger and George Marcus, Philadelphia and London 1983; *International Design Yearbook 1985/1986,* edited by Robert A. M. Stern, London 1985; *Finnish Industrial Design,* edited by Tua Pontasuo, Hel-

sinki 1987; *International Design Yearbook 1988/1989,* edited by Arata Isozaki, London 1988; articles—"Marimekko Oy" in *Domus* (Milan), October 1979; "The Spirit of Things" by U. Pallasmaa in *Form Function Finland* (Helsinki), no. 3/4, 1981; "Castle of the Winds" by B. Obermaier in *Mobilia* (Snekkersten), no. 298, 1981; "Marimekko Exports Know-how" by M. Vuorimaa in *Form Function Finland* (Helsinki), no. 2, 1983; "Design 87: Crosscurrents and Mutual Influences" by P. Gallo-Stenman in *Design in Finland* (Helsinki), 1987.

At the outset of designing a new collection, I work quite freely and spontaneously. My aim is to give expression to subjects that, at that very moment, interest me or are important to me. Finally, these personal ideas are communicated to other people, and it is time to see what kind of response my interests find. It is also essential that each new collection is up-to-date, fresh and novel.

My foremost object is to design fabrics that are suitable for everyday use, fabrics that are not too "artistic". The fabrics can (or should) of course be of high aesthetic quality, but they also have to be appropriate for practical use. Here lies the basic difference between art and design. I do not generally design my fabrics for any particular application—the fabrics are sold by the yard, and they can be used for almost any purpose (curtains, tablecloths, bedlinen, clothes, etc.). There is no "right" or "wrong" way of use.

Another important factor affecting the design process are the technical resources at hand. The design work has to be adjusted according to those printing methods that are available but, on the other hand, development of new techniques in collaboration with the manufacturer is one inspiring aspect of the work.

—Fujiwo Ishimoto

ISSIGONIS, Alec.

British car designer. Born Alexander Constantine Issigonis, in Smyrna (now Izmir), Turkey, 18 November 1906; emigrated to Britain in 1922. Educated privately in Smyrna, until 1921; studied engineering, at Battersea Polytechnic, London, 1924-27. Worked in the Edward Gillett design office, London, 1928-33; draughtsman, Rootes Motors, Coventry, 1934-36; suspension engineer, then chief engineer, Morris Motors, Cowley, Oxfordshire, 1937-52; designer, Alvis Car Company, Gloucestershire, 1953-56; deputy engineering co-ordinator and chief engineer, 1957-61, technical director, 1961, director of research and development, 1961-72, and consultant in advanced design, 1972-88, British Motor Corporation, and subsequently British Leyland (Austin-Morris). **Exhibitions:** Institute of Contemporary Arts, London, 1970; *Eye for Industry,* Victoria and Albert Museum, London, 1986. Recipient: Commander, Order of the British Empire, 1964; Royal Designer for Industry, 1964, Leverhulme Medal, 1966, and Fellow, 1967, Royal Society of Arts, London:

Knighthood, London, 1969. *Died* (in Edgbaston, Birmingham, England) *2 October 1988.*

Works:

Morris Minor saloon car, for Morris Motors, 1948.
Morris Mini Minor and Austin Seven car, for British Motor Corporation, 1957-59.
Morris 1100, for British Motor Corporation, 1962.
Austin 1800, for British Motor Corporation, 1967.

Publications:

On ISSIGONIS: books—*Transport Design* by Corin Hughes-Stanton, London and New York 1967; *Automobile Design: Great Designers and Their Work,* edited by Ronald Barker and Anthony Harding, Newton Abbot 1970; *Issigonis,* exhibition catalogue, London 1970; *The Library of Motoring: The Designers* by L. J. K. Setright, London 1976; *Mini* by Bob Golding, London 1979; *Design by Choice* by Reyner Banam, London 1981; *The Conran Directory of Design,* edited by Stephen Bayley, London 1985; *Eye for Industry: Royal Designers for Industry 1936–1986,* exhibition catalogue by Fiona MacCarthy and Patrick Nuttgens, London 1986.

Alec Issigonis was an engineer who thought small change of car stylists, saying that if the engineering is right, the car will look right. In designing the Mini, which was very much one man's car and not the product of a committee, the basic problem he wanted to solve was how to create a small car without the transmission tunnel taking up such a slice of the limited interior. His solution of placing the engine sideways was highly original, and the nature of the car flowed from that arrangement, which was an engineering solution, not an artistic one.

Issigonis thought he was making the car for the working man, but the working man is a pretty conservative animal, and it was the smart set who snapped up the Mini and made it the "in" car of the 1960s. The Mini was cheeky, for it could nip into a parking place which a lordly Rolls Royce was manoeuvring in vain to occupy, so the young loved it. A Mini fan club grew up to organize rallies and races for standard and souped-up Minis. Other versions came from Issigonis and his team: the Mini estate car, the Mini van, the Mini pickup, the Mini beach car for warm climates, and the military model Mini Moke. A Mini Cooper won the Monte Carlo rally in 1964. Peter Sellers ordered a special hatchback version, which is the ancestor of all today's hatchbacks. The Mini is so popular that many of its owners buy a second one when the first one has worn out. In 1983, Austin Morris stated that of their two best-selling models, the Issigonis Mini was still one, so they were going to increase its production still further. That is not bad going for a car which celebrated its thirtieth birthday in August 1989 and whose sales have totalled well over five million.

The qualities which Issigonis built into his car are permanent ones: fuel economy, manoeuvrability, ease of parking in city conditions, and fast acceleration. There have been modifications over the years, of course, such as larger headlamps and a new front grille, but the Mini's basic qualities will not go out of date for some time to come, and the Mini is certain to enter the record books as one of the longest-lasting vehicles in production.

—Diana de Marly

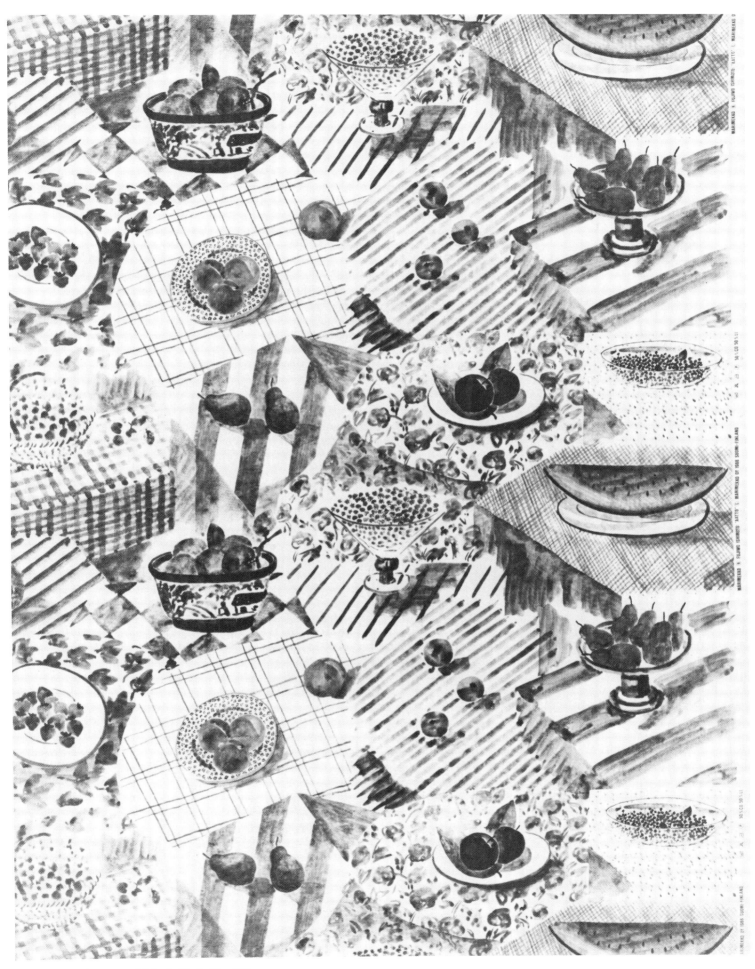

Fujiwo Ishimoto: *Aatto* **cotton fabric, for Marimekko, 1989**

ITO, Shima.

Japanese industrial designer. Born in Kobe, 3 September 1937. Studied art and design under Tsugiji Doi, at Kyoto Technical University, 1959–63: BS 1963; also postgraduate studies in architecture, 1963–64. Has worked for Matsushita Electric works, in Hikone, Shiga Prefecture, 1964–74, and in Osaka from 1974: designed household electrical appliances, 1964–74, and domestic products, 1974–80; consultant 1981–83, chief designer, 1983–85, and senior designer from 1985, in the Kinki Business Department. Lecturer, Shiga Women's Junior College, Otsu, Shiga Prefecture, 1979. Recipient: Machinery Design Prize, 1967; Matsushita President's Prize, 1974, 1979, 1982. Member: Japan Industrial Designers' Association, 1973; Japan Home Economists in Business Council, 1980; Japan Illuminating Engineering Society, 1982. Address: 11-16-2, Nisidemachi, Hyogo-ku, Kobe 652, Japan.

Publications:

By ITO: booklets—*A Thought from Lifestyle,* paper edited by Matsushita Electric Works, Osaka 1979; *Trend of Consumers Seen from the Show-Window,* paper edited by Matsushita Electric Works, Osaka 1983; articles—in *Denko Gijutsu* (Osaka), April 1970, February 1976, June 1977, December 1980; January–May 1987; *Matsushita News* (Osaka), January 1978–September 1981.

In today's industrialized world, man cannot live without "things." The world of "things" does not change basically, but their meaning and value vary according to the person and the time. Therefore, the timing and target for new production are important factors. "Things" cannot exist alone. They must have reason for being in their relations with man and environment. Therefore, things must be designed as elements of man's life.

Creation of things starts from frustration or dissatisfaction in life. The process of production of things is just the same as child-bearing and rearing. Just as in child care, full affection must be poured into the process.

What does society want now? What do people want to have at this very moment? For designers, it is indispensable to feel with all their senses what the real needs are and to see accurately the essence of products from the users' standpoint. This basic attitude will not change even if the environment of producing things may change.

Shima Ito: Battery-operated ladies' shaver with decoration by Kansai Yamamoto, for Matsushita, 1973

Ideology in design is, of course, important, but this alone does not produce things. The image of products must be given shape concretely, and that should be as simple and concise as possible. Superficially well designed products will soon disappear from the market. Such products made not for sale but made based on the consumers' needs will widely be accepted and sell well for a long period of time.

Perfect production is only an ideal. But at the least, a product should have "something" in it, something like the attractive personality of a person. Design activity, however small it may be can mobilize people, organization and the management of business. Here lies the mission and attractiveness of design.

Now that we are at the turning point from the age of mass-production to one of small-quantity production of diversified designs, we are questioning the methodology, uniformity, and fixity of ideas, the homogeneity of design caused by

equality of technological level, and the complexity and specialization caused by the advancement of technology.

The production system based on vertical structure within the company and on an efficiency-oriented way of thinking tends to restrict the horizon of designers, and they tend to fail to see things from the viewpoint of human life. In order to get free from such a closed way of thinking, coordinating and feedback efforts based on the spirit of service to a more humane environment are demanded of designers. In other words, designers must stand between consumers and business, have flexible and broad horizons, and create products from actual daily life. This is the work I undertake myself.

—Shima Ito

In conversation, Shima Ito often says, "As a woman, I think . . ." She clearly identifies herself as a woman designer, tries to be a spokesman of women consumers, and makes products from a woman's point of view. Though working for a big producer of electric appliances, she strives to make products based on what she observes in daily life rather than on design policy led by survey data or theoretical writings. Potential needs become explicit in living daily life, and she considers this as the substance of product design. In her mind, producers and users are not in conflict with each other; rather, both parties should cooperate to create a better life. She likens the relationship to that between a physician of a village and his patients. An able designer can integrate many factors, can see things in totality and reflect that in production. Ito fulfills this qualification from all aspects.

Through her product design and consulting, she has made proposals to make better use of living space in Japanese houses. Looking straight at reality, she says, "The design of living space in Japan is still in a transition period. Originality in design may be found, but it is of a poor level in general. What the producer can do now is to study and develop the basic function of the house and provide products in the form of prefabricated houses. However, considering total living environment, the lifestyle of users must be fully reflected in the design." In making Japanese housing which combines traditional techniques and advanced technology, as well as Japanese and Western styles, into a genuine expression of the culture, her flexible thinking will achieve great success.

—Kunio Sano

JACOBS, Sally.
British stage set and costume designer. Born Sally Rich, in London, 5 November 1932. Educated at Dalston County Grammar School, London, until 1946; studied at St. Martin's School of Art, London, 1946–47; Central School of Arts and Crafts, London, 1957–60. Married Alexander Jacobs in 1953 (died, 1979); son: Toby. Worked as a production secretary and continuity assistant on British feature films, 1951–57; scene painter, with Colchester Repertory Theatre, Essex, 1960; freelance set and costume designer, working with Peter Brook for the Royal Shakespeare Company, London, 1960–67, for the Mark Taper Forum, Los Angeles, 1967–68, for the Manhattan Theatre Club and the Shakespeare Festival, New York, 1979–82, for the English National Opera, Royal Opera House and others, in London, from 1982. Lecturer, California Institute of the Arts, Los Angeles, 1970–71, University of California at Los Angeles, 1977, Actors and Directors Laboratory, New York, 1978–79, Theatre Arts Department of Stage Design, New York, 1979–82, Rutgers University, New Brunswick, New Jersey, 1980–82, and Central School of Art and Design, London, 1982–88. **Exhibitions:** *Opera Design,* National Theatre, London, 1986; *British Theatre Design '83–87,* Riverside Studios, London, 1988. Recipient: *Plays and Players* Design Award, London, 1970; Drama Desk Best Design Award, New York, 1970; Obie Award, New York, 1980. Address: c/o Mrs. Emanuel Wax, A.C.T.A.C. Limited, 16 Cadogan Lane, London SW1, England.

Works:

Stage productions include—*Wildest Dreams* (musical), Cheltenham Everyman Theatre, 1960; *Five Plus One* (revue), at the Edinburgh Festival, 1961; *Women Beware Women* (sets only), for the Royal Shakespeare Company, Arts Theatre, London, 1962; *The Empire Builders,* for the Royal Shakespeare Company, Arts Theatre, London 1962; *Nothing But the Best* (film; costumes only), 1963; *The Day of the Prince,* Royal Court Theatre, London, 1963; *Theatre of Cruelty* (experimental theatre), for the Royal Shakespeare Company, Lamda Theatre, London, 1964; *The Formation Dancers,* Arts Theatre, London, 1964 (moved to the Globe Theatre, London); *The Screens* for the Royal Shakespeare Company, Donmar Theatre, London, 1964; *Marat/Sade,* for the Royal Shakespeare Company, Aldwych Theatre, London, 1964, adapted for the Martin Beck Theatre, New York, 1965, and film version by Peter Brook, 1966; *Love's Labour's Lost,* for the Royal Shakespeare Company, Stratford-upon-Avon, 1964; *Having a Wild Weekend* (film; costumes only), 1965; *Twelfth Night,* for the Royal Shakespeare Company, Stratford-upon-Avon, 1966; *Us,* for the Royal Shakespeare Company, Aldwych Theatre, London, 1966; *The Golden Fleece* and *Muzeeka,* Mark Taper Forum, Los Angeles, 1968; *A Midsummer Night's Dream,* for the Royal Shakespeare Company, Stratford-upon-Avon, 1970, adapted for the Aldwych Theatre, London, 1970, Billy Rose Theatre, New York, 1970, American tour, 1970, and world tour, 1972; designed for Peter Brook's International Centre for Theatre Research tour of West Africa, 1973; *The Conference of the Birds,* Peter Brook's Centre in Paris, 1973 (toured the United States, including Teatro Campesino, San Juan Battista, California and Brooklyn Academy, New York); *Mahagonny Songplay* and *The Measures Taken,* Mark Taper Forum, Los Angeles, 1973; *Ajax,* Forum Lab, Los Angeles, 1974; *Of Mice and Men,* San Francisco Opera, 1974; *Savages,* Mark Taper Forum, Los Angeles, 1974; *Il Trovatore,* Houston Grand Opera, 1974; *Oedipus at Colonus* (also director), Forum Lab, Los Angeles, 1975; *Cross Country, Where She Shops, Ashes* (sets only) and *Three Sisters* (4 repertory plays), Mark Taper Forum, Los Angeles, 1976; *Meetings with Remarkable Men* (film; costumes only), 1976; *Ascent of Mount Fuji* (sets only), Hollywood Television Theatre, Los Angeles, 1977; *Much Ado about Nothing,* Los Angeles Shakespeare Festival, 1977; *Gethsemane Springs* (sets only), Mark Taper Forum, Los Angeles, 1977; *Black Angel,* Mark Taper Forum, Los Angeles, 1978; *Antony and Cleopatra,* for the Royal Shakespeare Company, Stratford-upon-Avon, 1978, adapted for the Aldwych Theatre, London, 1979; *Conference of the Birds* (revival), for Peter Brook's Centre, Paris, at the Avignon Festival, 1979 (toured Europe and the United States); *Ice,* Manhattan Theatre Club, New York, 1979; *End Game,* Manhattan Theatre Club, New York, 1980, adapted for the American Centre, Paris, 1980; *Selma* (sets only), Theatre for the New City, New York, 1981; *Three Acts of Recognition* (sets only), at the New York Shakespeare Festival, 1981; *Antigone,* at the New York Shakespeare Festival, 1982; *Die Fledermaus,* Opera de Paris, 1982–83; *The Relapse,* Lyric Theatre-Hammersmith, London, 1983; *Turandot,* Royal Opera House, London, and Los Angeles, 1984; *Fidelio,* Royal Opera House, London, 1986; *Turandot,* touring production, Korea and Japan, 1986; *Eugene Onegin,* English National Opera, London, 1989; *Last Tango on the North Circular* (also directed), Royal Opera House, London, 1989.

Publications:

By JACOBS: article—in *Themes in Drama 2,* Cambridge 1980.

On JACOBS: books—*British Theatre Design '83–87,* with texts by Timothy O'Brien and David Fingleton, London 1988; *British Theatre Design,* edited by John Goodwin, London 1989.

I became a designer because I developed a passion for the theatre in the mid-1950s, when the Royal Court and the Theatre Royal Stratford East produced a stream of plays with a burst of new energy which is now a part of theatre history. I decided to study theatre design and have been devoted to the theatre ever since.

When I started work with Peter Brook in 1964, I was introduced to a more international theatre for the first time. We read the *Tulane Drama Review Happenings* and Artaud's *Theatre of Cruelty*—and this was the beginning of one of the most important relationships in all of my theatre experience. With Brook, I learned to question everything and to invent a unique visual language for each piece we produced.

When I went to live in Los Angeles in 1967, I experienced the shock and excitement of a complete break with tradition and familiar cultural patterns, out of which came the *Midsummer Night's Dream* with Brook in 1970. Also during this time in Los Angeles, I learned how to use the thrust stage while designing several productions for Gordon Davidson at the Mark Taper Forum—another cornerstone of my design experience. Eventually, I spent some years in New York also, teaching and working with two directors whose work I have always admired, Joseph Chaikin and Richard Foreman. No rules can be imposed on the theatre, and it is only in retrospect that I can see that I have tended to concern myself more with the dynamics of space than with pictorialization and that the collaborative process has been, for me, a continual source of investigation and creative freedom.

—Sally Jacobs

There is no question but that the formative influence on the design work of Sally Jacobs was her close association with Peter Brook, who throughout the 1960s and early 1970s espoused a modified and updated version of Artaud's Theatre of Cruelty, in which all his productions worked strongly to gain a simple, physical, direct relationship with the audience. In *Marat/Sade,* Jacobs' plain, dirty, inmate uniforms, coupled with costume pieces from the period of the French Revolution, created such a vivid impression that the audience felt that it could

Sally Jacobs: *Midsummer Night's Dream*, Royal Shakespeare Company, Stratford-upon-Avon, 1970

smell the stench of the asylum. In *A Midsummer Night's Dream,* her simple, white, empty box set with catwalk and trapeze, along with colorful tunics and exercise pants with tie-dyed accents, created a feeling of physical exuberance and euphoria, as if the audience might be ready to soar into the air with the actors.

Thus, more than almost any other contemporary designer, Jacobs has been influenced by and has presented those aspects of the visual arts of the 1960s and 1970s which were the outgrowth of happenings, environmental art, process art, and sculptural tableaux. She has broken with period style in her costumes to express the essence of character- or play-mood, just as she has removed time and place in her settings in favor of an interesting space within which the actors can physically and visually tell their story. It is also true that the productions with which Jacobs has been connected have been for the most part socially and politically oriented toward antiestablishment values.

In general, Jacobs has been committed to presenting a collage of costumes and scenic pieces that are interesting as shapes, colors, and textures in themselves and that can be used by the director and the actors to tell the story in a most vivid and physically direct way without the interference of a great deal of factual and historic information.

—Douglas A. Russell

JACOBSEN, Arne.

Danish architect, interior, furniture, textile and ceramics designer. Born in Copenhagen, 11 February 1902. Studied architecture at the Royal Academy of Arts, Copenhagen, 1924–28: Dip. Arch. 1928. Married; had 2 sons. Worked in the office of city architect Paul Holsoe, Copenhagen, 1927–30; in private architectural practice, Copenhagen, 1930–71; freelance furniture, textile and ceramics designer, Copenhagen, 1943–71: designed for Graucob Textilen, August Millech, C. Olesen, A. Michelsen, Fritz Hansen, Louis Poulsen Company, etc. Professor of architecture, Royal Academy of Arts, Copenhagen, 1956–71. **Exhibitions:** Royal Institute of British Architects, London, 1959; McLellan Galleries, Glasgow, 1968; Ministry of Cultural Affairs, Copenhagen, 1971. Recipient: Bellevue Seaside Development Prize, 1932; Eckersberg Medal, Copenhagen, 1936; Aarhus Town Hall Prize, 1937; Sollerod Town Hall Prize, 1939; Grand Prize, Sao Paulo Bienal, 1953. Honorary Doctorates: Oxford University 1966; Strathclyde University, Glasgow, 1968. Honorary Corresponding Member, Royal Institute of British Architects; Honorary Fellow, American Institute of Architects. *Died* (in Copenhagen) *24 March 1971.*

Works:

House of the Future, at the *Danish Building Exhibition,* Copenhagen, 1929 (with Flemming Lassen).
Bellevue Theatre and Gammel Bellevue Restaurant, Copenhagen, 1937.

Dockleaves printed fabric, for C. Olesen Company, 1942–43.
Reed printed fabric and wallcoverings, for C. Olesen Company, 1942–43.
Office interiors, for Poulsen and Company, Copenhagen, 1948.
Showroom and spares depot, for Massey-Harris, Copenhagen, 1952.
Stacking chair with 3 legs, for Fritz Hansen Company, 1952.
Desk, for the American-Scandinavian Foundation of New York, produced by Rudolf Rasmussen Company, 1952.
Ceiling lamp in opaline glass and brass, for Munkegaards School, produced by Louis Poulsen Company, 1955.
3100 Chair, for Fritz Hansen Company, 1955.
Stacking chair with 4 legs, for Fritz Hansen Company, 1957.
Cutlery in stainless steel, for A. Michelsen Company, 1957.
SAS Royal Hotel standard lamp in black varnished metal, produced by Louis Poulsen Company, 1957.
Chair in laminated wood, for Fritz Hansen Company, 1957.
Egg chair in upholstered plastic and steel, for Fritz Hansen Company, 1959.
Swan chair in steel and plastic with leather upholstery, for Fritz Hansen Company, 1959.
Cylinda range of tablewares, for Stelton Company, 1962.
Factories, for Novo Company, in Mainz and Chartres, 1969–70.

(for a complete list of Jacobsen's buildings and architectural projects, see *Contemporary Architects*)

Publications:

On JACOBSEN: books—*Arkitekten Arne Jacobsen* by J. Pedersen, Copenhagen 1954; *Danish Chairs,* edited by Nanna and Jorgen Ditzel, Copenhagen 1954; *Modern Danish Furniture* by Esbjorn Hiort, Copenhagen, New York and London 1956; *Arne Jacobsen: Architecture, Applied Art,* exhibition catalogue by Poul Erik Shriver, London 1959; *Modern Danish Textiles,* edited by Bent Salicath and Arne Karlsen, Copenhagen 1959; *Arne Jacobsen* by T. Faber, London 1964; *Arne Jacobsen at the McLellan Galleries, Glasgow,* exhibition catalogue, Glasgow 1968; *Arne Jacobsen* by Jorgen Kastholm, Copenhagen 1968; *Arne Jacobsen: A Danish Architect* by Poul Erik Shriver, Copenhagen 1972; *Arne Jacobsen* by Poul Erik Shriver and Ellen Waade, Copenhagen 1976; *Arne Jacobsen: Opera Completa 1909–1971* by Luciano Rubino, Rome 1980; *Modern Furniture Classics* by Miriam Stimpson, London 1987.

In all areas related to the arts, invention has become highly prized, and interpretation is frequently dismissed as of lesser value. And yet, inspired interpretation can equal or occasionally surpass an original, as Arne Jacobsen's work repeatedly proves. When we identify the sources of Jacobsen's classic chairs, Egg and Swan, we also identify his own creative abilities. Egg wraps its user in a protective shell of padded and upholstered fiberglass, while Swan takes its shape from the curved wing and neck of its drifting namesake. In both pieces, a minimal pedestal base allows curvilinear forms to float in space. Structurally and technologically, neither piece is original. One-piece bodies, developed by Eames and Saarinen, were widely used in America—although not, as yet, in Scandinavia—when Jacobsen incorporated them into his design vocabulary. The same can be said of the slender supports. Even the top line of Egg recalls the amoebic forms used by Finn Juhl in Denmark and, more especially, by Isamu Noguchi and Vladimir Kagan in the United States. Together, however, these borrowed elements are united by Jacobsen into forms that enlighten even as they explain, forms that establish him not only as a designer but as a sculptor of furniture.

Similar borrowings can be seen in the various versions of his molded-plywood, stacking chairs. Again, the material and approach come from Eames; but the subtle changes of the contours—as well as the unexpected wit—of these mass-produced designs come from Jacobsen alone. While he cannot be described as an originator, his power as an interpreter should lead us to realize the limitations of invention—unless it is potent enough to inspire others to internalize and surpass it.

—Reed Benhamou

JENKINS, George.
American stage and film designer. Born in Baltimore, Maryland, 19 November 1911. Studied architecture, at the University of Pennsylvania, Philadelphia, 1929–31. Married Phyllis Adams in 1955; daughter by previous marriage: Jane; stepdaughter: Alexandra. Worked as an interior designer and engineer, New York, 1932–36; assistant to stage designer Jo Mielziner, New York, 1937–41; freelance stage designer, New York, from 1942, and film and television designer from 1945: art director in charge of colour, CBS Columbia Broadcasting System, New York, 1953–54; designer and partner, Sugar Mill Inn, St. Vincent, West Indies, from 1954. Theatre consultant, University of Pennsylvania, Philadelphia, and professor of motion picture design, University of California at Los Angeles, from 1985. Theatre standards board mem-

Arne Jacobsen: Stacking chair in moulded plywood, for Fritz Hansen, 1953

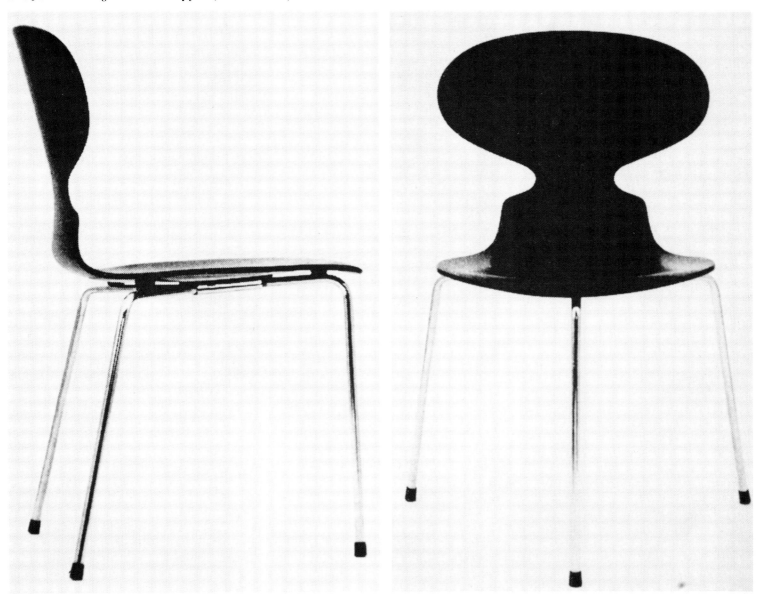

George Jenkins: Set design for Allan Pakula's *See You in the Morning*, 1989

ber, American National Theatre Association, from 1954. Recipient: Donaldson Award, New York, 1946; Academy Award, 1976. Addresses: 740 Kingman Avenue, Santa Monica, California 90402; Apt. A702, 200 East 66th Street, New York, New York 10021, U.S.A.

Works:

Stage productions (New York, unless noted) include *Early to Bed*, 1943; *Mexican Hayride*, 1944; *I Remember Mama*, 1944; *Dark of the Moon*, 1945; *Common Ground*, 1945; *Strange Fruit*, 1945; *Are You With It?*, 1945; *Lost in the Stars*, 1949; *Bell, Book, and Candle*, 1950; *Three Wishes for Jamie*, 1952; *Gently Does It*, 1953; *The Immoralist*, 1954; *The Bad Seed*, 1954; *Ankles Aweigh*, 1955; *The Desk Set*, 1955; *Too Late the Phalarope*, 1956; *The Happiest Millionaire*, 1956; *The Merry Widow*, 1957; *Rumple*, 1957; *Two for the Seesaw*, 1958; *Tall Story*, 1959; *The Miracle Worker*, 1959; *One More River*, 1960; *Critic's Choice*, 1960; *A Thousand Clowns*, 1962; *Jennie*, 1963; *Everybody Out, The Castle is Sinking*, 1964; *Catch Me If You Can*, 1965; *Wait Until Dark* (also London), 1966; *The Student Prince* (San Francisco), 1966; *Night Watch*, 1972; *Sly Fox*, 1976; films include—*The Best Years of Our Lives* (Wyler), 1946; *The Secret Life of Walter Mitty* (Penn), 1947; *The Bishop's Wife* (Koster), 1947; *A Song Is Born* (Hawks), 1948; *Enchantment* (Reis), 1948; *Little Women* (LeRoy), 1949; *Roseanna McCoy* (Reis), 1949; *At War with the Army* (Walker), 1950; *The San Francisco Story* (Parrish), 1952; *Monsoon* (Amateau), 1953; *The Miracle Worker* (Penn), 1962; *Mickey One* (Penn), 1965; *Up the Down Staircase* (Mulligan), 1967; *Wait Until Dark* (Young), 1967; *No Way to Treat a Lady* (Smight), 1968; *The Subject Was Roses* (Grosband), 1968; *Me, Natalie* (Coe), 1969; *The Angel Levine* (Kadar), 1970; *The Pursuit of Happiness* (Mulligan), 1971; *Klute* (Pakula), 1971; *1776* (Hunt), 1972; *The Paper Chase* (Bridges), 1973; *The Parallax View* (Pakula),

1974; *Funny Lady* (Ross), 1975; *Night Moves* (Penn), *All the President's Men* (Pakula), 1976; *Comes a Horseman* (Bridges), 1978; *The China Syndrome* (Bridges), 1978; *Starting Over* (Pakula), 1979; *Power* (Shear—for TV), 1980; *Rollover* (Pakula), 1981; *The Postman Always Rings Twice* (Rafaelson), 1981; *Sophie's Choice* (Pakula), 1982; *The Dollmaker* (Petrie—for TV), 1984; *Orphans*, 1987; *See You in the Morning* (Pakula), 1989; *Presumed Innocent* (Pakula), 1990.

Publications:

By JENKINS: article—in *Film Comment* (New York), May 1978.

On JENKINS: books—*Le Décor de Film* by Leon Barsacq, Paris 1970, as *Caligari's Cabinet and Other Grand Illusions*, Boston 1976; *The International Film Encyclopedia* by Ephraim Katz, New York and London 1980; *The International Dictionary of Films and Filmmakers*, Chicago and London 1987, 1991.

George Jenkins is a flexible designer, who has worked for theater, film, and television. His first work was on the settings and lighting of Broadway plays, and in 1946 he won an award for the intimate and homey sets of *I Remember Mama*.

Jenkins enjoyed designing for the stage because of the many points of view from which the audience sees the sets. His transition to film, however, was quite successful. He was brought to Hollywood in 1945 by Samuel Goldwyn to work for Goldwyn/RKO. The first film he designed (in collaboration with Perry Ferguson) was *The Best Years of Our Lives*, shot in deep focus by the cinematographer Gregg Toland and directed by William Wyler. The result of this happy collaboration is a beautiful film, full of interesting long shots through doorways, windows, and mirrored rooms. Wyler conferred with Jenkins on the types of living quarters that would suit the characters.

Throughout his career, Jenkins has displayed a knack for creating environments that perfectly fit the scenario. Often, his designs are based on careful research. His background in theater seems to have made him extremely propconscious; he selects the right objects to suit the setting and the character. Jenkins designed a setting for *Little Women* (1949) copied from Louisa May Alcott's own childhood home. (Though the sets of the 1949 version of *Little Women* are based on Jenkins' drawings he received no screen credit because the production was transferred from David O. Selznick to MGM.) For the film *The Miracle Worker*, Jenkins sought out a setting that would closely resemble Helen Keller's actual home in Georgia. For *Klute*, Jenkins designed a highly individualistic apartment for the prostitute-heroine, Bree Daniels.

In the 1970s, Jenkins made two films with newspaper settings. *Parallax View* (1974) revolved around a small-town newspaper. To achieve a convincing newsroom, Jenkins visited many such newspaper offices and combined their characteristics. For his award-winning *All the President's Men*, Jenkins sketched and photographed the *Washington Post* newsroom. For the sake of accuracy, he even collected discards from the reporters to be spread on the desks in the film set.

—Lois Miklas

JUHL, Finn.
Danish architect and industrial designer. Born in Copenhagen, 30 January 1912. Educated at Sanct Jørgens Gymnasium, Copenhagen, until 1930; studied architecture under Kay Fisker, at the Kunstakademiet, Copenhagen, 1930–34; mainly self-taught in industrial design. Worked in the architectural office of Vilhelm Lauritzen,

Copenhagen, 1934–45; freelance designer, establishing own office for exhibition and furniture design, Copenhagen, 1945–89: designed for Boex, France and Son, Baker Furniture, Georg Jensen, Bing and Grondahl, etc.; consultant designer to General Electric, Louisville, 1954, and IBM Typewriters, New York, 1960. Head of the School of Interior Design, Copenhagen, 1944–55; guest professor, Institute of Design, Illinois Institute of Technology, Chicago, 1965. **Exhibitions:** Corcoran Gallery of Art, Washington, D.C., 1963; *I Grandi Designers,* Cantu, Italy, 1973; *Finn Juhl: Møbler og Andre Arbejder,* Kunstindustrimuseum, Copenhagen, 1982 (traveled to Oslo); *Scandinavian Modern Design 1880–1980,* Cooper-Hewitt Museum, New York, 1982; *Design Since 1945,* Philadelphia Museum of Art, 1983. **Collections:** Victoria and Albert Museum, London; Kunstindustrimuseum, Copenhagen; Museum of Modern Art, New York. Recipient: Cabinetmakers Guild Annual Awards, Copenhagen, from 1937; Eckersberg Medal, Copenhagen, 1947; Diploma of Honour, 1954, and Gold Medals, 1954, 1957, Milan Triennale; Association of Industrial Designers Award, Chicago 1954; Danish State Art Foundation Annual Stipend, 1971–89. Member, Akademisk Arkitektforening, Copenhagen, 1940; Honorary Royal Designer for Industry, Royal Society of Arts, London, 1978. *Died* (in Copenhagen) *17 May 1989.*

Works:

Armchair in walnut with loose cushion, for Niels Vodder, 1945.
Shop and showrooms, for Bing and Grondahl, Copenhagen, 1946.
Sofa and matching armchair in mahogany with leather upholstery, for Niels Vodder, 1948.
Egyptian chair, for Niels Vodder, 1949.
Good Design exhibition layouts, for the Merchandise Mart, Chicago, and the Museum of Modern Art, New York, 1951.
Trustees Council Chamber interiors, for the United Nations building, New York, 1952.
Dining chair in beech with veneered seat and back, for Bovirke, 1953.
Easy chair in upholstered teak, for Niels Vodder, 1953.
Desk in teak and blue steel, for Bovirke, 1953.
Danish Silver exhibition layouts, for the Corcoran Gallery of Art, Washington, D.C., 1954.
Chair in teak with sprung upholstery, for France and Daverkosen, 1954.
European and Far East office interiors, and DC-8 airplane interiors, for Scandinavian Airlines System, from 1955.
Formes Scandinaves exhibition layouts, for the Musée du Louvre, Paris, 1958.
The Arts of Denmark exhibition layouts, for the Metropolitan Museum of Art, New York, 1960.

Publications:

On JUHL: books—*Dansk Møbelkunst* by Viggo Sten Moller and Svend Erik Moller, Copenhagen 1951; *Danish Chairs,* edited by Nanna and Jorgen Ditzel, Copenhagen 1954; *Finn Juhl and Danish Furniture,* pamphlet by Bent Salicath, Copenhagen 1955; *Modern Danish Furniture* by Esbjorn Hiort, Copenhagen, New York and London 1956; *Modern Scandinavian Furniture* by Ulf Hård af Segerstad, Stockholm and London 1963; *Danish Design,* edited by Svend Erik Moller, Copenhagen 1974; *En Kobenhavnsk Porcelaenfabriks Historie: Bing og Grondal 1853–1978* by Erik Lassen, Copenhagen 1978; *Finn Juhl: Møbler og Andre Arbejder,* exhibition catalogue with text by Erik Lassen, Copenhagen 1982; *Design Since 1945,* edited by Kathryn Hiesinger and George Marcus, Philadelphia and London 1983; *Modern Furniture Classics* by Miriam Stimpson, London 1987.

During the depression in the early 1930s, the members of the Copenhagen Cabinetmakers' Guild were in bad straits. They had their excellent skill, their small workshops, hardly any showrooms, and no sales.

Prompted by the architect Tyge Hvass, they decided on a last great effort, consisting of an invitation to all to a yearly competition of new designs, with very small awards, but with the splendid promise of producing at least one sample of each awarded design on the condition that the designer would arrange the presentation at the autumn-exhibitions at the Copenhagen Kunstindustrimuseum.

They were lucky to get Crown Prince Frederik and Crown Princess Ingrid as patrons, and they continued to be so when they were King and Queen. Especially during the Occupation, this combination of domestic design and royal patronage lead to a row of glorious events for the press, so that the designer of one chair might overnight be in the whole press with photographs of object and designer and the cabinetmaker hovering in the background.

The official School of Furniture at the Royal Academy was completely dominated by Professor Kaare Klint, who taught that the best furniture was the classical English or Chinese-inspired English. In many ways, it was an excellent school of furniture-making in traditional but functional design, although it lead to some inevitable epigonism and hardly any creativity. As I was not a student of Klint's, I had to play my David to his Goliath. Some of his surviving students are still disgusted with my audacity; for others, my efforts may have helped them to freedom. Were that the case, I would be happy.

My designs have been around so long that they cannot today appear rebellious, but so they were in an aesthetic sense, not in technique—after all, they were designed for my limited, handmade production to save the cabinetmakers' trade. Also, my displays were less realistic and tried to indicate that there was a connection between architecture, furniture, and other accessories and the contemporary free arts, just as there had been in former epochs, such as the Baroque, Empire, etc.

During World War II, few impulses came from abroad. We developed a kind of Danish design in almost all fields—silver, ceramics, glass, textiles, furniture. We worked as individualists but appeared after the war to the outer world as a homogenous group, which was an immense advantage for such a tiny country. At

Finn Juhl: Armchair produced in walnut, rosewood or mahogany, 1944

the same time, our being individualists made us more appealing to possible importers, as there was more to choose from. One success helped the other, so it was delightful being allowed to arrange the exhibitions abroad.

My furniture (also the latest designs for machine production) has often been called sculptural. Naturally it is three-dimensional, as is architecture, but I guess that it is more the continuation of one member into the other through a smooth joint and the varying, moulded sections of each member, plus the "readiness" to accept and support the sculptural human body with a great margin for movement, since sitting as well as sleeping involves a process of movements. I want my chairs to be comfortable. I also want them beautiful to look at, as we, in contrast to the Japanese, leave all our furniture "on stage," even when we need only one chair.

—Finn Juhl (1984)

Finn Juhl's work represents a high point in Scandinavian design during the 1950s, when America and Britain were influenced by the quality and strength of work coming from these countries. In the late 1940s, the Danish furniture industry had been revitalized by a new generation of designers that included Juhl and Hans Wegner. The country had not suffered major devastation during the war and was therefore able to pick up quickly its long and rich design tradition, a tradition reinforced in the 1930s by the Copenhagen Cabinet Makers' Guild, which, under the inspired leadership of Kaare Klint, had become a major centre for furniture design. It was Klint who had studied eighteenth-century English furniture for proportion and construction that could be adapted to a contemporary style, using the highest standards of craftsmanship. Klint's work and research made a deep impact on Juhl. If his work moved away from Klint's more functional orientation, the kind of furniture sculpture he developed, pushing wood as it did to the limits of its capacity, depended entirely on quality of craftsmanship for its success. The style he developed, with its curved contours, natural wood, and coarse-textured fabrics, was a combination that captured the 1950s and was quickly adapted and imitated all over the Western world.

Juhl believed his design work to be closely allied to fine art, and his furniture often explored the borderlines between fine and applied art. He looked for inspiration to African primitive art and the work of abstract artists, such as Henry Moore and Barbara Hepworth. In the craft area, his work includes some famous, wood bowls, usually in teak, showing the strong pattern of wood grain. In the 1950s, no avantgarde interior was seen without one. During the 1950s and 1960s, Juhl played a part in promoting Scandinavian design worldwide. He organized and exhibited in shows such as *Formes Scandinaves* at the Louvre in 1958 and the Milan *Triennale*.

—Catherine McDermott

JUHLIN, Sven-Eric.
Swedish industrial designer. Born in Horndal, 6 May 1940. Studied mechanical engineering, Katrineholm Technical School, 1958–61; sculpture and industrial design, National College of Art and Design, Stockholm, 1963–67. Married Siv Larsson in 1964; children: Oskar and Par. Worked as a constructor, AB Electrolux, Stockholm, 1961–63; industrial designer, AB Gus-

tavsberg, Sweden, 1967–76; partner, Ergonomi Design Gruppen, Bromma, since 1976: has collaborated with designer Maria Benktzon, since 1972. Instructor in Ergonomics and Design Methods, National College of Art and Design, Stockholm, 1970–73; also visiting lecturer at congresses and professional institutes in Europe, Japan and Canada, since 1983. Board Member, Swedish Society of Crafts and Design, Stockholm, 1970–76. **Exhibitions:** *A Society Open to All,* Kharkov, U.S.S.R., 1977 (toured the Soviet Union, Poland and Czechoslovakia); *Swedish Craft and Design,* Victoria and Albert Museum, London, 1980; *Scandinavian Modern Design 1880-1980,* Cooper-Hewitt Museum, New York, 1982; *Design Since 1945,* Philadelphia Museum of Art, 1983; *Contemporary Swedish Design,* Nationalmuseum, Stockholm, 1983; *International Design Exhibition,* Osaka, Japan, 1985; *Design in Sweden Now,* toured Canada and Australia, 1985–86; *Scandinavian Design: A Way of Life,* Toyama Museum of Modern Art, Japan, 1987; *Designs for Independent Living,* Museum of Modern Art, New York, 1988; *Faces of Swedish Design,* IBM Gallery, New York, 1988 (toured the United States); *Art and Design,* Internationales Design Zentrum, West Berlin, 1988. **Collections:** Nationalmuseum, Stockholm; Museum of Modern Art, New York; Design Museum, London. Recipient: Swedish Industrial Design Award, 1974, 1975; Gold Medal, *Bio 10* Biennale of Industrial Design, Liubliana, 1975; First International Design Award, 1982 (with Maria Benktzon), and International Design Competition Prize, 1985 (with Maria Benktzon and Håkan Bergkvist), Japan Design Foundation; Bruno Mathsson Prize, Sweden, 1984; Swedish Design Excellence Award, 1984, 1988. Address: Ergonomi Design Gruppen, Box 14021, 161 14 Bromma, Sweden.

Works:

Double-wall tablewares, for AB Gustavsberg, 1969.
Shopping basket, for AB Gustavsberg, 1970.
Gripping Tongs, for AB Gustavsberg, 1971.
Handles and Grips project, for Swedish Institute for the Handicapped, 1973.
Linie tableware set, for AB Gustavsberg, 1974.
Kitchen knife and cutting-board, for AB Gustavsberg, 1974.
Pots and pans project, for STU Swedish National Board for Technical Development, 1977.
Eating and drinking implements project, for Folksam Research Foundation/STU Swedish National Board for Technical Development, produced by RFSU Rehab, 1980.
Gripping tongs project, for STU Swedish National Board for Technical Development, produced by RFSU Rehab, 1985.
Fix food preparation board, for STU Swedish National Board for Technical Development, produced by RFSU Rehab, 1985.
Cane for arthritics, for Folksam Research Foundation/STU Swedish National Board for Technical Development, produced by RFSU Rehab, 1987.
Coffee- and teapot, for SAS Scandinavian Airlines System, 1988.
Knife for quadraplegics, for STU Swedish National Board for Technical Development, produced by RFSU Rehab, 1989.
Elbow Crutch, for STU Swedish National Board for Technical Development, produced by Etac, 1989.
Eating and drinking implements for multihandicapped children, for Swedish National Board for Technical Development, produced by RFSU Rehab, 1989.
Slaughterhouse knife, for Bahco Tools, 1989.

Publications:

By JUHLIN: articles—"Plast och miljö" in *Form* (Stockholm), no. 8, 1970; "Redskap for hander", with Maria Benktzon, in *Form* (Stockholm), no. 10, 1973; "What Can Design Contribute to the Human Society of the Near Future?", with Maria Benktzon, in *Design Quarterly* (Tokyo), no. 2, 1984.

On JUHLIN: books—*Konsthantverk, Konstindustri, Design 1875-1975* by Dag Widman, Stockholm 1975; *Form och Tradition i Sverige,* edited by Birgitta Walz, Stockholm 1982; *Scandinavian Modern Design 1880-1980,* edited by David Revere McFadden, New York 1982; *Contemporary Swedish Design,* exhibition catalogue by Monica Boman, Lennart Lindkvist and others, Stockholm 1983; *Design Since 1945,* edited by Kathryn Hiesinger and George Marcus, Philadelphia and London 1983; *Design Source Book* by Penny Sparke and others, London 1986, *Faces of Swedish Design,* exhibition catalogue edited by Monica Boman, Stockholm 1988.

See BENKTZON, Maria.

JUNG, Dora (Elisabet).
Finnish textile designer. Born in Helsinki, 16 October 1906. Studied textile design, Skola for Konstflit, Helsinki, 1932; also study-travels in Scandinavia, 1934, in England and France, 1937, 1950, and in the United States, 1958. Freelance textile designer, Helsinki, 1932–80: designed for the Tampella textile company, and for churches and other public buildings. Instructor in design, at Helsinki city schools, 1936–46. **Exhibitions:** Stockholm, 1948; Copenhagen, 1956; Helsinki, 1957, 1968, 1977; *D. Jung/K. Franck/B. Gardberg,* Göteborg, 1966; *Nordisk Industridesign,* Kunstindustrimuseet, Oslo, 1976; *Form und Struktur,* Osterreichisches Museum fur Angewandte Kunst, Vienna, 1980 (traveled to Nuremberg); *Scandinavian Modern Design 1880-1980,* Cooper-Hewitt Museum, New York, 1982; *Design Since 1945,* Philadelphia Museum of Art, 1983. Recipient: State Stipend for Design, Helsinki, 1934; Sverige Kulturforening Award, Stockholm, 1945, 1955; Grand Prize, Milan Triennale, 1951, 1954, 1959; Prince Eugene Medal, Stockholm, 1961; Cotil Prize, Copenhagen, 1962; Finnish State Design Prize, 1969; Svenska Folkskolans Vanner Culture Prize, Stockholm, 1970; Nordiska Craft and Design Prize, 1972; City of Helsinki Prize, 1972. Honorary Royal Academician, London, 1980. *Died* (in Helsinki) *in 1980.*

Publications:

On JUNG: books—*A Treasury of Scandinavian Design,* edited by Erik Zahle, New York 1961; *Modern Finnish Design* by Ulf Hård af Segerstad, London 1969; *New Design in Weaving* by Donald J. Willcox, New York and London 1970; *Finnish Design 1875-1975* by Timo Sarpaneva, Erik Bruun and Erik Kruskopf, Helsinki 1975; *Scandinavian Design: Objects of a Life Style* by Eileene Harrison Beer, New York and Toronto 1975; *Scandinavian Modern Design 1880-1980,* edited by David McFadden, New York 1982; *Contemporary Textile Art: Scandinavia* by Charles S. Talley, Stockholm 1982; *Design Since 1945,* edited by Kathryn Hiesinger and George Marcus, Philadelphia and London 1983; *The Conran Directory of Design,* edited by Stephen Bayley, London 1985.

K

KAMALI, Norma.

American fashion designer. Born Norma Arraez, in New York City, in 1944. Studied fashion illustration, at the Fashion Institute of Technology, New York, 1961–64. Married Mohammed (Eddie) Houssein Kamali in 1967 (divorced, 1972). Freelance fashion illustrator, New York, 1965–66; worked as an airlines reservation clerk, 1966–67; freelance fashion designer, and partner, with Eddie Kamali, in Kamali fashion imports and design shop on East 53rd Street, New York, 1968–74, and on Madison Avenue, New York, 1974–78; established OMO (On My Own) Norma Kamali store, and Norma Kamali Designs office, on West 56th Street, New York, from 1978: introduced ready-to-wear line, 1981; produced sportwear for Jones Apparel Group, 1981, children's sportswear for Empire Shield Company, 1982, Far East sportswear for Renown Incorporated of Japan, 1983, socks and tights for Camp Hosiery, 1983, shoes, sneakers and bags for Vittorio Ricci, 1983–84, headwear for Stetson Hats, 1983, and belts for Raymon Ridless, 1985. **Exhibition:** *Vanity Fair,* Metropolitan Museum of Art, New York, 1976. Recipient: Coty American Fashion Critics' Award, 1981, Return Award, 1982, and Hall of Fame Award, 1983; Council of Fashion Designers of America Outstanding Designer Award, 1983; Fashion Institute of Design and Merchandising Award, Los Angeles, 1984. Address: 11 West 56th Street, New York, New York 10019, U.S.A.

Publications:

On KAMALI: books—*Fairchild's Who's Who in Fashion,* edited by Ann Stegemeyer, New York 1980; *Fashion 2001* by Lucille Khornak, London 1982; *The Collector's Book of Twentieth Century Fashion* by Frances Kennett, New York and London 1983; *McDowell's Directory of Twentieth Century Fashion* by Colin McDowell, London 1984; *The Encyclopaedia of Fashion from 1840 to the 1980s* by Georgina O'Hara, London 1986.

American-Lebanese Norma Kamali opened in New York in the 1960s, first with the help of her husband and, subsequently, on her own, calling her shop OMO (On My Own). She wanted ordinary women to be able to afford designer-quality clothes, although this was unusual in New York. As she said, "In Europe, fashion is treated as an art form. There's appreciation for the art rather than for the dollar. Here, it's big business with mass appeal. I am almost a displaced person in the fashion world here. Yet, it's worked. I'm earning a living and liking what I'm doing." When she launched her cheapest range in 1981 with nothing over $80, the queue of women was a mile long. She was a pioneer in giving New Yorkers clothes of a signature and a cut previously exclusive to salons.

Just as the nineteenth-century, English sportsman's blazer and grey flannels became fashionable wear from the 1920s, so Kamali has taken twentieth-century sportswear and turned that into street attire, this time for women, now that looking sporty and healthy is no longer dubbed unfeminine. Taking old, military, grey cotton fleece, she turned it into sweatshirts and jogging suits for the town. By so doing, she has helped to alter the conservative attitude towards clothes found among Americans by encouraging individuality. So popular have her casual clothes become that she has been copied on an enormous scale by manufacturers in the United States and Europe. The quality of the fabric is not the same, nor the cut, but it is beyond the power of one designer to track down every imitation. Even the Parisian couturier Claude Montana has taken up Kamali's grey sweatshirts.

In addition to these loose garments, Kamali also creates a very slender range which she designs on the body. Her slinky gowns have the likes of Raquel Welch and Diana Ross after them, while her moulded swimsuits are considered daring in their sculptural sensuality. There is little doubt that Kamali is the most original designer in New York of the 1980s and 1990s. She displays the same total devotion to her work as other women couturieres, scorning the press and high society, for nothing must be allowed to interfere with the creation.

—Diana de Marly

KAMEKURA, Yusaku.

Japanese graphic designer. Born in Yoshidamachi, Nisha-Kambara, Niigata Prefecture, 6 April 1915. Educated at Nippon University high school, Tokyo, 1928–33; studied constructivist theory under Renshichiro Kawakita, at the Institute of New Architecture and Industrial Arts, Tokyo, 1935–37. Designer, 1937–40, and chief of the art department, 1940–60, Nippon Kobo (later re-named International Industrial Arts Information Company), Tokyo; co-founder and managing director, Nippon Design Center, Tokyo, 1960–62; freelance designer, establishing Kamekura Design Institute, Tokyo, from 1962: director, LD Yamagiwa Laboratory, Tokyo, from 1970; art director, *Nippon* magazine, from 1937, and *Commerce Japan* magazine, from 1949; editor-in-chief, *Kaupapu* magazine, from 1939; editorial staff member, *Collection of Commercial Designs* series, for the Evening Star Company, Tokyo, from 1951, and *Outline of Design* series, for David Publishing, Tokyo,

from 1954. Founder-member, Japan Advertising Art Club, Tokyo, 1951–70; founder-president, Japan Graphic Designers Association, 1978. **Exhibitions:** Chuokoron-sha Publishing House, Tokyo, 1953; Museum of Modern Art, Kamakura, 1953; *Graphic 55,* Tokyo, 1955 (travelled to Paris); *AGI International Exhibition,* Paris, 1955, London 1956, and Lausanne, 1957; Society of Typographic Arts, Chicago, 1956; *Kamekura: retrospective exhibition,* Tokyo, 1971; *Kamekura: Posters for Nikon,* Matsuya Department Store, Tokyo, 1982; *Designs by Yusaku Kamekura,* Matsuya Department Store, Tokyo, 1983; *Japon des Avant-Gardes,* Centre Georges Pompidou, Paris, 1986; *Works by Yusaku Kamekura,* Niigata, 1987, and Kirin Palace, Osaka, 1988. **Collections:** Museum of Modern Art, New York; Stedelijk Museum, Amsterdam. Recipient: Dentsu Advertising Award, 1955, 1956, 1961; Mainichi Design Award, 1955, 1957, 1963; Tokyo Art Directors Club Awards, 1957, 1958, 1959, 1960, 1961, 1962, 1963, 1964, 1965, 1966, 1967, 1968, 1969, 1972, 1983; Grand Prize, Japanese Ministry of Education, 1961; Graphics Awards, Warsaw Poster Biennale, 1966, 1968, 1988; Kodansha Culture Prize, 1970; Brazilian Coffee Institute Poster Prize, 1970; Japan Sign Design Association Awards, 1972, 1973, 1975, 1976, 1982; Japanese Ministry of Trade and Industry Prizes, 1975, 1981; Brno Graphics Biennale Awards, 1976, 1980, 1984; Gold Award of Merit, Japanese Red Cross Society, 1976; Asahi Prize, 1984; Lahti Poster Biennale Award, 1985; Japanese Order of the Sacred Treasure, Tokyo, 1985; International Cultural Design Prize, Tokyo, 1986; International Graphic Design Prize, Yugoslavia, 1987. Address: Recruit Building, 8-4-17 Ginza, Chuo-ku, Tokyo 104, Japan.

Works:

Poster series, for Nippon Kogaku, 1955.
Peaceful Uses of Atomic Energy poster, 1956.
Neon sign, for Meiji Confectionery Company, Tokyo, 1956.
Poster series, for Nikon Camera Company, from 1957.
Official poster, for the Tokyo Olympics, 1963.
Alfa chocolate packaging, for Meiji Confectionery Company, 1965.
Poster series, for Kokudokeikaju Ski Resort, 1969.
Signage and graphics, for the arcade of Matsuya Department Store, Tokyo, 1972.
Neon signage, for Yamagiwa Light Fixture Company, Tokyo, 1975.
Cover designs, for *Sogetsu* magazine, Tokyo, from 1976.
Performance Arts of Japan poster, for the University of California at Los Angeles, 1981.
Hiroshima Appeals '83 poster, 1983.
Cover design, for *Graphis,* no. 230, Zurich, 1984.

Norma Kamali: Denim, coat, jacket and jeans, with buffalo check shirt, 1983

Yusaku Kamekura: Official poster for *Design Expo '89*, **Nagoya, 1980**

Logotype symbol, for Nippon Telephone and Telegraph Corporation, 1985.

Official poster of *Expo '89,* Nagoya, for the World Design Exposition Association, 1988.

Publications:

By KAMEKURA: books—*Graphic Design,* with others, Tokyo 1954, 1957; *Photo Design,* Tokyo 1956; *Trademarks of the World,* editor, Tokyo and New York 1956; *Paul Rand,* Tokyo and New York 1959; *Trademarks and Symbols of the World,* editor, Tokyo and New York 1965; *Japanese Gardens,* with Teiji Ito and Takeji Iwamiya, Tokyo 1971, New Haven 1972; *Yusaku Kamekura: Graphic Works,* Tokyo and New York 1971; *Takeoff/Landing,* compiler, Tokyo 1972; *Three Men, Three Minds,* with Sofu Teshigahara and Ken Domon, Tokyo 1977; *The Minga of the Lee Dynasty,* editor, Tokyo 1982; *The Work of Yusaku Kamekura,* Tokyo 1983.

On KAMEKURA: books—*The New Graphic Design* by Karl Gerstner and Markus Kutter, Teufen and London 1959; *Packaging: An International Survey of Package Design,* edited by Walter Herdeg, Zurich 1961; *Design Coordination and Corporate Image* by F. H. K. Henrion and Alan Parkin, London and New York, 1967; *An International Survey of Packaging* by Wim Crouwel and Kurt Weidemann, London 1968; *History of the Poster* by Josef and Shizuko Muller-Brockmann, Zurich 1971; *The Graphic Design of Yusaku Kamekura* by Masaru Katsumie, Tokyo and New York 1973; *Who's Who in Graphic Art,* edited by Walter Amstutz, Dubendorf 1982; *A History of Graphic Design* by Philip B. Meggs, New York and London 1983.

Yusaka Kamekura belongs to a generation which first introduced the Japanese graphic message to international circulation, giving it the rank genuine art. The generation abounded in talents and outstanding individualities, such as Ikko Tanaka, Takashi Kono, Kazumasa Nagai or Makoto Nakamura. It is to them that credit goes for the interesting and promising symbiosis of Eastern and Western culture in the visual mass media, to this day resulting in intense exchange of material and intellectual goods. Though the coming together and interpenetration of the East and the West had its "prehistory" and latent stage, the process gained in impetus after World War II, in which graphic design performed the function of an ambassador. It is no overstatement to say that, just as the Japanese woodcut ukyi-oe was the harbinger of a peculiar, different way of modelling the world to the Europeans at the close of the 19th century, the appearance of Kamekura's first works in the west in the late 1950s heralded the onset of an original school of graphic design. Until then, the domain of the European spirit and the product of a long aesthetic evolution starting with Art Nouveau, it had to accept the historical challenge.

Kamekura has certainly been the key figure in the competition going on before our eyes. The critics have pointed out the influence on him that Cassandre and the Bauhaus style were on him at the outset of his career. Kamekura admits that this was really the case with him, which he does with quite considerable pride. This in turn reflects on his aesthetic leanings and priorities. Indeed, at an early stage, as at other times, concepts originating in Esprit Nouveau, Purism, Constructivism and Functionalism may be identified in his work. This is probably the source of his evident disinclination for ornamental or disintegrated forms in favour of order based on unchanging, apparently natural canons

of harmony. He is also consistent in discarding illusive spatiality on the plane and anecdotal interpretations of the subject, which precludes a banal illustrative approach. From the heritage of the post-Cubist avant-garde, Kamekura has assimilated certain techniques and formal devices, for instance the elaboration of the surface, masses, textures and colour arrangements. His favourite lay-out are based on crisp, compact forms, concentric or radial, or on full or open structures that may be reduced to geometric masses. He also finds delight in asymmetric compositions featuring diagonals, crossings and kinetic transformations, in optical illusions quickening perception. In this, he is like a magician conjuring up fantastic beings. Like the Constructivists, Kamekura has reduced his palette to several basic colours, but his favourite colour is black. He enriches his deliberately restricted colour-scheme, e.g., by means of an afterimage, a colour halo, as was the case in a series of his prints for the Corporation Yamagiwa Lamps.

The "European" quality of Kamekura's work remains in harmony with the Japanese roots of his vision and style. The Japanese quality is omnipresent in his posters, books, covers, and typography, and especially in his trademarks. His unforgettable, exquisitely beautiful signs and symbols (e.g., Expo '75, 1972; ICSID '73, 1972; Design Year 1973; East–West Culture Communication Association, 1960) make one think of the old Japanese tradition of family crests. The linking factor of all his works is their linear quality, deeply rooted in old and contemporary Japanese art. We may speak of the wealth and culture of lines in his work: they are expressive, symbolic, and distinct. The lines themselves, as well as their complexes, bands, streams and linear accents are orchestrated in an intricate way.

From my meetings with Kamekura in Tokyo and in Warsaw, where he was awarded the main prize at the International Poster Biennale in 1971, I remember the artist as one guided by ethical motives in his professional life. Here is what he has written about it: "No matter how much money I am offered, I will not do work that I am not convinced is right. This means that I refuse to do any work for political parties or religious groups, because I find that I usually cannot agree with their ideals and purposes . . . I simply cannot get an inspiration to do work that does not seem worthwhile or of interest to me. . . ."

—Szymon Bojko

KANTOR, Tadeusz.

Polish painter, graphic artist and stage designer. Born in Wielopole, 16 March 1915. Studied at the Academy of Fine Arts, Krakow, 1936–39. Served in the Polish Resistance, directing underground theatre, Krakow, 1940–44. Married Maria Stangret in 1962. Worked as a stage designer, in Krakow, Warsaw, and throughout Poland, 1944–55; also independent painter and graphic artist, in Krakow and Warsaw, from 1948: founder and director, Cricot 2 Theatre, Krakow, from 1955. Nominated professor, Academy of Fine Arts, Krakow, 1949, 1968; visiting professor, Academy of Fine Arts, Hamburg, 1961. **Exhibitions:** Galerie Po Prostu, Warsaw, 1956; Galerie Krzystofory Krakow, 1957, 1963, 1967, 1968; Muzeum Miejskie Lublin, 1958; Kunsthalle, Dusseldorf, 1959;

Galeria Foksal, Warsaw, 1965, 1967, 1968, 1970, 1971, 1973; Kunsthalle, Baden-Baden, 1966; Kunsthalle, Nuremberg, 1968; Musée des Arts Decoratifs, Lausanne, 1971; Henie-Onstad Kunstsenter, Oslo, 1971, 1976; Muzeum Sztuki, Lodz, 1975; Kulturhuset, Stockholm, 1975; Whitechapel Art Gallery, London, 1976; Riverside Studios, London, 1976, 1982. **Collection:** Muzeum Sztuki, Lodz. Recipient: Painting Prize, Sao Paulo Bienal, 1969; Premio Roma Medal, Rome, 1969; Tadeusz Boy-Zelenski Theatre Prize, Warsaw, 1977; Mayor's Medal, Rome, 1978; Cyprian Norwid Art Critic's Prize, Warsaw, 1978; Goethe Foundation Rembrandt Prize, 1978; Mayor's Medal, Milan 1979; Mayor's Medal, Florence, 1980; City of Gdansk Medal, 1980. Addresses: Theatre Cricot 2 (Cricoteca), Kanonisza Street 5, Krakow; Elblaska Street 6/11, Krakow, Poland.

Works:

Major productions and happenings include—*Sepia,* Galeria Krzystofory, Krakow, 1956; *The Cuttlefish,* Galeria Krzystofory, Krakow, 1956; *In a Small House,* Galeria Krzystofory, Krakow, 1961; *The Madman and the Nun,* Galeria Krzystofory, Krakow, 1963; *Cricotage,* Galeria Foksal, Warsaw, 1965; *Line of Division,* Galeria S.H.S., Krakow, 1966; *The Waterhen,* Galeria Krzystofory, Krakow, 1967; *Panoramic Seashore Happening,* Osieki, Baltic Seashore, 1967; *The Anatomy Lesson: After Rembrandt,* Kunsthalle Nuremberg, 1968; *Conference with Rhinoceros,* Kunsthalle, Nuremberg, 1968; *The Cobblers,* Malakoff Theatre, Paris, 1972; *Lovelies and Dowdies,* Galeria Krzystofory, Krakow, 1973; *The Dead Class,* Galeria Krzystofory, Krakow, 1975; *Où Sont les Neiges d'Antan,* Rome, 1978; *Wielopole, Wielopole,* Florence, 1980.

Publications:

By KANTOR: books—*Emballages,* Warsaw 1976; *La Théâtre de la Morte,* Paris 1978; *La Classa Morta,* with photos by Maurizio Buscarina, Milan 1981; *Wielopole, Wielopole,* Milan 1981.

On KANTOR: books—*Happening and Fluxus,* compiled by Hanns Sohm, Cologne 1970; *Tadeusz Kantor: Emballages,* exhibition catalogue with texts by Wieslaw Borowski and Ryszard Stanislawski, Lodz 1975; *Tadeusz Kantor: Emballages 1960–1976,* exhibition catalogue by Ryszard Stanislawski, London 1976; *Contemporary Polish Theatre* by Witold Filler, Warsaw 1977; *Tadeusz Kantor* by Wieslaw Borowski, Warsaw 1982.

The Renaissance artist is almost a forbidden species in our time. Everyone narrows his activities in the hope of mastering some single act of creativity. But not Tadeusz Kantor.

For more than forty years, he has struggled at an amazingly wide range of the arts. Always a front-runner on untested ground, for many years, he was misjudged and sometimes ridiculed.

This sketch must focus on Kantor's stage design, but it is impossible to separate this subject from the full panorama of Kantor's "life-theatre." Trained as a painter in the prewar Krakow Academy, but unable to practice his art, Kantor began experiments with the theatre—as he calls it, "closet-theatre"—in a mountain hide-out.

After the war, despite Stalinist social-realism governing Polish art during the 1950s, Kantor maintained a rare position: as one of very few, he never compromised his ideas. He tried some café theatre, he continued to paint. Having minimal contact with the world beyond the Iron Curtain and painting in his own style, to everybody's surprise, he was nevertheless in tune with current European styles.

But his independence didn't pay well, even after 1956, when Poland opened herself to the West. Kantor was freer to experiment, but mere abstract painting was not his joy. The early 1960s brought a new series of paintings, dramatic compositions, partially ready-made. With objects incorporated, they suggested stage sets. Simultaneously, theatrical ideas flourished. A little, cavernous cafe in the old town of Krakow, the headquarters of the unofficial "Krakow Group" of painters (lead by Kantor, of course), served as a theatre. It had no stage and only a few rows of wood chairs for the public, but it was enough. Here, he first gave his attention to the works of the great Polish playwright Stanislaw Ignacy Witkiewicz, then an almost forgotten, avant-garde figure from prewar Poland.

In the early 1970s, Kantor reached new frontiers. His adaptations of Witkiewicz's works, extremely personal as they were, limited his energy and self-realization. Now, for the first time, he created his own world, created all elements by himself. Only the music was not written by him but carefully selected and mixed to serve as Kantor's choice for Kantor's idea.

Two recent creations (*Dead Class*, 1975, and *Wielopole, Wielopole*, 1979) are truly masterpieces of Kantor's lifelong struggle. They put him at the very top of world theatrical achievements—past and present.

This sophisticated thinker, in touch with history, skillfully using the variety of actors' methods, this formidable director, "conducting" his team in every performance, this amazing creator of set, light, and music recreates scenes from his life (our own as well) and forces us into deep reflection about our basic existence. The artist builds his performances with mixtures of touching scenes in which the atmosphere is tense with music, light, formidable actors playing with life-size puppets, and sometimes found objects—all these elements are carefully orchestrated to create the world according to Tadeusz Kantor.

His mastery is most obvious when he freezes moments that are fast, loud, and full of running people, dust, and the scream of old Austrian military band music, so the spectator is struck by the beauty, strange and dramatic, of what seems to be an old photograph derived from a remote corner of everybody's mind. The antique, graying, sepia picture of man's fate, joy, and death, of the paranoia of switching borders, of religious ceremonies, of repeating holocausts, of births, weddings, sufferings, this picture of our ancestors and ourselves has an overwhelming effect. The whole spectacle in each case is built around a few painting-like scenes arranged carefully to the smallest detail, so that they call to mind the fading memory of childhood, the failure of our lives, Kantor's own autobiography—a Galician town with Poles and Jews, Catholic priests and rabbis, and armies, the rolling armies, every time a different color. Only soldiers remain the same—the father, the brothers, and you, too, maybe.

Kantor has achieved the dream of every theatrically oriented artist. He is able to catalyze all the aspects of visual spectacle into the very powerful and universal story of humanity. When you are watching his theatre, you are overwhelmed by his three-dimensional, live, monochromatic portraits of the human condition. They are as tragic and beautiful as the condition of all of us.

—Jan Sawka

KAPITZKI, Herbert W.

German graphic and industrial designer. Born in Danzig (now Gdansk, Poland), 24 February 1925. Studied at the Hochschule für Bildende Künste, Hamburg, 1946; Arbeitsgruppe für Bildende Künste, Bernstein, 1947–49; under Willi Baumeister, at the Akademie für Bildende Kunste, Stuttgart, 1949–53. Served in the German Army, 1940–43: prisoner of war, 1943–45. Married Line Pinnow in 1980; sons: Boris and Ivo. Exhibition designer, for the Landesgewerbeamt Baden-Württemberg, Stuttgart, 1955–65; freelance designer, West Berlin, from 1965: layout and installation design coordinator, for the Historisches Museum, Frankfurt, 1970–74, and for Firma Schering AG, West Berlin, 1974–78. Docent, Hochschule für Gestaltung, Ulm, 1964–68; professor of visual communications, Hochschule der Künste, West Berlin, from 1970. **Exhibitions:** *Kunst in Baden-Württemberg*, Kunsthalle, Baden-Baden, 1962; *Design: Herbert W. Kapitzki*, Hochschule für Bildende Künste, Hamburg, 1965; Landesgewerbeamt Baden-Württemberg, Stuttgart, 1965; Kunstschule, Offenbach, 1965; National Museum, Helsinki, 1965; *107 Grafici dell'AGI*, Castello Sforzesco, Milan, 1974 (travelled to Venice); *Korper/Zeichen/Bilder*, Galerie Behr, Stuttgart, 1980; *Konstruktive Tendenzen, Prinzip Reihe*, Galerie unterm Turm, Stuttgart, 1987; Deutsches Plakatmuseum, Essen, 1988; Galerie im Burgenlandzentrum, Stuttgart, 1989; *Plakate*, Hochschule der Künste, West Berlin, 1989. **Collections:** Staatliche Museen, Stuttgart; Deutsches Plakatmuseum, Essen; Museum of Modern Art, New York. Address: Nymphenburger Strasse 11A, 1000 Berlin 62 (West), Germany.

Works:

Dokumentation der Grafik exhibition layouts, for the Landesgewerbeamt Baden-Württemberg, Stuttgart, 1961.
Anton Stankowski exhibition layouts, for the Landesgewerbeamt Baden-Württemberg, Stuttgart, 1962.
Internationale Verpackungsausstellung exhibition layouts, for the Landesgewerbeamt Baden-Württemberg, Stuttgart, 1965.
German pavilion layouts, at *Expo 67*, Montreal, 1967.
Installation layouts, for the Historisches Museum, Frankfurt, 1970–74.
Signage systems, for the Verband Deutscher Flughafen, West Berlin, 1972.
Building layouts and interiors, for Firma Schering AG, West Berlin, 1974–78.
Signage system, for the IDZ International Design Centre, West Berlin, 1976.
Signage system, for the Senat Building, West Berlin, 1980.
Signage and graphics, for the Ausstellungs Messe Kongress GmbH, West Berlin, 1988–89.
Signage and graphic identity, for Galerie und Edition Schlichtenmaier, Datzingen, 1989.

Publications:

By KAPITZKI: books—*Programmiertes Gestalten*, Karlsruhe 1980; *Proportionen*, West Berlin 1981.

On KAPITZKI: books—*An International Survey of Press Advertising* by Kurt Weidemann, Stuttgart and London 1966; *German Advertising Art*, edited by Eberhard Holscher, Munich 1967; *Design with Type* by Carl Dair, London and Toronto 1967; *Modern Graphics* by Keith Murgatroyd, London 1969; *107 Grafici dell'-AGI*, with texts by Renzo Zorzi and Franco Grignani, Venice 1974; *Form und Kommunikation* by Walter Diethelm, Basel 1977; *Visual Transformation* by Walter Diethelm, Basel 1982; *Who's Who in Graphic Art*, edited by Walter Amstutz, Dubendorf 1982.

The design praxis that I have followed for three decades has always been determined by the realization that for every design project, a high degree of creativity to discover new relationships must be brought into play. Priority is given not to the arrangement of known elements but to the development of new areas of perception. From this point of view, a designer, whether he is active in the two- or in the three-dimensional field, must always examine his general design capabilities.

There is no doubt that in the long run this becomes increasingly difficult. In the visually experienced world of today, more and more pictures are produced and used. As the various broadcasting media in our technical world become increasingly complex, consumers demand more and more innovative visualizations. As a university teacher, I have become particularly aware in recent years that this also leads to other problems in society. It is clear that the greater the demands put on visual materials, the lower the creative (artistic-aesthetic) level tends to become. There are many reasons for this, among which ignorance of cultural responsibility of the people concerned, especially consumers, takes a prominent place. In most cases, design is treated purely as an economic factor. It is ignored that design is not only manipulation of form but also an expression of contents, even a manifestation of culture. However, our world of form and image is receiving more attention as a cultural factor than ever before.

In my own design, I try to develop images that appear rational on the basis of geometrically arranged factors but that nevertheless exhibit emotional levels of interpretation. The constructive design that develops from generative structures can provide many proportional relationships which can be employed for various semantic problems and which then can also be seen as harmonic aesthetic constellations.

—Herbert W. Kapitzki

Herbert Kapitzki's most important contributions have been the development of information communication and the use of comprehensive planning principles in solving graphic design problems.

Early in his career, from 1956 to 1964, Kapitzki designed a series of posters and numerous exhibitions for the Stuttgart Trade and Industry Office. Here, he often innovated in the translation of the rational vocabulary of Op and programmed art into graphics. Later in the 1960s, his engagement at the Hochschule für Gestaltung in Ulm proved to be decisive to his further development in both the theoretical and practical spheres. During his tenure there, he developed the Baden-Baden South West Radio image, which demonstrated his strength in the design of a flexible yet constructive system. In 1969, the year after the Hochschule closed, he designed a new logotype for the Bund Deutscher Gebrauchsgraphiker (which on his initiative changed its name to Bund Deutscher Graphic Designer).

From the beginning of Kapitzki's teaching activity in Berlin in 1970, his emphasis has been on "visual research." He introduced video into the curriculum and extended the traditional framework of graphic design to embrace the field of visual communication. During these same years, outstanding projects included his re-design of the Frankfurt historical museum in 1971 and his comprehensive design scheme for Schering AG in Berlin. His achievement at the

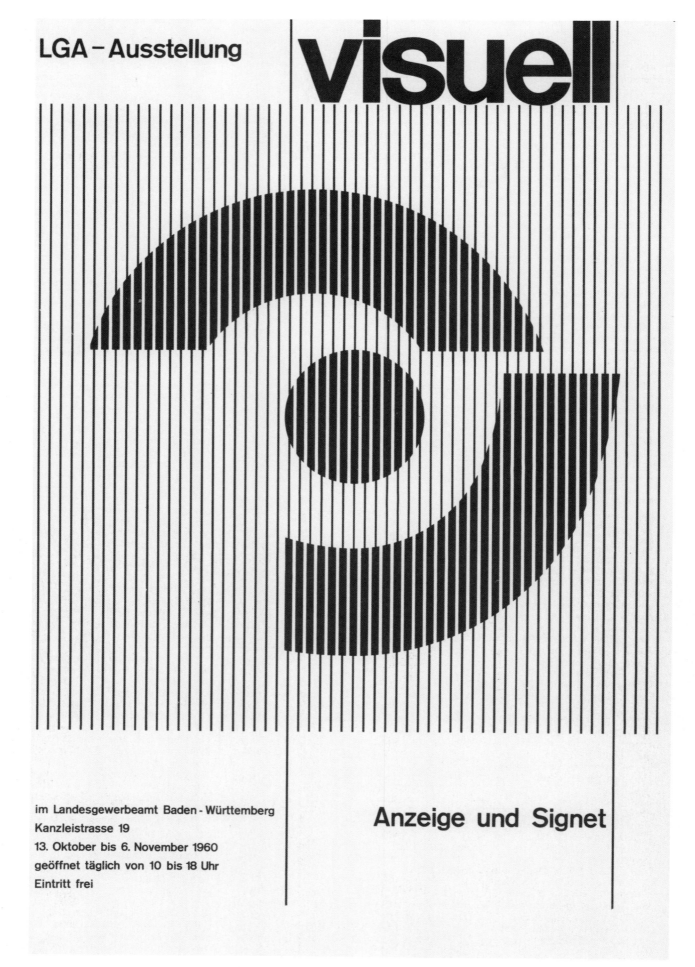

Herbert W. Kapitzki: *Visuelle-Anzeige und Signet* poster, for the Landesgewerbeamt Baden-Wurttemberg, 1960

museum pointed the way for many others, which have since adopted his communication system. Conceiving of an exhibition as an "information-bank," he enriched it with audio-visual media. Placards and reproductions provided comprehensive information, and the individual areas were coded by colour and symbol. For Schering, he not only designed a communication system, but determined also the interior decor and graphic image of the firm.

—M. Droste

KAPR, Albert.

German book and type designer. Born in Stuttgart, 20 July 1918. Apprenticed as a compositor, to Stahle und Friedel, Stuttgart, 1933–35, 1937–38; studied typography and book design under Ernst Schneidler, at the Akademie für Bildende Künste, Stuttgart, 1938–40, 1945–48. Served in the German Army, 1940–45. Married Fanny Schmid in 1947; sons: Johannes and Klaus. Independent calligrapher, type and book designer, from 1948: artistic director, Typoart typefoundry, Dresden, 1964–77. Assistant lecturer in typography, Technische Hochschule, Stuttgart, 1947–48; docent, Hochschule für Baukunst und Bildende Künste, Weimar, 1948–51; professor, 1951–56, head of the Institut für Buchkunst, 1951–78, and rector, 1959, 1966–73, Hochschule für Grafik und Buchkunst, Leipzig. **Exhibitions:** *International Book Design Exhibition,* London 1957, Leipzig, 1959, 1965, 1971, 1977, 1982; *Wort und Werk,* Leipzig, 1968, 1977; Pushkin Museum, Moscow, 1976; National Museum, Prague, 1978. **Collections:** Deutsche Bucherei, Leipzig; Klingspor Museum, Offenbach. Recipient: DDR Type Design Prize, Berlin, 1958; DDR National Prize, 1961; Gutenberg Prize, Leipzig, 1961; has also received more than 50 DDR Book of the Year Awards. PhD.: Akademie für Bildende Künste, Stuttgart, 1974. Address: Jacobstrasse 22, 7010 Leipzig, German Democratic Republic.

Works:

Faust-Antiqua typeface, for Typoart Foundry, Dresden, 1958.
Leipziger Antiqua typeface, for Typoart Foundry, Dresden, 1959.
Faust I and *Faust II* (Goethe) book designs, for Verlag der Kunst, Dresden, 1961.
Clarendon Neutra typeface, for Typoart Foundry, Dresden, 1965.
Totentanz von Basel (Grieshaber) book design, for Verlag der Kunst, Dresden, 1966.
Prillwitz-Antiqua typeface, for Typoart Foundry, Dresden, 1971.
Marx-Engels Gesamtausgabe book design, for Dietz Verlag, East Berlin, from 1972.
Garamond-Russisch typeface, for Typoart Foundry, Dresden, 1975.

Publications:

By KAPR: books (as author an designer)— *Deutsche Schriftkunst,* Dresden 1955, 1965; *Johann Neudörffer: Der grosse Schreibmeister der deutschen Renaissance,* Leipzig 1956; *Fundament zum rechten Schreiben,* Leipzig 1958; *Buchgestaltung,* Dresden 1963; *Schriftkunst: Geschichte, Anatomie und Schönheit der lateinischen Buchstaben,* Dresden 1971, 1976, 1983; *Hundertundein Sätze zur Buchgestaltung,* Leipzig 1973, 1976; *Typoart-Typenkunst,* with Hans Fischer, Leipzig 1973; *Gestaltung und Funktion der Typografie,* with Walter Schiller, Leipzig 1977, 1980, 1983; *Johannes Gutenberg,* Leipzig 1977; *Ästhetik der Schriftkunst,* Leipzig 1979; *Buchkunst der Gegenwart: Thesen und Marginalien,* Leipzig 1979; *Schrift- und Buchkunst,* Leipzig 1982; *Stationen der Buchkunst,* Leipzig 1984.

On KAPR: books—*Who's Who in Graphic Art,* edited by Walter Amstutz, Zurich 1962, Dubendorf 1982; *The Art of Written Forms* by Donald M. Anderson, New York 1969; *Gebrauchsgraphik in der DDR* by Helmut Rademacher, Dresden 1975.

Ever since my youth, I have felt myself drawn to type and book design. My first activity for the press consisted of an illegal pamphlet, which was directed against Hitler's war preparations.

I have Professor Ernst Schneidler—who headed the chair for typography and commercial art at the Akademie für Bildende Künste in Stuttgart—to thank for my artistic training.

During my more than thirty years of work in Leipzig, I have seen as my primary purpose to promote the good tradition of a center of publishing as well as to educate a particular breed of excellent book and type designer. The typeface, as an important element of every book, must even in its mature form, become more highly developed for still better readability and expression of modern times. Computers, now used in the development of type and in type

Albert Kapr: Book cover in *Leipziger Antiqua* typeface, for Fachbuchverlag Leipzig, 1982

manufacture, must not be allowed to become dictators of the technocrats and media concerns. The new technological advances in the production of books and journals must be governed by the needs of mankind, as well as by aesthetic sensibilities, and so governed that the moral and social progress of the culture is not hindered, but rather, advanced. Books earn more material support than the bomb, and require more ingenuity than advertisements for consumer goods and merchandise. Books, as a form and symbol of human culture, its technical and aesthetic quality, must be defended and be kept alive by creativity and intelligence.

—Albert Kapr

KARAN, Donna/DELL'OLIO, Louis.

American fashion designers. Donna Karan: born Donna Faske, in Forest Hills, New York, 2 October 1948. Studied at Parsons School of Design, New York. Married the menswear manufacturer Mark Karan; daughter: Gabrielle. Assistant designer, Anne Klein and Company, and Addenda Company, New York, 1966–68; designer, 1968–71, associate designer, 1971–74, and director of design in association with Louis Dell'Olio, from 1974, Anne Klein and Company, New York. Louis Dell'Olio: born in New York City, 23 July 1948. Studied at Parsons School of Design, New York, 1966–69: Normal Norell Scholarship, 1968. Assistant to designer Dominic Rompello, at Teal Traina, New York, 1969–71; chief designer, for the Georgini division of Originals, New York, 1971–74; director of design in association with Donna Karan, at Anne Klein and Company, New York, from 1974. Recipients: Coty Awards, New York, 1977, 1981. Members: Fashion Designers of America. Address: Anne Klein and Company, 205 West 39th Street, New York, New York 10018, U.S.A.

Publications:

On KARAN/DELL'OLIO: books—*The World of Fashion: People, Places, Resources* by Eleanor Lambert, New York and London 1976; *The Fashion Makers* by Bernardine Morris, New York 1978; *Fairchild's Who's Who in Fashion*, edited by Ann Stegemeyer, New York 1980; *Fashion 2001* by Lucille Khornak, London 1982; *The Collector's Book of Twentieth Century Fashion* by Frances Kennett, London and New York 1983; *McDowell's Director of Twentieth Century Fashion* by Colin McDowell, London 1984; *The Encyclopaedia of Fashion from 1840 to the 1980s* by Georgina Howell, London 1986.

The clothes created by Donna Karan and Louis Dell'Olio last not just for a season but for years. Like Anne Klein herself, with whom Karan was co-designer between 1971 and 1974, they do not believe in change for its own sake. While change is necessary, it occurs as a logical and gradual development in their work. The range of separates which they design today—interrelating skirts, blazers, pants, and shirts, and long, slim evening dresses—has changed little from those produced when Klein was alive. The lines are classic, but they have been subtly updated to suit the lifestyle of sophisticated, active women in the 1970s and 1980s.

The argyle sweater has grown to hip-length, its pattern has become larger and bolder, and it has been teamed with a slimline skirt, trilby hat, and gauntlet gloves. Their garments are deliberately understated to suit the needs of the wearer.

Karan and Dell'Olio have succeeded in making Anne Klein one of the top names in American ready-to-wear, along with Calvin Klein, Ralph Lauren, and Perry Ellis, by creating clothes for real people. It is not only the lines themselves, but also the versatility of their collections and the quality of the fabrics, which give their garments a style that is more than mere short-lived fashion. Particularly concerned with fabrics for their own sake, they use them to provide the inspiration for the shape of a garment. By using soft suedes, crepe, and silks, they have transformed casual wear into something soft and sophisticated. The importance of the fabric is made evident by Takihyo's translations of them. Here, a different fabric can change the look, even though the style of Anne Klein still comes through.

Karan and Dell'Olio are in touch with their times but believe in quality and longevity in fashion. The furs that they design for Michael Forrest can be seen as investments, but so can all their work. Casual dressing is the strong fashion force of the present and future, and Karan and Dell'Olio together lead the field with their uncluttered, classic lines. They continue the major contribution which American fashion designers have made to casual and sportswear since the 1950s.

—Hazel Clark

KATAYAMA, Toshihiro.

Japanese artist, environmental, exhibition and graphic designer. Born in Osaka, 17 July 1928. Self-taught in design. Married Atsumi Fukui in 1960. Designer, at the Japan Design Center, Tokyo, and at Geigy AG, Basel, 1963–66; freelance designer, establishing Atsumi & Toshihiro Katayama design office, in Arlington, Massachusetts, and in Tokyo, from 1966. Senior lecturer, Carpenter Center for the Visual Arts, Harvard University, Cambridge, Massachusetts, from 1966. **Exhibitions:** Herman Miller Showrooms, Basel, 1965; Galerie ABC, Winterthur, 1965; Galerie Aktuell, Bern, 1965; Herman Miller Showrooms, Zürich, 1966; American Institute of Graphic Arts, New York, 1968; Cooper and Beatty Gallery, Toronto, 1968; Gallery Plaza DIC, Tokyo, 1970; Harvard Graduate School of Design, Cambridge, Massachusetts, 1971; Brandeis University, Waltham, Massachusetts, 1971; Künstlerhaus, Vienna, 1977; Nantenshi Gallery, Tokyo, 1978, 1980, 1983, 1986; Sogetsu Kaikan, Tokyo, 1981; Clark Gallery, Lincoln, Massachusetts, 1982. **Collections:** Municipal Museum, Tokyo; Seibu Museum of Art, Tokyo; Municipal Museum, Toyama; Municipal Museum, Osaka; Museum of Modern Art, New York; Rose Art Museum, Brandeis University, Waltham, Massachusetts; Harvard Graduate School of Design, Cambridge, Massachusetts; Künstlerhaus, Vienna; Staatsgalerie, Stuttgart. Addresses: 16 Mystic Bank, Arlington, Massachusetts 02174, U.S.A.; 5-18-9 Inokashira, Mitaka-Shi, Tokyo 181, Japan.

Works:

Gund Hall banners, for Harvard Graduate School of Design, 1972.
Star mural and signage at State Street Station, for the Boston Subway, 1975 (with WFE Architects).
Josep Lluis Sert, Architect to the Arts exhibition layouts, for the Carpenter Center, Harvard University, 1978.
Midnight mural and environmental graphics, for Cronkhite Graduate Center, Radcliffe College, 1979.
Environmental graphics and signage at Alewife Station, for the Boston Subway, 1980 (with EMA Architects).
Rainbow Elevator graphics and marble Grand Floor, for the Sinjuku N.S. Building, Tokyo, 1982 (with Nikken Sekkei Architects).
Homage to the Crystal wall sculpture, for the Akasaka Prince Hotel, Tokyo, 1983 (with Kenzo Tange and Urtec Architects).
Reliefs, murals and environmental design, for Taisho Marine and Fire Insurance Company, Tokyo, 1984 (with Nikken Seiki Architects).
T sculpture-sign at Alewife Station, for the Boston Subway, 1985 (with EMA Architects).
Plaza, restaurant and fountain, for the Toho Company headquarters, Yuraku-Cho, Tokyo, 1985–87 (with Takenaka Construction Company).
Scarpitta: Recent Painting exhibition poster, for Carpenter Center, Harvard University, 1986.
Plaza and tapestries, for the Ohmiya Cultural Center, Tokyo, 1986–88 (with Nikken Seiki Architects).
Le Corbusier exhibition poster, for the Carpenter Center, Harvard University, 1987.
1988 calendar, for the Seibu Museum of Art, Tokyo, 1987.
1989 calendar, for the Seibu Museum of Art, Tokyo, 1988.
Poster design, for First Night, Boston, 1988.

Publications:

By KATAYAMA: books—*Twelve Persons in Graphic Design Today,* with others, Tokyo 1968; *Visual Poetry: 3 Notations/Rotations,* with Octavio Paz, New York 1974.

On KATAYAMA: books—*Who's Who in Graphic Art,* edited by Walter Amstutz, Zurich 1962, Dubendorf 1982; *Modern Graphics* by Keith Murgatroyd, London 1969; *The Work of Toshi Katayama,* with texts by Kenzo Tange, Josep Lluis Sert and others, Tokyo 1980.

There are no brushes or paints on my work desk. There is a scalpel. The rest are sharpened pencils and Kern drafting instruments. Instead of paints, I have at most eight different Color-aid papers. It would not be an exaggeration, therefore, to say that practically all my works have been produced with this Swiss surgical knife.

Actually, I do have brushes and paints. I put them, however, as far away as possible from my work desk, where I cannot find them. If they are not going to be used, they might as well be thrown away, but having them provides a feeling of security, much like having cold medicine on hand just in case; in fact there are occasions when I do use them, so I cannot throw them away. I keep them where I cannot see them to strengthen my will. I am afraid of having to have brushes and paints, a camera, countless books, and, on top of that, a number of collaborators to get work done. By not having brushes and paints and assistants—or rather, by not using them—I limit what I can do. By this I try to clarify what I am capable of doing and what my creative work, in a true sense, is.

Toshi Katayama: *Hommage to the Crystal* wall sculpture in stainless steel, for the Akasaka Prince Hotel, 1983

Recently I have come to believe that there are two types of creative processes, the positive and the negative. In the positive process, a person will collect as much information and as many tools as he can and then work with numerous collaborators. I work, however, by a negative process. The more I seek a purity of approach, the deeper I enter this negative world. I have come to respect the artist with his single-minded devotion to his own world more than the designer accustomed to doing group work. Superficially, it is true that the more one limits oneself, the fewer opportunities there seem to be; when the will is weak, the greater this feeling is. One must be patient. When the work is not going smoothly, one must try to keep one's will strong. Luckily, fate handed me this knife.

I came upon the knife in the spring of 1963 in Basel, Switzerland where I had been invited by Geigy AG and where I was to spend three years; in fact, it was on the day that I started work for Geigy. Designers put down their scalpels, which I had never seen or considered using in Japan, and shook hands with me. As I smiled, not being able to speak German or even English, my eyes were attracted strangely to the surgical knives. It was almost like being stabbed by them. In that moment I realized how the Swiss graphic designers, whom I had admired for a long time, were able to produce works of such quality and precision. From the knives I was able to intuit their source.

Men make tools, and tools may come to life depending on who uses them; tools accentuate a person's character. An artist ought to possess a tool he can call his own. If possible he should create it himself. Unless he creates his own tool or discovers a new material, it may be that no truly creative work is possible.

—Toshi Katayama

In recent years, much of Toshi Katayama's impressive work has been done not in his capacity as a designer, but rather as an individual artist. His painting exhibitions, which occur almost yearly, evidence this, as do his architectural wall reliefs.

For Katayama, life and design activities in Switzerland may have been ascetic and constricting, for after he arrived in the United States, he came to incorporate into his works, a freehand line and accidental form, such as that which is achieved with the Japanese ink technique.

Thus, Katayama, who has expressed geometric form perceptively and meticulously, may be seen to be attempting a freer mode of expression. His problem henceforth will be the extent to which is able to bring clarity and perfection to these works.

—Shukuro Habara

KEMÉNY, György.
Hungarian graphic designer. Born in Budapest, 25 May 1936. Apprentice in the poster design studio of Pal Gabor, Budapest, 1954–55; studied painting and design, at the Hungarian Academy of Art, Budapest, 1956–61. Freelance painter, environmental artist and graphic designer, Budapest, since 1964: art director, *Interpress* magazine, Budapest, from 1975. **Exhibitions:** Feszek Artists' Club, Budapest, 1968; Club Bercsenyi, Budapest, 1971; Galleri Kirjavintii, Helsinki, 1971; Blue Chapel, Balatonboglar, 1975; Mucsarnok Exhibition Hall, Budapest 1982; Little Gallery, Pecs, 1987. **Collections:** Hungarian National Gallery, Budapest; Museum Petofi, Budapest; Wilanow Poster Museum, Warsaw; Musée de l'Affiche, Paris. Recipient: Silver Medal, Casalecchio di Reno Poster Competition, 1969, 1971; Warsaw International Poster Competition Prize, 1975; Toyama Poster Triennale Prize, 1985; New York Art Directors Club Merit Awards, 1987, 1988. Address: Fodor utca 86, 1124 Budapest, Hungary.

Works:

Marat/Sade poster, for the National Theatre, Budapest, 1966.
Pretty Girls, You Musn't Cry film poster, for Mokep, 1971.
Too Much Drink Is Poison poster, for the National Alcoholism Prevention Committee, 1971.
Dodeskaden film poster, for Mokep, 1971.
Bumm record sleeve, for LGT Group, 1972.
Football of Old Times film poster, for Mokep, 1972.
Seven Dutch Artists exhibition poster, for the Mucsarnok Exhibition Hall, Budapest, 1977.
Le Cinema Hongrois exhibition layouts at the Centre Georges Pompidou, Paris, for Hungarofilm, 1979.
Saint George and the Dragon poster, for the National Theatre, Budapest, 1979.
Studio 80 television special environment, for Miklos Jancso, 1980.
Cabaret film poster, for Mokep, 1980.
Fiction and Objectivity exhibition poster, for Galerie Budapest, 1981.
Fact-Picture exhibition layouts and poster, for the Mucsarnok Exhibition Hall, Budapest, 1981.
101 Years of Hungarian Posters exhibition layouts and poster, for the Mucsarnok Exhibition Hall, Budapest, 1986.
Season of Monsters film poster, for Mokep, 1987.
Hanussen film logo and poster, for Mokep and Hungarofilm, 1988.
Mikyprint logo, for a silkscreen firm, Budapest, 1988.

Publications:

On KEMÉNY: books—*Muveszeti Kislexikon,* edited by Edit Latja, Budapest 1973; *Szora Birt Mutermek* by Janos Frank, Budapest 1975; *Fiuk-Lanyok Konyve* by Judit Fekete, Budapest 1976; articles—in *Graphis* (Zurich), no. 192, 1977; *Graphic Design* (Tokyo) December 1978; *Muveszet* (Budapest), April 1982, January 1986; *New Hungarian Quarterly* (Budapest), Summer 1983; *Creation* (Paris), February 1988.

In the previous edition of the present book I wrote very pessimistic sentences about the design's situation and its future prospects. It was reasonable at that time because economical recession was a characteristic phenomena all around the world, the tension between the two world systems seemed to culminate in a new, horrible world war. With the exception of some examples, design and aestheticism played an unimportant and overshadowed role everywhere. If I think of the recent past I remember bitterly that the most brilliantly designed objects of that period were actually the American and West European fighter planes.

However, there were unexpected changes in the last years such as the powerful economic development in numerous countries from Singapore to Turkey, fantastic technologies were set up in the world, and a part of the Eastern European block—containing the Soviet Union and my country as well—seem to move out from the deep political, economical and intellectual crisis. The growing activity of designers and graphic artists can be seen again all over the world involving Hungary, too. New commissions and claims appeared: up-to-date buildings, trendy dresses or the very emblems of new firms are born not only in New York but also in Budapest, though weaker in numbers. Satellites can broadcast even to Hungary the programs of different West European TV channels that contain, amongst others, aesthetical informations just like the traditional mediums of cultural exchanges: books, magazines, exhibitions. Our projects and designs can also be seen at other countries' exhibitions, in their books and magazines. I think that over and above politicians, scientists, engineers, it is the turn of us, designers—in the broadest sense of the word: artists—to come up mostly to requirements of the great challenge, to welcome worthily the new millennium. I can registrate again only the momentary situation: I am optimistic, I work.

—György Kemény

In all György Kemény's graphic compositions, in his posters, bookjackets, illustrations, record covers, and other contributions to mass media, an attentive observer can discern the imprint of the time and place of their origin. Certainly, his design is different from what is customary in the developed countries of the West, not so much in the formal aspect of his design as in his approach to reality. By selecting certain means and forms of communication, this Hungarian designer reveals a broad scale of moods and emotions, such as violence, pain, anger, hope, and despair, as his way of reacting to certain phenomena and events. Showing his disdain for estheticism, for a smooth, adorned picture of the world, he does not conceal his liking for certain models of mass or youth culture.

Under a thin layer of internationalism, it is easy to notice the national origin of Kemény's interests. He cannot and probably does not want to reject the burden of tradition because history, like geopolitics, is always present in this part of Europe. The quality of Kemény's design would be difficult to appreciate without regard for these conditions, restrictions, and suppressions, and so it is necessary to keep in mind the history and difficult experiences of the society and the individuals living in his country.

During the international poster competition organized in commemoration of the thirtieth anniversary of victory over fascism, Kemény shared the first prize. Presenting the story of his own World War II experience, when he faced evil and violence as a small boy, his poster shows two photographs taken from a family album; one depicts the face of nine-year-old György, and the second, György as a young man. Next to the pictures there is a typewritten text which is quoted here in full, as it is the most authentic testimony:

Gyorgy Kemény: Trade mark for the Mikyprint silkscreen company, 1988

I am György Kemény. I live in Budapest as a graphic designer. I work as everybody does. Thirty years ago, I was a Jewish boy of nine. My parents put me in an asylum to save my life. There, I was once shot at, but the bullet missed me. Next, I was taken to a mass execution at the river Danube, but an air raid dispersed my would-be murderers. When liberation came, I weighed thirty-four pounds. My mother still starts crying when remembering this. Today I live in Budapest. I am a graphic designer, and I work like everybody else.

There are very few similar examples of confession by means of the poster.

Although the author operates with a contemporary visual language and conventions that originated in conceptualism, yet he belongs among those Hungarian artists who in the past used mass prints as a tool of their individual, personal expressions. This is a group of expressionists—Bíró, Berény, Jeges, Pór, Uitz, as well as Kassak and Bortnyik. The participants in the big movement of Hungarian activism, they are the avant-garde, concentrated around the magazine *MA,* and associating themselves with new art in Europe, with Russian constructivism and Dutch neo-graphicism.

Kemény's preference for form which is flat, two-dimensional, rough, and expressionistic, has its source in the national tradition. His drawing, often in pencil or in feather-pen, exposes the brutal and almost praises the ugliness and aggressiveness of things surrounding us.

Plainness and negligence in Kemény's work are used to challenge the consumer ideal. In this respect, he refers to the esthetics of ugliness that was so popular in the period of the youth anti-culture, in the "underground" prints in England and the United States in the 1960s. These features are clearly evident in his record-cover designs made for the Hungarian producers of "pop music" (Lokomotiv). At that time under the strong influence of American Pop art, Kemény tried to transplant it to Hungarian territory. He did so with grace and talent, but it was for him a temporary and superficial artistic adventure.

—Szymon Bojko

KENZO.
Japanese fashion designer, Born Kenzo Takada, in Tokyo, 27 February 1939. Worked as a pattern designer, *Soen* magazine, Tokyo, 1960–64; freelance fashion designer, Paris, from 1965: established Jap boutique, Paris, 1970. Addresses: 3 Place des Victoires, 75001 Paris, France; 824 Madison Avenue, New York, New York 10021, U.S.A.

Publications:

On KENZO: books—*A History of Fashion* by J. Anderson Black and Madge Garland, London 1975, 1980; *The Changing World of Fashion: 1900 to the Present* by Ernestine Carter, London 1977; *In Fashion: Dress in the Twentieth Century* by Prudence Glynn, London 1978; *The Guinness Guide to 20th Century Fashion* by David Bond, Enfield 1981; *McDowell's Directory of Twentieth Century Fashion* by Colin McDow-

ell, London 1984; *The Conran Directory of Design,* edited by Stephen Bayley, London 1985; *The Encyclopaedia of Fashion from 1840 to the 1980s* by Georgina O'Hara, London 1986; *Japanese Design* by Penny Sparke, London 1987.

When Kenzo arrived in Paris in 1965, haute couture dominated fashion. Shocked by the perfection of the work of couturiers such as Dior, Cardin, and Chanel, Kenzo found his inspiration in the young people in the streets; for them, he began to create exciting, wearable clothes. By aiming at the new, young market which had become so apparent in the late 1960s, Jap led the explosion of ready-to-wear as the major influence from Paris in the 1970s.

Kenzo's work is witty, lively, and unpredictable. While he has been responsible for many innovations, it is virtually impossible to predict what he is going to do next. Soft, white cottons were followed by bright, school-girl tunics, which gave way to sombre, natural-coloured tweeds. His inspiration, drawn from all over, has captured or even preempted the mood of the times. It was he who, in 1973, introduced the peasant folkloric types, which foreshadowed the "return to nature" later in the 1970s. His functional, survival clothing of 1974 predicted a move to days of harder economy. This ability to know what is right at the time, plus the spirit of adventure and a desire to cater to a wide, young market, made him a fashion leader.

Many influences are plainly apparent in Jap's collections. Russian peasants, Chinese coolies, tribal Africans, red Indians, swashbuckling pirates, Buster Keaton, and Charlie Chaplin have all been reflected in his work, which never ceases to astonish. But beneath these ephemeral, yet influential changes runs a powerful force—Japan. While his early sweaters and kimonos were clearly derivative, his uses of oversize and layers are more subtle appropriations of traditional roots. Kenzo's love of volume, as seen clearly in his balloon dresses, owes as great deal to Japanese costume, in which the shape of the body is of little concern. Likewise, this approach is also apparent when he uses five or six garments to create an outfit, often mixing colours and textures along the way. Colour and fabrics, which he designs himself, are his initial inspiration, and these wonderful textures and hues set a Jap original apart from a copy. Whilst price makes his typical customer the woman of thirty, his individual, light-hearted looks have been copied internationally for the young. Most recently, Kenzo's collections have been less crazy than before but no less exciting. He is a master of the unpredictable; strong colours, bold shapes (seen recently in his sculpturally constructed, wrap dresses), embroidered tweeds, mixed plaids and stripes, frills, and layers all bear witness to this. Kenzo has shown that fashion as fun and fantasy can sell.

—Hazel Clark

KEPES, Gyorgy.
American painter, photographer, filmmaker, architectural, exhibition and graphic designer. Born in Selyp, Hungary, 4 October 1906; emigrated to the United States in 1937: naturalized, 1956. Studied under Istvan Csok, at the Academy of Arts, Budapest, 1924–28: MA 1928. Married Juliet Appleby in 1937; children: Juliet and Imre. Independent painter and filmmaker,

associating with the Munka Art Group, Budapest, 1929–30; freelance designer and teacher, working in Berlin, 1930–32, 1934–36, in London, 1936–37, in Chicago and New York, 1938–45, and in Cambridge, Massachusetts, from 1946: design consultant, to Travelers Insurance Company of Los Angeles, Container Corporation of America, Abbot Laboratories, *Fortune* magazine, etc., 1938–50. Head of the light and color department, New Bauhaus School (later, Institute of Design), Chicago, 1938–43; professor of design, North Texas State College, Denton, and Brooklyn College, New York, 1943–45; professor of visual design, 1946–66, founder-director of the Center for Advanced Visual Studies, 1967–70, and Institute professor, 1970–74, Massachusetts Institute of Technology, Cambridge; also visiting lecturer and professor at colleges and universities throughout the United States, from 1939. **Exhibitions:** Katherine Kuh Gallery, Chicago, 1939; Art Institute of Chicago, 1944; Currier Gallery of Art, Manchester, New Hampshire, 1951; San Francisco Museum of Art, 1952, 1954; Cranbrook Academy of Art, Bloomfield Hills, Michigan, 1954; Stedelijk Museum, Amsterdam, 1955; Everson Museum of Art, Syracuse, New York, 1957; Dallas Museum of Fine Arts, 1957, 1959; Baltimore Museum of Art, 1959; Massachusetts Institute of Technology, Cambridge, 1959, 1978; Houston Museum of Fine Arts, 1959; Phoenix Art Museum, Arizona, 1966; Phillips Exeter Academy, New Hampshire, 1967; Museum of Science, Boston, 1973; Künstlerhaus, Vienna, 1976; Mucsarnok Exhibition Hall, Budapest, 1976; Bauhaus-Archiv, West Berlin, 1977; International Center of Photography, New York, 1984. **Collections:** Museum of Modern Art, New York; Rhode Island School of Design, Providence; Boston Museum of Fine Arts; Art Institute of Chicago; San Francisco Museum of Modern Art; Massachusetts Institute of Technology, Cambridge; National Museum of Fine Arts, Budapest; Bauhaus-Archiv, West Berlin. Recipient: American Institute of Graphic Arts Typography Award, 1947; Guggenheim Fellowship, New York, 1960; Silver Medal, Architectural League of New York, 1961; American Institute of Architects Fine Arts Award, 1968; College Art Association of American Distinguished Teaching Award, 1982. Fellow, Rhode Island School of Design; American Academy of Arts and Sciences; Academician, National Academy of Design; Member, Hall of Fame, Art Directors Club of New York; National Institute of Arts and Letters. Address: 90 Larchwood Drive, Cambridge, Massachusetts 02138, U.S.A.

Publications:

By KEPES: books—*Tul a Valon,* with Gyorgy Dan, Budapest 1925; *Language of Vision,* Chicago 1944; *Graphic Forms: The Art as Related to the Book,* Cambridge, Massachusetts 1949; *The New Landscape in Art and Science,* Chicago 1956; *The Education of Vision,* editor, New York 1965; *Structure in Art and Science,* editor, New York 1965; *The Nature and Art of Motion,* editor, New York 1965; *Light as a Creative Medium,* with Bernard I. Cohen, Cambridge, Massachusetts 1965; *Module, Symmetry, Proportion, Rhythm,* editor, New York 1966; *Sign, Image, Symbol,* editor, New York 1966; *The Man-Made Object,* editor, New York 1966; *The Center for Advanced Visual Studies,* Cambridge, Massachusetts 1967; *Arts of Environment,* editor, New York 1972; *El Arte y la Technologia,* Bogota 1973; *Gyorgy Kepes Kialliasa,* with an introduction by Eva Korner, Budapest 1976; *Portfolio of Photographs by Gyorgy Kepes,* with an introduction by Philip

Hofer, Boston 1977; *Gyorgy Kepes Irasai*, edited by Ferenc Bodri, Budapest 1978; *Gyorgy Kepes: The MIT Years 1945-1977*, with text by Judith Wechsler and Jan Van der Marck, Cambridge, Massachusetts 1978; *Gyorgy Kepes: Lightgraphics*, with text by Anne Hoy, New York 1984.

On KEPES: books—*Posters: 50 Artists and Designers*, edited by W. H. Allner, New York 1952; *Advertising Directions*, edited by Edward M. Gottschall and Arthur Hawkins, New York 1959; *Art as Design/Design as Art* by Sterling McIlhany, New York and London 1970; *Gyorgy Kepes: Works in Review*, exhibition catalogue with texts by O. Piene, R. Arnheim and others, Boston 1973; *The Language of Graphics* by Edward Booth-Clibborn and Daniele Baroni, London 1980; *A History of Graphic Design* by Philip B. Meggs, New York 1983; *An Introduction to Design and Culture in the Twentieth Century* by Penny Sparke, London 1986; *The American Design Adventure 1940-1975* by Arthur J. Pulos, London and Cambridge, Massachusetts 1988.

The importance of Gyorgy Kepes to design lies not only in his work as a designer, but in his teaching, in his leadership of interdisciplinary efforts, in his collaborative projects, and in his deep sense of the opportunities for serving human values through design. Working in Chicago from 1937 as a teacher and graphic designer, he had an electrifying impact because in his teaching and in his lively, innovative graphic designs, he explored the possibilities opened by recent developments in painting and photography as well as psychology. His exhibition designs explored ways of involving and educating the viewer, as was seen in his work on such diverse themes as *Close-up of Tintoretto* at the Art Institute of Chicago in 1942 and *Light as a Creative Medium*.

His projects for "civic art" move beyond individual experience to works on an epic scale, embodying a unified understanding. For instance, for an unrealized Boston Harbor project of 1964-65, Kepes designed a mile-long, luminous wall with programmed light modulations, interacting with mirrored buoys. These buoys recall a proposal Kepes made in Chicago during World War II, when he called for decoy lights floating in Lake Michigan to confuse pilots should there be an air attack.

Although Kepes had no direct connection with the German Bauhaus, he became part of the Bauhaus circle through his long associations with László Moholy-Nagy and Walter Gropius. Moreover, in his own work in his teaching, Kepes recalls the Bauhaus masters by his experimental approach and by his interests in group effort and in links between design and architecture on the one hand and the arts and sciences on the other. *Language of Vision*, a basic text in many schools for nearly forty years, has done more to spread Bauhaus educational methods than any other publication. Significantly, in 1982, Kepes received the annual "Distinguished Teaching of Art" award of the College Art Association.

The New Landscape and the earlier exhibition on the same theme constitute a bold attempt to expand the imagery familiar to designers and artists. The same kind of broad cooperation which Kepes elicited for that project also was required for the *Vision and Value* series, which includes individual volumes on such subjects as *The Education of Vision* (1965) and *Arts of the Environment* (1972), and for the Center for Advanced Visual Studies, which was set up as a workshop where interdisciplinary and cooperative projects are undertaken on a continuing basis.

Commissions for collaboration with archi-

tects include faceted glass windows for St. Mary's Cathedral in San Francisco (1965), done with Pietro Belluschi, Luigi Nervi, and A. McSweeney, and a programmed light mural based on night aerial views of cities for the KLM office in New York City (1959, no longer in place), with L. L. Rado. The KLM mural, like the Boston Harbor project, recalls Kepes' experiences during World War II, when he flew over Chicago at night as part of his research to formulate recommendations for protecting the city through the use of camouflage. Kepes has also collaborated with Walter Gropius, W. W. Wurster, Karl Loch, Welton Beckett, and other architects.

Throughout his career Kepes has also been active as an artist, from the paintings he made as a youth through photographs and multimedia compositions of the 1930s and 1940s to his later paintings, characterized by tones and textures which suggest aspects of the natural landscape.

The social role of design and the arts has been central to Kepes' thinking since his youth, when he read the works of John Ruskin and William Morris and also became aware of social injustices inflicted on Hungarian peasants. His convictions were reinforced through his association with Lajos Kassak and other artists allied with the Hungarian political left.

—Lloyd C. Engelbrecht

KERZ, Leo.

German stage, film, exhibition and graphic designer. Born in Berlin, 1 November 1912. Studied at the Friedrich Ebert Oberrealschule, Berlin, 1928-32: BA 1932; Academy of Arts and Sciences, Berlin, 1933; also studied design with Bertholt Brecht, Laszlo Moholy-Nagy and Erwin Piscator, 1928-32, and with Traugot Mueller, 1930-33. Stage and film designer from 1932, television designer from 1949, and exhibition designer from 1955: worked for theatres in Berlin and Prague, 1932-37; founder, Pioneer Theatre, Johannesburg, 1937-42; art director, Pittsburgh Civic Light Opera Association, 1946-47, San Francisco Opera Association, and New York City Opera Company, 1956; staff designer, CBS Television, New York, 1949-54. Lecturer, University of Witwatersrand, Johannesburg, 1938-39, and New School for Social Research, New York 1943-44; visiting professor, Montana State University, Bozeman, 1964. Recipient: New York Music Critics Award, 1956; Outer Circle Award, 1961; United States Government Cultural Exchange Grant, 1963. *Died* (in New York City) *in 1976.*

Works:

Stage productions include—*The Threepenny Opera*, Pioneer Theatre, Johannesburg, 1938; *Miracle at Verdun*, Pioneer Theatre, Johannesburg, 1939; *Golden Boy*, Pioneer Theatre, Johannesburg, 1940; *The Cradle Will Rock*, Pioneer Theatre, Johannesburg, 1941; *The Hairy Ape*, Pioneer Theatre, Johannesburg, 1942; *The Rally of Hope*, Madison Square Garden, New York, 1946; *The Golden Doors*, Madison Square Garden, New York, 1946; *Antony and Cleopatra*, Martin Beck Theatre, New York, 1947; *A Long Way From Home*, Maxine Elliot's Theatre, New York, 1948; *Bravo*, Ly-

ceum, New York, 1948; *The Biggest Thief in Town*, Mansfield Theatre, New York, 1949; *The Gypsies Wore High Hats*, Cape Theatre, Dennis, Massachusetts, 1952; *The Victim*, President Theatre, New York, 1952; *The Sacred Flame*, President Theatre, New York, 1952; *Troilus and Cressida*, San Francisco Opera, 1954; *Macbeth*, San Francisco Opera, 1954; *Aida*, San Francisco Opera, 1955; *Lohengrin*, San Francisco Opera, 1955; *Der Rosenkavalier*, San Francisco Opera, 1956; *Parsifal*, Metropolitan Opera, New York, 1956; *The Magic Flute*, Metropolitan Opera, New York, 1956; *Landara*, Curtis Institute of Music, Philadelphia, 1956; *Orpheus in the Underworld*, New York City Center, 1956; *Susannah*, New York City Center, 1956; *The Tempest*, New York City Center, 1956; *Clerambard*, Rooftop Theatre, New York, 1957; *Listen to the Mockingbird*, Colonial Theatre, Boston, 1958 (toured); *Moonbirds*, Cort Theatre, New York, 1959; *Rhinoceros*, Longacre Theatre, New York, 1961; *Der Stellvertreter*, Theater am Kurfurstendamm, Berlin, 1963; films—*Extase* (Machaty), 1932; *Guilty Bystander* (Lerner), 1950; *Mr. Universe* (Lerner), 1951; *Teresa* (Zinnemann), 1951; *This is Cinerama*, 1952; *The Goddess* (Cromwell), 1958; *Middle of the Night* (Delbert Mann), 1959; *Odds Against Tomorrow* (Wise), 1959; *New York Confidential* (ABC Television), 1959; *In What America?* (television, for Esso World Theatre), 1964.

Publications:

On KERZ: books—*The Biographical Encyclopaedia and Who's Who of the American Theatre*, edited by Walter Rigdon, New York 1966; *Le Decor de Film* by Leon Barsacq, Paris 1970, as *Caligari's Cabinet and Other Grand Illusions*, Boston 1976.

When one tries to center on the core of Leo Kerz's work, one finds that the early influence of having worked with Irwin Piscator and Bertolt Brecht in Berlin left its mark on all his productions. Thus, he was always less interested in placing realistic or romantic facts on stage than in capturing how several enlarged and enhanced historical shapes could stand for an entire culture or how an open stage defined by a number of large set pieces could give direction and movement to a play or an opera's action. In many ways, he was a transitional figure in stage design, as he used historic information from the romantic and symbolist past but without stressing fuzzy mood and emotional feeling. He was more interested in giving size, movement, character definition, and spatial clarity to the scene, while allowing a few broad images to carry the weight of the historical or emotional action of the play or opera. For example, in his first Broadway production, *Antony and Cleopatra*, he created a great bank of Egyptian columns across the stage; against and within these, he created the play's scenes with a minimal use of properties and accessories.

Following the lead of his teacher, Piscator, he also made great use of films and projections when they seemed appropriate, used a constructivist methodology to define space and give definition to actor-movement, and made great use of texture as an integral and yet autonomous element in a stage setting. Thus, he combined the best of the past and present in the visual arts, using abstraction and spatial definition while still giving the audience a shorthand sense of place, time, and atmosphere. He also designed for industrial shows, pageants, and television and was a teacher at a number of United States schools and universities, where he spread the epic theatre theories of Piscator.

Though Kerz designed in all theatrical media

and may at first appear to have designed in all the artistic theatrical styles, with a little distance and perspective, one can say that his major contribution to theatrical scene design was to solidify, modify, and spread the visual ideals of epic theatre.

—Douglas A. Russell

KHANH, Emmanuelle.

French fashion designer. Born Renée Mezière, in Paris, 12 September 1937. Married the designer Quasar Khanh (Manh Khanh Nguyen) in 1957; children: Othello and Atlantique-Venus. Worked as a mannequin, for the fashion houses of Balenciaga and Givenchy, Paris, 1957–63; creator of collections for Belletete, Missoni, Dorothée Bis, Laura, Cacharel, Pierre d'Alby, Krizia, Max Mara, and Le Bistrot du Tricot, in Paris, 1963–69; founder-director, Emmanuelle Khanh fashion design company, Paris, from 1971. Address: Emmanuelle Khanh International, 39 Avenue Victor Hugo, 75116 Paris, France.

Publications:

On KHANH: books—*Fairchild's Dictionary of Fashion,* edited by Charlotte Calasibetta, New York 1975; *In Vogue: Sixty Years of Celebrities and Fashion,* edited by Georgina Howell, London 1975, 1978, New York 1976; *A History of Fashion* by J. Anderson Black and Madge Garland, London 1975, 1980; *The World of Fashion: People, Places, Resources* by Eleanor Lambert, New York and London 1976; *In Fashion: Dress in the Twentieth Century* by Prudence Glynn, London 1978; *Fairchild's Who's Who in Fashion,* edited by Ann Stegemeyer, New York 1980; *McDowell's Directory of Twentieth Century Fashion* by Colin McDowell, London 1984; *The Encyclopaedia of Fashion from 1840 to the 1980s* by Georgina O'Hara, London 1986.

The look that Emmanuelle Khanh created in the 1960s can be placed between the styles being inspired by the new London designers and those of Parisian couturiers such as Yves Saint Laurent. It was her beautifully produced, youthful garments which foreshadowed the rise of ready-to-wear as a real threat, in the 1970s, to the dominance of haute couture. Skillful cutting, seaming, the use of innovative detail, such as the petal and "spaniel's ears" collars, and a preference for natural fabrics have continued to distinguish her personal style. Hers is a young, classical image which has ranged from updated versions of the trench coat and the two-piece suit to the jaunty "Jules and Jim" caps and knickerbockers of the early 1960s. By the late 1960s, she had made an impact well beyond Paris and had developed her range to include knitwear, ski-wear, and the light, natural underwear which was important for the young look.

Despite the range of her designs, Khanh has created a predominantly feminine style, which epitomises her own relationship with clothes. The fact that she began her career in the fashion world as a model for such prominent houses as Balenciaga and Givenchy meant that she has been able, personally, to promote her new ideas, such as the show-stopping shorts of 1971. The fact that she wears her own designs has led her to concentrate on comfort, freedom of movement, looseness, and the draping of fabric to produce individual yet essentially wearable garments.

Her individuality does not mean isolation, however, for she is also involved with cooperative design projects as part of a closely knit team. Quasar Khanh, her husband and business associate, is an interior designer who also designs Quasar menswear, while his sister Be Khanh is a textile fashion coordinator. A business partnership with her friend Aimer Bruno led to the organisation of a firm which specialised in the use of Rumanian hand embroideries and then to the fashion firm Emmanuelle Khanh/-CINEC. This most recent use of hand embroidery on her dresses continues the emphasis on detail seen even in her earliest work.

As a female designer, Khanh works for an ideal of woman which she herself personifies. She has become a classic ready-to-wear designer whose attention to the specific, such as jewel-like effects by means of beading, marks her personal style.

—Hazel Clark

KIESER, Gunther.

German stage, exhibition, industrial and graphic designer. Born in Kronberg, 24 March 1930. Studied lithography and commercial design, at the Werkkunstschule, Offenbach am Main, 1947–50. Freelance designer, with Hans Michel, in Michel + Kieser design studio, Offenbach, 1950–63; established own design studio, in Frankfurt, from 1964: has designed for Concertbüro Lippman und Rau, R. Schulte-Bahrenberg, J. von Hasselt, Berliner Festwochen, Hessischer Rundfunk, Sudwest Rundfunk, Frankfurt Opera, etc. Instructor in lettering, College of Fine Arts, Frankfurt, from 1957; professor of communications design, Bergische Universität, Wuppertal, from 1980. **Exhibition:** Lincoln Center, New York, 1972. **Collections:** Museum of Modern Art, New York; Royal Ontario Museum, Toronto. Recipient: Best German Poster Award, 1956, 1957, 1958, 1959; Photokina Award, Cologne, 1958; New York Art Directors Club Award, 1966; Gold Medal, 1968, and Silver Medal, 1984, Warsaw Poster Biennale; Toulouse Lautrec Gold Medal, Essen Poster Triennale, 1982; Grand Prix, Lodz Jazz Poster Salon, 1985; Gold Medal, Brno Poster Biennale, 1986. Member: Alliance Graphique Internationale; Deutsche Werkbund; Berufsverband Bildenden Künstler, Munich. Address: Gunthers-burgallee 81, 6000 Frankfurt am Main 60, West Germany.

Publications:

On KIESER: books—*Who's Who in Graphic Art,* edited by Walter Amstutz, Zurich 1962, Dubendorf 1982; *Illustration: Aspects and Directions* by Bob Gill and John Lewis, London 1964; *The Poster: An Illustrated History from 1860* by Harold F. Hutchinson, London and Toronto 1968; *Graphis Record Covers,* edited by Walter Herdeg, Zurich, 1974; *Album Cover Album,* edited by Storm Thorgerson and Roger Dean, Limpsfield 1979.

KIMURA, Kazuo.

Japanese industrial designer. Born in Osaka, 24 July 1934. Studied at Tokyo University of Arts, 1954–58: BFA 1958. Married Seiko Kimura; son: Mitsuhiro. Chief designer, at Nissan Motor Company, Tokyo, 1958–72; freelance designer, Osaka, from 1972. Kyoto Conference Committee Member, 1972–74, and vice-president from 1980, ICSID International Council of Societies of Industrial Design; executive secretary, Japan Industrial Designers Association, from 1974; secretary general, Japan Design Foundation, from 1980. Contributor, *Industrial Design, Nikkei Architecture* and *Design Age* magazines, Tokyo. Address: c/o Japan Design Foundation, Senba Center Building no. 4, 2-2 Senba Chuo, Higashi-ku, Osaka 541, Japan.

Publications:

By KIMURA: book—*ICSID 73: Official Report,* edited, Tokyo 1973.

On KIMURA: book—*The Language of Graphics* by Edward Booth-Clibborn and Daniele Baroni, London 1980.

Most of my recent work has been devoted invisibly to promotion and development of industrial design in Japan because, in view of the development of our environment for better or worse, the role and responsibilities of industrial design seem extremely important. Therefore, I have endeavored to form organizations that promote design activities, to advance public relations at both the national and international levels, and to establish other professional activities with the help of the Japan Industrial Designers' association in the hope that these may also relate to other fields of design.

—Kazuo Kimura

The contemporary Japanese design movement, which was initiated in the early 1950s, can be said to have comprised three stages: study and experimentation; an autonomous period of growth; and the current internationalist stance. Among the many designers who guided this development—off stage, as it were—is Kazuo Kimura.

For fifteen years, Kimura was Chief Designer for Nissan Motors. But he then changed course, and since the early 1970s, he has been prominent in the administration of design organizations—to which he has made very substantial contributions. Kimura has great self-confidence as a designer, and he tries to promote his own philosophy of the value of the "hand-made"—but he is also a diplomat, a man held in great affection by his peers, and, essential to an administrator, he is always open-minded.

The conference of the International Council of Societies of Industrial Design held in Kyoto in 1973 was the first such conference to take place outside of Europe or North America, and it was organized on a grand scale. The results of the conference provoked great discussion both in Japan and abroad; in fact, its theme of "mind/material" came to dominate design philosophies in the next decade. And it was Kimura who served as Secretary General of the organizing committee of the conference.

His career as a design administrator has evolved from that first success. He was appointed Executive Secretary of the Japan Industrial Designers Association and became the champion on industrial designers suffering from the problems of low economic growth.

Then, in 1980, Kimura was appointed Secretary-General of the Japan Design Foundation, which was established under the auspices of the Ministry of International Trade and Industry actively to organize various international programs. Thus, Kimura is responsible for providing opportunities to industrial designers in Japan and other countries to share information and exchange opinions: in effect, Japan, through the foundation, acts as a coordinator. In one sense, Japan until now has been a recipient of design information. From now on, it intends to be a disseminator as well, an active contributor to the world community of design. Kimura hopes that the Foundation's activities will provoke not only important symposia but also new movements in design.

At about the same time, Kimura was also appointed Vice-President of ICSID; his position as an internationalist was confirmed. In both of these posts, Kimura continues to display his great competence and his abiding commitment to design.

—Kunio Sano

KINNEIR, (Richard) Jock.
British graphic designer. Born in Aldershot, Hampshire, 11 February 1917. Studied at Chelsea School of Art, London, 1935–39. Freelance graphic designer, from 1945. Formerly, Head of graphic design, at the Royal College of Art, London, and visiting lecturer, Aarhus School of Architecture, Denmark. **Exhibition:** *107 Grafici dell'AGI,* Castello Sforzesco, Milan, 1974. Recipient: Council of Industrial Design Award, London, 1967. Member: Alliance Graphique Internationale. Address: Hope House, Winderton, Brailes, Banbury OX15 5JQ, England.

Publications:

By KINNEIR: book—*Words and Buildings,* London 1980; articles—in *Architectural Review* (London), May 1966, April 1978; *Arkitektur* (Copenhagen), no. 3, 1969; *The Designer* (London), November 1970; *Design and Art* (London), July 1983.

On KINNEIR: books—*Modern Graphics* by Keith Murgatroyd, London 1969; *107 Grafici dell'AGI,* with texts by Renzo Zorzi and Franco Grignani, Venice 1974; *Industrial Design in Britain* by Noel Carrington, London 1976; *The Thames and Hudson Manual of Typography* by Ruari McLean, London 1980.

One of the early jobs of Jock Kinneir's practice—a system of labelling for the P & O Company—exemplifies on a small scale the character of his major contributions. The design of the system, of sets of elements to be assembled according to stated rules, emerged as the visual elements took the form of a coding system for information that was first analysed and sorted. A set of labels was an outcome, but what had been designed, more fundamentally, was a system. So with the signing systems: their success has depended as much on the initial work of analysis and on the final work of formulating instructions for implementation as on the design of the particular visual elements employed. Another vital procedure has been testing and modifying prototypes, as the signing systems have been tested for legibility.

Kinneir's first alphabets—sanserif, upper- and lower-case—were not easily accepted, and a counter-proposal for the motorway signs, of a roman (seriffed) alphabet of capital letters only, was seriously entertained by some parties. One might now see the acceptance of the Kinneir letterforms and symbols as part of the belated arrival of the modern movement in Britain—and these were also the years of the vogue for "Swiss," sanserif typography. But their place in the environment has proved more assured than an explanation on mere grounds of taste would allow.

The success of the road signs in particular (the most complex of the various systems) lies in an avoidance of any unthinking formalism. And the system shows the benefits of considerable typographic sophistication, in such details as its use of brackets and indentation, as well as in forms of letters and numerals and (crucially) in spacing. The succession of the signing alphabets seems to show a broad development, allowing for the clearly different functions of each. The Gatwick and also the road alphabets have what may seem oddities in certain characters. These disappear in the rail alphabet, which is a more homogenous set of forms. The most recent alphabet, for the Tyne and Wear Metro, has slab serifs; it has been developed by Margaret Calvert as a typeface for printing (Monophoto Calvert).

That the signing systems designed by Kinneir's practice are now taken for granted by their users is one measure of the achievement. The work is ubiquitous and necessary. In all this, and in the manner in which the tasks have been tackled, this work represents a new level of maturity in British design.

—Robin Kinross

KIRK, Mark-Lee.
American film designer. Designer, working mainly with supervising art director Richard Day, for 20th Century-Fox Film Studios, Hollywood, 1936–40; art director, with RKO Studios, Hollywood, 1940–44, and, working with Lyle Wheeler, at 20th Century-Fox Studios, Hollywood, 1945–59. *Died.*

Works:

Films include—*Wake up and Live* (Lanfield), 1937; *Young Mr. Lincoln* (Ford), 1939; *Drums Along the Mohawk* (Ford), 1939; *The Grapes of Wrath* (Ford), 1940; *My Favorite Wife* (Kanin), 1940; *They Knew What They Wanted* (Kanin), 1940; *The Magnificent Ambersons* (Welles), 1942; *Journey Into Fear* (Foster and Welles), 1943; *I'll Be Seeing You* (Dieterle), 1944; *A Bell for Adano* (H. King) 1945; *A Royal Scandal* (Preminger), 1945; *Moss Rose* (Ratoff), 1947; *The Iron Curtain* (Wellmann), 1948; *The Prince of Foxes* (H. King), 1949; *Way of a Gaucho* (Tourneur), 1952; *Kangaroo* (Milestone), 1952; *White Witch Doctor* (Hathaway), 1953; *Prince Valiant* (Hathaway), 1954; *The Tall Men* (Walsh), 1955; *Prince of Players* (Dunne), *The Revolt of Mamie Stover* (Walsh), 1956; *Bus Stop* (Logan), 1956; *The Sun Also Rises* (H. King), 1957; *The Bravados* (H. King), 1958; *The Best of Everything* (Negulesco), 1959; *Compulsion* (Fleischer), 1959.

Publications:

On KIRK: book—*Le Décor de Film* by Leon Barsacq, Paris 1970, as *Caligari's Cabinet and Other Grand Illusions,* Boston 1976.

Mark-Lee Kirk's reputation rested on his atmospheric period reconstructions. However, this wealth of well researched details transcended mere documentary display. Facts served as tools for revealing deeper insights into character and theme. For such philosophical art direction, one usually turned to Kirk's contemporary, Richard Day. Since the two collaborated on Kirk's earliest motion pictures, Day presumably influenced Kirk. However, Kirk alone served as art director on that masterpiece of "symbolic realism," *The Magnificent Ambersons* (1942).

The Amberson mansion, as designed by Kirk, played a more potent role than any member of the film's cast. With its genteel charm and ominous horror, it served at times as a sanctuary from reality, while in other instances it played the prison, trapping its owners in a gilded cage. As an intimidating baronial estate, the mansion's opulent decor encompassed Gothic, Victorian, and Edwardian styles, all emblems of the ruling class.

Neither Tara from the 1939 *Gone With the Wind* nor *Rebecca*'s Manderlay of 1940 rivaled Kirk's vision of the mansion. Only *Citizen Kane*'s Xanadu, from 1941, came close. The Amberson mansion surpassed its inhabitants in visual power. Isabel might be paralleled to the house, particularly with a zealous Freudian interpretation (with Eugene struggling to enter the doors and son George refusing to leave them), but her weak character undercuts the comparison.

As the audience first enters the mansion, it is swept (via camera), along with the other invited guests, from room to room, to marvel at the Ambersons' sparkling treasures. To enhance that sense of presence, Kirk added the illusion of all four walls, an impressive detail few films would bother including. This technical trick gave the mansion further structural credibility.

Kirk also built in the mansion an unusual staircase for interesting compositional and expressive effects. Characters hover over each other from banister to banister in sadistic domination. In another situation, the staircase provides a simile, as George and Lucy strolling on the upper levels echo the elder generation on the main floor.

Thematically, *The Magnificent Ambersons* considered the transitory nature of man's world. Kirk demonstrated this early in the picture by disrupting an idyllic, Currier-and-Ives snow scene with such vestiges of civilization as telephone wires. This image, more than correct historically, was prophetic. Later, as the small, midwestern town burst with urban blight, its clutter contrasted with the now empty, tomb-like mansion.

Kirk created more than the documentation of days gone by. He drew beyond the backdrops of life's activities. Although few may recognize that a world exists outside its inhabitants and that this world influences us even as we assuredly alter it, Kirk's observations and interpretations of such environments added depth to his characters' cinematic surroundings.

—Edith Cortland Lee

KJAERHOLM, Poul.
Danish architect, furniture and ceramic de-

signer. Born in Øster Vra, 8 January 1929. Studied design, at the Konsthantverkskolan, Copenhagen, 1949–52. Married the architect Hanne Dam in 1953. Freelance designer, working with Thorald Madsen, Fritz Hansen, E. Kold Christiansen companies, etc., in Copenhagen, 1953–80. Instructor, at the Konsthantverkskolan, Copenhagen, 1952–56; instructor, 1955–76, and professor, 1976–80, at the Kunstakademie, Copenhagen. **Exhibitions:** *Neue Form aus Danemark,* toured Germany, 1956–59; *Formes Scadinaves,* Paris, 1958; *The Arts of Denmark,* the United States, 1960–61; Stedelijk Museum, Amsterdam, 1966; *Les Assises du Siège Contemporain,* Musée des Arts Decoratifs, Paris, 1968; *Modern Chairs 1918–1970,* Whitechapel Art Gallery, London, 1970; *Classics,* Heal's Furniture Store, London, 1981; *Scandinavian Modern Design 1880–1980,* Cooper-Hewitt Museum, New York, 1982; *Design Since 1945,* Philadelphia Museum of Art, 1983; *The Lunning Prize,* Nationalmuseum, Stockholm, 1986. **Collection:** Kunstindustrimuseet, Copenhagen. Recipient: Grand Prize, Milan Triennale, 1957, 1960; Danish Society of Applied Arts Annual Prize, 1957; Lunning Prize, Copenhagen, 1960; Knud V. Engelhardt Prize, Copenhagen, 1965; Brno Critics' Prize, 1968; Copenhagen Industrial Design Prize, 1973; Copenhagen Furniture Makers Association Prize, 1977. *Died* (in Hillerod, Denmark) *18 April 1980.*

Works:

Chair in chrome steel and linen, 1951, produced by E. Kold Christiansen, from 1957.
Coffee table in steel and marble, for E. Kold Christiansen, 1956.
Candle-holders in matt chromed steel, for E. Kold Christiansen, 1956.
Stackable tables in steel and acrylic, for E. Kold Christiansen, 1957.
Modular sectioned room-screen in pine, for E. Kold Christiansen, 1957.
Number 24 chaise longue in steel and wicker with leather neck-rest, for E. Kold Christiansen, 1958.
Number 9 chair in chrome steel and glassfibre with leather upholstery, for E. Kold Christiansen, 1960.
Model 91 folding stool in chrome steel and leather, for E. Kold Christiansen, 1961.
Number 20 recliner chair in steel and leather, for E. Kold Christiansen, 1968.
Seating system and chairs, for the Louisiana Concert Hall, Humlebaek, 1973.

Publications:

On KJAERHOLM: books—*Danish Chairs* by Nanna and Jorgen Ditzel, Copenhagen 1954; *Dansk Keramik,* edited by Bredo L. Grandjean, David Westholm and Arthur Hald, Stockholm 1960; *Modern Scandinavian Furniture* by Ulf Hard af Segerstad, Copenhagen 1963; *Contemporary Danish Design,* edited by Arne Karlsen, Bent Salicath and Mogens Utzon-Frank, Copenhagen 1966; *34 Scandinavian Designers* by Svend Erik Moller, Copenhagen 1967; *Modern Chairs 1918–1970,* exhibition catalogue by Carol Hogben and others, London 1970; *The Modern Chair: Classics in Production* by Clement Meadmore, London 1974; *Twentieth Century Furniture* by Philippe Garner, London 1980; *Danish Design 1980,* edited by Jens Bernsen and Per Mollerup, Copenhagen 1980; *Scandinavian Modern Design 1880–1980,* edited by David Revere McFadden, New York 1982; *Contemporary Furniture* by Klaus-Jürgen Sembach, London 1982; *Design Since 1945,* edited by Kathryn Hiesinger and George Mar-

cus, Philadelphia and London 1983; *Mid-Century: Furniture of the 1950s* by Cara Greenberg, London 1984; *Industrial Design: Unikate Serienzeugnisse* by Hans Wichmann, Munich 1985; *Design Source Book* by Penny Sparke, London 1986; *Modern Furniture Classics* by Miriam Stimpson, London 1987.

Almost invariably, discussions of Poul Kjaerholm's work compare it to Mies van der Rohe's. Certainly, there are points of likeness in the approaches of these two architects. Both exhibit that elegance which can result only when all excess is banished. In their furniture, both favor flat, rather than tubular, steel frames, and they relied on the subtle stitching of leather upholstery to reinforce form.

But there are differences as well. Mies's work, however classic it has become, evinces a Germanic gravity that binds it to the floor. Kjaerholm's pieces, on the other hand, are more lightly tethered, their clearly articulated joins and imaginatively profiled frames implying an upward thrust. In Mies's famous Brno chair, for example, the cantilevered support promises a springing motion, but this is visibly denied by the uncompromising angle of seat and back. In contrast, the seductive sling of Kjaerholm's Chair 20 (1968) works with the elasticity of its C-curved base even as it provides a visual complement.

Another illustration of their differences is the contrast between Mies's X-framed Barcelona stool and Kjaerholm's X-framed Stool 91. Both draw on a folding-furniture tradition which goes back to Egypt, if not beyond. In Mies's version, the supporting X is drawn with exquisite elegance and deception: the stool does not fold. Stool 91 offers its own, equally elegant X, the quarter-turns of its frame shimmering in the light and introducing a sensation of movement. To this sensory impact is joined function: the stool folds. In historical terms, one might say that in these pieces the designers exemplify aspects of the Classic tradition—Kjaerholm exhibiting the honesty of Greece; Mies, the illusion of Rome.

Kjaerholm's use of the International Style's signature material, metal, sets him apart from the majority of his Scandinavian peers, most of whom remained committed to wood before the advent of the stylistic challenge of the Italians in the 1960s. Remaining as independent of the resulting move to plastics as he had been of traditional woodcraft, Kjaerholm continued his perfection of a machine esthetic. However, both the linear purity of his designs and his exploration of the subtleties to be drawn from his material enhance, rather than challenge, the comfort of the user. Kjaerholm's work meets the criteria of intellectual and structural honesty developed in the early years of the International Style and brings them into correspondence with the realities of the human experience.

—Reed Benhamou

KLEIN, Anne.
American fashion designer. Born Hannah Golofsky, in Brooklyn, New York, 7 June 1923. Studied art, at the Girls' Commercial High School, Brooklyn, until 1937; Traphagen School of Fashion, New York 1937–38. Married Ben Klein (divorced, 1958); then Matthew Rubinstein. Worked as a designer, for Varden Petites, New York, 1938–40; designer of wom-

en's fashions, for Maurice Rentner, New York, 1940–47; founder and partner, with Ben Klein, of Junior Sophisticates fashion firm, New York, 1948–66; established Anne Klein Studio design and fashion consultancy firm, New York, 1965; founder, with Matthew Rubinstein, and president, of Anne Klein and Company, New York, 1968–74. Founder-member and trustee, Council of Fashion Designers of America. Recipient: *Mademoiselle* Merit Award, New York, 1954; Coty American Fashion Critics Winnie Award, 1955, 1969, and Hall of Fame Award, 1971; Neiman-Marcus Award, New York, 1959, 1969; Lord and Taylor Award, New York, 1964; National Cotton Council Award, New York, 1965. *Died* (in New York City) *19 March 1974.*

Publications:

On KLEIN: books—*The Fashionable Savages* by John Fairchild, New York 1965; *The World of Fashion: People, Places, Resources* by Eleanor Lambert, New York and London 1976; *Birds of Paradise* by Rose Hartman, New York 1980; *McDowell's Directory of Twentieth Century Fashion* by Colin McDowell, London 1984; *The Encyclopedia of Fashion from 1840 to the 1980s* by Georgina O'Hara, London 1986.

Anne Klein is as important an influence to the American look in women's clothes as Coco Chanel is to the French. "Breezy," "crystalline," "sharp," "fluid" are words most often used to define her designs. She first worked out clothing designs for the shorter-figured woman and then did much to erase the all-too-fussy look of junior-sized clothing. While at the same time not sacrificing its girlish quality. The Anne Klein look came to be a happy marriage of the advantages of sportswear with the sophistication of more formal attire. Her informal clothing, cut more sophisticatedly and enriched with well-chosen detail, never lost its active quality. Her formal ware is as relaxed as her casual wear (hooded jersey dresses for evening, as an example). The merchandizing of her clothing and related accessories that could be worn in variable combinations, presented in special Anne Klein Rooms in stores across the United States, made possible, and with ease, the complete look which has become somewhat of a standard. Her related separates—blazers, skirts, pants, sweaters—by a change of fabric, color, or detail have broken the barriers between casual and formal attire. Thus through her, a number of fashion's dictates lost their sting.

In a comparatively short career, Klein made a definite impact on womenswear. At a time when the social role of women was changing dramatically, she provided clothes that were designed to complement these changes.

—Harlan Sifford

KLEIN, Calvin (Richard).
American fashion designer. Born in the Bronx, New York, 19 November 1942. Studied at the Fashion Institute of Technology, New York, 1959–62. Married Jayne Centre in 1964 (divorced, 1974); daughter: Marci. Assistant designer, with Dan Millstein, New York, 1962–64; independent designer, New York,

from 1964: formed Calvin Klein fashion company, in partnership with Barry Schwartz, New York, from 1968. Visiting critic, Parsons School of Design, New York, and Fashion Institute of Technology, New York. Member of the Council of Fashion Designers, New York. **Collections:** Museum of Modern Art, New York; Guggenheim Museum, New York; Whitney Museum, New York. Recipient: Coty American Fashion Critics' Winnie Award, 1973, 1974, 1975, and Hall of Fame Award, 1975. Address: 205 West 39th Street, New York, New York 10018, U.S.A.

Publications:

By KLEIN: article—in *Mademoiselle* (New York), September 1979.

On KLEIN: books—*Fashion Merchandizing* by Mary D. Troxell, New York 1971, 1976; *The Changing World of Fashion: 1900 to the Present* by Ernestine Carter, London 1977; *Fairchild's Who's Who in Fashion,* edited by Ann Stegemeyer, New York 1980; *Magic Names of Fashion* by Ernestine Carter, London 1980; *The Collector's Book of Twentieth Century Fashion* by Frances Kennett, London and New York 1983; *McDowell's Directory of Twentieth Century Fashion* by Colin McDowell, London 1984; *The Conran Directory of Design,* edited by Stephen Bayley, London 1985; *The Encyclopedia of Fashion from 1840 to the 1980s* by Georgina O'Hara, London 1986; *Design Source Book* by Penny Sparke and others, London 1986.

Calvin Klein has created the "Classic American Look" in both men's and women's fashions and has had considerable success in bringing good design to the mass market. His unique approach has made him one of America's most influential designers. Many of his designs acknowledge American emphasis on physical fitness, as he has created clothes that fit the body in fabrics that "feel good against the skin." In the mid-1970s, Klein extended this emphasis by expanding his line to include make-up and skin care products, thus creating a total fashion approach.

When Klein began designing for women, he found that they no longer sought to assert liberation by wearing a pair of pants with a man-tailored jacket. Klein accommodated this shift by designing clothes that were more feminine. By 1978, the American woman had had enough of fashion gimmickery and over-designed clothes. She was interested, instead, in simple and comfortable styles, and Klein shifted his focus from soft blouses and gathered skirts to simple and tailored sportswear. The 1983 spring/summer collection, for example, succeeds in providing the American woman tailored suiting and an authoritative image without the loss of a feminine quality.

Klein is also important for bringing the look of designer clothes to the general market. The application of designer labels, instigated by Calvin Klein jeans, has flooded the mass clothing market from jeans to sheets and from infant clothing to high couture. Klein was responsible for bringing what only the rich could afford down to the masses, thereby opening the doors for other designers, such as Halston, recently designing for J. C. Penney, to participate in the mass clothing market.

Klein is one of a small group of designers who have shifted the focus away from Europe to develop sportswear into a distinctly American design classic. The Calvin Klein look, leaning toward informality and practicality, became the uniform of the 1970s and now the 1980s. European designers are looking at Klein and American merchandising techniques to learn about designing clothes for the "way we live."

—Teal Ann Triggs

KLEMKE, Werner.
German painter, illustrator, graphic and typographic designer. Born in Berlin, 12 March 1917. Educated in Berlin; mainly self-taught in design, from 1937. Worked as animated cartoon draughtsman, Berlin, 1935–39; freelance illustrator and graphic designer, in East Berlin, from 1945: designed books for publishers Siebholts, Ulenspiegel, Volk und Welt, Verlag Neues Leben, Verlag Volk und Wissen, Verlag Stichnote, Dietz Verlag, Verlag Rutten und Loening, Aufbau-Verlag, Verlag Tribune, etc.; also designed record sleeves from 1952. Lecturer in book illustration, 1950–56, and professor of design and typography from 1956, Hochschule für Bildende und Angewandte Kunste, Berlin-Weissensee. Permanent contributor, *Das Magazin* journal, East Berlin. Founder-member, Pirckheimer-Gesellschaft, Deutscher Künstlerbund, East Berlin, 1956. **Exhibitions:** Mexico City, 1956; Kleine Galerie, Hoyerswerda, 1977; Moscow, 1986; Leningrad, 1988. **Collections:** Nationalgalerie, East Berlin; Kupferstichkabinett, East Berlin; Kupferstichkabinett, Dresden. Recipient: DDR Drawing Medal, Berlin, 1954, 1958, 1964; Children's Book Prize, DDR Ministry of Culture, 1957, 1962; Gutenberg Prize, Leipzig, 1962; DDR National Prize, 1962, 1969, 7; Gold Award, Gesellschaft für Deutsche-Sowjetische Freundschaft, 1966. Honorary citizen of Certaldo, Italy; Honorary member, USSR Academy of Fine Arts; Member, DDR Akademie der Künste, Bund Deutscher Künstler, and Alliance Graphique Internationale. Address: Tassostrasse 21, 1120 Berlin-Weissensee, German Democratic Republic.

Works:

Books illustrated include—*Schelmufskis Reisebeschreibungen* by Charles Reuter, Munich 1952, 1954; *Gargantua* by Rabelais, Munich 1954; *Till Eulenspiegel,* East Berlin 1955; *Leben und Abenteuer des Martin Chuzzlewit* by Charles Dickens, East Berlin 1956; *Tagebuch aus China* by Bodo Uhse, East Berlin 1956; *Das Rollwagenbuchlein* by J. Wickram, 1956; *Schule des Humors* by J. Hasek, East Berlin 1957; *Decameron* by Boccaccio, 1958; *Betrugslexikon* by G. P. Honn, 1958; *Candide* by Voltaire, Munich 1958; *Pont und Anna* by Arnold Zweig, East Berlin 1962; *Die Berliner Antigone* by Rolf Hochhuth, Reinbek 1964; *Hansel und Gretel* by Sarah Kirsche, Leipzig 1972; *Die Schreckliche Pulver-Explosion zu Harburg,* edited by Lukas Richter, East Berlin 1973; *Im Mittelpunkt das Buch* by Horst Kunze, Leipzig 1980.

Publications:

By KLEMKE: book—*Herbert Sandberg,* East Berlin 1958.

On KLEMKE: books—*Who's Who in Graphic Art,* edited by Walter Amstutz, Zurich 1962; *Buchgestaltung* by Albert Kapr, Dresden 1963; *Künstler der Gegenwart: Werner Klemke* by Bernhard Nowak, Dresden 1963; *Deutsche Grafik* by Georg Piltz, Leipzig, Berlin and Jena 1968; *Werner Klemkes Gesammelte Werk* by Horst Kunze, Dresden 1968, 1972, 1977; *Werner Klemke: Illustrationen und Plakate,* exhibition catalogue, Hoyerswerda 1977; *Werner Klemke* by Jelena Marchenko, Moscow 1986; *Werner Klemke* by Mikhail Liebman, Leningrad 1988.

KLIMOWSKI, Andrzej.
British illustrator, film, stage and graphic designer. Born in London, 1 July 1949. Studied painting, at St. Martin's School of Art, London, 1968–73: Dip.AD. 1972; studied poster design and film animation, under Henryk Tomaszewski and Kazimierz Urbanski, at the Academy of Fine Arts, Warsaw, 1973–75. Married Danusia Schejbal in 1974; children: Dominik and Natalia. Freelance designer, in Warsaw, 1973–80, and in London from 1980: designer, Film Polski, Warsaw, 1976–80; director, Semafor Short Film Studios, Lodz, 1980; art director, Artificial Eye Film Company, London, 1980–81; designer and art director, London Sinfonietta orchestra, 1986–87; also designed for Polish television; *Szpilki* magazine, Warsaw's National Theatre, Teatr Wielki and Teatre Ateneum, Hamburg Deutsches Schauspielhaus, Wroclaw Contemporary Theatre, Royal Shakespeare Company, etc. Visiting Lecturer, Canterbury College of Art, Kent, 1981–89, West Surrey College of Art, Farnham, 1982–84, and Royal College of Art, London, from 1983. **Exhibitions:** Contemporary Posters Gallery, Warsaw, 1978; Galeria Wielka, Poznan, 1980; Contemporary Theatre, Wroclaw, 1980; Galeria Grazyny Hase, Warsaw, 1981; South Hill Park Arts Centre, Bracknell, 1983; Vanessa Devereux Gallery, London, 1986, 1988. **Collections:** National Museum, Warsaw; National Museum Poznan; Stedelijk Museum, Amsterdam; Library of Congress, Washington, D.C.; California Museum of Science and Technology, Los Angeles. Recipient: *Hollywood Reporter* Key Art Award, 1977, 1978; Warsaw Film Poster Prize, 1978; Polish Poster Biennale Award, Katowice, 1981; *Campaign* Posters Silver Award, London, 1986; *Daily Telegraph* Press Advertisement Award, London 1988. Address: 105 Sutton Court, London W4 3EE, England.

Publications:

By KLIMOWSKI: books—*Montserrat 71,* with Zbigniew Szydlo, London and Barcelona 1971; *Klimowska/Klimowski,* exhibition catalogue, London 1988; films—*19 bis, Dreamstrasse,* 1973; *Dead Shadow,* 1980; *Sonata,* 1983.

On KLIMOWSKI: books—*The Polish Poster 1970–1978,* with introduction by Zdzislaw Schubert, Warsaw 1979; *Das Polnische Plakat,* West Berlin 1980; *Who's Who in Graphic Art,* edited by Walter Amstutz, Dubendorf 1982; *A History of Graphic Design* by Philip B. Meggs, London and New York 1983.

I have always been attracted to mass-media forms of communication, to everything that involves the creation of images for mass consumption. Contact with the streets is important, the pulse of city life. Yet this contact should be a warm one: I wish to maintain a human scale, just as when, in a letter to a friend or a loved

Andrzej Klimowski: *Mephisto* **poster, for the Royal Shakespeare Company, 1986**

one, I use the resources of the many possible metaphors, symbols, and signs that trigger human emotions as well as the intellect.

Of course, I realize that working through graphics I have to speak with a loud voice. Whispers and subtle reflections are futile—they cannot survive the fast and often aggressive momentum of urban life. Nevertheless, it is of vital importance to work to the human scale, embracing the very nature of man, and thus reflecting his weaknesses, fears, passions, his need for human contact, his anguish and solitude, his sense of humour, his vulnerability, etc.

I believe that, with the rapid advancement of technology, the sense of human scale is often lost. Figures and statistics become more important than people. This can prove disastrous in political life—something we are at present experiencing in the Western world. In this climate of monetarism and the worship of modern technology, where more and more decisions rely upon computers, there is an urgent need for individual voices which speak up for the individual.

The function of graphic artists and designers is similar to that of journalists. They are responsible for informing and educating a large public, using a language which is direct and unambiguous, yet charged with strong beliefs and convictions. Paradoxical? Maybe—but needed in an atmosphere of anonymity, where most graphics can be reduced to mere packaging and empty decoration, perfect in technical execution but nothing beyond that. There are strong traditions in the not-too-distant past to turn to for inspiration: designers of the calibre of Cassandre, for example, whose laconic concepts were executed with tremendous flair. His posters sang out in the streets.

This flair and dynamism in execution accompanied by an intellectual poignancy is sadly missing in much of the graphic design work that we see today. Designers all too often look to fashion and popular trends, re-shaping their bag of graphic tricks accordingly. What is lacking is the weight, both intellectual and spriritual, to the visual messages that designers are communicating to the public.

—Andrzej Klimowski

To put it frankly, almost every young graduate of the Warsaw Academy of Art dreams of going to the West—New York, Paris, London—and making it. Sure, why not London?

Andrzej Klimowski, born in London, the son of World War II emigrants, chose the opposite route. In the early 1970s, after graduating from art school in London, he left for Warsaw. His dream was simple—to go to the source and try himself in his dream discipline, the poster. For sure, no place could be better (except Tokyo perhaps). After refining his skills in Henryk Tomaszewski's studio at the Warsaw Academy, Klimowski began his real struggle as a professional.

From the start, his works were different from the mainstream of the Polish school. He has developed a happy mixture of the photographic way of thinking prevailing in western Europe and the more painterly and romantic Polish style. In the early works of his Warsaw period, his style was somewhat inspired by Roman Cieslewicz, but soon, Klimowski distanced himself from that most prominent photocollagist. Since then, the photographic base has been preserved in his work. But the compositions look more like painting because of the color, softened black-and-white shapes, and extensive use of various filters and films. Titles and all additional texts were integrated into the overall compositions, never contrasting aggressively with the pictures.

The dominant area of Klimowski's activity in Poland was theatrical and movie posters. Some of them, such as a poster for Robert Altman's *Nashville* are extremely accurate and dramatic, thanks to the artist's firsthand understanding of the West and its problems. On such occasions, his bi-cultural being pays off.

An important factor in Klimowski's work as a posterist is his private world of art, which, however, provides also many ideas for commercial work. He realizes himself best in a series of mostly silkscreen prints. Here, he creates his own little home-theatre, in which the heroine is usually his wife. As a model in specially created costumes, she plays a central role in Klimowski's "sets." Bursting with sexuality, sometimes posing as *la femme fatale,* she narrates the artist's story. The result is never overdone. The atmosphere of these delicate works of art is somewhat literary, following in the vein of England's great eighteenth- and nineteenth-century masters of graphic art. A happy mixture of delicate color and dark, mysterious compositions make them the best part of Klimowski's work today.

Now, back in London, Klimowski has taken off in a new struggle. He faces an uneasy future. His Polish achievements are much admired, but translating them into commercial commissions is not an easy task. Despite everything, I strongly believe this young artist will prevail. He's intelligent and flexible, has a decent intellectual capacity and energy. And he's home again.

It's not too bad to have two built-in cultures and two homes in which to settle. Good luck, Andrzej!

—Jan Sawka

KLING, Vincent G(eorge).

American architect and interior designer. Born in East Orange, New Jersey, 9 May 1916. Studied at Columbia University, New York, 1936–40: B.Arch. 1940; Massachusetts Institute of Technology, Cambridge, 1940–42: M.Arch. 1942. Married Caperton Booth in 1942; sons: Vincent and Robert. Designer, with architects Skidmore, Owings and Merrill, New York, 1943–46; in private architectural and design practice, Philadelphia, from 1946. Architectural Advisory Panel member, United States General Services Administration; Philadelphia Citizens' City Planning Council Member; Chester County Airport Authority Board Member. **Exhibition:** *47 Outstanding Examples of American Architecture,* Museum of Modern Art, New York, 1944. Recipient: National Honor Award, American Institute of Architects, 1954; Philadelphia Arts Festival Award, 1959; City of Quito Gold Medal, Ecuador, 1961; Samuel Finley Breese Morse Medal, National Academy of Design, 1968. Fellow, American Institute of Architects, 1960. Address: The Kling Partnership, 2301 Chestnut Street, Philadelphia, Pennsylvania 19103, U.S.A.

Publications:

On KLING: book—*Interior Spaces Designed by Architects,* edited by Barclay F. Gordon, New York, 1974; articles—in *Pencil Points* (New York), May 1945; *Architectural Forum* (New York), March 1953, December 1958; *Architectural Record* (New York), December 1953, August 1959, October 1959, February 1963, April 1965; *AIA Journal* (Washington, D.C.), May 1957, June 1960; *Architectural Review* (London), December 1961; *Progressive Architecture* (New York), January 1962, November 1964, September 1966; *Interiors* (New York), February 1972.

Vincent G. Kling sees the architect as a "generalist by training and practice" who, to serve his clients fully, offers a comprehensive service. This breadth of vision enabled him to secure major commissions and be prominent in the "rebirth" of downtown Philadelphia in the late 1950s, when he designed the master plan, six buildings, and two plazas at Penn Center, as well as other Philadelphia buildings, including the airport and the United States Mint.

While the office is known primarily as an architectural firm, Kling has always recognized interior design as integral to architecture: "What happens inside a building determines what happens outside." Thus, the firm was one of the first to establish an interior design department. Under the direction of Joseph Bobrowicz (1956–69), responsibility of the department expanded from selection of colors and materials to total coordination of design and installation. Although not always the practical reality, the philosophical principle was that the interior staff be part of the team from the beginning of the design process to assure that interior needs and organizational relationships would be an integral part of the total. In the 1950s, Kling's office was a leader in design of campus plans for corporate organizations. The Monsanto Company's national headquarters in St. Louis is an excellent illustration of total involvement of a number of disciplines, including interior design and landscape design. Simultaneity in development is most evident at Swarthmore College's Philip T. Sharples Dining Hall, where interior and exterior materials are one, and the internal volumes form the external shapes.

In keeping with Kling's generalist philosophy, the office was reorganized in 1971 as a multidisciplinary design partnership encompassing architecture, planning and landscape, interior design engineering, construction management, and computer services. Until reorganization, the interior design work had been carried out primarily in conjunction with architectural commissions, but the formation of Kling/Interior Design enabled the firm to compete for independent commissions, as well as work on buildings designed by Vincent G. Kling and Partners, the architectural division. Xerox's International Center for Training and Management Development in Leesburg, Virginia, is a joint architecture and interior design commission. The differentiation of separate lounge spaces and coordinated color-coding are critical elements in personalizing the six buildings which house 1000 persons for up to six weeks at a time. The American Telephone and Telegraph building in New Jersey, is a similar example of the successful coordination of the two divisions of the firm. The remodeling of Philadelphia's First Pennsylvania Bank executive offices into an exceptional, calm, thoroughly controlled sequence of expressively lighted spaces represents the work of Kling/Interior Design as an independent unit.

As an early and continued presence in the field of interior design, the department has trained many who are now principals in other interior design firms. Bobrowicz and Edward Semanko formed Semanko/Bobrowicz; Roland Gallimore became head of interior design at Geddes, Brecher, Qualla, Cunningham; Karen Daroff established Daroff Designs; Ralph Melick, Donald Kriebel, and Ann Sutphin each have offices; and Florinda Doelp was president of Interspace before returning to head Kling/Interior Design.

The Kling work could be labeled conservative; it certainly is not trendy. "High style is not our driver. We believe that the unique functional needs of each client should shape our design. Only by meeting these requirements can we fulfill our responsibilities to our clients." This response to owner and occupant of the 2,500 projects designed by the Kling offices and the straightforward quality of the work have brought many awards and repeat commissions from the corporate and institutional clients they serve.

—Marjorie Kriebel

KLOTZ, Florence.
American stage and film costume designer. Born in New York City, 1920. Studied at the Parsons School of Design, New York, 1940. Freelance stage costume designer, New York, from 1951, and film costume designer, in Germany, Austria and the United States, from 1969. Recipient: Antoinette Perry (Tony) Awards, New York, 1971, 1973, 1976, 1984; Drama Desk Award, New York, 1971, 1973, 1976, 1978; Los Angeles Drama Critics' Award, 1972, 1974; Carbonell Award, 1981. Address: 1050 Park Avenue, New York, New York 10028, U.S.A.

Works:

Stage productions (New York, unless noted) include—*A Call on Kuprin*, 1961; *Take Her, She's Mine*, 1961; *Never Too Late*, 1962; *On an Open Roof*, 1963; *Nobody Loves an Albatross*, 1963; *Everybody Out*, 1964; *The Castle is Sinking*, 1964; *One by One*, 1964; *The Owl and the Pussycat*, 1964; *The Mating Dance*, 1965; *The Best Laid Plans*, 1966; *This Winter's Hobby*, 1966; *It's a Bird . . . It's a Plane . . . It's Superman*, 1966; *Golden Boy*, 1968 (also coordinator of tour); *Norman, Is That You?*, 1970; *Paris is Out*, 1970; *Follies*, 1971; *A Little Night Music*, 1973; *Sondheim: A Musical Tribute*, 1973; *Dreyfus in Rehearsal*, 1974; *Pacific Overtures*, 1976; *Legend*, 1976; *Side by Side by Sondheim*, 1977; *On the Twentieth Century*, 1978; *Ice Dancing*, 1979; *Harold and Maude*, 1980; *Little Foxes*, 1981; *Madam Butterfly*, for the Chicago Lyric Opera, 1982; *Doll's Life*, 1982; *Dancin' in the Streets*, 1983; *Peg*, 1983; *Grind*, 1984; *Roza*, 1986; *Rags*, 1987; films—*Something for Everyone* (Prince), 1970; *A Little Night Music* (Prince), 1977.

Publications:

On KLOTZ: books—*Contemporary Stage Design USA*, edited by Elizabeth Burdick, Peggy Hansen and Brenda Zanger, Middletown 1974; *Who's Who in the Theatre*, edited by Ian Herbert, London and Detroit 1977.

Getting into any creative phase of the theatre is supposed to be terribly difficult—like aspiring to be a movie star. Yet, when I am asked whether I encountered any obstacles in entering my professional life and also about the difficulties for a woman trying to balance a private life and a profession, I have to confess. Actually, it has all been very easy. I became a costume designer mostly through sheer luck.

One day in 1941, I got a call from a friend to come "paint some materials" at Brooks Costume Company. In my ignorance, I didn't know that Brooks was, at that time, the most famous costume company in the theatre. I went, they gave me a paintbrush, and I was on my way.

The longer I was at Brooks, the more people I met. Soon I was accepted into the United Scenic Artists Union and began working as an assistant to some of the famous costume designers. I worked for and was greatly influenced by Lucinda Ballard, Miles White, and Irene Sharaff.

My first show as an assistant was the hauntingly beautiful *The King and I*. After that, I assisted on many musicals—*A Tree Grows in Brooklyn, Top Banana, Of Thee I Sing, Pal Joey, Pajama Game, Flower Drum Song, Juno, Carnival in Flanders, Jamaica, Pipe Dream, Mr. Wonderful, Wish You Were Here, Bells Are Ringing, The Music Man, The Sound of Music, Gay Life*—and plays—*Cat on a Hot Tin Roof, J.B., Kind Sir, Clearing in the Woods, Time Remembered*.

People began to know my work and ask for me. In the late 1950s I designed for the City Center such musicals as *Carousel, South Pacific*, and *Annie Get Your Gun*. In 1960, Harold Prince asked me to design *Take Her, She's Mine* and then many more plays for Broadway. My first musical was *Superman* (1966). My first movie was *Something for Everyone* (1969), made in Germany, with Angela Lansbury. My first Tony Award was in 1971 for *Follies*. I also won the Drama Desk Award and Los Angeles Drama Critics Award for that show. Nothing I have done in my life will ever compare with the fear, stagefright, and nerves I suffered on having to walk up and appear *before* instead of *behind* the footlights. I went on to win two more Tonys, several Drama Desk Awards, and an Oscar nomination for the movie of *A Little Night Music* with Elizabeth Taylor.

I still say success was made possible for me by a combination of luck, the adaptable skills I picked up, my basic artistic instincts, being in the right place (Brooks) at the right time, meeting and working for talented designers who helped me help myself while in their apprenticeship, and, finally, learning to go it alone. And I was fortunate in the people who believed in me and encouraged me.

—Florence Klotz

In the twenty-two years since her first Broadway design assignment, Florence Klotz has designed only about twenty-five productions on Broadway and a few films; she cannot be considered a prolific designer. From 1961 through 1970 she designed almost solely lightweight, contemporary-dress comedies. Although some of these were rather important plays of the time, their clothes could hardly be considered important design.

Klotz's career changed almost overnight when she was hired to design the costumes for Hal Prince's *Follies*, a complicated musical about a reunion of Ziegfeld Follies girls on the stage of a theatre in the process of being demolished. Each of them had come from a different era of the Ziegfeld Follies, and each was living a different sort of life. In addition, the action included flashbacks to each woman's day on the stage. Klotz's research was impeccable. Each character had her own rather moth-eaten look plus her glamorous recollection of herself. It was sophisticated, intelligent, and glorious design.

Follies, the first of the collaborative works of Klotz with Prince and Stephen Sondheim, was followed by *A Little Night Music, Pacific Overtures, Side by Side by Sondheim* and *On the Twentieth Century.* Each of the major Sondheim-Prince musicals had its distinctly different look, and thus they made very different demands on Klotz. Each required careful and specific research into complex worlds and periods: *Follies* reflected fifty years of clothing; *A Little Night Music*, turn-of-the-century Sweden; *Pacific Overtures*, nineteenth-century Japan; and *On the Twentieth Century*, 1930s American Art Deco. For each, she developed a unique design concept: dresses out of trunks for aging showgirls and black-and-white recollections of glamour; ethereal, almost surrealistic, costumes for Swedish eccentrics in the country; multi-patterned, Americanized Kabuki; and softly colored, 1930s movie glamour. Each concept, as well as each costume, was done with great style and flair. With only a few concessions to quick changes and other theatrical requirements, Klotz maintains correct silhouette in her designs, although frequently they are as contemporary as they are period-style.

Klotz's costumes, mostly made by Barbara Matera Ltd. for these four productions, have shown a mastery of fabric and trim in color and cut. One of Klotz's favorite techniques for getting the right texture and color in garments (used in both *Follies* and *A Little Night Music*) is to layer repeatedly one color over another, and then to bead, trim, or decorate over the layers. As a result, the costume costs for these productions were astronomical.

—John E. Hirsch

KNEEBONE, Peter (Jack George).
British-French illustrator, signage and graphic designer. Born in Middlesbrough, England, 28 April 1923; resident in France from 1975. Studied philosophy, politics and languages, at University College, Oxford, 1942–43, 1946–48: MA 1948. Served as British Naval Liaison Officer, in Italy, and as Naval Broadcasting Representative, in Cairo, Royal Naval Volunteer Reserve, 1943–46: Lieutenant. Married Catherine Shanks in 1958 (divorced, 1976); children: Anna, Jonathan, Sophie and Lucy; married Françoise Jollant in 1976. Assistant to the director of exhibitions, Festival of Britain, London, 1951; television producer, British Broadcasting Corporation, London, 1952–55; freelance designer, in Paris and London, 1952–90: illustrator for *News Chronicle, The Observer, Sunday Times, Radio Times, New Scientist*, Central Office of Information, National Economic Development Office, Institute of Directors, Imperial Chemical Industries, Shell, British Broadcasting Corporation, etc., 1953–75; signage consultant, Philips Corporation, Netherlands, 1969–76, and Ministry of Industry, Paris, 1974–77; design consultant, National Fund for Research into Crippling Diseases, London, 1969–74; Salle Pleyel concert halls, Paris, 1980–81, Ministry of Research, Paris, 1981–88, Centre National d' Art Contemporain, Villa Arson, Nice, 1983, and Europrospective conference, Paris, 1986–87. Head of complementary studies, at Kingston School of Art, Surrey, 1963–66; coordinator of postgraduate studies, Central School of Art and Design, London, 1967–74; visual communications coordinator, Ecole Nationale des Beaux-Arts, Nancy, 1980–89; also visiting tutor, University

Florence Klotz: Costume for Stephen Sondheim's *Follies*, 1971

of Paris VII, 1978–81, and Parsons School of Design, Paris, 1981–88. Secretary, 1963, secretary general, 1977–79, and president, 1979–81, ICOGRADA International Council of Graphic Design Associations. **Exhibitions:** *Funny Peculiar: Illustrations by Peter Kneebone,* Kilkenny, 1984; *Design Français 1960–1980: Trois Decennies,* Centre Georges Pompidou, Paris, 1988 (toured). Recipient: ICOGRADA President's Trophy, 1970; IBM Fellowship, Aspen Design Conference, Colorado, 1980. Fellow, Chartered Society of Designers, London; Society of Typographic designers, London, *Died* (in Paris) *30 January 1990.*

Works:

Old Possum's Book of Practical Cats television programme direction and illustration, for BBC Television, 1952.
Look Before You Elope book design and illustration, for Longmans, 1952.
Social commentary texts and illustrations, for *The Observer* newspaper, London, 1955.
Oiling the Wheels book design and illustrations, for Shell, 1955–58.
Corporate identity and graphics, for the National Fund for Research into Crippling Diseases, London, 1955–75.
Happy Families typeface calendar, for the Monotype Corporation, London, 1963.
English Pronunciation Illustrated book design and illustrations, for the Cambridge University Press, 1965.
Baby's Book design and illustrations, for Charles Letts, 1971.
Look Behind You alphabet design and illustrations, for Associated Business Programmes, 1973.
How to Interview and *How to Be Interviewed* conceptual illustrations, for the British Institute of Management, 1975–80.
Sign system, for the *3rd Architectural Psychology Conference,* at the University of Strasbourg, 1976.
Corporate identity and graphics, for the Salle Pleyel concert halls, Paris, 1980–81.
CPE Centre visual identity and publications design, for the Ministry of Research, Paris, 1981–89.
Visual identity and graphics, for *Europrospective* conference, at the International Conference Centre, La Villette, Paris, 1987.

Publications:

By KNEEBONE: books—*Look Before You Elope,* London 1952; *Sexes and Sevens,* London 1953; *Oiling the Wheels,* London 1957; *The Art of Afghanistan,* translator, London 1967; *How to Interview,* co-author, London 1975; *A Signature for Singapore,* Paris 1979; *How to Be Interviewed,* co-author, London 1980; *Signaletique,* Paris 1980; articles—in *Filmmaking in Schools and Colleges,* London 1966; *ICOGRADA: The First Five Years,* London 1968; *Print* (New York), special issue, 1969, March/April 1969, November/December 1969, March/April 1971; *The Designer* (London), September 1969, January 1970, May 1971, September 1971, March 1973; *Communication et Langages* (Paris), December 1969; *Icographic* (London), no. 5, 1973, no. 8, 1974, no. 3, 1982; *British Travel News* (London), Summer 1974; *Neuf* (Brussels), March/April 1977; *Industrijsko Oblikovanje* (Belgrade), no. 35, 1977; *Design* (London), February 1979, March 1980, November 1983, July 1987, May 1988; *Graphic Design* (Tokyo), June 1985; *France Graphique* (Paris), August 1985; *Art Press* (Paris), January 1987; *Typographic* (London), August 1987.

Peter Kneebone: "Do Boast Modestly" from *How To Be Interviewed,* for the British Institute of Management, 1980

On KNEEBONE: books—*Designers in Britain,* London 1951–71; *Drawing for the Radio Times* by R. D. Usherwood, London 1961; *Minerva at Fifty* by James Holland, London 1980; *Trademarks and Symbols of the World,* Tokyo 1987; *Trademarks Collection: Europe I,* Tokyo 1988; *Design Francais 1960–1980: Trois Decennies* by Margo Rouard and Françoise Jollant Kneebone, Paris 1988, London 1989.

I attempted to find apparently simple visual solutions to complex problems. "Apparently," because the aim of the simplicity is to make clear something that is not simple. This means a search not only for clarity but also for any answer that is satisfying because it works on more than a superficial level and that might be therefore more stimulating both for me and for the receiver/user of the message. In the case of my illustration design, this is usually done with some humour. Humour can make the message more immediate, more human. Wit can make it more memorable and, ideally, enhance its mnemonic value.

An autodidact, I slid gradually into graphic design because I liked drawing and did the school posters. Not having a conventional professional training has kept me open-minded about my work and open-ended about its direction—though not its spirit. It has also meant that I have been preoccupied with style and techniques as means rather than as ends. A great satisfaction comes from finding a fitting visual solution, one that communicates clearly, usefully, and, with luck, enjoyably and intellectually provocatively. This is why my greatest satisfaction lies in communicating concepts, ideas, and certain kinds of information. This is also why, apart from the illustration of concepts, I have been particularly interested in questions of visual identity, environmental communication, and information design.

Having been brought up with a combined English-French cultural background, and having studied languages, philosophy and politics, has meant that I have been attracted by a wide range of problems and concerned with the nature of problems, with that asking of questions, with the relationship between verbal and visual communication (very important this), and with human needs. This is a necessary position because we design for others, and we should ask ourselves, with some humility, "What are the aptitudes and qualities that I have that can best be applied to what problems, to my satisfaction and to that of others?" I am unique and so is every problem. If I am not, then someone else could well be asked to solve it. If it is not, then a solution doubtless exists already. A sense of curiosity, an ability to make connections, a critical and self-critical faculty are essential attributes for a designer.

—Peter Kneebone

Peter Kneebone will be remembered as the originator of the idea for a representative, international, non-governmental organization for graphic design, the International Council of Graphic Design Associations (ICOGRADA), founded in 1963 and dedicated to improving the practice of graphic design and to increasing the understanding and use of visual and graphic communications worldwide.

Kneebone was very interested in the use of drawing to explain verbal concepts and ideas, for an illustration can be remembered better than a lot of text. His style was full of detail in the 1950s, but since then, he aimed for increasing simplicity and discarded the inessential. He liked the simple shape for its direct impact, and employed humour to help messages get across, for he insisted that learning should be enjoyable. His training in philosophy, politics, and modern languages at Oxford taught him to be detached and analytical, and not tied to fashion in the way that some products of design colleges are. He wanted his drawings to encourage people to ask questions, rather than to assume that there is one doctrinal approach for everything.

As an educator himself, Kneebone was concerned with raising the standards of graphic design and with widening its ability to tackle a variety of communication problems. From this have come ICOGRADA's international student projects and the annual student design seminar in London, while the encouragement of innovation in graphic design has been established in the ICOGRADA-Phillips biennial award. Kneebone was very active in getting ICOGRADA recognised by UNESCO and by the council of Europe, and much involved in its activities. He saw his original concept blossom into a worldwide exchange of ideas and aims

—Diana de Marly

KNOLL, Florence.

American architect, interior, furniture and textile designer. Born Florence Schust, in Saginaw, Michigan, 24 May 1917. Studied Architecture under Eero Saarinen, at Kingswood School, and at Cranbrook Academy of Art, Bloomfield Hills, Michigan, 1932-39; Architectural Association, London, 1937-38; under Ludwig Mies van der Rohe, at the Illinois Institute of Technology, Chicago, 1940-41: B.Arch. 1941. Married the manufacturer Hans Knoll in 1946 (died, 1955); Harry Hood Bassett in 1958. Worked for architect Wallace K. Harrison in New York, and for Walter Gropius and Marcel Breuer in Boston, 1941-43; founder-director, with Hans Knoll, of the Knoll Planning Unit furniture and textiles firm, New York, 1943-55; president, Knoll International, New York, 1955-65; freelance designer, living in Florida and Vermont, from 1965. **Exhibitions:** *An Exhibition for Modern Living,* Museum of Modern Art, New York, 1949 (toured); *Die Gute Industrieform,* Kunstverein, Hamburg, 1955; *Knoll au Musée,* Musée des Arts Decoratifs, Paris, 1972; *A Modern Consciousness: D. J. DePree and Florence Knoll,* Smithsonian Institution, Washington, D.C., 1975; *Design in America: The Cranbrook Vision 1925-1950,* Detroit Institute of Art, 1983 (toured); *Design Since 1945,* Philadelphia Museum of Art, 1983. **Collections:** Museum of Modern Art, New York; Metropolitan Museum of Art, New York; Cranbrook Academy of Art, Bloomfield Hills, Michigan. Recipient: Good Design Award, Museum of Modern Art, New York, 1950, 1951, 1952, 1953, 1954; American Institute of Decorators International Design Award, 1954, and Citation of Merit, 1957; New York Art Directors Club Merit Award, 1954, 1956; American Institute of Architects Gold Medal, 1961; American Institute of Interior Designers International Design Award, 1962, and Total Design Award, 1977; Illinois Institute of Technology Professional Achievement Award, 1969, and Hall of Fame Award, 1982. DFA: Parsons School of Design, New York, 1979; Honorary Member, Industrial Designers Society of America, 1982; President's Fellow, Rhode Island School of Design, Providence, 1983. Address: Knoll Associates, 575 Madison Avenue, New York, New York 10022, U.S.A.

Works:

Chest in maplewood, for Knoll Planning Unit, 1947.
Stacking stool in steel and birchwood, for Knoll Planning Unit, 1947.
Cabinet in steel and rosewood veneer with marble top, for Knoll Planning Unit, 1950.
M. D. Anderson Cancer Research Hospital interiors, Houston, Texas, 1954.
CBS Columbia Broadcasting System headquarters interiors, New York, 1955.
Center for Advanced Study in Behavioral Sciences interiors, Palo Alto, California, 1955.
Southern Methodist University interiors, Dallas, Texas, 1956.
Refectory interiors, Rochester University, New York, 1956.
Dining and rest room interiors, Connecticut General Life Insurance Company, Hartford, 1957.
Oval table-desk in steel and teak veneer, for Knoll International, 1961.
Upholstered lounge chair in steel and hardwood with helical spring suspension, for Knoll International, 1962.

Publications:

On KNOLL: books—*An Exhibition for Modern Living,* exhibition catalogue edited by A. H. Girard and W. Laurie, New York and Detroit 1949; *Die Gute Industrieform,* exhibition catalogue by Hans Eckstein and Robert Gutmann, Hamburg 1955; *Public Interiors: An International Survey* by Misha Black, London 1960; *World Furniture,* edited by Helena Hayward, London 1965, 1981; *The Modern Chair: 1850 to Today* by Gilbert Frey, London and Niederteufen 1970; *Interior Design: An Introduction to Architectural Interiors* by Arnold Friedmann and others, New York and Amsterdam 1970, 1976; *Knoll au Musee,* exhibition catalogue by Christine Rae, Paris 1972; *A Modern Consciousness: D. J. DePree and Florence Knoll,* exhibition catalogue, Washington, D.C. 1975; *Twentieth Century Furniture* by Philippe Garner, London 1980; *Knoll Design* by Eric Larrabee and Massimo Vignelli, New York 1981; *Contemporary Furniture,* edited by Klaus-Jurgen Sembach, Stuttgart, London and New York 1982; *Design Since 1945,* edited by Kathryn Hiesinger and George Marcus, Philadelphia and London 1983; *Design Source Book* by Penny Sparke, London 1986; *The American Design Adventure 1940-1975* by Arthur J. Pulos, London and Cambridge, Massachusetts 1988.

Florence Knoll is an architect, interior space planner, and furniture designer. Her career is symbiotically linked with Knoll International, the furniture company founded by Hans Knoll who later became her husband. The Knolls shared the conviction that a market could be created for innovative, high-quality, modern furniture. To promote their idea, they established the Knoll Planning Unit, which offered a unique package of original furniture and professional design services to a growing number of important corporate clients. Florence Knoll, as head of this service, is substantially responsible for the postwar acceptance of modern design by American business.

Knoll studied at Cranbrook Academy under the tutelage of Eliel Saarinen, an admirer of Walter Gropius' Bauhaus movement. At Cranbrook, she discovered that everyone was interested in everything, from weaving, pottery, and furniture to architecture and city planning. Her studies continued in London at the Architectural Association and concluded with Ludwig Mies van der Rohe in Chicago.

She worked first for Wallace K. Harrison in New York and later for Gropius and Marcel Breuer in Boston. Her international training and her sympathy for the interdisciplinary approach produced in Knoll a firm, well-modulated esthetic which she brought to the Planning Unit. Her work on large-scale projects for clients such as Connecticut General Life Insurance and CBS conveys the self-assurance and sophistication which exemplified the best in postwar design in the United States and epitomizes the style of the 1950s.

In her planning, spaces interact in a relaxed but highly rational architectural integration. They are embellished with chastely elegant textiles and accented by vivid color contrasts and artful lighting. She designed much of the furniture her projects required and commissioned work from other designers such as Eero Saarinen, Mies van der Rohe, Harry Bertoia, Franco Albini, George Nakashima, and Isamu Noguchi, many of whom were friends or colleagues. Her own designs were frequently cited for awards, but she tended to think of them as relatively insignificant. "I designed the fill-in pieces that no one else was doing. . . . Eero and Bertoia did the stars. . . . I did it because I needed the piece of furniture for a job and it wasn't there."

Knoll's work with the Planning Unit and Knoll International's exceptional furniture products are now understood to have been responsible, in large measure, for initiating the modern corporate style of interior design which matured in the 1960s and, for a time, was referred to as "the Knoll look." *Architectural Forum* commented in 1957 that ". . . the Knoll interior is as much a symbol of modern architecture as Tiffany glass was a symbol of the architecture of the Art Nouveau."

—Kenneth Gaulin

Florence Knoll: Office furniture, for Knoll Associates, c.1954

KOIKE, Iwataro.
Japanese industrial designer. Born in Tokyo, 22
February 1913. Studied under Sanzo Wada,
Wajiro Kon and Kitaro Kunii, at Tokyo University
of Arts, 1930–35: Dip. 1935. Married
Taka Kinoshita in 1938; children: Natsuko,
Taiso and Yoko. Design technician, working in
Fukuoka City, 1935–39, and for the Industrial
Arts Institute and Ministry of International
Trade and Industry, in Sendai City, 1939–40;
chief of Renbo Ceramics Workshops, Naha
City, Okinawa, 1940–42; independent designer
and theorist, Tokyo, from 1942. Lecturer,
1942–49, associate professor, 1949–65, and
professor, 1965–79, at Tokyo University of
Arts. **Exhibitions:** *Works of Iwataro Koike,* Tokyo
University of Arts, 1979; *19 Designers:
30th Anniversary of the Japan Design Committee,*
Matsuya Department Store, Tokyo, 1982.
Recipient: Ministry of International Trade
and Industry Prize, Tokyo, 1939. Honorary Professor,
Tokyo University of Arts, 1980. Address:
4–21–10 Shimo Ochiai, Shinjuku-ku, Tokyo
160, Japan.

Publications:

By KOIKE: books—*Basic Design: Composition
and Formation,* Tokyo 1956; *Arts,* Osaka 1970;
Talk on Design: From Daily Life, Tokyo 1974.

I was born in 1913 in Tokyo, but my father,
who was a furniture craftsman, moved to Shikoku
Island in Kagawa Prefecture to be a
teacher of wood-craft in an industrial arts
school, so I grew up there. I, too, entered
wood-carving by my choice of course at school,
but then I became rather interested in design,
particularly in the form of bowls, dishes, and
other tableware, because there was a ceramic
workshop nearby.
In 1930, I proceeded to the Design Department
of the Tokyo University of Arts. The design
course then included commercial design,
decorative design, and industrial arts; there
were no specific majors. Japan at that time produced
excellent decorative craftwork, but the
design of useful things was slighted. I found
this unfortunate and decided to enter the design
field. Because there was no demand for industrial
designers in the private sector, I was employed
by Fukuoka prefectural government on
Kyushu Island as a technician for commerce
and industry. In 1939, I was transferred to Sendai
in Miyagi Prefecture, north of Tokyo, to
work for the Ministry of International Trade
and Industry, which was then promoting production
of exportable merchandise. While I was
working for these governmental agencies, I had
time to learn about the actual situation of industrial
design in Japan and in advanced countries.
Later, I was assigned as chief of the Renbo lac-

querware workshop in Okinawa, where I studied
design along with production and product
control.
Design has been said to be a product of science
and art, but I am of the opinion that the
preeminent element of design is to be found in
its ethics, based on the nature of society and
humanity. If ethics is included as part of philosophy,
then design is a product of philosophy,
science, and art, and it is basically the affectionate
heart which coordinates all these factors.
In any case, the product should not be the
advertising medium of the maker. Design is
ideal when the designers' and makers' desire
for self-manifestation is suppressed.

—Iwataro Koike

Iwataro Koike is the preeminent teacher of design
in Japan. He taught for forty years at the
Tokyo University of Arts and has written two
secondary-school textbooks in which he describes
"beauty in daily life." And in his book
Talk on Design—From Daily Life, he precisely
clarifies for his readers his concepts of design
in easy-to-understand terms.
Koike says: "Design is synonymous with
thinking; design starts from identifying a problem
in one's own life." Everyone should have a
"philosophy of life," a plan of how one will live
his life, and this philosophy should inform

Iwataro Koike: *Rock 'n Roll* sake bottle, for the Ozeki Brewing Company, 1979

one's view of life, means of livelihood, relation to society and nature, and the direction of one's desires. Design is a means of realizing these desires comprehensively and systematically—according to these aspects: science (truth); ethics (goodness); and aesthetics (beauty).

By "truth" Koike means that the design will be useful, efficient, and economical; it will not be frivolous. One's effort must be a scientific approach to the truth of the natural world. By "goodness" he means that the work will not be harmful or distressing to others. Design should strive to "make better" or "refine" the object. By "beauty" Koike means that the design should strive to be pleasing, comfortable, and attractive; it should reveal the *quest* for beauty. What Koike has done, in fact, is to link modern design to certain traditional Oriental values, and he has made a conscious effort to instill elements of good design in the minds of his readers, who are, of course, also consumers.

For the Japanese people, with a culture stretching back over centuries, the coming of universal industrial civilization has been difficult. Even after 100 years of industrialization, Japan has not yet managed to reconcile this new kind of civilization with her old culture. For a time, during the postwar period of rapid industrialization, "culture" was something of a catch phrase—but the reality of the time was the process from material paucity to material sufficiency. Koike's concern about present trends in design seems to be based on his reflection that Japan has evolved into a society in which man must keep moving—running, almost; his apprehension is about the way of life of the people in such a society. He reiterates the question: "What is our true culture?" As he suggests that man in the modern age must be a person who inquires, he himself is determined that he will continue advocating the claims of humanity, whatever the pressures or criticisms to the contrary.

In recent years, he has led a group of people devoted to "considering the colors of public amenities." One of their targets was the new color chosen for the public buses of Tokyo. With public support, Koike succeeded in mak-

ing the authorities change the color—proving that, even in Tokyo, there are still "human" beings.

—Kunio Sano

KOLTAI, Ralph.
British stage designer. Born in Berlin, Germany, 31 July 1924; emigrated to Britain in 1939: naturalized, 1947. Educated at the Waldschule Kaliski private school, Berlin, 1934–39; studied graphic design, at Epsom School of Art, Surrey, 1942–44; stage design, at the Central School of Arts and Crafts, London, 1948–51. Served in the Royal Army Service Corps, at the International Military Tribunal, Nuremberg, 1945–48. Married Annena Stubbs in 1956 (divorced, 1976). Worked as a window display artist, London, 1951–53; freelance stage designer, working mainly on operas, London, 1950–62; associate designer, Royal Shakespeare Company, in London and Stratford-on-Avon, 1962–66 and from 1976; also designed for Sadler's Wells Company (now the English National Opera), Scottish Opera, National Theatre, Chichester Festival Theatre, Royal Opera House/Covent Garden, London Opera Club, Welsh National Opera, Ballet Rambert, Sydney Opera House, Nederlands Opera, Aalborg Teater, etc. Head of theatre design, 1965–73, and external assessor for diplomas in art and design, 1981–83, Central School of Art and Design, London. **Exhibitions:** McLaurin Art Gallery, Ayr, 1980; *British Theatre Design '83–87*, Riverside Studios, London, 1988. **Collections:** British Council, London; Arts Council of Great Britain, London; Victoria and Albert Museum, London; University of Reading, Berkshire; Manchester

University, Lancashire. Recipient: London Drama Critics' Designer of the Year Award, 1976, 1977; Prague Quadriennale Gold Medal, 1975, 1979, and Silver Medal, 1987; Designer of the Year Award, London 1976, 1977; Society of West End Theatres Award, London, 1978. Commander, Order of the British Empire, 1983. Address: c/o MacNaughton Lowe Representation Limited, 200 Fulham Road, London SWIO 9PN, England.

Works:

Stage productions include—*Two Brothers*, Ballet Rambert, 1958; *Carmen*, English National Opera, 1961; *Murder in the Cathedral*, English National Opera, 1962; *Conflicts*, Ballet Rambert, 1962; *The Caucasian Chalk Circle*, Royal Shakespeare Company, 1962; *Mahagonny*, English National Opera, 1963; *The Travellers*, Ballet Rambert, 1963; *The Representative*, Royal Shakespeare Company, 1963; *Dul de Sac*, Ballet Rambert, 1964; *The Birthday Party*, Royal Shakespeare Company, 1964; *Don Giovanni*, Scottish Opera, 1964; *Endgame*, Royal Shakespeare Company, 1964; *The Jew of Malta*, Royal Shakespeare Company, 1964; *Otello*, Scottish Opera, 1964, 1975; *The Merchant of Venice*, Royal Shakespeare Company, 1965; *Boris Godunov*, Scottish Opera, 1965; *Timon of Athens*, Royal Shakespeare Company, 1965; *The Rake's Progress*, Scottish Opera, 1967; *As You Like It*, National Theatre, 1967; *Little Murders*, Royal Shakespeare Company, 1967; *Soldiers*, Albery Theatre, London, 1968; *Back to Methuselah*, National Theatre, 1968; *The Tempest*, Chichester Festival Theatre, 1968; *Major Barbara*, Royal Shakespeare Company, 1970; *Elegy for Young Lovers*, Scottish Opera, 1970; *Wagner Ring Cycle*, English National Opera, 1970–73; *Taverner*, Royal Opera House, 1972; *Duke Bluebeard's Castle*, English National Opera, 1972; *Oedipus Rex*, Chichester Festival Theatre, 1974; *Billy*, Drury Lane Theatre, London, 1974; *Too True To Be Good*, Royal Shakespeare Company, 1975; *Old World/Wild Oats*, Royal Shakespeare Company, 1976; *The Cruel Garden*, Ballet Rambert, 1977; *State of Revolution*, National Theatre, 1977; *Every Good Boy Deserves Favour*, Festival Hall and Mermaid Theatre, London, 1977; *The Seven Deadly Sins*, English National Opera, 1978; *Rosmersholm*, Haymarket Theatre, London, 1978; *The Ice Break*, Royal Opera House, 1978; *Brand*, National Theatre, 1978; *The Tempest*, Royal Shakespeare Company, 1978; *The Guardsman*, National Theatre, 1978; *Love's Labours Lost*, Royal Shakespeare Company, 1978; *Sons of Light*, Royal Shakespeare Company, 1978; *Hippolytus*, Royal Shakespeare Company, 1978; *Richard III*, National Theatre, 1979; *The Threepenny Opera*, Aalborg Teater, 1979; *Baal*, Royal Shakespeare Company, 1979; *The Wild Duck*, National Theatre, 1979; *Romeo and Juliet*, Royal Shakespeare Company, 1980; *Hamlet*, Royal Shakespeare Company, 1980; *The Love Girl and the Innocent*, Aalborg Teater, 1980; *Man and Superman*, National Theatre, 1981; *Terra Nova*, Aalborg Teater, 1981; *The Love Girl and the Innocent*, Royal Shakespeare Company, 1981; *The Carmelites*, Aalborg Teater, 1981; *Anna Karenina*, English National Opera, 1981; *Much Ado About Nothing*, Royal Shakespeare Company, 1982; *Moliere*, Royal Shakespeare Company, 1982; *Bugsy Malone*, Her Majesty's Theatre, London, 1983; *Cyrano de Bergerac*, Royal Shakespeare Company, 1983; *Custom of the County*, Royal Shakespeare Company, 1983; *Pack of Lies*, Lyric Theatre, London, 1983; *Les Soldats*, Opera de Lyons, 1983; *Mahagonny*, Aalborg Teater, 1984; *An Italian Girl in Algiers*, Opera de Geneve, 1984; *Troilus and*

Cressida, Royal Shakespeare Company, 1986; *Othello,* Royal Shakespeare Company, 1986; *Tannhaeuser,* Opera de Geneve, 1986; *The Flying Dutchman,* Hong Kong Arts Festival, 1987; *Pacific Overtures,* English National Opera, 1988; *Carrie,* Royal Shakespeare Company, Stratford and New York, 1988; *They Shoot Horses, Don't They,* Royal Shakespeare Company, 1988; *Metropolis,* Piccadilly Theatre, London, 1989.

Publications:

By KOLTAI: article—in *Design and Art Direction* (London), March 1983.

On KOLTAI: books—*Stage Design Throughout the World Since 1960,* edited by René Hainaux and Yves Bonat, Brussels 1972, London 1973; *Who's Who in the Theatre,* edited by Ian Herbert, London and Detroit 1977; *British Theatre Design '83–87,* with texts by Timothy O'Brien and David Fingleton, London 1988.

My work is very dependent on my development as an artist. I can't work like a painter, just pursuing one direction in a very single-minded way. I have a number of fascinations or directions. It might be kinetic art, it might be superhumanism, or Op art, or hard-edge painting or film. I'm very art motivated.

When I come to do a play, I try to steer one of my interests in its direction. I make a decision as to which of my avenues is suitable, because you mustn't be wilful. Finally, you've got to take the matter of the play as your brief, and you've got to be honest to that piece of work. But I use one of the areas of my own fascination to try to bring out the best in that play.

And what is best has to be best for that particular moment in time. The audience is conditioned to be on a particular wavelength, and you have to try to gauge that. Theatre is a progressive art form, and you can't have definitive productions. Maybe if you saw Peter Brook's *Midsummer Night's Dream* today, it wouldn't have the same effect. But in 1970, it was spot on right. I have sensed for the last couple of years that audiences are getting rather tired of the empty stage and spare decor and highly intellectualised productions. I think they actually want to see something for their money. I'm also bored with such productions. The minimalism with one chair in the middle of the stage has got rather tiresome. One could occasionally come back to it, but basically, at the moment, I'm inclined to be a little more exuberant, more colorful, more spectacular if you like. Not that I consciously think about being right for the moment in time. I'm hoping that I keep sufficiently abreast and alive to be automatically, subconsciously, intuitively in tune with the current mood.

I have problems turning a piece of work into an aesthetic object. I find it easier to create a piece of sculpture on which the actors perform than to create a mess which is a mess. My messes turn quite easily into being rather aesthetic messes. When I am aware that that is not what is required, I find it quite hard.

I think you have to be fiercely critical of yourself in order to produce anything that is worthwhile. It is quite easy to design a respectable show, but that would be a bore to me, and boredom is the greatest enemy. You don't get paid a lot of money in this business, so the only reason for doing it is the satisfaction of having explored a particular idea. There are some exciting moments—as when you are asked by a director you like and admire if you will do a particular play or opera. Then comes a period of calm, then a period of trauma when you don't seem able to solve the problem. And if it goes quite well, you are pleased for a moment. Maybe a day. Then you start on the next thing.

—Ralph Koltai

Koltai refers explicitly to his art-oriented approach and to his intuitiveness, both of which are most evident in those productions that reveal a sculptor's eye for shape, mass, texture, and space, usually abstractly stylized rather than realistic. *Tannhäuser* (Australia, 1973) had a smooth, raked floor unmarred except for two graceful segments that peeled up from is surface. The settings for Ibsen's *Brand* (National Theatre, 1978) and Ted Tally's *Terra Nova* (Denmark, 1981) represented landscapes of snow and ice: jagged sections of white plywood tilted up to suggest a cracking ice-field for *Brand,* while stainless steel on a gently curved base, echoed by the steel grill arching over part of the floor, captured the icescape of *Terra Nova.*

Fiberglass and plexiglas are typical of synthetic materials often employed by Koltai. Wagner's *Ring* (English National Opera, 1970–73) blended shimmering, splintery fiberglass with metallic, boulder-like spheres to create a fantasy landscape. Similarly striking effects were produced by panels of paint-sprayed and transparent plexiglas in *As You Like It* (National Theatre, 1976) and *Much Ado About Nothing* (Royal Shakespeare Company, 1982).

Koltai's sculptural scenography often blends with other techniques: for Brecht's *Baal* (Royal Shakespeare Company, 1979), he combined a rear wall in relief (created by protruding objects later to be used in the action) with projections that erased the effect of the relief surface during the scene changes; for Shaw's *Man and Superman* (National Theatre, 1981), a curving mirror formed the rear wall and reflected people and objects in the upstage part of the scene.

When the occasion demands, Koltai is able to be documentarily realistic, although that is not his natural heart, which inclines towards the metaphoric and imagistic. For Solzhenitsyn's *The Love Girl and the Innocent* (Royal Shakespeare Company, 1981, he constructed a barbed-wire freight yard including tracks, cars and

Ralph Koltai: Model set for Zimmermann's *Die Soldaten*, at the Opera Lyon, 1982

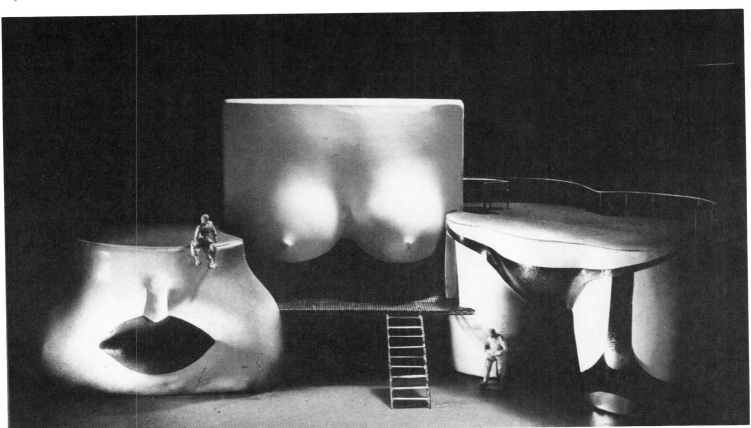

gantries with almost cinematic verisimilitude because the production concept demanded that approach.

Like Josef Svoboda, to whose work his own has been occasionally compared, Koltai demonstrates an ability to adapt contemporary technology to the needs of theatre art, as some of his most expressive scenography makes clear. Maxwell Davies' opera *Taverner* (Covent Garden, 1972) employed a large ring circumscribing a skeletal see-saw—capable of rotation and alternating vertical movement—to represent Renaissance science as well as the shifting fortunes of contending forces within the play. Shaw's *Back to Methuselah* (National Theatre, 1968), was more stylized and more consciously artistic. The creation of the universe and the earth was represented by a number of revolving travelling spheres in relation to a centrally suspended solar disk made luminous by lights concealed within its circumference.

Among his recent outstanding productions have been *Othello* (Royal Shakespeare Company), based on abstract configurations of fiber optics and transparent plastic—for which he was awarded a silver medal at the Prague Quadriennale; and the musical *Carrie* (Royal Shakespeare Company) in 1988. Koltai also extended his activities to include opera direction, with *The Flying Dutchman*, Hong Kong, 1987.

—Jarka M. Burian

KOPPEL, Henning.

Danish painter, sculptor, glass, ceramics and metalware designer. Born in Ostenvold, Copenhagen, 8 May 1918. Educated at Oregaards Gymnasium, Copenhagen, until 1934; attended the Bizzie Hoyer School of Drawing, Copenhagen, 1935–36; studied sculpture under Einar Utzon Frank, at the Kunstakademie, Copenhagen, 1936–37, and under Malfrey, at the Académie Ranson, Paris, 1938. Married Jytte Skouboe in 1941. Independent painter, stonemason, and freelance jewellery designer for the Svensk Tenn shop, Stockholm, 1942–45; contract silverware and jewellery designer, working with Harald Nielsen, for Georg Jensen Solvsmedie, Copenhagen, from 1945; also freelance ceramics designer, working mainly for Bing and Grondahl, Copenhagen, from 1961, and glass designer, for Holmgaards and Orrefors Glassworks, Sweden, from 1971. **Exhibitions:** Georg Jensen Inc., New York, 1966; *Scandinavian Modern Design 1880–1980*, Cooper–Hewitt Museum, New York, 1982; *Design Since 1945*, Philadelphia Museum of Art, 1983; *The Lunning Prize*, Nationalmuseum, Stockholm, 1986; *Scandinavia: Ceramics and Glass in the Twentieth Century*, Victoria and Albert Museum, London, 1989. Recipient: Gold Medal, Milan Triennale, 1951, 1954, 1957; National Art Gallery Drawing Prize, Copenhagen, 1953; Lunning Prize, Copenhagen, 1953; International Design Award, New York, 1963; Golden Spoon Award, Munich, 1963; Diamonds International Award, New York, 1966; ID Design Prize, Copenhagen, 1966; Gold Medal for Design, Florence, 1967; Exempla Gold Medal, Munich, 1970. *Died* (in Copenhagen) *27 June 1981*.

Works:

Bracelet with silver links, for Georg Jensen, 1947.

Fish dish and cover in silver, for Georg Jensen, 1954.

Wine jug in silver, for Georg Jensen, 1955.

Bowl with pedestal feet in silver, for Georg Jensen, 1958.

Serving jug in silver, for Georg Jensen, 1959.

Jug in white porcelain, for Bing and Gröndahl, 1962.

Koppel White tableware range in white porcelain, for Bing and Gröndahl, 1963.

Jug in white porcelain, for Bing and Gröndahl, 1965.

Publications:

On KOPPEL: books—*Henning Koppel: Tegningen*, Copenhagen 1938; *Modern Danish Silver* by Esbjørn Hiort, New York, London and Copenhagen 1954; *Fifty Years of Silver in the Georg Jensen Tradition* by Edgar J. Kaufmann, Erik Lassen and C. Detlev Reventlow, Copenhagen 1956; *Dansk Keramik*, edited by Bredo L. Grandjean, David Westholm and Arthur Hald, Stockholm 1960; *Modern Jewellery: An International Survey 1890–1964* by Graham Hughes, London 1963, 1964; *Henning Koppel* by Viggo Sten Moller, Copenhagen 1965; *34 Scandinavian Designers* by Svend Erik Moller, Copenhagen 1967; *Danish Design* by Svend Erik Moller, Copenhagen 1974; *International Modern Glass* by Geoffrey Beard, London 1976; *En Kobenhavnsk Porcelaenfabriks Historie: Bing och Gröndahl 1853–1978* by Erik Lassen, Copenhagen 1978; *Scandinavian Modern Design 1880–1980*, edited by David Revere McFadden, New York 1982; *Design Since 1945*, edited by Kathryn Hiesinger and George Marcus, Philadelphia and London 1983; *The Lunning Prize*, exhibition catalogue edited by Helena Dahlbäck Lutteman and Marianne Uggla, Stockholm 1986; *Scandinavia: Ceramics and Glass in the Twentieth Century* by Jennifer Hawkins Opie, London 1989.

Henning Koppel began his professional career as a silversmith in the post-World War II period, when the axiom "form follows function" was seriously being challenged by a generation who sought to forge connections between art and craft. Their objective was greater expressive freedom within the constraints of the utilitarian form.

Koppel consciously worked silver as a sculptural medium, employed no surface decoration, and concentrated entirely on producing pure, sensuous forms which invited the sense of touch. He was one of the leading figures, if not the most influential, in founding the new aesthetic which directed attention to the characteristics of silver, exploiting its reflective capacity and its high malleability.

His famous Fish Dish of 1954 has been displayed in museums around the world and is probably the best-known piece of modern Scandinavian metalwork. The hand grips formed at the ends of the cover have been designed to suggest the mouth of a fish, and this theme, carried out in flowing, asymmetrical forms, characterized much of Koppel's subsequent work. The problems of covers, spouts, and handles led to integrational considerations which freed the utilitarian vessel from strict symmetry and a central axis. His cutlery pattern Caravel (1957) was designed with top, back, and side views equally considered, thereby restoring this category of utensil to the realm of sculptural design from its more usual, rigid top view—or graphic—interpretation.

In 1965, for the ceramic company Bing and Gröndahl, Koppel designed the pattern White Koppel, which is completely devoid of decoration. Blue Koppel followed in 1975 and Comet in 1978. This latter pattern is again white and

decorated with a single-headed, blue line which diminishes to a fine tail. In 1973 he designed the stainless steel cutlery pattern New York.

Koppel's work was a powerful source of inspiration to American smiths during the 1950s and 1960s when this craft was undergoing revitalization in the art departments of colleges and universities across the country. More than any other designer of his generation, Koppel succeeded in striking a harmony between the objectives of the artist and the capacities of the virtuoso craftsman.

—Barbara Young

KORDA, Vincent.

British painter and film designer. Born Vincze Kellner, in Pusztaturpaszto, Hungary, in 1897; emigrated to Britain in 1932: naturalized, 1938. Educated in Turkeye, Kecskemet and Budapest, until 1909; studied at the College of Industrial Art, Budapest, 1910–12; also apprentice in an architect's office, Budapest, 1910–12; studied painting and drawing under Belya Avanyi Grunwald, at Kecskemet art colony, 1912–15; also studied painting in Vienna, Florence and Paris, 1919–25. Served in the Hungarian Army, 1916–18. Married the actress Gertrude Musgrove in 1933 (divorced, 1942); son: Michael. Independent painter, working in Kecskemet, Nagbanya and Budapest, 1919–26, and in Paris, 1927–32; film designer, working mainly for his brother, the producer-director Alexander Korda, in Paris, 1929–32, and in London and Hollywood, 1932–71: art director, London Films, Denham, Buckinghamshire, 1932–45, and British Lion Films, Shepperton, London, 1946–54. Recipient: Academy Award, 1940. *Died* (in London) *5 January 1979*.

Works:

Film productions include—*Marius* (A. Korda), 1931; *Men of Tomorrow* (Sagan and A. Korda), 1932; *Wedding Rehearsal* (A. Korda), 1933; *The Private Life of Henry VIII* (A. Korda), 1933; *The Girl from Maxim's* (A. Korda), 1933; *Catherine the Great* (Czinner), 1934; *The Private Life of Don Juan* (A. Korda), 1934; *The Scarlet Pimpernel* (Young), 1935; *The Ghost Goes West* (Clair), 1935; *Sanders of the River* (Z. Korda), 1935; *Moscow Nights* (Asquith), 1935; *Things To Come* (Menzies), 1935; *The Man Who Could Work Miracles* (Mendes), 1936; *Rembrandt* (A. Korda), 1936; *Men Are Not Gods* (Reisch), 1936; *Elephant Boy* (Flaherty and Z. Korda), 1937; *I, Claudius* (von Sternberg—unfinished), 1937; *Action for Slander* (Whelan), 1937; *The Squeaker* (Howard), 1937; *Paradise for Two* (Freeland), 1937; *Over the Moon* (Freeland), 1937; *21 Days* (Dean), 1937; *The Drum* (Z. Korda), 1938; *The Challenge* (Rosmer), 1938; *Prison Without Bars* (Hurst), 1938; *Q Planes* (Whelan), 1939; *The Spy in Black* (Powell), 1939; *The Lion Has Wings* (Powell, Hurst and Brunel), 1939; *The Conquest of the Air* (Z. Korda and others), 1940; *The Thief of Baghdad* (Berger, Powell and Whelan), 1940; *Old Bill and Son* (Dalrymple), 1940; *Major Barbara* (Pascal), 1941; *Lydia* (Duvivier), 1941; *That Hamilton Woman* (A. Korda), 1941; *To Be or Not to Be* (Lubitsch), 1942; *Jungle Book* (Z. Korda), 1942; *Perfect Strangers* (A. Korda), 1945; *An Ideal Husband* (A. Korda), 1947; *The Fallen Idol*

(Reed), 1948; *Bonnie Prince Charlie* (Kimmins), 1948; *The Third Man* (Reed), 1949; *Miracolo a Milano* (De Sica), 1950; *Outcast of the Islands* (Reed), 1951; *Home at Seven* (Richardson), 1952; *The Sound Barrier* (Lean), 1952; *The Holly and the Ivy* (O'Ferrall), 1952; *Malaga* (Sale), 1954; *Summer Madness* (Lean), 1955; *The Deep Blue Sea* (Litvak), 1955; *Scent of Mystery* (Cardiff), 1960; *The Longest Day* (Annakin, Marton and Wicki), 1962; *The Yellow Rolls Royce* (Asquith), 1964; *Nicholas and Alexandra* (Schaffner), 1971.

Publications:

By KORDA: article—in *Sight and Sound* (London), Spring 1934.

On KORDA: books—*Art and Design in the British Film* by Edward Carrick, London 1948; *Alexander Korda* by Paul Tabori, London 1959; *Le Decor de Film* by Leon Barsacq, Paris 1970, as *Caligari's Cabinet and Other Grand Illusions,* Boston 1976; *Alexander Korda* by Karol Kulik, New Rochelle 1975; *The Hollywood Exiles* by John Baxter, London 1976; *Charmed Lives* by Michael Korda, London 1979; *The International Dictionary of Films and Filmmakers,* London and Chicago 1987, 1991.

Vincent Korda, who took charge of the art department at Denham Film studios in the 1930s, brought to art direction there a quality far higher than that of the average designer in either theatre or film. His period as a painter in France made an imprint on both his personal set designs and those produced under his charge in the studio, while his strongly persuasive character and impatience dominated the work of those around him, from his fellow designers to carpenters and decorators who carried out the finished sets.

The ideal situation in set design is a cooperative, integrated effort between the film director, the cameraman, and the designer. In many instances, the role of the latter has been considered unimportant, but Korda never allowed this to happen. If anything, his art direction, with his strong personality, dominated the production. On the other hand, he insisted on emphasising the director's ideas and the cameraman's artistic and technical potential. Consequently, the end result was almost always satisfactory, well above average, and even when the film itself failed to gain acceptance, the set design received acclaim.

Such was the case with the film *Things to Come,* one of the first science fiction subjects brought to the screen by Denham Studios in 1936. The sets stunned with their functional, "Bauhaus" interiors and immensely distorted perspectives of exteriors. Korda pioneered the use of models for trick effects for this production, accentuating distances, and avoiding the flat, direct appearance of ordinary, dull reality.

Possibly his most memorable designs were the sets for the film *Rembrandt,* also made in 1926. As a former painter, he found a remarkable sympathy with Rembrandt and succeeded in recreating the background and atmosphere of the subject. His knowledge of architecture, combined with his pictorial sense and attention to minute detail, as well as—for a change—the money lavished on his production, resulted in one of the most satisfying achievements in the history of set design.

Korda's approach differed from Hollywood's. Instead of lavishing money on sets which did not reflect their cost on the screen, he spent little but made the sets look expensive. He strove frequently to save money and, with it, valuable time. He made his team work throughout the night on the production of *The Private*

Life of Henry VIII (1933), reusing many props to turn a bedroom into a banquet hall ready for the cameras the following morning. The next night, he turned the same set back into a reception room. He even saved (as his son maintains) the reusable nails and pasteboard structures to be used in another production. The success of this film included comments to the effect that no other film resembled such classic "Englishness" as *Henry VIII*.

He succeeded in applying his sense of period style in other films such as the unfinished *I Claudius* (1937), *That Hamilton Woman* (1941), and *The Thief of Baghdad* (1940), although the latter also demanded huge sets which proved to be almost beyond the technical resources of the British film industry at that time. In spite of his personal dislike of the style of the production, it won him an Oscar for art direction. Another production of great distinction was *The Drum* (1938), which once again gave proof of his unique sense of pictorial style, his talent for establishing the right atmosphere, and his technical perfection. Korda one of the most imaginative art directors the medium of film has had.

—John Halas

Markku Kosonen: Basket in willow, 1982

KOSONEN, Markku (Pekka).
Finnish craftsman, interior architect and designer. Born of Finnish parents, in Djupvik, Sweden, 22 January 1945. Studied at the School of Handicrafts, Punkaharju, Finland, 1960–61; Institute of Applied Arts, Helsinki, 1964–68. Married Tammi Outi in 1969; daughter: Emma. Independent craftsman and designer, establishing own workshop, Helsinki, from 1968: full-time freelance artist, since 1985. Instructor, University of Industrial Arts, Helsinki, 1968–78; planner and handicrafts instructor, National Board of Vocational Education, Helsinki, 1979–85; freelance critic and teacher, Helsinki, since 1985. Board Member, Ornamo Finnish Association of Designers, Helsinki, 1974–78 and since 1986. **Exhibitions:** *Five Finnish Artist Craftsmen,* Röhsska Konstslöjdmuseet, Göteborg, 1980; *Finland: Nature, Design, Architecture,* toured the United States, 1981; *Markku Kosonen/Kari Virtanen,* Artek, Helsinki, 1982; *Finnland Gestaltet,* Hamburg and Düsseldorf, 1983; *Design Finland,* Brighton, Sussex, 1987; *Markku Kosonen: Wood Objects,* Artek, Helsinki, 1987; *Markku Kosonen,* Konsthantverkana, Stockholm, 1988; *The Language of Wood,* American Craft Museum, New York, 1989; *Markku Kosonen: Easter,* Galleria

25, Helsinki, 1989. **Collections:** Museum of Applied Arts, Helsinki; Röhsska Konstslöjdmuseet, Goteborg; Nationalmuseum, Stockholm; Kunst₀industrimuseet, Oslo; Museum für Kunst₀ und Gewerbe, Hamburg; Museum für Kunst₀handwerk, Frankfurt. Recipient: Finnish State Prize for Industrial Art, 1981; Three-Year Finnish State Artist's Stipend, 1985–88. Address: Luotsikatu 4 A 2, 00160 Helsinki, Finland.

Works:

Pestle and mortar in curly birch, 1975.
Workbench in birch, 1980.
Baskets in rush and willow, 1988.

Publications:

On KOSONEN: articles—"Sense of Wood" in *Form Function Finland* (Helsinki), no. 1, 1988; "Av videung" by K. Wickman in *Form* (Stockholm), no. 5, 1988; "Only Brushwood?" by S. Parko in *Muoto* (Helsinki), no. 33, 1989.

The life of a tree is in its seed, which carries in its flight the heritage of its species. After falling to the ground and taking root, it stays there all the time. A tree attains its full height during the lifespan of a human being. After that, it grows wiser—provided it is allowed to remain standing. The growth of a tree can be compared to that of a person. Such is its educational purpose. Since it is a renewable natural resource, a tree is an example of the eternal cycle of life. As a material it does not last forever. Wood "lives" even after death—by shrinking, swelling, or rotting. Time and insects eat it; it cracks and finally disintegrates. Wood is new to every era. In using it, one must consider what it is needed for, and what kind of ideals are to be interpreted from it.

The forests are our lungs and our souls: they give life to the entire Earth. A chill to the soul follows from the destruction of our forests. The forest has given such good cover and protection to we Finns that it has even isolated us. From trees we have derived energy for both warmth and food. We fend off physical cold with the help of a cell-structure insulating the heat of the wood. It surrounds the sphere of our life like the shell of a building. As protection from the changing weather and as a mediator on behalf of Nature, the tree teaches us the wisdom of an ecological way of life.

—Markku Kosonen

There are 40 tree species growing in Finland. Of these, industry uses three: birch, spruce and pine. The rest can be left to artists and craftspeople.

Interior designer and craftsman Markku Kosonen has been working with wood for several years, using some of these 37 species left over by industry as his material. Birch, spruce and pine do not interest him because of their industrial character, but for example alder, apple, larch or willow offer somebody who can handle wood all kinds of fresh potential.

Markku Kosonen's wooden objects are mortars, chopping boards, dishes, baskets, boxes. For him, practical function is something he wants to stick to, although his 1987 exhibition at Artek in Helsinki also included some magnificent willow basket work, which was actually more like sculpture. "The willow is one of the visually most fascinating trees we have," says Markku Kosonen. "It constantly produces 'new' species. Each season of the year makes it look different. The colours of the trunks in the spring sun, ranging from yellow to dark brown, form a particularly beautiful sight."

The essential features of Markku Kosonen's work are his themes, developed out of the natural forms, the shapes, created using geometrical patterns with constant variation, and the beautifully finished treatment of the wood. When working with his hands, the artist has time to think and the thought gets conveyed to the object. The thought follows its own course, changing all the time, and the hand makes the next piece different, unique.

—Kristina Paatero

KROLL, Boris.
American textile designer. Born in Buffalo, New York, 11 October 1913. Apprenticed in family furniture manufacture business, New York, 1930–32; mainly self-taught in design. Served in the United States Army Corps of Engineers, in India, Burma, Philippines and Japan, 1943–45. Married Lynn Steyert in 1945; children: Geoffrey, Eric and Lisa. Freelance textile designer from 1932, and manufacturer, New York, from 1938: founder, president, chief executive and director of design, Cromwell Designs, 1938–61, Boris Kroll Fabrics from 1946, 220 East 51st Street Corporation, 1950–79, Boris Kroll Fabrics of Los Angeles, and Boris Kroll Prints, 1955–64, Boris Kroll Labs, and Boris Kroll Fabrics of Miami, 1957–64, Boris Kroll Fabrics of Illinois, 1959–64, Boris Kroll Jacquard Looms from 1959, and BK Land Corporation from 1968. President, Decorative Design Association, 1958; vice-president of the resources council, Association of Interior Designers, 1963; board member, Color Association of the United States, 1967; advisory committee member, SONA Handicrafts and Loom Export Corporation of India, 1967–70. **Exhibitions:** *Good Design*, Museum of Modern Art, New York, 1953; Seattle Art Museum, 1955; Detroit Institute of Arts, 1962, 1966; Victoria and Albert Museum, London, 1965; Purdue University, Lafayette, Indiana, 1970; Georgia State University, Atlanta, 1970; Guild Hall of East Hampton, New York, 1977; Fashion Institute of Technology, New York, 1980. **Collections:** Detroit Institute of Arts; Victoria and Albert Museum, London. Recipient: Museum of Modern Art Design Award, New York, 1953; American Institute of Interior Designers Award, New York, 1967; *Industrial Design* Award, New York, 1970; American Society of Industrial Designers Award, 1976. Honorary doctorate: Philadelphia College of Textiles, 1971. Address: Boris Kroll Fabrics, 979 Third Avenue, New York, New York 10022, U.S.A.

Publications:

By KROLL: article—in *Interiors* (New York), May/June 1968.

On KROLL: book—*Design Since 1945*, edited by Kathryn Hiesinger and George Marcus, Philadelphia and London 1983; articles—in *New York World Telegram*, 7 October 1939; *American Fabrics* (New York), Fall 1958; *House Beautiful* (New York), November 1964; *Interiors* (New York), January 1965, September 1969, January 1981, November 1981; *Seattle Times*, 17 April 1969; *San Francisco Chronicle*, 24 April 1969; *San Francisco Examiner*, 23 April 1969; *Atlanta Journal*, 21 April 1970; *Interior Design* (New York), February 1971, April 1982; *New York Times*, 16 January 1977.

A creative fabric is the result of the calculated integration of color, fiber, weave, and design. Design in fabrics is the answer.

Even as the structural integrity of any architectural undertaking is intrinsic to its beauty, so is the quality of the infinite number of components which go into its interiors. As a manufacturer of fabrics for interiors, I am aware of my responsibility to that end. Durability must be considered. The selection of a particular fiber—wool, silk, linen, or nylon—does not necessarily guarantee long life for the fabric. What gives it resistance to wear is the fabric designer's engineering of construction, involving such factors as staple length, spinning system, how many turns are specified in the yarn in relation to the size of the yarn (heavy yarn needs fewer turns, finer yarn needs more turns), or, if the yarn is a plied yarn made up of two yarns each with specific turns, then plied with what specific number of turns in creating a final two-plied yarn ready for use in weaving, etc. For filling, less twist is used or what is known as a filling twist. It is a misconception by interior designers that the type of fiber or raw material necessarily means better-wearing fabric. This is simply not true. Durability is achieved by selecting and engineering of yarns for warps. The number of ends per inch in the warp, the selection and combination of weaves, and the final determination of picks per inch are necessary factors in attaining the balance a fabric needs in order to affect the durability of the finished fabric. A heavy, bulky fabric is not necessarily long-wearing.

Superior resistance to the changes inevitably caused by exposure to sunlight, gas fading, crocking, water-spotting, and dry-cleaning is necessary in any contract fabric. Such superior resistance can only be achieved through the use of selected dyestuffs and chemicals and expert dyeing techniques—certain fibers must be dyed with certain types of dyes. Frequently, the fabric designer must compromise on the color desired in order to meet fastness standards. To achieve especially vibrant blues and greens and maintain a high degree of fastness to light, each fiber must be treated in an individual manner (i.e., linen—direct colors are used; cotton and rayon—direct and fiber reactive dyes; silk—directs and acids; wool—acid colors and modified reactives; orlon—poly disperse colors and basic colors). It is important to remember that within all these dyestuff categories, there are variations in the color fastness properties. A knowledgeable chemist and dyer will select and use only those that perform well. There are new and sophisticated machines to test the color fastness of dyes. Improper dyestuffs, or incorrect dyeing, may result in color that comes off when rubbed.

As in apparel fabrics, light and bright colors show the effects of soiling more rapidly than medium-value, neutral colors. Very dark colors frequently attract lint and show up dust particles more readily. The knowledgeable designer/specifier tries to avoid bright clear yellows and such color in areas subject to hard use. Design elements such as striae and multi-color effects will help reduce the visual effects of soiling. It is increasingly important that contract fabrics be engineered so that they can be cleaned with solvent dry-cleaning methods.

One of the biggest hazards a fabric must undergo is the stress and pull by the body which causes seam-slippage. I am constantly amazed at the fact that furniture designers are asked to design upholstered furniture which will hold snugly and securely to a petite feminine body

Boris Kroll: *Island Cloth Collection* (4 patterns), 1989

and which at the same time will hold a lineman from a football team who may weigh 280 pounds. The problems can be avoided by proper engineering of fabrics, size of warp yarn, selection of size and type of filling, selection of weaves, both face and back weaves in relation to warp yarns, ends per inch, and picks per inch in order to avoid unravelling of both warp and yarn filling.

My life is dedicated to designing and manufacturing the highest quality fabrics for interiors. I can produce the kind of fabrics that I described above both for residential use and for use in public places because I have complete control over all phases of production. They are designed under my supervision in the design studio of Boris Kroll Fabrics; the yarn is spun to my specifications; the construction is determined; experimental blankets are woven to find the most suitable yarns, weaves, wraps, fillings, etc.; dyeing is accomplished in the dye laboratories of Boris Kroll Fabrics; and, when everything is perfect, according to our specifications, it is woven in our own manufacturing center. My integrity of design can only be achieved because I have complete control over every phase of the manufacture of my fabrics.

—Boris Kroll

As a result of his sensitivity as a designer, weaver, and colorist, combined with his technological knowledge, Boris Kroll is a world leader in the professional field of fabric design and production. In 1930, he started working in his brother's modern-furniture factory in New York. When, to his dismay, he discovered that the range of fabrics suitable for such furniture was extremely limited, he learned to weave on a hand loom and mastered the intricate Jacquard loom. In 1936, he began to produce custom fabrics from yarns he sometimes dyed in his own bathtub.

During the 1930s, he was particularly concerned with fabrics using silks and rayons, and his hand-woven fabrics were commissioned for many luxury liners, including the *S.S. America*. Following World War II, Kroll turned his attention to the use of nylon in fabrics for interiors. His unique handling of pattern and texture blossomed in the 1950s, particularly in his Caribbean and Mediterranean collections, which were marked by saturated colors and flamboyant designs. In the 1960s, he received enormous attention for his collection of hard-edged, geometric Jacquards, as well as for his fabrics which were woven or printed with organic motifs. He produced a series of limited-edition Jacquard tapestries, including Banners and Confetti, during the 1970s. His fabrics for the 1980s, including Jacquard weaves, have a more subtle, toned-down approach to design and coloration.

Kroll exercises great control over his designs, sometimes producing five or six hand-woven samples before approving the final production sample. Quality control has a high priority in his business. He has enormous enthusiasm for his profession and is constantly searching for new fabric designs and technological solutions. While his production is distinctive, the variety in his design, weave, texture, and color is enormous. He is intrigued by the triangle and has worked its angular, diagonal appeal into a number of fabrics with great success. This is particularly true with his Jacquards, when he builds on intricate geometries to generate an illusion of complexity and depth. Like a composer, he is a master at taking a design theme and transforming it with either bold or subtle variations, sometimes through scale or color changes. For example, Bentley, a recent fabric with a subtle, zigzag linearity, is translated to Claridge, using lurex yarn in the figure for a change in fabric

character. He delights in working with different scales, and is as intrigued with small block designs as he is with supergraphics with repeats of forty-eight inches or more. His color palette has included the shocking as well as the subtle, and he is particularly adept at using a variety of colored yarns to produce fabrics with an overall grayed tone.

He has also produced handsome contemporary handscreened velvets, such as Peregrine and Refractions, as well as distinctive modern sheers, often with delicate prints of tropical leaves or shells. His fabrics, such as Pampas, drawn from African or Latin American sources, reflect his interest in interpreting traditional forms for modern design solutions. This was especially true in his Shibui collection of 1963.

Kroll works in a wide vein, and his insistence on design quality and fabric performance have earned him his leadership in the industry.

—Grant Greapentrog

KUKKAPURO, Yrjo.

Finnish interior, exhibition and furniture designer. Born in Viipuri, 6 April 1933. Studied at Imatra Art School, 1951–52; Institute of Crafts and Design, Helsinki, 1954–58. Married Irmeli Kukkapuro in 1956; daughter: Lisa. Freelance designer, establishing Studio Kukkapuro design firm, Helsinki, since 1959: has designed interiors and exhibits for Marimekko, SAS Scandinavian Airlines System, Rank Xerox, Finnish Design Center, Helsinki Ateneum Art Museum, etc., and furniture for Haimi, etc.; Avarte Oy company set up to produce Kukkapuro furniture, Helsinki, from 1980. Instructor, Institute of Crafts and Design, Helsinki, 1963–69, and Department of Architecture, Helsinki Polytechnic, 1969–74; Professor, 1974–80, and Rector, 1978–80, University of Industrial Arts, Helsinki. Chairman, State Committee on Arts and Crafts, and member of the Central State Art Committee, Helsinki, since 1977. **Exhibitions:** *Annual Design Exhibition,* Helsinki Art Hall, 1959; Milan Triennale, 1960, 1968; *Yrjo Kukkapuro: Furniture,* Finnish Design Centre, Helsinki, 1962; *75 Years of Finnish Design,* Liljevalchs Konsthall, Stockholm, 1963; *Art of Living,* Grand Palais, Paris, 1967; *The Modern Chair,* Victoria and Albert Museum, London, 1970; *100 Years of Finnish Design,* Ateneum Art Museum, Helsinki, 1975; *Metamorphoses Finlandaises,* Centre Georges Pompidou, Paris, 1978; *Form und Struktur,* Museum of Industrial Arts, Vienna, 1980; *Finnland Gestaltet,* Museum für Kunst und Gewerbe, Hamburg, 1981 (toured) *The Lunning Prize,* Nationalmuseum, Stockholm, 1986. **Collections:** Museum of Industrial Arts, Helsinki; Museum of Modern Art, New York; Victoria and Albert Museum, London. Recipient: Kaunis Koti Bursary, Finnish Society of Crafts and Design, 1961; Grand Prize for Arts and Literature, City of Helsinki, 1963; Lunning Prize, 1966; Design Award, Republic of Finland, 1970; First Prize, Furniture of the Year Competition, Helsinki, 1972; Illum Prize, Copenhagen, 1977; First Prize, *New York* Magazine Chairs Competition, 1974; Gold Medal, Brno International Fair, 1981; Artek Prize, Helsinki, 1982; Pro Finlandia Medal, Helsinki, 1983; Institute of Business Designers Award, New York, 1984. Member: SIO Interior Designers Association; Ornamo Finnish Associa-

tion of Designers. Address: Alppitie 25, 02700 Kauniainen, Finland.

Works:

Shop interiors, for Marimekko, in Helsinki, 1963–65.
Carousel 412 chair, 1965.
Finnish exhibit layouts, at the XIV Milan Triennale, 1968.
Ars 69 exhibition layouts, for the Ateneum Art Museum, Helsinki, 1969.
Finnish displays, Scandinavian Furniture Fair, 1969, 1970, 1971.
New York air terminal, for SAS Scandinavian Airlines System, 1971.
Rank Xerox head office interiors, Helsinki, 1972.
City Theatre interiors, Imatra, Finland, 1973.
City and main underground station interiors, Helsinki, 1973–77 and 1979–82.

Publications:

By KUKKAPURO: books—*New Form Furniture: Japan,* with others, Tokyo 1971.

On KUKKAPURO: books—*Scandinavian Design: Objects of a Life Style* by Eileene Harrison Beer, New York 1975; *Finnish Design 1875–1975* by Timo Sarpaneva, Erik Bruun and Erik Kruskopf, Helsinki 1975; *One Hundred Great Finnish Designs,* edited by Per Mollerup, Snekkersten 1979; *Finnland Gestaltet,* exhibition catalogue by Tapio Periainen, Simo Heikkila and others, Espoo 1981; *Finnish Vision,* with texts by P. Suhonen, J. Lintinen and others, Helsinki 1983; *The Conran Directory of Design,* edited by Stephen Bayley, London 1985; *International Design Yearbook 1985/86,* edited by Robert A. M. Stern, London 1985; *The Lunning Prize,* exhibition catalogue edited by Helena Dahlbäck Lutteman and Marianne Uggla, Stockholm 1986; *Finnish Industrial Design,* edited by Tua Pontasuo, Helsinki 1987; *International Design Yearbook 1988/89,* edited by Arata Isozaki, London 1988.

KUKKASJÄRVI, Irma.

Finnish textile designer. Born Irma Anneli Hilska, in Helsinki, 8 February 1941. Studied handicrafts, 1962–63, and weaving, 1963–64, Training College for Handicraft Teachers, Helsinki; textiles, Institute of Applied Arts, Helsinki, 1964–68. Married Kullervo Kukkasjärvi in 1966 (died, 1983); son: Sampo. Freelance textile designer, working for industry, hotels and public buildings, in Helsinki, since 1968: designer for the Commonwealth Trust India Limited, London, from 1982. Part-time instructor, University of Industrial Arts, Helsinki, 1975–80. **Exhibitions:** *Towards Industry,* Talli-Skanno, Helsinki, 1968; *Experimental Nordic Textile,* toured Norway, Sweden and Denmark, 1970–71; *Expressions Textiles Nordiques,* Angers, France, 1973; *Finnish Textile Art,* Stockholm, 1974; 7th International Textile Biennale, Lausanne, 1975; *Tapisserie Vivante,* Palais de Congrès, Paris, 1977; *Finnland Gestaltet,* Museum für Kunst und Gewerbe, Hamburg, 1981 (toured Germany and Netherlands); *Five Finnish Textile Artists,* toured Scandinavia, 1982–83; *Irma Kukkasjarvi: Textiles,* Kluuvin

Irma Kukkasjarvi: Stage curtain in linen and wool, for the Iisaliti Cultural Centre, 1989

Galleria, Helsinki, 1985; *Textile Artist Irma Kukkasjarvi,* Bronda Art Gallery, Helsinki, 1986; *Textiles in Space: Four Finnish Textile Artists,* Ontario Science Centre, Toronto, 1986 (travelled to Winnipeg and Montreal, 1987); *Art By Design: Reflections of Finland,* Katonah Gallery, New York, 1988. **Collections:** Museum of Applied Arts, Helsinki; Museum of Modern Art, Kyoto; Finnish House of Parliament, Helsinki; City Theatre, Lahti; City Theatre, Jyvaskyla; Finnish Embassy, Canberra; City of Angers, France; Baghdad Conference Palace, Iraq. Recipient: Finnish State Award for Applied Arts, 1978; Product Design Award, American Society of Interior Designers, 1978; Silver Medal, International Textile Triennale, Lodz, 1978; Textile Designer of the Year Award, Helsinki, 1984; Pro Finlandia Medal, Helsinki, 1985; Finnish Television Cultural Award, 1986. Address: Vyokatu 9 B 12, 00160 Helsinki, Finland.

Works:

Carpets and rya relief, for Baghdad Conference Palace, Iraq, 1978.
Interior textiles and rya relief, for the Parliament House Annex, Helsinki, 1978–79.
Stage curtain, for the City Theatre, Jyvaskyla, 1981–82.
Stage curtain and interior textiles, for the City Theatre, Lahti, 1981–83.
Forum collection of woven fabrics, for Marimekko, 1983–84.
Furnishing fabrics, curtains and carpets, for Eka Group Headquarters, Helsinki, 1985.
Interior textiles, for Villa Johanna, Helsinki, 1986.

Auditorium carpet and textiles, for Amer Oy Headquarters, Helsinki, 1987.
Carpets, for Skop-Rahoitus, Vantaa, 1988.
Carpet, for Mec Rastor, Espoo, 1988.
Carpet, for Tuko Oy, Helsinki, 1989.
Carpets and handwoven blinds, for Partek Oy, Helsinki, 1989.
Stage curtain, for Tampere Congress and Concert Centre, Finland, 1989–90.

Publications:

On KUKKASJÄRVI: books—*Finnland Gestaltet,* exhibition catalogue by Tapio Periainen, Simo Heikkila and others, Espoo 1981; *Finnish Vision,* with texts by P. Suhonen, J. Lintinen and others, Helsinki 1983; *Textiles in Space: Four Finnish Textile Artists,* exhibition catalogue with text by Marianne Aav, Helsinki 1986; *Art By Design: Reflections of Finland,* exhibition catalogue with texts by Tutta Runeberg and others, New York 1988; article—"Impressions of Irma" by M. L. Markkula in *Form Function Finland* (Helsinki), no. 1, 1987; films—*Irma Kukkasjärvi: Land of the Blue Flower,* Finnish television film by Kirsti Petajaniemi, Helsinki 1979; *Reflections of Light in the Arts* by Kirsti Petajaniemi, Helsinki 1989.

With respect to her manner of working Irma Kukkasjärvi carries on the tradition created by Dora Jung. Her works unite designing interior fabrics and continuous co-operation with industry in the decorative textiles produced at her own textile atelier.

Irma Kukkasjärvi graduated as a textile designer from the Institute of Applied Arts at the end of the 1960s, at a time when the impor-

tance of designing anonymous everyday objects was being stressed, and this factor is a source of the dualism which marks her work. She became interested in the traditional methods used to produce ryijy wall rugs when she was still a student, and she has undoubtedly developed into one of the leading ryijy designers in Finland. She has broken with established traditions of decorating ryijy rugs with different experiments involving both form and choice of material, as well as by using nap of various lengths in order to produce ryijy rugs with a relief effect.

Irma Kukkasjärvi does not consider it possible to draw any clear line between decorative textiles and the textiles used for interior decorating. In public premises so-called purely decorative textiles, such as ryijy wall rugs, may, in addition to having aesthetic characteristics also serve a functional purpose as noise abaters, and the whole created by well-designed interior textiles undoubtedly also provides a total artistic experience. The annex to the Finnish House of Parliament in Helsinki and the renovation of the older part of the building carried out during the late 1970s and early 1980s provided Irma Kukkasjärvi with a large, unified interior to be decorated.

A splendid example of how the design of textiles for normal and decorative purposes can complete and enrich an architectural whole is provided by the main curtain Irma Kukkasjärvi designed during 1981 and 1982 for the Jyväskylä City Theatre. The theatre is one of Alvar Aalto's creations, and the curtain was designed in close co-operation with the architect's office. Its simple vertical beam decorations continue the decorative elements used in the architecture, in addition to which they attempt in

Mervyn Kurlansky: Poster for the Museum of Modern Art, Oxford, 1988

some manner to emphasize the impression created by the low space.

During 1983 and 1984 Irma Kukkasjärvi designed a woven cotton collection of interior fabrics for Marimekko Oy which was given the name "Forum". In this collection the clear, timeless language of design was combined with the demands now made both on public premises and on the textiles used for home interior decorating.

—Marianne Aav

KURLANSKY, Mervyn (Henry).
British graphic designer. Born in Johannesburg, South Africa, 3 March 1936; emigrated to Britain in 1958. Educated at Highlands North High School, Johannesburg, until 1954; studied at Central School of Arts and Crafts, London, 1959-61. Design assistant to Peter Wildbur, at BDMW Design Associates, London, 1960-61; freelance designer, London, 1961-62; graphics director of the planning unit, for Interiors International (Knoll International, UK), London, 1962-67; freelance designer, London, 1967-69; partner, with Theo Crosby, Alan Fletcher and Colin Forbes, in Crosby/Fletcher/Forbes design studio, London, 1969-72; founder-partner, with Crosby, Fletcher, Forbes and Kenneth Grange, in Pentagram Design partnership, London, from 1972. **Exhibitions:** *107 Grafici dell'AGI,* Castello Sforzesco, Milan, 1974; *Forum Design,* Linz, Austria, 1980; *Libres d'Artista,* Spain, 1981; *Art and Design,* Plymouth College of Art, Devon, 1982; Reinhold Brown Gallery, New York, 1982; Israel Museum, Jerusalem, 1982; *Graphics UK,* Saint Martin's School of Art, London, 1982; Tyler School of Art, Philadelphia, 1983. Recipient: Design and Art Directors Association Silver Medal, London, 1972, 1973; Bronze Medal, Brno Graphics Biennale, 1978; Japanese Ministry of Trade and Industry Medal, 1978; Packaging Design Council Gold Medal, London, 1979. Member, Alliance Graphique Internationale, 1974; Fellow, Chartered Society of Designers, London, 1982, and Society of Typographic Designers, London, 1983. Address: Pentagram Design, 11 Needham Road, London W11 2RP, England.

Works:

Promotional campaign graphics, for Interiors International, 1965.
Book cover designs, for Penguin Books Limited, 1967-69.
Nobrium promotional campaign, for Roche, 1970.
Coffee canister designs, for Lyons, 1972.
Music and catalogue cover designs, for Boosey and Hawkes, 1972-80.
Corporate identity, technical and promotional graphics, for Reuters Limited, from 1972.
Promotional campaign and identity graphics, for Rotring UK, 1975.
Tactics men's cosmetics packaging, for Shiseido, 1977.
Prestel computer information service identity, for British Telecom, 1978.
John Barr whisky label and packaging, for John Walker and Sons, 1980.

Publications:

By KURLANSKY: books—*Pentagram: The Work of Five Designers,* with Pentagram partners, London 1972; *Watching My Name Go By,* designer, London 1973; *Living by Design,* with Pentagram partners, London and New York 1978; articles—in *Campaign* (London), July 1981; *American Fashion and Fabrics* (New York), no. 127, 1982; *Creative Review* (London), July 1982; *Typographic* (London), December 1982; *Jewish Chronicle* (London), June 1983.

On KURLANSKY: book—*107 Grafici dell'AGI,* with texts by Renzo Zorzi and Franco Grignani, Venice 1974; *The Conran Directory of Design,* edited by Stephen Bayley, London 1985.

Design serves for me a personal need to communicate. Earlier in my life, I tried to meet this need by making music and by painting. In music, I was quickly drawn to jazz, because of its immediate, expressive possibilities unfettered by the written score. In painting, my allegiances were futurist and abstract, with a strong attention to the industrial environment.

But neither of these avenues satisfied a second and equally powerful drive: to relate my creative work to the immediacy of everyday life. Design is inextricably bound up with the ordinary, living world. Its commercial basis, far from troubling me, bridges the gap between "art" and "life."

The teacher who influenced me most was a painter with an acute appreciation for visual language. I remember he compared looking at Malevich for the first time to hearing Japanese for the first time. You might "like" or "dislike" it, but until you had actually learned it, the new language would mean very little.

This sense of language informs my work in the way I use symbols, familiar images, even clichés—speaking to a particular audience in the visual vocabulary they already possess. I tend to prefer found objects to drawings, and like many of my contemporaries, I am completely eclectic in sources I use for both style and imagery.

I have an aversion to formulae and fixed styles, again like most present-day designers. In borrowing, I always alter the ideas I use—manipulating, recombining and adding, in order to communicate something new. In fact, I believe that all ideas, including those yet to be seen, already exist: We gain access to them by learning to attend in the right way. So, in a sense, every work of art and design is a "found object."

Ours is the age of information. We have instantly available to us not only the images of our own time but also the wealth of the past, which is constantly growing as more of it is uncovered. Indeed, the past has become a present resource, and I draw on it without any sense of nostalgia. It is my nature to live in the present and to look forward to the future. I welcome the arrival of computer technology, for the richness of communication and new knowledge that it promises.

At the heart of good design is pleasure—the pleasure the designer takes in his work and the pleasure he creates for his audience. Of special importance to me is the "sudden, unexpected intellectual pleasure" of wit. The intellectual component here is essential, for I relish complex problems which can be expressed in a visual solution of surprising simplicity.

Politically, I believe in being alive to new possibilities rather than allying myself with one system of ideas in opposition to another.

As for my work, I have no "plans" for its future development. With each new job, I start again, holding my mind open to fresh discoveries—prepared to find, to create, and to communicate.

—Mervyn Kurlansky

LAGERFELD, Karl (Otto).

German fashion designer. Born in Hamburg, 10 September 1938. Educated in Paris, until 1955. Worked as assistant to fashion designer Pierre Balmain, Paris, 1955–58; art director, Jean Patou fashion house, Paris, 1958–63; freelance fashion designer, working for Chloe, Krizia, Ballantyne, Timwear, Charles Jourdain, Mario Valentino, Fendi, Cadette, Max Mara, etc., in Paris, from 1964; director of collections and ready-to-wear fashions, Chanel Haute Couture, Paris, from 1983; established Karl Lagerfeld ready-to-wear fashion house, Paris, 1984, and KL ready-to-wear in Germany, from 1984; created fragrances Lagerfeld, for Elizabeth Arden, 1975, Chloe-Lagerfeld for men, 1978, KL for women, 1983, and KL for men, 1984. Also film and stage costume designer, and photographer. **Exhibitions:** *40 Years of Italian Fashion*, Trump Tower, New York, 1983; *Karl Lagerfeld: Fotografien*, Galerie Hans Mayer, Dusseldorf, 1989. Recipient: International Wool Secretariat Prize, Paris, 1954. Address: 10 rue du Colonel Bellando, 98000 Monaco-Ville, Principality of Monaco.

Publications:

On LAGERFELD: books—*Fairchild's Who's Who in Fashion*, New York 1975, 1980; *A History of Fashion* by J. Anderson Black and Madge Garland, London 1975, 1980; *The World of Fashion: People, Places, Resources* by Eleanor Lambert, New York and London 1976; *In Fashion: Dress in the Twentieth Century* by Prudence Glynn, London 1978; *French Style* by Suzanne Slesin and Stafford Cliff, New York and London 1982; *The Collector's Book of Twentieth Century Fashion* by Frances Kennett, London and New York 1983; *40 Years of Italian Fashion*, exhibition catalogue compiled by B. G. Aragno, Rome 1983; *McDowell's Directory of Twentieth Century Fashion* by Colin McDowell, London 1984; *The Conran Directory of Design*, edited by Stephen Bayley, London 1985; *The Encyclopaedia of Fashion from 1840 to the 1980s* by Georgina O'Hara, London 1986.

A Hamburger who trained under Pierre Balmain and Jean Patou, Karl Lagerfeld has described himself as a romantic, full of nostalgia for the seventeenth and eighteenth centuries. "Clothes should put back what's missing in a woman's life. I want them to have the eighteenth-century countryside, the Elysian fields, the *douceur de vie*," he stated. Lagerfeld wanted to recreate the paintings of Fragonard and Watteau by presenting modern women as shepherdesses. This is a very artificial concept of history, for the past was far from being Elysian to most women, and most flocks of sheep were watched over by shepherds, not girls. Lagerfeld revived so many historical looks that by April 1980 the *Sunday Times* was complaining that it was becoming boring and that he confused journalists and customers alike, for what was he mixing now, art nouveau and Art Deco? His clothes are a compound of the 1920s, 1930s, 1940s, 1950s and anything that went before. Skillfully made, they can be either in misty tones or in bright colour contrasts, such as black and yellow, but what is peculiarly Lagerfeld about them except the cut? He takes ideas from all sides, and his 1978 duster coat/dress had been featured in Sheridan Barnett's collection of 1974. This *omnium gatherum* approach is more theatrical entertainment than a serious attempt to contribute to mainstream fashion. Designers have always plundered the past, but it can be done more subtly than this.

In 1980, Lagerfeld stated, "The role of the designer is not to dictate length but to update," and proceeded to show no less than three hemlines, at mid-thigh mini, knee, and mid-calf lengths. However, trying to revive anything as recent as the mini could only fail, and it is the longer hemlines that have reached the High Street. It is clear that Lagerfeld has inherited some of the simplicity of line he received from Balmain after Molyneux, but lacking are that careful evolution and avoidance of dramatic change which those couturiers maintained as the fundamental principle of good design. What that requires is resolute self-discipline and a degree of modesty, but Lagerfeld is too fond of self-indulgence in fantasy. He lives surrounded by history in a château filled with state beds and wallpaper after Marie Antoinette frocks. One cannot imagine Lagerfeld feeling that the creation is more important than its creator, as do the best women designers. There are too many signs of the male ego at work.

Lagerfeld is so good at cut that really he does not need to strive for a sensational revival every season. He could produce the same classics every year, and they would still sell because of the beauty of the construction. Doubtless, Lagerfeld would reply that such absence of sensation would give no opportunity for his imagination, but of course genius could find opportunity in such a narrow field. That is the real challenge.

—Diana de Marly

LALANNE, Claude and Francois-Xavier.

French sculptors, furniture, jewellery and interior designers. Claude Lalanne: born in Paris. Studied architecture at the Ecole des Beaux-Arts, and the Ecole des Arts Décoratifs, Paris. Francois-Xavier Lalanne: born in Agen in 1927. Studied painting at the Académie Julian, Paris, 1945–47. The Lalannes, married in 1962, collaborated as interior and stage designers, Paris, 1952–64: have worked on electroplated copper and brass sculptures and furniture from 1964, porcelain works from 1965, plastic works from 1970, and concrete structures from 1971. **Exhibitions:** Galerie J, Paris, 1964; Galerie Alexandre Iolas, Paris, 1966, 1970, 1972, 1974, 1976; Art Institute of Chicago, 1967; Alexander Iolas Gallery, New York, 1967; Galleria Iolas, Milan, 1970; Eat-Art Galerie, Dusseldorf, 1970; Galerie Alexandre Iolas, Geneva, 1970; Galerie Paul Facchetti, Zurich, 1971; Galerie Zoumboulakis, Athens, 1971; Maison de la Culture, Amiens, 1972, 1974; Royal Scottish Academy, Edinburgh, 1974; Galerie Sweden, Paris, 1974; Centre National d'Art Contemporain, Paris, 1975; Museum Boymans-Van Beuningen, Rotterdam, 1975; Centre d'Art, Flaine, 1975; Whitechapel Art Gallery, London, 1976; Artcurial, Paris, 1983; Artcurial, Munich, 1989. **Collection:** Museum Boymans-Van Beuningen, Rotterdam. Address: 15 rue de Nemours, 77116 Ury, France.

Works:

Office interiors and furnishings, for Olivier de la Baume, Paris, 1965.
Flock of Sheep furniture—objects in wool, wood and other media, 1965.
Porcelain products, for Manufacture Nationale de Sèvres, 1966–72.
Hippopotamus cabinet-sculpture in copper and lead flux, 1968.
Labyrinth open-air fountain and maze, for the University of Pennylvania, 1969–74.
123-piece cutlery service in copper and silver, 1971.
Furniture range, for Daedalus Concepts, New York, 1971.
Crocodile armchair in galvanized copper, 1972.
Monumental head in stone and concrete, for CES Company, Ury, 1973.
Petit Poisson fish-sculpture in copper and bronze, 1974.
Mirrors in galvanized copper, bronze, lead and silver, 1975.

Publications:

By LALANNE: book—*Claude et Francois-Xavier Lalanne: Dessins*, Paris and Milan 1972.

On LALANNE: books—*Les Lalanne*, exhibition catalogue with text by James Metcalfe, Paris 1964; *Les Lalanne*, exhibition catalogue with text by Francois Nourissier, Paris 1966; *Claude et Francois-Xavier Lalanne*, exhibition catalogue with text by Jon Russell, Edinburgh 1974; *Les Lalanne: Domesticated Beasts and Other Creatures*, exhibition catalogue with text by John Russell, London 1976; *Twentieth Century Furniture* by Philippe Garner, London

Karl Lagerfeld: *Antiker Traum* photograph, 1987

1980; *French Style* by Suzanne Slesin and Stafford Cliff, New York and London 1982; *Les Années 60* by Anne Bony, Paris 1983.

LANCETTI, Pino.
Italian fashion designer. Born Giuseppe Lancetti, in Bastia Umbra, Perugia, 27 November 1932. Studied fine arts, at Bernardino di Betto Art Institute, Perugia, 1946-53; trained in fashion design with De Luca and Carosa, in Rome, 1956-61. Worked as ceramics painter for Santarelli, in Gualdo Tadino, 1952; independent painter, Rome, 1954-56; freelance fashion designer, working for Simonetta and Fabiani, Rome, 1956-59; founder-director, of Lancetti Creazioni fashion house, Rome, from 1961: opened "Shop in Shop" boutiques in Osaka, 1979, Tokyo, 1980, Sapporo and Kobe, 1981, Fukuoka, 1982, in Tokyo, Nagoya and Kyoto, 1983, and a boutique in Milan, 1983; designed kimono fabrics, for Ichida textile company, Tokyo, 1982. Also film costume designer, from 1962. Instructor in fashion design, Bernardino

di Betto Art Institute, Perugia, 1968-72, and Armando Diaz professional school, Rome, 1972-73. **Exhibitions:** *Il Disegno dell'Alta Moda Italiana dal 1940 al 1970*, National Institute of Graphic Arts, Rome, 1982 (toured); *Consequenze Impreviste*, Pretorio Palace, Prato, 1983; *Italian Fashion 1920-1980*, Daimaru Museum, Osaka, 1983 (toured); *40 Years of Italian Fashion*, Trump Tower, New York, 1983. Recipient: *La Stampa* Premio Speciale, Florence, 1964; Tiberio d'Oro Award, Capri, 1972; Cavaliere d'Onore, Rome, 1975. Addresses: Piazza di Spagna 93, 00187 Rome; Via Condotti 61, 00187 Rome; Via Bocca di Leone 25, 00187 Rome, Italy.

Works:

Film costumes include—*La Lebre e la Tartaruga*, 1962; *La Mia Signora*, 1964; *La Congiuntura*, 1964; *Three Bites of the Apple*, 1967; *La Lucertola dalla Pelle di Donna*, 1971; *La Luna*, 1979.

Publications:

On LANCETTI: books—*The World of Fashion: People, Places, Resources* by Eleanor Lambert, New York and London 1976; *I Mass-Moda: Fatti e Personaggi dell'Italian Look/The Who's Who of Italian Fashion*, with text by Adriana

Mulassano, Florence 1979; *Storie e Favole di Moda* by Nanda Calandri, Florence 1982; *Il Disegno dell'Alta Moda Italiana dal 1940 al 1960*, exhibition catalogue by Bonizza Giordani Aragno, Rome 1982; *Consequenze Impreviste*, exhibition catalogue by Rossana Bossaglia, Prato 1983; *Italian Fashion 1920-1980*, exhibition catalogue by Bonizza Giordani Aragno, Tokyo 1983; *40 Years of Italian Fashion*, exhibition catalogue compiled by Bonizza Giordani Aragno, Rome 1983; *McDowell's Directory of Twentieth Century Fashion* by Colin McDowell, London 1984; *The Encyclopaedia of Fashion from 1840 to the 1980s* by Georgina O'Hara, London 1986.

Every fashion designer has a personal style, but he should always be aware of the socio-economic situation and evolution of life.

In my creative activity, I usually draw my attention to painting and costumes of other countries, in particular when I study my new collections. When the ideas are clear, I begin to draw by myself the fabrics that will be produced by the textile industries in northern Italy. The last phase of my work is to transform the fancy weave into a high fashion dress, maybe the most glamorous. My woman remains the "real woman," very feminine for the evening and inspired to a masculine gender for the day—but always with a womanly grace.

About my work I can tell that it is now developing in a double way: on one side, the high fashion collections, my passion, that remain for an elite and for my prestige; on the other side, a business programme in having licencees of many products, such as knitwear, furs, men's and women's perfume and make-up, bags and leather accessories, ties, umbrellas, shoes, bathing costumes, T-shirts, bed-linen, table-linen, ceramic tiles, scarves, optical frames, leather clothes.

—Pino Lancetti

Lancetti can create great simplicity in crisply tailored coats and suits on the British model, but he cannot resist adorning them with embroidery, appliqué work, and panels. The 1930s are a strong influence on his daywear in particular. In 1973, he used not only 1930s motifs but also the look of the silent film vamp of the 1920s. His 1978 collection had Art Deco prints by D'Este and Etro, as in a blouson to hip level worn with a long fishtail skirt of distinctly 1930s style. He mixes 1930s pillbox hats with 1940s square shoulders on his wool suits.

Despite this historical influence, however, the biggest factor in Lancetti's style is brilliant colour in startling effects. He began the 1970s with white jackets contrasted with black skirts adorned by large appliquéd flowers in white and red jackets teamed with white skirts splashed with large, black flowers. This look was still available in his ready-to-wear line at the end of the decade. His fascination with lurid brocades also demonstrates his interest in brilliant contrast; his very full-skirted evening dresses of 1950s type look like glittering cascades of silver and gold. His Balkan-Caucasian look of 1976-80 showed frocks in multi-coloured prints with broad sashes, accompanied by coin jewellery in plenty. In brilliant brocades, it featured harem trousers, off-the-shoulder blouses, turbans, and little jackets heavy with embroidered jewels, very Arabic in character, and no doubt created with the Gulf states market in mind. In 1981, Lancetti decided on frills, and the brocades became even more elaborate. In contrast to all this extravaganza, in 1979-80, Lancetti showed quiet and simple tweed suits, which were very British; these proved that he is capable of restraint, which is usually overwhelmed by the brocade barrage.

Pino Lancetti: High-fashion dress, 1983

Full of Latin flamboyance, Lancetti is a very theatrical designer whose clothes can only be for the very rich. A gown of gold and silver is not for every woman, and it cannot be copied for the mass market to the same brilliance. Lancetti is a good tailor, but in his clothing the construction disappears beneath the splendour. He creates for a world where every day is a gala one—which is a long way from the real one.

—Diana de Marly

LANDOR, Walter (Joseph).

American corporate, environmental, industrial and graphic designer. Born in Munich, Germany, 9 July 1913; emigrated to the United States in 1940. Studied at the University of Munich, and University of London. Married Jo Landor. Founder-partner, Industrial Design Partnership, London, 1935–39; founder-president, then chairman, of Landor Associates design firm, San Francisco, from 1941: subsequently established regional offices in New York, Rome, Mexico City, Tokyo and Singapore, and affiliate company, Communications Research Center, San Francisco. Associate professor, California College of Arts and Crafts, Oakland, 1940. Member: Package Designers Council, New York; Pratt Institute Creative Packaging Center, New York. Honorary doctorate: California College of Arts and Crafts, 1957. Address: Landor Associates, 1001 Front Street, San Francisco, California 94111, U.S.A.

Works:

Planning and design programmes for—Chase Manhattan Bank, New York; Bank of America, San Francisco; Landesgirokasse Bank, Stuttgart; Sanwa Bank, Tokyo; Banco Nacional de Mexico, Mexico City; Caja de Pensiones La Caixa, Barcélona; Wells Fargo Bank, San Francisco; Montedison S.p.A., Milan; Atlantic Richfield Company, Los Angeles; Industria Italiana Petroli, Genoa; Jardine Matheson Company, Hong Kong; General Tire and Rubber Company, Ohio; Mercedes Benz of America, New York; Nissan Motor Company, Tokyo; Fiat-Fabbrica Italiana Automobili, Turin; Scandinavian Airlines System, Stockholm; Alitalia Airlines, Rome; Singapore Airlines, Singapore; Thai International, Bangkok; Iberia Airlines, Madrid; US Air, Washington, D.C.; Westin Hotels, Seattle; Royal Viking Lines, Oslo; Raffles Hotel, Singapore; Las Hadas, Mexico; Italcable, Rome; American Telephone and Telegraph, New York; Sony Corporation, Tokyo; 20th Century-Fox, Los Angeles; Fuji Photo Company, Tokyo; General Electric Company, Connecticut; Safeway Stores, San Francisco; Magazzini Standa S.p.A., Milan; Delaize, Brussels; Isetan Department Stores, Tokyo; Cote d'Or, Belgium; Cospar Lancôme et Cie/Guy Laroche, Paris; Nestle Group, Germany; General Foods Corporation, New York; Pillsbury Company, Minnesota; H. J. Heinz Company, Pennsylvania; Philip Morris International, New York; Seven-Up, Missouri; 3M Company, Minnesota; Levi Strauss, San Francisco; Coca-Cola Company, Georgia; Thomas J. Lipton, New Jersey.

Publications:

On LANDOR: books—*Package Design* by Milner Gray, London and New York 1955; *Advertising Directions,* edited by Edward M. Gottschall and Arthur Hawkins, New York 1959; *Letter Design in the Graphic Arts* by Mortimer Leach, New York 1960; *Design in America* by Ralph Caplan, New York 1969; *Packaging and Corporate Identity,* edited by Idea Publishers, Tokyo 1971; *Archigraphia: Architectural and Environmental Graphics,* edited by Walter Herdeg, Zurich 1978; *The American Design Adventure 1940–1975* by Arthur J. Pulos, London and Cambridge, Massachusetts 1988.

In his ingenious blending of old and new architectural details, designer Walter Landor turned an old ferryboat in San Francisco into the floating offices of Landor Associates. For Landor, the beautiful and imaginative as well as functional studio serves to stimulate the imaginations of his staff. A collection of old packages from around the world, which he uses as a reference source, is located on board, in his Museum of Packaging Antiques.

Landor has aligned his firm with a communications standpoint. As a result, he can provide a client company not only with a graphic identity, but also with a total, corporate image-building program. His design for a graphic "keystone," a bright, abstract device, suggestive of water and movement, for the Golden Gate Bridge Highway and Transportation District, was developed to help persuade the area's commuting population to accept the idea of public transportation. Landor emphasizes the importance of the color and design of these graphic symbols. They give companies new visual identifications to make their positions more effective in the marketplace.

Landor's approach to his design projects is research-oriented. By working with and reporting to the top management of his clients, he closely examines the problems and sets up the criteria to find solutions. For Allied Van Lines, which has as its primary communication medium the vehicle, Landor's design team was able to work out a symbol, which simultaneously served as a "highway" and the letter "A" and which was easily recognized as representing the company.

As one of the world's leading design firms, Landor Associates has offices located throughout Europe, the Far East, Africa, and Latin America, giving him a broad exposure to new kinds of problems. In repackaging Mexicali beer, Landor was faced with the problem of illiteracy. As a result, his design incorporated favorite Mexican emblems as a way of communicating to the people. It is this type of response to his foreign assignments that demonstrates Landor's flexibility in developing successful solutions. Whether Landor is working for companies in the United States, or abroad, his strategy for designing communication methods, corporate image-building programs, and brand identities is based on a full understanding of the goals of his client companies.

—Patricia A. Russac

LAPIDUS, Ted.

French fashion designer. Born Edmond Lapidus, in Paris, 23 June 1929. Educated at the Lycé Saint-Charles, Marseille, the Lycée Berthollet, Annecy, and the Lycée Voltaire, Paris, until 1945; studied medicine, at the University of Paris, 1945–49: Dip.Med. 1949; mainly self-taught in fashion design. Married Ursula Mai in 1970; children: Olivier, Thomas and Heloise. Part-time freelance fashion designer, Paris, 1945–49; tailor, for the Club de Paris, 1950; founder-manager, 1951–70, and president from 1970, Ted Lapidus Couture, Paris; administrator, Ted Lapidus International, from 1975. Instructor in clothing design, Industrial Arts College, Tokyo, 1961. Member, Chambre Syndicale de la Couture Parisienne. Address: 37 Avenue Pierre Premier de Serbie, 75008 Paris, France.

Publications:

On LAPIDUS: books—*Fairchild's Who's Who in Fashion*, New York 1975, 1980; *A History of Fashion* by J. Anderson Black and Madge Garland, London 1975, 1980; *The World of Fashion: People, Places, Resources* by Eleanor Lambert, New York and London 1976; *McDowell's Directory of Twentieth Century Fashion* by Colin McDowell, London 1984; *The Encyclopaedia of Fashion from 1840 to the 1980s* by Georgina O'Hara, London 1986.

LA PIETRA, Ugo.

Italian architect, exhibition and furniture designer. Born in Milan, in 1938. Studied architecture, at the Politecnico, Milan, 1957–61. Independent artist and designer, Milan, from 1962; founder-member, with Lucia, Ferrari, Sordini, Verga and Verni, of the Gruppo del Cenobio artist's group, Milan, 1963; organizer of numerous interdisciplinary exhibitions, in Milan, Brussels, Osaka, etc., from 1965. Instructor in architectural design, Politecnico, Milan, 1964–70. **Exhibitions:** Galleria Il Cenobio, Milan, 1963, 1967; Faculty of Architecture, Politecnico of Milan, 1964; Galleria Flaviana, Locarno, 1966, 1968; Galleria Cadario, Rome, 1967, 1969; Studio di Informazione Estetica, Turin, 1968; Galleria Toselli, Milan, 1970. **Collections:** Galleria Civica d'Arte Moderna, Turin; Museo Sperimentale d'Arte Contemporanea, Turin; American Crafts Museum, New York; Landesmuseum Joanneum, Graz. Recipient: MPI Study Scholarship, Milan, 1964, 1965; Premio Cesare da Sesto, Sesto Calende, 1968; Premio Castello Svevo, Termoli, 1970. Address: Via Garibaldi 50, 20121 Milan, Italy.

Works:

Pretenziosa armchair, for Busnelli, 1984.
Agevole sofa, for Busnelli, 1984.
Flessuosa sofa, for Busnelli, 1984.
Anterevole chairs, for Busnelli, 1985.
AT-Tese chair and table, for Busnelli, 1985.
Incrocio table and chair, for Busnelli, 1985.
Articolata chairs, Busnelli, 1986.

Publications:

By LA PIETRA: books—*La Ricerca Morfologica*, exhibition catalogue, Locarno 1966; *Il Sistema Disequilibrante*, exhibition catalogue, Milan 1970; *Recupero e Reinvenzione 1969–1976*, Milan 1976; *La Riappropriazione dell'-Ambiente*, Milan 1977.

On LA PIETRA: books—*Ugo La Pietra*, exhibition catalogue by Germano Celant, Bergamo 1967; *La Pietra*, exhibition catalogue by Tomasso Trini, Locarno 1968; *Italy: The New Domestic Landscape* by Emilio Ambasz, New York and Florence 1972; *Boutiquen, Shops und Schicke Laden* by Wolfgang Grub, Munich 1974; *Living Spaces*, edited by Franco Magnani, Milan 1977; *Design e Forme Nuove nell'Arredamento Italiano*, edited by Paolo Portoghesi and Marino Marini, Rome 1978; *The Hot House: New Wave Italian Design* by Andrea Branzi, London 1984; *Italian Design: 1870 to the Present* by Penny Sparke, London and New York 1988.

LARCHER, Jean.

French calligrapher and graphic designer. Born in Rennes, 28 January 1947. Educated at the Lycée Jacques Decourt, Rennes, 1958–62; studied typography and printing, at the Chambre de Commerce, Paris, 1962–65; also studied Spanish, from 1969. Served in the French Army, in West Germany, 1966–67: Sergeant. Freelance lettering artist and calligrapher, from 1973. Guest artist, Chambre de Paris, 1975–81, Ecole Supérieure de la Publicite, Paris, 1975–83, and Escuela Superior de Arquitec-

tura, Madrid, 1980; lecturer, Ecole des Beaux-Arts, Cergy-Pontoise, 1975, 1977, 1982–89. **Exhibitions:** Galerie Paul Marquet, Paris, 1973; MJC de Colombes, France, 1973; Centre International de Sejour, Paris, 1974; Caravanserail, Kus Adasi, 1974; Typogalerie Ere Nouvelle, Paris, 1974, 1975; Galerie Lurs, France, 1976; Galerie Sauvage-Moreau, Paris, 1976; Editions Retz, Paris, 1977; Librairie La Hune, Paris, 1977; Agence Belier, Paris, 1977; Librairie Artcurial, Paris, 1988; *10 Caligraphes Exposent*, Toulouse, 1988; *Kalligraphia V*, San Francisco Public Library, 1988; *Dressing Words Old and New*, Paperpoint Gallery, London, 1989. **Collections:** Bibliothèque Nationale, Paris; Musée de la Publicité, Paris; Museo de Arte Contemporaneo, Madrid; Victoria and Albert Museum, London. Address: 16 Chemin des Bourgognes, 95000 Cergy, France.

Works:

8 book designs, for Dover Press, New York, 1974–81.
ABC/XYZ Larcher exhibition poster, for Librairie La Hune, Paris, 1977.
8 calligraphic postcards, self-published, Paris, 1980.
Logo and corporate identity, for Studio Guillaume Tell music recording studio, Paris, 1981.
Pologne exhibition logo, for the Banque d'Images pour la Pologne, Paris, 1982.
Letraset calligraphic catalogue cover, for Letraset France, 1982.
6 calligraphic record sleeves, for Chant du Monde, Paris, 1983.
Equilibre sportswear manufacturer's logo, for the Brigitte Quakrat Agency, Paris, 1984.
Logo and masthead, for *Plaisir de la Maison* magazine, Paris, 1985.
Calligraphic New Year card, for fashion designer Emanuel Ungaro, 1986.
Atelier Du advertising agency logo, for J. P. Gauthier et Associes, Paris, 1986.
Logo and corporate identity, for fashion designer Paul Mercier, 1986.
Bicentenaire de la Revolution Française 1789–1989 silkscreened calligraphic poster, self-published, Paris, 1989.

Publications:

By LARCHER: books—*Graphismes Cinètiques*, Paris 1970; *Geometrical Designs and Optical Art*, New York 1974; *Op Art Coloring Book*, New York 1975; *Ecritures*, Paris 1976; *Fantastic Alphabets*, New York 1976; *Une Typographie Nouvelle*, Paris 1976; *The 3-Dimensional Alphabet Coloring Book*, New York 1978; *Op Message Postcards*, New York 1979; *Optical and Geometrical Allover Pattern*, New York 1979; *News Announcements*, New York 1981; *Calligraphies*, Paris 1984; *Allover Patterns with Letter Forms*, New York 1985; *Jean Larcher Calligraphe*, Rennes 1986; articles—in *Communication et Langages* (Paris), no. 33, 1977, no. 36, 1977, no. 39, 1978, no. 40, 1978, no. 50, 1981, no. 54, 1982; *Campana* (Madrid), no. 101, 1978, no. 103, 1978, no. 120, 1978, no. 123, 1979; *Visible Language* (Cleveland), no. 2 1979; *Bat* (Paris), nos. 14–15, 1979; *Arts et Metiers du Livre* (Paris), no. 140, 1986; *Calligraphy Review* (Norman), no. 2, 1987; *La Letra* (Barcelona), no. 1, 1988.

On LARCHER: books—*Pour une Semiologie de la Typographie* by Gerard Blanchard, Brussels 1979; *Sixty Alphabets*, with introduction by G. Briem, London 1986; *Trademarks Collection: Europe 1* by Yasaburo Kuwayama, Tokyo 1988; *L'Histoire de l'Ecriture* by Armand Colin, Paris 1990.

Jean Larcher: Silkscreen poster for the bicentenary of the French Revolution, 1989

Since I left my typography school (the Paris Chamber of Commerce) in 1965, I have never ceased to be an enthusiast and, indeed, even much more than that. I have literally devoted my whole existence to my graphic activities (painting, typography, calligraphy, articles, exhibitions, conferences, etc.) My own curiosity, my interest in this profession, the passion for the written and printed word which continually motivates me have brought me quite far, even very far, for I have published seven books with Dover Editions in New York, and it is rather exceptional for a Frenchman to make a breakthrough in the United States.

I have not contented myself with doing and carrying out things only for myself; I have written numerous articles and continue to do so on designers throughout the world who seemed interesting to me. I have organised nearly fifteen exhibitions in Paris (typography, illustration, and design) with one at an international level on the phenomenon of letterheads—*Letterheads from the Four Corners of the World* in April 1981—and I have myself actively taken part in some thirty exhibitions throughout the world, including ten personal exhibitions. My work, very eclectic at the start and now uniquely specialised in the field of calligraphy, shows well enough, I think, my personal development, an unceasing desire to progress, to improve myself, and to take part in an improvement in graphics in the widest sense of the word.

The first ten to twelve years of my work were quite hard, sometimes even very hard (including seven salaried years in various studios and advertising agencies.) Only for the last few years have my position, my research, my works been recognised in France, a country which unfortunately is not a graphic country and where typography and calligraphy are not taken into consideration—far from it. So everything remains to be done, but it is difficult, and the French are refractory in design and graphic matters. It is a question of education; our schools of design are of a very average level or even poor, and the results are felt much later in the profession and in the taste of the public, which is completely insensitive to graphics and very little interested in art in general.

For the present and future, I sincerely believe that faced with computers and with a certain abstraction in human relationships, if we still want to communicate in a natural and personal manner, graphics, illustration, photography, typography, calligraphy—everything that comes from the hand that is thought, realised, and carried out by a man or a woman—is very important. If we leave it to machines to carry out all these tasks in our place and are satisfied with watching, this is very dangerous. We must leave a large area to individual creation, to pleasure, to joy, to accident, to the imagination in all the fields of the visual arts, so that the professionals and the artists can express themselves instead of disappearing and so that the public in general may benefit in the environment in the broadest sense of the word. I decided to devote my life to the development of the aesthetics of printed matter so that my contemporaries may take part in it.

—Jean Larcher

All of Jean Larcher's graphic output is deeply imbued with a passion for lettering—lettering in an infinite profusion of forms, ranging from elegant copperplate flourishes to alphabets sculpted from Swiss cheese. Although trained in the canons of classical typography, Larcher disdains legibility, advocating imagination instead. His philosophy was articulated and dazzlingly illustrated in *Fantastic Alphabets* (1975), his third book for Dover Publications. In it he followed a "semantic approach to the letters, making use of specific themes," such as letters drawn in a variety of perspectives, letters created from objects, and letters inspired by Op Art. When properly conceived and executed, these letters are intended to function as "self-sufficient illustrations" of the messages they bear.

Larcher's concept of lettering as illustration is derived from several sources, most importantly the typographic work of Herbert Lubalin. Lubalin pioneered the notion of expressive typography with its emphasis on "wordgames" at the expense of readability. The other primary influences on Larcher's work in this realm have been Push Pin Studios and Robert Massin. The various Pop art alphabets, such as Baby Teeth and Buffalo, created by Push Pin's Milton Glaser and Seymour Chwast during the 1960s, are the immediate predecessors of *Fantastic Alphabets*. While the work of Lubalin, Glaser, and Chwast provided contemporary models for Larcher to follow, Massin's *Letter and Image* (1970) provided an historical basis for his theory of illustrative typography. Massin's landmark book chronicled the use of letters as pictures over the course of several centuries, from medieval manuscripts to nineteenth-century advertising art. In it were displayed alphabets created out of twigs, human figures, and animals, among other objects.

Larcher's other principal form of lettering is copperplate. Once again, it was Lubalin, through the work of his associates Tom Carnase and Tony DiSpigna, who was the main contemporary influence on Larcher. Carnase and DiSpigna led the revival of interest in script and copperplate letterforms in current graphic design. Yet, for Larcher, one of the few designers in France with a knowledge of calligraphy, the work of the seventeenth-century French writing masters Louis Barbedor and Lucas Materot has been equally important.

Both of Larcher's interests—in illustrative typography and in copperplate letterforms—are united by a common goal: to circumvent the increasing rationalization of "alphabetic codes" by new typesetting technologies. Larcher has insisted on the primacy of the artist's imagination and creativity in the design of letterforms for today and for the future.

—Paul Shaw

LARKIN, Anya.

American textile designer. Born Ann Seymour Larkin, in Washington, D.C., 30 July 1945. Studied at the Thomas School, Rowayton, Connecticut, Briarcliff College, and Silvermine College of Fine Arts, New Canaan, Connecticut; AFA. President and designer, Anya Larkin Limited textile design company, New York, from 1974: has designed fashion and furnishing fabrics for Henri Bendel, Mary McFadden, etc. **Collection:** Textile Museum, Smithsonian Institution, Washington, D.C. Address: 7 West 22nd Street, New York, New York 10010, U.S.A.

Publications:

On LARKIN: article—in *Fiberarts* (Asheville), January/February 1982.

A fabric design, like a painting, is no mere pattern sitting on the surface of the cloth. Rather, it has power and joy and is fascinating to the eye; it transforms the cloth into another dimension.

If the designer puts color together and combines unusual motifs to create action, the design is never flat or dead. It moves, it falls, it jumps if it has to, it twirls or is static and peaceful, or it is horizontal or vertical like a fresco, a frieze, or a woodblock. It has mystery and embodies the image of classical antiquity; it evokes memories and reminds you of something you can't quite put your finger on. It conjures up visions of other things (seen or felt)—imagery of the past. Its colors make your mouth water; they are pleasing to look at. It has life!

This design process is done best when it is done unconsciously, when it springs from the deep well of the subconscious—when it is not mapped out or planned, when there is no strategy or technique involved, only a moment of meditation before the creative process begins to happen, making a space for an action to take place. It is not an intellectual pursuit or exercise. It is only the art of tapping into the greater universal creative force.

—Anya Larkin

Anya Larkin began painting clothing for friends while working in the film industry in the early 1970s. Soon her napkins and painted suede jackets were being sold through Henri Bendel in Manhattan. She did not make a full commitment to the textile design business, however, until she began creating the fabrics for one of today's most successful American fashion designers, Mary McFadden. Since 1975, she has been producing all of McFadden's prints and stripes. As a result, her hand-painted silks, cottons, suedes, and challis have become quite recognizable.

Color is what Larkin's work is all about. Unable to find fabric suited to her own keen sense of color, she felt the need when quite young to create her own fabrics, using the colors she felt belonged together. She pairs color in unpredictable but wonderfully refreshing combinations. In the spirit of the *fauve* artists, her boldly stroked stripes and oversized prints remind one of a Kandinsky oil. Often, she will soften her palette a touch, working in more of an Impressionist mode, and she admits that Matisse is her greatest inspiration. "If you ever need a color, go to Matisse," she says. Her delicate pastels and bold brights are achieved through her own resist-wax method that is similar to batik. This technique, while very time-consuming, enables her to capture delicate, vivid hues.

In the past, she has dabbled in textile design for home furnishing. Now, she has decided to make this her main emphasis, while continuing to design dress fabric on the side. She will design a line of hand-woven textiles to be coordinated with her hand-painted ones. While she is adapting many of her fashion prints to fit the realm of home furnishing, all of her new creations are guaranteed to show the same fine quality and unique color sense as her previous work.

Why this change of focus? Larkin feels that the improving economy and the rage to own a home of one's own are being met with a revival in the home decorating industry. Consequently, people today will be investing in their homes. "Interior design just seems to be the proper direction in which to move for the moment," she states.

With her reputation firmly established as a textile designer, Larkin certainly can choose her area of concentration. Her success has shown that color is a very effective tool. Her combinations are exceptional; they are invigorating as well as comforting, and they undoubtedly move the spirit.

While the fashion and textile industries may determine the dominant color palette from one season to the next, it is the independent artist such as Larkin who provides an alternative to that palette as well as the impetus for subsequent color preferences. In this capacity, Larkin's sense of color will certainly endure as one of the most influential.

—Deirdre Kerr

LARSEN, Jack (John) Lenor.

American textile designer. Born in Seattle, Washington, 5 August 1927. Studied architecture and furnishing design, at the University of Washington, Seattle, 1945–47, 1949–50: BFA 1950; Cranbrook Academy of Art, Bloomfield Hills, Michigan, 1950–51: MFA 1951. Freelance textile designer, in Seattle, 1949–50, and in New York, 1952–53; founder-president, 1953, design director from 1953, and chairman of the board from 1975, of Jack Lenor Larsen Incorporated, New York; established Larsen Design Studio, New York, 1958, and Jack Lenor Larsen International, in Zurich, Stuttgart and Paris, 1963; acquired Thaibok Fabrics, 1972; established Larsen Carpets, Larsen Leather Division, New York, 1973, and Larsen Furniture, New York, 1974: United States consultant, grass weaving projects of Taiwan and Vietnam, 1957–59; United States commissioner and design director, Milan Triennale, 1964. Co-director of fabric design, Philadelphia College of Art, 1960–63; artist-in-residence, Royal College of Art, London, 1975; member of the board of overseers, Parsons School of Design, New York, 1980; visiting committee member, Metropolitan Museum of Art, New York, 1988–89. Vice-president, Architectural League of New York, 1966–67. **Exhibitions:** Portland Museum of Art, Oregon, 1949; M. H. de Young Memorial Museum, San Francisco, 1956; Stedelijk Museum, Amsterdam, 1968; Museum Bellerive, Zürich, 1970; Museum of Fine Arts, Boston, 1971; Smithsonian Institution, Washington, D.C.; Kunstindustrimuseet, Copenhagen, 1976; Fashion Institute of Technology, New York, 1978; Musée des Arts Décoratifs, Paris, 1981. **Collections:** Museum of Modern Art, New York; Metropolitan Museum of Art, New York; Cooper-Hewitt Museum, New York; Fashion Institute of Technology, New York; Philadelphia Museum of Art; Archives of American Art, Washington, D.C.; Art Institute of Chicago; Victoria and Albert Museum, London; Royal Scottish Museum, Edinburgh; Museum Bellerive, Zürich; Kunstindustrimuseet, Copenhagen; Musée d'Art Décoratif, Montreal; Stedelijk Museum, Amsterdam. Recipient: Gold Medal, Milan Triennale, 1964; American Institute of Architects Gold Medal, 1968; Elsie de Wolfe Award, American Institute of Interior Designers, 1971; American Print Designers Tommy Award, 1971; *House Beautiful* Pace Setter Award, 1973. Fellow: American Society of Interior Designers, 1978; American Crafts Council, 1978; Eliot Noyes Fellow: Aspen Design Conference, Colorado, 1978. Honorary Professor, University of Washington, Seattle, 1980; Honorary Royal Designer for Industry, Royal Society of Arts, London, 1983. Honorary doctorate: Parsons School of Design, New York, 1981; Rhode Island School of Design, Providence, 1982; Philadelphia College of Art, 1982. Address: 41 East 11th Street, New York, New York 10003, U.S.A.

Works:

Draperies, for Lever House, New York, 1952.
Fine Arts Collection of sheets and towels, for J. P. Stevens, New York, 1965.

Jack Lenor Larsen: *Homage to Jim Thompson* dyed and woven fabric, 1972

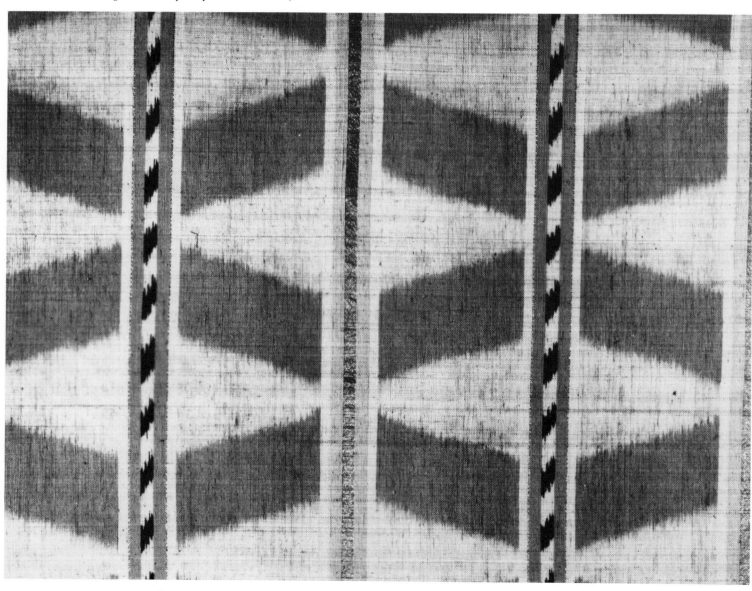

Wall Hangings exhibition layouts, for the Museum of Modern Art, New York, 1968.
Art curtain, for Filene Center for the Performing Arts, Vienna, Virginia, 1971.
Fabric program, for Braniff International Airlines, 1972–78.
Visiona IV exhibition layouts, for Bayer AG, Frankfurt, 1974.
Silk hangings, for Sears Bank and Trust Company, Chicago, 1978.
Theatre curtain, for St. Charles Cultural Center, Illinois, 1978.
Dinnerware range in porcelain, for Dansk International Designs, 1980.
Upholstery collections, for Cassina and Vescom, 1981.
The Art Fabric: Mainstream exhibition layouts, for the San Francisco Museum of Modern Art, 1981.

Publications:

By LARSEN: books—*Elements of Weaving,* with Azalea Thorpe, New York 1967; *Beyond Craft: The Art Fabric,* with Mildred Constantine, New York 1972; *Fabric for Interiors,* with Jeanne Weeks, New York 1975; *Dyer's Art: Ikat, Batik, Plangi,* with A. Buhler, A. and G. Solyom, New York 1977; *The Art Fabric: Mainstream,* with Mildred Constantine, New York 1981; *Interlace: On Plaiting and Related Techniques,* with Betty Freudenheim, New York 1984; *Material Wealth: Interior Fabrics for the 1990s,* London and New York 1989.

On LARSEN: books—*Interior Design: An Introduction to Architectural Interiors* by Arnold Friedmann and others, New York and Amsterdam 1970, 1976; *Objects: USA* by Lee Nordness, London 1970; *Jack Lenor Larsen: 30 Years of Creative Textiles,* exhibition catalogue by François Mathey, Mildred Constantine and others, Paris 1981; *Design Since 1945,* edited by Kathryn Hiesinger and George Marcus, Philadelphia and London 1983; *The Conran Directory of Design,* edited by Stephen Bayley, London 1985; *High Style: 20th Century American Design* by David Gebhard, Esther McCoy and others, New York 1985; *Eye for Industry: Royal Designers for Industry 1936–1986,* exhibition catalogue by Fiona MacCarthy and Patrick Nuttgens, London 1986; *The American Design Adventure 1940–1975* by Arthur J. Pulos, London and Cambridge, Massachusetts 1988.

Larsen Design Studio's mentors—William Morris, Louis Tiffany, Mario Fortuny, the weavers of pre-Columbian Peru and Sassanian Persia—belong to other centuries. This gave them unfair advantages: they not only were there first, but with an aristocratic support system unavailable today. Like us they looked to evolving needs, created within new and old technologies, and sustained quality and style.

We started out as revolutionaries, wanting only to make brave new designs for a contemporary society. Today our mission is to maintain the great tradition for luxurious quality as a buffer against mass production. And, of course, we are aware of the inheritance of all of history's art and technologies. These are riches not to be ignored.

Towards the future: The late Twentieth Century design challenge, for me, pivots on creating a civilized environment within the hostile indifference of mass culture. The challenge means a resolution of the present dilemma. Our society must make renewed efforts to allow for individual and rewarding expressions within our consumer culture.

We have not yet resolved design for an egalitarian lifestyle. Indeed, can we accept the challenge to do so? Can we achieve the equivalent of the ready-to-wear revolution in the area of furnishings? This is of prime importance, since it contributes to our basic sense of shelter and security—and more: personal environment must support our need for identity.

As more of us spend more time indoors in an urban environment, as commercial communication becomes even more cunningly aggressive, as security becomes rarer, personal environment must provide more than small space inside locked doors.

We have learned that what matters is how we feel in a space and how we move within it. Art and the social sciences must work in tandem to achieve a keener understanding of the conditions that evoke these emotional responses. And we can very well look to theatre for inspiration, technology to orchestrate light, and color to evoke mood.

We now control climate and sound within space; why not as readily the visual elements? It is time for projected color and pattern to come into its own.

I believe that the revolution coming to architecture will center on designing from the inside out. The starting point will be not merely facade nor available structure (as it has been since the time of cavemen).

As it becomes possible for architect and client alike to afford the luxury and detail of residential commissions, the solution may be similar to that used in converted industrial lofts: residents will take blocks of open and undifferentiated space to divide, compose, and personalize according to need and ability. Such spaces can be multiple in purpose and, more importantly, multiple in mood.

Still, most of us will live and work in spaces without a sense of structure, materials, or architectural detail. In other words, shoe boxes, dull in themselves and undifferentiated one from another.

What distinguishes these spaces will be the contents within them. The furniture, to be sure, but mostly the fabric of floors, walls, windows, and furniture covers will be the means to achieving variation in scale and pattern, color and texture.

Wall fabrics will become increasingly important; they relieve monotony with their plays of pattern and texture and with tactile and visual softness. Depending on application, wall fabrics will dull noise from adjoining spaces and modulate sound within.

We need a brave new vision and a new kind of environmental design team in which all of the design disciplines will contribute as a unit. Engineering and automation are but the means to realize the humanist message of social sciences. Poetic insight will remain basic to the exaltation of the individual. *Reprinted from* Jack Lenor: 30 ans de création textile/30 years of Creative Textiles, *Exhibition catalogue, Paris 1982.)*

—Jack Lenor Larsen

Jack Lenor Larsen treats fabric as a singular presence in our lives and our environment. In his fabric for interiors, for industrial use, in art, and in craft, he recognizes fabric as a tactile, visual, sensitive element in today's society. He is constantly aware of its relationship to people, to their bodies, and to the environment.

Beginning as a weaver, he produced as one of his earliest collections, Andean, which had been gestating since student days out of his admiration for pre-Columbian weaving. However, in such works as Conquistador, an authentic wax batik on heavy upholstery velvet, he avoided imitation or reproduction of ancient design.

The name of Larsen stands worldwide for serious design, luxurious quality, and courageous variety stemming from his global view. His knowledge of past generations and cultures throughout the world takes him beyond the limits of his own tradition. Through his travels, he finds what he needs in materials and inspiration, and his respect for other cultures and their accomplishments perpetuates a craft tradition. His fantastic color sense has been influenced by Shibui shades of Japan, by the colors of his native northwest, by the subdued pastels of China and by the brilliance of Brazilian sunlight.

The fascination of his work also lies in his use of today's resources, whatever they are and wherever they happen to be. His respect is equal for natural and man-made materials. All of his fabric innovations reflect the environmental harmony which he makes a central aim of all his work.

—Mildred Constantine

LAUREN, Ralph.
American fashion designer. Born Ralph Lifschitz, in the Bronx, New York, 14 October 1939. Studied business science, at the City College of New York, 1958–61. Married Ricky Low-Beer in 1965; children: Andrew, David and Dylan. Worked as a salesman, at Bloomingdales and Brooks Brothers, and as assistant buyer for Allied Stores, New York, 1962–65; New York representative, for Rivetz necktie manufacturers, 1965–66; founder and designer, Polo Neckwear Division of Beau Brummel, New York, 1967; founder, designer and chairman, Polo Fashions, New York, from 1968: established Polo Menswear Company, 1968, Ralph Lauren Womenswear, 1971, Polo Leather Goods, 1979, Polo/Ralph Lauren Luggage, 1982; launched fragrances *Polo* for men, and *Lauren* for women, 1978, *Chaps* for men, and *Tuxedo* for women, 1979, *Day, Night* and *Active* cosmetic lines for women, 1981. Also film costume designer, from 1974. **Exhibition:** Denver Art Museum, Colorado. **Collection:** Fashion Institute of Technology, New York. Recipient: Neiman-Marcus Distinguished Service Award, 1971; American Fashion Institute Award, New York, 1975; Council of Fashion Designers of America Award, 1981; Coty Hall of Fame Award, New York, 1981. Address: Polo/Ralph Lauren, 40 West 55th Street, New York, New York 10019, U.S.A.

Works:

Robes and swimwear collection, for Trylon Robes, 1968.
Polo/Ralph Lauren men's apparel range, for Seibu of Tokyo, 1969.
Polo/Ralph Lauren men's neckties, for Hishiya of Tokyo, 1970.
Chaps by Ralph Lauren men's clothing range, for L. Greid, 1970.
Chaps by Ralph Lauren men's shirts and sportswear, for C. F. Hathaway (division of Warnaco), 1971.
Ralph Lauren Active Sport women's wear, for Seibu of Tokyo, 1971.
Fur coats range, for Tepper Collection, 1972.
Women's dress designs, for Vogue Patterns, New York, 1973.
Polo by Ralph Lauren shirts and knits, for Holbrook Company 1978.

Ralph Lauren: Fair Isle shawl-collar sweater with suede dirndl, 1981

Ground and air personnel uniforms, for Trans World Airlines, 1978.
Polo by Ralph Lauren men's trousers, for Calvin Clothes, 1979.
Ralph Lauren Girl's Wear collection, for Oxford industries, 1979.
Ralph Lauren household textiles and accessories range, for J. P. Stevens Company, 1983.

Publications:

On LAUREN: books—*Fashion Merchandizing* by Mary D. Troxell, New York 1971, 1976; *The Changing World of Fashion: 1900 to the Present* by Ernestine Carter, London and New York 1977; *Fairchild's Who's Who in Fashion,* edited by Ann Stegemeyer, New York 1980; *Costume and Fashion* by James Laver, New York and Toronto 1983; *McDowell's Directory of Twentieth Century Fashion* by Colin McDowell, London 1984; *The Conran Directory of Design,* edited by Stephen Bayley, London 1985; *Fashion: The Inside Story* by Barbaralee Diamonstein, New York 1985; *The Encyclopaedia of Fashion from 1840 to the 1980s* by Georgina O'Hara, London 1986; *Design Source Book* by Penny Sparke and others, London 1986.

My clothing is anti-fashion. I design with the point of view that what I'm doing is for a person with a strong sense of style. I don't want anything I do to be this year's "hot look." I like things that will age—that will look better next year.

We all need different clothes for the different ways we live. We all go from office to dinner parties, from the city to the country, from the tennis court to the riding stable, and we all get actively involved in what we do. Even the wealthiest people take care of their own boats and horses and need clothing appropriate for all of these varied activities.

My inspiration comes from everything—from the books I read, the movies I see, the places I go. It comes from keeping my eyes open over the years, looking at photographs, seeing what appeals to me personally. I have always liked the look—the image—of certain people: Cary Grant, the Duke of Windsor, Anthony Eden, the look of the English aristocrat. It's the look, too, of the Harvard and Yale men of past decades, and by extension, of their female counterparts at the prestigious women's schools.

I believe that fashion is a function of lifestyle. I believe in clothes that are natural to the way people live today—clothes that are as easy and nonchalant as a pair of jeans, that mix well, and that don't go out of style tomorrow. I want my clothes to become more personal and special as they are worn. I use only natural fabrics, avoid gimmics, and concentrate on evolving and perfecting the classics. I strive for three things in the clothes I design: quality, simplicity, and longevity. The look I strive to achieve is anti-style—an untrendy, un-packaged individual look.

—Ralph Lauren

Style, as opposed to fashion, is the major imperative underlying Ralph Lauren's work. Initially a designer of the high-quality ties which started the Polo label, Lauren soon directed his talents to menswear. Inspired by such notable dressers as the Duke of Windsor, Cary Grant, and Fred Astaire, he began to produce classic lines derivative of the elegant man-about-town or the country squire of a bygone age. A love of the fashions of the F. Scott Fitzgerald era led him to introduce wide neckties and bold shirt patterns. In 1974, he achieved world acclaim as the designer of the men's fashions in the film version of Fitzgerald's novel, *The Great Gatsby*.

When he turned to women's wear, he applied the same qualities of timeless elegance to his designs. By using uniformly high-quality tweeds, by tailoring down men's trousers and jackets, and by producing shirts in finer cottons, Lauren created clothes for the active woman of the 1970s, as epitomised in the Annie Hall look. These classic, tailored garments have changed little since they were first introduced but continue to epitomise long-lasting quality and style.

Another side of Ralph Lauren is seen in his Roughwear. Directly inspired by the tradition of America's past, this takes the form of long tweed or plaid skirts combined with colourful, hand-knitted, Fair Isle or sampler sweaters, tartan scarves, trilby hats, and lumberjack's wind cheaters and brushed cotton shirts. The origins are easy to trace, but the result is an up-dated, truly American style. Romantic touches of Edwardian and Victorian times occur in lace-trimmed jabots and large collars delicately held together with aging cameo brooches. Shades of the classic English riding costume appear in his tailored tweed jackets. Lauren's contribution to fashion can perhaps be best summed up in the names which he gave to his cosmetics introduced in 1981—"Day," "Night," and "Active."

His skill and experience has enabled him to design for both men and women in all they do. As a native New Yorker, he has promoted a truly American casual style in his prairie look, whilst developing classic, uncluttered lines which have brought him international fame along with his colleagues Calvin Klein and Perry Ellis. For Ralph Lauren, fashion is something that lasts for more than one season. This timelessness, abetted by inspirations deep in the soil of America's past, distinguishes his work.

—Hazel Clark

LAVONEN, Maija (Sisko).

Finnish textile designer. Born Maija Luukela, in Ii, Oulun laani, 29 October 1931. Studied at the University of Helsinki, 1953–55; Institute of Applied Arts, Helsinki, 1953–56; Free Art School, Helsinki, 1956–57. Married Antti Ahti Lavonen in 1958 (died, 1970); children: Kuutti Johannes and Sussa Milona. Worked as fashion designer, Katinette dress manufacturers, Helsinki, 1956–58; industrial designer, Muoti-Tuote Oy, Helsinki, 1963; freelance industrial designer, working for Katinette dress manufacturers, Helsinki, 1963–65; founder-director and desinger, Poppi Boutique fabircs shop, Helsinki, 1967–68; freelance textile artist and designer since 1970, establishing own workshop in Helsinki, working for Forssa-Finlayson, 1970–74, Marimekko, 1971–76, Socota, 1972–74, OTK and SOK textile mills, 1972–76, Venilia Product and Griffine-Marechal wallpapers, 1972–77, Fiorete of Fino Mornasco, 1973–75, Rissanen Oy, 1973–77, Tampella, 1975, Almedahls, 1987; concentrated on spatial art textiles for architecture, from 1978. Instructor in fashion design, Girls' Vocational School, in Kotka and Karhula, 1958–61; instructor in textile design, University of Industrial Arts, Helsinki, 1985–87, and since 1989. Board Member, State Committee for Applied Arts, Helsinki, 1974–76; Board Member, Museum of Applied Arts, Helsinki, 1979–85. **Exhibitions:** Kluuvin Galleria, Helsinki, 1970; Galleria Haimi, Helsinki, 1976; Waino Aaltonen Museum, Turku, 1978; Oulu Art Museum, Finland, 1978; Lapinlahti Art Centre, Finland, 1978; Hvittrask Cultural Centre, Finland, 1978; Galerie Artek, Helsinki, 1980; Galleria Sculptor. Helsinki, 1981; Kemi Art Museum, Finland, 1981; Galerie Artek, Helsinki, 1983; Maltinranta Art Centre, Tampere, 1986; Galleria Pelin, Helsinki, 1986; Galleria 25, Helsinki, 1989. **Collections:** Museum of Applied Arts, Helsinki; Röhsska Konstslöjdmuseet, Goteborg; Pori Art Museum, Finland; Kemi Art Museum, Finland; Union Bank of Finland, Helsinki. Recipient: State Award for Industrial Design, Helsinki, 1981; 15-year State Grant for the Arts, 1982. Address: Ruoholahdenkatu 23 A 62, 00180 Helsinki, Finland.

Works:

Uudet tuulet/Fresh Winds multi-part textile, for Suomen Puhallintehdas, Helsinki, 1978.
Linjat/The Lines three-part tapestry, for Valio, Jyvaskyla, 1980.
City of the Sea and Industry two-part tapestry, for the City Theatre, Kemi, 1981.
Luonto lahteena/Nature as a Source two-part tapestry, for the Ministry of the Interior, Helsinki, 1982.
Textile in Three Levels tapestry, for the Finnish Parliament Building, Helsinki, 1982.
Ps. 18:3 multi-part tapestry, for Malmi Church, Helsinki, 1982.
Kalvikin ryijy two-part ryijy rug, for Kalvik Villa, Bank of Finland, 1983.
Karhumetsa/Bear Forest two-part ryijy rug, for Pohjola Insurance Company, Helsinki, 1984.
Haukivesi three-level textile, for the City Library, Varkaus, 1985.
Mutual Understanding multi-art textile, for Hässelby Castle, Stockholm, 1985.
Lahti tapestry, for the City Hall Council Chamber, Lahti, 1986.
Sininen kaari/Blue Vault textile, for the Finnish Slot-Machine Association, Espoo, 1987.
Double Beat tapestry, for the Main Post Office, Helsinki, 1987.
Hand-embroidered church textiles, for St. Michael's Lutheran Church, Helsinki, 1987–88.
Kivijalka/Corner Stone ryijy rug, for Villa Haka, Helsinki, 1988.
Kimmellys/Glimmer tapestry, for the Savings Bank of Etela-Karjala, Lappeenranta, 1989.
Blue Arch tapestry, for the Bank of Finland, Helsinki, 1989.
Forest textile hanging, for the Kemi Company, Kemi, 1989.

Publications:

By LAVONEN: articles—"The Picture as a Door to an Era—A Code Image of our Times" in *Kulttuurivihkot* (Helsinki), no. 1, 1982; "Textiles of Kaarina Church" in *Arkkitehti* (Helsinki), no. 7, 1984; "As I Saw It: The Fading Glimmer" in *Helsingin Sanomat* (Helsinki), 12 August 1984.

On LAVONEN: books—*La Tapisserie—Art du XX Siècle* by Madeleine Jarry, Fribourg 1974; *Scandinavian Modern Design 1880–1980*, edited by David Revere McFadden, New York 1982; *Maija Lavonen*, seminar discourse by Leena Kaseva, University of Helsinki 1983; *Form Finland*, edited by Marianne Aav and Kaj Kalin, Helsinki 1986; *Art By Design: Reflections of Finland*, exhibition catalogue by Barbro Kulvik and Antti Siltavuori, New York 1988; articles—"Maija Lavonen—An Artisan" by H. Vehkaoja in *Anna* (Helsinki), no. 45, 1970; "Maija Brings Nature Inside" by L. Korhonen in *Me Naiset* (Helsinki), no. 30, 1981; "Maija Lavonen" by U. Pallasmaa in *Form Function Finland* (Helsinki), no. 3, 1982; "For the Floor" by N. Znamierowski in *American Craft* (New York), April/May 1985; "An Explorer in Textiles" by L. Maunula in *Helsingin Sanomat* (Helsinki), 15 May 1986; "Maija Lavonen's Art—A Dialogue of Metal and Textiles" by T. Runeberg in *Anna* (Helsinki), no. 11, 1989.

*

I am interested in public spaces, where we work and conduct our daily business: offices, city traffic, all the information surrounding us. I think it is ever more important to create alternatives, deviations from standardized universal design, relaxing places of rest and calming interiors.

In my own work, which today mostly consists of designing and making textiles for architecture, I aim at taking into consideration the forms and materials of the building while including my own personal vision. It is my belief that an independent work that is not too restrained gives an enlivening touch to a space. I believe in the power of simple geometric lines and rhythms. Textile in itself is forcible and impressive as a material; I want the material to breathe, to avoid heaviness. Sometimes I include a supplementary metal element in my works—as a feature that contrasts with and purifies the material feel of the textile.

I have also designed textiles for household use, but I believe that my work has greater significance in so-called public spaces or places of work. I would like to think that people might want to linger awhile near them, or simply receive an uplifting or calming touch while passing by. My designs are therefore a reaction to today's stressful life rhythm. I like to use very simple techniques in my spatial works. I want them to get across to people because of their general appearance and content rather than technical flourishes.

For reasons of tradition, textile art has a special position of its own in Finland. Textiles have always been used in Finnish home for practical reasons alone, to fend off the cold. As building methods have changed, they are no longer needed in the same way. But now that textiles are becoming a part of architecture, I believe that the old functional tradition has largely helped to create a situation over the past twenty years where art textiles have become a relatively strong alternative to other visual arts. In Finland, unlike the rest of Europe, there is no tradition in tapestry: here, the ryijy rug has been the dominant textile. Tapestry in Finland is not set into one rigid pattern that continues to be imitated, but is very alive and open to variation. In Finland, the status of textiles has a firm basis.

My design work is based on feelings and observation of nature. I hope my works convey a suggestion of natural experience—perhaps of the bright light of noon, or the spatial experience of standing atop the crest of a rock. When I am at work choosing colours and materials, little things are important, such as the delicate hues and tints of colour. In taking natural observation as a starting point, I have wanted to bring to mind our right to experience nature, and stress the need to preserve it.

—Maija Lavonen

*

Maija Lavonen's breakthrough to the front rank of Finnish textile artists happened in 1978 when she exhibited a group of works that lent new vitality and a new appearance to the ryijy-rug which is so important in Finland. Lavonen's works, restrained yet full of feeling, transformed this classic of Nordic textile art in a propitious and balanced way. The transition from the tradition of the ryijy to the pictorial language of modern art had occurred without friction.

The transformation took place at a time when faith in the future of this warm woollen rug had almost been lost. For some time, artists had

Maija Lavonen: *Ledges of Rock* hand-dyed ryijy-relief in linen and wool, with sculptures in baked steel, 1989

been having difficulty with getting a new hold of it. The economic depression affecting industry in the 1970s cast its shadow over much applied art, including textiles; crafts also, with their genuine but expensive natural materials, were going through a crisis. Public commissions for art textiles were rare.

Maija Lavonen abandoned her career as fashion designer and became an experimenter and innovator in art textiles in 1970, after the death of her painter husband. From the start, her work has carried the mark of a boundary-breaking and experimental attitude while manifesting a firm belief in the functionalist rules of international modernism.

After her success with the ryijy, Lavonen began weaving linen into large, three-dimensional spatial works. With exhibitions of her work, she joined in the early 1980s topical debates concerning art in the civic environment, the role of ecology in the world of objects and the human alternative offered by handicraft.

As a textile artist, Lavonen constantly refuses all extravagance in the use of her yarns. She regards them as basic materials to which one should be faithful while subjecting them to artistic control. She does not limit herself to yarns and threads alone, however. Being a lively discoverer, Lavonen has incorporated into her spatial works indigenous Lapp marble as well as international neon lighting. All her materials, including linen and silk fibres, she uses frugally in order not to squander unique gifts of nature. Thus, even large works become light and airy, which aspect is further emphasized by the artist's preference for spare but fresh and always pure colours.

On the threshold of the 1990s, Lavonen has returned to the heavier and more material idiom of the ryijy. In her ryijy-rugs or in any other works, Lavonen tells no stories, yet she is able to tap profound feelings of the Finnish people's close relationship with nature and its strongly contrasting seasons. One of the hidden themes of her works is in fact an interpretation of the effect of the seasons in her native district on the shores of the Gulf of Bothnia, where the sea sparkles with light in summer and lies leaden and foreboding in winter.

Maija Lavonen's modern textiles have evolved side by side with the liberation of architecture's formal language, and she has been able to realize many large-scale works in civic buildings. For her one-woman shows, she has always preferred to find a new gallery each time in order to be able to build a fresh, carefully considered, exemplary work of art. Lavonen has done pioneering work by reinstating textile art in the civic environment. In their restraint and equilibrium, her works match well with contemporary Finnish architecture which also bases its transformation on the more moderate traditions of modernism.

The role of the artist in applied arts in Finland includes diversification. Lavonen has designed fabrics for industrial manufacturers such as the Finnish firm of Marimekko as well as international companies. Church art, which holds an important position in Finland, has also provided work. A major commission is a large multi-part spatial work in Kristian Gullichsen's Malmi church in a suburb of Helsinki. The central part of the tapestry is changed following changes of liturgical colours during the ecclesiastical year.

Teaching has also been a part of Lavonen's work. In addition to training students at the University of Industrial Arts, she has also supervised the activity of municipal workshops in the northern Lapp town of Kemi. In 1982 she received the first 15-year state grant awarded to an artist of the applied arts.

—Leena Maunula

LAX, Michael.

American exhibition and industrial designer. Born in New York City, 8 November 1929. Studied at Alfred University, New York, 1948–51: BFA 1951; Fulbright study fellowship to Finland, 1953–54. Freelance industrial designer, New York, from 1965: has designed for American Cyanamid, Copco, Champion International, Eastern Airlines, Formica, Lightolier, Mikasa, Salton, N. A. Christensen, Coquet, Faveka, Artemide, Takatsuki Diecasting, Gullaskrufs Glasbruks, etc.; also exhibit designs for the American Federation of Arts, Brooklyn Children's Museum, Ford Foundation, Metropolitan Museum of Art, Smithsonian Institution, and United States Information Agency. Lecturer, Pratt Institute, Brooklyn, New York, 1970–71, and Rhode Island School of Design, Providence, 1975–76. **Exhibitions:** *Good Design,* Museum of Modern Art, New York, 1952; Museum of Modern Art, New York, 1968; Nationalmuseum, Stockholm, 1975; Stedelijk Museum, Amsterdam, 1978; Musée des Arts Décoratifs, Paris, 1980; *Design Since 1945,* Philadelphia Museum of Art, 1983. Recipient: Rome Prize Fellowship, 1977. Member: Industrial Designers Society of America; American Institute of Graphic Arts. Address: 124 East 65th Street, New York, New York 10021, U.S.A.

Publications:

On LAX: books—*Design in America* by Ralph Caplan, New York 1969; *One Hundred Great Product Designs* by Jay Doblin, New York 1970; *Environment Design of the World,* Tokyo 1971; *Design Review* annual, New York and London 1978; *Design Since 1945,* edited by Kathryn Hiesinger and George Marcus, Philadelphia and London 1983.

LEACH, Bernard (Howell).

British potter and ceramics designer. Born, of British parents, in Hong Kong, 5 January 1887. Educated at schools in Hong Kong, Singapore and England, until 1902; studied drawing under Henry Tonks, at Slade School of Art, London, 1903–05, banking, at a commercial college, Manchester, 1906–08, etching under Frank Brangwyn, at London School of Art, 1908–09, and pottery under Ogata Kenzan, in Tokyo and Korea, 1909–20. Married Edith Muriel Hoyle in 1909; children: David, William, Edith, Ruth and Elizabeth; married Laurie Cookes in 1936; son: Maurice; married Jane Darnell in 1956. Independent potter, working with Ogata Kenzan, in Tokyo and Korea, 1909–20; founder with Shoji Hamada, and director of the Leach Pottery, St. Ives, Cornwall, 1920–79. Instructor in pottery, Dartington Hall, Devon, 1932, 1936; also visiting lecturer in the United States and Japan, from 1950. **Exhibitions:** Cotswold Gallery, London, 1922; Beaux-Arts Gallery, London, 1931, 1933, 1952; Arts Council Gallery, London, 1961; Osaka Museum, Japan, 1961; Galerie de France, Paris, 1964; Crane Kalman Gallery, London, 1967; Victoria and Albert Museum, London, 1977. Recipient: American Ceramic Society Binns Medal, 1950; World Crafts Council Award, Dublin, 1970; Japan Foundation Prize, 1974. Honorary doctorates: Manchester College of Art, 1960; University of Exeter, 1961. Commander, Order of the British Empire, 1962; Order of the Sacred Treasure, Japan, 1966; Freedom of the Borough of St. Ives, 1968; Companion of Honour, London, 1973. *Died* (in St. Ives, Cornwall) *6 May 1979.*

Publications:

By LEACH: books and pamphlets—*A Review*

Michael Lax: *Copco* tea kettle in enamelled steel and teak, 1982

1909-1914, Tokyo 1914; *A Potter's Outlook,* pamphlet, London 1928; *A Potter's Book,* London 1940, 1945, 1976, New York 1948, 1967; *The Leach Pottery,* pamphlet, London 1946; *A Potter's Portfolio: A Selection of Fine Pots,* London 1951; *A Potter in Japan 1952-1954,* London 1960, New York 1967; *Kenzan and His Tradition: The Life and Times of Koetsu, Sotatsu, Korin and Kanzan,* London 1966, New York 1967; *A Potter's Work,* London 1967, 1974, 1977; *The Unknown Craftsman: A Japanese Insight into Beauty,* editor, with Soetsu Yanagi, Tokyo and London 1972; *Bernard Leach: Drawings Verse and Belief,* Bath 1973; *Hamada, Potter,* Tokyo, New York and San Francisco 1975, London 1976; *A Potter's Challenge,* edited by David Outerbridge, New York 1975, London 1976; *Beyond East and West: Memoirs, Portraits and Essays,* London 1978.

On LEACH: books—*Design in the Home,* edited by Noel Carrington, London 1933; *The Work of the Modern Potter in England* by George Wingfield Digby, London 1952; *Artist Potters in England* by Muriel Rose, London 1955, 1970; *Bernard Leach: 50 Years a Potter,* exhibition catalogue by J. P. Hodin, London 1961; *Bernard Leach* by Soetsu Yanagi, Tokyo 1966; *Modern Ceramics* by Geoffrey Beard, London 1969; *The Art of Bernard Leach,* edited by Carol Hogben, London 1977, 1978; *Contemporary International Ceramics* by Hildegaard Storr-Britz, Cologne 1980; *The Conran Directory of Design,* edited by Stephen Bayley, London 1985.

During his lifetime, Bernard Leach was called "the greatest living Western potter," ranking with Japanese masters Shoji Hamada, Kenkichi Tomimoto, and Kanjiro Kawai as one of the four supreme masters of clay in modern times. A painter and graphic artist, Leach was drawn by chance to potterymaking while studying art in Japan in the early 1900s. Having participated in a party where Japanese raku vessels were being decorated and fired for use in the tea ceremony, Leach became fascinated with the application of ancient pottery techniques to contemporary needs. He studied raku under Ogata Kenzan VI, whose ancestors were potters in the raku tradition. Kenzan eventually gave Leach not only his glazing secrets but also bestowed on him the title Kenzan VII.

Upon his return to England in 1920, Leach established a studio in St. Ives, Cornwall with Shoji Hamada. Using local clay and glaze materials and firing with local wood, he sought to produce a truly contemporary British folk pottery. Leach's work, influenced by Mingei, or Japanese folk art, was in direct contrast to the shiny, hard, white translucency then fashionable in English ceramics. His one-of-a-kind pieces were based on traditional Chinese Sung Dynasty and Korean shapes and brush decoration. However, standard tableware produced at St. Ives largely adapted the British slipware tradition of jugs, beakers, sugar bowls, and creamers.

Leach is responsible for bringing handmade pottery back to British homes. During his lifetime, his studio at St. Ives was a mecca for pottery students and collectors alike. Apprentices from his studio, such as Warren MacKenzie and Byron Temple, have carried on the tradition of making by hand affordable tableware in their own studios in the United States.

Leach's reputation as a potter is rivaled today by his reputation as a thinker and writer. His long friendship with writer and museum organizer Soetsu Yanagi fueled a fifty-year dialogue on the anonymous craftsman and beauty in art. Besides his 1940 *Potter's Book,* he wrote memoirs, *Beyond East and West,* and a variety of treatises and analyses of pots, pointing the way

for future generations to understand the synthesis of Eastern and Western traditions. Once a Zen Buddhist, Leach ended his days as a devout member of the Baha'i faith.

In an age when mass production was a powerful influence, Bernard Leach advocated an appreciation of work by the human hand. He preached the virtues of innocence, modesty, and humility to a generation of Western students who listened and followed.

—Sarah Bodine

LEE, Eugene.
American stage, film and television designer. Born 9 March 1939. Studied at Carnegie-Mellon University, Pittsburgh, and Yale University, New Haven, Connecticut. Married Franne Newman; Brooke Lutz in 1981; children: William and Edward. Freelance designer, from 1965: worked for theatre companies in Philadelphia, New York, Washington, D.C., and Dallas; resident designer, Trinity Square Repertory Company, Providence, Rhode Island, from 1968; also designer of *Saturday Night Live* television programmes, 1974-80. Recipient: Drama Desk Award, New York, 1970; Antoinette Perry (Tony) Award, New York, 1974, 1979. Addresses: 31 Union Square West, New York, New York 10003; 292 Wayland Avenue, Providence, Rhode Island 02902, U.S.A.

Works:

Stage productions include—*A Dream of Love,* Theater of Living Arts, Philadelphia, 1966; *Belch,* Theater of Living Arts, Philadelphia, 1966; *The Threepenny Opera,* Studio Arena Theater, Buffalo, 1967; *The Imaginary Invalid,* Studio Arena Theater, Buffalo, 1967; *HMS Pinafore,* Studio Arena Theater, Buffalo, 1967; *Enrico IV,* Studio Arena Theater, Buffalo, 1967; *A Delicate Balance,* Studio Arena Theater, Buffalo, 1968; *World War 2 1/2,* Martinique Theatre, New York, 1969; *Slave Ship,* Brooklyn Academy of Music, 1969; *The Recruiting Officer,* Theater of the Living Arts, Philadelphia, 1970; *Harry Noon and Night,* Theater of the Living Arts, Philadelphia, 1970; *Wilson in the Promised Land,* ANTA Playhouse, New York, 1970; *Alice in Wonderland,* Extension Theater, New York, 1970; *Saved,* Brooklyn Academy of Music, 1970; *Mother Courage,* Arena Stage Theatre, Washington, D.C., 1970; *Son of Man and the Family,* Rhode Island School of Design Theatre, 1970; *Taming of the Shrew,* Rhode Island School of Design Theatre, 1970; *Love for Love,* Rhode Island School of Design Theatre, 1971; *The Threepenny Opera,* Rhode Island School of Design Theatre, 1971; *Dude,* Broadway Theatre, New York, 1972; *Candide,* Brooklyn Academy of Music, 1973; *Gabrielle,* Studio Arena Theatre, Buffalo, 1974; *The Skin of Our Teeth,* Kennedy Center for the Performing Arts, Washington, D.C., 1975; *It's Me, Sylvia,* Playhouse Theatre II, New York, 1981; *Agnes of God,* Music Box Theatre, New York, 1982; *Some Men Need Help,* 47th Street Theatre, New York, 1982; *The Ballad of Soapy Smith,* New York Shakespeare Festival, 1984; *Misalliance,* Dallas Theater Center, 1984; *Amadeus,* Dallas Theater Center, 1984; *A Christmas Carol,* Dallas Theater Center, 1984, 1985; *The Normal Heart,* New York Shakespeare Festival, 1985; *Passion Play,* Dallas Theater Center, 1985; *The Three Sisters,* Dallas Theater Center, 1985; *You Can't Take It With You,* Dallas Theater Center, 1985; *Good,* Dallas Theater Center, 1985; *The Skin of Our Teeth,* Dallas Theater Center, 1985; *The Marriage of Bette and Boo,* Dallas Theater Center, 1985; *The Glass Menagerie,* Dallas Theater Center, 1986; *The Tavern,* Dallas Theater Center, 1986; *The Ups and Downs of Theophilus Maitland,* Dallas Theater Center, 1986; *A Folk Tale,* Dallas Theater Center, 1986; *Kith and Kin,* Dallas Theater Center, 1986. At Trinity Square Theatre, Providence— *The Threepenny Opera,* 1967; *The Importance of Being Earnest,* 1967; *Year of the Locust,* 1968; *An Enemy of the People,* 1968; *Phaedra,* 1968; *Macbeth,* 1969; *The Homecoming,* 1969; *Billy Budd,* 1969; *Old Glory,* 1969; *Black/White,* 1969; *Wilson in the Promised Land,* 1969; *The Skin of Our Teeth,* 1970; *Lovecraft's Follies,* 1970; *You Can't Take It With You,* 1970; *Troilus and Cressida,* 1971; *Down by the River Where Waterlilies Are Disfigured Every Day,* 1971; *The Good and Bad Times of Cady Francis McCullum and Friends,* 1971; *Old Times,* 1972; *Royal Hunt of the Sun,* 1973; *Feasting with Panthers,* 1973; *Brother to Dragons,* 1973; *Ghost Dance,* 1973; *Aimee,* 1974; *Well Hung,* 1974; *A Man for All Seasons,* 1974; *Peer Gynt,* 1975; *Tom Jones,* 1975; *Seven Keys to Baldpate,* 1975; *El Grande de Coca-Cola,* 1980; *An Almost Perfect Person,* 1980; *Deathtrap,* 1980; *Arsenic and Old Lace,* 1980; *Betrayal,* 1980; *On Golden Pond,* 1980; *A Christmas Carol,* 1981, 1982, 1984, 1985; *The Iceman Cometh,* 1981; *Inherit the Wind,* 1981; *How I Got That Story,* 1981; *Whose Life Is It Anyway?,* 1981; *The Whales of August,* 1981; *Tintypes,* 1982; *The Crucifer of Blood,* 1982; *13 Rue de l'Amour,* 1982; *The Dresser,* 1982; *Translations,* 1982; *The Front Page,* 1983; *The Tempest,* 1983; *Pygmalion,* 1983; *The Web,* 1983; *Letters from Prison,* 1983; *Beyond Therapy,* 1984; *What the Butler Saw,* 1984; *Terra Nova,* 1984; *Passion Play,* 1984; *Tartuffe,* 1984; *Misalliance,* 1985; *And a Nightingale Sang,* 1985; *The Country Wife,* 1985; *Master Harold and the Boys,* 1985; *Present Laughter,* 1985; *The Marriage of Bette and Boo,* 1985; *Cat On a Hot Tin Roof,* 1985; *The Crucible,* 1986; *The Tavern,* 1986; *Life and Limb,* 1986; *Pasta,* 1986; *The Country Girl,* 1986; *Baby,* 1986; *Not By Bed Alone,* 1986.

Publications:

On LEE: books—*The Cambridge Guide to World Theatre,* edited by Martin Banham, Cambridge and New York 1988; *Contemporary Theatre, Film and Television no. 5,* Detroit 1988; articles—in *Theatre Design and Technology* (Charlottesville), Summer 1982; *Theatre* (New Haven), Winter 1982.

Eugene Lee's large, provocative, audience-involving settings are generally unlike those of any other mainstream American designer today. Elements of his style, of course, have corollaries in other theatre artists, but there is no clear influence from any one source, no overriding similarity to any other designer. Totally unlike his contemporaries and classmates of Yale University, the wellspring of much contemporary stage design, he is closest in spirit to European theatricalists such as Luca Ronconi or Patrice Chereau, but differences between European and American production styles, budgets, and repertoires preclude any extensive comparison. Lee admits to some influence from Peter Brook and Jerzy Grotowski—and indeed, his environmental designs began after seeing Grotowski's in Edinburgh—but the underlying esthetics are different.

The key to Lee's style is his feeling that the audience should be involved, that the only significant relationship is between the actor and the audience, and that the entire space of the theatre—not only the stage—should be considered in relation to the demands of the play. As a result, each play is approached with no preconceptions as to the style, space, or scope of the setting.

In the late 1960s and early 1970s, when experimentation and iconoclasm were more readily accepted, Lee could take the ideas he had developed at Trinity Square and move them to the theatres on and off Broadway. For the production of Amiri Baraka's *Slaveship* (1969), the normal seating area of the Chelsea Theatre was platformed over, and the cramped hold of a slave ship was constructed in the center of the space. The audience, on wood benches, very close to the "slaves," was, in turn, surrounded by other acting platforms and spaces. The audience was thus enveloped by the production, which achieved a sense of claustrophobia and fear. The same principle, on a more elaborate scale, was employed for *Billy Budd* at Trinity Square earlier the same year to create the impression that the audience was within a nineteenth-century sailing ship. For *Alice in Wonderland* (1970), the audience entered through a three-and-a-half-foot door into a space covered by a parachute.

Lee's work at Trinity and elsewhere is typified by environmental design (or "atmospheric" as he calls it). Ramps jut into the auditorium, performance areas are scattered throughout the audience space, scenic elements dangle above the heads of the spectators. In general, there is an attempt to eliminate the proscenium and encompass the audience. His fondness for natural, non-traditional materials is not only to supply texture but to help in the creation of an aural environment as well. *Son of Man and the Family* (1970) for example, was set in a prison, and the sound of the actor-prisoners marching on the steel mesh catwalks of the set could frequently be heard.

With the production of *Candide* (1974), Lee and director Harold Prince hoped to signal the end of the proscenium on Broadway and to establish at least one, ongoing, flexible theatre space for commercial productions. *Sweeney Todd* (1979) was originally envisioned for the same space. But economics and an increasingly conservative trend among theatre-goers and producers defeated this idea. Lee continues to incorporate as many of his ideas as possible within the confines of commercial theatre or under-budgeted regional theatre, but he is unhappy with the current state of theatre and its lack of opportunities for experimentation. It is this, he feels, that has pushed him toward film and television.

—Arnold Aronson

LEE, Ming Cho.

American painter and stage designer. Born in Shanghai, China, 3 October 1930; emigrated to the United States in 1949. Educated at schools in Shanghai and Hong Kong until 1948; studied at Occidental College Los Angeles, 1950–53: BA 1953; University of California, Los Angeles, 1953–54; also studied with watercolorist Kuo-Nyen. Married Elizabeth Rapport in 1958. Assistant designer to Jo Mielziner, New York, 1955–57; freelance designer, from 1958:

worked with the Peabody Arts Theatre operatic company, Peabody Institute, Baltimore, 1959–63; art director and resident designer, San Francisco Opera, 1961–62; principal designer, New York Shakespeare Festival, 1962–73, Juilliard Opera Theatre, and American Opera Center of the Juilliard School of Music, New York, from 1964; also designed for ballet companies of Jose Limon, Martha Graham, Gerald Arpino and Alvin Ailey; design consultant to the Performing Arts Center at the State University of New York, Purchase, the Cincinnati Music Hall, and the Patricia Corbett Pavilion of the University of Cincinnati School of Music. Instructor in set design, Yale University Drama School, New Haven, Connecticut, and the New York University Washington Square College. Member: Theatre Projects Committee, New York City Planning Commission; American Theatre Planning Board; United Scenic Artists, New York; California Watercolor Society. Address: 13 East 87th Street, New York, New York 10028, U.S.A.

Works:

Stage productions (New York unless noted) include—*The Crucible*, 1958; *Triad*, 1958; *The Infernal Machine*, 1958; *Mother Courage*, 1962 (also 1978); *King Lear*, 1962; *The Moon Besieged*, 1962; *Walk in Darkness*, 1963; *Conversations in the Dark*, 1963; *Slapstick Tragedy*, 1963; *Othello*, 1964; *Electra*, 1964; *Madame Butterfly*, 1965; *The Witch of Endor* (ballet), 1965; *A Time for Singing*, 1966; *Little Murders*, 1967; *Here's Where I Belong*, 1968; *Peer Gynt*, 1969; *Billy*, 1969; *La Strada*, 1969; *Gandhi*, 1970; *The Wars of the Roses (Henry VI, Parts I, II, and III)*, 1970; *Our Town* (Washington, D.C. and tour of the Soviet Union), 1972; *Inherit the Wind* (Washington, D.C. and tour of the Soviet Union), 1972; *Myth of a Voyage* (ballet), 1973; *Two Gentlemen of Verona*, 1973; *The Glass Menagerie* (Minneapolis), 1975; *Boris Gudonov*, 1975; *The Sea Gull*, 1975; *All God's Children Got Wings*, 1975; *Colored Girls*, 1976; *Much Ado about Nothing*, 1976; *The Shadow Box*, 1977; *I Puritani*, 1977; *Lohengrin*, 1978; *K2*, 1983.

Publications:

By LEE: article—in *Theater* (New Haven) Fall/Winter 1981.

On LEE: books—*The Biographical Encyclopaedia and Who's Who of the American Theatre*, edited by Walter Rigdon, New York 1966; *Stage Design* by Donald Oenslager New York 1975; *Who's Who in the Theatre* edited by Ian Herbert London and Detroit 1977; *The Cambridge Guide to World Theatre*, edited by Martin Banham, Cambridge and New York 1988.

Ming Cho Lee entered the world of professional design in the mid-1950s as an assistant to Jo Mielziner and, more briefly, to George Jenkins, Rouben Ter-Arutunian, and Boris Aronson. By the end of the decade, he was designing off-Broadway. His first production, *The Infernal Machine* (1958) at the Phoenix Theater, garnered favorable reviews which focused mainly on the decor and set his career in motion.

Early, Lee's preference in design tended toward the non-literal, with dance design being his favorite activity, followed closely by opera and Shakespeare. Now, he enjoys designing plays as well. Some of his critics accused him of a "too Brechtian" approach, but his emphasis on simplicity derived from an attempt to integrate the setting within the framework of the entire production. The sparseness was evident

in Martha Graham's dance work *The Witch of Endor* because the designer chose to use only two thrones and a metal configuration. Equally spare for the New York Shakespeare Festival, his approach, however, suited the situation, since his ingenious simplicity triumphed over budget restraints. He sometimes designed one basic structure which might be used for three separate summer shows, thus saving the expense of much scenery.

However, this type of multi-purpose setting was also effectively used (as for *The Shadow Box*) on Broadway, where budgets are not always a main concern. Lee's design of Brecht's *Mother Courage* (1978) prompted Mel Gussow of the *New York Times* to comment "Ming Cho Lee's set—an almost barren plane surmounted by Mother Courage's rustic wagon—is stark." Lee's intent was not to emphasize the setting, or to underplay its importance, but to blend it into the fabric of production so that the playgoer would experience what the designer refers to as "a total theatrical experience."

To his enjoyment, Lee's later career seems to be emphasizing more realistic, literal works, which he infuses with style. For *K2*, he reproduced a section of mountain, which actually replaced the stage, prompting Ted E. Kalem of *Time* to write, "Lee's awesome set is the playgoer's eye, restored to a 20/20 vision of the power, mystery, majesty and menace of undomesticated nature." Although realistic, Lee's *The Glass Menagerie* (in the words of the designer) "attempts to make connections between the verbal and the visual," resulting in an organic whole. He adds that this production was quite unlike the original that Jo Mielziner designed on Broadway.

His design process moves from the general to the specific. Reading the script only once, Lee keeps his mind open to interpretation until he meets the director. Although he has an initial, personal reaction to the play, not until he has conferred with the director does Lee decide on matters such as the basic approach or the construction materials.

Brought up through the Broadway ranks by Mielziner, Lee, as teacher at Yale's Drama School, now transmits his knowledge to future generations of designers. He feels an obligation to train his apprentices and pass along the crafts of his trade, while continuing to uphold a rigorous schedule of design activities.

—Tom Mikotowicz

LEEDS, Harold Eliot.

American architect and interior designer. Born in Meriden, Connecticut, 1 April 1919. Studied at Harvard University, Cambridge, Massachusetts, 1936–39: BA 1939; School of Architecture and Allied Arts, New York University, 1939–42: B.Arch. 1942. Designer, working in New York, from 1942: draftsman, at Skidmore, Owings and Merrill architectural firm; draftsman and designer, at Raymond Loewy Associates design firm; designer and director, at Donald Deskey Associates design firm, until 1946; founder and partner, of Warner/Leeds Associates, New York, 1947–55, and of Leeds Associates, New York, from 1955; freelance designer, in A. E. Leeds Design, New York, from 1970. Professor and chairman of the interior design department, Pratt Institute, Brooklyn, New York, 1959–69. Address: 64 Perry Street, New York, New York 10014, U.S.A.

Works:

Warner-Leeds design office interiors, New York, 1948.
Paris Theatre cinema interiors, New York, 1949.
Bonniers Bookstore interiors, New York, 1949.
Caribe Hilton Hotel interiors, San Juan, Puerto Rico, 1950.
Guest House interiors, St. Thomas, U.S. Virgin Islands, 1952.
Cerromar Beach Hotel, Dorado Beach, Puerto Rico, 1975–76.
Bedford Stuyvesant CABS Nursing Home interiors, Brooklyn, New York, 1976.

Publications:

By LEEDS: article—in *Interiors* (New York), November 1970.

On LEEDS: book—*Interior Design: An Introduction to Architectural Interiors* by Arnold Friedmann, John F. Pile and Forrest Wilson, New York and Amsterdam 1970, 1976; articles—in the *New Yorker*, 4 December 1948; *Architectural Forum* (New York), January 1949, March 1949, March 1950; *Interiors* (New York), August 1949, April 1950, January 1952, June 1969, November 1970, February 1976, December 1976; *Interior Design* (New York), July 1978.

Harold Leeds has made his strongest contribution to interior design as an educator. Under his chairmanship from 1959 to 1969, the Department of Interior Design at Pratt Institute in Brooklyn became the leading school in the field in the United States and most likely, the world. He assembled a group of experienced and dedicated faculty members, and he managed to attract the most talented students. The program he implemented there became the model for such courses throughout the United States. In 1970, upon completion of a sabbatical leave from Pratt, Leeds began to teach exclusively in the graduate interior design program, which had been initiated during his chairmanship. Perhaps the measure of Leeds' influence upon the world of design can best be expressed by the very large number of leading designers in many tip positions, as principals of major design firms and as recipients of numerous awards, who all were his students during his administration or even during the years before that when he was a design critic at Pratt Institute for seven years.

Leeds is an enormously talented designer, who produced a distinguished body of work prior to his teaching career and continues his professional work even now. After graduating from one of the finest architectural programs of the time, at New York University, he worked in several firms before establishing the Warner/Leeds partnership (1947–1955). Some of the most important projects done during those years were the Bonniers Shop and the Paris Theater in New York City and the Caribe Hilton Hotel in Puerto Rico. Warner-Leeds was so far ahead of other firms in the accomplishment of excellent interior design work that the projects remained as important twenty years later as they had been at completion. Subsequently, Leeds established an active design firm under the name of Leeds Associates, which numbered offices, hotels, and colleges among its commissions.

Leeds is not interested in publicity, even though a number of his design projects have been published. Perhaps the public at large is not familiar with his work, yet he has been widely recognized, has served on many distinguished design juries, has been made a consultant to New York City's Transit Authority by the mayor, and has served as a design consultant and critic in several countries. If a poll were to be taken among designers and architects to name a truly great twentieth-century interior designer, chances are that Leeds would be one of the most frequently mentioned names.

—Arnold Friedmann

LENICA, Jan.

Polish-French filmmaker, stage and graphic designer. Born in Poznan, Poland, 4 January 1928; emigrated to France in 1963: naturalized, 1981. Studied at the Architectural High School, Warsaw, 1947–52: Ing.Arch. 1952. Married Merja Alanen in 1969; children: Anneli and Maia. Independent poster artist, working in Warsaw, 1950–58, and in Paris from 1963; also animated film designer from 1957, and stage designer from 1972. Teaching assistant to Henryk Tomaszewski, at the Art Academy, Warsaw, 1954; professor, at the Kunstakademie Gesamthochschule, Kassel, 1979–85; professor of graphic design, at the Hochschule der Künste, West Berlin, from 1986; artist in residence, Carpenter Center for the Visual Arts, Harvard University, Cambridge, Massachusetts, 1974. **Exhibitions:** Club of Young Artists, Warsaw, 1948; Filmmuseum, Copenhagen, 1966; Filmmuseum, Arnhem, 1967; Museum Villa Stuck, Munich, 1968; Poster Museum, Warsaw, 1968; Museum des 20. Jahrhunderts, Vienna, 1971; National Museum, Poznan, 1973; Harvard University, Cambridge, Massachusetts, 1973; Centre Georges Pompidou, Paris, 1980; Deutsches Plakatmuseum, Essen, 1980, 1983; Katholische Akademie, Hamburg, 1981; Kunstverein, Kassel, 1981; High School of Graphic Arts, Vienna, 1982; Modern Art Museum, Tampere, 1988. **Collections:** Poster Museum, Warsaw; National Museum, Poznan; Deutsches Plakatmuseum, Essen; Kunstgewerbemuseum, Zurich; Museum of Modern Art, New York; Library of Congress, Washington, D.C. Recipient: Grand Film Prize, World's Fair, Brussels, 1958; Toulouse-Lautrec Prize, Paris, 1961; Warsaw Poster Biennale Prize, 1966; Max Ernst Award, Paris, 1966; Bundesfilm Prize, West Germany, 1969; City of Essen Prize, 1980; Jules Cheret Award, Paris, 1983; Alfred Jurzykowski Award, New York, 1987; Premio Grafico, Bologna, 1987. Address: 3 rue Saint Christophe, 75015 Paris, France.

Works:

Animated films include—*Strip-Tease*, 1957; *Once Upon a Time*, 1957; *Love Required*, 1957; *The House*, 1958; *Banner of Youth*, 1958; *Monsieur Tete*, 1959; *New Janko the Musician*, 1960; *Italia 61*, 1961; *Labyrinth*, 1962; *Rhinoceroses*, 1963; *A*, 1964; *Cul de Sac* (trailer for Polanski), 1964; *The Woman Flower*, 1965; *Weg zum Nachbarn*, 1966; *Adam 2*, 1969; *Still Life*, 1969; *Nature Morte*, 1970; *Fantorro, The Last Just Man*, 1972; *Landscape*, 1974; *King Ubu*, 1976; *Ubu and the Great Gidouille*, 1979.

Publications:

By LENICA: books—*Plakat Tadeusza Trepkowskiego*, Warsaw 1958; *Population Explosion*, with A. Sauvy, New York 1962; *Monsieur Tête*, with text by Eugene Ionesco, Munich 1970; *The Magic Bird*, Zurich 1986; *Theo the Snowman*, Zurich 1988; *Jan Lenica: Noir et Blanc*, Paris 1988.

On LENICA: books—*Jan Lenica* by Zygmunt Kaluzynski, Warsaw 1963; *Film and TV Graphics*, edited by Walter Herdeg, Zurich 1967; *History of the Poster* by Josef and Shizuko Müller-Brockmann, Zurich 1971; *Polish Poster Art Today* by Szymon Bojko, Warsaw 1972; *Full Length Animated Feature Films* by Bruno Edera, London and New York 1977; *Jan Lenica*, edited by Heinz-Jurgen Kristahn, West Berlin 1981; *Who's Who in Graphic Art*, edited by Walter Amstutz, Dubendorf 1982; *A History of Graphic Design* by Philip B. Meggs, New York and London 1983; *The International Dictionary of Films and Filmmakers*, Chicago and London 1984, 1991.

I have always enjoyed working on the peripheries of art, at the edge of styles, penetrating the distant lands of the principal currents and those which are, as it were, more noble. I have amused myself in opposing the rules in force in the different disciplines, in associating apparently distant or entirely dissimilar elements, in blurring the edges between neighbouring fields, in grafting more noble characteristics onto styles of "inferior rank"—in a word, I have enjoyed tacit diversion. Forms considered ordinary, scorned by those who work at more elevated levels, have always attracted me.

These remarks are perhaps surprising nowadays when there is general integration in the arts, emancipation in fields such as graphics, photography, and many others. But I remember the time when painters scorned graphics and when the name "graphic artist" had a disdainful aftertaste. Where are the snows of yesteryear? The doors of artistic salons wide open to graphics and those of the museum to the poster? Where nowadays is the dividing line between painting and graphics—and who today holds to "purity of style"?

During the 1950s, I was reproached for resorting, in the poster, to non-graphic techniques, supposedly incompatible with print technique, and for introducing particularly pictorial subjects—the portrait, for example. At present, there is no technique that the poster has not adopted or adapted to its own ends. The poster has freed itself from the utilitarian graphics which constrained it like a corset, it has released itself from prudish isolation, detached itself from its often servile functions to such a degree that even its definition has become unacceptable. The poster has returned to its roots, it has again become a picture—reproduced many times, a picture dealing with the "proposed subject."

I once believed that in the hands of an artist, the animated film could become an instrument with extraordinary possibilities. Film appeared to me as the most contemporary product, as an incomparable means of expression, as a vast and fertile field of activity. I did not see at the time the immense difficulties which face those who do not want to submit to the cinema's commercial system. The margin of creative liberty and of experiment which still existed recently—that is, in the short film—has almost entirely disappeared. No one needs it, there is no room for it in the cinema, and the festivals of shorts emit the melancholy of their past glory into a vacuum. As also in the socialist countries, it still has a raison d'être in the United States, where the distribution network in the universities and lecture halls (in a way, cinematographic libraries) assure its diffusion and audiences for it.

The cinema continues its development in the show-business tradition. As an artistic product,

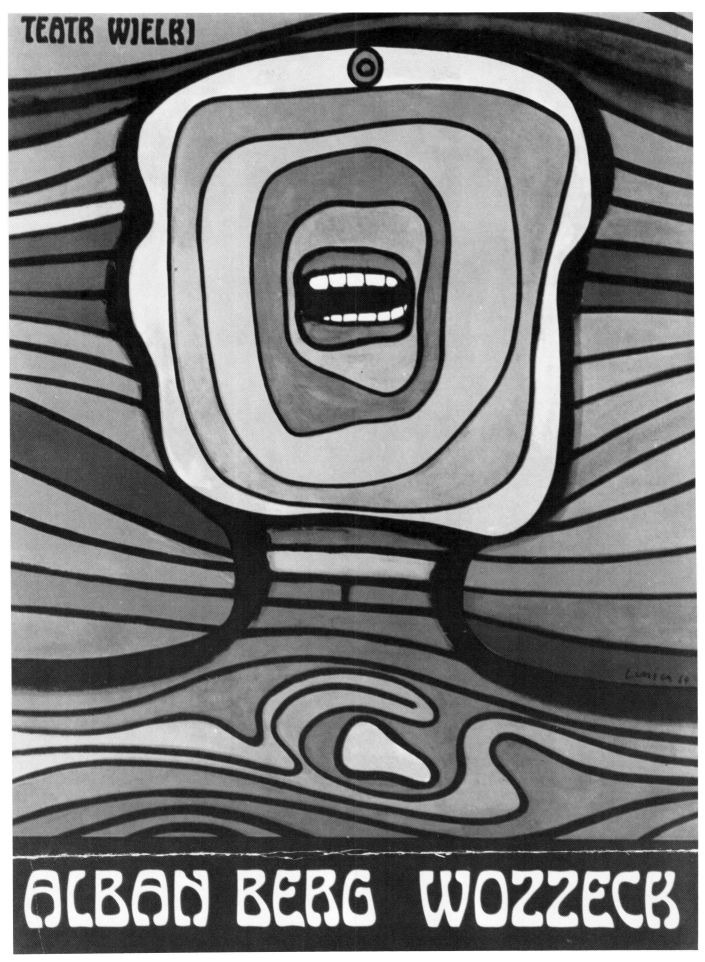

Jan Lenica: *Wozzeck* **poster, for the Teatr Wielki, Warsaw, 1964**

which can demonstrate the character of an objet d'art in time and movement, the cinema has still not found either its patron or its destined collector. I see its only chance in the development of modern means of reproduction, in the popularity of cassettes and video discs which must soon appear on the market. They can radically change the situation and assure the cinema of the same popularity which literary and musical works enjoy.

—Jan Lenica

Jan Lenica's reputation rests on his artistic versatility. His contribution to poster design, book illustration, animated film, and stage design has caused him to emerge as one of the most significant practitioners in European graphic art. As a poster designer, animated filmmaker and innovator in modern graphic techniques, Lenica demonstrates an unusual ability to interrelate the various media, thus enriching each of them.

In his posters, Lenica follows the highly respected tradition of Polish poster art but refreshes it. He has developed from realist representation to more and more subjective interpretation of themes as he has attempted to give poster art more freedom, more expressive power. At the same time, he recognizes that changes have taken place in the display of posters. Since he started designing, posters have lost their traditional location; they should now be planned for an intimate environment and for more subtle impact, as Lenica has done in his best posters, such as those for *Wozzeck, Faust, Othello,* and for the Olympic Games in Munich. Now, also, there are galleries and museums for poster design and many of his works are kept in fine art museums as examples of contemporary art.

Lenica maintains a similar approach to animated films. Using this entertaining form, he superimposes his own world, his own fantasies, his own fear, menace, and hallucinations in a surrealistic way to create a new, poetic, and fearful universe, a kind of graphics in motion. For him, animated film is a stepping stone toward visualizing his powerful imagination, as well as an admirable medium for the expression of an ideological view of man and society. To achieve these ends, Lenica uses various processes never before seen or tried in animation, such as hand-coloured fragments of engravings, bold typographic layouts synchronized to music effects, and stylized graphic designs with thick outlines, as seen previously only in poster design, combined with simply choreographed motion. The result is a contemporary graphic impact which gives his films richness and a new look. It also opens up the world of subconscious vision where objects and subjects behave like automata in an electronic hell. Films such as *Monsieur Tête* (1959), *Labyrinth* (1962), *Rhinoceros* (1963), *A* (1964), *Adam II* (1969), and *Ubu* (1977), all of which have won numerous awards, are among the many that carry his message and help to widen the vocabulary of animated film. In 1983 Lenica designed the posters and graphic presentation for the Annecy International Animated Film Festival.

—John Halas

LENK, Krzysztof.
Polish graphic designer. Born in Warsaw, 21 July 1936. Studied at the Academy of Fine Arts, Warsaw, 1954–57, and Krakow Academy of Fine Arts, in Katowice, 1957–61: MA 1961. Married Ewa Zembrzuska in 1963; children: Honorata and Jacek. Freelance graphic designer, in Warsaw, 1958–82, and in Providence, Rhode Island, from 1982: design director, *Polish Machinery News* magazine, Warsaw, 1965–66; creative art director, AGPOL state advertising agency, Warsaw, 1966–68; art director and designer, *Jeune Afrique* magazine, Paris, 1968–69; design director, *Perspektywy* magazine, Warsaw, 1969–72, and *Polish Art Review* magazine, Warsaw, 1971–73; deputy chairman and art director, 1973–76, and consultant designer, 1976–82, of KAW Publishing House, Warsaw; design director, *Animafilm* magazine, Warsaw, 1978–82; also designed for Provuost-Masurel Group, 1968; Erco Lighting Systems, 1972–73; WIFON records and cassettes, 1977–82; Polski Fiat cars, 1978–80; *Solidarnosc* newspaper, 1981–82. Assistant professor, 1973–76, and associate professor of graphic design from 1976, at the School of Design, Lodz; professor of graphic design, Rhode Island School of Design, Providence, from 1982; also visiting lecturer at numerous colleges throughout Europe and the United States from 1976. Education group member, ICOGRADA International Council of Graphic Design Associations. **Collections:** National Poster Museum, Warsaw; National Museum, Poznan; Museum Folkwang, Essen. Recipient: Polish Ministry of Culture Teaching Award, 1977, 1980; IBM Fellowship, Aspen Design Conference, Colorado, 1983. Addresses: Department of Graphic Design, Rhode Island School of Design, 2 College Street, Providence, Rhode Island 02903; 14 Imperial Place, Apt. 603, Providence, Rhode Island 02903, U.S.A.

Krzyzstof Lenk: Cover design for a book on energy cycles, Warsaw, 1974

Publications:

By LENK: articles—in *International Biennale of Graphic Design: Symposium,* Brno 1976; *AIGA Journal* (New York), Summer 1988.

On LENK: books—*Polish Poster Art Today* by Szymon Bojko, Warsaw 1972; *Penrose Annual,* London 1976; articles—in *Interpressgrafik* (Budapest), no. 1, 1975; *Projekt* (Warsaw), no. 5, 1976; *Literatura* (Warsaw), April 1978; *Solidarnosc* (Warsaw), November 1981; *Graphis* (Zurich), no. 238, 1985.

*

I am looking for emotional results using rather cool, logical tools.

—Krzysztof Lenk

*

The achievements of Krzysztof Lenk in design, thought and pedagogy pervade the field of visual communication. He is involved with models, processes, conditioning, and the technology of mass information—that is, with nonpersuasive communication, or that which is not emotionally motivated.

In Poland, he belongs to the first generation of graphic artists who, although educated in schools of fine arts, were self-educated in the system of concepts and the criteria of modern design. This was the case because until then, the late 1960s, applied graphics were treated as a branch of beaux arts, thanks to the imposing artistic reputation of Polish posters, which have been the domain of the artist's individual expression and his personal attitude toward the subject.

The poster figures in Lenk's artistic career only marginally, for after a short while, he realized that as civilization changes, the impetuous development of mass media would dictate the graphic artist's profession. The young graphic artist was able to shake off the burdens of traditionalism thanks to his Paris apprenticeship with SNIP, an agency well acquainted with current methods of designing for market needs, and to his work in the *Jeune Afrique* editorial office, where he witnessed for the first time modern industrial techniques of press production. Also, the general atmosphere favored all innovations at the time when electronics, such as color television and automated production, were beginning to pervade everyday life. It was also the beginning of youth anticulture, of the sexual revolution, of mass protest movements, and of the underground press. A new scientific discipline, semiotics, attempted to regulate theoretically phenomena of human communication and of the information system: "man-machine" and "machine-machine." Graphic artists reached for works of McLuhan, Barthès, Benze, Eco, Maldonado, Bonsiepe. They were interested in structuralism, topology, and the theory of perception as the means by which they could reinforce the designer's workshop with the achievements of scientific research.

Design was identified with the humanistic idea capable of opposing growing chaos in the world of things and of visual announcements. Against such a background, rationalistic tendencies flourished, while responding to the ideas of constructivism that were represented by Bauhaus, Vkhutemas, and Ulm. This trend encompassed the iconosphere—sign codes, functional topography, the language of identification and information, and mass media. From a philosophical standpoint, it was a confirmation of reason, efficiency, and the purposefulness of human actions. Revived once again was the vision of the 1920s avant-garde—constructivists, Suprematists, De Stijl artists—the vision of a wisely organized world and of universal harmony.

Such was the state of design, roughly when Lenk, after returning from Paris by the end of the 1960s, began to manifest his own ideas and creative concepts. His experimental field was the weekly magazine *Perspektywy,* for which he prepared a repeatable structure based on a module and adapted to the industrial environment but flexible enough to secure dramatic character for the pages. It was the Polish press's first example of the serial product that allowed for incidental solutions, a structure to be filled with new content with each issue.

After he decided to take a position at the university, Lenk managed, under specific Polish conditions, to make arrangements for further research on designing printed matter. Research was done on methodology and technology with regard to social requirements. Analysis was performed on the structures and systems applied in newspapers and periodicals and on the quality of their readability, with respect to the hierarchy of information and the power of press photography. Some original concepts of alternative magazines were born then—for instance, the soccer fan's weekly, which served as a measure of reading absorption during the thirty-minute interval in the game. Similarly, he tried to project a model of a newspaper suitable for commuting people, who read while standing in crowded, shaking trains.

In his teaching activity, Lenk represents a view that one cannot teach a student how to design, but one can steer his thinking and teach him to put questions and to look for their answers. According to Lenk, shaping the mentality and the character of the young designer should be the goal of teaching.

—Szymon Bojko

*

LENNON, (John) Dennis.

British architect, interior, furniture and stage designer. Born in London, 23 June 1918. Educated at the Merchant Taylor's School, London, until 1935; studied architecture, at University College, London, 1936–39. Served in the British Army Royal Engineers, in France, North Africa and Italy, 1939–45 (prisoner of war in France, 1940: escaped): Military Cross, 1942. Married Else Bull-Andersen in 1947: 3 sons. Assistant designer, in the architectural office of Maxwell Fry, London, 1946–48; director, Rayon Industry Design Centre, London, 1948–50; senior partner, Dennis Lennon and Partners architectural and design firm, London, from 1950: consultant architect, Royal Opera House, Covent Garden, London. Fellow, Royal Institute of British Architects; Chartered Society of Designers, London: Royal Society of Arts, London. Commander, Order of the British Empire, 1968. Addresses: (home) Hamper Mill, Watford, Hertfordshire; (office) Dennis Lennon and Partners, 3 Fitzhardinge Street, London W1, England.

Works:

Rayon Design Centre interiors, London, 1948.
Desk in oak and formica laminate, for Dunn's of Bromley, 1950.
Sofas and chairs, for Scottish Furniture Manufacturers Ltd., 1951.
Thomas Cook and Sons office interiors, Berkeley Street, London, 1953.
London Steak Houses interiors in London, for J. Lyons, 1953–70.
Vono wholesale showrooms, Grosvenor Street, London, 1954.
Jaeger shops interiors in Oxford, Glasgow, Manchester, Bristol and London, 1954–59.
Office furniture range, for Peter Jones Stores, London, 1957.
Hearing aid showroom and fitting center, for Ardente, London, 1958.
Bowater House showroom interiors, Knightsbridge, London, 1959.
Kayser Bondor boutique in Barker's Department Store, London, 1959.
White House restaurant and cocktail lounge interiors, Regent's Park, London, 1961.
L'Epée d'Or restaurant in the Cumberland Hotel, London, for J. Lyons, 1963.
Albany Hotel interiors, Glasgow, 1973.
Holiday Inn interiors, Swiss Cottage, London, 1974.
American Express Bank interiors in Moorgate, London, for Rothschild International, 1975.
Arts Club interiors, Dover Street, London, 1976.
Central dining hall interiors, for Harrow School, Middlesex, 1979.
Theatre Royal interiors, Bath, 1981.
Bank of Scotland interiors, Threadneedle Street, London, 1982.

Publications:

On LENNON: books—*British Furniture Today* by Erno Goldfinger, London 1951; *Design in British Industry: A Mid-Century Survey* by Michael Farr, Cambridge 1955; *Public Interiors: An International Survey* by Misha Black, London 1960; *Hille: 75 Years of British Furniture,* exhibition catalogue by Sutherland Lyall, London 1981.

*

Dennis Lennon clearly announced a design personality from his first work to be known to the public, the Rayon Design Centre (1948), which was the conversion of a largish Georgian house in Mayfair, London. It is notable for the overall design plan meticulously pursued without any visible conflict with the equally meticulous respect for the existing building. Indeed, the two were brought together by the sensitive colouring of the plasterwork, which was in turn related to the colours used for the furniture and furnishings. These qualities have continued to dominate the partnership which, for most of its lifetime, has remained small.

The thirty-seven London Steakhouses for J. Lyons, (1953–1970), shopfronts and interiors, along with work for the hotels of that same company and for Grand Metropolitan Hotels, Trust House Hotels, Forte, and Metropolis Hotels Group, demonstrate the partnership's particular approach: an appreciation of the precise nature of the commission and a careful satisfaction of the requirements in painstaking attention to detail without giving any laboured effect whatsoever. In many cases, these even preserve the freshness of Lennon's original sketches.

Though the partnership has produced a large number of interior designs, it has also been responsible for some quite considerable architectural schemes, of which Plumtree Court in the City of London merits close examination for its consistency of design through plans, elevations, accommodation to the site, details, and fittings. In view of the partnership's success with prestige office interiors for the Commercial Union, Sainsbury's, Vickers, Mercantile and General, Bank of America (the Dealers Room table especially worthy of notice), and Rothschild Intercontinental, one would not be surprised to learn that future tenants ask for its services.

It would be amiss not to comment upon the

nature of some of these office interiors. Rothschild's is notable for a staircase, clad in stainless steel and linking three floors. The use of stainless steel for Sainsbury's deserves mention, as do the revolving doors at the new entrance in Rennie Street the two columns that distinguish the waiting area on the ground floor, and the handrails to the steps leading up to the reception and waiting areas. Of course, their various dining rooms for directors and for staff are all meticulously conceived and executed, as is the case in the staff dining room for Sainsbury's, for example. Converted from a second basement cheese store, it was relined with London stock brick to give a forthright but welcoming air, underlined by the choice of furniture and subtly varied floor treatment, carpet, brick, and tiles.

The partners have a distinguished record in such conversions, which have shown in each case their appreciation of the qualities of the original building and a delicate bending of their repertoire of modern idiom to suit, without ever falling into eclecticism or mere revivalism. Their conversion of a mediaeval barn into a restaurant at Leeds Castle is an outstanding example.

—Toni del Renzio

LE QUERNEC, Alain.

French graphic designer. Born in Le Faouet, Morbihan, 15 November 1944. Educated at the Lycée Dupuy de Lome, Lorient, until 1961; studied art, at the Lycée Claude Bernard, Paris, 1961–64, and graphic design under Henryk Tomaszewski, at the Academy of Fine Arts, Warsaw, 1972. Served in the French Army, in Algeria, 1967–69. Married Czeslawa Sykut in 1973; children: Paul, Mathieu and Helene. Freelance poster designer, working in Quimper, from 1972. Art teacher, at the Lycée Brizeux, Quimper, from 1972. **Exhibitions:** Press Club, Kalisz, 1972; Galerie du Steir, Quimper, 1973; Press Club Gallery, Warsaw, 1973; Musée des Jacobins, Morlaix, 1975, 1988; Galerie Gloux, Concarneau, 1978; Musée des Arts Decoratifs, Nantes, 1981; Stadtische Galerie, Erlangen, 1984; Centre Culturel, Landerneau, 1986; Pecsi Galeria, Pecs, 1986; Musée de la Publicité, Paris, 1987; Musée Departemental Breton, Quimper, 1987; Hochschule der Künste, Offenbach, 1988; Deutsches Plakatmuseum, Essen, 1988; Palais des Congrès, Lorient, 1989; Musée La Cohue, Vannes, 1989. **Collections:** Museum of Modern Art, New York; Library of Congress, Washington, D.C.; National Poster Museum, Warsaw; Neue Sammlung, Munich; Deutsches Plakatmuseum, Essen; Bibliothèque Forney, Paris; Musée de la Publicité, Paris; Australian National Gallery, Canberra; Israel Museum, Jerusalem. Recipient: Prize of Distinction, Mons Triennale, Belgium, 1982; Zycie Warszawie Prize, Warsaw, 1984; Lahti Poster Biennale Award, 1985; Poster Award of Honour, Paris, 1986; Award of Honour, 1986; ICOGRADA Prize, 1988, Warsaw Poster Biennale: Cultural Poster Prize, Bibliothèque Nationale, Paris, 1988. Address: Trogour Huella, 29136 Plogonnec, France.

Publications:

By LE QUERNEC: articles—in *Bon a Tirer* (Paris), no. 7, 1978, no. 14, 1978, no. 28,

1980, no. 57, 1983; *Novum Gebrauchsgraphik* (Munich), no. 5, 1988.

On LE QUERNEC: books—*Sur les Murs de France* by Alain Gesgon, Paris 1979; *Il Linguaggio della Grafica Politica* by Robert Philippe, Milan 1981; *Alain Le Quernec: Affiches,* exhibition catalogue, Nantes 1981; *Affiches* by Alain Gesgon, Paris 1982; *Alain Le Quernec: Plakate,* exhibition catalogue, Erlangen 1984; *L'Affiche dans le Monde* by Alain Weill, Paris 1984; *Design Français 1960–1990: Trois Decennies,* exhibition catalogue by Margot Rouard and Françoise Jollant Kneebone, Paris 1988, London 1990.

For as long as I can remember, I have been attracted by poster design. This mysterious attraction has no other reason than seeking one's own childish pleasure—the pleasure of seeing or knowing that your picture has been printed several thousand times and pasted up all over a town or country; the pleasure of discovering that your last poster bloomed one night, brightening walls or billboards, covering former posters. But there is also the melancholy of seeing them vanish day after day in a rather short time due to their becoming torn or covered by other posters.

For me, the rectangular piece of paper is as blank as the painter's canvas. Nobody can make you draw that which you don't want to draw, unless you decide to do so. My work is far from that of the advertising poster. The advertising poster fascinates me in some ways and scares me in many others. Publicity has become such a profession, divided into so many distinct parts and using so many different people from the start of the idea to the final result, that creativity seems to be restricted from the outset—one's work in that case is already defined before one starts painting it. That is why I chose, once and for all, the cultural and social poster rather than the commercial one.

I owe a lot to the Polish school of poster design, and especially to Henryk Tomaszewski, a great professor with whom I studied for a year. The important lesson to get out of Poland is not to copy a kind of mannerism, but to understand the freedom of Polish design in pictures, lettering, and thinking. I consider our own commercial censure more frustrating than the official censure of the Polish.

I am lucky to live in a country where the poster is a medium still widely used. It allows those who so desire to project themselves onto the walls—I am just a street exhibitionist.

—Alain Le Quernec

Brittany—a stony corner of France, with its roaring Atlantic and sturdy, individualistic people, a country within a country. The city of Quimper plays a prominent role in the entire region. Of course, it's not Paris, not LeHavre nor Lyon, but it has its cultural life, politics, problems, and long tradition. And it has Alain Le Quernec.

After completing his education in Paris, this poster artist spent a year at the Warsaw Academy of Arts. Under Henryk Tomaszewski's eye, lets's say he didn't fool around. A big, burly man, he worked the way he looked, and early, he decided to master the skills of the poster in general, to learn how to approach every aspect rather than to concentrate on some narrow subject or visual style.

To the surprise of many friends, Le Quernec returned to Quimper, to his place, his sky and sea. With his Polish wife, he settled near the city and soon had established himself as the dominant posterist of the entire area. His poster-making activity reaches every aspect of life. From music concerts, art shows, and adver-

tising to politics, the hand of Le Quernec is visible. Somewhat shockingly, sometimes political rivals from opposing parties collide on the same wall—their images both set by Le Quernec's hand.

Despite his overwhelming grip on local "poster affairs," Le Quernec manages to survive as a fresh, changing, intelligent force. He keeps an eye on the world art market, updates his own style, and aggressively advertises his own case elsewhere. You can find his works in major poster publications as well as in various competitions and biennales, from Lahti to Colorado. On the other hand, Le Quernec makes an important contribution to his own place and people. Popular in Quimper, this energetic person plays a central role in the artistic community of Brittany. Frequently, the best graphic artists from the wide world exhibit in Quimper, lured and befriended by Le Quernec, of course.

Working and living far away from the center of the country's cultural life makes a strong point against the old theory that "nothing happens outside Paris, London or New York." Thanks to the happy combination of his energy, gift, ambition, and charm, he became a local master, joining the long tradition of cathedral-builders, carpenters, sculptors, and painters that have formed the history and rich tradition of Brittany. But there is one important difference: through his activity, he links his distant Quimper with the world for the good of all involved.

—Jan Sawka

LEU, Olaf.

German graphic designer. Born in Chemnitz, Saxony (now Karl-Marx-Stadt, East Germany), 28 July 1936. Educated at Volksschule and Gymnasium, 1942–51; apprenticed in a printing house, and studied typesetting at the Gewerbliche Berufsschule, Biberach-an-der-Riss, 1951–54. Married Eva Gutermann in 1977. Type director, at Bauer Typefoundry, Frankfurt, 1954–57; art director, Hanns W. Brose advertising agency, Frankfurt, 1957–59; freelance graphic designer, Wiesbaden, from 1960. Visiting lecturer and professor, at London College of Printing, 1964, Manchester College of Art and Design, 1968, State University of Chile, 1975–77, St. Martin's School of Art, London, 1982–84, and Akademie der Bildenden Künste, Stuttgart, 1985–86; instructor, Fachhochschule Rheinland-Pfalz, Mainz, from 1986. **Exhibitions:** Gewerbliche Berufsschule, Ulm, 1956; Akademie der Bildenden Kunste, Karlsruhe, 1957; London College of Printing, 1964; Brighton College of Art and Design, Sussex, 1964; Haus am Lutzowplatz, West Berlin, 1970; Museum der Stadt, Biberach-an-der-Riss, 1971; Museum of Contemporary Arts, Santiago de Chile, 1976; Kulturamt der Stadt, Wiesbaden, 1980; Bezalel Academy of Fine Arts, Jerusalem, 1981; International Typeface Corporation, New York, 1982; Akademie fur das Graphische Gewerbe, Munich, 1982; Wurttembergische Landesbibliothek, Stuttgart, 1985; Galerie von Oertzen, Frankfurt, 1985; Fachhochschule fur Gestaltung, Augsburg, 1987. **Collections:** Museum of Modern Art, New York; International Typeface Corporation Center, New York; Cooper Union, New York; Deutsches Plakat Museum, Essen; Stiftung Preussischer Kulturbesitz, West Berlin; Museum für Gestaltung, Zurich. Recipient: 58 Typographic Awards, Type Directors Club of New

 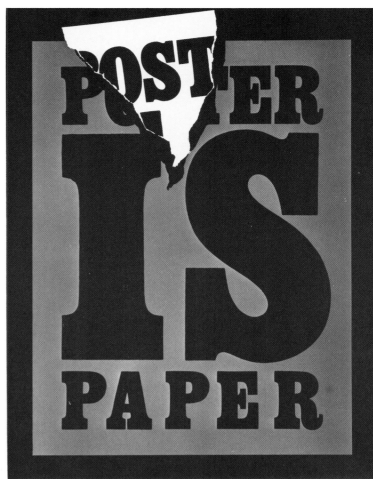

Alain Le Quernec: *Poster is Paper* **posters, 1982**

York, 1957–89; 50 International Calendar Awards, Stuttgart, 1969–89; Gold Medal, Philadelphia Art Directors Club, 1969; Brno Graphic Biennale Silver Medal, 1970, 1982; New York Art Directors Club Award, 1974, 1975; Tokyo Calendar Awards, 1981, 1982, 1983. Address: Lanzstrasse 18, 6200 Wiesbaden 1, West Germany.

Works:

Corporate design programme, for Gebruder Schmidt Druckfarben, Frankfurt, from 1960.
Zeitloser Glanz calendar, for Zanders Feinpapiere, Bergisch Gladbach, 1967.
Zahlen aus aller Welt calendar, for Roland Offsetmaschinenfabrik, Offenbach, 1970.
Hans-Peter Haas druckt New York calendar, for Hans-Peter Haas, Stuttgart, 1971.
Old Games calendar, for Roland Offsetmaschinenfabrik, Offenbach, 1975.
Corporate design programme, for Colonia Versicherung, Cologne, from 1981.
The LinoType Show promotion campaign, for LinoType AG, Eschborn, 1983.
Still-Life calendar, for Zanders Feinpapiere AG, Bergisch Gladbach, 1983.
Ford Futura calendar, for Ford Werke, Cologne, 1984.
Porsche calendar, for Porsche Sports Cars, 1985.
Seh-Felder calendar, for MAN-Roland Druckmaschinen AG, Offenbach, 1985.
Corporate design programme, for the Landesbank Rheinland-Pfalz, Mainz, from 1985.

Feuer, Wasser, Luft und Erde calendar, for Gebrüder Schmidt Druckfarben, Frankfurt, 1988.
Corporate design programme, for the BHF-Bank, Frankfurt, from 1988.
Pastorale calendar, for Gebrüder Schmidt Druckfarben, Frankfurt, 1989.

Publications:

By LEU: book—*Process Visual,* with Wolfgang Schmittel, Zurich 1978; articles—in *Novum Gebrauchsgraphik* (Munich), no. 6, 1981, no. 12, 1981, no. 1, 1982, no. 3, 1982, no. 6, 1982, no. 9, 1982, no. 12, 1982, no. 10, 1983, no. 12, 1984, no. 9, 1985, no. 3, 1986, no. 10, 1987, no. 8, 1989; *Print* (New York), July/August 1981; *Offsetpraxis* (Stuttgart), no. 4, 1982, no. 9, 1982, no. 4, 1983, no. 10, 1983, no. 1, 1984, no. 4, 1984, no. 10, 1984, no. 10, 1985, no. 1, 1986, no. 4, 1987, no. 11, 1988; *Deutscher Drucker* (Stuttgart), no. 27, 1984, no. 33, 1986, no. 1, 1987, no. 3, 1988; *Der Polygraph* (Frankfurt), no. 8, 1986.

On LEU: books—*Modern Graphics* by Keith Murgatroyd, London 1969; *Who's Who in Graphic Art,* edited by Walter Amstutz, Dubendorf 1982; articles—in *Gebrauchsgraphik* (Munich), no. 11, 1956, no. 4, 1961, no. 6, 1963, no. 12, 1971; *Print* (New York), May/June 1965, September/October 1982; *Graphis* (Zurich), no. 202, 1979, no. 253, 1988; *Deutscher Drucker* (Stuttgart), no. 16, 1985; *Der Polygraph* (Frankfurt), no. 24, 1986; *Novum Gebrauchsgraphik* (Munich), December 1987; *Grafik Design + Technik* (Munich), no. 2, 1988.

Above all, a project must be fun. For me this pleasurable aspect inspires a great deal of enthusiasm, which then is manifest in the solution of the problem at hand. In order to pass this pleasure on to others, I try to surround a striking idea with a "joyful" quality, so as to produce a positive atmosphere.

I think that graphic design is meant to create an intelligent, humane order, but one which can include fashionable elements. For this reason, I have never sworn allegiance to any one direction in style or school of fashion. Therefore, all of my works which have appeared since 1956 express my own individuality even as they reflect the directions that taste was taking at the time of their origin. Because taste signifies change and activity, not stagnation, good graphic design is, indeed must be, fashionable. Just as our lives and environment undergo change, so must graphic design.

Every artistic statement reflects temperament, intelligence, experience, and age. These various components add up to the maturity and universality of a work. Although graphic design is an individualistic profession, since individuality itself is so rare, there is little truly individualistic design. Individuality is equally as rare in the client as in the graphic designer. The rare circumstance that they should happen to meet results in what observers call "good" graphic design.

—Olaf Leu

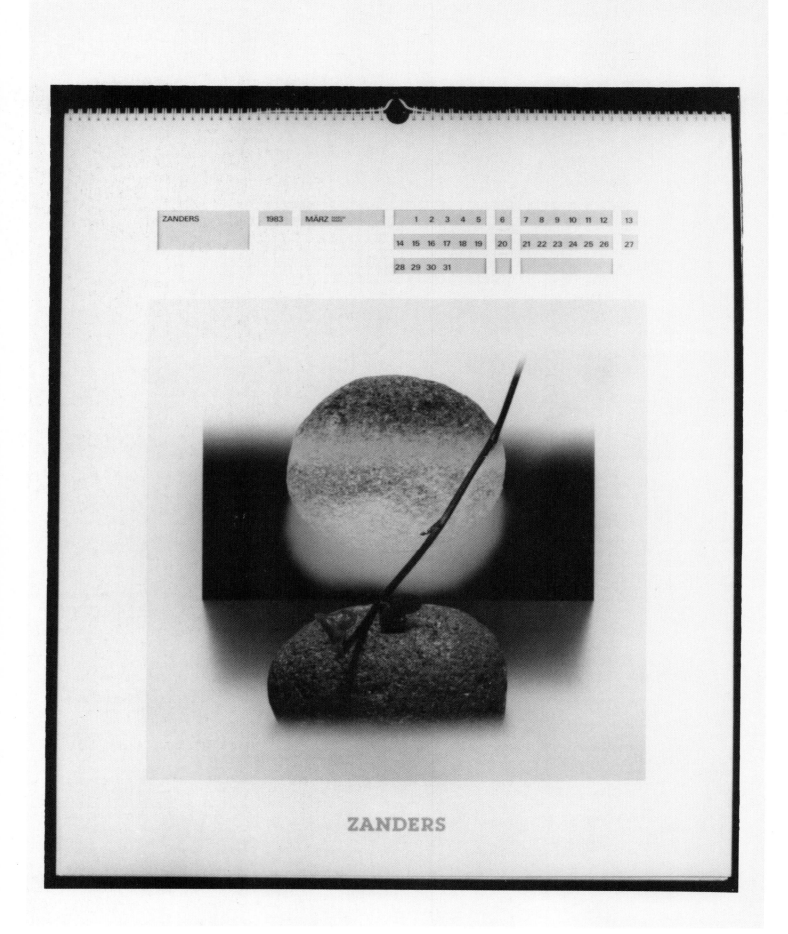

ZANDERS   1983   MÄRZ

		1	2	3	4	5		6		7	8	9	10	11	12		13
14	15	16	17	18	19		20		21	22	23	24	25	26		27
28	29	30	31												

ZANDERS

Olaf Leu: *Still Life* **calendar, for Zanders Paper Company, 1983**

LEUPIN, Herbert.

Swiss painter, illustrator, advertising and graphic designer. Born in Beinwil am See, 20 December 1916. Educated at Realgymnasium, Basel, until 1931; studied graphics under Paul Kammuller and Theo Eble, at the Allgemeine Gewerbeschule, Basel, 1932–35; also apprenticed in the Hermann Eidenbenz design studio, Basel, 1932–35; studied poster design, at the Ecole Paul Colin, Paris, 1936–37. Married in 1945; sons: Tommy and Charly. Graphic designer, in the Donald Brun studio, Basel, 1938; freelance designer, working in Basel, 1939–45, and in Augst, Baselland, from 1945: designed for Globi Verlag, Bata-Schuh AG, Roth-Handle Zigaretten, etc. Recipient: Foire de Paris Silver Medal, 1936; Schutzenfest Poster Prize, Lucerne, 1939; Poster of the Month Award, Munich and Vienna, 1952; Cicago Art Directors Club Medal, 1960; International Poster Prize, Toronto, 1961; Warsaw Poster Biennale Prize, 1968. Member: Alliance Graphique Internationale; Bund Grafischer Gestalter, Basel; Schweizerischer Werkbund. Address: Augustinergasse 1–3, Basel, Switzerland.

Publications:

By LEUPIN: books and portfolios—*Herbert Leupin—Placards and Posters,* portfolio with text by Manuel Gasser, Zürich and Frankfurt 1957, London 1959; books designed include—*Bruder Grimm Marchen,* Zürich; *Hansel und Gretel,* Zürich; *Des tapfere Schneide Hein,* Zürich; *Hans im Gluck,* Zürich, 1944; *Tischlein deck dich!,* Zürich; *Schneewittchen und die sieben Zwerge,* Zürich, 1945; *Der gestiefelte Kater,* Zürich, 1946; *Der Wolf und die sieben junger Giesslein,* Zürich, 1947; *Dornroschen,* Zürich, 1948; *Frau Holle,* Zürich, 1949.

On LEUPIN: books—*Posters: Fifty Artists and Designers,* edited by W. H. Allner, New York 1952; *Packaging: An International Survey of Package Design,* edited by Walter Herdeg, Zürich 1959; *The New Graphic Design* by Karl Gestner and Markus Kutter, Teufen and London 1959; *Who's Who in Graphic Art,* edited by Walter Amstutz, Zurich 1962, Dubendorf 1982; *Das Plakat* by Anton Sailer, Munich 1965; *History of the Poster* by Josef and Shizuko Muller-Brockmann, Zurich 1971; *Graphic Designers in Europe 2,* edited by Henri Hillebrand, London 1972; *The Language of Graphics* by Edward Booth-Clibborn and Daniele Baroni, London 1980.

For more than forty years, Herbert Leupin's posters have been injecting humor and novelty into the Swiss poster tradition. His simple and direct imagery is created with flat, cut-out forms. Copy is kept to an extreme minimum (just the name of the product or company), and colors are usually primaries. However, the playful arrangement of image, type, and color betrays an understated elegance and sophistication, as in his ingenious posters for Eptinger mineral water. One shows an outline of a bottle and glass formed by white dots on a bright blue background. The product's white-and-red label and logotype, affixed to the bottle, become the focus of this deceptively simple composition, which conveys a clear message. Another shows a large caricature of a clown-like figure shaped into the capital letter E and holding a glass of mineral water. The only copy is the product's name displayed in an equally whimsical type style.

His circus posters are another outlet for his playfulness. One depicts a seal poised confidently on a ball. On each outstretched flipper is a fish and a series of colored balls, one on top of the other, spelling out the name of the circus.

Again, the image is in broad areas of color, and copy is kept to a minimum. The sketch-like treatment, in an almost naive, child-like style adds tremendously to the vitality of the poster. Disarmingly simple, it has an impact reminiscent of Polish circus posters.

Leupin's work reflect a deep understanding of how and what communicates most thoroughly and effectively. His skillfully manipulated typography for the Suze beverage company poster and the cartoon-like figure used in the Agfa photographic materials poster demonstrate a style which enhances and complements the products. To enjoy and appreciate Leupin's creations fully, one must view them in their outdoor setting, in competition with other advertisements, where their light-hearted visual statements provide a welcome contrast and are a joy to behold.

—D. Ichiyama

LEVEN, Boris.

American painter and film designer. Born in Moscow, Russia, 13 August 1912; emigrated to the United States in 1927: naturalized, 1938. Studied architecture, at the University of Southern California, Los Angeles, 1927–32: B. Arch. 1932; Beaux-Arts Institute of Design, New York, 1932–33. Served in the United States Army Air Force, 1942–45: Staff Sergeant. Married Vera Gloushkoff in 1948. Sketch artist and designer, for Paramount Pictures, 1933–35, for Samuel Goldwyn Studios and David O. Selznick Productions, 1936, in Hollywood, California; assistant art director, Major Pictures Corporation, Hollywood, 1936; art director, at 20th Century-Fox Studios, Hollywood, 1937–38, 1941–42, 1945–46, and at Universal International Pictures, in Hollywood, 1947–48; freelance art director and production designer, Los Angeles, 1939–41 and from 1948. **Exhibitions:** Los Angeles County Museum of Art, 1952; Society of Motion Picture Art Directors, Los Angeles, 1963; *The Union Artist,* Los Angeles County Museum of Art, 1971; *The Art of Hollywood,* Victoria and Albert Museum, London, 1979; Hollywood Studio Gallery, California, 1980. Recipient: Emerson Architecture Prize, New York, 1932; Beaux Arts Ball Prize, New York, 1932; American Institute of Steel Construction Prize, 1932; National Scarab Watercolor Prize, 1933; Art Direction Prize, American Institute of Decorators, 1947; Photoplay Magazine Award, 1956; Academy Award, 1961. Member: Society of Motion Picture and Television Art Directors. Address: 527 Hanley Place, Los Angeles, California 90049, U.S.A.

Works:

Film productions include—*Alexander's Ragtime Band* (H. King), 1938; *Just Around the Corner* (Cummings), 1938; *Second Chorus* (Potter), 1940; *The Shanghai Gesture* (von Sternberg), 1941; *Tales of Manhattan* (Duvivier), 1942; *Life Begins at 8.30* (Pichel), 1942; *Hello, Frisco, Hello* (Humberstone), 1943; *Doll Face* (Seiler), 1945; *Home Sweet Homicide* (Bacon), 1946; *Shock* (Werker), 1946; *The Shocking Miss Pilgrim* (Seaton), 1947; *I Wonder Who's Kissing Her Now* (Bacon), 1947; *The Senator Was Indiscreet* (Kaufman), 1947; *Mr. Peabody and the Mermaid* (Pichel), 1948; *Criss Cross* (Siodmak), 1948; *The Lovable Cheat* (Oswald),

1949; *Search for Danger* (Bernhard), 1949; *House by the River* (F. Lang), 1949; *Woman on the Run* (Foster), 1950; *Quicksand* (Pichel), 1950; *Dakota Lil* (Selander), 1950; *Destination Murder* (Cahn), 1950; *Once a Thief* (W. Wilder), 1950; *The Second Woman* (Kern), 1951; *The Prowler* (Losey), 1951; *A Millionaire for Christie* (Marshall), 1951; *Two Dollar Better* (Cahn), 1951; *The Basketball Fix* (Feist), 1951; *Sudden Fear* (Miller), 1952; *Rose of Cimarron* (Keller), 1952; *The Star* (Heisler), 1953; *Invaders from Mars* (Menzies), 1953; *Donovan's Brain* (Feist), 1953; *The Long Wait* (Saville), 1954; *The Silver Chalice* (Saville), 1955; *Giant* (Stevens), 1956; *Courage of Black Beauty* (Schuster), 1957; *My Gun Is Quick* (White and Victor), 1957; *Zero Hour* (Bartlett), 1957; *Anatomy of a Murder* (Preminger), 1959; *Thunder in the Sun* (Rouse), 1959; *September Storm* (Haskin), 1960; *West Side Story* (Wise), 1961; *Two for the Seesaw* (Wise), 1962; *Strait-Jacket* (Castle), 1964; *The Sound of Music* (Wise), 1965; *The Sand Pebbles* (Wise), 1966; *Star* (Wise), 1968; *A Dream of Kings* (Daniel Mann), 1969; *The Andromeda Strain* (Wise), 1971; *Happy Birthday Wanda June* (Robson), 1971; *The New Centurions* (Fleischer), 1972; *Jonathan Livingston Seagull* (Bartlett), 1973; *Reflections of Murder* (Badham—for TV), 1974; *Shanks* (Castle), 1974; *Mandingo* (Fleischer), 1975; *New York, New York* (Scorcese), 1977; *The Last Waltz* (Scorcese), 1978; *Matilda* (Daniel Mann), 1978; *The King of Comedy* (Scorcese), 1983; *Fletch* (Ritchie), 1985.

Publications:

By LEVEN: articles—in *Film Index* (Mosman Bay), no. 15, 1973; *Film Comment* (New York), May/June 1978.

On LEVEN: books—*Hollywood in the Forties* by Charles Higham and Joel Greenberg, New York 1968; *Le Décor de Film* by Leon Barsacq, Paris 1970, as *Caligari's Cabinet and Other Grand Illusions,* Boston 1976; *The International Dictionary of Films and Filmmakers,* Chicago and London 1987, 1991.

What interests me the most in designing a film is the final look! I try to visualize what this "look" will be during the early readings of the script.

I believe that the early feelings with regard to mood and style and textures are vitally important and should be the guiding force during the development of the design. I believe that the greatest contribution to the film on the part of the production designer is the creation of visual continuity, balance, and dramatic emphasis.

I believe that if a setting is well designed, one should be able, at a glance, to tell what it represents, what transpires in it, and who are its occupants.

In designing an individual setting, I constantly keep in mind the style of the entire film and how this setting relates to the whole.

I believe in utmost simplicity. Simplicity is the key to my thinking, and it is my only approach to creative work. In my life and relations with others, I have always tried to be as honest as I am with myself.

—Boris Leven

Boris Leven graduated from the architecture school at the University of Southern California during the Depression. With little prospect of work in architecture, after another year of study in New York, he took a job in Paramount's art department, which was run by Hans Dreier.

Leven is one of few designers who benefited

Boris Leven: set for the film *West Side Story*, at Goldwyn Studios, 1961

from the training of the strictly-run big, Hollywood studio system, absorbed the eclecticism of styles prevalent in the 1930s and 1940s, survived the decline of the studios in the 1950s, and has flourished as an independent designer since the mid-1950s. He cannot be associated with the independent realist designers of the post-World War II period, for his approach is more tied to the eclecticism of William Cameron Menzies with whom he co-designed the 1953 *Invaders from Mars* (which Menzies also directed).

Leven's clear theory and method appear in a short definition of production design he wrote for a 1978 exhibition at the Museum of Modern Art. Like Harry Horner, who also acknowledges Menzies' influence, Leven stresses the twin components of research and the artistic of personal creative formulation of a design program.

As a designer, Leven mixes within a film actual locations and stylized or abstract sets. He is very conscious of these juxtapositions, and to avoid "visual discrepancies," he makes special studies of "textures, color and aging of each setting." His works also contain significant examples of expressive color programs. But most of all, Leven's designs reveal his architectural training in their masterful manipulations of planes and masses, whether in interior or exterior spaces or the integration of the two.

These architectonic sensibilities are found, for example, in *Giant* (1956, directed by George Stevens). The key set is the massive, Victorian mansion located on a vast, flat, Texas plain. Based in part on a painting by Edward Hopper, this imposing set is a visual character in its own right. Indeed, it gives the film a scale that the performers did not always bring to their roles. The great house helped to save the film and, as an imposing part of the production, gave the design program an overt but appropriate role. The *Giant*'s mansion belongs to the film history of the house-as-character; this includes Tara from *Gone With the Wind*, designed by Lyle Wheeler and Menzies, and Dr. Sloper's house from *The Heiress*, designed by Horner. Leven's mansion is closer than Horner's to Menzies' idealization and grandeur, whereas Horner's more authentically conceived house leans toward the best aspects of the realist school.

In *West Side Story*, Leven joined the realistic and the expressionistic by juxtaposing actual New York locations with abstractly conceived sets, some painted with highly saturated, tension-filled colors. Likewise eclectic is the film's blends of Shakespeare and the contemporary, urban, ethnic poor; of opera and jazz; and of modern ballet and realistic performance. Despite these mixed treatments of plot, character,

music, and dance, this film marks a high new standard for the film musical. Rarely since then have locations been effectively married to song and dance, largely because the new realist school of designers have not explored the powers of eclecticism, and do not understand how sets can relate to music or dance. Leven, who knows how to bring a set alive and give it character without it overpowering the actors, believes that a set can be noticed in a film, that it should have strong expressive meaning even without the performers.

Because Leven's architectural sense of the plane and of pictorial surface are so basic to his work, his use of the wide-screen format is noteworthy. Superior are his interior and exterior spaces' sensitivity to the broad, horizontal format in *The Silver Chalice* (1954), *Giant*, *West Side Story*, *The Sound of Music*, and *New York, New York* (1977). This latter film depends upon an unusual eclecticism in its boldly abstract sets, which are obviously painted and deliberately flat. While these make clear that Leven is not committed to authenticity, neither is his eclecticism arbitrary, for his first commitment is to overall structure.

—Norman Gambill

LE WITT, Jan.

British painter, illustrator, stage and graphic designer. Born in Czestochowa, Poland, 3 April 1907; emigrated to Britain in 1937: naturalized, 1947. Educated in Czestochowa until 1924; mainly self-taught in design, Warsaw, from 1927. Married Alina Prusicka in 1939. Freelance designer, Warsaw, 1927–33; partner with George Him, in LeWitt-Him design practice, in Warsaw, 1933–37, and in London, 1937–54: designed for Sadler's Wells Ballet, Murano Glassworks, the Festival of Britain, Ministry of Information, Home Office, General Post Office, etc; independent painter, London, from 1955. Executive Council member, Societe Europeenne de Culture, Venice, from 1961. **Exhibitions:** Society of Fine Arts, Warsaw, 1930; Lund Humphries, London, 1934; Zwemmer Gallery, London, 1947, 1953; Tate Gallery, London, 1950, 1952; Hanover Gallery, London, 1951; Galleria San Marco, Rome, 1952; AAA Gallery, New York, 1954; Galleria Apollinaire, Milan, 1957; Grosvenor Gallery, London, 1961; Musée d'Antibes, 1965; Narodni Museum, Warsaw, 1967; Galleria d'Arte, Venice, 1970; *Second World War Posters,* Imperial War Museum, London, 1972; Fitzwilliam Museum, Cambridge, 1989. **Collections:** Musée National d'Art Moderne, Paris; National Museum, Jerusalem; National Museum, Warsaw; Musée d'Antibes; Halifax Museum and Art Gallery, Yorkshire; British Council, London; Contemporary Art Society, London. Recipient: Gold Medal, Vienna, 1948; Gold Medal, Milan Triennale, 1954. Honorary Member, Centro Internazionale dell'Arte del Vetro, Venice; Fellow, International PEN Club, London, 1978. Member, Alliance Graphique Internationale, Paris, 1948. Address: 10 Highfield Avenue, Cambridge CB4 2AL, England.

Publications:

By LE WITT: books—*Locomotive,* with George Him. London 1937; *The Little Red Engine,* with George Him, London 1942; *Vegetabull,* London and New York 1956; *A Necklace for Andromeda,* London 1976.

On LE WITT: books—*British Achievement in Design,* edited by Noel Carrington and Muriel Harris, London 1946; *Posters: 50 Artists and Designers,* edited by W. H. Allner, New York 1952; *Jan Le Witt,* with texts by Pierre Emanuel, Herbert Read and others, London 1971; *Second World War Posters,* exhibition catalogue by Joseph Darracott and Belinda Loftus, London 1972; *The Language of Graphics* by Edward Booth-Clibborn and Daniele Baroni, London 1980.

See HIM, George

LINDAU, Borge.

Swedish interior and furniture designer. Born in Ahus, in 1932. Studied at the School of Arts and Crafts, Göteborg, 1957–61. Worked in an architect's office, Helsingborg, 1961–63; freelance designer, establishing Lindau and Lindekrantz design firm, with Bo Lindekrantz, in Helsingborg, from 1964: has designed principally for Lammhults Mekaniska AB, from 1965. **Exhibitions:** *Scandinavian Modern Design 1880–1980,* Cooper-Hewitt Museum, New York, 1982 (toured); *Contemporary Swedish De-

sign,* Nationalmuseum, Stockholm, 1983 (toured); *The Lunning Prize,* Nationalmuseum, Stockholm, 1985; *Faces of Swedish Design,* IBM Gallery, New York, 1988 (toured). Recipient: Lunning Prize, 1969; SID Society of Swedish Industrial Designers Prize, 1975. Address: Box 100, 296 Ahus, Sweden.

Works (with Bo Lindekrantz):

Opal stackable hook-on armchair, for Lammhults, 1964.
Ritz stackable armchair, for Lammhults, 1965.
Royal stackable chair, for Lammhults, 1966.
Joker nursery furniture, for Lammhults, 1966.
S-70 stackable chairs and stools in tubular steel, for Lammhults, 1967.
Peking stackable armchair, for Lammhults, 1970.
Hacken sectional sofa, for Lammhults, 1970.
City Library interiors, Norrköping, 1971.
Director's Chair in steel and canvas, for Lammhults, 1971.
X-75 collapsible tubular steel chairs and tables, for Lammhults, 1972.
Morris office chair, for Lammhults, 1977.
Armchair 88 hook-on chair in tubular steel, for Lammhults, 1980.
Duet 8 easy chair, for Lammhults, 1982.
Solo club armchairs, for Lammhults, 1983.
Trio stackable armchair, for Lammhults, 1985.
Planka chair in plywood and perforated metal, for Lammhults, 1985.

Publications:

On LINDAU/LINDEKRANTZ: books—*Konthantverk, Kontindustri, Design 1875–1975* by Dag Widman, Stockholm 1975; *Scandinavian Modern Design 1880–1980,* edited by David Revere McFadden, New York 1982; *Contemporary Swedish Design,* exhibition catalogue by Monica Boman, Lennart Lindkvist and others, Stockholm 1983; *Den Svenska Formen* by Monica Boman and others, Stockholm 1985; *The Lunning Prize,* exhibition catalogue edited by Helena Dahlback Lutteman and Marianne Uggla, Stockholm 1986; *Faces of Swedish Design,* exhibition catalogue edited by Monica Boman, Stockholm 1988.

See LINDEKRANTZ, Bo.

L&L plus L equals a long and faithful (but not long-winded) success story involving two designers and a manufacturer.

L&L are Börge Lindau and Bo Lindekrantz. They first met in the late 1950s at the Gothenburg School of Arts and Crafts. They were in the same class, and claim that they were drawn to each other because they felt so old. They happened to be five years older than their classmates. Afterwards they continued on to the same architect's office in Helsingborg and later set up on their own.

Two representatives from Lammhults, the third L, walked in one day and asked the two young designers if they could design a chair made of metal which would suit university students. The company was thinking of adding to its product range by manufacturing furniture.

Börge and Bo grandly proposed a condition: that they be allowed to design two chairs. These were the "Ritz" and "Royal," named after two rural cafés near the small town of Lammhult, in the province of Småland. The chairs became classics, and after 20 years are still among the best-selling models in the collection. Since then a unique collaboration has developed between the designers and manufacturer.

The major breakthrough for Lammhults and the designers came at the end of the 1960s,

with the S-70 collection: Bauhaus-inspired chairs, tables and clothes hangers of strong, painted tubes, and corduroy garments in gay colors. The S-70 furniture became popular for public environments which required modernity, youth, and a personal style.

But Börge and Bo also wanted to reach the public at home. The X-75 series of folding chairs and tables offered flexible interior design. The chairs can be folded into a "bicycle rack" to be taken out according to need. The model itself appears to be as old as the hills: it existed in the days of the Pharaohs, but Börge and Bo further developed it by radically changing the folding mechanism. In the X-75 you can sit comfortably and tuck your feet under the chair, in contrast to older versions. The X-75 has been greatly appreciated in public milieus as well—including museums—both as a seat and as a display object.

At the beginning of the 1980s Börge and Bo separated. After working in the same premises for over 20 years, they thought they had had enough. So Börge moved back to his childhood town of Ahus and Bo remained in Helsingborg. Since then they have remained like two partners in a happily separated marriage—where the separation works. They have continued to develop more intensely than ever. There is a sort of creative ping-pong competition going on between L&L and L—Börge, Bo, and Lammhults. The finals take place at the factory.

Börge and Bo like to regard themselves as redesigners. Their models are often inspired by some well-known classic. What makes them exciting is that they produce not merely an improvement, but an addition which is fresh and innovative.

One example is the rebirth of the club chair—first in the sectional sofa "The Hedge" in the early 1970s and later in the "Solo" family, which includes both sofas and armchairs. In an elegant way they reveal their source, yet the new form and function are a refined addition for the benefit of the user.

Börge and Bo have devoted themselves to several interesting experiments in furniture and design. There have been mobile storage units which have also been sculptures, flexible tabletops with varying heights and adaptable chairs, and "The Plank"—a seat and debating point in the discussion on ergonomics and materials. They have spent a lot of time thinking about how to be flexible with color and decoration, and how to give rational series production a new direction.

For Börge and Bo, there has also been the question of linking the human desire to recline and relax with the wish for an individual product.

Börge has also continued on his own with his "Blue Station"—a small collection of chairs, tables, and lamps, all having a laminated ring of birch as a common denominator. This is an experiment in carrying out a consistent theme using the greatest variety of approaches without sacrificing esthetic demands and technical construction.

Bo has returned to wood with renewed force. He continues to refine the tradition further.

—Hedvig Hedqvist

LINDBERG, Stig (Frederik Sigurd).

Swedish illustrator, graphic, textile, ceramics and glass designer. Born in Umeå, 17 August 1916. Educated in Jönköping, until 1935; studied at the Konstfackskolan, Stockholm, 1935–37; also studied in Denmark and at the Academie Colarossi, Paris, 1938–39. Married Gunnel Margareta Elisabet Jonsson in 1939 (died, 1975); children: Vibeke, Marita and Lars. Assistant to Wilhelm Kåge, 1937–40, staff designer, 1940–49, and art director, 1949–57, 1971–82, at the Gustavsberg Potteries, Varmolo, near Stockholm: founder, with Wilhelm Kåge, of Gustavsberg Studio for Ceramic Art, Stockholm, 1943; also designed for Maleras, Holmgaards, Heyman and Olsen, Mölnlycke Vefverd, Nordiska Kompaniet, Öberg and Son, De La Rue, etc. Senior lecturer in ceramics, at the Konstfackskolan, Stockholm, 1957–72. Chairman, Svenska Konsthantverkare och Industri-Formgivare, Stockholm. **Exhibitions:** Stockholm, 1941; *Gustavsberg Studio Works,* Stockholm, 1945; Georg Jensen, Copenhagen, 1947; Zürich, 1947; Copenhagen, 1949; Georg Jensen Inc., New York, 1951; West Berlin, 1952; Tokyo, 1959; London, 1961, 1966; Cologne, 1965; Amsterdam, 1968; National Museum, Stockholm, 1982. **Collections:** Victoria and Albert Museum, London; Museum of Modern Art, New York; Museum für Angewandte Kunst, Vienna; Arkiv för Dekorativ Konst, Lund; Röhsska Konstslöjdmuseet, Göteborg; National Museum, Stockholm; Malmö Museum, Sweden. Recipient: Gold Medal, 1948, 1957, Grand Prix, 1951, 1954, Milan Triennale; Ceramics Gold Medal, Cannes, 1955, California, 1958, Prague, 1962, Liubliana, 1965, Munich, 1966; Gregor Paulsson Award, Stockholm, 1957; Swedish State Art Award, 1967, 1968; Prins Eugen Medal, Stockholm, 1968. Fellow, Royal Society of Arts, London; Honorary Member, Swedish Designer-Craftsmen Association; Member, Alliance Graphique Internationale, and Swedish Industrial Designers Association. *Died* (in Italy) 7 April 1982.

Works:

Kadet ceramic wares, for Gustavsberg, 1939.
LB Service bone china tablewares, for Gustavsberg, 1945.
Spectrum Leaf painted earthenware range of bowls, for Gustavsberg, 1947.
SA Service bone china tablewares, for Gustavsberg, 1949.
Servus ceramic tableware range, for Gustavsberg, 1949.
Pungo white stoneware vases, for Gustavsberg, 1950.
Leaf salad bowl and dishes in earthenware, for Gustavsberg, 1950–52.
Pike painted bone china tablewares, for Gustavsberg, 1951.
Sagoland blue printed earthenware range, for Gustavsberg, 1951.
Spisa Ribb ceramic tableware service, for Gustavsberg, 1955.
Tema range of ceramic stonewares, for Gustavsberg, 1955–58.
Playing cards, for Öberg and Son, Eskilstuna, 1958.
Vit Bohås ceramic wares, for Gustavsberg, 1958–61.
Television set, for Luna Company, 1959.
Bensa tablewares, for Gustavsberg, 1960.
Aland tablewares, for Gustavsberg, 1961.
Brunus tablewares, for Gustavsberg, 1962.
Birka speckled stoneware range, for Gustavsberg, 1973.

Publications:

By LINDBERG: books illustrated—*Nyfiken i en strut* by L. Hellsing, Stockholm 1947; *Musikkussen* by L. Hellsing, Stockholm 1948; *Berättelser om koulek* by K. J. Radström, Stockholm 1951;

ABC-Book by E. G. Hallquist, Stockholm 1953; *Krakel Spektakel* by L. Hellsing, Stockholm 1954; *Daniel Doppsko* by L. Hellsing, Stockholm 1958.

On LINDBERG: books—*Contemporary Swedish Design: A Survey in Pictures* by Arthur Hald and Sven Erik Skawonius, Stockholm 1951; *A Treasury of Scandinavian Design,* edited by Erik Zahle, New York 1961; *Stig Lindberg: Swedish Artist and Designer* by Dag Widman, Stockholm 1962; *Svensk Keramik* by Per Palme and Eva Nordenson, Uddevalla 1965; *Serviser fran Gustavsberg* by Inga Arno-Berg, Vasteras 1971; *Design in Sweden* by Lennart Lindkvist, Stockholm 1972; *Stig Lindberg: Formgivare,* exhibition catalogue by Helena Dahlbäck Lutteman, Stockholm 1982; *Design Since 1945,* edited by Kathryn Hiesinger and George Marcus, Philadelphia and London 1983; *The Conran Directory of Design,* edited by Stephen Bayley, London 1985; *Scandinavia: Ceramics and Glass in the Twentieth Century* by Jennifer Hawkins Opie, London 1989.

LINDEKRANTZ, Bo.

Swedish interior and furniture designer. Born in Helsingborg, in 1932. Studied at the School of Arts and Crafts, Göteborg, 1957–61. Worked in an architect's office, Helsingborg, 1961–63; freelance designer, establishing Lindau and Lindekrantz design firm, with Borge Lindau, in Helsingborg, from 1964: has designed principally for Lammhults Mekaniska AB, from 1965. **Exhibitions:** *Scandinavian Modern Design 1880–1980,* Cooper-Hewitt Museum, New York, 1982 (toured); *Contemporary Swedish Design,* Nationalmuseum, Stockholm, 1983 (toured); *The Lunning Prize,* Nationalmuseum, Stockholm, 1986; *Faces of Swedish Design,* IBM Gallery, New York, 1988 (toured). Recipient: Lunning Prize, 1969; SID Society of Swedish Industrial Designers Prize, 1975. Address: Kullagatan 40, 252 20 Helsingborg, Sweden.

See LINDAU, Borge.

LINDSTRAND, Vicke (Viktor Emanuel).

Swedish glass and ceramics designer. Born in Göteborg, 27 November 1904. Studied at the Svensk Slöjdforenings Skola, Göteborg, 1924–27; also study-travels in France and Italy, 1933–37. Married Svea Kristina Frisch in 1929(divorced, 1945); son: Ola; married Marianne Lliesköld in 1946. Worked as a cartoonist and illustrator, for *Handelstidningen* newspaper, Göteborg, 1922–28; designer, with Edward Hald and Simon Gate, at Orrefors Glassworks, Sweden, 1928–41; artistic director, at Ekebybruk ceramics factory, Uppsala-Ekeby, 1942–50; design director, at Kosta Glassworks, Sweden, 1950–73: also designed glass sculptures from 1964. **Exhibitions:** Milan Triennale, 1933, 1951, 1957; Paris International Exposition, 1937, 1951; World's Fair, New York, 1939; *Orrefors 1917–42,* Nationalmuseum, Stockholm, 1942; *Scandinavia: Ceramics and Glass in the Twentieth Century,*

Victoria and Albert Museum, London, 1989. **Collections:** Nationalmuseum, Stockholm; Röhsska Konstslöjdmuseet, Goteborg; Smålands Museum, Växjö; Konsthantverkmuseet, Oslo; Museum für Kunst und Gewerbe, Hamburg; Musée du Louvre, Paris; Metropolitan Museum of Art. New York; British Museum, London; Victoria and Albert Museum, London. Recipient: International Design Prize, New York, 1963; Litteris et Artibus Award, Stockholm, 1976. *Died*(in Åhus, Sweden), 7 May 1983.

Works:

Samson and the Lion engraved bowl in green glass, for Orrefors, 1929.
See No Evil painted and etched vase in clear glass, for Orrefors, 1930.
Crowded Skies engraved vase in clear glass, for Orrefors, 1930.
Peach jug and tumbler in clear glass, for Orrefors, 1933.
The Diver engraved vase in clear and black glass, for Orrefors, 1934.
Nude and Fish engraved vase in clear and black glass, for Orrefors, 1934.
Trees in Mist vase in clear, white and black glass, for Kosta, 1950.
Bowl in clear and brown glass, for Kosta, 1953.
Bowl in clear glass with blue and brown stripes, for Kosta, 1954.
Vase in cut and sandblasted clear glass, for Kosta, 1954.
Laplander with Reindeer object in green glass, for Kosta, 1960.

Publications:

On LINDSTRAND: books—*Modern Glass* by Guillaume Janneau, London and New York 1931; *Orrefors 1917–1942,* exhibition catalogue edited by Elisa Hald-Steenberg, Stockholm 1942; *Modernt Svenskt Glas,* edited by Gregor Paulsson, Stockholm 1943; *The Beauty of Modern Glass* by R. Stennett-Wilson, London and New York 1958; *Forma Sueca* by Ake Stavenlow and Ake H. Huldt, Stockholm 1961; *Design in Sweden* by Lennart Lindkvist, Stockholm 1972; *Scandinavian Design: Objects of a Life Style* by Eileene Harrison Beer, New York and Toronto 1975; *Legend i Glas* by Lars Thor, Stockholm 1982; *Twentieth Century Design: Glass* by Frederick Cooke, London 1986; *Scandinavia: Ceramics and Glass in the Twentieth Century* by Jennifer Hawkins Opie, London 1989.

LIONNI, Leo.

American graphic designer. Born in Amsterdam, Netherlands, 5 May 1910; emigrated to the United States in 1939: naturalized, 1945. Studied at the University of Zurich, 1928–30; University of Genoa, 1931–35: Ph.D. 1935. Married Nora Maffi in 1931; sons: Louis and Paul. Freelance painter, illustrator, writer and designer, working in Milan, 1931–39, in Philadelphia, 1939–47, in New York, 1948–60, in San Bernardo and Radda in Chianti, Italy, from 1961: art director, Motta Company, Milan, 1933–35, N. W. Ayer and Son, Philadelphia, 1939–47, *Fortune* magazine, New York, 1949–61; design director, Olivetti Company of Amer-

Leo Lionni: Olivetti showroom interior, Chicago, 1956

ica, New York, 1950–57; editor, *Print* magazine, New York, 1955–59, *Panorama* magazine, for Time-Life, Milan, 1962–63. Instructor, Charles Morris Price School, Philadelphia, 1939–47, Black Mountain College, North Carolina, 1946, and Parsons School of Design, New York, 1954; George Miller visiting lecturer, University of Illinois, Urbana-Champaign, 1967; critic-in-residence, Cooper Union, New York, 1982–83. Co-founder, 1951, and chairman, 1953, of the Aspen Design Conference, Colorado. **Exhibitions:** Norlyst Gallery, New York, 1947; Philadelphia Print Club, 1949; Matsukoshi Gallery, Tokyo, 1954; American Institute of Graphic Arts, New York, 1957; Worcester Art Museum, Massachusetts, 1959 (toured); Galleria Il Naviglio, Milan, 1963; Galleria dell'Obelisco, Rome, 1963; Galleria dell'Ariete, Milan, 1966; Galleria Il Milione, Milan, 1972 (toured); Galleria Il Vicolo, Genoa, 1973; Baukunst Galerie, Cologne, 1974; Klingspor Museum, Offenbach, 1974; Galleria Ciak, Rome, 1975; Galleria dell'Oca, Rome, 1976; Staempfli Gallery, New York, 1977; Galleria Giulia, Rome, 1987. **Collections:** Metropolitan Museum of Art, New York; Museum of Modern Art, New York; Philadelphia Museum of Art; Israel Museum, Jerusalem; Bratislava Museum, Czechoslovakia. Recipient: U.S. Art Director of the Year Award, National Society of Art Directors, 1955; Gold Medal, Architectural League of New York, 1956; Citation of Honor, Philadelphia Museum College of Art, 1959; Deutscher Jugendpreis illustrated book award, Bonn, 1965; Golden Apple Award, Bratislava Biennale, 1967; Animated Cartoon Awards, Teheran Film Festival, 1967; Christopher Award, New York, 1967; Graham Foundation Grant, New York, 1967; New York Art Directors Club Hall of Fame Award, 1974; Japan Foundation Grant, 1981. Honorary Member, Society of Typographic Arts, Chicago; member; Alliance Graphique Internationale, Paris. Address: Porcignano, 52017 Radda in Chianti, Italy.

Publications:

By LIONNI: books—*The Family of Man*, designer, New York 1955; *Designs for the Printed Page*, New York 1960; *Taccuino di Leo Lionni*, Milan 1972; *Botanica parallela*, Milan 1976, as *Parallel Botany*, New York 1977, German edition, Cologne 1978, Japanese edition, Tokyo 1980, and French edition, Paris 1981; *The Book of Ma*, with Seigow Matsuoka, Tokyo 1981; picture-books for children—*Little Blue and Little Yellow*, New York 1959, Leicester 1962; *Inch by Inch*, New York 1961, London 1967; *On My Beach There Are Many Pebbles*, New York 1961, London 1977; *Swimmy*, New York 1963; *Tico and the Golden Wings*, New York 1964; *Frederick*, New York 1967, London 1977; *The Alphabet Tree*, New York 1968; *The Biggest House in the World*, New York 1968; *Alexander and the Wind-Up Mouse*, New York 1969, London 1971; *Fish Is Fish*, New York 1971, London 1972; *The Greentail Mouse*, New York 1973; *In the Rabbit-Garden*, New York 1975, London 1976; *A Colour of His Own*, London 1975, New York 1976; *Pezzettino*, New York 1975, London 1977; *I Want to Stay Here! I Want to Go There! A Flea Story*, New York 1977; *Geraldine, The Music Mouse*, London and New York 1979; *Let's Make Rabbits*, New York 1982; *Cornelius*, New York 1983; *Who? What? Where? When?*, New York 1983; *Frederick's Fables*, New York 1985; *It's Mine*, New York 1986; *Nicolas, Where Have You Been?*, New York 1987; *Six Crows*, New York 1988; *Tillie and the Wall*, New York 1989.

On LIONNI: books—*Posters: 50 Artists and Designers*, edited by W. H. Allner, New York 1952; *The Corporate Search for Visual Identity* by Ben Rosen, New York and London 1970; *Leo Lionni: Dipinti, Sculture, Disegni*, exhibition catalogue with text by F. Russoli, Milan 1972; *Leo Lionni: Plastiken, Olbilder, Zeichnungen, Druckgraphik*, exhibition catalogue with text by P. Creagh, Cologne 1974; *Illustrators of Children's Books 1967–1976*, compiled by L. Kingman, G. A. Hogarth and H. Quimby, Boston 1978; *Who's Who in Graphic Art*, edited by Walter Amstutz, Dubendorf 1982.

When, as a child, I was asked what I wanted to be when I grew up, my answer was simply, "an artist." During the seventy years that followed, I have remained loyal to that early promise. Now, when people ask me what I do, I know that they expect me to answer, "I am a designer" or "I am a sculptor" or "I am an author of picture books." The word "artist," alas, seems to have lost much of its meaning. How, then, should I define my work?

I am interested in the full range of artistic experience, of which design is an integral—not a separate—part. I believe that through first hand-experience in all the arts, the problems of vision, both real and imaginary, can be seen in a sharper focus and solved with greater freedom. There are no dividing lines, no no-man's-lands between the arts—each participates in the curses and blessings of the others. To be truly creative and vital, design cannot feed on itself. It must find its forms and meanings in the totality of our culture.

—Leo Lionni

Leo Lionni uses all the tools of his many-faceted creativity with supple grace. An artist working in sculpture, painting, drawing, and design, a writer who invents his own fables, he has a poetic imagination, full of ineffable spontaneity and character. His work in all media is totally interdependent within this broad range. Although the work stems from the sphere of the imaginary, it is nevertheless processed by rigorous discipline. His sense of order permits him to reduce complexity with graphic refinement that goes beyond illustration and possesses forms that have significance fusing ideas and feelings.

From his beginnings at N. W. Ayers and *Fortune*, he was certainly influenced by Bauhaus ideas, but he was not limited to functional austerity. Exposed to the seminal artists working in Europe and the United States, he included their work at times in his advertising assignments and often in the pages of the magazine. In American graphic design's breakthrough years from the 1930s through the 1950s, he was not only a practitioner but one who discovered and encouraged others in the field.

Wit and humor permeate his work, and his wide-ranging curiosity and experience give him the enormous perspective he needs to work in all the media he chooses to express himself. What he calls "the irresistable poetic charge" is in evidence in the nineteen children's books he has published. Just as he invents and illustrates his own fables, he also has invented a purely ficticious visual anthology of plants in his book *Parallel Botany*, a parody of scientific jargon and scholarship; this in turn led to the bronze castings and drawings of a nature not like any known biological order.

He has a passionate interest in the human face; ever mindful of the individuality of each human being, he records the quintessence with a restrained yet rich line. Many such drawings appear in his posters and designs. Maximum visual extension of his creativity can be seen in his sculpture and drawings devoted to the transformation of organic forms into visual metaphors. The true source of his creativity is more than talent—it is the amalgam of his questing mind and experience, imbued with an awareness of our socio-cultural environment.

—Mildred Constantine

LOEWY, Raymond (Fernand).

American industrial designer. Born in Paris, France, 5 November 1893; emigrated to the United States in 1919: naturalized, 1938. Studied at the University of Paris, 1910–12; Ecole de Lanneau, Paris, 1913–14, 1918: Dip.Ing. 1918. Served in the French Army Corps of Engineers, as liaison officer with the American Expeditionary Force, 1914–18: Captain, Interallied Medal, Croix de Guerre and Grand Officier of the Légion d'Honneur. Married Jean Tomson in 1931(divorced, 1945); Viola Erickson in 1948; daughter: Laurence. Freelance window display artist and fashion illustrator, working for *Vogue, Harper's Bazaar*, Macy's, Saks Fifth Avenue, etc., from 1919, and industrial designer, establishing Raymond Loewy Associates, New York, from 1929: art director, Westinghouse Electric Company, 1929; also design consultant to Hupp Motor Company, Studebaker Motor Company, Coca-Cola, United Airlines, Shell Oil, Exxon Oil Company, IBM International Business Machines, National Aeronautics and Space Administration, etc.; established Compagnie de l'Esthétique Industrielle, Paris, 1952. President, American Society of Industrial Designers, 1946, and French Chamber of Commerce of the United States, 1958; executive board member, Art Center College, Los Angeles; industrial design committee member, University of California, Los Angeles; vocational education board member, New York City Board of Education. **Exhibitions:** *An Exhibition for Modern Living*, Detroit Institute of Arts, 1949; *Le Design Français*, Centre de Création Industrielle, Paris, 1971; *The Designs of Raymond Loewy*, Smithsonian Institution, Washington, D.C., 1975; *Raymond Loewy: Living in Space*, Sotheby's, London, 1981; *Design Since 1945*, Philadelphia Museum of Art, 1983; *The Machine Age in America*, Brooklyn Museum, New York, 1986. Recipient: J. Gordon Bennett Medal, Paris, 1906; Gold Medal, Paris International Exposition, 1937; Lord and Taylor Design Award, New York, 1938; All-American Packaging Prize, Paris Exposition, 1939; *Sunday Times* 20th-Century Designer Award, London, 1969; American Academy of Achievement Hall of Fame Award, 1978; American Society of Industrial Designers Distinguished Achievement Award, 1978; President's Award, France, 1980; ICSID Grand Prize, 1981. Honorary DFA: University of Cincinnati, 1956, Art Center College of Design, Los Angeles, 1970. Fellow, American Society of Interior Design; American Academy of Achievement; American Society of Industrial Designers. Honorary Royal Designer for Industry, Royal Society of Arts, London, 1937; Honorary Citizen of France, 1969. *Died (in Monte Carlo) 14 July 1986.*

Works:

Gestetner 466S copying machine housing, for Gestetner Duplicating Machine Company, 1929.

Hupmobile streamlined car, for Hupp Motor Company, 1931–34.

S-1 steam locomotive, for the Pennsylvania Railroad, 1933.

Coldspot Super Six refrigerator, for Sears, Roebuck and Company, 1934.

International Harvester "Farmall" tractor, for McCormick-Deering, 1940.

Constellation passenger aircraft interiors, for Lockheed, 1945.

Scenicruiser coach, for Greyhound Bus Company, 1946.

Streamlined radio receivers, for Hallicrafter, 1947.

Studebaker Starlight coupé, for the Studebaker Motor Company, 1947.

Office interiors, for the Lever Brothers Building, New York, 1952.

Studebaker Starliner coupé, for the Studebaker Motor Company, 1953.

2000 china coffee service, for Rosenthal Studio Line China, 1954.

Studebaker Avanti car, for the Studebaker Motor Company, 1961–62.

Logotype symbol, for the Exxon Oil Corporation, 1966.

Logotype symbol, for the Shell Oil Company, 1967.

Skylab interiors, for National Aeronautic and Space Administration, 1967–73.

Publications:

By LOEWY: books—*The Locomotive: Its Esthetics*, London 1937; *Never Leave Well Enough Alone*, New York and Paris 1951; *Industrial Design*, London and Woodstock 1979.

On LOEWY: books—*Industrial Design: A Practical Guide* by Harold Van Doren, New York and London 1940; *An Exhibition for Modern Living*, catalogue edited by A. H. Girard and W. D. Laurie, Detroit 1949; *Packaging: An international Survey of Package Design*, edited by Walter Herdeg, Zurich 1959; *L'Esthétique Industrielle* by Denis Huisman and Goerges Patrix, Paris 1961; *An International Survey of Packaging* by Wim Crouwel and Kurt Weidemann, London 1968; *Le Design Français*, exhibition catalogue with introduction by Francois Mathey, Paris 1971; *Streamline: Art and Design of the Forties* by Marc Arsenaux, San Francisco 1975; *The Streamlined Decade* by Donald J. Bush, New York 1975; *The Library of Motoring: The Designers* by L. J. K. Setright, London 1976; *Twentieth Century Limited: Industrial Design in America 1925–1939* by Jeffrey L. Meikle, Philadelphia 1979; *The Machine Age in America 1918–1941* by Richard Guy Wilson and Dianne H. Pilgrim, New York 1986; *New American Design* by Hugh Aldersley-Williams, New York 1988; *The American Design Adventure 1940–1975* by Arthur J. Pulos, London and Cambridge, Massachusetts 1988.

To a degree unequaled by the names of any of the other founding fathers of industrial design, the name of Raymond Loewy radiates a charisma that has attracted public attention throughout the past half century. Loewy's flamboyant lifestyle has included at various times country homes outside Paris, in southern France, Mexico, Long Island, and Palm Springs, as well as luxurious urban apartments in Manhattan and Paris. The worldwide image has been reinforced by his design offices not only in New York, Chicago, and Los Angeles, but also in London, Paris, San Juan and São Paulo, among others.

This matter of image and style is important because—in combination with a keen business sense, a highly-developed imagination, and a rich design talent—it was an important element in generating a sense of excitement about, not only Raymond Loewy, but the new profession of industrial design itself.

Much has been written about the trial by fire the new profession underwent during the great Depression and how industrial design proved itself by demonstrating that in a shrinking market, the product "designed" by an industrial designer would win out over an otherwise similar and equal product. The office of Raymond Loewy provided more than its share of such demonstration cases—and did so with a flair that reflected credit on client firm and designer alike.

Loewy's design philosophy is not a deeply intellectual one. He summarized it with the acronym MAYA—most advanced, yet acceptable. The proliferation of clean, functional, and dynamic products that emerged from the Loewy offices throughout his long career provides testimony to his success in correctly making the prediction "most advanced, yet acceptable."

Examples of his designs that have become famous include the 1947 Studebaker Starlight Coupe, the 1953 Starliner Coupe and the 1961 Avanti—designs that generated a public interest and acceptance far out of proportion to the company's relative size in the industry; the 1947 line of Hallicrafter radio receivers that conveyed a crisp precision far ahead of their time; the 1929 Gestetner duplicating machine, the 1934 Sears Coldspot refrigerator, and the S-1 steam locomotive for the Pennsylvania Railroad—all landmark designs that were extremely successful and influential in establishing higher design standards in their respective product areas.

It is difficult to measure precisely Loewy's impact on our contemporary environment, but it has certainly been a dynamic and significant one. His vitality and international influence are demonstrated by his being retained as a major industrial design consultant in the 1970s by the government of the Soviet Union—this as he entered his eighties!

—James M. Alexander

LOGAN, Ian.

British packaging and graphic designer. Born in Gloucester, 12 July 1939. Studied art and design, at Bath Art School, Avon, 1952–55; textile design, at the West of England College of Art, Bristol, 1959–61; Central School of Art and Design, London, 1961–64: NDD 1964; Konstfackskolan, Stockholm, 1964–65. Married Deborah Hugh-Jones in 1966; children: Harriet and Barnaby. Worked as a draughtsman for the Westinghouse Corporation, London, 1956–59; founder and principal, with other Central School graduates, of JRM Designs, London, 1966–70; founder-partner, of Ian Logan Associates, from 1968; president of Ian Logan Design, and Ian Logan Wholesale-Export Company, London, from 1975: designed for the National Trust, Woods of Windsor, Harrod's, Macy's, Boots, the French Sugar Corporation, the Smithsonian Institution, Paraphernalia, Alan Spiegelman, etc.; consultant, Woods of Windsor toiletries, from 1979, and Helenware Household Textiles, from 1982. Visiting lecturer in textile design, Royal College of Art, London, and Hornsey College of Art, Middlesex; packaging juror, Royal College of Art Bursary, Designers and Art Directors Association, London, 1982–83. **Exhibitions:** Design Centre, London, 1981. **Collections:** Victoria and Albert Museum, London; Smithsonian Institution, Washington, D.C. Recipient: *Observer* Design Award, London, 1978. Fellow, Chartered Society of Designers, London, 1980. Address: 42 Charterhouse Square, London EC1N 6EU, England.

Publications:

By LOGAN: books—*Lost Glory,* London 1976; *Classy Chassy,* with Henry Nield, London 1977; article—in *The Designer* (London), March 1981.

On LOGAN: books—*Design and Art Directors Annual,* London 1980–83.

Design in every visual aspect has always excited me, I suppose from when I was a small boy. Although I was trained as a textile designer, I very quickly realised that a textile was not very important on its own without an interior, and with the wrong interior and lighting effect, the textile furnishing would be stone dead.

I have always been excited by functional industrial design and layout, particularly that of military equipment, because it is usually designed for a function. The layout of fighter aircraft cockpits are a prime example of what I mean. The design of railway locomotives in America from the 1930s to the 1950s have also always influenced me, particularly the experiments in streamlining, some of which are totally stunning, e.g., the Rock Island Rockets of the 1950s. Also the displays of graphic images on American trains of this time show a freedom of style that, I think, has yet to be matched. Many, I believe, were designed by employees of the railway companies in competitions.

Early graphic images of airlines also stimulate me. I feel that any designer in any field should be totally aware of all things around him—from the latest space vehicle to the latest jacket designed by Giorgio Armani, from a drawing pen to the latest piece of furniture designed by Vico Magistretti.

—Ian Logan

Ian Logan might be said to be a graphic designer who works in three as well as two dimensions. Images and colour, but images above all, are his stock in trade, and with a freedom characteristic of graphic designers, he regards humanity's creation and accumulation of an immense and endlessly various sign language, decade by decade, century by century, as being at his and our disposal. He sees a vast paintbox of images and styles which it would be wasteful not to use and to enjoy, but which cannot be used imaginatively without being extended and added to at the same time. A motif from Victorian times or the 1930s, for instance, reused today, at the very least finds itself transformed by its new context, quite apart from any transformation wrought upon it by the designer. What is wrong with "nostalgia" if nostalgia means, not vainly trying to escape into a past which has gone for ever, but enjoying and renewing what the past has bequeathed to us? This is the question with which Logan's artifacts rebuke the purist and the puritan.

Logan can get away with his joyful eclecticism because he specialises in the design of gifts and souvenirs, small things which would fail if they were not fun, and which would not be bought if they were not exquisitely tempting. A particular speciality, the manufacture of which he has helped to revive, is tinware—money-boxes, biscuit tins, tea caddies, tin eggs, tin rulers—permanently useful, permanently decorative "Packaging" which may come

Ian Logan: Tin tea caddies, for J. Sainsbury and Company, 1983

empty or with a first cargo of soap or sweets and which may itself be "packaged" in a distinctive point-of-sale display unit. Logan's products function dually—on the one hand to hold biscuits (or whatever), which they do splendidly, and on the other, to be enjoyed. Why should the concept of "functionalism" in design be tied to an unsmiling, humourless moral seriousness?

Logan is an important designer precisely because he has demonstrated that not only buildings and cars and furniture and washing machines can be well designed, but so also can the little things in our lives, if differently. He has moved into an area which other designers have chosen to ignore and which in consequence has been, and is, dominated by trash, and he has shown that gifts and mementoes do not have to be outrageously expensive, or expensive at all, to be desirable. In particular, his attitude toward the past—his refusal to see it either as something that has to be put away on its shelf and left to gather dust or a burden which must at all times weigh heavily upon us—has especially well equipped him to create souvenires for museums, and for instance, for the National Trust in England, which has set high standards in this field with the assistance of Logan, among others.

—Philip Pacey

LOIS, George (Harry)

American graphic designer. Born in the Bronx, New York, 26 June 1931. Studied at the High School of Music and Art, New York, 1945–49; Pratt Institute, Brooklyn, New York, 1949–50. Served in the United States Army, in Korea, 1951–53: Private 1st Class. Married Rosemary Lewandowski in 1951; son: Luke. Designer, at Reba Sochis, 1951, and CBS-TV, New York, 1954–56; art director, at Sudler and Hennessey, 1956–57, and at Doyle Dane Bernbach, New York, 1958–59; executive vice-president and creative director, of Papert Koenig Lois, New York, 1960–67; chairman and creative director, of Lois Holland Callaway, New York, from 1967, then president of Creamer Lois, and chairman and creative director of Lois Pitts Gershon, New York. Columnist, *Art Direction* magazine, 1961–63, and *Adweek,* New York, 1980–82. President, Art Directors Club of New York, 1972–73. **Collections:** Museum of Modern Art, New York; Cooper-Hewitt Museum, New York. Recipient: Alumni Award, High School of Music and Art, New York, and Pratt Institute, Brooklyn; Art Director of the Year Award, New York, 1963; Art Directors Hall of Fame Award, New York, 1978; Creative Hall of Fame Award, New York, 1984. DFA: Pratt Institute, Brooklyn, 1982. Address: Lois/GGK, 650 Fifth Avenue, New York, New York 10019, U.S.A.

Publications:

By LOIS: books—*George Be Careful,* with Bill Pitts, New York 1972; *The Art of Advertising,* with Bill Pitts, New York 1977; *The Dictionary of Visual Language,* New York 1980; articles—in *Photo/Design* (New York), August/September 1984; *Madison Avenue* (New York), November 1985; *Backstage* (New York), 12 October 1988.

On LOIS: books—*Advertising Directions,* edited by Edward M. Gottschall and Arthur Hawkins, New York 1959; *Typography* by Aaron Burns, New York 1961; *The Language of Graphics* by Edward Booth-Clibborn and Daniele Baroni, London 1980; *The Design Concept* by Allen Hurlburt, New York 1981; *A History of Graphic Design* by Philip B. Meggs, New York 1983; *Typographic Design: Form and Communication* by Rob Carter, Ben Day and Philip Meggs, New York 1985.

Any attempt to understand the art of advertising as a serious expression of a man's creative originality is usually overwhelmed by controversy over morality and ethics. We tend to equate art with virtue and commerce with sin. According to many critics who try to understand its massive impact on modern living, advertising is a twentieth-century love-potion; it arouses wants beyond means, it invites extreme consumption, it conjures a material paradise as life's goal.

It is not easy to explain the complexity of the ethos that inspires my life of creating ideas for selling. Since I was a youngster in public school, I lived to draw, design, and rearrange things. I knew I was going to be an *artist.* When I went to a specialized high school—the High School of Music and Art—I could draw better, design better, sculpt better, paint better, and do better in history of art courses than anyone in the school. But my special fascination was with that art that was expected to persuade, to sell. Like no other art I was studying, it required a cause-and-effect connection, or it simply couldn't work.

In high school, I worshipped the paintings of Stuart Davis, with his floating words jammed between objects and images, but the spontaneity of a Cassandre poster seemed even more thrilling by the merging of words and images into a wholly new language. There were more hints of this new way of communicating in the work of Paul Rand, who struck out boldly during the 1940s by visualizing copy in an individualistic manner. At sixteen, I started to get more kick out of listening to Cassandre and Rand talk to me than Picasso or Léger or O'Keeffe or Davis. I knew I was hooked.

From the role of artisan or craftsman or designer, the art director of our media age has come a distance, and I hope I've played a part in shoving him into modern times. An art director must be a communicator, or he's simply someone who rearranges elements in a layout or design. An art director must be someone who treats words with the same reverence that he accords graphics because the verbal and visual elements of modern communication are as indivisible as words and music in song. In retrospect, the pioneering of Paul Rand was an almost primeval advance, for he dealt, in the final analysis, with words and themes that were fragments of language related to him by copywriters, rather than with fully integrated visual/verbal concepts.

Talking to people on a page or in a television commercial requires what I call "street talk." It has nothing to do with literature, other than using today's language. Art and words are merely tools for communicating. But all the tools in the world are meaningless without an essential idea—an artist, or advertising man, or doctor, or lawyer, or electrician, or factory worker, without an idea is unarmed. When the original idea springs out of a communicator's head and intuitions, the mystical and artful blending—or even juxtaposition—of concept, image, words, and art can lead to magic, where one and one can indeed be three.

I had a lot of breaks in my life—including being raised in a hard-working Greek family and marrying the right woman—but three people recognized my talent and led me to what I do today: my public school art teacher, Miss Engle; my design teacher at Pratt Institute, Hershel Levit; and my first boss, Reba Sochis. After working for Reba Sochis and then for Bill Golden at CBS, I plunged into the mediocrity of the commercial world and got myself a reputation as the *enfant terrible* of advertising. I'm sure I deserved it, and I'm just as sure that without fighting for my work every second of my life, my work would be just as dull and uninspired as most of the so-called communications in the world—the bland leading the bland. To produce work I could be proud of, I've had to shove, push, cajole, persuade, wheedle, exaggerate, flatter, manipulate, be obnoxious, occasionally lie, and always *sell*. And with all those lucky breaks of mother and father and teachers and wife and sons and first jobs, I still believe a person decides his own fate, that he ordains what kind of work he wants to produce. He can decide that no client can make him run a bad ad! A client could kill and kill and kill what you think is right for him—the Abominable No-man—but he can't make you run bad work. (Your choice is to fight back with better work, or find better clients.)

Creative people in our business all speak of their "great ads" that remain on tissue paper in their dark file drawers. I say that you never did the job if you didn't sell it to the client. The accurate measure of a human being is what he actually gets done. In my life, I can't imagine any taste worse than the taste of sour grapes.

A work of art derives its identity from its visibility and from the response it evokes in others. I spend my spare moments drinking in that art created by generations of artists who have been the antennae of human sensibility—artists who understood that art of the past, but who broke with it according to the needs of their time. I see my own role as precisely that of an artist. But my kind of art has nothing to do with putting images on canvas. My concern is with creating images that catch people's eyes, penetrate their minds, warm their hearts, and cause them to act.

—George Lois

Before he was thirty, George Lois had created the first advertising agency headed by an art director. With his fifteen-hour-a-day energy, he invented advertising outrageous enough not to forget. Lois's humor in advertising, as evident in the work of more than twenty years as creative director of his agencies, is equally matched by an ability to simplify the message and sell the idea.

The notion that art directors could be suc-cessful businessmen was a revelation for the nature of the industry in the early 1960s as George and his associates startled the New York advertising community with a quality and visual brashness not before seen. But this advertising worked. Lois's accurate perception of the man-on-the-street within the American culture is a consistent element of his advertising fabric and strategy.

Visually recalling the spirit of film characters from his early childhood, Lois has often integrated the likes of Laurel and Hardy and the Marx brothers into television spot commercials in order to sell products through humor and appeal to the cinematic past. His humor, much like Lou Dorfsman's, is aimed at Everyman, while perhaps slightly chiding our culture and myths.

Whether in print ads or filmed spots for television, Lois's acuity for advertising is evident in an individuality of form and message, as seen in ideas ranging from caveman as businessman using a word processor to Frankenstein combing a beautiful head of hair for a men's hair-spray. His use of celebrities and star athletes set a trend in American advertising, and particularly influential was the manner in which he developed graphic and conceptual ideas as the art director for the covers of *Esquire* for a decade. Often incorporating the photographic skills of Carl Fisher, realistic, often humorous ideas reflecting the nature and spirit of the times candidly challenged the consumer to buy the magazine. To Lois, it was

George Lois: Advertisement for Mug Root Beer, 1989

nothing more than effective package design.

A strong belief that you have to love what you are doing, confidence in himself, and the desire to get things done and to sell characterize Lois personally as man and art director. His advertising energies are balanced by a supportive artist-painter wife and a collection of ancient and tribal masks from the Pacific and elsewhere; it is considered to be one of the finest collections in New York.

—Michael Robert Soluri

LOQUASTO, Santo.

American stage and film designer. Born in Wilkes Barre, Pennsylvania, 26 July 1944. Studied at King's College, Wilkes Barre, and at Yale University, New Haven, Connecticut: MFA 1969. Assistant, Williamstown Theatre Festival, Massachusetts, 1965–74; resident designer, Yale Repertory Theatre, New Haven, Connecticut, 1969–72, and Kreeger Theatre, Arena Stage, Washington, D.C., from 1971; principal designer, New York Shakespeare Festival, and Twyla Tharp Dance Foundation, New York, from 1971; also designed for the Tyrone Guthrie Theatre, Minneapolis, the San Diego Opera, California, the Opera Society of Washington D.C., and the San Francisco Spring Opera. Recipient: Drama Desk Award, New York, 1972, 1977; *Variety* New York Drama Critics Award, 1972; Antoinette Perry Award, New York, 1973, 1977; *Village Voice* Obie Award, New York, 1975; Joseph Maharam Award, New York, 1977. Address: c/o United Scenic Artists, 1540 Broadway, New York, New York 10036, U.S.A.

Works:

Stage productions include—*Push Comes to Shove and Other Dances*, American Ballet Theatre, New York, 1967; *Concerto*, American Ballet Theatre, New York, 1967; *The Hostage*, Hartford Stage Company, Connecticut, 1968; *The Rose Tattoo*, Hartford Stage Company, Connecticut, 1968; *Tiny Alice*, Long Wharf Theatre, New Haven, Connecticut, 1968; *The Bacchae*, Yale Repertory Theatre, 1969; *The Waltz Invention*, Hartford Stage Company, Connecticut, 1969; *The Homecoming*, Hartford Stage Company, Connecticut, 1969; *The Farce of Scapin*, Hartford Stage Company, Connecticut, 1969; *Narrow Road to the Deep North*, Charles Playhouse, Boston, 1969; *Tartuffe*, Williamstown Theatre Festival, Massachusetts, 1969; *Hedda Gabler*, Williamstown Theatre Festival, Massachusetts, 1969; *Rosencrantz and Guildenstern Are Dead*, Williamstown Theatre Festival, Massachusetts, 1969; *The Skin of Our Teeth*, Long Wharf Theatre, New Haven, Connecticut, 1970; *A Day in the Death of Joe Egg*, Hartford Stage Company, Connecticut, 1970; *Misalliance*, Hartford Stage Company, Connecticut, 1970; *The Trial of A. Lincoln*, Hartford Stage Company, Connecticut, 1970; *Anything Goes*, Hartford Stage Company, Connecticut, 1970; *Rosencrantz and Guildenstern Are Dead*, Hartford Stage Company, Connecticut, 1970; *Ring 'round the Moon*, Hartford Stage Company, Connecticut, 1970; *Three Philip Roth Stories*, Yale Repertory Theatre, 1970; *Cops and Horrors*, Yale Repertory Theatre, 1970; *The Revenger's Tragedy*, Yale Repertory Theatre, 1970; *The Story Theatre*, Yale Repertory Theatre, 1970; *The Unseen Hand*, Astor Place Theatre, New York, 1970; *Forensic and the Navigators*, Astor Place Theatre, New York, 1970; *The Little Mahagonny*, Yale Repertory Theatre, 1971; *Sticks and Bones*, Public Theatre, New York, 1971; *The Seven Deadly Sins*, Yale Repertory Theatre, 1971; *A Gun Play*, Hartford Stage Company, Connecticut, 1971; *A Long Day's Journey into Night*, Hartford Stage Company, Connecticut, 1971; *Henry V*, Hartford Stage Company, Connecticut, 1971; *Wipe-Out Games*, Arena Stage, Washington, D.C., 1971; *Pantagleize*, Arena Stage, Washington, D.C., 1971; *The Sign in Sidney Brustein's Window*, Arena Stage, Washington, D.C., 1971; *Sticks and Bones*, John Golden Theatre, New York, 1972; *That Championship Season*, Public Theatre, New York, 1972; *The House of Blue Leaves*, Arena Stage, Washington, D.C., 1972; *Uptight*, Arena Stage, Washington, D.C., 1972; *Old Times*, Mark Taper Forum, Los Angeles, 1972; *The Secret Affairs of Mildred Wild*, Ambassador Theatre, New York, 1972; *Sunset*, Chelsea Theatre Center, New York, 1972; *A Public Prosecutor Is Sick of It All*, Arena Stage, Washington, D.C., 1973; *Boom Boom Room*, Vivian Beaumont Theatre, New York, 1973; *La Dafne*, Spoleto Festival, Italy, 1973; *Siamese Connections*, Public Theatre, New York, 1973; *The Orphan*, Public Theatre, New York, 1973; *As You Like It*, Delacorte Theatre, New York, 1973; *King Lear*, Delacorte Theatre, New York, 1973; *The Tempest*, Mitzi Newhouse Theatre, New York, 1974; *King Richard III*, Mitzi Newhouse Theatre, New York, 1974; *Macbeth*, Mitzi Newhouse Theatre, New York, 1974; *What the Wine Sellers Buy*, Vivian Beaumont Theatre, New York, 1974; *Mert and Phil*, Vivian Beaumont Theatre, New York, 1974; *The Dance of Death*, Vivian Beaumont Theatre, New York, 1974; *Pericles, Prince of Tyre*, Delacorte Theatre, New York, 1974; *The Merry Wives of Windsor*, Delacorte Theatre, New York, 1974; *That Championship Season*, Garrick Theatre, London, 1974; *The Cherry Orchard*, Hartford Stage Company, Connecticut, 1974; *Sephardic Song*, American Ballet Theatre, New York, 1974; *A Midsummer Night's Dream*, Mitzi Newhouse Theatre, New York, 1975; *A Doll's House*, Vivian Beaumont Theatre, New York, 1975; *Hamlet*, Vivian Beaumont Theatre, New York, 1975; *The Comedy of Errors*, Delacorte Theatre, New York, 1975; *Kennedy's Children*, John Golden Theatre, New York, 1975; *Murderer Among Friends*, Biltmore Theatre, New York, 1975; *Legend*, Ethel Barrymore Theatre, New York, 1976; *Measure for Measure*, Delacorte Theatre, New York, 1976; *The Glass Menagerie*, Hartford Stage Company, 1976, 1983; *Landscape of the Body*, Public Theatre, New York, 1977; *Agamemnon*, Vivian Beaumont Theatre, New York, 1977; *The Cherry Orchard*, Vivian Beaumont Theatre, New York, 1977; *Miss Margarida's Way*, Ambassador Theatre, New York, 1977; *Golda*, Morosco Theatre, New York, 1977; *American Buffalo*, Ethel Barrymore Theatre, New York, 1977; *The Lower Depths*, Arena Stage, Washington, D.C., 1977; *Heartbreak House*, Arena Stage, Washington, D.C., 1977; *The Mighty Gents*, Ambassador Theatre, New York, 1978; *Curse of the Starving Class*, Public Theatre, New York, 1978; *Don Quixote*, American Ballet Theatre, New York, 1978; *The Play's the Thing*, Brooklyn Academy of Music, 1978; *Ice Dancing*, Felt Forum, New York, 1978; *Stop the World—I Want to Get Off*, New York State Theatre, 1978; *King of Hearts*, Minskoff Theatre, New York, 1978; *Sarava*, Broadway Theatre, New York, 1979; *Bent*, New Apollo Theatre, New York, 1979; *The Goodbye People*, Belasco Theatre, New York, 1979; *Ramonda*, American Ballet Theatre, New York, 1980; *The Member of the Wedding*, Hartford Stage Company, Connecticut, 1980; *The Suicide*, Academy Theatre, New York, 1980; *The Floating Light Bulb*, Vivian Beaumont Theatre, New York, 1981; *Field, Chair and Mountain*, American Ballet Theatre, New York, 1981; *Theme and Variations*, American Ballet Theatre, New York, 1981; *A Midsummer Night's Dream*, Brooklyn Academy of Music, 1981; *Crossing Niagara*, Manhattan Theatre Club, New York, 1981; *Short Stories*, Los Angeles Music Center, 1981; *The Tempest*, Tyrone Guthrie Theatre, Minneapolis, 1982; *Happily Ever After*, Joffrey Ballet, New York, 1982; *Gardenia*, Manhattan Theatre Club, New York, 1982; *The Wake of Jamey Foster*, Eugene O'Neill Theatre, New York, 1982; *Richard III*, Delacorte Theatre, New York, 1983; *The Three Sisters*, Manhattan Theatre Club, New York, 1983; *Little Malcolm and His Struggle Against the Eunuchs*, Yale Experimental Theatre, 1983; *Orgasmo Adulto Escapes from the Zoo*, Public Theatre, New York, 1983; *America Kicks Up its Heels*, Playwrights Horizons, New York, 1983; *Uncle Vanya*, La Mama Annex Theatre, New York, 1983; *In Trousers*, Promenade Theatre, New York, 1985; *Virginia*, Public Theatre, New York, 1985; *California Dog Fight*, Manhattan Theatre Club, New York, 1985; *Singin' in the Rain*, Gershwin Theatre, New York, 1985; film designs include—*Stop the World—I Want to Get Off* (Saville), 1979; *Simon* (Brickman), 1980; *Stardust Memories* (Allen), 1980; *So Fine* (A. Bergman), 1981; *The Fan* (Bianchi), 1981; *A Midsummer Night's Sex Comedy* (Allen), 1982; *Zelig* (Allen), 1983; *Falling in Love* (Grosbard), 1984; *Desperately Seeking Susan* (Seidelman), 1985; *Radio Days* (Allen), 1986; *September* (Allen), 1987; *Bright Lights, Big City* (Bridges), 1988.

Publications:

On LOQUASTO: book—*Contemporary Theatre, Film and Television: 6*, edited by L. S. Hubbard and O. O'Donnell, Detroit 1989; articles—in *Newsweek* (New York), March 1977; *People Weekly* (Chicago), 17 November 1980; *Theatre Design and Technology* (Charlottesville), Fall 1981.

*   *   *

Santo Loquasto is the logical heir to the tradition of American stage design that began with the simplification and abstraction of the New Stagecraft in the 1920s and the uses of textural materials and emblematic design that grew popular under Boris Aronson Ming Cho Lee in the 1950s and 1960s. An overview of Loquasto's work reveals the use of rough wood, erosion cloth, metal tubing, and other textural and constructivist elements typical of the past few decades, and in this, the influence of Lee is clearly evident, although Loquasto denies any intentional copying. His sets also display a strong use of vertical and horizontal lines in seeming opposition to the more common practice of asymmetry practiced by many designers.

A frequent Loquasto trademark in realistic sets is the use of "clutter." *American Buffalo* (1977), set in a junk shop, is the extreme example, but clutter occurs in many other designs as well. Loquasto states that it is not simply a thematic or decorative device but is there to break the stark, almost classic angularity of his sets. He uses texture to offset linearity. Loquasto considers himself a sculptural designer and, more than most other contemporary designers, he creates a strongly three-dimensional sense of space on the stage rather than a pictorial setting. This is a result of doing much of his work in arena and thrust spaces which, he says, force you to "push action forward and deal with space sculpturally."

Peter Lord: Arthur Young office and atrium, Bridewell Street, Bristol, 1987

Loquasto sees design as a unifying force in the production. The setting is the visual element that holds the production together through time. In fact, his sets have often helped to focus otherwise disjointed plays such as *Bent* (1982) or *Savara* (1978). Recently, like several other designers, he has begun to incorporate moving parts into his settings—not so much for spectacle, although this is important, as for their ability to alter and sculpt space fluidly. The moving back wall of *The Suicide* (1980), for instance, altered the space of the stage with both visual and psychological effect.

Loquasto has emerged as one of the best designers for the purpose of expressing subtleties of the play through setting, for creating and manipulating space and mood, and for deft use of color and texture. More than most designers, he is increasingly designing costumes as well as sets (something he has long done in ballet) to gain more visual control over the productions.

—Arnold Aronson

LORD, Peter (John).

British architect and interior designer. Born in London, 1 September 1929. Educated at Welwyn Garden City Grammer School, Hertfordshire, 1941–46; studied under Robert Furneaux Jordan, at the Architectural Association School, London, 1946–51: Dip.Arch. 1951. Served in the British Army Royal Engineers, and in the Army Emergency Reserve, 1951–53. Married Shirley Munday in 1956; daughter: Kathryn. Architect and designer, with J. M. Austin-Smith architects, London, 1953–56; partner, 1956–80, and senior partner from 1980, in Austin-Smith: Lord architects and designers, London. President, Chartered Society of Designers, London, 1969–70, and ICSID International Council of Societies of Industrial Design, 1985–87; Chairman, Association of Consultant Architects, London, 1989. Associate, 1952, and Fellow, 1959, Royal Institute of British Architects; Member, 1956, and Fellow, 1964, Chartered Society of Designers; Fellow, Royal Society of Arts, 1964; Honorary Member, Union des Designers en Belgique, 1974. Address: 10–12 Carlisle Street, London W1V 5RF, England.

Works:

Office and display warehouse interiors, for John Wright and Sons, London, 1956.

Shops, offices and warehouses, for Heffers Booksellers and Heffers Stationers, Cambridge, from 1965.

Office, warehouse and depot buildings, for IBM (UK) Limited, from 1969.

ABC Cinemas interiors, in Romford and Plymouth, 1970–71.

Office building and interiors, for Lloyds Bank, Oxford, 1972.

Headquarters office interiors, for the Central Electricity Generating Board, London, from 1980.

Manufacturing plant and office interiors, for Twentieth Century-Fox Video, Perivale, Middlesex, 1981.

Restaurants interiors, for Cranks Limited, from 1981.

Exhibit galleries, restaurant and cafeteria interiors, for the British Museum, London, from 1981.

Office interiors, for Twentieth Century-Fox, Soho Square, London, 1983.

Publications:

By LORD: books—*Materials Handling in Factories and Warehouses,* London 1963; *The Concept of Professionalism in the Field of Design,* London 1968; articles—in *The Designer* (London), September 1969, October 1969, October 1970, December 1970, October 1973; *Official Architect and Planning* (London), February 1970; *Management Today* (London), August 1972; *Interior Design* (London), October 1972, April 1973; *Housing Review* (London), August 1973; *Shopspec* (London), April 1982.

On LORD: book—*Architecture Guide to Cambridge and East Anglia Since 1970* by Charles McKean, London 1982; articles—in *Official Architect and Planning* (London), April 1967; *Architectural Review* (London), May 1971; *Architects' Journal* (London), May 1982.

My training as an architect and practice as an architect/designer in all fields from urban planning and landscape through to project design and associated graphics underlines my personal philosophy that design must be a consistent thread within a total environment.

When distortions in emphasis occur through failure to analyse the problem or resolve conflicts—or just the plain inability of the designer—a solution cannot have an elegance that transcends the ordinary, a quality which is essential for me. I find pleasure in the design process, which for me more often than not starts before putting pencil to paper, and which is a synthesis of a building with its inhabitants, a product design with its user, and overall, a demonstration of harmony and purpose.

—Peter Lord

Since Peter Lord began to practice in 1953, his work has included interiors for the *Times* newspapers, Unilever, IBM (UK), London Weekend Television, Lloyds Bank, W. H. Smith, the Inn on the Park, British government Job Centres, the British Museum, and some bookshops, namely, Heffers of Cambridge, Dillons University Bookshop in London, and Hatchards of Piccadilly. In his presidential address to the Society of Industrial Artists and Designers in October 1969, Lord stated: "Even if we only defined design as the part of a creative process concerned with the visual and aesthetic aspect as an essential element in a comprehensive process, we must still recognise it as only part of a creative process. The emphasis which we and our clients—individual, corporate and governmental—place on this aspect will vary from year to year, but it is our responsibility to see that this vital function is regarded from the outset as a criterion as important as utility and economy." Lord argued that the William Morris attempt to retreat from industrialisation was doomed to fail. Machines are here to stay, but there is no reason why industrial products cannot be well designed. He welcomed the institution of two A-level examination subjects in design as a major step in increasing the public understanding of design.

Lord regards himself as a pragmatist, not an idealist. Doing a good job within the brief allowed is what matters. The theoretical base must be sound, with a full understanding of cost-efficiency. Lord's style is one of functionalism which can be beautiful, not of beautiful concepts devoid of practicality. The beauty must work. He does not want his interiors to be too fashionable, for that would date them too quickly; rather, he strives to attain a durable

simplicity. This British reserve meshes very well with the Modern Movement, for it is the classic simplicity of Bauhaus designs that makes them still marketable sixty years later. Lord follows the same approach, aiming for a functional elegance that will remain efficient and useful for decades. For a theatre, the building and interior should not compete with the action on the stage, and the same applied to offices and shops. Lord is a modest designer who puts usability before any grandiose concepts, and that is why he is successful.

—Diana de Marly

LOURIÉ, Eugene.

American film designer. Born, of French parents, in Kharkov, Russia, in 1905; emigrated to the United States in 1941. Worked as an extra in Russian films, 1919; designed cinema publicity materials, in Istanbul, 1920; scenery painter and assistant to art director Lochakoff, at Albatross Film Studios, Paris, 1921–23; freelance film designer and art director, in Paris, from 1923, and in Hollywood, California, from 1943; also stage set and costume designer, working for the Ballets Russes de Monte Caro, the San Francisco Ballet, etc., from 1928; designed TV series *Kung Fu,* 1973–75.

Works:

Film designs include—*Le Brasier Ardent* (Mosjoukine), 1923; *Le Jouer d'Echecs* (Bernard), 1927; *Napoleon* (Gance), 1927; *Cagliostro* (Oswald), 1929; *Un Coupe de Téléphone* (Lacombe), 1931; *Madame Bovary* (Renoir), 1933; *La Porteuse du Pain* (Sti), 1934; *Jeanne* (Tourjansky), 1934; *Les Yeux Noirs* (Tourjansky), 1935; *Quand la Vie etait Belle* (Sti), 1935; *La Petite Sauvage* (de Limur), 1935; *Le Bébé de l'Escadrot* (Sti), 1935; *Crime et Chatiment* (Chenal), 1935; *Sous les Yeux d'Occident* (M. Allegret), 1936; *Baccara* (Mirandel), 1936; *Les Hommes Nouveaux* (L'Herbier), 1936; *Le Grand Refrain* (Siodmak), 1936; *Aventure à Paris* (M. Allegret), 1936; *Les Bas-Fonds* (Renoir), 1936; *La Grande Illusion* (Renoir), 1937; *L'Alibi* (Chenal), 1937; *Le Messager* (Rouleau), 1937; *Nuit de Feu* (L'Herbier), 1937; *La Bête Humaine* (Renoir), 1938; *Ramuntcho* (Barberis), 1938; *L'Affaire Lafarge* (Chenal), 1938; *Werther* (Ophuls), 1938; *La Tragédie Impériale* (L'Herbier), 1938; *Le Paradis de Satan* (de Gandera), 1938; *Les Nouveaux Riches* (Berthomieu), 1938; *La Régle du Jeu* (Renoir), 1938; *Sans Lendemain* (Ophuls), 1939; *L'Or du Cristobal* (Becker), 1939; *Une Fausse Alerte* (de Baroncelli), 1940; *Air Pur* (Clair—unfinished), 1940; *Three Russian Girls* (Ozep), 1943; *This Land Is Mine* (Renoir), 1943; *Sahara* (Z. Korda), 1943; *The Impostor* (Duvivier), 1944; *In Society* (Yarbrough), 1944; *The House of Fear* (Neill), 1944; *Uncle Harry* (Siodmak), 1945; *The Southerner* (Renoir), 1945; *The Diary of a Chambermaid* (Renoir), 1946; *The Long Night* (Litvak), 1947; *The Song of Scheherazade* (Reisch), 1947; *A Woman's Vengeance* (Z. Korda), 1948; *The River* (Renoir), 1951; *The Adventures of Captain Fabian* (Marshall), 1951; *Limelight* (Chaplin), 1952; *The Diamond Queen* (Brahm), 1953; *The Beast from 20,000 Fathoms* (also director), 1953; *So This Is Paradise* (Quine),

1954; *Napoleon* (Guitry), 1954; *Si Paris nous etait Conte* (Guitry), 1955; *The Colossus of New York* (also director), 1957; *The Giant Behemoth* (also director), 1958; *Confessions of an Opium Eater* (Zugsmith), 1961; *Gorgo* (also director), 1961; *Back Street* (Miller), 1961; *Shock Corridor* (Fuller), 1962; *The Strangler* (Topper), 1962; *Flight from Ashiya* (Anderson), 1962; *That Touch of Mink* (Delbert Mann), 1962; *The Naked Kiss* (Fuller), 1963; *Bikini Paradise* (Tallas), 1964; *A Crack in the World* (Marton), 1965; *Battle of the Bulge* (Annakin), 1965; *Custer of the West* (Siodmak), 1966; *Krakatoa, East of Java* (Kowalski), 1969; *Royal Hunt of the Sun* (Lerner), 1969; *Eliza's Horoscope* (Sheppard), 1971; *Death Takes a Holiday* (Butler—for TV), 1971; *The Delphi Bureau* (Wendkos—for TV), 1972; *What's the Matter with Helen?* (Harrington), 1972; *Kung Fu* (Thorpe—for TV), 1972; *Haunts of the Very Rich* (Wendkos—for TV), 1972; *What Are Best Friends For?* (Sandrich—for TV), 1973; *Carola* (Lloyd—for TV), 1973; *Burnt Offerings* (Curtiss), 1975; *Philemon* (Lloyd—for TV), 1975; *Time Travelers* (Singer—for TV), 1976; *Lacy and the Mississippi Queen* (Butler—for TV), 1978; *An Enemy of the People* (Schaeffer), 1978; *Supertrain* (Curtiss), 1979; *A Whale for the Killing* (Heffron—for TV), 1980; *Bronco Billy* (Eastwood), 1980; *Freebie and the Bean* (Auerback—for TV), 1980; *Breathless* (McBride), 1983.

Publications:

By LOURIÉ: books—*My Work in Films,* New York 1985; articles—in *Film Comment* (New York), May/June 1978; *American Film* (Washington, D.C.), January/February 1985.

On LOURIÉ: books—*Le Décor de Film* by Leon Barsacq, Paris 1970, as *Caligari's Cabinet and Other Grand Illusions,* Boston 1976; *Screen Series: France* by Marcel Martin, London and New York 1971; *The International Dictionary of Films and Filmmakers,* Chicago and London 1987, 1991; articles—in *Films and Filming* (London), February 1960, December 1961; *Monthly Film Bulletin* (London), January 1972; *Film Comment* (New York), May/June 1978; *Film Dope* (London), February 1987.

By far, Eugene Lourié's best work was done with director Jean Renoir, who closely controlled all aspects of his films, including the visual. Perhaps Renoir's best-known and best-liked film is *Grand Illusion,* about French soldiers held in a German prison. The prison, actually in a castle, shot at a combination of locations in Alsace, has a grimly realistic atmosphere. It contrasts with the light and airy atmosphere of the Swiss farm to which the prisoners flee. *The Human Beast,* based on a Zola novel, gives the impression of having been

shot on location, but the railyard and railwaymen's homes were all created by Lourié. The dark, ramshackle buildings are an effective accompaniment for this tale of human depravity. Renoir's tendency to show many planes of depth within one camera shot is especially apparent in *The Rules of the Game.* Lourié's busy rooms and long hallways of the villa in which the socialities' verbal thrusts and foils take place provide excellent backgrounds for the camera's juxtapositions of characters.

Much of Lourié's work in the United States was done for mediocre productions, and he actually directed several typical science-fiction films. The first, *The Beast from 20,000 Fathoms,* had the most inventive effects. In the United States, he also had the opportunity to work with Renoir again. *The River,* shot on location in India, is noted for a brilliant use of color. To arrive at the desired color compositions, Lourié moved clumps of flowers and repainted trees in slightly different shades of green. It was not the last time a director would repaint natural scenery to achieve a special color effect; Michelangelo Antonioni did the same in 1964 for his famous film, *The Red Desert.*

Lourié discovered the essence of art direction in scouting a location for Renoir's rendition of a William Faulkner novel, *The Southerner,* for which he chose a California location that perfectly suited the story. He had found that the town in Texas where the story had actually taken place did not look at all right for the film. Lourié's simple conclusion could be considered an art director's credo: "The real truth is never as truthful as the invented truth."

—Lois Miklas

LUBALIN, Herbert (Frederick).

American typographer and graphic designer. Born in New York City, 17 March 1918. Studied at Cooper Union, New York, 1936–39. Worked on New York World's Fair exhibits, for Display Counselors, New York, 1939; freelance book designer, New York, 1939–41; art director, at Deutsch and Shea Advertising, New York, 1941–42, for *Men's Wear* magazine, Fairchild Publications, New York, 1942–43, and at Reis Advertising, New York, 1943–45; director, of Herb Lubalin Incorporated design firm, New York, 1946–69; president, Lubalin-Smith-Carnase design firm, New York, 1969–75; LSC & P Design Group, New York, 1976–78, and Herb Lubalin Associates design firm, New York, 1978; chairman, Lubalin Peckolick Associates, New York, 1980; also es-

tablished subsidiary firms Lubalin Delpire, in Paris, Lubalin Maxwell in London, Good Book Publishing, in New York, and Aki-Lubalin in Hawaii. Founder, with Aaron Burns, of Lubalin-Burns and Company, New York, 1970, International Typeface Corporation, New York, 1970. *Upper and Lower Case* typography magazine, New York, 1973, and Design Processing International, New York, 1976. Instructor, Cornell University, New York, and Syracuse University, New York; visiting professor, Cooper Union, New York. President and board member, Art Directors Club of New York; board member, American Institute of Graphic Arts; international president, Alliance Graphique Internationale. **Exhibitions:** Society of Typographic Arts, Chicago, 1957; American Institute of Graphic Arts, New York, 1958; Philadelphia School of Design, 1961; Gallery 303, New York, 1961. **Collections:** Museum of Modern Art, New York; Smithsonian Institution, Washington, D.C. Recipient: Art Director of the Year Award, National Society of Art Directors, 1962; American Television Festival Cleo Award, 1963; Lotus Club Award, 1973; 3 Gold Medals, Advertising Club of New York; 9 Gold Medals, and Hall of Fame Award, 1977, Art Directors Club of New York; Cooper Union Alumnus of the Year Award, 1980; American Institute of Graphic Arts Medal, 1981. *Died*(in New York) *25 May 1981.*

Works:

Avant Garde Gothic typeface, for the International Typeface Corporation, 1967.
Serif Gothic typeface, for the International Typeface Corporation, 1974.
ITC Lubalin Graph typeface, for the International Typeface Corporation, 1974.

Publications:

By LUBALIN: book—*Folio II,* New York 1968; articles—in *Graphis*(Zurich), March 1959; *Print*(New York), January 1964, May/June 1979; *Communication Arts*(Palo Alto), August/September 1969; *Form*(Cologne), no. 1, 1971.

On LUBALIN: books—*The New Graphic Design* by Karl Gerstner and Markus Kutter, Teufen and London 1959; *Typography* by Aaron Burns, New York 1961; *Who's Who in Graphic Art,* edited by Walter Amstutz, Zürich 1962, Dubendorf 1982; *Graphic Designers in the USA: 1,* edited by Henri Hillebrand, London 1971; *The Language of Graphics* by Edward Booth-Clibborn and Daniele Baroni, London 1980; *The Design Concept* by Allen Hurlburt, New York 1981; *The Conran Directory of Design,* edited by Stephen Bayley, London 1985; *Typographic Design: Form and Communication*

Herb Lubalin: *Mother & Child* typogram, 1980

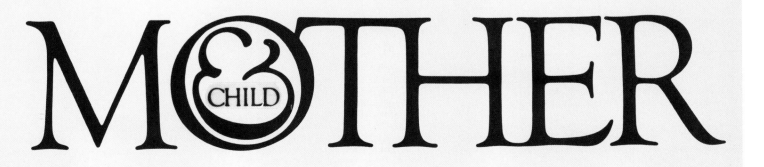

by Rob Carter, Ben Day and Philip Meggs, New York 1985.

One of the most influential American graphic designers, Herb Lubalin first achieved international acclaim during the 1950s for the originality of his typographic designs. Perhaps more than any other designer, Lubalin understood the design potential of phototypography, which during the 1960s, rapidly replaced hand-set metal type for display material and machine-set metal type for text matter. While metal type was constrained by limited sizes, fixed spacing between letters, and rigid geometric constraints, phototypography had the potential for large sizes, overlapping characters, distortions, and extremely tight line-, word-, or letter-spacing. Lubalin demonstrated for designers throughout the world how the new capabilities of photography could be used for both impact and communication. In Lubalin's most innovative work, message and visual form are inseparably united. Examples of this are Lubalin's typograms, or brief, visual, typographic poems. For example, in the proposed logo for "Mother & Child," the ampersand cradles the word "Child" inside the "O" of the word "mother" to symbolize the mother-and-child relationship.

Lubalin's Avant Garde family of typefaces was inspired by the logo that he designed for *Avant Garde* magazine. A geometric, sans serif type, it features capital ligatures that tightly interlock into unique alphabetic configurations.

Because typeface designs cannot be copyrighted, piracy often seriously erodes royalty compensation for them. To combat this problem, in partnership with phototypography pioneer Edward Rondthaler and typographer Aaron Burns, Lubalin established the International Typeface Corporation in 1970 to provide royalties to typeface designers while licensing and making fonts available to all manufacturers of typesetting equipment. This event dramatically expanded the production of original type designs. ITC published a bimonthly journal, *U&lc (Upper and Lower Case)* to publicize and demonstrate its typeface designs. Designed by Lubalin, *U&lc* had a complex, dynamic layout style that became a major graphic design influence during the 1970s. ITC typeface designs favored a large x-height (height of the lower-case x) and short ascenders and descenders to allow a larger optical size in text settings.

—Philip B. Meggs

LUSS, Gerald.
American interior designer. Born in Gloversville, New York, 7 October 1926. Studied at Rensselaer Polytechnic Institute, Troy, New York, 1945–48; Pratt Institute, Brooklyn, New York, 1946–48: BFA 1948. Married Ann Langhof in 1954(died, 1975); children: Jan, Jil, Gay and Jay; married Denise Feliziani in 1989; daughter: Jaclyn. Director of design and executive vice-president, at Designs for Business interior design firm, New York, 1948–65; founder-president and director of design, Luss/Kaplan and Associates, New York, 1965–87, and Gerald Luss and Associates, New York, from 1987. Formerly, visiting lecturer at Pratt Institute, Parsons School of Design, and Rhode Island School of Design. Addresses: 1060 Fifth Avenue, New York, New York 10128; 100 Truesdale Drive, Croton on Hudson, New York 10520, U.S.A.

Works:

Interior designs include—corporate office, for Capital Centre, Landover, Maryland; corporate office, for AVX Incorporated, New York; education facility, for K-12 Cerebral Palsy Foundation of Brooklyn, New York; corporate office, for Corning Glass, New York; Coney Island leisure facility, Brooklyn, New York; national headquarters, for the Federal Aviation Administration, Washington, D.C., and regional offices in Atlanta, Oklahoma City and Los Angeles; FAA Air Route Traffic Control Centers, in Hawaii, Atlanta, and Miami; corporate headquarters, for Focus Technologies Incorporated, Washington, D.C.; offices, for Geers Gross Advertising, New York; Institute for Geriatric Care, for Long Island Jewish Hospital, New York; underground security and living facilities, for Iron Mountain Incorporated, Hudson, New York; offices, for Israel Discount Bank, New York; television broadcast facilities and office in Flint, Miami, Nashville, Norfolk and Phoenix, for Knight-Ridder Incorporated; offices, for Maritime Overseas Corporation, New York; clubhouse and dining rooms, for Montauk Golf and Racquet Club, Long Island, New York; news bureaux in Atlanta, Boston, Los Angeles, New York, Washington and Paris, for NBC National Broadcasting Company; country club and corporate offices, for Nevada Equities Incorporated, Las Vegas; ten-year expansion program, for North Shore University Hospital, Manhasset, Long Island, New York; United States Headquarters, for Polly Peck International, New York; corporate headquarters, for Post-Newsweek Stations Incorporated, Washington, D.C.; offices, for Sam Minskoff and Sons Incorporated, New York; offices, for South Nassau Medical Center, New York; offices and banking facilities, for Sumitomo Bank, New York; offices, for Time Incorporated, New York; offices and studios, for WDIV Television, Detroit, corporate offices, for World Wide Volkswagen Corporation, New York; major residential developments in Bal Harbor, Bogota, Kings Point, Mexico City, Miami, New York, Palm Beach and Washington, D.C.

Publications:

On LUSS: books—*AIA Guide to New York,* edited by Norval White and Ellen Willenski, New York 1963; *Interiors Book of Offices,* New York and London 1965; *Offices/Office Space,* New York 1965; *Interior Design: An Introduction to Architectural Interiors* by Arnold Friedmann, John F. Pile and Forrest Wilson, New York and Amsterdam 1970, 1976.

I believe that the concept of order is to be most devoutly desired. In the quest for realization of such order, it is necessary that the function of every element—whether supportive or purely aesthetic—existing in any given environment be most clearly defined and in evidence in its purest state. To paraphrase, I believe that the two lines should not be used if one line will enunciate as clearly. This concept does not eliminate the desirability or inevitability of any given design expression or historic period as, for example, the most beautiful of the Victorian era in which the simplest expression was achievable only with a multiplicity of profusion of many single lines still representative of the most direct expression of that area.

I have endeavored to achieve two goals in my work as a designer: 1) a redefinition of interior design as interior architecture, in which capacity the designer is responsible for and responsive to all elements realizing the total environment, rather than responsive only to cosmetic declarations; 2)

the education of the client to the realistic necessity of the evolution of space on the basis of the final use of such space by its occupants, with the relegation of the design of the enveloping skin as simply the logical, final, creative step, rather than the reverse—in which the envelope-esthetics are conceived in a vacuum and the functional and esthetic environment is then forced to conform to this enclosure, which, in the vast majority of instances, cannot realize the full potential or expression of functional and environmental prerequisites.

—Gerald Luss

Gerald Luss is the driving force and the creative spirit of the firm Luss/Kaplan and Associates. Before forming his present company, he had gone straight from Pratt institute to Designs for Business, where he remained for seventeen years, bringing the firm to the forefront of American interior design and exerting an enormously strong influence upon design in the United States. Designs for Business was one of the largest and most highly respected firms during the 1950s and early 1960s. Under Luss's direction, the staff grew to more than 100 at peak periods, and just about every one of its major projects found its way into national design magazines. Luss was known as one of the stars in the field of contract design, and although he pioneered the team concept at Designs for Business, it was clearly his personal influence that determined the shape of every project. Some of the most important commisions included the huge Time-Life project, the Federal Aviation Agency, and the Internal Revenue Service.

Luss formed his own firm when he realized that a design firm can operate more efficiently when each job is assigned to a single designer, yet the high-quality work produced by Luss/Kaplan is very much controlled and influenced by Luss. Projects have included a number of health care facilities, large corporate offices, hotels, and governmental agencies. Since Luss/Kaplan does not engage in any promotional activities, all clients must find the firm on the basis of Luss's reputation.

Luss is a designer with a passion for order, clarity, and function. He insists upon making spaces work as background for their occupants. However, even though this Luss/Kaplan philosophy may consciously encourage understatement, each project turns out to be well solved, innovative, and esthetically satisfying. Luss is a working prodigy who puts in incredibly long hours, yet he has found time to lecture at Pratt Institute, the Parsons School of Design, and the Rhode Island School of Design.

—Arnold Friedmann

LUTZ, Hans-Rudolf.
Swiss typographer and graphic designer. Born in Zürich, 14 January 1939. Educated at primary and secondary schools in Zürich, 1946–54; apprenticed as typesetter to Orell Füssli printers, Zürich, 1955–58; studied under Emil Ruder and Robert Buchler, at the Allgemeine Gewerbeschule, Basel, 1963. Worked as a typesetter and printer, for Orell Füssli, Anton Schob and Arthur Kumin, in Zurich, 1959–60; freelance typesetter, typographer and designer, Zürich, from 1961: leader of Expression Typographique group, at Studio Hollenstein, Paris, 1964–66; founder-publisher, of Lutz Verlag

Gerald Luss: Royal National Bank interior, 1988

352 LUTZ

Die Geschichte aller bisherigen Gesellschaft ist die Geschichte von Klassenkämpfen. Freier und Sklave, Patrizier und Plebejer, Baron und Leibeigener, Zunftbürger und Gesell, kurz, Unterdrücker und Unterdrückte standen in stetem Gegensatz zueinander, führten einen ununterbrochenen, bald versteckten, bald offenen Kampf, einen Kampf, der jedesmal mit einer revolutionären Umgestaltung der ganzen Gesellschaft endete oder mit dem gemeinsamen Untergang der kämpfenden Klassen. In den früheren Epochen der Geschichte finden wir fast überall eine vollständige Gliederung der Gesellschaft in verschiedene Stände, eine mannigfaltige Abstufung der gesellschaftlichen Stellungen. Im alten Rom haben wir Patrizier, Ritter, Plebejer, Sklaven; im Mittelalter Feudalherren, Vasallen, Zunftbürger, Gesellen, Leibeigene und noch dazu in fast jeder von diesen Klassen wieder besondere Abstufungen. Die aus dem Untergang der feudalen Gesellschaft hervorgegangene moderne bürgerliche Gesellschaft hat die Klassengegensätze nicht aufgehoben. Sie hat nur neue Klassen, neue Bedingungen der Unterdrückung, neue Gestaltungen des Kampfes an die Stelle der alten gesetzt. Unsere Epoche, die Epoche der Bourgeoisie, zeichnet sich jedoch dadurch aus, dass sie die Klassengegensätze vereinfacht hat. Die ganze Gesellschaft spaltet sich mehr und mehr in zwei grosse feindliche Lager, in zwei grosse einander direkt gegenüberstehende Klassen: Bourgeoisie und Proletariat. Aus den Leibeigenen gingen die Pfahlbürger der ersten Städte hervor: daraus entwickelten sich Elemente der Bourgeoisie. Die Entdeckung Amerikas, die Umschiffung Afrikas schufen der Bourgeoisie neues Terrain. Der ostindische und chinesische Markt, die Kolonisierung von Amerika, der Austausch mit den Kolonien, die Vermehrung der Tauschmittel und der Waren überhaupt gaben dem Handel, der Schiffahrt, der Industrie einen nie gekannten Aufschwung und damit dem revolutionären Element in der zerfallenden feudalen Gesellschaft eine rasche Entwicklung. Die bisherige feudale oder zünftige Betriebsweise der Industrie reichte nicht mehr aus für den mit neuen Märkten anwachsenden Bedarf. Die Manufaktur trat an ihre Stelle. Die Zunftmeister wurden verdrängt durch den industriellen Mittelstand; die Teilung der Arbeit zwischen den verschiedenen Korporationen verschwand vor der Teilung der Arbeit in der einzelnen Werkstatt selbst. Aber immer wuchsen die Märkte, immer stieg der Bedarf. Auch die Manufaktur reichte nicht mehr aus. Da revolutionierten Dampfmaschinen die industrielle Produktion. An die Stelle der Manufaktur trat die moderne grosse Industrie, an die Stelle des industriellen Mittelstandes traten die industriellen Millionäre, die Chefs ganzer industrieller Armeen, die modernen Bourgeois. Die grosse Industrie hat den Weltmarkt hergestellt, den die Entdeckung Amerikas vorbereitete. Der Weltmarkt hat dem Handel, der Schiffahrt, den Landkommunikationen eine unermessliche Entwicklung gegeben. Diese hat wieder auf die Ausdehnung der Industrie zurückgewirkt, und in demselben Masse, worin Industrie, Handel, Schiffahrt, Eisenbahnen sich ausdehnten, in demselben Masse entwickelte sich die Bourgeoisie, vermehrte sie ihre Kapitalien, drängte sie alle vom Mittelalter her überlieferten Klassen in den Hintergrund. Wir sehen also, wie die moderne Bourgeoisie selbst das Produkt eines langen Entwicklungsganges, einer Reihe von Umwälzungen in der Produktions- und Verkehrsweise ist. Jede dieser Entwicklungsstufen der Bourgeoisie war begleitet von einem entsprechenden politischen Fortschritt. Unterdrückter Stand unter der Herrschaft der Feudalherren, bewaffnete und sich selbst verwaltende Assoziation in der Kommune, hier unabhängige städtische Republik, dort dritter steuerpflichtiger Stand der Monarchie, dann zur Zeit der Manufaktur Gegengewicht gegen den Adel in der ständischen oder in der absoluten Monarchie, Hauptgrundlage der grossen Monarchien überhaupt, erkämpfte sie sich endlich seit der Herstellung der grossen Industrie und des Weltmarktes im modernen Repräsentativstaat die ausschliessliche politische Herrschaft. Die moderne Staatsgewalt ist nur ein Ausschuss, der die gemeinschaftlichen Geschäfte der ganzen Bourgeoisklasse verwaltet. Die Bourgeoisie hat in der Geschichte eine höchst revolutionäre Rolle gespielt. Die Bourgeoisie, wo sie zur Herrschaft gekommen, hat alle feudalen, patriarchalischen Verhältnisse zerstört. Sie hat die buntscheckigen Feudalbande, die den Menschen an seinen natürlichen Vorgesetzten knüpften, unbarmherzig zerrissen und kein anderes Band zwischen Mensch und Mensch übriggelassen, als das nackte Interesse, als die gefühllose «bare Zahlung». Sie hat die heiligen Schauer der frommen Schwärmerei, der ritterlichen Begeisterung, der spiessbürgerlichen Wehmut in dem eiskalten Wasser egoistischer Berechnung ertränkt. Sie hat die persönliche Würde in den Tauschwert aufgelöst und an die Stelle der zahllosen verbrieften und wohlerworbenen Freiheiten die eine gewissenlose Handelsfreiheit gesetzt. Sie hat, mit einem Wort, an die Stelle der mit religiösen und politischen Illusionen verhüllten Ausbeutung die offene, unverschämte, direkte, dürre Ausbeutung gesetzt. Die Bourgeoisie hat alle ehrwürdigen und mit frommer Scheu betrachteten Tätigkeiten ihres Heiligenscheins entkleidet. Sie hat den Arzt, den Juristen, den Pfaffen, den Poeten, den Mann der Wissenschaft in ihre bezahlten Lohnarbeiter verwandelt. Die Bourgeoisie hat dem Familienverhältnis seinen rührend-sentimentalen Schleier abgerissen und es auf ein reines Geldverhältnis zurückgeführt. Die Bourgeoisie hat enthüllt, wie die brutale Kraftäusserung, die die Reaktion so sehr am Mittelalter bewundert, in der trägsten Bärenhäuterei ihre passende Ergänzung fand. Erst sie hat bewiesen, was die Tätigkeit der Menschen zustande bringen kann. Sie hat ganz andere Wunderwerke vollbracht als ägyptische Pyramiden, römische Wasserleitungen und gotische Kathedralen, sie hat ganz andere Züge ausgeführt als Völkerwanderungen und Kreuzzüge. Die Bourgeoisie kann nicht existieren, ohne die Produktionsinstrumente, also die Produktionsverhältnisse, also sämtliche gesellschaftlichen Verhältnisse fortwährend zu revolutionieren. Unveränderte Beibehaltung der alten Produktionsweise war dagegen die erste Existenzbedingung aller früheren industriellen Klassen. Die fortwährende Umwälzung der Produktion, die ununterbrochene Erschütterung aller gesellschaftlichen Zustände, die ewige Unsicherheit und Bewegung zeichnet die Bourgeoisepoche vor allen anderen aus. Alle festen, eingerosteten Verhältnisse mit ihrem Gefolge von altehrwürdigen Vorstellungen und Anschauungen werden aufgelöst, alle neugebildeten veralten, ehe sie verknöchern können. Alles Ständische und Stehende verdampft, alles Heilige wird entweiht, und die Menschen sind endlich gezwungen, ihre Lebensstellung, ihre gegenseitigen Beziehungen mit nüchternen Augen anzusehen. Das Bedürfnis nach einem stets ausgedehnteren Absatz für ihre Produkte jagt die Bourgeoisie über die ganze Erdkugel. Überall muss sie sich einnisten, überall anbauen, überall Verbindungen herstellen. Die Bourgeoisie hat durch ihre Exploitation des Weltmarktes die Produktion und Konsumation aller Länder kosmopolitisch gestaltet. Sie hat zum grossen Bedauern der Reaktionäre den nationalen Boden der Industrie unter den Füssen weggezogen. Die uralten nationalen Industrien sind vernichtet worden und werden noch täglich vernichtet. Sie werden verdrängt durch neue Industrien, deren Einführung eine Lebensfrage für alle zivilisierten Nationen wird, durch Industrien, die nicht mehr einheimische Rohstoffe, sondern den entlegensten Zonen angehörige Rohstoffe verarbeiten und deren Fabrikate nicht nur im Lande selbst, sondern in allen Weltteilen verbraucht werden. An die Stelle der alten, durch Landeserzeugnisse befriedigten Bedürfnisse treten neue, welche die Produkte der entferntesten Länder und Klimate zu ihrer Befriedigung erheischen. An die Stelle der alten lokalen und nationalen Selbstgenügsamkeit und Abgeschlossenheit tritt ein allseitiger Verkehr, eine allseitige Abhängigkeit der Nationen voneinander. Und wie in der materiellen, so auch in der geistigen Produktion. Die geistigen Erzeugnisse der einzelnen Nationen werden Gemeingut. Die nationale Einseitigkeit und Beschränktheit wird mehr und mehr unmöglich, und aus den vielen nationalen und lokalen Literaturen bildet sich eine Weltliteratur. Die Bourgeoisie reisst durch die rasche Verbesserung aller Produktionsinstrumente, durch die unendlich erleichterten Kommunikationen, auch die barbarischsten Nationen in die Zivilisation. Die wohlfeilen Preise ihrer Waren sind die schwere Artillerie, mit der sie alle chinesischen Mauern in den Grund schiesst, mit der sie den hartnäckigsten Fremdenhass der Barbaren zur Kapitulation zwingt. Sie zwingt alle Nationen, die Produktionsweise der Bourgeoisie sich anzueignen, wenn sie nicht zugrunde gehen wollen; sie zwingt sie, die sogenannte Zivilisation bei sich selbst einzuführen, d.h. Bourgeois zu werden. Mit einem Wort, sie schafft sich eine Welt nach ihrem eigenen Bilde. Die Bourgeoisie hat das Land der Herrschaft der Stadt unterworfen. Sie hat enorme Städte geschaffen, sie hat die Zahl der städtischen Bevölkerung gegenüber der ländlichen in sehr hohem Grade vermehrt und so einen bedeutenden Teil der Bevölkerung dem Idiotismus des Landlebens entrissen. Wie sie das Land von der Stadt, hat sie die barbarischen und halbbarbarischen Länder von den zivilisierten, die Bauernvölker von den Bourgeoisvölkern, den Orient vom Okzident abhängig gemacht. Die Bourgeoisie hebt mehr und mehr die Zersplitterung der Produktionsmittel, des Besitzes und der Bevölkerung auf. Sie hat die Bevölkerung agglomeriert, die Produktionsmittel zentralisiert und das Eigentum in wenigen Händen konzentriert. Die notwendige Folge hiervon war die politische Zentralisation. Unabhängige, fast nur verbündete Provinzen mit verschiedenen Interessen, Gesetzen, Regierungen und Zöllen wurden zusammengedrängt in eine Nation, eine Regierung, ein Gesetz, ein nationales Klasseninteresse, eine Douanenlinie. Die Bourgeoisie hat in ihrer kaum hundertjährigen Klassenherrschaft massenhaftere und kolossalere Produktionskräfte geschaffen als alle vergangenen Generationen zusammen. Unterjochung der Naturkräfte, Maschinerie, Anwendung der Chemie auf Industrie und Ackerbau, Dampfschiffahrt, Eisenbahnen, elektrische Telegraphen, Urbarmachung ganzer Weltteile, Schiffbarmachung der Flüsse, ganze aus dem Boden hervorgestampfte Bevölkerungen – welches frühere Jahrhundert ahnte, dass solche Produktionskräfte im Schosse der gesellschaftlichen Arbeit schlummerten. Wir haben also gesehn: Die Produktions- und Verkehrsmittel, auf deren Grundlage sich die Bourgeoisie heranbildete, wurden in der feudalen Gesellschaft erzeugt. Auf einer gewissen Stufe der Entwicklung dieser Produktions- und Verkehrsmittel entsprachen die feudale Gesellschaft produzierte und austauschte, die feudale Organisation der Agrikultur und Manufaktur, mit einem Wort die feudalen Eigentumsverhältnisse den schon entwickelten Produktivkräften nicht mehr. Sie hemmten die Produktion, statt sie zu fördern. Sie verwandelten sich in ebenso viele Fesseln. Sie mussten gesprengt werden, sie wurden gesprengt. An ihre Stelle trat die freie Konkurrenz mit der ihr angemessenen gesellschaftlichen und politischen Konstitution, mit der ökonomischen und politischen Herrschaft der Bourgeoisklasse. Unter unsern Augen geht eine ähnliche Bewegung vor. Die bürgerlichen Produktions- und Verkehrsverhältnisse, die bürgerlichen Eigentumsverhältnisse, die moderne bürgerliche Gesellschaft, die so gewaltige Produktions- und Verkehrsmittel hervorgezaubert hat, gleicht dem Hexenmeister, der die unterirdischen Gewalten nicht mehr zu beherrschen vermag, die er heraufbeschwor. Seit Dezennien ist die Geschichte der Industrie und des Handels nur die Geschichte der Empörung der modernen Produktivkräfte gegen die Eigentumsverhältnisse, welche die Lebensbedingungen der Bourgeoisie und ihrer Herrschaft sind. Es genügt, die Handelskrisen zu nennen, welche in ihrer periodischen Wiederkehr immer drohender die Existenz der ganzen bürgerlichen Gesellschaft in Frage stellen. In den Handelskrisen wird ein grosser Teil nicht nur der erzeugten Produkte, sondern der bereits geschaffenen Produktivkräfte regelmässig vernichtet. In den Krisen bricht eine gesellschaftliche Epidemie aus, welche allen früheren Epochen als ein Widersinn erschienen wäre – die Epidemie der Überproduktion. Die Gesellschaft findet sich plötzlich in einen Zustand momentaner Barbarei zurückversetzt; eine Hungersnot, ein allgemeiner Vernichtungskrieg scheinen ihr alle Lebensmittel abgeschnitten zu haben; die Industrie, der Handel scheinen vernichtet, und warum? Weil sie zuviel Zivilisation, zuviel Lebensmittel, zuviel Industrie, zuviel Handel besitzt. Die Produktivkräfte, die ihr zur Verfügung stehn, dienen nicht mehr zur Beförderung der bürgerlichen Eigentumsverhältnisse; im Gegenteil, sie sind zu gewaltig für diese Verhältnisse geworden, sie werden von ihnen gehemmt; und sobald sie dieses Hemmnis überwinden, bringen sie die ganze bürgerliche Gesellschaft in Unordnung, gefährden sie die Existenz des bürgerlichen Eigentums. Die bürgerlichen Verhältnisse sind zu eng geworden, um den von ihnen erzeugten Reichtum zu fassen. – Wodurch überwindet die Bourgeoisie die Krisen? Einerseits durch die erzwungene Vernichtung einer Masse von Produktivkräften; andererseits durch die Eroberung neuer Märkte und die gründlichere Ausbeutung alter Märkte. Wodurch also? Dadurch, dass sie allseitigere und gewaltigere Krisen vorbereitet und die Mittel, den Krisen vorzubeugen, vermindert. Die Waffen, womit die Bourgeoisie den Feudalismus zu Boden geschlagen hat, richten sich jetzt gegen die Bourgeoisie selbst. Aber die Bourgeoisie hat nicht nur die Waffen geschmiedet, die ihr den Tod bringen; sie hat auch die Männer gezeugt, die diese Waffen führen werden – die modernen Arbeiter, die Proletarier. In demselben Masse, worin sich die Bourgeoisie, d.h. das Kapital, entwickelt, in demselben Masse entwickelt sich das Proletariat, die Klasse der modernen Arbeiter, die nur solange leben, als sie Arbeit finden, und diese auch ausüben können, und die nur so lange Arbeit finden, als ihre Arbeit das Kapital vermehrt. Diese Arbeiter, die sich stückweise verkaufen müssen, sind eine Ware, wie jeder andere Handelsartikel, und daher gleichmässig allen Wechselfällen der Konkurrenz, allen Schwankungen des Marktes ausgesetzt. Die Arbeit der Proletarier hat durch die Ausdehnung der Maschinerie und die Teilung der Arbeit allen selbständigen Charakter und damit allen Reiz für den Arbeiter verloren. Er wird ein blosses Zubehör der Maschine, von dem nur der einfachste, eintönigste, am leichtesten erlernbare Handgriff verlangt wird. Die Kosten, die der Arbeiter verursacht, beschränken sich daher fast nur auf die Lebensmittel, die er zu seinem Unterhalt und zur Fortpflanzung seiner Rasse bedarf. Der Preis einer Ware also, auch der Arbeit, ist aber gleich ihren Produktionskosten. In demselben Masse, in dem die Arbeit wächst, nimmt daher der Lohn ab. Noch mehr, in demselben Masse, wie Maschinerie und Teilung der Arbeit zunehmen, in demselben Masse nimmt auch die Masse der Arbeit zu, sei es durch Vermehrung der Arbeitsstunden, sei es durch Vermehrung der in einer gegebenen Zeit geforderten Arbeit, beschleunigten Lauf der Maschinen usw. Die moderne Industrie hat die kleine Werkstube des patriarchalischen Meisters in die grosse Fabrik des industriellen Kapitalisten verwandelt. Arbeitermassen, so in der Fabrik zusammengedrängt, werden soldatisch organisiert. Sie werden als gemeine Industriesoldaten unter die Aufsicht einer vollständigen Hierarchie von Unteroffizieren und Offizieren gestellt. Sie sind nicht nur Knechte der Bourgeoisklasse, des Bourgeoisstaates, sie sind täglich und stündlich geknechtet von der Maschine, von dem Aufseher und vor allem von den einzelnen fabrizierenden Bourgeois selbst. Diese Despotie ist um so kleinlicher, gehässiger, erbitternder, je offener sie den Erwerb als ihren Zweck proklamiert. Je weniger die Handarbeit Geschicklichkeit und Kraftäusserung erheischt, d.h. je mehr die moderne Industrie sich entwickelt, desto mehr wird die Arbeit der Männer durch die der Weiber verdrängt. Geschlechts- und Altersunterschiede haben keine gesellschaftliche Geltung mehr für die Arbeiterklasse. Es gibt nur noch Arbeitsinstrumente, die je nach Alter und Geschlecht verschiedene Kosten machen. Ist die Ausbeutung des Arbeiters durch den Fabrikanten so weit beendigt, dass er seinen Arbeitslohn bar ausgezahlt erhält, so fallen die anderen Teile der Bourgeoisie über ihn her, der Hausbesitzer, der Krämer, der Pfandleiher usw. Die bisherigen kleinen Mittelstände, die kleinen Industriellen, Kaufleute und Rentiers, die Handwerker und Bauern, alle diese Klassen fallen ins Proletariat hinab, teils dadurch, dass ihr kleines Kapital für den Betrieb der grossen Industrie nicht ausreicht und der Konkurrenz mit den grösseren Kapitalisten erliegt, teils dadurch, dass ihre Geschicklichkeit von neuen Produktionsweisen entwertet wird. So rekrutiert sich das Proletariat aus allen Klassen der Bevölkerung. Das Proletariat macht verschiedene Entwicklungsstufen durch. Sein Kampf gegen die Bourgeoisie beginnt mit seiner Existenz. Im Anfangsstadium kämpfen die einzelnen Arbeiter, dann die Arbeiter einer Fabrik, dann die Arbeiter eines Arbeitszweiges an einem Ort gegen den einzelnen Bourgeois, der sie direkt ausbeutet. Sie richten ihre Angriffe nicht gegen die bürgerlichen Produktionsverhältnisse, sie richten sie gegen die Produktionsinstrumente selbst; sie vernichten die fremden konkurrierenden Waren, sie zerschlagen die Maschinen, sie stecken die Fabriken in Brand, sie suchen die untergegangene Stellung des mittelalterlichen Arbeiters wieder zu erringen. Auf dieser Stufe bilden die Arbeiter eine über das ganze Land zerstreute und durch die Konkurrenz zersplitterte Masse. Massenhaftes Zusammenhalten der Arbeiter ist nicht die Folge ihrer eigenen Vereinigung sondern die der Bourgeoisie, die zur Erreichung ihrer eigenen politischen Zwecke das ganze Proletariat in Bewegung setzen muss und es einstweilen noch kann. Auf dieser Stufe bekämpfen die Proletarier also nicht ihre Feinde, die Reste der absoluten Monarchie, die Grundeigentümer, die nichtindustriellen Bourgeois, die Kleinbürger. Die ganze geschichtliche Bewegung ist so in den Händen der Bourgeoisie konzentriert; jeder Sieg, der so errungen wird, ist ein Sieg der Bourgeoisie. Aber mit der Entwicklung der Industrie vermehrt sich nicht nur das Proletariat; es wird in grösseren Massen zusammengedrängt, seine Kraft wächst, und es fühlt sie mehr. Die Interessen, die Lebenslagen innerhalb des Proletariats gleichen sich immer mehr aus, indem die Maschinerie mehr und mehr die Unterschiede der Arbeit verwischt und den Lohn fast überall auf ein gleich niedriges Niveau herabdrückt. Die wachsende Konkurrenz der Bourgeois unter sich und die daraus hervorgehenden Handelskrisen machen den Lohn der Arbeiter immer schwankender; die immer rascher sich entwickelnde, unaufhörliche Verbesserung der Maschinerie macht ihre ganze Lebensstellung immer unsicherer; immer mehr nehmen die Kollisionen zwischen dem einzelnen Arbeiter und dem einzelnen Bourgeois den Charakter von Kollisionen zweier Klassen an. Die Arbeiter beginnen damit, Koalitionen gegen die Bourgeois zu bilden; sie treten zusammen zur Behauptung ihres Arbeitslohns. Sie stiften selbst dauernde Assoziationen, um sich für die gelegentlichen Empörungen zu verproviantieren. Stellenweis bricht der Kampf in Emeuten aus. Von Zeit zu Zeit siegen die Arbeiter, aber nur vorübergehend. Das eigentliche Resultat ihrer Kämpfe ist nicht der unmittelbare Erfolg, sondern die immer weiter um sich greifende Vereinigung der Arbeiter. Sie wird befördert durch die wachsenden Kommunikationsmittel, die von der grossen Industrie erzeugt werden und die Arbeiter der verschiedenen Lokalitäten miteinander in Verbindung setzen. Es bedarf aber bloss der Verbindung, um die vielen Lokalkämpfe von überall gleichem Charakter zu einem nationalen, zu einem Klassenkampf zu zentralisieren. Jeder Klassenkampf ist aber ein politischer Kampf. Und die Vereinigung, zu der die Bürger des Mittelalters mit ihren Vizinalwegen Jahrhunderte bedurften, bringen die modernen Proletarier mit den Eisenbahnen in wenigen Jahren zustande. Diese Organisation der Proletarier zur Klasse, und damit zur politischen Partei, wird jeden Augenblick wieder gesprengt durch die Konkurrenz unter den Arbeitern selbst. Aber sie ersteht immer wieder, stärker, fester, mächtiger. Sie erzwingt die Anerkennung einzelner Interessen der Arbeiter in Gesetzesform, indem sie die Spaltungen der Bourgeoisie selbst benutzt. So die Zehnstundenbill in England. Die Kollisionen der alten Gesellschaft überhaupt fördern mannigfach den Entwicklungsgang des Proletariats. Die Bourgeoisie befindet sich in fortwährendem Kampfe: anfangs gegen die Aristokratie; später gegen die Teile der Bourgeoisie selbst, deren Interessen mit dem Fortschritt der Industrie in Widerspruch geraten; stets gegen die Bourgeoisie aller auswärtigen Länder. In allen diesen Kämpfen sieht sie sich genötigt, an das Proletariat zu appellieren, seine Hilfe in Anspruch zu nehmen und es so in die politische Bewegung hineinzureissen. Sie selbst führt also dem Proletariat ihre eigenen Bildungselemente, d.h. Waffen gegen sich selbst, zu. Es werden ferner, wie wir sahen, durch den Fortschritt der Industrie ganze Bestandteile der herrschenden Klasse ins Proletariat hinabgeworfen oder wenigstens in ihren Lebensbedingungen bedroht. Auch sie führen dem Proletariat eine Masse Bildungselemente zu. In Zeiten endlich, wo der Klassenkampf sich der Entscheidung nähert, nimmt der Auflösungsprozess innerhalb der herrschenden Klasse, innerhalb der ganzen alten Gesellschaft, einen so heftigen, so grellen Charakter an, dass ein kleiner Teil der herrschenden Klasse sich von ihr lossagt und sich der revolutionären Klasse anschliesst, der Klasse, welche die Zukunft in ihren Händen trägt. Wie daher früher ein Teil des Adels zur Bourgeoisie überging, so geht jetzt ein Teil der Bourgeoisie zum Proletariat über, und namentlich ein Teil der Bourgeoisideologen, welche zum theoretischen Verständnis der ganzen geschichtlichen

Hans-Rudolf Lutz: *Communist Manifesto/Karl Marx* typographic design, 1968

publications, Zurich, from 1966; co-founder and publisher, *Verlagsgenossenschaft,* Zürich, 1971–80; visual director of UnknownmiX multimedia performance group, Zürich, from 1983. Contributor from 1966, and co-editor from 1980, of *Typographische Monatsblätter,* St. Gallen. Instructor in design, Cours 19 Evening School, Paris, 1964–66; instructor in typography, Kunstgewerbeschule, Zürich, 1966–70; founder of typography department, and instructor in design, at the Schule für Gestaltung, Lucerne, from 1968; guest instructor, at F + F Schule für Experimentelle Gestaltung, Zürich, University of Alberta, Edmonton, Ohio State University, Columbus, and Schule für Gestaltung, Zurich, from 1983. Address: Lessingstrasse 11, 8002 Zürich, Switzerland.

Works:

Zufall und Spiel kinetic poster, for the Allgemeine Gewerbeschule, Basel, 1963.
Univers type program advertisement and poster series, for the Monotype Corporation, Bern, 1964.
Die Varierung des Gleichen series of cover designs, for *Typographische Monatsblätter,* St. Gallen, 1965.
Communist Manifesto/Karl Marx poster, for Ernst Gloor Typesetter, Zurich, 1968.
Über die Russische Revolution/Rosa Luxemburg poster, for Helvetische Typografia, Basel, 1971.
Caractere Hollenstein typeface specimen series, for Hollenstein Phototype, Paris, 1972.

Kontinuierliche Stadtentwicklung book design, for Birkhauser Verlag, Basel, 1975.
Englersatz poster series, for Englersatz, Zurich, 1976.
Gestaltung ist Information series of cover designs, for *Typographische Monatsblätter,* St. Gallen, 1977.
My Edmonton Journal book design, for Lutz Verlag, Zurich, 1977.
CIAM: Congres International d'Architecture Moderne book design, for Birkhauser Verlag, Basel, 1979.
UX, Loops, Mix 3, Snacks, Whaba record sleeves and labels, for UnknownmiX/Recrec Music, Zurich, from 1983.
Herzblut, populare Gestaltung in der Schweiz exhibition poster, for the Museum fur Ges-

taltung, Zurich, 1987.
Ausbildung in typografischer Gestaltung book design, for Lutz Verlag, Zurich, 1987.
Britische Sicht, Fotografie aus England exhibition poster, for the Museum fur Gestaltung, Zurich, 1988.
UnknownmiX in Concert at the Fri-Son 60-minute video, for UX and Recrec Music, Zurich, 1989.
Die Verpackung der Verpackung der Verpackung book design, for Lutz Verlag, Zurich, 1989.

Publications:

By LUTZ: books—*Grafik in Kuba*, Zürich 1971; *Experiment F + F, 1965-71*, Zürich 1971; *Edmonton Journal*, Zürich 1977; *1979: Eine Art Gescichte*, Zürich 1980; *Bilderbuch 1: Menshen*, Zürich 1986; *Bilderbuch 2: Gesichter*, Zürich 1986; *Ausbildung in Typografischer Gestaltung*, Zürich 1987; audiovisuals—*Grakifer auf der Strasse*, 1979; *A. Zerfall, Unordnung: B. Reproduktion und Druck*, 1980; *Stadte für Tote: Stadte für Lebende*, 1980; *Über die fliessende Grenze zwischen verbalen und visuellen Information*, 1981.

On LUTZ: book—*Typography Today* by Helmut Schmid, Tokyo 1980; articles—in *Idée . . à Jour*(Basel), November 1988; *Der Alltag*(Zurich), February 1989.

LUZZATI, Emanuele.
Italian illustrator, filmmaker, stage and graphic designer. Born in Genoa, 3 June 1921. Studied at the Ecole des Beaux-Arts, Lausanne, 1940–45. Freelance stage and graphic designer, Genoa, from 1945, and animated film designer, from 1957. Professor of theatre design, Accademia di Arte Drammatica, Rome, 1967–82, and Centro Arti e Mestieri dello Spettacolo, Rome, 1982–83. **Exhibitions:** Venice Biennale, 1972; *107 Grafici dell'AGI*, Castello Sforzesco, Milan 1974; *Il Sipario Magico*, Galera Nazionale, Milan, 1982 (toured); Genoa, 1984; Pontremoli, 1985; Israel Museum, Jerusalem, 1986; Galleria Nuages, Milan, 1987; Comune di Parma, 1987; Galleria Giulia, Rome, 1988; Casa del Mantegna, Mantova, 1988; Teatro Nazionale, Budapest, 1989. Recipient: Ceramics Prize, Cannes, 1955; Bratislava Biennale Prize, 1967; Golden Rose Award, Albissola, 1970; Premio Andersen-Baia delle Favole, Sestrilevante, 1982; Ubu Award, Milan, 1982; Stage Production Prize, Verona and Milan, 1987. Member, Alliance Graphique Internationale. Address: Via Caffaro 12A, Apt. 7, 16125 Genoa, Italy.

Works:

Stage productions include—*Lea Lebowitz*, Teatro Nuovo, Milan, 1947; *Le Allegre Comari di Windsor*, Teatro dei Parchi, Nervi, 1949; *Peer Gynt*, Teatro d'Arte Italiano, 1950; *La Celestina*, Piccolo Teatro Eleonora Duse, Genoa, 1952; *La Diavolessa*, Teatro La Fenice, at the *Biennale*, Venice, 1952; *Il malato immaginario*, Piccolo Teatro Eleonora Duse, Genoa, 1953; *Tieste*, Teatro d'Arte Italiano, 1953; *Mefistofele*, Maggio Musicale Fiorentiono, 1953–54; *Colombe*, Piccolo Teatro Eleonora Duse, Genoa, 1954; *Nabucco*, Maggio Musicale Fiorentino, 1955; *Volpone*, Piccolo Teatro Eleonora Duse, Genoa, 1955; *Il figliol prodigo*, Maggio Musicale Fiorentino, 1957; *La Venere prigioniera*, Maggio Musicale Fiorentino, 1957; *Molto rumore per nulla*, Teatro Stabile, Trieste, 1957; *Renard*, Maggio Musicale Fiorentino, 1958; *Job*, Maggio Musicale Fiorentino, 1958; *Mavra*, Teatro Massimo, Palermo, 1959; *Il Cordovano*, Piccola Scala, Milan, 1959; *Giochi e favole per bambini: Girotondo, Gli abiti nuovi del re, Le lettere dell'alfabeto, Lo scoiattolo in gamba, Comica finale, La bambola malata, Ballettto, L'usignolo dell'imperatore*, and *Nardiello*, Teatro La Fenice, at the *Biennale*, Venice, 1960; *La Barraca*, Teatro del Lido, at the *Biennale*, Venice, 1960; *Santa Giovanna*, Teatro Mercadante, Naples, 1960; *La Cenerentola*, Teatro alla Scala, Milan, 1960; *Le Menage de Caroline*, La Borsa d'Arlecchino, Genoa, 1960; *Escurial*, La Borsa d'Arlecchino, Genoa, 1960; *Il rinoceronte*, Teatro Mercadante, Naples, 1961; *Le rossignol*, Teatro San Carlo, Naples, 1961; *Per un Don Chisciotte*, Piccola Scala, Milan, 1961; *La bisbetica domata*, Teatro Romano, Verona, 1962; *Il figliuol prodigo*, Teatro alla Scala, Milan, 1962; *Andorra*, Teatro Manzoni, Milan, 1962; *Un uomo e un uomo*, Teatro Stabile, Trieste, 1963; *Vita di Edoardo II d'Inghilterra*, Compagnia dei Quattro, 1963; *Il bugiardo*, Teatro Stabile, Turin, 1963; *Il flauto magico*, at the Glyndebourne Festival, England, 1963; *Il re muore*, Teatro Stabile, Turin, 1963; *Chout, il buffone*, Teatro alla Scala, Milan, 1963; *Macbeth*, at the Glyndebourne Festival, England, 1964; *Tamburi nella notte*, Teatro Stabile, Bologna, 1964; *Il mandarino meraviglioso*, Maggio Musicale Fiorentino, 1964; *Cesare o Cleopatra*, Teatro Stabile, Turin, 1964; *La dannazione di Faust*, Teatro San Carlo, Naples, 1964; *L'Anconetana e Bilora*, Teatro Stabile, Turin, 1965; *Carmina Burana*, Chicago Lyric Opera, 1965; *L'heure espagnole*, Chicago Lyric Opera, 1965; *La luna*, Teatro Comunale dell'Opera, Genoa, 1965; *La gazza ladra*, Maggio Musicale Fiorentino, 1965; *La locandiera*, at the *Biennale*, Venice, 1965; *Prometeo incatenato*, Teatro Romano, Trieste, 1965; *Zip lap lip vap mam crep scap plip trip scrap e la grande Mam alle prese con la societa contemporanea*, at the *Biennale*, Venice, 1965; *Coppelia, Orfeo*, and *Danze Polostane*, Staatsoper, Vienna, 1966; *I dialoghi*, Teatro Stabile, Turin, 1965; *Come vi piace*, Teatro Romano, Verona, 1966; *Arlecchino*, Teatro Comunale, Bologna, 1967; *A Midsummer Night's Dream*, English Opera Group, London, 1967; *Don Giovanni*, at the Glyndebourne Festival, England, 1967; *Il mercante di Venezia*, Teatro Romano, Verona, 1967; *Le diavolerie*, at the Festival dei Mundi, Spoleto, 1967; *Le vedova scaltra*, Teatro La Fenice, at the *Biennale*, Venice, 1967; *I dialoghi*, Teatro Olimpico, Vicenza, 1968; *Rosencrantz e Guildenstern sono morti*, Compagnia dei Quattro, 1968; *Le mosche*, Teatro Olimpico, Vicenza, 1968; *Elettra*, Teatro Greco, Siracusa, 1968; *Le Fenicie*, Teatro Greco, Siracusa, 1968; *Il ratto dal serraglio*, at the Glyndebourne Festival, England, 1968; *Titus Andronicus*, Teatro Romano, Verona, 1968; *Le rossignol*, Chicago Lyric Opera, 1968; *Il prigioniero*, Teatro Comunale, Florence, 1969; *Cosi fan tutte*, at the Glyndebourne Festival, England, 1969; *Cosi fan tutte*, Bayerische Staatsoper, Munich, 1969; *El amor brujo*, Chicago Lyric Opera, 1969; *La Cenerentola*, Scottish Opera, Edinburgh, 1969; *La dame aux camelias o Festa per la beatificazione di Margherita Gautier, santa di 2° categoria*, at the *Biennale*, Venice, 1970; *La Moscheta*, Piccolo Teatro, Milan, 1970; *Il Turco in Italia*, at the Glyndebourne Festival, England, 1970; *Don Chisciotte*, London Festival Ballet, 1970; *Elettra*, Teatro Greco, Siracusa, 1970; *Il signor Puntila e il suo servo Matti*, Teatro Stabile, Turin, 1970; *L'Italiana in Algeri*, Chicago Lyric Opera, 1970; *L'elisir d'amore*, Teatro alla Scala, Milan, 1970; *La Création du Monde*, Maggio Musicale Fiorentino, 1971; *Macbeth*, Teatro Romano, Verona, 1971; *La carriera di un libertino*, Teatro Regio, Turin, 1972; *Medea*, Teatro Greco, Siracusa, 1972; *Edipo Re*, Teatro Greco, Siracusa, 1972; *Sogno di una notte di mezza estate*, Gruppo della Rocca, 1972; *Peer Gynt*, Teatro Stabile, Turin, 1972; *Il mandarino meraviglioso*, Staatsoper, Vienna, 1972; *Elektra*, Teatro Massimo, Palermo, 1973; *L'anima buona di Se-Zuan*, Teatro di Roma, 1973; *Petruska*, Staatsoper, Vienna, 1973; *Schweyk nella II guerra mondiale*, Gruppo della Rocca, 1973; *La tarantella di Pulcinella*, Piccola Scala, Milan, 1974; *Divinas parablas*, Maggio Musicale Fiorentino, 1974; *Matilde di Shabran*, Teatro comunale dell'Opera, Genoa, 1974; *Il mercato di Malmantile*, Lincoln Center, New York, 1974; *O Cesare o nessuno!*, Teatro alla Pergola, Florence, 1974; *I due avari*, Teatro Comunale dell'Opera, Genoa, 1975; *Fuenteovejuna*, Teatro Stabile, Bolzano, 1975; *Il barbiere di Siviglia*, Teatro Comunale, Bologna, 1976; *Misura per misura*, Teatro di Roma, 1976; *Don Giovanni*, Teatro Comunale dell'Opera, Genoa, 1976; *La fantesca*, Teatro Stabile, Bolzano, 1976; *Le due giornate o Il portatore d'acqua*, Settimana Musicale Senese, 1976; *Gargantua-Opera*, Teatro della Tosse, Genoa, 1977; *Volpone*, Teatro di Roma, 1977; *Leonzio e Lena*, Teatro Stabile, Bolzano, 1977; *Ubu incatenato*, Teatro della Tosse, 1977; *Il pipistrello*, Teatro Comunale dell'Opera, Genova, 1978; *L'Histoire du soldat*, Estate Romana all'Arancera, 1978; *Arlecchino*, Teatro Massimo, Palermo, 1979; *Don Perlimplin*, Teatro Massimo, Palermo, 1979; *La donna serpente*, Teatro Stabile, Genoa, 1979; *Le nozze di Figaro*, Teatro Comunale dell'Opera, Genoa, 1979; *I corvi*, Teatro della Tosse, Genoa, 1980; *Salome*, Teatro Comunale dell'Opera, Genoa, 1980; *L'Azzurro non si Misura con la Mente*, Gruppo della Rocca, 1980; *Il Cavalier della Rosa*, Teatro dell'Ater, Modena, 1983; *Façade*, Teatro all Scala, Milan, 1983; *Don Quixote*, Teatro di Roma, 1983; *Satiri*, Teatro della Tosse, Genoa, 1983; *Il Turco in Italia*, Festival of Pesaro, 1983; *Lo Stratagemma dei Bellimbusti*, Veneto Teatro, Padua, 1983; *L'Italiana in Algeri*, Teatro la Fenice, Venice, 1984; *Gargantua*, Teatro Regio, Turin, 1984; *Les Esprit*, Camus Festival, Angers, 1984; *Opera Buffa*, Teatro della Tosse, Genoa, 1984; *Pulcinella*, Ater Balletto, Reggio Emilia, 1985; *Piero d'Angera*, Teatro della Tosse, Genoa, 1985; *Il Barbiere di Siviglia*, Bergen Festival, 1985; *Pinocchio*, Teatro Opera of Genoa, 1985; *Armida*, Teatro la Fenice, Venice, 1985; *Sticus*, Teatro Greco, Segesta, 1985; *Attila*, Teatro la Fenice, Venice, 1986; *Boîte à Joux Joux*, Teatro alla Scala, Milan, 1986; *Ballo in Maschera*, Staatsoper, Vienna, 1986; *Il Principe Felice*, Teatro alla Scala, Milan, 1987; *Pollicino*, Teatro Comunale, Florence, 1987; *Johnny Spieltauf*, Teatro Massimo, Palermo, 1987; *La Piovana*, Teatro Romano, Verona, 1987; *La Coscienza di Zeno*, Compagnia Bosetti, Rome, 1987; *Hamlet*, Teatro dela Tosse, Genoa, 1987; *La Scuola delle Mogli*, Teatro di Genova, Genoa, 1988; *La Pace*, Teatro della Tosse, Genoa, 1988; *Le Tre Sorelle*, Haifa Theatre, 1988; *Oberon*, opera Theatre of St. Louis, 1988; *La Scala di Seta*, Festival of Pesaro, 1988; *Lo Schiaccianoci*, Ater Balletto, Reggio Emilia, 1989; *La Mandragola*, National Theatre, Budapest, 1989.

Publications:

By LUZZATI: books—*Facciamo insieme tea-*

Emanuele Luzzati: *Il Re e il suo doppio,* 1982

tro, with T. Conte, Turin 1977; *Teatro Aperto '74,* edited with G. Rodari, Milan 1978; books written and illustrated—*Viaggio alla città di Safed,* Rome 1955; *I paladini di Francia,* with G. Rodari, Milan 1962; *La gazza ladra,* Milan 1964; *Ali Babà e i quaranta ladroni,* Milan 1968; as *Ali Baba and the Forty Thieves,* New York 1969; *Ronald and the Wizard Calico,* adaptor, London 1969; *The Magic Flute,* adaptor, Oxford, 1971, as *Il flauto magico,* Florence 1979; *La tarantella di Pulcinella,* Milan 1971, as *Punch and the Magic Fish,* New York 1972; *Dimbo recita,* with T. Conte, Milan 1974; *C'erano tre fratelli,* Milan 1977; *Orlando in guerra,* with G. Davico Bonino, Turin 1979; *La Cenerentola di Rossini,* Milan 1979; books illustrated—*Calendario columbiano,* Genoa 1953; *Chichibio e la gru* by Boccaccio, Rome 1961; *Castello di carte* by G. Rodari, Milan 1963; *Whistle, Mary, Whistle . . .* by Bill Martin Jr., New York 1970; *L'uccelino Tic Tic* by E. Poi, Turin 1972; *Il viaggio di Marco Polo* by D. Ziliotto, Turin 1972, as *The Travels of Marco Polo,* London 1975; *Voglio comperare una tazza gialla con una ochetta blu* by I. Lepscky, Turin 1974; *Il principe Granchio e altre fiabe italiane,* edited by I. Calvino, Turin 1974, as *Italian Folk Tales,* London 1975; *Il visconte dimezzato* by I. Calvino, Turin 1975; *Dodici Cenerentole in cerca d'autore* by R. Cirio, Conegliano, Italy 1976; *Walking and Talking with Yoav* by M. Sununit, Tel Aviv 1976; *Gli uomini del libro* by G. Limentani, Milan 1976; *Sundiata* by D. Ziliotto, Milan 1980; *Il vizio del faraone* by G. Limentani, Turin 1980; *I tre grassoni* by T. Conte, Rome 1980; *Filastrocche lunghe e corte* by G. Rodari, Rome 1981; *Oh che bel castello* by V. Savona,

Milan 1981; *La casa incantata* by F. Jesi, Milan 1982; *Atalanta* by G. Rodari, Rome 1982; *Belfagor arcidiavolo* by N. Macchiavelli, Genoa 1982; *A Tiresia* by S. Guidro, Rome 1983; *Il Libro dei Perche* by Gianni Rodari, Rome 1984; *Filastrocche da Cantare* by Gianni Rodari, Milan 1984; *Haggadah of Pessah,* Florence 1983; New York 1985; *Un Rabbi che Amava i Banchetti* by Enzo Bianchi, Milan 1985; *Habitat per un'Idea* by Licia Odisio, Genoa 1985; *Le Avventure di Tonio l'Invisibile,* by Gianni Rodari, Rome 1985; *Filastrocche per Tutto l'Anno* by Gianni Rodari, Rome 1986; *Fiabe Lunghe un Sorriso* by Gianni Rodari, Rome 1987; *I Sentieri della Notte* by Tonino Conte, Genoa 1988; *Fiabe Scelte* by J. and W. Grimm, Milan 1988; *The Monster of Jerusalem* by Meyr Shalev, Jerusalem 1989; animated films (with Giulio Gianini)—*I due guerrieri,* 1957; *Pulcinella: Il gioco dell'oca,* 1959; *I paladini di Francia,* 1960; *Castello di carte,* 1962; *La gazza ladra,* 1964; *L'Italiana in Algeri,* 1968; *Ali Baba,* 1970; *Il viaggio di Marco Polo,* 1971; *Pulcinella,* 1973; *Turandot,* 1974; *L'augellin belverde,* 1975; *Il flauto magico,* 1978; *I tre fratelli,* 1979; *La donna serpente,* 1979; *L'uccello di fuoco,* 1981; *Pulcinella e il pesce magico,* 1981; (with Jan Trmal)—*La ragazza cigno,* 1980; *La Palla d'Oro,* 1980; *Il Libro,* 1984; *Concerto per Gatti,* 1985.

On LUZZATI: books—*The Italian Cinema* by Pierre Leprohon, Paris 1966, London 1972; *Gianini e Luzzati: Animazione per Due* by N. Ivaldi, Castellanza 1971; *The Animated Film* by R. Stephenson, London and New York 1973; *Emanuele Luzzati: Scenografie 1947–1975* by G. Davico Bonino, Turin 1975; *Il Sipario Ma-*

gico di Emanuele Luzzati by S. Carandini and M. Fazio, Rome 1980; *Pastelli, Pupazzi e Siparietti: Il Cinema di Gianini e Luzzati* by Sara Cortellazzo, Genoa 1982; *Le Immagini di Emanuele Luzzati per La Tosse,* Genoa 1984.

I had a very happy childhood. I liked making up stories, drawing, fooling around with scraps of paper, paints, and puppets, and when I was seven, my little sister was born, providing the ideal audience for my puppet shows, my fairy tales and pictures. My parents often took me to the theatre to see the "plays," which I unfailingly went home and reproduced with puppets and stage sets to the speechless delight of my little sister. This went on for a long while, except for five years when I had to flee to Switzerland to escape the racial laws (my family is Jewish) and where, in Lausanne, I attended a school of applied arts.

When I came back to Italy I did as a professional the same things I had done as a little boy. I threw myself into the theatre—so far I have designed costumes and sets for more than 300 productions; I told stories in various ways, as an illustrator and also as a writer; I've made up all sorts of characters in ceramics and concocted wall panels that tell of paladins and knights and old legends; and then with Giulio Gianini, film technician and cameraman, we started telling stories in the form of animated cartoons, for me probably the most complete form of narrations, in which everything can be created from the beginning to the end; a story has to be made up, a script written, character and settings invented, music adapted—as I said, probably the most perfect way to tell a story visually. I hasten to add, however, that all these different activities are interlinked and interrelated. Actually, I do nothing but tell the same stories over and over again; all that changes is the vehicle of expression.

The subjects are relatively few: from the "Paladins," those legendary knights we studied in school in the poetic texts of Ariosto and Tasso and then recast in a popular form in the traveling puppet shows of Italy (in particular, the Sicilian "*pupi*" or marionettes); to the characters of the commedia dell'arte, with a personal preference for Pulcinella, he too a sort of puppet in embryo who, with his shrewish wife and his dread of carabinieri, has delighted thousands of children in public parks; down to the more refined, but in Italy highly popular, characters of the opera stage, like Figaro or Papageno, or to those in the fables of Carlo Gozzi in which commedia dell'arte characters are mingled with Oriental heroes and heroines from *The Arabian Nights*.

If you come right down to it, I don't think I've ever strayed very far from these subjects, whether my stories were told in a panel of painted terracotta, or I brought them to life on a stage, or, animated by Gianini, they appeared on a movie screen, or lastly were set down forever on the pages of a printed book.

Indeed, every book that I have written or illustrated has almost always appeared in the form of a stage work or an animated cartoon. Sometimes the book comes first, sometimes the animated cartoon, sometimes the stage work, but it is very rare that a given story with its characters and settings remains confined to only one of these three forms. . . .

I don't know if I'm a painter, a story-teller or a theaterman, nor do I know if what I do is more or less valid artistically. But I do know that when a mother tells me: "To get my little boy to eat his soup, I always have to read him the Paladins of France," I have been useful for at least something in life. There's always a little child who, thanks to me, has eaten his soup or been lulled to sleep by the nursery rhymes of Ali Baba. And for me that's enough. *(Excerpted from an address to an illustrators' convention in Boston, 1981.)*

—Emanuele Luzzati

Emanuele Luzzati is rare in being able to pursue two careers at the same time: stage design for the opera, ballet, and theatre, and animated film design for the movies and television. His own style of design is successfully conveyed in his characters for animated film. They are light, humorous figures, easily identifiable, defined with bold lines. Their simple shapes allow them to be easily given movement, which is carried out by his partner Giulio Gianini (born in Rome in 1927). Their co-operation in film animation dates to 1957 when Gianini began to animate Luzzati's figures and photograph them under the animation rostrum cameras, while Luzzati drew the characters, designed the backgrounds, and cooperated in the story development and the timing of the action. They chose the music together and fit their pictures afterwards.

Among Luzzati's animated films with Gianini, possibly the best known are (feature-length), *The Magic Flute*, *Ali Baba*, *The Paladins*, *Turandot*, and *The Thieving Magpie*. The latter was chosen by a panel of specialists as one of the fifteen most outstanding animated films of all time.

Luzzati's stage work has reached a dimension quite outstanding in the European theatre. He has designed more than 300 sets and costumes for La Scala in Milan, and for the operas in Rome, Naples, Venice, Florence, Vienna, Genoa, Munich, Lisbon, and Tel Aviv. Besides designing for the London Festival Ballet, and the Glyndebourne Opera House, he has worked extensively in Chicago where, among other operas, he designed the sets for Rossini's *Italian Girl in Algiers*. The American public, like the European, responded to his style with delight.

Luzzati's approach is based on a colourful, decorative expression. With a strong sense of pictorial projection, he can manipulate his dress designs to unify all the visual elements on the stage. His sets light up with pictorial beauty and with optimism which particularly helps some of the heavy operas.

Luzzati has also illustrated and written some of Europe's most popular children's books. He began his work as a ceramic artist some three decades ago at the Bianco Factory at Pozzo Garitta, and since that time he has produced art objects ranging from small, individual pieces to mural panels. In 1955, he received the first prize for ceramics at Cannes, and in 1970 he was awarded the Golden Rose at Albissola. He has created wall panels and tapestries for such transatlantic ships as the Leonardo da Vinci, the Michelangelo, and the Marco Polo. His graphic design work was represented in a show at the 1972 Venice *Biennale* in the experimental design section.

—John Halas

MAGISTRETTI, (Lodo)Vico.

Italian architect, interior and industrial designer. Born in Milan, 6 October 1920. Educated at the Liceo Parini, Milan, 1931–39; studied architecture, at the Politecnico, Milan, 1940–45: Dip.Arch. 1945. Served in the Italian Army, 1942–43. Freelance architect and designer, working in Milan, from 1946: designed for Artemide, Azucena, Cassina, Rosenthal Porzellanfabrik, Coran/Habitat, Knoll International, La Rinascente, De Padova ICF, Montina Fratelli, O-Luce, Oca Brasil, Asko, Poggi, Carrara e Matta, Spalding, etc. Commission member, for the Milan Triennale, 1960, 1964, and for the Compasso d'Oro Awards, Milan, 1959, 1960. Visiting lecturer, Architectural School, Venice, 1962, Colegio de Arquitectura, Barcelona, 1962–67, and Royal College of Art, London, from 1980. **Exhibitions:** Milan Triennale, 1948, 1951, 1954, 1960; Studio Marconi, Milan, 1971; *Knoll au Musée,* Musée des Arts Décoratifs, Paris, 1972; *One Hundred Modern Chairs,* National Gallery of Victoria, Melbourne, 1974; *Design e design,* Palazzo delle Stelline, Milan, 1979 (travelled to Venice); *Italian Re-Evolution,* La Jolla Museum of Art, California, 1982; *Design Since 1945,* Philadelphia Museum of Art, 1983; *New Design for Old,* Boilerhouse/Victoria and Albert Museum, London, 1986. **Collections:** Design Museum, London; Museum of Modern Art, New York. Recipient: Grand Prize, 1948, 1954, and Gold Medal, 1954, Milan Triennale; Vis Prize, Milan, 1950; Compasso d'Oro Award, Milan, 1967, 1980; Gold Medal, Society of Industrial Artists and Designers, London, 1985. Member, Accademia di San Luca, Rome, 1970; Honorary Fellow, Royal College of Art, London, 1983. Address: Via Conservatorio 20, 20121 Milan, Italy.

Works:

Torre Parco apartment building, Milan, 1956 (with Longoni).
Villa Arosio at Arenzano, near Genoa, 1959.
Marina Grande development at Arenzano, near Genoa, 1963.
Demetrio table in fibreglass and resin, for Artemide, 1964.
Cerruti department stores, in Paris, Tokyo and Vienna, 1967–76.
Stadio 80 table in fibreglass and resin, for Artemide, 1968.
Selene stacking chairs in fibreglass and resin, for Artemide, 1968–69.
New Town Hall, Cusano Milanino, Milan, 1969.
Caori table in black aluminium, for Knoll International, 1969.
Hotel and restaurant at Sarzana near La Spezia, 1973.
707 Fiandra sofas and chairs, for Cassina, 1975.
114 Nuvola Rossa bookshelves, for Cassina, 1977.

High school at San Daniele del Friuli, near Udine, 1977.
Maralunga sofas and chairs, for Cassina, 1979.
Cutlery in stainless steel, for Cleto Munari, 1979–80.
Kuta 250 table lamp, for O-Luce, 1980.
Sinbad seating range, for Cassina, 1981.
Veranda seating range, for Cassina, 1983.
Idomeneo lamp, for O-Luce, 1984.
Planet lamp, for Venini, 1986.

Publications:

By MAGISTRETTI: article—in *The Designer* (London), December 1982.

On MAGISTRETTI: books—*Mobili Tipo* by Robert Aloi, Milan 1956; *Recent Italian Architecture* by Agnoldomenico Pica, Milan 1959; *Public Interiors* by Misha Black, London 1960; *The Modern Chair: 1850 to Today* by Gilbert Frey, London and Niederteufen 1970; *History of Modern Furniture* by Karl Mang, Stuttgart 1978, 1989, London 1979; *Atlante del Design Italiano 1940/1980* by Alfonso Grassi and Anty Pansera, Milan 1980; *Knoll Design* by Eric Larrabee and Massimo Vignelli, New York 1981; *Design Since 1945,* edited by Kathryn Hiesinger and George Marcus, Philadelphia and London 1983; *Design Process Olivetti 1908–83,* with text by Renzo Zorzi, Milan 1983; *Modern Furniture Classics* by Miriam Stimpson, London 1987; *Italian Design: 1870 to the Present* by Penny Sparke, London and New York 1988; *Italian Modern: A Design Heritage* by Giovanni Albera and Nicolas Monti, New York 1989.

Profound changes are taking place in every aspect of design—in the products, the methods of production, and the distribution of them. Also in the words used. The famous "industrial design" no longer has the same mythical, liberating significance that it had in the 1960s.

We can see now that perhaps it hardly ever existed and that technology, the wicked fairy of industrial design, has not been the true protagonist of what it must already be time to call simply "Italian design." Technology is a means, never an end; you can make the finest design using the most complex of machinery to shape a brand new material, but you can also do it with pieces of wood if you use them in the right way.

Technology (the real technology of our times) has produced the Saturn rocket, not Italian design. Italian design was born and lives on as the result of a fortunate and quite casual meeting some twenty years ago between courageous small industries (craftsmen, almost) and designers.

After so great an interval of time, it is possible to say that, despite all the criticism and reserve on the ideological level, there is a positive result: a strong image, spread through the world, of Italian design and the birth—and I believe one can say this too without being

ashamed of that naughty word—of an Italian "Style," translated into plans for certain objects which make their mark on a period and last in time. I think that an object of good design should last forever, should be an archetype of permanent validity, not an object of fashion. The production of "fashionable" articles (based on the 1930s, Art Deco, various other revivals) is a fine way to kill the image of Italian design; we now have to design for a changed world, which has no use for the provisional, the throwaway, a better-informed and more cultured world which wants, and can identify with, not the ridiculous expensive "status symbol," but much more simply, something that in a harder—more exhausting—world is more authentic. This is the world which has emerged crippled from the "petrol war" and which can no longer afford the frivolities of the past but which will have an increasing need of a poetry of the authentic.

I think it is worthwhile recalling the antithesis that has emerged in recent years between the meaning of the words "design" and "styling." Out of this contrast there has come the idea that styling was in some way inferior to design. Styling has always been thought of as useless decoration, superimposition, superficial alteration, while design meant the search for the essential, the unambiguous quality of the only form possible, as if it was wished to endow design with some ethical value and styling with an aestheticizing value, to the clear detriment of the latter. I believe that it should be possible to share such a judgment only after establishing that we are talking of two entirely different things, not necessarily opposed, but rather complementary.

I think that today, given the demands and the limitations that this western civilization has to face, the time has come to reach a definition, albeit synthetically and approximately, that can be stated thus: design does not need drawing, but styling does. What I mean by this is that an object of design could be described, even to the person who has to produce it, by spoken or written words, because what materializes through the process is a precise function, and, in particular, a special use of the materials which, as a matter of principle, leaves all aesthetic questions out of consideration because the object is to achieve a precise practical aim. That does not of course mean that a precise image cannot be produced that will reflect and express "aesthetic" qualities proper to the new methodology used in the conception of the object.

Styling, on the other hand, has to be expressed by the most exact drawings, not because it disregards function but simply because it wraps that function in a cloak that essentially expressed qualities that are called "style" and that are decisive in making the quality of the object recognizable. Just think of the use of the world "styling" in the American motorcar industry, which perhaps coined the expression to justify superficial changes in each year's new

Vico Magistretti: *Gaudi* **armchair in ABS plastic, for Artemide, 1970**

model; the successive cars are identical in substance but slightly different in shape, that is to say in styling.

Once we make the distinction between design and styling, it should be possible to get rid of the negative premise of the world styling completely and say simply that the two words have different content, not in conflict with each other, but complementary in the creative definition of an object in which design and styling are two elements of which one or the other will prevail from time to time, thereby making it possible to define an object as an object of either design or styling. I believe one may say that nowadays you will much less often come across an object in which design is prevalent than an object in which styling prevails.

Going back to my earlier example, I should say that the American motorcar is a typical object of styling alone. I must add, to make my point clear, that such an object, simply because it is purely an object of styling, is a very negative example. On the application of design or styling to the needs of the contemporary world, or to future needs, I believe it is possible to express a choice by saying that today and tomorrow there will always be more need for design than for styling because in having to face, as we do, a shortage of means available to us, we shall have to cope with an increasingly emphatic demand for simplification and essentiality, most of all where the useful life of the object is concerned.

Scarcity of materials and impossibility of maintenance will lead increasingly to the cutting out of a tendency of the past two decades to produce "throwaway" articles, made not to last but to be easily replaceable. We shall be dealing with a society growing at the same time poorer and more sophisticated. This society, accustomed to enjoying collective or scientific services of great sophistication, will learn that it can no longer rely on that sophistication and will want objects that look strong and simple, that need no maintenance or as little as possible, and that will never be quickly or economically replaced.

Design, understood in this way, will have to face these new and urgent demands. I believe that this situation will be beneficial because, however attractive we may find the postmodernist slogan (a strictly pro-styling slogan) "less is a bore," we may well come to believe that Mies got it right in thinking that the best guarantee of durable quality lay in "less is more." I think perhaps the time has come to say: first we thought that what was useful was beautiful, but now we know that what is beautiful is useful.

—Vico Magistretti

Sculptural forms with organic shapes, rounded edges, and understated structure predominate in all of Magistretti's designs. Whether executed in hard materials, such as plastic, wood, or metal, or such soft materials as wool, leather, or cotton, all designs have a fluid and developing quality. For example, in lounge seating, chair and sofa surfaces seem malleable.

The 928 (1962), the Maralunga (1973), the 707 Fiandra (1975), and the Sinbad (1982) groups typify Magistretti's innovations: sculptural form, imaginative use of fabric, design for comfort, and adaptability. Stylistically, these four seating groups range from the 928, an ample, traditional chair and sofa with a conservative treatment of materials, to Sinbad, his boldest attempt at sculptural form in lounge seating. Sinbad's fabric cover is loosely applied to the structure by means of Velcro and a system of hidden clips so that the sculptural drape of the fabric becomes the design statement. The colorful, rectangular, removable covers approximate the ease of throwing a blanket over a worn sofa, an idea with which Magistretti first experimented in the 707 Fiandra system. The Maralunga, 707 Fiandra, and Sinbad seating designs also express Magistretti's growing interest in comfort and adaptability. In all three designs, single chairs and larger pieces have been structured to cushion the body in a gentle embrace. As for adaptability, the Maralunga's back cushion in both the armchair and the sofa, can be raised by a concealed steel armature from a folded height to a high lounge position. In the 707 Fiandra series, large-scale seating components were designed to be ganged in a variety of configurations. Pieces in the Sinbad collection change upholstery to match environmental conditions—cotton for summer, brushed wool or thick leather for the winter. The ability to change fabrics also facilitates maintenance, another concept first introduced by means of zippered covers in the 707 Fiandra series.

Magistretti is a prolific and consistent designer who has concentrated on reinterpreting traditional lines and forms. Throughout the last twenty years, ninety-five percent of Magistretti's designs have remained in production, a testimony to his consistency and his philosophy of timeless design. According to Magistretti, "Good design has nothing to do with fashion. Good design has to last years."

—Jan Jennings

MAGNUSSEN, Erik.

Danish industrial designer. Born in Copenhagen, 31 March 1940. Studied ceramics, School of Arts and Crafts (Kunsthandvaerkerskolan), Copenhagen, 1957–60. Married Jonna Dreyer in 1982. Furniture, ceramics and glass designer, from 1960. Ceramics designer for Bing and Grondahl porcelain factory, Copenhagen, from 1962; also designed for Stelton AS tablewares, Hellerup, from 1976, and for Georg Jensen Silversmithy AS, Copenhagen, from 1978. Instructor, Royal Academy of Fine Arts, Copenhagen, 1970–73. **Exhibitions:** *Bing og Grondahl 125 Ar*, Kunstindustrimuseet, Copenhagen, 1978; *Georg Jensen Silversmithy: 77 Artists, 75 Years*, Washington, D.C., 1980; *Scandinavian Modern Design 1880–1980*, Cooper-Hewitt Museum, New York, 1982; *Design Since 1945*, Philadelphia Museum of Art, 1983; *The Lunning Prize*, Nationalmuseum, Stockholm, 1986. **Collections:** Kunstindustrimuseet, Copenhagen; Statens Kunstfond, Copenhagen; Röhsska Konstslöjdmuseet, Goteborg; Victoria and Albert Museum, London. Recipient: Lunning Prize, 1967; ID Prize, Danish Design Council, 1972, 1977, 1987; Furniture Prize, Copenhagen, 1975; Danish Designer of the Year Award, 1983. Address: Strandvejen 630, 2930 Klampenborg, Denmark.

Works:

Termo tableware, for Bing and Gröndahl, 1965.
Chair Z, in steel and fabric, for Torben Orskov Company, 1968.
School furniture, for Kevi, 1969.
Hank tableware, for Bing and Grondahl, 1971.
Thermal Carafe, for Stelton AS, 1976.
Porcelouis porcelain lamps, for Louis Poulsen/ Bing and Gröndahl, 1983.
Bowls in steel and plastic, for Stelton AS, 1986.

Angle measurer, for Wernblad and Lokvig, 1988.
Servizz melamine tableware, for Rosti, 1988.
201 cabin lamp, for Harlang and Dreyer, 1988.
301 kerosene wall lamp in stainless steel, for Harlang and Dreyer, 1988.
351 kerosene suspension lamp in stainless steel, for Stelton AS, 1988.
Erik Magnussen Collection of tablewares, for Selangor Pewter of Malaysia, from 1988.
Chair and table, for Paustian, 1989.

Publications:

On MAGNUSSEN: books—*Dansk Brugskunst og Design*, edited by Landsföreningen DB+D, Copenhagen 1972; *Dansk Design/Danish Design* by Henrik Steen Moller, Copenhagen 1975; *En Kobenhavnsk porcelaenfabriks historie: Bing og Grøndahl 1853–1978* by Erik Lassen, Copenhagen 1978; *Bing og Grøndahl 125 Ar*, exhibition catalogue with introduction by Erik Clemmesen, Copenhagen 1978; *Scandinavian Modern Design 1880–1980*, edited by David Revere McFadden, New York 1982; *Design Since 1945*, edited by Kathryn Hiesinger and George Marcus, Philadelphia and London 1983; *International Design Yearbook 1985/ 1986*, edited by Robert A. M. Stern, London 1985; *The Lunning Prize*, exhibition catalogue edited by Helena Dahlbäck Lutteman and Marianne Uggla, Stockholm 1986; articles— "Thirty-four Lunning Prizewinners" in *Mobilia* (Snekkersten), September 1967; "Erik Magnussen" by S. E. Moller in *Mobilia* (Snekkersten), July/August 1973; "The Magnussen/Stelton Bowls" in *DD Bulletin* (Copenhagen), March 1987.

MAINBOCHER.

American fashion and costume designer. Born Main Rousseau Bocher, in Chicago, Illinois, 24 October 1890: adopted name Mainbocher in 1929. Studied at the Lewis Institute, Chicago, from 1907; studied piano under Claire Osborn Reed, at Columbia School of Music, Chicago, 1907; studied design, at Chicago Academy of Fine Arts, 1908–09, and at the Arts Students League, New York, 1909–11; attended University of Chicago, 1911, and Königliche Kunstgewerbemuseum, Munich, 1911–12; also studied painting with E. A. Taylor, Paris, 1913–14, piano with Frank La Forge, New York, 1914, opera under Henri Albers and Giulia Valda, in New York, 1917–21. Served in the American Ambulance Corps, and Intelligence Corps, Paris, 1917–18. Worked part-time as a lithographer, New York, 1909–11; fashion sketch artist, for clothing manufacturer E. L. Mayer, New York, 1914–17; illustrator, *Harper's Bazaar*, in Paris, 1917–21; fashion correspondent, then editor, *Vogue* French edition, Paris, 1922–29; established Mainbocher fashion house, Paris, 1930–39, and Mainbocher Incorporated fashion firm, New York, 1939–71; also designed stage costumes, from 1932. **Exhibition:** *Fashion: An Anthology*, Victoria and Albert Museum, London, 1971. **Collection:** New York Public Library. *Died (in New York City) 27 December 1976.*

Works:

United States WAVE uniform, 1942.
American Girl Scout uniform, 1946.

Erik Magnussen: Ship's cabin lamp, for Harland and Dreyer, 1988

American Red Cross uniform, 1948.
Nurses' uniforms, for Passavant Hospital, Chicago, 1949.
United States Marine Corps women's uniform, 1951.

Stage costumes (New York, unless noted) include—*La Fleur des Pois*, Théâtre de la Michodière, Paris, 1932; for Peggy Wood and Leonora Corbett in *Blithe Spirit*, Morosco Theatre, 1941; Katharine Cornell and Doris Dudley in pre-Broadway tryout of *Rose Burke*, Curran Theatre, San Francisco, 1942; Mary Martin in *One Touch of Venus*, Imperial Theatre, 1943; Ruth Chatterton in the pre-Broadway tryout of *A Lady Comes Home*, Nixon Theatre, Pittsburgh, 1943; Ruth Gordon in *Over Twenty-One*, Music Box Theatre, 1944; Betty Field in *Dream Girl*, Coronet Theatre, 1945; Jean Arthur in the pre-Broadway tryout of *Born Yesterday*, Shubert Theatre, New Haven, Connecticut, 1945; Tallulah Bankhead in *Private Lives*, Plymouth Theatre, 1948; Ethel Merman in *Call Me Madam*, Imperial Theatre,

1950; for *The Prescott Proposals*, Broadhurst Theatre, 1950; *Point of No Return*, Alvin Theatre, 1951; *Wish You Were Here* (as consultant), Imperial Theatre, 1952; for Rosalind Russell in *Wonderful Town*, Winter Garden Theatre, 1953; for *Kind Sir*, Alvin Theatre, 1953; for Libby Holman in part one of *Blues, Ballads and Sin Songs*, Bijou Theatre, 1954; Lynn Fontanne in *The Great Sebastians*, ANTA Theatre, 1956; Mary Martin in *The Sound of Music*, Lunt-Fontanne Theatre, 1955; and Irene Worth in *Tiny Alice*, Billy Rose Theatre, 1964; also designed Mary Martin's wardrobe for the television adaptation of *Born Yesterday*, NBC-TV, New York, 1956.

Publications:

On MAINBOCHER: books—*Always in Vogue* by Edna and Ilka Chase, London 1954; *Dressmakers of France* by Mary Brooks Picken and Dora Loues Miller, New York 1956; *The World in Vogue 1893-1963*, edited by Bryan Holmes

and others, New York and London 1963; *Fashion: An Anthology by Cecil Beaton*, exhibition catalogue compiled by Madeleine Ginsburg, London 1971; *American Fashion: The Life and Lines of Adrian, Mainbocher, McCardell, Norell, Trigere*, edited by Sarah Tomerlin Lee, New York 1975, London 1976; *In Vogue: Sixty Years of Celebrities and Fashion* by Georgina Howell, London 1975, 1978, New York 1976; *Magic Names of Fashion* by Ernestine Carter, London 1980; *Fairchild's Who's Who in Fashion*, edited by Ann Stegemeyer, New York 1980; *McDowell's Directory of Twentieth Century Fashion* by Colin McDowell, London 1984; *The Encyclopaedia of Fashion from 1840 to the 1980s* by Georgina O'Hara, London 1986.

As editor of French *Vogue* from 1922 to 1929, Mainbocher simplified the layout, removed decorative borders, and started the editorial "Vogue's Eye View." Such simplification he carried over to his clothes design when he opened as a couturier in 1929. However, Mainbocher was very conservative in his view that fashion was only for ladies who were famous and aristocratic. He did not approve of Paul Poiret's oriental fantasies or Gabrielle Chanel's bold, unladylike, classless look, and he was unaware of Sonia Delaunay's textiles. To keep out copiers and tourists, he was the first designer to charge a caution, a pledge to buy, of visitors to his collections. He based his approach on those of two of the then-leading couturiers—the royal dressmaker Edward Molyneux's classic restraint and Madeleine Vionnet's fluid, bias-cut style—imitating their elimination of superfluous detail and their avoidance of gimmicks and dramatic changes. He was fond of simple contrasts, such as a white evening gown with a black printed train, a black dress with white cravat and gloves, a black evening gown with white piqué jacket, a black dress with a red tie and red gloves. For evenings, trying to recreate the glamour of portraits by Winterhalter, Sargent, and Boldini, he used such historical items as overskirts and corsets. With his early training in opera, he liked to think of design as similar to music, with its variations on a theme, and he was not afraid to repeat ideas. He could have remained a quietly successful designer but for the arrival of fellow American Wallis Simpson, who gave him worldwide publicity by ordering her wedding dress from Mainbocher when she espoused the Duke of Windsor. Her determination to be the best-groomed woman in high society gave Mainbocher enormous opportunity and impact.

In 1939, he had to flee back to the United States, but as the first Parisian couturier to base himself in New York, he received much attention. He demanded the same standards as a Parisian couture house, despised Seventh Avenue's rag trade, and until his retirement in 1971, refused to touch wholesale production, remaining always an exclusive couturier for the rich. In 1942, he designed the WAVES uniform for the United States Navy, and the Mainbocher suit, with more echoes of Chanel than he would acknowledge, became a fashion stalwart. His operatic background gave him a fascination with the theatre, and he dressed Leonora Corbett in *Blithe Spirit* (1941), Mary Martin in *One Touch of Venus* (1943) and *The Sound of Music* (1955), Ethel Merman in *Call Me Madam* (1950), Rosalind Russell in *Wonderful Town* (1953), Lynn Fontanne in *The Great Sebastians* (1956), and Irene Worth in *Tiny Alice* (1964). Although Mainbocher was essentially a couturier on the pre-war model, he managed to continue operating in the very changeable post-war period.

—Diana de Marly

MALDONADO, Tomas.

Italian design theorist and industrial designer. Born in Buenos Aires, Argentina, 25 April 1922; emigrated to Italy in 1967; naturalized, 1976. Studied at the Academia de Bellas Artes, Buenos Aires, 1938–43. Independent painter, architectural and industrial designer, in Buenos Aires, 1944–54; freelance designer, working on electronic, medical, optical, agricultural and office products, in Ulm, 1954–66, and in Milan and Bologna, from 1967. Editor, *Nueva Vision* magazine, Buenos Aires, 1951; chief editor, *Casabella* magazine, Milan. Professor, 1954–66, and Rector, 1964–66, Hochschule für Gestaltung, Ulm; professor of environmental planning, University of Bologna, from 1967; visiting professor, Princeton University, New Jersey, 1967–70. Member, Arte Concreto-Invencion group of painters, Buenos Aires, 1945; executive committee president, ICSID International Council of Societies of Industrial Design, 1967–69. **Exhibitions:** Stedelijk Museum, Amsterdam, 1953; *6a. Biennale Internazionale della Grafica d'Arte*, Palazzo Strozzi, Florence, 1978. **Collection:** Stedelijk Museum, Amsterdam. Addresses: Via Manzoni 14, 20121 Milan; Via Zamboni 38, 40126 Bologna, Italy.

Publications:

By MALDONADO: books—*Max Bill*, Buenos Aires 1955; *Tomas Maldonado: Buenos Aires-Montevideo*, Montevideo 1964; *Universita: La Sperimentazione Dipartimentale*, with Omar Calabrese, Florence 1978.

On MALDONADO: books—*Il Disegno Industriale e la sua Estetica* by Gillo Dorfles, Bologna 1963; *What is a Designer?* by Norman Potter, London and New York 1969, Reading 1980; *The Aspen Papers: 20 Years of Design Theory*, edited by Reyner Banham, London 1974; *Die Geschichte des Design in Deutschland* by Gert Selle, Cologne 1978; *Industrial Design* by John Heskett, London 1980; *Moderno Postmoderno Millenario*, edited by Andrea Branzi, Milan 1980; *A History of Industrial Design* by Edward Lucie-Smith, Oxford 1983; *The Conran Directory of Design*, edited by Stephen Bayley, London 1985; *Design Source Book* by Penny Sparke and others, London 1986; *Italian Design: 1870 to the Present* by Penny Sparke, London 1988.

Although Tomas Maldonado has played a significant role in the burgeoning field of high-tech industrial design: computing equipment, typewriters, word processors, electro-medical, and optical equipment, his enduring achievement is tied to the Hochschule for Gestaltung, Ulm, West Germany, where, as Professor and later Rector, he was the school's guiding force from 1954–1966.

As a design theorist and educator, Maldonado spearheaded a revolt in design thinking that became synonymous with the school at Ulm, one that set a course in opposition to esthetic taste and functional problem-solving as the fundamental criteria for successful practice.

The school at Ulm was established in 1951 (closed in 1968), under Max Bill as its first director, with the goal of rejuvenating Bauhaus ideals and thus reestablishing Germany as the center of design after the war. Upon Maldonado's arrival in the mid-50s, from Argentina where he was a painter, designer, and editor, there was evidence of a radical shift in the educational philosophy at the school. Gone was the emphasis on form-building that marked the foundation of Bauhaus discipline, replaced by an emphasis on the social sciences, mathematics, and semiology. Gone also were the Fine and Graphic Art Departments, replaced by studies in visual and verbal communication. The hierarchy of architecture as the mother of the arts was dismantled in favor of a more egalitarian enterprise that embraced every facet of the designed environment.

Maldonado was a tireless advocate of the changes wrought at Ulm, as he proselytized throughout the design community against the pervasive ideology of formalism. He believed that the growing complexity of design problems could not be solved by a reliance on intuition or historical research of prototypes but in developing more sophisticated analytical tools. What Maldonado proffered was a systematic approach to design methodolgy—identified as "scientific operationalism"—that was more theory than prescription. Under his leadership, design at Ulm became allied with other social sciences in the study of human relationships that can be measured and tested in the communication of symbolic meanings.

Considering the technocratic overtones of this philosophy, there was an underlying humanism in the fulfillment of universal needs rather than idiosyncratic desires as the ultimate purpose of design. In this way, Ulm maintained a connection (in spirit) with its predecessor, the Bauhaus, and impelled a serious consideration of its experiments in the annals of design.

Currently, there is scant evidence of manufactured products that might attest to the success or failure of Maldonado's teachings. Maldonado, himself, had worked with German companies, most notably with Erbe of Tubingen, where he designed electronic surgical and radiation equipment that utilized concepts derived from mass-produced consumer goods. The best-known work that shows the influence of Ulm, however, were the electrical appliances produced by Braun, a company that maintained a close relationship with the school during Maldonado's tenure. These appliances were the epitome of Ulm's rationalist approach to design. Appropriate in the extreme, they focused on user needs without the interference of style. They were not visually aggressive nor did they intrude upon the user's perception of function. The clarity of expression and the precise relationships of material, engineering, and form dissolved in attempts at a democratized solution for the human dependency upon tools.

—Sarah Bodine

MALMSTEN, Carl (Per Hendrik).

Swedish interior, furniture and textile designer. Born in Stockholm, 7 December 1888. Educated at the Norra Realgymnasium, the Pahlmanns Handelsinstitut, and the Högskolan, Stockholm, until 1908; studied economics, in Lund, 1910; apprenticed in furniture workshops of Pelle Jonsson, Stockholm, 1910–12; studied handicrafts and architecture with Carl Bergsten, Stockholm, 1912–15. Served in the Royal Swedish Lifeguards, 1909–10. Married Siv Munthe in 1917; children Ulf, Kerstin, Egil, Vidar and Torgils. Freelance furniture and interior designer, in Stockholm, from 1916: established workshops at Tunnelgatan, 1916–19, at Arbetargatan, 1919–22, at Krukmakargatan, 1940–50, and at Renstiernagatan, 1950–72; director, Firma Carl Malmsten, Stockholm, 1933, and Carl Malmsten AB, Stockholm, 1944. Head of design, Nåäs Slöjdseminarium, Stockholm, 1922–25, and Sigtuna Skolan, 1926–34; workshop founder, Oloffskolan, Stockholm, 1928–32; handicrafts instructor, at Svolvaer, Bruksvallarna and Hedemora, 1933–40, and at the Konstfackskolan, Stockholm, 1948; also instructor at summer courses, Viggbyholmsskolan, 1946–47, and Capellagården School, 1958–72. Founder of Malmstens Handicrafts Union, Stockholm, 1930, Nyckelbrödernas Förbundet association, Stockholm, 1955, and of the Capellagårdens Förbund, Stockholm, 1961. **Exhibitions:** Blanchs Konstsalong, Stockholm, 1917; *Jubilee Exhibition* Goteborg, 1923; *Exposition des Arts Decoratifs*, Paris, 1925; *Jonsson-Malmsten-Munthe*, Liljevalchs Konsthall, Stockholm, 1928; *Swedish Arts and Crafts*, Dorland Gallery, London, 1930; *Malmsten/Måås-Fjetterström*, Konstslöjdmuseet, Göteborg, 1933; Liljevalchs Konsthall, Stockholm, 1934; *Swedish Exhibition*, Warsaw and Prague 1938; New York World's Fair, 1939; *Nyttokonstnären*, Nationalmuseum, Stockholm, 1943; *Carl Malmsten: Retrospective*, Nationalmuseum, Stockholm, 1944; *Svenska Stolar*, Nationalmuseum, Stockholm, 1963; *Scandinavian Modern Design 1880–1980*, Cooper-Hewitt Museum, New York, 1982. **Collections:** Röhsska Konstslöjdmuseet, Göteborg; Nationalmuseum, Stockholm; Metropolitan Museum of Art, New York. Recipient: Furniture Competition Prize, Stockholm, 1916; Grand Prize, Paris International Exposition, 1925; Litteris et Artibus Award, Stockholm, 1926; St. Erik and Prince Eugen Medals, Stockholm, 1945. *Died* (in Stockholm) *in 1972.*

Works:

Stadshusstolen chairs, for Stockholm Town Hall, 1916.
Konsert armchair, for Stockholm Concert Hall, 1923.
Jonas upholstered armchair, for KV Larsson Eftr., 1938.
Ingrid chair, for P. Holsten, 1944.
Widemar writing chair, for Andoman-Padouk, 1944.
Klyftan cupboard, for AB Fanerkompaniet, 1946.
Juni chair, for L. and L. Cederlöf, 1949.
Tidlösa grandfather clock, for Bröderna Holm AB, 1953.
Mittens Rike cupboard, for Feuk and Wilson, 1964.
Island sewing cabinet, for Bröderna Holm AB, 1964.
Sommar cupboard, for Bröderna Holm AB, 1964.

On MALMSTEN: books—*Modern Decorative Arts of Sweden* by Erik Wettergren, Malmö and London 1928; *Svenska Möbler* by Brynhof Hellner, Stockholm 1947; *Carl Malmsten: Swedish Furniture*, edited by Paul Artaria, Basel 1954; *A Treasury of Scandinavian Design*, edited by Erik Zahle, New York 1961; *Carl Malmsten: Pionjär och Traditionsbevarare* by Ulf Hård af Segerstad, Stockholm 1963; *Carl Malmsten hel och hallen* by Eric Wennerholm, Stockholm 1969; *Design in Sweden*, edited by Lennart Lindkvist, Stockholm 1972; *Scandinavian Design: Objects of a Life Style* by Eileene Harrison Beer, New York and Toronto 1975; *Twentieth Century Furniture* by Philippe Garner, London 1980; *Carl Malmstens Verkstadsskola 1930–1980* by P. O. Scote, S. Malmsten and others, Stockholm 1980; *Scandinavian Modern Design 1880–1980*, edited by David Revere McFadden, New York 1982; *The Conran Directory of Design*, edited by Stephen Bayley, London 1985; *Twentieth Century Design: Furniture* by Penny Sparke, London 1986.

MANASSEH, Leonard (Sulla).
British architect, environmental and interior designer. Born in London, 21 May 1916. Educated at Cheltenham College, Gloucestershire, until 1935; studied at the Architectural Association School, London 1936-40; Dip. Arch. 1940. Served as a Fleet Air Arm pilot, Royal Navy, 1943-46. Married in 1947 (divorced, 1956); 2 sons; married Sarah Delaforce in 1957; 2 sons, 1 daughter. Assistant architect, with C.R.E., North London, and Guy Morgan and Partners, London, 1941-43, and with Hertfordshire County Council, 1946-48; senior architect, Stevenage Development Corporation, Hertfordshire, 1948-50; in private architectural and design practice as Leonard Manasseh and Partners, in London and Bath, from 1950; with James Cubitt and Partners, established offices Cubitt Manasseh and Partners, in Singapore and Malaysia, 1953-54. Instructor, Kingston School of Art, Surrey, 1941-43, and Architectural Association School, London, 1941-43, 1951-59. Council member, 1959-66, and president, 1964-65, Architectural Association, London; member, Council of Industrial Design, London, 1965-68; council member, 1968-70, 1976-82, and honorary secretary, 1979-81, Royal Institute of British Architects; council member, National Trust, London, from 1977; member of the Ancient Monuments Board, London, 1978-84; president, Franco-British Union of Architects, 1978-79; board member, Chatham Historic Dockyard Trust, from 1984. Recipient: *News Chronicle* Schools Competition Prize, London, 1938; Festival of Britain Restaurant Competition Prize, London, 1950; *Financial Times* Industrial Architecture Award, London, 1967; Ministry of Housing and Local Government Gold Medal, 1970;

Royal Institute of British Architects Award, 1973; Structural Steel Design Award, London, 1974; National Heritage Award, London, 1974; *The Times*/Institute of Chartered Surveyors Conservation Award, London, 1975; European Architectural Heritage Year Award, 1975. Associate, 1941, and Fellow, 1964, Royal Institute of British Architects; Fellow, Chartered Society of Designers, London, 1965; Fellow, Royal Society of Arts, London, 1967; Member, Royal West of England Academy, Bristol, 1972; Associate, 1976, and Academician, 1979, Royal Academy of Art, London; Officer, Order of the British Empire, 1982. Addresses: 6 Bacon's Lane, London N6 6BL; Leonard Manasseh and Partners, 58 Bloomsbury Street, London WC1, England.

Works:

Luxury restaurant, for the Festival of Britain, South Bank, London, 1950-51.
Manasseh house, Highgate, London, 1958-59.
Rutherford Secondary School in Marylebone, London, for the London County Council, 1960.
Furzedown Training College, London, for the London County Council, 1964-65.
National Motor Museum in Beaulieu, Hampshire, for Montagu Ventures Limited, 1971.
Master Builder Hotel extensions, Buckler's Hard, Hampshire, 1972.
Wellington Country Park in Heckfield, Hampshire, for Stratfield Saye Estates Management, 1975.
Manasseh house in Merindol, Provence, France, 1981.

Publications:

By MANASSEH: books—*Office Buildings,* with Roger Cunliffe, London 1962, Tokyo 1964; *The Historic Core of King's Lynn,* report with E. U. Chesterton, London 1964; *Snowdown Summit: A Report,* London 1975; *Eastbourne Harbour Study,* report, London 1976.

On MANASSEH: books—*Public Interiors: An International Survey* by Misha Black, London 1960; *House and Garden: The Modern Interior,* edited by Robert Harling, London 1964; *The Practical Idealists: 25 Years of Designing for Industry* by Jon and Avril Blake, London 1969.

Manasseh became an associate of the Royal Institute of British Architects in 1941 but was obliged by the war to serve as a pilot in the Royal Naval Fleet Air Arm. From 1946 to 1948, he was an assistant architect at the Hertfordshire County Council and from 1948 to 1950, a senior architect at the Stevenage Development Corporation. Winning the Festival of Britain prize for a restaurant design encouraged him to open his own practice in 1950, and the partnership developed with work in housing and schooling such as the North Westminster School in London for the Westminster City Council.

An enormous brief arrived when Lord Montagu decided to rebuild and expand his motor museum, and the plan was agreed with Hampshire County Council in 1966. The client required the museum, an information centre, an administration block, a library, and a restaurant. Work began in 1970, and the complex was opened by the Duke of Kent two years later. The largest structure is the National Motor Mu-

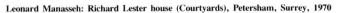

Leonard Manasseh: Richard Lester house (Courtyards), Petersham, Surrey, 1970

seum, a vast square crossed by two diagonal transepts which provide top lighting and form the entrance canopies. To unify the complex, materials were limited to steel, blockwork, and glazing, the idea of a glass building in a park being inspired by such English precedents as Paxton's Crystal Palace and Decimus Burton's glasshouses at Kew Gardens. (However, triangular glass roofs are a regular feature of the firm's designs, as in the house for the film producer Richard Lester.)

Impressed by the layout at Beaulieu, the Duke of Wellington asked Manasseh to design the information centre, restaurants, boating facilities, and museum at his new Wellington Country Park, Heckfield Hampshire. The west side of the park is for golf and riding, while the east side is organised into boating and fishing areas, nature trails, picnic sites, adventure areas for children, and a camping site. Manasseh based his designs on a six-metre structural grid to allow for future expansion, and pyramidal roofs dominate the buildings. He subscribes to Sir Henry Wotton's definition of architecture as "Firmness, Commodity and Delight," and says that scale is all-important. He believes in modern architecture as honest form, not as self-expression. With Roger Cunliffe, he is author of *Office Buildings*.

—Diana de Marly

MANDELLI, Mariuccia.

Italian fashion designer. Born in Bergamo, in 1933. Married Aldo Pinto. Worked as a teacher, Milan, 1952–54; designer and founder, with Flora Dolci, of Krizia fashion firm, Milan, from 1954; founded Kriziamaglia knitwear, 1966, and Kriziababy children's clothes, 1968: subsequently established Krizia boutiques, in Milan, Tokyo, London, New York, Detroit, Houston, etc. **Exhibitions:** *Italian Re-Evolution*, La Jolla Museum of Art, California, 1982; *40 Years of Italian Fashion*, Trump Tower, New York, 1983. Recipient: Fashion Press Award, Florence, 1964. Address: Via Agnelli 12, 20100 Milan, Italy.

Publications:

ON MANDELLI: books—*A History of Fashion* by J. Anderson Black and Madge Garland, London 1975, 1980; *The World of Fashion: People, Places, Resources* by Eleanor Lambert, New York and London 1976; *I Mass-Moda: Fatti e Personaggi dell'Italian Look* by Adrianna Mulassano, Florence 1979; *Fairchild's Who's Who in Fashion*, edited by Ann Stegemeyer, New York 1980; *Who's Who in Fashion*, edited by Karl Strute and Theodor Doelken, Zurich 1982; *The Collector's Book of Twentieth Century Fashion* by Frances Kennett, London and New York 1983; *40 Years of Italian Fashion*, exhibition catalogue compiled by B. G. Aragno, Rome 1983; *McDowell's Directory of Twentieth Century Fashion* by Colin McDowell, London 1984; *Design Source Book* by Penny Sparke and others, London 1986; *The Encyclopaedia of Fashion from 1840 to the 1980s* by Georgina O'Hara, London 1986.

The success of the Milanese boutique called Krizia, and, in fact, the prominence of Milanese fashion which has occurred during the past decade, are both largely due to the efforts to Krizia's founder and designer, Mariuccia Mandelli. Mandelli is one of the originators of the major contrast trend of Milan in which a simple, classic tailoring is punctuated with original and amusing accents to create a new face for stylish ready-to-wear fashion that is both eminently wearable and exuberantly youthful.

Among Krizia's early, important presentations was a showing at Orsini's on the invitation of Jean Rosenberg, vice-president of Bendel's. It was on this occasion that Mandelli was labeled "Crazy Krizia" by the fashion press for her combinations of simple shapes with madcap details. In 1976, Bergdorf Goodman featured stock by Krizia and other Milanese designers, providing the final step necessary for the Italians' rise to the forefront.

Representative of what has been called Krizia's "rough and sweet" look are Mandelli's 1977 outfittings consisting of nylon undershirts topped by matching rose-colored or dove-gray mohair bed-jackets or cardigans in open-knit weaves and worn with dropped-waist ballerina skirts of scalloped lace. Mandelli's daywear tends toward the practical; she has, for example, put elastic waistbands on her skirts for comfortable ease of movement, and her 1982 group of sport suits of loose tweeds and checks are plain, loose, and stylized. Mandelli's uses of her signature "improbable contrasts," however, abound most openly in her evening clothes, such as the mixes of satin skirts with sporty Angora sweaters which appeared in 1978. In that same year, she also presented her preferred simple slip dress accompanied by characteristic touches of humourous flamboyance such as a long, feathered stole or quilted jacket of satin faced in a different shade of the same color.

Mandelli has often used jodhpur pants. One 1977 outfit consisted of loose, draping jodhpurs in silk charmeuse worn with a lacy, mohair camisole, the whole enlivened by the glowing berry colors she featured that year. Also among Mandelli's original fashion accomplishments is her development of what she named "harmonica pleats" which combine vertical and horizontal pleatings.

Outstanding among Mandelli's designs are her knits which include items such as her 1977 lacy, mushroom-colored, evening sweater teamed with double-scarf of silk taffeta and eyelet taffeta and jodhpur pants. In 1981, she showed subtly sophisticated shiny knits and white angoras bedecked with yokes of pearls. Often appearing on Mandelli's knitwear are her signature animal motifs. In 1978, there was a jacquard crepe blouse with the front view of a tiger on its front and rear-tiger-view on its back. In her 1980 collection, there were colorful knits featuring parrots and toucans; short knit dresses included a one-piece version sporting the front half of a leopard and a two-piece style revealing the leopard's rear half. Not limiting herself to knitwear, Mandelli also put highly colorful birds and parrots on that season's summer tote bags and shoulder purses. For 1984, it's the dalmation, sharing the scene with more streamlined suits and double-dresses such as a back-buttoned flare over a little bit longer slim skirt.

From the start, Krizia's Mariuccia Mandelli has continuously based her highly original designs on nervy eccentricity and wit which have earned her a prominent place in the recent Milanese force that has successfully nudged ready-to-wear fashion in a new direction.

—Barbara Cavaliere

MANG, Karl.

Austrian architect, interior, exhibition and furniture designer. Born in Vienna, 5 October 1922. Educated at a high school in Vienna, 1933–41; studied engineering, at the Technical University, Vienna 1944–48: Dip.Ing. 1948; post-graduate studies, University of Rome, 1950–51. Served in the German Army, 1941–45: Lieutenant. Married the architect Eva von Frimmel in 1957; children: Bauxi, Carolina and Hannerl. Independent designer and architect. Vienna, from 1955: has designed for Thonet, Morawa, Wienerberger, Austrian Ministry of Science, Vienna Bundeskammer, Austrian Building Center, etc. Teaching assistant, Technical University, Vienna, 1948–54; instructor in furniture construction, Federal Trade School, Modling, 1954–59; lecturer, Academy of Applied Art, Vienna, 1963–72; guest professor, Staatliche Akademie der Bildenden Künste, Stuttgart, 1983; visiting professor, Universidad de Chile, Santiago, 1986. President, Österreichisches Institut für Formgebung, Vienna, 1972–83; permanent member of the Denkmalbeirat, Vienna, from 1980. **Exhibitions:** Künstlerhaus, Vienna, 1964; Schloss Walchen, Austria, 1976; Ursulinenhof, Linz, 1978; Ingenieurkammer, Vienna, 1987. Recipient: Communications Collaborative Certificate of Excellence, 1975; Chicago Book Clinic Award, 1975; Silver Medal of Honour, Vienna, 1981; and over 30 European architectural prizes, Titular professor, Vienna, 1977. Address: Baumannstrasse 9, 1030 Vienna, Austria.

Works:

Das Werk Michael Thonets travelling exhibition layouts, for the Austrian Center of Building, 1965.
Wienerberger variable pavilions in Graz, for Wienerberger, 1965, 1967.
Creative Austria travelling exhibition layouts, for the Bundeskammer, Vienna, 1970.
Thonet shops in Düsseldorf and Vienna, for Thonet, 1970–71.
Pocketbook shop, for Morawa, 1972.
Die Shaker travelling exhibition layouts, for the Neue Sammlung, Munich, 1974.
Kommunaler Wohnbau in Wien travelling exhibition layouts, for the City of Vienna, 1977.
Österreichische Architektur in Zeichnungen 1800–1900 travelling exhibition layouts, for the Kunstlerhaus, Vienna, 1981.
Vienna Imperial Treasury displays, for the Ministry of Science and Inquiry, 1981–87.
Austrian Embassy interiors, Baghdad, for the Foreign Ministry, 1982.
Austrian Theatre Museum interiors, for the Ministry of Science and Inquiry, from 1986.
Café Viennois interiors, for the Centre Georges Pompidou, Paris, 1986.

Publications:

By MANG: books—*Das Werk Michael Thonets*, exhibition catalogue, Vienna 1965; *Die Shaker*, exhibition catalogue, with Wend Fischer, Munich 1974; *Kommunaler Wohnbau in Wien, die Leistungen der zweiten Republik*, exhibition catalogue, Vienna 1978; *Kommunaler Wohnbau in Wien 1923–1934*, exhibition catalogue, Vienna 1978; *History of Modern Furniture*, Stuttgart 1978, London, New York and Tokyo 1979, Rome 1982; *Viennese Architecture 1860–1930 in Drawings*, with Eva Mang, Stuttgart, New York and London 1979; *Neus Wohnen, Wiener Innenraumgestaltung 1918–1938*, exhibition catalogue, Vienna 1980; *Moderne Verangenheit 1800–1900*, exhibition catalogue, Vienna 1981; *New Shops*, with Eva Mang, Stuttgart 1981, New York 1982; *Thonet Bugholzmöbel*, Vienna

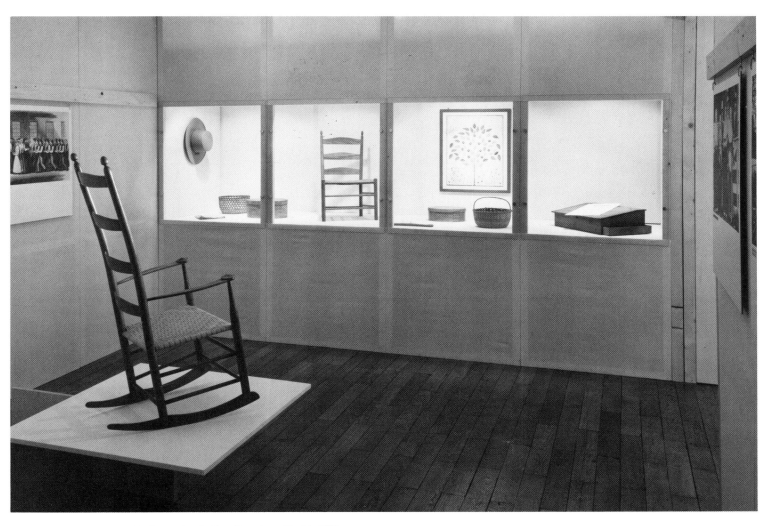

Karl Mang: *Die Shaker* exhibition layout, for the Neue Sammlung, Munich, 1974

1982, Tokyo 1985; *Moebel unserer Zeit: Fibel für die Einrichtung von Wohnungen,* with Eva Mang, Vienna 1984; *Wohnen in der Stadt: Ideen für Wien,* with Peter Marchant, Vienna 1988.

On MANG: books—*Mercati e Negozi* by Robert Aloi, Milan 1959; *International Shop Design* by Karl Kaspar, Stuttgart and London 1967; *Boutiquen, Shops und schicke Laden* by Wolfgang Grub, Munich 1974; *Industrial Design* by Bernd Lobach, Munich 1976; *Die Geschichte des Design in Deutschland von 1870 bis heute* by Gert Selle, Cologne 1978; *Shop Design* by Ingrid Wenz-Gahler, Leinfelden 1986.

Against the compulsion of consumer society to subject every product to rapid changes in fashion stands the design of a small but continually growing number of people to escape from this pressure and to become actively involved in creating their own personal home environments. Yet, a walk through any furniture fair, be it in Paris, Cologne, or Milan, should be enough to rob anyone of his illusions with respect to the true situation in the furniture market. It is safe to say that most furniture companies and retailers (not to mention most buyers) still prefer styles inspired by the past—prettily painted "peasant" furniture, for instance—perhaps as a way of compensating for the missing warmth in their daily lives. Rather than good contemporary designs, the stores offer fake Baroque, Spanish rustic, and the glib forms of a noncommittal modern.

Good modern furniture has been granted only a very modest corner in our civilization, and the interiors of tomorrow will not come without some serious re-thinking in the field of city planning. What is needed in the face of our rapidly disappearing countryside is an industrialized program of housing, based on higher population density and offering apartments with open floor plans. The greatest possible variability and mobility for every individual are just as important as the chance to design and plan one's own surroundings—in a word, participation in the design of housing, under the guidance of trained architects and planners.

An urban environment conceived in this way, modest but well designed, will require furniture that is not sensational but useful, and above all, flexible. It should be simple and human in form and designed for manufacture in large numbers at low prices. Furniture is basically always a child of its time, if only because the demands that people make on it change—and they often change several times even in the course of one lifetime. Nonetheless, this process should not be subject to the dictates of fashion alone. Then, too, many young people of today establish their households with very modest means. Having grown up in a rapidly shrinking world, they are accustomed to living in one apartment or city today and in another tomorrow. Rigid tradition has given way to a new, flexible style that, though it may express a greater social equality than ever before, is also characterized by an extremely individual view of interiors as personal environments. Light, versatile furniture makes it possible to furnish even today's tiny apartments in a pleasing way, even on a limited budget.

The variable furniture systems that have recently come on the market, often sold cash-and-carry to be assembled at home, are a good example of the kind of policy that is needed for the future. They provide an excellent means of supplementing, at a reasonable price, those single pieces which by reason of their aesthetic quality and their craftsmanship may still form the centre of gravity in any good contemporary interior.

Home furnishings of this type, if they are to be successful in the long run, will probably have to be accompanied by a program of consumer education. As long as most people's idea of formal quality swings back and forth between the poles of historicism and kitsch, a truly human and generally valid formal quality in home furnishings, as in architecture itself, will remain the dream of a few. There is reason to hope that a program of education in home furnishing, starting in the schools, might help people get over their status-consciousness and need for representation in choosing the objects they live with. If the mass media were to do their part, and if good, simple, modern furniture were made available at reasonable prices, then a change might truly come about. An architecture of quiet is going to have to follow the chaos of form and material of our consumer age, if we wish to continue existing reasonably with technology. Simple spaces for living, with clean well-designed furniture, will go far toward placing man in the center of his world again.

—Karl Mang

Angelo Mangiarotti: *Casta* centerpiece bowl in crystal, for the Colle Cristallo di Val d'Elsa, Siena, 1988

MANGIAROTTI, Angelo.

Italian architect, interior, exhibition and industrial designer. Born in Milan, 26 February 1921. Studied architecture, at the Politecnico, Milan, 1945–48: Dip.Arch. 1948. Architect and designer in partnership with Bruno Morassutti, Milan, 1955–60; freelance designer and architect in private practice, Milan, from 1960: design consultant to Porte Echappement Universel, La Chaux de Fonds, 1955–68, CGE of Milan, 1959, Alfa Romeo, Milan, 1960, and to Electrolux, Stockholm, 1961; art director, Colle Cristallo di Val d'Elsa, Siena, from 1987. Visiting professor, Institute of Design, Illinois Institute of Technology, Chicago, 1953–54, University of Hawaii, Honolulu, 1970, Ecole Polytéchnique Fédérale, Lausanne, 1975, University of Adelaide and South Australian Institute of Technology, Adelaide, 1976, and University of Sao Paulo, 1978; lecturer, Istituto Superiore di Disegno Industriale, Venice, 1963–64, and University of Florence, 1981–82. **Exhibitions:** *La Casa Abitata,* Florence, 1965; *Angelo Mangiarotti,* Zurich, 1966; *Angelo Mangiarotti,* Delft, 1966; *Ten Italian Architects,* Los Angeles, 1967; *Modern Chairs 1918–1970,* London, 1970; *Exposicion Internacional de la Vivienda,* Santiago de Chile, 1972; *Architettura 28/78,* Milan, 1978; *Design Since 1945,* Philadelphia, 1983; *Sammenhenger Angelo Mangiarotti,* Oslo, 1985; *Poiesis: Alabastri di Angelo Mangiarotti,* Milan, 1986; *Angelo Mangiarotti,* Genoa, 1988; *Poiesis: Sculture di Angelo Mangiarotti,* Milan, 1988. Recipient: Olimpiadi della Cultura Boy's Prize, Milan, 1952; Economic Development Center Prize, Trieste, 1953; Domus Formica Award, Milan, 1956; Gold Medal, Villa dell'Olmo, Como, 1957; Associazione Italiana Tecnico Economica del Cemento Award, 1962; In/Arch Lombardia Award, Milan, 1962; National Gulf of La Spezia Award, 1963; Associazione Italiana Prefabbricatori Award, 1972; Prix Européen de la Construction Métallique, 1979; World Architecture Biennial Medal, Sofia, 1986; Targa Alcan Award, Milan, 1988. Addresses: Via Cesare da Sesto 15, 20123 Milan; Stradela Valmarana 2, 36100 Vicenza, Italy.

Works:

Multi-Use furniture system, for Poltronova, 1955 (with Bruno Morassutti).
Secticon series of mantle clocks, for Porte Echappement Universel, 1957 (with Bruno Morassutti).
Sewing machines, for Salmoiraghi, 1957 (with Bruno Morassutti).
Series of bronze vases, for Bernini, 1962.
Cub8 furniture system, for Poltronova, 1967.
In/Out furniture system, for Knoll International, 1968.
Series of polyurethane armchairs and side chairs, for Zanotta, 1969.
Eros series of marble tables, for Skipper, 1971.
De Nos range of wood furniture, for Skipper, 1975.
Incas series of sandstone tables, for Skipper, 1978.
Egina wall and ceiling lamp, for Artemide, 1978.
Asolo series of granite tables, for Skipper, 1981.
Chicago fibreglass chair, for Chicago, 1983.
Clessidra and *Sorela* glass lamps, for Skipper, 1985.
Ice-Stopper crystal glasses, for Colle Cristallo di Val d'Elsa, 1986.
Anatis, Oinoche, Askos and *Kyatos* crystal pitchers, for Colle Cristallo di Val d'Elsa, 1987.
Series of blown glass vases, for Vistosi, 1988.

Techne halogen lamp, for Skipper, 1988.
Casta crystal centerpiece bowl, for Colle Cristallo di Val d'Elsa, 1988.

(for a complete list of Mangiarotti's buildings and architectural projects, see *Contemporary Architects.*)

Publications:

By MANGIAROTTI: book—*In Nome dell'Architettura,* Milan 1987; articles—in *Domus* (Milan), 1948–78; *Arts and Architecture* (Los Angeles), 1953–70; *L'Architecture d'Aujourd'hui* (Paris), 1953–73; *Casabella* (Milan), 1955–78; *L'Oeil* (Paris), 1956–72; *Architectural Forum* (New York), 1959–63; *Bauen und Wohnen* (Zurich), 1959–77; *Moebel Interior Design* (Stuttgart), 1960–75; *L'Industria Italiana del Cemento* (Rome), 1963–77; *Ottagono* (Milan), 1967–77; *Casa Vogue* (Milan), 1968–77; *Premiere* (Milan), 1987–88; *Design News* (Tokyo), 1984–88.

On MANGIAROTTI: books—*Italian Contemporary Architecture,* London 1952; *Mobili Tipo* by Robert Aloi, Milan 1956; *Angelo Mangiarotti,* Tokyo 1965; *Design Italiano: i mobili* by Enrichetta Ritter, Milan and Rome 1968; *Introduzione al Disegno Industriale* by Gillo Dorfles, Turin 1972; *History of Modern Furniture* by Karl Mang, Stuttgart, 1978, 1989, London 1979; *Angelo Mangiarotti: Il Processo del Costruire* by Enrico D. Bona, Milan 1980; *Il Design Italiano degli Anni '50* by Andrea Branzi and Michele De Lucchi, Milan 1981; *Contemporary Furniture* by Klaus-Jürgen Sembach, Stuttgart and New York 1982; *Furniture by Architects,* Tokyo 1982; *Angelo Mangiarotti,* Zurich 1985; *Bauten von Angelo Mangiarotti,* Stuttgart 1985; *Mangiarotti* by Enrico D. Bona, Genoa 1988.

Angelo Mangiarotti has worked with various collaborators, often in fairly lasting partnerships, but his strong design personality seems to sweep his partners along his chosen path, in which certain forms and materials seem predominant, notably cones, truncated cones, and shapes generated from them to support tables. Besides the characteristic 1955–56 desk and the important 1963 tables, the M1 table of 1969 used these forms, this time in marble. Over several years after 1957, they also appeared in a series of table clocks for the Swiss firm Porte Echappement Universel.

It must not be supposed, however, that he is a designer who uses a single form in all his work. Mangiarotti constantly senses new formal possibilities, a well as new uses of the forms he has employed in other situations, as can be seen, for example, in his apartment block at San Siro, Milan. Here, he used an ingenious arrangement of three cylinders that must have been thought out in three dimensions, although the coherence of the planning might suggest otherwise, and could have played a considerable role in the generation of the block. The general effect of the building, however, is so strikingly successful that the coherence must derive from the overall vision.

In the late 1950s in Milan, when a number of pioneer designers had virtually established the new shape of sewing machines, it took courage to accept such a commission and to stamp the design of the Salmoiraghi 44 with a character of its own, but this was exactly what Mangiarotti achieved. His sewing machine had a four-square look, forthright but suitably refined, with all corners and edges rounded. The final form was also admirably suited to the manufacturing process and assembly.

The storage and shelving units produced for

Knoll International developed ideas with which he had first experimented a few years earlier in the CUB8 component wall-system and free-standing assemblies, for Poltronova. This design, which had also used extruded plastic, interlocking joints, in its turn departed from some of the aspects of an even earlier series of mass-produced bedroom units for Mascheroni, though in 1955, the clever use of trestle supports had seemed more interesting. These concerns were also to be seen in his research in the mid-1960s into a pre-fabrication building system, though the formal preoccupations changed with the changing situations.

It would be difficult to sum up Mangiarotti's qualities as a designer and even more so to attempt to characterise his work in other than somewhat general terms. To be sure, however, he always manifests concern for formal possibilities, for precise use of materials and finishes, and for immaculate detailing, as well as devotion to the most pleasing effect with the most rational use of manufacturing possibilities.

—Tonio del Renzio

MANWARING, Michael

American graphic designer. Born in Palo Alto, California, 21 March 1942. Studied under James Robertson, Gordon Ashby and Barbara and Jack Stauffacher, at the San Francisco Art Institute, 1961–64: BFA 1964. Married Dixie Wells in 1960; children: Elizabeth and Christopher. Graphic designer, in the Gordon Ashby exhibition design studio, San Francisco, 1964, and in the Robertson/Montgomery graphic design studio, San Francisco, 1964–68; partner, in Reis and Manwaring graphic design studio, San Francisco, 1968–76; founder-president, The Office of Michael Manwaring, San Francisco, from 1976. Instructor in graphic design, California College of Arts and Crafts, Oakland, from 1976; visiting instructor in environmental graphic design, University of California, Berkeley, 1977. Co-founder, San Francisco chapter of the American Institute of Graphic Arts, 1982. **Collection:** Library of Congress, Washington, D.C. Recipient: San Francisco Society of Communicating Arts Medal, 1972, 1974, 1980, 1981, 1982; *Architectural Record* interiors award, 1972; New York Art Directors Club Gold Medal, 1980; Typographers International Association Award, 1982. Address: 1005 Sansome Street, San Francisco, California 94111, U.S.A.

Works:

Graphic signage, for the Oakland/Alameida Coliseum, California, 1967.
Theme exhibit, for *Hemisfair '68,* San Antonio, Texas, 1968.
Bookstore graphics, for the San Francisco Museum of Modern Art, 1973.
Environmental graphics, for California Street Cooking School, San Francisco, 1973.
Showroom displays and interior graphics, for Patrick Carpet Mills, San Francisco, 1976.
Indian Basin Industrial Park graphic signage, San Francisco, 1977.
Graphic signage, for Oakville Grocery Company, San Francisco, 1980.

Michael Manwaring: Poster for the Stanford Conference on Design, 1981

Centro Nuevo urban development graphics, Santiago de Chile, 1980.

Plaza Lyon urban development graphics, Santiago de Chile, 1981.

AIASFLOO exhibition graphics, for the American Institute of Architects, San Francisco, 1982.

Publications:

On MANWARING: books—*Letterheads of the World* by Yoshihisa Ishihara, Tokyo 1977; *Print Casebooks: Environmental Graphics* by Susan Braybrooke, Baltimore 1978, 1982; *Architectural Signing and Graphics* by John Follis and David Hammer, New York 1979; *Graphic Design for Our Environment* by Takenobu Igarashi, Tokyo 1980; *Print Casebook: Exhibition Design* by Susan Braybrooke, Baltimore 1983; *New American Design* by Hugh Aldersley-Williams, New York 1988.

*

Perhaps the most important factor regarding my design is that I am a native Californian. Our California graphic design source of influence is more Oriental than European, which gives our work intuitive, mystical, and sensual qualities, as contrasted with midwest or east coast design, which tends to be more literary, conceptual, and European.

I am for: contextual approach to graphic design, elegance, richness, sensuality, appropriate ambiguity, and graphic design as cultural contribution. I am against: dogmatic approach to graphic design, rigidity, pragmatism, international sign symbols, monoculture, and graphic design imitating art.

—Michael Manwaring

*

Michael Manwaring was trained in the 1960's at the San Francisco Art Institute, a school which has long emphasized personal expression. Manwaring's work never partook of the sometimes funky naivete typical of student work there, but he did absorb the emphasis on a personal symbolism and individual composition. Since he began his work as a graphic designer during the period of primacy of the Swiss style, with its grid system for composition; reductivist repertoire of hard-edged, geometric shapes; brilliant, flat color; and very large type contrasting with small, Manwaring's emphasis on texture, especially delicate pencil shading of pointillist dots, his precise and touching detail, soft and unusual colors, and freedom from the grid in compositional placement made his work seem quietly revolutionary. In fact, over the ten years from 1972 to 1982, his style has so influenced the designers of northern California that at least half of them could be said to belong to his "school."

One of the crucial elements of his style, the exquisitely modulated tonal range of his drawings, has proved to be inimitable. His unique color repertory of grayed blues, roses, and greens and pale yellows, is distinctive, but even more influential has been his choice of scale of compositional elements. Instead of large, flat components, he has scattered white or colored-powder patterns of dots through both foreground and background areas. While no one has equalled Manwaring's finesse with grayed hues, the use of ornamental dot grids and another of his innovations—the use of looping, monoweight lines with split-font color gradations—have been widely copied.

Manwaring moved from compass-drawn shapes to a modified realism, featuring softly rounded curves. The edge, still an important component in his design, became variable, sometimes torn into letters or animal shapes from paper. In subject matter, too, his work is unique, especially in his sensitive rendering of flowers, flora in general, and small animals. All testify to his understanding of the pleasures of attending to detail in small things, often overlooked by the harried, brash, or blasé observer. Manwaring's emphasis on images of quiet contemplation are appropriate to his clients—who generally sell especially well-made clothing or delectable foodstuffs—but they are equally appreciated by a public eagerly looking for the gentle and humane in graphic design.

—Frances Butler

MARDERSTEIG, Giovanni (Hans).

Italian typographer, book and typeface designer. Born in Weimar, Germany, 8 January 1892; emigrated to Italy in 1926. Studied law, at the universities of Bonn, Vienna, Kiel and Jena, until 1913: D.Jur. 1913. Co-editor, with C. G. Heine, of *Genius* biannual, for Kurt Wolff Verlag, Munich, 1917–22; freelance typographer and book designer from 1922, and type designer from 1937: typographic and technical consultant, to William Collins and Sons publishers, London and Glasgow, 1934–35; founder-director, of Officina Bodoni handpress, in Montagnola, Switzerland, 1923–27, and in Verona, Italy, 1927–77; founder-director, of Stamperia Valdonega typesetting and printing firm, Verona, 1947–77. **Exhibitions:** Musée Plantin, Antwerp, 1954; Museum fur Kunst und Gewerbe, Hamburg, 1954; British Museum, London, 1954; Biblioteca Comunale, Verona, 1956; Staatliche Graphische Sammlung, Munich, 1958; Gutenberg Museum, Bern, 1963; Bibliothèque Royale, Brussels, 1965. Recipient: First Prize, Gabriele D'Annunzio Competition, Rome, 1927. Order of the Grande Ufficiale, Rome; honorary member, Double Crown Club, London; member, Society of Typographical Artists, London, and Association Typographique Internationale. *Died* (in Verona, Italy) *December 1977.*

Works:

A Socratic Dialogue by Plato book design, for The Pleiad, Paris, 1926.

Damianus Moyllus: Treatise on Classic Letter Design book design, for the Pegasus Press, Paris, 1927.

Zeno typeface, 1936.

Griffo typeface, 1939.

Paul Valery/C. Day Lewis: Le Cimetière Marin book design, for Secker and Warburg, London, 1946.

Dylan Thomas: 26 Poems book design, for J. M. Dent, London, 1949.

Dante typeface, 1955.

Pacioli typeface, 1956.

T. S. Eliot: Four Quartets book design, for Faber and Faber, London, 1960.

T. S. Eliot: The Waste Land book design, for Faber and Faber, London, 1961.

Publications:

By MARDERSTEIG: books include—*Felice Feliciano Veronese: Alphabetum Romanum,* editor, Verona, Italy 1960; *Das Werkbuch der Officina Bodoni,* Wetzlar, West Germany 1960; *The Remarkable Story of a Book Made in Padua in 1477,* translated by Hans Schmoller, London 1967; *Ein Leben der Buchern gewidmet,* Mainz 1968; *Manuale typografico di Giovanni B. Bodoni,* editor, Verona, Italy 1968; *Libre del Officina Bodoni 1954–1968,* Verona, Italy 1968; *Francesco Alunno di Ferrara,* Florence 1970; *Liberale ritrovato nell'Esopo Veronese del 1479,* Verona, Italy 1973.

On MARDERSTEIG: books—*L'Officina Bodoni: Biblioteca Civica di Verona 1923–62,* exhibition catalogue, Verona 1962; *Buchgestaltung* by Albert Kapr, Dresden 1963; *The Officina Bodoni 1923–62,* exhibition catalogue, Bern 1963; *Officina Bodoni, Verona: Catalogue Raisonne 1923–1964,* edited by Franco Riva and Luc Indestege, Verona 1965; *Giovanni Mardersteig: An Account of his Work* by John Dreyfus, New York 1966; *Ein beispielhaftes Lebenswerk: Laudatio auf Giovanni Mardersteig* by Rudolf Hafelstange, Mainz 1968; *Officina Bodoni* by John S. Ryder, Pinner 1972; *In Fair Verona,* edited by Nicholas Barber, Cambridge 1972; *Giovanni Mardersteig, the Officina Bodoni: An Account of the Work of a Hand Press 1923–1977* by Hans Schmoller, Verona 1980.

*

Having been impressed as an adolescent in Weimar, Germany by the Kelmscott and Doves Press books, Giovanni Mardersteig as a young man worked for Kurt Wolff Verlag, the influential publisher of the German avant-garde. But the necessity of living in the more salutary climate of the Italian Alps (Mardersteig's lungs were fragile) propelled him into establishing his own press, the Officina Bodoni, in Montagnola in 1923 and then in Verona in 1927. In more than fifty years, he produced almost 200 books on a handpress, all scrupulously edited and designed, and from 1945 to 1977, larger editions of books printed by offset lithography at the Stamperia Valdonega.

Mardersteig's insistence on the highest standards of scholarship in his texts and, above all, on the most appropriate and the best-quality materials and meticulous workmanship constitutes the basis of one component of his reputation as a pre-eminent private publisher of the twentieth century. The other aspect of his work, famed in Italy and throughout Europe, was the simplicity of his typographic composition, recalling the spare perfection of the typography of his inspiration, the eighteenth-century master printer, Giambattista Bodoni, but not limited to imitation of any one format. Through this work, Mardersteig reactivated interest in Bodoni's design and Bodoni's types. (He was allowed to use Bodoni's matrices to cast types for the printing of Gabriele d'Annunzio's complete works, commissioned by the Italian Government.) His use of the sparkling Bodoni types, which called for princely generosity of format—wide leading, large type relative to the page, and lavish margins—continued the esthetic introduced by T. J. Cobden-Sanderson and Emery Walker through their Doves Press and added an element of grandeur more reflecting Italian book models. Eventually, he reset, from newly cast type, the monumental pages of Bodoni's *Manuale tipografico.*

However, Mardersteig also used other faces extensively and was responsible, working closely with the French punch-cutter Charles Malin, for the design of the typefaces Zeno, Griffo, Dante, and Pacioli Titling for his own use. All of these faces were based on the earliest roman types, cut in Italy 200 years before Bodoni, and they attest to the primacy of the Italian model—open, legible, elegant—in Mardersteig's imagination. In return for this Italian gift, Mardersteig renewed Italian pride in their heritage, and his book design remains influential there, as is seen in the work of both small presses (such as that of Franco Maria Ricci) and large publishing houses. His design influence continues, too, in the Stamperia Valdonega, directed now by his son Martino Mardersteig.

—Frances Butler

MARI, Enzo.

Italian artist, illustrator, graphic, textile and industrial designer. Born in Novara, 27 April 1932. Studied classics and literature, at the Accademia di Brera, Milan, 1952–56; mainly self-taught in design from 1952. Independent visual artist and researcher from 1952, and freelance designer, Milan, from 1956: designed for Danese, Driade, Gabbianelli, Gavina, Artemide, Zanotta, etc. Co-ordinator of Nuova Tendenza group of artists, Milan, 1963. Instructor, at the Scuola Umanitaria, Milan, 1963–66, Institute of Art, Rome, 1970, Centro Sperimentale di Cinematografia, Rome, 1971, Centro Studi di Comunicazione Visiva, University of Parma, 1972. **Exhibitions:** Galleria San Fedele, Milan, 1953; Studio B24, Milan, 1957; Galleria Danese, Milan, 1959, 1961, 1972, 1974; Muzej za Umjetnosti, Zagreb, 1962; Centro Arte Viva, Trieste, 1966; Stedelijk Museum, Amsterdam, 1966; Galleria del Naviglio, Milan, 1968; Musée des Arts Decoratifs, Paris, 1970; Museo di Castelvecchio, Verona, 1970; Galleria Nazionale d'Arte Moderna, Rome, 1970; Galleria Milano, Milan, 1972, 1973, 1974; Galleria Uxa, Verona, 1974; Palazzo Reale, Milan, 1984; Galleria Civica, San Marino, 1988. **Collections:** Museum of Modern Art, New York; Philadelphia Museum of Art; Moderna Museet, Stockholm; Stedelijk Museum, Amsterdam; Museum für Kunst und Gewerbe, Hamburg; Galleria Nazionale d'Arte Moderna, Rome. Recipient: Premio San Fedele, Milan, 1952, 1954; Premio Villa dell'Olmo, Como, 1957; Domus/Inox Prize, Milan, 1962; In/Arch Prize, Rome, 1963; Liubliana Graphics Biennale Prize, 1964, 1966; Premio Convegni di Rimini, 1965; Premio Michetti, Francavilla al Mare, 1967; Compasso d'Oro Award, Milan, 1967, 1979, 1986; Youth Book Prize, Bonn, 1971; International Design Center Prize, New York, 1987. Address: Piazzale Baracca 10, 20123 Milan, Italy.

Works:

16 Animali educational game in wood or plastic, for Danese, 1957.
Putrelle containers in welded sheet metal, for Danese, 1958.
Paros containers in marble, for Danese, 1960.
Natural Fruit serigraph print series, for Danese, 1960–72.
Camicia flower vases in aluminium and glass, for Danese, 1961.
Celebes wastebin, *Mascarene* umbrella stand, and *Kerguelen* hat-stand in plastic, for Danese, 1962–68.
Glifo adjustable bookcase in plastic, for Gavina, 1967.
Serie Elementare majolica ceramic tile system, for Gabbianelli, 1968.
Day-Night divan bed, for Driade, 1973.
Samos containers in handmade porcelain, for Danese, 1973.
Frate, Fratelle and *Cugino* series of tables in crystal, cast iron and wood, for Driade, 1974.
Box folding chair in plastic, for Anonima Castelli, 1975.

Aggregato lighting system, for Artemide, 1976.
Tonietta chair in cast aluminium, for Zanotta, 1985.
Salina desk accessories in pressed glass, for Danese, 1985.
Opasis tablewares in stainless steel, for Zani e Zani, 1986.
Paolina chair in walnut, for Pozzi e Verga, 1986.
Smith e Smith kitchen tools and fittings in cast steel, for Zani e Zani, 1987.
Resegone, Hot-Dog and *Altino* series of tables in wood, for Lema, 1988.
Toscolano range of table cutlery in cast steel, for Zani e Zani, 1989.

Publications:

By MARI: books—*La Funzione della Ricerca Estetica*, Milan 1970; *The Appel and the Butterfly*, with Lela Munari, London 1970; *Falce e Martello*, Milan 1973; *Proposta per un'Autoprogettazione*, Milan 1974; *Romanzo Storico*, with Carla Vasio, Milan 1975; *Ipotesi di Rifondazione del Progetto*, Milan 1978; *Dove' e l'Artigiano*, Florence 1981; *Tre Palazze del Duomo*, Milan 1984.

On MARI: books—*Enzo Mari* by Max Bill and Bruno Munari, Milan 1959; *Il Disegno Industriale e la sua Estetica* by Gillo Dorfles Bologna 1963; *Il Design in Italia 1945–1972* by Paolo Fossati, Turin 1972; *Enzo Mari, Designer* by Renato Pedio, Bari 1980; *Contemporary Furniture*, edited by Klaus-Jürgen Sembach, Stuttgart and New York 1982; *Enzo Mari* by Arturo Carlo Quintavalle, Parma 1983; *Italian Design: 1870 to the Present* by Penny Sparke, London and New York 1988; *Enzo Mari: Modelli del Reale* by F. Leonetti, F. Menna and R. Pedio, Milan 1988; *Italian Modern: A Design Heritage* by Gianni Albera and Nicolas Monti, New York 1989.

Like some of his product designs, Enzo Mari is an enigma. Following his studies at the Accademia di Brera, in 1952 he started his theoretical research into the psychology of vision, systems of perception, and the methodology of design. In the following years, three-dimensional models of linear elements, planes, and other shapes were produced. Mari soon discovered one reason that this esoteric work must be interrupted: he needed to produce some income, since he was not independently wealthy. There followed a series of product designs.

Probably the most notable are the objects and games that he conceived for the Italian firm Danese. The objects included vases, bowls, pen- and pencil-holders, and ashtrays, primarily in ABS and other plastics, in forms that could be easily mass-produced while still being beautiful to look at, tactile, and, of course, functional. Mari professed a "rational" design philosophy in which he defined "rational" as "elaborated or constructed in a way that corresponds exactly to the purpose or function."

Mari once contemplated the design of an ashtray for more than a year (while doing other things) before finally producing an extraordinarily handsome design that had one major drawback—its design was so carefully thought out and so inherently different from other designs that an uncomprehending public caused it to be unsuccessful in the marketplace. The project did, however, have a positive contribution to Mari's own lifestyle—by the end of the process he had abandoned his two-packs-a-day smoking habit!

Mari's games and game cards have usually been intended as communicative (instructional) instruments as well as tactile objects. Il Gioco dell Favole [The fable game] was a series of

twelve tablets slotted to interlock and portraying forty-five animals, the sun, moon, etc. These invited the user to "re-discover the pleasure of recognizing the symbols of his imagination," while inventing his own story as the cards were played. Some of the images (a sleeping bear, the head of a duck) were also enlarged into another form of object—a wall-hanging print—still another form of visual communication. Another series of cards provided a few lines—an idea upon which users could build (actually draw on the surface of the card) by themselves.

Curiously, Mari, himself the designer of many beautiful objects, does not believe that the task of designing objects has any significance in today's society. He believes that the designer's role should be in the field of communication and, more important, that the designer should be politically active and responsive to the needs of contemporary society. It is not by accident that the pieces of 44 Valuations, in spite of the curvy, irregular shapes, when assembled together produce a hammer and sickle—one symbol of social revolution. Recently, Mari's "objects" have grown into a variety of furniture designs for various manufacturers. All of them continue his "rational" approach.

—William Victor Kriebel

MARISCAL, (Francisco) Javier (Errando).

Spanish fashion, textile, graphic and industrial designer. Born in Valencia, 9 February 1950. Educated in Valencia, until 1967; studied philosophy, at the Universidad de Valencia, 1967–70; graphic design, at the Escuela de Grafismo Elisava, Barcelona, 1971–73. Served in the Spanish Army, 1974. Worked as a gardener and handyman, in Ibiza, 1975–76; freelance designer, in Barcelona, from 1976: has designed for Memphis furniture, BD Ediciones de Diseno, Marieta textiles, etc. **Exhibitions:** Galeria Mec-Mec, Barcelona, 1977; Sala Vincon, Barcelona, 1979, 1981, 1982; Galeria Central, Madrid, 1980; Galeria Local, Madrid, 1980; Galeria Moriarti, Madrid, 1981; Galeria Fucares, Almagro, 1982; Galeria Temple, Valencia, 1983; Galeria Rene Metras, Barcelona, 1983; Galerie Actuel, Paris, 1983. **Collection:** Philadelphia Museum of Art. Addresses: Valencia 264, 08007 Barcelona, Spain; c/o BD Ediciones de Diseno, 291 Mallorca, 08037 Barcelona, Spain.

Works:

Textile collections, for Marieta, 1978–83.
Duplex bar stool, for BD Ediciones de Diseno, 1980.
Bar-Cel-Ona poster, for the City of Barcelona, 1980.
Duplex Bar interiors and furnishings, Barcelona, 1980.
The Garriris comic strip, for *El Vibora* magazine, 1980–82.
Carnaval poster, for the City of Barcelona, 1981.
Hilton food trolley, for Memphis, 1981.
Arana lamp, for BD Ediciones de Diseno, 1983 (with Pepe Cortes).
Garraf lamp, for BD Ediciones de Diseno, 1983 (with Pepe Cortes).
Valencia lamp, for BD Ediciones de Diseno, 1983 (with Pepe Cortes).

Enzo Mari: *Tonietta* side chair in welded aluminium, for Zanotta, 1985

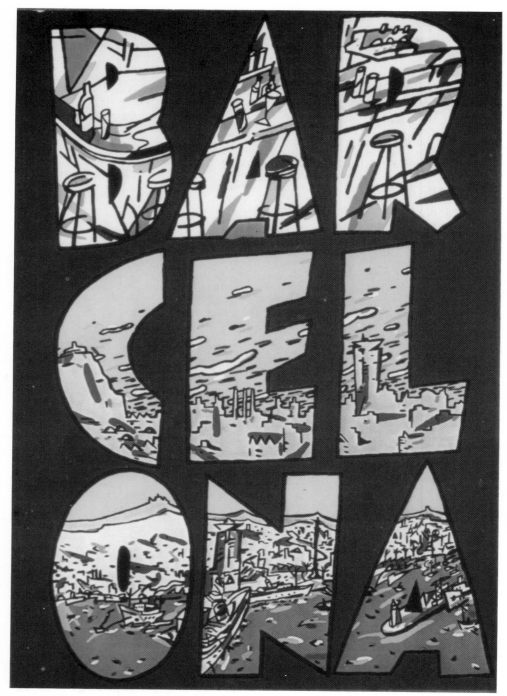

Javier Mariscal: *Bar-Cel-Ona* pictographic poster, 1980

Publications:

By MARISCAL: books—*ABC.DARI IL.LUS-TRAT,* Barcelona 1979; *Apuntes,* Barcelona 1983; *Mariscal,* Paris 1983.

On MARISCAL: books—*Memphis: The New International Style,* edited by Barbara Radice, Milan 1981; *Design Since 1945,* edited by Kathryn Hiesinger and George Marcus, Philadelphia and London 1983; *Design Source Book* by Penny Sparke and others, London 1986; *Nouvelles Tendances,* with introduction by Francois Burkhardt, Paris 1987; *International Design Yearbook 1988/89,* edited by Arata Isozaki, London 1988; articles—in *El Pais* (Madrid), 8 January 1978, 21 September 1978; *Ajoblanco* (Barcelona), March 1978; *Graphic Design* (Tokyo), no. 76, 1979; *New York Times,* 16 October 1980; *Casa Vogue* (Milan), August 1981; *Modo* (Milan), September 1981, December 1986; *Diagonal* (Barcelona), March 1982; *La Vanguardia* (Barcelona), 5 October 1982; *Bon a Tirer* (Paris), September 1985, January 1987; *Blueprint* (London), December/January 1986; *Form* (Stockholm), January 1987; *Design* (London), January 1988.

A designer is a person who plans objects for particular uses. The designs, the objects that are interesting to me are those that have—in addition to and in spite of their usefulness—a special charm, something that makes them a little mysterious, magical, poetic, or simply pleasant. I love it when they're beautiful because the shapes, colors, and textures are in agreement with the internal philosophy of the object. This makes them esthetically pleasing, natural, and harmonious.

—Javier Mariscal

MARTIN, Noel.

American exhibition and graphic designer. Born in Syracuse, Ohio, 19 April 1922. Studied painting, drawing and printmaking, Art Academy of Cincinnati, Ohio, 1939–41, 1945–47; mainly self-taught in typography and design, from 1947. Served in camouflage and information units, U.S. Army, 1942–45: Sergeant. Married Coletta Ruchty in 1942; children: Dana and Reid. Display and graphic designer, Cincinnati Art Museum, since 1947; also freelance graphic designer and art director, working for the Mortgage Corporation of Detroit, Cincinnati Contemporary Arts Center, Abraham and Strauss, Standard Oil of New Jersey, *Atlantic Monthly, New Republic,* etc., in Cincinnati, from 1949: design consultant, Champion International, 1959–82, Xomor Corporation from 1961, Federated Department Stores, 1962–83, and Hebrew Union College from 1969. Assistant to the Director, Cincinnati Art Museum, 1947–55. Instructor, Cincinnati Art Academy, 1951–57; Adjunct Professor and Designer-in-Residence, University of Cincinnati, 1968–73. Advisory Board Member, Carnegie-Mellon University, Rhode Island School of Design, Cincinnati Symphony Orchestra, American Institute of Graphic Arts, and Aspen Design Conference. **Exhibitions:** *Four American Graphic Designers: Martin, Matter, Lionni, Shahn,* Museum of Modern Art, New York, 1954; Contemporary Arts Center, Cincinnati, 1954, 1971; Rhode Island School of Design, Providence, 1955; Society of Typographic Arts, Chicago, 1956; Cornell University, Ithaca, New York, 1956; American Institute of Graphic Arts, New York, 1958; Cooper and Beatty, Toronto, 1971. **Collections:** Museum of Modern Art, New York; Cincinnati Art Museum, Ohio; Cincinnati Historical Society, Ohio; Boston Museum of Fine Arts; Library of Congress, Washington, D.C.; Stedelijk Museum, Amsterdam. Recipient: Art Directors Club Award, Philadelphia, 1957; Sachs Award, Cincinnati, 1973. Member: Alliance Graphique Internationale; International Center of Typographic Arts. Address: 6226 Robinson Road, Cincinnati, Ohio 45213, U.S.A.

Publications:

By MARTIN: book illustrated—*The Afternoon in Dismay* by P. Wild, Cincinnati 1968; articles—"Tschichold's Position Today" in *Modern Graphic Design* (New York?), Spring 1957; "Modern Art and Graphic Design" in *Printing Progress: A Mid-Century Report,* Cincinnati 1959.

On MARTIN: books—*Who's Who in Graphic Art,* edited by Walter Amstutz, Zurich 1962, Dubendorf 1982; articles—"Noel Martin: A Designer in the Midwest" by E. H. Dwight in *Print* (New York), October/November 1954.

Noel Martin is known for the range of his work as a graphic designer, encompassing catalogs, brochures, books, posters and advertisements for cultural, commercial and industrial institutions, and for his exhibition designs. Martin is also an educator, in the broadest sense, because his work as a graphic designer made the Cincinnati area community aware of the expanded possibilities arising from new technical means and progressive concepts.

Born in a small river town in southeastern Ohio, Martin moved to Cincinnati as a young boy and spent the rest of his life there (except for military service). From 1939–1941 he studied at the Cincinnati Art Academy, where his teachers included the painter Ralston Crawford. He spent 39 months in the U.S. Army Air Force during World War II, assigned to camouflage and educational units, where he worked with fellow artists making drawings, models and filmstrips. While on assignment in New York he became familiar with a wider range of modern art than he had been able to see in Cincinnati.

In 1945 Martin returned to his studies at the Cincinnati Art Academy, where he remained until 1947. While still a student, he began working in the nearby Cincinnati Art Museum. His duties included building display cases, mounting sculpture, and assisting in the installation of temporary exhibitions. Meanwhile he continued his own work as a painter. He fell into the profession of graphic design by being asked to design some small printed pieces for the Museum. His interest in graphic design grew, in spite of what he later called his "art school snobbery." The Museum had its own print shop, and Martin spent a lot of time with the Museum printer, a skilled craftsperson, who taught him the basic mechanics of printing. Beyond this, Martin thinks of himself as a self-taught graphic designer. He asked a lot of questions, studied type books, and learned from some of his mistakes. He also began his lifelong practice of working very closely with the craftspersons who actually carry out his designs. And he studied the work of other graphic designers of the past and present.

Martin supplemented what could be learned locally and from publications by corresponding with other designers and meeting with designers who visited Cincinnati, and by attending sessions of the International Design Conference at Aspen, Colorado.

From the first there was nothing parochial about Martin's designs, as evidenced by the fact that he began to receive national recognition as early as 1954 when the Museum of Modern Art in New York included his work in its exhibition, "Four American Graphic Designers" (with Leo Lionni, Ben Shahn and Herbert Matter). Later the same year he had his first one-person exhibition, at the Contemporary Arts Center in Cincinnati. Other one-person exhibitions followed, including those at the Rhode Island School of Design in Providence, in 1955, at the Society of Typographic Arts in Chicago in 1956, and at the American Institute of Graphic Arts in New York in 1958.

From his base in the Cincinnati Art Museum, where he has designed most of the Museum's catalogs, posters and brochures since 1947, Martin went on to become designer for many leading cultural, commercial and industrial institutions in Cincinnati and surrounding communities. In doing so he expanded local awareness of the possibilities inherent in progressive concepts in graphic design, and in advances in printing technology. Cincinnati had once been a leader in the fine arts and in ceramics; it had also been a leader in the printing arts, due to the lithographic firms which rose to prominence there during the nineteenth century. But by the 1940s Cincinnati had become a backwash, and had generally remained unmoved by new developments in art and in graphic design.

The pioneering role in bringing new concepts in art and design to Cincinnati was taken by the Modern Art Society, founded in 1939 (and renamed the Contemporary Arts Center in 1954). The Modern Art Society is best known as co-organizer (with the Museum of Modern Art) of the 1941 exhibition, "Organic Design in Home Furnishings," and for staging, in 1946, the only one-person showing of the work of Laszlo Moholy-Nagy in the United States during his lifetime. The Modern Art Society also showed the work of Fred Lewy, an immigrant from Germany (via Spain), who did most of its early graphic design work, and who was a pioneer in bringing the concepts of European Modernism to Cincinnati. Lewy, of course, and the Modern Art Society generally, were strong influences

on Martin. Thus Martin may be said to have consolidated some of the influence the Modern Art Society had on the community, and to have extended and intensified it in the area of graphic design.

Another influence on Martin was his friend and collaborator, the late photographer George S. Rosenthal, who had studied with Moholy in Chicago.

Martin began working as a free-lance designer in 1949, while continuing his work for the Cincinnati Art Museum, where he held the title of assistant to the director from 1947 to 1955. He taught at the Cincinnati Art Academy from 1951 to 1957, and was an adjunct professor at the University of Cincinnati from 1968 to 1973.

The range of Martin's work is due to his location in Cincinnati and to his pioneering role there. He has worked for cultural institutions such as the Cincinnati Symphony Orchestra, Contemporary Arts Center and Hebrew Union College, for merchandisers such as Federated Department Stores, has provided graphic and exhibition designs for XomoX Corporation, an international valve company, since 1961, and served as an advisor to Champion Papers from 1959 to 1980. Clients outside the Cincinnati area have included the Museum of Modern Art, Alfred Knopf, *The Atlantic Monthly,* the *New Republic,* Abraham & Straus, and Standard Oil of New Jersey. Martin has said that he will accept any kind of project, provided he is convinced that he will be allowed to do a good job.

Noel Martin maintains a small office, and usually has only one or two assistants at any given time. Most often these are his wife, Coletta, his son Reid, or his daughter Mrs. Dana Wolfe.

One of Martin's finest achievements, and one he looks back on with a great deal of pleasure, was, significantly, a project with a large dose of community education. This was a 1975–1976 exhibition at the Cincinnati Art Museum, "Change of Pace: Contemporary Furniture 1925–1975," which he co-organized with Carol Macht, then the Museum's curator of decorative arts. In addition to designing the installation and the catalog, Martin designed a poster/mailer based on a photograph of a Marcel Breuer chair, printed in black on a brown ground, with lettering showing through from the bright white paper stock. The result conveys the basic information about the exhibition at a glance, but also allows the subtle image of the chair to emerge more slowly.

—Lloyd C. Engelbrecht

MARX, Enid (Crystal Dorothy)

British graphic and textile designer. Born in London, 20 October 1902. Educated at Roedean School, Sussex, until 1919; studied at the Central School of Arts and Crafts, London, 1920–21, and at the Royal College of Art, London, 1922–25. Apprentice technician and designer, in the Phyllis Barron and Dorothy Larcher textile studio, London, 1925–26; established own textile design and printing studio, London, 1927–39; freelance graphic and textile designer, London, from 1939: textile consultant, under Gordon Russell, Board of Trade Utility Furniture Advisory Committee, London, 1944–47; designed for London Transport, Whatajoy Luggage, Chatto and Windus publishers, Dunbar Hay Textiles, Penguin Books, Morton Sundour Fabrics, Aspinall Brothers, General Post Office, Harrisons of High Wy-

combe, etc. Instructor in wood-engraving, Ruskin School of Art, Oxford, 1931–33; design instructor, Bromley School of Art, Kent, 1935–39; head of dress, textiles and ceramics, Croydon College of Art, London, 1965–70. **Exhibitions:** *Utility Furniture and Fashion 1941–51,* Geffrye Museum, London, 1974; *Thirties: British Art and Design Before War,* Hayward Gallery, London, 1979; *Enid Marx: Retrospective,* Camden Arts Centre, London, 1979; *The Maker's Eye,* Crafts Council Gallery, London, 1981; *Design Since 1945,* Philadelphia Museum of Art, 1983; *Eye for Industry,* Victoria and Albert Museum, London, 1986. **Collections:** Victoria and Albert Museum, London; Sheffield Art Gallery, Yorkshire; Scottish Arts Council Gallery, Glasgow; Musée des Arts Décoratifs, Paris; Museum of Fine Arts, Boston. Royal Designer for Industry, Royal Society of Arts, London, 1945; Honorary Fellow, 1982, and Senior Fellow, 1987, Royal College of Art, London; Fellow, Chartered Society of Designers, London. Address: 39 Thornhill Road, Barnsbury Square, London N1 1JS, England.

Publications:

By MARX: books as author and illustrator—*When Victoria Began to Reign,* compiler, with Margaret Lambert, London 1937; *A Book of Nursery Rhymes,* compiler, London 1938; *Bulgy the Barrage Balloon,* London 1941; *Nelson the Kite of the King's Navy,* London 1942; *The Little White Bear,* London 1945; *Quiz,* London 1945; *English Popular and Traditional Art,* with Margaret Lambert, London 1946; *The Pigeon Ace,* London 1946; *Menagerie Cut Out,* London 1946; *Slithery Sam,* London 1947; *English Popular Art,* with Margaret Lambert, London 1951; *Sam and Arry, or Thereby Hangs Two Tails,* London 1972; books illustrated—*A Childhood* by Francesca Allinson, London 1937; *An Almanac* by Norman Douglas, London 1945; *Tom Thumb,* London and New York 1946; *A Book of Rigmaroles, or Jingle Rhymes,* London 1946.

On MARX: books—*Design in the Home,* edited by Noel Carrington, London 1933; *British Textile Designers Today* by H. G. Hayes Marshall, Leigh-on-Sea 1939; *British Textiles* by Frank Lewis, Leigh-on-Sea 1951; *Design in British Industry: A Mid-Century Survey* by Michael Farr, Cambridge 1955; *Utility Furniture and Fashion 1941–1951,* exhibition catalogue by Jeffery Daniels, John Vaizey and others, London 1974; *Enid Marx,* exhibition catalogue by Zuleika Dobson, Margaret Lambert and others, London 1979; *Design Since 1945,* edited by Kathryn Hiesinger and George Marcus, Philadelphia and London 1983; *The Conran Director of Design,* edited by Stephen Bayley, London 1985; *Eye for Industry: Royal Designers for Industry 1936–1986,* exhibition catalogue by Fiona McCarthy and Patrick Nuttgens, London 1986.

When the British Craft Council opened a lavish new gallery in London in 1981, they celebrated the event with a major exhibition called *The Makers Eye,* to which distinguished craftsmen were asked to contribute; it was no surprise that Enid Marx was included. For more than fifty years she has remained an indefatigable and highly respected maker. Originally trained as a painter, in 1925 she worked in the Hampstead craft workshop of weavers Phyllis Barron and Dorothy Larcher, who influenced her with their traditional methods of production—using, for example, vegetable and mineral dyes such a quercitron, madder red, and walnut. Marx believed in these production ethics throughout her

Enid Marx: *Shell* hand-block print on velvet, c.1930

life. "Craft," she wrote in 1982, "is for quality and not quirks." She did not, however, ignore or disapprove of industrial methods of production. In 1937, she produced small scale, abstract moquette patterns (which owed something of their inspiration to Paul Nash) for London tube train seats, and in 1941 she developed this work for the Utility scheme, where her style of limited colour ranges and small pattern repeats lent itself admirably to wartime constraints. She went on to design printed furnishing fabrics for the distinguished textile firm of Morton Sundour, set up by Alistair Morton. Her design achievement over this period was recognised by her election as Royal Designer for Industry in 1945.

After the war, publishers Chatto and Windus commissioned book covers and illustrations; the best known of her books is the whimsical and and decorative *English Popular and Traditional Art,* written by herself and Margaret Lambert in 1946. Captivated by the exuberance and power of peasant art, as seen in corn dollies, inn signs, and decorated barges, she drew heavily on these influences, and images from traditional English life gave her work great strength. Though in the postwar period her style remained rather static, it was always fresh and lively, as she turned her hand to stamp designs for the post office, to advertising posters for Shell and London Transport, and to teaching and lecturing, which won her the respect and admiration of a new generation.

—Catherine McDermott

MASSEY, John (Vincent).

American painter and graphic designer. Born in Chicago, Illinois, 14 February 1931. Studied at the University of Illinois, Urbana-Champaign, 1950–54: BFA 1954.. Married Barbara Massey in 1971; children: Timothy, Stephanie, Scott and Guy. Freelance graphic designer, Chicago, from 1955: director of corporate design and communication, Container Corporation of America, Chicago, 1957–83; founder-director, of the Center for Advanced Research in Design, Chicago, 1967–79; president, John Massey Incorporated design firm, Chicago, from 1983; has designed posters and graphics for the Field Museum of Natural History, Chicago Lakefront, Adler Planetarium, Lincoln Park, and for the cities of Boston and San Francisco. Instructor in design, at the Institute of Design, Illinois Institute of Technology, Chicago. Advisory board member, Design Management Institute, Chicago. **Exhibitions:** Art Center College of Design, Pasadena, 1980; Rochester Institute of Technology, New York, 1981; University of Tennessee, Knoxville, 1982. **Collection:** Museum of Modern Art, New York. Recipient: Art Director of the Year, National Society of Art Directors, 1967; Gold Medal, Art Directors Club of New York, 1979; Gold Medal, Leipzig Book Fair, 1982. DFA: Art Center College of Design, Pasadena, 1980; Fellow, Rhode Island School of Design, Providence. Address: 2131 North Cleveland, Chicago, Illinois 60614, U.S.A.

Publications:

By MASSEY: book—*Great Ideas of the West-* *ern World: Container Corporation of America,* editor, Chicago 1976.

On MASSEY: books—*Communication by Design: A Study in Corporate Identity* by James Pilditch, Maidenhead 1970; *Who's Who in Graphic Art,* edited by Walter Amstutz, Dubendorf 1982; articles—in *Graphis* (Zurich), no. 135, 1968; *Industrial Design* (New York), November 1970; *Print* (New York), July/August 1971; *Projekt* (Warsaw), no. 5, 1974; *Communication Arts* (Palo Alto), March 1976; *Idea* (Tokyo), November 1978.

The obligation of a designer is to create a vehicle to transfer a thought, concept, or idea from one mind to another. The concept to be transferred may range from a simple one to one of intricate complexity. As an example, a rather simple idea might be a poster to promote a theatre production. A more complex concept would be the transfer of the philosophy, products, and services of a multinational corporation from the corporation to the corporation's employees, customers, potential customers, media, shareholders, and local and national governmental agencies. In either case, it is the designer's responsibility to understand each problem as completely as possible and to develop a customized design solution accordingly.

Every solution must be relevant and to the point. It must be understood by the audiences for which it is intended, must have impact and recall through innovation, and must be void of extraneous or superficial elements.

If the designer is able to clarify thoughts and transmit them visually to the proper audiences, then the designer can provide a valuable com-

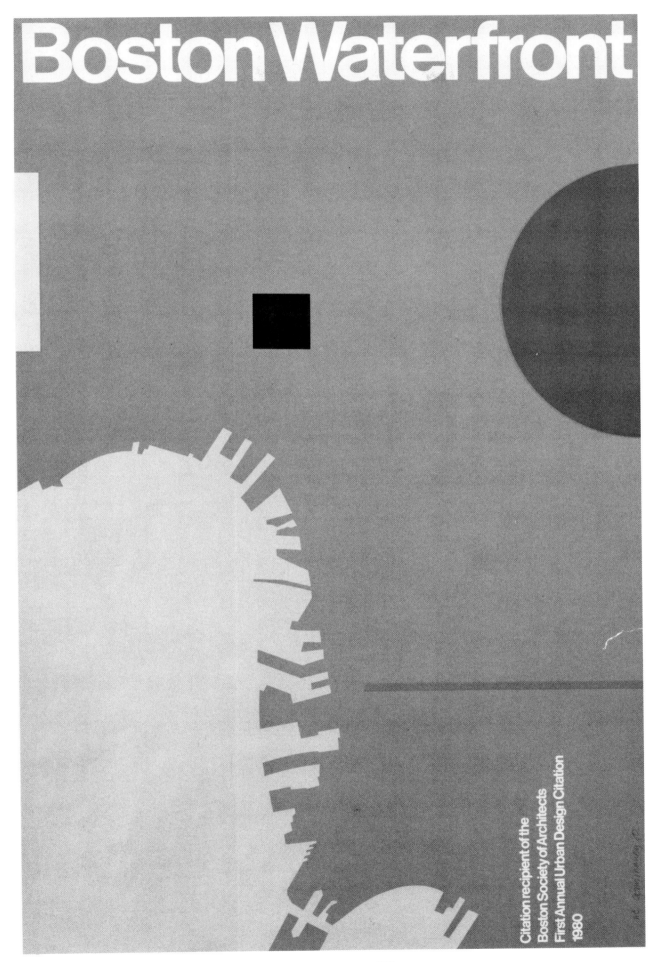

Citation recipient of the
Boston Society of Architects
First Annual Urban Design Citation
1980

John Massey: *Boston Waterfront* silkscreen poster, for the Boston Society of Architects, 1980

munication service for the overall social and economic infrastructure.

—John Massey

John Massey's appointment as Director of Communication at Container Corporation of America was important because it allowed Massey to develop a visual identification program for the firm, one that would in the following years act as a model for other similar ones. These programs provided cohesive, visual identification and publication formats that reflected Massey's views on a "total environment." Massey applied the concept of corporate identification to the federal government in 1974 when he completed the first federal graphic standards manual for the Department of Labor; later, this was utilized as a model for other federal departments and agencies. The manual specified consistent publication formats, including sizes, typography, grid systems, papers, and colors. Massey had earlier developed for Atlantic Richfield (ARCO) a similar corporate system for which he had recognized the existing program and worked with marketing to develop new selling tools.

Massey's approach to creating unified programs extended to his designs for America's first civic cultural communication program, which consisted of posters and banners calling attention to areas and events in Chicago. The program was designed to convert areas such as the Chicago Civic Center Plaza from the "business environment of the day to a scene of festive aura in the evening." The simple posters and banners utilized abstract symbols and bold, primary colors. Feeling that the business-industrial elite must embrace graphic design, Massey has stated, "They have a vital stake in improving the environment. . . . Conservation of human resources through the enrichment of man's surroundings is probably the most vital problem facing us today." His banners promote this view, as they provide visual excitement no less than information.

—Teal Ann Triggs

MASSIN, Robert (Charles Joseph).
French graphic designer. Born in Boisvillette, Erue-et-Loir, 13 October 1925. Self-taught in design. Married Huguette Hedouin in 1958; children: Laure and Julie. Freelance graphic designer and art director, in Paris, from 1948: designer, Club Français du Livre, 1948–52; art director, Club du Meilleur Livre, 1952–58, and Gallimard publishers, 1958–78; director, Hachette-Realités, 1979, and Hachette/Massin, 1980; editor, Editions Denoel, from 1981. Recipient: Prix des Graphistes, Paris, 1970. Address: 69 rue du Montparnasse, 75014 Paris, France.

Publications:

By MASSIN: books—*Vignettes français fin de siècle*, preface, edited by Deberny and Peignot, Paris 1966; *L'Amour la ville*, with François Guiot, Maurice Pech and Marcel Viguier, Paris 1968; *La Lettre et l'image,* Paris 1970; as *Letter and Image,* New York and London 1970, as *Buchstabenbilder und Buchalphabete,* Ravensburg, West Germany 1970; *Une Enfance ordinaire* (by Claude Menuet, pseudonym), Paris 1972; *Le Pensionnaire* (by Claude Menuet, pseudonym), Paris 1974; *Les Cris de la ville,* Paris and Munich 1978; *Zola Photographe,* with François Emile Zola, Paris, Munich and Milan 1979; *Les Célébrités de la rue,* Paris 1981; *Le Branle des Voleurs* (novel), Paris 1983; books designed—*Cent Mille Millards de Poèmes* by Raymond Queneau, Paris 1961; *Exercises de style* by Raymond Queneau, Paris 1963; *La Cantatrice chauve* by E. Ionesco, Paris 1964, as *The Bald Soprano,* New York 1965, as *The Bald Prima-Donna,* London 1966; *Conversation-Sinfonietta* by Jean Tardieu, Paris 1966; *Delire à Deux* by E. Ionesco, Paris 1966.

On MASSIN: books—*Design with Type* by Carl Dair, London and Toronto 1967; *Art Without Boundaries 1950–1970,* edited by Gerald Woods, Philip Thompson and John Williams, London 1972; *The Language of Graphics* by Edward Booth-Clibborn and Daniel Baroni, London 1980.

In his book *Letter and Image,* Massin relates his role as graphic designer to that of stage director: translating and visually presenting the atmosphere, the movement, the speeches and the silences, indicating time and space through the interplay of image and text.

While working with the Gallimard Press in Paris, Massin designed the graphics for Eugene Ionesco's play *La Cantatrice chauve (The Bald Soprano).* The characters in the play are represented by Henry Cohen's photographs from the Nicolas Bataille production. The words to be spo-

Massin: Typographic interpretation of Ionesco's *La Cantatrice Chauve*

ken by the characters are set in a wide variety of typefaces, depending on who is speaking and what is being said. By juxtaposing different typefaces on one page, Massin reiterates Ionesco's message that language has lost its ability to communicate.

Nevertheless, Massin's pages do communicate, but through their overall design: the primary message is received at a glance, not word by word. Whispers are shown in delicate, small letters: and shouts, in large, bold letters. Overlapping letters of various sizes, at disparate angles, indicate confrontations; boring passages become visually boring pages. Having rejected standard, horizontal line placement, Massin is free to place his words at any angles appropriate to illustrating the text. Space is likewise important. While some pages are busy with words, others are quiet and spare.

Among his other works, Massin created a "vocal calligram" as a tribute to Edith Piaf in *Evergreen Review*. The letterforms, printed on latex, are distorted to emulate the volume, range, and timbre of Piaf's voice.

Designing for a different purpose, Massin arranged the six voices in Jean Tardieu's *Conversation-Sinfonietta*, an approximation of dialogue set to music, according to the musical register. High voices are placed high on the page and set in slender, sans serif letterforms. Successively lower voices are lower on the page and are set in successively broader and heavier letterforms.

Massin did not attend art school, but learned his trade from his father, a sculptor and graphic designer. He also worked with Pierre Faucheux, a typographer associated with French avant-garde poets.

Influences on Massin's graphic work include Guillaume Apollinaire's *Calligrammes,* which are letterforms arranged in a design, and Stéphane Mallarmé's use of space in *Coup de dés (The Throw of the Dice).* Massin's work is also related to the Futurists' concept that writing and/or typography could become a concrete and expressive visual form.

Regardless of the topic of a work, Massin's primary concern has been to give visual reality to the literary content. He accomplished this through his innovative use of letters and letterforms, their selection and placement.

—Nancy House

MATHSSON, Bruno.

Swedish interior and furniture designer. Born in Värnamo, 13 January 1907. Studied furniture-making with his father Karl Mathsson, in Värnamo, 1923–31. Married Karin Margareta Sward in 1943. Furniture designer, working mainly for Firma Karl Mathsson, Varnamo, from 1933. **Exhibitions:** Röhsska Konstslöjdmuseet, Göteborg, 1936; *Svenska Stolar,* Nationalmuseum, Stockholm, 1963; *Nordisk Industridesign,* Kunstindustrimuseet, Oslo, 1976; *Kunsthandwerk und Industrieform,* Staatliche Kunstsammlungen, Dresden, 1976; *Scandinavian Modern Design 1880–1980,* Cooper-Hewitt Museum, New York, 1982; *Design Since 1945,* Philadelphia Museum of Art, 1983; *Faces of Swedish Design,* IBM Gallery, New York, 1988 (toured). **Collections:** Röhsska Konstslöjdmuseet, Göteborg; Museum of Industrial Arts, Prague; Konstindustrimuseet, Copenhagen; Museum of Modern Art, New York; Victoria and Albert Museum, London. Recipient: Gregor Paulsson Medal, Stockholm, 1955. Honorary Royal Designer for Industry, Royal Society of Arts, London, 1978. *Died* (in Värnamo, Sweden) *17 August 1988.*

Works:

Eva workchair in laminated wood with leather upholstery, 1934, produced by Dux Moebel AB.
Annika coffee table in grained birch, 1936, produced by Dux Moebel AB.
Pernilla upholstered chair and chaise longue with laminated beech frame, 1944, produced by Dux Moebel AB.
Linda table in birch with beech frame, 1948, produced by Dux Moebel AB.
Glass House (Bruno Mathsson residence), in Varnamo, Sweden, 1950.
Superellipse table, 1964, produced by Dux Moebel AB (with Piet Hein).
Jetson chair in steel with suspended leather seat, 1966, produced by Dux Moebel AB.
Karin chair in tubular steel with suspended canvas or leather seat, for Dux Moebel AB, 1969.
Ulla bed in tubular steel, for Dux Moebel AB, 1973.
Mirja conference chair in chrome tubular steel and padded leather upholstery, for Mathsson International AB, 1975.
Sonja sectional sofa in tubular steel with leather cushions, for Dux Moebel AB, 1976.
Ingrid chair, for Dux Moebel AB, 1976.
Milton High executive and conference swivel chair with padded leather upholstery, for Mathsson International AB, 1980.
Kuggen executive desk and conference table in beech veneer and chromed steel, for Mathsson International AB, 1983.
Computer workstation and desk with arm supports, for Mathsson International, 1983.
Minister upholstered swivel chair in tubular steel, for Mathsson International AB, 1987.

Publications:

On MATHSSON: books—*Svenska Möbler* by Brynholf Hellner, Stockholm 1947; *Contemporary Swedish Design: A Survey in Pictures* by Arthur Hald and Sven Erik Skawonius, Stockholm 1951; *A Treasury of Scandinavian Design,* edited by Erik Zahle, New York 1961; *Svenska Stolar,* exhibition catalogue by Dag Widman, Åke Huldt and others, Stockholm 1963; *Modern Scandinavian Furniture* by Ulf Hård af Segerstad, Copenhagen 1963, London 1964; *The Modern Chair: 1850 to Today* by Gilbert Frey, London and Niederteufen 1970; *Design in Sweden,* edited by Lennart Lindkvist, Stockholm 1972; *Scandinavian Design: Objects of a Life Style* by Eileen Harrison Beer, New York and Toronto 1975; *Contemporary Furniture,* edited by Klaus-Jürgen Sembach, Stuttgart and London 1982; *Mid-Century: Furniture of the 1950s* by Cara Greenberg, London 1984; *Modern Furniture Classics* by Miriam Stimpson, London 1987; *Faces of Swedish Design,* exhibition catalogue edited by Lennart Lindkvist and Monica Boman, Stockholm 1988.

With a self-confident and outgoing personality, Bruno Mathsson learnt the craft of furniture design the hard way, as an apprentice in his father's carpentry workshop. It was, however, a background that gave him a thoroughly practical feeling for form and structure and a knowledge of wood. In the early 1930s, when Mathsson began to design furniture, the area was attracting a great deal of interest and debate in Sweden. Something of a battle had developed between modernists and those who thought along more traditional lines, based on the Arts and Crafts movement. This split is best demonstrated by an incident at the famous 1930 Stockholm exhibition: Carl Malmsten, then Sweden's best-known furniture designer, refused to exhibit, in protest over Gunnar Asplund's steel-and-glass pavilion architecture. Allying himself with the new school, Mathsson began a series of experiments that culminated in a one-person show at the Rohsska Museum in Göteborg in 1936. The design principles he demonstrated there remained constant in his work for the next thirty years.

The immediate impression of a Mathsson chair is one of lightness, achieved with minimal structural parts and fabric support. The materials are unstained, bent beech with natural-coloured, canvas webbing or leather. The shapes, sculpturally moulded to fit the human body, reflect Mathsson's belief in function combined with maximum comfort. He has always based his designs on detailed anatomical studies, thus showing an early concern for ergonomic considerations. The result of this commitment to serious design principles was the evolution in the postwar period of an ergonomically sound range of seating furniture using laminated woods, usually beech or native woods, and because of its proportion, requiring little or no upholstery. In the general assessment of Scandinavian design, these have come to represent a standard of what can be produced with care, attention to detail, and a belief in form and function, an achievement recognised by consistent backing from the Swedish government, which in the 1950s and 1960s featured Mathsson's work in the Swedish Consumers Association handbook *Mobelrad* (Furnishing Suggestions) and in exhibitions at home and abroad. Between 1945 and 1958, Mathsson's principles were extended into simple architectural projects, most notably summer vacation houses using the simplest possible construction of wood frames and concrete.

—Catherine McDermott

MATSUBA, Minoru.

Japanese industrial designer. Born in Osaka, 20 February 1929. Studied at Osaka Prefectural Fuse Industrial School, 1942–48. Married Toyoko Yamanishi in 1953; children: Yoko, Masakazu and Yumi. Display designer, for Nomural Design Company, Osaka, 1951–54; has worked for the Tokyo Sanyo Electric Company from 1954: industrial designer, 1954–56, and chief of radio design section, 1956–62, at the Osako Radio Plant; chief of the rotary machine design section, in Hokujo, 1962–66; chief of the wireless radio section, 1966–67, deputy director of the design department, 1967–70, director of the design department, 1970–82, and director of the design center from 1982, at the Gumma works. Design committee deputy chairman, 1975, and chairman, 1976, Japan Electronic Industries Association; council member, Japan Machinery Design Center, from 1979. Address: 30–6 Kanamaya-cho, Ota-shi, Gumma Prefecture, Japan.

Publications:

On MATSUBA: books—*Japan Design Annual,* Tokyo 1965, 1966; *International Design Festival, Osaka,* Osaka 1983.

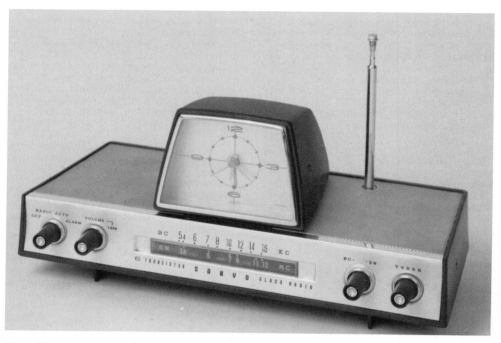

Minoru Matsuba: Portable transistor clock/radio, for Sanyo, 1961

Before becoming an industrial designer, I dreamed of being an aircraft design engineer. Airplanes excited me as man's most intelligent product, filled with romantic and adventurous feeling. Unfortunately, I could not realize my dream because of Japan's defeat in the war, but the image of the airplane has never ceased to occupy my mind as a beautiful crystal of advanced technology and functional utility.

During this period, I read Raymond Loewy's *From Lipstick to Locomotive*, which showed me the way I should take. By adding an esthetic sense to already acquired aviation engineering and architectural engineering, it would be possible to develop areas in which I could exhibit my ability. Wouldn't it be wonderful if I could share the fruits with users? With such an idea, I started collecting and reading books on industrial design.

In 1954, I took advantage of a chance which changed the course of my career from display design to industrial design. The Sanyo Electric Company, which started right after the war as a producer of electric appliances for the home, was looking for radio-designers. Young and ambitious, I made the effort to sell myself (in spite of my ability), and fortunately, I was given a workroom in the radio factory.

The basic knowledge that I possessed in technical engineering was useful in order to integrate industrial design with the technology. Our work went relatively smoothly because the role and the area of speciality of each staff member were identified. The technicians who thought that designers were artists were surprised when I submitted a structure plan along with a rendering. This experience made clear to me how important it is for designers to have a common means of communication with the partners on a job.

In the last thirty years, industrial designers have come to be indispensable to the production system, and the many new products developed have influenced the daily lives of people. Thus, industrial designers are playing a significant part in creating a more comfortable and cozier life.

From its beginning with five designers, the design section of the Sanyo Electric Group has now expanded to exceed 300 designers who respond to diverse needs of consumers in electric appliances in for the home. But the development of products can never be achieved by industrial designers alone. They must cooperate with those involved in research and analysis, graphics, photography, and other related areas.

In the decade of 1980s, a shift has taken place, along with the development of industry and economy, from an industrialized society to an information society, or in other words, from a materialistic value system to a quality-oriented one. The work of industrial designers should be reoriented from the production of things to the creation of lifestyle.

Although advanced technology today promotes the materialization of various functions of human life at a surprising speed, there is no guarantee that those products serve to create a happy life for people. Rather, they can lead to dehumanization. It is therefore important for designers to make use of the advanced technology as a means to a positive and desirable life.

Making proposals for more dynamic and higher-quality life and designing products to realize such a life are the tasks of designers. Humanity should not be forgotten as the basis of designers' work.

—Minoru Matsuba

Japan's reconstruction after World War II and its ensuing economic growth were both made possible by increased industrial production, the driving force of which was the "new technology." But a country such as Japan, with few natural resources, if it was to continue to develop, had to sell its products abroad—and Japan first recognized the usefulness of good industrial design when it was seen to aid the export effort. Forty years after the end of the war, the strategies can be seen to have worked: eighty percent of the population now say that they belong to the middle class. And now, material prosperity achieved, the Japanese people have begun talking about "culture." Industrial design is seen to have a new role.

Until recently, because manufacturers were concerned about other matters, Japanese companies did not try to express a particular philosophy or design policy (as many European and American corporations do): the catch phrase has been, "high-quality products at a cheap price." Now, too, designers in these companies are interested in "culture."

It is a theme that preoccupies Minoru Matsuba. He has worked for thirty years for the Tokyo Sanyo Electric Company, one of Japan's major producers of audio equipment and electrical appliances for the home. His career has gone through stages that, in a sense, reflect major concerns in design: how to make design recognized within a company; the search for method; the development of new techniques; the concentration and integration of design sections, to enhance the influence of designers within a company; the expansion of good design through marketing; and, finally, the problem of culture, the response of a company to the changing consciousness of consumers. It would not be an exaggeration to say that such stages have been common to the careers of other Japanese industrial designers—yet much still depends on the individual designer. If Matsuba's career is typical, his work is of high quality, and his future is likely to be promising.

Matsuba is now most notable in his approach to the theme of the "fusion of civilization and culture." He says: "I recognize, as a premise, high technology: it can make people happier, more dynamic, more active, and richer. However, when I design things using the new technology, I would like to create not just individual, independent pieces but parts of an integrated lifestyle. We now make scenarios of different lifestyles—business executive, TV director, artist, schoolteacher, etc., and attempt to create products that integrate with that scenario. The designer can be the 'motivator' in such an enterprise."

Behind this apparently optimistic vision is Matsuba's belief that "just as the term 'consensus' became rooted in contemporary Japanese society, so the new age will create a new standard that cannot be measured by out-of-date concepts."

—Kunio Sano

MATSUMOTO, Takaaki.
Japanese graphic and product designer. Born in Kanazawa, 2 November 1954; emigrated to the United States in 1974. Studied graphics at the Art Center College of Design, Los Angeles, 1976–80: BFA 1980. Married Julie Losch in 1989. Designer, Gips and Balkind Associates, Inc., New York, 1980–82; Art Director, Knoll International, New York, 1982–87; Founder-Director, with Michael McGinn, of M Plus M Incorporated design firm, working for *Art in America, National Geographic,* Jack Lenor Larsen, Wacoal Interior Fabric, Sazaby Inc., Fashion Institute of Technology, Museum of Modern Art, Pratt Institute, etc., in New York, since 1987. Visiting Lecturer, American Institute of Graphic Arts, New York, 1987, and University of Akron, Ohio, 1988. **Exhibitions:** *Takaaki Matsumoto: Square Installation and Graphic Designs,* University of Akron, Ohio, 1988; *Takaaki Matsumoto: Design Plus Square,* Fashion Institute of Technology, New York, 1989. **Collections:** Library of Congress, Washington, D.C. Recipient: Silver Merit Award, Art Directors Club of New York, 1983, 1984, 1985, 1986; Award of Excellence, *Communication Arts* magazine, Palo Alto, 1983, 1985, 1986; Award of Excellence, American Institute of Graphic Arts, New York, 1983, 1984, 1985, 1986, 1987, 1988; Award of Excellence, *Graphis* magazine, Zurich, 1983, 1986, 1988; Merit Award, Type Directors Club, New York,

Takaaki Matsumoto: Catalogue for Knoll International, 1984

1983, 1986, 1987, 1988; Award of Excellence, *Industrial Design* magazine, New York, 1984, 1985, 1986; Merit Award, Art Directors Club of Los Angeles, 1985, 1986; Award of Excellence, Society of Typographic Arts, Chicago, 1985, 1986; Award of Excellence, *Print* magazine, New York, 1986; Award of Excellence, American Federation of Arts, San Francisco, 1988; Artist Grant, Art Matters Inc., New York, 1989. Address: M Plus M Incorporated, 17 Cornelia Street, New York, New York 10014, U.S.A.

Works:

Making Paper lithograph, for the American Craft Museum, New York, 1982.
Design Message from Japan exhibition catalogue, for Gallery 91, New York, 1983.
Newsletter 84, for Knoll International, 1984.
Catalogue, for Knoll International, 1984.
Venturi lithographed poster, for Knoll International, 1985.
Matsumoto Moving lithographed announcement, 1987.
Uzuro photo book, for Livro Porto Publishing, 1987.
Wristwatches, for Sointu USA, 1987.
Furniture catalogue, for Comme des Garçons, 1987.
Square lithographed poster, for the University of Akron, 1988.
Square installation, for the University of Akron, 1988, and the Fashion Institute of Technology, 1989.
Silkscreen series, for Serigrafia Ltd., 1989.

Publications:

On MATSUMOTO: articles—"A Very Graphic Business" in *Metropolis* (New York), January 1985; "Takaaki Matsumoto" in *Portfolio Design* (Tokyo), January 1986; "Takaaki Matsumoto" in *FP Design* (Tokyo), January 1987; "Square Installation" in *Sho-kukan Design* (Tokyo), April 1989; "How Does Your Plastic Grow?" in the *New York Times*, 13 April 1989.

The best way I know of to describe my ideas on design is to tell you a brief story which summarizes ever so simply and succinctly the way I approach my work. It goes something like this . . .
There was a blind boy in a hospital. One day, his doctor told him that his eyes would be cured. A week later, the boy's eye operation was completed and his doctor said, "I am going to take the bandages off your eyes tonight. It will be easier for you in the moonlight." Later that evening, the doctor guided the boy out into the night. Gently, he removed the bandages from the boy's eyes. The boy stared up at the perfect quarter moon and said to his doctor, "That is not the quarter moon I imagined. I imagined that a quarter moon would be shaped like a piece of pie."

—Takaaki Matsumoto

Born into an art papermaking family from Kanazawa, a centre of traditional Japanese arts, Takaaki Matsumoto brings to his fluency in the international design vocabulary a particularly Japanese concept of *shibui*—extraordinary refinement in the guise of apparent simplicity. In his graphic as well as his product designs, Matsumoto's signature is not the stridency of the bold stroke, but rather the harmony of the impeccably considered detail.
As the art director of Knoll International and as a co-founding partner in the design firm M Plus M, Matsumoto has created a body of graphics predicated on modernist intentions. But the essential utility and communicative functions of his designs are always cloaked in the accumulation of precise aesthetic judgements. Typically, Matsumoto's work mediates the reductive and the decorative, the elemental and the refined. His style of quiet but assertive elegance has successfully reflected the identities of such bastions of contemporary design and high culture as the American Craft Museum, the Museum of Modern Art and *Art in America*.
Matsumoto has suggested that he combines something of the formalism of the Bauhaus with a concept-oriented approach. He is both, and neither: his designs frequently evoke a Swiss classicism, but they avoid the rigidity of modernist ideology; his work is often imbued with a witty conceptual twist, but the humour is subtle and stops short of the populist. As a designer he is on high ground, but remains deliberately outside the ivory tower.
Much of Matsumoto's graphic work requires the active manipulation of his pieces for a full understanding of his concept. Closed or folded, his designs seem complete and readily apprehended, but this first comprehension is invariably partial. Only in the opening and unfolding of his work does one confront the fuller intentions of the piece. This transformative possibility extends to Matsumoto's product designs. The jagged Art Moderne hands of a watch become, at 12, the outline of the Empire State Building. On another, the markings of the watch face have been displaced to the crystal; the discrete units of time are enhanced by their own shifting shadows on the watch's blank face.
Given the terse gestures of his style, Matsumoto's choice of materials takes on significant aesthetic weight. Often surprisingly industrial, they are, however, always selected in faintly muted variation: corrugated plastic is given a translucent vinyl skin, aluminium sheeting a matte rather than polished finish, or black granite a dulled, almost porous, surface. The effect is at once strong and veiled. Matsumoto is a modernist with a poetic core that precludes the extreme resolutions of minimalism or functional brutalism.
Because Matsumoto enjoys the challenge of possibilities within defined limitations, he has been involved in an ongoing manipulation of the square in a series of graphics. By conforming to a rigid, formulistic use of modules, he has created his most distinctive work. Aided by a computer, his "Square" images have an astonishing freedom, affirming his contention that creativity is reliant less on limitless options than on simple but original perspectives.

—Harold Koda

MATTER, Herbert.

Swiss photographer and graphic designer. Born in Engelberg, in 1907; settled in the United States, 1936. Studied painting in Geneva, 1925–27, and at the Académie Moderne, Paris, 1928–29. Married Mercedes Matter; son: Alex. Freelance designer and photographer, working with poster artist A. M. Cassandre, architect Le Corbusier, for Deberny et Peignot printing company, Paris, 1929–32, and for the Swiss National Tourist Board, Zurich, 1932–36; freelance photographer, working for *Harper's Bazaar, Vogue*, etc., in New York, 1936–46; staff photographer, Condé Nast Publications, New York, 1946–57; freelance photographer and graphic designer, New York, 1956–84; design consultant, to Knoll International, 1946–66, New Haven Railroad, 1954–55, Guggenheim Museum and Houston Museum of Fine Arts, 1958–68, and New York Studio School, 1964–78. Professor of photography, Yale University, New Haven, Connecticut, 1952–82. **Exhibitions:** Pierre Matisse Gallery, New York, 1943 (toured); American Institute of Graphic Arts, New York, 1962; Yale University, New Haven, Connecticut, 1978; Kunsthaus, Zurich, 1978; Marlborough Gallery, New York, 1979. **Collections:** Kunstgewerbemuseum, Zurich; Musée des Arts Décoratifs, Paris; International Museum of Photography at George Eastman House, Rochester, New York. Honorary Royal Designer for Industry, Royal Society of Arts, London, 1982. *Died* (in Southampton, New York) *8 May 1984*.

Publications:

By MATTER: books—*13 Photographs: Alberto Giacometti and Sculpture*, portfolio with Ives Stillman, New York 1978; *Alberto Giacometti*, with text by Mercedes Matter, New York 1987; film—*The Works of Calder*, 1949.

ON MATTER: books—*Die neue Fotografie in des Schweiz*, exhibition catalogue by Georg Schmidt and Peter Meyer, Zurich 1932; *Herbert Matter: Photographs*, exhibition catalogue with text by James Johnson Sweeney, New York 1943; *Advertising Directions*, edited by Edward M. Gottschall and Arthur Hawkins, New York 1959; *The New Graphic Design* by Markus Kutter and Karl Gertstner, Teufen and London 1959; *History of the Poster* by Josef and Shizuko Muller-Brockmann, Zurich 1971; *Herbert Matter: A Retrospective*, exhibition catalogue with text by Paul Rand, New Haven 1978; *The Vogue Book of Fashion Photography* by Polly Devlin, London 1979; *Knoll Design* by Eric Larrabee and Massimo Vignelli, New York 1981; *Who's Who in Graphic Art*, edited by Walter Amstutz, Dubendorf 1982; *The 20th-Century Poster: Design of the Avant-Garde* by Dawn Ades, New York 1984; *Eye for Industry: Royal Designers for Industry 1936–1986*, exhibition catalogue by Fiona MacCarthy and Patrick Nuttgens, London 1986; *New American Design* by Hugh Aldersley-Williams, New York 1988; *Typographic Communications Today* by Edward M. Gottschall, New York 1989; *American Typography Today* by Rob Carter, New York 1989.

For the past half century, Herbert Matter's photography and design has resulted in some of the period's most exciting and beguiling advertisements. Influenced early by Fernand Leger and Amedee Ozenfant at the Académie Moderne in Paris, he later worked with the architect Le Corbusier and the great French posterist A. M. Cassandre, both of whom deeply affected his work.
Matter is perhaps best known for his Swiss travel posters, which were created in the 1930s. Demonstrating his photographic vision and flair for the dramatic, these compositions rely particularly on scale and space. (All Swiss posters are uniform in size, approximately thirty-six by fifty-one inches.) The famous *Pontresina* poster with a huge, sunglassed head shows a bold contrast in scale and space between figure and ground. A diagonally-placed, larger-than-life head dominates the poster, while the background is a greatly reduced figure of a skier in a Swiss landscape. The type in the foreground (*Pontresina*), which occupies the entire width of the poster, is positioned on a slight incline. With the added impact of color, the total effect is highly active and dramatic.

Another classic example is a poster titled *All Roads Lead to Switzerland,* also done for the Swiss tourist office. As in the *Pontresina* poster, there are three distinct sections that form a coherent, overall composition. The base of the poster with the title leads immediately to the large, straight road penetrating the space and occupying seventy percent of it. It converges to a series of winding roadways which lead to the summit of the poster and the ever-present Alps.

For twenty years, from 1946–1966, Matter was design consultant to Knoll Associates, where his innovative advertising designs became models that other emulated. Containing vestiges from his earlier posters in their play of forms, shapes, and space, the more abstract and playful Knoll advertisements exemplify the sophistication and sense of style that have permeated all of Matter's work.

For a quarter of a century, Matter was Professor of Photography at Yale University, where he trained a generation of graphic designers from 1952–1976. In 1977, he completed photographing the works of Alberto Giacometti, and a decade later, they were published posthumously. Andrew Forge, then Dean of Yale School of Art, writes in the Introduction, *Herbert Matter's photographs of Giacometti's sculptures are not only beautiful and moving in themselves, but very intelligent and totally convincing paraphrases of the sculptures as well.*

—Dennis Ichiyama

MATTHIES, Holger.
German photographer and graphic designer. Born in Hamburg, 26 May 1940. Trained in colour lithography, at Druckerei Baruth printing works, Hamburg, 1957–60; studied design, at the Werkkunstschule, Hamburg, 1961; studied graphics and design under Erwin Krubeck and Hans Michel, at the Hochschule für Bildende Kunste, Hamburg, 1962. Married Gabriele Hoffmann in 1967. Freelance graphic designer, with own studio, Hamburg, from 1965: has designed for the Hamburg Deutsches Schauspielhaus, Hamburg Thalia Theater, Berlin Schiller Theater, Münster Städtische Buhnen, Wuppertaler Bühnen, Kiel Stadttheater, Saarbrucken Saarländisches Staatstheater, Polydor International, Deutsche Grammophon, Teldec, Philips, Hamburg Museum für Kunst und Gewerbe, etc. Guest professor, 1970–72, and professor of communications design from 1983, at the Fachhochschule für Gestaltung, Hamburg. **Exhibitions:** Städtische Bühnen, Dortmund, 1969; Fachhochschule für Gestaltung, Hamburg, 1970, 1978, 1985; Stedelijk Museum, Amsterdam, 1971; Stadttheater, Hildesheim, 1971; Theatre der Stadt, Schweinfurt, 1971; Stadtmuseum, Emmerich, 1972; Theater Baden-Baden, 1973; Bühnen der Landeshauptstadt Kiel, 1973; Museum für Kunst und Gewerbe, Hamburg, 1976; Musée de Marseille, 1976 (toured); Centre Culturel Allemand, Paris, 1980; Thalia Theater, Hamburg, 1980; Stadtmuseum, Oberhausen, 1981 (toured); Stadtmuseum, Lüneberg, 1982; Stadtmuseum, Kaltenkirchen, 1983; Museum of Bucharest, 1983; Colorado State University, 1983; Kunstindustrimuseum, Copenhagen, 1985; Art Poster Gallery, Lambsheim, 1986; Centre Culturel Allemand, Marseille, 1986 (toured); Theater der Stadt Gutersloh, 1989. **Collections:** Deutsches Plakat-

museum, Essen; Museum of Modern Art, New York; Colorado State University, Fort Collins; Museum für Kunst und Gewerbe, Hamburg. Recipient: Brno Graphics Biennale Prize, 1970; Deutsches Plakatmuseum Gold Medal, Essen, 1976; Warsaw Poster Biennale Medal, 1980; Edwin-Scharff-Prize, Hamburg, 1981; Colorado Poster Exhibition Medal, 1981; Japan Graphic Designers Prize, 1982; Toulouse-Lautrec Medal, Essen, 1984; New York Art Directors Club Merit Award, 1987. Address: Wrangelstrasse 13, 2000 Hamburg 20, West Germany.

Publications:

On MATTHIES: books—*Book Jackets and Record Sleeves,* edited by Kurt Weidemann, Stuttgart and London 1969; *Monografie des Plakats: Entwicklung, Stil, Design* by Herbert Schindler, Munich 1972; *Holger Matthies,* exhibition catalogue with text by Axel von Saldern, Hamburg 1976; *Who's Who in Graphic Art,* edited by Walter Amstutz, Dubendorf 1982; *A History of Graphic Design* by Philip B. Meggs, New York and London 1983; *Les Années 60* by Anne Bony, Paris 1983.

Designing posters is marvellous. Designing posters is agony.

The antagonism which lies in each relationship, which is performed with passion and obsession, which signifies heaven and hell, if one enters into it fully, will also on this branch line of "relationships" (shapes and surfaces) influence, change, sometimes destroy people.

I do not want to be overly solemn and maintain that this is a matter of life and death. Certainly not, but the silent scream of the empty surfaces produces echoes which will pursue you into your dreams.

The virginal quality of the untouched DIN format has a whiteness that makes mind and soul pale.

Splendour and misery are close neighbours. The muse whose kiss of enlightenment is so highly valued can also be a moody lady. She

Holger Matthies: Poster for the Schauspielhaus, Kiel, 1978

doesn't always kiss and certainly not everyone.

First of all, the vertical or horizontal format is a challenge and enticement! The DIN as vertical format lies taut, disciplined, and essential before you. The horizontal format stretches out seductively and invitingly, offering you the full broadside. Now let's go!

Cut into it; that makes the viewer giddy. Photograph it in all poses; don't worry, she likes that. Spray it with colour; that cheers the spectator. Do not forget she has a public that can read. Inscribe it, fold it, divide it, tear it up, only don't do it awkwardly.

If you let everyone look at it, do not be mean; give this or that one a little, tender, loving touch.

Rough or smooth, stamped or varnished, matt or neon-bright, on ordinary or fine-art paper, it must hit you in the eye and explode in the head. At any price!

If it is ignored, the message is ignored, and you are ignored.

That is the nightmare of the poster.

—Holger Matthies

After World War II, it took a long time for the German poster to regain its strength. Two vital sources of inspiration were gone, as with a wind. The expressionistic ways personified in Käthe Kollwitz's political woodcuts directed at propaganda issues, as well as constructivist Bauhaus ideas, disappeared, smashed by Nazism.

Slowly, in the 1960s a new generation took charge, as the time of painful national confession, of terrible convulsion was replaced by new voices, new ideas. Though almost mortally wounded, the culture began to regain its strength with new films, new literature, a theatre, and at last, the western part of this divided nation opened at her sources to new winds.

Especially in theatrical life, the harvest was very rich. Not surprisingly, posters for this institution were innovative and almost totally free of commercial restrictions. In some major cultural centers of West Germany, a few new masters began to show in the 1960s. Among the best of this group was the Hamburg-based artist Holger Matthies. Now, thirty years later, he is not only still a leader in the German poster field, but he also counts on the international scene.

His great power rests on two important capacities. One is his brilliance in the technology of photography, printing, and the use of photomontage. The second is his enormous gift of mind, his happy marriage of a designer's eye for reduction and selection with a freewheeling sense of surrealism and dadaism.

Sometimes metaphysical and demanding a certain intelligence of the viewer, his ideas are clearly realized technically. Carefully arranged, ready-made objects play different roles from those they have served. His skilful touch of montage or collage doesn't show how they were rearranged; they state *why* the rearrangement took place. Subtle colors only add to the clarity. They don't shock. Rather, they slow your pace, as if to say, "Think what we have to say to you. . . ." Matthies' theatrical posters reflect the playwright's message in an intelligent and intellectually well-developed way. These clients are fortunate to have him to do their posters, for Matthies carefully mixes the sense of a play and the way a director stages it with our common understanding of the world and its culture as it is today. He demonstrates how good theatre can be served by the artist by exemplifying the sensible person who understands his role to be that of go-between in the delicate balance of playwright, actor, director, and sometimes totally unaware public. Matthies tries not to play his own game, displaying mastery and technical tricks. Rather, he chooses a calm way of communicating between two worlds.

But when you see his work arranged together, you can enjoy the rich talent of a well-cultivated person with a strong, magical, surrealistic eye eagerly interpreting the marvels of the art of others—writers, musicians, actors. A true artist, he is the best example of regained cultural health in his native Germany.

—Jan Sawka

MAVIGNIER, Almir (da Silva).
German painter and graphic designer. Born in Rio de Janeiro, Brazil, 1 May 1925; emigrated to West Germany in 1953. Studied painting with an abstract art group in Brazil, from 1945; studied visual communications, at the Hochschule für Gestaltung, Ulm, 1953–58. Married Sigrid Quarch in 1965; son: Delmar. Freelance poster and graphics designer, with own studio, in Ulm, 1959–65, and in Hamburg from 1965. Professor, Hochschule für Bildende Kunste, Hamburg, from 1965. **Exhibitions:** Pfälzische Landesgewerbeanstalt, Kaiserslautern, 1961; Ulmer Museum, Ulm, 1962; Casa do Brasil, Rome, 1962; Museu de Arte Moderna, Rio de Janeiro, 1962; *Mavignier/Kapitzki,* Library of Congress, Washington, D.C., 1965; Zacheta Museum, Warsaw, 1967; Kestner Gesellschaft, Hannover, 1968; Galerie Denise René-Hans Mayer, Düsseldorf, 1973; Kunstgewerbemuseum, Zurich, 1974; Die Neue Sammlung, Munich, 1975; Museu de Arte, Sao Paulo, 1977; Museum fur Kunst und Gewerbe, Hamburg, 1981; Deutsches Plakatmuseum, Essen, 1982. **Collections:** Ulmer Museum, Ulm; Kunstmuseum, Dusseldorf; Museum für Kunst und Gewerbe, Hamburg; Museum of Modern Art, New York; Museu de Arte Moderna, Sao Paulo. Address: Schöne Aussicht 35, 2000 Hamburg 76, West Germany.

Publications:

By MAVIGNIER: books—*Permutationen,* exhibition pamphlet, Ulm 1962; statements in *Almir Mavignier,* exhibition catalogue, Düsseldorf 1973; *Struktur in Rotation,* portfolio with serigraphs, Düsseldorf 1980.

On MAVIGNIER: books—*Signals of Functional Poster Design* by Eckhard Neumann, Milan 1963; *The Poster* by Harold F. Hutchinson, London and Toronto 1968; *Deutsche Kunst: Eine Neue Generation* by Rolf-Gunter Dienst, Cologne 1970; *History of the Poster* by Josef and Shizuko Müller-Brockmann, Zurich 1971; *Deutsche Kunst der 60er Jahre* by Juliane Roh, Munich 1971; *Almir Mavignier,* exhibition catalogue with text by Max Bense, Düsseldorf 1973; *Almir Mavignier: Plakatretrospektiv,* exhibition catalogue, Hamburg 1981.

Like the actor, the poster designer must play different roles. If in so doing, he only represents himself in order to achieve a particular "style," he is in danger of losing the interest of his audience. He must win public approval with form and metaphor, and he will discover his particular style by means of personal attitudes towards an esthetic concept.

Like the actor, he works for an immediate audience, unlike the painter, whose audience is not necessarily directly influenced. The painter must await his audience and, more often than not, does not become closely acquainted with it.

The format of the poster changes with time. Toulouse-Lautrec would, for example, design his sketches differently today. Not only the content of the message but also the media of different times strongly affect the designer. For example, the modern billboard is suitable for communicating with the automobile driver. Rate of speed is also an important factor for the designer to consider—the faster the vehicle is travelling, the less time the driver has to concentrate on the billboard and, particularly, on its printed message. Basically, these things have to date influenced both the form and written content of the advertisement, and they will continue to do so. The advertisements for today's air passengers, for example, are futuristic.

—Almir Mavignier

Almir Mavignier is, with equal intensity, both a painter and a graphic designer whose disciplined work leaves nothing to chance. His is a European rationale spiced with the Latin American magic of his native Brazil.

Trained in the Hochschule für Gestaltung in Ulm, West Germany, he is a true disciple of Max Bill but was influenced as well by the color theories of the constructivists and Joseph Albers. This background imbued in him a demanding concern for logic with an emphasis on light and the interplay between surface and depth. He also recognizes the milestones in the development of abstract painting made by the pioneers: Malevich, Mondrian, and Van Doesburg.

His work is almost hypnotic in effect, due to his optical experimentation with a variety of techniques and his visual play. Sometimes he used overall geometric patterns; sometimes he clusters his design in the center of page or canvas. Sometimes within a single work, he shifts from planar to three-dimensional effects to create dynamic illusions.

At first influenced by the Op art movement of the 1960s, he later became a more formalized exponent of the concrete art movement, but with a difference. This difference is manifest in his unorthodox (from the concrete art point of view) handling of color and use of a palette which is more exotic and less rigid. His color instrumentations are eye boggling. His work therefore flashes like signals, particularly in the posters, the perfect graphic medium for the effective broadcasting of documentation, information, and propaganda.

Although in his paintings and serigraphs his main esthetic is close to the geometry of concrete art, in his posters he often uses photographs and other illustrative material. Even in these, there is an emphasis on light and the interplay between surface and depth. Often, a subtle, tactile quality is to be found, especially in the sea of polka dots made of three-dimensional colored points of paint; although they adorn his work, they are not reduced to embellishments but placed to provide a tactile quality and to galvanize the eye. This stems from the degree of saturation of color tones and the position in which the dots are placed in relation to other tones.

Beyond the verbal information which it imparts, Mavignier's work has much to say to the spectator about *how* this information—an art for human experience—is stated; this separates his work from the countless images with which we are surrounded.

—Mildred Constantine

Almir Mavignier: Poster for the Kleine Galerie, Schwenningen, 1962

Mary McFadden: Bridal gown with ruffled bustle and embroidered bib, 1989

McFADDEN, Mary.

American fashion designer. Born in New York City, 1 October 1938. Studied at the Ecole Lubec, and at the Sorbonne, Paris, 1955–57; Traphagen School of Design, New York, 1957–58; sociology, at Columbia University, New York, and at the New School for Social Research, New York, 1958–60. Married Philip Harari in 1965 (divorced); Frank McEwan in 1968; daughter: Justine. Director of public relations, at Christian Dior, New York, 1962–64; merchandising editor, *Vogue* magazine, South Africa, 1964–65; travel and politics columnist, *Rand Daily Mail,* South Africa, 1965–68; founder, Vukutu sculpture workshop, Rhodesia, 1968–70; also freelance editor, for *My Fair Lady,* Cape Town, and *Vogue,* Paris, 1968–70; special projects editor, American *Vogue,* New York, 1970; freelance fashion and jewelery designer, New York, from 1973; founder and president, of Mary McFadden Incorporated, New York, from 1976. Has designed for Henri Bendel, Jon Lakis Furs, Roscoe, Kirk-Brummel, Martex, etc. Director of the Fashion Group, New York, 1981–82; president and board member, Council of Fashion Designers of America, New York; design panel member, National Endowment for the Arts; advisory committee member, Steuben Glass, Kent State University, Cooper-Hewitt Museum, and Traphagen School. **Exhibition:** *The Golden Eye,* Cooper-Hewitt Museum, New York, 1985. Recipient: Coty American Fashion Critics' Design Award, 1976, 1978, and Hall of Fame Award, 1979; Audemars Piquet Fashion Award, 1976; Rex Award, 1977; Moore College of Art Award, Philadelphia, 1977; Pennsylvania Governor's Award, 1977; Roscoe Award, 1978; Presidential Fellows Award, Rhode Island School of Design, 1979; Neiman Marcus Award of Excellence, 1979. DFA: Miami International Fine Arts College, Florida, 1984. Address: 240 West 35th Street, New York, New York 10001, U.S.A.

Publications:

By McFADDEN: articles—in *Vogue* (New York), August 1970–October 1972, December 1977; *House and Garden* (New York), October 1978.

On McFADDEN: books—*Fairchild's Who's Who in Fashion,* edited by Ann Stegemeyer, New York 1980; *McDowell's Directory of Twentieth Century Fashion* by Colin McDowell, London 1984; *Fashion: The Inside Story* by Barbaralee Diamonstein, New York 1985; *The Encyclopaedia of Fashion from 1840 to the 1980s* by Georgina O'Hara, London 1986.

The major ingredient in the high-fashion designs of Mary McFadden is a unique synthesis of the simple forms and proportions of Oriental, African, Greek, and other primitive civilizations with contemporary techniques of silkscreening and tie-dyeing. McFadden has revitalized the feel and flow of ancient robes and drapery by using new technology to achieve colors and prints of refinement and splendor.

Fabric is central to her designs. It may be Eastern silk or hand-painted, silk batik; it may be light and filmy, pleated or quilted, but the overall effect is always one of exotic sophistication, delicacy, and austerity, whether in a jumpsuit bound in ribbon with jacket of hand-painted suede or in a quilted jacket worn over a dress of abstract patterning. Taking their inspiration from the peasants' costumes of the Middle East, China, and Russia, McFadden's quilted coats and jackets with moleskin linings are stunningly cosmopolitan with their stitching running vertically for the thin look or outlined for a fuller sensation. Unintimidated by either the clinging jersey or the layered taffeta styles prominent when she began to work, McFadden practiced her preference for the lean, long tunic over pants or long skirt which became prevalent during the late 1970s. When she found that her unevenly hemmed tunic designs were being widely copied, she turned toward the creation of longer jackets over ankle-length skirts in combinations of rich colors and patterns based on various kinds of ancient and primitive abstract decorations and symbols.

At a time when costume jewelry was experiencing something of a downswing in popularity, McFadden began fashioning her own jewelry, suggestive of sculptural reliefs, beginning with gold-washed, abstract medallions, and she started making such accessories a central element of her overall style. The jewelry is plastic, modelled after antiquity like the clothing but always endowed with her flair for the contemporary. A medallion may be hung from a necklace of beads or coral, sometimes worn asymmetrically so that it hangs over one arm. Archaic symbols, leaf patterns, and the like abound on necklaces and bracelets; there are belt buckles like pre-Colombian idols which become integral ingredients in the total outfittings. Prints from McFadden's dresses have been adapted for wall paper and upholstery fabrics and for table coverings, and she added perfume to her repertoire in 1979.

McFadden's fashions are closely related to the art she admires. As research for her work, she takes photographs of museum collections all around the world. She designs for a special, exclusive, and elite clientele, which sees her work as a wearable artform.

—Barbara Cavaliere

MELLOR, David.

British industrial designer. Born in Sheffield, Yorkshire, 5 October 1930. Studied at Sheffield College of Art, 1946–48; Royal College of Art, London, 1950–54; British School, Rome, 1953–54. Served in the British Army, 1948–49. Married Fiona MacCarthy in 1966; children: Corin and Clare. Silversmith, designer, manufacturer and retailer: established David Mellor industrial design workshop, Sheffield, 1954; installed cutlery workshops in the historic Broom Hall, Sheffield, 1975, and in new factory at Hathersage, Derbyshire, 1988; opened shops in Sloane Square, London, 1969, in Manchester, 1980, and in Covent Garden, London, 1981: design consultant to Walker and Hall, Abacus Municipal, Glacier Metal, Post Office, International Telephone and Telegraph, British Rail, James Neill Tools, and the Department of the Environment. Chairman, Design Council Committee on Design Standards, 1981–83; National Advisory Board Member, Art and Design Working Group, from 1982; chairman, Crafts Council, London, 1982–84. **Exhibitions:** Stedelijk Museum, Amsterdam, 1968; Welsh National Museum, Cardiff, 1972; *Design Since 1945*, Philadelphia Museum of Art, 1983; *New Design for Old*, Boilerhouse/Victoria and Albert Museum, London, 1986; *Eye for Industry*, Victoria and Albert Museum, London, 1986. **Collections:** Worshipful Company of Goldsmiths, London; Victoria and Albert Museum, London; Sheffield City Museum, Yorkshire; Museum of Modern Art, New York; Philadelphia Museum of Art. Recipient: Royal College of Art Silver Medal, London, 1953; Design Council Award, London, 1957, 1959, 1962, 1965, 1966, 1974, 1977; Architectural Heritage Year Award, London, 1975; Royal Society of Arts Presidential Award, London 1981; Chartered Society of Designers Medal, London, 1988. D.Litt: Sheffield University, 1986. Honorary Designer, 1954, and Honorary Fellow, 1966, Royal College of Art, London; Royal Designer for Industry, Royal Society of Arts, London, 1962; Fellow, Chartered Society of Designers, London, 1964; Honorary Fellow, Sheffield Polytechnic, 1979; Liveryman, Worshipful Company of Goldsmiths, London, 1981; Freeman, Cutlers' Company, London, 1981; Order of the British Empire, 1981. Address: Broom Hall, Broomhall Road, Sheffield S10 2DR, England.

Works:

Street lighting column, for Abacus Municipal, 1957.
Pride silverplate cutlery, for Walker and Hall, 1958, now produced by David Mellor.
Campden stainless steel cutlery, for David Mellor, 1958.
Bus shelter system, for Abacus Municipal, 1960.
Symbol cutlery, for Walker and Hall, 1962.
Embassy sterling silver cutlery, for British Embassies, 1963.
Thrift basic stainless steel cutlery, for government canteens, 1965.
Road traffic signals, for the Department of the Environment, 1965–70.
Pillar box, for the General Post Office, 1968.
Automatic half-barrier crossing, for the Department of the Environment, 1969.
Provençal stainless steel cutlery, for David Mellor, 1973.
Chinese stainless steel cutlery, for David Mellor, 1975.
Plane stainless steel cutlery, for David Mellor, 1978.
Flute stainless steel cutlery, for David Mellor, 1983.
Classic stainless steel cutlery, for David Mellor, 1984.
Hoffmann stainless steel and silverplate cutlery, for David Mellor, 1985.
Café stainless steel cutlery, for David Mellor, 1985.
Odeon stainless steel cutlery, for David Mellor, 1986.
Cutlery range for the disabled, for the Hamlyn Foundation, 1987.
Savoy silverplate cutlery, for David Mellor, 1988.

Publications:

By MELLOR: articles—in *The Guardian* (London), 11 October 1972; *The Designer* (London) November 1981.

On MELLOR: books—*Design in British Industry: A Mid-Century Survey* by Michael Farr, Cambridge 1955; *Modern Silver Throughout the World 1880–1967* by Graham Hughes, London and Toronto 1967; *Modern Design in Metal* by Richard Stewart, London 1979; *Design Since 1945*, edited by Kathryn Hiesinger and George Marcus, Philadelphia and London 1983; *The Conran Directory of Design*, edited by Stephen Bayley, London 1985; *Eye for Industry: Royal Designers for Industry 1936–1986* by Fiona MacCarthy and Patrick Nuttgens, London 1986; *New Design for Old*, exhibition catalogue by Helen Hamlyn, Eric Midwinter and others, London 1986; *International Design Yearbook 1987/88*, edited by Philippe Starck, London 1987.

*

Having trained as a silversmith, I tend to think of myself primarily as a maker. My work as an industrial designer, developing prototypes for quantity production, has been balanced by my work as a craftsman, making special one-off pieces of silver. My approach to design is still, to some extent, that of a craftsman, in my involvement in directing all the detail and in making a design concept work from end to end.

In the early 1970s, after long experience with the cutlery industry as a design consultant, I took the major step of beginning to manufacture my own cutlery designs in my own factory. I acquired Broom Hall, a large historic building in central Sheffield, and gradually restored it to make purpose-designed workshops and also to provide living accommodation for myself and my family, for it is part of my idea as a designer that work and leisure should merge almost imperceptibly and also that the same design standards should apply to industrial and domestic environments.

However, expansion plans made the premises at Broom Hall no longer viable, so in 1988 the cutlery factory moved out to a rural site at Hathersgate in Derbyshire. The new building is circular, built on the site of a gas holder. It is constructed in natural stone with a lead roof, combining traditional materials with the most modern structural techniques. The workshops are highly mechanized, with some of the most modern equipment in the industry; some of the machinery has been purpose-built—designed and made in our development workshop. Our principle has been to get away from traditional production procedures, with each worker doing a single operation, and to introduce a more flexible method of manufacturing, whereby every cutler is gradually trained to use all the machines.

Almost simultaneously with becoming a designer-manufacturer, I also became a designer-retailer, opening three shops successively—two in London and one in Manchester—which sell my own designs as well as many other designs which I have selected, using the dual criteria of functional efficiency and visual quality. I feel strongly that the creative skill of choosing is an underrated aspect of designing.

For me, in all aspects of my activity—from the choice of our buildings, the selection of our office equipment, right down to the choice of the right rivets for my cutlery—to aim for the highest visual standards has been paramount, and perfecting this skill has been one of the main aims of my life as a designer.

—David Mellor

*

Trained as a silversmith, David Mellor has specialized in cutlery. Always concerned with industrial production, nonetheless in his early consultancy work, he completed various private and government commissions, including work for the Post Office, British Rail, and the Department of the Environment. In 1965, he was commissioned by the Ministry of Public Buildings and Works to design a contemporary pattern for both cutlery and holloware to be used in British embassies, and in 1966, he was commissioned by the same agency to produce a low-cost pattern, Thrift, to be manufactured in volume and used in government institutions. Concurrently with his industrial design activities throughout the years, Mellor has designed and executed numerous private commissions, which include those for the Worshipful Company of Goldsmiths; the Cutlers' Company; Southwell Minister, Essex University; Darwin College, Cambridge; and others.

His most important innovations have been in the organizational methods he has devised in his own cutlery workshop at Broom Hall in Sheffield. Accomplishing this at a time when the Sheffield cut-

David Mellor: *Hoffmann* cutlery in stainless steel, 1985

lery industry has been contracting, he has attempted to introduce a flexible method of manufacturing and avoid specialization. Each of his employees learns to perform all operations involved in the manufacture of his cutlery from start to finish. This has required a high degree of mechanization and investment in machines that are geared to perform specific operations required for each design. While the firm is still growing, Mellor sees the ultimate size of his work cell as about thirty employees, at which time some modifications would be required for his system of production.

The first David Mellor shop, opened in Sloane Square, London in 1969, offered a comprehensive collection of equipment for cooking and eating, with a special emphasis on cutlery. This was followed by the David Mellor shop in Manchester (1980) and, more recently, by his second London shop in Covent Garden. His shops have given the designer scope to develop new products in special collections of pottery, woodware, basketware, and woven textiles. In these activities, Mellor acts as the entrepreneur able to promote individual craftsmen's work designed for volume production. Philosophically,

Mellor sees this relationship of the craftsman to industry as being more realistic and economically feasible in the foreseeable future than the fine art/craftsman approach. He is perhaps the single figure in Britain who has been successful in combining the activities of craftsman and designer with those of the entrepreneur and businessman.

—Barbara Young

MENTULA, Perttu.

Finnish architect, interior, graphic and industrial designer. Born in Lappeenranta, 5 March 1936. Educated at Helsingin Kaksoisyhteislyseo high school, Helsinki, 1948–56; studied interior design, at the College of Industrial Arts, Helsinki, 1958–60. Served in the Finnish Army Reserve Officers School, 1956–57. Married Marika Tamme in 1983; children: Arttu, Atte and Toomas. Interior and product development designer, in the studios of Antti Nurmesniemi, Timo Sarpaneva, Toivo Korhonen and Reino Lamminsoila, in Helsinki, 1958–60; freelance designer, with own studio, Helsinki, from 1960; director, Studio Perttu Mentula Oy, Helsinki, from 1977: design consultant to Wärtsila shipyards, Helsinki, 1964–66; design manager, Keriland Project, Kerimaki, from 1982; project chief for Arlandstad airport city scheme, from 1988. Board member from 1968, and chairman of the assessment committee, 1970, 1978–80, Ornamo Federation of Industrial Arts, Helsinki; fine art commission member, Helsinki Festival, from 1974; chairman, SIO Interior Architects Society, Helsinki, 1978–80; arts commission and ideas group member, 1978, and vice-president, 1980–83, International Federation of Interior Designers; advisory committee member, Art Center College of Design/Europe, Switzerland, from 1985. **Exhibitions:** *Total Environment,* Finnish Design Centre, Helsinki 1966; *Textile Space,* PMK Showrooms, Helsinki, 1972; *Uniform-Project,* Milan, 1975; *Wood and Textile,* Savonlinna Opera Festival, 1977; *Design by Perttu Mentula,* Copenhagen, 1977; *Scolt Lapp Culture,* Cathedral Crypt, Helsinki, 1978; *Finnish Design,* Finlandia Hall, Helsinki, 1980. Recipient: Lighting Competition Prize, Helsinki, 1961; Export Furniture Competition Prizes, Helsinki, 1963; Silver Medal, Milan Triennale, 1964; Restaurant Furniture Competition Prize, Helsinki, 1966; Finnish travel and study grants, 1971, 1972, 1973, 1977, 1982–85; Tokyo Lighting Competition Awards, 1972; Scandinavian Environment and Furniture Prize, Copenhagen, 1973; Kerimaki Community Development Competition Prize, 1981; Research grant, Finnish Dwelling Fair Fund, 1988. Honorary Professor, Helsinki University of Industrial Design, 1981; Honorary member, AIPI Italian Interior Architects Association, 1983. Address: Huvilakatu 8 A 2, 00150 Helsinki 15, Finland.

Works:

Wood furniture, for Varjosen Puunjalostus Oy, Uusikyla, 1960–63.
Kick sledge, for Velsa Oy, Kurikka, 1964.
Naval architecture, passenger liners and ice-breakers, for Wärtsila Shipyards, Helsinki, 1964–67.
Interior Collection printed fabrics, for Tampella Oy, Tampere, 1969–75.
Ringside furniture range, for Decembre Oy, 1969–79, and for Avitom Oy, 1979.
Uniform furniture range, for De Padova, Milan, 1973–74.
Space Balk office and exhibition systems, for Tampella Oy, Tampere, 1975.
Visitors' Building interiors, for Haka Building Company, Obbnas, 1978.
Edison de Lux light fittings, for Airam Oy, Helsinki, 1981–83.
Parkstreet furnishing system, for Pohjoiskalotti Oy, Rovaniemi, 1983.
Playground constructions in wood, for Lappset Production, 1983–84.
Glass table collection, for Juvonen Glass Industries, 1989.

Publications:

By MENTULA: articles—in *Architect* (Helsinki), no. 2, 1961, no. 6, 1964, no. 7, 1970, no. 8, 1970, no 6, 1972; *Launis Koti* (Helsinki), no. 5, 1963; *Engineer News* (Helsinki), no. 1, 1965; *Rank Xerox Magazine* (Helsinki), no. 1, 1972; *Abitare* (Milan), no. 10, 1972; *Ottagono* (Milan), no. 3, 1974; *Nyketekstiili*

(Helsinki), no. 1, 1976; *Architect News* (Helsinki), no. 12, 1978; *Journal of Interior Design Education and Research* (New York), no. 1, 1979; *Muoto* (Helsinki), no. 1, 1980; *Finnish Furniture* (Helsinki), no. 1, 1981.

On MENTULA: books—*Modern Finnish Design* by Ulf Hard af Segerstad, New York 1969; *New Design in Wood* by Donald J. Willcox, New York and London 1970.

The internationalism . . . which I criticize is the internationalism that lacks self-criticism and feeling. . . . The architects we have to thank for this similarity characteristic of today's built-up environment are those responsible for the Bauhaus style and school of rationalism and functionalism which held sway from 1919 to 1928. . . .

It is . . . paradoxical that constructivism and functionalism are rarely rational in modern architecture which tends to represent visual constructivism. . . . Designers today tend mainly to create impressions of things rather than structural realities. The Bauhaus architects had a message, but that message has come across too effectively and has been misinterpreted. It has led to an all-embracing conformity and similarity, an environmental democracy against which I protest. . . .

A national tradition which takes local environmental realities into account may develop into high-quality architecture which in turn gives rise to internationalism with a lasting culture and historical significance. Environmental design which starts out from internationalism generally leads to transient, poor-quality architecture which rarely takes local environmental phenomena into account. The same, I think, applies to furniture and interior design. *(Excerpted from the* Journal of Interior Design Education and Research, *1979.)*

—Perttu Mentula

Perttu Mentula's design ideology originates from his native soil, from those vital impulses that contributed to the creation of the cultural ethos of "the country of a thousand lakes." The Finns, for generations and to a greater extent than their neighbors, have had an inherent respect for nature—wood, stone, sand, water, and air—for all that may be transformed with the artist's hands into objects that are economical, practical, and functionally harmonious with the natural environment. Because of their sober attitude toward life, the Finns have a higher appreciation for things that are lasting, reliable, and modest but noble in appearance than for those of sophisticated form. It seems as though every Finn bears within himself a germ of forms and appearances which fill the sphere of his imagination. As these forms exist in a collective imagination, in the community, they are not imposed from outside by a designer or producer, but they constitute a part of the Finn's world, such as a forest, rocks, the lake surface, or a loaf of bread. Perhaps deriving from the Protestantism of the North, the Finnish humbleness toward nature and alliance with it constitute a philosophical basis of sensible design. As a symbol of this philosophy, the sauna, like the tea ceremony in Japan, plays a cultural role. Although it is a physical treatment concerning human body and its fitness, at the same time, it reaches the spheres of spiritual and metaphysical experience. A parallel tendency to unify practical with esthetic elements, function with form, is characteristic of Finnish designers.

Mentula, like other Finns, has strongly emphasized the national factor in his designing. In his 1978 paper "The Role of Nationalism and Internationalism in Design," delivered at a conference in Washington, D.C., Mentula stated: "I am becoming . . . convinced that the national factors and local environmental conditions constitute an extremely important part of design and the built-up environment. This is . . . because I am concerned about deterioration in the quality of architecture and building and the lack of environmental values. I consider it important to be aware of the local environment, to know where we are and what the environmental realities are."

According to Mentula, the national and international factors do not oppose each other; on the contrary, they are considered to be different points of view which, when unified, lead the way to the universal. What has been brought

Perttu Mentula: Sauna stool in pine, for Varjosen Punnjalostus Oy, 1963

from outside may be compared to the wind that contributes to the pollination of flowers. Such was the case in the architecture and design of Eero Saarinen and Alvar Aalto, who may serve as examples of designers that integrated local and international styles. In the same category, from among Mentula's works are a series of hanging chairs (1971–74), a sauna stool (1961), and some solutions in environmental design.

The portrait of Mentula's creative work would not be complete without emphasizing his indefatigable energy, which has been manifest in his numerous activities that were stimulating to designers, architects, and to those professions whose work has a formative influence on the environment.

Occasionally, Mentula has an opportunity to show off his talents in organizing and programming teamwork. I had a chance to observe it while participating in an international creative workshop, organized with the aim of preparing a program, "Challenges of Kerimäki," for a small community, beautifully located among lakes and forests, away from the tourist trails. Mentula's enthusiasm for the idea of animating this region was so contagious that it encompassed everybody around, including some important economic officials. But perhaps the most important thing was that he demonstrated in practice his broad and progressive understanding of the concept of design.

—Szymon Bojko

METSOVAARA, Marjatta.

Finnish fashion and textile designer. Born in Abo, 29 November 1927. Studied textile design, at the Konstindustriella Läroverket, Helsinki, 1949; also studied in the United States, 1961, 1964. Married Kaj Erik Nyström in 1948; Albert Van Havere in 1965; children: Kai, Katariina, Patrick and Barbara. Fashion designer, for Suomen Malto Oy, Helsinki, 1949–53; founder and chief designer from 1954, and managing director from 1957, of Metsovaara Oy textile firm, Helsinki; managing director, Marjatta Metsovaara Designs, Helsinki, from 1962: designed for Team Oy Finn-Flare, Oy Finnra AB, Oy Tampella AB, Villayhtyma Oy, NV Albert Van Havere of Belgium, Lusotufo of Portugal, Firth Carpets of England, etc. **Exhibitions:** Artek Showrooms, Helsinki, 1957; Konsthall, Helsinki, 1963, 1966, 1969; *Finnland Gestaltet,* Museum für Kunst und Gewerbe, Hamburg, 1981 (toured); *Design Since 1945,* Philadelphia Museum of Art, 1983. Recipient: Gold Medal, Milan Triennale, 1960; Ornamo Silver Bowl Award, Helsinki, 1964; Signe d'Or Award, Brussels, 1968. Address: Puistokatu 3 A 4, 00140 Helsinki, Finland.

Publications:

On METSOVAARA: books—*Scandinavian Design* by Ulf Hård af Segerstad, Stockholm and London 1961; *A Treasury of Scandinavian Design,* edited by Erik Zahle, New York 1961; *Modern Finnish Design* by Ulf Hård af Segerstad, London and New York 1969; *New Design in Weaving* by Donald J. Willcox, New York and London 1970; *Finnish Design: Facts and Fancy* by Donald J. Willcox, New York 1973; *Scandinavian Design: Objects of a Life Style* by Eileene Harrison Beer, New York and Toronto 1975; *Finnland Gestaltet,* exhibition catalogue by Tapio Periainen, Simo Heikkila and others, Espoo 1981; *Design Since 1945,* edited by Kathryn Hiesinger and George Marcus, Philadelphia and London 1983.

*

The long tradition of peasant weaving and rugmaking in Finland did not develop into formal textile design until Eeva Anttila became the country's first teacher of the subject in 1926. Marjatta Metsovaara was born in the following year; in her lifetime, work in textiles has grown to be one of the most important areas of Finnish design. Finland was the first European country to give women the vote; the majority of textile designers there today are women, and it is perhaps not too fanciful to perceive a link between a traditional women's craft and the sensitivity of contemporary designs.

Metsovaara's imagination seems to be freshly fired with each new design, not only by the technical means at her disposal but also by the (to her) unlimited possibilities offered by the traditional materials of her craft and their combination with new and in some cases very unlikely alternatives. As early in her career as 1960, she made a curtain using polished copper strip and linen thread, with the fine linen thickened at intervals into patches of glowing colour reflected and enriched by the copper. Brightly coloured plastic strip or cable, metal wire or tape, even splinters of metal and wood all find their way into her work. Her upholstery and clothing fabrics, carpets, blankets, shawls, and wall hangings incorporate every technique from flat weaves to pile fabrics to embossed jacquards.

Some of Metsovaara's most striking and successful work has been as the designer of integrated fabrics for furnishings and floor and wall coverings in cooperation with interior designers. Perhaps the most striking, indeed startling, of these was the carpet used for both floor and walls of the night club in the Hesperia Hotel in Helsinki; the eight colours of its design included two with a phosphorescent glow in the club's special lighting.

Her work as a designer for printed textiles is secondary but complementary to her woven designs; these fabrics appear not only in Finland but worldwide. Her career is studded with successful exhibitions and international awards. When writing about her work, one cannot, as with most designers, concentrate on one or two major achievements because her variety and originality, her adventurous use of all possible combinations of colour and texture, and her continually successful experiments have continued throughout her working life. Like many of her countrymen, she has constantly enlarged and enriched her national traditions.

—Gordon Steele

MEYER, Grethe.

Danish architect, ceramic, furniture and industrial designer. Born in Svendborg, 8 April 1918. Studied architecture, at the Royal Academy of Fine Arts, Copenhagen, until 1947. Architect, working for the State Institute for Building Research, Copenhagen, 1955–60; freelance designer and architect in private practice, Horsholm, from 1960: designed for Kastrup Glassworks, Royal Copenhagen Porcelain, C. M. Madsen Furniture, etc. **Exhibitions:** *Nordisk Industridesign,* Kunstindustrimuseet, Oslo, 1976; *Scandinavian Modern Design 1880–1980,* Cooper-Hewitt Museum, New York, 1982; *Design Since 1945,* Philadelphia Museum of Art, 1983; *Scandinavia: Ceramics and Glass in the Twentieth Century,* Victoria and Albert Museum, London, 1989. Recipient: Kaj Bojesen Grant, Copenhagen, 1960; Silver Medal, Faenza, 1965; Nordic Crafts Council Award, Copenhagen, 1973; ID Danish Industrial Design Award, 1976; Binnesbolle Award, Copenhagen, 1982. Address: Ved Stempedammen 23, 2970 Horsholm, Denmark.

Works:

Boligens Byggeskabe storage units, for C. Danel and FDB Danish Consumers' Co-operative, 1952.
Table and chair set in beechwood, for C. Madsen A/S, 1957 (with Borge Morgensen).
Stub og Stamme glassware series, for Kastrup and Holmegaard Glassworks, 1959–60 (with Ibi Trier Morch).
Blåkant/Blue Line earthenware ceramic table range, for Royal Copenhagen Porcelain, 1964–65.
Hvidpot ceramic tablewares, for Royal Copenhagen Porcelain, 1971.
Ildpot ceramic tablewares, for Royal Copenhagen Porcelain, 1976.
Rodtop ceramic tablewares, for Royal Copenhagen Porcelain, 1981.
Glas i Glas glasswares, for Kastrup Glassworks, 1982.
Picnic porcelain tableware, for Royal Copenhagen Porcelain, 1982–83 (with Ole Kortzau).

Publications:

On MEYER: books—*Made in Denmark* by Arne Karlsen and Anker Tiedemann, Copenhagen 1960; *Modern Scandinavian Furniture* by Ulf Hård af Segerstad, Copenhagen 1963, London 1964; *Contemporary Danish Design,* edited by Arne Karlsen, Bent Salicath and others, Copenhagen 1966; *Danish Design,* edited by Svend Erik Moller, Copenhagen 1974; *Scandinavian Design: Objects of a Life Style* by Eileene Harrison Beer, New York and Toronto 1975; *Danish Design 1980,* edited by the Danish Design Foundation, Copenhagen 1980; *Contemporary Furniture,* edited by Klaus-Jürgen Sembach, Stuttgart, London and New York 1982; *Scandinavian Modern Design 1880–1980,* edited by David Revere McFadden, New York 1982; *Design Since 1945,* edited by Kathryn Hiesinger and George Marcus, Philadelphia and London 1983; *Kongelig Dansk Porcelain 1884–1980* by Bredo L. Grandjean, Copenhagen 1983; *Scandinavia: Ceramics and Glass in the Twentieth Century* by Jennifer Hawkins Opie, London 1989.

*

One of my main theses when working with design is that the object should not rule the person. In all my work, I try to reach the point where the design is very simple and at the same time very complex. Let me give you an example. When I was given the task of designing a series of ovenware for the Royal Copenhagen Porcelain Factory, it began with a purely technical specification: the ovenware must be able to be transferred directly from the freezer to the oven without cracking. This resulted in the factory developing a new type of clay for stoneware. With this material in my hands, I designed a simple, sensible, and undecorated range of ovenware suitable for a wide range of purposes. Each unit was designed for typical portion sizes, in dimensions to fit into the racks of a normal oven. They are good to handle and

Grethe Meyer: Earthenware bowls, for Royal Copenhagen Porcelain

are easily stacked for storage. The more you use it, the more beautiful it becomes.

Whenever I design objects, I never think of market sales. I simply design things that I like myself and say, "This is my offer to the market." I cannot force people to use my things, and I could not dream of criticising those who prefer articles decorated with flowers and strawberries. I can only say that I think a particular design is right; then I try to make things that people can afford. I feel it is important to buy things that you really like and want. Instead of going out and buying a lot of bad quality items all at once, one should buy fewer items of better quality. Quality is the thread running through all my work.

—Grethe Meyer

MEYNELL, Francis (Meredith Wilfrid).
British publisher, typographic and book designer. Born in Palace Gate, London, 12 May 1891. Educated at Downside School, Bath, until 1909; studied at Trinity College, Dublin, 1909–11. Married Hilda Saxe in 1914 (divorced); daughter: Cynthia; married Vera Mendel in 1923 (divorced); son: Benedict; married Alix Hester Kilroy in 1946. Head of design, at Burns and Oates Catholic publishers, London 1911–13; founder and director, Pelican Press, London, 1916–18, 1921–22; founder-director, with David Garnett and Vera Mendel, of the Nonesuch Press, London, 1923–35, 1953–75 (Press taken over by Limited Editions Club of New York, 1935–51); also advertising designer, working for United Artists, Gaumont British Picture Corporation, Charles W. Hobson Lim-

ited, etc., 1935–39, and for the Ministry of Food, 1940–45: board member, Mather and Crowther advertising agency, London, 1939–60, and The Bodley Head publishers, London 1960–75. Freelance journalist, 1914–16, staff writer, 1916–18, assistant editor and director, 1918–20, of the *Daily Herald* newspaper, London; editor, *The Communist* newspaper, London, 1921; columnist, *News Chronicle* newspaper, London, 1934–35. Founder, Union of Democratic Control anti-war body, London, 1914, No-Conscription Fellowship, London, 1915, Guild of the Pope's Peace, London, 1916, and Anglo-Russian Democratic Alliance, London, 1917. Advisor on consumer needs, Board of Trade, London, 1940–45; alternate chairman of The Brains Trust, British Broadcasting Corporation, London, 1942–43; member of the Council of

Industrial Design, London, 1944-48; advisory council member, Victoria and Albert Museum, London 1945-48; director general, Cement and Concrete Association, London, 1946-58; advisory council member, The Royal Mint, London, 1954-70; president, Society of Typographic Designers, London, 1958-62; advisory council member, Royal Society of Arts, London, 1959-61; vice-president, Poetry Society, London, 1960-65. **Exhibitions:** First Editions Club, London, 1933; Wolverhampton Polytechnic, 1973; Cambridge University Library, 1973; Gainsborough House, Sudbury, 1974; Manchester Polytechnic, 1979. Royal Designer for Industry, Royal Society of Arts, London, 1945; Knighthood, London, 1946; D.Litt: University of Reading, Berkshire, 1964. *Died* (in London) *9 July 1975.*

Publications:

By MEYNELL: books—*Typography,* London 1923; *The Week-End Book,* editor, London 1923; *George Herbert: The Temple,* editor, London 1927; *Bee-dome: Poems,* editor, London 1928; *The Typography of Newspaper Advertisements,* London 1929; *The Nonesuch Century,* London 1936; *Seventeen Poems,* London 1945; *English Printed Books,* London 1946; *The New Week-End Book,* editor, London 1955; *The Typography of Advertising,* London 1960; *Poems and Pieces,* London 1961; *By Heart,* London 1965; *My Lives* (autobiography), London 1971; *Fleuron Anthology,* editor, with Herbert Simon, London and Toronto 1973; articles—contributor of numerous writings on typography to *The Times, The Sunday Times, The Manchester Guardian, The Listener, Time and Tide, Encyclopedia Britannica,* etc.

On MEYNELL: books—*British Achievement in Design,* edited by Noel Carrington and Muriel Harris, London 1946; *Modern Book Design* by Ruari McLean, London 1958; *The Typographic Book 1450-1935* by Stanley Morison and Kenneth Day, London 1963; *Introduction to Typography* by Oliver Simon, London 1964; *Industrial Design in Britain* by Noel Carrington, London 1976; *Francis Meredith Wilfrid Meynell* by Alix Meynell, Burford 1977; *Typography: Design and Practice* by John Lewis, London 1978; *Sir Francis Meynell and the Nonesuch Press,* exhibition catalogue by Ian Rogerson, Manchester 1979; *A History of the Nonesuch Press* by John Dreyfus, London 1981; *Eye for Industry: Royal; Designers for Industry 1936-1986* by Fiona MacCarthy and Patrick Nuttgens, London 1986.

Francis Meredith Wilfrid Meynell justifiably titled his autobiography *My Lives,* so varied were his talents and activities—poet, editor, publisher, wit, advertising designer, games enthusiast, and civil servant—but it will be as a typographer and book designer that he will be best remembered. He was born in 1891 into a family where literature was the common interest. His father, Wilfrid Meynell, was a distinguished journalist and editor. His mother Alice was a poet (at one time backed for the Laureate) and friend of Coventry Patmore, Meredith, and Browning. Both she and her husband were Catholic converts. Francis Thompson, whom they had rescued from destitution and established as a poet, was godfather of their youngest child, Francis.

As a Catholic, Francis was educated at Downside and Trinity College, Dublin. He entered the book trade in his father's Catholic publishing firm, Burns and Oates in 1910. He and Stanley Morison worked together there and also on the two books printed on Meynell's

handpress, the Romney Street Press, which he had set up in his house. In 1916, Meynell founded the Pelican Press, where Morison also joined him. Its aim was to do for "jobbing printing" (catalogues, posters, press advertisements, etc.) what his hero Bruce Rogers, the great American typographer, had done for book design in America. He could boast that the Pelican always had in use some type held by no other printer.

Meynell was a socialist and a follower of George Lansbury, with whom he worked on the early *Daily Herald.* A conscientious objector in World War I, when called up by conscription, he suffered a self-imposed hunger and thirst strike almost to death. Meynell retained his socialist faith throughout his life, but in 1923 he extricated himself from politics to renew his career as printer and publisher. The Nonesuch Press which he founded in that year with the help of a small capital provided by Vera Mendel (who became his second wife) and with the literary advice of David Garnett, was not a private press on the model of William Morris's Kelmscott. He did maintain a small handpress, a compositor, and a wide range of typefaces for the experimental setting of title or sample pages, but his books were printed by firms with modern machinery, though every detail of type, paper, and binding were to his own fastidious design. The number printed for each edition was more than usual for works produced by private presses, sometimes four or five hundred, often into four figures, but they were almost always over-subscribed by the booksellers. Occasionally, Nonesuch issued an unlimited edition, such as *The Week-End Book,* which achieved best-seller status.

The choice of titles lay with the partners, aided by editors such as Geoffrey Keynes. They included neglected classics including the poems of John Donne and works of the Restoration playwrights, but of their publishing policy Meynell wrote, "We chose the books we wanted to have on our own shelves, and for those among collectors who also use books for reading."

Though Nonesuch was able to celebrate publication of its hundredth book within its first twelve years, it had not generated enough capital to weather the economic storm of the 1930's, and he had to make over the press to George Macy in America while retaining the design of books printed in England in his own hands. In 1951, with the help of Max Reinhardt, he restarted Nonesuch in England and continued to run it till his death. Nonesuch Press was one of the most influential enterprise of the present century in the world of books: an enterprise small in itself and its staffing, but large in the number and quality of publications and in its effect on book production throughout the English-speaking world.

—Noel Carrington

MIELZINER, Jo.

American stage designer. Born in Paris, France, 19 March 1901. Educated at the Ethical Culture School, New York, until 1917; studied at the National Academy of Design, New York, the Art Students League of New York, Pennsylvania Academy of Fine Arts, Philadelphia; also studied in Paris and Vienna. Served in the United States Marine Corps,

1918-19, and as a camouflage specialist in the United States Army Air Force, 1942-45: Major. Married Annie Laurie Witzel (divorced); Maryana Mannes (divorced); Jean Macintyre in 1938 (divorced); children: Michael, Neil and Jennifer. Actor and scene designer, Jessie Bonstelle Stock Company, Detroit, Michigan, 1921-22; actor, assistant manager and apprentice designer under Lee Simonson, at the Theatre Guild, New York, 1923; freelance stage designer, New York, from 1924: designed for the Lincoln Center Repertory Theatre, Los Angeles Music Center Forum Theatre, University of Illinois Krannert Center, University of Michigan Theatre, American National Theatre and Academy, Washington Square Theatre, etc. Chairman, American Theatre Planning Board; board member, United States Institute for Theatre Technology. **Exhibitions:** Lincoln Center, New York, 1966; Brandeis University, Waltham, Massachusetts, 1966; Coffee House Club of New York, 1966; Virginia Museum of Fine Arts, Richmond, 1967; International Exhibition Foundation touring exhibitions, 1968, 1969; Toneelmuseum, Amsterdam, 1972; Amherst College, Massachusetts, 1973. Recipient: Donaldson Awards, New York, 1945, 1947, 1950, 1952; *Variety* Critics Poll Award, New York, 1945, 1946, 1948, 1949, 1950, 1951, 1952, 1953; Academy Award, Los Angeles, 1955; New York Drama Critics Award, 1956; New England Theatre Conference Award, 1957; Charlotte Cushman Award, 1958; Ford Foundation Award, 1960; Lotus Club Award of Merit, 1961; Brandeis University Creative Arts Award, 1963; Maharam Awards, New York, 1970; Drama Desk Award, New York, 1970; American Theatre Association Award, 1975. DFA: Fordham University, 1947, University of Michigan, 1971; HHD: Otterbein College, 1967, University of Utah, 1972. Benjamin Franklin Fellow, Royal Society of Arts, London. *Died* (in New York City) *15 March 1976.*

Works:

Stage productions (New York, unless noted) include—*The Guardsman,* 1924; *Nerves,* 1924; *That Awful Mrs. Eaton,* 1924; *Mrs. Partridge Presents,* 1925; *First Flight,* 1925; *Caught,* 1925; *The Call of Life,* 1925; *The Enemy,* 1925; *Luck Sam McCarver,* 1925; *The Wild Duck,* 1925; *Little Eyolf,* 1926; *Masque of Venice,* 1926; *Unseen,* 1926; *Seed of the Brute,* 1926; *Pygmalion,* 1926; *Saturday's Children,* 1927; *Right You Are If You Think You Are,* 1927; *Mariners,* 1927; *The Second Man,* 1927; *Marquise,* 1927; *The Doctor's Dilemma,* 1927; *Fallen Angels,* 1927; *Cock Robin,* 1928; *The Grey Fox,* 1928; *The Jealous Moon,* 1928; *The Lady Lies,* 1928; *A Most Immoral Lady,* 1928; *Strange Interlude,* 1928; *The Amorous Antic,* 1929; *Karl and Anna,* 1929; *Street Scene,* 1929; *The Sky Rocket,* 1928; *Judas,* 1929; *Meet the Prince,* 1929; *Young Alexander,* 1929; *The First Little Show,* 1929; *Jenny,* 1929; *First Mortgage,* 1929; *Dread,* 1929; *Mrs. Cook's Tour,* 1929; *Uncle Vanya,* 1930; *Mr. Gilhooley,* 1930; *Solid South,* 1930; *Sweet and Low,* 1930; *The Second Little Show,* 1930; *The Barretts of Wimpole Street,* 1931; *Of Thee I Sing,* 1931; *I Love an Actress,* 1931; *Brief Moment,* 1931; *Anatol,* 1931; *The House Beautiful,* 1931; *Billy Rose's Crazy Quilt,* 1931; *The Third Little Show,* 1931; *Distant Drums,* 1931; *Gay Divorce,* 1932; *Never No More,* 1932; *Bloodstream,* 1932; *Bridal Wise,* 1932; *Biography,* 1932; *Emperor Jones* (opera), 1933; *Champagne Sec,* 1933; *A Divine Drudge,* 1933; *I Was Waiting for You,* 1933; *The Dark Tower,* 1933; *The Lake,* 1933; *By Your Leave,* 1934; *Dodsworth,* 1934; *Yellow Jack,* 1934; *Merrily*

We Roll Along, 1934; Spring Song, 1934; Romeo and Juliet, 1934; Accent on Youth, 1934; The Pure in Heart, 1934; Merrymount (opera), 1934; Bird of Our Fathers (tour), 1934; It's You I Want, 1935; De Luxe, 1935; Panic, 1935; Winterset, 1935; Flowers of the Forest, 1935; Jubilee, 1935; Pride and Prejudice, 1935; A Room in Red and White, 1935; Co-Respondent Unknown, 1935; The Postman Always Rings Twice, 1935; Saint Joan, 1935; Daughters of Atreus, 1935; The Women, 1935; Ethan Frome, 1936; On Your Toes, 1936; St. Helena, 1936; Hamlet, 1936; The Wingless Victory, 1936; Hell Freezes Over, 1936; High Tor, 1937; The Star Wagon, 1937; Susan and God, 1937; Father Malacky's Miracle, 1937; Antony and Cleopatra, 1938; Barchester Towers, 1937; Your Obedient Husband, 1938; On Borrowed Time, 1938; Save Me the Waltz, 1938; Sing Out the News, 1938; Abe Lincoln in Illinois, 1938; Knickerbocker Holiday, 1938; I Married an Angel, 1938; The Boys from Syracuse, 1938; Mrs. O'Brien Entertains, 1939; Stars in Your Eyes, 1939; No Time for Comedy, 1939; Key Largo, 1939; Too Many Girls, 1939; Mornings at Seven, 1939; Christmas Eve, 1939; Two on an Island, 1940; Higher and Higher, 1940; The Little Dog Laughed (tour), 1940; Journey to Jerusalem, 1940; Pal Joey, 1940; Flight to the West, 1940; Mr. and Mrs. North, 1941; The Talley Method, 1941; Watch on the Rhine, 1941; The Wookey, 1941; Best Foot Forward, 1941; The Land is Bright, 1941; Candle in the Wind, 1941; The Seventh Trumpet, 1941; Solitaire, 1942; Pillar of Fire (ballet), 1942; By Jupiter, 1942; Foolish Notion, 1945; The Firebrand of Florence, 1945; Carousel, 1945; Hollywood Pinafore, 1945; Carib Song, 1945; Beggars Are Coming to Town, 1945; The Rugged Path, 1945; The Glass Menagerie, 1945; The Dream Girl, 1945; Jeb, 1946; Annie Get Your Gun, 1946; Windy City, 1946; Happy Birthday, 1946; Another Part of the Forest, 1946; The Big Two, 1947; The Street Scene, 1947; Finian's Rainbow, 1947; The Chocolate Soldier, 1947; Barefoot Boy with Cheek, 1947; Command Decision, 1947; Allegro, 1947; A Streetcar Named Desire (London), 1947; Mister Roberts, 1948; Shadow of the Wind (ballet), 1948; Sleepy Hollow, 1948; Summer and Smoke, 1948; Anne of the Thousand Days, 1948; Death of a Salesman, 1949; South Pacific, 1949; The Man, 1950; The Innocents, 1950; The Wisteria Trees, 1950; Burning Bright, 1950; Dance Me a Song, 1950; The Real McCoy, 1950; Guys and Dolls, 1950; The King and I, 1951; A Tree Grows in Brooklyn, 1951; Top Banana, 1951; Point of No Return, 1951; Flight into Egypt, 1951; Wish You Were Here, 1952; The Gambler, 1952; A Month of Sundays (tour), 1952; Picnic, 1953; Can-Can, 1953; Me and Juliet, 1953; Tea and Sympathy, 1953; Kind Sir, 1953; By the Beautiful Sea, 1954; All Summer Long, 1954; Fanny, 1954; Silk Stockings, 1955; Cat on a Hot Tin Roof, 1955; Island of Goats, 1955; Pipe Dream, 1955; The Lark, 1955; Middle of the Night, 1956; The Most Happy Fella, 1956; Happy Hunting (also produced), 1956; Maiden Voyage, 1957; Miss Lonelyhearts, 1957; The Square Root of Wonderful, 1957; Look Homeward, Angel, 1957; Oh, Captain!, 1958; The Day the Money Stopped, 1958; Handful of Fire, 1958; The World of Suzie Wong, 1958; The Gazebo, 1958; Whoop-Up, 1958; Rashomon (lighting), 1959; Sweet Bird of Youth, 1959; The Gang's All Here, 1959; The World of Suzie Wong (London), 1959; Gypsy, 1959; Silent Night, Lonely Night, 1959; There Was a Little Girl, 1960; The Best Man, 1960; Christine, 1960; Little Moon of Alban, 1960; Period of Adjustment, 1960; White Alice (tour), 1960; The Devil's Advocate, 1961; A Short Happy Life, 1961; Everybody Loves Opal, 1961; All American, 1962; Mr. President, 1962; The Milk Train Doesn't Stop Here Anymore, 1963; After the Fall, 1964; But for Whom Charlie, 1964; The Owl and the Pussycat, 1964; Danton's Death, 1965; The Playroom, 1965; Venus Is, 1966; Don't Drink the Water, 1966; My Sweet Charlie, 1966; The Paisley Convertible, 1967; That Summer . . . That Fall, 1967; Daphne in Cottage D, 1967; Mata Hari, 1967; The Prime of Miss Jean Brodie, 1968; I Never Sang for My Father, 1968; The Seven Descents of Myrtle, 1968; Slaughter on Tenth Avenue (ballet), 1968; Possibilities, 1968; Kingdom on Earth, 1968; 1776, 1969; The Conjuror, 1969; Galileo, 1969; The Girls Upstairs, 1969; Child's Play, 1970; Georgy, 1970; Look to the Lillies, 1970; 1776 (London), 1970; Who Cares? (ballet), 1970; Child's Play (London), 1971; Father's Day (also lighting), 1971; Love Me, Love My Children, 1971; Children! Children! (also lighting), 1972; Voices (also lighting), 1972; The Crucible (also lighting), 1972; Out Cry (also lighting), 1974; In Praise of Love (also lighting), 1974; Miss Moffat (also lighting; Philadelphia), 1974; Don Giovanni (opera), 1974.

Publications:

By MIELZINER: books—Designing for the Theatre: A Memoir and Portfolio, New York 1965; The Shapes of Our Theatre, New York 1970; Theatre Check List: A Guide to the Planning and Construction of Proscenium and Open Stage Theatres, editor, with Edward F. Kook and Henry Hewes, Middletown, Connecticut, 1970.

On MIELZINER: books—The Biographical Encyclopedia and Who Who's of the American Theatre, edited by Walter Rigdon, New York 1966; Contemporary Stage Design USA, edited by Elizabeth Burdick, Peggy Hansen and Brenda Zanger, Middletown 1974; Stage Design: Four Centuries of Scenic Invention by Donald Oenslager, New York 1975; The Cambridge Guide to World Theatre, edited by Martin Banham, Cambridge 1988.

In his memoir and portfolio Designing for the Theatre, Jo Mielziner states that he was born with an inherited gift for painting and drawing. His remarkable success as a designer of costumes, settings, and lighting supports this statement, but it is also true that Mielziner possessed remarkable taste, judgment, and imagination. All of these elements began to be seen in the theatre with his first productions in 1924, following his association with the great designers Joseph Urban, Lee Simonson, and Robert Edmond Jones. Urban and Jones helped Mielziner to learn the intricacies of what was then known as the New Stagecraft, a modern approach which revolutionized the way plays were produced, while Simonson introduced Mielziner to the power of light on the stage. These men particularly helped Mielziner to establish a design point of view upon which he steadily built throughout his career.

Through trial and error, Mielziner eventually discovered the significant relationship between the setting and the actor which he soon espoused as a fundamental dictum of theatrical design. It is in this regard, as much as in the beauty and appropriateness of his designs, that Mielziner became an example for designers who have followed him. While seeing to the needs of the actor, Mielziner also demonstrated a frequently remarkable sensitivity to the play. Two of his most significant sets, for Maxwell Anderson's Winterset and Death of a Salesman by Arthur Miller, differed radically from the authors' original specifications. It was

Mielziner's thorough and sensitive understanding of these plays which persuaded the authors to his point of view to the benefit of both plays in their initial productions.

Lighting early became a major interest for Mielziner, and he eventually designed lighting for all his settings. Unusually sensitive to light and color, he constantly experimented with colors and their combinations, spending long hours in a specially designed light laboratory in his studio. His interest led to the improvement of old lighting instruments and the invention of new devices through his close association with Edward F. Kook, a founder of Century Lighting Company. Despite Mielziner's strong advocacy of the need for a scene designer to light his own settings, this combination of skills remains rare.

Because so many of Mielziner's settings were associated with the greatest plays in American literature, he became a major influence on design throughout the United States. In the process, he raised the quality of American scene design to the position of superiority it maintains today.

—David W. Weiss

MIHO, James (Noboru).
American graphic designer. Born in Gridley, California, 20 November 1933. Studied at Pasadena City College, California, and Woodbury College, Los Angeles: BS 1952; studied painting under Lorser Feitelson, at the Art Center College of Design, Pasadena: BFA 1957; studied video design, at Philadelphia Museum College, 1958; also attended Wayne State University, Detroit. Served in the United States Army, in Korea, 1950–51: M/Sergeant. Married Tomoko Kawakami in 1956 (divorced, 1977); married Judith M. in 1978; stepdaughter: Jane. Art director, at N. W. Ayer advertising agency, Philadelphia and Detroit, 1959–63; founder-partner of James Miho Incorporated design office, Los Angeles, 1964-65; creative director, Needham Harper and Steers, Chicago, 1965–67, and vice-president of Needham Harper and Steers, New York, 1967–69; freelance designer, working in New York, 1970–82, in Redding, Connecticut, 1982–88, and in Pasadena, California, from 1988: design consultant to Chrysler Corporation, 1957–60, Atlantic Richfield, 1970–72, Xerox Corporation, 1970–72, Denise Rene Gallery of New York, 1972, Danish Embassy, 1973–81. Lecturer in graphic design, Cooper Union, New York, 1983–88; chairman of graphic and packaging design, Art Center College of Design, Pasadena, from 1988. Alumni Board Member, Art Center College of Design, Pasadena, 1982–83. **Exhibition:** Toppan Printing Company, Tokyo, 1973. **Collections:** Museum of Modern Art, New York; Library of Congress, Washington, D.C.; National Air and Space Museum, Smithsonian Institution, Washington, D.C.; Museu de Arte Moderno, Sao Paulo; Poster Museum, Warsaw. Recipient: Gold Award, Cannes Film Festival, 1968, 1980; Advertising Campaign Award, Type Directors Club of New York, 1972; Industrial Film Award, Chicago Film Festival, 1981; and numerous New York, Cincinnati, Connecticut, Chicago, Philadelphia and Boston Art Directors Club awards. Address: 1200 Chateau Road, Pasadena, California 91105, U.S.A.

Works:

Great Ideas of Western Man poster series, for the Container Corporation of America, 1962–63.

Imagination poster series, for Champion International Paper Division, from 1965.

Poster designs, for the National Air and Space Museum, Smithsonian Institution Washington, D.C., from 1975.

AIGA Annual book designs, for the American Institute of Graphic Arts, New York, 1980–87.

Computer designs, for IBM Video Division, from 1982.

Book designs, for Connecticut Historical Society, from 1982.

Design concepts and posters, for American Bell, from 1983.

New American Paper Works exhibition and catalogue design, for the Albright-Knox Art Gallery, Buffalo, New York, 1984.

Fun and Games promotional design, for Champion International Paper Division, 1986.

1640–1940: Furniture Design in New Mexico book design, for the Folk Art Museum of New Mexico, Santa Fe, 1987.

Artists as Photographers exhibition catalogue, for the Aldrich Museum of Contemporary Art, Ridgefield, Connecticut, 1988.

Political Graphics in America book design, for the University of Hartford, Connecticut, 1988.

Rossetti Associates, Architects book design, for Rosetti Associates, Santa Monica, California, 1989.

Publications:

By MIHO: articles—in *Communication Arts* (Palo Alto), 1970, 1973; *Lamp* (New York), 1970; *Print* (New York), September/October 1972.

On MIHO: articles—in *Communication Arts* (Palo Alto), April/May 1969; *Idea* (Tokyo), September 1970, December 1972.

*

It is time that designers not look to the top the mountain, but look to the valleys and forests where human life begins and lives. Conquering mountains does not solve the real issues. Exploring the rich abundance of life in the forests and preserving its variety is more important.

—James Miho

In these days of inexorable technological change, it is important not to lose sight of the things that make us human. Corporations also must increasingly recognize their environmental and social responsibilities and accept obligations which cannot help but have a positive effect on their public image. To this end, James Miho has worked to turn business communication into progressive public information. His work is an expression of the wonder of nature and a celebration of human potential and imagination. He has helped a number of corporations and institutions not only to express their educational and aesthetic concerns, but also to establish their presences as socially responsible, creative organizations.

In 1959, Miho took his first job out of school with the N. W. Ayer and Son agency, where he worked with Herbert Bayer on the "Great Ideas of Western Man" series for the Container Corporation of America. Bayer, who remains Miho's greatest influence, had already established a precedent of using artists such as Cassandre, Léger, Kepes, Matter, and Shahn to interpret the words and ideas of some of the world's

greatest thinkers. Miho searched for new talent and brought, among others, Rauschenberg, Dine, Warhol, and Kane to the series.

Shortly after leaving Ayer, Miho was contacted U.S. Plywood and Champion Paper. Inspired by Container Corporation's example, they had begun a promotion to show the creative use of their paper products. At his suggestion, a travel theme was established for these booklets. Since that time, Miho has literally traveled around the world producing the "Imagination" series for what is now Champion International. His approach to the series is evidence of Miho as an intelligent, responsible, and visually articulate person. Before he begins each piece, he reads and researches extensively. He then spends months at a time on location gathering information, working with local photographers and illustrators and formulating the idea for the final design. Though he works closely with writers on these projects, in the finished piece, the story that is told is primarily pictorial. For "Imagination XV" on Scandinavia, for example, struck by the idea of a Scandinavian smorgasbord, he used this concept in the booklet by showing a chronology of architectural styles with die cuts allowing old and new to be shown simultaneously. This work serves well the needs of his client by taking full advantage of creative work on paper. As many as thirty different production techniques may be used in a single booklet.

For a person who has explored our world so extensively, what new travels will the future bring? What new frontiers? Perhaps his personal interest in outer space is a clue.

—Barbara Sudick

*

MIHO, Tomoko.
American graphic designer. Born Tomoko Kawakami, in Los Angeles, California, in 1933. Studied at Minneapolis College of Design, 1951; studied art under Mary Sheridan, Lorser Feitelson, Bernyce Polifka and Gene Fleury, at the Art Center College of Design, Los Angeles, 1952–56: BA 1956. Married James Noboru Miho in 1956 (divorced, 1977). Designer, 1960–63, and head of graphics department, 1963–64, at George Nelson and Company, New York; founder-partner of Miho Design, Los Angeles, 1964–65; designer, Container Corporation's Center for Advanced Research in Design, Chicago, 1966–67, and design manager, Center for Advanced Research in Design, New York, 1967–74; freelance designer, New York, from 1974: has designed for Champion International Corporation, Stendig International, Herman Miller, Atlantic Richfield, Neiman-Marcus, etc. Board Member, Alliance Graphique Internationale, Paris, 1979–82. **Exhibitions:** *Word and Image,* Museum of Modern Art, New York, 1968 (toured); *International Poster Biennale,* Warsaw, 1970; Toppan Printing Company, Tokyo, 1973; *Images of an Era,* Corcoran Gallery of Art, Washington, D.C., 1976 (toured); *AGI Posters,* Place Ville-Marie, Montreal, 1982; *The Modern Poster,* Museum of Modern Art, New York, 1988; *AGI 88 Tokyo,* G7 Gallery and Ginza Graphic Gallery, Tokyo, 1988. **Collections:** Museum of Modern Art, New York; Library of Congress, Washington, D.C., Recipient: awards from Art Directors Club of New York, Advertising Club of New York, American Institute of Graphic Arts, Society of Typographic Arts, *Industrial*

Design magazine, and Art Directors Club of Los Angeles. Address: 1045 Fifth Avenue, New York, New York 10028, U.S.A.

Works:

Tower Suite and Hemisphere Club identity programs, for Restaurant Associates, New York, 1961.

ARCO corporate identity program, for the Atlantic Richfield Corporation, 1967–72.

Identity program and literature, for Omniplan Architects, from 1970.

Great Ideas of Western Man poster, for the Container Corporation of America, Chicago, 1972.

Signage and graphics, for Andersen's Food Emporium, Hiroshima, 1978.

Concentration posters, for the Whitney Museum of American Art, New York, 1980.

United States pavilion banners and symbols, at the *Energy Expo,* Knoxville, Tennessee, 1982.

Borrowed Landscape poster, for the Herman Miller Ethospace System, 1984.

Environmental graphics, for Herman Miller showrooms in Los Angeles, New York City and Long Island City, 1984–87.

The Isamu Noguchi Garden Museum book design, for Harry N. Abrams, 1987.

Identity program, for Roberdeau Companies, Dallas, 1987.

Publications:

On MIHO: books—*Word and Image,* exhibition catalogue, New York 1968; *Signet, Signal, Symbol* by Walter Diethelm, Zurich 1970; *History of the Poster* by Josef and Shizuko Müller-Brockmann, Zurich 1971; *AGI: Alliance Graphique Internationale Posters,* edited by Rudolph deHarak, New York 1986; *Letterheads: A Collection from Around the World* by Takenobu Igarashi, Tokyo 1986; *Planning and Design* by Larry Klein, New York 1986; *The Modern Poster,* exhibition catalogue, New York 1988.

*

Space defines substance.
Substance defines space.
The two are inseparable.
They are one.

Design is a oneness that
reveals space and substance
in relationship to one another.

As a designer, I feel an
assignment is finished

only when I have finally
joined space and substance
in honest harmony.

It is that harmony that
creates the ringing clarity
of statement that we
sense as an experience, as
a meaningful whole, as
a oneness—as good
design.

—Tomoko Miho

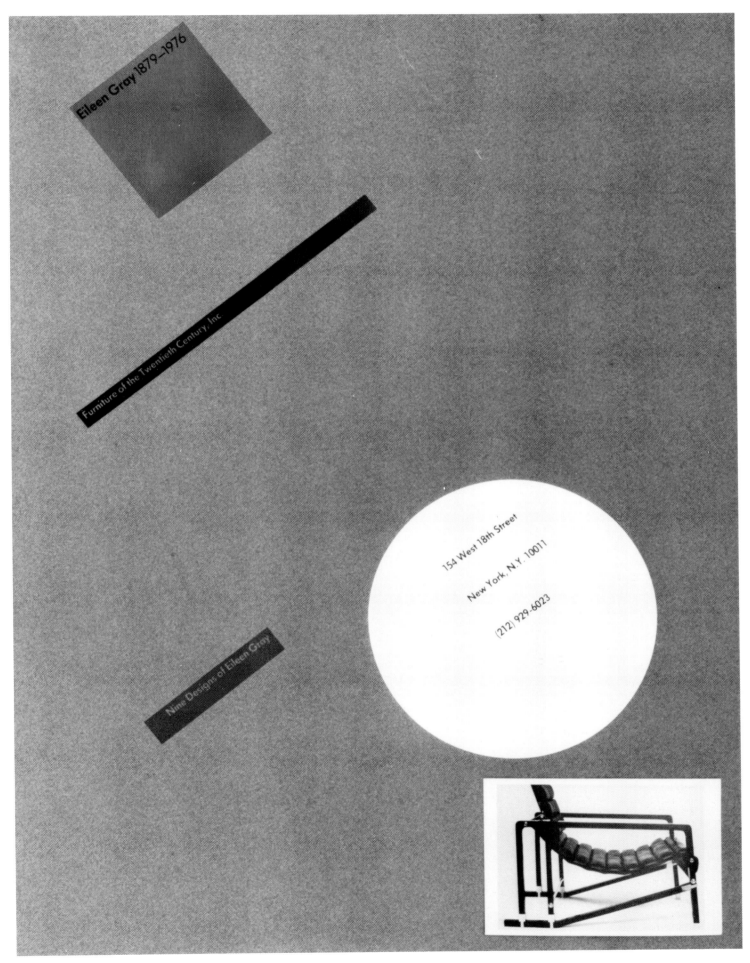

Eileen Gray 1879–1976

Furniture of the Twentieth Century, Inc.

Nine Designs of Eileen Gray

154 West 18th Street

New York, N.Y. 10011

(212) 929-6023

James Miho: *Eileen Gray* **poster, for Furniture of the Twentieth Century Incorporated, New York, 1989**

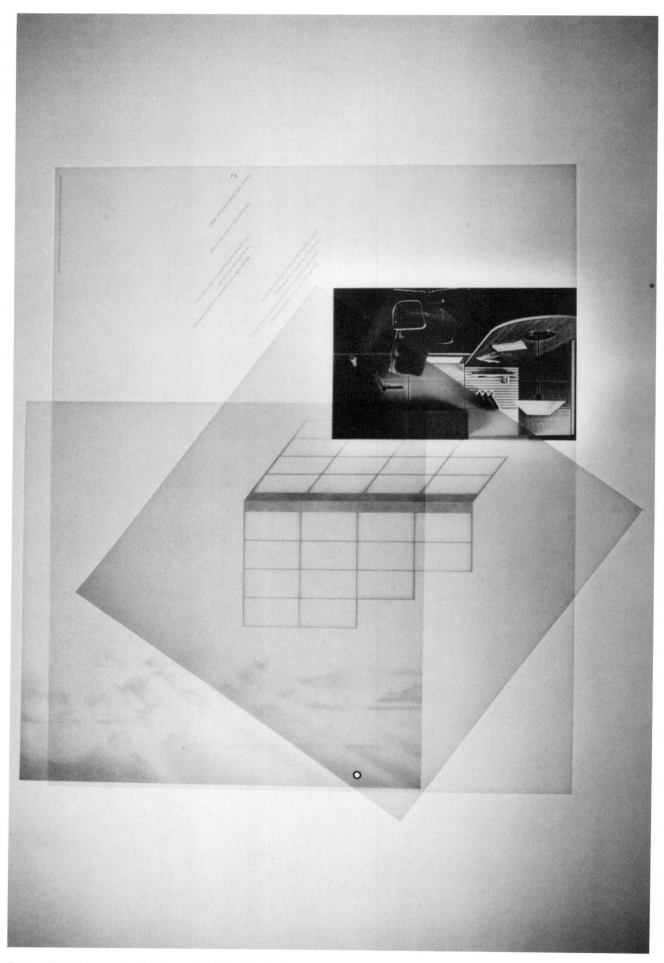

Tomoko Miho: *Ethospace* **poster, for Herman Miller Incorporated, 1984**

MINAGAWA, Masa.

Japanese industrial designer. Born in Tokyo, 23 December 1917. Studied under Takao Miyashita, at the Tokyo Higher Industrial Arts School (now Chiba University), 1936–40: Inumaru Prize, 1940. Served in the Japanese Army, in Tokyo, 1942–45. Married Akiko Kimura in 1946 (died, 1980); daughters: Hiromi and Yoshiko; married Masue Matsumoto in 1982. Staff designer, at Toko Electric Company, Tokyo, 1940–54; freelance lighting and electrical appliance designer, establishing Masa Minagawa Design studio, Tokyo, from 1954. Professor, Kuwasawa Design Institute, Tokyo, 1953–65; lecturer, Chiba University, Tokyo, 1957–63; dean of the industrial design department, Tokyo University of Arts and Design, 1963–83. Founder-member, Japan Industrial Designers Association, Tokyo, from 1953; judge for the Mainichi Shimbun Industrial Design Competition, Tokyo, from 1962; organizing committee member of Design Year, from 1973, coordinating committee chairman, 1973, and design promotion council chairman, 1978–80, Ministry of International Trade and Industry, Tokyo. Recipient: Blue Ribbon Medal, Japanese Government, 1978. Address: 5-12-4 Kita Asagaya, Suginami-ku, Tokyo 166, Japan.

Publications:

By MINAGAWA: books—*Lighting Practice of Japan*, vols. 1–6, Tokyo 1957; *Design Collection: Metal and Non-Ferrous Metal*, 2 vols., Tokyo 1965; article—in *Industrial Design* (Tokyo), August 1983.

When I was about seventeen years old, I used to pass a river on my way to school. One day I saw two flowerpots on the boat of a family that lived on the water because the father was a water-transport worker. At that time, it occurred to me that those with little income too have a desire for beautiful things, and I thought even cheap tools, such as tea cups and chopsticks, should be easy to use and beautiful in shape. This was my motivation for entering Tokyo Higher Industrial Arts School.

In my philosophy of today, I believe in
—products of good quality, of beautiful shape, of inexpensive price for wide use. Designers should be involved in basic layout and should endeavor to make easy-to-use products by pollution-free processes.
—efforts to reduce production costs—for example, reduction of the number of parts and use of parts common to various products.
—ease of assembly—for example, reduction of the number of screws.
—ease and safety of handling.
—beauty. The design should be as simple as possible and should make use of the natural flavor of materials.

—Masa Minagawa

Masa Minagawa worked in the design department of Toko Electric Company from 1940 until 1954 and achieved prominence as one of the first noteworthy industrial designers of electrical appliances in Japan. He opened his own design firm in 1954, when there were few such independent design offices; he has continued to specialize in appliance as well as lighting-systems design. Minagawa was also founding member of the Japan Industrial Designers Association and for twenty years (until his retirement in 1983) he was the Dean of the Industrial Design Department at Tokyo University of Arts and Design.

The Delta fan, designed by Minagawa in 1966, is typical of his work. He replaced the traditional, heavy, molded leg with light,

chrome-plated iron pipe, and the fan is so designed that it can either stand on the floor or be hung on the wall. The light, fresh style creates a clear image of that kind of civilized life-style that Japanese industrial designers have tried to suggest to a public still suffering the "hangover" of postwar chaos. Minagawa's design has far-reaching effects: the Delta fan served as a prototype not only for later fans but also for other electrical appliances for the home.

In his work, Minagawa attempts to follow three rules:
1) A designer should be concerned with economy, with creating good products at cheap prices so that they can be available to the maximum number of consumers. Profit margins are not the responsibility of the designer.
2) A designer should strictly check whether his product is easy to handle, safe, and not a pollutant. These criteria are the designer's responsibility.
3) A designer should not be concerned with just the external form of a product but should also be committed to the design of the basic layout of parts.

According to Minagawa, rational thinking can produce products that are universally useful. For example, his oil filter for cars was manufactured for sixteen years, and more than 160 million copies were produced.

Referring to the present environment for design, Minagawa says: "In order for better design to happen, good design must receive more recognition from the public." As for designers themselves, he advises: "Don't insist too much on yourself, your own personality; put yourself in an objective position when designing." His view, finally, is that the essence of design lies in honesty and sincerity, and his own products are obviously in conformity with that goal.

—Kunio Sano

MINALE, Marcello.

British graphic, interior and industrial designer. Born of Italian parents, in Tripoli, Libya, 15 December 1938. Studied at the Istituto Tecnico, Naples, 1957–60. Married Roberta M; sons: Marcello, Manlio and Massimo. Designer at the Taucker advertising agency, and art director of the Makkinointi Uierjuuri agency, Helsinki, 1960–62; design director, Young and Rubicam agency, London, 1962–64; founder-partner,

Masa Minagawa: *Delta* **electric fan, 1958**

British Airports

Marcello Minale: Advertisement for the British Airports Authority, 1978

with Brian Tattersfield, of Minale Tattersfield and Partners design firm, London, from 1964. President, Designers and Art Directors Association, London, 1982. **Exhibitions:** Design Centre, London, 1979; *Penguin Books,* Manchester Polytechnic, 1981; Museo d'Arte Contemporanea, Milan, 1983. **Collections:** Poster Museum, Warsaw; Victoria and Albert Museum, London; Museum of Modern Art, New York. Recipient: Silver Medals, Design and Art Directors Association, London, 1972–82; Gold Medal, Art Directors Club of New York, 1977. Fellow, Chartered Society of Designers, London. Address: Minale Tattersfield and Partners, The Courtyard, 37 Sheen Road, Richmond, Surrey TW9 1AJ, England.

Publications:

By MINALE: books—*Minale Tattersfield,* vols. 1–4, co-editor with Brain Tattersfield, London 1965–72; *Creatures Great and Small,* London 1973; *The Black Pencil,* London 1974; *The Tree That Could Fly,* London 1976; *Tomo the Water Dragon,* London 1977; *Minale Tattersfield Designers,* edited by Edward Booth-Clibborn London 1977.

On MINALE/TATTERSFIELD: books—*Graphic Design Britain,* edited by Frederick Lambert, London 1967; *Modern Graphics* by Keith Murgatroyd, London 1969; *European Designers: England, France, Italy* by Idea Publishers, Tokyo 1970; *Minale Tattersfield Designers* by Idea Publishers, Tokyo 1978; *Penguin Books: The Pictorial Cover 1960–1980,* exhibition catalogue by Evelyne Green, Manchester 1981; *Who's Who in Graphic Art,* edited by Walter Amstutz, Dubendorf 1982; *Contemporary Furniture,* edited by Klaus-Jurgen Sembach, Stuttgart and New York 1982; *Design Source Book* by Penny Sparke and others, London 1986; *International Design Yearbook 1987/88,* edited by Philippe Starck, London 1987.

These are my three basic principles of design:
1. Keep it simple even if it is complicated.
2. Think before designing instead of designing before thinking.
3. The duty of every designer is never to bore the audience.

—Marcello Minale

See TATTERSFIELD, Brian.

The Minale Tattersfield corporate identity symbol is a soft black pencil scribble, a gentle poke at the cool Swiss formalism that constituted good graphics in the 1960s, but absolutely right for a company whose work is noted for its flair, originality, and wit. Marcello Minale and Brian Tattersfield met at Young and Rubicam in the early 1960s when New York-inspired ideas were transforming British advertising agencies. But frustrated with a lack of client contact, they set up a partnership, adopting the practical business lessons they had learned along with a fresh approach, a philosophy summed up by Minale as "expressing the maximum possible with the simplest means." With the reputation of being slightly crazy as well as avant-garde, they did at first find it hard to attract clients. A major breakthrough came with the commission to update Harrod's conventional, "establishment" image with a sortie into the swinging sixties boutique style. With new retailing methods, Pop art images, coffer bars, and subdued lighting, it caught the mood of the time perfectly.

In 1972, they were appointed graphic design consultants to Milton Keynes, with a brief to help soften the hard qualities of new town architecture. Other commissions include De Beers offices, a new logo for the London furniture store Heal's, and work for a range of Italian clients, including Alitalia, Star, and Buitoni Perugina.

Sadly, because of financial cutbacks in 1979, some of their most brilliant work—the redesign of fifteen tube stations on London Transport's Northern Line—was never executed. Since its pioneering work in the 1930s, London Transport has unfortunately declined, and Minale Tattersfield's strong and exciting visual identity would have done a great deal to revive a flagging image. What might have been is suggested by a full-scale mock-up of a ceiling vault for Oval Station and a Kings Cross subway decorated with the word "smile" in large, colourful letters.

Their design achievement has been recognised by a major retrospectives in London and Milan. Contemporary Alan Fletcher of Pentagram summed them up: "They represent to the world of graphics what Laurel and Hardy, Rodgers and Hammerstein, Romeo and Juliet, Gilbert and Sullivan, Young and Rubicam represent in their respective worlds."

—Catherine McDermott

MINKS, Wilfried.

Czechoslovak stage designer. Born in Binai, 21 February 1930. Studied at the Meisterschule für Angewandte Kunst, Leipzig, 1950–54; stage design under Willy Schmidt, at the Akademie der Bildende Künste, Berlin, 1955–57. Assistant to Gerd Richter, at the Staatstheater, Stuttgart, 1957–58; resident designer, at the Stadttheater, Pforzheim, 1958–59, Städtische Bühnen, Ulm, 1959–62, and at the Stadttheater, Bremen, 1962–71; freelance designer and stage director, Frankfurt, from 1971: board member, Schauspiel, Frankfurt, 1980–81. Professor, Hochschule für Bildende Kunste, Hamburg, from 1970. **Exhibitions:** *Die Neue Buhne,* Städtisches Museum, Leverkusen, 1967; Studio F, Ulm, 1967; Kunsthalle, Bremen, 1968. Address: c/o Schauspiel Frankfurt, Städtische Bühnen, 6000 Frankfurt 1, West Germany.

Works:

Stage productions include—*The Hostage,* Stadttheater, Bremen, 1964; *The Quare Fellow,* Stadttheater, Bremen, 1964; *Spring Awakening,* Stadttheater, Bremen, 1965; *Hamlet,* Stadttheater, Bremen, 1965; *Macbeth,* Stadttheater, Bremen, 1966; *The Robbers,* Stadttheater, Bremen, 1966; *War of the Roses,* Stadttheater, Bremen, 1967; *Tasso,* Stadttheater, Bremen, 1969; *The Tempest,* Stadttheater, Bremen, 1969; *Bremer Freiheit,* Concordia Cinema, Bremen, 1971.

Publications:

On MINKS: books—*Die Neue Buhne,* exhibition catalogue, Leverkusen 1967; *Die Bühne von Wilfried Minks,* exhibition catalogue, Bremen 1968; *Stage Design Throughout the World Since 1960,* edited by René Hainaux and Nicole Leclercq, Brussels 1972, London 1973; *Stage Design Throughout the World 1970-1975,* edited by René Hainaux and Nicole Leclercq, Brussels and London 1976.

Wilfried Minks first invigorated German design through a return to bold realism in his designs for Peter Zadek's productions to Brendan Behan's plays in the early 1960's *(The Hostage, The Quare Fellow).* He was instrumental in shaking design out of a benign formalism, represented most clearly to Minks by the work of Franz Mertz in the 1950s. Minks advocated a "tougher" design, one that used real materials and made reference to contemporary reality, either social or esthetic.

By 1965, his work had developed in an eclectic direction, borrowing heavily from tendencies in the visual arts, especially Pop Art. For Zadek's production of Schiller's *The Robbers,* he blew up a painting by Roy Lichtenstein into a full stage backdrop and clothed the characters in comic strip costumes. For a production of *The Tempest* in 1969, he covered the entire stage floor with sand and erected a fluorescent rainbow over it. In creating works like these, Minks espoused a design that borrowed unabashedly from what were, in his mind, the more aggressive arts of contemporary painting and sculpture to make a visual comment and connection between the time in which the play was written and the contemporary world.

Gradually, Minks designs gathered a strength of expression that rivaled the actor and playwright for attention. In 1970, he said that design "should have the self-sufficiency of landscapes." This tendency in German design, originated by Minks, was pushed to an extreme by later designers (Achim Freyer and Erich Wonder) who considered some of their designs independent visual statements, complete without actors. Minks was also instrumental in encouraging designers to seek out alternative spaces for their settings. For a production of Fassbinder's *Bremer Freiheit* in 1971, he transformed an old movie theater (the Concordia) into a complete audience-stage space. This design tendency was developed much further by Minks colleague in Bremen, Karl-Ernst Herrmann, when he became the chief designer at the Schaubühne am Halleschen Ufer in Berlin.

Around 1972, Minks turned his attention away from design toward directing; by this time, his legacy could be seen throughout West Germany, where many of his former students, working in the major state theaters, were creating audacious stage designs that drew heavily on contemporary visual arts for inspiration. If Caspar Neher had shown how scene design could have a dramaturgical function, Minks made clear how it could make a purely visual comment on the text.

—Richard V. Riddell

MISSONI, Ottavio.

Italian fashion designer. Born in Ragusa, Yugoslavia, 11 February 1921. Educated in Zara, Italy, until 1938, in Trieste, 1930–40, and in Milan, 1941–42. Served in the Italian Army (prisoner of war, Egypt, 1942–46). Married Rosita Jelmini in 1953; children: Vittorio, Luca and Angela. Designer and manufacturer of knitwear, from 1948: established knitwear factory, with Giorgio Oberweger, in Trieste, 1948–53; partner, with Rosita Missoni, in knitwear design and manufacturing firm, in Gallarate, Italy, 1953–68, and in Missoni S.p.A. workshop and factory, in Sumirago, Italy, from 1968: designed clothing and household fabrics for Biki, American Fieldcrest, Saporiti, T. e J. Vestor, etc.; launched *Missoni* women's perfume, 1981, and *Missoni Uomo* men's fragrance, 1983. Also an athlete: Italian 400-metre champion, Milan, 1939; World Student Champion, Vienna, 1939; Olympic Games 400-metre finalist, London, 1948. **Exhibitions:** *Missoni and the Magic Machine,* Galleria del Naviglio, Venice, 1975; *Missoni Retrospective,* La Rotonda di Via Besana, Milan, 1978 (toured); *Italian Re-Evolution,* La Jolla Museum of Art, California, 1982; *Icontri Venezia,* Venice, 1982; *40 Years of Italian Fashion,* Trump Tower, New York, 1983. Recipient: Neiman Marcus Award, 1973; Tommy Award, American Printed Fabrics Council, 1976; Fragrance Foundation Award, 1982. Address: Missoni S.p.A., Via Luigi Rossi, 21040 Sumirago, Varese, Italy.

Publications:

On MISSONI: books—*20th Century Fashion: A Scrapbook* by Ernestine Carter, London 1975; *In Vogue: Sixty Years of Celebrities and Fashion* by Georgina Howell, London 1975, 1978, New York 1976; *Missoni and the Magic Machine,* exhibition catalogue by Guido Ballo, Venice 1975; *In Fashion: Dress in the Twentieth Century* by Prudence Glynn, London 1978; *I Mass-Moda: Fatti e Personaggi dell'Italian Look* by Adriana Mulassano, Florence 1979; *Italian Re-Evolution: Design in Italian Society in the Eighties,* exhibition catalogue edited by Piero Sartogo, La Jolla 1982; *40 Years of Italian Fashion,* exhibition catalogue compiled by B. G. Aragno, Rome 1983; *McDowell's Directory of Twentieth Century Fashion* by Colin McDowell, London 1984; *The Conran Directory of Design,* edited by Stephen Bayley, London 1985; *Design Source Book* by Penny Sparke and others, London 1986; *The Encyclopaedia of Fashion from 1840 to the 1980s* by Georgina O'Hara, London 1986; *Italian Design: 1870 to the Present* by Penny Sparke, London 1988.

See MISSONI, Rosita.

Ottavio Missoni was born in Yugoslavia to a sea captain and a Dalmatian countess. While enjoying athletic triumph in England in 1948, he met Rosita Jelmini from Lombardy, then a student at Hampstead. At that time, he had already begun a small knitwear business in Trieste with partner Giorgio Oberweger. After the Missonis married, they began to develop women's knitwear in a small factory at Gallarate, outside Milan. Unfortunately for the sports world, after an injury, Tai retired from competition to devote all his time to experiments and to merchandizing the ready-to-wear line. He did admit, though, that in this field he would continue to compete: "The formula remains the same—an amazing pace, serious preparation and a masterpiece in style."

Initially, while developing and refining knitting techniques by machine, the Missonis approached the problem of designing the patterns and colors with open minds. By concentrating on the material, they became famous for multicolored, brilliant hues, as well as muted, rich shades. Their garments are vehicles for these patterns, which they carry in simple, graceful lines. Their styles, introduced in collections twice a year, are yet classic and able to be worn at any age, during any season, and they can be beautifully mixed and matched (an innovative idea of theirs years ago).

About 1962 their famous flame-stitch pattern was introduced; variations included hard, soft, or curved lines in addition to the rainbow flame-stitch. In 1972, see-through net was introduced, to be followed by netted stripes in 1973, the zig-zag knit, as well as the shaded horizontal stripe and the wavy diagonal stripe. In 1975, the chenille knit was introduced, then printed on woolen shawls in 1976. The shaded herring-bone was created in soft colors, and the tartan-plaid knit followed in 1978.

As a guest, I was very impressed when Vitto-

Ottavio and Rosita Missoni: Straight-cut high-collar coat with matching hat, 1983

rio Missoni, now in charge of production and sales, brother Luca, a pattern and color technician, and sister Angela, who creates accessories and organizes shows, hosted me and a group of fashion students. The entire family welcomed us into their modern factory and laboratories in the tranquil, wooded hills at Sumirago, north of Milan. Besides being thoroughly charmed, we were inspired. Typically, the Missoni family follows everything directly, overseeing 200 workers creating approximately 1,000 garments a day to supply fewer than 200 clients.

In his laboratory, Tai creates surrounded by stacks of samples, swatches, skeins, reels of wool and silk, paint pots, multitudes of colored felt-tip pens, and graph paper. Also at hand are a test-knitting machine and bits and pieces of fabrics collected from travels to serve as inspiration. In her workroom, Rosita concentrates on research influenced by her purchases at flea markets. She explained that their work is really their hobby. It expresses influences from travel, books, art, and music. They truly feel that they are not fashion creators but a private, happy family working together as artisans.

—Gillion Skellenger

MISSONI, Rosita.

Italian fashion designer. Born Rosita Jelmini, in Golasecca, 20 November 1931. Studied modern languages, at the Collegio Rosetum, Besozzo, 1948–51. Married Ottavio Missoni in 1953; children: Vittorio, Luca and Angela. Worked as a design assistant in her parents' loungewear and furnishing fabrics factory, Vestor, 1950–53; partner, with Ottavio Missoni, in knitwear design and manufacturing workshop and factory, in Gallarate, 1953–68, and in Missoni S.p.A. knitwear design and manufacturing firm, in Sumirago, from 1968: designed for Biki, American Fieldcrest, Saporiti, T. e J. Vestor, etc.; launched *Missoni* women's perfume, 1981, and *Missoni Uomo* men's fragrance, 1983. **Exhibitions:** *Missoni and the Magic Machine,* Galleria del Naviglio, Venice, 1975; *Missoni Retrospective,* La Rotonda di Via Besana, Milan, 1978 (toured); *Italian Re-Evolution,* La Jolla Museum of Art, California, 1982; *Incontri Venezia,* Venice, 1982; *40 Years of Italian Fashion,* Trump Tower, New York, 1983. Recipient: Neiman Marcus Award, 1973; Tommy Award, American Printed Fabrics Council, 1976; Fragrance Foundation Award, 1982. Address: Missoni S.p.A., Via Luigi Rossi, 21040 Sumirago, Varese, Italy.

Our philosophy since we went into business has been that a piece of clothing should be like a work of art. It should not be bought for a special occasion or because it's in fashion, but because a woman likes it, finds it suits her needs and feels she could wear it forever.

—Rosita Missoni

See MISSONI, Ottavio.

MIYAKE, Issey.

Japanese fashion designer. Born Kazumaru Miyake, in Tokyo, 22 April 1939. Studied at Tama Art University, Tokyo, 1959–63, and at La Chambre Syndicale de la Couture Parisienne, Paris, 1965. Assistant to designer Guy Laroche, Paris, 1966–68, and to Hubert de Givenchy, Paris, 1968–69; designer, for Geoffrey Beene ready-to-wear fashion firm, New York, 1969–70; freelance designer, establishing Miyake Design Studio, Tokyo, from 1970; also director of Issey Miyake International, Tokyo, Issey Miyake and Associates, Tokyo, Issey Miyake Europe, Paris, Issey Miyake USA, New York, and Issey Miyake On Limits, Tokyo. Executive adviser and planner, First Japan Culture Conference, Yokohama, 1980. **Exhibitions:** *Issey Miyake in the Museum,* Seibu Museum of Art, Tokyo, 1977; *Escape-Temps du Japon,* Musée des Arts Décoratifs, Paris, 1978; *Intimate Architecture: Contemporary Clothing Design,* Massachusetts Institute of Technology, Cambridge, 1982. **Collections:** Metropolitan Museum of Art, New York; Victoria and Albert Museum, London. Recipient: Japan Fashion Editors Club Award, 1974; Mainichi Design Prize, Tokyo, 1977; Pratt Institute Design Excellence Award, New York, 1979. Address: 3-5-27 Roppongi, Minato-ku, Tokyo, Japan.

Publications:

By MIYAKE: books—*Issey Miyake East Meets West,* edited by Kazuko Koide and Ikko Tanaka, Tokyo 1978; *Issey Miyake Bodyworks,* edited by Shozo Tsurumoto, Tokyo, 1983.

On MIYAKE: books—*25 Ans de Marie-Claire de 1954 a 1979,* compiled by Francoise Mohrt, Paris 1979; *Fashion 2001* by Lucille Kornak, London 1982; *Intimate Architecture: Contemporary Clothing Design,* exhibition catalogue, Cambridge, Massachusetts 1982; *McDowell's Directory of Twentieth Century Fashion* by Colin McDowell, London 1984; *New Fashion Japan* by Leonard Koren, Tokyo and New York 1984; *The Conran Directory of Design,* edited by Stephen Bayley, London 1985; *Design Source Book* by Penny Sparke and others, London 1986; *The Encyclopedia of Fashion from 1840 to the 1980s* by Georgina O'Hara, London 1986; *Japanese Design* by Penny Sparke, London 1987.

For Issey Miyake, the kimono is a perfect garment which epitomises the Oriental concept of clothing. It is in the East that we find the roots of his designs which have proved a radical departure from the established Western traditions of haute couture. Miyake does not conform to the Western mode of tailoring garments to fit the body, but produces large, geometric shapes, unadorned with additional detail, which rely on the quality of the fabric for their effect.

Having studied the traditions of his craft, both in Japan and in Europe, he broke away to produce loose, free styles which were sympathetic to the freedom demanded from their clothes by young people in the 1970s. By concentrating on the space between body and clothes, he has utilised the manner in which fabric reacts with the human form. To this effect, he admits that his thinking was influenced by the work of Madeleine Vionnet, who employed the bias cut for her most famous garments, produced in the 1920s and 1930s. The result was that her dresses glided over the surface of the body, rather than clinging to the silhouette. In order to achieve a similar feeling, Miyake has been influenced by traditional Japanese techniques which simplify cutting to a minimum and utilize the natural width of the fabric. The traditional influences do not stop

there, for many of his garments have been adapted from time-honoured prototypes. The basic shape of the kimono, of course, underlies many of his forms. The *sashiko* labourers' garment and the uniforms worn for the martial arts such as Judo or Kendo have been adapted from their hand-sewn originals and recreated in industrially produced fabrics. The long, hooded *tanzen* lounging robe has become a loose, wrap-around coat. Even the dull, functional uniform of the Japanese student was updated, using bright, exciting prints, in 1973. Fabrics too look to tradition for their inspiration. This is the wellspring of his "folklore" or "countryside" stripe, his indigo dyed cottons, and his Balinese checked weaves.

While influences upon him are apparent, he used them with great innovation which he hopes will stimulate the imagination of the wearer. His clothes do not have to be worn in a precisely defined manner, and by changing a belt or a manner of wrapping, they can be adapted by the individual. These large expanses of fabric are like canvases to which are applied the most stunning or subtle designs, influenced by both Eastern and Western cultures. In his first New York collection in 1970, Miyake featured prints influenced by Japanese tattoos but devoted to the memories of Jimi Hendrix, Janis Joplin, and Marilyn Monroe. Later, his design team produced the more obviously Eastern patterns—The Spinnaker in Indian Magic, Mantra and Tantra. The cooperative work between the Issey Miyake Design Studio and a Japanese dye printer led in 1977 to the invention of laser-beam printing to produce beautiful, geometric patterns of graduated colors. Through his experiments with the new and revitalisation of the old, Miyake has shown us the importance of fabrics for the clothes of the future.

—Hazel Clark

MLODOZENIEC, Jan (Lukasz).

Polish cartoonist, illustrator and graphic designer. Born in Warsaw, 8 November 1929. Studied poster design under Henryk Tomaszewski, at the Academy of Fine Arts, Warsaw, 1948–55. Married Monika Ruszewska in 1953; sons: Stanislaw and Piotr. Poster designer and illustrator, working with the publishers Czytelnik, Iskry, WAG, KAW, PIW, Polfilm, and the magazine *Poland,* in Warsaw, from 1952. Contributor to *Miesiecznik Literacki* magazine, 1966–81, and *Film* magazine, 1973–77. **Exhibitions:** Kordegardaa Gallery, Warsaw, 1962; Galerie in der Biberstrass, Vienna, 1963; Polish Cultural Centre, Prague, 1966; Galerie d'Art, Poitiers, 1968; Gallery Ruch, Lublin, 1969; District Museum, Przemysl, 1971; Dum Pana, Brno, 1975; Vystavnisin Hollar, Prague, 1975; Galerie am Prater, Berlin, 1978; National Museum, Poznan, 1979; Polska Institutet, Stockholm, 1981; BWA Gallery, Zamosc, 1981; Poster Museum, Wilanow, 1984; Maison Gerbolier, La Salle, Italy, 1985; BWA Gallery, Zakopane, 1986; Teatr Nowy Gallery, Warsaw, 1986; Polnisches Kulturzentrum, Leipzig, 1988; Librairie Polonaise, Paris, 1988. **Collections:** Poster Museum, Wilanow; National Museum, Poznan; Stedelijk Museum, Amsterdam; Museum of Decorative Arts, Prague; Kunstgewerbe museum, Zurich; Musée de l'Affiche, Paris; Bibliothèque Forney, Paris; Biblioteka

Jan Mlodozeniec: *Generations: Páinters from Warsaw* **exhibition poster, 1988**

Narodowa, Warsaw; Israel Museum, Jerusalem. Recipient: Internationale Buchkunst Ausstellung Medal, Leipzig, 1965, 1971; Poster of the Year Award, Warsaw, 1965, 1966, 1970, 1972, 1973, 1979, 1981, 1983, 1985, 1987; Warsaw Poster Biennale Prize and Medal, 1980; Katowice Poster Biennale Medal, 1981; Lahti Poster Biennale Prize, 1983. Member: Zwiazek Polskich Artystow Plastykow, Warsaw; Alliance Graphique Internationale, Paris. Address: Naruszewisza 3, m.7, 02-627 Warsaw, Poland.

Works:

Birth Certificate film poster, for CWF, 1961.
Slawomir Mrozek: Le Dindon poster, for Teatr Dramatyczny, Warsaw, 1961.
Paul Hindemith: Quatre Temperaments poster, for the Warsaw Opera, 1962.
Cyrk (elephant) circus poster, for WAG, 1965.
F. Durrenmatt: Meteor poster, for Teatr Dramatyczny, Warsaw, 1966.
Jean Genet: The Maids poster, for Teatr Ateneum, Warsaw, 1967.
Giancarlo Menotti: Konsul poster, for Teatr Wielki, Warsaw, 1972.
Cyrk (dancing horse) circus poster, for KAW, 1972.
Ruggiero Leoncavallo: I Pagliacci poster, for the Wroclaw Opera, 1974.
Cromwell film poster, for Polfilm, 1974.
The Conformist film poster, for Polfilm, 1974.
Klute film poster, for Polfilm, 1975.
New York, New York film poster, for Polfilm, 1979.
Igor Stravinsky: l'Histoire d'un Soldat poster for Teatr Wielki, Warsaw, 1983.
Zamosc Shakespeare Festival poster for BWA Zamosc, 1985.
Molière: School for Wives poster, for Teatr Polski, Szczecin, 1985.

Publications:

By MŁODOZENIEC: books illustrated—*Perla* [The Pearl] by John Steinbeck, Warsaw 1956; *The Taming of the Shrew* by William Shakespeare, Warsaw 1972; *The Stories of Cronopios and Famas* by Cortazar, Warsaw 1973; *Le Diable au Corps* by Radiguet, Warsaw 1979; *L'École des Femmes* by Molière, Warsaw 1983.

On MŁODOZENIEC: book—*Who's Who in Graphic Art,* edited by Walter Amstutz, Zurich 1962, Dubendorf 1982; *The Polish Poster* by Jerzy Wasniewsky and Jozef Mroszczak, Warsaw 1968, 1972; *Polish Poster Art Today* by Szymon Bojko, Warsaw and London 1972; *Modern Polish Posters* by Janina Fijalkowska, Paris 1974; *Contemporary Polish Posters,* edited by Joseph S. Czestochowski, New York 1979; *Jan Młodozeniec,* exhibition catalogue with text by Zdzislaw Schubert, Poznan 1979; *Posters by Member of the Alliance Graphique Internationale,* edited by Rudolph deHarak, New York 1986; *Jan Młodozeniec,* exhibition catalogue with text by Edmund Lewandowski, Warsaw 1986; *World Graphic Design 1: Posters* by Yusaku Kamekura and Ikko Tanaka, Tokyo 1988.

*

Posters, book jackets, illustrations—the knot on Pegasus' tail, hand-painted clothes of Venus de Milo.

From Altamira, the line progresses through the Greek vase, the blackness of the grid of Rembrandt lines, secessionally along the shorelines of Japan, through a Toulouse-Lautrec drawing to the galleries: SUBWAY, WALL, FENCE.

Posters. Colour is flowing through the town.

Flashes of ART amidst the monotony of the photographic sentences of commerce. Painterly Esperanto in the Importunate Ocean of advertising publicity. François, Fukuda, Chwast, Tomaszewski. The masterpieces.

The poster is an IDEA, COLOUR, LAYOUT, DRAWING, LETTERING, all of them close-knit, each accorded the same significance.

The graphic designer, tailor, shoemaker . . . SUBJECT MATTER, FORMAT, DEADLINE.

A *placard-frac* for Monsieur Verdi, a jacket for Monsieur Beckett's book, "a pair of boots" for Fellini's *La Strada*.

The book—daughter of Gutenberg. Its author and title on the cover. Image, word, typography.

The illustration—wife of the printed text: concise, equivocal, peripheral, and fantasy, synthesis, and decoration in between.

The THEATRE, POETRY, CINEMA, MUSIC, PAINTING are worth promoting and recommending.

Questing . . .

—Jan Młodozeniec

If we want to understand the artist's way of thinking, it is important to note that Jan Młodozeniec is the son of a prominent Polish poet. A word, the power of writing, the beauty of a letter, its shape and weight—these particularly interest him. Yet, this leader in the Polish Poster School is also the master of drawing. His is simple, linear, realized with speed and energy mixed with accurate decisiveness.

Many of his early posters, in the 1950s, were large-scale drawings with lettering incorporated into the overall composition. Although very personal, they were always easily readable. At the same time, in his illustrations, Młodozeniec worked in almost an etcher's style, retaining the traditional Central European approach toward graphic art, as formulated in Munich and Vienna at the beginning of the century. The maze of lines, with heavy areas of black and white, produced a very expressionistic mood.

Slowly, his compositions, posters, private drawings, and illustrated books began to change. The artist reduced the illustrations to purely linear drawings, full of air and lightness. Despite this simplicity, they offer a nearly three-dimensional effect. His "purification" of the poster went even further. The role of details and ornament diminished, but the use of color became more extensive. The posters of the last fifteen years are built on a basis of black, linear compositions separating flat, deep colors. The effect is very powerful. Despite flatness, the colors fight aggressively, making the posters vibrate with energy.

This virtuoso at hand-lettering has developed his own style of integrating text with picture in his posters and has, as well, sometimes even successfully used his skills to make entire short books of poetry by hand. Some popular poetry books, priced at around fifty cents and printed by the hundreds of thousands, were "illuminated" by Młodozeniec in the fashion of medieval monks—but available for all.

Some critics have, at times, claimed that Młodozeniec was declining. They were wrong. The artist is developing his own distinctive style, his tides rising according to natural progress. He doesn't seek stardom. Calm, closed within himself, Młodozeniec lives in his own world of color, line, and ever-important words. He tries to improve, despite early success in the 1950s, knowing his abilities as well as his limitations and flaws, and he continues to master the good, eliminate the bad. This unusual self-discipline and enormous talent put him at the very top of the Polish graphic-art elite, then and now.

—Jan Sawka

MOGENSEN, Børge (Vestergård).

Danish furniture and textile designer. Born in Aalborg, 13 April 1914. Apprenticed to a cabinet maker in Aalborg, 1934–36; studied at the Konsthandvaerkskolan, Copenhagen, 1936–38; studied furniture design under Kaare Klint, at the Royal Danish Academy of Arts, Copenhagen, 1938–41. Married Alice Kluver Krohn in 1942. Worked as an assistant to Mogens Koch, Kaare Klint and other designers, in Copenhagen, 1938–42; furniture designer and head of the FDB Danish Consumers Cooperative, Copenhagen, 1942–50; freelance designer, Copenhagen, from 1950: design consultant, with Lis Ahlmann, to C. Olesen textile company, from 1953; designed for Soborgs Moebelfabrik, Fredericia Stolefabrik, Karl Andersson, Erhard Rasmussen, P. Lauritzen, Fritz Hansen, I. Christiansen, Jacob Kjaer, Ove Lander, L. Pontoppidan, Rudolf Rasmussens Snedkerier, Boligens Byggeskabe, etc. Assistant to Kaare Klint, 1945–47, and professor from 1947, at the Royal Danish Academy of Arts, Copenhagen. **Exhibitions:** Danish Cabinetworkers Guild exhibitions, Copenhagen, 1939–62; *Die Gute Industrieform,* Kunstverein, Hamburg, 1955; *Two Centuries of Danish Design,* Victoria and Albert Museum, London, 1968 (toured); *Modern Chairs,* Whitechapel Art Gallery, London, 1970; *Børge Morgensen: Mobler/Lis Ahlmann: Tekstiler,* Kunstindustrimuseet, Copenhagen, 1974; *Nordisk Industridesign,* Konstindustrimuseet, Oslo, 1976; *Scandinavian Modern Design 1880–1980,* Cooper-Hewitt Museum, New York, 1982; *Design Since 1945,* Philadelphia Museum of Art, 1983; *Design au Danemark 1950–1987,* Château de Brion, Dordogne, 1987. **Collections:** Kunstindustrimuseet, Copenhagen; Statens Kunstfond, Copenhagen; Louisiana Museum, Humelbaek. Recipient: Bissens Stipend, Copenhagen, 1945; Eckersberg Medal, Copenhagen, 1950; Silver Medal, Danish Trade Fair, Copenhagen, 1953; Cabinetmakers Guild Award of Honour, Copenhagen, 1958; Furniture Manufacturers Association Prize, Copenhagen, 1971; C. F. Hansen Medal, Copenhagen, 1972. Honorary Royal Designer for Industry, Royal Society of Arts, London, 1972. *Died* (in Gentofte) *5 October 1972.*

Works:

Drop-sided sofa in beech with woollen cushions, 1945, produced by Fritz Hansen, from 1962.
Chair in natural beech with plaited hessian seat, for FDB Danish Consumers' Co-operative, 1947.
Chair in oak or oiled beechwood with woven cane seat, for FDB Danish Consumers' Co-operative, 1948.
Easy chair in oak with natural leather seat and back, for Erhard Rasmussen, 1950.
Table in oak with black slate top, for Erhard Rasmussen, 1951.
Adjustable tilting armchair in oak with stretched leather seat and back, for Erhard Rasmussen, 1955.
Dining chair in oak with woven cane seat, for P. Lauritzen, 1957.
Cotil Collection cotton drapery fabric, for C. Olesen, 1957 (with Lis Ahlmann).
Spanish Chair in natural oak with oxhide seat and back, for Fredericia Stolefabrik, 1958.
End-table and armchair with footstool in oak, for Fredericia Stolefabrik, 1960.
Cotil Collection rug, for C. Olesen, 1960 (with Lis Ahlmann).
Asserbo 504 chair, for Karl Andersson, 1964.

Publications:

On MOGENSEN: books—*Dansk Mobelkunst* by Viggo Sten Møller and Svend Erik Møller, Copenhagen 1951; *Danish Chairs*, edited by Nanna and Jørgen Ditzel, Copenhagen 1954; *Modern Danish Furniture* by Esbjørn Hiort, New York, London and Stuttgart 1956; *Modern Danish Textiles*, edited by Bent Salicath and Arne Karlsen, Copenhagen 1959; *Modern Scandinavian Furniture* by Ulf Hård af Segerstad, Copenhagen 1963, London 1964; *Furniture Designed by Børge Mogensen* by Arne Karlsen, Copenhagen 1968; *Modern Chairs 1918-1970*, exhibition catalogue with texts by Carol Hogben and others, London 1970; *Børge Mogensen: Møbler/Lis Ahlmann: Tekstiler*, exhibition catalogue, Copenhagen 1974; *History of Modern Furniture* by Karl Mang, Stuttgart 1978, London 1979; *Scandinavian Modern Design 1880-1980*, edited by David Revere McFadden, New York 1982; *Twentieth Century Design: Furniture* by Penny Sparke, London 1986; *Modern Furniture Classics* by Miriam Stimpson, London 1987.

MOISEIWITSCH, Tanya.

British stage designer. Born in London, 3 December 1914. Studied at the Central School of Arts and Crafts, London, 1928-32. Married Felix Krish in 1942 (died). Stage designer, working for repertory theatre, from 1934, and for the opera, from 1947: designed for the Abbey Theatre, Dublin, 1935-39, Q Theatre and Duchess Theatre, London, 1940, the Oxford Playhouse, 1941-44, the Old Vic Company in Liverpool and Bristol, 1944-46, New Theatre, London, 1945-46, Shakespeare Memorial Theatre, Stratford upon Avon, from 1949, Shakespeare Festival productions in Stratford, Ontario, from 1953, the National Theatre Company at the Old Vic, London, 1968-75, etc. Principal designer, Tyrone Guthrie Theatre, Minneapolis, from 1963; consultant designer, Crucible Theatre, Sheffield, 1971-73; associate director, Stratford Festival Stage, Ontario, from 1974. Recipient: Diploma of Honour, Canadian Conference of Arts. Honorary Doctorates: Birmingham University, 1964; University of Waterloo, Ontario, 1977; University of Toronto, Ontario, 1988. Commander, Order of the British Empire, 1976; Honorary Fellow, Ontario College of Art, Toronto, 1979. Address: 17B St. Alban's Studios, St. Alban's Grove, London W8 5BT, England.

Works:

Stage productions include—*The Faithful*, Westminster Theatre, London, 1934; *Deuce of Jacks*, Abbey Theatre, Dublin, 1935; *The Golden Cuckoo*, Duchess Theatre, London, 1940; *Dr. Faustus*, Old Vic Company at Liverpool Playhouse, 1944; *John Gabriel Borkman*, Old Vic Company at Liverpool Playhouse, 1944; *The School for Scandal*, Old Vic Company at Liverpool Playhouse, 1945; *The Beaux Stratagem*, Old Vic Company at Theatre Royal, Bristol, 1945; *Twelfth Night*, Old Vic Company at Theatre Royal, Bristol, 1945; *Point Valaine*, Old Vic Company at Liverpool Playhouse, 1945; *Uncle Vanya*, Old Vic Company at the New Theatre, London, 1945; *The Critic*, Old Vic Company at the New Theatre, London,

1945; *Weep for the Cyclops*, Old Vic Company at Theatre Royal, Bristol, 1946; *Time of Your Life*, Lyric Theatre Hammersmith, London, 1946; *Cyrano de Bergerac*, Old Vic Company at the New Theatre, London, 1946; *Bless the Bride*, Adelphi Theatre, London, 1947; *Peter Grimes*, Royal Opera House/Covent Garden, London, 1947; *The Beggar's Opera*, English Opera Group, Aldeburgh, 1948; *Lady Rohesia*, Sadler's Wells Opera, London, 1948; *The Cherry Orchard*, Old Vic Company at the New Theatre, London, 1948; *Henry VIII*, Shakespeare Memorial Theatre, Stratford upon Avon, 1949; *Don Giovanni*, Sadler's Wells Opera, London, 1949; *A Month in the Country*, Old Vic Company at the New Theatre, London, 1949; *Treasure Hunt*, Apollo Theatre, London, 1949; *Captain Carvallo*, St. James's Theatre, London, 1950; *The Holly and the Ivy*, Duchess Theatre, London, 1950; *Home at Seven*, Wyndham's Theatre, London, 1950; *Romersholm*, Winter Garden Theatre, London, 1950; *Richard II*, Shakespeare Memorial Theatre, Stratford upon Avon, 1950; *The Passing Day*, Lyric Theatre Hammersmith, London, 1951; *A Midsummer Night's Dream*, Old Vic Theatre, London, 1951; *Henry IV*, parts 1 and 2, Shakespeare Memorial Theatre, Stratford upon Avon, 1951; *Henry V*, Shakespeare Memorial Theatre, Stratford upon Avon, 1951; *Othello*, Shakespeare Memorial Theatre, Stratford upon Avon, 1952; *Timon of Athens*, Old Vic Theatre, London, 1952; *The Deep Blue Sea*, Globe Theatre, London, 1952; *Julius Caesar*, Old Vic Theatre, London, 1953; *Henry VIII*, Old Vic Theatre, London, 1953; *The Matchmaker*, Theatre Royal, London, 1954; *Oedipus Rex*, Shakespeare Festival Stage, Stratford, Ontario, 1954; *A Life in the Sun*, Assembly Hall, Edinburgh, 1955; *The Cherry Orchard*, Piccolo Teatro, Milan, 1955; *Measure for Measure*, Shakespeare Memorial Theatre, Stratford upon Avon, 1956; *The Two Gentlemen of Verona*, Old Vic Theatre, London, 1957; *Much Ado About Nothing*, Shakespeare Memorial Theatre, Stratford upon Avon, 1958; *The Merchant of Venice*, Habimah Theatre, Tel Aviv, 1958; *Biederman and the Fire-raisers*, Habimah Theatre, Tel Aviv, 1958; *All's Well That Ends Well*, Shakespeare Memorial Theatre, Stratford upon Avon, 1959; *The Wrong Side of the Park*, Cambridge Theatre, London, 1960; *Ondine*, Royal Shakespeare Company at the Aldwych Theatre, London, 1961; *Coriolanus*, Shakespeare Festival Stage, Stratford, Ontario, 1961; *The Alchemist*, Old Vic Theatre, London, 1962; *Hamlet*, Tyrone Guthrie Theatre, Minneapolis, 1963; *The Miser*, Tyrone Guthrie Theatre, Minneapolis, 1963; *The Three Sisters*, Tyrone Guthrie Theatre, Minneapolis, 1963; *Saint Joan*, Tyrone Guthrie Theatre, Minneapolis, 1964; *Volpone*, Tyrone Guthrie Theatre, Minneapolis, 1964; *The Way of the World*, Tyrone Guthrie Theatre, Minneapolis, 1965; *The Cherry Orchard*, Tyrone Guthrie Theatre, Minneapolis, 1965; *As You Like It*, Tyrone Guthrie Theatre, Minneapolis, 1966; *Skin of Our Teeth*, Tyrone Guthrie Theatre, Minneapolis, 1966; *The House of Atreus*, Tyrone Guthrie Theatre, Minneapolis, 1967; *Peter Grimes*, Metropolitan Opera, New York, 1967; *Volpone*, National Theatre Company at the Old Vic, 1968; *Uncle Vanya*, Tyrone Guthrie Theatre, Minneapolis, 1969; *Cymbeline*, Shakespeare Festival Stage, Stratford, Ontario, 1970; *The Barber of Seville*, Brighton Festival, Sussex, 1971; *The Government Inspector*, Tyrone Guthrie Theatre, Minneapolis, 1973; *The Misanthrope*, National Theatre Company at the Old Vic, 1973; *The Imaginary Invalid*, Shakespeare Festival Stage, Stratford, Ontario, 1974; *Phaedra Britannica*, National Theatre Company at the Old Vic, 1975; *The Voyage of Edgar Allan Poe*, Minne-

sota Opera Company, Minneapolis, 1976; *Rigoletto*, Metropolitan Opera, New York, 1977; *All's Well That Ends Well*, Shakespeare Festival Stage, Stratford, Ontario, 1977; *The Double Dealer*, National Theatre, London, 1978; *Red Roses for Me*, Abbey Theatre, Dublin, 1980; *La Traviata*, Metropolitan Opera, New York, 1981; *The Clandestine Marriage*, Compass Theatre Company at Albery Theatre, London, 1984 (and tour); *The Government Inspector*, Festival Theatre, Stratford, Ontario, 1985.

Publications:

On MOISEIWITSCH: books—*Showcase* by Roy Newquist, New York 1966; *The Biographical Encyclopaedia and Who's Who of the American Theatre*, edited by Walter Rigdon, New York 1966; *Stage Design Throughout the World 1970-1975* by René Hainaux and Nicole Leclercq, Brussels and London 1976; *British Theatre Design*, edited by John Goodwin, London 1989.

Moiseiwitsch began her career at the Abbey Theatre in Dublin on a stage that demanded that less be more. She thus developed a sense of design in which—once she and the director had decided on the visual metaphor of the production—she was able to sweep away the rich, multiple effects often intended by other designers in favor of a bold and very clear visual picture in both sets and costumes. Never allowing these supports for a play to interfere with or obscure the playing of the production, she learned to paint her visual effects with a large brush so that a larger-than-life world was created, and when she was able to design her own theatre stage in consultation with Tyrone Guthrie, she created a bold thrust stage on which her costumes could be sculpted by light coming from widely divergent angles. If one were to think of a single phrase to describe her sense of the actor moving against a setting, it would be moving "sculpture in space." All Moiseiwitsch's settings are designed to create a spatial world for the actor, and all of her costumes are sculptures of fabric, trim, and color; they boldly present both the character of the actor and the world that he inhabits.

Because of the publicity given to *Oedipus Rex* and *The House of Atreus*, she also came to be known for the brilliance of her Greek masks, heightened and subtly exaggerated to give exactly the right expression that she and Guthrie had decided upon for the production. At the present time, when a certain almost Victorian heavy-handedness and complexity in costume design has begun to be popular, it is instructive to look back at the best of Moiseiwitsch's work and see the basic simplicity and focus of her esthetic, even when she was designing rich, larger-than-life productions. She is a theatrical designer who has always worked for the essence of the play rather than surface display.

—Douglas A. Russell

MOLLINO, Carlo.

Italian architect, photographer, interior, exhibition and industrial designer. Born in Turin, 6 May 1905. Studied architecture at the University of Turin, 1927-31: Dip. Arch. 1931. Architectural designer, working with his engineer father Enrico Mollino, Turin, 1928-31; freelance architect from 1931, exhibition and furniture designer from 1935, and car and aeronautical designer, from 1954. Professor, Accademia di San Lucca, Turin, and Politecnico of Turin. **Exhibitions:** *Carlo Mollino: Aeronautica e Architettura,* and the Venice Biennale, 1978; *Architettura 28-78: Carlo Mollino,* Palazzo delle Stelline, Milan, 1979; *Omaggio a Mollino: Dal Design all'Habitat,* Fiera del Levante, Bari, 1982; *Carlo Mollino: Premier Designer des Années '50,* Galerie Denis Bosselet, Paris, 1984; *From Mackintosh to Mollino,* Barry Friedman Gallery, New York, 1985; *Caro Mollino: Architettura, Mobili e Ambientazioni,* Spazio Trau, Turin, 1985; *Carlo Mollino: Cronaca,* Fulvio Ferrari Gallery, Turin, 1985; *Carlo Mollino: Primo Designer,* Southern California Institute of Architecture, Vico Morcote, Switzerland, 1985; Centre de Creation Industrielle, Paris, 1989. *Died* (in Turin) *in 1973.*

Works:

Headquarters offices and interiors, for the Societa Ippica Torinese, Turin, 1937.
Furniture, for Lisa and Gio Ponti, Milan, 1940.
L'Elettrica shop interiors, Turin, 1941.
Radiogram, for Deaglio, Turin, 1941.
Furniture, for the San Giuseppe College, Turin, 1941.
Trademark logo, for Varda leather goods, 1944.
Offices and interiors, for Apelli e Varesio, Turin, 1945.
Offices and interiors, for Einaudi publishing house, Turin, 1945.
Lamp with counterweight, for P. Foa, Turin, 1947.
Furniture, for La Vigna Gallery, Florence, 1948.
Furniture, for the Underwood office, Turin, 1949.
Singer store interiors, Turin, 1950.
Offices and interiors, for the Lattes publishing house, Turin, 1951.
Exhibition stand at the Turin Motor Show, for AGIP-Supercortemaggiore, 1953.
Bar furnishings, for the Societa Lombardia Petroli, Turin, 1955.
Colour scheme of the De Havilland-Heron aircraft, 1956.
Cutlery range, for Reed and Barton, 1960.
Montanaro camera shop interiors, Turin, 1962.
Writing desk, pendulum clock and table sculpture, for Ada Minola, Turin, 1966.
Furnishings and interiors, for the Teatro Regio, Turin, 1970.

Publications:

By MOLLINO: books—*Completa y Veridica Historia de Picasso y el Cubismo,* Turin 1945; *Il Messaggio della Camera Oscura,* Turin 1945; *Architettura, Arte e Tecnica,* with F. Valdacchino, Turin 1947; *Il Linguaggio dell'Architettura: Il Volto della Citta,* Turin 1949; *Introduzione al Discesismo,* Rome 1951; *Istruzione ad Uso dei Candidati ed Asporanti alla Qualifica di Maestro Scelto,* with G. Segni, Milan 1953.

On MOLLINO: books—*Ritratti Ambientati di Carlo Mollino* by E. Scopinich, Milan, 1945; *Italy at Work: Her Renaissance in Design Today,* exhibition catalogue by Meyric Rogers, Rome 1950; *Furniture for Modern Interiors* by Mario Dal Fabro, New York 1954; *World Furniture,* edited by Helena Hayward, London 1965, 1981; *Carlo Mollino: Architecture as Autobiography* by G. Brino, Milan 1979, London 1987; *A Century of Chair Design,* edited by

Frank Russell, London 1980; *Carlo Mollino: Premier Designer, Dernier Artisan des Années '50* by G. Brino, Turin and Paris 1984; *Mid-Century: Furniture of the 1950s* by Cara Greenberg, London 1984; *Carlo Mollino: Cronaca* by F. Ferrari, Turin 1985; *Polaroid Carlo Mollino* by G. Arpino and D. Palazzoli, Turin 1986; *Italian Design: 1870 to the Present* by Penny Sparke, London and New York 1988; *Italian Modern: A Design Heritage* by Giovanni Albera and Nicolas Monti, New York 1989; *L'Etrange Univers de l'Architecte Carlo Mollino,* Paris 1989.

MONGUZZI, Bruno.

Swiss graphic and exhibition designer. Born in Mendrisio, Ticino, 21 August 1941. Studied at the Ecole des Arts Décoratifs, Geneva, St. Martin's School of Art, London, and the London College of Printing, 1956-61: Prix Cailler and Swiss Federal Diploma, 1960. Married Anna Boggeri in 1969; children: Nicolas and Elisa. Graphic designer, in the Studio Boggeri, Milan, 1961-63; freelance designer, working in Milan and London, 1963-65; designer, at Gagnon and Valkus studio, in New York and Montreal, 1965-67; freelance designer, in Milan, from 1968: has collaborated on exhibition design with Roberto Sambonet and Giancarlo Ortelli, in Milan, from 1972. Lecturer in typographic design and gestalt psychology, at the Cini Foundation, Venice, 1963-65; professor of typographic design and the psychology of perception, at the School of Applied arts, Lugano, from 1971; IBM Fellow, Aspen Design Conference, Colorado, 1981; visiting professor, Cooper Union, New York, 1982, 1987. **Exhibitions:** Museo de Arte, Sao Paulo, 1974; Artek Gallery, Helsinki, 1976; *Della Pazzia,* Galleria d'Arte, Milan, 1977; Casa del Mantegna, Mantua, 1978; Palazzo Bagatti Valsecchi, Milan, 1980; *Lo Studio Boggeri 1933-81,* at the Milan Triennale, 1981; *Il Progetto Grafico,* Milan, 1981; New York Public Library, Pound Ridge, 1982; *L'Italie d'Aujourd'hui,* Nice, 1985; *Bio 11,* Liubliana, 1986; *L'Image de la Lettre,* Centre Georges Pompidou, Paris, 1987; Art Directors Club, New York, 1987, 1989; XIII Brno Graphics Biennale, 1988. **Collections:** Centre Georges Pompidou, Paris; Stedelijk Museum, Amsterdam; Museum of Modern Art, New York. Recipient: Bodoni Prize, 1971. Member, Alliance Graphique Internationale, Paris, 1979. Address: 6866 Meride, Switzerland.

Works:

Processo per il Museo exhibition design, for the Accademia di Brera, Milan, 1976.
Della Pazzia portfolio of drawings, for the Galleria d'Arte, Milan, 1977.
Lo Studio Boggeri 1933-1981 exhibition catalogue design, for the Milan Triennale, 1981.
Signage, for the new Museo Cantonale d'Arte, Lugano, 1987.
Il Ticino e i suoi Fotografi exhibition poster, for the Museo Cantonale d'Arte, Lugano, and the Kunsthaus, Zürich, 1987.
Oskar Schlemmer/Igor Strawinsky: Les Noces exhibition poster, for the Museo Cantonale d'Arte, Lugano, 1988.
Flavio Paolucci/Alberto Flammer exhibition design, poster and catalogues, for the Museo Cantonale d'Arte, Lugano, 1988.

Photographie aus der Sowjetunion poster, for the Kunsthaus, Zürich, 1989.

Publications:

By MONGUZZI: books—*Note per una Tipografia Informativa,* Venice 1964; *Lo Studio Boggeri 1933-1981,* Milan 1981; *Piet Zwart: The Typographical Work 1923-1933,* Milan 1983.

On MONGUZZI: books—*Due Dimensioni,* Milan 1964; *Who's Who in Graphic Art,* edited by Walter Amstutz, Dubendorf 1982; *Top Graphic Design* by F. H. K. Henrion, Zurich 1983; *12 Grafici dell'AGI,* edited by the Alliance Graphique Internationale, Milan 1984; *Posters by Member of the Alliance Graphique Internationale,* edited by Rudolph deHarak, New York 1986; *Alle Radici della Comunicazione Visiva Italiana* by Heinz Waibl, Como 1988; *Basic Typography: Design with Letters* by Rudi Ruegg, Zurich 1989.

Perfection was not enough. What was to me the end was to him the beginning. And I would walk back to the desk to look for the right mistake. One day he had explained to me the spider's web theory. Most Swiss design was only perfect, like the spider's web. And useless. The web became useful only when injured by the entangled fly. It is there, with Antonio Boggeri, that the hunt began.

—Bruno Monguzzi

That appropriate visual forms can arise only in response to careful analysis of a problem is not an obscure idea in the late twentieth century; however, many lesser designers who purport to practice this concept in actuality bow to the dictates of fashion and produce little more than stylistic affectation—rarely the answer to a client's needs. Bruno Monguzzi, however, conscientiously and successfully tailors solution to problem. He is as at home with three-dimensional design for exhibitions as he is with two-dimensional catalogues, posters, and printed ephemera, and the entire scope of his work, though broad, reflects his careful consideration of each detail in relation to the desired communication. For example, in his poster "Di mano in mano, da uomo a uomo," the purpose of which was to request volunteers to aid the victims of the 1980 Irpinia earthquake, Monguzzi used a subtle gray rectangle surprinted over the main image to act as a soft veil, building a psychological distance between the viewer and the powerful, black image of the mourners. Such emotive power he achieved amid typographic elements interacting structurally with two squares and a rectangle which in turn overlap on a golden-section grid!

A rationalist by character, his Swiss training in the late 1950s introduced him to the typography of El Lissitzky and Piet Zwart, as well as the pioneers of the Swiss school. Later, his visual vocabulary was enriched, and the rigidity of Swiss formalism, softened as a result of his associations with Italian design, most notably with Studio Boggeri, and with the early 1960s New York school of Herb Lubalin, Gene Federico, and Louis Dorfsman. These influences yielded a hybrid which is as logical in approach as the Swiss but at the same time humanist.

By his own admission, Monguzzi is an outsider among his peers in the design field. He welcomes the role of intermediary in the process of public communication. In exercising this role, he insists on selecting appropriate tools to fulfill the criteria of a problem and generally operates intentionally outside the stifling

Bruno Monguzzi: Poster for Arte Grafiche Nidasio printing firm, Milan, 1982

confines of current trends. He gets right to the point—succinct communication. As Monguzzi himself says, "I find our society a bit noisy. I just would like to contribute a little silence."

—Ken Carls

MONO, Rune (Gotthard).
Swedish industrial, graphic and interior designer. Born in Helsingborg, 4 June 1920. Educated at Karolinska Läroverket, Örebro, until 1937; Tekniska Gymnasiet, Örebro, 1938–41; mainly self-taught in industrial design, from 1941. Married Irene Mary Gustavsson in 1943; children: Ralph and Elisabeth. Worked as an engineering planner and draughtsman, SAAB Aeroplanaktiebolaget, Linköping, 1941–43; head of interior and graphic draughting studio, ABA/SAS Aktiebolaget Aerotransport/Scandinavian Airlines System, Stockholm, 1943–49; freelance draughtsman and product designer, Täby, 1949–57; industrial design consultant, establishing firm AB Industridesign, Stockholm, 1957–64, and AB Rune Mono Industridesign (now AB Rune Mono Design), Täby, from

1964: designed for LKB-Produkter, 1952–88, Alweg monorail company, 1954–57, Skagersviks Industrier, 1960–69, ICA-Forbundet, 1962–72, BT Bygg och Transportekonomi, 1965–73, Draco, 1972–79, Dynapac, 1973–80, Arcu Armaturindustri, 1978–86, Stiga, 1979–85, etc. Guest instructor, at the Konstfackskolan, Stockholm, the Högskolan for Design och Konsthantverk, Göteborg, and other schools in Sweden and Norway, since 1970. Co-founder, 1957, and President, 1957–61, SID Society of Swedish Industrial Designers; Copyright Panel Member, 1976, and Board Member, 1979–85, Svensk Form Society of Crafts and Design, Stockholm. **Exhibitions:** *Hemmets redskap,* Östermans, Stockholm, 1958; *Svenska Industridesigner,* Nordiska Kompaniet, Stockholm, 1959; *Unga Nordiska Formgivare,* Röhsska Konstslöjdmuseet, Göteborg, 1962; *Swedish Industrial Design,* Design Centre, London, 1966; *Schwedische Form,* Design Center, Stuttgart, 1969; *Industridesign i Norden,* Kunstindustri Museet, Oslo, 1976; *Fran Revolution till nya uttryck,* Nationalmuseum, Stockholm, 1988. **Collection:** Nationalmuseum, Stockholm. Recipient: First Prize, SAS Aircraft Emblem Competition, 1947; Svensk Form-God Form Award, Stockholm, 1961; Prize of Honour, Svensk Form, Stockholm, 1964; Gute Industrieform Award, West Germany, 1964; Best International Product Award, Toronto, 1984; Utmärkt Svensk Form Award, Stockholm, 1985. Address: AB Rune Mono Design, Box 2023, 183 02 Täby, Sweden.

Works:

Aircraft logotypes, interior and exterior designs, for SAS, 1945–64.

Logotypes and electronic medical instruments, for LKB-Produkter, 1952–88.

Monorail train and railway installation designs, for Alweg, 1954–57.

Grinding machine, for Ulvsunda Verkstader, 1958.

Petrol gauge, for Ljungmans Verkstader, 1959.

Intercommunications system, for Centrum Radio, Stockholm, 1960.

Stainless steel dishes, for Olofström, 1960–61.

Kitchen designs, for Skagersviks Industrier, 1960–69.

Kalmar lightweight car, for Swedish Post Office Administration, produced by Kalmar Verkstader, 1961.

Logotypes and corporate design programme, for ICA-Forbundet, 1962–72.

Television apparatus, for ITT Stockholm, 1963–65.

Printing machine, for Grafiska Maskinaktiebolaget, 1964–67.

Elevating pallet trucks, for BT Bygg- och Transportekonomi, 1965–73.

Asthma inhalers, for Draco, 1972–79.

Trucks and roadwork machinery, for Dynapac, 1973–80.

Design function analysis system, for Sveriges Mekanförbund, 1974.

Clinical chemistry multi-purpose analysers, for Clinicon, 1978–79.

Colorado bathroom and kitchen sink mixers, for Arcu Armaturindustri, 1978–86.
Lawnmowers, for Stiga, 1979–85.
Packaging machines, for Norden Packaging Machinery, 1985–86.

Publications:

By MONO: books—*Mekanresultat 65024: Designarbete*, with others, Stockholm 1965; *Mekanresultat 71018: Modeller och modellarbete*, with others, Stockholm 1971; *Mekanresultat 74203: Analys och vardering av designfunktioner*, Stockholm 1974; *Produktdesign*, Lund 1975; *Mekanresultat 76006: Maskiners anpassning till människan*, with others, Stockholm 1976; *Mekanresultat 76205: Maskiners form och gestalt*, Stockholm 1976; *Närmare*, Stockholm 1981; *Designutredning*, report, Stockholm 1982; *Ting till synes*, with others, Stockholm 1985; *Njutningen av att akta tag*, Stockholm 1988.

On MONO: books—*Forma Sueca* by Åke Stavenow and Åke H. Huldt, Göteborg 1961; *Konsthantverk, Konstindustri, Design 1875–1975* by Dag Widman, Stockholm 1975; *Den Svenska Formen* by Monica Boman and others, Stockholm 1985; articles—"Firma for form" in *Industria* (Stockholm), no. 5, 1958; "Firma for produktveckling" in *Form* (Stockholm), no. 8, 1963; "God design och formgivning" in *Jern og Industrien* (Copenhagen), no. 7, 1972; "Designern far koll pa tyckandet" in *Industria* (Stockholm), June 1972; "Från patent till produkt" in *Form* (Stockholm), no. 8, 1983.

Knowledge, imagination and skill are essential to the industrial designer. The way he uses them differs according to who he is, the object concerned, the situation as well as current trends and ideas in society.

To me, professional rules and philosophies can be summed up in one particular concept. Having started my design career at a time when to fight against superficial 'styling' seemed necessary, and later trying to establish the profession in industry without locking it into doctrinaire functionalism, I see the word "honesty" as a guideline towards technique without dogmatism, an attractiveness without formalism.

It should be self-evident (but to some people it is not) that the purpose of industrial design lies outside the designer. It is hidden in the needs of human beings he will never know personally. He has to fulfil that purpose, making his way through a jungle of industrial technologies and economic conditions. He will succeed if he looks upon them as challenges rather than limitations. He has to leave prestige and the free artist's ideas of self expression behind, and be very clear about the specific role of his own profession.

The education of future industrial designers—trying to give them knowledge, imagination and skill—is still, in 1989, in its childhood, but is developing and growing. Their need for a comprehensive capacity is continuously increasing. Industrial design, however, can never be fully established as an integral part of product development until information about design practice and teaching in design management are incorporated into the education of future leaders in industry and commercial society. Industrial design has to be regarded as just as important as technology and marketing.

—Rune Mono

When a special edition of a leading industrial journal was published in the autumn of 1988 with the title "Survival through Design", it went without saying that Rune Monö's name would be among the collaborators. Almost as obvious was the title of his article: "A little catechism for collaboration in design". Mono is namely not only one of Sweden's leading industrial designers, but is also one of the profession's idealogists. As an idealogist he is above all a champion of good work ethics.

Rune Monö's ideology is anchored in the idealistic post-war period, when a new and better world for all was to be built, and where an industrial designer would have a key role. He was strongly influenced by objective philosophy that supported Scandinavian Design, which at this time was enjoying its greatest period. Mono wished to convey across its train of thought about the good life in a beautiful home to a more pronounced engineering design.

Today, during the less idealistic 1980's, Rune Monö adheres even closer to his original attitude that good design can only develop from a basis of good morale. As a veteran within the profession, he is assuredly concious that successful activity demands great adaptiveness and willingness to compromise, but at the same time he rigorously maintains that there are prin-

Rune Mono: Ultramicrotome equipment, for LKB-Produkter, 1983

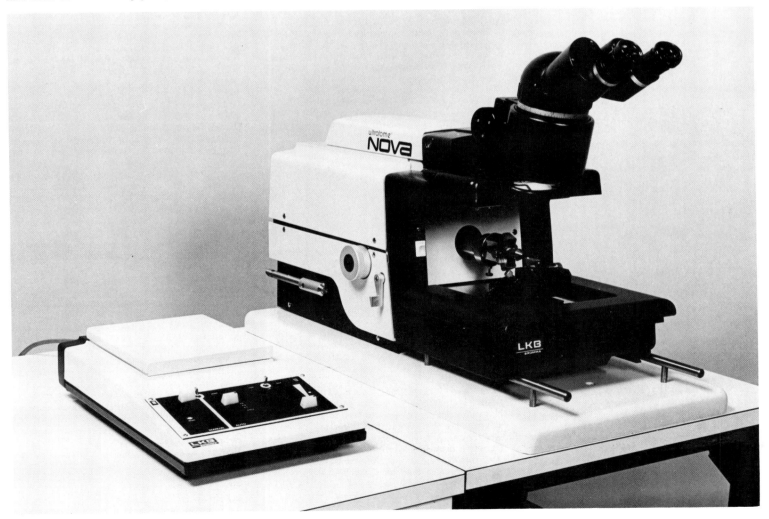

ciples that the good designer must never renounce. With this attitude Rune Monö has captured an undisputed position as one of the most honest of design's representatives, not only form the viewpoint of the patron, but also that of the customer's.

This is not the place to give a detailed account of Rune Monö's design catechism. But its significance is: absolute honour. For instance, you must never work with competing products. You should have a clear purpose and always work with clearly defined goals. In all areas you should give decipherable instructions and clear justifications. You should be prepared to collaborate with your patron during the entire length of the product's life. Regard others with appreciation and yourself with humour.

Rune Monö represents, both in theory and in practice, the classical attitude that aesthetics and ethics are inseparably bound with each other; that beauty and morals cannot be divided; that good industrial form is also honourable!

—Ulf Hård af Segerstad

MONTANA, Claude.

French fashion designer. Born in Paris in 1949. Began freelance design of fashion jewellery, in London 1971–72; fashion designer, for Mac-Douglas leathers, Complice menswear, Ferrer y Sentis knitwear, etc., in Paris, from 1975; founded Claude Montana fashion company, with shops on the rue de Grenelle, Paris, 1977: launched *Montana Pour Femme* fragrance, 1986. Address: 31 rue de Grenelle, 75001 Paris, France.

Publications:

On MONTANA: books—*Mode im 20. Jahrhundert* by Ingrid Loschek, Munich 1978; *Fairchild's Who's Who in Fashion*, edited by Ann Stegemeyer, New York 1980; *The Collector's Book of Twentieth Century Fashion* by Frances Kennett, London and New York 1983; *McDowell's Directory of Twentieth Century Fashion* by Colin McDowell, London 1984; *Design Source Book* by Penny Sparke and others, London 1986; *The Encyclopaedia of Fashion from 1840 to the 1980s* by Georgina O'Hara, London 1986.

Claude Montana came to the field of fashion design rather offhandedly. In London and in need of money in 1971, he began making rhinestone-encrusted, papier-mâché jewelry which caught on, encouraging him to pursue his new-found direction. By 1974, Montana was freelancing, learning as he went along. The work he did for the French leather firm of Mc-Douglas was to form an important basis for his future, as Montana has continued to make wide use of leathers, especially a type called cuir de plongée, a spongy soft variety.

In 1977, Montana presented a leather line which included motorcycle hats and metal chains as well as honey-colored leather vests with long fringes. He was immediately accused of being "Nazi-like," a claim that was to wrap him in controversy and that unjustifiably ignored the dissimilarities of his creations to Nazi garb and also brushed aside his simultaneous showing of white cotton spencers with full trousers.

However, 1978 was another story. Montana's showing at Bergdorf Goodman was a smash success with its black, floor-length, leather dresses, sequined jeans, and concentration on the wide-shouldered look. His fall presentation included Montana's signature broad-shouldered jacket and narrow skirt, sailor costumes of white and navy linen with metallic tassels and middy collars, and characteristic jumpsuits which had big, big shoulders and puffed sleeves and which narrowed from the tight belt down. This time the press called Montana "strong, gutsy, refined, for women with an eye for quality."

The following year brought equally strong items and equally strong success. Among the most outstanding numbers were Montana's pantsuit of taupe herringbone linen with extended shoulders, worn with matching taffeta peplum blouse, and a group of futuristic sharp-shouldered jumpsuits, ultra-slick and svelte, worn with longish jackets with wing collars, high-heeled pumps, and wonderful, flat-brimmed hats, which had quarter-moons jutting out from one side and were intended to be worn at a jaunty angle. Montana favored this style of hat and showed a wider-brimmed version with another 1979 outfit, a black and white, geometric faille jacket accompanied by silk brushstroke crepe de chine blouse, peplum, and silk skirt.

In the fall of 1980, Montana featured terry cloth in offerings such as a large bathrobe coat, worn with linen pants. Montana's silhouette at this time seemed to be softening, with shoulders not so pronounced. His pantsuits of spring 1981 featured pleated trousers with slim, double-breasted jackets. In a marvelously fitted suit of 1982, Montana found a happy medium, maintaining the broad look softly fluid to the waist and moving down into a closely-fitted skirt. This black cotton outfit outlined in white also exemplified Montana's continual preference for this sharply contrasting color combination and, it should be added, pointed up his resemblance to the young Milanese designers who came to fame during the mid-1970s.

Montana's individualistic touch, however, continued to shine through in fall 1983 designs such as his flowing tunics, deeply draped across the chest and long, worn with white linen cropped pants, and his sensuous combination of big, loose, ribbed sweater with matching ribbed skirt sporting a slit to the top of the thigh.

—Barbara Cavaliere

MOORE, (Charles) Gene.

American photographer, display, exhibition and stage designer. Born in Birmingham, Alabama, 10 June 1910. Studied painting under Louise Cone, Birmingham, Alabama, (1930–33?); Academy of Fine Arts, Chicago, 1934–35; mainly self-taught in design, from 1936. Worked in New York as delivery man, cafeteria bus boy, and as a waiter on a cruise ship to South America, 1935–36; display assistant, at I. Miller, 1936–38, and at Bergdorf Goodman store, New York, 1938–45; display manager, Bonwit Teller store, New York, 1945–55; display manager and divisional vice-president, of Tiffany and Company, New York, from 1955; also freelance designer from 1955, working for Clarence House, Seagram Building, Delmar Shoe Salon, Madison Avenue Bookstore, Bonwit Teller, American Museum of Natural History, Museum of Modern Art, Castelli Gallery, London Old Vic Theatre Company, Paul Taylor Dance Company, etc. Recipient: Lumen Award, Illuminating Engineering Society, New York, 1976; American Society of Interior Designers Award, 1988; New York Municipal Arts Society Award, 1989. Address: c/o Tiffany and Company, 727 Fifth Avenue, New York, New York 10022, U.S.A.

Publications:

By MOORE: book—*My Time at Tiffany's*, with Jay Hyams, New York 1990.

On MOORE: books—*Window Display 2*, edited by Walter Herdeg, Zurich 1961; *Windows* by Michael Emory, Chicago 1977; *The American Store Window* by Leonard Marcus, New York 1978; *Windows at Tiffany's: The Art of Gene Moore* by Judith Goldman, New York 1980; *Show Windows* by Barry James Wood, New York 1982.

About twenty-five years ago, I happened to see the windows at Tiffany and Company for the first time. They were a revelation to someone who had grown up in Buffalo and was used to seeing jewelry displayed on velvet-covered props with artificial flowers lurking in the background. Years later, I was informed that the magician behind the windows at Tiffany's is Gene Moore. He's been a hero of mine ever since.

Display, recently given the more important-sounding name of "visual merchandising," is one of those fields in which the output is short-lived and the designers, mainly anonymous. Nevertheless, among these previously most underpaid and underappreciated people in retailing, the talented ones are some of the most inventive, insightful, and unorthodox designers ever known. In this group, Moore is at the top. His work makes us think.

While Moore's work at Bonwit's and other New York stores was exceptionally fine, he is more clearly identified with Tiffany's, where he has generated ingenious displays in a series of windows so cramped that they would try any designer's patience. Tiffany's and Moore were made for each other. There is less snobbishness than one would expect from the best-known jewelry store in the world, and an unusually sensitive management allows Moore to concentrate freely on producing beautiful windows to express the store's personality, rather than solely to sell merchandise.

Because of its scale, jewelry is one of the most difficult items to display. Moore understands this in a way that few people do, partly because he scrupulously avoids the phony and the pretentious. He never talks down to us. Seeing beauty in both the common and the rare, he is as intrigued by a paper bag, a ball of twine, a mound of sand as by a ruby bracelet or gold watch. In his juxtaposition of the ordinary and the rare, each element in his display ornaments the other. Moore's connection with the human is something that moves behind the surface of his other displays and activates whatever memories, understanding, or humor may exist within the viewer. You don't just pass his works by. You stop, look, and think. His use of deliberate mistakes, his wit, and his lightheartedness reveal his world. Aware of music, dance, literature, science, and nature, he offers more than meets the eye. He can make a cultural or social comment through his displays without resorting to shock. He makes us smile, he makes us learn, he helps us to make peace with the world.

Moore's connection with the human also allows him to animate the inanimate. He has a strong feeling for spatial and scale considerations, and his sensitive use of lighting integrates spaces, objects, and emotions. Over the years, his work has become more spare, yet not

Gene Moore: Jewellery display with butterflies, eggs and grass, for Tiffany's, New York

arid, and he constantly returns to nature for inspiration, reminding us that the natural object must be considered as crucial and beautiful as the man-made artifact. To date, his skill and brilliance in visual merchandising have not been surpassed.

—Grant Greapentrog

MORI, Hanae.

Japanese textile, costume and fashion designer. Born in Tokyo, 8 January 1926. Studied literature, at Tokyo Christian Women's College, 1945–48. Married to Ken Mori; 2 children. Freelance fashion and film costume designer, designing for over 1,000 films, Tokyo, from 1951: established Hanae Mori fashion shop, in Shinjuku, Tokyo, 1955, and Hanae Mori International headquarters office and boutiques building, in Omote-sando, Tokyo, 1978; also established offices in Paris and New York. Recipient: Neiman-Marcus Award, 1973. Member, la Chambre Syndicale de la Couture Parisienne, Paris, 1978. Addresses: 6-1, 3 Chome, Kita-Aoyama, Minato-ku, Tokyo, Japan; 17–19 Avenue Montaigne, 75008 Paris, France; 27 East 79th Street, New York, New York 10021, U.S.A.

Publications:

On MORI: books—*The World of Fashion: People, Places, Resources* by Eleanor Lambert, New York and London 1976; *Quest for the Best* by Stanley Marcus, New York 1979; *Fairchild's Who's Who in Fashion,* edited by Ann Stegemeyer, New York 1980; *McDowell's Directory of Twentieth Century Fashion* by Colin McDowell, London 1984; *The Conran Directory of Design,* edited by Stephen Bayley, London 1985; *The Encyclopaedia of Fashion from 1840 to the 1980s* by Georgina O'Hara, London 1986; *Jap-*

Hanae Mori: Chiffon dress with pleated top and printed skirt, 1989

anese Design by Penny Sparke, London 1987.

Long before her work was known in the West, Hanae Mori had designed costumes for more than 1,000 Japanese movies. In order to satisfy the Japanese cultural traditions of dress, she solved the problem of creating appropriate costumes by using unusual colours to satisfy dramatic requirements. This work provided her with an introduction to the Japanese people and to the world of fashion. Since then, she has built up an international enterprise in partnership with her son and husband, a textile manufacturer who provided her with the initial impetus to design fabric.

While Mori produces Western styles, her textiles, which are woven, dyed, and printed specially, reveal her heritage. Her vivid colours and linear patterns are reminiscent of the work of Japan's Edo period. Recognising that everyone needs colour in their lives, she keeps her boldest and brightest tones for her evening wear. Stunning combinations, as seen in the violet, blue, green, yellow, and black striped creation from her 1979 Paris collection, bring to mind her earlier work for films. Her work reveals the excitement which colour and pattern bring to garment design. Floral and butterfly motifs—the Japanese symbols of femininity—occur frequently in her prints, and on occasion, she returns to adaptations of the traditional kimono shapes for the simple lines which best display her lively prints.

By successfully combining the influences of East and West, she proved herself worthy to show with the top Parisian couturiers. In the late 1970s, an evening outfit comprising a quilted satin jacket over a long, bias-cut dress with a halter neck in the same fabric evidenced both cultures. Likewise, in spring 1979, she showed asymmetrical hemlines and kimono jackets in the same collection as padded shoulders, bare shoulders, ruffles, and taffeta dresses. Mori has skilfully taken ideas from the East and the West in order to create classically elegant garments which have a wide appeal. In her ready-to-wear she has proved herself very aware of the practical needs of contemporary women. While her shapes are easy to wear, they are also elegant and feminine, and her fabrics provide an excitement that sets her garments apart.

—Hazel Clark

MOULTON, Alex(ander Eric).
British vehicle engineer and designer. Born in Stratford-upon-Avon, Warwickshire, 9 April 1920. Studied at Marlborough College, Wiltshire, 1933–37; King's College, Cambridge, 1938–39, 1947–49: MA 1949. Worked in the engine research department, 1939–44, and as assistant to Sir Roy Fedden, 1940–42, at Bristol Aeroplane Company, Bristol, Gloucestershire; works manager and technical research director, at George Spencer Moulton and Company family firm, Bradford-on-Avon, Wiltshire, 1945–56; founder chairman, 1956–67, and managing director from 1967, Moulton Developments Limited design development engineers, Bradford-on-Avon; chairman and managing director, 1962–67, and director from 1967, of Moulton Bicycles, Nottingham; director of Alex Moulton Limited, Bradford-on-Avon, and of Bicycle Consultants Limited, Nottingham, from 1967. Chairman of

Alex Moulton: *AM2/Alex Moulton* bicycle, 1983

the Committee on Engineering Design Education, Design Council, London, 1975–76; Master of the Faculty of Royal Designers for Industry, Royal Society of Arts, London, 1982–83. **Exhibition:** *Eye for Industry,* Victoria and Albert Museum, London, 1986. **Collection:** National Motor Museum, Beaulieu, Hampshire. Recipient: Design Centre Award, London, 1964; Bidlake Memorial Cycling Award, London, 1964; Queen's Award to Industry, London, 1967; Society of Industrial Artists and Designers Medal, London, 1976; Clayton Prize, Crompton-Lanchester Medal, and Hawksley Medal, Institute of Mechanical Engineers, London, 1979. Honorary doctorates: Royal College of Art, London, 1967; University of Bath, 1971. Royal Designer for Industry, Royal Society of Arts, London, 1968; Commander, Order of the British Empire, 1976; Fellow, Institute of Mechanical Engineers, 1980. Address: The Hall, Bradford-on-Avon, Wiltshire BA15 1AJ, England.

Works:

Flexitor vehicle suspension, 1957.
Hydrolastic vehicle suspension, 1962.
Moulton compact pedal bicycle, 1962.
Moulton motor coach, 1968–70.
Hydragas vehicle suspension, 1973.
Alex Moulton pedal bicycle, 1983.

Publications:

On MOULTON: books—*Automobile Design:*

The Great Designers and Their Work, edited by Ronald Barker and Anthony Harding, Newton Abbot 1970; *The Moulton Bicycle* by Tony Hadland, Reading 1980; *Design By Choice* by Reyner Banham, London 1981; *British Design Since 1880: A Visual History* by Fiona MacCarthy, London 1982; *Eye for Industry: Royal Designers for Industry 1936–1986,* exhibition catalogue by Fiona MacCarthy and Patrick Nuttgens, London 1986.

MOURGUE, Olivier.

French industrial designer. Born in Paris, 15 April 1939. Educated at the Lycée Pasteur, Paris, 1946–54; studied interior design, at the Ecole Boulle, Paris, 1954–58: Dip.Arch.Int. 1958; Ecole Nationale Supérieure des Arts Décoratifs, Paris, 1958–60: Dip. 1960. Served in the French Army, 1960–62. Married Christina Sanders in 1967 (divorced, 1980); sons: Thomas and Mikael; married Anne Turlan in 1981; sons: Armel and Gaetan. Freelance designer from 1959, establishing studio in the rue Campagne-Première, Paris, 1966–76, and in Keralio, Brittany, from 1976: worked with architectural designer Maurice Holland, at Nordiska Kompaniet, Stockholm, 1960; interior designer, for Agence d'Architecture Intérieure Gautier-Delaye, Paris, 1963; also designed for Airborne, 1964–66, Atelier de Création du Mobilier National from 1966, Societé Pierre

Charron, 1967, Societé Disderot, 1967, Bayer fabrics, 1971, Societé Clairitex, 1972. Professor, Institut de Geo-Architecture, Ecole des Beaux-Arts, Brest, from 1976. **Exhibitions:** *Expo 67,* Montreal, 1967; *Euro Design,* Nancy, 1969; *Eurodomus,* Milan, 1970, 1972; *Expo 70,* Osaka, 1970; *Design Francais,* Musee des Arts Decoratifs, Paris, 1971; *Portable World,* American Museum of Contemporary Crafts, New York, 1973; *S'Asseoir,* Musee de Peintures et de Sculptures, Grenoble, 1974; *Design en France,* Design Centre, Brussels, 1975; *Olivier Mourgue: Retrospective,* Musee des Arts Decoratis, Nantes, 1976; *Design Since 1945,* Philadelphia Museum of Art, 1983; *Design Francais 1960–1990,* Centre Georges Pompidou, Paris, 1988 (toured). **Collection:** Museum of Modern Art, New York. Recipient: International Design Award, New York, 1968; Eole 74 Prix d'Honneur, Paris, 1974. Address: Keralio par Plougiel 22220, France.

Works:

Joker low-back armchair in chrome steel with leather upholstery, for Airborne, 1959–63.
Djinn chaise longue in tubular steel with jersey upholstery, for Airborne, 1964–65.
Whist Dos à Dos chair with metal frame and leather seat, for Airborne, 1964–65.
Montreal shell-structure armchair in polyester with loose cushions, for Airborne, 1966.
Fleur lamp series in chromed metal and aluminium, for Editions Pierre Disderot, 1967.
Trestle table in lacquered wood, for Editions Charron, 1967.

Olivier Mourgue: *Le Cri des Oiseaux* beach lounger and windbreak, 1981

Cubic armchair with polyester shell and loose jersey cushions, for Airborne, 1968.

Bouloum chaise longue in polyester and jersey, for the French pavilion at *Expo 70,* Osaka, 1968–70.

Five-pillar bookcase in natural wood with lacquered metal fixings, for Prisunic, 1969.

Games and *Forest* ranges of textiles and carpets in synthetic fibres, for Bayer, 1972.

Hold-all storage systems (models A-D) in unbleached cotton, for Editions Clairitex, 1972.

Rosita Hernandez sofa in wood and fabric with mirrors and pompoms, for Editions Cedac-Minvielle. 1975–76.

Publications:

By MOURGUE: book—*Hexa For,* exhibition catalogue, Paris 1975.

On MOURGUE: books—*The Modern Chair: 1850 to Today* by Gilbert Frey, London and Neiderteufen 1970; *Portable World,* exhibition catalogue with texts by Paul J. Smith and Barbara Bullock, New York 1973; *S'Asseoir,* exhibition catalogue by Maurice Besset, Grenoble 1974; *Olivier Mourgue,* exhibition catalogue with text by P. R. Chaigneau, Nantes 1976; *Contemporary Furniture* by Klaus-Jurgen Sembach, Stuttgart and London 1982; *Designers' Workplaces* by Beverly Russell, New York 1983; *Les Annees 60* by Anne Bony, Paris 1983; *Mid-Century: Furniture of the 1950s* by Cara Greenberg, London 1984; *The Conran Directory of Design,* edited by Stephen Bayley, London 1985; *Modern Furniture Classics* by Miriam Stimpson, London 1987; *Design Francais 1960-1990: Trois Decennies,* exhibition catalogue by Margo Rouard and Francoise Jollant Kneebone, London 1990.

Like others on the Continent, but particularly like his compatriot Pierre Paulin, Olivier Mourgue manipulates the synthetic materials of the day to reawaken us to the sculptural and utilitarian possibilities of line. This is especially evident in the Djinn stool and chaise. Viewed from the side, as they are in advertisements, they appear first as line in space. Only later do we realize that these lines can also serve our needs for support and relaxation.

The Djinn chair, on the other hand, is always shown head on, so that we see it not only as a form but as a persona, a supposedly inanimate object with the jinni's ability to animate and deceive. These double meanings made it an appropriate choice to appear in *2001: A Space Odyssey.* Furthermore, we thought at the time that this was what the next century would be: clean, linear, artificially intelligent. (It is perhaps no coincidence that at the time Mourgue was designing his furniture for the future, another French designer, André Courrèges, was clothing charmingly dehumanized mannequins in space-boots and figure-skimming shifts beneath bubbles of hair like space helmets.)

Mourgue's work also looks backward, however. Structurally, its past lies in the metal tubing so frequently used by Breuer and Mart Stam (although there is little of their Bauhaus-inspired joy in material). Psychically, his furniture returns to that misty age when people lived surrounded by gods and assumed the existence of a spirit in every natural object. Both Djinn and Bouloum force us to recall that chairs are something we create in our own image; that they share our body parts of head, leg, arm, seat, foot, back; and that their forms can communicate spiritual and temporal power, as witness the bishop's chair and the sovereign's throne.

Mourgue's ability to combine myth, symbol, and esthetic and to express multiple meanings within a twentieth-century idiom has earned him a place in the pantheon of contemporary designers. One is left only to ask why such achievement now occurs so rarely in France, a country that once dominated furniture design, and why the French capture of the spirit of the 1960s could not inspire a return to dominance.

—Reed Benhamou

MROSZCZAK, Jozef.

Polish illustrator, exhibition and graphic designer. Born in Podhale, Nowy Targ, 11 May 1910. Educated in Nowy Targ, until 1926; studied law, at the University of Krakow, 1927–28; design, under Bukowski and Uziembo, at the Academy of Fine Arts, Krakow, 1929–32; graphics and advertising, at the Kunstgewerbeschule, the Graphische Lehr- und Versuchanstalt, and at a local commercial art school, Vienna, 1933–36. Married; son: Marcin. Freelance illustrator and designer from 1937, and exhibition designer from 1947, working in Katowice, 1937–40, 1945–53, in Nowy Targ, 1940–45, and in Warsaw, 1953–75: head of the graphic art department, at WAG graphic art publishers, Warsaw, from 1953; co-founder and editorial board member, of *Projekt* magazine, Warsaw, 1956–75. Instructor, at the Commercial Secondary School, Katowice, 1937–38, the Giermynski Free School of Painting and Drawing, Katowice, 1938–40, and at the Secondary Commercial School, Nowy Targ, 1940–45; organizer and head of the applied graphic art department, Polish College of Art, Katowice, 1947–53; instructor, 1953–55, and professor, 1955–73, at the Academy of Arts, Warsaw. Organizer of the Silesian section, Polish Union of Plastic Artists, 1945–46; Polish section chairman, ICOGRADA International Council of Graphic Design Associations; organizing committee chairman, Warsaw Poster Biennale. **Exhibitions:** *Vier Polnische Plakat Künstler*, Deutsches Plakatmuseum, Essen, 1971; *107 Grafici dell'AGI*, Castello Sforzesco, Milan, 1974. **Collection:** Poster Museum, Wilanow. Recipient: Polish Government Graphic Art Prize, 1953; Warsaw National Poster Prize, 1953; Polish State Prize for Artistic Achievement, 1953, 1968; Leipzig Book Fair Gold Medal, 1965; Brno Poster Biennale Prize, 1974. Honorary member, Dutch Union of Graphic Artists; member, Parma Academy of Fine Art, and Alliance Graphique Internationale. *Died* (in Warsaw) *in 1975.*

Works:

King Solomon's Mines (C. Bennett) film poster, for Polfilm, 1954.
Die Blumen Volkspolens poster, for the Polish national holiday, 1954.
Aida poster, for the State Opera, Warsaw, 1958.
Boris Godunov poster, for the State Opera, Warsaw, 1959.
Bettelstudent poster, for the Warsaw Operetta, 1961.
Don Carlos poster, for the State Opera, Warsaw, 1963.
Word and Picture exhibition poster, for the State Ethnographical Museum, Warsaw, 1967.
The Icon in Poland exhibition poster, for the Ethnographical Museum, Warsaw, 1967.
Opening Exhibition poster, for the Poster Museum, Wilanow, 1968.
Cabal and Love (Schiller) poster, for the Polish Theatre, Warsaw, 1969.
Landscape After a Battle (A. Wajda) film poster, for Polfilm, 1970.

Publications:

By MROSZCZAK: book—*Polnische Plakatkunst*, Dusseldorf 1966.

On MROSZCZAK: books—*Das Polnische Plakat*, Warsaw 1952; *Who's Who in Graphic Art*, edited by Walter Amstutz, Zurich 1962; *Buchgestaltung* by Albert Kapr, Dresden 1963; *Das Plakat* by Anton Sailer, Munich 1965; *Vier Polnische Plakatkunstler*, exhibition catalogue by H. Schardt, Essen 1971; *Polish Poster Art Today* by Szymon Bojko, London 1972; *Contemporary Polish Posters*, edited by Joseph Czestochowski, New York 1979; *The Polish Poster 1970–1978*, with introduction by Zdzislaw Schubert, Warsaw 1979.

If I had been asked to write about Jozef Mroszczak fifteen years ago, it would have been quite a difficult task. For years, he was regarded as one of two major "lions" of the Polish Poster School, sharing the position with Henryk Tomaszewski. It was the official cliché. Now that he is long ago gone, Mroszczak's position can be seen from a different angle.

As a designer, he was a very good one. No question about it. But it would be foolish to equate him with Tomaszewski, indisputably the master of his craft. Also, when pure craft, skill, and innovation are counted, quite a large group of younger colleagues outdid him. On this point, a little reflection: In many other countries, Mroszczak would have been number one as a posterist. But in Poland, the competition is greatest. The achievements, too.

Mroszczak himself was instrumental in creating this situation. It sounds paradoxical: Why would somebody build the competition against himself? But Mroszczak did, to such a point that years later, anybody was able to separate the pure designer from the great administrator and organizer. In the stormy, dark, late 1940s and early 1950s, Mroszczak persuaded the Communists that the poster must be the leading art form of the new regime. Of course, their goals differed greatly. Mroszczak had to fight for the quality of art, to save his discipline from the overwhelming Stalinization of cultural life. They, on the other hand, like the revolutionaries of 1918 in Moscow, sought a great tool of propaganda in the poster.

How Mroszczak managed to succeed, nobody will ever know. He keeps the whole truth to himself, forever. But we know that he engineered the Polish Poster School, GraphicAgency, *Projekt* graphic-art magazine, the poster museum at Wilanow, near Warsaw, and—his biggest victory—Warsaw's *International Poster Biennale*, which took place for the first time in 1966. After a long, sneaky route, with double-goals and half-truths, the Polish poster achieved its global position. Not only did it dominate the domestic market as the premier art form, the poster museum was the first major one of its kind in the world, and the *Biennale* was established as the first such exhibition, and it is still the most important.

Step by step, Mroszczak achieved all of this, with the help of many, but against many, too. He was a controversial figure all his life, overpraised by officials, underrated by society. But now, almost ten years after his death, nobody can question his achievements. He was a first-rate designer, an excellent professor at the Academy, and the most crucial figure backing the rise and overwhelming success of his beloved child, the poster. Thank you, Jozef, for the job well done.

—Jan Sawka

MROSZCZAK, Marcin (Jan).

Polish illustrator, photographer, stage and graphic designer. Born in Katowice, 10 January 1950. Studied graphics under Henryk Tomaszewski, at the Academy of Fine Arts, Warsaw, 1968–73. Married Maria Glinska in 1979; son: Mateusz. Designer, Arte Graphica Silva agency, Parma, 1970, Pentagram Design studio, London, 1971, and Tel Design agency, The Hague, 1972; freelance designer, working with Andrzej Krauze, in Warsaw, 1971–75, and with photographer Tomasz Sikora, Warsaw, 1976–82; art director, Apport Infoplan agency (McCann-Erickson), Brussels, 1983–86; founder-partner, with Kris Lenaerts, of Corporate Images design studio, Brussels, from 1986: has designed for the Warsaw National Theatre, Warsaw Theatre Powszechny, Lodz Theatre Jaracza, and for films of Andrzej Wajda and Roman Polanski. Art Director, *Le Théâtre en Pologne* magazine from 1972, and *Theatre* review, Warsaw, 1975–77. Instructor in graphic design, at the Academy of Fine Arts, Poznan, 1980, and the Académie Royale des Beaux-Arts, Ghent, from 1980. **Exhibitions:** Galeria Plakatu, Warsaw, 1978; BWA Gallery, Poznan, 1978; Author's Gallery, Amsterdam, 1979; Galeria On, Poznan, 1980; Galeria Wielka 19, Poznan, 1980. **Collections:** Museum of Contemporary Art, Lodz; Poster Museum, Warsaw; National Museum, Poznan; Stedelijk Museum, Amsterdam; Deutsches Plakatmuseum, Essen; Musée d'Art Moderne de la Ville, Paris. Recipient: Katowice Poster Biennale Award, 1975, 1977; President's Medal, Warsaw Poster Biennale, 1978. Address: Corporate Images, Rue Faider 55, 1050 Brussels, Belgium.

Publications:

On MROSZCZAK: books—*Who's Who of European Designers: Belgium, Spain, Czechoslovakia, Poland*, edited by Idea Publishers, Tokyo 1972; *The Polish Poster 1970–1978*, with introduction by Zdzislaw Schubert, Warsaw 1979; *Who's Who in Graphic Art*, edited by Walter Amstutz, Dubendorf 1982.

I always work to order; that means that the problem to be solved is set by someone else. This already excludes any kind of theory because each time the problem I face is very different. An interesting theatre poster and an advertising campaign which fulfills its role belong to two different worlds, though one and the other serve the same purpose: communication.

—Marcin Mroszczak

It would be easy but unfair to state that Marcin Mroszczak has nothing to do with Jozef Mroszczak—maybe the name only. No, it is true that Marcin is the son of Jozef Mroszczak—one of the most important poster designers of postwar Poland and the main builder of the poster's fame and position. This acknowledgment will help us to understand the younger Mroszczak's ups and downs as an artist. Of course, to be the son of such a powerful figure in small Warsaw makes your life an instant success. And a nightmare, as well.

Growing up under his father's umbrella, Marcin had all ways, all doors and windows, wide open. He knew everybody important because almost every body wanted to know his father. However, this privileged position and the older Mroszczak's sometimes blind desire to see his son as the leading poster artist, as the best of the best, made his life quite difficult. He had to face friendships that were built on self-interest and that quickly disappeared when Marcin Mroszczak set up as a freelance designer of books, posters, magazines, record sleeves, and practically anything with a graphic arts application in Warsaw in 1972. Best known for his work in the entertainment field, working on theatre and film posters, Mroszczak also be-

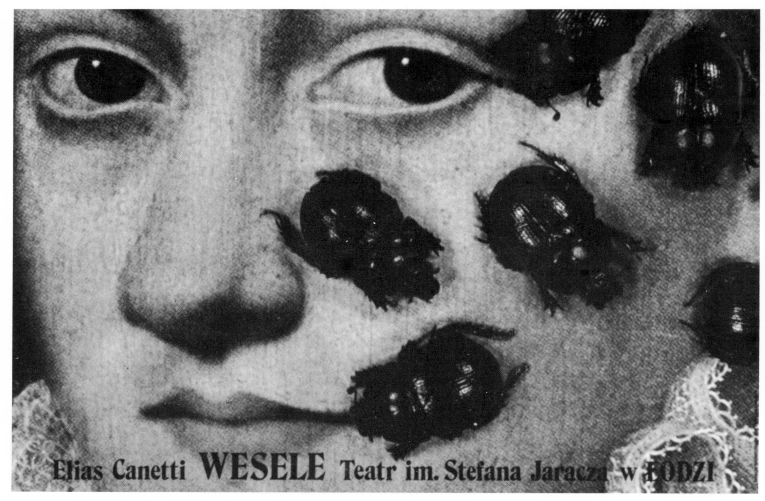

Marcin Mroszczak: *The Wedding* (Canetti) poster, for Theatre Jacaracza, Lodz

gan designing stage sets for the theatre. In collaboration with the photographer Tomasz Sikora, he has designed and illustrated two—as yet unpublished—picture books: *Album* and Lewis Carroll's *Alice in Wonderland*. His skill at photographic montage and trompe-l'oeil imagery is best evidenced in his posters for the National Theatre, Warsaw, and the Jacaracza Theatre in Łódź. He has also acted as art director of the magazines *Le Theatre en Pologne* and *Theatre Review* and, more recently, moved to Belgium as art director for a branch of the prestigious McCann-Erickson advertising agency.

Marcin's connections and power had been "used," as well as the stiffening competition of his generation of artists who did all they could to outdo the "Mroszczak-baby." Another obstacle was how to develop his own style. Like anyone else, he was criticized for copying, for borrowing, or simply for lacking his own style. Yesterday's friends, now turned major enemies, claimed it was their achievement but Marcin's signature.

Slowly, Mroszczak began to develop his own style. Knowing that drawing and painting are not his most formidable tools, he decided to use photography. When his technique had improved, he experimented with something which was not pure collage but not yet an object. Rather, these were pre-arranged situations, carefully staged, photographed, and afterward incorporated into poster compositions.

And, at this point, the real *Marcin* Mroszczak was born. Very theatrical, intelligent, and visually almost perfect posters appeared. The influence of theatre was obvious. Mroszczak likes film and theatre, and in the latter he feels at home. The atmosphere of theatre, its stage,

set-design, hundreds of requisites, enriches Mroszczak's mind. His constructions, or, better, his arrangements, are never heavy-handed. He organizes them intelligently, reserving to the public a delicate margin of interpretation of various allusions and the possibility of finding its own language of understanding. As time has passed, Mroszczak has developed his own image, style, posture.

People now do not see him as the offspring of the old one—the past disappears and old wounds heal fast. Hard times of struggling alone, no longer the young lion with daddy's help, have crystallized the best from Mroszczak. Perhaps, as his father wished, he will one day be the best of the best.

—Jan Sawka

MUGLER, Thierry.

French fashion designer. Born in Strasbourg, Alsace, in 1946. Educated in Strasbourg until 1964. Worked as a ballet dancer with the Opéra du Rhin, Strasbourg, 1965–66; assistant clothing designer in the Gudule boutique, Paris, 1966–67; designer of fashion collections for André Peters, London, 1968–69; freelance designer, in Amsterdam and Paris, 1970–71; created *Café de Paris* fashion collection, Paris

1971; founded Thierry Mugler fashion firm, Paris, from 1973: also established Thierry Mugler Diffusion ready-to-wear company, with distribution in United States outlets including Saks Fifth Avenue, Bergdorf Goodman, Neiman-Marcus, Marshall Field, John Wanamaker, Bloomingdale's, and in Japan via Takashimaya department stores; opened boutiques on the Place des Victoires, and on Avenue Montaigne, Paris. Address: 130 rue du Faubourg Saint Honoré, 75008 Paris, France.

Publications:

By MUGLER: books—*Thierry Mugler, Photographer,* Paris and London 1988.

On MUGLER: books—*Fashion and Anti-Fashion* by Ted Polhemus and Lynn Proctor, London 1978; *25 Ans de Marie-Claire de 1954 a 1979,* compiled by Françoise Mohrt, Paris 1979; *Fairchild's Who's Who in Fashion,* edited by Anne Stegemeyer, New York 1980; *Fashion 2001* by Lucille Khornak, London 1982; *McDowell's Directory of Twentieth Century Fashion,* London 1984, 1987; *The Encyclopaedia of Fashion from 1840 to the 1980s* by Georgina O'Hara, London 1986; *Design Source Book* by Penny Sparke and others, London 1986.

Sharp, pointed, wide shoulders, sharply defined waistlines, tight, sensuously fitted skirts or pants, simple shapes and colors, no hint of the past or folksiness: these are the elements of costumes Thierry Mugler creates for the 1980s. He likes the idea of the "uniform," so that everyone will look the same; it links people together, he says, both men and women. Mugler himself wears a broad-shouldered jumpsuit which suggests a cross between space cadet and race-driver. His silhouettes are not unrelated; note, for example, his 1979 dress with the exaggeratedly widened triangular shoulders and large, stiff, triangular hip-pockets with belt to match. Although his clothes are quite futuristic, they are never busy but rather are simplified, incorporating a minimum of details.

Mugler spent two years of his youth as a classical ballet dancer, a brief career which, he believes, has been a primary source for his designs—first, for the architectural element and second, for his emphasis on the shoulders to give a sense of height and grandeur to the figure. His showings are notoriously elaborate extravaganzas, like Kenzo's before him and also like those of his contemporaries Claude Montana and Jean-Claude de Luca. These tend to lend his clothes a far-out feeling, more science fiction-like than they seem in normal circumstances. Mugler's 1979 herringbone plaid pants suit, for example, with short jacket, padded shoulders, and buttoned pocket accents, is less wild when seen alone. Even his uses of accessories, such as his 1979 visor sunglasses, gladiator bracelets, and belts decorated with geometric shapes (triangles, diamonds) and pointed tips, come across more as contemporary classical than as theatrical or elaborate.

A look at some of Mugler's designs from the past few years shows him remaining true to the style he developed about a decade ago. His 1980 above-the-knee dress has a basic look, accented starkly by a sharply pointed waistband with two tails flowing down from the tie and matching triangular hemline; the accompanying shoes have similarly pointed insteps and wraparound, calf-height ties. In 1982, Mugler showed long, belted jackets with circle skirts and wide-legged pants in navy gabardine, an updating of a well-known classic look. His fall 1983 clothes for men included basic turtlenecks, thigh-length "car coat" jackets, slim pants, and "Perry Como" cardigans of mohair plush with ribbed-wool details, and worn over simple, mock turtleneck sweaters, the emphasis being on loose, roomy, soft shoulders and sleeves. In middle age, Mugler seems to have found his style and located some of the very refined variations upon which he hopes to elaborate in the future.

—Barbara Cavaliere

MUIR, Jean (Elizabeth).
British fashion designer. Born in London in 1933. Educated at Dame Harper School, Bedford, 1945–50. Married Harry Leuckert in 1955. Worked in a solicitor's office, London, 1951; salesgirl and fashion sketcher, Liberty's department store, London, 1952–55; designer, for Jacqmar, London, 1955, and for Jaeger dress and knitwear collections, London, 1956–63; founder-director, Jane and Jane fashion company, London, 1962–66; founder-partner, with Harry Leuckert, and chief designer, of Jean Muir Limited, London, from 1966. **Exhibitions:** *Fashion: An Anthology,* Victoria and Albert Museum, London, 1971; *Eye for Industry,* Victoria and Albert Museum, London, 1986. **Collection:** Museum of Costume, Bath. Recipient: British Fashion Writers Dress of the Year Award, 1964; Ambassador Achievement

Award, 1965; Harper's Bazaar Trophy, 1965; Maison Blanche Rex International Fashion Award, New Orleans, 1967, 1968, 1974; Churchman's Fashion Designer of the Year Award, 1970; Neiman Marcus Award, 1973; Mayor's Citation Award, Philadelphia, 1977; British Fashion Industry Award, 1984; Federation Francaise du Prêt-à-Porter Feminin Award, 1985; Design Medal, Chartered Society of Designers, London, 1987. Honorary Doctorate: Royal College of Art, London, 1981. Royal Designer for Industry, Royal Society of Arts, London, 1972; Fellow, Chartered Society of Designers, London, 1978; Commander, Order of the British Empire, 1984. Address: 59/61 Farringdon Road, London EC1M 3HD, England.

Publications:

By MUIR: book—*Jean Muir,* London 1981.

Jean Muir: Culotte suit in matte jersey, 1971

On MUIR: books—*The Fashion Makers* by Leonard Halliday, London 1966; *Fashion: An Anthology* by Cecil Beaton, exhibition catalogue compiled by Madeleine Ginsburg, London 1971; *In Vogue: Sixty Years of Celebrities and Fashion* by Georgina Howell, London 1975, 1978, New York 1976; *A History of Fashion* by J. Anderson Black and Madge Garland, London 1975, 1980; *McDowell's Directory of Twentieth Century Fashion* by Colin McDowell, London 1984, 1987; *The Encyclopaedia of Fashion from 1840 to the 1980s* by Georgina O'Hara, London 1986; *Eye for Industry: Royal Designers for Industry 1936–1986,* exhibition catalogue by Fiona MacCarthy and Patrick Nuttgens, London 1986; *Design Source Book* by Penny Sparke and others, London 1986.

"Fashion is not Art, it is Industry. There are too many designers and not enough workers,"

says Jean Muir, who regards herself as a crafts-woman before a designer. Glamorous ideas are worthless if one cannot turn them into a working pattern, and Muir is critical of colleges which turn out designers who cannot even cut and sew. The engineering is the basis of the art, and Muir insists on excellence in handwork as the foundation without which no fashion house can operate. Fashion is business, a production line, and Muir is now involved in ensuring that fashion students understand this.

Her approach to design is equally fundamental, for clothes must start on the body, not in abstract concepts. It is how the fabric flows on the human form which rules her talents, and she continues the approach of the greatest women couturières—Chanel, Grès, and Vionnet. Like them, she is fascinated by the fluidity of jersey on the female form, which produces a liquid sculpture echoing every movement. She is also fond of suede, and the same toile will be worked out and applied to both types of material to produce the different but related effects that characterize her collections. "I am a traditionalist with a sense of evolution, someone who loves evolving continuity. I prefer evolution or organic growth to revolution or grand idealistic concepts," she states, thereby showing that she is also a representative of the British approach to design taught by Edward Molyneaux.

Obvious tricks, such as plunging necklines and skirts slit up to the hip, are vulgar. A reserved design can achieve a lasting quality and be infinitely more seductive in a subtle way. No Muir gown exposes a woman, but her soft lines are full of physical appeal. Customers will wear a Muir creation for years because its effect does not fade, and it is too well made to wear out. Carol Channing, Lauren Bacall, Elaine Stritch, and Glenda Jackson typify her clientele, who collect her clothes like treasures. Because Muir avoids major changes every year, her clothes rise above fashion to exist on that plateau with gowns by Grès; such simplicity has a classical durability. They represent the modern movement at its very best.

—Diana de Marly

MÜLLER, Rolf Felix.

German illustrator, cartoonist and graphic designer. Born in Lobenstein, 22 July 1932. Educated at Grundschule, Lobenstein, 1939–47; apprentice lithographer, Gera, 1948–51; studied lettering and book design under Egon Pruggmayer, at the Hochschule für Grafik und Buchkunst, Leipzig, 1952–57. Married Marie-Luise Kahle in 1957; son: Thomas. Freelance designer, in Gera, from 1957: has designed and illustrated books for Greifen Verlag, Insel-Verlag, Eulenspiegel, Reclam, Union, Urania-Verlag, Kinderbuchverlag, etc. Head of graphic design from 1985, and professor from 1987, at the Hochschule fur Grafik und Buchkunst, Leipzig. **Exhibitions:** Haus des Lehrers, East Berlin, 1964; Schloss Heidecksburg, Rudolstadt, 1973; Sommerpalais, Greiz, 1973, 1982; Kleine Galerie, Unterwellenborn, 1974; Schauspielhaus, Karl-Marx-Stadt, 1975; Galerie Gucke, Bad Kostritz, 1976, 1981; Kunstgalerie, Gera, 1977; Studentenclub, Weimar, 1978; Kulturzentrum DDR, Warsaw, 1979; Kulturzentrum DDR, Budapest, 1980; Kreiskulturhaus, Meerane, 1981; Kunstsammlung, Cottbus, 1981; Galerie am Markt, Gera, 1981; Haus der Kultur, Gera,

1982; Klubhaus Wema Union, Gera, 1984; Theater der Stadt, Rostow am Don, 1984; Kulturband-Galerie, Lobenstein, 1985; Galerie ans Steger, Zeulenroda, 1986; Kulturhaus Wilhelm Pieck, Schwarza, 1986; Staatliches Museum, Burgk, 1988. **Collections:** Museum für Deutsche Geschichte, East Berlin; Kunstbibliothek, East Berlin; Galerie Kunstsammlung, Kottbus; Mahrische Galerie, Brno; Museum Wilanow, Warsaw. Recipient: Kunstpreis der Stadt Gera, 1959; Kunstpreis des Bezirkes Gera, 1964, 1970; Deutscher Turn und Sport Art Prize, 1972; Kunstpreis der DDR, 1973; DDR Medal of Merit, 1979; DDR National Prize, 1987. Address: Oststrasse 8 6500 Gera, German Democratic Republic.

Works:

Giacomo Casanova: Neunundneunzig Abenteuer book design, for Greifenverlag, Rudolstadt, 1958.
Georg Christoph Lichtenberg: homo sapiens book design, for Eulenspiegel Verlag, Berlin, 1961.
Hansgeorg Stengel: Seegang Satan Sansibar book design, for Eulenspiegel Verlag, Berlin, 1970.
Hartmut Biewald: Tonca book design, for Der Kinderbuchverlag, Berlin, 1974.
Die feine stenglische Art: Epigramme von Hansgeorg Stengel book design, for Eulenspiegel Verlag, Berlin, 1977.
Hans Lowe: Leben ist Lernen book design, for Urania-Verlag, Leipzig, 1978.
Hansgeorg Stengel: Gedichte und Epigramme book design, for Eulenspiegel Verlag, Berlin, 1981.
Lilo Hardel: Nadja, mein Liebling book design, for Der Kinderbuchverlag, Berlin, 1982.
Hansgeorg Stengel: Poesiealbum 186 book design, for Verlag Neues Leben, Berlin, 1983.
Carlo Collodi: Pinocchios Abenteuer book design, for Verlag Philipp Reclam, Leipzig, 1986.
Kleines Ratbuch fur Kinder book design, for Der Kinderbuchverlag, Berlin, 1987.
Johannes Lehmann: Kurzweil durch Mathe book design, for Urania-Verlag, Leipzig, 1988.

Publications:

On MÜLLER: books—*Gebrauchsgraphik in der DDR* by Hellmuth Rademacher, Dresden 1975; *Rolf F. Müller: Das Plakat als Kunstgegenstand*, exhibition catalogue, Rostock 1980; *Plakate Rolf F. Müller*, exhibition catalogue with text by V. Waallenberg, Kottbus 1980; *Who's Who in Graphic Art*, edited by Walter Amstutz, Dubendorf 1982; *Rolf Felix Müller: Arbeit fur das Buch*, exhibition catalogue with texts by Lothar Lang, Axel Bertram and others, Burgk/Saale 1988.

Next to book illustration, the theatre poster has a particular place in my work. If the poster is often described as the favourite child of commercial graphics, I consider cultural advertising and the art poster as one of the noblest and enticing tasks I can think of. The theatre poster draws its charm not least from its relationship to its surroundings. It brings something meditative, a breath of poetry, into the everyday life of our towns, for the cultural atmosphere of a town is influenced by its billboards. Ideas and events are made visual in signs and images which challenge the thinking observer. It is here that the poster has its chance, along with its aesthetic and educational functions, to stimulate thoughtful attitudes.

—Rolf Felix Müller

MÜLLER-BROCKMANN, Josef.

Swiss graphic designer. Born Josef Mario Müller, in Rapperswil, St. Gallen, 9 May 1914; adopted name Müller-Brockmann, 1942. Studied architecture, design and art history, at the Abendgymnasium Juventus, the ETH Eidgenossische Technische Hochschule, the University of Zürich and at the Kunstgewerbeschule, Zürich. Married Verena Brockmann in 1942 (died, 1964); son: Andreas; married Shizuko Yoshikawa in 1967. Assistant designer to graphics and advertising consultant Walter Diggelmann, Zurich, 1934–36; freelance graphic and stage designer, in Zurich, from 1936: design consultant, IBM Europe, Paris, from 1966; founder and co-editor, of *Neue Grafik* magazine, Zurich, 1958–65; founder, Galerie 58 (later, Galerie Seestrasse), Rapperswil, 1965. Professor of graphic design, at the Kunstgewerbeschule, Zürich, 1956–59; guest lecturer, University of Arts, Osaka, from 1961, Hochschule für Gestaltung, Ulm, 1963, and Carlton University, Ottawa, 1972. President, Verband Schweizerische Graphiker, 1956–59; jury member, *Gute Form* committee, Bonn, from 1979. **Exhibitions:** Amerika Haus, Munich, 1952 (toured); Kongresshaus, Zürich, 1958; Institut für Auslandbezieungen, Stuttgart, 1958; Matsuya Department Store, Tokyo, 1961 (toured); Gewerbemuseum, Winterthur, 1963; AIGA Gallery, New York, 1967; BMW Pavilion, Munich, 1969; Feierabendhaus der Rosenthal, Selb, 1971; Galerija Studenstskog Centra, Zagreb, 1973; Plakanda Gallery, Zurich, 1974; Osaka Art Center, Japan, 1975; Ryder Gallery, Chicago, 1977; Reinhold-Brown Gallery, New York, 1980; Engadiner Kollegium, St. Moritz, 1981; Plakat Galerie, Bern, 1982. **Collections:** Kunstgewerebemuseum, Zürich; Deutsches Plakatmuseum, Essen; Stedelijk Museum, Amsterdam; Gemeentemuseum, The Hague; Poster Museum, Warsaw; Museum of Modern Art, New York. Member, Alliance Graphique Internationale, Paris. Address: Enzianweg 4, 8048 Zürich, Switzerland.

Publications:

By MÜLLER-BROCKMANN: books—*Gestaltungsprobleme des Grafikers,* Teufen 1961; *History of Visual Communication,* Teufen 1971; *History of the Poster,* with Shizuko Müller-Brockmann, Zürich 1971; *Grid-System,* Teufen 1981.

On MÜLLER-BROCKMANN: books—*Posters: 50 Artists and Designers,* edited by W. H. Allner, New York 1952; *The New Graphic Design* by Karl Gerstner and Markus Kutter, Teufen and London 1959; *Modern Graphics* by Keith Murgatroyd, London 1969; *Graphic Designers in Europe 1,* edited by Henri Hillebrand, London 1971; *Design* by Jocelyn de Noblet, Paris 1974; *Who's Who in Graphic Art,* edited by Walter Amstutz, Dubendorf 1982; *Josef Müller-Brockmann: Typographie und Photographie in Konstruktiven Plakat,* exhibition catalogue by Willy Rotzler, Bern 1982; *The 20th-Century Poster: Design of the Avant-Garde* by Dawn Ades, New York 1984; *Typographic Design: Form and Communication* by Rob Carter, Ben Day and Philip Meggs, New York 1985.

The use of the grid as an ordering system is the expression of a certain mental attitude inasmuch as it shows that the designer conceives his work in terms that are constructive and oriented to the future. This is the expression of a professional ethos: the designer's work should have the clearly intelligible, objective, functional and aesthetic quality of mathematical thinking.

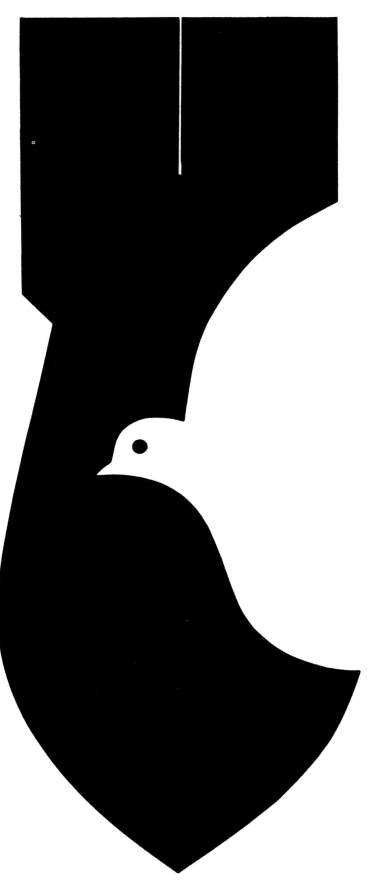

Rolf Felix Muller: Anti-war poster

juni-festwochen zürich 1959

tonhalle grosser saal
dienstag, 2. juni 1959
20.15 uhr

1. konzert der tonhalle-
gesellschaft zürich
leitung:
hans rosbaud
solisten:
maria stader, anton fietz,
pierre fournier

frank martin
ouverture en hommage
à mozart
willy burkhard
cellokonzert, op. 60
rolf liebermann
capriccio für sopran,

violine und orchester
arthur honegger
dritte sinfonie ‹liturgique›

karten fr. 5.50 bis 16.50
vorverkauf: tonhalle
hug, jecklin, kuoni

Josef Muller-Brockmann: Concert poster for the Zurich Tonhalle, 1959

His work should thus be a contribution to general culture and itself form part of it.

Constructive design which is capable of analysis and reproduction can influence and enhance the taste of a society and the way it conceives forms and colours. Design which is objective, committed to the common weal, well composed, and refined, constitutes the basis of democratic behaviour. Constructivist design means the conversion of design laws into practical solutions. Work done systematically and in accordance with strict formal principles makes those demands for directness, intelligibility, and the integration of all factors which are also vital in socio-political life.

Working with the grid system means submitting to laws of universal validity. The use of the grid system implies the will to systematize, to clarify; the will to penetrate to the essentials, to concentrate; the will to cultivate objectivity instead of subjectivity; the will to rationalize the creative and technical production processes; the will to integrate elements of colour, form, and material; the will to achieve architectural dominion over surface and space; the will to adopt a positive, forward-looking attitude; and the recognition of the importance of education and the effect of work devised in a constructive and creative spirit.

Every visual creative work is a manifestation of the character of the designer. It is a reflection of his knowledge, his ability, and his mentality. What is the purpose of the grid? The grid is used by the typographer, graphic designer, photographer, and exhibition designer for solving visual problems in two and three dimensions. The graphic designer and typographer use it for designing press advertisements, brochures, catalogues, books, periodicals, etc., and the exhibition designer, for conceiving his plan for exhibitions and show-window displays.

By arranging the surfaces and spaces in the form of a grid, the designer is favourably placed to dispose his texts, photographs, and diagrams in conformity with objective and functional criteria. The pictorial elements are reduced to a few formats of the same size. The size of the pictures is determined according to their importance for the subject. The reduction of the number of visual elements used and their incorporation in a grid system creates a sense of compact planning, intelligibility, and clarity and suggests orderliness of design. This orderliness lends added credibility to the information and induces confidence.

Information presented with clear and logically set out titles, subtitles, texts, illustrations, and captions will not only be read more quickly and easily, but the information will also be better understood and retained in the memory. This is a scientifically proved fact, and the designer should bear it constantly in mind. The grid can be successfully used for the corporate identities of firms. This includes all visual media of information from the visiting card to the exhibition stand, all printed forms for internal and external use, advertising matter, vehicles for goods and passenger transport, name-plates, lettering on buildings, etc.

—Josef Müller-Brockmann

In order to appreciate the achievement of Josef Müller-Brockmann, it is necessary to set his clear, concise designs in the context of Swiss design generally. Although the Bauhaus moved from Germany to the United States, it may be said that the country that followed its achievements most closely was Müller-Brockmann's Switzerland. Two factors isolated this nation from the rest of the world at the time the designer was a young man. These were first, the economic depression which had originated in the United States and later, World War II, in which Switzerland remained neutral but became encircled. In this situation, with the help of the Swiss Ministry of the Interior, the design profession—and Müller-Brockmann—developed with a concentration on the precision long associated with Swiss craftsmanship.

This talented artist had exactly the skill and perception to provide a series of remarkable posters for the Zürich Tonhalle concerts just before 1960. As he explained, the posters, which were designed with strict formal elements, were intended as "the symbolic expression of the innate laws of music." Thus, for him, "thematic, dynamic, rhythmic and metrical factors in music" have a corresponding form in the composition of the poster. In order to retain the economy and clarity he desired and yet provide the required information relating to the performances, all visual imagery based on the orchestra was dropped, and the essential musical element, conveyed solely in terms of typography. The resulting posters show lettering slanted diagonally in rhythmic intervals to produce images analogous to musical scores; equivalent to the disciplines of music, they are yet exciting visual experiences. Müller-Brockmann has also made a number of powerful posters for safety on the road; in these, he has combined the expressive typography demonstrated in the concert posters with dramatic photomontage imagery. Unlike the informationally oriented posters of the concert performances, these have the necessary single visual impact from which the entire message can be assimilated at a glance.

—John Barnicoat

MUNARI, Bruno.
Italian painter, sculptor, photographer, exhibition, graphic and industrial designer. Born in Milan, 24 October 1907. Studied at the Technical Institute, Naples, 1924; mainly self-taught in art and design. Married Dilma Carnevali in 1934; son: Alberto. Independent painter and sculptor, associating with Futurist groups, in Milan and Rome, from 1927, photographer and graphic designer from 1932, and industrial designer from 1948: designed for Danese, Olivetti, Pirelli, Mondadori, Einaudi, La Rinascente, Robots, IBM, Campari, Cinzano, etc. Professor, at the Scuola Politecnica di Design, Milan; visiting professor of design, at Harvard University, Cambridge, Massachusetts, 1970–71. **Exhibitions:** Galleria Tre Arti, Milan, 1933; Galleria Milano, Milan, 1934; Galleria Borromini, Milan, 1948; Galleria Cavallino, Venice, 1949; Galleria Elicottero, Milan, 1950; Museum of Modern Art, New York, 1954; Galleria Montenapoleone, Milan, 1958; Galleria Danese, Milan, 1959, 1961, 1963, 1965, 1968, 1980, 1981; Olivetti, Milan, 1962; Isetan, Tokyo, 1965; Galleria Obelisco, Rome, 1966; National Museum of Modern Art, Tokyo, 1966; Howard Wise Gallery, New York, 1966; Allgemeine Gewerbeschule, Basel, 1968; Galleria Sincron, Brescia, 1969, 1974, 1975, 1976, 1980, 1981, 1983; Galleria Uxa, Novara, 1970; Galleria San Fedele, Milan, 1971; Italian Cultural Institute, Copenhagen, 1972; Italian Cultural Institute, Stockholm, 1972; Galeria Cadaques, Spain, 1975; Galleria Portello, Genoa, 1976; Galleria Mercato del Sale, Milan, 1976; Pinacoteca di Brera, Milan, 1977; University of Parma, 1979; Centro Culturale Olivetti, Ivrea,

1980; Galleria Apollinaire, Milan, 1980. **Collections:** Galleria Nazionale d'Arte Moderna, Rome; Kaiser Wilhelm Museum, Krefeld; Museum of Modern Art, New York; Philadelphia Museum of Art. Recipient: Gold Medal, Milan Triennale; Compasso d'Oro Award, Milan, 1954, 1955, 1979. Address: Via Vittoria Colonna 39, 20149 Milan, Italy.

Works:

Zizi the Monkey flexible toy, produced by Pigomma, 1953.
Ice bucket, produced by Tre A, 1955.
Cubic ashtray, produced by Danese, 1957.
Cube suspension lamp, produced by Danese, 1958.
Book designs, for Einaudi publishers, 1960s.
X Hour limited edition (50 examples) multiple, produced by Danese, 1963.
Falkland tubular lamp in aluminium and elastic knit, produced by Danese, 1964.
Flexy creative toy, produced by Danese, 1968.
Lipari ashtray in melamine and anodised aluminium, produced by Danese, 1971.
Abitacolo toy dwelling in steel, produced by Robots, 1971.
Panarea candlestick in stainless steel, produced by Danese, 1973.
Datillo lamp in plastic and iron, produced by Danese, 1978.
Hanging tensile bookshelf, produced by Robots, 1979.
Poster series, for Campari, from 1984.

Publications:

By MUNARI: books—*I Libri Munari*, Milan 1945; *Libro Illegibile*, Milan 1949, New York 1967; *The Lorry Driver*, London 1953; *What I'd Like To Be*, London 1953; *Nella notte buia*, Milan 1956, as *In the Dark of the Night*, New York 1961; *Animals for Sale*, New York 1957; *Who's There? Open the Door!*, New York 1957; *Tic, Tac, Toc*, New York 1957; *The Birthday Present*, New York 1958; *The Elephant's Wish*, New York 1959; *Jimmy Has Lost His Cap, Where Can It Be?*, New York 1959; *Bruno Munari's ABC*, New York 1960; *Alfabetiere secondo il metodo attivo*, Turin 1960; *Il quadrato/The Square*, New York 1960, as *Discovery of the Square*, New York 1963; *Vetrine, negozi italiani/Modern Design for Italian Shop-Windows*, Milan 1961; *Good Design*, Milan and New York 1963; *Supplemento al dizionario italiano/Supplement to the Italian Dictionary*, Milan and New York 1963; *Bruno Munari's Zoo*, New York 1963; *Il cerchio*, Milan 1964, as *Discovery of the Circle*, New York 1965; *Arte come mestiere*, Bari, Italy 1966, as *Design as Art*, London 1971; *Libro illeggibile NY 1*, New York 1967; *Design e communicazione visive*, Bari, Italy 1968; *Nella nebbia di Milano*, Milan 1968, as *Circus in the Mist*, New York 1969; *Design italiano: Mobili*, editor, Rome 1968; *Campo urbano: interventi estetici nella dimensione collettiva urbana*, editor, with others, Milan 1969; *Artista e designer*, Rome 1971; *Codice ovvio*, Turin 1971; *Da lontano era un'isola*, Milan 1971, as *From Afar It Is An Island*, New York 1972; *Cappuccetto verde*, Turin 1972; *Cappuccetto giallo*, Turin 1972; *Alfabetiere*, Turin 1972; *Search for a Stone*, Milan and London 1972; *A Flower with Love*, London 1974; *12 Prelibri* (for children who do not know how to read), Milan 1980; *Da cosa nasce cosa*, Bari, Italy 1981; *Rose nell'insalata*, Turin 1982; *Made in Italia: Selezione dei Marchi Italiani*, editor, with G. Giugiaro, Bologna 1988.

On MUNARI: books—*The New Graphic De-*

sign by Karl Gerstner and Markus Kutter, Teufen and London 1959; *Design Coordination and Corporate Image* by F. H. K. Henrion and Alan Parkin, London and New York 1967; *Munari 71*, exhibition catalogue by Paolo Fossati and others, Milan 1971; *Il Design in Italia 1945–1972* by Paolo Fossati, Turin 1972; *Design e Forme Nuove nell'Arredamento Italiano*, edited by Paolo Portoghesi and Marino Marini, Rome 1978; *Bruno Munari*, exhibition catalogue by Giulio Carlo Argan and Alessandro Mendini, Parma 1979; *Atlante del Design Italiano 1940/1980* by Alfonso Grassi and Anty Pansera, Milan 1980; *L'Arte Anomala di Bruno Munari* by A. Tanchis, Bari 1981; *Design Since 1945*, edited by Kathryn Hiesinger and George Marcus, Philadelphia and London 1983; *Bruno Munari: From Futurism to Post-Industrial Design* by A. Tanchis, London 1987; *Italian Modern: A Design Heritage* by Giovanni Albera and Nicolas Monti, New York 1989.

Bruno Munari began his career at the age of nineteen in the engineering studio of an uncle in Milan. Although he quickly became involved in the Futurist movement, the experience in his uncle's studio was important for having convinced him that his artistic work should always be approached as a job rather than a stylistic undertaking, thereby eliminating financial dependence on an art market characterized by continuously changing taste. Munari's work might be described as lacking any definable style. Over the course of nearly seventy years of making art he has experimented with, and been influenced by, a wide range of movements and individuals. But defining his own "style" is the essence of correctness of the design for the particular purpose. He believes that "if the form of an object turns out to be 'beautiful' it will be thanks to the logic of its construction, and to the precision of the solutions found for its various components. It is 'beautiful' because it is just right."

Munari participated in the Futurist exhibitions in Milan from 1927 to 1936. Few works from this period survive due to the perishable materials used for their construction, but his work showed a devotion to nature and an interest in the human figure which has been sustained throughout his career. His Futurist work led to experimentation with abstraction, but it was an abstraction free of formalist dogma. The *Useless Machines* which he designed in the 1930s developed out of his interest in the machine combined with his desire to create machines which were pacific, representing only themselves through their colors and the movement of forms. The idea for the *Useless Machines* arose from Munari's desire to free abstract forms from the painter's canvas and "let them share our surroundings with us, sensitive to the true atmosphere of reality . . ." Made of ordinary materials and mass producible, they were one of the earliest examples of kinetic sculpture.

Beginning in 1929 Munari worked as a graphic designer in a number of advertising studios, including Cassio's IPC where he pioneered the use of animated cartoons in Italian advertising. He also worked as a designer and illustrator for several magazines. In 1930 he opened a graphic design studio with Riccardo Ricas. His designs of the period show the influence of Enrico Prampolini, a Futurist, and Herbert Bayer. They often make reference to the human figure. His work in the 1930s and early 1940s ranged from painting to sculpture, photography (including photomontages and film), and set design, both for European and traditional Nō theatre. This range of experience with varied media no doubt facilitated his success in industrial design after World War II. In fact, Munari had worked in industrial design to a

limited extent prior to the war, designing ceramic tiles, furniture (in which the pieces were painted in the style of his paintings), interior designs, and fabric designs.

One of Munari's greatest lifelong concerns has been communication, but not only visual communication. A prolific writer of essays, articles, poems, manifestoes, and books, he has strived to educate a broad audience, from children to adults, from artists to lay persons. Some of his writing, such as *Le Macchine di Munari* (1945) which contains imaginary machines like the "tail wagger for lazy dogs," displays an acute sense of humor in addition to didactic information.

In an effort to reconcile architecture, industrial design, and the visual arts, in 1948 Munari founded the Movimento Arte Concreta with Gillo Dorfles and Gianni Monnet. Their attempt to synthesize the arts was filled with disagreement and lasted only ten years, but during this time Munari worked on a series of paintings designed to challenge optical perceptions. His *Negative positives* were composed of nonobjective shapes which alternately advance and recede, each capable of appearing to be either background or foreground. In the same way that his *Useless Machines* were an attempt to break with the ground, so too did the *Negative positives* attempt to break out of the confines of the plane of the painting.

This fascination with breaking the plane and with reducing a design to its simplest form can be seen in his industrial designs of the 1950s and 1960s. His designs for the *Tubular Falkland Lamp* of 1964 are the essence of simplicity. Made of knit fabric with aluminum rings of various sizes inserted to give them shape, the lamps break down easily into two dimensions when the rings are collapsed together. His candlesticks and ashtrays, produced by Danese in the 1970s, are exceedingly simple forms which are appealing precisely because of that simplicity. These and virtually all products which he designs are made of unadorned materials, often steel or aluminum. They are so simple as to appear anonymous, in keeping with his belief that the objects are in fact incomplete until influenced by the owner's additions to the object or his placement of it with other objects. Munari has said, "It is always a question of clarity, of simplicity. There is much work to do that involves taking away, instead of adding. Taking away the superfluous in order to give exact information, instead of adding to and complicating the information." The imposition of the designer's style is seen by Munari as inappropriate because it is not essential to the function of the designed object. An excellent example is the *Abitacolo* of 1971. A multipurpose structure made of lightweight steel components assembled in a grid system, it is the ultimate living structure for a child, providing him with his own dwelling inside a dwelling. With components that may be rearranged at will, the *Abitacolo* incorporates into one structure bed, lamp, table, shelving, bins, and elements for hanging objects. It is essentially transparent, indestructible, completely devoid of any style. Its style becomes whatever the child makes it with his possessions.

In the 1940s Munari began to design and write for children, the artistic contribution for which he may be best known to the average person since, unlike his industrial designs, the work bears his name. Disturbed by the lack of educational books available to his son he began writing and illustrating his own books and designing his own toys. Intended not just to amuse, but to improve the quality of a child's learning experience, his books and toys are, like his industrial designs, incomplete until the child interacts with them.

In the 1960s, convinced that children are less

culturally conditioned and therefore show more potential for creativity than adults, Munari shifted his focus largely to educating the young. He has travelled in Europe, Japan, and South America to conduct workshops with children. Anti-authoritarian in his approach to education, Munari's work with children in pre-schools, museum workshops, and elementary schools demonstrates his belief that experimentation with only limited direction is the key to the creative process.

—Sheila Klos

MUSSER, Tharon.
American stage lighting designer. Born in Roanoke, Virginia, 8 January 1925. Studied at Berea College, Kentucky, 1943–46: BA 1946; Yale University, New Haven, Connecticut, 1946–50: MFA 1950. Independent stage lighting designer, working in the United States and abroad, from 1949: staff designer, Center Theatre Group, Mark Taper Forum, Los Angeles, from 1970; advisor to the Chicago Auditorium, 1971, Los Angeles Shubert Theatre, 1971, and Dallas Music Hall, 1972; worked for Province Town Playhouse, Jose Limon Dance Company, Phoenix Theatre Company, American Theatre Festival Company, National Repertory Theatre Company, Boston Arts Festival, Dallas Civic Opera, Miami Opera Guild, Wolf Trap Foundation, etc. Lecturer, Yale University, New Haven, Connecticut, 1962, 1969, Bridgeport University, Connecticut, 1968, State University of New York, 1969, Bucknell University, Pennsylvania, 1973, Harvard University, Cambridge, Massachusetts, 1974–76. Recipient: Los Angeles Drama Critics Circle Award, 1970, 1972, 1977, 1979; Antoinette Perry (Tony) Award, New York, 1971, 1975, 1981; Distinguished Alumnus Award, Berea College, Kentucky, 1973; United States Institute of Theatrical Technology Award, 1976; Theatre Hall of Fame Award, New York, 1984. Honorary Doctorates: Berea College, Kentucky, 1979; Emerson College, Boston, 1980. Address: 21 Cornelia Street, New York, New York 10014, U.S.A.

Works:

Lighting designs include (in New York, unless specified) *The Father*, 1949; *Naked*, 1950; *Lucky Sam McCarver*, 1950; *Long Day's Journey into Night*, 1956; *Shinbone Alley*, 1957; *Much Ado About Nothing*, Stratford, Connecticut, 1957; *Monique*, 1957; *The Makropoulos Secret*, 1957; *The Chairs*, 1958; *The Lesson*, 1958; *The Infernal Machine*, 1958; *The Firstborn*, New York and Tel Aviv, 1958; *The Entertainer*, 1958; *The Shadow of a Gunman*, 1958; *A Midsummer Night's Dream*, Stratford, Connecticut, 1958; *Murder in the Cathedral*, 1958; *JB*, 1958; *The Beaux' Stratagem*, 1959; *The Rivalry*, 1959; *Once upon a Mattress*, 1959; *Romeo and Juliet*, *A Midsummer Night's Dream*, and *The Merry Wives of Windsor*, all Stratford, Connecticut, 1959; *The Great God Brown*, 1959; *Only in America*, 1959; *Five Finger Exercise*, 1959; *Peer Gynt*, 1960; *The Long Dream*, 1960; *The Tumbler*, 1960; *Twelfth Night*, *The Tempest*, and *Antony and Cleopatra*, all Stratford, Connecticut, 1960; *As You Like It* and *Macbeth*, both Stratford, Connecticut, 1961; *The Garden of Sweets*, 1961; *The Turn of the Screw*, *Anatol*, and *Elizabeth the Queen*, all at the American Theatre Festival, Boston, 1961; *Advise and Consent*, on tour, 1961; *Mary Stuart* and *Elizabeth the Queen*, both National Repertory Theatre tours, 1961; *The Skin of Our Teeth*, *The Glass Managerie*, and *The Miracle Worker*, all American Repertory Company State Department-sponsored tours, 1961; *Giants, Sons of Giants*, 1962; *Calculated Risk*, 1962; *Nowhere to Go But Up*, 1962; *HMS Pinafore* and *Androcles and the Lion*, both at the American Theatre Festival, Boston, 1962; *Andorra*, 1963; *Mother Courage and Her Children*, 1963; *King Lear*, *The Comedy of Errors*, and *Henry V*, all Stratford, Connecticut, 1963; *Here's Love*, 1963; *Marathon '33*, 1963; *Ring Round the Moon*, *The Seagull*, and *The Crucible*, all National Repertory Theatre tours, 1963; *Any Wednesday*, 1964; *Much Ado About Nothing*, *Richard III*, and *Hamlet*, all Stratford, Connecticut, 1964; *Golden Boy*, 1964; *Alfie*, 1964; *Hedda Gabler*, 1964; *Liliom*, 1964; *She Stoops to Conquer*, National Repertory Theatre tour, 1964; *Kelly*, 1965; *All in Good Time*, 1965; *Flora*, 1965; *The Red Menace*, 1965; *Coriolanus*, *Romeo and Juliet*, *The Taming of the Shrew*, and *King Lear*, all Stratford, Connecticut, 1965; *Mais Oui*, Beirut, 1965; *Minor Miracle*, 1965; *Rivals*, *The Madwoman of Chaillot*, and *The Trojan Women*, all National Repertory Theatre tours, 1965; *Malcolm*, 1966; *The Great Indoors*, 1966; *The Lion in Winter*, 1966; *Mame*, 1966; *Twelfth Night*, *Falstaff*, *Julius Caesar*, and *Murder in the Cathedral*, all Stratford, Connecticut, 1966; *A Delicate Balance*, 1966; *Tonight at 8:30*, *A Touch of the Poet*, and *The Imaginary Invalid*, all National Repertory Theatre tours, 1966; *Hallelujah, Baby!*, 1967; *A Midsummer Night's Dream*, *Antigone*, and *The Merchant of Venice*, all Stratford, Connecticut, 1967; *The Birthday Party*, 1967; *After the Rain*, 1967; *The Promise*, 1967; *Everything in the Garden*, 1967; *John Brown's Body* and *The Comedy of Errors*, both National Repertory Theatre tours, 1967; *House of Flowers*, 1968; *Catch My Soul*, Los Angeles, 1968; *Golden Boy*, Palladium, London, 1968; *As You Like It* and *Androcles and the Lion*, both Stratford, Connecticut, 1968; *The Lovers*, 1968; *Maggie Flynn*, 1968; *The Fig Leaves Are Falling*, 1969; *The Gingham Dog*, 1969; *Spofford*, on tour, 1969; *Mame*, Drury Lane, London, 1969; *Fedora*, Dallas Civic Opera, 1969; *Blood Red Roses*, 1970; *Applause*, 1970; *The Boy Friend*, 1970; *The Dream on Monkey Mountain* and *Rose Bloom*, both Los Angeles, 1970; *The Merry Widow*, *Madama Butterfly*, *Il Tabarro*, and *Carmina Burana*, all Dallas Civic Opera, 1970; *L.A. under Siege*, 1970; *The Trial of the Catonsville Nine*, Los Angeles, 1970; *Follies*, 1971; *The Trial of the Catonsville Nine*, 1971; *Who Wants to Be the Lone Ranger*, Los Angeles, 1971; *On the Town*, 1971; *The Prisoner of Second Avenue*, 1971; *Major Barbara*, Los Angeles, 1971; *Fidelio*, Dallas Civic Opera, 1971; *Night Watch*, 1972; *The Creation of the World and Other Business*, 1972; *The Great God Brown*, 1972; *Don Juan*, 1972; *The Sunshine Boys*, 1972; *Old Times*, Los Angeles, 1972; *The Dream on Donkey Mountain*, Munich, 1972; *Applause*, Her Majesty's Theatre, London, 1972; *A Little Night Music*, 1973; *Forget Me Not Lane*, Los Angeles, 1973; *Sondheim: A Musical Tribute*, 1973; *The Orphan*, 1973; *The Good Doctor*, 1973; *Andrea Chenier*, Dallas Civic Opera, 1973; *Candide*, 1974; *Saint Joan* and *The Last Charlatan*, both Los Angeles, 1974; *God's Favorite*, 1974; *Mack and Mabel*, 1974; *Good News*, 1974; *The Pearl Fishers*, Miami Opera Guild, 1974; *Lucrezia Borgia*, Dallas Civic Opera, 1974; *Mignon*, Dallas Civic Opera, 1974; *The Wiz*, 1975; *Same Time, Next Year*, 1975; *A Chorus Line*, 1975; *Me and Bessie*, 1975; *Tales of Hoffman*, Dallas Civic Opera, 1975; *The Flying Dutchman*, Miami Opera

Guild, 1975; *Pacific Overtures*, 1976; *Otello*, Miami Opera Guild, 1976; *1600 Pennsylvania Avenue*, 1976; *California Suite*, 1976; *A Chorus Line*, London, 1976; *Hooray U.S.A.!*, Miami Bicentennial Pageant, 1976; *Romeo and Juliet*, London Ballet Festival, 1977; *Doktor Faust*, Wolf Trap Foundation, Vienna, Virginia, 1977; *Chapter Two*, 1977; *The Act*, 1977; *Tribute*, 1978; *Ballroom*, 1978; *They're Playing Our Song*, 1979; *They're Playing Our Song*, London, 1979; *Terra Nova*, 1979; *Romantic Comedy*, 1979; *Whose Life Is It, Anyway?*, 1979; *1940's Radio Hour*, 1979; *Last Licks*, 1979; *The Roast*, 1980; *Children of A Lesser God*, 1980; *I Ought to Be in Pictures*, 1980; *42nd Street*, 1980; *Dreamgirls*, 1981; *Children of a Lesser God*, London, 1981; *Fools*, 1981; *Moony Shapiro's Songbook*, 1981; *Hoagy, Bix and Wolfgang*, Los Angeles, 1981; *Tales of Hollywood*, Los Angeles, 1982; *Special Occasions*, 1982; *Merlin*, 1983; *Brighton Beach Memoirs*, 1983; *Private Lives*, 1983; *The Real Thing*, 1984; *Open Admissions*, 1984; *Biloxi Blues*, 1985; *Odd Couple*, 1985; *Jerry's Girls*, 1985; *Broadway Bound*, 1986; *A Month of Sundays*, 1987; *Teddy and Alice*, 1987; *Rumors*, 1988; *Ziegfeld*, Paladium, London, 1988; *Dutch Landscape*, Los Angeles, 1989.

Publications:

On MUSSER: books—*The Biographical Encyclopaedia and Who's Who of the American Theatre*, edited by Walter Rigdon, New York 1966; *Contemporary Theatre, Film and Television 2*, Detroit 1986; *The Cambridge Guide to World Theatre*, edited by Martin Banham, Cambridge 1988; articles—in *Theatre Crafts* (New York), November/December 1974, November/December 1975, March/April 1979, August/September 1982; *Lighting Dimensions* (New York), June 1977; *Diversion* (New York), June 1982; *Christian Science Monitor* (Boston), 12 July 1982; *Popular Computing* (New York), August 1983.

Lighting design is a most difficult art to verbalize on. I am afraid the work must speak for itself. I am first, last, and always a designer, not a speaker or writer. Thanks to our technology, I believe theatre design in this country, particularly on Broadway, is the best in the world, and still improving.

—Tharon Musser

Tharon Musser is not only the most prolific lighting designer in American theatre history, she is also a pioneer. Since her first professional job as a designer off-Broadway in 1949, her work has brought respect to the lighting designer as a theatre professional. While helping to open a field previously closed to women, she has pioneered the practice of the lighting designer being part of a collaborative artistic team, working from the beginning of a production with the scenic designer, costume designer, and director. Finally, she has, almost singlehandedly, brought modern technology to the Broadway stage by initiating computerized lighting control.

At the American Shakespeare Festival, Musser has designed lighting for more than twenty-five productions, including *Much Ado About Nothing*, *A Midsummer Night's Dream*, *The Merry Wives of Windsor*, *Romeo and Juliet*, *Antony and Cleopatra*, *Twelfth Night*, *The Tempest*, *As You Like It*, *Macbeth*, *Henry V*, *Comedy of Errors*, *King Lear*, *Richard III*, *Hamlet*, *The Taming of the Shrew*, *Julius Caesar*, and *The Merchant of Venice*. Her versatility is exemplified by her very different work on Broadway with musicals such as *Hallelujah, Baby!*, *Applause*, *The Boy Friend*, *Follies*, *A Little Night Music*, *Mack and Mabel*, *Good News*, *The Wiz*, *Pacific Overtures*, *The Act*, *42nd Street*, *Ballroom*, and *A Chorus Line*. Moreover, Musser

is just as comfortable with contemporary plays as she is with Shakespeare and musical theatre. She designed the lighting for *Any Wednesday*, *A Delicate Balance*, *California Suite*, *Travesties*, *The Sunshine Boys*, *The Prisoner of Second Avenue*, *Chapter Two*, *Whose Life Is It Anyway?*, and *Same Time, Next Year*.

Musser's talent lies in her ability to paint with color and light, using the stage like a canvas in order to create subtleties of atmosphere and mood. Although she sees each production as an individual entity, one can see some telltale "brush-marks" in her work. For example, she prefers many lamps with a great many cues (e.g., more than 260 lighting cues in *Ballroom*); she experiments with new kinds of lamps and equipment to achieve special effects; she is well known for her preference for a "no-color green" gel and for her fast moving changes of lighting, which are now accomplished through computerized lighting panels. These computerized controls used in the majority of productions today, as a result of her innovation, permit faster, smoother changes of lights; they allow the technicians to run the production from in front of the stage, where they can see what is happening, rather than as before, from a black box off to the side backstage where they could only hear; and they make it possible for one or two technicians to run a show, where as previously it took many more.

Musser constantly experiments with new equipment and new methods of using lights in the theatre. In *Ballroom*, for example, she utilized new three-and-one-half-inch units with 750-watt lamps (rather than the approved 500-watt lamps) to replace the standard six-inch lamps for which she did not have room. She also used color-wheels and an old-fashioned mirror-ball to transform the ballroom into a place of magic. In *Dreamgirls*, Musser exploited all the techniques and technologies of lighting design to create a quickly moving world of showbusiness with lights everywhere; the lighting helps to shift the constantly changing locations of the musical's fast-paced action.

—John E. Hirsch

MYKKANEN, (August) Martti.
Finnish illustrator and graphic designer. Born in Iisalmi, 15 November 1926. Studied at the Central School of Design Arts, Helsinki, 1946–51, and as an exchange artist, in Basel, Switzerland, 1952. Married Raija Liisa Vuorela in 1954 (divorced, 1986); daughters: Raili and Riitta. Graphic artist, working with the Cooperative Chain, Helsinki, 1946–52; illustrator, *Uusi Kuvalehti* weekly magazine, Helsinki, 1953–54; freelance graphic designer, working for Gummerus, Tammi, WSOY, Lahti Art Museum, Talja Traffic Safety Association, OKO Bankers consumer magazine, *Look at Finland* magazine, etc., in Helsinki, since 1955. **Exhibitions:** *Martti Mykkanen: Posters of the 1950s and 1960s*, Lahti Art Museum, Finland, 1989. **Collections:** Stedelijk Museum, Amsterdam; Royal Ontario Museum, Toronto; Poster Museum, Warsaw; Lahti Art Museum, Finland. Recipient: First Prize, Book Cover Competition, Helsinki, 1957, 1958, 1959; Ulkomainos Oy Scholarship, Helsinki, 1966; City of Helsinki Scholarship, 1970; Gold Medal, Travel Poster Competition, Catania, 1971; Goldene Reisekutsche Award, Darmstadt, 1973; State Industrial Design Award, Helsinki, 1979; Björn

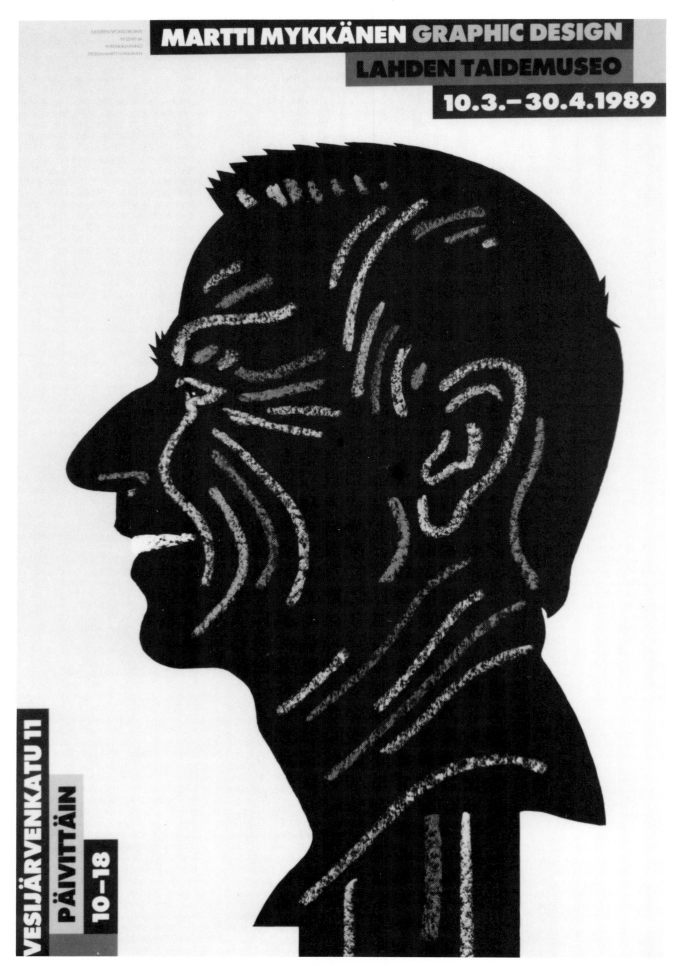

Martti Mykkanen: Exhibition poster for the Lahti Poster Museum, 1989

Landström Award, Helsinki, 1986; Czech Peace Council Award, Brno, 1988. Member, Alliance Graphique Internationale, 1966. Address: Mannerheimintie 146 A 32, 00270 Helsinki, Finland.

Works:

The Lamb (F. Mauriac) book cover, for WSOY, 1955.
The Winter (F. Griese) book cover, for WSOY, 1955.
Small Gods (R. Wright) book cover, for WSOY, 1955.
Alberte Is Alone (C. Sandel) book cover, for Gummerus, 1955.
The Red Room (A. Strindberg) book cover, for Gummerus, 1955.
Story of the Seven Hanged (L. Andrejev) book cover, for Gummerus, 1957.
Starvelin Artist (F. Kafka) book cover, for Gummerus, 1959.
Beggar's Novel (B. Brecht) book cover, for Tammi, 1959.
Love of the Old Prince (F. Dostojevski) book cover, for Gummerus, 1960.
Too Late, Water Swallow (A. Paton) book cover, for WSOY, 1963.
Ulysses (J. Joyce) book cover, for Tammi, 1963.
Poster, for the Finnish Heart Disease Association, 1967.
Remember the Danger When Driving Fast poster, for Talja Traffic Safety Association, 1967.
Gallery of the Street poster, for Ulkomainos Oy, 1969.
Design '81 poster, for the Helsinki Design Congress, 1981.
5th Poster Biennale poster, for Lahti Art Museum, 1982.
Finnish Graphic Planning poster, for Association of Graphic Artists, 1983.
Finnish Graphic Design in Oslo poster, for Graphic Designers Association, 1986.
Martti Mykkanen: Graphic Design poster, for Lahti Art Museum, 1989.

Publications:

On MYKKANEN: books—*Poster Design* by Tom Eckersley, London 1954; *Posters of Protest and Revolution* by Maurice Rickards, Milan 1970; *History of the Poster* by Josef and Shizuko Muller-Brockman, Zurich 1971; *Den Massproducerade Bilden* by Lena Johannesson, Stockholm 1978; *Who's Who in Graphic Art*, edited by Walter Amstutz, Dubendorf 1982; *The Modern Poster* by Stuart Wrede, Barcelona 1988; *Martti Mykkanen: Posters of the 1950s and 1960s*, exhibition catalogue with text by Riitta Niskanen, Lahti 1989; articles—"Martti Mykkanen—Finland" by Ludwig Ebenhoh in *Gebrauchsgraphik* (Munich), no. 11, 1957; "From Pure Art to Poster War" by Osmo Pasanen in *Form Function Finland* (Helsinki), no. 1/2, 1980; "The Poster—A Mini-Scandal" by Ullamaria Pallasmaa in *Look at Finland* (Helsinki), no. 1, 1983.

NAGAI, Kazumasa.

Japanese graphic designer. Born in Osaka, 20 April 1929. Studied sculpture, at Tokyo National University of Fine Arts and Music, 1949–51. Married Setsuko Sakuma in 1978; son: Kazufumi. Worked as a graphic designer, for Daiwa Spinning Company, Osaka, 1951–60; founder-designer from 1960, president, 1975–86, and representative director from 1986, of the Nippon Design Center, Tokyo: has designed for Asahi Breweries, Sapporo Winter Olympics, Suruga Bank, *Space Design* magazine, Toyama Museum of Modern Art, Takashimaya Department Stores, Tenri Religious Organization, etc. Member, Tokyo Designer's Space, from 1976; executive vice-president, Japan Graphic Designers Association, Tokyo, from 1980. **Exhibitions:** Museum of Modern Art, Warsaw, 1968; Ichibankan Gallery, Tokyo, 1968, 1970; Imabashi Gallery, Osaka, 1968, 1975; Plaza Dick, Tokyo, 1971; Fuma Gallery, Tokyo, 1975; Tokyo Designer's Space, 1975, 1978, 1981; Green Collections, Tokyo, 1975; Mikimoto Gallery, Tokyo, 1978; Nick Gallery, Fukuoka, 1978; Matsuya Department Store, Tokyo, 1978; Ikeda Museum, Ito City, 1980; Ginza Itoya Gallery, Tokyo, 1982; Gallery Coco, Kyoto, 1982; Gallery Tableaux 5, Takamatsu, 1982; Parco Gallery, Tokyo, 1982; Gallery Eme, Tokyo, 1983; University of Quebec, Montreal, 1985; Inax Gallery, Tokyo, 1985; Machida Municipal Print Museum, Tokyo, 1988; Gallery Aries, Tokyo 1988; Municipal Museum, Himeji, 1988. **Collections:** National Museum of Art, Tokyo; Ikeda 20th Century Museum, Ito City; Poster Museum, Warsaw; Museum of Modern Art, New York; Konstindustrimuseet, Copenhagen; Musee de la Publicite, Paris; Kunstgewerbemuseum, Zurich; Australian National Gallery, Canberra; Israel Museum, Jerusalem. Recipient: Tokyo Art Directors Club Award, 1962, 1983; Warsaw Poster Biennale Medals, 1966, 1968; Japanese Advertising Artists Club Prize, 1966; Mainichi Design Prize, Tokyo, 1966, 1983; Asahi Advertising Prize, Tokyo, 1966; National Museum of Modern Art Prize, Tokyo, 1968; Yamana Prize, Tokyo, 1980; Japan Graphic Design Exhibition Prize, New York, 1981, 1984; Brno Graphic Design Biennale Award, 1984, 1988; Japanese Ministry of Art Prize, 1988. Member: Art Directors Club of Tokyo, 1965; Japan Design Committee, Tokyo, 1975; Alliance Graphique Internationale, Paris, 1984. Address: c/o Nippon Design Center, Chuo-Daiwa Building, 1–13–13 Ginza Chuo-ku, Tokyo 104, Japan.

Works:

Growth poster, for Time-Life science book series, 1966.

Expo '75 poster, for the Okinawa International Ocean Exposition Organizing Committee, 1972.

GQ print magazine poster, for GQ Publishing Company, 1974.

Wallpaper poster, for Kawakichi Company, 1974.

Posters for Adonis Printing Company, 1976.

Kazumasa Nagai exhibition poster, for Mikimoto Hall, Tokyo, 1978.

The World of Kazumasa Nagai exhibition poster, for Ikeda Museum of 20th Century Art, Ito City, 1980.

Kazumasa Nagai touring exhibition poster, for the Gallery Nurihiko, Tokyo, 1982.

Contemporary Japanese Posters exhibition poster, for the Museum of Modern Art, Toyama, 1982.

Shuzo Takiguchi and His Favorite Postwar Arts exhibition poster, for the Museum of Modern Art, Toyama, 1982.

Tradition et Nouvelles Techniques: 12 Graphistes Japonais exhibition poster, for the French Ministry of Culture, 1984.

Georges Rouault's Prints exhibition poster, for the Museum of Modern Art, Toyama, 1984.

Hiroshima Appeals '87 poster, for the Hiroshima International Cultural Foundation/ Japan Graphic Designers Association, 1987.

4–G.D., Posters and Marks exhibition poster, for the Four Graphic Designers Exhibition Executive Committee, Tokyo, 1987.

Japan posters, for the Four Graphic Designers Exhibition Executive Committee, Tokyo, 1987.

Japan posters, for the JAGDA Japan Graphic Designers Association, 1988.

Images Internationales pour les Droits de l'Homme et du Citoyen poster, for the French Revolution Bicentenary Mission, Paris, 1988.

Publications:

By NAGAI: books—*Art Direction,* Tokyo 1968; *On Contemporary Design,* with others, Tokyo 1968; *Twelve Graphic Designers,* with others, Tokyo 1968; *Brief History of Japanese Design,* with others, Tokyo 1970; *Graphic Design in the World,* with Hideo Mukai and Yusuke Kaji, Tokyo 1974; *Posters by Kazumasa Nagai,* Tokyo 1976; *Japan's Art Direction,* with Seiichiro Arai, Yusuke Kaji and Ikko Tanaka, Tokyo 1977; *Ads Change; Change Ads,* with others, Tokyo 1979; *The Works of Kazumasa Nagai,* Tokyo 1985.

On NAGAI: books—*An International Survey of Press Advertising,* edited by Kurt Weidemann, Stuttgart and London 1966; *An International Survey of Packaging* by Wim Crouwel and Kurt Weidemann, London 1968; *History of the Poster* by Josef and Shizuko Müller-Brockmann, Zürich 1971; *Ten Print Artists* by Shozo Kawai, Tokyo 1976; *Graphic Designers* by Seiichiro Arai, Tokyo 1981; *Who's Who in Graphic Art,* edited by Walter Amstutz, Dubendorf 1982.

*

Over the past several years, I have been striving to bring out my own personal, individual consciousness in my design work. I have been doing this because stereotyped advertising and designs are ineffective in this age of wave after wave of information. Although there seem to be certain effective styles that have been established for use in mass communication media, I can never simply repeat such styles.

What I have gained confidence in, however, is something very similar to "personal communication," or, so to speak, the transmitting of ideas to specific individuals. In the ultimate analysis, this is like talking to oneself.

Can I be allowed to have such an idea, however? Most probably, I can't. This is because each poster design—which is usually printed in a volume of several thousand—is viewed by many people. Although I consider poster art the best form of expression that I can trust, on close examination, however, it's impossible to expect every one of the scores of thousands of people who look at a poster to get so much out of it that that poster would be remembered or that everyone would get an identical feeling and effect from seeing that poster. Any such expectation would be merely a fruitless delusion.

A design produced from such a delusive expectation would have to be composed of the most common elements, and such a design would surely quickly disappear into the overflowing sea of information without leaving a trace. Instead of entertaining such false expectations, the artist would do better to express himself to the very best of his ability by aiming at only a few select individuals, perhaps a couple of dozen people who will definitely gain a strong impression from his poster design. In this way, the artist will be sure to effect at least some communication.

I'm afraid the world—especially Japan—has been working too hard for economic success. Most corporations have been seeking material wealth by making profits their major goal, for the just cause that they might eventually offer such material richness to all. Advertising and design, too, have been playing a strong role as a detached force at the commercial warfront for corporate purposes. As a result, we have to realize that something valuable has gone down the drain. An alarm bell has begun to peal its warning that the way companies are racing faster and faster in search of profits, all humanity may be ruined. The environment and culture in which corporations are located deserve more serious consideration. We must discover the way in which our spirit and human mind can peacefully exist in today's society, where materialism has achieved a dominant place. The money Japan has spent on culture in this sense, compared with that of other advanced countries, is so petty and infinitesimal that we should feel ashamed.

Some Japanese corporations are well aware that their future existence may not be permitted without attempts to improve the local environ-

Kazumasa Nagai: *Japan* poster for the *Four Graphic Designers* exhibition, Tokyo, 1988

ment, culture and the arts. And, it is true that some of them have recently begun concrete activities for such community purposes. Still, most corporations are not aware of the importance of returning some portion of their business profits to society.

Concrete, coordinated, cultural and artistic activities for corporate image-building are badly needed both in Japan and around the world. That, I think, is becoming an important role for today's graphic designers. I hope to take a leading part in this activity.

—Kazumasa Nagai

The ability to skillfully combine abstract expression and realistic demands has been a characteristic feature of Kazumasa Nagai's work. Nagai states that it is easier to express his inner self with abstraction, but that no doubt has something to do with the fact that he studied sculpture as a student. Nagai's graphic expression is not something which presses one urgently; rather, it persuades quietly. At the same time, however, his modeling shows firmness. In early works, he pursued form, but in recent years, he has added the techniques of color and collage, and his works have gained a certain liveliness.

Nagai has, on the one hand, for quite some time directed a business as president of a design production company, while on the other, he also practices art, particularly printmaking. In addition, he is in a position of leadership in the Japan Graphic Designers Association.

—Masaaki Tanaka

NAKAMURA, Makoto.

Japanese graphic designer. Born in Iwate, 9 May 1936. Studied design, at the University of Arts, Tokyo, 1944–48. Married Shoko Nakamura in 1953; son: Seiichi. Staff designer, 1948–83, and advertising and design manager from 1983, at Siseido Cosmetics Company, Tokyo. **Exhibitions:** Mona Lisa Smile Exhibition, Tokyo, 1972; International Posters, Musée des Arts Décoratifs, Paris, 1972; Warsaw Poster Biennale, 1978; Makoto Nakamura: Posters, Art Directors Club of New York, 1983. **Collections:** Musée des Arts Décoratifs, Paris; Museum of Modern Art, New York. Recipient: Japan Advertising Art Association Award, Tokyo; Tokyo Art Directors Club Award; Ministry of International Trade and Industry Awards, Tokyo; Dentsu Advertising Art Award, Tokyo; Warsaw Poster Biennale Award; Kinugasa Award, Tokyo; Yamana Award, Tokyo. Member of the Art Directors Club of Tokyo, and the Art Directors Club of New York. Address: 1403 Hongo House, 1-28-7 Hongo, Bunkyo-ku, Tokyo, Japan.

Publications:

By NAKAMURA: book—One Hundred Smiles of Mona Lisa, Tokyo 1971.

On NAKAMURA: books—Art Directors Club Yearbook, Tokyo 1980; Ten Poster Artists of the World by Idea editors, Tokyo 1982; Makoto Nakamura: Poster Works, exhibition folder, with text by Kazumasa Nagai, New York 1983.

I like to create a cheerful and happy picture

through graphic design in advertising. I hope that the advertisements will be enjoyed by the consumers who view them and that they will have a positive influence on their lives. I hope my work contributes to the culture of everyday life. Further, I wish to express the beauty of Japanese women in pictures through advertising.

—Makoto Nakamura

Makoto Nakamura came to maturity within the enterprise of Shiseido, which has had a tradition ever since its founding as one of the most prominent advertisers in Japan and at which many designers are directly employed because the company does not rely on agencies for its design.

Not surprisingly, therefore, Nakamura is not the type of designer who possesses a strong individuality; rather, as art director and as head of the department of design in that company, he exhibits a well-rounded personality. He often collaborates with photographers and his skillful layouts of those photographs always have great freshness.

—Masaaki Tanaka

NAPIER, John.

British stage designer. Born in London, 1 March 1944. Studied at Hornsey College of Art, London, 1961–62; Central School of Arts and Crafts, London, 1962–66. Married Andreane Neofitou: 3 children; married Donna King: 1 son. Freelance stage designer, working with the Phoenix Theatre, Leicester, 1967–68, London West End theatres from 1968, the National Theatre, London, from 1973, and the Royal Shakespeare Company in London and Stratford-upon-Avon, from 1974. **Exhibition:** British Theatre Design 83–87, Riverside Studios, Hammersmith, London, 1988. Recipient: Society of West End Theatres Award, London, 1977, 1978, 1980; Antoinette Perry (Tony) Award, New York, 1981, 1982, 1987. Member, British Society of Theatre Designers; associate member Royal Shakespeare Company, London. Address: c/o McNaughton Lowe Representation, 200 Fulham Road, London SW10, England.

Works:

Stage productions (London, unless noted) include—A Penny for a Song, Phoenix Theatre, Leicester, 1967; Fortune and Men's Eyes, 1968; The Ruling Class, 1969; The Fun War, 1969; Muzeeka, 1969; Cancer, 1970; Isabel's A Jezebel, 1970; Mister, 1971; The Foursome, 1971; The Lovers of Viorne, 1971; Lear, 1971; Jump, 1972; Sam, Sam, 1972; Big Wolf, 1972; The Devils, Sadlers Wells Theatre, 1973; Equus, Old Vic, 1973; The Party, Old Vic, 1973; Knuckle, 1974; King John, Shakespeare Memorial Theatre, Stratford, 1974; Richard III, Shakespeare Memorial Theatre, Stratford, 1974; Cymbeline, Shakespeare Memorial Theatre, Stratford, 1974; MacBeth, Shakespeare Memorial Theatre, Stratford, 1974; Richard II, Shakespeare Memorial Theatre, Stratford, 1974; Hedda Gabler, 1975; A Midsummer Night's Dream, Royal Shakespeare Company, 1977; As You Like It, Royal Shakespeare Company, 1977; Twelfth Night, Royal Shakespeare Company, 1978; Three Sisters, Royal Shake-

speare Company, 1978; Comedy of Errors, Royal Shakespeare Company, 1978; Nicholas Nickleby, Royal Shakespeare Company, 1980; Cats, 1981 (also Winter Garden Theatre, New York, 1982); Henry IV, Royal Shakespeare Company, Barbican Theatre, 1982; Starlight Express, 1984 (and Broadway, New York, 1987); Les Miserables, 1985 (and Broadway, New York, 1987); Time, 1986; Miss Saigon, 1989; The Baker's Wife, 1989.

Publications:

By NAPIER: book—William Shakespeare: Cymbeline, illustrator, London 1976; article—in The Designer (London), April 1981.

On NAPIER: books—Who's Who in the Theatre, edited by Ian Herbert, London 1977; British Theatre Design 83–87, with texts by Timothy O'Brien and David Fingleton, London 1988; Contemporary Theatre, Film and Television, Detroit 1988; British Theatre Design, edited by John Goodwin, London 1989.

John Napier does not see himself as a pictorial or decorative artist working with abstract forms in a studio remote from the theatre. Instead, he seeks intensively cooperative work, much of which evolves on stage during rehearsals. Preferring productions of human-centered action, he reflects the general tendency of recent art towards neo-realism. Napier's realism, however, dispenses with traditional forms of scenic illusion in favor of assemblages of materials and found objects. "I don't care if it's not naturalistic, but I can't believe in artificiality," he has asserted. Moreover, in his drive for fuller audience involvement with a production, he has often altered the interiors of theatres to create forms of environmental staging: for Equus (National Theatre, 1973), he sat part of the audience at the rear and sides of a proscenium stage; for Nicholas Nickleby (1980) and Cats (1981), he joined audience and acting areas by ramps and bridges.

His background and special interests have lead to two distinct types of scenography. One reflects a spare, highly selective side of his sculpture training as well as a minimalist tradition in modern British staging, largely associated with the Royal Court Theatre. In Royal Shakespeare Company productions such as A Midsummer Night's Dream (1977), As You Like It (1977), Twelfth Night (1978), and Chekhov's Three Sisters (1978), relatively few scenic elements were carefully composed within a large space. Conversely, productions such as the Royal Shakespeare Company's Comedy of Errors (1978), Nicholas Nickleby, and Cats reflect a more flamboyant part of Napier's talent—his urge to fill the stage with objects and structures, some found, some hammered or chiseled out of unfinished materials.

Here, echoes of pop art and environmental art of the 1960s combine with his sculptural feel for space and matter, as well as his attraction to tangible reality, no matter how unusually organized. For Shakespeare's Henry IV, the initial production at the Royal Shakespeare Company's new Barbican Theatre in 1982, for example, he created mobile sculptures in the form of four huge towers on wheels; these seemingly random artifacts of the fifteenth century evoked an entire age with great vitality. In another example, for the New York production of Cats (1982), he broke through the roof of the Winter Garden Theatre to erect an inclined track for the spectacular, rocket-like heavenly ascension of one of the characters at the climax of the musical's action.

—Jarka M. Burian

NELSON, George.

American architect and industrial designer. Born in Hartford, Connecticut, 29 May 1908. Studied at Yale University, New Haven, Connecticut, 1926-31: BA 1928, BFA 1931; Catholic University of America, Washington, D.C., 1932; American Academy in Rome, 1932-34. Freelance architect and designer, in partnership with William Hamby, New York, 1936-41; president, George Nelson Associates industrial design firm, New York, from 1946: design director, Herman Miller Furniture Company, Zeeland, Michigan, from 1946; partner, Nelson and Chadwick architects, New York, from 1953. Instructor in design, Yale University, New Haven, Connecticut, 1931-32, Columbia University, New York, 1941-44; design consultant, University of Georgia, Athens, 1952-55, Boston Museum School of Fine Arts, 1968-69; visiting critic in architecture, Harvard University, Cambridge, Massachusetts, 1972-73; visiting professor, Pratt Institute, Brooklyn, New York, 1975-77. Associate editor, 1935-43, co-managing editor, 1943-44, and consultant, 1944-49, of *Architectural Forum* magazine, New York; head of *Fortune-Forum* experimental department, Time Incorporated, New York, 1944-45; editor, *Interiors* magazine, New York, 1948-75; editor-in-chief, *Design Journal*, New York, 1968-73. Member, Conseil Superieur de la Creation Esthetique Industrielle, Paris, and New York State Council on Architecture, 1968-75; board member, Industrial Designers Society of America, 1969-76, and Aspen Design Conference, Colorado, from 1965; committee member, Centre de Creation Industrielle, Paris, 1970. **Exhibition:** *Nelson/Eames/Girard/Probst: Design at Herman Miller,* Walker Art Center, Minneapolis, 1975. **Collections:** Museum of Modern Art, New York; Brooklyn Museum, New York; Philadelphia Museum of Art; Musee des Arts Decoratifs, Montreal. Recipient: American Institute of Architects Industrial Design Medal, 1964, and Medal of Honor, 1979; Industrial Designers Society of America Award, 1974, 1981; American Society of Interior Designers Elsie de Wolfe Award, 1975, DFA: Parsons School of Design, New York, 1979, Minneapolis College of Art and Design, 1980. Fellow, American Institute of Architects, 1963, Industrial Designers Society of America, 1968; Honorary Royal Designer for Industry, Royal Society of Arts, London, 1973. *Died* (in New York City) *5 March 1986.*

Works:

Storagewall cupboard and shelving system, for Herman Miller, 1944 (with Henry Wright).
Basic Cabinet storage system series, for Herman Miller, 1947.
Herman Miller showrooms, in Chicago, 1948, New York, 1953, 1966, and in Washington, D.C., 1964.
Wall clock with brass and birch housing, for Howard Miller Clock Company, 1949.
Bubble lamp, for Howard Miller Clock Company, 1952.
Florence Ware table service in melamine, for Prolon, 1955.
Kangaroo upholstered club chair with steel legs, for Herman Miller, 1956.
Omni System furniture, for Structural Products, 1956.
Marshmallow Sofa in steel with leather-covered foam upholstery, for Herman Miller, 1956.
Fire alarm unit, for Acme Fire Alarm Company, 1958.
Design Today in America and Europe touring exhibition design, for the Government of India, 1958.

Swag-legged chair with fiberglass shell, for Herman Miller, 1958.
Loeb Student Center interiors in La Guardia Place, for New York University, 1959.
Herman Miller factory, Zeeland, Michigan, 1962-66.
U.S.—Us Show touring exhibition design, for Herman Miller Company, 1963.
Industrial Design USA touring exhibition design, for the United States Information Agency, 1967.
AO2 Action Office furniture system, for Herman Miller, 1968 (with Robert Propst).
Rosenthal Studio showrooms in New York, for Rosenthal Porcelain, 1968.
The First Two Hundred Years touring exhibition design, for the American Bicentennial Administration, 1974-76.
Design Since 1945 exhibition design, for Philadelphia Museum of Art, 1983.

(for a complete list of Nelson's buildings and architectural projects, see *Contemporary Architects*)

Publications:

By NELSON: books—*Industrial Architecture of Albert Kahn Inc.,* New York 1939; *Tomorrow's House,* with Henry Wright, New York 1946; *Living Spaces,* editor, New York 1952; *Chairs,* editor, New York 1953; *Display,* editor, New York 1953; *Storage,* New York 1954; *Problems of Design,* New York 1957, Tokyo 1960; *How To See: Visual Adventures in a World God Never Made,* Boston 1978; *George Nelson on Design,* New York 1979.

On NELSON: books—*Public Interiors* by Misha Black, London 1960; *Art and Design in Home Living* by F. M. Obst, New York and London 1963; *Design in America,* edited by Ralph Caplan, New York 1969; *Interior Design: An Introduction to Architectural Interiors* by Arnold Friedmann, John F. Pile and Forrest Wilson, New York and Amsterdam 1970, 1976; *The Modern Chair: Classics in Production* by Clement Meadmore, London 1974; *In Good Shape: Style and Design in Industrial Products Since 1960* by Stephen Bayley, London 1979; *Industrial Design* by John Heskett, London 1980; *Contemporary Furniture* by Klaus-Jurgen Sembach, Stuttgart and London 1982; *Mid-Century: Furniture of the 1950s* by Cara Greenberg, London 1985; *Modern Furniture Classics* by Miriam Stimpson, London 1987; *Office Furniture* by Lance Knobel, London 1987; *New American Design* by Hugh Aldersley-Williams, New York 1988; *The American Design Adventure 1940-1975* by Arthur J. Pulos, London and Cambridge, Massachusetts 1988.

During my undergraduate years, a chance exposure to an exhibit of student drawings created a strong desire to become an architect. It took some years to discover that what had attracted me was architecture as expression rather than technique. I enjoyed these years enormously and even more, the two subsequent years at the American Academy in Rome, which provided an almost explosive expansion of awareness.

Returning to New York at the bottom of the Depression provided a very different experience, and I had prepared for unemployment by writing a series of articles on the leading modern architects of Europe. These were published and led to a job with *Architectural Forum,* which again provided a series of invaluable experiences. During this period an association with William Hamby brought me back into architectural work, culminating in a townhouse for Sherman Fairchild; this drastically revised the traditional plan by splitting the house into two elements with a court and glassed-in ramp in between. The house was finished in 1941,

when the war broke out, terminating architectural activity for a number of years.

Work at *Architectural Forum* led to a book assignment, *Tomorrow's House* (with Henry Wright), and this in turn triggered the creation of the Storagewall, a device which quickly became a standard element in dwellings and offices. Publications of this project came to the attention of Herman Miller, a Michigan furniture manufacturer, and an association developed which has continued to the present. An office was opened in 1946, and in subsequent years a very broad range of work—furniture design, graphics, packaging, corporate identity, exhibitions, commercial interiors, products and architecture—was carried out.

During the period from 1946 to the present, many changes have taken place. There were no schools for industrial design at the beginning; now a large network turns out hundreds of graduates each year. The typical client has changed radically, from a hands-on manufacturer to management more concerned with marketing, promotion, and the bottom line than the product. In the society itself, the direction can perhaps be best described as a lack of direction, accompanied by steadily reduced standards of living, greatly reduced literacy, and a general decline in morale. At the same time, this period has been one of great creative activity in science, notably cosmology, paleontology, molecular biology, and subatomic physics.

This paradoxical coexistence of increasing dehumanization and alienation, characteristic of a technological society in its later stages, and vigorous work and brilliant accomplishment in a limited number of disciplines is, of course, the mark of a society in a state of radical, massive transformation.

It is thus possible to say, not for the first time in our short and turbulent history, that we are living in the best of times and the worst. If humanity survives the present series of crises, a great leap towards maturity is a possibility.

—George Nelson

In the infancy of the industrial design profession, George Nelson came from an education as an architect, as did Eliot Noyes and Charles Eames, to become one of the most important design theorists and practitioners. During the prewar years in Europe, Nelson's interviews with modern European architects marked an early consummation of his skills at analytical thought and expository writing. Curiosity about the future implications of a designed world led him to investigate further the growth of American architecture and design in his work on the editorial staff of *Architectural Forum* and later in two books: *The Industrial Architecture of Albert Kahn,* and, with Henry Wright, *Tomorrow's House.*

Nelson's accomplishments in both the theory and practice of design reflect an enduring curiosity about process. He continually asks why (or, more often, why not), and then seeks out answers. This procedure can be traced through the successes of his career. Why do we need more verbiage on the history of architecture when there is so much happening today in Europe?—which led to an editorial career. Why can't walls be used as more than partitions?—which led to his storagewall concept. Why is design necessary to modern society?—which led to his own continuing series of essays on such topics as "Design as Communication," "Obsolescence," "The Future of Packaging," and "A New Profession?"

Nelson has worked in association with some of the leaders of contemporary industrial design, including Charles Eames and Alexander Girard at Herman Miller and Buckminster Fuller, and he has collaborated with other de-

George Nelson: Plastic exhibit umbrellas, for the *American National Exhibition*, Moscow, 1959

signers in the search for the ultimate "Seating Tool" and with the British design group Pentagram. From inside the design profession, he has focused a critical eye on the role of design as it contends with function, technology, and social values. He has illuminated through insightful, often humorous prose the responsibilities of the designer first to comprehend and then possibly adjust the modern world. In this activity, he emphasizes process rather than dwelling on discreet objects, which leads him to such definitions as "good design is the mani-

festation of the capacity of the human spirit to transcend its limitations." A predictor of the future trends, Nelson foresaw in the 1950s the breaking down of arbitrary lines between art and design disciplines; he saw that industry and the "real world" would have an impact on education in the 1960s; and he saw the office revolution as affecting society as a whole in the 1970s and 1980s. This thinking has profoundly influenced the first and subsequent generations of industrial designers to examine and reexamine their profession and its goals. At the same

time, Nelson debunks the myth of industrial design as magical process by showing that designers are people.

—Sarah Bodine

NEUBURG, Hans.

Swiss industrial, display and graphic designer. Born in Grulich, Czechoslovakia, 20 March 1904; emigrated to Switzerland in 1910: naturalized, 1954. Educated at Elementarschule, Hamburg, 1909–10, and at schools in Zurich, 1910–18; studied at the Art Institut Orell Füssli, Zürich, 1919–22. Married Stefi Kovacic in 1934. Worked as a copywriter and text editor, Max Dalang design agency, Zurich, 1928–29; freelance publicity specialist, working with Max Bill, Anton Stankowski, Herbert Matter, Heiri Steiner and others, in Zürich, 1930–31; propaganda chief, for AWZ, Basel, 1931–32; advertising manager, Jean Haecky Import, Basel, 1932–36; freelance advertising and graphic designer, Zurich, from 1936: designed for Leibig, Gebrüder Sulzer, Von Roll, Von Moos, Bern Hyspa Exhibition, International Red Cross, Basel Mustermesse, etc. Editor, *Industrie-Werbung* magazine, Basel, 1933–37; picture editor, *Actualis* daily, Zurich, 1941; founder-editor, *Chamaleon* magazine, Zurich, 1946; sports journalist, *Die Tat* and *Weltwoche*, Zurich, 1950; editor, *Camera* magazine, Lucerne, 1952–53; art critic, for *Weltwoche*, *Werk*, *Neue Zurcher Zeitung* and *Tagenanzeiger* periodicals, Zürich, 1958, and *Zürcher Woche*, 1962; founder-editor, with Richard Paul Lohse, Josef Müller-Brockmann and Carlo Vivarelli, of *Neue Grafik* magazine, Olten, 1958; picture editor and layout artist, *Woche* magazine, Olten, 1963. Director, Arts and Crafts Museum, Winterthur, 1962–64. Instructor, Hochschule für Gestaltung, Ulm, from 1963; instructor in abstract art, Migros Klubschule, Zurich. Ortsgruppe president from 1959, and central president from 1960, Verband Schweizer Grafiker, Zurich; vice-president, ICOGRADA International Council of Graphic Design Associations, 1963. **Exhibition:** *107 Grafici dell'AGI,* Castello Sforzesco, Milan, 1974. Extraordinary member, Schweizerischer Werkbund, 1962; honorary president, Verband Schweizerischer Grafiker; member, Alliance Graphique Internationale, Paris. *Died* (in Zürich) *in 1983.*

Publications:

By NEUBURG: books—*Moderne Werbe- und Gebrauchsgraphik,* Ravensburg 1960; *Rund um den Buchdruck,* Zürich 1962; *Richard Paul Lohse: 60 Geburtstag,* editor, Teufen 1962; *Fritz Krebs,* Zürich 1973.

On NEUBURG: books—*The New Graphic Design* by Karl Gerstner and Markus Kutter, Teufen and London 1959; *Who's Who in Graphic Art,* edited by Walter Amstutz, Zürich 1962, Dubendorf 1982; *Hans Neuburg,* with texts by Max Bill, Anton Stankowski and others, Teufen 1964; *Das Plakat* by Anton Sailer, Munich 1965; *Signet, Signal, Symbol: Handbook of International Signs* by Walter and Marion Diethlem, Zürich 1970; *History of the Poster* by Josef and Shizuko Müller-Brockmann, Zürich 1971; *107 Grafici dell'AGI,* exhibition catalogue with texts by Renzo Zorzi and Franco Grignani, Venice 1974; *Les Années 60* by Anne Bony, Paris 1983; *A History of Graphic Design* by Philip B. Meggs, New York and London 1983.

NEUMEISTER, Alexander.

German industrial designer. Born in Berlin, 17 December 1941. Educated at Saint Theresa's Academy, Boise, Idaho, 1955–56, and at schools in Germany, 1957–62; studied industrial design, at the Hochschule fur Gestaltung, Ulm, 1963–67, and at Tokyo University of Arts, 1968–69. Married Gudrun Heinle in 1969; daughters: Sarah and Laura. Freelance designer and head of Neumeister Design, Munich, from 1969; partner, in Axis Design Rio industrial design firm, Rio de Janeiro, from 1988: has designed medical equipment, transport and data communication systems for German Federal Railways, AEG Magnetbahn, Loewe Opta, MBB, Dornier Medical Division, Thyssen Henschel, PCS, Kontron, etc. Lecturer in industrial design, Fachhochschule, Munich, 1975–80. Group coordinator for design in developing countries, VDID German Association of Industrial Designers, 1975–87; vice-president, ICSID International Council of Societies of Industrial Design, 1985–87. Recipient: Carozzeria Bertone Sports Car Design Prize, Turin, 1968; Table 80 Design Prize, Hamburg, 1971; Gesika Office Furniture Design Prize, Hannover, 1973; Brunel Design Award, 1988; plus numerous Stuttgart Design Center and Hannover Gute Industrieform awards. Address: Neumeister Design, von Goebel Platz 8, 8000 Munich 19, West Germany.

Works:

Maglev Transrapid TR06 magnetic levitation train, for Thyssen Henschel, 1982.
ICE intercity experimental train, for German Federal Railways, 1985.
Medilas 30 medical laser, for MBB, 1987.
VideoCom video-conference unit, for MBB Erno, 1988.
Maglev Transrapid TR07 magnetic levitation train, for Thyssen Henschel, 1988.
City trolleybus, for VOV, 1988–90.
MoDiC mobile diagnosis computer, for MBB Gelma/BNW, 1989.
Lithotripter-Compact medical diagnostic equipment, for Dornier Medical Division, 1989.
Aircraft seating, for Recaro, 1989.
Passenger transfer train, for AEG-Magnetbahn, 1989–90.

Publications:

By NEUMEISTER: book—*Design Promotion: Facts and Arguments,* with Gudrun Neumeister, Munic 1981; articles—in *Form* (Opladen), no. 71, 1975, no. 83, 1978, no. 99, 1982; *Design*

Alexander Neumeister: *Maglev Transrapid TRO6* magnetic levitation train, for Thyssen Henschel, 1982

News Japan (Tokyo), no. 144, 1981, no. 135, 1982; *Design Quarterly* (Tokyo), no. 2, 1982.

On NEUMEISTER: articles—in *Domus* (Milan), no. 598, 1979, no. 616, 1981; *Industrial Design* (New York), September 1979; *Design News Japan* (Tokyo), no. 1, 1980; *Technique and Design in USSR* (Moscow), no. 3, 1983.

Right from the beginning of my professional career, I have chosen to specialize in the design of investment goods, namely transportation systems, medical equipment, and electronics products, as I am deeply suspicious of the still popular version of the "genial designer" who designs a flower vase today and an airplane tomorrow and whose intuition leads him to the perfect answer despite vast differences in technical complexity and special know-how.

With the kind of products I am working on, development is a constant team effort, with the designer contributing his special know-how on human factors, ergonomics, and aesthetics. I have found it to be absolutely necessary that, within such a team, the designer be able to speak the language of his counterpart—meaning that in my case I need to have a sound knowledge of engineering and of electronics as well. Only in this way can technical possibilities be exploited to the fullest and innovative solutions rising from teamwork be realised.

It is not the breathtaking design model presented to management by the designer which constitutes the quality of a design or of a designer as such, but what remains of it when the final prototype has gone through testing. As a designer, I am in the unique position, in various stages of a development, of being able to blend all factors of influence, technical restraints, and components with their specific limitations into a three-dimensional object and to work it out, down to the details. This three-dimensional puzzle, especially when it is a complex project such as the Magnetic Levitation train, for instance, is what has always fascinated me in design and what will probably continue to do so for a long time.

—Alexander Neumeister

NILSSON, Barbro.

Swedish textile designer. Born Barbro Lundberg, in Malmo, 18 July 1899. Educated in Lidingo, 1910–13; studied textile design under Johanna Brunsson and Alma Jakobsson, at Brunssons Vavskola, Stockholm, 1913–17, at the Tekniska Skolan, Stockholm, 1917–20, and at the Hogre Konstindustrielle Skolan, Stockholm, 1920–24. Married the sculptor Robert Nilsson in 1928; son: Pal-Nils. Independent textile designer, Stockholm, 1924–42; art director, Marta Maas-Fjetterstrom textile workshops, Bastad, from 1942. Instructor, at Johanna Brunnstroms Vavskolan, Stockholm, 1919–41, the Kunstindustri Skolan, Kunstindustri Dagskolan, and Kunstindustri Aftonskolan, Stockholm, 1934–45; director and chief instructor, with Maria Nordenfelt, of the Craft and Design Seminarium, Goteborg, 1924–25; also visiting instructor, at the Konstfackskolan, Stockholm, and the Konsthantverkskolan, Copenhagen. **Exhibition:** *Scandinavian Modern Design 1880–1980,* Cooper-Hewitt Museum, New York, 1982. **Collections:** Nationalmuseum, Stockholm; Nordisk Museum, Oslo;

Dansk Kunstindustrimuseum, Copenhagen. Recipient: Litteris et Artibus Medal, Stockholm, 1948; Prince Eugene Medal, Stockholm, 1954; Lengetz Prize, Stockholm, 1969. *Died* (in Stockholm) *11 October 1983.*

Works:

Tunes at the Marketplace tapestry hanging, for the Concert Hall, Goteborg, 1935–39 (with Sven Erixson).
Goteborg Harbour tapestry, for Swedish-American lines ship *M/S Stockolm,* 1938 (with Sven Erixson).
The Snails rya rug, 1943.
Harlequins Returning Home tapestry, 1943 (with Endre Nemes).
Berry-Pattern rya rugs, 1946.
The Falursquare rya rug, 1952.
Tree of Life flossa rug, for the Storkyrkan, Stockholm, 1955.
Tribute to Boras Textile Crafts tapestry, for Boras Town Hall, 1956–57 (with Olle Nyman).
Danish Peasant Woman tapestry, for the Folketinget, Copenhagen, 1957–58 (with William Scharff).
Gustaf Vasa tapestry, for Vasteras Town Hall, 1960–61 (with Sixten Lundbom).
Series of ten tapestries, for the Marcus Church, Stockholm, 1961 (with Robert Nilsson).
Violets rya rug, for the Svenska Handelsbanken, Stockholm, 1961.
Equestrians' Battle tapestry hanging, for the Svenska Handelsbanken, Stockholm, 1961–62 (with Olle Nyman).
Pomona tapestry hanging, for the Skandinavska Banken, Stockholm, 1964–65 (with Olle Nyman).
Series of five tapestries, for the Gustaf Adolf Church, Helsingborg, 1965.
Portokalli rya rug, for the Hotel Anglais, Stockholm, 1966.
Series of seven tapestries, for the Southern Energy Company, Malmo, 1966.
Wine Master tapestry hanging, 1969 (with Olle Nyman).

Publications:

On NILSSON: books—*Contemporary Swedish Design: A Survey in Pictures* by Arthur Hald and Sven Erik Skawonius, Stockholm 1951; *Scandinavian Design* by Ulf Hard at Segerstad, Stockholm and London 1961; *Svensk Form,* edited by Ake Stavenlow and Ake H. Huldt, Stockholm 1961; *Marta Maas-Fjetterstrom och Vav-Verkstaden i Bastad* by Tyra Lundgren, Stockholm 1968; *Design in Sweden,* edited by Lennart Lindkvist, Stockholm 1972; *En Bok om Barbro Nilsson* by Viggo Sten Moller, Stockholm 1977; *Scandinavian Modern Design 1880–1980,* edited by David Revere McFadden, New York 1982; *Tryckta Tyger fran 30-tal till 80-tal* by Inez Svensson, Stockholm 1984; *Design in Sweden,* edited by Monica Boman, Stockholm 1985.

Barbro Nilsson possesses all the characteristics of a great master. Her craftsmanship is impressive, grounded in clarity of self; she knows and can do so much that she can allow herself to let go; she recognizes her position in the history of the textile crafts, and thus she is humble; her work is simple, playful, with the sure rhythm of dancing patterns on the surface. And moreover, she has humor. When last I met her, she received me lying in bed after a difficult eye-operation; eighty-four years of age, she was beautiful in a way that expressed itself in her shining eyes and extended into her white hair, which was like a glowing crown around her head. Her strong hands were resting—for the

time being. As soon as she was well, she assembled a new weave. Her voice was like that of a young woman, melodic and laughing, carefully avoiding anything pretentious.

Why have I described Nilsson so carefully? Because her work as a pioneer of the Swedish textile crafts is so integrated with her personality. Nilsson is an unusually powerful and active woman. She is gifted with a rich imagination which apparently never runs dry. Her energy has allowed her to work on her own personal creations as well as to direct Sweden's most prestigious textile mill, AB Märta Maas-Fjetterström, and for several years, to retain the position of principal instructor in the textile subjects at the Academy for Arts and Crafts in Stockholm.

Her combination of humility and confidence has made it possible for her to learn not only from the tradition of indigenous Swedish textiles but also from ancient Coptic fabrics. She has the ability to cooperate, and she quickly uncovers the essential concept embedded in several artists' designs. And yet, she has always remained herself, a formidable artist untouched by surrounding trends.

Her most lasting contribution to Swedish textile tradition is probably her production of rugs, exquisite works of art as well as useful items. It was not at all easy for the young, gifted artist suddenly to take over and become responsible for the legendary Märta Maas-Fjetterström textile mill, to maintain its tradition of many unique and strongly established patterns, and simultaneously, to introduce new concepts into the mill's work. But Nilsson succeeded and apparently without strenuous effort. Her patterns (The Woodpecker, The Snails, Seaweed, Berries) adhere to a fine tradition; they are rhythmic and very decorative, like all indigenous patterns; they are often created in an unpretentious way around a small detail from nature; and yet, they are highly expressive of a strong personality, of a unique sense of color and a confident knowledge of form. Nilsson can place a light red and a turquoise next to each other and yet achieve a sense of harmony; she can let a rug consist of zig-zag patterns and small medallion shapes—all of different sizes and yet render it so unbound by time as to be used for decades (Seaweed). She always seeks out nature as her inspiration, avoiding reproducing it but rather creating abstractions—interpreting nature through her medium.

One could say so many more wonderful things about her—not the least about her work as a pedagogue. While she was an instructor at the Academy for Arts and Crafts, her importance for the generation of women who were the genesis of the movement bringing Swedish textile crafts to its present level of worldwide recognition cannot be overestimated. Here, the unique artist changed into a humorous and attentive helper towards the young, aspiring talents. One cannot perceive her students as less accomplished copies of her; rather one knows they are Nilsson's students because of their knowledge of earlier textile traditions, their feeling for quality, and their confidence in their own crafts—this is what she succeeded in conveying to them.

—Gertrud Gustafsson

NOORDA, Bob.

Dutch graphic, display and industrial designer. Born in Amsterdam, 15 July 1927. Studied at the Instituut voor Kunstnijverheidsonderwijs, Amsterdam, 1944–47. Worked as a layout artist on Dutch government military publications, in Jakarta, Indonesia, 1947–50; freelance designer, working in Amsterdam, 1950–52, and in Milan from 1952; art director, for Pirelli Company, Milan, from 1961; co-founder and senior vice-president, Unimark International design and marketing corporation, Milan, from 1965; has designed for Montecatini, Farmitalia, Remington Rand Italia, Alfa Romeo, Philips, Agip, Mitsubishi, Spear and Jackson, Stella-Artois, Upim, Chiari e Forti, Feltrinelli, Mondadori, Total, Shiseido, Olivetti, etc. Commission member, ICSID International Council of Societies of Industrial Design, 1968–70; general secretary, 1969–70, and national president from 1979, ADI Associazione Disegno Industriale, Milan; scientific committee member, Istituto Superiore per il Disegno Grafico, Urbino, from 1975. **Exhibitions:** Milan Triennale, 1957; *Manifesti Italiani,* Lugano, 1959; Composing Room, New York, 1960; *107 Grafici dell'AGI,* Castello Sforzersco, Milan, 1974; *Design e design,* Palazzo delle Stelline, Milan, 1979 (toured). Recipient: Gold Medal, Rimini, 1973; Compasso d'Oro Awards, Milan, and Gold Medal, 12th Milan Triennale. Addresses: (office) Via Santa Maria Fulcorina 20, 20123 Milan; (home) Via Leopardi 28, 20123 Milan, Italy.

Publications:

On NOORDA: books—*Packaging: An International Survey of Package Design,* edited by Walter Herdeg, Zurich 1959; *Who's Who in Graphic Art,* edited by Walter Amstutz, Zurich 1962, Dubendorf 1982; *An International Survey of Packaging* by Wim Crouwel and Kurt Weidemann, London 1968; *Mongrafie des Plakats* by Herbert Schindler, Munich 1972; *Arcigraphia: Architectural and Environmental Graphics,* edited by Walter Herdeg, Zurich 1978; *Modern Furniture* by John F. Pile, New York and Toronto 1979; *Atlante del Design Italiano 1940/1980* by Alfonso Grassi and Anty Pansera, Milan 1980; *The Conran Directory of Design,* edited by Stephen Bayley, London 1985; *Italian Modern: A Design Heritage* by Giovanni Albera and Nicolas Monti, New York 1989.

In the 1950s Bob Noorda appeared in Milan, where he worked for some of the Italian companies most known for their enlightened patronage of design, such as Pirelli and Montecatini. His most outstanding work for this latter company was the design of the graphics for the pavilion at the Milan Samples Fair in 1963; here, he indicated his abilities to handle a range of solutions, which carefully differentiated the various purposes within an overall concept while maintaining a family likeness. For Pirelli, perhaps his most remembered work is the 1956 advertisement for the Cinturato tyre, with its startling graphic adaption of the pattern of the tread and its bold typography.

All Noorda's work of the early period combined clear and bold layout with highly imaginative imagery, rational and effective. With the Milan Metropolitana subway system, however, imagery had scarcely a role to play. There, he organized all the graphics to convey the appropriate message directly and unambiguously but always with deceptively easy elegance, with no laboured effect that might have arisen from the deep preparation for the work. Everything was subject to his own rigorous tests within a logical appreciation of what a passenger would expect. The lettering style was the result of an investigation into legibility under the conditions that would prevail on the system, while the position-ing of station names on the platforms resulted from a study of the visual restrictions upon a passenger seated in one of the coaches, so that no one might miss or mistake a station. Similar considerations affected the disposition of the exit signs both from the platform and from the underground concourses to the various streets, as well as traffic in the other direction, particularly in the street-level indications of stations and entrances. It is a measure of Noorda's integration into the culture of Milan that his achievements with the Metropolitana were seen as an expression of the best that could be done by that culture, as, in fact, an addition to and an extension of it.

Probably no other work by Noorda has risen quite to the level reached with the graphics for the Metropolitana, but other works have demonstrated the imaginative qualities he has been able to bring to the design of posters, advertisements, exhibition stands, and pavilions. Often, his approach has been to reduce an image to its essential graphic quality, enhanced by a dramatic viewpoint. This has meant, frequently, distancing himself from any naive representation and seizing, rather, upon the indexical signs existentially linked to an object, transforming such signs into magic symbols, as he did perhaps most effectively in the Pirelli Cinturato tyre advertisement, in which the tread pattern was rendered in stark black-and-white patterning.

—Toni del Renzio

NORELL, Norman.

American fashion designer. Born Norman David Levinson, in Noblesville, Indiana, 20 April 1900. Studied illustration, at Parsons School of Fine and Applied Arts, New York, 1919; figure drawing and fashion design, at the Pratt Institute, Brooklyn, New York, 1920–22. Worked as a costume designer for Paramount Pictures, at Astoria Studio, Long Island, New York, 1922–23; stage costume designer, for Brooks Costume Company, Charles Armour dress manufacturer, and for burlesque, vaudeville and revues, in New York, 1924–28; designer, Hattie Carnegie custom-order dresses, New York, 1928–40; founder-designer and partner, with wholesale manufacturer Anthony Traina, of Traina-Norell company, New York, 1941–60; director, Norman Norell fashion company, New York, 1960–72. Instructor, Parsons School of Design, New York. President, Council of Fashion Designers of America. **Exhibitions:** *The Art of Fashion,* Metropolitan Museum of Art, New York, 1967; *Fashion: An Anthology,* Victoria and Albert Museum, London, 1971; *Norman Norell: Retrospective,* Metropolitan Museum of Art, New York, 1972. Recipient: Coty American Fashion Critics Award, 1943, 1951, 1956, 1966, and Hall of Fame Award, 1958; *Sunday Times* International Fashion Award, London, 1963; City of New York Bronze Medallion, 1972. DFA: Pratt Institute, Brooklyn, New York, 1962. *Died* (in New York City) *25 October 1972.*

Publications:

By NORELL: article—in the *New York Times,* 15 October 1972.

On NORELL: books—*Fashion Is Our Business* by Beryl Epstein, New York 1945; *The Wheels of Fashion* by Phyllis Lee Levin, New York 1965; *The Beautiful People* by Marilyn Bender, New York 1967; *Fashion: An Anthology by Cecil Beaton,* exhibition catalogue compiled by Madeleine Ginsburg, London 1971; *American Fashion: The Life and Lines of Adrian, Mainbocher, McCardell, Norell, Trigere,* edited by Sara Tomerlin Lee, New York 1975, London 1976; *In Fashion: Dress in the Twentieth Century* by Prudence Glynn, New York 1978; *Fairchild's Who's Who in Fashion,* edited by Ann Stegemeyer, New York 1980; *McDowell's Directory of Twentieth Century Fashion* by Colin McDowell, London 1984; *The Encyclopaedia of Fashion from 1840 to the 1980s* by Georgina O'Hara, London 1986.

Norman Norell, known as "the dean of American fashion," was the one American designer regarded as an equal by French couturiers. He selected basic American elements and pared them down to their essentials, producing a concise, recognizable style. His success with Traina-Norell during World War II encouraged other American designers to disavow the myth of American fashion inferiority.

Starting with the sailor's middy, the shirtdress, the chemise, and the blazer, Norell brought out his clean lines with substantial fabrics and careful tailoring. For forty years, he reinterpreted these well-chosen classics in new lengths, new proportions, and in different fabrics, with crisper or softer tailoring, depending upon fashion's prevailing mood.

The son of an Indiana haberdasher, Norell designed daytime cardigans, blazers, and shirts in the functional, classic spirit of American menswear. For evening, his theatrical costuming experience surfaced in vivid lace; bouffant, Southern-Belle organdies with candy-box bows; and the famous, sequined, "mermaid" sheath. The sailor's middy blouse of his childhood inspired at least one nautical design in each Norell collection. His chemise dress, accessorized with simple pumps, plain hose, and neat hairdo, was his idealized version of the 1920s, a fashion period he admired.

As a teacher at Parsons School of Design, he taught from his own experience that a designer should be able to do everything, just in case the need should arise. A perfectionist, Norell oversaw every aspect of production, from the choosing of fabrics through the making of duplicate samples to the inspection of final details.

A master of the constructed look, he was at the fashion forefront and self-avowedly at the top of his form during the 1960s, when his clothes were frequently copied. This bothered him mainly because cheap copies were bound to be poorly made. When his 1960 culotte suit (preceding even European couture in showing divided garments for ladies' daytime wear) was copied, he offered the pattern to the press so that at least the cheap knockoff would be properly made.

Called the Rolls-Royces of fashion, his clothes were expensive because one jacket could take a week to tailor. Norell believed in uncompromising quality, wanting women to appreciate the practicality of looking great in a few perfect pieces they could wear for years, rather than buying lots of cheap, throw-away clothes. Wearing simple blazers and cardigans over skirts or trousers, whether they were tailored in wool or paved with sequins, Norell's customer could count on the same nonchalant luxury for day and night, never having to think twice about being well-dressed.

The Metropolitan Museum's twenty-five-year retrospective of his clothes opened, sadly, the week before his death but proved beyond any doubt that there is such a thing as American style and that, at its best, it is great.

—Sandra Michels Adams

NOYES, Eliot (Fette).
American architect and industrial designer. Born in Boston, Massachusetts, 12 August 1910. Studied at Phillips Academy, Andover, Massachusetts, 1926–28; Harvard College, Cambridge, Massachusetts, 1928–32; BA 1932; architecture, Harvard University, Cambridge, Massachusetts, 1932–35, 1937–38: M.Arch. 1938; Eugene Dodd Medal, 1935; Alpha Rho Chi Medal, 1938; AIA Medal, 1938. Served in the United States Air Force, 1942–45: Major. Married Mary Duncan Weed in 1938; children: Mary, Eliot, Frederick and Margaret. Worked as an architect on the University of Chicago's Iranian archaeological expedition, 1935–37; draftsman, in the office of Coolidge, Shepley, Bulfinch and Abbot, in Boston, 1938, and in the office of Walter Gropius and Marcel Breuer, in Cambridge, Massachusetts, 1939–40; director of the department of industrial design, Museum of Modern Art, New York, 1940–42, 1945–46; design director, at Norman Bel Geddes and Company, New York, 1946–47; in private architectural and design practice as Eliot Noyes and Associates, New Canaan, Connecticut, 1947–77: design consultant to IBM, 1956–77, Mobil Oil, 1964–77, Westinghouse Electric, 1960–76, Pan American World Airways, 1969–72, and Massachusetts Institute of Technology, 1972–77. Exhibition curator and associate professor of architecture, Yale University, New Haven, Connecticut, 1948–53. President, Aspen Design Conference, Colorado, 1965–70. **Exhibition:** *Design Since 1945,* Philadelphia Museum of Art, 1983. Recipient: *Progressive Architecture* Design Award, New York, 1954; *Architectural Record* Award, New York, 1956, 1957, 1959, 1974; American Institute of Architects Honor Award and Centennial Medal, 1957, Industrial Arts Medal, 1965; *House and Home* Award, New York, 1957; United States Department of Housing Merit Award, 1968; American Society of Landscape Architects Award, 1970; Society of Industrial Artists and Designers Medal, London, 1971; AIA/Connecticut Society of Architects Honor Award, 1975; *Industrial Design* Award, New York, 1975. DFA: Carnegie-Mellon University, Pittsburgh, 1969. Fellow, American Institute of Architects, Industrial Designers Society of America, and Royal Society of Arts, London. Associate, National Academy of Design. *Died* (in New Canaan, Connecticut) *18 July 1977.*

Works:

IBM Model A Electric typewriter, for International Business Machines, 1947.
Wonder Home exhibit, for the General Electric Corporation, 1954.
IBM Selectric typewriter, for International Business Machines, 1961.
IBM American Branch Offices, for International Business Machines, 1961–72.
IBM 1440 data processing system for International Business Machines, 1962 (with W. Furcani and J. Stinger).
300/Marine Diesel powerboat, for Cummins Engine Company, 1963.
Time Capsule Pavilion at the New York World's Fair, for Westinghouse Electric, 1964.
IBM Aerospace Building in Los Angeles, for International Business Machines, 1964–65.
Gasoline Service Station prototypes, for Mobil Oil, 1965 (55 built).
Showroom interior in New York, for the Xerox Corporation, 1965.
Showroom and Sales Office in Toronto, for General Fireproofing Company, 1967.
United Nations Pavilion at *Expo 67,* Montreal, 1967.
IBM Pavilion at San Antonio *Hemisfair,* for In-

ternational Business Machines, 1968.
Sales and Service Building prototypes, for Cummins Engine Company, 1969.
Refinery Administration Building in Joliet, Illinois, for Mobil Oil, 1970.
Portuguese Headquarters Building in Lisbon, for Mobil Oil, 1971.
Passenger Terminal interiors at Kennedy Airport, New York, for Pan American World Airways, 1971.
IBM Headquarters lobby interiors in Armonk, New York, for International Business Machines, 1972.

(for a full list of Noyes' buildings and architectural projects, see *Contemporary Architects*)

Publications:

By NOYES: books—*Organic Design and Home Furnishing,* New York 1941; *Symposium on the Esthetics of Automobile Design,* New York 1950.

On NOYES: books—*Inside Today's Home* by Ray and Sarah Faulkner, New York 1954, 1975; *Design Coordination and Corporate Image* by F. H. K. Henrion and Alan Parkin, London and New York 1967; *Design in America* by Ralph Caplan, New York 1969; *The Corporate Search for Visual Identity* by Ben Rosen, New York 1970; *Interior Design: An Introduction to Architectural Interiors* by Arnold Friedmann, John F. Pile and Forrest Wilson, New York and Amsterdam 1970, 1976; *In Good Shape: Style and Design in Industrial Products Since 1960* by Stephen Bayley, London 1979; *Industrial Design* by John Heskett, London 1980; *Design Since 1945,* edited by Kathryn Hiesinger and George Marcus, Philadelphia and London 1983; *Design Source Book* by Penny Sparke and others, London 1986; *The American Design Adventure 1940–1975* by Arthur J. Pulos, London and Cambridge, Massachusetts 1988; *New American Design* by Hugh Aldersley-Williams, New York 1988.

Once called "an industrial designer with a conspicuous conscience," Eliot Noyes, when he was Director of Industrial Design at the Museum of Modern Art, wrote:

A design . . . is a harmonious organization of the parts within the whole, according to structure, material and purpose. Within this definition there can be no vain ornamentation or superfluity, but the part of beauty is nonetheless great in ideal choice of material, in visual refinement and in the rational elegance of things intended for use.

This philosophy enunciated in 1941 was confirmed and influenced by Bauhaus theories through Noyes' association with Walter Gropius and Marcel Breuer, with whom he had studied and worked as draftsman.

Noyes ascertained that it was the designer's responsibility to define the real character of a company for which he designed and then to express this character, not merely as "corporate identity" in a superficial sense, but throughout the corporation's entire entity: architecture, interiors, graphics, advertising, and products. Believing that good design was good business, Noyes insisted that the entire company had to be considered. He turned down prospective clients who would not be committed to ongoing assignments. Although he consulted with outside experts when necessary, Noyes reserved all final design decisions for himself. The team approach he used in his office was influenced by both Gropius' working methods and by the Olivetti Company's organization.

Noyes' methods are evident in the history of a product for the Cummins Engine Company. When the company decided to go into the small

boat field in 1963 with the 300/Marine Diesel, Noyes was commissioned as a designer. Company engineers submitted working drawings for the new diesel, and Noyes had a model made in his office. He realized that the engine must continue the reputation for quality and reliability that Cummins had gained in its large engines for trucks. He deduced the basic requirements of the small boat engine to be: 1) comparability in size and weight with spark-ignition engines of similar power and usage; 2) elimination of exterior tubing where possible to avoid danger of breakage; 3) accessibility for easy maintenance within the confinement of small boats. Confronted with drawings and model, Noyes decided that repositioning of some basic parts of the engine was necessary. Changes were made in consultation with staff engineers. Even the heavy lead logo, bolted to the housing, was eliminated. The metal housing was refined, and the result was a handsome design which solved all requirements of the assignment and fulfilled his own belief that "good design, whether of a building, an office machine, or of a company's operating statement derives from the nature of the problem; when the design problems have been solved, the end products will have in common a clarity and appropriateness of form.

The scope of Noyes' work is vast. He practiced both design and architecture throughout his career, considering both in the same terms. He designed exhibitions, computers, houses, and railroad vehicles. He was president of the International Design Conference from 1965 to 1970, he taught at Yale for several years, and he acted as design consultant to the president of M.I.T., as well as to IBM, Mobil, and Westinghouse.

—Nina Bremer

NURMESNIEMI, Antti (Aarre).
Finnish interior, exhibition, graphic and industrial designer. Born in Hameenlinna, 30 August 1927. Studied interior design, at the Institute of Industrial Arts, Helsinki, 1947–50. Served in the Finnish Army, 1950–51: Ensign. Married Vuokko Eskolin in 1953. Worked as a furniture designer, Stockmann design office, Helsinki, 1949–50; interior designer, in the Viljo Revell architectural office, Helsinki, 1951–56, and in the Giovanni Romano architectural office, Milan, 1954–55; freelance designer, establishing Studio Nurmesniemi, Helsinki, from 1956. Instructor in interior and furniture design, Institute of Industrial Arts, Helsinki, 1962–68; visiting lecturer, at the Industrial Art Institute, Tokyo, 1965, Kingston Polytechnic, London, 1974, and Tokyo Designers College, 1978. President, SIO Finnish Association of Interior Designers, 1960–63, and Ornamo Association of Finnish Designers, 1977–82; chairman, Institute of Industrial Arts, Helsinki, 1968–73, and Museum of Applied Art, Helsinki, from 1975; board member, Centenary Foundation of Finnish Design, Helsinki, 1975, and ICSID International Council of Societies of Industrial Design, 1979–83; council member, European Foundation for Science, Art and Culture, Paris, from 1982. **Exhibitions:** Artek Showroom, Helsinki, 1957, 1964; Kunstnernes Hus, Oslo, 1960; Hameenlinna Museum of Art, 1967; Kluuvin Gallery, Helsinki, 1971; Norden Hus, Reykjavik, 1975 (toured); Het Meesterteken, Oirschot, 1976; Carelia Studio, Milan, 1980. **Collections:** Finnish Museum of Applied Art,

Antti Nurmesniemi: *Chair 006* in lacquered birch, for Vuokko Oy, 1986

Helsinki; Museum of Modern Art, New York; Metropolitan Museum of Art, New York; Philadelphia Museum of Art; Röhsska Konstslöjdmuseet, Göteborg; Malmö Museum; Stedelijk Museum, Amsterdam; Royal Scottish Museum, Edinburgh; Die Neue Sammlung, Munich; Norske Kunstindustrimuseum, Oslo; Seibu Museum of Art, Tokyo. Recipient: Lighting competition award, Helsinki, 1948; Finnish Society of Crafts and Design Award, Helsinki, 1955; Helsinki City Art and Literature Award, 1957; Milan Triennale Silver Medal, 1957, 1976, Grand Prize, 1960, 1964, and First Prize, 1963; Lunning Prize, Copenhagen, 1959; Pro Finlandia Medal, 1960; Merivaara Furniture Prize, Helsinki, 1967; Interdesign Competition Award of Honor, 1968; Finnish State Design Award, 1976, 1979; Finnish Artist-Professorship Award, 1978; Society of Industrial Artists and Designers Medal, London, 1981; SIO Best Interior Award, Helsinki, 1984; State Professorship, Helsinki, 1988. Honorary Royal Designer for Industry, Royal Society of Arts, London, 1986. Address: Hopeasalmentie 27, 00570 Helsinki, Finland.

Works:

Hallapyora Restaurant interiors, Hameenlinna, 1958.

KOP Finnish National Bank branch office interiors, in Lahti, Turku, Jyvaskyla, etc., from 1960.

Olavinlinna Fortress interiors, furniture and visual communications system, 1962–75.

Amer-Yhtma head office interiors, Hyryla, 1964–65, 1978.

Vuokko shops interiors, Helsinki, from 1965.

Kanta-Hame Savings Bank interiors, Hameenlinna, 1966–67, 1976.

001 Chaise Longue in fiberglass, foam rubber and steel, for Vuokko Oy, 1967.

Railway carriage interiors, for the President of Finland and the State Council, 1968–70.

IBM managing director's office interiors, Helsinki, 1970.

Finnjet Car Ferry interiors and visual communications system, 1975–76.

Jet Hamburger Restaurant interiors, Helsinki, 1976.

Helsinki Rail Station restoration, from 1980.

006 Chair in lacquered birch, for Vuokko Oy, 1986.

Publications:

By NURMESNIEMI: book—*Omakotijirja/Small House Book,* Helsinki 1960.

On NURMESNIEMI: books—*A Treasury of Scandinavian Design,* edited by Erik Zahle, New York 1961; *Modern Scandinavian Furniture* by Ulf Hård af Segerstad, Copenhagen 1963, London 1964; *34 Scandinavian Designers* by Svend Erik Moller, Copenhagen 1967; *Modern Finnish Design* by Ulf Hård af Segerstad, London 1969; *Scandinavian Design: Objects of a Life Style* by Eileene Harrison Beer, New York and Toronto 1975; *History of Modern Furniture* by Karl Mang, Stuttgart 1978, London 1979; *Scandinavian Modern Design 1880–1980,* edited by David Revere McFadden, New York and London 1982; *Design Since 1945,* edited by Kathryn Hiesinger and George Marcus, Philadelphia and London 1983; *The Conran Directory of Design,* edited by Stephen Bayley, London 1985; *Design Source Book* by Penny Sparke and others, London 1986; *Finnish Industrial Design,* edited by Tuula Pontasuo, Helsinki 1987.

My "official" degree is in interior design, but during my professional activity, I have worked in very many areas of design. Perhaps this variety stems from the quality of design education at the turn of the 1940s–1950s in Finland; I was exposed to broad-minded teachers, teaching programs that ignored professional borders, and an atmosphere of creativity. In the background, of course, there is my own will, too, to look at the events of the world from the greatest possible number of angles. And not only to look, but to work and create.

I could not operate in my profession without being in close contact with photography, filmmaking, and freehand drawing. I have never liked professional limits because they are not, in my opinion, conducive to creative work or design activity. From my point of view, professional limits would mean non-professionalism.

Before starting my design education, I was building gliders and working as a carpenter, too, so I learned to know the nature of wood. I also was an apprentice in a metal shop and an aeroplane factory; there, I learned to know the hardness of metal. In addition, during my studies, I was an assistant to a scenographer in a film studio, and I learned to love the atmosphere of making films. I believe that all this has helped me enormously when planning spaces, objects, structures, exhibitions, and practical and visual environments.

—Antti Nurmesniemi

Antti Nurmesniemi's design lies closer to that of the rest of Europe than the work of any other Finnish interior designer. It may be that his year in Italy influenced him out of proportion to his time there; certainly some of his early work, for instance the display at the 1960 *Triennale,* has a refinement and spatial clarity reminiscent not only of contemporary Italian work but even seeming to hark back to the sparseness and controlled simplicity of Rietveld and De Stijl. Nevertheless, he has always been able to combine this with typical Finnish toughness; for instance, the Hälläpyörä restaurant of the same period sets this elegance firmly and successfully into the native tradition of strongly used, natural materials.

Likewise, the enamelled and cast-iron cooking utensils he designed in the 1960s show the same ability to impart to traditional shapes a greater simplicity and almost classical refinement than is found in the work of many of his contemporaries. This quality is particularly noticeable in his chair design. The chair in the *Triennale* exhibition, a steel frame with the seat and back covered in leather, exploits the structural potential of the material to its utmost. In the same way, his lounge chair of 1979, in steel tube and canvas, although it may be inspired by Le Corbusier and Marcel Breuer, shows again Nurmesniemi's ability to propose a minimal statement.

By contrast, he is equally successful when using traditional materials in traditional ways, but with the same refined simplicity. His garden seat, designed as a self-assembly kit in 1982, eschews advanced timber technology and reverts to simple, straightforward joinery. Strongly reminiscent of some of Saarinen's furniture of eighty years before, it nevertheless shares with other work the sensitivity to the nature and potential of the material that characterises all that he does.

Although Nurmesniemi in no sense would consider himself the founder of a school, his influence on younger designers has been considerable, not only through his work but by his continuous involvement in national and international design associations and competition juries and by his teaching and lecturing in Finland, Britain, Japan, and many other countries. History may well show that Nurmesniemi, the quiet man of Finnish design, will prove to be a major if indirect influence.

—Gordon Steele

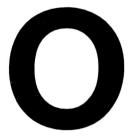

O'BRIEN, Timothy (Brian).

British stage and exhibition designer. Born of British parents, in Shillong, Assam, India, 8 March 1929. Educated at Wellington College, Crowthorne, Berkshire, 1942–47; Corpus Christi College, Cambridge, 1949–52: MA 1952; studied stage design under Donald Oenslager, at Yale University, New Haven, Connecticut, 1952–53. Served in the British Army Intelligence Corps, Austria, 1948–49: Sergeant. Design Assistant, BBC Television, London, 1954–55; designer, Associated Rediffusion Television, London, 1955–56; head of design, ABC Television, London, 1956–66; associate designer, Royal Shakespeare Company, Stratford-upon-Avon, Warwickshire, from 1966; designer, National Theatre, London, 1974–77; has worked in collaboration with designer Tazeena Firth, since 1961. Lecturer, Royal College of Art, London, 1966–67. Chairman, Society of British Theatre Designers, London, since 1984. **Exhibition:** *British Theatre Design '83–87,* Riverside Studios, London, 1988. **Collections:** Victoria and Albert Museum, London; Theatre Museum, Goteborg. Recipient: Gold Medal, Prague Quadriennale, 1975. Address: 33 Lansdowne Gardens, London SW8 2EQ, England.

Publications:

By O'BRIEN: book—*British Theatre Design '83–87,* with David Fingleton, London 1988.

The aim is to create a world, its people and their circumstances, in the service of a production and its ideas. The best result is the illumination of life, provoking thought and arousing strong feelings. A designer in the theatre needs good collaborators, since he works in a social art. In particular, his relationship with his director and the script or score is all-important. Design may come easily, even the design of beautiful things, but it has to be relevant. The work has to be understood and its ideas clearly grasped, if they are to be clearly expressed. Design has first to persuade the freshly-arrived audience to clear their minds.

Good design is contemporary in that it seeks to remove stale associations. But contemporary design is no good if fashion obscures content. An audience in the theatre is never free of the artificiality of its surroundings. But the designs are a concrete reality and must arrive at the right degree of abstraction or the figurative. Preconception is dangerous, as the designs should evolve with the production; and when the work is on stage, the opening design statement, however effective, should permit of development and during the performance accumulate effects altogether larger than the means employed. Things connect. Borkman stands, self-imprisoned in his upstairs room. A hidden door in a faded tapestry of a nymph and her shepherd opens to admit the woman he loved and then forsook when he married her sister for worldly advantage. The audience shivers afresh at the consequences.

—Timothy O'Brien

See FIRTH, Tazeena.

ODERMATT, Siegfried.

Swiss typography and graphic designer. Born in Neuheim, Zug, 13 September 1926. Educated at schools in Neuheim, 1933–42; studied at the Kunstgewerbeschule, Zurich, 1942–44; mainly self-taught in design from 1944. Worked in the Georg Vetter industrial design studio, Zurich, 1944–45; freelance designer, in collaboration with Hans Falk, Zurich, 1946–48; designer, in the Paul Zurrer advertising agency, Wadenswil, 1948–50; freelance designer, establishing Siegfried Odermatt studio, Zurich, 1950–68; partner, with Rosmarie Tissi, in Odermatt and Tissi design studio, Zurich, from 1968: has designed for City Druck AG, BP Benzin und Petroleum, Grammo Studio, Apotheke Sammet, Schelling Wellpappen, Univac, Mettler and Company, Union Safe Company, Kimo, Reinhard, etc. **Exhibitions:** Visual Graphic Gallery, New York, 1966; ICTA Knauer Expo, Stuttgart, 1967; ICTA German Section, Wuppertal, 1968; Stadtische Berufschule, Hof-Saale, 1972. Recipient: Typomundus Award, 1965, 1970; Type Directors Club Award, New York, 1966; 4th Calendar Competition Award, West Germany, 1972. Member: Alliance Graphique Internationale, Paris, and International Center for Typographic Arts, New York. Address: Odermatt and Tissi, Schipfe 45, 8001 Zurich, Switzerland.

Works:

Promotional brochures and leaflets, for Neuenburger Versicherung insurance company, 1960.
Advertisements and brochures, for Univac Computers, 1963–70.
Advertisements, for E. Lutz and Company blockmakers, 1964.
Logotype, advertisements and promotional brochures, for the Union Safe Company, 1966–75.
Help Prevent Fire poster, for Beratungsstelle fur Brantverhutung, Bern, 1968.
Trademark logotype, for Mettler and Company Textiles, 1969.
Antiqua Classica typeface, for Englersatz AG, 1971.
Sonora typeface, for Englersatz AG, 1972.
Marabu typeface, for Englersatz AG, 1972.
Sinalog typeface, for Englersatz AG, 1972.
Mindanao typeface, for Englersatz AG, 1975.
Advertisements, for Crypto, 1977–78.
Brochures, for BBC Brown Boverie et Cie, 1978–83.
It's Time for Prime poster, for Prime Computer AG, 1980.
Trademark logotype, for Kupferschmid Papers, 1980.
Economical Development in Germany 1950–2000 exhibition poster, for Wirtschaft Woche, Dusseldorf, 1982.

Publications:

On ODERMATT/TISSI: books—*An International Survey of Packaging* by Wim Crouwel and Kurt Weidemann, London 1968; *Signet, Signal, Symbol* by Walter Diethelm, Zurich 1970; *International Trademark Design* by Peter Wildbur, London 1979; *Architectural Signing and Graphics* by John Follis and Dave Hammer, New York and London 1979; *Who's Who in Graphic Art,* edited by Walter Amstutz, Zurich 1982; *A History of Graphic Design* by Philip B. Meggs, London and New York 1983.

We have deliberately kept our team small in order to keep a limited field of graphic design under close personal control. Graphic design is to both of us a vehicle of communication, and we generally limit ourselves to the media of typography, photography, and technical drawing. What we stress in our work is a conceptual idea which we try to develop in our design. Thus, we use our media in the manner of elements, assembling them into an informative whole. Generally, we arrive at the solutions of our design-problems by means of what could be called a dialectical process: we try to analyse the given content of the intended message into segments which can be translated into the various media we use and then form a synthesis accordingly.

Although we both work in the same manner, we often arrive at startlingly different solutions. Although our manner of work may seem rather intellectual, intuition inevitably plays a distinctive role. As we complement each other in this often argumentative process, many of our works cannot be fairly attributed to either one of us; they are the product of a team. However, many years of collaboration have led us to rather intimate knowledge of our "graphic brains".

Generally speaking, we tend to use simple, distinctive patterns of design and thus often arrive at signal-type solutions which can easily be remembered and individually recognized. Our main differences are congenial; while Rosmarie Tissi has a more playful approach to graphic problems, Siegfried Odermatt prefers the disciplined mental probing. However, both our work

Siegfried Odermatt: Advertisement for the Union Safe Company, 1967

has developed in the same direction and thus bears the marks of a common style.

—Siegfried Odermatt and Rosmarie Tissi

See TISSI, Rosmarie.

OENSLAGER, Donald.

American stage designer. Born in Harrisburg, Pennsylvania, 7 March 1902. Studied at Phillips Exeter Academy, New Hampshire, 1919-20; Harvard University, Cambridge, Massachusetts, 1921-23: BA 1923; also studied in Europe on Sachs travel grant, 1923-24. Served in the United States Air Force, 1942-45: Major; Bronze Star. Married Mary Osborne Polak in 1937. Stage designer, working in New York and in New Haven, Connecticut, 1925-75: consultant to the American Pavilion Theatre at the Brussels World's Fair, 1958; Montreal Cultural Center, 1961; Broadmoor International Center, 1961; Philharmonic Hall of the Lincoln Center, New York, 1962, 1969; New York State Theatre, 1964; Scott Theatre at Fort Worth Performing Arts Center, 1965; John F. Kennedy Center for Performing Arts, Washington, D.C., 1969; Meeting Center of Albany South Mall Project, 1969, etc. Instructor in scenic design, Middlebury College, Vermont, 1925; instructor and professor, 1925-71, and emeritus, 1971-75, Yale University, New Haven, Connecticut; professor of theatre, City University of New York, 1971-72. Vice-president, 1962-69, and board member, American National Theatre and Academy. Member of New York Mayor La Guardia's Art Committee of One Hundred, 1934; President's Advisory Committee on the Arts, 1960-62; United States National Commission for UNESCO, 1963-68; Art Commission of New York, 1965-75. **Exhibitions:** *Donald Oenslager: A Retrospective Exhibition,* Detroit Institute of Arts, 1956; *Russian Stage and Costume Designs from the Lobanov-Rostovsky, Oenslager, and Riabov Collections,* Metropolitan Museum of Art, New York, 1967 (toured); *Changing Concepts in Stage Design from the Donald Oenslager Collection,* Finch College, New York, 1971; *Four Centuries of Scenic Invention from the Donald Oenslager Collection,* International Exhibitions Foundation, Washington, D.C., 1974 (toured). **Collections:** Metropolitan Museum of Art, New York; Museum of Modern Art, New York; Museum of the City of New York; Museum of Fine Arts, Boston; Detroit Institute of Arts. Recipient: American School of Design Scroll of Honor Award, 1939; Pennsylvania Ambassador Award, 1950; Antoinette Perry Award, New York, 1959; Ford Foundation Grant, 1960. DFA: Colorado College, 1953. Honorary Member, American Federation of Arts; Royal Society of Arts, London; Master Drawing Association; Association Internationale de Bibliophile; Master Drawing Society; Municipal Art Society of New York. *Died* (in Bedford, New York) *21 June 1975.*

Works:

Stage productions include—*Sooner or Later,* 1925; *Morals,* 1925; *A Bit o' Love,* 1925; *Pinwheel,* 1927; *Good News,* 1927; *Anna,* 1928; *L'Histoire du Soldat,* 1928, *The New Moon,* 1928; *Follow Thru'* (also co-director), 1929; *Girl Crazy,* 1930; *Overture,* 1930; *The Winter's Tale,* 1931; *Free for All,* 1931; *Singin' the Blues,* 1931; *East Wind,* 1931; *The Emperor Jones,* 1931; *Whistling in the Dark,* 1932; *Adam Had Two Sons,* 1932; *A Thousand Summers,* 1932; *Forsaking All Others,* 1933; *Keeper of the Keys,* 1933; *Jezebel,* 1933; *Uncle Tom's Cabin,* 1933; *Salome,* 1934; *The Lady from the Sea,* 1934; *Dance with Your Gods,* 1934; *Divided by Three,* 1934; *Tristan and Isolde,* 1934; *Anything Goes,* 1934; *Gold-Eagle Guy,* 1934; *Rosenkavalier,* 1934; *The Farmer Takes a Wife,* 1934; *Something Gay,* 1935; *First Lady,* 1935; *Tapestry in Gray,* 1935; *Stage Door,* 1936; *Ten Million Ghosts,* 1936; *Sweet River,* 1936; *Red, Hot and Blue!,* 1936; *200 Were Chosen,* 1936; *Johnny Johnson,* 1936; *Russet Mantle,* 1936; *Matrimony Pfd.,* 1936; *You Can't Take It With You,* 1936; *Miss Quis,* 1937; *Robin Landing,* 1937; *Edna, His Wife,* 1937; *Otello,* 1937; *Of Mice and Men,* 1937; *A Doll's House,* 1937; *I'd Rather Be Right,* 1937; *The Circle,* 1938; *The Fabulous Invalid,* 1938; *Amelia Goes to the Ball,* 1938; *I Am My Youth,* 1938; *Spring Thaw,* 1938; *The Good,* 1938; *A Woman's a Fool to Be Clever,* 1938; *From Vienna,* 1939; *The American Way,* 1939; *Off to Buffalo,* 1939; *Skylark,* 1939; *The Man Who Came to Dinner,* 1939; *Margin for Error,* 1939; *I Know What I Like,* 1939; *Young Couple Wanted,* 1939; *My Dear Children,* 1940; *Beverly Hills,* 1940; *Retreat to Pleasure,* 1940; *The Old Foolishness,* 1940; *My Sister Eileen,* 1940; *The Lady Who Came to Stay,* 1941; *Mr. Big,* 1941; *Claudia,* 1941; *The Doctor's Dilemma,* 1941; *Theatre,* 1941; *Spring Again,* 1941; *Pie in the Sky,* 1941; *The Flowers of Virtue,* 1942; *Hairpin Harmony,* 1943; *Pygmalion,* 1945; *Born Yesterday,* 1946; *Three to Make Ready,* 1946; *On Whitman Avenue,* 1946; *Loco,* 1946; *La Traviata,* 1946; *Present Laughter,* 1946; *The Abduction from the Seraglio,* 1946; *Park Avenue,* 1946; *The Fatal Weakness,* 1946; *Years Ago,* 1946; *Land's End,* 1946; *Lovely Me,* 1946; *The Eagle Has Two Heads,* 1947; *Message for Margaret,* 1947; *Portrait in Black,* 1947; *Fidelio,* 1947; *How I Wonder,* 1947; *Eastward in Eden,* 1947; *Angel in the Wings,* 1947; *The Men We Marry,* 1948; *Cosi Fan Tutte,* 1948; *Life with Mother,* 1948; *Goodbye, My Fancy,* 1948; *Town House,* 1948; *The Leading Lady,* 1948; *The Smile of the World,* 1949; *At War with the Army,* 1949; *The Father,* 1949; *The Rat Race,* 1949; *The Velvet Glove,* 1949; *The Liar,* 1950; *Springboard to Nowhere,* 1950; *The Live Wire,* 1950; *Second Threshold,* 1951; *The Small Hours,* 1951; *Peer Gynt,* 1951; *The Constant Wife,* 1951; *Paris '90,* 1952; *Candida,* 1952; *To Be Continued,* 1952; *La Bohème,* 1952; *Horses in Midstream,* 1953; *Dido and Aeneas,* 1953; *Sabrina Fair,* 1953; *Escapade,* 1953; *Madam Will You Walk,* 1953; *The Prescott Proposals,* 1953; *Coriolanus,* 1954; *Dear Charles,* 1954; *The Wooden Dish,* 1955; *Janus,* 1955; *A Roomful of Roses,* 1955; *Major Barbara,* 1956; *The Ballad of Baby Doe,* 1956; *Four Winds,* 1957; *Mary Stuart,* 1957; *Nature's Way,* 1957; *A Shadow of My Enemy,* 1957; *The Girls in 509,* 1958; *The Pleasure of His Company,* 1958; *The Man in the Dog Suit,* 1958; *The Marriage-Go-Round,* 1958; *J.B.,* 1958; *A Majority of One,* 1959; *The Mikado,* 1959; *The Pink Jungle,* 1959; *The Highest Tree,* 1959; *Orpheus and Eurydice,* 1959; *Dear Liar,* 1960; *Orfeo,* 1960; *The Prisoner,* 1960; *A Far Country,* 1961; *A Call on Kuprin,* 1961; *Blood, Sweat and Stanley Poole,* 1961; *The Wings of the Dove,* 1961; *First Love,* 1961; *Venus at Large,* 1962; *The Irregular Verb to Love,* 1963; *A Case of Libel,* 1963; *One by One,* 1964; *Madame Butterfly,* 1964; *Lady From Colorado,* 1964; *Carmen,* 1966; *The Italian Lady from Algiers,* 1966; *Tosca,* 1966; *Love in E Flat,* 1966; *Der Rosenkavalier,* 1967; *Antigone,* 1967; *The Merry Widow* 1967; *Don Pasquale,* 1963; *Spofford,* 1967; *Avanti!,* 1968; *The Mikado,* 1968; *Don Carlos,* 1968; *The Wrong Way Light Bulb,* 1969.

Publications:

By OENSLAGER: books—*Scenery Then and Now,* New York 1936; *Theatre of Bali,* booklet, 1940; *Four Centuries of Theatre Design: Drawings from the Donald Oenslager Collection,* New Haven, Connecticut 1964; editor, *Four Centuries of Scenic Invention: Drawings from the Collection of Donald Oenslager,* New York 1974; *Stage Design: Four Centuries of Scenic Invention,* New York and London 1975; *The Theatre of Donald Oenslager,* Middletown, Connecticut 1978.

On OENSLAGER: books—*Donald Oenslager: Stage Designer and Teacher: A Retrospective Exhibition,* catalogue, Detroit, Michigan 1956; *Russian Stage and Costume Designs for the Ballet, Opera, and Theatre: A Loan Exhibition from the Lobanov-Rostovsky, Oenslager and Riabov Collections,* catalogue, Washington, D.C. 1967; *Changing Concepts in Stage Design: Drawings from the Donald Oenslager Collection,* New York 1971.

Donald Oenslager came to the theatre through study in playwriting with Professor George Pierce Baker at Harvard; thus he always placed his theatrical design work at the service of the script. Time in Europe in 1921 introduced him to the work of Gordon Craig, Adolphe Appia, and many other decorative or impressionistic symbolists, and these influences inhabited his design approach throughout his career. He was also greatly influenced by the work of Robert Edmond Jones, with whom he apprenticed on his return to the United States and for whom he always had the greatest respect. Another powerful factor in his life was his acceptance of a design post at Yale University after Baker was invited to open a professional school of dramatic art there in 1925. Oenslager as a teacher of young designers always perceived his role as that of the Renaissance master working with talented apprentices, and he always saw his own professional designs on Broadway within the great, historic continuum of artists, craftsmen, and designers to royalty from medieval times to the present. As the only major Broadway designer until the 1960s who was also a teacher, his immense influence through his students always led in the direction of professionalism, a sense of respect for the play to be designed, and a sense of theatrical vision that harked back to the visual dreams of Gordon Craig and the poetic outlook of Robert Edmond Jones.

The essence of Oenslager's teaching lay in his call for student designers to probe a play and the culture within which it was written to find underlying principles of structure and rhythm that could then be embodied in a contemporary stylistic approach for a particular theatre and audience. He did not relate particularly well to the concept of the stage setting as a projector of social or intellectual ideas, nor to the concept of the setting as a junk-art collage. He was a person of taste and a certain elegance who preferred these qualities in his designs, and the designs that he admired the most in his personal historical collection were those that presented a striking and evocative beauty. Even among his own designs, those that he remembered with the most pleasure were those with a Baroque elegance and decorative flamboyance.

—Douglas A. Russell

OHL, Herbert (Karl).
German architect and industrial designer. Born in Mannheim, 26 August 1926. Studied painting and graphics, at the Akademie der Bildenden Kunste, Karlsruhe, 1947–49; architecture under Egon Eiermann, at the Technische Hochschule, Karlsruhe, 1947–52: Dip.Ing. 1952; architecture, at the Politecnico, Milan, 1968: D.Arch. 1968. Assistant architect to Egon Eiermann, Karlsruhe, 1951–53; chief architect in an architectural office, Saarbrucken, 1953–56; freelance architect and designer, in Ulm, 1956–69, Frankfurt, 1969–74, and in Darmstadt from 1974; partner, with Gino Valle, in Valle-Ohl architectural and design office, Milan, 1966–69: has designed for La Rinascente, Renus AG, Metzeler AG, Max Braun, Hoechst AG, Korrekta-Werke, Danzer KG, Elements Minvielle, Canadian Plywood Association, Krupp,

Esso, Fiat, Fantoni, Brionvega, etc. Professor, 1956–68, and chairman of the industrial building department, 1960–68, and director, 1964–68, Hochschule fur Gestaltung, Ulm; guest professor, Columbia University, New York 1960–62, Carnegie-Mellon University, Pittsburgh, 1960, University of Illinois at Urbana-Champaign, 1961, Harvard University, Cambridge, Massachusetts, 1961, University of California at Los Angeles, 1963, Texas A and M University, College Station, 1963–64, and Instituto Nacional de Technologia Industrial, Buenos Aires, 1965. Director, Institut fur Industrialisiertes Bauen, Frankfurt, 1969–74; committee member, Pio Manzu Research Centre, Rimini, from 1969, and Bau und Wohnform Commission, Bonn, 1971–74; section chief, Rat fur Formgebung, Darmstadt, from 1974; planning and development chief, Gute

Form prize commission, Bonn and Darmstadt, from 1975; executive committee member, 1975–77, and honorary treasurer, 1977–79, ICSID International Council of Societies of Industrial Design. **Exhibitions:** Columbia University, New York, 1960, 1961; *Fertigbau-Ausstellung,* Ulm, 1963; *Expo 67,* Montreal, 1967; Milan Triennale, 1968; Galleria del Naviglio, Milan, 1971; Centro Internazionale Ricerche Pio Manzu, Rimini, 1971, 1972. **Collection:** Museum of Modern Art, New York. Recipient: Gold Medal, Rimini, 1968; United Nations Low-Cost Housing Prize, New York, 1969; Bundesministerium Integra Building Prize, Bonn, 1973; Gute Form Prize, Darmstadt, 1983. Address: Frankensteinerstrasse 86, 6100 Darmstadt 13, West Germany.

Herbert Ohl: Pedestal chairs, for O-Linie, 1970

Works:

Exhibition design and concept at the Milan Triennale, for the Hochschule fur Gestaltung, Ulm, 1960.

Multipli furniture system, for Fantoni 1965–73.

German pavilion displays at *Expo 67,* Montreal, for the Bundesministerium, Bonn, 1967.

OSI 1/2/3, BCCF Basic Concept car, and *Auto-Bisensi-Trinic* car, for Fiat, 1973–83.

Seating system, for O-Linie, 1974–79.

Design diagnosis and evaluation system, for the German Rat fur Formgebung, Darmstadt, 1974–83.

Publications:

By OHL: books—*Wandverkleidungen aus Hostalit Z Polyfaltplatten,* Frankfurt 1964; *Die Adequate Wohnform, Stadtebauder Zukunft,* Düsseldorf 1969; *Centro di tempo libero,* Verucchio, Italy 1970; *Tempo libero e potere dell'audiovisivo,* Verucchio, Italy 1971; *Flexibles Wohnen,* Bad Godesberg, West Germany 1972.

On OHL: book—*Talk About Design* by James Pilditch, London 1976; *Design e Forme Nuove nell'Arredamento Italiano* by Paolo Portoghesi and Marino Marini, Rome 1978.

Even if the designer works in a rational and resolutely functional manner, his designs will show a surprising and distinctive expression and sometimes will even touch on other realms, such as those of beauty or truth. Transcending the rational detachment of product analysis, this expression produces an emotionally direct and spontaneous relation between user and product. Thus it is that while design responds to material imperatives, it may nonetheless minister to the spiritual needs of people.

—Herbert Ohl

Herbert Ohl is as well-known for his teaching at the Hochschule für Gestaltung in Ulm as he is for his precise and elegant solutions to architectural and industrial design problems. It was during his directorship at Ulm (1964–68) that he also worked with the renowned Italian architect Gino Valle, one of that roster of building architects who expresses a common sense in the face of a general rush toward the outlandishly exceptional. Ohl, who had already made a name for himself as head of Ulm's industrial building department, was much influenced by his contact with Valle's work based on a methodology of design more than on a vocabulary of forms. This experience happily tied in with Ohl's formative studies under the equally-renowned architect Egon Eiermann (in whose office Ohl had subsequently worked), a person whose widely publicized support of rationalism had caused him to be placed in the same critical category as Mies van der Rohe, Walter Gropius, and the Bauhaus. At this time, the early 1950s, Eiermann was executing industrial buildings for Ciba pharmaceuticals, the State silk factories, and technical structures for university complexes, including the Technical School in Karlsruhe where Ohl had met him.

Ohl's subsequent work both in architectural and industrial fields bears Eiermann's stamp and displays a plastic power and elegance unique in Germany. In his designs for low-cost housing, prefabricated building systems, adaptable hospital facilities, modular packaged furniture, seating systems, and radical new conceptions for automobiles, Ohl focuses on the realization of a "catalogue" of required elements, a catalogue that includes modules of human activity as well as modules of form. These compositional elements are laboriously investigated, scrutinized, and

related to the framework of their environment. The results, however, are relatively independent of programmatic limits and recognize the need to relate human functions to architectural and product design—without which they have little reason to exist. His inheritance of rationalist common sense gives his works a remarkable degree of technical and visual durability.

—George Walsh

OKADA, Tomoji.

Japanese industrial designer. Born in Tokyo, 21 November 1936. Educated at Tokyo Metropolitan Technical High School, until 1955; studied at Nihon University, Tokyo, 1958–61, Kuwazawa Design School, Tokyo, 1961–62, and under Jay Doblin, at Illinois Institute of Technology, Chicago, 1965–68: MS 1968. Married Kaoru Katayama in 1968; children: Sanae and Takuya. Worked as a mechanical engineer, Nihon Camera, Tokyo, 1960–65; design researcher, at the Trade Center, Chicago, 1965–67; chief industrial designer, Nikon Camera, Tokyo, 1967–70; industrial design manager, 1970–75, technical support manager, 1975–78, audio products manager, 1978–82, automation manufacturing manager 1982–83,

Tomoji Okada: *Nikkorex 8* movie camera, for Nikon, 1962

and vice-president for automation from 1983, at General Electric, Tokyo. Instructor, Kuwazawa Design School, Tokyo, 1968, and Nihon University, Tokyo, 1970. Recipient: Japan External Trade Organization Award, 1962; Mainichi Industrial Design Award, Tokyo, 1962; Japanese Government Study Grant, 1965. Address: 40–29 Todoroki, 2-chome, Setagaya-ku, Tokyo 158, Japan.

Publications:

By OKADA: thesis—*Still Camera,* Chicago 1968; articles—in *Industrial Art News* (Tokyo), August 1963, September 1968; *Japan Design House* (Tokyo), August 1968; *Machine Design* (Tokyo), July 1975.

On OKADA: article—in *Industrial Design* (Tokyo), November 1980.

Tomoji Okada creates the impression of being very much his own man.

After graduating in mechanical engineering from Nihon University, he went to work for the world-famous camera maker Nikon, then took a leave of absence to study at the Kuwazawa Design School: the intention was that he would later return to Nikon to establish an industrial design department. While at Kuwazawa, he heard a lecture by Jay Doblin, who so impressed him that he decided to go to America to study with Doblin at the Illinois Institute of Technology in Chicago. After receiving an M.S. at I.I.T., he returned to Nikon, established the promised design section, then resigned and became manager of industrial design at General Electric Japan; he is now Vice-President of General Electric Industrial Automation. In the meantime, he has also lectured in industrial design.

In Japan, there are two kinds of designers: those who are specialists and those who are generalists. Okada seems to rise above such either/or designations. A good description of him might be that he is "a unique management executive and an original industrial designer."

Okada is now in charge at General Electric Industrial Automation's computer-aided design department established in January 1983. He was entirely responsible for its creation—from finding staff to implement the systems to finding a plant to house the operation. In creating the department, he applied the methodology of industrial design. In fact, he later commented that the total process (identifying problems; searching for solutions; evaluation; implementation) was surprisingly similar to the design process.

Okada is also active as an international businessman. He often faces "tense situations, whether to persuade or to be persuaded by others," and, again, he considers that the stages of the design process are effectively applicable. For example, he points out that the final evaluation of a business proposal (like a design proposal) should be avoided while it is still an abstract concept. And he points out that, in general, the ability to grasp the substance of any business problem can be developed through the application of precepts learned in design work.

Given his example, one would have to agree. One would also have to add that Okada's success has something to do with his qualities as a person—because success at his kind of work also demands a great deal of creativity.

Design methodology, then, has become Okada's second nature. He says: "I may be an exceptional case in Japan, but I think that it is desirable that designers go into other fields of work. Instead of having social contacts only among themselves, they should go out to breathe the air of the outside world. The time has now come for such a change."

Because his background is shared by few persons in Japan, Okada must inevitably become the leading proponent of what he preaches.

—Kunio Sano

P

PALMQVIST, Sven.

Swedish glass designer. Born in Lenhovda, Smaland, 4 September 1906. Studied at Orrefors Glass Engraving School, Sweden, 1928–30; Tekniska Skolan, Stockholm, 1931–33; Kungliga Konsthogskolan, Stockholm, 1934–36; under Paul Connet, at the Academie Ranson, Paris, 1937–39; also studied in Germany and Czechoslovakia, 1934, and in Italy, Denmark, Holland, Belgium and the United States, 1937–39. Served in the Swedish Home Guard, 1939–45. Married Gertrud Brolin in 1942 (died, 1969); children: Jonas, Petter, Maria and Andreas. Designer, working with Simon Gate and Edward Hald, at Orrefors Glassworks, Sweden, 1928–72; retired to Valdemarsvik and Orrefors, 1972–81, and to Paris, 1981–84. **Exhibitions:** *Swedish Arts and Crafts,* New York World's Fair, 1939; *Orrefors 1917–42,* Nationalmuseum, Stockholm, 1942; German Crafts Fair, Munich, 1955; Milan Triennale, 1957; *Sven Palmqvist,* at the Venice Biennale, 1976; *Nordisk Industridesign,* Kunstindustrimuseet, Oslo, 1976; Royal Academy of Art, Stockholm, 1982; *Scandinavian Modern Design 1880–1980,* Cooper-Hewitt Museum, New York, 1982; *Design Since 1945,* Philadelphia Museum of Art, 1983; *Scandinavia: Ceramics and Glass in the Twentieth Century,* Victoria and Albert Museum, London, 1989. **Collections:** Philadelphia Museum of Art; Victoria and Albert Museum, London. Recipient: Schwedisches Schaffen Heute Design Prize, Zurich, 1949; German Crafts Fair Award, Munich, 1955; Grand Prize, Milan Triennale, 1957; State of California Gold Medals, 1953–61; Gold Medal, Liubliana Biennale, 1964; American Institute of Interior Designers Award, New York, 1967; Wasa Order, Stockholm, 1977; Prince Eugen Medal, Stockholm, 1977. *Died* (in Paris) *6 February 1984.*

Works:

Fasett vase in blue tinted glass with cut decoration, for Orrefors, 1941.
Kantara bowl in white semi-opaque glass, for Orrefors, 1944.
Kraka glassware series, for Orrefors, 1944–50.
Ravenna glassware series in blue with stained red and blue interior pattern, for Orrefors, 1948–53.
Girl with Spring Flowers vase in blue tinted glass with cut decoration, for Orrefors, 1949.
Christening font, for Vantors Church, 1959.
Glass wall, for the International Telecommunications Building, Geneva, 1961.
Glass wall, for the Swedish Broadcasting and Television Corporation, Stockholm, 1961.
Monumental glass decorations, for the Government Building of Dubai, 1981.
Glass sculpture, for the Hospital of Saint Sigfrid, Vaxjo, 1981.
Ceiling decoration, for the Government Assembly Hall, Rosenbad, Stockholm, 1981.

Publications:

On PALMQVIST: books—*Orrefors 1917–1942,* exhibition catalogue edited by Elisa Hald-Steenberg, Stockholm 1942; *Modernt Svenskt Glas,* edited by Gregor Paulsson, Stockholm 1943; *Orrefors* by Carl Hernmarck, Stockholm 1951; *The Beauty of Modern Glass* by R. Stennett-Willson, London and New York 1958; *Modern Glass* by Ada Polak, London 1962; *Svenskt Glas* by Elisa Steenberg, Stockholm 1964; *Scandinavian Design: Objects of a Life Style* by Eileene Harrison Beer, New York and Toronto 1975; *International Modern Glass* by Geoffrey Beard, London 1976; *Sven Palmqvist, Orrefors,* exhibition folder by Dag Widman, Stockholm 1982; *Design Since 1945,* edited by Kathryn Hiesinger and Goerge Marcus, Philadelphia and London 1983; *Design in Sweden,* edited by Monica Boman, Stockholm 1985; *Twentieth Century Design: Glass* by Frederick Cooke, London 1986; *Scandinavia: Ceramics and Glass in the Twentieth Century* by Jennifer Hawkins Opie, London 1989.

During my work as a glass designer, I have found that no material is closer to the light. With glass you can sculpt with light, paint with the spectral colours through the aid of the sun. Glass will express so much more than other materials; it will never be affected—it is eternal, unchangeable. The air bubble born in the heat of a sudden improvisation, locked up forever in the crystal block—a moment of eternity in the wide space of the universe.

—Sven Palmqvist (1983)

Sven Palmqvist: Glass wall for the Swedish Broadcasting and Television Corporation, Stockholm, 1961

PANTON, Verner.

Danish architectural, interior, textile and industrial designer. Born in Gamtofte, 13 February 1926. Studied at the Technical School, Odense, 1944–47; Royal Academy of Fine Arts, Copenhagen, 1947–51; also study travels in Holland, Germany, France and Italy, 1953–55. Served in the Danish Army, 1947. Married Marianne Pherson in 1964; daughter: Carin. Worked with the architect Arne Jacobsen, Copenhagen, 1950–52; freelance architect and designer, working in Denmark, 1955–62, in France, 1962, and in Switzerland from 1963: designed for Bayer, Spiegel publishing, Gruner and Jahr, Fritz Hansen Herman Miller, Cassina, Thonet, Louis Poulsen, Unika-Vaev, Mira-X, etc. Visiting professor of industrial design, Hochschule fur Gestaltung, Offenbach, 1984. **Exhibitions:** Dansk Kobstaevne, Fredericia, 1958; Bauzentrum, Hamburg, 1961; Musee des Arts Decoratifs, Paris, 1969; Galerie Interieur, Kortrijk, 1978; Bella Center, Copenhagen, 1988. Recipient: Poul Henningsen Prize, Copenhagen, 1967; Rosenthal Studio Prize, Selb, 1967; Eurodomus Award, Milan, 1968; Osterreichisches Bauzentrum Medal, Vienna, 1968; International Furnishing Salon Award, Vienna, 1969; Gute Form Prize, Bonn, 1972, 1986; Mobelprisen, Copenhagen, 1978; International Design Award, New York, 1963, 1968, 1981; Design Center Awards, Stuttgart, 1981, 1982, 1984; Sadolin Colour Prize, Copenhagen, 1986. Fellow, Royal Society of Arts, London. Member: Medlem Akademisk Arkitektforbund, Denmark; Danske Arkitekters Landsforbund; Industrielle Designere Danmark; Schweizerischer Werkbund. Address: Kohlenberggasse 21, 4051 Basel, Switzerland.

Works:

Bachelor Chair in tubular steel and leather, for Fritz Hansen, 1955.
Cone Chair in upholstered steel, for Plus Linje, 1957.
Topan Lamp in aluminium, for Louis Poulsen, 1959.
Geometri wool carpet, for Unika Vaev, 1961.
Wire Chair in upholstered steel wire, for Plus Linje, 1961.
S-Chair in laminated wood, for Thonet, 1966.
Panton Chair in plastic, for Herman Miller, 1967.
Living Tower upholstered furniture, for Herman Miller, 1969.
Panthella lamps series in plastic and metal, for Louis Poulsen, 1970.
1.2.3 furniture system in upholstered tubular steel, for Fritz Hansen, 1973.
Emmenthaler upholstered furniture, for Cassina, 1979.
Pantheon upholstered sofa, for Erik Jorgensen, 1986.
Bowl in crumpled silver, for Georg Jensen, 1988.

Publications:

By PANTON: book—*Verner Panton*, Copenhagen 1986.

On PANTON: books—*Brugskunst: Mobler, Textiler, Lamper* by Birgit and Christian Enevoldsen, Copenhagen 1958; *Modern Scandinavian Furniture* by Ulf Hard af Segerstad, Copenhagen 1963, London 1964; *World Furniture,* edited by Helena Hayward, London 1965, 1981; *Danish Design,* edited by Svend Erik Moller, Copenhagen 1974; *The Modern Chair: Classics in Production* by Clement Meadmore, London 1974; *Contemporary Furniture* by Klaus-Jurgen Sembach, Stuttgart and London 1982; *Design Since 1945*, edited by Kathryn Hiesinger and George Marcus, Philadelphia and London 1983; *Mid-Century: Furniture of the 1950s* by Cara Greenberg, London 1984; *Twentieth Century Design: Furniture* by Penny Sparke, London 1986; *Modern Furniture Classics* by Miriam Stimpson, London 1987.

The main purpose of my work is to provoke people into using their imaginations. Most people spend their lives dwelling in dreary, grey-beige conformity, mortally afraid of using colours. By experimenting with lighting, colours, textiles, and furniture and utilizing the latest technologies, I try to show new ways, to encourage people to use their fantasy and make their surroundings more exciting.

Some thoughts on chairs and on sitting: Observe children, how they sit—right on the edge of the chair, barely reaching for the floor with their toes, or messy all over the chair, kneeling on the seat, or crouching on their heels. Then the grown-ups say, "Sit properly, sit decently, sit straight." I'm asking why should this be? The king sits upon his throne, guests sit around the table, music-lovers sit in a concert, the old woman slouches in her easy-chair, the poor sinner sits bent-over on a bench. Is sitting a theatrical game? Do you only have to look at the chairs to know what is going to take place on them? To disturb this game of chairs and sitting is a real temptation. It could lead to making chairs on which you sit right, no matter how or why you sit: with your knees over the side, the arm around the back of the chair, slouching or bravely straight. It would also lead to making chairs which, as long as they are empty, do not tell about the purpose for which they were put there. Will people sit on them to eat or play cards or even quarrel? The chairs should be, while useful, objects in their own right, and, when arranged next to each other, should form a kind of chair-landscape, which refuses to be just functional.

Another thought: Steel tubes, foam, springs, and covers have been so developed technically that we can create forms which were unthinkable just a few years ago. Designers should now use these materials to create objects which up to now they could only see in their dreams. Personally, I'd like to design chairs which exhaust all the technical possibilities of the present in which I also live.

—Verner Panton

Verner Panton: *Wire Chair*, **for Plus Linje, 1969**

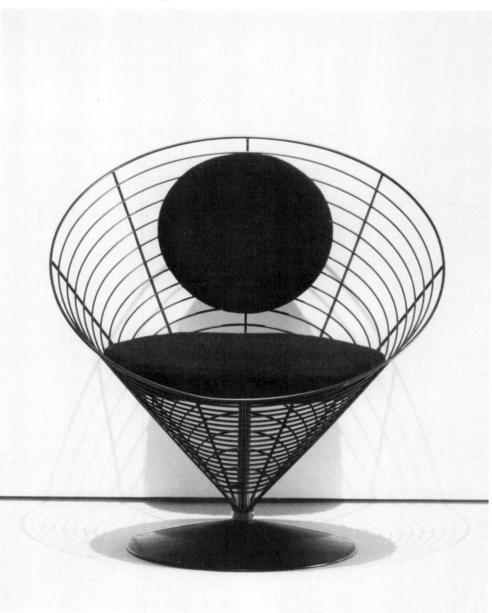

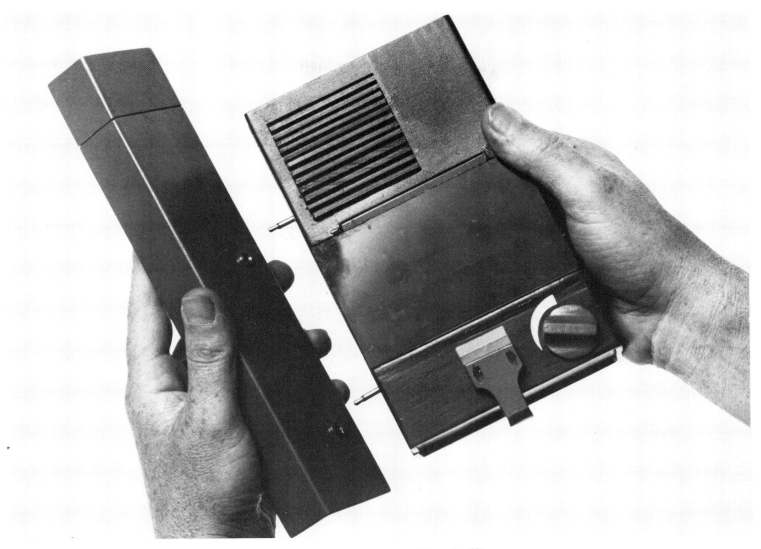

Victor Papanek: *Batta-Koya (Talking Teacher)* tape cassette player, for the governments of Nigeria and Tanzania, 1981

PAPANEK, Victor.

American product designer. Born in Vienna, Austria, 22 November 1925; emigrated to the United States in 1939; naturalized, 1946. Studied industrial design, at Cooper Union, New York, 1942–48; also studied at Frank Lloyd Wright's Taliesin and Taliesin West, 1949, Massachusetts Institute of Technology, 1954, 1955, Chicago Institute of General Semantics, 1956, and at other universities, 1950–57. Served in the camouflage unit of the United States Army, in Alaska and the Aleutian Islands, 1944–45. Married Winifred Higginbotham in 1950 (divorced, 1957); daughter: Nicolette; married Jean Parker in 1957 (divorced, 1964); Harlanne Herdman in 1966; daughter: Jennifer. Independent product development designer, from 1964: design consultant to Volvo A/B, Dartington Industries, Planet Products, World Health Organization, Midwest Applied Science Corporation, etc. Instructor, Ontario College of Art, University of Toronto, 1954–59; associate professor of art and design, State University of New York at Buffalo, 1959–62; associate professor and head of product design department, North Carolina State College, Raleigh, 1962–64; associate professor, 1964–68, professor and chairman of environmental and industrial design department, 1968–70, Purdue University, Lafayette, Indiana; professor, 1970–71, and dean of the school of design, 1971–72, California Institute of the Arts, Valencia; professor and chairman of the design department, Kansas City Art Institute, 1976–81; J. L. Constant pro-

fessor of design, University of Kansas, Lawrence, from 1981; also visiting professor and lecturer at Rhode Island School of Design, Providence, 1959, Penland School of Crafts, North Carolina, 1963–67, Kunstakademiets Arkitektskole, Copenhagen, 1972–73, Manchester Polytechnic, 1973–75, Carleton University, Ottawa, 1975–76, etc. Developing Countries Working Group Member, ICSID International Council of Societies of Industrial Design, from 1973; founder-member, Developing Countries Design Information Group, from 1973. **Exhibitions:** *Visionary Architecture,* Museum of Modern Art, New York, 1962; *Do-It-Yourself Design,* International Design Centre, West Berlin, 1973; *Papanek: Work and Theories,* Galerij Grada, Zagreb, 1974. **Collections:** Centre Georges Pompidou, Paris. Recipient: Gold Medal, Indianapolis Art Directors Club, 1968; UNESCO Design Award, 1963; ICSID/Philips Design Award, 1978; Kyoto Honours Award, 1981; Dartington/Watershed Speaker Award, 1982; August St. Gaudens Medal, Cooper Union, New York, 1987; National Endowment for the Arts Distinguished Designer Fellowship, Washington, D.C., 1988. Honorary Doctorate: Marycrest College, Davenport, Iowa, 1983; University of Zagreb, 1986. Fellow, Creative Leadership Council, 1962, Creative Education Foundation, 1962, Chartered Society of Designers, 1974; honorary fellow, American Scandinavian Foundation, 1966, Industrial Designers Society of Mexico, 1975; member, Industrielle Designere Den-

mark, 1972, U.S. Federal Design Council, 1977, Industrial Design Institute of Australia, 1978. Address: School of Architecture and Urban Design, University of Kansas, Lawrence, Kansas 66045, U.S.A.

Works:

Candle-heat powered tin can radio, for the United Nations in Bali and Indonesia, 1958.

Exercise environment for children with cerebral palsy, 1967 (with Finnish student team).

24-pod midrange hi-fi speaker clusters, for Altec-Lansing Corporation, 1970–74.

Exercise bicycles for handicapped children, for Ritter Surgical Supplies, St. Louis, 1970–88.

Work enrichment scheme components for foreign guest-workers, for Volvo A/B, Goteborg, 1972–75 (as member of design team).

Do-it-yourself play environment in mixed media, for the American Cerebral Palsy Association, 1973.

Auto-diagnostic medical equipment for developing countries, for the World Health Organization, from 1975.

Medical lamps and task lighting in aluminium, steel and brass, for Planet Products, Australia, 1978.

Bata-Koya (Talking Teacher) cassette tape player, for the governments of Tanzania and Nigeria, 1979.

High-altitude geodesic tents in canvas, plastic and aluminium, for Trans-World Expedition Gear, Berkeley, 1979.

Solar-powered refrigerator with lithium bromide coolant, for the World Health Organization, 1982.

Custom-designed surgical scalpels in steel, for Ritter Surgical Supplies, St. Louis, 1982.

Mobile and adjustable exhibition structures in wood, metal, glass and plastics, for Koch-Multivac Corporation, Kansas City, 1982.

High-performance emergency flashlights in plastic and metal, for Croatia Corporation, Zagreb, 1984.

Exercise environment for multi-handicapped children, for New York Presbyterian Hospital, 1985.

Modular electric heating carpet in wool, cotton or plastic fibres, for Yamasaki Company, Osaka, 1986.

Musicians' ergonomic chairs in hardwood and steel, for Pro Musica Company, San Diego, 1987.

Publications:

By PAPANEK: books—*Creative Engineering,* Hamilton 1961; *Miljon och Miljonerna,* Stockholm 1970; *Design for the Real World,* New York, 1971, London 1972, 1985, Chicago 1985; *Big Character Poster no. 1: Work Chart for Designers,* Copenhagen 1973; *Nomadic Furniture 2,* with Jim Hennessey, New York, 1974; *How Things Don't Work,* with Jim Hennessey, New York 1977; *L'Arredamento Mobile 1 e 2,* Milan 1978; *Design for Human Scale,* New York 1983; *Viewing the World Whole,* Lawrence 1983; *Nomadic Furniture 1 and 2,* Zagreb 1983; *Design and Society,* with others, London 1984; *Kansas Communities,* with others, Lawrence 1986; *The Other Side of Design,* with others, Amsterdam 1988.

On PAPANEK: books—*The Conran Directory of Design,* edited by Stephen Bayley, London 1985; *Design Source Book* by Penny Sparke and others, London 1986; *New American Design* by Hugh Aldersley-Williams, New York 1988.

As a working designer, I feel that product design *excludes* large numbers of people. Most design is routinely performed for middle-class income, predominantly white populations in Eastern and Western Europe, North America, and Australia. These mythical consumers are envisaged as young, in good health, and with a decent income. Product design has helped industry manipulate people's desires into wants and needs. Furthermore, design, through forced obsolescence, has created dissatisfaction and irritation among consumers.

To fulfill its social and moral obligation, design must be turned around to re-examine its performance in three specific ways:

(1) The true needs of the elderly, the handicapped and retarded, children, babies, and the poor, as well as many other sub-groups must be taken into consideration. Members of the consumer group must become part of the design team. This team must be cross-disciplinary.

(2) The problems of people in developing countries must be met by designers, by helping the capable talent now existing in the third world to develop their own goals. This will mean: appropriateness of scale, local autonomy, independence from international and multinational corporations, the use of alternative energy, decentralization, and research into appropriate technology on village levels.

(3) Product and graphic design must also change to fit in with the realities of the 1980s. This means an increase in quality in all consumer products. It furthermore means that products must be designed to be safe, easy to maintain and repair, simple to understand and learn to use, and beautiful in appearance. They must be designed to last long, use renewable resources in their construction, and be prudent in energy usage. They must make participation by consumers possible and still bring long-lasting delight to the people who use them.

This combination of ideal function with common sense and aesthetic excellence can be described by the phrase "frugal sensuousness." (Since my first book appeared in 23 languages and I have worked and taught in many countries, I have seen the beginnings of this change, specifically in Denmark, Sweden, Finland, and Holland, and, to a lesser degree, in the United Kingdom, Canada, and Australia.)

—Victor Papanek

Born in Vienna, Victor Papanek came to New York at the age of fourteen. He studied industrial design at Cooper Union, engineering at the Massachusetts Institute of Technology, and architecture with Frank Lloyd Wright, whom he considers a major influence on his ideas.

While working briefly for Raymond Loewy and, later, Helena Rubenstein, he became critical of advertising and contacted the United Nations which appointed him a design expert to help developing countries. During this period, he also began his career in teaching. During his years at Purdue University, 1965–70, he started writing his first major book, *Design for the Real World,* which brought much recognition and controversy, since it attacked the very premises of American design—conspicuous consumption and planned obsolescence.

This book established Papanek as a design critic at a time when most designers were more concerned with enhancing their images than defining an ideology for responsible design. *Design for the Real World* became a primer of many design students around the world and remains popular today. In the mid-1970s, while he was teaching widely in the United States and abroad, he co-authored with Jim Hennessey three additional books, *Nomadic Furniture, Nomadic Furniture II,* and *How Things Work.* These "how-to-do-it" books were a necessary extension of his first book, since at that time, most manufacturers were insensitive to the needs of an increasingly mobile society. Since moving to the University of Kansas, he has published *Design for Human Scale* and *Viewing the Whole World.*

His recent commissions have included architectural concepts for the dock area of Bristol, England and the design of the Greenshade Studio C Lamp which is manufactured in Australia. The lamp utilizes a double parabolic shade to reduce heat and to maximize light from a less powerful bulb.

—Al Gowan

PARISI, Ico.

Italian architect, painter, stage and industrial designer. Born in Palermo, Sicily, 23 September 1916. Studied building construction in Como, 1931–35; architecture under Alberto Sartoris, at the Instituto Atheneum, Lausanne, 1948–52: Dip.Arch. 1950. Served in the Italian Army, 1940–43: Major, 2 war crosses. Married Luisa Aiani in 1947. Worked in the studio of architect Giuseppe Terragni, Como, 1935–36; independent filmmaker, Como, 1937–38, and stage designer, Como, 1939; freelance designer and visual artist, and founder with Luisa Parisi, of Studio La Ruota, Como, from 1945: has designed for Artecasa, Bonacina, Cassina, A. Colombo, Mobili Italiana Moderni, etc. **Exhibitions:** Villa Olmo, Como, 1937, 1957, 1979; Fondazione La Masa, Venice, 1943; Galerie Germain, Paris, 1974; In-Arch, Rome, 1974; Serre Ratti, Como, 1977; Palazzo delle Prigioni, Venice, 1978; Galleria La Colonna, Como, 1978, 1982; Centro Proposte, Salerno, 1979; Galleria d'Arte Moderna, Rome, 1979; Museum of Art, Slonenj Gradec, 1979; Scuola Caprin, Trieste, 1980; Musee d'Ixelles, Brussels, 1980; Palazzo dei Diamanti, Ferrara, 1980, 1981; Galleria La Boite, Salerno, 1981; Italian Cultural Institute, 1984; Centre Culturel ADF, Lille, 1984; Galleria La Chiocciola, Padua, 1985. Recipient: Film Prize, Como, 1937; Silver Medal, Milan Triennale, 1954; Compasso d'Oro Award, 1955; Color and Form exhibition medals, Como, 1957; Lurago d'Erba Gold Medal, 1959; Knight of Mark Twain Award, Kirkwood, 1971; Premio Marco Aurelio, Rome, 1974. Member: Art Club di Milano, 1952; ADI Associazione Disegno Industriale, Milan, 1956. Address: Studio La Ruota, Via Diaz 24, 22100 Como, Italy.

Works:

Roll-top desk in rosewood, for Artecasa, 1951.

Unio wall unit with interchangeable cabinets and shelves, for MIM Mobili Italiani Moderni, 1952.

Chintz-upholstered armchair and table, for A. Colombo, 1953.

Armchair in metal and plywood, for Cassina, 1955.

Chair in cane with slung leather seat, for Bonacina, 1959.

Contenitoriumani human womb-environment, 1968.

Ipotesi per una Casa Esistenziale dwelling project, 1973.

Operazione Arcevia existential community project, 1976.

Publications:

By PARISI: books—*Padiglione Soggiorno,* Como 1954, Milan 1955; *Biblioteca al Parco,* Milan 1955; *Immagine per una Industria,* Como 1969; *Ipotesi per una Casa Esistenziale,* Rome 1974; *Operazione Arcevia,* Como 1975; *Utopia Realizzabile,* Milan 1978; *Architecture en Papier,* exhibition catalogue, Paris 1984.

On PARISI: books—*Gute Mobel—Schone Raume,* edited by Mia Seeger, Stuttgart 1953; *Art in European Architecture* by P. Damaz, New York 1956; *Catalogo Bolaffi dell'Architettura Italiana 1963–1966,* edited for Pier Carlo Santini and G. L. Marini, Turin 1966; *Design e Forme Nuove nell'Arredamento Italiano,* edited by Paolo Portoghesi and Marino Marini, Rome 1978; *Ico Parisi: Operazione Arcevia,* exhibition catalogue by G. de Marchis, Rome 1979; *Ico Parisi,* exhibition catalogue by Pierre Restany, Brussels 1980; *Contemporary Furniture,* edited by Klaus-Jurgen Sembach, Stuttgart and London 1982; *Mid-Century: Furniture of the 1950s* by Cara Greenberg, London 1984; *Ico Parisi: L'Officina del Possibile* by F. Gualdoni, Milan 1986: Como nel Disegno exhibition catalogue by L. Caramel, Como 1987.

A creative crisis in the current situation—with regard to industrial design—has led to an aesthetic levelling of the objects produced. My analysis sees the following as the decisive causes:

The obligation of almost all designers to con-

Ico Parisi: *Contenitore Umano Numero 2*, **1968**

centrate on forms dictated more by fashion than by the functional requirements, repetitive even in the most difficult conditions, doing formal violence to the object.

The growing numbers of points of production for the same ranges of products. This results in deliberate imitation of designs, with consequent commercial confusion between one product and another.

The readiness to follow the lead of the consumerist population that believes in the new object and will put up with the formal variations imposed by producers. This forces industries to change the form of the same model ever more frequently to make sure that it will be exchanged, a phenomenon that does not allow an object to be usefully improved aesthetically, economically, or commercially. Such improvement can occur only if the model has a period of steady production.

To my mind, what is needed is a more severe professional approach by the designer, who can then defend us from industrial speculations so as to revalue his creativity, personality, and professionalism.

—Ico Parisi

Leo Parisi and his wife Luisa have been responsible for a long line of designs, chiefly furniture, which have been remarkable for the exploration of the formal and structural possibilities of different sorts of material, including plywood, metal, marble, glass, basketware, cane, leather, and plastic. Typical of their approach is the 1954 villa with its extraordinary front elevation of two overlapping facades or the 1950 Egg easychair, a sort of half-shell supported by splayed legs. All their work is informed by a masterful sense of geometry, which they call upon to articulate their unconventional proposals. One calls to mind such notions as a free-standing, outdoor fireplace, surmounted by a metal hood and accompanied by a log basket utilising a frame formed of a double spiral of cane, or the table in rosewood on a white mar-

ble base; in the latter, the table top and its support are made of an up-turned cone, with sides curving in to meet the flat, marble circle of the base. The arrangement of cane circles for the 1959 chair for Bonacina further exemplifies this imaginative geometry, as do also the curves of a 1954 lamp.

These geometric forms are always so consonant with the natural structure of the materials they use that it is difficult to pinpoint the exact source of their originality, yet their work is always individual and unmistakable without ever being perverse or eccentric. In a certain sense, they continue within a rationalist scheme of designing without reducing their designs to functionalism pure and simple, and their geometry contributes an elegance of form and concept, becoming thus expressive means.

One can understand how Ico Parisi reacted to the architectural and design situation in the early 1970s when what he came to call the "survival necessities" were given a subordinate role in the making of design decisions and given only the limited attention strictly required to make things work. Other and deeper considerations of human needs were to be dominant. "This project, on which I have been working for two years, does not mean to resolve nowadays architectural problems but rather propose a living space free from all possible bonds. Man and his existential problems are here the subject," he wrote in 1974. In a sense, he suggests that it is human problems that the designer addresses and not any problem of design as such. Certainly, he does not imagine that there are unique solutions to "design problems." In some ways, his position relates to the attitudes of the Memphis designers in the 1980s but with a quite different outcome.

—Toni del Renzio

PAUL, Art(hur).

American graphic and exhibition designer. Born in Chicago, Illinois, 18 January 1925. Studied at the Art Institute of Chicago, 1940–43; Institute of Design, Illinois Institute of Technology, Chicago, 1946–50. Served in the United States Army Air Force, 1943–46: Master Sergeant. Married Beatrice Miller in 1950 (divorced, 1971); children: William, Fredric and Nina; married Suzanne Seed in 1975. Freelance illustrator and designer, Chicago, 1950–54; art director, *Playboy* magazine, Chicago, 1954–82; vice-president and art director, Playboy Enterprises, Chicago, 1962–82; freelance designer and president of Art Paul Design, Chicago, from 1982. Guest instructor, Illustrators Workshop, Tarrytown, New York, 1978. Alumni association board member, Illinois Institute of Technology, Chicago, 1978–79; trustee, Museum of Contemporary Art, Chicago; advisory board member, Moraine Valley College, Illinois, 1980, and University of Illinois School of Art and Design, 1981. **Exhibitions:** Etc. Gallery, Chicago, 1949; Gallery 500D, Chicago, 1957; University of Illinois, Chicago, 1965; *Beyond Illustration: The Art of Playboy,* Milan, 1971 (toured); *The Art of Playboy: The First 25 Years,* Cultural Center, Chicago, 1978 (toured). **Collection:** Art Institute of Chicago. Recipient: Artists Guild of Chicago Award, 1962; Norfolk Art Directors Club Award, 1962; St. Louis Art Directors Club Medal, 1963; Society of Typographic Arts Special Award, Chicago, 1964; Philadelphia Art Directors Club Creative Achievement Award, 1964, and Polycube Award, 1975; Dallas Art Directors Club Award, 1964; Boston Art Directors Club Award, 1964; City of Milan Gold Medal, 1971; *Art Direction* Magazine Award, 1975; Midwest Commercial Association of Direct Marketing Prize, 1979; New York Art Directors Club Gold Medal, 1980; Illinois Institute of Technology Professional Achievement Award, 1983; Art Directors Hall of Fame Award, 1986. Honorary Member: Artists Guild of Chicago, 1965, and Society of Publication Designers, 1980. Member: Chicago Society of Communicating Arts, 1960; Chicago 27 Designers, 1976; Alliance Graphique Internationale, 1978. Address: 175 East Delaware Place, Suite 7511, Chicago, Illinois 60611, U.S.A.

Works:

Playboy Bunny logo, for Playboy Enterprises, 1953.

Playboy magazine design and layout, for Playboy Enterprises, 1953–79.
Corporate identity program, for Playboy Enterprises, 1953–82.
Television commercial advertisements, for Playboy Enterprises, 1965–82.
Beyond Illustration: The Art of Playboy travelling exhibition layouts, for Playboy Enterprises, 1971.
Poster, for the Chicago International Film Festival, 1980.
Logotype symbol, for Golda's hot dog stands, Chicago, 1986.

Publications:

By PAUL: books—*Beyond Illustration: The Art of Playboy,* exhibition catalogue, Chicago 1971; *The Art of Playboy: The First 25 Years,* exhibition catalogue with preface by Ted Hearne, Chicago 1978.
On PAUL: books—*Playboy Illustration,* exhibition catalogue, Edmonton 1976; *Beyond Illustration,* exhibition catalogue, Madison 1978; *Who's Who in Graphic Art,* edited by Walter Amstutz, Dubendorf 1982; *Playboy Art Exhibit,* exhibition catalogue, Lafayette 1983; *The Art of Playboy,* with text by Ray Bradbury, Chicago 1985.

Most of my career has been with one magazine, *Playboy.* I designed the first issue and the rabbit symbol in 1953 and retired from the corporation in 1982.
Before 1953, I freelanced illustration and de-

sign for various clients. Today I do much the same thing—but more selectively.
Looking at the best of my past work, I would interpret it as being bold and risky. I believe in taking chances in design and illustration because I feel communication is helped by it.

—Art Paul

Art Paul has been credited with leading the "Illustration Liberation Movement." This distinction came from a propitious set of circumstances beginning when Paul, a rebellious art student, found himself questioning the notion of a difference between high and low art. Such nonprejudicial instincts allied him, perhaps unconsciously at first, with the democratic and experimental approach of Bauhaus teaching. His obstinacy about seeing a hierarchy in art was reinforced on his return from World War II when he attended the Institute of Design in Chicago, which had become a modern mecca of graphic design, and especially the Bauhaus philosophy, with the influx of such Bauhaus teachers as Moholy-Nagy.
Uncharacteristically, in a volatile and changeable profession, Paul's notoriety has come from one client—*Playboy* magazine. Hired by publisher/editor Hugh Hefner when the magazine was founded and given free rein, Paul fashioned a highly original and nonconformist view of men's entertainment in magazine format. This freedom allowed him to indulge his "grand plan" for what a magazine should be in the bland commercialism of the 50s. This plan viewed the raw material of illustration, an area

Art Paul: *Rabbit* symbol, for the Playboy Corporation, 1953

in which Paul had freelanced prior to his employment at *Playboy,* as important in its own right, as editorial art, to provoke the reader and to establish a mood for the story. At first, unable to persuade painters to work for him in this capacity, he created his own constructions and collages to enliven the magazine's visuals as well as to convince artists that this was a respectable exercise in originality. His insertion of die-cuts and pop-ups between pages, techniques previously employed in children's books, made illustration kinetic. In this, he broke the lock that the grid had held on modern layout and humanized the look of the page. This highly conceptual approach may seem uncharacteristic for a magazine that has a reputation of dealing with men's prurient interests, but it meshed with Hefner's desire for a mix of urbanity and liveliness.

The debonair image carried over to Paul's design of a corporate logo for *Playboy,* the now internationally recognized rabbit symbol, introduced in 1953. The stylized rabbit head with its dignified profile and formal bowtie is set slightly out of kilter by the roguish slant of the ears. It could be compared to the suave and sophisticated, yet somewhat foppish gentleman who graces the pages and annually the cover of *The New Yorker.* However, in contrast, except for the first issue, the rabbit has been seen on every cover of *Playboy* and has graced hundreds of products of the Playboy corporation. This seemingly ageless corporate logo epitomized the daring, exciting and risky venture of *Playboy,* on both a practical and conceptual level.

As the founding art direct of *Playboy,* Art Paul not only supported new talent and reversed the tendency to conformity in mass magazines, but he also added credibility and legitimacy to a men's magazine and the taboo content within. Both were avant garde but in different ways— Art Paul's work was legitimate art whereby *Playboy*'s intentions were purely risqué.

—Sarah Bodine

PAWLOSKI, Andrzej.

Polish exhibition, stage, film, graphic and industrial designer. Born in Wadowice, 20 July 1925. Educated at high school and unofficial "underground" school, in Tarnow, 1937–42; studied at the Jagiellonian University, Krakow, 1942–45, and at the Academy of Fine Arts, Krakow, 1945–50. Served in the Polish Home Army, Krakow, 1942–54. Married Wanda Grochowalska in 1950: children: Maciej, Marcin and Marek. Independent painter, sculptor and designer, in Krakow, from 1950: kinetic artist, working with the Cricot 2 theatre company, Krakow, 1956–57; design specialist for the Prozamet industrial building company, Krakow, from 1960; consultant to the Krakow Metal Products Company, 1963; research consultant on car ergonomics, for the Bielsko-Biala factory, 1978–80. Assistant professor of interior design, 1948–54, dean, 1954–63 and from 1981, chairman of the industrial design department, 1963–71, senate member from 1963, chairman of industrial form department, 1964–66, chairman of the product design and visual communications department, 1966–68, chairman of the design methodology department from 1968, professor of industrial design from 1971, and president of the senate committee on publishing, 1978–80, at the Academy of Fine Arts, Krakow. Chairman, 1965–69, vice-

chairman, 1973–75, and board member, 1975–79, Association of Industrial Designers, Warsaw; executive vice-president, 1967–69, executive board member, 1969–71, and congress coordinator, 1975, 1979, ICSID International Council of Societies of Industrial Design. **Exhibitions:** Cricot 2 Theatre, Krakow, 1957; KMPIK Gallery, Warsaw, 1957; Gallery Krzysztofory, Krakow, 1964, 1988; National Museum, Krakow-Peiskowa Skala, 1966; BWA Gallery, Lublin, 1966; Art Gallery of Zakopane, 1966; BWA Galleries of Koszalin, Radawica and Slupsk, 1973; Desa Gallery, Krakow, 1974; Omamy Gallery, Krakow, 1978; Form Gallery, Warsaw, 1980. Recipient: Silver Cross of Merit, Krakow, 1952; Polish Ministry of Art and Culture Award, 1963, 1964, 1966, 1970, 1977; Polish Industrial Design Award, 1966; Polish Knight's Cross, 1969; Order of Polonia Restituta, 1970; Knight's Cross of Honour, 1976; City of Krakow Cultural Award, 1976; Gold Medal for Services to Krakow, 1977; Polish Teachers Union Medal, 1977. Member: Union of Polish Graphic Artists, 1953; Association of Industrial Designers, Warsaw, 1965; Union of Polish Artist-Photographers, Warsaw, 1979. Address: 18-Stycznia 60/11, 30 045 Krakow, Poland.

Works:

Young Plastic Arts exhibition layouts, for the BWA Gallery, Krakow, 1956.
Telephone apparatus, for the Telecommunications Company, Radom, 1959.
Automatic loading, wire-cutting, and moulding machines, for the Prozamet Company, Krakow, 1960.
West sewing machine, for Polna Przemysl, 1961.
Art in Krakow 1350–1550 exhibition layouts, for the Jagiellonian University, Krakow, 1964.
Lightweight roofing structure in polyester resin, for Stockznia-Ustka, 1972.
500 Years of Printing in Krakow exhibition layouts, for the MN Gallery, Krakow, 1974.
Fiat 126 ergonomic car seating, for the Bielsko-Biala Factory, 1979.
Fiat KL1000 ergonomic car seating, for the Bielsko-Biala Factory, 1980.
The History of Jewish Culture exhibition layouts, for the Historical Museum, Krakow, 1980.

Publications:

By PAWLOWSKI: book—*Initiation: On Art, Design, and Design Teaching,* edited by Janusz Krupinski, Warsaw 1987; articles—in *Zycie Literackie* (Krakow), no. 49, 1961; *Architektura* (Warsaw), no. 11, 1968; *Polska* (Warsaw), no. 6, 1970; *Suggestions* (Warsaw), no. 1, 1970, no. 2, 1970; *ZPAP Bulletin* (Warsaw), no. 1, 1973; *Wiadomosci IWP* (Warsaw), no. 3/4, 1974, no. 3/4, 1975; *Technicheskaya Estetika* (Moscow), no. 7, 1975; *Projekt* (Warsaw), no. 4, 1987.
On PAWLOWSKI: books—*Design for the Real World* by Victor Papanek, New York, 1971; *To See and to Understand,* exhibition catalogue, Warsaw 1975; *Andrezej Pawlowski,* exhibition catalogue by Mieczyslaw Porebski, Krakow 1988.

During the last dozen or so years in Poland, numerous terms were coined for the field that now can be spoken of as: industrial pattern design, designing industrial forms, graphic arts of industrial forms, industrial artistic design, industrial design, artistic construction, esthetics of industrial production, industrial art, product

design, form-making, or industrial form design.

There is no other field that released such an out-burst of language fancy and imagination. However, it may be that there are some reasons for it. Perhaps there are different branches within the field of design. But so far, these differences have not been determined, and any attempts to do that have been drowned in the ocean which is proudly called "art integration."

The main reason for such a state is that design is always considered an artistic activity. The means of activity cannot be substituted for the ends of it. A disregard of this basic rule has become a common sin of many graphic artists-designers.

As soon as industrial design developed, there appeared an ardent debate on the question: "Who am I? A graphic artist or an engineer?" A question of this type explains in itself the situation that exists in this field. One cannot ask an Egyptian: "Are you English or Spanish?"

In design, we have to do with such factors as economic, constructive, technological, aesthetic, and utilitarian. These factors are examined during the process of design by teams of experts. It is obvious that the economist (E) examines the constructive (k), technological (t), aesthetic-graphic (p) and utilitarian (u) factors mainly from the economic point of view:

$$E - \frac{k \cdot t \cdot p \cdot u}{e}$$

The constructor (K) examines the above factors with regard to the construction:

$$K - \frac{e \cdot t \cdot p \cdot u}{k}$$

The technologist (T) examines these factors from the technological point of view:

$$T - \frac{e \cdot k \cdot p \cdot u}{t}$$

While the graphic designer (P) examines them from the point of view of his profession and interests, i.e. of graphic arts:

$$P - \frac{e \cdot k \cdot t \cdot u}{p}$$

A question arises: who in the design team is to determine the utilitarian qualities of the product? Is it possible that these qualities are less essential than the other ones? Or, is the determining of the utilitarian qualities so simple that it can be done by any of the above mentioned experts?

The industrial designer (U) examines the economic, constructive, technological, and graphic factors from the utilitarian point of view:

$$U - \frac{e \cdot k \cdot t \cdot p}{u}$$

The design of the utilitarian form of industrial products is a separate profession which requires expert knowledge and qualifications. The emancipation of this profession is necessary for actual realization of social needs.

To state that the utilitarian aspect of the product can be handled while the graphic and visual factors are examined introduces illusion and mystification, which lead to the domination of the graphic form over the function of the product. It is in the interest of industrial design that all the adjoining fields develop harmoniously, visual design, craftsmanship, and art industry included. Also, a modern graphic art can and should be expected to give many valuable inspirations if it is independent and progressive.

However, we should not attempt to identify industrial design with graphic arts and vice versa. Only the neophytes who have not experienced well the taste of either field can presume that both fields are the same. Let us not mix salt with sugar merely because they look alike. Putting an equation mark between these two professions will doom one of them to failure. (*Excerpted from a paper delivered in 1972 during the Conference of Artists and Designers Union of Poland and the U.S.S.R., in Moscow.*)

—Andrzej Pawlowski

Andrzej Pawlowki's philosophical views are rooted in the rationalism of European science and in an intellectual orientation in arts. His strict, analytical mind is turned toward tomorrow. His personality was shaped not by the past but by expectations and anticipations of new events and new insoluble questions.

The idea of an active attitude toward life, as preached by the Greek philosophers, directed Pawlowski to Descartes, Kant, Marx, and finally, to the Polish thinker Tadeusz Kotarbiński, the author of praxeology, i.e., the theory of effective action. This philosophy, with its main features of rationalism, realism, and activism, accorded with his own world view. He has also relied on his sound judgment of reality. This attitude, which he might have inherited from his peasant ancestors, has allowed him to confront, under specific Polish conditions, an ideal, theoretical model with life itself. He was reinforced in this attitude by the experiences of his youth, first his activity in the resistance movement, an underground education in agriculture, then his employment in a metallurgic plant.

Unlike most other people in the art world, Pawlowski has had regular contact with centers of science and has participated in scholarly councils, e.g., in the Ergonomic Committee of the Polish Academy of Sciences. He is also a member of the Committee on Scientology and of the editorial office of the journal *Designing and Systems* at the same Academy.

His simultaneous participation in scientific research and art has sometimes confused his critics. Once I asked him myself about his opinion on this association of two functions. His answer was: "I am trying to objectivize the creative process, but only in designing. I do not favor rationalization of artistic creativity, in spite of such tendencies existing in art. It is a coincidence that I work in both designing and art. For example, the concept of form naturally shaped is the result of my interest in praxeology and precisely in the principle of minimalization which I still consider very inspiring but unexploited either by designers or by artists."

Pawlowski has strongly emphasized the distinctiveness of design as a creative discipline and its independence of fine arts and applied arts. Hence, his reluctance to consider himself an artist and to misue this word. However, the dilemma—art or design—becomes pointless in front of works by such creators as Gropius, Itten, Albers, Lissitzky, Eames, Aalto, Ekuan, or Sottsass. Pawlowski's work also shows a unity of artistic and scientific elements.

The division into art and design was not accepted in the past. The Greek term *techne* comprises technics, art, and science. The Latin term *ars* referred to both—to technical and what is today called "artistic" production. A Polish philosopher, Wladyslaw Tatarkiewicz, emphasized that the ancient Greeks and Romans "had not intended to separate technics from arts nor arts from science. There was a deeper thought or instinct involved in their association, i.e., that their essence is the same and that all the

three branches—technics, arts, and science—are nothing other than skillful production: *ars est systema praeceptorum.*"

That explains why Pawlowski's work is as indivisible as is Eames's heritage. His *Kineform*, which open up the secrets of motion and light, and the biomorphic *Manekiny*, his museum exhibits, and his designs humanizing man's work and raising his purposeful effort to the level of creativity are all based on the same mental attitude and confidence in logic and the cognitive potentialities of intellect. It is surprising that current times, so strongly marked by scepticism, have not undermined that attitude in Pawlowski's mind.

—Szymon Bojko

PENTAGRAM DESIGN.

British architectural, interior, graphic and product design partnership. Founded by Theo Crosby, Alan Fletcher, Colin Forbes, Kenneth Grange and Mervyn Kurlansky, in London, 1972; subsequently joined by current partners John McConnell in 1974, David Hillman in 1978, Peter Harrison in 1979, Kit Hinrichs, Linda Hinrichs and Neil Shakery in 1986, Etan Manasse in 1987, and Woody Pirtle in 1988. Offices established in New York, 1978, and in San Francisco, 1986. Major designs include corporate identities for Lloyd's of London, Nieman Marcus, Reuters, Lucas Industries, Solaglas; alphabets for Arup Associates, IBM Europe, Cunard, Nissan, Rank Xerox; promotional graphics for American Express, British Olivetti, Chase Manhattan Bank, Pirelli, Polaroid Corporation, Roche; industrial designs for British Rail, General Electric, Ideal-Standard, Kenwood, Kodak, Parker, Platignum, Shiseido, Wilkinson Sword, etc. **Collections:** Museum of Modern Art, New York; Stedelijk Museum, Amsterdam; Centre Georges Pompidou, Paris; Musee de la Publicite, Paris: Victoria and Albert Museum, London. **Addresses:** 11 Needham Road, London W11, England; 212 Fifth Avenue, New York, New York 10110, U.S.A.; 620 Davies Street, San Francisco, California 94111, U.S.A.

Works:

High-speed train, for British Rail, 1976 (Grange).
Unilever House interiors, London, for Unilever, 1979–83 (Crosby).
Company identity and book-jacket designs, for Faber and Faber, from 1981 (McConnell).
IRM: Information and Resource Management magazine design, for Ericsson Information Systems, 1983–85 (Hillman).
AIGA Teapot poster, for the American Institute of Graphic Arts, 1985 (Pirtle).
Yesterday's Tomorrows exhibition layouts, for the Smithsonian Institution, Washington, D.C., 1986 (Manasse).
100 Years of the Motor-Car poster, for Daimler-Benz, 1985 (Fletcher).
Near Eastern Gallery interiors, for the Metropolitan Museum of Art, New York, 1986 (Manasse).
Vegetables book design, for Chronicle Books, 1986 (K. Hinrichs).
Identity, signage and promotional materials, for the Museum of Modern Art, New York, from 1987 (Kurlansky).

Corporate logotype, for Toray, 1987 (Forbes).
Children's Hospital at Stanford Capital campaign brochure, for Lucile Salter Packard, 1987 (L. Hinrichs).
Fannie Mae: Fifty Years of Opening Doors . . . book design, for Fannie Mae, 1988 (Harrison).
UCLA Summer Sessions poster, for the University of California at Los Angeles, 1989 (Pirtle).

Publications:

By PENTAGRAM: books—*Pentagram: The Work of Five Designers*, London 1972; *Living by Design*, London 1978; *Ideas on Design*, London and Boston 1986.

On PENTAGRAM: books—*The Conran Directory of Design*, edited by Stephen Bayley, London 1985; *An Introduction to Design and Culture in the Twentieth Century* by Penny Sparke, London 1986: *The Design Source Book* by Penny Sparke and others, London 1986; articles—in *Design* (London), June 1972, February 1978, January 1988; *Die Verpackung* (Zurich), September 1972; *Cree* (Paris), May 1974; *Idea* (Tokyo), September 1974; *Novum Gebrauchsgraphik* (Munich), March 1976, February 1977, January 1981; *Graphic Design* (Tokyo), September 1984; *Graphis* (Zurich), January/February 1986; *Print* (New York), January/February 1989.

Pentagram came about through the amalgamation of Crosby/Fletcher/Forbes (of which Mervyn Kurlansky had become a partner) and Kenneth Grange's industrial design practice. Pentagram seemed a more interesting solution to the name problem than a string of surnames. Inevitably, some of the members' individual reputations have stuck with them, and so have clients, and developments under Pentagram have continued trends they had already initiated. Nevertheless, there is a quality about the work they do that is now recognisably Pentagram's without in any way being just a set of exercises in a house style. This quality stems from a sort of commitment everyone at Pentagram, not just the senior partners, feels about design. They live *to* design as well as *by* it.

This sense of a "life-style" is reinforced by another aspect of Pentagram's activity, one which has been criticised both for being self-indulgent and self-seeking! This is their publishing program, which has issued the *Pentagram Papers* and the book *Living by Design*, which, to be sure, are overwhelmingly full of work of the group. Linked to this is the impresario-like role they have assumed in presenting the work of photographers such as Enzo Ragazzini and Bruce Davidson.

Another aspect of the partnership's work has been the design of exhibitions, in which area Theo Crosby has tended to be dominant. Indeed, it was his British section at the 1964 Milan Triennale that brought together the relationships that were to be the basis for Pentagram. Some of the outstanding achievements of Pentagram in this field have been *British Genius* (1977), a tented exhibition in Battersea Park, *The Environment Game* (1973), and the British Industry Pavilion at the 1967 Montreal World's Fair.

Given the nature of Pentagram and the interests and commitment of its partners and members, it is not at all surprising to discover that *Living by Design*, should characterise the practice of design under headings which, while not particularly unconventional, do demonstrate an intellectually rigorous analysis and an attention to aspects often ignored. Thus, under the main heading, "Environment Design," conservation

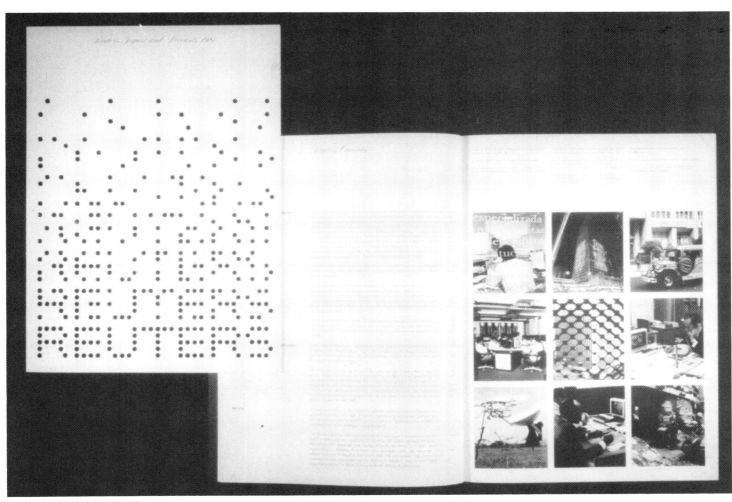

Pentagram Design: Graphics for Reuters, 1978

is identified as "Grooming white elephants." Perhaps the sometimes sharp wit and the often gentle irony are as much the consequence of Pentagram's lifestyle as contributory factors to it.

—Toni del Renzio

STUDIO PER.
Spanish architectural, industrial and graphic design firm. Founded by Pep Bonet (born 1941), Cristian Cirici (born 1941), Lluis Clotet (born 1941), and Oscar Tusquets (born 1941), in Barcelona, 1965; also established BD Ediciones de Diseno furniture and interior products firm, Barcelona, 1972: designed for Feria de Barcelona, Profitos, Bazan, Zanotta, Polinax, Alessi, Cleto Munari, Matteo Grassi, Casas, Quartett, Artespana, Carlos Jane, Ceramicas Bidasoa, Escofet, Aleph, etc. **Exhibitions:** *Arquitectura de Studio Per,* Colegio de Arquitectos, Lerida, 1971; *Arquitectura y Lagrimas,* Sala Vincon, Barcelona, 1975; *Transformations in Modern Architecture,* Museum of Modern Art, New York, 1979; *The House As Image,* Louisiana Museum, Humlebaek, 1981; *Ten Buildings,* Institute of Contemporary Arts, London, 1983; *Contemporary Spanish Architecture,* Architectural League of New York, 1986; *Documenta,* Kassel, 1987. **Collections:**

Centre Georges Pompidou, Paris; Museum of Modern Art, New York. Recipient: Premio FAD, Barcelona, 1965, 1970, 1972, 1978, 1979, 1987; Premio Azulejo de Deo, Barcelona, 1970; Delta de Oro Industrial Design Prize, Barcelona, 1974, 1979, 1980, 1986; Creu de Sant Jordi Award of Catalunya, 1987. Address: Caspe 151, 08013 Barcelona, Spain.

Works:

Girafa standard lamp, for Polinax, 1967.
Miro Otro exhibition layouts, for the Centro Joan Miro, Barcelona, 1968–69.

Factory building and interiors at Polinya, Barcelona, for Profitos, 1973.
Transparent bookcase and shelving, for BD Ediciones de Diseno, 1973.
Portrait of Mae West as a Living Room exhibit, for the Salvador Dali Museum, Figueras, 1974.
La Balsa restaurant interiors, Barcelona, 1978–79.
Catalano armchair and coffee-table, for BD Ediciones de Diseno, 1979.
Hipostila bookcase, for BD Ediciones de Diseno, 1980.
Oronda teapot, for Alessi, 1980–83.
Serpent fruit bowl, for Cleto Munari, 1983.

Studio Per: *Sevilla* **table and chair, for B. D. Ediciones de Diseno, 1981**

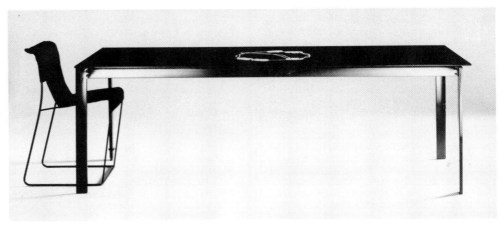

Varius armchair, for Casas, 1984.
Alada table, for Casa, 1985.
Gaulino chairs, for Carlos Jane, 1986–87.
Metalastica chair, for BD Ediciones de Diseno, 1986–87.
Sofanco seating, for Escofet, 1988.
Astrolabio table, for Aleph, 1988.
Nipon ceramic jug, for Bidaso, 1988.

(for complete lists of Studio Per buildings and architectural projects, see *Contemporary Architects*)

Publications:

By PER: books designed by Clotet and Tusquets—*Neutral Corner,* Barcelona 1965; *Arquitectura Gotica Catalana,* Barcelona 1968; *Arquitectura y Lagrimas,* exhibition catalogue, Barcelona 1975.
On PER: books—*El Studio Per o los Confines de la Arquitectura Actual* by J. Muntanola, Barcelona 1976; *Contemporary Furniture,* edited by Klaus-Jurgen Sembach, Stuttgart and London 1982; *Clotet, Tusquets* by Claudia Mann, Barcelona 1983; *Spanish Contemporary Architecture* by E. Bru and J. L. Mateo, Barcelona 1984; *Industrial Design* by Hans Wichmann, Munich 1985.

PERSSON, Sigurd.
Swedish industrial designer. Born in Helsingborg, 22 November 1914. Studied handicrafts with his father S. F. Persson, Helsingborg, 1928–37; Akademie fur Angewandte Kunst, Munich, 1937–39; Konstfackskolan, Stockholm, 1939–42. Married Iris Flodell in 1942; sons: Stefan and Jesper. Freelance industrial designer, gold- and silversmith, Stockholm, from 1942: founded own industrial design office, Stockholm, 1949; designer, Kosta Glassworks, 1968–82; independent glass designer, at Transjo Glass Studio, from 1984: designed for Silver och Stal, Kockums Jernverk, Kooperativa Forbundet, Norplasta, Alghults Glasbruk, AB Kronborsten, Folksam, Ary Stalmobler, Sunnex, Sporrongs, Ron-Produkter, etc. Also independent sculptor: founded Galleri Sigurd Persson, Helsingborg, 1970, and Argentum Gallery, Stockholm, 1976. Member of the Swedish State Advisory Group on Culture, 1963–68, and of KUS Commission into the Education of Artists and Designers, 1967–77. **Exhibitions:** Waldenstrom Art Dealers' Gallery, Stockholm, 1950; Nordenfjeldske Museum, Trondheim, 1957; Konstindustrimuseet, Oslo, 1959; *68 Rings,* Liberty's, London, 1961; *Sigurd Persson Design,* Malm Museum, Sweden, 1961; *7 × 7,* Nordiska Kompaniet, Stockholm, 1963; *Stakar,* Hantverket, Stockholm, 1963; *The Eloquent Jewels of Sigurd Persson,* Georg Jensen Inc., New York, 1964; *Sigurd Persson Design,* toured Sweden, 1966–68; *Kosta Glas och Silver,* Galleri Sigurd Persson, Helsingborg, 1972; *New Jewellery by Sigurd Persson,* Nordiska Kompaniet, Stockholm, 1974; *Glass,* Illums Bolighus, Copenhagen, 1975; *Guld, Silver och Gammal Vals,* Helsingborg, 1977; *Sigurd Persson Shuffles and Deals,* Hoganas Museum, Sweden, 1984; *Sigurd Persson in Retrospect,* Vikingsberg Museum, Helsingborg, 1985; *Sigurd Persson's Golden Wedding with Silver,* Helsingborg and Stockholm, 1987; *Glass,* Galleri Argo, Stockholm, 1989. **Collections:** Nordiska Museet, Stockholm; Nationalmuseum, Stockholm; Rohsska Konstslojdmuseet, Goteborg; Helsingborgs Museum; Nordenfjeldske Konstindustrimuseum, Trondheim; Konstindustrimuseet, Oslo; Neue Sammlung, Munich; Kestner Gesellschaft, Hannover; Victoria and Albert Museum, London; Museum of Modern Art, New York; Philadelphia Museum of Art. Recipient: Diploma of Honour, 1951, Silver Medal, 1954, 1957, 1960, Milan Triennale; Gold Ring of Honour, Stockholm, 1955; Gregor Paulsson Prize, Stockholm, 1958; SAS Cutlery Prize, Stockholm, 1959; Swedish Form/Good Form Diploma, 1961; Gold Medal and Diplomas, Liubliana Biennale, 1964, 1966; Helsingborgs Kulturpris, 1965; Swedish State Life Stipend, 1967; St. Eligius Prize, Stockholm, 1969; Prince Eugen Medal, Stockholm, 1980; Sydsvenska Dagbladet Kulturpris, 1972; Helsingborg Medal, 1983; Vi Magazine Design Prize, 1985; Excellent Swedish Design Prize, 1986. Honorary Member, Worshipful Company of Goldsmiths, London, 1965; Titular Professor, Stockholm, 1985; Honorary Royal Designer for Industry, Royal Society of Arts, London, 1987. Addresses: Hogbergsgatan 11, 116 45 Stockholm, Djurgardsslatten 78, 115 21 Stockholm, Sweden.

Works:

Soup tureen in stainless steel, for Silver och Stal, 1950.
Servus cutlery in stainless steel, for Kooperativa Forbundet, 1953–55.
Saucepans in enamelled cast iron, for Kockums Jernverk, 1954.
Servus Svart knife in stainless steel with nylon handle, for Kooperativa Forbundet, 1957–66.
Jet-line cutlery in stainless steel, for SAS Scandinavian Airlines System, produced by Kooperativa Forbundet, 1959.
Dinner service, coffee- and tea-set in melamine, for SAS Scandinavian Airlines System, produced by Norplasta, 1959.
Easy chair in steel with velvet upholstery, for Ary Stalmobler, 1964.
Restaurant glasses, for Sara-Bolaget, produced by Alghults Glasbruk, 1965.

Sigurd Persson: Dustpan and broom, for Kronborsten, 1985

Flag design, for Folksam Insurance Company, 1965.

Electric cooker, for Kockums Jernverk, 1966.

Armchair in tubular steel and plywood with leather upholstery, for Ary Stalmobler, 1968.

Compressed air nozzle in plastic, for Sunnex, 1974.

Charlotte frying pans in cast iron with stainless steel lids, for Ron-Produkter, 1979.

Colombina coffee pot in stainless steel, for Hackman, 1979.

Pots in cast iron with stainless steel lids, for Ron-Produckter, 1982.

Dustpan and brush in plastic and aluminium, for AB Kronborsten, 1985.

Publications:

By PERSSON: books—*Modern Swedish Silver*, editor, Stockholm 1951; *Sigurd Persson Silver*, Stockholm 1979; *Sigurd Persson Smycken*, Stockholm; *Sigurd Persson Skulptur*, Stockholm 1983; *Sigurd Persson Design*, Stockholm 1986.

On PERSSON: books—*Contemporary Swedish Design: A Survey in Pictures* by Arthur Hald and Sven Erik Skawonius, Stockholm 1951; *Swedish Silver* by Erik Andren, Stockholm 1960; *A Treasury of Scandinavian Design*, edited by Erik Zahle, New York 1961; *Design in Sweden*, edited by Lennart Lindkvist, Stockholm 1972; *Scandinavian Design: Objects of a Life Style* by Eileene Harrison Beer, New York and Toronto 1975; *Contemporary Furniture*, edited by Klaus-Jurgen Sembach, Stuttgart and London 1982; *Scandinavian Modern Design 1880–1980*, edited by David Revere McFadden, New York and London 1982; *Design Since 1945*, edited by Kathryn Hiesinger and George Marcus, Philadelphia and London 1983; *Design in Sweden*, edited by Monica Boman, Stockholm 1985; *Twentieth-Century Jewelry* by Barbara Cartlidge, New York 1985; *Faces of Swedish Design*, exhibition catalogue edited by Monica Boman, Stockholm 1988.

*

Designing for industry is taking part in teamwork. The technicians have their points of view, the economists theirs, and the designer his or hers. Each one must take the others into consideration. I like to say that a designed object is the result of a compromise. But that doesn't mean it is bad! Bad designing is when an object looks like something that it is not. You can imagine a bowl which looks heavy but which weighs hardly anything. There is no congruity between what the bowl seems to be and what it really is.

In every well-designed object, it is not just the function that is described in the form. Something else is there, too—we might call it an expression of the times. A Baroque chair, of course, expresses something more than that it is an object to sit on. There is something which is specifically for the seventeenth century. You had to sit straight-backed and stiffly. For various reasons, people liked the pompous, and the chair shows it. We perhaps imagine today that our chairs are only functional, but that is quite wrong. The expression of the times is there in just as great a degree. We just can't see it as clearly since it is so close to us.

—Sigurd Persson

*

In the 1920s, Sigurd Persson began a traditional silversmithing education under the tutelage of his father, Fritiof Persson. Continuing to work in this medium, he is today perhaps the finest metalsmith in Sweden. His career virtually matches the profile of the growth and de-

velopment of the interdependence between craft and industry which has transpired in Sweden, as in all Scandinavian countries, over the past fifty to sixty years.

Early in his career, Persson was interested in reviving techniques and processes which had fallen into disuse; these included enamelling, granulation, and niello. Philosophically, he was deeply influenced by the pioneers of the modern movement, which was officially encouraged by the Swedish Society for Industrial Design. Throughout his career he has held the personal convictions that through good craft, good taste is instilled in people and that individuals are capable of exercising independent judgment as to what constitutes work of merit. Through such belief in the designer's responsibility to the buyer, he adheres to the fundamentally moralistic tenets of modern Scandinavian design.

Aesthetically, Persson works as a sculptor, in the round, producing powerful, tectonic forms. Even his small-scale articles, such as rings or bracelets, at times attain monumentality. As a whole, his formally elegant jewelry is unusually extroverted and dramatic for Scandinavia, which has many practitioners more concerned with understatement.

In his strictly functional design, he works with economy and restraint. This can be seen in his 1958 prize-winning cutlery for the Scandinavian Airlines System, as well as in the tableware he later designed to go with it. More recently, he has designed pots and pans in stainless steel for the company Silver and Steel, In the 1970s, Persson worked as a freelance designer for the glass company Kosta-Boda, creating simple glass forms in bright, primary colors with sparse decorations in the form of signs. For this same company, he collaborated with the graphic designer Lisa Bauer in creating the engraved crystal bowl Wild Strawberries.

He has designed, or rather redesigned, the badges for the Swedish Army uniforms. Understandably, here he was required to draw heavily on traditional symbolism, but nonetheless, he succeeded in executing them in spirited, modernistic imagery.

Persson's handcrafted silverwork, both jewelry and vessels, has been a vital source of inspiration to American craftsmen in the period since World War II, especially from the 1960s onward, when the craft of metalsmithing was being revitalized in the art departments of colleges and universities across the United States.

—Barbara Young

PERSSON-MELIN, Signe.

Swedish ceramics and glass designer. Born Signe Persson, in Tomelilla, 19 June 1925. Trained with potter Nathalie Krebs, in Saxbo, Denmark, 1946–47; School of Handicrafts, Copenhagen, 1947–48; with Robert Nilsson, National College of Art, Craft and Design, Stockholm, 1948–50. Married the designer John Melin in 1955: 3 sons. Independent ceramics designer, establishing own studio in Malmo, since 1951: designer, for Kosta-Boda glassworks, 1967–77, for Boda Nova, from 1970, and for Rorstrand, from 1980. Professor, National College of Art, Craft and Design, Stockholm, since 1985. **Exhibitions:** Galerie Moderne, Stockholm, 1953; *Design from Scandinavia*, toured the United States, 1954; *H55*, Helsingborg, 1955; *Hantverkets, 60-tal*, Nationalmuseum, Stockholm, 1968; *Design in*

Scandinavia, National Gallery of Victoria, Melbourne, 1968 (toured); *Adventure in Swedish Glass*, toured Australia, 1975; *Scandinavian Modern Design 1880–1980*, Cooper-Hewitt Museum, New York, 1982 (toured); *Contemporary Swedish Design*, Nationalmuseum, Stockholm, 1983 (toured); *The Lunning Prize*, Nationalmuseum, Stockholm 1986; *Faces of Swedish Design*, IBM Gallery, New York, 1988 (toured); *Scandinavia: Ceramics and Glass in the Twentieth Century*, Victoria and Albert Museum, London, 1989. **Collections:** Nationalmuseum, Stockholm; Malmo Museum, Sweden; Rohsska Konstslojdmuseet, Goteborg; Kunstindustrimuseum, Copenhagen; Victoria and Albert Museum, London; Museum of Modern Art, New York, Recipient: T-Centralen Station Design Prize, Stockholm, 1956 (with Anders Osterlin); Lunning Prize, 1958; Gregor Paulsen Statuette, Stockholm, 1973; SDS Culture Prize, Stockholm, 1989. **Address:** Sanekullavagen 16, 217 74 Malmo, Sweden.

Works:

Ceramic murals, for T-Centralen underground station, Stockholm, 1956 (with Anders Osterlin).

Ruben glassware, for Kosta Boda, 1966.

Original souffle dish in ovenproof glass and cork, for Boda Nova, 1970.

Nova tableware in ovenproof stoneware, for Boda Nova, 1970–86.

Ice bucket in cork with metal lining, for Boda Nova, 1971.

Hot teapot and cups in ovenproof glass, for Boda Nova, 1974.

Corkline serving cutlery in stainless steel and cork, for Boda Nova, 1974.

Facette tableware in ovenproof glass, for Boda Nova, 1980.

Primeur tableware in feldspar porcelain, for Rorstrand, 1980.

Gourmet cutlery in stainless steel, for Boda Nova, 1981 (with John Melin).

A La Carte tableware in feldspar porcelain, for Rorstrand, 1981.

Chess tableware in feldspar porcelain, for Boda Nova, 1985.

Tradition tableware in ovenproof stoneware, for Hoganas, 1989.

Publications:

On PERSSON-MELIN: books—*Svensk Form/ Forma Sueca* by Ake Stavenlow and Ake H. Huldt, Stockholm 1961; *Konsthantverk, Konstindustri, Design* by Dag Widman, Stockholm 1975; *Glasboken: Historia, Teknik och Form* by Carl F. Hermelin and Elsebeth Welander, Boras 1980; *Scandinavian Modern Design 1880–1980*, edited by David Revere McFadden, New York, 1982; *Generationers arbete pa Boda Glasbruk*, edited by Boda Glassworks, Jonkoping 1982; *Form och Tradition i Sverige* by Birgitta Walz, Stockholm 1982; *Contemporary Swedish Design*, exhibition catalogue by Monica Boman, Lennart Lindkvist and others, Stockholm 1983; *The Lunning Prize*, exhibition catalogue edited by Helena Dahlback Lutteman and Marianne Uggla, Stockholm 1986; *Made in Sweden: Art, Handicrafts, Design* by Anja Notini, London 1987; *Faces of Swedish Design*, exhibition catalogue edited by Monica Boman, Stockholm 1988; *Scandinavia: Ceramics and Glass in the Twentieth Century* by Jennifer Hawkins Opie, London 1989.

Signe Persson-Melin has tried and mastered a great variety of materials ranging from clay and glass to cork, steel, fibrous cement and iron

Signe Persson-Melin: Teapot in salt-glazed porcelain, for Boda Nova, 1985

netting. She is an ingenious and highly original designer. She has gained assurance from a firm, practical training with no deviations, and also—presumably—from the early encouragement she received from her father, Erik Sigfrid Persson, a master builder with an original turn of mind. Like his daughter, he was unusually fond of experimentation and devoid of inhibition in his manner of working.

This is not to say that Signe is afraid of traditions. She dares to follow them as well. She says that pottery, stoneware, means the most to her. Clay is the material she loves best. This is the material she returns to after all her excursions elsewhere. And she is more interested in clay than in glazes. If she glazes the clay body, it is only to lend even more sensual prominence to the naked parts of the clay itself. She has always been quite actively concerned with design as such, but in her heart of hearts she is a craftsperson—a potter ("I don't feel like a designer"). Sometimes she has dug the clay with her own hands, beaten it, soaked it, screened it . . .

Signe Persson-Melin grew up in Skåne, Sweden's southernmost province, a region of rich soil and groaning tables. To her, food is very much of a piece with craftsmanship, art and civilization.

Everything she makes, even unique pieces, can be used—be it teapots, salad bowls or the walls of subway stations. Such is the way her mind works. Everything must be durable, useful, humane, easy to look after, suitable for children. Above all it must not be mean or petty-minded.

But then, of course, she received some of her training in Denmark, Scandinavia's land of Goshen. She studied first with Nathalie Krebs, the Grand Old Lady of Pottery, and then at the School of Handicraft in Copenhagen.

In 1956, together with the artist Anders Österlin, she won a competition for decorating some of the walls of the new Central Station on Stockholm's subway line. Her battle honors include a number of other major decorative commissions, such as the big wall of the Folkets Hus convention hall in Stockholm, an assignment she shared with Anders Liljefors.

By collaborating with her husband John Melin, a graphic designer and advertising man, she began working with, and thinking in terms of, materials other than clay. First came the "Ruben" glass designed for Kosta Boda and named after an old master blower at the glassworks. It has the individuality and charm of hand-blown glass. When Boda Nova launched its program for the set table, Signe Persson-Melin was an obvious candidate for the design group. It was she who introduced cork as a natural material for table settings. Nobody had designed with it in such a way before. Now Signe showed that cork and flameproof glass make an excellent combination which is both beautiful and practical. Food can be put straight onto the table, where it simmers and keeps warm. And its delicious colors can be viewed through the glass.

The absolutely plain stoneware service with the gentle backward-turned "rolled" brims, which she produced for Boda Nova over ten years ago is already a classic. Signe Persson-

Melin also sets her table with knives, kitchen utensils and other flatware having handles of pottery, steel or cork. All these various table-laying items display an unmistakable family likeness.

Boda Nova's first stoneware service later acquired a younger cousin, "Chess." It is made of porcelain and is a little slimmer and lighter in shape. The bowls and serving dishes are ovenproof. The "checkered" glaze has been allowed to spread unevenly.

Signe Persson-Melin's admirable capacity for alternating between different expressions of design and materials can be seen from her latest contribution to the set table: the "A la Carte" and "Primeur" services designed for Rörstrand. They are more brittle and "classy" in character than the tableware designed for Boda Nova. A la Carte, in feldspar porcelain, comes in all white or else white with a brown, pink or blue stripe. Primeur is exactly the same in shape but has a very fine color decoration in pale blue or gold.

"These services are rather on the smart side," says Signe, "and completely different from the others I have designed. But it's fun working with different kinds of assignments, and on such completely different terms."

Since Signe became professor of ceramics and glass at the National College of Art and Design in 1985, she has devoted much of her creative energy to improving the quality of teaching and the workshops. A new, highly advanced glassblowing shop was completed in 1987. When it was inaugurated, a large glass workshop was held to which glass artists were invited from the United States and Europe.

"I want to open the school to the world," says Signe Persson-Melin.

But now she longs for her potter's wheel in her studio at home. She says she has "a teapot in my head . . ."

—Carin Sjölander

PESCE, Gaetano.

Italian architectural, interior, industrial and graphic designer. Born in La Spezia, 8 November 1939. Studied architecture, at the University of Venice, 1959-65; Institute of Industrial Design, Venice, 1961-65. Married Francesca Lucco in 1969; chlildren: Tata and Tato. Independent artist and filmmaker, working with programmed, kinetic and serial art, and co-founder of Gruppo N art group, in Padua, 1959-67; freelance designer, in Padua, 1962-67, and in Venice from 1968: designed for Cassina, Bracciodiferro, Bernini, C & B Italia, Expansion, Knoll, Parisotto, Venini, Vittel, etc. Professor of architectural planning, University of Strasbourg, from 1975; also visiting professor and lecturer at Ohio State University, Columbus, 1974, Cooper Union, New York, 1975, 1979, 1980, 1983, 1985, 1986, Pratt Institute, New York, 1979, 1980, 1984, Ecole des Beaux-Arts, Nancy, 1981, University of Technology, Compiegne, 1981, Yale University, New Haven, Connecticut, 1983, Universities of Quebec and Montreal, 1984, Polytechnic of Hong Kong, 1985, Domus Academy, Milan, 1986, 1987, University of Sao Paulo, 1987, etc. **Exhibitions:** Galleria Bevilacqua La Masa, Venice, 1961; Hochschule fur Gestaltung, Ulm, 1964; Finnish Design Centre, Helsinki, 1964; Keski Suomen Museum, Jyvsakyla, 1965; Galleria Il Canale, Venice, 1966; Galleria La Carabaga, Genoa, 1966; Galleria La Chioccola, Padua, 1966; Linea Sud Gallery, Naples, 1967; Atelier d'Urbanisme at Architecture, Paris, 1969; Galleria Luca Palazzoli, Milan, 1974; Musee des Arts Decoratifs, Paris, 1975; Architectural Association, London, 1978; JDC Gallery, Tokyo, 1978; Museum of Modern Art, New York, 1979; Carnegie-Mellon University, Pittsburgh, 1980; Centro de Arte y Communicacion, Buenos Aires, 1981; Yale University, New Haven, Connecticut, 1983; Museum of Decorative Arts, Montreal, 1984; Harvard University, Cambridge, Massachusetts, 1985; University of Architecture, Hong Kong, 1985; Musee d'Art Moderne, Strasbourg, 1986; Galerie Leptien 3, Frankfurt, 1988; Deutsches Architekturmuseum, Frankfurt, 1988; Max Protetch Gallery, New York, 1989; Sapporo Brewery, Tokyo, 1989; University of Quebec, Montreal, 1989. **Collections:** Museum of Modern Art, New York; Centre Georges Pompidou, Paris; Musee des Arts Decoratifs, Paris; Keski Suomen Museum, Helsinki; Museo d'Arte Moderna, Turin. Recipient: Locarno Film Festival Award, 1968; Tokyo Lighting Design Competition Award, 1973; Parc de la Villette Award, Paris, 1982; Office Furniture Competition Award, Paris, 1983. Addresses: San Toma 2775, Venice, Italy; 67 Boulevard Brune, 75014 Paris, France.

Works:

Carlotta furnishing fabric, for Cassina, 1967.

Up self-inflating chairs in polyurethane foam and synthetic jersey, for C & B Italia, 1969.
Golgotha series of tables and chairs, for Bracciodiferro, 1974.
Sit-Down upholstered seating group in polyurethane foam and dacron, for Cassina, 1975.
Dalila chairs in hard polyurethane with coloured epoxy finish, for Cassina, 1980.
Tramonto a New York upholstered three-seat sofa in plywood, polyurethane foam and dacron, for Cassina, 1980-83.
Cannaregio asymmetrical sofa units in plywood with polyurethane foam padding, for Cassina, 1983.
Prospect Park chair in urethane, for Cassina, 1983-89.
Greene Street chair in steel and polyester, for Edition Vitra, 1984-87.
Sansone polychrome tables in moulded polyester resin, for Cassina, 1985.
Les Ateliers sideboard/cupboards in beechwood with lacquer finish, for Cassina, 1985.
Feltri armchairs in felt and resin with quilted upholstery, for Cassina, 1986.
People fabric, for Cassina, 1987.
Table in rubber, silicone and metal, for Basia Rossignol, 1988.

Publications:

By PESCE: articles—in *Keski-Suomen* (Jyvaskyla), June 1965; *Mobilia* (Snekkersten), no. 173, 1969; *l'Architecture d'Aujourd'hui* (Paris), no. 155, 1971; *Cree* (Paris), no. 18, 1972, no. 24, 1973, no. 9, 1977; *Space Design* (Tokyo), no. 6, 1972, no. 8, 1973; *Japan Interior Design* (Tokyo), no. 159, 1972; *Casabella* (Milan), no. 375, 1973, no. 378, 1973, no. 383, 1973; *Opus International* (Paris), no. 47, 1973; *Industrial Design* (New York), September/October 1981.
On PESCE: books—*Modern Chairs 1918-1970*, exhibition catalogue by Carol Hogben, Dennis Young and Reyner Banham, London

1970; *Italy: The New Domestic Landscape,* edited by Emilio Ambasz, New York and Florence 1972; *Gaetano Pesce: The Future Is Perhaps Past,* exhibition catalogue with texts by Francois Barre, Alessandro Mendini and others, Paris and Florence 1974; *The Modern Chair: Classics in Production* by Clement Meadmore, London 1974; *Design e Forme Nuove nell'Arredamento Italiano,* edited by Paolo Portoghesi and Marino Marini, Rome 1978; *Contemporary Furniture,* edited by Klaus-Jurgen Sembach, Stuttgart and London 1982; *The Hot House: Italian New Wave Design* by Andrea Branzi, London and Cambridge, Massachusetts 1984; *Modern Furniture Classics* by Miriam Stimpson, London 1987; *Italian Design: 1870 to the Present* by Penny Sparke, London and New York 1988; *Italian Modern: A Design Heritage* by Giovanni Albera and Nicolas Monti, New York 1989; *Gaetano Pesce: Architecture, Design, Art* by France Vanlaethem, London 1989.

Gaetano Pesce studied both architecture and industrial design in Venice. He is best known for the radical furniture and interior spaces he creates, designed for a specific audience.

In 1969, Pesce designed the *Up 1* chair, a polyurethane foam shape covered with stretch nylon and wool jersey. It came compressed in a package and expanded to the correct size and shape when opened. The design of the *Up 1* chair, places Pesce's design work in the mainstream of Italian design. During the 60's Italian designers rejected the concepts of functionalism, finding its theories of mass production and concern for aesthetic value too limiting. They worked instead for a more personal market, utilizing new technologies and concepts of design. The *Up 1* chair was one of the first in a series of original furniture designs.

Pesce worked in close association with the manufacturer which allowed him to develop his more expressive styles. This also gave him the capacity to produce one of a kind or small

Gaetano Pesce: *Sit-Down* chair, for Cassina, 1975

quantities of objects such as furniture and lamps. The *Sit Down* series of sofas and chairs are of foam polyurethane padding injected into tufted dacron over a plywood base. Because of this process the shapes vary from one chair or sofa to another. The *Golgotha* chair appears soft, as if fabric somehow magically was formed into a chair like shape, and would collapse if any weight were put on it. However, the chair is formed of fiberglass cloth and resin and quite rigid, capable of supporting a person. Because each seat is individually contoured by someone sitting in them before they dry completely, the chairs are each a distinct form. Colors vary, shapes are not specific, and surfaces which seem soft are hard. Amorphic shapes are created utilizing the latest technology. His designs challenge the viewer. They are not for everyone, but for a small, more personal market.

For an exhibit *Italy, a New Domestic Landscape,* held at the Museum of Modern Art in New York City, Pesce created an Archeological Environment. This is a subterranean habitation from the period of the great contaminations or 2000 A.D. Not only has Pesce created a site, but one which exists years in the future, discovered by civilization of a much later date. Though the furnishings made of wood and fabric have disintegrated, the stone structure, which used the square and the rectangle as fundamental forms remained. Discovery of this space with its enigmatic meanings poses many questions for contemporary designers which Pesce raises in an essay accompanying the exhibit. Though based on this specific site, Pesce raises questions about the purpose of space and its design, both interior and exterior, and how it effects man's behavior. These are the same questions a designer in contemporary society considers during the design process.

In a later design for a skyscraper formed of expanded polyurethane foam blocks which are exactly alike on five sides but vary on the sixth, Pesce creates a 'soft' or modern architecture. It is a building of the future, of contemporary building materials.

Questions are raised by many of Pesce's designs. Questions about historical references in design, the codes which govern lives, and what the future holds. He challenges the purpose of the designer and architect. He challenges the methodology of the designer and architect. He challenges accepted concepts of good design. Pesce writes of design, and is involved in design proceedings. He was molded by the Italian post war design practices which turned away from the functionalism of the Bauhaus, reaching towards an individualized design based on the needs of the individual rather than mass marketing.

—Nancy House

PINELES, Cipe.

American graphic designer. Born in Slovita, Austria-Hungary (now Poland), 23 June 1910; emigrated to the United States in 1923. Educated at Bay Ridge High School, Brooklyn, New York, 1924–27; studied at the Pratt Institute, Brooklyn, New York, 1927–31; Louis Comfort Tiffany Foundation, New York, 1930, 1931. Married the designer William Golden in 1941 (died, 1959); son: Thomas; married the designer Will Burtin in 1961 (died, 1972); adopted daughter: Carol. Designer, in the Contempora industrial design studio, New York, 1931–33; assistant to art director Mehemed Fehmy Agha, at *Vogue* magazine, New York, 1933–36; associate editor and art director, British *Vogue,* London, 1936–38; art director, of *Glamour,* New York, 1938–45, *Overseas Woman,* Paris, 1945–46, *Seventeen,* New York, 1947–50, *Charm,* New York, 1950–58, and of *Mademoiselle,* New York, 1958–59; freelance designer from 1959, working mainly for Will Burtin design studio, New York, 1961–72: graphics consultant and designer, Lincoln Center for the Performing Arts, New York, 1965–72; director of publication design, Parsons School of Design, New York, from 1970. Instructor, Parsons School of Design, New York, from 1963; Andrew Mellon Professor, Cooper Union, New York, 1977. Member of the visiting committee, Harvard University, Cambridge, Massachusetts, from 1978. Recipient: Art Directors Hall of Fame Award, New York, 1975; Society of Publication Designers Award of Excellence, New York, 1978. Member: American Institute of Graphic Arts, New York: Alliance Graphique Internationale, Paris. Address: 40 East 10th Street, New York, New York 10003, U.S.A.

Publications:

By PINELES: books—*Bread,* editor, New York 1973, as *Parsons Bread Book,* New York 1974; *Cheap Eats,* editor, New York 1976; *Parsons T-Shirt Book,* editor, New York 1979.
By PINELES: book—*Magazine USA,* exhibition catalogue, New York 1965; articles—in *Studio News* (New York), March 1950; *Print* (New York), September 1955; *AIGA Journal* (New York), January 1959; *New York Times,* 28 November 1975.

As a designer as well as a teacher of graphic design, my approach to solving a problem has remained the same since my years of basic training—that is, to understand the objective of the message, be it an annual report for Lincoln Center, a school catalogue for Parsons, or a book on bread; to know the audience I am addressing; and to limit my scheme to the time allowed. My intention is to make the type very readable and good-looking; to involve illustrators, artists, photographers of exceptional quality, preferably the ones who have not handled such assignments before; to seek for the most direct and simple solutions to complicated problems; and to pay constant attention to every detail of the job from its inception to its coming off the press, to the packaging of the final product. I was pleased to hear from one of my students that he chose Parsons over other schools because the application forms came to him in a red envelope.

—Cipe Pineles

The role of art director is most enigmatic in the graphic arts. As an auteur, driving the creative process, the art director employs the diverse talents of artists, photographers, typographers and graphic designers in service to a unitary vision. Though that vision is legitimately credited to the art director, for it to be successful, it must be a cooperative effort, synonymous with the content of the publication.

Cipe Pineles learned this lesson well as her apprenticeship was taken under the inestimable Dr. M. F. Agha at *Vogue* magazine, where she worked from 1933–36. More than anyone, Agha established the art director as the editor's partner in the formation of style and the control of visual communication. Under Agha, Pineles learned to focus on the big picture, foregoing a craftsman's preoccupation with the details and forging an expansive idea that was consonant with editorial purpose. Pineles got her first op-portunity to test her newly acquired skills in 1938 when she was hired to art direct *Glamour,* another Condé Nast publication aimed at young women. Although this job provided her with a strong sense of her own priorities and the ability to experiment, it wasn't until after the war in 1947, when she was hired to art direct *Seventeen* that Pineles made her important contribution to magazine design.

During the years at *Glamour,* she married William Golden, then working at *House and Garden,* who pushed her to envision layout, and especially typography, as a sort of adventure, to be sensitive to the way the final outcome is conditioned by opportunities inherent to each component. Design was never considered to be just problem solving but an expression of the copy.

At *Seventeen,* Pineles instituted a new approach to the illustration of fiction. The artwork she commissioned from the likes of Ben Shahn, Robert Gwathmey and Raphael Soyer was not meant to grace the page as decoration but to successfully interpret the copy as a narrative in its own right. She encouraged artists to consider their work as integral to the overall effect of editorial content. Further, she bought only reproduction rights to the art, returning the original after publication.

In 1950, Pineles moved with editor Helen Valentine to *Charm,* a fledgling publication aimed at the new breed of female, the working woman. To be one is to know one, and Pineles eagerly embarked on an impassioned eight-year stint at *Charm,* parlaying her staunch views about respect for the readership through illustration as art, fashion photography as practical reality for the everyday woman and layout as reflective of the aspirations and goals of women in the workforce.

Her second marriage to Will Burtin, a proponent of Swiss Modernist typography, challenged further her goals of expressive clarity and effective communication, and, subsequently, she joined Burtin's studio as a freelance designer. Her dedicated approach to graphic design bred of these influences became most apparent in her work as consultant and graphic designer for the Lincoln Center for the Performing Arts and as Director of Publications for Parsons School of Design, a position she currently holds. Also as a teacher at Parsons since 1963, she has focused on content, pointing to the basic communication need as the ultimate problem, demanding that students discard complicated concepts that might obfuscate the message. She stresses designing from the inside out, consideration of the copy as the inspirational catalyst for visual efficacy. Being natural and comfortable with the medium means avoiding a style that will distinguish the graphic component from its context. Hers is an integrated approach to art direction that reinforces the notion of the art director, learned from Agha and carried on by Pineles as the vortex of imaginative design.

Not the least of Pineles's accomplishments was her example as the first woman to be elected a member of the Art Director's Club of New York and, ostensibly, the first woman art director to head an educational program. She is a model for all women in the profession aspiring to enter positions long dominated by men. Not a feminist per se, nor are there indications of this in her designs, she nonetheless exhibits an expansive tolerance and extraordinary openness to contributions and experiences of a collaborative process. It just may be that her anomaly within the history of the profession was a contributive factor to the freedom she was afforded. No matter, once gained, she fiercely holds to this freedom and continues to instill it in others.

—Sarah Bodine

Pininfarina: *Peugeot 205* 5-door hatchback, 1982

PININFARINA.

Italian automobile design firm. Founded by Battista "Pinin" Farina (1893–1966) in Turin, 1930. Current president: Sergio (Pinin)Farina (born 1926), since 1966. New works established at Grugliasco, near Turin, 1965: aerodynamic body-styling department created in 1965; automated calculation and draughting centre created in 1967; aerodynamic wind-test tunnel completed in 1972. Pininfarina has designed cars for Nash, 1952–54, Alfa Romeo and Lancia, from 1953, Fiat, 1954–74, Ferrari and Peugeot from 1955, Cadillac, from 1958, BMC, 1958–68, Nissan, 1965–66, Rolls-Royce, 1975, Jaguar, 1978, and Honda, 1984; also wristwatches for Orfina, and sunglasses for Ratti Industria Ottica, 1981–82. **Exhibitions:** *Bolide Design,* Musee du Louvre, Paris, 1970; *Car Body Styling Prototypes,* Tokyo, 1977 (toured); *Carrozzeria Italiana,* Palazzino della Promotrice delle Belle Arti, Turin, 1978 (toured); *Die Nutzlichen Kunste,* Messegelande am Funkturm, West Berlin, 1981; *Italian Re-Evolution,* La Jolla Museum of Art, California, 1982; *Dal Cucchiaio all Citta,* Milan, 1983. **Collections:** Museo Alfa Romeo, Arese; Museo dell'Automobile, Turin; Museo dei Trasporti, Lucerne; Museo dell'Automobile, Le Mans; Museum of Modern Art, New York. Ad-dress: Pininfarina S.p.A., Via Lesna 78/80, 10095 Grugliasco (Turin), Italy.

Works

Cisitalia GT 2-seater sports coupe, for Cisitalia, 1947.
Lancia Aurelia B20 2-door coupe, for Lancia, 1951.
Alfa Romeo Giulietta spider sports car, for Alfa Romeo, 1954.
Peugeot 403 Prototipo 4-door saloon, for Peugeot, 1955.
Ferrari 250 GT berlinetta, for Ferrari, 1961.
Fiat 124 Sport spider, for Fiat, 1966.
Alfa Romeo 1600 spider duetto, for Alfa Romeo, 1966.
Ferrari GTB 4(Daytona) 2-seater berlinetta, for Ferrari, 1968.
Ferrari GT4 BB 2-seater berlinetta, for Ferrari, 1971.
Rolls-Royce Camargue 4-seater coupe, for Rolls-Royce, 1974.
Ferrari 308 GTB 2-seater coupe, for Ferrari, 1975.
Lancia Gamma 4-door/4-seater saloon, for Lancia, 1976.
Peugeot 205 saloon, for Peugeot, 1983.

Ferrari Testarossa 2-seater berlinetta, for Ferrari, 1984.
Cadillac Allante 2-seater convertible, for Cadillac, 1986.
Alfa Romeo 164 4-seater sedan, for Alfa Romeo, 1987.
Ferrari F40 2-seater belinetta, for Ferrari, 1987.
Peugeot 405 4-seater sedan, for Peugeot, 1987.
ETR 500 high-speed train, for Ferrovie dello Stato, Italy, 1987.
Pininfarina/Lancia HIT 2-door/2-seater sports coupe, for Lancia, 1988.

Publications:

By PININFARINA: books—*Cara Automobile,* Turin 1968; *Nato per l'Automobile,* Turin 1968; *La Vaporiera,* Turin 1970; *Ricerca Teorico Sperimentale di una Forma Aerodinamica Ideale,* report, Turin 1979; *Il lessico della Carrozzeria,* Turin 1979; *Pininfarina Cinquantanni,* with texts by Sergio Pininfarina and Renzo Carli, Turin 1980; *Pininfarina Figurini,* Turin 1983; *La Galleria del Vento,* Turin 1984; *Filosofia e Progetto,* Turin 1985; *Ingegneria del Prodotto e della Produzione,* Turin 1987; *Il Processo Produttivo,* Turin 1989.

On PININFARINA: books—*l'Esthetique Indus-trielle* by Denis Huisman and Georges Patrix, Paris 1961; *Le Ferrari Pininfarina* by Bernabo and Cornil, Milan 1966; *Transport Design* by Corin Hughes-Stanton, London and New York 1967; *The Library of Motoring: The Designers* by L. J. K. Setright, London 1976; *Pinin-farina: Master Coachbuilder/Architect of Cars*, 2 vols., by Michael Frostick, London 1977–78; *Carrozzeria Italiana*, exhibition catalogue by A. T. Anselmi, Milan 1978; *Pininfarina 1930–1980: Prestige and Tradition* by Didier Merlin, Lausanne 1980; *Pininfarina* by A. Alfieri, Tu-rin 1982; *Le Ferrari di Pininfarina* by Tito An-selmi, Turin 1988; *Ferrari e Pininfarina* by Gianni Rogliatti, Turin 1988.

Aspects of my activity include studies of new shapes carried out from experience in the aero-dynamic field; studies in the field of passive and active safety; researches for the utilization of new materials in automobiles.

The philosophy of my life and work is in-spired by that of my father. In our work, we are seeking a purity of line, harmony of propor-tions, but above all functionalism. We avoid os-tentation. A handle is not valuable because it is gold: it is, if it works well and is made of light material. A car is an extraordinary object, and to design one means living a double experience: for the exterior, so that it has an attractive and aggressive enough personality to act as the main standard-bearer for sales promotion; for the interior, which must confirm the potential buyer's impression that the car is a good buy and make him feel that the vehicle has been made to measure for him—especially if he is going to be using it for several hours a day. Few objects have influenced our way of life and even the landscape around us more than the car. And we designers have an extremely important task: to introduce a little order into the chaos which surrounds us and to make everyday life a little easier and more pleasant.

—Sergio Pininfarina

In the work of Sergio Pininfarina, we see the development in the industrial sense of the great craft tradition of coachwork design of which his father was one of the great protagonists; Giovan Battista was a pioneer in the very idea of auto-mobile coachwork design, introducing into the field a formal conception with strong reference to the arts as traditionally understood. Pinin-farina's cars have for years been synonymous with sculpture, modelled on a precise formal idea, artistic expression in themselves.

Into this tradition Sergio has brought the idea of more advanced technology as a means of bringing the product up to date formally and functionally; he has thus moved on from the creation of form-automobiles that sprang from a craftsman's skill in design and modelling to ve-hicles planned to give maximum performance on the basis of precise scientific criteria.

The Pininfarina wind tunnel, the first in Italy, made it possible to give rigorous tests to the formal ideas the designer's mind produced; there has now been added to it one of the first Italian computer-aided design centres, with which it has been possible not only to automate the traditional procedures of design but also to study automobile design in terms of every phase in the process of production. Pininfarina thus represents the most progressive phase of modernization and "industrialization" in a long tradition at once artisanal and artistic.

However, the highly advanced technology is not used exclusively for formal ends but also to make effective progress in the quality of the product. The cabs for agricultural factors, for instance, are studied in the light of the condi-tions in which the driver works; advanced ma-

terials and technology are employed to give the vehicle biotechnological features that will en-sure the comfort and safety of the driver.

Thus, Pininfarina does not confine himself to the use of existing technology but tries to evolve technical knowledge through his own scientific research. One result of this effort is the experi-mental vehicle produced in collaboration with the Italian National Centre for Research to test the theory of a car whose form is designed ex-clusively to reduce wind resistance while still retaining the seating capacity of a current mass-produced interior. The vehicle thus produced enables fuel consumption to be reduced by as much as fifteen percent. With this type of ex-periment, Pininfarina contributes to research that aims to apply design to the solution of general problems as well as to the traditional role of generating ideas for new forms and functions.

—Stefano Casciani

PINTORI, Giovanni.

Italian display, graphic and industrial designer. Born in Tresnuraghes, Sardinia, 14 July 1912. Studied design, at the Istituto Superiore per le Industrie Artistiche, Monza, 1930–36. Worked as a typist, in Sardinia, 1927–29; graphic de-signer, 1936–50, and head of publicity, 1950–67, at Olivetti Company, Milan; freelance designer, establishing own studio in Milan, from 1968: also designed for magazines *Stile Industria* and *Fortune*. **Exhibitions:** *Giovanni Pintori: Graphic Designs*, Museum of Modern Art, New York, 1952; *Olivetti Design*, Musee du Louvre, Paris, 1954; *Alliance Graphique In-ternationale*, in Paris, 1955, London, 1956, Lausanne, 1957, and Milan, 1961; *Giovanni Pintori*, Tokyo, 1967. Recipient: Palma d'Oro Award, Milan, 1950; Grand Prize, Milan Triennale, 1957. Member: Alliance Graphique Internationale, Paris. Addres: Via Baracchini 10, Milan, Italy.

Works:

Studio 42 and Studio 44 advertising campaign, for Olivetti, 1937–39 (with I. Sinisgalli).
The Rose and the Inkwell poster, for Olivetti, 1939.
The Bands That Fly poster, for Olivetti, 1939.
Abacus poster, for Olivetti, 1947.
Numbers in Relief poster, for Olivetti, 1947.
Numbers poster, for Olivetti, 1949.
Lettera 22: The Boat poster, for Olivetti, 1955.
Lexikon: The Ball poster, for Olivetti, 1955.
Tetractys: The Arrows poster, for Olivetti, 1956.
Divisumma: Boat from America poster, for Olivetti, 1957.
Graphika electric typewriter, for Olivetti, 1957.
Electrosumma 22 poster, for Olivetti, 1958.
Olivetti 1908–1958 book jacket, for Olivetti, 1958.
Summa Prima 20 posters, for Olivetti, 1960.
Raphael electric typewriter, for Olivetti, 1961.
Showroom interiors in Milan, for Olivetti, 1963.
Three-colour ribbons poster series, for Olivetti, 1965.

Publications:

On PINTORI: books—*Posters: 50 Artists and Designers*, edited by W. H. Allner, New York 1952; *Olivetti 1908–1958*, with texts by Adri-ano Olivetti, Libero Bigiaretti and Franco Forlini, Turin 1958; *The New Graphic Design* by Karl Gerstner and Markus Kutter, Teufen and London 1959; *Lettering Today*, edited John Brinkman, London 1964; *History of the Poster* by Josef and Shizuko Muller-Brockmann, Zu-rich 1971; *Graphic Designers in Europe 2*, edited by Henri Hillebrand, London 1972; *Design Process Olivetti 1908–83*, with text by Renzo Zorzi, Milan 1983.

Giovanni Pintori has been in the forefront of Italian graphic design for nearly fifty years, during which time he contributed much to the distinctive graphic style that has characterised Olivetti publicity material almost from the be-ginning. Perhaps to him was due their aware-ness of contemporary art and the adoption of its techniques and effects for advertising, a strat-egy by which was asserted the modernity of the whole Olivetti enterprise.

Already in the late 1930s and early 1940s, Pintori had designed advertisements for Olivetti that took as their point of departure the business machine itself, typewriter or calculator, sleek and modern-looking, usually represented in the final advertisement by a cut-out photograph, to which was added the minimum of written mes-sage, often only the name of the firm, some-times the name of the model as well. To this was added some image derived from an aspect of the machine's purpose or function or mecha-nism. This simple "formula" was capable of infinite, sophisticated variation, which Pintori investigated without loss of invention over the years and to which he brought his enthusiasm for the achievements of modern art, particularly juxtapositions of style, technique, and content. In one of those early advertisements, the type-writer is shown on a pale ground within a shape derived from curved brackets, and this in turn is on a night sky where the stars have been re-placed by letters and numbers of differing type styles and sizes. Another shows an overhead view of the typewriter against a ground painted like a sky, while curved and folded sheets of paper elegantly float around the machine. In yet another variation of this theme with the paper more in scrolls, the typewriter has been re-duced to a row of keys. Extending this direction even further was the famous 1956 poster with the array of coloured digits freely and densely scattered all over a black ground.

In many of these images, however, there was, further, a sensitivity to letter-forms and to the characteristics of the different typefaces, to, in fact, the distinguishing features between fonts and letters and, therefore, to the unifying ele-ments within fonts. This kind of sensibility un-derlay such enterprises as the skilful design made of the letters of the name "Olivetti," start-ing with the large, white, capital "O" and so on.

The developments in Pintori's work, for all the consistency and coherence displayed, reflect his continuing interest and involvement in the innovations of contemporary art. One can read in his work the gradual displacement in the 1950s of, for example, surrealism (which had supplied much of the impetus towards unlikely associations) by a more turbulent and all-over effect, as in the scattering of coloured digits, due to his appreciation of contemporary paint-ing, later still, newer trends led him to a redis-covery of his own past, from which he was able to launch himself anew.

—Toni del Renzio

PIRI, Markku.

Finnish textile, fashion and industrial designer. Born in Kauhava, 23 January 1955. Studied at Parsons School of Design, New York, 1973; fashion and textiles, University of Industrial Arts, Helsinki, 1975–79. Printed textile designer, Marimekko Oy, Helsinki, 1979–81; senior designer, China Seas Inc. textile and housewares company, New York, 1981–82; independent textile, housewares and menswear designer, working with ITC, Finlayson, Petritex, Imperial Wallcoverings, Osaka Nishikawa, Burlington Industries, Spring Mills, Reko, Wakabayashi, etc., since 1983; founder, Markku Piri Inc., New York, from 1983, and Markku Piri Oy, Helsinki, from 1986. Also stage costume designer, for Jorma Uotinen, Arja Saijonmaa Cabaret, the Swedish Cullberg Ballet, and Brooklyn Academy of Music, 1978–86. Guest Instructor in Printed Textiles, Parsons School of Design, New York, 1982; also visiting lecturer, at colleges and professional institutes, in Europe, Canada, Japan and the United States, from 1981. **Exhibitions:** Kluuvi Gallery, Helsinki, 1981, 1986; Gallery Bronda, Helsinki, 1984; Piri Atelje, Helsinki, 1988; Galeria Alfa 38, Lisbon, 1989; Galleria 25, Helsinki, 1989. **Collections:** Museum of Applied Arts, Helsinki; Art Collection of the City of Helsinki. Recipient: Scholarship, Parsons School of Design, New York, 1973; Hoover Foundation Grant, 1978, 1981, 1982; Finnish Culture Foundation Grant, 1980, 1984; Design Award, *Jugend Gestaltet* exhibition, Munich, 1981; Ornamo Finnish Association of Designers Grant, 1981, 1983; City of Helsinki Grant, 1981, 1986; Design Award, Republic of Finland, 1986; Central Organization for the Arts Grant, Helsinki, 1988. Addresses: Markku Piri Oy, Nervanderinkatu 7 C, 00100 Helsinki, Finland; Markku Piri Inc., 496 La Guardia Place, Suite 403, New York, New York 10012, U.S.A.

Works:

Printed interior fabrics collection, for Marimekko, 1980–81.
Home furnishing fabrics collection, for ITC-Corporation, 1982.
First collection of household textiles and printed interior fabrics, for Finlayson, 1983.
Second collection of household textiles and printed interior fabrics, for Finlayson, 1984.
Wallcoverings and co-ordinated fabrics, for Imperial Wallcoverings, 1985.
Summer 87 menswear collection, for Petritex and Finnwear, 1986.
Bed linen, pyjamas, towels and blankets collection, for Osaka Nishikawa, 1988.
Three collections of household textiles and interior fabrics, for Finlayson, 1988.
First printed silk scarves collection, for Wakabayashi, 1988.
First men's shoes collection, for Reko/Rentto, 1988 (with Janne Renvall).
Second printed silk scarves collection, for Wakabayashi, 1989.
Menswear collection, for Petritex, 1989 (with Janne Renvall).
Second men's shoes collection, for Reko/Rentto, 1989 (with Janne Renvall).
First jacquard terry towels and bathrobes collection, for Egeria, 1989.

Publications:

By PIRI: book—*Vuosi/Year,* Helsinki 1988; articles—"New York Art Deco" in *Muoto* (Helsinki), no. 2, 1984; "Essay on Kyoto, Japan" in *Suomen Kuvalehti* (Helsinki), no. 50, 1985; "Clothing for the Future" in *Image* (Helsinki), no. 2, 1986; "Helsinki: Summer Streets and

Markku Piri: *Sytytys* **jacquard terry towels, for Finlaysson, 1988**

City Planning" in *Suomen Kuvalehti* (Helsinki), no. 30, 1987; "First Collection of Piri Men's Shoes" in *Design Forum* (Helsinki), September 1989.
On PIRI: book—*Finnland Gestaltet*, exhibition catalogue by T. Periainen, S. Heikkila and others, Espoo 1981; articles—"Markku Piri at Kluuvi Gallery" by L. Maunula in *Helsingin Sanomat* (Helsinki), 18 October 1981; "Markku Piri's Recent Work" by L. Uusiniitty in *Suomen Kuvalehti* (Helsinki), no. 49, 1983; "New Piri Shirts" by J. Kuikka in *Suomen Kuvalehti* (Helsinki), no. 18, 1984; "I Think That's The Year" in *Design in Finland* (Helsinki), 1986; "Piri Autumn 86 Menswear Collection" by C. Enbom in *Hufvudstadsbladet* (Helsinki), 27 January 1986; "Ecoute Optique" by K. Kalin in *Muoto* (Helsinki), no. 2, 1986; "Markku Piri Exhibition and Book" by C. Enbom in *Helsingin Sanomat* (Helsinki), 16 November 1988; "Markku Piri: 10 Years" by H. Rantala in *Suomen Kuvalehti* (Helsinki), no. 30, 1989; "Ten Spiritual Years" by K. Valtonen in *Design in Finland* (Helsinki), 1990.

*

If there weren't colours, I would go mad. With colours, I happily do so. Colour is the basis for my work. I react to colour very emotionally, and to all of my work with passion. Yet, creating colour harmonies and atmospheres is also a rational process.

I am intrigued by patterns, ornaments. The Japanese textile culture has had a great influence on the way that I create textile collections, coordinated collections, or combine shapes and materials. Harmonious wholes can be composed with contrasting rhythms, seemingly clashing colours. I consider my jacquard woven terry towels to be graphic art, soft, mass-produced for the consumers . . .

The border between fine and applied art can be thin: original paintings can be reproduced with impeccable technique: my discharge printed silk scarves for Japan.

The elements of the vulgar and the elegant overlap. I would rather take the risk, as long as my designs convey a sense of life (if not speed), sensuality and . . . fun.

—Markku Piri

*

Markku Piri is a young designer who has always made well-considered and conscious choices. Although obstacles may force him to consider alternative routes, his determined aim remains constant and his final direction proceeds with sure strides. Following his schooling under an inspiring arts teacher and a year as an exchange student in the United States, Piri's course became clear. It was in his first year at the University of Industrial Arts in the mid-1970s that he resolved to work for the textile firm of Marimekko. He became an unsalaried summer apprentice so that he could pursue a relatively independent line. Then, following an urge to travel in Japan, he wrote a convincing grant application that yielded the desired result.

His professional career also began at Marimekko—a firm large enough to encompass the entire production process through all its stages, yet remaining positive in its attitude to design and experiment. There, Piri was exposed to an exceptional market within the Finnish context, but Marimekko was also directed outwards and internationally. It was a direction eagerly taken by the young designer. After two years, he saw it was time to test his abilities in a wider environment, and went to New York to become head designer at China Seas Inc. He had already created collections for licensed manufacture in Japan whilst at Marimekko, and now continued this activity for the new enterprise. Although still under thirty, Piri had a worldwide network of contacts. In 1983, Markku Piri Inc. was founded, while Markku Piri Oy, the Finnish equivalent, was created three years later.

A significant part of Piri's design production has been an innumerable series of furnishing textiles for a variety of firms in different countries. A survey of his creations over the years reveals a marvellously rich panoply of colour, pattern, character and design configuration—but a common and unifying thread indicates that the same person is behind them all. This indefinable factor may be characterized as style, honesty, sensitivity, or simply an assured artistic sense.

Early on in Piri's American travels, he realized that most things can be done in many ways in a multicultural society not constrained by such narrow customs as Finland's. He made himself open to the challenge of vigorous competition, difficult and unusual commissions, and learned the necessity of communicating his own opinion. But it was in Japan that he perceived the high value placed on quality. Visiting Kiyoto to meet kimono master Moriguchi—a man regarded as a living national treasure—Piri observed how timeless techniques produced divinely beautiful prints. There was also the fascination of Kabuki theatre costume where the richness and multiplicity of up to thirteen fabric layers shone through one another. This coordination of different patterns within a unified whole where clearly demarcated areas of strong graphic pattern harmonize with stripes and squares has become characteristic of Piri's own textile designs.

A remarkable feature of all Piri's activities is his openness and enthusiasm for new forms of expression. He has a keen sense of visual effect, and endeavours to carry his own style—via photography, layout, presentation and display—throughout production up to the final point of sale. Having created the costumes for several theatre publications, Piri often presents his clothing and textile collections in the form of a multivisual performance.

Clothing was a logical development from textile design. Piri's menswear has a uniquely personal feel constructed from a basis of unified colour scale. The clothes have a lightness and an elegance that follows neither temporal fashion nor tradition.

Being an artist who uses industry as his main means of expression, Piri nonetheless has a definite leaning toward the unique artwork—in writing and painting. In 1988 he held his first exhibition of paintings comprising a series of gouache and serigraph portraits of friends. With seismographic sensitivity, Piri registered essential relationships and rendered them in sparkling crystal colours accented by dark masses and sweeping line. These painted rhythms were later redeveloped in the creation of patterns for fabrics. Concurrent with his painting exhibitions, Piri also published an autobiographical novel drawn from his diary kept during a year of illness, in which he sharply analyses the world around him. Of all his work, Piri believes his exhibitions and book are the most important so far.

Having worked as a designer for over ten years, Markku Piri has produced a body of work impressive both in range and quality. At his recent exhibition, however, he declared no inclination to review his past work, preferring instead to present what was yet to come. Attention was focussed on the latest additions to his repertoire—a range of men's shoes and a collection of silk scarves printed in Japan. Markku Piri continues to strengthen his position as Finland's most international designer.

—Carla Enbom

PLATNER, Warren.

American architect, interior and furniture designer. Born in Baltimore, Maryland, 18 June 1919. Studied at Cornell University, Ithaca, New York, 1938–41: B.Arch. 1941. Married Joan Payne in 1945; children: Bronson, Joan, Sharon and Madeleine. Worked in the architectural and design offices of Raymond Loewy, I. M. Pei and Kevin Roche/John Dinkeloo, 1945–50; associate architect and designer, at Eero Saarinen and Associates, Birmingham, Michigan, 1950–65; freelance architect and designer, in practice as Warren Platner Associates, New Haven, Connecticut, from 1965: designed for Knoll International, Lehigh-Leopold, Georg Jensen, Steelcase Partnership, etc. **Exhibitions:** *Knoll au Musee*, Musee des Arts Decoratifs, Paris, 1972; *Design Since 1945*, Philadelphia Museum of Art, 1983. **Collection:** Philadelphia Museum of Art. Recipient: Rome Prize for Architecture, 1955; Fulbright Research Award, 1955; Graham Foundation Award, 1962; Designers Lighting Forum Award, 1975. Fellow: American Academy in Rome: American Institute of Architects; Rhode Island School of Design. Address: Warren Platner Associates, 18 Mitchell Drive, New Haven, Connecticut 06511–2595, U.S.A.

Works:

CBS Building restaurant interiors and equipment, New York, 1964.
Lounge chairs and tables with steel-rod supports, for Knoll, 1965.
Executive furniture, for the Ford Foundation Building, New York, 1967.
Design Center interiors, for Georg Jensen Inc., New York, 1968.
Executive furniture range, for Knoll, 1969.
Prospect Center faculty club building, for Princeton University, New Jersey, 1970.
Kent Memorial Library, Suffield, Connecticut, 1972.
Interiors and furnishings, for the Mortgage Guarantee Investment Corporation, Milwaukee, Wisconsin, 1973.
Showroom in the Chicago Merchandise Mart, for Steelcase Partnership, 1974.
American Restaurant interiors, Kansas City, Missouri, 1974.
Windows on the World top-floor restaurant, for the World Trade Center, New York, 1975.
Shopping mall interiors, for Water Tower Place, Chicago, 1977.
Sea Containers Corporation world headquarters building, London, 1982.

Publications:

By PLATNER: article—in *Industrial Design* (New York), June 1969.
On PLATNER: books—*Inside Today's Home* by Ray and Sarah Faulkner, New York, 1954, 1975; *Knoll au Musee*, exhibition catalogue by Christine Rae, Paris 1972; *Modern Furniture* by John F. Pile, New York and Toronto, 1979; *Interior Spaces Designed by Architects*, edited by Charles K. Hoyt, New York and London 1981; *Knoll Design* by Eric Larrabee and Massimo Vignelli, New York 1981; *Contemporary Furniture*, edited by Klaus-Jurgen Sembach, Stuttgart and London 1982; *Interior Design: The New Freedom* by Barbaralee Diamonstein, New York 1982; *Design Since 1945*, edited by Kathryn Hiesinger and George Marcus, Philadelphia and London 1983; *Furniture by Architects* by Marc Emery, New York 1983; *Modern Furniture Classics* by Miriam Stimpson, London 1987; *The American Design Adventure 1940–1975* by Arthur J. Pulos, London and Cambridge, Massachusetts 1988.

Warren Platner: Sea Containers House, London, 1982

Warren Platner, trained in architecture, found his true metier as an interior designer. His attitude toward building is that one must not relegate the "people space" to the status of afterthought, that is what's left after the building "package" and its internal systems have been organized. He has assumed the humanistic posture which requires that a building grow organically, from the inside out, reflecting the uses to which the space will be put and the feelings it ought to inspire. Kent Memorial Library and the Prospect Center at Princeton, similar glass-enclosed pavilions, are typical of Platner's ability to use architecture as a bridge between internal space and the surrounding landscape.

Platner's work is distinguished by the comprehensiveness of his approach and the virtuosity of his attention to detail. Not content simply to design the architectural space and its fixtures, lighting, and surface finishes, he frequently, as with Mortgage Guarantee Investment Coproration, creates original furniture, designs the art work, and selects even the small, ornamental accessories (vases, lamps, ashtrays, etc.). In fact, his acceptance of a project is sometimes contingent on a client's willingness to support this level of involvement.

Commissioned in 1974 to create a restaurant of unprecedented opulence atop the 107-story World Trade Center in New York, Platner evinced the full-blooded response that characterizes his best efforts and dramatically illustrates the richness of his visual imagination. The well-known result, Windows on the World, was conceived as an "entertainment" wherein the element of dining would be but a part of the total experience. In the textural richness deployed throughout this remarkable restaurant—tasselled silk wall coverings, faceted mirrors,

marble edging, brass railing, gilding, glazing, stenciling, and floral patterning—Platner takes issue with the arid value-system of the International Style. Although, strictly speaking, not a post modernist, Platner exhibits in his project an impatience with the modern movement's disdain for purely ornamental detailing. At Windows on the World, he has indulged in what he un-apologetically calls "interior decorating," albeit with an architect's discipline, to achieve a rich, almost "period" ambience. Without actually using devices such as carved mouldings, for instance, he has panelled walls in overlapping layers of material to achieve a similar effect, creating what Olga Gueft of *Interiors* magazine called "subliminal associations of traditional grandeur without the prototype."

Speaking of his chair designs for Knoll International, Platner says, "I felt there was room for the kind of decorative, gentle, graceful kind of design that appeared in a period style like Louis XV. . . . It is important that if you design a chair you produce something that enhances the person in it." A noble ambition in an ignoble age; this assessment could well be applied to the entire body of Platner's work.

—Kenneth Gaulin

PLUMB, William Lansing.
American industrial designer. Born in Malone, New York, 13 July 1932. Studied at Cornell University, Ithaca, New York, 1950–54: BFA 1954; Politecnico, Milan, 1957–59. Served in the United States Navy, in Korea, 1954–57. Married Catherine Olden in 1973; children: Abigail and Christian. Freelance designer, working with Gio Ponti and Gianfranco Frattini, in Milan, 1957–59: design consultant to La Rinascente stores, Milan, 1957–59; senior designer in the office of Eliot Noyes, New Canaan, Connecticut, 1959–63; founder and president, Plumb Design Group, New York, 1963–88; principal, Plumb Pearson Inc. design firm, New York, from 1988: has designed for Savin, Dictaphone, Thermo Electric, Bussman/McGraw Edison, Apple Computer, American Telephone and Telegraph, Corning Glass, Citibank, Matsushita Electric Company, Du Pont, Sharp, etc. Editorial board member, *Industrial Design* magazine, New York, from 1978. Lecturer, Rhode Island School of Design, Providence, and Philadelphia College of Art. **Exhibitions:** Museum of Modern Art, New York; Philadelphia Museum of Art; Smithsonian Institution, Washington, D.C.; Whitney Museum, New York; American Crafts Museum, New York; Brooklyn Museum, New York; Gallery 91, New York. **Collection:** Museum of Modern Art, New York. Recipient: *Industrial Design* Magazine Award, New York; Gute Form Prize, Hannover; American Institute of Graphic Arts Award, New York; Communication Arts Magazine Award, Palo Alto; IEA Focus Award, New York; Prix de Rome, 1985. Fellow: Industrial Designers Society of America; American Academy in Rome. Address: Plumb Pearson Inc., 57 East 11th Street, New York, New York 10003, U.S.A.

William Lansing Plumb: AM/FM stereo radio/cassette player, for Sharp, 1987

Works:

IBM Model D typewriter, for International Business Machines, 1960 (with Eliot Noyes).
IBM Selectric I/O typewriter, for International Business Machines, 1961 (with Eliot Noyes).
IBM 214 dictating machine, for International Business Machines, 1963 (with Eliot Noyes).
Corporate identity and design program, for the Savin Corporation.
Corporate identity and design program, for the Thermo Electric Company.
Office interiors, graphics and Buss bus mobile sales training units, for Bussman Division of McGraw Edison.
Stereo Spread portable radio, for J. C. Penney.
World Timer quartz alarm clock, for Copal of Japan.
Pillminder programmable electronic pillbox, for Greenwich Electronic Time.
PXL-6 word-processing printer, for AM International.
Centor transcutaneous nerve stimulator, for IPCO Hospital Supply Corporation.
Portable AM/FM stereo radio/cassette player, for Sharp, 1987.

Publications:

On PLUMB: book—*International Design Yearbook 1988/89*, edited by Arata Isozaki, London 1988; article—in *Industrial Design* (New York), September 1972.

PLUNKETT, Walter.

American film and stage costume designer. Born in Oakland, California, 5 June 1902. Studied at the University of California, Berkeley. Worked as a vaudeville and stock actor, designing first stage costumes for touring vaudeville chorus, 1923–26; head-of wardrobe department, 1926–30, 1932–35, and film costume designer, 1936–39, at FBO Studios (later, RKO), Hollywood; freelance film costume designer, working in Hollywood; 1939–47; designer, Metro-Goldwyn-Mayer film studios, Hollywood, 1947–66; also designed for the Metropolitan Opera and Broadway stage shows, New York. **Exhibition:** *Romantic and Glamorous Hollywood Costume Design*, Metropolitan Museum of Art, New York, 1974. Recipient: Academy Award, 1951. *Died 8 March 1982.*

Works:

Film productions include—*Ain't Love Funny?* (Andrews), 1926; *One Minute to Play* (Wood), 1926; *Red Hot Hoofs* (DeLacy), 1926; *A Regular Scout* (Kirkland), 1926; *Boy Rider* (L. King), 1927; *Clancy's Kosher Wedding* (Gillstrom), 1927; *The Gingham Girl* (Kirkland), 1927; *Her Summer Hero* (Dugan), 1927; *Legionnaires in Paris* (Gillstrom), 1927; *Lightning Lariats* (DeLacy), 1927; *The Magic Garden* (Meehan), 1927; *Shanghaied* (R. Ince), 1927; *Hard Boiled Haggerty* (Brabin), 1927; *The Bandit's Son* (Fox), 1927; *Sinners in Love* (Melford), 1928; *Bantam Cowboy* (L. King), 1928; *Captain Careless* (Storm), 1928; *Chicago After Midnight* (R. Ince), 1928; *Circus Kid* (Seitz), 1928; *Headin' for Danger* (Brad-

bury), 1928; *Hey Rube* (Seitz), 1928; *Hit of the Show* (R. Ince), 1928; *Phantom of the Range* (Dugan), 1928; *Sally of the Scandals* (Shores), 1928; *Son of the Golden West* (Forde), 1928; *Tropic Madness* (Vignola), 1928; *Wallflowers* (Meehan), 1928; *When the Law Rides* (DeLacy), 1928; *Wizard of the Saddle* (Clark), 1928; *Stolen Love* (Shores), 1928; *Stocks and Blondes* (Murphy), 1928; *The Red Sword* (Vignola), 1929; *Love in the Desert* (Melford), 1929; *Air Legion* (Glennon), 1929; *Amazing Vagabond* (Fox), 1929; *The Big Diamond Robbery* (Forde), 1929; *Come and Get It* (Fox), 1929; *Dance Hall* (M. Brown), 1929; *Delightful Rogue* (Shores), 1929; *Freckled Rascal* (L. King), 1929; *Gun Law* (DeLacy), 1929; *Half Marriage* (Cowen), 1929; *Hardboiled* (R. Ince), 1929; *The Jazz Age* (Shores), 1929; *Laughing at Death* (Fox), 1929; *The Little Savage* (L. King), 1929; *Night Parade* (St. Clair), 1929; *Outlawed* (Fogwell), 1929; *The Pride of Pawnee* (DeLacy), 1929; *Seven Keys to Baldpate* (Barker), 1929; *Street Girl* (Ruggles), 1929; *Syncopation* (Glennon), 1929; *Tanned Legs* (Neilan), 1929; *Vagabond Lover* (Neilan), 1929; *The Very Idea* (Rosson), 1929; *Voice of the Storm* (Shores), 1929; *Queen Kelly* (Von Stroheim), 1929; *The Woman I Love* (Melford), 1929; *The Case of Sergeant Grischa* (Brenon), 1930; *The Cuckoos* (Sloane), 1930; *Dixiana* (Reed), 1930; *The Fall Guy* (Pearce), 1930; *Half Shot at Sunrise* (Sloane), 1930; *Lawful Larceny* (Sherman), 1930; *Leathernecking* (Cline), 1930; *Love Comes Along* (Julian), 1930; *Midnight Mystery* (Seitz), 1930; *Second Wife* (Mack), 1930; *Cimarron* (Ruggles), 1931; *Night after Night* (Mayo), 1932; *The Conquerors* (Wellman), 1932; *The Phantom of*

Crestwood (Ruben), 1932; *Secrets of the French Police* (Sutherland), 1932; *The Past of Mary Holmes* (Thompson), 1933; *Double Harness* (Cromwell), 1933; *Morning Glory* (Sherman), 1933; *The Right to Romance* (Santell), 1933; *Ace of Aces* (Ruben), 1933; *Aggie Aplleby, Maker of Men* (Sandrich), 1933; *Ann Vickers* (Cromwell), 1933; *Blind Adventure* (Schoedsack), 1933; *Chance at Heaven* (Seiter), 1933; *Christopher Strong* (Arzner), 1933; *Cross Fire* (Brower), 1933; *Emergency Call* (Cahn), 1933; *The Great Jasper* (Ruben), 1933; *Lucky Devils* (R. Ince), 1933; *Melody Cruise* (Sandrich), 1933; *Midshipman Jack* (Cabanne), 1933; *No Marriage Ties* (Ruben), 1933; *No Other Woman* (Ruben), 1933; *One Man's Journey* (Robertson), 1933; *Professional Sweetheart* (Seiter), 1933; *Rafter Romance* (Seiter), 1933; *Scarlet River* (Brower), 1933; *The Silver Cord* (Cromwell), 1933; *Sweepings* (Cromwell), 1933; *Tomorrow at Eight* (Enright), 1933; *Little Women* (Cukor), 1933; *Flying Down to Rio* (Freeland), 1933; *The Little Minister* (Wallace), 1934; *Spitfire* (Cromwell), 1935; *Finishing School* (Tuchock and Nicholls), 1934; *Sing and Like It* (Seiter), 1934; *Where Sinners Meet* (Ruben), 1934; *Stingaree* (Wellman), 1934; *The Life of Vergie Winters* (Santell), 1934; *Bachelor Bait* (Stevens), 1934; *Cockeyed Cavaliers* (Sandrich), 1934; *Strictly Dynamite* (Nugent), 1934; *The Age of Innocence* (Moeller), 1934; *The Fountain* (Cromwell), 1934; *His Greatest Gamble* (Robertson), 1934; *We're Rich Again* (Seiter), 1934; *Down to Their Last Yacht* (Sloane), 1934; *The Gay Divorcee* (Sandrich), 1934; *Anne of Green Gables* (Nicholls), 1934; *Kentucky Kernels* (Stevens), 1934; *The Silver Streak* (Atkins), 1934; *Wednesday's Child* (Robertson), 1934; *By Your Leave* (Corrigan), 1934; *Dangerous Corner* (Rosen), 1934; *Lightning Strikes Twice* (Holmes), 1934; *The Crime Doctor* (Robertson), 1934; *Gridiron Flash* (Tyron), 1934; *A Hat, a Coat, and a Glove* (Miner), 1934; *Keep 'em Rolling* (Archainbaud), 1934; *Long Lost Father* (Schoedsack), 1934; *Man of Two Worlds* (Ruben), 1934; *Meanest Gal in Town* (Roberts), 1934; *Of Human Bondage* (Cromwell), 1934; *Romance in Manhattan* (Roberts), 1934; *Success at Any Price* (Ruben), 1934; *Their Big Moment* (Cruze), 1934; *This Man is Mine* (Cromwell), 1934; *Woman in the Dark* (Rosen), 1934; *Mary of Scotland* (Ford), 1935; *Hooray for Love* (W. Lang), 1935; *The Informaer* (Ford), 1935; *The Arizonian* (C. Vidor), 1935; *Jalna* (Cromwell), 1935; *Alice Adams* (Stevens), 1935; *Hot Tip* (McCarey and Gleason), 1935; *Freckles* (Killy and Hamilton), 1935; *His Family Tree* (C. Vidor), 1935; *The Three Musketeers* (Lee), 1935; *The Rainmakers* (Guiol), 1935; *To Beat the Band* (Stoloff), 1935; *Hi, Gaucho* (Atkins), 1935; *The Return of Peter Grimm* (Nicholls), 1935; *Annie Oakley* (Stevens), 1935; *Another Face* (Cabanne), 1935; *Captain Hurricane* (Robertson), 1935; *Chasing Yesterday* (Nicholls), 1935; *A Dog of Flanders* (Sloman), 1935; *Enchanted April* (Beaumont), 1935; *Grand Old Girl* (Robertson), 1935; *Murder on a Honeymoon* (Corrigan), 1935; *Seven Keys to Baldpate* (Hamilton and Killy), 1935; *Strangers All* (C. Vidor), 1935; *Sylvia Scarlett* (Cukor), 1935; *Village Tale* (Cromwell), 1935; *The Plough and the Stars* (Ford), 1936; *The Soldier and the Lady* (Nicholls), 1936; *Chatterbox* (Nicholls), 1936; *Quality Street* (Stevens), 1937; *The Woman I Love* (Litvak), 1937; *Nothing Sacred* (Wellman), 1937; *The Adventures of Tom Sawyer* (Taurog), 1937; *Allegheny Uprising* (Seiter), 1939; *Stagecoach* (Ford), 1939; *The Story of Vernon and Irene Castle* (Potter), 1939; *Gone With the Wind* (Fleming), 1939; *The Hunchback of Notre Dame* (Dieterle), 1939; *Abe Lincoln in Illinois* (Cromwell), 1939;

Virgil in the Night (Stevens), 1939; *The Corsican Brothers* (Ratoff), 1941; *Lydia* (Duvivier), 1941; *Ladies in Retirement* (C. Vidor), 1941; *Sundown* (Hathaway), 1941; *Go West, Young Lady* (Strayer), 1941; *Lady for a Night* (Jason), 1941; *To Be or Not to Be* (Lubitsch), 1942; *Commandos Strike at Dawn* (Farrow), 1943; *In Old Oklahoma* (Rogell), 1943; *The Heat's On* (Ratoff), 1943; *Knickerbocker Holiday* (H. Brown), 1943; *Can't Help Singing* (Ryan), 1944; *A Song to Remember* (C. Vidor), 1944; *Along Came Jones* (Heisler), 1945; *Song of Love* (C. Brown), 1946; *Because of Him* (Wallace), 1946; *My Brother Talks to Horses* (Zinnemann), 1947; *Duel in the Sun* (K. Vidor), 1947; *Sea of Grass* (Kazan), 1947; *Summer Holiday* (Mamoulian), 1947; *Green Dolphin Street* (Saville), 1947; *Fiesta* (Thorpe), 1947; *The Three Musketeers* (Sidney), 1948; *The Kissing Bandit* (Benedek), 1948; *Little Women* (LeRoy), 1948; *The Secret Garden* (Wilcox), 1949; *Madame Bovary* (LeRoy), 1949; *That Forsyte Woman* (Bennett), 1949; *Adam's Rib* (Cukor), 1949; *Ambush* (Wood), 1949; *Black Hand* (Thorpe), 1949; *The Outriders* (Rowland), 1949; *Stars in My Crown* (Tourneur), 1950; *Annie Get Your Gun* (Sidney), 1950; *Devil's Doorway* (A. Mann), 1950; *Father of the Bride* (Minnelli), 1950; *The Happy Years* (Wellman), 1950; *Summer Stock* (Walters), 1950; *Toast of New Orleans* (Taurog), 1950; *King Solomon's Mines* (Bennett and Marton), 1950; *The Miniver Story* (Potter), 1950; *Two Weeks With Love* (Rowlands), 1950; *The Magnificent Yankee* (J. Sturges), 1950; *Payment on Demand* (Bernhardt), 1950; *Vengeance Valley* (Thorpe), 1950; *Soldiers Three* (Garnett), 1950; *Mr. Imperium* (Hartman), 1950; *Kind Lady* (J. Sturges), 1951; *Man with a Cloak* (Markle), 1951; *Show Boat* (Sidney), 1951; *The Law and the Lady* (Knopf), 1951; *An American in Paris* (Minnelli), 1951; *Across the Wide Missouri* (Wellman), 1951; *Westward the Women* (Wellman), 1951; *Singin' in the Rain* (Kelly and Donen), 1952; *Carbine Williams* (Thorpe), 1952; *Plymouth Adventure* (C. Brown), 1952; *The Prisoner of Zenda* (Thorpe), 1952; *Million Dollar Mermaid* (LeRoy), 1952; *Young Bess* (Sidney), 1953; *Scandal at Scourie* (Negulesco), 1953; *Ride, Vaquero* (Farrow), 1953; *The Actress* (Cukor), 1953; *All the Brothers Were Valiant* (Thorpe), 1953; *Kiss Me Kate* (Sidney), 1953; *Seven Brides for Seven Brothers* (Donen), 1954; *The Student Prince* (Thorpe), 1954; *Valley of the Kings* (Pirosh), 1954; *Athena* (Thorpe), 1954; *Deep in My Heart* (Doenen), 1954; *Jupiter's Darling* (Sidney), 1954; *The Glass Slipper* (Walters), 1954; *Many Rivers to Cross* (Rowland), 1954; *Moonfleet* (F. Lang), 1955; *The Scarlet Coat* (J. Sturges), 1955; *The King's Thief* (Leonard), 1955; *Diane* (Miller), 1955; *Forbidden Planet* (Wilcox), 1955; *Tribute to a Bad Man* (Wise), 1955; *Lust for Life* (Minnelli), 1956; *The Wings of Eagles* (Ford), 1956; *The Fastest Gun Alive* (Rouse), 1956; *Gun Glory* (Rowlands), 1957; *Raintree County* (Dymytryk), 1957; *The Brothers Karamazov* (Brooks), 1957; *Merry Andrew* (Kidd), 1957; *The Sheepman* (Marshall), 1958; *The Law and Jake Wade* (J. Sturges), 1958; *Some Came Running* (Minnelli), 1958; *Home from the Hill* (Minnelli), 1959; *Pollyanna* (Swift), 1960; *Bells Are Ringing* (Minnelli), 1960; *Cimarron* (A. Mann), 1960; *Pocketful of Miracles* (Capra), 1961; *The Four Horsemen of the Apocalypse* (Minnelli), 1961; *Two Weeks in Another Town* (Minnelli), 1962; *How the West Was Won* (Ford, Marshall and Hathaway), 1963; *Marriage on the Rocks* (Donohue), 1965; *Seven Women* (Ford), 1966.

Publications:

By PLUNKETT: article—in *The Velvet Light Trap* (Madison), Spring 1978.
On PLUNKETT: books—*Romantic and Glamorous Hollywood Costume Design,* exhibition catalogue by Diana Vreeland, New York 1974; *Hollywood Costume Design* by David Chierichetti, London 1976; *Costume Design in the Movies* by Elizabeth Leese, New York 1976; *In a Glamorous Fashion: The Fabulous Years of Hollywood Costume Design* by W. Robert LaVine, Boston and London 1981.

Walter Plunkett lacked the knack of high couture. He could not compete in the world of super-rich chic with Paris-trained Adrian or Travis Banton. Instead, Plunkett excelled in designing glorious garments of days gone by. With the fervor of a nineteenth-century archeologist, Plunkett worked to make his name virtually synonymous with the "period" picture.

Originally an actor, Plunkett prepared as if trained by Stanislavski. Endowing his costumes with presence and character, even the humblest handmade, as seen in *Little Women* (1948), was seamed with integrity. Plunkett worked especially well with Katharine Hepburn at RKO because both artists aimed for veracity in character and era. Because Plunkett's dresses were assuredly accurate even in basic construction, Hepburn rehearsed in costume to achieve proper movement. She insisted on learning how to maneuver hoops and how to turn her head in stiffly starched ruffs as if such movements were natural to her in order to insure that costume and characterization became one. Plunkett also was responsible for the Fred Astaire–Ginger Rogers look. Their dance attire, integral to that "carefree" image, depended on Plunkett's elegant lines, as they inhibited or released areas of mobility. Astaire, of course, insisted on comfort and optimum freedom. Rogers preferred glamour and gimmicks to catch the eye.

For David Selznick's *Gone With the Wind* (1939), Plunkett chronicled the fall and rebirth of the South through Scarlett O'Hara's well-researched wardrobe, which marked her passage from selfish innocence to hardened maturity. For example, the famous "dining room curtains" dress, ornamented with jaunty tassels and a smart, one-shoulder cape, illustrated Scarlett's spunky calculation in the face of adversity. As one of the first technicolor movies, *Gone With the Wind* dazzled with picture-postcard color. Plunkett had already worked within the limited range of the two-color process at RKO, but now he filled the screen with sapphire, dusty rose, antique blue, claret red, and infinite shades of green. Still remembered today, the gowns of this film reflected an emerging post-depression fashion trend. However, World War II aborted the cinch waist and wide, fabric-consuming skirt symbolic of prosperity and the romantic ideal of womanhood; only after the war were they resurrected as Dior's postwar "New Look."

Plunkett's later pictures echoed some interesting modern trends. His *American in Paris* (1951) sequence depicted the artists' ball of abstract blacks and whites, more like the flamboyant visions of Adrian than traditional Plunkett. They splashed the screen abstractly as if flung from Jackson Pollock's paint brush.

Throughout the 1950s, Plunkett continued his successful "period" creations. At the same time, he began to mimick the very popular culture that he and other designers had created. His mannerish garb for Judy Garland's *Summer Stock* (1950), for example, recalls Travis Banton's collaborations with Marlene Dietrich. Plunkett's greatest homage to the silver screen however was *Singin' in the Rain* (1952). Exaggerated American motifs paid glorious tribute to those brash Hollywood musicals of his earlier days in the business.

—Edith C. Lee

POLIDORI, Gi(ov)anni.

Italian painter, stage and film designer. Born in Rome, 7 November 1923. Studied painting, under Renato Guttuso, 1941–43, Vittorio Grassi, 1945–46, and Corrado Cagli, 1947–49, in Rome: stage design, at the Accademia di Belle Arti, Rome, 1945–46; film design, at the Centro Sperimentale di Cinematografia, Rome, 1947–48. Served as a photographer, in the Italian Air Force, 1943, and the military information service, 1944–45. Married Marisa D'Andrea in 1950; daughers: Silvia and Carlotta. Professional designer for stage and film from 1946, and for television from 1959: worked on films of Alessandro Blasetti, Jean Renoir, King Vidor, Luchino Visconti, Michelangelo Antonioni, Alberto Lattuada, Vittorio Gassman, Franco Rossi, Eduardo De Filippo, Nanni Loy, Terence Young, Elio Petri etc., and on stage productions of Gianfranco De Bosio, Aurel Milloss, Giancarlo Sbragia, Luigi Squarzina, Marco Sciaccaluga, etc. Instructor, Centro Sperimentale di Scenografia, Rome, 1967–68; Accademia Nazionale d'Arte Drammatica, Rome, 1969–71; associate professor of scenography, Universita degli Studi, Bologna, 1971–86. Technical director, Teatro di Genova, Genoa, 1980–82; planning consultant, Carlo Felice Theatre, Genoa, and the Teatro Cavour, Imperia, 1982–83; founder, with Emanuele Luzzati of the Politecnico G. Byron school of scenography and visual communications, Genoa, 1983. **Exhibitions:** Galleria Schneider, Rome, 1956; Galleria La Medusa, Rome, 1958; Galleria Passeggiata di Ripetta, Rome, 1960; Galleria Il Fiore, Florence, 1965; Galleria La Sferna, Modena, 1965; Grafica dei Greci, Rome, 1980; Studio Firma, Genoa, 1983; Galleria Ellequadro, Genoa, 1988. Recipient: Premio San Genesio, Milan, 1957. Address: Via L. Montaldo 55/35, 16137 Genoa, Italy.

Works:

Film productions include—*Due Moglie sono Troppe*, 1949; *Bellissima*, 1951; *La Signora senza Camellie*, 1952; *La Carrozza d'Oro*, 1952; *Il Cappotto*, 1952; *I Vinti*, 1952; *Amore in Citta*, 1953; *Siamo Donne*, 1953; *Il Sole negli Occhi*, 1953; *Il Seduttore*, 1954; *Guerra e Pace*, 1955; *Le Amiche*, 1955; *Kean*, 1956; *Un Ettaro di Cielo*, 1957; *Il Mondo di Notte*, 1960; *Maciste contro il Vampiro*, 1961; *Il Mondo di Notte 2*, 1960; *I Moschettieri del Mare*, 1961; *Le Quattro Giornate di Napoli*, 1962; *Violenza Segreta*, 1962; *Liola*, 1963; *Una Rosa per Tutti*, 1965; *Spara Forte . . . Piu Forte: Non Capisco*, 1966; *L'Avventuriero*, 1966; *Come, Quando, Perche . . .*, 1968; *Riusciranno i Nostri Eroi a Ritrovare il Loro Amico Misteriosamente Scomparso in Africa?*, 1968; *Il Commissario Pepe*, 1969; *Rosolino Paterno Soldato*, 1969; *La Supertestimone*, 1970; *Detenuto in Attesta di Giudizia*, 1971; *La Proprieta non e piu un Furto*, 1973; *Il Mio Nome e Nessuno*, 1973. Stage productions include— *Woyzeck*, Teatro Eliseo, Rome, 1946; *All My Sons*, Teatro Quirino, Rome, 1948; *Death of a Salesman*, Teatro Eliseo, Rome, 1951; *The Power and the Glory*, San Miniato, 1955; *Anne Frank*, Teatro Eliseo, Rome, 1957; *I Demoni*, Teatro Duse, Genoa, 1957; *Hin und Zuruck*, Teatro Massimo, Palermo, 1959; *The Miracle Worker*, Teatro Odeon, Milan, 1960; *Le Diable et le Bon Dieu*, Teatro Duse, Genoa, 1962; *Hamlet*, Teatro Romano, Verona, 1963; *Johnny Spielt Auf*, Teatro della Pergola, Florence, 1964; *Seeschlacht*, Teatro della Pergola, Florence, 1964; *Troilus and Cressida*, Teatro Duse, Genoa, 1964; *The Iceman Cometh* Politeana Genovese, Genoa, 1965; *Julius Caesar*, Music Hall, Kansas City 1965; *Se Questo e' un Uomo*, Teatro Carignano, Turin, 1966; *The Bacchae*, Teatro della Pergola, Florence, 1968; *Don Carlos*, Teatro Romano, Verona, 1969; *Caligola*, Teatro Carignano, Turin, 1970; *Il Visio Assurdo*, Teatro Verdi, Padua, 1974; *Our Town*, Teatro Verdi, Padua, 1975; *Lucia di Lammermoor*, Arena, Verona, 1976; *Minnie la Candida*, Piccolo Teatro, Milan, 1980; *Volki i*

Gianni Polidori: Set design for Archibald McLeish's *J. B.: A Play in Verse*, **1958**

Ovcy, Teatro Duse, Genoa, 1980; *She Stoops to Conquer,* Teatro Duse, Genoa, 1981; *The Twin Rivals,* Teatro Duse, Genoa, 1982; *Bertoldo,* Teatro Dehon, Bologna, 1983; *Gli Accidenti di Constantinopoli,* Parco di Nervi, Genoa, 1984; *Otello,* Teatro Romano, Verona, 1985; *Affabulazione,* Teatro Manzoni, Pistoia, 1986; *Trois Poemes de Mallarme,* Villa Imperiale, Genoa, 1987; *Dario Fo: Two Farces,* Teatro del Filodrammatici, Milan, 1988; *Front Page,* Teatro del Giglio, Lucca, 1988.

Publications:

On POLIDORI: books—*Das Buhnebild* by Ottmar Schubert, Munich 1956; *Scenografia* by Guido Frette, Milan 1956; *Dizionario del Cinema Italiano 1945-1969* by Gianni Rondolino, Turin 1969; *Le Decor de Film* by Leon Barsacq, Paris 1970, as *Caligari's Cabinet and Other Grand Illusions,* Boston 1976; *Scenografia in Italia Oggi* by Roberto Rebora, Milan 1974; *Stage Design Throughout the World 1970-1975* by Rene Hainaux and Nicole Leclercq, Brussels and London 1976; *I'Illusione Alternativa* by Franco Mancini, Turin 1980.

Nowadays you can put on a play without scenery, without a theatre, without actors. Not without an audience. In the final analysis, it is the public that has determined the ways in which a play can be produced. It always has been that way, at every period in our civilization. Today, however, we are trying—at the moment of our creative activity—to orient, to pilot, and sometimes to record both our attitudes and our use (sometimes actually the philological use) of the techniques and materials in an area of research organized so as to accept, by absorbing them, the faculties and intentions of human nature and of life. The play can probably never be produced—never again—according to the rules of the original understanding, of tradition. The almost obsessional search for new and "unpublished" theatrical fields, the evocation of the single gesture/symbol, of the impossible pure sound, of a new total protagonist, the actor-spectator, are simple confirmation of this endeavour.

The designer of scenery is no longer a decorator, an architect, a painter. For at least the past fifty years, he has been simply a person who is irremediably compromised, the clearest victim in the "new world of active vision and presence"; he is no longer the *grandemagosololuiautorizzato,* the one great self-authorized wizard, of the stage. He is, perhaps, just an anthropologist who studies and records the science of motivations. From A to Z.

—Gianni Polidori

Polidori's training in design was a concerted effort, embracing several disciplines: painting, theatre, and film. As a young man, during World War II, he studied painting with the famous artists Renato Guttuso, and Vittorio Grassi, and later, after the war, with Corrado Cagli. No less auspicious was his schooling in stage design from 1945 to 1946 at the Accademia di Belle Arti, located in Rome. Soon after, he enrolled in the prestigious Centro Sperimentale di Cinematografia, also in Rome, completing the film design program in 1948. His design work in all of these fields has been distinctive, and has led to a long, illustrious career. Additionally, in 1959 he expanded his training in design by working in television.

In film, Polidori's work is well known because he has designed for such international film directors as Michelangelo Antonioni, Alessandro Blasetti, Vittorio Gassman, Alberto Lattuada, Franco Rossi, King Vidor, and Lu-

chino Visconti. Starting out as an assistant designer to Chiari for *La Carozzo d'oro (The Golden Coach)* (1952), Polidori soon made his mark on the international film community by designing Visconti's neorealistic picture, *Bellissima* (1952). This film concerns a stage mother who shuttles her daughter to audition after audition. Polidori provided sets that went from, "beauty parlor to ballet and to sound stages," according to the New York Times review. Afterwards, he worked on Lattuada's production of Gogol's *Il Cappotto (The Overcoat)* (1953). His work with Antonioni in *I vinti (The Vanquished)* (1953), *La Signora senza Camellie* (1953), and *Le Amiche (The Girl Friends)* (1955), was equally impressive. León Barsacq, in *Le Decor de Film,* calls his settings "simple and incisive, a style that perfectly suited Antonio's films." Polidori continued his designs for film into the sixties with such works as *Il mondo di notte 2* (1960), and *Liola* (1963); and into the seventies with *La proprieta'non e' piu' un furto* (1971), and the "spaghetti western," *Il mio nome e' nessuno* (released in the U.S. as *My Name is Nobody*) (1973). The latter, produced by Sergio Leone and starring Henry Fonda, was shot on location in New Mexico, Colorado, and Spain.

Polidori's stage designs have spanned five decades and range from drama and opera to ballet. He has variously functioned as set, lighting, and costumer designer, and has worked with well-known Italian stage directors such as Giancarlo Sbragia, Luigi Squarzino, and Luchino Visconti, among others. His first professional design was for Buchner's *Woyzeck* (1946), and showed a natural talent for correlating the visual elements of the set with the text in a simple manner. This production was followed by *L'Uomo e il fucile* (1947), and Arthur Miller's *All My Sons* (1947). In 1950, he married Misa D'Andrea, a costumer with whom he had worked on Ibsen's *The Master Builder* and *Enemy of the People* (both 1950).

Polidori has designed many American and British plays that were produced in Italy: Miller's *Death of a Salesman* (1951 in Italy with the Mirelli-Stoppa Company), in which he used Jo Mielziner's original backdrop, and *The Diary of Anne Frank* (1957), for which he created the split-scene attic set against a backdrop of a devastated Rotterdam. Other designs include Archibald MacLeish's *J.B.* (1958), M. V. Gazo's *Hatful of Rain* (1956), John Van Druten's *I Am A Camera* (1957), O'Neill's *The Iceman Cometh* (1965), John Osborne's *Look Back in Anger* (1957), Thornton Wilder's *Our Town* (1975), and Ben Hecht's and Charles McArthur's *The Front Page* (1988). Polidori's success at capturing an American ambience within the designs have been noted by various critics.

He has also designed plays for contemporary Italian playwrights. His sets for *Affabulazione* (1986) by Pier Paolo Pasolini and *Two Farces* (1988) by Dario Fo are among his most recent. Equally adept at designing for the classical theatre, Polidori has applied his craft to such standard works as Moliere's *The Bourgeois Gentleman* (1953), Shakespeare's *Measure for Measure* (1957), *Hamlet* (1963), and *Julius Caesar* (presented at the Kansas City Music Hall in Missouri, 1965), and finally Goldsmith's *She Stoops to Conquer* (1981). Also, he has designed the ballets, *Il Cappello a tre punte* and *Scarlattiana* (1954), both choreographed by T. Wallmann.

Polidori's technique for design begins with an analysis of the text, from which the design derives its form. As a result of his classical training, his style is distinctive, relying upon strong composition, and sufficient detail. He has, however, worked on a wide range of productions, designing abstract as well as realistic sets. His style, therefore, is best described as eclectic. Further, perhaps because of his in-

volvement with film design, he has sometimes employed projections and lighting effects in his productions similar to those of Czechoslovakian scenographer, Josef Svoboda. One example was in his production of *Il Vizio Assurdo* (1974) by Diego Fabbri, produced at the Teatro Verdi in Padua. For this production, he created a set that was a constructivist arrangement of steps, platforms, and back panels on which vast projections appeared.

His illustrious design career encompasses a multitude of other activities such as theatre consulting, exhibiting his paintings, and teaching. He has consulted on the laboratory theatre at the Nazionale d'Arte Drammatica Art in Rome, the Carlo Felice Theatre in Genoa, and the Teatro Cavour in Imperia, to name only a few examples. His paintings have been shown at major galleries, primarily in Italy. And, he has taught scenography at the Centro Sperimentale di Cinematographia in Rome in 1967-68, and has taught as Associate Professor of Scenography at the Universitá degli Studi in Bologna since 1971. This last position he retired from in 1986. Dedicated to teaching, in 1983 he and Emmanuele Luzzati founded the Polytechnico 'G. Byron' Scuola di Communicazione visiva e scenografia in Genoa.

Philosophizing on the role of the scenographer in the theatre, Polidori's definition goes well beyond that of merely a decorator or architect. He sees the scenographer as an anthropologist. Specifically, a person who is engaged in the study of human motivation and how it relates to the "new world of active vision and presence." To Polidori, the scenographer of today must have a thorough understanding of this world, and infuse it into the design.

—Tom Mikotowicz

POND, Edward (Charles).
British painter, textile, graphic and industrial designer. Born in London, 12 March 1929. Educated at Royal Liberty School, Romford, Essex, until 1946; studied textiles and lithography, at Southeast Essex Technical College, Dagenham, 1951-55: NDD 1955; Royal College of Art, London, 1955-58: Des.RCA 1958. Served in the British Army Parachute Regiment, 1947-49. Married Grace Sparks in 1954; children: Christopher, Rebecca and Hannah. Design director, at Bernard Wardle (Everflex), North Wales, 1958-62, Bernard Wardle Fabrics, Derbyshire, 1962-65, and at The Wallpaper Manufacturers, London, 1965-76; founder-chairman of Edward Pond Associates design firm, London, from 1976: has designed for Crown Wallpapers, Heals Fabrics, Tomkinson Carpets, Edinburgh Weavers, Ford Motor Company, Antiference Limited, Reed Paper Group, Marley Tiles, etc. Also director of Polycell Products, London, 1968-71, Polypops Products, London, 1969-71, Paperchase Products, London 1969-82, and Panache, London, 1972-76. President, Chartered Society of Designers, London, 1981-83. **Exhibitions:** Portmeirion North Wales, 1960: Scott-Howard, London, 1987; Bournemouth College of Art, Hampshire, 1988; Medway College of Art, Kent, 1988. **Collections:** Victoria and Albert Museum, London: Whitworth Art Gallery, Manchester. Recipient: Royal College of Art Silver Medal, London, 1958; Design Council Award, London, 1959; Public Arts Develop-

Edward Pond: *Armada* ceramic mural, Plymouth, 1988

ment Trust Prize, London, 1988; Packaging Association of America Award, 1988. Fellow, Chartered Society of Designers, London, and Royal Society of Arts, London. Address: Edward Pond Associates, 9 Alfred Place, London WC1E 7EB, England.

Works:

Printed swimsuit fabric, for Clutsom and Kemp, 1958.
Harlequin range of textiles and wallcoverings, for Bernard Wardle, 1958–59.
Piazza printed PVC fabric, for Bernard Wardle, 1960.
Scene Collection range of wallcoverings, for Crown Wallpapers, 1966.
Britannia printed metal serving tray, for Poly-pops Products, 1969.
Irish tweed suiting fabrics, for Foxford Woollens, 1977.
Wool upholstery fabrics, for Yorkshire Tweed, 1978.
Cosmetic products and packaging, for Boots the Chemist, from 1983.
Screenprinted fabric wall panels at Heathrow, for the British Airports Authority, 1984.
Network Southeast murals and line brand insignia, for the British Railways Board, 1987–88.
Murals panels in melamine laminate, for British Rail/Public Arts Development Trust, 1988.

Armada 400 ceramic mural, for the City of Plymouth, 1988.

Publications:

By POND: books—*Anti-Rationalists,* London 1960; *A. H. Mackmurdo: His Life and Work,* thesis, London 1962; *Historic Wallpapers in the Whitworth Gallery,* Manchester 1972; articles—in *The Designer* (London), July/August 1975, December 1982; *The Times* (London), 3 July 1980, 1 June 1981, 12 June 1981.
On POND: books—*Designers in Britain 5,* edited by Herbert Spencer, London 1957; *Did Britain Make It? British Design in Context 1946–86,* edited by Penny Sparke, London 1986; articles—in the *Financial Times* (London), 22 August 1975; *Greenville News* (South Carolina), 12 April 1978; *The Designer* (London), June 1978, May 1981.

*

Colour, pattern, and texture are the ingredients of what we wear, use, and live with. They are the basic component parts used by designers who design for products as diverse as furnishings, carpets, wallpapers, bed linen, gift wrap, and so on. As such, they are subject for commercial success to the vagaries of fashion—not fashion in the simple, dress sense, but the changes in the design scene which move with the Zeit Geist.

My interest as stylist, producer, coordinator, or what you will, has been to define marketing objectives for design collections, to brief designers, to find designs, and to make it all work. The best recent example of this is the Zambezi Collection (1982), for a manufacturer printing in Zimbabwe: a range of all-cotton furnishing fabrics with a distinct local look—but not ethnic—yet all designed in England. On the same basis, I have produced design collections on special themes for Japan, the United States, South Africa, and Australia.

The best designers are always part of a collection, and collections are at their best when planned. In this way, the best individual characteristics of designers can be used to advantage, as in casting the actors in a play. Viable design statements can be formulated to set trends and influence design worldwide. Good examples are the Palladio Wallpaper Collections, no longer in production, which set out to interpret trends in painting, as large-scale, and sometimes very large-scale, wallcoverings. For twenty years, from 1955–75, these collections moved through tachism, Op art, Pop art, "new" art nouveau, decorative romanticism, and a few styles that never quite "made it." Palladio, along with Heals Fabrics, were without doubt the greatest incentives to the creative ingenuity of British designers during this period, and I was fortunate enough to be involved with both.

It is these design/marketing concepts which

interest me in particular. Other specific examples of commercial successes are Harlequin for Bernard Wardle (1958), and the Scene Collection for Crown Wallcoverings (1966).

For some years, my design involvement has been in the coordination of wide ranges of domestic products and now includes the incorporation of packaging, graphics, and promotional materials.

—Edward Pond

In a business where designers often take a low profile, Edward Pond is a colourful personality with an eighteenth-century ebullience and a determination to succeed. His reputation as a designer derives from his combination of ability to interpret modern style and a strong sense for what will actually sell. On leaving art school, he was quickly promoted to chief designer with Bernard Wardle, a company committed to 1950s contemporary taste. Then invited to design textiles for Heal's, the London furniture store, he benefited from their policy of promoting young talent (a tactic that was helping British textile designers to achieve an international reputation). Inevitably, London design of the 1960s made a deep impact on his work. This period looked very closely at stylistic revivals, particularly art nouveau, which became the score for many of his patterns. Pond followed through on this interest with the publication of his thesis on the late nineteenth-century designer A. H. Mackmurdo.

Some of his most innovative work was for Palladio Wallpaper, a company whose design policy set out to interpret trends in fine art, and the designs he produced there remain a case study of style throughout the period, including as they do a range from Op- and Pop- inspired patterns, to a more decorative romanticism. Style was not, however, his only concern, and Pond has worked closely with the new developments in technology affecting post-war textiles. For the Reed Paper group, he worked on experimental uses for non-woven fabric; for Northern Bedding, the development of coated fabrics for mass-produced upholstered fabrics; for Bernard Wardle, stretch covers.

Since he set up Edward Pond Associates in 1976, his design interests have widened to include packaging, graphics, and design consultancy. Some examples of his company's projects include the 1982 Zambezi collection of cotton furnishing fabrics, designed with a local feel for a manufacturer printing in Zimbabwe, and the design of toiletries, packaging, logo, and graphics for the major retailer and manufacturer Boots the Chemists.

—Catherine McDermott

PONNELLE, Jean-Pierre.
French film and stage designer. Born in Paris, 19 February 1932. Studied philosophy and art history, at the Sorbonne, Paris, 1949-52. Served in the French Army, in Algeria, 1959-61. Married Margit Saad in 1957; son: Pierre-Dominicq. Freelance designer from 1952, and stage director from 1961: designed productions for the Hannover Opera, New York Metropolitan Opera, Vienna State Opera, Munich State Opera, Dusseldorf Schauspielhaus, Zurich Opera, Covent Garden Opera, San Francisco Opera, Chicago Lyric Opera, and for the Salzburg and Bayreuth Festivals. *Died* (in Munich, West Germany) *11 August 1988.*

Works:

Major stage productions include—*Boulevard Solitude,* Hannover Opera, 1952; *Il Barbiere di Siviglia,* Salzburg Festival, 1968; *Pelleas et Melisande,* Munich State Opera, 1978; *Contes d'Hoffmann,* Salzburg Festival, 1980-82; *Don Giovanni,* Lyric Opera, Chicago, 1980; *Tristan und Isolde,* Bayreuth Festival, 1981; *Lear,* San Francisco Opera 1981; *I Pagliacci,* Houston Opera, 1982; *Idomeneo,* Metropolitan Opera, New York, 1982; *Mitridate,* Zurich Opera, 1983; *Liebesverbot,* Munich State Opera, 1983; *Cosi Fan Tutte,* Paris Opera, 1983; *Parsifal,* Cologne Opera, 1983; *Idomeneo,* Salzburg Festival, 1983; *Fidelio,* Berlin Opera, 1984; *Nozze di Figaro,* Paris Opera, 1984; *Aida,* Royal Opera House, London, 1984; *Clemenza di Tito,* Metropolitan Opera, New York, 1984; *Cavalliera/Pagliacci,* Vienna State Opera, 1984. Films include—*Carmina Burana, Nozze di Figaro, Il Barbniere di Siviglia, Clemenza di Tito, Madama Butterfly, Incoronazione di Poppea, Ritorno d'Ulisse in Patria, Orfeo, Tristan und Isolde, La Cenerentola, Rigoletto.*

Publications:

On PONNELLE: books—*Who's Who in Opera,* edited by Maria F. Rich, New York 1976; *Who's Who in Arts and Literature,* edited by Karl Strute and Theodor Doelken, Zurich 1982; *The Cambridge Guide to World Theatre,* edited by Martin Banham, Cambridge 1988.

Ponnelle began his career just in theatrical design, but he soon came to realize that in opera he could give the production his own, personal stamp only if he also acted as the stage director. His first great international success was as the director-designer of *Il Barbiere de Siviglia* at Salzburg in 1968, and this reputation was solidified by his 1973 Munich production of *Pelléas et Mélisande,* a masterpiece of poetry and symbolism, a feast for both eye and ear. Though most critics have felt that he is at his best with the great, romantic, Italian operas by Rossini, Verdi, and Donizetti, he has also achieved success with Mozart.

Ponnelle's approach is to put aside the history of an opera's production and the writings on how it should be interpreted and to look at the story and listen to the music as if they had never been read or heard before. Then, he slowly and carefully develops a personal interpretation that he hopes will make the audience also hear and see the opera as if for the first time. Sometimes, this means shifting emphases or even scenes, a practice which frequently creates sharp controversy, but his end result is always theatrically effective. For Mozart's *Idomeneo,* he took the design of one of the large, Mannerist stone masks of a god from the Tivoli Gardens outside Rome, enlarged it to tremendous size, and placed it on stage to brood over the mythological events transpiring on the stage below, as if it embodied the power of the Greek god Poseidon. He designed the costumes in a mixture of eighteenth-century and Greek fashions, thus reflecting both the nature of the Greek story and the eighteenth-century character of the music.

Always Ponnelle looks for the visual metaphor that will make an opera visually vivid and theatrically pleasurable. He is very aware that opera operates on an audience as much visually as aurally, and he is determined that in his productions there will be no separation between the two. Therefore, once he has worked out the setting and costumes for an opera, he directs the stage movement to enhance in every way the visual metaphor of the production. Despite critics' objections to Ponnelle's approach, his visual production is always at the service of the composer and his music. Thus, Ponnelle's greatest influence on the contemporary opera scene has been to make the visual production match and equal the musical component in the appreciation of the audience.

—Douglas A. Russell

PONTI, Gio(vanni).
Italian architect, interior, exhibition and industrial designer. Born in Milan, 18 November 1891. Studied architecture, at the Politecnico, Milan, 1918-21: Dip.Arch. 1921. Served in the Italian Army, 1916-18: War Cross and Military Medal. Married Giulia Vimercati in 1921; four children. Worked in the architectural studio of Mino Fiocchi and Emilio Lancia, Milan, 1921; designer and product renovator, at the Richard Ginori factory, in Milan and Florence, 1923-30; partner, with Emilio Lancia, in Studio Ponti e Lancia architectural firm, Milan, 1927-33; with Antonio Fornaroli and Eugenio Soncini, in Studio Ponti/Fornaroli/Soncini architectural firm, Milan, 1933-45; with Fornaroli and Alberto Rosselli, in Studio Ponti/Fornaroli/Rosselli architectural firm, Milan, 1952-76: designed for La Pavoni, La Visa, Argenteria Krupp, Fraser, Greco, Cassina, Edison, Singer, Gallieni, Marazza, Ideal Standard, Nordiska Kompaniet, La Luma, Christofle, Rima, Colombi, Arredoluce, Knoll, etc. Founder, 1928, and editor, 1928-41, 1948-79, of *Domus* magazine, Milan; director, *Stile* magazine, Milan, 1941-47. Executive director of the Monza Biennale, subsequently the Milan Triennale, 1933-79; general supervisor of the *Italia 61* exhibition in Turin, 1961, and of the *Eurodomus* exhibitions in Genoa and other Italian cities, 1966-69. Professor of architecture, Politecnico, Milan, 1936-61; president, Collegio Lombardo degli Architetti, Milan, 1957-60, and the International Museum of Modern Architecture, Milan, 1961. **Exhibitions:** Florence, 1937; Galleria Gianferrari, Milan, 1939, 1951; Galleria dell'Obelisco, Rome, 1950; Institute of Contemporary Art, Boston, 1954 (toured); Galleria La Bussola, Turin, 1955; AB Ferdinand Lundquist, Goteborg, 1956; Galleria del Sole, Milan, 1956; Christofle, Paris, 1957; Liberty's, London, 1957; Galleria del Disegno, Milan, 1959; University of California at Los Angeles, 1966 (toured); Galleria de Nieubourg, Milan, 1967; Galleria Toselli, Milan, 1978; Centro Internazionale di Brera, Milan, 1982; University of Padua, 1989. Recipient: University of Padua English Building Prize, 1934; Art Prize, Accademia d'Italia, 1945; Compasso d'Oro Award, Milan, 1956; Academie d'Architecture Gold Medal, Paris, 1968. Honorary doctorate: Royal College of Art, London, 1958. Corresponding member, Royal Institute of British Architects; honorary associate, American Institute of Architects; member, Accademia di San Luca, Rome. *Died* (in Milan) *in September 1979.*

Works:

Grotesque tableware in white porcelain with blue and gold decoration, for Richard Ginori/Doccia, 1923-35.

The Classic Conversation bowls, vases and lamps in porcelain, for Richard Ginori/Doccia, 1924–28.
Orfeo costumes and scenery, for Teatro alla Scala, Milan, 1949.
Self-illuminating furniture, for the Casa Cremaschi, Milan, 1949.
Espresso coffee machines, for La Pavoni, 1949.
Leggera wooden chair with woven rush seat, for Cassina, 1951.
Tables and upholstered chairs, for the Singer Company of New York, 1952.
Distex armchair, for Cassina, 1953.
Sanitary fittings, for Ideal Standard, 1953.
Superleggera wooden chair with woven rush seat, for Cassina, 1955.
Cutlery and silverwares, for Christofle, 1955, 1958.
Desk in metal, for Rima, 1955.
Pirelli skyscraper building, Milan, 1956 (with Nervi, Danuso, Fornaroli, Roselli, Valtolina and dell'Orto).
Italia 61 exhibition layouts, Turin, 1961 (with Nervi).
Pavilion at the *Milan Fair,* for Montecatini, 1962.
Armchair 1215 in walnut with rattan seat, for Knoll International, 1964.
De Bijenkorf shopping center, Eindhoven, 1967 (with Boosten, Negri and Gast).
Lamps in plastic, for Guzzini, 1968.
Cathedral of Taranto, Italy, 1971.
Denver Museum of Modern Art, Colorado, 1972 (with Sudler and Cronenwett).

(for a complete list of Ponti's buildings and architectural projects, see *Contemporary Architects*).

Publications:

By PONTI: books—*La Casa all'Italiana,* Milan 1933; *Italiani,* with Leonardo Sinisgalli, Milan 1937; *Il Coro,* Milan 1944; *Cifre Parlanti,* Milan 1944; *Politica dell'Architettura,* Milan 1944; *Ideario,* Milan 1945; *L'Architettura e un Cristallo,* Milan 1945; *Verso la Casa Esatta,* Milan 1945; *Ringrazio Iddio che le Cosi non vanno a Mode Mio,* Milan 1946; *Paradiso Perduto,* Milan 1956; *Amata l'Architettura,* Genoa 1957, as *In Praise of Architecture,* New York 1960; *Milano Oggi,* Milan 1957; *Nuvole sono Immagini,* Milan 1968.
On PONTI: books—*Mobili Tipici Moderni* by G. C. Palanti, Milan 1933; *Espressione di Giovanni Ponti* by James S. Plaut, Milan 1954; *Forme Nuove in Italia* by Agnoldomenico Pica, Milan and Rome 1957; *Ponti: Summing Up* by Mario Labo, Milan 1958; *World Furniture,* edited by Helena Hayward, London 1965, 1981; *The Modern Chair: 1850 to Today* by Gilbert Frey, London and Niederteufen 1970; *Design e Forme Nuove nell'Arredamento Italiano,* edited by Paolo Portoghesi and Marino Marini, Rome 1978; *Atlante del Design Italiano 1940/1980* by Alfonso Grassi and Anty Pansera, Milan 1980; *Gio Ponti alla Manifattura di Doccia* by Paolo Portoghesi and Anty Pansera, Milan 1982; *Mid-Century: Furniture of the 1950s* by Cara Greenberg, London 1984; *The Hot House: Italian New Wave Design* by Andrea Branzi, London 1984; *Modern Furniture Classics* by Miriam Stimpson, London 1987; *Italian Design: 1870 to the Present* by Penny Sparke, London and New York 1988; *Italian Modern: A Design Heritage* by Giovanni Albera and Nicolas Monti, New York 1989; *Gio Ponti, Designer: Padova 1936–1941* by Mario Universo, Padua 1989.

It is impossible to assess Gio Ponti's contribution as a design professional independent from his work as a founder and the primary editor of the journal *Domus,* which is devoted to architecture, interiors, industrial design, and art—all of which he himself cherished. However, he did consider himself first and foremost an architect: "Think [about architecture] at night, and work [on architecture] during the day." It is important to note that the original title of his major book was *Amate L'Architettura* [Love Architecture], a more definitive command than the English translation *In Praise of Architecture.*

Graduated in 1921 from Milan's prestigious Politecnico School of Architecture and somewhat stifled by unsuccessful participation in several architectural competitions, Ponti turned to other forms of cultural expression; he developed what would become a life-long interest in painting and concurrently produced ceramic and porcelain designs for one of the largest Italian manufacturers. Appointed a director of the *Second Biennial Exposition of Decorative Arts* at Monza, and reappointed to succeeding expositions, he eventually helped to expand the fair and move it to Milan in 1933 as the *Fifth Triennial Exhibition of Modern Art and Modern Architecture* (thereafter, "Ponti's Triennale"). Ponti continued with the sixth and seventh *Triennials* thereby establishing the groundwork for exhibitions that are still held regularly, enjoy an international reputation, and contribute to Italian prominence in design.

Ponti's first architectural commission (1926) was for a house, outside of Paris, for the President of Christofle, a firm for which he eventually designed some tableware. His architectural designs in these early years expressed the neoclassical overtones which were the mode of the day in Italy—a "modern" style which would eventually be dubbed "fascist" as a political system attempted to clothe itself in contemporary dress.

Ponti's first major commission (1936) was for the first of two buildings (the other was commissioned in 1951) for the expansion of the facilities for the Montecatini company, Italy's major chemical concern. Its design marked a change from the earlier work but still presented a rather formal, stone facade perforated with individual window units in a regular, somewhat scale-less manner, presenting a design problem which Ponti did not completely resolve until twenty years later. The building appeared as if it could be expanded laterally and/or vertically ad infinitum; it had no definite limits. At this same time, he began teaching at his former school.

Four years later, architectural work waned in Italy, as in the rest of the world when war intervened, but the desire for housing after the war and the obvious need to rebuild facilities destroyed in the conflict presented major opportunities for many architects, Ponti among them. In the early 1950s, Ponti also became involved in the design of the interiors of several Italian steamships, including some for the ill-fated *Andria Doria.* Industrial design products, including an espresso coffee maker with the sleek lines and chrome of a modern automobile, sewing machines, and, of course, furniture, including the now classic La Leggera chair—a simple study in wood with a rush seat—filled in and rounded out the oeuvre of this multi-faceted person.

Ponti's unrealized proposal for the Italian-Brazilian Center in São Paulo (1953) narrowed his search for a definitive form. An attempt was made here to limit the facade and the shape of the building and to define it as a complete entity. In a similar manner, his designs for Ideal Standard's sanitary fixtures remolded the basic shape and derived their final form from a purely functional esthetic. "I am not a tailor, I am an architect. I am not interested in the fashionable novelty," he stated.

In the Pirelli office building, the search and experimentation culminated. This thirty-two story office tower for a rubber manufacturing firm is perched atop a plaza on an irregularly shaped plot. The plaza itself houses a parking facility for 2,000 cars and provides separation of visitor and employee entrances as well as the necessary service access facilities, all planned around a careful analysis of the functional requirements of circulation and traffic flow. The floors above are supported by a unique structural system designed in collaboration with the masterful Italian engineer Pier Luigi Nervi; concrete fingers thrusting upward to carry the floors and roof.

However successful the functional and structural organization, however, in the visual form of the building lies Ponti's innovation. In the hands of lesser designers, this form might have again been an endless rectangular prism, but as it is, in plan it tapers at its ends, clearly suggesting that no further extension is possible, and in elevation the tapers form solids to bracket the bands of glass windows, while the whole is capped by a broad, sheltering, cantilevered roof—a "hat"—which terminates the vertical extension. Ponti had achieved his forma finita.

Ponti's designs in the 1960s took a different tack apparently an exploration of the enclosure as a "screen"; these experiments led to less successful solutions. From a high-rise apartment in Milan to a department store in Holland to the cathedral in Taranto to the Denver Art Museum, exterior walls play the fantasy of irregularly perforated masks, often disguising completely the role of the space beyond. Somewhat Middle-Eastern in form and character, they clearly denied the structural and functional role of the volumes they enclosed. Ponti's search for form had perhaps become a psychedelic experience: "Imagination is the ecstasy of a vision."

Throughout his career, Ponti was, from its founding in 1928 (with the exception of the wartime period 1941–47) until his death in 1979, the editor and motivating source from behind the successful and highly influential magazine *Domus.* He was quick to detect (and in some cases helped to establish) trends and directions in art, architecture, and design. Just as in his office or at school, talented young artists and designers received his support and encouragement; through pages rich in color and line, they were welcomed into homes, offices, and schools throughout the world. A large portion of Ponti's energies was directed to helping, influencing, and stimulating others. The late Charles Eames once commented on Ponti's "willingness and need to be completely involved in anything he does. His masteries of skill are those that seem to come automatically to the special few who have the capacity for really caring."

—William Victor Kriebel

PORSCHE, Ferdinand (Alexander).
German/Austrian automobile and product designer. Born in Stuttgart, Germany, 11 December 1935. Apprenticed in engineering, at the Bosch Company, Stuttgart; studied at the Hoch-

Ferdinand Porsche: Alternative motorcycle, for *Motorrad* magazine, 1979

schule fur Gestaltung, Ulm; apprenticed in engineering and design studios, at Porsche AG, Stuttgart-Zuffenhausen. Married Brigitte Porsche in 1960; children: Ferdinand, Kai and Mark-Philipp. Head of design, 1961–72, and vice-president, 1969–72, of Porsche AG, Stuttgart-Zuffenhausen; founder and director of Porsche Design, in Stuttgart, 1972–75, and in Zell am See, Austria, from 1975: has designed for Yashica, Puch, Roemer, Carrera, British Broadcasting Corporation, etc. **Collections:** Kunstgewerbemuseum, Zurich; Museum of Modern Art, New York. Recipient: International Automobile Industry Trophy, 1968; Austrian Design Prize, 1979, 1980. Address: Porsche Design, Flugplatzstrasse 29, 5700 Zell am See, Austria.

Works:

Porche 804 Formula 1 racing car, for Porsche AG, 1961.
Porsche 904 racing/sports car, for Porsche AG, 1963.
Porsche 91 and *Taga* version sports limousine, for Porsche AG, 1963.
Contax camera, for Yashica, 1974.
Cobra motorcycle, for Steyr-Puch, 1976.
Motorcycle helmet, for Roemer, 1976.
Model 911 sunglasses with interchangeable lenses, for Carrera, 1977.
Experimental racing bicycle, for Steyr-Puch/ America, 1977.
Servogor 281 and *Servogor 460* electronic plotting instruments, for the British Broadcasting Corporation, 1978–80.
AMK alternative motorcycle project, for *Motorrad* magazine, 1979.
Telephone, for NEC-Tokyo, 1981.

Publications:

On PORSCHE: books— *Automobile Design: Great Designers and Their Work,* edited by Ronald Barker and Anthony Harding, Newton Abbot 1970; *Deutsche Autos 1945–1975* by Werner Oswald, Stuttgart 1976; *The Library of Motoring: The Designers* by I. J. K. Setright, London 1976; *Das grosse Buch der Porsche-Typen* by Lothar Boschen and Jurgen Barth, Stuttgart 1977, as *The Porsche Book,* Cambridge 1978, 1983; *In Good Shape: Style in Industrial Products Since 1960* by Stephen Bayley, London 1979; *Industrial Design* by John Heskett, London 1980; *Porsche Past and Present* by Denis Jenkinson, London 1983; *Les Annees 60* by Anne Bony, Paris 1983; *The Conran Directory of Design,* edited by Stephen Bayley, London 1985; *Porsche: Portrait of a Legend* by Ingo Seiff, London 1985, 1989; *Design Source Book* by Penny Sparke and others, London 1986.

Product design, intended to maintain its appeal beyond today and tomorrow, must follow a number of essential maxims, without which any design becomes mere formalism, and creativity, a useless formula. The problem is to achieve the right balance between principal objectives that seem to compete with each other—e.g., "economy" as opposed to "beauty"—without giving in to a one-sided, intolerant design philosophy.

Correct product design means several things: domination of the whole product over its individual parts; functional styling from the inside, instead of external styling of an article following completion; realism in detecting what is possible; concentration on an assessable future instead of utopian speculation; development of

new technologies and products to meet market potentials; and, last but not least, a genuine team spirit to accumulate the knowledge of specialists. Our primary objective is to improve the quality of human life by allowing design and function to complement, not to obstruct, each other, and by concentrating equally on aesthetic, technical, and practical function.

Typical of our approach is the development of our alternative motorcycle concept (AMK) as the result of a competition with such designers as Hans A. Muth and Giorgetto Giugiaro for the *Motorrad* magazine in Germany. It was conceived for a society with limited traffic space and limited energy resources.

The vehicle of the future is a motorcycle— but a rather special motorcycle, with its chassis, engine, and wheels enclosed in aerodynamic body panels for the rider's greater comfort and safety. My vehicle is based on the Yamaha SR 500 motorcycle. The glass-reinforced, plastic body panels that were added to the standard motorcycle help to keep a rider clean without the need for special protective clothing. The body panels also allow the owner to clean the machine with a hose without fear of soaking exposed mechanical parts. For safety, the leg supports—or fairings, as they are called—have built-in knee protectors and are designed to throw a rider clear of the handlebars in the event of a crash. Beneath all this futuristic body work, the Porsche design incorporates convenience features that lift motorcycle riding out of the limited realm of enthusiasts and into the reach of people who desire basic transportation. The bike has an automatic transmission, a car-like pedal-brake, adjustable handlebars and seat, and built-in hand-warmers.

—Ferdinand Alexander Porsche

Anthony Powell: Costume for Raj Singh in Stephen Spielberg's *Indiana Jones and the Temple of Doom*, 1984

POWELL, Anthony.
British film, stage and interior designer. Born in Chorlton-cum-Hardy, Lancashire, 2 June 1935. Educated at William Hulme's Grammar School, Manchester, 1940–46, and Saint Andrew's College, Dublin, 1946–53; studied under Norah Waugh, Margaret Woodward, Ruth Keating and Alan Davie, at the Central School of Art and Design, London, 1955–58. Served in the Royal Corps of Signals, British Army on the Rhine, 1953–55. Costume designer, Oxford Playhouse, 1958–60; freelance stage designer from 1960, film designer from 1968, and interior designer from 1978; also assistant to Cecil Beaton and Oliver Messel for galas and theatrical events in London, 1958; consultant, to Sabre Sportswear, Jantzen Swimwear, and others, London, 1960–69. Lecturer in theatre design, Central School of Art and Design, London, 1958–71. **Collection:** Victoria and Albert Museum, London. Recipient: Royal Society of Arts Travel Scholarship, London, 1958; Antoinette Perry Award, New York, 1963; Academy Award, Hollywood, 1972, 1979, 1981; Los Angeles Drama Critics Award, 1979. Address: c/o The London Company, Panton House, 25 Haymarket, London SW1N 4EN, England.

Works:

Stage productions include—*Rinaldo,* for Sadlers Wells, London, 1960 (and for Komisches Oper, East Berlin, for the Handel Festival, Halle, East Germany, and for the Leipzig Opera House); *School for Scandal,* for the Haymarket Theatre, London, 1961 (toured the United States); *Women Beware Women,* for the Royal Shakespeare Company, Arts Theatre, London, 1961; *Comedy of Errors,* for the Royal Shakespeare Company, Stratford-upon-Avon and London, 1962 (and world tour); *La Belle Helene,* for the Sadlers Wells, London, 1962; *Capriccio,* for the Glyndebourne Opera, Sussex, 1963; *Il Seraglio,* for Sadlers Wells, London, 1963; *Martin's Lie,* for American television, 1965; *The Rivals,* for the Haymarket Theatre, London, 1966; *Fish Out of Water,* London, 1971; *Private Lives,* for the Queen's Theatre, London, 1972; (toured the United States); *Ring Around the Moon,* for the Ahmansan Theatre, Los Angeles, 1975; and *Amadeus,* for the Theatre Marigny, Paris, 1982; film costume designs include *Royal Hunt of the Sun,* 1968; *Joe Egg,* 1969; *A Town Called Bastard,* 1970; *Nicholas and Alexandra,* 1971; *Travels with My Aunt,* 1972; *Papillon,* 1973; *That Lucky Touch,* 1974; *Buffalo Bill and the Indians,* 1975; *Sorcerer,* 1976; *Death on the Nile,*
1977; *Tess,* 1978–79; *Priest of Love,* 1980; *Evil under the Sun,* 1981; *Indiana Jones and the Temple of Doom,* 1983.

Publications:

By POWELL: book illustrated—*William Shakespeare: The Comedy of Errors,* London 1969. On POWELL: books—*Designing and Making Stage Costumes,* London 1964; *International Film and Television Yearbook 1979–80,* edited by Peter Noble, London 1979; articles—in *Women's Wear Daily* (New York), 1979; *Denver Post,* 4 March 1982; *Los Angeles Times,* 12 March 1982; *New York Times,* 12 May 1983.

As I see it, the job of the designer in theatre, cinema, or television is essentially an interpretive one—to give visual expression or emphasis to the intentions of the writer/composer, the director, and the performer. This demands not only creative and imaginative ability but a sympathetic understanding of others' points of view in order to achieve a cohesive whole, whilst still being able to make a positive statement of one's own. A talent for designing is, in itself, only fifty percent of the job.

—Anthony Powell

PREMSELA, Benno.

Dutch interior, exhibition and industrial designer. Born in Amsterdam, 4 May 1920. Studied interior design, under A. Bodon, at the Nieuwe Kunstschool, Amsterdam, 1937–41. Worked as a display designer with Martin Visser, at De Bijenkorf department store, Amsterdam, 1949–51; textile designer, in the studio of Bueno Mesquita, Florence, 1951–53; freelance designer, Amsterdam, from 1953, collaborating with architect Jan Vonk from 1956; partner in Buro Premsela Vonk, 1963–72, design studio Premsela Vonk, 1972–73, and Premsela Vonk BV architectural firm from 1973. Head of window display, De Bijenkorf department store, Amsterdam, 1956–63, and consultant to Van Besouw NV from 1967, Vescon BV from 1972, and Gerns + Gahler from 1975. Board member from 1953, and chairman, 1964–71, Nederlandse Vereiniging tot Integratie van Homosexualiteit COC, Amsterdam; chairman, Gerrit Rietveld Institute, Amsterdam, 1972–80; governor, Kroller-Muller Foundation, Otterlo, 1975; chairman, Amsterdam Council for the Arts, 1980; member: advisory committee for the Applied Arts, Amsterdam, 1961–67; visual art and architecture section of the Council for the Arts, Amsterdam, 1964–70; committee for exhibitions abroad, Amsterdam, 1965–81; Council for Industrial Design, Amsterdam, 1969–75; advisory board for the Museum Fodor, Amsterdam, 1979–80; acquisitions committee of the Stedelijk Museum, Amsterdam, 1980. **Exhibitions:** *Benno Premsela—onder anderen*, Stedelijk Museum, Amsterdam, 1981; *Design Since 1945*, Philadelphia Museum of Art, 1983. **Collections:** Stedelijk Museum, Amsterdam; Israel Museum, Jerusalem. Recipient: Bergoss Carpet Competition Prize, 1956; Knight of the Order of the Oranje Nassau. Address: Herengracht 569, 1017 CD Amsterdam, Netherlands.

Works:

Furniture ranges, for Spectrum Company, Bergeyk, 1956–62.
Carpet designs, for Koninklijk Fabrieken Bergoss, from 1956.
Pioneers of Today exhibition layouts, for De Bijenkorf store, Amsterdam, 1961.
Creative Thinking in Plastics exhibition layouts, for the Centre for Industrial Design, Amsterdam, 1967.
Sieraad 1900–1972 exhibition layouts, for the Zonnehof, Amsterdam, 1972.
Malton and *Lungi* wallcoverings, for Vescom BV, Deurne, 1973.
Design standardization programme, for the Amro Bank, Amsterdam, 1974.
Rice Grain and *Venezuela* textiles, for Aupin BV, Deventer, 1975–76.
Tetuan and *Volkswagen* upholstery fabrics, for Gerns + Gahler, 1978–79.
Exhibition stand at the Utrecht Spring Fair, for Pulsar Time Europe, 1981.

Publications:

By PREMSELA: book—*Fotopocket Florence*, with Cas Oorthuys, Amsterdam 1953.
On PREMSELA: books—*Window Display 2*, edited by Walter Herdeg, Zurich 1961; *An International Survey of Press Advertising*, edited by Kurt Weidemann, Stuttgart and London 1966; *International Window Display*, edited by Karl Kaspar, Stuttgart and London 1966; *Benno Premsela—onder Anderen*, exhibition catalogue with texts by Martin Visser, Jan Vonk and others, Amsterdam 1981; *Design Since 1945*, edited by Kathryn Hiesinger and George Marcus, Philadelphia and London 1983.

My training was dominated by the Bauhaus ideas: my great teacher was the architect Bodon, who taught me awareness of the points of departure. "Form follows function" was the motto, and although that statement is not suitable (there is always more than one solution to a single problem), I was attracted by the unassuming aspect and the sober tone. That's another thing by which I have always tried to be guided, and it is best expressed in the industrial products for which I am responsible. There is an obvious reason for that. Industries often have eyes only for their own products as unique, as the only important thing, while those products end up in an environment where they naturally meet other products. And so I think that sobriety is one of the most important elements, also to meet the criterion of longevity. Being an industrial designer myself, I don't know who is going to arrange different products together—so in such situations I opt for reticence in the visual information. Leaving room for others—I think you can probably see that in everything I do.

Also, as regards interiors as a whole, we are not concerned with displaying our fabulous designs to the world; that's not our object. We believe that our work is to render services, and that's why you'll see more of the client than of us in our work. We consider that a compliment. The more restricting factors there are, the more interesting it all becomes. My departure from Bijenkorf had something to do with that. I had so much freedom there that the excitement wore off. In interior architecture—and certainly in the industrial sector—the restrictions are so compelling that the challenge is tremendous. I think that sharpens creativity. And then, I must also add that working together with people is one of the things I enjoy most of all—I haven't been collaborating with Jan Vonk the past twenty-five years for nothing. The tensions that arise from collaboration, and the possibilities they offer in their turn, are an inspiration to me. Besides, I consider coordinating and guiding a group of designers just as creative as designing in my own right.

—Benno Premsela

Benno Premsela: *Carpet 5401* in linen, for Van Besouw Interior, 1979

PRESTINI, James.

American industrial designer. Born in Waterford, Connecticut, 13 January 1908. Studied mechanics, at Yale University, New Haven, Connecticut, 1927–30; BS 1930; Yale School of Education, 1932; University of Stockholm, 1938; Institute of Design, Chicago, 1939; also studied sculpture in Italy, 1953–56. Development engineer, Sargeant Lock and Hardware Manufacturing Company, New Haven, Connecticut, 1930–31; research engineer, at the Armour Institute, Illinois Institute of Technology, Chicago, 1943–53: consultant to Midwest Research Institute, Kansas City, 1946; Museum of Modern Art, New York, 1946–51; Albright Art Gallery, Buffalo, 1947; Institute of Contemporary Art, Washington, D.C., 1948–49; Knoll International, Zurich, 1953–54; American Craftsmens Council, New York, 1957; University of California Department of Architecture, Berkeley, 1958–65; West German Government, Bonn, 1962; Indian National Institute of Design, Ahmedabad, 1962–63; United States Office of Science and Technology, Washington, D.C., 1964; University of Washington College of Architecture, Seattle, 1964; University of California School of Architecture, Los Angeles, 1965; University of New Mexico Department of Architecture, Albuquerque, 1966; University of Idaho Department of Architecture, Moscow, 1967; California Institute of the Arts, Valencia, 1967; University of Waterloo School of Architecture, Ontario, 1971; Fulbright-Hayes Program, Washington, D.C., 1972; Institute of International Education, 1973. Instructor in mathematics, Lake Forest Academy, Illinois, 1933–42; instructor in design, Institute of Design, Chicago, 1939–46, 1952–53; lecturer, 1956–62, professor of design, 1962–75, and professor emeritus from 1975, University of California, Berkeley; research professor, Bauhaus-Archiv, West Berlin, 1977. **Exhibitions:** Lake Forest Academy, Illinois, 1934–42, 1983; Currier Gallery of Art, Manchester, New Hampshire, 1938; Toledo Museum of Art, Ohio, 1938; Butler Art Institute, Youngstown, Ohio, 1940; Dallas Museum of Fine Arts, 1940; Milwaukee Art Institute, 1940; Seattle Art Museum, Washington, 1940; Smithsonian Institution, Washington, D.C., 1940; Dayton Art Institute, Ohio, 1941; Cincinnati Art Museum, Ohio, 1944; Institute of Contemporary Art, Washington, D.C., 1949; University of California, Berkeley, 1957, 1971, 1975; Ahmedabad Museum, India, 1963; San Francisco Museum of Art, 1969; Arts Club of Chicago, 1975. **Collections:** Cooper-Hewitt Museum, New York; Museum of Modern Art, New York; Metropolitan Museum of Art, New York; Boston Museum of Fine Arts; Philadelphia Museum of Art; Art Institute of Chicago; San Francisco Museum of Modern Art; Smithsonian Institution, Washington, D.C.; Musee des Arts Decoratifs, Montreal; Bauhaus-Archiv, West Berlin. Recipient: Los Angeles County Fair Crafts Prize, 1951, 1952; Honour Award, Milan Triennale, 1954, 1973; Furniture Award, Cantu, 1955; U.S. Department of State Citation, 1958; Graham Foundation Award, Chicago, 1962; Ford Foundation Fellowship, 1962–63; American Steel Institute Award, 1971, 1973; Guggenheim Fellowship, New York, 1972–73; American Institute of Architects R. S. Reynolds Award, 1972; University of California Berkeley Award, 1975; German Academic Exchange Fellowship, 1977; National Woodturning Conference Award, 1985; Lake Forest Academy Hall of Fame Award, 1987. Address: 2324 Blake Street, Berkeley, California 94704, U.S.A.

Publications:

By PRESTINI: articles—in *The Frontier* (Chicago), March 1948; *Armour Research Foundation Report* (Chicago), September 1948, October 1949, April 1950, January 1953; *Congressional Record* (Washington, D.C.), no. 51, 1950; *Technical Cooperation Administration*

James Prestini: Salad set in Cuban and Honduras mahogany, 1939

Report (Chicago), December 1950, December 1951; *Industrial Design* (New York), May 1964; *Bauhaus-Archiv* (West Berlin), September 1977.

On PRESTINI: books—*Prestini's Art in Wood* by Edgar Kaufmann Jr., Lake Forest 1950; *Prize Designs for Modern Furniture,* exhibition catalogue by Edgar Kaufmann Jr., New York 1950; *Chairs* by George Nelson, New York 1953; *Shaping America's Products* by Don Wallance, New York 1956; *Twentieth Century Design from the Museum of Modern Art,* exhibition catalogue by Arthur Drexler and Greta Daniel, New York 1959; *Creative Design in Wood* by Dona A. Meilach, New York 1968; *Man the Designer* by Helen Marie Evans, New York 1973; *Innovative Furniture in America from 1800 to the Present* by David A. Hanks, New York 1981; *Design Since 1945,* edited by Kathryn Hiesinger and George Marcus, Philadelphia and London 1983; *The Art of Turned Wood Bowls* by Edward Jacobson, New York 1985; *Woodturning: The Modern Movement* by David Ellsworth, New York 1986; *The American Design Adventure 1940–1975* by Arthur J. Pulos, London and Cambridge, Massachusetts 1988.

To create a humanistic future environment is the chief problem confronting the artist in a technological age. If the art of the future—and particularly its sculpture—is to fulfill man aesthetically, rather than overwhelm him with hollow technical feats, it must express the most humane significance of the new technologies which, precisely because they are so new, complex, and imperfectly understood, have led to confusion and demoralization, instead of enrichment, of the modern environment. One reaction to this problem has been a revival of Luddism—the machine-breaking protest of the early Industrial Revolution. Yet, history would indicate that it is the responsibility of the artist to make technology humane, as the heroic nineteenth-century engineers did, rather than to destroy or ignore the life-enhancing potentialities of applied science. Thus, a humane art of the future inevitably must incorporate the technologies of the future, just as the finest art of the past expressed the most advanced technologies of its own time and place. Furthermore, this new art—in the highest sense a socially responsible public art—must be at the scale of the future. To paraphrase a famous statement of Mies van der Rohe: technology reaches its real fulfillment when it transcends itself in becoming art.

—James Prestini

James Prestini was born in Waterford, Connecticut, the son of a skilled stone-carver who had emigrated from Italy. The younger Prestini chose mechanical engineering as his profession and after earning the B.S. degree in that field at Yale University in 1930, worked as a development engineer for a lock and hardware firm.

Prestini soon turned to teaching by accepting a position at Lake Forest Academy, a preparatory school in suburban Chicago. There, from 1933 to 1942 he taught mathematics and, in addition, served as supervisor of the school's workshop, where he began experimenting with lathe-turned wooden bowls. He also became interested in the student-oriented design pedagogy of László Moholy-Nagy through reading *The New Vision.* His interest in design was quickened by his close observation of the construction of the nearby Winnetka, Illinois Crow Island School, designed by Eliel Saarinen and his son Eero (in association with Perkins and Will) and completed in 1939. The innovative wooden furniture for the school was designed by the Saarinens (in association with Carleton Washburne).

The interests in design, in design education, and in wood-turning, which Prestini had acquired, converged into his activity as a maker of lathe-turned wooden bowls: he decided to use manual work as a resource to teach himself design. His idea was that he would make an object, draw it, think about it, and then make it again, so that the process, rather than the product, would be important. As he once explained, he was "not interested in turning a good looking bowl," but rather in what one must learn in order to turn a bowl. He added that he felt "reverence not for wood, but for work."

There was no category into which Prestini's bowls might readily fit. They are not craft work, if that term is used to mean the revival of vestigial skills or practices peculiar to a locality, and in any case, the production of lathe-turned, wooden kitchen utensils (except for rolling pins) ceased during the nineteenth century. Rather, Prestini created a new category. Many of the bowls seem to be made for use, but function is nearly always suggested rather than literal. Thus, even a 1939 mahogany salad set, consisting of a tray, a large bowl, and six smaller bowls, was made with such precision that the bowls may be placed so that they touch each other while just fitting within the raised lip of the tray; it was donated to the Metropolitan Museum of Art in 1975, and then reluctantly, because Prestini considered it "to be one of my very best designs."

Prestini began to exhibit his bowls in 1934, first at Lake Forest Academy, then more widely. Because of their light weight, their shell-like, thin walls, and their finish of clear lacquer, which preserved the natural, unstained appearance of the grain of the woods from which they were made (usually cherry, walnut, birch, or mahogany), the bowls were widely acclaimed. They were exhibited in many parts of the United States, and museums began collecting them in 1940. Henry van de Velde, one of the pioneer architects and designers of the modern movement, owned one of Prestini's bowls and assured him, in a letter of 1950, of "the admiration with which an object of such pure and infinite beauty and one made with such perfect execution is held by one of the old pioneers of 'pure forms.' . . . I have rarely been able to touch an object that has awakened in me a more intense and deep pleasure." At about the same time Edgar Kaufmann, Jr. wrote about Prestini's bowls and other objects in *Prestini's Art in Wood,* describing "the serenity, refinement and purity of his turned forms."

Today Prestini's bowls and other wooden objects are seen in numerous public and private collections in the United States and Western Europe, and many have been widely published. As one result, Prestini's work has had an influence on factory-produced items, such as salad bowls. He has also influenced the revival of the craft of wood-turning, which began about 1960 and continues to gather momentum into the 1980s. But Prestini remains aloof from the newer generation of wood turners, whose interests only partially coincide with his, because wood turning has been only a means to an end for Prestini, and thus only a part-time activity.

During the summer of 1938, Prestini worked with Carl Malmsten as an apprentice furniture designer and craftsman at the University of Stockholm. The following year, he was a part-time student at Moholy-Nagy's School of Design in Chicago, and shortly after enrolling he was asked to become a part-time member of the faculty. In 1942 he taught at North Texas State College in Denton, but he returned to Chicago the following year to resume teaching at the School of Design in Chicago (renamed the Institute of Design in 1944) and to work as a research engineer at the Armour Research Foundation of the Illinois Institute of Technology.

The exercises in wood which Prestini encountered in the foundation course at the School of Design in Chicago led to a series of "design experiments" in which qualities of wood not revealed by the use of the lathe were explored. These experiments resulted in pieces such as spirals and wood springs in which the resilience of wood was exploited. At the same time there were abstract, asymmetrical forms which exploited the visual qualities of grain in ways not possible when using the lathe.

Prestini left Chicago in 1953 to go to Italy, where he organized the manufacture of furniture in Milan for Knoll International and conducted a survey of the Italian furniture industry for Knoll, while also finding time to study sculpture. He returned to the United States in 1956 to teach design in the Architecture Department of the University of California in Berkeley, from which he retired as Professor of Design twenty-one years later.

Prestini's research on production methods for low-cost furniture included work as part of a team on a project funded by a grant to the Armour Research Foundation from the Museum of Modern Art. The team's research was the basis for its entry in the Museum of Modern Art's 1949 *International Competition for Low-cost Furniture Design,* in which it won a prize for the best research report. The team's entry was a one-piece chair made of resin-impregnated wood fiber. It was suggested by a series of drawings made in the early 1940s by Ludwig Mies van der Rohe as studies for a conchoidal-form chair (suggested by the conch shell). Although only a prototype of the Armour Research team project was produced, it has had a great influence on mass-produced furniture, especially one-piece, molded, thermoplastic chairs.

In his nickel-plated steel sculpture, begun in 1967, Prestini initially used structural steel elements, such as I-beams and cylindrical pipes, which were fused together, coated with nickel, and finally polished, using industrial methods, to the point of transparency. Gradually, more and more of the work was taken over by assistants, enabling Prestini to abandon the I-beams and other structural elements for the freedom of working with solid plate and to confine his own role to the making of wooden models to guide his assistants. The high degree of polish of Prestini's metal sculpture results in surfaces so reflective they seem to be a microcosm of the surroundings.

Prestini's most important achievement is his demonstration that there need be no barriers between technology and art or between art and utilitarian objects.

—Lloyd C. Engelbrecht

PUCCI, Emilio.

Italian fashion designer. Born Marchese Emilo Pucci di Barsento, in Naples, 20 November 1914. Educated at the Liceo Galileo, Florence, until 1933; studied at the University of Milan, 1933–35; University of Georgia, Athens, 1935–36; Reed College, Portland, Oregon, 1936–37: MA 1937; University of Florence, 1938–41: Ph.D. 1941. Served as a bomber pilot in the Italian Air Force, 1938–42. Married Cristina Nannini di Casabianca in 1959; children: Laudomia and Alessandro. First designed women's skiwear for *Harper's Bazaar* photographer Toni Frissell, 1947; freelance fashion designer, establishing studio in Florence, from 1949: now president of Emilio Pucci S.r.l., Florence, and Emilio Pucci Limited, New York; has also designed clothing and accessories for Qantas Airlines, Formfit Rogers, Parker Pen Company, Ford Motor Company, Dandolo e Primi, Akerman, Grasset et Pittion, Rosenthal, etc. Member of Parliament for the Florence Liberal Party, 1963–72, and head of the Liberal Group of Palazzo Vecchio, 1963–80; City Councillor, Florence, from 1964; also proprietor of the Castelli di Cerreto, Granaiolo and Coiano wine-producing estates. President: National Association of Shoe Stylists, Shoe Fair Consulting Group, Associazione Proprieta Edilizia, Societa San Giovanni Battista, Antico Setifico Fiorentino, Societa Fiorentina Corse Cavalli, and Societa San Giovanni di Dio Cinqecento Fiorentino; board member, SINA Hotels and Finanziaria Banca Popolare di Novara. **Exhibitions:** *Fashion: An Anthology,* Victoria and Albert Museum, London, 1971; *40 Years of Italian Fashion,* Trump Tower, New York, 1983. Recipient: Neiman-Marcus Fashion Award, 1954, 1967; *Sports Illustrated* Designers Award, 1955; *Sunday Times* Fashion Award, London, 1963; ADI Association of Industrial Design Award, Milan, 1968; Drexel Annual Award 1975; Italy-Austria Award, 1977. Knighthood, Rome, 1982. Address: Palazzo Pucci, via de'Pucci 6, Florence, Italy.

Publications:

On PUCCI: books—*Vogue's Book of Houses, Gardens, People,* with text by Valentine Lawford, New York and London 1968; *Fashion: An Anthology by Cecil Beaton,* exhibition catalogue compiled by Madeleine Ginsburg, London 1971; *A History of Fashion* by J. Anderson Black and Madge Garland, London 1975, 1980; *In Fashion: Dress in the Twentieth Century* by Prudence Glynn, London 1978; *I Mass-Moda: Fatti e Personnaggi dell'Italian Look* by Adriana Mulassano, Florence 1979; *Magic Names of Fashion* by Ernestine Carter, London 1980; *The Collector's Book of Twentieth Century Fashion* by Frances Kennett, New York and London 1983; *40 Years of Italian Fashion,* exhibition catalogue compiled by B. G. Aragno, Rome 1983; *McDowell's Directory of Twentieth Century Fashion* by Colin McDowell, London 1984; *The Encyclopaedia of Fashion from 1840 to the 1980s* by Georgina O'Hara, London 1986.

PULOS, Arthur J.
American industrial designer. Born in Vandergrift, Pennsylvania, 3 February 1917. Studied under Alexander Kostellow, Peter Muller-Munk and F. Clayter, at the Carnegie Institute of Technology, Pittsburgh, 1935–39; BA 1939; under Victoria Avakian, Fred Cuthbert and Robert Motherwell, at the University of Oregon, Eugene, 1939–41: MFA 1942. Served in the United States Air Force, 1944–46: First Lieutenant. Married Elizabeth Jane McQueen in 1944; children: Cristofer, Maria and Demetra. President, Pulos Design Associates product design firm, Syracuse, New York, 1958–88. Associate professor of design, University of Illinois, Urbana, 1946–55; chairman, 1955–82,

and professor emeritus from 1982, Department of Design, Syracuse University, New York. Trustee, American Craftsman's Council, 1955–57; president, chairman of the board and fellow, Industrial Designers Society of America, 1973–77; policy panel member, National Endowment for the Arts, 1979–81; president, ICSID International Council of Societies of Industrial Design, Brussels, 1980–84. **Collections:** Museum of Modern Art, New York; Newark Museum of Fine Art, New Jersey; Walker Art Center, Minneapolis; Detroit Institute of Arts; University of Wisconsin, Madison. Recipient: Associate Artists of Pittsburgh Award, 1939, 1940, 1942, 1947; Wichita Art Association Award, 1947, 1950; Ford Foundation Fellowship, 1952–53; Detroit Institute of Arts Award, 1953; Brooklyn Museum of Art Award, 1953; Art Institute of Chicago Award, 1954; Syracuse University Chancellor's Citation, 1982; National Endowment for the Arts Distinguished Design Fellowship, 1984; World Design Award, New York, 1988. Address: 3 The Orchard, Fayetteville, New York 13066, U.S.A.

Publications:

By PULOS: books—*Contact: Selling Design Services,* Ottawa 1975; *Opportunities in Industrial Design,* Skokie 1978; *American Design Ethic: A History of Industrial Design to 1940,* Cambridge, Massachusetts 1983; *The American Design Adventure 1940-1975,* London and Cambridge, Massachusetts 1988.
On PULOS: book—*Design in America* by Ralph Caplan, New York 1969.

I have always had a deep interest in all forms of human expression. I respect and am stimulated by music, dance, theatre, literature, the plastic arts and architecture. At the same time, I do not consider myself to be so much an artist as a designer. The difference between the two lies in the fact that the artist is properly committed to self-expression, answerable only to inner compulsion. The designer, on the other hand, is dedicated to human service. He is sensitive to the needs and desires of others and the quality of the man-made environment that serves them. He is pained by any discordances between human beings and the products that have been built or manufactured for them and strives to establish a state of environmental harmony. In this sense, the designer serves as the humane conscience of industry. Still, as a designer, I realize that there is aesthetic quality trapped in my work that will be released after its utility has been consumed, as has been the case for all of man's artifacts in the past.

For more than forty years, my philosophy has been heated in the fire of daily practices of design, shaped against the anvil of university teaching, and tempered by a generation of questioning young minds. It has become clearer to me that industrial design is one of the new generalist professions that reaches beyond the narrow specializations of the past to realize that technics, aesthetics, and humanics are vested in every man-made object and must be brought into sensible balance.

I realize that profound changes are underway on this globe as both developed and underdeveloped nations learn how to tame threatening social and technological forces. I am aware that a new morality of things is emerging by which the tyranny of runaway production may be tempered by a democracy of products and product services that is sympathetically matched to the needs of the people.

—Arthur Pulos

Since the industrial revolution, nineteenth- and twentieth-century European theorists, such as William Morris and Walter Gropius, have struggled with the relationship of hand versus industrial production. Arthur Pulos is the first American to put into perspective the alliance between crafts and industrial designs in United States history. From his 1952 study of Colonial silversmithing in New England, he concluded that Colonial smiths were not so much craftsmen as the first industrialists, who used the most advanced tools and processes available to them to meet their client's needs. The industrial design profession grew out of this attitude. Pulos defines design in the United States as the imaginative development of manufactured products to meet both the physical needs and psychological desires of the consumer in a democratic society.

Pulos was a member of the generation—trained as both craftsmen and designers—who pioneered in the industrial design as a profession. As a silversmith in the 1940s and 1950s, he hand-produced silver holloware, flatware, and jewelry, influenced by the *moderne* style, which had been introduced into the United States by earlier twentieth-century European émigré silversmiths, such as Peter Muller-Munk. The fine finish of his silverwork, which did not show signs of the hand that made it, allied it with the industrial design esthetic. Pulos continued to work in both worlds throughout his post-war career, when he taught both designs and crafts, first at the University of Illinois and later at Syracuse University. At first, these courses were justified primarily as occupational therapy for returning veterans, but as demand for consumer goods grew, crafts made the shift from therapy and recreation to a profession.

Pulos realized that the few pieces he could make by hand were inadequate to growing demand. However, breaking into American industry as a craftsman/designer was almost impossible, as industry discouraged new designs because of the high cost of start-up. Therefore, in the late 1950s Pulos established his own design firm. With this move, he proved that the craftsmen and industrial designer are not far apart in the creation of technically sound, appropriate, and useful objects, the major difference being that the craftsman is oriented toward material and process while the designer is oriented toward product. For industry, he has designed diagnostic instruments for Welch Allyn, portable power tools for Rockwell Manufacturing, and dictation machines for Dictaphone.

Pulos advocated industrial design as a profession, free from the dominance of architecture. He felt that industrial designers should apply craftwork to manufactured goods for a mass market. His ongoing research into the roots of the industrial design profession in the United States has resulted in the first history of American Industrial design to 1940. In *American Design Ethic,* published in 1983, he champions the growth and development of design in America for its democratic approach and ability to synthesize esthetics and function in designed objects.

—Sarah Bodine

PUOTILA, Ritva.
Finnish textile and glass designer. Born Ritva Soilikki Sairanen, in Viipuri, 7 June 1935.

Arthur Pulos: Riding lawn-mower, for Porter-Cable Company, 1960

Studied at the Institute of Applied Arts, Helsinki, 1954–59. Married Pauli Kalevi Puotila in 1955; children: Jukka, Antti and Mikko. Freelance textile designer, from 1959: established own studio in Helsinki, 1960, working for Dansk International Design Ltd., from 1961, Oy Tampella Ab, 1961–86, Dembo Ab, 1967–75, Made In Ab, 1976–86, Partek Oy, 1977–78, Gefjun Ab, 1978–87, Neste Oy, 1979, etc.; founder-designer, Woodnotes Oy design firm, Helsinki, and Studio Ritva Puotila unique textiles workshop, Helsinki, from 1987; also experimental glass designer, for Hadeland of Norway, from 1987. Design Consultant for Thailand silk products, United Nations International Trade Centre, Geneva, 1988; Consultant to the Finnish Handicrafts Association, 1989. **Exhibitions:** Industrial Arts Museum, Copenhagen, 1962; Studio of the Friends of Finnish Handicrafts, Helsinki, 1965; City Library, Espoo, 1976; Gallery Otso, Espoo, 1986; Craft Museum, Jyvaskyla, 1988 (with Markku Kosonen); Nordisk Mobel Gallery, Oslo, 1989. **Collections:** Museum of Applied Arts, Helsinki; Industrial Art Museum of Finland, Helsinki; Victoria and Albert Museum, London; Industrial Arts Museum, Copenhagen. Recipient: First Prize, Villayhtyma Oy Fabric Competition, Helsinki, 1960; Gold Medal, Milan Triennale, 1960; Finnish State Award for Industrial Arts, 1981; Paper Textiles Prize, *Finn Form 6*, Helsinki, 1987; Paper Textile Collection Prize, French National Association of Interior Architects, Paris, 1988. Address: Hiiralankaari 25 C, 02160 Espoo, Finland.

Works:

Carpet designs, for Finnrya Oy, 1959–80.
Zeus ryijy-rug, for the Milan Triennale, made by Friends of Finnish Handicrafts, 1960.
Woollen fashion fabrics, for Villayhtyma Oy, 1960.
Linen and cotton household textiles, for Tampella Oy, 1961–86.
Linen table textile collection, for Dansk International Design, 1963.
Colour scale of enamel household wares, for Dansk International Design, 1964.
Unique textile piece, for Hasselby Castle, Stockholm, 1964.
Unique linen textile piece, for the City of Espoo, 1975.
Fashion fabric collections, for Made In Ab, 1976–81.
Unique textile piece, for Essen Town Hall, West Germany, 1980.
Unique textile piece, for Neste Company, in Moscow, 1986.
Paper textile collection, for Woodnotes Oy, 1987.
Experimental glass pieces, for Hadeland Glasverk, 1987.

Publications:

On PUOTILA: books—*Tapisseries finlandaises*, exhibition catalogue with text by Jacques Lassaigne, Paris 1972; *Finnish Industrial Design* by Tua Pontasuo, Helsinki 1987; articles—"Way Out Colors" in the *San Francisco Examiner*, October 1963; "Varikas loyto Suomesta" in *Suomen Kuvalehti* (Helsinki), 1963; "Designer Inspired by Dreams in Color" in the *New York Times*, 22 October 1963; "Ritva Puotila" in *Graphis* (Zurich), no. 111, 1964; "Weaving with Paper and String" in *Design in Finland* (Helsinki), 1988; "Papier und Baumwolle" in *MD Moebel Interior Design* (Hamburg), July 1989; "Papier pa gulvet" in *Textil Forum* (Oslo), no. 6, 1989.

*

We are sitting on Ritva Puotila's cozily unpretentious porch where sunlight filters through a white woven linen and paper curtain and the floor is covered with cream and white paper carpets. Grandchildren play around, and we drink tea from glasses she has designed. Conversation ranges over several subjects, and we talk about the designer's responsibility in improving the human environment and the role of textile materials as an essential part of people's lives.

Ritva Puotila regards being able to make a handtowel suitable for all as more significant than concentrating on the creation of artworks for museums. She talks of cooperation with weavers and glassblowers, which must be based on mutual respect. She speaks of the advantage of having her own studio where she can make her own decisions, experiment, develop and renew her ideas, and where, in all phases of the work, she can stick to her own line—since this is the reason the client has chosen her to design his products. We talk about travel and impres-

Ritva Puotila: Household textile in woven paper, for Woodnotes Oy, 1988

sions of foreign lands, which at home are transformed by her own experience and nature's influences—finally to become something that is genuinely her own. In Finland there is still a pureness and space that opens up all possibilities. On the subject of textile craft traditions, which in Finland has become banal and tired, we discuss how it is no longer possible to produce the fine qualities of a hundred years ago. But in this connection, one cannot but note that Ritva Puotila herself has contributed to a development based both on tradition and a widening of the textile concept.

From the beginning, Ritva Puotila was drawn towards an artistic career. At school she devoted herself seriously to oil painting, and would have liked to become a painter. At home, however, it was regarded important to learn a profession first, so she chose to study at the department of decorative painting and scenography of the Institute of Applied Arts in Helsinki. Finland in the 1950s showed a positive and open attitude towards design, and students participated in a lot of competitions in all fields of design both in and outside school. It was a prize in textile design that influenced Ritva Puotila's future direction. Just one year after leaving school, in 1960, she was awarded a gold medal at the Milan Triennale for a rya rug designed for the Friends of Finnish Handicraft. The rich collec-

tion of rya weavings she has designed since include compositions ranging from the strong and assured to the most tenderly delicate. It is in these works that Puotila has been able to most closely approach painting.

In 1961 Ted Nierenberger arrived in Scandinavia looking for designers he could recruit to his firm Dansk Design. At the Friends of Finnish Handicraft, he picked out six rugs, and asked to meet the artists who had designed them. All six were by Ritva Puotila. This was the start of a collaboration that has lasted up to the present day. Primarily she has designed collections for the table, but has also had extensive commissions as colour coordinator. For a long time the Finnish company Tampella had produced textiles for sale in the United States; Puotila worked out a broad colour chart that in its freshness differed totally from the colour ranges to which the American market had been accustomed. Tampella's export figures rose impressively. For Made In AB, where she created textiles for fashion garments, Puotila noticed how indistinct were differences between seasonal collections and how superficial were the attempts at innovation—ultimately, there was never any real innovation. She demonstrated that true designing meant giving the product new qualities instead of merely modifying the look.

In her own studio, Ritva Puotila has not only continued to develop and re-create her design, but she has also experimented with different techniques and materials. Her paper products are a result of such experimentation, something that has come about as a result of her own initiative and not from a client's commission.

As raw material she uses natural Finnish products, beautiful and strong. When Tampella began spinning paper and the first table mats were ready, they were called *Pine Weaves* because of their direct use of the Finnish forest. Puotila's paper textiles are beautiful and durable. The limited range of black, white and natural colour creates calm and harmonious surfaces in a rhythmic texture. The smoothness of the surface gives a feeling of cleanness, and the material is non-allergenic. The product combines the practical with the aesthetic. Technical problems are invariably resolved in an artistically acceptable manner, which is a constant feature of her work.

In 1987, Hadeland's glass factory of Norway invited designers from different fields to create a glass collection. Ritva Puotila was assigned to design unique pieces, large sculptural vases, and production tablewares. The simple glasses are decorated with a raspberry motif and the bottoms of smooth plates are ribbed. Fine colour stripes appear in the delicate facets of the vases. Even in glass Ritva Puotila shows an acute sensitivity for the possibilities of the material.

—Carla Enbom

PUTMAN, Andree.
French interior and furniture designer. Born Andree Christine Aynard, in Paris, 23 December 1925. Educated at the College d'Hulst, Paris; studied piano under Francis Poulenc, at the Conservatoire, Paris; mainly self-taught in design from 1960. Married Jacques Putman (divorced); children: Cyrille and Olivia. Worked as a journalist for *Femina* magazine, Paris 1950–52; design columnist, *Elle* magazine, Paris, 1952–58; interiors editor at *L'Oeil* magazine, Paris, 1960–64; stylist, for Prisunic stores Paris, 1958–67; designer, with Arnodin and Denise Maime Fayolle's M.A.F.I.A. publicity agency, Paris, 1968–71; founder-member, with Didier Grumbach, of Createurs et Industriels fashion and furniture designers' group, and director of Createurs store, Paris, 1971–76; founder-manager, of Ecart S.A. furniture and interior design company, Paris, from 1978, and Ecart International, Paris, from 1983: has produced classic furniture re-editions of designs by Eileen Gray, Mariano Fortuny, Jean-Michel Frank, Robert Mallet-Stevens, Michel Dufet, etc., and interiors for Thierry Mugler, Karl Lagerfeld, Mendes S.A., Tan Giudicelli, Chanel, etc. **Exhibition:** *Design Francais 1960–1990,* Centre Georges Pompidou, Paris, 1988. Recipient: *Interior Design* Hall of Fame Award, New York, 1987. Officer des Arts et des Lettres, France. Address: Ecart International, 111 Rue Saint Antoine, 75004 Paris, France.

Works:

Thierry Mugler boutique, Place des Victoires, Paris, 1979–80.
Yves Saint Laurent boutiques (15), in the United States, 1980–84.
Karl Lagerfeld boutiques and showrooms, in Paris, New York, Melbourne and Toronto, 1980–85.
Morgans Hotel interiors, New York, 1984.
Palladium nightclub interiors, New York, 1984 (with Arata Isozaki).
Museum of Contemporary Art conversion, Bordeaux, 1984.
Azzedine Alaia showroom, Paris, 1985.
Jack Lang office interiors, Ministry of Culture, Paris, 1985.
World headquarters interiors in New York, brand image, advertising, exhibits and boutiques, for Ebel, 1986–91.
Saint James Club Hotel interiors, Paris, 1987.
Ferrari exhibition layouts, for the Cartier Foundation, Paris, 1987.
Corporate re-design programme, for Balenciaga, from 1989.
Rights of Man Foundation headquarters in the Grande Arche de la Defense, Paris, from 1990.

Publications:

By PUTMAN: articles—in *Passion* (Paris), 15 April 1982; *F. Magazine* (Paris), June 1983.
On PUTMAN: books—*French Style* by Suzane Slesin and Stafford Cliff, New York and London 1982; *Les Annees 60* by Anne Bony, Paris 1983; *Design Francais 1960–1990: Trois Decennies,* exhibition catalogue by Margo Rouard and Francoise Jollant Kneebone, Paris 1988; *International Design Yearbook 1988/89* edited by Arata Isozaki, London 1988; articles—in *Metropolitan Home* (New York) April 1984; *Vogue* (New York), September 1984; *Decoration Internationale* (Paris), March 1985, May 1985, September 1985 September 1986; *House and Garden* (New York), October 1985, April 1986; *Maison Francaise* (Paris), April 1986, December 1986, January 1987, December 1987, September 1988; *Interiors* (New York), June 1986, December 1987; *House and Garden* (London) November 1986; *Interior Design* (New York), February 1987; *Domus* (Milan), November 1987; *Progressive Architecture* (New York), March 1988.

Mary Quant: *Q4200* **leisure wear, 1988**

QUANT, Mary.

British fashion, housewares and product designer. Born in London, 11 February 1934. Educated at schools in England, until 1951; studied art and design, at Goldsmith's College of Art, University of London, 1952–55. Married Alexander Plunket Greene in 1957 (died, 1990); son: Orlando. Fashion designer, London, from 1955: established Bazaar fashion clothing shop and Alexander's Restaurant, in Chelsea, London, 1955, and Bazaar shop, in Knightsbridge, London, 1957; founder-director, Mary Quant Ginger Group wholesale clothing design and manufacturing firm, and Mary Quant Limited, London, 1963, and Mary Quant Japan franchise shops, throughout Japan, 1983: has designed for J. C. Penney, Puritan Fashions, Alligator Rainwear, Kangol, Dupont Europe, Dorma, Berg River Textiles, Model Toys, Staffordshire Potteries, Polaroid, Templeton Carpets, K. Shoes, Radici Sud, Pollyanna Childrenswear, etc.; also director of Mary Quant Wine Shippers, London, 1974–78. Member: Design Council, London, from 1971; British/US Bicentennial Commission, 1973–76; Advisory Council of the Victoria and Albert Museum, London, 1976–78. **Exhibitions:** *Fashion: An Anthology,* Victoria and Albert Museum, London, 1971; *Mary Quant's London,* London Museum, 1973; *Eye for Industry,* Victoria and Albert Museum, London, 1986. Recipient: Woman of the Year Award, London, 1963; *Sunday Times* Design Award, London, 1963; Maison Blanche Rex Award, 1964; Piavola d'Oro Award, Italy, 1966; Chartered Society of Designers Medal, London, 1966. Officer, Order of the British Empire, 1966; Fellow, Chartered Society of Designers, London, 1967; Royal Designer for Industry, Royal Society of Arts, London, 1969. Address: Mary Quant Limited, 3 Ives Street, London SW3 2NE, England.

Works:

Fashion collections, for J. C. Penney, 1962.
Dress collections, for Puritan Fashions, 1964.
Mary Quant hosiery, for the Nylon Hosiery Company, 1965.
Berets and hats, for Kangol, 1967.
Bedwear and curtains, for Dorma, 1972.
Axminster carpets, for Templetons, 1978.
Mary Quant shoes, for K Shoes/Mocci Shoes, 1982.

Mary Quant wallcoverings, for Worley, 1984.
Mary Quant rainwear, for Fultons, 1985.
Mary Quant clothing, for Great Universal Stores/Kays, 1987.

Publications:

By QUANT: books—*Quant by Quant,* London 1966, Bath 1974; *Colour by Quant,* with Felicity Greene, London 1984; *Quant on Make-Up,* with Vicci Bestley, London 1986.
On QUANT: books—*The Fashion Makers* by Leonard Halliday, London 1966; *Fashion: An Anthology by Cecil Beaton,* exhibition catalogue compiled by Madeleine Ginsburg, London 1971; *Mary Quant's London,* exhibition catalogue by Brian Morris and Ernestine Carter, London 1973; *The World of Fashion: People, Places, Resources* by Eleanor Lambert, London and New York 1976; *Fashion in the 60s* by Barbara Bernard, London and New York 1978; *Magic Names of Fashion* by Ernestine Carter, London 1980; *The Collector's Book of Twentieth Century Fashion* by Frances Kennett, London and New York 1983; *Les Annees 60* by Anne Bony, Paris 1983; *McDowell's Directory of Twentieth Century Fashion* by Colin McDowell, London 1984; *The Conran Directory of Design,* edited by Stephen Bayley, London 1985; *The Encyclopaedia of Fashion from 1840 to the 1980s* by Georgina O'Hara, London 1986; *Eye for Industry: Royal Designers for Industry 1936–1986* by Fiona MacCarthy and Patrick Nuttgens, London 1986.

Mary Quant born into a musical Welsh family, knew from her earliest days that she wanted to design clothes and early manifested her individuality by attending—and leaving—thirteen schools. But her parents insisted on a conventional education, and she finally did her studies at the Goldsmith's College, London: as recompense for this compliance, she was allowed to attend evening classes in the cutting and construction of clothes. She was only twenty-one when, in 1955, she opened her first shop, Bazaar, in London's artist-quarter, Chelsea. This instantaneous success was followed by a sister shop of the same name in the prestigiously fashionable Knightsbridge.

In 1957 she married Alexander Plunkett Greene, son of a famous musical family, and together they went to America where they caused a sensation and were quickly signed by

J. C. Penney to design clothes and underwear for the wholesale market. The following year, Quant was nominated "Woman of the Year," won the Sunday *Times* International Award, and founded her Ginger Group, whose aim was to make prototypes for the wholesale market to copy and sell to the retail.

In 1964, she made an agreement with Puritan Fashions of New York to design dresses for the American wholesale market and another to design for the worldwide Butterick Paper Patterns. A born innovator, Quant was the first to explore the possibilities of P.V.C. and the first designer of tights for the Nylon Hosiery Company, soon followed by a collection of swimwear. In 1966, she began to produce a range of cosmetics (since taken over by Max Factor) which have a global distribution and have been particularly successful in Japan. The same year she was given the Order of the British Empire, won the Piavola d'Oro award of Italy, and published her autobiography, *Quant by Quant.*

In 1969, Quant was elected Royal Designer for Industry, but activities did not prevent her bearing a son, Orlando, in 1970. Nineteen seventy-three saw a special exhibition of *Mary Quant's London* at the London Museum, and during the next eighteen months, Quant was the pivot of two important promotional campaigns, one for the International Wool Secretariat and the other for I.C.I.'s new dress fabric, Crimpelene. In these and the ensuing years, Quant continued to widen her range to include toys, dolls, sunglasses, pottery mugs for Staffordshire, carpets for Axminster, berets, scarves, uniforms for stewardesses, and household goods.

Nineteen eighty-three has seen "Mary Quant at Home" launched in the United States. Under this program, a dozen carefully chosen firms have agreed to manufacture their products in correlated colours chosen by Quant, so that any one item of household furnishings can be selected with the certain knowledge that all other household necessities—wall-papers, soft furnishings, carpets, china, etc.—can be obtained in matching colours but in a wide range of designs.

At present, she has sixteen current licences, including one for wine, and continues from strength to strength. Just the name Quant conjures up her individual flair for design to anyone with any knowledge of fashion.

—Madge Garland

R

RAACKE, Peter.

German sculptor, interior and industrial designer. Born in Hanau, 27 September 1928. Studied metal and glass design under Elisabeth Teskow, at the Ecole des Beaux-Arts, Paris, 1942; metal and enamelwork, at the Staatliche Zeichenakademie, Hanau, 1942–48; metal and glass design, at the Werkschule, Cologne, 1950. Served in the German Army, 1944–45. Married Ingrid Kauffmann in 1952; children: Gordian, Dominic, Katarina and Roman. Freelance furnishing and household appliance designer, working in Saarbrucken and Kassel, 1953–58, in Ulm, 1963–68, and in Hamburg, from 1968: has designed for Faltmobel Ellen Raacke, Hessische Metallwerke, ITT, Dunlop, Rasch, etc. Assistant instructor in metal construction, State Technical Art School, Darmstadt, 1951–53; instructor in metal design, State Technical Art School, Saarbrucken 1953–58; head of production design course, State Technical Art School, Kassel, 1958–61; instructor in product design, University of Design, Ulm, 1963–66; professor of industrial design, Hochschule fur Bildende Kunste, Hamburg, from 1968. Founder and co-editor, of *Szene* magazine, Hamburg; founder-member, Vereinigung Deutscher Industrie Designer. **Exhibitions:** *Gold und Silber,* Gewerbemuseum, Nuremberg, 1971; *1. Detuscher Designertag,* Karlsruhe, 1977; *Design Since 1945,* Philadelphia Museum of Art, 1983. **Collections:** Musee des Arts Decoratifs, Paris; Museum of Modern Art, New York; Philadelphia Museum of Art. Recipient: Gold Medal, Milan Triennale, 1964; National German Industry Award, 1971, 1974; Gute Form Prize, Darmstadt, 1973. Address: Innocentiastrasse 44, 22 Hamburg 13, West Germany.

Works:

Mono range of cutlery and kitchen equipment, for Hessische Metallwerke, from 1958.
Papp cardboard furniture, for Faltmobel Ellen Raacke, 1967.
Voko office furniture range.
Dunlopillo beds in foam construction, for Dunlop.
Telephones and electronic equipment, for ITT Business Systems.

Publications:

On RAACKE: books—*Stahlmobel* by Gustav Hassenpflug, Dusseldorf 1960; *The Modern Chair: 1850 to Today* by Gilbert Frey, London and Niederteufen 1970; *Contemporary Furniture,* edited by Klaus-Jurgen Sembach, Stuttgart and London 1982; *Design Since 1945,* edited by Kathryn Hiesinger and George Marcus, Philadelphia and London 1983.

RABANNE, Paco.

Spanish fashion designer. Born Francisco Rabaneva-Cuervo, in San Sebastian, 18 February 1934; emigrated to France in 1939. Educated at the College of Morlaix, France, 1940–45, and the Lycee de Sables d'Olonne, France, 1945–50; studied architecture, at the Ecole Nationale Superieure des Beaux-Arts, Paris, 1952–64. Designer of accessories for the fashion houses of Balenciaga, Givenchy, Dior, etc., in Paris, 1960–64; freelance fashion designer, working in plastics, paper and metal, from 1965: established Paco Rabanne fashion house, Paris, in 1967, and Maison Paco Rabanne furnishings company, Paris, 1981; launched perfumes *Calandre,* 1966, *Paco,* 1973, and *Metal,* 1979; also film costume designer from 1964. Founder of Groupe Verseau modern aesthetics group, Paris, 1966, and Theatre Panique group, Paris, 1967. Recipient: Sculpture Prize, Paris Biennale, 1963; Tibere d'Or Fashion Award, Capri. 1967; Beaute-Industrie Award, Institut d'Esthetique Industrielle, Paris, 1969; International Oscar Award for perfume, New York, 1975; Golden Needle Award, Paris, 1977. Address: 7 rue du Cherche-Midi, 75006 Paris, France.

Publications:

By RABANNE: article—in *Maison Francaise* (Paris), May 1983.
On RABANNE: books—*Design Through Discovery* by Marjorie Elliott Bevlin, New York 1977; *In Vogue: Sixty Years of Celebrities and Fashion,* edited by Georgina Howell, London 1975, 1978, New York 1976; *The World of Fashion: People, Places, Resources* by Eleanor Lambert, New York and London 1976; *Quest for the Best* by Stanley Marcus, New York 1979; *The Collector's Book of Twentieth Century Fashion* by Frances Kennett, London and New York 1983; *Les Annees 60* by Anne Bony, Paris 1983; *McDowell's Directory of Twentieth Century Fashion* by Colin McDowell, London 1984; *The Encyclopaedia of Fashion from 1840 to the 1980s* by Georgina O'Hara, London 1986.

The clothes produced by Paco Rabanne in the 1960s brought a new meaning to the word "couture," as he replaced traditional textiles with plastic, aluminum, and paper, while hand and machine sewing gave way to welding and moulding. Rabanne's creations could be termed "wearable sculptures," for the materials and methods used to produce them had closer similarities to developments in contemporary sculpture and kinetic art than to those used in fashion at the time. His first designs, made of plastic and feathers, were in fact shown in a Paris art gallery as Pop sculptures.

The image he created was shockingly futuristic but serious in intent. To Rabanne, fashion is a reflection of the world in which it is created.

If his designs of the 1960s still appear to be bizarre, sci-fi fantasies today, they must, at the same time, be recognized as products of their age. They helped to draw attention to the potential of new fabrics, such as synthetics, and to the widest colour ranges which were becoming available to the world of fashion. The fluorescent and neon effects new to sculpture were suddenly shown to have potential for dressing; with them, came new methods of construction. Welding and boning are now accepted methods for uniting plastic fabrics which have since become so popular, particularly for rainwear. This gave scope for the introduction of new, freer shapes which, for Rabanne, indicate the future of developments in clothing.

It was probably Rabanne's architectural training that impelled him to design clothes which were built up of individual elements such as plastic and metal discs. These discs produced a vogue for huge, bright, plastic earrings which became a commercial fashion in the late 1960s. Ever since, plastic has had a considerable role to play in modern jewelry design. Rabanne's work in the 1960s helped plastics and synthetics to become respected in their own right, rather than being treated as shoddy alternatives to other materials. He also opened up the scope for experiment with more traditional fabrics such as leather and fur.

Rabanne has brought a fresh approach to fashion by showing that there is much to be learned by looking beyond established methods and techniques. The fact that during the 1970s and 1980s, he has widened his interests emphasizes that his view of fashion is broad and that this is no respecter of seasonal changes of style.

—Hazel Clark

RAMBOW, Gunter.

German graphic designer. Born in Neustrelitz, 2 March 1938. Studied glass painting at the Staatliche Glasfachschule, Hadamar, 1954–58; graphics under Hans Hillmann, at the Hochschule fur Bildende Kunste, Kassel, 1958–64. Founder-partner, with Gerard Lienemeyer, of the Rambow + Lienemeyer graphic design studio, in Kassel, 1960–64, in Stuttgart, 1964–67, and in Frankfurt, 1967–73; partner, with Lienemeyer and Michael Van de Sand, in Rambow/Lienemeyer/Van de Sand studio, Frankfurt, 1972–88; partner, in Rambow/Rambow/Van de Sand studio, Frankfurt, from 1988; also founder, with Gerhard Lienemeyer,

Paco Rabanne: Coat in enamelled grey fur with leather flamingoes, 1984   photo: George Tourdjman

of Kohlkunst Verlag publishing company, Frankfurt, 1967. Professor of graphic design, Gesamthochschule, Kassel, 1974–87; professor of visual communications, University of Kassel, from 1987. **Exhibitions:** *Plakate von Rambow, Lienemeyer, Van de Sand,* Deutsches Plakatmuseum, Essen, 1983; *Rambow, Lienemeyer, Van de Sand,* Wilanow Poster Museum, Warsaw, 1984; *Posters from Rambow, Lienemeyer, Van de Sand,* Galerie Bruno Oldani, Oslo, 1985; *Rambow, Lienemeyer, Van de Sand: Affiches,* 7 Allee Georges Braque, Paris, 1985; *Posters from Lenica, Hillmann, Rambow,* New York Gallery, New York, 1986; *Rambow a la Bibliotheque,* Bibliotheque Nationale, Paris, 1988; *Rambow: Plakate 1960–1988,* Museum, Wiesbaden, 1988; *Plakatwerke von Rambow,*

Akademie de Kunste der DDR, Berlin, 1989. **Collections:** Deutsches Plakatmuseum, Essen; Staatliche Kunstsammlungen, Kassel; Stedelijk Museum, Amsterdam; Bibliotheque Nationale, Paris; Musee de l'Affiche, Paris; Wilanow Poster Museum, Warsaw; Library of Congress, Washington, D.C.; Museum of Modern Art, New York. Recipient: 49 national poster prizes, West Germany, 1960–83; Warsaw Poster Biennale Bronze Medal, 1968, and Gold Medal, 1980; Colorado Poster Exhibition Prize, Fort Collins, 1979, 1985; Brno Graphic Design Biennale Gold Medal, 1982, and Critics' Prize, 1986; Lahti Poster Biennale Grand Prize, 1985; Political Poster Prize, Mons, 1988. Address: Kronberger Strasse 32, 6000 Frankfurt am Main 1, West Germany.

Works:

Charlie Chaplin, Goldrausch poster, for Atlas Film, Duisburg, 1962.
Onkel Onkel poster, for the Theater der Altstadt, Stuttgart, 1967.
Stop poster, for *Egoist* magazine, 1968.
It's Time to Fly to Hanoi poster, for Kohlkunstverlag, 1968.
Hand and Book poster series, for S. Fischer Verlag, Frankfurt, 1976–79.
Antigone poster series, for the Schauspiel Frankfurt, 1978.
Othello poster, for the Schauspiel Frankfurt, 1978.
Zum Raum wird ier die Zeit . . . poster series, for Galerie Rene Block, Berlin, 1981.

Gunter Rambow: Poster for GEW, 1988

P.E.N. im Exil poster, for the Deutsche Bibliothek, Frankfurt, 1983.
Schauspiel im Fruhling poster, for the Schauspiel Frankfurt, 1985.
Nachtlicht poster, for Hessischer Rundfunk, 1987.
Nur Wissen schafft keine Kunst poster, for the University of Kassel, 1988.
Sudafrikanisches Roulette poster, for the Staatstheater, Stuttgart, 1988.

Publications:

By RAMBOW: books—*Der Glockner von Notre Dame und die Madonna der sieben Monde,* Frankfurt 1976; *Das sind eben Bilder der Strasse,* Frankfurt 1979; *Ein Plakat ist eine Flache die ins Auge springt,* Frankfurt 1979.
On RAMBOW: books—*German Advertising Art,* edited by Eberhard Holscher, Munich 1967; *The Poster: An Illustrated History from 1860* by Harold F. Hutchinson, London and Toronto 1968; *Who's Who in Graphic Art,* edited by Walter Amstutz, Dubendorf 1982; *A History of Graphic Design* by Philip B. Meggs, London and New York 1983; *Top Graphic Design* by F. H. K. Henrion, Zurich 1983; *Rambow: Plakate 1960–1988,* exhibition catalogue edited by Volker Rattemeyer, Wiesbaden 1988.

Audio 1/2 stereo unit, for Braun AG, 1962.
Studio 1000 stereo systems, for Braun AG, 1965.
T2 cylindrical table lighter, for Braun AG, 1968.
HLD 4 hairdryer, for Braun AG, 1970.
TG 1000/1020 tape recorder, for Braun AG, 1970.
Audio 308 stereo units, for Braun AG, 1973.
Control ET 44 pocket calculator, for Braun AG, 1978.
Atelier P1, T1, A1 and *C1* hi-fi components, for Braun AG, 1980.

Publications:

By RAMS: articles—in *Management* (Tokyo), Marc 1974; *Form* (Seeheim), January 1976; *Werk und Archithese* (Stuttgart), April 1977; *Format* (Karlsruhe), May 1977; *The Designer* (London), September 1978; *Design Age* (Tokyo), November 1979; *Werk und Zeit* (Berlin), April 1979.

On RAMS: books—*Zeitgemasse Form* by Joann Klockner and others, Munich 1967; *One Hundred Great Product Designs* by Jay Doblin, New York 1970; *Made in Germany* by Hans Wichmann, Munich 1970; *In Good Shape: Style in Industrial Products Since 1960* by Stephen Bayley, London 1979; *Contemporary Furniture,* edited by Klaus-Jurgen Sembach, Stuttgart and London 1982; *A History of Industrial Design* by Edward Lucie-Smith, London 1983; *Design Since 1945,* edited by Kathryn Hiesinger and George Marcus, Philadelphia and London 1983; *The Conran Directory of Design,* edited by Stephen Bayley, London 1985; *Design Source Book* by Penny Sparke and others, London 1986.

I think that a good designer must always be an avant-gardist. Always one step ahead of the times. He should—and he must—question everything generally thought to be obvious. He must have an intuition for people's changing attitudes, for the reality in which they live, for their dreams, their desires, their worries, their needs, their living habits. He must also be able to assess realistically the opportunities and the bounds of technology.

—Dieter Rams

Dieter Rams: *862 Programm* chair, for Vitsoe, 1986

RAMS, Dieter.
German industrial designer. Born in Wiesbaden, 20 May 1932. Studied architecture and interior design, at the School of Art, Wiesbaden, 1947–48, 1951–53; apprenticed as a carpenter, in Kelkheim, 1948–51. Married Ingeborg Kracht in 1967. Worked in the Otto Appel architecture office, Frankfurt, 1953–55; architect and interior designer, 1955–56, product designer, 1956–60, director of design, 1960–80, and board member from 1980, at Braun AG, Frankfurt; also furniture designer for Otto Zapf (now Wiese Vitsoe), Frankfurt, from 1957. Professor, Hochschule fur Bildende Kunste, Hamburg, from 1981. President, German Design Council, Frankfurt, 1987. **Exhibitions:** *Modern Chairs,* Whitechapel Art Gallery, London, 1971; International Design Centre, West Berlin, 1980 (toured); *Design Since 1945,* Philadelphia Museum of Art, 1983. **Collection:** Museum of Modern Art, New York. Recipient: Interplast Design Award, London, 1961, 1963; Gold Medal, Milan Triennale, 1964; Gold Medal, Liubliana Design Biennale, 1964; Gold Medal, Vienna Furnishing Salon, 1969; Gute Form Award, Vienna, 1969, 1970, 1973; Society of Industrial Artists and Designers Medal, London, 1978. Honorary Royal Designer for Industry, Royal Society of Arts, London, 1968. Address: Braun Aktiengesellschaft, Frankfurter Strasse 145, 6242 Kronberg (Taunus), West Germany.

Works:

Phonosuper SK4 stereo unit, for Braun AG, 1956.
H1/H2D heater-ventilators, for Braun AG, 1959.
606 shelving system, for Wiese Vitsoe, 1960.
D 40 slide projector, for Braun AG, 1961.
T 1000 multiband radio, for Braun AG, 1962.
620 lounge chair program, for Wiese Vitsoe, 1962.

As head designer for one company for almost three decades, Dieter Rams would seem less independent than his peers. However, at Braun, he has attained the respect and trust of management and has built a team which can work with unusual freedom. Moreover, Rams has a reputation for drawing engineers to the furthest limits of their possibilities.

In Rams's admiration for Japanese lacquer ware is seen a reflection of his own design concerns—simple yet sleek, stackable yet individually complete, comfortable yet visually stimulating, seamlessly joined yet easily dismantled. Continuity in design development and product families, where several products are interconnected, supplementing and complementing each other, are the hallmarks of the Rams design approach. In both Braun products and Vitsoe furniture, Rams has focused on creating complete systems, which are both functional and combinable. His audio components, with tape deck, stereo turntable, and television capable of being either stacked vertically or aligned horizontally, exemplify this flexibility and ingenuity. Portability in television sets, radios, record players, hair dryers, clocks, and shavers is a highly developed mode in the Braun line, thanks to another aspect of the Rams philosophy. Not only do the designs make efficient use of material and technology, but they are also sensitive to user need—such as frequent travel, frequent moves from one living space to another, faster pace of life. His solutions are streamlined, lightweight, durable everyday objects. In a tribute to the appropriateness of his designs, all the Vitsoe furniture systems, including shelving, stacking units, and wall paneling, which have come on the market since 1958 are still available today.

Rams believes that design should not intrude or be visually aggressive. His product design, therefore, while similar in clarity of expression, precise relationships of volumes and shapes, and minimalist skin to modern twentieth-century architecture, such as that of Bruno Taut or Erich Mendelsohn, is concerned with the potential of material, engineering, and contemporary technology in its application to user need.

Rams first considers utility; next, practicality; and third, esthetics. This pragmatic approach, as much as the actual products—which rely on a simple range of neutrals: black, white, and gray; and basic geometric volumes: cubes, cylinders, and spheres—has given presence and success to his designs. Rams has brought a high level of design to a large number of people and influenced the democratization of present-day material culture.

—Sarah Bodine

RAND, Paul.
American graphic designer. Born in New York City, 15 August 1914. Studied at the Pratt Institute, Brooklyn, New York, 1930–32; Parsons School of Design, New York, 1932; under George Grosz, at the Art Students League, New York, 1939. Married Marion Swannie Hall in 1975; daughter: Catherine. Assistant designer in the studio of George Switzer, New York, 1932–35; art director of *Esquire* and *Apparel Arts* magazines, New York, 1937–41; creative director, William H. Weintraub advertising agency, New York, 1941–54; freelance designer, New York, from 1955: consultant to IBM, Cummins Engine Company, and Westinghouse Electric Corporation, from 1956. Instructor in graphic design, at Cooper Union, New York, 1938–42, and at the Pratt Institute, Brooklyn, New York, 1946; professor of graphic design, Yale University School of Art, New Haven, Connecticut, from 1956; instructor, Yale Summer Program, Brissago, Switzerland, from 1977. **Exhibitions:** *Advance Guard of Advertising Artists,* Katharine Kuh Gallery, New York, 1941; Composing Room, New York, 1947; Philadelphia Museum of Art, 1948; Boston Museum School of Fine Arts, 1951; University of Florida, Gainesville, 1958; American Institute of Graphic Arts, New York, 1958; Art Directors Club of Tokyo, 1958; School of the Visual Arts, New York, 1964; Carnegie Institute, Pittsburgh, 1964; Temple University, Philadelphia, 1968; Louisiana Arts and Science Center, Baton Rouge, 1969; Virginia Museum of Fine Arts, Richmond, 1970 (toured); *107 Grafici dell'AGI,* Castello Sforzesco, Milan, 1974 (toured); Wichita State University, Kansas, 1977; Pratt Manhattan Center, New York, 1977; Philadelphia College of Art, 1979; Reinhold Brown Gallery, New York, 1982; William Paterson College, Wayne, New Jersey, 1982. **Collections:** Museum of Modern Art, New York; Smithsonian Institution, Washington, D.C.; Library of Congress, Washington, D.C.; Kunstgewerbemuseum, Zurich. Recipient: Philadelphia College of Art Citation, 1962; American Institute of Graphic Arts Medal 1966; New York Art Directors Club Hall of Fame Award, 1972; Florence Prize for Visual Communication, 1987. Honorary Professor, Tama University, Tokyo, 1958; honorary master of arts, Yale University; honorary doctorates: Philadelphia College of Art, Parsons School of Design, University of Hartford, and Kutztown University. Honorary Royal Designer for Industry, Royal Society of Arts, London, 1973. Address: 87 Goodhill Road, Weston, Connecticut 06883, U.S.A.

Publications:

By RAND: books—*Thoughts on Design,* New York 1946, 1970, London 1970; *The Trademarks of Paul Rand,* New York 1960; *Design and the Play Instinct,* New York 1965; *Paul Rand: A Designer's Art,* New Haven and London 1985.
On RAND: books—*Posters: 50 Artists and Designers,* edited by Walter Allner, New York 1952; *Paul Rand: His Work from 1946–58* by Yusaku Kamekura and others, New York and Tokyo 1959; *The New Graphic Design* by Karl Gerstner and Markus Kutter, Teufen and London 1959; *An International Survey of Packaging* by Wim Crouwel and Kurt Weidemann, London 1968; *Design in America* by Ralph Caplan, New York 1969; *The Corporate Search for Visual Identity* by Ben Rosen, New York and London 1970; *Communication by Design: A Study in Corporate Identity* by Gerald Woods and others, London 1972; *In Good Shape: Style in Industrial Products Since 1960* by Stephen Bayley, London 1979; *Who's Who in Graphic Art,* edited by Walter Amstutz, Dubendorf 1982; *Advertising: Reflections of a Century* by Bryan Holme, London 1982; *The Conran Directory of Design,* edited by Stephen Bayley, London 1985; *The American Design Adventure 1940–1975* by Arthur J. Pulos, London and Cambridge, Massachusetts 1988; *New American Design* by Hugh Aldersley-Williams, New York 1988.

When Paul Rand began his career, graphic communication was dominated by traditional narrative illustration, and page design often consisted of a symmetrical arrangement of isolated elements: picture, headline, trademark, etc. Seeing the space instead as a visual unit, Rand pushed the separate elements into a dynamic equilibrium and played an important role in introducing the visual language of cubism, constructivism, de Stijl, and the Bauhaus into American design. Also, he further contributed by forging his modernist approach into a graphic design style that was highly personal and uniquely American. From European modern art, Rand learned the use of color, texture, collage, montage, gesture, and visual contrasts as expressive means. His work reflects his understanding of the communicative power of abstract and pictographic symbols, and many of Rand's designs have a disarming simplicity that grows from his ability to comprehend the essence of the subject matter, then project it to the viewer with an economy of means. Always interested in the totality of graphic design, he seeks the strongest possible unity of the visual form with content, which, for him, is conceptual expression rather than narrative matter.

The work that Rand did for IBM, beginning with the 1956 trademark, had a seminal influence upon the evolution of corporate graphic communications. The logo is composed of capital initials developed from a geometric, slab-serif typeface, City Medium. Rand applied this to packaging and corporate literature with a consistency that established a strong and memorable image. The 1958 annual report that Rand designed for IBM set the tone and approach for this type of publication for many years. Photographic closeups of electronic circuitry, products, and employees in work environments have simple, elegant design qualities that project an image of an efficient, technologically advanced corporation. Lucid and restrained typography is achieved through the use of wide outer margins and quiet, relatively small headings that depend on weight and placement rather than large size for their contrast with the text.

In other circumstances, Rand has not hesitated to use humor and whimsy as design approaches. He recognizes that the "play instinct," both for the designer searching for a viable solution and for the spectator decoding and responding to the communication, is a vital aspect of effective visual communications.

—Philip B. Meggs

RASMUSSEN, Jorgen.
Danish architect, industrial and graphic designer. Born in Odense, 26 April 1931. Studied architecture, Royal Danish Academy of Fine Arts, Copenhagen, 1950–55. Married Hanne Ringsted in 1957 (divorced, 1972); children: Soren, Maja, Sophie and Pauline. Freelance architect and designer, establishing studio with his twin brother Ib Rasmussen, in Vedbaek, since 1957: has designed for Knoll International, Herman Miller, Kevi, Louis Poulsen, etc. Instructor in architecture, Royal Academy of Fine Arts, Copenhagen, 1960–75; Guest Professor, University of Trondheim, 1961; also guest lecturer at Boston University School of Architecture, 1988. **Exhibitions:** *Knoll au Musee,* Musee des Arts Decoratifs, Paris, 1972; *Scandinavian Modern Design 1880–1980,* Cooper-Hewitt Museum, New York, 1982; *New Design for Old,* Boilerhouse/Victoria and Albert Museum, London, 1986. **Collections:** Museum of Applied Arts, Copenhagen. Recipi-

Paul Rand: Rebus poster for IBM, 1981

Jorgen Rasmussen: Double-wheel furniture castors, for Kevi, 1989

ent: Neuhausen Competition Prize, Copenhagen, 1957; Gold Medal, Royal Academy of Fine Arts, Copenhagen, 1959; ID Danish Design Council Prize, Copenhagen, 1969; Traeprisen Architecture Prize, Copenhagen, 1974; Gute Form Prize, West Germany, 1978; Goed Industriele Ontwerp Prize, Netherlands, 1987. Address: Vedbaek Station, 2950 Vedbaek, Denmark.

Works:

Square lamp, for Louis Poulsen, 1960.
Office chairs, for Kevi, 1960–89.
Logos, for Kevi, 1964.
Double-wheel furniture castors, for Kevi, 1967–89.
The Rasmussen Chairs, for Knoll International, 1968.
Kitchen, for Grona Garden exhibition, Sweden, 1968.
Tables and filing systems, for Kevi, 1970–75.
Old Man's Wicker Chair, for *New Design for Old* exhibition, Boilerhouse, London, 1986.
Simple seating in laminated wood, for Herman Miller, 1989.

Publications:

By RASMUSSEN: book—*Gamle Teglvaerker*, Copenhagen 1968; article—"Streetscape and its Furniture" in *Havne og Stadsingenioren* (Copenhagen), no. 3, 1989.

On RASMUSSEN: books—*Dansk Brugskunst og Design*, edited by Landsforeningen DB+D, Copenhagen 1972; *Knoll au Musee*, exhibition catalogue with text by Christine Rae, Paris 1972; *50 Designers* by Marc Lavrillier, Novara 1978; *Knoll Design*, edited by Eric Larrabee and Massimo Vignelli, New York 1979; *Scandinavian Modern Design 1880–1980*, edited by David Revere McFadden, New York 1982; *New Design for Old*, exhibition catalogue with texts by Helen Hamlyn, Eric Midwinter and others, London 1986; articles—in *Mobilia* (Snekkersten), vol. 134, 1966, and vol. 194, 1971.

I was educated as an architect, but have always worked in several fields of design—from town and landscape planning to housing and industrial design.

Thirty years ago, one of my house clients asked me to redesign a whole programme of office chairs, and I have continued working on it for Kevi A/S ever since. Around 1968, I designed "The Rasmussen Chair" for Knoll International, and for it I designed a new double-wheel castor, which was not only functionally perfect, but also had a neat geometrical appearance. These castors are now produced all over the world in a quantity of twelve million a year, and copy versions must number around three hundred million annually.

I think it a pleasure to have contributed to a higher standard of design worldwide, although my work is only a small detail of the whole. The drive for good design is for me the same as the urge to go on living; I assume that some-

where hidden is a better way of doing things. I am a little scared of many recent designs and the approach of some designers to their work. I think design should be timeless and functional—not haute couture or art-for-art's-sake. Form is not the aim of our work, but an end result.

—Jorgen Rasmussen

REID, John (Robson).
British architect, exhibition, and industrial designer. Born in Northampton, 1 December 1925. Educated at Wellingborough School, Northamptonshire, until 1941; studied architecture at the Regent Polytechnic, London, 1942–44, 1948–50: Dip.Arch. 1950. Served in the Green Howards, British Army, 1944–47: Captain. Married Sylvia Payne in 1948; 3 children. Freelance architect and designer, in partnership with Sylvia Reid, London, from 1951: consultant to Thorn Lighting, Rotaflex lighting, Stag Furniture, British Rail, the Post Office, and the United Nations Industrial Development Organization. Dean of art and design, Middlesex Polytechnic, London, 1975–78. Advisory committee member to Central School of Arts and

Crafts, London, Leeds College of Art and Design, Newcastle School of Art and Design, and Carleton University, Ottawa; governor, Hornsey College of Art, London. President, Society of Industrial Artists and Designers, London, 1965–66, and of ICSID International Council of Societies of Industrial Design, 1969–71; vice-president, Illuminating Engineering Society, London, 1969–71; chairman, National Inspection Council for Electrical Installations, London, 1972–73; pageantmaster to the Lord Mayors of London, from 1972. Recipient: Design Council Awards, London; Milan Triennale Medals. Fellow, Chartered Institution of Building Services, London. Address: Arnoside House, 5 The Green, Old Southgate, London N14 7EG, England.

Works:

The Champion pub interiors, Wells Street, London, 1955.
Modular storage units in veneered teak, for Stag Furniture, 1960.
Dining chairs in steel and afromosia with leather upholstery, for Stag Furniture, 1962.
Fineline bedroom furniture range in birch and metal, for Stag Furniture, 1966.
Hooper Beach House, Anglesea, Victoria, 1972.
Westminster Arts Theatre office additions, London, 1973.
West Lodge Park Hotel extension, Hadley Wood, 1974.
The Pyramid pub, Pin Green, Stevenage, Hertfordshire, 1975.

Publications:

By REID: books—*International Code of Professional Conduct*, London 1969; *A Guide to Conditions of Contract for Industrial Design*, London 1971; *Design in India, Pakistan, Egypt and Turkey*, London 1978.
On REID: Books—*Public Interiors* by Misha Black, London 1960, *Looking at Furniture* by Gordon Russell, London 1964; *Furniture in Britain Today* by Dennis and Barbara Young, London 1964; *Industrial Design and the Community* by Ken Baynes, London 1967; *Twentieth Century Furniture* by Philippe Garner, London 1980.

It was Paul Rickley (now Lord Rickley) then director of the Design Council in 1971 who brought John Reid together with me; each of us heading then the two international design associations. Him as President of the International Council of Societies of Industrial Design, and me as President of the International Council of Graphic Design Associations. My favourite reaction to him as a man confirmed my admiration of his talent as a designer. Competence, professionalism and imagination. In post-war Britain these qualities were badly needed and were somewhat in short supply. No wonder that such a large organisation like Thorn Lighting engaged him to design their light fittings and industrial products, as their Design Consultant; and other organisations like Telecom, Savoy Hotel, the New Barbican Art Centre among others, to carry out major architectural interior designs. His work eventually expanded over a variety of products, architectural and furniture designs, each actively benefiting the other with a typical Reid's touch which could be described as an excellent feel for the right type of material to be used for a product and a good sense of space, making the best of limitations by which a location is handicapped. Since his approach to a problem proceeds with such a fundamental research to an assignment and the solution is

not only pleasing but inventive, his achievements have a permanency which is not often to be found. The complex theoretical problems are well researched prior to the start of any work, and this is one of the reasons why Reid's is so much in demand in countries like India, Pakistan and Egypt, as well as Japan, USA and many other locations round the world.

—John Halas

RHODES, Zandra (Lindsey).

British fashion and textile designer. Born in Chatham, Kent, 19 September 1940. Studied textiles, design and printmaking, at Medway College of Art, Chatham, 1959–61; textile design, at the Royal College of Art, London, 1961–64; Des.RCA 1964. Established textile design and printing studio, with Alexander McIntyre, London, 1965, and dressmaking firm, with Sylvia Ayton, London, 1966; partner and designer, Fulham Clothes Shop, London, 1967–68; freelance fashion designer, London, 1968–75; director, Zandra Rhodes UK Limited, and Zandra Rhodes Shops Limited, from 1975: launched ready-to-wear collections, in Australia, 1979, and in Britain, 1984. **Exhibitions:** Oriel Gallery, Cardiff, 1978; Texas Gallery, Houston, 1981; Otis Parsons Institute, Los Angeles, 1981; La Jolla Museum of Art, San Diego, 1982; Barbican Centre, London, 1982; School of the Art Institute of Chicago, 1982; Parsons School of Design, New York, 1982; Art Museum of Santa Cruz, California, 1983; El Paso Museum of Art, Texas, 1984. **Collections:** Victoria and Albert Museum, London; City Museum, Stoke on Trent; Bath Museum of Costume, Avon; Royal Pavilion Museum, Brighton; City Art Galley, Leeds; Metropolitan Museum of Art, New York; Chicago Historical Society; La Jolla Museum of Art, California; Smithsonian Institution, Washington, D.C.; Royal Ontario Museum, Toronto. Recipient: English Fashion Designer of the Year Award, London, 1972; Moore College of Art Award, Philadelphia, 1978; City of Philadelphia Award, 1978; Emmy Award, New York, 1984. DFA: International Fine Arts College of Miami. Royal Designer for Industry, Royal Society of Arts, London, 1977. Address: 87 Richford Street, Hammersmith, London W6 7HJ, England.

Works:

Bedlinens, for Wamsutta USA, 1976.
Interior patterns, for CVP Designs, 1977.
Carpets and rugs, for Regal Rugs, 1977.
Headscarves, for Baar and Beard Incorporated, 1978.
Kitchen textiles and accessories, for Sari Fabrics, 1979.
Printed silk dresses and blouses, for Jack Mulqueen, 1980.
Jeans and T-shirts, for Falmers, 1981.
Knitted silk lingeries, for Courtaulds, 1981.
Cashmere knitwear, for Lyle and Scott, 1982.
ZR perfume, for Faberge Incorporated, 1984.
Designs on Legs hosiery, for Jambetex, 1984.
Shoes, for Pentland Industries, 1984.
Bedlinens, for Monitor Designs, 1985.

Publications:

By RHODES: book—*The Art of Zandra*

Rhodes, with Anne Knight, London 1984, New York 1985.

On RHODES: Books—*Fashion: An Anthology by Cecil Beaton*, exhibition catalogue compiled by Madeleine Ginsburg, London 1971; *20th Century Fashion: A Scrapbook* by Ernestine Carter, London 1975; *Zandra Rhodes: A Retrospective with Artworks*, exhibition catalogue, Santa Cruz 1983; *McDowell's Directory of Twentieth Century Fashion* by Colin McDowell, London 1984; *Eye for Industry: Royal Designers for Industry 1936–1986* by Fiona MacCarthy and Patrick Nuttgens, London 1986; *The Encyclopaedia of Fashion from 1840 to the 1980s* by Georgina O'Hara, London 1986; *Design Source Book* by Penny Sparke and others, London 1986.

I am a person driven by extreme ambition with the desire to make an original contribution to society. My individual statement is made mainly by my prints and the way in which they are transformed into dresses. I believe in the excitement of dressing up and making a woman feel beautiful. Every woman has something wonderful about her, no matter what her size. I enjoy finding the key to each individual in order to enhance her looks.

I am an artist working through the medium of my prints and dresses. I produce specially designed screen prints that set the theme and express my own particular handwriting. The inspiration in these prints comes mainly from artist friends, travel and landscape, and from my life and where it leads me.

I like to work in the print room with a variety of fabrics: e.g., chiffon, felt, velvet, taffeta, and suede, my arms elbow-deep in dye until I am satisfied by the design and colour. This is where and when I am happiest in my work.

I love to specialise in making evening dresses, but I also like to cover the full spectrum of a woman's daily wardrobe, enabling her to feel "special" at any hour of the day or night.

I do not like to copy the past—my work must represent the present. Retrospective influences are used but not copied.

—Zandra Rhodes

Imaginative, rhythmic, mysterious—one might use these words to describe the art of Zandra Rhodes. Looming out of the late 1960s, she emerged in our world like a painter of dreams, her fantasy illuminating new escape routes from a confused, dizzy world of drugs and nostalgia. Rhodes put fashion with poetic vision into a new dimension. Her colors flow rhythmically through a room and over the wearer's body. Her patterns and prints defy criticism, as lipsticks, teardrops, and teddybears cover organdy, while cacti the colors of the New Mexico desert decorate chiffon. One becomes lost in the dreamlike world as a swoosh of tulle and silk takes one to some mystical place.

Whereas others of the 1960s English movement died in 1971, when Yves Saint Laurent opened Rive Gauche and Paris once again took the crown of fashion, Rhodes continued to grow. She has developed a personal look through painting fabrics and originating garments that sometimes tests the limits of the three-dimensional. A tireless worker, she has labored long to create a vocabulary of intensely personal forms that speak softly of intimacy and nature. By infusing the abstract with natural shapes, she evokes poetic echoes. As a designer, she is breaking new ground, not only by introducing a fantasy, a delicate and lyrical content into her designs, but by daring to experiment with new techniques of finishings and application of materials.

Zandra Rhodes: Circular dress in quilted satin with knitted pattern, 1971 photo: Clive Arrowsmith

Her personal appearance is part of her extravagant art form. Rainbows color her hair and her make-up is quite extraordinary. Electric zigzags are where brows used to be. Colors mix and surprise on "tatooed" fingernails. Yet, joined with this eccentricity is a sensitive, bright, calculating spirit, sometimes mystical and erotic, often lyrical, and always creative.

—Andrea Arsenault

RISOM, Jens.

American furniture and product designer. Born in Copenhagen, Denmark, 8 May 1916; emigrated to the United States in 1939: naturalized, 1944. Educated at Kreb's School, Copenhagen until 1928, and St. Anne Vester School, Copenhagen, 1929–32; studied at Niels Brock's Business School, Copenhagen, 1932–34; furniture and interior design, at the School of Arts and Crafts, Copenhagen, 1935–38. Served in the United States Third Army, in Europe, 1943–45. Married Iben Haderup in 1939 (died, 1977); children: Helen, Peggy, Thomas and Sven; married Henny Panduro in 1979. Interior and furnishings designer, in the Ernst Kuhn architectural office, Copenhagen, 1937–38; design director and furnishing textiles designer, at Dan Cooper Incorporated, New York, 1939–41; freelance furniture, interior and textile designer, New York, 1941–43; founder and chief executive, of Jens Risom design, New York, 1946–73, and of Design Control, New Canaan, Connecticut, from 1973: has designed for Knoll International, Georg Jensen Incorporated, Howe Furniture, etc. Trustee, Rhode Island School of Design, Providence, 1970–76. Address: 103 Chichester Road, New Canaan, Connecticut 06840, U.S.A.

Works:

Easy chair in wood with webbing seat, for Knoll Associates 1941.
600 Line range of cabinets and furniture in cherrywood, for Knoll Associates, 1942.
Knoll Associates showroom interiors, Madison Avenue, New York, 1947.
Model Home interiors and furniture in the Rockefeller Center, New York, for *Collier's* magazine, 1940 (with Edward Durell Stone).
Risom/Burr range of folding-leg tables in tubular steel with oak or walnut tops, for Howe Furniture Corporation, 1977 (with Alan Burr).

Publications:

On RISOM: books—*Design in America* by Ralph Caplan, New York 1969; *Modern Furniture* by John F. Pile, New York and Toronto 1979; *Knoll Design* by Eric Larrabee and Massimo Vignelli, New York 1981; *Contemporary Furniture*, edited by Klaus-Jurgen Sembach, Stuttgart and London 1982; *Mid-Century: Furniture of the 1950s* by Cara Greenberg, London 1984; *The American Design Adventure 1940–1975* by Arthur J. Pulos, London and Cambridge, Massachusetts 1988.

Jens Risom, son of a well-respected Danish architect, determined in his youth to create modern furniture appropriate to both residential and commercial modern architecture. In Scandinavia, since the Stockholm Workshops exhibition of 1930, modern furniture has been accepted as the norm, so Risom's decision was not radical except perhaps in its architectural orientation. After completing business school, he took his degree from the School of Arts and Crafts in Copenhagen, where he came under the influence of Kaare Klint. Klint reinforced Risom's aim to consider furniture as part of the architectural space, rather than as an isolated sculptural entity, and Klint's teachings led him to seek simplicity and fitness to purpose above any particular style.

In 1939, Risom came to the United States, intending to study or work for a year. Here, he found virtually no interest either in training modern designers or in manufacturing modern furniture. American markets preferred Grand Rapids imitation of older styles, and what the market demanded, the schools and manufacturers supplied. Nevertheless, Risom, armed with introductions to influential people at the Museum of Modern Art in New York, soon met architects and others who encouraged him, and he decided to remain in the United States. Briefly, he worked with textile designer Dan Cooper, for whom he was head of studio, producing designs for printed fabrics and arranging displays of home-like settings with his own furniture designs. In 1940, *Colliers* magazine commissioned Edward D. Stone to design a model home in Rockefeller Center, and Risom was placed in charge of interiors throughout.

This was his first chance to introduce his modern, residential furniture to a broad public. By the next year, he was designing for private clients, for Hans Knoll, a young entrepreneur friend, and for Georg Jensen.

In 1946 Risom formed his own company, in which he remained always the sole designer. From the start, Risom explored production of his designs in components, so his furniture could be individualized either for space requirements or for specific tastes and needs of individual users. Selling mostly through architects and interior planners, his furniture presented an assortment of options available within any line of furniture.

Risom sought to accommodate his designs to the changing styles of life at home and in the work place. By the early 1960s, he concentrated mostly upon furniture for the office, targeting middle- and upper-level executives as his users. He found that they no longer occupied positions as in the past, no longer required static, throne-like chairs nor heavy desks behind which to barricade themselves. Risom realized that office size, being at a premium, is usually smaller than it used to be, and that the democratic open-planning now standard in most offices must be taken into account when designing furniture. Sofas, low tables, and comfortable chairs, which occur in groupings to accommodate conferences, make office and home more alike.

Among leaders in modern furniture design after World War II, the Herman Miller Com-

Jens Risom: *U440* low armchair, for Risom Design Inc., 1960

pany and Knoll International were most radically innovative. Both displayed consistently high quality, and Knoll's designers were particularly identified with avant-garde, Bauhaus, metal and molded furniture. By contrast, Risom designs of finely crafted woods appealed to a more conservative taste. Today, with the widespread acceptance of modern spaces, particularly in offices and institutions, Risom designs mingle with authentic Chippendale and Bauhaus modern.

—Nina Bremer

ROBBINS, Carrie.

American stage designer. Born Carrie Mae Fishbein, in Baltimore, Maryland, 7 February 1943. Studied at Pennsylvania State University, University Park, 1960–64: BA, BS 1964; Yale University School of Drama, New Haven, Connecticut, 1964–67: MFA 1967. Married Richard D. Robbins in 1969. Freelance stage costume and scenic designer, New York, from 1967, and company uniform designer from 1987: has designed productions for the New York Shakespeare Festival, Lincoln Center

Repertory Theatre, Chelsea Theatre Center, Vivian Beaumont Theatre, Martin Beck Theatre, and uniforms for the Rockefeller Center Rainbow Room, Aurora Grill, Empress Court of Las Vegas, etc. Instructor in costume design, 1971–84, and master teacher from 1984, at New York University; visiting lecturer, University of Illinois, Urbana, 1977–78. Steering committee member of the league of Professional Theatre Training Programs, and of the United States Institute of Theatre Technology Costume Commission. **Exhibition:** Central Falls Gallery, New York, 1980. Recipient: Drama Desk Award, New York, 1971, 1973; Maharam Award, New York, 1975; Surface Design Award, Fashion Institute of Technology, New York, 1980; Novi Sad Theatre Design Triennale Award, 1981; Drama-logue Critics' Choice Award, Los Angeles, 1982. Address: Carrie Robbins Designage Incorporated, 11 West 30th Street, New York, New York, 10001, U.S.A.

Works:

Stage productions include—*Bells are Ringing*, Schwab Auditorium, University Park, Pennsylvania, 1962; *Leda Had a little Swan*, Cort Theatre, New York, 1968; *Inner Journey* Forum Theatre, New York, 1969; *The Year Boston Won the Pennant*, Forum Theatre, New York, 1969; *The Time of Your Life*, Vivian Beaumont Theatre, New York, 1969; *The Good Woman of*

Setzuan, Vivian Beaumont Theatre, New York, 1970; *Look to the Lilies*, Lunt-Fontanne Theatre, New York, 1970; *An Enemy of the People*, Vivian Beaumont Theatre, New York, 1971; *Narrow Road to the Deep North*, Vivian Beaumont Theatre, New York, 1972; *The Crucible*, Vivian Beaumont Theatre, New York, 1972; *Grease*, Eden Theatre, New York, 1972; *The Hostage*, Good Shepherd-Faith Church, New York, 1972; *Sunset*, Chelsea Theatre Center, New York, 1972; *The Beggar's Opera*, Chelsea Theatre Center, New York, 1972; *The Secret Affairs of Mildred Wild*, Ambassador Theatre, New York, 1972; *Let Me Hear You Smile*, Biltmore Theatre, New York 1973; *The Plough and the Stars*, Vivian Beaumont Theatre, New York, 1973; *Molly*, Alvin Theatre, New York, 1973; *The Iceman Cometh*, Circle in the Square, New York, 1973; *The Beggar's Opera*, Billy Rose Theatre, New York, 1973; *Over Here*, Shubert Theatre, New York, 1974; *Merry Wives of Windsor*, New York Shakespeare Festival, 1974; *Yentl, the Yeshiva Boy*, Chelsea Theatre Center, New York, 1974; *Polly*, Chelsea Theatre Center, New York, 1975; *The Boss*, Chelsea Theatre Center, New York, 1976; *Rebel Women*, New York Shakespeare Festival, 1976; *The Misanthrope*, New York Shakespeare Festival, 1977; *The Creditors*, Public Theatre, New York, 1977; *The Stronger*, Public Theatre, New York, 1977; *Happy End*, Martin Beck Theatre, New York, 1977; *Old Man Joseph and His Family*, Chelsea Westside Theatre, New York, 1978; *Fearless*

Carrie Robbins: Costume designs for Leonard Bernstein's *Mass*, 1989

Frank, Princess Theatre, New York, 1980; *Frankenstein*, Palace Theatre, New York, 1981; *El Bravo*, Entermedia Theatre, New York, 1981; *The First*, Martin Beck Theatre, New York 1981; *Agnes of God*, Music Box Theatre, New York, 1983; *The Boys of Winter*, Biltmore Theatre, New York, 1985; *The Octette Bridge Club*, Music Box Theatre, New York, 1985; *Twelfth Night*, Alaska Repertory Theatre, Anchorage, 1986; *The Mass*, Boston Opera Company, 1989.

Publications:

By ROBBINS: articles—in *Theatre Crafts*(New York), September 1967, January/February 1974, November/December 1977, January 1981.

On ROBBINS: books—*Encyclopedia of Collectibles*, Alexandria, Virginia 1980; *Fabric Painting and Dyeing for the Theatre* by Deborah Dryden, New York 1981; *Costume Design* by Barbara and Cletus Anderson, New York 1983; articles—in *Theatre Design and Technology*(New York), Winter 1987; *Manhattan Inc.*(New York), December 1987; *New York Magazine*, 8 February 1988; *GQ*(New York), March 1988; *Theatre Crafts*(New York), November 1988.

*   *   *

Carrie Robbins' distinctive style results directly from her rich and obsessive personal vision of period and modern costumes in all their complexity and detail. In *Who's Who in The Theatre* under the heading of recreation, she lists "fighting insomnia and workaholism," and these personal characteristics become very significant in helping to explain her distinctive personal style. She admits to being obsessed with visions of the complex parts and details of her costumes when she is designing a production and often sketches ideas and costume details in the middle of the night. The results on stage are rich and overpowering in their visual complexity. For a production of *The Little Foxes* for the American Conservatory Theatre of San Francisco, Robbins created wonderfully rich and detailed costumes in which as much time and thought had been placed on the subtle heading on Regina Giddon's gowns as upon the individual costume silhouettes. For the San Francisco Opera's *Samson et Dalila*, she evoked an overpoweringly sumptuous Mesopotamian world that reminded one of the great de Mille Biblical epics or Griffith's *Intolerance*. To create these complex visual worlds on stage, Robbins calls upon the costume technicians who work on her productions to use every technique of construction, decoration, and texturing in present use, as well as to experiment with many new techniques.

Unlike some costume designers for whom the costume sketch is a mere suggestion or initial plan for costume shop construction, Robbins' sketches are masterpieces of rich complexity in color, line, and texture, with full attention to all costume detail. In an age when the impressionistic simplicity of a Gordon Craig or a Robert Edmond Jones is no longer in vogue and there is a fond nostalgia for the rich complexities of the Victorian Age, Robbins' richly complex style is most appealing to opera and theatre audiences throughout the major theatres in the United States. She takes her inspiration for sketching techniques from the graphic artists and painters of the later nineteenth century—people such as Gustave Moreau, Edward Burne-Jones, Dante Gabriel Rosetti, and Gustave Doré. But her rich, personal style is in every way an expression and fulfillment of her individual vision.

—Douglas A. Russell

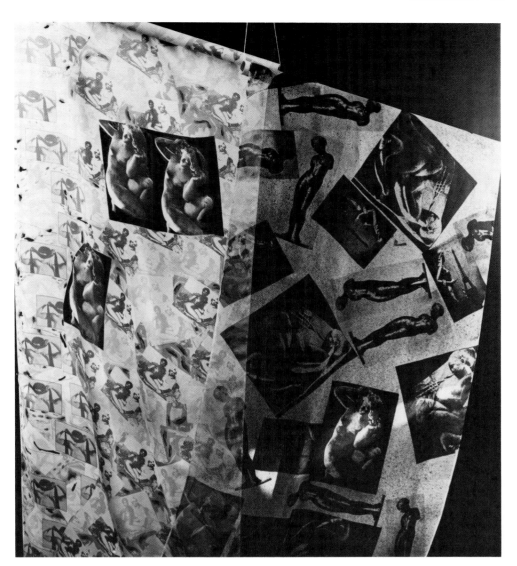

M. Clark Robertson: *Twin Borders* and *Hellenistic Models* printed fabrics, 1983

ROBERTSON, M(alcolm) Clark.
American textile and furniture designer. Born in Texas, 17 September 1955. Studied at Texas Christian University, Fort Worth, 1974–76; textile and interior design, at the University of Kansas, Lawrence, 1976–79: BFA 1979; Kansas City Art Institute, Missouri, 1979. Worked as a textile colorist, at Brewster Finishing and Design, New York, 1979; design consultant, China Seas Incorporated, New York, 1980–82; freelance textile and home furnishings designer, New York, from 1983. Teaching assistant, Navosota High School, Texas, 1974, and University of Kansas, Lawrence, 1979; guest lecturer at the Fashion Institute of Technology, New York, 1982–83, Rhode Island School of Design, Providence, 1983, Cooper-Hewitt Museum, New York, 1983; instructor in textile design, Parsons School of Design, New York from 1983. **Exhibitions:** Handcrafters Gallery, Fort Worth, Texas, 1976; Kerby Gallery, Austin, Texas, 1976; World Trade Center, Dallas, 1976; Brilezyay Gallery, Omaha, 1977; Pacific Basin School of Textile Arts, Berkeley, 1979; China Seas Showroom, New York, 1981; World Trade Center, New York, 1982; Ophelia Gallery, Miami, 1982; Roscoe Resource Council, New York, 1982; *Contemporary Continuous Pattern Design*, Cooper-Hewitt Museum, New York, 1983; *Textiles for the Eighties*, Rhode Island School of Design, Providence, 1984. **Collection:** Cooper-Hewitt Museum,

New York. Address: 474 Broadway, 2nd floor, New York, New York 10013, U.S.A.

Publications:

On ROBERTSON: book—*Textiles for the Eighties*. exhibition catalogue with texts by Sheila Hicks and Maria Tulokas, Providence 1984.

*   *   *

The textile designer M. Clark Robertson applies pigment to cashmere and silk alike through a combination of processes which include hand-painting, photo-silkscreening, and resist techniques. The results are alluring pastiches of socially poignant imagery on fabric.

His textiles are not created solely for ornamentation, for although they are undoubtedly decorative, they are much more. Robertson's designs contain elements of dissonance and sarcasm. Whether considering Viet Nam, androgyny, or the haunting possibility of suicide, a curious sense of lightheartedly delivered unrest pervades his work.

Twin Borders, a piece of silk chameuse, which appeared in the 1983 exhibit *Contemporary Continuous Pattern* at the Cooper-Hewitt Museum, contains scattered, floating images of contemporary as well as historical figures—male, female, solitary, coupled, black, and white. In this, as in much of his work, color and texture act as a sugarcoating, to camouflage some very serious questions Robertson raises about racism, sexuality, and the human condition.

Robertson does not confine himself solely to textile design, however. He designs tables that are stylistically considered contemporary Pop and that resemble pieces of Lego. He works with marble, glass, and formica, modeling his pieces after anything but the conventional table—the ancient Chinese clog and inverted table being just two examples.

His most recent endeavors extend to the arena of fine art, where his approach is much like that of his textile designs, but he transfers his work to canvas as a way of asking whether his work will hold up in yet one more medium. Will his message read the same when stretched on canvas, mounted on the wall as a painting?

Regardless of his medium, Robertson's sensitivity to color and texture and his dedication to incorporating meaning into the work he produces remain constant. Eschewing formalism, he produces work that is chaotic, unsettling, and laden with questions. His designs challenge tradition by asking, why can't an object do more than serve its immediate function? Can an object be esthetically pleasing and conceptually challenging at the same time?

While Robertson's work in part denies convention, his expressions of discontent and confusion are skillfully couched in finely blended colors and sensuous surfaces, making both his inquiries and his assertions extremely palatable.

—Dierdre Kerr

T. H. Robsjohn-Gibbings: Armchair, for Widdicomb Furniture, 1948

ROBSJOHN-GIBBINGS, Terrence Harold.

American furniture and interior designer. Born in London, England, in 1905; emigrated to the United States in 1930: naturalized, 1945. Apprenticed as an architectural draughtsman, London, then studied architecture, at the University of Liverpool, and London University: BS. Head designer, at Ashby Tad Limited, London, 1925–26; art director, British International Pictures film company, Elstree, Essex, 1927; worked for Charles Duveen (Charles of London) antiques and furniture firm, London, 1928–29, and in New York, 1930–35; established Robsjohn-Gibbings Limited interior design firm, New York, 1936–64: sole designer, for Widdicombe Furniture, Grand Rapids, Michigan, 1943–56, and for Saridas company, Athens, from 1960. **Exhibitions:** Sotheby Parke-Bernet, New York, 1980, 1981; *High Style: 20th Century American Design*, Whitney Museum, New York, 1985. Recipient: Waters Award, New York, 1950; Elsie de Wolfe Award, New York, 1962. *Died* (in Athens, Greece) *20 October 1976.*

Works:

Console table in carved gilt-wood and nickel-plate steel, for Peterson Studios, 1937.
Armchairs in carved oak with loose seat cushions, for Peterson Studios, 1937.
Dining-table in French walnut, for Schmieg-Hungate and Kotzean, 1937.
Large stool in walnut with splayed supports and loose cushion, for Peterson Studios, 1937.
Upholstered sofa in carved Canadian birch, for Peterson Studios, 1937.

Palm-tree pedestal end table in harewood and American walnut, for Peterson Studios, 1937.
Writing table in bleached oak, for Peterson Studios, 1937.
Side chair in wood and leather, for Tifal Limited, 1939.
Wall-backed settee with butterfly table, for Widdicombe Furniture, 1948.
Sectional upholstered sofa, for Widdicombe Furniture, 1949.
Coffee table in walnut and brass with glass top, for Widdicombe Furniture, 1950.
Bathroom of 1960, for *Look* magazine, New York, 1951.

Publications:

By ROBSJOHN-GIBBINGS: books—*Furniture Today*, New York n.d.; *Goodbye Mr. Chippendale*, New York 1944; *Mona Lisa's Mustache: A Dissection of Modern Art*, New York 1947; *Homes of the Brave*, New York 1954; *Furniture of Classical Greece*, with C. W. Pullin, New York 1963.
On ROBSJOHN-GIBBINGS: books—*Neo-Classical Art Moderne Furniture Designed by T. H. Robsjohn-Gibbings*, catalogue, New York 1980; *Architecture and Interior Design* by Victoria Kloss Ball, New York 1980; *Mid-Century: Furniture of the 1950s* by Cara Greenberg, London 1984; *High Style: 20th Century American Design*, exhibition catalogue by David Gebhard, Esther McCoy and others, New York 1985; *The American Design Adventure 1940–1975* by Arthur J. Pulos, London and Cambridge, Massachusetts 1988.

There is a tendency among contemporary critics to spurn reproduction of period furniture, but without the work of T.H. Robsjohn-Gibbings, we could not know the power of the furniture of ancient Greece. Styles as unlike as art nouveau and English neoclassic have incorporated, sometimes consciously, more often self-consciously, the dramatic arc of the shoulder-high cresting rail that characterizes the distinctive Greek chair form, the klismos. Designers as disparate as Thomas Hope in early nineteenth-century England and Ole Wanscher in mid-twentieth-century Denmark have executed ponderous (as in the case of Hope) or sensitive (Wanscher) adaptations of the Greek model. Before Robsjohn-Gibbings completed his project, however, time had assured that our only practical contact with the source would be through its interpretations.

Those who have been privileged to see pieces from this collection have been witness to more than impeccable scholarship. Robsjohn-Gibbings' reproductions—so finely executed as to qualify as recreations—have an immediate emotional and esthetic impact, which can be summed up only by the word "presence." One is struck first of all by the unexpectedly large scale. (Robsjohn-Gibbings extrapolated the measurements from vase drawings and existing fragments; his accuracy was proven when a re-created klini, or chaise with a klismoid back, fit exactly into the impressions left by a similar, original couch at the Sanctuary of Artemis, near Athens.) The next impression is of awe at the daring of those ancient artisans whose chairs defied the natural grain and strength of wood as they balanced on the sweeping curves of the out-thrust legs. The diphroi, or stools, exhibit less structural hubris; but with the chairs and the rectangular, three-legged tables, or trapezai, they seem, like genius, to have sprung mature from the brow of Zeus. Each object is characterized by a unity so complete that it could be thought to serve as the Platonic ideal for its genre.

Excellent though they are, Robsjohn-Gibbings' own designs now appear dated. Although one appreciates them intellectually as among the best of their type, that type no longer holds general appeal. But in his patient re-creation of the furnishings used four to six hundred years before Christ, Robsjohn-Gibbings established his reputation and made an unequalled contribution to design.

—Reed Benhamou

ROCH, Ernst.

Canadian graphic and environmental designer. Born, of Austrian parents, in Osijek, Yugoslavia, 8 December 1928; emigrated to Canada in 1953: naturalized, 1973. Educated in Osijek, 1935–44, and in Graz, 1944–48 studied graphic design under Hans Wagula and Rudolf Szyszkowitz, at the Meisterschule fur Angewandte Kunst, Graz, 1948–53. Married Helene Salchenegger in 1952(divorced, 1977); children: Ursula, Uli and Barbara. Designer with Rapid Grip and Batten, Montreal, 1953–54, and with Y and M Studio, Montreal, 1954–59; design director, James Valkus office, Montreal, 1960; founder-principal of Roch Design, Montreal, 1960–65, Design Collaborative, Montreal, 1965–77, and of Roch Design, Montreal, from 1977; also founder of Signum Press, Montreal, from 1973. Member of the Postage Stamp Design Advisory Committee, Canadian Post Office, Ottawa, 1975–80; advisory board member, International Institute for Information Design, Vienna, 1988. Lecturer, School of the Museum of Fine Arts, Montreal, 1956–58; guest lecturer, Sir George Williams(Concordia) University, Montreal, McGill University, Montreal, and Nova Scotia College of Art and Design, Halifax, 1967–77; visiting lecturer, Ohio State University, Columbus, 1980. **Exhibitions:** Goethe Institut, Montreal, 1963, 1977; Goethe Institut, Toronto, 1964; Museum of Fine Arts, Montreal, 1970; Museum of Fine Art, Belgrade, 1973; Museum of Art and Design, Zagreb, 1973; Landesmuseum, Oldenburg, 1974; Hochschule fur Bildende Kunste, Braunschweig, 1974; National Library, Ottawa, 1977(toured). **Collections:** National Library, Ottawa; Museum of Modern Art, New York; Library of Congress, Washington, D.C.; National Poster Museum, Warsaw. Recipient: numerous awards from the American Institute of Graphic Arts, Lahti Poster Biennale, Leipzig Book Fair, Brno Graphic Biennale, and Warsaw Poster Biennale. DFA: Nova Scotia College of Art and Design, 1988. Address: P. O. Box 1056, Station B, Montreal, Quebec H3B 3K5, Canada.

Works:

Queen Elizabeth II set of 5 postage stamps, for the Government of Canada, 1962.
Trademark and visual identity program, for Standard Desk Limited, 1962–66.
Trademark and visual identity program, for Kruger Pulp and Paper Company, 1963–64.

Symbol and visual identity program, for William S. Merrell Company, 1963–64.
Symbol and visual identity program, for the New Brunswick Telephone Company, 1964–66.
Symbol, signage and visual identity program, for the National Arts Center, Ottawa, 1965–68.
Sir Oliver Mowat commemorative postage stamp, for the Government of Canada, 1967.
Visual identity program, for Imasco Limited, from 1970.
The Visual Image of the Munich Olympic Games exhibition layouts, for the Museum of Fine Arts, Montreal, and the Art Gallery of Ontario, Toronto, 1972.
Canadian passport and citizenship certificate, for the Government of Canada, 1974(project).
Official poster of the 1976 Montreal Olympic Games, for the Organizing Committee of the Olympic Games, 1974.
Quebec Canada poster and annual report, for Imasco Limited, 1979.
Symbol and visual identity progam, for the Federal Business Development Bank of Montreal, 1980–82.
AGI Posters exhibition layouts, for the Alliance Graphique Internationale, in Montreal, 1982.
Early Canadian Locomotives set of 16 commemorative postage stamps, for the Canada Post Corporation, 1983–86.
Paper Zoo paper folding kit, produced by Signum Press, 1974, and the Museum of Modern Art, New York, 1976–87.
Arts of the Eskimo: Prints book design, for Signum Press/Oxford University Press/Barre Publishing Company, 1974.
Canadian Mushrooms set of 4 commemorative postage stamps, for the Canada Post Corporation, 1989.

Publications:

By ROCH: books edited—*Farmer's Year*, Montreal 1973; *Arts of the Eskimo: Prints*, Montreal 1974; *Paper Zoo*, booklet, Montreal 1974.
On ROCH: books—*Who's Who in Graphic Art*, edited by Walter Amstutz, Zurich 1962, Dubendorf 1982; *Trademarks and Symbols of the World* by Yusaku Kamekura, Tokyo and New York 1965; *Signet, Signal, Symbol* by Walter Diethelm, Zurich 1970; *107 Grafici dell'AGI*, with texts by Renzo Zorzi and Franco Grignani, Venice 1974, Toronto 1975; *Graphic Design by Rolf Harder and Ernst Roch* by Allan Harrison and Hans Neuburg, Montreal 1977.

Design is a function of man's intelligence, and of his need to control his environment. The designer actively contributes to the shaping of the human environment in an attempt to make people's lives more agreeable, harmonious, and enjoyable.

The designer's task is not to decorate or beautify; neither is it self-expression, as in the case of the "fine artist." Although imagination and the mastery of form and colour are indeed crucial to him, the designer is above all a realist who is able to penetrate to the essence of a given problem, devise solutions, and give form to these solutions. He is bound by a sense of social responsibility to make our increasingly complex world more intelligible to human beings.

It is the business of the designer to enrich and enhance human life by promoting communication between man and his environment.

—Ernst Roch

Ernst Roch is recognized as a pioneer of Canadian "international" or "new" graphic design,

Ernst Roch: *Paper Zoo* paper-folding kit, for Signum Press, 1974

with its emphasis on rational thinking and formal clarity. This functionalist approach, a product of his Austrian training, which he adapted and applied to the Canadian situation, has retained its elan and humanistic integrity through three decades of work in this country. With wit and sensitivity, Roch has helped shape the visual environment of his adopted homeland by producing a number of influential and memorable designs for government and industry. From symbols and postage stamps to books and posters, his clean, incisive style has left its mark.

Roch's work begins with a thorough and many-faceted investigation of the client's requirements. His designs, which are always based on a painstaking and systematic analysis, are planned and rendered with imagination and a joyful sense of experimentation. This disciplined, methodical approach produces work of enduring symbolic power, Though immediate, accurate communication is his prime concern, the work evinces a purity and universality approaching the timeless. Through the conscientious organization of form, striking aesthetic values emerge in Roch's award-winning designs, the purpose, of which, according to one writer, is "to say the most with the least."

—Anne McLean

ROSSELLI, Alberto.
Italian architect, product and industrial designer. Born in Palermo, Sicily, 21 June 1921. Studied engineering, 1938–39, and architecture, 1945–47, at the Politecnico, Milan: Dip.Arch. 1947. Freelance designer, Milan, 1950–76: partner, with Gio Ponti and Antonio Fornaroli, in the Ponti-Fornaroli-Rosselli architectural and design studio, Milan, 1952–76; design consultant to Arflex, Saponiti, and Fiat-Orlandi. Founder-director, *Stile Industria* magazine, Milan, 1953–63; also contributor to *Design, Domus,* and *Architecture d'Aujourd'hui,* from 1952. Professor of industrial design, at the Politecnico, Milan, 1963–76. Founder-member and president, 1956, and council member, 1967–68, of the ADI Associazione Disegno Industriale, Milan; vice-president, ICSID International Council of Societies of Industrial Design, 1961–63. **Exhibitions:** *Modern Chairs,* Whitechapel Art Gallery, London, 1970; *Italy: The New Domestic Landscape,* Museum of Modern Art, New York, 1972; *28/78 Architettura,* Palazzo delle Stelline, Milan, 1979; *Design Since 1945,* Philadelphia Museum of Art, 1983. **Collection:** Philadelphia Museum of Art. Recipient: Gold Medals, Milan Triennale, 1954, 1957, 1960; Compasso d'Oro Award, Milan, 1957. *Died (in Milan) in 1976.*

Works:

Desk with tubular steel frame and glass top, for Vis, 1950.
Desk in moulded wood laminate with glass top, for RIV, 1953.
Chair in laminated bentwood with moulded plywood seat and back, for Cassina, 1954.
Cupboards in laminated wood, for Lips Vago, 1960.
Corriere della Sera office building, Milan, 1960–65.

Brasilia coffee machine, for Pavone, 1962.
Associazione Industriale Lombardi headquarters building, Milan, 1963–64.
Tables and trolleys in ABS plastic, for Kartell, 1968.
Jumbo furniture range in plastic, for Saponiti, 1970.
Pullman car interiors, for the Dutch Railways, 1970.
Modular container furniture in plastic with castors, for Kartell, 1972.
Mobile House, for Carrozzerie Boneschi-Orlandi, 1972.
Open-space office systems, for Facomet, 1973.
Pack 1 collapsible chair in polyfoam with dacron and sailcloth upholstery, for Bonacina, 1975.

Publications:

By ROSSELLI: books—*Los Spazio Aperto: Ricerca e Progettazione tra Design e Architettura,* Milan 1974; *Alberto Rosselli: Stile Industria,* edited by Giovanni Klaus Koenig, Parma 1981. On ROSSELLI: books—*Mobili Tipo* by Robert Aloi, Milan 1956; *Mercati e Negozi* by Robert Aloi, Milan 1959; *Il Disegno Industriale e la sua Estetica* by Gillo Dorfles, Bologna 1963; *Design Italiano: I Mobili,* edited by Enrichetta Ritter, Milan and Rome 1968; *Modern Chairs 1918-1970,* exhibition catalogue with texts by Carol Hogben and others, London 1970; *Il Design in Italia 1945-1972* by Paolo Fossati, Turin 1972; *Italy: The New Domestic Landscape,* edited by Emilio Ambasz, New York and Florence 1972; *History of Modern Furniture* by Karl Mang, Stuttgart 1978, London 1979; *Atlante del Design Italiano 1940/1980* by Alfonso Grassi and Anty Pansera, Milan 1980; *Contemporary Furniture,* edited by Klaus-Jurgen Sembach, Stuttgart and London 1982; *Design Since 1945,* edited by Kathryn Hiesinger and George Marcus, Philadelphia and London 1983; *The Hot House: Italian New Wave Design* by Andrea Branzi, London 1984; *Italian Design: 1870 to the Present* by Penny Sparke, London and New York 1988.

ROTH, Ann.
American stage and film costume designer. Educated at Carnegie-Mellon University, Pittsburgh. Freelance stage costume designer from 1958, and film costume designer from 1964: has worked in New York for the Playhouse Theatre, Circle in the Square, Entermedia Theatre, Helen Hayes Theatre, Majestic Theatre, Imperial Theatre, John Golden Theatre, Music Box Theatre, etc. Recipient: British Academy Award, 1976. Address: c/o United Scenic Artists Union, local 829, AFL-CIO, 575 Eighth Avenue, New York 10018, U.S.A.

Works:

Stage productions(New York, unless noted) include—*Maybe Tuesday,* 1958; *Edward II,* 1958; *Make a Million,* 1958; *The Disenchanted,* 1958; *A Desert Incident,* 1959; *The Cool World,* 1960; *Gay Divorce,* 1960; *Ernest in Love,* 1960; *Face of a Hero,* 1960; *A Far Country,* 1961; *Purlie Victorious,* 1961; *Look: We've Come Through,* 1961; *We Comrades Three* (sets only), 1962; *This Side of Paradise,*

1962; *Isle of Children,* 1962; *Venus at Large,* 1962; *A Portrait of the Artist as a Young Man,* 1962; *The Barroom Monks,* 1962; *Natural Affection,* 1963; *Hey You, Light Man!,* 1963; *Children from Their Games,* 1963; *A Case of Libel,* 1963; *In the Summer House,* 1964; *The Last Analysis,* 1964; *Slow Dance on a Killing Ground,* 1964; *I Had a Ball,* 1964; *The Odd Couple,* 1965; *Romeo and Juliet,* 1965; *The Impossible Years,* 1965; *The Wayward Stork,* 1966; *The Star-Spangled Girl,* 1966; *The Deer Park,* 1967; *The Beard,* 1967; *Something Different,* 1967; *Happiness Is Just a Little Thing Called a Rolls Royce,* 1968; *Play It Again, Sam,* 1969; *My Daughter, Your Son,* 1969; *Tiny Alice,* 1969; *The Three Sisters,* 1969; *Gantry,* 1970; *Purlie,* 1970; *What the Butler Saw,* 1970; *The Engagement Baby,* 1970; *Father's Day,* 1971; *Prettybelle* (Boston), 1971; *Fun City,* 1972; *Rosebloom,* 1972; *Twelfth Night,* 1972; *Children! Children!,* 1972; *6 Rms Riv Vu,* 1972; *Enemies,* 1972; *Purlie,* (revival), 1972; *The Merchant of Venice,* 1973; *Seesaw,* 1973; *The Women,* 1973; *The Royal Family,* 1975; *The Heiress,* 1976; *The Importance of Being Earnest,* 1977; *Do You Turn Somersaults?,* 1978; *The Best Little Whorehouse in Texas* 1978; *The Crucifer of Blood,* 1978; *First Monday in October,* 1978; *They're Playing Our Song,* 1979; *Strangers,* 1979; *Lunch Hour,* 1980; *Gardenia,* 1982; *Kaufman at Large,* 1982; *Present Laughter,* 1982; *The Misanthrope,* 1983; *Yankee Wives,* Old Globe Theatre, San Diego, 1983; *Open Admissions,* 1984; *Hurlyburly,* Goodman Theatre, Chicago, 1984; *Design for Living,* 1984; *Biloxi Blues,* Ahmanson Theatre, Los Angeles, 1984; *Arms and the Man,* 1985; *Juno's Swans,* 1985; film productions include—*The World of Henry Orient*(G.R. Hill), 1964; *A Fine Madness*(Kershner), 1966; *Up the Down Staircase*(Mulligan), 1966; *Pretty Poison*(Black), 1968; *Sweet November*(R. Miller), 1968; *Midnight Cowboy*(Schlesinger), *The Owl and the Pussycat*(Ross), 1970; *The People Next Door*(Greene), 1970; *Klute*(Pakula), 1971; *The Pursuit of Happiness*(Mulligan), 1971; *They Might Be Giants*(Harvey), 1971; *The Valachi Papers*(Young), 1972 *Day of the Locust*(Schlesinger), 1975; *Murder By Death*(Moore), 1976; *California Suite*(Ross), 1978; *Hair*(Forman), 1979; *The Island*(Ritchie), 1980; *Honky Tonk Freeway*(Schlesinger), 1981; *Only When I Laugh*(G. Jordan), 1981; *Rollover*(Pakula), 1981; *The World According to Garp*(G.R. Hill), 1982.

Publications:

On ROTH: book—*Contemporary Theatre, Film and Television 4,* Detroit and London 1987; article—in the *Herald-Examiner*(Los Angeles), 7 February 1974.

Ann Roth was associated with a group of brilliant, Carnegie-Mellon University students, who were fascinated by the richness, elegance, and style to be found in certain classic and modern plays. In working with this group (two of whom, William Ball and Ellis Rabb, have become major figures in preserving this tradition in their own productions), Roth also developed a taste for elegant theatricality. She has been little interested in the theatre of rags and distressed clothing and has usually been associated with productions that placed an emphasis on elegance and sophistication.

Even her Shakespearean productions have been noted for their elegant sophistication, rather than for weight, painted texture, or larger-than-life formality. For example, when she designed the costumes for Rabb's production of *The Merchant of Venice* in modern dress, the emphasis was on Via Veneto elegance and sophisticated charm, and the same gentle worldliness was apparent in her designs for *Twelfth Night*. Similar precepts guided her designs for the revivals of *The Heiress* and *The Importance of Being Earnest*. Even in such a famous musical as *The Best Little Whorehouse in Texas*, which dealt with the nether side of society, the costumes for the brothel girls came across with their own flashy elegance. Much the same is true for her best-remembered films. There was a kind of sleazy grace to *Midnight Cowboy* and a west-coast chic in *California Suite*.

Thus, her inspiration comes from elegant designers of the past, such as Rex Whistler, Adrian, Cecil Beaton, and Edith Head rather than from the Brechtian designers who have proliferated in the past two decades. Roth's costumes enhance the characters in a play or film so that an audience sees what normally might be mundane or even ugly with certain patina of glamour.

—Douglas A. Russell

ROWLANDS, Martyn (Omar).

British industrial designer. Born in Penarth, Glamorgan, Wales, 27 July 1923. Educated at Eltham College, London, 1931–40; studied at the Central School of Arts and Crafts, London, 1946–49. Served as an engine fitter in the Royal Air Force, in India and Burma, 1941–46. Married Ann Patricia Black in 1951(died, 1974); children: Ceinwen, Glyn and Dylan; remarried in 1978(divorced, 1986). Designer, for Bakelite plastics company, London, 1950–54; head of design, Ekco Plastics, Southend-on-Sea, Essex, 1954–59; founder-director of MRDC Martyn Rowlands Design Consultants, London and Essex, from 1959: has designed for Rantan and Company, Standard Telephones and Cables, Thermos, British Airways, Boots Company, IMI/Opella, Fisons Pharmaceuticals, etc. President, Society of Industrial Artists and Designers, London, 1974–75. **Collection:** Victoria and Albert Museum, London. Recipient: Design Council Award, London, 1958, 1961, 1966, 1969, 1971. Fellow, Chartered Society of Designers, London, 1960; Plastics and Rubber Institute, London, 1973. Address: Parndon Mill, Harlow, Essex CM20 2HP, England.

Works:

Moulded baby bath and stand, for Ekco Plastics, 1957.
Moulded watering can in nestable parts, for Ekco Plastics, 1958.
Chemical toilet in high-density polythene, for Ekco Plastics, 1960.
Children's tablewares in melamine, for Rantan and Company, 1960.
Trimphone and *Deltaline* lightweight telephones, for STC Standard Telephones and Cables, 1964.
Intal drug inhaler, for Fisons Pharmaceuticals, 1967.
500 Series domestic water taps in moulded plastic, for IMI/Opella, 1969.
Boots Preview Screen in plastic, for The Boots Company, 1970.
Airline meals servicewares in disposable plastics, for British European Airways, 1972.
Thermos vacuum flask jug in plastic, for Thermos, 1973.

Nursery products range in polypropylene, for The Boots Company, 1979.
Kitchen mixer tap monobloc in moulded plastics, for IMI/Opella, 1980.

Publications:

By ROWLANDS: articles—in *The Designer*(London), September 1971. November 1975, May 1979; *Plastics Today*(London), May 1976.
On ROWLANDS: books—*The Business of Product Design* by James Pilditch and Douglas Scott, London 1965; *All Things Bright and Beautiful: Design in Britain, 1830 to Today* by Fiona MacCarthy, London 1972; *Les Annees 60* by Anne Bony, Paris 1983.

I feel one can only design well if one fully understands the materials and the manufacturing techniques to be used in the product you are designing. I have specialised in design for the plastics industry, and the technology for this industry is developing very fast and provides exciting design opportunities to completely rethink the product. My views are perhaps best illustrated by part of an article in the ICI house journal *Plastics Today*, and I quote from this:

First and foremost, the designer must know and understand exactly why he is undertaking a particular design brief. This is, indeed, one of his most important activities before even beginning to consider visual concepts. A remarkably wide range of influences affect industrial design, and that is especially so where plastics are concerned due to the interrelation between designer, toolmaker, processor and, frequently, the assembler of component parts. For example, when considering a design for the first time, one must analyse its function and decide what material or materials should be used to make it. If it is to be a redesign of an existing article, either as a simple substitute or as an improvement, one naturally considers carefully what materials were used before and why, and whether the use of new material is relevant and what the implications of such a change will be. Today that new material is likely to be one of the wide range of plastics. But caution is necessary. Many of the past failures of products made from plastics can be attributed to a simple desire to make them in plastics—whether the material is suitable for the job or not. Nor does the problem end with manufacture; it continues into use in service and, probably, some kind of maintenance during the life of the product. These latter considerations may be termed the "system" in which the product is used, and it is just as important to study that system as it is to consider the design of the product itself.

If one is designing a product intended to be disposable—say, cutlery for use in a cafeteria—it is obviously important to understand why such a product is wanted in the first place. Probably, the principal reason put forward is that it is uneconomic to have people doing the washing-up, or there may have been problems of loss of valuable cutlery and inexpensive substitutes are required. Note that here the system of usage is to be changed: items are to be used once only. Hence the problem that arises is one of disposal of a quantity of plastics material—either by destruction or by recycling in a sane and sensible manner. As an aside, it may be mentioned that one must make sure that the

Martyn Rowlands: Monobloc kitchen water tap, for IMI Opella, 1988

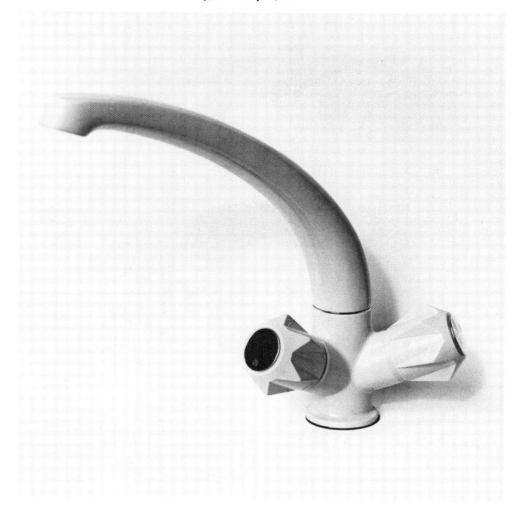

system is changed in practice; otherwise, there will be accusations of inadequate design should the product be used in the old manner.

Almost every design product has influences on it other than simple aesthetics of the product itself. There are hosts of reasons for the designer to make a critical analysis of the product—from whether it gives "value for money", is "safe" to use and is ergonomically satisfactory, to its visual attractiveness and its sales appeal. While not wishing to play down these important matters, I feel it is worthwhile to isolate one other that is particularly important in any discussion on design in plastics. It is what in the past may have been described as "validity of the craftsmanship": having decided to use a material—in the present instance, plastics—are the forms chosen relevant to the material and to the process of manufacture? Most people would recognise these attributes in a piece of pottery, or carved wood, or even in blown glass. The touch of the hand and intellect can be seen—at first hand, as it were. The casual movement of the thumb that presses the soft clay form of a handle onto a jug is easy to appreciate. The precise, logical cutting of steel to make a mould for plastics that will later form millions of moulded products is not so easy to discern. It is there, for all that.

One cannot judge the success of a design on just one facet of its make-up. The overall success comes from a skilful blending of them all. Whilst it is important to appreciate these subtle factors, they would certainly be meaningless if the product did not work. Too much "craft" and no "art" is as bad as the other way round.

—Martyn Rowlands

In the 1940s, Martyn Rowlands studied in the first industrial design course at the Central School of Arts and Crafts in London and was attracted to the brand-new field of plastics. His first job was with Bakelite; after that, he headed the design department at Ekco Plastics. Subsequently, he founded his own firm.

Rowlands believes that the manufacturing process is the root of good design. While his career has seen many new polymers being invented, he has insisted on learning all the processes involved, and he will not design something which he does not know how to make himself. To him, the designer must have total control of a product, be able to prevent technicians from messing up his creation, and not be helpless where the quality of the final achievement is concerned. Thus, Rowlands is very much in the craft tradition, and his approach would have been applauded by William Morris, albeit that his materials and machinery are completely different. How interesting it is that one of the exponents of the new art of designing plastics should approach his work in the traditional manner.

His style is one of great simplicity, with few decorative flourishes. Plastic can be moulded into forms as ornate as anyone could wish, so it is not the medium which restricts Rowland's style; it is his own design philosophy, which contains a firm measure of functionalism. He admires the Bauhaus products, which have been an influence, to which he has added a belief in the honest simplicity of the good craftsman as applied to industrial processes.

—Diana de Marly

RUDER, Emil.

Swiss typographer, exhibition and graphic designer. Born in Zurich, 20 March 1914. Apprenticed as a type-compositor, Zurich, 1929–33; studied graphics, in Paris, 1938–39; lettering and book design under Alfred Willimann and Walter Kaech, at the Kunstgewerbeschule, Zurich, 1941–42. Married I. S. Schwartz in 1950; sons: Martin and Daniel. Freelance poster, book and typographic designer, in Basel, 1942–70: postage stamp design advisor to the Swiss Post Office, 1961. Instructor in typography, 1942–47, head of arts and crafts, 1947–65, and director, 1965–70, at the Allgemeine Gewerbeschule, Basel; director of the Kunstgewerbemuseum, Basel, 1965–70. Contributor to the periodicals *Schweizerische Lehrerzeitung, Typographische Monatsblätter, Werk, Form und Technik,* and *Der Druckspiegel.* Basel group chairman, 1948, central committee member, 1956, and vice-chairman, 1966, of the Schweizerischer Werkbund; Swiss regional delegate, ATYPI Association Typographique Internationale 1959; member of the Federal Commission for Fine Arts, Basel, 1961; founder-member, International Center for Typographic Arts, New York, 1962. **Exhibitions:** *Der Mensch und die Dinge,* Basel, 1955; *Die Gute Form,* Basel, 1956; *Typographie,* Kunstgewerbemuseum, Basel, 1960; *Schweizerische Landesausstellung* Lausanne, 1964. **Collection:** Kunstgewerbemuseum, Basel. *Died* (in Basel) *13 March 1970.*

Publications:

By RUDER: book—*Typographie,* Teufen 1967, New York 1981; articles—in *Typographische Monatsblätter*(St. Gallen), no.2, 1952, nos. 2

and 5, 1958, no. 4, 1959, no. 6, 1959, no. 1 1961; *Graphis*(Zurich), no. 85, 1959, no. 146, 1969; *Neue Graphik*(Zurich), no. 2, 1959.

On RUDER: books—*The New Graphic Design* by Karl Gerstner and Markus Kutter, Teufen and London 1959; *Who's Who in Graphic Art,* edited by Walter Amstutz, Zurich 1962; *Buchgestaltung* by Albert Kapr Dresden 1963; *The Art of Written Forms* by Donald M. Anderson, New York 1969; *Typography Today* by Helmut Schmid, Tokyo 1980.

Emil Ruder understood typography in the classical sense, as a serving art, as the shaping of given contents and meanings, as a means that finds completeness in its unobtrusiveness. As he put it, "*Es ist unser Beruf, der sprache Form zu geben, ihr dauer zu verleihen und sie in die Zukunft hinüberzuretten. Oft sind wir uns gar nicht bewusst, dass wir diese aufgabe nur mittels der Form bewältigen können.*" As teacher and, later, as director at the Gewerbeschule in Basel, Ruder's imprint on Swiss-style typography is fundamental to the apprentice of typography and, as contributor to the Swiss professional magazine *TM (Typografische Monatsblätter),* to the profession in general. Ruder's works are not monuments. Rather, they speak a clear, meditative form-language in which form and counterform, printed and unprinted each have their important parts in the message. One of his purest typographic works is a political poster, in which where the message is grouped and arranged in such a way that connected text-groups form rhythmical flow from top to bottom.

While his earlier period was dominated by a typography of order, his later period was ruled by organic and natural arrangement of texts.

Emil Ruder: *Typographie* book jacket, 1967

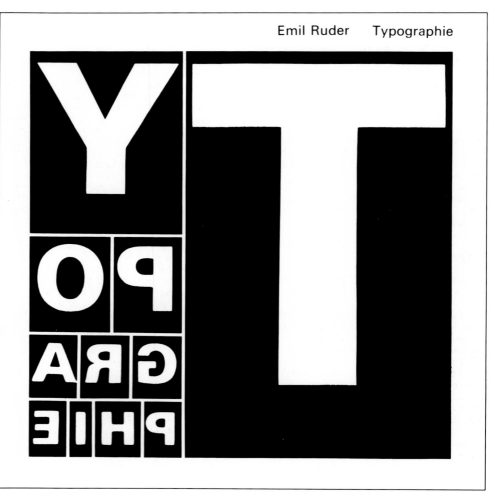

While the typography of order was the purification of the typography of the 1920s and early 1930s, his organic typography arose with the typeface Univers. In the Univers special issue of *TM* in 1961, Ruder reduced the text per page to a readable amount and created a typography of lightness and elegance, which made Swiss-Zürich-style typography look heavy and dated. Ruder's familiarity with Univers since its creation enabled him to bring out the beauty of proportion in the letters by the beauty of proportion in his typography.

Ruder was an ardent believer in the educative value of good typography and honestly styled everyday goods as contributions to the improvement of our environment. His lasting impetus to good typography is the design manual *Typographie*. Here, Ruder tells and shows us that the difference between good and anemic design is often just the difference of a small detail. Further, as he points out. "Contemporary typography is not based primarily on the flash of inspiration and striking idea. It is based on the grasp of the essential underlying laws of form on thinking in connected wholes, so that it avoids on the one hand turgid rigidity and monotony and on the other unmotivated arbitrary interpretation."

—Helmut Schmid

Cinzia Ruggeri: *Magathon* chair, 1987

RUGGERI, Cinzia.

Italian fashion and industrial designer. Born in Milan, 1 February 1945. Studied design, at the Accademia Arti Applicati, Milan, 1963-65. Freelance designer, Milan, from 1966. **Exhibitions:** Galleria del Prisma, Milan, 1963; Venice Biennale, 1981; *Italian Re-Evolution*, La Jolla Museum of Contemporary Art, California, 1982; *Per un Vestire Organico*, Palazzo Fortuny, Venice, 1983; *Italia: The Genius of Fashion*, Fashion Institute of Technology New York, 1985; *Dopo Gondrand: Cinzia Ruggeri/ Denis Santachiara*, Il Luogo di Corrado Levi, Milan, 1986; *Extra Vacanze di Cinzia Ruggeri*, Galleria Tucci Russo, Turin, 1986; *Internationale Mobel Messe*, Cologne, 1987; *Fashion and Surrealism*, Fashion Institute of Technology, New York, 1987(toured); *Pianeta Italia*, Kaufhof Stores, Cologne, 1988; *Salon del Mobile*, Milan, 1988. **Collection:** Museo della Moda, Parma. Recipient: Fil d'Or Award, Confederation Internationale du lin, 1981, 1982, 1983. Address: Via Crocefisso 21, 20122 Milan, Italy.

Publications:

By RUGGERI: article—in *Casa Vogue*(Milan), April 1980.

On RUGGERI: books—*Vestire Italiano* by Paola Amendola, Rome 1983; *The Hot House: Italian New Wave Design* by Andrea Branzi London 1984; *Il Genio Antipatico* by Pia Soli, Milan 1984; *La Materia dell'Invenzione* by Ezio Manzini, Milan 1986; *Fashion and Surrealism* by Richard Martin, New York and London 1987; *Pranzo alle 8* by Pia Soli, Milan 1988; *Fashion Illustrators of Europe* by Isao Yajima, Tokyo 1989.

Cinzia Ruggeri's work belongs to the recent tendency in Italian design towards "transdisciplinary" activity, in which designers of industrial products, fashion designers, scenic artists, and interior decorators exchange their experiences with each other and collaborate in the creation of new typologies of objects.

The artistic avant-gardes of the twentieth century have certainly been the decisive influence on this kind of attitude to design; the inspiration of Cinzia Ruggeri's frocks is, in fact, strictly abstract in character, with forms and patterns of geometrical types; cubism, futurism, constructivism, and the Bauhaus School are the historical precedents for this kind of work, And it is from the same avant-gardes that Ruggeri gets her interest in the "theatrical" appearance of fashion design; her frocks are often introduced in actual performances, with light and music playing essential parts.

Her interest in sophisticated techniques has led her to introduce directly into her models elements that react so as to change the look of the dress under the influence of light or temperature. She therefore makes great use of liquid crystals, which enable her to create from a single model a number of variants of colour and pattern with each change of temperature. In her own words, "The frock is a changeable and ephemeral entity; the same model worn by different people will give out different messages." This statement makes clear her anthropological view of fashion as connected with the problems of individual expression of whoever "is being dressed." In this sense, her professional practice influences (and is influenced by) the theories that go to make up the "neo-modern" ideologies of design, which see in makeup, in the decoration of objects as well as of buildings and of the body, the possibility of a recovery of formal qualities in design but also of a real quality of existence.

Her collaboration with Alessandro Mendini and the Studio Alchimia are part of this phenomenon, and in this, too, Ruggeri is an exception in the world of fashion stylists; while they are continually extending their activities into many different fields (furnishing, cars, etc.) she keeps her interest exclusively for the design of dresses but elaborates it with an element of high industrial technology and transforms it into something new, a machine/object/performance.

—Stefano Casciani

RUSSELL, (Sydney) Gordon.

British furniture designer. Born in Gricklewood, London, 20 May 1892. Educated in London and in Repton, Derbyshire, until 1904, and in Chipping Campden, Gloucestershire, 1904-07. Served in the British Army Worcester Regiment, 1914-19: Military Cross, 1918; also served as Special Police Officer, London, 1939-45. Married Constance Elizabeth Jane Vere(Toni) Denning in 1921; children: Michael, Robert, Kate and Olive. Worked as a purser on the *S.S. Veronese*, to the River Plate, 1908; furniture restorer and manager in his father's antique business, Broadway, Worcestershire, 1908-14; partner, in Russell and Sons furniture makers, Broadway, Worcestershire, 1919-46; also founder-director, 1926-66, and

Gordon Russell: Armchair with upholstered seat and back, 1928

chairman, 1967–77, of Gordon Russell Limited furniture makers, Chipping Campden, Gloucestershire; founder-director of Gordon Russell design studio, in Kingcombe, Gloucestershire, 1960–80. Assessor, 1938–53, and council member, 1961–68 National Council for Diplomas in Art and Design, London; chairman, Board of Trade Utility Furniture Design Panel, London, 1943–47; council member, Royal Society of Arts London, 1947–49 1951–55; director, 1947–59, and life member, 1960–80, Council of Industrial Design, London; arts panel member, Arts Council, of Great Britain, London, 1948–53; fine arts committee member, British Council, London, 1948–58; council member, Royal College of Art, London, 1948–51, 1952–63; executive committee member, Festival of Britain, London, 1951; design panel member, British Railways Board, London, 1956–66; president, Design and Industries Association, London, 1959–62; member of the Crafts Advisory Council, London, 1971–74.
Exhibitions: *Utility Furniture and Fashion 1941–1951,* Geffrye Museum, London, 1974; *Thirties: British Art and Design Before the War,* Hayward Gallery, London, 1979. Recipient: Gold and Silver Medals, *Exposition des Arts Decoratifs,* Paris, 1925; Society of Industrial Artists and Designers Medal, London 1959; Royal Society of Arts Medal, London, 1962.

Honorary doctorates: Birmingham University, 1960; University of York, 1969. Royal Designer for Industry, 1940, and Master of the Faculty, 1947–49, Royal Society of Arts, London; fellow, Society of Industrial Artists, London, 1945; honorary designer, Royal College of Art, London, 1952; honorary associate, Institute of Landscape Architects, London, 1955; fellow, Royal Institute of British Architects, 1965. Commander, Order of the British Empire, 1947; Knight Bachelor, Britain, 1955; Officer of the Order of the Vasa, Stockholm, 1954; Commander, Norwegian Royal Order of Saint Olav. Oslo, 1957. *Died* (in Chipping Campden, Gloucestershire) *7 October 1980.*

Publications:

By RUSSELL: books—*Furniture Making: 12 Cards for Wall Display,* London 1947; *Things We See: Furniture,* London 1947, 1953; *The Story of Furniture,* London 1947, 1967; *How to Buy Furniture,* London and Glasgow 1951; *How To Furnish Your Home,* with Alan Jarvis, London 1953; *Looking at Furniture,* London 1964; *Designer's Trade: Autobiography of Gordon Russell,* London 1968.

On RUSSELL: books—*Modern English Furni-* *ture* by J. C. Rogers, London and New York 1930; *A Survey of British Industrial Arts* by Henry G. Dowling, Benfleet 1935; *British Achievement in Design,* edited by Noel Carrington and Muriel Harris, London 1946; *British Furniture Today* by Erno Goldfinger, London 1951; *World Furniture,* edited by Helena Hayward, London 1965, 1981; *Utility Furniture and Fashion 1941–1951,* exhibition catalogue by Jeffrey Daniels and others, London 1974; *Industrial Design in Britain* by Noel Carrington, London 1976; *In Good Shape: Style in Industrial Products 1900–1960* by Stephen Bayley, London 1979; *Gordon Russell* by Ken and Kate Baynes, London 1981; *The Conran Directory of Design,* edited by Stephen Bayley, London 1985; *Eye for industry: Royal Designers For Industry 1936–1986,* exhibition catalogue by Fiona MacCarthy and Patrick Nuttgens, London 1986; *Twentieth Century Design: Furniture* by Penny Sparke, London 1986.

When Sidney Russell moved in 1904 from Derbyshire to Broadway Worcestershire to take over the Lygon Arms Hotel, he sent his boys to the grammar school at neighbouring Chipping Campden. It was not surprising that Gordon, the eldest, should there acquire an interest in craftsmanship because it was at Campden that C.R. Ashbee had set up his Guild of Craftworkers, which he had first formed in the East End of London and later persuaded to migrate (150 men, women, and children) to the Cotswolds to be closer to nature. On leaving school, Gordon was drafted into the workshop which his father had set up to repair antique furniture. It had been discovered that antiques were a profitable sideline to sell to the guests of the hotel, especially to the Americans who flocked to this attractive Cotswold village.

Came the First World War in which Russell served with distinction. In the trenches, before he was seriously wounded, he often dreamed of the furniture he would design if and when he returned. On demobilisation, he did return to find a warehouse full of old furniture only waiting to be repaired. However, once having set up a workshop for himself, he started designing what he felt was more appropriate for his own generation. He also found that the younger craftsmen were eager to work with him. But when his newly designed pieces were set alongside the antiques in the showroom window at Broadway, they met with derision, such was the craze then for "period style and reproductions". Gordon's reaction was to publish a booklet, "Honesty and the Crafts," in which he questioned the workship of things simply because they were old and claimed that the practice engendered an "army of swindlers faking what a deluded public demanded."

He found support in a body called "Design and Industries," itself a secession from the Arts and Crafts Movement but differing in that its members accepted machine-production. To Gordon, the machine was just a special tool, more powerful than a chisel or saw, but a tool the nature of which the designer must have constantly in mind. He never lost his respect for fine, individual craftsmanship, but his mission was to design for his own age. Not till 1929, ten years later, was he able to offer a dining room suite, planned for continuous production. Its reception gave him courage to open his showrooms in the West End of London where his work could be shown in company with the best contemporary textiles, pottery, or glass. Here his wife Toni, whom he married in 1921 proved an invaluable help.

In the early 1930s the great American slump caused a serious setback because trade with America had been an important factor in the firm's success. Fortunately, an unforseen chance, as he wrote, "shipwrecked us into health again." Frank Murphy, an ex-Post Office engineer, was making radio sets for the craze of the "wireless." He was dissatisfied with the cabinets then on offer from the trade, which had persuaded itself that this new invention must be disguised behind a mass of fretwork. Murphy, having seen some of Russell's furniture, approached him for a design.

For months, the radio engineers hammered out their problem with Russell and his younger architect-brother. Murphy found their cabinet logical and seemly as a solution, but when he offered it to a sales conference it was greeted as unsaleable and nicknamed by one wit as "Pentonville". However, Murphy stood by his convictions and the set became a public favourite. Its sale outstripped the capacity of the Broadway workshops, thereby necessitating installation of a separate factory in West London for its production. This model was only the first of a series for Murphy Radio.

Thenceforward, until World War II, Gordon Russell enterprises prospered. He was able to recruit a team of young designers, including several architects and, as buyer for the shops, Nicholas Pevsner, refugee from Nazism and later to be known as a brilliant scholar of European architecture. The war's shortage of timber meant difficulties at Russell's workshops, but in 1942, the Board of Trade asked Russell to field a team which could design and make the simplest furniture to replace that lost in bombed-out homes. The result, known as the Utility line, though hardly to the taste of the trade, was serviceable and soundly made. It remained in use for several years after the war and may have done much to wean the public from the reproduction vogue and to prepare the way for the revolutionary designs that appeared at the Festival of Britain in 1951.

Gordon Russell's role by this time became largely that of a public servant. As director of the Design Council, with its showrooms and changing exhibitions, he was able to influence all the trades producing durable consumer goods. One of the original Royal Designers for Industry, he was also honoured with knighthood. Nevertheless, he retained his habit of walking around daily to keep in touch personally with his staff, just as he had done with his workers at Broadway—a habit, as he used to tell me, he had formed in the trenches.

After leaving the Design Council post in 1959, he was still in demand as a consultant by the government for many years. On one such mission, he made an extended tour of India. There, he advised its new government on setting up an institution to maintain the vitality of crafts, for Russell still maintained his respect for handicrafts and secured them government support, too, in Britain. When he finally retired to the home he had built for himself at Campden, he was able to resume what had been his first love, working with his own hands, which he now devoted to masonry, garden design, and carving fine lettering in stone.

—Noel Carrington

RUUHINEN, Erkki (Antero).

Finnish advertising, graphic and typographic designer. Born in Toivakka, 3 September 1943. Studied graphic design, at the School for Advertising Design, Helsinki, 1964-66. Designer and art director in the agencies Mainosyhtyma Oy, 1966-68, SEK Advertising, 1968-75, and Anderson and Lembke Oy, 1975-85, in Helsinki; founder and managing director, Erkki Ruuhinen Design, Helsinki, since 1983: has designed for the Pohjole Insurance Group, Finnish Sugar Corporation, KOP Bank, Alko Finnish State Alcohol Company, etc. Chairman, Finnish Society of Graphic Artists, 1970-71. **Exhibitions:** *International Poster Exhibition*, London, 1967; *UNICEF Help the Children Posters*, Paris, 1969; *Typomundus 2*, Munich 1970; *International Poster Biennale*, Warsaw, 1970, 1972; *International Graphics Biennale*, Brno, 1970, 1974, 1978; *Filmexpo*, Ottawa, 1972; *Creativity Awards*, New York, 1978, 1979, 1980, 1982; *Erkki Ruuhinen: Graphics*, Lahti, 1979; *Clio Awards*, New York, 1979, 1981, 1983; *Calligraphy Today*, New York, 1980, 1981; *Posters of the Year*, Helsinki, 1982, 1983, 1984, 1985. **Collections:** Lahti Poster Museum, Finland; Stedelijk Museum, Amsterdam; International Poster Museum, Warsaw; Musee d'Affiche, Paris; Poster Museum of Musashino Art University, Tokyo. Recipient: Finnish State Award for Craftsmanship, 1969; Poster of the Year Award, Helsinki, 1971, 1972, 1973, 1976, 1978, 1981, 1982, 1983; Gold Medal, Rizzoli Advertising Competition, New York, 1972; Film Expo Award, Ottawa, 1972; Communication Arts Gold Medal, Palo Alto, 1978; New Clio First Awards, New York, 1979, 1980, 1982, 1983; Best of the Year Award, Helsinki, 1981, 1982, 1983, 1984, 1985; Type Directors Club Awards, New York, 1982, 1983, 1984, 1989; Special Platinum Award for Advertising and Graphic Design, Helsinki, 1986; Finnish State Prize for Applied Arts, 1989. Member: Finnish Society of Graphic Artists; Finnish Graphic Designers Association; Finnish Marketing Association; Type Directors Club, New York; International Center for Typographic Arts, New York; Society of Scribes, New York. Address: Juustilanpolku 7, 00150 Helsinki, Finland.

Works:

Film posters, for Jorn Donner Productions, 1967-88.
Annual reports, for IBM Finland, 1983-88.
Posters, for Kuopio Dance and Music Festival, 1984-85.
Posters, for Pori Jazz Festival, 1985-87.
Annual reports, for Enso-Gutzeit Oy, 1986-88.
Annual reports, for Valio Dairies, 1986-88.
Corporate identity program, for the Amos Anderson Art Gallery, Helsinki, 1987.
Corporate identity program, for the Helsinki Stock Exchange, 1987.
Corporate identity program, for Libris Printing Company, 1988.
Corporate identity program, for Heureka Finnish Science Center, 1988.
Corporate identity program, for Enso-Gutzeit forestry industry group, 1989.
Corporate identity program, for Ilmarinen Pension Insurance Company, 1989.
Corporate identity program, for Tampere Civic Center, 1989.
Corporate identity program, for Turve Insurance Company, 1989.

Publications:

By RUUHINEN: book—*Ruuhinen Design*, Helsinki 1987.
On RUUHINEN: books—*Who's Who in Graphic Art*, edited by Walter Amstutz, Dubendorf 1982; *Finnish Industrial Design*, edited by Tua Pontasuo, Helsinki 1987; articles—in *Graphis* (Zurich), *Graphis Photo* (Zurich), *Poster Publicity* (London), *Idea* (Tokyo), *Communication Arts* (Palo Alto), *Upper and Lower Case (New York)*, *Novum Gebrauchsgraphik* (Munich), etc.

Erkki Ruuhinen has been instrumental in developing modern Finnish graphic design. As well as running his own design studio, he works tirelessly to improve professional advertising standards in Finland by lecturing, writing articles and serving on professional bodies and award panels. Almost everywhere you look there are examples of his work—work that has achieved widespread domestic and international recognition. Recently he was elected the first Graphic Artist of the Year in Finland and was also awarded a state artist's prize for his contribution to the graphic arts. In addition, out of the 130 awards he has received, over half have been international. What is so remarkable for someone from such a small country is that these awards have come from all areas—posters, advertisement campaigns, corporate design programs, direct mail, packaging, typography, calligraphy, and even copy.

An early interest in letters, logos and signs led Ruuhinen into the study of graphics, calligraphy and typography as well as a thorough investigation of the relationship between colour, space and composition. Because he firmly believes that designers should be able to understand their clients' background to provide effective design services, he also started business and marketing studies. After qualifying as a graphic artist, Ruuhinen worked through the late 1960s and 1970s in two of Finland's leading advertising agencies. The first was SEK, which had a reputation for outstanding creativity. Ruuhinen worked on a variety of consumer accounts there before switching to the business-to-business sector and the newly opened Finnish branch of the Swedish Anderson and Lembke chain. In all, he spent eight years there, becoming a board member and helping Anderson and Lembke establish itself as one of the pioneers of business-to-business in Scandinavia and the rest of Europe by combining in-depth strategic planning with exceptional creativity.

During this period, Ruuhinen continued to carry out special graphic design commissions—posters, logos, trademarks, etc.—and played with the idea of setting up his own graphic design company. The final impetus came from one of Ruuhinen's prime sources of inspiration—Herb Lubalin. Whilst in Helsinki to judge the Finnish advertising awards, Lubalin asked why Ruuhinen had not yet set up on his own and predicted he would do so within five years. Only two years later and Erkki Ruuhinen Design was opening its doors. To date, the company has carried out corporate design programs and projects for many of Finland's leading concerns and institutions, including Enso-Gutzeit, the KOP Bank, Postipankki, the former Finnish Sugar Corporation, and Labsystems. Nevertheless, Ruuhinen is not simply concerned with the giants; just as many small newly-begun companies turn to him for their design needs.

Over the years, Ruuhinen has become increasingly interested in the basic elements of art—space, form, colour and composition. He believes there are examples of internationally oriented thinking and tradition to be found in Finnish architecture and design, the best known practitioners being the architect Alvar Aalto and the glass designers Tapio Wirkkala and Timo Sarpaneva. Representative through their work in the United States are the architects Eliel and Eero Saarinen; via their teaching at the Cranbrook Academy of arts, they spread the Finnish design gospel and exerted a significant influence on the development of American de-

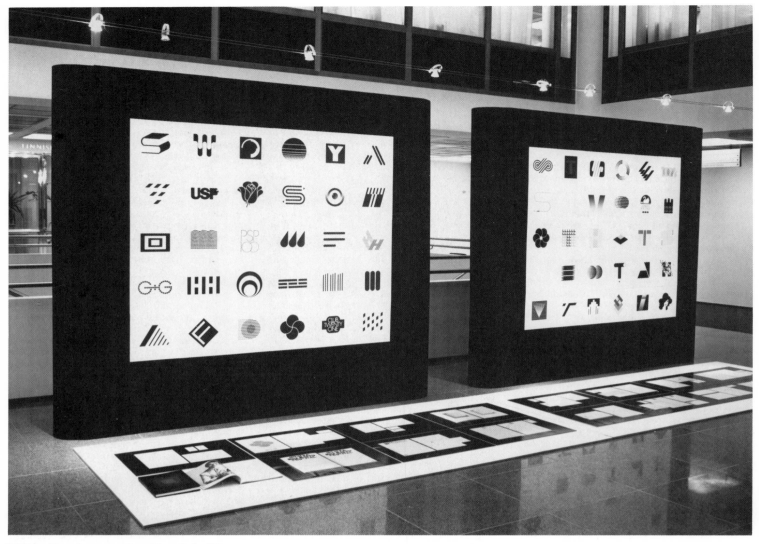

Erkki Ruuhinen: Logotype and graphic symbols, 1979

sign in the early decades of this century.

Ruuhinen has also studied the teachings of the Bauhaus movement as well as the Russian avantgarde, and admires their influence on the subsequent development of art, design and architecture. As a consequence, he has come to believe that the development of graphic design is tied to the "traditional movements" in modern art. He illustrates this by pointing out that Josef Albers' work on the use of colour can still help open the eyes not only of painters, architects and textile designers, but also of graphic artists. In a similar vein, he cites the work of Paul Klee, Wassily Kandinsky, Marcel Breuer, Mies van der Rohe and other Bauhaus designers and students. Recognition of influences is very important to Ruuhinen, since he holds that "we are all only messengers on the long road of art, irrespective of which areas of arts or design we work in. Indeed, the part we play in the overall development of art depends on how significant future generations regard our contribution." Certainly Ruuhinen's work reflects his interest—clear, unadorned designs with bold use of colour, but with an originality all their own.

—Richard Hayhurst

RYKIEL, Sonia.

French fashion, interior and accessories designer. Born Sonia Flis, in Paris, 25 May 1930. Educated at a girls' school, Neuilly-sur-Seine, until 1949; mainly self-taught in design. Married; children: Nathalie and Jean-Philippe. Worked as a stylist, at the Boutique Laura, Paris, 1962–68; founder and president, Sonia Rykiel fashion company, Paris, from 1968: launched the perfume *7e Sense*, 1979; first knitwear collection licensed for United States and Canada, 1982. Vice-president, Chambre Syndical du Pret-a-Porter des Couturiers et des Createurs de Mode, Paris, from 1973. Contributor to *Femme* magazine, Paris, from 1983. **Exhibitions:** *Woman of the Year 2000*, Forum des Halles, Paris, 1979; *Tables en Fetes*, International Centre of Tableware, Paris, 1979. Recipient: Oscar de la Mode, Paris. Chevalier de la Legion d'Honneur; Chevalier des Arts et des Lettres. Address: 175 Boulevard Saint-Germain, 75006 Paris, France.

Works:

Shopping bag designs, for Galeries Lafayette, Bloomingdale's, Macy's, and Seibu, 1979.
Tablewares and menu designs, for Lutetia and Terminus Saint-Lazare Hotels, Paris, 1979.
Notebooks, diaries and stationery accessories, for Galeries Lafayette, Paris, 1980.
Leather accessories range, for Japan, 1981.

Hotel de Crillon interior renovations, Paris, 1982.

Publications:

By RYKIEL: book—*Et Je la Voudrais Nue*, Paris 1979, Tokyo 1981.
On RYKIEL: books—*A History of Fashion* by J. Anderson Black and Madge Garland, London 1975, 1980; *In Fashion: Dress in the Twentieth Century* by Prudence Glynn, London 1978; *25 Ans de Marie-Claire de 1954 a 1979*, compiled by Francoise Mohrt, Paris 1979; *The Collector's Book of Twentieth Century Fashion* by Frances Kennett, London and New York 1983; *McDowell's Directory of Twentieth Century Fashion* by Colin McDowell, London 1984; *The Encyclopaedia of Fashion from 1840 to the 1980s* by Georgina O'Hara, London 1986.

*

I say that I am mad, that I wanted to create a space between them and myself.

They, the other women, all those who were not me, my skeleton, my silhouette. That I wanted to put a distance between what they were and the desire I had to be different, contrary, hallowed, other.

I am certain that I did not want to build an eyrie for these strangers but a special appearance for myself, a deviation from a system that I knew well and that was the uniform, the envelope in which I drowned myself, rolled myself, lost myself.

I thought that I could hide myself inside the dress, but I soon knew that it was I who shaped it, gave it life, supported it.

As a spectator, I witnessed my transformation and that of this dress which became invisible, transparent, while my body assumed increasing importance. At the same time, I worked on this dress. It had become a profession.

I made it fold, obey. I treated it like an infant, seduced it like a mistress, padded it sometimes to make it larger, to give it volume, or I undid it simply to understand.

I turned it inside out to see if it would resist me. It accepted the ideal on one condition, that from then on we would say that the wrong side is as good as the right side.

I even went further. I affirmed that the other side of the garment, that which touches the skin, the wrong side, was much more beautiful because it was emphasized by the seams (now visible) like the beams of a house or the columns of a cathedral.

I gave it symbolic value.

"You have put your sweater on inside out, you'll certainly get a present."

A present, like the wrong side, is a celebration; it is living twice for a few moments, the second living being inside the packet.

I remember a very beautiful phrase of Tonino Guerra: "Every time I make up a parcel, I rediscover myself inside."

Every time I make a garment, I rediscover myself inside it. I give it my form, my strength, my soul. I condition it, I show it, I gauge it. Standing in front of the mirror, I judge it, hate it, and adore it. (*Excerpted from* Et Je la Voudrais Nue, *1979.*)

—Sonia Rykiel

Although she has never had any formal training in fashion design, Sonia Rykiel has succeeded in creating classic, comfortable clothes which cater more to the wearer than to the vagaries of fashion. Rykiel has a practical and realistic approach; she designs as a woman for women. Her long, soft lines are not only visually attractive, but free from clutter, they accentuate the natural movement of the body. This is achieved by the use of knitted wools and fabrics such as crepe, which drape naturally. Her concentration on layers means that her garments can be mixed and matched according to the wishes of the individual. While her vertical lines have a timeless quality, her emphasis on coordination is essentially modern.

It is Rykiel's belief that women should not have to spend too much time selecting what they will wear. Her own dissatisfaction with what was available as ready-to-wear led her to become a designer. By creating garments for herself, she found that she was appealing to other women. Her original style is reminiscent of the early 1920s with its calf-length skirts, broad hip sashes, and tiny hats.

Rykiel's work stands apart from that of her contemporary designers, most of whom change their style frequently. She produces two collections a year, each containing only four new models, with perhaps a change to one detail, such as a belt, a handbag, or a pair of glasses.

Sonia Rykiel: Dresses from the Winter Collection, 1985

It is not her intention to seduce her customer with novelty. She finds the visual arts, literature, and music more inspiring to her than the ever-changing world of fashion. Colour enlivens her creations, and she will spend up to two months selecting the most suitable combinations for a collection. Like a painter, she instinctively knows where to place a vibrant band of bright colour in order to create maximum impact. Practically too, the use of limited colourways, usually consisting of a basic tone plus a contrast, gives a visual cohesion to her multi-layered creations. She is a subtle innovator whose work is consciously relaxed and understated. Her clothes wrap themselves around the body, leaving it unrestricted. Knitwear has been stimulated by her utilisation of the soft, natural qualities of wool. An understanding of what women demand from their clothes enabled Rykiel to eschew fashion and produce some of the most classic designs of the 1970s.

—Hazel Clark

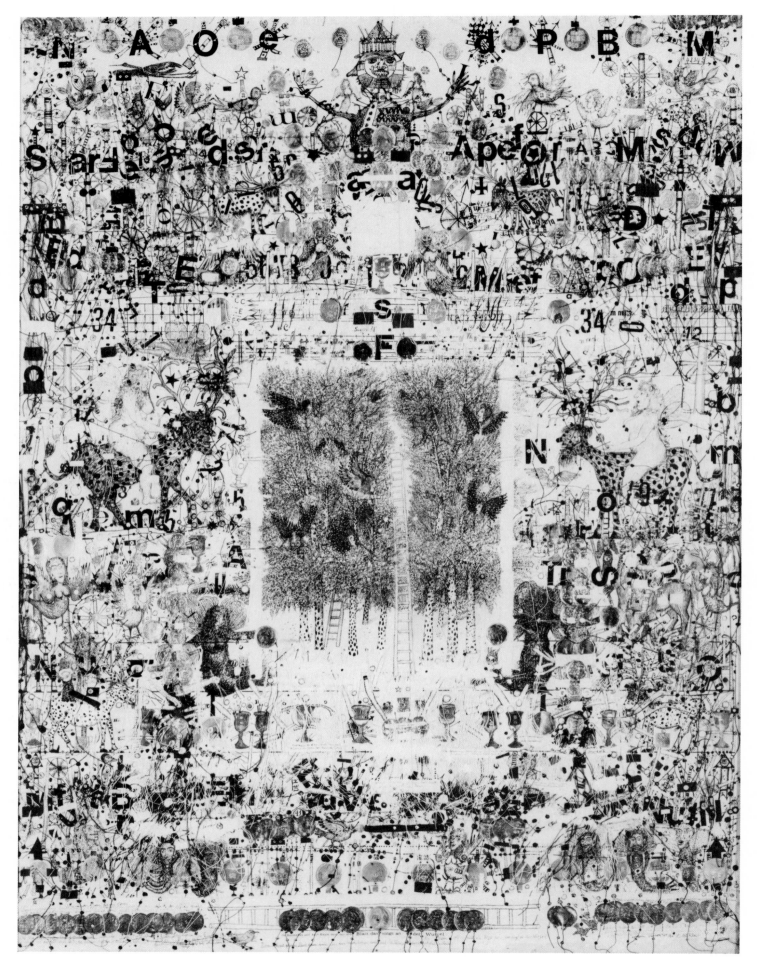

Horst Sagert: *Grosses Amulett* collage and graphic work, 1975–77

SAGERT, Horst.

German painter, medallist and stage designer. Born in Dramburg, 13 October 1934. Educated in Hagenow, Mecklenburg, until 1953; studied under Heinrich Kilger, at the Kunstschule, Berlin-Weissensee, 1953–58: Dip. 1958. Married Eva Stengel in 1963; daughter: Anna. Freelance stage designer, East Berlin, from 1958: has designed for the Deutsches Theater, Deutsches Staatsoper, Berliner Ensemble, Freie Volksbuhne of West Berlin, the Zurich Schauspielhaus, and the Buhnen der Stadt Koln. **Exhibitions:** Zentrum fur Kunstausstellungen der DDR, East Berlin, 1979; Galerie Oben, Karl-Marx-Stadt, 1983. **Collections:** Staatliche Museen, East Berlin; Staatliche Kunstsammlungen, Dresden. Recipient: Quadriennale Prize, 1971, and Gold Medal, 1979, Prague; Critics Prize, Venice Biennale, 1971. Address: Knaackstrasse 45, 1058 Berlin, German Democratic Republic.

Works:

Stage productions include—
Der Drache, Deutsches Theater, Berlin, 1965; *Oedipus Tyrann*, Deutsches Theater, Berlin, 1967; *Horizons*, Arbeiter Theater Schwedt, 1968; *Turandot oder der Kongress der Weisswascher*, Zurich Schauspielhaus, 1969 (also director); *Dona Rosita bleibt ledig oder die Sprache der Blumen*, Deutsches Theater, Berlin, 1970 (also director); *Die Komodie von Konig Bamba*, Deutsches Theater, Berlin, 1972 (also director); *A Midsummer Night's Dream*, Cologne, 1976; *Medea*, Deutsches Theater, Berlin, 1977 (also director); *The Taming of the Shrew*, West Berlin, 1981.

Publications:

By SAGERT: book—*Die Krahe und die Taube: Ein Todeszauber in der Art der Kinderspiele*, Karl-Marx-Stadt 1983.

On SAGERT: books—*Horst Sagert: Buhnenbilder und Figurinen zu Jewgeni Schwarz Der Drache* by Lothar Lang, Leipzig 1971; *Stage Design Throughout the Word Since 1960*, edited by Rene Hainaux and Yves Bonnat, Brussels 1972, London 1973; *Gebrauchsgraphik in der DDR* by Hellmut Rademacher, Dresden 1975; *Horst Sagert: Buhnenbilder und Bilder*, exhibition catalogue by Ursula Riemann-Reyher and others, Berlin 1979; *Horst Sagert—Bilder, Buhnenbilder und Medaillen*, exhibition catalogue, Karl-Marx-Stadt 1983.

The number of Horst Sagert's works for the stage is not large, for he has often taken long breaks during which he has worked as a painter, graphic artist, and medalist. However, an international breakthrough' in his career resulted from his designs for Benno Besson's 1965 production of *Der Drache* at the Deutsches Theater Berlin. Here, the essential elements of Sagert's approach came together in a synthesis of great originality.

Sagert's art is influenced on the one hand by the socio-critical impulses of Brechtian theater, but on the other hand, it is close to surrealism and Russian constructivism. His work employs suggestions of so-called naive painting (recalling Friedrich Schroder-Sonnenstern) but also of modern graphic script. The works of his teacher in Berlin, Heinrich Kilger, had a strong influence on Sagert's development. In method, too, Sagert is linked to the achievements of the Brechtian stage, particularly (as in the work of Caspar Neher and Karl von Appen) to the importance attributed to design. What is new in Sagert's work is that he has regained an integrated idea of space; new also are the magical-fantastic element and the eminent subtlety of his draftsmanship, including the handling of script, which functions as a particularly attractive graphic system and makes explicit the literary connection of Sagert's work. From an artistic point of view, Sagert's theatre design was a starting point for the total theatrical work of art which the stage designer controls now as director, now as scriptwriter. With drama to which music is added, he approaches idea opera in the German romantic sense: integration of the arts in a poetic theatrical cosmos.

This artist's obsession for detail—present in his designs on paper and also finding its way through paint room and costume workshop to the stage—is free from naturalistic representation. The precision of detail contributes to the high style of the whole; there results a single, theatrical, poetic world which does not close its eyes to the real world but includes its freedom. At one time, when the quotation stage of the Brechtian school was popular and often devolved on dogmatism and formalism, Sagert again called attention to the totality of the stage space; from the description of apparent social totalities, he achieved new opportunities in spatial relations on the stage—a coherence that revealed itself precisely in its denseness, in its fragility.

—Friedrich Dieckmann

SAINT LAURENT, Yves (Henri Donat Mathieu).

French fashion designer. Born in Oran, Algeria, 1 August 1936. Educated at the Lycee d'Oran, until 1953; studied at the Ecole de la Chambre, Syndicale de la Couture, Paris, 1954. Independent clothing stylist, Paris, 1953–54; designer and partner, 1954–57, and chief designer, 1957–60, Christian Dior fashion house, Paris; founder and managing director of Societe Yves Saint Laurent fashion firm, Paris, from 1962; also stage designer from 1959, and film costume designer from 1962. **Exhibitions:** *Fashion: An Anthology*, Victoria and Albert Museum, London, 1971; *Franzosisches Kunsthandwerk Heute*, Overstolzenhaus, Cologne, 1981; *Yves Saint Laurent*, Metropolitan Museum of Art, New York, 1983; *Yves Saint Laurent et le Theatre*, Musee des Arts Decoratifs, Paris, 1986; *Yves Saint Laurent: 28 Ans de Creation*, Musee des Arts de la Mode, Paris, 1986. Recipient: International Wool Secretariat Prize, 1954; Neiman-Marcus Fashion Oscar, Dallas, 1958; *Harper's Bazaar* Award, New York, 1966. Addresses: (office) 5 Avenue Marceau, 75016 Paris; (home) 55 rue de Babylone, 75007 Paris, France.

Publications:

By SAINT LAURENT: books—*Yves Saint Laurent*, with others, New York and London 1984; *Yves Saint Laurent par Yves Saint Laurent*, Paris 1986; book illustrated—*La Vilaine Lulu*, Paris 1967.

On SAINT LAURENT: books—*The Fashionable Savages* by John Fairchild, New York 1965; *Fashion: An Anthology by Cecil Beaton*, exhibition catalogue compiled by Madeleine Ginsburg, London 1971; *In Vogue: Sixty Years of Celebrities and Fashion*, edited by Georgina Howell, London 1975, 1978, New York 1976; *Living for Design: The Yves Saint Laurent Story* by Axel Madsen, New York 1979; *Magic Names of Fashion* by Ernestine Carter, London 1980; *McDowell's Directory of Twentieth Century Fashion* by Colin McDowell, London 1984; *Yves Saint Laurent et le Theatre*, with preface by Edmonde Charles-Roux, Paris 1986; *The Encyclopaedia of Fashion from 1840 to the 1980s* by Georgina O'Hara, London 1986.

The name of Yves Saint Laurent must, deservedly, be one of the best known within and outside the world of fashion today. It it often difficult to recall how many of our "basics" first came from his pen. He has helped to create a fundamental, functional, women's wardrobe, consisting of jacket, trousers, and suit, styles which he constantly updates in his own collections.

Always aware of what is happening about him, he produces garments which reflect the feelings of their time. By introducing Pop art to fashion and opening his Rive Gauche ready-to-wear boutique in 1966, he anticipated the breakdown of social barriers and the emergence of young, liberated styles. Masterminded by his financial partner Pierre Berger, Rive Gauche

set the trend for boutique shopping. Like his great influence, Chanel, Saint Laurent believes that clothes should be easy and pleasant to wear. The apparent simplicity of his work is, however, deceptive. While his Trapeze line may have become the standard maternity dress and his Mondrian shift was immediately copied, nothing ever hung as well, or was as well cut, as the originals.

Despite his successes in couture, ready-to-wear, theatre, and film by the later 1960s, he never lost touch with the world at large. His 1968 collection featuring fur duffle coats, fringed buckskins under fox coats, and plaited headbands showed sympathy, in couture terms, with the student demonstrations and anti-Vietnam marches. Likewise his maxi-skirts of 1969 indicated a hippie influence and prefigured the ethnic looks of the 1970s. Saint Laurent had introduced a number of themes, such as his Carmen and Dr. Zhivago looks, in the 1960s, ahead of their time. They returned to make their impact in the 1970s. Having established his reputation and his practical attitude to dressing, he was able to indulge in the fantasy revealed in his love of ethnic costume. In 1970, he returned to Russia for inspiration, then to China, India, Morocco, Japan, and back to Spain in 1976 for his Carmen ready-to-wear collection and his Rich Peasant couture look. The splendour of Diaghilev's Ballets Russes provided the pattern for the sumptuous gold, the brilliant colours, and the full, swirling skirts shown in 1979.

Call it escapism if you like, but the 1970s saw Saint Laurent bring gaiety into fashion. Throughout his career to date, he has been at various times practical, revolutionary, and sensational. His ideas are never static; they capture the feeling of the moment.

—Hazel Clark

Yves Saint-Laurent: Jacket and skirt in black and white spot cotton, 1990

SAKASHITA, Kiyoshi.

Japanese industrial designer. Born in Osaka, 23 March 1933. Studied industrial design, at Tokyo Art University, 1953–57. Married Eiko Tani in 1958; son: Shiu. Staff designer, 1957–60, home appliances design manager, 1960–63, New York research and marketing manager, 1963–66, audio and tape systems manager, 1966–73, corporate design manager from 1973, and corporate director and board member from 1979, at the Sharp Corporation, Osaka. Board member, Japan Industrial Designers' Association, Tokyo, from 1975, and Japan Package Design Association, Tokyo, from 1979; adviser, Japan Industrial Design Promotion Organization, Tokyo, from 1980, and Japan Design Foundation, Osaka, from 1981. **Collection:** Museum of Modern Art, New York. Address: Corporate Design Group, Sharp Corporation, 22–22 Nagaikecho, Abenoku, Osaka 545, Japan.

Works: (as design supervisor)

18C-D13E colour television, for Sharp, 1983.
VC-180 video cassette recorder, for Sharp, 1983.
VP-1000 video disc player, for Sharp, 1983.
SA-V500 stereo receiver, for Sharp, 1983.
RT-V500 stereo cassette deck, for Sharp 1983.
RP-V500 stereo record player, for Sharp, 1983.
CP-V500 speaker system, for Sharp, 1983.
R-527 microwave oven, for Sharp, 1983.

Kiyoshi Sakashita: *EC-553* vacuum cleaner, for the Sharp Corporation, 1983

SJ-26K3A fridge/freezer, for Sharp, 1983.
ES-320C washing machine, for Sharp, 1983.
EC-553 vacuum cleaner, for Sharp, 1983.
SS-209 electric razor, for Sharp, 1983.
OK-263V kerosene fan heater, for Sharp, 1983.
WD-800 word processor, for Sharp, 1983.
EI-8152 electronic calculator, for Sharp, 1983.
PA-7050 electronic graph, for Sharp, 1983.
SF-755 plain paper copier, for Sharp, 1983.

Publications:

By SAKASHITA articles—in *Design Quarterly* (Tokyo), no. 1, 1980, no. 3, 1981, no. 2, 1983.

On SAKASHITA books—*Structure of Dexterity: Industrial Design Works in Japan*, Tokyo 1983; *World Design Today*, Tokyo 1983.

Kiyoshi Sakashita is a corporate director and the general manager of the Design Center of the Sharp Corporation of Japan. His company has been a leader in the design of electrical home appliances and office automation equipment. Besides being notable for his own work in these fields, many of his colleagues admit that it is Sakashita's vitality that provides the driving force for their own work.

Sakashita is a product of the industrial design milieu of postwar Japan. His logic is clear-cut; his attitudes about abstracting future themes from the present are persuasive; and he is one of those speakers who can mobilize a large audience. But his accomplishment is more than simply having been a product of his time.

The revolution in electronics caused by micro-computers has been remarkable, and that revolution has, to a great extent, changed the consciousness of consumers. Some years ago the Sharp Corporation was in the forefront of helping to effect this change: it created a "new life merchandizing strategy" before it occurred to anyone else, impressing the public with its vision of a new lifestyle. As the person responsible for the design section of the Sharp Corporation, Sakashita has since been concerned, as well, with creating an "integrated style" in personal computers, electronic appliances, and office equipment—concerned, that is, not just with the design of individual products but with the design of complete systems—and, further, with the entire design image of his company. He seems to be intent on creating a corporate style that will permeate to all employees.

Sakashita is a sophisticated international businessman, the sort of person who grasps the realities of commerce, yet he has also been concerned about the role of design in modern society. He has been outspoken about the obligations of corporations to respond to the needs of users through enlightened industrial design. Though ideas and methods will obviously vary from one designer to another, Sakashita believes that linking consumer needs to effective product design is a reasonable, worthwhile goal.

The core of his design philosophy, as he expresses it, is the "humanization of scientific technology—that is, humanware design." This principle is shared by his co-workers, but it is Sakashita to whom they look for inspiration and direction.

—Kunio Sano

SALADINO, John F.
American interior, furniture and textile designer. Born in Kansas City, Missouri, 23 July 1939. Educated at Rockhurst Preparatory High School, Kansas City, until 1957; studied fine arts, at Notre Dame University, Indiana, 1958–60: BFA 1960; painting and sculpture under Josef Albers, at Yale University, New Haven, Connecticut, 1960–63: MFA 1963; also studied in the studio of architect Piero Sartogo, Rome, 1968–69. Married Virginia Hendrick in 1969; son: John. Freelance interior designer, as John F. Saladino Incorporated, New York, from 1972. Board member, Parsons School of Design, New York, and Formica Corporation, New York. Recipient: Illuminating Engineering Society Award, New York, 1976; *Interiors* Magazine Designer of the Year Award, New York, 1980; Daphne Award, New York, 1982; American Society of Designers Distinction Award, New England, 1982; Chicago Design Sources Committee Award, 1982; Euster Merchandise Mart Award, 1982. Address: 305 East 63rd Street, New York, New York 10021, U.S.A.

Works:

Thonet showroom interiors at the Decorative Arts Center, New York, 1980.
Sectioned Column table, for Saladino Incorporated, 1981.
Chaus showroom interiors, New York, 1981.
Pavilion sofa, for Saladino Incorporated, 1981.
Papyrus chair, for Saladino Incorporated, 1981.
Almay office interiors, New York, 1981.
Corolla chair, for Saladino Incorporated, 1982.
Model 404-29 tripod end table, for Saladino Incorporated, 1986.
Chase Manhattan Bank office interiors, New York, 1987.
Amphora table lamp, for Saladino Incorporated, 1987.
The Arch chair, for Saladino Incorporated, 1988.
The Tuscan end table, for Saladino Incorporated, 1988.
NutraSweet headquarters interiors, Deerfield, Illinois, 1988.
Horseshoe chair, for Saladino Incorporated, 1988.

Publications:

By SALADINO: article—in *Interior Design* (New York), April 1982.

On SALADINO: books — *Living Spaces*, edited by Franco Magnani, Milan 1977, New York and London 1978; *Hi-Tech: The Industrial Style*

John Saladino: Office reception area, Long Island, New York, 1983

and Resource Book for the Home by Joan Kron and Suzanne Slesin, New York 1978, London 1979; *Interior Views* by Erica Brown, London 1980; *Interior Design: The New Freedom* by Barbaralee Diamonstein, New York 1982; *Designers' Workplaces* by Beverly Russel, New York 1983; *Modern Furniture Classics* by Miriam Stimpson, London 1987; *International Design Yearbook 1988/89*, edited by Arata Isozaki, London, 1988.

"Juxtapositions" might be the single-word title of a book by John Saladino, in which he would start, of course, with the old and the new, the grand and the humble, and move into the more subtle areas of shadow and light, solid and void, even of architecture versus interior design. For Saladino is constantly pushing the frontier of interior design further toward the fine arts, toward architecture, as well as toward the refinement of space itself.

Color is one of the designer's most important contributions to interiors in the 1980s, colors such as mauve, aqua, terra cotta, tones that the designer has pointed out he was using considerably earlier than postmodernist architects. But again, juxtaposition is part of the context here, because Saladino will take the lightest and prettiest of hues and counter it with, say, a round, natural, plywood surface. Walls of scratch-coat plaster will be a background for an exquisitely lacquered cabinet. Saladino achieves an effect of piquant and slightly perverse luxury through the use of such devices, as well as through his multifarious references to the classical past. He believes that a cultural context is absolutely necessary for successful design and considers himself with "one foot in Europe, the other in America." A year spent in Rome made an enormous impression on him, embuing in him a lasting love for weathered or even corroded surfaces, as well as adding the fondness for fragmentation and fractured perspective that makes his work unique.

"Miniature theatre" is another term he has used to describe his effects, and indeed there is a set-like quality to many of his rooms, especially in their exploitation of dramatically enlarged, classical fragments, their characteristically dynamic lighting, and perhaps most important, the sense that there is something going on *beyond* the room. A scrim-like shade across a window, or a trellis running across a length of a room to suggest a mysterious additional space beyond—these are among the visual aids Saladino uses in his work. He feels that his work manifests an essentially existential attitude toward design, for he believes in hesitancy, incompletion, at least in an intellectual sense. To a selective eye, however, his rooms look very complete indeed. Complete and assured, occupying a fascinating space between two sensibilities in contemporary design, the reductionist and the enriching, and explaining them both well.

—Peter Carlsen

SALOVAARA, (Aki Heikki) Juhani.
Finnish industrial designer. Born in Kokkola, 16 March 1943. Educated at Kokkola High School, until 1961; studied at the Institute of Industrial Design, Helsinki, 1962–67: Dip. 1967. Designer, Upo Oy household apparatus, Helsinki, 1967, N. V. Philips, Eindhoven, Netherlands, 1968, and Wallac Oy, Turku, Finland, 1970; Managing Director, Ergonomiadesign Oy, Turku, since 1973; Chairman of the Board, Jobat Oy, Turku, from 1982: has designed for Martela, Nokia, Sohlberg, Treston, Tunturi, etc. Instructor in interior design, 1979–80, and instructor in industrial design from 1983, University of Applied Arts, Helsinki. Committee Member, 1971–73, Board Member, 1973–76, Hungarian Interdesign Congress Coordinator, 1979, and Deputy Chairman of Helsinki Design Integration Congress, 1981, ICSID International Council of Societies of Industrial Design; Foreign Affairs Committee Member, 1972–77, Chief of Cooperative Projects with Berlin Design Council, 1977–79, Scandinavian Cooperation Chief, 1980–83, Chairman of TKO Industrial Designers Section Board, 1988–89, and First Deputy Chairman, 1988–89, Ornamo Association of Finnish Designers; Scientific-Technical Committee Member, Academy of Finland, 1977–80; Member, Finnish Design Council, 1983–84; Editorial Board Member, *Design in Finland*, Helsinki, from 1985. **Exhibitions:** *Finnland Gestaltet*, Museum for Kunst und Gewerbe, Hamburg, 1981 (toured). **Collections:** Museum of Applied Arts, Helsinki; Museum of Modern Art, New York. Recipient: Institute of Applied Arts Scholarship, Helsinki, 1967; Keski-Pohjanmaa County Cultural Foundation Scholarship, 1967; *Kaunis Koti* magazine design grant, 1972; Finnish State Industrial Art Prize, 1973, 1975; Internationales Design Zentrum Prize, West Berlin, 1974; Finnish Cultural Foundation Design Grant, 1977; Gute Industrieform Recognition Award, 1981, 1983; Ergodesign Award, Montreux, 1984; Finnish Design Council Honorary Diploma, 1985; Finnish State Artist's Grant, 1985; Saab-Valmet Ergonomics Prize, 1988. Address: Tervaskuja 72, 1110 Naantali, Finland.

Publications:

By SALOVAARA: books—*Playthings*, editor with others, Helsinki 1976; *Preliminary Study on the Needs and Conditions of Work Environment Planning*, with Y. Kukkapuro and A. Sotamaa, Helsinki 1977; *Playthings for Play*, with others, Helsinki and West Berlin, 1979; *Ergonomy of Hairdressing*, report with others, Helsinki 1985; *Working Station of Haircare*, report, Helsinki 1986.

On SALOVAARA: book—*Finnland Gestaltet*, exhibition catalogue by Tapio Periainen, Simo Heikkila and others, Espoo 1981.

SAMBONET, Roberto.
Italian painter, architectural, graphic, display and industrial designer. Born in Vercelli, 20 October 1924. Studied architecture, at the Politecnico, Milan, 1942–45; mainly self-taught in art and design. Independent painter, furnishing and textile designer, working with Pietro Maria Bardi, at the Museu de Arte, Sao Paulo, 1948–53, and with Alvar Aalto in Finland, 1953; freelance designer, working in Vercelli and Milan, from 1953: has designed for La Rinascente, Tiffany's, Einaudi, Alfieri e Lacroix, Carlo Bestetti, Galleria Il Milione, Baccarat, Bing och Grondahl, Richard Ginori, etc. Art director, *Zodiac* magazine, Milan, 1957–66. Technical Committee Member of the Milan Triennale, 1960. President, Italian section of the Alliance Graphique Internationale. **Exhibitions:** Galleria Cardazzo, Venice, 1948; Museu de Arte, Sao Paulo, 1949, 1974; Museu de Arte Moderna, Rio de Janeiro, 1949; Galleria Il Milione, Milan, 1950, 1952, 1969; Artek Gallery, Helsinki, 1956, 1976; Biblioteca Comunale, Milan, 1957; Galleria Il Disegno, Milan, 1960; Palazzo dei Centori, Vercelli, 1962; Galleria Profili, Milan, 1963; Galleria Pater, Milan, 1966; *Italian Design*, Hallmark Gallery, New York, 1969; *Italy: The New Domestic Landscape*, Museum of Modern Art, New York, 1972; *Design Italiano degli Anni '50*, Centrokappa, Milan, 1977; Casa del Mantegna, Mantua, 1978; *Design Since 1945*, Philadelphia Museum of Art, 1983; *Italia: Disegno*, Museo Rufino Tamayo, Mexico City, 1986. **Collections:** Design Archive, University of Parma; Museu de Arte, Sao Paulo; Museum of Modern Art, New York; Philadelphia Museum of Art. Recipient: Compasso d'Oro Award, Milan, 1956, 1970, 1979; Grand Prize, Milan Triennale, 1960; Art Directors Club Prize, Milan, 1977. Address: Foro Bonaparte 44/A, 20121 Milan, Italy.

Works:

Pesciera fish dish with bivalve lid in stainless steel, for Sambonet S.p.A., 1957.
Center Line stackable cooking pans in stainless steel, for Sambonet S.p.A., 1965–71.
Caviar glass dessert cup and ice container, for Compagnie des Cristalleries de Baccarat, 1971.
Stackable picnic cutlery in stainless steel, for Sambonet S.p.A., 1971.
TIR Series glass tumblers, for Compagnie des Cristalleries de Baccarat, 1971.
Center Line Pan double-function frying pan and griddle with detachable handle in stainless steel, for Sambonet S.p.A., 1972.
Empilage stackable glass tumblers, for Compagnie des Cristalleries de Baccarat, 1972.
845 Flatware cutlery in stainless steel, for Sambonet S.p.A., 1973.
Menage cruet-set in stainless steel, crystal and wood, for Sambonet S.p.A., 1975–76.
Prehistoire hemispheric glass vases, for Compagnie des Cristalleries de Baccarat, 1975–77.
Glass corner vases, for Compagnie des Cristalleries de Baccarat, 1975–77.
Square stackable oven pans with detachable handles in stainless steel, for Sambonet S.p.A., 1977.

Publications:

By SAMBONET: books—*Il Disegno come Doppio: 61 Disegni 1956–1972*, with text by Paolo Fossati, Milan 1974; *l'Arte in Tavola*, Milan 1988.

On SAMBONET: books — *Sambonet: 22 Cause + 1*, exhibition catalogue by E. Villa, Milan 1952; *Forme Nuove in Italia* by Agnoldomenico Pica, Milan and Rome 1957; *Il Disegno Industriale e la sua Estetica* by Gillo Dorfles, Bologna 1963; *Forme Disegnate da Roberto Sambonet per la Sambonet S.p.A.* by Pier Carlo Santini, Milan 1970; *Baccarat: Nuove Forme di Art Design di Roberto Sambonet* by R. Guiducci, Milan 1972; *Roberto Sambonet: Ricerca e Strutture '49–74*, exhibition catalogue by P. M. Bardi and Paolo Fossati, Sao Paulo 1974; *Album Progetto Mangiare* by Mario Bellini, Milan 1980; *Il Disegno Industriale Italiano 1928–1981* by Enzo Frateili, Turin 1983; *l'Italia del Design* by Alfonso Grassi and Anty Pansera, Casale Monferrato 1986; *World Graphic*

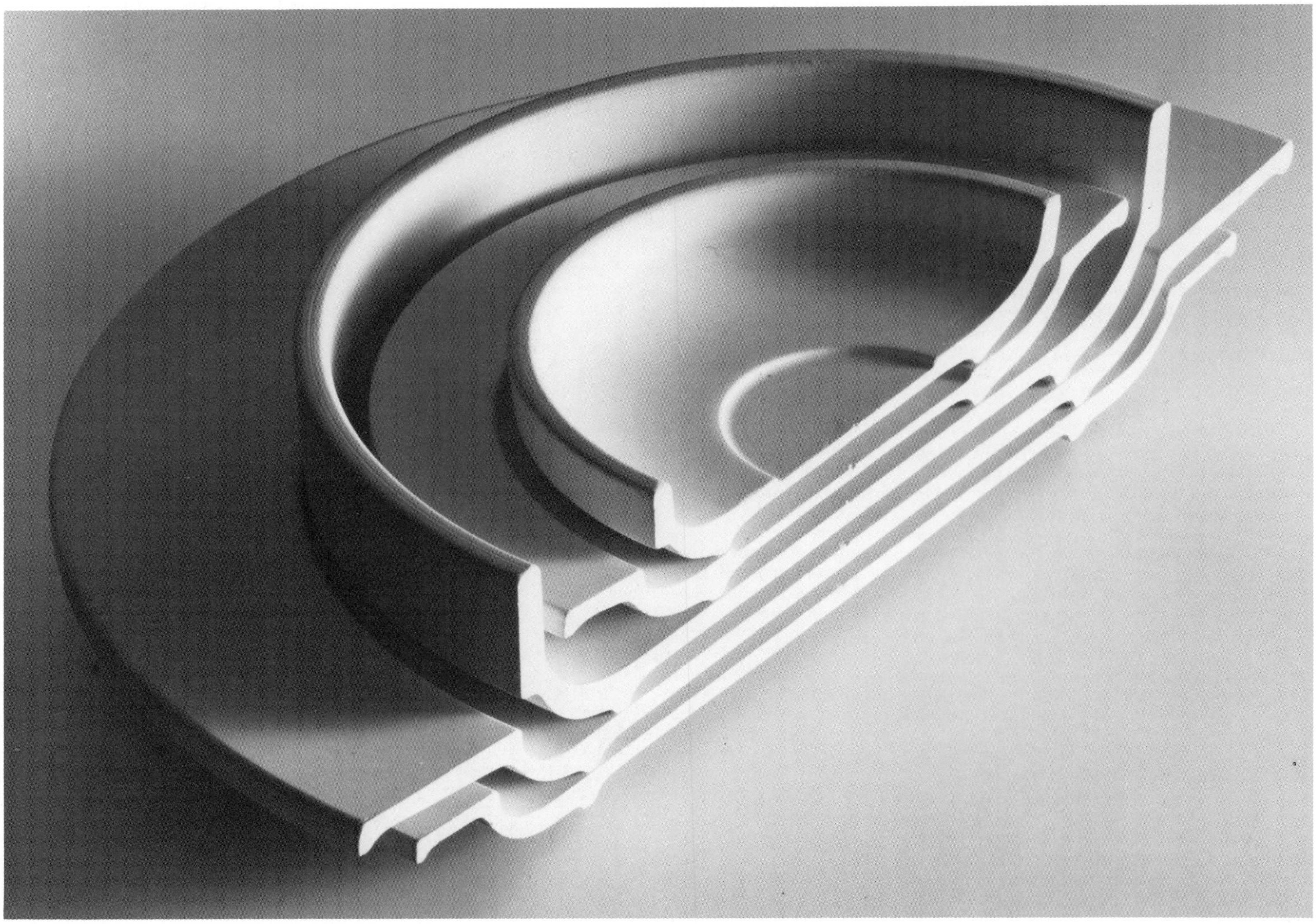

Roberto Sambonet: Plaster models of stacking porcelain tableware, for Richard Ginori, 1979

Design Now by Katsuo Kimura and Shin Matsunaga, Tokyo 1988.

Despite the increasing number and quantity of international schools of design and graphics, in this post-industrial and service-oriented second half of the century, we see a progressive decadence in contemporary design, both that of its own period and that inherited from the great cultural movements of the second and third decades of the century. The political world, the world of contractors and managers, the great masses, and consumerism generally are, with a few exceptions (Adriano Olivetti, for example), more and more hostile to what is needed for evolution and innovation, giving no thought to such extraordinary, unique achievements in the history of mankind as we see in space travel, especially in the United States and the Soviet Union. After more than thirty years of idealistic and polemical activity, work that was often unpaid, such as my contributions to public bodies and museums and to the Milan *Triennale*, along with marvellous designers from all over the world, I now feel that I must devote as much time as possible to "research" in the expectation that the decadence will end and a recovery set in. After my objectivist designs of the 1950s and 1960s and of the 1970s—not, I hope, formalistic but rather poetic in intention—I now feel an increasing need for contact with social reality and the requirements of collective life, which can be developed in the studio and in town planning.

—Roberto Sambonet

SANDBERG, Willem (Jacob Henri Berend).
Dutch graphic and exhibition designer. Born in Amersfoort, 24 October 1897. Educated in Assen, until 1917; studied at the Amsterdam Art Academy, 1919–20; independent pictorial studies in Vienna, Berlin and Dessau, 1927; psychology student and assistant to F. Roels, Utrecht, 1930–35. Served as coastguard in the Dutch Army, in Assen and Breda, 1917–19. Married C. A. Frankamp in 1920 (divorced, 1929); daughter: Helga; married Alida Augustin Swaneveld in 1937 (died, 1974); stepchildren: Paula and Sven. Worked as a typesetter for a printing company, Heidelberg, 1921; founder and director of the Madaznan spiritual healing centre, in Paris and Amsterdam, 1923–26; freelance professional graphic designer, Amsterdam, from 1927; chief graphic and publications designer for the Stedelijk Museum, Amsterdam, 1945–62; also designed for Ploegsma Publishing Company, State Insurance Bank, Economic Information Service, Dutch Post Office, Nijgh en Van Ditmar publishers, etc. Curator of modern art, 1937–41, and director, 1945–62, Stedelijk Museum, Amsterdam; director, Fodor and Willet Museums, Amsterdam, 1949–62; organizer and planner of the Historical Museum, Amsterdam, from 1938 (opened, 1962). Co-editor, *Open Oog* magazine, Amsterdam, from 1946; founder and co-editor, *Form* magazine, Amsterdam. Chairman, Architecture and Related Arts Exhibition Council, Amsterdam, 1945–48; vice-chairman, Dutch Arts Council, Amsterdam, 1948–60; executive committee chairman, Israel Museum, Jerusalem, 1964–68, 1971–72. Erasmus Lecturer, Harvard University, Cambridge, Massachusetts, 1969–70. **Exhibitions:** Steendrukkerij De Jong, Hilversum, 1958; Gemeentemuseum, The Hague, 1965; Musee des Arts Decoratifs, Paris, 1973; *107 Grafici dell'AGI*, Castello Sforzesco, Milan, 1974. Recipient: Werkman Prize, Amsterdam, 1959; Gold Medal, City of Amsterdam, 1962; Dutch Award for Art and Architecture, 1968; Progressiven Deutschen Kunsthandler Prize, Cologne, 1973; Erasmus Prize, Amsterdam, 1975. Honorary Doctorate: University of Buffalo, New York, 1962. Honrary member, American Institute of Graphic Arts, 1962; honorary fellow, Israel Museum, Jerusalem, 1975. *Died* (in Amsterdam) *April 1984.*

Works:

Duitse Kunst na 1945 exhibition catalogue, for the Stedelijk Museum, Amsterdam, 1954.
Vijf Amerikanen in Europa exhibition catalogue, for the Stedelijk Museum, Amsterdam, 1955.
Museumjournaal magazine designs, for the Stedelijk Museum, Amsterdam, 1956–63.
Vitality in Art exhibition catalogue, for the Palazzo Grassi, Venice, 1959.
Art Since 1950 exhibition catalogue, for the Seattle World's Fair, 1962.
De Collectie Sandberg book design, for Uitgeverij Meulenhoff, Amsterdam, 1962.
Logotype symbol, for the Israel Museum, Jerusalem, 1965.

Heart for Harvard poster, for Harvard University, 1970.
Le Corbusier: Vers un Architecture book design, for Stichting de Roos, Utrecht, 1971.
Wilhelm Wagenfeld exhibition poster and catalogue, for the Kunstgewerbemuseum, Cologne, 1973.
Cobra and Contrast exhibition poster and catalogue, for the Detroit Institute of Arts, 1974.
Paribas poster, for the Banque de Paris et des Pays-Bas, 1977.

Publications:

By SANDBERG: books — *Kwadrattbladen: Nu-midden in de XXe euw*, Hilversum 1959; *Sleutelwoorden/Keywords: Piet Zwart*, The Hague 1965; *Nu 2*, Hilversum 1968; *Experimenta Typographica 1943–1968*, Nijmegen 1969.

On SANDBERG: books—*Advertising Directions*, edited by Edward M. Gottschall and Arthur Hawkins, New York 1959; *Typography* by Aaron Burns, New York 1961; *De Collectie Sandberg*, with introduction by Gerrit Kouwenaar, Amsterdam 1962; *Design Co-ordination and Corporate Image* by F. H. K. Henrion and Alan Parkin, London and New York 1967; *Sandberg Designe*, exhibition catalogue with introduction by Edy de Wilde, Paris 1973; *Sandberg: A Documentary*, compiled by Ad Petersen and Pieter Brattinga, Amsterdam 1975; *Typography: Design and Practice* by John Lewis, London 1978; *A History of Graphic Design* by Philip B. Meggs, New York and London 1983.

While studying psychology in Vienna during the late 1920s, Sandberg became interested in the system of pictorial statistics, called Isotype, which Otto Neurath was then developing there. Returning to Amsterdam, he was commissioned by the Stedelijk Museum to prepare pictorial statistics for an exhibition, *Work for the Disabled*, in 1928. From his first contact with the museum developed the relationship that was to dominate his life; he was appointed curator in 1937 and director in September 1945. A major exhibition of the work of van Gogh in 1945 was followed by a major retrospective of the work of H. N. Werkman, the printer-painter who was shot by the Germans a few days before the liberation of Groningen but whose influences can be traced in many of Sandberg's robust typographic designs.

Sandberg's catalogue and poster designs have had a far-reaching effect on European and American museum publications and publicity. He made extensive use of bold typography, often incorporating large wooden type, torn paper shapes, and interesting paper textures. The use of coarse wrapping papers and other similar cheap materials give many of his catalogues an unusual, tactile quality.

His innovative use of materials and colour is also evident in *Experimente Typographica*, the series of eighteen booklets of experimental typography which he produced during the war. His output of typographic works, especially given his heavy national and international commitments as director of a major museum, is remarkable both for its quantity and for the standard he maintained.

—Mafalda Spencer

SANT'ANGELO, Giorgio.

American fashion designer. Born Count Giorgio Imperiale de Sant'Angelo, in Florence, Italy, 5 May 1933; emigrated to the United States in 1962. Studied architecture in Buenos Aires, industrial design in Barcelona, and Fine Arts at the Sorbonne, Paris. Worked as a cartoonist for Walt Disney Studios, Hollywood, California, 1962–63; fashion stylist, furnishings and textile designer, working for Cohn-Hall-Marx and Marcus Brothers fabric firms, and for E. I. Du Pont, 1963–67; independent fashion

Giorgio Sant'Angelo: Coat in mohair with platinum sequins over a cashmere dress, 1983

designer, establishing Sant-Angelo ready-to-wear, New York, from 1967 and Sant'Angelo Incorporated, New York, 1968: designed for Marjer, Gabar, Ed Rosenthal Neckwear, Eagle Clothing, Charles of the Ritz, Wamsutta, Lane Furniture, Regal Rugs, etc. Recipient: Coty American Fashion Critics' Winnie Award, New York, 1968, 1970; Inspiration Home Furnishings Award, New York, 1978; Knitted Textile Association Designer Award, New York, 1982; Fashion Designers of America Award, New York, 1988. *Died* (in New York City) *29 August 1989.*

Publications:

On SANT'ANGELO: books—*The World of Fashion: People, Places, Resources* by Eleanor Lambert, New York and London 1976; *The Fashion Makers* by Bernardine Morris, New York 1978; *Fairchild's Who's Who in Fashion,* edited by Anne Stegemeyer, New York 1980; *McDowell's Directory of Twentieth Century Fashion* by Colin McDowell, London 1984; *The Encyclopaedia of Fashion from 1840 to the 1980s* by Georgina O'Hara, London 1986.

Giorgio Sant'Angelo began with startling colour contrasts. Early in his career, concentrating on Lycra spandex stretch fabric for jackets and trousers, he created a moulded look. In 1981, he looked to metallic effects, as were seen in his gold lurex trouser suit and a suede jacket appliquéd with metal shapes after Miro. His strong colour was still evident in a red matte jersey evening gown with bright gold shoulder and bow. Metal beads were applied to pullovers in tones of bronze and green brass. He aimed for striking effects.

Sant'Angelo was born in Italy but spent much of his boyhood in Argentina and Brazil, where his family owned estates. In South America, his grandparents taught him to notice colour and shape before he was sent back to Europe to take a degree in architecture and industrial design. He then began to design furniture and, eventually, clothes for the people who sat in his chairs. He never saw himself as a dress designer but rather as someone who applied his talents to a universal range. Thus, he produced womenswear, menswear, children's clothes, swimwear, furniture and rugs.

Acknowledging that his dramatic creations are not the clothes for every woman and that they require a lot of self-confidence to wear, he maintained that he was not trying to design for everybody. His customers included the singer Lena Horne and the socialite Bianca Jagger—striking individuals who want to look different. Sant'Angelo rarely planned far ahead or sought to establish a design policy. He preferred the excitement of not knowing where he would move next. He would often use the same pattern in a dress and a rug, and which range might dominate in any one year was a matter of chance.

—Diana de Marly

SAPPER, Richard.

German industrial designer. Born in Munich, 30 May 1932. Studied philosophy, anatomy, graphics, engineering and economics, at the University of Munich, 1952–56. Married Dorit Polz in 1963; children: Carola, Mathias and Cornelia. Designer, Mercedes-Benz car styling department, Stuttgart, 1956–57; freelance designer, working in the studio of Alberto Rosselli and Gio Ponti, Milan, 1957–59, and in the studio of Marco Zanuso, Milan, 1959–75; established own design studio in Stuttgart, from 1970: design consultant to Fiat car company and Pirelli tyre company, 1970–76, and to IBM Corporation from 1980; has designed for Lorenz, Kartell, Gavina, Brionvega, Terraillon, Italora, Artemide, B & B Italia, Unifor, Batavus, Knoll, Alessi, etc. Founder, with Gae Aulenti, Urban Transport systems study group, Milan, 1972. Professor of industrial design, at the Stuttgart Academy of Fine Arts, and the Vienna Hochschule fur Angewandte Kunst, from 1986. **Exhibitions:** Milan Triennale, 1968, 1979, 1986; *Italy: The New Domestic Landscape,* Museum of Modern Art, New York, 1972; *Italienische Moebel,* Stadtmuseum, Cologne, 1980; *Design Since 1945,* Philadelphia Museum of Art, 1983; *Richard Sapper: 40 Design Projects 1958–1988,* Sala Vincon, Barcelona, 1988. **Collections:** Museum of Modern Art, New York; Philadelphia Museum of Art. Recipient: Compasso d'Oro Award, Milan, 1960, 1962, 1964, 1967, 1979, 1986; Gute Form Prize, West Germany, 1969, 1983; Premio

Richard Sapper: *Tizio* desk lamp, for Artemide, 1972

SMAU, Milan, 1969, 1981, 1986; Gold Medal, Liubliana Industrial Design Biennale, 1973, 1979. Honorary Royal Designer for Industry, Royal Society of Arts, London, 1988. Addresses: Via Vignino 2, 6926 Montagnola, Ticino, Switzerland; Loewenstrasse 96, 7000 Stuttgart 70, West Germany.

Works:

Static electronic table-clock, for Lorenz, 1960.
K-1340 children's chair in polyethylene, for Kartell, 1963 (with Zanuso).
Lambda chair in sheet metal, for Gavina, 1963 (with Zanuso).
Algol portable television set, for Brionvega, 1965 (with Zanuso).
Black Box portable television set, for Brionvega, 1969 (with Zanuso).
Tantalo electric table-clock, for Artemide, 1971.
Genia bookshelf system, for B & B Italia, 1971–72.
Tizio table lamp, for Artemide, 1972.
Misura office furniture system, for Unifor, 1974.
Bicycle in sheet metal, for Batavus, 1976.
Espresso coffee-maker in stainless steel, for Alessi, 1978.
Sappercollection office chairs, for Knoll International, 1979.
Whistling kettle in stainless steel, for Alessi, 1983.
System 25 office chair, for Comforto, 1984.
Nena folding armchair, for B & B Italia, 1984.
PC Convertible laptop computer, for IBM, 1986.
From 9 to 5 office furniture system, for Castelli, 1986.
Argo tracklighting system, for Artemide, 1988.

Publications:

By SAPPER: article—in *Design* (London), September 1980.

On SAPPER: books—*Italy: The New Domestic Landscape* by Emilio Ambasz, New York and Florence 1972; *Design e Forme Nuove nell'Arredamento Italiano*, edited by Paolo Portoghesi and Marino Marini, Rome 1978; *Atlante del Design Italiano 1940/1980* by Alfonso Grassi and Anty Pansera, Milan 1980; *Knoll Design* by Eric Larrabee and Massimo Vignelli, New York 1981; *Design Since 1945*, edited by Kathryn Hiesinger and George Marcus, Philadelphia and London 1983; *The Conran Directory of Design*, edited by Stephen Bayley, London 1985; *Modern Furniture Classics* by Miriam Stimpson, London 1987; *Italian Design: 1870 to the Present* by Penny Sparke, London and New York 1988; *Richard Sapper: 40 Progetti di Design 1958–1988*, exhibition catalogue with preface by Roberto Sambonet, Milan 1988; *Italian Modern: A Design Heritage* by Giovanni Albera and Nicolas Monti, New York 1989.

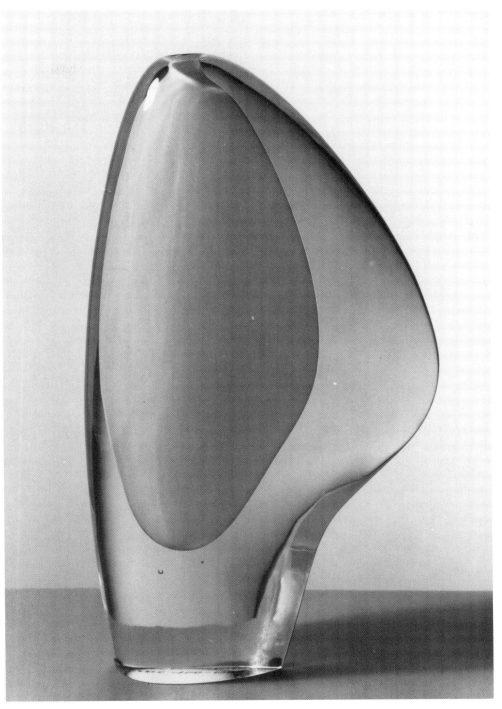

Timo Sarpaneva: Vase in clear and opaque white glass, for Iitala, 1954   Courtesy Victoria and Albert Museum, London

SARPANEVA, Timo (Tapani).

Finnish painter, sculptor, exhibition, graphic, textile and industrial designer. Born in Helsinki, 31 October 1926. Studied graphics, at the Central School of Industrial Design, Helsinki, 1941–48: influenced by interior designer Arttu Brummer. Married Ann-Mari(Pi) Holmberg in 1954 (divorced, 1970); sons: Tom and Markus; lives with Marjatta Svennevig from 1971; children: Johanna and Aleksei. Freelance designer, from 1950: artistic director, Porin Puuvilla cotton mill, Pori, 1955–66, and AB Kinnasand textile mill, Kinnasand, 1964–72; designed for A. Ahlstrom glass company, Littala, from 1950, Villayhtyma woollen rugs, 1960–62, Rosenlew cast iron, 1961–70, Primo building equipment from 1963, Rosenlew paper, 1964–70, Opa stainless steel, and Rosenthal porcelain and cutlery from 1970. Instructor in textile printing and design, Central School of Industrial Design, Helsinki, 1953–57. **Exhibitions:** *Fins Glas*, Stedelijk Museum, Amsterdam, 1972 (toured); *Nordisk Industridesign*, Kunstindustrimuseet, Oslo, 1976; *Form und Struktur*, Museum fur Angewandte Kunst, Vienna, 1980 (toured); *Scandinavian Modern Design 1880–1980*, Cooper-Hewitt Museum, New York, 1982; *Design Since 1945*, Philadelphia Museum of Art, 1983; *Timo Sarpaneva: Glaszeit*, Museum fur Angewandte Kunst, Dortmund 1985; *The Lunning Prize*, Nationalmuseum, Stockholm, 1986; *Scandinavia: Ceramics and Glass in the Twentieth Century*, Victoria and Albert Museum, London, 1989. **Collections:** Museum of Applied Arts, Helsinki; Nationalmuseum, Stockholm; Det Danske Kunstindustrimuseum, Copenhagen; Nordenfjeldske Kunstindustrimuseum, Trondheim; Stedelijk Museum, Amsterdam; Kunstmuseum, Dusseldorf; Victoria and Albert Museum, London; Museum of Modern Art, New York; National Gallery of Victoria, Melbourne. Recipient: Gold and Silver Medals, Milan Triennale, 1954, 1957; *House Beautiful* Award, New York, 1954; Museum of Contemporary Crafts Prize, New York, 1956; Lunning Prize, Copenhagen and New York, 1956; International Design Award, New York, 1963, 1969; Eurostar Packaging Award, The Hague, 1965; Gold Medal, Faenza Ceramics Competition, 1976. Honorary Doctorate: Royal College of Art, London, 1967; Honorary Professor, Helsinki, 1976. Honorary Royal Designer for Industry, Royal Society of Arts, London, 1963. Address: Via Navegna 7, Minusio, Locarno, Switzerland.

Works:

Lansett II sculpture in clear and opaque white glass, for Iittala Glass, 1952.
Orkidea sculpture in clear glass, for Iittala Glass, 1954.
Nukkuva Lintu sculpture in steam-blown clear and blue glass, for Iittala, 1957.
Stacking bottles in red, blue or clear glass, for Iittala Glass, 1959.
Covered cooking pot in cast iron and wood, for Rosenlew, 1959.
Purkaus sculpture in mould-blown and cast clear glass, for Iittala Glass, 1964.
Festivo candlesticks in textured and moulded clear glass, for Iittala Glass, 1967.
Bolero printed cotton fabric, for Tampella, 1968.
Satula glassware, for Iittala Glass, 1969.
Covered casserole dish in stainless steel, for Opa, 1970.
Cooking platter and pot in stainless steel, for Opa, 1970.
Jurmo series of glasswares in blue and white glass, for Iittala Glass, 1972.
Suomi table service in porcelain and stainless steel, for Rosenthal, 1974.
Arkipelago drinking glasses and candleholders in mould-blown clear glass, for Iittala Glass, 1978.
Koh-I-Noor sculpture-vase in cast and cut clear glass, for Iittala, 1982.
Claritas sculptures in free-blown clear glass, for Iittala Glass, 1983–86.
Lancett-35, II sculpture in clear glass and granite, for Iittala Glass, 1985.

Publications:

By SARPANEVA: books—*Finnish Decorative Art 1950–54*, co-editor, Helsinki 1955; *History of the Cotton Mill Porin Puuvilla*, editor, with Jukka Pellinen, Helsinki 1957; *Finnish Design 1875–1975*, editor, with E. Bruun and E. Kruskopf, Helsinki 1975.

On SARPANEVA: books—*Finnish Designers of Today* by Oili Maki, Helsinki 1954; *Packaging: An International Survey of Package Design*, edited by Walter Herdeg, Zurich 1959; *A Treasury of Scandinavian Design*, edited by Erik Zahle, New York 1961; *Modern Glass* by Ada Polak, London 1962; *34 Scandinavian Designers* by Svend Erik Moller, Copenhagen 1967; *Modern Finnish Design* by Ulf Hard af Segerstad, New York 1969; *Fins Glas*, exhibition catalogue by Hugh Wakefield, Amsterdam 1972; *Scandinavian Design: Objects of a Life Style* by Eileene Harrison Beer, New York and Toronto 1975; *Industrial Design* by John Heskett, London 1980; *Design Since 1945*, edited by Kathryn Hiesinger and George Marcus, Philadelphia and London 1983; *Timo Sarpaneva*, with text by Kaj Kalin, Helsinki 1986; *The Lunning Prize*, exhibition catalogue edited by Helena Dahlback Lutteman and Marianne Uggla, Stockholm 1986; *Scandinavia: Ceramics and Glass in the Twentieth Century* by Jennifer Hawkins Opie, London 1989.

Like many of his generation, Timo Sarpaneva has worked in a wide range of media and styles,

yet his versatility and excellence are almost unparalleled. His success in these fields has brought him numerous awards, exhibitions, and commissions. Sarpaneva's inventiveness and experimentation have acquired for him a reputation for artistic creativity and independence.

In the mid-twentieth century, the debate continued over the production of functional, mass-produced objects for the general public versus catering to the artistic preferences of the elite. It is generally acknowledged that of all the Scandinavian countries, Finnish design at mid-century was generally more inclined to be of service to the upper classes. Many of Sarpaneva's early glass designs, such as his vase of 1953 in the collection of the Metropolitan Museum of Art in New York, exhibit just such a sophisticated elegance and delicacy. His vase of 1964 in the Iittala Museum shows a technique he developed in the later 1950s and 1960s for making "sculptured" glass. The glass is formed in wood molds that are permitted to burn during blowing, giving the finished glass strong patterns and varying textures. Sarpaneva's works from this period show a much greater concern for developing visually interesting, "natural" forms, and some of his latest works have become even more intricate and complex by combining multiple media and processes.

However, Sarpaneva has also made significant contributions to functional, applied art. He has designed extremely popular lines of Scandinavian metal cookware and tableware, glassware, ceramic wares, printed cloths and textiles, and industrial packaging. The range of his widely varying forms and textures is clearly shown by comparing his 1961 Rosenlew cooking pot, with its simplified lines and removable, sculptured handle, with his gleaming, stainless steel cookware manufactured by Opa in 1970. The ease with which Sarpaneva moves from glass to cast iron to stainless steel reflects his underlying concern to show the usefulness and beauty of all the materials he chooses to work with.

He is an artist who has the remarkable ability to pull selectively from historic repertoires and then combine these past ideas with new design inspirations. Often, however, he is totally original. Sarpaneva's works have evolved from purely traditional modes of Scandinavian design to express his adventuresome, artistic nature.

—Virginia A. Rose

SAWKA, Jan.
American graphic and stage designer. Born in Zabrze, Poland, 10 December 1946; emigrated to the United States in 1977; naturalized, 1989. Studied architecture, at the Polytechnic Institute, Wroclaw, 1964–72; Fine Arts Academy, Wroclaw, 1967–72. Married Hanna Maletz in 1974; daughter: Hanna. Freelance artist and graphic designer from 1970: artistic director, Barn Gallery, Warsaw, and F.A.M.A. Summer Art Festival on the Baltic coast, 1973–74; has designed for the Wroclaw Jazz Festival, Barn Art Center in Warsaw, *New York Times*, Harold Clurman Theatre, Samuel Beckett Theatre, Jean Cocteau Repertory Theatre, etc. **Exhibitions:** Wilanow Museum, Warsaw, 1976, 1980; Galerie Noire, Paris, 1977; Pulchri Studio, The Hague, 1977; Centre George Pompidou, Paris, 1978; Ankrum Gallery, Los Angeles, 1979, 1981; Andre Zarre Gallery,

New York, 1982; Deutsch Gallery, New York, 1983, 1985; Di Laurenti Gallery, New York, 1988; Dorsky Gallery, New York, 1989; State University of New York, New Paltz, 1989. **Collections:** Museum of Modern Art, New York; Library of Congress, Washington, D.C.; Centre Georges Pompidou; Paris; Deutsches Plakatmuseum, Essen; Stedelijk Museum, Amsterdam; Tokyo Museum of Modern Art; Israel Museum, Jerusalem. Recipient: Best Young Artist Award, Katowice Poster Biennale, 1974; Ministry of Culture Special Award, Warsaw, 1974; International Painting Festival Award, Cagnes-sur-Mer, 1975; Warsaw Poster Biennale Award, 1978; Lahti Poster Biennale Award, 1980. Address: R.D. 2, Box 14A, High Falls, New York 12440, U.S.A.

Works:

A Conversation installation, for the Deutsch Gallery, New York, 1983.
A Book of Fiction 25 prints, for Clarkson N. Potter Incorporated, 1986.
Krapp's Last Tape installation, for the Samuel Beckett Theatre, New York, 1986.
The Shoemakers (Witkacy) set design, for the Cocteau Theatre, New York, 1987.
The Trial (Kafka) set design, for the Cocteau Theatre, New York, 1987.
Macbeth (Shakespeare) set design, for the Cocteau Theatre, New York, 1989.
Grateful Dead touring concert stage sets, for The Grateful Dead band, 1989.
The Room installation, for the Dorsky Gallery, New York, 1989.
Dead Set book design, for Viking-Penguin, 1990.

Publications:

On SAWKA: books — *Contemporary Polish Posters in Full Color*, edited by Joseph S. Czestochowski, New York 1979; *Polish Posters 1970–1980* by Zdzislaw Schubert, Warsaw 1982; *Who's Who in Graphic Art*, edited by Walter Amstutz, Dubendorf 1982; *Visual Design Exhibition*, catalogue by Giovanni Brunazzi, Aosta 1988; articles—in *Cree* (Paris), October 1974, November 1976; *Projekt* (Warsaw), no. 4, 1974, no. 4, 1975, no. 4, 1976, no. 3, 1979; *Art and Artists* (London), June 1976; *Idea* (Tokyo), July 1977, March 1982; *Novum* (Munich), June 1978; *Artnews* (New York), September 1983, October 1984; *Backstage* (New York), March 1989.

My poster career evolved from my early involvement in the so-called "counter-culture" movement, particularly strong in Poland in the late 1960s and early 1970s. Of course, I don't divide art into two narrow categories—fine and applied. Every work I do I try to make the best—private tensions, dreams, desires. I treat my paintings, poetry illustrations, and theatrical posters equally seriously.

I'm sure I know why and what I paint. It's something like a feeling of warmness in your head: a half-ready answer is waiting. But when I *must* put it down, my God, it's not so easy.

From the very beginning, childhood, something was wrong with me (oversensitivity, the family physician stated). Books and reading interested me first. As far as I can remember, drawing was somehow regarded as natural, not respected at all—like eating or playing with toys. My parents' house was overwhelmed by books and discussions during those dark, Stalin years. Little groups of friends gathered over the bridge table, not so much to play but mostly to talk.

Jan Sawka: Stage setting for the Grateful Dead tour of the United States, 1989

Up to the last moment before entering higher education, I was unsure what to choose—philology at the university or fine arts at the academy. But the "oldies" decided to push me toward some "practical" career—architecture, engineering. And that *was* the beginning of my way to the current painting. Nothing fitted me properly, the frustrations built up; now I understand it was very positive, this sneaky, many-times-forced way.

Disillusioned by technical training in architecture, I began desperately to add something more to this boring existence. The relatively lively cultural life of city students lured me quickly. Jazz, "nightlife," cabarets, theatre—I lived for it, waiting nervously every day at the drawing rooms of school. Troubles built; I hardly managed to pass all the exams. Finally, after two years, without resigning from my engineering school, I joined the Fine Arts Academy, trying to cope with two problems. But my "off-duty" activity didn't cease; it even grew. Although extremely hectic, it was a far more exciting life. The next event, which shaped my entire life, was not designed by me but the "Reds." Nineteen sixty-eight: student riots, Zionists, Revisionists, tanks rumbling down Prague streets. It was a time of extreme tensions and simple "yes" or "no."

After the amnesty was granted by the government to all (almost all) unruly students, I tried to rebuild. But the amnesty was mainly on paper. Practically, I was eliminated. However, some brave people fought back, and by 1969 I had a carefully constructed, multi-media study program, which protected me from being pushed out of the schools but gave me a mad

schedule. Staying at the architecture faculty, I studied mostly design, while I worked also at the history of art institute as a junior researcher in my free time, restoring churches, etc. To keep "them" happy, I worked around the clock.

My "post-school" activities had grown serious. By the early 1970s, I was among those who had rejected the "Socialist way" and tried to pursue "free culture" (read: "counter-Red establishment"). My real companions were theatre, poetry, cabaret, visual arts—and I did anything that was needed. Thank God, it paid well, not in money but in far more important bonuses: I travelled abroad, all over Western Europe. You don't understand how hungry somebody can be to see the normal, civilized life of the Western world. During this time, I worked on those hard-to-formulate, private tensions—my private world.

Now, how do I say *what* I paint? Maybe it sounds megalomaniacal, but I try to discuss the world I see and feel. I try to care about the composition, shape, color, the so-called "form," of course. I try to execute painting in the best possible way—no easy tricks, no airbrushes, no copying from slides—all hand, pure hand.

But, most important, I try to communicate with all, concerned and unconcerned. I have no idea which trend of art I represent. Nothing interests me less. Of course, I'm sensitive to many currents of modern art, but I try to understand art as a whole. I love Old Masters but try to put their work into a larger context, not to separate their canvases from literature, music, society. I listen to music during my

work. I read. I try to know a little of everything. They did the same, I think. You cannot close yourself in a personal shell. Or maybe you can. I can't. *(Adapted from an interview published in Arts Magazine (New York), May 1983.)*

—Jan Sawka

Perhaps Jan Sawka is a visionary of our times. In 1980, he designed a poster titled "Car of the Year" which won first prize at the *Eighth International Poster Biennale* in Warsaw. It pictures a new-style, Russian tank rolling down a city street. On December 13, of the next year, tanks did indeed roll in Poland as a show of strength behind the government-imposed martial law. Sometime before that fateful day, Sawka had also been requested by the leaders of Solidarnosc to design the official Solidarnosc poster which would express, among other things, the hopes of the Polish people. The design for the poster showed the sun of Solidarnosc shining down forever on the hopes and dreams of a colorful landscape of the Polish people below. The original artwork for the poster was secretly transported into Poland and proudly displayed in the headquarters of Solidarnosc until it was destroyed by the Polish government. The poster however, could not be suppressed. Sawka recently recreated it in New York, and the AFL-CIO has exhibited and distributed it worldwide.

As a student, Sawka had participated in the political underground, but being a talented and gifted artist, he was rescued from any serious repercussions. He was a student of design and the fine arts at the time of his emergence into the Polish poster movement. Realizing that acceptance into the Polish poster school would have to be step-by-step up the already established ladder, he set out designing posters according to his own rules, artistic expertise, and available technique. His first poster was a linoleum cut for a student musical group; after that, he was asked to design other posters for various music clubs and student groups. By the time of his diploma show for graduation, Sawka had thirty posters to exhibit, as well as his paintings, prints, and drawings.

Later, Sawka moved to Krakow, which he considered the cultural center of Poland. There, he was asked to be art director for the renowned Polish avant-garde theater, STU. Although he received no salary, he was given a free hand to design whatever he chose.

In his student days, he had studied all aspects of design in order to understand all the processes and fine art of culture. By understanding the varied aspects of culture, Sawka believes that he can then better understand the relationships and complexities of mankind. He attempts to express this in his work.

As an artist who developed during the 1960s, Sawka reveals the influence of the psychedelic in both his compositions and in his use of colors. While his designs are always—without exception—powerful, they are also satirical, symbolic, humorous, bursting with energy, and imaginatively created. The colours he uses are combined in an explosive mélange. The lasting and overall effect is one of total honesty. Sawka converses in his language—art—succinctly, truthfully, and creatively. He does not compromise his ideas or designs for expediency. His images cause one to confront oneself, to examine one's thinking, one's way of life, one's hopes and dreams.

A versatile artist, Sawka paints, draws, and designs what he sees and what he believes in. His graphics reveal his insights into every phase of life—culture, politics, society, history, etc. He considers the poster a personal statement about the problem or subject. When designing a poster, he uses the medium he is working on at the time. If he is working on a print, the poster will look like a print; if a painting, the poster will look like a painting. Having studied architecture, his work naturally includes many architectural elements. He displays talent in every medium: etching, engraving, stencil, linocut, drypoint, etc. From miniatures to wall-size works, he works on masonite, paper, plywood, etc., using gouache, crayon, felt-tip, ball point, and acrylic—in any combination.

While in the United States, Sawka has become recognized not only for his expertise as a painter, but also as an illustrator. He has made more than 200 illustrations for the op-ed pages of the *New York Times* and the Boston *Globe*. These assignments have helped Sawka to understand the United States. Before he could execute the commission, he had to understand the current political or social situation he was to interpret. He has a knack for reducing each complex assignment to its simplest common denominator. His social comments on "the system" are artfully and delightfully drawn.

Freedom, as one can imagine, is very important to this designer, and he has expressed this through his graphics. His designs warrant more than one look, for although the exuberance is apparent, the real meaning, which is often biting, is sometimes concealed, often in narratives in the form of the comic strip, revealing the message which has been interwoven through the design.

Sawka's first major international award was won in 1975 in Cagnes-sur-Mer for a painting. The painting consisted of 216 smaller pictures that give the illusion of being prints and drawings. Now in New York City, he has once again

turned his creativity to painting. Sawka's achievements and zest serve as an inspiration to other young designers throughout the world. As Sawka himself has said of his life so far in this country: 'I am successful, I do what I want, I shall stay my old self, I, Jan Sawka."

—Elena Millie

SCARPA, Carlo (Alberto).
Italian architect, interior, exhibition and industrial designer. Born in Venice, 2 June 1906. Studied architecture, at the Accademia di Belle Arti, Venice, 1921–26: Dip.Arch. 1926; student and assistant to Guido Girilli, at the Institute of Architecture, University of Venice, 1926–27. Married Onorina Lazzari in 1934: son: Tobia. Assistant to the architect Vincenzo Rinaldi, Venice, 1922–24; freelance architect, designer and graphic artist, in Venice, 1927–62, in Asolo, 1962–72, and in Vicenza, 1972–78: artistic consultant to Murano Cappellin and Company Glassworks, Venice, 1972–30, and to Venini Glassworks, Venice, 1933–47; design consultant to the Venice Biennale from 1941, and to Cassina and B & B Italia furniture companies, 1969. Assistant teacher, 1926–29, 1932–33, professor, 1933–76, and director, 1970–78, at the Istituto Universitario di Architettura, Venice; head of design course, Istituto Artistico Industriale, Venice, 1945–47; head of visual studies, Istituto Superiore di Disegno Industriale, Venice, 1960–61. **Exhibitions:** *Carlo Scarpa*, at the Milan Triennale, 1960; *Museum Architecture*, Museum of Modern Art, New York, 1966; Royal Institute of British Architects, London, 1972; Accademia Olimpica, Vicenza, 1974; Institut de l'Environnement, Paris, 1975; Palazzo delle Stelline, Milan, 1978; Galeria I.D., Madrid, 1978; Accademia di San Luca, Rome, 1979; Istituto Statale di Architettura, Reggio Calabria, 1981; Museo Castelvecchio, Verona, 1982; Italian Cultural Institute, Paris, 1983; Galleria dell'Accademia, Venice, 1984. Recipient: Diploma of Honour, 1934, and Grand Jury Prize, 1960, Milan Triennale; Olivetti National Award, Turin, 1956; Ministry of Public Information Medal, Rome, 1962; In-Arch National Award, Rome, 1962; Regional Architecture Award, Verona, 1964; President's Architecture Prize, Rome, 1967; Accademia dei Lincei Prize, 1971. D.Arch.: Istituto Universitario di Architettura, Venice, 1978. Honorary member, British Institute of Design, 1970, and Pierre Chareau Foundation, Paris, 1975; member, Accademia Olimpica, Vicenza, 1974; Academician, Accademia di San Luca, Rome, 1976. *Died* (in Sendai, Japan) *28 November 1978.*

Works:

Onion-shaped decanter in smoked glass, for Cappellin and Company, 1927.
Sfriso silverware shop interiors, Campo San Toma, Venice, 1932.
Drinking glasses in double-layered black and green glass, for Venini, 1936.
Oval bottle in textured red and black glass, for Venini, 1940.
Il Cavallino modern art gallery interiors, Riva degli Schiavoni, Venice, 1942.
Dish in azure and violet glass with mauve circular decoration, for Venini, 1942.

Giovanni Bellini exhibition layouts, Palazzo Ducale, Venice, 1948.
Public telephones in Venice, for the Twelve Company, 1950.
Piet Mondrian exhibition layouts, Valle Giulia, Rome, 1956.
Olivetti shop interiors, St. Mark's Square, Venice, 1957.
Gavina shop (now Simon shop) interiors, via Altabella, Bologna, 1961.
Doge table in steel and glass, 1968.
Florentine Frescoes exhibition layouts, Hayward Gallery, London, 1969.
Orseolo writing table in treated wood and black lacquer, 1973.
Le Corbusier exhibition layouts, Querini-Stampalia, Venice, 1973.
Toledo range of beds in turned wood with leather headboards, 1975.
Logotype sign, for the Banca Popolare of Verona, 1977.
Cutlery set in gold and silver, for Cleto Munari, 1977–78.

(for a complete list of Scarpa's buildings and architectural projects, see *Contemporary Architects*)

Publications:

By SCARPA: book—*Memoriae Causa*, editor, Verona 1977; article—in *Modo* (Milan), January/February 1979.

On SCARPA: books—*Carlo Scarpa: Architetto Poeta* by Sergio Los, Venice 1967; *Carlo Scarpa: Architetto Poeta*, exhibition catalogue by Sherban Cantacuzino, London 1974; *Carlo Scarpa*, exhibition catalogue by Neri Pozza, Vicenza 1974; *Carlo Scarpa*, exhibition catalogue by Luciana Miotto-Muret, Paris 1975; *Carlo Scarpa* by Neri Pozza, Padua 1978; *Carlo Scarpa per Bernini*, edited by G. Scarpa, Venice 1979; *Carlo Scarpa: Venezia 1906—Sendai 1978—I Sette Foglie Giapponese*, edited by G. Scarpa, Venice 1979; *Carlo Scarpa a Castelvecchio*, exhibition catalogue edited by L. Magnagnato, Milan 1982; *Carlo Scarpa* by M. A. Crippa, Milan 1984; *Carlo Scarpa 1906–1978*, edited by Francesco Dal Co and Giuseppe Mazzariol, Milan 1984; *Carlo Scarpa: Theory, Design, Projects* by Maria Antonietta Crippa, Milan 1984, Cambridge, Massachusetts 1986.

SCARPA, Tobia.
Italian architect, furniture and product designer. Born in Venice, 1 March 1935: son of the architect Carlo Scarpa. Studied architecture, at the Instituto Universitario di Architettura, Venice, 1953–57: Dip. Arch. 1957. Married the designer Afra Bianchini. Designer, at the Venini Glassworks, Murano, Venice, 1958–61; freelance designer, in partnership with Afra Scarpa, in Montebelluna, from 1960; designed for C & B, Stildomus, Maxalto, B & B Italia, Unifor, Flos, Cassina, Knoll, Gavina, etc. Lecturer, School of Industrial Design, Venice. **Exhibitions:** Milan Triennale, 1960, 1964, 1968; *Selection 66*, Museum fur Angewandte Kunst, Vienna, 1966; *Italian Furniture Design*, Furniture Salon, Tokyo, 1968; *Modern Chairs*, Whitechapel Art Gallery, London, 1970; *One Hundred Modern Chairs*, National Gallery of Victoria, Melbourne, 1974; *Design and Design*,

Tobia Scarpa: *Soriana* chair, for Cassina, 1969

Palazzo delle Stelline, Milan, 1979 (toured); *Design Since 1945*, Philadelphia Museum of Art, 1983. **Collections:** Museum of Modern Art, New York; Philadelphia Museum of Art. Recipient: Compasso d'Oro Award, Milan, 1970; American Society of Interior Designers Award, New York, 1979. Address: Corso Manzini 10, Montebelluna, Treviso, Italy.

Works:

Pigreco armchair in moulded plywood with leather or cloth seat, 1959–60, produced by Santabona, Gavina and Knoll.
Bastiano 2- or 3-seat sofa in wood, steel and leather, 1961, produced by Gavina and Knoll.
Seky-Han fluorescent floor lamp in wood and metal, 1963, produced by Flos.
Nibai extending table in wood and metal, 1963, for Gavina.
915 and *923* sofas in metal with polyfoam and leather upholstery, 1964, produced by Cassina.
Torcello container system of furniture, 1964, produced by Stildomus.
Coronado armchair, divan and pouf in tubular steel with foam and leather upholstery, 1966, produced by C & B Italia and B & B Italia.
Ciprera armchair in polyurethane foam with reinforced polyester covering, 1968, produced by Cassina.
Soriana armchair, divan and pouf in metal, polyfoam, polyester and dacron, 1969, produced by Cassina.
Pozzetto armchair in pre-formed resin, 1970, produced by C & B Italia and B & B Italia.
TL 59 Circular table in aluminium and glass, 1972, produced by Roberto Poggi.
Crispino and *Bordo* ceramic tableware, 1973, produced by Galvani.
Mix upholstered swivel office chair, 1975, produced by Unifor.

Artona range of furniture, 1975–79, produced by Maxalto.
Miro modular storage furniture units, 1981, produced by Molteni & Cie.
Abatina table lamp, 1981, produced by Flos.
Serenda armchairs in wood with upholstered seats, 1983, produced by Stildomus.

Publications:

On SCARPA: books—*Modern Furniture* by Ella Moody, London 1966; *Design Italiano: I Mobili*, edited by Enrichetta Ritter, Milan and Rome 1968; *Modern Chairs 1918–1970*, exhibition catalogue with texts by Carol Hogben and others, London 1970; *The Modern Chair: Classics in Production* by Clement Meadmore, London 1974; *One Hundred Modern Chairs*, exhibition catalogue by Terence Lane, Melbourne 1974; *Knoll Design* by Larrabee and Massimo Vignelli, New York 1981; *Contemporary Furniture*, edited by Klaus-Jurgen Sembach, Stuttgart and London 1982; *Design Since 1945*, edited by Kathryn Hiesinger and George Marcus, Philadelphia and London 1983; *Afra and Tobia Scarpa, Architetti e Designers* by Antonio Piva, Milan 1985; *Modern Furniture Classics* by Miriam Stimpson, London 1987; *Designed by Architects in the 1980s* by Juli Capella and Quim Larrea, London 1988; *Italian Modern: A Design Heritage* by Giovanni Albera and Nicolas Monti, New York 1989.

After Tobia Scarpa graduated with an architectural degree in Venice, he went to work as a designer at the Murano glass works. Two years later, in 1958, he started to work for Paolo Venini, also in glass design. In 1960, he opened his own office in collaboration with his wife, Afra.

It was about this time that the first of many successful furniture designs, Bastiano, was conceived. Architecturally detailed in matte fin-

ished rosewood, the cushions crisply finished in fine leather, the seating units would soon become classic in the furniture world.

There followed a succession of innovative designs from this team. Nuvola, a cocoon hanging light in spun fiberglass over a metal frame, and Fantasma Piccolo, a floor-mounted version; Coronado, an upholstered armchair and sofa; Juker, a spun-aluminum table lamp with a tilting shade that creates a "personality" for an otherwise inanimate object; Fior di Loto and Nictea, mushroom-like hanging lamps in polished metal; Ciprea, an upholstered polyurethane foam design that simultaneously conveys the character of a stuffed Victorian chair and a front seat from a modern automobile; and Foglio, an incredibly simple, wall-mounted light fixture which conveys the notion of a metal bracelet encircling the lamps and screening them from direct view. They also produced some unique uses of precast concrete, as in the Maglieria factory, where long, x-shaped (cross-section) beams are interspaced with roof glazing panels to provide natural daylighting for the interior, and in the C+B Furniture factory, where vertical and horizontal elements are interlocked like a gigantic children's puzzle.

A favorite design is Soriana, armless seating in tufted fabric or leather over multi-density polyurethane foam and dacron fiberfill, the marshmallow-like forms girdled by a chrome-plated, spring-steel, external skeleton which holds the forms in shape and provides the necessary finishing detail. The chair was the winner of the 1970 Compasso d'Oro and, together with a leather-covered, molded-plywood and wood chair, called simply 925, is included in the permanent design collection of the Museum of Modern Art in New York.

Possibly reflecting his training at the glass works, Biagio, a table lamp made from two pieces of hollowed-out, white marble, somewhat resembles a space-age or sports (or perhaps, religious) headdress. Recently, Bollo and Papillona halogen wall and floor lighting fixtures appeared.

Most recently, the pair has produced the Master range of modular office furniture components, which can also function as individual pieces. Finely detailed in leather-edged woods on a painted aluminum structure, the inherent design and precision manufacturing (one-tenth millimeter tolerance) destine this line to become another classic.

—William Victor Kriebel

SCHEICHENBAUER, Mario.
Italian architectural and industrial designer. Born in Milan, 31 May 1931. Studied architecture, at the Politecnico, Milan, 1957. Freelance designer, specialising in plastics and solar-energized structures, Milan, from 1954: has designed for Societa RPD, Montedison, Marini e Sordelli, ENI, Milani Resine, etc. President, Associazione Progamma ERG, Milan. **Exhibitions:** Battersea College of Technology, London, 1970; Guildford School of Art, Surrey, 1973; Faculty of Architecture, University of Bucharest, 1974; Faculty of Architecture, University of Sofia, 1975; University of Moscow, 1981. Member, Associazione degli Architetti di Milano. Address: Via Vincenzo Bellini 11, 20122 Milan, Italy.

Mario Scheichenbauer: City-car in ABS plastic, for Marini e Sordelli, 1973

Works:

Ogamma system plastic roofed buildings, in Lugano and Varese, for Societa RPD, 1965.
Montenapo upholstered armchair in moulded white plywood, for Zanotta, 1967.
Monoblock bathroom units, for Societa RPD, 1968.
Beach cabins in GF-UP plastics, for Brianza Plastica, 1969.
Experimental plastic-construction building, for Montedison, 1972.
Beach cabins in ABS plastic, for Marini e Sordelli, 1972.
City car in ABS plastic, for Marini e Sordelli, 1973.
Experimental thermoplastic building materials, for ENI, 1973–78.
Prefabricated buildings in thermoplastics, for ENI, 1977.
Extruded plastic flooring, for Milani Resine, 1980.
Thermoplastic solar panels, for Milani Resine, 1981.

Publications:

By SCHEICHENBAUER: books—*A. Campanini, Architetto*, Milan 1968; *Il Poliestere Rinforzato*, Milan 1972; *La Termoformatura*, Milan 1979; *Il Libro della Casa Solare*, translator, Rome 1980; *Sintesi dei Corsi sull'Energia Solare*, Milan 1981; *Bilancio Energetico dell' Abitazione*, Milan 1982.

On SCHEICHENBAUER: books — *Catalogo Bolaffi dell'Architettura Italiana 1963–66*, edited by Pier Carlo Santini and Giuseppe Luigi

Marini, Turin 1966; *Design Italiano: I Mobili*, edited by Enrichetta Ritter, Milan and Rome 1968; *Idee per la Casa/Modern Interiors* by Franco Magnani, Milan and London 1969; *Design e Forme Nuove nell'Arredamento Italiano* by Paolo Portoghesi and Marino Marini, Rome 1978; *Storia e Cronaca della Triennale* by Anty Pansera, Milan 1978; *Da Cosa Nasce Cosa* by Bruno Munari, Bari 1981.

New ideas spring from new problems or new ways of solving them. Industrial design and planning have to tackle (and translate the answers into form-language) the problems connected with industrial production (including products for the building industry), the problems derived from the new awareness of energy and ecology, and the new means available for solving these problems (new materials such as plastics, new technologies such as pressings, programming, marketing).

—Mario Scheichenbauer

SCHLEGER, Hans.
British corporate, exhibition and graphic designer. Born in Kempen, Germany, 29 December 1898; settled in Britain in 1932: naturalized, 1938. Studied painting and drawing, at

the Kunstgewerbescule, Berlin, 1918–21. Served in the German Army 1916–18. Married Pat Maycock in 1956; daughters: Maria and Lalli. Publicity manager and film set designer for Karl Hagenbeck, Berlin, 1921–24; magazine layout artist and freelance advertising designer, establishing own Madison Avenue studio under the name "Zero", New York, 1924–29; designer, in the German branch office of W. S. Crawford advertising agency, Berlin, 1929–32; freelance designer, London, 1932–76; founder-director, Hans Schleger and Associates design studio, London, 1953–76; designed corporate images for MacFisheries, Associated Electrical Industries, Imperial Chemical Industries, Fisons, Jaeger, Finmar Furniture, Grants Whisky, British Sugar, British Rail, Edinburgh International Festival, Manchester Polytechnic, etc. Visiting lecturer at the Chelsea School of Art, London, Royal College of Art, London, and at the Regional College of Art, Manchester; visiting associate professor, Institute of Design, Chicago, 1950–51. **Exhibitions:** Lund Humphries, London, 1934; Institute of Design, Chicago, 1951; Manchester Polytechnic, 1977; North Staffordshire Polytechnic, 1978. **Collections:** Victoria and Albert Museum, London; London Transport Museum; British Railway Museum, York; Imperial War Museum, London; National Gallery of Australia, Canberra. Recipient: Royal Designer for Industry, Royal Society of Arts, London, 1959; Fellow, Society of Industrial Artists and Designers, London. Member, Alliance Graphique Internationale, Paris; Designers and Art Directors Association, London. *Died* (in London) *18 September 1976.*

Works:

Plain or Fancy newspaper advertisements, for Weber and Heilbroner, 1927–29.
Bus stop designs, for London Transport, 1935.
The Highway Code exhibition layout and poster, for the Ministry of Transport, London, 1937.
These Men Use Shell poster, for Shell Oil Company, 1938.
Trade mark, for the Coal Utilisation Council, 1947.
Hands at Your Service posters, for London Passenger Transport Board, 1947.
With Gin This Is It promotional poster, for Martini Vermouth, 1949.
Logo and corporate identity programme, for MacFisheries, 1952–59.
Trade mark, for Finmar, 1953.
Terylene: Handle and Drape press advertisements, for Imperial Chemical Industries, 1954.
Symbol, for the Design Centre, London, 1955.
Standfast triangular whisky bottle, for W. Grant and Sons, 1956.
Stop for Super Shell and Go poster, for Shell Oil Company, 1958.
Fisons Pest Control manuals and advertisements, for Fisons, 1959–64.
Corporate identity programme, for the British Sugar Corporation, 1961–75.
Hardback book symbol, for Allen Lane/The Penguin Press, 1966.
Unified design programme, for the Edinburgh International Festival, 1966–75.

Publications:

By SCHLEGER: book—*The Practice of Design*, with others, London 1946; articles—in *Arts and Industry* (London), March 1949; *Advertising Review* (London), nos. 1–4, 1954–55, no. 8, 1956, no. 18, 1958; *Idea* (Tokyo), no. 43, 1960.

On SCHLEGER: books—*Line Drawing for Reproduction* by Ashley Havinden, London 1933, 1941; *Lettering Today*, edited by C. G. Holme, London and New York 1937, 1948; *The New Graphic Design* by Karl Gerstner and Markus Kutter, Teufen and London 1959; *Who's Who in Graphic Art*, edited by Walter Amstutz, Zurich 1962; *Graphic Design in Britain*, edited by Frederick Lambert, London 1967; *An International Survey of Packaging* by Wim Crouwel and Kurt Weidemann, London 1968; *107 Grafici dell'AGI*, with texts by Renzo Zorzi and Franco Grignani, Venice 1974; *Archigraphia: Architectural Graphics*, edited by Walter Herdeg, Zurich 1978; *Thirties: British Art and Design Before the War*, exhibition catalogue with texts by Ian Jeffrey and others, London 1979; *Eye for Industry: Royal Designers for Industry 1936–1986* by Fiona MacCarthy and Patrick Nuttgens, London 1986.

Hans Schleger's German background and his early experience in the United States seem very much present in his British work and may partly account for its assurance and easy grasp of modernist principles. He embodied the foreign influences that fostered a native, belated, British modernism, and his work played a leading role in the development from "commercial art" of the prewar period to "graphic design" proper, as it emerged in the 1950s and 1960s. In Schleger's case, the passage is from the artist Zero to the design practice Hans Schleger and Associates. It is a development that can be seen also, for example, in the career of F. H. K. Henrion, another of the pioneer graphic designers in Britain and also an émigré.

Schleger first became known in Britain for his posters and work in press advertising. At this stage, he was already a sophisticated artist; his early work, often employing montage, shows the tendency towards simplification and integration of text and image that characterizes his postwar work in graphic design. This process reaches a culmination in the trade symbols that he designed. Here, as in his earlier drawing, especially from the years in New York, the forms are subtle and not at all tempted by crude geometry.

The postwar work in corporate identity, in which Schleger was among the early leaders in Britain, shows the breadth of his talents. His trademarks take their place in the design of a whole range of items. Schleger showed a special interest in package design, as is clear from the Finmar work and also in his whisky bottle for Grant's. It seems typical of his approach that he found a fresh form for the bottle itself and dispensed with the traditional label. (The client retained the bottle's form, but applied a label, not of Schleger's design.)

Apart from the inevitably ephemeral products of this graphic design work, standing as more lasting testimony to Schleger's talent is the book *The Practice of Design* (1946), a compilation of essays predominantly by members of the Design Research Unit; it includes a short written contribution by Schleger on "designing this book." The volume is still a distinguished object (reminiscent of the best American work of the period) and must have stood out sharply from the normal level of book production in postwar Britain.

As his published statements suggest, Schleger became interested in the human aspects of design (which figure largely in work of the scale he came to tackle) as much as in the purely visual or formal problems. Aware of the need to fuse both aspects of a task satisfactorily, he approached the project, as well as its visual forms, in a way that can properly be described as elegant, sensitive, refined.

—Robin Kinross

SCHMIDT, Douglas W.

American stage designer. Born in Cincinnati, Ohio, 4 October 1942. Educated at High Mowing School, Wilton, New Hampshire, until 1960; studied at the School of Fine and Applied Arts, Boston University, 1961–64. Designer and stage manager, Monmouth Repertory Theatre, Maine, 1961; assistant to designer Ming Cho Lee, in New York, 1964–67; freelance stage designer, New York, from 1965, and television designer from 1974: resident designer, Lincoln Center Repertory Theatre, New York, from 1969; also designed for the Cincinnati Playhouse-in-the-Park, Juilliard Opera Theatre, Juilliard Dance Company, New York Shakespeare Festival, East Side Playhouse, 41st Street Theatre, Ethel Barrymore Theatre, etc. Lecturer, New York Center for Field Studies. Board member, Studio and Forum of Stage Design, New York. Recipient: New York Drama Desk Award, 1973, 1974; Obie Award, New York, 1977; Joseph Maharam Award, New York, 1977. Member, American Society of Interior Designers. Address: 1501 Broadway, Suite 1606, New York, New York 1036, U.S.A.

Works:

Stage productions (New York, unless noted) include—*The Caretaker* (for Playhouse-in-the-Park, Cincinnati), 1964; *La Bohème* (first design for New York production, for Juilliard Opera Theatre), 1965; *The Ox Cart*, 1966; *To Bury a Cousin*, 1967; *Father Uxbridge Wants to Marry*, 1967; *The Memorandum*, 1968; *Huui-Huui*, 1968; *Twelfth Night*, 1969; *The Time of Your Life*, 1969; *The Good Woman of Setzuan*, 1970; *Operation Sidewinder*, 1970; *Landscape and Silence* (double-bill; also designed costumes), 1970; *The Disintegration of James Cherry*, 1970; *Paris is Out!* 1970; *Play of the Western World*, 1971; *Landscape*, 1971; *Silence*, 1971; *An Enemy of the People*, 1971; *Antigone*, 1971; *Play Strindberg*, 1971; *The Merry Wives of Windsor* (Stratford, Connecticut), 1971; *Pictures in the Hallway*, 1971; *Mary Stuart*, 1971; *People are Living There*, 1971; *The Wedding of Iphigenia*, 1971; *Iphigenia in Concert*, 1971; *The Losers*, 1971; *Huckleberry Finn*, 1971; *Narrow Road to the Deep North*, 1972; *The Love Suicide at Schofield Barracks*, 1972; *Grease*, 1972; *Twelfth Night*, 1972; *The Country Girl*, 1972; *The School for Scandal*, 1972; *The Hostage*, 1972; *Women Beware Women*, 1972; *Lower Depths*, 1972; *Enemies*, 1972; *Happy Days*, 1972; *Act Without Words I*, 1972; *Krapp's Last Tape*, 1972; *Not I*, 1972; *Macbeth* (Stratford, Connecticut), 1973; *The Plough and the Stars*, 1973; *A Streetcar Named Desire*, 1973; *A Breeze from the Gulf*, 1973; *Veronica's Room*, 1973; *The Three Sisters*, 1973; *Measure for Measure*, 1973; *An American Millionaire*, 1974; *Fame*, 1974; *Kid Champion*, 1974; *Who's Who in Hell*, 1974; *Over Here!*, 1974; *The Three Sisters*, 1975; *Our Late Night*, 1975; *The Robber Bridegroom*, 1975; *Edward II*, 1975; *The Time of Your Life*, 1975; *Angel Street*, 1975; *Truckload*, 1975; *Threepenny Opera*, 1976; *Let My People Come*, 1976; *Herzl*, 1976; *The Crazy Locomotive*, 1977; *Agamemnon*, 1977; *Sunset* (Los Angeles), 1977; *Stages*, 1978; *Runaways*, 1978; *They're Playing Our Song*, 1979; *The Most Happy Fella*, 1979; *Romantic Comedy*, 1979; *Frankenstein*, 1981; *The Death of von Richtofen as Witnessed from Earth*, 1982; *The Skin of Our Teeth*, 1983; *Porgy and Bess*, 1983; *Chaplin*, 1983; *Detective Story*, 1984; *Black Comedy*, 1984; *Scapino*, 1984; *The Loves of Don Perlimpin*, 1984; *Dancing in the End Zone*, 1985; *Palladium Club Phase 1*, 1985.

Publications:

On SCHMIDT: books—*Who's Who in the Theatre*, vol. 17, London and Detroit 1981; *Contemporary Theatre, Film and Television*, Detroit 1986.

Since the beginning of the twentieth century, when set designers were elevated to the level of creative artists, it has been assumed that a good designer would have a distinctive style. Douglas Schmidt, by his own admission is eclectic. Yet, he is one of the most successful Broadway designers. Basically, he is a theatricalist in the nineteenth-century tradition. His sets are large, often pictorial, with their own theatrical quality—moving elements, multiple units, and special effects. It is because of his fascination with theatricality and presentationism that he is drawn to nineteenth-century opera, for which he has designed *Aida* and *Samson and Delilah*, among many others. Although he assisted Ming Cho Lee in the early 1960s at the New York Shakespeare Festival, and his early work shows Lee's influence, Schmidt's real influence comes from his teachers at Boston University, Raymond Sovey and Horace Armistead—both traditional Broadway designers from the pre-World War II era. As a result, his design proclaims itself as such, rather than as naturalistic illusion or subtle thematic statement.

Almost inadvertently, then, Schmidt has become the quintessential designer of the 1980s because American theatre now lacks distinguished play-writing and outstanding actors and has come to be dominated by spectacle. Design is the innovative aspect of current theatre, and Schmidt is in the forefront. He thrives on unabashed theatricality, slickness, invention, and spectacle. In this, he is like fellow designers Robin Wagner and John Lee Beatty. It is significant that in the past decade, opera has become a focal point for innovation in design and directing.

Besides the flying airplane in *The Death of von Richtofen as Witnessed from Earth*, Schmidt's mechanisms have included audience seating sections moving on air casters (*Agamemnon*, 1977), interlocking steel pieces of a backdrop (*Macbeth*, 1973), a revolving garden that allowed the audience to view each scene from a different angle (*Enemies*, 1972), moving walls (*Threepenny Opera*, 1976, and *Stages*, 1978), multiple sets for which the changes became a spectacle in itself (*They're Playing Our Song*, 1979), and a treadmill (*Over Here!*, 1974). He has stated that scenery should play the part of an actor and be as entertaining as the play itself. Interestingly, he is an admirer of the work of avant-garde director Richard Foreman for whom he has designed two shows on Broadway. Foreman's work contains moving sets or set pieces which are as important as the performers, and Schmidt considers Foreman not only a significant director but a major designer as well.

The high point of Schmidt's career to date was the ill-fated *Frankenstein*. Despite the show's critical and box-office failure, it was one of the most spectacular productions on Broadway in this century. Eight gothic sets moved on and off the stage to conclude in a cataclysmic scene in which the laboratory was reduced to rubble. The curtain descended on the scene only to rise within five seconds on a totally bare stage. The show was a potpourri of scenographic tricks and spectacle reminiscent of nineteenth-century staging.

Schmidt's sets do not evolve from artistic theory, they make no subtle statements; rather, they delight in their own presentation and serve the needs of the play.

—Arnold Aronson

SCHMOLLER, Hans (Peter).
British typographer and book designer. Born in Berlin, Germany, 9 April 1916; emigrated in 1938: naturalized British citizen, 1946. Educated at the Kaiser-Friedrich-Schule, Berlin-Charlottenburg, until 1933; apprenticed as a compositor in a printing firm, Berlin, 1933–37; part-time studies in calligraphy and lettering, at the Hohere Graphische Fachschule, Berlin, 1935–36. Married Dorothee Wachsmuth in 1947 (died, 1948); daughter: Monica; married Tatyana Kent in 1950; son: Sebastian. Assistant manager, Morija Printing Works, Lesotho, 1938–46; assistant to Oliver Simon, at the Curwen Press, London, 1947–49; typographer, 1949–56, head of production, 1956–76, director, 1960–76, and consultant, 1976–80, at Penguin Books publishers, Harmondsworth, Middlesex. Chief examiner in typography, City and Guilds Institute, London, 1956–57; president, Double Crown Club, London, 1968–69; council member, Royal Society of Arts, London, 1979–85. **Exhibitions:** *British Book Design* exhibitions, National Book League, London, from 1951; *Penguin Production and Design*, Monotype Corporation, London 1951; *Eye for Industry*, Victoria and Albert Museum, London, 1986. Recipient: Gold Medal, Leipzig Book Fair, 1971; Francis Minns Award, London, 1974. Royal Designer for Industry, Royal Society of Arts, London, 1976. Corresponding member, Bund Deutscher Buchkunstler, 1965. *Died* (in London) *25 September 1985.*

Works:

Painting in Britain 1530 to 1790 (E. K. Waterhouse) book design, for Penguin Books, 1953.
The Art and Architecture of India (B. Rowland) book design, for Penguin Books, 1953.
Silas Marner (G. Eliot) book design, for The Limited Editions Club, New York, 1953.
Gargantua and Pantagruel (F. Rabelais) book design for Penguin Books, 1955.
The Penguin Story 1935–1956 (W. E. Williams) book design, for Penguin Books, 1956.
The Fairy Tales of Charles Perrault book design, for Penguin Books, 1957.
The Twelve Caesars (Suetonius/R. Graves) book design, for Penguin Books, 1957.
The Story of an African Farm (O. Schreiner) book design, for the Limited Editions Club, New York, 1961.
C. A. Mace: A Symposium book design, for Methuen and Company, and Penguin Books, 1962.
Without Prejudice: One Hundred Letters from Frederick William Rolfe to John Lane book design, for Allen Lane, 1963.
Concerning Architecture: Essays Presented to Nikolaus Pevsner book design, for Allen Lane/The Penguin Press, 1968.
The Complete Pelican Shakespeare book design, for Penguin Books Incorporated and Allen Lane/The Penguin Press, 1969.
Camden's Britannia: Surrey and Sussex book design, for Hutchinson and Company, 1977.

Publications:

By SCHMOLLER: books—*Giovanni Mardersteig: Die Officina Bodoni 1923–77*, editor, Hamburg 1979, Verona 1980; *Mr. Gladstone's Washi*, Newtown 1983; articles—in *Penrose Annual* (London), no. 52, 1958; *Der Druckspiegel* (Stuttgart), no. 6, 1959; *The Book Collector* (London), no. 2, 1982.

On SCHMOLLER: books—*Modern Book Design* by Ruari McLean, London 1958; *Magazine Design* by Ruari McLean, New York and Toronto 1959; *Who's Who in Graphic Art*, edited by Walter Amstutz, Zurich 1962, Dubendorf 1982; *Eye for Industry: Royal Designers for Industry 1936–1986*, exhibition catalogue by Fiona MacCarthy and Patrick Nuttgens, London 1986.

*

Hans Schmoller seems to have been perfectly suited for his job at Penguin Books. Knowing about typography in an absolutely practical way from his apprenticeship in Berlin and his work in Africa, then at the Curwen Press, he could deal confidently with printers. He also brought with him a background of German culture, with its craft traditions in book production better maintained than those in Britain. He thus shared many of the same assumptions as his predecessor at Penguin, Jan Tschichold. Care taken over the smallest details (of letter-spacing or word-division, say) is a chief characteristic of this approach. Success in these things depends on the quality of layouts and specifications; Schmoller's directions to printers have been notable for their precision but also for knowing what can and what cannot be exactly instructed; the "voice" of these instructions is an understanding one.

Outside the special field of mass-produced paperbacks—in the design of cased or hardback books—Schmoller's concern for the book as a working object becomes fully evident. Because of careful choice of materials and vigilant attention to presswork and finishing processes, the final products of Schmoller's typography have a physical distinction unusual among British books. His typographic manner, most obvious in display work, shows his allegiances—perhaps "neo-classical" (though averting its glance from late-nineteenth-century excess), but willing to work with new techniques. One might place his work in the tradition to which C. E. Poeschel or Jakob Hegner belong.

A particular strength of Schmoller's work has been its treatment of editorially complex text matter. This is evident in the Penguin reference books and in editions of texts with annotations. The design of *The Complete Pelican Shakespeare* (1969) may be his most successfully achieved single work. The edition provides consistently satisfactory settings of the different verse and prose forms, along with related notes on each page, and welds these pages, with supplementary editorial matter, into a visually coherent, useable, and attractive book.

Schmoller's writings on the history of printing and typography have followed from his design work. They have been confined to occasional articles and to translating and editing. His subjects have included the history of paperbacks, patterned papers, the work of other typographers. His writing shows qualities that correspond to his typography: a relish for detail and for clarification of complexity, along with humane presentation.

—Robin Kinross

SCHUITEMA, (Geert) Paul (Hendrikus).
Dutch painter, photographer, exhibition, furniture and graphic designer. Born in Groningen, 27 February 1897. Educated in the Hague and Rotterdam, until 1914; studied painting and drawing, at the Akademie van Beeldende Kunsten en Technische Wetenschappen, Rotterdam, 1915–17, 1919–20. Served in the Dutch Army, 1917–18. Married Elly van Dobben in 1936. Independent painter, establishing studio with his brother E. B. W. Schuitema, in Rotterdam, 1922–25; graphic and industrial designer from 1925, photographer and filmmaker from 1928, working in Rotterdam, 1925–36, The Hague, 1936–39, and in Wassenaar, 1940–73: head of publicity, NC Mij. van Berkel's Patent company, Rotterdam, 1927–31; founder and director of the steel furniture co-operative workshops, Rotterdam, 1930–31; co-founder, Nederlandische Werkgemeenschap voor Filmproductie, Wassenaar, 1945; typographic designer, *Cement* magazine, for Verkoopassociatie Enci-Cemij NV, Wassenaar, 1948–67; also designed for C. Chevalier printing company, Boel and Van Eesteren, I. J. van Ettinger, Philip Dekker, Philips, Eternit, Algemeene Kunstzijde Unie, Dutch Posts and Telecommunications, etc. Chief editor, *De Fakkel* magazine, Rotterdam, 1926; contributor to *Filmliga magazine*, Rotterdam, 1932–33, and *De 8 en Opbouw* magazine, Rotterdam, 1933–36. Chairman, Centrale van Bonden van Leerligen en Oud-Leerligen van Kunstscholen Nederland, Rotterdam, 1926; secretary, Opbouw group, Rotterdam, 1928–34; advisory council member, Nederland-Nieuwe Russland association, Rotterdam, 1932–33; cultural advisory commission member, Nederlandse Bioskoopbond, Wassenaar, 1946. Instructor in publicity design, Akademie van Beeldende Kunsten, The Hague, 1930–62; guest professor, West of England College of Art, Bristol, 1966. **Exhibitions:** C. Chevalier print showroom, Rotterdam, 1935; Stedelijk Museum, Amsterdam, 1965; Kunstgewerbemuseum, Zurich, 1967. Recipient: Dutch Royal State Subsidy, 1923–25; Award of Honour, Concours du Meilleur Siege in Aluminium, Paris, 1933; Dutch Ministry of Culture Stipend, 1970. Honorary member, Gebonden Kunsten Federatie, The Hague, 1963. *Died* (in Wassenaar) *25 October 1973.*

Publications:

By SCHUITEMA: book—*Syst-o-Colour*, 2 vols., The Hague 1966; articles—in *i 10* (Leiden), no. 16, 1928; *Schoonheid en Opvoeding* (Amsterdam), January 1929; *Links Rechten* (Rotterdam), February 1933; *De Reclame* (Amsterdam), November 1933; *Neue Grafik* (St. Gallen), December 1961.

On SCHUITEMA: books—*Die Neue Typografie* by Jan Tschichold, Berlin 1928; *Foto-Auge* by Franz Roh and Jan Tschichold, Stuttgart 1929; *Eine Stunde Druckgestaltung* by Jan Tschichold, Stuttgart 1930; *Pismo a Fotografie v Reklame* by Z. Rossmann, Brno 1938; *The New Graphic Design* by Karl Gerstner and Markus Kutter, Teufen and London 1959; *Functional Graphic Design in the 20s* by Eckhard Neumann, New York 1967; *A History of the Dutch Poster 1890–1960* by Dick Dooijes and Pieter Brattinga, Amsterdam 1968; *Pioneers of Modern Typography* by Herbert Spencer, London 1969; *Paul Schuitema 1897–1973*, dissertation by Flip Bool, Amsterdam 1974; *Fotografie in Nederland 1920–1940*, exhibition catalogue by Flip Bool and Kees Broos, The Hague 1979.

*

Paul Schuitema, with G. Kiljan and Piet Zwart, formed a trinity of Dutch modernist designers, practising (to different degrees) across the whole field of design but now regarded principally as graphic designers. Zwart's pre-World War II graphic work, notable for its inventiveness, has come to overshadow that of the other two (and Kiljan is still almost unknown outside The Netherlands). In comparison with Zwart's,

Paul Schuitema: Advertisement for the Berkel Auto-Scale Company, 1930 Courtesy Haags Gemeentemuseum

Schuitema's work is more direct and plainer. His work of the late 1920s and early 1930s, for Berkel and for the printers Chevalier (two of his major clients), shows all the qualities of the *nieuwe zakelijkheid* of that moment; it belongs to the specifically Duch variety of functionalism evident also in the work of contemporaneous architects in the groups around the publication *De 8 en Opbouw* (for which Schuitema did some graphic work). By contrast, the German and Central European modernists—Tschichold, above all, of course—followed a path of increasing sophistication, particularly in employing the more refined sanserif typefaces (such as Futura), as they became available. The Dutch seemed to prefer the slightly crude, older sanserifs, perhaps for their very lack of sophistication.

Schuitema's production of these years exhibits an air of great confidence and assurance. In the case of the work for Berkel, one may attribute some of this to what must have been the privileged status accorded to Schuitema by the firm. Concerned as he was with all aspects of design, including that of their weighing and meat-cutting machines, his role prefigures the emergence of the "consultant designer." (Peter Behrens at AEG, in the early years of the century, would be the progenitor for this kind of designer.)

Schuitema was a committed socialist and took part, for example, in the workers' photography movements in The Netherlands in the 1930s. For books and magazines of the left, he designed covers that embody both the formal and social principles of modernism: formal and social revolutions are implied as inseparable. The spirit of this work was well evoked by Schuitema years later in his text "New Typographical Design in 1930," published in 1961 with extensive reproduction of the Berkel jobs: "The form was not predetermined but was the outcome of an attitude to life. And life itself took on form when it was given a new meaning..." By the same token, the impetus and confidence of the modern movement would desert it as the late 1930s wore on. Schuitema began to teach graphic design and to practice less, but he remained a lively presence. As a younger designer reported of him in 1966, following his teaching visit at the West of England College of Art, he was "instantly recognizable as a colleague, not a monument."

—Robin Kinross

SERAFINOWICZ, Leokadia.
Polish stage designer. Born in Janow, 23 February 1915. Studied fine arts, at Copernicus University, Torun. Artistic director and general manager, of the Marcinek Theatre, Poznan, 1960–75. Recipient: Gold Medal, Prague Quadriennale of Scenography, 1971. Address: Lipowa 13/2, 62–041 Puszczykowo, K-Poznan, Poland.

Works:

Stage productions include—*Ball at Professor Baczynski's*, Poznan, 1961; *Little Tiger*, Poznan, 1963; *Nightingale*, Poznan, 1965; *Bath*, Poznan, 1967; *Misterium Buffo*, Plovdiv, 1968; *Kathy Who Lost Her Geese*, Poznan, 1969; *Hobby-Horse*, Poznan, 1969; *Wanda*, Poznan, 1970; *Tigrisorul*, Timisoara, 1970; *Hefajstos*, Lublin, 1974; *Ojczyzna*, Poznan, 1974; *Wkole*, Poznan, 1974; *Pani Koch*, Poznan, 1975; *Janosik*, Poznan, 1975; *Petrushka's Theatre*, Poznan, 1976.

Publications:

On SERAFINOWICZ: book—*Contemporary Polish Stage Design* by Zenobiusz Strzelecki, Warsaw 1983.

Leokadia Serafinowicz: Set and costumes for Goethe's *Reineke Fuchs*, Theater fur Kinder, Hamburg, 1980

The puppet theatre is above all a theatre of the plastic arts. The practitioner of such an art plays a very important role in it, the more so if, like Leokadia Serafinowicz, she happens to be the director as well as the general manager of a theatre. A repertoire for children as well as for adults offered her great creative possibilities for ambitions in both directions, while the theatre which she led belonged to a narrow elite of the very best in Poland. In part, this is also due to the services of artistic director Wojciech Wieczorkiewicz and artist Jan Berdyszek, thanks to whom the Theatre Marcinek has a decidedly artistic and modern face.

Here folklorism makes its appearance: This tendency within Polish scenography consists of analogies to folk art—so rich and alive in Poland—to its sculpture, painting, and architecture. Serafinowicz, however, does not copy or imitate, but only follows principles, those of facture and material, and usually utilizes wood, straw, linen cloth—as, for example, in *Kasis, co gaski zgubila* [Kathy who lost her geese], in *Lajkonik* [Hobby-horse], in *Wanda*. The latter spectacle—in which the puppets are roughly chiseled wood blocks and the set, just cloth strips—participates in the creation of a monumental Polish theatre.

Serafinowicz's devices are very rich: in *Teatr Pietrushki* [Petrushka's theatre], she alludes to the Russian folk theatre; in *Tygrysek* [Little tiger], the live actor wears a metal mesh mask with a design of coloured sponge; in *Balwanowa bajka* [Snowman's tale], the figures are of styrofoam, the birds, formed into expressive designs, are wire; in *Bath*, some of the puppets are made of feathers, others from rags (as if to delineate characteristics of the play's two worlds simply by means of facture). One also encounters experiments in the area of stage space. There may be a screen (as is usual in a puppet theatre) or none at all (in other words, no mystification); or sometimes, a center stage (as in *Nightingale*), while at other times, the whole theatre becomes a stage.

One should also take into account Serafinowicz's directorial work—such as for Witkiewicz's *Matwa* [The Cuttlefish] and *Szalona lokomotywa* [The crazy locomotive], Wyspianski's *Wesele* [Wedding], Milobedzka's *Siala baba mak* [She sowed poppies]—in which her love for a new, poetic, synthetic, metaphoric, theatrical form finds expression, and in which she leaves much room for the spectator's—child's and adult's—imagination.

—Zenobiusz Strzelecki

Raul and Ronald Shakespear: Logos for Cafetal coffeemakers, Harrod's of Buenos Aires and Vega menswear, 1975–76

SHAKESPEAR, Raul (Lorenzo).
Argentinian graphic designer. Born in Buenos Aires, 7 July 1947. Studied at Raggio Polytechnic School, Buenos Aires, 1960–65. Married Silvia Paez in 1971; children: Victoria and Andres. Freelance graphic designer and art director, Buenos Aires, 1965–72; designer, in the Guillermo Gonzalez Ruiz and Ronald Shakespear design studio, Buenos Aires, 1972–73; co-director, with Ronald Shakespear, of Shakespear Brothers Design Team, Buenos Aires, from 1973. Permanent graphic design contributor, *Summa* magazine, Buenos Aires. Committee member, Centro de Arte y Comunicacion, Buenos Aires. **Exhibitions:** Galeria Espanola, Buenos Aires, 1977; Teatro Munici-

pal General San Martin, Buenos Aires, 1980; Centro de Arte y Comunicacion, Buenos Aires, 1981; *Dal Cucchiaio al Citta*, Centro Kappa, Milan, 1983. **Collection:** Museo de Arte Moderno, Mar del Plata. Member, Asociacion Disenadores Graficos, and Centro de Investigacion del Disegno Industrial y Grafico, Buenos Aires. Address: Shakespear Studio, Juan Jose Diaz 594, San Isidro, 1642 Buenos Aires, Argentina.

See SHAKESPEAR, Ronald.

SHAKESPEAR, Ronald.
Argentinian graphic designer. Born in Rosario, Sante Fe Province, 18 September 1941. Studied at Raggio Polytechnic School, Buenos Aires, 1954–58: influenced by Romulo Maccio, Juan Carlos DiStefano, and Alan Fletcher. Served in the Argentine Army, 1962. Married Elena Peyron in 1968; children: Lorenzo, Barbara, Juan,

Maria and Sofia. Freelance graphic designer and art director, Buenos Aires, 1960–67; partner, with Guillermo Gonzales Ruiz, in Ruiz and Shakespear design studio, Buenos Aires, 1967–73; co-director, with Raul Shakespear, of Shakespear Brothers Design Team, Buenos Aires, from 1973. Permanent graphic design contributor, *Summa* magazine, Buenos Aires. Committee member of the Centro de Arte y Comunicacion, Buenos Aires. **Exhibitions:** Galeria Espanola, Buenos Aires, 1977; Teatro Municipal General San Martin, Buenos Aires, 1980; Centro de Arte y Comunicacion, Buenos Aires, 1981; *Dal Cucchiaio al Citta*, Centro Kappa, Milan, 1983. **Collection:** Museo de Arte Moderno, Mar del Plata. Member, Asociacion Disenadores Graficos, and Centro de Investigacion del Disegno Industrial y Grafico, Buenos Aires. Address: Shakespear Studio, Juan Jose Diaz 594, San Isidro, 1642 Buenos Aires, Argentina.

Works:

Sign system and unified identity programme, for the City of Buenos Aires, 1971–73 (Ruiz and Shakespear).
Symbol and logotype, for Corp women's clothing firm, 1973 (Shakespear Studio).

Symbol and logotype, for Argemac toolmakers, 1975 (Shakespear Studio).

Super-graphics environmental design, for Marby building and metallurgy company, 1975 (Shakespear Studio).

Symbol, logotype and signage, for Harrod's, Buenos Aires, 1975 (Shakespear Studio).

Newspaper advertisements, for Fate tyre company, 1975–77 (Shakespear Studio).

Symbol and logotype, for Cafetal coffee makers and importers, Buenos Aires, 1976 (Shakespear Studio).

Symbol and logotype, for Vega men's clothing, Buenos Aires, 1976 (Shakespear Studio).

Total signage system and visual identity, for Buenos Aires hospitals, from 1980 (Shakespear Studio).

Publications:

By SHAKESPEAR: books—*Ronald and Raul Shakespear: 20 Years of Design in Argentina*, Buenos Aires 1976; *Trademarks: Shakespear Studio*, Buenos Aires 1981.

On SHAKESPEAR: books — *Illustration: Aspects and Directions* by Bob Gill and John Lewis, London 1964; *Archigraphia: Architectural Graphics*, edited by Walter Herdeg, Zurich 1978; *Top Symbols of the World*, edited by Franco Maria Ricci, Milan 1979; *The Shakespear Brothers* by Jorge Glusberg, Buenos Aires 1980; *Who's Who in Graphic Art*, edited by Walter Amstutz, Dubendorf 1982.

The visual style of the work of Ronald and Raul Shakespear is rooted in the work of Josef Müller-Brockman, Armin Hofmann, and Herb Lubalin. The almost typographical character of the Shakespears' images (e.g., Sports Centre, Buenos Aires), the interaction between figure and ground which are equal in their abstract and expressive power, and the monumentality of their conceptions cause the designs to overflow their initial informational objective. This monumentality—deriving not only from size but also from proportion—creates vitality, energy, and optimism in its environments and communicates these qualities to their inhabitants (e.g., Maternity Hospital, Buenos Aires). In signage, where this level of communication is normally and willfully reduced or neglected, the Shakespears' approach is especially praiseworthy. In their approach, graphic communication, in addition to informing the public, forms the environment.

Simplicity, abstractness, and monumentality appear in Ronald Shakespear's early work, continues during his association with Guillermo Gonzalez Ruiz, and develops to its present maturity in the Shakespears' own studio. In their design conception, form follows function, a non-reductionist function that recognizes, along with the primary objective of a given project, the general and specific requirements of the human environment. In the Shakespears' hands, graphic design becomes architecture, art, and cityscape.

Although many designers have been influenced by the Shakespears' work of the 1960s and 1970s, this influence might initially have been attributed to those designers who had previously influenced the Shakespears. But their recent work is not only qualitatively comparable to the best produced anywhere (as Ronald's has been since 1963), but it has also ceased to follow any other designer; Müller-Brockman, Hofmann, Lubalin, Fletcher, and DiStefano, among others, no longer look at us through the Shakespears' works. The high quality of the Shakespears' corporate identity work is unquestionable, but their historical significance derives from their signage projects.

The work of the Shakespears represents a fourth stage in the evolution of graphic design, a profession where the first stage was craft-oriented, the second was artistic/intuitive, and the third, in an attempt to control reality, was rational/reductionist. In this fourth stage, the Shakespears integrate freedom and control, function and expression, performance and pleasure, as a consequence of their understanding of the complexity of communication problems, along with their ability to deal with them. This ability makes their studio one of the most exciting working today.

—Jorge Frascara

SHAMASK, Ronaldus.

Dutch fashion designer. Born in Amsterdam, 24 November 1945. Self-taught in design, from 1960. Window display artist, in Melbourne, Australia, 1963–66; fashion illustrator, working for *The Times* and *Observer* newspapers, London, 1967–68; freelance stage set and costume designer for ballet, opera, and for Company of Man multimedia artists' group, in Buffalo, New York, 1968–71; freelance interior and clothing designer, New York, 1971–77; founder-partner, with Murray Moss, of Moss Shamask fashion company, New York, from 1978; opened Moss boutique on Madison Avenue, New York, 1979. **Exhibition:** *Intimate Architecture: Contemporary Clothing*, Massachusetts Institute of Technology, Cambridge, 1982. **Collection:** Smithsonian Institution, Washington, D.C. Recipient: Coty Fashion Award, New York, 1981; Fil d'Or Award, Conference Internationale du Lin, 1982. Address: Moss Shamask, 39 West 37th Street, New York, New York 10018, U.S.A.

Publications:

On SHAMASK: books—*McDowell's Directory of Twentieth Century Fashion* by Colin McDowell, London 1984; *Fashion: The Inside Story* by Barbaralee Diamonstein, New York 1985; articles—in *Daily News* (New York), March 1979, September 1979; *New York Times*, 1 March 1979, 8 February 1981, 16 August 1981; *Gentleman's Quarterly* (New York), November 1979; *San Francisco Chronicle*, 6 December 1979; *Women's Wear Daily* (New York), 3 November 1980, 26 April 1982; *People Weekly* (Chicago), 24 August 1981; *Vogue* (New York), June 1982.

In recent years, something of a cult has grown up around the clothes of Ronaldus Shamask. His grave and hieratic presentations have made it clear that he sees a fashion show as a theatrical event, in the way many Japanese designers also conceive of these presentations. Music by Philip Glass and severe minimalist backgrounds are all suggestive of Shamask's sensibilities. But of course, it is by his clothes that a fashion designer must be judged, and as far as Shamask is concerned, the verdict is essentially—or will be, in the course of time—that what he really creates are wearable works of art. Contemplative, austere, yet luxurious in their very denial of overt pattern, and highly refined, they attract a woman who has a connoisseur's eye for fabric and quality and who is not afraid of the abstraction of Shamask's shapes.

Shamask dresses an elite—the largely self-

---

appointed elite comprising the devotees of high style. Certainly, his work is part of a way of life that is bound up with living in Manhattan; his clothes are meant to be worn in lofts, to downtown openings, are meant to signal to other members of what might be called the esthetic establishment their wearers' good standing in its ranks. Which is not to be negative; every city in its prime, or during one of the many bloomings it may undergo, has its definers of esoteric style. What Charles James was to 1940s New York, Shamask was to the late 1970s and early 1980s—a quintessence of the stern discipline which is always at the heart of high style, no matter whether it be the strict and complicated construction of a James creation or the seemingly more effortless silhouette of a Shamask.

—Peter Carlsen

SHARAFF, Irene.

American stage and film costume designer. Born in Boston, Massachusetts, in 1910. Studied at the School of Fine and Applied Arts, New York, the Art Students League, New York and at the Academie de la Grande Chaumiere, Paris. Assistant to stage designer Aline Bernstein, at the Civic Repertory Theatre Company, 1928–30; freelance stage costume designer, working for New York Broadway shows, Ballet Russe de Monte Carlo, New York City Ballet, Joffrey Ballet, Royal; Ballet, etc., from 1932; film costume designer, mainly for Metro-Goldwyn-Mayer, in Hollywood, California, from 1942. **Exhibition:** *Romantic and Glamorous Hollywood Design*, Metropolitan Museum of Art, New York, 1974. Recipient: Academy Award, 1951, 1956, 1961, 1963, 1966. Address: c/o Gloria Safier, 677 Madison Avenue, New York, New York 10021, U.S.A.

Works:

Stage productions (New York, unless noted) include—*Alice in Wonderland* (also sets), 1932; *As Thousands Cheer*, 1933; *Life Begins at 8:40*, 1934; *The Great Waltz*, 1934; *Crime and Punishment*, 1935 (also sets), *Parade*, 1935; *Jubilee*, 1935; *Rosmersholm*, 1935 (also sets); *Idiot's Delight*, 1936; *On Your Toes*, 1936; *White Horse Inn*, 1936; *Virginia, I'd Rather Be Right*, 1937; *The Boys from Syracuse*, 1938; *The American Way*, 1939; *Gay New Orleans*, 1939; *Streets of Paris*, 1939; *Boys and Girls Together*, 1940; *All in Fun*, 1940; *Lady in the Dark*, 1941; *The Land Is Bright*, 1941; *Sunny River*, 1941; *Banjo Eyes*, 1941; *By Jupiter*, 1942; *Star and Garter*, 1942; *Count Me In*, 1942; *Billion Dollar Baby*, 1945; *The Would-Be Gentleman*, 1946; *GI Hamlet*, 1946; *Bonanza Bound*, 1948; *Montserrat*, 1949; *Dance Me a Song*, 1950; *Mike Todd's Peep-Show*, 1950; *The King and I*, 1951; *A Tree Grows in Brooklyn*, 1951; *Of Thee I Sing*, 1952; *Me and Juliet*, 1953; *The King and I*, 1953 (London); *On Your Toes*, 1954; *By the Beautiful Sea*, 1954; *Shangri-La*, 1956; *Candide*, 1956; *Happy Hunting*, 1956; *West Side Story*, 1957; *Small War on Murray Hill*, 1957; *Flower Drum Song*, 1958; *Juno*, 1959; *Do Re Mi*, 1960; *Jenny*, 1963; *The Girl Came to Supper*, 1963; *The Boys from Syracuse*, 1963 (London); *Funny Girl*, 1964; *The King and I*, 1964 (revival); *Sweet Charity*, 1965; *Hallelujah, Baby!*, 1967; and *Irene*, 1972. Films include—*Girl Crazy* (Taurog), 1943; *I Dood It*

(Minnelli), 1943; *Madame Curie* (LeRoy), 1943; *Broadway Rhythm* (Del Ruth), 1943; *Meet Me in St. Louis* (Minnelli), 1944; *Bathing Beauty* (Sidney), 1944; *Yolanda and the Thief* (Minnelli), 1945; *The Best Years of Our Lives* (Wyler), 1946; *The Dark Mirror* (Siodmak), 1946; *Ziegfeld Follies* (Minnelli), 1946; *The Bishop's Wife* (Kosta), 1947; *The Secret Life of Walter Mitty* (McLeod), 1947; *A Song Is Born* (Hawks), 1947; *Every Girl Should Be Married* (Hartman), 1948; *An American in Paris* (Minnelli), 1951; *Call Me Madam* (W. Lang), 1953; *A Star Is Born* (Cukor), 1954; *Brigadoon* (Minnelli), 1954; *Guys and Dolls* (Mankiewicz), 1955; *The King and I* (W. Lang), 1956; *Porgy and Bess* (Preminger), 1959; *Can-Can* (W. Lang), 1960; *Flower Drum Song* (Koster), 1961; *West Side Story* (Wise and Robbins), 1961; *Cleopatra* (Mankiewicz), 1963; *The Sandpiper* (Minnelli), 1965; *Who's Afraid of Virginia Woolf?* (Nichols), 1966; *The Taming of the Shrew* (Zeffirelli), 1967; *Funny Girl* (Ross), 1968; *Hello Dolly* (Kelly), 1969; *Justine* (Cukor), 1969; *The Great White Hope* (Ritt), 1970; *The Way We Were* (Pollack), 1974; *Mommie Dearest* (Perry), 1981.

Publications:

By SHARAFF: book—*Broadway and Hollywood: Costumes Designed by Irene Sharaff*, New York 1976; article—in *Metropolitan Museum of Art Bulletin* (New York), November 1967.

On SHARAFF: books—*Romantic and Glamorous Hollywood Design*, exhibition catalogue by Diana Vreeland, New York 1974; *Hollywood Costume Design* by David Chierichetti, London 1976; *In a Glamorous Fashion: The Fabulous Years of Hollywood Costume Design* by W. Robert La Vine, Boston and London 1981; *McDowell's Directory of Twentieth Century Fashion* by Colin McDowell, London 1984; *International Dictionary of Films and Filmmakers*, Chicago and London 1987, 1991.

Making motion pictures often demands more from an artist than the duties suggested by an official title. Had "costume designer" Irene Sharaff merely sketched pretty dresses for stunning starlets, prestigious Metro-Goldwyn-Mayer studios would have slammed shut the pages of her drawing pad. But Sharaff's talent included a strong intellect, a fine eye, intuitive insights, and ingenious ability for original adaption, and an integrating mind that united all into workable designs.

Sharaff succeeded quickly as a New York stage designer. She showed a clever use of color in her costumes for Irving Berlin's "Easter Parade" from play *As Thousands Cheer* (1933). For this stage revue, various shades of browns, tans, and other neutrals mimicked the pages of the *New York Times* rotogravure. Sharaff's designs for *Alice in Wonderland* (1932) won acclaim as reconstructions of the original Tenniel illustrations. These successes caught the attention of MGM filmmakers who hoped to translate Sharaff's theatrical skills into money-making Hollywood ventures. Specifically, they sought a suitable designer to deal with the new technicolor process. Irene Sharaff did not disappoint them after she joined the staff in 1942.

MGM designated Sharaff's skills to the Freed unit, which made some of the world's most memorable musicals. Almost immediately, Sharaff's touch turned projects into screen gold. *Meet Me in St. Louis* (1944), for instance, was a nostalgic valentine of lace, swiss dots, and ruffles. But the *American in Paris* (1951) ballet sequence proved Sharaff's finest hour, as it

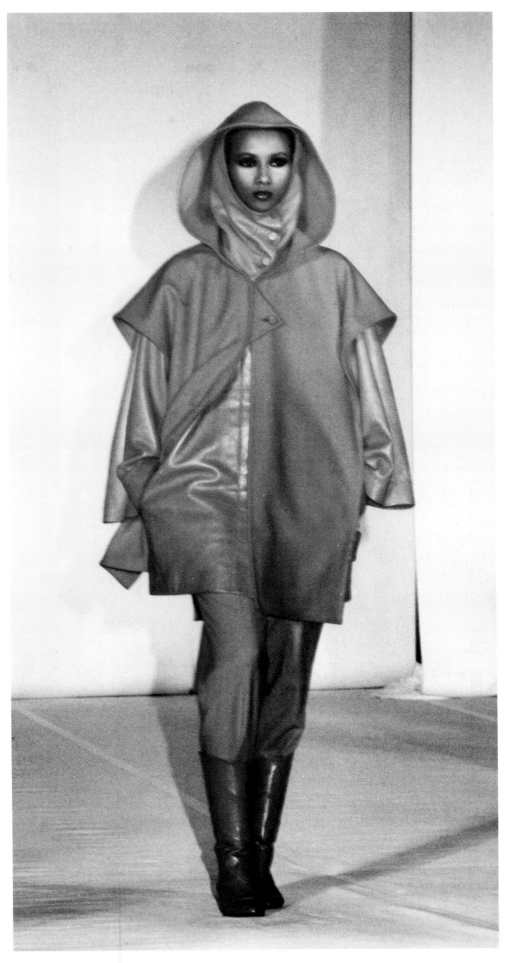

Ronaldus Shamask: Rainwear, 1983

utilized a multitude of her varied talents. For this ballet, Sharaff based her visuals on a number of famous French painters. Paying homage to the impressionists and several post-impressionists, she translated the colors and techniques of individual artists to set design and costume, even as she facilitated Gene Kelly's dances with garments constructed specifically for movement. Even the fabrics flowed with harmonizing rhythms.

Sharaff's career displayed considerable variety. *The King and I* (1956) sparkled with exotic ethnic dress. *Can-Can* (1960) offered an imaginative "Adam and Eve" ballet complete with guise from animal to insect. In 1961, *West Side Story* glorified the uniforms of working-class New York toughs. A few years later, *The Sandpiper* (1965) peopled the beaches of Big Sur with contemporary bohemians. Sharaff often dressed Elisabeth Taylor, be it as Egyptian queen (*Cleopatra*, 1963), a brilliant but testy Renaissance jewel (*Taming of the Shrew*, 1967), or an overweight, aging slob (*Who's Afraid of Virginia Woolf?*, 1966).

Whatever her script, Sharaff's quality continued. She translated her visions from stage to screen, using all the artistries of the world as inspiration. Understanding the natures of film, the stage, and ballet, she recognized their similarities and differences. Starting with this knowledge, she splashed it with just the right colors and elevated each creation to optimum advantage. Sharaff took the superficial show out of show business and replaced it with the depth of fine art.

—Edith Cortland Lee

SIMPSON, Adele.

American Fashion designer. Born Adele Smithline, in New York City, 28 December 1904. Studied dressmaking, at the Pratt Institute of Design, Brooklyn, New York, 1921–22. Married textile manufacturer Wesley William Simpson in 1930 (died); children: Jeffrey and Joan. Assistant designer, 1922, then head dress designer, 1923–26, at Ben Gershel's ready-to-wear fashion house, New York; chief designer, William Bass, New York, 1927–28; designer of Adele Simpson fashions, at Mary Lee Fashions, New York, 1929–49; president and director of Adele Simpson Inc. (bought out Mary Lee Fashions), New York, from 1949. Member of the New York Couture Group; treasurer and board member, Fashion Group, New York; co-founder and board member, Fashion Designers of America. **Collections:** Brooklyn Museum, New York; Metropolitan Museum of Art, New York; Dallas Public Library, Texas. Recipient: Neiman-Marcus Award, 1946; Coty American Fashion Critics Winnie Award, New York, 1947. Address: 530 Seventh Avenue, New York, New York 10018, U.S.A.

Publications:

On SIMPSON: books—*Fairchild's Who's Who in Fashion*, edited by Ann Stegemeyer, New York 1980; *Les Annees 60* by Anne Bony, Paris 1983; *McDowell's Directory of Twentieth Century Fashion* by Colin McDowell, London 1984; *The Encyclopaedia of Fashion from 1840 to the 1980s* by Georgina O'Hara, London 1986.

Adele Simpson: Fur-trimmed suit in pinstripe wool jersey with chiffon blouse, 1983

Adele Simpson has long been in the center of the world of fashion and the clothing industry. Never a designer to startle by bizarre innovations, she has used her awareness of new ideas to design wearable clothes. Her travels and collecting of historic and native costumes and fabrics have added a richness to her clothing, especially in the use of fabrics, which are not selected only for their surface decoration but are considered as well in construction and design. Her designs are more often created directly on the model than from sketches. Simpson has also, with a touch of light-heartedness, removed longstanding fashion prejudices, as for instance those against cotton and boots for evening wear. Critics, when speaking of her contributions to the field of clothing design, always mention wearability, richness, and appropriateness for the active woman. Designing for the ready-to-wear market, mostly in the higher-priced lines, she has maintained high standards in all aspects of her work, which is always conservative with flair, feminine, and carefully constructed.

Her work is consistently acclaimed for the thoughtful coordination of the complete costume from underwear out, an idea most commonplace currently, but perhaps not so much so when Simpson entered the design field. The long history of her continuing success gives reason for her influence on fashion and clothing design. She removes pretense and replaces it with good design sense and wearability.

As Simpson continues her business with her daughter Joan and son-in-law Richard Raines, she remains, as always, responsible to design institutions; she serves on many boards, for example, and has given her own resource collections to the Fashion Institute of Technology. A designer who has never taken the fashion world by surprise, she has consistently produced clothes that have quietly and tastefully expressed the quality of carefully chosen materials structured through good design and that consider the needs of the person who will wear them.

—Harlan Sifford

SMITH, Jack Martin.

American film designer. Studied architecture, University of Southern California, Los Angeles. Worked as sketch artist, then designer, at Metro-Goldwyn-Mayer film studios, Hollywood, California, 1938–53; designer, 1953–61, and supervising art director, 1961–75, at 20th Century-Fox film studios, Hollywood: worked on films of Robert Aldrich, George Cukor, Stanley Donen, Victor Fleming, Walter Lang, Mervyn LeRoy, Rouben Mamoulian, Joseph Mankiewicz, Vincente Minnelli, Nicholas Ray, etc. Recipient: Academy Award, 1963, 1966, 1969. Address: c/o Twentieth Century-Fox Film Corporation, Post Office Box 900, Beverly Hills, California 90213, U.S.A.

Works:

Films include—*The Wizard of Oz* (Fleming), 1939; *Meet Me in St. Louis* (Minnelli), 1944; *Yolanda and the Thief* (Minnelli), 1945; *Holiday in Mexico* (Sidney), 1946; *Ziegfeld Follies* (Minnelli), 1946; *The Pirate* (Minnelli), 1948; *Summer Holiday* (Mamoulian), 1948; *Easter Parade* (Walters), 1948; *Words and Music* (Taurog), 1948; *Madame Bovary* (Minnelli), 1949; *On the Town* (Kelly and Donen), 1949; *Nancy Goes to Rio* (Leonard), 1950; *Summer Stock* (Walters), 1950; *Royal Wedding* (Donen), 1951; *Show Boat* (Sidney), 1951; *An American in Paris* (Minnelli), 1951; *The Belle of New York* (Walters), 1952; *Million Dollar Mermaid* (LeRoy), 1952; *I Love Melvin* (Weis), 1953; *Dangerous When Wet* (Walters), 1953; *Easy to Love* (Walters), 1953; *Valley of the Kings* (Pirosh), 1954; *White Feather* (Webb), 1955; *Soldier of Fortune* (Dymytryk), 1955; *Seven Cities of Gold* (Webb), 1955; *Carousel* (H. King), 1956; *The Man in the Gray Flannel Suit* (Johnson), 1956; *Bigger Than Life* (Ray), 1956; *Bandido* (Fleischer), 1956; *Teenage Rebel* (Goulding), 1956; *Boy on a Dolphin* (Negulesco), 1957; *An Affair to Remember* (McCarey), 1957; *Peyton Place* (Robson), 1957; *The Barbarian and the Geisha* (Huston), 1958; *Woman Obsessed* (Hathaway), 1959; *The Best of Everything* (Negulesco), 1959; *Can-Can* (W. Lang), 1960; *North to Alaska* (Hathaway), 1960; *All Hands on Deck* (Taurog), 1961; *The Comancheros* (Curtiz), 1961; *Marines, Let's Go* (Walsh), 1961; *Pirates of Tortuga* (Webb), 1961; *Return to Peyton Place* (J. Ferrer), 1961; *Sanctuary* (Richardson), 1961; *The Second Time Around* (V. Sherman), 1961; *Snow White and the Three Stooges* (W. Lang), 1961; *Voyage to the Bottom of the Sea* (Allen), 1961; *Wild in the Country* (Dunne), 1961; *Bachelor Flat* (Tashlin), 1962; *Five Weeks in a Balloon* (Allen), 1962; *Hemingway's Adventures of a Young Man* (Ritt), 1962; *Mr. Hobbs Takes a Vacation* (Koster), 1962; *State Fair* (J. Ferrer), 1962; *Tender Is the Night* (H. King), 1962; *Cleopatra* (Mankiewicz), 1963; *Move Over, Darling* (Gordon), 1963; *The Stripper* (Schaffner), 1963; *Take Her, She's Mine* (Koster), 1963; *Fate Is the Hunter* (Nelson), 1964; *Goodbye Charlie* (Minnelli), 1964; *The Pleasure Seekers* (Negulesco), 1964; *Rio Concho* (Douglas), 1964; *Shock Treatment* (Sanders), 1964; *What a Way to Go* (Lee Thompson), 1964; *The Agony and the Ecstasy* (Reed), 1965; *Dear Brigitte* (Koster), 1965; *Do Not Disturb* (Levy), 1965; *John Goldfarb, Please Come Home* (Lee Thompson), 1965; *Morituri* (Wicki), 1965; *The Reward* (Bourguignon), 1965; *Von Ryan's Express* (Robson), 1965; *Batman* (Martinson), 1966; *Fantastic Voyage* (Fleischer), 1966; *I Deal in Danger* (Grauman), 1966; *Our Man Flint* (Daniel Mann), 1966; *Smoky* (G. Sherman), 1966; *Stagecoach* (Douglas), 1966; *Way . . . . Way Out* (Douglas), 1966; *Caprice* (Tashlin), 1967; *Doctor Dolittle* (Fleischer), 1967; *A Guide for the Married Man* (Kelly), 1967; *Hombre* (Ritt), 1967; *In Like Flint* (Douglas), 1967; *Tony Rome* (Douglas), 1967; *The St. Valentine's Day Massacre* (Corman), 1967; *Valley of the Dolls* (Robson), 1967; *The Flim-Flam Man* (Kershner), 1967; *Bandolero* (McLaglen), 1968; *The Boston Strangler* (Fleischer), 1968; *The Detective* (Douglas), 1968; *Planet of the Apes* (Schaffner), 1968; *Pretty Poison* (Black), 1968; *The Sweet Ride* (Hart), 1968; *The Secret Life of an American Wife* (Axelrod), 1968; *Butch Cassidy and the Sundance Kid* (Hill), 1969; *Che* (Fleischer), 1969; *Hello, Dolly* (Kelly), 1969; *Justine* (Cukor), 1969; *Daughter of the Mind* (Grauman—for TV), 1969; *Beneath the Planet of the Apes* (Post), 1970; *Beyond the Valley of the Dolls* (Meyer), 1970; *Cover Me, Babe* (Black), 1970; *M*A*S*H* (Altman), 1970; *Move* (Rosenberg), 1970; *Myra Breckinridge* (Sarne), 1970; *Tora-Tora-Tora* (Fleischer, Masuda and Fukasaku), 1970; *The Challenge* (Smithee—for TV), 1970; *Tribes* (Sargent—for TV), 1970; *Escape from the Planet of the Apes* (Taylor), 1971; *Powderkeg* (Hayes—for TV), 1971; *Fireball Forward* (Chomsky—for TV), 1972; *The Culpepper Cattle Company* (Richards), 1972; *Ae Eli and Rodger of the Skies* (Erman), 1973; *Emperor of the North Pole* (Aldrich), 1973; *Rhinoceros* (Horgan), 1974; *The Reincarnation of Peter Proud* (Lee Thompson), 1975; *Bug* (Szwarc), 1975; *Strange New World* (Butler—for TV, 1975; *The Great Scout and Cathouse Thursday* (Taylor), 1976.

Publications:

By SMITH: article—in *Film Comment* (New York), May/June 1978.

On SMITH: books—*Le Decor de Film* by Leon Barsacq, Paris 1970, as *Caligari's Cabinet and other Grand Illusions*, Boston 1976; *Don't Say Yes Until I Finish Talking* by Mel Gussow, New York 1971; *The World of Entertainment: Hollywood's Greatest Musicals* by Hugh Fordin, New York 1975; *Dance in the Hollywood Musical* by Jerome Delamater, Ann Arbor 1981; *International Dictionary of Films and Filmmakers*, Chicago and London 1987, 1991.

Jack Martin Smith's training in architecture at the University of Southern California prepared him well for his film design career, which had its high point in the fifteen-year period he spent at MGM designing the popular musicals produced by Arthur Freed. At MGM, Smith had the good fortune to work with the director Vincente Minnelli who was also visually oriented because of his own background as a stage designer. For Minnelli's fable-like *Yolanda and the Thief*, Smith drew upon the eighteenth-century paintings of Tiepolo; a dream sequence in the same film was patterned after Salvador Dali paintings. Elsewhere, Smith's film designs were inspired by baroque and rococo art, as was, apparently, the curvilinear ballroom furniture in Minnelli's famous *An American in Paris* (1951).

Smith's greatest talent as a designer is his technical finesse. His skill has saved film producers thousands of dollars, since they were able to film in his settings on the studios' back lots in lieu of costly on-location shooting. Smith's recreations of reality are many. At MGM, Smith designed film sets resembling turn-of-the-century Kensington Avenue for *Meet Me in St. Louis*, the top of the Empire State Building for *On the Town*, Fifth Avenue for *Easter Parade* (1948), and a full-scale paddle-wheeler for *Show Boat* (1951). Smith continued this trend at 20th Century-Fox, where he rebuilt a small Maine town for *Peyton Place* (1957) and first century B.C. Rome and Egypt for *Cleopatra*.

Just as Smith's architectural training helped him accurately to reproduce real and historical settings, it also allowed him to devise technical tricks which add to a film's visual impact. For example, he surrounded Esther Williams with blue, yellow, and red smoke in *Million Dollar Mermaid* (1952) by placing smoke pots in the swimming tank, and for this effect, he designed the necessary adjunct—an air evacuation system. For *Royal Wedding* (1951), Smith conceived the famous room in which Fred Astaire appears to be dancing on the walls and ceiling. To achieve this strange and convincing illusion, Smith put the room inside a revolving barrel and affixed the light sources, camera, and camera operator to the set.

Smith's career has illustrated a combination of skills. His sets at MGM, especially, exhibit a flair for design and a knowledge of art and historical sources. He was also gifted with the technical talent to fashion any trick or illusion that a director could desire.

—Lois Miklas

SMITH, Oliver (Lemuel).

American stage and film designer. Born in Wawpawn, Wisconsin, 13 February 1918. Studied at Pennsylvania State University, University Park, 1936–39: BA 1939. Freelance stage designer, New York, from 1941, and film designer from 1953: co-director, with Lucia Chase, of the American Ballet Theatre, New York, 1948–51; has designed for the Metropolitan Opera, Cuevas International Ballet, Biltmore Theatre, Adelphi Theatre, Playhouse Theatre, Belasco Theatre, Booth Theatre, New York City Center, etc.; also designed interiors for the Waldorf-Astoria Ballroom, New York, 1962. Master instructor in scene design, School of the Arts, New York, from 1972. Member of the National Council for the Arts, Washington, D.C., 1965–70. Recipient: Donaldson Award, New York, 1946, 1947, 1949, 1953; New York Drama Critics Award, 1956, 1957, 1959, 1960, 1964; Antoinette Perry "Tony" Award, New York, 1957, 1958, 1960, 1961, 1964, 1965; Sam S. Shubert Theatre Award, New York, 1961; Pennsylvania State University Distinguished Alumnus Award, 1962; Handel Medallion, New York, 1975. Address: 70 Willow Street, Brooklyn, New York 11201, U.S.A

Works:

Stage productions (New York, unless noted) include—*Saratoga* (ballet for Leonid Massine), 1941; *Rodeo* (ballet for Agnes DeMille), 1942; *Rosalinda*, 1942; *Fancy Free* (ballet for Jerome Robbins), 1944; *The New Moon*, 1944; *The Perfect Marriage*, 1944; *Rhapsody*, 1944; *On the Town* (also co-produced), 1944; *Billion Dollar Baby* (also co-produced), 1945; *On Stage* (ballet for Michael Kidd), 1945; *Twilight Bar*, 1946; *No Exit* (also co-produced), 1946; *Beggar's Holiday*, 1946; *Brigadoon*, 1947; *High Button Shoes*, 1947; *The Medium* (opera), 1947; *Topaz*, 1947; *Look, Ma, I'm Dancin'!*, 1948; *Me and Molly*, 1948; *Fall River Legend* (ballet for Agnes DeMille), 1948; *Along Fifth Avenue*, 1949; *Miss Liberty*, 1949; *No Exit*, 1949; *Bless You All*, 1949; *Gentlemen Prefer Blondes* (also co-produced), 1949; *Paint Your Wagon*, 1951; *Pal Joey*, 1952; *Carnival in Flanders*, 1953; *At Home with Ethel Waters*, 1953; *In the Summerhouse*, 1953; *The Burning Glass*, 1954; *On Your Toes*, 1954; *Will Success Spoil Rock Hunter?*, 1955; *Mr. Wonderful*, 1956; *My Fair Lady*, 1956; *Auntie Mame*, 1956; *The Amazing Adele*, 1956; *Candide*, 1956; *A Clearing in the Woods* (also co-produced), 1957; *Eugenia*, 1957; *Visit to a Small Planet*, 1957; *The Saturday-Night Kid* (co-produced), 1957; *Carousel* (revival), 1957; *The Carefree Heart*, 1957; *West Side Story*, 1957; *Jamaica*, 1957; *Time Remembered*, 1957; *Nude with Violin*, 1957; *La Traviata* (for the Metropolitan Opera), 1957; *Present Laughter*, 1958; *Winesburg, Ohio*, 1958; *My Fair Lady* (London), 1958; *Say Darling*, 1958; *Flower Drum Song*, 1958; *West Side Story* (London), 1958; *Juno* (also co-produced), 1959; *Destry Rides Again*, 1959; *Chéri*, 1959; *Take Me Along*, 1959; *The Sound of Music*, 1959, *Five Finger Exercise*, 1959; *Juniper and the Pagans*, 1959; *Goodbye, Charlie*, 1959; *Flower Drum Song* (London), 1960; *A Taste of Honey*, 1960; *Becket*, 1960; *The Unsinkable Molly Brown*, 1960; *Under the Yum-Yum Tree*, 1960; *Camelot*, 1961; *Martha* (for the Metropolitan Opera), 1961; *Show Girl* (also co-produced), 1961; *Mary, Mary*, 1961; *The Sound of Music* (London), 1961; *The Night of the Iguana*, 1961; *Sail Away*, 1961; *The Gay Life*, 1961; *Oh Dad, Poor Dad, Mama's Hung You in the Closet and I'm Feelin' So Sad* (London), 1961; *Daughter of Silence*, 1961; *Romulus*, 1962; *Sail Away* (London), 1962; *Come on Strong*, 1962; *Lord Pengo*, 1962; *Tiger, Tiger, Burning Bright* (also co-produced), 1962; *Natural Affection* (also co-produced), 1963; *Children from Their Games*, 1963; *On the Town* (London, also co-produced), 1963; *The Time of the Barracudas*, 1963; *110 in the Shade*, 1963; *Barefoot in the Park*, 1963; *The Girl Who Came to Supper*, 1963; *The Chinese Prime Minister*, 1964; *Hello, Dolly!* (also national and international companies and Australian production), 1964; *Dylan*, 1964; *In the Summerhouse* (revival), 1964; *Beckman Place*, 1964; *Ben Franklin in Paris*, 1964; *I Was Dancing*, 1964; *Luv*, 1964; *Bajour*, 1964; *Slow Dance on a Killing Ground*, 1964; *Poor Richard*, 1964; *Kelly*, 1965; *Baker Street*, 1965; *The Odd Couple*, 1965; *The Great Waltz*, 1965; *On a Clear Day You Can See Forever*, 1965; *Hot September*, 1965; *Cactus Flower*, 1965; *Barefoot in the Park* (London), 1965; *Hello, Dolly!* (London), 1965; *The Best Laid Plans*, 1966; *This Winter's Hobby*, 1966; *Show Boat*, 1966; *I Do! I Do!*, 1966; *The Star-Spangled Girl*, 1966; *The Odd Couple* (London), 1966; *110 in the Shade* (London), 1967; *Cactus Flower* (London), 1967; *Illya Darling*, 1967; *A Certain Young Man* (co-produced), 1967; *Swan Lake* (ballet re-created by David Blair), 1967; *Stephen D* (co-produced), 1967; *Niggerlovers* (co-produced), 1967; *Song of the Grasshopper*, 1967; *How Now, Dow Jones*, 1967; *Darling of the Day*, 1968; *Plaza Suite*, 1968; *Weekend*, 1968; *The Exercise* (also co-produced), 1968; *I Do! I Do!* (London), 1968; *Collision Course* (co-produced), 1968; *Dear World*, 1969; *But Seriously...*, 1969; *Come Summer*, 1969; *Adaptation and Next* (co-produced), 1969; *A Patriot for Me*, 1969; *Indians* (also co-produced), 1969; *Jimmy*, 1969; *Last of the Red Hot Lovers*, 1969; *Alice in Wonderland* (co-produced), 1970; *Lovely Ladies, Kind Gentlemen*, 1970; *Four on a Garden*, 1971; *Prettybelle* (tour), 1971; *Candide* (tour), 1971; *Lost in the Stars*, 1972; *The Little Black Book*, 1972; Leonard Bernstein's *Mass*, 1972; *The Time of Your Life* (Washington D.C.), 1972; *Doctor Selavy's Magic Theatre* (co-produced), 1972; *The Mother of Us All* (co-produced), 1972; *Tricks*, 1973; *The Women*, 1973; *Gigi*, 1973; *Alice in Wonderland* (co-produced), 1974; *Endgame* (co-produced), 1974; *Perfect Pitch* (co-produced, Washington D.C.), 1974; *Present Laughter* (tour), 1975; *Don't Call Back*, 1975; *Hello, Dolly!* 1975; *The Royal Family*, 1975; *Contredances* (ballet for Glenn Tetley), 1979; *Carmelina*, 1979; *Summer Hotel*, 1980. Films include—*Band Wagon* (Minnelli), 1953; *Oklahoma* (Zinnemann), 1955; *Guys and Dolls* (Mankiewicz), 1955; *Porgy and Bess* (Preminger), 1959; *Sound of Music* (Wise), 1965.

Publications:

By SMITH: articles—in *Dance Magazine* (New York), March 1967; *Harper's Bazaar* (New York), September 1971.

On SMITH: books—*The Biographical Encyclopaedia and Who's Who of the American Theatre*, edited by Walter Rigdon, New York 1966; *Le Decor de Film* by Leon Barsacq, Paris 1970, as *Caligari's Cabinet and Other Grand Illusions*, Boston 1976; *Who's Who in the Theatre 17*, edited by Ian Herbert, Detroit 1981.

*   *   *

Oliver Smith's beginnings in design were through the ballet, an association which he keeps to this day. For American Ballet Theatre, he designed classic works such as *Swan Lake*, *Giselle*, and *Sleeping Beauty*, but his main function, early on, was to design new works. As a result, he was actively involved in helping to create American ballet, which had previously been predominantly European in style. The sets for *Rodeo*, *Fancy Free*, and *Fall River Legend*, which are still used today, exemplify Smith's artistic contribution.

Smith's theory of design focuses on the dialectic between "painterly" and "sculptural" settings—that is, between two-dimensional backdrops, which are derived from the easel painting tradition, and three-dimensional "plastic" or architectural elements. His settings use either one of these forms or, more often, an admixture to create designs that range from romantic realism to abstraction. Examples of his predominantly sculptural settings for the theater include the designs for *Dylan*, *Indians*, and *Night of the Iguana*, while many of his other designs, although including "sculptural" elements, make use of the "painterly" approach. The backcloths of the ballets *Rodeo* and *Fancy Free* and the backdrops for the musical comedies *Hello, Dolly!* and *Baker Street* indicate the latter approach.

Smith believes that, in general, musicals should visually entertain the audience through bright, lively, attractive colors and forms, which should change rapidly and beautifully. "The design is not something to be looked at just as a static thing in itself.... It's really part of the choreography," he has stated.

This concept is evident in DeMille's ballet *Fall River Legend*, for which the setting is intrinsic to the dance movement. Through the reassembly of the main house unit, the dancers create a gallows, a church, and variations on the house. The dancers even revolve the unit 360 degrees in full view of the audience. In other examples, the colorful sets for *Hello, Dolly!* moved rapidly, but gracefully, from the feed store to the millinery shop to the Harmonia Gardens Restaurant, while in *West Side Story*, the scenes dissolved one into the other in front of the audience, yet unobtrusively. There is no doubt, to anyone who has seen these productions that the sets were choreographed into the shows to become intrinsic to the presentation. Smith elevates decor to a level equal to music and dance, thereby creating harmonious combinations.

Through all of his work, however, runs a concept which he often states to his students: that a setting should be simple, free from unnecessary details and fussiness. Smith continues to influence new generations of designers through his teaching, and, ultimately, through the example of his work, which is ubiquitous in many revivals, as well as shows that he continues to design.

—Tom Mikotowicz

SNYDER, Jerome.

American muralist, illustrator and graphic designer. Born in New York City, 20 April 1916. Educated in New York City schools; mainly self taught in art and design. Served in the United States Army, in Europe, 1942–46: Captain. Married Gertrude Goodrich; sons: Rowan and Todd. Muralist, working for the Federal Art Project, New York, 1939–41; freelance artist and graphic designer, New York, 1946–76: art director and associate editor, 1954–60, special projects director and consultant from 1960, *Sports Illustrated* magazine, New York; art director, *Scientific American* magazine, New York, from 1961. Recipient: National Mural Competition Honour Award, San Francisco, 1940; United Nations Poster

Prize, New York, 1946; Art Directors Gold Medal, New York, 1956, and Merit Award, 1960; also numerous awards from the New York Art Directors Club and the Society of Illustrators. *Died* (in New York City) *2 May 1976.*

Works:

A Politician's Map of the Farm Problem magazine layout, for *Fortune*, New York, March 1954.
Mozart record sleeve series, for the Haydn Society, Boston, 1958–59.
Boxed programme promotional kit, for CBS Radio, New York, 1959.
The Lives and Times of Peter Cooper (M. Gurko) book design, for Crowell, New York, 1959.
Days to Remember (W. Lipkind) book design, for Obolensky, New York, 1960.
A Day in Ancient Rome (G. Kirtland) book design, for Harcourt Brace, New York, 1961.
Umbrellas, Hats and Wheels (A. Rand) book design, for Harcourt Brace, New York, 1961.
One Day in Elizabethan England (G. Kirtland) book design, for Harcourt Brace, New York, 1962.
Scientists and Scoundrels (R. Silverberg) book design, for Crowell, New York, 1965.
Why the Sun Was Late (B. Elkin) book design, for Parents' Magazine Press, New York, 1966.

Publications:

By SNYDER: book — *The Underground Gourmet*, with Milton Glaser, New York 1967; articles—in *Graphis* (Zurich), no. 126, 1966, no. 133, 1967, no. 142, 1969, no. 143, 1969, no. 161, 1972, no. 163, 1972, no. 174, 1974, no. 177, 1975, no. 179, 1975, no. 182, 1975; *Print* (New York), January 1969; *American Artist* (New York), October/December 1970.

On SNYDER: books—*Posters: 50 Artists and Designers*, edited by W. H. Allner, New York 1952; *Illustration: Aspects and Directions* by Bob Gill and John Lewis, London 1964; *Graphis Record Covers*, edited by Walter Allner, Zurich 1974; *The Language of Graphics* by Edward Booth-Clibborn and Daniele Baroni, London 1980.

Well-known for his extensive, diversified talents, self-taught Jerome Snyder established himself as an important, innovative graphic artist and illustrator. Born in New York City, Snyder embodied all the dynamic qualities of that city: respect, intelligence, wit, and determination.

Before World War II, he painted murals for the WPA Federal Art Project, then served in the United States Army for four years as a captain in an infantry unit in Europe. After teaching art for two years at the Army University in Biarritz, France, Snyder returned to the United States to enter the commercial art field and teach, influence, and inspire students at such institutions as Parsons School of Design, Cooper Union, New York's Workshop School of Advertising and Editorial Art, Pratt Institute, and Yale University.

Intelligence and humor characterize Snyder's works, including the intricate and whimsical line drawings for which he was especially known. Reminiscent of the work of such artists as Joan Miro and Paul Klee, these renderings, despite intricately detailed patterns, paradoxically create a certain simplicity, as seen on the record covers for Boston's Hayden Society. His elementary, blocky forms and figures are embellished with a brocade of lines, spirals, and circles, yet they are not lost in this complexity, partly because colors create decorative patterns. His intelligent playfulness is particularly well exemplified in his witty Mark Cross Christmas catalogue cover depicting Santa Claus at each month of the year.

Snyder correlated the complexity of his art with the complexity of postwar man and society. However, he believed that form should be enhanced, not dominated, by this complexity.

As an art director and writer, Snyder combined his knowledge with practical artistic experience. In 1954, as the first art director of *Sports Illustrated*, Snyder designed the magazine's graphic format, then went on to become art director for *Scientific American* in 1961. As a writer, Snyder wrote intelligent, informative articles for such magazines as *Graphis*; however, he is more widely known as the co-author of the popular *Underground Gourmet*. Written with designer Milton Glaser, the book had as its goal to inform the public of inexpensive but good New York restaurants.

—Eumie Imm

SOLOVIEV, Yuri.

Russian industrial designer. Born in Kostroma, 12 January 1920. Studied design, Poligraphic Institute, Moscow, 1938–43. Married Ksenia Moskalenko in 1945; daughter: Ksenia. Professional industrial, transport and furniture designer, Moscow, from 1945. Founder-Director and Chief Designer of the Architectural and Art Bureau, at the Ministry for Transport Industry, Moscow, 1946–56; Director and Chief Engineer, Central Design Bureau of the Ministry for Shipbuilding, Moscow, 1956–59; Expert on Design, State Committee for Science and Technology of the USSR, Moscow, 1959–62; Founder-Director, USSR Research Institute of Industrial Design (VNIITE), Moscow, 1962–87; Director and Editor-in-Chief, *Tekhnicheskaya Estetika* magazine, Moscow, since 1964. Organizer, ICSID Interdesign Seminar, Minsk, 1971; Vice-President, 1969 and 1976, President, 1977–80, and Senate Member since 1981, International Council of Societies of Industrial Design (ICSID); President, Society of Soviet Designers, Moscow, since 1987. People's Deputy, Soviet Parliament, Moscow, 1989. Recipient: Best Design Project Prize, USSR Council of Ministers, 1980; DDR State Prize for Outstanding Merit in Design, Berlin, 1980; Design Development Prize, Mexico City, 1987; International World Design Prize, Washington, D.C. 1988; International Design Award, Japan Design Foundation, Tokyo, 1989. Address: Society of Soviet Designers, Arbatskaya Square 1/2, Moscow 121019, U.S.S.R.

Works:

All-metal passenger rail carriage, for the Kalinin Coach Plant, 1946 (with Y. Somov, G. Lebedev and I. Kulakov).
Noiseless tram, for the Riga Factory, 1950.
City trolleybus, for the Uritsky Factory, 1951.
Moskva-Rostov fleet diesel-electric passenger flagship, 1951 (with G. Botcharov).
Convertible wardrobe/desk/bed furniture set, 1953 (with S. Logginiva).
Combined desk/bookcase/bed furniture set, 1953 (with S. Logginiva).
MKS-1 collapsible motor boat, 1953.
MK-3 motor boat, 1954.
Tissa motor boat, 1956.
Lenin atomic-powered icebreaker ship, 1956.
Festival motor boat, 1957.
Plastic motor boat for mass-production, 1958.
Official sea yacht, 1959.

Publications:

By SOLOVIEV: books — *Industry's Requirements from the Projects of Artists and Designers*, VNIITE report, Moscow 1964; *Mutual Influences of the Arts and Sciences in the Context of Contemporary Scientific and Technological Thought*, UNESCO symposium paper, Paris 1968; *Methodologies of Design*, editor, Moscow 1983; articles—"On Combined Furniture" in *Wood and Timber Products Industry Journal* (Moscow), no. 8, 1954; "The International Design Conference in Aspen" in *Man: Problem Solver*, Chicago 1961; "On a Variety of Domestic Goods" in *Tekhnicheskaya Estetika* (Moscow), no. 6, 1966; "Yuri Solovieve: Russian Industrial Designer" in *Communication Arts* (Palo Alto), September 1961; "All-Union Industrial Design Conference" in *Journal of the Industrial Design Society of America* (Great Falls, New York), no. 1, 1971; "Organization as Design" in *Industrial Design* (New York), no. 4, 1971; "Soviet Design of the Last Ten Years" in *Tekhnicheskaya Estetika* (Moscow), no. 5, 1972; "Industrial Design in the USSR" in *Design Industrie* (Paris), no. 110, 1973; "On Neglected Methods of Protecting the Environment", with K. M. Yakuolevas-Matenkis, in *Tekhnicheskaya Estetika* (Moscow), no. 9, 1974; "Design Problems in the Creation of the Urban Environment" in *Tekhnicheskaya Estetika* (Moscow), no. 9, 1978; "Evolution of Industrial Design in Developed Countries" in *UNIDO-ICSID India 79: Design for Development*, Ahmedabad 1979; "Soviet Design: Progress and Problems" in *Tekhnicheskaya Estetika* (Moscow), no. 4, 1982.

On SOLOVIEV: books—*Industrial Design* by John Heskett, London 1980; articles—"Russian Institute Pushes Product Planning" by H. Rausch in *Product Engineering* (New York), 1 January 1968; "That was the Beginning" by S. Sylvestrova in *Design Issues* (Chicago), Spring 1986.

People are lazy by nature, and life is constantly creating difficulties which they have to overcome. With this in mind, I try to design for convenience. In the majority of cases, people would like to get more for what they are prepared to pay. I believe this is a natural human characteristic, and therefore try to design things to be easily produced. All people, consciously or unconsciously, like beautiful things; hence I make this a prime consideration in my design.

In practice, I prefer designing complex objects (passenger ships, for example), where all objects in one spatial interior are designed to help each other to better fulfil their function, and together require less space and render better service whilst affording aesthetic pleasure.

Our world is full of unnecessary or superfluous things. To produce them, we waste a lot of manpower, material and time. I think that the designer's task is to reduce to the minimum the number of such items, to help regain a feeling of delight from contact with nature, whilst utilizing the comfort provided by scientific and technical advances to enrich our lives.

On the whole, I consider that the designer has a great responsibility in society. His professional duty is to present those proposals and

Yuri Soloviev: *Lenin* atomic-powered icebreaker, 1956

solutions that would safeguard ecology and preserve national resources.

—Yuri Soloviev

In 1945 among the most critical problems facing the Soviet Union was restoration of the nation's severely war-damaged transportation system. When the Minister of Transport Machine Building, V. M. Malyshev, selected the Kalinin Railway Coach Company to replace old wooden passenger coaches with ones that provide maximum comfort with minimum materials the company in turn assigned Yuri Soloviev, a 25 year old graduate from the Polytechnic Institute in Moscow and a Doctor of Science, to head up the project. The result was an all-metal coach that borrowed heavily from aircraft technology to build a product that in competition with another proposal made by the original coach builder was judged superior and was approved for production. Soloviev and his associates had gone beyond technological problems to propose a concept that was not only attractive but also considered ergonomic factors that were often simply passed over in the past. Forty years later the same design with minor modifications was still in service in the Soviet Union as well as the German Democratic Republic.

As a result of this demonstration—that technical, aesthetic and ergonomic considerations could be put into balance—the Architectural-Artistic Bureau was set up in 1946 within the ministry with Soloviev as director. At the time designers were called "craftsmen" because the term "designer" was considered to be seditious. Soloviev put together a team of fellow designers and technicians that began to concentrate on products to be mass-produced rather than custom-built, employing principles of comfort,

economy, appearance and production logic that are now standard practice for professional industrial designers. In short order, their assignments also included river passenger ships, excursion launches, city trolley buses as well as furniture and interior design for the nation's atomic-powered ice-breaker. These transportation projects were further expanded into other areas to include the design of interiors, furniture and appliances for comfortable one family flats. To assist him Soloviev called upon students from Moscow's schools of architecture, art and engineering thus setting the basis for industrial design education in the Soviet Union.

In 1959 the State Committee for Science and Technology invited Yuri Soloviev to propose a plan for the expansion of design to a national scale. In the course of developing his proposal Lord Paul Reilly, Director of the British Design Council, and Raymond Loewy, a major American industrial designer, were invited to visit the Soviet Union and share their experiences with him as well as others. As a result of his proposal in 1962 the government established the USSR Research Institute of Industrial Design, VNIITE, with Soloviev as director. In 1965 the first All-Union Exhibition of Industrial Design was organized followed by the first All-Union conference on industrial design, organized by VNIITE, with participation of designers from socialist countries. VNIITE has since grown into a statewide system of research laboratories and applied studios for industrial design practice. There are now some twelve branch offices of VNIITE across the various republics as well as 1500 design studios in industries across the country.

After the Soviet Union and the United States signed a Cultural Exchange Agreement, also in 1962, the American government sent three design exhibitions to the Soviet Union over the

next six years, the first one on graphics, the second on tools and machines and a third on industrial design. In 1967, while serving as a specialist with the last exhibition in Leningrad the author was invited to visit VNIITE in Moscow to lecture on industrial design practice and education in the United States. Later that year on the initiative of Soloviev with support of UNESCO the Soviets conducted an international seminar in Tbilisi on the subject of Art and Technology. In 1969 VNIITE became a member of the International Council of Societies of Industrial Design and, in 1975, under his leadership the biannual Congress of ICSID was staged in Moscow, with the title, "Design for Man and Society". Soloviev was elected President of ICSID for the 1978–79 term and is now a Senator of that organization.

Soloviev was the pioneer in organizing and holding international working seminars on design that are unique to ICSID. Called "Interdesigns" they bring together a team of foreign specialists to work with the host country team on a design problem of global interest. In 1971 Yuri Soloviev organized the first one in Minsk on the subject of baking bread and has since staged others, more than any other country, on subjects as diverse as the design of a self-sufficient small town and watch-making. Over the years Soloviev has served as a jury member of a number of international design competitions. He has been honored for his accomplishments by the German Democratic Republic, the Mexican Academy of Design as well as receiving the WORLDESIGN Award from the Industrial Designers Society of America.

In 1988 Yuri Soloviev left his position at VNIITE to become founding member and the first President of the Society of Soviet Designers, the only voluntary self-governing creative organization that amalgamates professional designers in the Soviet Union. Its some 2000 members are free to take on private contracts for design service to government agencies and industries. Its purpose, as stated in its charter, is "to promote designer's creative activity in aesthetic and functional perfectioning of the subject area in order to improve labor, living and leisure conditions of the Soviet people."

With his election to the Council of Ministers of the Soviet Union in 1989 he will be able to play an even greater part in the design quality of products and their impact on the economy and well-being of the citizens of his country as well as its entry into international markets.

—Arthur J. Pulos

SOPRANI, Luciano.

Italian fashion designer. Born in Reggiolo, Reggio Calabria, 12 April 1946. Educated in Guastalla, until 1959; studied at agricultural college, Guastalla, 1960–65; mainly self-taught in design. Assistant stylist, 1967–70, and designer, 1970–74, at Achille Maramotti's Max Mara fashion company, in Reggio Emilia and Milan; freelance fashion designer, working for Dorian, Helyett, Pims, Gruppo Finanziario Tessile, etc., in Reggio Emilia and Milan, 1975–81; founder and director of Luciano Soprani SRI fashion company, Milan, from 1981: has designed collections for Basile and Gucci. **Exhibition:** *Florida Salute to Basile*, Jordan Marsh Store, Miami, 1981; **Collection:** Museo della Moda, Parma. Recipient: Fil d'Or Award, Festival du Lin, 1981, 1982, 1983. Address: Via Santo Spirito 24, 20121 Milan, Italy.

Publications:

On SOPRANI: books—*I Mass-Moda: Fatti e Personaggi dell'Italian Look* by Adriana Mulassano, Florence 1979; *Leaders in Fashion* by Maria Vittoria Alfonsi, Bologna 1983; *The Fashion Year* by Brenda Polan, London 1983; *McDowell's Directory of Twentieth Century Fashion* by Colin McDowell, London 1984; *The Encyclopaedia of Fashion from 1840 to the 1980s* by Georgina O'Hara, London 1986.

I was born into a big peasant family, a truly patriarchal family like the ones Bertolucci describes in *Novecento*. All the branches of the tree, all the generations were together, from grandparents to grandchildren. In the golden years, there were twenty-four of us around the table. The house no longer exists, but Reggiolo, a little village near Reggio Emilia, is still there, with its mediaeval castle in the middle, its air of by-gone revolutions, its cooperatives, its workers' associations, the socialist playing cards with the priest. And on Sundays, Sunday best; on feast days, new clothes. Respect for oneself and for others, no signs of exhibitionism. I owe my love for music to my grandfather, who was a keen Verdi fan, my love for drawing to my grandmother, who used to buy me exercise books and pencils and would stand for hours and watch me sketching figures, heads, hats, clothes.

But after I had completed secondary school at Guastalla, I had to go to agricultural school and get a diploma. I worked in this sector for a few months but was fixated on fashion. I don't know why. Maybe I had inherited this passion

Luciano Soprani: Tuxedo outfit in wool crepe, 1983

from my mother who adored beautiful lingerie and nice clothes. I remember some brocades, some wools, some lovely soft silks, and then I remember going to the dressmaker with my mother. As my mother was against it, I had to learn by myself, copying clothes from magazines. Once, twice, three times. Changing, inventing, adding, taking away. And then, after a letter to Achille Maramotti, the owner of Max Mara, I went to Reggio Emilia with a folder full of sketches. I answered his questions very shyly, and the next day at nine o'clock in the morning, I was on the job. He had hired me. This was in March 1967. I was nineteen years old. For month after month, I did nothing but study, take part in the fittings, learn the secrets of designing and cutting. And within two years, I had designed seven Max Mara collections out of fourteen.

I stayed with Max Mara until 1974. I liked it there, and I learned a lot. I took my time and let things mature, which is a typical country habit I learned from my grandfather. Then I gradually took off on my own: two years of freelance consulting, then new experiences. I wanted to find out who I was, what I was doing, and what I could do. I divided my time between Milan and Reggio Emilia until 1978, when I made my final move to Milan, for that was where my future was. In fact after Pims', my first complete adventure—also from the point of view of image and press relations—I met Gigi Monti and Basile, who represented tradition, reliability, and international fashion styles. I prepared a spring/summer 1980 collection, and it was a great success. This led in 1981 to the beginning of the Luciano Soprani signature. And it is slowly but surely being completed: shoes, accessories, spectacles, everything but leather which is going to be presented next season with a well-balanced, refined touch. And in winter 1985, the man's line I have been working on for some time. Because I still think I have something to say.

I am fascinated by the seasons, by the birth of animals, by the passing of time. Everything that is real, natural, precise. Definite outlines, no uncertainties. It's my peasant origin: I want wool to be wool, cotton to be cotton. I don't mix fibres, I don't exasperate them. You must be able to recognize them, they must be known. And I love the colours of the earth, the greys, whites, and neutral shades. They are reassuring. They are the other side of my undeniable love: the 1920s, Art Deco, the Bloomsbury group, Vita Sackville-West. And I like travelling: South America, the Far East, India, but I also like coming home.

—Luciano Soprani

In 1981, Luciano Soprani, designer of high-style ready-to-wear fashions, presented the first collection under his own label. The collection assured Soprani a distinct place in recent Italian design circles, including as it did so many outstanding outfits. There were wonderful coats with fur shoulders, coats and capes in tweeds, plaids, flannels, and loden. There was his individualistic use of the layered look, with knee-pants and finely tailored jackets in variations of the safari and blouson under outer layers of coat or cape. There were the poncho layerings with quietly patterned plaids and tweeds intermixed with Soprani's characteristic duck print and black and white or browns and grays. There was the so-called "choir girl look" and the "preppy" tuxedo blouse worn with short skirt. There were short, blousy pants in satins of stripes and solids.

In 1982, Soprani was busy with his vivacious, yellow and red, draped and wrapped gabardine jackets, his leather and brown tweed jackets

under olive and marine-green, short, hooded coats and his blouses with puffy sleeves worn with sleeveless jackets of leather and tweed. Among the designs he created for Basile during that same year is his combination of sable jacket under brown hooded and sleeveless blouson. It was also for Basile that Soprani came up with a stunning, all white sports outfit composed of wool challis shirt and wide-wale corduroy pants worn with undyed wool vest, wool hopsack jacket, and cosy leg warmers.

Nineteen eighty-three saw Soprani in a more romantic mood in his linen dresses but continuing the layered look in his light wool gabardine jacket with pants and in his suede jacket over floral and bayadere prints for Basile. Also for the Basile collection, Soprani came up with a line of tailored clothes and sportswear which begins with the essentials of the Basile style and locates new variations for an updated feeling. For example, he adds new pocket treatments and one-inch cuffs to the characteristically loose-fitting Basile trousers, widens the cut of blousons and jackets and enlarges collars on topcoats. This collection is a fine representation of Soprani's place in the Milanese style of the comfortable, loose, and easy-layered feel which maintains a body-consciousness in the silhouettes by draping or fitting over the form to result in a subtle sense of the sensuous shape underneath.

—Barbara Cavaliere

SORENSEN, Johnny.
Danish architect, interior and furniture designer. Born in Helsingor, 3 February 1944. Studied furniture design, School of Arts and Crafts (Kunsthandvaerkskolan), Copenhagen, 1963–67: Dip. 1967. Married Lis Ostergard Berthelsen. Freelance furniture designer, establishing design firm with Rud Thygesen, in Copenhagen, since 1967: has designed for Mogens Kold, Domus Danica, Erik Boisen, Per Jorgensen, Textil Lassen, Magnus Olesen, Zon International, etc. **Exhibitions:** Den Permanente, Copenhagen, 1972; Danske Kunstindustrimuseum, Copenhagen, 1976; *Scandinavian Modern Design 1880–1980*, Cooper-Hewitt Museum, New York, 1982 (toured); *Denmark in Britain: Design and Architecture*, Business Design Centre, London, 1989. **Collections:** Nordenfjeldske Kunstindustrimuseum, Trondheim; Statens Kunstfond, Copenhagen; Kunstindustrimuseet, Copenhagen. Recipient: First Prize, Society of Cabinetmakers Exhibition, Copenhagen, 1966, 1968; Central Bank Jubilee Awards, Copenhagen, 1969, 1975; Alex Foss Industrifond Award, 1976. Address: Ostergade 26 C, 1100 Copenhagen K, Denmark.

Works:

Cafe chair and table in laminated beech, for Magnus Olesen, 1982.
8000 range of furniture, for Magnus Olesen, 1983.

Publications:

On SORENSEN/THYGESEN: books — *Rud Thygesen and John Sorensen: Industri og Design* by Henrik Sten Moller, Copenhagen 1976; *Scandinavian Modern Design 1880–1980*,

edited by David Revere McFadden, New York 1982; *International Design Yearbook 1985/86* edited by Robert A. M. Stern, London 1985; *Objects One: An Account of Danish Arts and Crafts 1985/86*, edited by the Objects Group, Copenhagen 1986; *International Design Yearbook 1987/88*, edited by Philippe Starck, London 1987; *Denmark in Britain: Design and Architecture*, exhibition catalogue with texts by Per Bernsen and others, Copenhagen 1989.

See THYGESEN, Rud.

SOTTSASS, Ettore, Jr.
Italian architect, interior, exhibition and industrial designer. Born, of Italian parents, in Innsbruck, Austria, 14 September 1917. Educated in Trento and Turin until 1934; studied architecture, at the Politecnico, Turin, 1935–39: Dip.Arch. 1939. Served in the Italian Army, in Montenegro and Sargiaccato, 1942–45. Married Fernanda Pivano in 1949; lived with Eulalia Grau, 1970–75, and with Barbara Radice from 1976. Worked as a writer, associating with designer Luigi Spazzapan, in Turin, 1937–40, and with Giuseppe Pagano's group of architects, Turin, 1945; freelance architect and designer, Milan, from 1945: worked in studio of designer George Nelson, New York, 1956; design consultant, Olivetti company, Turin, from 1958; founder-member, Global Tools group, Milan, 1975, and Studio Alchymia design group, Milan, 1979; founded Sottsass Associati architectural design partnership, Milan, 1980, and Memphis design co-op, Milan, 1981. **Exhibitions:** Milan Triennale, from 1954; *Italy: The New Domestic Landscape*, Museum of Modern Art, New York, 1972; Internationales Design Zentrum, West Berlin, 1976 (toured); Centre de Creation Industrielle, Paris, 1976; Cooper-Hewitt Museum, New York, 1976; *Design Process Olivetti 1908–78*, University of California, Los Angeles, 1979; *Italian Re-Evolution*, La Jolla Museum of Art, California, 1982; *Design Since 1945*, Philadelphia Museum of Art, 1983. **Collections:** Philadelphia Museum of Art; Museum of Modern Art, New York. Recipient: Compasso d'Oro Award, Milan, 1959. Honorary Doctorate: Royal College of Art, London, 1968. Address: Via Manzoni 14, 20121 Milan, Italy.

Works:

Oggetti per la Casa exhibition layouts, at the Milan Triennale, 1947.
Side table in marble and brass alloy, for Italia Disegno, 1956.
Italian Glass exhibition layouts, at the Milan Triennale, 1957.
Elea 9003 electronic computer, for Olivetti, 1959.
Prime Materials exhibition layouts, at *Italia '61*, Turin, 1961.
Tekne 3 electric typewriter, for Olivetti, 1962 (with Hans von Klier).
Praxis 48 electric typewriter, for Olivetti, 1964 (with Hans von Klier).
Lucrezia bench with tip-up seat in walnut and white lacquer, for Poltronova, 1964–65.
Asteroide lamp in two-coloured perspex and aluminium, for Poltronova, 1968.
Olivetti display stand, at *La Macchina della Informazione*, Turin, 1968.

Nefertiti desk in plywood with white and green striped laminate, for Poltronova, 1968.

Lettera 36 portable electric typewriter, for Olivetti, 1969.

Valentine portable typewriter in red ABS plastic housing, for Olivetti, 1970 (with Perry King).

Mickey Mouse table in ABS plastic and chair with stain-proof upholstery, for BBB Bonacina, 1971.

Synthesis 45 office furniture system, for Olivetti, 1971–73.

Flying Carpet armchair with carpet footrest, for Bedding Brevetti, 1974–75.

Sign system and graphics programme, for Fiumicino Airport, Rome, 1977.

Consolle table in plastic laminate, for Croff Centro Casa, 1978–79.

Beverly sideboard in root-wood and plastic laminate, produced by Memphis for Renzo Brugola, 1981.

Park Lane circular coffee table in fibreglass and marble, produced by Memphis for Up & Up, 1983.

(for a list of Sottsass's buildings and architectural projects, see *Contemporary Architects*)

Publications:

By SOTTSASS: books — *Europe e America*, exhibition catalogue, Turin 1946; *Arte Astratta e Concreta*, exhibition catalogue, Rome 1948; *Ceramiche dell'tenebre*, exhibition catalogue, Milan 1963; *Miljo for en Ny Planet*, exhibition catalogue, Stockholm 1969; *De l'Objet Fini a la Fin de l'Objet*, exhibition catalogue, Paris 1977; *Esercizio Formale*, Crusinallo 1979; *Esercizio Formale II*, Milan 1980; *Alcantara*, with others, Milan 1983; *Memphis Milano 1986: The Firm*, Milan 1986; *Sottsass Associati*, with others, New York 1988.

On SOTTSASS: books—*Forme Nuove in Italia* by Agnoldomenico Pica, Milan and Rome 1957; *Design Italiano: I Mobili*, edited by Enrichetta Ritter, Milan and Rome 1968; *Italy: The New Domestic Landscape* by Emilio Ambasz, New York and Florence 1972; *Il Design in Italia 1945–72* by Paolo Fossati, Turin 1972; *Sottsass's Scrapbook*, edited by Frederica Di Castro, Milan 1976; *Il Design di Ettore Sottsass*, thesis by Milena Fornari, University of Turin 1978; *Ettore Sottsass*, exhibition catalogue by Izzika Gaon, Jerusalem 1978; *Ettore Sottsass Jr.: Ipotesi di Controdesign*, thesis by Simona Riva, University of Parma 1978; *History of Modern Furniture* by Karl Mang, Stuttgart 1978, London 1979; *Atlante del Design Italiano 1940/1980* by Alfonso Grassi and Anty Pansera, Milan 1980; *Memphis: The New International Style* by Barbara Radice, Milan 1981; *Ettore Sottsass Jr.* by Penny Sparke, London 1982; *Design Process Olivetti 1908–83*, with text by Renzo Zorzi, Milan 1983; *Ettore Sottsass Jr.*, thesis by Philippe Thome, University of Geneva 1984; *Ettore Sottsass: Mobili e Qualche Arredamento*, edited by Guia Sambonet, Milan 1985; *Ettore Sottsass: Design Metaphors*, edited by Barbara Radice, Milan 1987; *Designed by Architects in the 1980s* by Juli Capella and Quim Larrea, London 1988; *Italian Modern: A Design Heritage* by Giovanni Albera and Nicolas Monti, New York 1989.

As a leading figure philosophically, as well as in terms of sheer output of design ideas and products, in Italy today, Ettore Sottsass, Jr. has a profound influence, one that has been particularly dramatic in the past four years, ever since he became involved with the Memphis group. In his deliberate veering away from "serious" design to a vocabulary that is anarchic, colorful, and witty. Sottsass is attempting to return a sense of life and adventure to furniture design. When asked recently what he thought were the key properties of good design, Sottsass was quoted as replying: "This is a question that supposes a Platonic view of the situation, that is that somewhere, somehow, there is a place where GOOD DESIGN is deposited. The problem then is to come as close as possible to that 'good design.' My idea instead is ... to design keeping as near as possible to the anthropological state of things, which, in turn is to be as near as possible to the need a society has for an image of itself."

Sottsass further suggests that the only design that is not valid for contemporary conditions is that which attempts to be timeless, to offer a permanent solution to a given problem—certainly the moral and metaphysical mission of the Bauhaus and of modernism in general. Thus, Sottsass must be seen as rebel against the tradition of the pure, the functional and as seeker after a richer and more poignant relationship between the consumer and the artifact.

Another important component of Sottsass' recent output has been its conscious historicism, for Memphis is a surrealistic kaleidoscope of many cultures and period styles. Art Deco interacts with freeform shapes of the 1950s, with Egyptian, neo-Classical, and elements that can only be described as kitsch. This too is consistent with Sottsass' world view that brings together many civilizations and ideologies. It is a tribute to the extraordinary synthesizing talent of the man that what has emerged is not a chaotic mish-mash of non-style but a smooth, glamorous, highly knowing hybrid *style*. One suspects that if it becomes the most characteristic style of the 1980s, Sottsass would be well satisfied. Certainly, it is the hitherto most colorful marriage between high design and consumer culture, the ultimate consummation of the former's twenty-year flirtation with popular culture and the ironic coda to this century's search for an appropriate style suited to industrial society.

—Peter Carlsen

SPACE DESIGN GROUP.
American architectural, interior and graphic design firm. Founded by Marvin B. Affrime (born 1925), in New York City, 1958. President: Marvin B. Affrime; Senior Vice-President for Design: Frank R. Failla; Senior Vice-President for Projects: Leonard F. Pepi; Senior Vice-President for Planning: Gerard L. Krush; Executive Vice-President for Finance: Jules I. Lasky; Vice-President for Furnishings: Connie Mack Locklin; Vice-President for Production: George Como; Vice-President for Construction: Richard Rockstuhl. The Space Design Group has designed for Johns-Manville Corporation, IBM, International Paper Company, National Westminster Bank, Eastman Kodak, Air France, Lippincott & Margulies, McCann-Erickson, etc. Recipient: *Interior Design* 100 Giants Award, 1981, and Hall of Fame Award, 1986; and numerous Fifth Avenue Association awards, New York. Address: The Space Design Group, 8 West 40th Street, New York, New York 10018, U.S.A.

Works:

Benton and Bowles headquarters, New York, 1969.
Philadelphia National Bank public facility, 1971, and offices, 1977.
Touche Ross and Company headquarters, New York, 1971.
Johns-Manville computer center and offices, and headquarters, 1971–77.
Clarendon Bank and Trust Company headquarters, Virginia, 1976.
All-Steel showrooms, New York, 1978.
Philadelphia National Corporation headquarters, 1979.
IBM data processing headquarters, White Plains, New York, 1979.
Sterling Sound graphic image programme, New York, 1980.
Morgan Finnegan Pine Foley & Lee law offices, New York, 1980.
The Itkins graphic image programme, New York, 1982.
International Paper Company headquarters and public plaza, New York, 1982–83, 1988.
Hotel Riverparc graphic image programme, Miami, 1983.
First American Bank of Virginia headquarters, Fairfax, 1983.
Porchester Partners offices and public lobby, Pittsburgh, 1983.
National Westminster Bank North American headquarters, New York, 1983.
BBDO Worldwide headquarters, New York, 1987.
First American Metro Corporation headquarters, Virginia, 1989–90.

Publications:

On SPACE DESIGN GROUP: books — *Lighting and Its Design* by Leslie Larson, New York 1964; *Shops and Showrooms* by Karl Kaspar, New York 1967; *Interiors Book of Offices*, edited by Jon F. Pile, New York 1969, 1976; *The Office Book*, New York 1982; *Corporate Design*, New York 1983.

The list of clients of The Space Design Group includes some of the most prestigious corporations in the United States. Although the most significant contribution to interior design has been made by the firm's superior corporate offices, clients have included firms in banking, travel, and advertising.

The firm's founding president, Marvin B. Affrime, is the key person in the organization. However, several of his associates have been with him from the firm's inception—and some even in a prior venture. The firm is lean in size, if measured by its influence and quantity of work. Several key associates, together with Affrime, function as a team. The firm is well organized yet consciously avoids the internal corporate structure that is the norm for large design firms. Every project is so thoroughly researched that Affrime often surprises his clients with the knowledge and understanding that he acquires in the course of his interviews and subsequent research.

One cannot characterize the resulting work in a particular esthetic category. Every project seems to be elegant, beautiful, and unique in some way, yet totally functional. A recent project, the executive offices for the International Paper Company, was given the almost unheard-of coverage of twenty-eight pages in the magazine *Interior Design*. More than any other interior design firm, The Space Design Group has achieved its goal of creating buildings from the inside outward. Two of the firm's most renowned projects are the interiors of the Johns-Manville World Headquarters in Denver

Space Design Group: National Westminster Bank headquarters, New York, 1983

and of the First American Bank of Virginia Headquarters in Fairfax, Virginia. In both cases, the firm worked closely with the architects and essentially determined the shape of the buildings with them. Both projects were exceptionally successful because their programs originated in the people-oriented research upon which Affrime insists.

In a recent article on Affrime, the magazine *Contract* referred to him and his firm as being at the pinnacle of design. It is an opinion widely shared by critics and design professionals alike.

—Arnold Friedmann

SPENCE, Basil (Urwin).

British architect, interior, exhibition and furniture designer. Born, of British parents, in Bombay, India, 13 August 1907. Studied at George Watson's College, Edinburgh, 1920–25; Heriot-Watt University School of Architecture, Edinburgh, 1925–29; Bartlett School of Architecture, University College, London, 1929–30. Served in the British Army, 1939–45; Major. Married Mary Joan Ferris in 1934; children: Milton and Gillian. Worked as assistant in the office of architect Edward Lutyens, London, 1929–30; architect, working with William Kininmonth, in the office of Rowland Anderson and Paul, Edinburgh, 1931–33; partner, Rowland Anderson and Paul, Edinburgh, 1934–37; in private architectural and design practice, Edinburgh, 1937–39, as Basil Spence and Partners, Edinburgh, 1946–63; partnership divided into Sir Basil Spence, London 1964–76, Spence Glover and Furguson, Edinburgh, 1964–74, and Spence Bonnington and Collins, London, 1964–70; Sir Basil Spence International (now The Sir Basil Spence Partnership), London, established 1974. Adviser to the Board of Trade for the British Industries Fair, London, 1947, 1948 and 1949; planning consultant to the universities of Edinburgh, Southampton and Nottingham, and to Basildon New Town. Hoffman Wood Professor of Architecture, University of Leeds, 1955–56; professor of architecture, Royal Academy, London, 1961–68. Council member, 1952, vice-president, 1954–55, honorary secretary, 1956, and president, 1958–60, Royal Institute of British Architects; member of the Fine Art Commission, London, 1956–70; treasurer, Royal Academy, London, 1962–64. **Exhibition:** *Eye for Industry*, Victoria and Albert Museum, London, 1986. Recipient: Festival of Britain Award, London, 1951; Coventry Cathedral Competition Prize, 1951; Saltire Society Award, 1952; Royal Institute of British Architects Bronze Medal, 1962; City of Coventry Merit Award, 1970; Academie d'Architecture Gold Medal, Paris, 1974. Honorary Doctorate: University of Leicester, 1963; University of Manitoba, 1963; University of Southampton, 1965. Fellow, Royal Institute of British Architects, 1947; Associate of the Royal Scottish Academy, 1952; Associate, 1953, and Academician, 1960, Royal Academy of Art, London; Royal Designer for Industry, Royal Society of Arts, London, 1960; Honorary Fellow, Royal College of Art, London, 1962, and American Institute of Architects, 1963; Honorary Member, Accademia di San Luca, Rome, 1973. Knighted, 1960; Order of Merit, London, 1962. *Died* (in Eye, Suffolk) *19 November 1976.*

Works:

Britain Can Make It exhibition layouts, Victoria and Albert Museum, London, 1946.
Enterprise Scotland exhibition layouts, Edinburgh, 1947.
Scottish Industries Exhibition layouts, Glasgow, 1949.
Allegro chair, produced by H. Morris, 1949.
Heavy Industries exhibition layouts, at the *Festival of Britain*, South Bank, London, 1951.
Sea and Ships pavilion, at the *Festival of Britain*, South Bank, London, 1951.
British pavilion, at *Expo 67*, Montreal, 1967.
Cathedral of Saint Michael, Coventry, 1962.
British Embassy Chancery Building, Rome, 1971.

(for a complete list of Spence's buildings and architectural projects, see *Contemporary Architects*)

Publications:

By SPENCE: books—*Exhibition Design*, with others, London 1950; *The Cathedral of St. Michael, Coventry*, London 1962; *Phoenix at Coventry: The Building of a Cathedral*, London 1962, 1964; *Out of the Ashes: A Progress Through Coventry Cathedral*, with Henk Snoek, London 1963; *The Idea of a New University: An Experiment in Sussex*, with others, London 1964; *New Buildings in Old Cities*, Southampton 1973.

On SPENCE: books — *British Furniture Today*, by Erno Goldfinger, London 1951; *Design in British Industry: A Mid-Century Survey* by Michael Farr, Cambridge 1955; *Furniture in Britain Today* by Dennis and Barbara Young, London 1964; *Case di Abitazione* by Giampiero Aloi, Milan 1971; *A Century of Chair Design*, edited by Frank Russell, London 1980; *A Broken Wave: The Rebuilding of England 1940–1980* by Lionel Esher, London 1981; *Contemporary Furniture*, edited by Klaus-Jurgen Sembach, Stuttgart and London 1982; *Eye for Industry: Royal Designers for Industry 1936–1986* by Fiona MacCarthy and Patrick Nuttgens, London 1986.

SPENCER, Herbert.

British painter, photographer and graphic designer. Born in London, 22 June 1924. Married Marianne Mols in 1954; daughter: Mafalda. Freelance designer, London, from 1945: editor of *Typographica* magazine, London, 1949–67, and of the *Penrose Annual*, London, 1964–73; advisor to the Post Office Stamp Design Committee, London, from 1968, and to the British Telecom Design Committee, 1981–83; design consultant to W. H. Smith Limited from 1973, Tate Gallery, London, from 1981, and British Rail, 1984–86; also consultant designer to the Westminster Press newspapers, Lund Humphries printers, University of Leeds, University of East Anglia, Imperial War Museum, and the Royal Institute of British Architects. Director, Lund Humphries publishers, London, from 1970. Lecturer, Central School of Arts and Crafts, London, 1949–55; senior resident fellow, 1966–78, and professor of graphic arts, 1978–85, Royal College of Art, London; master of the faculty of Royal Design-

ers for Industry, Royal Society of Arts, London 1979–81; governor, Bath Academy of Art, Corsham, 1982–83. International president, Alliance Graphique Internationale, Paris, 1971–74; vice-president, Royal Society of Arts, London, 1979–81. **Exhibitions:** Zwemmer Gallery, London, 1953; *107 Grafici dell'AGI*, Castello Sforzesco, Milan, 1974; *Eye for Industry*, Victoria and Albert Museum, London, 1986; Bleddfa Trust, Wales, 1986. *Collection:* Victoria and Albert Museum, London. Recipient: Fellow, Society of Industrial Artists, London, 1947; Royal Designer for Industry, Royal Society of Arts, London, 1965; honorary doctorate, 1960, and honorary fellow, 1985, Royal College of Art, London. Address: 75 Deodar Road, Putney, London SW15 2NU, England.

Works:

Catalogue layout and cover design, for Common Ground Limited, 1951.
Letterhead and stationery design, for Chamberlin Powell & Bon, 1954.
Letterhead and symbol, for Lund Humphries, London, 1964.
Train timetable re-design, for British Railways, 1961–62.
Logotype symbol, for Span Developments, 1965.
5 Young Artists exhibition catalogue design, for the British Council, 1966.
Recent British Painting exhibition catalogue design, for the Peter Stuyvesant Foundation, 1967.
Annual Report layout and cover design, for Bovis Holdings, 1969.
Logotype symbol, for Hamish Hamilton publishers, London, 1971.
Vordemberge-Gildewart exhibition catalogue design, for Annely Juda Fine Art, London, 1974.

Publications:

By SPENCER: books—*Design in Business Printing*, London 1952; *Designers in Britain*, no. 4 and no. 5, London 1954, 1957; *London's Canal*, London 1961; *Printers and Designers*, London 1963; *The Visible World*, London and New York 1969; *Pioneers of Modern Typography*, London 1969, New York 1970, London and Cambridge, Massachusetts 1983; *Words, Words, Words*, London and Cologne 1972; *New Alphabets A to Z*, with Colin Forbes, London and New York 1973, Paris 1974; *The Book of Numbers*, with Mafalda Spencer, London 1977; *The Liberated Page*, London 1987.

On SPENCER: books—*Graphic Design Britain*, edited by Frederick Lambert, London 1967; *107 Grafici dell'AGI*, with texts by Renzo Zorzi and Franco Grignani, Venice 1974; *The Thames and Hudson Manual of Typography* by Ruari McLean, London 1980; *Who's Who in Graphic Art*, edited by Walter Amstutz, Dubendorf 1982; *Eye for Industry: Royal Designers for Industry 1936–1986* by Fiona McCarthy and Patrick Nuttgens, London 1986.

No matter how great the author's wisdom or how vital the message or how remarkable the printer's skill, unread print is merely a lot of paper and a little ink. The true economics of printing must be measured by how much is read and understood and not by how much is produced. (*Reprinted from* The Visible Word, *1969.*)

—Herbert Spencer

Herbert Spencer's first jobs as a freelance

Vordemberge-Gildewart

Herbert Spencer: Exhibition catalogue cover, for Annely Juda Fine Art, London, 1974

SPOHN, Jurgen.

German illustrator and graphic designer. Born in Leipzig, 10 June 1934. Studied under Hans Leistikow, at the Hochschule fur Bildende Kunste, Kassel, 1956–61. Freelance designer, Berlin, from 1961: has designed for Taschenbucher/Harenberg, Siegbert Mohn Verlag, Bertelsmann Verlag, Verlag Beltz & Gelberg, Thienemann Verlag, Neuer Finken Verlag, Otto Maier Verlag, Bibliophilen Taschenbucher, Nishi Nura, Running Press, etc. Professor of visual communications, Technische Universitat, Berlin, 1961–72; professor of graphic design, Hochschule der Kunste, Berlin, from 1972. **Exhibitions:** Haus am Lutzowplatz, Berlin, 1967, 1969; Galerie Saucke, Hamburg, 1969; Neuer Berliner Kunstverein, Berlin, 1972; Theater Foyer, Munster, 1973; Kunstamt, Berlin-Zehlendorf, 1976; Martinihalle, Emmerich, 1976; Berliner Festspiele Galerie, Berlin, 1983; Goethe Institute, Madrid, 1985; Berliner Bank City Service, Berlin, 1987. **Collections:** Kunstbibliothek, Berlin; Museum of Modern Art, New York; Koniglijke Academie voor Kunst en Vormgeving, Den Bosch. Recipient: Poster Prize, *Expo 67*, Montreal, 1967; Graphik Design Deutschland Poster Prize, 1968; Golden Apple Award, 1969, and Plakette Award, 1987, Bratislava Biennale of Illustration; Bronze Medal, 1970, and Albatross-Prize, 1972, 1980, Brno Graphic Biennale; Silver Medal, Leipzig Book Fair, 1971; Deutscher Jugendliteraturpreis, 1981; German Post Office Stamp Design Prize, 1983; Graphics Prize, Bologna Children's Book Fair, 1986. Address: Tapiauer Allee 21, 1000 Berlin 19, Germany.

Works:

Der Spielbaum book design, for Siegbert Mohn Verlag, 1966.
Eledil & Krokofant book design, for Siegbert Mohn Verlag, 1967.
Der Mini-Mini-Dusenzwerg book design, for Bertelsmann Verlag, 1971.
Nanu book design, for Verlag Beltz & Gelberg, 1975.
Der Papperlapapp-Apparat book design, for Annette Betz Verlag, 1978.
Herzlich grusst... book design, for Taschenbucher/Harenberg, 1982.
Vom Kochen book design, for Taschenbucher/Harenberg, 1983.
Oh, Manhatten book design, for Taschenbuucher/Harenberg, 1983.
10 Jahre BRD in den Vereinten Nationen postage stamp, for the German Post Office, 1983.
Augenreise duch die Provence book design, for Taschenbucher/Harenberg, 1984.
Nocturno Veneziano book design, for Taschenbucher/Harenberg, 1984.
London Life book design, for Taschenbucher/Harenberg, 1985.
Das Schnepfenkofferchen book design, for Thienemann Verlag, 1985.
Circus Quatsch book design, for Neuer Finken Verlag, 1987.
Moritz kann book design, for Otto Maier Verlag, 1987.
Drauf & Dran book design, for Carlsen Verlag, 1988.
Flausensausen book design, for Verlag Ravensburger, 1989.
Villen und Landhauser in Berlin book design, for Verlag Nicolai, 1989.

Publications:

On SPOHN: books—*German Advertising Art*, edited by Eberhard Holscher, Munich 1967; *Plakate der Kasseler Schule*, Kassel 1979;

designer show him applying the lessons of Jan Tschichold's new typography, and his book, *Design in Business Printing*, echoes Tschichold's *Typographische Gestaltung* in both form and content. Spencer's modernism, here as throughout his work, is not doctrinal and has been expressed in forms that are accessible to a wide section of designers, printers, and print-buyers. His cumulative achievement has been to diffuse, through a number of channels, reformed and enlightened practice.

A leading theme of his first book was its concern for non-book ("business") printing, and Spencer has acted as an encouraging sponsor to the generation of graphic designers emerging in the 1950s and 1960s. His journal *Typographica* was important here for its publication of work by foreign designers, of both earlier and contemporary generations. (The work of the pre-war Continental modernists was brought together in *Pioneers of Modern Typography*.) If historical articles came to predominate in *Typographica*—from around the time when Spencer became editor of *Penrose Annual*—the journal had served, in a critical period, as a forum for discussion and had let fresh (foreign) air into the rather stuffy British situation. The two exhibitions *Purpose and Pleasure* (1952) and *Typography in Britain today* (1963), organized at Lund Humphries under Spencer's direction and published in *Typographica*, were significant focussing events in British graphic design.

The attempt to find empirically tested grounds for practice, at which he had hinted in *Design in Business Printing*, was taken up in the research conducted under Spencer's direction at the Royal College of Art. Perhaps for the first time, experimental research in this field was directed by a designer, and the published results (though inevitably limited) have had a corresponding pertinence for practising designers. *The Visible Word* was an early, widely distributed product of this work; it provided a well-ordered presentation of the results of previous research and of current issues of legibility. Spencer has since gone on within the Royal College of Art to introduce more critical, information-oriented approaches to graphic design.

Spencer's own design work has been firmly rooted in typography and book design, though it extended to graphic design of all kinds. It is an achievement of consistent quality.

—Robin Kinross

Kurschner's Graphiker Handbuch, West Berlin 1967; *Modern Publicity*, annual, London 1980; *Who's Who in Graphic Art*, edited by Walter Amstutz, Dubendorf 1982.

Graphic design is whatever you use it for. It can consist of pretty pictures (delicious), it can serve commercial purposes, or it can try to make life and circumstances different from what they used to be. This choice is what expresses your personality. If you are lucky enough, you will find a creative metaphor that puts you in touch with people. I, for myself, try to stimulate imagination, and because of this adventure, I "can't help" but be a graphic designer.

—Jurgen Spohn

STAECK, Klaus.

German illustrator and graphic designer. Born in Pulsnitz, near Dresden, 28 February 1938. Educated at schools in Biterfeld, Halle/Saale, 1944–56; studied law, at the universities of Heidelberg, Hamburg and West Berlin, 1957–62: Dip. 1969. Married Ingeborg Karst in 1982. Independent artist, book and graphic designer, Heidelberg, from 1964: founder of Edition Tangente (now Edition Staeck) press, Heidelberg, 1965; founder and co-editor, with Peter Knorr and Siegfried Mehnert, of *Tangente-Report* magazine, Heidelberg, 1965. Founder, Politischer Arbeitskreises student association, Heidelberg, 1961; candidate, SPD Social Democratic Party, West Germany, 1967; chairman, lawyer and graphics editor, Freie Hochschule fur Kreativitat und Interdisziplinare Forschung, Dusseldorf, 1973. Art tutor, Studenthochhausen, Klausenpfad, Heidelberg, 1967–69; guest professor, Gesamthochschule, Kassel, 1971, and at the Gesamthochschule, University of Essen, 1981–82; professor, Kunstakademie, Dusseldorf, 1986–88. **Exhibitions:** Viola Gallery, Prague, 1965; Kunsthalle, Dusseldorf, 1973; Van Abbemuseum, Eindhoven, 1975; Kunstverein, Frankfurt, 1978 (toured); Wilhelm Lehmbruck Museum, Duisburg, 1979; Henie-Onstad Kunstsenter, Oslo, 1983; Konsthall, Malmo, 1985; Kunsthalle, Darmstadt, 1986. **Collections:** Kunstverein, Heidelberg; Kunstverein, Dusseldorf; Kunsthalle, Cologne; Kaiser-Wilhelm Museum, Krefeld; Kunstmuseum, Basel; Museum des 20. Jahrhunderts, Vienna; Van Abbemuseum, Eindhoven; Mahnsche Galerie, Brno; Kulturhuset, Stockholm; Poster Museum, Warsaw. Recipient: Pratt Center Prize, New York, 1968; Zille Prize, Berlin, 1970; Verkehrsburo Prize, Graphic Biennale, Vienna, 1972; Forderpreis, Intergrafik Biennale, Berlin, 1976; Kritikerpreis, West Berlin, 1979; Gold Medal, Gridziadz Photomontage Biennale, Poland, 1979; Lahti Poster Biennale Prize, Finland, 1979. Address: Ingrimstrasse 3, Postfach 102063, 6900 Heidelberg, West Germany.

Works:

Konsumgedenktage '68 calendar, for Edition Tangente, 1967.
NPD/SIEG/HEIL object-book, for Edition Tangente, 1969.
Pornografie book design, for Anabas Verlag, 1971.

Plakate abreissen verboten book design, for Steidl Verlag, 1972.
Die Reichen mussen noch reicher werden book design, for Rowohlt Verlag, 1973.
Gedichte/Collagen (Boll/Staeck) book design, for Lamuv-Verlag, 1975.
Die Kunst findet nicht im Saale statt book design, for Rowohlt Verlag, 1976.
Der Bonner Bildersturm book design, for Steidl Verlag, 1976.
Worte des Statthalters Kohl book design, for Steidl Verlag, 1976.
Eine Zensur findet gelegentlich statt book design, for Steidl Verlag, 1977.
Briefe zur Verteidigung der Republik book design, for Steidl Verlag, 1977.
Brief zur Verteidigung der burgerlichen Freiheit book design, for Rowohlt Verlag, 1978.
Einschlagige Worte des kandidaten Strauss book design, for Steidl Verlag, 1979.
Die Gedanken sind frei book design, for Eulenspiegel-Verlag, 1981.
Verteidigt die Republik book design, for Steidl Verlag, 1983.

Klaus Staeck: *Die Gedanken sind frei* poster, 1979

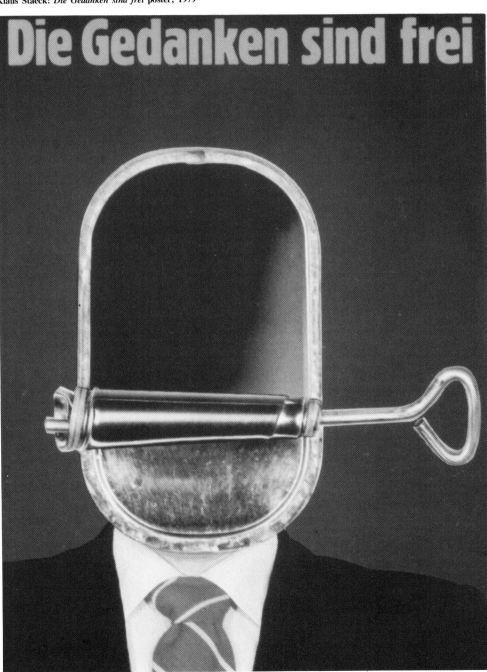

Publications:

By STAECK: books — *Intermedia 69*, exhibition catalogue, Heidelberg 1969; *Befragun der Dokumenta*, editor, Gottingen 1972; *Der Fall Staeck*, Gottingen 1975; *Staeck's Umwelt*, Gottingen 1984.

On STAECK: books — *Kunst und Politik*, exhibition catalogue by Robert Kudielka and others, Karlsruhe 1970; *Mail Art* by Jean-Marc Poinsot, Paris 1971; *Deutsche Kunst der 60er Jahre* by Jurgen Morschel, Munich 1972; *Demonstrative Fotografie*, exhibition catalogue by Hans Gercke, Heidelberg 1974; *Klaus Staeck: Ruckblick in Sachen Kunst und Politik*, exhibition catalogue by Dieter Adelmann and others, Frankfurt 1978; *Images de la Revolte 1965–1975*, exhibition catalogue by Steef Davidson, Paris 1982.

Anton Stankowski: *Progression* graphic study, 1930

STANKOWSKI, Anton.

German painter, advertising and graphic designer. Born in Gelsenkirchen, 18 June 1906. Apprenticed as a church painter and decorator, Dusseldorf, 1921–26; studied painting under Max Burchartz, at the Folkwangschule, Essen, 1927–29. Served in the German Army, 1940–45: prisoner-of-war, 1945–48. Married Else Hetzler in 1933. Freelance painter and graphic designer, working in Zurich, 1929–37, and in Stuttgart, 1937–40; head of typography, *Stuttgarter Illustrierte* magazine, Stuttgart, 1949–51; freelance advertising and graphic designer, Stuttgart, 1951–70; partner, with Karl Duschek and O. S. Rechenauer, in Stankowski + Partner design studio, Stuttgart, from 1970: head of visual design, 20th Olympic Games, Munich, 1972. Guest instructor in visual communications, Hochschule fur Gestaltung, Ulm, 1964. **Exhibitions:** Landesgewerbemuseum, Stuttgart, 1962 (toured); Retrospective, New York, 1962 (toured); Reuchlinhaus, Pforzheim, 1962; London College of Printing, 1968; Rosenthal AG, Selb, 1971; Stadtische Galerie Die Fahre, Saulgau, 1973; Kunstgewerbemuseum, Zurich, 1973; Galerie Schloss Remseck, Neckarrems, 1974, 1979; Kunstbibliothek, West Berlin, 1976; Kunsthalle, Tubingen, 1979; Kunsthaus, Zurich, 1979; Salon Sztuki, Lodz, 1979 (toured); Galerie Teufel, Cologne, 1980; Institut fur Technische Form, Darmstadt, 1982; Deutsches Plakatmuseum, Essen, 1983; Orangerie, Kassel, 1986; Neues Rathaus, Leonberg, 1987; Stadtisches Galerie Altes Theater, Ravensburg, 1988; Wilhelm-Hack-Museum, Ludwigshafen, 1988. **Collections:** Galerie Schloss Remseck, Neckarrems; Kunstgewerbemuseum, Zurich; Staatsgalerie, Stuttgart; Museum of Modern Art, New York. Recipient: Bavarian Advertising Association Medal, Munich, 1958, 1959; Billa Massimo Prize, Rome, 1982; Anton Stankowski Foundation and Prize established, Stuttgart, 1985. Member, Alliance Graphique Internationale, Paris; Verband Bildender Kunstler; Bund Deutscher Graphiker. Address: Menzelstrasse 92, 7000 Stuttgart 1, West Germany.

Works:

Advertising and graphics, for Standard Elektrik, 1955–65.
Advertising and graphics, for Pausa AG, 1954–74.
Graphic programmes and publicity, for IBM, 1956–66.
Advertising and promotional graphics, for Viessmann, 1960–83.
Unified graphics programme, for the 1972 Olympic Games, Munich, 1970–72.
Visual identity programme and graphics, for the Deutsche Bank, 1972–80.
Logo and graphics programme, for the Stadthaus, Bonn, 1976.
Graphics programme and signage, for the Klinik Gottingen, 1976.
Emblem and graphics programme, for the Savag Insurance Company, from 1978.

Publications:

By STANKOWSKI: books and portfolios — *Spiel und Gleichnis 1958*, print portfolio, Stuttgart 1958; *Funktion und ihre Darstellung in der Werbegrafik*, Teufen 1960; *Gipfel*, print portfolio, Stuttgart 1968; *Augenblick: ein Bildebuch vom Sehen und Drucken*, with O. S. Rechenauer, Düsseldorf 1969; *Kunst und Umwelt, Band 1: Der Pfiel—Spiel, Gleichnis, Kommunikation*, with Joachim Stankowski and Eugen Gomringer, Starnberg 1972; *Anton Stankowski: 6 Serigraphien von 1931–1972*, graphics portfolio, Stuttgart 1973; *Magnet Multiple*, book/object, Stuttgart 1973; *Signet Bilder*, print portfolio, Stuttgart 1974.

On STANKOWSKI: books—*Layout: Complete Introduction to the Fundamentals of Layout* by Franz Herman Wills, Dusseldorf 1957, 1960, New York and London 1965; *The New Graphic Design* by Karl Gerstner and Markus Kutter, Teufen and London 1959; *Moderne Werbe- und Gebrauchs-Graphik* by Hans Neuburg, *An International Survey of Press Advertising*, edited by Kurt Weidemann, Stuttgart and London 1966; *Design Coordination and Corporate Image* by F. H. K. Henrion and Alan Parkin, London and New York 1967; *Konkretes von Anton Stankowski* by Gunther Wirth and Eugen Gomringer, Stuttgart 1974; *Signale and Zeichen: Funktionelle Grafik 1927–1976 — Anton Stankowski*, exhibition catalogue by Eckhart Berckenhagen and Manfred Kroplein, Dusseldorf 1976; *Anton Stankowski: Das Gesamtwerk 1925–82*, with text by Stephan Wiese and others, Stuttgart 1982; *A History of Graphic Design* by Philip B. Meggs, New York and London 1983.

Famed as a pioneer of modern advertising and graphic design, Anton Stankowski has engaged in all aspects of visual communications for half a century. After his formative studies under Max Burchardt at Essen's Folkwangschule, Stankowski spent the 1930s in Zürich where he soon established himself as a leader of experimental photography and constructive art. Not only the most influential typographer of his time, he emerged as the forerunner and precursor of the New Photography and the Zürich school of Concrete Art. In postwar Stuttgart, he worked under exacting circumstances as a designer of trademarks, logos, sign systems, and advertising, as well as continuing his highly original studies in painting—but most importantly, he became Chief Editor responsible for the typographic and visual layout of the outstanding picture magazine *Stuttgarter Illustrierte*.

His first important comprehensive graphic information production was the design of publicity materials for the provisions company Hill AG in Hattingen-an-der-Ruhr. From corporate signature to company stationery, packaging, posters, advertising, and other announcements, Stankowski gave visual definition to every aspect of this retail business's identity. It was at the time not so much a company identity as a real family characterisation—a unity of all visual programming. He went on to develop this precise and definitive treatment of design systems in work for Standard Elektrik, Pausa AG, International Business Machines, the Savag Insurance Company, the Deutsche Bank, and others. During the 1950s and 1960s, Stankowski began working with the Graphics Atelier on architectural information systems, colour concepts, and laminated reliefs in buildings throughout Germany. In numerous retrospective exhibitions from 1970, a unity of these apparently disparate paths of free and applied art emerges more clearly. It is now seen that the varied ideals he inherited from the Bauhaus, Russian constructivism, and De Stijl have for half a century in no way compromised this unity.

—George Walsh

STARCK, Philippe (Patrick).

French architect, interior, exhibition and industrial designer. Born in Paris, 18 January 1949. Studied in the Institution Notre-Dame de Saint-Croix, Neuilly-sur-Seine, until 1966; Ecole Nissim de Camondo, Paris, 1966–68. Married Brigitte Laurent in 1977; daughter: Ara. Designer from 1968: Founder-director, with Lino Ventura, Perce-Neige inflatable dwellings company, Paris, 1969–70; Art Director, Pierre Cardin fashion house, Paris, 1971–72; Chalet du Lac nightclub, Paris, 1973–74, and Centre Ville restaurant, Paris, 1974. Founder-director, Starck Product, design company, designing for Dorothee Bis, Kansai Yamamoto, Creeks Fashion Shop, Habitat, Baleri, Driade, Kartell, Casatec, Vuitton, Alessi, Sasaki, Owo, etc., in Montfort l'Amaury, France, since 1979; Artistic Director, XO furniture company, Paris, since 1985, and Centre Culturel des Arts Plastiques, Paris, since 1986. Instructor, Domus Academy, Milan, since 1986, and Ecole des Arts Decoratifs, Paris, since 1987. **Exhibitions:** *Art et Industrie*, Musee des Monuments Francais, Paris, 1985; *Nouveaux Plaisirs d'Architecture*, Centre Georges Pompidou, Paris, 1985; Kyoto Museum of Art, Japan, 1985; Seibu Museum of Art, Tokyo, 1985; Kadewe, West Berlin, 1986; *Neocone 18*, Chicago, 1986; Maison Descartes, Amsterdam, 1987; *Starck Mobilier*, Marseille, 1987; *Les Cent Chaises*, Boulogne, 1987; *Nouvelles Tendances*, Centre Georges Pompidou, Paris, 1987. **Collections:** Musee des Arts Decoratifs, Paris. Recipient: Oscar du Luminaire, Paris, 1980; Creator of the Year, Paris, 1985; 3 furniture prizes, *Neocone 18*, Chicago, 1986; Delta de Plata Award, Barcelona, 1986; Chair Fair Award, New York, 1986; Platinum Circle Award, Chicago, 1987; *Design 87* Award, Tokyo, 1987; Grand Prix National de la Creation Industrielle, Paris, 1988. Chevalier des Arts et des Lettres, France, 1985. Address: Starck Product, 4 rue de Dion, 78490 Montfort l'Amaury, France.

Works:

La Main Bleue nightclub interiors, Paris 1976.
Les Bains-Douches nightclub interiors, Paris, 1978.
President's Office and Apartment interiors, Elysee Palace, Paris, 1982.
Starck Club interiors, Dallas, Texas, 1982.
Lecture Room interiors, La Villette Museum of Sciences, Paris, 1984.
Cafe Costes interiors, Paris, 1984.
Printemps department store interiors, Paris, 1986.
Manin Restaurant interiors, Tokyo, 1986.
Lemoult House, Paris, 1987.
Royalton Hotel interiors, New York, 1988.
Arango Restaurants interiors, Madrid and Barcelona, 1988.
Laguiole Cutlery Factory, France, 1988.
Naninant Apartment Block, Tokyo, 1988.
Asahi Beer Headquarters Building, Tokyo, 1988.

Publications:

By STARCK: articles—"Cafe Costes" in *Passion* (Paris), February 1985; "Philippe Starck: the world's hottest designer interviewed" in *Blueprint* (London), November 1985.

On STARCK: books—*Le Mobilier Francais 1965–1979*, edited by Gilles de Bure, Paris 1983; *Le Mobilier Francais 1980...*, edited by Sophie Anagyros, Paris 1983; *International Design Yearbook 1988/89*, edited by Arata Isozaki, London 1988; *Starck* by Christine Colin, Liege 1988; articles—"Starck" by G. de Bure

Philippe Starck: Stacking chairs, for Kartell, 1988

and O. Fillion in *Architecture Cree* (Paris), February/March 1982; "Les Habits neufs de l'Elysee" by M. Champenois in *Le Monde* (Paris), November 1983; "Temps, les sharks de Starck" by C. Colin in *L'Evenement du Jeudi* (Paris), 8 November 1984; "Starck Contrasts" in *Progressive Architecture* (New York), September 1985; "Designing Furniture in the Fast Lane" by C. Smart in the *Christian Science Monitor* (Boston), 24 December 1985; "Starck Treatment" in *Homes and Gardens* (London), April 1986; "Starck and Stardom" by H. Aldersley-Williams in *Industrial Design* (New York), May/June 1987; "Paris" by I. Grant in *Interior Design* (New York), March 1988.

STAROWIEYSKI, Franciszek (von Biberstein).

Polish illustrator, stage, film, television, mural and graphic designer. Born in Krakow, 8 July 1930; pseudonym: Jan Byk. Studied painting and graphics under Wojciech Weiss and Adam Mareczynski, at the School of Arts and Crafts, Krakow, 1949–52, and under Michael Bylina, at the Academy of Art, Warsaw, 1952–55. Freelance designer, Warsaw, from 1958: worked the Kosciuszko Foundation, New York, from 1974. Visiting professor, Hochschule der Kunste, East Berlin, 1980. **Exhibition:** *107 Grafici dell'AGI*, Castello Sforzesco, Milan, 1974. Recipient: Polish State Graphics Prize, Warsaw, 1953; Film Poster Prize, Warsaw Poster Biennale, 1970; Graphics Prize, Bienal de Sao Paulo, 1973; Film Poster Prize, Cannes, 1974; Annual Key Art Award, Los Angeles, 1978. Member, Polish Artists Association, Warsaw; Alliance Graphique Internationale, Paris. Address: Bernardynska 23, m.75, 02–804 Warsaw, Poland.

Publications:

By STAROWIEYSKI: books—*Plakat Polski: slownik artystow plastykow*, Warsaw 1972; *Affiches et dessins*, exhibition catalogue, Quimper 1979; books illustrated —*Varciavski slad* by L. Kruczkowski, Warsaw 1955; *Taszent Niasto chleba* by A. Niewievow, Warsaw 1956; *Karnawal* by S. Dygat, Warsaw 1968; *Dziecko Przez Prysniesione* by A. Kijowski, Warsaw 1968; *Chwila ulotna* by D. Vivant de Non, Warsaw 1969; *Nagrobek czlekoksztaltny* by W. Sadurski, Warsaw 1970; *Niebo Piekto* by E. Biatous, Warsaw 1976; *Czarny Pajak*, Warsaw 1976; film—*Bykowi chwala*, 1971.

On STAROWIEYSKI: books—*Polnische Plakatkunst* by Jozef Mroszczak, Vienna and Dusseldorf 1962; *Who's Who in Graphic Art*, edited by Walter Amstutz, Zurich 1962, Dubendorf 1982; *Plakat Polski* by Jerzy Wasniewski, Warsaw 1968; *Polski Plakat Filmowy 1947–1967* by Zdzislaw Schubert, Poznan Warsaw 1969; *A Concise History of Posters* by John Barnicoat, London 1972; *Polish Poster Art Today* by Szymon Bojko, Warsaw 1972; *Contemporary Polish Posters in Full Color*, edited by Joseph S. Czestochowski, New York 1979; *The Polish Poster 1970–1978*, with introduction by Zdzislaw Schubert, Warsaw 1979; *Polish Graphic Artists: Franek Starowieyski*, Warsaw 1981; *A History of Graphic Design* by Philip B. Meggs, New York and London 1983.

Franciszek Starowieyski.

Or Franek von Byk.

1768.

Maybe 1882.

A myth. A legend.

It seems impossible in the rigid, Communist, police-state of Poland to have an individual such as Starowieyski moving around freely.

A flamboyant, handsome man dressed with the nonchalance of a Parisian bohemian of the 1910s—with a whiff of Bavarian baron from the nineteenth century—"Franek von Byk" sits over the cafe table reeling off his new fairytales about his adventures, aristocratic titles, his castles on the Loire, the princesses begging for his favors, purchases of antique swords and china, and so on and on. You know he's not a prince, his collection is a bit smaller than Elizabeth II's, his Maserati turns out to be a battered Fiat, and his castle is located on the top floor of an old Warsaw apartment building. But you love his stories. They overwhelm you, and everything seems true in his mouth. Moreover, his pose is an integral part of his creativity.

He lives in his own world, half Kafkaesque, half Borgesian, or from another angle, the naive world of turn-of-the-century tales about princes, castles, hunting, Monte Carlo casinos, and grand prix races. The entire picture is richly colored by the Renaissance flavour of an old master born 400 years too late. O.K., you say, but why do the Commies tolerate such an animal in a golden cage—this first-rate example of the enemy of the proletariat, self-advertising himself wildly? It is only thanks to an even wilder and more obvious talent and vision that he has.

By western standards, the Polish poster in general can hardly be treated as an applied art; it is too freewheeling and non-commercial. Starowieyski's work is even further apart, insofar as personal freedom, style, and total lack of limits are concerned. Since his beginnings, he has set his own standards. He is unbeatable, impossible to copy with any success. He competes against himself, goes his own ways, and in the end, he's the sole representative of the curious style he has created.

The conclusion after some twenty-five years of Starowieyski's activity: He's creating one gigantic poster, a mosaic of hundreds and thousands of pieces of the same vision. The "movie" continues, despite all his shifts, meanders, ups, and downs; it's one world—or one hell, as you like—the same formula. Yet, his amazing fantasy creates new mini-worlds in the general galaxy of Starowieyski's mind. Confronted by hundreds of his works from many years, we drown helplessly in his dreamy, illusory, crazy, out-of-time ocean, made by Starowieyski or von Byk, now or a hundred years ago, who knows?

Many lesser artists try to base their work on surreal and Old Master schemes. Almost all end fatally, producing kitschy, cheap copies of something nobody can copy or follow. Starowieyski walks his high rope in a risky manner. But he doesn't fall, thanks to really masterful skills in drawing and painting, deep understanding of traditional techniques and the rules of anatomy, knowledge of calligraphy, and enormous control over color, shadow, shape, and composition. He even gets better, which is another mystery of the *enfant terrible* Franciszek Starowieyski.

A twin brother of von Byk.

Born, Florence, 1741; re-born, Bavaria, 1820; actually living in Warsaw, 1980s.

—Jan Sawka

STEINER, Alberto.

Italian display and graphic designer. Born in Milan, 15 November 1913. Mainly self-taught in art and design, from 1930. Married to Lica Steiner. Freelance designer, working for Olivetti, RAI Radiotelevision Italiana, Pirelli, Lark, Agfa, Bertelli, etc., in Milan, from 1933: director of display, La Rinascente stores, Milan, 1950–54; also consultant to the publishers Einaudi, Avanti, Feltrinelli, Zanichelli, C.E.I., and Vangelista. Art director, *Il Politecnico* magazine, Milan 1945; technical editor, *Costruyamos* magazine and architectural publications, Mexico City, 1947; also designer and contributor to the magazines *Realismo, Linea Grafica* and *Il Contemporanea*, Milan. Member of the Taller de Grafica Popular, Mexico City, 1946–48; research commission member, Milan Triennale, from 1947; experimental graphics commission member, Venice Biennale, 1972. Instructor, University of Mexico, 1946–48, and Convitto Rinascita school, Milan, 1948–58; director Scuola dell'Libro Umanitaria, Milan, 1958–74; instructor in graphics, Istituto d'Arte, Urbino, 1962–70. **Exhibitions:** Milan Triennale, 1940, 1951, 1954; *107 Grafici dell'AGI*, Castello Sforzesco, Milan, 1974. Recipient: Grand Prize, 1951, and Gold Medal, 1954, Milan Triennale; Gold Medal, Milan Trade Fair, 1956. Member: Alliance Graphique Internationale, Paris; Associazione Disegno Industriale, Milan. *Died* (in Raffaderi, Italy) *7 August 1974.*

Publications:

By STEINER: book—*Fotografia*, Milan 1943.

On STEINER: books—*The New Graphic Design* by Karl Gerstner and Markus Kutter, Teufen and London 1959; *Moderne Werbe- und Gebrauchs-Grafik* by Hans Neuburg, Ravensburg 1960; *Buchgestaltung* by Albert Kapr, Dresden 1963; *History of the Poster* by Josef and Shizuko Muller-Brockmann, Zurich 1971; *Monografie des Plakats: Entwicklung, Stil, Design* by Herbert Schindler, Munich 1972; *107 Grafici dell'AGI*, with texts by Renzo Zorzi and Franco Grignani, Venice 1974; *Archigraphia: Architectural and Environmental Graphics*, edited by Walter Herdeg, Zurich 1978; *The Language of Graphics*, by Edward Booth-Clibborn and Daniele Baroni, London 1980; *Atlante del Design Italiano 1940/1980* by Alfonso Grassi and Anty Pansera, Milan 1980.

STEINER, Henry.

American graphic designer. Born Hans Steiner, in Vienna, Austria, 13 February 1934; emigrated to the United States in 1939: naturalized, 1945. Studied under William Baziotes, Doug Kingman and Robert Motherwell, at Hunter College, New York, 1951–55: BFA 1955; under Josef Albers, Armin Hoffman annd Paul Rand, at Yale University, New Haven, Connecticut, 1955–57: MFA 1957; Sorbonne University Paris, 1958–59. Served in the United States National Guard, in New York and New Haven, 1952–58. Married Leela Singh in 1963; sons: Karl and Kurt. Design assistant, at Brownjohn, Chermayeff and Geismar, New York, 1957; designer, with Irving Miller Incorporated, New York, 1958; art director, Societe Nationale

HENRY STEINER: EAST/WEST DESIGN DIALOGUES

First Asia/Pacific Design Conference Australia 1988   Mildura 31 July-2 August

Henry Steiner: Poster for the Asia/Pacific Design Conference, 1988

Industrielle Publicitaire, Paris, 1959–60; design director, *Asia Magazine*, Hong Kong, 1961–63; managing director of Graphic Communication design studio, Hong Kong, from 1963. Lecturer, Hong Kong University, from 1965; chairman of the design advisory committee, Hong Kong Polytechnic, from 1973; founder, The Communication School, Hong Kong, 1985. Vice-president, American Chamber of Commerce in Hong Kong, 1986–88. Recipient: Typomundus 20 Award of Excellence, 1966; Asian Advertising Congress Creative Award, 1969, 1971, 1972, 1974; Mead Library Award of Excellence, 1969, 1970, 1973, 1974, 1975, 1977, 1981, 1983; Hong Kong Governor's Award, 1970; Brno Graphic Biennale Medal, 1972; Warsaw Poster Biennale Award, 1972, 1976; *The Times* Financial Advertising Award, London, 1974; *Communication Arts* Award of Excellence, Palo Alto, 1974, 1975, 1976, 1977, 1978, 1980, 1982; Worldstar Packaging Award, 1974; Hong Kong Designers Association Award, 1975, 1976, 1977, 1978, 1979, 1980; Tehran Biennale Asian Graphics Award, 1978; Society of Typographic Arts Award of Excellence, New York, 1978, 1979, 1980; Type Directors Club Award, New York, 1979, 1981, 1987; TTF Paper Gold Award, Hong Kong, 1988; Association of Accredited Advertising Agents Award, Hong Kong, 1988. Fellow, Chartered Society of Designers, London, 1982; honorary member, New Zealand Society of Designers, 1989. Member: American Institute of Graphic Arts, 1970; Alliance Graphique Internationale, 1980; Art Directors Club of New York, 1988. Address: Graphic Communication Limited, 28C Conduit Road, Hong Kong.

Works:

Corporate identity programme and advertising, for *The Asia Magazine*, Hong Kong, 1960–63.
Hotel corporate identity programme, for the Hongkong Hilton, 1963.
Departmennt store corporate identity, for the Lane Crawford Company, 1964.
Ocean Terminal architectural graphics, for Hong Kong & Kowloon Wharf, 1967.
Annual reports, for the HongkongBank, 1956–84.
Corporate identity programme, for The Hong Kong Land Company, 1969.
Amoy Peanut Oil package design, for the Amoy Canning Corporation, 1972.
Connaught Centre architectural graphics, for The Hong Kong Land Company, 1973.
Corporate identity programme, for Duty Free Shoppers International, 1974.
Banknote designs, for the Standard Chartered Bank, 1976–83.
Corporate Identity programme, for The Hong Kong Telephone Company, 1978.
Idea magazine cover design, for Seibundo Shinkosha Publishing Company, 1980.
Logo and cover designs, for *Asiaweek* magazine, 1980–82.
Corporate identity programme, for the Dairy Farm Company, 1982.
Four commemorative gold coins, for the Singapore Mint, 1982.
Corporate identity programme, for the Hong-kongBank, 1983.
Logo and magazine redesign, for the *Far Eastern Economic Review*, 1984, 1989.
Bond Centre architectural graphics, for First Pacific Davies (HK) Limited, 1988.
Supermarket corporate identity programme, for the Wellcome Company, 1988.
Ssangyong Corporation corporate identity programme, for DesignFocus Incorporated, Korea, 1989.

Publications:

By STEINER: articles — in *Typographica* (London), no. 13, 1966; *Icographic* (London), no. 8, 1974; *Design Intercourse* (Hong Kong), March 1988; *Monthly Design* (Seoul), August 1988; *The English Journal* (Tokyo), December 1988.

On STEINER: books — *Penrose Annual*, edited by John Anstey, London 1964; *Hong Kong Album*, compiled by P. C. Lee, Hong Kong 1965; *Graphic Design of the World*, by Hideyuki Oka, Tokyo 1974; *Form and Communication* by Walter Diethelm, Zurich 1975; *Who's Who in Graphic Art*, edited by Walter Amstutz, Dubendorf 1982; *World Trademarks and Logotypes* by Takenobu Igarashi, Tokyo 1983, 1987; *World Graphic Design Now*, vols. 1, 3, 4 and 5, Tokyo, 1987–89; *Graphis Posters*, edited by Walter Herdeg, Zurich 1988; *Shopping Bags and Wrapping Paper*, edited by Seiko Okuda, Tokyo, 1988; *Photographic Art*, Hong Kong 1989.

*

I can recall nothing from Vienna, but in New York there were wonderfully drawn comic books; they taught me to read English and today I see in them the influence of Ukiyo-e prints. Then there were playful subway posters and package designs by Paul Rand (his graphics led me to try my first cigar—an El Producto!), the wit and elegance of Henry Wolf's *Esquire* covers, and the tightly organized titles of Saul Bass (more exciting than the films appended to them). Overseas, there were confirmations of what I was learning: the Lettera-perfect typographic authority of Basel's illuminated shop signs; the modesty, utter correctness and clarity of the *Guides Michelin*; endlessly varied and subtle match boxes of Tokyo.

Gabor Peterdi, my print-making teacher at Hunter and Yale showed me how, in a multicolor print, no single block should be self-contained; each had to be incomplete and interdependent. Josef Albers taught me how to get the most effect with the least means: take one square out of a checkerboard pattern and you get a cross. Both the figure and the ground have to work. (When we criticized designs at school we spoke not of how good they looked but how they *worked*.) From Rand himself, I learned the value of analysis and the need for a clearly stated idea before beginning to sketch. He also taught me that contrast, visual and psychological, is the life-blood of a successful design.

The remarkable thing about my working life is that most of it has been spent in Hong Kong—the place you come out when you dig straight down from New York. At first, my work disseminated the attitudes then current in New York and New Haven. Later, I decided to embrace the "exotic" visual vocabulary of Asia. By analyzing and respecting it, I have been able to restore to what have seemed quaint Oriental visual clichés a dignity and conviction which has influenced a younger generation of indigenous designers.

When I first came to Hong Kong, printing was primitive and the range of typefaces (Roman and Chinese), restricted. This brought out a talent for improvisation and a preference for the challenge of working with a limited technical palette. The best of Asian art, it seems to me has always involved lavish effort and frugal means.

My exposure to the twin vulgarities of developing world commercialism and socialist realism has reinforced a distaste for cute conventions and received, undigested styles. As much as is feasible, I avoid a patronizing tone in my work. I try to bring to bear on a project the full experience of my matured self.

The struggle begun in the fifties for recognition of graphic design as a profession is over: we are no longer commercial artists. Ironically, we are now in danger of becoming stuffy, making pronouncements about "market positioning," and losing sight of the basic quality which is the charm of our work—the enhancement of the quotidian.

We are here to make ordinary objects extraordinary—pleasant, useful, witty, and sometimes inspiring. Using our powers of observation and working with economy and improvisation, we battle the enemies: mediocrity, cynicism, neglect.

What matters is to send through our craft modest messages which others will receive as saying: somebody cared about this.

—Henry Steiner

*

One of the distinctions of the career of Henry Steiner is the many years he has worked in a culture foreign to his European-American training. Hong Kong is not totally Asiatic, being an outpost of the West and a focal point for a great deal of the international trade and communications in the Pacific Basin; however, Hong Kong's proximity to the Asian mainland and to the various island cultures that ring the continent have had a notable impact on Steiner's work. He has plumbed the symbology of the Orient but not allowed it to dominate. Nor has he embraced the ubiquitous international style with the fervor of many of the contemporary designers of the countries of modern Asia. Steiner's way is eclectic, picking out useful cultural emblems to enrich his work. The thought process is no doubt the accepted designer approach, but Steiner has the overlay of the East-West interplay to his advantage.

For all of this, a most significant feature of Steiner's work is his use of the natural ingredients of a situation. He likes to create his pictures without the traditional pen-and-pencil, two-dimensional art work. For example, the cover of an annual report for a textile company is a photograph of the back of a model who wears a jacket on which are stitched the words which otherwise might have been set in type. Charts and graphs in the report are photographs of stitchery on contrasting pieces of fabric. For the Hong Kong and Shanghai Hotel annual report, Steiner had chefs at each of the group's hotels create pastry models of the hotels, then used photographs of these in the publication. Steiner designs photographs of a chalk drawing (a handsome illustration) on a brick wall, baggage and identification tags on a businessman's briefcase, toys, hand tools, anything that falls naturally into the situation. He sees richness in the world around him and makes use of all of it.

—Jerry Steimle

STEPHENSEN, Magnus (Laessoe).
Danish architectural and industrial designer. Born in Copenhagen, 12 October 1903. Studied at the Royal Academy of Fine Arts, Copenhagen, 1925–30. Married Else Widding in 1939; children: Karl, Jens, Snorre and Hannes. Freelance architect and industrial designer from 1930: designed for Kaj Bojesen, Georg Jensen,

Magnus Stephensen: Teapot and water-jug in stainless steel, for Georg Jensen, 1953

Royal Copenhagen Porcelain, Fritz Hansen, Ernst Dahl, etc. **Exhibitions:** *Nordisk Industridesign*, Kunstindustrimuseet, Oslo, 1976; Statens Kunstfond, Copenhagen, 1978; *Scandinavian Modern Design 1880–1980*, Cooper-Hewitt Museum, New York, 1982; *Design Since 1945*, Philadelphia Museum of Art, 1983. **Collections:** Louisiana Museum, Humlebaek; Kunstindustrimuseum, Copenhagen; Kunstindustrimuseet, Oslo; Nordenfjeldske Kunstindustrumuseum, Trondheim; Vesterlandske Museet, Bergen; Rohsska Konstslojdmuseet, Goteborg; Staatliches Museum, Munich; Museum fur Angewandte Kunst, Munich; Kunstgewerbemuseum, Zurich; Victoria and Albert Museum, London; Metropolitan Museum of Art, New York; Museum of Modern Art, New York. Recipient: Eckersberg Medal, Copenhagen, 1948; Gold Medal, 1952, and Grand Prize, 1954, Milan Triennale. Honorary member, IDD Industrielle Designere Danmark, 1971. Address: Hellebopark 37, 3000 Helsingor, Denmark.

Works:

Dan chair, for Fritz Hansen, 1931.
Chair in elm wood and leather, for Villadsen, c.1935.
Child's high chair, for Kaj Bojesen, 1938.
Bregner carpet, for Ernst Dahl's Tapetfabrik, 1943.
Coffee service in silver, for Kaj Bojesen, 1949.
Shades glassware, for Holmegaards Glassworks, 1950.

Covered marmalade pot in silver and cane, for Georg Jensen, 1951.
Coffee service in stainless steel, for Georg Jensen, 1952.
Teapot and covered water-jug in stainless steel, for Georg Jensen, 1953.
Teapot in sterling silver and ivory, for Georg Jensen, 1953.
Casserole dish and lid in silver, for Georg Jensen, 1954.
Tuja cutlery in stainless steel, for Georg Jensen, 1955.
Fondue dish and trivet in silver, for Georg Jensen, 1956.
Patella ceramic tablewares, for Royal Copenhagen Porcelain, 1957.
Ice bucket in stainless steel, for Georg Jensen, 1959.
Prunella china tableware, for Royal Copenhagen Porcelain, 1960.
Timiana china tableware, for Royal Copenhagen Porcelain, 1960.
Fregat cutlery in silver, for Georg Jensen, 1961.

Publications:

By STEPHENSEN: book — *Brugsting fra Japan*, with Snorre Stephensen, Copenhagen 1969.

On STEPHENSEN: books—*Moderne Danske Kunsthandvaerk* by Mogens Koch, Copenhagen 1948; *Esempi de Decorazione Moderna de Tutto il Mondo* by Roberto Aloi, Milan 1951; *Dansk Mobelkunst* by Viggo Sten Moller and Svend

Erik Moller, Copenhagen 1951; *Modern Danish Silver* by Esbjorn Hiort, Copenhagen, New York and London 1954; *Fifty Years of Danish Silver in the Georg Jensen Tradition* by Edgar J. Kaufmann Jr. and others, Copenhagen 1956; *Made in Denmark* by Arne Karlsen and Anker Tiedmann, Copenhagen and New York 1960; *A Treasury of Scandinavian Design*, edited by Erik Zahle, New York 1961; *Contemporary Danish Design*, edited by Arne Karlsen and others, Copenhagen 1966; *Mobilia: Georg Jensen 1866–1966* by Svend Erik Moller, Copenhagen 1966; *Dansk Kunstindustri 1900–1950* by Viggo Sten Moller, Copenhagen 1970; *Scandinavian Design: Objects of a Life Style* by Eileene Harrison Beer, New York and Toronto 1975; *Magnus Stephensen: Arbejder 1930–1978*, exhibition catalogue by Esbjorn Hiort, Copenhagen 1978; *History of Modern Furniture* by Karl Mang, Stuttgart 1978, London 1979; *Scandinavian Modern Design 1880–1980*, edited by David Revere McFadden, New York 1982; *Design Since 1945*, edited by Kathryn Hiesinger and George Marcus, Philadelphia and London 1983.

Magnus Stephensen is dually notable for his architectural achievements and his work in metal and ceramics. Each field, though, exhibits stylistic concerns of particular importance to this designer. In the 1940s, Stephensen was constructing low-income housing blocks in Denmark, such as his row houses at Husum (1948), which clearly illustrate his preference for structurally visible horizontals and verticals, economical materials, and open, repetitive floor plans. His silver designs for Kay Bojesen also show this pure, simple emphasis on line and on tangible volumes and spaces, and his restrained teapots of the late 1930s allow the viewer, and the user, to concentrate on the inherent beauty of the material and the ease with which they fulfill their function.

Stephensen's ardent interest in the Oriental arts is also reflected in his forms. His architecture often contains the same accent on projecting horizontal and vertical members that is characteristic of Japanese architecture. Many of his silver works have handles wrapped in bamboo, and his design shapes are often reminiscent of Japanese and Chinese ceramic forms. He worked at the Royal Copenhagen porcelain factory following a period in which it produced works of an extreme Oriental flavor, and undoubtedly the impact of this work, along with his subsequent research and travels in the Far East, accounts for the Oriental character of his works.

His later works for Georg Jensen, including his 1951 serving bucket and salad set, show greater individuality. His technical excellence and important stature in the Scandinavian design world increasingly led to a freedom that aided him in producing works which could be recognized at first sight as his alone, not merely the work of one designer among many in a workshop. These later works were distinguished by more pronounced curves and more clearly defined edges, for instance. Like other important Scandinavian designers of the 1930s, 1940s, and 1950s, Stephensen helped to mend the gap between the forces of straightforward functionalism and those of artistic elegance. In his works, the two ideas went hand in hand.

—Virginia A. Rose

STEVENS, Richard (William).

British industrial designer. Born in Dorking, Surrey, 1 October 1924. Educated at the County Grammar School, Dorking, 1935–40; studied physics at Regent Street Polytechnic, London, 1941–46: BSc. 1946. Married Anne Clara Hammond in 1947; children: Paul and Nicole. Technician, at Siemens Lamps and Supplies Limited, London, 1942–53; designer, for Metropolitan Vickers, London, 1953–54; designer, then chief of design, Atlas Lighting, London, 1954–63; industrial design manager, Standard Telephones and Cables, London, 1963–69; design manager, Post Office Telecommunications (now British Telecom), London, 1969–83; Richard Stevens Design Associates, London, from 1987. Index committee member, Council of Industrial Design, London, 1960–62; president, Society of Industrial Artists and Designers, London, 1972–73; treasurer and executive board member, ICSID International Council of Societies of Industrial Design, 1973–77; governor, Croydon College of Design and Technology, Surrey, 1975–79. **Exhibition:** *Eye for Industry*, Victoria and Albert Museum, London, 1986. Recipient: Gold Medal, Milan Triennale, 1957; three Design Centre Awards, London, 1959–60. Fellow, Chartered Society of Designers, London, 1960; Royal Designer for Industry, Royal Society of Arts, London, 1973; Fellow, Chartered Institution of Building Services, London, 1977. Address: Hazel Cottage, Ewood Lane, Newdigate, Dorking, Surrey R5 5AR, England.

Works:

Injection-moulded acrylic plastic street light units, for Atlas Lighting, 1955.
Fluorescent road lanterns in opal plastic and aluminium, for Thorn Electrical Industries, 1957.
Hermetically-sealed sodium road lantern in injection-moulded plastic, for Thorn Electrical Industries, 1957.
Decorative domestic lighting units, for Atlas Lighting, 1958.
Street light units with integrated support column, for Atlas Lighting, 1959.
Radio receiver units, for Ferguson Radio, 1961.
Programmable laboratory power supply unit, for Standard Telephones and Cables, 1972.
Young Scientist of the Year Award trophy, 1976.

Publications:

By STEVENS: articles—in *Transactions of the Illuminating Engineering Society* (London), no. 18, 1953, no. 25, 1960; *The Designer* (London), September 1971, April 1973, December 1978; *Institute of Electrical Engineers Journal* (London), November 1974.

On STEVENS: books—*Designers in Britain*, vols. 5–7, 1957–71; *Industrial Design and the Community* by Ken Baynes, London 1967; *British Design Since 1880* by Fiona MacCarthy, London 1982; *Eye for Industry: Royal Designers for Industry* by Fiona MacCarthy and Patrick Nuttgens, London 1986.

Product designers share common ground with engineers and artists. Engineers assume, wrongly, that the missing element provided by those with an arts background is concern primarily for visual aspects—aesthetics. In fact, the difference (and only difference) between an industrial designer and an engineering designer is that the latter aims to be wholly objective in his approach, whereas the former is entirely happy dealing with those aspects of design that may be regarded as subjective—including (but not only) aesthetics. The value of an arts training is that it gives confidence to one making decisions based on subjective judgements. In truth, much engineering is also based on subjective assessment, but it is deprecated by engineers who regard it as a weakness. Much effort is expanded in reducing the subjective element, so that all decisions may become wholly objective. The engineer would like this to apply to the industrial design contribution and cannot understand why this is not possible nor indeed desirable.

A facility for making subjective judgements—intuitive thinking—is also conducive to creativity, and, although not an attribute of which industrial designers have a monopoly it is perhaps an asset they may have in greater measure. Now, subjective judgements depend in the end on dogmatic assumptions—deeply held convictions on matters that are essentially irrational and not necessarily shared with others, although those who do share them are strongly drawn together, as in religion or politics. It is important to designers that they should be aware of their own dogmas, especially if they wish to be wholly professional in designing for others whose convictions they may not share.

My personal dogma—reinforced by Robert Pirsig in his book *Zen and the Art of Motorcycle Maintenance*—is that judgement on whether or not a design solution is acceptable depends on the degree to which it may be recognized as having a measure of quality, not only in an objective sense (nor subjective either) but in that special sense of a value recognizable yet undefinable, where the total value is greater

Richard Stevens: 400-watt fluorescent street lantern, for Atlas Lighting, 1958

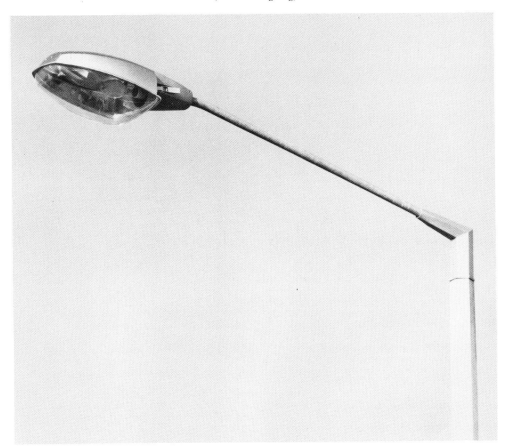

than the sum of the components, as was so well described by Pirsig. A satisfying design is one in which one may perceive this special kind of quality in the solution of the complex problems inherent in the design task.

—Richard Stevens

Richard Stevens took his degree in physics and then moved into design, a subject that he learned by doing it. He believes the big difference between an engineer and an industrial designer is that the former has to be very objective, whereas the latter has to have a good understanding of the subjective. An engineer can say a bridge must look this way or it will fall down; a designer can modify a creation to please the customer. Stevens says the good professional designer should be able to satisfy a customer whose tastes he does not condone himself. There is no room for the ego in this approach. Stevens strongly disapproves of the designer who wants to put his own stamp on everything and who wants every product to shout his own name. That is bad design, for it is not putting the job before the personality. Stevens' modest approach is very British, but he considers that the United States has had an influence on him through the designer Walter Dorwin Teague and Robert Pirsig's book *Zen and the Art of Motorcycle Maintenance*, which emphasises the importance of quality in everything, not that the West needs to borrow from Japan when it already has the Protestant work ethic.

While Stevens' prizes have been for lighting, he also designed telephones and associated equipment to create that variety of telephones on offer as part of the new look, now that Post Office Telecommunications has been separated from the Post Office as British Telecom. Pushbutton models, one-piece earpiece-and-dialling instruments, new tone types, all came from Stevens' department. His style is above all one of simplicity, but without sharp corners, for his telephone stands are smoothed at the edges to prevent accidents. Such consideration shows a careful approach, producing a product that will perform safely in addition to working properly and looking nice. A good creation, to Stevens, is one that can be used almost without being noticed. It should do its job and no more, and Stevens tries to do his best without attracting more attention than the job deserves.

—Diana de Marly

STONE, (Alan) Reynolds.
British painter, illustrator, calligrapher, typographer and graphic designer. Born in Eton, Buckinghamshire, 13 March 1909. Educated at Durnsford School, Furbeck, and at Eton School, Buckinghamshire, 1919–26; studied history, at Magdalen College, Cambridge University, 1926–30. Served as a photo-interpreter, in the Royal Air Force, 1941–45. Married Janet Woods in 1938; children: Emma, Phillida, Edward and Humphrey. Apprentice type compositor under Walter Lewis, at the Cambridge University Press, 1930–32; type compositor, Barnicott and Pearce printers, Taunton, Somerset, 1932–34; freelance typographer and book designer from 1934, and calligrapher from 1939, working in Codicote, Hertfordshire, 1934–51, and in Litton Cheney, Dorset, 1952–79. Con-

tributor to the *Times Literary Supplement* weekly, London. **Exhibitions:** Aldeburgh Festival, Suffolk, 1958; Art Council Gallery, London, 1959 (toured); Agnew's Gallery, London, 1965, 1969; Abbot Hall Art Gallery, Kendal, 1972; New Grafton Gallery, London, 1972, 1975, 1978; Fitzwilliam Museum, Cambridge, 1978; St. Paul's School Library, London, 1981; Dorset County Museum, Dorchester, 1981; *Eye for Industry*, Victoria and Albert Museum, London, 1986. Recipient: Commander, Order of the British Empire, 1953; Royal Designer for Industry, 1956, and Fellow, 1964, Royal Society of Arts, London. *Died* (in Dorchester, Dorset) *23 June 1979*.

Works:

Nonesuch Shakespeare Anthology chapter headings for the Nonesuch Press, 1935.
Heraldic arms, for Cambridge University, 1946.
Three pence victory commemoration postage stamp, for the General Post Office London, 1946.
Heraldic device, for the British Council, London, 1946.
Heraldic device, for the Rampant Lions Press, 1947.
Clock device, for *The Times* newspaper, London, 1948–51.
Logotype device, for Dolcis Shoes, 1951.
Minerva typeface, for the Linotype Corporation, 1954.
Heraldic device, for the Oxford University Press, 1955.
Engraved design of the £5 banknote, for the Royal Mint, London, 1961.
Logotype device, for Blackwell's Bookshop, Oxford, 1963.
Janet alphabet and typefount, privately produced, 1965.

Publications:

By STONE: books—*A Book of Lettering*, London 1935; *Wood Engravings of Thomas Bewick*, London 1953; *The Wood Engravings of Gwen Raverat*, London 1959; *Concerning Book Labels*, with Philip Beddingham and Will Carter, London 1963; *Reynolds Stone: Engravings*, London 1977.

On STONE: books—*Reynolds Stone: His Early Development as an Engraver on Wood* by J. W. Goodison, London 1947; *Reynolds Stone* by Myfanwy Piper, London 1951; *Graphic Design* by John Lewis and John Brinkley, London 1954; *Modern Book Design* by Ruari McLean, London 1958; *Reynolds Stone: An Exhibition of Engravings and Designs*, catalogue with introduction by Kenneth Clark, London 1959; *Calligraphy Today* by Heather Child, London 1963, 1976; *Schriftkunst* by Albert Kapr, Dresden 1971; *Paintings and Drawings by Reynolds Stone*, exhibition catalogue with introduction by M. E. Burkett, Kendal 1972; *Reynolds Stone 1909–1979* exhibition catalogue by J. W. Goodison and Ruari McLean, Dorchester 1979; *Eye for Industry: Royal Designers for Industry 1936–1986*, exhibition catalogue by Fiona MacCarthy and Patrick Nuttgens, London 1986.

English craftsman and designer Reynolds Stone was an uncomplicated man. He produced a large volume of work based on letterforms and nature, with great precision and skill.

Stone's early career centered on lettering and wood engraving. In the wood engraving process lines are incised across the end grain of a piece of wood, usually producing a negative form.

The result is a high contrast black and white image. Stone learned this craft as an apprentice at the Cambridge University Press. He became acquainted with the work of Stanley Morison who called for a revival of the pure classic lettering style of the Renaissance, and its passion for precise geometric forms with additive flourishes which surround the letterforms. The revival Morison called for is evident in Stone's work based on the 26 letters of the Roman alphabet. The simple, pure letters are crafted with precision, and demonstrates sensitivity to the correct proportions between the height and width and the intersection of curved and straight sections. Stone adds flourishes which enhance the basic letter form, and often decorates spaces surrounding the letters, but never the letter. Sometimes the form was planned and drawn out on the wood. At other times, Stone followed where the chisel led, letting the flourishes emerge from the wood.

Early in his career, Stone also began collecting the books of Thomas Bewick, an 18th-century wood engraver, known for his accurate representations of nature. Knowledge of these illustrations reinforced Stone's reverence for nature. Love of nature is evident in his illustrations where he shows idylic landscapes with perfect forms and textures. His bookplates combine letter forms with these natural shapes in a decorative manner. The influence of Bewick's nature illustrations, and Morison's love of the classic Roman letter forms, is seen in Stone's work. Though he is known primarily as a wood engraver, Stone also practiced the art of stone cutting and water-color painting.

Books illustrated by Stone range from *The Shakespeare Anthology* for Nonesuch Press, to *Omoo*, by Herman Melville for Heritage Press. Stone designed bookplates for various members of the British Royal Family; the Five Pound note for the bank of England; stamps for the Post Office, and logotypes for Bally Shoes, the London Library Label and Dolcis. He created devices for the University Presses of Oxford and Cambridge. He carved Winston Churchill's memorial stone in Westminster Abbey. This is but a partial listing of his oeuvre. Yet, Stone never appeared interested in developing a following or cult. He never made a statement of belief. Though he lectured at the Royal College of Art, he did not find joy in public speaking. He was rarely involved with commercial design problems such as designing books. He was not an experimenting artist. He was an artist who sought to perfect his craft.

Stone collected hand letter presses, some in working order and used these to print small editions of a book or pamphlet such as the 125 copies of Kenneth Clark's *The Other Side of the Alde* in 1968. He used the typeface Janet for the first time on this 16 page booklet. This was a typeface he designed and retained for private use. It worked well with his wood engraved illustrations. Minerva was the name of the type he designed for the Linotype Company in 1953. This was used for article headings and the New Statesman until discontinued in 1970.

Reynolds Stone died in 1979. He left behind a large volume of work. He was a quiet man, who produced a quiet art. His work, deceptively simple with its black and white forms based on twenty six letters of the Roman alphabet and nature, is beautiful in its precision, and grace.

—Nancy House

Giotto Stoppino: *Arlette* chaise longue, for Living, 1988

STOPPINO, Giotto.

Italian industrial designer. Born Luigi Stoppino, in Vigevano, Pavia, 30 April 1926. Studied architecture, at the University of Milan, 1945–50, and at the University of Venice, 1955–57. Married Deda Boccalini in 1965. Partner, in Stoppino/Gregotti/Meneghetti design firm, in Novara, 1952–63, and Milan, 1964–68; independent designer, Milan, from 1968: has designed for Poltrona Frau, Arteluce, Kartell, Bernini, Acerbis International, Zanotta, Rexite, Porro, etc. Visiting lecturer in architectural history, at the Italian Studies Centre of the University of Oregon, Pavia, 1963–69. President, Associazione Disegno Industriale, Milan, 1982–84, and ICSID Congress, Milan, 1983. **Exhibitions:** Galleria Arte Borgogna, Milan, 1983; Pentagono Arredamenti, Lugano, 1984; *Design Furniture from Italy*, Tokyo, 1984. **Collections:** Staatliches Museum fur Angewandte Kunst, Munich; Victoria and Albert Museum, London; Museum of Contemporary Art, Chicago; Museum of Modern Art, New York; City Hall, Shanghai. Recipient: Grand Prize, Milan Triennale, 1964; First Prize, Trieste Concorso, 1968; Compasso d'Orgo Award, Milan, 1979; Bio 9 Gold Medal, Liubliana, 1981; Business Designers Product Design Award, New York, 1981. Address: Via Argelati 30/A, 20143 Milan, Italy.

Works:

Cavour chair series in upholstered heartwood, produced by S.I.M., 1955, and by Poltrona Frau, 1988 (with Gregotti and Meneghetti).
537 Table Lamp in turned aluminium, for Arteluce, 1967.

Set of three nesting tables in ABS plastic, for Kartell, 1968.
Maia furniture range in tubular steel and wood, for Bernini, 1969.
Mobile serving table in injection-moulded ABS plastic, for Kartell, 1970.
Tic-Tac table lamp in injection-moulded plastic, for Kartell, 1970.
Magazine rack with integral handle in injection-moulded ABS plastic, for Kartell, 1971.
Jot Chair in metal and leather, for Acerbis International, 1976.
Sheraton Program cupboards in metal and lacquered wood, for Acerbis International, 1977.
Brooklyn Bookcase in steel rod with suspended shelves, for Acerbis International, 1977.
Hilton System modular furniture in enamelled wood and plastic, for Acerbis International, 1978.
Liuba Chair in plywood, steel rod and beechwood, for Zanotta, 1979.
Biblio cassette racks in injection-moulded ABS plastic for Rexite, 1981.
Menhir Tables in disc-welded steel, for Acerbis International, 1983.
Soffio di Vento adjustable storage and shelving system, for Acerbis International, 1986.
Elba Series sofa and armchair in steel and elasticated polyurethane with leather or fabric upholstery, for Rossi di Albizzate, 1987.
Mugello Table in leather-clad aluminium with crystal top, for Acerbis International, 1987.
Amadeus sideboard/cupboard with hinge-column supports, for Porro, 1987.
Arlette chaise longue in tubular steel and padded leather upholstery, for Living, 1988.

Publications:

By STOPPINO: books—*Italienisches Mobel* with others, Milan 1980; *La Sedia Italiano*, with others, Rome 1983.

On STOPPINO: books—*Mercati e Negozi* by Robert Aloi, Milan 1959; *Design Italiano: I Mobili*, edited by Enrichetta Ritter, Milan and Rome 1968; *Plastics as Design Form* by T. R. Newman, New York 1972; *Design e Forme Nuove nell'Arredamento Italiano*, edited by Paolo Portoghesi and Marino Marini, Rome 1978; *Atlante del Design Italiano 1940/1980* by Alfonso Grassi and Anty Pansera, Milan 1980; *Contemporary Furniture*, edited by Klaus-Jurgen Sembach, Stuttgart and London 1982; *Mobel aus Italien* by E. J. Auer and F. Burkhardt, Milan 1983; *Giotto Stoppino: d'all'Architettura al Design* by Daniele Baroni and Gillo Dorfles, Milan 1983; *The Hot House: Italian New Wave Design* by Andrea Branzi, London 1984; *The Conran Directory of Design*, edited by Stephen Bayley, London 1985; *Italian Design: 1870 to the Present* by Penny Sparke, London and New York 1988; *Designed by Architects in the 1980s* by Juli Capella and Quim Larrea, London 1988; *Italian Modern: A Design Heritage* by Giovanni Albera and Nicolas Monti, New York 1989.

My activities began in 1951 with my participation in the ninth Milan *Triennale* and continued over the next eighteen years with the formation of a professional studio with my partners Gregotti and Meneghetti. We turned out some significant work, particularly in the architectural field, but I shall not be talking of architecture here; rather, of my work as a designer.

An important date is the year 1968, which marks the start of my independent activities and of my collaboration with the firm of Kartell, with the stackable, plastic coffee tables which won a prize at the year's Trieste *Concorso* as objects for distribution by department stores.

The application of plastics technology to furniture was then still quite new. Research into these materials was based at that time on the need to produce materials for low-cost housing, so as make them available to consumers at every social level. The interest of design in this sector depended on the specific characteristics of the plastic materials (I mean in particular ABS plastic and other analogous materials moulded by the injection technique). These considerations could be summed up in four essential points:

(1) Form, understood as an aesthetic expression.

(2) Structure, in the sense of the rigidity of the moulded object in relation to its shape.

(3) The conception of the useful function in relation to the purpose of the object.

(4) The colour intrinsic to the actual material of the product.

The expressive possibilities of an object made from a plastic material were moreover closely linked to the limitations imposed by logic and by the economy of the injection press and to the weight-cost of the finished product.

Taking all these factors into account, planning in the field of plastic materials meant to me following what was almost the paradigmatic line of design research. From that time until 1974, my work on design with Kartell had a look of continuing collaboration in the study of a number of products, some of which are still in production. Of course, during that period, many other items of furniture designed in Italy used a great variety of materials, from wood to glass and metal, sometimes in combination with synthetic materials.

The success of Italian furniture design from the 1950s on has been due to three essential factors. In the first place, there was the development of a number of concerns created with the explicit purpose of studying products with designers involved throughout and of applying the latest technologies that emerge from the evolution of the use of the materials. These included Arflex, Kartell, Artemide, Poltronova, Zanotta, Anonima Castelli. Similarly important was the evolution of concerns which have a tradition of high-class work in wood but which are nonetheless ready to consider new ideas; these include Poggi, Cassina, and Bernini.

The success of Italian furniture design on an international level was to be crowned by the great 1972 show, *Italy: The New Domestic Landscape*, at the Museum of Modern Art in New York. It is interesting to note that of the 153 products exhibited there, sixty-nine were carried out entirely in plastic materials and twenty-two in plastics to such an extent as to be decisive for the object's appearance.

After the New York exhibition, and especially after the oil crisis in 1973, we saw a rethinking of the use of plastic materials both for economic reasons and on ecological grounds, from the point of view of the materials' degradability. I must add, however, that the products studied most carefully, those in which there is the most coherent relationship between object and material, still retain their place on the international market. At present, the tendency is to use every kind of material available from industrial production, taking care, of course, to use the right material in the right place.

The second factor was the establishment of design as an independent discipline, with a precise structure, quite separate from architectural research. One might even say that the chronic difficulties of architecture have directed Italian creativity towards the field of design, not only in the sector of furniture but also in the other sectors, as can be seen from the products of firms such as Olivetti, Brionvega, Solari, and Necchi, and above all, the motor industry.

The third factor, which must not be underestimated, is the existence of an uncommon number of specialized journals, which have helped to propagate the image of new products and, in some cases, to emphasize the significance of the new profession of design, understood as a process that can be integrated with the complex processes of industrial production. Here, too, the list is quite long, extending from the traditional *Domus*, *Casabella*, and *Architettura* through new titles such as *Abitare*, *Interni*, *Casa Vogue*, *Ottagono* and *Rassegna*, up to the more recent *Modo* and *Gran Bazar*. During the time of the economic boom, the idea began to spread of furnishing houses following models in the magazines, thus obliging the furniture manufacturers to turn out adequate products.

Another decisive date in this survey is the year 1976, when I began to collaborate with the Acerbis International company. I worked closely with Lodovico Acerbis, aiming to give the firm a new image. This business was founded more than 100 years ago, in 1870, as a workshop for craft woodwork; it has gone through remarkable changes in the course of three generations to reach its present industrial form, which aims to apply the most advanced design to the production of furniture. There were essentially three points that encouraged involvement in this industry:

(1) The relationship between technology and design.

One might say that creativity in design is always closely related to technology. Living in continual contact with the actual production of the firm, we tried to make as much use as possible of the potentialities of our own machinery, and only when that was not possible did we turn to materials produced by other industries. The unifying factor of these apparently disparate elements was, and still is, design, understood as research, perfected through successive stages by a considerable number of tests and prototypes in a process of development that sometimes lasts as much as two years for a single product.

(2) Synthetic ductility.

In order to appeal to the greatest number of potential users, we have naturally made a study of furniture that can be assembled in very different ways. New methods of assembly allow the furniture to be put together in the shortest possible time without using screws or other traditional means of fixing.

(3) Wood and synthetic lacquers.

With wood continuing to be the main material used in production, we tried to enhance its quality with extremely accurate work, or, in certain cases, with lacquers, using polyesters. This brought out the relationship with established tradition, going back to the ancient Chinese lacquers. In design research, color has always been a primary problem. The world around us is filled with colours, and not at random; nature expresses itself with an infinite palette of chromatic tones, and the rainbow, which appears only in special atmospheric conditions, is like a revelation of the colours of the universe arranged in a geometrical form.

(4) The last aspect to which we gave special importance was the application of sources of artificial light to furniture. It is generally recognized that social relationships in homes generally flower in the evening, and consequently we wanted our pieces of furniture to have a life of their own on those occasions, too, to create special effects and a characteristic atmosphere. This research resulted in such items of furniture as Brooklyn, Sheraton, Hilton, Madison, Axton, and Solemio, which have not only been widely taken up by the market but have also won remarkable recognition, winning, for instance, the Compasso d'Oro prize in 1979, the gold medal at Ljubljana in 1981, and the Product Design Award in New York in the same year, as well as being on permanent exhibition at the Victoria and Albert Museum in London.

But it is not those prizes of which I am most proud; what matters to me most of all is that by constant research, by work that always aimed at maintaining the characteristics of innovation and beauty at the highest level, I have made a small contribution to the efforts to improve the quality of life.

—Giotto Stoppino

STUMPF, William (Eugene).
American industrial, furniture and environmental designer. Born in St. Louis, Missouri, 1 March 1936. Studied at the School of the Art Institute of Chicago, 1954–56; University of Chicago, 1954–57; industrial design, University of Illinois, Urbana, 1957–59: BFA 1959; environmental design, University of Wisconsin, Madison, 1966–68: MS 1968. Served in the United States Naval Reserve, 1955–60. Married Sharon Rose Ford in 1957; children: Carol, Jon and Erich. Designer, Peter Muller-Munk Associates, Pittsburgh, 1959–62; Manager of Advanced Industrial Design, Franklin Division, Studebaker Industries, Minneapolis, 1962–67; Vice-President, Herman Miller Research Corporation, Ann Arbor, Michigan, 1970–72; Design Consultant, Herman Miller Inc., Zeeland, Michigan, since 1972. Director, William Stumpf and Associates, in Madison, Wisconsin, 1972–76, Winona, Minnesota, 1976–85, and Minneapolis since 1985. Also design consultant work for General Mills, 1966; American Telephone and Telegraph, 1969; Knape and Vogt, 1988. Lecturer and Design Consultant, Zeeland Planning Commission, Michigan, 1970–72. Assistant Professor of Environmental Design, University of Wisconsin, Madison, 1968–69; Assistant Professor of Product Design, Institute of Design, Illinois Institute of Technology, Chicago, 1969–70; Professor, Minneapolis College of Art and Design, 1982–83, 1983–84; Visiting Lecturer: Minneapolis College of Art and Design, 1970; Aquinas College, Grand Rapids, Michigan, 1972, 1973, 1974; University of Minnesota, Minneapolis, 1973; Kansas City Art Institute, 1974; Rhode Island School of Design, Providence, 1974; University of Illinois, Urbana, 1974; University of Wisconsin, Madison, 1975; University of Cincinnati, 1975–76; Cranbrook Academy of Art, Bloomfield Hills, Michigan, 1983; Taliesin East, Spring Green, Wisconsin, 1985–86. **Exhibitions:** *Design in Michigan 1967/1977*, Cranbrook Academy of Art, Bloomfield Hills, Michigan, 1978 (toured); *Please Be Seated*, University of Minnesota, St. Paul, 1984; *A Serious Chair*, Walker Art Center, Minneapolis, 1984 (toured); *The Art of Design*, University of Wisconsin, Milwaukee, 1988 (travelled to Chicago, 1989). Recipient: Motorola Design Scholarship, 1958; University of Illinois Award in Design, 1959; Alcoa Design Award, 1959; American Society of Industrial Design Award, 1959, 1976; University of Wisconsin Fellowship, 1967; Design Michigan Award, 1976; Designer of the 1970s Award, 1979, Annual Design Award, and Design Excellence Award, 1985, Industrial Design Society; Art Directors Club of Los Angeles

William Stumpf: *Equa* **chair, for Herman Miller Incorporated, 1984**

Award, 1984; IBD Gold Award, 1984, 1985; Stuttgart Design Centre Award, 1987. Member: Industrial Designers Society of America; Human Factors Society; Design Management Institute. Address: William Stumpf and Associates Inc., 128 North Third Street, Minneapolis, Minnesota 55401, U.S.A.

Works:

Harlem Preparatory School interiors, Harlem, New York, 1968.
Ergon office chair, for Herman Miller, 1976.
Equa chair, for Herman Miller, 1984 (with Don Chadwick).
Ethospace office system, for Herman Miller, 1986.
Ergon 2 chair, for Herman Miller, 1988.

Publications:

By STUMPF: books—*Leisure: A Study of Man and the Environment*, Chicago 1970; *Environmental Quality*, Madison, Wisconsin 1970; *The High School: The Process and the Place*, New York 1971; *Products: A Design Premise*, with Michael Wodka, Cambridge, Massachusetts 1972; *Design Quarterly 104: Julia Child's Kitchen—A Design Anatomy*, with the Walker Art Center, Cambridge, Massachusetts 1976; *Design Quarterly 126: A Serious Chair*, with the Walker Art Center, Cambridge, Massachusetts 1984; articles—"Conference: Environmental Bases for Design" in *Office Design* (New York), March 1969; "The Junkyard Backlash" in *Design* (London), April 1977; "Home Sweet Office" in *Ideas* (Zeeland, Michigan), 1978; "Design/Big Wheels" in *Parenting* (New York), May 1987; "The Crisis of Comfort" in *Arts* (Minneapolis), June 1987; "Reflections on the Urban Street" in *Inform* (Minneapolis), May 1989.

On STUMPF: books—*Design in Michigan 1967/1977* by Katherine McCoy, Detroit 1978; articles—"Mobile Housing" in *Look* (New York), February 1960; "Supermarket School" in *Progressive Architecture* (New York), February 1971; "The Resources General Store" by R. Weinstock in *Educational Facilities Newsletter* (New York), March 1971; "The Perfect Chair" by M. Mittelbach in *Republic* (New York), February 1986; "Looking Good Is Not Enough" by K. Andersen in *Time* (New York), 24 March 1986; "Designing Serendipity" by C. Kent in *Metropolis* (New York), November 1986; "Antidote to Ho-Hum Designs—A Sense of Playfulness" in *Design News* (Newton, Massachusetts), 3 November 1986; "Ethos Office System by Bill Stumpf for Herman Miller" in *Abitare* (Milan), April 1987; "Nine to Five and After" by G. Hollington in *Blueprint* (London), April 1987; "Furniture Designer Refuses to Sit on Laurels" by A. Patterson in *The Arizona Republic* (Phoenix), 31 May 1987; "Civil Liberties" by P. Dormer in *IQ* (London), Spring 1988; "The Ultimate Office Chair" by V. May in *Progressive Architecture* (New York), May 1988; "Chairs That Work" by K. Lanpher in the *Chicago Tribune*, 19 June 1988; "Industrial Ingenuity Takes On An Identity" by D. Wascoe in the *Minneapolis Star and Tribune*, 31 June 1988.

Working from a design perspective that has always involved a deep love affair with things that are animated versus things that are static such as structures and buildings, I view my work as a challenge to temper the machine to mankind. I see industrial design as a discipline compatible with the domestic realm of the home, as a benign but a pro-active force towards a clean environment, and as a primary extension of man's toolmaking ability and culture. I see my work as neither a subset of architecture, the so-called mother of the arts, nor a puppet of economics and marketing. I see it essentially as an extension of toolmaking, an art, and a craft. Industrial design has yet to find its legitimate place in the world.

I see man's fundamental need to play vested in his ability to make and manipulate machines and tools; the pursuit of the frivolous as well as the profound is critical to both pleasure and survival. The best of industrial design provides an admixture of play and physicality in objects; the best of my work, I hope, is comfortable, playful, accessible, and resistant to arbitrary obsolescence.

Like Blanche DuBois in *A Streetcar Named Desire*, I have always depended on the kindness of strangers. In an increasingly impersonal global and industrial milieu, it is precisely the quality of this kindness on which we all depend. Industrial design is, in my opinion, an activity devoted to being kind to strangers. By strangers, I mean us.

—William Stumpf

About a dozen years ago I walked into Herman Miller's New York showroom and was impressed not so much by the furniture, with which I was familiar, as by the weight and breadth of the books and magazines scattered around the place. I was familiar with most of those too, but I had never encountered their like in furniture showrooms, where what is grandly called "literature" is merely a device for what is prosaically called "accessorizing product." Books are chosen for this purpose irrespective of content, since their only function is to show a bookshelf in use. Periodicals are intended to provide "context," which means that, if the product is office furniture, a copy of *Fortune* or *The Wall Street Journal* is ubsubtly laid on a credenza for effect. Otherwise, the only magazines on display are the trades.

The publications in this showroom were different. These were books to be read—books, as E. M. Forster said, that *had* to be read, for it was the only way of finding out what was in them. Who in a furniture company, I wondered, read books like this? Who, in a furniture company, even knew there *were* books like this? Where had they come from, and why?

They had come, I was told, from a reading list provided by a designer named Bill Stumpf. No product of his had yet made its way into the Herman Miller line, but his thinking had. And Stumpf's thinking is his principal contribution to his clients and to industrial design.

Not that there is anything theoretical about Stumpf's design approach. Or anything bookish about his thinking, which is less evocative of *academe* than of general stores, barber shops, garages and baseball clubhouses—places where real work gets done.

Which is not a bad way to describe the William Stumpf Associates office: it is a place where real work gets done. One can tell a lot from the ambience of a design office. Some look corporate, like their clients. Others look cautiously arty, as if to say they are *in* business but not of it. One in Toronto that I particularly like has its kitchen front and center in the belief that, at work as at home, it is the most productive gathering place. There are design offices with no entrances as such at all, their front doors opening directly onto drafting tables in a self-conscious insistence that this is a no-nonsense operation. Stumpf's office is dominated by the shop, which gives the premises the ambience of a small-run manufacturing business. This is no coincidence, for making things, rather than making statements, is what the office is engaged in.

A design office so blatantly involved in the work process is appropriately concerned with products for the workplace, and that is where Stumpf has had his strongest influence. The design of the Ergon chair, which appeared in 1976, began with a serious study both of contemporary office work and of the kind of support the human body requires while sitting. Ergon, introduced in 1976, was a contract chair designed to support a variety of bodies, housing a variety of minds, performing various levels of work in offices. It was an effective interpretation for end users of what Stumpf had learned from human factors experts, physiologists, orthopedists and other specialists.

Through such projects Bill Stumpf has become known as "research oriented," which is technically accurate, I suppose, but misleading. The frame-and-tile office system called Ethospace is a case in point. As densely researched as any office furniture product on the market, it nevertheless reflects at every point the proclivities of the designer himself. "Given a choice, wouldn't anyone rather have a window?" Stumpf asked rhetorically, before incorporating the sense of that choice into the product. Even the best panel systems available at the time communicated a temporary feeling. Was there a way to combine the physicality, the *presence* of a room with the openness, flexibility and economy of a partitioned space?

As it turned out, there wasn't. That is, there wasn't any *one* way. But by introducing a combination of features—e.g., walls that are thick and strong but light—Stumpf was able to address the problem humanely. The result is a product that introduced to the open office the feeling of interior solidity that had heretofore been the exclusive province of rooms with dry walls.

Among Stumpf's current interests is a series of products for the elderly and the disabled. Here again, the research is deep and broad, but at every point subordinate to common sense. The actor John Barrymore once portrayed a man with a severe limp. An admirer asked how he had trained himself to limp so authentically. "I didn't," Barrymore retorted. "I trained myself to think like a man who limps. Then I tried as hard as I could to walk normally."

Some end users are disabled by genetics or accident or age. Many more of us are disabled by the built environment. The process of designing for them is the same for Bill Stumpf. He identifies first with the user's humanity, *then* with his or her problems.

Then he tries as hard as he can to walk normally.

—Ralph Caplan

SUGIURA, Kohei.
Japanese exhibition and graphic designer. Born in Tokyo, 8 September 1932. Studied at the University of Arts and Architecture, Tokyo, 1951–55: Dip. 1955. Married Fumiko Hasegawa in 1957 (died, 1982). Freelance book, magazine, poster, logotype and graphic designer, Tokyo, from 1955, and exhibition designer and organizer, from 1966: art director of the Tokyo magazines *Space Design*, 1966–70, *Toshi Jutaku*, 1967–70, *Ginka* from 1968, *Yu,*

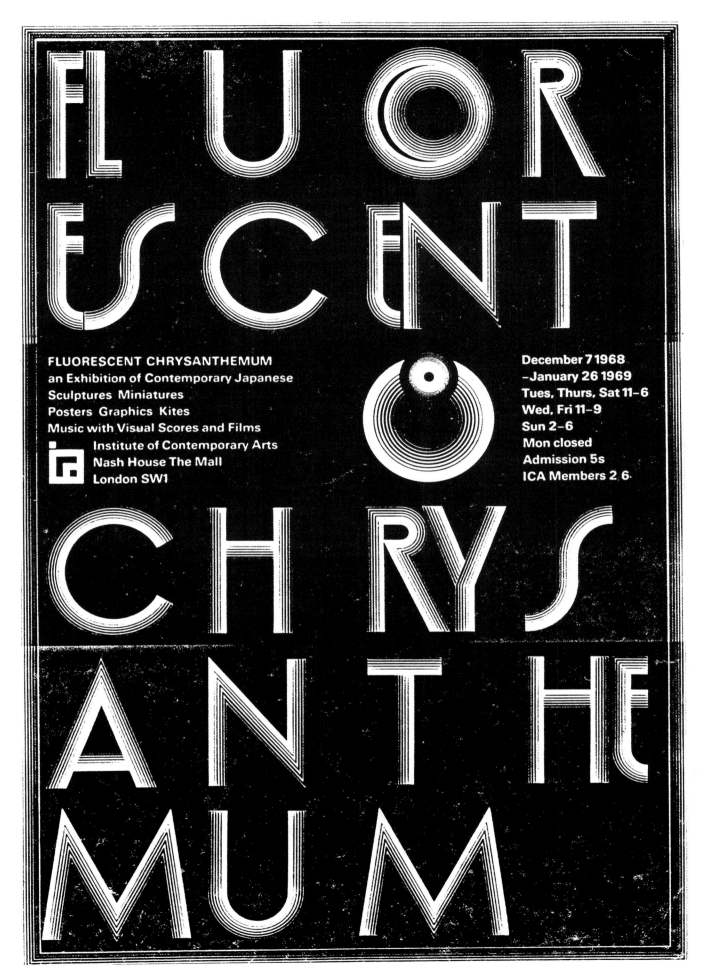

Kohei Sugiura: *Fluorescent Chrysanthemum* poster, for the Institute of Contemporary Arts, London, 1968

1971–80, *Asian Culture* from 1972, and *Episteme*, 1975–79. Guest professor, Hochschule fur Gestaltung, Ulm, 1964–65 and 1966–67; assistant professor, Zokei University, Tokyo, 1968–70; lecturer, Kyushu University of Art and Technology, Fukuoka, from 1978. Recipient: Mainichi Design and Industry Prize, Tokyo, 1961; Kodansha Publishing and Cultural Award, Tokyo, 1970; Gold Medal, Leipzig Book Fair, 1978, 1982; Japanese Ministry of Education Prize, 1982. Address: 3-3-10-507 Shiyuba, Shiyuba-ku, Tokyo, Japan.

Works:

Fluorescent Chrysanthemum exhibition layout and catalogue, for the Institute of Contemporary Arts, London, 1969.
Mandala—Now You See, Now You Don't exhibition layouts, for the Seibu Museum of Art, Tokyo, 1980.
The Mysterious World of Asian Masks exhibition layouts and posters, for the Seibu Museum of Art, Tokyo, 1981.
Asian Cosmology touring exhibition layouts, for La Foret Museum, Tokyo, and the Kyoto Shinbun Museum, Kyoto, 1982.
Venus Urania Pandemos exhibition layouts and catalogue, for the Ginza Art Gallery, Tokyo, 1983.

Publications:

By SUGIURA: books—*Visual Communication*, with others, Tokyo 1976; *Venus Urania Pandemos*, exhibition catalogue, Tokyo 1982; books designed—*The Map*, with K. Kawata, Tokyo 1965; *Still Time*, with I. Narahara, Tokyo 1966; *Zen Uchu-si, Summa Cosmologica*, Tokyo 1973–78; *Denshingonin Ryokai Mandala*, with Y. Ishimoto, Tokyo 1978; *Seven Photographs from Ikko*, with I. Narahara, Tokyo 1978; *The Rivers*, with J. Morinaga, Tokyo 1979; *Mandala, nishi-Tibet no Nukkyo Bijutso*, with K. Kato, Tokyo 1980; *Portici di Luche—Piazza San Marco*, with I. Narahara, Tokyo 1981; *Chinese Peking Opera*, with H. Tomiyama, Tokyo 1981; *Ajia no Uchukan—Kosumosu Mandala, Tokyo 1982; *Mandala no Sekai*, Tokyo 1983; *139 Sheets of Tibetan Mandalas of the Sakya Sect*, Tokyo 1983; *Bali—Devassphere, Ashrassphere, Fatassphere*, with H. Suga, Tokyo 1983.

On SUGIURA: book—*Typography Today*, edited by Helmut Schmid, Tokyo 1981; articles—in *Graphic Design* (Tokyo), no. 34, 1969; *Typography* (Tokyo), January 1974; *Design* (Tokyo), November 1977; *Idea* (Tokyo), September 1979.

*

Kohei Sugiura is an architect of information design. He has given contemporary editorial design new life and new meaning by creating faces of contents rather than make-up. His information starts on the cover, as a magazine is observed at first glance by letting the pages run through the fingers. His covers, extracts of ideas, quotations, and illustrative materials are two-dimensional with a three-dimensional effect. His interest in time and space makes him positively accept the baptism of the reflecting medium (TV), since a book "is not a thing which sticks to the congealing moment to become a still life, but a thing which structurizes and vectorizes the surroundings to become a dynamic element." Sugiura has invented what might be called "talking typography," which has revolutionized editorial design in Japan. Since the advent of his covers for the magazine *Space Design* in 1966, Sugiura has created many epochal works which shock at first sight but which unfold themselves as having been clearly and conceptually planned and executed. His use of type-size contrasts, for example, are not just the result of his design considerations but his invitation to the reader to enjoy multiple reading distances in order to contact the surface and smell of the paper. The smell of the paper is recently almost always a smell of printing ink. In his book design for *Summa Cosmographica*, the pages are of entirely solid black ink, with text and material in stardust-like white. Here, he even designed the book edge: bent to the left, Andromeda nebula appears, bent to the right, a constellation table is visible. Sugiura uses the four-colour printing process to its limit. His black colour, as used on the covers for the magazine *Yu*, is the precise accumulation of three process-colours. "Colours are in black. Black contains all the spectrum in it," he points out.

Sugiura has recently added a new material to visual art—air. In this book design for *Age of Human Dolls*, a seven-millimeter hole is punched through the whole book, symbolizing "a breathing duct for the prana of the cosmos."

—Helmut Schmid

SUMITA, Yoichi.
Japanese industrial designer. Born in Ishikawa Prefecture, 22 April 1924. Studied at the Ishikawa Prefectural Industrial School, 1937–42: Vanzato Prize, 1942: studied under Teizo Hano and Matsugoro Hirokawa, at the University of Arts, Tokyo, 1942–47. Served in the Second Army for Reserve Officers, at Kurume Military Academy, 1945: Sergeant-Major. Married Waka Iwai in 1951; sons: Masaaki and Kazuya. Designer, for the Technology Institute of the Ministry of Trade and Industry, Tokyo, 1947–52, Tokyo Electric Company, 1952–56, and Yao Electric Company, Kanagawa, 1956–63; freelance designer, working at the Toyoguchi Design Institute, Tokyo, 1963–77; independent designer, working mainly with the Telecommunication Institute and the Japan Telecommunication and Telephone Corporation, Tokyo, from 1977. Professor of design, Tokyo University of Arts from 1977; also visiting lecturer, at Iwate University, Morioka, from 1979, Kyushu Arts and Technology College, Fukuoka, from 1981, and Kanazawa Arts and Design College from 1982. Director, 1967–81, and director-general from 1982, Japan Industrial Designers Association, Tokyo; industrial design secretary, Japan Human Engineering Academy, Tokyo; trustee, Japan Design Academy, Tokyo, from 1977. **Exhibition:** Tokyo University of Arts, 1977. **Collection:** Postage and Telecommunications Museum, Tokyo. Recipient: Japan Electrical Industries Prize, Tokyo, 1975. Address: 6-23-12 Okusawa, Seatagya-ku, Tokyo 158, Japan.

Works:

Zuiko Pearlcorder micro-cassette tape recorder, for Olympus Optical Company, 1968.
Gastrocamera GT-6 medical camera, for Olympus Optical Company, 1970.
BH Series microscope, for Olympus Optical Company, 1975.
Xenon 16mm sound projector, for Hokushin Electric Company, 1975.
Car telephone, for Japan Telecommunication and Telephone, 1976.
Mini push-button telephone, for Japan Telecommunication and Telephone, 1976.
Mini-Type push-button telephone, for Japan Telecommunication and Telephone, 1978.
Loll paper holder, for Pultex Japan Limited, 1989.

Publications:

By SUMITA: books—*Complete Collection of Industrial Design*, vols. 2–6, Tokyo 1982–84; articles—in *Design News* (Tokyo), no. 6, January 1950, no. 1, 1951, no. 64, 1976; *Industrial Design* (Tokyo), no. 12, 1959, no. 112, 1981; *Modern Living* (Tokyo), no. 3, 1967; *Journal of the Japan Industrial Designers Association* (Tokyo), no. 5, 1972; *Mainichi Shimbun* (Tokyo), 14 January 1975; *Den Den Kensetsu* (Tokyo), no. 94, 1978.

On SUMITA: articles—in *Design News* (Tokyo), no. 10, 1955; *Living Design* (Tokyo), no. 6, 1955, no. 4, 1958; *Japan Illuminating Engineering Society Bulletin* (Tokyo), no. 3, 1956; *Industrial Design* (Tokyo), Summer 1961.

*

I was fortunate to have been employed by the Industrial Arts Institute of the Ministry of International Trade and Industry (MITI) in 1947 when Japan was lacking in basic human needs and when there were few openings for graduates from industrial design school. The Institute, established in 1928, was a national institute to make studies of design of local industries and to promote production of merchandise to be exported. It played a great part in the promotion of industrial design in Japan before modern concepts were introduced.

My assignment during the early period of this employment decided my future course. In the third year, I was given the theme of the container with a spout for serving liquid, such as water or soybean sauce, and was supposed to design safeguards against the overflow of liquid when pouring. In the near absence of reference materials, I devised experimental instruments, tested some samples, and expressed the data numerically. This outcome, published in 1950, was well received and led me into the world of industrial design even before Japan had received modern ideas in this field.

Based on my initial experiences, I came to conclude that objects of everyday life should be beautiful in shape, as well as, easy and pleasant to use for a long time. By identifying what the product should be like and grasping the needs of consumers correctly, designers can offer better products—which, in turn, will bring greater social recognition to designers.

Japan's present material affluence could never have been imagined three decades ago. However, the present situation leads to uniformity of individual lives because of mass-production, whereas man at present has reached the stage of seeking self-realization and individuality. Designers now should search for ways of satisfying the diversified desires of the future, when no one can foresee how to cope with the various possibilities that the advancement of technology may bring about.

Means for identifying the needs of people and for grasping the new lifestyle in the bud and mechanisms for mobilizing those involved in the work are essential problems today. I would like to do my best to make both the ideals and the practical role of designers effective in the problem-solving process.

—Yoichi Sumita

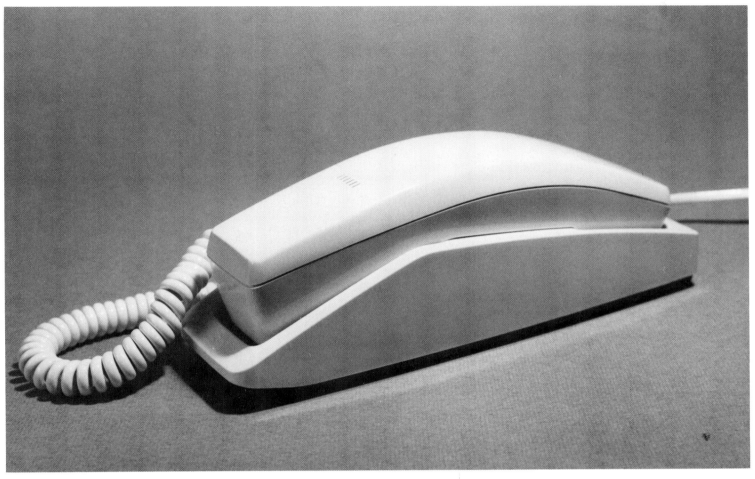

Yoichi Sumita: *Mini-type* push-button telephone, for Japan Telecommunication and Telephone, 1978

The consistency found in Yoichi Sumita's work derives from his "research and design" approach. In the 1950s, he tackled research on functions of containers with a spout. He took as his main problem how to prevent liquid in the container from running out, and he studied this by developing methodology and methods for testing. Significantly, his study was accomplished right before the modern concept of industrial design was introduced to Japan. Later, he was employed by a maker of illumination and lighting apparatuses, and he drew public attention which his non-symmetric fluorescent desk stands. He then moved to a firm that made electrical appliances for the home, and here he devoted himself more to organizational work and management.

In 1963, he became a freelance designer at the Toyoguchi Design Institute, where his major work was the development of telephones for the Japan Telecommunication and Telephone Corporation. Here again, he displayed his "research and design" approach to its full extent. His basics are "observation of product sample in use," in which human engineering is adopted, and "knowing the usefulness of something to hold by holding it yourself." His logical and verifiable method, which he put to use in designing public utilities is of epoch-making importance, for the Japanese in general tend to be sentimental, emotional, and conceptual even when making things.

He believes that design is "the making of high-quality products," and that "the making of long-lived products takes long preparation." At present committed to bettering the design of public utilities/facilities, he is making approaches to governmental offices, so that government workers might be well aware of the importance of design. Sumita also teaches at the Tokyo University of Arts and has been Director General of the Japan Industrial Designers' Association since 1981.

—Kunio Sano

SVENSSON, Inez (Gudrun Linnea).
Swedish textile and ceramics designer. Born in Mariestad, 28 March 1932. Studied fashion and textile design, Anders Beckman's School, Stockholm, 1951–53; School of the Art Institute of Chicago, 1956. Worked under Astrid Sampe, Nordiska Kompaniet textile design studio, Stockholm, 1954; textile designer, Stobo-Textil company, Stockholm, 1954–55; Head of Design, Boras Wafveri cotton mills, Sweden, 1957–67; founder-director, with Gunila Axen, Britt-Marie Christoffersson, Carl Johan De Geer, Susanne Grundell, Lotte Hagerman, Birgitta Hahn, Tom Hedqvist, Ingela Hakansson and Tage Moller, of Tio-Gruppen (Group of Ten) textile design company, Stockholm, since 1970; also freelance designer, for Ikea, from 1964, for Boras, from 1967, and for Rorstrand, from 1988. Fashion illustrator and reporter, to *Dagens Nyheter, Vi, Expressen, Form*, etc., Stockholm, from 1961; co-founder and director, with Carl Butler, of Svensson and Butler cookshop and restaurant, Stockholm, from 1968; Product Development Expert, United Nations Industrial Design Organization (UNIDO), in Pakistan, 1974–75. Board Member, National Association of Swedish Handicraft Societies, 1984–88, and the Statens Konstmuseer, Stockholm, since 1989. **Exhibitions:** *H55 International Design Exhibition*, Halsingborg, Sweden, 1955; *Design in Scandinavia*, toured the United States, 1955; *Scandinavian Modern Design 1880–1980*, Cooper-Hewitt Museum, New York, 1982; *Contemporary Swedish Design*, Nationalmuseum, Stockholm, 1983; *Design in Sweden*, Swedish Institute, Paris, 1987 (toured); *Tio-Gruppen: retrospective*, Stockholm Cultural Centre, 1987. **Collections:** Nationalmuseum, Stockholm; Rohsska Konstslojdmuseet, Goteborg; Staatliches Museum fur Angewandte Kunst, Munich. Recipient: SIDA Swedish Aid Grant, Stockholm, 1978. Address: Vikingagatan 13, 11342 Stockholm, Sweden.

Works:

Kally fabric, for Stobo-Textil, 1954.
Strix and *Strax* fabrics, for Ikea, 1971.
Cuba fabric, for Tio-Gruppen, 1972.
Pensel fabric, for Boras, 1977.
Banana Split fabric, for Tio-Gruppen, 1979.
Amadeus and *Zero* fabrics, for Boras, 1983.
Ultra fabric, for Tio-Gruppen, 1983.
Ratsch printed cotton, for Boras, 1983.
MM fabric, for Boras, 1985.
Tam-Tam fabric, for Tio-Gruppen, 1986.
Havanna fabric, for Tio-Gruppen, 1986.
Break-Dish ceramic plates, for Rorstrand, 1988.
A Taste of Lemon ceramic plates, for Rorstrand, 1988.
Trumf and *Trix* fabrics, for Boras, 1988.
Sang printed cotton, for Boras, 1988.

Inez Svensson: *Trumf*, *Trix* and *Sang* cotton fabrics, for Boras, 1988

Publications:

By SVENSSON: books—*Tryckta Tyger, fran 30-tal till 80-tal*, Stockholm 1984; *Den Svenska Formen*, with others, Stockholm 1985; *Formgivarnas Stickbok*, Stockholm 1986.

On SVENSSON: books—*Forma Sueca* by Ake Stavenow and Ake H. Huldt, Goteborg 1961; *Svensk Textilkonst/Swedish Textile Art* by Edna Martin and Beate Sydhoff, Stockholm 1980; *Form och Tradition i Sverige*, edited by Birgitta Walz, Stockholm 1982; *Scandinavian Modern Design 1880–1980*, edited by David Revere McFadden, New York 1982; *Contemporary Swedish Design*, exhibition catalogue by Monica Boman, Lennart Lindkvist and others, Stockholm 1983.

I nearly always work with geometrical patterns with delicate shifts of nuance. Early functionalism is one of my sources of inspiration. I hate patterns that float out into nothingness. Patterns must be tangible, and sound like music—jazz or pop.

Design should always be about searching for quality. Printed textile is a sort of mass-produced art. I believe in the old slogan from 1919: "More Beautiful Things for Everyday Life."

But it is easier said than done: design has become a tool of industry, instead of industry being a tool for the designer.

It takes a lot of fighting.

—Inez Svensson

The patterns are like visualized jazz on the white or black surfaces of the cotton fabrics. The air is filled with impertinent signals, whirring and roaring. The shapes spin and streak like comets. Amoeba-like and futuristic. We are clattering and chattering into tomorrow. Such is The Group of Ten's latest collection, *Megaphone*, from 1883, an obvious descendent of such early 20th-century avant-garde figures as Kandinsky and Mayakovsky.

How can multiprint sold here by the yard be as concentrated and expressive as art pictures? Perhaps the pattern units are a work of art in some sort of way. The Group of Ten have broken the bounds of the "permissible" in most things they have undertaken. Their patterns have migrated to streets and squares, three-piece suites, kitchen tables, sheets and pillowcases and walls. Both skinny teenage legs and adult corporations have been made much more fun to look at. In all modesty, The Group of Ten have fulfilled the dreams of the avant-garde pioneers of this century. They have taken art to the masses. To understand how this was possible, one has to think back into the 1960s. The new Swedish School of Arts, Crafts and Design in Stockholm (built in 1958) had a printed fabrics department. Young students acquired a new opportunity of selfexpression: hand printing, using silk-screen frames. (Until then, only woven pictures had been considered presentable.)

The School also had a printer, Richard Kunzl, who knew most of what there was to know about dyes, recipes and printing techniques. He would never allow himself to be put off by difficulties; every problem had a solution. If it had not been for Richard, The Group of Ten would probably never have existed. He has backed them up over the years with information and advice. For although The Group of Ten's fabrics are woven industrially at Boras Wäfveri, craft knowledge is an essential foundation. And although their products may seem avant-garde, they have a source of inspiration in the exuberance of Swedish folk art.

But there are many reasons why The Ten became what they became. Inez Svensson, one of the members of the group, was employed in the mid-sixties as Art Director at Boras Wäfveri. She managed to convince the management that they needed a "free pattern quota." The patterns in this collection were allowed to be bigger and bolder than the rest of the product range, most of which consisted of turgid, run-of-the-mill floral designs. The new fabrics appeared on department store counters like cheerful, cheeky exclamation marks. Fresh, bright colours, clear, sweeping, humorous patterns. They felt like a present and a release. This is what one's own home could be made to look like, as opposed to itsy-bitsy conservatism and a colour scheme as romantic as brown Windsor soup. Some of the patterns became best-sellers: Gunila Axen's *Cloud* fabric (1966) and Brigitta Hahn's *Poppy* (1968), for example. But the collection was still dependent on seasonal sales. A pattern had just about three months in which to gain the consumers' approval, otherwise it would disappear from the collection, no matter how good it was. In addition, many pattern designers saw their ideas being travestied by industry. Colour schemes were changed, and outlines lost their sharpness. The artists were mentioned by name, but they were not always willing to be associated with the end product. Suppose the artist could also take charge of production, deciding independently what the color schemes were to be and how long the patterns were to remain in production? Inez Svensson had an idea—a group of ten pattern designers who were capable of working together and of turning out patterns that would really catch on. She was as good as her word. It took a few years, but by 1970 she had mobilized ten pattern designers: Gunila Axen, Britt-Marie Christoffersson, Carl Johan De Geer, Susanne Grundell, Lotta Hågerman, Brigitta Hahn, Tom Hedqvist, Ingela Håkansson, Tage Möller and Inez Svensson. Together they printed a poster in English, offering their services: "We are ten Swedish designers working with textiles, paper and plastic. Swedish textile manufacturing is in a state of crisis. This concerns us too. We feel isolated and we want to reach out. If you're interested in good Swedish design, please get in touch with us whether you are passing through Sweden or not ..."

Many people did get in touch, in the belief that the fabrics shown in the poster were commercially available. But some of them did not even exist as yet. It was time to start production, and Boras Wäfveri undertook to print the fabrics. Ten fabrics altogether. (Finlayson had previously backed out. "Nobody could possibly want to buy such eccentric fabrics!")

In 1973 the group opened a shop of its own in Gamla Brogatan, Stockholm. But its biggest success was scored outside Sweden. Henri Deconinch, head of Boras Wäfveri's European office, has always been full of encouragement. The group's exhibitions have been given jubilant receptions in Paris and Italy. One French fashion designer, France Andre Vie, has brought out three collections using fabrics produced by The Ten.

Now at last the group is beginning to receive the attention it deserves in Sweden as well. Boras Wäfveri displays their fabrics at international trade fairs. Nordiska Kompaniet has recently added a number of their fabrics to its range, and in Stockholm itself the group's patterned garments are beginning to be seen on the streets, mostly in the younger age group. A glance back at the 1970s will suffice to show what pioneers the group have really been, not only through their patterns but also through their attitude to interior design. In museums and galleries all over the country, they have put on impudent and unconventional exhibitions. They have upholstered furniture and produced interiors of a kind which Italy has only come to match in very recent years. They have provided collective, hand-printed decorations for eighteen dining rooms and restrooms at the National Prison and Probation Administration and the National Administration of Shipping and Navigation in Norrkoping. They have produced magnificent pictures in a kind of patchwork technique (*skarvsöm*), in which the basic patterns acquire completely different qualities of expression. They have displayed unique pictures at art galleries, and they have produced joint collections for Ikea (a hypermarket chain dealing in furniture and furnishings) and the Duro wallpaper factory.

Their versatility is unrivalled in the textile design profession. They have a knack of doing what one least expects, boldly and cheerfully. Their shop window displays in Gamla Brogatan are a thing apart. They paint furniture like dainty suites and they devise gismos and combinations way ahead of the commercial trendsetters. *Festival*, *Space* and *Jazz* are pattern names which say a great deal about the way they work. They have loyally supported one another, sharing proceeds and outgoings, ups and downs. They are a strong team and each individual member is good at his or her particular thing. Separately they would never have made it. They always start by working out the general concept, what they want to achieve in a new collection, what different types of pattern it should contain so that the recipients can get as much out of it as possible. They are currently working on their seventh pattern collection. Four large, expressionist patterns with two striped fabrics in between, "like a sort of glue." The first manifestation, the second basic collection, the third (entitled *Marine*), the fourth (in black and white) and the fifth (entitled *Jamaica*) included many patterns which are still being manufactured. This if anything shows that patterns are capable of surviving more than one season, and that we consumers are not always on the look-out for something new; we can stick to old friends as well. The Ten are thin end of the wedge for commercialism. Living proof that things can be done differently.

—Kerstin Wickman

SVOBODA, Josef.
Czechoslovak stage, film and exhibition designer. Born in Caslav, 10 May 1920. Educated at a gymnasium, Caslav, until 1938; studied carpentry and cabinetmaking with his father, Caslav, 1935–37; philosophy, at Charles University, Prague, 1939; carpentry, at a vocational school, Prague, 1940–41; interior design, at the Industrial and Technical School, Prague, 1941–43; architecture, at the School of Fine and Applied Arts, Prague, 1945–50: Dip. Arch. 1950. Married Libuse Hrubesova in 1948. Amateur stage designer, Prague, 1941–45; founder-member and designer, 1945, technical director and chief designer, 1946–48, at the Grand Opera of the Fifth of May, Prague; technical supervisor and deputy designer, 1948–50, chief designer and technical director from 1950, at the Smetana Theatre and National Theatre, Prague; artistic director, Laterna Magica experimental studio of the National Theatre, Prague, from 1973. Founder-member, New Group of theatre writers and artists, Prague, 1943–45; general secretary, International Organization of

Scenographers and Theatre Technicians, from 1971. Instructor in scenography, Theatre Academy, Prague, 1952–58; professor, Academy of Fine and Industrial Arts, Prague, from 1969. **Exhibitions:** National Theatre, Prague, 1961; Theatre Institute, Prague, 1966, 1969. Recipient: Czech State Prize, Prague, 1954; Industrial Design Award and Gold Medals, World's Fair, Brussels, 1958; Scenography Award, Bienal of Sao Paulo, 1961; Sikkens Prize, Amsterdam, 1969. Merited Artist of the CSSR, Prague, 1966; National Artist of the CSSR, Prague, 1968; Honorary Royal Academician, London, 1969. Address: Filmarska 535/17, 15200 Prague, Czechoslovakia.

Works:

Stage productions include—*Empedokles*, Smetana Museum, Prague, 1943; *The Bride*, Smetana Museum, Prague, 1943; *The Fox Trap*, Municipal Chamber Theatre, Prague, 1944; *Manon Lescaut*, Municipal Theatre, Teplice, 1946; *Tales of Hoffman*, Grand Opera, Prague, 1946; *Andre and the Dragon*, Horacka Theatre, Jihlava, 1946; *The Bartered Bride*, Grand Opera of 5 May, Prague, 1946; *Insect Comedy*, National Theatre, Prague, 1946; *Aida*, Grand Opera of 5 May, Prague, 1947; *The Mayor of Stilmond*, Theatre of 5 May, Prague, 1947; *The Purge*, Satire Theatre, Prague, 1947; *The Little Foxes*, National Theatre, Prague, 1948; *El Amor Brujo*, Grand Opera of 5 May, Prague, 1948; *The Rogue's Ballad*, Grand Opera 5 May, Prague, 1948; *Marysa*, National Theatre, Prague, 1948; *The Czech Manager*, Smetana Theatre, Prague, 1949; *The Flaming Border*, Tyl Theatre, Prague, 1949; *The Bride of Chod*, Tyl Theatre, Prague, 1949; *The 11th Commandment*, State Film Theatre, Prague, 1950; *Der Freischutz*, Smetana Theatre, Prague, 1952; *The Robber*, Tyl Theatre, Prague, 1954; *A High Summer Sky*, Tyl Theatre, Prague, 1955; *Janosik*, State Opera, Dresden, 1956; *The Entertainer*, Tyl Theatre, Prague, 1957; *Rusalka*, Teatro La Fenice, Venice, 1958; *The Flying Dutchman*, Smetana Theatre, Prague, 1959; *The Seagull*, Tyl Theatre, Prague, 1960; *Intoleranza 1960*, Teatro La Fenice, Venice, 1961; *The Story of a Right Man*, National Theatre, Prague, 1961; *Julietta*, National Theatre, Prague, 1963; *La Sonnambula*, The National Ballet, Amsterdam, 1964; *The Whirlpool*, National Theatre, Prague, 1964; *Hamlet*, Belgian National Theatre, Brussels, 1965; *Atomtod*, Teatro La Scala, Milan, 1965; *The Makropulos Affair*, National Theatre, Prague, 1965; *The Storm*, National Theatre, London, 1966; *The Three Sisters*, National Theatre, London, 1967; *Delibor*, National Theatre, Prague, 1967; *One-Ended Rope*, Theatre Behind the Gate, Prague, 1967; *Faust*, State Theatre, Wiesbaden, West Germany, 1968; *The Soldiers*, State Opera, Munich, 1969; *The Fiery Angel*, Municipal Theatre, Frankfurt, 1969; *Pelléas et Mélisande*, Royal Opera House/Covent Garden, London, 1969; *The Clown*, Municipal Theatre, Düsseldorf, 1970; *Waiting for Godot*, State Theatre, Salzburg, 1970; *Idomeneo*, State Opera, Vienna, 1971; *Tannhäuser*, Royal Opera House/Covent Garden, London, 1973; *Tristan and Isolde*, Bayreuth, 1974; *The Ring*, Royal Opera House/Covent Garden, London, 1974–76; *Die Soldaten*, Hamburg, 1976; *The Queen of Spades*, Prague, 1976; *The Magic Circus*, Prague, 1977; *Idomeneo*, Prague, 1982; *Hamlet*, Prague, 1982; *Antigone*, Zurich, 1983; *Saint Joan at the Stake*, Zurich, 1983; *Six Characters in Search of an Author*, Louvain, 1984; *Break of Noon*, Louvain, 1984; *The Sea Gull*, Prague, 1986; *Ghetto*, Oslo, 1986; *Nabucco*, Zurich, 1986; *Odysseus*, Prague 1987; *Vivisection*, Prague, 1987; *Ring Cycle*, Orange, France, 1988; *Faust*, Milan, 1989; *Minotaur*, Prague, 1989.

Publications:

By SVOBODA: articles—in *Informacni Zpravy Scenograficke Laboratore* (Prague), September 1958; *Divadlo* (Prague), no. 1, 1964, no. 5, 1966, no. 8, 1967, no. 2, 1968; *Opera* (New York), August 1967; *Acta Scenographia* (Prague), January 1969.

On SVOBODA: books—*Le Theatre en Tchecoslovaquie: Scenographie*, edited by Vladimir Jindra, Prague 1962. *Josef Svoboda*, exhibition catalogue by Denis Bablet, Prague 1966; *Laterna Magica*, edited by Jiri Hrbas, Prague 1968; *The Art of Stage Lighting*, by Frederick Bentham, London 1968, 1980; *Josef Svoboda* by Denis Bablet, Turin and Lausanne 1970; *The Scenography of Josef Svoboda* by Jarka Burian, Middletown 1971, 1974; *Teatr Josefa Svobody* by V. Berjozkin, Moscow 1973.

Josef Svoboda's creativity may be viewed as an evolution of the major non-realistic movements in Western theatre of the last century. Without having studied their work, he is the heir of Adolphe Appia and Gordon Craig; his work also reflects many aspects of futurism, constructivism, and the Bauhaus approach, and he drew from the work of his own countrymen, especially E. F. Burian, Frantisek Tröster, and Alfred Radok. He has, however, gone beyond the work of these partial prototypes to create new archetypes in scenography for the twentieth century.

Svoboda prefers the term "scenographer" to "scene designer" because the latter has traditionally been associated with easel painting and decoration, whereas the scenographer is concerned with many other means of bringing a script and production concept to life on stage. A scenographer is primarily concerned with spatial relations not only on stage but also in relation to total theatre space. Moreover, a scenographer relies not only on painted decor but on sound and lighting, including projections; not only on static scenery but its expressive movement. Science and technology are not alien mysteries to a scenographer, but sources of enriched stage performance.

For Svoboda, the total stage environment does not merely establish a passive "place" for the dramatic action but provides a dynamic element of the total theatrical creation, an element capable of expressing (in its own "language") the meanings of the play with a force equal to the spoken or mimed parts of the action. In short, scenography becomes another actor in the total performance, and, like the actor, the scenography must be capable of transformation during the performance in response to the flow of the action, whether materially by kinetics or insubstantially by lighting, projections, sound, or other special means.

Svoboda most often seeks a relatively abstract, architectonic, and metaphoric expression for his scenography. He does not reject realism as a valid method for certain works, but he prefers to eliminate literal detail and fanciful decoration in favour of highly selective, figurative, and dramatically functional forms. His creative process involves a search for the scenographic "system" that will most fully convey a play's meanings as interpreted by the mutual deliberations of director and designer. The system may be a fundamentally architectonic configuration of plastic forms, or it may be based on combinations of technical instruments and special materials. Whatever the system, it will be determined by considerations of both func-

tion and design, it will probably involve contemporary materials and instruments, and it will certainly reflect a contemporary sensibility rather than reproduce or echo past traditions. The ultimate goal is the achievement of a scenographic instrument that offers the greatest opportunities for the expression of the central production concept.

A few of Svoboda's key productions illustrate the range of his scenography. Smetana's opera *Dalibor* (Prague, 1967) involved two huge towers on separate turntables plus specially designed, high-intensity lighting instruments to create curtains of light. F. Hrubin's *A Sunday in August* (Prague, 1958) had also made use of these lighting instruments in conjunction with frontal and rear projectors casting light and images onto a specially arranged series of scrims and opaque screens. Wagner's *Ring* at Covent Garden (1974–76) had as its central scenographic component a square platform capable of rising, sinking, rotating, and tilting; its mirrored undersurface reflected action below stage, while the top surface contained sections of stairs that automatically adjusted their position depending on the angle of the platform. In this production, Svoboda also made use of filmed laser projections in conjunction with scene changes.

Literally miles of strung cords filled much of the stage for *Tristan and Isolde* (Bayreuth, 1974) to create an effect of three-dimensional color as the cords received pointillistic, frontal-and-rear-projected images from a battery of high-powered instruments. Similar, originally created and projected color images were used in *Tannhäuser* (Covent Garden, 1973) in conjunction with suspended panels and mirrors above a series of inflated forms at stage level to create the erotic Venusberg scene. For Alois Zimmerman's opera *Die Soldaten* (Hamburg, 1976), Svoboda used the series of multi-tiered stage lifts of the theatre to create simultaneous performing areas in multiple planes and elevations. On more than one occasion, most notably for a Prague *Don Giovanni* (1969), Svoboda built on stage a background that was a mirror-like reproduction of the auditorium of the theatre. For this *Giovanni*, it heightened the significance of the theatre building itself (the site of the opera's premiere) and added to the essential theatricality of the performance.

Svoboda's protean creativity continued to explore the parameters of scenography in the 1980s. Several productions exhibited his talents in no-proscenium spaces: Orff's *Antigone* and Honegger's *Saint Joan at the Stake*, both in 1983 in Zurich's Congress Palace; Joshua Sobol's *Ghetto* in a complete arena staging in Oslo, 1986; and Verdi's *Nabucco* in 1986 in Zurich's Hallenstadion. Other productions employed highly poetic projections in conjunction with architectonic forms in studio productions: Pirandello's *Six Characters in Search of the Author* and Claudel's *Break of Noon*, both in Louvain, 1984.

Of special interest is Svoboda's multi-media production of *Odysseus*, a highly expressive combination of live choreography, complex projections of documentary, live, and animated material, and multi-track stereophonic sound. The whole production is the product of the Laterna Magika team, now part of the National Theatre and headed by Svoboda. Since its opening in Prague's Cultural Palace in 1987 it has also played in Munster, GFR, and plans are being made to tour to other parts of Europe.

In the summer of 1988 Svoboda designed his third Wagner *Ring* cycle, this time in the spacious antique Roman theatre in Orange, France. The scenography was based on a huge geodesic quarter globe lined with perforated material to take projections but also allow sight of the sculpturesque Roman scenic wall behind it. Laterally movable platform elements beneath the globe reflected the concave shape of the Orange auditorium itself.

Currently Svoboda is closely collaborating on productions with two other internationally celebrated theatre artists: with Georgio Strehler he is working on a production of Goethe's *Faust* in Milan; and after teaming with Friedrich Durrenmatt on the premiere of the latter's *Achterloo* (1988) in West Germany, he premiered Durrenmatt's new work, *Minotaur*, presented in Prague.

—Jarka M. Burian

SWIERZY, Waldemar.

Polish Graphic designer. Born in Katowice, 9 September 1931. Studied graphics, at the Academy of Fine Arts, Krakow, 1947–51. Married Magdalena Karaskiewicz in 1981; daughter: Dorota. Freelance poster and graphics designer, Warsaw, from 1952. Assistant, 1965–67, lecturer, 1967–88, and professor from 1988, at the Higher School of Fine Arts, Poznan. Polish section chairman, Alliance Graphique Internationale, from 1974; president, International Poster Biennale, Warsaw, from 1978. **Exhibitions:** Alexanderplatz, East Berlin, 1959; Polish Cultural Centre, Budapest, 1959; Polish Cultural Centre, Prague, 1959; Biberstrasse Galerie, Vienna, 1960; *Soyuz Chudoznikow*, Moscow, 1965; Bienal of Sao Paulo, 1969; Casa de las Americas, Havana, 1970; Kungliga Biblioteket, Stockholm, 1976; Poliforum Siqueiros, Mexico City, 1980; Oxe Galleri, Copenhagen, 1982; Art Gallery, Pecs, Hungary, 1984; Muzeum Sztuki, Poznan, 1986; Museo d'Aosta, Italy, 1987. **Collections:** Poster Museum, Warsaw; Pushkin Museum, Moscow; Stedelijk Museum, Amsterdam; Galleria d'Arte Moderna, Venice; Museum of Modern Art, New York. Recipient: Prix Toulouse-Lautrec, Paris, 1959, 1962; Gold Medal, Katowice Poster Biennale, 1965, 1971, 1975; Gold Medal, Bienal of Sao Paulo, 1969; Silver Medal, Warsaw Poster Biennale, 1972, 1976; *Hollywood Reporter* Prize, California, 1975, 1985; Gold Medal, Lahti Poster Biennale, Finland, 1977. Address: ul. Piwna 45/47, m.14, 00-264 Warsaw, Poland.

Works:

Mazowsze poster, for WAG, Warsaw, 1954.
Czerwona Oberza poster, for CWF, Warsaw, 1955.
Matka Joanna od Aniolow poster, for CWF, Warsaw, 1961.
Cyrk poster, for WAG, Warsaw, 1970.
Budowniczy Solness poster, for Teatr Klasyczny, Warsaw, 1971.
Biesy poster, for Teatr Stary, Krakow, 1972.
Tadeusz Brzozowski poster, for KAW, Poznan, 1974.
Jimi Hendrix poster, for KAW, Warsaw, 1974.
Szepty i krzyki poster, for CWF, Warsaw, 1974.
Stanislaw Teisseyre poster, for CBWA, Warsaw, 1975.
Charlie Parker poster, for KAW, Warsaw, 1975.
Jozef Mroszczak poster, for Galeria PP, Desa, 1976.
Jazz Jamboree 76 poster, for PSJ, Warsaw, 1976.
Psy Wojny poster, for Polfilm, 1984.

Count Basie poster, for Plakat Polski, 1985.
Majakowski poster, for Teatr Nowy, Warsaw, 1988.
Jazz Jamboree 88 poster, for PSJ, Warsaw, 1988.

Publications:

By SWIERZY: articles—in *Projekt* (Warsaw), February 1976, February 1977.

On SWIERZY: books—*The New Graphic Design* by Karl Gerstner and Markus Kutter, Teufen and London 1959; *Polnische Plakatkunst* by Jozef Mroszczak, Vienna 1962; *The Poster: An Illustrated History from 1860* by Harold F. Hutchinson, London and Toronto 1968; *Polish Poster Art Today* by Szymon Bojko, Warsaw 1972; *Circus Posters* by Jack Rennert, New York 1974; *Contemporary Polish Posters in Full Color*, edited by Joseph S. Czestochowski, New York 1979.

*   *   *

To hear doesn't necessarily mean to listen, but to see, you are bound to look at something. A poster is not designed for the purpose of a particular exhibition, but rather for the street, the place which is least suited for contemplation. A poster designer cannot depend on the goodwill of a passerby and one's immediate acceptance of the work. Thus, to achieve the desired effect, the artist must employ extreme means to arrest the viewer's attention.

Aggression and impudence are a poster's qualities. A poster must be observed unconsciously, even against one's will. It must attract a whole range of one's sensibilities, and it must also clearly communicate its basic impact in as loud a "voice" as possible.

I speak of the poster designer, for it is the only creative discipline in which I am interested. I began my gamble of missing spectators' attention thirty years ago, and I still find myself overwhelmed by poster design and under its spell.

—Waldemar Swierzy

*   *   *

"The ultimate poster machine"—this simple description best characterizes Waldemar Swierzy.

Now in his early fifties, Swierzy has produced more than 1,200 posters; some would say, two thousand. Inflated figures? Real ones. Since the mid-1950s when this incredible locomotive

Waldemar Swierzy: Exhibition poster for the Muzeum Sztuki, Poznan, 1986

waldemar świerzy – plakaty

began to gain steam, an unbroken flood of posters has come from his studio to all corners of Poland as well as to several Western European countries. He creates all kinds of posters—film, theatrical, political advertising, art, social, music, jazz, holiday, tourist. Anything which demands the publishing of a poster can count on Swierzy's skills and overwhelming versatility.

If someone could assemble all this amazing mass of paper designed by Swierzy in one place (perhaps Madison Square Garden would not be big enough), one would see there the changing panorama of world art styles ranging from the 1950s to today. Early, his work was painterly, typical of the Polish poster school. This was followed by the 1960s Art Deco, Pop art, and psychedelic themes and then by 1970s New Figuration portraits. Although Swierzy's creations show an amazingly wide range, don't think that he simply changes his hand or style like a chameleon. True, Swierzy's posters differ dramatically if seen from the distance of a decade, but remember, the poster is a short-lived butterfly of the street. It serves a day's, maybe a month's duty only to be destroyed by the next wave of new ones or the rain or simply a hostile hand.

Swierzy's magic lies in his sense of our times, in the actuality of his work being created today for tomorrow. The film poster for *The Wedding*, a romantic play by the early twentieth-century writer Wyspianski, repeats all the nostalgia, struggle, and craziness of the times, as recreated on the silver screen. Jimi Hendrix's high-flying, psychedelic, and fluorescent poster serves its hero ideally, suggesting the madness of his days, the music, the dust of Woodstock. Painter Tadeusz Brzozowski's retrospective poster, beautifully painted (yes, painted) by his friend Swierzy relates closely to its subject's style. No other poster artist changes style with such ease, and yet he focuses right on target, almost never misses.

Some of his friends are unhappy that Swierzy never seriously tried to become a "real" painter of oil on canvas. But he rebukes them, saying his joy is not to create pure-art "nonsense" for its own sake but rather to communicate thousands of ideas directly to the public. Like colorful video-recordings, his posters tirelessly show the kaleidoscope of trends, fancies, horrors, and dreams, all of them magically transformed from the simple light in Swierzy's mind to street displays available to all without cost.

—Jan Sawka

SYLBERT, Richard.

American film designer. Born in Brooklyn, New York, in 1928. Studied at Tyler School of Art, Philadelphia, 1946–50. Television art director, New York, 1951–53; freelance film designer, Hollywood, California, 1953–75; head of production, Paramount Pictures, Hollywood, 1975–78; independent film designer, from 1979. Recipient: Academy Award, 1966. Address: c/o Paramount Pictures Corporation, 5555 Melrose Avenue, Hollywood, California 90038–3197, U.S.A.

Works:

Film productions include—*Crowded Paradise* (Pressburger), 1956; *Baby Doll* (Kazan), 1956; *A Face in the Crowd* (Kazan), 1957; *Edge of the City* (Ritt), 1957; *Wind Across the Everglades* (Ray), 1958; *The Fugitive Kind* (Lumet), 1960; *Murder Inc.* (Balaban and Rosenberg), 1960; *Mad Dog Coll* (Balaban), 1961; *Splendor in the Grass* (Kazan), 1961; *The Young Doctors* (Karlson), 1961; *Walk on the Wild Side* (Dymytryk), 1962; *The Manchurian Candidate* (Frankenheimer), 1962; *The Connection* (Clarke), 1962; *Long Day's Journey into Night* (Lumet), 1962; *All the Way Home* (Segal), 1963; *Lilith* (Rossen), 1964; *How to Murder Your Wife* (Quine), 1965; *The Pawnbroker* (Lumet), 1965; *What's New Pussycat?* (Donner), 1965; *Who's Afraid of Virginia Woolf?* (Nicols), 1966; *Grand Prix* (Frankenheimer), 1966; *The Graduate* (Nichols), 1967; *Rosemary's Baby* (Polanski), 1968; *The April Fools* (Rosenberg), 1969; *The Illustrated Man* (Smight), 1969; *Catch-22* (Nichols), 1970; *Carnal Knowledge* (Nichols), 1971; *Fat City* (Huston), 1972; *The Heartbreak Kid* (May), 1972; *The Day of the Dolphin* (Nichols), 1973; *Chinatown* (Polanski), 1974; *The Fortune* (Nichols), 1975; *Shampoo* (Ashby), 1975; *Last Hours Before Morning* (Hardy—for TV), 1975; *Players* (Harvey), 1979; *Reds* (Beatty), 1981; *Partners* (Burrows), 1982; *Frances* (Clifford), 1982; *Breathless* (McBride), 1983; *The Cotton Club* (Coppola), 1984; *Under the Cherry Moon* (Prince), 1986; *Dick Tracy* (Beatty), 1990.

Publications:

By SYLBERT: articles—in *Film Heritage* (Dayton, Ohio), fall 1975; *Film Comment* (New York), January/February 1982; *Stills* (London), May 1985; *American Film* (Washington, D.C.), December 1985.

On SYLBERT: book—*International Dictionary of Films and Filmmakers*, Chicago and London 1987, 1991.

*   *   *

Sylbert's choices for the lush, wealthy worlds of contemporary Los Angeles in *Shampoo* also ring true as actual locations, although the design program is based mostly on color and pattern. The key characters, especially the women of the story, each have distinctive houses, offices, or bedrooms. The comfortable spaces are characterologically conceived: dark, warm forms are contrasted with bright, cheerier ones and each character-space is identified with socioeconomic details. Moreover, the slightly exaggerated inconography of the design is appropriate to the Pop, comic caricatures of the plot.

Chinatown's Los Angeles, a dusty one of the 1930s, is a different universe, a drought-stricken world; it would be hard to imagine that this was created by the designer of the Los Angeles in *Shampoo*. Just as the narrative of *Chinatown* is a mystery, the design program wears a disguise which unravels subtly during the story. Again, color and light are programmatically used. At the beginning of the film Sylbert stresses dry, brown desert-tones as the detective becomes involved in the murder-mystery. The screen is eventually sparked by bright, vibrant blues as the major clues appear. This color program is tied to the basic plot, in that the murder-mystery is mixed with a search for control of Los Angeles water supply. As the blue appears, so does the path to the murderer. This design program combines form and iconography with a masterful esthetic efficiency.

Sylbert's most ambitious historical film is *Reds*. Never departing from his personally selective authenticity, Sylbert boldly juxtaposed a large number of socioeconomic environments in this bio-picture of John Reed, the American writer and communist. Oregon, New York, and the Soviet Union—seen in many different aspects—share little, and Sylbert stresses their differences through color, light, and texture, thereby expanding the picture to give it a complicated, episodic scope. The scale of the Russian sequences also enlarges because of the number of people and largeness that history requires. These encyclopedic details of the design are kept in control visually by the camera's close views of the main characters and by the color program, with red dominating, of course, in the Soviet Union sequences.

Interestingly, *Reds'* design program is noteworthy for what it does *not* use. Sylbert does not imitate the historical period's famous visions whether in filmic or graphic media, whether in realistic or modernist styles. For example, *Reds* does not look like paintings of the Ash Can School or the Constructivists, nor like the films of Griffith or Eisenstein. Just as *Chinatown* does not imitate the *noir* mystery films on which its story is based, *Reds* evokes but does not mimic; through Sylbert's own view of the past, the film gives a demythologized, artful, realistic vision. He has made an original history picture, offering a personalized, artistic realism like that of the Romantic painters Gericault or Daumier.

Examining the great range in the images of Sylbert's film designs leads me to conclude that he designs more often from his responses to plot than to character. He is looking rationally for a way to design the overall drama to create a holistic design, a film's vision. He sets strict conceptual limits for himself, a tight rule or design program for each film story. He never decorates because he designs within structural definitions, and he has succeeded best with directors who give him visual control or the opportunity for creative collaboration.

—Norman Gambill

SZAJNA, Jozef.

Polish painter, theatre director, stage and graphic designer. Born in Rzeszow, 13 March 1922. Served in Polish resistance: prisoner-of-war in concentration camps at Auschwitz and Buchenwald, 1940–45. Studied graphics and stage design, at the Academy of Fine Arts, Krakow, 1949–53. Married Bozena Sierowslawska: one son. Stage designer, 1955–63, managing director and head of stage design, 1963–66, at the Ludowy Theatre, Nowy Huta; freelance designer, working with the Stary Theatre, Krakow, the Slaski Theatre, Katowice, the Wspolczesny Theatre, Szczecin, the Polish Theatre, Warsaw, etc., 1966–71; manager and artistic director of the Studio Theatre Gallery (formerly, Klasyczny Theatre), Warsaw, 1971–82; freelance designer and teacher, Warsaw, from 1982. Lecturer, 1954–65, head of scenography, 1972–78, and professor from 1972, at the Academy of Fine Arts, Warsaw. **Exhibitions:** BWA Gallery, Krakow, 1958, 1962, 1966, 1968, 1970, 1974; Pergola Theatre, Florence, 1965, 1973; Atelier 212, Belgrade, 1967; Artaud Club, Nice, 1968; Venice Biennale, 1970; Ernst Museum, Budapest, 1975; Kunstverein, Frankfurt, 1978; Studio Gallery, Warsaw, 1979, 1982, 1987; Institute of Polish Culture, Stockholm, 1979; Bienal of Sao Paulo, 1979; Polish Cultural Centre, Sofia, 1981; Kunstmuseum, Bochum, 1985; Studio Gallery, Krakow, 1986; Polish Cultural Centre, Paris, 1987. **Collections:** National Museum, Warsaw; Theatre Museum,

Jozef Szajna: Polyekran projections in a production of *Dante*, 1973

Warsaw; Studio Art Centre, Warsaw; National Museum, Krakow; Muzeum Sztuki, Lodz; Kunstmuseum, Recklinghausen; Stadtmuseum, Oberhausen; Kunstmuseum, Bochum; Konstindustrimuseet, Goteborg; Pushkin Museum, Moscow; Accademia Italia delle Arte e del Lavoro, Salsomaggiore. Recipient: Artistic Award, Nowa Huta, 1956; Polish Film Festival Prize, Krakow, 1962; City of Krakow Award, 1971; Gold Medal, Prague Quadriennale, 1971; Gold Medal, Warsaw Art Festival, 1972; Exempla Medal, Munich, 1974; Council of Ministers Prize, Warsaw, 1979; Golden Centaur Prize, Salsomaggiore Terme, 1982, 1987; Gold Medal, International Parliament, U.S.A., 1983; Oscar d'Italia, 1985; Special Ministry Prize, Warsaw, 1988. Order of the Builder, Nowa Huta, 1959; Order of Polonia Restituta Knight's Cross, 1969, and Commander's Cross, 1979; Merited Cultural Activist, Warsaw, 1975; 30th and 40th Anniversaries of the Polish Republic Medals, 1975, 1984; Letter of Honour, Polish Ministry of Foreign Affairs, 1978. Address: Spasowskiego 14/8, 00–389 Warsaw, Poland.

Works:

Stage productions include—*Princess Turandot*, 1956; *Of Mice and Men*, 1956; *Jacobowsky and Colonel*, 1957; *The State of Siege*, 1958; *Pantegleize*, 1958; *The Madman and the Nun*, 1959; *In a Small Country House*, Warsaw, 1959; *Leonce and Lena*, Warsaw, 1962; *The Fore-*

fathers, 1962; *Acropolis*, Theatre of 13 Rows, Opole, Poland, 1962; *The Inspector-General*, 1963; *The Empty Field*, Florence, 1965; *The Castle*, 1965; *The Buffo Mystery*, 1966; *Death on a Pear Tree*, 1966; *They, New Liberation*, 1967; *Bathhouse*, Kraków, 1967 (and in Belgrade, 1968); *Macbeth*, Sheffield, England, 1970; *Faust*, Polski Theatre, Warsaw, 1971; *Replika*, Studio Theatre Gallery, Warsaw, 1971 (and world tour 1972–79); *Witkacy*, 1972 (and in Italy, 1973, in West Germany, 1975, and in the Netherlands, 1977); *Gulgutiera*, 1973; *Dante*, 1973 (and in Florence and West Germany, 1974, in the Netherlands, 1975, in the United States, 1976, in West Germany and France, 1977, in Britain, 1979, and in Dubrovnik, Yugoslavia, 1982); *Cervantes*, 1976 (and in Mexico, 1980); *Mayakovsky*, 1978 (and in Finland, 1979); *Death on a Pear Tree*, 1978.

Publications:

By SZAJNA: articles—in *Dialog* (Warsaw), no. 10, 1958, no. 1, 1978, no. 7, 1982; *Zycie Literackie* (Krakow), no. 51, 1962, no. 1, 1978, no. 14, 1982, no. 43, 1985, no. 12, 1987; *Wspolczesnosc* (Warsaw), no. 22, 1971; *Kierunki* (Warsaw), no. 22, 1972; *Ekran* (Warsaw), no. 19, 1973; *Kultura* (Warsaw), no. 44, 1974, no. 30, 1986; *Fakty* (Warsaw), no. 32, 1977, no. 21, 1980; *Argumenty* (Warsaw), no. 8, 1978; *Scena* (Warsaw), no. 8, 1978, no. 3, 1979; *Literatura* (Warsaw), no. 48, 1979; *Projekt* (War-

saw), no. 2, 1980; *Teatr* (Warsaw), no. 22, 1980, no. 10, 1984, no. 10, 1987; *Tu i Teraz* (Warsaw), no. 11, 1982.

On SZAJNA: books—*Fine Arts in the Polish Theatre* by Zenobiusz Strzelecki, Warsaw 1963; *Jozef Szajna* by Jerzy Madeyski, Krakow 1970; *Talks with People of the Theatre*, edited by Andrzej Hausbrandt, Krakow 1973; *Szajna* by Maria Czanerle, Gdansk 1974; *Jozef Szajna: Plastyka, Teatr* by Jerzy Madeyski and Elzbieta Morawiec, Krakow 1974; *Maske und Kostume* by Stanislaw Kaszynski, Vienna 1977; *Contemporary Polish Theatre* by Witold Filler, Warsaw 1977; *Word and Image in Jozef Szajna's Theatre* by Ewa Wronska, Lodz 1978; *Familiar Strangers* by Teresa Krzemien, Warsaw 1978; *Directors of the Polish Theatre* by August Grodzicki, Warsaw 1979; *Talks About the Theatre* by Zbigniew Tananienko, Warsaw 1981; *Dimmed Lights* by Konstantyn Puzyna, Warsaw 1982; *Jozef Szajna and his Theatre* by Zofia Watrak, Warsaw 1985; *Sztuke Szajny* by Jerzy Madeyski and Andrzej Zurowski, Warsaw 1988.

Shaping man's imagination is a duty and not only a privilege of people dealing with art . . .

   Art means reducing the distance between known phenomena and merely suspected ones, between our ignorance and probability; it reaches universal time and meanings that live longer than the present and our today. To show only one side of reality means to tell just a part of the truth, that is, nothing is to be revealed.

Art does not like divisions; it aims at synthesis—hence, the need to find its own language, to determine its own philosophy. A constant dialogue with time, expressed in the play of signs and meanings, means a selection of meanings and elements. A continuous confrontation in an attempt to surprise oneself with new phenomena, to negate oneself. Art is also a risk: of taking responsibility for the situation which we create....

These values I try to convey in my creative work: the structure and relations of facts proceeding beyond illustrative literalism, place, and time....

The actor is often restricted to playing the part of an object. He is absorbed by the artisted reality. He livens an inanimate space and the reverse: he becomes an object of action. Taken out of the background-surrounding, he undergoes simultaneous reification. The barrow leads the man, the man wheels the barrow, the man sets the wheel, the wheel destroys the man....

(Excerpted from an address given in 1978 in Caracas.)

—Jozef Szajna

The experience of being a youthful inmate of concentration camps in World War II left an indelible impression on Jozef Szajna; as he repeatedly asserts, he is obsessed by the memory of the camps and man's dehumanization of man. Reflecting that preoccupation, the grotesque has played a constant, major role in his work, as have recurrent symbols of torture, aggression, and deformity, especially since the early 1970s when he began to be responsible for the texts or scenarios of his works as well as for their design. Even before that, however, surrealistic images dominated his idiosyncratic stage settings, even for traditional scripts directed by others, as was the case for Witkiewicz's *In a Small Country House* (Warsaw, 1959), Büchner's *Leonce and Lena* (Warsaw, 1962), Steinbeck's *Of Mice and Men* (Wroclaw, 1962), and Mayakovsky's *The Bathhouse* (Kraków 1967). Although he was trained as a painter, even his relatively traditional scenography showed the influence of constructivist sculpture and architecture.

Szajna's concentration camp experience was vividly embodied in his scenography for a production of Wyspianski's *Akropolis* (Opole, 1962), freely adapted and directed by Jerzy Grotowski; the set consisted of stove pipes strung on wires at eccentric angles throughout a central space surrounded by the audience. Even more striking was Szajna's production of *Replika* (Warsaw, 1971) which he has performed in several versions throughout Europe and abroad. It is a "spatio-visual composition" with no text and little traditional action. From a mound of earth littered with battered scraps of western civilization, mutilated survivors emerge to mime actions that metaphorically recapitulate humanity's destructiveness and yet also, its eternal revival. Like many of Szajna's other celebrated, subsequent creations, the work most nearly echoes the tradition of Antonin Artaud, as both men perceive theatre as an art of images rather than words. In productions such as *Dante* (1973) or *Mayakovsky* (1978), traditional stage design was rejected in favor of highly subjective groupings of seemingly random objects and artifacts in conjunction with carefully evolved gestures and movements of the performers, who relate themselves organically to the scenic elements and objects. The action may occur in all parts of the theatre, not only on a conventional stage. Strange sounds and *musique concrète* become as important as words. The text that remains consists of fragmentary passages that stress vocal dynamics and rhythms or suggestive verbal images as much as rational discourse. When compared to traditional theatre or scenography, Szajna's productions may seem haphazard and cryptic, perhaps self-indulgent, but there is no denying the power of their unorthodox, often shocking imagery and their thematic and esthetic coherence.

—Jarka M. Burian

T

TAC INTERIOR ARCHITECTURE AND GRAPHIC COMMUNICATION.

American interior and graphic design firm. The Architects Collaborative (TAC) was founded by Walter Gropius, Norman Fletcher, Jean B. Fletcher, John Harkness, Sarah Pillsbury Harkness, Robert MacMillan, Louis McMillen and Benjamin Thompson, in Cambridge, Massachusetts, 1945; TAC International established in 1960; TAC Incorporated established in 1964. Recipient: Boston Arts Festival Award, 1954, 1956, 1959, 1960, 1963, 1964; Parker Medal, Boston Society of Architects, 1961, 1973, 1978; American Institute of Architects Award, 1964, 1966, 1967, 1970, 1971, 1972, 1974, 1976, 1977, 1978, 1979; Prestressed Concrete Institute Award, 1966, 1983; American Society of Landscape Architects Award, 1967; United States Department of Housing and Urban Development Award, 1968; American Concrete Institute Award, 1972, 1984; United States General Services Administration Award, 1973; Johns Manville Competition Prize, Colorado, 1973; Connecticut Society of Architects Award, 1974; Arab Investment Company Competition Prize, 1976; Abu Dhabi Library Competition Prize, 1976; American Institute of Steel Construction Award, 1979; Owens-Corning Energy Conservation Award, 1982; Passive Solar Design Award, 1982; United States Department of Consumer Affairs White House Award, 1983; Concrete Industry Board of New York Prize, 1984. Addresses: 46 Brattle Street, Cambridge, Massachusetts 02138; 639 Front Street, San Francisco, California 94111, U.S.A.

Works:

Interior designs include—AIA Headquarters Building, Washington, D.C.; Amathus Resort Hotel, Limassol, Cyprus; Bahrain Chancery, Washington, D.C.; Basrah Sheraton Hotel, Basrah, Iraq; Blue Cross/Blue Shield of Connecticut, Corporate Headquarters, North Haven; Government Service Insurance System Headquarters Building, Manila, Philippines; Hotel Bernardin Resort, Piran, Yugoslavia; Indonesian Embassy Addition, Washington, D.C.; Institute of Public Administration, Riyadh, Saudi Arabia; Kuwait Fund Headquarters, Kuwait City, Kuwait; Lahey Clinic Medical Center, Burlington, Massachusetts; Maine State Office Building, Augusta; New York State Veterans Home, Oxford; Petra Hotel, Petra, Jordan; Shawmut Bank of Boston; Southern Illinois University, Edwardsville; St. Joseph's Hospital, Tampa, Florida; St. Mary's Hospital, Kansas City, Missouri; University of Baghdad, Baghdad, Iraq; graphics—signage systems for Charlestown Savings Bank, Boston; Childrens Hospital Medical Center, Boston; Harvard University Athletic Facilities, Cambridge, Massachusetts; Institute of Public Administration, Riyadh, Saudi Arabia; Ishtar Sheraton Hotel, Baghdad, Iraq; Johns Manville World Headquarters, Denver; Petra Hotel, Petra, Jordan; University of Baghdad, Baghdad, Iraq; Architectural Graphics for IBM Offices, East Fishkill, New York; Josiah F. Quincy Elementary School, Boston; Kuwait Investment Co., Souk al Manakh and Souk al Safat, Kuwait City, Kuwait; Smith College Gymnasium, Northampton, Massachusetts; printwork for Adelphi University, Garden City, New York; Amathus Hotel, Limassol, Cyprus; Copley Place, Boston; Government Service Insurance System, Manila, Philippines; Healthcare International, Boston; King Faisal University, Al Hasa Campus, Saudi Arabia; Kuwait Foundation for the Advancement of Sciences, Kuwait City, Kuwait.

Publications:

By TAC: books—*Town Plan for the Development of Selb* by Walter Gropius and TAC, Cambridge, Massachusetts 1970; *A Design Manual for Parking Garages* by Sergio Brizzi and TAC, Cambridge, Massachusetts 1975; *Streets: A Program to Develop Awareness of the Street Environment*, Boston 1976; *Building without Barriers* by Sarah P. Harkness and James N. Groom Jr., New York 1976.

On TAC: books—*The Architects Collaborative 1945–1965*, edited by Walter Gropius and others, Teufen 1966; *The Architects Collaborative 1945–1972*, Barcelona 1972; *The Architects Collaborative (TAC): A Bibliography of Books and Articles 1945–83* by Edward Teague, Monticello, Illinois 1984.

*

Our main concern has always been the person and society for which we design. This often complicates the actual design process. It may, for example, dictate offering several alternative office furnishings selections as a choice for a corporate staff, although one uniform selection for everybody would be preferable as a design concept. It also means throwing a brilliant idea overboard if it doesn't fully satisfy the needs of a particular project.

Uncovering those needs involves much probing beyond the surfaces of, for instance, an abstract corporate image, the official design policy of a university, the directions of a hospital administration, or the traditions of another society. One way we at TAC try to isolate the real design is by involving actual users of the building as much as possible in the design process: the patients as well as the nurses, the hotel guests, and the office workers. Although it is time-consuming and often frustrating, this is one of the most rewarding experiences of design.

Another way of making sure that the design solution really fits the client is in-house design reviews by our peers—a rather unique process initiated by Gropius as part of the overall collaborative philosophy at TAC. The design integrity which can easily be the loser in such a review process is maintained by giving the designer the last word.

We try to avoid following designs or fads, unless we are sure our client can shed his interior architecture as easily as last year's car or clothing. This responsibility towards our client is supplemented by our responsibility towards society. Energy-conscious design is one of the constant concerns for all of our projects. We attempt to utilize renewable energy resources and to reduce pollution and dependence on yet untamed nuclear energy without compromising the quality of the indoor environment.

Design is constantly evolving as new psychological, social and technological criteria develop so that the most rewarding project is always the next one.

—TAC Interior Architecture and
Graphic Communication

*

TAC Interior Architecture's reputation and, indeed, its standards of excellence in design are so closely intertwined with those of its parent company, The Architect's Collaborative, that it is difficult to separate the two. In any case, that is perhaps the largest compliment one can pay to interior design: that one cannot tell where architecture left off and interior design began—or possibly the other way around. TAC Interior Architecture carries out work which epitomizes the best of contemporary design. Its handling of space is dramatic—colors are subtle yet bold—and its solutions are functional yet elegant. Work is carried out with emphasis on the collaborative method of teamwork, which was the original concept of the company. The interior design department, which also deals with graphic design, can call upon the resources of the parent company and use the company's computer-based design system. The department thus can handle every aspect of interior design from feasibility studies to programming and space planning to producing working drawings and details.

The department has completed many large commissions, including government, municipal, corporate, and medical facilities. The meticulous care that is given to large projects is also given to small ones, such as restaurants and office spaces. Some of the more outstanding projects designed by TAC Interior Architecture include the Hotel Bernardin Resort in Yugoslavia, the Shawmut Bank of Boston, and the AIA Headquarters building in Washington, D.C.

Since 1974 the Interior Architecture and Graphic Communication department has been headed by Klaus E. Muller, whose wide experience included the work of international scope done in several leading firms. If one cannot refer to a particular stylistic expression for TAC Interior Architecture, nevertheless one thread

TAC Interior Architecture and Graphic Communication: Institute of Public Administration, Riyadh, Saudi Arabia, 1982

running through all the projects is the unfailing quality in design.

—Arnold Friedmann

TALLON, Roger.
French environmental, graphic and industrial designer. Born in Paris, in 1929. Studied electrical engineering, Paris, 1947–50. Designer, with Studio Avas, Paris, 1951–53; freelance designer, working for Dupont Europe, Caterpillar, General Motors, Thompson Company, etc., in Paris, 1953–62; designer, in collaboration with Jacques Vienot, 1962–63, then director of design research, 1963–73, at Technes design agency, Paris; founder and director of Design Programmes S.A. design agency, Paris, from 1973; collaborates with Vignelli Associates of New York: consultant to Frigidaire, General Motors and SNCF French Railways; also designed for Edition Lacloche, Blaupunkt, Salomon Shoes, Lip, Cetrina, Métro de Mexico, French Post Office, Elf Petroleum, Erco Systems, Testut, Société Buyss, Eurosit, Laboratoires Goupil, Cineco, etc. Instructor in design, Ecole Nationale Supérieure des Arts Décoratifs, Paris, from 1964. Founder-member and commission member of ICSID International Council of Societies of Industrial Design,

1964–69; founder-member, Collectif Enseignants-Chercheurs pour l'Environnement, Paris. **Exhibitions:** *l'Objet*, Musée des Arts Décoratifs, Paris, 1968; *Qu'est-ce que le Design?*, Musée des Arts Decoratifs, Paris, 1969; *Modern Chairs 1918–1970*, Whitechapel Art Gallery, London, 1970; *Le Design Français*, Centre de Création Industrielle, Paris, 1971; *Paris 1937–57*, Centre Georges Pompidou, Paris, 1981; *Design Since 1945*, Philadelphia Museum of Art, 1983; *Design Français 1960–1990: Trois Décennies*, Centre Georges Pompidou, Paris, 1988 (toured). Recipient: Silver Medal, Milan Triennale, 1960. Honorary Royal Designer for Industry, Royal Society of Arts, London, 1973. Address: 13 Avenue de la Bourdonnais, 75007 Paris, France.

Works:

Véronique ciné cameras, for SEM, 1957, 1961.
Coffee grinder, for Peugeot, 1957–58.
Teleavia television set, for Thompson, 1960.
Typewriter, for Japy, 1960.
Frigearia domestic refrigerator, for Frigidaire, 1964.
Stool in aluminium and polyester foam, for Edition Lacloche, 1965.
Spiral staircase, for Edition Lacloche, 1966–70.
Bulle Urbaine city bubble-car, for Technes, 1968.
Urbatrican electro-magnetic city overcraft, for Technes, 1969.
Crystal glasswares, for Daum, 1970.
Tableware and cutlery range, for Sola, 1970.
Corail high-speed train, for SNCF, 1970–75.
lamp, for Erco Systems, 1972–73.

Wrist watches, for lip, 1973.
Stereophonic record player, for Cineco, 1975.
TGV Atlantique train, for Alsthom and SNCF, 1990.

Publications:

On TALLON: books—*L'Esthétique Industrielle* by Denis Huisman and Georges Patrix, Paris 1961; *Modern Chairs 1918–1970*, exhibition catalogue with texts by Carol Hogben and others, London 1970; *Le Design Français*, exhibition catalogue with introduction by Francois Mathey, Paris 1971; *Twentieth Century Furniture* by Philippe Garner, London 1980; *Design Since 1945*, edited by Kathryn Hiesinger and George Marcus, Philadelphia and London 1983; *Le Mobilier Français 1965–1979* by Gilles de Bure, Paris 1983; *Les Années 60* by Anne Bony, Paris 1983; *The Conran Directory of Design*, edited by Stephen Bayley, London 1985; *Design Source Book* by Penny Sparke and others, London 1986; *Design Français 1960–1990: Trois Décennies*, exhibition catalogue by Margo Rouard and Françoise Jollant Kneebone, Paris and London 1990.

Roger Tallon is one of the few pioneers of industrial design in both its theoretical and practical aspects of the postwar years in France. French industry was slow to accept the professional designer, and although he was to create products for SEM, Peugeot, Japy, and others, his principal commissions were foreign; his most important work was done as consultant to General Motors for their range of Frigidaire refrigerators, whilst he also designed for the multinational companies Caterpillar and Dupont. His work of this period bears the stamp of his close cooperation with Jacques Vienot at the Technès agency, where he designed cine cameras, milling machines, motorcycles, chairs, tables, lighting equipment, coat-stands, stools, etc. Tallon's favourite subject, however, is private and public transport. In 1968, he designed a small car, the Bulle Urbaine, with universal drive. In 1969, in cooperation with the French Society for Studies and Realization of City Transport, he carried out studies on the underground system in Mexico. In 1970, he constructed the model of a vehicle based on the invention of Maurice Barthelon, namely, the Urbatrican—an electromagnetic hovercraft for communication within cities.

Tallon founded his own design company, Design Programmes S.A., in 1973. During its relatively short period of activity, it has won a prominent position among European enterprises of the kind. The bureau has undertaken literally hundreds of various programmes for the design of objects and sets of objects, such as office equipment, telephones, watches, furniture—in short, everything in industrial design from trademarks to the overall production policy of a given enterprise. Employing experts representing the mass media, typography, industrial production, the building sector, and the economy, Design Programmes operates in working groups cooperating, according to need, with specialists of all disciplines. Among the studies carried out in these conditions were those on the Corail train, a recent acquisition to SNCF rolling-stock, the prototype of which was first presented to the French public in March 1975. The daring design, which utilized central corridors with seats on either side, incorporated numerous re-designs for seat profile, air conditioning, lighting systems, signalling, luggage racks, rubbish bins, recreation areas, shops, and bars—all projected in conjunction with a renewal of railway station facilities and equipment.

The starting point for Tallon's works has always been to combine the function of an object with the conveniences of the user. This very concrete premise requires that industrial design differ from industrial aestheticizing, the main objective of which is not the structure nor the construction of an object but its appearance. Tallon was never satisfied with such a role, and has expressed this both as a designer and a teacher.

—George Walsh

TANAKA, Ikko.
Japanese display, corporate identity and graphic designer. Born in Nara City, 13 January 1930. Studied at the City College of Fine Arts, Kyoto, 1947–50. Textile designer, at Kanegafuchi Spinning Company, Kyoto, 1950–52; graphic designer, at Sankei Shinmbun Press, Tokyo, 1952–57, and at Light Publicity Limited, Tokyo, 1957–59; co-founder and art director, Nippon Design Centre, Tokyo, 1960–63; founder and director of Tanaka Design Atelier, Tokyo, 1963–76, and of Ikko Tanaka Design Studio, Tokyo, from 1976; also co-founder of Off-Design typographic studio, Tokyo, from 1972; creative director, Seibu department stores, Tokyo, from 1972; graphics art director, Seibu Museum of Art, Tokyo, from 1975; consultant, *Ryuko Tsushin* fashion magazine,

Tokyo, from 1976; creative director, Seiyu Store, Tokyo, from 1978. Founder-member, Tokyo Designers Space, Tokyo, from 1976. Lecturer, Kuwazawa Institute of Design, Tokyo, from 1961. **Exhibitions:** Steendrukkerij De Jong, Hilversum, 1965; Imabashi Gallery, Osaka, 1973 (toured), 1974; Green Collections, Tokyo, 1976, 1979; Galleria Grafica, Tokyo, 1977; Tokyo Designers Space, Tokyo, 1981. **Collections:** Museum of Modern Art, New York; Kunstgewerbemuseum, Zurich. Recipient: Japan Advertising Association Award, 1959; Tokyo Art Directors Club Medal, 1960, 1961, 1963, 1970, 1973; Mainichi Industrial Design Award, Tokyo, 1966, 1973; Warsaw Poster Biennale Award, 1968, 1970, 1972; Japan Sign Design Association Award, 1972, 1973, 1974, 1975, 1979, 1980; All-Japan Calendar Exhibition Awards, Tokyo, 1973, 1974, 1978, 1979; Kodansha Cultural Award, Tokyo, 1973; Japanese Ministry of Trade and Industry Prize, 1979; Japanese Ministry of Education Artists' Award, 1980. Address: AY Building, 3-2-2 Kita-Aoyama, Minato-ku, Tokyo 107, Japan.

Works:

Logotype symbol and medals, for the Tokyo Olympiad, 1964.
Japanese Government Pavilion displays, at *Expo 70*, Osaka, 1970.
Corporate identity programme, for Hanae Mori International, Tokyo, 1970.
Announcement cards and medals, for the Winter Olympiad, Sapporo, 1970.
Oceanic Cultural Museum displays, at *Ocean Expo 75*, Okinawa, 1975.
Roots of Contemporary Clothing exhibition layouts, for the Museum of Modern Art, Kyoto, 1975.
Issey Miyake in the Museum exhibition layouts, for the Seibu Museum of Art, Tokyo, 1977.
Mandala: Photos by Yasuhiro Ishimoto exhibition layouts, for the Seibu Museum of Art, Tokyo, 1977.
Corporate identity programme, for the Seiyu Store, Tokyo, 1978.
The World of Tamasaburo exhibition layouts, for the Seibu Department Store, Tokyo, 1978.
Japan Style exhibition layouts, for the Victoria and Albert Museum, London, 1980.

Publications:

By TANAKA: books—*Japanese Patterns*, with others, Tokyo 1968; *Modern Design Series: Color Scheme and Design*, Tokyo 1969; *The Work of Ikko Tanaka*, Tokyo 1977; *Surroundings of Design: Essays*, Tokyo 1980.

On TANAKA: books—*The Poster: An Illustrated History from 1860* by Harold F. Hutchinson, London and Toronto 1968; *Modern Graphics* by Keith Murgatroyd, London 1969; *Book Jackets and Record Sleeves*, edited by Kurt Weidemann, Stuttgart and London 1969; *History of the Poster* by Josef and Shizuko Müller-Brockmann, Zurich 1971; *Monografie des Plakats: Entwicklung, Stil, Design* by Herbert Schindler, Munich 1972; *The Language of Graphics* by Edward Booth-Clibborn and Daniele Baroni, London 1980; *Who's Who in Graphic Art*, edited by Walter Amstutz, Dubendorf 1982; *Les Années 60* by Anne Bony, Paris 1983; *Japanese Design* by Penny Sparke, London 1987.

Probably the person who had the most influence on Ikko Tanaka as a designer was Yoshio Hayakawa. Recollecting that time

around 1952–53, Tanaka has written "When one passes through the Ikomayama tunnel of the Kintetsu train line linking Nara and Osaka, the whole expanse of the Kawachi Plains spreads out before one like an aerial photograph. I stole the scene that appears at the small station which lies at the entrance to the second short tunnel for the 'Poster of the Shúsai Group of Yoshio Hayakawa' (1964)."

Another influence was modern jazz. While under the spell of Hayakawa's illustrations, with their delicate sense of color, and of the bold American jazz of the time, Tanaka governed form and meaning by the intellectual manipulation of shape. Eventually, he became aware of the vibrant, lively form and music seen in such forms as the Noh theater, which at first glance appear to be static, and this awareness came to be expressed in his own form and color. The beauty of his work wafts forth and fascinates me, like the karma of nirvana released from a mandala painting.

Tanaka's bold, clear form and sense of coloration are wonderful. In many of his works, each color is painted flatly, without gradation, on top of forms or letters which have been transformed into indeterminate shapes. His works show both the sadness and the brightness of startled surprise which are characteristic of the Kansai area of Japan.

Tanaka is also skilled at writing. His book *The Environs of Design* [*Dezain no shuhen*] is a collection of the essays he has written over the years. The prose has a lustre to it, and the work is an excellent place to learn about Tanaka's erudition.

—Shukuro Habara

TANAKA, Masaaki.
Japanese graphic designer. Born in Tokyo, 14 March 1931. Studied graphic design, at the National University of Arts, Tokyo, 1949–53: BA 1953; independent design education studies in the United States and Europe, 1962–63, and research studies at the Illinois Institute of Technology, Chicago, 1981. Married Reiko Toyozumi in 1956; daughter: Eriko. Worked as a graphic designer, at Bijutsu-Shuppan Publishing Company, Tokyo, 1953–56; freelance designer and consultant, Tokyo, from 1956. Lecturer, National University of Arts, Tokyo, from 1965; associate professor, 1966–76, and professor from 1976, Women's College of Art, Tokyo; special lecturer, Sookmyung Women's University, Seoul, 1982. Director, Japanese Society for the Science of Design, Tokyo, from 1964; chairman, Typography Society of Japan, Tokyo, from 1977. Address: 1-17-1-110 Ishikawa-cho, Ohta-ku, Tokyo 145, Japan.

Publications:

By TANAKA: books—*Outline of Graphic Design*, 5 vols., editor, Tokyo 1960; *Design Techniques: Layout*, Tokyo 1964; *Design Techniques: Lettering and Typography*, with others, Tokyo 1965; *Outline of Design Education: Visual Design*, Tokyo 1967; *Letters and Printing*, Tokyo 1970; *Graphic Design*, Tokyo 1971; *Contemporary Graphic Design*, 3 vols., Tokyo 1971; *Graphic Design of the World: Editorial Design*, Tokyo 1975; *Introduction to Western Alphabet*, Tokyo 1978; *Japanese Typography*

Design, Tokyo 1978; *Practical Art Education: Visual Communications Design*, Tokyo 1982.

In 1962–63, Masaaki Tanaka observed the state of affairs throughout the world in institutions of higher education specializing in design and reviewed these institutions in numerous journals. As a result, he became the leading authority on design education in Japan. Moreover, he has a broad knowledge of graphic design itself. In particular, his scholarship on nineteenth-century typography and Bodoni printing is extensive. Particularly illustrative of his erudition is his writing in which he explains the history and structure of European literature, as well as its beauty, to the Japanese in a manner that is both interesting and easy to understand.

As Director of the Society of Japanese Design, Tanaka is a key figure in the management of the society. His balanced judgement and demeanour have been indispensable to the governing of the society, which on occasion becomes one-sided in its viewpoint.

Overall, the basis of Tanaka's research and thought with regard to his design is a common sense combined with a world view. His papers, many of his introductory articles, and his attitude toward life all display democratic common sense as the ideal. This may just be the natural process of thinking for an educator who has researched many European and American schools and who furthermore knows the history of design. His idea of design education is that it is "something which does not go along with the current of the time, but will cultivate a spirit that will discern what is correct for modern production, communication, and environment; in other words, something that will develop critical minds that will learn in order to become the creators of the culture of the future and something that cultivates a sense of the plastic arts which respect individuality." This philosophy may well be a healthy one for a professor to hold.

—Shukuro Habara

TAN GUIDICELLI.
Vietnamese fashion designer. Born in Haiphong, 12 November 1934; settled in France, 1955. Studied at the Ecole de La Chambre Syndicale de la Couture, Paris, 1956–57. Apprentice designer, Christian Dior fashion house, Paris, 1957–59; assistant to Jules Francois Crahay, at Nina Ricci fashion studio, Paris, 1959–61; assistant, studio of Jacques Heim, Paris, 1961–62; freelance fashion designer, working for Chloe, Trell, etc., Paris, from 1962: chief stylist for Gunther Sachs of MicMac, Saint-Tropez, 1968–73; founder-director of Tan Guidicelli ready-to-wear fashions, Paris, from 1974; launched perfumes *T-Vert* and *T-Fumé*. Address: 45 rue de Babylone, 75007 Paris, France.

Publications:

On TAN GUIDICELLI: books—*Fairchild's Dictionary of Fashion*, edited by Charlotte Calasibetta, New York 1975; *The World of Fashion: People, Places, Resources* by Eleanor Lambert, New York and London 1976; *25 Ans de Marie-Claire de 1954 a 1979*, compiled by Françoise Mohrt, Paris 1979; *Fashion 2001* by Lucille Khornak, London 1982; *McDowell's Directory of Twentieth Century Fashion* by Colin McDowell, London 1984.

Many young designers go overboard for an extreme style because restraint is more characteristic of maturity. By declaring that women's clothes are plumage, Tan Guidicelli was saying that fashion is theatre before it is reality. Of course, among wild animals and many primitive tribes, plumage is the monopoly of the males, as it was also their privilege in western society until the rise of the middle classes in the nineteenth century when, under the influence of the puritan ethic, the male handed his plumage to his wife and told her to be his social advertisement. Women did literally wear the plumage during the *belle époque*, but since then, with more and more women working, they, too, follow the puritan ethic, and occasions for plumage have decreased. As Jean Muir has pointed out, young designers, suckers for glamour, produce cocktail dresses and teagowns without first asking just how many women still lead that sort of life. Tan Guidicelli appears to be of this fraternity, considering the show more exciting than the real routine. While a number of rich women can still afford plumage, even they simplify the greater part of their wardrobe because they travel so much, if only from resort to resort.

If Tan Guidicelli is to be a successful businessman in addition to a designer, he must learn to create models which can be reproduced for the mass market, where occasions for plumage are limited to wedding days. However, the young usually have to learn the hard way, and too many designers do not appreciate that fashion is ruthless business; it is easier to be a flash in the pan than it is to become a lasting presence. It is one thing to win a royal order and another to retain royal patronage thereafter, as the makers of a recent royal wedding gown have discovered. Tan Guidicelli has lasted for a decade, but how much he has learnt in that time remains to be seen. He can create such good designs when he keeps the look simple, but there have also been some ill-disciplined concoctions. Which will win, purity or extravagance?

—Diana de Marly

TAPIOVAARA, (Yrjo) Ilmari.
Finnish exhibition, film, interior and industrial designer. Born in Helsinki, in 1914. Apprenticed with furniture manufacturers in Helsinki, 1933–35; studied interior design, at the Central School of Industrial Design, Helsinki, 1933–37; University of London, 1936–37; apprentice in the studio of architect Le Corbusier, Paris, 1937. Married Iris Annikki Hyvarinen in 1939 (died, 1972); children: Timo, Eva and Lassi; married Riitta Kurikka in 1972. Art director, Asko Tehtaat Oy furniture manufacturers, Lahti, 1937–40; founder and designer, Keravan Puuteollisuus Oy furniture firm, Kerava, 1949–50; freelance designer, working for Marva Production, Knoll International, Thonet, Edsbyverk, Asko Konsern, Lukkiseppu, Oy Skanno Ab, Laukaan Puu, Hackmann Oy, Stockmann Orno, etc., in Helsinki from 1951. Head, 1950–52, and chairman of interior design department, 1953–56, at the Central School of Industrial Design, Helsinki; visiting professor, Illinois Institute of Technology, Chicago, and Art Institute of Chicago, 1952–53, and at the University of Technology, Helsinki, from 1965. Finnish representative, ICSID International Council of Societies of Industrial Design; member of the Finnish State Commission for Foreign Programmes, Helsinki, chairman Central Organization of Industrial Design, Helsinki, 1959–68. **Exhibitions:** Milan Triennale, from 1951; *Design in Scandinavia*, Museum of Modern Art, New York, 1954 (toured); *Formes Scandinaves*, Musée des Arts Decoratifs, Paris, 1958; *Finlandia*, Kunstgewerbemuseum, Zurich, 1961 (toured); *Modern Chairs 1918–1970*, Whitechapel Art Gallery, London, 1970; *Scandinavian Modern Design 1880–1980*, Cooper-Hewitt Museum, New York, 1982; *Design Since 1945*, Philadelphia Musem of Art, 1983; *Ilmari Tapiovaara*, Museum of Applied Arts, Helsinki, 1984. Recipient: Good Design Award, Chicago, 1950; Museum of Modern Art Low-Cost Furniture Prize, New York, 1951; Gold Medal, Milan Triennale, 1951, 1954, 1957, 1966; American Interior Design Award, New York, 1963; National Furniture Prize, Milan, 1968; Furniture Prize, Cantu, 1970. Honorary Royal Designer for Industry, Royal Society of Arts, London, 1969. Address: Itaranta 6, 02100 Espoo 10 Finland.

Works:

Domus stackable wooden chair, for the Domus Accademica hostel, Helsinki, 1946, produced by Wilhelm Schauman, 1946–65.
Olivetti showroom interiors, Helsinki, 1954.
Corvair and Caravelle aircraft interiors, for Finnair, 1957.
Children's furniture range, for Heal's, 1960.
Kiki upholstered stackable wooden chairs, for Merivaara, 1960.
Polar cutlery in stainless steel, for Hackmann Oy, 1963.

Publications:

By TAPIOVAARA: book—*Finnish Decorative Art: 13th Yearbook*, editor, Helsinki 1949; article—in *Form Function Finland* (Helsinki), 1983.

On TAPIOVAARA: books—*Prize Designs for Modern Furniture* by Edgar Kaufmann Jr., New York 1950; *Gute Möbel—Schöne Raume*, edited by Mia Seeger, Stuttgart 1953; *Mobili Tipo* by Robert Aloi, Milan 1956; *A Treasury of Scandinavian Design*, edited by Erik Zahle, New York 1961; *Scandinavian Domestic Design*, edited by Erik Zahle, Copenhagen 1961, London 1963; *Modern Finnish Design* by Ulf Hard af Segerstad, London 1969; *Modern Chairs 1918–1970*, exhibition catalogue with texts by Carol Hogben and others, London 1970; *Scandinavian Design: Objects of a Life Style* by Eileene Harrison Beer, New York and Toronto 1975; *History of Modern Furniture* by Karl Mang, Stuttgart 1978; *One Hundred Great Finnish Designs*, edited by Per Mollerup, Snekkersten 1979; *Twentieth Century Furniture* by Philippe Garner, London 1980; *Knoll Design* by Eric Larrabee and Massimo Vignelli, New York 1981; *Scandinavian Modern Design 1880–1980*, edited by David Revere McFadden, New York 1982; *Contemporary Furniture*, edited by Klaus-Jürgen Sembach, Stuttgart, London and New York 1982; *Design Since 1945*, edited by Kathryn Hiesinger and George Marcus, Philadelphia and London 1983; *Finnish Vision*, with texts by Pekka Suhonen and others, Helsinki 1983; *The Conran Directory of Design*, edited by Stephen Bayley, London 1985; *Mid-Century: Furniture of the 1950s* by

Cara Greenberg, London 1985; *Twentieth Century Design: Furniture* by Penny Sparke, London 1986.

"Being a designer is rather like being a doctor; once you have the professional skill, you can practise wherever you like. If what you do is good, it's good everywhere." These words from Ilmari Tapiovaara sum up his philosophy and his career. The experience of working as a young man with Aalto and Le Corbusier, and later with Mies van der Rohe, fostered his own professionalism; rather than indulging in high-flown theory, he has seen the designer's task as making the object right for its job, efficient and economic but with "a sense of dimension and intellectual readiness." His almost accidental involvement after the war with mass-produced furniture for export led him to extend the principle of economic fitness to the economics of packaging; this additional element of design led in its turn to such things as the Domus chair which is packable, stackable, economic in its use of timber technology, and, above all, comfortable to use and good to look at. With 750,000 made between 1946 and 1965 this is a piece of furniture worthy to rank with the best of Aalto, Breuer, and Mies van der Rohe.

Some fifteen years after the Domus chair came another, even more refined use of wood—the Wilhelmina chair of 1959. Perhaps the most elegant of all his designs, it is a superb combination of use and economy. Tapiovaara's ingenuity was by now in full spate; simultaneously with the Wilhelmina chair, he produced the Kiki range of stools, chairs, and tables, all based on a simple steel frame with seat and back covered in leather or fabric, widely variable and still capable of easy packing and stacking.

It was about the time of these designs that Tapiovaara, through his work with the International Labour Office, first became concerned with aiding underdeveloped countries by designing ranges of furniture for export using native materials, exploiting and adapting high-quality hand-craftsmanship. From projects in Paraguay and Mauritius, his commitment to this service has become worldwide. He believes fervently in the value of international design cooperation, and this is arguably his greatest contribution. His own example of economic design, inspired by sensitivity to materials and to the product in use, is now mainly devoted to the furtherance of international aid—to "the process of renewal that's going on in the world. The world uses goods up rapidly because it wants a more rational environment. Fortunately, we're moving from excess towards economy and at the same time towards better quality, a higher standard of living." he asserts.

—Gordon Steele

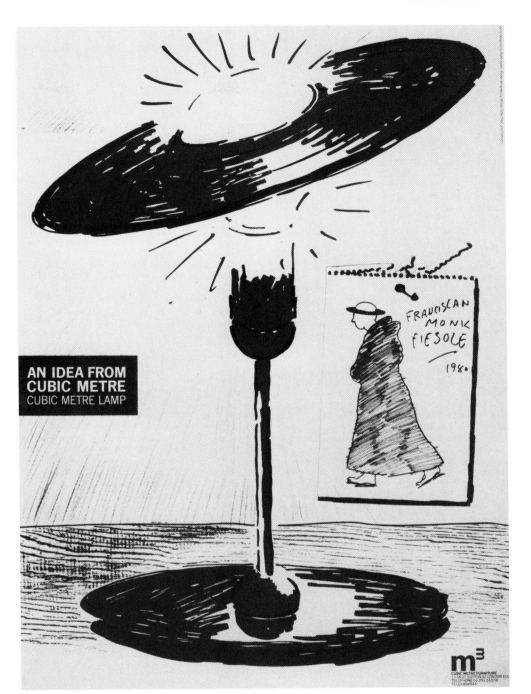

Brian Tattersfield: Poster for Cubic Metre Furniture, London, 1980

TATTERSFIELD, Brian.

British graphic, interior and industrial designer. Born in Heckmondwike, Yorkshire, 12 April 1936. Educated at Heckmondwike Grammar School, until 1953; studied at Batley School of Art, Yorkshire, 1953–57: NDD 1957; Royal College of Art, London, 1959–62: ARCA 1962. Served in the Royal Air Force, 1957–59. Married Mary Wakelin in 1964; daughters: Jane and Emma. Art director, at Young and Rubicam agency, London, 1962–63; designer, at Fletcher/Forbes/Gill design partnership, in Geneva, 1963–64; founder-partner, with Marcello Minale, of Minale Tattersfield and Partners design firm, London, from 1964. Visiting lecturer, Royal College of Art, London; governor, Norwich School of Art, Norfolk. **Exhibitions:** Design Centre, London, 1979; *Penguin Books*, Manchester Polytechnic, 1981; Museo d'Arte Contemporanea, Milan, 1983. **Collections:** Poster Museum, Warsaw; Museum of Modern Art, New York; Victoria and Albert Museum, London. Recipient: Silver Medals, Design and Art Directors Association, London 1972–82; Gold Medal, Art Directors Club of New York, 1977. Fellow, Chartered Society of Designers, London. Address: Minale Tattersfield and Partners, The Courtyard, 37 Sheen Road, Richmond, Surrey TW9 1AJ, England.

I firmly believe that good design should touch the lives of everyone, not only in the form of expensively tasteful objects, but in everyday things like knives and forks, comfortable chairs, cornflake packets.

Too much design concerns itself with nostalgia, or the fantasy of tomorrow, instead of making the realities of today more bearable.

—Brian Tattersfield

See MINALE, Marcello.

TAVOULARIS, Dean.

American film designer. Born in Lowell, Massachusetts, in 1932. Studied architecture, at Otis Art Institute, Los Angeles, 1950–54. Worked in the animation department, then on live production films, at Walt Disney Studios, Hollywood, California, until 1963; assistant designer, then art director, at Columbia Studios and Warner Studios, Hollywood, from 1964. Recipient: Academy Award, 1974. Address: c/o Academy of Motion Picture Arts and Sciences, 8949 Wilshire Boulevard, Beverly Hills, California 90211, U.S.A.

Works:

Film productions include—*Ship of Fools* (Kramer), 1965; *Inside Daisy Clover* (Mulligan), 1965; *Bonnie and Clyde* (Penn), 1967; *Candy* (Marquand), 1968; *Petulia* (Lester), 1968; *Zabriskie Point* (Antonioni), 1970; *Little Big Man* (Penn), 1970; *The Godfather* (Penn), 1972; *The Conversation* (Coppola), 1974; *The Godfather Part II* (Coppola), 1974; *Farewell, My Lovely* (Richards), 1975; *Apocalypse Now* (Coppola), 1978; *The Brink's Job* (Friedkin), 1978; *One From the Heart* (Coppola), 1982; *The Escape Artist* (Deschanel), 1982; *Hammett* (Wenders), 1982; *The Outsiders* (Coppola), 1983; *Rumble Fish* (Coppola), 1983; *Testament* (Littman), 1983.

Publications:

By TAVOULARIS: article—in *Positif* (Paris), September 1979.

On TAVOULARIS: books—*Le Décor de Film* by Leon Barsacq, Paris 1970, as *Caligari's Cabinet and Other Grand Illusions*, Boston 1976; *International Dictionary of Films and Filmmakers*, Chicago and London 1987, 1991.

TER-ARUTUNIAN, Rouben.

American stage designer. Born of Armenian parents, in Tiflis, Russia, 24 July 1920; emigrated to the United States in 1951: naturalized, 1957. Educated at schools in Berlin, 1927–38; studied piano, Berlin, from 1939; studied design, at the Reimann Art School, Berlin, 1939–41; film music, at the Musik Hochschule, and art history and theatre arts, at the Friedrich Wilhelm University, Berlin, 1941–43; University of Vienna, 1943–45; painting and sculpture, at the Ecole des Beaux-Arts, Académie Julien and at the Académie de la Grande Chaumière, Paris, 1945–50. Designer of stage sets and costumes, and club interiors, for the United States Third Army Special Services, in Heidelberg, 1945–47; jewellery designer for Harry Winston, New York, 1951; sketch artist, at Staples and Smith display firm, New York, 1951; staff designer, at CBS Television, 1951–53, ABC Television, 1953, and at NBC Television, New York, 1954–57; freelance stage, film and television designer, New York, from 1957. **Exhibitions:** Wright/Hepburn/Webster Gallery, New York, 1968; Canyon Road Art Gallery, Santa Fe, New Mexico, 1968; Vincent Astor Gallery, Lincoln Center, New York, 1970. **Collections:** Museum of Modern Art, New York; Houghton Library, Harvard University, Cambridge, Massachusetts; Library and Museum of Performing Arts, Lincoln Center, New York. Recipient: Emmy Award, New York, 1957; Outer Critics' Circle Award, New York, 1958; Armenian Bicentennial Award, 1976. Address: 360 East 55th Street, Apt. 15, New York, New York 10022, U.S.A.

Works:

Set and costume designs (New York, unless noted) include—*King John* and *Measure for Measure*, 1956; *Othello*, *Merchant of Venice*, and *Much Ado About Nothing*, 1957; *Twelfth Night* and *Antony and Cleopatra*, 1960, all at *The American Shakespeare Festival*, Stratford, Connecticut; *New Girl in Town*, 1957; *Who Was That Lady I Saw You With?*, 1958; *Redhead*, 1959; *Advise and Consent*, 1960; *A Passage to India*, 1962; *Arturo Ui*, 1963; *The Milktrain Doesn't Stop Here Anymore*, 1964; *The Deputy*, 1964; *The Devils*, 1965; *Ivanov*, London, 1965, and New York, 1966; *Medea*, Rome, 1966; *Exit the King*, 1967; *All Over*, 1971; *Leibelei*, 1972, and *Anatol*, 1973, both at Akademie Theater, Vienna; *Good Time Charley*, 1975; *The Lady from the Sea*, 1976; *The Lady from Dubuque*, 1980; opera and lyric presentations—*The Bartered Bride*, Volksoper, Dresden, 1943; *Salome*, Volksoper, Vienna, 1944; *Bluebeard's Castle*, and *L'Heure Espagnole*, 1952, *La Cenerentola*, 1953, and *The Trial*, 1953, all New York City Opera; *Maria Golovin*, at the World's Fair, Brussels, 1958 (travelled to Teatro all Scala, Milan); *Blood Moon*, San Francisco Opera, 1961; *Orpheus and Euridice*, Staatsoper, Hamburg, 1963; *The Play of Herod*, New York Pro Musica, The Cloisters of the Metropolitan Museum of Art, 1963; *Pelléas et Melisande*, at the *Festival of Two Worlds*, Spoleto, Italy, 1966; *The Bassarids*, 1968 (sets only), and *The Devils of Loudun*, 1969, both Santa Fe Opera; *Pelléas et Mélisande*, Teatro alla Scala, Milan, 1973 (travelled to Teatro La Fenice, Venice, 1973, and Teatro all'Opera, Rome, 1974); *Pelléas et Mélisande*, Opéra de Monte Carlo, 1976 (travelled to Teatro Regio, Turin, 1979); *Dido and Aeneas*, New York City Opera, 1979; *Die Liebe der Danae*, Santa Fe Opera, 1982; dance—costume designs for soloists of the Berlin State Opera Ballet, 1941; *Getantze Malerei*, Vera Mahlke Ballet Company, Dresden and Berlin, 1942; *Concerto*, Ballet of the Opéra Comique, Paris, 1950; *Souvenirs*, 1955 and *Seven Deadly Sins*, 1958, both New York City Ballet; *Fibers*, Paul Taylor Dance Company, 1960; *Samson Agonistes*, Martha Graham Company, 1961; *Pierrot Lunaire*, Glen Tetley Company, 1962; *The Nutcracker*, 1964 (sets only), and *Harlequinade*, 1965, both New York City Ballet; *Ricercare*, American Ballet Theatre, 1966; *Firebird*, Harkness Ballet, 1967; *Requiem Canticle*, New York City Ballet, 1968; *Transitions*, Operhaus, Cologne, 1969; *The Unicorn, the Gorgon, and the Manticore*, at the Festival of Two Worlds, Spoleto, Italy, 1970; *Chronochromie*, Staatsoper, Hamburg, 1971; *The Song of the Nightingale*, *Symphony of Psalms*, and special decor for closing night, all for the New York City Ballet, at the *Stravinsky Festival*, 1972; *Laborintus*, Royal Opera House, London, 1972; *Chopiniana*, New York City Ballet, 1972 (not produced); *Remembrances*, City Center Joffrey Ballet, 1973; *Voluntaries*, Stuttgart Ballet, 1973; *Dybbuk Variations*, and *Coppelia*, both New York City Ballet, 1974; *Pulcinella*, reconstruction of Picasso designs, City Center Joffrey Ballet, 1974; *The Real McCoy*, Eliot Feld Ballet, 1975; *The Mooche*, Alvin Ailey Dance Theater, 1975 (sets only); *Union Jack*, New York City Ballet, 1976; *Vienna Waltzes*, New York City Ballet, 1977 (sets only); *Sphinx*, American Ballet Theatre, 1977 (sets only); *Pierrot Lunaire*, BBC-TV, 1978; *L'Après-Midi d'un faune*, Joffrey Ballet and London Festival Ballet, 1979; *Night Piece*, Maggio Musicale, Florence, 1979; *Robert Schumann's Davidsbündlertänze*, New York City Ballet, 1980; *Souvenir de Florence*, *Mozartiana* (costumes only), and *Adagio Lamentoso*, all for New York City Ballet, at the Tchaikovsky Festival, 1981; *Noah and the Flood*, for the New York City Ballet, at the Stravinsky Centennial Celebration, 1982; *Sphinx*, National Ballet of Canada, 1983; *Romantic Pieces*, San Francisco Ballet, 1983; *Components*, National Ballet of Canada, 1984; *Ballet Imperial*, American Ballet Theatre, Chicago, 1988. Television—*This Is Show Business* (sets only), 1951; *The Bert Parks Show*, (sets only), 1952; *Toast of the Town* (sets only), 1952; and *Studio One*, 1952–53, all series for CBS-TV; *The Abduction from the Seraglio*, NBC Opera, 1954; *The Magic Flute*, NBC Opera, 1956; *The Taming of the Shrew*, for Hallmark Hall of Fame series, NBC, 1956; *Twelfth Night*, for Hallmark Hall of Fame series, NBC, 1957; *Swing into Spring*, CBS, 1958; *The Tempest*, for Hallmark Hall of Fame series, NBC, 1959; *Maria Golovin*, NBC Opera, 1959; *A Musical Bouquet for Maurice Chevalier* (sets only), CBS, 1960; *Noah and the Flood*, CBS, 1962; *The Art of the Prima Donna*, (for Bell Telephone Hour), NBC, 1966; *Marlene Dietrich: I Wish You Love*, BBC and CBS, 1973; *Rachel La Cubana*, NET Opera, 1973; *Other Dances* (sets only), for Dance in America series, NET-TV, 1979; films—*The Loved One*, MGM/Filmways, (production and costume design), 1964–65; *Such Good Friends* (production design only), Paramount Pictures, 1971.

Publications:

On TER-ARUTUNIAN: books—*Stravinsky and the Dance*, New York 1962; *Stravinsky and the Theatre*, New York 1963; *Rouben Ter-Arutunian: Theater Designs*, exhibition catalogue with preface by Gian Carlo Menotti, New York 1970; *From Script to Stage* by Randolph Goodman, New York 1971; *Stage Design* by Howard Bay, New York 1974; *Designing and Planning for the Theatre* by Lynn Pektal, New York 1976; *Stage Design Throughout the World 1970–1975* by Rene Hainaux and Nicole Leclercq, Brussels and London 1976; *Theatrical Evolution 1776–1976* by Kenneth Spritz, New York 1976; *Spotlight: Four Centuries of Ballet Costume* by Richard Buckle and others, London 1981.

I have searched to find a visual complement to drama, poetry, music, and movement by means of organization of the cubic space of the stage and the dressing of the human body—hopefully with simplicity, clarity, and a certain element of mystery.

—Rouben Ter-Arutunian

Although born in Tiflis, Soviet Georgia, internationally famous Rouben Ter-Arutunian is a distinctly American set and costume designer for stage, film, and television. Fifteen at the time, he became enamoured of his future profession while viewing Colonel de Basil's Ballets Russes as the company toured the Diaghilev repertoire through Europe in the 1930s. Due in part to this stimulus, he subsequently studied the humanities at the Universities of Berlin and Vienna and also classical painting at the Ecole des Beaux Arts in Paris. After World War I, he worked for the Special Services division of the United States Third Army. Soon after coming to America, Ter-Arutunian began his professional life by designing commercials and soap operas for CBS Television in 1951.

In considering the possibilities for design in the service of dance, Ter-Arutunian came to distinguish four basic approaches: "the classic," employs a decor-les stage; "the romantic," which uses realistic-illusionistic devices; "the sculptural," which uses three-dimensional scenery; and "the decorative," which derives from the easel-painting tradition. In practice, Ter-

Rouben Ter-Arutunian: Set for George Balanchine's ballet *The Nutcracker*, **New York City Ballet, 1964.**

Arutunian has designed settings which range from "the decorative" to "the sculptural," combining "romantic" and "classic" principles.

Ter-Arutunian's now-legendary *Nutcracker* for the New York City Ballet, an organization for which he is especially fond of working, exemplifies a primarily "decorative" approach, as do his designs for *Coppelia*. His production for Glenn Tetley's *Ricercare*, which was produced for American Ballet Theater, is an example of "the sculptural," his preferred mode at its best. When the curtain opens, the audience is confronted with a half-moon-shaped object, in which the dancers lay down. It is a symbolic, minimal object which summarizes the meaning of the dance but does not dominate the stage or "crowd" the dancers. Ter-Arutunian believes that plenty of space on stage should be organized around minimal scenery. His concern for the use of space, no doubt, led him to design the permanent stage for the American Shakespeare Festival.

Ter-Arutunian's work on Edward Albee's *All Over* on Broadway shows the creative approach which the designer employs. Instead of designing the realistic interior originally specified by the playwright, he decided to begin at the essence of the situation, using only those pieces of furniture which were necessary. Clive Barnes, in the *New York Times*, remarked,

"The staging was perfect in its sensibility, Rouben Ter-Arutunian's setting has exactly the same sparse elegance as the play." In the ballet *Vienna Waltzes*, Ter-Arutunian's strength of imagination was evident in his use of mylar-mirrored, crystal chandeliers which were transformed out of the trees of a forest. In the hundreds of designs credited to Ter-Arutunian, the mark of his genius is that he never repeats himself.

—Tom Mikotowicz

TERRAZAS (de la Pena), Eduardo.
Mexican architect, interior, exhibition and graphic designer. Born in Guadalajara, Jalisco, 5 March 1936. Studied architecture, at the Universidad Nacional Autonoma de Mexico, Mexico City, 1954–58; Cornell University, Ithaca, New York, 1958–59: M.Arch. 1959; University of Rome, 1959–60; Centre Scientifique et Tech-

nique du Bâtiment, Paris, 1961–62. Worked as an architect in the offices of Howell, Killick and Partridge, London, 1961, Candilis, Josic and Woods, Paris, 1962, Pedro Ramirez Vazquez and Rafael Mijarez, New York, 1963–64, and office George Nelson, New York, 1965; founder-director, Eduardo Terrazas y Asociados, Mexico City, from 1966: technical director, INDECO National Institute for Community Development and Housing, Mexico City, 1971, and AURIS Institute for Urban Action and Social Integration, Mexico City, 1972–73; consultant to the City Development Authority, Karachi, and to the Capital Development Authority, Islamabad, 1974. Director of the New Alternatives Institute, Mexico City; co-founder and secretary general, Centro Tepotztlan, Mexico, 1980. Professor of architectural design Columbia University, New York, 1963–66; visiting lecturer at design institutions and congresses in Mexico, Canada, United States, India, etc.. from 1969. **Exhibitions:** Palacio Nacional de Bellas Artes, Mexico City, 1971; Knoll International, Paris, 1973; Museo Nacional de Bellas Artes, Santiago, 1973; Museo Nacional de Arte, La Paz, 1973; Galeria Fundacion Eugenio Mendoza, Caracas, 1974; Benjamin Franklin Library, Mexico City, 1975 (with Arnaldo Coen); Museo de Alhondiga de Granaditas, Guanajuato, 1975 (with Arnaldo

Coen). Address: Eduardo Terrazas y Asociados, Cordoba 23N, Mexico 7, D.F., Mexico.

Works:

Masterpieces of Mexican Art touring exhibition layouts, in the Soviet Union, Poland and France, 1961–62.
Mexican Pavilion, at the 1964 World's Fair, New York, 1963–64.
Mexican Pavilion, at the XIV Milan Triennale, 1968.
Mexico 68 publications and unified identity programme, for the Olympic Games, Mexico City, 1966–69.
Mexican Image city-wide exhibition displays, Mexico City, 1969.
Logotype symbol, for the IX World Cup Football Championship, Mexico City, 1969.
Visual identity graphics, for the Secretariat of Press and Propaganda, Mexico City, 1975–76.
Family Planning publicity campaign, for the United Nations, 1976.
Architecture of Public Spaces urban roads and signage program, for Alternativas XXI Incorporated, Mexico City, 1979.
Macro Plaza urban renewal plan, for the City of Monterrey, 1981.
Logotype, visual identity programme and conference hall design, for the North-South International Cooperation Congress, Cancun, 1981.

Publications:

On TERRAZAS: books—*World Architecture One*, edited by John Donat, London 1964; *Art of the Environment*, edited by Gyorgy Kepes, New York 1972; *Spazio e Società*, edited by Giancarlo de Carlo, Milan 1978; *Archigraphia: Architectural and Environmental Graphics*, edited by Walter Herdeg, Zurich 1978; *The language of Graphics* by Edward Booth-Clibborn and Daniele Baroni, London 1980.

Eduardo Terrazas is a many-faceted creative planner, architect, painter, and designer whose wide experience and activities have led to important interactions with his own culture in Mexico, as well as with other countries and cultures. His many innovative and seminal programs have influenced the thinking and planning of wide-ranging activities reflecting the advancing industrialization and the social and cultural life of Mexico.

On the occasion of the opening of the Mexico Metro system, his exhibition *Imagen Mexico* was a spectacular testimony to his graphic imagination. In the poster for it, silkscreened on aluminized paper, with a multicolored background of arrows, the letters which make up the title are dropped out so that they make an overall pattern which reveals the aluminum. Thus, the viewer is reflected in the poster and becomes part of the image. This was produced in a single size (12″ × 12″) and used in multiples of up to four feet square.

At times working independently in his own office, Alternativas XXI, at times working for the Government of Mexico, he has been a true cultural ambassador by serving, for instance, as the Director of Technical Assistance provided by Mexican Government to the government of Tanzania for the design and construction of its new capital city Dodoman. This project included urban design, an architectural system for schools, and renovation of existing settlements. At home, he has combined his urban and graphic concerns in such projects as the System of Urban Furnishings, Signs, Symbols and Gardens for the orderly circulation system

through the streets of Mexico City and the Dialogue North-South for the Cancun Conference.

His disciplines are never separate. Prolific and richly gifted, he is at once theoretician, teacher, and artist in his analytical projects which have application to his own country as well as to other expanding and developing nations.

—Mildred Constantine

TESTA, Armando.
Italian graphic designer. Born in Turin, 23 March 1917. Apprenticed to a locksmith, 1928–29, sheet metal worker, 1930, and typesetter, Turin, 1931–33; studied under Ezio d'Errico, at the Vigliardi Paravia School of Graphic Arts, Turin, 1932–34. Served as an aerial photographer in the Italian Air Force, 1940–43. Married Lidia de Barberis in 1945; children: Delfina, Marco and Antonella; married Gemma de Angelis in 1978. Freelance designer, establishing own graphics studio, Turin, 1946–56, and Armando Testa S.p.A. advertising agency, Turin, from 1956: designed for Martini & Rossi, Carpano, Pirelli, Borsalino, Punt e Mes, Antonetto, Citterino, Euchessina, Simmenthal, San Pellegrino, *Graphicus*, *Publitransport*, etc. Instructor in graphic design and contemporary art, at the Polytechnic Institute, Turin, 1965–75. **Exhibitions:** Poster Museum, Warsaw, 1972; *Italian Re-Evolution*, La Jolla Museum of Art, California, 1982; Padiglione d'Arte Contemporanea, Milan, 1984; *Italie d'Aujourd'hui*, Villa Arson, Nice, 1985; Mole Antonelliana, Turin, 1985; Maison Gerbollier, La Salle, 1986; Parsons School of Design, New York, 1987; Niccoli Art Gallery, Parma, 1987; *Reklama 88*, Moscow, 1988; Otis Parsons School of Design, Los Angeles, 1988; Circulo de Bellas Artes, Madrid, 1989. **Collections:** Poster Museum, Trento; Communications Archive, University of Parma; Kunstmuseum, Munich; Stedelijk Museum, Amsterdam; Poster Museum, Warsaw; Moravian Gallery, Brno; Colorado State University, Fort Collins; Rufino Tamayo Museum, Mexico City. Recipient: ICI Poster Competition Prize, Milan, 1937; Olympic Games Poster Competition Prize, Rome, 1960; Italian Ministry of Culture Medal, 1968; Warsaw Poster Biennale Prize, 1970; Federazione Italiana Pubblicita Medal, Milan, 1974; Poster Prize, Associazione Aziende Pubblicitarie Italiene, Milan, 1982. Address: Corso Quintino Sella 56, 10131 Turin, Italy.

Works:

ICI Industria Colori e Inchiostri poster project, for ICI Printing Inks, Milan, 1937.
Martini Rooster poster, for Gallo Martini, 1948.
"Elephant" poster, for Pirelli Tyres, 1954.
Giochi della XVII Olimpiade poster, for the 1960 Rome Olympics, 1959.
Globe-and-a-half poster, for Punt e Mes, 1960.
Caballero and *Carmencita* television commercial characters modelled in plaster, for Cafe Paulista, 1965.
Pippo television commercial hippopotamus dummy in polyurethane resin, for Lines diapers, 1966–67.
Plast 72 poster, for the plastics exhibition, Milan, 1969.
"Finger in Water" cover design, for *Graphicus* magazine, 1969.

Trademark, for Perugina Candies, 1971.
"Shadow-figure" poster, for Amnesty International, 1979.
Trademark, for Urama Simmonds mechanical engineering company, 1982.
Poster and trademark, for *Avanti* newspaper, 1983.
Magia exhibition poster, for the Municipality of Milan, 1984.
Torino Ufficio exhibition poster, for the Annual Office Furniture Show, Turin, 1985.
Trademark and symbol, for Sanlorenzo haute couture, 1987.
Logotype symbol, for the Castello di Rivoli museum of contemporary art, Turin, 1988.
MACAM poster, for the Museum of Contemporary Art, Magliano, 1988.
Linea 3 billboard poster series, for the new Milan underground train line, 1989.

Publications:

By TESTA: articles—in *Campaign Europe* (London), December 1979; *Publirama Italiano 1979* (Milan), 1980; *Pubblicità Domani* (Milan), March 1982; *Campaign* (Milan), November/December 1982; *Il Giornale dell'Arte* (Turin), May 1983, June 1983; *Graphicus* (Turin), March 1985; *Epoca* (Milan), June 1987.

On TESTA: books—*Packaging: An International Survey Package Design*, edited by Walter Herdeg, Zurich 1959; *Window Display, 2*, edited by Walter Herdeg, Zurich 1961; *The Poster: An Illustrated History from 1860* by Harold F. Hutchinson, London and Toronto 1968; *Armando Testa* by Gillo Dorfles and others, Milan 1984; *Armando Testa: Il Segno e la Pubblicità*, exhibition catalogue by Omar Calabrese and others, Turin 1985; *Armando Testa: 40 Years of Italian Creative Design* by Gillo Dorfles and Arturo Carlo Quintavalle, Turin 1987; *Alle Radici della Comunicazione Visiva Italiana* by Heinz Waibl, Milan 1988.

As an artist I never wanted to have a personal style. I preferred to explore all the paths of visual communication using, without distinction, painting, drawing, or photography. Although I admired the great poster designers of the past, I have always felt drawn to every new avant-garde experience which I have tried to apply in advertising.

In the first year of my advertising activity, I had to temper my love for avant-garde art in order to create more direct and synthetic messages which could reach prospects' minds in a stronger way. I started an activity that became a real poster and advertising school for young designers in Italy.

In my "free"—not advertising—works I like to elaborate visually and make use of the same materials I must everyday enhance in my ads or posters. So I designed such things as the "ham-armchair" which was published in *Life* magazine, or the "sausage-eye" and the "putto."

After many years of photographs, of outlined images, of strong and direct advertising messages, I wish today to be a bit more ambiguous and to be able to return to painting with the same energy I used in my life as a poster designer.

—Armando Testa

Armando Testa is a person with intense interest in the world around him. This type is unique in the world of design, where talented people are constantly questioning how things are put together and striving for new and better ways to do things. Nevertheless, Testa manages to be a leading example of the voracious appetite for new experiences.

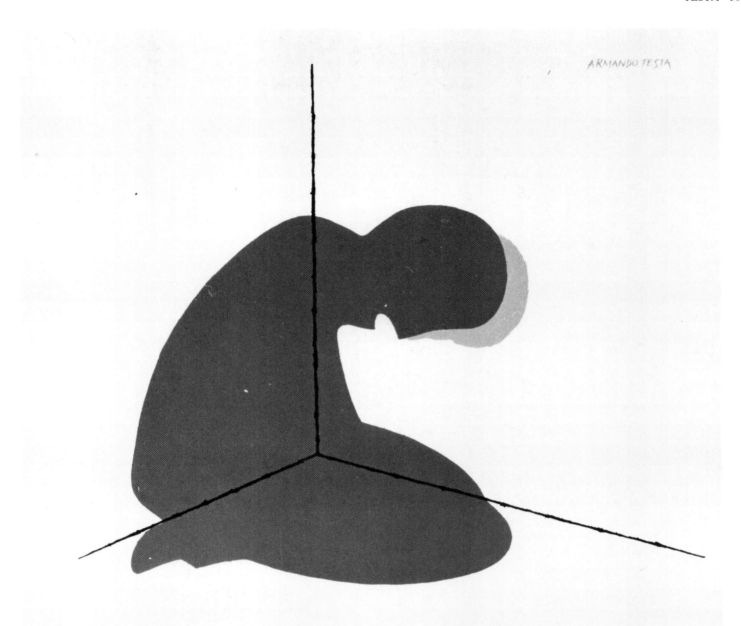

Armando Testa: Poster for Amnesty International, 1979

Very little passes by Testa that does not set his mind to work. Whatever he sees that he admires, he would like to have been the one who did it. Testa would, for example, be just as pleased to be doing medieval liturgical paintings as his playful, modern posters. In fact, that he would do either or both would satisfy his great motivation to "do it all."

As head of one of Italy's leading advertising agencies, Testa is involved with the full range of promotion. This has taken him into all media, which presents him with constant opportunity to do the same old things in different and unusual ways. But at the same time, it limits his time to do the other-Testa things, works that are expressions of his own personal interests and tastes.

In these things, here again, Testa is Testa, off in his own world, carefully distilling the essence of every situation, applying his own thought processes, and developing unique solutions. Bizarre is better than banal with Testa.

He can play with a single idea in endless variations. His exploration of the uses, some really far-fetched, of the tip of a finger (the pointer finger) have exploited just about every possibility. Testa has put his "fingers" to work in non-commercial serigraphs, personal greeting cards, promotion for his agency, and in advertisements for his clients.

In Testa's eye, the view is just a bit different. Throughout Italy, designers recognize Testa's individuality and divide into camps, for and against. His work does not encourage apathy.

—Jerry Steimle

THOMASS, Chantal.

French fashion designer. Born Chantal Genty, in Malakoff, Seine, 4 September 1947. Mainly self-taught in design. Married Bruce Thomass in 1967; children: Louise and Robin. Worked as a secretary, Paris, 1965–66; freelance clothing designer, selling to Dorothée Bis in Paris, and Le Café des Arts in Saint-Tropez, 1966–68; partner, with Bruce Thomass, in Ter et Bantine fashion company, Paris, 1968–76; founder-director, Société Chantal Thomass fashion firm, Paris, from 1976. Member, Chambre Syndicale de la Couture, Paris, from 1981. Chevalier des Arts et Lettres, France. Addresses: (office) 100 rue du Cherche-Midi, 75006 Paris; (home) 12 rue Armangaud, 92210 Saint-Cloud, France.

Publications:

On THOMASS: books—*Fairchild's Who's Who in Fashion*, edited by Anne Stegemeyer, New York 1980; *Fashion 2001* by Lucille Khornak, London 1982; *French Style* by Suzanne Slesin and Stafford Cliff, New York and London 1982; *McDowell's Directory of Twentieth Century Fashion* by Colin McDowell, London 1984; *The Encyclopaedia of Fashion from 1840 to the 1980s* by Georgina O'Hara, London 1986.

Of this husband-and-wife team, Bruce Thomass was the one with training at the Ecole des Beaux Arts, while Chantal herself was a secretary who grew bored with her job and wanted to do something creative, although she did not know a pattern from a toile. She may be regarded as an instinctive designer rather than one with an intellectual approach. Prettiness is important to her, as is typified by her lingerie which includes silk petticoats and lashings of lace. She says she designs for the young woman who wants to look young and who is feminine and reasonably romantic, so her concept of woman is very conservative.

There have not been any important attempts in her work to discover a new look; rather, she reinterprets many existing styles, as can be seen in her North African pantaloons, oriental embroidered black taffeta gowns, the hacking habit presented in rose-pink wool, Victorian lace hemlines on embroidered satin dresses, a Scottish kilt and jacket done in huge checks, a 1950s shawl collar on a lambswool coat, and a 1950s siren look in a cerise cotton frock bedecked with too many rows of white beads. Regularly featured in her collections are trousers, such as the 1978 blue pantaloons with T-shirt, the 1979 print trousers with matching long coat, and the clinging cotton jersey overalls, more subtly seductive than revealing. Accordingly, Thomass is a safe designer, who is not trying to overthrow the existing order, but who tries to create attractive versions of current garments.

This traditional path is one that has proved successful for many designers to follow, for what revolutionary designers often forget is that the customers who can afford to buy original creations are usually women in their middle ages or over. Thus, while Chantal may have young women in mind, her clothes will be bought mainly by their mothers who prefer a traditional approach. A reputation for invention is not all-important in dress design, for a traditional garment presented in a different material or colour from usual will appeal to many. A slight variation can be novelty enough.

—Diana de Marly

THOMPSON, Bradbury.

American graphic designer. Born in Topeka, Kansas, 25 March 1911. Studied at Washburn University, Topeka, 1930–34: BA 1934. Served as a designer in the United States Office of War Information, 1942–45. Married Della Deen Dodge in 1939; children: Leslie, Mark, David and Elizabeth. Art director, for Capper Publishers, 1934–38, and for Rogers-Kellogg-Stilson agency, 1938–42; freelance graphic designer and art director, New York, from 1945: consultant to *Art News*, Westvaco Corporation, Pitney-Bowes, Famous Artists Schools, Time-Life Books, McGraw-Hill, Field Enterprises, Cornell University, etc. Visiting critic, Yale School of Art and Architecture, New Haven, Connecticut, from 1956. Advisory board member, Parsons School of Design, New York, 1945–55; governing board member, Philadelphia Museum College of Art, 1956–59; board member, Perrot Memorial Library, from 1966; member of the First Federal Design Assembly, 1973, and the University American Arbitration Association, 1976–78; trustee, Washburn University, Topeka, from 1972.

Former vice-president, Art Directors Club of New York. **Exhibitions:** American Institute of Graphic Arts, New York, 1959, 1975; Washburn University, Topeka, Kansas, 1964; Cornell University, Ithaca, New York, 1969; Harvard University, Cambridge, Massachusetts, 1965; Yale University, New Haven, Connecticut, 1976; Museum of Modern Art, New York, 1977. **Collection:** Museum of Modern Art, New York. Recipient: New York Art Directors Club Medal, 1945, 1947, 1951, 1955, and Hall of Fame Award, 1973; American Institute of Graphic Arts Award, 1948 and Gold Medal, 1975; National Society of Art Directors Gold T-square Award, 1950; Silver Medal, 1963, and Gold Medal, 1965, Bienal of Sao Paulo. Address: Jones Park, Riverside, Connecticut 06878, U.S.A.

Works:

Westvaco Inspirations magazine design and layouts, for the West Virginia Pulp and Paper Company, 1938–62.
Mademoiselle magazine design and layouts, New York, 1945–49.
Art News magazine and annual design and layouts, New York, 1945–72.
Freedom of the American Road single-issue magazine design, for Ford Motor Company, 1955.
Print magazine cover design, New York, January/February 1962.
Harvard Business Review magazine design and layouts, Cambridge, Massachusetts, 1965–67.
Library of America book design, for Time-Life Books, New York, 1966.
Food of the World book design, for Time-Life Books, New York, 1966.
The Swing Era book design, for Time-Life Books, 1970.
The Washburn Bible book design, for Washburn University Press, Topeka, 1982–83.

Publications:

By THOMPSON: books—*The Monalphabet*, New York 1945; *Modern Painting and Typography*, New York 1947; *Alphabet 26*, New York 1950.

On THOMPSON: books—*Posters: 50 Artists and Designers*, edited by W. H. Allner, New York 1952; *The New Graphic Design* by Karl Gerstner and Markus Kutter, Teufen and London 1959; *The Design Concept* by Allan Hurlburt, New York 1981; *Who's Who in Graphic Art*, edited by Walter Amstutz, Dubendorf 1982; *A History of Graphic Design* by Philip B. Meggs, New York and London 1983; *Typographic Design: Form and Communication* by Rob Carter, Ben Day and Philip Meggs, New York 1985; *Nine Pioneers in American Graphic Design* by Roger R. Remington and Barbara Hodik, Cambridge, Massachusetts 1989.

The elegant and quiet work of Bradbury Thompson very much reflects the person. His influence on the printed page carries on a noble and distinguished tradition. The design of a book often tests the abilities and skills of a designer, yet Thompson has made that medium his art form and has created innumerable classics, culminating in the recently completed *Washburn Holy Bible*.

In 1958, the West Virginia Paper and Pulp Company began production of a series of limited edition books based on great American classics. This unique series served the two-fold purpose of demonstrating the quality of Westvaco's papers and of serving as Christmas souvenirs to its customers and friends. Each six by nine-and-one-half-inch volume is slip-cased, creating an elegant effect, along with additional touches such as head bands, end sheets, and a colophon. One of the editions of Edgar Allen Poe contains four of his tales, each designed in an unusual and individual way. Thompson carefully integrated type, paper, color, and illustration to achieve an attractive and cohesive balance between the visual and written elements. In the tale of "The Great Balloon Hoax," the entire layout is treated like a newspaper article of the period, with the text, arranged in columns, accompanied by appropriate headlines and line drawings. Color, texture of paper, and illustration add richness to the page and story.

Drama plays a special part in Thompson's creation for Stephen Crane's *Red Badge of Courage*, which displays an unusual but appropriate graphic element—a bullet hole! After much historical research experimentation, Thompson felt this rather violent symbol would serve as an effective device to represent the horrors of war. The effect was attained with a carefully drilled hole through the volume.

Westvaco's edition of Benjamin Franklin's writing is another marvelous example of typographic experimentation. The treatment is appropriate to the subject, and Thompson's use of large type creates a harmonious, overall pattern. Full-page Diderot engravings beautifully complement the opposing text pages to produce highly textual and effective spreads.

The overall mood created in each of the twenty-four volumes is very special. The visual effects do not in any way impede reading but rather, enhance the enjoyment and appreciation of these classics. The foreword to each issue contains a concise analysis of the design concept and so invites the reader to observe the mind of the designer.

—D. Ichiyama

THYGESEN, Rud.

Danish architect, interior and furniture designer. Born in Saeby, 15 August 1932. Studied at the Handels-school, Copenhagen, 1953–57; School of Arts and Crafts (Kunsthandvaerkskolan), Copenhagen, 1962–66: Dip. 1966. Married to Lillian Simonsen. Freelance furniture designer, establishing design studio with Johnny Sørensen, in Copenhagen, from 1967; has designed for Mogens Kold, Domus Danica, Erik Boisen, Per Jorgensen, Textil Lassen, Magnus Olesen, Zon International, etc. **Exhibitions:** Den Permanente, Copenhagen, 1972; Danske Kunstindustrimuseum, Copenhagen, 1976; Museum of Contemporary Crafts, Chicago, 1977; *Scandinavian Modern Design 1880–1980*, Cooper-Hewitt Museum, New York, 1982 (toured); *Denmark in Britain: Design and Architecture*, Business Design Centre, London, 1989. **Collections:** Nordenfjeldske Kunstindustrimuseum, Trondheim; Statens Kunstfond, Copenhagen; Kunstindustrimuseet, Copenhagen. Recipient: First Prize, Society of Cabinetmakers Exhibition, Copenhagen, 1866, 1968; Central Bank Jubilee Award, Copenhagen, 1969, 1975; Alex Foss Industrifond Award, Copenhagen, 1976. Address: Ostergade 26 C, 1100 Copenhagen K. Denmark.

See SØRENSEN, Johnny.

Rosmarie Tissi: Logo for an architect's office, 1980

TISSI, Rosmarie.

Swiss typography and graphic designer. Born in Scaffhausen, 13 February 1937. Studied design, at the Kunstgewerbeschule, Zurich, 1954–55. Apprentice, 1955–59, and designer, 1959–68, in Siegfried Odermatt design studio, Zurich; partner, with Siegfried Odermatt, in Odermatt and Tissi design studio, Zurich, from 1968: has designed for City Druck AG, Burlet AG, Baumgartner, AG, Cliche Lutz, Univac, Telelift, Union Safe Company, Mettler and Company, Benz AG, Elektrowatt AG, etc. **Exhibitions:** Visual Graphic Gallery, New York, 1966; ICTA Knauer Expo, Stuttgart, 1967; ICTA German Section, Wuppertal, 1968; Städtische Berufsschule, Hof-Saale, 1972. Recipient: Typomundus Award, New York, 1965, 1970; Type Directors Club Award, New York, 1966; 4th Calendar Competition Award, West Germany, 1972. Member: Alliance Graphique Internationale, Paris, and International Center for Typographic Arts, New York. Address: Odermatt and Tissi, Schipfe 45, 8001 Zurich, Switzerland.

See ODERMATT, Siegfried.

TOIKKA, Oiva (Kalervo).

Finnish ceramics and glass designer. Born in Viipuri, 29 May 1931. Studied ceramics, 1953–56, and art education, 1959–60, at the Institute of Applied Arts, Helsinki. Designer, at Oy Wärtsilä AB Arabia ceramics firm, Helsinki, 1956–59, at Marimekko Textiles, Helsinki, 1959, and at Oy Wärtsilä Nuutajärvi, Glass firm, Finland, from 1963; also designed stage sets and costumes for the Finnish National Theatre and National Opera, Helsinki. Instructor, Sodankyla Secondary School, 1960–63, and at the Institute of Applied Arts, Helsinki, 1961–63. **Exhibitions:** Helsinki, 1956, 1963, 1965, 1972, 1981, 1984, 1987; Stockholm, 1967, 1974, 1985; Malmo, 1967; London, 1968; Amsterdam, 1976, 1986; Finnish Glass Museum, Riihimaki, 1988; Museum of Science and Industry, Los Angeles, 1989. **Collections:** Museum of Applied Arts, Helsinki; City Art Collection, Helsinki; National Museum, Helsinki; Sara Hilden Art Museum, Tampere; Finnish Glass Museum, Riihimaki; Nationalmuseum, Stockholm; Nordenfjeldske Kunstindustrimuseum, Trondheim; Leerdam Museum, Amster-

dam; Kunstgewerbemuseum, Hamburg; Museum für Kunstgewerbe, Frankfurt; Victoria and Albert Museum, London; Museum of Modern Art, New York; Corning Glass Museum, New York; Hokkaido Museum of Modern Art, Japan. Recipient: Internationales Kunsthandwerk Diploma, Stuttgart, 1969; Finnish State Scholarship, 1969, 1975; Lunning Prize, 1970; Alfred Kordelin Foundation Scholarship, 1980; Pro Finlandia Medal, 1980; Prize of Honour, *World Glass Now*, Hokkaido, Japan, 1985. Address: c/o Nuutajärvi Glass, 31160 Nuutajärvi, Finland.

Works:

Kurkkupurkki pickle jar in grey-brown blown glass, for Nuutajärvi, 1963.
Kastehelmi range of decorated tablewares in pressed glass, for Nuutajärvi, 1964.
Pioni range of tablewares in pressed glass, for Nuutajärvi, 1967.
Lollipop Isle sculpture in coloured glass, for Nuutajärvi, 1969.
Lasimetsa balloon-sculptures in coloured glass, for Nuutajärvi, 1972.
Vuosikuutiot series of nine coloured glass sculptures in clear glass cubes, for Nuutajärvi, 1977.
Snow Castle sculpture in opaque white glass, for Nuutajärvi, 1980.

Publications:

On TOIKKA: books—*Scandinavian Design: Objects of a Life Style* by Eileene Harrison Beer, New York 1975; *Finnish Design 1875–1975* by Timo Sarpaneva, Erik Bruun and Erik Kruskopf, Helsinki 1975; *Nordisk Kunsthandverk og Design* by Fredrik Wildhagen and others, Oslo 1981; *Finnland Gestaltet*, exhibition catalogue by Tapio Periainen, Simo Heikkila and others, Espoo 1981; *Glas: Unikate Finnische Künstler*, exhibition catalogue by Helmut Ricke, Düsseldorf 1982; *Scandinavian Modern Design 1880–1980*, edited by David Revere McFadden, New York 1982; *Finnish Vision*, with texts by P. Suhonen, J. Lintinen and others, Helsinki 1983; *The Lunning Prize*, exhibition catalogue edited by Helena Dahlbäck Lutteman and Marianne Uggla, Stockholm 1986; *Form Finland*, edited by Marianne Aav and Kaj Kalin, Helsinki 1986; *Finnish Industrial Design*, edited by Tua Pontasuo, Helsinki 1987.

TOMASZEWSKI, Henryk.

Polish illustrator, stage and graphic designer. Born in Warsaw, 10 June 1914. Studied graphics under Mieczyslaw Kotarbinski, at the Academy of Fine Arts, Warsaw, 1934–39. Freelance designer, working in Warsaw, from 1945: has designed for PIW, KAW and Czytelnik publishers, and for the Teatr Ateneum, Teatr Powszechny, Teatr Nowy and Teatr Narodowy. Head of poster design department from 1951, and professor of graphic design from 1955, at the Academy of Fine Arts, Warsaw. **Exhibitions:** *International Poster Exhibition*, Vienna, 1948; Bienal of Sao Paulo, 1963, 1979; Kongresshaus, Biel-Beinne, 1969; *Vier Polnische Plakatkunstler*, Deutsches Plakatmuseum, Essen, 1971; Vilanov Poster Museum, Warsaw, 1972; *International Design Biennale*, Wroclaw,

1978; *Das Polnische Plakat voin 1892 bis Heute*, Hochschule der Künste, West Berlin, 1980; *Graphic Arts Biennale*, Brno, 1982; Gallery A. and B. Wahl, Warsaw, 1984. **Collections:** National Museum, Warsaw; Deutsches Plakatmuseum, Essen; Stedelijk Museum, Amsterdam; Museum of Applied Arts, Stockholm; Museum of Modern Art, Kamakura; Museu de Arte Moderno, Sao Paulo; Museum of Modern Art, New York. Recipient: 5 First Prizes, *International Poster Exhibition*, Vienna, 1948; Polish National Art Prize, 1953; Poster and Illustration Prize, Warsaw, 1955; First Prize, *Polish Posters Exhibition*, Vienna, 1956; Poster of the Month Award, Vienna, 1957; *Przeglad Kulturalny* Satirical Drawing Prize, Warsaw, 1960; Graphics Prize, Bienal de Sao Paulo 1963; Advertising Poster of the Year Award, Warsaw, 1963, 1965, 1967; Gold Medal, Leipzig Book Fair, 1965; Gold Medal, 1967, 1970, 1988, Warsaw Poster Biennale; Lahti Poster Biennale Prize, 1979; Colorado Poster Exhibition Prize, Fort Collins, 1981; Alfred Jurzykowski Foundation Award, New York, 1984; ICOGRADA Special Prize, International Council of Societies of Graphic Design, 1986. Honorary Royal Designer for Industry, Royal Society of Arts, London, 1976. Address: Jazgarzewska Street 13, 00-730 Warsaw, Poland.

Publications:

By TOMASZEWSKI: book—*Book of Complaints*, Warsaw 1961.

On TOMASZEWSKI: books—*The Graphic Arts in Poland 1945–1955* by Jan Bialostocki, Warsaw 1956; *Henryk Tomaszewski* by Barbara Kwiatkowska, Warsaw 1959; *Buchgestaltung* by Albert Kapr, Dresden 1963; *Das Plakat* by Anton Sailer, Munich 1965; *The Poster: An Illustrated History from 1860* by Harold F. Hutchinson, London and Toronto 1968; *Polski Plakat Filmowy 1947–1967*, exhibition catalogue by Zdzislaw Schubert, Poznan 1969; *Polska Sztuka Plakatu* by Szymon Bojko Warsaw 1971; *Vier Polnische Plakatkunstler*, exhibition catalogue by H. Schardt, Essen 1971; *Monografie des Plakats: Entwicklung, Stil, Design* by Herbert Schindler, Munich 1972; *The Polish Poster 1970–1978*, with introduction by Zdzislaw Schubert, Warsaw 1979; *The Language of Graphics* by Edward Booth-Clibborn and Daniele Baroni, London 1980; *Das Polnische Plakat von 1892 bis Heute*, exhibition catalogue by Jan Bialostocki and others, West Berlin 1980; *Top Graphic Design* by F. H. K. Henrion, Zurich 1983; *A History of Graphic Design* by Philip B. Meggs, New York and London 1983; *Les Années 60* by Anne Bony, Paris 1983.

The famed Polish poster school is now almost forty years old. Many scholars and observers have counted its ups and downs—its early periods, heroic 1960s, 1970s and crisis, recently more international outlook, etc. In this history, there are many names—from the founders to the recent third or fourth generation. But Henryk Tomaszewski belongs to all of it. one of the founders just after the war, he is still one of the youngest. A paradox? Not at all. In the incredible competition of the small, crowded market of several dozen really top-class designers, he is the towering figure.

More than simply a designer, Tomaszewski is a living legend. Always the front-runner, crisp critic, the joker, he is the clown of a gray rigid, unhappy country, a diplomat and educator, a great one.

His intellectual power mixes with an outstanding sense of humour. He unbeatably selects the important from "decor" or empty ornamentalism. If we were able to remove him from his Warsaw studio and his times, he could easily have been a great conceptual artist of the Soho galleries in the late 1960s. Tomaszewski uses a word, a phrase, a meaning as the basis of creation. His best works are manifestoes of the idea, of the concept—pure intellectual marvels. Removed from the poster frame, his simple, colored-paper cut-outs would rank with the best dadaistic works. Or, in drawings, his lines are nervous, sharp, close to abstract painting. It is almost an impossible task to complete this giant poster-designer's portrait.

When all the bits and pieces are compiled and organized on the white board of his poster space, the effect is stirring. A simple peace dove, a tragic circus clown pedaling a bicycle that is breaking apart, Henry Moore's name formed like his own sculptures, a cheap official slogan, "To work better," transformed into a powerful message, endless magnificent theatrical posters that create their own theater of allusions and concepts—this is Tomaszewski in his prime. And nobody can surpass him in the longevity of his prime. Every discussion among young students who make their first steps in the poster field must focus on "Professor Henryk's" work.

Again and again, the lightning strikes from a blue sky. New work by Tomaszewski, fresh, original, refined, cutting harder. He's a real poet of the poster.

His unique personality and lasting enthusiasm toward his lifelong love, the poster, make him a formidable teacher. Even the laziest student is forced to think in Tomaszewski's Warsaw Academy studio. In this demanding training program, wit must work quickly; the simplest and most direct realization of the concept counts most. Everybody dreams of being accepted to his classes. Half of them are foreign students. Even the Japanese are hovering around.

This rare sample of a big artist, this flamboyant, individual and caring teacher, Tomaszewski shapes the past, present, and future well-being of his country's favorite art form—the poster.

—Jan Sawka

TOMS, Carl.
British stage, film, exhibition, interior and graphic designer. Born in Kirkby-in-Ashfield, Nottinghamshire, 29 May 1927. Educated at High Oakham School, Mansfield, Nottinghamshire, until 1945; studied at Mansfield College of Art, Nottinghamshire, 1946–49; Royal College of Art, London, 1949–53; Old Vic Theatre School, London, 1954–57. Freelance stage designer, working for the Royal Shakespeare Company, Old Vic Theatre, Young Vic, Welsh National Opera, New York State Opera, Edinburgh Festival, Glyndebourne Opera, Chichester Festival, Aldeburgh Festival, etc., from 1957; head of design and associate director, for the Young Vic at the National Theatre, London, from 1970; redesigned and decorated the Theatre Royal, Windsor, 1965, Theatre Royal, Bath, 1982, Garrick Theatre, London, 1986, and the Cambridge Theatre, London, 1987; design consultant, for the investiture of the Prince of Wales, Caernarvon Castle, 1969; also film designer from 1954, and television designer from 1959. **Exhibition:** *British Theatre Design '83–87*, Riverside Studios, London, 1988. Recipient: Antoinette Perry Award, New York, 1974–75; Drama Desk Award, New York, 1975; Society of West End Theatres Design Award, London 1980. Officer, Order of the British Empire, 1969. Address: The White House, Beaumont, near Wormley, Broxbourne, Hertfordshire EN10 7QJ, England.

Works:

Stage productions include *Apollo de Bellac*, Royal Court Theatre, 1957; *Beth*, London, 1958; *Something to Hide*, London, 1958; *The Complaisant Lover*, London, 1959; *The Seashell*, Edinburgh Festival, 1959; *No Bed for Bacon*, Bristol, 1959; *The Merry Wives of Windsor*, London, 1959; *La Cenerentola*, Sadler's Wells Theatre, London, 1959; *New Cranks*, Lyric Theatre, London, 1960; *A Midsummer Night's Dream*, Aldeburgh Festival, 1960; *The Barber of Seville*, Sadler's Wells Theatre, London, 1960; *Camille*, Old Vic Theatre, London (and world tour), 1961; *Iphigenie en Tauride*, Royal Opera House/Covent Garden, London, 1961; *Write Me a Murder*, London, 1962; *A Time to Laugh*, London, 1962; *Who'll Save the Plowboy?*, London, 1963; *The Importance of Being Earnest*, Nottingham, 1963; *Ballet Imperial*, Royal Opera House/Covent Garden, London, 1963; *Our Man in Havana*, Sadler's Wells Theatre, London, 1963; *The Merchant of Venice*, British Council touring production, 1964; *A Midsummer Night's Dream*, British Council touring production, 1964; *A Singular Man*, London, 1965; *Public Mischief*, London, 1965; *The Trojan Women*, Pop Theatre, London, 1966; *The Winter's Tale*, Pop Theatre, London, 1966; *Die Frau ohne Schatten*, Royal Opera House/Covent Garden, London, 1967; *The Burglar*, London, 1967; *Fallen Angels*, London, 1967; *The Tricks of Scapin*, Pop Theatre, London, 1967; *A Midsummer Night's Dream*, Pop Theatre, London, 1967; *The Soldier's Tale*, Pop Theatre, London, 1967; *Edward II*, National Theatre, London, 1968; *Love's Labour's Lost*, National Theatre, London, 1968; *The Magistrate*, London (and Chichester Festival Theatre), 1969; *Antony and Cleopatra*, Chichester Festival Theatre, 1969; *Girlfriend*, London, 1970; *Sleuth*, London (also New York and Paris), 1970, *Vivat! Vivat Regina!*, London, 1970; (also Chichester Festival Theatre, 1970, and New York, 1972); *The Alchemist*, Chichester Festival Theatre, 1970; *Cyrano de Bergerac*, National Theatre, London, 1970; *The Rivals*, Chichester Festival Theatre, 1971; *Caesar and Cleopatra*, Chichester Festival Theatre, 1971; *Reunion in Vienna*, Chichester Festival Theatre, 1971; *The Beheading*, London, 1972; *Reunion in Vienna*, London, 1972; *Dear Love*, London, 1973; *Section Nine*, London, 1973; *Fanfare for Europe*, Royal Opera House/Covent Garden, London, 1973; *Peter Grimes*, San Francisco Opera, 1973; *Sherlock Holmes*, London (and New York), 1974; *Travesties*, London, 1974; (also New York, 1975, and Vienna, 1976); *Waltz of the Toreadors*, London, 1975; *Die Meistersinger von Nürnberg*, New York City Opera, 1975; *Murderer*, London, 1976; *Thais*, San Francisco Opera, 1976; *Norma*, San Diego Opera, 1976; *La Traviata*, San Diego Opera, 1976; *Long Day's Journey into Night*, Los Angeles, 1977; *Man and Superman*, Malvern Festival (and London), 1977; *The Devil's Disciple*, Los Angeles, 1977 (and New York, 1978); *Travesties*, National Theatre, Vienna, 1977; *The Marriage of Figaro*, New York City Opera, 1977; *The Voice of Ariadne*, New York City Opera, 1977; *The Merry Widow*, San Diego Opera, 1977; *Look After Lulu*, Chichester Festival Theatre (and Haymarket Theatre, London), 1978; *Night and*

Carl Toms: Stage set for Tom Stoppard's *Rough Crossing*, National Theatre, London, 1984

Day, Phoenix Theatre, London, 1978 (and New York, 1979); *She Stoops to Conquer*, National Theatre, Vienna, 1978; *Betrayal*, National Theatre, Vienna, 1978; *Thais*, Metropolitan Opera, New York, 1978; *Hamlet*, San Diego Opera, 1978; *Stage Struck*, Vaudeville Theatre, London, 1979; *For Services Rendered*, National Theatre, London, 1979; *The Guardsman*, National Theatre, Vienna, 1979; *Playbill*, National Theatre, London, 1980; *The Provok'd Wife*, National Theatre, London, 1980; *Night and Day*, National Theatre, Vienna, 1980; *On the Razzle*, National Theatre, London, 1981; *The Second Mrs. Tanqueray*, National Theatre, London, 1981; *Der Freischutz*, New York City Opera, 1981; *Windy City*, Victoria Palace, London, 1982; *Swan Lake*, Festival Ballet, London, 1982; *Macbeth*, Vienna State Opera, 1982; *Romeo and Juliet*, San Diego Opera, 1982; *The Rehearsal*, Yvonne Arnaud Theatre, Guildford, 1982; *The Real Thing*, Strand Theatre, London, 1982; *A Patriot for Me*, Chichester Festival, 1983; *The Winslow Boy*, Lyric Theatre/Hammersmith, London, 1983; *Hay Fever*, Queens Theatre, London, 1983; *The Italian Girl in Algiers*, Geneva, 1983; *The Hot House*, Burgtheater, Vienna, 1983; *The Real Thing*, Burgtheater, Vienna, 1983; *Amadeus*, Burgtheater, Vienna, 1984; *The Aspern Papers*, Theatre Royal/Haymarket, London, 1984; *Rough Crossing*, National Theatre, London, 1984; *Faust*, State Opera, Vienna, 1985; *The Dragon's Tail*, Apollo Theatre, London, 1985; *Lucia di Lammermoor*, Cologne Opera, 1985; *Jumpers*, Aldwych Theatre,

London, 1985; *Where She Danced*, Yvonne Arnaud Theatre, Guildford, 1985; *The Happiest Days of Your Life*, Royal Shakespeare Company/Barbican, London, 1985; *Wildfire*, Phoenix Theatre, London, 1986; *The Magistrate*, National Theatre, London, 1986; *Blithe Spirit*, Vaudeville Theatre, London, 1986; *Brighton Beach Memoirs*, National Theatre, London, 1986; *Noel and Gertie*, Donmar Warehouse, London, 1986; *Oberon*, Edinburgh Festival, 1986; *Dalliance*, National Theatre, London, 1986; *Fanfare for Elizabeth*, Royal Opera House/Covent Garden, London, 1986; *Six Characters in Search of an Author*, National Theatre, London, 1987; *The Importance of Being Ernest*, Royal Theatre, Copenhagen, 1987; *Carry On, Jeeves*, Wyndham's Theatre, London, 1987; *The Importance of Being Ernest*, Royalty Theatre, London, 1987; *Ting Tang Mine*, National Theatre, London, 1987; *The Living Room*, Royalty Theatre, London, 1987; *Hapgood*, Aldwych Theatre, London, 1988; *Rigoletto*, New York State Opera, 1988; *Playbill*, Royalty Theatre, London, 1988; *Richard II* Phoenix Theatre, London, 1988; *Artist Descending a Staircase*, Duke of York's Theatre, London, 1988; *Richard III*, Phoenix Theatre, London, 1989; *Hapgood*, Doolittle Theatre, Los Angeles, 1989. Films include *Rocket to the Moon*, 1954; *She*, 1965; *The Quiller Memorandum*, 1966; *One Million Years B.C.*, 1967; *Prehistoric Women*, 1967; *Those Fantastic Flying Fools*, 1967; *The Winter's Tale*, 1968; *The Lost Continent*, 1968; *The Vengeance of She*, 1968, *Moon Zero Two*, 1970.

Publications:

By TOMS: books—*The Winter's Tale* (stage designs), London 1975; *The Tricks of Scapin* (stage designs), London 1975.

On TOMS: books—*Who's Who in Opera*, edited by Maria F. Rich, New York 1976; *Notable Names in the American Theatre*, Clifton, New Jersey 1976; *Who's Who in the Theatre*, edited by Ian Herbert, London 1977; *International Who's Who in Music and Musicians' Directory*, edited by Adrian Gaster, Cambridge 1977, 1980; *International Film & TV Year Book 1979–80*, edited by Peter Noble, London 1979; *British Theatre Design '83–87*, with texts by Timothy O'Brien and David Fingleton, London 1988; *British Theatre Design: The Modern Age*, edited by John Goodwin, London 1989.

Going to the Old Vic School from the Royal College of Art, Carl Toms singlemindedly dedicated himself to the theatre, and in this has lain his strength. Though susceptible to much that has gone on in contemporary art, he has brought to his theatre designs a sense of style rather than a style to impose. His work has thus been genuinely of the theatre without any slide into Camp theatricality except where, as in *New Cranks*, for example, it was required in an ironic sense which he marvellously satisfied, and reacting creatively to John Cranko's requirements, Toms made his Scarlatti ballet a little gem.

In much the same way, his work for television has been relentlessly tailored to the demands of the medium, so he avoided many of the difficulties that arise when designs are primarily conceived behind the proscenium arch. Indeed, his television *Twelfth Night* is utterly unlike his other Shakespeare productions for the theatre, except, of course, for the evidence of his careful attention to requirements and his respect for the play and the director. However, this is not to say he merely carried out instructions; he is far too imaginative for that.

His first major design was for *Apollo de Bellac* at the Royal Court Theatre in 1957. It immediately announced that an important talent had appeared, but it also put Toms in touch with some of the liveliest minds in stage production. He was able to profit from these contacts, but he was also equal to their demands. This first work had none of the shortcomings that so often mar a young designer's debut, though, to be sure, it left room for development, which indeed has been the most outstanding characteristic of his subsequent career.

It is difficult to pick out any one design as the masterpiece. Rather, one recalls so many magical moments in the theatre, particularly at the outset, when his achievement was not always to be taken for granted. Then, the success seemed the more enjoyable, and in this respect, memorable occasions include that Royal Court production of 1957, the ballet *La Reja* and *The Merry Wives of Windsor* in 1959, and, of course, *New Cranks* the following year.

Finally, in the renewal of a Victorian manor for the Nevills, Toms has taken a new departure, one that has called upon quite different resources. The interiors are theatrical in a way none of the stage sets are, perhaps because Toms is working to an unknown drama, indeed to a drama still to be written or, rather, improvised.

—Toni del Renzio

TRAUNER, Alexandre.
French film and stage designer. Born Sandor Trauner, in Budapest, Hungary, 3 September 1906; emigrated to France in 1929: naturalized, 1944. Studied painting, at the School of Fine Arts, Budapest, 1925–29. Assistant to film designer Lazare Meerson, Paris, 1929–36; freelance art director, working on films of Rene Clair, Julien Duvivier, Marcel Carne, Jacques Feyder, Marc Allegret, Billy Wilder, Fred Zinnemann, Howard Hawks, Anatole Litvak, Stanley Donen, Joseph Losey, etc., in France and the United States, from 1937; also stage designer, Paris, from 1953. Founder-member, Cinématèque Française, Paris, 1936. **Exhibitions:** Mucsarnok Gallery, Budapest, 1928; National Gallery, Budapest, 1982. **Collections:** Musée du Cinema, Paris; National Gallery, Budapest. Recipient: Academy Award, 1960; César Award, Paris, 1978, 1979; Grand Prix National du Cinema, Paris, 1983. Member, Académie du Cinema, Paris, Address: c/o Aline Dumontet, 4 rue de la Planche, 75007 Paris, France.

Works:

Film productions include—*Sous les Toits de Paris* (Clair), 1930; *David Golder* (Duvivier), 1930; *Jean de la Lune* (Choux), 1931; *A Nous la Liberté* (Clair), 1931; *Le Million* (Clair), 1931; *L'Affaire est dans le Sac* (P. Prevert), 1932; *Quatorze Juillet* (Clair), 1932; *Danton* (Roubaud), 1932; *Ciboulette* (Autant-Lara), 1933; *Amok* (Ozep), 1933; *Faut Réparer Sophie* (Ryder), 1933; *L'Hotel du libre-Echange* (M. Allegret), 1934; *Sans Famille* (M. Allegret), 1934; *La Kermesse Héroique* (Feyder), 1935; *Gribouille* (M. Allegret), 1937; *La Dame de Malacca* (M. Allegret), 1937; *Drôle de Drame* (Carne), 1937; *Mollenard* (Siodmak), 1937; *Quai des Brumes* (Carne), 1938; *Entrée des Artistes* (M. Allegret), 1938; *Hôtel du Nord* (Carne), 1938; *Le Jour se Lève* (Carne), 1939; *Soyez les Bienvenus* (de Baroncelli), 1940; *Remorques* (Gremillon), 1941; *Le Soleil a Toujours Raison* (Billon), 1941; *Les Visiteurs du Soir* (Carne), 1942; *Lumière d'Ete* (Gremillon), 1943; *Les Enfants du Paradis* (Carne), 1945; *Les Malheurs de Sophie* (Audry), 1945; *Les Portes de la Nuit* (Carne), 1946; *Reves d'Amour* (Stengel), 1946; *Voyage Surprise* (P. Prevert), 1946; *La Fleur de l'Age* (Carne), 1947; *La Marie du Port* (Carne), 1949; *Maneges* (Y. Allegret), 1950; *Les Miracles n'ont Lieu qu'une Fois* (Y. Allegret), 1950; *Juliette, ou laClé des Songes* (Carne), 1951; *The Green Glove* (Mate), 1951; *Othello* (Welles), 1952; *Les Sept Peches Capitaux* (Y. Allegret), 1952; *La Jeune Folle* (Y. Allegret), 1952; *Un Acte d'Amour* (Litvak), 1953; *Land of the Pharaohs* (Hawks), 1954; *Du Rififi chez les Hommes* (Dassin), 1955; *L'Amant de Lady Chatterley* (M. Allegret), 1955; *The Happy Road* (Kelly), 1956; *En*

Alexandre Trauner: Film set design for Marcel Carne's *Hotel du Nord*, 1938

Effeuillant laMarguerite (M. Allegret), 1956; *Love in the Afternoon* (Wilder) 1957; *Witness for the Prosecution* (Wilder), 1958; *The Nun's Story* (Zinnemann), 1958; *Le Secret du Chevalier d'Eon* (Audry), 1959; *Once More with Feeling* (Donen), 1960; *The Apartment* (Wilder), 1960; *Romanoff and Juliet* (Ustinov), 1961; *Paris Blues* (Ritt), 1961; *Aimez-Vous Brahms* (Litvak), 1961; *One, Two, Three* (Wilder), 1961; *Le Couteau dans la Plaie* (Litvak), 1962; *Irma La Douce* (Wilder), 1963; *Behold a Pale Horse* (Zinnemann), 1963; *Kiss Me, Stupid* (Wilder), 1964; *How to Steal a Million* (Wyler), 1966; *The Night of the Generals* (Litvak), 1967; *La Puce a l'Oreille* (Charon), 1967; *Uptight* (Dassin), 1968; *The Private Life of Sherlock Holmes* (Wilder), 1970; *Les Maries de l'An II* (Rappenau), 1970; *La Promesse de l'Aube* (Dassin), 1971; *L'Impossible Objet* (Frankenheimer), 1972; *Grandeur Nature* (Berlanga), 1972; *The Man Who Would Be King* (Huston), 1975; *La Première Fois* (Berri), 1976; *Mr. Klein* (Losey), 1977; *Les Routes du Sud* (Losey), 1977; *Fedora* (Wilder), 1978; *Don Giovanni* (Losey), 1979; *The Fiendish Plot of Dr. Fu Manchu* (Haggard), 1979; *Coup de Torchon* (Tavernier), 1981; *The Trout* (Losey), 1982; *Subway* (Besson), 1985.

Publications:

On TRAUNER: books—*Ragionamenti sulla Scenografia* by Baldo Bandini and Glauco Viazzi, Milan 1945; *Les 1001 Métiers du Cinema* by Pierre Leprohon, Paris 1947; *La Scenografia nel Film* by Mario Verdone, Rome 1956; *Dictionnaire des Cinéastes* by Georges Sadoul, Paris 1964; *The Cinema as Art* by Ralph Stephenson and R. Debrix, London 1965; *Le Décor de Film* by Leon Barsacq, Paris 1970, as *Caligari's Cabinet and Other Grand Illusions*, Boston 1976; *The World Encyclopedia of Film*, edited by Tim Cawkwell and John M. Smith, London 1972; *International Dictionary of Films and Filmmakers*, London and Chicago 1987, 1991.

When I told Alexandre Trauner I was writing this piece about him, he gave a start and said with a slight, malicious frown: "We'll have to do it with humour!" His vast career is mentioned and analysed in all books about production design, but he has remained modest and dislikes to talk about his skills. "I work in the shadow of the authors, and it's just as well," he says, "A designer is a manipulator, he makes believe . . . and makes audiences believe. And as a magician, he should not reveal too much of his tricks!"

What kind of tricks has Trauner used, for instance, to build houses, towns, atmospheres that have become for millions of people throughout the world, *the* houses, *the* towns, *the* atmospheres of Paris, London, or the Pharaohs' Egypt? Even those who don't precisely remember the docks in *Quai des Brumes* or the boulevard in *Children of Paradise* imagine them just as Trauner has designed them.

"What makes my job most interesting," says Trauner, "is that there are no two identical films, even though producers would like to repeat indefinitely the same success. Every time I start working on a movie, I try to forget all that I have experienced."

He claims that invention is the one and only acceptable rule. That's trick number one. Another of his tricks I might call friendship. The best of his work has been done with people who have become his friends: poet and screenwriter Jacques Prévert, directors Billy Wilder, Orson Welles, Joseph Losey, composer Maurice Jaubert, designers Ray and Charles Eames, actors Jean Gabin, Yves Montand, Jack Lemmon, and others.

"Shooting a film is collective work," says Trauner, and that is obviously something he enjoys. "Each member of the team contributes, everything is important, but what's decisive for me is to have an adventure in common!"

Trauner's sets are immediately recognisable. During World War II, when France was occupied and he worked undercover, everyone in the profession felt his touch and knew that he had designed Grémillon's *Lumière d'été* or Carné's *Les Visiteurs du soir*, for his style is unmistakable. The basic trick is simplicity. He banishes the picturesque and loathes the decorative. "It's useless," says he, "to fill the screen with superfluous things. Come to think about it, what a designer refrains from doing is almost more important that what he actually does. He's like a sculptor who eliminates material from the marble block. He cannot show everything; he chooses the significant elements, the unexpected ones, and these must look true, they must sound right."

That is how Trauner achieves the sturdiest, the most meaningful and imaginative of sets. He created the Paris that many people have in their minds, but he believes that movies become interesting when they don't stick to reality. Showing reality is not enough: the picture must be new and surprising. Only then does it become real. "It's a question of point of view, just as painting is a question of vision, and from Far Eastern to European painting, there are many different visions!" says Trauner.

Painting, since his beginnings at the Fine Arts School of Budapest, has remained essential for him. He is. the best known of production designers, the most ignored of painters. Only his close friends, Prévert or Picasso, knew about it, as he was always too modest or careless to do or let do anything about it; his set designs turn out to be fascinating pieces of painting. They are made with paint and a brush, just as the sets are made of plaster, wood, and sunlight. They are made by a person whose trick, all said and done, is to have no tricks—only an incisive eye, a keen understanding of people and places, and talent, as they say.

—André Pozner

TRIGÈRE, Pauline.

American fashion designer. Born in Paris, France, 4 November 1912; emigrated to the United States in 1937: naturalized, 1942. Educated at Victor Hugo Collège, Paris, 1923–28; apprenticed as trainee clothing cutter, at Martial et Armand, Place Vendôme, Paris, 1928–29. Married; children: Jean-Pierre and Philippe. Assistant cutter and fitter in her father's tailoring business, Paris, 1929–32; freelance fashion designer and clothing cutter, Paris, 1933–36; design assistant to Travis Banton, at Hattie Carnegie fashion house, New York, 1937–42; founder and partner, with her brother Robert, in House of Trigère fashion firm, New York, from 1942. Critic and board member, Fashion Institute of Technology, New York. Recipient: Coty American Fashion Critics' Winnie Award, New York, 1949, 1951, and Hall of Fame Award, 1959; Neiman-Marcus Award, New York, 1950; National Cotton Council of America Award, New York, 1951; Filene Award, 1959; Silver Medal, City of Paris, 1972. Address: 550 Seventh Avenue, New York, New York 10018, U.S.A.

Publications:

On TRIGÈRE: books—*The Fashionable Savages* by John Fairchild, New York 1965; *The Wheels of Fashion* by Phyllis Lee Levin, New York 1965; *American Fashion: The Life and Lines of Adrian, Mainbocher, McCardell, Norell, Trigère*, edited by Sarah Tomerlin Lee, New York, 1975; *Quest for the Best* by Stanley Marcus, New York 1979; *Fairchild's Who's Who in Fashion*, edited by Anne Stegemeyer, New York 1980; *McDowell's Directory of Twentieth Century Fashion* by Colin McDowell, London 1984; *Fashion: The Inside Story* by Barbaralee Diamonstein, New York 1985; *The Encyclopaedia of Fashion from 1840 to the 1980s* by Georgina O'Hara, London 1986.

Pauline Trigère, born into a French tailoring family, began her own clothing business in 1942 out of economic necessity. Practicality in an elegant guise has continued to distinguish her designs for the wives of wealthy American businessmen. She creates flattering, couture-quality clothes, investments her customers can depend upon season after season. Living the same active and social life as her customers, her design approach is based on personal experience.

A master fitter, she designs without toile or paper pattern. With a surgeon's skill, she cuts directly into the final fabric, shaping it on a live model until every detail has been perfected. Her use of bias-cut and princess seaming has resulted in designs such as the one she calls Everybody's Dress, a simple, jersey dress which skims the mature figure gracefully. Cowls and scarves soften necklines. Trigère daytime ensembles allow a busy woman to be completely well-dressed with no bother. Full-cut Greatcoats are chic and warm. Her variations of the cape swing dramatically with the wearer's every gesture. Her showy evening gowns, frequently trimmed with fur, sequins, or feathers, offer imaginative but ladylike elegance beyond fashion's changes. In all, her handling of fabrics is superb, from carefully-matched woolen plaids to spectacularly bold silk prints.

Trigère travels with her collections to the prestigious American shops which carry her clothes. She enjoys meeting with salespeople and customers, helping them select fabrics from the swatches which accompany each garment. Her own enthusiastic commentary at her fashion shows includes formulas for efficient elegance, such as the Trigère Plan, a suggested basic wardrobe of one color for simplified traveling. This individualized attention allies Trigère's approach more closely with couture than with ready-to-wear.

Her busy schedule includes teaching, both at the Fashion Institute of Technology, and through student visits to her workrooms, where she stresses to would-be designers the necessity of hard work and high standards. She enjoys entertaining in her eclectically elegant city and country homes, amidst her collection of the turtle objects which are her symbols of good luck and longevity. The turtle motif recurs in her perfume packaging, jewelry, and line of serving pieces.

Through four decades of devotion to her work, she has won the respect of fellow designers and the continuing loyalty of her satisfied customers. Trigère brings a woman designer's realistic approach to elegance.

—Sandra Michels Adams

TROIKE, Gero.

German stage designer. Born Gero Brauner, in Schönheide, Erzgebirge, 29 June 1945. Educated at the Oberschule, Berlin-Köpenick, 1959–63; geology and mineralogy laboratory assistant, at Humboldt-Universität, Berlin, 1963–64; mainly self-taught in design. Married Angela Troike in 1966; daughters: Anne and Sara. Worked for VEB Bero-Kaffee, Berlin, 1964, and Saint-Laurentius Cemetery, Berlin-Kopenick, 1965–66; stagehand, set painter and assistant stage designer, working for the Volksbuhne, Berlin, 1964–65, 1969–71, 1972–81, for the Maxim Gorki Theatre, Berlin, 1967–69, and for the Komische Oper, Berlin, 1971–72; resident stage set and costume designer, for the Deutsches Theatre, Berlin, from 1981; also independent painter. **Exhibitions:** Galerie am Prater, Berlin, 1976; Galerie im Schloss Kopenick, Berlin, 1977. Address: Dahmestrasse 1, 1180 Berlin, Germany.

Works:

Stage productions include—*The Chairs*, Volksbühne, Berlin, 1974; *Die Schlacht*, Volksbühne, Berlin, 1975; *Pauline*, Deutsches Theatre, Berlin, 1976; *The Burger General*, Volksbühne, Berlin, 1977; *Horribilicribrifax*, Deutsches Theatre, Berlin, 1978; *Leonce and Lena*, Volksbühne, Berlin, 1978; *King Lear*, Ro-Theater, Amsterdam, 1978; *Midsummer Night's Dream*, Deutsches Theatre, Berlin, 1980; *Maria Stuart*, Deutsches Theatre, Berlin, 1980; *Maria Magdalena*, Kai Theatre, Brussels, 1980; *Dick Hunt*, Municipal Theatre, Dresden, 1981; *The Birds*, Municipal Theatre, Dresden, 1981; *The Sad Story of Frederick the Great*, Deutsches Theatre, Berlin, 1982; *Faust II*, Deutsches Theatre, Berlin, 1983.

Publications:

By TROIKE: article—in *Bauten der Kultur* (Berlin), March 1983.

On TROIKE: book—*Malerei und Grafik in der DDR* by Lothar Lang, Leipzig 1978; articles—in *Sibylle* (Berlin), June 1977; *Der Morgen* (Berlin), May 1983.

*   *   *

The stage designer Gero Troike did not attend any arts academy; he is self-taught, or rather, he acquired artistic and technical skills by assisting the leading designers of the German Democratic Republic, Reinhart Zimmerman and Pieter Hein. He modelled himself on the Old Masters of Germany, on the Romantic Caspar David Friedrich, and on Otto Dix, but he was stimulated more by the working methods of leading directors Benno Besson, Manfred Karge, Matthias Langhoff, and Alexander Lang than by painterly techniques. Even his interest in the work of designer Karl von Appen was mainly directed toward the style of his methods, its thoroughness and culture. With these major theatre artists, Troike learned to respect responsible collaboration and to understand that genuine teamwork is an integral component of theatrical activity.

In his own designs, Troike aims at symbolic expression via simple, sparse, and very functional effects, whilst his stage spaces create concrete acting opportunities for the players.

In these designs, he introduced specific stage movement recommendations, whereby the conceptual intent of the producer/director and the designer is evidenced in relationships of the stage space to the actors.

Troike uses the period of the play's original production as an artistic inspiration for the creation of his images (Baroque, Shakespearian, classic theatre of Goethe, etc.), his techniques varying according to the type of play under production. His first, major, independent production was the design of Georg Hirschfeld's piece *Pauline* at the Deutsches Theater in Berlin. The action of the play takes place in Berlin at the turn of the century, the precise location being an elegant kitchen in which the resolute serving-girl Pauline lives. For this setting, Troike built a kitchen with a tiled floor and everything bright, clean, precise, and well-kept. Every item of lovingly researched period detail, such as little spice cupboards, pots, and ladles, told of the neat habits of its user. With minimal technical outlay, the kitchen was transformed into an old Berlin tavern where Pauline goes dancing once a week—a scene of poetic realism which creates for the actors a space in which they can live.

For Goethe's *Bürgergeneral* at the Berlin Volksbühne, Troike built another kitchen, again neat and bright—and yet of another world. The compact and heavy furniture, the Thuringian landscape of the poet Goethe, and the atmosphere of rural life dominate the scene. Such realistic poetry, which creates its own idyll, makes historical detachment possible. On the other hand, his attempt to illustrate a social pyramid with a triple-staggered stage, for the Baroque writer Gryphius's *Horribilicribifax*, was a failure. The stage design was too heavily "statuesque," precluding any relationship between the actors themselves or between actors and scenic space.

Gero Troike: Set and costumes for Heinrich Mann's *The Sad Story of Frederick the Great*, Deutsches Theater, Berlin, 1982

Troike's genius and originality, however, were to surface again in the production of Shakespeare's *A Midsummer Night's Dream*, for which he created a dramatically luminous, red space merely from three simple walls with a single doorway cut into each, the forest setting being conceived as within the characters themselves. The apogee of his creative work has been reached in recent productions of Heinrich Mann's *The Sad Story of Frederick the Great*, for which the stage was covered in tiles and punctuated by economically selected items of furniture to represent Prussian asceticism, and of Goethe's *Faust II*, both for the Berlin Deutsches Theater.

—Ingeborg Pietzsch

TROXLER, Niklaus.
Swiss graphic designer. Born in Willisau, 1 May 1947. Studied graphics, at the Kunstgewerbeschule, Lucerne, 1968–71. Married Ems Baettig in 1973; daughters: Kathrin, Annik and Paula. Art director, at Hollenstein Creation agency, Paris, 1972–73; freelance graphic designer, establishing Niklaus Troxler Grafik-Studio, Willisau, from 1973: has designed for the Willisau Jazz Festival, Lucerne Little Theatre, German Industrial Design Association, Zurich Kunstgewerbemuseum, Circus Knie, Autosalon Geneva, etc. **Exhibitions:** Galerie Raeber, Lucerne, 1978; Plakat-Galerie Migros, Bern, 1981; Artcurial, Paris, 1981; *Poster Triennale*, Deutsches Plakatmuseum, Essen, 1987; *The Big Show: The Modern Poster*, Museum of Modern Art, New York, 1988. *Collection:* Kunstgewerbemuseum, Zurich. Recipient: Vestag Kulturpreis, Lucerne, 1977; Swiss Poster of the Year Award, 1977, 1978, 1979, 1980, 1982, 1984, 1985, 1986, 1987, 1988; Swiss Art Directors Club Silver Award, 1979, 1980, 1981, 1982, 1983, 1984, 1985, 1986, 1987, 1988, and Gold Award, 1981, 1982; Innerschweizer Kulturpreis, 1982; Toulouse-Lautrec Gold Medal, Essen, 1987. Address: Bahnhofstrasse 22, 6130 Willisau, Switzerland.

Works:

McCoy Tyner Sextet poster, for Jazz in Willisau, 1980.
Arthur Blythe Quartet poster, for Jazz in Willisau, 1982.
Hermeto Pascoal: Brazilian Jazz poster, for Jazz in Willisau, 1985.
A Tribute to the Music of Thelonious Monk poster, for Jazz in Willisau, 1986.
Funk Night: Willisau poster for Jazz in Willisau, 1987.
Maria Joao-Aki Takase: Concert poster, Jazz in Willisau, 1988.
Entweder-oder poster, for the Madtheater, Bern, 1988.
OLMA: Fair of Eastern Switzerland poster, for Olma, St. Gallen, 1988.
Wirz ist auf Talentsuche poster, for Wirz Publicity, Zurich, 1988.
Luzerner Unwelt- und Besinnungstage poster, for Forum Neuland, 1988.
African Echoes poster, for Jazz in Willisau, 1988.
Vaterland series of 9 posters, for *Vaterland* newspaper, Lucerne, 1988–89.

Niklaus Troxler: *American Echoes* poster, for Jazz in Willisau, 1988

Bobby Burri Quartet poster, for Jazz in Willisau, 1989.
Anthony Braxton Trio poster, for Jazz in Willisau, 1989.

Publications:

By TROXLER: book—*Jazz-Plakate von Niklaus Troxler*, Willisaw 1978.

On TROXLER: books—*Graphis Posters*, annuals edited by Walter Herdeg, Zurich 1975, 1979, 1980, 1982, 1983; *Jazz in Willisau*, Lucerne 1978; *Modern Publicity 48*, annual, London 1979; *Art Directors Club of Switzerland*, annuals, Zurich 1979, 1980, 1981, 1982, 1983; *The Dictionary of Visual Language* by Philip Thompson and Peter Davenport, London 1980; *Romeo und Julia in Willisau*, Zurich 1982; *Swiss Posters 1970–1980*, edited by Idea Publishers, Tokyo 1982; *The Modern Poster* by Stuart Wrede, New York 1988.

My "graphic design" should be a surprise. It should suit the thing it advertises. It should have humour. The design should be striking and different from everything else. But it should be honest and shouldn't bluff.

It may confuse, it may perplex. It should in any case bear my own signature. My design should now and again be a sign of the times, as well.

—Niklaus Troxler

George Tscherny: Advertisement for San Francisco Clothing, 1988

TSCHERNY, George.

American graphic designer. Born in Budapest,
Hungary, 12 July 1924; emigrated to the United
States in 1941: naturalized, 1943. Studied at
Newark School of Fine and Industrial Arts,
New Jersey, 1946–47; Pratt Institute, Brooklyn,
New York, 1947–50. Served in the United
States Army, in Europe, 1943–45: Corporal.
Married Sonia Katz in 1950; daughters: Nadia
and Carla. Staff designer, at Donald Deskey
and Associates, New York, 1950–53; associate
and head of graphic design, at George Nelson
and Associates, New York, 1953–55; founder
and president of George Tscherny Incorporated
graphic design studio, New York, from 1955:
designed for Johnson and Johnson, Pan American, Public Broadcasting System, Mobil, IBM,
Texasgulf, Aluminium Association, Air
Canada, General Dynamics, etc. Instructor, at
the Pratt Institute, Brooklyn, New York,
1956–57, and the School of Visual Arts, New
York, 1956–64; Mellon visiting professor,
Cooper Union, New York, 1976. Curriculum
consultant, Philadelphia College of Art,
1967–68; advisory board member, Pratt Institute, Brooklyn, New York, 1979. President,
American Institute of Graphic Arts, 1966–68.
Exhibitions: School of Visual Arts, New York,
1959; Landesgewerbeamt, Stuttgart, 1962;
Galerie Intergraphis, Munich, 1967; Pratt Institute, Brooklyn, New York, 1972; *107 Grafici
dell'AGI*, Castello Sforzesco, Milan, 1974; *Images of an Era: The American Poster
1945–1975*, Corcoran Gallery of Art, Washington, D.C., 1975; *The Modern Poster*, Museum
of Modern Art, New York, 1988. **Collections:**
Museum of Modern Art, New York; Cooper-
Hewitt Museum, New York; Library of Congress, Washington, D.C. Recipient: Silver
Medal, Warsaw Poster Biennale, 1976; American Institute of Graphic Arts Gold Medal,
1988; plus numerous other awards from the
American Institute of Graphic Arts, New York
Art Directors Club, and Type Directors Club.
Address: 238 East 72nd Street, New York, New
York 10021, U.S.A.

Works:

Series of advertisements, for Herman Miller
    Furniture Company, 1950–53.
Theater program designs, for Marcel Marceau,
    Martha Graham, Benny Goodman, and
    others, New York, 1954–56.
Appointment calendar designs, for the Museum
    of Modern Art, New York, 1957–60.
Annual reports and publication designs, for the
    Ford Foundation, 1958–61.
Subway poster series, for the School of Visual
    Arts, New York, 1960–62.
Jose de Rivera exhibition catalogue, for the
    American Federation of Arts, 1961.
Imagination 10: Trains and Railroads brochure,
    for Champion Papers, 1967.
Lark, *Chesterfield*, and *L&M* modular cigarette
    pack designs, for Liggett and Myers Tobacco
    Company, 1968.
Oceanography poster series, for General
    Dynamics Corporation, 1969.
Destinations modular displays, for Pan Amer-
    ican Airways, 1971.
Corporate identity program and publications,
    for W. R. Grace and Company, from 1974.
Happy Birthday USA bicentennial poster, for
    Davis-Delaney-Arrow, 1975.
Telephone Centenary commemorative postage
    stamp, for the U.S. Postal Service, 1976.
Series of exhibition posters, for Goethe House,
    New York, 1977–80.
Connections poster, for the Simpson Paper
    Company, 1982.
IBM Yesterday and Today illustrated book
    design, for IBM, 1984.

Swim for Breath poster, for the Cystic Fibrosis
    Foundation, 1985.
Logotype, packaging and advertising, for San
    Francisco Clothing, 1987.
1989 appointment calendar, for Sandy-Alexan-
    der Incorporated, 1988.
Progress in Skin Care report, for Johnson and
    Johnson, 1989.

Publications:

By TSCHERNY: articles—in *Communication
Arts* (Palo Alto), February 1962; *High Quality*
(Munich), no. 4, 1986.

On TSCHERNY: books—*Packaging: An International Survey of Package Design*, edited by
Walter Herdeg, Zurich 1959; *Who's Who in
Graphic Art*, edited by Walter Amstutz, Zurich
1962, Dubendorf 1982; *The Poster: An Illus-
trated History from 1860* by Harold F. Hutchin-
son, London and Toronto 1968; *107 Grafici
dell'AGI*, with texts by Renzo Zorzi and Franco
Grignani, Venice 1974; *The Language of
Graphics* by Edward Booth-Clibborn and
Daniele Baroni, London 1980; *A History of
Graphic Design* by Philip B. Meggs, New York
1983; *Thirty Centuries of Graphic Design* by
James Craig and Bruce Barton, New York
1987; *Contemporary Graphic Artists*, edited by
Maurice Horn, Detroit 1988; *Annual Report
War Stories*, edited by Simpson Paper Com-
pany, San Francisco 1988.

*

Although the pioneering phase of the modern
design movement took place largely in the
1920s and 1930s, it became a popular and accepted style only in the 1950s and 1960s. Despite having been very much a part of this
second phase, I never felt a dogmatic allegiance
to the International Style. It was, I suppose,
simply not wanting to be too closely identified
with any style or movement. Moreover, I had
my differences with many of my colleagues during those years: their fascination with man-
made, ersatz materials, the sterile
"one-typeface" ideology of some, and the typographic gluttony of others. Nor will I miss the
typographic acrobatics that followed the introduction of film type. My joys in typography
were not derived from squeezing, pulling, and
otherwise manipulating type, nor by "killing
widows." Still, surprisingly, I share little of the
general disillusionment with modernism which
has overtaken designers today.
    Why then did I not eagerly embrace post-
modernism as an alternative? Although, historically, protest movements have tended to be
destructive rather than constructive, the novel
aspect of postmodernism was that it recycled, in
large part, the very past it was repudiating.
Here, I must give credit to the fashion designers
who aptly called their parallel movement
"Retro." Moreover postmodernism chose to
celebrate the most trivial and pedestrian aspects
of the past; it never rose above its mannerisms.
The purported goal of injecting humanism was
never implemented or even honestly pursued.
Fortunately, protest movements are shortlived.
About the only legacy postmodernism has left
us is a refreshing color palette.
    I don't know what is next. I do know what I
would wish for. I would wish for a truly human
and humane period in design. For sure, it will
have to be called "Post-Mortem" design. I have
already detected beginnings of this human
touch in illustrations. We are done with the
noodled, air-brushed, embalmed faces that
dominated much of illustration in the 1970s. I
am looking for an indication that the brush or
pencil was held by a human hand.
    The big unknown in our future is the com-
puter. Will it be an aid or a hindrance? I know

it will make me design faster; I am not sure it
will make me design better.

—George Tscherny

George Tscherny does not fit the mold of most
professional graphic designers. Even though his
career began within design offices such as
Donald Deskey's and George Nelson's in the
1950s, he has devoted the majority of his career
to maintaining a flourishing, small, independent
office. He has said that there are no revolutionaries in design today and adds, "In my
generation, in school, we were stirred by a still-
developing art. We had our idols in such men
as Lester Beall, Charles Eames, and Paul
Rand."
    But in the more than thirty years of Tscher-
ny's career, how has he been innovative in his
creative design? He claims that he pursues two
opposite directions in design. He sometimes
extracts the essence of a subject and presents it
simply and dramatically, as in the *Triennale*
poster and the *Art Auction* publication.
Alternatively, he utilizes a more pluralistic,
scrapbook technique when that approach seems
useful in order to intensify or deepen communication. This method is exemplified in the
Champion Papers *Imagination Book on Railroads*, the poster on nineteenth-century Germany and the Simpson Paper Company
"Connections" poster. With either method, he
attempts to avoid being timid or predictable.
Tscherny is a keen and intelligent analyst who
finds answers to design problems within the
natures of the problems themselves. The problem establishes the form, and he uses whatever
solution appears appropriate to enhance the
content in the simplest, most communicative
manner. He feels that "the designer" is the
creator of his own visual vocabulary, and the
recycled form is a denial of that commitment.
His delightful graphic solutions evidence integration, surprises, economy of means, and a
special elegance of orchestration.
    By reason of its subtle ingenuity, self-
possession, and intellectual maturity his work
offers an invigoratingly distinctive oasis of
achievement. His versatility has kept him independent and vice versa, as his practice has
engaged in wide-ranging types of projects,
including corporate identity, advertising, posters, displays, stamps, annual reports, displays,
and more. Tscherny's work has been influential
in that he is consistently producing graphic
design that is different and fresh. His work is
logical, and he insists on doing nothing more or
less than what serves the interests of the
"unmistakable design."
    Tscherny has said that in his design he
attempts to "zig when everyone else zags." He
is indeed one of the select few of contemporary
graphic designers who have evolved an authentic and unique American style.

—R. Roger Remington

TSCHICHOLD, Jan.

Swiss typographer, lettering, typeface and book
designer. Born in Leipzig, Germany, 2 April
1902; emigrated to Switzerland in 1933: naturalized, 1942. Studied at the Teacher Training
College, Grimma, near Leipzig, 1916–19; private studies in graphics and typography, at the
Hall of Culture, Leipzig, 1915–19; studied

graphic design under Hermann Delitsch, at the Academy for Graphic Arts and Book Production, Leipzig, 1919–21; under Heinrich Wieynck, at the School of Arts and Crafts, Dresden, 1921. Married Edith Kramer in 1926; son: Peter. Typographer, at Poeschl und Trepte printing firm, Leipzig, 1922; freelance typographer and graphic designer, working for Fischer und Wittig and Insel-Verlag publishers, in Leipzig, 1923–25, for Phoebus-Palast cinemas in Berlin and Munich, 1926–33, for Verlag Benno Schwabe, Verlag Holbein, and Uhertype, in Basel, 1933–46; design chief, Penguin Books, Harmondsworth, Middlesex, 1947–49; freelance typography and design consultant to German and Swiss publishers, in Basel, from 1950: design consultant to F. Hoffman-La Roche, Basel, 1955–67; retired to Berzona, near Locarno, 1968–74. Assistant in charge of evening classes, under Walter Tiemann, Academy for Graphic Arts and Book Production, Leipzig, 1921–22; instructor, at Paul Renner's German Master Printing School, Munich, 1925–33, and at the Kunstgewerbeschule, Basel, 1933–46. **Exhibitions:** Lund Humphries, London, 1935; *Commercial Typography*, Victoria and Albert Museum, London, 1936; St. Bride Printing Library, London, 1975; Kunstgewerbemuseum, Zurich, 1976; National Library of Scotland, Edinburgh, 1982. **Collections:** Lund Humphries, London; Victoria and Albert Museum, London. Recipient: American Institute of Graphic Arts Gold Medal, New York, 1954; Gutenberg Prize, Leipzig, 1965. Honorary member, Double Crown Club, London, 1949; Honorary Royal Designer for Industry, Royal Society of Arts, London, 1965; Honorary corresponding member, Akademie der Kunste, West Berlin, 1966. *Died* (in Locarno) *11 August 1974.*

Publications:

By TSCHICHOLD: books—*Die neue Typographie*, Berlin 1928; *Foto-Auge; 76 Fotos der Zeit*, with Franz Roh, Stuttgart 1929, New York 1973; *Eine Stunde Druckgestaltung* Stuttgart 1930; *Das neue Plakat*, 1930; *Fototek 1: L. Moholy-Nagy—60 Fotos*, designer, Berlin 1930; *Schriftschreiben für Setzer*, Frankfurt am Main 1931; *Typographische Entwurfstechnik*, Stuttgart 1932; *Typographische Gestaltung*, Basel 1935, Copenhagen and Stockholm 1937, Amsterdam 1938, as *Asymmetric Typography*, New York, Toronto and London 1967; *Der frühe chinesische Farbendruck*, Basel 1940, New York and London 1953; *Geschichte der Schrift in Bildern*, Basel 1941, London 1946; *Gute Schriftformen*, Basel 1941; *Schriftkunde, Schreibungen und Skizzieren für Setzer*, Basel 1942; *Chinesische Farbendruck der Gegenwart*, Basel 1944; *Schatzkammer der Schreibkunst*, Basel 1945; *Im Dienst des Buches*, St. Gallen, Switzerland, New York and Copenhagen 1951; *Meisterbuch der Schrift*, Ravensburg, West Germany 1952, New York 1966; *Formenwandlungen der Et-Zeichen*, Frankfurt 1953; *Schonste, liebe mich*, compiler and designer, Heidelberg 1957; *Der Chinesische und der Japanesische mehrfarbige Holztafeldruck, technische*, Basel 1959; *Erfreuliche Drucksachen durch gute Typography*, Ravensburg, West Germany 1960; *Zur Typographie der Gegenwart*, Bern 1960; *Die Bildersammlung der Zehnbambushalle*, Erlebach 1970; *Ausgewählte Aufsätze über Fragen der Gestalt des Buches und der Typographie*, Basel 1975; *Leben und werk des Typographen Jan Tschichold* (with bibliography), Dresden 1977.

On TSCHICHOLD: books—*Lettering of Today*, edited by C. G. Holme, London and New York 1937, 1949; *Design in British Industry: A Mid-Century Survey* by Michael Farr, Cambridge 1955; *Modern Graphic Design 2: The Typography of Jan Tschichold*, Cincinnati 1957; *Modern Book Design* by Ruari McLean, London 1958; *The New Graphic Design* by Karl Gerstner and Markus Kutter, Teufen and London 1959; *The Typographic Book 1450–1935* by Stanley Morison and Kenneth Day, London 1963; *Functional Graphic Design in the 20s* by Eckhard Neumann, New York and London 1967; *Pioneers of Modern Typography* by Herbert Spencer, London 1969; *History of the Poster* by Josef and Shizuko Muller-Brockmann, Zurich 1971; *Jan Tschichold*, exhibition catalogue with foreword by James Mosley, London 1975; *Jan Tschichold, Typographer* by Ruari McLean, London 1975; *J.T.: Johannes Tschichold, Iwan Tschichold, Jan Tschichold*, edited by Philipp Luidl, Munich 1976; *The Thames and Hudson Manual of Typography* by Ruari McLean, London 1980; *Jan Tschichold: Typographer and Type Designer*, exhibition catalogue, Edinburgh 1982; *Typographic Design; Form and Communication* by Rob Carter, Ben Day and Philip Meggs, New York 1985.

The son of a sign-writer, trained in calligraphy and book-production, Jan Tschichold was grounded in a knowledge of production processes. Unlike artist-typographers, he could communicate his intentions precisely. Among other characteristic features of all his mature work (both "new" and "traditional") are sensitivity to physical materials and to letterforms, as also to the semantic content of text and image; great care in the smallest details of visual placing; and a willingness to experiment within quite severely defined constraints.

By his own testimony, Tschichold experienced a sudden conversion to modernism in 1923, on seeing the exhibition of the Weimar Bauhaus. His achievement was to absorb and refine principles suggested by slightly preceding modernists (Lissitzky and Moholy-Nagy, for example), then to propagate them within the printing trade.

The seriousness with which Tschichold practised typography can be seen in the arguments that surrounded his break with modernism. He explained that he had come to see parallels between the absolutism of his advocacy of a new typography and the totalitarianism of National Socialism; on a lesser plane, he suggested that new typography could not deal adequately with the complexities of book design. However, his mature new typography such as his work for Social-Democratic "Bücherkreis"' club or the content and design of *Typographische Gestaltung*, suggests that such an explanation should be questioned. In any case, it is this phase of his work (roughly 1930–35) that has been most influential for younger generations of typographers.

Tschichold turned away from modernism, but he continued to work with the tasks and technologies of the modern world. Penguins were a new kind of book: mass produced paperbacks, cheap, but serious and worthwhile in content. In less than two years of intensive work, Tschichold was able to obtain high standards of text composition from undistinguished printers, as well as lay down new standards for the design of the text and covers of the whole range of books.

Tschichold's historical research and writing ranged widely and often meshed with his practise. He produced notable contributions on Chinese colour printing, on systems of page proportion, and more generally on the history of written and printed letterforms. His writing always had a polemical, rather authoritarian edge. It was typical that he should have supplied his own pseudonymous account of his work, "Jan Tschichold: Praeceptor Typographiae" (reprinted in the posthumous *Leben und Werk* that he planned and designed). Subsequent historians may adjust and expand this account, but the importance of Tschichold's typography will remain undeniable.

—Robin Kinross

TYE, Alan.
British architect and industrial designer. Born in London, 18 September 1933. Studied architecture, at Regent Street Polytechnic, London, 1952–60: Dip.Arch. 1960. Married Anita Birgitta Goethe in 1966; children: Madeleine, Nicholas and Kevin. Assistant architect, in the office of Arne Jacobsen, in Copenhagen, 1960–62; freelance designer, as Alan Tye Design RDI Limited, in London and Hertfordshire, from 1962; partnership with Knud Holscher, as Holscher-Tye Architects, London and Copenhagen, from 1964: has designed for Adamsez, Allgood, Headway-Syncronol, Apple, Mallinson-Denny, Sissons, Domaine International, etc. Tutor, at the Royal College of Art, London, 1978–83; also visiting lecturer, at the Ceramic Society, London, 1974, and the Royal Institute, London, 1976, 1978. Design selection committee member, Council of Industrial Design, London, 1967; assessor, Civic Trust Awards, London, 1968–69; juror, Royal Society of Arts, London, 1980; specialist advisor to the Council for National Academic Awards, London, 1980; architectural awards assessor, Royal Institute of British Architects, London, 1981, 1988; Young Designers in Industry juror, Royal Society of Arts, London, 1986–89; advisor to the Wuxi University Industrial Design School, China, 1987; external degrees examiner, Royal College of Art, London 1987–89. **Exhibitions:** Design Society, Copenhagen, 1972; Design Centre, London, 1979; *New Design for Old*, Victoria and Albert Museum, London, 1985 (toured); *Eye for Industry*, Victoria and Albert Museum, London, 1986. **Collections:** Victoria and Albert Museum, London; Ringling Museum, Sarasota, Florida. Recipient: International Bathroom Design Prize, Rome, 1962; Council of Industrial Design Award, London, 1965, 1966; Guild of Architectural Ironmongers Award, London, 1966, 1969, 1971, 1976; British Aluminium Industry Design Award, 1966, and Eros Trophy, 1973; Stainless Steel Development Association Prize, London, 1966; Silver Cup for Exhibition Display, London, 1969; *Observer* Design Award, London, 1969; Ringling Museum Design Award, Sarasota, 1969; Star Design Award and Gold Medal, London, 1970; Building Centre Exceptional Merit Award, London, 1970; *Architects' Journal* Graphic Design Award, London, 1976; Interbuild Gold Lion Award, 1978, Design Award, 1981, and Exhibition Award, 1983, 1985, London and Birmingham; Roscoe Design Award, New York, 1988. Fellow, 1974, and Royal Designer for Industry, 1986, Royal Society of Arts, London; Fellow, Chartered Society of Designers, London, 1975; member, Royal Institute of British Architects, 1965. Address: Great West Plantation, Tring, Hertfordshire HP23 6DA, England.

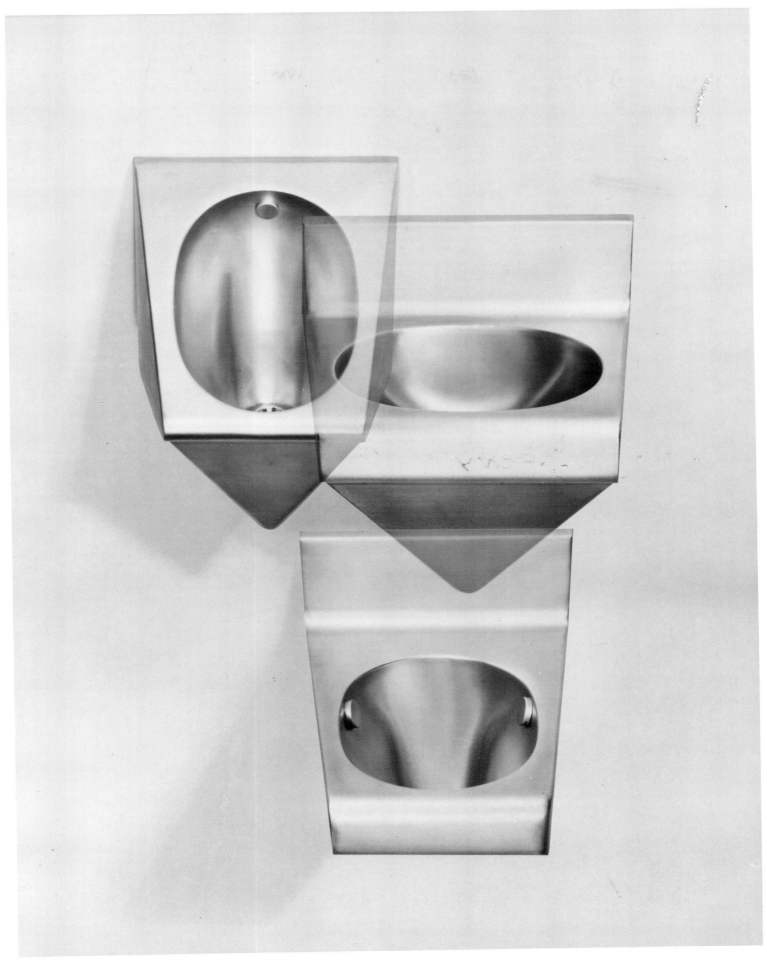

Alan Tye: *System 94* sanitary wares in stainless steel, for Sissons, 1981

Works:

Meridian ceramic sanitary fittings, for Adamsez, from 1965.
Hedway signposting system in stainless steel, for Syncronol Industries Limited, from 1970.
Modric Limbar hospital rails and handle in aluminium and steel, for G. and S. Allgood Limited, from 1972.
Modric cloakroom system in aluminium, for G. and S. Allgood Limited, from 1973.
Computer disc storage furniture in plastic laminate, for Data Efficiency, from 1976.
Barrier rail system in stainless steel, for Marler Haley, 1977.
Office furniture system, for Hille International, 1979.
Intravenous operation workstation in stainless steel and plastic, for Travenol, 1979.
Wood-burning stove in cast iron and brass, for a private client, 1979.
System 94 anti-vandal sanitary fittings in aluminium, for W. G. Sissons, from 1981.
Cubicle and washroom system in laminated aluminium and steel, for Mallinson-Denny and Brooke Bond Liebig, from 1981.
Mirror storage system in wood, glass and metal, for Finnmirror, 1981.
Security system in thermoplastic mouldings, for Reed International, 1983.
Vallum ceiling tile system in perlite, for Thermo-Acoustic Products, from 1983.
Low-voltage light fittings, for Concord, 1984.
Conservatory in wood, glass and cemfil, for Pilkington, 1984.
Min table system in brass, glass, wood and cast iron, for Messin Oy, 1985–88.
Modric Spectra electrostatic paint colour system, for G. and S. Allgood Limited, from 1986.
Modric Unilite hardware in photoluminescent plastic, for G. and S. Allgood Limited, from 1988.
Sport changing cubicles in stainless steel and solid laminate, for Bushboard Parker-Celcon, from 1988.

Publications:

By TYE: articles—in *The Architect* (London), March 1976; *Architects' Journal* (London), 1 December 1976; *Architectural Review* (London), May 1978; *The Designer* (London), November 1978.

On TYE: books—*Modern Design in Metal* by Richard Stewart, London 1979; *New Design for Old*, exhibition catalogue with texts by Helen Hamlyn, Eric Midwinter and others, London 1986; *Eye for Industry: Royal Designers for Industry 1936–1986* by Fiona MacCarthy and Patrick Nuttgens, London 1986; *International Design Yearbook 1988/89*, edited by Arata Isozaki, London 1988; articles—in *Architectural Review* (London), October 1976; *House and Garden* (London), March 1977; *MD: Moebel Interior Design* (Leinfelden), March 1977; *RIBA Journal* (London), August 1977, August 1978; *Architecture + Urbanism* (Tokyo), February 1979; *Ville Giardini* (Milan), September 1981; *Building* (London), 16 April 1982; *Building Enquirer* (London), June 1988.

*

Only 1/200ths of the weight of coffee is the oil which gives coffee its lovely smell and taste. Without this, it is just blackish caffeine-water.

Design is like that. It takes very little to make or spoil it, and very few people can honestly provide that special ingredient which makes all the difference.

What is the origin of this quality?

I do not see it coming from value analysis, ease of manufacture, doing what the wholesaler wants, ergonomics, or market research. The answer is so simple that it seems too easy; yet it is easy, and also profound. The following poem from our Christmas card of 1975 explains:

WHY IS THIS SO BEAUTIFUL?
IT HAS NO STYLE
NO AESTHETICS.
IT'S PURPOSEFUL
NOT ARTFUL.

Fortunately, the client doesn't have to understand the working of the designer, but just let the right designer get on with it for him.

—Alan Tye

*

The 1950s in Britain were an exciting time for young architects and designers. The opportunity to build after more than ten years of inactivity, combined with the development of design-consciousness fostered by the Council of Industrial Design and given sudden impetus by the 1951 Festival of Britain, stimulated a new and enterprising school of designers. Ready to look anew at accepted solutions, as well as to experiment with and exploit the technological developments of wartime industry, they saw themselves as builders of a new Britain.

Alan Tye, like most students of his generation, was strongly influenced by Scandinavian designers, in his case, by the Danish and, in particular, by Arne Jacobsen, for whom he later worked. He claims also to have been influenced by James Stirling, who was one of his teachers; Stirling's direct and uncompromising attitude may be discernible in Tye's approach, but to it must be added the refinement and visual suavity characteristic of the Danish designers.

Tye's first notable success was the 1965 Meridian range of bathroom fittings for Adamsez. Washbasins, WC's, and the like had seldom if ever been the subject of either ergonomic or aesthetic consideration; most were inefficient or ugly, or both. Tye evolved fittings which were not only easy and comfortable to use, easy to clean and maintain, and simple to manufacture and install, but they also looked good. Thus, for the first time, bathroom fittings became a considered part of house furniture.

His outstanding achievement came in the following year. Hitherto, British architects could get an integrated range of building ironmongery (door handles, window catches, locks, letter plates, etc.) only by importing from Denmark or Germany, a costly and frequently slow process, and by no means a complete solution. In these circumstances, Paul Shirville, managing director of the ironmongery firm of G & S Allgood and chairman of the newly formed Guild of Architectural Ironmongers, asked Tye to design a fully integrated line. Close cooperation between designer, manufacturer, and merchant from the beginning rapidly resulted in the Modric range, based on a modular grid but by no means purely a cold, mathematical exercise. For instance, the standard door handle, carefully calculated ergonomic design though it may appear to be, was evolved from a fat candle carved out until it looked good, fitted the grid system, and was easy and comfortable in use. The Modric range completely transformed the British market. It alone can stand as an example of Tye's philosophy of design: not visual design for its own sake, but design whose beauty is inherent in its fitness for its purpose.

—Gordon Steele

UNGARO, Emanuel (Matteotti).

French fashion designer. Born, of Italian parents, in Aix-en-Provence, 13 February 1933. Educated at the Lycée, Aix-en-Provence, 1943–50. Worked in his father's tailoring business, Aix-en-Provence, 1951–54; stylist, at Maison Camps tailoring company, Paris, 1955–57; designer, at Balenciaga fashion house, in Paris, 1958–64, and head of design at Balenciaga's Madrid headquarters, 1959–61; designer, at Courrèges fashion house, Paris, 1964–65; established own couture firm, Paris, from 1965: launched Ungaro Parallèle women's ready-to-wear fashion range, 1968, and menswear range, 1975. **Exhibition:** *Fashion: An Anthology*, Victoria and Albert Museum, London, 1971. Recipient: Neiman Marcus Award, Dallas, 1969. Address: 2 Avenue Montaigne, 75008 Paris, France.

Publications:

On UNGARO: books—*The Fashion Makers* by Leonard Halliday, London 1966; *Fashion: An Anthology by Cecil Beaton*, exhibition catalogue compiled by Madeleine Ginsburg, London 1971; *Paris Fashion: The Great Designers and Their Creations*, edited by Ruth Lynam, London 1972; *In Vogue: Sixty Years of Celebrities and Fashion* by Georgina Howell, London 1975, 1978, New York 1976; *A History of Fashion* by J. Anderson Black and Madge Garland, London 1975, 1980; *25 Ans de Marie-Claire de 1954 a 1979*, compiled by Françoise Mohrt, Paris 1979; *Fashion 2001* by Lucille Khornak, London 1982; *The Collector's Book of Twentieth Century Fashion* by Frances Kennett, London and New York 1983; *Les Années 60* by Anne Bony, Paris 1983; *McDowell's Directory of Twentieth Century Fashion* by Colin McDowell, London 1984; *The Encyclopaedia of Fashion from 1840 to the 1980s* by Georgina O'Hara, London 1986.

*

Memories from my childhood of Aix-en-Provence: sunshine, pink stone and fountains. What many people call *joie de vivre*. A privileged place to grow up. Where there is beauty. And gravity too. Aix is a capital city of classical culture. It is also the mountain of Sainte-Victoire, Cézanne: Impressionism is there.

I learned my trade with my father. A feeling for work well done, the perfect garment: this I owe to him. At 22, I enter the House of Balenciaga as a "qualified tailor's assistant." In my six years with this *grand couturier*, I discover perseverance, pride in my job, and a frenzied taste for work; and freedom, too, of the kind qualified by constraint and respect for restrictions. A feeling for clothes worn and lived in, a sense of movement, all this I learn from him. After these six years, I launch out fully armed, or should I say disarmed, as an artist is when he dares to be himself.

Fashion defines itself, and I pave the way for it. The dress designer in me is at one and the same time humble, purposeful, and terribly proud. Pride in colour and treatment of colour. I love whatever sings to me. I love Debussy and jazz, Uccello and Motherwell, Proust and Handke, colours, colour values, every kind of Impressionism; I love the warmth of the South and the rigours of the North. In this, I am fundamentally European, a Westerner, constantly torn between my Mediterranean origins and my aspirations, which are Nordic, Saxon, Germanic. As for music, I was about to forget the School of Vienna. I love dissonances, the superimposition of tones, the interaction of pattern and line.

In reality, every woman creates the dress she wears. A designer worth his salt, who deserves the name of couturier, has to capture her verve and interpret her desires. That's my metier.

—Emanuel Ungaro

*

It is not surprising that Emanuel Ungaro's first collection, presented in 1965, acknowledged debts both to Cristobal Balenciaga and to André Courrèges, since the Parisian fashion designer had spent six years apprenticed to the widely influential Balenciaga and had worked with Courrèges. From the beginning of his career, Ungaro's has been a combination of the geometric silhouette and minidressed Courrèges look with a more classic and less faddish touch, stressing the feminine and recalling his connections with Balenciaga.

Exemplary of Ungaro's designs of the late 1960s for day and evening wear for women are A-line minidresses with tone-on-tone inserts, Bermuda shorts under shifts or minidresses, jumpers in rabbit fur, and pleated print shirts with long jackets in suedes and wool. He was making wide use of leather and the pantsuit in outfits such as his flared, long, leather jacket teamed with calfskin pants of 1969. Always, Ungaro incorporated a variety of accessories, such as white, knee-length socks and black, patent-leather shoes to help achieve the youthful, freedom-loving mood he desired. He wanted to create outfittings which were "more than a dress" for women of individual personality with a vivacious flair. During this period, Ungaro became known for his quirky combinations of patterns, textures, and colors, mingled together and layered in outfits which blend contemporary flavor with clean-lined elegance.

As he moved into the decade of the 1970s, Ungaro had slowly but surely tempered the stiffness and toughness of his work from the previous decade, evolving toward a more graceful, feminine tone, using soft fabrics such as crepe, satin, and Qiana and concentrating on a more flowing line and liquid silhouette. For a period during the 1970s, entranced by the man-tailored look which was then coming into vogue, Ungaro designed outfits such as knickers with high boots accompanied by canvas coat and big-brimmed hat. But the characteristic fusion with classic line and individualistic flavor persisted and came to the fore again toward the end of the decade, showing itself in Ungaro's 1977 flared plaid coat superimposed by a soft, large shawl of another plaid.

During the past few years, Ungaro has enjoyed a resurgence in acclaim, giving a boost in America to Parisian couture and gaining such significant recognition as to bring him comparisons with Yves Saint Laurent, to whom he is said to be running "a close second." Ungaro's 1983 collection is precisely cut, attuned to the very feminine woman, vibrantly colorful and patterned, and geared for flowing movement and sex appeal. There are daring cocktail dresses, draped and hitched in several places, in cobblestone-patterned silk jacquard. One is worn with a square-cut coat in fuchsia mohair with seaming visible. Among the many jackets are one which is yoked of black, cream, and gray wool and another which is lightly quilted with asymmetric opening of plum and sea-blue wool. There are ample touches of flamboyance in a number of fox boas and slightly wild hats, and, most dramatically, in the Belle Epoque gown with puffed sleeves and swept-up skirt of diagonal stripes, worn with a boa around the neck. Ungaro's latest work shows him reaching a mature style which has evolved steadily through longtime study and practice into a unique synthesis which lends contemporary vigor to the tradition of Parisian high fashion for women.

—Barbara Cavaliere

URBANIEC, Maciej (Jerzy).

Polish graphic designer. Born in Zwierzyniec, 1 September 1925. Studied at the School of Fine Arts, Wroclaw, 1952–54; Academy of Fine Arts, Warsaw, 1954–58. Served in Polish resistance, Warsaw uprising, 1944. Married Maria Kotarbinska in 1952; daughter: Barbara. Freelance poster, advertisement and graphic designer, Warsaw, from 1958. Lecturer, at the School of Fine Arts, Wroclaw, then head of the graphics department, at the Academy of Fine Arts, Warsaw. **Exhibitions:** Dom Artysty Plastyka, Warsaw, 1958; WAG Gallery, Szczecin, 1969; Biuro Wystaw Artystycznych, Radom, 1975; Biuro Artystycznych, Poznan, 1975; Galeria Dom Wojska Pokskiego, Warsaw, 1975; Biuro Wystaw Artystycznych, Kielce, 1976. **Collections:** Vilanov Poster Museum, Warsaw; National Museum, Poznan; Centre Georges Pompidou, Paris; Stedelijk Museum, Amster-

Emanuel Ungaro: Multicoloured silk jacquard suit, 1982

dam. Recipient: Tadeusz Trepkowski Prize, Warsaw, 1958; Social Poster of the Year Awards, Warsaw, 1964–82; Five Gold Medals, Katowice Poster Biennale, 1967–78; Silver Medal, Brno Graphics Biennale, 1970, 1974; Bronze Medal, Leipzig Book Fair, 1970, 1982. Member: Zwiazek Polskich Artystow Plastykow, Warsaw; Alliance Graphique Internationale, Paris. Address: Academicka 3, m.94, 02-038 Warsaw, Poland.

Publications:

By URBANIEC: article—in *Projekt* (Warsaw), no. 3, 1974.

On URBANIEC: books—*Polish Poster Art Today* by Szymon Bojko, Warsaw 1972; *107 Grafici dell'AGI*, with texts by Renzo Zorzi and Franco Grignani, Venice 1974; *100 Years of Circus Posters* by Jack Renner, New York 1974; *Glad Konst* by Sten Mollerstrom and Bra Becker, Hoganas 1975; *Contemporary Polish Posters in Full Color*, edited by Joseph S. Czestochowski, New York 1979; *The Polish Poster 1970–1978*, with introduction by Zdzislaw Schubert, Warsaw 1979; *The Language of Graphics* by Edward Booth-Clibborn and Daniele Baroni, London 1980; *Who's Who in Graphic Art*, edited by Walter Amstutz, Dubendorf 1982.

I am a poster designer. My idea is the synthetic expression of thoughts. If I could better express my thoughts in words than in images, I would not make posters but would have become a writer. Forgive me that my statement is so modest; however, the older a man is, the shorter his biography because many events lose their significance. I have executed more than 300 posters, which after I have painted them, begin a life of their own, and I am unable to follow their plights.

—Maciej Urbaniec

Let us take two posters and hang them together. The first attacks us with vulgar colors and, even more, with its shocking subject—a circus performer in a somewhat forced, unnatural position with raised, crossed legs. She has the torso of the *Mona Lisa*, Leonardo's famous lady. The top of this poster bears the word "circus." After a moment of confusion, you have to laugh. All those trivial colors and the obviously cheap trick with the *Mona Lisa* don't offend; rather, they play together so well that we draw some conclusions immediately. One: the artist is blinking his eye on the real cheapness of the circus as an art form. Another: He makes a point about his own discipline by suggesting the question "Is a poster truly art?"

The second poster we discuss is a world apart from the previous one. It is a simple composition of letters composed of thick, brutal, raw rope against a clear, glowing red background. The rope letters spell "The Wedding," the title of a play by Stanislaw Wyspianski, famous Polish playwright of the beginning of the twentieth century. *The Wedding* is a traumatic, agonizing discussion about the fate of Poland, the struggle for freedom, lost hopes, futile dreams, the faults of national character, lack of ideology. Every Pole remembers this message, keeps it in the corner of his mind, for it is still very accurate almost a century later.

Both of these posters are signed by Maciej Urbaniec, one of the true masters of the Polish school. His approach differs from that of such colleagues as Tomaszewski or Starowieyski, whose works are recognizable at a first glance, because Urbaniec has the ease of the great

Maciej Urbaniec: Poster for the Warsaw Poster Biennale, 1974

craftsman. He could paint anything in an almost Renaissance manner. But he sees no point in working in one style on every poster he does. His major concern is to reach "the target" in the simplest and most powerful way. Every subject is carefully studied by the artist in order to choose the best way to convey the message. Among the techniques he uses are assemblage, collage, tempera painting, and colored-paper cut-outs, but despite this versatility, Urbaniec never overdoes his work, and his solutions are always intelligent.

Another important factor is humor in all possible cases. His *Mona Lisa*'s, "Renaissance" madonnas making faces, somewhat too serious looking "icons" that are almost better done than Andrei Rublëv's originals—many of his works make us smile, help to distance ourselves from the not-too-happy reality of daily life. When matters are serious, he's sharp, strikes to

a painful point, no gimmicks, no smoky allusions. In every other situation, he tries to find the optimistic side of the problem, make a little face on you, on himself, on the subject.

A formidable teacher, Urbaniec is loved by his students. He doesn't act flamboyantly, and the atmosphere in his studio doesn't resemble the master-pupil scheme. The pressure to learn and perform well and think fast is not evident after a short time. He tries to keep a rather low-key, intimate communication with his "chickens." Day after day, the conversation continues on equal terms. Literature, theatre, the movies, art, jokes, everyday happenings, a little gossip—that's it. Meanwhile, a relationship is growing. The student doesn't feel it at the beginning, but he's slowly lured into thinking about the artist and society, about the graphic designer and the variety of arts problems. Slowly, everyone is trapped by Urbaniec's method and comes to know something very important, that after graduating from the Academy, he has a friend, a true guide, defender, and the best advisor in the difficult, fresh years of real professional testing of every young artist.

—Jan Sawka

URBAŃSKI, Leon.
Polish typographer and graphic designer. Born in Tarnow, 11 September 1926. Studied at the High School of Fine Arts, Warsaw, 1946–48; Academy of Fine Arts, Warsaw, 1948–59. Married Krystyna Urbański in 1952; children: Jacek, Marek and Dorota. Freelance book and graphic designer, Warsaw, from 1959: art director, Arkady Publishers, Warsaw. Associate professor of graphic arts, Academy of Fine Arts, Warsaw, 1977–82. Juror, Leipzig Book Fair, 1977–82; secretary of the executive council, Association of Polish Artists, Warsaw. **Collections:** Plock Scientific Society Collection, Muzeum Ksiazki, Wroclaw; Regional Museum, Sanok;

Leon Urbanski: Book design, 1971

Deutsche Bucherei, Leipzig. Recipient: Gold Medal, Polish Association of Book Publishers; Leipzig Book Fair Medal, 1959, 1965, and Grand Prize, 1971; Teaching award, Academy of Fine Arts, Warsaw, 1978, 1980. Knight of the Order of Polonia Restituta, Warsaw; Merited Activist in Culture, Warsaw. Address: ul. Gagarina 33, m.25, 00-595 Warsaw, Poland.

Publications:

On URBÁNSKI: book—*Grafika Polska* by Danuta Wroblewska, Warsaw 1983.

I work in a narrow branch of graphic arts. My main interest is the world in every form, from an exclamation to an epic poem, and the ways by which it reaches its audience. I wish for the reception of words to bring enjoyment and to be like the touch of a hand in today's mechanized world. I would like to work for a million people. I hate bibliophiles, rare books, and elitism. I want to do things for everybody. My tastes are somewhat traditional, and I would like to preserve in this crazy desensitized world something that has an old-fashioned name—beauty, which can be found in the unique perfume label, in a sound commercial, in the seriousness of a monument, or in the esthetic appearance of a book.

I have to admit that I have never considered my work an art but, rather, a kind of a social service. I am only a designer. It will be possible

to classify my work as an art only if the work of the engineer Eiffel or of the technicians who built the American cosmic pendulum can be considered as great art.

Jan Tschichold said some time ago that only two in a thousand graphic designers have an ideal sense of proportion, and they become typographers.

How am I different from my colleagues? Most of the time, they already have the shape for their word when they begin. For me, the word form comes much later because I wait for the word to suggest it. Sometimes it comes immediately, but other times, it takes a long time. That is why I am so sensitive to the text. I never work on poorly formulated or bad sounding texts.

The reason that I have never wanted to exhibit my works is that the intention of my design manifests itself best in its natural function: a book, when it is being read; a sign, when it is warning; a diploma, when in the hands of someone who earned it. If they were displayed, all these objects would look dead. If I ever do arrange an exhibit of my work, it will be one in which my prints will be passed from hand to hand or one that will show all stages of my work.

I love my work, and at the same time I hate it. I also love music, and I think that the two of them have something in common.

I am a perfectionist; i.e., I am satisfied only with my own work. When I stand by the type case or when I work on book-binding, I know

Hymny Rigwedy

*Przełożył z sanskrytu,
wstępem i komentarzem opatrzył
Franciszek Michalski
Ossolineum 1971*

Lud, który w odległych wiekach wysnuł z otaczającego go świata własny panteon i zaklął go w hieratycznej poezji *Rigwedy*, należał do tej samej rodziny językowej indoeuropejskiej co my, co Litwini, Grecy, Italowie, Germanie, Celtowie, Hetyci czy Irańczycy. Wszystkie te ludy białej rasy stanowiły w dalekiej przeszłości jedność, ale epoka ich jedności, ich późniejszego rozbicia i rozpłynięcia się po świecie zasłana jest dotąd mrokiem tajemnicy. [Na podstawie skąpych śladów epoki przedhistorycznej dadzą się

5

that I have a full command of my work. The work of others has always less spirit for me.

I regret that in Poland it is not customary to have a private assistant. Although I dream of one, I am aware that he would have a hard time with me.

—Leon Urbański

As much as typography in general is a field for industrious people, Leon Urbański's nature makes it a benedictine task. Being a technical perfectionist forces him to devote to each project more plans of form and arrangement, more studies of coloring than are usually done. Besides that, Urbański is an ambitious man, full of a sense of his own independence. This genetic inheritance from mountaineer ancestors allied with a line of Austro-Hungarian, Galician gentry gives him a strong sense of identity, a strong foundation in the center of an expressive historical culture.

It is difficult to say what is most interesting in Urbański: his own powerful creativity, his penetrating and analytic understanding of plastic and word forms (the twin means of communication), or his didactic passion for opening the talents of others. As a typographer, he does not close himself in specialization. Rather, he responds to contemporary art and technology, he understands literature and music, he is interested in linguistic knowledge. However, as a humanist, he feels the weight of technology on culture.

Working in almost every field of graphic design, he believes, above all else, in the power of the book as the basic means for the transfer of thoughts, independent of time, space, and all adversity of fate. He believes in its culturally creative force. He also sees that its architecture and form are a condensation of the characteristics of the reality which shapes it. All the elements of the book ripened in full between the sixteenth and eighteenth centuries; the sequel consists just of delicate mutations. In letter design, says Urbański, there are no old or new forms, just bad and good ones. The printer's sign will always be supported by that which has already been catalogued. He is, however, interested in the new possibilities of computer technology and electronic recording because these contain different possibilities of expression.

At the Academy of Fine Arts, Urbański was the pupil of professor Andrzej Rudziński, a good graphic artist and sensitive book artist. From him, he took a classical orientation, which he strengthened with his own sense of harmony. In the European milieu, the views of Jan Tschichold and the Swiss typographers were closest to his own, though his outlook was much broader. Urbański's creativity, though contained within the golden canon of the European esthetic of print, introduces into it a certain lightness and romanticism. The best example of these characteristics, as well as the most beautiful connection of the letter with free composition, are to be found in his little volumes of Far Eastern poetry. The lesson learned during his Asian trips showed how consonant had been his earlier intuitions with the oriental art of the sign.

Urbański's work as a teacher lasted not quite five years. In such a short time, he was able to accomplish the most difficult thing imaginable in the Department of Graphic Arts of the Academy of Fine Arts: in the exceedingly modest conditions of school work, he awoke a great typographical sensitivity in the young people, who were hitherto unconscious of it. He did not so much teach typography per se, as open students to the essence of the sign and all of its functions and contexts. In general, he directed them to the culture of form. In 1981, at the Leipzig *Internationale Buchkunstausstellung*, his students received the gold medal for their collective work. A year later, his great achievement was a portfolio of typographical exercises with the texts of Czesław Miłosz. This explains the unprecedented case of such a young teacher being awarded two rector's prizes in so short a span of time.

—Danuta Wróblewska

VALENTINO (Garavani).
Italian fashion designer. Born in Voghera, near Milan, 11 May 1932. Studied French and fashion design, Milan, until 1948; studied at the Chambre Syndicale de Couture, in the Ecole des Beaux-Arts, Paris, 1949–51. Assistant designer, in Jean Desses fashion house, Paris, 1950–55, and in Guy Laroche fashion house, Paris, 1956–58; founder and partner, with Giancarlo Giammetti, of Valentino fashion house, Rome, from 1960, and of Valentino Più interior decor, textile and gift company, Rome, from 1973; opened ready-to-wear fashion boutiques in Rome, 1972, 1988, Milan, 1979, and in London 1987; established Rome headquarters in the newly-restored Palazzo Gabrielli, from 1987. Also film costume designer from 1964. **Exhibitions:** *Fashion: An Anthology*, Victoria and Albert Museum, London, 1971; *Italian Re-Evolution*, La Jolla Museum of Art, California, 1982; Metropolitan Museum of Art, New York, 1982; *40 Years of Italian Fashion*, Trump Tower, New York, 1983; *Atelier delle Illusioni*, Castello Sforzesco, Milan, 1985; Royal Academy of Arts, London, 1989. Recipient: Neiman Marcus Award, Dallas, 1967, 1988. Address: Piazza Mignanelli 22, 00187 Rome, Italy.

Publications:

On VALENTINO: books—*Fashion: An Anthology* by Cecil Beaton, exhibition catalogue compiled by Madeleine Ginsburg, London, 1971; *Fashion Merchandizing* by Mary D. Troxell, New York, 1971, 1976; *Fairchild's Dictionary of Fashion* by Charlotte Calasibetta, New York, 1975; *The World of Fashion: People, Places, Resources* by Eleanor Lambert, New York and London, 1976; *Quest for the Best* by Stanley Marcus, New York, 1979; *I Mass-Moda: Fatti e Personaggi dell'Italian Look* by Adriana Mulassano, Florence, 1979; *Fashion 2001* by Lucille Khornak, London, 1982; *Italian Re-Evolution: Design in Italian Society in the Eighties*, exhibition catalogue edited by Piero Sartogo, La Jolla, 1982; *Valentino*, edited by Franco Maria Ricci, Milan, 1982; *The Collector's Book of Twentieth Century Fashion* by Frances Kennett, London and New York, 1983; *40 Years of Italian Fashion*, exhibition catalogue compiled by B. G. Aragno, Rome, 1983; *McDowell's Directory of Twentieth Century Fashion* by Colin McDowell, London, 1984; *Valentino che Veste di Nuovo* by Marina Cosi, Milan, 1984; *The Encyclopaedia of Fashion from 1840 to the 1980s* by Georgina O'Hara, London, 1986.

On the pages of many fashionable magazines, prestigious women of the world are often featured wearing the feminine, glamorous, and flattering dresses of Valentino. Among them are Consuelo Crespi, Christina Ford, Gloria Guinness, Audrey Hepburn and Jacqueline Onassis. The advertisements for various Valentino franchises are exquisitely photographed, often by the French and Japanese, to create a world one imagines to be exclusively of the upper classes.

I often note his dramatic use of floral fabrics, fluidly patterned, occasionally incorporating butterflies, petals, leaves, tropical themes, and some geometrics. Generally, his fabrics are created by such Italian companies as Setarium, Lucchini, Gandini, Taroni, Stucchi, Clerici, and Rainbow. The patterns always complement the feminine lines of the dresses and are often printed in mysterious black with touches, to dramatize, of white or bright colors. Recently, I met a young child wearing a black velveteen Valentino smock with a white pique collar and ribbon trim.

Valentino showed little interest in formal education until he arrived at the Chambre Syndicale in Paris to study cutting and sewing. He left his first position with Jean Desses to work with Guy Laroche until he returned to Rome, where he opened his first atelier. High fashion, though, it seemed was really happening on the runways of the Pitti Palace in Florence. His first collection, introduced there in 1962, was praised and purchased by I. Magnin. At the beginning of the 1970s, he introduced a more accessible ready-to-wear line and opened the first of many boutiques. Today, there are more than 100 throughout the United States, Europe, and Japan, where he is enjoying a flurry over anything he designs.

The Valentino empire comprising couture, ready-to-wear, fashion accessories, lingerie, the home furnishing line Valentino Più, cosmetics, and most recently, the fragrance Valentino by Valentino has flourished with the help of 260 employees as well as the guidance and friendship of partner Giancarlo Giametti.

—Gillion Skellenger

VALLIEN, Bertil (Erik).
Swedish glass, ceramics and metalware designer. Born in Stockholm, 17 January 1938. Studied under Stig Lindberg, School of Art, Craft and Design, Stockholm, 1957–61; also studied in the United States and Mexico, 1961–63, Married Ulrica Hydman in 1963; children: Hampus and Markus. Glass designer, since 1963, and Head of Design, 1983–86, Afors Glasbruk (Kosta Boda Group), Eriksmala; established Rebus Design AB company, working with sandblast sculpture and art glass, Eriksmala, from 1986; also freelance industrial, ceramics and cutlery designer, working for Boda Nova, Gense, Rorstrand, Alfa-Laval, etc. Instructor in Glass Design, University of Stockholm (Konstfackskolan), 1967–83; Pilchuk Glass Center, Washington, 1980–89; Artist-in-Residence, Rhode Island School of Design, Providence, 1985; also guest lecturer throughout Britain, the United States and Canada, from 1973. **Exhibitions:** Ryder Gallery, Los Angeles, 1963; Bonniers, New York, 1966; George's Gallery, Melbourne, 1968, 1980; Heal's Gallery, London, 1974; Nordiska Kompaniet, Stockholm, 1976; Seibu Gallery, Tokyo, 1980, 1982; David Jones Gallery, Sydney, 1980; Konsthantverkarna, Stockholm, 1980; Galleri Gamla Stan, Stockholm, 1983; Atelier d'Amon, Paris, 1983; Heller Gallery, New York, 1983, 1985, 1987; Norrkoping Museum, Sweden, 1984; Gallery Takanawa-Kai, Tokyo, 1984; Galleri Ikaros, Goteborg, 1985; Galerie Rosenthal, Hamburg, 1986; Collier Gallery, Phoenix, Arizona, 1986; The Works Gallery, Philadelphia, 1987; Gallery Malen, Helsingborg, 1987; Betsy Rosenfield Gallery, Chicago, 1988; Travers-Sutton Gallery, Seattle, Washington, 1988; Smalands Museum, Vaxo, Denmark, 1988. **Collections:** Nationalmuseum, Stockholm; Rohsska Konstslojdmuseet, Goteborg; Vaxjo Glassmuseum, Sweden; Art Institute of Chicago; Corning Glass Museum, New York; Musee des Arts Decoratifs, Paris; Victoria and Albert Museum, London. Recipient: Swedish Royal Scholarship, 1961; Young Americans Prize, 1962; Illum Prize, Copenhagen, 1967; Swedish State Major Award for Design, 1970; Most Influential Artist Award, *Japan Interior Design* magazine, 1981; First Prize for Swedish Design, Nationalmuseum, Stockholm, 1983; Silver Medal, International Art Competition, New York, 1985; Coburger Glass Prize, West Germany, 1985; Formland Prize, Denmark, 1988. Address: Afors Glasbruk, 351 04 Eriksmala, Sweden.

Works:

Husar glassware, for Kosta Boda, 1965.
Spiral candle-holders, for Dansk Design, 1967.

Bertil Vallien: *Spin* glass jugs, for Kosta Boda, 1983

Network decorative blown glass on iron netting, for Kosta Boda, 1977.
Artist's Collection range of glass stemware, for Kosta Boda, 1977–89.
Oktav glass stemware, for Kosta Boda, 1978.
Chateau optically-blown glass stemware, for Kosta Boda, from 1981.
Oktav cutlery, for Gense, 1981.
Ships sandcast glass sculptures, for Kosta Boda, 1985.
Next cutlery, for Boda-Nova, 1986.
Petit Point cutlery, for Gense, 1987.
Glass with rubber details, for Kosta Boda, 1987.
Provence glassware, for Kosta Boda, 1988.
Blue Water decorative glassware, for Kosta Boda, 1988.
Apostrof glassware, for Kosta Boda, 1989.
Separator, for Alfa-Laval, 1989.

Publications:

On VALLIEN: books—*Glasboken: Historia, Teknik och Form* by Carl F. Hermelin and Elsebeth Welander, Boras 1980; *Scandinavian Modern Design 1880–1980*, edited by David Revere McFadden, New York 1982; *Form och Tradition i Sverige*, edited by Birgitta Walz, Stockholm 1982; *Bertil Valliens Glass, Sand-casted* by Ulf Thomas Moberg and Ole Terje, Stockholm 1983; *Contemporary Swedish Design*, exhibition catalogue by Monica Boman, Lennart Lindkvist and others, Stockholm 1983; *Den Svenska Formen* by Monica Boman and others, Stockholm 1985; *Kosta* by Ann Marie Herlitz-Gezelius, Lund 1987; *Faces of Swedish Design*, exhibition catalogue edited by Monica Boman, Stockholm 1988; *Bertil Vallien* by Gunnar Lindqvist, Stockholm 1990.

*   *   *

Bertil Vallien belongs to the generation which received its training at the end of the 1950s, when Swedish design was at its height. He studied pottery at the National College of Art and Design in Stockholm under the legendary Kåge disciple, Prof. Stig Lindberg, who died in 1982. Graduating in 1961, Bertil Vallien spent two years in the U.S., where he worked as a designer at a small factory. At the same time his duties included practical pottery. Designer or sculptor? That was the question. He opted for both. He has always given himself a free hand with pottery, and the free Scandinavian style in ceramics was his model.

One profoundly symbolic piece of work, which today ranks as the apogee and turning point of a period, is a large earthenware sphere at the National Museum in Stockholm, painted in red lacquer! That was in 1968, the year of rebellion. To Bertil Vallien, who had been teaching at the National College of Art and Design since his return home from America, it was an emancipation from the "Scandinavian Design" which had enclosed him like well-tailored armour plating, obstructing any kind of expansion—the tyranny of good taste.

For almost 20 years now Bertil Vallien has been a designer at the Åfors glassworks, part of the Kosta Boda Group. Services, single pieces and art collections have taken shape in his hands in a never-ceasing flow. There was heavier, more rustic glasswear in the 1960s and thinner designs in the '70s with the highly successful "Octav." Thin-walled octagonal shapes, blown in an iron mold, classic and yet new in design. The serving pieces especially had many exciting new variations of form.

Personal expression has always been a strong point with Bertil Vallien, without being contrived or far-fetched. This is particularly true of his unique and ever-flowing output, not only in glassware. New techniques such as sand-molding glass, netted mold-blowing. etc. have given him a firm profile.

As a glassware artist he has always been a rebel and transgressor. Where others utilize the brilliance and reflective power of glass, Vallien creates glass that "eats light," cast in sand molds to have a rough surface and magical, arcane content.

One of the distinguishing qualities of his glassware has been his admirable capacity for getting the glassworkers on his side, and making them active participants in the process. He has always tried to give free rein to their knowledge, and this too is the idea behind the "Artists' Collection." He wanted to be part of the great activity constituted by a glassworks—not so much a conductor as the first violinist. "Glass as a material has difficulty in conveying anything," he says. "It is sufficient unto itself."

Bertil Villien's dilemma is that glass in itself is so beautiful. But he has never hesitated to express profound seriousness even in glass. Using simple and sometimes almost excessively distinct symbols, he can make the décor of his unique glass compositions convey a profounder dimension: the dynamics of the waterfall, the wistful searchings of the flying man. The reindeer as an emblem of nature. The key and the keyhole.

The boats which he has cast in glass during the '80s give the impression of having reached a climax. They are small, large, or huge, all of them inscribed with secret symbols. Hovering, floating, inaccessible—uniting all the symbolic ships created by human mythology from the Ship of Dreams to Charon's ferry. It is like peering into the universe and trying to solve its eternal mystery of When and Where: a macrocosmos within a microcosmos. That is where Bertil Vallien is today—a classicist with new forms of expression.

Clay seems to be his most intimate material, often in bold combinations. He was the first artist in Sweden to use feathers in sculpture. There is something about Bertil Vallien's interminable flow of creativity that feels like immense, uncomplicated generosity.

And I have still not mentioned his public sculptures, cutlery, wrought ironwork, etc.

A truly profound and somewhat diffident seriousness combined with an infinite warmth of feeling which also contains a great deal of sensuality and sensuousness, plus a tremendous capacity for giving of himself—this is how I would like to characterize Bertil Vallien as a personality and artist.

—Åke Livstedt

VAN DEN AKKER, Koos.

American fashion designer. Born in The Hague, Netherlands, 16 March 1939; emigrated to the United States in 1968; naturalized, 1982. Studied at the Royal Academy of Arts, The Hague, 1956–58; Ecole Guerre Lavigne, Paris, 1961. Served in the Royal Dutch Army, 1958–60. Worked as an apprentice designer, in the Christian Dior fashion house, Paris, 1963–65; freelance designer, establishing own custom fashion boutique, The Hague, 1965–68; designer, in the Eve Stillman lingerie company, New York, 1969–70; freelance designer, establishing own boutiques on Columbus Avenue, New York, 1971–75, and on Madison Avenue, New York, from 1975; also established separate showrooms on Seventh Avenue, New York, from 1978; has designed clothing for Bill Cosby, Erica Jong, Barbara Walters, Diahann Carroll, Marilyn Horne, Glenn Close, Ringo Starr, Madonna, George Benson, etc. **Collections:** Kostum Museum, The Hague; Metropolitan

Museum of Art, New York. Recipient: Gold Coast Award, 1978; American Printed Fabrics Council Tommy Award, 1982. Address: Koos Van den Akker Couture Incorporated, 234 West 39th Street, New York, New York 10018, U.S.A.

Works:

Collaged fur coat range, for Ben Kahn Furs, from 1981.
Handbag range, for Meyers Manufacturing, 1986–88.
Couture lingerie collections, for La Lingerie stores, from 1987.
Collaged upholstery furniture ranges, for James II Galleries, from 1988.

Publications:

On VAN DEN AKKER: books—*Fashion 2001* by Lucille Khornak, London 1982; *The Encyclopaedia of Fashion from 1840 to the 1980s* by Georgina O'Hara, London 1986.

I paint with fabrics, as a painter paints with paint. Fabrics are where it all starts. I create my own fabrics by collages and combinations.

—Koos van den Akker

VASSOS, John.

American illustrator, graphic, display, interior and industrial designer. Born of Greek parents, in Bucharest, Romania, 23 October 1898; emigrated to the United States in 1919: naturalized 1924. Studied at Robert College, Constantinople, 1912–14; Fenway Art School, Boston, 1920; with the painter John Singer Sargent, Boston Museum of Fine Arts School, 1921; with George Bridgman, John Sloan, Charles Hawthorne and Louis Bouché, Art Student's League, New York, 1921–22; New York School of Design, 1923. Served with the British Army, in Gallipoli, 1916–18, and with the United States Army intelligence unit, in North Africa, 1942–45: Lieutenant-Colonel. Married Ruth Carriere in 1923 (died, 1965). Worked as assistant stage designer to Joseph Urban, Boston Opera Company, and promotional graphics designer, Columbia Records, Boston, 1921; freelance commercial illustrator, muralist and display designer, working for *Harper's Bazaar*, Macy's, Saks Fifth Avenue, Namm's Lord and Taylor, Best and Company, Bonwit Teller, Packard, French Lines, etc., in New York, from 1923; industrial designer, for Waterman, Remington, Dupont, Savage Arms, Imperial Cutlery, Perey Turnstiles, Egli Lighting, American Telephone and Telegraph Company, etc., in New York, from 1926; established New York Display Company design studio, New York, 1924; Design Consultant, RCA Victor Company, New York, 1932–74. Lecturer, Pratt Institute, Brooklyn, New York, Syracuse University, New York, and Vassar College, Poughkeepsie, New York. Founder-President, Industrial Design Institute, New York, 1938–41. **Exhibitions:** New York Public Library; Toledo Public Library, Ohio; New School for Social Research, New York; Riverside Museum, New York; Silvermine Art Guild, Connecticut, 1977; *Art Deco*, Finch Col-

lege Museum, New York; *High Style: 20th Century American Design*, Whitney Museum, New York, 1985; *The Machine Age in America 1918–1941*, Brooklyn Museum, New York, 1986. **Collections:** Athens Museum, Greece; Athens Public Library, Greece; Syracuse University, New York; Greek Museum, Washington D.C. Recipient: Greek Cross of the Golden Phoenix, 1945; Industrial Designers Institute Award, New York, 1955, 1961, 1968; Paidea Award, Hellenic University Club of New York, 1964; American Society of Neo-Hellenic Studies Award, New York, 1973. Fellow, Silvermine Guild of Artists, Connecticut, 1973. *Died* (in Norwalk, Connecticut) *6 December 1985*.

Works:

Mural for Rivoli Cinema, New York, c.1928.
Sound and Fury mural for Riviera Cinema, New York, c.1928.
Lucite fountain pen, for Waterman, 1928.
"Passimeter" turnstile, for Perey Company, 1929.
"Magic Lock" adjustable table and standard lamps, for Egli Company, 1929.
Mural for United Artists Egyptian Theater, Los Angeles, c.1930.
Chromium flatware cutlery, for Wallace Silverware Company, 1930.
Mural for WCAU Radio Station, Philadelphia, 1932.
Electron microscope housing, for RCA, 1934.
Kitchen utensils, for Remington Dupont, 1934.
Plastic radio with horizontal tuning dial, for RCA, 1934.
RCA Victor Special portable phonograph, 1935.
Eternal Quest of Electronics mural for RCA office, Washington, D.C., c.1935.
Mural for Military Electronic Center, Van Nuys, California, c.1950.
U.S. Pavilion, New Delhi Trade Fair, 1955.
U.S. Pavilion, Karachi Trade Fair, 1955.
Refrigerated 400-cup Coca-Cola dispenser, 1956.
Undersea mural for Condado Beach Hotel, San Juan, Puerto Rico, c.1958.

Publications:

By VASSOS: books—*Contempo: This American Tempo*, with Ruth Vassos, New York 1929; *Ultimo: An Imaginative Narration of Life Under the Earth*, with Ruth Vassos, New York 1930; *Phobia*, New York 1931; *Humanities*, with Ruth Vassos, New York 1935; *Contempo, Phobia, and Other Graphic Interpretations*, with foreword by P. K. Thomajan, New York 1976; books illustrated—*Salome* by Oscar Wilde, New York 1927; *The Ballad of Reading Gaol* by Oscar Wilde, New York 1928; *The Harlot's House and Other Poems* by Oscar Wilde, New York 1929; *Elegy in a Country Churchyard* by Thomas Gray, New York 1931; *Kubla Khan* by Samuel Taylor Coleridge, New York 1933; articles—"Controlled Light" in *Interiors* (New York), February 1948.

On VASSOS: books—*American Design Ethic* by Arthur J. Pulos, London and Cambridge, Massachusetts 1983; *High Style: 20th Century American Design*, exhibition catalogue by David Gebhard, Esther McCoy and others, New York 1985; *An Introduction to Design and Culture in the Twentieth Century* by Penny Sparke, London 1986; *The Machine Age in America 1918–1941*, exhibition catalogue by Richard Guy Wilson and Dianne H. Pilgrim, New York 1986; articles—"A half-century of design" in *Industrial Design* (New York), June 1971; "John Vassos: Master Designer" in *Fair-*

Koos van den Akker: Sweater top and globe skirt in wool tweed, 1981

John Vassos: United States pavilion at the Delhi Trade Fair, 1955

press (Fairfield, Connecticut), 10 October 1973; "Obituary: John Vassos" in the *New York Times*, 10 December 1985.

By all the accounts of his time and many since, John Vassos is a growing legend of American art and industrial design. He was a handsome Greek, medium in height, a solidly built man always with a sparkle in his eyes. Dynamically eloquent, he tended by sheer logic and tenacity to convince his audiences to his point of view be they corporate executives, engineers, marketing types, educators and even fellow designers.

Excelling in practically every facet of the arts, he seemed to always find time to involve himself in salvaging local art groups, creating the Industrial Designer's Institute, the first society of industrial designers to spearhead a legal effort to achieve professional licensing for industrial designers, while losing the battle to inspire local zoning boards to choose better design. And always, he found time to provide a plethora of free design services to several Greek Hellenic Societies. He even designed the medals they later awarded him. These are but a partial listing of his revolving activities through the years. Whatever the cause, it always seemed that John Vassos ended up being President and the driving force of the endeavor. Perhaps the deep moral idealism and compassion

for his fellow man first became manifest in the underlying themes of his superb Gouache in Black, White and shades of Gray. Whether advertising art or illustrations for his nine books written often with his wife, Ruth Carriere, his theme was always the smallness of man against the soaring, inescapable size of the universe be it infinity or his struggle against his immediate and overwhelming environment.

In his major work, *Phobia*, all his pent up compassison for humans became summed up in over twenty Gouache's, "Interpretations", as he called them. Written with Dr. Harry Stack Sullivan, he graphically delineated in his hard edge style, the major phobias of human kind. Not only has the book become an art and medical classic, it more than any other Vassos activity clearly identified the compassion of the innermost man.

By the 1920s and 1930s, he discovered his talent for what was to be industrial design. Without losing interest in past involvements, industrial design for the next sixty years was to become the focal point of his life.

Initially he designed with the Art Deco trends. Furniture, store windows, the first open front fast food operation and then products. A turnstile and dispensers for Coca Cola among others. Except for the turnstile, that became a classic, these were not noteworthy designs and Vassos reassessed his work. Interestingly, he returned to designing in terms of human needs

and product functionalism at a time when his peers were happily embracing "streamlining," on stationary objects.

In the early 1930s, Vassos found the answer to a designer's prayer in his long affiliation with RCA. Here a new vista of involvement occurred; first with corporate management, then with the mechanical functions of product electronics. He adjusted to team management while creating a long list of mechanical and design patents that frequently revolutionized the appearance of the company's many products. Visibly back again and evident in the products and environments he designed was his compassion for how people related to their surroundings. We now call it, human factors or ergonomics, or better yet, the "friendly look and feel" of a product. By whatever name we now identify the result, in Vassos's world it was building into a product or environment his compassion for those who must use or work in a man made world.

Vassos was one of the small handful of founders of United States Industrial Design, who, as consultants provided corporate wide product, exhibitions, human factor, graphic and design education for the corporate executives and sales staffs or their clients. Of this small group Vassos was the only designer who, on the drafting board, personally originated and developed the concepts, then executed or oversaw the developments to the market levels. Others amassed large staffs and quite often became directors of design, rather than the originators of designs that many were during the infancy of industrial design.

This has been but a glimpse of this remarkable man. Perhaps his own public description of an industrial desginer for an educational film tells much: "Leonardo de Vinci was the first industrial designer—he could paint pictures, design tools, guns, fortifications, water systems, air-planes, even clothes for his patrons. The perfect example of the Renaissance Man and the industrial designer."—as was John Vassos.

Finally, the greatest compliment to an individual's professional career and life can come only from his peers. Thus, Raymond Loewy's description of John Vassos to *Industrial Design* editor, Rodger Gillfoyle: "John Vassos's is unsung and unsullied." Hopefully to become sung about, he will remain unsullied.

—Raymond Spilman

sonality, Versace is low-keyed. It is only the closer look that yields the critical detail, which that year pushes clothing a little further in the direction one assumes he would wish to see it. He is more of a historicist, however, than a revivalist. Versace will be intrigued by a particular school of painting, rather than, say, the look affected by French socialites of 1930. In a fashion world where so much is simply an endless cycle of repeated ideas about past *clothing* history, Versace is more interested in using the broader context of the past, its furniture, its architecture, to suggest a new way of dressing for the present. This is not to say that Versace is merely an essayist in nostalgia; it is simply to say that as a romantic, he is naturally attracted to a lush and visionary view of clothing, rather than a purely architectural or utilitarian one. At his most successful, such as in his experiments with neo-Grecian tunic dresses, he achieves a superbly limpid and supple elegance which can

truly be called timeless, with none of the rather fatigued overtones that epithet can have.

Versace at his most inspired does suggest a realistic futurism, a pleasant Arcadia equally as remote from the morbid vampire fantasies of Claude Montana as it is from the slowly fossilizing, beaded visions of the older French couturiers. On a more meaningful level, however, that is to say in the day-to-day chronology of changing fashion, Versace generates consistently, more than any other designer, those small and telling gestures that, by expanding a line here or contracting one there, change the course of style. His widening of the hips and narrowing of the calf on his men's trousers had a great impact on the silhouette of men's clothing of the 1980s, for instance, just as the aforementioned tunic dresses have had on women's clothing.

—Peter Carlsen

Gianni Versace: Drawing for woman's jacket and skirt, 1984

VERSACE, Gianni.

Italian fashion designer. Born in Reggio Calabria, 2 December 1946. Studied architecture, at a technical school, Reggio Calabria, 1964–67; mainly self-taught in fashion design. Worked as a fashion buyer in Paris and London, for his mother's dressmaking studio, Reggio Calabria, 1968–72; freelance fashion designer, working for Callaghan, Complice and Genny companies, Milan, 1972–77; established Gianni Versace fashion company, Milan, from 1978; first womenswear collection, 1978, menswear collection, 1979, and first fragrance, 1981. Also stage costume designer, for La Scala Opera and Bejart Ballet, from 1982. **Exhibitions:** Galleria Rizzardi, Milan, 1982; Studio La Citta, Verona, 1983; *Italian Fashion*, Civic Museum, Osaka, 1983; Galerie Focus, Munich, 1983; *It's Design*, Padiglione d'Arte Contemporanea, Milan, 1983; *40 Years of Italian Fashion*, Trump Tower, New York, 1983. **Collections:** Museo Civico, Parma; Rijksmuseum, Amsterdam; Metropolitan Museum of Art, New York. Recipient: Revlon Golden Eye Award, Milan, 1982; Cutty Sark Award, Philadelphia, 1983. Address: Via della Spiga 25, 20121 Milan, Italy.

Publications:

By VERSACE: article—in *Vogue* (New York), November 1983.

On VERSACE: books—*A History of Fashion* by J. Anderson Black and Madge Garland, London 1975, 1980; *I Mass-Moda: Fatti e Personaggi dell'Italian Look* by Adriana Mulassano, Florence 1979; *The Collector's Book of Twentieth Century Fashion* by Frances Kennett, London and New York 1983; *40 Years of Italian Fashion*, exhibition catalogue compiled by B. G. Aragno, Rome, 1983; *McDowell's Directory of Twentieth Century Fashion* by Colin McDowell, London 1984; *The Encyclopaedia of Fashion from 1840 to the 1980s* by Georgina O'Hara, London 1986.

In many ways, Gianni Versace is the most visionary of the current generation of designers dominating Italian fashion. Yet his style is deceptively calm, smooth, and undemonstrative. Both in terms of his work and his per-

VIGNEAULT, Nelson.
Canadian photographer and graphic designer. Born in Sept-Iles, Quebec, 16 November 1951. Studied graphic communication, at Laval University, Quebec, 1973–76: BACC 1976; independent photography and design studies, Quebec, 1976–77; studied photography, at the Banff Centre, Alberta, 1978–79; photography, graphics and painting, at Rochester Institute of Technology, New York, 1979–81: MFA 1981. Freelance photographer and graphic designer, Calgary, Alberta, from 1981: vice-president, Paperworks Press, Calgary. Instructor, at Rochester Institute of Technology, New York, 1981, Banff Centre, Alberta, 1981–82, and at the Visual Art Centre, Montreal, 1983. **Exhibitions:** *Nelson Vigneault: Laser Scan Photos*, Peter Whyte Gallery, Banff, 1981; *Solos de Imagem: Visao Americana*, Museu da Imagem e do Som, Brasilia, 1982 (toured); *Bundesfotoschau 83*, Wurzburg, 1983; *Alternative Scans*, Stephens College, Missouri, 1983. Recipient: Printing Industries of America Prize, 1981; American Institute of Graphic Arts Excellence Award, 1981; Western Canadian Art Association Award, 1982, 1983; Toronto Art Directors Silver Award, 1982; International Society of Performing Art Administrators Award of Excellence, New York, 1982. Address: 2943 19th Street N.E., Calgary, Alberta T2E 7A2, Canada.

Publications:

By VIGNEAULT: books designed—*1981 Techmila: 150 Years of Celebration* by Tom Grotta, Rochester, New York 1981; *William Townsend in Alberta* by Karyn Elizabeth Allen, Calgary, Alberta 1982; *A Delicate Wilderness* by Edward Cavell, Banff, Alberta 1983; *Legacy in Ice* by Edward Cavell, Banff, Alberta 1983; *Calgary: Places and People* by Harry Palmer, Calgary, Alberta 1983; *Barbara Astman* by Karen Allen, Calgary, Alberta 1983; *Inese Birstins and Anne Pixley* by Lorne Falk, Banff, Alberta 1983.

VIGNEAULT: book—*Creative Source:*, 4th edition, Toronto 1983; article—"News" in *Graphic Arts Buyer* (New York), March/April 1981.

My special area of interest is the production of graphic work for the fine arts community. Because most people's experience of works of art is through printed documentation and not through contact with original works, the designer/graphic artist is charged with the responsibility of defining an appropriate translation of a work of art or capturing the essential nature of a field of artistic endeavor.

The goal is not to reproduce the works of art, as this cannot be done, but to provide access to that interpretation which is most consistent with the intentions of the artist, or at least to suggest that many interpretations are possible and to provoke the viewer to seek out the original work. The point is that the viewer must not be fooled into imagining that experiencing the design is an adequate substitute for the experience of the original art. The emotional impact of the design should trigger or reinforce the emotional essence of the art. The designer must have a well-developed visual, technical, and critical sensibility in order to evolve a visual concept that will translate this essence to the intended viewer.

—Nelson Vigneault

Nelson Vigneault: Page from *The Europeans* calendar, 1983

VIGNELLI, Lella (Elena).
Italian graphic and industrial designer. Born Lella Valle, in Udine, in 1936. Studied at the School of Architecture, Massachusetts Institute of Technology, Cambridge, 1955–58, and at the School of Architecture, University of Venice, 1960–62: D.Arch. 1962. Married Massimo Vignelli in 1957: children: Luca and Valentina. Worked as a designer, at Skidmore, Owings and Merrill architectural firm, Chicago, 1959–60; founder and principal, Lella and Massimo Vignelli Office of Design and Architecture, Milan, 1960–64; interior designer, at Unimark International, New York, 1965–71; executive vice-president of Vignelli Associates, New York, from 1971; president, Vignelli Designs, New York, from 1978. Board member, Artemide U.S.A., New York, from 1980. **Exhibitions:** *Knoll au Musée*, Musée des Arts Décoratifs, Paris, 1972; *107 Grafici dell'AGI*, Castello Sforzesco, Milan, 1974; Kansas City Art Institute, Missouri, 1978; Art Center Col-

Massimo Vignelli: Covers for *Skyline* magazine, New York, 1979

lege of Design, Pasadena, 1979; Padiglione d'Arte Moderna, Milan, 1980; Parsons School of Design, New York, 1981; *Design Since 1945*, Philadelphia Museum of Art, 1983; *The Twentieth Century Poster*, Walker Art Center, Minneapolis, 1984; *New Design for Old*, Boilerhouse/Victoria and Albert Museum, London, 1986. Recipient: American Institute of Architects Industrial Arts Medal, 1973; American Institute of Graphic Arts Gold Medal, 1983; *Interiors* Magazine Special Award, New York, 1982. Honorary Member, Women in Design, New York, 1981. Member: Ordine degli Architetti, Milan, 1962; Decorators Club of New York, 1982. Address: Vignelli Associates, 475 Tenth Avenue, New York, New York 10018, U.S.A.

See VIGNELLI, Massimo.

VIGNELLI, Massimo.
Italian graphic and industrial designer. Born in Milan, 10 January 1931. Studied at the Brera Academy of Art, Milan, 1948–50, at the Politecnico, Milan, 1950–53, and at the School of Architecture, University of Venice, 1953–57. Married Lella Elena Valle in 1957; children:

Luca and Valentina. Founder and principal, of Lella and Massimo Vignelli Office of Design and Architecture, Milan, 1960–64; director and vice-president for design at Unimark International, New York, 1965–71; president of Vignelli Associates, New York, from 1971; chairman, Vignelli Designs, New York, from 1978. President, American Institute of Graphic Arts, New York, 1976–77; trustee, Institute for Architecture and Urban Studies, New York, from 1978. **Exhibitions:** *Knoll au Musée*, Musée des Arts Décoratifs, Paris, 1972; *107 Grafici dell'AGI*, Castello Sforzesco, Milan, 1974; Kansas City Art Institute, Missouri, 1978; Art Center College of Design, Pasadena, 1979; Padiglione d'Arte Moderna, Milan, 1980; Parsons School of Design, New York, 1981; *Design Since 1945*, Philadelphia Museum of Art, 1983; *The Twentieth Century Poster*, Walker Art Center, Minneapolis, 1984; *New Design for Old*, Boilerhouse/Victoria and Albert Museum, London, 1986. **Collections:** Museum of Modern Art, New York; Tel Aviv Museum. Recipient: Towle Silversmiths Fellowship, 1957; Moholy-Nagy Fellowship, Chicago Institute of Design, 1958; American Institute of Architects Industrial Arts Medal, 1973; New York Art Directors Club Hall of Fame Award, 1982; American Institute of Graphic Arts Gold Medal, 1983; National Associated Schools of Art and Design Annual Award, 1983; Presidential Design Award, Washington, D.C., 1985. Member: American Institute of Graphic Arts; Industrial Designers Society of America; Architectural League of New York; Alliance Graphique Internationale, Paris. Address: Vignelli Associates, 475 Tenth Avenue, New York, New York 10018, U.S.A.

Works:

Posters and graphics, for the Venice Biennale, 1962, 1964.
Stacking dinner and tableware ranges in ceramic and melamine, for Heller, 1964.
Corporate identity program, for Knoll International, 1966.
Logotype symbol, for American Airlines, 1967.
Nuts and Bolts series of toiletry containers in glass and plastic laminates, for Colton/Gillette, 1970.
Cocktail bar accessories in stainless steel, for Sanlorenzo, 1971.
Lotogype symbol and identity, for Bloomingdale's Department Store, 1972.
Gallery and office interiors, for the Minneapolis Institute of Fine Arts, 1974.
Cookwares in ovenproof glass, for Heller, 1975.
St. Peter's Church interiors, New York, 1975.
Corporate identity program, for Lancia automobiles, 1978.
Corporate identity program, for Ciga Hotels, 1979.
Publications program, for the United States National Parks Administration, 1983–85.

Publications:

By VIGNELLI: books—*Graphic Design for Nonprofit Organizations*, New York 1980; *Knoll Design*, with Eric Larrabee, New York 1981; articles—in *Journal of Graphic Design* (New York), November 1982; *Upper and Lower Case* (New York), December 1982.

On VIGNELLI: books—*An International Sur-*

vey of Packaging by Wim Crouwel and Kurt Weidemann, London 1968; *Knoll au Musée,* exhibition catalogue by Christine Rae, Paris 1972; *107 Grafici dell'AGI,* with texts by Renzo Zorzi and Franco Grignani, Venice 1974; *Design: Vignelli* by Emilio Ambasz, New York 1980; *The Language of Graphics* by Edward Booth-Clibborn and Daniele Baroni, London 1980; *Who's Who in Graphic Art,* edition by Walter Amstutz, Dubendorf 1982; *Design Since 1945,* edited by Kathryn Hiesinger and George Marcus, Philadelphia and London 1983; *The Twentieth Century Poster: Design of the Avant-Garde* by Dawn Ades, New York 1984; *The Conran Directory of Design,* edited by Stephen Bayley, London 1985; *New Design for Old,* exhibition catalogue with texts by Helen Hamlyn, Eric Midwinter and others, London 1986; *New American Design* by Hugh Aldersley-Williams, New York 1988.

Our design philosophy is based on discipline—intended as methodology and attitude; appropriateness—intended as the search for the specific; and ambiguity—intended as a plurality of meaning.

We believe in improving the visual quality of our environment and in the commitment to achieve this goal; in design dignity and its influence on people; and in timelessness and change, in consistency and contradiction, and in classicism and friendliness. We love to affect design and affect others by design. We love to create and to transform until projects, objects, and ideas become "things."

—Massimo and Lella Vignelli

See VIGNELLI, Lella.

Lella and Massimo Vignelli are total designers whose work enhances our physical and emotional environment with a subtle combination of mind and eye. Their design work is varied and ubiquitous, including furniture, glassware, and silverware, exhibitions, showrooms and stores, interiors, books and other publications, posters, transportation graphics, and corporate identity programs. Theirs is a multi-layered bond, personal and professional.

If their "style" is to be defined, it is one of erudition and elegance: a Euclidian approach articulating geometry in two- and three-dimensional form. They carry their stylistic momentum into our contemporary lives, absorbing the history of art, architecture, and design, while elaborating it significantly. The esthetic imports is of first consideration, whether for a poster, a book, a chair, or an interior. They do not disregard functional requirements but always eschew the austere and the merely decorative.

No rigid formula keeps down their quest for solutions, often now with flashes of randomness; however focused and refined, they are rendered with an emotional élan, a simplicity born of abstracting from complexities and redundancies. Theirs has been a gradual metamorphosis away from formal visual language which sometimes plays with the past. With perceptual shifts and ambiguities, their work titilates our vision with a careful selection of particular values. The balancing of myriad intangibles and unconscious mental force produces a judgmental act which adds up to tangible works of art. One of their strong points is their ability to break even their own rules, so that their "style" evolves, bringing in new principles that bring in transformations.

In graphics, Massimo Vignelli's most distinctive successes are achieved through brilliant use of typography and the grid. With his masterful use of the grid as structures, he has altered the look of both the single page and full publi-

cations while emphasizing the legibility of the message. He has made lettering itself a means of expression by using contrasts of scale, typesize and weight, color, texture, and spacing to create powerful patterns with emotional value. Close coordination of image and typography carries the message with potent force. Derived from the Swiss, the Vignelli devotion to the grid produces results which are clear and ordered; the design principles are applied vigorously, effectively, but never slavishly.

These two extraordinary, talented people have pooled their innermost resources to endow our visual world with tangible and unmistakable character. Theirs has been a great journey of discovery wherein people and process are of utmost concern.

—Mildred Constantine

VIONNET, Madeleine (Marie Valentine).

French fashion designer. Born in Chilleurs-aux-Bois, Loiret, 22 June 1876. Educated at the Ecole Communale, Chilleurs-aux-Bois, until 1888. Married in 1893 (divorced, 1894); 1 child (died); married Dmitri Netchvolodov in 1925 (divorced, 1955). Apprenticed to a dressmaker, Aubervilliers, 1888–93; dressmaker, in House of Vincent fashion company, Paris, 1893–95; cutter, then head of workshops, at Kate Reilly fashion house, London, 1895–1900; saleswoman, at Bechoff David fashion company, Paris, 1900–01; head of studios, under Marie Gerber, at Callot Soeurs fashion house, Paris, 1901–05; designer, in Robert Doucet fashion house, Paris, 1905–11; founder and director of Maison Vionnet fashion house, in the Rue de Rivoli, Paris, 1912–14, 1919–22, and in the Avenue Montaigne, 1922–39; retired, 1940. **Exhibitions:** *Exposition Internationale des Arts Décoratifs,* Paris, 1925; *Grands Couturiers Parisiens 1910–1939,* Musée Carnavalet, Paris, 1965; *Fashion: An Anthology,* Victoria and Albert Museum, London, 1971; *The Tens, Twenties and Thirties,* Metropolitan Museum of Art, New York, 1974; *Art and Fashion 1900–1939,* Victoria and Albert Museum, London, 1975. **Collections:** Centre de Documentation du Costume, Paris; Metropolitan Museum of Art, New York; Victoria and Albert Museum, London. Recipient: Chevalier de la Légion d'Honneur, France. *Died* (in Paris) *2 March 1975.*

Publications:

On VIONNET: books—*Dressmakers of France* by Mary Brooks Picken and Dora Loues Miller, New York 1956; *Paris a la Mode* by Celia Bertin, Paris and London 1956; *Kings of Fashion* by Anny Latour, Stuttgart 1956, London 1958; *The World in Vogue 1893–1963,* edited by Bryan Holme and others, New York and London 1963; *Grands Couturiers Parisiens 1910–1939,* exhibition catalogue edited by Madeleine Delpierre and Henriette Vanier, Paris 1965; *Fashion: An Anthology by Cecil Beaton,* exhibition catalogue compiled by Madeleine Ginsburg, London 1971; *Couture,* edited by Ruth Lynam, New York 1972; *In Vogue: Sixty Years of Celebrities and Fashion,*

edited by Georgina Howell, London 1975, 1978, New York 1976; *A History of Fashion* by J. Anderson Black and Madge Garland, London 1975, 1980; *The World of Fashion: People, Places, Resources* by Eleanor Lambert, London and New York 1976; *Inventive Paris Fashions 1909–1939* by Diana Vreeland, New York and London 1977; *Magic Names of Fashion* by Ernestine Carter, London 1980; *Fairchild's Who's Who in Fashion,* edited by Anne Stegemeyer, New York 1980; *McDowell's Directory of Twentieth Century Fashion* by Colin McDowell, London 1984; *The Encyclopaedia of Fashion from 1840 to the 1980s* by Georgina O'Hara, London 1986.

*

Madeleine Vionnet said that she designed not fashions but harmonies. As a talented young designer in Paris at the turn of the century, she was influenced by avant-garde notions of physical freedom and the romantic classicism popularly expressed by dancer Isadora Duncan. By 1907 a skilled modiste for the prestigious House of Doucet, she boldly insisted that models remove the black cotton underdress then worn for the sake of modesty. She wanted the clothes to be shown as customers would wear them. Her first collection for Doucet consisted of *deshabille,* the loose "tea gowns" accepted for at-home wear, at that time the only kind of garment a lady would wear without corseting. But in a radical attempt at dress reform not appreciated by Doucet's conservative clients, Vionnet intended her designs for street wear.

With the support of friends and demimondaines who favored emancipated dress, Vionnet opened her own couture house in Paris in 1912 and developed her unique contribution to garment technology, the bias-cut. Working with the actual fabric custom-woven two yards longer than usual, she turned it diagonal to the straight grain and draped it on a small-scale, wood mannequin. Exploiting the fabric's natural elasticity, her mathematically precise cuts and intricate seams molded the fabric to the female form like a second skin. Surface embellishment was totally integrated with design, always serving to amplify line and motion. Technique had been wedded to philosophy. As Vionnet said, "The dress must accompany its wearer, and when a woman smiles, the dress must smile with her."

While Vionnet worked to create gowns of individual beauty and timeless proportions, her designs nevertheless kept pace with changes in fashion, expressing what she called "harmonic variations on a given theme." Asymmetrical handkerchief-points fluttered gracefully from her silk dresses of the late 1920s. She offered classically-draped gowns popular in the early 1930s and molten satin evening sheaths, which became archetypical movie-star glamor, in the mid-1930s. At the decade's end, her interpretation of the Victorian revival was accomplished not with stiff crinolines but with knowing manipulation of crisp taffeta. What mattered to Vionnet most was not fashion but the behavior of the fabric and its enhancement of the body beneath it.

By the time World War II caused her to close her business, her clientele included the royal and social aristocracy of Europe. After retirement, she served as a frequent consultant to the French couture industry. While her intricate designs were difficult to copy, the bias-cut had become the basic garment construction method of the 1930s. Vionnet's singular technique has come into standard usage by contemporary designers creating comfortable, body-conscious clothes.

—Sandra Michels Adams

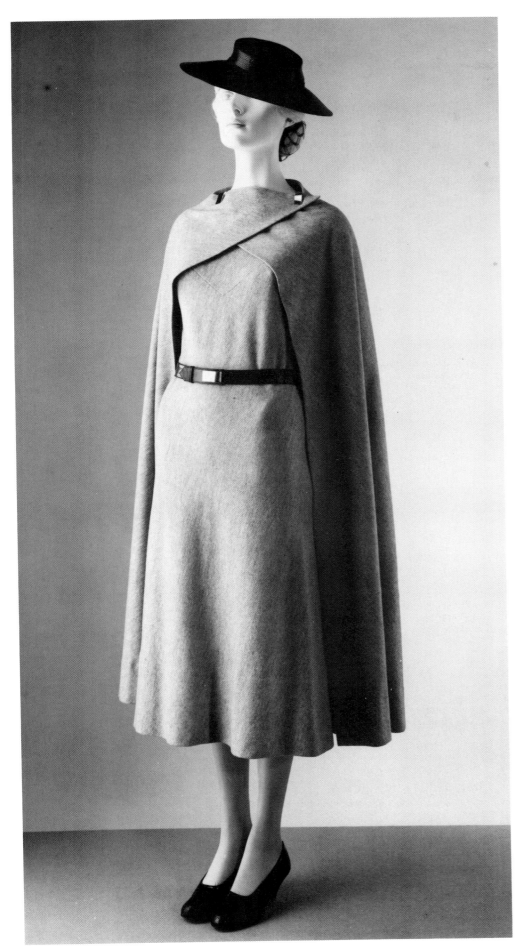

Madeleine Vionnet: Day dress and cape in wool jersey, 1935 Courtesy Victoria and Albert Museum, London

VON APPEN, Karl.

German painter and stage designer. Born in Dusseldorf, 12 May 1900. Educated at schools in Krefeld, Hamburg and Frankfurt, 1906–15; apprenticed as a chemigraph, Frankfurt, 1915–18; apprentice scene painter, under Ludwig Sievert, at the Schauspielhaus, Frankfurt, 1918–22; studied painting and graphics under F. K. Delavilla, at the Kunstgewerbeschule, Frankfurt, and under Max Beckmann, at the Stadelsches Institut, Frankfurt, 1922–24. Married Manja Behrens. Worked as a stage decor designer, at the Kunstlertheater fur Rhein und Main, Frankfurt, 1924–27; independent painter and graphic artist, Berlin, 1927–30; stage designer, at the Stadttheater, Wurzburg, 1930; freelance designer and painter, working in Dresden, from 1930; joined Communist Party and forbidden to work, 1935–40; scene painter, at the Staatstheater, Dresden, 1940–41; arrested as a resistance group member and imprisoned at camp in Niederroden, near Frankfurt, 1941–45; head of design 1945–54, and art director, 1947–49, at the Staatstheater, Dresden; chief stage designer, for the Berliner Ensemble, Berlin, 1954–81; worked with producers Heinz Arnold, Bertolt Brecht, Benno Besson, Erich Engel, Manfred Karge, Matthias Langhoff, Joachim Tenschert, etc. **Exhibitions:** East Berlin, 1975, 1982; Leipzig, 1976; Warsaw, 1976; Bratislava, 1978; Prague, 1978; Stockholm, 1978; Venice, 1980; Dresden, 1983. **Collections:** Graphic collections of the State Galleries of Berlin and Dresden. Recipient: DDR National Prize, German Democratic Republic, 1956, 1969; DDR National Order of Merit, 1965; Gold Medal, Prague Quadriennale, 1967. State Professor of the DDR, 1960; Member of the Akademie der Künste, Berlin, 1961; DDR Order of Karl Marx, 1975; Honorary President, Organization Internationale des Scenographes et des Techniciens du Theatre. *Died* (in East Berlin) *21 August 1981.*

Works:

Stage productions include—for the Schauspielhaus, Frankfurt—*Herzog Blaubarts Burg*, 1922; *Der holzgeschnitzte Prinz*, 1922; for the Staatstheater, Dresden—*Die Zauberflöte*, 1946; *Die Flut*, 1947; *Die Kluge*, 1947; *Salome*, 1947; *Rusalka*, 1948; *Cosi fan tutte*, 1948; *Fidelio*, 1948; *Antigonae*, 1950; *Des Simplicius Simplicissimus Jugend*, 1950; *Carmen*, 1951; *Die Brücke des Lebens*, 1952; *Die Liebe der Danae*, 1952; for the Berliner Ensemble, East Berlin—*Katzgraben*, 1953; *Der kaukasische Kreidekreis*, 1954; *Winterschlacht*, 1955; *Pauken und Trompeten*, 1955; *The Playboy of the Western World*, 1956; *Furcht und Elend des Britten Reiches*, 1957; *Der gute Mensch von Sezuan*, 1957; *Optimistische Tragödie*, 1958; *Der aufhatsame Aufstieg des Arturo Ui*, 1959; *Die Dreigroschenoper*, 1960; *Frau Flinz*, 1961; *Die Tage der Commune*, 1962; *Coriolanus*, 1964; *Der Brotladen*, 1967; *Die heilige Johanna der Schlachthofe*, 1968; *Turandot oder der Kongress der Weisswascher*, 1973; *Der Unbedeutende*, 1976; for the Deutsches Theater, East Berlin—*Wallenstein*, 1959; *Die Sommerfrische*, 1974; in Halle—*Polly oder Die Bataille am Bluewater Creek*, 1965.

Publications:

By VON APPEN: book—*Karl Von Appen , Altes und Neues: Bilder und Text*, edited by Friedrich Dieckmann, Berlin 1975.

On VON APPEN: books—*The Theatre of Bertolt Brecht* by John Willett, London 1969, 1967, 1977; *Bertolt Brecht: Der Brotladen* by

Karl von Appen: Stage design for Brecht's *The Caucasian Chalk Circle*, at the Berliner Ensemble, 1954

Manfred Karge and Matthias Langhoff, Frankfurt 1967; *Notate: Zur Arbeit des Berliner Ensembles 1956–1966* by Manfred Wekwerth, Berlin and Weimar 1967; *Buhnenbildarbeit in der Deutschen Demokratische Republik*, edited by Friedrich Dieckmann, Berlin 1971; *Karl Von Appens Buhnenbilder am Berliner Ensemble* by Friedrich Dieckmann, Berlin 1971, 1973; *Monografie des Plakats: Entwicklung, Stil, Design* by Herbert Schindler, Munich 1972; *Gebrauchsgraphik in der DDR* by Hellmut Rademacher, Dresden 1975; *Die Schauspieltheater der DDR und das Erbe 1970–1974*, edited by Manfred Nossig, Berlin 1976; *Streifzuge: Aufsatze und Kritiken* by Friedrich Dieckmann, Berlin and Weimar 1977.

Most of Karl von Appen's work prior to 1945 was destroyed by the Nazi terror and the war. The paintings from this period reveal the artist's sympathy with the Neue Sachlichkeit, a number of his graphic works exhibiting a pungent sociocritical accent. In the stage designs, a strong sense of color liberated from the confines of illusionism makes itself felt.

His post-1945 Dresden stage work is marked by a spirit of penetrating honesty with a sure sense of spatial and colour effects to give the director appropriate possibilities of action. The meeting with Brecht in 1953 had a decisive influence on von Appen and soon led to a close relationship with the Berliner Ensemble. With Brecht, von Appen discovered the theoretical and materially practicable bases for those

efforts which had only begun to be effective in his previous work in Dresden. Von Appen adapted the achievements of epic theatre to his own artistic temperament—a temperament of quiet, painterly ingenuity, which the Brechtian stage used as a means of individualising the scenic element. The solution of integrated illusion or "symbol scene" pursued by Brecht and Caspar Neher in the 1920s and early 1930s was adapted by von Appen according to changes in the social situation, a method by which the empty space acted both as a dividing and unifying element. The method was described and praised by Brecht in "Chinese Painting."

Von Appen also gave adequate expression to the dialectical realism of the later Brecht, who regarded von Appen's stage sketches for *Katzgraben* as having, for the first time in the theatre, revealed the face of the working class. In von Appen's subsequent work, there was a physiognomic certainty not previously seen in the realm of stage design. By means of the stage movement and layout drawings, the designer influences the work of the director; this preferred instrument of the epic theatre was exactly adapted by von Appen to the demands of the piece and used as a starting point for his work on the decor and costumes. The objectively distanced perusal of historical stage settings plays a large role in von Appen's own productions of classical pieces. Among his most famous productions are The *Caucasian Chalk Circle* (1954), *Kettle Drums and Trum-*

pets (1955), *The Good Woman of Sezuan* (1957), *Optimistic Tragedy* (1958), *The Incredible Rise of Arturo Ui* (1959), and *The Threepenny Opera* (1960).

—Friedrich Dieckmann

VUORI, Pekka (Vaino Johannes).
Finnish illustrator and graphic designer. Born in Kiikka, 12 November 1935. Studied graphic design, Institute of Industrial Arts, Helsinki, 1953–56. Married Sirkka Marjatta Nupponen in 1963; children: Joonas and Julia. Worked as a magazine and newspaper layout artist, Helsinki, 1959–73; freelance illustrator and graphic designer, working for *Lipas, Suomen Kuvalehti, Helsingin Sanomat, Form Function Finland*, and the publishers Kirjasieppo, SKS, WSOY, Tammi and Kustannuskiila, in Helsinki, since 1973. **Exhibitions:** Pinx Gallery, Helsinki, 1963, 1964; SKS Gallery, Helsinki, 1978; Vellamo Gallery, Helsinki, 1982; AKK Gallery, Helsinki, 1985, 1986, 1987; Rotunda Gallery, Helsinki, 1988; Ruka Art Gallery, Finland, 1989. Recipient: Church Film Award, Helsinki, 1969 (with Seppo Saves); Rudolf Koivu Awards.

Helsinki, 1972, 1978, 1982; Finnish State Award for Applied Arts, 1972, 1983; Well Done Book Award, Tokyo, 1985; GRAFIA Graphic Artist of the Year Award, Helsinki, 1987; Finnish State Literature Award, 1988. Address: Vyokatu 10 B 22, 00160 Helsinki, Finland.

Works:

Kapalamaki/Folk Tales book illustrations, for Kirjasieppo, 1977.
Helsingin Sanomat newspaper illustrations, from 1978.
Form Function Finland magazine design, from 1980.
Jattilaiset/Folk Tales book illustrations, for SKS, 1981.
Kotimainen Krokotiili (Jukka Parkkinen) book illustrations, for WSOY, 1981.
Sydameni Laulu (Aleksis Kivi) book illustrations, for SKS, 1984.
Lintukotolaiset/Folk Tales book illustrations, for SKS, 1985.
Treasures of the Orthodox Church Museum book design, for Kustannuskiila, 1985.
Viktor Barsokevitsch: Photos 1893–1927 book design, for Kustannuskiila, 1987.
Joe-Seta/Uncle Joe (Veikko Huovinen) book illustrations, for WSOY, 1988.
Suomalaisia Nykykirjailijoita/Modern Finnish Writers (Pekka Tarkka) book illustrations, from Tammi, 1989.

Publications:

By VUORI: books—*Otto Ja Ville*, Helsinki 1972; *Into Parrakas Vauva*, with text by K. Helakisa, Helsinki 1985; *Kadonneet Alushameet*, Helsinki 1987; *Ei Housut Lainissa Parane*, Helsinki 1989.

On VUORI: books—*Parhaat Pilapiirtajat*, Helsinki 1979; *Finnish Industrial Design*, edited by Tua Pontasuo, Helsinki 1987; *Finnish Illustrators of Children's Books*, Helsinki 1989; article—"Graphic Artist of the Year" in *Form Function Finland* (Helsinki), no. 1, 1987.

*

As an illustrator and graphic artist, Pekka Vuori's varied output and use of line put him in the front rank of Finns in his field. Vuori skilfully combines numerous talents. His all-round ability and creativity are shown by the fact that he has written and illustrated several much-admired and award-winning children's books, illustrated works on children's culture and folk traditions in the 1970s and 1980s, designed books and jackets for publishers from the 1960s onwards, and created the layout of many major illustrated works and historical books over a period of three decades.

Vuori also illustrated and designed the visual aspects of many Finnish newspapers and periodicals, including *Lipas* magazine (published for children by the Savings Bank), the prestigious *Suomen Kuvalehti*, and served Finland's leading daily newspaper, *Helsingin Sanomat*, as an illustrator under the signature "Pekka" from 1978. Since 1980, he has been responsible for the look of the high-class *Form Function Finland* magazine, which deals with the arts and industrial design and is distributed internationally. During the late 1960s, Vuori also made short films and animated movies.

The fine arts have been strongly represented in Pekka Vuori's output since he painted his first canvas in oils at the age of twelve. More recently, he has concentrated on drawings and serigraphy. As well as participation in survey shows of illustrators in Finland and abroad, exhibitions of Vuori's paintings, drawings and illustrations have been presented in Helsinki since 1963.

Pekka Vuori has worked on many children's projects for the Manerheim League for Child Welfare and several banks, and was the first Finn to make a UNICEF card. Among his books of fairy tales are *Into, the Bearded Baby* (1985), and *The Lost Petticoats* (1987). The latter was also published in Japanese, Danish and Italian.

He has also illustrated about twenty-five different books. One of these was a collection of folk tales entitled *Jattilaiset* (*The Giants*), a large edition of which was published in Japanese. Among his recent illustration work are Veikko Huovinen's stories of Stalin, *Uncle Joe* (1988), and Pekka Tarkka's *Modern Finnish Writers* (1989).

Vuori's work in designing illustrated volumes and historical books has received recognition.

Pekka Vuori: *The Giants* book illustration, for SKS Publishers, **1981**

To date, the eighteen such works he has designed have been the recipients of numerous Book of the Year diplomas, awarded annually by the Finnish Book Design Selection Committee.

—Jukka Sorjo-Smeds

VYCHODIL, Ladislav.

Czechoslovak stage designer. Born in Hacky, 28 February 1920. Educated at secondary school in Olomouc, 1931–38; studied geometric drawing and design under Oldrich Blazicek, Cyril Bouda and A. Pokorny, at the University of Architecture, Prague, 1938–39, 1945. Married Vera Krausova in 1944; children: Ivana, Daniela and Ladislav. Chief stage designer, at the Slovak National Theatre, Bratislava, from 1945. Head of the scenography department, 1952–83, and professor from 1983, at the University of Theatre Arts, Bratislava. **Exhibitions:** Bratislava, 1965; Bienal of Sao Paulo, 1965; Paris, 1966; Brighton, Sussex, 1967; Sofia, 1967; Budapest, 1968; Vienna, 1969; Santa Barbara, California, 1974; Berlin, 1975; Venice, 1976. **Collections:** Slovak National Gallery, Bratislava; Smetana Museum, Prague; Toneel Museum, Amsterdam; University of Texas, Austin. Recipient: Czech State Prize, Prague, 1951, 1960; Gold Medal, Bienal of Sao Paulo, 1965. Merited Artist, Prague, 1966; National Artist, Prague, 1975; Order of Work, Prague, 1980. Address: Prokopa Velkeho 15, 811 04 Bratislava, Czechoslovakia.

Works:

Stage productions, for the Slovak National Theatre, include—*Tartuffe*, 1946; *Ivan the Terrible*, 1947; *Boris Godunov*, 1954; *Optimistic Tragedy*, 1957; *Galileo*, 1959; *A View from the Bridge*, 1959; *Atlantida*, 1961; *Twelfth Night*, 1962; *Hamlet*, 1963; *The Play of Love and Death*, 1964.

Publications:

By VYCHODIL: article—in *Acta Scenographica* (Prague), no. 9, 1961; *Theatre Design and Technology* (Charlottesville), no. 10, 1974; and regular column, in *Slovak National Theatre Bulletin* (Bratislava), 1946–67.

On VYCHODIL: books—*Ladislav Vychodil* by Miroslav Kouril, Bratislava 1963; *Soucasna*

Slovenska Scenografia by Ladislav Lajcha, Bratislava 1977; *Ladislav Vychodl* by Ladislav Lajcha, Bratislava 1980; *The Cambridge Guide to World Theatre*, edited by Martin Banham, Cambridge 1988.

During my forty-year career, I have designed approximately 350 sets for both drama and opera. In my opinion, scenography is a space discipline, not one related to painting. Despite this, I think it would be a pity to exclude painting and colour from scenography. However, I do not use them in their primary form—I use colour as light and painting as material.

When a scenographer works in theatre, he must belong to the team of stage director-author-dramaturgist-scenographer-actor. Each scenographer works in a certain dependence on this team, and this is one of the differences from being an "independent" artist. A scenographer must take the influence of these disciplines into account, as well as that of light, theatre technology, etc.

Scenography can be compared to the background of a figural painting. Let's use the famous Rembrandt work *Return of the Prodigal Son* for comparison. We shall have the image of scenography if we take out the figures. How does this "stage" look? As to space, the background is not too well articulated; the artist has taken into account that the quality of space will enter the picture along with the figures. As to colour, the "stage" (background) is neutral. The costumes are in most attractive colours. As to light, it falls on the furniture and on the figures (now absent). Without the figures, the picture is incomplete; the figures are necessary to provide the picture as a whole. The "stage" (background) is made in such a way that the figures (actors) dominate the picture. The costuming is achieved similarly. It is realized as a background that underlines and emphasizes the actor's face, which is the carrier of the action.

Scenography is a discipline developing in space and time (similar to theatre). This means that it should not contain constant, invariable elements. Its nature should change as time passes. The scenographer should not be limited to one kind of acting (e.g., drama). Even a tragedy begins as a conversational play, and there are some comic elements as well. Scenography must take these facts and requirements into account, and it must change according to them.

—Ladislav Vychodil

Ladislav Vychodil's scenography falls between two main devices—scene painting and architecture—of stage design as an indicator of place. For him, the question of architectonic space is central, but color as produced by lighting (rather than paint), on varying materials, textures, and forms is also highly significant. With regard to style, Vychodil inclines toward the lyrical and emotive, but with restraint, economy, and grace rather than force or distortion.

The logical extension of this tendency is a suppression of traditional stage decor and increased emphasis on properties and related scenographic elements. Vychodil is also conservative with regard to reliance on technical innovations, which he de-emphasizes as primary sources of striking effects.

Vychodil's career evolved in several places. In the early postwar years, he showed the influence of his mentor, Frantisek Tröster. Then, a preoccupation with architectonic, abstract forms, often against an indefinite, darkened background was exemplified by *Tartuffe* (1946) and Tolstoy's *Ivan the Terrible* (1947). In the early 1950s, when socialist realism dominated east European arts, Vychodil turned to more traditional techniques of scene painting and realistic detail, as in *Boris Gudonov* (1954). In the late 1950s, as if in reaction to such literalness, Vychodil's work suggested an effort to sweep the stage clean of both the illusion of actuality and conventional decor. The emphasis was on economy, function, and the actor (Vishnevsky's *Optimistic Tragedy*, 1957). Vychodil also began to make increasing use of the cyclorama and special lighting, including projections, to convey both mood and information (Brecht's *Galileo* and Miller's *A View from the Bridge*, both 1959). In the 1960s, his settings once again became more expressive and emotive, made so chiefly by more complex patterns of suspended elements in layers and by more complex lighting effects on textured surfaces (*Twelfth Night*, 1962; *Hamlet*, 1963).

In the 1960s, Vychodil also began to work with Alfred Radok, co-inventor of the Laterna Magika form of blending live and filmed action for the stage. They did not employ this technique per se but its poetic essence: the juxtaposition of seemingly disparate elements to present ironic, metaphoric insights about reality. Traditional scenography was subordinated to a collage of actors and carefully chosen properties, furniture, and other "signs" that took on various functions and meanings. By far the most striking example of this approach occurred in Rolland's *The Play of Love and Death* (1964), for which Vychodil created a setting that had no basis in the text: a metaphoric, rough-hewn bull ring in which French aristocrats played out their destinies during Revolution. Vychodil's subsequent work has consisted of variations and refinements of these last phases, with a consistent attention to textured, layered backgrounds that establish the quality or mood of a piece and to an often ironic interplay of actors and scenic objects.

In recent years, Vychodil has increasingly worked in Scandinavia and North America. Especially noteworthy has been his scenography based on simultaneous settings for *Crime and Punishment* (Stockholm, 1984), *Romeo and Juliet* (Oslo, 1985), and *Dr. Jekyll and Mr. Hyde* (San Diego, 1986).

—Jarka M. Burian

Ladislav Vychodil: Set design for *Atlantida*, **Bratislava, 1961**

WAGENFELD, Wilhelm.

German metalsmith, glass, ceramic and industrial designer. Born in Bremen, 15 April 1900. Apprenticed as a draughtsman, in Koch und Bergfeld silverware factory, Bremen, 1915–18; studied design at the Kunstgewerbeschule, Bremen, 1916–18; Staatliche Zeichenakademie, Hanau, 1919–21; studied privately in Bremen and Worpswede, 1921–22; studied metalwork under Laszlo Moholy-Nagy, at the Staatliche Bauhaus, Weimar, 1923–24. Served in the German Army, 1942–45. Freelance designer, working in Weimar and Dessau, 1926–30, in Berlin, 1931–35, in Weisswasser, 1935–47, in West Berlin, 1947–50, and in Stuttgart from 1950: designer for Schott und Genossen glassworks, Jena, and in the Thuringer Wald glassworks, 1930–32; artistic director, for Vereinigte Lausitzer Glaswerke, Weisswasser, for Fürstenberg china works, Weser, and for Rosenthal porcelain factory, Selb, 1934–37; design consultant, to Württembergische Metalware factory, Geisslingen, and to the Württembergische Landesgewerbeamt, Stuttgart, 1949–51. Assistant metalwork instructor, Bauhochschule, Weimar, 1926; head of metalwork classes, Staatliche Bauhaus, Dessau, 1929; instructor, at the Kunsthochschule, Berlin, 1931–35, and at the Institut fur Bauwesen, West Berlin, 1947–48; instructor in standardisation, Leibnitz-Akademie, West Berlin, 1947–49; professor of industrial design, Hochschule fur Bildenden Kunste, West Berlin, 1948–49; founder-director of his own design workshops, Stuttgart, from 1954. **Exhibitions:** Neue Sammlung, Munich, 1939, 1961; Kunstmuseum, Gorlitz, 1939; Kunstgewerbemuseum, Breslau, 1940; Kunstdienst, Berlin, 1940; Kunsthalle, Mannheim, 1941, 1956; Museum fur Kunst und Gewerbe, Hamburg, 1941; Kunstmuseum, Bautzen, 1942; Kunstgewerbemuseum, Zurich, 1960; Stedelijk Museum, Amsterdam, 1961; Akademie der Bildende Kunste, West Berlin, 1962; Landesgewerbeamt, Stuttgart, 1965; Landesmuseum, Oldenburg, 1965; Kunstkreis, Hameln, 1965; Kunstgewerbemuseum, Cologne, 1973 (toured); Musee des Arts Decoratifs, Paris, 1975; Württembergisches Landesmuseum, Stuttgart, 1980. **Collection:** Philadelphia Museum of Art. Recipient: Grand Prize, Paris Exposition, 1937; Bronze Medal, 1937, Grand Prize, 1940, 1957, Milan Triennale; Berliner Kunstpreis, West Berlin, 1968; Heinrich Tessenow Medal, Technische Universitat, Hannover, 1968; Gute Form Prize, Bonn, 1969. Honorary Member, Staatliche Akademie der Kunste, Stuttgart, 1962; Honorary Senator, Technische Universitat, Stuttgart, 1964; Extraordinary Member, Akademie der Kunste, West Berlin, 1965; Guest of Honor, Villa Massimo, Rome, 1968. Address: Heidehofstrasse 2, 7000 Stuttgart 1, West Germany.

Works:

Bauhaus table lamp in stainless steel and opalescent glass, 1923–24, reproduced by Tecnolumen, Bremen, 1980.
Metalwares and lamps, for Walter and Wagner, 1926–30.
Tea service in clear glass, for Schott und Genossen, 1932.
Oberweimar table service in glass, for Vereinigte Lausitzer Glaswerke, 1935.
Kubus refrigerator storage wares in pressed glass, for Vereinigte Lausitzer Glaswerke, 1938.
Beakers in tourmaline-coloured crystal, for Württembergische Metallwarenfabrik, 1949.
Form 3600 cutlery in stainless steel, for Württembergische Metallwarenfabrik, 1952.
Bremen light-fitting, for Peill and Putzler, 1953–54.
Portable radio, for Braun AG, 1954.
Atlanta cutlery, for Württembergische Metallwarenfabrik, 1954–55.
Tablewares in melamine, produced by Johannes Buchsteiner, for Lufthansa German Airlines, 1955.
Hotel tea service in silverplate, for Württembergische Metallwarenfabrik, 1956–58.
Mirror-light in porcelain and opalescent glass, for Lindner, 1958.
Osiris light-fitting, for Peill und Putzler, 1958.
Wine glasses, for Peill und Putzler, 1961.

Publications:

By WAGENFELD: books—*Wesen und Gestalt der Dinge um Uns*, Potsdam 1948; *Deutsche Industrie fur Industrielle Standardform*, Stuttgart 1950; *Z: Diskussionsgestellt*, Stuttgart 1950.

On WAGENFELD: books—*Wilhelm Wagenfeld*, exhibition catalogue by O. Eberle, Munich 1939; *Die Gute Industrieform*, exhibition catalogue by Hans Eckstein and Robert Gutmann, Hamburg, 1955; *Wilhelm Wagenfeld: Ein Kunstler in der Industrie*, exhibition catalogue by Siegfried Asche, Mannheim 1957; *Industrieware von Wilhelm Wagenfeld 1930–1960*, exhibition catalogue edited by Hans Fischli and Willy Rotzler, Zurich 1960; *Wagenfeld: Ontwerpen en Fabriek Werken voor Dagelijks Gebruiek*, exhibition catalogue by Willem Sandberg, Amsterdam 1961; *Wilhelm Wagenfeld: 30 Jahre Kunstlerische Mitarbeit in der Industrie*, exhibition catalogue by Hans Eckstein, Munich 1961; *Wilhelm Wagenfeld: Zusammenarbeit mit Fabriken 1930–1962*, exhibition catalogue by Herta Elisabeth Killy, Hans Scharoun and Johanna Hofmann, West Berlin, 1962; *Moderne Deutsche Industrieform* by Heinz Spielmann, Hamburg 1962; *Wilhelm Wagenfeld: Vom Bauhaus in die Industrie*, exhibition catalogue by Eduard Leuze and J. A. Thuma, Stuttgart 1965; *Crafts of the Weimar Bauhaus 1919–1924* by Walther Scheidig, Leipzig 1966, London 1967; *Laudatio fur Wilhelm Wagenfeld* by Wilhelm Hofmann, Hamburg 1968; *Wilhelm Wagenfeld: 50 Jahre Mitarbeit in Fabriken*, exhibition catalogue by Brigitte Klesse and others, Cologne 1973; *International Modern Glass* by Geoffrey Beard, London 1976; *Classics of Modern Design*, exhibition catalogue by Barnard Gay, London 1977; *In Good Shape: Style in Industrial Products 1900–1960* by Stephen Bayley, London 1979; *Wilhelm Wagenfeld: Schone Form, Gute Ware*, exhibition catalogue, Stuttgart 1980; *Design Since 1945*, edited by Kathryn Hiesinger and George Marcus, Philadelphia and London 1983; *The Conran Directory of Design*, edited by Stephen Bayley, London 1985; *Twentieth Century Design: Glass* by Frederick Cooke, London 1986.

A pioneer of industrial design, Wilhelm Wagenfeld belongs also among its most important representatives since the 1920s. His particular achievements lie in metal and glass work. With a consistency hardly matched by any other Bauhaus graduate, he converted into fact the Bauhaus slogan "Art and technology—a new unity." His Bauhaus Lamp of 1923 suited contemporary taste as much as it embodied the spirit of the early Bauhaus, whilst Wagenfeld himself described Moholy-Nagy as his most important teacher there.

From his earliest activities at the Weimar Bauhochschule, Wagenfeld consistently worked with industry. It is not the single product which is characteristic of his work but the long-term collaboration with a few firms and the renovation of whole production processes. Wagenfeld's products were consistently successful, frequently being marketed for decades after their original design. His intense preoccupation with manufacturing processes often led him to new and unusual design solutions: his first discovery was of modern and practical forms for hollow and compressed glass (tea and coffee services, baking dishes, and the Kubus storage wares). The glass products of the Vereinigte Lausitzer Glaswerke gained an international reputation through his designs. The diamond shape introduced by Wagenfeld soon developed into a mark of quality. Among the designers introduced to the factory by Wagenfeld were Heinz Loffelhardt, Hermann Gretsch, Walter Dexel, Josef Hoffmann, and Wolfgang von Wesin.

In the postwar period, the chief accent was on metalwork for the Württembergische Metallwarenfabrik. This firm's production was also marked for decades by Wagenfeld's stamp. Their shapes developing out of the material itself, his Cromagan utensils are characterized by simplicity, beauty of form, and superb fitness to their purposes. Wagenfeld's long-standing design work for industry rests on an ethos that vetoes any expression of the artist's individuality in the product design. His belief in the moral strength of a well-designed form has marked his professional attitude throughout.

—Magdalena Droste

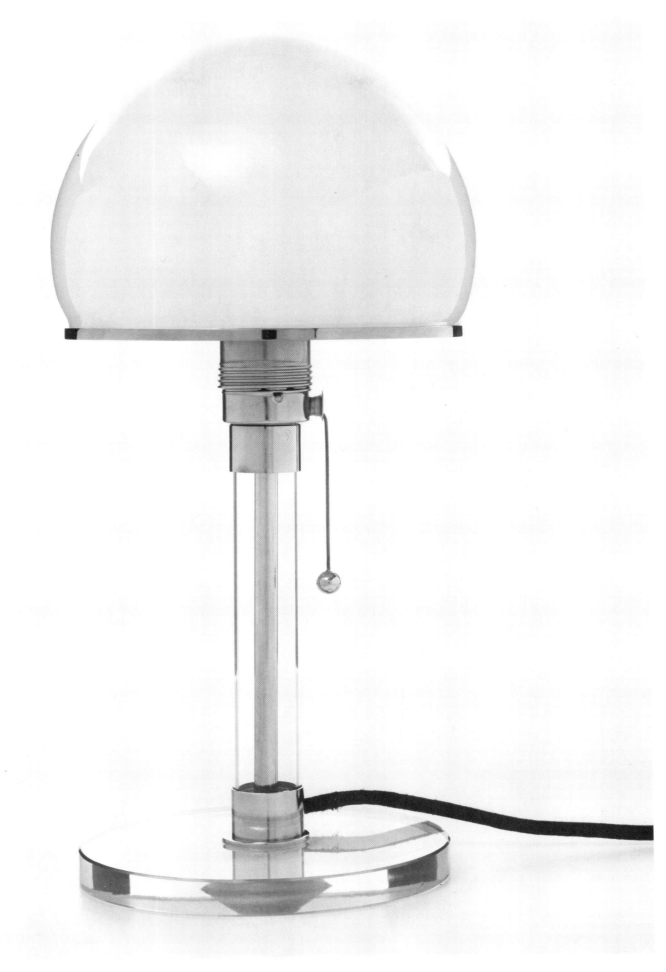

Wilhelm Wagenfeld: *Bauhaus Lamp*, 1924, produced by Technolumen, 1980

WAGNER, Robin (Samuel Anton).

American stage designer. Born in San Francisco, California, 31 August 1933. Educated at Balboa High School, San Francisco, until 1952; studied at the California School of Fine Arts, San Francisco, 1952–54. Married Joyce Marie Workman in 1959 (divorced); children: Kurt, Leslie and Christie. Freelance stage set designer, working in San Francisco, 1953–59, and in New York from 1959; also film designer from 1970. Theatre Advisory Council Member, New York; board member, Corporate Fund for Theatre; steering committee member, League of Professional Theatre Training Programs. Recipient: Drama Desk Award, New York, 1971, 1978; Joseph Maharam Award, New York, 1973, 1975, 1981; Lumen Award, New York, 1975; Outer Circle Critics Award, New York, 1978; Antoinette Perry "Tony" Award, New York, 1978. Member, United Scenic Artists. Address: 890 Broadway, 6th floor, New York, New York 10003, U.S.A.

Works:

Stage productions include: for the Golden Gate Opera Workshop, San Francisco—*Don Pasquale*, 1953; *Amahl and the Night Visitors*, 1953; *Zanetto*, 1953; for the Theatre Arts Colony, San Francisco—*Tea and Sympathy*, 1954; for the Encore, San Francisco—*The Immoralist* and *Dark of the Moon*; for the Actors Workshop, San Francisco—*Waiting for Godot*, 1957, *The Miser*, 1958; *The Ticklish Acrobat*, 1958; *The Plaster Bambino*, 1959; for the San Francisco Ballet Company—*The Filling Station*, 1958; all in New York unless indicated—*And the Wind Blows*, 1959; *The Prodigal*, 1960; *Between Two Thieves*, 1960, *Borak*, 1960; *A Worm in Horseradish*, 1961; *Entertain a Ghost*, 1962; *The Days and Nights of Beebee Fenstermaker*, 1962; *The Playboy of the Western World* (for the Irish Players), 1962; *Cages*, 1963; *In White America*, 1963; *The Burning*, 1963; *The White Rose and the Red*, 1964; *Dark of the Moon*, (for the Arena Stage, Washington, D.C.), 1964; *Galileo* (for the Arena Stage, Washington, D.C.), 1964; *A View from the Bridge*, 1965; *An Evening's Frost*, 1965; *The Condemned of Altona*, 1966; *Galileo*, 1967; *The Trial of Lee Harvey Oswald*, 1967; *A Certain Young Man*, 1967; *Love Match* (in Los Angeles), 1967; *Hair*, 1968; *Lovers and Other Strangers*, 1968; *The Cuban Thing*, 1968; *The Great White Hope*, 1968; *Promises, Promises*, 1968; *Hair* (at the Shaftesbury Theatre, London), 1968; *The Watering Place*, 1969; *My Daughter, Your Son*, 1969; *Promises, Promises* (in London), 1969; *Gantry*, 1970; *Mahagonny*, 1970; *The Engagement Baby*, 1970; *Lenny*, 1971; *Jesus Christ Superstar*, 1971; *Inner City*, 1971; *Sugar*, 1971; *Lysistrata*, 1972; *Seesaw*, 1973; *Full Circle*, 1973; *Mack and Mabel*, 1974; *Sergeant Pepper's Lonely Hearts Club Band on the Road*, 1974; *A Chorus Line*, 1975; *The Red Devil Battery Sign* (in Boston), 1975; *Les Troyens* (for the Vienna State Opera), 1976; *Hamlet Connotations* (for the American Ballet Theatre), 1976; *West Side Story* (for the Hamburg State Opera), 1977; *On the Twentieth Century*, 1978; *Ballroom*, 1978; *Comin' Uptown*, 1979; *Swing*, 1980; *42nd Street*, 1980; *One Night Stand*, 1980; *Semmelweiss*, 1981; *Dreamgirls*, 1981; *Barber of Seville* (for the Metropolitan Opera), 1962; *Mahalia*, 1982; *Rolling Stones Concert* (Madison Square Garden), 1982; *Merlin*, 1983; *Three Dances* (for Eliot Field Ballet), 1983; *Jewels* (for New York City Ballet), 1983; *Song and Dance*, 1985; *Teddy and Alice*, 1986; *Chess* (London production), 1987; *Chess* (New York production), 1988; *Jerome Robbins' Broadway*, 1989.

Publications:

On WAGNER: books—*The Biographical Encyclopaedia and Who's Who of the American Theatre*, edited by Walter Rigdon, New York 1966; *Who's Who in the Theatre*, edited by Ian Herbert, Detroit 1981; *Contemporary Theatre, Film and Television*, edited by Monica M. O'Donnell, Detroit 1986; *The Cambridge Guide to World Theatre*, edited by Martin Banham, Cambridge 1988.

*

Since he designed *Hair*, the breakthrough musical that altered the look of American theatre in the late 1960s, Robin Wagner's personal style of large-scale, fast-moving, automated scenery has set a standard for contemporary design in America. During the 1970s Wagner designed the scenery for *Lenny*, *Jesus Christ Superstar*, *Sugar*, *Seesaw*, *Mack and Mabel*, *A Chorus Line*, *On the Twentieth Century* and *Ballroom*; since 1980, he has designed the musicals *42nd Street* and *Dreamgirls*. These have won him all of the major theatre design awards. In addition to his work on Broadway, Wagner has designed scenery for the Vienna State Opera, the Hamburg State Opera, the American Ballet Theatre, the Arena Stage in Washington, D.C., and the American Shakespeare Festival in Stratford, Connecticut, as well as for television, film, and rock group tours.

Robin Wagner's structural, sometimes minimal, technologically exciting, visually simulating, and kinetic work will be remembered as the classic scenic design of the 1970s and 1980s. He is not a set designer in the old-fashioned sense of the term. He is not painterly; he does not design traditional box sets or painted drops. His work cannot be called delicate or decorative. He does not sketch pretty pictures for the scene shop, but rather, builds models of good scale, models that work, models that show how the scenery works.

The most memorable facet of Wagner's scenery is that it moves. Automation plays a key role in all of his designs, which are in constant motion—movement that is full of surprises. No one who saw *Jesus Christ Superstar* can forget the floor slowly rising in the back as though it were hinged at the footlights, then bodies beginning to crawl, and finally the floor continuing to rise almost straight upwards. And what about the excitement of the train speeding across the night sky in *On the Twentieth Century* and then, three-dimensionally, the train, with its headlight gleaming, heading down the track right towards the audience? and in *Dreamgirls*, constantly moving light towers created different spaces as they pivoted and moved back and forth across the stage.

The second memorable aspect of Wagner's scenery is its scale: the larger structural scenery in *Lenny*, the tall light towers in *Dreamgirls*, the cavernous spaces in *A Chorus Line* and in *Ballroom*. Also, he seems to work well with lighting designers, and his scenery allows for the theatricality of light. His sets are filled with lights—not the lighting designer's lamps hung from rails or at the sides of the stage, nor footlights, nor follow spots, but lights that are part of the scenery, lights that can be seen from the audience, lights that are part of the action of the show. The train lights in *On the Twentieth Century* not only lit the stage, they were part of the moving scenery. The theatrical lights of *A Chorus Line* and *Dreamgirls* similarly served a dual purpose. The lights surrounding the Stardust Ballroom created the space and mood of *Ballroom*.

Finally, Wagner's scenery has substance; it never consists of painted canvas flats. There is wood and metal and weight. The act "curtain" in *On the Twentieth Century*, made of contemporary materials such as formica-covered plywood, weighed 6,000 pounds.

—John E. Hirsch

WALLANCE, Don.

American industrial designer. Born in New York City, 26 September 1909. Studied at New York University, 1926–30: BA 1930; Design Laboratory, New York, 1935–39. Served as a technologist in the United States Army, Washington, D.C., 1942–43, 1945, and in the United States Air Force, in Alaska, 1943–44: Staff Sergeant. Married Shula R. Cohen in 1941 (died, 1979); sons: Gregory and David. Design and technical director, National Youth Administration, New Orleans, 1940–41; freelance designer, working in Washington, D.C., 1946–50, and in Croton-on-Hudson, New York, from 1950. Visiting lecturer, University of Illinois, Urbana-Champaign, 1964, and Rhode Island School of Design, Providence, 1980. **Exhibitions:** *A Designer's Case History of a Product*, Aspen Design Conference, Colorado, 1955; *Design Since 1945*, Philadelphia Museum of Art, 1983. **Collections:** Museum of Modern Art, New York; Philadelphia Museum of Art; Musee des Arts Decoratifs, Montreal; Centre de Creation Industrielle, Centre Georges Pompidou, Paris. Recipient: Museum of Modern Art Research Grant, New York, 1948; Golden Form Award, Utrecht, 1954. Address: 56 Mount Airy Road, Croton-on-Hudson, New York 10520, U.S.A.

Works:

Design 1 cutlery in stainless steel, for H. E. Lauffer Company, 1954, now produced by Towle Manufacturing Company.
Design 2 cutlery in stainless steel, for H. E. Lauffer Company, 1957, now produced by Towle Manufacturing Company.
ALCOA Forecast Collection of cooking and serving wares in aluminium, for the Aluminum Corporation of America, 1962.
Hospital furniture in steel and plastics, for the Hard Manufacturing Company, 1965.
Auditorium seating in steel and upholstered polyurethane foam, for the Philharmonic Hall of the Lincoln Center, New York, produced by the American Seating Corporation, 1965.
Palisander cutlery in stainless steel and rosewood, for H. E. Lauffer Company, 1969, now produced by Towle Manufacturing Company.
Magnum cutlery in stainless steel, for H. E. Lauffer Company, 1970, now produced by Towle Manufacturing Company.
Design 10 cutlery in coloured plastics, for H. E. Lauffer Company, 1971, now produced by Towle Manufacturing Company.

Publications:

By WALLANCE: book—*Shaping America's Products*, New York 1956.

On WALLANCE: books—*Industrial Design* by John Heskett, London 1980; *Design Since 1945*, edited by Kathryn Hiesinger and George Marcus, Philadelphia and London 1983; *American*

Don Wallance: *Magnum* stainless steel cutlery, for H. E. Lauffer, 1970

Design Classics by Joan Wessel and Nadia Westerman, New York 1985; *The American Design Adventure* by Arthur J. Pulos, London and Cambridge, Massachusetts 1988; *Dictionary of Twentieth Century Design* by John Pile, New York 1989; *Design in Plastics* by Douglas Cleminshaw, New York 1990.

As the practise of industrial design has become more comprehensive, it has involved such diverse functions as ergonomics, product planning, product engineering, market analysis, and, most recently, computer-aided design. But the essential core of the design process remains the creation of forms that have an esthetic vitality which is communicable to other people. Design in this sense is the function of a designer who has creative skill, inner conviction, technical competence, and esthetic sensibility and who is attuned to the needs and aspirations of his fellow human beings.

I work as an industrially oriented craftsman, concerned with every detail of a project from initial concept to technical specifications and, wherever possible, I fabricate my own product models.

—Don Wallance

After World War II, the mandate for American industrial designers was to fulfill the promise of the good life in the manufacture of better designed consumer goods. This mandate entailed styling that was simple, elegant and modern, coupled with advances in technology and industrial materials that facilitated mass production and distribution. Of the many pioneers who emerged during this period of frenetic design activity to make important contributions, Don Wallance is credited with establishing stainless steel flatware as a suitable replacement for silver as the conventional domestic service.

The shift from silver to steel was rapid and effective. At first, silver-plating alloys, like those designed by Garth and Ada-Louise Huxtable, were being accepted in restaurants, as was crude stainless steel in the home, although, for the most part, it was perceived as a temporary substitute until fine silver could be purchased. But, with the application of stamping and embossing techniques, this sheet metal flatware acquired an intricacy of decoration that challenged silver for a permanent place on the table. Working within this technology, Russel Wright had simplified designs, producing the first American expression of minimal, reductive, yet organically pleasing, stainless steel flatware.

With Don Wallance's designs of the 1950s, there was a radical break in the evolution of flatware. Forging, the traditional method of producing fine sterling silver flatware was found applicable to the mass production of stainless steel. Wallance, who staunchly defended and proselytized for the retention of a craftsman's esthetic in industrial methods, saw forging as a method for maintaining the sculptural solidity and dimensional feel that was prized in classic handforged silver. His designs that employed deep forging procedures came closest to replicating the clean, fluid lines, the satin finish, the fully rounded bowls that were virtuous in their respect for the material's nature. The absence of superficial styling was more than compensated for by the harmony of form that rendered the designs the epitome of classic modernism.

Wallance's dedication in forcing a craftsman's esthetic onto the field of industrial design extended beyond flatware into other consumer products, as well as various educational activities. Most notable in this regard was Wallance's seminal "*Study of Design and Craftsmanship in*

Today's Products," sponsored jointly by the Walker Art Center in Minneapolis, and the American Craftsmen's Council in New York, later developed into a traveling exhibition, and the book *Shaping America's Products* (1956). In his study, Wallance examined large-scale manufacturers like Bell Laboratories, Corning Glass, small-scale industry like Herman Miller and Lauffer as well as independent craftsmen-designers in pottery and jewelry with an eye on the contribution that the human instinct for workmanship can and must make the full benefit of mechanization. As a seminal effort to establish the relationship between craftsmanship and industry and its confluence in the modern industrial design, Wallance's study stands as the earliest treatment of the ethic and esthetic of the design process since the Arts and Crafts Movement.

—Sarah Bodine

WARM, Hermann.

German painter, stage and film designer. Born in Berlin, 5 May 1889. Studied design, at the Kunstgewerbeschule, Berlin, 1905–07; trained in stage design at the Szenograph, Berlin, 1908–09, and at the Schauspielhaus, Dusseldorf, 1910–11. Independent painter, associating with Der Sturm expressionist artists, Berlin; film set designer, under contract to Vitaskop, then working for Union, Decla-Bioskop, Greenbaum film company, etc., Berlin, 1912–60; freelance architect and set designer, working in Hungary, France and Britain, 1924–33, and in Switzerland, 1941–44: collaborated with designers Walter Rohrig, Walter Reimann, Otto Hunte, Carl Kirmse, Ernst Meivers, Erich Czernowski, Rudolf Bamberger, Gustav Knauer, Franz Schroedter, Ferdinand Ballen, Mathieu Osterman, Bruno Morden, Robert Herlth, Kurt Herlth, Alfons Windau, Erik Grave, Paul Markwitz and Fritz Maurischat, in Berlin and Munich, from 1919. Died (in Berlin) *in 1976*.

Works:

Film productions include—*Der Shylock von Krakau* (Wilhelm), 1913; *Menschen und Masken* (Piel), 1913; *Der Letzte Tag* (Mack), 1913; *Wo ist Coletti?* (Mack), 1913; *Der Konig* (Mack), 1913; *Die Blaue Maus* (Mack), 1913; *Der Andere* (Mack), 1913; *Die Geschichte der Stillen Muhle* (Oswald), 1914; *Pauline* (Etievant), 1914; *Der Hund von Baskerville* (Oswald), 1914; *Der Spion* (Schmidt-Hasler), 1914; *Die Beiden Rivalen* (Etievant), 1914; *Die Millionen-Mine* (Piel), 1914; *Totentanz* (Rippert), 1919; *Der Volontar* (Neuss), 1919; *Die Pest von Florenz* (Rippert), 1919; *Der Tunnel* (Meinert and Wauer), 1919; *Die Spinnen* (Lang), 1920; *Das Kabinett von Dr. Caligari* (Wiene), 1920; *Die Toteninsel* (Froelich), 1920; *Masken* (Wauer), 1920; *Das Blut der Ahnen* (Gerhardt), 1920; *Das Haupt des Juarez* (Guter), 1920; *Der Richter von Zalamea* (Berger), 1920; *Kamfende Herzen* (Lang), 1920; *Der Mude Tod* (Lang), 1921; *Der Ewige Flug* (Wendhausen), 1921; *Die Fliegenden Briganten* (Felmy), 1921; *Die Jagd nach dem Tode* (Gerhardt), 1921; *Schloss Vogelod* (Murnau), 1921; *Zirkus des Lebens* (Guter), 1921; *Phantom* (Murnau), 1922; *Das Spiel der Konigin* (Berger), 1923; *Der Kaufmann von Venedig*

(Flener), 1923; *Quarantine* (Mack), 1923; *Grafin Donelli* (Pabst), 1924; *Rosenmontag* (Meinert), 1924; *Konigsliebschen* (Schall), 1924; *Madels von Heute* (Friesler), 1925; *Die Rote Maus* (Meinert), 1925; *Soll Man Heiraten?* (Noa), 1925; *Das Susse Madel* (Noa), 1926; *Der Student von Prag* (Galeen), 1926; *Fraulein Josette, meine Frau* (Ravel), 1926; *Die Frau ohne Namen* (Jacoby), 1926; *Die Flucht in die Nacht* (Palermi), 1926; *Die Frauen von Folies Bergeres* (Obal), 1926; *Die Insel der Verbotenen Kusse* (Jacoby), 1926; *Liebe* (Czinner), 1926; *Parkettsessel 47* (Ravel), 1926; *Die Liebe Jeanne Ney* (Pabst), 1927; *Die Jagd nach der Braut* (Jacoby), 1927; *Colonialskandal* (Jacoby), 1927; *Millionenraub im Rivieraexpress* (Delmont), 1927; *La Passion de Jeanne d'Arc* (Dreyer), 1928; *Eine Nacht in London* (Pick), 1928; *Priscillas fahrt ins Gluck* (Asquith), 1928; *Die Weissen Rosen von Ravensnberg* (Meinert), 1929; *Masken* (Meinert), 1929; *Fundvogel* (Hoffmann-Harnisch), 1929; *Das Erlebnis einer Nacht* (Brignone), 1929; *Freiheit in Fesseln* (Wolff), 1929; *Vertauschte Gesichter* (Randolf), 1929; *Dreyfus* (Oswald), 1930; *Es Kommt alle Tage vor . . .* (Natge), 1930; *Der Mann, der den Mord Beging* (Bernhardt), 1931; *Der Herr Finanzdirektor* (Friedmann-Frederich), 1931; *Vampyr* (Dreyer), 1932; *Friederike* (Friedmann-Frederich), 1932; *Gehetzte Menschen* (Feher), 1932; *Hochzeit am Wolfgangsee* (Behrendt), 1933; *Wenn am Sonntagabend die Dorfmusik Spielt* (Schundler), 1933; *Peer Gynt* (Wendhausen), 1934; *Wenn ich Konig War* (Hubler-Kahla), 1934; *Musik im Blut* (Waschneck), 1934; *Peter, Paul und Nanette* (Engels), 1934; *Pappi* (Rabenalt), 1934; *Zigeunerblut* (Klein), 1934; *Der Student von Prag* (Robison), 1935; *Mazurka* (Forst), 1935; *Ich Liebe alle Frauen* (Lamac), 1935; *Krach im Interhaus* (Harlan), 1935; *Ein Hochzeitstraum* (Engel), 1936; *Madchenjahre einer Konigin* (Engel), 1936; *Die Nacht mit Kaiser* (Engel), 1936; *Gefahrliches Spiel* (Engel), 1937; *Ein Volksfeind* (Steinhoff), 1937; *Die Warschauer Zitadelle* (Buch), 1937; *Jugend* (Harlan), 1938; *Verwehte Spuren* (Harlan), 1938; *Das Unsterbliche Herz* (Harlan), 1939; *Die Geierwally* (Steinhoff), 1940; *Le Corbeau* (Clouzot), 1943; *Wozzeck* (Klaten), 1947; *Morituri* (York), 1948; *Vors uns Liegt das Leben* (Rittau), 1948; *Tragodie einer Leidenschaft* (Meisal), 1949; *Konigskinder* (Kautner), 1950; *Sehnsuchte des Herzens* (Martin), 1950; *Das Ewige Spiel* (Cap), 1951; *Herz der Welt* (Braun), 1952; *Cuba Cabana* (Buch), 1952; *Die Privatsekretarin* (Martin), 1953; *Hokuspokus* (Hoffmann), 1953; *Der Raub des Sabinerinnen* (Hoffmann), 1954; *Verrat an Deutschland* (Harlan), 1955; *Hannusse Hanussen* (Fischer), 1955; *Konigswalzer* (Tourjansky), 1955; *Dany, Bitte Schreiben Sie* (von Borsody), 1956; *Helden* (Wirth), 1959; *Die Nackte und der Satan* (Trivas), 1959; *Die Wahrheit uber Rosemarie* (Jugert), 1959; *Die Botschafterin* (Braun), 1960.

Publications:

By WARM: articles—in *Filmkunst* (Vienna), no. 43, 1965; *Film* (Hannover), July 1965; *Kosmorama* (Copenhagen), October 1965.

On WARM: books—*Ragionamenti sulla Scenografia* by Baldo Bandini and Glauco Viazzi, Milan 1945; *From Caligari to Hitler: A Psychological History of the German Cinema* by Siegfried Kracauer, Princeton 1947; *La Scenografia nel Film* by Mario Verdone, Rome 1956; *Murnau* by Lotte H. Eisner, Paris 1964, London 1973; *The Haunted Screen: Expressionism in the Cinema* by Lotte H. Eisner, Berkeley 1969, 1973; *Film in the Third Reich* by David Stewart Hull, Los Angeles 1969; *Le Decor de Film* by Leon Barsacq, Paris 1970, as *Caligari's Cabinet*

Hermann Warm (with Rohrig and Reimann): Set for Wiene's *Cabinet of Dr. Caligari*, 1919

and Other Grand Illusions, Boston 1976; *Schopferische Filmarchitektur* by Walter Kaul, West Berlin 1971; *The German Cinema* by Roger Manvell and Heinrich Fraenkel, London 1971; *Caligari's Children: The Film as Tale of Terror* by S. S. Prawer, New York and Oxford 1980; *German Expressionist Film* by John D. Barton, Boston 1982; *International Dictionary of Films and Filmmakers*, Chicago and London 1987, 1991.

Hermann Warm had been designing films for several years when the script of *The Cabinet of Dr. Caligari* was handed to him in 1919. He called in Walter Reimann and Walter Röhrig, fellow designers who were also employed by Decla-Bioscop Studios. Together they decided upon an expressionistic mode and made rough sketches of the film setting. The designers' methodical approach was unusual in early film; *Caligari* is one of the first films in which the visual program was completely planned in advance by the designers.

The Cabinet of Dr. Caligari jolted critics and audiences at that time because of its unreal appearance and lack of illusionistic space. Warm articulated the concept underlying this style when he said, "The cinema image must become an engraving." Warm's statement recognizes the fact that film is a two-dimensional art form and explains, in part, why the designers looked to expressionist painting for inspiration.

Warm organized the art direction of Fritz Lang's *destiny*, just as he had done for *The Cabinet of Dr. Caligari*. The film has several parts: Röhrig designed the prologue and epilogue; Robert Herlth, the Chinese segment; and Warm, the Venetian and Arabian segments. Warm's work in this film is not expressionistic. The glow of torchlight against the cloaked figures of Renaissance Venice are reminiscent of Max Reinhardt's Deutsches Theatre productions, which were quite popular in Berlin from 1907 to 1919.

One of the most successful of the many films based on romantic literature is Henrick Galeen's *Student of Prague* of 1926. Warm's sets are faithful to the early nineteenth-century period of the story. His use of looming shadows and hazy light filtering through windows imbues the film with a romantic aura. Warm's sets appear to have been based on paintings by the German romantic painter Caspar David Friedrich.

Warm's greatest accomplishment after *The Cabinet of Dr. Caligari* was his setting for *The Passion of Joan of Arc*. For Danish director Carl Dreyer, Warm and theatrical designer Jean Hugo reproduced an entire medieval town. Although they based their construction on medieval painting, the town is somewhat abstract, with smooth, neutral walls. The set was not shot in its entirety but used as a backdrop to the close-ups of the characters' faces and the silhouetted implements of torture that are seen in the famous montage at the end of the film.

Warm's long and varied career as an art director indicates not only his technical skills but also his ability to carry out research on historical periods and his adaptability to various material and directors.

—Lois Miklas

WATANABE, Tokuji.
Japanese industrial designer. Born in Nagoya, 8 May 1934. Studied at Aichi Prefectural College of Education, Okazaki City, 1956–60: BA 1960. Married Mioko Futamura in 1957; children: Osamu, Makoto and Yoko. Freelance industrial designer, establishing UNI Design Office, in Nagoya, from 1960. Instructor in art, Tempaku Junior High School, Nagoya, 1960–63; lecturer in design, Miye University, Tsu City, 1973–77, Ministry of Trade and Industry Design Administration Section, Tokyo, 1975, and Aichi Prefecture College of Arts, Nagakute-machi, 1975–76. Executive director, Central Japan Designers' Association, from 1970; director general, Miye Prefecture Designers and Crafts-

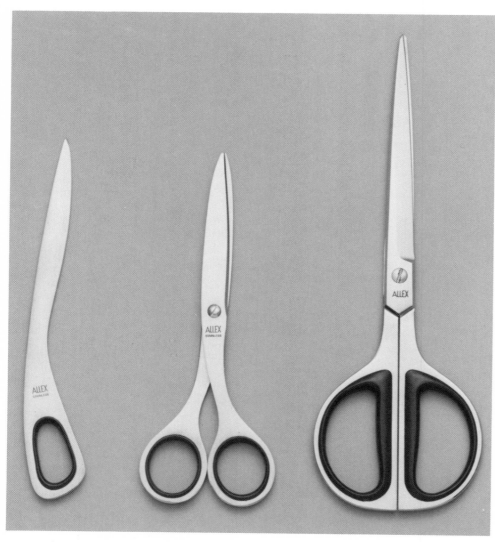

Tokuji Watanabe: Allex scissors and paper knife, 1973

and insight must be the minimum requirements for qualified designers in the coming age.

—Tokuji Watanabe

Tokuji Watanabe is best known as a designer of scissors—produced under the Allex brand and notable for the beauty of their forms. The scissors were first put on the market in 1973, and at that time such high quality, small-size scissors were not available in Japan. In the last ten years more than five million of these scissors have been produced. They have achieved an international reputation, and are now the world's best seller.

The Allex scissors are made of pressed stainless plate. Soft plastic rings are inserted within the finger holes. Polishing the finger holes to make them smooth is usually the most difficult part of making ordinary scissors: the plastic rings in the Allex scissors solved the problem —and the rings, done in a variety of shades, create an agreeable and colorful accent.

The success of Watanabe's scissors demonstrated several "lessons." Watanabe showed that, for local industries, it made more sense— that is, produced a better result—to work with an "indigenous product" than to attempt to produce what one imagined would have international appeal. Ironically, he also showed that a traditional product, produced by a local industry, could achieve international fame if it were well designed. And it occurred not only to other designers but also to other manufacturers that the simplest products can be well designed and that such well-designed products have great commercial appeal.

Watanabe has always said that designers should be good members of society if they wish to be good designers. If the role of the industrial designer is defined as "creative activity to produce materials and an environment that will satisfy man's natural and spiritual desires to live a humane life," then the actual circumstances in Japan seem to be very far from the ideal. Moreover, designers have tended to be too much involved in just one sector of society; they know very little about society as a whole. Watanabe has tried to be what he preaches: he has spoken out on many occasions about the world's limited resources, the energy crisis, pollution, and environmental problems, and, as a designer, he has advocated good design for public amenities.

Watanabe strives to achieve quality in both his life and his art: in fact, it could be said that he attempts to "design" his life and to make design a reflection of his larger concerns.

—Kunio Sano

men's Association, 1977–79; advisor on design development and promotion, Japan Industrial Design Promotion Society, Tokyo, 1976; Design Promotion Council member, Miye Prefecture, 1980–82; City Landscape Council member, Nagoya, 1980–83; Town Scenery Review Committee member, Aichi Prefecture, 1982. **Exhibition:** Yamagiwa Showroom, Nagoya, 1981. **Collection:** Die Neue Sammlung, Munich. Recipient: Kunii Kitaro Industrial Design Prize, 1981. Member: Japan Industrial Designers Association; Miye Local Industry Design Promotion Council; Central Japan Designers Association; Miye Designers and Craftsmen's Association. Address: UNI Design, 1–341 Kameiri, Tashiro-cho, Chikasu-ku, Nagoya 464, Japan.

Publications:

By WATANABE: book—*Scissors ABC*, Seki City 1980; articles—in *Design News* (Tokyo), January 1973, January 1980; *Chunichi Shimbun* (Nagoya), November 1977; *Industrial Design* (Tokyo), November 1979; *Chibu Designers Research Report* (Anjo City), April 1980.

On WATANABE: book—*Japanese Design* by Penny Sparke, London 1987; article—in *Interior* (Tokyo), June 1981.

The 1980s and 1990s may be the decades when

drastic solutions must be found for the problems raised during the 1960s and 1970s; these include considerations of energy, resources, food, nationalism, big business, controlled society, and human alienation. Moreover, in the daily life of people, changes are taking place in the value system, as is suggested by the phrases "from quantity to quality" and "from material to heart."

Although Japanese product design now holds a high international reputation as a result of improvements in tools and home appliances during the last three decades, if you turn your eyes to products for public use, such as tableware for school lunch, trains and other public transportation facilities, furniture used in hospitals and other public facilities, they reveal an imbalance in design, if the design is defined as "activity to satisfy the material and spiritual desires of man to live a cozy, humane life." This fact indicates that designers have forgotten their role in society; they are too much concerned about desirable relations between products and consumers.

The mainstream of our present lifestyle consists of a consumerism created when energy and other resources were obtained cheaply. This lifestyle must be totally revamped in the 1980s. Now, desirable relations among products, consumers, and nature must be demanded of designers. When the meaning of making things and of marketing and consuming products is questioned, then the meaning of creating must also be questioned. Courage, mental toughness,

WEALLEANS, Jon.
British architectural, interior and furniture designer. Born in Yorkshire, 10 February 1946. Studied at the Architectural Association School, London, 1966–67; Royal College of Art, London, 1967–70: MA 1970. Married Jane Hill in 1970. Designer, in the Building Partnership, Manchester and London, 1969–70, and with Foster Associates, London, 1970–71; freelance designer, London, 1971–85; creative director, Crighton Limited design group, London, from 1985: interior design consultant to Rock Townsend Architects, London, 1973–78. Unit staff lecturer, Architectural As-

sociation School, London, 1982–83; senior lecturer in three-dimensional design, Kingston Polytechnic, Surrey, from 1983. Addresses: 9 Grange Walk, London SE1; Crighton Limited, 10 New Oxford Street, London WC1A 1EE, England.

Works:

Bank of England headquarters interiors, Leeds, Yorkshire, 1969–70.
IBM Building interiors, Havant, Hampshire, 1971.
Roscoes Restaurant interiors, Soho, London, 1973.
Furniture, for Luna BV, Milan, 1973–78.

Publications:

On WEALLEANS: book—*The Contemporary Decorative Arts from 1940 to the Present Day* by Philippe Garner, London 1980; *Twentieth Century Furniture* by Philippe Garner, London 1981; *Restaurants: Architektur und Ambiente* by Egon Schirmbeck, New York 1982; *Fireplaces* by Nicholas Hills, London 1983; *Street Style* by Catherine McDermott, London 1988.

It is a fact—and important to me—that I do not have a particular style or hallmark other than an emphasis on detail design and the establishment of whether or not a (potential) client *needs* an architect and then whether or not I am the correct choice. I don't normally work with lavish budgets and, indeed, I am not uninterested in small-scale projects or budgets.
My criteria for accepting a commission are the same as those of Eliot Noyes: Potential clients should be in agreement with my design philosophy; they should allow adequate time for each project; and the programme and the budget should be in scale with one another.

—Jon Wealleans

Jon Wealleans describes himself as an eclectic designer without a strong sense of personal style, but with, however, a clear philosophy behind his design work. He believes that the designer should adapt his talents to the requirements of individual commissions, with the result that this work has been diverse. He is careful to take only briefs demanding innovative work, not pastiches, and only clients with sufficient finances and time to produce good work. This policy, which ensures that both client and designer have decided on the right person, has lost him work but gained him a great deal of respect. The question of pastiche is critical because he is inspired by design individualists such as Charles Rennie Mackintosh, Frank Lloyd Wright, Ettore Sottsass, and Robert Stern. It's a mixture explained by Wealleans' background, as one of a group of talented designers who graduated from the Royal College of Art in the 1960s, and who contributed to a feeling of excitement in British design during that period. His list of design inspirations is a classic 1960s amalgam of avant-garde Italian radicalism, images from popular culture, and stylistic motifs from previously unfashionable art nouveau designers. Not surprisingly, some of his work from this early period reflects a Pop design ethic.
His most important designs include the famous Mr. Freedom boutique in Kensington Church Street (1969) and, in the early 1970s, a house for a member of the rock group Led Zeppelin. Designed as a backdrop for the musician's collection of Art Deco, this interior features pink and cream colour, decorative inlays, etched glass, and painted troupe l'oeil perspec-

tives. More recently, in the design of the IBM interior at Edinburgh, he has adapted Mackintosh's work to a modern idiom. Wealleans' style of creatively transforming the work of other designers can be best seen in his own flat, featured in *Abitare* in May 1983. Using a standard Arts and Crafts formula of black floor and cream walls, doors, and curtains, he then added Liberty, Breuer, OMK, and his own furniture designs. The effect is comfortable, stylish, and very impressive. Wealleans is also developing as a serious design commentator, appearing on television programmes and in design magazines.

—Catherine McDermott

WECKSTRÖM, Björn (Ragnar).
Finnish sculptor, jewellery, glass and metalwork designer. Born in Helsinki, 8 February 1935. Studied at the Goldsmith's School, Helsinki, 1953–56: Dip. 1956. Married Britta Berg in 1957 (divorced, 1983); Leila Viljanen in 1989; children: Joachim and Cecilia. Freelance professional goldsmith and jewellery designer, Helsinki, 1956–67; designer, for Hopeakontu Oy, Helsinki, 1957, and for Lapponia Jewellery Oy, Helsinki, from 1963; also glass designer, for Wartsila-Nuutajarvi Glassworks, from 1967. Established own gallery in Helsinki, from 1958; concentrated on sculpture, in Agnano, Italy, from 1981. **Exhibitions:** Rohsska Konstslojdmuseet, Goteborg, 1967; Finland House, London, 1969; Amos Anderson Art Museum, Helsinki, 1973; David Jones Gallery, Sydney, 1975; Galerie der Greef, Brussels, 1977; Waino Aaltonen Museum, Turku, Finland, 1978; Sculpture Galleria, Palm Beach, Florida, 1978; Mikimoto Gallery, Tokyo, 1979; Boardwalk Gallery, Houston, 1979; Vestlandske Kunstindustrimuseum, Bergen, 1982; Kunstmuseum, Cologne, 1984; Stadtpark, Dortmund, 1985; Goldsmith's Hall, London, 1986; Nationaal Museum, Utrecht, 1987; *30th Anniversary Exhibition*, Galerie Bjorn Weckstrom, Helsinki, 1988; Ekenas Museum, Finland, 1989. **Collections:** Museum of Arts and Crafts, Helsinki; Finnish Glass Museum, Riihimaki; Victoria and Albert Museum, London; Royal Scottish Museum, Edinburgh; Rohsska Konstslojdmuseet, Goteborg; Vestlandske Kunstindustrimuseum, Bergen. Recipient: Medal, Milan Triennale, 1960; Purchase Prize, Norstaal Contest, Oslo, 1964; Grand Prix, International Jewellery Contest, Rio de Janeiro, 1965; Finnish Goldsmith's Medal of Honour, 1967; Lunning Prize, 1968; Pro Finlandia Medal, 1971; Illum Prize, 1972. Honorary Professor, Helsinki, 1986. Addresses: Marjaranta 12, 002260 Esbo, Finland; Via Settembrini 18, Agnano, Pisa, Italy.

Publications:

On WECKSTRÖM: books—*Finnish Design 1875–1975* by Timo Sarpaneva, Erik Bruun and Erik Kruskopf, Helsinki 1975; *Finland Creates*, edited by Jack Fields and David Moore, Jyvaskyla 1977; *Björn Weckström*, with texts by Christer Kihlman and Marika Hausen, Helsinki 1980; *Glas: Unikate finnische Kunstler*, exhibition catalogue by Helmut Ricke, Dusseldorf 1982; *Scandinavian Modern Design 1880–1980*, edited by David Revere McFadden, New York 1982; *The Lunning Prize*, exhibition catalogue edited by Helena Dahlback Lutteman and Mar-

ianne Uggla, Stockholm 1986; articles—"New Line of Jewellery for Lapponia Oy, Finland" in *Aurum* (Geneva), Summer 1987.

WEGNER, Hans J(orgensen).
Danish architectural, interior and furniture designer. Born in Tonder, Jutland, 2 April 1914. Educated in Tonder until 1926; apprenticed as a cabinet-maker, Tonder, 1927–31; studied at the Danish Institute of Technology, Copenhagen, 1936; studied furniture design under O. Moelgaard Nielsen, at the School of Arts and Crafts, Copenhagen, 1936–38. Married Inga Helbo in 1940. Furniture designer, working in the office of architects Flemming Lassen and Erik Moller, Aarhus, 1939, and office of Erik Moller and Arne Jacobsen, Aarhus, 1940–43; freelance interior and furniture designer, in Aarhus, 1943–46, and in Copenhagen from 1946: designed for Johannes Hansens Mobelsnedkeri, Fritz Hansen, Tarm Stole- og Mobelfabrik, RY-Mobler, Carl Hansen, Andreas Tuck, AP Stolen, Getama, PP Mobler, Erik Jorgensen, etc. Assistant to Palle Suenson, 1946–48, and instructor in design, 1946–53, at the School of Arts and Crafts, Copenhagen. **Exhibitions:** Cabinetmakers Guild Exhibitions, Copenhagen, 1938–67; *The Arts of Denmark*, toured the United States, 1960; *Modern Chairs 1918–1970*, Whitechapel Art Gallery, London, 1972; *Scandinavian Modern Design 1880–1980*, Cooper-Hewitt Museum, New York, 1982; *Design Since 1945*, Philadelphia Museum of Art, 1983. **Collections:** Museum of Modern Art, New York; Metropolitan Museum of Art, New York; Philadelphia Museum of Art; Victoria and Albert Museum, London; Die Neue Sammlung, Munich; Rohsska Konstslojdmuseet, Goteborg; Nationalmuseum, Stockholm; Kunstindustrimuseet, Oslo; Kunstindustrimuseet, Copenhagen. Recipient: Lunning Prize, 1951; Grand Prix, 1951; Gold Medal, 1954; Silver Medal, 1957; Diploma, 1957, Milan Triennale; Eckersberg Medal, 1956; Danish Trade Fair Medal, 1956; Cabinetmakers Guild Prize, Copenhagen, 1959, 1965; Citation of Merit, Pratt Institute, New York, 1959; American Institute of Decorators Award, 1961; Prince Eugen Medal, Stockholm, 1961; American Institute of Interior Designers Prize, 1967, and Citation of Merit, 1968; Danish Furniture manufacturers Prize, 1980; C. F. Hansen Medal, 1982; IDD Industrial Design Prize, Copenhagen, 1987. Honorary Royal Designer for Industry, Royal Society of Arts, London, 1959; Knight of the Dannebrog, 1984. Address: Tinglevej 17, 2820 Gentofte, Denmark.

Works:

Rocking Chair J 16 in beech with woven cord seat, for Tarm Stole- og Mobelfabrik, 1944.
Chinese Chair PP 66 in ash with woven string seat, for PP Mobler, 1944.
Chinese Chair FH 4283 in cherrywood with leather cushion, for Fritz Hansen, 1944.
Peacock Chair JH 550 in ash, oak and woven cord, for Johannes Hansen, 1947.
Folding Chair JH 512 in oak and woven cane, for Johannes Hansen, 1949.
Classic Chair JH 501 in oak and woven cane, for Johannes Hansen, 1949.

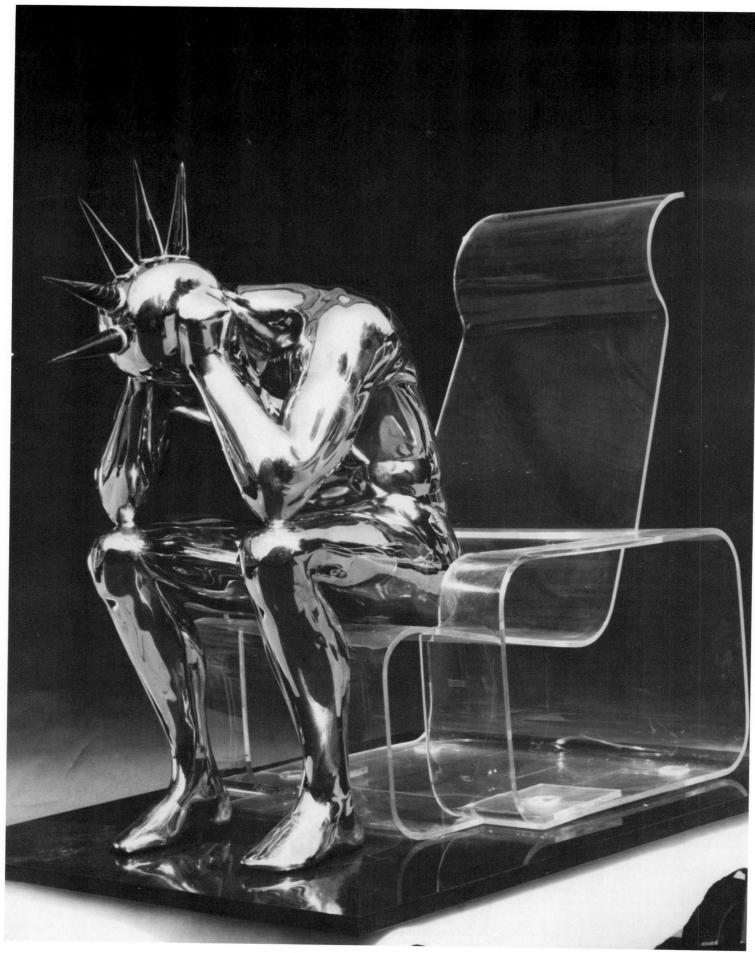

Bjorn Weckstrom: *The Thinker* sculpture in bronze, acrylic and glass, 1989

Wishbone Chair CH 24 in oak with woven string seat, for Carl Hansen and Son, 1950.

Flag Haliyard Chair upholstered steel-frame chair, for Getama, 1950.

Valet Chair PP 250 in pine and teak, for PP Mobler, 1953.

Swivel Chair JH 502 in tubular steel and teak with leather seat and wheels, for Johannes Hansen, 1955.

Easy Chair JH 40 in tubular steel with leather upholstery, for Johannes Hansen, 1958.

Armchair JH 518 in teak and wickerwork, for Johannes Hansen, 1961.

Easy Chair CH 44 in oak and beech with woven cord seat, for Carl Hansen and Son, 1965.

Chair JH 701 in steel and maple with leather upholstery, for Johannes Hansen, 1965.

Bull Chair EJ 100 in chrome steel with leather upholstery, for Erik Jorgensen, 1968.

Chair PP 201 in ash with woven string seat, for PP Mobler, 1969.

Chair PP 112 in ash with woven string seat, for PP Mobler, 1978.

Rocking Chair PP 124 in ash with rope seat and back, for PP Mobler, 1983.

Easy Chair PP 130 in laminated ash with woven seat and back, for PP Mobler, 1986.

Easy Chair JH 478 in laminated ash with upholstered back and seat, for Johannes Hansen, 1986.

Publications:

On WEGNER: books—*Dansk Mobelkunst* by Viggo Sten Moller and Svend Erik Moller, Copenhagen 1951; *Danish Chairs*, edited by Nanna and Jorgen Ditzel, Copenhagen 1954; *Modern Danish Furniture* by Esbjorn Hiort, Copenhagen, New York and London, 1956; *Made in Denmark* by Arne Karlsen and Anker Tiedemann, Copenhagen 1960; *A Treasury of Scandinavian Design*, edited by Erik Zahle, New York 1961; *Scandinavian Domestic Design*, edited by Erik Zahle, Copenhagen 1961, London 1963; *Wegner: En Dansk Mobelkunstner* by Johann Moller-Nielsen, Copenhagen 1965; *Contemporary Danish Design*, edited by Arne Karlsen and others, Copenhagen, 1966; *34 Scandinavian Designers* by Svend Erik Moller, Copenhagen 1967; *Modern Chairs 1918–1970*, exhibition catalogue with texts by Carol Hogben and others, London 1970; *The Modern Chair: Classics in Production* by Clement Meadmore, London 1974; *Scandinavian Designs: Objects of a Life Style* by Eileen Harrison Beer, New York and Toronto 1975; *History of Modern Furniture* by Karl Mang, Stuttgart 1978, London 1979; *Tema med Variationer: Hans J. Wegner's Mobler* by Henrik Sten Moller, Tonder 1979; *Twentieth Century Furniture* by Philippe Garner, London 1980; *A Century of Chair Design*, edited by Frank Russell, London 1981; *Knoll Design* by Eric Larrabee and Massimo Vignelli, New York 1981; *Contemporary Classics: Furniture by the Masters* by Charles D. Gandy and Susan Zimmerman-Stidham, New York, 1981; *Contemporary Furniture*, edited by Klaus-Jurgen Sembach, Stuttgart and London 1982; *Design Since 1945*, edited by Kathryn Hiesinger and George Marcus, Philadelphia and London 1983; *Industrial Design: Unikate Serienzeugnisse* by Hans Wichmann, Munich 1985; *Mid-Century: Furniture of the 1950s* by Cara Greenberg, London 1985; *Modern Furniture Classics* by Miriam Stimpson, London 1987.

Hans Wegner exemplifies the prolific designer, one comparable to an author who produces best-sellers year after year. And yet, to parallel Wegner's output, this would have to be a novelist who also turns out histories, biographies,

Hans J. Wegner: *PP 130* easy chair in laminated ash and woven cord, for P P Mobler, 1986

and even an occasional volume of verse. Over the years, Wegner has produced an extensive line of furnishings: storage systems and storage pieces; wood-framed and fully upholstered seating; lamps and wallpapers; tables of every type; pieces for the home and, more recently, for public spaces; and, of course, chairs. His approach is literally that of the artist-craftsman, with prototypes developed in his basement workshop and tested in the home he designed for himself outself Copenhagen before being given over to the firm that produces his work.

Again indicative of his mastery of many genres is the fact that although he appears to prefer wood to other materials, he is also willing to experiment with metals, as he did in the steel-framed "hammock" chair which is innovatively upholstered with 230 meters of flag cord anchored with an obvious knot at one end.

It is not for his versatility that Wegner is celebrated, however. It is for his wood chairs—his poetry. As counterpoint to his other designs, which are united more by a general level of craft and utility than by stylistic similarities, Wegner's wood chairs have consistently explored subtle sculptural relationships. Their origins are frequently Oriental—the back rails often wrapping into the front uprights—and occasionally traditional, as in the examples of the Boston rockers and Windsor-like Peacock. Seats frequently appear to float on their supporting rails, and both joins and combinations

of woods and materials break from the expected.

Wegner exhibits the poet's ability to interpret and reinterpret a theme, to make statements which are complete without being final. Moreover, his chairs are beyond the mainstream. Their complexity prevents their being readily copied. Thus, they avoid being cheapened by imitations (as happened to other Danish designs in the 1950s, for example, as they were insensitively transformed into "Danish modern" by American manufacturers).

—Reed Benhamou

WEINGART, Wolfgang.

German graphic and typographic designer. Born in 1941. Apprenticed as a hand-typesetter, Basel; mainly self-taught in design. Freelance designer and teacher, in Basel, from 1968. Founder of *TM/Communication* and *Typographic Process*, in collaboration with *Typographische Monatsblatter*, St. Gall. Instructor,

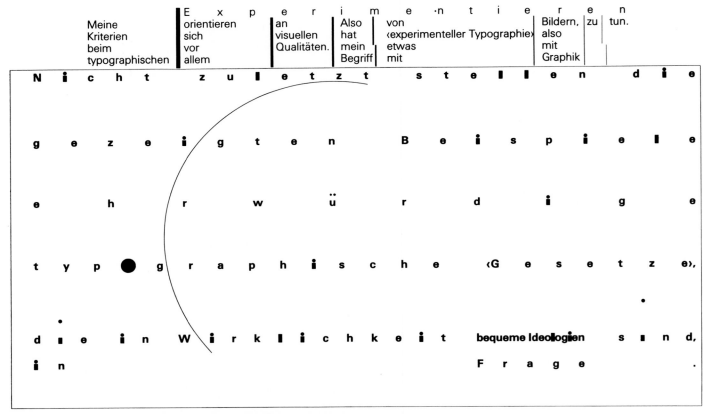

Meine Kriterien beim typographischen **E**orientieren sich vor allem **x**p**e**r**i**m**e**n·**t**i**e**r**e**n an visuellen Qualitäten. Also hat mein Begriff von ‹experimenteller Typographie› etwas mit Bildern, also mit Graphik zu tun.

Nicht zuletzt stellen die gezeigten Beispiele ehrwürdige typographische ‹Gesetze›, die in Wirklichkeit bequeme Ideologien sind, in Frage.

Durch das Experiment suche ich neue Gestaltungselemente und nicht nur die bekannten neu zu arrangieren.
Zu diesem Begriff ‹Experiment› gehört, daß die klassischen Spielregeln der Typographie aufgehoben sind.

Wolfgang Weingart: *Text Interpretation*, **1969**

Kunstgewerbeschule, Basel, from 1968; also visiting lecturer throughout Europe and the United States, from 1972. **Exhibition:** *The Twentieth Century Poster: Design of the Avant-Garde*, Walker Art Center, Minneapolis, 1984. Recipient: numerous poster and graphics prizes from the Swiss Department of Cultural Affairs. Member: Alliance Graphique Internationale, Paris. Address: Postfach 2235, 4001 Basel, Switzerland.

Works:

Typographische Monatsblatter magazine covers, St. Gall, 1972–73, 1976.
Kunstkredit posters in B2 format, 1977–83.
Idea no. 12 magazine cover, Tokyo, 1979.
Projekte/Projects book jacket design, for Verlag Arthur Niggli, 1979.
Didacta booklets and folders, 1980–81.
Didacta poster in B2 format, 1981.
Schreibkunst poster in B2 format, 1981.
The Swiss Poster book jacket design, for Birkhauser Verlag, 1983.
The Swiss Poster promotion poster in B2 format, 1983.

Publications:

By WEINGART: books—*How Can One Make Swiss Typography*, Basel 1972, London 1987; *Projects: Typographic Research at the Basel School of Design*, Niederteufen 1979; articles—in *Typographische Monatsblatter* (St. Gall), 1968–85; *Design Quarterly* (Minneapolis), no. 1, 1985.

On WEINGART: books—*Top Graphic Design* by F. H. K. Henrion, Zurich 1983; *The Twentieth Century Poster: Design of the Avant-Garde* by Dawn Ades, New York 1984; articles — in *Typographische Monatsblatter* (St. Gall), January 1970, November 1970, October 1973, December 1976; *Idea* (Tokyo), no. 1, 1978; *Graphis* (Zurich), no. 227, 1983.

The use of sans serif typography, rigid adherence to a grid system, asymmetrical balance, and flush left/ragged right type settings characterized the universal and harmonious typographic style that emerged from Switzerland and found advocates throughout the world. Just as this approach started to harden into a formula, Weingart began to teach at Basel and to challenge prevailing concepts of typographic design. Wide letterspacing of type, the swelling of typography through photographic overexposure, and the mixing of type sizes and weights in the same design (or even in the same word) were explored in an effort to revitalize and invigorate typography. Rather than use traditional means to indicate paragraphs, such as indenting the first line or separating paragraphs with a space, Weingart invented new devices to serve this function. For example, he placed paragraphs throughout the page in one advertisement, using arrows and numbers to direct the reader through the information. In another project, paragraphs had stepped geometric shapes and were locked together like a puzzle. Numerals informed the reader of their reading order.

As Weingart's design innovations from the early 1970s (including step-rules, size and weight contrasts, letterspaced type, and fine

rules moving through the space to link elements together) were widely emulated during the late 1970s. Weingart moved on to create collage-like compositions by layering film positives of images and type. This innovative technique enabled Weingart to juxtapose and overlay complex visual information. During this period, Weingart delighted in contrasts. Type, images, moiré and halftone patterns, torn collage elements, and linear patterns are densely layered and stacked into rich, tonal graphic expressions.

—Philip B. Meggs

WEITZ, John.
American fashion and industrial designer. Born in Berlin, Germany, 25 May 1923; emigrated to Britain in 1934, then to the United States in 1940; naturalized, 1943. Educated at The Hall School, and at St. Paul's School, London, 1935–39; apprenticed to fashion designer Edward Molyneux, Paris, 1939–40. Served in the United States Army, 1943–46: Captain. Married the actress Susan Kohner in 1964; children: Robert, Karen, Paul and Christopher. Designer of women's sportswear, working with several companies in London and New York, until 1954; founder-designer and chairman of John Weitz Incorporated men's fashion designs,

New York, from 1954. Vice president, Old Pauline Club, London, and Skeeters 21 union, New York; board member: Allen-Stevenson School, New York; Phoenix House, New York; Raoul Wallenberg Committee; William J. Donovan Foundation; Council of Fashion Designers of America; Leo Baeck Institute; Education Foundation for the Fashion Industries; Veterans of the OSS, New York. Council member, Museum of the City of New York. **Collection:** Smithsonian Institution, Washington, D.C. Recipient: *Sports Illustrated* Award, 1959; *NBC Today* Award, 1960; Philadelphia Museum of Art Award, 1960; Caswell-Massey Awards, 1963–66; *Harper's Bazaar* Medallion, 1966; Moscow Diploma, 1967; International Best Dressed List Hall of Fame Award, 1971; Coty American Fashion Critics Award, 1974; Cartier Award, 1981; Mayor's Liberty Medal, New York, 1986; Cutty Sark Career Achievement Award, 1986; First Class Order of Merit, West Germany, 1988. Address: 600 Madison Avenue, New York, New York 10022, U.S.A.

Publications:

By WEITZ: books—*Sports Clothes and Cars*, New York 1959; *The Value of Nothing*, New York and London 1970; *Man in Charge*, New York 1974; *Friends in High Places*, New York 1982.

On WEITZ: books—*Dress Optional* by Bennett-England, London 1967; *The Fashion Makers* by Vecchio and Riley, New York 1968; *The Beautiful People* by Marilyn Bender, New York 1968; *Esquire's Encyclopedia of Men's Fashions*, New York 1973; *Mature Man's Guide to Style* by Gale, New York 1980; *Fairchild's Who's Who in Fashion*, edited by Anne Stegemeyer, New York, 1980; *Inside the Fashion Business* by Jarrow, Judelle and Goerreiro, New York 1981; *McDowell's Directory of Twentieth Century Fashion* by Colin McDowell, London 1984.

Obviously, form follows function and fashion follows form. Therefore, I have always tried to think of function first, be it technical, physical, or emotional.

—John Weitz

Although born in Germany, John Weitz, the son of a well-to-do textile manufacturer, was educated in England in the late 1930s (safe from the Nazis). The combination of an English education and an apprenticeship with the famous couturier Edward Molyneaux, whose classic style was legendary, developed in Weitz a taste for the classically tailored.

His early work as a designer in America was in women's sportswear—a relatively new field after World War II. Weitz innovatively introduced men's tailored sportswear to American women, thereby setting a style for the rest of the fashion world. His "second career" as a menswear designer in the 1960s and 1970s brought him even greater success. While most designers were experimenting in the men's market with outlandish colors and fabrics and extreme cuts, Weitz made an important name for himself with conservatively designed clothing, such as navy blue flannel blazers, oxford cloth tailored shirts, and classically "English" ties—a style once called Ivy League, but now called Preppy—in the moderate price range that non-Preppy young men can afford.

As much a businessman as he is a designer, he was one of the first American designers to put his signature on the exterior of the menswear he designed. With the success of the John Weitz signature, he licensed his name to manufacturers of many different kinds of products, ranging from traditional clothing for men, women, and boys, to accessories such as scarves, gloves, and handbags and to non-clothing articles like cigar boxes and ice buckets.

Though Weitz has won many awards for his designs, including the Coty which is the *grand prix* of American fashion awards, one of his most prestigious awards is the 1981 Cartier

Design Award for an all-aluminium sports car, the X-600 (nicknamed the Weitzmobile). Weitz believes that a man should wear his car as he would wear his clothes; the X-600 fits the well-dressed man in the same manner that his classically tailored clothes should fit. Although Weitz designs only a very small percentage of the clothing (and other articles) produced under his name, he supervises most of the licensed articles, so he can veto those things which do not conform to his taste.

—John E. Hirsch

WELCH, Robert (Radford).
British silversmith and product designer. Born Hereford, 21 May 1929. Educated at Hanley Castle Grammar School, Worcestershire, 1941–46; studied under Victor Moody, at Malvern School of Art, Worcestershire, 1946–47, 1949: Charlotte Jacob Prize 1950; under C. J. Shiner and R. Baxendale, at Birmingham College of Art, 1950–52: Charles Foye Scholarship 1951; under Robert Gooden, at the Royal College of Art, London, 1952–55: RCA Prize and Medal, 1955. Served as a wireless operator in the Royal Air Force, 1947–49. Married Patricia Marguerite Hinksman in 1959; children: Alice, Alan and Leonard. Independent silversmith and metalware designer, with workshop in Chipping Campden, Gloucestershire, from 1955, and studio shop in Chipping Campden, from 1969: design consultant to J. and J. Wiggin Old Hall Tableware, Bloxwich, from 1955. Lecturer, at the Central School of Art and Design, London, 1956–59, and at the Royal College of Art, London, 1960–71. **Exhibitions:** Foyles Art Gallery, London, 1956; Heal and

John Weitz: X600 aluminium-body sports car, 1980

Robert Welch: stainless steel cutlery

Sons, London, 1964; Skjalm Petersen Shop, Copenhagen, 1967; Leeds Art Gallery, Yorkshire, 1969; Crafts Advisory Council, London, 1974; *Design Since 1945*, Philadelphia Museum of Art, 1983; *Eye for Industry*, Victoria and Albert Museum, London, 1986. **Collections:** Victoria and Albert Museum, London; Worshipful Company of Goldsmiths, London; Bir-

mingham Museum; Leeds Museum, Yorkshire; Bergen Museum, Norway; Museum of Decorative Art, Copenhagen; Stedelijk Museum, Amsterdam; Museum of Modern Art, New York; Philadelphia Museum of Art. Recipient: Design Centre Award, London, 1958, 1963, 1964, 1965; Silver Medal, Milan Triennale, 1958; Silver Medal, Jerusalem Art Book Bien-

nale, 1975. Fellow, Chartered Society of Designers, London, 1962; Royal Designer for Industry, Royal Society of Arts, London, 1965; Honorary Fellow, Royal College of Art, London, 1972; Member, Order of the British Empire, 1980; Liveryman, Worshipful Company of Goldsmiths, London, 1982. Address: The White House, Alveston Leys, Alveston,

Stratford-upon-Avon, Warwickshire, England.

Works:

Toast rack in stainless steel, for Old Hall Tableware, 1958.
Campden cutlery in stainless steel, for David Mellor, 1958.
S.S. Oriana dishes and cutlery, for Old Hall Tableware, 1963.
Electric alarm clock, for Westclox, 1964.
Alveston cutlery in stainless steel, for Old Hall Tableware, 1965.

Publications:

By WELCH: books—*The Design and Production of Stainless Steel*, thesis, Royal College of Art, London 1955; *Robert Welch: Design in a Cotswold Workshop*, London 1973; *Hand and Machine*, London 1986.

On WELCH: books—*Modern Jewelry: An International Survey 1890–1964* by Graham Hughes, London 1963, 1964; *Modern Silver Throughout the World 1880–1967* by Graham Hughes, London and Toronto 1967; *Industrial Design and the Community* by Ken Baynes, London 1967; *All Things Bright and Beautiful: Design in Britain 1830 to the Present Day* by Fiona MacCarthy, London 1972; *The Contemporary Decorative Arts from 1940 to the Present Day* by Philippe Garner, London 1980; *A History of Industrial Design* by Edward Lucie-Smith, Oxford 1983; *Design Since 1945*, edited by Kathryn Hiesinger and George Marcus, Philadelphia and London 1983; *Eye for Industry: Royal Designers for Industry 1936–1986* by Fiona MacCarthy and Patrick Nuttgens, London 1986.

For the first two years of my training, I studied drawing, painting, and silversmithing. Product design came much later in my career. In fact, not until my last year at the Royal College of Art, in 1955, did I consider the possibility of designing for industrial production. From the beginning of my workshop in 1955 to the present day, I continue to pursue two roles—silversmith and product designer. I believe that this dual development is mutually beneficial to both pursuits, especially so in the area of product design, that the silversmithing craft really has no limitations on the objects that can be made, and the finished result is a complete entity in its own right.

—Robert Welch

Of particular interest in Robert Welch's career is his successful combination of silversmithing with designing for industry. He was one of the group of Royal Group of Art-trained silversmiths who revived the craft in the late 1950s and early 1960s. Like David Mellor and others, he set up an independent workshop on leaving the college in the mid-1950s and, like them, benefited from the boom in sales of individually made goods after the war.

Welch's most successful designs for silver demonstrate his particular attention to craftsmanship and materials—legacies of the Arts and Crafts movement. His ability to achieve impressive results from apparently simple elements gives many of his designs their classic quality. Some more elaborate pieces, such as his silver candelabrum of 1970 for Goldsmiths' Hall and the cigar box with radial ribs of 1974, show his interest in surface texture and decoration, often achieved after experimentation with unorthodox techniques.

Welch initially turned towards industrial design as a result of the influence of Scandinavian domestic products in stainless steel; these had been developed during the war by Sigurd Persson and by designers for Gense and Georg Jensen. Welch's study of this work led to his early design consultancy for J. & J. Wiggin (marketing under the name of "Old Hall"), the only manufacturers of stainless steel domestic products in Britain at the time. Through this association, he pioneered the introduction of stainless steel in Britain for domestic wares. Welch sees himself as having also been "nudged" towards industrial design by two other factors: the difficulty of surviving on special commissions for silver during the 1960s and the prevalent early 1960s ideology favouring the combination of a craft with designing for production.

In his early craft and industrial work, the then-current preoccupation with organic forms, as seen not only in Scandinavian design but also in the contemporary sculpture of Hepworth and Moore, is evident, as exemplified by the Alveston range of cutlery. But this influence was quickly modified by his preference for symmetry. A retention of flowing elements, however, can be seen in some of Welch's most recent cutlery, designed for Yamazaki of Japan.

Welch's proficiency in his designs for stainless steel and cast-iron is clear. His Bistro range of 1966 was the first stainless steel cutlery with laminated wood handles. In his cast-iron cookware for Lauffer, his attention to problems of manufacturers is demonstrated by the ease with which the flash can be removed from the ribs and the pieces hung from the handles for enamelling.

—Karen Moon

WHEELER, Lyle.
American film designer. Born in Woburn, Massachusetts, 2 February 1905. Studied at the University of California, Los Angeles, 1923–26. Worked as a magazine illustrator and industrial designer, Los Angeles, 1927–35; film designer, Los Angeles, from 1936: art director for David O. Selznick, Los Angeles, 1938–42, and for Metro Goldwyn Mayer Studios, 1945–47; supervising art director, at 20th Century-Fox film studios, Hollywood, 1947–60; freelance production designer, working for Columbia studios and others, 1961–75. Recipient: Academy Award, Hollywood, 1939, 1946, 1953, 1956, 1959. *Died* (in Los Angeles, California) *10 January 1990.*

Works:

Film productions include—*The Garden of Allah* (Boleslawsky), 1936; *A Star Is Born* (Wellman), 1937; *The Prisoner of Zenda* (Cromwell), 1937; *Nothing Sacred* (Wellman), 1938; *The Young in Heart* (Wallace), 1938; *The Adventures of Tom Sawyer* (Taurog), 1938; *Gone With the Wind* (Fleming), 1939; *Made for Each Other* (Cromwell), 1939; *Intermezzo* (Ratoff), 1939; *Rebecca* (Hitchcock), 1940; *That Hamilton Woman* (A. Korda), 1941; *Keeper of the Flame* (Cukor), 1942; *The Jungle Book* (Z. Korda), 1942; *Cairo* (Van Dyke), 1942; *Bataan* (Garnett), 1943; *Laura* (Preminger), 1944; *Dragon Seed* (Conway and Bucquet), 1944; *Thirty Seconds Over Tokyo* (LeRoy), 1944; *Winged Victory* (Cukor), 1944; *Wing and a Prayer* (Hathaway), 1944; *Hangover Square* (Brahm), 1945; *Leave Her to Heaven* (Stahle), 1945; *A Tree Grows in Brooklyn* (Kazan), 1945; *The Dolly Sisters* (Cummings), 1945; *The House on 92nd Street* (Hathaway), 1945; *Fallen Angel* (Preminger), 1945; *Anna and the King of Siam* (Cromwell), 1946; *Cluny Brown* (Lubitsch), 1946; *My Darling Clementine* (Ford), 1946; *Centennial Summer* (Preminger), 1946; *Wake Up and Dream* (Bacon), 1946; *Dragonwyck* (Mankiewicz), 1946; *Daisy Kenyon* (Preminger), 1947; *Forever Amber* (Preminger), 1947; *The Foxes of Harrow* (Stahl), 1947; *Gentlemen's Agreement* (Kazan), 1947; *Kiss of Death* (Hathaway), 1947; *Nightmare Alley* (Goulding), 1947; *Call Northside 777* (Hathaway), 1948; *The Art Director* (documentary), 1948; *That Lady in Ermine* (Lubitsch), 1948; *Unfaithfully Yours* (P. Sturges), 1948; *The Iron Curtain* (Wellman), 1948; *Cry of the City* (Stodmak), 1948; *Give My Regards to Broadway* (Bacon), 1948; *The Snake Pit* (Litvak), 1948; *Street With No Name* (Keighley), 1948; *Thieves' Highway* (Dassin), 1949; *Whirlpool* (Preminger), 1949; *Pinky* (Kazan), 1949; *Chicken Every Sunday* (Seaton), 1949; *Twelve O'Clock High* (H. King), 1949; *Mother is a Freshman* (Bacon), 1949; *Slattery's Hurricane* (De Toth), 1949; *I Was a Male War Bride* (Hawks), 1949; *House of Strangers* (Mankiewicz), 1949; *The Fan* (Preminger), 1949; *A Letter to Three Wives* (Mankiewicz), 1949; *Dancing in the Dark* (Reis), 1949; *Down to the Sea in Ships* (Hathaway), 1949; *Panic in the Streets* (Kazan), 1940; *Cheaper by the Dozen* (W. Lang), 1950; *All About Eve* (Mankiewicz), 1950; *Broken Arrow* (Daves), 1950; *American Guerrilla in the Philippines* (F. Lang), 1950; *Two Flags West* (Wise), 1950; *When Willie Comes Marching Home* (Ford), 1950; *No Way Out* (Mankiewicz), 1950; *Where the Sidewalk Ends* (Preminger), 1950; *Fourteen Hours* (Hathaway), 1951; *Bird of Paradise* (Davies), 1951; *The House on Telegraph Hill* (Wise), 1951; *David and Bathsheba* (H. King), 1951; *Halls of Montezuma* (Milestone), 1951; *Fixed Bayonets* (Fuller), 1951; *Rawhide* (Hathaway), 1951; *The Guy Who Came Back* (Newman), 1951; *Golden Girl* (Bacon), 1951; *The Frogmen* (Bacon), 1951; *The Day the Earth Stood Still* (Wise), 1951; *Call Me Mister* (Bacon), 1951; *Anne of the Indies* (Tourneur), 1951; *People Will Talk* (Mankiewicz), 1951; *Love Nest* (Newman), 1951; *The Thirteenth Letter* (Preminger), 1951; *You're in the Navy Now* (Hathaway), 1951; *The Desert Fox* (Hathaway), 1951; *Deadline: USA* (Brooks), 1952; *My Cousin Rachel* (Koster), 1952; *Viva Zapata* (Kazan), 1952; *The President's Lady* (Levin), 1952; *The Snows of Kilimanjaro* (H. King), 1952; *Five Fingers* (Mankiewicz), 1952; *Monkey Business* (Hawks), 1952; *Return of the Texan* (Daves), 1952; *The Model and the Marriage Broker* (Cukor), 1952; *Red Skies of Montana* (Newman), 1952; *Diplomatic Courier* (Hathaway), 1952; *My Pal Gus* (Parrish), 1952; *Pony Soldier* (Newman), 1952; *Something for the Birds* (Wise), 1952; *Way of a Gaucho* (Tourneur), 1952; *The Robe* (Koster), 1953; *Call Me Madam* (W. Lang), 1953; *Titanic* (Negulesco), 1953; *Gentlemen Prefer Blondes* (Hawks), 1953; *The Farmer Takes a Wife* (Levin), 1953; *Man in the Attic* (Fregonese), 1953; *Treasure of the Golden Condor* (Daves), 1953; *Dangerous Crossing* (Newman), 1953; *How to Marry a Millionaire* (Negulesco), 1953; *Pickup on South Street* (Fuller), 1953; *White Witch Doctor* (Hathaway), 1953; *The I Don't Care Girl* (Bacon), 1953; *Niagara* (Hathaway), 1953; *King of the Khyber Rifles* (H. King), 1953; *River of No Return* (Preminger), 1954; *Three Coins in the Fountain* (Negulesco), 1954; *Garden of Evil* (Hathaway), 1954; *The Egyptian* (Curtiz), 1954; *Desiree* (Koster), 1954; *Hell and High Water*

(Fuller), 1954; *The Siege at Red River* (Mate), 1954; *Demetrius and the Gladiators* (Daves), 1954; *There's No Business Like Show Business* (W. Lang), 1954; *Love Is a Many-Splendored Thing* (H. King), 1955; *The Racers* (Hathaway), 1955; *The Girl in the Red Velvet Swing* (Fleischer), 1955; *Daddy Long Legs* (Negulesco), 1955; *The Seven Year Itch* (Wilder), 1955; *Violent Saturday* (Fleischer), 1955; *House of Bamboo* (Fuller), 1955; *The Tall Men* (Walsh), 1955; *The Left Hand of God* (Dymytryk), 1955; *Bus Stop* (Logan), 1956; *Teenage Rebel* (Goulding), 1956; *The King and I* (W. Lang), 1956; *The Bottom of the Bottle* (Hathaway), 1956; *Carousel* (H. King), 1956; *The Lieutenant Wore Skirts* (Tashlin), 1956; *The Man in the Gray Flannel Suit* (Johnson), 1956; *The Revolt of Mamie Stover* (Walsh), 1956; *Bigger Than Life* (Ray), 1956; *The Lazy Wagon* (Daves), 1956; *The Girl Can't Help It* (Tashlin), 1956; *Between Heaven and Hell* (Fleischer), 1956; *The Sun Also Rises* (H. King), 1957; *A Hatful of Rain* (Zinnemann), 1957; *Peyton Place* (Robson), 1957; *Will Success Spoil Rock Hunter?* (Tashlin), 1957; *An Affair to Remember* (McCarey), 1957; *Stopover Tokyo* (Breen), 1957; *The Three Faces of Eve* (Johnson), 1957; *Kiss Them for Me* (Donen), 1957; *No Down Payment* (Ritt), 1957; *South Pacific* (Logan), 1958; *A Certain Smile* (Negulesco), 1958; *The Young Lions* (Dymytryk), 1958; *From Hell to Texas* (Hathaway), 1958; *Ten North Frederick* (Dunne), 1958; *The Bravados* (H. King), 1958; *The Long Hot Summer* (Ritt), 1958; *The Hunters* (D. Powell), 1958; *The Barbarian and the Geisha* (Huston), 1958; *These Thousand Hills* (Fleischer), 1958; *The Fiend Who Walked the West* (Douglas), 1958; *Rally 'round the Flag Boys* (McCarey), 1958; *Compulsion* (Fleischer), 1959; *Blue Denim* (Dunne), 1959; *Journey to the Center of the Earth* (Levin), 1959; *A Farewell to Arms* (C. Vidor), 1959; *The Diary of Anne Frank* (Stevens), 1959; *The Sound and the Fury* (Ritt), 1959; *Woman Obsessed* (Hathaway), 1959; *Say One for Me* (Tashlin), 1959; *Hound Dog Man* (Siegel), 1959; *The Man Who Understood Women* (Johnson), 1959; *The Story on Page One* (Odets), 1959; *From the Terrace* (Robson), 1960; *Wild River* (Kazan), 1960; *Wake Me When It's Over* (LeRoy), 1960; *Seven Thieves* (Hathaway), 1960; *Can-Can* (W. Lang), 1960; *Advise and Consent* (Preminger), 1962; *The Cardinal* (Preminger), 1963; *The Best Man* (Schaffner), 1964; *In Harm's Way* (Preminger), 1965; *The Big Mouth* (Lewis), 1967; *The Swimmer* (Perry), 1968; *Where Angels Go . . . Trouble Follows* (Neilson), 1968; *Marooned* (J. Sturges), 1969; *Tell Me That You Love Me, Julie Moon* (Preminger), 1970; *The Love Machine* (Haley), 1971; *Doctor's Wives* (Schaefer), 1971; *Bless the Beasts and the Children* (Kramer), 1972; *Stand Up and Be Counted* (Cooper), 1972; *Posse* (K. Douglas), 1975.

Publications:

By WHEELER: article—in *Film Comment* (New York), May 1978.

On WHEELER: books—*Le Décor de Film* by Leon Barsacq, Paris, 1970, as *Caligari's Cabinet and Other Grand Illusions*, Boston 1976; *The World Encyclopedia of Film*, edited by Tim Cawkwell and John M. Smith, London 1972; *The International Film Encyclopedia* by Ephraim Katz, New York and London 1980; *International Dictionary of Films and Filmmakers*, Chicago and London 1987, 1991.

Lyle Wheeler began his career in art direction on a high note, precociously winning an Academy Award for *Gone With the Wind* (1939). His role was to execute the sets which were painstakingly sketched by William Cameron Menzies, the production designer. Wheeler's talent for creating historically accurate sets is not only evident in this epic but is also seen in his later films, such as *That Hamilton Woman* (1941, with Vincent Korda), about the lives of Lord Nelson and Lady Hamilton, and *The Robe*.

Wheeler's black-and-white films are characterized by a sharp, clean look. In the contemporary psychological thrillers *Rebecca* (1940, directed by Alfred Hitchcock) and *Laura* (1944, directed by Otto Preminger), the sharp shadows cast on and around the characters became more overbearing during tense moments. Though Wheeler's black-and-white films are much admired, he regretted that some of them could not have been made in color. The Academy Award-winning *Anna and the King of Siam* (1946) was made in black-and-white because of a painter's strike. To compensate for the lack of color, Wheeler built the sets of plaster treated to appear in varying values. The result is a black-and-white film so vivid that it almost convinces the audience that it was shot in color.

Wheeler's color films are as beautiful as his black-and-white. He was able to design the "Anna and the King" story in bold, stunning colors when he worked on the musical version, *The King and I*. Wheeler even made the unusual decision to shoot one of the *noir* films, *Leave Her to Heaven* (1947), in color. Instead of the dark, rain-soaked streets typical of that genre, this tale of deception is set effectively against bright country lawns and sunny skies.

From 1945 to 1960, Wheeler was Supervising Art Director at 20th Century-Fox. As such, he oversaw the visual aspects of each film from its inception, as he worked with the writer, scouted locations with the art director assigned to each film, and approved all sketches.

During his career as an art director, Wheeler was in on the ground floor of many advances in film technology. He experimented with Technicolor as early as 1936 when he worked on *The Garden of Allah* with producer David O. Selznick. He led 20th Century-Fox through the transition from black-and-white to color production and from the standard shot-size to CinemaScope.

—Lois Miklas

WHITLOCK, Albert.
British film effects artist and designer. Born in London in 1915; emigrated to the United States in 1954. Mainly self-taught in scenic design and matte painting, from 1934. Worked at a variety of jobs in the British film industry, 1934–40, then title designer and backdrop artist, 1935–54; worked at Walt Disney Studios, Hollywood, California, 1954–61; freelance film designer and matte artist, Hollywood, 1961–63; contract designer, at Universal Studios, Hollywood, from 1963. Former board member, Academy of Motion Picture Arts and Sciences, Beverly Hills, California. Recipient: Academy Award, Hollywood, 1974, 1975. Associate member, American Society of Cinematographers. Address: Department of Special Effects, Universal International Films, 100 Universal City Plaza, North Hollywood, California 99608, U.S.A.

Works:

Film productions include—*The Man Who Knew Too Much* (Hitchcock), 1955; *Greyfriars Bobby* (Chaffey), 1961; *The Birds* (Hitchcock), 1963; *Captain Newman MD* (Miller), 1963; *I'd Rather Be Rich* (Smight), 1964; *Marnie* (Hitchcock), 1964; *Island of the Blue Dolphins* (Clark), 1964; *Mirage* (Dmytryk), 1965; *Shenandoah* (McLaglen), 1965; *Ship of Fools* (Kramer), 1965; *That Funny Feeling* (Thorpe), 1965; *The War Lord* (Schaffner), 1965; *Beau Geste* (Hayes), 1966; *Blindfold* (Dunne), 1966; *Munster, Go Home* (Bellamy), 1966; *The Rare Breed* (McLaglen), 1966; *Torn Curtain* (Hitchcock), 1966; *The King's Pirate* (Weis), 1967; *The Reluctant Astronaut* (Montagne), 1967; *Rough Night in Jericho* (Laven), 1967; *Tobruk* (Hiller), 1967; *Thoroughly Modern Millie* (Hill), 1967; *The War Wagon* (Kenedy), 1967; *The Ballad of Josie* (McLaglen), 1968; *Counterpoint* (Nelson), 1968; *Hellfighters* (McLaglen), 1968; *In Enemy Country* (Keller), 1968; *P. J.* (Guilermin), 1968; *The Shakiest Gun in the West* (Rafkin), 1968; *The Learning Tree* (Parks), 1969; *Topaz* (Hitchcock), 1969; *Catch-22* (Nichols), 1970; *The Forbin Project* (Sargent), 1970; *Skullduggery* (Douglas and Wilson), 1970; *Diamonds Are Forever* (Hamilton), 1971; *Short Walk to Daylight* (Shear—for TV), 1972; *The Sting* (Hill), 1973; *The Questor Tapes* (Colla—for TV), 1974; *Killdozer* (London—for TV), 1974; *Earthquake* (Robson), 1974; *Day of the Locust* (Schlesinger), 1975; *The Hindenburg* (Wise), 1975; *The Man Who Would Be King* (Huston), 1975; *Bound for Glory* (Ashby), 1976; *The Car* (Silverstein), 1977; *MacArthur* (Sargent), 1977; *High Anxiety* (Brooks), 1977; *Airport '77* (Jameson), 1977; *Exorcist II: The Heretic* (Boorman), 1977; *Dracula* (Badham), 1979; *The Prisoner of Zenda* (Quine), 1979; *The Wiz* (Lumet), 1979; *Cheech and Chong's Next Movie* (Chong), 1980; *The Blues Brothers* (Landis), 1980; *Ghost Story* (Irvin), 1981; *Heartbeeps* (Arkush), 1981; *History of the World, Part I* (Brooks), 1981; *Missing* (Costa Gavras), 1982; *The Thing* (Carpenter), 1982; *Cat People* (Schrader), 1982; *The Best Little Whorehouse in Texas* (Higgins), 1982; *Psycho II* (Franklin), 1983; *The Lonely Guy* (Hiller), 1984; *Dune* (Lych), 1984; *Greystoke: The Legend of Tarzan* (Hudson), 1984; *Red Sonja* (Fleischer), 1985; *Clue* (Lynn), 1985.

Publications:

By WHITLOCK: articles—in *Filmmakers' Newsletter* (Ward Hill), October 1974; *American Cinematographer* (Los Angeles), November 1974, November 1978; *Super-8 Filmmaker* (San Francisco), May 1977; *Cinefantastique* (New York), February 1982; *Cahiers du Cinema* (Paris), June 1982.

On WHITLOCK: book—*The Saga of Special Effects* by Ron Fry and Pamela Fourson, Englewood Cliffs 1977; articles—in *Variety* (New York), 20 April 1977; *New Times* (New York), 29 May 1978; *New York Times Magazine*, May 1980; *Starburst* (London), no. 56, 1983; *American Cinematographer* (Los Angeles), January 1986.

Artificially created backgrounds—painted or filmed—have been exploited to the full in movies other than cartoons. This is due to the fact that movie-makers today tend to concentrate on big films that make vast sums, so in contrast to earlier times, long, experienced careers do not develop. Spielberg and Lucas are, of course, the obvious exceptions. They endure.

Nevertheless, matte painting will also endure,

as it is without doubt *the* cost-saving technique in movie visuals. With little cost, one can construct a scene and, with good preparation, matte or black out part of it later to replace the matte area with another subject. This description perhaps oversimplifies the technique, but faced with this simple premise, a designer has the world, in the movie sense, at his disposal. A process using painting or photography can be used to show movement, as of clouds, water, etc. *Bound for Glory* had a three-dimensional duststorm integrated into the painted area. *The Learning Tree* had a sequence of matte shots with a tornado forming and then moving away over the scene.

Such work can be done by applying the work to the original negative (the method I favor) or when copying the original film. The latter is most often done on a larger negative, Vista Vision of 65mm film, so as to recoup definition lost during copying or duplicating. As with illustrations, the reduction of size improves the quality.

Narrative generally deals with characters in stationary positions, and their environs are our domain. However, chases will always occur, and movement is necessary, but in these cases, the matte technique can always be applied, and the technique can work for all movies. Hitchcock summarised it to me: "You plan the master scene with the needed image and design the sequence around it." As always with Hitchcock, the problem well stated is half solved. His summary is in itself design.

—Albert Whitlock

The space and science fiction films of the late 1970s and 1980s have focused attention on special effects artists in Hollywood. Generally, these effects are obvious ones, involving other planets, prehistoric times, fantastic robots, or organic creatures. These kind of effects do not interest Albert Whitlock, whose idea of a great effect is one that the public does not recognize as one. Whitlock's art furthers the illusion that what is seen on the screen is "real" and causes the thrill that often accompanies such illusionism. Whitlock is an artist of the natural world, creating images of things that cannot be filmed realistically because of their violent nature, such as an earthquake or a dust-storm (*Bound for Glory*, 1976) or because of their cost to build, such as an entire castle (*Dracula* and *The Prisoner of Zenda*, both 1979) or a mountaintop city (*The Man Who Would Be King*, 1975).

Whitlock's art makes movies cheaper to produce. His is a world of matte paintings, models, and filming at different speeds. In his emphasis on illusionism, Whitlock can be seen as part of an artistic tradition going back to the Italian Renaissance and the invention of perspective to make two-dimensional pictures appear to be windows on the world. In his painting style, however, he considers himself closer to Impressionism than to academic painting because he is more interested in the study of phenomena and the effects of light than in objects themselves.

In the late 1950s, Whitlock was influenced by working under Peter Ellenshaw Sr., an effects supervisor for Disney studios. He has been associated with Universal since 1963 and has worked with a number of art directors, including Robert Boyle (*The Birds*, 1963). Though his work may go unrecognized because it is so convincing, Whitlock's artistry with special effects is important in understanding three concepts: the collaboration necessary in movie-making, the need to use effects for budgetary reasons, and the fact that film is a two-dimensional illusionistic medium.

—Floyd W. Martin

WIERCHOWICZ, Zofia.

Polish stage designer. Born in Deblin, Lublin Province, 30 December 1924. Studied design, at the Higher School of Fine Arts, Warsaw, 1948–54. Resident stage designer, at the Teatr Ziemi Mazowieckiej, Warsaw, 1955–56, and at the Jaracz Theatre, Olsztyn, 1956–58; freelance designer, working for the Teatr Beltycki, Koszalin, Teatr Powszechny, Warsaw, Opera House of Poznan, Boguslawski Theatre, Kalisz, Teatr Polski, Poznan, and the Chamber Opera, Warsaw, 1959–78. **Exhibitions:** Artists' Union, Warsaw, 1975; Zapiecek Gallery, Warsaw, 1978; *Contemporary Stage Design*, Berlin, 1978. **Collections:** Wielki Theatre Museum, Warsaw; Centre of Polish Stage Design, Gdansk; National Museum, Warsaw. Recipient: Gold Medal, Novi Sad Triennale, 1969; Gold Medal, Prague Quadriennale, 1971. *Died* (in Warsaw) *8 January 1978.*

Works:

Stage productions include—*Much Ado About Nothing.* Teatr Ziemi Mazowieckiej, Warsaw, 1956; *Twelfth Night*, Teatr Baltycki, Koszalin, 1957; *Hamlet*, Teatr Baltycki, Koszalin, 1960; *Romeo and Juliet*, Teatr Baltycki, Koszalin, 1962; *War and Peace*, Teatr Powszechny, Warsaw, 1963; *Henry VI*, Teatr in Bydgoszcz, 1964; *The Apothecary*, Chamber Opera, Warsaw, 1965; *Polish Amphitryon*, Chamber Opera, Warsaw, 1965; *Charlatan*, Opera, Warsaw, 1965; *Prince Igor*, Wroclaw Opera, 1966; *Othello*, Teatr Polski, Szczecin, 1966; *Richard III*, Teatr Polski, Szczecin, 1966; *La Bohème*. Warsaw Opera, 1967; *Tannhauser*, Poznań Opera, 1968; *The Queen of Spades*, Poznań Opera, and in Oslo, Norway, 1969; *Tristan und Isolde*, Poznań Opera 1968; *Salomea's Silver Dream*, Boguslawski Theatre, Kalisz, 1969; *Apollo the Lawgiver*, Chamber Opera, Warsaw, 1969; *Knovanshtchina*, Poznań Opera, 1969; *Henry IV*, Teatr Polski Szczecin, 1969; *Romeo and Juliet* ballet, Teatr Wielki, Warsaw, 1970; *La Traviata*, Teatr Wielki, Warsaw, 1971; *L'Incoronazione di Poppea*, Teatr Wielki, Warsaw, 1971 and in Yugoslavia, 1976; *Waiting for Godot*, Teatr Ateneum, Warsaw, 1971; *Othello*, Novi Sad, Yugoslavia, 1972; *Spartacus*, Wroclaw Opera, 1972; *The Tempest* (also director), Boguslawski Theatre, Kalisz, 1972; *Timon of Athens* (also director), Theatre in Grudziadz, 1975; *Dusk*, Jewish Theatre, Warsaw, 1976; *Don Giovanni*, Teatr Wielki, Warsaw, 1976; *Richard III* (also director), Teatr Ziemi Pomorskiej, Grudziadz, 1976; *King Roger*, Krakow Opera, 1976; *Comedy of Errors* (also director), Teatr Ziemi Mazowieckiej, Warsaw 1976; *La Nozze di Figaro*, Krakow Opera 1978; *Narciso*, Teatr Wielki, Warsaw, 1978.

Publications:

By WIERCHOWICZ: article—in *Poland* (Warsaw), September 1970.

On WIERCHOWICZ: books—*Polish Stage Design* by Zenobiusz Strzelecki, Warsaw 1963; *Trends in Contemporary Stage Design* by Zenobiusz Strzelecki, Warsaw 1970; *Zofia Wierchowicz*, exhibition catalogue by A. Oseka, Warsaw 1978; *Contemporary Polish Stage Design* by Zenobiusz Strzelecki, Warsaw 1983.

*   *   *

Zofia Wierchowicz was primarily interested in two types of theatre: Shakespearean and musical, although many different dramaturgies interested her, as long as they were worthwhile. However, she designed sets and costumes for fourteen Shakespearean plays, while many plays by other authors, including Polish ones, she placed in settings similar to those which she had designed for the Elizabethan theatre. Towards the end of her life (so short—54 years), she herself began directing, precisely and only Shakespearean dramas. For the two types of theatre that preoccupied her, she created two different plastic conceptions: for the one, functional constructions—stark, wooden, blackened—and costumes, often leather, also blackened; for the other, painterly decorations and costumes, sparkling with colors.

Those Shakespearean sets which are most characteristic of Wierchowicz are not reconstructions of the Globe's stage. Rather, they feature a podium supported by posts (an equivalent of the Elizabethan balcony), the height of two stories, which at the stage's central axis connects with the level of the floor by means of a staircase. This arrangement could be adapted to the needs of a particular dramatic scene by the addition of arcades, doors, or other functional forms, whereas the lower level could be given bars or metal doors fastened to the posts which support the podium (as in *Othello*). Sometimes the wood construction was covered by rusted iron sheets (*Richard III*); sometimes the stage was covered with dirt, forming something akin to a trough hollowed out in the earth for *Hamlet*; this also could be Caliban's territory in the *Tempest*, while Prospero and Ariel act on the podium.

In her early work, costumes are the skins of animals which are born "armed." Helmets, cuirasses, whole armours form an integral part of the "body," are fused with man from birth—such is his fate: to kill, and because of that, he was endowed with "fangs and claws." In a later period of the artist's life, the tragedy of Shakespearean characters was moved more into the interior; it exists in the soul and seems to tear apart Hamlet, Richard, Othello. Towards the end of her life, she felt the need to enliven her dead world of sets and costumes and undertook directing. Among others, she produced *Timon of Athens*, in which, on the universe of the stage, out of the whole world, only a clump of earth remains—a tragic vision of humanity's or her own fate.

Her operatic scenography encompassed a wide range from Monteverdi through Wagner, from nineteenth century verists to smaller musical forms, often of Polish or little-known composers. In it, appears the Polish tendency towards painterly scenography, for which she utilized the experiences of new plastic directions—among others, "action painting." This offered both in the sets, as well as (more interestingly) in the costumes, a richness of factures and colors. (The costumes were often painted, not dyed one hue; colors were "entered," utilizing the so-called "degrade" method.) A kind of equivalent for the sublime music and poetics resulted.

Wierchowicz, like many Polish scenographers, also attempted painting. Disquieting birds in flight were a common motif.

A solemn artist, seriously and responsibly practicing her profession, she was honored for many of her scenographies at national theatrical festivals.

—Zenobiusz Strzelecki

Zofia Wierchowicz: Production of Shakespeare's *Henry VI*, Teatr Polski, Bydgoszcz, 1964

WIESE, Bruno K(arl).

German graphic designer. Born in Berlin, 7 April 1922. Studied under O. H. W. Hadank, at the Staatliche Hochschule fur Bildende Kunste, Berlin, 1945–49. Served as a military cartographer in the German Army, 1942–45. Married Ruth Kern in 1954; daughter: Carola. Assistant designer in the graphics studio of O. H. W. Hadank, Hamburg, 1949–54; freelance designer, establishing own graphic design studio, Hamburg, from 1954: designed for the United Nations Postal Administration, Federal German Post Office, D. Stempel AG, Kristinus Cigarette Company, Inlettweber GmbH, Kieler Woche, Stalling-Filmsatz AG, Zanders Feinpapiere AG, S. Fischer Verlag, etc. Instructor in communications design, 1978–80, and Professor from 1980, at the Fachhochschule, Kiel.
Exhibitions: *B. K. Wiese: Visual Design*, Kiel, 1987 (toured). Recipient: Henkell Packaging Competition Prize, Wiesbaden, 1970; Kieler Woche Poster Prize, Kiel, 1970; German Aeronautics and Astronautics Institute Prize, 1975; United Nations Stamp Prize, 1977; Kieler Woche Visual Programme Prize, Kiel, 1982; Industrial Designers Society of America Prize, 1983; Toulouse-Lautrec Silver Medal, Essen, 1983; City of Hamburg Arts and Crafts Award, 1987. Member: Alliance Graphique Internationale, Paris; Deutscher Werrkbund; Bund Deutscher Graphiker. Address: Allhornweg 7, 2000 Hamburg 67, West Germany.

Works:

Henkell-Sekt packaging, for Sektkellerei Henkell, 1966.
Logotype symbol, for Stalling-Filmsatz AG, 1972
Lotus cigarette packaging and promotional graphics, for Kristinus, 1973.
Combat Racism postage stamp, for the UN Postal Administration, 1977.
Neujahrsblatt New Year card, for D. Stempel AG, 1979.
United Nations Peace-Keeping Operations postage stamp, for the UN Postal Administration, 1980.
100 Jahre Kieler Woche posters and visual identity, Kiel, 1982.
Kammer Jazz Ensemble poster, for the Kiel Jazz Ensemble, 1986.
Es geht um gute Werbe-Nasen promotional design, for Zanders Feinpapiere AG, 1986.
Europa Marke postage stamps, for the Deutsche Bundespost, 1987.
Gute Designer braucht das Land exhibition poster, for the Fachhochschule, Kiel, 1987.

Publications:

By WIESE: articles—in *Graphis* (Zurich), no. 199, 1978; *Form* (Seeheim), no. 92, 1980.

On WIESE: books—*An International Survey of*

Packaging by Wim Crouwel and Kurt Weidemann, London 1968; *Top Symbols and Trademarks of the World*, edited by Franco Maria Ricci, Milan, 1973, 1978; *Who's Who in Graphic Art*, edited by Walter Amstutz, Dubendorf 1982; *B. K. Wiese: Visual Design*, exhibition catalogue with texts by Harald Kohne and Fritz Seitz, Kiel 1987.

If one starts from the position that communications design is to be understood as the intellectual and material mastery of a given problem, there are two stages in the solution of such a problem. First, there is the conceptual phase, both non-material and material; via discovery of ideas and visual trials, this leads to the decision. Second comes the realization phase, with the formulation of a prototype and the development of a working copy for presentation and reproduction. Therefore, the intellectual phase of the problem-solving process lies at the beginning. At this point, the designer has to analyze the informative and psychological content of the message in a thought process which is already broadly directed toward the investigation of the content of items, which can lead to a meaningful visualization.

As a result of the synthesis of this investigation, the solution will rest on what is discovered as the particularity of an important "special aspect" of the content. This process will logically penetrate and encircle the problem

in order to produce a convincing image-idea that—in the ideal case—is neither inter-change-able nor repeatable. Simply stated, the solution is immanent to the content of the message; it needs to be sought out, to be set free.

After possible modification of the result at that stage with regard to its use or to the socio-logical structure of the group at which it is aimed, the second phase begins. In this phase of objectivization, the material concept is worked out and the coding of the message is achieved. Insofar as it is not specified, the medium must then be chosen. This choice of a vehicle for conveying the message depends upon an analysis of the general and particular possibilities of the medium and tests of its adaptability with respect to the previously dis-covered image-idea.

The repertoire of symbols from which the image is formulated—that is, the visual lan-guage—must be suited to the understanding of the groups at which it is aimed. Those individ-uals must be able to decode it. Only then can communication take place.

The concrete work-up of the image then fol-lows by a process that takes into account a spe-cial catalogue of criteria which will not be discussed here. In a number of stages, the weight and correlation of iconic and typo-graphic signs will be tested, selected, and cor-rected. Finally, a decision is taken, and the conceptual stage is complete.

The non-material and material conceptual stages described above can be seen as creativity operating systematically. Such a process does not, as one might assume, exclude intuition. Indeed, it leads directly to it—particularly in the stage of thought process. Originality and innovation have their roots here. Plagiarism, even unconscious, will hardly ever be found in this kind of search for ideas. Creativity—in relation to communication design—comes poss-ibly in the use of the intellect, in the presence of artistic sensibility and through specific experience.

The realization of the concept, the final visual formulation of the prototype, should demon-strate a logical correspondence to the facts of the case, adequacy and precision in the reper-toire of signs, perfect organizations of the sur-face through form and colour, and, not last, originality and power of conviction in the visualized message.

—Bruno K. Wiese

WIRKKALA, Tapio (Veli Ilmaari).
Finnish sculptor and industrial designer. Born in Hango, 2 June 1915. Studied sculpture, at the School of Industrial Arts, Helsinki, 1933–36. Served in the Finnish Army, in Kare-lia, 1940–45: Lieutenant. Married Rut Bryk in 1945; children: Sami and Maaria. Glass designer, for Karhula-Iitala, 1946–85: founder and director of Tapio Wirkkala Design Studio, Helsinki, from 1955: designed for Soinneek, Venini, Hackmann, Airam, Rosenthal, etc. Art director, School of Industrial Arts, Helsinki, 1951–54. Chairman, Finnish Government In-dustrial Arts Commission, Helsinki, 1968–73.
Exhibitions: Kunstnernes Hus, Oslo, 1952; Jablonec Glass Exhibition, Czechoslovakia, 1965; Goldsmith's Hall, London, 1972; Stede-lijk Museum, Amsterdam, 1976; *Six Masters of Glass*, Venice Biennale, 1976; *Europaische*

Keramik, Museum fur Kunst und Gewerbe, Hamburg, 1979 (toured); Museum of Architec-ture, Moscow, 1981 (toured); *Scandinavian Modern Design 1880–1980*, Cooper-Hewitt Mu-seum, New York, 1982; *Design Since 1945*, Phi-ladelphia Museum of Art, 1983; IBM Gallery, New York, 1985; *The Lunning Prize*, Nation-almuseum, Stockholm, 1986; *Scandinavia: Ceramics and Glass in the Twentieth Century*, Victoria and Albert Museum, London 1989.
Collections: Finnish Glass Museum, Riihimaki: Nationalmuseum, Stockholm; Nordenfjeldske Kunstindustrimuseet, Trondheim; Kunstindus-trimuseum, Copenhagen; Die Neue Sammlung, Munich; Staatliche Kunstsammlung, Dresden; Stedelijk Museum, Amsterdam; Kunstgewerbe-museum, Zurich; Museum of Modern Art, Tokyo; Victoria and Albert Museum, London; Museum of Modern Art, New York; Metro-politan Museum of Art, New York; Philadel-phia Museum of Art. Recipient: Bank of Finland Banknote Prize, 1947; Grand Prize, 1951, 1954, 1960, Gold Medal, 1960, Silver Medal, 1963, Milan Triennale; Lunning Prize, 1951; *House Beautiful* Award, New York, 1951; Olympic Games Stamps Prize, Helsinki, 1952; Department Store Competition Prize, Brussels World's Fair, 1957; Society of Industrial Artists Medal, London, 1958; Museum of Contempor-ary Crafts Silver Cutlery Prize, New York, 1960; Badische Anilin- und Soda-Fabrik Prize, 1962; Domus Golden Obelisk Award, Milan, 1963; International Ceramics Gold Medal, Faenza, 1963, 1966, 1967, 1973; Premio Inter-nazionale, Vicenza Ceramics Competition, 1963, 1966, 1967; Finnish Culture Foundation Prize, 1968; Finnish Composers Copyright Bureau Medal, 1980; Prince Eugene Medal, Stockholm, 1980. Honorary Doctorate: Royal College of Art, London, 1971. Honorary Royal Designer for Industry, Royal Society of Arts, London, 1964; Honorary Associate, Worshipful Company of Goldsmiths, London, 1971; Honorary Academician, Helsinki, 1972; Honor-ary Member, Asociacion Disenadores Indus-triales, Mexico, 1982; Honorary Academician, Academia Mexicana de Diseno, 1982. Knight of the Order of the White Rose, Finland. *Died* (in Helsinki) *19 May 1985.*

Works:

Kantarelli vases in clear blown and cut glass, for Iitala, 1946.
Jaavuori vase in clear mould-blown glass, for Iitala, 1950.
Jaapal vase in clear mould-blown glass, for Iitala, 1950.
Platter in laminated birch, for Soinneek Kni, 1951.
Tuonen Virta vase in clear glass with vertical cut lines, for Iitala, 1951.
Tokio vase in clear mould-blown glass with bubble insert, for Iitala, 1954.
Paaderin jaa sculpture in clear mould-blown glass, for Iitala, 1960.
Wirkkala hanging lamps, for Airam and Idman, 1960.
Composition cutlery in stainless steel, for Rosenthal, 1963.
Puukko hunting knife in stainless steel, brass and polyamide, for Hackmann, 1963.
Ultima Thule jars and tumblers in clear moulded glass, for Iitala, 1968–70.
Finlandia vodka bottles in clear mould-blown glass, for Iitala, from 1969.
Bolla vase in decorated glass, for Venini, 1970.
Kartano drinking glasses in clear glass, for Iitala, 1978.
Primavera drinking glasses in clear glass, for Iitala, 1978–79.
Viva jugs and tumblers in clear mould-blown glass, for Iitala, 1980–84.

Pallas vase in clear moulded glass with rib and bubble decoration, for Iitala, 1983.
Kelo jugs and tumblers in clear textured glass, for Iitala, 1984.

Publications:

By WIRKKALA: book—*Finnish Decorative Art: 13th Yearbook*, editor, Helsinki 1941; arti-cle—in *Domus* (Milan), July/August 1981.

On WIRKKALA: books—*Finnish Designers of Today* by Oili Maki, Helsinki 1954; *The Beauty of Modern Glass* by R. Stennett-Willson, London and New York 1958; *Introduction to Twentieth Century Design* by Arthur Drexler and Greta Daniel, New York 1959; *A Treasury of Scandinavian Design*, edited by Erik Zahle, New York 1961; *Modern Glass* by Ada Polak, London 1962; *Modern Scandinavian Furniture* by Ulf Hard at Segerstad, Copenhagen 1963, London 1964; *34 Scandinavian Designers* by Svend Erik Moller, Copenhagen 1967; *Modern Finnish Design* by Ulf Hard af Segerstad, London 1969; *New Design in Wood* by Donald J. Willcox, London and New York 1970; *Fin-nish Design: Facts and Fancy* by Donald J. Willcox, New York 1973; *Finnish Design 1875–1975* by Timo Sarpaneva and others, Hel-sinki 1975; *Scandinavian Design: Objects of a Life Style* by Eileene Harrison Beer, New York and Toronto 1975; *International Modern Glass* by Geoffrey Beard, London 1976; *Europaische Keramik seit 1950*, exhibition catalogue edited by Heinz Spielmann and Hans Thiemann, Hamburg 1979; *Tapio Wirkkala*, Helsinki 1981; *Scandinavian Modern Design 1880–1980*. edited by David Revere McFadden, New York and London 1982; *Design Since 1945*, edited by Kathryn Hiesinger and George Marcus, Phila-delphia and London 1983; *Les Annees 60* by Anne Bony, Paris 1983; *The Conran Directory of Design*, edited by Stephen Bayley, London 1985; *Twentieth Century Design: Glass* by Fred-erick Cooke, London 1986; *The Lunning Prize*, exhibition catalogue edited by Helena Dahlback Lutteman and Marianne Uggla, Stockholm 1986; *Scandinavia: Ceramics and Glass in the Twentieth Century* by Jennifer Hawkins Opie, London 1989.

Tapio Wirkkala entered the Scandinavian design scene in the postwar era when function-alism had become "organic"—less severe and dogmatic than it had been in the 1930s. He was a product of an age in Scandinavia when the ideal came to be commonly held that ordinary people had a right to a comfortable home that was both functional and esthetically pleasing. Although developing his designs through craft techniques, he sought to work with industry to bring these designs to a large public. His 1951 laminated-wood serving pieces were some of the first examples of this type of collaboration. While exploring laminated wood for sculptural purposes, he arrived at leaf-shaped, functional trays and platters, which were then produced at Soinne et Kni in Helsinki. He also ventured into more mundane household items, such as oddly shaped light bulbs which transformed the bulb into its own fixture.

Wirkkala created his award-winning design for the Finnish exhibition at the 1951 Milan *Triennale* in the beginning of an era when the outside world became aware of "Scandinavian Modern" as a style. Although each country in Scandinavia had contributed at varying rates and quantities to this style, its general character became known as primarily functionalist, with simple, geometric lines and exposed materials and construction. Such recognition meant a large export market to an influential and afflu-ent public; in turn, this meant growing oppor-

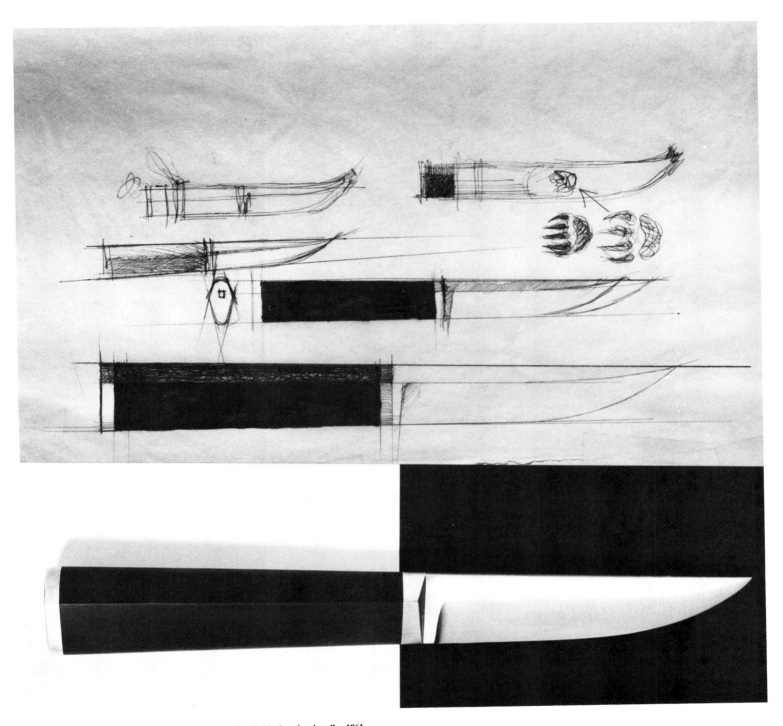

Tapio Wirkkala: *Pukko* **hunting knife in stainless steel with black nylon handle, 1961**

tunities for Scandinavian designers within industry. Along with other new designers, such as Arne Jacobsen and Henning Koppel in Denmark, Wirkkala was hired by industry to design products in wood, glass, silver and ceramic.

In both his production lines and one-of-a-kind ware, Wirkkala is perhaps best known for his art glass, a Finnish industry dating back to the seventeenth century. Influenced by art nouveau and by natural forms, Wirkkala investigates both the integral structure of the material and its optical qualities. For example, he uses layers of color to refract light, curved upper surfaces, and interior lines to resemble melting ice, or rippled effects to connote liquid in the bottom of a goblet. Control over the metamorphosis of an abstract idea to create a product from modern material with modern production methods is the essence of Wirkkala's contribution to design. This subtle under-

standing of material and technique has made many of his products classics of Finnish modern design.

—Sarah Bodine

WOLF, Henry.
American painter, photographer and graphic designer. Born in Vienna, Austria, 23 May 1925; emigrated to the United States in 1941; naturalized, 1943. Educated at the Lycee

Hoche, Versailles, France, 1938–41; studied at the School of Industrial Art, New York, 1941–42, and at the New School for Social Research, New York, 1947–50. Served in the United States Army 32nd Division, 1943–46: Sergeant. Married Renate Vogel in 1951 (divorced, 1956); Macha Gagarine in 1960 (divorced, 1960). Graphic designer, working in New York, from 1946: designer, at Arnold Studios, New York, 1946–47; art director, at Geer duBois and Company, New York, 1947–51, United States Department of State, 1951–52, *Esquire* magazine, New York, 1952–58, *Harper's Bazaar* magazine, New York, 1958–61, and *Show* magazine, New York, 1961–64; creative director, at Jack Tinker and Partners, and at McCann Erickson advertising agency, New York, 1964–66; vice-president and creative director, Tahey Advertising, New York, 1966; executive vice-president and partner, Trahey-

Wolf Advertising, New York, 1966–71; president of Henry Wolf Productions, New York, from 1971. Instructor, at Cooper Union, New York, 1955–64, and at the School of Visual Arts, New York, 1964–74. President, American Institute of Graphic Arts, New York, 1970–72; Board member, International Design Conference, Aspen, Colorado. Recipient: New York Art Directors Club Gold Medal, 1956, 1957, 1959, 1961, 1963, and Hall of Fame Award, 1981; American Institute of Graphic Arts Gold Medal, 1976. Benjamin Franklin Fellow, Royal Society of Arts, London, 1971. Member: American Institute of Graphic Arts; Alliance Graphique Internationale, Paris. Address: Henry Wolf Productions Incorporated, 167 East 73rd Street, New York, New York 10021, U.S.A.

Publications:

By WOLF: books—*Automobile and Culture*, with text by Gerald Silk, New York 1987; *Visual Thinking: Methods for Making Images Memorable*, New York 1988; articles—in *Graphics* (Zurich), no. 149, 1970; *American Photographer* (New York), February 1983.

On WOLF: books—*Who's Who in Graphic Art*, edited by Walter Amstutz, Zurich 1962, Dubendorf 1982; *Designers in the USA: Volume 1*, edited by Henri Hillebrand, London 1971; *Art Without Boundaries 1950–1970*, edited by Gerald Woods and others, London 1972; *The Language of Graphics* by Edward Booth-Clibborn and Daniele Baroni, London 1980; *The Design Concept* by Allen Hurlburt, New York 1981; *Great Magazine Covers* by Pat Kerry, New York 1983; *The Art of Persuasion* by Robert Sobieszek, New York 1987.

*

A designer is a problem-solver. I have no philosophy about it, except to do the best possible design and still get published. No philosophy could span all the assignments I have undertaken.

We are not artists who gratify their own obsessions but professionals who help clients with their visual problems.

—Henry Wolf

*

Wherever this multi-talented, creative professional in graphic design, art direction, photography, and publication design puts his creative energy, excellence results. Henry Wolf emerged as a force in the magazine publishing business in the 1940s. Extending earlier traditions established by Dr. M. F. Agha at Condé Nast, William Golden, and Paul Rand, Wolf has been influenced particularly by Alexey Brodovitch and his work at *Harper's Bazaar*. Wolf has said of Brodovitch, "The man was the most informative and self-contradictory person I have ever met, and yet in his own strange way, the most stimulating."

During the heyday of the magazine publishing business, Wolf consistently designed and produced magazines of unmatched quality. Beginning in 1952, his work at *Esquire* showed the blending of an artistic eye with the pragmatics of the editorial/journalistic milieu. After 1958, he brought *Harper's Bazaar* to a point of high refinement with his special vision as it was directed toward the fashion world. In 1961, as art director of *Show* magazine, he began a new arts-oriented magazine from scratch. Its photography, layouts, covers, editorial stance, and overall fresh, innovative look stand in combination, to this day, as a benchmark in magazine design. In spite of its short life span, *Show* was well ahead of its time in both form and content.

Wolf has been innovative in the way in which he has blended several disciplines together in a particularly unique way. He is a graphic designer with a controlled method and a working knowledge of the pragmatics of structure, economics, etc. As an art director, he widens an eye for the editorial and an understanding of the communication requirements of mass media. Above all, he has shown in his photography a concern for the message and for the appropriate visual way to achieve the goal of this medium. Wolf's photographic vision is strongly perceptual, reminding one of the paintings of René Magritte with playfulness and ambiguity in the arrangement of elements. His work is simple and direct but maintains a human touch.

His career has shown him to be a prolific producer in whatever field he is working. His total creative energies, as directed toward *Show*, for example, pushed the boundaries of photography, layout, typography, and editorial art to new heights of quality. Wolf has been very influential in stimulating directions in photography, graphic design, and magazine publishing. The products of his career have greatly improved our collective visual environment and continue as a testament to what is possible by a very talented, sensitive man with great vision and skill.

—R. Roger Remington

WOLFF, Ann.

Swedish artists and glass and ceramics designer. Born Ann Schaefer, in Lubeck, Germany, 26 February 1937; adopted mother's family name Wolff in 1985. Studied drawing, Meisterschule fur Mode, Hamburg, 1953–54; visual communications, under Tomas Maldonado, Hochschule fur Gestaltung, Ulm, 1956–59. Married Swedish glass designer Goran Warff in 1960 (divorced, 1972); daughters: Hanna and Amanda; lives with glass artist Dirk Bimberg since 1973; daughter: Lina. Designer, at Pukebergs Glassworks, Nybro, 1960–64, and at Kosta Boda, 1964–78; independent glass artist, establishing own studio in Transjo, Kosta, since 1978: founder, with Wilke Adolfsson, of Studioglashutte Stenhytta, Transjo, 1978; founder-director, with Jan Erik Ritzman, Sven Ake Carlsson and Dirk Bimberg, of Studioglashutte Transjo Kulturarbetare i Glas, Transjo, 1982–84. Also painter, sculptor and graphic artist, since 1982. Guest instructor, at California College of Arts and Crafts, Fullerton University, Vanderbilt University, Penland School of Crafts, in the United States, 1976; Guest Professor, Pilchuk Glass Center, Stanwood, Washington, 1977, 1979, 1984, 1986; also visiting teacher at other schools in Europe, Japan and the United States, from 1974. **Exhibitions:** Varbergs Museum Sweden, 1966, 1985; Norrkopings Museum, Sweden, 1967; Galerie Wulff, Helsinki, 1968; Galerie Doktor Glas, Stockholm, 1976, 1979, 1984, 1987, 1988; Galerie SM, Frankfurt, 1978; Seibu Store, Tokyo, 1978; Galerie der Kunsthandwerker, Hamburg, 1979; Yamaha Gallery, Kyoto, 1980; Galerie Mors Mossa, Goteborg, 1981; Essener Galerie, Essen, 1981; Heller Gallery, New York, 1982, 1987; Ivor Kurland Glass Art Gallery, Los Angeles, 1983; Holsten Galleries, Palm Beach, Florida, 1983, 1986; Galerie Lietzow, West

Berlin, 1984; Galerie Gamla Stan, Stockholm, 1985; Galerie Arti-choque, Velp, 1985; Galerie Belle, Vasteras, 1985; Kilkenny Art Gallery, Ireland, 1985; Maurine Littleton Gallery, Washington, D.C., 1985; Gotlands Fornsal, Visby, 1986; Kurland Summers Gallery, Los Angeles, 1987; Galleri F15, Moss, 1987; Galerie Kaplanen, Visby, 1987; Vaxjo Konstnarscentrum, Sweden, 1988; Stockholm Art Fair, 1988; Karlshamn Museum, Sweden, 1988; Galerie Gottschalk Betz, Frankfurt, 1988; Galerie Clara Scemini, at Chicago Art Fair, 1988; Mejeriet, Alskog, 1989; Konstmuseum, Visby, 1990. **Collections:** Nationalmuseum, Stockholm; Rohsska Konstslojdmuseet, Goteborg; Danske Kunstindustrimuseet, Copenhagen; Museum fur Kunst und Gewerb, Hamburg; Stedelijk Museum, Amsterdam; Musee des Arts Decoratifs, Paris; Corning Museum of Glass, New York; Metropolitan Museum of Art, New York. Recipaient: Lunning Prize, 1968; Coburger Glass Prize, 1977; Central Swiss Glass Prize, 1980; Award of Honor, *Glaskunst 81*, Kassel, 1981; Glass Prize, World Crafts Exhibition, Bratislava, 1984; Gold Medal, Bayrischer Staatspreis, Munich, 1988. Address: Transjo, 35052 Kosta, Sweden.

Works:

Household and tableware series, for Pukebergs Glassworks, 1960–64.
Children's toys in wood, for Boda, 1964.
Chair in wood, for Stockaryds Stolfabrik, 1973.
Household and tableware series *Party, Garden, Grape, Brava, Krinolin, Snowball*, etc., for Kosta Boda, 1964–78.
Litet Fro relief in metal, for Djurangsskola, Kalmar, 1969.
Kontrapunkt relief in wood, for the Volvo dining-room, Goteborg, 1971.
Flanorens Dag relief in metal, for the Restaurant Flanor, Gavle, 1971.
Staircase reliefs, for Stena Lines transit hall, Goteborg, 1971.
Staircase reliefs in metal and glass, for Umea Karhus, 1971.
Pladsk relief in metal for Norrkoping Swimming Hall, 1971.
Livets Tra reliefs in etched glass and iron, for Dalsjofors Old People's Home, 1972.
Vitliv, Bla och Scenen three reliefs in wood and glass, for the Scandinavska Enskilda Banken, Goteborg, 1973.
Hurlig ar orden relief in metal, for the Hogbyskola, Jarfalla, 1975.
Hyttorgel sculptures in glass, for the Lansstyrelsen, Vaxjo, 1976.
Glass wall, for Nybro Kommunhus, 1981.
Panels and reliefs in glass, for the Kontorshus VBB, Vaxjo, 1982.
Gaster hos Verkligheten wall in stained glass, for the Lansstyrelsen, Kalmar, 1983.
Vid Floden five panels in stained glass, for Trelleborg Library, 1983.
Tradgard full av Liv sculpture in stained glass, for Laolms Library, 1984.

Publications:

On WOLFF: books—*I Glasrike* by Bertil Palmqvist, Lund 1979; *Ann Warff*, exhibition catalogue with texts by Helga Hilschenz and Barbro Werkmaster, Malmo 1982; *Geschichte des Studioglases* by Christian Sellner, Frankfurt 1984; *Scandinavia: Ceramics and Glass in the Twentieth Century* by Jennifer Hawkins Opie, London 1989; articles—*Glass Studio* (New York), January/February 1978; *Form* (Stockholm), no. 605, 1981; *Horizon* (New York), 25 July 1982; *American Craft* (New York), February 1983.

Some of us have more finely developed nesting instincts than others.

Henry Wolff: Advertisement for Karastan Rug Mills, 1986

WOUDHUYSEN, Lewis.

British architectural, exhibition, graphic and industrial designer. Born in the Netherlands, 15 September 1912; emigrated to Britain in 1940: naturalized. Studied architecture in Delft, 1930–34, graphic design in Amsterdam, 1936–37, and book design in Leipzig, 1938. Art director, working for J. Walter Thompson agency, and for Adprint, London 1949–53; freelance designer from 1953, establishing Woudhuysen Consultant Designers, London, from 1955: designed for the Clydesdale Bank, Department of Health and Social Security, Manpower Services Commission, Shenley Trust, EMI Laboratories, William Mallinson and Sons, Courtaulds, Plessey, Arbuthnot Factors, Acme Signs and Displays, Advance Electronics, Bass Charrington, Bertorelli, British Petroleum, Cape Building Products, Castrol, General Post Office, Lambert Chemical Company, Rootes Limited, Scottish Brewers, Twinlock, United Linen Services, etc. Fellow, Society of Industrial Artists and Designers, London; Associate, Designers and Art Directors Association, London; Member, Institute of Packaging, London. *Died* (in London) *12 November 1985.*

Publications:

By WOUDHUYSEN: articles—in *The Designer* (London), November 1970, December 1975.

On WOUDHUYSEN: books—*Designers in Britain*, edited by Herbert Spencer, London 1954, 1957; *The Silent Salesman: Packaging*

That Sells by James Pilditch, London 1961; *Design Co-ordination and Corporate Image* by F. H. K. Henrion and Alan Parkin, London and New York 1967; *An International Survey of Packaging* by Wim Crouwel and Kurt Weidemann, London 1968; *All Things Bright and Beautiful: Design in Britain 1830 to Today* by Fiona MacCarthy, London 1972.

*

Lewis Woudhuysen read architecture at Delft and graphics at Amsterdam and Liepzig. On the outbreak of war, he escaped by rowing boat to England in 1940. There, he became art director for J. Walter Thompson and, in 1949, for Adprint. In 1955, he founded his own Woudhuysen Design Group, which covered corporate identity programmes, marketing, public relations schemes, product innovation, product consultancy, design packaging, brand images, beer labels, advanced instrumentation design research, and modular systems.

Woudhuysen was a down-to-earth type designer. Design is a job, and he had little time for high-flown concepts. As he saw it, the first duty is to make an object which is fit for its purpose. One should listen to what the customer wants and then advise him on the best way to achieve his goal. Thinking that some designers overrate their own importance, Woudhuysen preferred to believe that the designer creates part of the ordinary furniture of life, not some romantic monument to his own importance. To Woudhuysen, the commercial requirement was the dominating concern, but he would allow moral considerations to enter if, say, an order came from South Africa; that he would refuse, despite knowing the language. Woudhuysen's

practicality has been recognised by his awards, including four from the Design Council, for his products do what is required of them.

—Diana de Marly

WRIGHT, Russel.

American stage, interior and industrial designer. Born in Lebanon, Ohio, 3 April 1904. Studied under Frank Duveneck, at Cincinnati Academy of Art, Ohio, 1921–22, and under Leo Lentell and Kenneth Hayes Miller, at the Art Students League, New York, 1922; studied law and theatre, at Princeton University, New Jersey, 1922–24; Columbia University School of Architecture, New York, 1923; New York University School of Architecture, 1938–39. Married Mary Small Einstein in 1927 (died, 1952; daughter: Eve. Stage set and costume designer, working with Norman Bel Geddes, New York, 1925–26; stage manager, at the Theatre Guild, Neighborhood Playhouse, and the Group Theatre, New York, 1926–30; freelance stage prop, furnishings and product designer, establishing own workshops in New York, from

1930; established Russel Wright Associates designer furniture firm, New York, 1943–67: designed for Sears Roebuck, Colgate Aircraft Corporation, Acme Fluorescent, Amplex Corporation, Steubenville Pottery, Sterling China, Paden City Pottery, Edwin M. Knowles Pottery, American Cyanamid, Ideal Toy Company, John Hull Cutlery, Imperial Glass, Century Metalcraft, Duraware Corporation, General Electric, Simtex Mills, etc. Consultant, United States Technical Aid Missions to Cambodia, Vietnam and Taiwan, 1956–60; crafts consultant to the Government of Japan, 1957–58, and to the Government of Barbados, 1970. President, Society of Industrial Designers of America, 1952–53; director, Summer in the Parks Program, Washington, D.C., 1968, and Nature Center of the Nature Conservatory, Manitoga, New York, 1975–76. **Exhibitions:** *Russel Wright, American Designer*, Hudson River Museum, Yonkers, New York, 1983; *Design Since 1945*, Philadelphia Museum of Art, 1983; *High Style: 20th Century American Design*, Whitney Museum, New York, 1985; *The Machine Age in America 1918–1941*, Brooklyn Museum, New York, 1986. **Collections:** Museum of Modern Art, New York; Metropolitan Museum of Art, New York; Cooper-Hewitt Museum, New York; Arents Research Library, Syracuse University, New York. Recipient: Tiffany Sculpture Competition Prize, 1921; Museum of Modern Art Good Design Award, New York, 1950, 1952, 1953; Home Furnishings League Trailblazer Award, New York, 1951; Society of Industrial Designers Medal, New York; Beautification Committee Citation, Washington, D.C., 1968. *Died* (in New York City) *21 December 1976.*

Works:

Modern Living/American Modern upholstered furniture, for Conant Ball Company, 1935.
American Modern ceramic dinnerware, for Steubenville Pottery, 1937–39.
American Way furniture range, for Monitor Company, and Sprague and Carleton Company, 1940.
Knockdown furniture range, for Sears Roebuck, 1942.
Alcohol stove and coffee-maker, for Silex Corporation, 1942.
Meladur melamine plastic dinnerware, for American Cyanamid and General American Transportation, 1945–49.
Cutlery range in stainless steel and plastic, for Englishtown Cutlery, 1946.
American Modern table linen range, for Lecock and Company, 1946–48.
Stove-to-Table aluminium serving wares, for the Aluminum Goods Manufacturing Corporation, 1946–48.
Swivel lamp, for Amplex Corporation, 1949.
Flair tumblers in clear, coloured and seed glass, for Imperial Glass, 1949.
Easier Living wooden furniture range, for Statton Furniture Company, 1950.
Samsonite folding metal chairs and tables, for Shwayder Corporation, 1950.
American Modern stainless steel cutlery, for John Hull Cutlery, 1951.
Broil Quick electric cooking appliance, for Peerless Electric, 1955.
Idealware polyethylene plastic dinnerwares, for Ideal Toy Company, 1955.
Esquire Collection ceramic dinnerware, for Edwin M. Knowles Pottery, 1956.
Electro-thermal serving trays, for Cornwall Corporation, 1958–61.
Big Top Peanut Butter jar and label, for Procter and Gamble, 1959.
Trays, buckets and colanders in plastic, for Duraware Corporation, 1964–65.

Publications:

By WRIGHT: books—*Home Furnishings at the Fair*, booklet, New York 1939; *A Guide to Easier Living*, with Mary Wright, New York 1951; articles—in *American Home* (New York), January 1934; *Arts and Decoration* (New York), February 1935; *Architectural Forum* (New York), October 1937, September 1942; *House and Garden* (New York), April 1938; *Country Life* (New York), May 1938; *Design* (New York), March 1941; *Interiors* (New York), June 1943, December 1951, April 1955, August 1956; *Better Homes and Gardens* (New York), September 1944, February 1945; *Woman's Home Companion* (New York), September 1956.

On WRIGHT: books—*A History of American Furniture*, edited by N. I. Bienenstock, East Stroudsburg 1936; *The Story of Modern Applied Art* by Rudolph Rosenthal and Helena Ratzka, New York 1948; *The Consultant Designer in American Industry*, thesis by Jerry Streichler, New York University 1963; *Depression Modern: The 30s Style in America* by Martin Greif, New York 1975; *The Streamlined Decade* by Donald Bush, New York 1975; *Twentieth Century Limited: Industrial Design in America 1925–39* by Jeffrey Meikle, Philadelphia 1979; *Industrial Design* by John Heskett, London 1980; *Russel Wright, American Designer*, exhibition catalogue by James Hennessey, Cambridge, Massachusetts 1983; *Design Since 1945*, edited by Kathryn Hiesinger and George Marcus, Philadelphia and London 1983; *High Style: 20th Century American Design*, exhibition catalogue by David Gebhard, Esther McCoy and others, New York 1985; *Mid-Century: Furniture of the 1950s* by Cara Greenberg, London 1985; *The Machine Age in America 1918–1941* by Richard Guy Wilson and Dianne H. Pilgrim, New York 1986; *The American Design Adventure 1940–1975* by Arthur J. Pulos, London and Cambridge, Massachusetts 1988.

*

Russel Wright, as a student at Princeton in the 1920s, was strongly enough influenced by the work of Norman Bel Geddes to leave school and enter the design field. He began by designing theater sets and costumes with his mentor. By the early 1930s, his interest in the design of theatrical environments had expanded into the domestic arena. Here, Wright distinguished himself as a breed apart from his noteworthy peers among whom it was fashionable to design consumer products only to assure their commercial desirability, by placing a premium on style and modernity.

Wright, on the other hand, revealed a strong commitment to improving daily life for American families. He devoted the remainder of his life to developing an American national style based on modern, functional simplicity brought into line with the needs, materials, and technology of the twentieth century. He rejected many aspects of the austere formalism of European modernists, recognizing early a need for a more humanistic approach to the domestic landscape. Wright subscribed to a philosophy, recurrent since the mid-nineteenth century, that improvement of environments in which people live and work improves the quality of those people's lives.

Wright's recognition of the designer's role as both a mirror and arbiter of taste yielded great commercial success for his products. His American Modern furniture of 1935 was widely accepted and brought "blonde," solid-wood furniture into the mainstream as it paved the way for the Scandinavian Modern taste of several decades later. As late as 1976, in the design of his own house and grounds, Dragon Rock,

north of New York City, he still sought to prove that contemporary design could be as liveable, romantic, and sentimental as traditional design.

Wright's analysis of living spaces (he defined living areas for specific activities such as relaxing, eating, cleaning, etc.) changed the way middle-class Americans perceived their needs and defined their priorities. For example, his experiments with spun aluminium and informal dinnerware pioneered the stove-to-table concept of serving meals and were influential by virtue of altered function in redefining the needs for dining space. The culmination of this drive for improvement of daily life was the 1950 *Guide to Easier Living*, co-authored by his wife, Mary Einstein Wright. In the book, the Wrights outlined their philosophy for socially based design. In so doing, they described a generation of Americans.

—Ken Carls

WYMAN, Lance.

American graphic designer. Born in Newark, New Jersey, 2 July 1937. Educated in public schools, Kearny, New Jersey, 1943–55; studied advertising, at Fairleigh Dickinson College, Rutherford, New Jersey, 1955–56; design, at Pratt Institute, Brooklyn, New York, 1956–60: BA 1960. Served in the United States Army Reserve, 1960–61, in the Michigan National Guard, 1961–63, and in the New York National Guard, 1963–66: Staff Sergeant. Married Neila Cohalan in 1966; daughter: Stacey. Designer, at General Motors Corporation, Detroit, 1960–61, William M. Schmidt Associates, Detroit, 1961–63, and with George Nelson and Company, New York, 1963–66; partner in Lance Wyman/Peter Murdoch design studio, New York, Mexico City and London, 1966–68; graphic design director, in Mexico City, 1966–70; president of Wyman and Cannan Limited, New York, 1971–79, and Lance Wyman Limited, New York, from 1979. Instructor, Parsons School of Design, New York, from 1973. **Exhibitions:** *Trademarks USA*, National Design Center, Chicago, 1964; *World Poster Art*, Museum of Modern Art, New York, 1968; *Graphics of the Mexican Olympics*, American Institute of Graphic Arts, New York, 1968; *L'Espace Collectif*, Centre de Creation Industrielle, Paris, 1970; *Mexican Stamps by Lance Wyman*, Smithsonian Institution, Washington, D.C., 1971; *Work by Lance Wyman and Bill Cannan*, Pratt Institute, Brooklyn, New York, 1973; *Wyman and Cannan Company*, Kutztown State College, Pennsylvania, 1976; *Environmental Design*, American Institute of Graphic Arts, New York, 1978; *Abecedarian Art*, Camino Real Gallery, Mexico City, 1979; *Lance Wyman*, La Chinche Gallery, Mexico City, 1981; *Artists Against Nuclear Madness*, Parsons Exhibit Center, New York, 1982. **Collections:** Museum of Modern Art, New York; Cooper-Hewitt Museum, New York; Smithsonian Institution, Washington, D.C.; Poster Museum, Warsaw. Recipient: Gold Plaque, Milan Triennale, 1968; Pratt Institute Achievement Award, New York, 1968; *Creativity Magazine* Prize, Mexico City, 1979; New York Art Directors Club Silver Medal, 1981; *Time* Magazine Best of the Year Award, New York, 1982. Honorary Professor, University of Guadalajara, Mexico, 1979. Address:

118 West 80th Street, New York, New York 10024, U.S.A.

Works:

Olympic graphics and signage program, for the
    Mexican Olympics Committee, 1966–68.
Graphics program, for the Camino Real Hotel,
    Mexico City, 1968.
Graphics program, for the Mexico City Metro
    System, 1969.
Soccer World Cup poster, Mexico City, 1971.
Maps and signage, for the Washington Metro
    System, 1974.
Graphics system, for the National Zoo, Wash-
    ington, D.C., 1975.
Graphics and signage, for Jeddah International
    Airport, Saudi Arabia, 1978.
Architectural signage system, for Capitol Hill,
    Washington, D.C., 1979.
Central de Abasto graphics system, for the new
    market, Mexico City, 1982.

Publications:

On WYMAN: books—*Word and Image* by
Mildred Constantine and Alan M. Fern, New
York 1968; *Signet, Signal, Symbol* by Walter
Diethelm, Zurich 1972; *Urban Spaces* by David
Kenneth Specter, New York 1974; *Public
Transportation Systems*, edited by the Institute
of Business Administration, Tokyo 1976; *Archi-
tectural Signing and Graphics* by John Follis and
Dave Hammer, New York 1979; *Visual Puns in
Design* by Eli Kince, New York 1982.

In looking back over my career as a graphic designer, I find that my work has ranged from postage stamps to a ten-ton architectural sign. However, my most significant designing has probably been that of graphic symbols in the form of trademarks, logos, and pictograms. I have designed or directed the design of some 300 graphic symbols, ranging from complete systems, such as the forty symbols that identified the sporting and cultural events of the Mexican Olympic Games, to the symbol that identifies our West 80th Street Block Association here in New York. I love designing symbols and figuring out interesting ways of using them, not only for international projects such as airports and Olympic Games, where graphic symbols bridge multi-language gaps, but in general. Graphic symbols can add a different kind of order and personality to a subway system, a zoo, or a city market place, where most people speak the same language.

Of course, I use words, too. I've designed more than thirty typefaces for making words, but my heart is with graphic symbols. They are one of our most ancient forms of communication, and we are still learning how to design and use them. If a picture is worth a thousand words, then a symbol, such as the Red Cross, for example, is certainly worth a thousand pictures. Sometimes the simple, direct expression of a graphic symbol works better than anything else to identify a corporation or an institution, to mark a trail at the zoo, or to give directions. The directional arrow, probably our most used graphic symbol, can tell us which way to go without saying a word. Einstein once said that "everything should be made as simple as poss-

Lance Wyman: Poster for the Olympic Games in Mexico City, 1968

ible, but not simpler." I think this is good advice for a graphic designer.

—Lance Wyman

The graphic communications system designed by Lance Wyman for the XIX Olympiad is a bellwether project in the evolution of graphic design. Wishing to create an image that could evoke the spirit of the host nation, Mexico, Wyman made extensive study of Mexican folk art and Aztec relics, which led him to two motifs: repeated multiple lines to form patterns and bright color. Using them, Wyman developed an alphabet composed of five bands or ribbons to be used for the logo, "MEXICO 68," and all titling on brochures, signage, etc. To accommodate a multilingual audience, Wyman used pictographs and color-coding to communicate with visitors from nations around the world. A set of twenty sports pictographs communicated nonverbally through images of the equipment while an additional twenty pictographs symbolized cultural events. Colour coding and pictographs conveyed information on tickets. A pictographic clock, for example, communicated the time for an event to all visitors regardless of their language. Because the XIX Olympiad was held in facilities located in and around one of the world's largest cities, rather than in a specially constructed facility,

Wyman created an environmental signage system using modular components. A rainbow of colors was used on the official maps, and color bands were painted onto the curbs of the corresponding streets. The design system of pictographs and color-coding was so effective that the *New York Times* observed that a visitor to the Mexico Olympics could "be illiterate in all languages as long as you are not colorblind." The complex exterior environmental system developed by Wyman and Murdoch was composed of modular and interchangeable parts, which included directional signs, clocks, mailboxes, telephones, and maps. Thirty informational kiosks, placed at strategic locations throughout Mexico City, were covered with the sports pictographs printed in bright, vibrant colors. In addition to providing information to thousands of visitors from all over the world, the totality of Wyman's design system for the XIX Olympiad provided a joyous, celebratory aspect that commemorated the Olympic games and provided a source of national pride for Mexico, an emerging nation that was striving toward a more progressive and prominent role in the community of nations. Since his return to New York, Wyman has applied his knowledge and experience to visual identification and systems design for numerous clients.

—Philip B. Meggs

Y

YAMAMOTO, Kansai.
Japanese fashion designer. Born in Yokohama in 1944. Studied civil engineering, at Yokohama High School, 1959–62; studied English literature at Nippon University, Tokyo, 1962–65. Worked as an assistant designer, in Hisashi Hosono Studio, Tokyo, 1966–70; freelance designer, establishing his own fashion company, Tokyo, from 1971: now produces ready-to-wear men's clothing, bags, household linens and stationery. **Exhibition:** *Fashion: An Anthology*, Victoria and Albert Museum, London, 1971. **Collection:** Victoria and Albert Museum, London. Address: Kansai Yamamoto Company Limited, Tokyo Central Apt., 4-3-15 Jingumae, Shibuya-ku, Tokyo, Japan.

Publications:

On YAMAMOTO: books—*Fashion: An Anthology by Cecil Beaton*, exhibition catalogue compiled by Madeleine Ginsburg, London 1971; *The World of Fashion: People, Places, Resources* by Eleanor Lambert, New York and London 1976; *In Vogue: Sixty Years of Celebrities and Fashion*, edited by Georgina Howell, New York 1976; *Fashion 2001* by Lucille Khornak, London and New York 1982; *McDowell's Directory of Twentieth Century Fashion* by Colin McDowell, London 1984; *New Fashion: Japan* by Leonard Koren, Tokyo, New York and San Francisco 1984; *The Encyclopaedia of Fashion from 1840 to the 1980s* by Georgina O'Hara, London 1986; *Japanese Design* by Penny Sparke, London 1987; *Advancing Towards the Future*, Tokyo 1988.

The fashion press has commented that some of Kansai Yamamoto's creations have the appeal of collector's items, due to his exquisite attention to detailed decoration. These views, expressed in 1981, harken back to his first English collection of 1971, which was based on Japanese Kabuki costume. The clothes did not sell but were widely talked about because of their rich colours and fabrics. He has built on that experience to produce clothes which combine Japanese and Western influences, function and fantasy. He now has three different, though mutually influential, lines: one Japanese, one international, and one futuristic—Kansai 2000. Not hard to find is the inspiration for an embroidered dragon motif or for the huge mohair sweater with the simple moon-and-mountain motif seen in Paris in summer 1977. However, sources of his designs are by no means always Japanese. His layered, oversize look of 1974 was perhaps as much Peruvian as Oriental. In 1976, he introduced white and brightly coloured miniskirts, some with small front panels, which had a distinctly Egyptian flavour.

The particular quality that unifies his designs is an adventurous approach to colour and surface effects. Quite simple shapes have become canvases for brightly abstract and complex naturalistic designs. His love of beading, appliqué, embroidery, and rich fabrics has made his garments expensive, but these clothes have produced ideas which have been adapted for ready-to-wear, printed T-shirts, and separates. for him, the T-shirt dress is an ideally simple, sensible garment, which reflects his concern with the functional role of clothing. Despite their often dazzling surfaces, his clothes are created to be easy to wear.

His space-age suits show that his thoughts are on the future. Theatrical in appearance, with their large, pointed shoulders and often metallike surfaces, these suits show an awareness of a need for future change in clothing concepts. While his backless, transparent, plastic rainsuits shown in 1977 might have been dismissed as pure fantasy at the time, the future may reveal the innovative power of such garments. He proved himself one of the exciting Japanese designers of the 1970s and may turn out to be an even greater fashion force in years to come.

—Hazel Clark

YANAGI, Sori.
Japanese industrial designer. Born in Tokyo, 29 June 1915. Studied at the National University of Arts, Tokyo, 1936–40; apprenticed as a designer, in the office of architect Junzo Sakakura, Tokyo, 1940–42. Married Fumiko Nakanishi in 1981; children: Shinichi, Mariko, Muneaki and Michiko. Assistant to designer Charlotte Perriand, Tokyo, 1942; designer, working for various agencies, Tokyo, from 1946; founder and director of Yanagi Industrial Design Office, Tokyo, from 1952: designed for Matsumura, Tendo-mokko, Kotobuki, Mitsuiseiki, Shussai Potteries, Tajimi Ceramic Institute, Kyoto-Gojozaka Kilns, Yamaya Glass, Hakusan-toki, Akita-mokko, Aoki Ceramics Japan, etc. Director, Japan Folk Crafts Museum, Tokyo, from 1977. Lecturer, Women's College of Art, Tokyo, 1953–54; professor, Kanazawa University of Arts and Crafts, from 1954; visiting professor, Staatliche Werkkunstschule, Kassel, 1961–62. Member of the Japan Committee on International Design, Tokyo, 1953; executive committee member, World Design Conference, Tokyo, 1960. **Exhibitions:** Matsuya Department Store, Tokyo, 1956; *Documenta*, Kassel, 1964; Padigilione d'Arte Moderna, Milan, 1980; Italian Cultural Center, Tokyo, 1983. **Collections:** Musée du Louvre, Paris; Stedelijk Museum, Amsterdam; Metropolitan Museum of Art, New York; Museum of Modern Art, New York. Recipient: Japanese Industrial Design Competition Prize, Tokyo, 1951; Gold Medal, Milan Triennale, 1957. Honorary Member, Accademia Tiberina, Rome, 1978; Honorary Member, Finnish Designers Association, Helsinki, 1981; Order of the Purple Ribbon, Tokyo, 1981. Address: Yanagi Design Office, 8 Honshio cho, Shinjuku-ku, Tokyo, Japan.

Works:

Stacking ashtray in ironstone china, for Matsumura China Company, 1950.
Butterfly Stool in plywood and steel, for Tendomokko Company, 1954.
Stacking stool in polyester plastics, for Kotobuki Company, 1954.
Orient three-wheeled car, for Mitsu-seiki Company, 1956.
Teapot in porcelain with bamboo handle, for Tajimi Ceramic Institute, 1956.
Teapot in black ironglaze with bamboo handle, for Kyoto-Gojozaka Kiln, 1958.
Casserole in black ironglaze, for Shussai Kiln, 1960.
Stacking chair in polypropylene and tubular steel, for Kotobuki Company, 1965.
Water jug in clear glass, for Yamaya Glass Company, 1967.
Stacking chairs and tables in moulded beech, for Akita-mokko Company, 1967.
Sacred fire plinth in bronze, for the Winter Olympics, Sapporo, 1972.
Sales kiosk with hood shutter, for the Yokohama Subway, 1973.
Small teapot in porcelain, for Hakusan-toki Company, 1975.
Armchair in solid beech, for Tendo-mokko Company, 1978.
Sound-absorbing screen-panel, for the Tomei super highway, Tokyo, 1980.
Dinnerwares in porcelain, for Ceramic Japan Company, 1988.

Publications:

By YANAGI: books—*Sori Yanagi: Design*, with introduction by Charlotte Perriand, Tokyo, 1983.

On YANAGI: books—*New Furniture 6*, edited by Gerd Hatje, Stuttgart and London 1962; *Il Disegno Industriale e la sua Estetica* by Gillo Dorfles, Bologna 1963; *The Modern Chair, 1860 to Today* by Guilbert Frey, London and Niederteufen 1970; *Contemporary Furniture*, edited by Klaus Jurgen Sembach, Stuttgart and London 1982; *Japanese Design* by Penny Sparke, London 1987.

Sori Yanagi: Soundproofing screens on the Tomei Superhighway, Tokyo, 1980

The most important factor in "design" must be one's mind.

In the real sense of the word, "design" does not exist without creation. That is the reason something lacking creativity is mere imitation and cannot be called true design. Creative design does not concern itself with superficial alterations in outward appearance. Rather, it works out original means of reforming the inner structure. The beauty of design cannot be achieved by mere cosmetic change. It must exude from within.

Whether a design results in success or not, its quality hinges upon the process by which it is made. Here, the workshop has a central role. Basic concepts and beautiful forms do not come from the drawing board alone.

Scientific technique is helpful for creating design images and undoubtedly contributes to developing fresh artistic presentations. But needless to say, each scientific technique has its own characteristics and respectively has its own limits. Therefore, scientific techniques can go against the design's intrinsic nature, depending on how it is utilized. It must also be remembered that scientific knowledge can work as a brake upon design creativity.

So-called market research is little help in the production of a good design. In fact, for the creative designer, it is an inhibiting factor. Market research consists of the analysis of past data, whereas the primary mission of the designer whose aim is creative work, lies in bringing forth something superior to anything that has existed in the past. On the other hand, the cooperation of flexible minded, forward-looking, skilled techniques is vital. Success or failure in producing a good design depends in large upon finding such well-qualified associates and also upon the way in which they are allowed to contribute to the work. Another person who must share with the designer the credit for a good design is the business executive who is able to recognize a good design and who commissions a qualified designer to create it. Well designed products are born under the patronage of the business executive who regards his products with a genuine pride and love. The "productmanship" of such a person is equivalent to the craftsmanship which goes into the creation of handmade articles.

The articles which sell well today are not necessarily well designed, and conversely, well designed articles do not necessarily sell well. For today's designer, it is not enough to work merely with the aim of creating good designs. He must also take into consideration what is likely to sell. That means he must discover the point at which good design and saleability come together. The majority of today's designs bow subserviently to current tastes. But true design consists in challenging the prevailing fashion.

At the heart of folk crafts, it is possible for us to see the fundamental circumstances of human existence. Their purity enables us to drink at the fountain-head of beauty. Such folk crafts make us consider the meaning of modernization. Tradition exists in the cause of creation. Good design without tradition and creation is inconceivable.

Sound designs are found in a sound society. Such a society can be defined as one that is held together by the principle of *gemeinschaft*. When people are unified in such a common spirit, designs that attempt to deceive the public will probably not be produced. With the depleting of the earth's limited resources, a more acute problem by the day, the curtain will be coming down hard and fast upon designs that merely fuel the fires of economic growth and promote high stock turnover and consumerism. For the survival of civilization, man will have to turn back, re-examine his roots, and reflect deeply on the course he is to take. As for design, the problem is very similar. Time has come for us to take a step back and think over the ultimate question: What is design?

—Sori Yanagi

Sori Yanagi is an internationally-known designer who has established his own context in industrial design in Japan. A designer of products, particularly domestic products, he has been strongly influenced by Walter Gropius and the Bauhaus philosophy; he also inherited purely modern design concepts from Charlotte Perriand.

His father, Soetsu Yanagi, was the first advocate in Japan of applying artistic concepts to individual items used in the average home; his interest was in utensils, the instruments of daily life. His concept—"what is useful is beautiful"—was not so different in its artistic philosophy from that which informs Western functionalism; as well, it reflects traditional Japanese views on the making of goods and Japanese aesthetics and ethics.

Growing up in such an environment, Yanagi absorbed his father's principles, but he established his own unique, modern individuality when still quite young. As early as the 1950s, Yanagi was already his own man, and his works from then until now are glorious. They are all handmade, and each work has a presence and beauty of form that is appropriate to the modern world but that revitalizes the essence of traditional Japanese forms.

Industrial society in Japan enjoyed its greatest growth in the 1960s. There were, of course, many positive results, but such rapid growth also revealed and created new problems. Industrialists placed the highest priority on economy and on efficiency in production—and design itself was too often judged according to such criteria. Yanagi has been openly critical of such attitudes. He believes that designers should be autonomous, that they should resist becoming the servants of materialism or of the worst aspects of modern industrialism. Among his targets have been showy designs, the bastardization of the arts, the intrusion of government in setting design policies in developing countries, the degradation of design techniques by commercialism, and the countless products churned out by industries obviously oblivious to the ways in which people actually live.

His attitude is best expressed in his own words:

Design is a culture of mankind as a whole. As design finds itself moving with vigorous momentum through the changing and merging of various regional cultures toward an ever-lasting unit and a future world culture, the timing will no doubt come when the authenticity of an integrated human culture can be established. At present, however, amid the confusion caused in the transition from the age of handicrafts to the age of the machine, and with the many contradictions that emerge suddenly with the advance of modernization, it is not yet possible.

What is needed, in Yanagi's view, is that designers must stand their ground: They must, coolly, contemplate the alternative, then resolve to become the leaders, not the blind followers, of industrial progress—and never consider compromise until that brave new world he describes has come to pass.

—Kunio Sano

YANG, Jay.

American textile and furnishings designer. Born in Hsin-Chu, Taiwan, in 1946; emigrated to the United States in 1967; naturalized, 1977. Studied under Neil Welliver, at the University of Pennsylvania, Philadelphia, 1967–70: MFA 1970. Married Myra Hines in 1973. Worked as an illustrator, New York, 1970–73; freelance textile and home furnishings designer, New York, from 1973; founder and president of Jay Yang Designs Limited, New York, from 1975. Recipient: Paritex Design Award, Paris, 1980; Editeurs-Créateurs Design Award, Paris, 1982. Address: Jay Yang Designs Limited, 41 Madison Avenue, New York, New York 10010, U.S.A.

Works:

Victoria and Albert: Rowena glazed chintz fabric, for Anstoetz, 1985.
Victoria and Albert: Ivanhoe glazed chintz fabric, for Anstoetz, 1985.
Victoria and Albert: Chatterley glazed chintz fabric, for Anstoetz, 1985.
Victoria and Albert: Lancelot glazed chintz fabric, for Anstoetz, 1985.
Victoria and Albert: Camelot glazed chintz fabric, for Anstoetz, 1985.
Victoria and Albert: Fairlawn glazed chintz fabric, for Anstoetz, 1986.
Victoria and Albert: Hampton Court glazed chintz fabric, for Anstoetz, 1986.
Victoria and Albert: Abington glazed chintz fabric, for Anstoetz, 1986.
Victoria and Albert: Chelsea glazed chintz fabric, for Anstoetz, 1986.
Victoria and Albert: Sandringham glazed chintz fabric, for Anstoetz, 1986.
Victoria and Albert: Kensington glazed chintz fabric, for Anstoetz, 1986.
Versailles Collection: Fontain Bleau glazed chintz fabric, for Chanee, 1987.
Versailles Collection: Marie Antoinette glazed chintz fabric, for Chanee, 1987.
Versailles Collection: Pompadour glazed chintz fabric, for Chanee, 1987.
Versailles Collection: Josephine glazed chintz fabric, for Chanee, 1987.
Versailles Collection: Orangerie glazed chintz fabric, for Chanee, 1987.
Versailles Collection: Strie glazed chintz fabric, for Chanee, 1987.

Publications:

By YANG books illustrated—*The Pai-Pai Pig* by Joy Anderson, New York 1967; *Hai-Yin, The Dragon Girl* by Joy Anderson, New York 1970; *Tales That People Tell in China*, New York 1971; *The Wooden Cat Man* by Flishman, Boston 1972.

If I have, indeed, made a contribution in the field since I started designing fabrics in 1973, much of the credit goes to the American consumer in whose innate good taste I strongly believe. In fact, I have always designed *up* to the consumer, not down. During my first few years as a novice designer in the United States, I worked with exclusive fabric houses which sold only to decorators who, in turn, reached a very limited, and generally affluent, audience. My fabric designs sold very well, but I was not satisfied. My goal was—and is—to bring a "decorator look" to a broad consumer market and give the customers who buy at department stores and other open retail outlets an opportunity to buy fine fabric designs, whether on upholstery and drapery materials or on sheets, pillows, table linens, etc. Creative Designs. In fresh palettes. That's exactly what I've striven

Jay Yang: *Allegro* **pattern printed on combed sateen cotton, 1988**

to do since I opened my own business in 1975. My contribution? I hope I've helped to raise the general level of design in the American home.

My philosophy of design might be called "historical eclecticism." "Historical," because I believe that tradition is the base for renewal and radical innovation can come only from those steeped in tradition. "Eclecticism" because my designs are a synthesis of different times and places. My belief is that if the proportions are right, diverse styles from past and present can live together esthetically. My own country house started as a small farmhouse to which different generations of people have added, wing by wing. I'm adding on, too, blending the old parts of the house with the new, in happy harmony that's all the richer because of the "time blocks" that reach back into the past, bespeak the present, and move forward to the future.

—Jay Yang

First achieving prominence through his Orient Express collection, with this and other work, Jay Yang helped place P. Kaufman's firmly in the volume design market in the mid-70s. He demonstrated considerable energy by free-lancing at the same time for Clarence House and Brunschwig et Fils. His designs often included unusual features, such as more than a dozen colors per pattern and patterns that were uneven and off-center.

The founding of his own company, Jay Yang Designs, allowed him to broaden his base. He licensed designs for soft goods, fine china for International China, and, most recently, furniture for Bernhardt. His furniture, like all his work, embodies his dictum that design is a trade, not an art. The furniture is basically functional, incorporating the classic simplicity of Chinese lines, with the minimum of detailing that gives it an Art Deco look. His Chinese touch has also been employed in designing a commemorative collection of fabrics for England's Brighton Pavilion, which houses the best in Chinoiserie interior design and objets d'art. His historical sensitivity was sought out by the Louvre's Musée des Arts Décoratifs, for which he designed a collection based on 18th- and 19th-century documents. Through his converting company, Fabriyaz, he has also been responsible for bringing Givenchy designs to the American market.

An important part of the Yang philosophy is his belief in "designing up" to consumer taste, rather than down to it. He would like his own company to be a medium through which "good, clean design" can be made available to everyone. He has never underestimated the public's ability to appreciate the unusual and unexpected in design. For instance, his 1976 Imari design for P. Kaufman displayed random, uncentered patterns, with both geometric and floral motifs. His willingness to take chances, to explore the unusual, has been a part of his success. His decorator fabrics have been lapped up by the consumer, and his designs for Wamsutta caused theirs to be the world's best-selling sheets.

While his designs have won recognition for their individuality and sheer beauty, he has still remained true to historical traditions. His acquisitive eye for the beautiful has enabled him to draw ideas from many sources. His designs for the Musée des Arts Décoratifs, which have been introduced at fine stores around the country, demonstrate his understanding of forms and colors suitable for contemporary American living, while keeping the charm and spirit of the classic French motifs. Yet, his interest in history and his own background in Taiwan have not rendered him incapable of the odd surprise on his own account. In the Made in USA collection, he departed from the "oriental floral" pigeonhole to celebrate his new homeland by featuring American and contemporary materials. Designs such as Apple Pie, Yankee Doodle Dandy, and Pop Corn, employed American folk art geometrics, ikats, contemporary solids and prints, and applique and patchwork looks. His designs are tailored to the environment, and he is sensitive to the society that has matured his talent.

While Yang designs are numerous, he strictly confines himself to the inteior design market and rejects many chances to broaden his scope, feeling that to evolve as a designer of too many things is to dilute one's talent. Similarly, even though schooled in the fine arts, he shuns the artist's label. He sees himself as a tradesman and is very involved in the running of his two companies.

In 1984, he is producing a tenth anniversary collection consisting of his most successful lines, updated to suit contemporary trends and tastes, and some new ones. He posits that something

good will always be so and that one should be careful just how he tries to improve it.

—Augustine Hope

YOH, Shoei (Hamura).

Japanese architect, interior and industrial designer. Born, of Chinese parents, in Kumamoto, Japan, 7 March 1940: naturalized, 1975. Studied at Keio Gijuku University, Tokyo, 1958–62: BA 1962; studied design, at Wittenberg University, Springfield, Ohio, 1962–63. Married Kimiko Nakakita in 1966; children: Masaaki, Kaori and Motoki. Project designer, for International Design Associates, Tokyo, 1964–67, and for NIC, Fukuoka, 1967–69; freelance architect, interior and furniture designer, Fukuoka, from 1970. Chairman, Kyushu Design Committee, Fukuoka, 1974–76. **Exhibitions:** *Transformation from Space to Space*, Japan Design Commission, Tokyo, 1980; *WXYZ Chairs*, Tokyo Designers Space, 1982; *Light Architecture*. Tokyo Designers Space, 1982; *Forms in Wood*, Japan Design Commission, Tokyo, 1985; *Interface Design*. Gallery MA, Tokyo, 1987. **Collection:** International Art Museum, Osaka. Recipient: Lighting Design Competition Silver Award, Tokyo, 1973; Japan Interior Designers Association, Award, 1980; Japan Architects Association Award, 1983; Mainichi Design Award, Tokyo, 1983; Architectural Excellence Award, Kumamoto City, 1984; Commercial Space Design Award, Tokyo, 1984; Commercial Environment Design Award, Tokyo, 1985, 1986; Architectural Culture Award, Kita Kyushu City, 1987; Architectural Institute of Japan Award, 1988. Address: 1-12-30 Heiwa, Minami-ku, Fukuoka 815, Japan.

Works:

Free-form microwave-powered lamps, 1976.
Ingot coffee shop in the form of a glass prism, Tokyo, 1977.
Kinoshita Clinic in structural plastics, Fukuoka City, 1979.
Stainless steel house with latticed lights, 1981.
WXYZ Chairs in photobonded glass, 1982.
Egami Clinic building in aluminium, 1982.
Laforet Museum of Art, Akasaka, 1982–86.
Pavilion shopping centre, Kumamoto City, 1983.
Aluminium house with sundial, 1984.
House with illuminated cross-of-light structure, 1985.
Music atelier, Kumamoto Prefecture, 1986.
Aspecta outdoor theatre, Mount Aso, Kumamoto Prefecture, 1987.
Bus Station building in glass, Oguni, 1987.
Forestry Centre, Oguni, 1987.
Gymnasium in wooden structure, Oguni, 1988.
Seibu Gas Museum, Tokyo, 1989.

Publications:

By YOH: articles—in *Japan Architect* (Tokyo), no. 209, 1974, no. 210, 1974, no. 246, 1977, no. 252, 1978, no. 263, 1980, no. 267, 1981, no. 300, 182, no. 302, 1982; *Space Design* (Tokyo), February 1980.

On YOH: books—*Decorative Art and Modern Interiors*, 5 vols., London 1975–79: *Transformations in Modern Architecture* by Arthur Drexler, New York 1979; articles—in *Domus*

(Milan), no. 506, 1972, no. 584, 1978, no. 586, 1978, no. 588, 1978, no. 608, 1980, no. 625, 1982, no. 640, 1983; *Global Architecture* (Tokyo), no. 4, 1978, no. 14, 1983; *Architecture d'Aujourd'hui* (Paris), September 1980; *Architectural Review* (London), April 1981; *AIA Journal* (Washington, D.C.), August 1962; *Progressive Architecture* (New York), May 1983.

Simple form, materials, and details express my belief that unconscious design is the best, which makes me feel free from all of the restrictions such as gravity and process of evolution. Design is the creation of an object in a form that has never existed in the past. The new form is derived from evaluation which goes far back to the root of the process of development of our time. The technology for men to control nature is really only the means to borrow a part of nature temporarily. It has nothing to do with conquering or taming nature.

My designs begin with the recognition of mutual relationships among men, technology, and nature. Unlike Icarus in the Greek myth, the Solar Challenger could cross the straits of Dover using solar energy, by borrowing 15,000 solar batteries from NASA. It was not the sun but man who was challenged. Dedicated to our great designers, my WXYZ glass chairs, which are photobonded through ultra-violet rays while standing in the sunlight, will be found someday fallen into hundreds of pieces of glass shining in the morning sun.

Professor Teijiro Muramatsu of Tokyo University speaks of my work as the handmade architecture of a highly industrial technology. He points out the importance of enthusiasm in enterprising, technological achievement by making things with the highest quality of industrial materials available in our time, just as the old carpenters used to select and handle wood. After all, the ceramic tile cladding on the United states space shuttle was attached piece by piece with hands! Advanced technology has always been tested by hands through many trials and failure. I see nothing but beauty in making an effort to make these experiments possible.

—Shoei Yoh

Shoei Yoh has received the prestigious Japan Architects Association Award for 1983. It was given in recognition of his achievements in building design, but in his case, architecture is simply one aspect of a remarkably coherent design oeuvre. "High-tech" inadequately describes his approach, which is characterized, rather, by an overriding concern for minimalism—in both the sense of primary geometric forms and the sense of minimal physical substance. Matter is seemingly stretched to its limits in order to enfold the greatest volume of space.

A transparent or translucent membrane enveloping a pristine volume has consistently been his solution to problems at quite different scales, from lamps to entire buildings. Structure is reduced to the most slender members possible. His works thus have both delicacy (of membrane) and boldness (of form), a combination that distinguishes him from most of the so-called avant-garde architects and designers in Japan. He has quite obviously been influenced by traditional Japanese elements such as the *shoji* screens, but that influence has perhaps been filtered through the Western sensibility of designers such as Eames. Yoh's works are surreal objects in the interior and exterior landscape. These poetic and scrupulously detailed works have earned hima unique place among contemporary Japanese designers.

—Hiroshi Watanabe

Shoei Yoh: Kinoshita Clinic, Fukuoka City, 1979

YOKOO, Tadanori.
Japanese painter, printmaker and graphic designer. Born in Nishiwaki City, Hyogo Prefecture, 17 June 1936. Educated at Nishiwaki High School until 1954. Married Yasue Tani in 1958; children: Ei and Mimi. Worked as a block copy artist, at Seibundo Printing Company, Kakogawa City, 1954–56; graphic artist, at Kobe Shimbun-sha newspaper company, Kobe, 1956–59; designer, at the National Advertisement Laboratory, Osaka, 1959–60, and at the Nippon Design Center, Tokyo, 1960–64; co-founder and director, with Akira Uno and Chunao Harada, of Studio Illfill graphic design firm, Tokyo, 1964–65; freelance designer, Tokyo, from 1965: founder and partner, with Masamichi Oikawa, of The End Studio graphic design firm, Tokyo, 1968–71; in private design practice as Tadanoro Yokoo Design Studio, Tokyo, from 1971; has designed books for Shinshokan, Kodansha, Gakugeishorin, Chikumashobo, Kawadeshobo, Bungeishunju, Shobunsha, Tokyo Ongakusha, Shiya-soshosha, Hirakawa Shuppansha, etc. **Exhibitions:** Matsuya Department Store, Tokyo, 1965; Nantenshi, Gallery, Tokyo, 1966, 1982, 1984; Museum of Modern Art, New York, 1972; Museum fur Kunst und Gewerbe, Hamburg, 1973, 1982; Stendelijk Museum, Amsterdam, 1974; Okayama Museum, Japan, 1980; Otani Memorial Art Museum, Nishinomiya City, 1983; Musee de la Publicite, Paris, 1983; Otis Parsons Gallery, Los Angeles, 1984; Palazzo Bianco, Genoa, 1985; Falcone Theatre, Genoa, 1985; Kunstlerhaus Bethanien, West Berlin, 1985; Laforet Museum, Harajyuku, Tokyo, 1985; Japanese-American Cultural Center, Los Angeles, 1985; Nishimura Gallery, Tokyo, 1985; Roberta English Gallery, San Francisco, 1986, Roy Boyd Gallery, Los Angeles, 1986; Seibu Museum of Art, Tokyo, 1987; Carnegie-Mellon University, Pittsburgh, 1987; Galerie Silvia Menzel, West Berlin, 1988. **Collections:** Museum of Modern Art, New York; Museum of Fine Art, Boston; Walker Art Center, Minneapolis; Library of Congress, Washington, D.C.; Stedelijk Museum, Amsterdam; Musee de la Publicite, Paris; Museum fur Kunst und Gewerbe, Hamburg; Museum of Modern Art, Vienna; Kunstgewerbemuseum, Zurich; Poster Museum, Warsaw; Israel Museum, Jerusalem; Konstindustrimuseet, Copenhagen; Metropolitan Art Museum, Tokyo; National Museum of Modern Art, Tokyo; National Library, Tokyo, Municipal Museum of Art, Kyoto; Museum of Industrial Encouragement, Toyama; Ohara Museum of Art, Okayama. Recipient: Japan Advertising Artists Club Prize, 1957; Tokyo Art Directors Club Prize, 1961, 1962, 1971, 1973, 1974, 1975, 1980; Grand Print Prize, Paris Biennale, 1969; Warsaw Poster Biennale UNESCO Prize, 1972, and Gold Medal, 1974; Brno Graphic Biennale Prize, 1972 1974, 1984; Hyogo Museum of Modern Art Prize, 1974; Mainichi Design Prize, Tokyo, 1974; Hollywood Reporter Key Art Prize, 1976; Kodansha Cultural Award, Tokyo, 1978; Lahti Poster Biennale Prize, 1979; Hyogo Prefecture Cultural Award, 1987. Address: 4-19-7 Seijo, Setagaya-ku, Tokyo, Japan.

Works:

A la Maison de M. Civecawa poster, for the Garmera Company, 1965.
Tadanori Yokoo: Persona exhibition poster, for the Matsuya Department Store, Tokyo, 1965.
The City and Design book promotion poster, for Kajima Institute Publishing Company, 1965.
Koshimaki-Osen poster, for the Jyokyo Gekijyo Troupe, 1966.
A Ballad Dedicated to a Small Finger Cutting Ceremony book promotion poster, for Yakuza Shobo Publishing, 1966.
Tenjo Sajiki poster, for Shuji Terayama and the Tenjo Sajiki Troupe, 1967.
Word and Image exhibition poster, for the Museum of Modern Art, New York, 1968.
Chinzei Yumihari-Zuki poster, for the National Theater, Tokyo, 1969.
Punishment by Roses (Y. Mishima) book illustrations, for Shuei-Sha Publishing Company, 1970.
Pavilion design at *Expo 70*, Osaka, for Japan Textiles, 1970.

Tadanori Yokoo: Poster, 1986

Wonderland poster, for Shimojima seaside resort, 1971.

The Beatles poster, for Apple Records and Toshiba Records, 1972.

Santana Amigos record Sleeve, for CBS Sony, 1974.

Suntry campaign posters, for the Suntry Brewery, 1978.

Chiyonofuji sumo wrestling sash/belt, for Kokonoe-Beya, 1981.

Bow Wow Wow publicity poster, for RCA Records, 1982.

Tadanori Yokoo exhibition poster, for the Musee de la Publicite, Paris, 1984.

Issey Miyake: Body Works exhibition poster, for the Victoria and Albert Museum, London, 1985.

JASRAC poster, for the Japanese Society for the Rights of Authors, Composers and Publishers, 1988.

Yamatotakeru poster, for the Tokyo Electric Company, 1989.

Publications:

By YOKOO: books—*The 170cm Blues*, Tokyo 1968; *Tadanori Tokoo's Posthumous Works*, Tokyo 1968; *The Complete Tadanori Yokoo*, Tokyo, 1970, as *Tadanori Yokoo*, Woodbury, New York 1977; *An Escape to Incompletion*, Tokyo 1970; *Contemporary Prints—Tadanori Yokoo*, Tokyo 1971; *Push*, Tokyo 1972; *Groping in the Dark*, Tokyo 1973; *Yearning for Millenium*, Tokyo 1974; *Why I am Here*, Tokyo 1976; *To India*, Tokyo 1977; *Tadanori Yokoo's Collage Design*, Tokyo 1977; *A Dove Flying from the Ark*, Tokyo 1977; *My Zen Apprenticeship*, Tokyo 1978; *100 Posters of Tadanori Yokoo*, Tokyo and New York 1978; *Haragyate*, Tokyo 1978; *YFO Revolution*, Tokyo 1979; *My Dream Diary*, Tokyo 1979; *A Child of Aquarius*, Tokyo 1979; *Gleaming Woman*, Tokyo 1980; *Cosmic Meditation*, Tokyo 1980; *Yesterday I Was, Today I Am*, Tokyo 1980; *Get Up 8:00am, Fine*, Tokyo 1980; *Bigeiko*, Tokyo 1981; *Paintings, Prints and Drawings by Tadanori Yokoo*, Tokyo 1981; *Tadanori Yokoo*, Kobe, Japan 1982.

On YOKOO: books—*Modern Graphics* by Keith Murgatroyd, London 1969; *Graphis Record Covers*, edited by Walter Herdeg, Zurich 1974; *Japan: Tradition und Gegenwart* by Jurgen Harten, Joseph Love and others, Dusseldorf 1974; *Art in Japan Today*, edited by S. Takashima and others, Tokyo 1974; *Album Cover Album: The Book of Record Jackets*, edited by Storm Thorgerson and Roger Dean, Limpsfield 1979; *The Language of Graphics* by Edward Booth-Clibbborn and Daniele Baroni, London 1980; *Album Cover Album 2* by Roger Dean and David Howells, New York 1982; *A History of Graphic Design* by Philip B. Meggs, New York and London 1983; *Les Années 60* by Anne Bony, Paris 1983; *The Twentieth Century Poster: Design of the Avant-Garde* by Dawn Ades, New York 1984; *Japanese Design* by Penny Sparke, London 1987.

*

It is my principle not to have a definite style for my work. I always rely on my instincts. What scares me most is creating images with ideology. I do not know where I came from or where I am going. I do not even who who I am. How could I possibly adopt one style as my own?

—Tadanori Yokoo

Since the 1960s, Tadanori Yokoo has been an advertising designer, poster artist, printmaker, architect, actor, and author, and in Japan he achieved the kind of celebrity usually accorded rock musicians and film stars. It is his work as a poster artist, however, that brought him to international attention.

The great poster artist A. M. Cassandre likened the poster-maker to the telegraph operator whose sole duty is to transmit a client's message. Yokoo has exemplified the reverse. The poster in his hands became a vehicle for personal opinion, social and political commentary, and personal revelation.

As a student and young designer, Yokoo was both fascinated by and resentful of the increasing influence of the West on Japanese life and on the growing internationalism of its art and design. In 1965, he was commissioned to produce for Tatsumi Hijikta's modern dance company. Hijikata shared Yokoo's concern for restoring an indigenous imagery and sensibility to Japanese design. The result was a startling poster filled with rising suns, Hiroshige-like ocean waves, a mixture of Japanese and English text, deliberately obscure phrases, and unabashed eroticism.

This eclectic, audacious poster struck a responsive chord with the Tokyo intellectual community, and Yokoo was soon commissioned to design posters for exhibitions, publications, and the theatre and given the same freedom of expression. Yokoo's clients themselves unknowingly became allies in his subversion of the traditional well-made poster. It is precisely the personal nature of his work and its notoriety that attracts them. Although their messages might become obscured or incidental, a Yokoo poster is never ignored. Yokoo's work is saved from its own iconoclasm and self-indulgence by the over-all creative intelligence, brilliance of execution, and underlying seriousness of purpose.

Yokoo was commissioned to design the Textile Pavilion for *Expo 70* in Osaka. This project also became an opportunity for Yokoo's comment. In its finished state, the building still appeared to be under construction—even the scaffolding remained intact. Yokoo's explanation: "The precise moment when the building can first be said to have been completed will be the moment when the act of living there is denied us and it has become a ruin. Therefore, the fact that I turned the significance of what would be the ultimate fate of the building into the very building itself can be considered as representing my attitude towards architecture and my creative work."

—Mildred Constantine

Z

ZANUSO, Marco.

Italian architect, exhibition, interior and industrial designer. Born in Milan, 14 May 1916. Studied architecture, at the Politecnico, Milan, 1935–39: Dip.Arch. 1939. Served in the Italian Navy, 1940–45: Lieutenant; Cross of Valour. Married Marialisa Pedroni in 1944; daughters: Federica, Lorenza and Susanna. Freelance architect and designer, Milan, from 1945: has designed for Olivetti, Necchi, Edgards, IBM, Arflex, Elam, Brionvega, Moretti e Bianchi, Gavina, Bonacina, Techniform, Kartell, Lumenform, Zanotta, Mim Mobili, Anic, Lanerossi, Fiat, Poggi, Borletti, Siemens, Fusital, Villeroy e Boch, etc. Editor, *Casabella* magazine, Milan, from 1947; councillor, 1956–60, building commission member, 1961–63, and planning commission member from 1961, City of Milan; president, ADI Associazione Disegno Industriale, Milan, 1957–59, 1966–74; council member, Milan Triennale, from 1977; regional councillor, IN/ARCH building institute, Milan, from 1977. Professor of industrial design from 1965, professor of the development of materials, 1966–68, Athens Commission member, 1980–82, president of the planning and production department from 1981, and president of the council of address from 1982, at the Politecnico, Milan. **Exhibitions:** *Marco Zanuso*, at the Spoleto Festival of Two Worlds, 1967; *Italy: The New Domestic Landscape*, Museum of Modern Art, New York, 1972; *Design Since 1945*, Philadelphia Museum of Art, 1983. **Collections:** Museum of Modern Art, New York; Philadelphia Museum of Art. Recipient: Grand Prize, 1948, 1954, Gold Medal, 1951, 1954, 1957, 1964, Silver Medal, 1960, Milan Triennale; Compasso d'Oro Award, Milan, 1956, 1962, 1964, 1967, 1979; Villa Olmo Silver Medal, Como, 1957; La Casa Abitata Gold Award, Florence, 1965; Interplas Award, London, 1965; Bio 2 Biennale Gold Award, Liubliana, 1966; Estetica Sperimentale Gold Medal, Rimini, 1966; Industrial Design Gold Medal, Yverdon, 1969; Associazione Italiana per Edilizia Industrializzata Prize, Milan, 1971; Bolaffi Prize, Turin, 1972. Address: Via Laveno 6, 20148 Milan, Italy.

Works:

MOMA armchair, for Moretti e Bianchi, 1949.
Lady armchair, for Arflex, 1951.
Sleep-o-matic sofa bed, for Arflex, 1954.
1100/2 sewing machine, for Borletti, 1956.
Carosello coffee-maker, for Girmi/Subalpina, 1958.
Lambda chair in sheet steel, for Gavina, 1958–62.
Doney television set, for Brionvega, 1962.
Springtime armchair, sofa and table, for Arflex, 1964.
Grillo television, for Auso/Siemens, 1966.
Marcuso table, for Zanotta, 1969.

ST/201 black television set, for Brionvega, 1970.
575 sewing machine, for Necchi, 1972.
Ariante ventilator fan with slatted plastic housing, for Vortice, 1974.
Eta Beta table, for Zanotta, 1978.
SD 60 upholstered chair, for Poggi, 1979.
Medical pacemaker programmer, for Sorin Biomedica, 1981.
Monobloc bathroom unit, for Villeroy e Boch, 1982.
Caraffa teapot, for Cleto Munari, 1983.
Due Z cutlery and hardware, for Fusital, 1985.
Laveno table, for Zanotta, 1986.

(for a list of Zanuso's buildings and architectural projects, see *Contemporary Architects*)

Publications:

By ZANUSO: books—*La Macchina per Cucire*, exhibition catalogue, Milan 1962; *Elemtni di Tecnologia dei Materiali come Introduzione allo Studio del Designs*, Milan 1967; *La Progettazione e L'Organizzazione degli Ambiente di Lavoro*, with Pierluigi Nicolin, Milan 1974; articles—in *Domus* (Milan), no. 197, 1944, no. 1, 1988; *Stile Industria* (Milan), no. 21, 1959, no. 2, 1962; *Rivista Ideal Standard* (Milan), no. 59, 1961; *Abitare* (Milan), no. 10, 1962; *La Repubblica* (Milan), no. 18, 1979.

On ZANUSO: books—*Prize Designs for Modern Furniture* by Edgar Kaufmann Jr., New York 1950; *Gute Möbel: Schöne Räume*, edited by Mia Seeger, Stuttgart 1953; *Mobili Tipo* by Robert Aloi, Milan 1956; *Design for Modern Living* by Gerd and Ursula Hatje, Munich 1961, London 1962; *Il Nuovo Arredamento* by Morris Alfieri, Venice 1964; *The Modern Chair: 1850 to Today* by Gilbert Frey, London and Niederteufen 1970; *Zanuso*, edited by Trevor Wilson, Melbourne 1971; *Marco Zanuso: Designer* by Gillo Dorfles, Rome 1971; *Italy: The New Domestic Landscape* by Emilio Ambasz, New York and Florence 1972; *Il Design in Italia 1945–1972* by Paolo Fossati, Turin 1972; *Design e Forme Nuove nell'Arredamento Italiano*, edited by Paolo Portoghesi and Marino Marini, Rome 1978; *History of Modern Furniture* by Karl Mang, Stuttgart 1978, London 1979; *Atlante del Design Italiano 1940/1980* by Alfonso Grassi and Anty Pansera, Milan 1980; *Industrial Design* by John Heskett, London 1980; *Il Design Italiano degli Anni '50*, edited by Andrea Branzi and Michele De Lucchi, Milan 1981; *Contemporary Furniture*, edited by Klaus-Jurgen Sembach, Stuttgart and London 1982; *Design Since 1945*, edited by Kathryn Hiesinger and George Marcus, Philadelphia and London, 1983; *Design Process Olivetti 1908–1983*, with text by Renzo Zorzi, Milan 1983; *Mid-Century: Furniture of the 1950s* by Cara Greenberg, London 1984; *Twentieth Century Design: Furniture* by Penny Sparke, London 1986; *Modern Furniture Classics* by

Miriam Stimpson, London 1987; *Italian Design: 1870 to the present* by Penny Sparke, London and New York 1988; *Designed by Architects in the 1980s* by Juli Capella and Quim Larrea, London 1988.

ZAPF, Hermann.

German calligrapher, lettering, typeface and book designer. Born in Nuremberg, 8 November 1918. Studied as an apprentice retoucher in a printing works, Nuremberg, 1934–38; also private studies in lettering, from manuals of Edward Johnston and Rudolf Koch, 1935–37; studied at Paul Koch's Haus zum Fursteneck type workshop, Frankfurt, 1938. Served in a geographic unit of the German Army, 1941–45. Type director, at D. Stempel typefoundry, Frankfurt, 1947–56; design consultant, at Mergenthaler Linotype Company, Brooklyn, New York, and Frankfurt, 1957–74; consultant to Hallmark International, Kansas City, Missouri, 1966–73; vice-president, Design Processing International, New York, from 1977. Instructor in Lettering, Werkkunstschule, Offenbach, 1947–50; professor of graphic design, Carnegie Institute of Technology, Pittsburgh, 1960; instructor in typography, Technische Hochschule, Darmstadt, 1972–82; professor of typographic computer programs, Rochester Institute of Technology, New York, 1977–87; also visiting lecturer at colleges throughout the United States and Europe. **Exhibitions:** Cooper Union, New York, 1951 (with Fritz Kredel); Book Club of California, San Francisco, 1953, 1961, 1972, 1977; University of California, Los Angeles, 1957; Carnegie Institute of Technology, Pittsburgh, 1960 (toured); Bibliothèque Albert I, Brussels, 1962 (toured); Stadtbibliothek, Nuremberg, 1963 (with Rudolf Koch); Gutenberg Museum, Mainz, 1964, 1974; Hallmark Incorporated, Kansas City, 1967 (toured); Rijksmuseum Meermanno-Westreenianum, The Hague, 1968; Musée de Nice, France, 1969; University of Texas, Austin, 1970; Museo Civico, Saluzzo, 1972; Technische Hochschule, Darmstadt, 1973; Museo Bodoniano, Parma, 1975; University of Kentucky, Lexington, 1976; Stanford University, California, 1960; Rochester Institute of Technology, New York, 1980; National Museum, Tokyo, 1982 (toured). **Collections:** Pierpont Morgan Library, New York; Newberry Library, Chicago; Harvard University, Cambridge, Massachusetts; San Francisco Public Library; Bibliothèque Royale, Brussels; Klingspor Museum, Offenbach; Gutenberg Museum, Mainz. Recipient: Silver Medal, Belgian Ministry of Information, 1962; Brno Graphics Bien-

Hermann Zapf: *Time Flies – Seize the Day* **three-dimensional letters in aluminium, 1984**

nale Typography Prize, 1966; Type Directors Club Gold Medal, New York, 1967; Goudy Award, Rochester Institute of Technology, New York, 1969; Silver Medal, Leipzig Book Fair, 1971; Gutenberg Prize, Mainz, 1974; Museo Bodoniano Gold Medal, Parma, 1975; Merck Award, Darmstadt, 1978; National Composition Award, 1986; Robert II. Middleton Award, 1987. Honorary citizen, State of Texas, 1970; Honorary Royal Designer for Industry, Royal Society of Arts, London, 1985. Honorary Member: Type Directors Club of New York; Society of Typographic Arts, Chicago; Association of Stanford University Libraries; Double Crown Club, London; Society of Scribes and Illuminators, London; Societe Typographique de France; Grafiska Institutet, Stockholm; Society of Typographic Designers, Toronto; The Typophiles, New York; Art Directors Club of Kansas City; Society for Calligraphy, Los Angeles; Washington Calligraphers Guild; Typographers International Association, Washington, D.C.; Estonian Calligraphers Union, Tallinn; Alpha Beta Club, Hong Kong; Wynkyn de Worde Society, London; Bund Deutscher Buchkunstler. Address: Seitersweg 35, 6100 Darmstadt, West Germany.

Works:

Typeface designs include—*Gilgengart*, 1938–41; *Alkor*, 1939–40; *Novalis*, 1946–47; *Melior*, 1948–49; *Virtuosa*, 1948–49; *Palatino*, 1948–50; *Festival Figures*, 1948–50; *Primavera Ornaments*, 1948–50; *Michelangelo Titling*, 1949–50; *Zodiac Signs*, 1950; *Sistina Titling*, 1950; *Saphir*, 1950; *Linotype Janson*, 1951; *Kompakt*, 1952; *Linotype Aldus*, 1952–53; *Optima*, 1952–58; *Attika Greek*, 1953; *Artemis Greek*, 1953; *Phidias Greek*, 1953; *Heraklit Greek*, 1953; *Frederika Greek*, 1953; *Linotype Mergenthaler*, 1953; *Alahram Arabic*, 1954; *Magnus San Serif*, 1956–58; *Trajanus Cyrillic*, 1957; *Linofilm Venture*, 1960–67; *Hunt Roman*, 1961–63; *Hallmark Jeannette Script*, 1966–67; *Hallmark Firenze*, 1967–68; *Hallmark Textura*, 1968–69; *Linofilm Medici*, 1969; *Orion*, 1974; *ITC Zapf Book*, 1976; *Comenius*, 1976; *Digiset Marconi*, 1976; *ITC Zapf International*, 1977; *Digiset Edison*, 1978; *ITC Zapf Chancery*, 1979; *AMS Euler*, 1983; *Aurelia*, 1984; *Pan-Nigerian*, 1985; *Zapf Renaissance Roman*, 1985; *URW Roman*, 1985; *Sans Serif*, 1985; *AT&T Garamond*, 1988.

Publications:

By ZAPF: books—*William Morris: Sein Leben und Werk*, Lubeck 1949; *Das Blumen-ABC*, Frankfurt 1949; *Feder und Stichel*, Frankfurt 1950, 1952, as *Pen and Graver*, New York 1952; *Manuale Typographicum*, Frankfurt 1954, 1968, New York 1968, London and Cambridge,

Massachusetts 1970; *About Alphabets*, Frankfurt and New York 1960, London and Cambridge, Massachusetts 1970; *Typographische Variationen*, Frankfurt 1963, London and New York 1964, New Rochelle 1980; *Hunt Roman: The Birth of a Type*, Pittsburgh 1965; *Orbis Typographicus*, Prairie Village, Kansas 1980; *Hermann Zapf: Hora Fugit—Carpe Diem*, Darmstadt and Hamburg 1984; *Hermann Zapf and His Design Philosophy*, Chicago 1987.

On ZAPF: books—*Modern Lettering and Calligraphy*, edited by Rathbone Holme and Kathleen Frost, London and New York 1954; *Modern Book Design* by Ruari McLean, London 1958; *Hermann Zapf: Calligrapher, Type-Designer and Typographer*, exhibition catalogue by Noel Martin, Cincinnati 1960; *Who's Who in Graphic Art*, edited by Walter Amstutz, Zurich 1962, Dubendorf 1982; *Calligraphie et Typographie de Hermann Zapf*, exhibition catalogue, Brussels 1962; *Buchgestaltung* by Albert Kapr, Dresden 1963; *Design With Type* by Carl Dair, London and Toronto 1967; *Hermann Zapf: Kalligrafie, Drukletters en Typografische Verzorging*, exhibition catalogue by C. Reedijk, The Hague 1968; *The Salesman's Herald, Book 39: Dedicated to the Work of Hermann Zapf* by Edward Russell and David Brown, Stamford, Connecticut 1978; *The Thames and Hudson Manual of Typography* by Ruari McLean, London 1980; *A History of Graphic Design* by Philip B. Meggs, New York and London 1983; *Les Annees 60* by Anne Bony, Paris 1983; *Typographic Design: Form and Communication* by Rob Carter, Ben Day and Philip Meggs, New York 1985; *Eye for Industry: Royal Designers for Industry 1936-1986* by Fiona MacCarthy and Patrick Nuttgens, London 1986.

*

We don't create heroic things to earn fame. No scratches we put on the globe; perhaps with our gentle art, we add a few little dabs of joy into life, in a nicely written praise of the Lord, written with the complete engagement of our heart.

Calligraphy is a peaceful and noble art, done by well-educated human beings who do their work with full commitment, with intense concentration. For we want to put into our letters a little of our own feelings, of our personality and mood. Letters should have grace and beauty in themselves.

We see everywhere a growing interest is calligraphy. In the future, people will work fewer hours a day and hopefully, some may use their free time to do something creative with their hands.

A few more facts about us. No calligrapher is polluting rivers with his ink or is poisoning the air we breathe. Calligraphy makes no noise. We don't fight with arms nor with our pens, but we want to convince sometimes with a handwritten message of special importance in which we believe.

Of course, we know we are not the navel of the world; merely, we like to make nice things with our given talent. And we have a burden of responsibility, the heritage of the great masters of the past, the tradition of the scribes of the Middle Ages, of the royal and imperial ancestors in Europe and Asia. Calligraphy is still a royal activity.

—Hermann Zapf

*

As a typographer and type-designer, Hermann Zapf is probably most significant for his reintroduction of calligraphic detail and difference into the shapes and spacing of roman type design. More precisely, he has translated many of the qualities of Fraktur type—variety in the swell of the letter stroke, attention to the balance of curved and straight elements in each letter, and fluidity and vigor in line quality—into the more restricted forms of the Latin alphabet. Zapf's first type design was a Fraktur, Gilgengart, but his roman types, especially Palatino and Optima, display in their graceful swells and their slightly squared-off curves a mixture of past and present proportions that has led the way to a late-twentieth-century re-evaluation of the appropriateness of the serif type for virtually all aspects of typography, display as well as text.

Both Zapf's roman and sans serif faces emphasize varied letter widths, a fact that represents an innovative stance in the postwar period, which tended to be dominated by redesigns of the nineteenth-century grotesque sans serifs, which were characterized by, to quote Zapf, "a thoroughgoing equalization of all the letter-widths, rendering them to a certain degree uniform." Zapf's variety in both line quality and letter shape allowed a more active interaction between the paper and the printed letter, while large counters, the open letter spacing required by varied letter widths, and generous leading produced a distinctive German page, spacious and quiet, which has continued to typify German books and has influenced book design throughout the world.

Zapf also designed a Cyrillic face and an Arabic type, as well as display faces and a redrawing of Nicholas Kis's Janson type. He has continued to produce relevant designs for each of the new developments in the rapidly changing technology of the twentieth-century, designing for lead, for phototype (faces for International Typeface Corporation include Zapf Book and Zapf International), and now digital type design. He is working closely with the mathematician Donald Knuth on the Metafont program, which will allow computer generation of new letterforms, and their first face, for use mathematical publications, is named Euler. That Zapf works for a maximum of technical efficiency while maintaining as much non-technical variety as possible reflects his understanding of the value of innovation and of the human capacity to pay attention and to learn from distinctive detail, not uniformity.

—Frances Butler

ZEFFIRELLI, (Gian)Franco (Corsi).

Italian stage and film director and designer. Born in Florence, 12 February 1923. Educated at schools in Florence until 1939; studied painting, at the Accademia di Belle Arti, Florence, 1939–40; architecture, at the University of Florence, 1941–46. Worked as a radio and stage actor, appearing with the Morelli Stoppa Company, in Florence and Rome, 1946–47; film actor and designer, working with Luchino Visconti, Michelangelo Antonioni and Vittorio de Sica, in Rome, 1947–53; freelance stage director and designer, mainly of operas and Shakespearian plays, from 1951; film director and designer from 1957; contract director to Paramount Pictures, 1967–71. Member, Directors Guild of America. Address: Via Due Macelli 1, 00180 Rome, Italy.

Works:

Stage productions include—*A Streetcar Named Desire*, Morelli Stoppa Company, Rome, 1949; *Troilus and Cressida*, Morelli Stoppa Company, Rome, 1949; *The Three Sisters*, Morelli Stoppa Company, Rome, 1951; *La Cenerentola*, La Scala, Milan, 1953; *Lucia di Lammermoor*, Covent Garden, London, 1959; *Cavalliera Rusticana*, Covent Garden, London, 1959; *Romeo and Juliet*, Old Vic, London, 1960; *Othello*, Royal Shakespeare Company, Stratford-upon-Avon, 1961; *Falstaff*, Covent Garden, London, 1961; *L'Elisir d'Amore*, Glyndebourne Opera, Sussex, 1961; *Don Giovanni*, Covent Garden, London, 1962; *Alcina*, Covent Garden, London, 1962; *Romeo and Juliet*, City Center, New York, 1962; *The Lady of the Camellias*, Winter Gardens, New York, 1963; *Who's Afraid of Virginia Woolf?* Festival de Teatro, Venice, 1963; *After the Fall*, Rome, 1964; *Hamlet*, Old Vic, London, 1964; *Tosca*, Covent Garden, London, 1964; *Rigoletto*, Covent Garden, London, 1964; *Much Ado About Nothing*, Old Vic, London, 1965; *Norma*, Paris Opera, 1965; *The She Wolf*, Aldwych Theatre, London, 1969; *Don Giovanni*, Staatsoper, Vienna, 1972; *Otello*, Metropolitan Opera, New York, 1972; *Un Ballo in Maschera*, La Scala, Milan, 1972; *Pagliacci*, Covent Garden, London, 1973; *Saturday, Sunday, Monday*, Old Vic, London, 1973; *Antony and Cleopatra*, Metropolitan Opera, New York, 1973; *Otello*, La Scala, Milan, 1976; *Lorenzaccio*, Comedie Francaise, Paris, 1976; *Filumena*, Lyric Theatre, London, 1977; *Carmen*, Staatsoper, Vienna, 1978; *Turandot*, Metropolitan Opera, New York, 1987. Films include—*Giorni de Distruzione* (for TV), 1966; *Taming of the Shrew*, 1967; *Romeo and Juliet*, 1968; *Beethoven's Fidelio* (for TV), 1970; *Beethoven's Missa Solemnis* (for TV), 1970; *Brother Sun, Sister Moon*, 1973; *Jesus of Nazareth* (for TV), 1977; *The Champ*, 1979; *Endless Love*, 1981; *La Traviata*, 1982; *I Pagliacci* (for TV), 1984; *Otello*, 1986.

Publications:

By ZEFFIRELLI: books—*Jesus*, Paris and Montreal 1978: *Zeffirelli*, London 1986; articles—in *Films and Filming* (London), April 1973, August 1979; *Filmmakers Newsletter* (Ward Hill), September 1973.

On ZEFFIRELLI: books—*The Biographical Encyclopaedia and Who's Who of the American Theatre*, edited by Walter Rigdon, New York 1966; *The World Encyclopaedia of Film*, edited by Tim Cawkwell and John M. Smith, London 1972; *The Oxford Companion to Film*, edited by Liz-Anne Bawden, London and New York 1976; *Stage Design Throughout the World 1970–1975* by Rene Hainaux and Nicole Leclercq, Brussels and London 1976; *The International Film Encyclopedia* by Ephraim Katz, New York and London 1980; *International Dictionary of Films and Filmmakers*, Chicago and London 1984, 1991; *The Cambridge Guide to World Theatre*, edited by Martin Banham, Cambridge and New York 1988.

*

The important influences on the work of Franco Zeffirelli, aside from the cinematic style of his early mentor Luchino Visconti, have been the great artists of Italy's past from the Renaissance through the nineteenth century. From his early work as an actor, Zeffirelli gained a sense of a performance in action against a rich visual setting, and from his early apprenticeship in films, he learned the importance of the visual envelope that surrounds the actor. He soon began to practice his craft in the theatres and opera houses of Italy, and after his work for the Old Vic, he fully established his mature style of rich, romantic opulence of production. For example, in his production of *Romeo and Juliet*, he made the audience feel as if it were enveloped within the dust, light, color-atmosphere, and texture of Renaissance Verona. The same elements were at work when he filmed the production, and they were fully operative in the films *The Taming of the Shrew* and *Brother Sun, Sister Moon*. During the 1960s and 1970s, Zeffirelli's work came to be synonymous with richness and romantic opulence, and audiences looked forward to becoming a part of past times and faraway places as they watched the tapestry of his vision unroll upon the stage.

Zeffirelli is not an innovator but a conservator, a designer who takes the best from the great artists of Italy's past and recreates their esthetic for modern audiences. He projects no political or social values in his work, no innovative artistic ideals from the contemporary art world. He is a director-designer wedded to presenting a unified visual and aural vision of past times for modern audiences, hoping to make them appreciate with a new awareness the values of Baroque, Renaissance, and Romantic art as a basis for theatrical production. When one attends a Zeffirelli film or a Zeffirelli production of an opera or play, one has the sense that the artist at work on the stage is a direct inheritor of the vision of Titian, Rubens, or Guardi.

—Douglas A. Russell

ZEISEL, Eva.

American ceramic, furniture and product designer. Born Eva Polanyi Stricker, in Budapest, Hungary, in 1906; emigrated to the United States in 1938: naturalized, 1944. Studied painting under Vaszari, at the Royal Academy of Fine Arts, Budapest, 1923–25; apprenticed at Karapanscik's pottery, Budapest, 1924–25. Married Hans Zeisel in 1938; children: Jean and John. Ceramics designer, at Kispester Earthenware Factory, Budapest, 1926–27, Hansa Kunstkeramik, Hamburg, 1927, Schramberger Majolika Fabrik, Schramberg, 1928–30, Christian Carstens Kommerzial, Berlin, 1930–32; freelance designer and art director, working for the Lomanossova Porcelain Factory, Dulevo Porcelain Factory and the China and Glass Industry of the U.S.S.R., Leningrad, 1932–37; freelance designer, in New York and Chicago, from 1938: designed for Bay Ridge Specialty Company, Castleton China Company, Red Wing Pottery, Riverside Ceramic Company, Hall China Company, Rosenthal Porcelain, General Mills Company, Sears Roebuck, Loza Fina, Federal Glass Company, Mancioli, Noritake, Nikkon Toki, Zsolnay Factory, etc. Instructor in industrial design, Pratt Institute, Brooklyn, New York, 1939–55; professor, Rhode Island School of Design, Providence, 1954–55; guest lecturer, Royal College of Art, London, 1987–89. **Exhibitions:** Museum of Modern Art, New York, 1946; Walker Art Center, Minneapolis, 1947; Akron Art Institute, Ohio, 1947; Florida Gulf Coast Art Center, Clearwater, 1950; Brooklyn Museum, New York, 1957, 1984; Art Institute of Chicago, 1985; Flint Institute of Art, Michigan, 1985; New Jersey State Museum, Trenton, 1985; St. Louis Art Museum, Missouri, 1985; Everson Museum of Art, Syracuse, New York, 1986; Musée des Arts Decoratifs, Montreal, 1986; Museum of Decorative Arts, Budapest, 1987; Museum für Angewandte Kunst, Vienna, 1987; Konstindustrimuseum, Helsinki, 1987; Museum of Decorative Arts, Amersfoort, 1988; Stadt-

museum, Schramberg, 1988; Staatsmuseum, Karlsruhe, 1989; Keramik Museum, Metleach, 1989. **Collections:** Museum of Modern Art, New York; Victoria and Albert Museum, London. Recipient: Hungarian Exhibition Honor Award, Philadelphia, 1926; National Endowment for the Arts Senior Grant, Washington, D.C., 1982. Hungarian Order of the Star, Budapest, 1984; Honorary Doctorate, Royal College of Art, London, 1988. Address: 5825 South Dorchester Avenue, Chicago, Illinois 60637, U.S.A.

Works:

Pitcher in earthenware, for Schramberger Majolika Fabrik, 1929–30.
Tea service in yellow and red glazed porcelain, for Dulevo Porcelain Factory, 1934–36.
Tea service in black, yellow and orange underglazed porcelain, for Dulevo Porcelain Factory, 1934–36.
Diamond Design tea service in black and red underglazed porcelain, for Dulevo Porcelain Factory, 1934–36.
Museum dinner service in clear glazed porcelain, for Castleton China Company, 1942–43.
Town and Country earthenware dinner service, for Red Wing Pottery, 1945.
Hallcraft Tomorrow's Classic white glazed earthenware dinner service, for Hall China Company, 1949–50.
Chair in tubular steel, for Chicago Metalcraft/Richards Morgenthau and Company, 1950–51.
Stoneware dinner service, for Western Stoneware Company, 1952.
Hallcraft Century white glazed earthenware dinner service, for Hall China Company, 1955.
Form Eva white glazed porcelain dinner service, for Rosenthal Glas und Porzellan, 1957–58.
Lidded casserole, teapot and creamer in white and blue glazed porcelain, for Noritake, 1963.
Lidded bottle in porcelain, for Zsolnay Porcelain Factory, 1983.
Vase in porcelain, for Zsolnay Porcelain Factory, 1983.
Set of majolica bowls, for the Staatliche Majolika Manufaktur, 1989.

Publications:

By ZEISEL: articles—in *Die Schaulade* (Bamberg), February 1932; *Legkaia Industriia* (Moscow), 4 April 1936; *China, Glass and Lamps* (New York), June 1940, June 1941, May 1942; *Interiors* (New York), November 1941, July 1946; *Ceramic Age* (Olmsted), July 1942; *Crockery and Glass Journal* (New York), September 1945, February 1958; *Everyday Art Quarterly* (Minneapolis), Fall 1946.

On ZEISEL: books—*Modern China: New Designs by Eva Zeisel*, exhibition catalogue, New York 1946; *The Art of Interior Design* by Victoria Kloss Ball, New York 1960; *World Ceramics*, edited by Robert J. Charleston, London 1968, 1981; *One Hundred Great Product Designs* by Jay Doblin, New York 1970; *Design Since 1945*, edited by Kathryn Hiesinger and George Marcus, Philadelphia and London 1983; *Eva Zeisel: Designer for Industry* by Martin Eidelberg and others, Montreal and Chicago 1984; *The American Design Adventure 1940–1975* by Arthur J. Pulos, London and Cambridge, Massachusetts 1988.

My ideas on contemporary design? Too much has been written, too much, forbidden; too many principles have inhibited too much playfulness and have introduced too many idiosyncracies into the gentle endeavor of making beautiful and practical things, which can also be produced by our contemporary method of production. To design such things is a comfortable activity, one that has been enjoyed since time immemorial. But this activity flourished in a tacit atmosphere, a tolerant one, a joyful one—giving pleasure to the maker and his audience. The less said, the less written, the more pleasurable, the more practical will be our surroundings. Let's forget the word "functional" and the form-language for which it now stands.

—Eva Zeisel

For forty years, from the late 1920s to the late 1960s, Eva Zeisel held a position at the top of her profession as a china and glassware designer for industry. The list of factories that employed her includes the most prestigious and most prolific in the business—Schramberg and Rosenthal in Germany, Doulevo in the U.S.S.R., Universal, Red Wing, Castleton, and Hallcraft in the United States.

Although an intellectual working in Austria and Germany in the late 1920s and early 1930s, Zeisel did not join any academic group, such as the Bauhaus, as she preferred to work from inside industry rather than impose a set of values and standards from the outside. Her conviction that good design should be based on communication with an audience, as well as usefulness and esthetics, differentiated her attitude from the strictly functionalist philosophy of modernism.

Throughout her career, Zeisel continued as an independent designer, applying her talents to the problems at hand and seeking solutions which communicated with her audience. In an era inspired by machine iconography, Zeisel formulated a design philosophy based on familiar and friendly associations for the greatest number of people. For example, she examined the associations of lines and shapes with form and line in nature, with human proportions or reminiscences of classic forms, or with the order of geometry. Small deviations from these she felt could make the viewer uncomfortable.

During the postwar era in the United States, when a premium was placed on design of consumer goods for the home, Zeisel designed a broad range of wares. The most elegant of these, and the one that drew most acclaim, was a dinnerware set designed in collaboration with New York's Museum of Modern Art and Castleton China. This unusual circumstance was a result of the MOMA design department's orientation, under the direction of Eliot Noyes, both to raise quality and bring good design to the American public. The first contemporary, translucent, porcelain dinnerware produced in the United States for a general audience, the Museum White line competed with those of traditional European porcelain manufacturers such as Rosenthal. Its design relied on the company's technical proficiency for its thick-to-thin development from foot to rim and its blemish-free, shiny white glaze.

Throughout her career, Zeisel's designs have shown influences from the shapes and decoration of her native Hungary's traditional, handmade peasant pottery. Although drawn to both classic design and geometry, she brought an inventive playfulness to her work, which distinguished it from the stark geometry of her European contemporaries. Zeisel used the possibilities of industrial production to create complex relationships of shapes in families of ceramic forms. She sought to synthesize humanistic functionalism in timely designs, which were both pleasant to touch and easy to use.

As a teacher at Pratt Institute for many

Eva Zeisel: *Hallcraft Classic* ceramic tableware, for Hall China Company, 1952

years, Zeisel endorsed a design approach that drew on human resources and communication through objects. She relished making things for the pleasurable use of others, and those pursuits made her designs classics of their time.

—Sarah Bodine

ZIMMERMANN, Reinhardt.

German stage designer. Born in Erfurt, 1 March 1936. Trained as a stage set painter, at the Stadtische Buhnen, Erfurt, 1952–54, and as a set designer, at the Landestheater, Halle an der Saale, 1954–57. Married Nadeshda Denissowa in 1973; daughter: Sophie-Marija. Assistant to designer Rudolf Heinrich, 1957–61, resident designer, 1961–63, and head of stage design from 1963, at the Komische Oper, East Berlin. Chairman of the DDR section, Organisation Internationale des Scenographes et des Techniciens de Theatre. **Exhibitions:** Prague Quadriennale of Scenography, 1967, 1971, 1976, 1979, 1983. **Collection:** Markisches Museum, Berlin. Recipient: *Berliner Zeitung* Critics' Prize, 1976; DDR National Prize, Berlin, 1976. Address: Kustrinerstrasse 65, 1125 Berlin, German Democratic Republic.

Works:

Stage productions (at the Komische Oper, Berlin, unless noted) include—*Cosi fan Tutte*, 1962; *Der fliegende Holländer*, Opernhaus, Leipzig, 1962 (travelled to Bolschoi Theater, Moscow, 1963); *Boris Godunow*, Opernhaus, Leipzig, 1964; *Jenufa*, 1964, Königliche Oper, Stockholm, 1972, Opéra de Paris, 1980; *Lohengrin*, Opernhaus, Leipzig, 1965; *Heimkehr des Odysseus*, 1966; *Don Giovanni*, 1966; *Der junge Lord*, 1968; *Simone Boccanegra*, Königliches Theater, Copenhagen, 1968; *Salome*, Theater der Freien Hansestadt, Bremen, West Germany, 1968; *Aida*, 1969, and at Holland Festival, Amsterdam, 1973; *Falstaff*, Norske Opera, Oslo, 1969, and at Holland Festival, Amsterdam, 1972; *Porgy and Bess*, 1969; *Der tolle Tag*, Deutsches Theater, Berlin, 1970; *Hoffmanns Erzähhungen*, for GDR television, Berlin, 1970, Norske Opera, Oslo, 1974; *Eugen Onegin*, Königliches Theater, Copenhagen, 1970; *Undine*, 1970; *Macht des Schicksals*, 1971; *Troubadour*, Königliches Theater, Copenhagen, 1971; *Don Quichotte*, 1971; *Romeo and Juliet*, 1972; *Hary Janos*, 1973; *Die Wahlverwandtschaften*, DEFA film studio, East Berlin, 1973; *Figaros Hochzeit*, 1975; *Moses und Aron*, Staatsoper, Dresden, 1975; *Lulu*, 1975, complete version, 1980; *Aufstieg und Fall der Stadt Mahagonny*, 1977; *Erdgeist und Büchse der Pandora*, Schauspielhaus, Graz, Austria, 1977; *Madame Butterfly*, 1978 (travelled to the Welsh National Opera, Cardiff); *Nachtasyl*, Schauspielhaus, Graz, Austria, 1978; *Fidelio*, English National Opera, London, 1980; *Peter Grimes*, 1981; *La Bohème*, 1982; *Lear*, 1983.

Publications:

By ZIMMERMAN: articles—in *Jahrbuch der Komische Oper*, Berlin 1968, 1969; *Walter Felsenstein Inszeniert Mozart: Die Hochzeit des Figaro*, Berlin 1981.

On ZIMMERMAN: article—in *Opernwelt Jahrbuch*, Berlin 1970.

Just as the actors, singers, dancers, words, music, gestures, costumes and lighting all are parts, stage design is a part, but only a part, of the complete artistic performance. To achieve a unified whole, it is necessary to have the creative cooperation of many people, all of whom must want the same thing, namely, to make the work comprehensible to the public. The director and stage designer, as equal authorities in charge of the production, must devote themselves to this task.

The director should be able to envision the finished product, while the stage designer must be able to comprehend clearly the thoughts of the director. Both should attempt to develop their ideas out of the work itself and to test the results again and again on the work. They should be able to recognize and understand what the author—or composer—was trying to achieve, to comprehend his times and state of existence, and to know where they now find themselves and what is happening around them. Only then can a unification of a faithfulness to the work and contemporaneity occur and be successfully transmitted to the audience.

—Reinhart Zimmermann

For two decades, Reinhart Zimmermann has counted among the leading stage designers of the German Democratic Republic in the field of musical theatre. He was decisively influenced by his work as assistant to the important stage designer Rudolf Heinrich. One finds traces of this collabortion chiefly in Zimmermann's fundamentally intellectual and aesthetic attitude: a hallmark of his work is the opulent balance between fantasy and energy of form, stemming

Reinhart Zimmermann: Stage set for Puccini's *La Boheme*, Komische Oper, Berlin, 1982

from a basic dramaturgic analysis. In his best works, which arise mainly from his collaboration with leading producers, such as Walter Felsenstein (*Don Giovanni, Hary Janos, The Marriage of Figaro*) Joachim Herz (*The Young Lord, Lulu, Peter Grimes*), Götz Friedrich (Siegfried Matthus's *The Last Shot, The Return of Odysseus*, Massenet's *Don Quixote*), and Harry Kupfer (*Moses and Aaron* in Dresden, *La Bohème*, and Reimann's *Lear*), Zimmermann's creative energy and ability are clearly evident, making specific and cohesive connections with the work. The most creative principle in Zimmermann's design work is to assist the expression of a production's spirit and essence. His works are understood as functionally and aesthetically integrated into the total artistic performance. Zimmermann is concerned with strong synthetic effect, based on a meaningful dovetailing of production, musical interpretation, performance, and decor. As a designer, he does not strive for any symbolic encoding of the scene but for clarity of staging which effectively speeds the action, for a precisely registered social atmosphere and interpretative accent.

—Wolfgang Lange

ZIPPRODT, Patricia.

American stage and film costume designer. Born in Evanston, Illinois, in 1925. Studied at Wellesley College, Massachusetts, 1943–46: BA 1946; School of the Art Institute of Chicago, 1946–49; Art Students League, New York, 1950–52; Fashion Institute of Technology, New York, 1952–53. Worked as an assistant to stage designers Rouben Ter-Arutunian, William and Jean Eckart, Boris Aronson, Robert Fletcher and Irene Sharaff, in New York, 1953–57; freelance costume designer, New York, from 1957: artistic advisor to the Ballet Hispanico, New York, from 1975. Professor of theatre design, University of Utah, Salt Lake City; also visiting lecturer at colleges and universities throughout the United States. **Exhibitions:** Wright Hepburn Gallery, London, 1966; Capricorn Gallery, New York, 1968; Museum of the City of New York, 1972; University of California, San Diego, 1974; *International Stage Design*, Toneel Museum, Amsterdam, 1975; *American Stage Design*, Lincoln Center, New York, 1975 (toured); *American Ballet Theatre*, New York, 1976 (toured). **Collection:** Museum of the City of New York. Recipient: Antoinette Perry Tony Award, New York, 1964, 1966, 1984; Drama Desk Award, New York, 1968, 1972, 1978; Emmy Television Award, New York, 1969; Wellesley College Alumnae Achievement Award, 1971; New England Theatre Conference Award of Excellence, 1973; Fashion Institute of Technology Ritter Award, New York, 1977; Joseph P. Maharam Award, New York, 1969, 1983, 1984; Southeastern Theatre Conference Career Award, 1985. Address: 29 King Street, New York, New York 10014, U.S.A.

Works:

Stage productions (New York, unless noted) include—*The Potting Shed*, 1957; *A Visit to a Small Planet*, 1957; *The Virtuous Island*, 1957; *The Apollo of Bellac*, 1957; *Miss Lonely-hearts*, 1957; *The Rope Dancers*, 1957; *The Crucible*, 1958; *Back to Methuselah*, 1958; *The Night Circus*, 1958; *Our Town*, 1958; *The Gang's All

Here, 1959; *The Balcony*, 1960; *Camino Real*, 1960; *Period of Adjustment*, 1960; *The Blacks*, 1961; *The Garden of Sweets*, 1961; *Laurette*, 1961; *Sunday in New York*, 1961; *Madame Aphrodite*, 1961; *Ah Dad, Poor Dad, Mama's Hung You in the Closet and I'm Feelin' So Sad*, 1962; *A Man's a Man*, 1962; *The Matchmaker*, 1962; *Step on a Crack*, 1962; *The Dragon*, 1963; *She Loves Me*, 1963; *Morning Sun*, 1963; *Next Time I'll Sing to You*, 1963; *Too Much Johnson*, 1964; *Fiddler on the Roof*, 1964; *The Tragical Historie of Dr. Faustus*, 1964; *Anya*, 1965; *Pousse-Café*, 1966; *Cabaret*, 1966; *The Little Foxes*, 1967; *Fiddler on the Roof* (London), 1967; *Plaza Suite*, 1968; *Zorba*, 1968; *Gianni Schicchi* (opera), 1969; *The Tale of Kasane*, 1969; *Blueprints*, 1969; *1776*, 1969; *Georgy*, 1970; *Scratch*, 1971; *Pippin*, 1972; *The Mother of Us All* (opera), 1972; *Waiting for Godot* (Minneapolis, Minnesota), 1973; *Pippin* (London), 1973; *Dear Nobody*, 1974; *Mack and Mabel*, 1974; *All God's Chillun Got Wings*, 1975; *Chicago*, 1975; *Poor Murderer*, 1976; *Four Saints in Three Acts*, National Theatre of the Deaf, 1976; *Tannhauser*, 1977; *Naughty Marietta*, 1978; *Stages*, 1978; *King of Hearts*, 1978; *Swing*, 1979; *One Night Stand*, 1980; *Kingdoms*, 1981; *Fools*, 1981; *Whodunnit*, 1982; *The Barber of Seville*, 1982; *Alice in Wonderland*, 1982; *Don Juan*, Tyrone Guthrie Theatre, Minneapolis, 1982; *Sunset*, 1983; *Brighton Beach Memoirs*, 1983; *The Glass Menagerie*, 1983; *Accidental Death of an Anarchist*, 1984; *Anna Christie*, Central Theatre Institute, Beijing, 1984: *Sunday in the Park with George*, 1984; *The Loves of Don Perlimplin*, San Francisco Opera, 1984. Ballets—*Les Noces*, American Ballet Theatre, 1965; *La Sonnambula*, National Ballet, 1965; *Watermill*, New York City Ballet, 1972; *Dumbarton Oaks*, New York City Ballet, 1973; *Bybbuk Variations*, New York City Ballet, 1974; *The Leaves Are Fading*, American Ballet Theatre, 1975; *Tres Cantos*, Ballet Hispanico, 1976; *Caprichos*, Ballet Hispanico, 1976; *Estuary*, American Ballet Theatre, 1983; *Llamada*, Ballet Hispanico, 1983; *Tito on Tambales*, Ballet Hispanico, 1984.

Publications:

By ZIPPRODT: articles—in *Contemporary Stage Design USA*, New York 1974; *Theatre Crafts* (New York), 1971, 1973, 1974, 1977.

On ZIPPRODT: books—*Contemporary Theatre, Film and Television 2*, Detroit 1986; *The Cambridge Guide to World Theatre*, edited by Martin Banham, Cambridge and New York 1988.

Patricia Zipprodt might be considered a director's designer because she epitomizes the ideal, so often preached in conservatories and schools of design, that the costume designer should subordinate personal design preferences or stylistic approaches to those of the play and the director. She is thus unlike Robert Edmond Jones, Leon Bakst, and Gordon Craig, who are known for developing personal styles and personal philosophic approaches to theatrical design.

When the work of Jean Genet was very little known in this country, she designed the original New York production of *The Balcony* and *The Blacks* and created such distinctive costumes that they have come to be accepted as the "right" way to interpret the intertwined, mirror-reflecting realities of this absurdist. When Zipprodt worked on the musical *Pippin*, she faced, with the director and the choreographer, the seemingly insoluble problem of creating breast-plates and armor for an extremely active chorus. Not to be deterred, she worked with one of

the costume profession's finest craftsmen on a new form of completely flexible, rubber latex to make armor that broke new ground for costuming. In this case, the new product dictated the nature of her designs rather than the reverse. When she worked on the original production of *Fiddler on the Roof* for Broadway, she let the nature of the material, the background stories behind the libretto, and the music lead her to a collaboration with the director, choreographer, librettist, and composer to produce a completely cohesive visual whole in which the costumes presented the Russian texture and ethnic Jewish flavor that seemed absolutely appropriate. Other examples as well would demonstrate that Zipprodt never appears to have a distinctive, personal style because she always subordinates herself to explorations and decisions made in consultation. Her artistic position is clear: Costume design today is a collaborative art.

—Douglas A. Russell

ZWART, Piet.

Dutch photographer, architectural, interior and graphic designer. Born in Zaandijk, 28 May 1885. Studied at the Rijksschool voor Kunstnijverheid, Amsterdam, 1902–07; Technische Hogeschool, Delft, 1913–14. Served in the Dutch Army, 1908, 1914–17. Married Nel Cleyndert: 4 children. Furniture and interior designer from 1911, photographer and designer from 1919, and typographer from 1921, working in Leeuwarden, 1909–13, in Voorburg, 1913–26, and in Wassenaar, 1927–77; assistant in the office of architect Jan Wils, 1919–21, and in the office of H. P. Berlage, The Hague, 1921–27; designed for Dutch Posts and Telecommunications, Lagafabriek flooring, Nederlandsche Kabelfabriek, Bruynzeel Company, Kristal Unie, Scheveningen Radio, Trio Printers, etc. Instructor in drawing and art history, at the Industrie- en Huishoudschool voor Meisjes, Leeuwarden, 1909–19; instructor in design and ornament, Academie voor Beeldende Kunsten en Technische Wetenschappen, Rotterdam, 1919–23; visiting instructor, Technische Hogeschool, Delft, 1929, and at the Staatliche Bauhaus, Dessau, 1931. Architecture correspondent, *Het Vaderland* newspaper, Amsterdam, 1925–28; president, De 8 en Opbouw architects' group, Amsterdam, 1931–37. **Exhibitions:** Drukkerij Trio, The Hague, 1933; Stedelijk Museum, Amsterdam, 1961; Haags Gemeentemuseum, The Hague, 1968, 1973 (toured), 1985; Wassenaarse Galerie-Bibliotheek, Wassenaar, 1974; Ex Libris, New York, 1980. **Collections:** Piet Zwart Archive, Prentenkabinet, Leiden University; Haags Gemeentemuseum, The Hague; Stedelijk Museum, Amsterdam; Museum Folkwang, Essen; Kestner-Gesellschaft, Hannover. Recipient: Quellinus Typography Prize, 1959; David Roell Prize, 1964. Honorary Royal Designer for Industry, Royal Society of Arts, London, 1966. *Died (in Leidschendam) 24 September 1977.*

Publications:

By ZWART: books—*Filmreclame*, Rotterdam, 1933; *Documents in the Visual Arts, Vol. 1: Piet Zwart*, with texts by F. Muller and P. E. Althaus, Teufen 1966; *Piet Zwart: 12 Fotografien*,

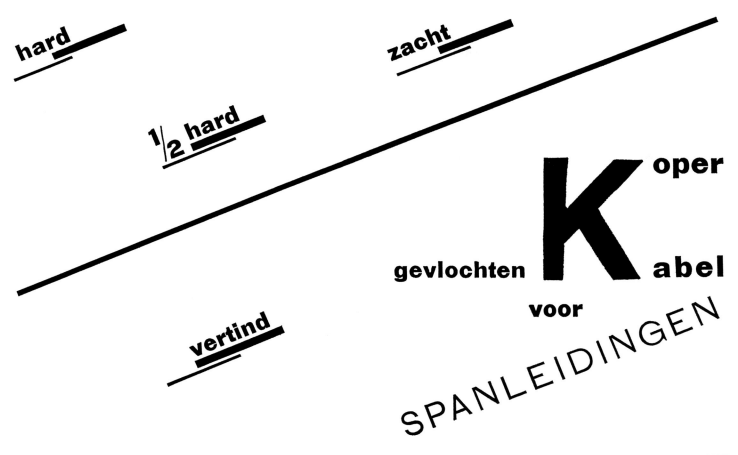

N.V. NEDERLANDSCHE KABELFABRIEK DELFT

Piet Zwart: Advertisement for Nederlandsche Kabelfabriek, 1928

portfolio, with an introduction by Kees Broos, Cologne 1974. books designed—*De Absolute Film* by Ter Braaks, Rotterdam 1931; *De Techniek van de Kunstfiilm* by Mannus Franken and Joris Ivens, Rotterdam 1931; *Wij Slaven van Suriname* by Anton de Kok, Rotterdam 1934; and other books in the series *Monografien over Filmkunst*, for W. L. & J. Brusse Publishers, Rotterdam 1931–34; also numerous publications for Nederlandse Kabelfabriek, Delft; the Dutch PTT, The Hague; Bruynzeel Company, Zaandam; Drukkerij Trio, The Hague; Nijgh & Van Ditmar, Rotterdam; De 8 en Opbouw, Amsterdam.

On ZWART: books—*Die Neue Typografie* by Jan Tschichold, Berlin 1928; *Eine Stunde Druckgestaltung* by Jan Tschichold, Stuttgart 1930; *The New Graphic Design* by Karl Gerstner and Markus Kutter, Teufen and London 1959; *Piet Zwart: Typotekt*, exhibition catalogue designed by Otto Treumann and Wim Crouwel, Amsterdam 1961; *Sleutelwoorden/Keywords: Piet Zwart*, edited by Jurrian Schrofer and Will Sandberg, The Hague 1965; *Piet Zwart* by Fridolin Muller, New York 1966; *Piet Zwart en PTT*, exhibition catalogue by Karst Zwart, The Hague 1968; *Pioneers of Modern Typography* by Herbert Spencer, London 1969; *A History of Visual Communication* by Josef Muller-Brockmann, New York 1971; *Piet Zwart*, exhibition catalogue by Kees Broos, The Hague 1973; *Fotografie in Nederland 1920–1940*, exhibition catalogue by Flip Bool and Kees Broos, The Hague 1979; *Tub-*

ular Steel Furniture, edited by Barbie Campbell-Cole and Tim Benton, London 1979; *Piet Zwart: Typotekt*, exhibition catalogue with introduction by Arthur Cohen, New York 1980; *Retrospective Fotografie: Piet Zwart* by Kees Broos, Dusseldorf 1981; *Piet Zwart 1885–1977* by Kees Broos, Amsterdam 1982; *The Twentieth-Century Poster: Design of the Avant-Garde* by Dawn Ades, New York 1984; *Typographic Design: Form and Communication* by Rob Carter, Ben Day and Philip Meggs, New York 1985.

Before joining Jan Wils, a member of the de Stijl group, as an assistant in 1919 at the age of 34, Piet Zwart had already carried out a few minor furniture designs in the style of Berlage, Dijsselhof, and Bazel. The influence of de Stijl can clearly be seen in the first typographical design (a letterhead for Wils) which he executed at that time. In 1921, Zwart became assistant to the famous Dutch architect, H. P. Berlage, with whom he collaborated on the construction of a Christian Science church and on early designs for a municipal museum, both in the Hague. While working in Berlage's office, Zwart produced his first advertisement designs, for a firm of flooring manufacturers in the Hague, and carried out his first commissions for industrial design. About this time, too, he designed a brochure for Fortoliefabriek in Utrecht. Berlage then introduced Zwart to one of his relatives who was manager of the Nederlandsche Kabelfabriek (NKF) at Delft, and by 1925, at the age of forty, Zwart had begun to

devote the greater part of his time to typography. During the next few years, he produced many hundreds of designs for advertisements and catalogues for the Nederlandsche Kabelfabriek. These designs, like the earlier Wils letterhead, make use of heavy rules and strong contrasts.

Zwart had an extraordinary ability to organise layout so that essential information could be grasped by the reader with the minimum of effort. He made increasingly effective use of imaginative photography (after 1938, his own), and this became a major interest for him. Photography plays an important part in much of the graphic design, including stamps, he executed for the Dutch Post Office from 1928 onwards.

Zwart's designs for Nederlandse Kabelfabrick catalogues and booklets and for the Dutch post office are full of vigorous and imaginative surprises. His colours are those of de Stijl—primary blue, yellow, and red—but Zwart's clever use of words, his ingenious manipulation of type and printer's rules, his dramatic use of strong-contrast photographs and of negative reproductions, the dexterity with which he superimposed photographs in one strong colour over other photographs in other colours, his use of transparent materials, of cut-out shapes and clever folds, and, indeed, the whole uninhibited, pioneering enthusiasm of his attack suddenly charged the printed page with a new power, a new tension and gave it in effect a new dimension.

—Herbert Spencer

NOTES ON ADVISERS AND CONTRIBUTORS

AAV, Marianne. Essayist. Principal Curator, Museum of Applied Arts, Helsinki. Author of several catalogues on twentieth-century Finnish craft and design. **Essay:** Kukkasjarvi.

ADAMS, Sandra Michels. Essayist. Instructor in History of Costume, School of the Art Instutute of Chicago; clothing designer, in the collaboration Dress Code; and freelance costume specialist (exhibit consultant, lecturer, and teacher), all since 1982. Display designer and fashion coordinator, Marshall Field and Company, Oak Park, Illinois, 1976–79; Assistant to the Curator of Costumes, Chicago Historical Society, 1979–82. **Essays:** Balenciaga, Galanos, Norell, Trigère, Vionnet.

ALEXANDER, James M. Essayist. Professor of Industrial Design, since 1947, and head of Industrial Design, 1948–76. University of Cincinnati, Ohio; also freelance architect and designer. Detailer, designer, and planner, Raymond Loewy Associates, New York, 1942, 1946–47; director, Design Research Collaborative, University of Cincinnati, 1964–75. Author of numerous articles in professional journals. **Essay:** Loewy.

ARONSON, Arnold. Essayist. Professor of Drama, University of Virginia; co-editor, *Theatre Design and Technology.* Professional Stage manager, 1969–75; assistant editor, *The Drama Review,* 1974–76. Author of *The History and Theory of Environmental Scenography,* 1981. **Essays:** Eugene Lee, Loquasto, Schmidt.

ARSENAULT, Andrea. Adviser and essayist. Fashion instructor, School of the Art Institute of Chicago; also freelance fashion designer **Essays:** Ashley, de Castelbajac, Rhodes.

ASHWIN, Clive. Essayist. Dean of the Faculty of Education and Performing Arts, Middlesex Polytechnic. Editor of *Art Education: Documents and Policies,* 1975; author of *Drawing and Education in German-Speaking Europe 1800–1900,* 1975; *Encyclopaedia of Drawing,* 1982; and *History of Graphic Design and Communication: A Source Book,* 1983. **Essays:** Eckersley, Havinden, Holland.

AUBÖCK, Carl. Essayist and entrant. See his own entry. **Essay:** Ekuan.

BARNICOAT, John. Essayist. Principal, Chelsea School of Art, London, since 1980. Senior tutor in painting, Royal College of Art, London, 1976–80. Author of *A Concise History of Posters,* 1972. **Essays:** Aldridge, Brattinga, Carlu, Chwast, Colin, Edelmann, Fletcher, Games, Glaser, Müller-Brockmann.

BENHAMOU, REED. Essayist. Professor of Interior Design, Purdue University, West Lafayette, Indiana, since 1978; editorial board member. *Journal of Interior Design Education and Research,* since 1979. **Essays:** Deskey, Graves, Kjaerholm, Jacobsen, Mourgue, Robsjohn-Gibbings, Wegner.

BLAUENSTEINER, Charlotte. Essayist. Secretary General, Osterreichisches Institut für Formgebung, Vienna, since 1958. **Essay:** Auböck.

BODINE, Sarah. Essayist. Freelance editor and writer; lecturer, University of the Arts, Philadelphia, since 1968; editor, *Documents of American Design,* since 1985; contributor, *AIGA Journal, Design Book Review, Industrial Design* and *American Ceramics* magazines. Exhibition coordinator, Andrew Dickson White Museum of Art, Cornell University, Ithaca, New York 1970–71, and Leonard Hutton Gallery, New York, 1971–73; craft editor, Watson-Guptil publications, 1973–76; senior editor, Whitney Library of Design, 1976–79; contributing editor to *Metropolis* magazine, 1980–87. **Essays:** Agha, Agnes B., Ambasz, Grotell, Leach, Maldonado, Nelson, Paul, Pineles, Pulos, Rams, Wallance, Wirkkala, Zeisel.

BOJKO, Szymon. Essayist. Freelance art and design critic, Warsaw. Board member, responsible for design education, State Council of Industrial Design, Warsaw, 1960–67; editorial board member, *Projekt* magazine, Warsaw, 1969–74; editor, *Polish Art Review,* Warsaw, 1971–72; also formerly visiting lecturer in visual communication, School of Design, Lódź, Poland. Author of *Art of the Polish Poster,* 1972; *New Graphic Design in Revolutionary Russia,* 1972; *The Polish Poster,* 1973; co-author of *Mass Culture,* 1976; editor of *Art as Environment,* 1972; also contributor to many art and design journals in Poland and abroad. **Essays:** Balicki, Danziger, Duszek, Folon, Górowski, Kamekura, Kemény, Lenk, Mentula, Pawlowski, Telingater, Zamecznik.

BOMAN, Monica. Essayist. Freelance editor and writer, Stockholm. Editor, *Form* magazine, 1973–76; also worked for the HSB Housing cooperative, and the Swedish National Board for Consumer Politics. Editor of *Design in Sweden,* 1985; *Design Art,* 1988. **Essay:** Axelsson.

BREMER, Nina. Essayist. Instructor, University of Bridgeport, Connecticut, since 1979. Formerly, instructor, Lehman College, Bronx, New York, and Hunter College, New York; freelance lecturer for Museum of Modern Art, New York, for Knoll International, for United Nations groups, and for other museums. **Essays:** Breuer, Chermayeff and Geismar Associates, Federico, Noyes, Risom.

BURIAN, Jarka M. Essayist. Professor, Department of Theatre, State University of New York at Albany, since 1955. Formerly, producer and artistic director, Albany Arena Theatre. Author of *Americke Drama a Divadelnictvi* [American drama and theatre], 1966; *The Scenography of Josef Svoboda,* 1971; *Svoboda: Wagner,* 1983. **Essays:** Bury, Farrah, Herbert, Koltai, Napier, O'Brien/Firth, Svoboda, Szajna, Vychodil.

BUTLER, Frances. Essayist and entrant. See her own entry. **Essays:** Manwaring, Mardersteig, Zapf.

BYRNE, Elizabeth Douthitt. Essayist. Librarian and Head of the Environmental Design Library, University of California at Berkeley, since 1984. Head of the Art Library, University of Louisville, Kentucky, 1970–71; Assistant Head of Fine Arts, Detroit Public Library, 1972–76; Head of the Design, Architecture, Art and Planning Library, University of Cincinnati, Ohio, 1978–84. Co-author of *Great Cooks of the Western World,* 1977. **Essays:** Butler, Colombo, de la Renta.

CAPLAN, Ralph. Essayist. Freelance writer and communication design consultant, New York. Editor in Chief, *Industrial Design* magazine, 1958–62. Author of *Design in America,* 1969; *The Design Necessity,* 1972; *The Design of Herman Miller,* 1976; *Chair,* 1978; *By Design,* 1982. **Essay:** Stumpf.

CARLS, Ken. Essayist. Professor of Graphic Design, University of Illinois at Urbana-Champaign, since 1978. **Essays:** Monguzzi, Wright.

CARLSEN, Peter. Essayist. Freelance writer and commentator on design, fashion, and the visual arts, New York City, for the *New York Magazine, New York, Architectural Digest, Gentlemen's Quarterly, Art News,* and others. Author of *Manstyle* compendium of men's fashion, 1978, and *Design Quarterly* monograph on Joseph Paul D'Urso, 1984. **Essays:** Ellis, Ferré, Hipp, Saladino, Shamask, Sottsass, Versace.

CARRINGTON, Noel (died, 1989). Essayist. Retired former editor and art consultant to Penguin Books, Roxe Publications, and others. Member, Design Council, London, 1948–55. Author of *Design*, 1935; *Design in the Home*, 1938; *The Shape of Things*, 1939; *Colour in the Home*. 1947; *Industrial Design in Britain*, 1976; co-author of *The Face of the Land*, 1930; *Popular English Art*, 1944; *Life in the English Village*, 1949; and others. **Essays:** Meynell, Russell.

CASCIANI, Stefano. Essayist. Freelance writer on art and design, Milan. **Essays:** Bonetto, Pininfarina, Ruggeri.

CAVALIERE, Barbara. Essayist. Freelance writer on art and design, New York City. Associate editor, *Womanart* magazine (New York), 1976–78; contributing editor, *Arts Magazine* (New York), 1976–83. Fellowship in art criticism, National Endowment for the Arts, 1979–80. Author of exhibition catalogues for *Abstract Expressionism: The Formative Years*, Ithaca, New York, 1978; *William Baziotes: A Retrospective*, Newport Beach, California, 1978; *Stamos: Paintings 1958–60*. New York, 1981; *Theodoros Stamos: On the Horizon of Mind and Coast*, Aachen, West Germany, 1984. Contributor to *Flash Art, Soho Weekly News, High Performance*, and other magazines, to *Contemporary Artists* edited by Muriel Emmanuel and others, 1983, and to *Academic American Encyclopedia*. **Essays:** Albers, Armani, Basile, Bill, Blass, Cardin, de Givenchy, Donati, du Bois, Fiorucci, Fuller, Gibb, Hardwick, Head, Mandelli, McFadden, Montana, Mugler, Soprani, Ungaro.

CLARK, Hazel. Essayist. Assistant Registrar for Art and Design, Council for National Academic Awards. Research assistant in design history, Brighton Polytechnic, 1978–82; Lecturer in Design, Fashion and Textile History, Brighton Polytechnic and Ravensbourne College of Art, Kent, 1981–83. Founder-committee member, Textile Society, since 1982. **Essays:** Bohan, Collier/Campbell, Courrèges, Erté, Karan/Dell'Olio, Kenzo, Khanh, Lauren, Miyake, Mori, Rabanne, Rykiel, Saint Laurent, Yamamoto.

CONSTANTINE, Mildred. Essayist. Independent consultant on art, architecture, and design to museums, universities, and industry. Assistant to the Director, secretary of traveling exhibitions, and editorial assistant on the *Art Bulletin* and *Parnassus*. College Art Association, New York, 1930–37; Curator, Department of Architecture and Design and Special Assistant to the Director, Museum of Modern Art, New York, 1948–71. Author or editor of *Art Nouveau*, 1959; *Sign Language*, 1961; *Lettering by Modern Artists*, 1963; *The Object Transformed*, 1963; *Word and Image*, 1967; *Wall Hangings*, 1969; *Beyond Craft: The Art Fabric*, 1973; *Soviet Film Posters*, 1974; *Tina Modotti: A Fragile Life*, 1975, 1978; and *The Art Fabric: Mainstream*, 1981. **Essays:** Delaunay, Dreyfuss, Hurlburt, Larsen, Lionni, Mavignier, Terrazas, Vignelli, Yokoo.

CONWAY, Hazel. Essayist. Principal Lecturer in Design History, Leicester Polytechnic, since 1980. Open University Course Tutor in History of Architecture and Design, 1975–76; Chairman, Design History Publications Sub-Committee of the Association of Art Historians, 1978–81. Author of *Ernest Race*, 1982. **Essay:** Eileen Gray.

COULSON, Anthony J. Essayist. Liaison Librarian (Arts), Open University Library, since 1970. Author of *A Bibliography of Design in Britain, 1851–1970*, 1979, and of project, literature, and library guides for Open University published courses. **Essays:** Archer, Bawden, Black, Design Research Unit, Milner Gray.

CURRIER, Catherine L. Essayist. Graduate student in art history (special program in history of design), University of Cincinnati, Ohio. Editor, Providence College art journal *Interface*, 1983. **Essay:** Crouwel.

DAHLBACK LUTTEMAN, Helena. Essayist. Keeper of the Department of Applied Art, at the Nationalmuseum, Stockholm. Author of *Svenskt Porslin/Svensk Keramix*, 1980; *Majolika fran Urbino*, 1981; *Svenskt Silver*, 1989. **Essays:** Bjorquist, Bulow-Hube, Cyren, Hoglund.

DAVID-WEST, Haig. Essayist and entrant. See his own entry. **Essay:** Betanova.

DEL RENZIO, Toni. Essayist. Director and Professor, British Studies Centre of the Institute of American Universities, since 1982. Principal lecturer in charge of the Department of History of Art/Design and Complementary Studies, Canterbury College of Art, 1975–80; has also taught at the Camberwell School of Arts and Crafts, Bath Academy of Art, and Chelsea School of Art, London. Author of numerous articles on art and design in *Architectural Design, Architectural Review, Art and Artists, Art International, Che Fare, Horizon, Interior Design, Studio International, Art Monthly*, and others. **Essays:** Franco Albini; Bega; Bertoia; Cadbury-Brown; Carmi; Livio Castiglioni; Chamberlin, Powell and Bon; Chessa; Confalonieri; Frattini; Fronzoni; Gill; Giugiaro; Gregotti; Heckroth; Huber; Lennon, Mangiarotti; Noorda; Parisi; Pentagram; Pintori; Toms.

DE MARLY, Diana. Essayist. Regular guest lecturer, Department of History of Dress, Courtauld Institute of Art, University of London, since 1970. Lecturer, London College of Fashion, 1971–73; Croydon College of Art, 1973–75; Susette Taylor Research Fellow, Lady Margaret Hall, University of Oxford, 1977–78, and guest of the German Academic Exchange. Author of *The History of Haute Couture 1850–1950*, 1980; *Charles Frederick Worth, A Biography*, 1980; and *Costume on the Stage; Reform Movements in Relation to Artistic Theory, 1600–1940*, 1982. **Essays:** Adolfo, Asquith, Balmain, Barrie, Bates, Beene, Beretta, Burrows, Chadwick, Chanel, Conran, de Luca, Duffy-Eley-Giffone-Worthington, Grès, Halston, Issigonis, Kamali, Kneebone, Lagerfeld, Lancetti, Lord, Mainbochen, Manasseh, Muir, Noble, Rowlands, Sant'Angelo, Stevens, Tan Guidicelli, Thomass, Woudhuysen.

DIECKMANN, Friedrich. Essayist. Writer, East Berlin. Dramaturge, Berliner Ensemble, 1972–76. Author of *Karl von Appens Bühnenbilder am Berliner Ensemble*, 1971; *Streifzüge*, 1972, and *Theaterbilder*, 1979; editor of *Bühnenbilder der DDR*, 1978. **Essays:** Sagert, von Appen.

DROSTE, M. Essayist. Research assistant, Bauhaus-Archiv, Berlin, since 1980. Author of exhibition catalogues for *Klee and Kandinsky*, Stuttgart, 1979; *George Muche; Das künstlerische Werk, 1912–1927*, Berlin, 1980; and *Herbert Bayer; Das künstlerische Werk, 1912–1938*, Berlin, 1981. **Essays:** Bayer, Blase, Kapitzki, Wagenfeld.

EKUAN, Kenji. Adviser and entrant. See his own entry.

ENBOM, Carla. Essayist. Freelance writer on design and applied arts, Stockholm. **Essays:** Piri, Puotila.

ENGELBRECHT, Lloyd C. Essayist. Professor of History of Design, Art History Department, University of Cincinnati, Ohio, and Curator of the Design Archives, Archives and Rare Books Department, University of Cincinnati Libraries. Professor, Bradley University, Peoria, Illinois, 1970–73; Indiana State University, Terre Haute, 1973–77; Wichita State University, Kansas, 1977–78. Author, with June F. Englebrecht, of *Henry C. Trost: Architect of the Southwest*, 1981. **Essays:** Aalto, S. Chermayeff, Eames, Kepes, Martin, Prestini.

FERRABEE, Lydia. Essayist. Instructor, Bishops University, Lennoxville, Quebec, since 1978. Formerly, instructor, Nova Scotia College of Art and Design and Concordia University, and contributing editor, *Canadian Interiors*. Author of numerous articles on design and design education for *Design* (London). *From* (Opladen, West Germany). *Abitare* (Milan), *Form* (Stockholm), *Créé* (Paris), *Industrial Design* (New York), and others. **Essay:** Gersin.

FRASCARA, Jorge. Essayist. Professor, since 1977, and Chairman, since 1981, Department of Art and Design University of Alberta, Edmonton; Associate Editor, *Icographic* magazine, since 1982. Vice-President, International Council of Graphic Design Associations, 1979–81; member, National Council, Society of Graphic Designers of Canada, 1979–81. Author of *Introduction to Aesthetic Evaluation*, 1969; *Drawing as a Teaching Aid*, 1972; and *Art in General Education*, 1973. **Essays:** Frutiger, Gonzalez, Ruiz, Shakespear.

FRIEDMANN, Arnold. Adviser, essayist and entrant. See his own entry. **Essays:** Associated Space Design, D'Urso, Environetics International, ISD (Interior Space Design), Leeds, Luss, Space Design Group, TAC Interior Design and Graphic Communication.

GAMBILL, Norman. Adviser and essayist. Head of the Art Department, South Dakota State University, Brookings, since 1984. Professor, Department of Art and Design, University of Illinois at Urbana-Champaign, 1966–83; also previously guest curator, International Museum of Photography at George Eastman House, Rochester, New York, and consultant. Learning Museum Program. Indianapolis Museum of Art, Indiana. **Essays:** Horner, Leven, Sylbert.

GARLAND, Madge (died, 1990). Essayist. Freelance writer on fashion, architecture, design, and travel, London. Formerly, Fashion Editor, English *Vogue*; Professor of Fashion Design, Royal College of Art, London. Author of *The Changing Face of Beauty*, 1957; *The Changing Face of Childhood*, 1963; *The Indecisive Decade*, 1968; *The Changing Form of Fashion*, 1970; *The Small Garden in the City*, 1974; *A History of Fashion*, with J. Anderson Black, 1975, 1980; and others. Contributor to *Apollo, Country Life, Harpers, The Saturday Book*, and others. **Essays:** Fratini, Quant.

GAULIN, Kenneth. Essayist. Design writer and consultant, Boston. Formerly, sales representative, Knoll International; consultant-designer, Haffenreffer Museum, Brown University, Bristol,

Rhode Island, and Education Development Center, Newton, Massachusetts; technical director, New York University Medical Center. **Essays:** Aulenti, Diffrient, Knoll, Platner.

GOWAN, Al. Essayist. Chairman, Design department, Massachusetts College of Art, Boston, since 1979. Instructor in graphic design, Indiana University Bloomington, 1964–66; Professor and Head of Visual Design, Purdue University, West Lafayette, Indiana, 1966–70; Professor and Head of Graphic Design, Boston University, 1970–74; Director, Cambridge Arts Council, Massachusetts, 1964–77; Designer-in-Residence, City of Cambridge, Massachusetts, 1977–78. Founder-editor, *Design-course*, an international design quarterly, 1968–70. Author of *Nuts and Bolts, Case Studies in Public Design*, 1980. **Essays:** Beltrán, Cooper, Papanek.

GREAPENTROG, Grant. Essayist. Professor, Design Department, Drexel University, Philadelphia, since 1979. College Department, Appleton-Century-Crofts, 1964–71, and Harcourt Brace Jovanovich, 1971–79. **Essays:** Bellinger, Fields, Kroll, Moore.

GUSTAFSSON, Gertrud. Essayist. Editor, *Paletten* (Göteborg, Sweden), since 1981; correspondent, *Form* (Stockholm), since 1980. **Essay:** Nilsson.

HÀBARA, Shukuro. Essayist. Design editor, *SD (Space Design)* art and architecture journal, since 1975; lecturer, Tama University of Fine Arts. Editor-in-chief, *Design* (Tokyo), 1962–68; Professor, Tokyo University of Arts, 1968–74. Co-author of *Introduction to Modern Art*, 1970; *The Origin of Design*; *The Philosophy and Background of Braun & Co. Design*, 1978; and *The Secret of a Musician—Dedication to Glenn Gould*, 1978. **Essays:** Awazu, Katayama, Ikko Tanaka, Masaaki Tanaka.

HALAS, John. Essayist. Co-producer and director of more than 2,000 animated and live-action films. Founder and Creative Director, Halas and Batchelor Animation, 1940–81. Founder and Creative Director, Educational Film Centre; President and Chairman of the Research and Development Commission, ASIFA (International Animated Film Association); President, British Federation of Film Societies. Graphic Design correspondent, *Novum Gebrauchsgraphik*. Author of *How to Cartoon*, with Bo Privett, 1959; *Design in Motion*, 1962; *Film and TV Graphics*, with Walter Herdeg, 1968; *The Technique of Film Animation*, with Roger Manvell, 1969; *Art in Movement*, with Roger Manvell, 1970; *Computer Animation*, 1974; *The Great Movie Cartoon Parade*, with David Rider, 1976; *Visual Scripting*, 1975; *Film Animation: A Simplified Approach*, 1976; *Full Length Animated Feature Film*, with Bruno Edera, 1977; *Timing for Animation*, with Harold Whitaker, 1981; *Graphics in Motion*, 1981. **Essays:** Adam, Bozzetto, Casson, de Majo, Gardner, Henrion, Lewitt/Him, Korda, Lenica, Luzzati, Reid.

HÅRD af SEGERSTAD, Ulf. Essayist. Art and design critic, *Svenska Dagbladet* newspaper, Stockholm. Editor, *Form* magazine, Stockholm, 1957–60; design consultant to Philips, Sweden, 1964–67; vice president, International Council of Societies of Industrial Design, 1967–71; visiting professor, at the University of Minnesota, 1975, and at the Danish Royal Academy of Fine Arts, 1979. Author of *Bildkomposition*, 1952; *Scandinavian Design*, 1961; *Modern Scandinavian Furniture*, 1963; *Modern Svensk Textilkonst*, 1963; *Design in Finland*, 1968; *Keramik*, 1976. **Essay:** Mono.

HAYHURST, Richard. Essayist. Freelance writer, London. Director of the Hayhurst, Conington and Cripps advertising agency. Copywriter, at AC-Mainos, Helsinki, 1984–87; marketing and communications manager, Labsystems, Helsinki, 1987–89. **Essay:** Ruuhinen.

HIRSCH, John E. Essayist. Instructor, Department of English, New York University, since 1980; also theatrical costume designer and director. Writer of theatrical reviews and feature articles, *The Villager* (New York), 1977–80. **Essays:** Klotz, Musser, Robin Wagner, Weitz.

HOPE, Augustine. Essayist. Editor, *Encyclopedia of Light and Color* for Color Association of the United States. Formerly, Associate Editor, *American Fabrics and Fashions* (New York) and Editor, *Cherwell Magazine* (United Kingdom). **Essay:** Yang.

HOUSE, Nancy. Essayist. Freelance writer on art and design, Marblehead, Massachusets. **Essays:** Aicher, Forbes, Hillmann, Massin, Pesce, Stone.

ICHIYAMA, D. Essayist. Professor, Visual Communications Design, Purdue University, West Lafayette, Indiana, since 1980. **Essays:** Gerstner, Hofmann, Keller, Leupin, Matter, Thompson.

IMM, Eumie. Essayist. Graduate student in art history, University of Cincinnati, Ohio. **Essay:** Snyder.

INKO-DOKUBO, Alaboigoni. Essayist. Film producer and editor, 1977–78, and Head of Film Centre, since 1978, Directorate of Information and Public Relations, Port Harcourt, Nigeria; culture and art columnist for various Nigerian newspapers, since 1977; Chairman, Seiyefa Publishing Company, Port Harcourt, Nigeria. Author of *Rivers of My Passion*, 1982; *Go to the Ants*, 1982; and *Songs of the Eagle*, 1982. **Essay:** David-West.

JENNINGS, Jan. Essayist. Visiting Professor, College of Design, Iowa State University, Ames; Principal, Jennings, Gottfried, Check design consultants, Ames, Iowa. Planner, Tulsa Metropolitan Area Planning Commission, Oklahoma, 1969–73; Director, Tulsa Historic Preservation Office, Oklahoma, 1977–79; formerly instructor at several universities in interior design, housing, planning, and urban design. Author, with Herbert Gottfried, of *American Vernacular: A Design Handbook*, 1984. **Essay:** Magistretti.

KERR, Deirdre. Essayist. Pseudonym of an assistant editor at *Harpers' Bazaar* and freelance writer for *Gentlemen's Quarterly*. Formerly, intern. Costume Institute, Metropolitan Museum of Art, New York, and Apprentice to fashion designer Yeohlee Teng. **Essays:** Larkin, Robertson.

KINROSS, Robin. Essayist. Freelance typographer and writer. Lecturer, Department of Typography, University of Reading, Berkshire, 1977–82. **Essays:** Froshaug, Garland, Kinneir, Schmoller, Spencer, Tschichold.

KLOS, Sheila. Essayist. Librarian and Head of the Architecture and Allied Arts Library, University of Oregon; book review coordinator for *Art Documentation*, since 1988. Associate Curator of slides and photographers, Brown University, 1977–83; Serials Librarian, Cleveland Museum of Art, 1983–85. Co-editor, *Historical Bibliography of Art Museum Serials*, 1987. **Essay:** Munari.

KODA, Harold. Essayist. Curator of the Edward C. Blum Design Laboratory, Fashion Institute of Technology, New York. Author of *Jocks and Nerds*, 1989; *The Historical Mode*, 1989. **Essay:** Matsumoto.

KRIEBEL, Marjorie. Essayist. Professor of Design, Drexel University, Philadelphia, since 1975; also registered architect, Philadelphia. Member, Board of Directors, National Council for Interior Design Qualifications, since 1982. **Essays:** Friedmann, King.

KRIEBEL, William Victor. Essayist. Instructor, Department of Interiors and Graphic Studies, Colege of Design Arts, Drexel University, Philadelphia; also a Registered Architect in independent private practice. **Essays:** Bellini, A. Castiglioni, P.G. Castiglioni, De Lucchi, Hollein, Mari, Ponti, C. Scarpa, T. Scarpa.

LANGE, Wolfgang. Essayist. Writer on theatre, East Berlin. **Essay:** Zimmermann.

LARSEN, Jack Lenor. Adviser and entrant. See his own entry.

LEE, Edith Cortland. Essayist. Freelance writer and consultant on film and video, Chicago. **Essays:** Carrick, Richard Day, Ferguson, Margaret Furse, Roger Furse, Hipgnosis, Kirk, Plunkett, Sharaff.

LINDGREN, Maud. Essayist. Freelance writer and public relations consultant, Stockholm. **Essay:** Huldt.

LINDKVIST, Lennart. Adviser and essayist. Managing director and board member, Foreningen Svensk Form, Stockholm. Editor-in-chief, *Form* magazine, 1963–73. Editor, *Design in Sweden*, 1977. **Essays:** Ahlstrom and Enrich, Benktzon and Juhlin.

LIVSTEDT, Ake. Essayist. Freelance art critic and lecturer, Stockholm. Curator, at the Nationalmuseum, Stockholm, 1971–77. **Essay:** Vallien.

LUNDAHL, Gunilla. Essayist. Freelance architecture and design critic, Stockholm. Editor, *Nordisk Funktionalism*, 1980; *Recent Developments in Swedish Architecture 1983; Memory of a Landscape*, 1984; *Swedish Textile Art*, 1987. **Essays:** Bohlin, Dessau.

MARTIN, Floyd W. Essayist. Professor of art history, University of Arkansas at Little Rock, since 1982. Visiting lecturer in art history, University of Illinois at Urbana-Champaign, 1981–82. **Essays:** Box, Boyle, Gherardi, Grot, Whitlock.

MAUNULA, Leena. Essayist. Architecture and design critic of *Helsingin Sanomat* newspaper, Helsinki, since 1968. **Essay:** Lavonen.

McDERMOTT, Catherine. Essayist. Senior Lecturer in History of Design, Kingston Polytechnic, Kingston upon Thames, Surrey. Chairman, Design History Society, 1981–84. **Essays:** Crosby, Lucienne Day, Franck, Goldfinger, Juhl, Marx, Mathsson, Minale/Tattersfield, Pond, Weallans.

McLEAN, Anne. Essayist. Freelance writer on design. **Essay:** Roch.

MEGGS, Phillip B. Essayist. Professor, since 1968, and Chairman, since 1974, Department of Communication Arts and Design, Virginia Commonwealth University, Richmond. Senior Designer, Reynolds Metals Company, 1965–66; Art Director, A.H. Robins Company, 1966–68. Author of *A History of Graphic Design*, 1983, and *Typographic Design*, with Robert C. Carter and Ben Day, 1984. **Essays:** Bass, Binder, Brodovich, Cieslewicz, Greiman, Lubalin, Odermatt/Tissi, Rand, Weingart, Wyman.

MENARD, Gloria. Essayist. Principal of Gloria Menard and Associates communications consultants, Montreal; contributing editor, *MacLean's* magazine. Formerly manager of internal communications, for Alcan Aluminium Limited, and editor of *Alcan News*. **Essay:** Harder.

MERZDORF, Russell. Essayist. Professor, Department of Creative Arts, Purdue University, West Lafayette, Indiana. **Essay:** Colley.

MIKLAS, Lois Irene. Essayist. Intern, 1982–83, and assistant to the Program Coordinator, 1983–84, Children's Museum, Indianapolis, Indiana; also participant-interpreter, Conner Prairie Pioneer Settlement, Noblesville, Indiana. **Essays:** Carré, Clark, Jenkins, Lourié, Jack Martin Smith, Warm, Wheeler.

MIKOTOWICZ, Tom. Essayist. Assistant Professor of Theatre, University of Maine. Associate editor, *Theatre Design and Technology* magazine, 1985–89. **Essays:** Aronson, Fisher, Ming Cho Lee, Polidori, Oliver Smith, Ter-Arutunian.

MILLIE, Elena G. Essayist. Curator, Poster Collection, Library of Congress, Washington, D.C., since 1970. **Essays:** Allner, Sawka.

MOLLERUP, Per. Adviser. Freelance writer on design. Director, Designlab ApS, Denmark. Author of *The Corporate Design Programme*, 1987.

MOON, Karen. Essayist. Design Assistant (Visual Effects) with BBC Television, London, 1974–78 (1975–78, soleiy on Open University productions); lecturer, History of Art and Design Department, Kingston Polytechnic, Kingston upon Thames, Surrey, 1978–79. **Essays:** Grange, Welch.

NEUMANN, Eckhard. Design Promotion Manager, Rat für Formgebung (German Design Council), Darmstadt, since 1975. Formerly, Advertising Manager, Swissair-Germany; creative director for an advertising agency; and Manager of Communication Design for Braun AG, Kronberg; also teacher at several design schools. Founder and co-editor of the annual *Werbung in Deutschland*, since 1964; author of *Functional Graphic Design in the 20's*, 1967; editor of *Bauhaus and Bauhaus People*, 1970. **Essay:** Friedl.

OLSON, Ronald C. Essayist. Director of Marketing, Kliegl Brothers stage lighting, Long Island City, New York, since 1978. Lighting Specialists, Strand Century Incorporated, 1964–78. Officer, United States Institute for Theatre Technology, since 1971, and President, 1982–84. **Essay:** Rosenthal.

PAATERO, Kristina. Essayist. Researcher at the Museum of Finnish Architecture in Helsinki. Assistant editor, *Form Function Finland* magazine, 1980–88. Co-author, *The Things Around Us*, 1981; *Arabia*, 1987. **Essay:** Kosonen.

PACEY, Philip. Essayist. Art Librarian, Preston Polytechnic, Lancashire, since 1975. **Essay:** Logan.

PALLASMAA, Juhani. Essayist. Freelance writer and architect, Helsinki. Exhibitions Curator, 1968–72, and Director, 1983–83, Museum of Finnish Architecture, Helsinki; Rector, Institute of Industrial Arts, Helsinki, 1970–72; Associate Professor, Haile Selassie University, Addis Ababa, 1972–74; State Artist and Professor, Helsinki, 1983–88. Editor, *Alvar Aalto*, 1977; *Tapio Wirkkala*, 1977; *Alvar Aalto: Furniture*, 1984; *Phenomenon Marimekko*, 1986; *Hvittrask: The Home as a Work of Art*, 1987; *The Language of Wood*, 1987. **Essay:** Bryk.

PELLINEN, Jukka. Adviser. Designer, Helsinki. Editor of *ORNAMO 1950–1954: Finnish Decorative Art*, with Kaj Franck, Timo Sarpaneva and others, 1955, and *History of the Cotton Mill Porin Puuvilla*, with Timo Sarpaneva, 1957.

PERIÄINEN, Tapio. Adviser and essayist. Managing Director of the Finnish Society of Crafts and Design. Architect in private practice, Helsinki, 1955–75; Research assistant at the Academy of Finland's Council for Social Sciences, 1965–68; Adviser to the Mannerheim League for Child Welfare, 1969–71, and Head of the Children's Environmental Project, 1972–75. Author of *Nature, Man, Architecture*, 1969; *Goals for Housing Policy*, 1971; *Recommendations for Playgrounds*, 1972. **Essay:** Eskolin-Nurmesniemi.

PIETZSCH, Ingeborg. Essayist. Editor and theatre critic. *Theatre der Zeit* magazine, East Berlin, since 1967. Author of *Werkstatt Theatre*, 1975, and *Gardenbengespräche*, 1982. **Essays:** Finke, Hein, Troike.

POZNER, André. Essayist. Writer and journalist, Chécy, France. **Essay:** Trauner.

PULOS, Arthur J. Adviser, essayist and entrant. See his own entry. **Essays:** Blaich, Soloviev.

REMINGTON, R. Roger. Essayist. Professor of Graphic Design, Rochester Institute of Technology, New York. Author of *Nine Pioneers in American Graphic Design*, 1989. **Essays:** Tscherny, Wolf.

RIDDELL, Richard V. Essayist. Professor, University of California, San Diego, since 1978; freelance scene and lighting designer, since 1976. Contributing Editor, *Theatre Crafts*, 1980. Author of articles on German theatre for *Theatre Crafts* and other publications. **Essays:** Freyer, Herrmann, Minks.

ROSE, Virginia. Essayist. Instructor of art and architectural history. Beirut University College, Lebanon, since 1983. **Essays:** Sarpaneva, Stephensen.

RUSSAC, Patricia A. Essayistl Freelance writer on art and design. **Essays:** Bernadotte, Fossella, Grear, Landor.

RUSSELL, Douglas A. Essayist. Professor of Drama, Stanford University, California, since 1961; trainer and educational consultant to the American Conservatory Theatre of San Francisco, since 1973. Director of costume, Oregon Shakespeare Festival, Ashland, 1948–61; also formerly costume designer for the Missouri Repertory Theatre, for The Old Globe in San Diego, California, and for the Berkeley, California, Shakespeare Festival. Vice-Commissioner of Costume, 1978–82, and board member, United States Institute of Theatre Technology. Author of *Stage Costume Design*, 1973; *Theatrical Style: A Visual Approach to the Theatre*, 1976; *Period Style for the Theatre*, 1980; *An Anthology of Austrian Drama*, 1982; and *Costume History and Style*, 1983. **Essays:** Aldredge, Bay, Gorelik, Heeley, Jacobs, Kerz, Moiseiwitsch, Oenslager, Ponnelle, Robbins, Roth, Zeffirelli, Zipprodt.

SANO, Kunio. Essayist. Director, Joint Design System since 1972; lecturer, Kuwazawa Design School, since 1977. Information and Planning Committee Chairman, Japan Industrial Designers Association, since 1983; editorial committee member, since 1970, and chairman, 1978–79, *Industrial Design* (Tokyo). Author of *Maker, User and Designer*, 1975, and "Image and Industrial Design," monthly column in *Industrial Engineering* (Tokyo), 1977; editor of *The Futurology of Rice*, 1977, and *The Structure of Dexterity* (Japan Industrial Designers Association thirtieth-anniversary commemorative publication), 1983. **Essays:** Ito, Kimura, Koike, Matsuba, Minagawa, Okada, Sakashita, Sumita, Watanabe, Yanagi.

SAWKA, Jan. Entrant and essayist. See his own entry. **Essays:** Fukuda, Hilscher, Kantor, Klimowski, Le Quernec, Matthies, Mlodozeniuec, Jozef Mroszczak, Marcin Mroszczak, Starowieyski, Swierzy, Tomaszewski, Urbaniec.

SCHEINMAN, Pamela. Essayist. Adjunct Professor, Department of Fine Arts, Montclair Stage College, New Jersey. Publications Editor, Philadelphia Museum of Art, 1975; Crafts Instructor, Tyler School of Art, Elkins Park, Pennsylvania, 1976–79; Mexico City Correspondent, *Craft International* magazine, 1984–85. Contributor to *Threads, Surface Design, Craft International* and *American Craft*. **Essay:** Hernmarck.

SCHMID, Helmut. Essayist. Typographer, designer, and art director, living in Japan. Editor and designer of *Typography Today*, 1980, and special issue on Japanese typography, *Typografische Monatsblätter* (St. Gallen, Switzerland), 1973. **Essays:** Ruder, Sugiura.

SHAW, Paul. Essayist. Freelance calligrapher, letterer, and designer. Instructor, School of Visual Arts, New York; New York Institute of Technology, Metro Campus; and Long Island University, Brooklyn, New York. Contributor, *Calligraphy Quarterly*, 1978–81, and *Printing News*. Author of articles on calligraphy and printing for *Scripsit, A.B. Bookman's Weekly, Fine Print*, and others. **Essays:** Bernhard, Larcher.

SIFFORD, Harlan. Essayist. Art librarian, University of Iowa City, since 1962. Professor of Art, Furman University, Greenville, South Carolina, 1953–54; Shorter College, Rome, Georgia, 1954–60. Author of *The Alcock Collection of Silver Plate in the University of Iowa Museum of Art*, 1978, and of silver catalogues for *The Owen and Leone Elliott Collection; Selected Works*, Iowa City, 1964 and *The Owen and Leone Elliott Collection*, Iowa City, 1969. **Essays:** Erni, Gernreich, Girard, Anne Klein, Simpson.

SJÖLANDER, Carin. Essayist. Staff journalist, *Dagens Nyheter* Newspaper, Stockholm. Formerly, art critic, *Sydsvenska Dagbladet* newspaper, Malmo, 1965–71; editorial staff member, *Form* magazine, Stockholm, 1970–72. **Essay:** Persson-Melin.

SKELLENGER, Gillion. Essayist. Freelance wallpaper and fabric designer, Chicago; instructor in Fashion Department, School of the Art Institute of Chicago, since 1977. **Essays:** Walter Albini, Biagiotti, Fendi, Missoni, Valentino.

SOLURI, Michael Robert. Essayist. Professor in photography, Rochester Institute of Technology, Rochester, New York, since 1979; also freelance photographer. **Essays:** Dorfsman, Lois.

SORJO-SMEDS, Jukka. Essayist. Copywriter, in T:mi Mainosideointi Leena Serlachius advertising agency, Helsinki. Author of *Odours of the Wind*, 1983. **Essay:** Vuori.

SPENCER, Herbert. Entrant and essayist. See his own entry. **Essay:** Zwart.

SPENCER, Mafalda. Essayist. Typographic designer and lecturer on design history, London. Author of *The Book of Numbers*, with Herbert Spencer, 1974. **Essay:** Sandberg.

SPILMAN, Raymond. Essayist. Director, Raymond Spilman Industrial Design, Connecticut. Staff designer, General Motors, Detroit, 1935–40; product designer, office of Walter Dorwin Teague, New York, 1940–42; director and product designer, at Johnson-Cushing-Nevell, New York, 1942–46. Chairman, President and Director, American Society of Industrial Designer, 1950–62; Director, Inter Society Color Council, 1970–72, 1978–78. **Essay:** Vassos.

STEELE, Gordon. Essayist. Open University tutor and lecturer on art, architecture, and design history. Education Secretary to the Building Centre Trust, 1965–74. Author of articles, mainly on architecture in the Nordic countries and on housing there and in Britain, for architectural journals in Britain and the Netherlands. **Essays:** Aarnio, Metsovaara, Nurmesniemi, Tapiovaara, Tye.

STEIMLE, Jerry. Essayist. Freelance writer, Palo Alto, California. Author of articles for *Communication Arts* (Palo, Alto, California) and *Graphis* (Zürich). **Essays:** François, Henry Steiner, Testa.

STRANGER, Ivar. Essayist. Keeper, West Norway Museum of Applied Art, Bergen, from 1988. Assistant Keeper, National Gallery, Oslo, 1981–82; Curator, Vest-Agder County Museum, Kristiansand, 1982–88. Author of *Norwegian Studio Ceramics 1890–1914*, 1981. **Essay:** Eckhoff.

STRZELECKI, Zenobiusz. Essayist. Specialist in theatrical set and costume design, Warsaw. Author of *Wspólczesna Scenografia Polska/Contemporary Polish Stage Design*, 1983. **Essays:** Gurawski, Serafinowicz, Wierchowicz.

SUDICK, Barbara. Essayist. Designer-partner, Nightswander-Sudick design firm, New Haven, Connecticut. Instructor in graphic design, University of New Haven, 1982; University of Hartford, 1982–83. **Essays:** Geissbuhler, James Miho.

TANAKA, Masaaki. Essayist and entrant. See his own entry. **Essays:** Hayakawa, Igarashi, Nagai, Nakamura.

TAYLOR, Benjamin de Brie. Essayist. Professor, since 1973, and Director, 1973–75, Institute of Design, Illinois Institute of Technology, Chicago. Instructor, Pratt Institute, Brooklyn, New York, 1960–68; Dean, Parsons School of Design, New York, 1968–70; Dean, Herron School of Art, Indiana University, Indianapolis, 1970–73. Author of *Design Lessons from Nature*, 1974. **Essay:** Doblin.

TRIGGS, Teal Ann. Essayist. Designer, University of Texas Press, Austin, since 1983. **Essays:** Calvin Klein, Massey.

TULOKAS, Maria. Essayist. Head of the Textile Design Department, Rhode Island School of Design, Providence. Author of *Fabrics for the 80s*, 1985. **Essay:** Arai.

VOTOLATO, G. Essayist. Head of Art History, Buckinghamshire College, High Wycombe, since 1980. **Essay:** Basevi.

WALSH, George. Essayist. Freelance art and design critic and writer, Chicago. **Essays:** Grapus, Ohl, Stankowski, Tallon.

WATANABE, Hiroshi. Essayist. Architect and writer, Tokyo. Member of Kenchiku Keikaku Kobo [Architectural Planning Workshop], Tokyo. Author of *The Japanese Conception of Space*. **Essay:** Yoh.

WEISS, David W. Essayist. Professor of Drama, since 1954, and Chairman, 1966–75 and 1978-83. Department of Drama, University of Virginia, Charlottesville. Member, Board of Directors, United States Institute of Theatre Technology, 1966–67, and American Theatre Association, 1976–79; President, Southeastern Theatre Conference, 1972–73. **Essay:** Mielziner.

WIDMAN, Dag. Essayist. Director, Prins Eugens Waldemarsudde art gallery, Stockholm. Director of Svensk Form society of industrial design, Stockholm, 1963–65; Keeper of the Applied Art and Design Department, at the Nationalmuseum, Stockholm, 1966–80. Author of *Cezanne*, 1957; *Stig Lindberg*, 1962; *Konsthantverk, Konstindustri, Design 1895–1975*, 1975. **Essay:** Hasselberg-Olsson.

WRÓBLEWSKA, Danuta. Essayist. Writer on art and design, and adviser on contemporary arts to the Archdiocese Museum, Warsaw. Staff member, *Projekt* art and design magazine, Warsaw, 1956–83. Author of books on Polish graphic art and weaving. **Essay:** Urbański.

WYLIE, Liz. Essayist. Lecturer in Art History, University of Saskatchewan, Saskatoon. Instructor, York University, Toronto, 1980–81, and Brock University, St. Catharine's, Ontario, 1981–82; editorial assistant, *Artmagazine*, Toronto, 1980–81. Author of reviews and articles for *Artscanada* (Toronto), *Arts Magazine* (New York), *Artmagazine* (Toronto), *The Journal of Canadian Art History* (Montreal), *Photo-Communique* (Toronto), *Vanguard* (Vancouver), and others. **Essays:** Fleming, Grottschalk and Ash International.

YOUNG, Barbara. Essayist. Head, Art Department, California Polytechnic State University, San Luis Obispo, since 1983. Senior Lecturer, Sheffield City Polytechnic, England, 1980–83. **Essays:** Brandt, Robin Day, Koppel, Mellor, Persson.

X1.91